PHILIP'S

CONCISE
WORLD
ATLAS

D MAP PAGES

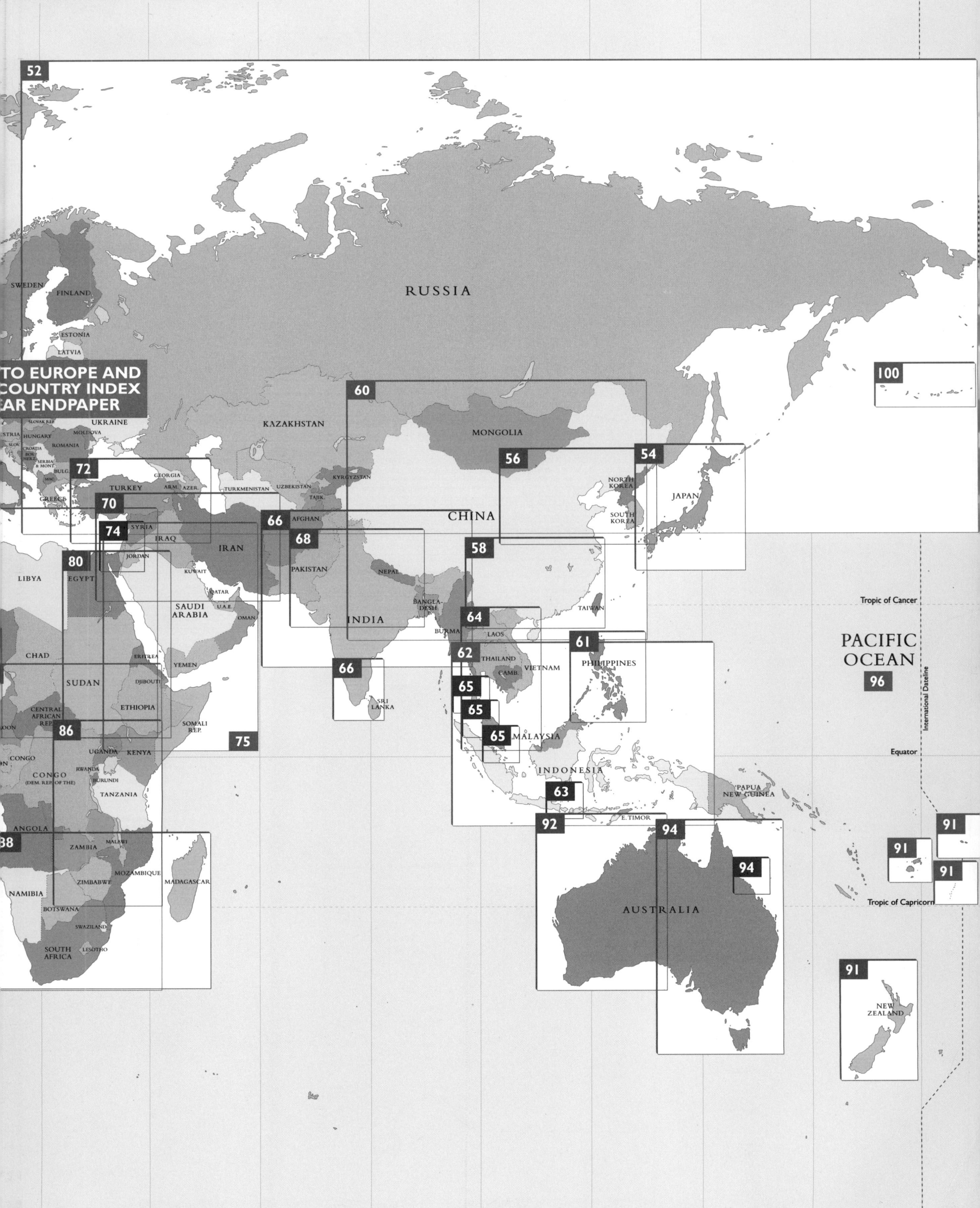

52

RUSSIA

SWEDEN
FINLAND
ESTONIA
LATVIA

TO EUROPE AND
COUNTRY INDEX
AR ENDPAPER

SLOVAK REP.
UKRAINE
STRIA HUNGARY MOLDOVA
SLOV. ROMANIA
CROATIA
BOSS.
SERBIA
HER. & MONT. BULG.
GREECE

72

GEORGIA
TURKEY ARM. AZER.
70
SYRIA
74 IRAQ
JORDAN
80
EGYPT
KUWAIT
QATAR
U.A.E.
SAUDI
ARABIA
OMAN

LIBYA

CHAD

ERITREA
YEMEN
SUDAN
DJIBOUTI
ETHIOPIA
CENTRAL
AFRICAN
REP.
SOMALI
REP.
OON

86
UGANDA KENYA
CONGO
CONGO
(DEM. REP. OF THE) RWANDA
BURUNDI
TANZANIA

ANGOLA
38
ZAMBIA MALAWI
ZIMBABWE MOZAMBIQUE MADAGASCAR
NAMIBIA
BOTSWANA
SWAZILAND
SOUTH LESOTHO
AFRICA

KAZAKHSTAN

60

MONGOLIA

56
54
NORTH
KOREA
JAPAN
KYRGYZSTAN
SOUTH
UZBEKISTAN KOREA
TURKMENISTAN
TAJIK.
66 AFGHAN. CHINA
68
58
PAKISTAN
NEPAL
BANGLA- TAIWAN
DESH
64
INDIA BURMA LAOS
61
66 THAILAND
62 VIETNAM PHILIPPINES
SRI CAMB.
LANKA **65**
65
65 MALAYSIA
INDONESIA
PAPUA
NEW GUINEA
63
E. TIMOR
92
94

100

Tropic of Cancer

PACIFIC
OCEAN
96

94

AUSTRALIA

91

91

91

Tropic of Capricorn

91

NEW
ZEALAND

PHILIP'S

CONCISE
WORLD
ATLAS

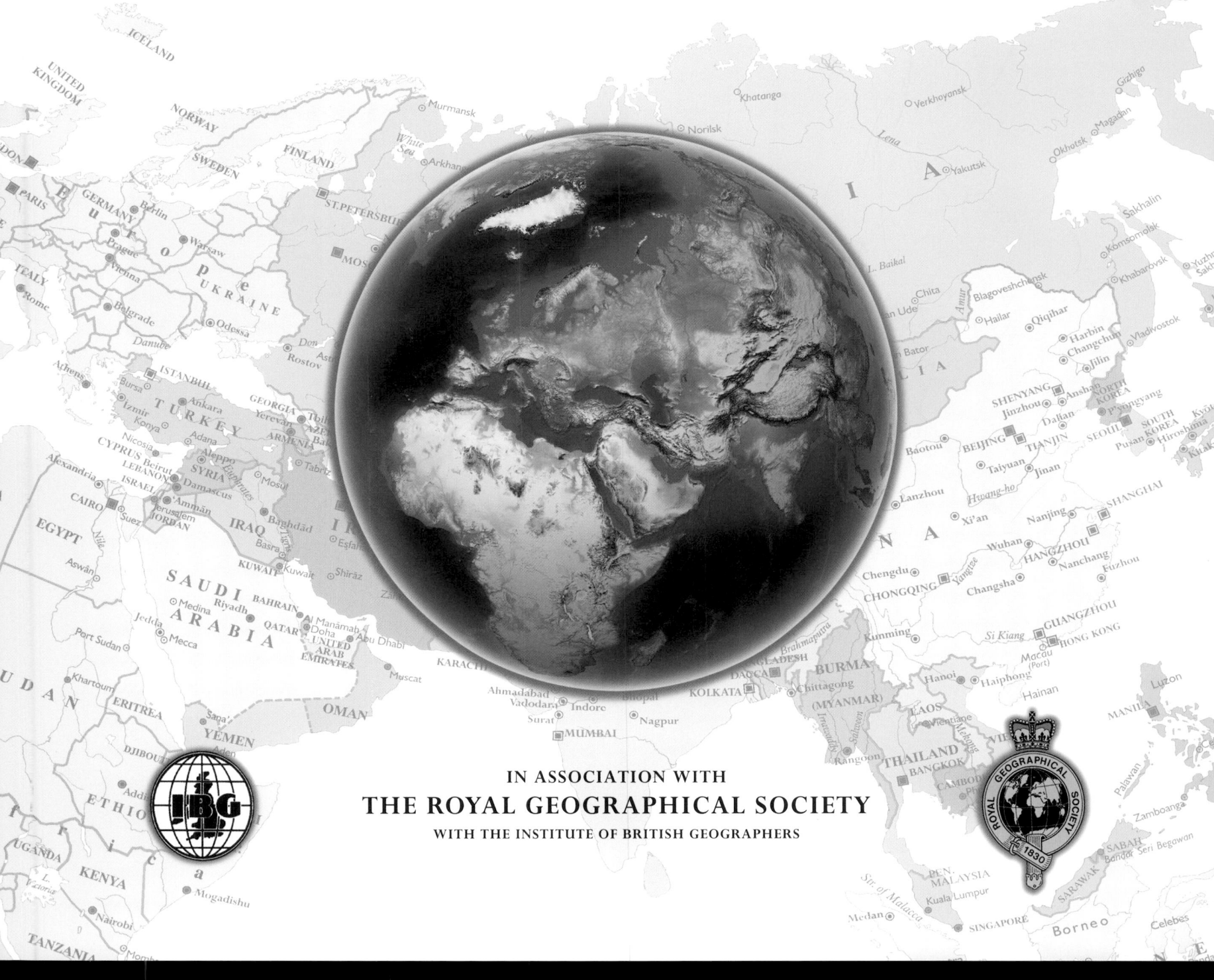

IN ASSOCIATION WITH
THE ROYAL GEOGRAPHICAL SOCIETY
WITH THE INSTITUTE OF BRITISH GEOGRAPHERS

THE EARTH IN SPACE
Cartography by Philip's

Text
Keith Lye

Illustrations
Stefan Chabluk

Star Charts
Wil Tirion

PICTURE ACKNOWLEDGEMENTS
Mike Brown 46 (top left), 48 (top left), 50 (top left), 56 (top left), 60 (top left)
Corbis /Ed Eckstein 58 (bottom), /Colin Garratt; Milepost 92 1/2 60 (bottom), /Aaron Horowitz
40 (top left), /Wolfgang Kaehler 37, /Manoocher/Webistan 48 (top right), /Kevin R. Morris 48
(bottom), /Galen Rowell 62 (bottom), /Royalty-Free 36 (top left), 44 (top left), 47, 52 (top left),
54 (top left), 58 (top left), 62 (top left), /Peter Turnley 51, /Nik Wheeler 46 (bottom), /Tim Wright 61
Corbis Saba /Shepard Sherbell 56 (bottom)
Corbis Sygma /Thorne Anderson 63
Michael P. Doukas/USGS/CVO 32 (top left)
Akira Fujii/David Malin Images 27
Getty Images/The Image Bank /Peter Hendrie 36 (top right), /Pete Turner 55
Getty Images/Stone /James Balog 32 (bottom), /Simeone Huber 49, /Gary John Norman 52 (bottom),
/Frank Oberle 41 (top), /Dennis Oda 33, /Donovan Reese 34–5, /Michael Townsend 45
Robert Harding Picture Library /Bill Ross 57, /Adam Woolfitt 59
Images Colour Library Limited 31
NASA 18 (top left), 20 (top left), 22 (top left), 24 (top left), 26 (top left), 26 (bottom), /Jacques
Descloitres, MODIS/GSFC 28 (top left), /ESA, S. Beckwith (STScI) and the HUDF Team 18 (bottom),
/GSFC 24 (top right), /Hubble Heritage Team (STScI/AURA)/R.G. French (Wellesley College)/J. Cuzzi
and J. Lissauer (NASA/Ames Research Center)/L. Dones (SwRI) 25 (bottom left), /JPL 24 (centre left),
24 (bottom left), 25 (top right), 25 (centre right), /JPL/Univ. Arizona 25 (top left), /JPL/USGS
24 (bottom right), /JSC 38 (top left), 42 (top left), /Hal Pierce/GSFC 40 (top right), /A. Stern (SwRI),
M. Buie (Lowell Observatory)/ESA 25 (bottom right), /Reto Stöckli, Robert Simmon/GSFC 17
NPA Group, Edenbridge, UK 28 (bottom), 29, (top), 29 (bottom), 64
Caroline O'Hara 34 (top left)
Christopher Rayner 30 (top left), 35 (top)
Rex Features /Sipa 50 (bottom)
Science Photo Library /Martin Bond 30 (bottom), /CNES, 1992 Distribution SPOT Image 43 (top),
/Luke Dodd 19, 21, /Earth Satellite Corporation 41 (bottom), /Simon Fraser 54 (bottom), /NASA 38
(bottom), 39, /David Parker 42 (bottom), /Peter Ryan 43 (bottom), /Jerry Schad 20 (bottom)
Still Pictures /François Pierrel 44 (bottom)
Tony Stone Images /Nigel Press 53

Front cover photographs:
Corbis /Royalty-Free (top left, bottom left, top right, bottom right)
NASA /Holland Ford (JHU), the ACS Science Team and ESA (top centre)

Published in Great Britain in 2005
by Philip's,
a division of Octopus Publishing Group Limited,
2–4 Heron Quays, London E14 4JP

Copyright © 2005 Philip's

Cartography by Philip's

ISBN-13 978–0–540–08697–9
ISBN-10 0–540–08697–5

A CIP catalogue record for this book is available from the British Library.

Printed in Hong Kong

Details of other Philip's titles and services can be found on our website at:
www.philips-maps.co.uk

Philip's World Atlases are published in association with
The Royal Geographical Society (with The Institute of
British Geographers).

The Society was founded in 1830 and given a Royal
Charter in 1859 for 'the advancement of geographical
science'. It holds historical collections of national and
international importance, many of which relate to
the Society's association with and support for scientific
exploration and research from the 19th century onwards.
It was pivotal in establishing geography as a teaching and
research discipline in British universities close to
the turn of the century, and has played a key role in
geographical and environmental education ever since.

Today the Society is a leading world centre for
geographical learning – supporting education, teaching,
research and expeditions, and promoting public
understanding of the subject.

The Society welcomes those interested in geography
as members. For further information, please visit the
website at: www.rgs.org

PHILIP'S WORLD MAPS

The reference maps which form the main body of this atlas have been prepared in accordance with the highest standards of international cartography to provide an accurate and detailed representation of the Earth. The scales and projections used have been carefully chosen to give balanced coverage of the world, while emphasizing the most densely populated and economically significant regions. A hallmark of Philip's mapping is the use of hill shading and relief colouring to create a graphic impression of landforms: this makes the maps exceptionally easy to read. However, knowledge of the key features employed in the construction and presentation of the maps will enable the reader to derive the fullest benefit from the atlas.

MAP SEQUENCE

The atlas covers the Earth continent by continent: first Europe; then its land neighbour Asia (mapped north before south, in a clockwise sequence), then Africa, Australia and Oceania, North America and South America. This is the classic arrangement adopted by most cartographers since the 16th century. For each continent, there are maps at a variety of scales. First, physical relief

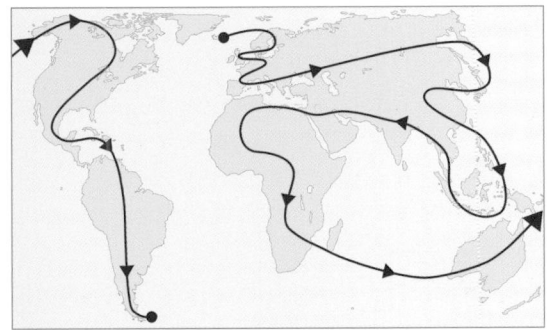

and political maps of the whole continent; then a series of larger-scale maps of the regions within the continent, each followed, where required, by still larger-scale maps of the most important or densely populated areas. The governing principle is that by turning the pages of the atlas, the reader moves steadily from north to south through each continent, with each map overlapping its neighbours.

MAP PRESENTATION

With very few exceptions (for example, for the Arctic and Antarctica), the maps are drawn with north at the top, regardless of whether they are presented upright or sideways on the page. In the borders will be found the map title; a locator diagram showing the area covered; continuation arrows showing the page numbers for maps of adjacent areas; the scale; the projection used; the degrees of latitude and longitude; and the letters and figures used in the index for locating place names and geographical features. Physical relief maps also have a height reference panel identifying the colours used for each layer of contouring.

MAP SYMBOLS

Each map contains a vast amount of detail which can only be conveyed clearly and accurately by the use of symbols. Points and circles of varying sizes locate and identify the relative importance of towns and cities; different styles of type are employed for administrative, geographical and regional place names to aid identification. A variety of pictorial symbols denote landscape features such as glaciers, marshes and coral reefs, and man-made structures including roads, railways, airports, canals and dams. International borders are shown by red lines. Where neighbouring countries are in dispute, for example in parts of the Middle East, the maps show the *de facto* boundary between nations, regardless of the legal or historical situation. The symbols are explained on the first page of the *World Maps* section of the atlas.

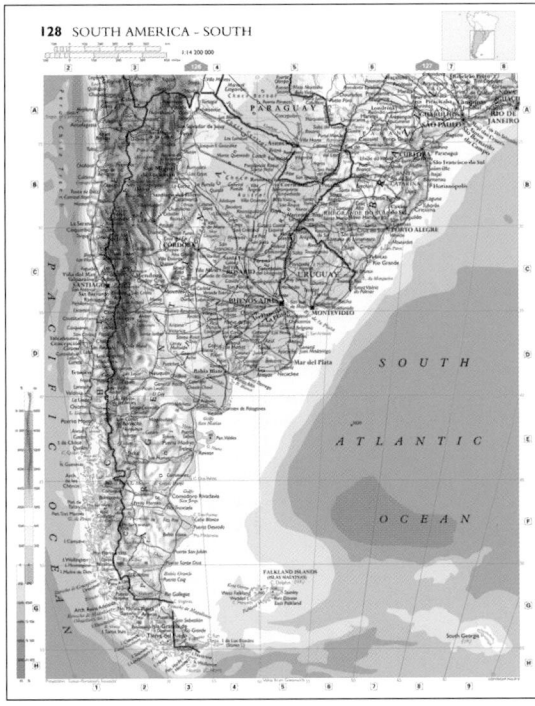

MAP SCALES

1:16 000 000
1 inch = 252 statute miles

The scale of each map is given in the numerical form known as the 'representative fraction'. The first figure is always one, signifying one unit of distance on the map; the second figure, usually in millions, is the number by which the map unit must be multiplied to give the equivalent distance on the Earth's surface. Calculations can easily be made in centimetres and kilometres, by dividing the Earth units figure by 100 000 (i.e. deleting the last five 0s). Thus 1:1 000 000 means 1 cm = 10 km. The calculation for inches and miles is more laborious, but 1 000 000 divided by 63 360 (the number of inches in a mile) shows that 1:1 000 000 means approximately 1 inch = 16 miles. The table below provides distance equivalents for scales down to 1:50 000 000.

LARGE SCALE		
1:1 000 000	1 cm = 10 km	1 inch = 16 miles
1:2 500 000	1 cm = 25 km	1 inch = 39.5 miles
1:5 000 000	1 cm = 50 km	1 inch = 79 miles
1:6 000 000	1 cm = 60 km	1 inch = 95 miles
1:8 000 000	1 cm = 80 km	1 inch = 126 miles
1:10 000 000	1 cm = 100 km	1 inch = 158 miles
1:15 000 000	1 cm = 150 km	1 inch = 237 miles
1:20 000 000	1 cm = 200 km	1 inch = 316 miles
1:50 000 000	1 cm = 500 km	1 inch = 790 miles
SMALL SCALE		

MEASURING DISTANCES

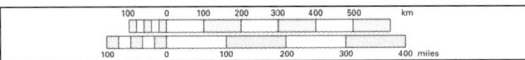

Although each map is accompanied by a scale bar, distances cannot always be measured with confidence because of the distortions involved in portraying the curved surface of the Earth on a flat page. As a general rule, the larger the map scale (that is, the lower the number of Earth units in the representative fraction), the more accurate and reliable will be the distance measured. On small-scale maps such as those of the world and of entire continents, measurement may only be accurate

along the 'standard parallels', or central axes, and should not be attempted without considering the map projection.

MAP PROJECTIONS

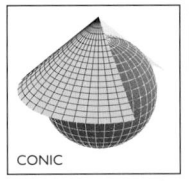  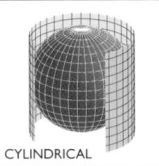

Unlike a globe, no flat map can give a true scale representation of the world in terms of area, shape and position of every region. Each of the numerous systems that have been devised for projecting the curved surface of the Earth on to a flat page involves the sacrifice of accuracy in one or more of these elements. The variations in shape and position of landmasses such as Alaska, Greenland and Australia, for example, can be quite dramatic when different projections are compared. For this atlas, the guiding principle has been to select projections that involve the least distortion of size and distance. The projection used for each map is noted in the border. Most fall into one of three categories – conic, azimuthal or cylindrical – whose basic concepts are shown above. Each involves plotting the forms of the Earth's surface on a grid of latitude and longitude lines, which may be shown as parallels, curves or radiating spokes.

LATITUDE AND LONGITUDE

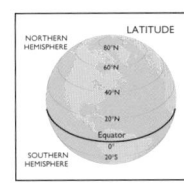 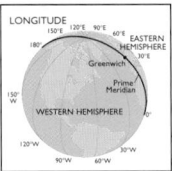 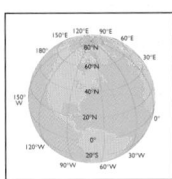

Accurate positioning of individual points on the Earth's surface is made possible by reference to the geometrical system of latitude and longitude. Latitude *parallels* are drawn west–east around the Earth and numbered by degrees north and south of the equator, which is designated 0° of latitude. Longitude *meridians* are drawn north–south and numbered by degrees east and west of the *prime meridian*, 0° of longitude, which passes through Greenwich in England. By referring to these co-ordinates and their subdivisions of minutes (1/60th of a degree) and seconds (1/60th of a minute), any place on Earth can be located to within a few hundred metres. Latitude and longitude are indicated by blue lines on the maps; they are straight or curved according to the projection employed. Reference to these lines is the easiest way of determining the relative positions of places on different maps, and for plotting compass directions.

NAME FORMS

For ease of reference, both English and local name forms appear in the atlas. Oceans, seas and countries are shown in English throughout the atlas; country names may be abbreviated to their commonly accepted form (for example, Germany, not The Federal Republic of Germany). Conventional English forms are also used for place names on the smaller-scale maps of the continents. However, local name forms are used on all large-scale and regional maps, with the English form given in brackets only for important cities – the large-scale map of Russia and Central Asia thus shows Moskva (Moscow). For countries which do not use a Roman script, place names have been transcribed according to the systems adopted by the British and US Geographic Names Authorities. For China, the Pin Yin system has been used, with some more widely known forms appearing in brackets, as with Beijing (Peking). Both English and local names appear in the index, the English form being cross-referenced to the local form.

CONTENTS

WORLD STATISTICS

COUNTRIES	10
CITIES	11
CLIMATE	12–13
PHYSICAL DIMENSIONS	14–15
REGIONS IN THE NEWS	16

THE EARTH IN SPACE

THE UNIVERSE	18–19
THE CONSTELLATIONS	20–21
STAR CHARTS	22–23
THE SOLAR SYSTEM	24–25
THE EARTH: TIME AND MOTION	26–27
THE EARTH FROM SPACE	28–29
THE DYNAMIC EARTH	30–31
EARTHQUAKES AND VOLCANOES	32–33
FORCES OF NATURE	34–35
OCEANS AND ICE	36–37
THE EARTH'S ATMOSPHERE	38–39
CLIMATE AND WEATHER	40–41
WATER AND LAND USE	42–43
THE NATURAL WORLD	44–45
THE HUMAN WORLD	46–47
LANGUAGES AND RELIGIONS	48–49
INTERNATIONAL ORGANIZATIONS	50–51
AGRICULTURE	52–53
ENERGY AND MINERALS	54–55
WORLD ECONOMIES	56–57
TRADE AND COMMERCE	58–59
TRAVEL AND COMMUNICATIONS	60–61
THE WORLD TODAY	62–63

WORLD MAPS

MAP SYMBOLS	1
THE WORLD: POLITICAL 1:84 000 000	2–3
ARCTIC OCEAN 1:31 100 000	4
ANTARCTICA 1:31 100 000	5

EUROPE

EUROPE: PHYSICAL 1:17 800 000	6
EUROPE: POLITICAL 1:17 800 000	7
SCANDINAVIA 1:4 400 000 Iceland 1:4 400 000 Færoe Islands 1:4 400 000	8–9
DENMARK AND SOUTHERN SWEDEN 1:2 200 000	10–11
IRELAND 1:1 800 000	12
SCOTLAND 1:1 800 000 Orkney Islands 1:1 800 000 Shetland Islands 1:1 800 000	13

ENGLAND AND WALES
1:1 800 000
Isles of Scilly 1:1 800 000

14–15

BRITISH ISLES
1:4 400 000

16

NETHERLANDS, BELGIUM AND LUXEMBOURG
1:2 200 000

17

NORTHERN FRANCE
1:2 200 000

18–19

SOUTHERN FRANCE
1:2 200 000

20–21

CENTRAL EUROPE
1:4 400 000

22–23

GERMANY AND SWITZERLAND
1:2 200 000

24–25

AUSTRIA, CZECH REPUBLIC
AND SLOVAK REPUBLIC
1:2 200 000

26–27

HUNGARY, ROMANIA AND THE LOWER DANUBE
1:2 200 000

28–29

POLAND AND THE SOUTHERN BALTIC
1:2 200 000

30–31

BALTIC STATES, BELARUS AND UKRAINE
1:4 400 000

32–33

THE VOLGA BASIN AND THE CAUCASUS
1:4 400 000

34–35

WESTERN SPAIN AND PORTUGAL
1:2 200 000

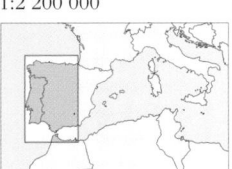

36–37

EASTERN SPAIN
1:2 200 000
Menorca 1:2 300 000

38–39

NORTHERN ITALY, SLOVENIA AND CROATIA
1:2 200 000

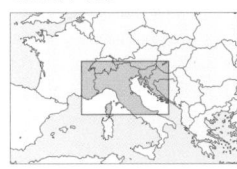

40–41

SOUTHERN ITALY
1:2 200 000

42–43

SERBIA AND MONTENEGRO, BULGARIA
AND NORTHERN GREECE
1:2 200 000

44–45

SOUTHERN GREECE AND WESTERN TURKEY
1:2 200 000

46–47

THE BALEARICS, THE CANARIES AND MADEIRA
1:900 000 / 1:1 800 000

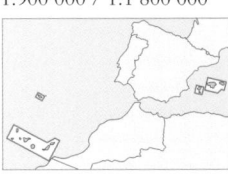

48

MALTA, CRETE, CORFU, RHODES AND CYPRUS
1:900 000 / 1:1 200 000

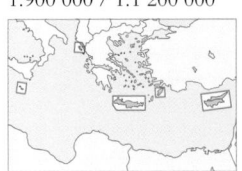

49

ASIA

ASIA: PHYSICAL
1:44 400 000   **50**

ASIA: POLITICAL
1:44 400 000   **51**

RUSSIA AND CENTRAL ASIA
1:17 800 000

52–53

JAPAN
1:4 400 000
Ryukyu Islands 1:4 400 000

54–55

NORTHERN CHINA AND KOREA
1:5 300 000

56–57

SOUTHERN CHINA
1:5 300 000

58–59

CHINA
1:17 800 000

60

THE PHILIPPINES
1:6 700 000

61

INDONESIA AND THE PHILIPPINES
1:11 100 000
Java and Madura 1:6 700 000
Bali 1:1 800 000

62–63

MAINLAND SOUTH-EAST ASIA
1:5 300 000
Ko Phuket 1:900 000
Ko Samui 1:900 000
Pinang 1:900 000
Singapore 1:900 000

64–65

SOUTH ASIA
1:8 900 000

66–67

NORTHERN INDIA AND NEPAL
1:5 300 000
Jammu and Kashmir 1:5 300 000

68–69

THE MIDDLE EAST
1:6 200 000

70–71

TURKEY AND TRANSCAUCASIA
1:4 400 000

72–73

THE NEAR EAST
1:2 200 000

74

ARABIA AND THE HORN OF AFRICA
1:13 300 000

75

AFRICA

AFRICA: PHYSICAL
1:37 300 000   **76**

AFRICA: POLITICAL
1: 37 300 000   **77**

NORTHERN AFRICA
1:13 300 000

78–79

THE NILE VALLEY
1:7 100 000
The Nile Delta 1:3 600 000

80–81

WEST AFRICA
1:7 100 000

82–83

CENTRAL AND SOUTHERN AFRICA
1:13 300 000
Madagascar 1:13 300 000

84–85

EAST AFRICA
1:7 100 000

86–87

SOUTHERN AFRICA
1:7 100 000
Madagascar 1:7 100 000

88–89

AUSTRALIA AND OCEANIA

AUSTRALIA AND OCEANIA:
 PHYSICAL AND POLITICAL
1:44 400 000   **90**

NEW ZEALAND
1:5 300 000
Samoan Islands 1:10 700 000
Fiji and Tonga 1:10 700 000

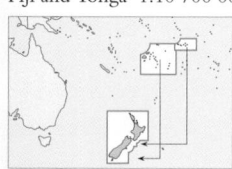
                                                91

WESTERN AUSTRALIA
1:7 100 000

                                              92–93

EASTERN AUSTRALIA
1:7 100 000
Whitsunday Islands 1:2 200 000
Tasmania 1:7 100 000

                                              94–95

PACIFIC OCEAN
1:48 000 000   **96–97**

NORTH AMERICA

NORTH AMERICA: PHYSICAL
1:31 100 000   **98**

NORTH AMERICA: POLITICAL
1:31 100 000   **99**

CANADA
1:13 300 000
Alaska 1:26 700 000

                                            100–101

WESTERN CANADA
1:6 200 000

                                            102–103

EASTERN CANADA
1:6 200 000

                                            104–105

UNITED STATES
1:10 700 000
Hawai'i 1:8 900 000

                                            106–107

WESTERN UNITED STATES
1:5 300 000

                                            108–109

CENTRAL AND SOUTHERN CALIFORNIA
 AND WESTERN WASHINGTON
1:2 200 000

                                            110–111

MIDDLE UNITED STATES
1:5 300 000

                                            112–113

EASTERN UNITED STATES
1:5 300 000

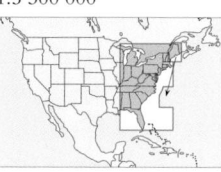
                                            114–115

NORTH-EASTERN UNITED STATES
1:2 200 000

                                            116–117

MEXICO
1:7 100 000

                                            118–119

CENTRAL AMERICA AND THE WEST INDIES
1:7 100 000
Jamaica 1:2 700 000
Guadeloupe 1:1 800 000
Martinique 1:1 800 000
Puerto Rico 1:2 700 000
Virgin Islands 1:1 800 000
St Lucia 1:890 000
Barbados 1:890 000

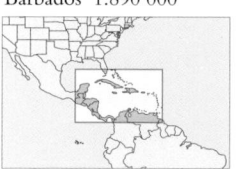
                                            120–121

SOUTH AMERICA

SOUTH AMERICA: PHYSICAL
1:31 100 000   **122**

SOUTH AMERICA: POLITICAL
1:31 100 000   **123**

SOUTH AMERICA – NORTH
1:14 200 000
Trinidad and Tobago 1:2 200 000

                                            124–125

CENTRAL SOUTH AMERICA
1:7 100 000

                                            126–127

SOUTH AMERICA – SOUTH
1:14 200 000

                                               128

INDEX TO WORLD MAPS
                                            129–224

World Statistics: Countries

This alphabetical list includes the principal countries and territories of the world. If a territory is not completely independent, the country it is associated with is named. The area figures give the total area of land, inland water and ice. The population figures are 2004 estimates where available. The annual income is the Gross Domestic Product per capita† in US dollars. The figures are the latest available, usually 2002 estimates.

Country/Territory	Area km² Thousands	Area miles² Thousands	Population Thousands	Capital	Annual Income US $
Afghanistan	652	252	28,514	Kabul	700
Albania	28.7	11.1	3,545	Tirana	4,400
Algeria	2,382	920	32,129	Algiers	5,400
American Samoa (US)	0.20	0.08	58	Pago Pago	8,000
Andorra	0.47	0.18	70	Andorra La Vella	19,000
Angola	1,247	481	10,979	Luanda	1,700
Anguilla (UK)	0.10	0.04	13	The Valley	8,600
Antigua & Barbuda	0.44	0.17	68	St John's	11,000
Argentina	2,780	1,074	39,145	Buenos Aires	10,500
Armenia	29.8	11.5	2,991	Yerevan	3,600
Aruba (Netherlands)	0.19	0.07	71	Oranjestad	28,000
Australia	7,741	2,989	19,913	Canberra	26,900
Austria	83.9	32.4	8,175	Vienna	27,900
Azerbaijan	86.6	33.4	7,868	Baku	3,700
Azores (Portugal)	2.2	0.86	236	Ponta Delgada	15,000
Bahamas	13.9	5.4	300	Nassau	15,300
Bahrain	0.69	0.27	678	Manama	15,100
Bangladesh	144	55.6	141,340	Dhaka	1,800
Barbados	0.43	0.17	278	Bridgetown	15,000
Belarus	208	80.2	10,311	Minsk	8,700
Belgium	30.5	11.8	10,348	Brussels	29,200
Belize	23.0	8.9	273	Belmopan	4,900
Benin	113	43.5	7,250	Porto-Novo	1,100
Bermuda (UK)	0.05	0.02	65	Hamilton	35,200
Bhutan	47.0	18.1	2,186	Thimphu	1,300
Bolivia	1,099	424	8,724	La Paz/Sucre	2,500
Bosnia-Herzegovina	51.2	19.8	4,008	Sarajevo	1,900
Botswana	582	225	1,562	Gaborone	8,500
Brazil	8,514	3,287	184,101	Brasília	7,600
Brunei	5.8	2.2	365	Bandar Seri Begawan	18,600
Bulgaria	111	42.8	7,518	Sofia	6,500
Burkina Faso	274	106	13,575	Ouagadougou	1,100
Burma (= Myanmar)	677	261	42,720	Rangoon	1,700
Burundi	27.8	10.7	6,231	Bujumbura	500
Cambodia	181	69.9	13,363	Phnom Penh	1,600
Cameroon	475	184	16,064	Yaoundé	1,700
Canada	9,971	3,850	32,508	Ottawa	29,300
Canary Is. (Spain)	7.2	2.8	1,682	Las Palmas/Santa Cruz	19,900
Cape Verde Is.	4.0	1.6	415	Praia	1,400
Cayman Is. (UK)	0.26	0.10	43	George Town	35,000
Central African Republic	623	241	3,742	Bangui	1,200
Chad	1,284	496	9,539	Ndjaména	1,000
Chile	757	292	15,824	Santiago	10,100
China	9,597	3,705	1,298,848	Beijing	4,700
Colombia	1,139	440	42,311	Bogotá	6,100
Comoros	2.2	0.86	652	Moroni	700
Congo	342	132	2,998	Brazzaville	900
Congo (Dem. Rep. of the)	2,345	905	58,318	Kinshasa	600
Cook Is. (NZ)	0.24	0.09	21	Avarua	5,000
Costa Rica	51.1	19.7	3,957	San José	8,300
Croatia	56.5	21.8	4,497	Zagreb	9,800
Cuba	111	42.8	11,309	Havana	2,700
Cyprus	9.3	3.6	776	Nicosia	13,200
Czech Republic	78.9	30.5	10,246	Prague	15,300
Denmark	43.1	16.6	5,413	Copenhagen	28,900
Djibouti	23.2	9.0	467	Djibouti	1,300
Dominica	0.75	0.29	69	Roseau	5,400
Dominican Republic	48.5	18.7	8,834	Santo Domingo	6,300
East Timor	14.9	5.7	1,019	Dili	500
Ecuador	284	109	13,213	Quito	3,200
Egypt	1,001	387	76,117	Cairo	4,000
El Salvador	21.0	8.1	6,588	San Salvador	4,600
Equatorial Guinea	28.1	10.8	523	Malabo	2,700
Eritrea	118	45.4	4,447	Asmara	700
Estonia	45.1	17.4	1,342	Tallinn	11,000
Ethiopia	1,104	426	67,851	Addis Ababa	700
Faroe Is. (Denmark)	1.4	0.54	47	Tórshavn	22,000
Fiji	18.3	7.1	881	Suva	5,600
Finland	338	131	5,215	Helsinki	25,800
France	552	213	60,424	Paris	26,000
French Guiana (France)	90.0	34.7	191	Cayenne	14,400
French Polynesia (France)	4.0	1.5	266	Papeete	5,000
Gabon	268	103	1,355	Libreville	6,500
Gambia, The	11.3	4.4	1,547	Banjul	1,800
Gaza Strip (OPT)*	0.36	0.14	1,325	–	600
Georgia	69.7	26.9	4,694	Tbilisi	3,200
Germany	357	138	82,425	Berlin	26,200
Ghana	239	92.1	20,757	Accra	2,000
Gibraltar (UK)	0.006	0.002	28	Gibraltar Town	17,500
Greece	132	50.9	10,648	Athens	19,100
Greenland (Denmark)	2,176	840	56	Nuuk (Godthåb)	20,000
Grenada	0.34	0.13	89	St George's	5,000
Guadeloupe (France)	1.7	0.66	445	Basse-Terre	9,000
Guam (US)	0.55	0.21	166	Agana	21,000
Guatemala	109	42.0	14,281	Guatemala City	3,900
Guinea	246	94.9	9,246	Conakry	2,100
Guinea-Bissau	36.1	13.9	1,388	Bissau	700
Guyana	215	83.0	706	Georgetown	3,800
Haiti	27.8	10.7	7,656	Port-au-Prince	1,400
Honduras	112	43.3	6,824	Tegucigalpa	2,500
Hong Kong (China)	1.1	0.42	6,855	–	27,200
Hungary	93.0	35.9	10,032	Budapest	13,300
Iceland	103	39.8	294	Reykjavik	30,200
India	3,287	1,269	1,065,071	New Delhi	2,600
Indonesia	1,905	735	238,453	Jakarta	3,100
Iran	1,648	636	69,019	Tehran	6,800
Iraq	438	169	25,375	Baghdad	2,400
Ireland	70.3	27.1	3,970	Dublin	29,300
Israel	20.6	8.0	6,199	Jerusalem	19,500
Italy	301	116	58,057	Rome	25,100
Ivory Coast (= Côte d'Ivoire)	322	125	17,328	Yamoussoukro	1,400
Jamaica	11.0	4.2	2,713	Kingston	3,800
Japan	378	146	127,333	Tokyo	28,700
Jordan	89.3	34.5	5,611	Amman	4,300
Kazakhstan	2,725	1,052	15,144	Astana	7,200
Kenya	580	224	32,022	Nairobi	1,100
Kiribati	0.73	0.28	101	Tarawa	800
Korea, North	121	46.5	22,698	Pyŏngyang	1,000
Korea, South	99.3	38.3	48,598	Seoul	19,600
Kuwait	17.8	6.9	2,258	Kuwait City	17,500
Kyrgyzstan	200	77.2	5,081	Bishkek	2,900
Laos	237	91.4	6,068	Vientiane	1,800
Latvia	64.6	24.9	2,306	Riga	8,900
Lebanon	10.4	4.0	3,777	Beirut	4,800
Lesotho	30.4	11.7	1,865	Maseru	2,700
Liberia	111	43.0	3,391	Monrovia	1,000
Libya	1,760	679	5,632	Tripoli	6,200
Liechtenstein	0.16	0.06	33	Vaduz	25,000
Lithuania	65.2	25.2	3,608	Vilnius	8,400
Luxembourg	2.6	1.0	463	Luxembourg	48,900
Macau (China)	0.02	0.007	445	–	18,500
Macedonia (FYROM)	25.7	9.9	2,071	Skopje	5,100
Madagascar	587	227	17,502	Antananarivo	800
Madeira (Portugal)	0.78	0.30	241	Funchal	22,700
Malawi	118	45.7	11,907	Lilongwe	600
Malaysia	330	127	23,522	Kuala Lumpur/Putrajaya	8,800
Maldives	0.30	0.12	339	Malé	3,900
Mali	1,240	479	11,957	Bamako	900
Malta	0.32	0.12	397	Valletta	17,200
Marshall Is.	0.18	0.07	58	Majuro	1,600
Martinique (France)	1.1	0.43	430	Fort-de-France	10,700
Mauritania	1,026	396	2,999	Nouakchott	1,700
Mauritius	2.0	0.79	1,220	Port Louis	10,100
Mayotte (France)	0.37	0.14	186	Mamoundzou	600
Mexico	1,958	756	104,960	Mexico City	8,900
Micronesia, Fed. States of	0.70	0.27	108	Palikir	2,000
Moldova	33.9	13.1	4,446	Chişinău	2,600
Monaco	0.001	0.0004	32	Monaco	27,000
Mongolia	1,567	605	2,751	Ulan Bator	1,900
Montserrat (UK)	0.10	0.04	9	Plymouth	3,400
Morocco	447	172	32,209	Rabat	3,900
Mozambique	802	309	18,812	Maputo	1,100
Namibia	824	318	1,954	Windhoek	6,900
Nauru	0.02	0.008	13	Yaren District	5,000
Nepal	147	56.8	27,071	Katmandu	1,400
Netherlands	41.5	16.0	16,318	Amsterdam/The Hague	27,200
Netherlands Antilles (Neths)	0.80	0.31	218	Willemstad	11,400
New Caledonia (France)	18.6	7.2	214	Nouméa	14,000
New Zealand	271	104	3,994	Wellington	20,100
Nicaragua	130	50.2	5,360	Managua	2,200
Niger	1,267	489	11,361	Niamey	800
Nigeria	924	357	137,253	Abuja	900
Northern Mariana Is. (US)	0.46	0.18	78	Saipan	12,500
Norway	324	125	4,575	Oslo	33,000
Oman	310	119	2,903	Muscat	8,300
Pakistan	796	307	159,196	Islamabad	2,000
Palau	0.46	0.18	20	Koror	9,000
Panama	75.5	29.2	3,000	Panamá	6,200
Papua New Guinea	463	179	5,420	Port Moresby	2,100
Paraguay	407	157	6,191	Asunción	4,300
Peru	1,285	496	27,544	Lima	5,000
Philippines	300	116	86,242	Manila	4,600
Poland	323	125	38,626	Warsaw	9,700
Portugal	88.8	34.3	10,524	Lisbon	19,400
Puerto Rico (US)	8.9	3.4	3,898	San Juan	11,100
Qatar	11.0	4.2	840	Doha	20,100
Réunion (France)	2.5	0.97	766	St-Denis	5,600
Romania	238	92.0	22,356	Bucharest	7,600
Russia	17,075	6,593	143,782	Moscow	9,700
Rwanda	26.3	10.2	7,954	Kigali	1,200
St Kitts & Nevis	0.26	0.10	39	Basseterre	8,800
St Lucia	0.54	0.21	164	Castries	5,400
St Vincent & Grenadines	0.39	0.15	117	Kingstown	2,900
Samoa	2.8	1.1	178	Apia	5,600
San Marino	0.06	0.02	29	San Marino	34,600
São Tomé & Príncipe	0.96	0.37	182	São Tomé	1,200
Saudi Arabia	2,150	830	25,796	Riyadh	11,400
Senegal	197	76.0	10,852	Dakar	1,500
Serbia & Montenegro	102	39.4	10,826	Belgrade	2,200
Seychelles	0.46	0.18	81	Victoria	7,800
Sierra Leone	71.7	27.7	5,884	Freetown	500
Singapore	0.68	0.26	4,354	Singapore City	25,200
Slovak Republic	49.0	18.9	5,424	Bratislava	12,400
Slovenia	20.3	7.8	2,011	Ljubljana	19,200
Solomon Is.	28.9	11.2	524	Honiara	1,700
Somalia	638	246	8,305	Mogadishu	600
South Africa	1,221	471	42,719	C. Town/Pretoria/Bloem.	10,000
Spain	498	192	40,281	Madrid	21,200
Sri Lanka	65.6	25.3	19,905	Colombo	3,700
Sudan	2,506	967	39,148	Khartoum	1,400
Suriname	163	63.0	437	Paramaribo	3,400
Swaziland	17.4	6.7	1,169	Mbabane	4,800
Sweden	450	174	8,986	Stockholm	26,000
Switzerland	41.3	15.9	7,451	Bern	32,000
Syria	185	71.5	18,017	Damascus	3,700
Taiwan	36.0	13.9	22,750	Taipei	18,000
Tajikistan	143	55.3	7,012	Dushanbe	1,300
Tanzania	945	365	36,588	Dodoma	600
Thailand	513	198	64,866	Bangkok	7,000
Togo	56.8	21.9	5,557	Lomé	1,400
Tonga	0.65	0.25	110	Nuku'alofa	2,200
Trinidad & Tobago	5.1	2.0	1,097	Port of Spain	10,000
Tunisia	164	63.2	9,975	Tunis	6,800
Turkey	775	299	68,894	Ankara	7,300
Turkmenistan	488	188	4,863	Ashkhabad	6,700
Turks & Caicos Is. (UK)	0.43	0.17	20	Cockburn Town	9,600
Tuvalu	0.03	0.01	11	Fongafale	1,100
Uganda	241	93.1	26,405	Kampala	1,200
Ukraine	604	233	47,732	Kiev	4,500
United Arab Emirates	83.6	32.3	2,524	Abu Dhabi	22,100
United Kingdom	242	93.4	60,271	London	25,500
United States of America	9,629	3,718	293,028	Washington, DC	36,300
Uruguay	175	67.6	3,399	Montevideo	7,900
Uzbekistan	447	173	26,410	Tashkent	2,600
Vanuatu	12.2	4.7	203	Port-Vila	2,900
Vatican City	0.0004	0.0002	1	Vatican City	N/A
Venezuela	912	352	25,017	Caracas	5,400
Vietnam	332	128	82,690	Hanoi	2,300
Virgin Is. (UK)	0.15	0.06	22	Road Town	16,000
Virgin Is. (US)	0.35	0.13	109	Charlotte Amalie	19,000
Wallis & Futuna Is. (France)	0.20	0.08	16	Mata-Utu	2,000
West Bank (OPT)*	5.9	2.3	2,311	–	800
Western Sahara	266	103	267	El Aaiún	N/A
Yemen	528	204	20,025	Sana'	800
Zambia	753	291	10,462	Lusaka	800
Zimbabwe	391	151	12,672	Harare	2,100

*OPT = Occupied Palestinian Territory   N/A = Not available

† Gross Domestic Product per capita has been measured using the purchasing power parity method. This enables comparisons to be made between countries through their purchasing power (in US dollars), showing real price levels of goods and services rather than using currency exchange rates.

World Statistics: Cities

This list shows the principal cities with more than 750,000 inhabitants. The figures are taken from the most recent census or estimate available, usually 2000, and as far as possible are the population of the metropolitan area or urban agglomeration (for example, greater New York, Mexico or Paris). All the figures are in thousands. Local name forms have been used for the smaller cities (for example, Thessaloniki).

City	Population
AFGHANISTAN	
Kabul	2,602
ALGERIA	
Algiers	1,722
ANGOLA	
Luanda	2,697
ARGENTINA	
Buenos Aires	12,024
Córdoba	1,368
Rosario	1,279
Mendoza	934
San Miguel de Tucumán	792
ARMENIA	
Yerevan	1,407
AUSTRALIA	
Sydney	4,086
Melbourne	3,466
Brisbane	1,627
Perth	1,381
Adelaide	1,096
AUSTRIA	
Vienna	1,807
AZERBAIJAN	
Baku	1,792
BANGLADESH	
Dhaka	12,519
Chittagong	3,651
Khulna	1,442
Rajshahi	1,035
BELARUS	
Minsk	1,717
BELGIUM	
Brussels	964
BOLIVIA	
La Paz	1,487
Santa Cruz	1,035
Cochabamba	797
BRAZIL	
São Paulo	17,962
Rio de Janeiro	10,652
Belo Horizonte	4,224
Pôrto Alegre	3,757
Recife	3,346
Salvador	3,238
Fortaleza	3,066
Curitiba	2,562
Brasília	2,051
Belém	1,658
Manaus	1,467
Campinas	1,434
Santos	1,270
Goiânia	1,117
São José dos Campos	972
São Luís	968
Maceió	886
Teresina	848
Campo Grande	821
Natal	806
BULGARIA	
Sofia	1,187
BURKINA FASO	
Ouagadougou	831
BURMA (MYANMAR)	
Rangoon	4,393
Mandalay	770
CAMBODIA	
Phnom Penh	1,070
CAMEROON	
Douala	1,642
Yaoundé	1,420
CANADA	
Toronto	4,881
Montréal	3,511
Vancouver	2,079
Ottawa	1,107
Calgary	972
Edmonton	957
CHILE	
Santiago	5,467
CHINA	
Shanghai	12,887
Beijing	10,839
Tianjin	9,156
Hong Kong	6,860
Wuhan	5,169
Chongqing	4,900
Shenyang	4,828
Guangzhou	3,893
Chengdu	3,294
Xi'an	3,123
Changchun	3,093
Harbin	2,928
Nanjing	2,740
Zibo	2,675
Dalian	2,628
Jinan	2,568
Guiyang	2,533
Linyi	2,498
Taiyuan	2,415
Qingdao	2,316
Zhengzhou	2,070
Zaozhuang	2,048
Liupanshui	2,023
Handan	1,996
Jinxi	1,821
Lu'an	1,818
Hangzhou	1,780
Tianmen	1,779
Changsha	1,775
Wanxian	1,759
Lanzhou	1,730
Nanchang	1,722
Kunming	1,701
Yantai	1,681
Tangshan	1,671
Xuzhou	1,636
Xiantao	1,614
Shijiazhuang	1,603
Heze	1,600
Yancheng	1,562
Yulin	1,558
Xinghua	1,556
Tai'an	1,503
Pingxiang	1,502
Anshan	1,453
Luoyang	1,451
Jilin	1,435
Qiqihar	1,435
Suining, Sichuan	1,428
Ürümqi	1,415
Fushun	1,413
Fuzhou	1,397
Neijiang	1,393
Changde	1,374
Zhanjiang	1,368
Huainan	1,354
Yiyang	1,343
Xintai	1,325
Baotou	1,319
Dongguan	1,319
Nanning	1,311
Weifang	1,287
Wenzhou	1,269
Hefei	1,242
Huaian	1,232
Yueyang	1,213
Suqian	1,189
Tianshui	1,187
Suzhou	1,183
Shantou	1,176
Ningbo	1,173
Yuzhou	1,173
Datong	1,165
Jingmen	1,153
Leshan	1,137
Shenzhen	1,131
Wuxi	1,127
Xiaoshan	1,124
Zaoyang	1,121
Yixing	1,108
Yongzhou	1,097
Chifeng	1,087
Huzhou	1,077
Daqing	1,076
Zigong	1,072
Mianyang	1,065
Nanchong	1,055
Fuyu	1,025
Jining, Shandong	1,019
Hohhot	978
Xinyi, Guangdong	973
Benxi	957
Jixi	949
Liuzhou	928
Xiangxiang	908
Yichun, Heilongjiang	904
Xianyang	896
Linqing	891
Changzhou	886
Zhangjiagang	886
Zhangjiakou	880
Jiamusi	874
Yichun, Jiangxi	871
Zhaotong	851
Yuyao	848
Jinzhou	834
Xuanzhou	823
Huaibei	814
Xinyu	808
Mudanjiang	801
Hengyang	799
Jiaxing	791
Anshun	789
Fuxin	785
Tongliao	785
Hunjiang	772
Kaifeng	769
COLOMBIA	
Bogotá	6,771
Medellín	2,866
Cali	2,233
Barranquilla	1,683
Bucaramanga	937
Cartagena	845
Cúcuta	772
CONGO	
Brazzaville	1,306
CONGO (DEMOCRATIC REPUBLIC OF THE)	
Kinshasa	5,054
Lubumbashi	965
Mbuji-Mayi	806
COSTA RICA	
San José	961
CROATIA	
Zagreb	1,067
CUBA	
Havana	2,256
CZECH REPUBLIC	
Prague	1,203
DENMARK	
Copenhagen	1,332
DOMINICAN REPUBLIC	
Santo Domingo	2,563
Santiago de los Caballeros	804
ECUADOR	
Guayaquil	2,118
Quito	1,616
EGYPT	
Cairo	9,462
Alexandria	3,506
Shubrâ el Kheima	937
EL SALVADOR	
San Salvador	1,341
ETHIOPIA	
Addis Ababa	2,645
FINLAND	
Helsinki	937
FRANCE	
Paris	9,630
Lyons	1,353
Marseilles	1,290
Lille	991
Nice	889
Toulouse	761
Bordeaux	754
GEORGIA	
Tbilisi	1,406
GERMANY	
Berlin	3,387
Hamburg	1,705
Munich	1,195
Cologne	963
GHANA	
Accra	1,868
GREECE	
Athens	3,116
Thessaloniki	789
GUATEMALA	
Guatemala City	3,242
GUINEA	
Conakry	1,232
HAITI	
Port-au-Prince	1,769
HONDURAS	
Tegucigalpa	949
HUNGARY	
Budapest	1,819
INDIA	
Mumbai	16,086
Kolkata	13,058
Delhi	12,441
Chennai	6,353
Bangalore	5,567
Hyderabad	5,445
Ahmedabad	4,427
Pune	3,655
Surat	2,699
Kanpur	2,641
Jaipur	2,259
Lucknow	2,221
Nagpur	2,089
Patna	1,658
Indore	1,597
Vadodara	1,465
Bhopal	1,425
Coimbatore	1,420
Ludhiana	1,368
Cochin	1,340
Visakhapatnam	1,309
Agra	1,293
Varanasi	1,199
Madurai	1,187
Meerut	1,143
Nashik	1,117
Jabalpur	1,100
Jamshedpur	1,081
Asansol	1,065
Bhilainagar-Durg	1,049
Dhanbad	1,046
Allahabad	1,035
Faridabad	1,018
Vijayawada	999
Rajkot	974
Amritsar	955
Srinagar	954
Ghaziabad	928
Trivandrum	885
Calicut	875
Aurangabad	868
Gwalior	855
Solapur	853
Ranchi	844
Tiruchchirapalli	837
Jodhpur	833
Guwahati	797
Chandigarh	791
Hubli-Dharwad	776
Mysore	776
INDONESIA	
Jakarta	11,018
Bandung	3,409
Surabaya	2,461
Medan	1,879
Palembang	1,422
Ujung Pandang	1,051
Bandar Lampung	915
Malang	787
Semarang	787
Tegal	762
Bogor	761
IRAN	
Tehran	6,979
Mashhad	1,990
Esfahan	1,381
Tabriz	1,274
Karaj	1,200
Shiraz	1,124
Qom	888
Ahvaz	871
Bakhtaran	771
IRAQ	
Baghdad	4,865
Basra	1,338
Mosul	1,131
Irbil	840
IRELAND	
Dublin	985
ISRAEL	
Tel Aviv-Yafo	2,001
ITALY	
Rome	2,649
Milan	1,183
Naples	993
Turin	857
IVORY COAST (CÔTE D'IVOIRE)	
Abidjan	3,790
JAPAN	
Tokyo	12,064
Yokohama	6,427
Osaka	2,599
Nagoya	2,172
Sapporo	1,922
Kobe	1,493
Kyoto	1,468
Fukuoka	1,341
Kawasaki	1,250
Hiroshima	1,126
Kitakyushu	1,011
Sendai	1,008
Chiba	887
Sakai	792
JORDAN	
Amman	1,148
KAZAKHSTAN	
Almaty	1,130
KENYA	
Nairobi	2,233
KOREA, NORTH	
Pyŏngyang	3,124
Hamhung	821
KOREA, SOUTH	
Seoul	9,888
Pusan	3,830
Inch'on	2,884
Taegu	2,675
Taejŏn	1,522
Kwangju	1,379
Sŏngnam	1,353
Ulsan	1,340
Ansan	984
Puch'on	900
Suwŏn	876
P'ohang	790
KUWAIT	
Kuwait City	879
LATVIA	
Riga	811
LEBANON	
Beirut	2,070
LIBYA	
Tripoli	1,733
Benghazi	829
MADAGASCAR	
Antananarivo	1,603
MALAYSIA	
Kuala Lumpur	1,379
MALI	
Bamako	1,114
MEXICO	
Mexico City	18,066
Guadalajara	3,697
Monterrey	3,267
Puebla	1,888
Toluca	1,455
Tijuana	1,297
León	1,293
Ciudad Juárez	1,239
Torreón	1,012
San Luis Potosí	857
Mérida	849
Querétaro	798
Mexicali	771
Culiacán	750
MONGOLIA	
Ulan Bator	764
MOROCCO	
Casablanca	3,357
Rabat	1,616
Fès	907
Marrakesh	822
MOZAMBIQUE	
Maputo	1,094
NEPAL	
Katmandu	1,176
NETHERLANDS	
Amsterdam	1,105
Rotterdam	1,078
NEW ZEALAND	
Auckland	1,102
NICARAGUA	
Managua	1,009
NIGER	
Niamey	775
NIGERIA	
Lagos	8,665
Ibadan	1,549
Ogbomosho	809
NORWAY	
Oslo	779
PAKISTAN	
Karachi	10,032
Lahore	5,452
Faisalabad	2,142
Rawalpindi	1,521
Gujranwala	1,325
Multan	1,263
Hyderabad	1,221
Peshawar	1,066
Islamabad	791
PANAMA	
Panamá	1,173
PARAGUAY	
Asunción	1,262
PERU	
Lima	7,443
PHILIPPINES	
Manila	9,950
Davao	1,146
POLAND	
Warsaw	1,626
Lódz	815
PORTUGAL	
Lisbon	3,861
Porto	1,940
PUERTO RICO	
San Juan	2,217
ROMANIA	
Bucharest	2,001
RUSSIA	
Moscow	8,367
Saint Petersburg	4,635
Nizhniy Novgorod	1,332
Novosibirsk	1,321
Yekaterinburg	1,218
Omsk	1,174
Samara	1,132
Ufa	1,102
Kazan	1,063
Chelyabinsk	1,045
Perm	1,014
Rostov	1,012
Volgograd	1,000
Voronezh	918
Saratov	881
Simbirsk	864
Krasnoyarsk	840
Togliatti	771
SAUDI ARABIA	
Riyadh	3,180
Jedda	1,490
Mecca	770
SENEGAL	
Dakar	2,078
SERBIA & MONTENEGRO	
Belgrade	1,673
SIERRA LEONE	
Freetown	822
SINGAPORE	
Singapore City	4,131
SOMALIA	
Mogadishu	1,162
SOUTH AFRICA	
Johannesburg	2,950
Cape Town	2,930
Durban / eThekwini	2,391
Pretoria / Tshwane	1,590
Port Elizabeth	1,006
SPAIN	
Madrid	3,017
Barcelona	1,527
SUDAN	
Khartoum	2,742
SWEDEN	
Stockholm	1,612
Gothenburg	778
SWITZERLAND	
Zürich	939
SYRIA	
Aleppo	2,229
Damascus	2,144
Homs	811
TAIWAN	
Taipei	2,550
Kaohsiung	1,463
T'aichung	950
TANZANIA	
Dar es Salaam	2,115
THAILAND	
Bangkok	7,372
TUNISIA	
Tunis	1,892
TURKEY	
Istanbul	8,953
Ankara	3,203
Izmir	2,250
Bursa	1,184
Adana	1,133
Gaziantep	862
Konya	761
UGANDA	
Kampala	1,213
UKRAINE	
Kiev	2,621
Kharkov	1,521
Dnepropetrovsk	1,122
Donetsk	1,065
Odessa	1,027
Zaporozhye	863
Lvov	794
UNITED ARAB EMIRATES	
Abu Dhabi	928
Dubai	886
UNITED KINGDOM	
London	8,089
Birmingham	2,373
Manchester	2,353
Liverpool	852
Glasgow	832
UNITED STATES OF AMERICA	
New York	17,800
Los Angeles	11,789
Chicago	8,308
Philadelphia	5,149
Miami	4,919
Dallas–Fort Worth	4,146
Boston	4,032
Washington	3,934
Detroit	3,903
Houston	3,823
Atlanta	3,500
San Francisco	3,229
Phoenix	2,907
Seattle	2,712
San Diego	2,674
Minneapolis–St Paul	2,389
St Louis	2,078
Baltimore	2,076
Tampa–St Petersburg	2,062
Denver	1,985
Cleveland	1,787
Pittsburgh	1,753
Portland	1,583
San Jose	1,538
San Bernardino	1,507
Cincinnati	1,503
Norfolk–Virginia Beach	1,394
Sacramento	1,393
Kansas City	1,362
San Antonio	1,328
Las Vegas	1,314
Milwaukee	1,309
Indianapolis	1,219
Providence	1,175
Orlando	1,157
Columbus	1,133
New Orleans	1,009
Buffalo	977
Memphis	972
Austin	902
Stamford	889
Salt Lake City	888
Jacksonville	882
Louisville	864
Hartford	852
Richmond	819
Charlotte	759
URUGUAY	
Montevideo	1,324
UZBEKISTAN	
Tashkent	2,148
VENEZUELA	
Caracas	3,153
Maracaibo	1,901
Valencia	1,893
Maracay	1,100
Ciudad Guayana	966
Barquisimeto	923
VIETNAM	
Ho Chi Minh City	4,619
Hanoi	3,751
Haiphong	1,676
YEMEN	
Sana'	1,327
ZAMBIA	
Lusaka	1,653
ZIMBABWE	
Harare	1,791
Bulawayo	824

WORLD STATISTICS: CLIMATE

Rainfall and temperature figures are provided for more than 70 cities around the world. As climate is affected by altitude, the height of each city is shown in metres beneath its name. For each location, the top row of figures shows the total rainfall or snow in millimetres, and the bottom row the average temperature in degrees Celsius; the average annual temperature and total annual rainfall are at the end of the rows. The map opposite shows the city locations.

CITY	JAN.	FEB.	MAR.	APR.	MAY	JUNE	JULY	AUG.	SEPT.	OCT.	NOV.	DEC.	YEAR
EUROPE													
Athens, Greece	62	37	37	23	23	14	6	7	15	51	56	71	402
107 m	10	10	12	16	20	25	28	28	24	20	15	11	18
Berlin, Germany	46	40	33	42	49	65	73	69	48	49	46	43	603
55 m	−1	0	4	9	14	17	19	18	15	9	5	1	9
Istanbul, Turkey	109	92	72	46	38	34	34	30	58	81	103	119	816
14 m	5	6	7	11	16	20	23	23	20	16	12	8	14
Lisbon, Portugal	111	76	109	54	44	16	3	4	33	62	93	103	708
77 m	11	12	14	16	17	20	22	23	21	18	14	12	17
London, UK	54	40	37	37	46	45	57	59	49	57	64	48	593
5 m	4	5	7	9	12	16	18	17	15	11	8	5	11
Málaga, Spain	61	51	62	46	26	5	1	3	29	64	64	62	474
33 m	12	13	16	17	19	29	25	26	23	20	16	13	18
Moscow, Russia	39	38	36	37	53	58	88	71	58	45	47	54	624
156 m	−13	−10	−4	6	13	16	18	17	12	6	−1	−7	4
Odesa, Ukraine	57	62	30	21	34	34	42	37	37	13	35	71	473
64 m	−3	−1	2	9	15	20	22	22	18	12	9	1	10
Paris, France	56	46	35	42	57	54	59	64	55	50	51	50	619
75 m	3	4	8	11	15	18	20	19	17	12	7	4	12
Rome, Italy	71	62	57	51	46	37	15	21	63	99	129	93	744
17 m	8	9	11	14	18	22	25	25	22	17	13	10	16
Shannon, Ireland	94	67	56	53	61	57	77	79	86	86	96	117	929
2 m	5	5	7	9	12	14	16	16	14	11	8	6	10
Stockholm, Sweden	43	30	25	31	34	45	61	76	60	48	53	48	554
44 m	−3	−3	−1	5	10	15	18	17	12	7	3	0	7
ASIA													
Bahrain	8	18	13	8	<3	0	0	0	0	0	18	18	81
5 m	17	18	21	25	29	32	33	34	31	28	24	19	26
Bangkok, Thailand	8	20	36	58	198	160	160	175	305	206	66	5	1,397
2 m	26	28	29	30	29	29	28	28	28	28	26	25	28
Beirut, Lebanon	191	158	94	53	18	3	<3	<3	5	51	132	185	892
34 m	14	14	16	18	22	24	27	28	26	24	19	16	21
Colombo, Sri Lanka	89	69	147	231	371	224	135	109	160	348	315	147	2,365
7 m	26	26	27	28	28	27	27	27	27	27	26	26	27
Harbin, China	6	5	10	23	43	94	112	104	46	33	8	5	488
160 m	−18	−15	−5	6	13	19	22	21	14	4	−6	−16	3
Ho Chi Minh, Vietnam	15	3	13	43	221	330	315	269	335	269	114	56	1,984
9 m	26	27	29	30	29	28	28	28	27	27	27	26	28
Hong Kong, China	33	46	74	137	292	394	381	361	257	114	43	31	2,162
33 m	16	15	18	22	26	28	28	28	27	25	21	18	23

CITY	JAN.	FEB.	MAR.	APR.	MAY	JUNE	JULY	AUG.	SEPT.	OCT.	NOV.	DEC.	YEAR
ASIA (continued)													
Jakarta, Indonesia	300	300	211	147	114	97	64	43	66	112	142	203	1,798
8 m	26	26	27	27	27	27	27	27	27	27	27	26	27
Kabul, Afghanistan	31	36	94	102	20	5	3	3	<3	15	20	10	338
1,815 m	−3	−1	6	13	18	22	25	24	20	14	7	3	12
Karachi, Pakistan	13	10	8	3	3	18	81	41	13	<3	3	5	196
4 m	19	20	24	28	30	31	30	29	28	28	24	20	26
Kazalinsk, Kazakhstan	10	10	13	13	15	5	5	8	8	10	13	15	125
63 m	−12	−11	−3	6	18	23	25	23	16	8	−1	−7	7
Kolkata (Calcutta), India	10	31	36	43	140	297	325	328	252	114	20	5	1,600
6 m	20	22	27	30	30	30	29	29	29	28	23	19	26
Mumbai (Bombay), India	3	3	3	<3	18	485	617	340	264	64	13	3	1,809
11 m	24	24	26	28	30	29	27	27	27	28	27	26	27
New Delhi, India	23	18	13	8	13	74	180	172	117	10	3	10	640
218 m	14	17	23	28	33	34	31	30	29	26	20	15	25
Omsk, Russia	15	8	8	13	31	51	51	51	28	25	18	20	318
85 m	−22	−19	−12	−1	10	16	18	16	10	1	−11	−18	−1
Shanghai, China	48	58	84	94	94	180	147	142	130	71	51	36	1,135
7 m	4	5	9	14	20	24	28	28	23	19	12	7	16
Singapore	252	173	193	188	173	173	170	196	178	208	254	257	2,413
10 m	26	27	28	28	28	28	28	27	27	27	27	27	27
Tehran, Iran	46	38	46	36	13	3	3	3	3	8	20	31	246
1,220 m	2	5	9	16	21	26	30	29	25	18	12	6	17
Tokyo, Japan	48	74	107	135	147	165	142	152	234	208	97	56	1,565
6 m	3	4	7	13	17	21	25	26	23	17	11	6	14
Ulan Bator, Mongolia	<3	<3	3	5	10	28	76	51	23	5	5	3	208
1,325 m	−26	−21	−13	−1	6	14	16	14	8	−1	−13	−22	−3
Verkhoyansk, Russia	5	5	3	5	8	23	28	25	13	8	8	5	134
100 m	−50	−45	−32	−15	0	12	14	9	2	−15	−38	−48	−17
AFRICA													
Addis Ababa, Ethiopia	<3	3	25	135	213	201	206	239	102	28	<3	0	1,151
2,450 m	19	20	20	20	19	18	18	19	21	22	21	20	20
Antananarivo, Madag.	300	279	178	53	18	8	8	10	18	61	135	287	1,356
1,372 m	21	21	21	19	18	15	14	15	17	19	21	21	19
Cairo, Egypt	5	5	5	3	3	<3	0	0	<3	<3	3	5	28
116 m	13	15	18	21	25	28	28	28	26	24	20	15	22
Cape Town, S. Africa	15	8	18	48	79	84	89	66	43	31	18	10	508
17 m	21	21	20	17	14	13	12	13	14	16	18	19	17
Jo'burg, S. Africa	114	109	89	38	25	8	8	8	23	56	107	125	709
1,665 m	20	20	18	16	13	10	11	13	16	18	19	20	16

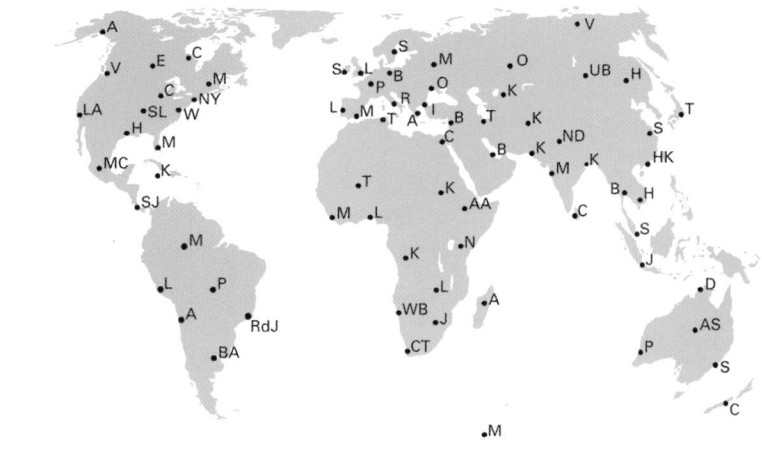

CITY	JAN.	FEB.	MAR.	APR.	MAY	JUNE	JULY	AUG.	SEPT.	OCT.	NOV.	DEC.	YEAR
AFRICA (continued)													
Khartoum, Sudan	<3	<3	<3	<3	3	8	53	71	18	5	<3	0	158
390 m	24	25	28	31	33	34	32	31	32	32	28	25	29
Kinshasa, Congo (D.R.)	135	145	196	196	158	8	3	3	31	119	221	142	1,354
325 m	26	26	27	27	26	24	23	24	25	26	26	26	25
Lagos, Nigeria	28	46	102	150	269	460	279	64	140	206	69	25	1,836
3 m	27	28	29	28	28	26	26	25	26	26	28	28	27
Lusaka, Zambia	231	191	142	18	3	<3	<3	0	<3	10	91	150	836
1,277 m	21	22	21	21	19	16	16	18	22	24	23	22	21
Monrovia, Liberia	31	56	97	216	516	973	996	373	744	772	236	130	5,138
23 m	26	26	27	27	26	25	24	25	25	25	26	26	26
Nairobi, Kenya	38	64	125	211	158	46	15	23	31	53	109	86	958
820 m	19	19	19	19	18	16	16	16	18	19	18	18	18
Timbuktu, Mali	<3	<3	3	<3	5	23	79	81	38	3	<3	<3	231
301 m	22	24	28	32	34	35	32	30	32	31	28	23	29
Tunis, Tunisia	64	51	41	36	18	8	3	8	33	51	48	61	419
66 m	10	11	13	16	19	23	26	27	25	20	16	11	18
Walvis Bay, Namibia	<3	5	8	3	3	<3	<3	3	<3	<3	<3	<3	23
7 m	19	19	19	18	17	16	15	14	14	15	17	18	18
AUSTRALIA, NEW ZEALAND AND ANTARCTICA													
Alice Springs, Aust.	43	33	28	10	15	13	8	8	8	18	31	38	252
579 m	29	28	25	20	15	12	12	14	18	23	26	28	21
Christchurch, N.Z.	56	43	48	48	66	66	69	48	46	43	48	56	638
10 m	16	16	14	12	9	6	6	7	9	12	14	16	11
Darwin, Australia	386	312	254	97	15	3	<3	3	13	51	119	239	1,491
30 m	29	29	29	29	28	26	25	26	28	29	30	29	28
Mawson, Antarctica	11	30	20	10	44	180	4	40	3	20	0	0	362
14 m	0	−5	−10	−14	−15	−16	−18	−18	−19	−13	−5	−1	−11
Perth, Australia	8	10	20	43	130	180	170	149	86	56	20	13	881
60 m	23	23	22	19	16	14	13	13	15	16	19	22	18
Sydney, Australia	89	102	127	135	127	117	117	76	73	71	73	73	1,181
42 m	22	22	21	18	15	13	12	13	15	18	19	21	17
NORTH AMERICA													
Anchorage, USA	20	18	15	10	13	18	41	66	66	56	25	23	371
40 m	−11	−8	−5	2	7	12	14	13	9	2	−5	−11	2
Chicago, USA	51	51	66	71	86	89	84	81	79	66	61	51	836
251 m	−4	−3	2	9	14	20	23	22	19	12	5	−1	10
Churchill, Canada	15	13	18	23	32	44	46	58	51	43	39	21	402
13 m	−28	−26	−20	−10	−2	6	12	11	5	−2	−12	−22	−7
Edmonton, Canada	25	19	19	22	43	77	89	78	39	17	16	25	466
676 m	−15	−10	−5	4	11	15	17	16	11	6	−4	−10	3
Honolulu, USA	104	66	79	48	25	18	23	28	36	48	64	104	643
12 m	23	18	19	20	22	24	25	26	26	24	22	19	22
Houston, USA	89	76	84	91	119	117	99	99	104	94	89	109	1,171
12 m	12	13	17	21	24	27	28	29	26	22	16	12	21

CITY	JAN.	FEB.	MAR.	APR.	MAY	JUNE	JULY	AUG.	SEPT.	OCT.	NOV.	DEC.	YEAR
NORTH AMERICA (continued)													
Kingston, Jamaica	23	15	23	31	102	89	38	91	99	180	74	36	800
34 m	25	25	25	26	26	28	28	28	27	27	26	26	26
Los Angeles, USA	79	76	71	25	10	3	<3	<3	5	15	31	66	381
95 m	13	14	14	16	17	19	21	22	21	18	16	14	17
Mexico City, Mexico	13	5	10	20	53	119	170	152	130	51	18	8	747
2,309 m	12	13	16	18	19	19	17	18	18	16	14	13	16
Miami, USA	71	53	64	81	173	178	155	160	203	234	71	51	1,516
8 m	20	20	22	23	25	27	28	28	27	25	22	21	24
Montréal, Canada	72	65	74	74	66	82	90	92	88	76	81	87	946
57 m	−10	−9	−3	−6	13	18	21	20	15	9	2	−7	6
New York City, USA	94	97	91	81	81	84	107	109	86	89	76	91	1,092
96 m	−1	−1	3	10	16	20	23	23	21	15	7	2	11
St Louis, USA	58	64	89	97	114	114	89	86	81	74	71	64	1,001
173 m	0	1	7	13	19	24	26	26	22	15	8	2	14
San José, Costa Rica	15	5	20	46	229	241	211	241	305	300	145	41	1,798
1,146 m	19	19	21	21	22	21	21	21	21	20	20	19	20
Vancouver, Canada	154	115	101	60	52	45	32	41	67	114	150	182	1,113
14 m	3	5	6	9	12	15	17	17	14	10	6	4	10
Washington, DC, USA	86	76	91	84	94	99	112	109	94	74	66	79	1,064
22 m	1	2	7	12	18	23	25	24	20	14	8	3	13
SOUTH AMERICA													
Antofagasta, Chile	0	0	0	<3	<3	3	5	3	<3	3	<3	0	13
94 m	21	21	20	18	16	15	14	14	15	16	18	19	17
Buenos Aires, Arg.	79	71	109	89	76	61	56	61	79	86	84	99	950
27 m	23	23	21	17	13	9	10	11	13	15	19	22	16
Lima, Peru	3	<3	<3	<3	5	5	8	8	8	3	3	<3	41
120 m	23	24	24	22	19	17	17	16	17	18	19	21	20
Manaus, Brazil	249	231	262	221	170	84	58	38	46	107	142	203	1,811
44 m	28	28	28	27	28	28	28	29	29	29	29	28	28
Paraná, Brazil	287	236	239	102	13	<3	3	5	28	127	231	310	1,582
260 m	23	23	23	23	23	21	21	22	24	24	24	23	23
Rio de Janeiro, Brazil	125	122	130	107	79	53	41	43	66	79	104	137	1,082
61 m	26	26	25	24	22	21	21	21	22	23	23	25	23

WORLD STATISTICS: PHYSICAL DIMENSIONS

Each topic list is divided into continents and within a continent the items are listed in order of size. The bottom part of many of the lists is selective in order to give examples from as many different countries as possible. The order of the continents is as in the atlas, Europe through to South America. The world top ten are shown in square brackets; in the case of mountains this has not been done because the world top 30 are all in Asia. The figures are rounded as appropriate.

WORLD, CONTINENTS, OCEANS

THE WORLD	km²	miles²	%
The World	509,450,000	196,672,000	–
Land	149,450,000	57,688,000	29.3
Water	360,000,000	138,984,000	70.7
Asia	44,500,000	17,177,000	29.8
Africa	30,302,000	11,697,000	20.3
North America	24,241,000	9,357,000	16.2
South America	17,793,000	6,868,000	11.9
Antarctica	14,100,000	5,443,000	9.4
Europe	9,957,000	3,843,000	6.7
Australia & Oceania	8,557,000	3,303,000	5.7
Pacific Ocean	155,557,000	60,061,000	46.4
Atlantic Ocean	76,762,000	29,638,000	22.9
Indian Ocean	68,556,000	26,470,000	20.4
Southern Ocean	20,327,000	7,848,000	6.1
Arctic Ocean	14,056,000	5,427,000	4.2

SEAS

PACIFIC	km²	miles²
South China Sea	2,974,600	1,148,500
Bering Sea	2,268,000	875,000
Sea of Okhotsk	1,528,000	590,000
East China & Yellow	1,249,000	482,000
Sea of Japan	1,008,000	389,000
Gulf of California	162,000	62,500
Bass Strait	75,000	29,000

ATLANTIC	km²	miles²
Caribbean Sea	2,766,000	1,068,000
Mediterranean Sea	2,516,000	971,000
Gulf of Mexico	1,543,000	596,000
Hudson Bay	1,232,000	476,000
North Sea	575,000	223,000
Black Sea	462,000	178,000
Baltic Sea	422,170	163,000
Gulf of St Lawrence	238,000	92,000

INDIAN	km²	miles²
Red Sea	438,000	169,000
Persian Gulf	239,000	92,000

MOUNTAINS

EUROPE		m	ft
Elbrus	Russia	5,642	18,510
Mont Blanc	France/Italy	4,807	15,771
Monte Rosa	Italy/Switzerland	4,634	15,203
Dom	Switzerland	4,545	14,911
Liskamm	Switzerland	4,527	14,852
Weisshorn	Switzerland	4,505	14,780
Taschorn	Switzerland	4,490	14,730
Matterhorn/Cervino	Italy/Switzerland	4,478	14,691
Mont Maudit	France/Italy	4,465	14,649
Dent Blanche	Switzerland	4,356	14,291
Nadelhorn	Switzerland	4,327	14,196
Grandes Jorasses	France/Italy	4,208	13,806
Jungfrau	Switzerland	4,158	13,642
Barre des Ecrins	France	4,103	13,461
Gran Paradiso	Italy	4,061	13,323
Piz Bernina	Italy/Switzerland	4,049	13,284
Eiger	Switzerland	3,970	13,025
Monte Viso	Italy	3,841	12,602
Grossglockner	Austria	3,797	12,457
Wildspitze	Austria	3,772	12,382
Monte Disgrazia	Italy	3,678	12,066
Mulhacén	Spain	3,478	11,411
Pico de Aneto	Spain	3,404	11,168
Etna	Italy	3,340	10,958
Zugspitze	Germany	2,962	9,718
Musala	Bulgaria	2,925	9,596
Olympus	Greece	2,917	9,570
Triglav	Slovenia	2,863	9,393
Monte Cinto	France (Corsica)	2,710	8,891
Galdhøpiggen	Norway	2,469	8,100
Ben Nevis	UK	1,342	4,403

ASIA		m	ft
Everest	China/Nepal	8,850	29,035
K2 (Godwin Austen)	China/Kashmir	8,611	28,251
Kanchenjunga	India/Nepal	8,598	28,208
Lhotse	China/Nepal	8,516	27,939
Makalu	China/Nepal	8,481	27,824
Cho Oyu	China/Nepal	8,201	26,906
Dhaulagiri	Nepal	8,167	26,795
Manaslu	Nepal	8,156	26,758
Nanga Parbat	Kashmir	8,126	26,660
Annapurna	Nepal	8,078	26,502
Gasherbrum	China/Kashmir	8,068	26,469
Broad Peak	China/Kashmir	8,051	26,414
Xixabangma	China	8,012	26,286
Kangbachen	India/Nepal	7,902	25,925
Jannu	India/Nepal	7,902	25,925
Gayachung Kang	Nepal	7,897	25,909
Himalchuli	Nepal	7,893	25,896
Disteghil Sar	Kashmir	7,885	25,869
Nuptse	Nepal	7,879	25,849
Khunyang Chhish	Kashmir	7,852	25,761
Masherbrum	Kashmir	7,821	25,659
Nanda Devi	India	7,817	25,646
Rakaposhi	Kashmir	7,788	25,551
Batura	Kashmir	7,785	25,541
Namche Barwa	China	7,756	25,446
Kamet	India	7,756	25,446
Soltoro Kangri	Kashmir	7,742	25,400
Gurla Mandhata	China	7,728	25,354
Trivor	Pakistan	7,720	25,328
Kongur Shan	China	7,719	25,315
Tirich Mir	Pakistan	7,690	25,229
K'ula Shan	Bhutan/China	7,543	24,747
Pik Kommunizma	Tajikistan	7,495	24,590
Demavend	Iran	5,604	18,386
Ararat	Turkey	5,165	16,945
Gunong Kinabalu	Malaysia (Borneo)	4,101	13,455
Yu Shan	Taiwan	3,997	13,113
Fuji-San	Japan	3,776	12,388

AFRICA		m	ft
Kilimanjaro	Tanzania	5,895	19,340
Mt Kenya	Kenya	5,199	17,057
Ruwenzori (Margherita)	Uganda/Congo (D.R.)	5,109	16,762
Ras Dashen	Ethiopia	4,620	15,157
Meru	Tanzania	4,565	14,977
Karisimbi	Rwanda/Congo (D.R.)	4,507	14,787
Mt Elgon	Kenya/Uganda	4,321	14,176
Batu	Ethiopia	4,307	14,130
Guna	Ethiopia	4,231	13,882
Toubkal	Morocco	4,165	13,665
Irhil Mgoun	Morocco	4,071	13,356
Mt Cameroun	Cameroon	4,070	13,353
Amba Ferit	Ethiopia	3,875	13,042
Pico del Teide	Spain (Tenerife)	3,718	12,198
Thabana Ntlenyana	Lesotho	3,482	11,424
Emi Koussi	Chad	3,415	11,204
Mt aux Sources	Lesotho/South Africa	3,282	10,768
Mt Piton	Réunion	3,069	10,069

OCEANIA		m	ft
Puncak Jaya	Indonesia	5,029	16,499
Puncak Trikora	Indonesia	4,730	15,518
Puncak Mandala	Indonesia	4,702	15,427
Mt Wilhelm	Papua New Guinea	4,508	14,790
Mauna Kea	USA (Hawai'i)	4,205	13,796
Mauna Loa	USA (Hawai'i)	4,169	13,678
Aoraki Mt Cook	New Zealand	3,753	12,313
Mt Balbi	Solomon Is.	2,439	8,002
Orohena	Tahiti	2,241	7,352
Mt Kosciuszko	Australia	2,230	7,316

NORTH AMERICA		m	ft
Mt McKinley (Denali)	USA (Alaska)	6,194	20,321
Mt Logan	Canada	5,959	19,551
Pico de Orizaba	Mexico	5,610	18,405
Mt St Elias	USA/Canada	5,489	18,008
Popocatépetl	Mexico	5,452	17,887

NORTH AMERICA (continued)		m	ft
Mt Foraker	USA (Alaska)	5,304	17,401
Iztaccihuatl	Mexico	5,286	17,343
Lucania	Canada	5,226	17,146
Mt Steele	Canada	5,073	16,644
Mt Bona	USA (Alaska)	5,005	16,420
Mt Blackburn	USA (Alaska)	4,996	16,391
Mt Sanford	USA (Alaska)	4,940	16,207
Mt Wood	Canada	4,848	15,905
Nevado de Toluca	Mexico	4,670	15,321
Mt Fairweather	USA (Alaska)	4,663	15,298
Mt Hunter	USA (Alaska)	4,442	14,573
Mt Whitney	USA	4,418	14,495
Mt Elbert	USA	4,399	14,432
Mt Harvard	USA	4,395	14,419
Mt Rainier	USA	4,392	14,409
Blanca Peak	USA	4,372	14,344
Longs Peak	USA	4,345	14,255
Tajumulco	Guatemala	4,220	13,845
Grand Teton	USA	4,197	13,770
Mt Waddington	Canada	3,994	13,104
Mt Robson	Canada	3,954	12,972
Chirripó Grande	Costa Rica	3,837	12,589
Pico Duarte	Dominican Rep.	3,175	10,417

SOUTH AMERICA		m	ft
Aconcagua	Argentina	6,962	22,841
Bonete	Argentina	6,872	22,546
Ojos del Salado	Argentina/Chile	6,863	22,516
Pissis	Argentina	6,779	22,241
Mercedario	Argentina/Chile	6,770	22,211
Huascarán	Peru	6,768	22,205
Llullaillaco	Argentina/Chile	6,723	22,057
Nudo de Cachi	Argentina	6,720	22,047
Yerupaja	Peru	6,632	21,758
N. de Tres Cruces	Argentina/Chile	6,620	21,719
Incahuasi	Argentina/Chile	6,601	21,654
Cerro Galan	Argentina	6,600	21,654
Tupungato	Argentina/Chile	6,570	21,555
Sajama	Bolivia	6,520	21,391
Illimani	Bolivia	6,485	21,276
Coropuna	Peru	6,425	21,079
Ausangate	Peru	6,384	20,945
Cerro del Toro	Argentina	6,380	20,932
Siula Grande	Peru	6,356	20,853
Chimborazo	Ecuador	6,267	20,561
Alpamayo	Peru	5,947	19,511
Cotapaxi	Ecuador	5,896	19,344
Pico Cristóbal Colón	Colombia	5,800	19,029
Pico Bolivar	Venezuela	5,007	16,427

ANTARCTICA		m	ft
Vinson Massif		4,897	16,066
Mt Kirkpatrick		4,528	14,855
Mt Markham		4,349	14,268

OCEAN DEPTHS

ATLANTIC OCEAN	m	ft	
Puerto Rico (Milwaukee) Deep	9,220	30,249	[7]
Cayman Trench	7,680	25,197	[10]
Gulf of Mexico	5,203	17,070	
Mediterranean Sea	5,121	16,801	
Black Sea	2,211	7,254	
North Sea	660	2,165	
Baltic Sea	463	1,519	
Hudson Bay	258	846	

INDIAN OCEAN	m	ft	
Java Trench	7,450	24,442	
Red Sea	2,635	8,454	
Persian Gulf	73	239	

PACIFIC OCEAN	m	ft	
Mariana Trench	11,022	36,161	[1]
Tonga Trench	10,882	35,702	[2]
Japan Trench	10,554	34,626	[3]
Kuril Trench	10,542	34,587	[4]
Mindanao Trench	10,497	34,439	[5]
Kermadec Trench	10,047	32,962	[6]

PACIFIC OCEAN (continued)

		m	ft	
Peru–Chile Trench		8,050	26,410	[8]
Aleutian Trench		7,822	25,662	[9]

ARCTIC OCEAN

		m	ft	
Molloy Deep		5,608	18,399	

LAND LOWS

		m	ft
Caspian Sea	Europe	−28	−92
Dead Sea	Asia	−411	−1,348
Lake Assal	Africa	−156	−512
Lake Eyre North	Oceania	−16	−52
Death Valley	North America	−86	−282
Valdés Peninsula	South America	−40	−131

RIVERS

EUROPE

		km	miles	
Volga	Caspian Sea	3,700	2,300	
Danube	Black Sea	2,850	1,770	
Ural	Caspian Sea	2,535	1,575	
Dnepr (Dnipro)	Black Sea	2,285	1,420	
Kama	Volga	2,030	1,260	
Don	Black Sea	1,990	1,240	
Petchora	Arctic Ocean	1,790	1,110	
Oka	Volga	1,480	920	
Belaya	Kama	1,420	880	
Dnister (Dniester)	Black Sea	1,400	870	
Vyatka	Kama	1,370	850	
Rhine	North Sea	1,320	820	
N. Dvina	Arctic Ocean	1,290	800	
Desna	Dnepr (Dnipro)	1,190	740	
Elbe	North Sea	1,145	710	
Wisla	Baltic Sea	1,090	675	
Loire	Atlantic Ocean	1,020	635	

ASIA

		km	miles	
Yangtze	Pacific Ocean	6,380	3,960	[3]
Yenisey–Angara	Arctic Ocean	5,550	3,445	[5]
Huang He	Pacific Ocean	5,464	3,395	[6]
Ob–Irtysh	Arctic Ocean	5,410	3,360	[7]
Mekong	Pacific Ocean	4,500	2,795	[9]
Amur	Pacific Ocean	4,442	2,760	[10]
Lena	Arctic Ocean	4,402	2,735	
Irtysh	Ob	4,250	2,640	
Yenisey	Arctic Ocean	4,090	2,540	
Ob	Arctic Ocean	3,630	2,285	
Indus	Indian Ocean	3,100	1,925	
Brahmaputra	Indian Ocean	2,900	1,800	
Syrdarya	Aral Sea	2,860	1,775	
Salween	Indian Ocean	2,800	1,740	
Euphrates	Indian Ocean	2,700	1,675	
Vilyuy	Lena	2,650	1,645	
Kolyma	Arctic Ocean	2,600	1,615	
Amudarya	Aral Sea	2,540	1,575	
Ural	Caspian Sea	2,535	1,575	
Ganges	Indian Ocean	2,510	1,560	
Si Kiang	Pacific Ocean	2,100	1,305	
Irrawaddy	Indian Ocean	2,010	1,250	
Tarim–Yarkand	Lop Nor	2,000	1,240	
Tigris	Indian Ocean	1,900	1,180	

AFRICA

		km	miles	
Nile	Mediterranean	6,670	4,140	[1]
Congo	Atlantic Ocean	4,670	2,900	[8]
Niger	Atlantic Ocean	4,180	2,595	
Zambezi	Indian Ocean	3,540	2,200	
Oubangi/Uele	Congo (D.R.)	2,250	1,400	
Kasai	Congo (D.R.)	1,950	1,210	
Shaballe	Indian Ocean	1,930	1,200	
Orange	Atlantic Ocean	1,860	1,155	
Cubango	Okavango Delta	1,800	1,120	
Limpopo	Indian Ocean	1,770	1,100	
Senegal	Atlantic Ocean	1,640	1,020	
Volta	Atlantic Ocean	1,500	930	

AUSTRALIA

		km	miles
Murray–Darling	Southern Ocean	3,750	2,330
Darling	Murray	3,070	1,905
Murray	Southern Ocean	2,575	1,600
Murrumbidgee	Murray	1,690	1,050

NORTH AMERICA

		km	miles	
Mississippi–Missouri	Gulf of Mexico	6,020	3,740	[4]
Mackenzie	Arctic Ocean	4,240	2,630	
Mississippi	Gulf of Mexico	4,120	2,560	
Missouri	Mississippi	3,780	2,350	
Yukon	Pacific Ocean	3,185	1,980	
Rio Grande	Gulf of Mexico	3,030	1,880	

NORTH AMERICA (continued)

		km	miles	
Arkansas	Mississippi	2,340	1,450	
Colorado	Pacific Ocean	2,330	1,445	
Red	Mississippi	2,040	1,270	
Columbia	Pacific Ocean	1,950	1,210	
Saskatchewan	Lake Winnipeg	1,940	1,205	
Snake	Columbia	1,670	1,040	
Churchill	Hudson Bay	1,600	990	
Ohio	Mississippi	1,580	980	
Brazos	Gulf of Mexico	1,400	870	
St Lawrence	Atlantic Ocean	1,170	730	

SOUTH AMERICA

		km	miles	
Amazon	Atlantic Ocean	6,450	4,010	[2]
Paraná–Plate	Atlantic Ocean	4,500	2,800	
Purus	Amazon	3,350	2,080	
Madeira	Amazon	3,200	1,990	
São Francisco	Atlantic Ocean	2,900	1,800	
Paraná	Plate	2,800	1,740	
Tocantins	Atlantic Ocean	2,750	1,710	
Orinoco	Atlantic Ocean	2,740	1,700	
Paraguay	Paraná	2,550	1,580	
Pilcomayo	Paraná	2,500	1,550	
Araguaia	Tocantins	2,250	1,400	
Juruá	Amazon	2,000	1,240	
Xingu	Amazon	1,980	1,230	
Ucayali	Amazon	1,900	1,180	
Uruguay	Plate	1,610	1,000	
Maranón	Amazon	1,600	995	

LAKES

EUROPE

		km²	miles²
Lake Ladoga	Russia	17,700	6,800
Lake Onega	Russia	9,700	3,700
Saimaa system	Finland	8,000	3,100
Vänern	Sweden	5,500	2,100
Rybinskoye Res.	Russia	4,700	1,800

ASIA

		km²	miles²	
Caspian Sea	Asia	371,000	143,000	[1]
Lake Baikal	Russia	30,500	11,780	[8]
Aral Sea	Kazakhstan/Uzbekistan	28,687	11,086	[10]
Tonlé Sap	Cambodia	20,000	7,700	
Lake Balqash	Kazakhstan	18,500	7,100	
Lake Dongting	China	12,000	4,600	
Lake Ysyk	Kyrgyzstan	6,200	2,400	
Lake Orumiyeh	Iran	5,900	2,300	
Lake Koko	China	5,700	2,200	
Lake Poyang	China	5,000	1,900	
Lake Khanka	China/Russia	4,400	1,700	
Lake Van	Turkey	3,500	1,400	

AFRICA

		km²	miles²	
Lake Victoria	East Africa	68,000	26,300	[3]
Lake Tanganyika	Central Africa	33,000	13,000	[6]
Lake Malawi/Nyasa	East Africa	29,600	11,430	[9]
Lake Chad	Central Africa	25,000	9,700	
Lake Turkana	Ethiopia/Kenya	8,500	3,290	
Lake Volta	Ghana	8,480	3,270	
Lake Bangweulu	Zambia	8,000	3,100	
Lake Rukwa	Tanzania	7,000	2,700	
Lake Mai-Ndombe	Congo (D.R.)	6,500	2,500	
Lake Kariba	Zambia/Zimbabwe	5,300	2,000	
Lake Albert	Uganda/Congo (D.R.)	5,300	2,000	
Lake Nasser	Egypt/Sudan	5,200	2,000	
Lake Mweru	Zambia/Congo (D.R.)	4,900	1,900	
Lake Cabora Bassa	Mozambique	4,500	1,700	
Lake Kyoga	Uganda	4,400	1,700	
Lake Tana	Ethiopia	3,630	1,400	

AUSTRALIA

		km²	miles²
Lake Eyre	Australia	8,900	3,400
Lake Torrens	Australia	5,800	2,200
Lake Gairdner	Australia	4,800	1,900

NORTH AMERICA

		km²	miles²	
Lake Superior	Canada/USA	82,350	31,800	[2]
Lake Huron	Canada/USA	59,600	23,010	[4]
Lake Michigan	USA	58,000	22,400	[5]
Great Bear Lake	Canada	31,800	12,280	[7]
Great Slave Lake	Canada	28,500	11,000	
Lake Erie	Canada/USA	25,700	9,900	
Lake Winnipeg	Canada	24,400	9,400	
Lake Ontario	Canada/USA	19,500	7,500	
Lake Nicaragua	Nicaragua	8,200	3,200	
Lake Athabasca	Canada	8,100	3,100	
Smallwood Reservoir	Canada	6,530	2,520	
Reindeer Lake	Canada	6,400	2,500	
Nettilling Lake	Canada	5,500	2,100	
Lake Winnipegosis	Canada	5,400	2,100	

SOUTH AMERICA

		km²	miles²
Lake Titicaca	Bolivia/Peru	8,300	3,200
Lake Poopo	Bolivia	2,800	1,100

ISLANDS

EUROPE

		km²	miles²	
Great Britain	UK	229,880	88,700	[8]
Iceland	Atlantic Ocean	103,000	39,800	
Ireland	Ireland/UK	84,400	32,600	
Novaya Zemlya (N.)	Russia	48,200	18,600	
W. Spitzbergen	Norway	39,000	15,100	
Novaya Zemlya (S.)	Russia	33,200	12,800	
Sicily	Italy	25,500	9,800	
Sardinia	Italy	24,000	9,300	
N.E. Spitzbergen	Norway	15,000	5,600	
Corsica	France	8,700	3,400	
Crete	Greece	8,350	3,200	
Zealand	Denmark	6,850	2,600	

ASIA

		km²	miles²	
Borneo	South-east Asia	744,360	287,400	[3]
Sumatra	Indonesia	473,600	182,860	[6]
Honshu	Japan	230,500	88,980	[7]
Sulawesi (Celebes)	Indonesia	189,000	73,000	
Java	Indonesia	126,700	48,900	
Luzon	Philippines	104,700	40,400	
Mindanao	Philippines	101,500	39,200	
Hokkaido	Japan	78,400	30,300	
Sakhalin	Russia	74,060	28,600	
Sri Lanka	Indian Ocean	65,600	25,300	
Taiwan	Pacific Ocean	36,000	13,900	
Kyushu	Japan	35,700	13,800	
Hainan	China	34,000	13,100	
Timor	Indonesia	33,600	13,000	
Shikoku	Japan	18,800	7,300	
Halmahera	Indonesia	18,000	6,900	
Ceram	Indonesia	17,150	6,600	
Sumbawa	Indonesia	15,450	6,000	
Flores	Indonesia	15,200	5,900	
Samar	Philippines	13,100	5,100	
Negros	Philippines	12,700	4,900	
Bangka	Indonesia	12,000	4,600	
Palawan	Philippines	12,000	4,600	
Panay	Philippines	11,500	4,400	
Sumba	Indonesia	11,100	4,300	
Mindoro	Philippines	9,750	3,800	

AFRICA

		km²	miles²	
Madagascar	Indian Ocean	587,040	226,660	[4]
Socotra	Indian Ocean	3,600	1,400	
Réunion	Indian Ocean	2,500	965	
Tenerife	Atlantic Ocean	2,350	900	
Mauritius	Indian Ocean	1,865	720	

OCEANIA

		km²	miles²	
New Guinea	Indonesia/Papua NG	821,030	317,000	[2]
New Zealand (S.)	Pacific Ocean	150,500	58,100	
New Zealand (N.)	Pacific Ocean	114,700	44,300	
Tasmania	Australia	67,800	26,200	
New Britain	Papua New Guinea	37,800	14,600	
New Caledonia	Pacific Ocean	19,100	7,400	
Viti Levu	Fiji	10,500	4,100	
Hawai'i	Pacific Ocean	10,450	4,000	
Bougainville	Papua New Guinea	9,600	3,700	
Guadalcanal	Solomon Is.	6,500	2,500	
Vanua Levu	Fiji	5,550	2,100	
New Ireland	Papua New Guinea	3,200	1,200	

NORTH AMERICA

		km²	miles²	
Greenland	Atlantic Ocean	2,175,600	839,800	[1]
Baffin Is.	Canada	508,000	196,100	[5]
Victoria Is.	Canada	212,200	81,900	[9]
Ellesmere Is.	Canada	212,000	81,800	[10]
Cuba	Caribbean Sea	110,860	42,800	
Newfoundland	Canada	110,680	42,700	
Hispaniola	Dominican Rep./Haiti	76,200	29,400	
Banks Is.	Canada	67,000	25,900	
Devon Is.	Canada	54,500	21,000	
Melville Is.	Canada	42,400	16,400	
Vancouver Is.	Canada	32,150	12,400	
Somerset Is.	Canada	24,300	9,400	
Jamaica	Caribbean Sea	11,400	4,400	
Puerto Rico	Atlantic Ocean	8,900	3,400	
Cape Breton Is.	Canada	4,000	1,500	

SOUTH AMERICA

		km²	miles²
Tierra del Fuego	Argentina/Chile	47,000	18,100
Falkland Is. (East)	Atlantic Ocean	6,800	2,600
South Georgia	Atlantic Ocean	4,200	1,600
Galapagos (Isabela)	Pacific Ocean	2,250	870

WORLD: REGIONS IN THE NEWS

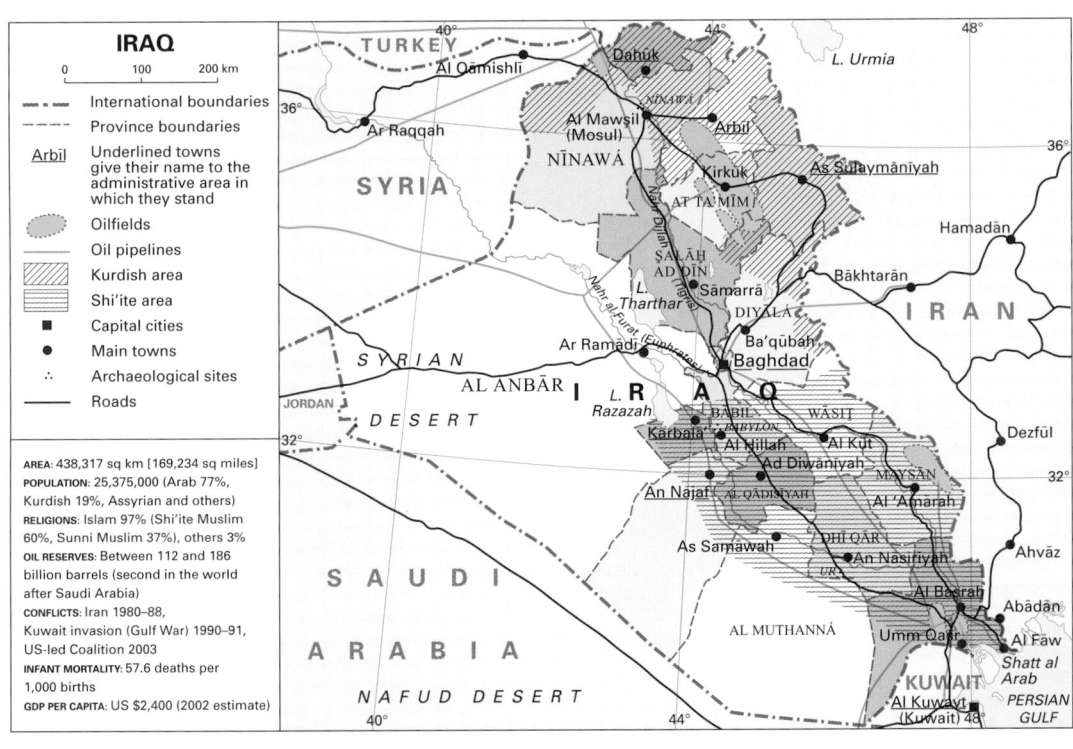

IRAQ

0   100   200 km

- – – – International boundaries
- – – – Province boundaries
- Arbil — Underlined towns give their name to the administrative area in which they stand
- Oilfields
- Oil pipelines
- Kurdish area
- Shi'ite area
- ■ Capital cities
- ● Main towns
- ∴ Archaeological sites
- — Roads

AREA: 438,317 sq km [169,234 sq miles]
POPULATION: 25,375,000 (Arab 77%, Kurdish 19%, Assyrian and others)
RELIGIONS: Islam 97% (Shi'ite Muslim 60%, Sunni Muslim 37%), others 3%
OIL RESERVES: Between 112 and 186 billion barrels (second in the world after Saudi Arabia)
CONFLICTS: Iran 1980–88, Kuwait invasion (Gulf War) 1990–91, US-led Coalition 2003
INFANT MORTALITY: 57.6 deaths per 1,000 births
GDP PER CAPITA: US $2,400 (2002 estimate)

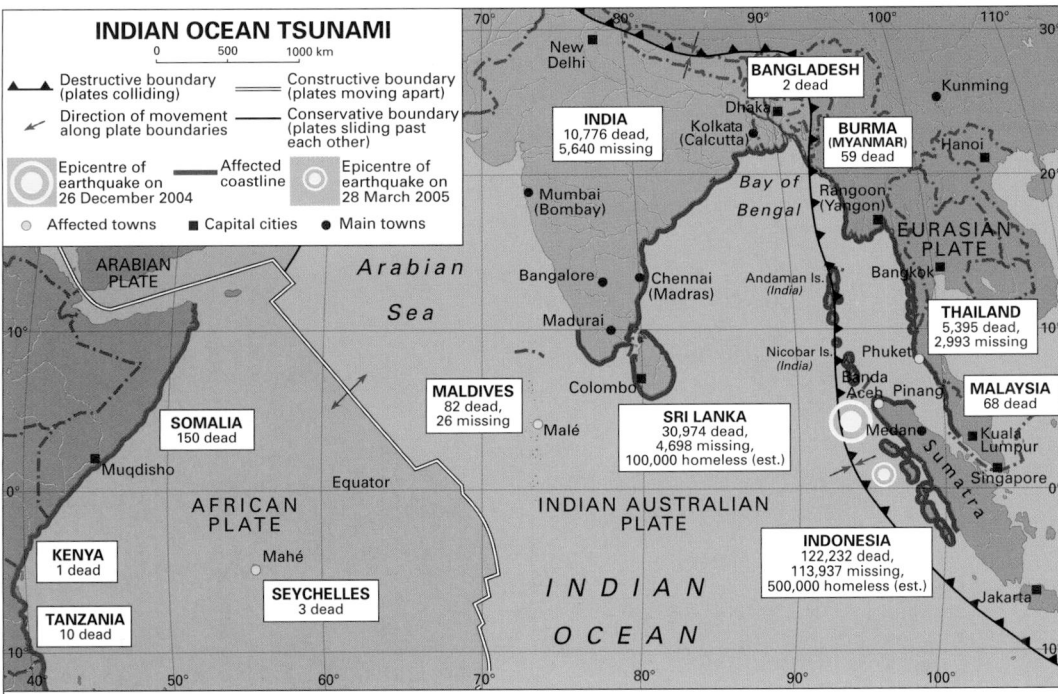

INDIAN OCEAN TSUNAMI

0   500   1000 km

- ▲ Destructive boundary (plates colliding)
- — Constructive boundary (plates moving apart)
- ↙ Direction of movement along plate boundaries
- — Conservative boundary (plates sliding past each other)
- ◎ Epicentre of earthquake on 26 December 2004
- — Affected coastline
- ◉ Epicentre of earthquake on 28 March 2005
- ○ Affected towns
- ● Capital cities
- ● Main towns

BANGLADESH 2 dead
INDIA 10,776 dead, 5,640 missing
BURMA (MYANMAR) 59 dead
THAILAND 5,395 dead, 2,993 missing
MALAYSIA 68 dead
MALDIVES 82 dead, 26 missing
SRI LANKA 30,974 dead, 4,698 missing, 100,000 homeless (est.)
SOMALIA 150 dead
INDONESIA 122,232 dead, 113,937 missing, 500,000 homeless (est.)
KENYA 1 dead
TANZANIA 10 dead
SEYCHELLES 3 dead

Total death toll: 169,752 dead, 127,294 missing

The 26 December 2004 earthquake measured 9.3 on the Richter Scale, whereas the earthquake on 28 March 2005 measured 8.7. The Richter Scale is a logarithmic scale, so in terms of energy released, the earthquake on 26 December was five times larger than the one on 28 March and was the second largest in recorded history. The December earthquake generated waves that, once they reached the land, were up to 20 m [65 ft] in height.

Timeline:
26 December 2004
0100 GMT Earthquake occurs
0130 GMT Tsunami hits Sumatra
0230 GMT Thailand hit
0300 GMT Sri Lanka and India hit
0430 GMT Maldives hit
0700 GMT East Africa hit

Aid Recipients:

Recipient	Pledges	Donations received (at 22 March 2005)
Indonesia	US $929 million	US $220.8 million
Sri Lanka	US $413.5 million	US $249 million
India	US $57.9 million	US $56.7 million
Thailand	US $13.3 million	US $7.5 million
Somalia	US $9.4 million	US $3 million

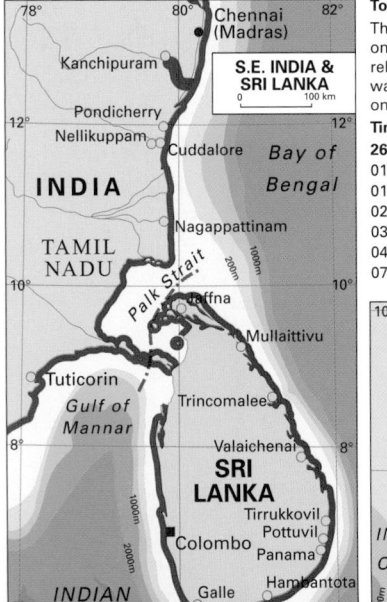

S.E. INDIA & SRI LANKA
0   100 km

THAILAND
0   100 km

S. THAILAND

W. INDONESIA
0   100 km

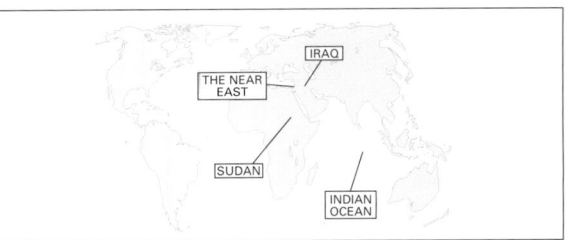

THE NEAR EAST

0   25   50 km

- – – – 1949 Armistice Line
- – – – 1950 Armistice Line
- – – – 1974 Cease-fire Line
- ☐ Palestinian control
- ▨ Joint Israeli/Palestinian control
- ● Efrata Main Jewish settlements
- ☐ Halhul Main Palestinian Arab towns
- — Israeli security fence completed
- — Israeli security fence under construction or planned

ISRAEL
POPULATION: 6,199,000 (inc. Israeli settlers in West Bank, Gaza Strip and Golan Heights)
INFANT MORTALITY: 6.2 deaths per 1,000 births
GDP PER CAPITA: US $19,500 (2002 estimate)

West Bank
POPULATION: 2,311,000 (Muslim 75%, Jewish 17%)
INFANT MORTALITY: 21.2 deaths per 1,000 births
GDP PER CAPITA: US $800 (2002 estimate)

Gaza Strip
POPULATION: 1,325,000 (Muslim 98.7%, Christian 0.7%, Jewish 0.6%)
INFANT MORTALITY: 24.8 deaths per 1,000 births
GDP PER CAPITA: US $600 (2002 estimate)

JORDAN
POPULATION: 5,611,000 (Palestinian Arab 50%)

LEBANON
POPULATION: 3,777,000 (Palestinian Arab 11%)

SUDAN

0   500   1000 km

- – – – Regional boundaries
- ■ Capital cities
- ● Main towns

AREA: 2,505,813 sq km [967,494 sq miles]
POPULATION: 39,148,000 (Black 52%, Arab 39%, Beja 6%, others)
RELIGIONS: Islam 70% (mainly Sunni Muslim), traditional beliefs 25%, Christianity 5%
BIRTH RATE: 35.79 births per 1,000 population
DEATH RATE: 9.37 deaths per 1,000 population
INFANT MORTALITY: 64.05 deaths per 1,000 births
GDP PER CAPITA: US $1,400 (2002 estimate)

Sudan has more internally displaced people than any other country (4.4 million in 2004). Up to 1.6 million people have left their homes and 70,000 are estimated to have been killed since conflict began in the Darfur region in early 2003.

The largest country in Africa, Sudan is one quarter the size of the USA, or 10 times the size of the UK. The country's inhabitants are divided into three main groups: those in the north, consisting of Muslim Arab and Nubian peoples; those in the south, consisting of traditional Nilotic and Bantu peoples; and those in the west, most of whom immigrated from western Africa in the 20th century.

THE EARTH
IN SPACE

THE UNIVERSE 18

THE CONSTELLATIONS 20

STAR CHARTS 22

THE SOLAR SYSTEM 24

THE EARTH: TIME AND MOTION 26

THE EARTH FROM SPACE 28

THE DYNAMIC EARTH 30

EARTHQUAKES AND VOLCANOES 32

FORCES OF NATURE 34

OCEANS AND ICE 36

THE EARTH'S ATMOSPHERE 38

CLIMATE AND WEATHER 40

WATER AND LAND USE 42

THE NATURAL WORLD 44

THE HUMAN WORLD 46

LANGUAGES AND RELIGIONS 48

INTERNATIONAL ORGANIZATIONS 50

AGRICULTURE 52

ENERGY AND MINERALS 54

WORLD ECONOMIES 56

TRADE AND COMMERCE 58

TRAVEL AND COMMUNICATIONS 60

THE WORLD TODAY 62

THE UNIVERSE

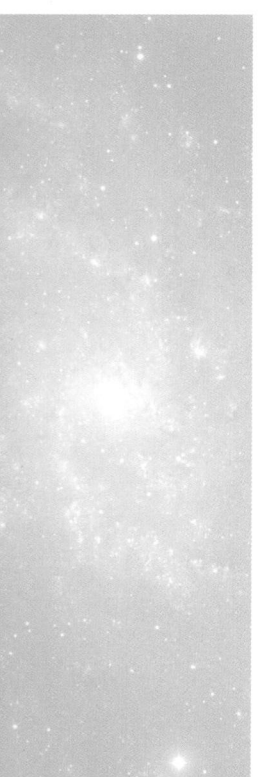

In early 2003, NASA scientists produced an image of the Universe as it was about 380,000 years after its creation. The image was produced by an American satellite called the Wilkinson Microwave Anisotropy Probe (WMAP), which was launched in June 2001.

The probe measures small variations in the cosmic microwave background (CMB) radiation, left over from the creation of the Universe. By measuring the size of hot and cold spots in the CMB, scientists have calculated how far away they are, and this data has enabled them to calculate the age of the Universe. It has also established the proportions of its three ingredients, namely 4% ordinary matter (made up of atoms), 23% of 'cold dark matter', whose nature is unknown, and 73% of the mysterious 'dark energy', which seems to be accelerating the expansion of space.

▼ *The depths of the Universe*
In this segment of sky, just one-tenth the area of the full Moon, the Hubble Space Telescope recorded an estimated 10,000 galaxies in 2003–4.

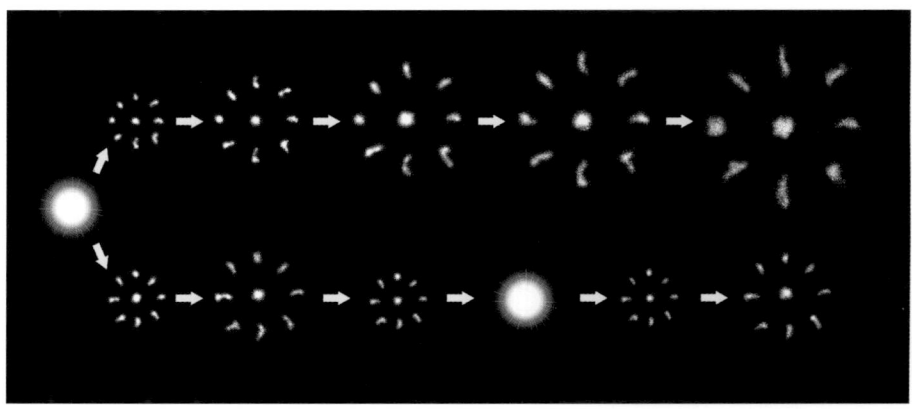

Scientists have established that our Universe was created, or 'time' began, about 13.7 billion years ago (disproving earlier estimates that ranged from 8 billion to 24 billion years), that it is flat, and that the first stars did not appear until it was 200 million years old.

THE BIG BANG

Most scientists agree that the Universe was formed by a colossal explosion, called the 'Big Bang'. In the first millionth of a second after the Big Bang, the Universe expanded from a dimensionless point of infinite mass and

▲ *The end of the Universe*
The diagram shows two theories concerning the fate of the Universe. One theory, top, suggests that the Universe will expand indefinitely, becoming an immense dark graveyard. Another theory, bottom, suggests that the galaxies will fall back until everything is again concentrated in one point in a so-called Big Crunch. This might then be followed by a new Big Bang.

THE NEAREST STARS

*The 22 nearest stars, excluding the Sun, with their distance from the Earth in light-years.**

Proxima Centauri	4.2
Alpha Centauri A	4.4
Alpha Centauri B	4.4
Barnard's Star	5.9
Wolf 359	7.8
Lalande 21185	8.3
Sirius A	8.6
Sirius B	8.6
UV Ceti A	8.7
UV Ceti B	8.7
Ross 154	9.7
Ross 248	10.3
Epsilon Eridani	10.5
HD 217987	10.7
Ross 128	10.9
L789-6	11.2
61 Cygni A	11.4
Procyon A	11.4
Procyon B	11.4
61 Cygni B	11.4
HD 173740	11.5
HD 173739	11.7

* *A light-year is about 9,500 billion km [5,900 billion miles].*

density into a fireball about 30 billion km [19 billion miles] across. The Universe has been expanding ever since, as demonstrated in the 1920s by Edwin Hubble, the American astronomer after whom the Hubble Space Telescope, which has also been shedding light on the origins of the Universe, was named.

The temperature at the end of the first second was perhaps 10 billion degrees – far too hot for composite atomic nuclei to exist. As a result, the fireball consisted mainly of radiation mixed with microscopic particles of matter. Almost a million years passed before the Universe was cool enough for atoms to form.

In regions where matter was relatively dense, atoms began, under the influence of gravity, to move together to form protogalaxies – masses of gas separated by empty space. The proto-galaxies were dark, because the Universe had cooled. But 200 million years after its creation, stars began to form within the protogalaxies as particles were drawn together. The internal pressure produced as matter condensed created the high temperatures required to cause nuclear fusion. Stars were born and later destroyed. Each generation of stars fed on the debris of extinct ones. Each generation produced larger atoms, increasing the number of different chemical elements.

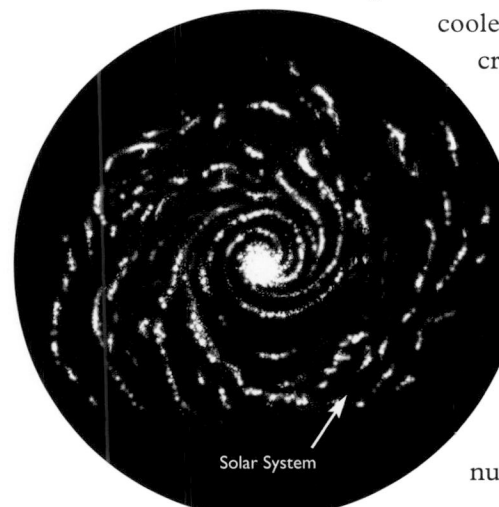

▲ *The Home Galaxy*
This schematic plan shows that our Solar System is located in one of the spiral arms of the Milky Way galaxy, a little less than 30,000 light-years from its centre. The centre of the Milky Way galaxy is not visible from Earth. Instead, it is masked by light-absorbing clouds of interstellar dust.

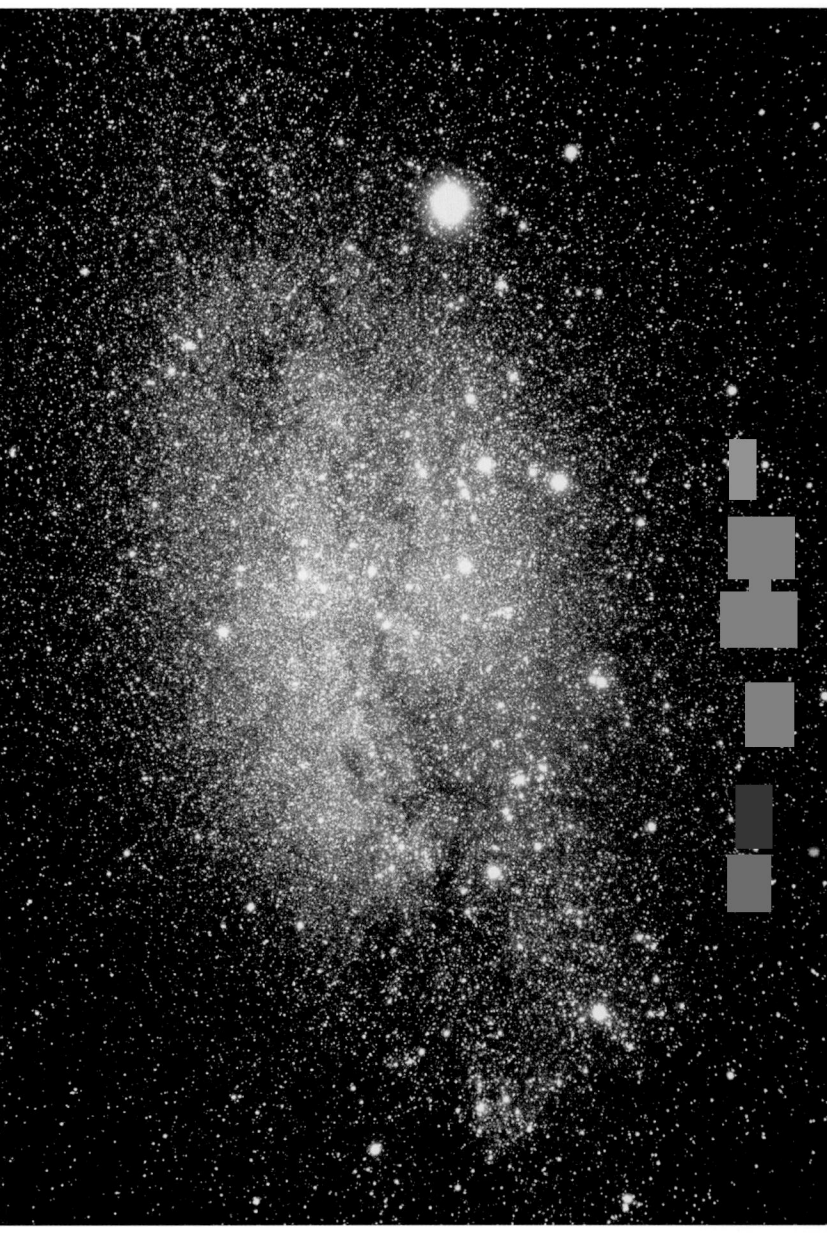

▲ *The Milky Way*
This section of the Milky Way is dominated by Sirius, the Dog Star, top centre, in the constellation of Canis Major. Sirius is the brightest star in the sky.

THE GALAXIES

At least a billion galaxies are scattered through the Universe, though the discoveries made by the Hubble Space Telescope suggest that there may be far more than once thought, and some estimates are as high as 100 billion. The largest galaxies contain trillions of stars, while small ones contain less than a billion.

Galaxies tend to occur in groups or clusters, while some clusters appear to be grouped in vast superclusters. Our Local Cluster includes the spiral Milky Way galaxy, whose diameter is about 100,000 light-years; one light-year, the distance that light travels in one year, is about 9,500 billion km [5,900 billion miles]. The Milky Way is a huge galaxy, shaped like a disk with a bulge at the centre. It is larger, brighter and more massive than many other known galaxies. It contains about 100 billion stars, which rotate around the centre of the galaxy in the same direction as the Sun does.

One medium-sized star in the Milky Way galaxy is the Sun. After its formation, about 5 billion years ago, there was enough leftover matter around it to create the planets, asteroids, moons and other bodies that together form our Solar System. The Solar System rotates around the centre of the Milky Way galaxy approximately every 225 million years.

Stars similar to our Sun are known to have planets orbiting around them. By the start of 2005, over a hundred of these extrasolar planets had been reported, and evidence from the Hubble Space Telescope suggests that the raw materials from which planets are formed is common in dusty disks around many stars. This raises one of the most intriguing questions that has ever faced humanity: if other planets exist in the Universe, are they home to living organisms?

Before the time of Galileo, people thought that the Earth lay at the centre of the Universe. But we now know that our Solar System and even the Milky Way galaxy are tiny specks in the Universe as a whole. Perhaps our planet is also not unique in its ability to support intelligent life.

THE CONSTELLATIONS

On a clear night, under the best conditions and far away from the glare of city lights, a person in northern Europe can look up and see about 2,500 stars. In a town, however, light pollution can reduce visibility to 200 stars or fewer. Over the whole celestial sphere it is possible to see about 8,500 stars with the naked eye and it is only when you look through a telescope that you begin to realize that the number of stars is countless.

SMALL AND LARGE STARS

Stars come in many sizes. Some, called neutron stars, are compact, with the same mass as the Sun but with diameters of only about 20 km [12 miles]. Larger than neutron stars are the small white dwarfs. Our Sun is a medium-sized star, but many visible stars in the night sky are giants with diameters typically 20 times that of the Sun, or supergiants with diameters from 50 to several hundred times that of the Sun.

Two bright stars in the constellation Orion are Betelgeuse (also known as Alpha Orionis) and Rigel (or Beta Orionis). Betelgeuse is an orange-red supergiant, whose diameter is about 500 times that of the Sun. Rigel is also a supergiant. Its diameter is about 50 times that of the Sun, but its luminosity is estimated to be 40,000 times that of the Sun.

The stars we see in the night sky all belong to our home galaxy, the Milky Way. This name is also used for the faint, silvery band that arches across the sky. This band, a slice through our galaxy, contains an enormous number of stars.

▼ *The Plough*

The Plough, or Big Dipper, seen above glowing yellow clouds lit by city lights. It is part of a larger group called Ursa Major, one of the best-known constellations of the northern hemisphere. The two bright stars to the lower right of the photograph (Merak and Dubhe) are known as the Pointers because they show the way to the Pole Star.

THE CONSTELLATIONS

The constellations and their English names. Constellations visible from both hemispheres are listed.

Andromeda	Andromeda	Delphinus	Dolphin	Perseus	Perseus
Antlia	Air Pump	Dorado	Swordfish	Phoenix	Phoenix
Apus	Bird of Paradise	Draco	Dragon	Pictor	Easel
Aquarius	Water Carrier	Equuleus	Little Horse	Pisces	Fishes
Aquila	Eagle	Eridanus	River Eridanus	Piscis Austrinus	Southern Fish
Ara	Altar	Fornax	Furnace	Puppis	Ship's Stern
Aries	Ram	Gemini	Twins	Pyxis	Mariner's Compass
Auriga	Charioteer	Grus	Crane	Reticulum	Net
Boötes	Herdsman	Hercules	Hercules	Sagitta	Arrow
Caelum	Chisel	Horologium	Clock	Sagittarius	Archer
Camelopardalis	Giraffe	Hydra	Water Snake	Scorpius	Scorpion
Cancer	Crab	Hydrus	Sea Serpent	Sculptor	Sculptor
Canes Venatici	Hunting Dogs	Indus	Indian	Scutum	Shield
Canis Major	Great Dog	Lacerta	Lizard	Serpens*	Serpent
Canis Minor	Little Dog	Leo	Lion	Sextans	Sextant
Capricornus	Sea Goat	Leo Minor	Little Lion	Taurus	Bull
Carina	Ship's Keel	Lepus	Hare	Telescopium	Telescope
Cassiopeia	Cassiopeia	Libra	Scales	Triangulum	Triangle
Centaurus	Centaur	Lupus	Wolf	Triangulum Australe	Southern Triangle
Cepheus	Cepheus	Lynx	Lynx	Tucana	Toucan
Cetus	Whale	Lyra	Lyre	Ursa Major	Great Bear
Chamaeleon	Chameleon	Mensa	Table Mountain	Ursa Minor	Little Bear
Circinus	Compasses	Microscopium	Microscope	Vela	Ship's Sails
Columba	Dove	Monoceros	Unicorn	Virgo	Virgin
Coma Berenices	Berenice's Hair	Musca	Fly	Volans	Flying Fish
Corona Australis	Southern Crown	Norma	Level	Vulpecula	Fox
Corona Borealis	Northern Crown	Octans	Octant		
Corvus	Crow	Ophiuchus	Serpent Bearer		
Crater	Cup	Orion	Hunter		
Crux	Southern Cross	Pavo	Peacock	** In two halves: Serpens Caput, the*	
Cygnus	Swan	Pegasus	Winged Horse	*head, and Serpens Cauda, the tail.*	

THE BRIGHTEST STARS

The 15 brightest stars visible from northern Europe. Magnitudes are given to the nearest tenth.

Sirius	−1.4
Arcturus	0.0
Vega	0.0
Capella	0.1
Rigel	0.2
Procyon	0.4
Betelgeuse	0.4
Altair	0.8
Aldebaran	0.9
Spica	1.0
Antares	1.0
Pollux	1.2
Fomalhaut	1.2
Deneb	1.2
Regulus	1.4

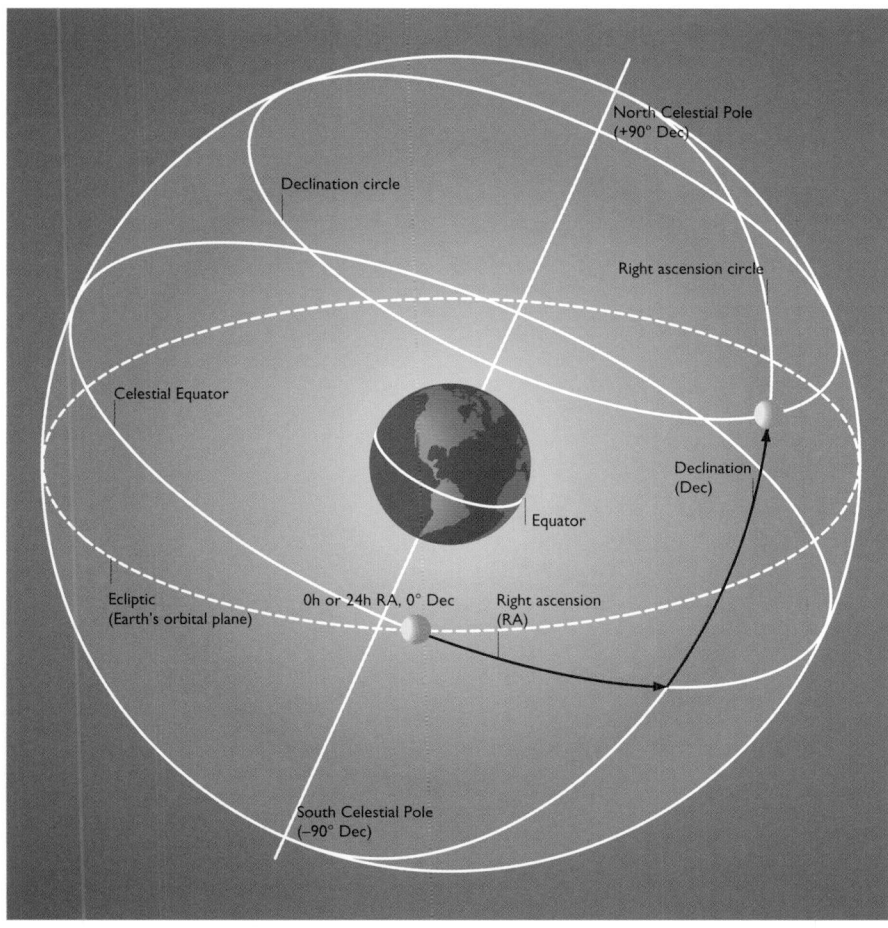

the apparent magnitude it would have if it could be placed 32.6 light-years away. So Deneb, with an apparent magnitude of 1.2, has an absolute magnitude of –8.7.

The brightest star in the night sky is Sirius, the Dog Star, with a magnitude of –1.4. This medium-sized star is 8.6 light-years distant but it gives out about 20 times as much light as the Sun. After the Sun and the Moon, the brightest objects in the sky are the planets Venus, Mars and Jupiter. For example, Venus has a magnitude of up to –4. The planets have no light of their own, however, and shine only because they reflect the Sun's rays. But while stars have fixed positions, the planets shift nightly in relation to the constellations, following a path called the ecliptic (shown on the star charts overleaf). As they follow their orbits around the Sun, their distances from the Earth vary, and therefore so also do their magnitudes.

While atlas maps record the details of the Earth's surface, star charts are a guide to the heavens. An observer at the equator can see the entire sky over the course of a year, but an observer at one of the poles can see only the stars in a single hemisphere.

The nucleus of the Milky Way galaxy cannot be seen from Earth. Lying in the direction of the constellation Sagittarius in the southern hemisphere, it is masked by clouds of dust.

THE BRIGHTNESS OF STARS

Astronomers use a scale of magnitudes to measure the brightness of stars. The brightest visible to the naked eye were originally known as first-magnitude stars, ones not so bright were second-magnitude, down to the faintest visible, which were rated as sixth-magnitude. The brighter the star, the lower the magnitude. With the advent of telescopes and the development of accurate instruments for measuring brightnesses, the magnitude scale has been refined and extended. Very bright bodies, such as Sirius, Venus and the Sun, have negative magnitudes. The nearest star is Proxima Centauri, part of a multiple star system, which is 4.2 light-years away. Proxima Centauri is very faint and has a magnitude of 11.0. Alpha Centauri A, one of the two brighter members of the system, is the nearest visible star to Earth. It has a magnitude of 1.7.

These magnitudes are known as apparent magnitudes – measures of the brightnesses of the stars as they appear to us. These are the magnitudes indicated on the star charts on pages 22–23. But the stars are at very different distances. The star Deneb, in the constellation Cygnus, for example, is 3,200 light-years away. So astronomers also use absolute magnitudes – measures of how bright the stars really are. A star's absolute magnitude is

STAR CHARTS

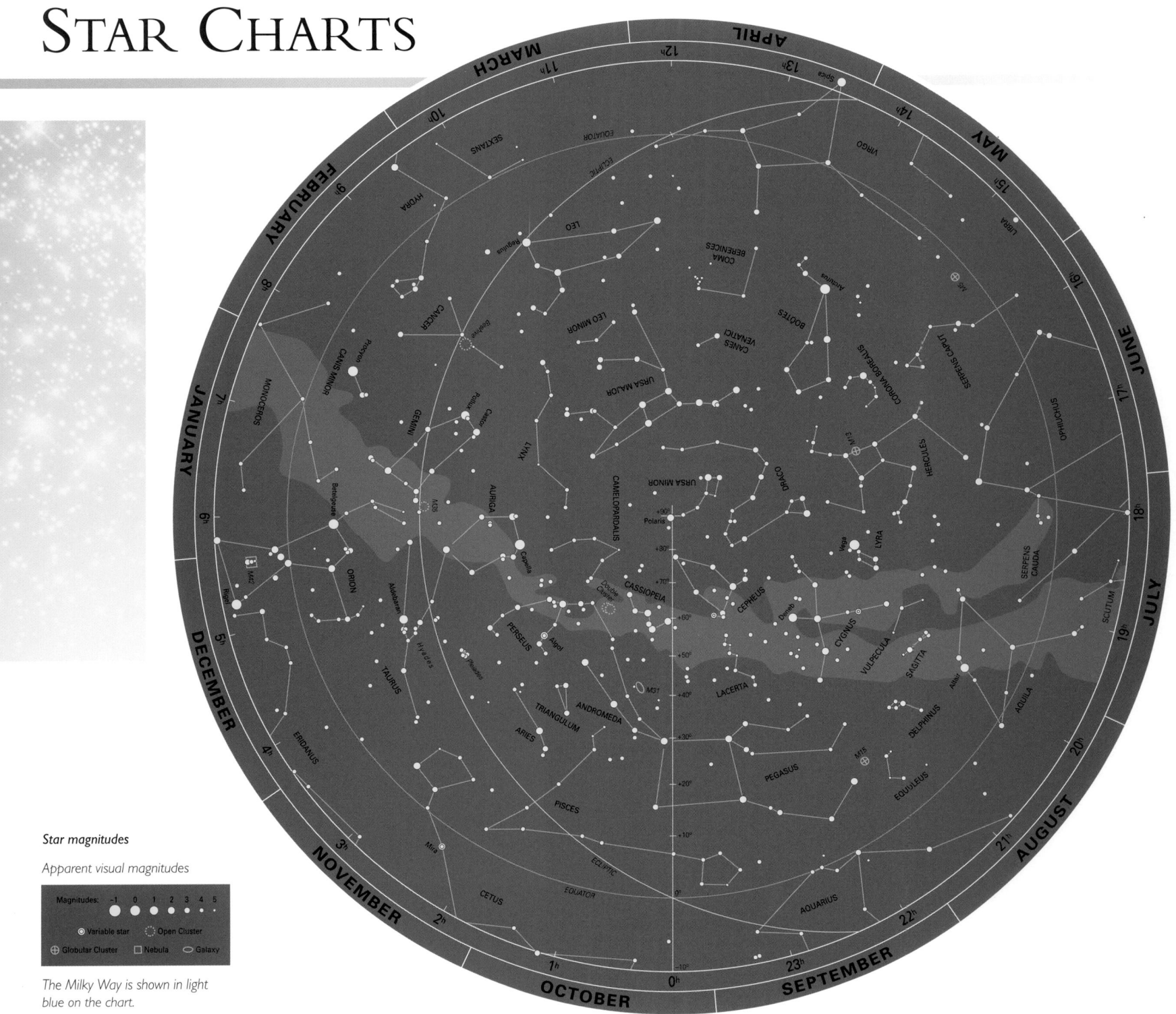

Star magnitudes

Apparent visual magnitudes

Magnitudes: -1 0 1 2 3 4 5

⊙ Variable star ⊙ Open Cluster
⊕ Globular Cluster ☐ Nebula ◯ Galaxy

The Milky Way is shown in light blue on the chart.

These pages show a star chart for each hemisphere. The northern hemisphere chart is centred on the North Celestial Pole, while the southern hemisphere chart is centred on the South Celestial Pole.

In the northern hemisphere, the North Pole is marked by the star Polaris, or Pole Star. Polaris lies within a degree of the point where an extension of the Earth's axis meets the sky. Polaris appears to be almost stationary, and navigators throughout history have used it as a guide. Unfortunately, the South Celestial Pole has no convenient reference point.

Star charts of the two hemispheres are bounded by the celestial equator, an imaginary line in the sky directly above the terrestrial equator. Astronomical co-ordinates, which give the location of stars, are normally stated in terms of

▲ **Star chart of the northern hemisphere**

When you look into the sky, the stars seem to be on the inside of a huge dome. This gives astronomers a way of mapping them. This chart shows the sky as it would appear from the North Pole. To use the star chart above, an observer in the northern hemisphere should face south and turn the chart so that the current month appears at the bottom. The chart will then show the constellations on view at about 11 p.m. Greenwich Mean Time. The map should be rotated clockwise 15° for each hour before 11 p.m. and anticlockwise for each hour after 11 p.m.

right ascension (the equivalent of longitude) and declination (the equivalent of latitude). Because the stars appear to rotate around the Earth every 24 hours, right ascension is measured eastwards in hours and minutes. Declination is measured in degrees north or south of the celestial equator.

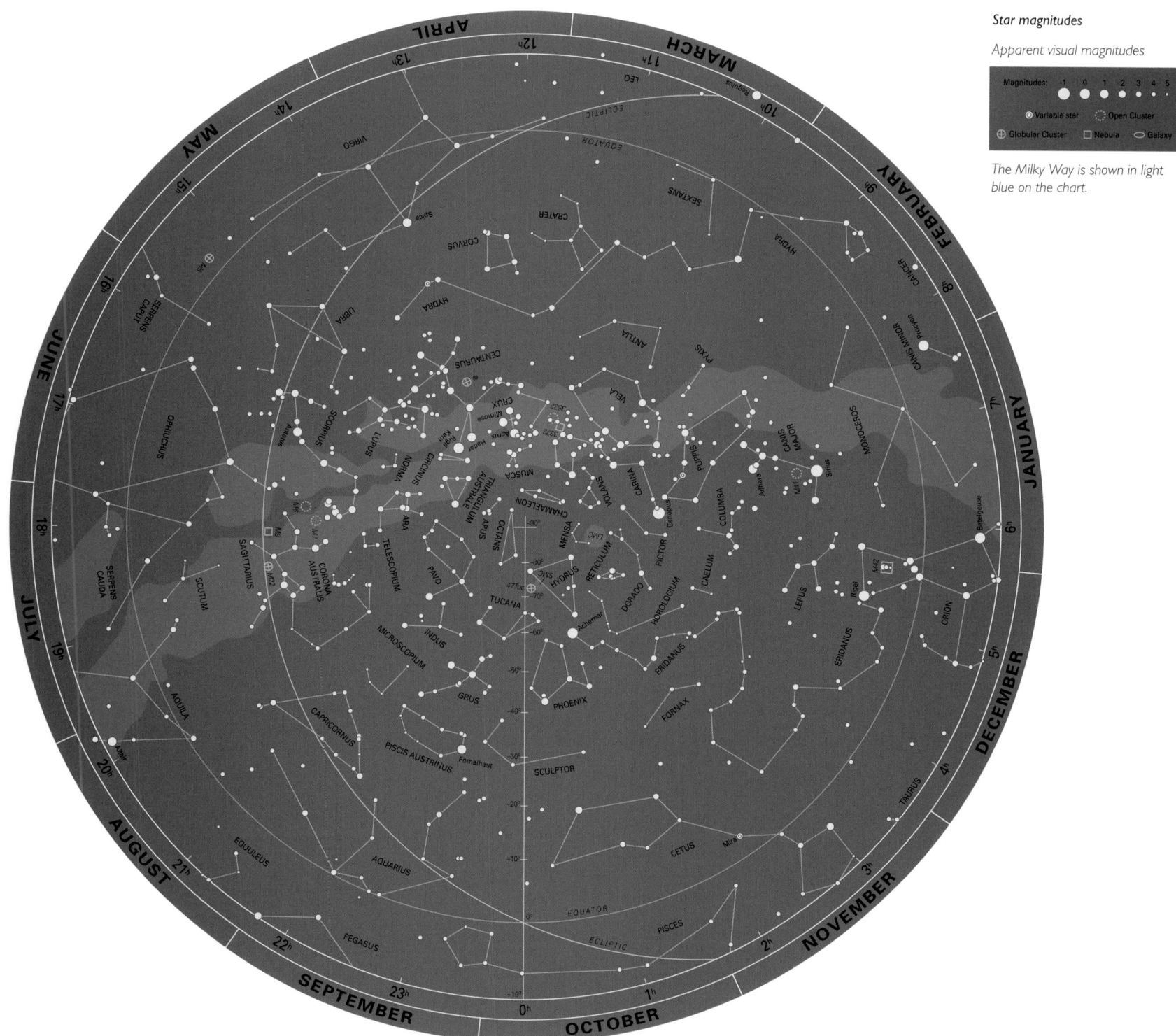

CONSTELLATIONS

Every star belongs to a particular constellation. There are 88 constellations, many of which were named by the ancient Greeks, Romans and other early peoples after animals and mythological characters, such as Orion and Perseus. More recently, astronomers invented names for constellations seen in the southern hemisphere, in areas not visible from around the Mediterranean Sea.

Some groups of easily recognizable stars form parts of a constellation. For example, seven stars form the shape of the Plough, or Big Dipper, within the constellation Ursa Major. Such groups are called asterisms.

The stars in constellations lie in the same direction in space, but normally at vastly different distances. Hence, there is no real connection

▲ *Star chart of the southern hemisphere*

Many constellations in the southern hemisphere were named not by the ancients but by later astronomers and thus have modern names. The Large and Small Magellanic Clouds (LMC, SMC) are small 'satellite' galaxies of the Milky Way. To use the chart, an observer in the southern hemisphere should face north and turn the chart so that the current month appears at the bottom. The map will then show the constellations on view at about 11 p.m. Greenwich Mean Time. The chart should be rotated clockwise 15° for each hour before 11 p.m. and anticlockwise for each hour after 11 p.m.

between them. The positions of stars seem fixed, but in fact the shapes of the constellations are changing slowly over very long periods of time. This is because the stars have their own 'proper motions', which because of the huge distances involved are imperceptible to the naked eye.

THE SOLAR SYSTEM

Although the origins of the Solar System are still a matter of debate, many scientists believe that it was formed from a cloud of gas and dust, the remains of a previous generation of stars. Around 5 billion years ago, material was drawn towards the hub of the rotating disk of gas and dust, where it was compressed to thermonuclear fusion temperatures. A new star, the Sun, was born, containing 99.8% of the mass of the Solar System.

The remaining material later gathered together to form the planets and the other bodies in the Solar System. Spacecraft, manned and unmanned, have greatly increased our knowledge of the Solar System since the start of the Space Age in 1957, when the Soviet Union launched the satellite Sputnik 1.

THE PLANETS

Mercury is the closest planet to the Sun and the fastest moving. Space probes have revealed that its surface is covered by craters, and looks much like the Earth's Moon. Mercury is a hostile place, with no significant atmosphere and temperatures ranging between 400°C [750°F] by day and −170°C [−275°F] by night. It seems unlikely that anyone will ever want to visit this planet.

Venus is much the same size as Earth, but it is the hottest of the planets, with temperatures reaching 475°C [885°F], even at night. The reason for this scorching heat is the atmosphere, which consists mainly of carbon dioxide, a gas that traps heat thus creating a greenhouse effect. The density of the atmosphere is about 90 times that of Earth, and dense clouds permanently mask the planet's surface. Active volcanic regions discharging sulphur dioxide may account for the haze of sulphuric-acid droplets in the upper atmosphere. Seen from Earth, Venus is brighter than any other star or planet and is

easy to spot. It is often the first object to be seen in the evening sky and the last to be seen in the morning sky. It can even be seen in daylight.

Earth, seen from space, looks blue (because of the oceans which cover more than 70% of the planet) and white (a result of clouds in the atmosphere). The atmosphere and water make Earth the only planet known to support life. The Earth's hard outer layers, including the crust and the top of the mantle, are divided into rigid plates. Forces inside the Earth move the plates, modifying the landscape, and causing earthquakes and volcanic activity. Weathering and erosion also change the surface.

Mars has many features in common with the Earth, including an atmosphere with clouds and polar caps that partly melt in summer. Scientists once considered that it was the most likely planet on which other life might exist, but the two Viking space probes that went there in the 1970s found only a barren rocky surface, with no trace of water. But, in 2004, two NASA Mars rovers – Spirit and Opportunity – sent back evidence that Mars was once wet and potentially habitable, at least by simple microbes.

PLANETARY DATA

Planet	Mean distance from Sun (million km)	Mass (Earth=1)	Period of orbit (Earth days/yrs)	Period of rotation (Earth days)	Equatorial diameter (km)	Average density (water=1)	Surface gravity (Earth=1)	Number of known satellites*
Sun	–	332,946	–	25.38	1,392,000	1.41	27.9	–
Mercury	57.9	0.06	87.97d	58.65	4,879	5.43	0.38	0
Venus	108.2	0.82	224.7d	243.02	12,104	5.24	0.91	0
Earth	149.6	1.00	365.3d	1.00	12,756	5.52	1.00	1
Mars	227.9	0.11	687.0d	1.029	6,792	3.94	0.38	2
Jupiter	778	317.8	11.86y	0.411	142,984	1.33	2.36	63
Saturn	1,427	95.2	29.45y	0.428	120,536	0.69	0.91	46
Uranus	2,871	14.5	84.02y	0.720	51,118	1.27	0.89	27
Neptune	4,498	17.2	164.8y	0.673	49,528	1.64	1.13	13
Pluto	5,906	0.002	247.9y	6.39	2,390	1.8	0.07	1

* Number of known satellites at mid-2005

Asteroids are small, rocky bodies. Most of them orbit the Sun between Mars and Jupiter, but some small ones can approach the Earth. The largest is Ceres, 913 km [567 miles] in diameter. There may be around a million asteroids bigger than 1 km [0.6 miles].

Jupiter, the giant planet, lies beyond Mars and the asteroid belt. Its mass is almost three times as much as all the other planets combined and, because of its size, it shines more brightly than any other planet apart from Venus and, occasionally, Mars. Jupiter is made up mostly of hydrogen and helium, covered by a layer of clouds. Its Great Red Spot is a high-pressure storm. The planet also has a faint ring system. The four largest moons of Jupiter were discovered by Galileo. They are worlds in their own right: Io is the most volcanic body yet discovered; Europa and Ganymede have icy surfaces, perhaps with liquid oceans below; and Callisto has an ancient, cratered terrain. Jupiter made headline news when it was struck by fragments of Comet Shoemaker–Levy 9 in July 1994, creating huge fireballs that caused scars on the planet that remained visible for months after the event.

Saturn is structurally similar to Jupiter but it is best known for its rings. The rings measure about 270,000 km [170,000 miles] across, yet they are no more than a few hundred metres thick. Seen from Earth, the rings seem divided into three main bands of varying brightness,

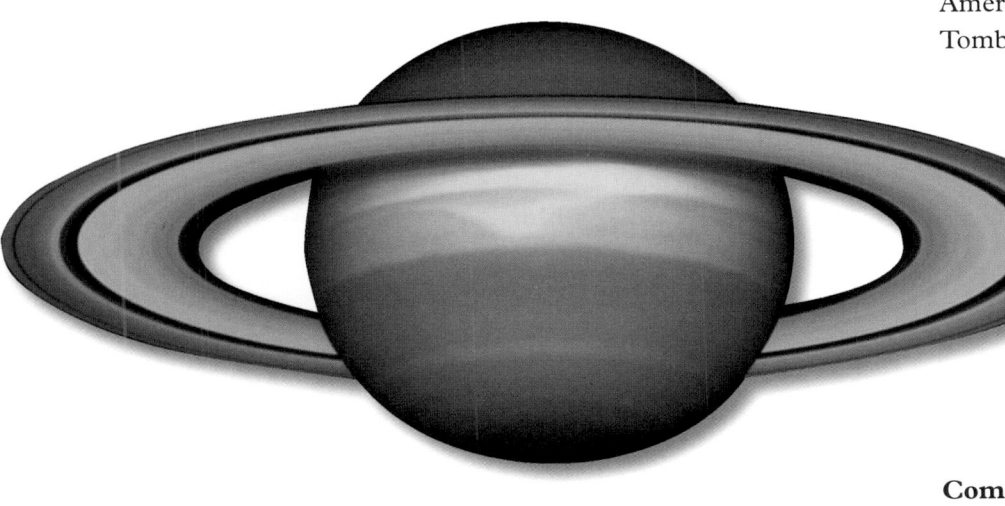

but photographs sent back by space probes showed that they are broken up into thousands of thin ringlets composed of ice particles ranging in size from a snowball to an iceberg. The origin of the rings is still a matter of debate.

Uranus was discovered in 1781 by William Herschel, who first thought it was a comet. It is broadly similar to Jupiter and Saturn in composition, though its distance from the Sun makes its surface even colder. Uranus is circled by thin rings which were discovered in 1977. Unlike the rings of Saturn, the rings of Uranus are black, which explains why they cannot be seen from Earth.

Neptune, named after the mythological sea god, was discovered in 1846 as the result of mathematical predictions made by astronomers to explain irregularities in the orbit of Uranus, its near twin. Little was known about this distant body until Voyager 2 came close to it in 1989. Neptune has thin rings, like those of Uranus. Its atmosphere features blue-green clouds and the occasional prominent dark spot.

Pluto is the smallest planet in the Solar System, even smaller than the Earth's Moon. The American astronomer Clyde Tombaugh discovered Pluto in 1930. Its orbit is odd and it sometimes comes closer to the Sun than Neptune. The Kuiper Belt is a vast region beyond the orbit of Neptune which contains many icy, asteroid-sized objects. Pluto and its solitary moon, Charon, are two of the largest objects in the Kuiper Belt.

Comets are small icy bodies that orbit the Sun in highly elliptical orbits. When a comet swings in towards the Sun some of its ice evaporates, and the comet brightens and may become visible from Earth. The best known is Halley's Comet, which takes 76 years to orbit the Sun.

THE EARTH: TIME AND MOTION

The Earth is constantly moving through space like a huge, self-sufficient spaceship. First, with the rest of the Solar System, it moves around the centre of the Milky Way galaxy. Second, it rotates around the Sun at a speed of more than 100,000 km/h [60,000 mph], covering a distance of nearly 1,000 million km [600 million miles] in a little over 365 days. The Earth also spins on its axis, an imaginary line joining the North and South Poles, via the centre of the Earth, completing one turn in a day. The Earth's movements around the Sun determine our calendar, though accurate observations of the stars made by astronomers

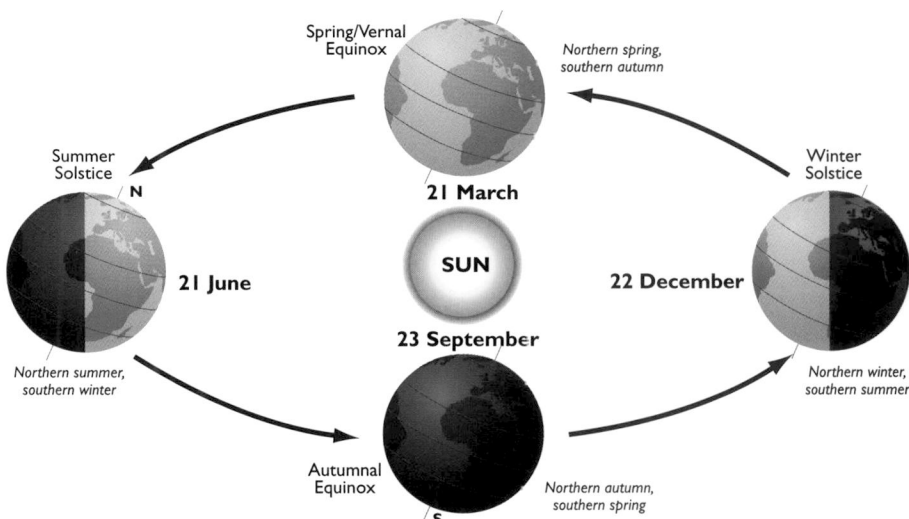

▼ *The Earth from the Moon*

In 1969, Neil Armstrong and Edwin 'Buzz' Aldrin, Jr, were the first people to set foot on the Moon. This photograph of the Earth was taken by the crew of Apollo 11 as they orbited the Moon.

help to keep our clocks in step with the rotation of the Earth around the Sun.

THE CHANGING YEAR

The Earth takes 365 days, 6 hours, 9 minutes and 9.54 seconds to complete one orbit around the Sun. We have a calendar year of 365 days, so allowance has to be made for the extra time over and above the 365 days. This is allowed for by introducing leap years of 366 days. Leap years are generally those, such as 1992 and 1996, which are divisible by four. Century years, however, are not leap years unless they are divisible by 400. Hence, 1700, 1800 and 1900 were not leap years, but the year 2000 was one. Leap years help to make the calendar conform with the solar year.

Because the Earth's axis is tilted by approximately 23½°, the middle latitudes enjoy four distinct seasons. On 21 March, the vernal or spring equinox in the northern hemisphere, the Sun is directly overhead at the equator and everywhere on Earth has about 12 hours of daylight and 12 hours of darkness. But as the Earth continues on its journey around the Sun, the northern hemisphere tilts more and more towards the Sun. Finally, on 21 June, the Sun is overhead at the Tropic of Cancer (latitude 23½° North). This is the summer solstice in the northern hemisphere.

▲ *The Seasons*

The approximate 23½° tilt of the Earth's axis remains constant as the Earth orbits around the Sun. As a result, first the northern and then the southern hemispheres lean towards the Sun. Annual variations in the amount of sunlight received in turn by each hemisphere are responsible for the four seasons experienced in the middle latitudes.

▼ *Tides*

The daily rises and falls of the ocean's waters are caused by the gravitational pull of the Moon and the Sun. The effect is greatest on the hemisphere facing the Moon, causing a 'tidal bulge'. The diagram below shows that the Sun, Moon and Earth are in line when the spring tides occur. This causes the greatest tidal ranges. On the other hand, the neap tides occur when the pull of the Moon and the Sun are opposed. Neap tides, when tidal ranges are at their lowest, occur near the Moon's first and third quarters.

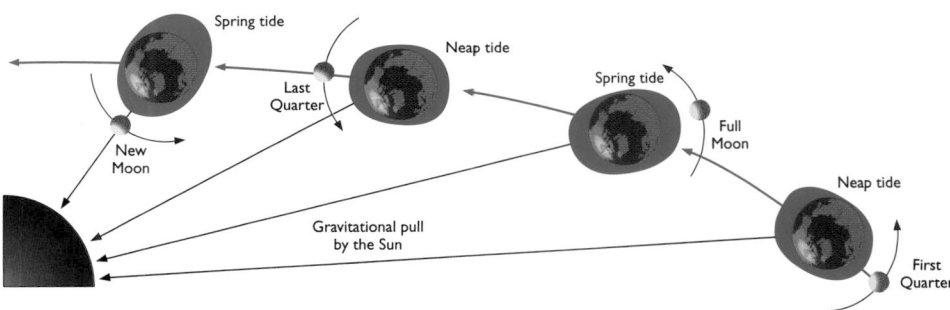

SUN DATA

DIAMETER	1.391×10^6 km
VOLUME	1.412×10^{18} km³
VOLUME (EARTH=1)	1.303×10^6
MASS	1.989×10^{30} kg
MASS (EARTH=1)	3.329×10^6
MEAN DENSITY (WATER=1)	1.409
ROTATION PERIOD:	
AT EQUATOR	25.4 days
AT POLES	about 35 days
SURFACE GRAVITY	
(EARTH=1)	28
MAGNITUDE:	
APPARENT	−26.9
ABSOLUTE	+4.71
TEMPERATURE:	
AT SURFACE	5,500°C [5,800 K]
AT CORE	15×10^6 K

MOON DATA

DIAMETER	3,475 km
MASS (EARTH=1)	0.0123
DENSITY (WATER=1)	3.34
MEAN DISTANCE FROM EARTH	384,401 km
MAXIMUM DISTANCE (APOGEE)	406,700 km
MINIMUM DISTANCE (PERIGEE)	356,400 km
SIDEREAL ROTATION AND REVOLUTION PERIOD	27.322 days
SYNODIC MONTH (NEW MOON TO NEW MOON)	29.531 days
SURFACE GRAVITY (EARTH=1)	0.165
MEAN DAYTIME SURFACE TEMPERATURE	+117°C [390 K]
MEAN NIGHTTIME SURFACE TEMPERATURE	−163°C [110 K]

▶ *Phases of the Moon*

The Moon rotates more slowly than the Earth, making one complete turn on its axis in just over 27 days. This corresponds to its period of revolution around the Earth and, hence, the same hemisphere always faces us. The interval between one full Moon and the next (and also between new Moons) is about 29½ days, or one lunar month. The apparent changes in the appearance of the Moon are caused by its changing position in relation to the Earth. Like the planets, the Moon produces no light of its own. It shines by reflecting the Sun's rays, varying from a slim crescent to a full circle, and back again.

The overhead Sun then moves south again until, on 23 September, the autumnal equinox in the northern hemisphere, the Sun is again overhead at the Equator. The overhead Sun then moves south until, on around 22 December, it is overhead at the Tropic of Capricorn. This is the winter solstice in the northern hemisphere, and the summer solstice in the southern, where the seasons are reversed.

At the poles, there are two seasons. During half of the year, one of the poles leans towards the Sun and has continuous sunlight. For the other six months, the pole leans away from the Sun and is in continuous darkness.

Regions around the equator do not have marked seasons. Because the Sun is high in the sky throughout the year, it is always hot or warm. When people talk of seasons in the tropics, they are usually referring to other factors, such as rainy and dry periods.

DAY, NIGHT AND TIDES

As the Earth rotates on its axis every 24 hours, first one side of the planet and then the other faces the Sun and enjoys daylight, while the opposite side is in darkness.

The length of daylight varies throughout the year. The longest day in the northern hemisphere falls on the summer solstice, 21 June, while the longest day in the southern hemisphere is on 22 December. At 40° latitude, the length of daylight on the longest day is 14 hours, 30 minutes. At 60° latitude, daylight on that day lasts 18 hours, 30 minutes. On the shortest day, 22 December in the northern hemisphere and 21 June in the southern, daylight hours at 40° latitude total 9 hours and 9 minutes. At latitude 60°, daylight lasts only 5 hours, 30 minutes in the 24-hour period.

Tides are caused by the gravitational pull of the Moon and, to a lesser extent, the Sun on the waters in the world's oceans. Tides occur twice every 24 hours, 50 minutes – one complete orbit of the Moon around the Earth.

▲ *Total eclipse of the Sun*

A total eclipse is caused when the Moon passes between the Sun and the Earth. With the Sun's bright disk completely obscured, the Sun's corona, or outer atmosphere, can be viewed.

The highest tides, the spring tides, occur when the Earth, Moon and Sun are in a straight line, so that the gravitational pulls of the Moon and Sun are combined. The lowest, or neap, tides occur when the Moon, Earth and Sun form a right angle. The gravitational pull of the Moon is then opposed by the gravitational pull of the Sun. The greatest tidal ranges occur in the Bay of Fundy in Canada. The greatest mean spring range is 14.5 m [47.5 ft].

The speed at which the Earth is spinning on its axis is gradually slowing down, because of the movement of tides. As a result, experts have calculated that, in about 200 million years, the day will be 25 hours long.

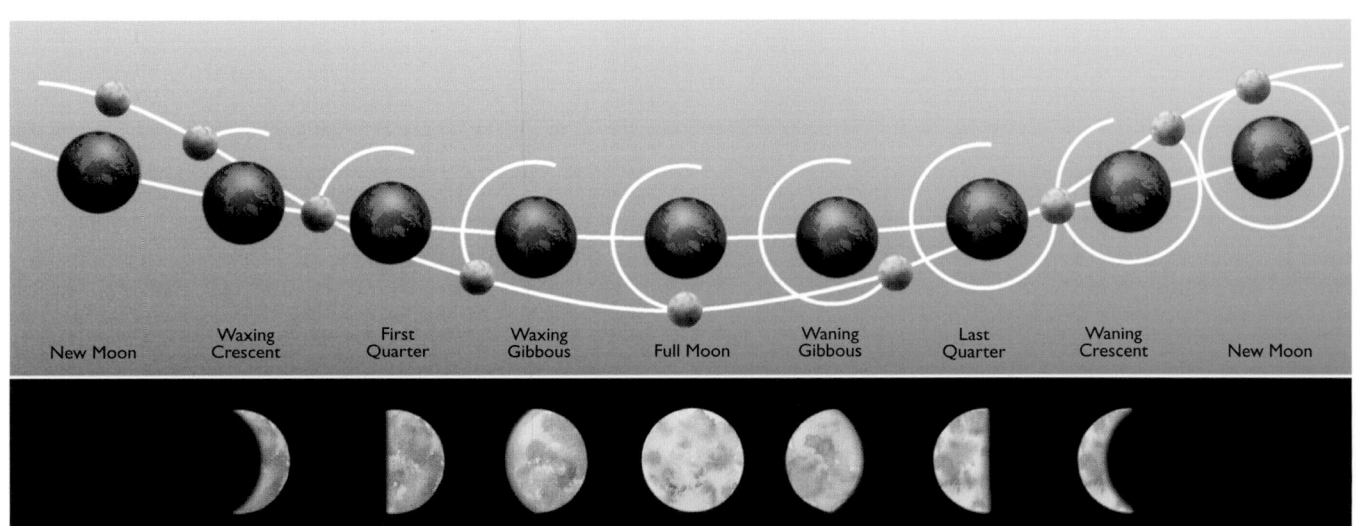

New Moon	Waxing Crescent	First Quarter	Waxing Gibbous	Full Moon	Waning Gibbous	Last Quarter	Waning Crescent	New Moon

THE EARTH FROM SPACE

Any last doubts about whether the Earth was round or flat were finally resolved by the appearance of the first photographs of our planet taken at the start of the Space Age. Satellite images also confirmed that map- and globe-makers had correctly worked out the shapes of the continents and the oceans.

More importantly, images of our beautiful, blue, white and brown planet from space impressed on many people that the Earth and its resources are finite. They made people realize that if we allow our planet to be damaged by such factors as overpopulation, pollution and irresponsible over-use of resources, then its future and the survival of all the living things upon it may be threatened.

VIEWS FROM ABOVE

The first aerial photographs were taken from balloons in the mid-19th century and their importance in military reconnaissance was recognized as early as the 1860s during the American Civil War.

Since the end of World War II, photographs

▼ *Mount Etna, Sicily*

The most active volcano in Europe, Mount Etna, 3,323 m [10,906 ft] high, is shown here during the 2002–3 eruption, its plume of ash and smoke spreading southwards over the Mediterranean, east of Malta.

taken by aircraft have been widely used in map-making. The use of air photographs has greatly speeded up the laborious process of mapping land details and they have enabled cartographers to produce maps of the most remote parts of the world.

Aerial photographs have also proved useful because they reveal features that are not visible at ground level. For example, circles that appear on many air photographs do not correspond to visible features on the ground. Many of these mysterious shapes have turned out to be the sites of ancient settlements previously unknown to archaeologists.

IMAGES FROM SPACE

Space probes equipped with cameras and a variety of remote-sensing instruments have sent back images of distant planets and moons. From these images, detailed maps have been produced, rapidly expanding our knowledge of the Solar System.

Images from space are also proving invaluable in the study of the Earth. One of the best known uses of space imagery is the study of the atmosphere. Polar-orbiting weather satellites that circle the Earth, together with geostationary satellites, whose motion is synchronized with the Earth's rotation, now regularly transmit images showing the changing patterns of weather systems from above. Forecasters use these images to track the development and the paths taken by hurricanes, enabling them to issue storm warnings to endangered areas, saving lives and reducing damage to property.

Remote-sensing devices are now monitoring changes in temperatures over the land and sea, while photographs indicate the melting of ice sheets. Such evidence is vital in the study of global warming. Other devices reveal polluted areas, patterns of vegetation growth, and areas suffering deforestation.

In recent years, remote-sensing devices have been used to monitor the damage being done to the ozone layer in the stratosphere, which prevents most of the Sun's harmful ultraviolet radiation from reaching the surface. The discovery of 'ozone holes', where the protective layer of ozone is being thinned by chlorofluorocarbons (CFCs), chemicals used in the manufacture of such things as air conditioners and refrigerators, has enabled governments to take concerted action to save our planet from imminent danger.

EARTH DATA

MAXIMUM DISTANCE FROM SUN (APHELION)
152,096,150 km

MINIMUM DISTANCE FROM SUN (PERIHELION)
147,099,590 km

LENGTH OF YEAR – SOLAR TROPICAL (EQUINOX TO EQUINOX)
365.24 days

LENGTH OF YEAR – SIDEREAL (FIXED STAR TO FIXED STAR)
365.26 days

LENGTH OF DAY – MEAN SOLAR DAY
24 hours, 3 minutes, 56 seconds

LENGTH OF DAY – MEAN SIDEREAL DAY
23 hours, 56 minutes, 4 seconds

SUPERFICIAL AREA
510,000,000 sq km

LAND SURFACE
149,000,000 sq km (29.2%)

WATER SURFACE
361,000,000 sq km (70.8%)

EQUATORIAL CIRCUMFERENCE
40,074 km

POLAR CIRCUMFERENCE
40,008 km

EQUATORIAL DIAMETER
12,756 km

POLAR DIAMETER
12,714 km

EQUATORIAL RADIUS
6,378 km

POLAR RADIUS
6,357 km

VOLUME OF THE EARTH
1,083,230 × 10^6 cu km

MASS OF THE EARTH
5.97×10^{24} kg

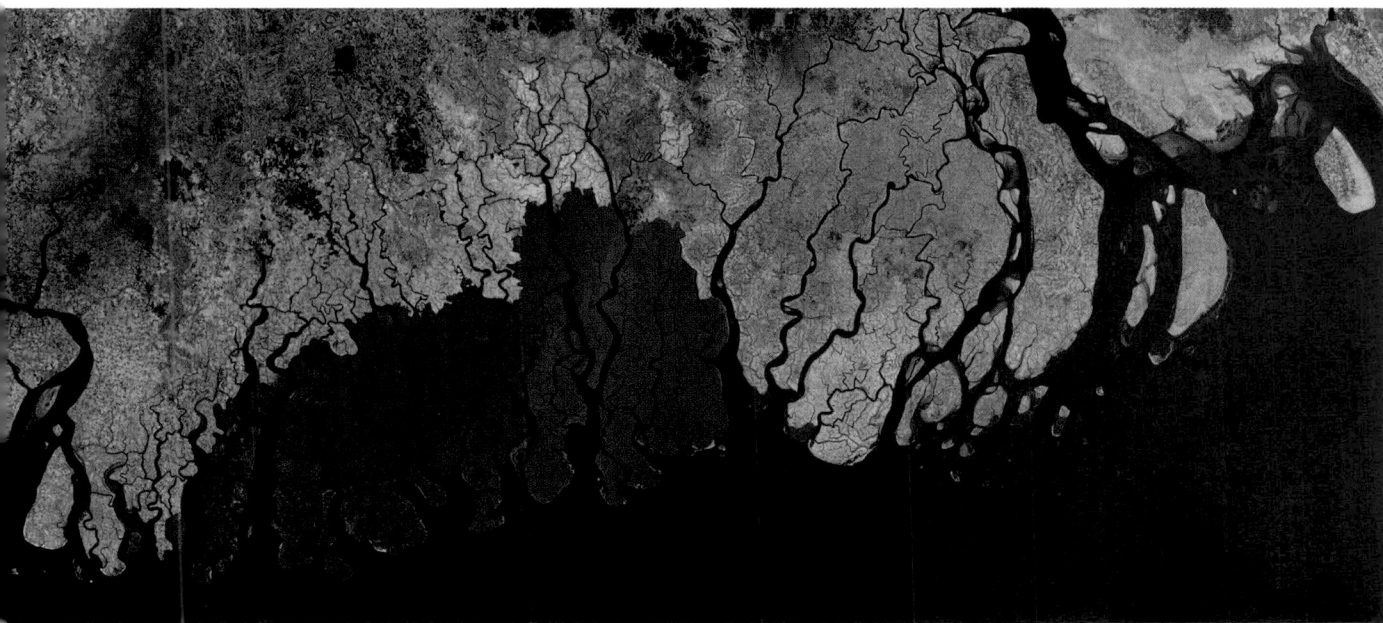

◄ *Ganges Delta, India/Bangladesh*
Over 300 km [186 miles] wide, this
is the world's largest delta, created by
the River Ganges depositing sediment
it has carried from the Himalayas.
It is extremely vulnerable to frequent
cyclones and tidal surges, but is
densely populated because of the
fertile land. On the western side of
the image is the mouth of the Hugli,
with the elongated city of Kolkata
(Calcutta) showing as dark grey just to
the north. The large red area indicates
the presence of mangrove forests and
swamps, and is divided between the
countries of India and Bangladesh.

► *Imperial Valley, USA/Mexico*
The Salton Sea is the dark area
at the top left of the image.
It was inadvertently created in
1905 during an attempt to divert
the flow of the Colorado River for
irrigation. It lies 72 m [236 ft]
below sea level and is very saline.
To the south is a large area of
productive land, showing bright
red on this image. The abrupt
colour change towards the
bottom of this area marks
the US–Mexico boundary.

THE DYNAMIC EARTH

The Earth was formed about 4.6 billion years [4,600 million years] ago from the ring of gas and dust left over after the formation of the Sun. As the Earth took shape, lighter elements, such as silicon, rose to the surface, while heavy elements, notably iron, sank towards the centre.

Gradually, the outer layers cooled to form a hard crust. The crust enclosed the dense mantle which, in turn, surrounded the even denser liquid outer and solid inner core. Around the Earth was an atmosphere, which contained abundant water vapour. When the surface cooled, rainwater began to fill hollows, forming the first lakes and seas. Since that time, our planet has been subject to constant change – the result of powerful internal and external forces that still operate today.

THE HISTORY OF THE EARTH

From their study of rocks, geologists have pieced together the history of our planet and the life forms that evolved upon it. They have dated the oldest known crystals, composed of the mineral zircon, at 4.2 billion years. But the oldest rocks are younger, less than 4 billion years old. This is because older rocks have been recycled or weathered away by natural processes.

The oldest rocks that contain fossils, which are

▼ *Lulworth Cove, southern England*
When undisturbed by earth movements, sedimentary rock strata are generally horizontal. But lateral pressure has squeezed the Jurassic strata at Lulworth Cove into complex folds.

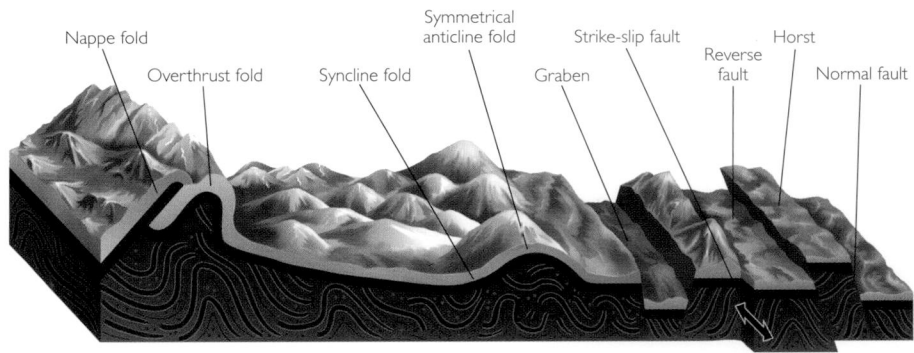

evidence of once-living organisms, are around 3.5 billion years old. But fossils are rare in rocks formed in the first 4 billion years of Earth history. This vast expanse of time is called the Precambrian. This is because it precedes the Cambrian period, at the start of which, about 590 million years ago, life was abundant in the seas.

The Cambrian is the first period in the Paleozoic (or ancient life) era. The Paleozoic era is followed by the Mesozoic (middle life) era, which witnessed the spectacular rise and fall of the dinosaurs, and the Cenozoic (recent life) era, which was dominated by the evolution of mammals. Each of the eras is divided into periods, and the periods in the Cenozoic era, covering the last 65 million years, are further divided into epochs.

THE EARTH'S CHANGING FACE

While life was gradually evolving, the face of the Earth was constantly changing. By piecing together evidence of rock structures and fossils, geologists have demonstrated that around 250 million years ago, all the world's land areas were grouped together in one huge landmass called Pangaea. Around 180 million years ago, the supercontinent Pangaea began to break up. New oceans opened up as the continents began to move towards their present positions.

Evidence of how continents drift came from studies of the ocean floor in the 1950s and 1960s. Scientists discovered that the oceans are young features. By contrast with the continents, no part of the ocean floor is more than 200 million years old. The floors of oceans older than 200 million years have completely vanished.

Studies of long undersea ranges, called ocean ridges, revealed that the youngest rocks occur along their centres, which are the edges of huge plates – rigid blocks of the Earth's lithosphere, which is made up of the crust and the solid upper layer of the mantle. The Earth's lithosphere is split into six large and several smaller plates. The ocean ridges are 'constructive' plate margins, because new crustal rock is being

▲ *Mountain building*
Lateral pressure, which occurs when plates collide, squeezes and compresses rocks into folds. Simple symmetrical upfolds are called anticlines, while downfolds are synclines. As the pressure builds up, strata become asymmetrical and they may be tilted over to form recumbent folds. The rocks often crack under the intense pressure and the folds are sheared away and pushed forward over other rocks. These features are called overthrust folds or nappes. Plate movements also create faults along which rocks move upwards, downwards and sideways. The diagram shows a downfaulted graben, or rift valley, and an uplifted horst, or block mountain.

Nappe fold • Overthrust fold • Syncline fold • Symmetrical anticline fold • Strike-slip fault • Graben • Reverse fault • Horst • Normal fault

The geological time scale was first constructed by a study of the stratigraphic, or relative, ages of layers of rock. But the absolute ages of rock strata could not be fixed until the discovery of radioactivity in the early 20th century. Some names of periods, such as Cambrian (Latin for Wales), come from places where the rocks were first studied. Others, such as Carboniferous, refer to the nature of the rocks formed during the period. For example, coal seams (containing carbon) were formed from decayed plant matter during the Carboniferous period.

formed there from magma that wells up from the mantle as the plates gradually move apart. The deep-ocean trenches are 'destructive' plate edges where two plates are pushing against each other. One plate descends beneath the other into the mantle where it is melted. These areas are called 'subduction zones'.

A third type of plate edge is called a transform fault. Here two plates are moving alongside each other. The best known of these plate edges is the San Andreas fault in California, which separates the Pacific plate from the North American plate.

Slow-moving currents in the partly molten asthenosphere, which underlies the solid lithosphere, are responsible for moving the plates, a process called plate tectonics.

MOUNTAIN BUILDING

The study of plate tectonics has helped geol-

▲ *The Himalayas seen from Nepal*

The Himalayas are a young fold mountain range formed by a collision between two plates. The earthquakes felt in the region testify that the plate movements are still continuing.

ogists to understand the mechanisms that are responsible for the creation of mountains. Many of the world's greatest ranges were created by the collision of two plates and the bending of the intervening strata into huge loops, or folds. For example, the Himalayas began to rise around 50 million years ago, when a plate supporting India collided with the huge Eurasian plate. Rocks on the floor of the intervening and long-vanished Tethys Sea were squeezed up to form the Himalayan Mountain Range.

Plate movements also create tension that cracks rocks, producing long faults along which rocks move upwards, downwards or sideways. Block mountains are formed when blocks of rock are pushed upwards along faults. Steep-sided rift valleys are formed when blocks of land sink down between faults. For example, the basin and range region of the south-western United States has both block mountains and downfaulted basins, such as Death Valley.

Pre-Cambrian	Lower		Paleozoic (Primary)			Upper		Mesozoic (Secondary)			Cenozoic (Tertiary, Quaternary)							Era
Pre-Cambrian	Cambrian	Ordovician	Silurian	Devonian	Carboniferous	Permian	Triassic	Jurassic	Cretaceous	Paleocene	Eocene	Oligocene	Miocene	Pliocene	Quaternary			System
			CALEDONIAN FOLDING		HERCYNIAN FOLDING							LARAMIDE FOLDING	ALPINE FOLDING					Orogeny
600	550	500	450	400	350	300	250	200	150	100	50							

Millions of years before present

EARTHQUAKES AND VOLCANOES

On 26 December 2003, a powerful earthquake measuring 6.7 on the Richter scale devastated the city of Bam in south-eastern Iran when most people were asleep. The official death toll was 26,271. About 80% of the buildings in Bam and nearby areas collapsed, and much of the medieval fortress outside Bam was also destroyed. In 2005, a 6.5-magnitude earthquake struck a rural area 190 km [118 miles] north-west of Bam, killing more than 400 people.

THE RESTLESS EARTH

Earthquakes can occur anywhere, whenever rocks move along faults. But the most severe and most numerous earthquakes occur near

▼ *San Andreas Fault, United States*
Geologists call the San Andreas fault in south-western California a transform, or strike-slip, fault. Sudden movements along it cause earthquakes. In 1906, shifts of about 4.5 m [15 ft] occurred near San Francisco, causing a massive earthquake.

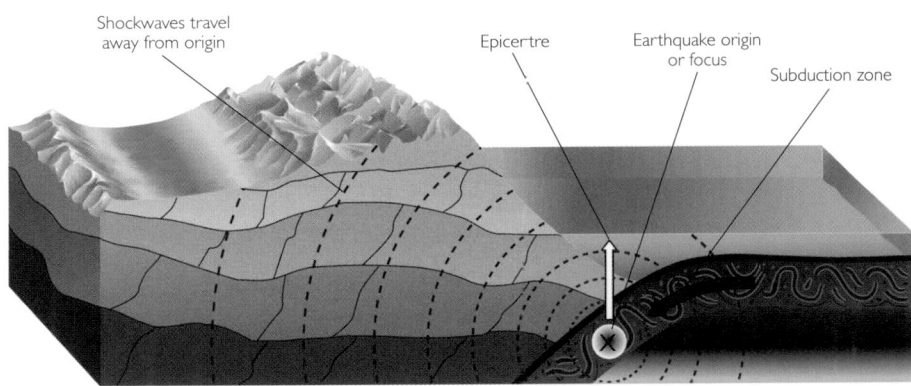

the edges of the plates that make up the Earth's lithosphere. Japan, for example, lies in a particularly unstable region above subduction zones, where plates are descending into the Earth's mantle. It lies in a zone encircling the Pacific Ocean, called the 'Pacific ring of fire'.

Plates do not move smoothly. Their edges are jagged and for most of the time they are locked together. However, pressure gradually builds up until the rocks break and the plates lurch forwards, setting off vibrations ranging from slight tremors to terrifying earthquakes. The greater the pressure released, the more destructive the earthquake.

Earthquakes are also common along the ocean trenches where plates are moving apart, but they mostly occur so far from land that they do little damage. Far more destructive are the earthquakes that occur where plates are moving alongside each other. For example, the earthquakes that periodically rock south-western California are caused by movements along the San Andreas Fault.

The spot where an earthquake originates is called the focus, while the point on the Earth's surface directly above the focus is called the epicentre. Two kinds of waves, P-waves or compressional waves and S-waves or shear waves, travel from the focus to the surface where they make the ground shake. P-waves travel faster than S-waves and the time difference between their arrival at recording stations enables scientists to calculate the distance from a station to the epicentre.

Earthquakes are measured on the Richter scale, which indicates the magnitude of the shock. The most destructive earthquakes are shallow-focus, that is, the focus is within 60 km [37 miles] of the surface. A magnitude of 7.0 is a major earthquake, but lower magnitude 'quakes can cause great damage if their epicentres are close to densely populated areas.

Scientists have been working for years to find effective ways of forecasting earthquakes but

▲ *Earthquakes in subduction zones*
Along subduction zones, one plate is descending beneath another. The plates are locked together until the rocks break and the descending plate lurches forwards. From the point where the plate moves – the origin – seismic waves spread through the lithosphere, making the ground shake. The earthquake in Mexico City in 1985 occurred in this way.

NOTABLE EARTHQUAKES
(since 1900)

Year	Location	Mag.
1906	San Francisco, USA	8.3
1906	Valparaiso, Chile	8.6
1908	Messina, Italy	7.5
1915	Avezzano, Italy	7.5
1920	Gansu, China	8.6
1923	Yokohama, Japan	8.3
1927	Nan Shan, China	8.3
1932	Gansu, China	7.6
1934	Bihar, India/Nepal	8.4
1935	Quetta, India[†]	7.5
1939	Chillan, Chile	8.3
1939	Erzincan, Turkey	7.9
1964	Anchorage, Alaska	8.4
1968	N. E. Iran	7.4
1970	N. Peru	7.7
1976	Guatemala	7.5
1976	Tangshan, China	8.2
1978	Tabas, Iran	7.7
1980	El Asnam, Algeria	7.3
1980	S. Italy	7.2
1985	Mexico City, Mexico	8.1
1988	N. W. Armenia	6.8
1990	N. Iran	7.7
1993	Maharashtra, India	6.4
1994	Los Angeles, USA	6.6
1995	Kobe, Japan	7.2
1995	Sakhalin Is., Russia	7.5
1996	Yunnan, China	7.0
1997	N. E. Iran	7.1
1998	N. Afghanistan	6.1
1998	N. E. Afghanistan	7.0
1999	Izmit, Turkey	7.4
1999	Taipei, Taiwan	7.6
2001	El Salvador	7.7
2001	Gujarat, India	7.7
2002	Afyon, Turkey	6.0
2002	Baghlan, Afghanistan	6.1
2003	Mexico	7.8
2003	Bam, Iran	6.7
2004	N. Morocco	6.5
2004	Sumatra, Indonesia	9.1

[†] *now Pakistan*

with limited success. But in the early 2000s, some scientists claimed that they had successfully forecast eruptions by identifying tremors, called 'long-period events'. They believe these relatively minor but long-lasting tremors are caused when magma surges up underground passages but fails to reach the surface.

VOLCANIC ERUPTIONS

Most active volcanoes also occur on or near plate edges. Many undersea volcanoes along the ocean ridges are formed from magma that wells up from the asthenosphere to fill the gaps created as the plates, on the opposite sides of the ridges, move apart. Some of these volcanoes reach the surface to form islands. Iceland is a country which straddles the Mid-Atlantic Ocean Ridge. It is gradually becoming wider as magma rises to the surface through faults and vents. Other volcanoes lie alongside subduction zones. The magma that fuels them comes from the melted edges of the descending plates.

A few volcanoes lie far from plate edges. For example, Mauna Loa and Kilauea on Hawai'i are situated near the centre of the huge Pacific plate. The molten magma that reaches the surface is created by a source of heat, called a 'hot spot', in the Earth's mantle.

Magma is molten rock at temperatures of about 1,100°C to 1,200°C [2,012°F to 2,192°F]. It contains gases and superheated steam. The chemical composition of magma varies. Viscous magma is rich in silica and superheated steam, while runny magma contains less silica and steam. The chemical composition of the magma affects the nature of volcanic eruptions.

Explosive volcanoes contain thick, viscous magma. When they erupt, they usually hurl clouds of ash (shattered fragments of cooled magma) into the air. By contrast, quiet volcanoes emit long streams of runny magma, or lava. However, many volcanoes are intermediate in type, sometimes erupting explosively and sometimes emitting streams of fluid lava. Explosive and intermediate volcanoes usually have a conical shape, while quiet volcanoes are flattened, resembling upturned saucers. They are often called shield volcanoes.

One dangerous type of eruption is called a *nuée ardente*, or 'glowing cloud'. It occurs when a cloud of intensely hot volcanic gases, dust particles, and superheated steam are exploded sideways from a volcano, often following a violent explosion which hurls ash high into the air. Pyroclastic surges and flows are similar. The clouds sweep downhill, destroying all in their paths. Pyroclastic surges and flows killed many people during the Vesuvius eruption in AD 79. The bodies were later buried by ash falls.

▲ *Cross-section of a volcano*

Volcanoes are vents in the ground, through which magma reaches the surface. The term volcano is also used for the mountains formed from volcanic rocks. Beneath volcanoes are pockets of magma derived from the semi-molten asthenosphere in the mantle. The magma rises under pressure through the overlying rocks until it reaches the surface. There it emerges through vents as pyroclasts, ranging in size from large lumps of magma, called volcanic bombs, to fine volcanic ash and dust. In quiet eruptions, streams of liquid lava run down the side of the mountain. Side vents sometimes appear on the flanks of existing volcanoes.

▲ *Kilauea Volcano, Hawai'i*

The volcanic Hawaiian islands in the North Pacific Ocean were formed as the Pacific plate moved over a 'hot spot' in the Earth's mantle. Kilauea on Hawai'i emits blazing streams of liquid lava.

FORCES OF NATURE

On 26 December 2004, a sudden movement of the plates beneath the Indian Ocean triggered a magnitude 9.1 earthquake. The 'quake created a tsunami, a fast-moving wave that battered the coasts of southern and south-eastern Asia, and was even felt in East Africa. Entire communities were wiped out and the death toll was about 280,000. The worst damage occurred in Indonesia, Thailand, Sri Lanka and India. Such events remind us of the great forces that operate inside our planet. But other forces are operating continuously, forever changing the landscape.

The chief forces acting on the surface of the Earth are weathering, running water, ice and winds. The forces of erosion seem to act slowly. One estimate suggests that an average of only 3.5 cm [1.4 inches] of land is removed by natural processes every 1,000 years. But over millions of years, the highest mountains are eroded away.

WEATHERING
Weathering occurs in all parts of the world, but the most effective type of weathering in any area depends on the climate and the nature of the

▼ *Grand Canyon, Arizona, at dusk*
The Grand Canyon in the United States is one of the world's natural wonders. Eroded by the Colorado River and its tributaries, it is up to 1.6 km [1 mile] deep and 29 km [18 miles] wide.

RATES OF EROSION

	SLOW	WEATHERING RATE	FAST
Mineral solubility	low (e.g. quartz)	moderate (e.g. feldspar)	high (e.g. calcite)
Rainfall	low	moderate	heavy
Temperature	cold	temperate	hot
Vegetation	sparse	moderate	lush
Soil cover	bare rock	thin to moderate soil	thick soil

Weathering is the breakdown and decay of rocks in situ. It may be mechanical (physical), chemical or biological.

rocks. For example, in cold mountain areas, when water freezes in cracks in rocks, the ice occupies 9% more space than the water. This exerts a force which, when repeated over and over again, can split boulders apart. By contrast, in hot deserts, intense heating by day and cooling by night causes the outer layers of rocks to expand and contract until they break up and peel away like layers of an onion. These are examples of what is called mechanical weathering.

Chemical weathering involves chemical reactions in various rocks. These reactions usually involve water. For example, rainwater containing carbon dioxide dissolved from the air or soil is a weak acid that reacts with limestone, wearing out pits, tunnels and complex networks of caves. Water also combines with some minerals, such as feldspar in granite, to create kaolin, a soft white clay.

▲ *Rates of erosion*
The chart shows that the rates at which weathering takes place depend on the chemistry and hardness of rocks, climatic factors, especially rainfall and temperature, the vegetation and the nature of the soil cover in any area. The effects of weathering are increased by human action, particularly the removal of vegetation and the exposure of soils to the rain and wind.

RUNNING WATER, ICE AND WIND

In moist regions, rivers are effective in shaping the land. They transport material worn away by weathering and erode the land. They wear out V-shaped valleys in upland regions, while vigorous meanders widen their middle courses. The work of rivers is at its most spectacular when earth movements lift up flat areas and rejuvenate the rivers, giving them a new erosive power capable of wearing out such features as the Grand Canyon. Rivers also have a constructive role. Some of the world's most fertile regions are deltas and flood plains composed of sediments periodically dumped there by such rivers as the Ganges, Mississippi and Nile.

▼ *Glaciers*

During Ice Ages, ice spreads over large areas but, during warm periods, the ice retreats. The chart shows that the volume of ice in many glaciers is decreasing, possibly as a result of global warming. Experts estimate that, between 1850 and the early 21st century, more than half of the ice in Alpine glaciers has melted.

ANNUAL FLUCTUATIONS FOR SELECTED GLACIERS

Glacier name and location	Changes in the annual mass balance†		
	1970–1	1990–1	2000–2001
Alfotbreen, Norway	+940	+790	−50
Careser, Italy	−650	−1,730	−1,860
Djankuat, Russia	−230	−310	−1,760
Grasubreen, Norway	+470	−520	−30
Gries, Switzerland	−970	−1,480	−902
Hintereisferner, Austria	−600	−1,325	−806
Place, Canada	−343	−990	−690
Sarennes, France	−1,100	−1,360	−1,160
Storglaciaren, Sweden	−190	+170	−115
Ürümqi, China	+102	−706	−1,170
Wolverine, USA	+770	−410	−480

† *The annual mass balance is defined as the difference between glacier accumulation and ablation (melting) averaged over the whole glacier. Balances are expressed as water equivalent in millimetres. A 'plus' indicates an increase in the depth or length of the glacier; a 'minus' indicates a reduction.*

▲ *Juneau Glacier, Alaska*

Like huge conveyor belts, glaciers transport weathered debris from mountain regions. Rocks frozen in the ice give the glaciers teeth, enabling them to wear out typical glaciated land features.

Running water in the form of sea waves and currents shapes coastlines, wearing out caves, natural arches, and stacks. The sea also transports and deposits worn material to form such features as spits and bars.

Glaciers in cold mountain regions flow downhill, gradually deepening valleys and shaping dramatic landscapes. They erode steep-sided U-shaped valleys, into which rivers often plunge in large waterfalls. Other features include cirques, armchair-shaped basins bounded by knife-edged ridges called *arêtes*. When several glacial cirques erode to form radial *arêtes*, pyramidal peaks like the Matterhorn are created. Deposits of moraine, rock material dumped by the glacier, are further evidence that ice once covered large areas.

The work of glaciers, like other agents of erosion, varies with the climate. In recent years, global warming has been making glaciers retreat in many areas, while several of the ice shelves in Antarctica have been breaking up.

Many land features in deserts were formed by running water at a time when the climate was much rainier than it is today. Water erosion also occurs when flash floods are caused by rare thunderstorms. But the chief agent of erosion in dry areas is wind-blown sand, which can strip the paint from cars, and undercut boulders to create mushroom-shaped rocks.

OCEANS AND ICE

In 2005, Tim Barnett of the Scripps Institution of Oceanography presented a paper to the American Association for the Advancement of Science showing that the upper waters of the oceans had markedly warmed up in the last 65 years, dramatic evidence of global warming.

Oceanography is a major science, but, only about 50 years ago, little was known of the dark world beneath the waves. But through the use of modern technology, including echo-sounders, magnetometers, research ships equipped with huge drills, and satellites, many of the oceans' secrets have been unravelled. Scientists have visited the ocean ridges in submersibles. There, they found hot vents, or 'black smokers' – chimney-like structures made up of minerals deposited from the hot water. Around them, are swarms of bacteria – the base of a food chain that includes strange creatures, many unknown to science, such as giant worms, eyeless shrimps and white clams. These discoveries have led some to speculate that the first living organisms on Earth may have evolved in such conditions on ancient ocean floors.

The study of the ocean floor led to the discovery that the oceans are geologically young features – no more than 200 million years old. It also revealed evidence as to how oceans form and continents drift because of the action of plate tectonics.

THE BLUE PLANET

Water covers almost 71% of the Earth, which makes it look blue when viewed from space. Although the oceans are interconnected, geographers divide them into four main areas: the Pacific, Atlantic, Indian and Arctic oceans. The average depth of the oceans is 3,370 m [12,238 ft], but they are divided into several zones.

Around most continents are gently sloping continental shelves, which are flooded parts of the continents. The shelves end at the continental slope, at a depth of about 200 m [656 ft]. This slope leads steeply down to the abyss. The deepest parts of the oceans are the trenches, which reach a maximum depth of 11,022 m [36,161 ft] in the Mariana Trench in the western Pacific.

Most marine life is found in the top 200 m [656 ft], where there is sufficient sunlight for plants, called phytoplankton, to grow. Below this zone, life becomes more and more scarce, though no part of the ocean, even at the bottom of the deepest trenches, is completely without living things.

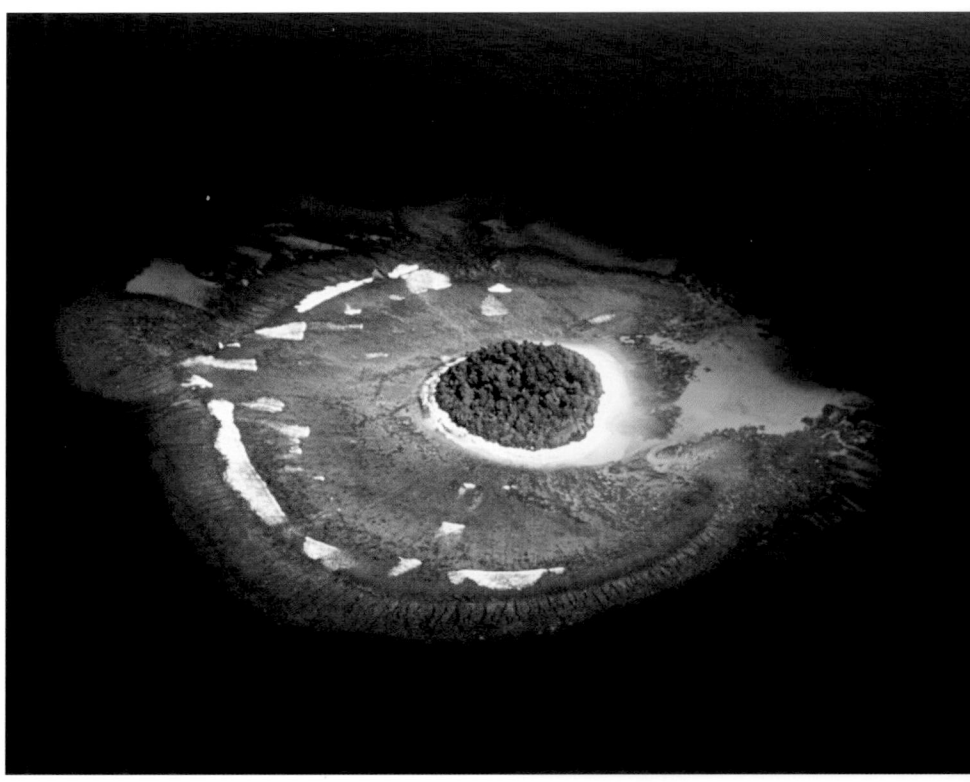

▲ *Vava'u Island, Tonga*
This small coral atoll in northern Tonga consists of a central island covered by rainforest. Low coral reefs washed by the waves surround a shallow central lagoon.

Continental islands, such as the British Isles, are high parts of the continental shelves. For example, until about 7,500 years ago, when the ice sheets formed during the Ice Ages were melting, raising the sea level and filling the North Sea and the Strait of Dover, Britain was linked to mainland Europe.

By contrast, oceanic islands, such as the Hawaiian chain in the North Pacific Ocean, rise from the ocean floor. All oceanic islands are of volcanic origin, although many of them in warm parts of the oceans have sunk and are capped by layers of coral to form ring- or horseshoe-shaped atolls and coral reefs.

OCEAN WATER

The oceans contain about 97% of the world's water. Seawater contains more than 70 dissolved elements, but chloride and sodium make up 85% of the total. Sodium chloride is common salt and it makes seawater salty. The salinity of the oceans is mostly between 3.3–3.7%. Ocean water fed by icebergs or large rivers is less saline than shallow seas in the tropics, where the evaporation rate is high. Seawater is a source of salt but the water is useless for agriculture or drinking unless it is desalinated. However, land areas get a regular

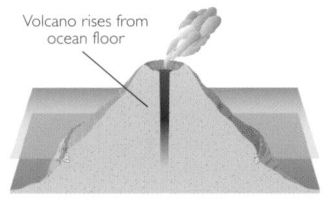
Volcano rises from ocean floor

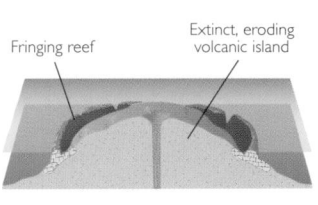
Fringing reef — Extinct, eroding volcanic island

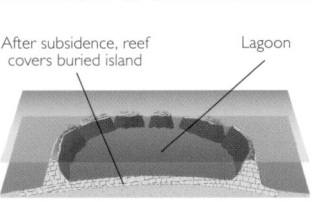
After subsidence, reef covers buried island — Lagoon

▲ *Development of an atoll*
Some of the volcanoes that rise from the ocean floor reach the surface to form islands. Some of these islands subside and become submerged. As an island sinks, coral starts to grow around the rim of the volcano, building up layer upon layer of limestone deposits to form fringing reefs. Sometimes coral grows on the tip of a central cone to form an island in the middle of the atoll.

▲ *The ocean depths*

The diagram shows the average depths (in dark blue) and the greatest depths in the four oceans. The North Pacific Ocean contains the world's deepest trenches, including the Mariana Trench, where the deepest manned descent was made by the bathyscaphe Trieste *in 1960. It reached a depth of 10,916 m [35,813 ft].*

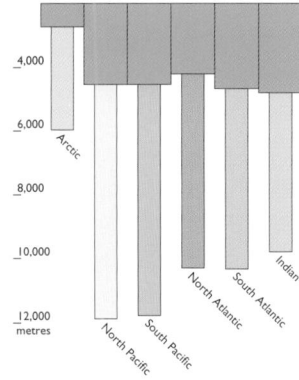

Relative sizes of the world's oceans:

PACIFIC 49% ATLANTIC 26%
INDIAN 21% ARCTIC 4%

Some geographers distinguish a fifth ocean, the Southern or Antarctic Ocean, but others regard these waters as the southern extension of the Pacific, Atlantic and Indian oceans.

supply of fresh water through the hydrological cycle (see page 42).

The density of seawater depends on its salinity and temperature. Temperatures vary from –2°C [28°F], the freezing point of seawater at the poles, to around 30°C [86°F] in parts of the tropics. Density differences help to maintain the circulation of the world's oceans, especially deep-sea currents. But the main cause of currents within 350 m [1,148 ft] of the surface is the wind. Because of the Earth's rotation, currents are deflected, creating huge circular motions of surface water – clockwise in the northern hemisphere and anticlockwise in the southern hemisphere.

Ocean currents transport heat from the tropics to the polar regions and thus form part of the heat engine that drives the Earth's climates. Ocean currents have an especially marked effect on coastal climates, such as north-western Europe. Some scientists are concerned that global warming may radically alter climates by weakening currents, such as the Gulf Stream, which is responsible for the mild winters in north-western Europe.

Ice Sheets, Ice Caps and Glaciers

Of the world's two ice sheets, the largest, covering most of Antarctica, has maximum depths of 4,800 m [15,748 ft]. Its volume is about nine times greater than the Greenland ice sheet. The ice sheets, together with smaller ice caps and glaciers, account for about 2% of the world's water. However, in many parts of the world, the ice is melting and many scientists think the cause is global warming. In March 2002, the vast Larsen ice shelf bordering the Antarctic peninsula collapsed and broke up into icebergs. Some scientists thought this was evidence of global warming, though some attributed the event to local factors.

Only about 11,000 years ago, during the final phase of the Pleistocene Ice Age, ice covered much of the northern hemisphere. The Ice Age, which began about 1.8 million years ago, was not a continuous period of cold. Instead, it consisted of glacial periods when the ice advanced and warmer interglacial periods when temperatures rose and the ice retreated.

Some scientists believe that we are now living in an interglacial period, and that glacial conditions will recur in the future. Others fear that global warming, caused mainly by pollution, may melt the world's ice, raising sea levels by up to 55 m [180 ft]. Many fertile and densely populated coastal plains, islands and cities would vanish from the map.

▼ *Icebergs float past the Antarctic Peninsula*

The Antarctic peninsula overlooks the Weddell Sea. The Weddell Sea and the Ross Sea are largely covered by huge ice shelves, which are extensions of the continental ice sheet. Many scientists are concerned that warmer weather is melting the ice sheets. In 2002, parts of the Larsen Ice Shelf, which adjoins the Antarctic Peninsula, collapsed and split up into icebergs.

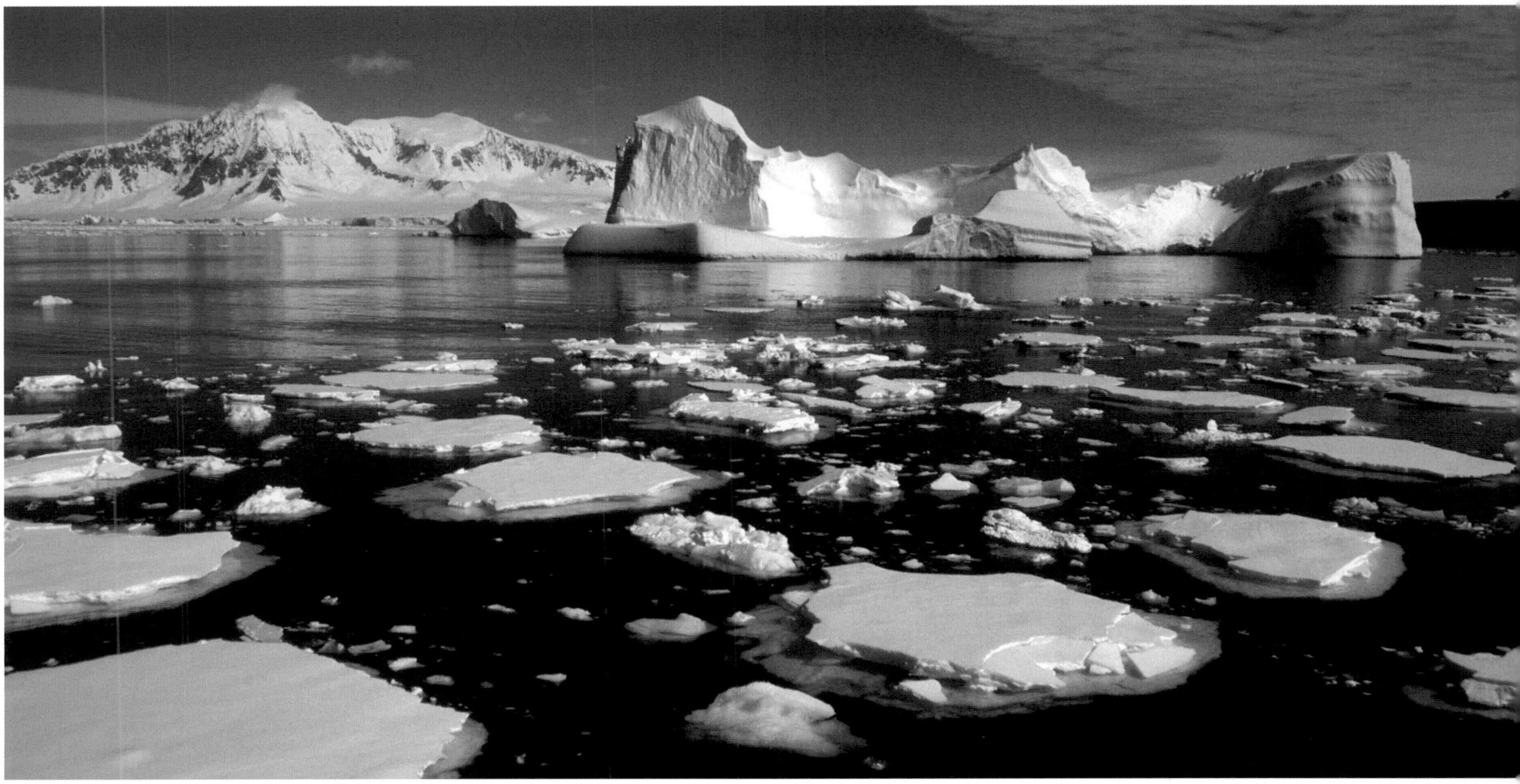

THE EARTH'S ATMOSPHERE

Since the discovery in 1985 of a thinning of the ozone layer, creating a so-called 'ozone hole', over Antarctica, many governments have worked to reduce the emissions of ozone-eating substances, notably the chlorofluorocarbons (CFCs) used in aerosols, refrigeration, air-conditioning and dry cleaning.

Following forecasts that the ozone layer would rapidly repair itself as a result of controls on these emissions, scientists were surprised in early 1996 when a marked thinning of the ozone layer over the northern hemisphere was recorded. In 2003, scientists reported that the situation over Antarctica was as serious as in the record year of 2000, while 2005 saw a marked thinning of the ozone layer over the Arctic region. Many predicted that it might take more than 50 years before the ozone layer made a full recovery.

The ozone layer in the stratosphere blocks out most of the dangerous ultraviolet B radiation in the Sun's rays. This radiation causes skin cancer and cataracts, as well as harming plants on the land and plankton in the oceans. The ozone layer is only one way in which the atmosphere protects life on Earth. The atmosphere

▼ *Moonrise seen from orbit*

This photograph taken by an orbiting Shuttle shows the crescent of the Moon. Silhouetted at the horizon is a dense cloud layer. The reddish-brown band is the tropopause, which separates the blue-white stratosphere from the yellow troposphere.

also provides the air we breathe and the carbon dioxide required by plants. It is also a shield against meteors and it acts as a blanket to prevent heat radiated from the Earth escaping into space.

LAYERS OF AIR

The atmosphere is divided into four main layers. The troposphere at the bottom contains about 85% of the atmosphere's total mass, where most weather conditions occur. The troposphere is about 15 km [9 miles] thick over the equator and 8 km [5 miles] thick at the poles. Temperatures decrease with height by approximately 1°C [2°F] for every 100 m [328 ft]. At the top of the troposphere is a level called the tropopause where temperatures are stable at around −55°C [−67°F]. Above the tropopause is the stratosphere, which contains the ozone layer. Here, at about 50 km [30 miles] above the Earth's surface, temperatures rise to about 0°C [32°F].

The ionosphere extends from the stratopause to about 600 km [373 miles] above the surface. Here temperatures fall up to about 80 km [50 miles], but then rise. The aurorae, which occur in the ionosphere when charged particles

CIRCULATION OF AIR

HIGH PRESSURE

LOW PRESSURE

WARM AIR

COLD AIR

SURFACE WINDS

CLOUDS

▲ *The circulation of the atmosphere can be divided into three rotating but interconnected air systems. These systems, or cells, are responsible for redistributing heat from the warm regions to the cold, and back again.*

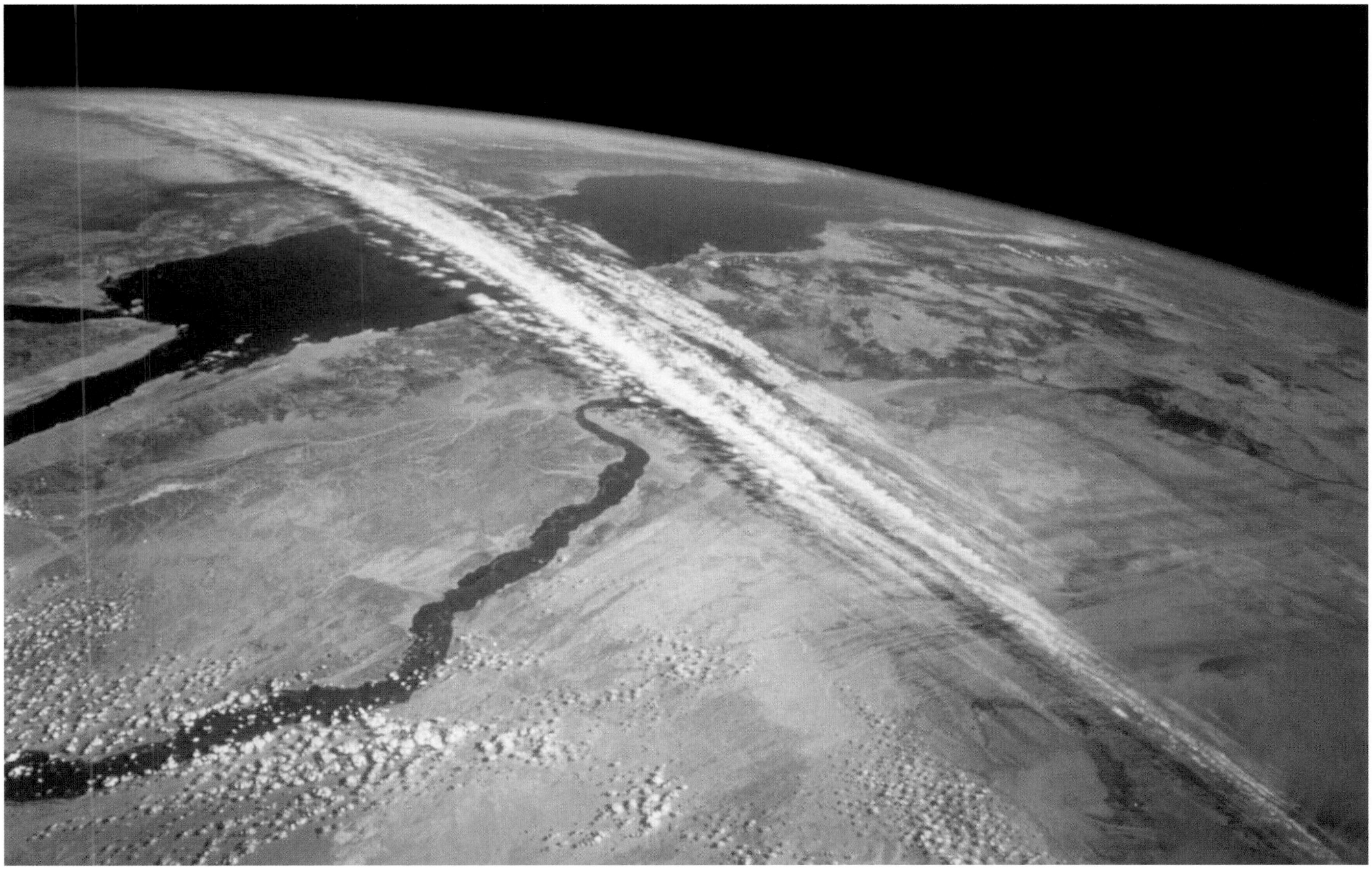

Jetstream from space photograph.

▶ **Classification of clouds**

Clouds are classified broadly into cumuliform, or 'heap' clouds, and stratiform, or 'layer' clouds. Both types occur at all levels. The highest clouds, composed of ice crystals, are cirrus, cirrostratus and cirrocumulus. Medium-height clouds include altostratus, a grey cloud that often indicates the approach of a depression, and altocumulus, a thicker and fluffier version of cirrocumulus. Low clouds include stratus, which forms dull, overcast skies; nimbostratus, a dark grey layer cloud which brings almost continuous rain and snow; cumulus, a brilliant white heap cloud; and stratocumulus, a layer cloud arranged in globular masses or rolls. Cumulonimbus, a cloud associated with thunderstorms, lightning and heavy rain, often extends from low to medium altitudes. It has a flat base, a fluffy outline and often an anvil-shaped top.

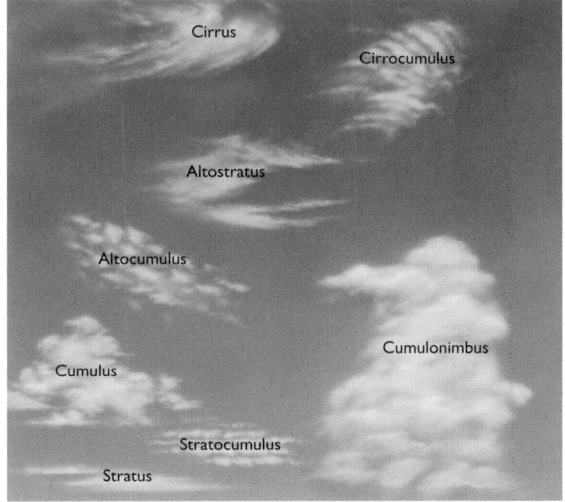

▲ **Jetstream from space**

Jetstreams are strong winds that normally blow near the tropopause. Cirrus clouds mark the route of the jet stream in this photograph, which shows the Red Sea, North Africa and the Nile valley, which appears as a dark band crossing the desert.

from the Sun interact with the Earth's magnetic field, are strongest near the poles. In the exosphere, the outermost layer, the atmosphere merges into space.

CIRCULATION OF THE ATMOSPHERE

The heating of the Earth is most intense around the equator where the Sun is high in the sky. Here warm, moist air rises in strong currents, creating a zone of low air pressure: the doldrums. The rising air eventually cools and spreads out north and south until it sinks downwards around latitudes 30° North and 30° South. The zones of high air pressure caused by the sinking air are called the 'horse latitudes'.

From the horse latitudes, trade winds blow back across the surface towards the equator, while westerly winds blow towards the poles. The warm westerlies finally meet the polar easterlies (cold dense air flowing from the poles). The line along which the warm and cold air streams meet is called the polar front. Depressions (or cyclones) are low-air-pressure frontal systems that form along the polar front.

COMPOSITION OF THE ATMOSPHERE

The air in the troposphere is made up mainly of nitrogen (78%) and oxygen (21%). Argon makes up more than 0.9% and there are also minute amounts of carbon dioxide, helium, hydrogen, krypton, methane, ozone and xenon. The atmosphere also contains water vapour, the gaseous form of water, which, when it condenses around minute specks of dust and salt, forms tiny water droplets or ice crystals. Large masses of water droplets or ice crystals form clouds.

CLIMATE AND WEATHER

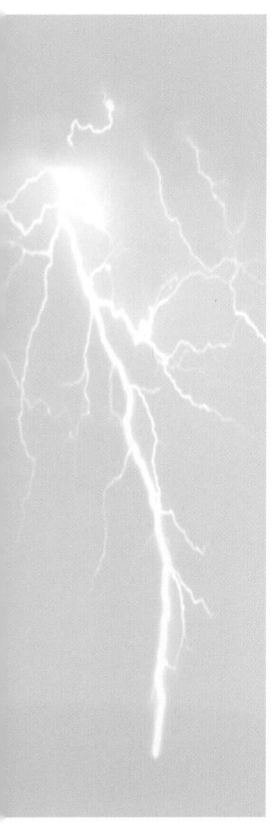

The year 2004 brought a record number of hurricanes, typhoons and tropical cyclones. These storms are similar, but different names are used in different regions. A record ten typhoons hit Japan. Hurricane Charley, which accounted for 32 deaths, was, in terms of the damage it caused, the second most costly ever to hit the United States. North America was also hit by Hurricane Frances, Hurricane Ivan, which destroyed 90% of all the buildings in Grenada, and Hurricane Jeanne, which caused floods that left more than 2,000 Haitians dead.

Every year, exceptional weather conditions cause disasters around the world. Modern forecasting techniques now give people warning of advancing storms, but the toll of human deaths continues as people are powerless in the face of the awesome forces of nature.

Weather is the day-to-day condition of the atmosphere. In some places, the weather is normally stable, but in other areas, especially the middle latitudes, it is highly variable, changing with the passing of a depression. By contrast, climate is the average weather of a place, based on data obtained over a long period.

▲ *Satellite image of Hurricane Floyd in 1999*
Hurricanes form over warm oceans north and south of the equator. Their movements are tracked by satellites, enabling forecasters to issue advance warnings. North American forecasters identify them with boys' and girls' names.

CLIMATIC FACTORS

Climate depends basically on the unequal heating of the Sun between the equator and the poles. But ocean currents and terrain also affect climate. For example, despite their northerly positions, Norway's ports remain ice-free in winter. This is because of the warming effect of the North Atlantic Drift, an extension of the Gulf Stream which flows across the Atlantic Ocean from the Gulf of Mexico.

By contrast, the cold Benguela current which flows up the coast of south-western Africa cools the coast and causes arid conditions. This is because the cold onshore winds are warmed as they pass over the land. The warm air can hold more water vapour than cold air, giving the winds a drying effect.

The terrain affects climate in several ways. Because temperatures fall with altitude, high-

CLIMATIC REGIONS

Tropical rainy climates
All mean monthly temperatures above 18°C [64°F].

RAINFOREST CLIMATE
MONSOON CLIMATE
SAVANNA CLIMATE

Dry climates
Low rainfall combined with a wide range of temperatures.

STEPPE CLIMATE
DESERT CLIMATE

Warm temperate rainy climates
The mean temperature is below 18°C [64°F] but above −3°C [26°F], and that of the warmest month is over 10°C [50°F].

DRY WINTER CLIMATE
DRY SUMMER CLIMATE
CLIMATE WITH NO DRY SEASON

Cold temperate rainy climates
The mean temperature of the coldest month is below 3°C [37°F] but the warmest month is over 10°C [50°F].

DRY WINTER CLIMATE
CLIMATE WITH NO DRY SEASON

Polar climates
The temperature of the warmest month is below 10°C [50°F], giving permanently frozen subsoil.

TUNDRA CLIMATE
POLAR CLIMATE

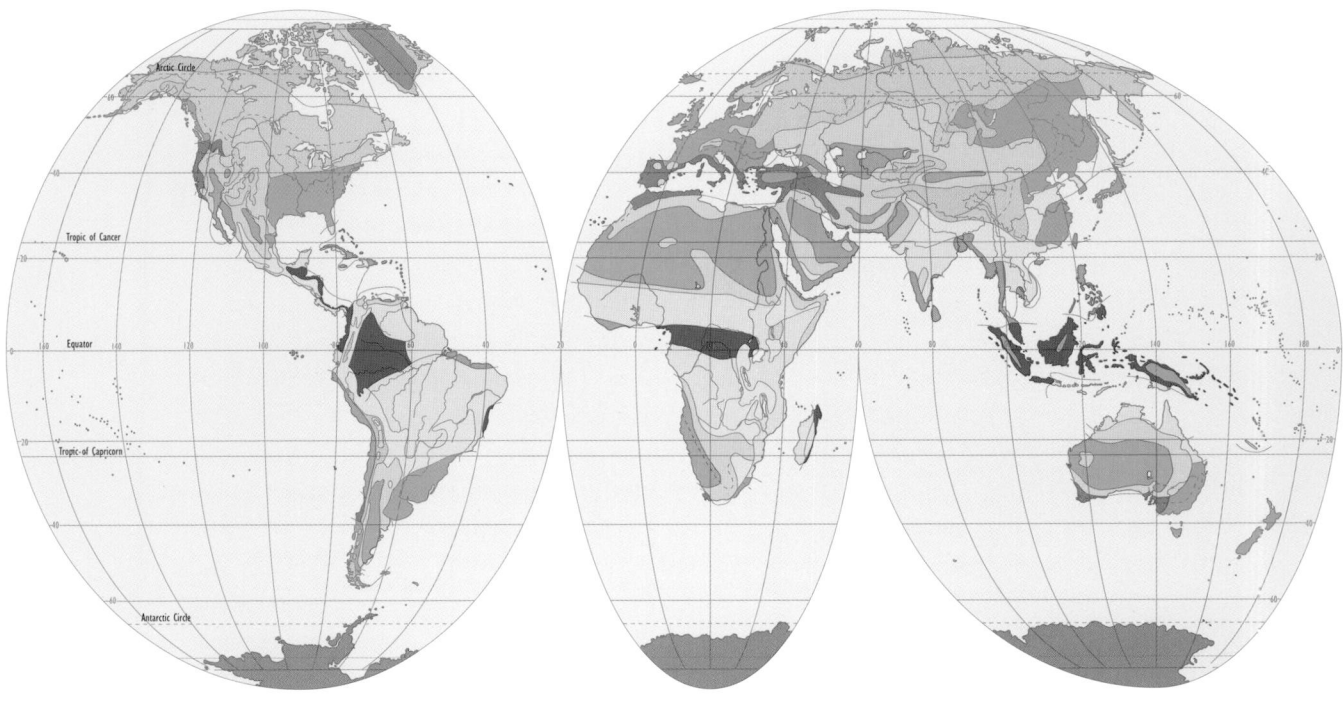

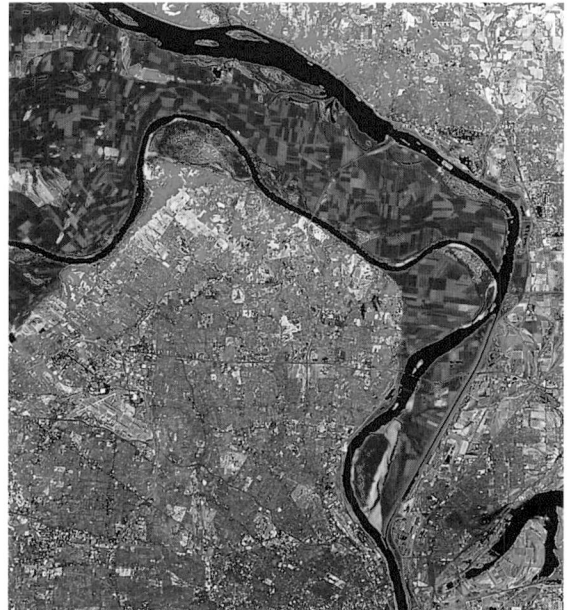

▶ **Floods in St Louis, USA**

The satellite image, right, shows the extent of the floods at St Louis at the confluence of the Mississippi and the Missouri rivers in June and July 1993. The floods occurred when very heavy rainfall raised river levels by up to 14 m [46 ft]. The floods reached their greatest extent between Minneapolis in the north and a point approximately 150 km [93 miles] south of St Louis. In places, the width of the Mississippi increased to nearly 11 km [7 miles], while the Missouri reached widths of 32 km [20 miles]. In all, more than 28,000 sq km [10,800 sq miles] were inundated and hundreds of towns and cities were flooded. Damage to crops was estimated at $8 billion.
The US was hit again by flooding in early 1997, when heavy rainfall in North Dakota and Minnesota caused the Red River to flood. The flooding had a catastrophic effect on the city of Grand Forks, which was inundated for months.

lands are cooler than lowlands at the same latitude. Terrain also affects rainfall. When moist onshore winds pass over mountain ranges, they are chilled as they are forced to rise and the water vapour they contain condenses to form clouds, which bring rain and snow. Beyond the mountains, the air descends and is warmed. These drying winds create rain-shadow (arid) regions on the lee side of mountains.

▲ **Flood damage in the United States**

In June and July 1993, the Mississippi River basin suffered record floods. The photograph shows a sunken church in Illinois. The flooding along the Mississippi, Missouri and other rivers caused great damage, amounting to about $12 billion. At least 48 people died in the floods.

CLIMATIC REGIONS

The two major factors that affect climate are temperature and precipitation, including rain and snow. In addition, seasonal variations and other climatic features are also taken into account. Climatic classifications vary because of the weighting given to various features. Yet most classifications are based on five main climatic types: tropical rainy climates; dry climates; warm temperate rainy climates; cold temperate rainy climates; and very cold polar climates. Some classifications also allow for the effect of altitude. The main climatic regions are sub-divided according to seasonal variations and also to the kind of vegetation associated with the climate. With rain throughout the year, rainforest climates differ from monsoon and savanna climates, which have dry seasons, while desert climates differ from steppe climates, which have enough moisture for grasses to grow.

WATER AND LAND USE

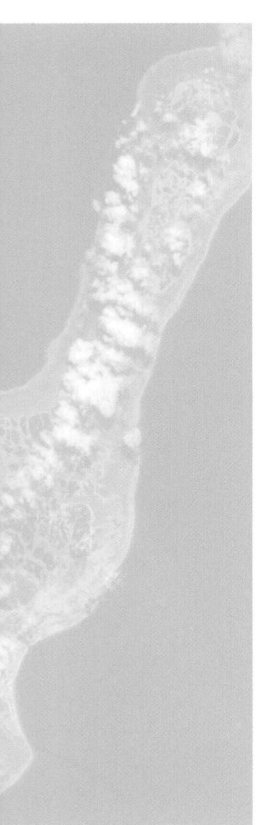

All life on land depends on fresh water. Yet about 80 countries now face acute water shortages. The world demand for fresh water is increasing by about 2.3% a year and this demand will double every 21 years. About a billion people, mainly in developing countries, do not have access to clean drinking water and around 10 million die every year from drinking dirty water. This problem is made worse in many countries by the pollution of rivers and lakes.

UN experts predict that water is becoming the most pressing environmental and development issue facing the world. By 2003, heavily populated regions in 26 countries were suffering serious water shortages. In 20 years, this number

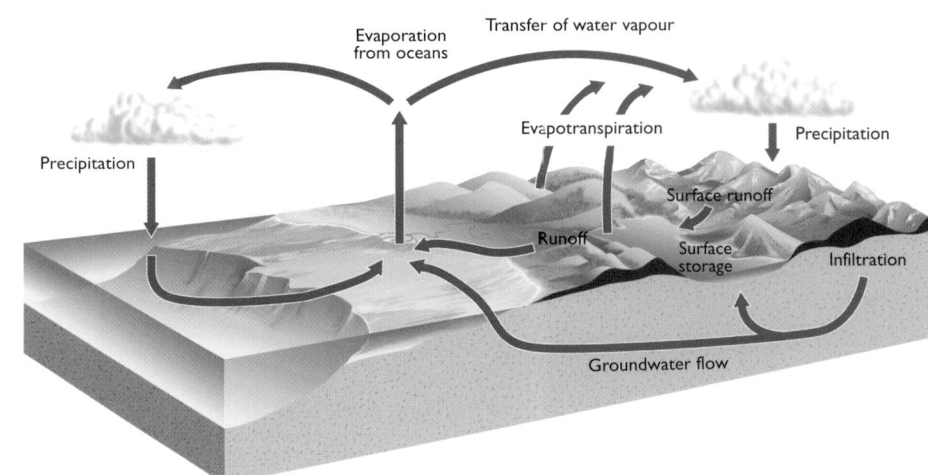

▼ Hoover Dam, United States

The Hoover Dam in Arizona controls the Colorado River's flood waters. Its reservoir supplies domestic and irrigation water to the south-west, while a hydroelectric plant produces electricity.

will probably rise to 65. Further, the United Nations estimated in 2005 that 1.1 billion people lack sufficient clean water for drinking and bathing. However, experts stress that while individual countries face water crises, there is no global crisis. The chief global problems are the uneven distribution of water and its inefficient and wasteful use.

THE WORLD'S WATER SUPPLY

Of the world's total water supply, 99.4% is in the oceans or frozen in bodies of ice. Most of the rest circulates through the rocks beneath our feet as groundwater. Water in rivers and lakes, in the soil and in the atmosphere together make up only 0.013% of the world's water.

The freshwater supply on land is dependent on the hydrological, or water, cycle which is driven by the Sun's heat. Water is evaporated from the oceans and carried into the air as invisible water vapour. Although this vapour averages less than 2% of the total mass of the atmosphere, it is the chief component from the standpoint of weather.

When air rises, water vapour condenses into visible water droplets or ice crystals, which eventually fall to earth as rain, snow, sleet, hail or frost. Some of the precipitation that reaches the ground returns directly to the atmosphere through evaporation or transpiration via plants. Much of the rest of the water flows into the rocks to become groundwater, or across the surface into rivers and, eventually, back to the oceans, so completing the hydrological cycle.

WATER AND AGRICULTURE

Only about a third of the world's land area is used for growing crops, while another third consists of meadows and pasture. The rest of the world is unsuitable for farming, being too dry, too cold, too mountainous, or covered by dense

▲ The hydrological cycle

The hydrological cycle is responsible for the continuous circulation of water around the planet. Water vapour contains and transports latent heat, or latent energy. When the water vapour condenses back into water (and falls as rain, hail or snow), the heat is released. When condensation takes place on cold nights, the cooling effect associated with nightfall is offset by the liberation of latent heat.

WATER DISTRIBUTION

The distribution of planetary water, by percentage.

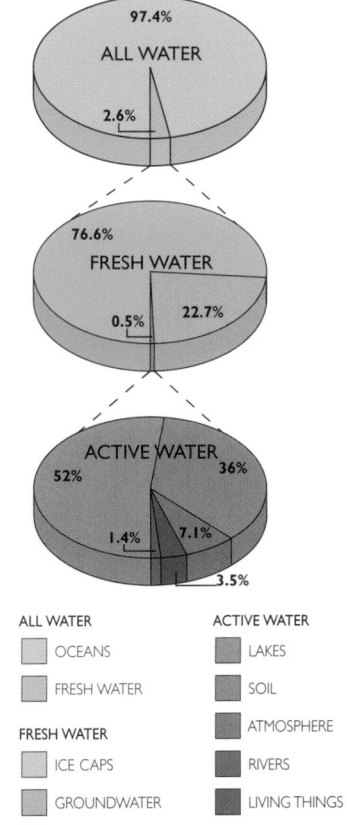

97.4%
ALL WATER
2.6%

76.6%
FRESH WATER
0.5% 22.7%

ACTIVE WATER
52% 36%
1.4% 7.1%
3.5%

ALL WATER
☐ OCEANS
☐ FRESH WATER

FRESH WATER
☐ ICE CAPS
☐ GROUNDWATER
☐ ACTIVE WATER

ACTIVE WATER
☐ LAKES
☐ SOIL
☐ ATMOSPHERE
☐ RIVERS
☐ LIVING THINGS

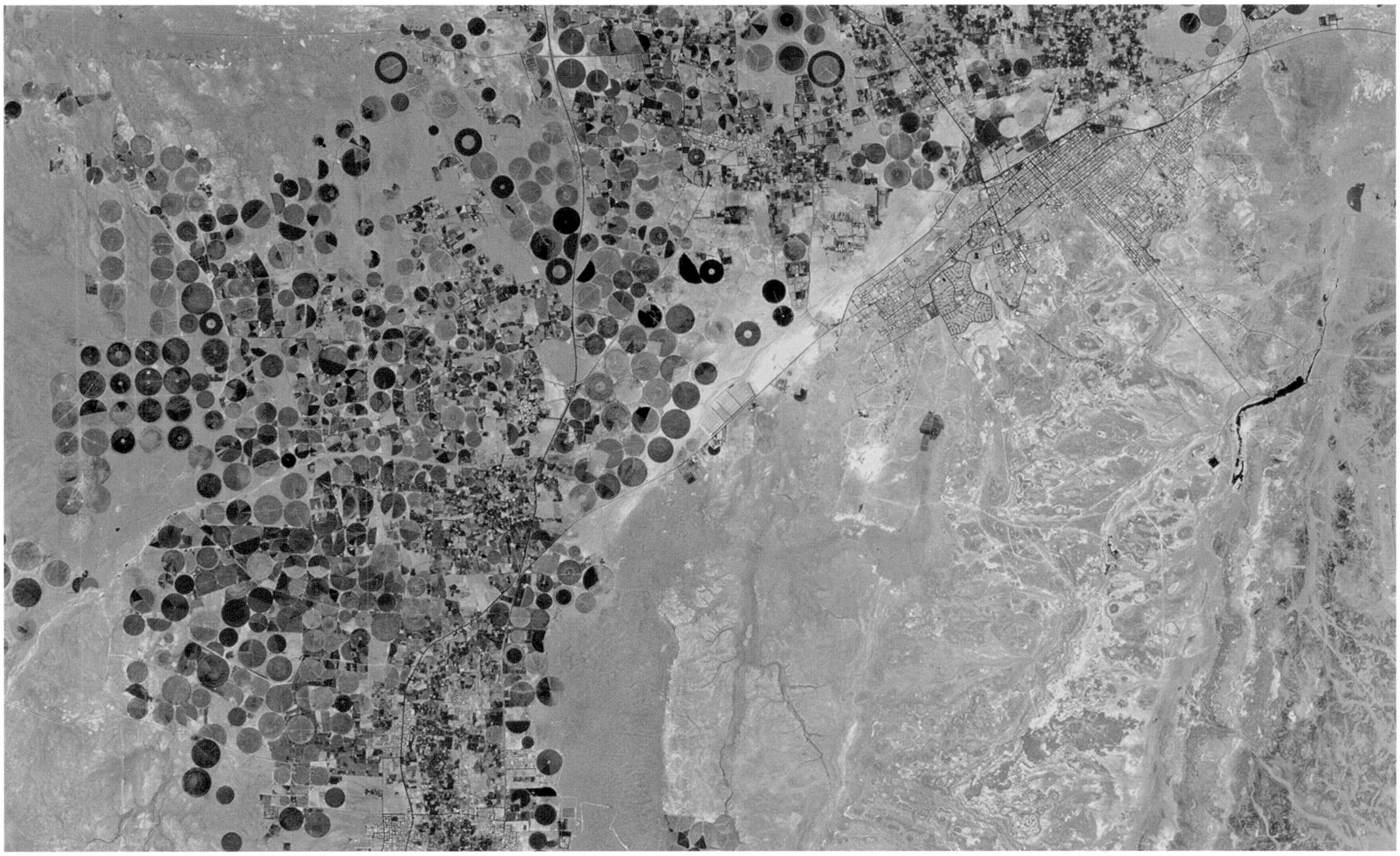

▶ Irrigation boom

The photograph shows a pivotal irrigation boom used to sprinkle water over a wheat field in Saudi Arabia. Irrigation in hot countries often takes place at night so that water loss through evaporation is reduced. Irrigation techniques vary from place to place. In monsoon areas with abundant water, the fields are often flooded, or the water is led to the crops along straight furrows. Sprinkler irrigation has become important since the 1940s. In other types of irrigation, the water is led through pipes which are on or under the ground. Underground pipes supply water directly to the plant roots and, as a result, water loss through evaporation is minimized.

▲ Irrigation in Saudi Arabia

Saudi Arabia is a desert country that gets its water from oases, which tap groundwater supplies, and desalination plants. The sale of oil has enabled the arid countries of south-western Asia to develop their agriculture. In the above satellite image, vegetation appears as brown and red circles, generated by centre-pivot irrigation systems.

forests. Although the demand for food increases every year, problems arise when attempts are made to increase the existing area of farmland. For example, the soils and climates of tropical forest and semi-arid regions of Africa and South America are not ideal for farming. Attempts to work such areas usually end in failure. To increase the world's food supply, scientists now concentrate on making existing farmland more productive rather than farming marginal land.

To grow crops, farmers need fertile, workable land, an equable climate, including a frost-free growing period, and an adequate supply of fresh water. In some areas, the water falls directly as rain. But many other regions depend on irrigation.

Irrigation involves water conservation through the building of dams which hold back storage reservoirs. In some areas, irrigation water comes from underground aquifers, layers of permeable and porous rocks through which groundwater percolates. But in many cases, the water in the

aquifers has been there for thousands of years, having accumulated at a time when the rainfall was much greater than it is today. As a result, these aquifers are not being renewed and will, one day, dry up.

Other sources of irrigation water are desalination plants, which remove salt from seawater and pump it to farms. This is a highly expensive process and is employed in areas where water supplies are extremely low, such as the island of Malta, or in the oil-rich desert countries around the Persian Gulf, which can afford to build huge desalination plants.

LAND USE BY CONTINENT (2000)

	Forest	Permanent pasture	Permanent crops	Arable	Non-productive
N. & C. America	25.7%	17.2%	0.4%	12.1%	44.6%
S. America	50.5%	28.7%	1.1%	5.5%	14.2%
Europe	46.0%	8.0%	0.7%	12.8%	32.5%
Africa	21.8%	30.2%	0.9%	6.1%	41.0%
Asia	17.8%	35.8%	1.9%	15.7%	28.8%
Oceania	23.3%	49.3%	0.4%	6.2%	20.8%

THE NATURAL WORLD

In 2004, a report by the International Union for the Conservation of Nature released its Red List of 15,560 plant and animal species that are threatened with extinction – more than 1,000 species than in 2003. Human activities, ranging from habitat destruction to the introduction of alien species from one area to another, are the main causes of this devastating reduction of our planet's biodiversity, which might lead to the loss of unique combinations of genes that could be vital in improving food yields on farms or in the production of drugs to combat disease.

Extinctions of species have occurred throughout Earth's history, but today the extinction rate is estimated to be about 10,000 times the natural average. Some scientists have even compared it with the mass extinction that wiped out the dinosaurs 65 million years ago. However, the main cause of today's high extinction rate is not some natural disaster, such as the impact of an asteroid a few kilometres across, but it is the result of human actions, most notably the destruction of natural habitats for farming and other purposes. In some densely populated areas,

▼ *Rainforest in Rwanda*

Rainforests are the most threatened of the world's biomes. Effective conservation policies must demonstrate to poor local people that they can benefit from the survival of the forests.

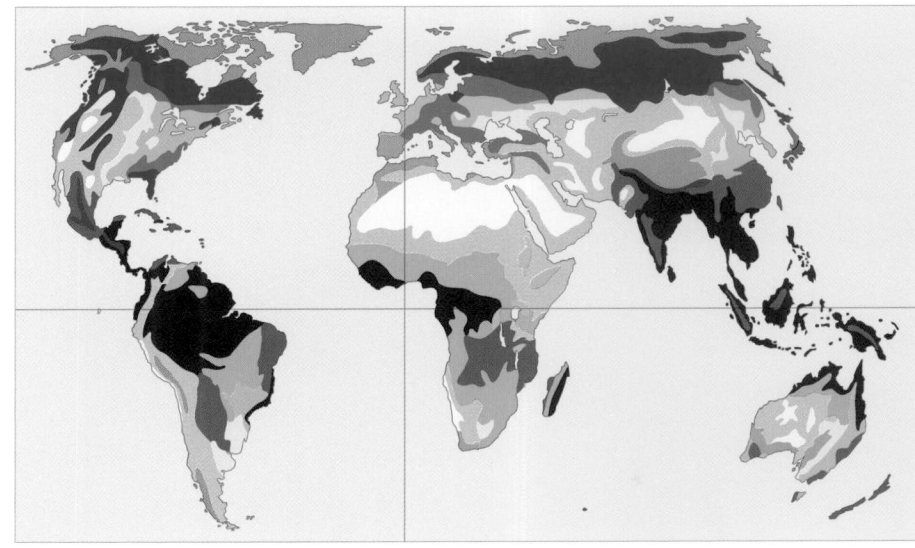

such as Western Europe, the natural habitats were destroyed long ago. Today, the greatest damage is occurring in tropical rainforests, which contain more than half of the world's known species.

Modern technology has enabled people to live comfortably almost anywhere on Earth. But most plants and many animals are adapted to particular climatic conditions, and they live in association with and dependent on each other. Plant and animal communities that cover large areas are called biomes.

THE WORLD'S BIOMES

The world's biomes are defined mainly by climate and vegetation. They range from the tundra, in polar regions and high mountain regions, to the lush equatorial rainforests.

The Arctic tundra covers large areas in the polar regions of the northern hemisphere. Snow covers the land for more than half of the year and the subsoil, called permafrost, is permanently frozen. Comparatively few species can survive in this harsh, treeless environment. The main plants are hardy mosses, lichens, grasses, sedges and low shrubs. However, in summer, the tundra plays an important part in world animal geography, when its growing plants and swarms of insects provide food for migrating animals and birds that arrive from the south.

The tundra of the northern hemisphere merges in the south into a vast region of needle-leaf evergreen forest, called the boreal forest or taiga. Such trees as fir, larch, pine and spruce are adapted to survive the long, bitterly cold winters of this region, but the number of plant and animal species is again small. South of the boreal forests is a zone of mixed needleleaf evergreens and broadleaf deciduous trees, which shed their leaves in winter. In warmer areas, this

NATURAL VEGETATION

◼ TUNDRA & MOUNTAIN VEGETATION

◼ NEEDLELEAF EVERGREEN FOREST

◼ MIXED NEEDLELEAF EVERGREEN & BROADLEAF DECIDUOUS TREES

◼ BROADLEAF DECIDUOUS WOODLAND

◻ MID-LATITUDE GRASSLAND

◼ EVERGREEN BROADLEAF & DECIDUOUS TREES & SHRUBS

◻ SEMI-DESERT SCRUB

◻ DESERT

◼ TROPICAL GRASSLAND (SAVANNA)

◼ TROPICAL BROADLEAF RAINFOREST & MONSOON FOREST

◼ SUBTROPICAL BROADLEAF & NEEDLELEAF FOREST

▲ *The map shows the world's main biomes. The classification is based on the natural 'climax' vegetation of regions, a result of the climate and the terrain. But human activities have greatly modified this basic division. For example, the original deciduous forests of Western Europe and the eastern United States have largely disappeared. In recent times, human development of some semi-arid areas has turned former dry grasslands into barren desert.*

mixed forest merges into broadleaf deciduous forest, where the number and diversity of plant species is much greater.

Deciduous forests are adapted to temperate, humid regions. Evergreen broadleaf and deciduous trees grow in Mediterranean regions, with their hot, dry summers. But much of the original deciduous forest has been cut down and has given way to scrub and heathland. Grasslands occupy large areas in the middle latitudes, where the rainfall is insufficient to support forest growth. The moister grasslands are often called prairies, while drier areas are called steppe.

▼ *The net primary production of eight major biomes is expressed in grams of dry organic matter per square metre per year. The tropical rainforests produce the greatest amount of organic material. The tundra and deserts produce the least.*

NET PRIMARY PRODUCTION OF EIGHT MAJOR BIOMES

- ■ TROPICAL RAINFORESTS
- ■ DECIDUOUS FORESTS
- ■ TROPICAL GRASSLANDS
- ■ CONIFEROUS FORESTS
- ■ MEDITERRANEAN
- ■ TEMPERATE GRASSLANDS
- ■ TUNDRA
- ■ DESERTS

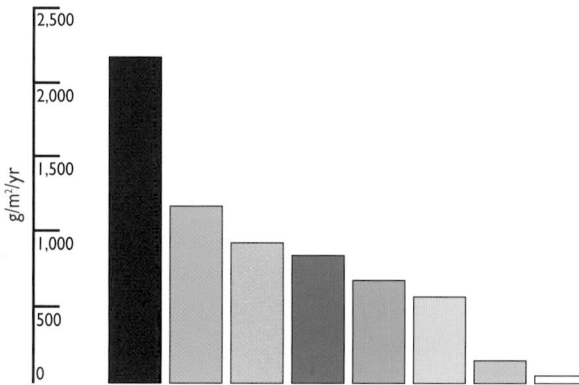

▲ *Tundra in subarctic Alaska, United States*
The Denali National Park, Alaska, contains magnificent mountain scenery and tundra vegetation that flourishes during the brief summer. The park is open between 1 June and 15 September.

The tropics also contain vast dry areas of semi-desert scrub that merges into desert, as well as large areas of tropical savanna, which is grassland, ranging from luxuriant to sparse, with scattered shrubs and trees, whose growth is limited by a marked dry season. Savanna regions support a wide range of animals.

Tropical and subtropical regions contain three types of forest biomes. The tropical rainforest, the world's richest biome measured by its plant and animal species, experiences rain and high temperatures throughout the year. Similar forests occur in monsoon regions, which have a season of very heavy rainfall. They, too, are rich in plant species, though less so than the tropical rainforest. A third type of forest is the subtropical broadleaf and needleleaf forest, found in such places as south-eastern China, south-central Africa and eastern Brazil.

THE HUMAN WORLD

Every minute, the world's population increases by more than 100. Predictions of future growth vary. In 1999, UN demographers stated that the population, which passed the 6 billion mark in October 1999, would reach 8.9 billion. It would level out after 2200, when it would peak at 11 billion. But, in 2004, UN demographers predicted that the world's population would peak at 9.1 billion in 2050 and then could start to decline. However, while some European countries are concerned about declining birth rates, all experts agree that the fastest rates of population increase will occur in developing countries – the places least able to afford the high costs arising from a rapidly growing population.

▼ *Quito, capital city of Ecuador*
In common with world trends, the annual growth rate in the population of Ecuador is declining, while urbanization is increasing rapidly.

Average world population growth rates are expected to decline from 1.6% per year in 1975–2001 to 1.1% in 2001–15. This is partly due to a decline in fertility rates – that is, the number of births to the number of women of child-bearing age – especially in developed countries where, as income has risen, the average size of families has fallen.

Declining fertility rates were also evident in many developing countries. Even Africa shows signs of such change, though its population is expected to triple before it begins to fall. Population growth is also dependent on death rates, which are affected by such factors as famine, disease and the quality of medical care.

THE POPULATION EXPLOSION

The world's population has grown steadily throughout most of human history, though certain events triggered periods of population growth. The invention of agriculture, around 10,000 years ago, led to great changes in human society. Before then, most people had obtained food by hunting animals and gathering plants. Average life expectancies were probably no more than 20 years and life was hard. However, when farmers began to produce food surpluses, people began to live settled lives. This major milestone in human history led to the development of the first cities and early civilizations.

From an estimated 8 million in 8000 BC, the world population rose to about 300 million by AD 1000. Between 1000 and 1750, the rate of world population increase was around 0.1% per year, but another period of major economic and social change – the Industrial Revolution – began in the late 18th century. The Industrial Revolution led to improvements in farm technology and increases in food production. The world population began to increase quickly as industrialization spread across Europe and into North America. By 1850, it had reached 1.2 billion. The 2 billion mark was passed in the 1920s, and then the population rapidly doubled to 4 billion by the 1970s.

POPULATION FEATURES

Population growth affects the structure of societies. In developing countries with high annual rates of population increase, the large majority of the people are young and soon to become parents themselves. For example, in Kenya, which had until recently an annual rate of population growth of around 4%, about 42% of the population is under 15 years of age, as

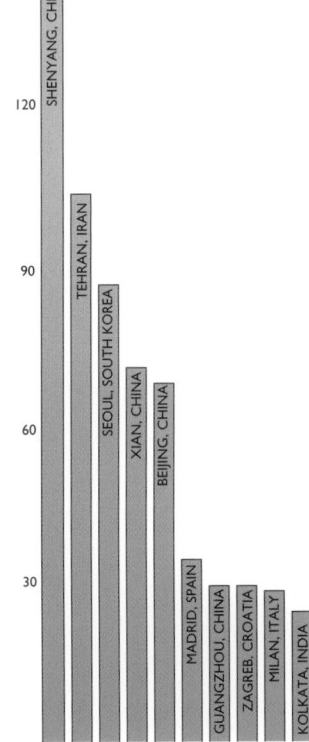

▲ *Urban air pollution*
This diagram of the world's most polluted cities indicates the number of days per year when sulphur dioxide levels exceed the WHO threshhold of 150 micrograms per cubic metre.

compared with 21% in the United States. Most developed countries have a fairly even spread across the age groups.

Such differences are reflected in average life expectancies. In a rich country, such as the USA, the average life expectancy in 2001 was 77 years (74 for men and 80 for women; women live longer, on average, than men). As a result, an increasing proportion of the people are elderly and retired. The reverse applies in many poor countries, where average life expectancies are below 60 years. In the early 21st century, life expectancies were falling in parts of southern Africa because of the spread of HIV and AIDS. However, overall, the world population is ageing. In 2003, demographers predicted that the average age of the world's people will rise from 28 to 40 years.

Paralleling the population explosion has been a rapid growth in the number and size of cities. Urban areas contained nearly half the world's people in the early 2000s. This proportion is expected to rise to nearly two-thirds by 2025.

Urbanization occurred first in areas under-

▲ Hong Kong's business district
By contrast with the picturesque old streets of Hong Kong, the business district of Hong Kong City, on the northern shore of Hong Kong Island, is a cluster of modern high-rise buildings. The glittering skyscrapers reflect the success of this tiny region, which has one of the strongest economies in Asia.

going the industrialization of their economies, but today it is also a feature of the developing world. In developing countries, people are leaving impoverished rural areas hoping to gain access to the education, health and other services available in cities. But many cities cannot provide the facilities necessitated by rapid population growth. Slums develop and pollution, crime and disease become features of everyday life.

The population explosion poses another problem for the entire world. No one knows how many people the world can support or how consumer demand will damage the fragile environments on our planet. The British economist Thomas Malthus argued in the late 18th century that overpopulation would lead to famine and war. But an increase in farm technology in the 19th and 20th centuries, combined with a green revolution, in which scientists developed high-yield crop varieties, has greatly increased food production since Malthus' time.

However, some modern scientists argue that overpopulation may become a problem in the 21st century. They argue that food shortages leading to disastrous famines will result unless population growth can be halted. Such people argue in favour of birth-control programmes. China, one of the two countries with more than a billion people, introduced a one-child family policy. Its action has slowed the growth of China's huge population.

POPULATION CHANGE
The projected population change for the years 2004–2050.

- OVER 125% POPULATION GAIN
- 100–125% POPULATION GAIN
- 50–100% POPULATION GAIN
- 25–50% POPULATION GAIN
- 0–25% POPULATION GAIN
- LOSS OR NO CHANGE
- NO DATA AVAILABLE

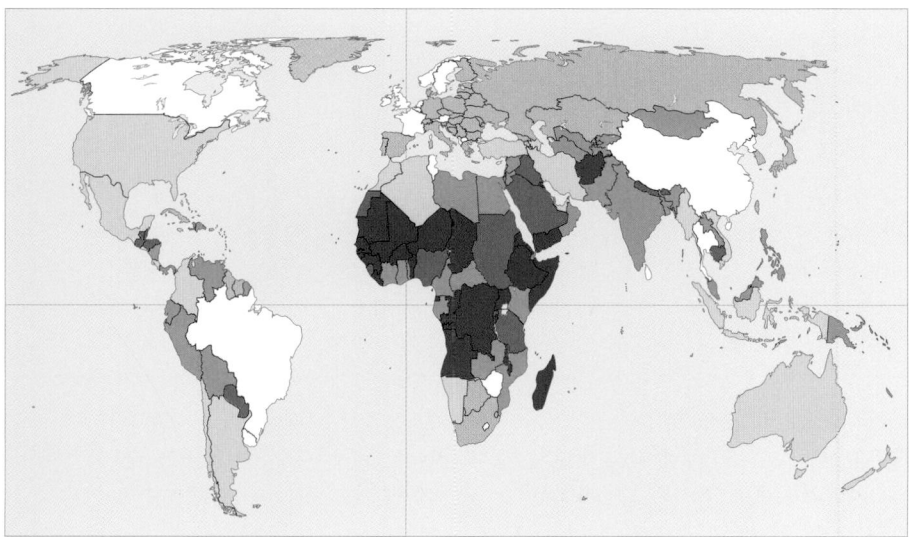

LANGUAGES AND RELIGIONS

In 1995, 90-year-old Edna Guerro died in northern California. She was the last person able to speak Northern Pomo, one of about 50 Native American languages spoken in the state. Her death marked the extinction of one of the world's languages. This event is not an isolated incident. Language experts regularly report the disappearance of languages and some of them predict that up to 90% of the world's languages will no longer exist by the end of the 21st century.

Improved transport and communications are partly to blame, because they bring people from various cultures into closer and closer contact. Many children no longer speak the language of their parents, preferring instead to learn the language used at their schools. The pressures on children to speak dominant rather than minority languages are often great. In the first part of the 20th century, Native American children were punished if they spoke their native language.

The disappearance of a language represents the extinction of a way of thinking, a unique expression of the experiences and knowledge of a group of people. Language and religion together give people an identity and a sense of belonging. However, there are others who argue that the disappearance of minority languages is a step towards international understanding and economic efficiency.

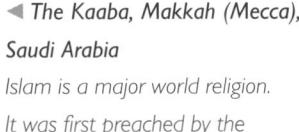

◀ *The Kaaba, Makkah (Mecca), Saudi Arabia*
Islam is a major world religion. It was first preached by the Prophet Muhammad who was born in Makkah (or Mecca) in Saudi Arabia in about AD 570. Its holiest shrine is the Kaaba, a black, square building in the Great Mosque in Makkah. Every adult Muslim must, if possible, make at least one pilgrimage (or hajj) to Makkah. More than a million Muslims make the pilgrimage every year. The pilgrims walk or run around the Kaaba seven times, praying or reciting verses from the Koran, the scared book of the Muslims.

THE WORLD'S LANGUAGES

Definitions of what is a language or a dialect vary and, hence, estimates of the number of languages spoken around the world range from about 3,000 to 6,000. But whatever the figure, it is clear that the number of languages far exceeds the number of countries.

RELIGIOUS ADHERENTS

Number of adherents to the world's major religions, in millions (2003).

Christianity	2,070
Roman Catholic	1,093
Protestant	364
Orthodox	217
Anglican	80
Independent	406
Others	110
Islam	1,254
Sunni	1,041
Shi'ite	201
Others	12
Secular/Atheist/Agnostic/ Non-religious	933
Hinduism	837
Chinese folk	398
Buddhism	362
Ethnic religions	373
New religions	105
Sikhism	24
Judaism	14
Spiritism	13
Baha'i	7
Confucianism	7
Jainism	3
Shintoism	3

◀ *Statues of the Buddha, Wat Yai Chai Mongkol, Thailand*
Buddhism is a major religion in South-east Asia, Sri Lanka and Japan. The statues of the Buddha in the photograph are swathed in saffron robes. They surround the main chedi, or Golden Mount Pagoda, at Wat Yai Chai Mongkol, a World Heritage site near the ancient city of Ayutthaya, north of Bangkok.

Countries with only one language tend to be small. For example, in Liechtenstein, everyone speaks German. By contrast, more than 860 languages have been identified in Papua New Guinea, whose population is only about 5.4 million people. Hence, many of its languages are spoken by only small groups of people. In fact, scientists have estimated that about a third of the world's languages are now spoken by less than 1,000 people. By contrast, more than half of the world's population speak just seven languages.

The world's languages are grouped into families. The Indo-European family consists of languages spoken between Europe and the Indian subcontinent. The growth of European empires over the last 300 years led several Indo-European languages, most notably English, French, Portuguese and Spanish, to spread throughout much of North and South America, Africa, Australia and New Zealand.

English has become the official language in many countries which together contain more than a quarter of the world's population. It is now a major international language, surpassing in importance Mandarin Chinese, a member of the Sino-Tibetan family, which is the world's leading first language. Without a knowledge of English, businessmen face many problems when conducting international trade, especially with the United States or other English-speaking countries. But proposals that English, French, Russian or some other language should become a world language seem unlikely to be acceptable to a majority of the world's peoples.

MOTHER TONGUES
First-language speakers of the major languages, in millions.

- MANDARIN CHINESE 885M
- SPANISH 332M
- ENGLISH 322M
- BENGALI 189M
- HINDI 182M
- PORTUGUESE 170M
- RUSSIAN 170M
- JAPANESE 125M
- GERMAN 98M
- WU CHINESE 77M

OFFICIAL LANGUAGES:
% OF WORLD POPULATION

English	27.0%
Chinese	19.0%
Hindi	13.5%
Spanish	5.4%
Russian	5.2%
French	4.2%
Arabic	3.3%
Portuguese	3.0%
Malay	3.0%
Bengali	2.9%
Japanese	2.3%

▶ *Polyglot nations*

The graph shows countries of the world with more than 200 languages. Although it has only about 5.4 million people, Papua New Guinea holds the record for the number of languages spoken.

Brazil (210)
Congo (DR) (220)
Australia (230)
Mexico (240)
Cameroon (275)
India (410)
Nigeria (470)
Indonesia (701)
Papua New Guinea (862)

WORLD RELIGIONS

Religion is another fundamental aspect of human culture. It has inspired much of the world's finest architecture, literature, music and art. It has also helped to shape human cultures since prehistoric times and is responsible for the codes of ethics by which most people live.

The world's major religions were all founded in Asia. Judaism, one of the first faiths to teach that there is only one god, is one of the world's oldest. Founded in south-western Asia, it influenced the more recent Christianity and Islam, two other monotheistic religions which now have the great-

▲ *The Church of San Giovanni, Dolomites, Italy*
Christianity has done much to shape Western civilization. Christian churches were built as places of worship, but many of them are among the finest achievements of world architecture.

est number of followers. Hinduism, the third leading faith in terms of the numbers of followers, originated in the Indian subcontinent and most Hindus are now found in India. Another major religion, Buddhism, was founded in the subcontinent partly as a reaction to certain aspects of Hinduism. But unlike Hinduism, it has spread from India throughout much of eastern Asia.

Religion and language are powerful creative forces. They are also essential features of nationalism, which gives people a sense of belonging and pride. But nationalism is often also a cause of rivalry and tension. Cultural differences have led to racial hatred, the persecution of minorities, and to war between national groups.

INTERNATIONAL ORGANIZATIONS

Twelve days before the surrender of Germany and four months before the final end of World War II, representatives of 50 nations met in San Francisco to create a plan to set up a peace-keeping organization, the United Nations. Since its birth on 24 October 1945, its membership has grown from 51 to 191 in 2005.

Its first 60 years have been marked by failures as well as successes. For example, because of the UN policy of neutrality, the Blue Berets, as UN troops are called, have been sometimes forced to stand by when atrocities have occurred. As a result, the UN Secretary-General, Kofi Annan, announced a reform plan in 2005.

THE WORK OF THE UN

The United Nations has six main organs. They include the General Assembly, where member states meet to discuss issues concerned with peace, security and development. The Security Council, containing 15 members, is concerned with maintaining world peace. The Secretariat, under the Secretary-General, helps the other organs to do their jobs effectively, while the Economic and Social Council works with specialized agencies to implement policies concerned with such matters as development, education and health. The International Court of Justice, or World Court, helps to settle disputes between member nations. The sixth organ of the UN, the Trusteeship Council, was designed to bring 11 UN trust territories to independence. Its task has now been completed.

The specialized agencies do much important

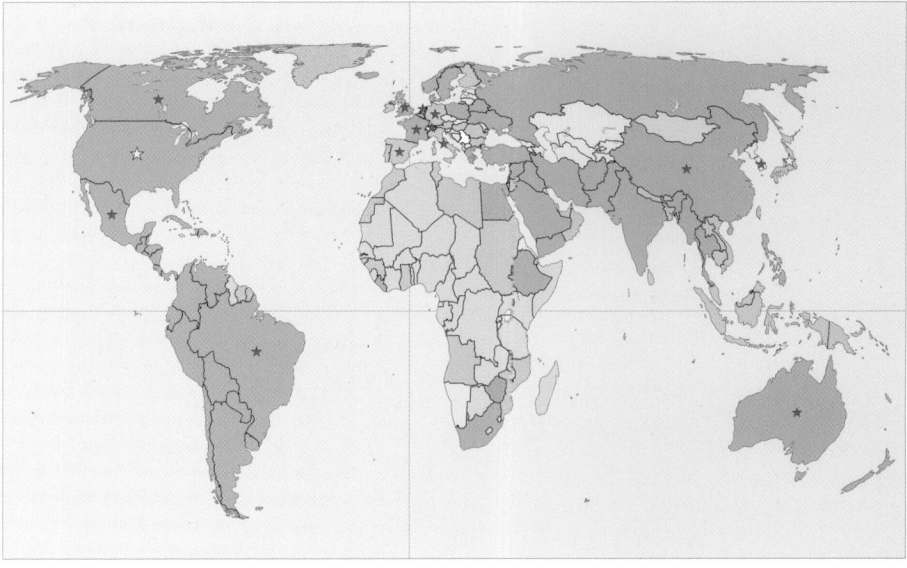

▼ *UN peace-keeping missions*

In the 1990s, a UN peace-keeping mission worked to restore peace to Bosnia-Herzegovina, following the Dayton Peace Accord of 1995. By 2005, hopes of long-term stability were high and refugees were returning home in large numbers.

work. For example, UNICEF (United Nations International Children's Fund) has provided health care and aid for children in many parts of the world. The ILO (International Labour Organization) has improved working conditions in many areas, while the FAO (Food and Agricultural Organization) has worked to improve the production and distribution of food. Among the other agencies are organizations to help refugees, to further human rights, and to control the environment. The latest agency, set up in 1995, is the WTO (World Trade Organization), which took over the work of GATT (General Agreement on Tariffs and Trade).

OTHER ORGANIZATIONS

In a world in which nations have become increasingly interdependent, many other organizations have been set up to deal with a variety of problems. Some, such as NATO (the North Atlantic Treaty Organization), are defence alliances. In the early 1990s, the end of the Cold War suggested that NATO's role might be finished, but the civil war in the former Yugoslavia showed that it still has a role in maintaining peace and security.

Other organizations encourage social and economic co-operation in various regions. Some are NGOs (non-governmental organizations), such as the Red Cross and its Muslim equivalent, the Red Crescent. Other NGOs raise funds to provide aid to countries facing major crises, such as famine.

Some major international organizations aim at economic co-operation and the removal of trade barriers. For example, in 2003, the European Union had 15 members, of which 12 had adopted a single currency, the euro, on 1 January 2001. On 1 May 2004, another ten countries in

MEMBERS OF THE UNITED NATIONS
Year of joining:

- ■ 1940s
- □ 1950s
- □ 1960s
- □ 1970s
- ■ 1980s
- □ 1990s
- □ 2000s
- ■ NON–MEMBERS

★ 1% – 10% CONTRIBUTION TO FUNDING

☆ OVER 10% CONTRIBUTION TO FUNDING

INTERNATIONAL AID AND GNP
Aid provided as a percentage of GNP, with total aid in brackets (latest available year).

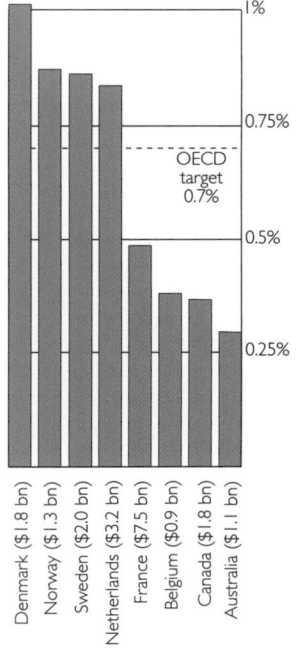

5 1

eastern and southern Europe joined the EU, bringing the total membership to 25. Further expansion is anticipated in the next decade.

Other groupings include ASEAN (the Association of South-east Asian Nations) which aims to reduce trade barriers between its members (Brunei, Burma [Myanmar], Cambodia, Indonesia, Laos, Malaysia, the Philippines, Singapore, Thailand and Vietnam). APEC (the Asia-Pacific Co-operation Group), founded in 1989, aims to create a free-trade zone between the countries

▲ *Refugee camp, Sudan*
In the late 20th and early 21st centuries, many people in the Horn of Africa and Sudan were displaced by war. Here, and in other parts of the world, refugees from war depend largely on aid from international organizations and NGOs.

of eastern Asia, North America, Australia and New Zealand by 2020. Meanwhile, Canada, Mexico and the United States have formed NAFTA (the North American Free Trade Agreement), while other economic groupings link most of the countries in Latin America. Another grouping with a more limited but important objective is OPEC (the Organization of Oil-Exporting Countries). OPEC works to unify policies concerning trade in oil on the world markets.

Some organizations exist to discuss matters of common interest between groups of nations. The Commonwealth of Nations, for example, grew out of links created by the British Empire. In North and South America, the OAS (Organization of American States) aims to increase understanding in the Western hemisphere. The African Union (formerly the Organization of African Unity) has a similar role in Africa, while the Arab League represents Arab nations.

COUNTRIES OF THE EUROPEAN UNION

Country	Total land area (sq km)	Total population (2004 est.)	Year of accession to the EU	Country	Total land area (sq km)	Total population (2004 est.)	Year of accession to the EU
Austria	83,859	8,175,000	1995	Latvia	64,600	2,306,000	2004
Belgium	30,528	10,348,000	1958	Lithuania	65,200	3,608,000	2004
Cyprus	9,251	776,000	2004	Luxembourg	2,586	463,000	1958
Czech Republic	78,866	10,246,000	2004	Malta	316	397,000	2004
Denmark	43,094	5,413,000	1973	Netherlands	41,526	16,318,000	1958
Estonia	45,100	1,342,000	2004	Poland	323,250	38,626,000	2004
Finland	338,145	5,215,000	1995	Portugal	88,797	10,524,000	1986
France	551,500	60,424,000	1958	Slovak Republic	49,012	5,424,000	2004
Germany	357,022	82,425,000	1958	Slovenia	20,256	2,011,000	2004
Greece	131,957	10,648,000	1981	Spain	497,548	40,281,000	1986
Hungary	93,032	10,032,000	2004	Sweden	449,964	8,986,000	1995
Ireland	70,273	3,970,000	1973	United Kingdom	241,857	60,271,000	1973
Italy	301,318	58,057,000	1958				

AGRICULTURE

Ever since 1798, when the British economist Thomas Robert Malthus published his view that populations would outgrow food supply, leading to famine and war, food production and distribution, and agricultural technology have been subjects of debate. The situation is complicated by the fact that, in rich countries, food is cheaper than ever, yet obesity has been identified as a major health hazard. On the other hand, malnutrition is rife in Africa, where local farmers cannot compete with the flood of subsidized food from the richer nations.

From the 1950s, the 'green revolution' greatly increased food production. By using new crop varieties, irrigation, and the extensive use of fertilizers and pesticides, India, once a food importer, became self-sufficient in food.

In the early 2000s, many people placed hopes in the use of genetically modified crops. Sup-

▼ *Rice harvest, Bali, Indonesia*

More than half of the world's people eat rice as their basic food. Rice grows well in tropical and subtropical regions, such as in Indonesia, India and south-eastern China.

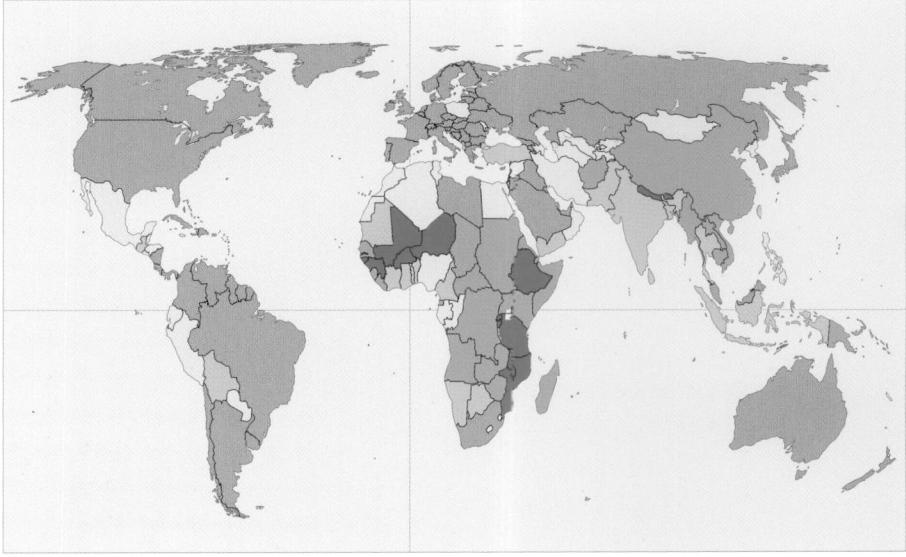

porters argued that GM crops could be one of the greatest advances ever in farming. But critics of GM crops voiced serious environmental and health concerns. The lack of conclusive scientific evidence led to strong consumer resistance in some parts of the world, notably in Western Europe. Even some developing countries were doubtful. For example, in 2004, Angola, a country badly in need of food aid, joined several other southern African countries in rejecting offers of GM foods.

FOOD PRODUCTION

Agriculture, which supplies most of our food, together with materials to make clothes and other products, is the world's most important economic activity. But its relative importance has declined in comparison with manufacturing and service industries. As a result, the end of the 20th century marked the first time for 10,000 years when the vast majority of the people no longer had to depend for their living on growing crops and herding animals.

However, agriculture remains the dominant economic activity in many developing countries in Africa and Asia. For example, in the early 21st century, 80% or more of the people of Bhutan, Burundi, Nepal and Rwanda depended on farming for their living.

Many people in developing countries eke out the barest of livings by nomadic herding or shifting cultivation, combined with hunting, fishing and gathering plant foods. A large proportion of farmers live at subsistence level, producing little more than they require to provide the basic needs of their families.

The world's largest food producer and exporter is the United States, although agriculture employs around 1.4% of its total workforce.

IMPORTANCE OF AGRICULTURE

Agricultural workforce as a percentage of the total workforce (2001).

- OVER 80%
- 60–80%
- 40–60%
- 20–40%
- UNDER 20%

	Food	Population
AUSTRALASIA	1.2%	0.4%
EUROPE	27.6%	15.5%
ASIA	44.5%	58.3%
SOUTH AMERICA	6.5%	6.7%
NORTH AMERICA	13.8%	7.1%
AFRICA	6.7%	12.0%

A comparison of world food production and population by continent.

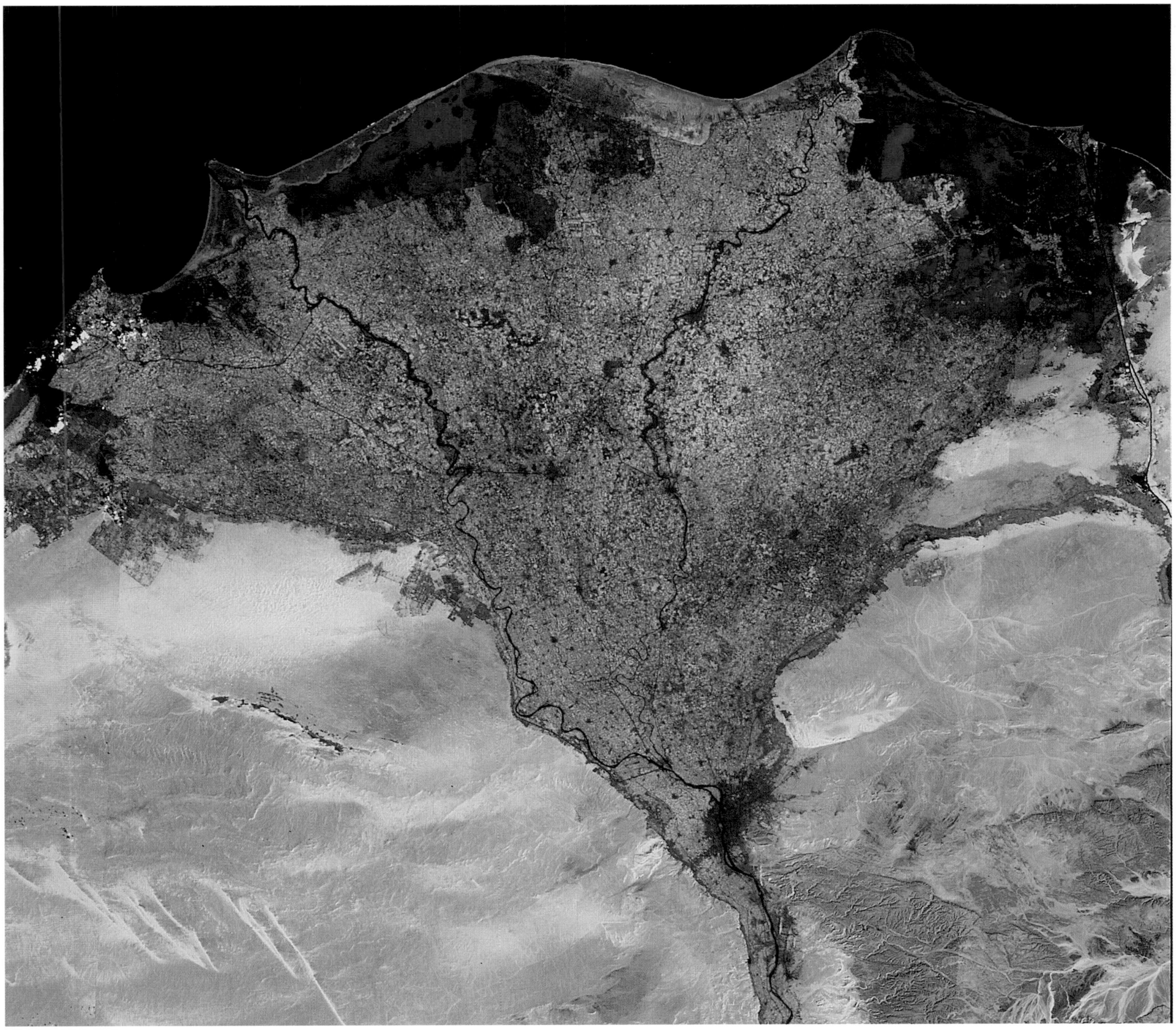

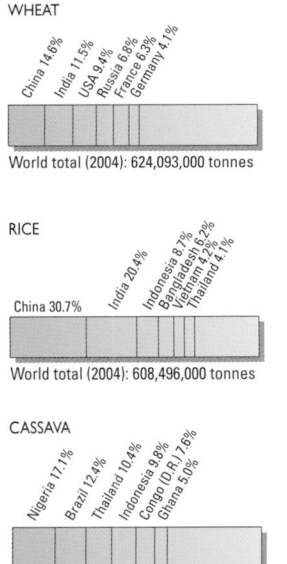

The high production of the United States is explained by its use of scientific methods and mechanization, which are features of agriculture throughout the developed world.

INTENSIVE OR ORGANIC FARMING

In the early 21st century, some people were beginning to question the dependence of farmers on chemical fertilizers and pesticides. Many people became concerned that the widespread use of chemicals was seriously polluting and damaging the environment.

Others objected to the intensive farming of animals to raise production and lower prices. For example, the suggestion in Britain in 1996 that BSE, or 'mad cow disease', might be passed on to people causing CJD (Creuzfeldt-Jakob Disease) caused widespread alarm. Such

▲ *Landsat image of the Nile delta, Egypt*

Most Egyptians live in the Nile valley and on its delta. Because much of the silt carried by the Nile now ends up on the floor of Lake Nasser, upstream of the Aswan Dam, the delta is now retreating and seawater is seeping inland. This eventuality was not foreseen when the Aswan High Dam was built in the 1960s.

factors, combined with the debate about the safety issues surrounding GM foods, have caused much concern.

Some farmers have returned to organic farming, which is based on animal-welfare principles and the banning of chemical fertilizers and pesticides. Organic foods are more expensive to produce than those produced by intensive farming, but an increasing number of consumers are demanding them.

WHEAT

China 14.6% · India 11.5% · USA 9.4% · Russia 6.8% · France 6.3% · Germany 4.1%

World total (2004): 624,093,000 tonnes

RICE

China 30.7% · India 20.4% · Indonesia 8.7% · Bangladesh 6.2% · Vietnam 6.2% · Thailand 4.7%

World total (2004): 608,496,000 tonnes

CASSAVA

Nigeria 17.1% · Brazil 12.4% · Thailand 10.4% · Indonesia 9.8% · Congo (D.R.) 7.6% · Ghana 5.0%

World total (2004): 195,574,000 tonnes

ENERGY AND MINERALS

In August 2004, a serious accident occurred when a pipe carrying superheated steam exploded at Mihama nuclear power plant, 80 km [50 miles] north of Kyoto, Japan. Four people were killed and seven injured. No nuclear contamination occurred, but the accident further weakened public confidence in the industry. Nuclear power provides about 17% of the world's electricity, but the industry's future is clouded by concerns about safety and high costs. The European Union, the world's leading nuclear generator, produces 32% of its electricity by this means. But, by the early 2000s, five member states were committed to phasing out nuclear energy.

FOSSIL FUELS

Huge amounts of energy are needed for heating, generating electricity and for transport. In the

▼ *Wind farms in California, United States*

Wind farms using giant turbines can produce electricity at a lower cost than conventional power stations. But in many areas, winds are too light or too strong for wind farms to be effective.

early years of the Industrial Revolution, coal, formed from organic matter buried beneath the Earth's surface, was the leading source of energy. It remains important as a raw material in the manufacture of drugs and other products, and also as a fuel, despite the fact that burning coal causes air pollution and gives off carbon dioxide, an important greenhouse gas.

However, oil and natural gas, which came into wide use in the 20th century, are cheaper to produce and easier to handle than coal, while, kilogram for kilogram, they give out more heat. Oil is especially important in moving transport, supplying about 97% of the fuel required.

In the 1990s, proven reserves of oil were sufficient to supply the world, at current rates of production, for 43 years, while supplies of natural gas stood at about 66 years. Coal reserves are more abundant and known reserves would last 200 years at present rates of use. Although these figures must be regarded with caution, because they do not allow for future discoveries, it is clear that fossil fuel reserves will one day run out.

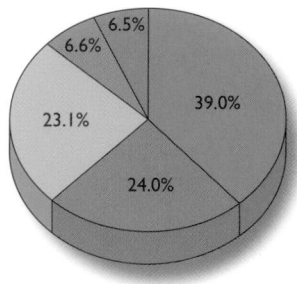

WORLD ENERGY CONSUMPTION

■ OIL
■ COAL
■ GAS
■ HYDRO
■ NUCLEAR

▲ *The diagram shows the proportion of world energy consumption in 2003 by form. Total energy consumption was 10,376 million tonnes of oil equivalent. Wood, peat and animal wastes, plus renewable forms, such as wind power, are locally important but they comprise only 0.8% of the total.*

SELECTED MINERAL PRODUCTION STATISTICS
(percentage of world total output, 2003)

Bauxite		Diamonds	
Australia	35.9%	Australia	20.7%
Brazil	11.9%	Botswana	20.2%
Guinea	11.0%	Congo (D.R.)	19.3%
Jamaica	8.7%	Russia	16.0%
China	7.1%	S. Africa	8.4%

Gold		Iron ore	
S. Africa	14.8%	China	21.1%
Australia	11.2%	Brazil	18.9%
USA	11.0%	Australia	17.2%
China	8.3%	India	9.7%
Russia	6.8%	Russia	7.4%

Manganese		Zinc	
China	23.2%	China	19.6%
S. Africa	14.4%	Australia	16.1%
Ukraine	11.1%	Peru	14.9%
Brazil	11.1%	Canada	8.6%
Australia	10.3%	USA	8.0%

▼ MINERAL DISTRIBUTION

The map shows the richest sources of the most important minerals. Major mineral locations are named. Undersea deposits, most of which are considered inaccessible, are not shown.

▽ GOLD
◠ SILVER
◆ DIAMONDS
▽ TUNGSTEN
● IRON ORE
■ NICKEL
◡ CHROME
▲ MANGANESE
□ COBALT
▲ MOLYBDENUM
■ COPPER
▲ LEAD
● BAUXITE
▽ TIN
◆ ZINC
◡ MERCURY

ALTERNATIVE ENERGY

Other sources of energy are therefore required. Besides nuclear energy, the main alternative to fossil fuels is water power. The costs of building dams and hydroelectric power stations are high, though hydroelectric production is comparatively cheap. But the creation of reservoirs uproots people and destroys natural habitats. Water power is also suitable only in areas with plenty of rivers and steep slopes, such as Norway.

In Brazil, alcohol made from sugar has been used to fuel cars. Initially, this government-backed policy met with success. However, it proved to be expensive and the production of ethanol-fuelled cars was halted until Brazil struck a deal with Germany in the early 2000s.

▲ *Potash mines in Utah, United States*

Potash is a mineral used mainly to make fertilizers. Much of it comes from mines where deposits formed when ancient seas dried up are exploited. Potash is also extracted from salt lakes.

Battery-run electric cars have been developed in the United States, but regular and time-consuming recharging is a major drawback.

Other forms of energy, which are renewable and cleaner than fossil fuels, are winds, sea waves, the rise and fall of tides, and geothermal power. In many Western countries seeking to reduce carbon dioxide emissions, these forms of energy seem to have a bright future.

MINERALS FOR INDUSTRY

In addition to energy, manufacturing industries need raw materials, including minerals, and these natural resources, like fossil fuels, are being used in such huge quantities that some experts have predicted shortages of some of them before long.

Manufacturers depend on supplies of about 80 minerals. Some, such as bauxite (aluminium ore) and iron, are abundant, but others are scarce or are found only in deposits that are uneconomical to mine. Many experts advocate a policy of recycling scrap metal, including aluminium, chromium, copper, lead, nickel and zinc. This practice would reduce pollution and conserve the energy required for extracting and refining mineral ores.

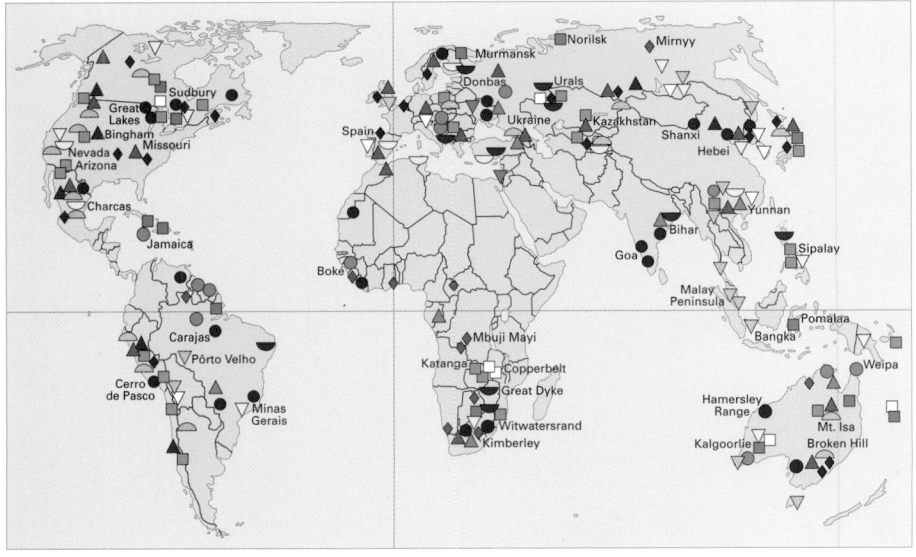

WORLD ECONOMIES

In 2003, Ethiopia had a per capita GNI (Gross National Income) of US$90, as compared with Norway, whose per capita GNI stood at $43,350, according to the World Bank. These figures indicate the vast gap between the economies and standards of living of the two countries.

The GNI includes the GDP (Gross Domestic Product), which consists of the total output of goods and services in a country in a given year, plus net exports – that is, the value of goods and services sold abroad less the value of foreign goods and services used in the country in the same year. The GNI divided by the population gives a country's GNI per capita. In low-income developing countries, agriculture makes a high contribution to the GNI. For example, in Ethiopia, 45% of the GDP came from agriculture. On the other hand, industry was small scale and contributed only 12% of the GDP. By comparison, in high-income economies, the percentage contribution of manufacturing far exceeds that of agriculture.

▼ Hard-disk assembly factory

The manufacture of computer equipment and computer software is a fairly new industrial phenomenon. In Asia, high-tech industries have developed quickly, helping relatively poor developing countries to achieve rapid economic growth.

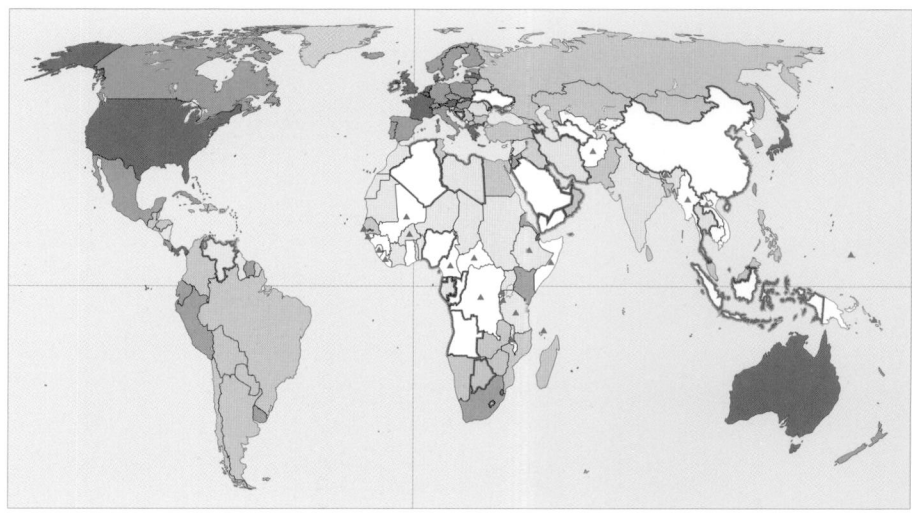

INDUSTRIALIZATION

The Industrial Revolution began in Britain in the late 18th century. Before that time, most people worked on farms. But with the Industrial Revolution came factories, using machines that could manufacture goods much faster and more cheaply than those made by cottage industries that already existed.

The Industrial Revolution soon spread to several countries in mainland Europe and the United States and, by the late 19th century, it had reached Canada, Japan and Russia. At first, industrial development was based on such areas as coalfields or ironfields. But in the 20th

IMPORTANCE OF THE SERVICE INDUSTRY
Percentage of total GDP from the service sector (2003).

- OVER 70%
- 60–70%
- 50–60%
- 40–50%
- UNDER 40%
- NO DATA AVAILABLE
- OVER 40% OF TOTAL GDP FROM THE INDUSTRIAL SECTOR
- ▲ OVER 40% OF TOTAL GDP FROM THE AGRICULTURAL SECTOR

GROSS NATIONAL INCOME PER CAPITA IN US$ (2003)		
1	Luxembourg	$43,940
2	Norway	$43,350
3	Switzerland	$39,980
4	United States	$37,610
5	Japan	$34,510
6	Denmark	$33,750
7	Iceland	$30,810
8	Sweden	$28,840
9	United Kingdom	$28,350
10	Finland	$27,020
11	Ireland	$26,960
12	Austria	$26,720
13	Netherlands	$26,310
14	Belgium	$25,820
15	Germany	$25,520
16	France	$24,770
17	Canada	$23,930
18	Australia	$21,650
19	Italy	$21,560
20	Singapore	$21,230

century, the use of oil, which is easy to transport along pipelines, made it possible for industries to be set up anywhere.

Some nations, such as Switzerland, became industrialized even though they lacked natural resources. They depended instead on the specialized skills of their workers. This same pattern applies today. Some countries with rich natural resources, such as Mexico (with a per capita GNI in 2003 of US$6,230), lag far behind Japan ($34,510) and Cyprus ($12,320), which lack resources and have to import many of the materials they need to sustain their manufacturing industries.

SERVICE INDUSTRIES

Experts often refer to high-income countries as industrial economies. But manufacturing employs only one in six workers in the United States, one in five in Britain, and one in three in Germany and Japan.

▲ *New cars awaiting transportation, Los Angeles, USA*
Cars are the most important single manufactured item in world trade, followed by vehicle parts and engines. The world's leading car producers are Japan, the United States, Germany and France.

In most developed economies, the percentage of manufacturing jobs has fallen in recent years, while jobs in service industries have risen. For example, in Britain, the proportion of jobs in manufacturing fell from 37% in 1970 to 12.8% in 2003, while jobs in the service sector rose from just under 50% to 78.6%. While change in Britain was especially rapid, similar changes were taking place in most industrial economies. Service industries now account for well over half the jobs in the generally prosperous countries that made up the OECD (Organization for Economic Co-operation and Development). Instead of being called the 'industrial' economies, these countries might be better named the 'service' economies.

Service industries offer a wide range of jobs and many of them require high educational qualifications. These include finance, insurance and high-tech industries, such as computer programming, entertainment and telecommunications. Service industries also include marketing and advertising, which are essential if the cars and television sets made by manufacturers are to be sold. Another valuable service industry is tourism; in some countries, such as the Gambia, it is the major foreign-exchange earner. Trade in services plays a crucial part in world economies. Service industries now account for more than a fifth of world trade.

THE WORKFORCE
Percentage of men and women over 15 years old in employment, selected countries (2001).

■ MEN
■ WOMEN

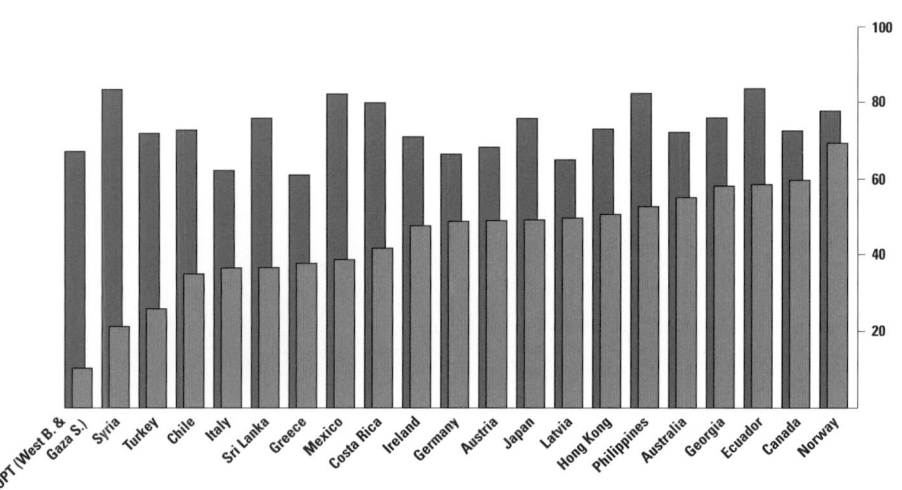

TRADE AND COMMERCE

The establishment of the WTO (World Trade Organization) on 1 January 1995 was the latest step in the long history of world trade. The WTO was set up by the eighth round of negotiations, popularly called the 'Uruguay round', conducted by the General Agreement on Tariffs and Trade (GATT). This treaty was signed by representatives of 125 governments in April 1994. By early 2005, the WTO had 148 members.

GATT was first established in 1948. Its initial aim was to produce a charter to create a body called the International Trade Organization. This body never came into being. Instead, GATT, acting as an *ad hoc* agency, pioneered a series of agreements aimed at liberalizing world trade by reducing tariffs on imports and other obstacles to free trade.

▼ *New York City Stock Exchange, United States*

Stock exchanges, where stocks and shares are sold and bought, are important in channelling savings and investments to companies and governments. The world's largest stock exchange is in Tokyo, Japan.

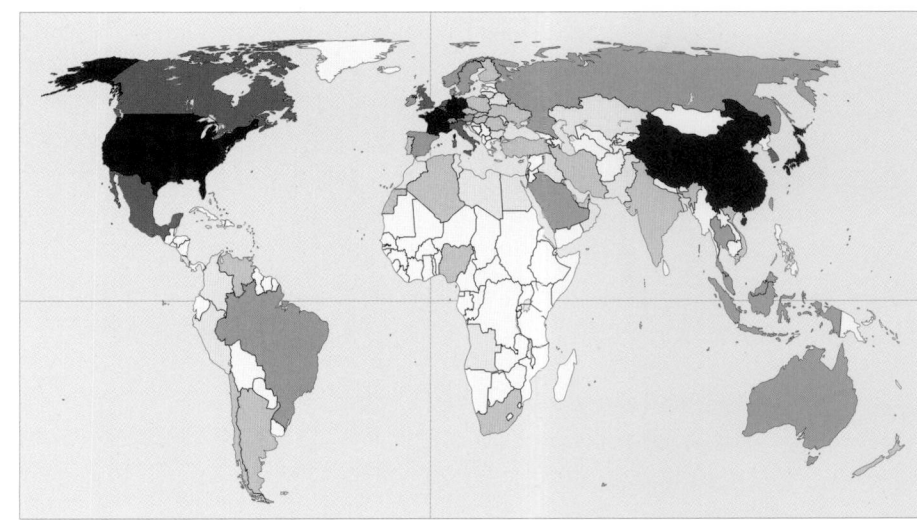

GATT's objectives were based on the belief that international trade creates wealth. Trade occurs because the world's resources are not distributed evenly between countries, and, in theory, free trade means that every country should concentrate on what it can do best and purchase from others goods and services that they can supply more cheaply. In practice, however, free trade may cause unemployment when imported goods are cheaper than those produced within the country.

Trade is sometimes an important factor in world politics, especially when trade sanctions are applied against countries whose actions incur the disapproval of the international community. For example, in the 1990s, world-wide trade sanctions were imposed on Serbia because of its involvement in the civil war in Bosnia-Herzegovina.

CHANGING TRADE PATTERNS

The early 16th century, when Europeans began to divide the world into huge empires, opened up a new era in international trade. By the 19th century, the colonial powers, who were among the first industrial powers, promoted trade with their colonies, from which they obtained unprocessed raw materials, such as food, natural fibres, minerals and timber. In return, they shipped clothes, shoes and other cheap items to the colonies.

From the late 19th century until the early 1950s, primary products dominated world trade, with oil becoming the leading item in the latter part of this period. Many developing countries still depend heavily on the export of one or two primary products, such as coffee or iron ore, but overall the proportion of primary products in world trade has fallen since the 1950s. Today the most important elements

WORLD TRADE

Percentage share of total world exports by value (2003).

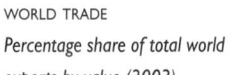
- OVER 5%
- 2.5–5%
- 1–2.5%
- 0.25–1%
- 0.1–0.25%
- UNDER 0.1%
- NO DATA AVAILABLE

The world's leading trading nations, according to the combined value of their exports and imports, are the United States, Germany, Japan, France and the United Kingdom.

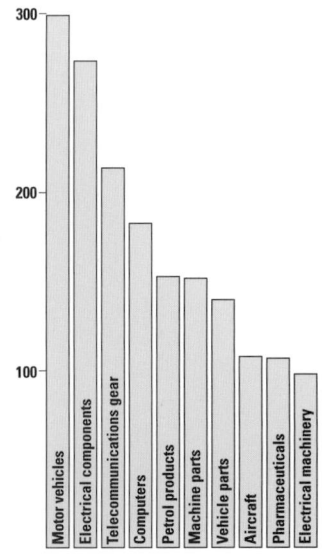

TRADED PRODUCTS

The diagram shows major manufactures traded by value in billions of US$. Manufactures in total comprise 74% of the world's total trade, the value of which was $7,294 billion in 2003.

in world trade are manufactures and semi-manufactures, exchanged mainly between the industrialized nations.

THE WORLD'S MARKETS
Private companies conduct most of world trade, but government policies affect it. Governments which believe that certain industries are strategic, or essential for the country's future, may impose tariffs on imports, or import quotas to limit the volume of imports, if they are thought to be undercutting the domestic industries.

For example, the United States has argued that

▲ *Rotterdam, Netherlands*
World trade depends on transport. Rotterdam, the world's largest port, serves not only the Netherlands, but also industrial areas in parts of Germany, France and Switzerland.

Japan has greater access to its markets than the United States has to Japan's. This might have led the United States to resort to protectionism, but instead the United States remains committed to free trade despite occasional disputes.

Other problems in international trade occur when governments give subsidies to its producers, who can then export products at low prices. Another difficulty, called 'dumping', occurs when products are sold at below the market price in order to gain a market share. One of the aims of the newly-created WTO is the phasing out of government subsidies for agricultural products, though the world's poorest countries will be exempt from many of the WTO's most severe regulations.

Governments are also concerned about the volume of imports and exports, and most countries keep records of international transactions. When the total value of goods and services imported exceeds the value of goods and services exported, then the country has a deficit in its balance of payments. Large deficits can weaken a country's economy.

DEPENDENCE ON TRADE
Value of exports as a percentage of GDP (2003).

■ OVER 50% GDP FROM EXPORTS
■ 25–50% GDP FROM EXPORTS
□ 10–25% GDP FROM EXPORTS
□ 5–10% GDP FROM EXPORTS
□ UNDER 5% GDP FROM EXPORTS
□ NO DATA AVAILABLE

TRAVEL AND COMMUNICATIONS

By the early 21st century, millions of people were linked to an 'information super-highway' called the Internet. Equipped with a personal computer, an electricity supply, a telephone and a modem, people are able to communicate with others all over the world. People can now send messages by e-mail (electronic mail), they can engage in electronic discussions, contacting people with similar interests, and engage in 'chat lines', which are the latest equivalent of telephone conferences.

These new developments are likely to affect the working lives of people everywhere, enabling them to work at home whilst having many of the facilities that are available in an office. The Internet is part of an ongoing and astonishingly rapid evolution in the fields of communications and transport.

TRANSPORT

Around 200 years ago, most people never travelled far from their birthplace, but today we are much more mobile. Cars and buses now provide convenient forms of transport for many millions of people, huge ships transport massive cargoes around the world, and jet airliners, some travelling faster than the speed of sound, can transport high-value goods as well as holiday-makers to almost any part of the world.

Land transport of freight has developed greatly since the start of the Industrial Revolution.

▼ *Eurostar travel*
High-speed Eurostar services connect London to Paris and Brussels via the $15 billion Channel Tunnel, linking the UK to mainland Europe. Only ten years after the tunnel opened in 1994, Eurostar carried about 7.3 million passengers per year.

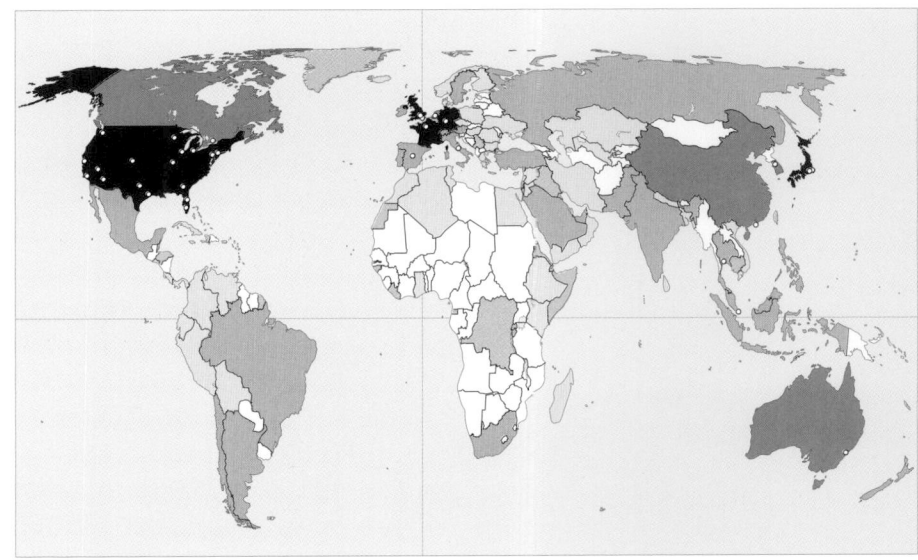

Canals, which became important in the 18th century, could not compete with rail transport in the 19th century. Rail transport remains important, but, during the 20th century, it suffered from competition with road transport, which is cheaper and has the advantage of carrying materials and goods from door to door.

Road transport causes pollution and the burning of fuels creates greenhouse gases that contribute to global warming. Yet privately owned cars are now the leading form of passenger traffic in developed nations, especially for journeys of less than around 400 km [250 miles]. Car owners do not have to suffer the inconvenience of waiting for public transport, such as buses, though they often have to endure traffic jams at peak travel times.

Ocean passenger traffic is now modest, but ships carry the bulk of international trade. Huge oil tankers and bulk grain carriers now ply the oceans with their cargoes, while container ships carry mixed cargoes. Containers are boxes built to international standards that contain cargo. Containers are easy to handle, and so they

AIR TRAVEL – PASSENGER KILOMETRES*
FLOWN *(latest available year)*.

- ■ OVER 100,000 MILLION
- ■ 50,000–100,000 MILLION
- ■ 10,000–50,000 MILLION
- □ 1,000–10,000 MILLION
- □ UNDER 1,000 MILLION
- ■ NO DATA AVAILABLE

○ MAJOR AIRPORTS (HANDLING OVER 25 MILLION PASSENGERS IN 2001)

* Passenger kilometres are the number of passengers (both international and domestic) multiplied by the distance flown by each passenger from the airport of origin.

SELECTED NEWSPAPER CIRCULATION FIGURES (2002)

France		**Russia**	
Le Monde	389,200	*Argumenty i Fakty*	2,900,000
Le Figaro	352,700	*Pravda*	674,000
		Izvestia	218,000
Germany			
Bild	4,100,000	**Spain**	
Süddeutsche Zeitung	427,000	*El Pais*	578,000
India		**United Kingdom**	
The Times of India	2,145,000	*The Sun*	3,541,000
The Hindustan Times	1,857,000	*Daily Mail*	2,343,000
		Daily Mirror	2,148,000
Italy		*The Daily Telegraph*	924,000
Corriere della Sera	690,000	*Daily Express*	916,000
La Repubblica	624,000		
La Stampa	398,000	**United States**	
		USA Today	2,100,000
Japan		*The Wall Street Journal*	1,801,000
Yomiuri Shimbun	14,500,000	*The New York Times*	1,113,000
Asahi Shimbun	12,600,000	*Los Angeles Times*	966,000

reduce shipping costs, speed up deliveries and cut losses caused by breakages. Most large ports now have the facilities to handle containers.

Air transport is suitable for carrying goods that are expensive, light and compact, or perishable. However, because of the high costs of air freight, it is most suitable for carrying passengers along long-distance routes around the world. Through air travel, international tourism, with people sometimes flying considerable distances, has become a major and rapidly expanding industry.

COMMUNICATIONS

After humans first began to communicate by using the spoken word, the next great stage in the development of communications was the invention of writing around 5,500 years ago.

The invention of movable type in the mid-15th century led to the mass production of books and, in the early 17th century, the first newspapers. Newspapers now play an important part in the mass communication of information, although today radio and, even more important, television have led to a decline in the circulation of newspapers in many parts of the world.

The most recent developments have occurred in the field of electronics. Artificial communications satellites now circle the planet, relaying radio, television, telegraph and telephone signals. This enables people to watch events on the far side of the globe as they are happening. Electronic equipment is also used in many other ways, such as in navigation systems used in air,

▲ *Commercial jet airliners, Washington, DC, United States*
Air travel has transformed world tourism. However, the terrorist attacks by suicide bombers on the United States on 11 September 2001 led to greater security checks at airports. Falls in passenger numbers were another consequence of the hijackings.

sea and space, and also in modern weaponry, as shown vividly in the television coverage of such military action as that in Iraq in 2003–4.

THE AGE OF COMPUTERS

One of the most remarkable applications of electronics is in the field of computers. Computers are now making a huge contribution to communications. They are able to process data at incredibly high speeds and can store vast quantities of information. For example, the work of weather forecasters has been greatly improved now that computers can process the enormous amount of data required for a single weather forecast. They also have many other applications in such fields as business, government, science and medicine.

Through the Internet, computers provide a free interchange of news and views around the world. But the dangers of misuse, such as the exchange of pornographic images, have led to calls for censorship. Censorship, however, is a blunt weapon, which can be used by authoritarian governments to suppress the free exchange of information that the new information superhighway makes possible.

TOP TOURIST DESTINATIONS

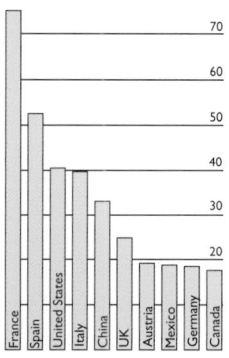

International tourist arrivals in millions (2003)

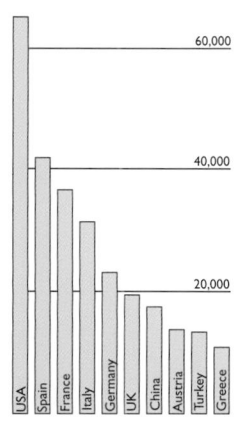

Countries receiving the most from overseas tourism, US$ million (2003).

THE WORLD TODAY

The early years of the 20th century witnessed the exploration of Antarctica, the last uncharted continent. Today, less than 100 years later, tourists are able to take cruises to the icy southern continent, while almost no part of the globe is inaccessible to the determined traveller. Improved transport and images from space have made our world seem smaller.

A DIVIDED WORLD

Between the end of World War II in 1945 and the late 1980s, the world was divided, politically and economically, into three main groups: the developed countries or Western democracies, with their free enterprise or mixed economies; the centrally planned or Communist countries; and the developing countries or Third World.

This division became obsolete when the former Soviet Union and its old European allies, together with the 'special economic zones' in eastern China, began the transition from centrally planned to free enterprise economies. This left the world divided into two broad camps: the prosperous developed countries and the poorer developing countries. The simplest way of distinguishing between the groups is with reference to their per capita GNPs (Gross National Products).

The World Bank divides the developing countries into three main groups. At the bottom are the low-income economies, including India and most of sub-Saharan Africa. In 2003, this group contained about 2.3 billion people, but the

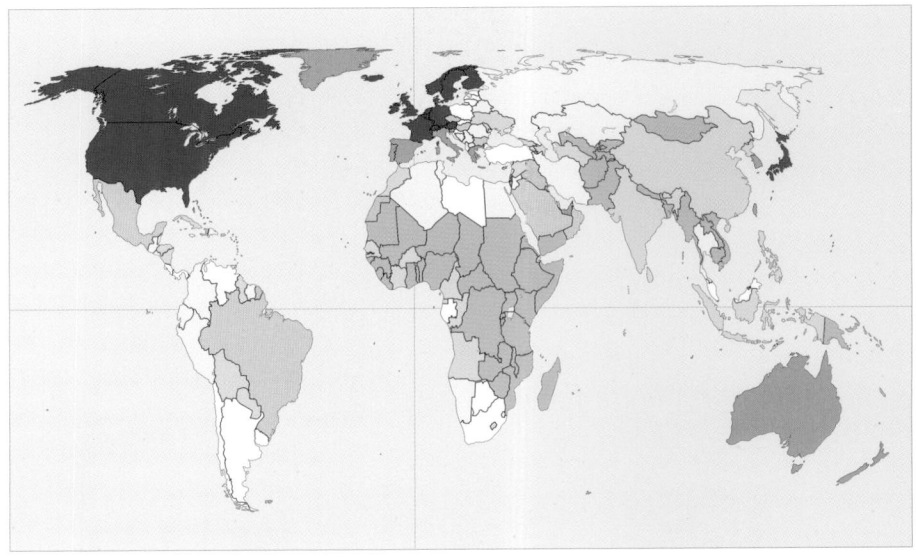

average annual income was only US$450, with some countries as low as $90. Two other groups, with a combined population of 3 billion people, are the lower-middle-income economies, with a per capita GNI (Gross National Income) of between $766 and $3,035, and the upper-middle-income economies with a per capita GNI between $3,306 and $9,385. The high-income economies, with 971 million people, have an average (and rising) per capita GNI of $28,550.

ECONOMIC AND SOCIAL CONTRASTS

Economic differences are coupled with other factors, such as rates of population growth. For example, around the turn of the century, the low- and middle-income economies had a high population growth rate of 1.7%, while the growth rate in high-income economies was about 0.1%. In high-income economies, youths made up only 18% of the population and people over 65, 14%.

Stark contrasts exist worldwide in the quality of life. Generally, the people in Western Europe

GROSS NATIONAL INCOME PER CAPITA
The value of total income divided by the population (2003).

- OVER 400% OF WORLD AVERAGE
- 200–400% OF WORLD AVERAGE
- 100–200% OF WORLD AVERAGE
- 50–100% OF WORLD AVERAGE
- 25–50% OF WORLD AVERAGE
- 10–25% OF WORLD AVERAGE
- UNDER 10% OF WORLD AVERAGE
- NO DATA AVAILABLE

RICHEST COUNTRIES
(GNI PER CAPITA, 2003)

Luxembourg	US$43,940
Norway	US$43,350
Switzerland	US$39,980
United States	US$37,610
Japan	US$34,510

POOREST COUNTRIES
(GNI PER CAPITA, 2003)

Ethiopia	US$90
Congo (Dem. Rep.)	US$100
Burundi	US$100
Liberia	US$130
Guinea-Bissau	US$140

▼ *East African tourism*

Improved transport, including the use of four-wheel drive vehicles, has led to a boom in tourism in many developing regions, such as East Africa. But terrorist incidents may slow down the development of tourism in some areas.

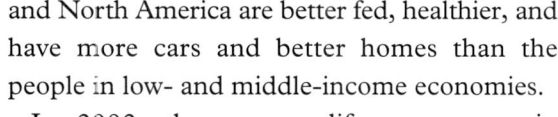

and North America are better fed, healthier, and have more cars and better homes than the people in low- and middle-income economies.

In 2002, the average life expectancy in sub-Saharan Africa was less than 55 years. By contrast, the average life expectancy in the United States was 77 years. While nearly half of all the people in low-income economies are illiterate, the illiteracy rate for women is more than 50%. But in the high-income economies, illiteracy is rare for both sexes.

FUTURE DEVELOPMENT

In the last 50 years, despite all the aid supplied to developing countries, much of the world still suffers from poverty and economic backwardness. Some countries are even poorer now than they were a generation ago while others have become substantially richer.

However, several factors suggest that poor countries may find progress easier in the 21st century. For example, technology is now more readily transferable between countries, while improved transport and communications make it easier for countries to take part in the world economy. But industrial development could lead to an increase in global pollution. Hence, any strategy for global economic expansion must also take account of environmental factors.

▲ *Operation Enduring Freedom, Afghanistan*
A joint patrol of US Marines and Army soldiers is seen here patrolling through the village of Cem, Afghanistan, some 10 km [6 miles] from the airport near Kandahar, in January 2002.

A WORLD IN CONFLICT

The end of the Cold War held out hopes of a new world order. But ethnic, religious and other rivalries have subsequently led to appalling violence in places as diverse as the Balkan peninsula, Israel and the Palestinian territories, and Rwanda–Burundi. Then, on 11 September 2001, the attack on those symbols of the economic and military might of the United States – the World Trade Center and the Pentagon Building – demonstrated that nowhere on Earth is safe from attack by extremists prepared to sacrifice their lives in pursuit of their aims.

The danger posed by terrorist groups, such as al Qaida, or by rogue states, possibly in possession of nuclear or biological weapons, has forced many countries into new alliances to combat the terrorists and the governments that give them shelter. Many people also recognize a pressing need to correct the wrongs, real or perceived, that lead people to acts of martyrdom or murderous destruction, while simultaneously tackling the problems of world poverty.

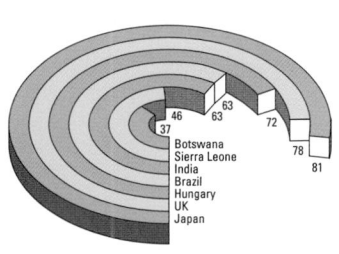

▲ *Years of life expectancy at birth, selected countries (2001).*
The chart shows the contrasting range of average life expectancies at birth for a range of countries, including both low-income and high-income economies. Generally, improved health services are raising life expectancies. On average, women live longer than men, even in the poorer developing countries.

WORLD MAPS

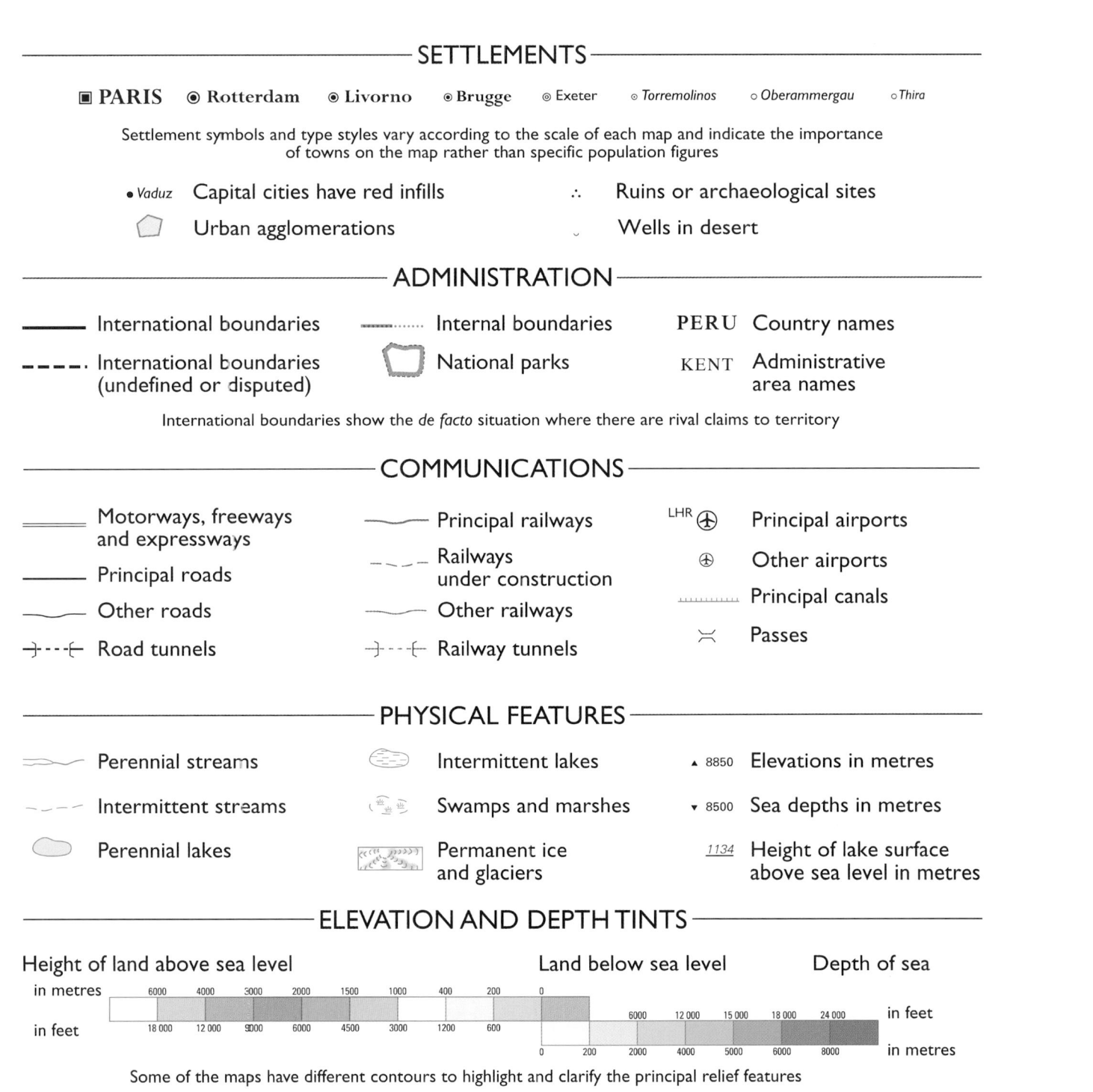

─── SETTLEMENTS ───

■ **PARIS**　◉ **Rotterdam**　◉ **Livorno**　◉ **Brugge**　◉ Exeter　○ Torremolinos　○ Oberammergau　○ Thira

Settlement symbols and type styles vary according to the scale of each map and indicate the importance of towns on the map rather than specific population figures

• Vaduz　Capital cities have red infills

∴　Ruins or archaeological sites

⬠　Urban agglomerations

ᵕ　Wells in desert

─── ADMINISTRATION ───

──────　International boundaries

─ ─ ─ ·　International boundaries (undefined or disputed)

▬▬▬▬　Internal boundaries

⬡　National parks

PERU　Country names

KENT　Administrative area names

International boundaries show the *de facto* situation where there are rival claims to territory

─── COMMUNICATIONS ───

═════　Motorways, freeways and expressways

─────　Principal roads

──╮──　Other roads

╾┼╌╌┼╼　Road tunnels

─────　Principal railways

─ ╌ ─　Railways under construction

──╮──　Other railways

╾┼╌╌┼╼　Railway tunnels

ᴸᴴᴿ ✈　Principal airports

✈　Other airports

╌╌╌╌╌╌　Principal canals

≍　Passes

─── PHYSICAL FEATURES ───

∼∼∼∼　Perennial streams

─ ╌ ─　Intermittent streams

⬭　Perennial lakes

⬭　Intermittent lakes

⬭　Swamps and marshes

▦　Permanent ice and glaciers

▲ 8850　Elevations in metres

▼ 8500　Sea depths in metres

1134　Height of lake surface above sea level in metres

─── ELEVATION AND DEPTH TINTS ───

Height of land above sea level　　　Land below sea level　　　Depth of sea

in metres

6000	4000	3000	2000	1500	1000	400	200	0						
									6000	12 000	15 000	18 000	24 000	in feet

in feet

18 000	12 000	9000	6000	4500	3000	1200	600							
								0	200	2000	4000	5000	6000	8000	in metres

Some of the maps have different contours to highlight and clarify the principal relief features

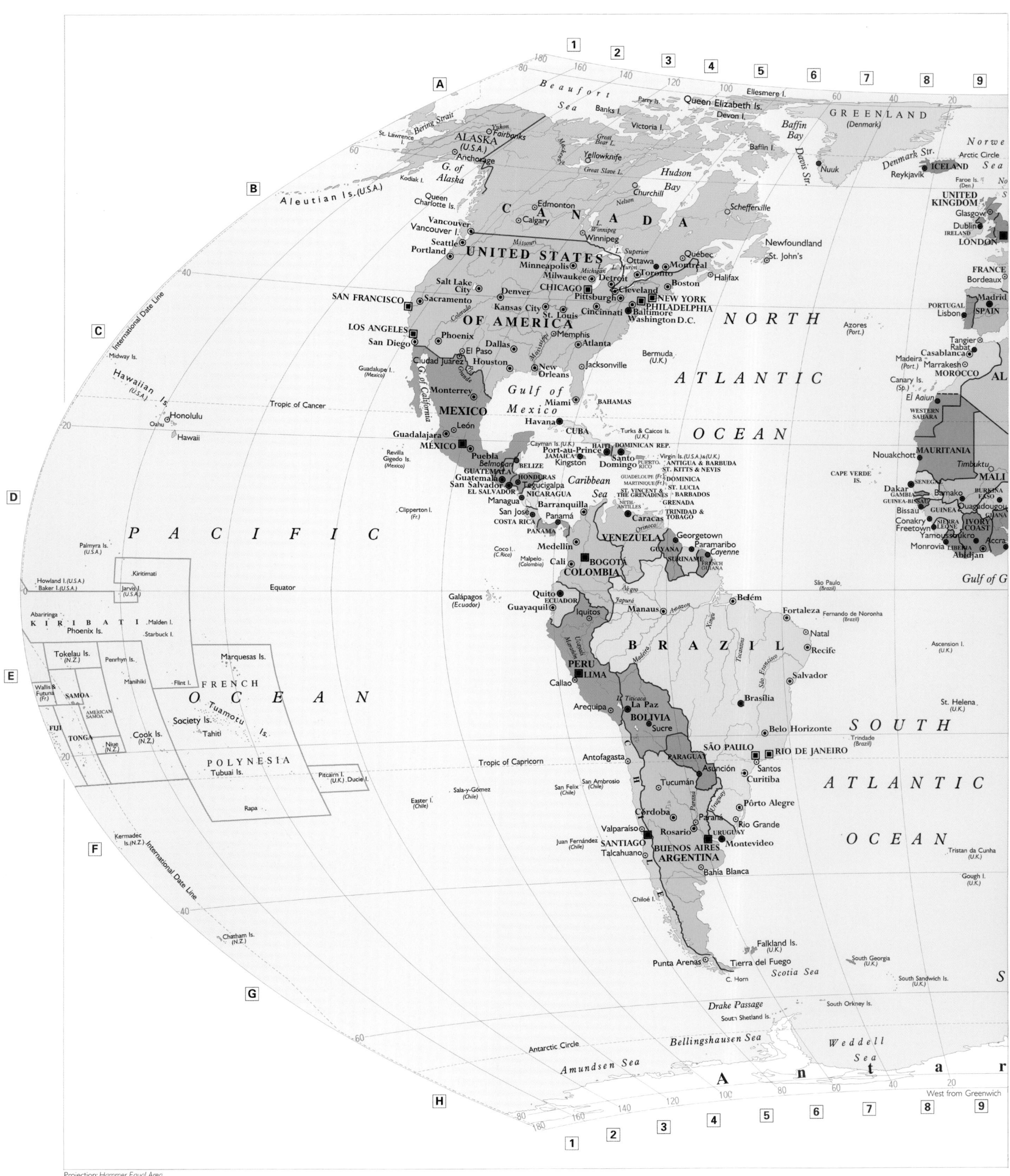

Projection: Hammer Equal Area

Hanoi ● Capital Cities

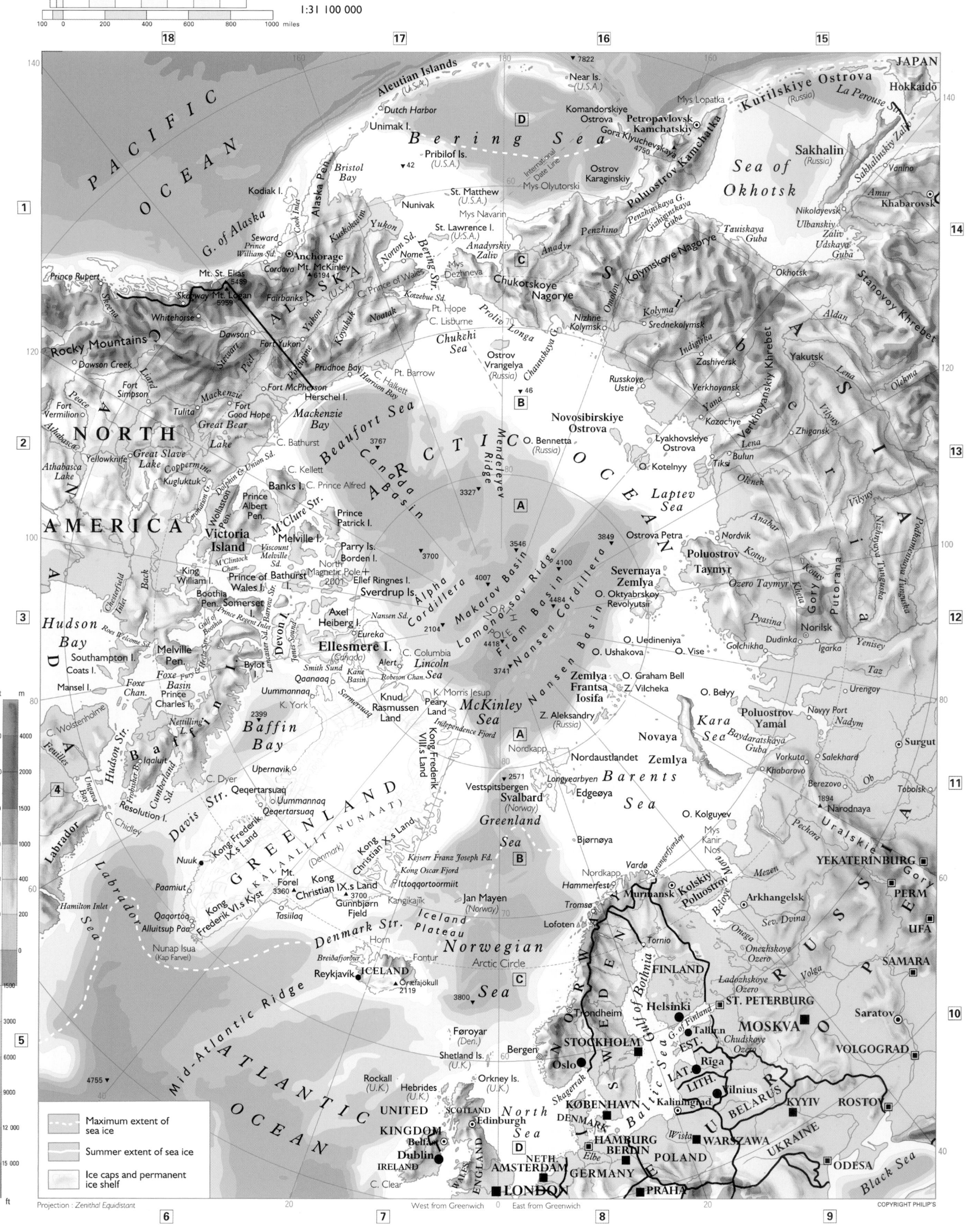

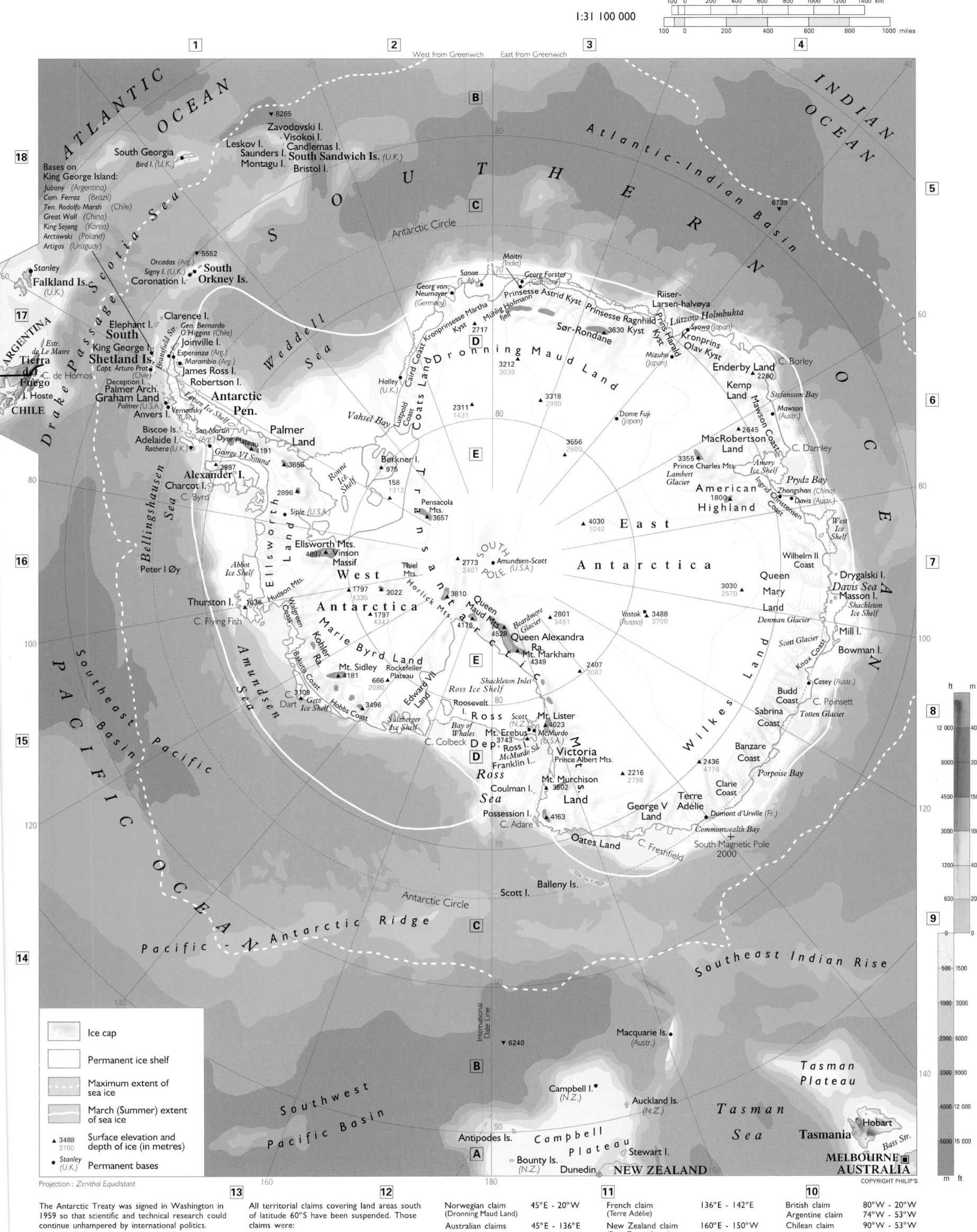

1:31 100 000

100 0   200   400   600   800 1000 1200 1400 km

100 0   200   400   600   800   1000 miles

ATLANTIC OCEAN

INDIAN

OCEAN

Atlantic-Indian Basin

S O U T H E R N

8265

Zavodovski I.
Visokoi I.
Candlemas I.
South Sandwich Is. (U.K.)
Montagu I.
Bristol I.

Leskov I.
Saunders I.

6739

South Georgia
Bird I. (U.K.)

Bases on
King George Island:
Jubany (Argentina)
Com. Ferraz (Brazil)
Ten. Rodolfo Marsh (Chile)
Great Wall (China)
King Sejong (Korea)
Arctowski (Poland)
Artigas (Uruguay)

S C O T I A

Antarctic Circle

Maitri
(India)

Sanae
(S. Afr.)

Georg Forster
(Germany)

Riiser-
Larsen-halvøya

Holmbukta

Lützow

5552

Orcadas (Arg.)
Signy I. (U.K.)
Coronation I.

South
Orkney Is.

Prinsesse Astrid Kyst
Georg von
Neumayer
(Germany)

Prinsesse Ragnhild
Kyst

Prins Harald
Kyst

Syowa (Japan)

O C E A N

Stanley

Falkland Is.
(U.K.)

Clarence I.

Elephant I.
South
King George I.
Shetland Is.

Gen. Bernardo
O'Higgins (Chile)
Esperanza (Arg.)
Marambio (Arg.)

Kronprinsesse Martha
Kyst

Mühlig Hofmann
fjell

2717

Sør-Rondane

3630

Kronprins
Olav Kyst

Enderby Land

C. Borley

ARGENTINA

Tierra
del
Fuego
C. de Hornos
I. Hoste

CHILE

Estr.
de Le Maire

Joinville I.
James Ross I.
Robertson I.
Deception I.

Capt. Arturo Prat
(Chile)

Caird Coast

Dronning Maud Land

3212
3039

Dome Fuji
(Japan)

Mizuho
(Japan)

Kemp
Land

2280

Stefansson Bay

Mawson
(Austr.)

2645

Palmer Arch.
Graham Land
Anvers I.

Palmer (U.S.A.)
Vernadsky (U.K.)

Antarctic
Pen.

Halley
(U.K.)

Coats Land

3318
2990

MacRobertson
Land

C. Darnley

San Martín
(Arg.)

Palmer
Land

Vahsel Bay

2311
1431

3656
2600

3355

Prince Charles Mts.

Amery
Ice
Shelf

Prydz Bay

Biscoe Is.
Adelaide I.

Dyer Plateau

Rothera (U.K.)

George VI Sound

4191

Berkner I.

975

Lambert
Glacier

Zhongshan (China)

Davis (Austr.)

Ingrid Christensen Coast

2987

3658

158
1312

Pensacola
Mts.
3657

American

Highland

1800

West
Ice
Shelf

Alexander I.

Charcot I.
C. Byrd

2896

Siple (U.S.A.)

4030
1040

East

Wilhelm II
Coast

Peter I Øy

Ellsworth Mts.
4897
Vinson
Massif

Thiel
Mts.

2773
2407

South
Pole

Amundsen-Scott
(U.S.A.)

Antarctica

Queen
Mary
Land

Drygalski I.
Davis Sea
Masson I.

3030
2570

Thurston I.

1936

West

Antarctica

1797
4335

3022

Horlick Mts.

3810

4116

Queen
Maud Mts.

4528

Beardmore
Glacier

2801
3491

Vostok
(Russia)

3488
3700

Shackleton
Ice Shelf

Mill I.

C. Flying Fish

1797
4347

Queen Alexandra
Ra.
Mt. Markham
4349

Scott Glacier

Bowman I.

Marie Byrd Land

Denman Glacier

Budd
Coast

Casey (Austr.)

Knox Coast

Kohler
Ra.

Mt. Sidley
4181

666
2080

Rockefeller
Plateau

2407
3087

Totten Glacier

C. Poinsett

Hudson Mts.

Bakutis Coast

Edward VII
Land

Shackleton Inlet

Sabrina
Coast

Getz
Ice Shelf

Dart

3709

3496

Sulzberger
Ice Shelf

Ross Ice Shelf

80

Banzare
Coast

Hobbs Coast

Roosevelt
I.

Ross

Scott
(N.Z.)

Mt. Lister
4023

Victoria

Prince Albert Mts.

Porpoise Bay

Clarie
Coast

Bay of
Whales

C. Colbeck

Mt. Erebus
3743
Ross I.

McMurdo Sd.
McMurdo
(U.S.A.)

2216
2798

2436
4776

Ross

Sea

Franklin I.

Land

Dep.

Coulman I.

Mt. Murchison
3502

George V
Land

Terre
Adélie

Dumont d'Urville (Fr.)

Possession I.

C. Adare

4163

Oates Land

C. Freshfield

Commonwealth Bay

South Magnetic Pole
2000

Balleny Is.

Scott I.

Antarctic Circle

Pacific – Antarctic Ridge

Southeast Indian Rise

International Date Line

6240

Macquarie Is.
(Austr.)

Tasman
Plateau

Southwest
Pacific Basin

Campbell I.
(N.Z.)

Auckland Is.
(N.Z.)

Tasman

Sea

Tasmania

Hobart

MELBOURNE
AUSTRALIA

Antipodes Is.

Campbell
Plateau

Stewart I.

Bounty Is.
(N.Z.)

Dunedin

NEW ZEALAND

COPYRIGHT PHILIP'S

Projection: Zenithal Equidistant

Legend:

Ice cap

Permanent ice shelf

Maximum extent of sea ice

March (Summer) extent of sea ice

3488
3700 Surface elevation and depth of ice (in metres)

Stanley
(U.K.) Permanent bases

ft   m

12 000   4000

6000   2000

4500   1500

3000   1000

1200   400

600   200

0   0

500   1500

1000   3000

2000   6000

3000   9000

4000   12 000

5000   15 000

m   ft

The Antarctic Treaty was signed in Washington in 1959 so that scientific and technical research could continue unhampered by international politics.

All territorial claims covering land areas south of latitude 60°S have been suspended. Those claims were:

Norwegian claim (Dronning Maud Land)	45°E – 20°W
Australian claims	45°E – 136°E
	142°E – 160°E
French claim (Terre Adélie)	136°E – 142°E
New Zealand claim (Ross Dependency)	160°E – 150°W
British claim	80°W – 20°W
Argentine claim	74°W – 53°W
Chilean claim	90°W – 53°W

100 0 100 200 300 400 500 600 700 800 km
1:17 800 000
100 0 100 200 300 400 500 miles

COPYRIGHT PHILIP'S

Projection: Bonne

ROCKALL   Sea areas named in weather forecasts

Ob

U r a l   M o u n t a i n s

Ural

Caspian Depression

Volga

Caspian Sea

Kama

Obshchi Syrt

Pechora

Volga Hts.

Volga

N. Dvina

Oka

Don

Donets

Donets Basin

Central Russian Uplands

Sea of Azov

Str. of Kerch

Crimea

Black Sea

Caucasus

Elbrus 5642

Pontine Mts.

Armenia

Kurdistan

Mesopotamia

Tigris

Euphrates

L. Van

L. Urmia

Taurus Mts.

Anatolia (Asia Minor)

Cyprus

Rhodes

C. Matapan

Morea

Ionian Is.

Ionian Sea

Str. of Otranto

Pindus

Olympus 2917

Aegean Sea

Dardanelles

Mt. Ida 1766

Sea of Marmara

Bosporus

Rhodope

Balkans

Wallachia

Transylvanian Alps

Plain of Hungary

Tisza

Danube

Prut

Dniester

Carpathians

Tatra 2655

Sudeten

Moravian Hts.

Bohemian Forest

Erzgebirge

Odra

Harz

Kattegat

Skagerrak

Jutland

Weser

Elbe

GERMAN BIGHT

Helgoland

North Sea

Ems

Rhine

Vosges

Jura

Black Forest

Hunsrück

Mt. Ardenne

Massif Central

Puy de Sancy 1885

Rhône

Loire

Seine

Garonne

Dordogne

Gironde

Bay of Biscay

Brittany

Ushant

Channel Is.

English Channel

Plymouth

WIGHT

PORTLAND

Land's End

Thames

THAMES

HUMBER

Humber

TYNE

FORTH

CROMARTY

Ben Nevis 1343

Great Britain

British Isles

Snowdon 1085

Irish Sea

Ireland

HEBRIDES

Hebrides

Orkney Is.

Shetland Is.

FAIR ISLE

Faroe Is.

FAEROES

Iceland

Hekla 1491

Öræfajökull 2119

Arctic Circle

SOUTH EAST ICELAND

NORTH UTSIRE

SOUTH UTSIRE

Lindesnes

FISHER

VIKING

FORTIES

DOGGER

FORTH

TYNE

CROMARTY

BAILEY

ROCKALL

Rockall

FASTNET

SHANNON

SOLE

LUNDY

C. Clear

Celtic Sea

FITZROY

C. Finisterre

C. Ortegal

Bay of Biscay

BISCAY

Cantabrian Mts.

Old Castile

New Castile

Douro

Tagus

Ebro

Iberian Peninsula

Pyrenees

Pico de Aneto 3404

Balearic Is.

Minorca

Majorca

Ibiza

Andalusia

Sierra Morena

Sierra Nevada

Mulhacén 3478

Guadalquivir

Guadiana

Serra da Estrela

C. de São Vicente

C. de Roca

Str. of Gibraltar

Africa

Plateau of the Shotts

Mediterranean Sea

Malta

Pantelleria

C. Bon

Sicily

Etna 3340

Str. of Messina

Calabria

Tyrrhenian Sea

Sardinia

Corsica

Str. of Bonifacio

Ligurian Sea

Apennines

Gran Sasso d'Italia

Vesuvius 1277

Tiber

Po

Mont Blanc 4807

Alps

Dinaric Alps

Adriatic Sea

Save

Drava

Inn

Bakony Forest

Danube

Norwegian Sea

Vesterålen

Lofoten

Scandinavia

Kjølen

Galdhøpiggen 2469

Glittertind 2481

Kebnekaise 2117

Lapland

Kola Pen.

White Sea

Inari

Torne

Ume

Indals

Onega

L. Onega

L. Ladoga

Svir

Rybinsk Res.

L. Chudskoye

Finland

Gulf of Finland

Aland

Sea of Bothnia

Gulf of Bothnia

European Plain

North European Plain

Pripet

Bug

Niemen

W. Dvina

Dnieper

Ukraine

Tsimlyansk Res.

Manych

Terek

Kuma

Kuban

Gotland

Öland

Bornholm

Baltic Sea

Vänern

Vättern

Mälaren

Kanin Pen.

Mezen

North Cape

Nordkinn

Norwegian Sea

ATLANTIC OCEAN

West from Greenwich

East from Greenwich

ft m
5000 15 000
4000 12 000
6000
3000
1200 400
200 600
0

m ft
200 600
1000 3000
2000 6000
4000 12 000

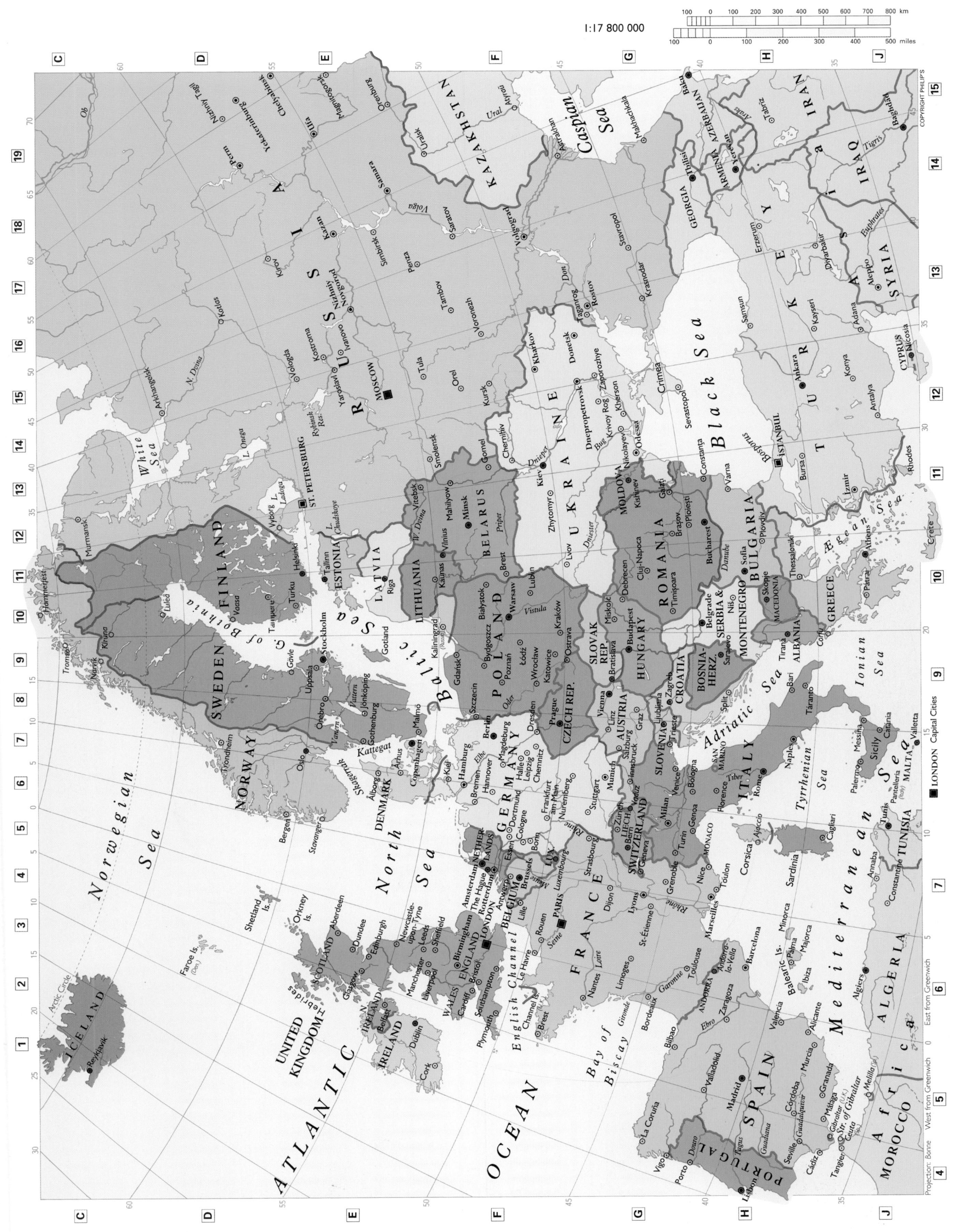

1:17 800 000

100 0 100 200 300 400 500 600 700 800 km
100 0 100 200 300 400 500 miles

ICELAND
Reykjavik

Arctic Circle

Norwegian Sea

ATLANTIC

OCEAN

Faroe Is. (Den.)

Shetland Is.

Orkney Is.

UNITED KINGDOM
SCOTLAND
Aberdeen
Dundee
Glasgow
Edinburgh
Newcastle-upon-Tyne
N. IRELAND
Belfast
IRELAND
Dublin
Cork
Hebrides
Leeds
Sheffield
Liverpool
Manchester
ENGLAND
WALES
Cardiff
Bristol
Birmingham
LONDON
Southampton
Plymouth
English Channel
Channel Is.
Brest

NORWAY
Tromsø
Narvik
Hammerfest
Trondheim
Bergen
Stavanger
Oslo

SWEDEN
Kiruna
Luleå
Umeå
Vaasa
Sundsvall
Uppsala
Stockholm
Örebro
Jönköping
Gothenburg
Malmö

FINLAND
Helsinki
Turku
Tampere

White Sea
Murmansk
Arkhangelsk
L. Onega
N. Dvina
L. Ladoga

Gulf of Bothnia

Baltic Sea
Gotland

ST. PETERSBURG
Vyborg
Tallinn
ESTONIA
LATVIA
Riga
LITHUANIA
Kaunas
Vilnius
Kaliningrad (Russia)

RUSSIA
MOSCOW
Pskov
Novgorod
Rybinsk Res.
Yaroslavl
Vologda
Kostroma
Ivanovo
Nizhniy Novgorod
Tula
Orel
Kursk
Voronezh
Tambov
Penza
Simbirsk
Kazan
Saratov
Samara
Ufa
Volga
Don
Kotlas

Ob
Nizhniy Tagil
Yekaterinburg
Chelyabinsk
Magnitogorsk
Kurgan
Ural

KAZAKHSTAN
Uralsk
Atyrau

Caspian Sea
Astrakhan
Makhachkala

GEORGIA
Tbilisi
ARMENIA
Yerevan
AZERBAIJAN
Baku
Aras

IRAN
Tabriz

IRAQ
Baghdad
Tigris
Euphrates

SYRIA
Aleppo

TURKEY
Ankara
Izmir
Konya
Adana
Kayseri
Samsun
Erzurum
Diyarbakir
Antalya

CYPRUS
Nicosia

Rhodes
Crete

Black Sea
Constanţa
Varna
Bosporus
ISTANBUL
Bursa

Aegean Sea

GREECE
Athens
Patra
Thessaloniki
Corfu

Ionian Sea

BELARUS
Minsk
Vitebsk
Mahilyow
Homel
W. Dvina
Pripet

UKRAINE
Kiev
Kharkov
Donetsk
Dnepropetrovsk
Zaporozhye
Krivoy Rog
Nikolayev
Odessa
Kherson
Lvov
Zhytomyr
Chernihiv
Dniester
Dnieper
Crimea
Sevastopol
Rostov
Taganrog
Krasnodar
Stavropol
Bug

MOLDOVA
Kishinev

ROMANIA
Bucharest
Cluj-Napoca
Timişoara
Braşov
Galaţi
Ploieşti
Danube

BULGARIA
Sofia
Plovdiv

SERBIA & MONTENEGRO
Belgrade
Niš

MACEDONIA
Skopje

ALBANIA
Tirana

BOSNIA-HERZ.
Sarajevo

CROATIA
Zagreb

SLOVENIA
Ljubljana
Trieste

HUNGARY
Budapest
Debrecen
Miskolc

SLOVAK REP.
Bratislava

CZECH REP.
Prague

AUSTRIA
Vienna
Linz
Salzburg
Innsbruck
Graz

POLAND
Warsaw
Łódź
Kraków
Wrocław
Poznań
Gdańsk
Szczecin
Bydgoszcz
Białystok
Lublin
Katowice
Ostrava
Brest
Vistula
Oder

GERMANY
Berlin
Hamburg
Munich
Cologne
Frankfurt am Main
Stuttgart
Dortmund
Essen
Düsseldorf
Bremen
Hannover
Magdeburg
Leipzig
Dresden
Nuremberg
Halle
Chemnitz
Bonn
Kiel
Elbe
Rhine

NETHERLANDS
Amsterdam
The Hague
Rotterdam

BELGIUM
Brussels
Antwerp

LUX.
Luxembourg

FRANCE
PARIS
Lyons
Marseilles
Lille
Strasbourg
Nantes
Bordeaux
Toulouse
Nice
Dijon
Rouen
Le Havre
St-Étienne
Limoges
Grenoble
Toulon
Rennes
Loire
Seine
Rhône
Garonne

SWITZERLAND
Bern
Zurich
Geneva
LIECH.

ITALY
Rome
Milan
Naples
Turin
Genoa
Venice
Bologna
Florence
Palermo
Catania
Messina
Bari
Taranto
Cagliari
Tiber

SAN MARINO
MONACO

Sardinia
Corsica (Fr.)
Sicily

Adriatic Sea
Tyrrhenian Sea
Ionian Sea
Mediterranean Sea

MALTA
Valletta
Pantelleria

SPAIN
Madrid
Barcelona
Valencia
Seville
Zaragoza
Málaga
Bilbao
Murcia
Córdoba
Granada
Valladolid
Alicante
La Coruña
Vigo
Ebro
Guadalquivir
Guadiana

Balearic Is.
Minorca
Majorca
Ibiza

ANDORRA
Andorra-la-Vella

PORTUGAL
Lisbon
Porto
Tagus
Douro

Gibraltar (U.K.)
Str. of Gibraltar
Ceuta (Sp.)
Melilla (Sp.)
Tangier

MOROCCO
ALGERIA
Algiers
Oran
Annaba
Constantine

TUNISIA
Tunis

Africa

Bay of Biscay

North Sea
Skagerrak
Kattegat

DENMARK
Copenhagen
Ålborg
Århus
Odense

Black Sea

East from Greenwich
West from Greenwich

Projection: Bonne

COPYRIGHT PHILIP'S

■ LONDON Capital Cities

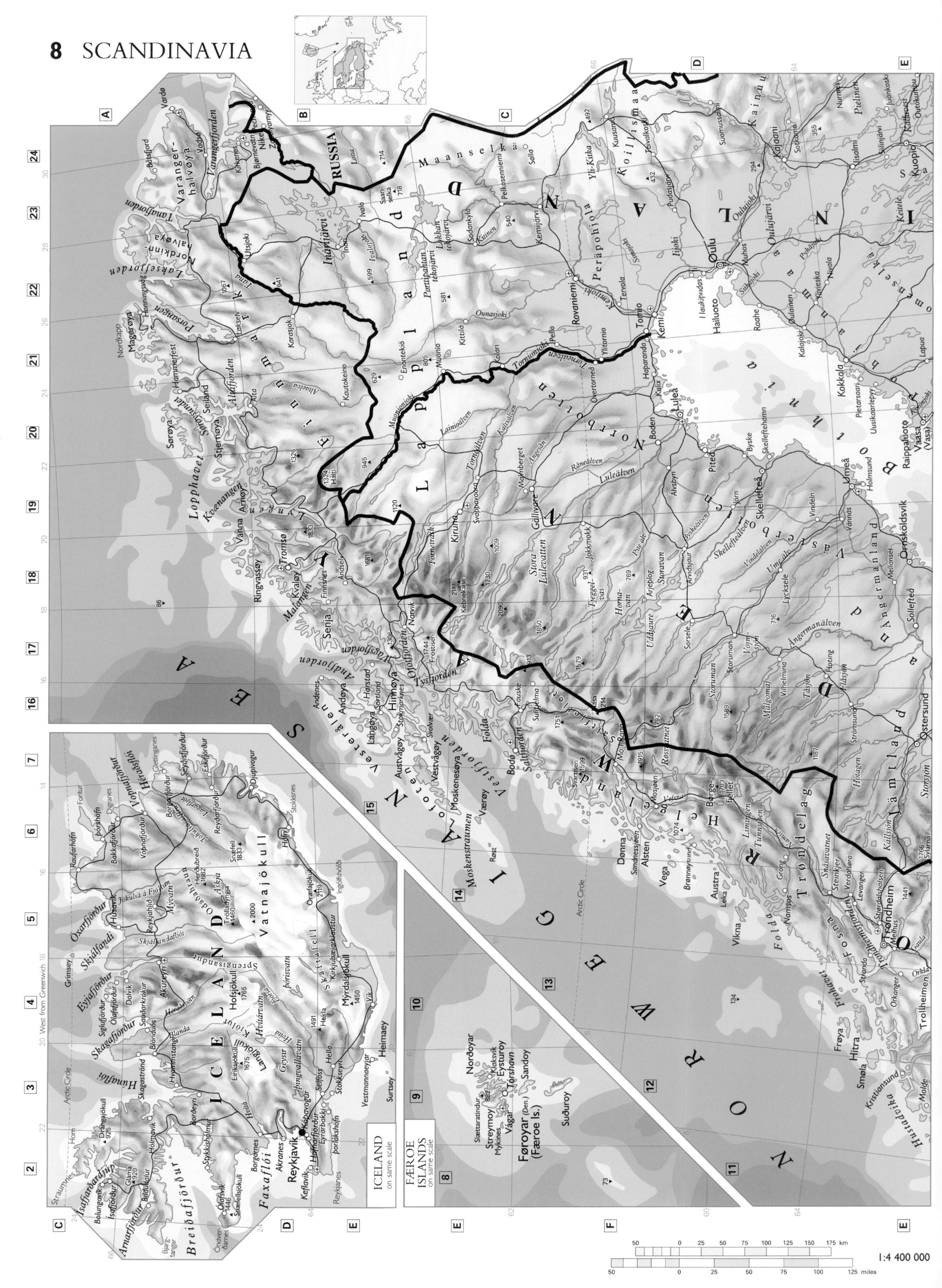

ICELAND on same scale

FEROE ISLANDS on same scale

1:4 400 000

East from Greenwich

Projection: Conical with two standard parallels

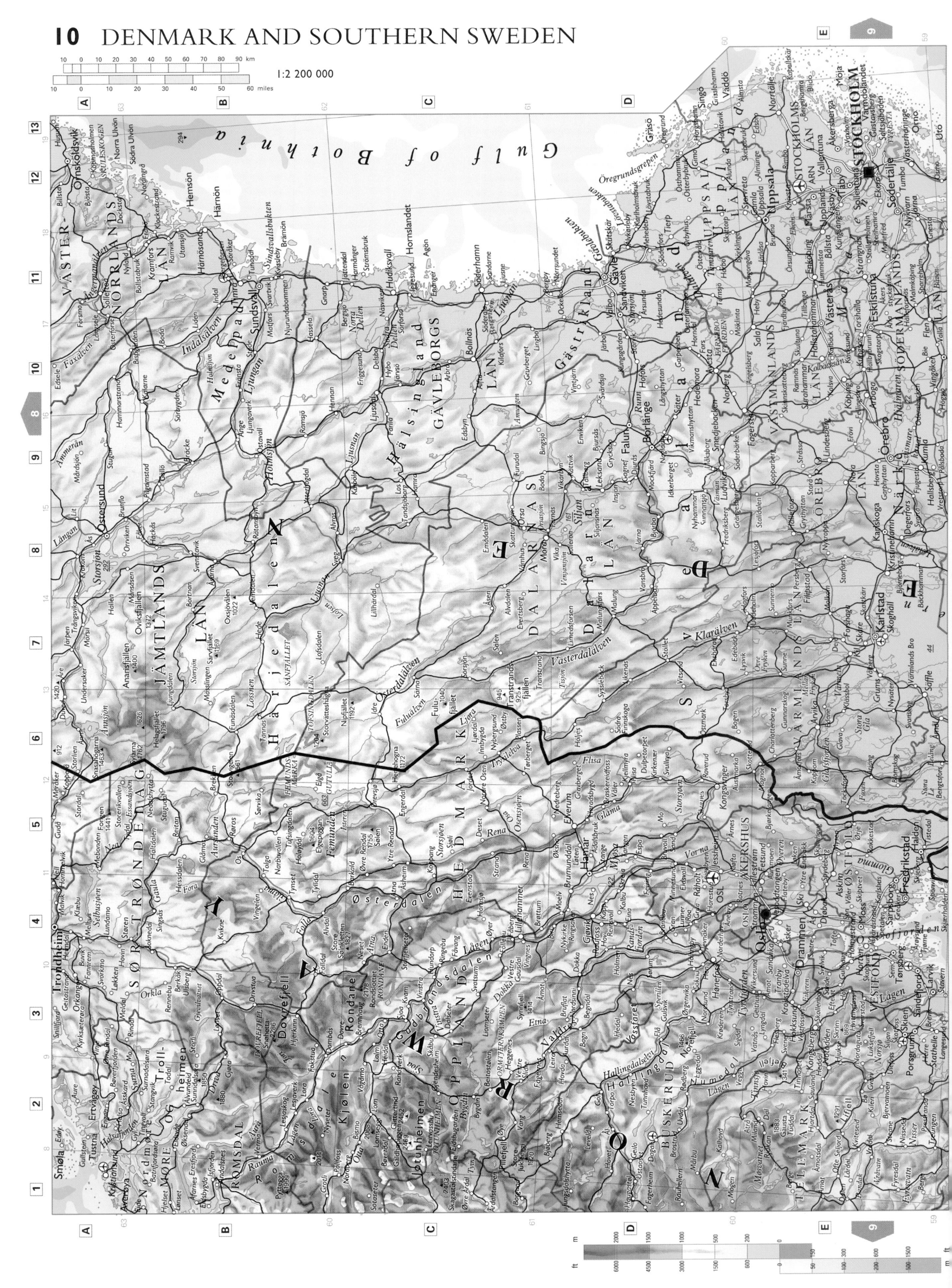

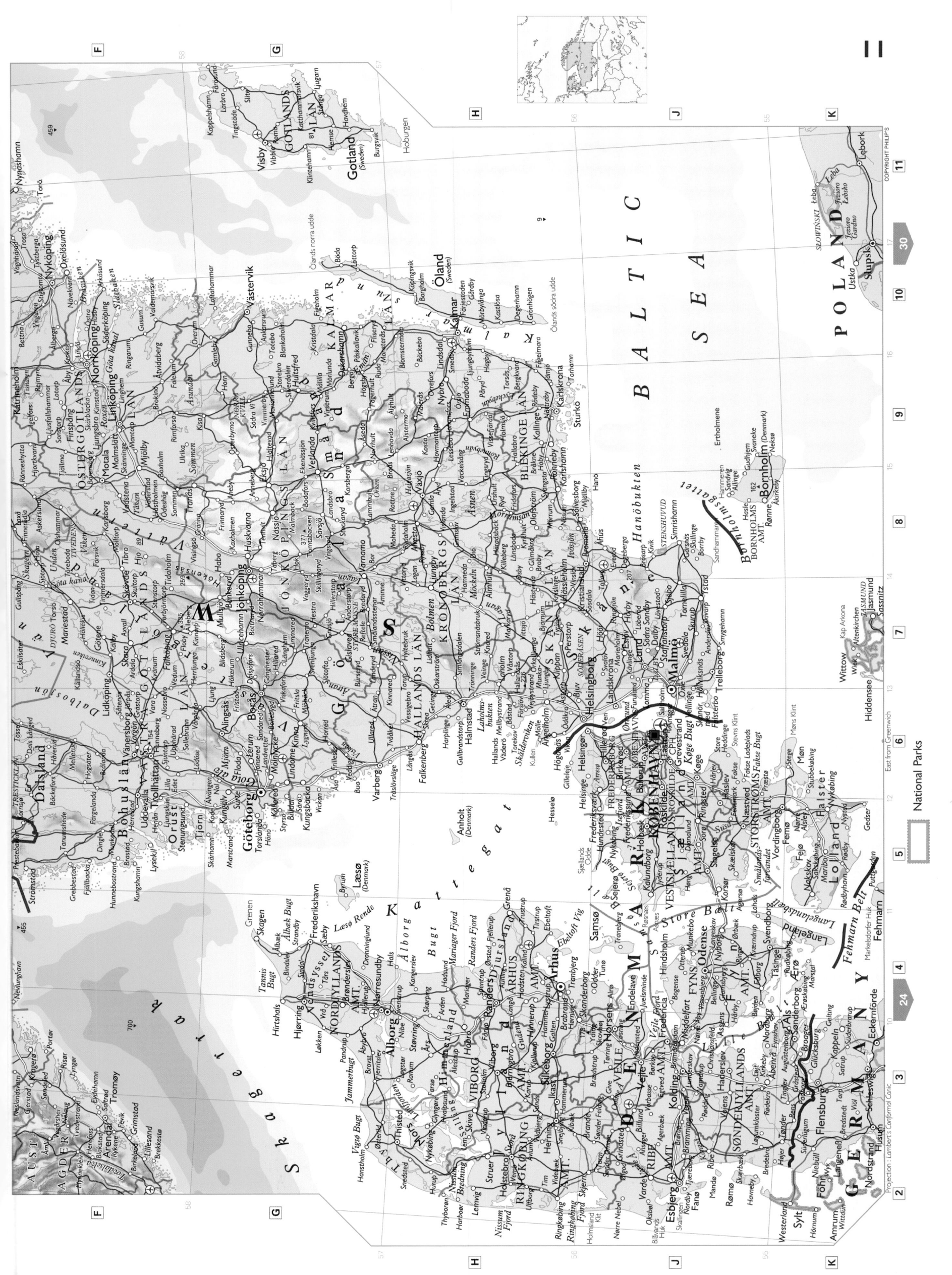

1:1 800 000

10 0 10 20 30 40 50 60 70 80 km
10 0 10 20 30 40 50 miles

13

SCOTLAND
Kintyre
Mull of Oa
Mull of Kintyre
Campbeltown
Brodick
Arran
Firth of Clyde
Ailsa Craig

A T L A N T I C   O C E A N

Inishtrahull
Malin Hd.
Lough Swilly
Fanad Hd.
Malin Pen.
Carndonagh
Moville
Inishowen Pen.
Buncrana
Portstewart Portrush
Giants Causeway
Ballycastle
Rath in I.
Cairnryan
Stranraer
Portpatrick

Sleep Haven
Mulroy B.
Horn Hd.
Tory I.
Bloody Foreland

Inishfree B.
Gweedore
Errigal 752
Rathmelton
L. Foyle
Coleraine
Limavady
Ballymoney
Garron Pt.
554
Trostan
L. Ryan

Aran I.
The Rosses
Crohy Hd.
Derryveagh Mts.
GLENVEAGH
683
Letterkenny
Lifford
Strabane
Londonderry
LONDONDERRY
Roe
Mts. of Antrim
GLENARIFF
269
Larne

DONEGAL
Glenties
Finn
Sion Mills
Newtownstewart
Sawel Mt. 683
Spean Mts.
Moneymore
Magherafelt
Randalstown
Ballyclare
Ballymena
Antrim
Carrickfergus
Donoghadee
Bangor
Newtownards

Gweebarra B.
Dawros Hd.
Lavagh More 676
Castlederg
Omagh
Cookstown
Coalisland
Lough Neagh
Belfast L.
Belfast
Lisburn
Comber
Newtownabbey

Rossan Pt.
601
Killybegs
Slieve League
Donegal
Ballyshannon
Bundoran
Derg
TYRONE
U l s t e r
Dromore
Dungannon
Craigavon
Lurgan
Portadown
Armagh
Lagan
Banbridge
Dromore
DOWN
Downpatrick
Ballyquintin Pt.
Ards Pen.
Strangford L.

St. John's Pt.
Donegal Bay
Lower L. Erne
Enniskillen
FERMANAGH
Upper L. Erne
Irvinestown
Clones
MONAGHAN
Castleblaney
Monaghan
Middletown
Keady
Newry
577 Slieve Gullion
Mourne Mts.
852 Slieve Donard
Warrenpoint
Greenore
Kilkeel
Newcastle
St. John's Pt.
Dundrum B.

Downpatrick Hd.
Killala B.
Sligo Bay
Sligo
Dromore West
544
Collooney
NORTHERN IRELAND
Belturbet
Annalee
Cootehill
Carrickmacross
Dundalk
Carlingford L.
Dundalk Bay
Clogher Hd.

Broad Haven
Erris Hd.
Mullet Pen.
Belmullet
Inishkea North
Inishkea South
Blacksod Bay
Ballina
Killala
Sligo
Ballymote
S L I G O
L. Arrow
LEITRIM
Leitrim
L. Allen
CAVAN
L. Gowna
L. Sheelin
Cavan
Kingscourt
Oldcastle
Ceanannus Mor (Kells)
Blackwater
LOUTH
Ardee
Dunleer
Drogheda

Achill Hd.
672
Achill I.
Corraun Pen.
Clare I.
Newport
Castlebar
Knock
M A Y O
Swinford
Charlestown
Ballaghaderreen
Boyle
Carrick-on-Shannon
Granard
LONGFORD
Longford
Castlepollard
MEATH
An Uaimh (Navan)
Boyne
Balbriggan

Clew Bay
Westport
Nephin 806
L. Conn
Moy
Slieve Gamph
544
ROSCOMMON
Castlerea
Roscommon
Athboy
Trim
Rush
Lambay I.
Malahide
Howth Hd.

Inishturk
Croagh Patrick 765
819
Ballinrobe
Claremorris
Ballyhaunis
Glennamaddy
I R E L A N D
Mullingar
WESTMEATH
Royal Canal
Swords
DUBLIN
Dublin
Dun Laoghaire

Inishbofin
Inishshark
Killary Harbour
Mweelrea 819
Lough Mask
Tuam
L e i n s t e r
Moate
Brosna
Edenderry
Maynooth
Clondalkin
Bray
Greystones
123

Connemara
CONNEMARA
C o n n a c h t
Lough Corrib
Oughterard
Loughrea
Athlone
Ballinasloe
Clara
Tullamore
Grand Canal
Bog of Allen
Naas
Droichead Nua
KILDARE
Kippure 754
WICKLOW MTS.
Wicklow

Clifden
Slyne Hd.
Galway
GALWAY
Galway Bay
Athenry
OFFALY
Portarlington
Kildare
Monasterevin
Athy
Poulaphouca Res.
WICKLOW
Lugnaquilla 926
Rathdrum
Wicklow Hd.

Aran Is.
Inishmore
Inishmaan
Inisheer
Black Hd.
Galway Bay
Gort
Slieve Aughty
368
Portumna
Shannon
Birr
Mountmellick
Port Laoise
Athy
Carlow
Tullow
Shillelagh
Gorey
Arklow
Mizen Hd.

Cliffs of Moher
Hags Hd.
Liscannor Bay
BURREN
Ennistimon
Tulla
Lough Derg
Nenagh
Roscrea
Slieve Bloom
Slievenaman 529
Arderin
Mountrath
Durrow
LAOIS
Carlow
CARLOW
Muine Bheag
Mt. Leinster 796
Bunclody
Enniscorthy

Mal Bay
Mutton I.
C L A R E
Ennis
Sixmilebridge
Killaloe
Templemore
Thurles
Kilkenny
KILKENNY
Callan
Nore
WEXFORD

Loop Hd.
Kilkee
Kilrush
Mouth of the Shannon
Foynes
Shannon Airport
Limerick
Keeper Hill 694
TIPPERARY
Golden Vale
Tipperary
Cashel
Carrick-on-Suir
Clonmel
New Ross
Wexford Harbour
Rosslare
Rosslare Harbour
Greenore Pt.

Kerry Hd.
Ballybunion
LIMERICK
Newcastle West
Kilmallock
M u n s t e r
Galtymore 920
Galty Mts.
Caher
Comeragh Mts. 792
Carsore Pt.

Brandon B.
Smerwick Harbour
Brandon Mt. 953
Dingle
Slieve Mish 853
Tralee B.
Tralee
Newmarket
Rath Luirc
Mitchelstown
Fermoy
Knockmealdown Mts.
Lismore
Dungarvan
Tramore
Dungarvan Harbour
Tramore B.
Waterford Harbour
Hook Hd.
Saltee Is.

Great Blasket I.
Dunmore Hd.
Dingle
Dingle Bay
Inishvickillane
KERRY
Maine
Castleisland
Kanturk
Buttevant
Mallow
Blackwater
WATERFORD
Waterford
Youghal
Midleton
Cobh
Youghal B.
St. David's Hd.
St. David's
St. Brides Bay

Valencia I.
Cahersiveen
Puffin I.
Great Skellig
Killorglin
Killarney
L. Leane
Carrauntoohill 1041
Macgillycuddy's Reeks
Boggeragh Mts. 646
CORK
Blarney
Cork
Passage West
Cork Harbour
Old Head of Kinsale
115

Ballinskelligs B.
Scariff I.
Kenmare
Caha Mts. 666
Glengarriff
707
Lee
Macroom
Bandon
Kinsale
WALES

Dursey I.
Crow Hd.
Bear I.
Bearhaven
Castletown
Bantry Bay
Bantry
Dunmanway
Clonakilty
Clonakilty B.

Dunmanus B.
Skull
Long I.
Mizen Hd.
Baltimore
Sherkin I.
Clear I.
Skibbereen
Galley Hd.
C. Clear
Fastnet Rock

C E L T I C   S E A

St. George's Channel
I R I S H   S E A
North Channel

West from Greenwich

Projection: Lambert's Conformal Conic

COPYRIGHT PHILIP'S

□ National Parks

ft m
1500 500
600 200
300 100
0 0
50 150
100 300
200 600
500 1500
1000 3000
2000 6000
m ft

1:1 800 000

10   0   10   20   30   40   50   60   70   80 km
10   0   10   20   30   40   50 miles

ORKNEY IS. on same scale

SHETLAND IS. on same scale

Key to Scottish unitary authorities on map

1 CITY OF ABERDEEN	8 EAST RENFREWSHIRE
2 DUNDEE CITY	9 NORTH LANARKSHIRE
3 WEST DUNBARTONSHIRE	10 FALKIRK
4 EAST DUNBARTONSHIRE	11 CLACKMANNANSHIRE
5 CITY OF GLASGOW	12 WEST LOTHIAN
6 INVERCLYDE	13 CITY OF EDINBURGH
7 RENFREWSHIRE	14 MIDLOTHIAN

Projection: Lambert's Conformal Conic

West from Greenwich

COPYRIGHT PHILIP'S

Forest Parks in Scotland

1:1 800 000

Key to English unitary authorities on map

25 HARTLEPOOL
26 DARLINGTON
27 STOCKTON-ON-TEES
28 MIDDLESBROUGH
29 REDCAR AND CLEVELAND
30 BLACKPOOL
31 BLACKBURN WITH DARWEN
32 HALTON
33 WARRINGTON
34 KINGSTON UPON HULL
35 NORTH EAST LINCOLNSHIRE
36 NORTH LINCOLNSHIRE
37 TELFORD AND WREKIN
38 STOKE-ON-TRENT
39 DERBY CITY
40 CITY OF NOTTINGHAM
41 LEICESTER CITY
42 RUTLAND
43 PETERBOROUGH
44 MILTON KEYNES
45 LUTON
46 NORTH SOMERSET
47 CITY OF BRISTOL
48 BATH AND NORTH EAST SOMERSET
49 SWINDON
50 READING
51 WOKINGHAM
52 WINDSOR AND MAIDENHEAD
53 SLOUGH
54 BRACKNELL FOREST
55 THURROCK
56 SOUTHEND-ON-SEA
57 MEDWAY
58 PLYMOUTH
59 TORBAY
60 POOLE
61 BOURNEMOUTH
62 SOUTHAMPTON
63 PORTSMOUTH
64 BRIGHTON AND HOVE

Key to Welsh unitary authorities on map

15 SWANSEA
16 NEATH PORT TALBOT
17 BRIDGEND
18 RHONDDA CYNON TAFF
19 MERTHYR TYDFIL
20 CAERPHILLY
21 BLAENAU GWENT
22 TORFAEN
23 CARDIFF
24 NEWPORT

NORTH SEA

IRISH SEA

North Channel

NORTHERN IRELAND

SCOTLAND

ENGLAND

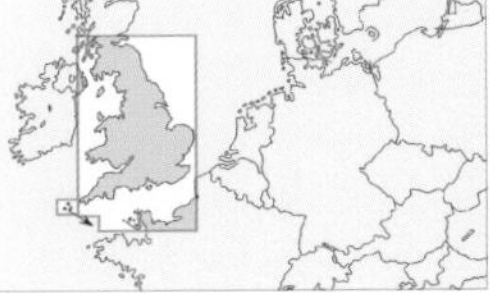

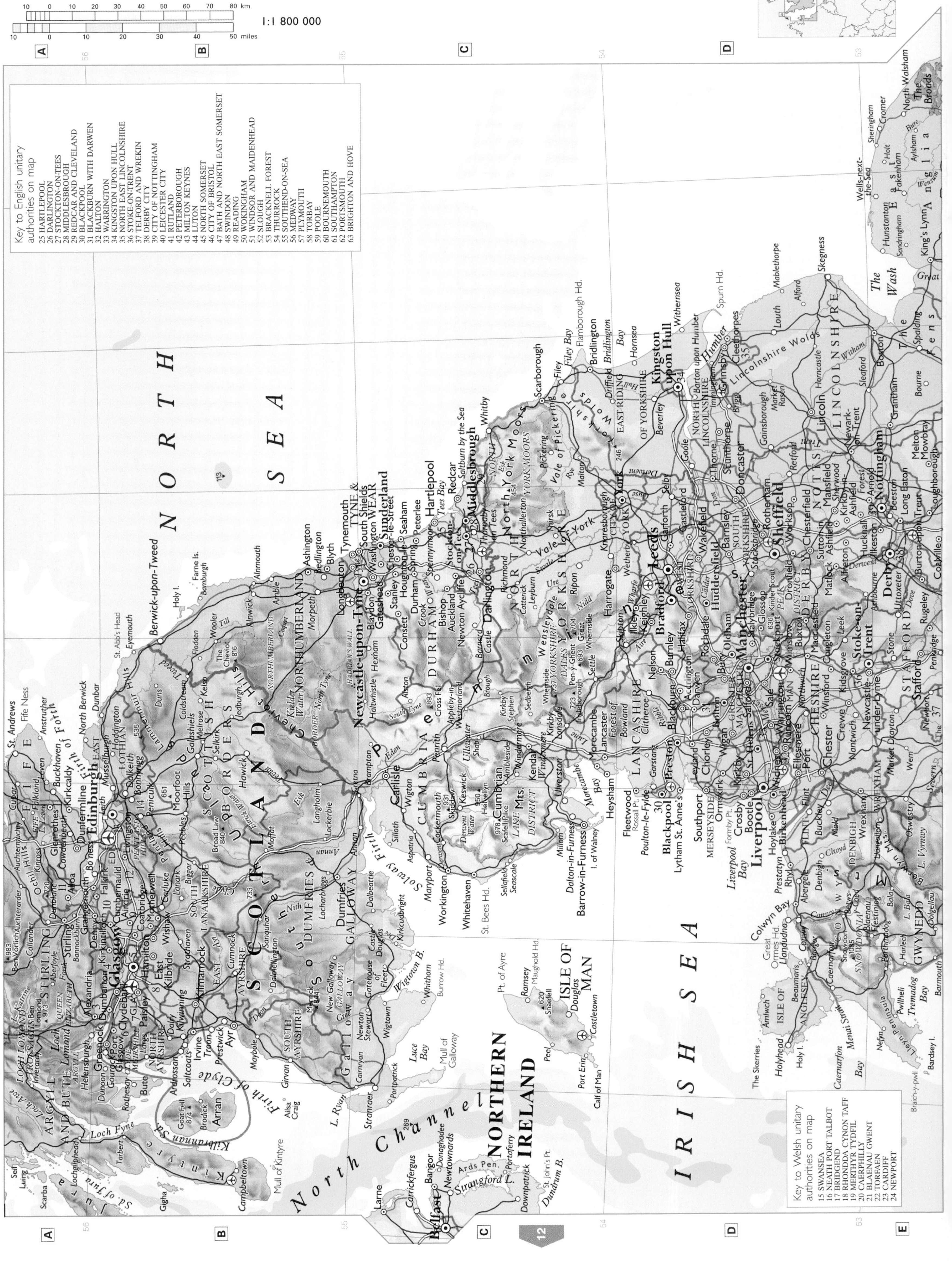

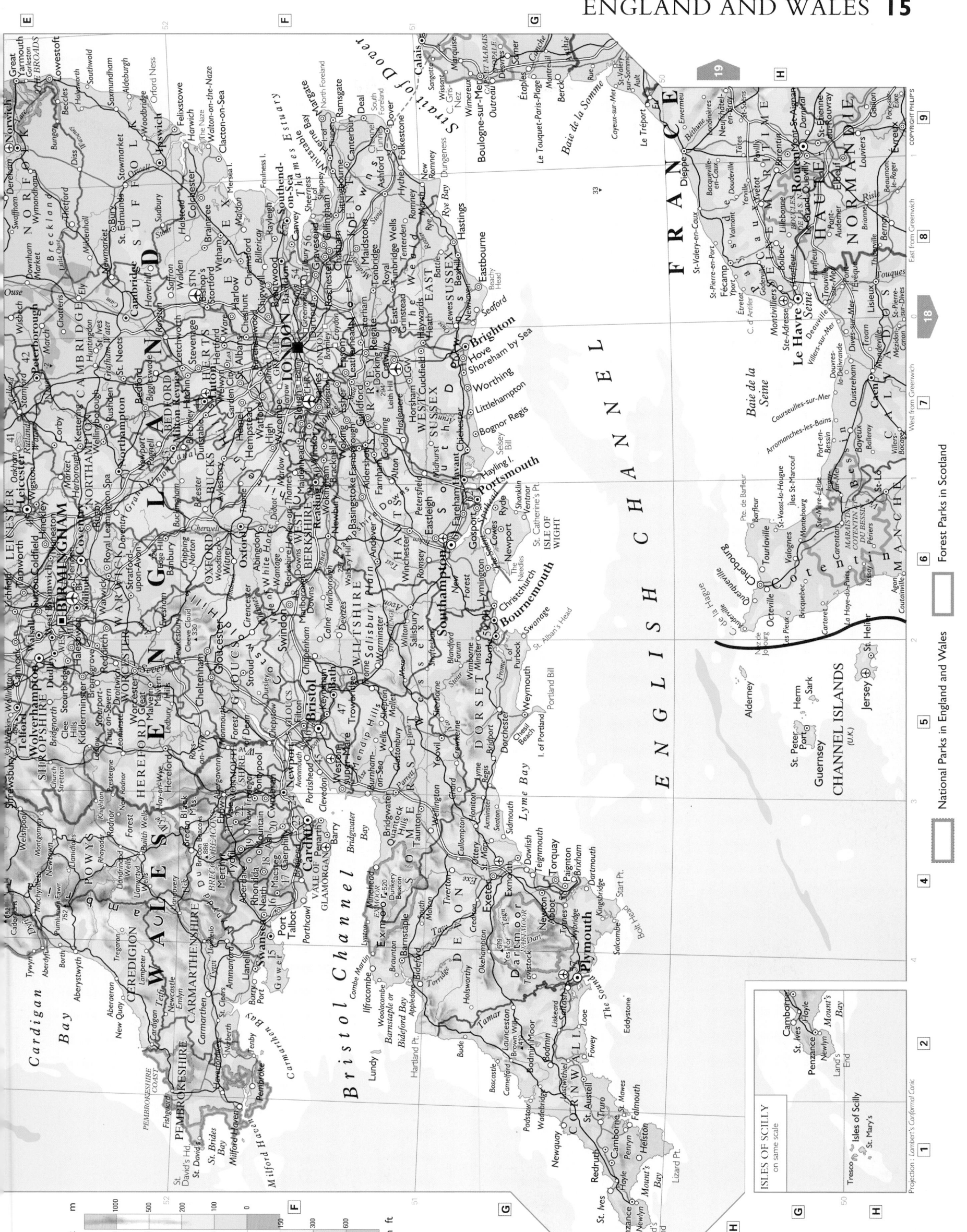

National Parks in England and Wales

Forest Parks in Scotland

ISLES OF SCILLY
on same scale

Projection: Lambert's Conformal Conic

COPYRIGHT PHILIP'S

50 0 25 50 75 100 125 150 175 km

50 0 25 50 75 100 125 miles

1:4 400 000

Projection: Conical with two standard parallels

COPYRIGHT PHILIP'S

ATLANTIC OCEAN

NORWAY
Bergen
Askøy
Osøyro
Stord
Leirvik
Bømlo
Haugesund
Kopervik
Åkrahamn
Stavanger
Sandnes
Bryne
Nærbø

NORTH SEA

Shetland Is.
Yell
Unst
Fetlar
Foula
Mainland
Lerwick
Fair Isle

Orkney Is.
Westray
Sanday
Mainland
Stronsay
Hoy
Kirkwall
South Ronaldsay

1224

316

C. Wrath
Pentland Firth
Thurso
Wick
Helmsdale

Lewis
Stornoway
North Minch
Outer Hebrides
Harris
St. Kilda
789
North Uist
Benbecula
South Uist
Barra

Ullapool
Lairg
Golspie
Tain
Invergordon
Dingwall
Nairn
Inverness
L. Ness
Aviemore
Elgin
Buckie
Banff
Fraserburgh
Huntly
Peterhead
Inverurie
Don
Aberdeen
Dee
Ballater
Stonehaven

Moray Firth

North West Highlands
Skye
Rhum
Eigg
Coll
Mallaig
Fort William
Ben Nevis
1342
Glen More
1182

SCOTLAND
Grampian Mts.
1311
1242

Inner Hebrides
Sea of the Hebrides
Tiree
Mull
Tobermory
Oban
1214
L. Awe
L. Fyne
Colonsay
Jura
Islay
Campbeltown

Tay
Perth
Forfar
Arbroath
Montrose
Dundee
St. Andrews
Glenrothes
Kirkcaldy
Stirling
L. Lomond
Dunfermline
973
Dunbar
Greenock
Dumbarton
Paisley
Glasgow
Edinburgh
East Kilbride
Motherwell
Hamilton
Berwick-upon-Tweed
Irvine
Kilmarnock
Southern Uplands
Galashiels
Arran
Ayr
Jedburgh
816
Hawick
Cheviot Hills
840
Girvan
Dumfries
Annan
Alnwick

238

NORTH SEA

16

Malin Hd.
Buncrana
Coleraine
Letterkenny
Londonderry
Ballymena
Larne
Donegal
Lifford
Omagh
NORTHERN IRELAND
Antrim
Bangor
Bundoran
Lough Erne
Enniskillen
Lower L. Erne
Portadown
Lisburn
Belfast
Lurgan
Sligo
Leitrim
Cavan
Armagh
Newry
Clones
Castleblayney
Ballina
Achill I.
L. Conn
Castlebar
Roscommon
Longford
Ceanannus Mor
Drogheda
Dundalk

North Channel
Stranraer
Kirkcudbright
Mull of Galloway
Whitehaven
Workington
Carlisle
Hexham
893
Darlington

Newcastle-upon-Tyne
South Shields
Sunderland
Gateshead
Durham
Hartlepool
Redcar
Middlesbrough
Stockton-on-Tees
Scarborough

Cumbrian Mts.
978
Barrow-in-Furness
Douglas
I. of Man
Lancaster
Harrogate
York
Bridlington
Beverley
Kingston upon Hull

UNITED KINGDOM

IRISH SEA

Lough Mask
Connemara
Galway B.
Galway
Aran Is.
Lough Corrib
Ballinasloe
Athlone
Tullamore
Mullingar
Lough Ree
Lough Derg
Ennis
Westport
Birr

Dublin
Dun Laoghaire
Bray
Holyhead
Anglesey
Bangor
Liverpool
Warrington
Stockport
Manchester
636
Oldham
Sheffield
Blackpool
Preston
Blackburn
Bolton
Burnley
Halifax
Huddersfield
Barnsley
Leeds
Bradford
Doncaster
Rotherham
Grimsby
Scunthorpe
Lincoln
Louth
Skegness
Boston
Cromer

Limerick
Nenagh
Thurles
Tipperary
Portlaoise
Athy
Carlow
Kilkenny
Listowel
953
Tralee
Dingle
Carrauntoohill
1041
Killarney
Macgillycuddy's Reeks
Mallow
Blackwater
Valencia I.
99
Kilrush
Shannon
Bandon
Cóbh
Kinsale
Bantry
C. Clear
Cork
Youghal
Dungarvan
Clonmel
Carrick-on-Suir
Waterford
Wexford
Rosslare
Wicklow Mts.
926
Arklow

Fishguard
St. George's Channel
Cardigan Bay
Aberystwyth
Snowdon
1085
Pwllheli
Colwyn Bay
Chester
Crewe
Wrexham
Cambrian Mts.
Welshpool
Shrewsbury
Stoke-on-Trent
Stafford
Telford
Derby
Nottingham
Mansfield
Chesterfield

ENGLAND

King's Lynn
The Wash
Great Yarmouth
Norwich
Lowestoft
Thetford
Peterborough
Leicester
Corby
Rugby
Coventry
Nuneaton
Northampton
Bedford
Cambridge
Bury St. Edmunds
Ipswich
Harwich
Felixstowe
Colchester

WALES
Carmarthen
886
Brecon
Merthyr Tydfil
Llanelli
Neath
Rhondda
Cwmbran
Swansea
Port Talbot
Newport
Barry
Cardiff

Hereford
Worcester
Redditch
BIRMINGHAM
Wolverhampton
Royal Leamington Spa
Gloucester
Cheltenham
Cotswold Hills
Oxford
High Wycombe
Hemel Hempstead
Luton
Milton Keynes
Stevenage
Harlow
Chelmsford
Southend-on-Sea
36

Bristol Channel
Barnstaple
Bude
Exmoor
618
Dartmoor
Weston-super-Mare
Bath
Bristol
Newbury
Swindon
Reading
Slough
LONDON
Thames
Basildon
Maidstone
Chatham
Canterbury
Margate

IRELAND

Bantry
Taunton
Yeovil
Salisbury
Basingstoke
Guildford
Reigate
Crawley
As hford
Folkestone
Str. of Dover

CELTIC SEA

Newquay
Truro
St. Austell
Falmouth
Penzance
Land's End
Isles of Scilly
Plymouth
Torbay
Exmouth
Torquay
Weymouth
Poole
Bournemouth
Southampton
Portsmouth
Fareham
Havant
Isle of Wight
Newport
Worthing
Brighton
Eastbourne
Hastings

English Channel

Alderney
C. de la Hague
Pte. de Barfleur
Guernsey
St. Peter Port
Sark
Channel Is.
(U.K.)
St. Helier
Jersey
33

NETHERLANDS
Texel
Den Helder
Alkmaar
Haarlem
's-Gravenhage
(Den Haag)
ROTTERDAM
Dordrecht
Hoek van Holland
Vlissingen
Zeebrugge
Oostende
Brugge
Gent
Antwerpen
Mechelen
BELGIUM
Brussel
Bruxelles
Tournai

FRANCE
Calais
Gris Nez
Boulogne-sur-Mer
Le Touquet-Paris-Plage
St-Omer
Béthune
Lens
Bruay-la-Buissière
Arras
Lille
Roubaix
Valenciennes
Cambrai
Dunkerque
Picardie
Fécamp
Pays de Caux
Le Havre
Rouen
Le Tréport
Dieppe
Abbeville
Amiens
St. Quentin
Laon
Cherbourg
Valognes
Trouville-sur-Mer
Bayeux
Cotentin
Caen
Lisieux
Elbeuf
Seine

East from Greenwich

West from Greenwich

1
2
3
4
5
6
7
8
9
17
18
19

1:2 200 000

NORTH SEA

UNITED KINGDOM

NETHERLANDS

BELGIUM

LUXEMBOURG

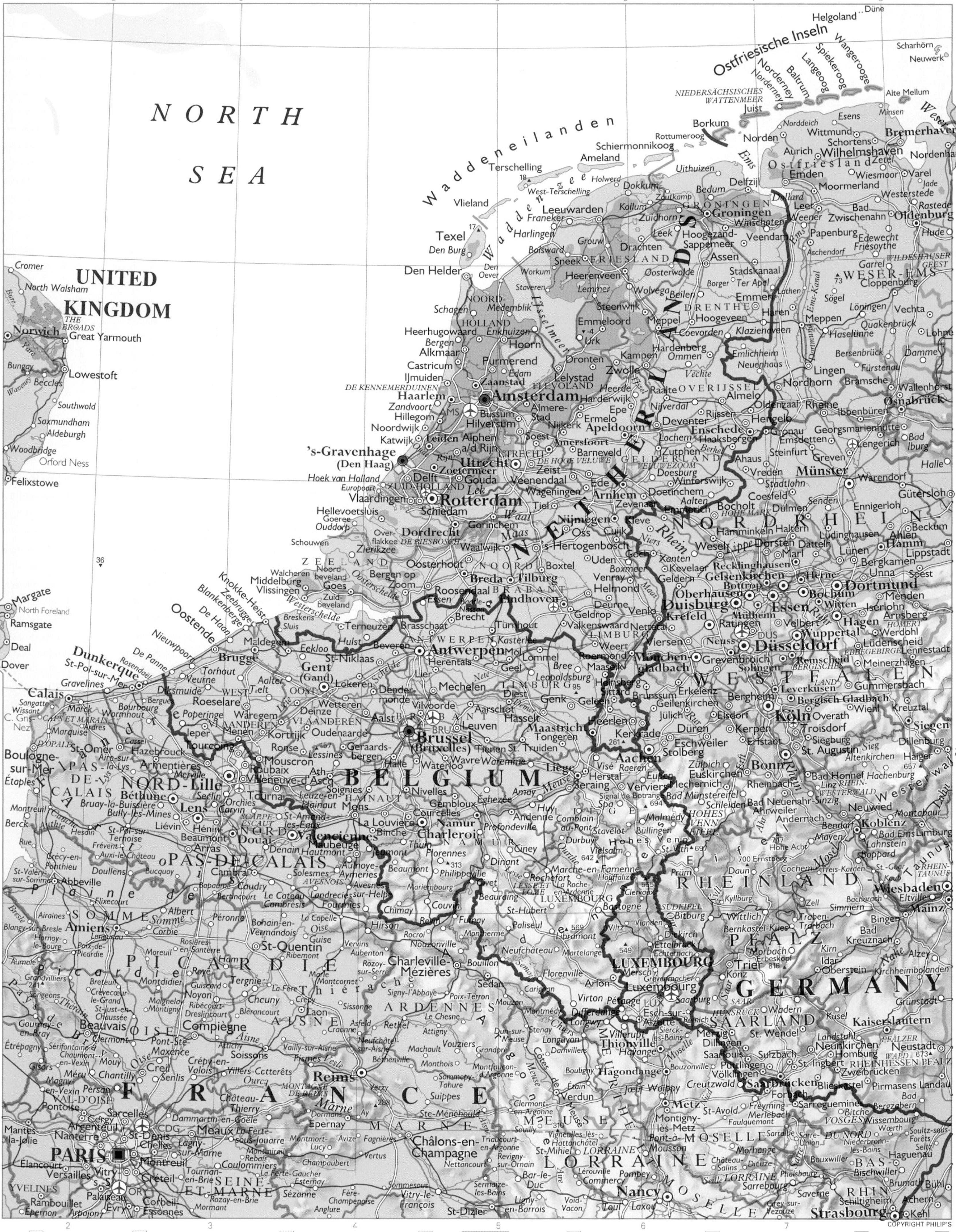

FRANCE

GERMANY

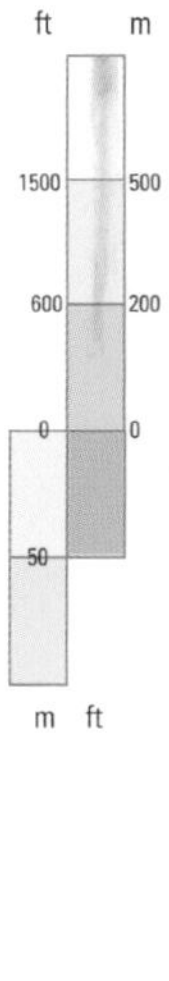

National Parks

Underlined towns give their name to the administrative area in which they stand.

COPYRIGHT PHILIP'S

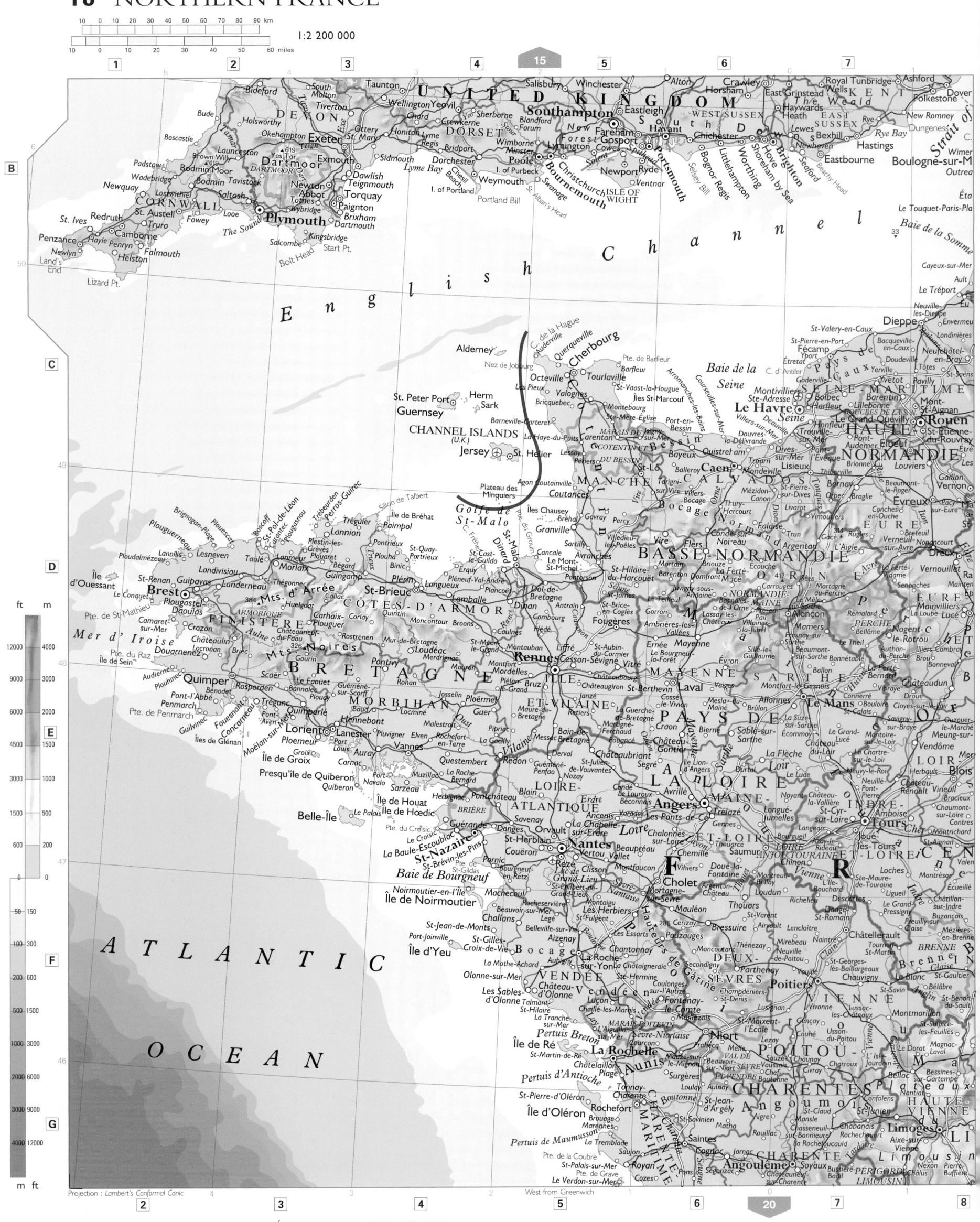

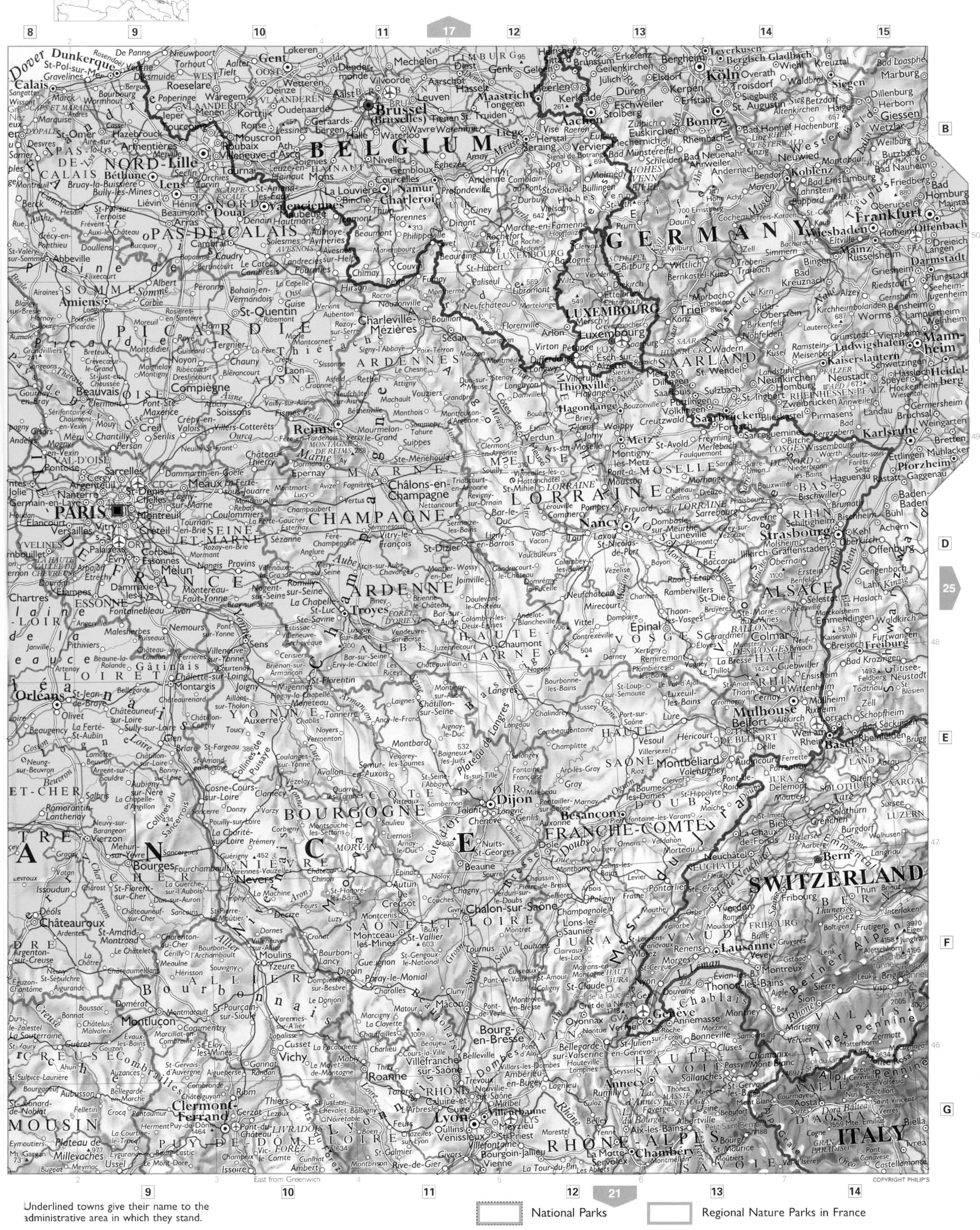

Underlined towns give their name to the
administrative area in which they stand.

National Parks   Regional Nature Parks in France

COPYRIGHT PHILIP'S

1:2 200 000

Projection : Lambert's Conformal Conic

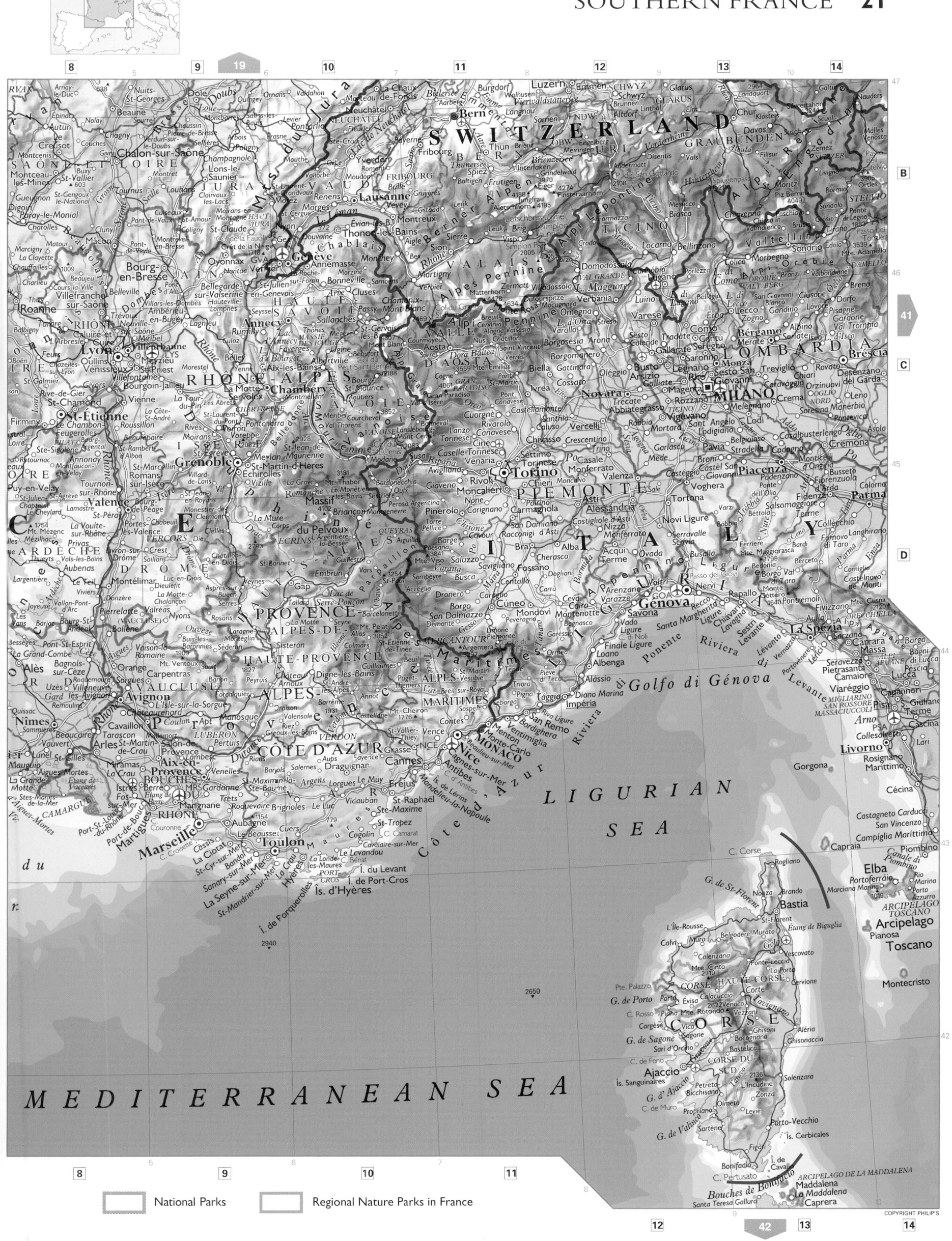

National Parks   Regional Nature Parks in France

1:4 400 000

Projection: Conical with two standard parallels

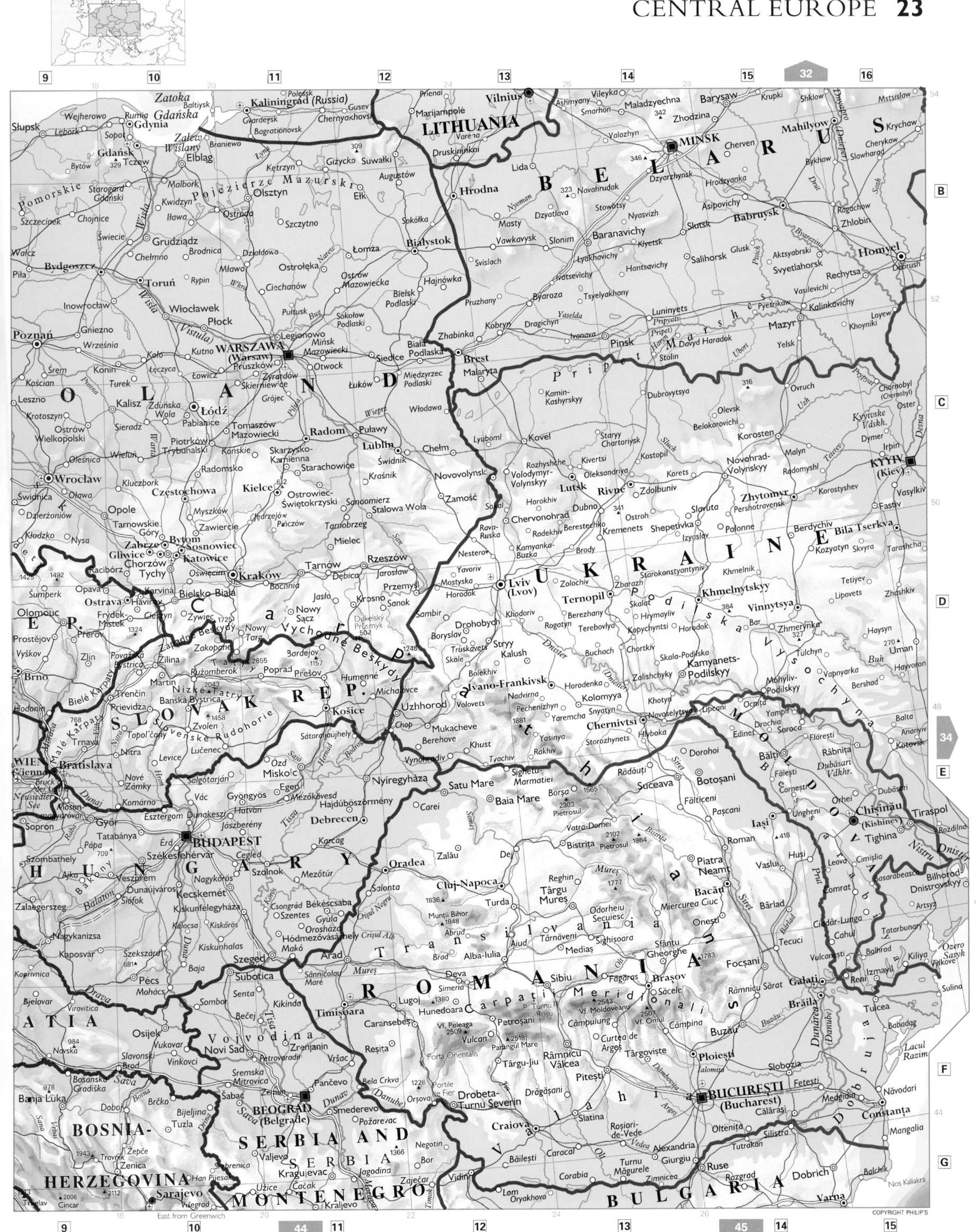

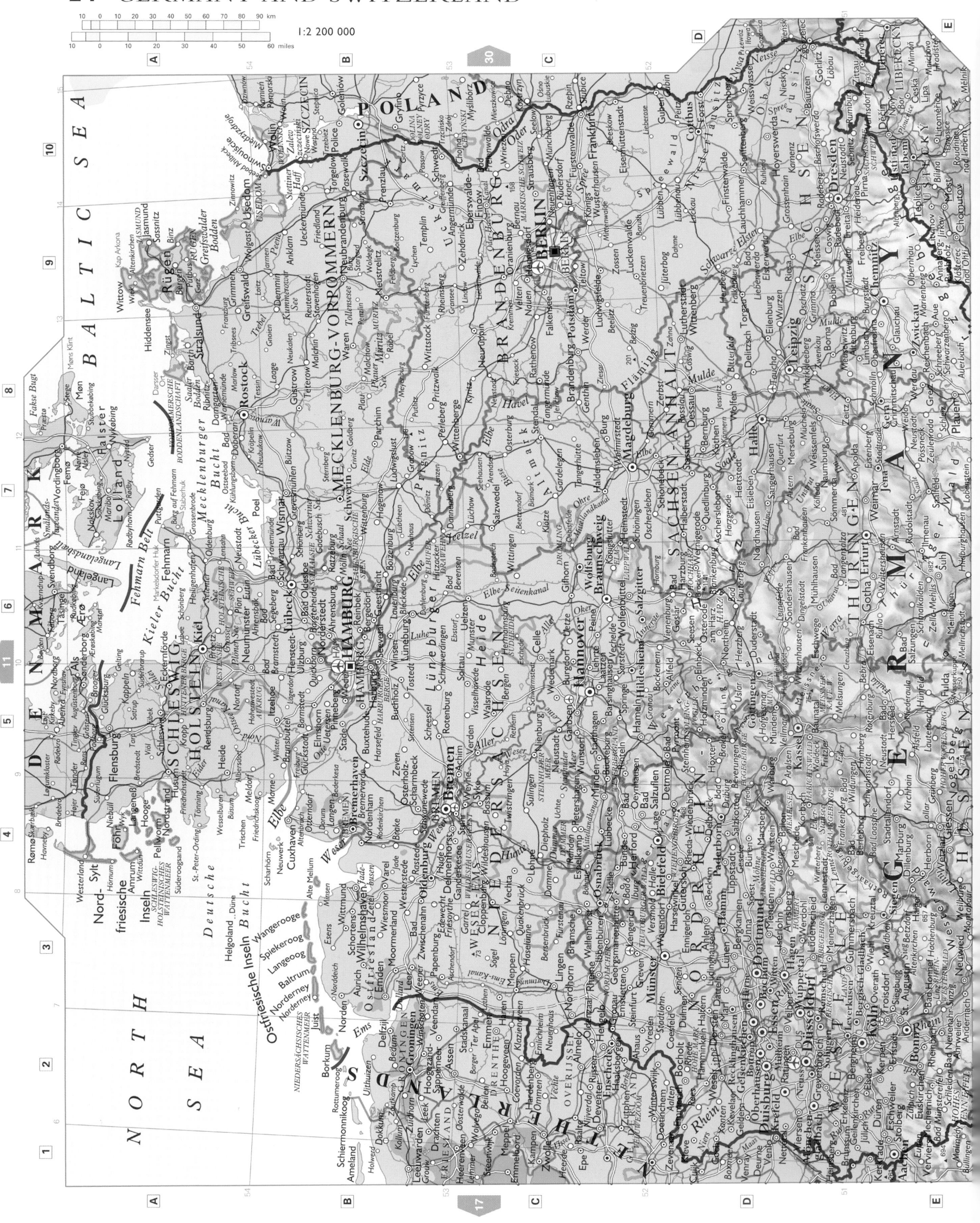

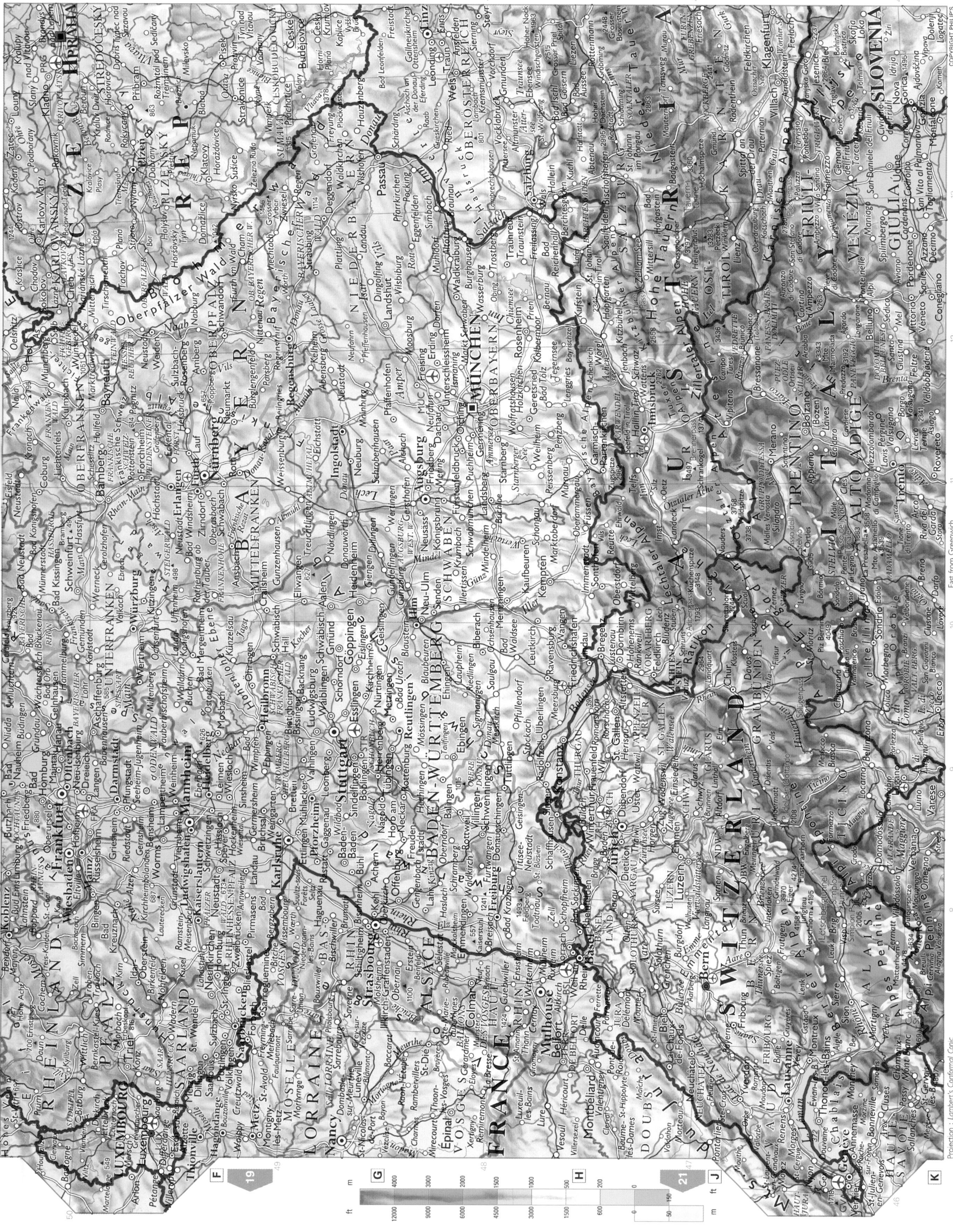

Nature Parks in Germany

National Parks

Underlined towns give their name to the administrative area in which they stand.

Projection : Lambert's Conformal Conic

COPYRIGHT PHILIP'S

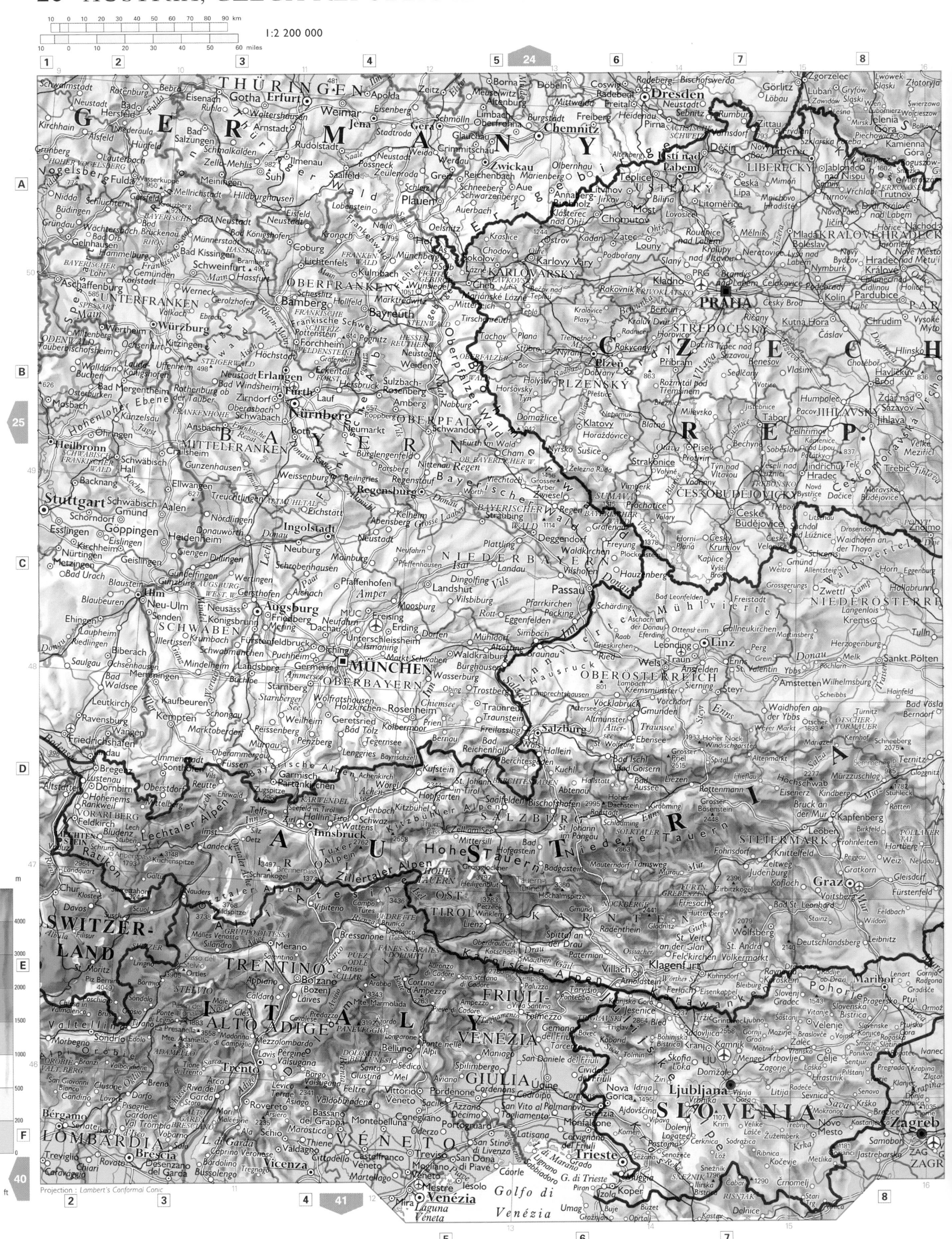

National Parks

Underlined towns give their name to the administrative area in which they stand.

1:2 200 000

Projection : Lambert's Conformal Conic

Administrative divisions in Croatia:
1 Brodsko-Posavska   5 Osječko-Baranjska   9 Vukovarsko-Srijemska
2 Koprivničko-Križevačka 6 Požeško-Slavonska
4 Medimurska   8 Virovitičko-Podravska

Inter-entity boundaries as agreed
at the 1995 Dayton Peace Agreement

National Parks

Underlined towns give their name to the
administrative area in which they stand.

COPYRIGHT PHILIP'S

1:2 200 000

10 0 10 20 30 40 50 60 70 80 90 km
10 0 10 20 30 40 50 60 miles

Gulf of Riga

LATVIA

LITHUANIA

KALININGRAD (Russia)

WARMIŃSKO-MAZURSKIE

POMORSKIE

ZACHODNIO-POMORSKIE

KUJAWSKO-

BALTIC SEA

SWEDEN

Gotland (Sweden)

Öland (Sweden)

GOTLANDS LÄN

KALMAR LÄN

BLEKINGE LÄN

Bornholm (Denmark)
BORNHOLMS AMT.

Hanöbukten

Riga
Jūrmala
Liepāja
Ventspils
Klaipėda
Palanga
Kaunas
MARIJAMPOLE
Šiauliai
Kaliningrad
Gdańsk
Gdynia
Sopot
Elbląg
Słupsk
Koszalin
Szczecin
Visby
Kalmar
Karlskrona
Jönköping

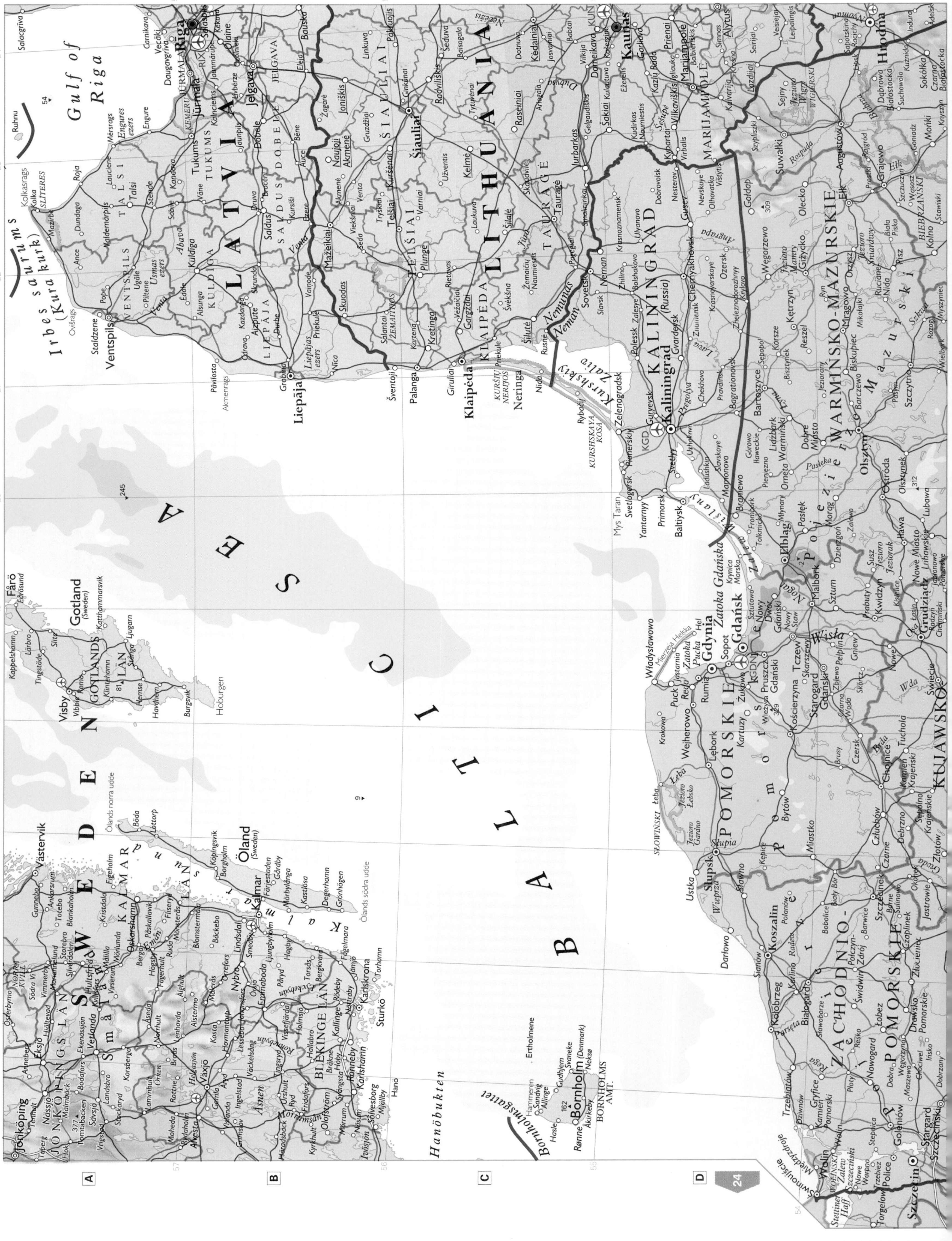

Irbes saurums (Kura kurk)

Kuršių Zalte
Kurshskiy Zaliv
KURSHSKAYA KOSA
KURŠIŲ NERIJOS

Neman
Nemunas

Wisła

Underlined towns give their name to the administrative area in which they stand.

National Parks

Projection: Lambert's Conformal Conic

East from Greenwich

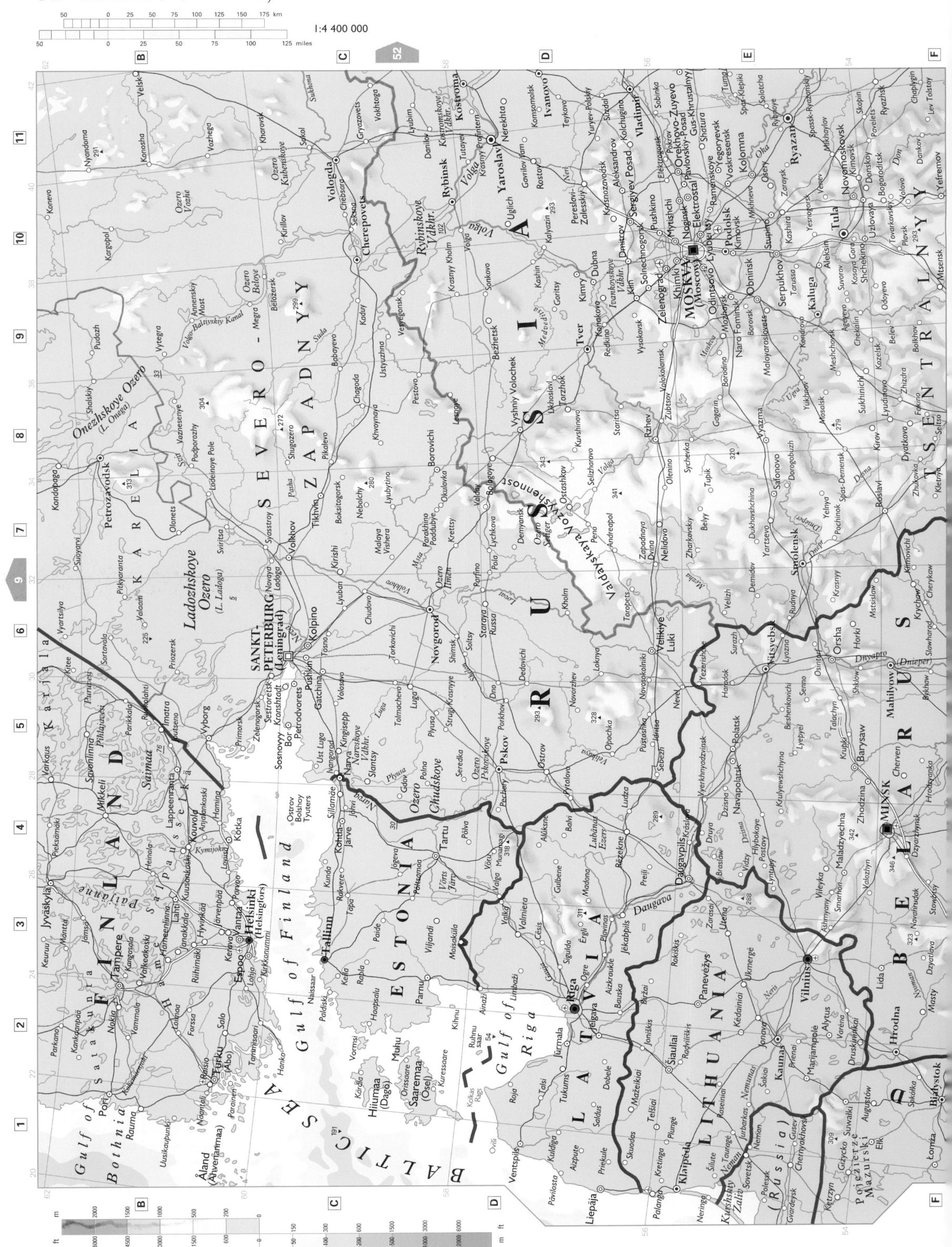

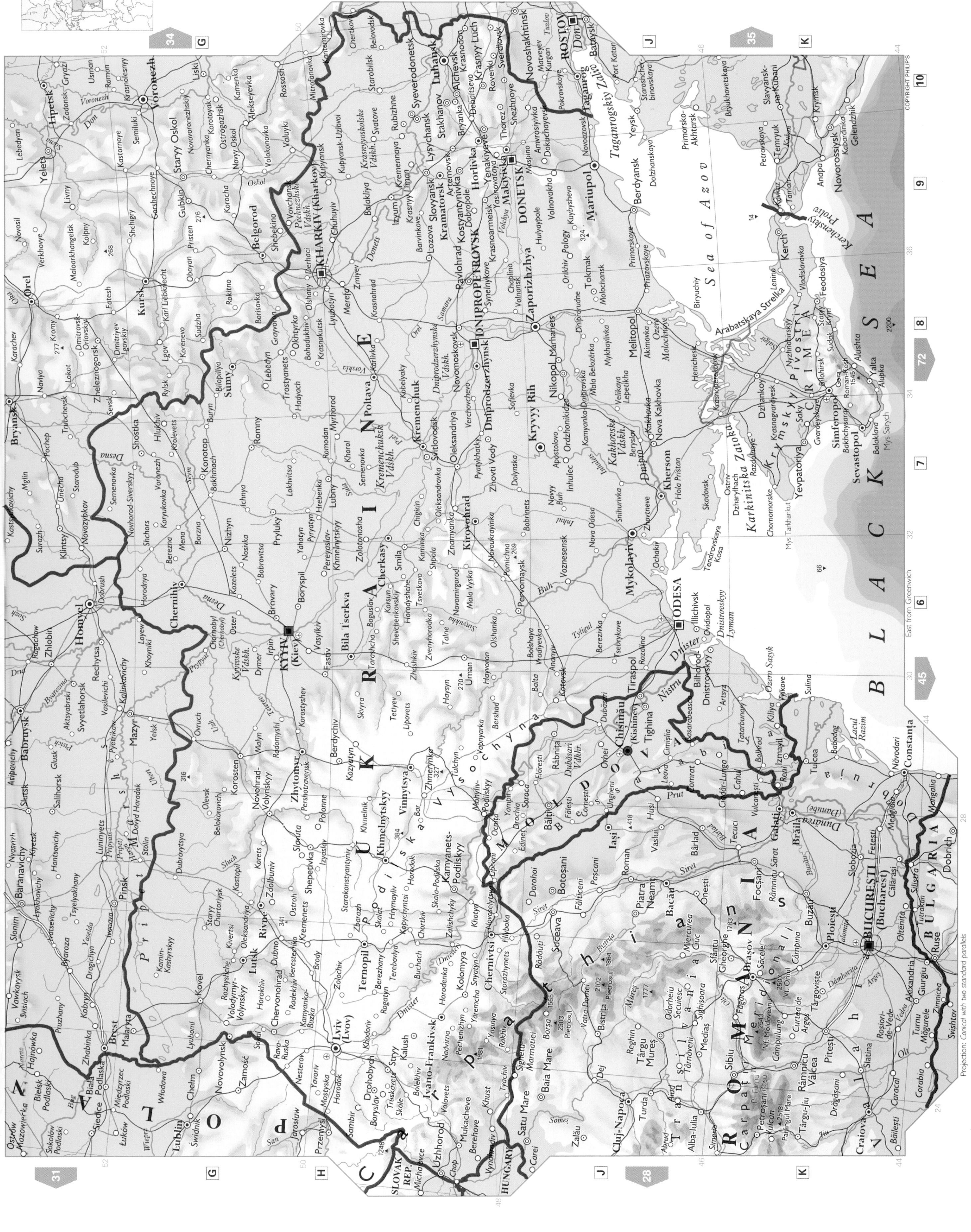

U K R A I N E

MOLDOVA

ROMANIA

BULGARIA

SLOVAK REP.

HUNGARY

CRIMEA

Sea of Azov

BLACK SEA

Taganrogskiy Zaliv

Kerchenskiy Proliv

R0STOV

KHARKIV (Kharkov)

KYIV (Kiev)

ODESA

DNIPROPETROVSK

DONETSK

Mariupol

Zaporizhzhya

Kryvyy Rih

Kherson

Mykolayiv

Luhansk

Simferopol

Sevastopol

Yalta

Chişinău (Kishinev)

Tiraspol

BUCUREŞTI (Bucharest)

Constanța

Lviv (Lvov)

Homyel

Babruysk

Brest

Pinsk

Chernihiv

Sumy

Poltava

Cherkasy

Kirovohrad

Zhytomyr

Vinnytsya

Ternopil

Rivne

Lutsk

Ivano-Frankivsk

Khmelnytskyy

Kamyanets-Podilskyy

Chernivtsi

East from Greenwich

Projection: Conical with two standard parallels

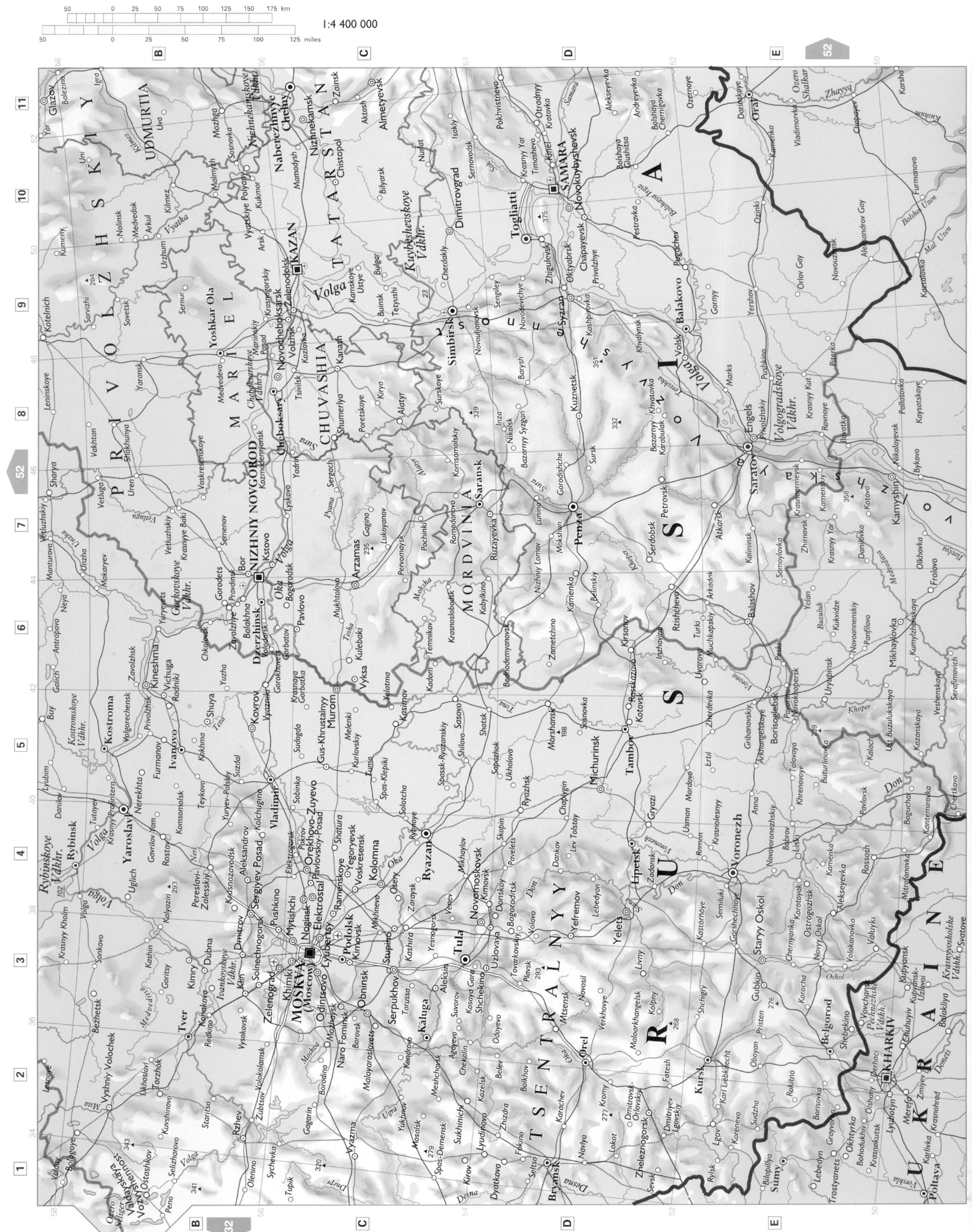

1:4 400 000

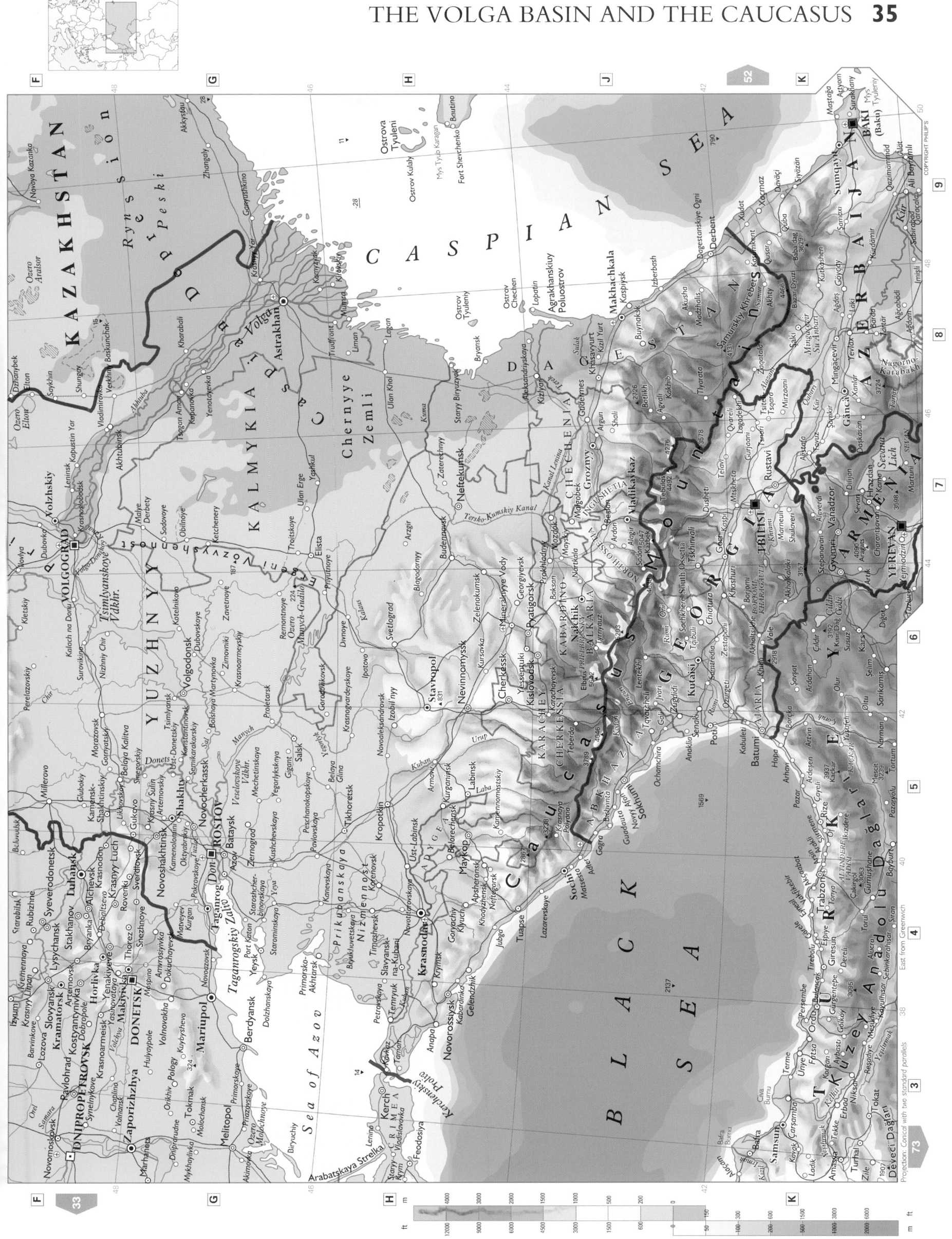

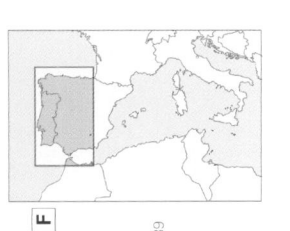

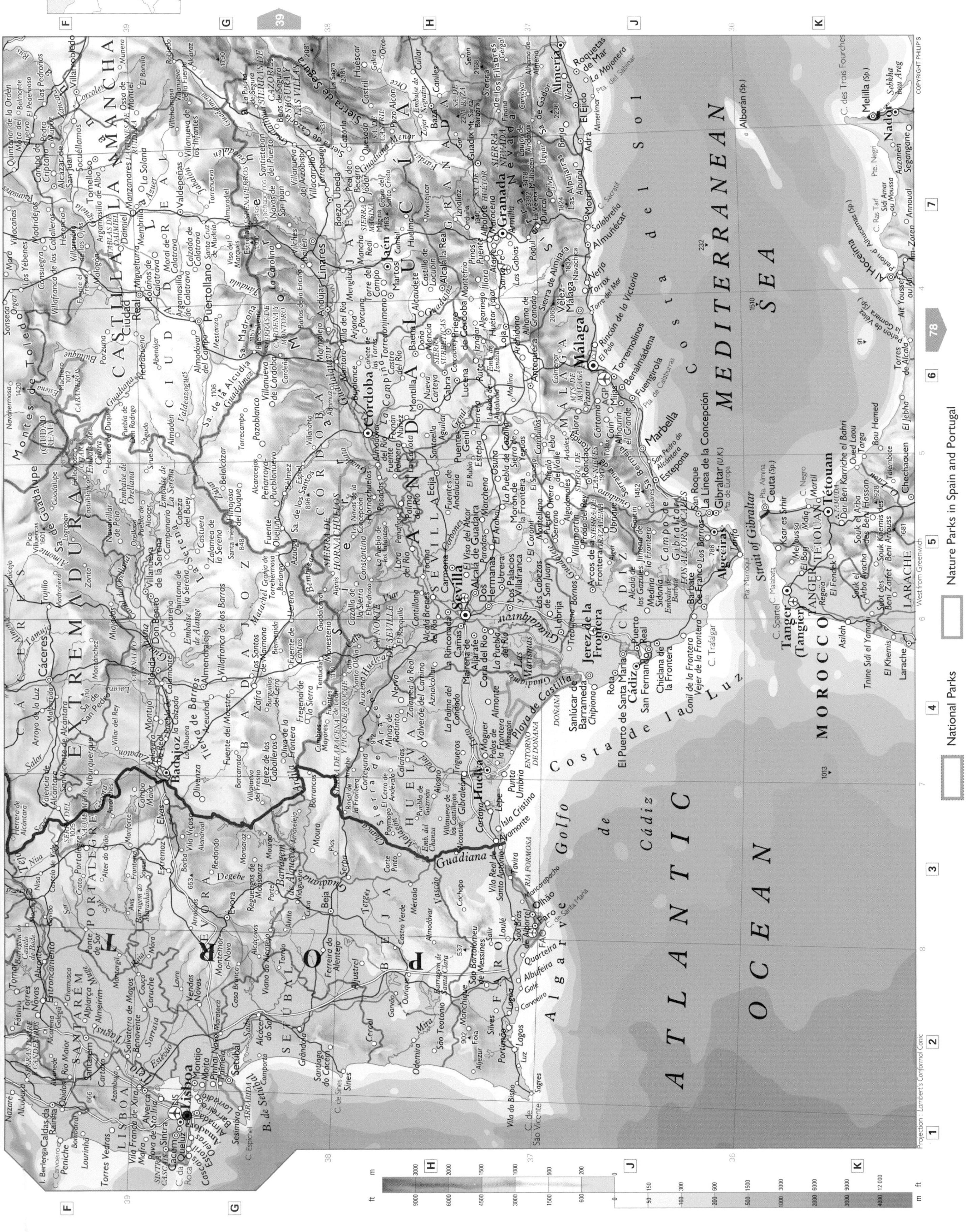
ATLANTIC OCEAN
MEDITERRANEAN SEA
Golfo de Cádiz
Costa de la Luz
Costa del Sol
Strait of Gibraltar
EXTREMADURA
CASTILLA-LA MANCHA
ANDALUCÍA
PORTUGAL
MOROCCO
Lisboa
Sevilla
Córdoba
Granada
Málaga
Cádiz
Huelva
Badajoz
Cáceres
Ciudad Real
Jaén
Almería
Gibraltar (U.K.)
Ceuta (Sp.)
Melilla (Sp.)
Tanger (Tangier)
Tétouan
National Parks
Nature Parks in Spain and Portugal
Projection : Lambert's Conformal Conic
West from Greenwich
COPYRIGHT PHILIP'S

1:2 200 000

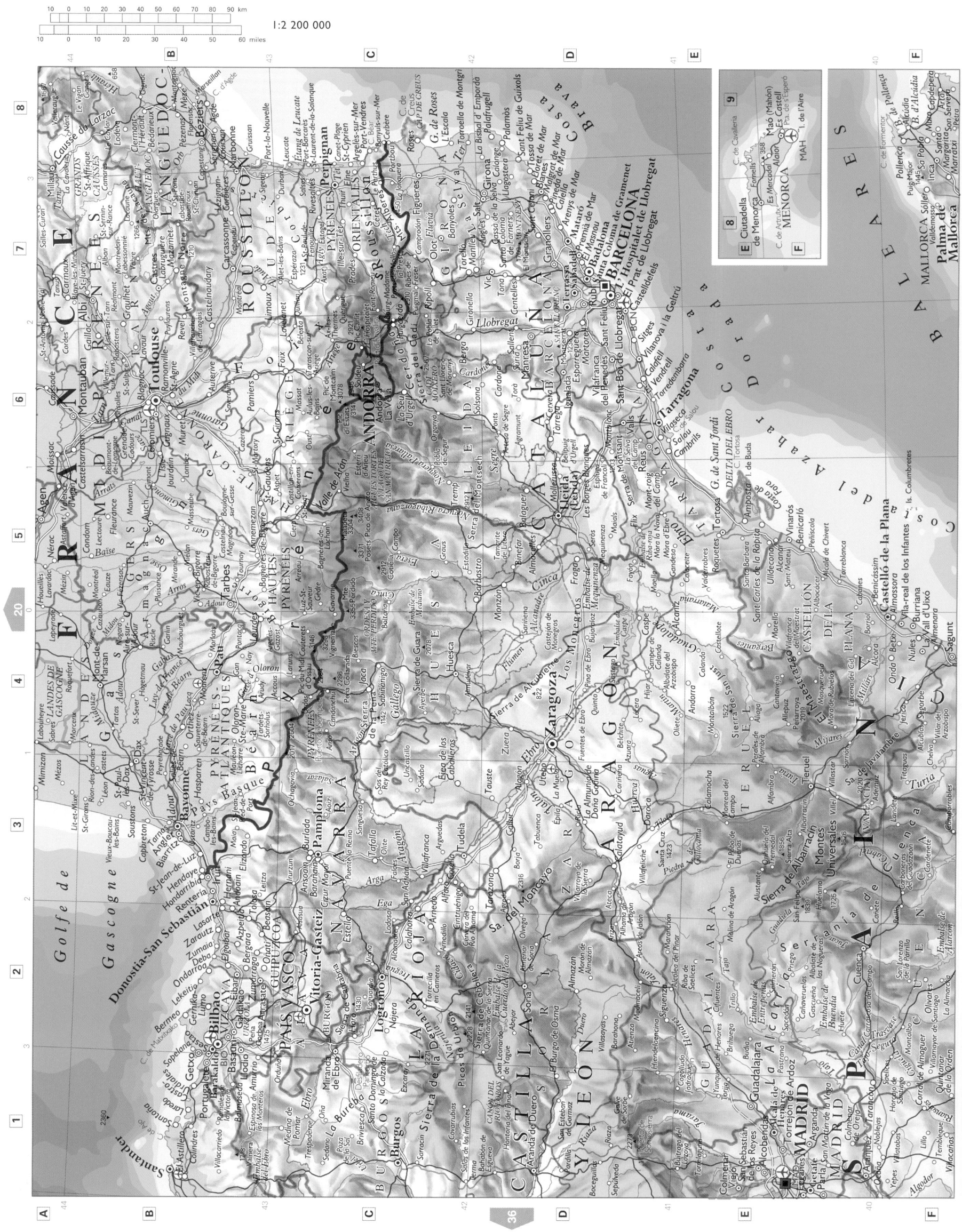

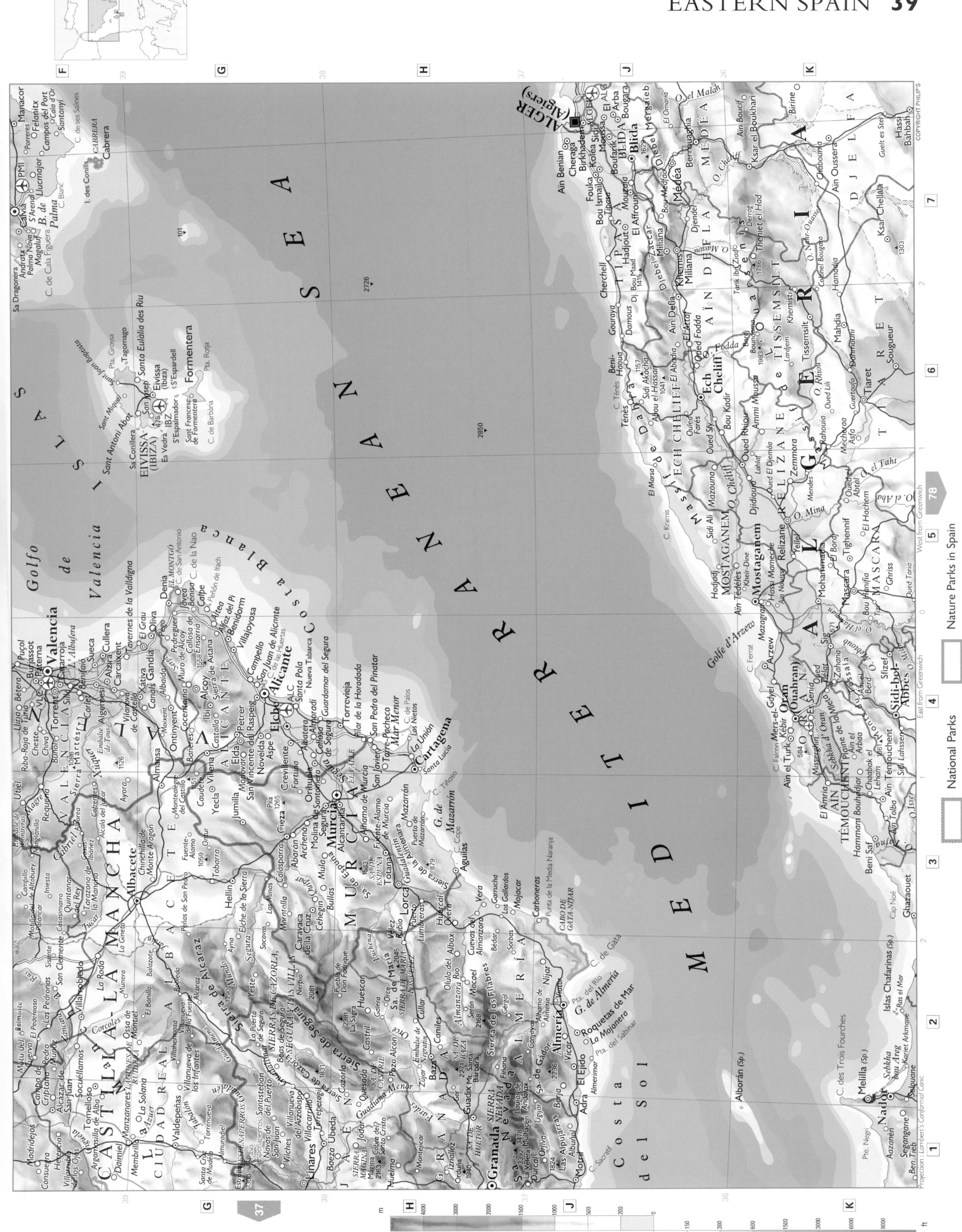

National Parks

Nature Parks in Spain

Projection : Lambert's Conformal Conic

1:2 200 000

National Parks

Underlined towns give their name to the administrative area in which they stand.

Projection : Lambert's Conformal Conic

East from Greenwich

Administrative divisions in Croatia:
1 Brodsko-Posavska 4 Medimurska 8 Virovitičko-Podravska
2 Koprivničko-Križevačka 6 Požeško-Slavonska 10 Zagreba čka
3 Krapinsko-Zagorska 7 Varaždinska

☐ Nature Parks in Italy

– – – – Inter-entity boundaries as agreed at the 1995 Dayton Peace Agreement

COPYRIGHT PHILIP'S

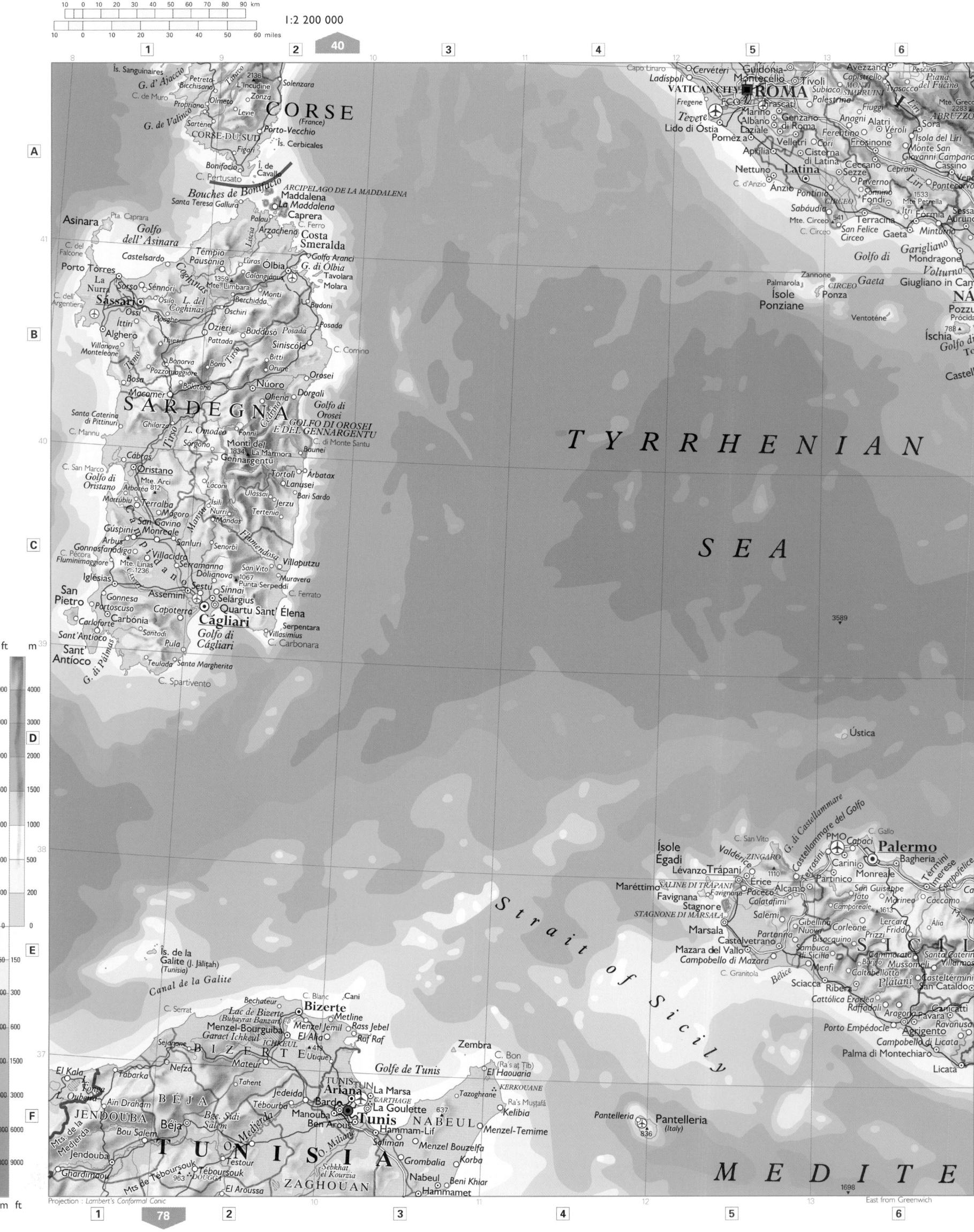

10 0 10 20 30 40 50 60 70 80 90 km

1:2 200 000

10 0 10 20 30 40 50 60 miles

Projection : Lambert's Conformal Conic

East from Greenwich

A D R I A T I C   S E A

I O N I A N   S E A

R R A N E A N   S E A

Nature Parks in Italy   National Parks   Underlined towns give their name to the administrative area in which they stand.

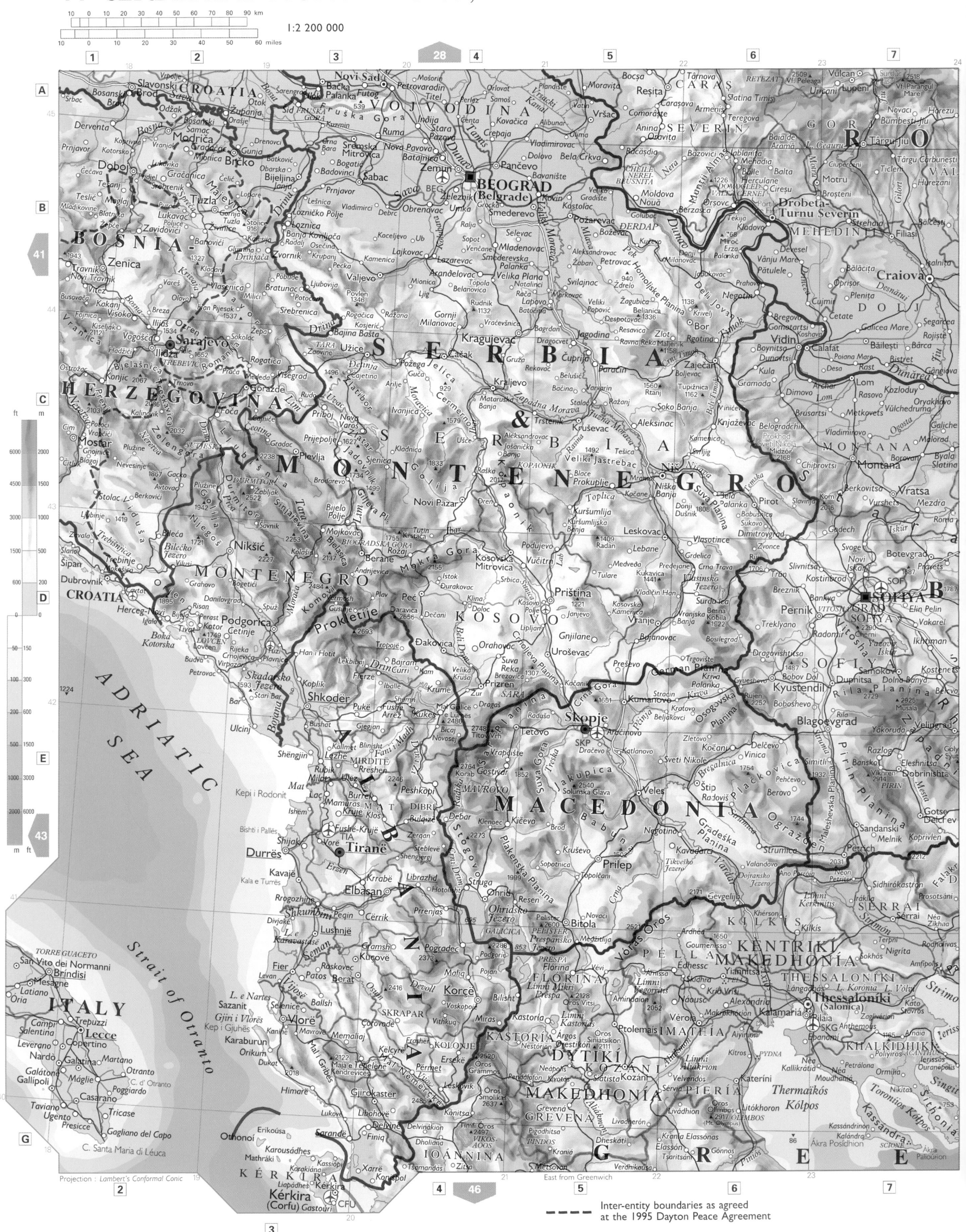

1:2 200 000

Projection: Lambert's Conformal Conic

East from Greenwich

- - - - Inter-entity boundaries as agreed
at the 1995 Dayton Peace Agreement

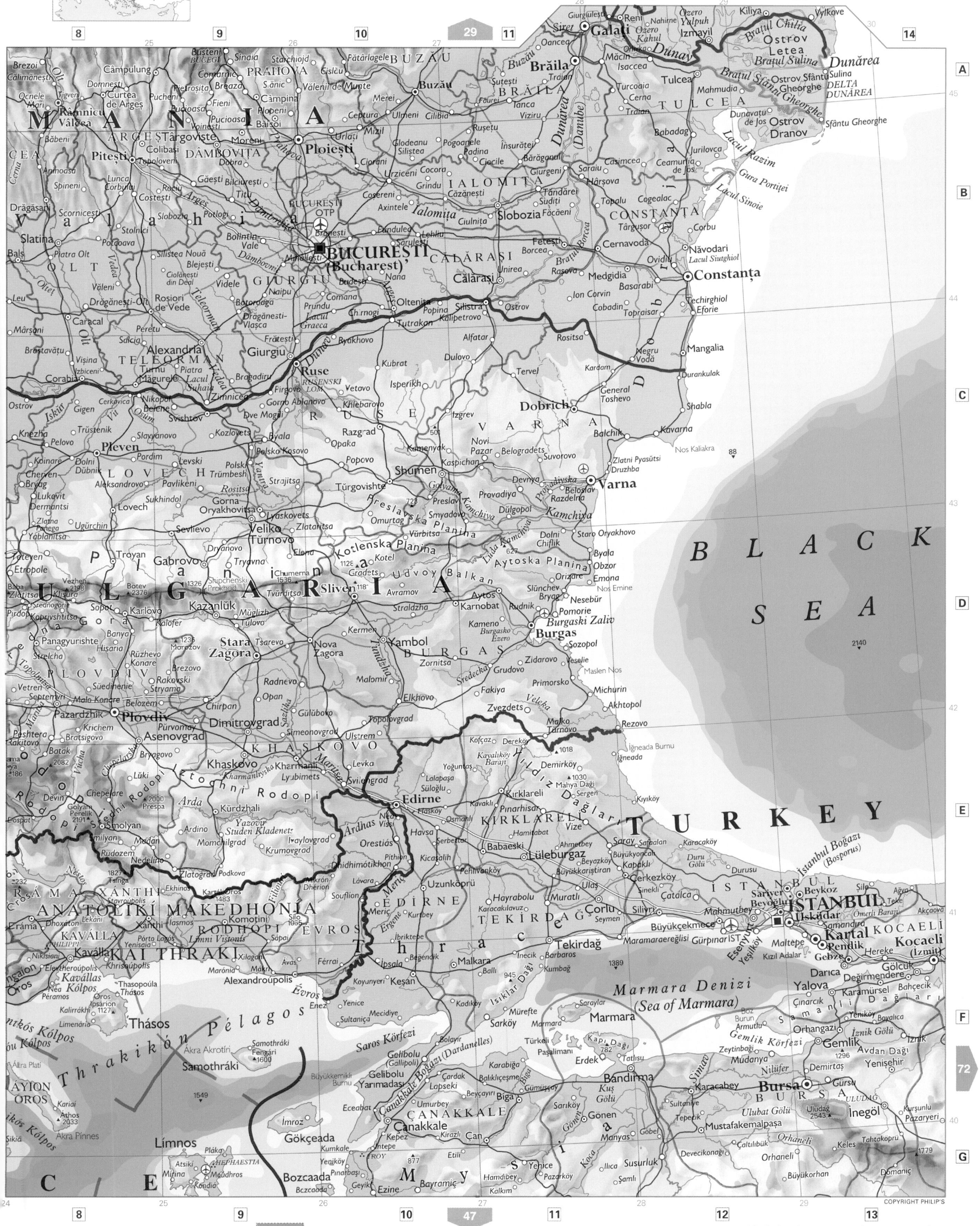

BLACK SEA

TURKEY

BULGARIA

ROMANIA

Bucureşti (Bucharest)

Ploieşti

Ruse

Varna

Burgas

Plovdiv

Stara Zagora

Edirne

İstanbul

Üsküdar

Bursa

Marmara Denizi (Sea of Marmara)

Çanakkale Boğazı (Dardanelles)

Gelibolu (Gallipoli)

Constanţa

Galaţi

Brăila

Buzău

Piteşti

Râmnicu Vâlcea

Dunărea

Thrakikón Pélagos

Kaválla

Alexandroúpolis

Samothráki

Límnos

National Parks

Underlined towns give their name to the
administrative area in which they stand.

COPYRIGHT PHILIP'S

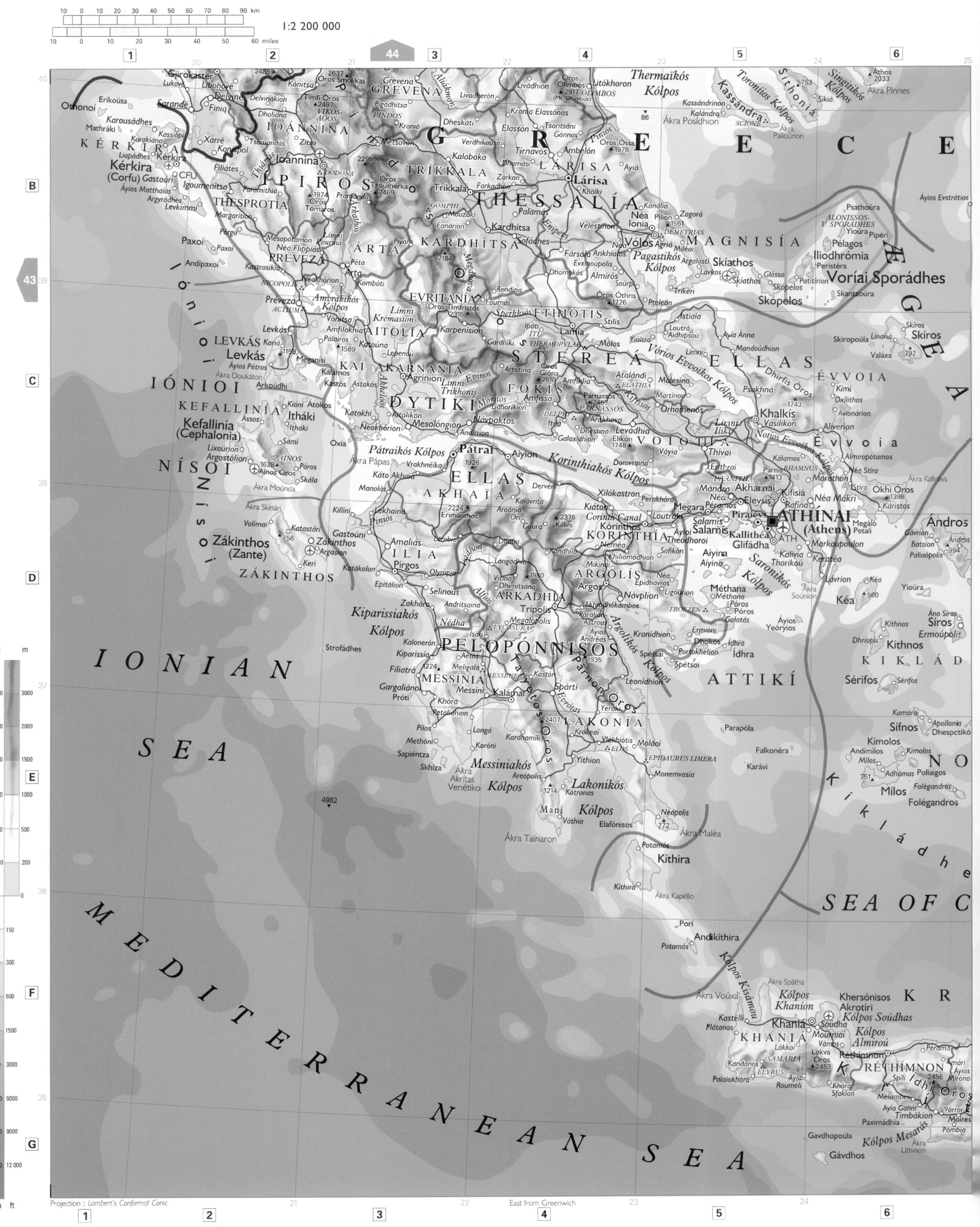

1:2 200 000

Projection : Lambert's Conformal Conic

East from Greenwich

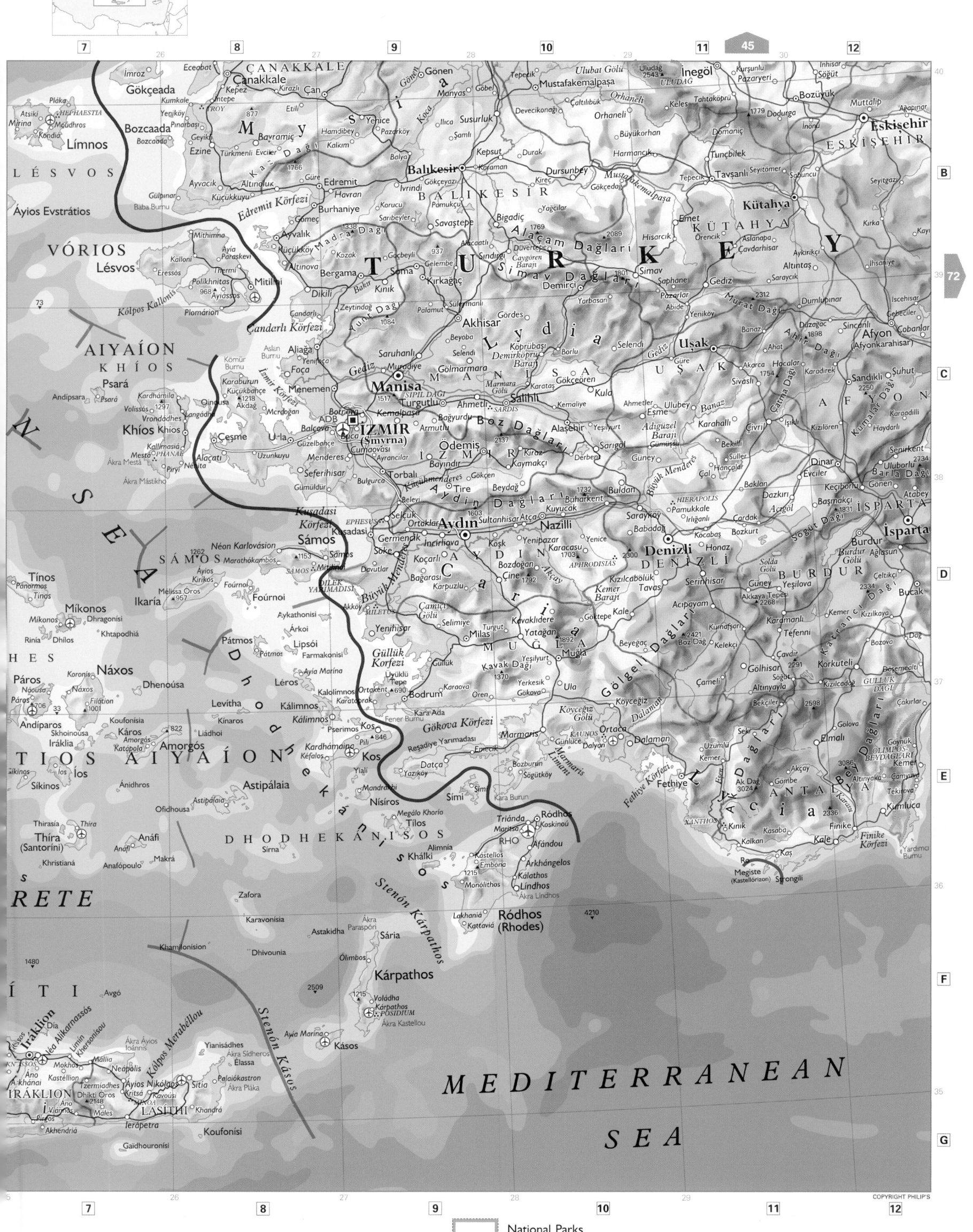

National Parks

ISLAS BALEARES *(Spain)*

Menorca (Minorca)

Mallorca (Majorca)

MEDITERRANEAN SEA

BALEARIC ISLANDS LOCATOR MAP
1:15 800 000

Menorca
Mallorca
Eivissa

BALEARIC ISLANDS
1:900 000

Eivissa (Ibiza) *(Spain)*

Formentera

MADEIRA
1:900 000

Madeira *(Portugal)*

ATLANTIC OCEAN

Funchal

CANARY ISLANDS
1:1 800 000

ISLAS CANARIAS *(Spain)*

Lanzarote

Fuerteventura

Gran Canaria

Las Palmas

Tenerife

Santa Cruz de Tenerife

Gomera

La Palma

Hierro

National Parks

Projection: Lambert's Conformal Conic
COPYRIGHT PHILIP'S

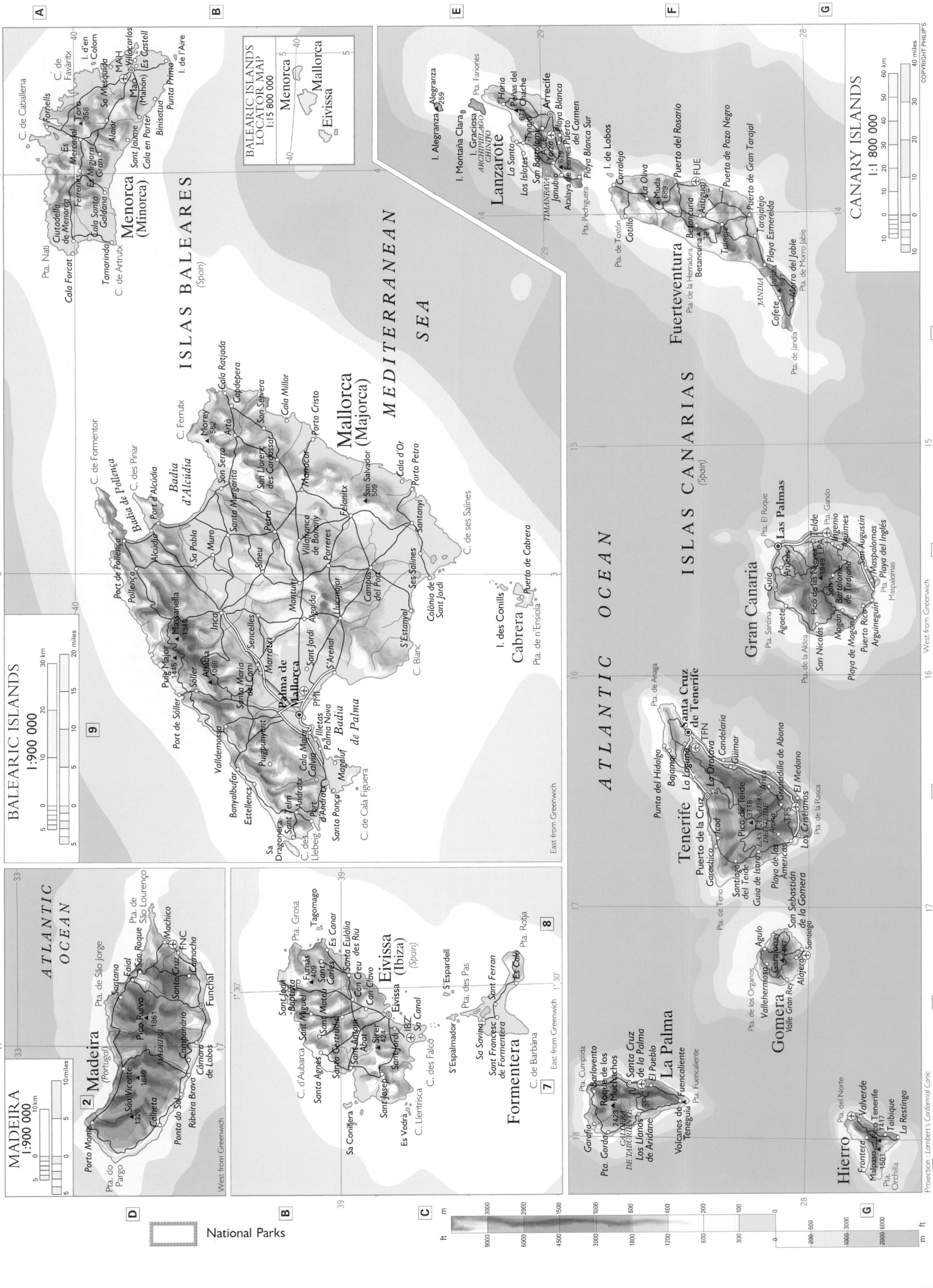

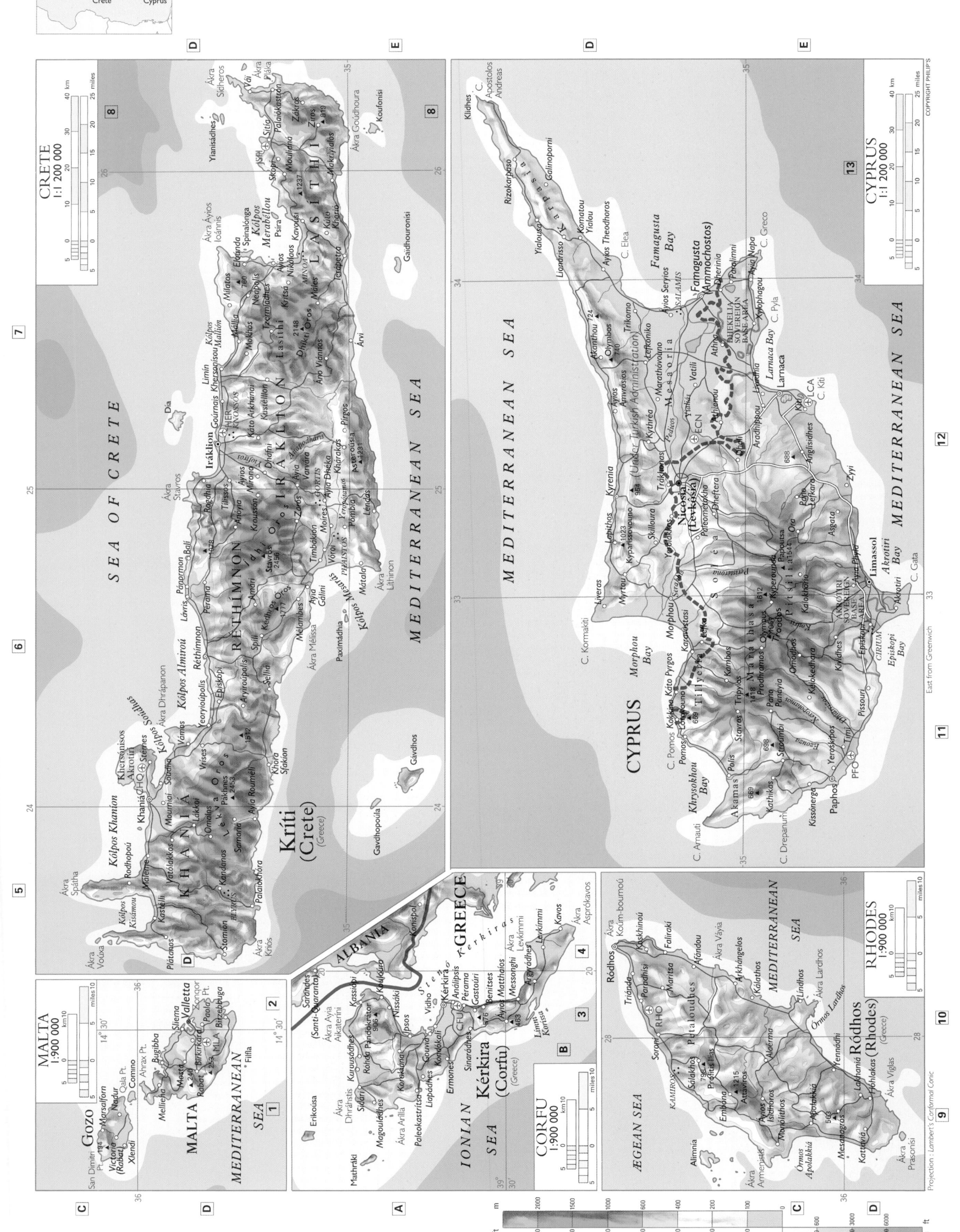

500   0   250 500 750 1000 1250 1500 1750 km

1:44 400 000

500   0   250 500 750 1000 1250 miles

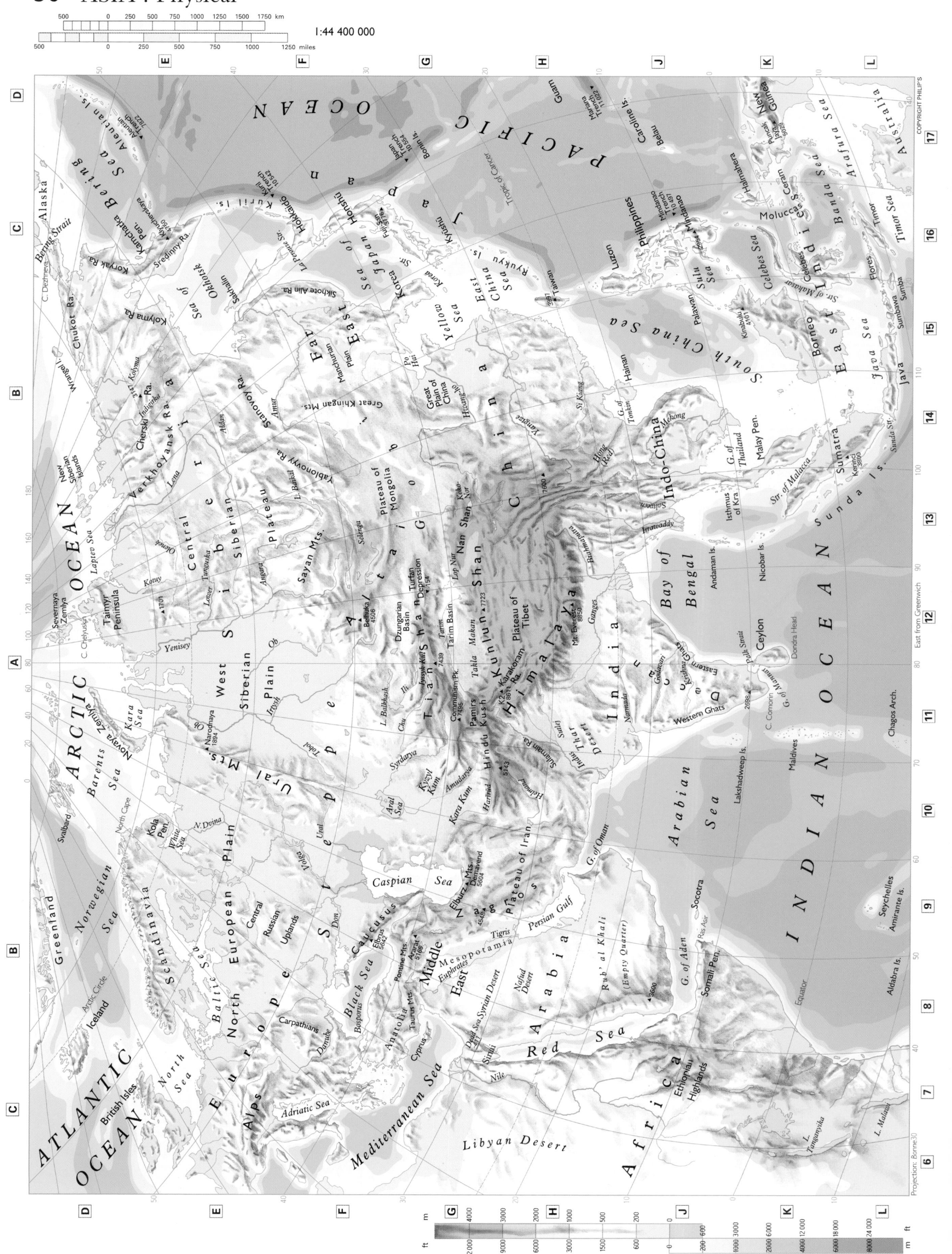

m 4000 3000 2000 1000 500 200 0 -200 -600

ft 12 000 9000 6000 3000 1500 600 0

ft 4000 6000 12 000 18 000 24 000

m 2000 6000 4000 6000 8000

Projection: Bonne Borne30

COPYRIGHT PHILIP'S

East from Greenwich

1:44 400 000

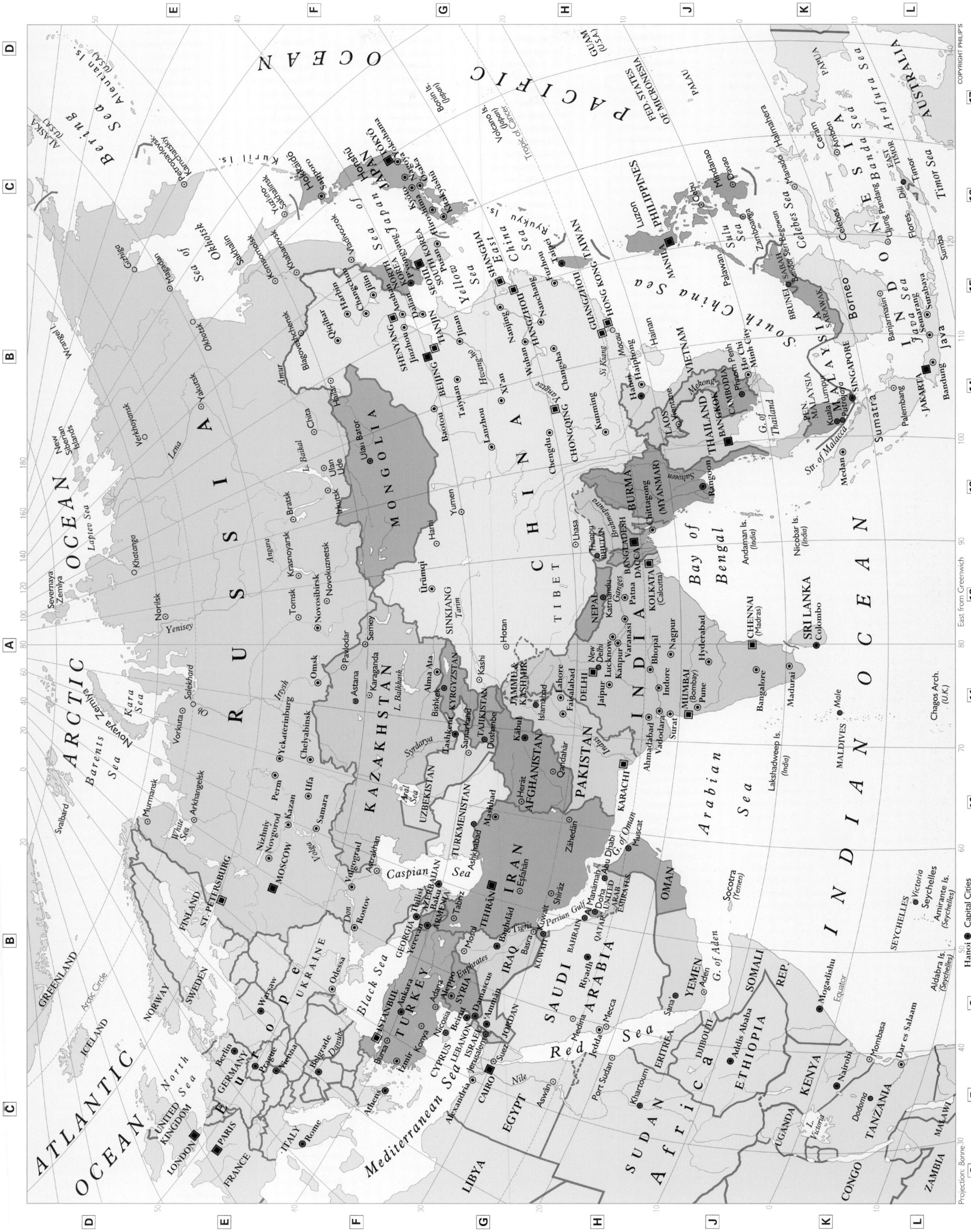
ARCTIC OCEAN
PACIFIC OCEAN
INDIAN OCEAN
ATLANTIC OCEAN
R U S S I A
C H I N A
I N D I A
I N D O N E S I A
M A L A Y S I A
MONGOLIA
KAZAKHSTAN
UZBEKISTAN
TURKMENISTAN
KYRGYZSTAN
TAJIKISTAN
AFGHANISTAN
PAKISTAN
IRAN
IRAQ
SAUDI ARABIA
YEMEN
OMAN
TURKEY
SYRIA
JORDAN
ISRAEL
LEBANON
CYPRUS
GEORGIA
ARMENIA
AZERBAIJAN
KUWAIT
QATAR
BAHRAIN
UNITED ARAB EMIRATES
NEPAL
BHUTAN
BANGLADESH
BURMA (MYANMAR)
THAILAND
LAOS
CAMBODIA
VIETNAM
PHILIPPINES
TAIWAN
JAPAN
NORTH KOREA
SOUTH KOREA
SRI LANKA
MALDIVES
SINGAPORE
BRUNEI
EAST TIMOR
SEYCHELLES
E u r o p e
A f r i c a
EGYPT
SUDAN
ETHIOPIA
ERITREA
DJIBOUTI
SOMALI REP.
KENYA
TANZANIA
UGANDA
LIBYA
CONGO
ZAMBIA
MALAWI
UKRAINE
FINLAND
SWEDEN
NORWAY
ICELAND
GREENLAND
UNITED KINGDOM
FRANCE
GERMANY
ITALY
AUSTRALIA
PAPUA
Bering Sea
Sea of Okhotsk
Sea of Japan
Yellow Sea
East China Sea
South China Sea
Bay of Bengal
Arabian Sea
Caspian Sea
Black Sea
Red Sea
Mediterranean Sea
Persian Gulf
Java Sea
Banda Sea
Arafura Sea
Timor Sea
Celebes Sea
Sulu Sea
Kara Sea
Barents Sea
Laptev Sea
North Sea
MOSCOW
BEIJING
TOKYO
SHANGHAI
DELHI
MUMBAI (Bombay)
KOLKATA (Calcutta)
CHENNAI (Madras)
KARACHI
TEHRAN
ISTANBUL
CAIRO
JAKARTA
MANILA
BANGKOK
SEOUL
HONG KONG
ST. PETERSBURG
LONDON
PARIS
Tropic of Cancer
Arctic Circle
Equator
Hanoi ● Capital Cities
COPYRIGHT PHILIP'S
Projection: Bonne
East from Greenwich

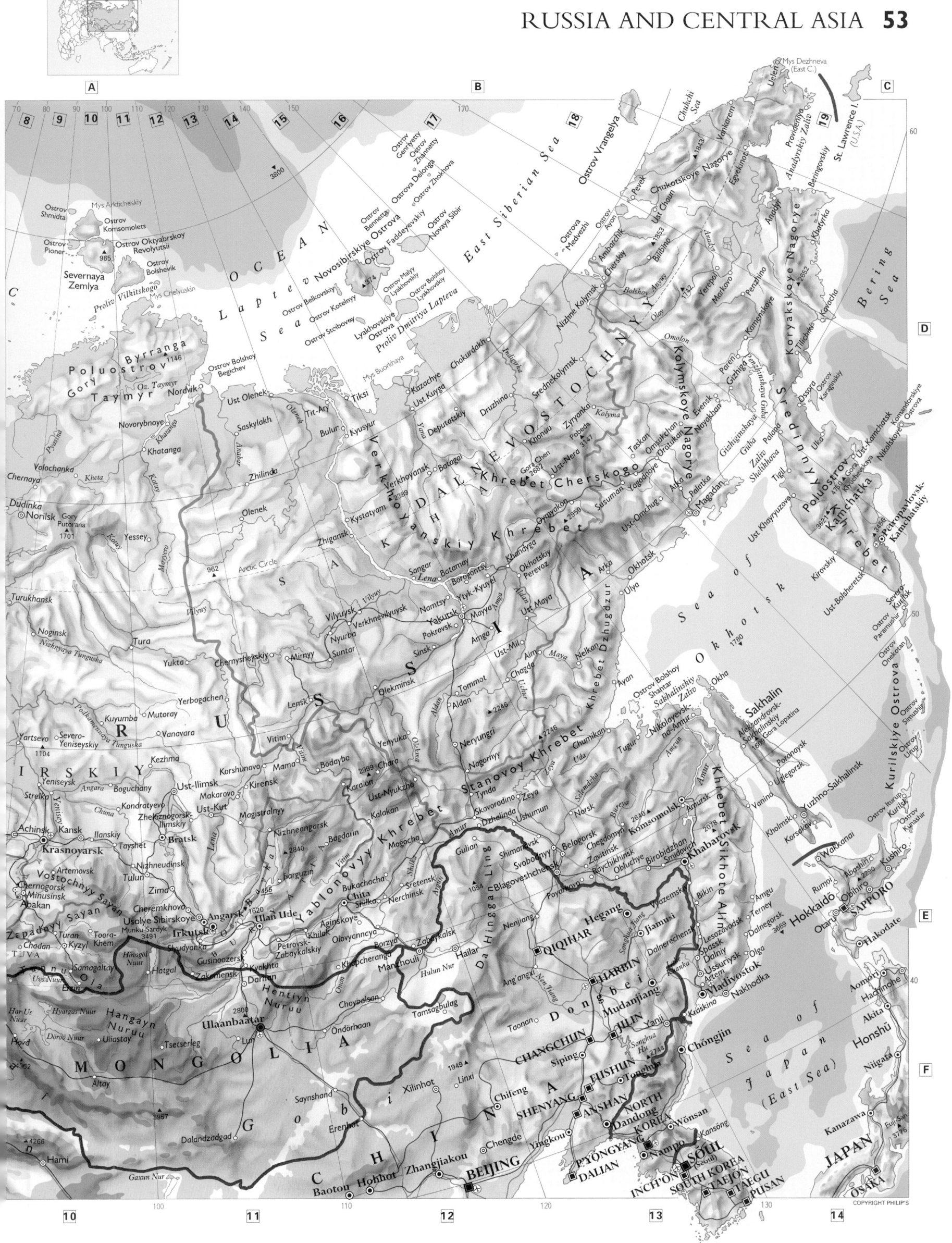

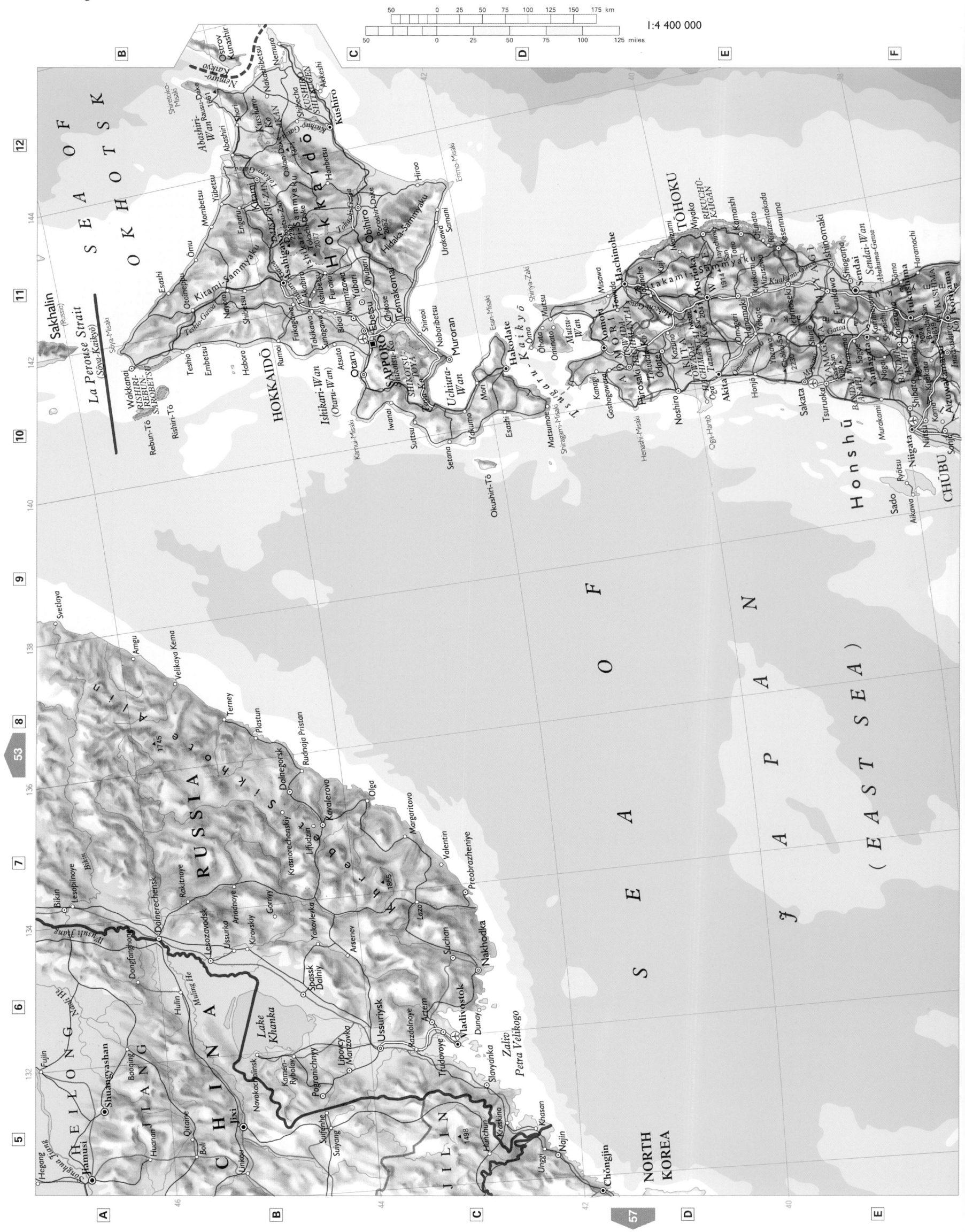

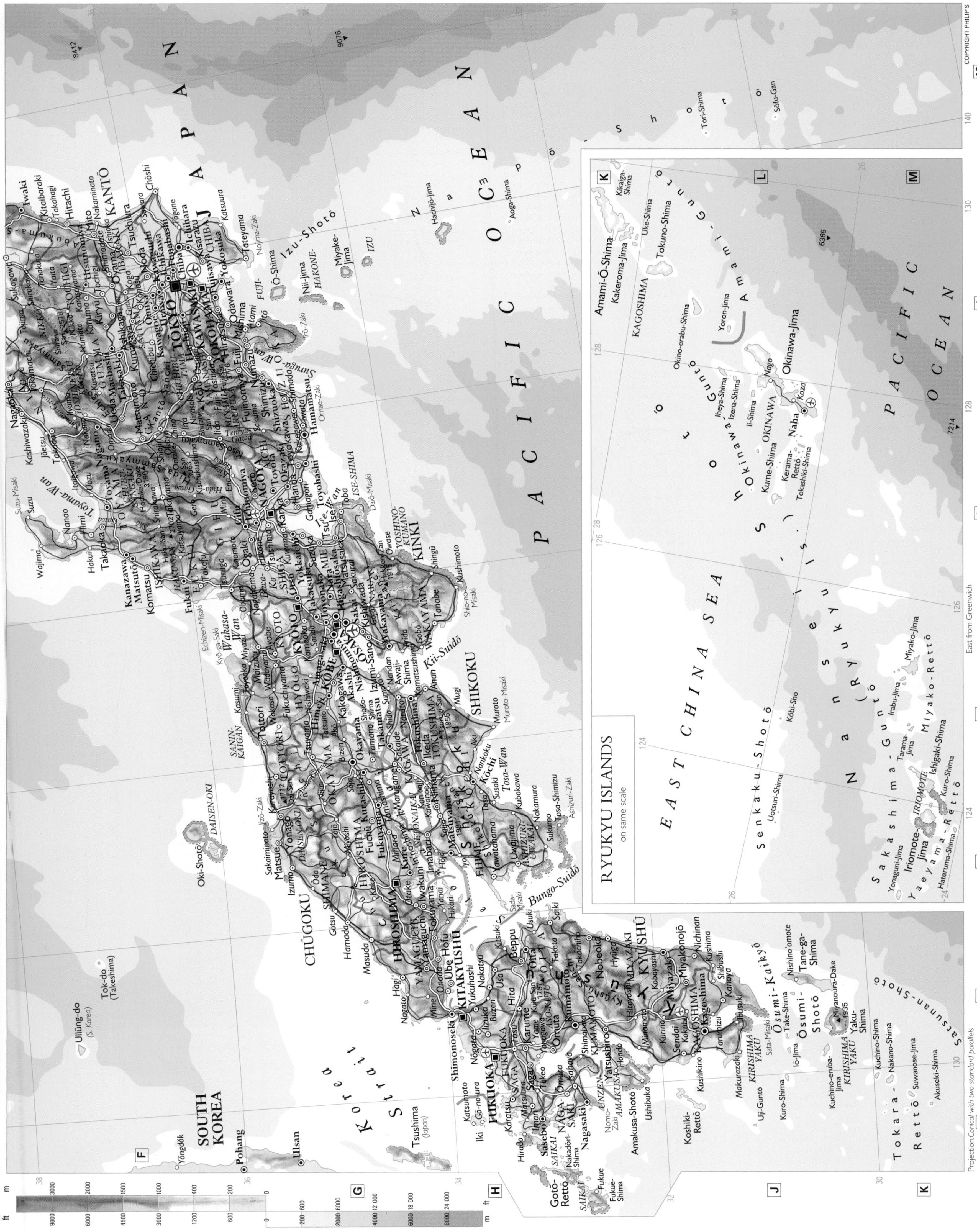

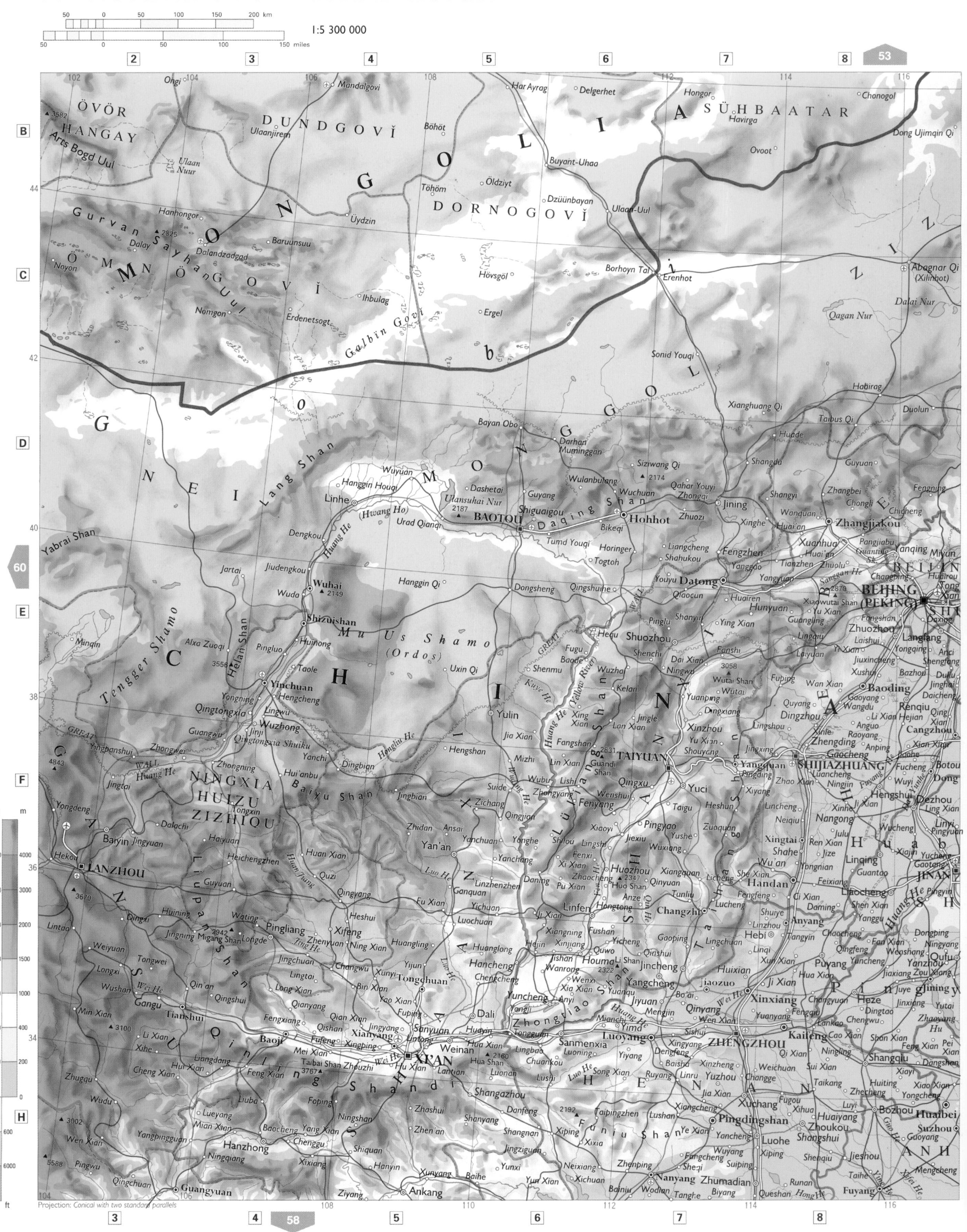

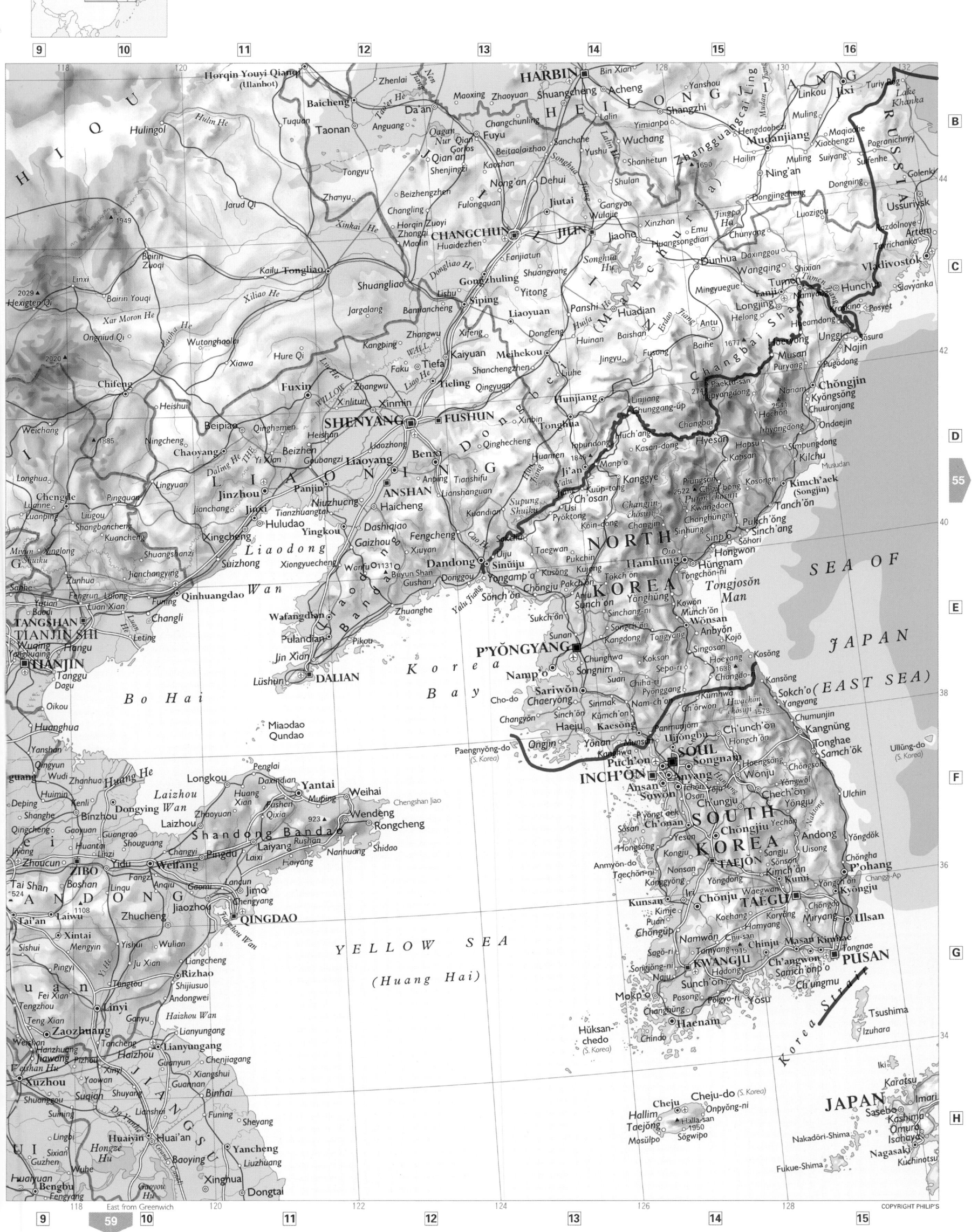

50 0 50 100 150 200 km
1:5 300 000
50 0 50 100 150 miles

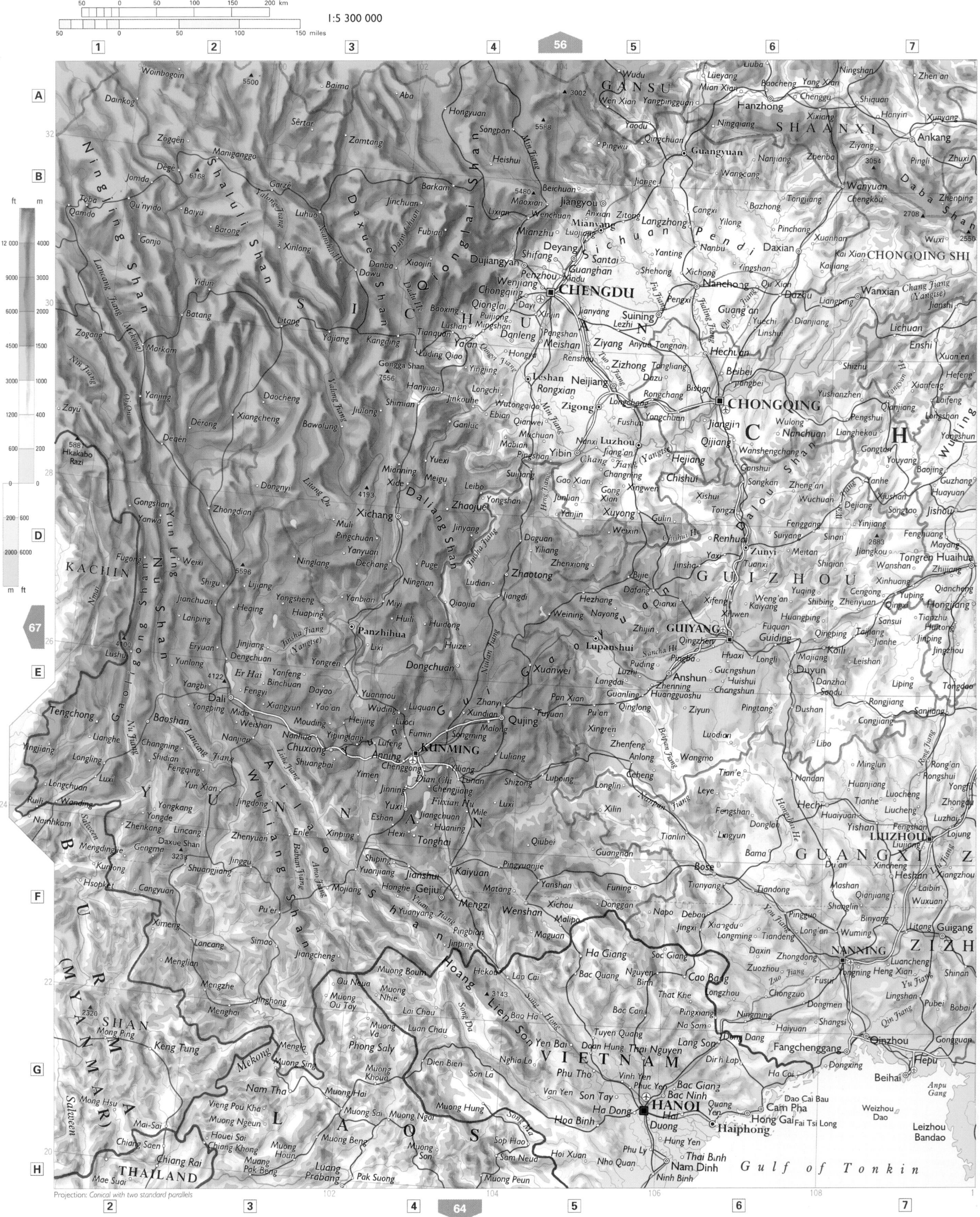

Projection: Conical with two standard parallels

57
HENAN
HUBEI
ANHUI
JIANGSU
SHANGHAI SHI
ZHEJIANG
JIANGXI
HUNAN
FUJIAN
GUANGDONG
TAIWAN
WUHAN
NANJING
SHANGHAI
HANGZHOU
NANCHANG
CHANGSHA
FUZHOU
GUANGZHOU
HONG KONG (XIANGGANG)
T'AIPEI
KAOHSIUNG
Hefei
Macau
Shenzhen
Shantou
Xiamen
Ningbo
Wenzhou
Chang Jiang (Yangtse)
Poyang Hu
Dongting Hu
Tai Hu
Taiwan Strait
Luzon Strait
SOUTH CHINA SEA
Tropic of Cancer
Dongsha Dao (Pratas I.) (China)
East from Greenwich
COPYRIGHT PHILIP'S
61

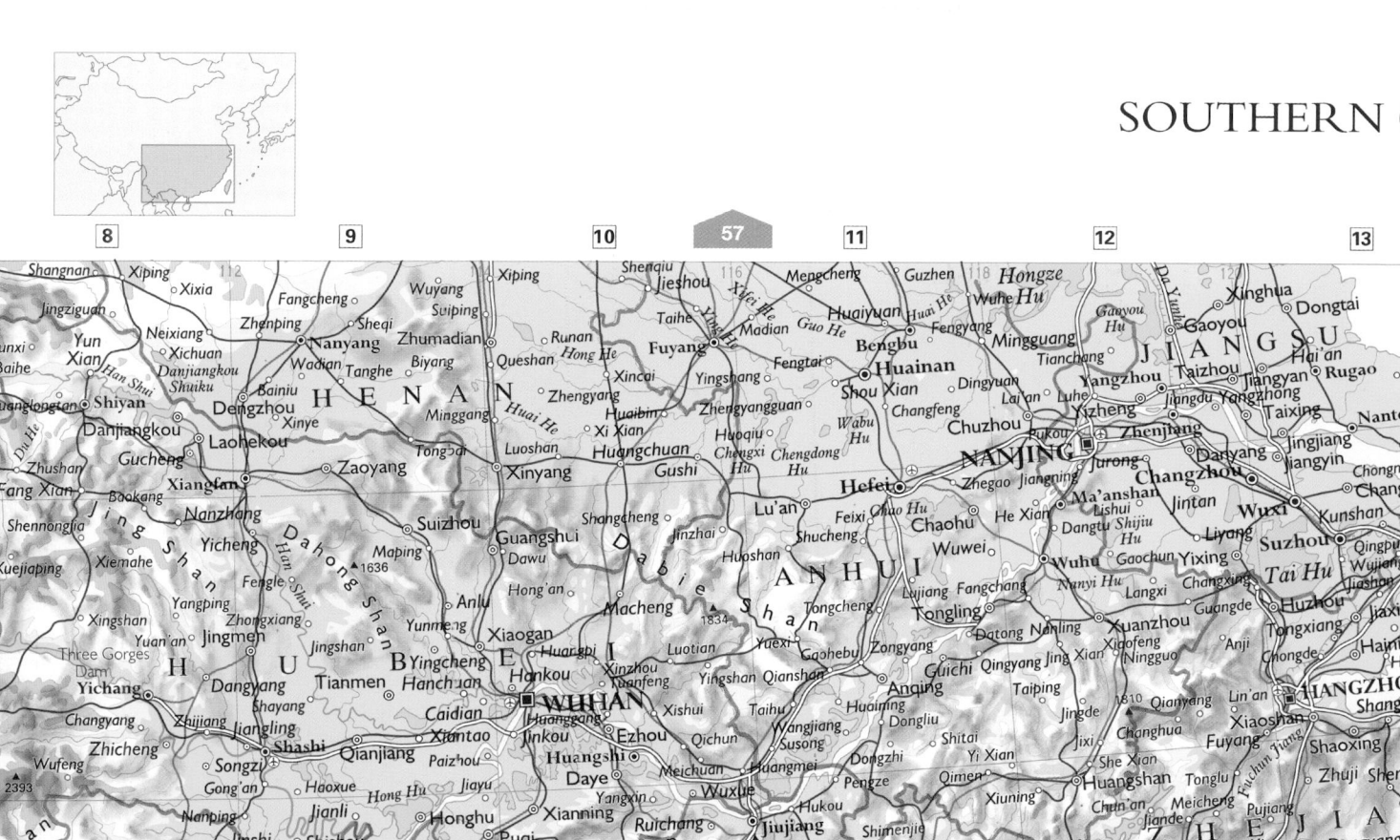

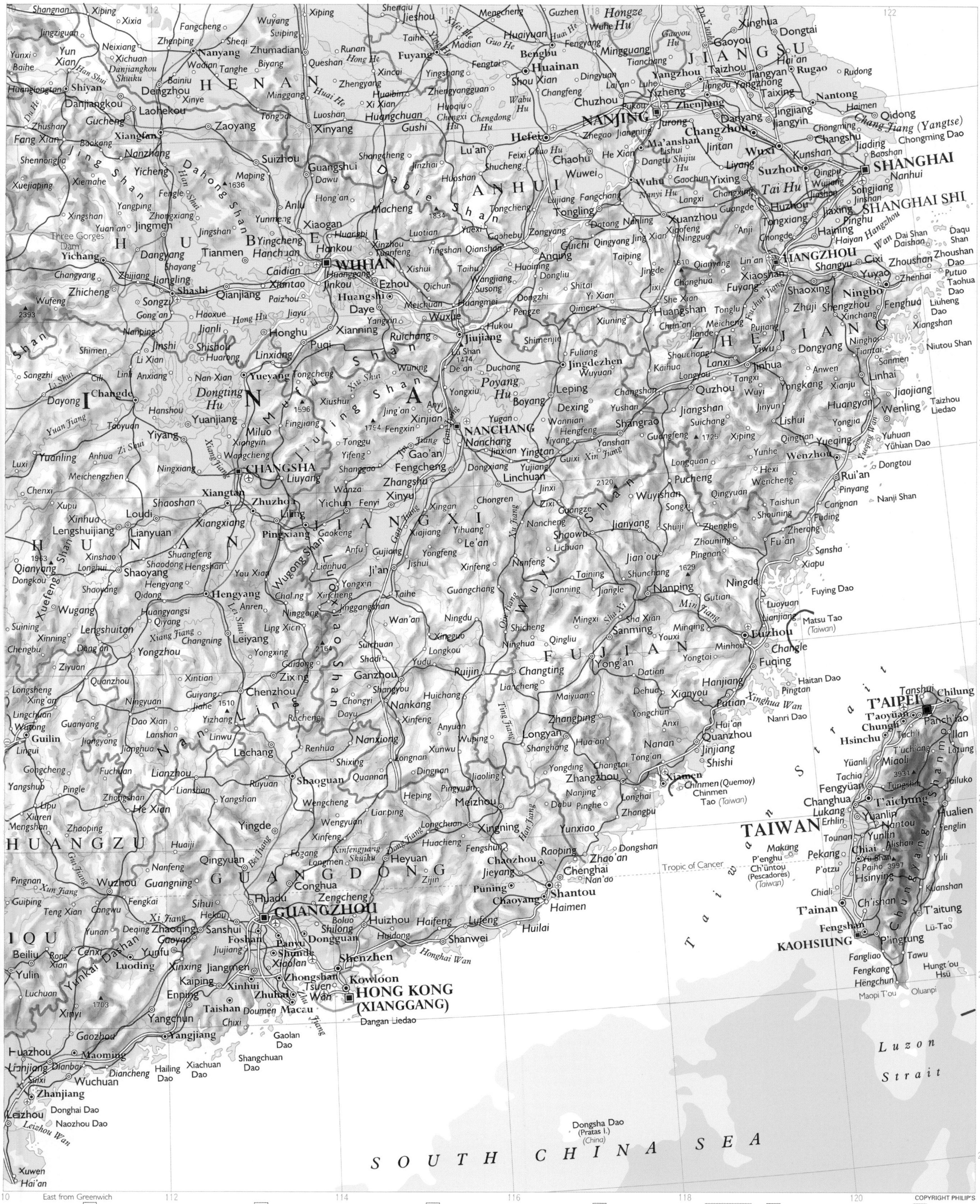

1:17 800 000

COPYRIGHT PHILIP'S

Projection: Bonne

East from Greenwich

R U S S I A

K A Z A K H S T A N

M O N G O L I A

Ulaanbaatar

NEI MONGGOL (INNER MONGOLIA)

HEILONGJIANG

JILIN

LIAONING

HARBIN

QIQIHAR

CHANGCHUN

SHENYANG

NORTH KOREA

PYONGYANG

SOUTH KOREA

SEOUL

PUSAN

JAPAN

FUKUOKA

BEIJING (PEKING)

TIANJIN

HEBEI

SHANXI

SHANDONG

JINAN

QINGDAO

DALIAN

YELLOW SEA

Bo Hai

SHIJIAZHUANG

TAIYUAN

HENAN

JIANGSU

SHANGHAI

NANJING

ANHUI

HEFEI

HUBEI

WUHAN

HANGZHOU

ZHEJIANG

NINGBO

EAST CHINA SEA

XINJIANG UYGUR ZIZHIQU (SINKIANG)

ÜRÜMQI

Tarim Pendi

Taklimakan Shamo

XIZANG ZIZHIQU (TIBET)

Lhasa

QINGHAI

Xining

GANSU

LANZHOU

NINGXIA HUIZU ZIZHIQU

Yinchuan

SHAANXI

Xi'an

SICHUAN

CHENGDU

CHONGQING

GUIZHOU

GUIYANG

YUNNAN

KUNMING

GUANGXI ZHUANGZU ZIZHIQU

NANNING

GUANGDONG

GUANGZHOU (CANTON)

HONG KONG

Macau

HAINAN

FUJIAN

FUZHOU

JIANGXI

NANCHANG

HUNAN

CHANGSHA

TAIWAN (FORMOSA)

TAIPEI

KAOHSIUNG

SOUTH CHINA SEA

PHILIPPINES

VIETNAM

HANOI

HAIPHONG

LAOS

BURMA (MYANMAR)

THAILAND (SIAM)

Mandalay

BANGLADESH

DHAKA

BHUTAN

NEPAL

Katmandu

I N D I A

KOLKATA (CALCUTTA)

BAY OF BENGAL

KYRGYZSTAN

Bishkek

ALMATY

Qaraghandy

KASHMIR

Tropic of Cancer

YELLOW SEA

Korea Bay

Ryukyu-retto

Mt Everest 8848

K2 8611

Tannu Ola

Altai

Da Hinggan Ling

Qilian Shan

Kunlun Shan

Huang He

Chang Jiang

1:6 700 000

50 0 100 150 200 250 300 km
50 0 50 100 150 200 miles

A

Dongsha Dao
(China)

Itbayat I.
Batan Is.
Batan I.

P A C I F I C

20

B

Balintang Channel

Calayan I.   Babuyan I.
Dalupiri I.   Babuyan
        Islands   Camiguin I.
           Fuga I.
Mayraira Pt.   *Babuyan Channel*

O C E A N

Bangui
Bacarra Claveria   Santa Ana
San Nicolas Laoag Kabugao Gonzaga
Batac Abulug Aparri Gattaran

18

C

Cabugao Tuao Tuguegarao
Vigan Bangued
Santa 2360
  Maria Ilagan
Candon   *Cordillera Central* Mt. Cresta 1685
Tagudin   Bontoc   Santiago Palanan Pt.
Balaoan Roxas   San Mateo   Palanan
San Fernando BATAC Mt. Pulog 2928 Cagayan
Lingayen Solano Santiago Cosiguran *Luzon*
Bolinao HUNDRED Baguio Cordon C. San Ildefonso
Alaminos ISLANDS Rosario Mt. Anacuan 1852

16

P H I L I P P I N E

Lingayen   Dagupan   San Manuel
San Carlos Bayambang San Jose Baler Bay
Santa Cruz Moncada Cuyapo Baler
Masinloc Camiling Victoria AURORA MEMORIAL
Iba 2037 Tarlac La Cabanatuan
Concepcion Paz Gapan Dingalan
1780 Angeles
Mt. Pinatubo San Fernando Polillo Is.
San Antonio   Malabon Patnanongan I.
Olongapo   Caloocan Jomalig I.
  Orani Quezon City
Bataan Manila MANILA Lamon Bay
Mariveles Bay Pasay Santa Cruz Paracale
Cavite   Lucban Labo
Dasmariñas QUEZON Alabat I.
Tagaytay Atimonan Daet Pandan
Nasugbu San Lucena Calauag Viga Catanduanes
Balayan Pablo   BICOL Calabanga San Andres
Lemery Lipa   Lopez Mt. Isarog 1976
Batangas Catanauan Naga Virac
Lubang Lobo Tayabas Bay 1242 Iriga Tabaco Rapu Rapu I.
Is. Verde I. Pass Baac   Nabua Mayon Vol.
C. Calavite Calapan Marin- Ligao Legazpi
Mamburao LAKE duque Donsol Sorsogon
NAUJAN Victoria   Magallanes Gubat
Mindoro Pinamalayan *SIBUYAN* Bulan San Bernardino Str.
Mt. Baco Sablayan Romblon Bulan Irosin Allen
  2487 Bongabong Sibuyan I. Ticao I. Laoang
APO REEF Roxas Tablas I. Aroroy Masbate Mondragon
San Jose Odiongan Mandaon Gamay
Busuanga I. Ilin I. *SEA* Masbate Catarman Arteche
  Oras
Culion I. Calamian Placer Catbalogan Paranas Oras
  Group Pandan Kalibo VISAYAN Bilinan I. Cabiran I. Santa Borongan
Linapacan Str. Roxas SEA Calubian Rita Llorente *Samar*
Linapacan I. Dao Nilar Bantayan Carigara Basey General MacArthur
Cuyo I. Tibiao 2117 Ajuy Calubian Palompon Leyte Tacloban Guiuan
Taytay Bugasong Panay Passi Cadiz Bogo Ormoc Leyte Gulf Homonhon I.
Cuyo Pototan Silay Victorias Tuburan Dulag
Cuyo West Pass San Jose Iloilo Sagay Baybay
Dumaran I. Guimaras Jordan San Carlos Danao Camotes Is.
Palawan Himamaylan La 2460 CENTRAL Mandaue San Juan Dinagat I.
ST PAUL Binalbagan Carlota CEBU Cebu Bato
1593 Kabankalan Sea Carcar Maasin Dinagat
Irahuan Honda Bay Sipalay Argao Bohol Panaon I. Siargao I.
Puerto Princesa Cagayan Is. Hinoba-an Bais RAJAH Surigao Bucas Grande I.
  Tanjay SIKATUNA Carrascal
Mt. Mantalingajan *Negros* Dumaguete BOHOL Cabadbaran Lanuza
  2085 Bayawan Tagbilaran Maliu Jandag
C. Buliluyan Bugsuk I. Siaton Zamboanguita Camiguin I. 2012 Tago
Balabac I. Siquijor I. Talisayan Butuan Bayugan Marihatag
  SEA Nasipit Lianga
Balabac Strait Dapitan Balingasag Hinatuan
Balambangan Bangi Dipolog Iligan Alubilid Cagayan de Oro Bislig
Banggi Manukan Oroquieta Bay Talacogon
Cagayan Sulu I. Sindangan Dpol MT. OZAMIZ Iligan Malaybalay
SABAH Labason Liloy MALINDANG 2938 Marawi City Bunawan
Kudat Sandakan Siocon Pagadian Tubod L. Lanao *Mindanao* Cateel
Langkon Kabasalan Malabang 2815 Tagum
Tenghilan Kota Belud Suba Talan Sibuca Parang Midsayap Baganga
Kota Kinabalu Turtle Is. Olutanga Illana Cotabato Panabo Manay
4101 MALAYSIA Pangutaran Moro Gulf Bay Datu Piang Mt. Apo Pantukan
Papar *Borneo* Group Pilas Zamboanga Talayan 2954 Davao Mati
Keningau Isabela Group Pikit Digos San Isidro
Melalap Tg. Labian Basilan Str. Kalamansig Koronadal Davao
Kuamat Jolo Basilan I. Lamitan Lebak Gulf Malita
Silam Parang Group Samales Palimbang 2083 General
Teluk Darvel Siasi I. Jolo Group Kiamba Santos C. San Agustin
Semporna Tapul Pata I. *CELEBES* Sarangani Bay Tinaca Pt.
Sibutu Tawi-tawi Tapul *Sulu Archipelago* INDONESIA Kep. Talaud Sarangani Is.
Group Group *SEA*

SOUTH

CHINA

SEA

SULU

SEA

Mindoro Strait

Tablas Strait

Sibuyan Sea

Panay

Guimaras Strait

PHILIPPINES

Mindanao Trench 10 497 ▼

TUBBATAHA REEFS

Projection: Lambert's Conformal Conic

East from Greenwich

COPYRIGHT PHILIP'S

National Parks

ft m
9000 3000
6000 2000
4500 1500
3000 1000
1200 400
600 200
0 0
200 600
4000 12 000
8000 24 000
m ft

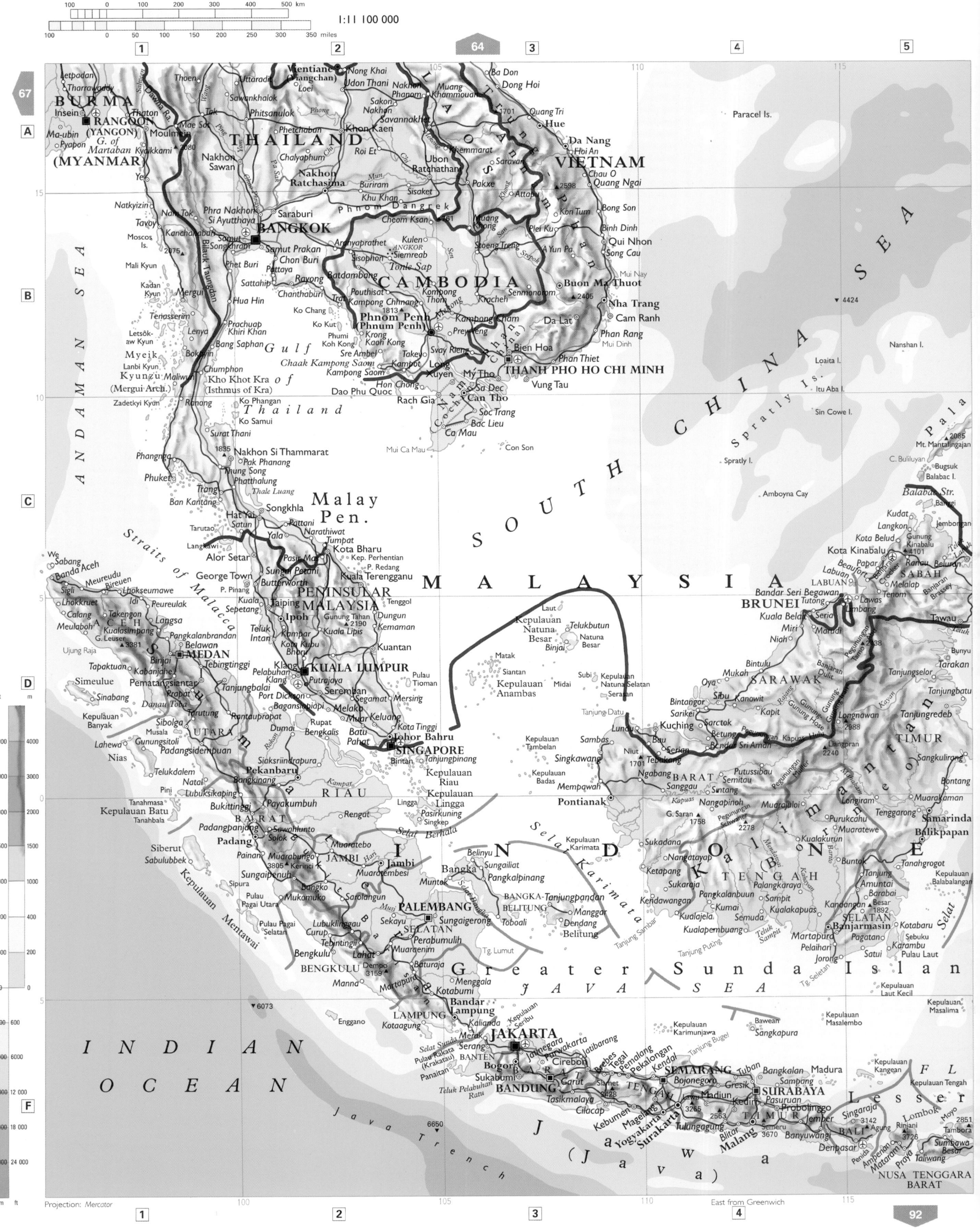

1:11 100 000

Projection: Mercator

East from Greenwich

JAVA AND MADURA
1:6 700 000

50 0 50 100 150 200 250 300 km
50 0 50 100 150 200 miles

BALI
1:1 800 000

10 0 10 20 30 km
10 0 10 20 miles

PHILIPPINE

Claveria · Babuyan Chan. · C. Engaño
Laoag · Bacarra · Aparri · Tuguegarao
Vigan · Bangued · Bayombong · Ilagan · Palanan Pt.
Tuao · 2048 · Solano · Palanan
San Fernando · Angeles · Casiguran
Lingayen G. · Baguio · 2929
Bolinao · Bayombong
Lingayen · Tarlac · 1799 · San Jose · C. San Ildefonso
Dagupan · Cabanatuan
Iba · San Jose · **Luzon**
Mt. Pinatubo · San Fernando · Polillo Is.
Olongapo · QUEZON CITY
Bataan · **MANILA** · Lamon Bay
Manila B. · Cavite · Santa Cruz
Lubang I. · Batangas · Lucena · Daet · Virac
Calatagan · Calauag · Catanduanes
Mamburao · Calapan · Naga · Tabaco · Legazpi · Sorsogon
Mindoro · 2586 · Marinduque · Mayon Volcano · 2462
Busuanga · Sibuyan · Burias · Bulan · Catarmon · Oras
Calamian Group · San Jose · Romblon Is. · Masbate · Samar
Culion · Tablas · Masbate · Calbayog · Taft · General MacArthur
Cuyo Is. · Panay · Roxas · Borongan
Taytay · San Jose de · Buenavista · Pototan · Iloilo · Tacloban · Guiuan
Imurian · Dumaran · Cadiz · Leyte · Baybay
Puerto Princesa · Bacolod · San Carlos · Maasin · Dinagat · 10 497
Negros · Tanjay · Mandaue · **Cebu** · Talibon · Surigao · Siargao
5576 · Dumaguete · Bohol · Tagbilaran · Butuan · Cagayan · Tandag
Dipolog · Oroquieta · de Oro · 2012 · Llanga
Siocon · Ozamis · Iligan · Malaybalay · Cateel · Bagania
Zamboanga · Pagadian · Parang · Tagum · 2804 · Mati
Isabela · Cotabato · Talayan · Davao · 2954 · Digos
Basilan · Lebak · Koronadal · Mt. Apo · C. San Agustin
Jolo · General Santos · 2083 · Kiamba · Malita
Siasi · Samales Group · Saranggani B. · Tinaca Pt.
Tapul Group · 5824 · Sarangani Is.
Tawitawi · Kepulauan Nanusa · Karakelong
Sandakan · Kepulauan Kawio · Karakelong
Semporna · Sibutu · Beo · Kepulauan Talaud · Merir (Palau)
Kepulauan Sangihe · Kaburuang

SULU SEA · **MINDANAO** · Mindanao Trench
CELEBES SEA · **SULU ARCH.** · **PHILIPPINE TRENCH**

JAKARTA · Merak · Bekasi · Karawang · Pamanukan
Anyer · Serang · Kandanghaur · Indramayu · Kepulauan Karimunjawa
Pulau Rakata · Bogor · Purwakarta · Subang · Cirebon · Pekalongan · Kendal · Demak · Kudus · Rembang · Tuban · **Madura**
BANTEN · Rangkasbitung · Cianjur · Sumedang · Kuningan · Brebes · Tegal · Pemalang · Pati · Blora · Bojonegoro · Bangkalan · Sampang · Sumenep
Pelabuhanratu · Sukabumi · **BANDUNG** · Ciamis · Banyumas · Batang · **SEMARANG** · Ngawi · Mojokerto · **SURABAYA** · Pamekasan
Teluk Pelabuhan Ratu · Pengalengan · Garut · Tasikmalaya · Purwokerto · Wonosobo · Salatiga · Madiun · Sidoarjo · Pasuruan
Genteng · Sindangbarang · Cijulang · Cilacap · Kebumen · Magelang · Boyolali · **Surakarta** · 3142 · Kediri · Malang · 3676 · Probolinggo · Bondowoso
Nusa Kambangan · Bantul · **YOGYAKARTA** · Ponorogo · Lawu · Blitar · Semeru · Pasirian · Jember · Banyuwangi
Pacitan · Trenggalek · Tulungagung · Wlingi · Rambipuji
Nusa Barung · Bali

G. BARAT · TENGAH · TIMUR · H · J · K

BALI
Tanjung Batugondang · Singaraja · Kubutambahan · Tejakula
Banyuwangi · Gilimanuk · Gerokgak · Bayun · Tianyar · Songan
Glagah · Cekik · Lovina · Seririt · Kintamani · Batur · Kubu
Jambewangi · Melaya · 1385 · Gunung Merbuk · Busungbiu · Batukau · 2153 · Amed
Beluki · Kabat · Negara · **BALI** · Pupuan · 2276 · Baturiti · Gunung Agung · Tirtagangga
Rogojampi · Srono · Mendoyo · Yehbuah · Belimbing · Tegallalang · Rendang · Saren · **Karangasem (Amlapura)** · **Lombok**
Genteng · Tegalsari · Tjuring · Muncar · Perancak · Pekutan · Pasar · Sembung · Ubud · Bangli · Candi Dasa · Pamenang
Grajagan · Bajatrejo · **Bali** · Tabanan · Sibang · Gianyar · Klungkung · Manggis · Montongbuwoh · Ampenan · **Mataram** · Lembuak
Tanjung Kucur · **Denpasar** · Sukawati · Sanur · Padang · Sampalan · Teluk Terang · Lembar
Jawa · Semenanjung Blambangan · Danginpur · **Kuta** · Jimbaran · Toyapakeh · 530 · Suwana · Gerung
Tanjung Purwo · Uluwatu · **DPS** · Nusa Dua · Bukit Badung · Nusa Penida · Tanjung Abah · Blongas
Tanjung Mebulu · Tanjung Pangga · Tanjung Tampa

17 INDIAN OCEAN 18

PACIFIC OCEAN

Maratua · Tahulandang · Biaro · Doi · Galela · Morotai
Manado · Bangka · Ibu · Jailolo · 1325 · Tobelo · Akelamo
Kema · Mayu · Ternate · **Halmahera** · Kepulauan Asia · Kepulauan Mapia
Amurang · Kotamobagu · **UTARA** · Tidore · Teluk Buli · Kepulauan Ayu · Waigeo
GORONTALO · Tilamuta · Gorontalo · Makian · Teluk Weda · Patani · Waibeem · Manokwari · Supiori · Biak
Teluk Tomini · Kayoa · Wosi · Umera · Sorong · Salawati · 2452 · Kwoka · Kaironi · Numfoor · Warsa · Bosnik
Donggala · Poh · Peleng · Kepulauan Bacan · Gani · Batanta · Selat Sorong · Jazirah Doberai · Ransiki · Wariap · Biak · Padaido
Palu · Toboli · **TENGAH** · Luwuk · Banggai · Obilatu · Bisa · Misool · Kofiau · Sailolo · Seget · Teminabuan · 2926 · Wasior · Yapen · Bonoi · Sarmi
Tojo · 2630 · Kolonodale · Kepulauan Banggai · Kawasi · Sesepe · Fluk · Kepulauan Sula · Adua · Inanwatan · Bintuni · Nabire · Kumamba
Lariang · Danau Poso · Poso · Todeli · Mangole · Sanana · Teluk Berau · Fakfak · Kokas · Wenut · Susunu · Waghete · Enarotali · Ansudu
SULAWESI (Celebes) · Mamasa · Malili · Taliabu · Buru · 2736 · Piru · Wahai · **Seram (Ceram)** · Waru · Kwatisore · Genyem · Jayapura
SELATAN · Makale · Mekongga · Kendari · Namlea · Tifu · 3019 · Amahai · Saparua · Weri · Ibonma · Karufa · **Pegunungan Van Rees** · Sentani
Palopo · Mondeodo · Manui · Wamulan · Kayeli · Namrole · Lima · Ambon · Geser · Karubaga · Teluk Kamrau · **PAPUA** · Krau
Majene · Singkang · Kolaka · Monse · Wowoni · **MALUKU** · Kepulauan Gorong · Manggawitu · Adi · **Pegunungan Maoke** · Wamena
Parepare · Pampanua · Buapinang · Buton · Kepulauan Banda · Kepulauan Watubela · Uta · Tembagapura · Trikora · 4730
Pangkajene · Watampone · Pising · Raha · Lawele · Bandanaira · 4702 · Mandala · Oksibil
Ujung Pandang · Lompobatang · Muna · Baubau · Wangiwangi · Tual · Kai Besar · Gumzai · Agats · Mindiptana
2871 · Bulukumba · Kabaena · Binongko Tukangbesi · 7440 · Kai Kecil · Dobo · Wokam · Sewer · Pirimapun · Tanahmerah
Bantaeng · Benteng · Batuata · Kepulauan Kai · Wangal · Rebi · Kepulauan Aru · Gomogomo · Kepi
Salayar · Kepulauan Bonerate · 5888 · Gunungapi · Nila · Serua · Molu · Trangan · Tafermaar · Pulau Dolak · Bade · Muting
Tanahjampea · Bonerate · Damar · Teun · Daya · Wuliaru · Larat · Kepulauan Tanimbar · Tanjung Ngabordamlu · Kimaam · Okaba
Sunda Is. · Kalaotoa · Wesiri · Romang · Barat · Tepa · Babar · Selu · Alusi · Saumlaki · Kimaan · Komoran · Merauke
FLORES SEA · BANDA SEA · ARAFURA SEA · PAPUA NEW GUINEA

Sumbawa · Sangeang · 5123 · Wetar · Ilwaki · Kisar · Moa · Lakor · Elase · Sermata · Masela · Tanjung Vals
Bima · Raba · Komodo · Rinca · Labuanbajo · Ruteng · **Flores** · 2350 · Aimere · Ende · Alor · Kalabahi · Pantar · Baucau · Tutuala · Viqueque · Nikiniki
Pa-ado · Sumba · 2371 · Maumere · Solor · Adonara · Lomblen · Larantuka · **Dili · EAST TIMOR** · Atapupu · Kefamenanu
Selat Sumba · Membora · **NUSA TENGGARA TIMUR** · Macas · Pante · Atambua · 2963
Waikabubak · Waingapu · Sawu · **Sawu Sea** · Kupang · Roti
Woikelo · Baing · Melolo · Raijua · Dana · Baa

EQUATOR · **94**

1:5 300 000

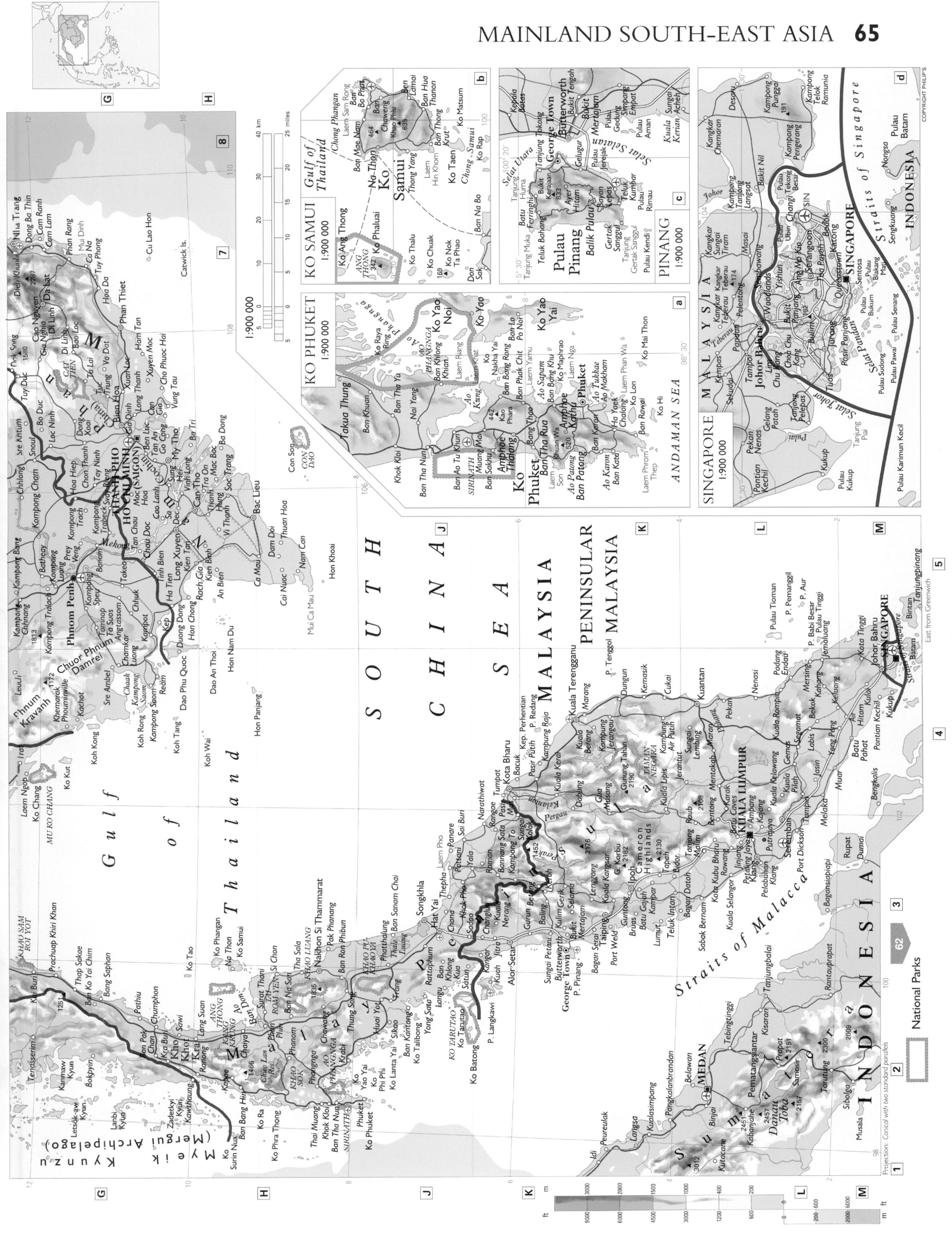

COPYRIGHT PHILIPS

Gulf of Thailand

KO SAMUI
1:900 000

ANG THONG

Ko Samui

KO PHUKET
1:900 000

Ko Phangnga

Ko Yao Noi

Ko Yao Yai

ANDAMAN SEA

Takua Thung

Ko Phuket

PINANG
1:900 000

George Town

Pulau Pinang

Straits of Singapore

SINGAPORE
1:900 000

MALAYSIA

SINGAPORE

Johor Bahru

INDONESIA

Selat Johor

G

H

SOUTH

CHINA

SEA

Gulf

of

Thailand

MU KO CHANG

MALAYSIA

PENINSULAR MALAYSIA

KUALA LUMPUR

Straits of Malacca

Straits of Singapore

SINGAPORE

INDONESIA

Phnum Kravanh

Chuor Phnum Damrei

HO CHI MINH (SAIGON)

Phnom Penh

Mekong

Kyunzu (Mergui Archipelago)

Myeik (Mergui Archipelago)

Sumatera

Danau Toba

MEDAN

National Parks

Projection: Conical with two standard parallels

East from Greenwich

62

1 2 3 4 5

m ft

1:8 900 000

Projection: Conical with two standard parallels

Continuation Southwards
on same scale

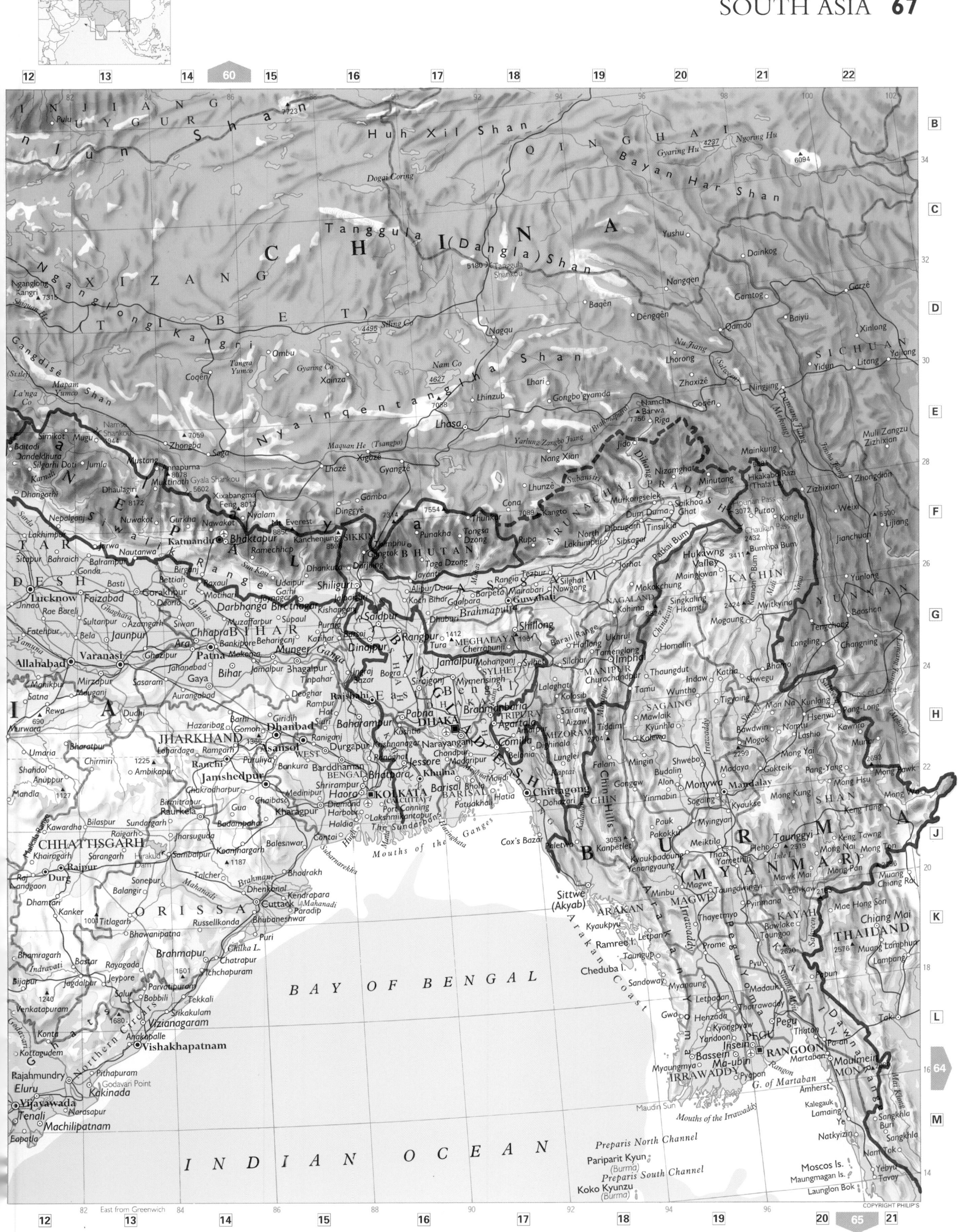

BAY OF BENGAL

INDIAN OCEAN

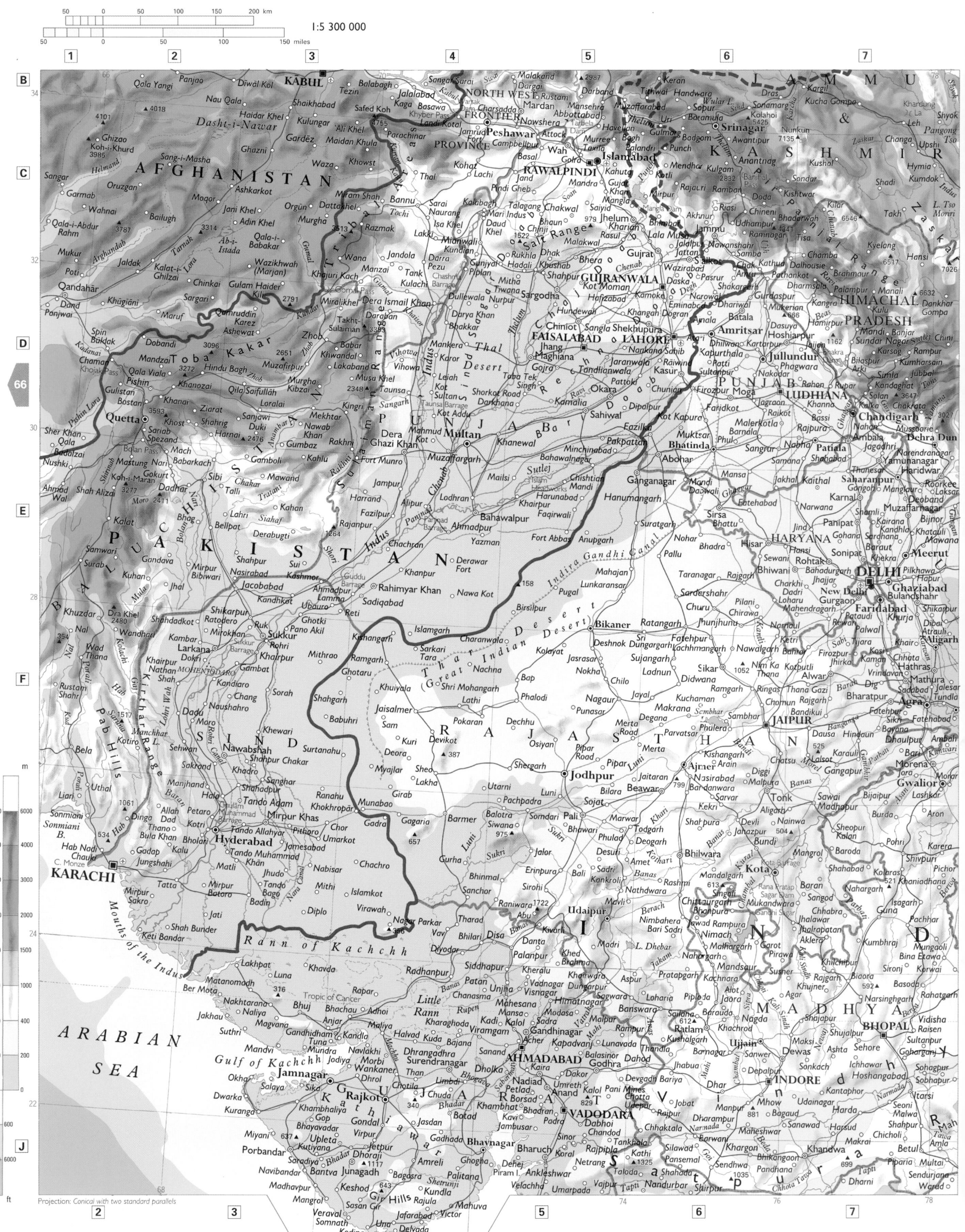

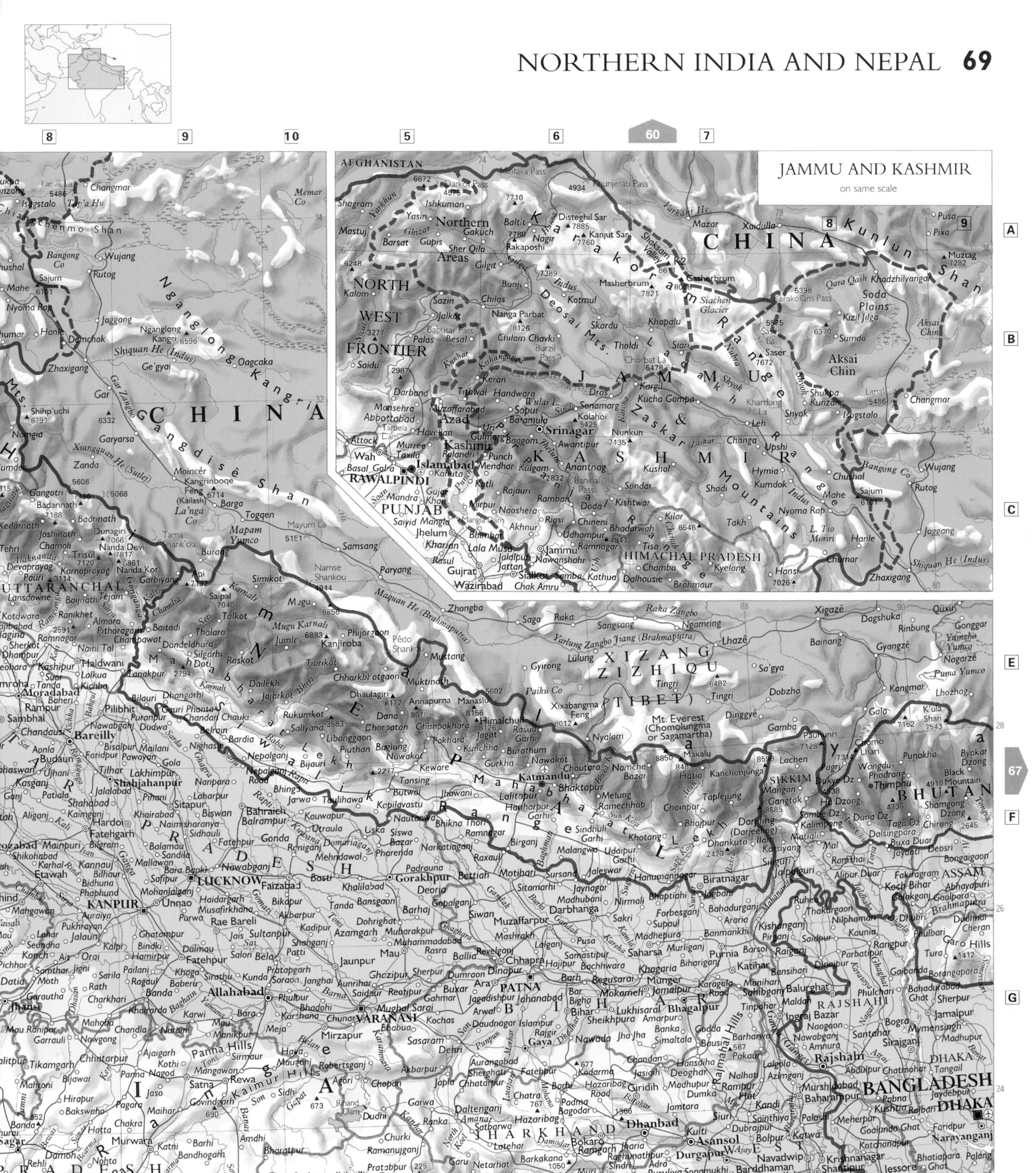

JAMMU AND KASHMIR
on same scale

50 0 50 100 150 200 250 300 km
50   0   50   100   150   200 miles

1:6 200 000

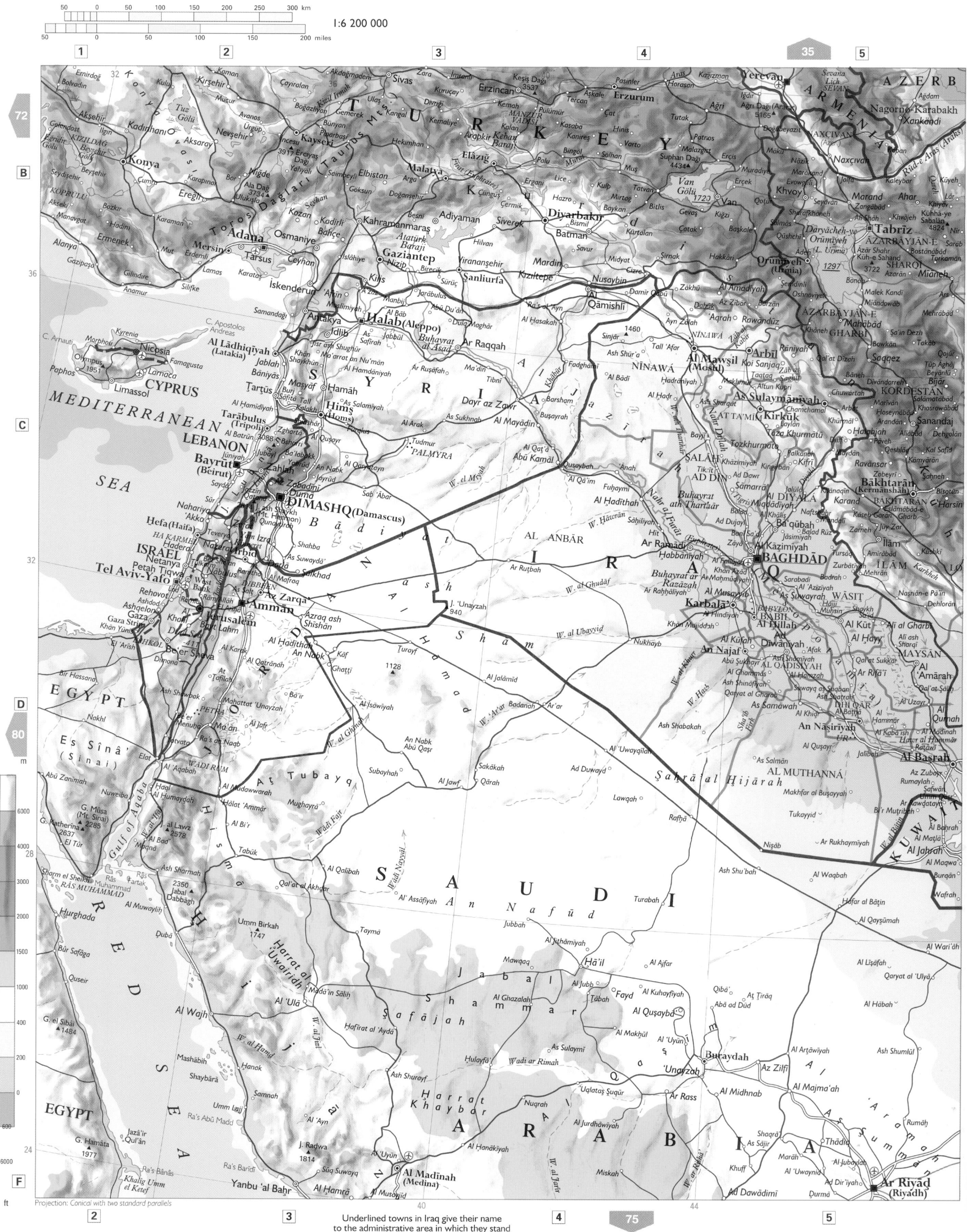

Underlined towns in Iraq give their name
to the administrative area in which they stand

TURKMENISTAN
Kara Kum
Kopet Dagh
CASPIAN SEA
IRAN
Dasht-e Kavīr
Dasht-e Lūt
Reshteh-ye Kūhhā-ye Alborz
Zāgros
AFGHANISTAN
PAKISTAN
PERSIAN GULF
Gulf of Oman
UNITED ARAB EMIRATES
OMAN
QATAR
BAHRAIN
Ashgabat
TEHRĀN
Mashhad
Eşfahān
Shīrāz
Yazd
Kermān
Zāhedān
Herāt
Bandar-e Abbās
Abū Ẓaby (Abu Dhabi)
Dubayy (Dubai)
Ad Dawḩah (Doha)
Al Kuwayt (Kuwait)
BAKI (Baku)
Str. of Hormuz
Tropic of Cancer
East from Greenwich
COPYRIGHT PHILIP'S

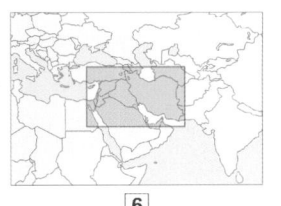

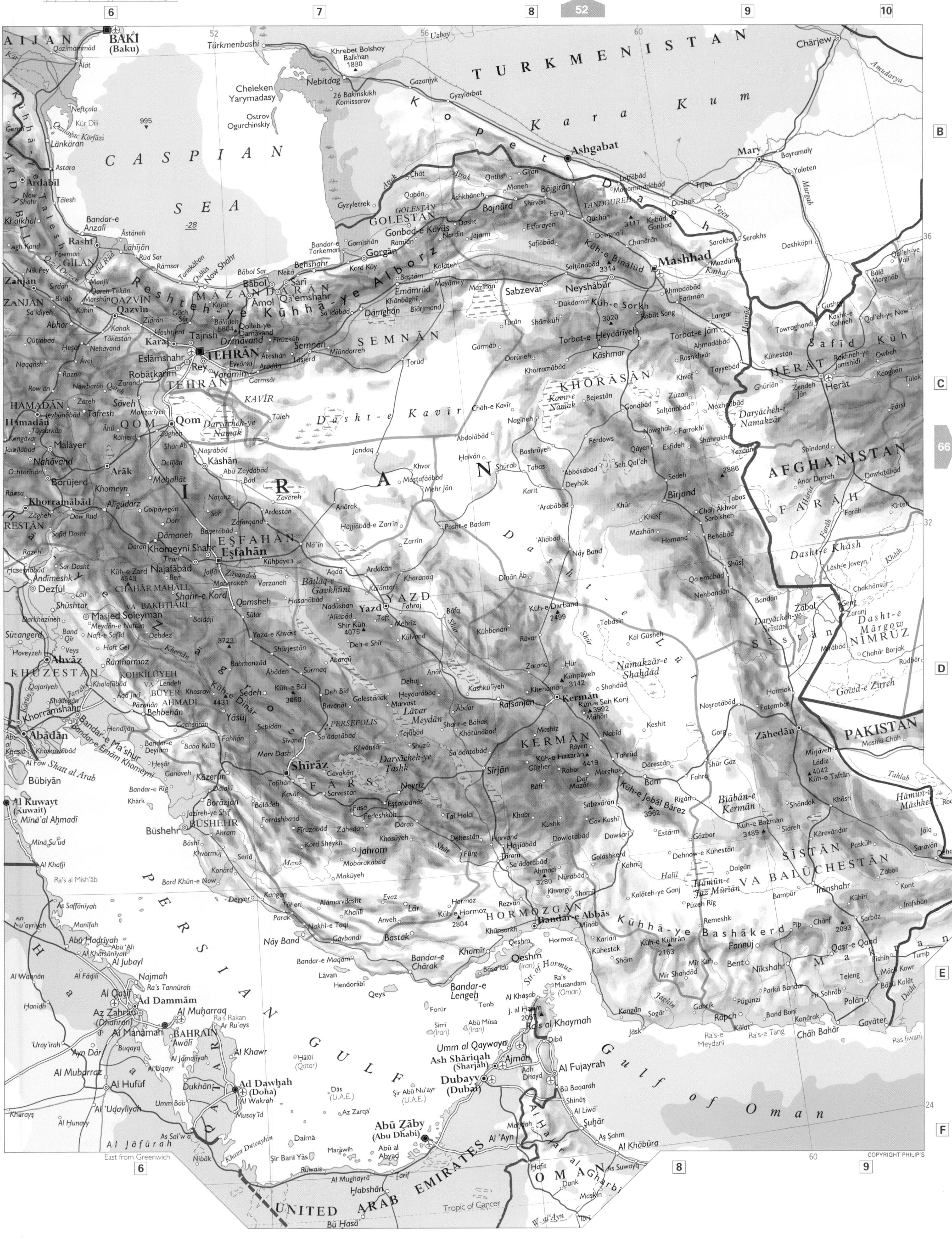

1: 4 400 000

50 0 25 50 75 100 125 150 175 km

50 0 25 50 75 100 125 miles

| 1 | 2 | 3 | 4 | 33 | 5 | 6 | 7 |

BULGARIA

B L A C K   S E A

A

Stara Zagora · Aytos · Burgas
Yambol · Nos Emine
Elkhovo · Michurin

B

Kırklareli · İğneada Burnu
Edirne · Pınarhisar · Vize · Saray · Çerkezköy
Orestiás · Babaeski · Lüleburgaz
Uzunköprü · Hayrabolu · Muratlı · Çatalca
İstanbul Boğazı (Bosporus)
Kilimli · Zonguldak · Ereğli · Kozlu · Çaycuma
Amasra · Cide · İnebolu · Abana · Ayancık · Sinop · Gerze
Kerempe Burnu · İnce Burun · Bafra Burnu · Civa Burnu
Bartın · Küre · Kastamonu · Taşköprü · Daday
Karabük · Safranbolu · Araç
Samsun · Terme · Ünye · Persembe

İSTANBUL · Kocaeli (İzmit) · Sakarya (Adapazarı)
Kartal · Gebze · Darıca · Gölcük · Hendek · Düzce · Bolu
Şile · Kandıra · Karasu · Akçakoca · Devrek · Gerede · Çerkeş
Amasya · Çarşamba · Kavak
Merzifon · Havza · Ladik · Tekke
Gümüşhacıköy · Suluova · Turhal

Marmara Denizi (Sea of Marmara)
Tekirdağ · Şarköy · Mudanya · Bandırma
Bursa · İznik Gölü · İnegöl · Uludağ 2543

ANKARA · Kırıkkale · Kalecik · Elmadağ
Eskişehir · Bozüyük · Bilecik · Söğüt
Kütahya · Tavşanlı · Emet

C

Lésvos · Manisa · Akhisar · Demirci · Gediz · Simav · Uşak
Balıkesir · Soma · Bergama · Bigadiç
Ak Dağ · Sivas · Yozgat · Sorgun
Kırşehir · Nevşehir · Kayseri
İzmir (Smyrna) · Menemen · Salihli · Alaşehir · Banaz · Afyon (Afyonkarahisar)
Çeşme · Urla · Torbalı · Ödemiş · Sandıklı

D

Söke · Aydın · Nazilli · Denizli · Isparta
Burdur · Eğirdir Gölü · Beyşehir Gölü · Konya
Ereğli · Karaman · Niğde · Bor
Muğla · Fethiye · Antalya · Manavgat · Alanya
Marmaris · Datça · Köyceğiz · Dalaman
Kahramanmaraş · Gaziantep · Nizip
Adana · Tarsus · Mersin (İçel) · Osmaniye
İskenderun · Antakya · **HALAB (Aleppo)**

GREECE
Ródhos (Rhodes) · Kárpathos · Kásos

Antalya Körfezi

MEDITERRANEAN SEA

CYPRUS
Nicosia · Kyrenia · Morphou · Famagusta · Larnaca
Troodos 1951 · Limassol · Paphos · Episkopi

E

Al Lādhiqīyah (Latakia) · Jablah · Baniyās
Hamāh · Tartūs · Himş (Homs)
S Y (RIA)

F

Tarābulus (Tripoli) · **LEBANON**
BAYRŪT (Beirut) · Saydā · Zahlah
DIMASHQ (Damascus)

G

ISRAEL · Hefa (Haifa) · Nazerat · Netanya
Tel Aviv-Yafo · West Bank
Jerusalem · **AMMAN** · **JORDAN** · Az Zarqā

| 80 | 3 | 4 | 5 | 74 | 6 | 7 |

Projection: Conical with two standard parallels

- - - Division between Greeks and Turks in Cyprus; Turks to the North.

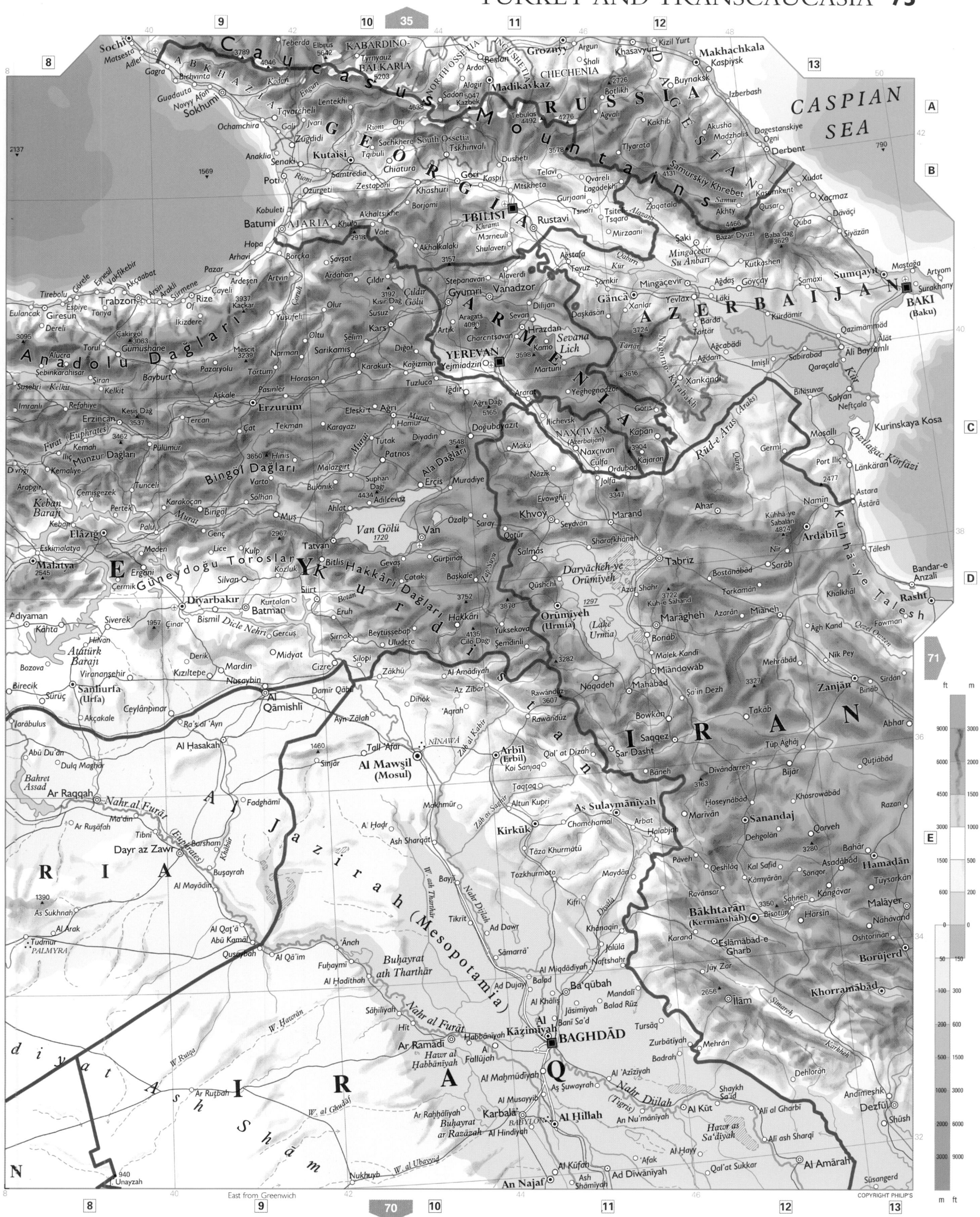

10 0 10 20 30 40 50 60 70 80 100 km

10 0 10 20 30 40 50 60 miles

1:2 200 000

CYPRUS

Paphos
Episkopi
Limassol
Akrotiri Bay
Episkopi Bay
C. Gata

M E D I T E R R A N E A N

S E A

Al Ḥamīdīyah
Ḥims (Homs)
Shinshār
Furqlus
Kalakh
Halbā
Al Qusayr
Al Mīnā'
ASH SHAMĀL
Ṭarābulus (Tripoli)
Zgharta
Al Ḥirmil
HIMS
Qurnat as Sawdā' 3088
Al Buḍayj 2464
Al Qaryatayn
Al Baṭrūn
Bsharri
Jubayl
Qarṭabā
Al Labwah
Bi'r Ghadīr
Ibrāhīm
AL BIQĀ'
2616
Ba'labakk
Yabrūd
An Nabk

BAYRŪT (Beirut)
'Alayḥ
2628
J. Sannīn
Sirghāyā
SYRIA
Ash Shuwayfāt
Ad Dāmūr
JABAL LUBNĀN
Zaḥlah
Ḥawsh
Al Qutayfah
Dūmā
Khān Abū Shāmat
LEBANON
1942
J. al Bārūk
Az Zabadānī
DIMASHQ
DIMASHQ (Damascus)
DAM
Saydā (Sidon)
Jazzīn
Ash Shaykh (Mt. Hermon) 2814
Dārayyā
Al Hājānah
An Nabaṭīyah at Taḥtā
Marj 'Uyūn
Al Kiswah
Burāq
AL JANŪB
Ṣūr (Tyre)
Qiryat Shemona
Al Qunayṭirah
As Sanamayn
AS SAFĀ
Naharīyya
Me'ona
1157
Ar Rafīd
DAR'Ā
'Akko (Acre)
Ḥagalil
Zefat
Fiq
Shaykh Miskīn
Izra'
Shahbā
JABAL AD DURŪZ
Mifraẓ Ḥefa
Qiryat Karmi'el
HAZAFON
Yam Kinneret -210
Saham al Jawlān
Der'ā
AS SUWAYDĀ
Ḥefa (Haifa)
Qiryat Ata
Teverya (Tiberias)
1600
As Suwaydā
Sālah
Ḥaifn
Nazerat (Nazareth)
Yarmūk
IRBID
Dāliyat el Karmel
HA KARMEL
Afula
Tayiba
'Ajlūn
Der'ā
Malaḥ
Salkhad
TEL MEGIDDO
Umm el Faḥm
Jenīn
Bet She'an
J. Umm ad Daraj
Al Mafraq
Umm al Qittayn
CAESAREA
ISRAEL
Hadera
Ḥanna-Karkur
SHOMRON
SAMARIA
Ṭūbās
'AJLŪN 1247
Jarash
AL MAFRAQ
Pardes
Netanya
Tulkarm
Nābulus
N. az Zarqā
Herzliyya
HAMERKAZ
Kefar Sava
W. al Fār'ā
JARASH
Benē Beraq
Petah Tiqwa
SHILO
AL BALQĀ'
Tel Aviv-Yafo
Ramat Gan
As Salṭ
Az Zarqā
Bat Yam
West Bank
Wādī as Sīr
AMMĀN
Rishon le Ziyyon
Lod
Azraq ash Shīshān
Yavne
Ramla
Rām Allāh
Karama
AMM
AZ ZARQĀ
Rehovot
El Arīḥā (Jericho)
Naẓir
'AMMĀN
Ashdod
-289
At Tunayb
Qiryat Mal'akhi
Bet Shemesh
Jerusalem (Yerushalayim) (Al Quds)
Ma'daba
Ashqelon
Qiryat Gat
Bayt Laḥm (Bethlehem)
MA'DABA
W. Ḥaydān
Gaza
TEL
Al Khalīl (Hebron)
Dhībān
Gaza Strip
N. Shiqma
Sederot
Az Ẓāhirīya
Arad
Al Karak
Khān Yūnis
Be'er Sheva (Beersheba)
Sedom
1305
Al Mazār
Rafaḥ
ESHKOL
AL KARAK
El Daheir
-411
Bor Mashash
W. al Ḥasā
W. Bā'ir
Bûr Sa'îd (Port Said)
Dimona
W. al Ghadaf
Bûr Fu'ad
Rås Burûn
Sabkhet el Bardawîl
El 'Arîsh
HADAROM
-335
AT ṬAFĪLAH
Khalig el Tîna
Bi'r el 'Abd
-121
Bā'ir
Râmâni
Bîr Qaṭia
W. 'Arîsh
Bîr Lahfân
Qezi'ot
JORDAN
Bîr el Duweidar
Bîr el Garârât
Birein
At Ṭafīlah
El Qantara
Bîr el Jafir
Sedé Boqér
Nijil
Mahaṭṭa 'Unayzah
Wâhid
Bîr Madkûr
Ismâ'ilîya
Talâta
Muweilih
Mizpe Ramon
Rujm Tal'at al Jamā'ah 1738
Ash Shawmari
ISMÂ'ILÎYA
Khamsa
SHAMĀL SÎNÎ
El Quseima
PETRA
El Buheirat el Murrat el Kubra (Bitter Lakes)
Bîr Hasana
H a n e g e v
Wādī Mūsā
Al Jafr
Qa'el Jafr
Gineifa
G. Yi 'Allaq 1094
Bîr Beiḍa
N. Paran
Ma'ān
892
El 'Agrûd
892
MA'ĀN
EGYPT
Bîr el Thamâda
W. el Brûk
El Quṣeima
N. Ḥiyyon
Bîr al Mārī
El Suweis (Suez)
Bûr Taufîq
Bîr Gebeil Hisn
W. Maḥasham
Ra's an Naqb
Adabiya
Uyûn Mûsa
Nakhl
'En 'Evrona
Ain Sudr
AL 'AQABAH
Mahaṭṭat ash Shīdīyah
948
G. el Kabrit
El Thamad
Bîr al Buṭayyḥāt
Bîr al Qaṭṭār
SÎNÂ (Sinai)
Yotvata
El Wabeira
Ghubbet el Bûs
Gebel el Tîh
1435
Ra's an Naqb
1272
JANŪB SÎNÎ
Elat
1592
1754
WADI RUM
SAUDI
EL SUWEIS
Bîr el Biârât
Bîr el Taba
Rum
Baṭn al Ghūl
ARABIA
Bîr Abu Şandûq
Bîr el Heisi
Al 'Aqaba
At Tubayq
1165
1754
Al Mudawwarah
Haql

Projection: Polyconic

East from Greenwich

COPYRIGHT PHILIP'S

═══ 1974 Cease Fire Lines

☐ National Parks

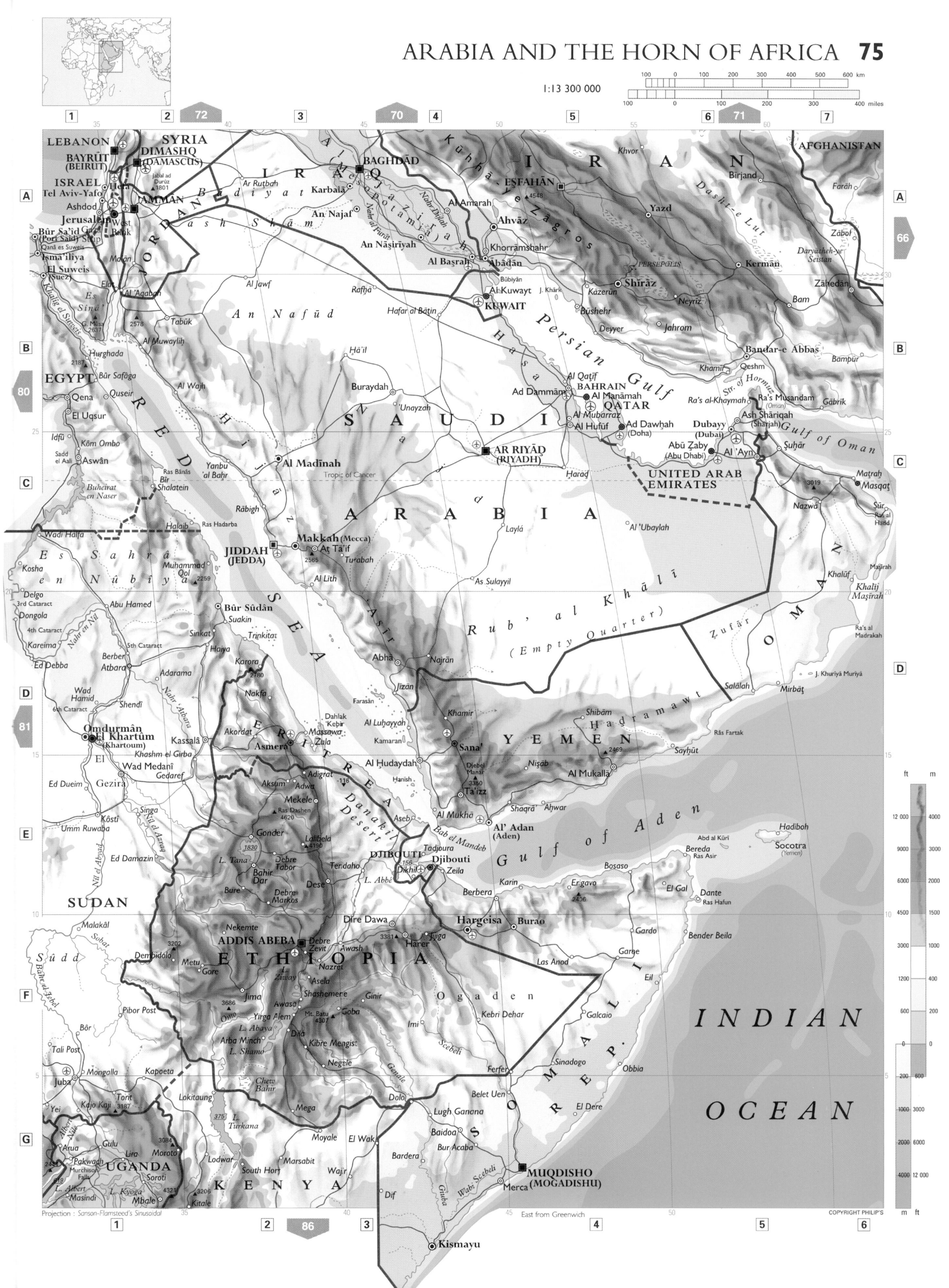

1:13 300 000

Projection : Sanson-Flamsteed's Sinusoidal

East from Greenwich

COPYRIGHT PHILIP'S

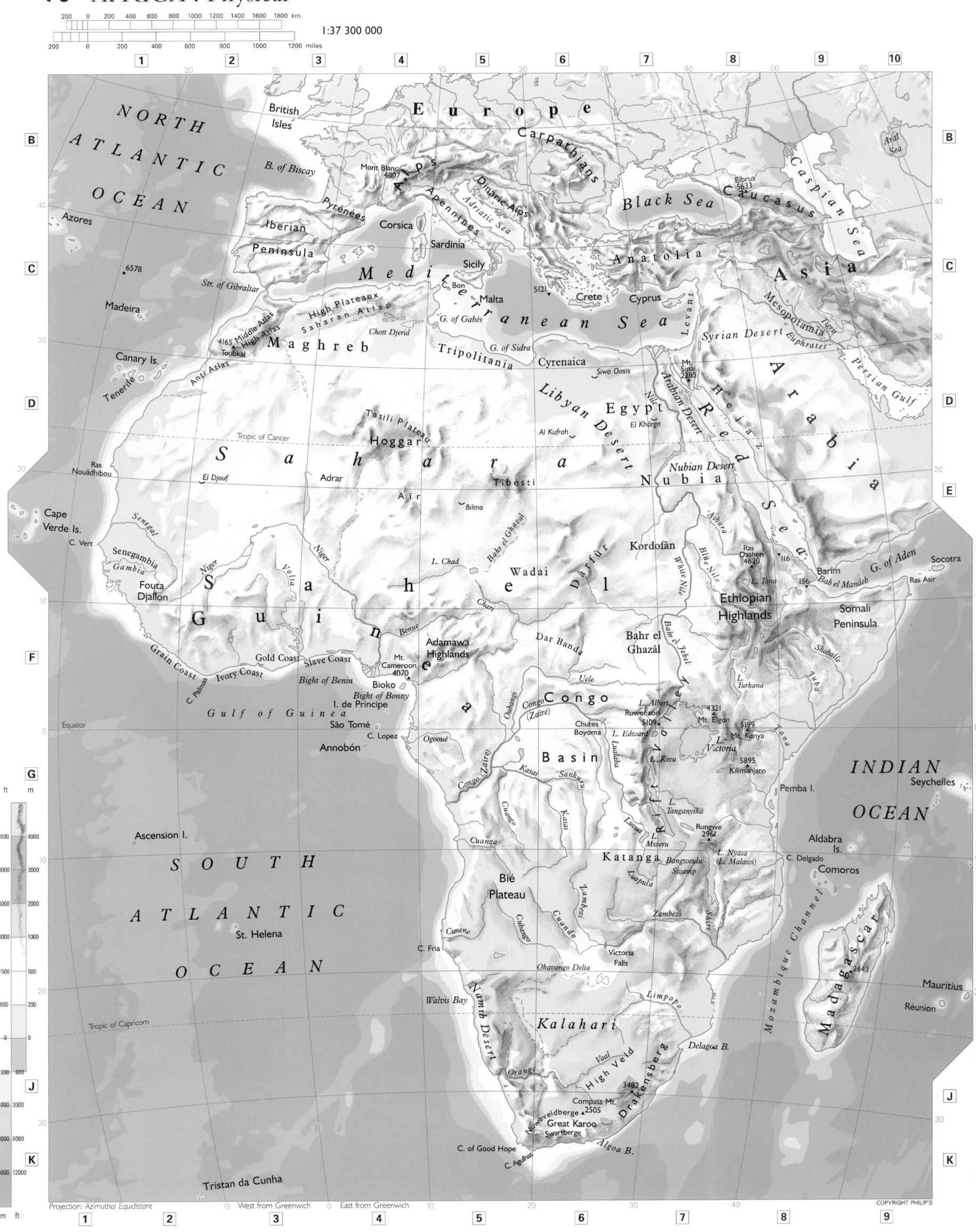

1:37 300 000

Projection: Azimuthal Equidistant

COPYRIGHT PHILIP'S

1:37 300 000

● Dakar Capital Cities

100   0   100   200   300   400   500   600 km

1:13 300 000

100   0   100   200   300   400 miles

1 | **2** | **3** | **4** | **5** | **6** | **7**

Azores
(Port.)

A T L A N T I C

SPAIN
Cabo de
São Vicente
Cádiz   **Málaga**   Almería
Str. of Gibraltar   Gibraltar (U.K.)
Tanger   Ceuta (Sp.)
Tétouan   Al Hoceima
Melilla (Sp.)
Ksar el Kebir   Nador
Kenitra   Taza
Salé
Rabat   **Fès**
Meknès
Khemisset
CASABLANCA
El Jadida   Khouribga
Settat   Beni Mellal
Safi
Ras Beddouza
Marrakech
Essaouira
Dj. Toubkal
4165▲
C. Rhir   Taroudannt
Agadir

ALGER
(ALGIERS)   Blida
Tizi-
Ouzou   Bejaia
Skikda   Annaba
Ech Cheliff   Constant
Mostaganem   Médéa   M'sila   Sétif
Oran   Mascara   Tiaret   Batna
Sidi-bel-Abbès   Chott el Hodna   Khenchela
Tlemcen   Aflou   Messad   Biskra   2328▲
Oujda   Chott ech Chergui   El Bayadh   Djelfa
Aïn-Sefra   Laghouat   Tozeur
Figuig   Berriane   El Oued
Béchar   Ghardaïa   Ouargla   Hassi Messaoud
Abadla   El Goléa   Grand Erg Oriental

MOROCCO
Khouribga   Moyen Atlas   Haut Atlas
Ar Rachidiya
Ouarzazate
2359▲   Anti Atlas
Ifni
Goulimine
Tan-tan

Madeira
(Port.)   Funchal
Porto Santo

O C E A N

ALGERIA

Kerzaz   Timimoun   Ohanet
Plateau du Tademaït
Bordj Fly   In Salah   Bordj Omar Driss
Ste. Marie
Zaouiet   Illizi
Reggane
Ouallene   Arak   2158▲
Tassili n Ajjer
Bordj-in-Eker   Djanet

Tarfaya
El Aaiún
Smara
Bu Craa
C. Bojador
Ain Ben Tili
Chegga
Erg Iguidi
Erg Chech   A h a g g a r
Tahat
2918▲
Tamanrasset

Islas Canarias
(Sp.)
Lanzarote
La Palma
Santa Cruz
de Tenerife   Arrecife
Gomera   3718▲   Fuerteventura
Tenerife   Las
Hierro   Palmas
Gran
Canaria
C. Juby

WESTERN

Dakhla

SAHARA

Tropic of Cancer

Zouîrat
Fdérik

El Djouf

S a h a r a

Taoudenni

Tanezrouft

Adrar
598▲
Tessalit
Adrar
des Iforas

Tenere

 Râs Nouâdhibou   Nouâdhibou
Atâr   Chinguetti
Akjoujt   Adrar
Râs Timirist   Rachid   Tidjikja
Nouakchott
MAURITANIA
Aoukâr

Arlit
Iférouâne
Agadez
1900▲

N I G

SAHEL
Tombouctou   Niger   Bourem
Gao   Ansongo   Ménaka
Hombori
Famalé
Tahoua
Tanout

12 000   4000
9000   3000
6000   2000
4500   1500
3000   1000
1200   400
600   200
0   0
200   600
1000   3000
2000   6000
4000   12000
m   ft

Nema
Tichit
'Ayoûn el 'Atroûs
Néma

St. Louis
Dagana   Kaédi   Kiffa
Rosso   Senegal   Matam
Mboro   Louga   Linguère   Sélibabi
C. Thiès   Tivaouane   Bakel   Nara   Nioro du Sahel
Vert   Kayes
DAKAR   Kaolack   Tambacounda   Bafoulabé
SENEGAL   Janjanbareh   Kita
Banjul   **GAMBIA**
Ziguinchor   Sédhiou   Gaoual   Labé
GUINEA   Satadougou
BISSAU   Fouta
Bissau   Diallon   Bafing   Siguiri
Arq. dos   Dabola
Bijagós   **G U I N E A**
C. Verga   Kindia   Dalaba   Dabola
Dubréka   Mamou   Faranah   Kankan
Conakry   Kabala   Kissidougou   Fabala
Port Loko   **SIERRA**   Kenema   Koro
Freetown   **LEONE**   Yonibana   Nzérékoré
Sherbro I.   Bonthe   Sanniquellie   Man
Sulima   Yekepa   Ghonta   Danané   Duékoué
Gbanga   Tapeta   Tabou

Diafarabé
Mopti   Dori
Ségou   Tougan   Kaya   Birni Nkonni   Zinder
San   **BURKINA**
Bamako   Sikasso   **Ouagadougou**   Dosso
Bobo   **FASO**   Fada-N-   **Niamey**   Maradi
Dioulasso   Koudougou   Gourma   Gaya   Katsina
Gaoua   Bawku   Dapaong   Birnin Kebbi   Gusau
Tingréla   Tumu   Mango   Jega   **Kano**
Odienné   Korhogo   Natitingou   Kontagora   Funtua
Boundiali   Bouna   Bembéréké   Kaduna
Ferkéssédougou   Kong   Savelugu   Parakou   Minna   Jos
Katiola   Bondoukou   Tamale   Bida   **Abuja**   Kafanchan
IVORY   Salaga   Sokodé   Shaki   Ilorin   Keffi   Lafia
Bouaké   Wenchi   Lake   Ogbomosho   Bida   Makurdi
Séguéla   Berekum   Volta   Oyo   Oshogbo   Offa
COAST   Kumasi   Abomey   **Ibadan**   Ikare   Benin
Bouaflé   Obuasi   Koforidua   Ife   Ilesha   Owo   City
Yamoussoukro   Asamankese   Abeokuta   Akure
Divo   Agboville   **Lomé**   **Porto-Novo**
Gagnoa   Adzopé   Tema   Cotonou   **LAGOS**
ABIDJAN   **Accra**   Onitsha
Grand   Cape Coast
Bassam   Sekondi-Takoradi
Axim   Slave
C. Three Points   Coast
Gold   Bight of
Coast   Benin

GHANA   **TOGO**   **NIGERIA**
Black Volta   Volta   Lake Volta
White Volta

Port Harcourt   Calabar
Aba
Uyo   Bamenda
Warri   CA
Buru   Mt. Cameroun   Dou
4070▲
Rey Malabo
Bioko   Limbe
2850▲

LIBERIA
Grain Coast
Monrovia
Buchanan
River   San Pédro
Cess   Harper
C. Palmas
Daloa   Sassandra
Lakota
Soubré   Tabou

West from Greenwich   0   East from Greenwich

Projection : Sanson-Flamsteed's Sinusoidal

2 | **3** | **4** | **5** | **6** | **7**

MEDITERRANEAN SEA
GREECE
TURKEY
CYPRUS
SYRIA
LEBANON
IRAQ
ISRAEL
JORDAN
SAUDI ARABIA
LIBYA
EGYPT
SUDAN
CHAD
CENTRAL AFRICAN REPUBLIC
ERITREA
ETHIOPIA
TUNISIA
Sahara
Sicilia
MALTA
Valletta
Kriti
Iráklion
Ródhos
Antalya
ADANA
HALAB
Antakya
Al Lādhiqiyah
Nicosia
Ḩimş
Tarābulus
BAYRŪT (BEIRUT)
DIMASHQ (DAMASCUS)
Jabal ad Durūz 1801
Ar Rutbah
Bādiyat ash Shām
Haifa
Tel Aviv-Yafo
Ashdod
Jerusalem
'AMMĀN
West Bank
Ma'ān
Nahr al Furāt
Bizerte
CARTHAGE
Ariana
TUNIS
Béja
Nabeul
Sousse
Kairouan
Mahdia
Gafsa
Sfax
Golfe de Gabès
Gabès
Île de Djerba
Médenine
Zarzis
Zuwārah
Tarābulus (Tripoli)
Tatahouine
Az Zāwiyah
Al Khums
Misrātah
Gharyān
968
Dehibat
Mizdah
Tripolitania
Daraj
Ghudāmis
Surt
Khalīj Surt
Banghāzī
Zāwiyat al Baydā
Darnah
Al Marj
Sulūq
Tubruq
Bardiyah
Salūm
Ajdābiya
Cyrenaica
Al Jaghbūb
Awjilah
Hūn
Zillah
Idehan Awbārī
Brach
Sabhah
Awbārī
Marzūq
Fezzan
Ghat
Al Qaţrūn
Wāw al Kabīr
1200
Şahrā' Rebiana
Al Jawf
Al Kufrah
Şahrâ' Lîbîya
EL ISKANDARÎYA (ALEXANDRIA)
Marsā Matrûh
El Alamein
Sîwa
Munkhafed el Qattâra
-133
El Mahalla el Kubra
Damanhûr
Dumyât
Bûr Sa'îd
Tanta
Zagazig
El Mansûra
Qanâ es Suweis
Ismâ'iliya
EL GÎZA
EL QÂHIRA (CAIRO)
El Suweis
Helwân
El Faiyûm
Beni Suef
Maghâgha
El Minyâ
Mallawi
Manfalût
Asyût
Tahta
Sohâg
Girga
Qena
THEBES
KARNAK
El Uqsur
Es Sahrâ Esh Sharqîya
Nahr en Nîl
Khalîg el Suweis
Es Sinâ'
G. Mûsa 2637
Elat
Al 'Aqabah
2578
Tabūk
Al Muwaylih
Hurghada
Bûr Safâga
Quseir
Qasr Farâfra
Mût
El Wâhât el-Dakhla
El Khârga
El Wâhât el-Khârga
Idfû
Kom Ombo
Aswân
Sadd el Aali
Buheirat en Naser
ABU SIMBEL
RED SEA
Al Wajh
Hijaz
Yanbu 'al Bahr
Rābigh
Ras Bânâs
Bîr Shalatein
Halaib
Ras Hadarba
1082
J. Uweinat 1893
Ma'ţan as Sarra
Aozou Strip
Tummo
Madama
Bardai
Aozou
Pic Toussidé 3265
3150 Tarso Emissi
Tibesti
Zouar
Emi Koussi 3415
Chirfa
Bilma
Fachi
Grand Erg du Bilma
Borkou
Faya-Largeau
Ounianga Sérir
Dépression du Mourdi
Fada
Ennedi
1310
Erg du Djourab
Zagaoua
Oum Chalouba
Wadi Halfa
El Wâhât el Selîma
Es Sahrâ en Nûbîya
Kosha
Delgo
3rd Cataract
Dongola
Abu Hamed
Muhammad Qol
2259
Bûr Sûdân
Suakin
Sinkat
Trinkitat
Haiya
Karora
2780
Nakfa
Akordat
Bir 'Atrun
Kareima
4th Cataract
5th Cataract
Berber
Atbara
Ed Debba
Adarama
Nahr 'Atbara
Wad Hamid
Shendi
6th Cataract
Omdurmân
El Khartûm (Khartoum)
Kassalâ
Khashm el Girba
El Wuz
Wâd Medanî
Gedaref
El Gezira
Sodiri
Ed Dueim
Malha
1954
Kutum
Al Junaynah
Umm Keddada
El Fâsher
Djebel Mara 3088
Dârfûr
Zalingei
Nyâlâ
El Obeid
Kôstî
Singa
Nîl el Azraq
Umm Ruwaba
Er Rahad
En Nahud
El Odaiya
Abu Zabad
Kordofân
1325
Kâdugli
Ed Damazin
Nîl el Abyad
Gonder
1830
L. Tana
Bahir Dar
Bure
Debre Markos
Nekemte
3202
Dembidolo
Metu
Gore
Jima
3086
Omo
L. Abaya
Arba Minch
L. Shamo
Chew Bahir
L. Turkana
375
Lokitaung
Kapoeta
Boultoum
Nguigmi
Mao
Zigey
Bahr el Ghazal
Lac Tchad
Moussoro
Biltine
Abéché
Oum Hadjer
Ati
Bosso
Massakory
Gashua
Nguru
Geidam
Maiduguri
Ndjamena
Kousseri
Bokoro
Mongo
Goz Beïda
Potiskum
Massenya
Abou-Deïa
Am-Timan
Bama
Chari
Bongor
Gombe
Bajoga
Kumo
Biu
Mubi
Maroua
Guider
Numan
Garoua
Yola
Logone
Lai
Pala
Moundou
Sarh
Koumra
Doba
Birao
Bahr el Arab
Songo
1276
Ndélé
Sa'id Bundas
Bahr el Ghazâl
Raga
Jur
Sûdd
Gogriâl
Wâw
Tonj
Bahr el Jebel
Rumbêk
Malakâl
Sobat
Pibor Post
Bôr
Baïbokoum
Ngaoundéré
Gashaka
Banyo
Adamawa Highlands
Paoua
Kaga Bandoro
Bossangoa
Bozoum
Bouar
Bétaré Oya
Yaloga
Ippy
Sibut
Bambari
Bakouma
Toinya
Amadi
Tali Post
El Istiwa'iya
Obo
Foumban
Yoko
CAMEROON
Carnot
Bossembélé
Bertoua
Batouri
Nsangamba
Sanaga
Nanga-Eboko
Abong-Mbang
Berbérati
Bangui
Zongo
Bosobolo
Mobaye
Mobayi
Ubangi
Bangassou
Bomu
Bondo
Uele
Ango
Dungu
Faradje
Yambio
Yei
Juba
Mongalla
Kajo Kaji
Torit
3187
Libenge
Mbaïki
Yaoundé
Mala
75
84
86
COPYRIGHT PHILIPS

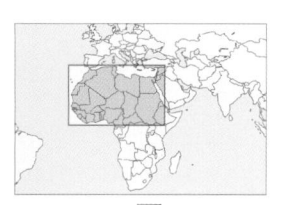

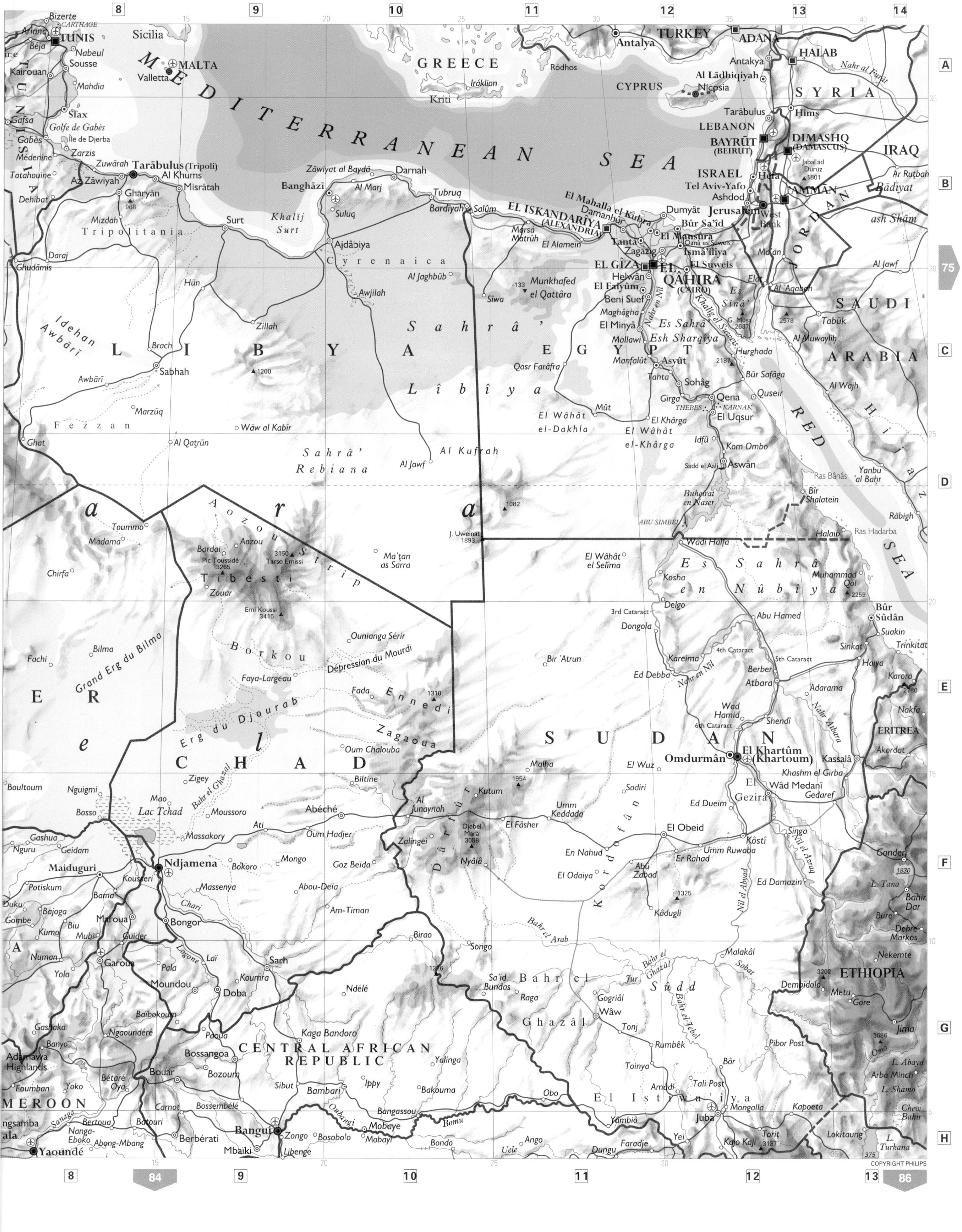

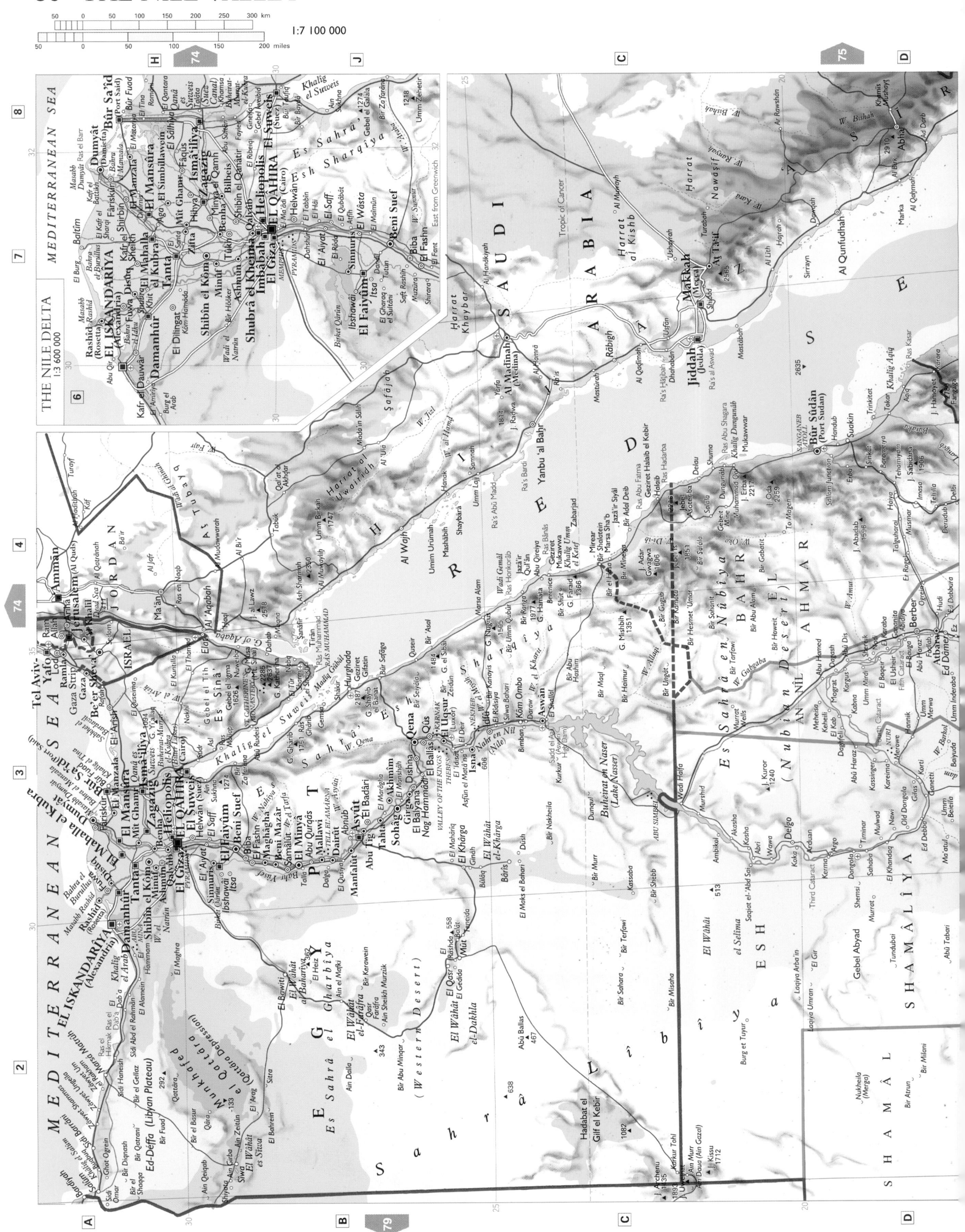

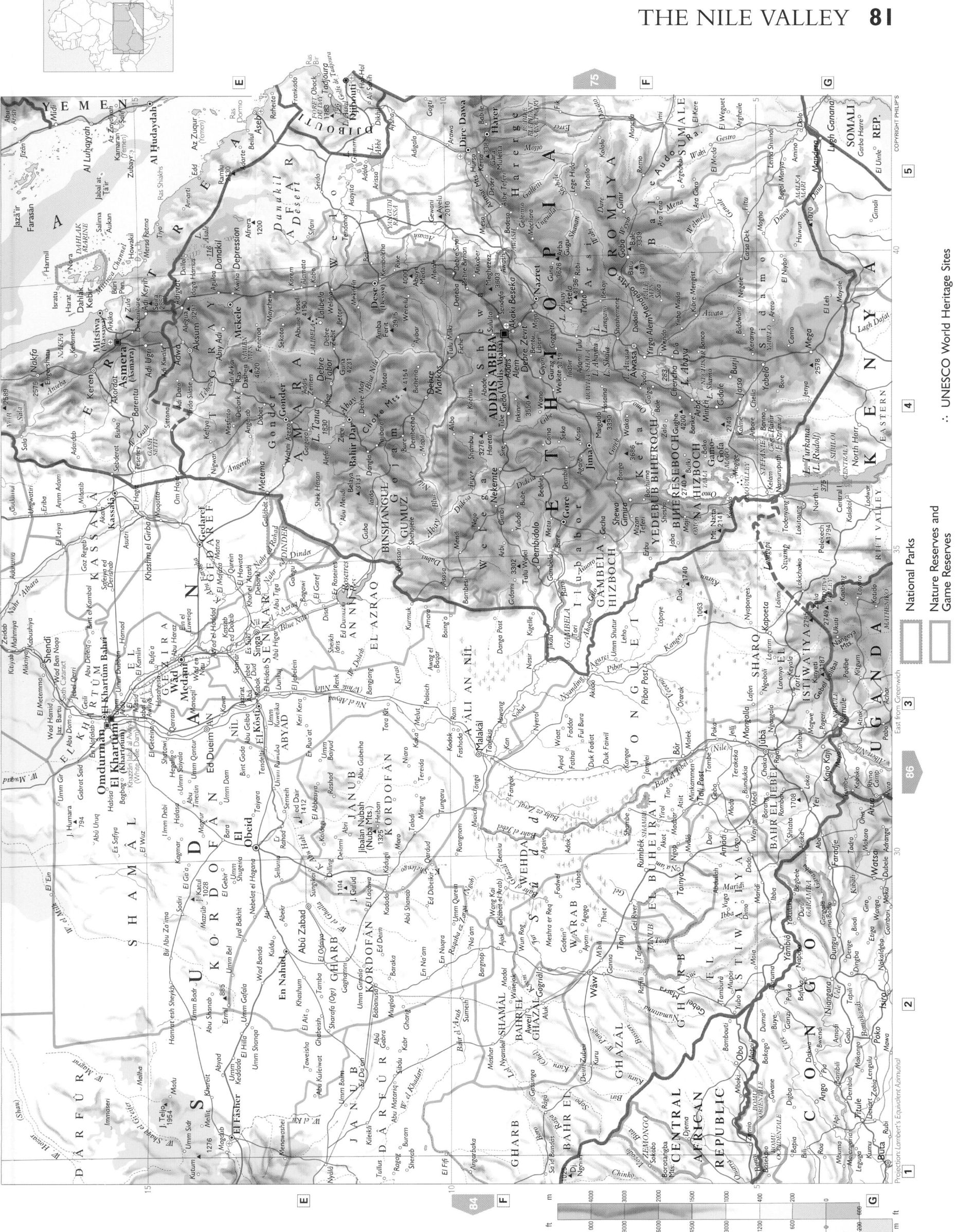

:: UNESCO World Heritage Sites

National Parks

Nature Reserves and
Game Reserves

Projection: Lambert's Equivalent Azimuthal

East from Greenwich

1:7 100 000

Projection: Lambert's Equivalent Azimuthal

West from Greenwich

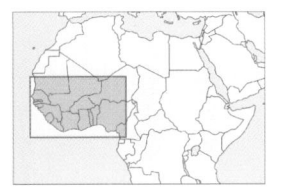

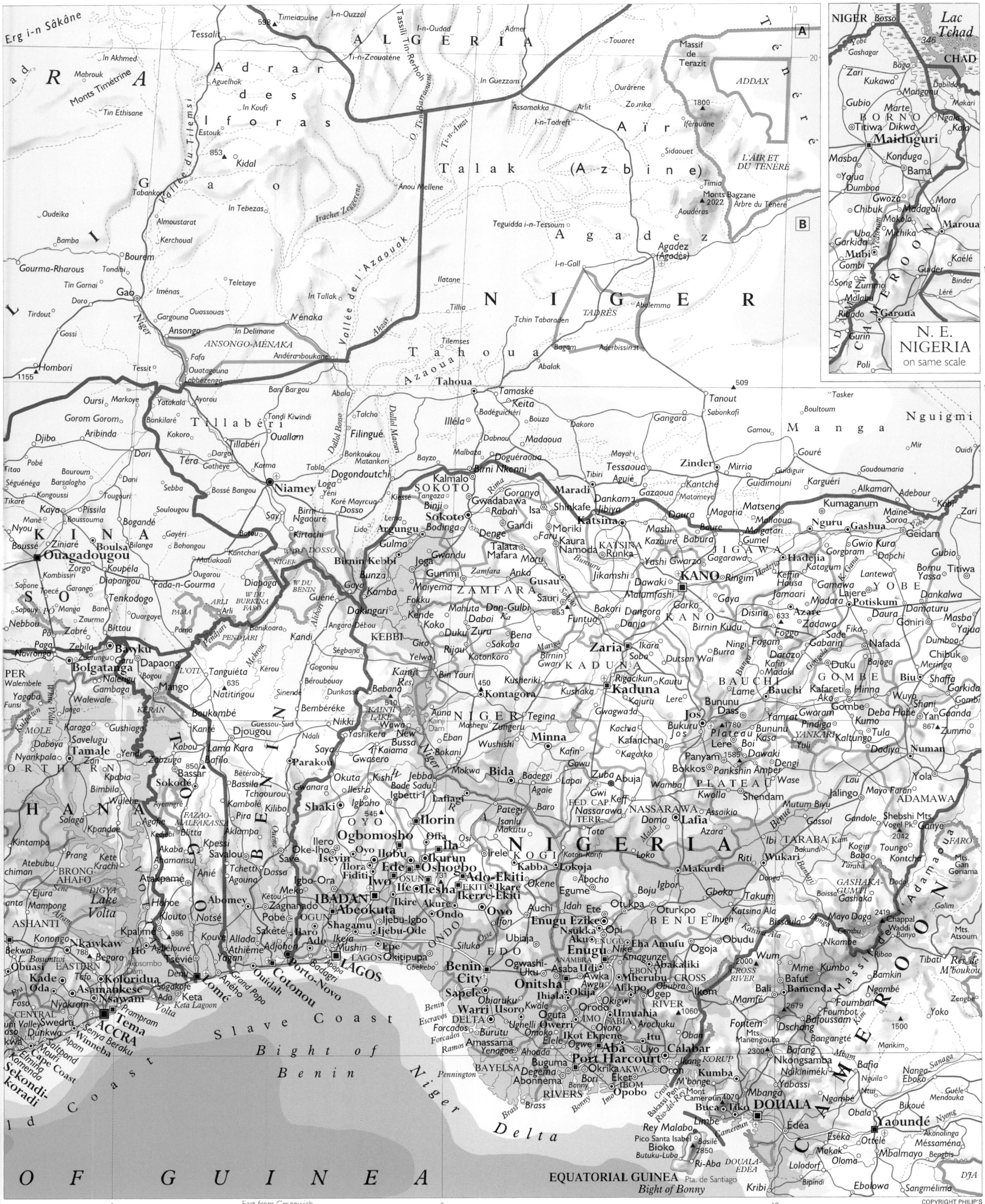

National Parks

Nature Reserves and Game Reserves

∴ UNESCO World Heritage Sites

COPYRIGHT PHILIP'S

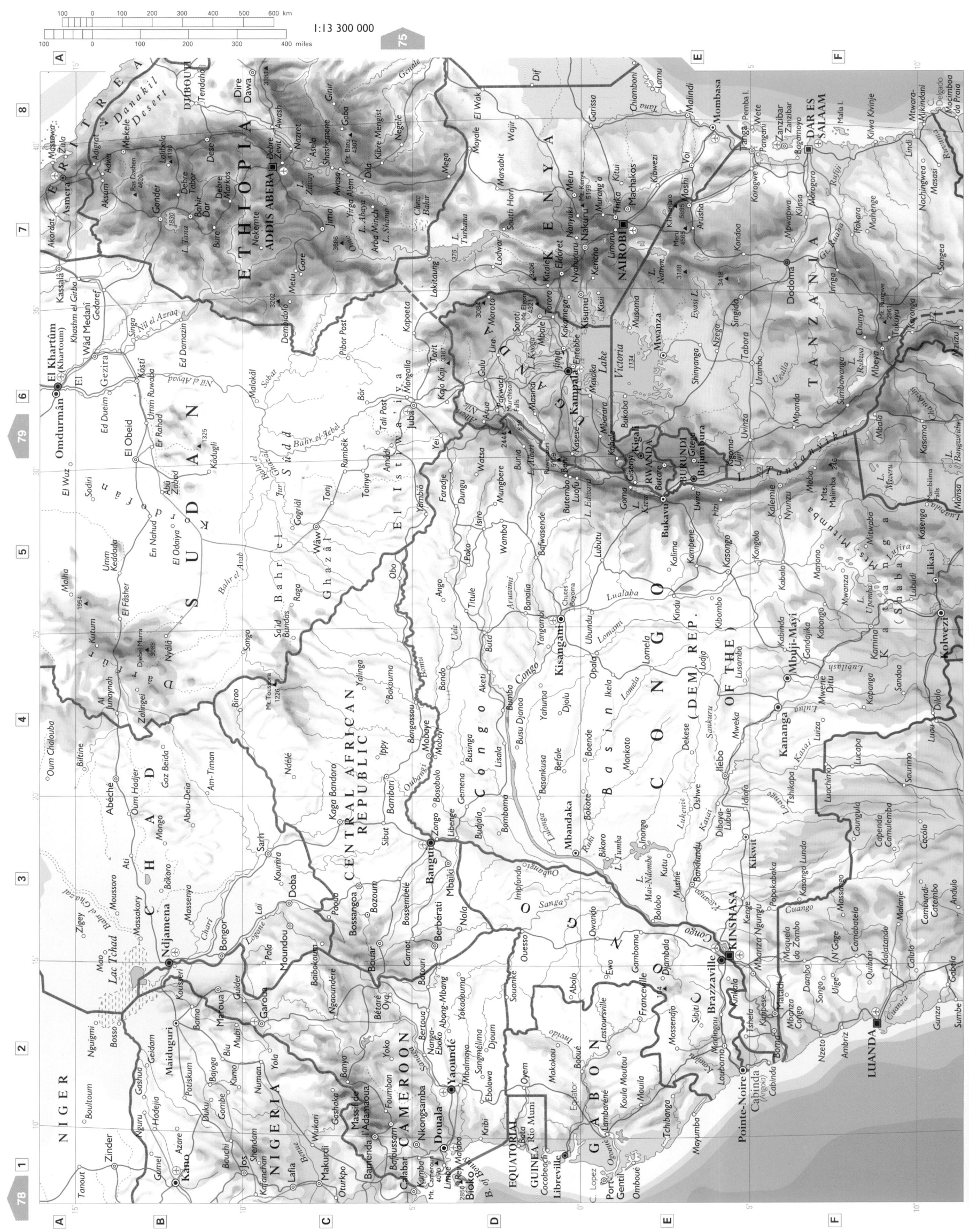

1:13 300 000

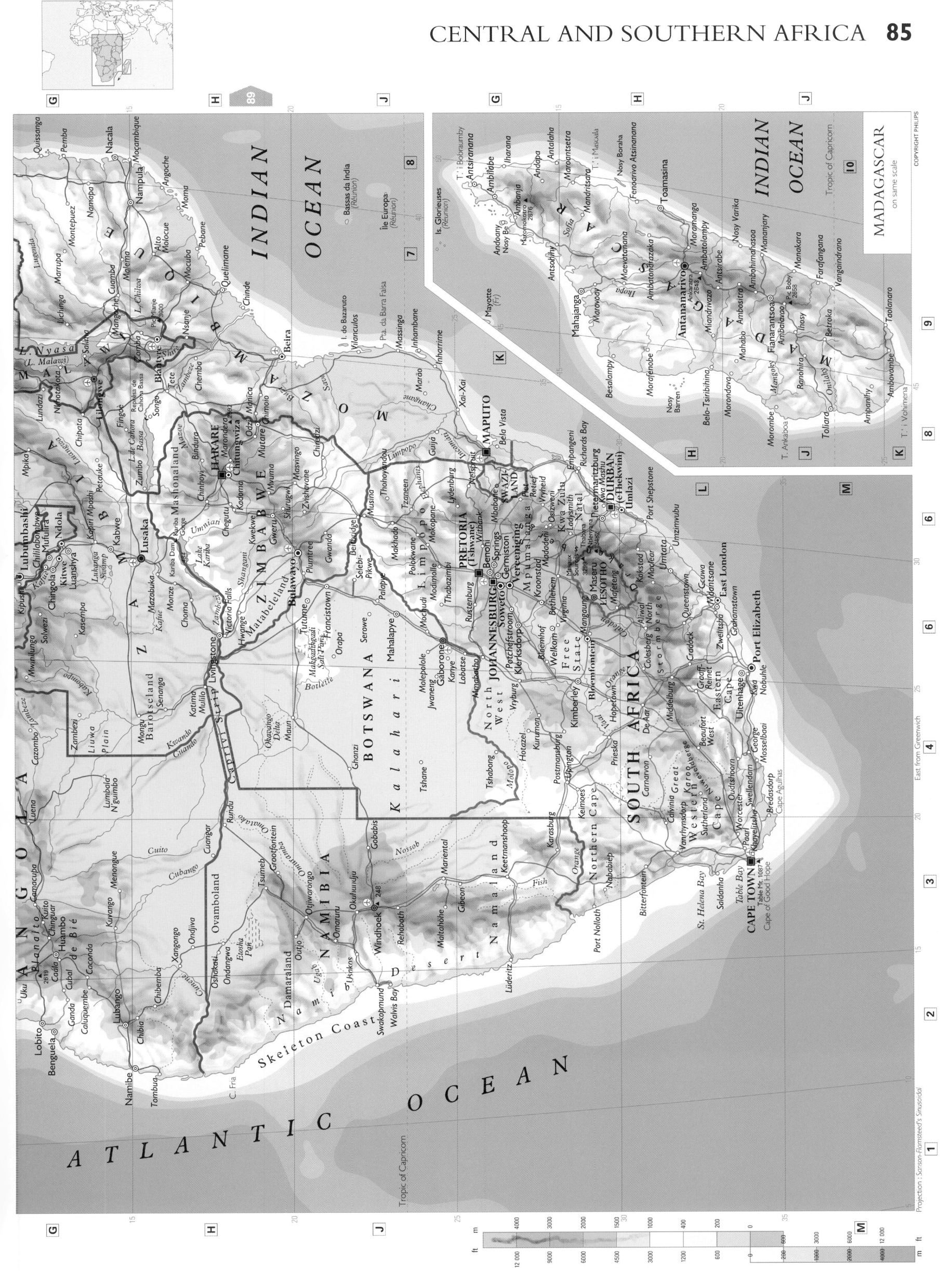

MADAGASCAR
on same scale

INDIAN

OCEAN

INDIAN

OCEAN

Tropic of Capricorn

ATLANTIC OCEAN

Tropic of Capricorn

East from Greenwich

Projection: Sanson-Flamsteed's Sinusoidal

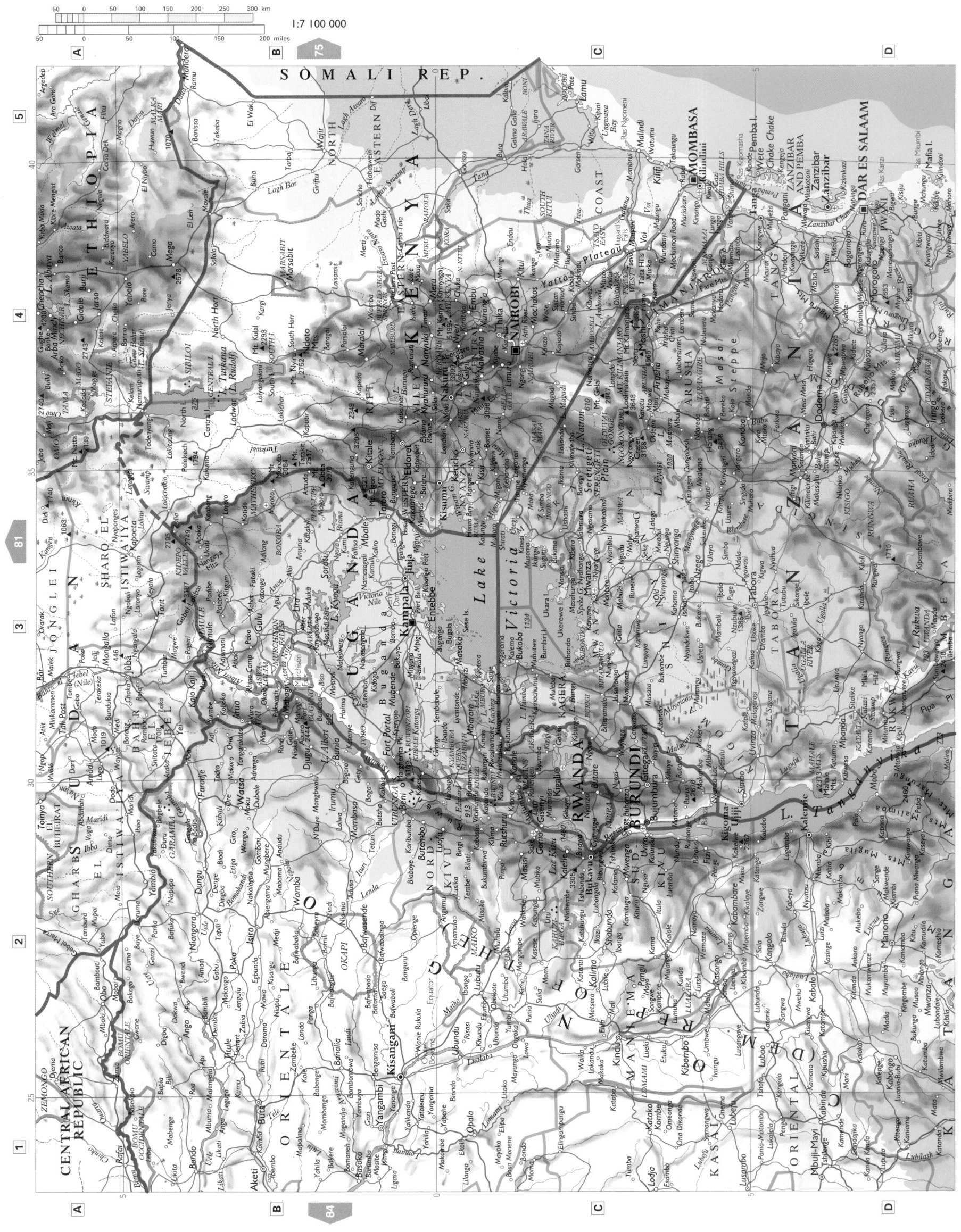

1:7 100 000

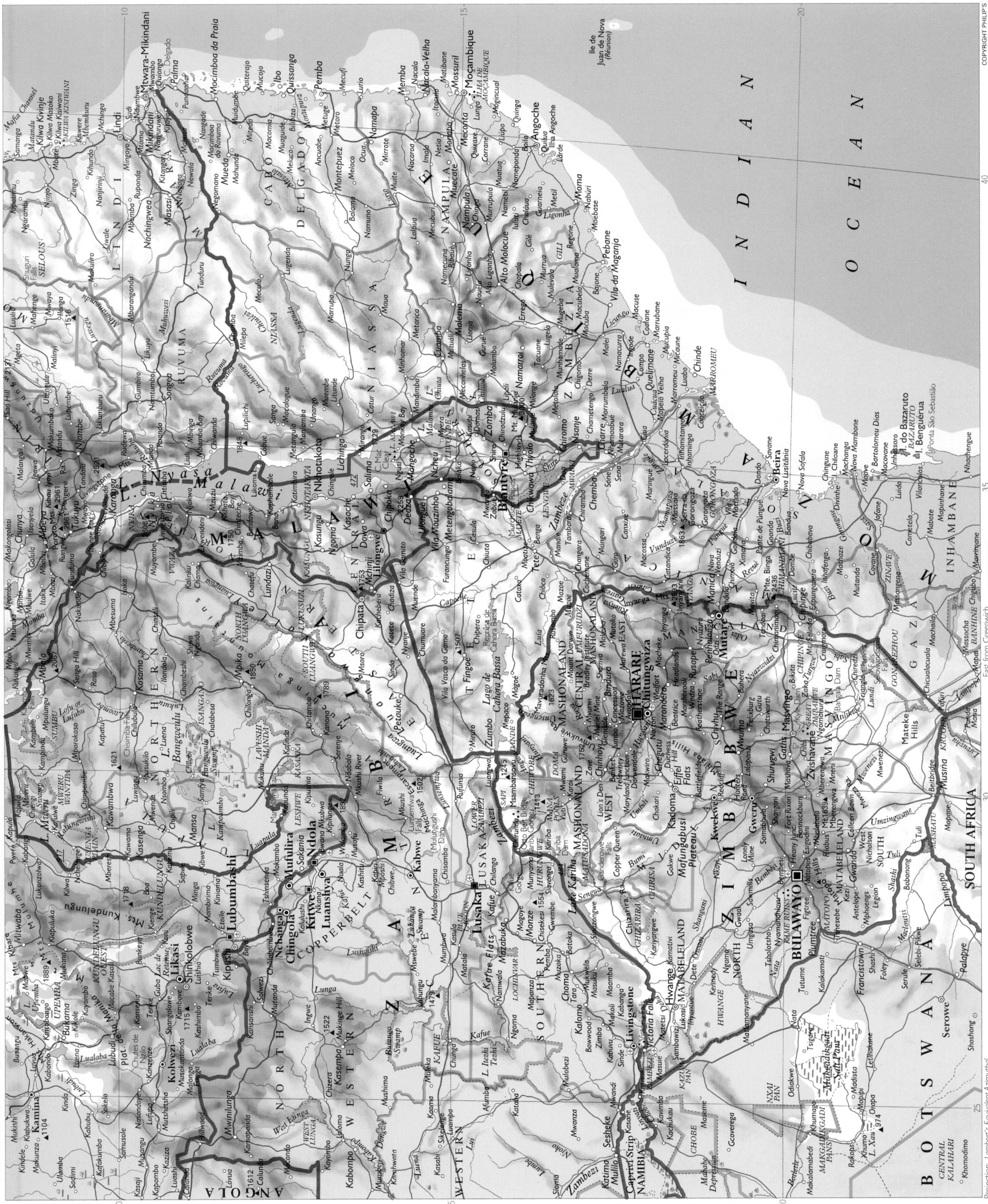

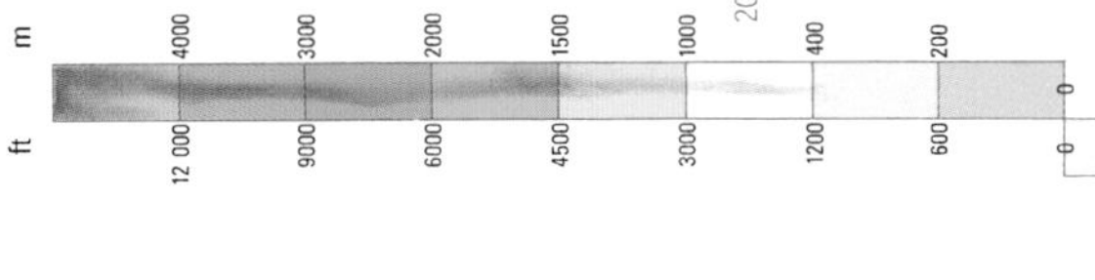

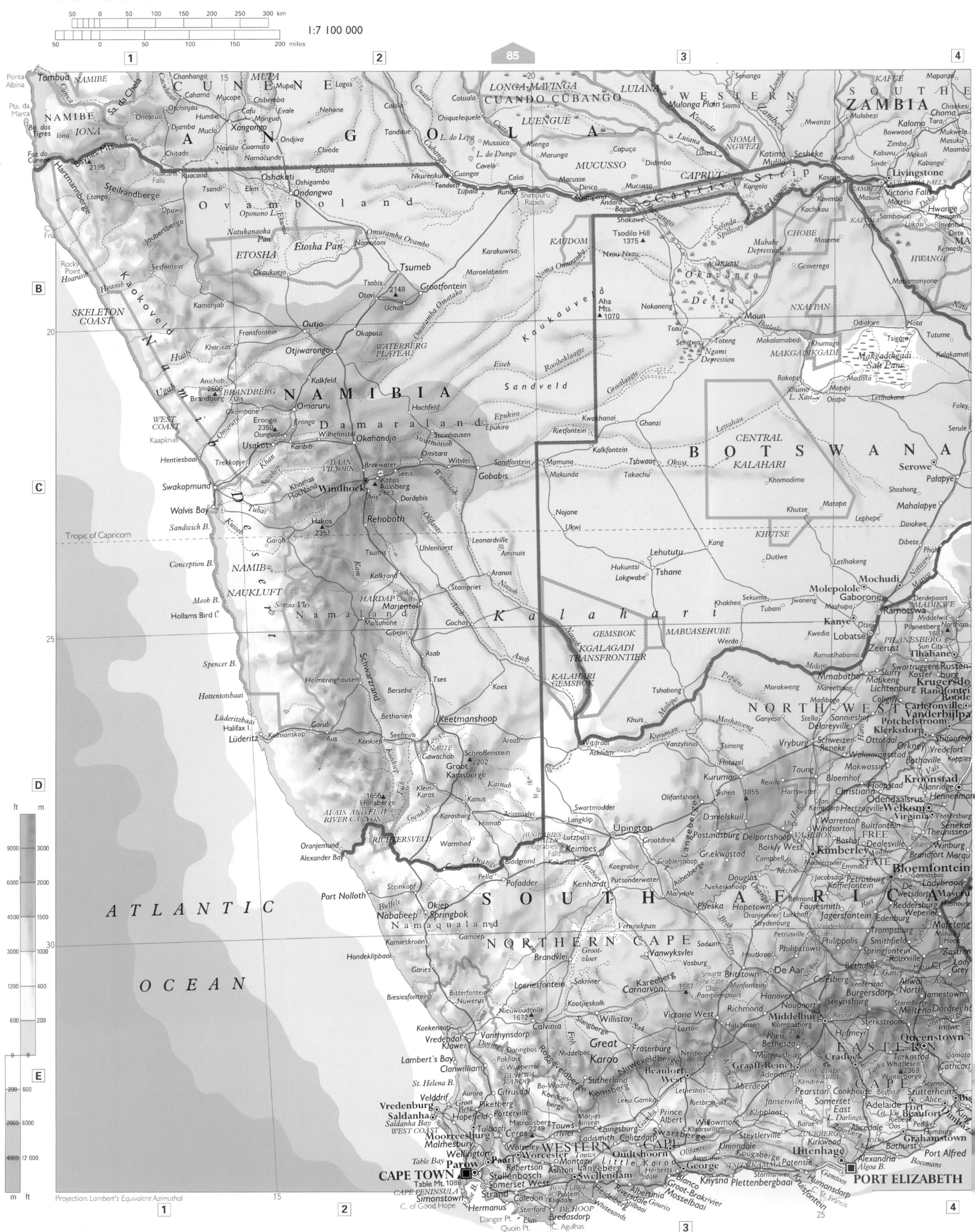

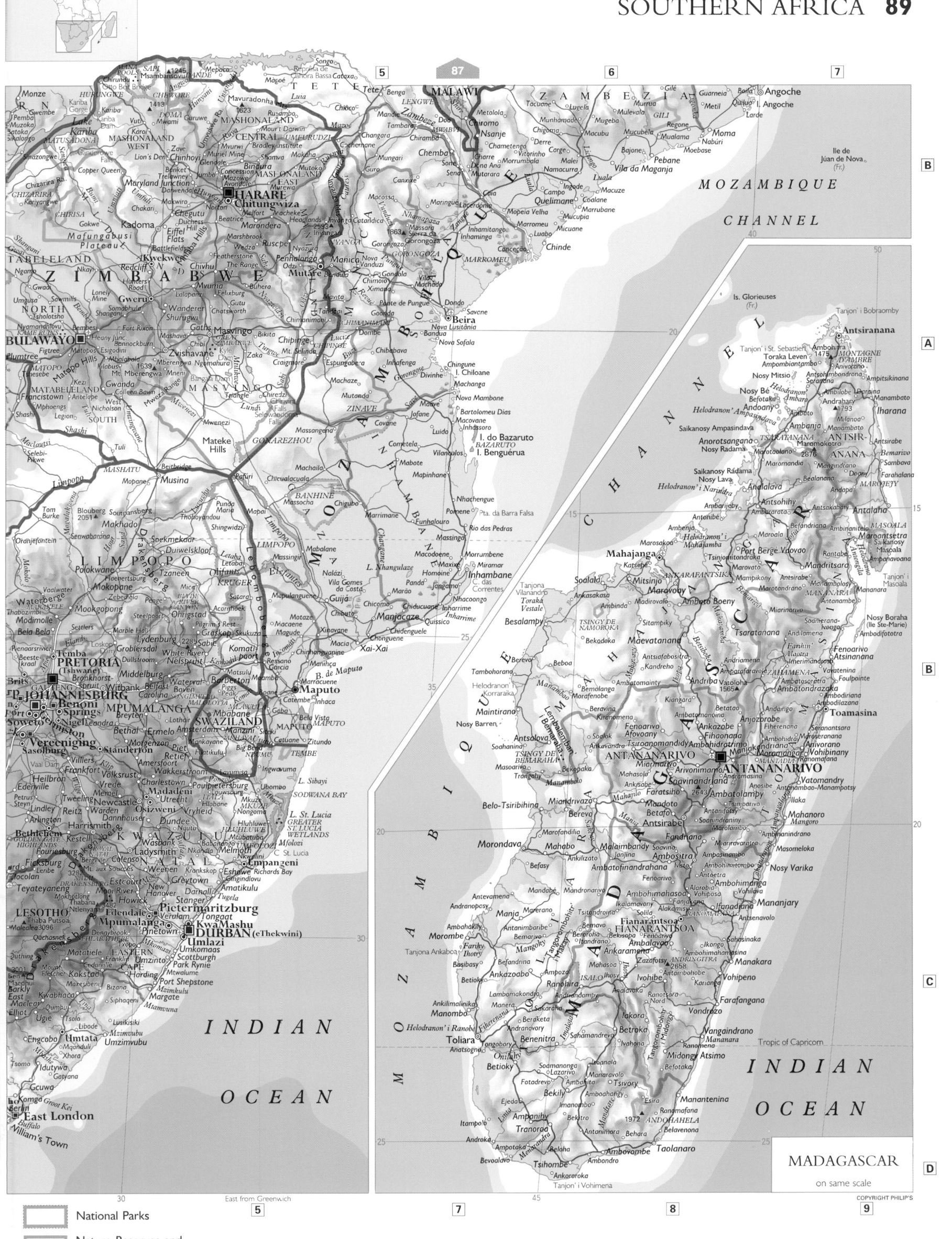

MOZAMBIQUE CHANNEL

MADAGASCAR

INDIAN OCEAN

INDIAN OCEAN

ZIMBABWE

LIMPOPO

MOZAMBIQUE

LESOTHO

SWAZILAND

MPUMALANGA

MALAWI

ZAMBEZIA

TETE

JOHANNESBURG
PRETORIA (Tshwane)
Maputo
DURBAN (eThekwini)
East London
HARARE
BULAWAYO
Gweru
Beira
Antananarivo
ANTANANARIVO
Mahajanga
Toamasina
Fianarantsoa
Toliara

Tropic of Capricorn

East from Greenwich

MADAGASCAR
on same scale

COPYRIGHT PHILIP'S

National Parks

Nature Reserves and Game Reserves

∴ UNESCO World Heritage Sites

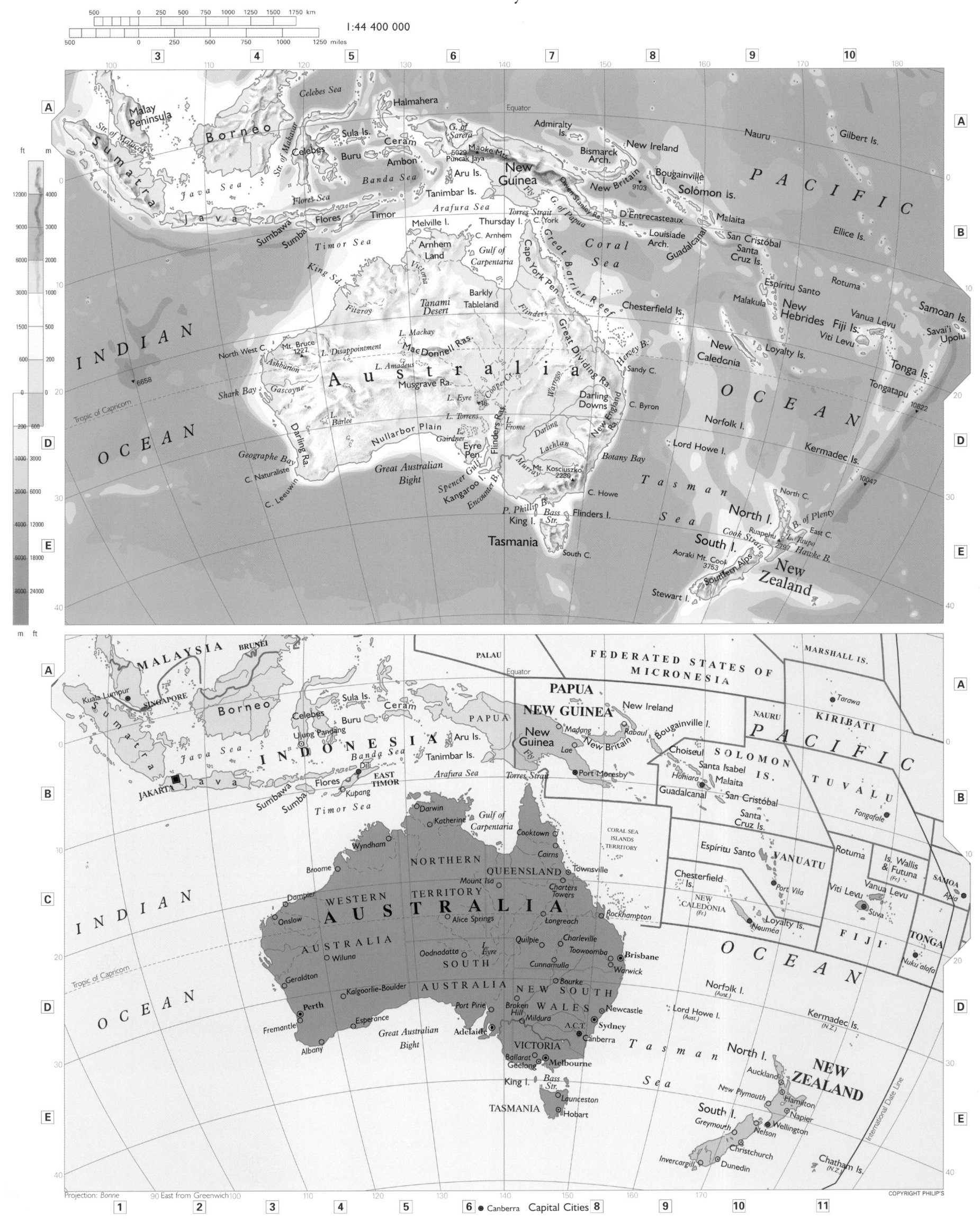

Projection: Bonne

6 ● Canberra   Capital Cities

1:5 300 000

50 0 50 100 150 200 km
50 0 50 100 150 miles

NEW ZEALAND

C. Reinga
C. Maria van Diemen
North C.
Houhora Heads
Ranganui B.
Doubtless B.
Mangonui
Ahipara B.
Whangaroa Harb.
Kaitaia
Tauroa Pt.
Okaihau
Waitangi
C. Brett
Opua
Rawene
B. of Islands
Kaikohe
Hikurangi
Hokianga Harbour
Whangarei
Whangarei Harb.
Waipoua
Forest
Bream Hd.
Bream B.
Dargaville
Waipu
Little
Barrier I.
Great Barrier I.
Kaipara Harbour
Warkworth
C. Rodney
C. Colville
Cuvier I.
Helensville
Hauraki Gulf
Coromandel
Whitianga
Takapuna
AUCKLAND
Manukau
Papakura
Thames
Whangamata
Mayor I.
Waiuku
Pukekohe
Waihi
Tauranga Harb.
Mercer
Paeroa
Whakaari
(White I.)
Waikato
Te Aroha
Huntly
Morrinsville
Tauranga
Mount
Maunganui
Bay of Plenty
Runaway
Hamilton
Cambridge
Whakatane
Te Puke
East C.
Raglan
Te Awamutu
Rotorua
Opotiki
Raukumara Ra.
Hikurangi
1753
Kawhia Harbour
Otorohanga
L. Rotorua
Tikitere
UREWERA
Waipiro
Kawhia
Waitomo
Caves
Te Kuiti
Tokoroa
Kinleith
L. Tarawera
Murupara
Ruatoria
Motu
Tolaga Bay
Mokau
Mokai
Wairakei
Waikaremoana
Ormond
North Taranaki
Bight
Ongarue
L. Taupo
Rangitaiki Mts.
Ruatahuna
Gisborne
Waitara
Taumarunui
Turangi
Tarawera
Poverty Bay
New Plymouth
WHANGANUI
Whangamomona
Kaimanawa Mts.
Ruahaka
Inglewood
Mt. Taranaki or Mt. Egmont
EGMONT
TONGARIRO
Waikokopu
C. Egmont
2518
Stratford
Ohakune
Ruapehu 2797
Waiouru
Wairoa
Mahia Pen.
Opunake
Kaponga
Eltham
Raetihi
Bay
View
Hawera
Waverley
Taihape
Ruahine Ra.
Napier
South Taranaki
Bight
Pctea
Mangaweka
C. Kidnappers
Hawke Bay
Wanganui
Hunterville
Hastings
Marton
Halcombe
Waipawa
Bulls
Feilding
Dannevirke
Tararua Ra.
Woodville
Waipukurau
Palmerston North
Foxton
Pahiatua
Shannon
Eketahuna
Levin
C. Farewell
Otaki
Golden B.
D'Urville I.
Paraparaumu
Masterton
Collingwood
Takaka
Kapiti I.
ABEL TASMAN
Tasman
Carterton
KAHURANGI
Tasman
Mts.
Motueka
Featherston
Greytown
Karamea
Pelorus Snd.
Upper Hutt
Martinborough
Karamea
Bight
Nelson
Havelock
Petone
L. Wairarapa
Richmond
Picton
Lower Hutt
Seddonville
Wakefield
Cook Str.
Wellington
Granity
Tadmor
Motueka
Eastbourne
Maitai R.
Blenheim
Westport
Lyell
Murchison
Seddon
NELSON LAKES
Ward
Inangahua
Wairau
2885 Tapuae-o-Uenuku
PAPAROA
Reefton
L. Rotoroa
Mt. Travers 2338
Punakaiki
Lewis Pass
Spenser
Mts.
Kaikoura
Blackball
Greymouth
Hanmer
Springs
Runanga
Stillwater
Waiau
Kaikoura
Kumara
L. Brunner
Jacksons
Clarence
Hokitika
Culverden
ARTHUR'S PASS
Waikari
Waiau
Ross
Arthur's Pass
Hurunui
Coleridge
Waipara
Amberley
Oxford
Pegasus Bay
Abut Hd.
WESTLAND
Rangiora
Waimakariri
Kaiapoi
Springfield
New Brighton
TASMAN SEA
Aoraki
Mt. Cook
3753
Whitecliffs
Christchurch
Riccarton
South Island
Westland Bight
Jackson B.
Okuru
Haast
Mount Cook
COOK
Methven
Staveley
Lincoln
Lyttelton
Banks Pen.
Akaroa
Castle Hill
Little River
L. Ellesmere
MOUNT ASPIRING
Mt. Aspiring 3027
Southern Alps
(Tiritiri o te Moana)
Geraldine
Rakaia
Rakaia
Canterbury Plains
Milford Sd.
Mt. Earnslaw 2818
L. Pukaki
Fairlie
Sutherland Falls
L. Wanaka
L. Tekapo
Temuka
Bligh Sound
Milford
Sound
Wanaka
Pleasant Point
Timaru
George Sound
Arrowtown
St. Andrews
Secretary I.
Cromwell
Dunstan Mts.
Kurow
Waimate
Doubtful Sd.
Queenstown
Clyde
Canterbury Bight
FIORDLAND
L. Anau
Kingston
Alexandra
Tokarahi
Ngapara
Breaksea Sd.
L. Te Anau
Eyre Mts.
Roxburgh
Naseby
Oamaru
Resolution I.
Garvie Mts.
Waikouaiti
Dusky Sd.
Manapouri
L. Mavora
Mossburn
Lumsden
Umbrella Mts.
Maheno
Hampden
Danback
Palmerston
L. Southland
Ohai
Edievale
Lawrence
Port Chalmers
Otago Harbour
Chalky
Inlet
Nightcaps
Waipahi
Milton
Mosgiel
Preservation
Inlet
Te Waewae B.
Tuatapere
Hedgehope
Gore
Clinton
C. Saunders
Dunedin
Orepuki
Winton
Mataura
Kaitangata
Solander I.
Riverton
Invercargill
Wyndham
Balclutha
FOVEAUX STR.
Bluff
Tokanui
Owaka
Nugget Pt.
Halfmoon Bay
Oban
Takahopu
Stewart I.
(Rakiura)
RAKIURA
South West C.
Port Pegasus

TASMAN SEA

South Island

PACIFIC OCEAN

SAMOAN ISLANDS
1:10 700 000

SAMOA
Savai'i
Apia
Upolu
AMERICAN SAMOA
Pago Pago
Tutuila
West from Greenwich

FIJI AND TONGA
1:10 700 000

50 0 50 100 150 200 km
50 0 50 100 150 miles

Wallis & Futuna (Fr.)
Futuna
Niuafo'ou
(Tonga)
Thikombia
Labasa
Vanua Levu
Yasawa Group
Taveuni
Koro
Vanua Balavu
Lautoka
Nandi 1323
Levuka
Viti Levu
Ovalau
Lakeba
Koro Sea
Lau Group
Suva
Gau
Vava'u
FIJI
Moala
Kandavu
PACIFIC OCEAN
Vatoa
Tofua
TONGA
(Friendly Is.)
Tongatapu
Nuku'alofa

West from Greenwich
East from Greenwich

Projection : Conical with two standard parallels
COPYRIGHT PHILIP'S

National Parks

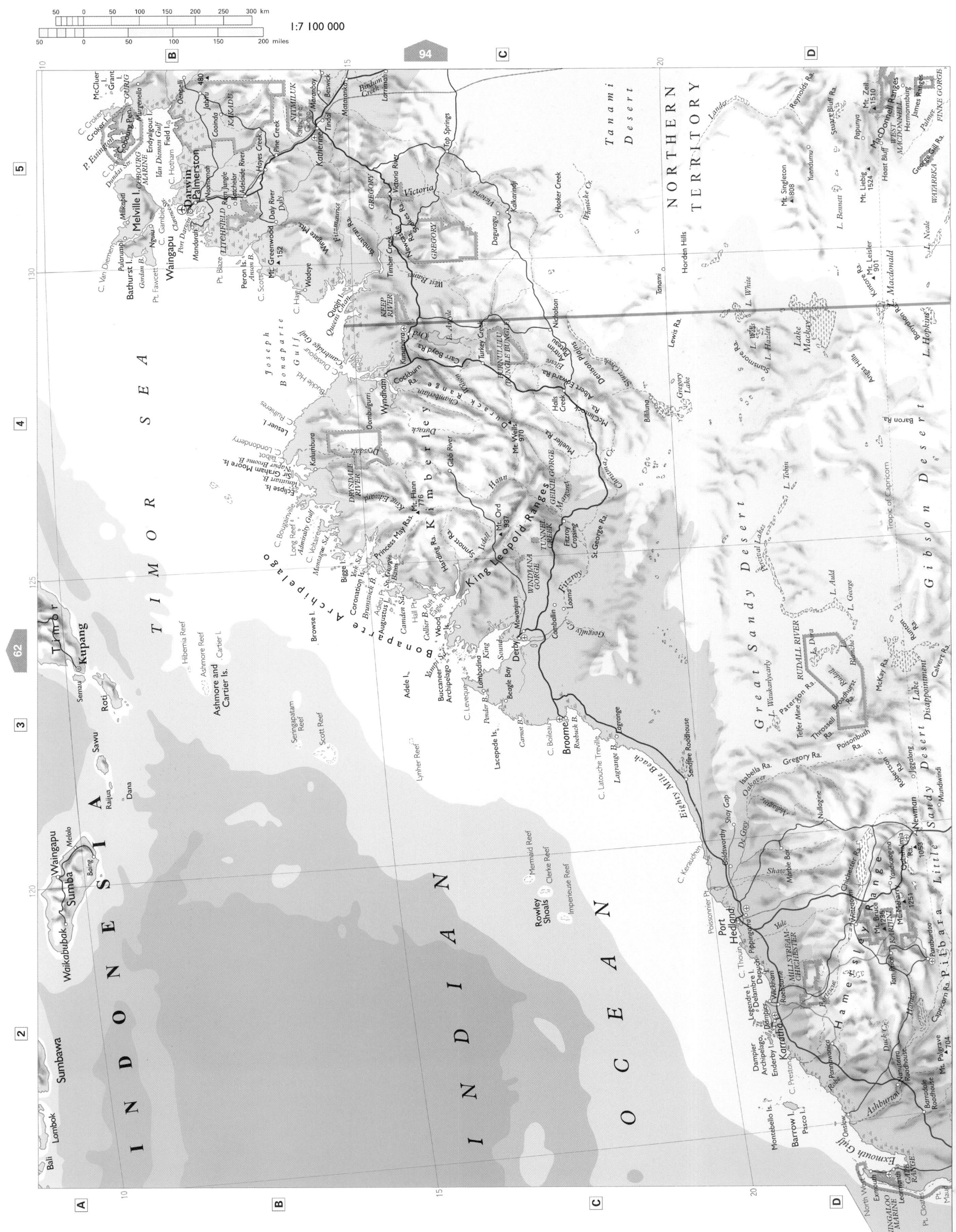

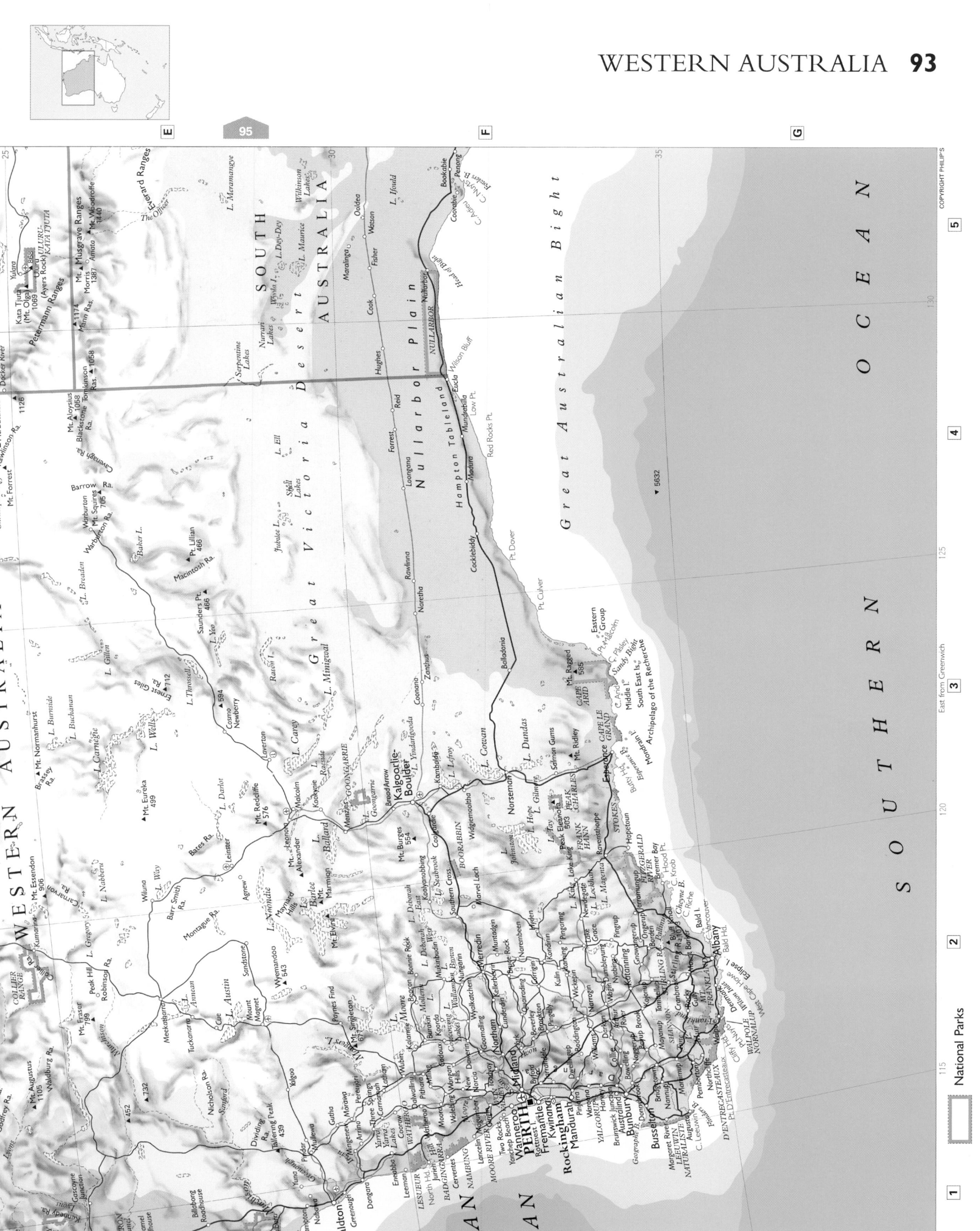

WESTERN AUSTRALIA

SOUTH AUSTRALIA

INDIAN OCEAN

SOUTHERN OCEAN

Great Australian Bight

Nullarbor Plain

Hampton Tableland

Great Victoria Desert

Kata Tjuta (Mt. Olga) 1069
ULURU-KATA TJUTA
Ayers Rock 868
Petermann Ranges
Musgrave Ranges
Everard Ranges
Mt. Woodroffe 1440

PERTH
Fremantle
Rockingham
Mandurah
Bunbury
Busselton
Albany
Geraldton
Kalgoorlie-Boulder
Coolgardie
Norseman
Esperance
Carnarvon
Kalbarri

SHARK BAY MARINE
FRANÇOIS PERON

National Parks

East from Greenwich

COPYRIGHT PHILIP'S

Projection: Bonne

m
3000
1200
600
200
0
ft

ft
12 000
6000
2000
600
400
200
0
m

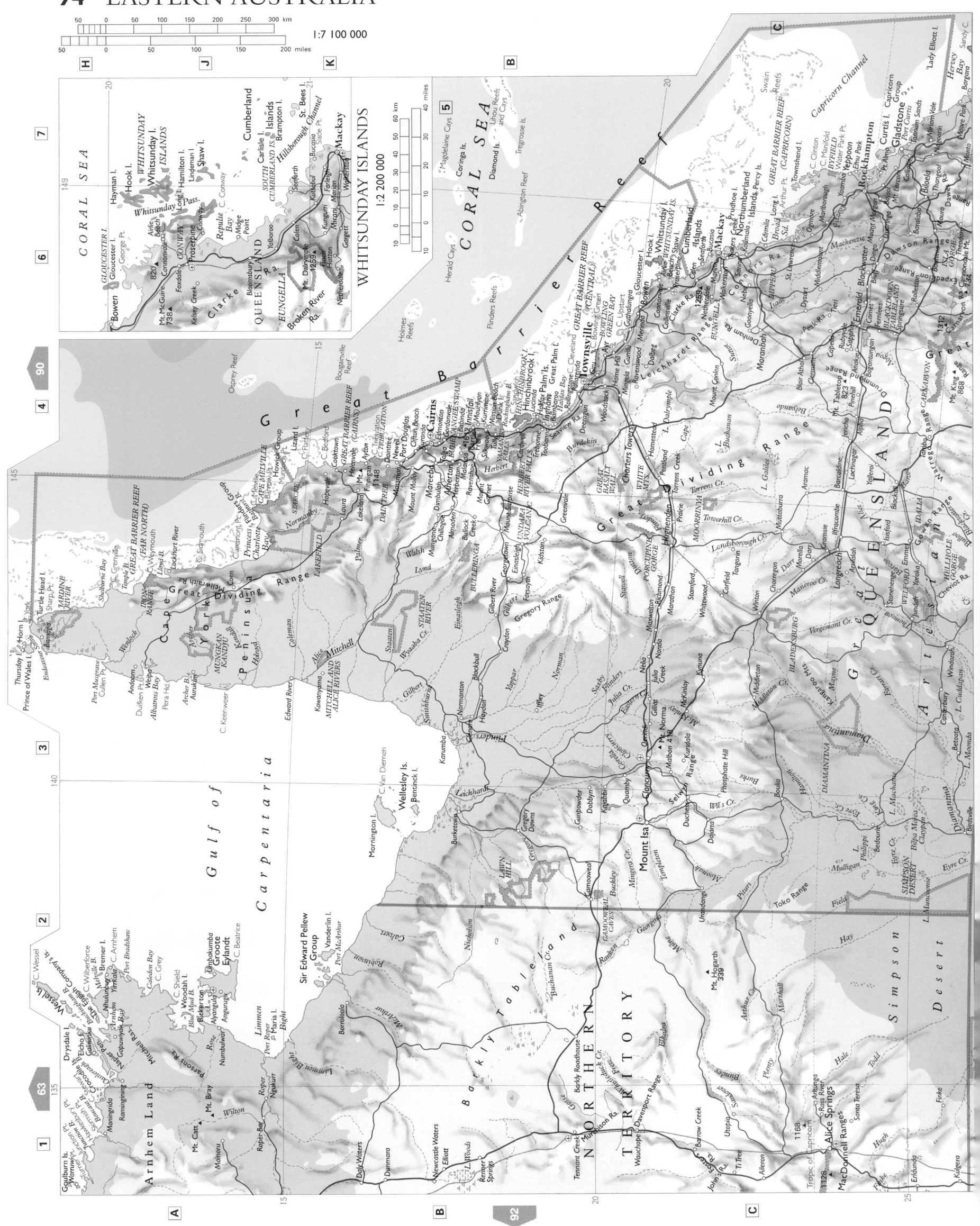

Scale 1:7 100 000

WHITSUNDAY ISLANDS
1:2 200 000

CORAL SEA

CORAL SEA

Gulf of Carpentaria

Great Barrier Reef

QUEENSLAND

Great Dividing Range

NORTHERN TERRITORY

Arnhem Land

Cape York Peninsula

Great Artesian Basin

Simpson Desert

Barkly Tableland

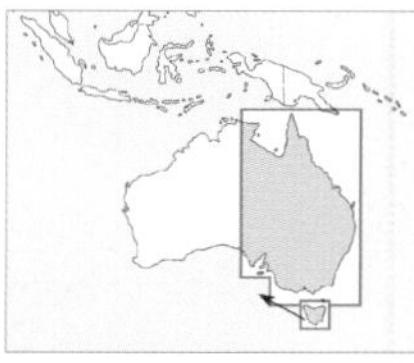

SOUTH AUSTRALIA

NEW SOUTH WALES

BRISBANE

Gold Coast

Sunshine Coast

Newcastle

SYDNEY

Gosford

Wollongong

Canberra

MELBOURNE

ADELAIDE

Broken Hill

TASMANIA

Hobart

Launceston

TASMAN SEA

Bass Strait

Lake Eyre

Lake Torrens

Lake Gairdner

Kangaroo I.

Flinders Island

King Island

Furneaux Group

Cape Barren I.

Sturt Stony Desert

Darling Range

National Parks

on same scale

East from Greenwich

Projection: Bonne

m ft

Equatorial Scale 1:48 000 000

RUSSIA

Yekaterinburg
Tomsk
Novosibirsk
MOSKVA
Astana (Aqmola)
Semey
Irkutsk
Chita
Oz. Baykal
Ulaanbaatar
Ob'
Lena
Volga

Okhotsk
Sea of Okhotsk
Poluostrov Kamchatka
Komandorskiye Ostrova (Russia)
Near Is. (U.S.A.)
Andreanof Is.
Bering Sea

KAZAKHSTAN
Aral Sea
Balqash Köl
Almaty
Ürümqi
MONGOLIA
Altai
Blagoveshchensk
Khabarovsk
Sakhalin
Petropavlovsk-Kamchatskiy
Kuril Trench
Aleutian
Aleutian Trench
7822

Toshkent
KYRGYZSTAN
Harbin
Changchun
SHENYANG
Vladivostok
Sapporo
Hakodate
La Pérouse Str.
Kurilskiye Ostrova (Russia)
10,542
Emperor Seamount Chain

TAJIKISTAN
BEIJING
TIANJIN
Taiyuan
Dalian
SOUL
NORTH KOREA
SOUTH KOREA
Sea of Japan
Sendai
TOKYO
Fuji-San 3776

CHINA
Lanzhou
Xi'an
Qingdao
Nagoya
Kyoto
Yokohama
JAPAN
Osaka
Shikoku
10,554
Midway Is. (U.S.A.)
Hawaii

Kabul
Srinagar
PAKISTAN
Lahore
DELHI
Kanpur
XIZANG
Kunlun Shan
Lhasa
Everest 8850
Himalaya
CHONGQING
Wuhan
Nanjing
SHANGHAI
HANGZHOU
Changsha
Yellow Sea
Kitakyūshū
Kyūshū
East China Sea
Japan Trench
Ogasawara Gunto (Japan)
Minami-Tori-Shima (Japan)
Lisianski I. (U.S.A.)

INDIA
KOLKATA (Calcutta)
DHAKA
BANGLADESH
BURMA
Mandalay
NEPAL
Ganga
Brahmaputra
Kunming
Fuzhou
GUANGZHOU
HONG KONG
Macau
Taipei
Ryūkyū-rettō (Japan)
TAIWAN
Hainan
Kazan-Rettō (Japan)
Marcus Ridge
Necker Ridge
Wake I. (U.S.A.)
South Honshu Ridge

Hyderabad
Bay of Bengal
Rangoon
CHENNAI (Madras)
THAILAND
BANGKOK
LAOS
VIETNAM
Hanoi
Salween
Mekong
C. Engano
Luzon
Paracel Is.
MANILA
PHILIPPINES
Mariana Trench
NORTHERN MARIANAS (U.S.A.)
Saipan
GUAM (U.S.A.) 11,022
MARSHALL IS.
Enewetak Atoll
Bikini Atoll
PA

SRI LANKA
Colombo
Andaman Is. (India)
CAMBODIA
Phnom Penh
G. of Thailand
Thanh Pho Ho Chi Minh
Nicobar Is. (India)
MALAYSIA
South China Sea
Mindoro
Samar
Palawan
10,497
Sulu Sea
Mindanao
Mindanao Trench
4101
Celebes Sea
Yap
Koror
PALAU
Caroline Is.
Truk
Micronesia
FEDERATED STATES OF MICRONESIA
Pohnpei
Paukir
Jaluit I.
Dalap-Uliga-Darrit
Butaritari
Tarawa
Gilbert Is.
Banaba
Howland I. (U.S.A.)
Baker I. (U.S.A.)
Phoenix Is.
Abariringa
Enderbury
KIR

Kuala Lumpur
WEST MALAYSIA
EAST MALAYSIA
SINGAPORE
INDONESIA
Sumatera
Sunda Islands
BRUNEI
SABAH
SARAWAK
77
Borneo
Palembang
Ujung Pandang
Sulawesi
Halmahera
Buru
Seram
Banda Sea
Puncak Jaya 5029
PAPUA
New Guinea
Admiralty Is.
Bismarck Arch.
New Ireland
Rabaul
New Britain
Bougainville
PAPUA NEW GUINEA
NAURU
Melanesia
SOLOMON IS.
Fongafale
TUVALU
Tokelau Is. (N.Z.)

JAKARTA
Java Sea
Flores Sea
Surabaya
Bali
Sumbawa
Flores
Sumba
EAST TIMOR
Timor
7440
Arafura Sea
Java Trench
Torres Strait
C. York
Lae
Port Moresby
Honiara
Guadalcanal
Santa Cruz I. 9165
Rotuma
Espíritu Santo
Vanua Levu
Is. Wallis & Futuna (Fr.)
SAMOA
Apia

Cocos Is. (Austral.)
Christmas I. (Austral.)
C. Arnhem
Darwin
Gulf of Carpentaria
Cairns
Townsville
Coral Sea
Great Barrier Reef
Louisiade Arch.
Is. Chesterfield
VANUATU
Port Vila
7570
Viti Levu
Suva
FIJI
Nuku'alofa
TONGA

INDIAN OCEAN
Broome
North West C.
AUSTRALIA
Alice Springs
Mount Isa
L. Eyre
Great Dividing Ra.
Rockhampton
Brisbane
Darling
NEW CALEDONIA (Fr.)
Nouméa
Is. Loyauté
Lord Howe Rise
Norfolk I. (Austral.)
10,822
Tonga Trench

Geraldton
Perth
Albany
Great Australian Bight
Adelaide
Murray
Canberra
Sydney
Mt Kosciuszko 2230
Bass Str.
Tasman Sea
Lord Howe I. (Austral.)
Kermadec Is. (N.Z.)
Kermadec Trench 10,047
NEW ZEALAND

Nouvelle Amsterdam (Fr.)
I. St. Paul (Fr.)
Melbourne
Tasmania
Hobart
Aoraki Mt Cook 3753
Auckland
Christchurch
Chatham Is. (N.Z.)
Wellington
Cook Strait
Dunedin
Invercargill
Bounty Is. (N.Z.)

Is. Crozet (Fr.)
Kerguelen (Fr.)
Heard I. (Austral.)
Mid-Indian Ridge
Auckland Is. (N.Z.)
Antipodes Is. (N.Z.)
Campbell I. (N.Z.)
Macquarie Is. (Austral.)

ft m
12 000 4000
9000 3000
6000 2000
3000 1000
1500 500
600 200
0 0
200 600
1000 3000
2000 6000
4000 12 000
6000 18 000
8000 24 000
m ft

Projection: Mollweide's Homolographic
East from Greenwich

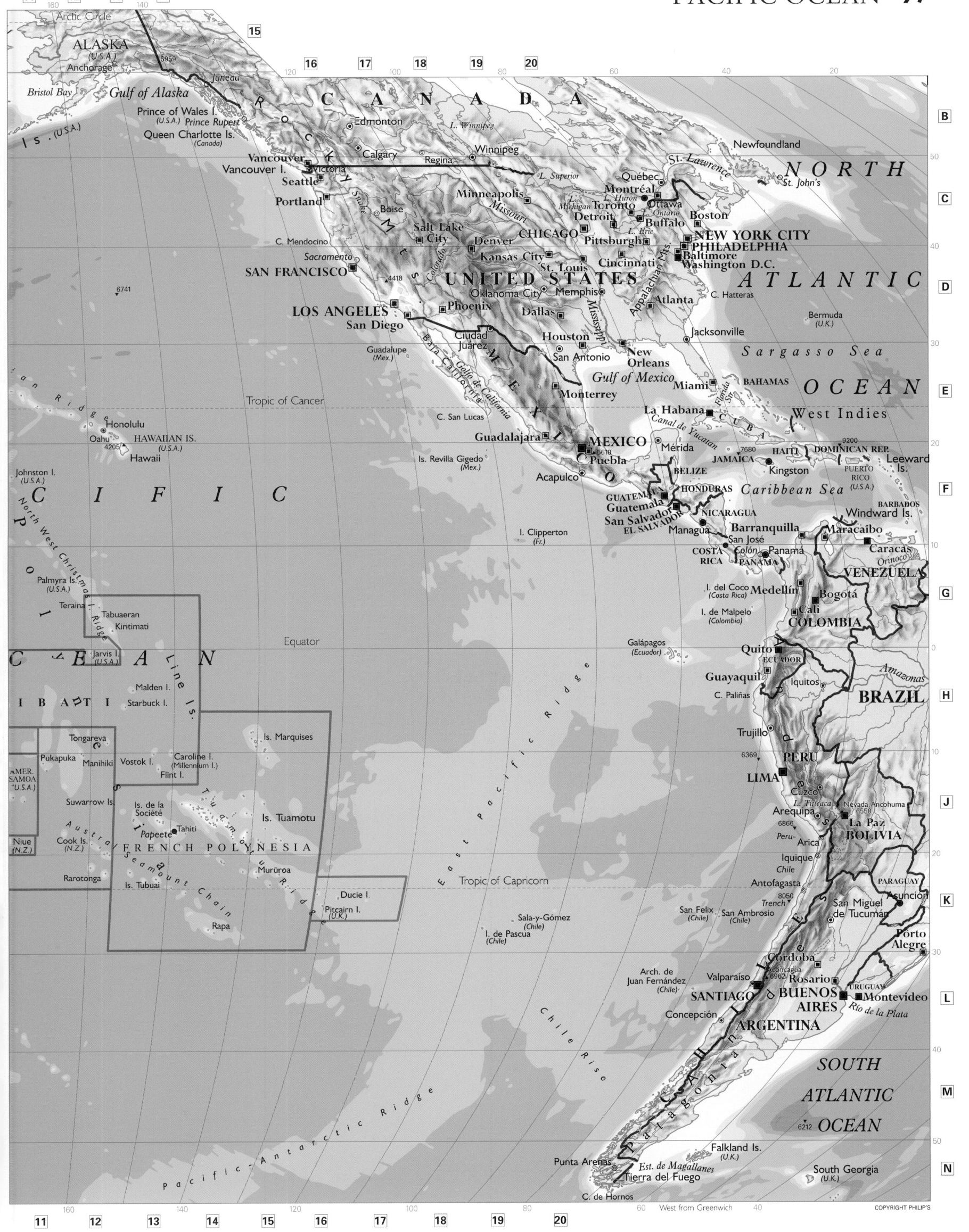

11 12 13 14

15

ALASKA
(U.S.A.)
Anchorage

Bristol Bay

Gulf of Alaska

Juneau

5959

160 140

Arctic Circle

Prince of Wales I.
(U.S.A.) Prince Rupert
Queen Charlotte Is.
(Canada)

Is. (U.S.A.)

C A N A D A

16 17 18 19 20

120 100 80

40 20

Edmonton

Calgary

Winnipeg

Regina

L. Winnipeg

Newfoundland

St. Lawrence

St. John's

B

Vancouver
Vancouver I.
Victoria
Seattle
Portland
Boise

Minneapolis

L. Superior

L. Huron
L. Michigan

L. Ontario
L. Erie

Québec

Montréal
Toronto Ottawa
Detroit Buffalo Boston

50

N O R T H

C

C. Mendocino

Sacramento

SAN FRANCISCO

Salt Lake
City

Denver

Kansas City

CHICAGO

St. Louis

Cincinnati

Pittsburgh

Washington D.C.

NEW YORK CITY
PHILADELPHIA
Baltimore

40

A T L A N T I C

D

6741

4418

UNITED STATES

LOS ANGELES
San Diego

Phoenix

Oklahoma City

Memphis

Dallas

Houston

San Antonio

Atlanta

C. Hatteras

Jacksonville

Bermuda
(U.K.)

30

O C E A N

Guadalupe
(Mex.)

Ciudad
Juárez

New
Orleans

Gulf of Mexico

Miami

Sargasso Sea

Tropic of Cancer

C. San Lucas

Monterrey

La Habana

BAHAMAS

West Indies

E

Honolulu

Oahu HAWAIIAN IS.
(U.S.A.)
4205
Hawaii

I. Revilla Gigedo
(Mex.)

Guadalajara

5610

MEXICO
Puebla

Acapulco

Mérida

Canal de Yucatán

CUBA

7680

JAMAICA

9200

HAITI

Kingston

DOMINICAN REP.
PUERTO
RICO
(U.S.A.)

Leeward
Is.

20

C

C I F I C

Johnston I.
(U.S.A.)

Palmyra Is.
(U.S.A.)

Teraina

Tabuaeran
Kiritimati

BELIZE

GUATEMALA
Guatemala
San Salvador
EL SALVADOR

HONDURAS

NICARAGUA

Managua

San José

COSTA
RICA

Barranquilla

Colón
Panama

PANAMA

Caribbean Sea

BARBADOS

Windward Is.

Maracaibo

Caracas

Orinoco

VENEZUELA

F

North West Christmas I. Ridge

P O L I

Jarvis I.
(U.S.A.)

Malden I.

Starbuck I.

Equator

I. Clipperton
(Fr.)

I. del Coco
(Costa Rica)

Medellín

I. de Malpelo
(Colombia)

Bogotá

Cali

COLOMBIA

G

O C E A N

I B A T I

Tongareva

Pukapuka Manihiki

Is. Marquises

Caroline I.
(Millennium I.)
Flint I.

Malden I.

Vostok I.

Galápagos
(Ecuador)

Quito

ECUADOR

Guayaquil

Iquitos

C. Paliñas

Amazonas

BRAZIL

0

H

AMER.
SAMOA
(U.S.A.)

Niue
(N.Z.)

Suwarrow Is.

Cook Is.
(N.Z.)

Is. de la
Société

Papeete Tahiti

Is. Tuamotu

FRENCH POLYNESIA

Trujillo

6369

PERU

LIMA

Cuzco

10

J

Rarotonga

Is. Tubuai

Mururoa

Rapa

Austral / Seamount Chain

Ducie I.

Pitcairn I.
(U.K.)

Tropic of Capricorn

Sala-y-Gómez
(Chile)

I. de Pascua
(Chile)

San Felix
(Chile)

San Ambrosio
(Chile)

8050

Trench

L. Titicaca

6866

Arequipa

Peru-
Chile

Arica

Iquique

Chile

Antofagasta

Nevada Ancohuma
6550

La Paz

BOLIVIA

PARAGUAY

San Miguel
de Tucumán

Asunción

20

K

Porto
Alegre

30

East Pacific Ridge

Cordoba

Aconcagua
6962

Valparaíso

Arch. de
Juan Fernández
(Chile)

Rosario

URUGUAY

SANTIAGO BUENOS
AIRES

Montevideo

Rio de la Plata

Concepción

Chile Rise

ARGENTINA

L

40

SOUTH

M

Pacific-Antarctic Ridge

Falkland Is.
(U.K.)

6212

South Georgia
(U.K.)

ATLANTIC

OCEAN

50

N

Punta Arenas

Est. de Magallanes
Tierra del Fuego

C. de Hornos

160 140 120 100 80

60 West from Greenwich 40

11 12 13 14 15 16 17 18 19 20

100 0 200 400 600 800 1000 1200 1400 km
100 0 200 400 600 800 1000 miles

1:31 100 000

ft m
9000 3000
6000 2000
3000 1000
1500 500
600 200
0 0
200 600
1000 3000
2000 6000
4000 12000
6000 18000
8000 24000
m ft

Projection: Bonne

West from Greenwich

COPYRIGHT PHILIP'S

1:31 100 000

100 0   200   400   600   800   1000 1200 1400 km

100 0   200   400   600   800   1000 miles

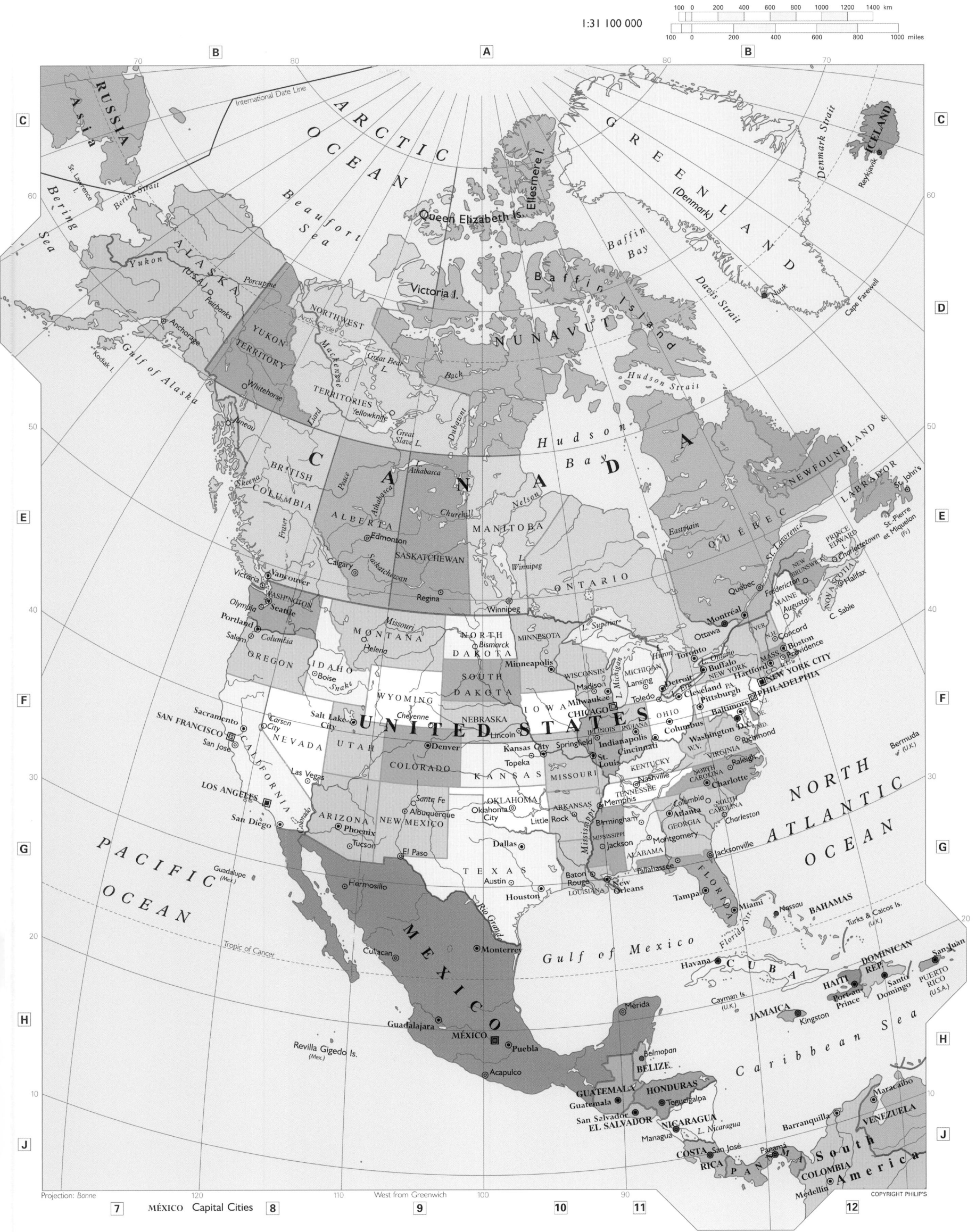

RUSSIA

ASIA

ARCTIC OCEAN

International Date Line

St. Lawrence I.

Bering Strait

Beaufort Sea

GREENLAND
(Denmark)

Denmark Strait

ICELAND

Reykjavik

Bering Sea

Queen Elizabeth Is.

Ellesmere I.

Baffin Bay

ALASKA
(U.S.A.)

Yukon

Fairbanks

Anchorage

Gulf of Alaska

Kodiak I.

Porcupine

Arctic Circle

Victoria I.

NORTHWEST

Baffin Island

NUNAVUT

Davis Strait

Nuuk

Cape Farewell

D

YUKON TERRITORY

Whitehorse

Mackenzie

Great Bear L.

Juneau

TERRITORIES

Yellowknife

Back

Hudson Strait

Great Slave L.

CANADA

BRITISH COLUMBIA

Skeena

Peace

Athabasca

L. Athabasca

Churchill

Hudson Bay

Fraser

Edmonton

ALBERTA

SASKATCHEWAN

Calgary

Saskatchewan

Regina

MANITOBA

Nelson

L. Winnipeg

ONTARIO

Eastmain

QUÉBEC

St. Lawrence

NEWFOUNDLAND & LABRADOR

St. John's

E

Victoria

Vancouver

WASHINGTON

Seattle

Olympia

Portland

Salem

Columbia

OREGON

IDAHO

Boise

Snake

MONTANA

Missouri

Helena

Bismarck

NORTH DAKOTA

MINNESOTA

Winnipeg

Minneapolis

L. Superior

WISCONSIN

Madison

Milwaukee

Ottawa

Toronto

L. Michigan

MICHIGAN

Lansing

L. Huron

L. Ontario

Buffalo

Detroit

Cleveland

Toledo

Montréal

Québec

Fredericton

NEW BRUNSWICK

PRINCE EDWARD

Charlottetown

St-Pierre et Miquelon (Fr.)

NOVA SCOTIA

Halifax

C. Sable

MAINE

Augusta

VER.

Concord

N.H.

Boston

MASS.

Providence

Hartford

NEW YORK

PA.

Pittsburgh

NEW YORK CITY

PHILADELPHIA

F

Sacramento

SAN FRANCISCO

San Jose

CALIFORNIA

Carson City

NEVADA

Salt Lake City

UTAH

WYOMING

Cheyenne

SOUTH DAKOTA

NEBRASKA

IOWA

UNITED STATES

CHICAGO

ILLINOIS

INDIANA

Indianapolis

Springfield

Lincoln

Denver

Kansas City

Topeka

OHIO

Columbus

Cincinnati

St. Louis

Baltimore

Washington D.C.

W.V.

Richmond

VIRGINIA

MD.

Las Vegas

COLORADO

KANSAS

MISSOURI

KENTUCKY

Nashville

TENNESSEE

NORTH CAROLINA

Raleigh

Bermuda (U.K.)

NORTH

LOS ANGELES

San Diego

ARIZONA

Phoenix

Tucson

Santa Fe

Albuquerque

NEW MEXICO

El Paso

Colorado

OKLAHOMA

Oklahoma City

ARKANSAS

Little Rock

Memphis

Mississippi

Birmingham

ALABAMA

GEORGIA

Atlanta

Columbia

SOUTH CAROLINA

Charlotte

Charleston

ATLANTIC

G

PACIFIC OCEAN

Guadalupe (Mex.)

Hermosillo

TEXAS

Dallas

Austin

Houston

Baton Rouge

LOUISIANA

Jackson

Montgomery

Tallahassee

Jacksonville

FLORIDA

OCEAN

Tropic of Cancer

MEXICO

Culiacan

Monterrey

Rio Grande

Gulf of Mexico

New Orleans

Tampa

Miami

Florida

Nassau

BAHAMAS

Turks & Caicos Is. (U.K.)

San Juan

H

Revilla Gigedo Is. (Mex.)

Guadalajara

MÉXICO

Puebla

Acapulco

Mérida

Havana

CUBA

Cayman Is. (U.K.)

HAITI

Port-au-Prince

DOMINICAN REP.

Santo Domingo

PUERTO RICO (U.S.A.)

JAMAICA

Kingston

Caribbean Sea

BELIZE

Belmopan

GUATEMALA

HONDURAS

Tegucigalpa

Guatemala

San Salvador

EL SALVADOR

NICARAGUA

Managua

L. Nicaragua

Barranquilla

VENEZUELA

Maracaibo

J

COSTA RICA

San José

Panamá

PANAMA

COLOMBIA

South America

Medellín

MÉXICO Capital Cities

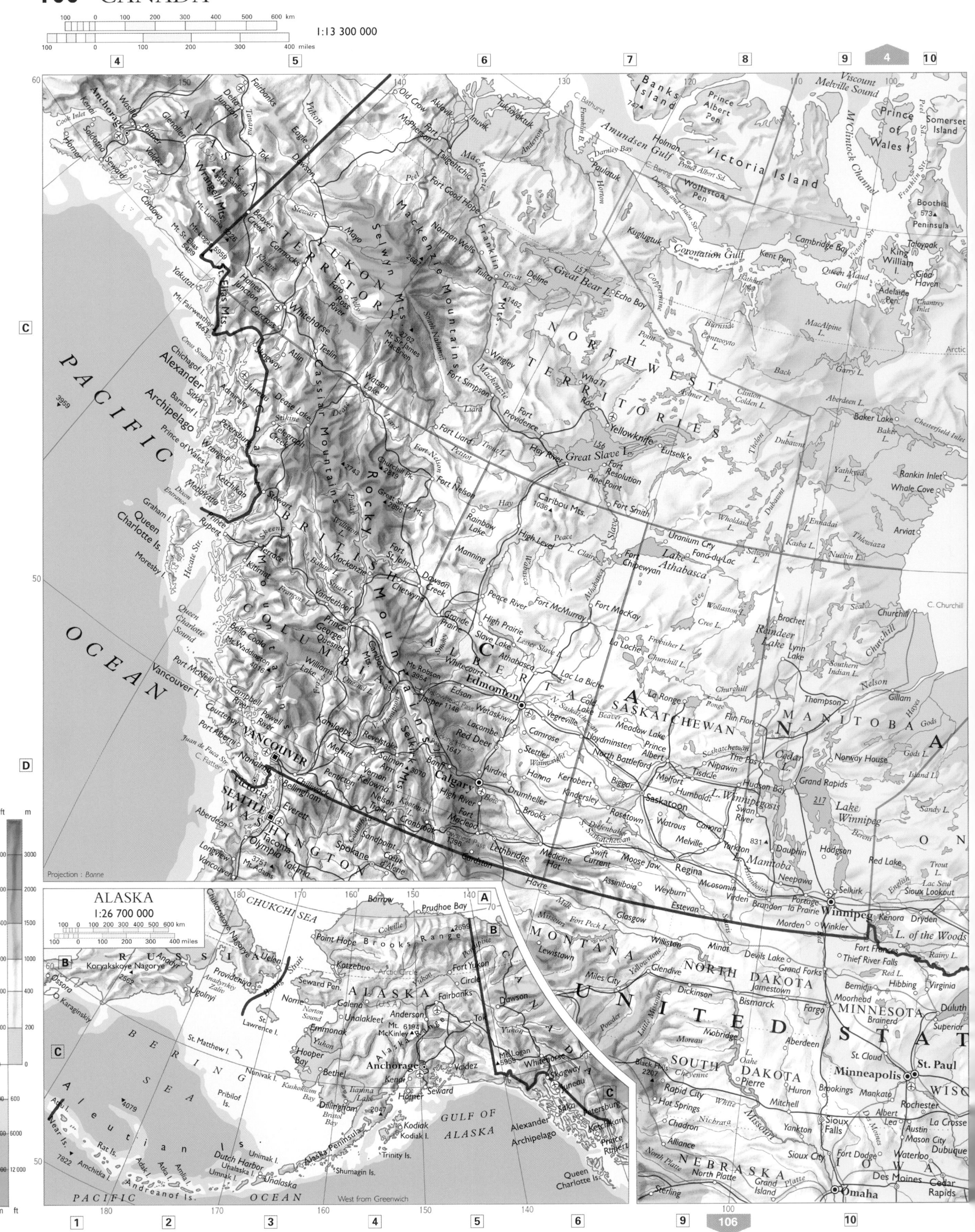

100 200 300 400 500 600 km

1:13 300 000

100 0 100 200 300 400 miles

PACIFIC OCEAN

ALASKA

YUKON TERRITORY

BRITISH COLUMBIA

ALBERTA

SASKATCHEWAN

MANITOBA

NORTHWEST TERRITORIES

Victoria Island

Prince of Wales I.

Banks Island

Great Bear L.

Great Slave L.

Lake Athabasca

Reindeer Lake

Lake Winnipeg

VANCOUVER

CALGARY

Edmonton

Winnipeg

WASHINGTON

MONTANA

NORTH DAKOTA

SOUTH DAKOTA

NEBRASKA

MINNESOTA

IOWA

WISC

UNITED STATES

Minneapolis

St. Paul

Omaha

Projection : Bonne

ft m

9000 3000
6000 2000
4500 1500
3000 1000
1200 400
600 200
0 0
200 600
2000 6000
4000 12 000
m ft

ALASKA

1:26 700 000

100 0 100 200 300 400 500 600 km

100 0 100 200 300 400 miles

CHUKCHI SEA

RUSSIA

ALASKA (U.S.A.)

Brooks Range

Anchorage

BERING SEA

Aleutian Is.

GULF OF ALASKA

PACIFIC OCEAN

West from Greenwich

11
12
13
14
15
16
B
C
D
E
Devon I.
Lancaster Sound
Bylot I.
Arctic Bay
Nanisivik
Borden Pen.
Pond Inlet
Brodeur Peninsula
Gulf of Boothia
Baffin Bay
Baffin Island
Clyde River
C. Adair
C. Raper
Home B.
Fury and Hecla Str.
Igloolik
Hall Beach
Simpson Pen.
Kugaaruk
Melville Peninsula
Committee B.
Foxe Basin
Prince Charles I.
Air Force I.
Cumberland Peninsula
Qikiqtarjuaq
C. Dyer
Pangnirtung
Hoare B.
Cumberland Sd.
C. Mercy
Nettilling L.
Rae Isthmus
Repulse Bay
NUNAVUT
C. Dorchester
Amadjuak L.
Foxe Pen.
Cape Dorset
Iqaluit
Meta Incognita Peninsula
Kimmirut
Hall Peninsula
Frobisher Bay
Resolution I.
Wager B.
Roes Welcome Sd.
Southampton I.
Coral Harbour
Bell Pen.
Foxe Channel
Salisbury I.
Nottingham I.
Hudson Strait
Chesterfield Inlet
Coats I.
Mansel I.
Ivujivik
Salluit
Kangiqsujuaq
Quaqtaq
Akpatok I.
C. Chidley
Péninsule d'Ungava
Kangirsuk
Ungava Bay
Kangiqsualujjuaq
Hebron
Puvirnituq
L. Payne
Arnaud
Hudson Bay
Ottawa Is.
Feuilles
Koksoak
Kuujjuaq
Baleine
George
Nain
Inukjuak
Mélèzes
Caniapiscau
L. Minto
Sleeper Is.
King George Is.
Baker's Dozen Is.
Sanikiluaq
Belcher Is.
C. Tatnam
L. à l'Eau Claire
Grande Baleine
L. Bienville
Kuujjuarapik
Schefferville
Petitsikapau L.
Smallwood Res.
Labrador
North West River
Happy Valley-Goose Bay
Churchill Falls
Churchill
Esker
Hopedale
C. Harrison
Rigolet
Cartwright
NEWFOUNDLAND & LABRADOR
Port Hope Simpson
Belle Isle
C. Bauld
St. Anthony
Str. of Belle Isle
Labrador City
Fermont
Ashuanipi
Gagnon
L. Caniapiscau
Peawanuck
Winisk
Severn
C. Henrietta Maria
Pte. Louis XIV
Chisasibi
Lanaaupscow
La Grande
Big Trout L.
Attawapiskat
James Bay
Akimiski I.
Wemindji
Eastmain
Charlton I.
Fort Albany
Waskaganish
Rupert
Moosonee
Albany
Nottaway
Harricana
Missinaibi
L. St. Joseph
Nakina
Kenogami
QUÉBEC
Rés. Manicouagan
Moisie
Romaine
Natashquan
St-Augustin
Havre-St-Pierre
Sept-Îles
Port-Cartier
Î. d'Anticosti
Mistassini
L. Mistassini
L. Albanel
Péribonka
Chibougamau
Baie-Comeau
Gulf of St. Lawrence
Cabot Str.
Gaspé
Pen. de la Gaspésie
Matane
Rimouski
Campbellton
Bathurst
Îs de la Madeleine
Chicoutimi
Dolbeau-Mistassini
St-Jean
Roberval
Jonquière
Matagami
L. Matagami
Rés. Gouin
Hearst
Cochrane
Abitibi L.
Amos
Kapuskasing
Greenstone
L. Nipigon
Nipigon
Marathon
Oba
Timmins
Kirkland Lake
Rouyn-Noranda
Val-d'Or
La Tuque
Québec
Lévis
Thetford Mines
Rivière-du-Loup
Edmundston
Grand Falls
NEW BRUNSWICK
Moncton
Fredericton
Saint John
Woodstock
Chatham
PR. EDWARD I.
Summerside
Charlottetown
Northumberland Str.
NOVA SCOTIA
Cape Breton I.
Sydney
Glace Bay
Port Hawkesbury
Antigonish
New Glasgow
Truro
Amherst
Kentville
Dartmouth
Halifax
Digby
Bridgewater
Liverpool
Yarmouth
C. Sable
B. of Fundy
Sable I. (Nova Scotia)
Newfoundland
St. John's
Carbonear
Bonavista
Gander
Lewisporte
Grand Falls-Windsor
Corner Brook
Deer Lake
Baie Verte
Notre Dame B.
Trinity B.
Placentia
Placentia B.
Marystown
C. Race
Stephenville
Channel-Port aux Basques
ST-PIERRE et MIQUELON (Fr.)
C. North
C. Ray
Thunder Bay
Lake Superior
Chapleau
Wawa
New Liskeard
Sudbury
Sault Ste. Marie
Elliot Lake
L. Nipissing
North Bay
Parry Sound
Georgian Bay
Manitoulin I.
Lake Huron
Owen Sound
Barrie
Huntsville
Pembroke
Ottawa
Hull
Outaouais
MONTRÉAL
Mont-Laurier
Rés. Cabonga
Shawinigan
Trois-Rivières
Joliette
St-Hyacinthe
Sherbrooke
Granby
Cornwall
Kingston
Belleville
Peterborough
Oshawa
TORONTO
Hamilton
Kitchener
London
Sarnia
Windsor
DETROIT
Lake Ontario
L. Erie
Niagara Falls
Buffalo
Rochester
Syracuse
Albany
NEW YORK
VERMONT
Montpelier
Burlington
L. Champlain
NEW HAMPSHIRE
Concord
Manchester
MAINE
Bangor
Augusta
Lewiston
Portland
MASS.
BOSTON
Springfield
Hartford
CONN.
R.I.
Providence
C. Cod
New Haven
Bridgeport
NEW YORK
Scranton
Binghamton
Elmira
Jamestown
Erie
CLEVELAND
Toledo
PENNSYLVANIA
Newark
N.J.
Allentown
Trenton
OHIO
INDIANA
ILLINOIS
CHICAGO
Gary
South Bend
Lansing
Flint
Saginaw
Grand Rapids
MICHIGAN
L. Michigan
Milwaukee
Racine
Kenosha
Madison
Rockford
Sheboygan
Appleton
Green Bay
Wausau
Rhinelander
Menominee
Escanaba
Manistique
Petoskey
Traverse City
Cadillac
Marquette
Houghton
Ironwood
WISCONSIN
ONTARIO
Davis Strait
Labrador Sea
ATLANTIC OCEAN
GREENLAND (KALAALLIT NUNAAT) (Denmark)
Nunavik
Uummannaq
Qeqertarsuaq
Qeqertarsuup Tunua
Ilulissat
Qasigiannguit
Kangerlussuaq
Sisimiut
Maniitsoq
Nuuk
Qeqertarsuatsiaat
Paamiut
Arsuk
Qaqortoq
Nanortalik
Alluitsup Paa
Nunap Isua
Kong Frederik VI's Kyst
Ammassalik
2136
1890
2591
2850
3809
1652
257
1135
814
1190
183
6309
174
75
90
80
70
60
50
40
30
West from Greenwich
COPYRIGHT PHILIP'S
11
107
12
13
14

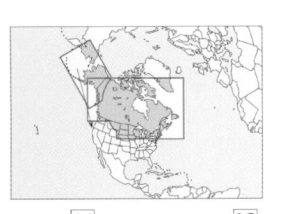

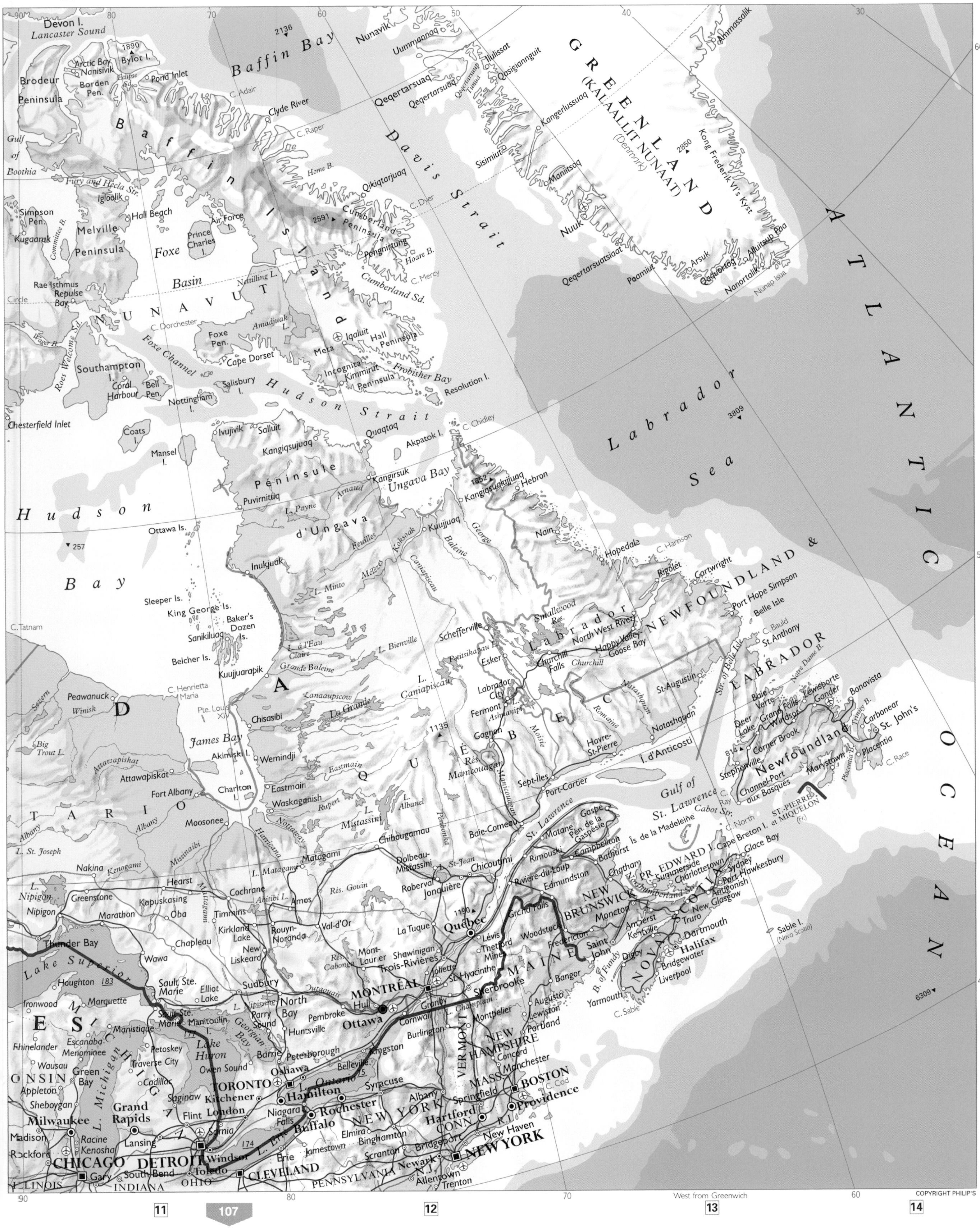

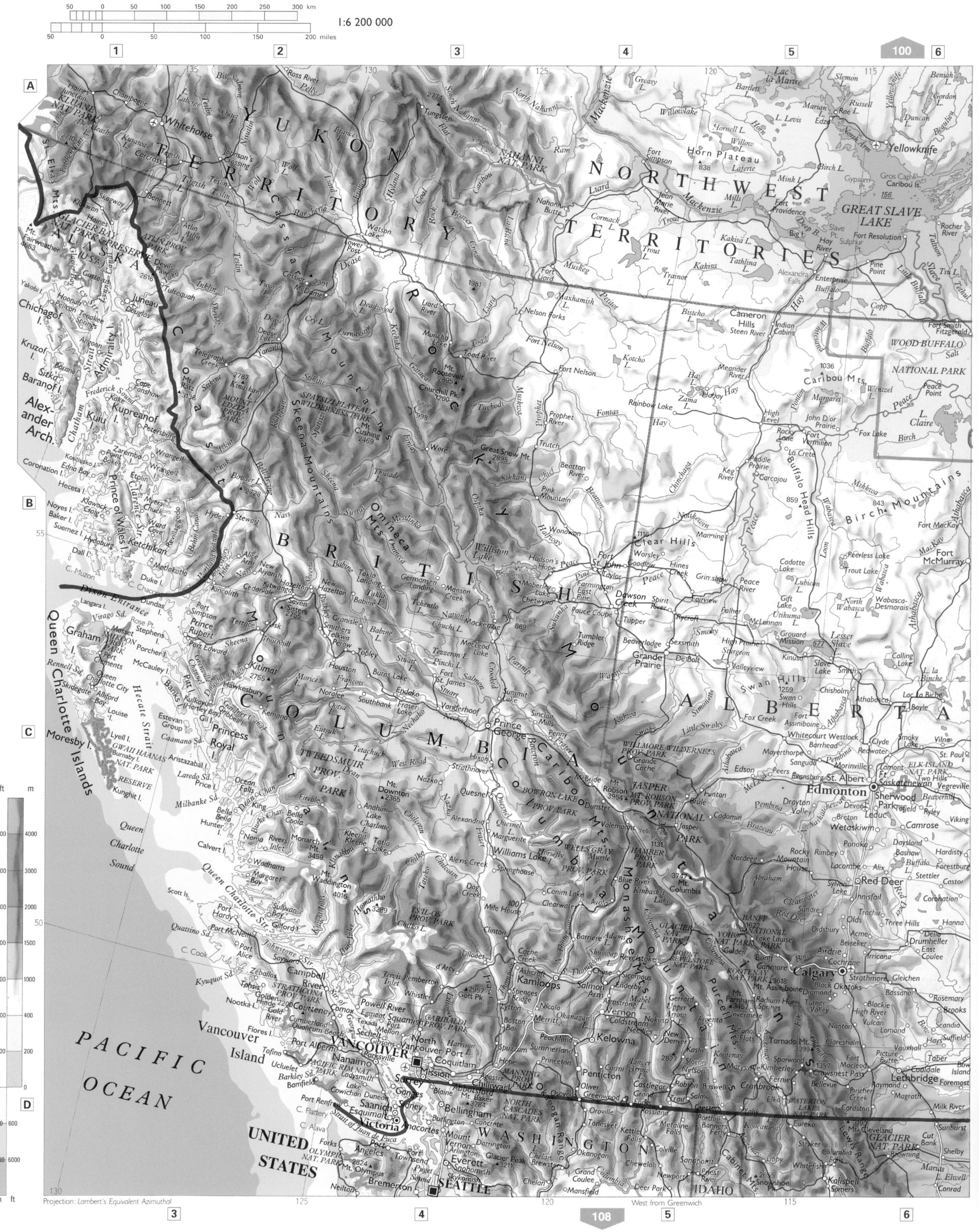

1:6 200 000

Projection: Lambert's Equivalent Azimuthal

West from Greenwich

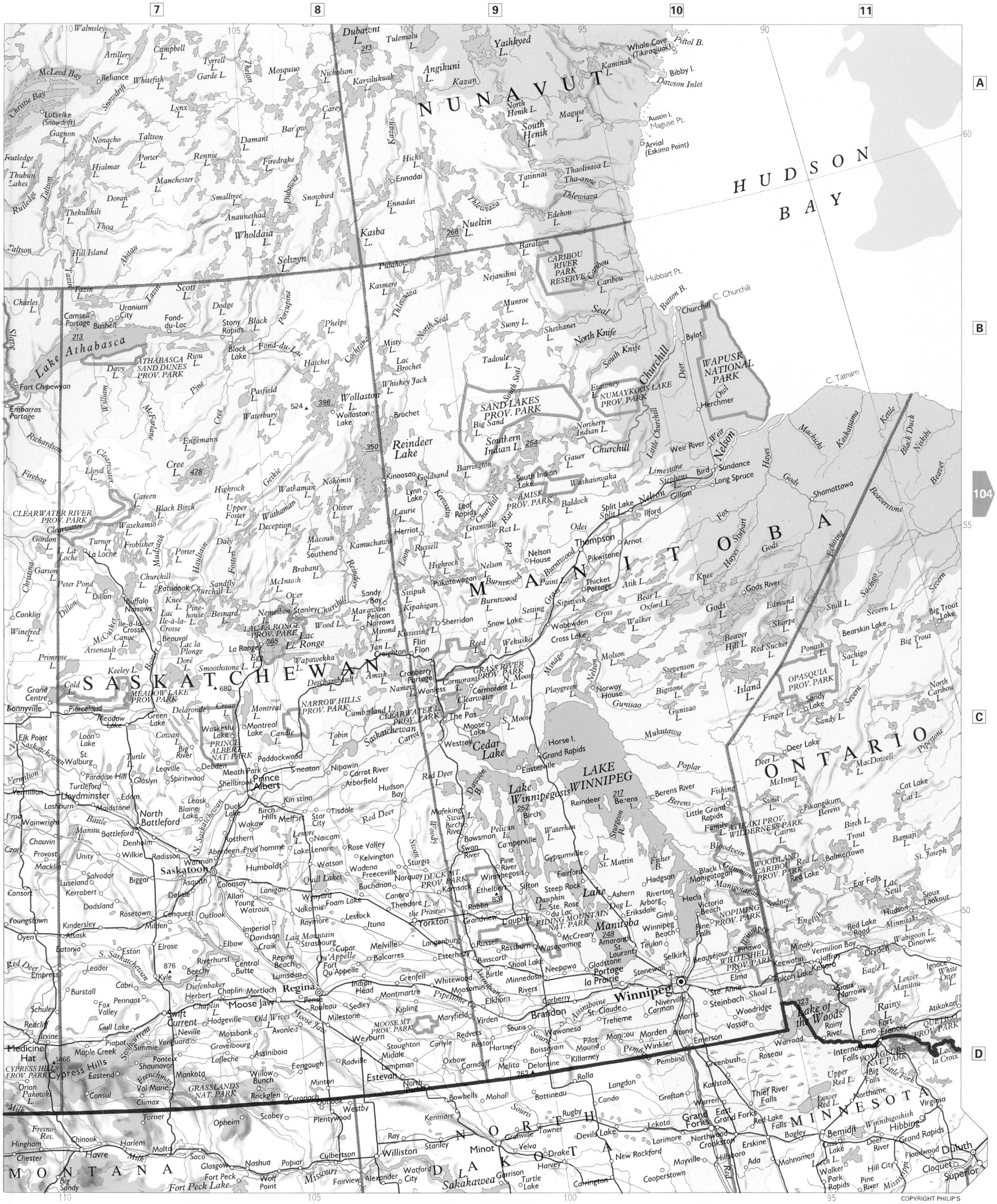

National Parks

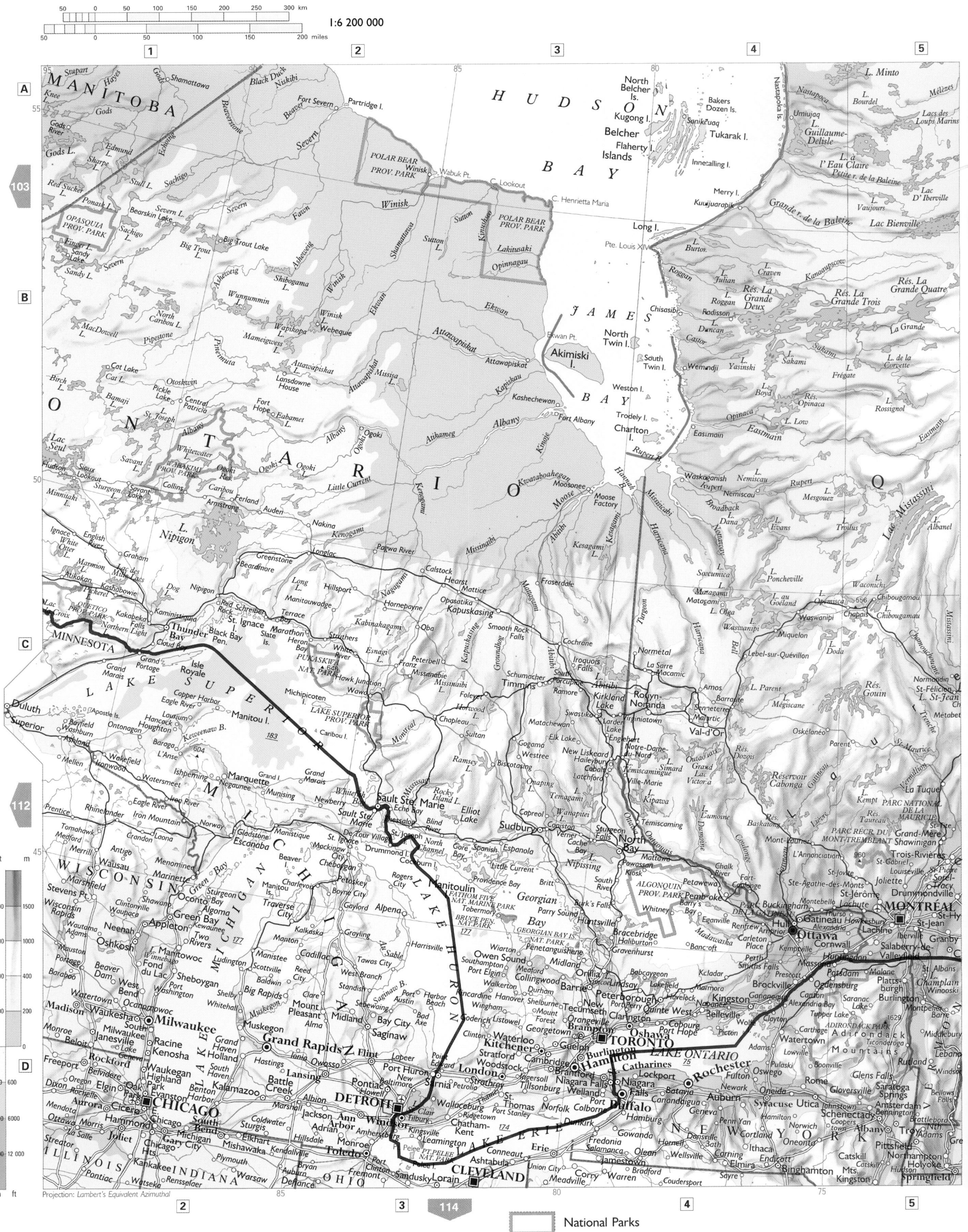

50 0 50 100 150 200 250 300 km

50 0 50 100 150 200 miles

1:6 200 000

National Parks

Projection: Lambert's Equivalent Azimuthal

6 101 7 8 9

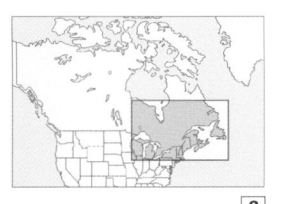

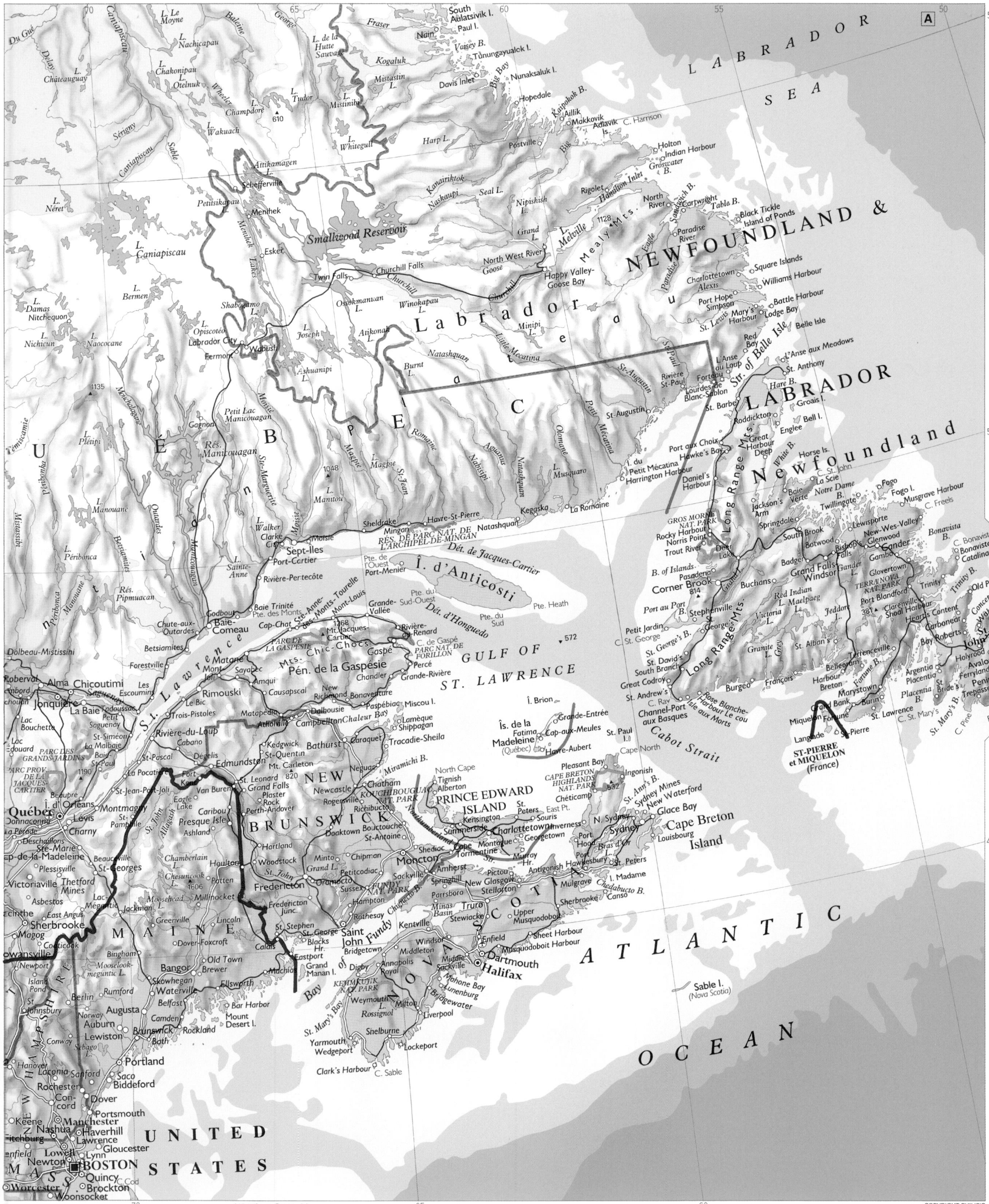
LABRADOR SEA
NEWFOUNDLAND & LABRADOR
Labrador Plateau
QUÉBEC
Newfoundland
Smallwood Reservoir
Churchill Falls
Happy Valley-Goose Bay
North West River
Nain
Hopedale
Makkovik
Postville
Cartwright
Labrador City
Wabush
Fermont
Schefferville
Sept-Îles
Port-Cartier
Baie-Comeau
Havre-St-Pierre
Natashquan
Kegaska
La Romaine
St-Augustin
Blanc-Sablon
Str. of Belle Isle
St. Anthony
Long Range Mts.
Corner Brook
Stephenville
Gander
Grand Falls-Windsor
St. John's
Avalon Peninsula
Marystown
ST-PIERRE et MIQUELON (France)
Cabot Strait
Î. d'Anticosti
GULF OF ST. LAWRENCE
Îs. de la Madeleine
Pén. de la Gaspésie
Gaspé
Rimouski
Matane
Chicoutimi
Jonquière
Québec
Lévis
Sherbrooke
Trois-Pistoles
Rivière-du-Loup
Edmundston
NEW BRUNSWICK
Fredericton
Saint John
Moncton
Bathurst
Campbellton
PRINCE EDWARD ISLAND
Charlottetown
Summerside
Cape Breton Island
Sydney
NOVA SCOTIA
Halifax
Dartmouth
Truro
Yarmouth
Bay of Fundy
Sable I. (Nova Scotia)
MAINE
Bangor
Augusta
Portland
Manchester
Concord
BOSTON
Worcester
UNITED STATES
ATLANTIC OCEAN
West from Greenwich

6 7 8

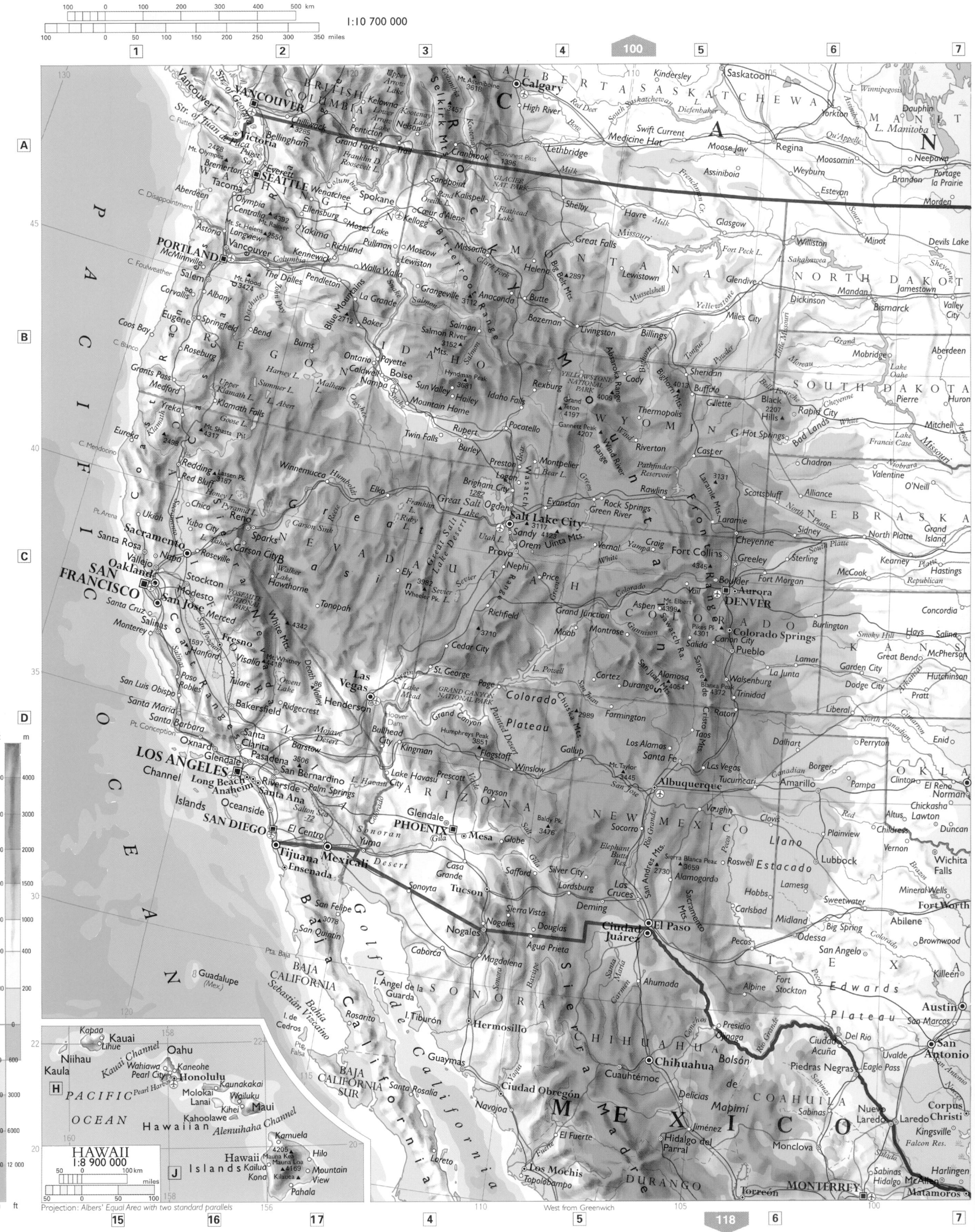

1:10 700 000

HAWAII
1:8 900 000

Projection: Albers' Equal Area with two standard parallels

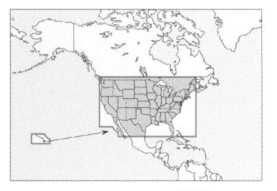

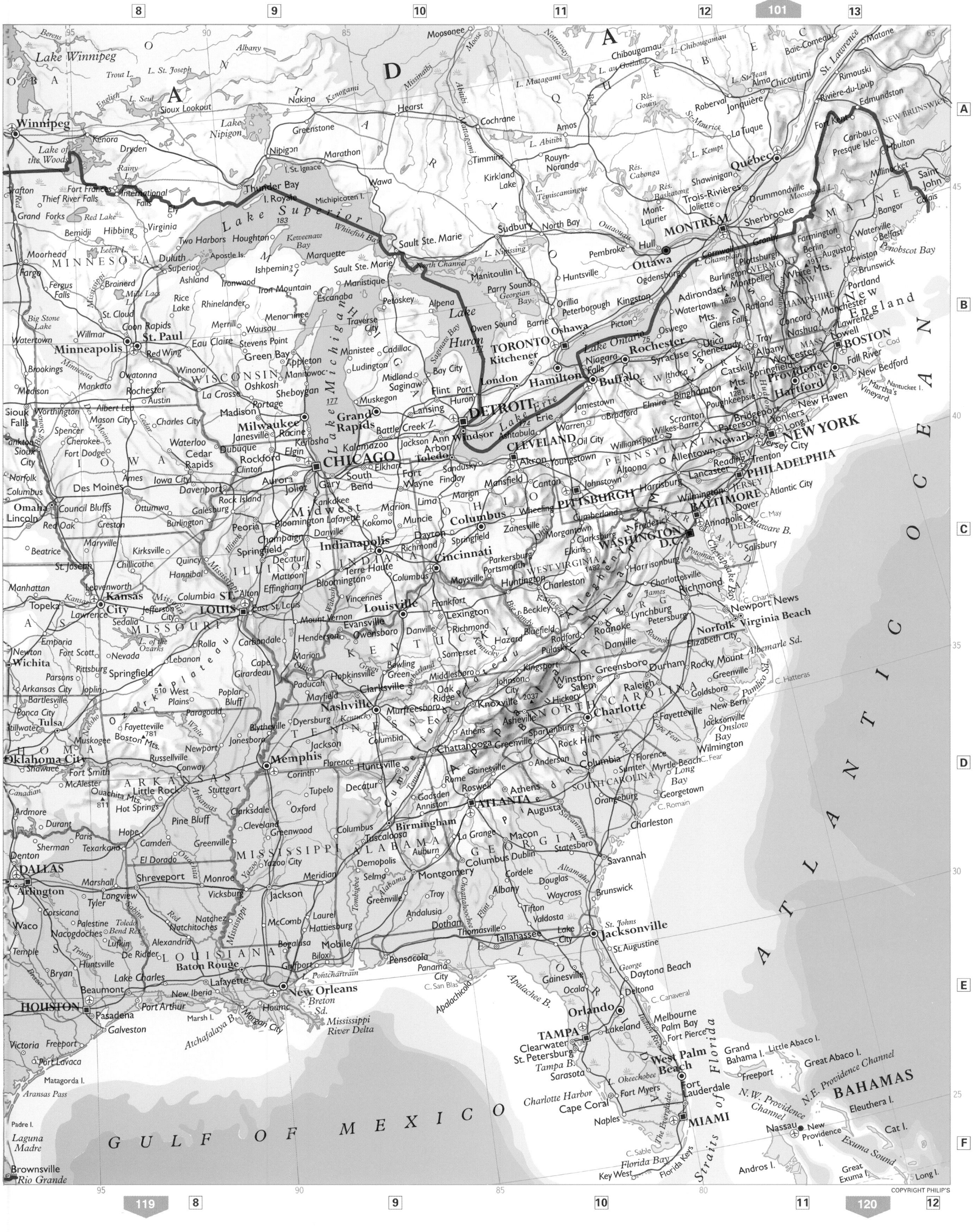

101
119
120
Lake Winnipeg
Winnipeg
Lake of the Woods
Lake Superior
Lake Michigan
Lake Huron
Lake Erie
Lake Ontario
CHICAGO
DETROIT
TORONTO
MONTRÉAL
Ottawa
Québec
NEW YORK
PHILADELPHIA
BOSTON
BALTIMORE
WASHINGTON D.C.
PITTSBURGH
CLEVELAND
Minneapolis
St. Paul
Milwaukee
Indianapolis
Cincinnati
Louisville
Nashville
Memphis
Kansas City
ST. LOUIS
Atlanta
Charlotte
Jacksonville
New Orleans
HOUSTON
DALLAS
Oklahoma City
Orlando
TAMPA
MIAMI
BAHAMAS
MINNESOTA
WISCONSIN
IOWA
MISSOURI
ILLINOIS
INDIANA
OHIO
KENTUCKY
TENNESSEE
MISSISSIPPI
ALABAMA
GEORGIA
FLORIDA
SOUTH CAROLINA
NORTH CAROLINA
WEST VIRGINIA
PENNSYLVANIA
NEW YORK
VERMONT
NEW HAMPSHIRE
MAINE
NEW BRUNSWICK
ARKANSAS
LOUISIANA
ATLANTIC OCEAN
GULF OF MEXICO
Straits of Florida
New England
Midwest
Appalachian Mts.
Ozark Plateau
Cumberland Plateau
Mississippi River Delta

50   0   50   100   150   200 km

50   0   50   100   150 miles

1:5 300 000

112

102

A   B   C   D   E   F

10   9   8   7   6   5   4   3   2   1

SASKATCHEWAN

ALBERTA

BRITISH COLUMBIA

MONTANA

WYOMING

IDAHO

OREGON

WASHINGTON

NEVADA

UTAH

VANCOUVER

SEATTLE

PORTLAND

Sacramento

Salt Lake City

Great Salt Lake

Bighorn Mountains

Absaroka Range

Wind River Range

Medicine Bow Mts.

Bitterroot Range

Salmon River Mountains

Sawtooth Range

Lewis Range

Swan Range

Cabinet Mountains

Blue Mountains

Wallowa Mts.

Columbia Basin

Uinta Mountains

Sierra Nevada

Coast Ranges

Warner Mts.

Great Salt Lake Desert

Columbia Plateau

Harney Basin

PACIFIC RANGES NAT. PARK

Strait of Juan de Fuca

Olympic Mts.

YELLOWSTONE NAT. PARK

GRAND TETON NAT. PARK

GLACIER NATIONAL PARK

CRATER LAKE NAT. PARK

Great Falls

Billings

Helena

Butte

Bozeman

Missoula

Boise

Spokane

Yakima

Olympia

Tacoma

Everett

Bellingham

Victoria

Nanaimo

New Westminster

Medicine Hat

Lethbridge

Reno

Carson City

Eugene

Salem

Eureka

Redding

Klamath Falls

Pocatello

Idaho Falls

Ogden

Provo

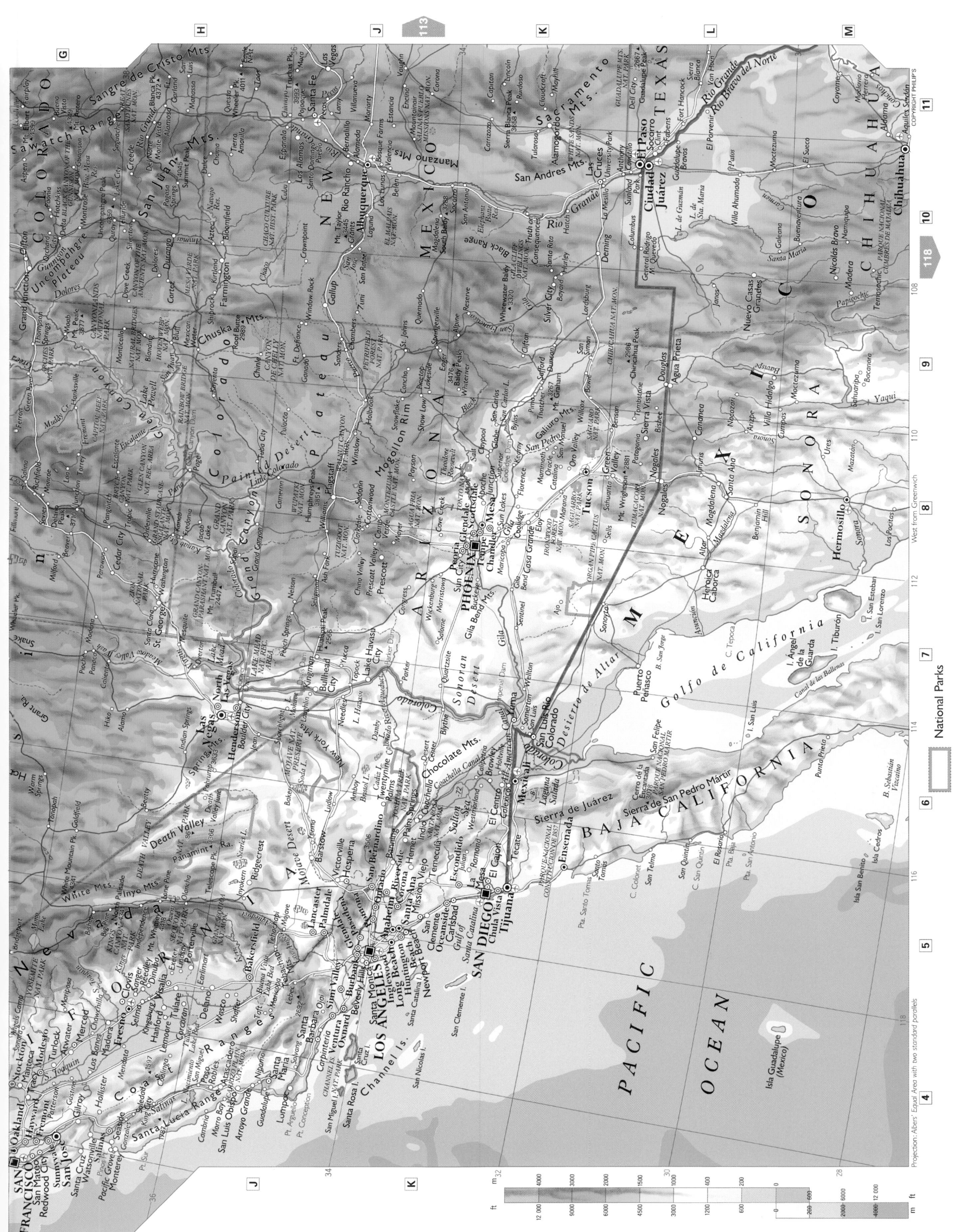

Projection: Albers' Equal Area with two standard parallels

West from Greenwich

National Parks

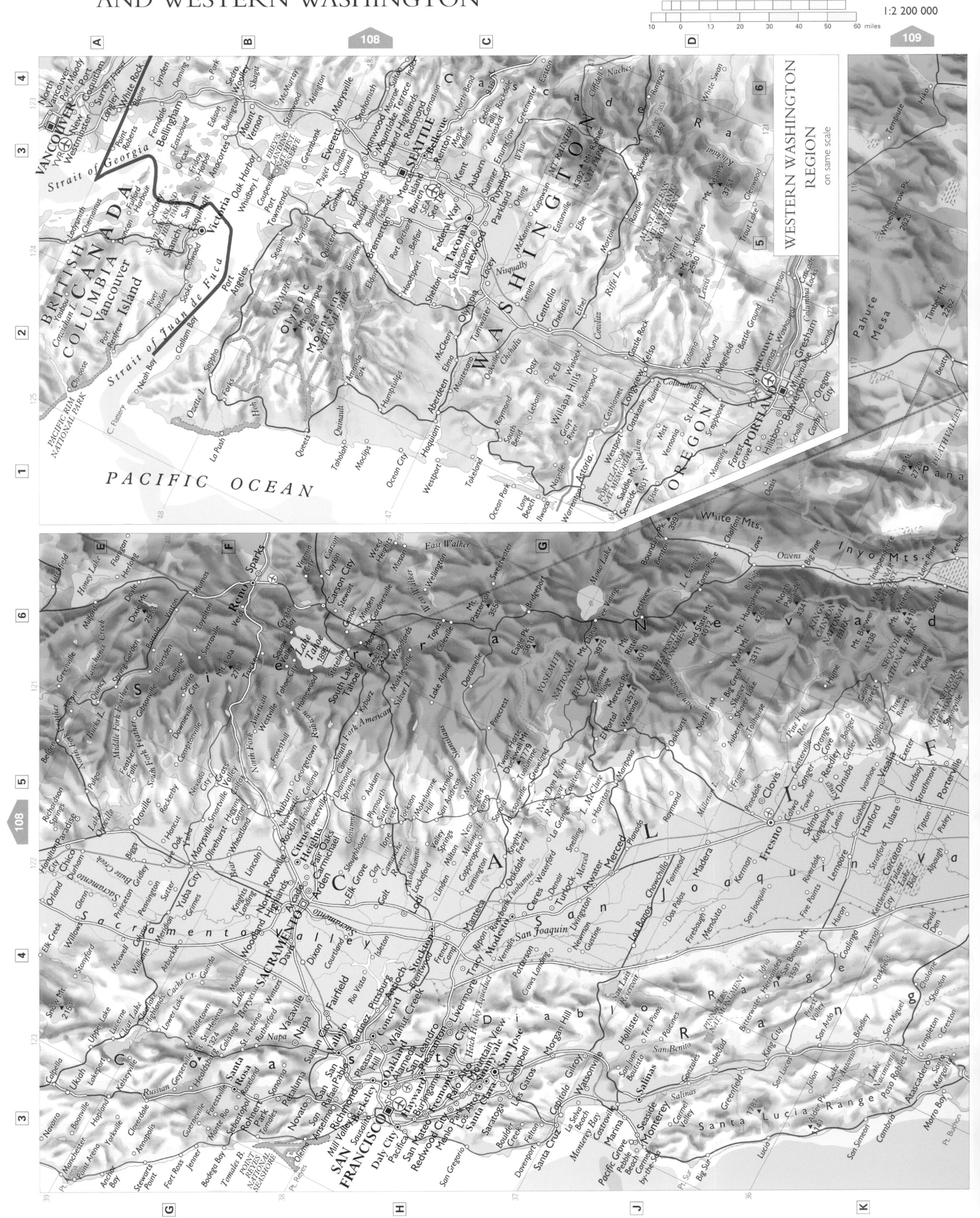

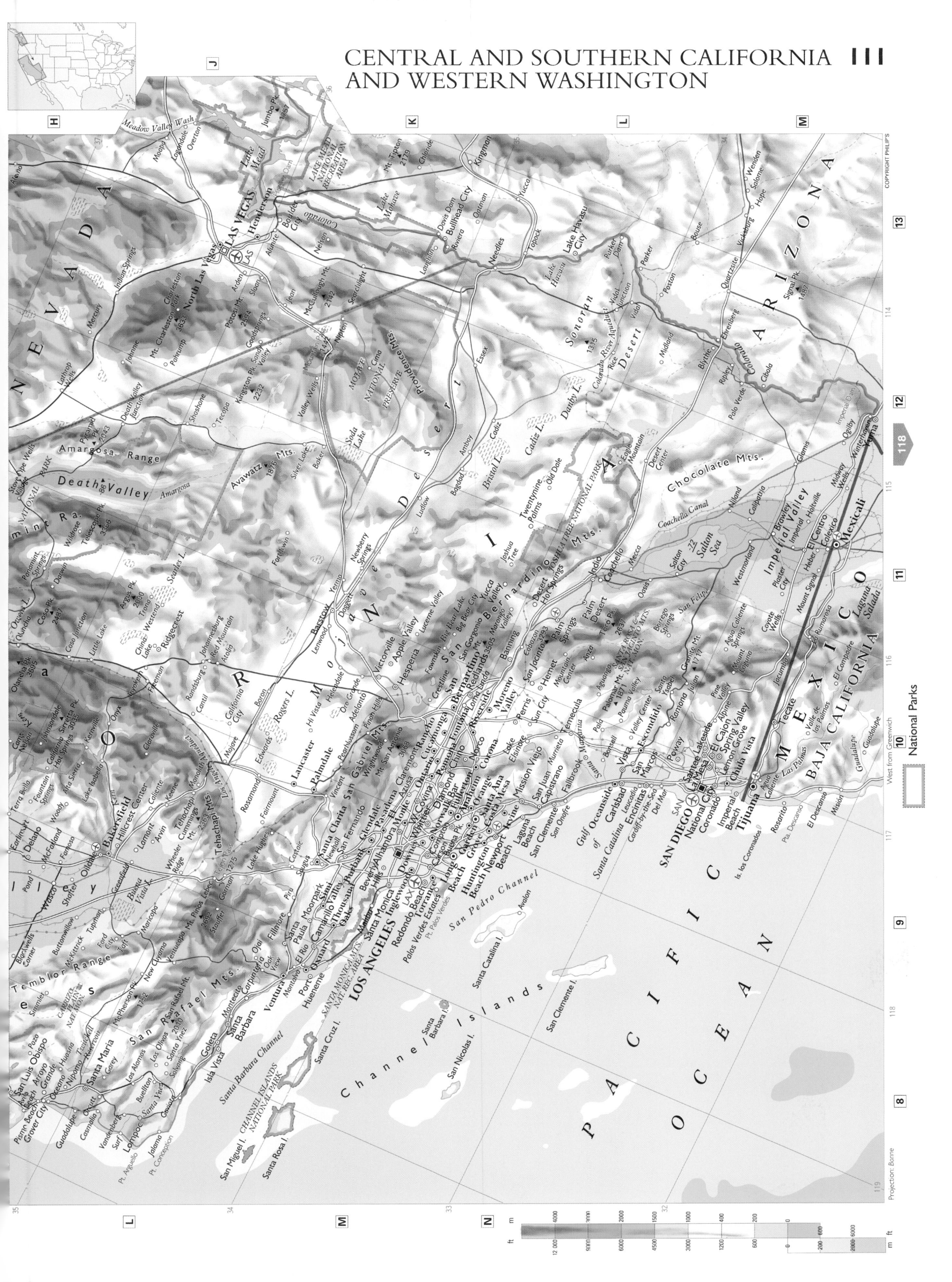

COPYRIGHT PHILIP'S

West from Greenwich

National Parks

Projection: Bonne

1:5 300 000

50   0   50   100   150   200 km
50   0   50   100   150 miles

CANADA

LAKE SUPERIOR

MICHIGAN

WISCONSIN

MINNESOTA

NORTH DAKOTA

SOUTH DAKOTA

MONTANA

WYOMING

NEBRASKA

IOWA

ILLINOIS

MISSOURI

KANSAS

COLORADO

CHICAGO

Milwaukee

Minneapolis
St. Paul

Duluth
Superior

Des Moines

Sioux City

Sioux Falls

Omaha

Lincoln

Kansas City

St. Joseph

Topeka

St. Louis

Springfield

Denver

Colorado Springs

Pueblo

Cheyenne

Rapid City

Bismarck

Fargo

Grand Forks

Thunder Bay

ISLE ROYALE NAT. PARK

BADLANDS NAT. PARK

THEODORE ROOSEVELT NAT. PARK

WIND CAVE NAT. PARK

Black Hills

Sand Hills

Smoky Hills

Coteau des Prairies

Missouri

Mississippi

Iowa

James

White

Platte

North Platte

South Platte

Red

Laramie Mountains

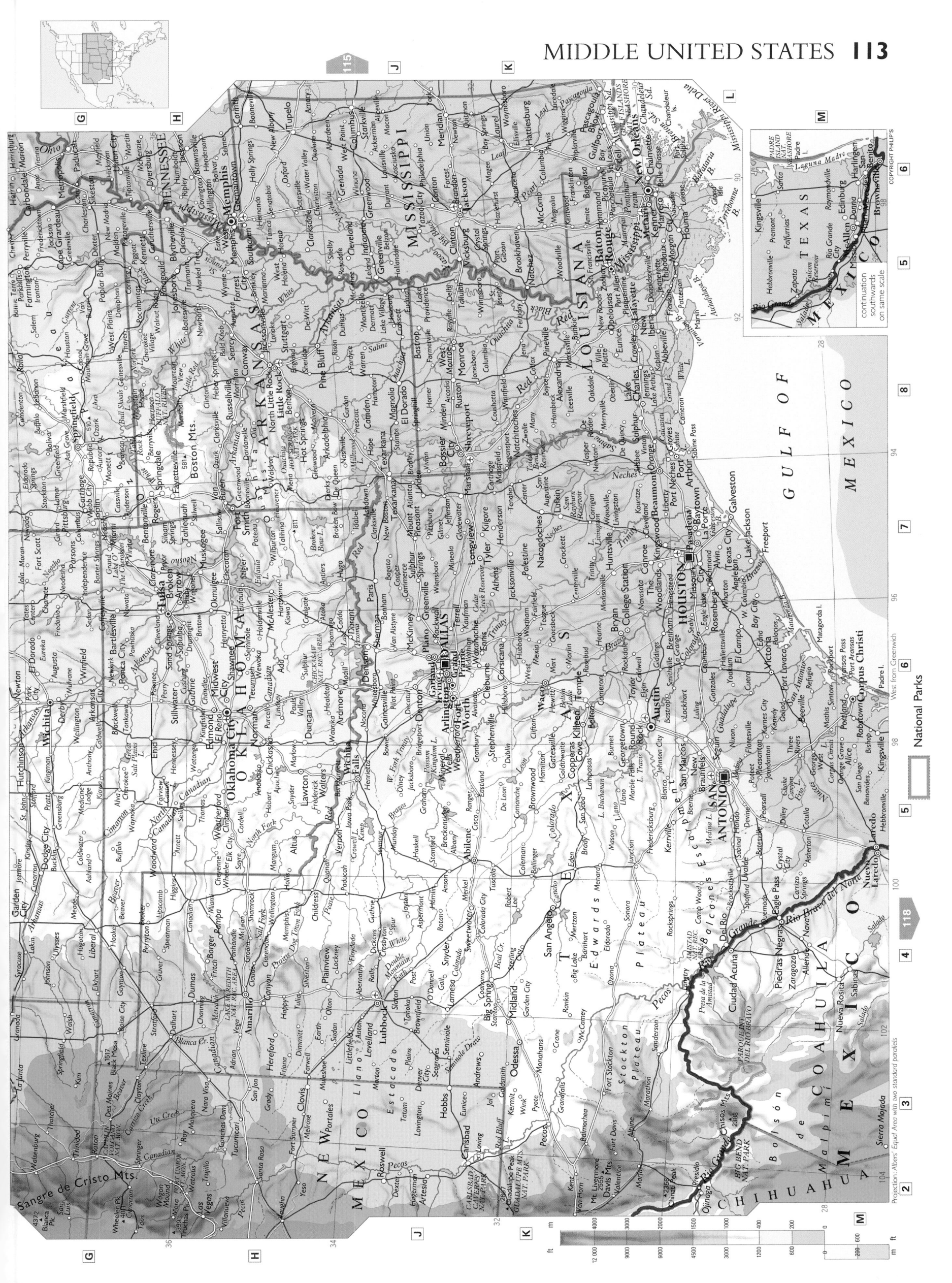

COPYRIGHT PHILIP'S

continuation southwards on same scale

National Parks

Projection: Albers' Equal Area with two standard parallels

West from Greenwich

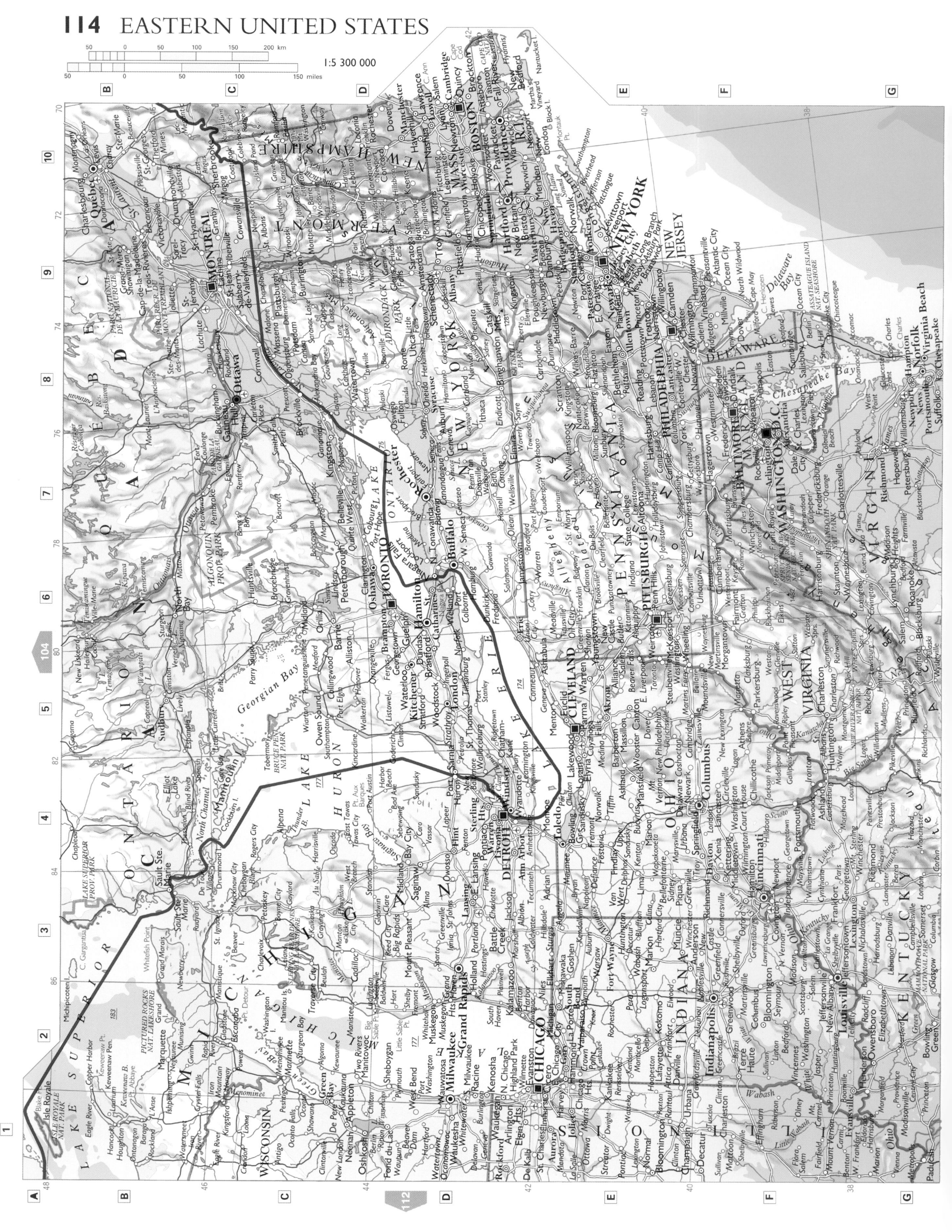

1:5 300 000

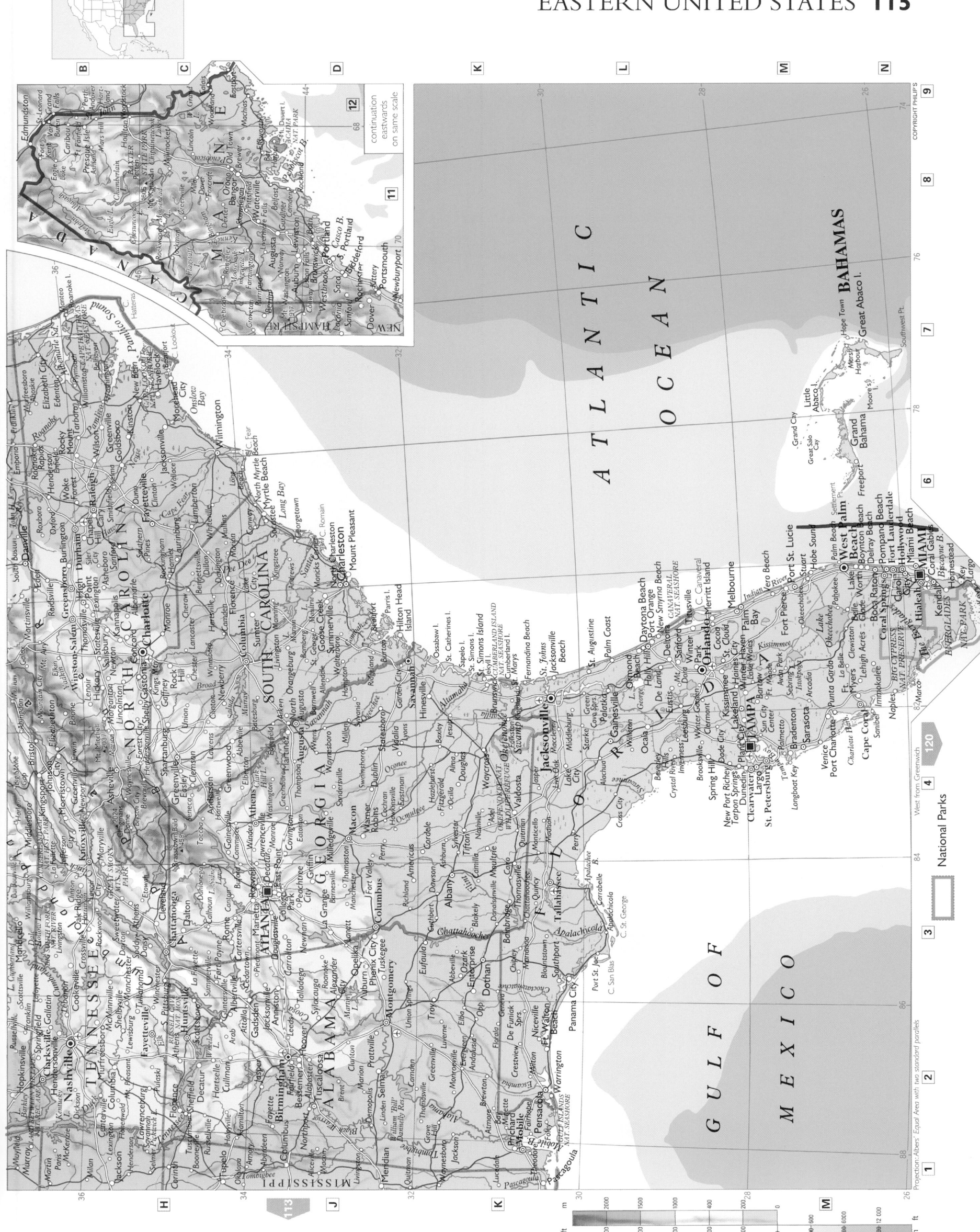

ATLANTIC OCEAN

GULF OF MEXICO

BAHAMAS

FLORIDA

GEORGIA

ALABAMA

MISSISSIPPI

TENNESSEE

NORTH CAROLINA

SOUTH CAROLINA

MAINE

CANADA

NEW HAMPSHIRE

National Parks

continuation eastwards on same scale

COPYRIGHT PHILIP'S

Projection: Albers' Equal Area with two standard parallels

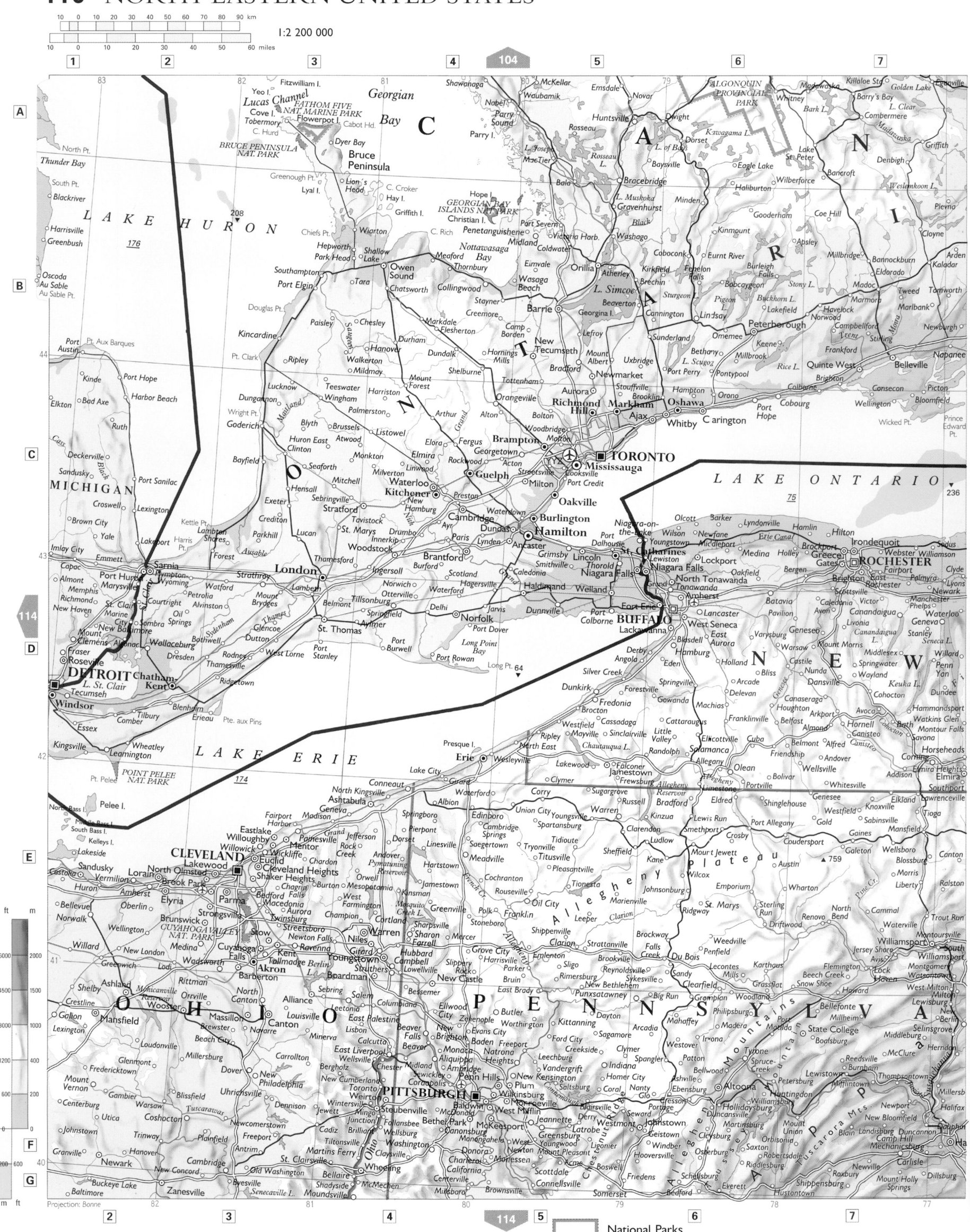

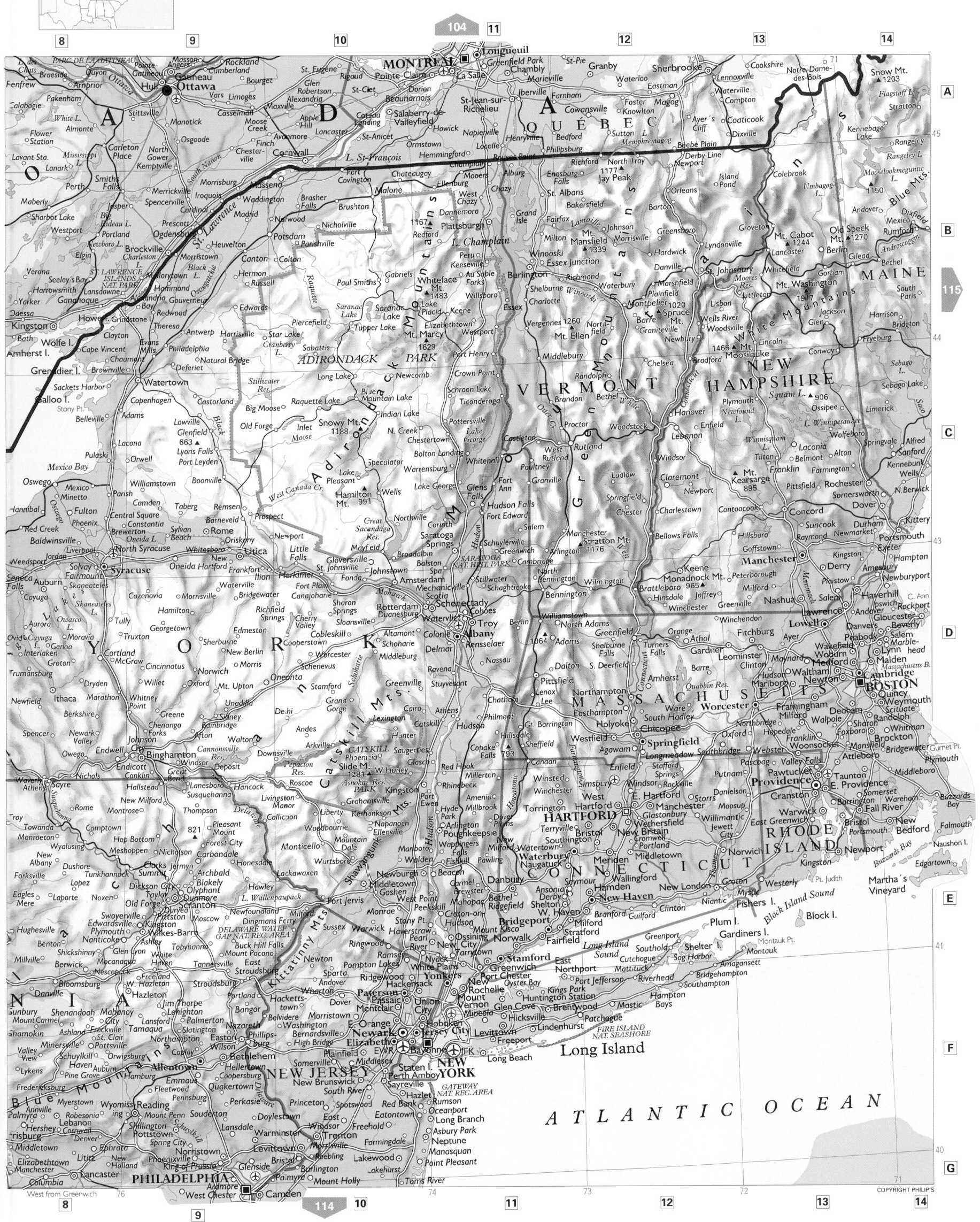

A

B

115

C

D

E

F

G

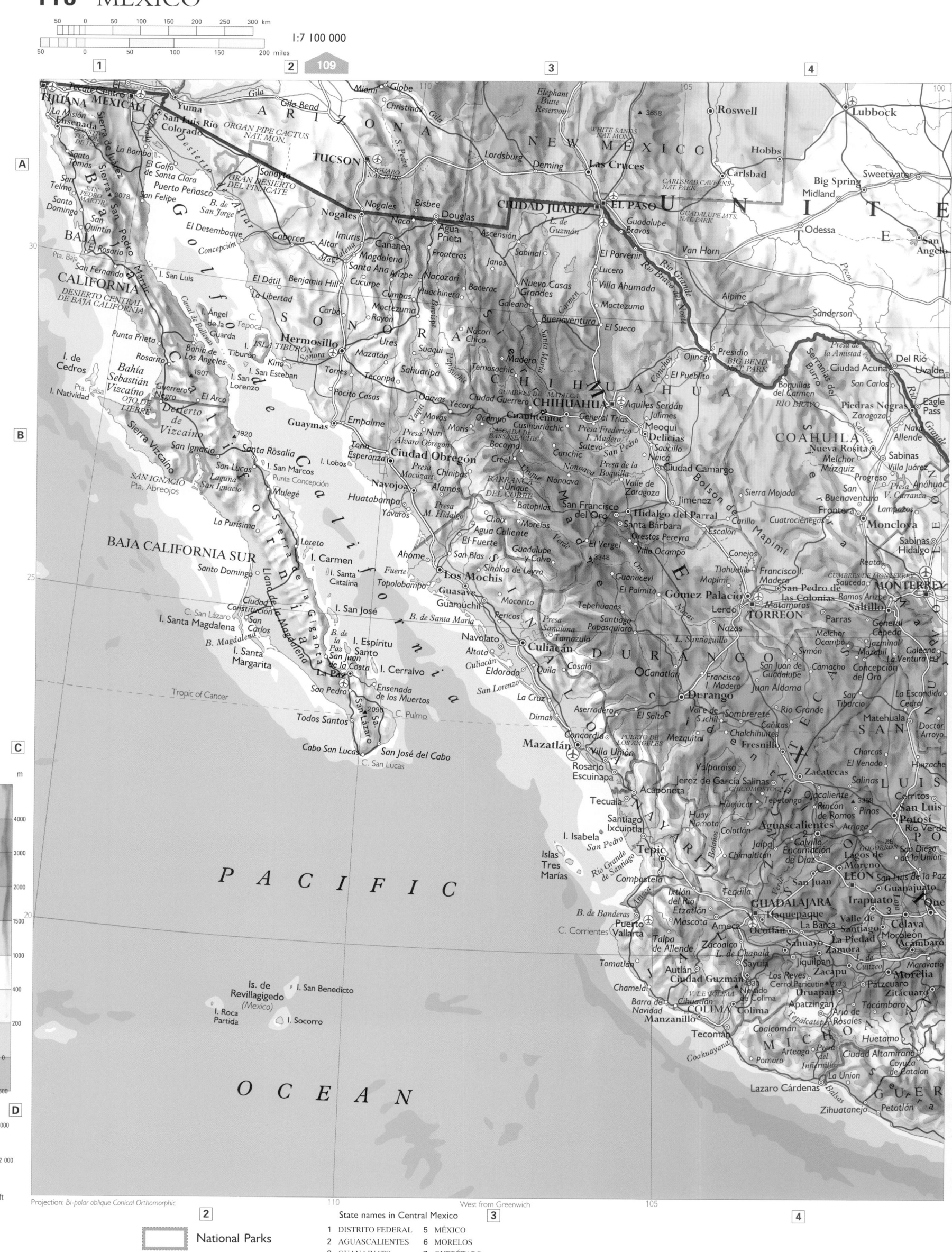

National Parks

State names in Central Mexico
1 DISTRITO FEDERAL
2 AGUASCALIENTES
3 GUANAJUATO
4 HIDALGO
5 MÉXICO
6 MORELOS
7 QUERÉTARO
8 TLAXCALA

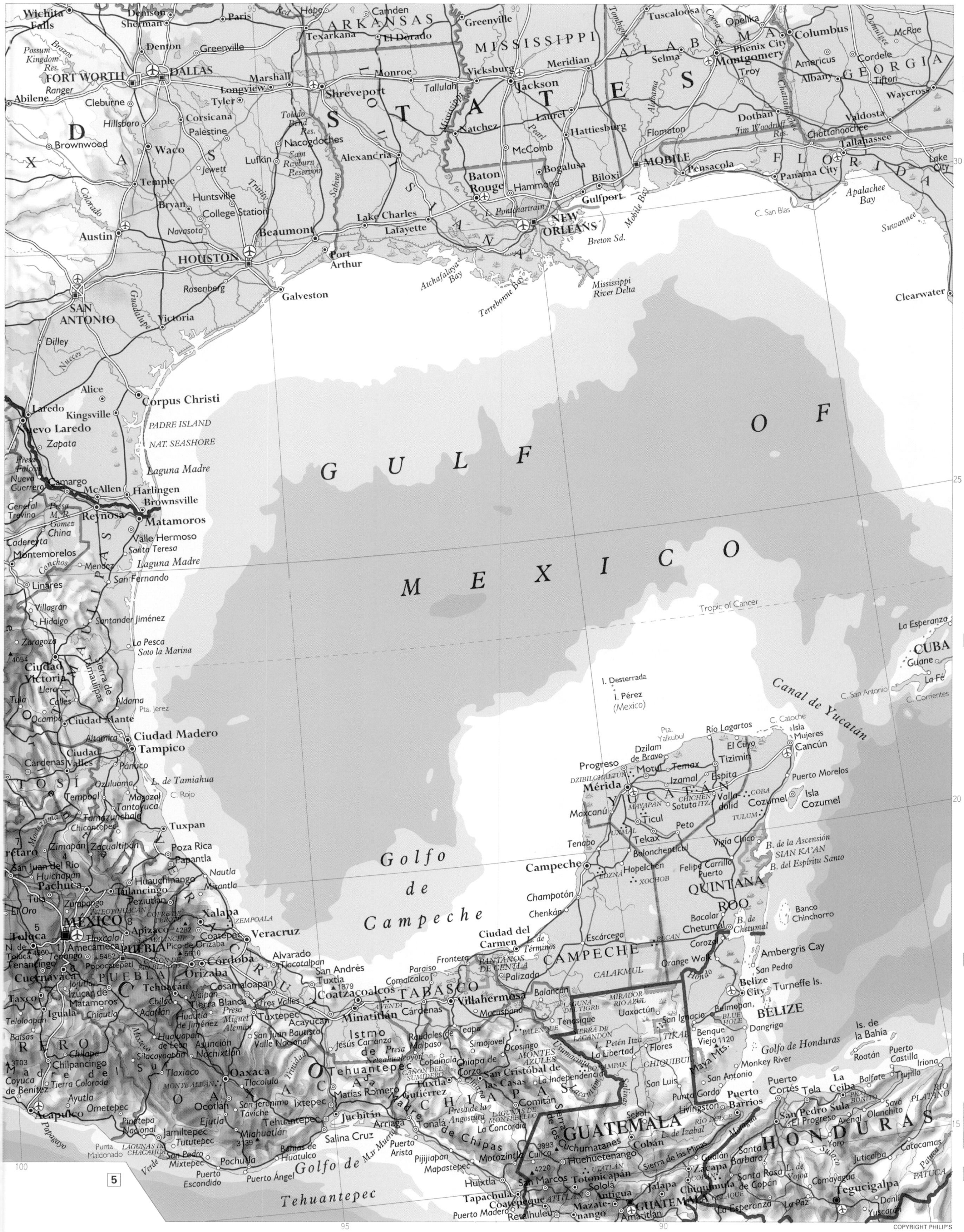

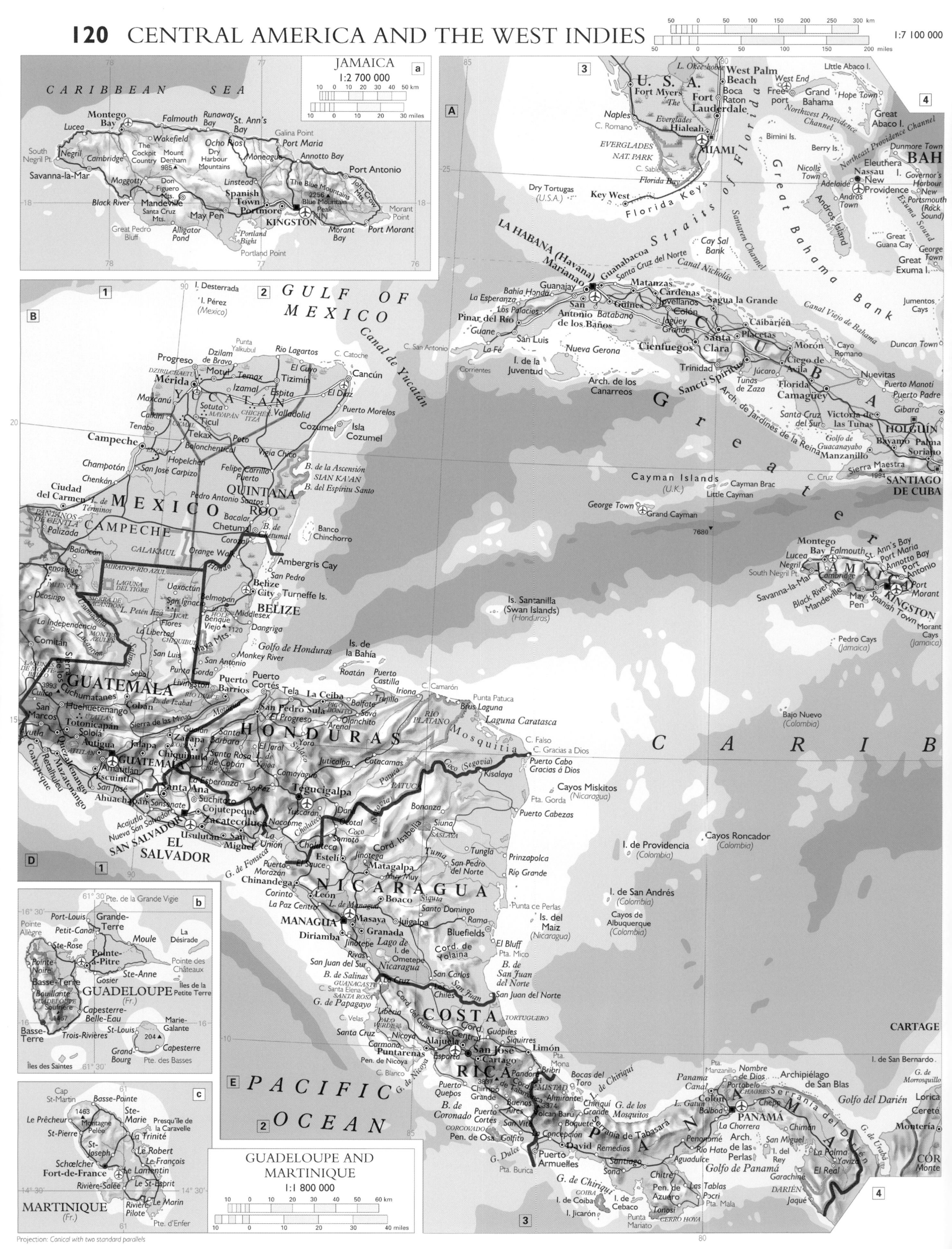

PUERTO RICO
1:2 700 000

VIRGIN ISLANDS
1:1 800 000

ST. LUCIA
1:890 000

BARBADOS
1:890 000

ATLANTIC OCEAN

CARIBBEAN SEA

BAHAMAS

HAITI — PORT-AU-PRINCE

DOMINICAN REP. — SANTO DOMINGO

PUERTO RICO (U.S.A.)

Virgin Is. (U.K.) / **Virgin Is.** (U.S.A.)

Greater Antilles — *Hispaniola*

Lesser Antilles — *Leeward Islands* — *Windward Islands*

ST. KITTS & NEVIS — Basseterre
ANTIGUA & BARBUDA — St. John's
Montserrat (U.K.)
GUADELOUPE (Fr.) — Basse-Terre
DOMINICA — Roseau
MARTINIQUE (Fr.) — Fort-de-France
ST. LUCIA — Castries
ST. VINCENT & THE GRENADINES — Kingstown
BARBADOS — Bridgetown
GRENADA — St. George's
TRINIDAD & TOBAGO — Port of Spain

COLOMBIA — Santa Marta, Barranquilla, Riohacha

VENEZUELA — Maracaibo, Caracas, Barquisimeto, Ciudad Bolívar, Ciudad Guayana

Aruba (Neth.), Curaçao, Bonaire — **NETH. ANTILLES** — Willemstad

Puerto Rico Trench — Milwaukee Deep 9200

West from Greenwich

National Parks

COPYRIGHT PHILIP'S

100 0 200 400 600 800 1000 1200 1400 km
1:31 100 000
100   200   400   600   800   1000 miles

Projection: Lambert's Azimuthal Equal Area

COPYRIGHT PHILIP'S

Tropic of Cancer

NORTH ATLANTIC OCEAN

Yucatán Channel
Cuba
Greater Antilles
Turks & Caicos Is.
Gulf of Campeche
Yucatán Peninsula
Hispaniola
9200
Puerto Rico
Isthmus of Tehuantepec
G. de Honduras
Jamaica
Guadeloupe
Dominica
Martinique
Lesser Antilles
St. Lucia
St. Vincent
Barbados
C. Gracias a Dios
Caribbean Sea
Grenada
Tobago
Trinidad
Guatemala Trench
L. Nicaragua
Panama Canal
C. de la Aguja
5800
Sierra Nevada de Santa Marta
L. Maracaibo
I. Margarita
G. of Darién
Gulf of Panamá
Cordillera Occidental
Cordillera Central
Cordillera Oriental
Cord. de Mérida
Orinoco
Llanos
Guiana Highlands
C. Orange
Meta
2810
Mt. Roraima
Sierra Pacaraima
Serra Tumucumaque
Serra Parima
Guaviare
Branco
Negro
C. de San Francisco
Caquetá
Equator
Marajó I.
Galapagos Is.
Cotopaxi 5897
Chimborazo 6267
Napo
Putumayo
Japurá
Amazon
Tocantins
Amazon
C. de São Roque
G. of Guayaquil
Marañón
Selvas
Juruá
Purus
Madeira
Tapajós
Xingu
Araguaia
Parnaíba
Pta. Pariñas
Pta. Negra
Ucayali
Juruá
Aripuanã
Roosevelt
Teles Pires
São Francisco
Plat. of Borborema
Huascarán 6768
Madre de Dios
Guaporé
Arinos
Brazilian Highlands
Chincha Alta
Titicaca
Mamoré
Plateau of Mato Grosso
Nevado Ancohuma 6550
Bolivian Plateau
L. de Poopó
PACIFIC
OCEAN
Gran Chaco
Paraguay
Paraná
Serra da Mantiqueira
2890 Pico da Bandeira
Tropic of Capricorn
8050
Atacama Desert
Andes
Chile Peru Trench
Pilcomayo
Paraguay
Entre Ríos
Iguaçu Falls
Uruguay
Serra do Mar
C. Frio
San Félix
San Ambrosio
Cerro Ojos del Salado 6863
Salado
Paraná
L. dos Patos
Abrolhos Bank
Salinas Grandes
Mt. Aconcagua 6962
Sierra de Córdoba
L. Mar Chiquita
Rio de la Plata
SOUTH
ATLANTIC
OCEAN
Arch. de Juan Fernández
Pampas
Colorado
Bahía Blanca
Negro
G. San Matias
Valdés Peninsula
Argentine Basin
Chile Rise
Chiloé I.
Chonos Archipelago
Mte. San Valentín 4058
Gulf of San Jorge
Taitao Peninsula
Gulf of Penas
Patagonia
6212
Wellington I.
Madre de Dios I.
Falkland Is.
West Falkland
East Falkland
Magellan's Str.
Santa Inés I.
Tierra del Fuego
Staten I.
South Georgia
Canal Cockburn
Canal Beagle
C. Horn

West from Greenwich

1:31 100 000

100 0   200   400   600   800   1000 1200 1400 km

100   0   200   400   600   800   1000 miles

1 ■ LIMA Capital Cities

Projection: *Lambert's Azimuthal Equal Area*

60 *West from Greenwich* 50

COPYRIGHT PHILIP'S

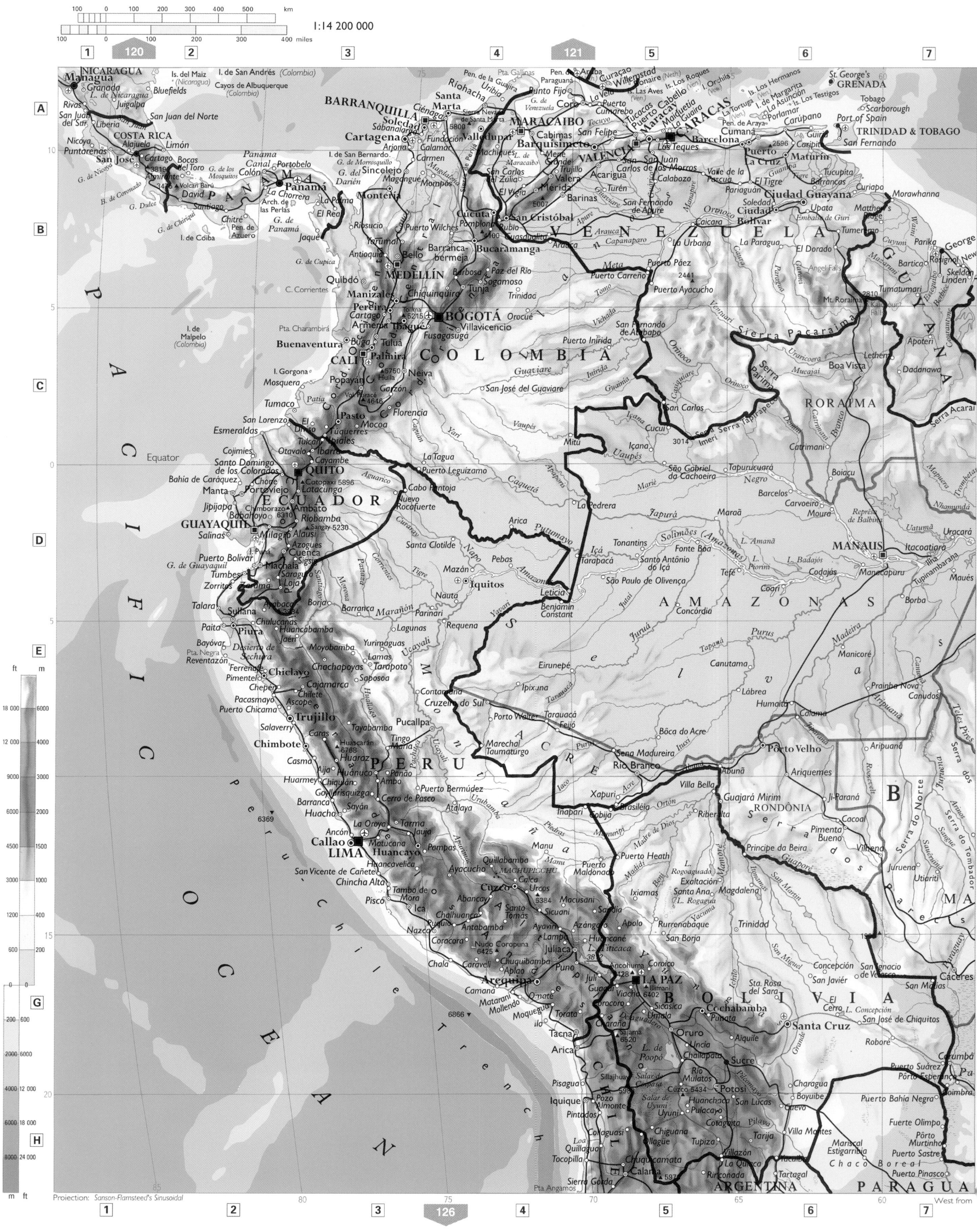

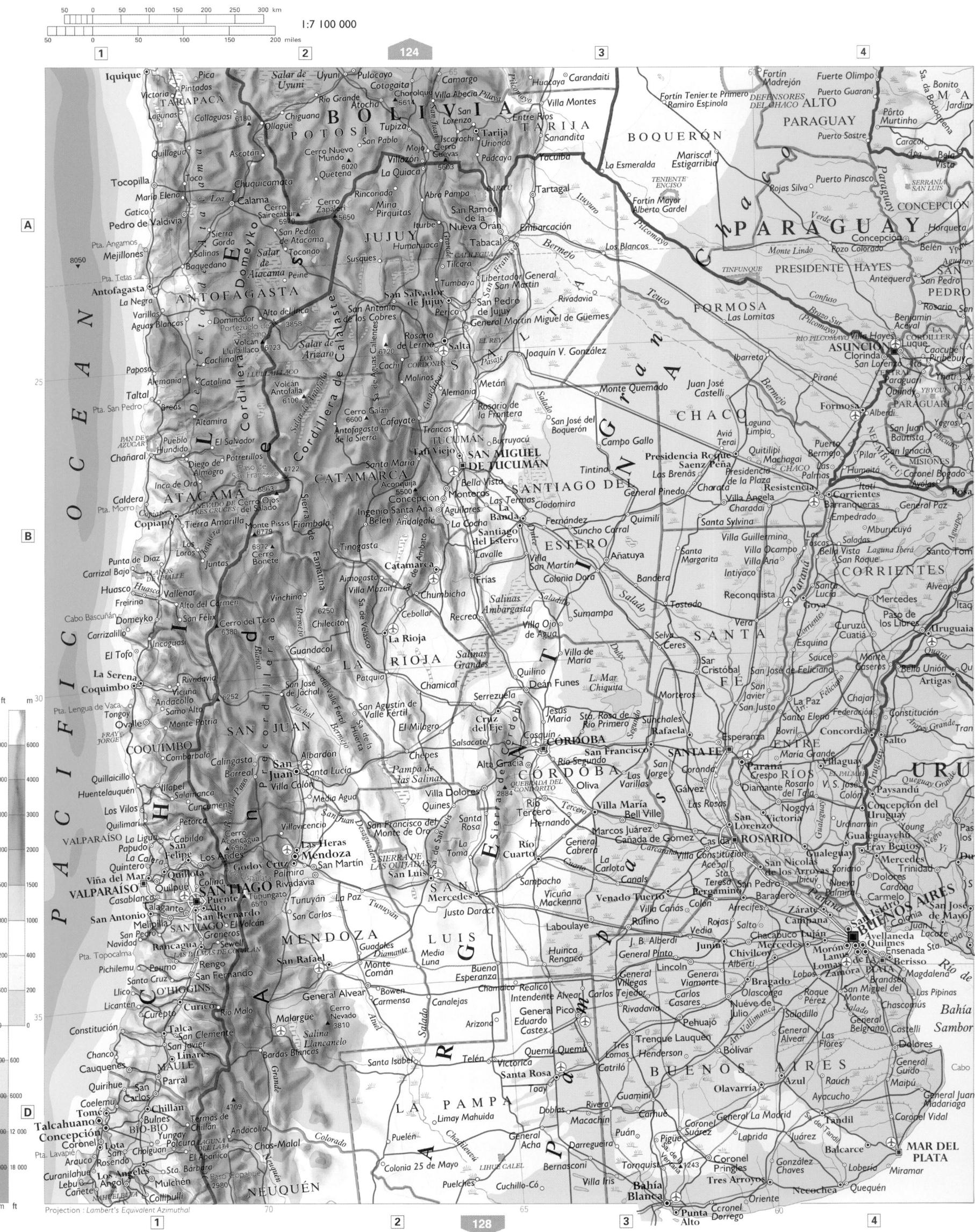

Projection : Lambert's Equivalent Azimuthal

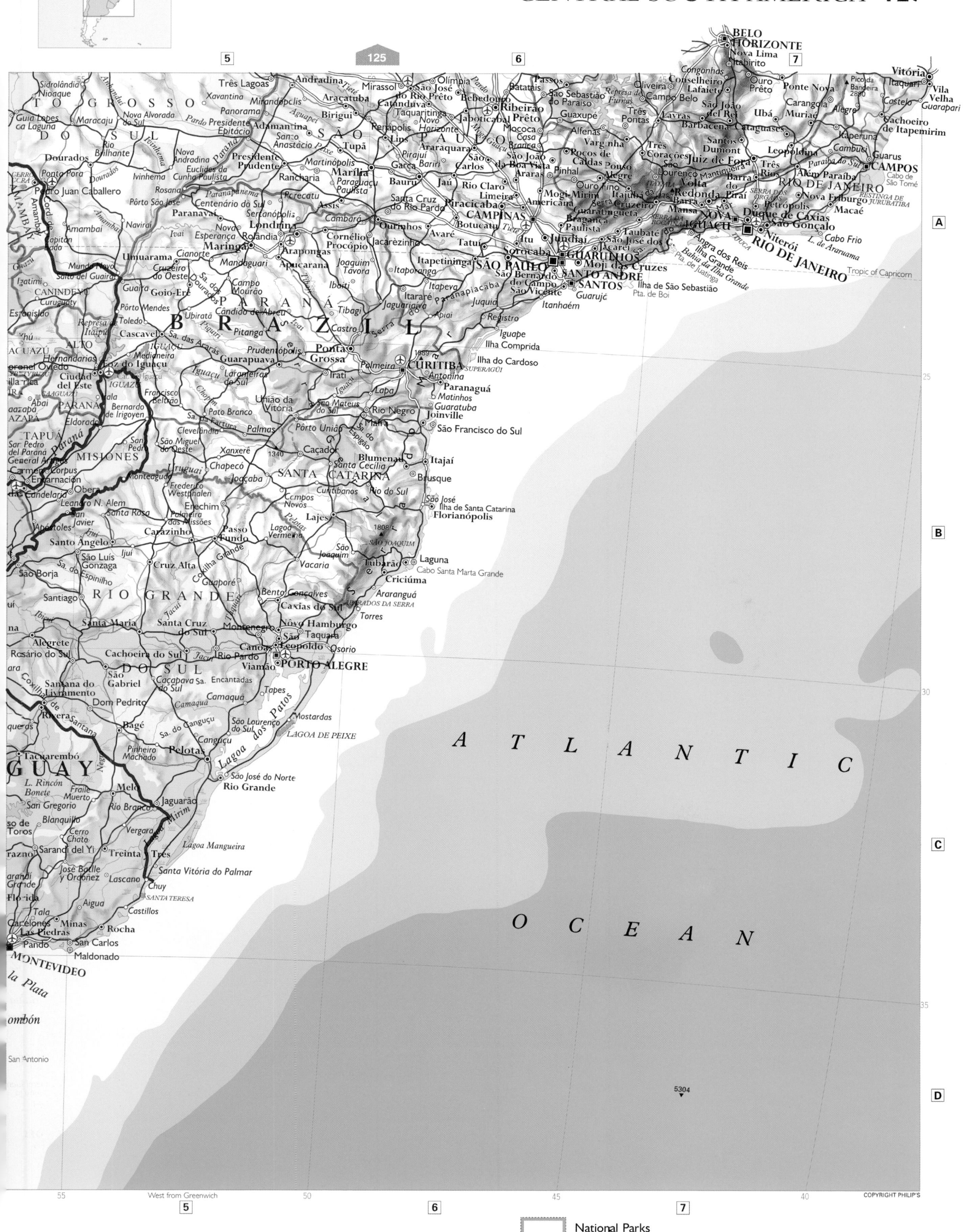

National Parks

1:14 200 000

100 0 100 200 300 400 500 km
100 0 100 200 300 400 miles

Projection: Sanson-Flamsteed's Sinusoidal

West from Greenwich

COPYRIGHT PHILIP'S

PARAGUAY

BRAZIL

URUGUAY

ARGENTINA

CHILE

PACIFIC OCEAN

SOUTH ATLANTIC OCEAN

Tropic of Capricorn

Peru–Chile Trench

Major places and features:

São Paulo · RIO DE JANEIRO · NOVA IGUAÇU · GHARULHOS · CURITIBA · Florianópolis · PORTO ALEGRE · Pelotas · Rio Grande · Ribeirão Prêto · Campinas · Santos · São Bernardo do Campo · Joinville · Blumenau · Caxias · Londrina · Maringá · Foz do Iguaçu

ASUNCIÓN · Concepción · Villarrica · Encarnación · Posadas · Formosa · Resistencia · Corrientes

MONTEVIDEO · Mercedes · Paysandú · Salto · Durazno · Rocha · Maldonado · Treinta y Tres

BUENOS AIRES · La Plata · Avellaneda · Rosario · CÓRDOBA · Santa Fe · Paraná · Mar del Plata · Bahía Blanca · Neuquén · San Juan · MENDOZA · San Luis · Río Cuarto · San Miguel de Tucumán · Santiago del Estero · Salta · San Salvador de Jujuy · La Rioja · Catamarca · Resistencia · Río Gallegos · Comodoro Rivadavia · Puerto Madryn · Trelew · Rawson · Viedma · San Carlos de Bariloche · Esquel

SANTIAGO · Valparaíso · Viña del Mar · Rancagua · Talca · Concepción · Talcahuano · Temuco · Valdivia · Osorno · Puerto Montt · Castro · Coihaique · Punta Arenas · Antofagasta · Calama · Chuquicamata · Copiapó · La Serena · Coquimbo · Chañaral · Taltal

Salar de Atacama · Puna de Atacama · Cerro Aconcagua · Ojos del Salado

FALKLAND ISLANDS (ISLAS MALVINAS) (U.K.)
West Falkland · East Falkland · Stanley · Port Darwin · Weddell I. · King George B.

South Georgia (U.K.)

Tierra del Fuego · Estrecho de Magallanes (Magellan's Str.) · Ushuaia · C. de Hornos (C. Horn) · Río Grande · Punta Arenas · I. de Los Estados (Staten I.)

I. de Chiloé · Arch. de los Chonos · Pen. de Taitao · G. de Penas · Golfo San Jorge · Golfo San Matías · Pen. Valdés · Bahía Grande · Estrecho de Magallanes

Río de la Plata · Río Colorado · Río Negro · Río Chubut · Río Deseado · Río Santa Cruz · Río Gallegos · Pilcomayo · Paraguay · Paraná · Uruguay

INDEX TO WORLD MAPS

How to use the index

The index contains the names of all the principal places and features shown on the World Maps. Each name is followed by an additional entry in italics giving the country or region within which it is located. The alphabetical order of names composed of two or more words is governed primarily by the first word and then by the second. This is an example of the rule:

Mīr Kūh, *Iran*	....	**71 E8**
Mīr Shahdād, *Iran*	....	**71 E8**
Mira, *Italy*	....	**41 C9**
Mira por vos Cay, *Bahamas*	..	**121 B5**
Miraj, *India*	....	**66 F2**

Physical features composed of a proper name (Erie) and a description (Lake) are positioned alphabetically by the proper name. The description is positioned after the proper name and is usually abbreviated:

Erie, L., *N. Amer.* **116 D4**

Where a description forms part of a settlement or administrative name however, it is always written in full and put in its true alphabetic position:

Mount Morris, *U.S.A.* **116 D7**

Names beginning with M' and Mc are indexed as if they were spelled Mac. Names beginning St. are alphabetised under Saint, but Sankt, Sint, Sant', Santa and San are all spelt in full and are alphabetised accordingly. If the same place name occurs two or more times in the index and all are in the same country, each is followed by the name of the administrative subdivision in which it is located. For example:

Jackson, Ky., *U.S.A.*	....	**114 G4**
Jackson, Mich., *U.S.A.*	....	**114 D3**
Jackson, Minn., *U.S.A.*	....	**112 D7**

The number in bold type which follows each name in the index refers to the number of the map page where that feature or place will be found. This is usually the largest scale at which the place or feature appears.

The letter and figure which are in bold type immediately after the page number give the grid square on the map page, within which the feature is situated. The letter represents the latitude and the figure the longitude. A lower case letter immediately after the page number refers to an inset map on that page.

In some cases the feature itself may fall within the specified square, while the name is outside. This is usually the case only with features which are larger than a grid square.

Rivers are indexed to their mouths or confluences, and carry the symbol ➣ after their names. The following symbols are also used in the index: ■ country, ☑ overseas territory or dependency, ☐ first order administrative area, △ national park, ◠ other park (provincial park, nature reserve or game reserve), ✈ (LHR) principal airport (and location identifier).

How to pronounce place names

English-speaking people usually have no difficulty in reading and pronouncing correctly English place names. However, foreign place name pronunciations may present many problems. Such problems can be minimised by following some simple rules. However, these rules cannot be applied to all situations, and there will be many exceptions.

1. In general, stress each syllable equally, unless your experience suggests otherwise.
2. Pronounce the letter 'a' as a broad 'a' as in 'arm'.
3. Pronounce the letter 'e' as a short 'e' as in 'elm'.
4. Pronounce the letter 'i' as a cross between a short 'i' and long 'e', as the two 'i's in 'California'.
5. Pronounce the letter 'o' as an intermediate 'o' as in 'soft'.
6. Pronounce the letter 'u' as an intermediate 'u' as in 'sure'.
7. Pronounce consonants hard, except in the Romance-language areas where 'g's are likely to be pronounced softly like 'j' in 'jam'; 'j' itself may be pronounced as 'y'; and 'x's may be pronounced as 'h'.
8. For names in mainland China, pronounce 'q' like the 'ch' in 'chin', 'x' like the 'sh' in 'she', 'zh' like the 'j' in 'jam', and 'z' as if it were spelled 'dz'. In general pronounce 'a' as in 'father', 'e' as in 'but', 'i' as in 'keep', 'o' as in 'or', and 'u' as in 'rule'.

Moreover, English has no diacritical marks (accent and pronunciation signs), although some languages do. The following is a brief and general guide to the pronunciation of those most frequently used in the principal Western European languages.

		Pronunciation as in
French	é	day and shows that the e is to be pronounced; e.g. Orléans.
	è	mare
	î	used over any vowel and does not affect pronunciation; shows contraction of the name, usually omission of 's' following a vowel.
	ç	's' before 'a', 'o' and 'u'.
	ë, ï, ü	over 'e', 'i' and 'u' when they are used with another vowel and shows that each is to be pronounced.
German	ä	fate
	ö	fur
	ü	no English equivalent; like French 'tu'
Italian	à, é	over vowels and indicates stress.
Portuguese	ã, õ	vowels pronounced nasally.
	ç	boss
	á	shows stress
	ô	shows that a vowel has an 'i' or 'u' sound combined with it.
Spanish	ñ	canyon
	ü	pronounced as w and separately from adjoining vowels.
	á	usually indicates that this is a stressed vowel.

Abbreviations

A.C.T. – Australian Capital Territory
A.R. – Autonomous Region
Afghan. – Afghanistan
Afr. – Africa
Ala. – Alabama
Alta. – Alberta
Amer. – America(n)
Arch. – Archipelago
Ariz. – Arizona
Ark. – Arkansas
Atl. Oc. – Atlantic Ocean
B. – Baie, Bahía, Bay, Bucht, Bugt
B.C. – British Columbia
Bangla. – Bangladesh
Barr. – Barrage
Bos.-H. – Bosnia-Herzegovina
C. – Cabo, Cap, Cape, Coast
C.A.R. – Central African Republic
C. Prov. – Cape Province
Calif. – California
Cat. – Catarata
Cent. – Central
Chan. – Channel
Colo. – Colorado
Conn. – Connecticut
Cord. – Cordillera
Cr. – Creek
Czech. – Czech Republic
D.C. – District of Columbia
Del. – Delaware
Dem. – Democratic
Dep. – Dependency
Des. – Desert
Dét. – Détroit
Dist. – District
Dj. – Djebel
Domin. – Dominica
Dom. Rep. – Dominican Republic
E. – East

E. Salv. – El Salvador
Eq. Guin. – Equatorial Guinea
Est. – Estrecho
Falk. Is. – Falkland Is.
Fd. – Fjord
Fla. – Florida
Fr. – French
G. – Golfe, Golfo, Gulf, Guba, Gebel
Ga. – Georgia
Gt. – Great, Greater
Guinea-Biss. – Guinea-Bissau
H.K. – Hong Kong
H.P. – Himachal Pradesh
Hants. – Hampshire
Harb. – Harbor, Harbour
Hd. – Head
Hts. – Heights
I.(s). – Île, Ilha, Insel, Isla, Island, Isle
Ill. – Illinois
Ind. – Indiana
Ind. Oc. – Indian Ocean
Ivory C. – Ivory Coast
J. – Jabal, Jebel
Jaz. – Jazīrah
Junc. – Junction
K. – Kap, Kapp
Kans. – Kansas
Kep. – Kepulauan
Ky. – Kentucky
L. – Lac, Lacul, Lago, Lagoa, Lake, Limni, Loch, Lough
La. – Louisiana
Ld. – Land
Liech. – Liechtenstein
Lux. – Luxembourg
Mad. P. – Madhya Pradesh
Madag. – Madagascar
Man. – Manitoba

Mass. – Massachusetts
Md. – Maryland
Me. – Maine
Medit. S. – Mediterranean Sea
Mich. – Michigan
Minn. – Minnesota
Miss. – Mississippi
Mo. – Missouri
Mont. – Montana
Mozam. – Mozambique
Mt.(s) – Mont, Montaña, Mountain
Mte. – Monte
Mti. – Monti
N. – Nord, Norte, North, Northern, Nouveau
N.B. – New Brunswick
N.C. – North Carolina
N. Cal. – New Caledonia
N. Dak. – North Dakota
N.H. – New Hampshire
N.I. – North Island
N.J. – New Jersey
N. Mex. – New Mexico
N.S. – Nova Scotia
N.S.W. – New South Wales
N.W.T. – North West Territory
N.Y. – New York
N.Z. – New Zealand
Nac. – Nacional
Nat. – National
Nebr. – Nebraska
Neths. – Netherlands
Nev. – Nevada
Nfld. & L. – Newfoundland and Labrador
Nic. – Nicaragua
O. – Oued, Ouadi
Occ. – Occidentale
Okla. – Oklahoma

Ont. – Ontario
Or. – Orientale
Oreg. – Oregon
Os. – Ostrov
Oz. – Ozero
P. – Pass, Passo, Pasul, Pulau
P.E.I. – Prince Edward Island
Pa. – Pennsylvania
Pac. Oc. – Pacific Ocean
Papua N.G. – Papua New Guinea
Pass. – Passage
Peg. – Pegunungan
Pen. – Peninsula, Péninsule
Phil. – Philippines
Pk. – Peak
Plat. – Plateau
Prov. – Province, Provincial
Pt. – Point
Pta. – Ponta, Punta
Pte. – Pointe
Qué. – Québec
Queens. – Queensland
R. – Rio, River
R.I. – Rhode Island
Ra. – Range
Raj. – Rajasthan
Recr. – Recreational, Récréatif
Reg. – Region
Rep. – Republic
Res. – Reserve, Reservoir
Rhld-Pfz. – Rheinland-Pfalz
S. – South, Southern, Sur
Si. Arabia – Saudi Arabia
S.C. – South Carolina
S. Dak. – South Dakota
S.I. – South Island
S. Leone – Sierra Leone
Sa. – Serra, Sierra
Sask. – Saskatchewan

Scot. – Scotland
Sd. – Sound
Serbia & M.. – Serbia & Montenegro
Sev. – Severnaya
Sib. – Siberia
Sprs. – Springs
St. – Saint
Sta. – Santa
Ste. – Sainte
Sto. – Santo
Str. – Strait, Stretto
Switz. – Switzerland
Tas. – Tasmania
Tenn. – Tennessee
Terr. – Territory, Territoire
Tex. – Texas
Tg. – Tanjung
Trin. & Tob. – Trinidad & Tobago
U.A.E. – United Arab Emirates
U.K. – United Kingdom
U.S.A. – United States of America
Ut. P. – Uttar Pradesh
Va. – Virginia
Vdkhr. – Vodokhranilishche
Vdskh. – Vodoskhovyshche
Vf. – Vîrful
Vic. – Victoria
Vol. – Volcano
Vt. – Vermont
W. – Wadi, West
W. Va. – West Virginia
Wall. & F. Is. – Wallis and Futuna Is.
Wash. – Washington
Wis. – Wisconsin
Wlkp. – Wielkopolski
Wyo. – Wyoming
Yorks. – Yorkshire

A

A 'Âli an Nîl □, *Sudan* 81 F3
A Baña, *Spain* 36 C2
A Cañiza, *Spain* 36 C2
A Coruña, *Spain* 36 B2
A Estrada, *Spain* 36 C2
A Fonsagrada, *Spain* 36 B3
A Guarda, *Spain* 36 D2
A Gudiña, *Spain* 36 C3
A Rúa, *Spain* 36 C3
Aachen, *Germany* 24 E2
Aalborg = Ålborg, *Denmark* 11 G3
Aalen, *Germany* 25 G6
Aalst, *Belgium* 17 D4
Aalten, *Neths.* 17 C6
Aalter, *Belgium* 17 C3
Äänekoski, *Finland* 9 E21
Aarau, *Switz.* 25 H4
Aarberg, *Switz.* 25 H3
Aare →, *Switz.* 25 H4
Aargau □, *Switz.* 25 H4
Aarhus = Århus, *Denmark* 11 H4
Aarschot, *Belgium* 17 D4
Aba, *China* 58 A3
Aba, *Dem. Rep. of the Congo* 86 B3
Aba, *Nigeria* 83 D6
Âbâ, Jazîrat, *Sudan* 81 E3
Abaco I., *Bahamas* 120 A4
Abadab, J., *Sudan* 80 D4
Ābādān, *Iran* 71 D6
Abade, *Ethiopia* 81 F4
Ābādeh, *Iran* 71 D7
Abadin, *Spain* 36 B3
Abadla, *Algeria* 78 B5
Abaetetuba, *Brazil* 125 D9
Abagnar Qi, *China* 56 C9
Abah, Tanjung, *Indonesia* 63 K18
Abai, *Paraguay* 127 B4
Abak, *Nigeria* 83 E6
Abakaliki, *Nigeria* 83 D6
Abakan, *Russia* 53 D10
Abala, *Niger* 83 C5
Abalak, *Niger* 83 B6
Abalemma, *Niger* 83 B6
Abana, *Turkey* 72 B6
Abancay, *Peru* 124 F4
Abano Terme, *Italy* 41 C8
Abarán, *Spain* 39 G3
Abariringa, *Kiribati* 96 H10
Abarqū, *Iran* 71 D7
Abashiri, *Japan* 54 B12
Abashiri-Wan, *Japan* 54 C12
Abaújszántó, *Hungary* 28 B6
Abava →, *Latvia* 30 A8
Ābay = Nîl el Azraq →, *Sudan* 81 D3
Abay, *Kazakhstan* 52 E8
Abaya, L., *Ethiopia* 81 F4
Abayita-Shala Lakes △, *Ethiopia* 81 F4
Abaza, *Russia* 52 D9
Abbadia di Fiastra ⌓, *Italy* 41 E10
Abbadia San Salvatore, *Italy* 41 F8
'Abbāsābād, *Iran* 71 C8
Abbay = Nîl el Azraq →, *Sudan* 81 D3
Abbaye, Pt., *U.S.A.* 114 B1
Abbé, L., *Ethiopia* 81 E5
Abbeville, *France* 19 B8
Abbeville, *Ala., U.S.A.* 115 K3
Abbeville, *La., U.S.A.* 113 L8
Abbeville, *S.C., U.S.A.* 115 H4
Abbiategrasso, *Italy* 40 C5
Abbot Ice Shelf, *Antarctica* 5 D16
Abbottabad, *Pakistan* 68 B5
Abd al Kūrī, *Yemen* 75 E5
Ābdar, *Iran* 71 D7
'Abdolābād, *Iran* 71 C8
Abdulpur, *Bangla.* 69 G13
Abéché, *Chad* 79 F10
Abejar, *Spain* 38 D2
Abekr, *Sudan* 81 E2
Abel Tasman △, *N.Z.* 91 J4
Abengourou, *Ivory C.* 82 D4
Abenójar, *Spain* 37 G6
Åbenrå, *Denmark* 11 J3
Abensberg, *Germany* 25 G7
Abeokuta, *Nigeria* 83 D5
Aber, *Uganda* 86 B3
Aberaeron, *U.K.* 15 E3
Aberayron = Aberaeron, *U.K.* 15 E3
Aberchirder, *U.K.* 13 D6
Abercorn, *Australia* 95 D5
Aberdare, *U.K.* 15 F4
Aberdare △, *Kenya* 86 C4
Aberdare Ra., *Kenya* 86 C4
Aberdeen, *Australia* 95 E5
Aberdeen, *Canada* 103 C7
Aberdeen, *S. Africa* 88 E3
Aberdeen, *U.K.* 13 D6
Aberdeen, *Ala., U.S.A.* 115 J1
Aberdeen, *Idaho, U.S.A.* 108 E7
Aberdeen, *Md., U.S.A.* 114 F7
Aberdeen, *S. Dak., U.S.A.* 112 C5
Aberdeen, *Wash., U.S.A.* 110 D3
Aberdeen, City of □, *U.K.* 13 D6
Aberdeenshire □, *U.K.* 13 D6
Aberdovey = Aberdyfi, *U.K.* 15 E3
Aberdyfi, *U.K.* 15 E3
Aberfeldy, *U.K.* 13 E5
Aberfoyle, *U.K.* 13 E4
Abergavenny, *U.K.* 15 F4
Abergele, *U.K.* 14 D4
Abernathy, *U.S.A.* 113 J4
Abert, L., *U.S.A.* 108 E3
Aberystwyth, *U.K.* 15 E3
Abhā, *Si. Arabia* 75 D3
Abhar, *Iran* 71 B6
Abhayapuri, *India* 69 F14
Abia □, *Nigeria* 83 D6
Abide, *Turkey* 47 C11
Abidiya, *Sudan* 80 D3
Abidjan, *Ivory C.* 82 D4
Abilene, *Kans., U.S.A.* 112 F6
Abilene, *Tex., U.S.A.* 113 J5
Abingdon, *U.K.* 15 F6
Abingdon, *U.S.A.* 115 G5
Abington Reef, *Australia* 94 B4
Abitau →, *Canada* 103 B7
Abitibi →, *Canada* 104 B3
Abitibi, L., *Canada* 104 C4
Abiy Adi, *Ethiopia* 81 E4
Abkhaz Republic = Abkhazia □, *Georgia* 35 J5
Abkhazia □, *Georgia* 35 J5
Abminga, *Australia* 95 D1
Abnûb, *Egypt* 80 B3
Åbo = Turku, *Finland* 9 F20
Abocho, *Nigeria* 83 D6
Abohar, *India* 68 D6
Aboisso, *Ivory C.* 82 D4
Abomey, *Benin* 83 D5
Abong-Mbang, *Cameroon* 84 D2
Abonnema, *Nigeria* 83 E6
Abony, *Hungary* 28 C5
Aboso, *Ghana* 82 D4
Abou-Deïa, *Chad* 79 F9
Aboyne, *U.K.* 13 D6
Abra Pampa, *Argentina* 126 A2
Abraham L., *Canada* 102 C5
Abrantes, *Portugal* 37 F2
Abreojos, Pta., *Mexico* 118 B2
Abri, *Esh Shamâliya, Sudan* 80 C3
Abri, *Janub Kordofân, Sudan* 81 E3
Abrolhos, Banka, *Brazil* 122 E7
Abrud, *Romania* 28 D8
Abruzzo □, *Italy* 41 F10
Absaroka Range, *U.S.A.* 108 D9
Abtenau, *Austria* 26 D6
Abu, *India* 68 G5
Abū al Abyad, *U.A.E.* 71 E7
Abū al Khaşīb, *Iraq* 71 D6
Abū 'Alī, *Si. Arabia* 71 E6
Abū 'Alī →, *Lebanon* 74 A4
Abu Ballas, *Egypt* 80 C2
Abu Deleiq, *Sudan* 81 D3
Abu Dhabi = Abū Ẓāby, *U.A.E.* 71 E7
Abu Dis, *Sudan* 80 D3
Abu Dom, *Sudan* 81 D3
Abū Du'ān, *Syria* 70 B3
Abu el Gairi, W. →, *Egypt* 74 F2
Abu Fatma, Ras, *Sudan* 80 C4
Abu Gabra, *Sudan* 81 E2
Abu Ga'da, W. →, *Egypt* 74 F1
Abu Gelba, *Sudan* 81 E3
Abu Gubeiha, *Sudan* 81 E3
Abu Habl, Khawr →, *Sudan* 81 E3
Abū Ḩadrīyah, *Si. Arabia* 71 E6
Abu Hamed, *Sudan* 80 D3
Abu Haraz, *An Nîl el Azraq, Sudan* 80 D3
Abu Haraz, *El Gezira, Sudan* 81 E3
Abu Haraz, *Esh Shamâliya, Sudan* 80 D3
Abu Higar, *Sudan* 81 E3
Abū Kamāl, *Syria* 70 C4
Abu Kuleiwat, *Sudan* 81 E2
Abū Madd, Ra's, *Si. Arabia* 70 E3
Abu Matariq, *Sudan* 81 E2
Abu Mendi, *Ethiopia* 81 E4
Abū Mūsā, *U.A.E.* 71 E7
Abū Qaşr, *Si. Arabia* 70 D3
Abu Qir, *Egypt* 80 H7
Abu Qireiya, *Egypt* 80 C4
Abu Qurqâs, *Egypt* 80 B3
Abu Shagara, Ras, *Sudan* 80 C4
Abu Shanab, *Sudan* 81 E2
Abu Simbel, *Egypt* 80 C3
Abū Şukhayr, *Iraq* 70 D5
Abu Sultân, *Egypt* 80 H8
Abu Tabari, *Sudan* 80 D2
Abu Tig, *Egypt* 80 B3
Abu Tiga, *Sudan* 81 E3
Abu Tineitin, *Sudan* 81 E3
Abu Uruq, *Sudan* 81 D3
Abu Zabad, *Sudan* 81 E2
Abū Ẓāby, *U.A.E.* 71 E7
Abū Zeydābād, *Iran* 71 C6
Abuja, *Nigeria* 83 D6
Abukuma-Gawa →, *Japan* 54 E10
Abukuma-Sammyaku, *Japan* 54 F10
Abunā, *Brazil* 124 E5
Abunã →, *Brazil* 124 E5
Abune Yosef, *Ethiopia* 81 E4
Aburo, *Dem. Rep. of the Congo* 86 B3
Abut Hd., *N.Z.* 91 K3
Abuye Meda, *Ethiopia* 81 E4
Abwong, *Sudan* 81 F3
Åby, *Sweden* 11 F10
Aby, Lagune, *Ivory C.* 82 D4
Abyad, *Sudan* 81 E2
Åbybro, *Denmark* 11 G3
Acadia △, *U.S.A.* 115 C11
Açailândia, *Brazil* 125 D9
Acajutla, *El Salv.* 120 D2
Acámbaro, *Mexico* 118 D4
Acanthus, *Greece* 44 F7
Acaponeta, *Mexico* 118 C3
Acapulco, *Mexico* 119 D5
Acarai, Serra, *Brazil* 124 C7
Acarigua, *Venezuela* 124 B5
Acatlán, *Mexico* 119 D5
Acayucan, *Mexico* 119 D6
Accéglio, *Italy* 40 D4
Accomac, *U.S.A.* 114 G8
Accous, *France* 20 E3
Accra, *Ghana* 83 D4
Accrington, *U.K.* 14 D5
Acebal, *Argentina* 126 C3
Aceh □, *Indonesia* 62 D1
Acerra, *Italy* 43 B7
Aceuchal, *Spain* 37 G4
Achalpur, *India* 66 J10
Acheng, *China* 57 B14
Achenkirch, *Austria* 26 D4
Achensee, *Austria* 26 D4
Acher, *India* 68 H5
Achern, *Germany* 25 G4
Achill Hd., *Ireland* 12 C1
Achill I., *Ireland* 12 C1
Achim, *Germany* 24 B5
Achinsk, *Russia* 53 D10
Acıgöl, *Turkey* 47 D11
Acıpayam, *Turkey* 47 D11
Acireale, *Italy* 43 E8
Ackerman, *U.S.A.* 113 J10
Acklins I., *Bahamas* 121 B5
Acme, *Canada* 102 C6
Acme, *U.S.A.* 116 F5
Aconcagua, Cerro, *Argentina* 126 C2
Aconquija, Mt., *Argentina* 126 B2
Açores, Is. dos, *Atl. Oc.* 78 A1
Acornhoek, *S. Africa* 89 C5
Acquapendente, *Italy* 41 F8
Acquasanta Terme, *Italy* 41 F10
Acquasparta, *Italy* 41 F9
Acquaviva delle Fonti, *Italy* 43 B9
Ácqui Terme, *Italy* 40 D5
Acraman, L., *Australia* 95 E2
Acre = 'Akko, *Israel* 74 C4
Acre □, *Brazil* 124 E4
Acre →, *Brazil* 124 E5
Acri, *Italy* 43 C9
Acs, *Hungary* 28 C3
Actium, *Greece* 46 C2
Acton, *Canada* 116 C4
Acuña, *Mexico* 118 B4
Ad Dammām, *Si. Arabia* 71 E6
Ad Dāmūr, *Lebanon* 74 B4
Ad Dawādimī, *Si. Arabia* 70 E5
Ad Dawḩah, *Qatar* 71 E6
Ad Dawr, *Iraq* 70 C4
Ad Dir'īyah, *Si. Arabia* 70 E5
Ad Dīwānīyah, *Iraq* 70 D5
Ad Dujayl, *Iraq* 70 C5
Ad Duwayd, *Si. Arabia* 70 D4
Ada, *Ghana* 83 D5
Ada, *Serbia & M.* 28 E5
Ada, *Minn., U.S.A.* 112 B6
Ada, *Okla., U.S.A.* 113 H6
Adabiya, *Egypt* 74 F1
Adair, C., *Canada* 101 A12
Adaja →, *Spain* 36 D6
Adak I., *U.S.A.* 100 C2
Adamaoua, Massif de l', *Cameroon* 83 D7
Adamawa □, *Nigeria* 83 D7
Adamawa Highlands = Adamaoua, Massif de l', *Cameroon* 83 D7
Adamello ⌓, *Italy* 40 B7
Adamello, Mte., *Italy* 40 B7
Adami Tulu, *Ethiopia* 81 F4
Adaminaby, *Australia* 95 F4
Adams, *Mass., U.S.A.* 117 D11
Adams, *N.Y., U.S.A.* 117 C8
Adams, *Wis., U.S.A.* 112 D10
Adams, Mt., *U.S.A.* 110 D5
Adam's Bridge, *Sri Lanka* 66 Q11
Adams L., *Canada* 102 C5
Adam's Peak, *Sri Lanka* 66 R12
Adamuz, *Spain* 37 G6
Adana, *Turkey* 70 B2
Adanero, *Spain* 36 E6
Adapazarı = Sakarya, *Turkey* 72 B4
Adar Gwagwa, J., *Sudan* 80 C4
Adarama, *Sudan* 81 D3
Adare, C., *Antarctica* 5 D11
Adarte, *Eritrea* 81 E5
Adaut, *Indonesia* 63 F8
Adavale, *Australia* 95 D3
Adda →, *Italy* 40 C6
Addis Ababa = Addis Abeba, *Ethiopia* 81 F4
Addis Abeba, *Ethiopia* 81 F4
Addis Alem, *Ethiopia* 81 F4
Addis Zemen, *Ethiopia* 81 E4
Addison, *U.S.A.* 116 D7
Addo, *S. Africa* 88 E4
Addo △, *S. Africa* 88 E4
Adebour, *Niger* 83 C7
Ādeh, *Iran* 70 B5
Adel, *U.S.A.* 115 K4
Adelaide, *Australia* 95 E2
Adelaide, *S. Africa* 88 E4
Adelaide I., *Antarctica* 5 C17
Adelaide Pen., *Canada* 100 B10
Adelaide River, *Australia* 92 B5
Adelaide Village, *Bahamas* 120 A4
Adelanto, *U.S.A.* 111 L9
Adele I., *Australia* 92 C3
Adélie, Terre, *Antarctica* 5 C10
Adelie Land = Adélie, Terre, *Antarctica* 5 C10
Adelsk, *Belarus* 30 E10
Ademuz, *Spain* 38 E3
Aden = Al 'Adan, *Yemen* 75 E4
Aden, G. of, *Asia* 75 E4
Adendorp, *S. Africa* 88 E3
Aderbissinat, *Niger* 83 B6
Adh Dhayd, *U.A.E.* 71 E7
Adhoi, *India* 68 H4
Adi, *Indonesia* 63 E8
Adi Arkai, *Ethiopia* 81 E4
Adi Daro, *Ethiopia* 81 E4
Adi Keyih, *Eritrea* 81 E4
Adi Kwala, *Eritrea* 81 E4
Adi Ugri, *Eritrea* 81 E4
Adieu, C., *Australia* 93 F5
Adieu Pt., *Australia* 92 C3
Adigala, *Ethiopia* 81 E5
Adige →, *Italy* 41 C9
Adigrat, *Ethiopia* 81 E4
Adıgüzel Barajı, *Turkey* 47 C11
Adilabad, *India* 66 K11
Adilcevaz, *Turkey* 73 C10
Adirondack ⌓, *U.S.A.* 117 C10
Adirondack Mts., *U.S.A.* 117 C10
Adis Abeba = Addis Abeba, *Ethiopia* 81 F4
Adıyaman, *Turkey* 73 D8
Adjohon, *Benin* 83 D5
Adjud, *Romania* 29 D12
Adjumani, *Uganda* 86 B3
Adjuntas, *Puerto Rico* 121 d
Adlavik Is., *Canada* 105 B8
Adler, *Russia* 35 J4
Admer, *Algeria* 83 A6
Admiralty G., *Australia* 92 B4
Admiralty I., *U.S.A.* 102 B2
Admiralty Is., *Papua N. G.* 96 H6
Adnan Menderes, İzmir ✈ (ADB), *Turkey* 47 C9
Ado, *Nigeria* 83 D5
Ado-Ekiti, *Nigeria* 83 D6
Adok, *Sudan* 81 F3
Adola, *Ethiopia* 81 E5
Adonara, *Indonesia* 63 F6
Adoni, *India* 66 M10
Adony, *Hungary* 28 C3
Adour →, *France* 20 E2
Adra, *India* 69 H12
Adra, *Spain* 37 J7
Adrano, *Italy* 43 E7
Adrar, *Mauritania* 78 D3
Adrar des Iforas, *Algeria* 78 C5
Ádria, *Italy* 41 C9
Adrian, *Mich., U.S.A.* 114 E3
Adrian, *Tex., U.S.A.* 113 H3
Adriatic Sea, *Medit. S.* 6 G9
Adua, *Indonesia* 63 E7
Adwa, *Ethiopia* 81 E4
Adygea □, *Russia* 35 H5
Adzhar Republic = Ajaria □, *Georgia* 35 K6
Adzopé, *Ivory C.* 82 D4
Ægean Sea, *Medit. S.* 47 C7
Aerhtai Shan, *Mongolia* 60 B4
Ærø, *Denmark* 11 K4
Ærøskøbing, *Denmark* 11 K4
Aëtós, *Greece* 46 D3
'Afak, *Iraq* 70 C5
Afándou, *Greece* 49 C10
Afar □, *Ethiopia* 81 E5
Afghanistan ■, *Asia* 66 C4
Afikpo, *Nigeria* 83 D6
Aflou, *Algeria* 78 B6
Afragóla, *Italy* 43 B7
Afram →, *Ghana* 83 D4
Afrera, *Ethiopia* 81 E5
Africa 76 E6
'Afrīn, *Syria* 70 B3
Afşin, *Turkey* 72 C7
Afton, *N.Y., U.S.A.* 117 D9
Afton, *Wyo., U.S.A.* 108 E8
Afuá, *Brazil* 125 D8
'Afula, *Israel* 74 C4
Afyon, *Turkey* 47 C12
Afyon □, *Turkey* 47 C12
Afyonkarahisar = Afyon, *Turkey* 47 C12
Aga, *Egypt* 80 H7
Agadès = Agadez, *Niger* 83 B6
Agadez, *Niger* 83 B6
Agadir, *Morocco* 78 B4
Agaete, *Canary Is.* 48 F4
Agaie, *Nigeria* 83 D6
Again, *Sudan* 81 F2
Agalega Is., *Mauritius* 3 E12
Ağapınar, *Turkey* 47 B12
Agar, *India* 68 H7
Agaro, *Ethiopia* 81 F4
Agartala, *India* 67 H17
Agăş, *Romania* 29 D11
Agassiz, *Canada* 102 D4
Agats, *Indonesia* 63 F9
Agawam, *U.S.A.* 117 D12
Agbélouvé, *Togo* 83 D5
Agboville, *Ivory C.* 82 D4
Ağcabädi, *Azerbaijan* 35 K8
Ağdam, *Azerbaijan* 35 L8
Ağdaş, *Azerbaijan* 35 K8
Agde, *France* 20 E7
Agde, C. d', *France* 20 E7
Agdzhabedi = Ağcabädi, *Azerbaijan* 35 K8
Agen, *France* 20 D4
Agerbæk, *Denmark* 11 J2
Agersø, *Denmark* 11 J5
Ageyevo, *Russia* 32 E9
Aggteleki △, *Hungary* 28 B5
Āgh Kand, *Iran* 71 B6
Aghireşu, *Romania* 29 D8
Aginskoye, *Russia* 53 D12
Ağlasun, *Turkey* 47 D12
Agly →, *France* 20 F7
Agnew, *Australia* 93 E3
Agnibilékrou, *Ivory C.* 82 D4
Agnita, *Romania* 29 E9
Agnone, *Italy* 41 G11
Agofie, *Ghana* 83 D5
Agogna →, *Italy* 40 C5
Agogo, *Sudan* 81 F2
Agön, *Sweden* 10 C11
Agon Coutainville, *France* 18 C5
Ágordo, *Italy* 41 B9
Agori, *India* 69 G10
Agouna, *Benin* 83 D5
Agout →, *France* 20 E5
Agra, *India* 68 F7
Agrakhanskiy Poluostrov, *Russia* 35 J8
Agramunt, *Spain* 38 D6
Agreda, *Spain* 38 D3
Agri, *Turkey* 73 C10
Agri →, *Italy* 43 B9
Ağrı Dağı, *Turkey* 70 B5
Ağri Karakose = Ağri, *Turkey* 73 C10
Agriá, *Greece* 46 B5
Agrigento, *Italy* 42 E6
Agrínion, *Greece* 46 C3
Agrópoli, *Italy* 43 B7
Ağstafa, *Azerbaijan* 35 K7
Agua Caliente, *Baja Calif., Mexico* 111 N10
Agua Caliente, *Sinaloa, Mexico* 118 B3
Agua Caliente Springs, *U.S.A.* 111 N10
Água Clara, *Brazil* 125 H8
Agua Fria ⌓, *U.S.A.* 109 J8
Agua Hechicero, *Mexico* 111 N10
Agua Prieta, *Mexico* 118 A3
Aguadilla, *Puerto Rico* 121 d
Aguadulce, *Panama* 120 E3
Aguanga, *U.S.A.* 111 M10
Aguanish, *Canada* 105 B7
Aguanus →, *Canada* 105 B7
Aguapey →, *Argentina* 126 B4
Aguaray Guazú →, *Paraguay* 126 A4
Aguarico →, *Ecuador* 124 D3
Aguaro-Guariquito △, *Venezuela* 121 E6
Aguas →, *Spain* 38 D4
Aguas Blancas, *Chile* 126 A2
Aguas Calientes, Sierra de, *Argentina* 126 B2
Aguascalientes, *Mexico* 118 C4
Aguascalientes □, *Mexico* 118 C4
Agudo, *Spain* 37 G6
Águeda, *Portugal* 36 E2
Agueda →, *Spain* 36 D4
Aguelhok, *Mali* 83 B5
Aguié, *Niger* 83 C6
Aguila, Punta, *Puerto Rico* 121 d
Aguilafuente, *Spain* 36 D6
Aguilar, *Spain* 37 H6
Aguilar de Campóo, *Spain* 36 C6
Aguilares, *Argentina* 126 B2
Aguilas, *Spain* 39 H3
Agüimes, *Canary Is.* 48 G4
Aguja, C. de la, *Colombia* 122 B3
Agujereada, Pta., *Puerto Rico* 121 d
Agulaa, *Ethiopia* 81 E4
Agulhas, C., *S. Africa* 88 E3
Agulo, *Canary Is.* 48 F2
Agung, Gunung, *Indonesia* 63 J18
Agur, *Uganda* 86 B3
Agusan →, *Phil.* 61 G6
Ağva, *Turkey* 45 E13
Agvali, *Russia* 35 J8
Aha Mts., *Botswana* 88 B3
Ahaggar, *Algeria* 78 D7
Ahamansu, *Ghana* 83 D5
Ahar, *Iran* 70 B5
Ahat, *Turkey* 47 C11
Ahaus, *Germany* 24 C2
Ahipara B., *N.Z.* 91 F4
Ahir Dağı, *Turkey* 47 C12
Ahiri, *India* 66 K12
Ahlat, *Turkey* 73 C10
Ahlen, *Germany* 24 D3
Ahmad Wal, *Pakistan* 68 E1
Ahmadabad, *India* 68 H5
Aḩmadābād, *Khorāsān, Iran* 71 C9
Aḩmadābād, *Khorāsān, Iran* 71 C8
Aḩmadī, *Iran* 71 E8
Ahmadnagar, *India* 66 K9
Ahmadpur, *Pakistan* 68 E4
Ahmadpur Lamma, *Pakistan* 68 E4
Ahmar, *Ethiopia* 81 F5
Ahmedabad = Ahmadabad, *India* 68 H5
Ahmednagar = Ahmadnagar, *India* 66 K9
Ahmetbey, *Turkey* 45 E11
Ahmetler, *Turkey* 47 C11
Ahmetli, *Turkey* 47 C9
Ahoada, *Nigeria* 83 D6
Ahome, *Mexico* 118 B3
Ahoskie, *U.S.A.* 115 G7
Ahr →, *Germany* 24 E3
Ahram, *Iran* 71 D6
Ahrax Pt., *Malta* 49 D1
Ahrensbök, *Germany* 24 A6
Ahrensburg, *Germany* 24 B6
Āhū, *Iran* 71 C6
Ahuachapán, *El Salv.* 120 D2
Ahun, *France* 19 F9
Åhus, *Sweden* 11 J8
Ahvāz, *Iran* 71 D6
Ahvenanmaa, *Finland* 9 F19
Aḩwar, *Yemen* 75 E4
Ahzar →, *Mali* 83 B5
Ai →, *India* 69 F14
Ai-Ais, *Namibia* 88 D2
Ai-Ais and Fish River Canyon △, *Namibia* 88 C2
Aichach, *Germany* 25 G7
Aichi □, *Japan* 55 G8
Aigle, *Switz.* 25 J2
Aignay-le-Duc, *France* 19 E11
Aigoual, Mt., *France* 20 D7
Aigre, *France* 20 C4
Aigua, *Uruguay* 127 C5
Aigueperse, *France* 19 F10
Aigues →, *France* 21 D8
Aigues-Mortes, *France* 21 E8
Aigues-Mortes, G. d', *France* 21 E8
Aigües Tortes y Lago San Mauricio △, *Spain* 38 C4
Aiguilles, *France* 21 D10
Aiguillon, *France* 20 D4
Aigurande, *France* 19 F8
Aihui, *China* 60 A7
Aija, *Peru* 124 E3
Aikawa, *Japan* 54 E9
Aiken, *U.S.A.* 115 J5
Ailao Shan, *China* 58 F3
Aileron, *Australia* 94 C1
Aillant-sur-Tholon, *France* 19 E10
Aillik, *Canada* 105 A8
Ailsa Craig, *U.K.* 13 F3
Aim, *Russia* 53 D14
Aimere, *Indonesia* 63 F6

Aimogasta, *Argentina* 126 B2
Ain □, *France* 19 F12
Ain ➤, *France* 21 C9
Aïn Ben Tili, *Mauritania* 78 C4
Ain Dalla, *Egypt* 80 B2
Ain el Mafki, *Egypt* 80 B2
Ain Girba, *Egypt* 80 B2
Ain Murr, *Sudan* 80 C2
Ain Qeiqab, *Egypt* 80 B1
Aïn Sefra, *Algeria* 78 B5
Ain Sheikh Murzûk, *Egypt* .. 80 B2
Ain Sudr, *Egypt* 74 F2
Ain Sukhna, *Egypt* 80 J8
Ain Zeitûn, *Egypt* 80 B2
Ainaži, *Latvia* 9 H21
Aínos Óros, *Greece* 46 C2
Ainsworth, *U.S.A.* 112 D5
Aiquile, *Bolivia* 124 G5
Aïr, *Niger* 83 B6
Air Force I., *Canada* 101 B12
Air Hitam, *Malaysia* 65 M4
Airaines, *France* 19 C8
Airdrie, *Canada* 102 C6
Airdrie, *U.K.* 13 F5
Aire ➤, *France* 19 C11
Aire ➤, *U.K.* 14 D7
Aire, I. de l', *Spain* 48 B11
Aire-sur-la-Lys, *France* 19 B9
Aire-sur-l'Adour, *France* 20 E3
Airlie Beach, *Australia* 94 J6
Airvault, *France* 18 F6
Aisch ➤, *Germany* 25 F6
Aisne □, *France* 19 C10
Aisne ➤, *France* 19 C9
Ait, *India* 69 G8
Aitana, Sierra de, *Spain* 39 G4
Aitkin, *U.S.A.* 112 B8
Aitolía kai Akarnanía □, *Greece* . 46 C3
Aitolikón, *Greece* 46 C3
Aiud, *Romania* 29 D8
Aix-en-Provence, *France* 21 E9
Aix-la-Chapelle = Aachen,
  Germany 24 E2
Aix-les-Bains, *France* 21 C9
Aixe-sur-Vienne, *France* 20 C5
Aíyina, *Greece* 46 D5
Aiyínion, *Greece* 44 F6
Aíyion, *Greece* 46 C4
Aizawl, *India* 67 H18
Aizenay, *France* 18 F5
Aizkraukle, *Latvia* 9 H21
Aizpute, *Latvia* 9 H19
Aizuwakamatsu, *Japan* 54 F9
Ajaccio, *France* 21 G12
Ajaccio, G. d', *France* 21 G12
Ajai △, *Uganda* 86 B3
Ajaigarh, *India* 69 G9
Ajalpan, *Mexico* 119 D5
Ajanta Ra., *India* 66 J9
Ajari Rep. = Ajaria □, *Georgia* . 35 K6
Ajaria □, *Georgia* 35 K6
Ajax, *Canada* 116 C5
Ajdābiyā, *Libya* 79 B10
Ajdovščina, *Slovenia* 41 C10
Ajibar, *Ethiopia* 81 E4
Ajka, *Hungary* 28 C2
'Ajlūn, *Jordan* 74 C4
'Ajlūn □, *Jordan* 74 C4
'Ajmān, *U.A.E.* 71 E7
Ajmer, *India* 68 F6
Ajnala, *India* 68 D6
Ajo, *U.S.A.* 109 K7
Ajo, C. de, *Spain* 36 B7
Ajok, *Sudan* 81 F2
Ajuy, *Phil.* 61 F5
Ak Dağ, *Turkey* 47 E11
Ak Dağları, *Muğla, Turkey* ... 47 E11
Ak Dağları, *Sivas, Turkey* ... 72 C7
Akaba, *Togo* 83 D5
Akabira, *Japan* 54 C11
Akagera △, *Rwanda* 86 C3
Akaki Beseka, *Ethiopia* 81 F4
Akala, *Sudan* 81 D4
Akamas, *Cyprus* 49 D11
Akan △, *Japan* 54 C12
Akanthou, *Cyprus* 49 D12
Akarca, *Turkey* 47 C11
Akaroa, *N.Z.* 91 K4
Akasha, *Sudan* 80 C3
Akashi, *Japan* 55 G7
Akbarpur, *Bihar, India* 69 G10
Akbarpur, *Ut. P., India* 69 F10
Akçaabat, *Turkey* 73 B8
Akçadağ, *Turkey* 72 C7
Akçakale, *Turkey* 73 D8
Akçakoca, *Turkey* 72 B4
Akçaova, *Turkey* 45 E13
Akçay, *Turkey* 47 E11
Akçay ➤, *Turkey* 47 D10
Akdağ, *Turkey* 47 C8
Akdağmadeni, *Turkey* 72 C6
Akelamo, *Indonesia* 63 D7
Åkers styckebruk, *Sweden* ... 10 E11
Åkersberga, *Sweden* 10 E12
Aketi, *Dem. Rep. of the Congo* .. 84 D4
Akhaïa □, *Greece* 46 C3
Akhalkalaki, *Georgia* 35 K6
Akhaltsikhe, *Georgia* 35 K6
Akharnaí, *Greece* 46 C5
Akhelóös ➤, *Greece* 46 C3
Akhendriá, *Greece* 47 G7
Akhisar, *Turkey* 47 C9
Akhladhókambos, *Greece* ... 46 D4
Akhnur, *India* 69 C6
Akhtopol, *Bulgaria* 45 D11
Akhtuba ➤, *Russia* 35 G8
Akhtubinsk, *Russia* 35 F8
Akhty, *Russia* 35 K8
Akhtyrka = Okhtyrka, *Ukraine* . 33 G8
Aki, *Japan* 55 H6
Akimiski I., *Canada* 104 B3

Akimovka, *Ukraine* 33 J8
Åkirkeby, *Denmark* 11 J8
Akita, *Japan* 54 E10
Akita □, *Japan* 54 E10
Akjoujt, *Mauritania* 82 B2
Akka, *Mali* 82 B4
Akkaya Tepesi, *Turkey* 47 D11
Akkeshi, *Japan* 54 C12
'Akko, *Israel* 74 C4
Akköy, *Turkey* 47 D9
Aklampa, *Benin* 83 D5
Aklavik, *Canada* 100 B6
Aklera, *India* 68 G7
Akmenė, *Lithuania* 30 B9
Akmenrags, *Latvia* 30 B8
Akmonte = Almonte, *Spain* .. 37 H4
Akō, *Japan* 55 G7
Ako, *Nigeria* 83 C7
Akôbô, *Sudan* 81 F3
Akobo ➤, *Ethiopia* 81 F3
Akola, *India* 66 J10
Akonolinga, *Cameroon* 83 E7
Akor, *Mali* 82 C3
Akordat, *Eritrea* 81 D4
Akosombo Dam, *Ghana* 83 D5
Akot, *Sudan* 81 F3
Akoupé, *Ivory C.* 82 D4
Akpatok I., *Canada* 101 B13
Åkrahamn, *Norway* 9 G11
Akranes, *Iceland* 8 D2
Akreïjit, *Mauritania* 82 B3
Akrítas Venétiko, Ákra, *Greece* . 46 E3
Akron, *Colo., U.S.A.* 112 E3
Akron, *Ohio, U.S.A.* 116 E3
Akrotiri, *Cyprus* 49 E11
Akrotíri, Ákra, *Greece* 45 F9
Akrotiri Bay, *Cyprus* 49 E12
Aksai Chin, *China* 69 B8
Aksaray, *Turkey* 70 B2
Aksay, *Kazakhstan* 52 D6
Akşehir, *Turkey* 70 B1
Akşehir Gölü, *Turkey* 72 C4
Aksu, *China* 60 B3
Aksu ➤, *Turkey* 72 D4
Aksum, *Ethiopia* 81 E4
Aktash, *Russia* 34 C11
Aktogay, *Kazakhstan* 52 E8
Aktsyabrski, *Belarus* 33 F5
Aktyubinsk = Aqtöbe,
  Kazakhstan 52 D6
Aku, *Nigeria* 83 D6
Akure, *Nigeria* 83 D6
Akureyri, *Iceland* 8 D4
Akuseki-Shima, *Japan* 55 K4
Akusha, *Russia* 35 J8
Akwa-Ibom □, *Nigeria* 83 E6
Akyab = Sittwe, *Burma* 67 J18
Akyazı, *Turkey* 72 B4
Al 'Adan, *Yemen* 75 E4
Al Ahsā = Hasa □, *Si. Arabia* . 71 E6
Al Ajfar, *Si. Arabia* 70 E4
Al Amādīyah, *Iraq* 70 B4
Al 'Amārah, *Iraq* 70 D5
Al 'Aqabah, *Jordan* 74 F4
Al 'Aqabah □, *Jordan* 74 F4
Al Arak, *Syria* 70 C3
Al 'Aramah, *Si. Arabia* 70 E5
Al 'Arṭāwīyah, *Si. Arabia* ... 70 E5
Al 'Āṣimah = 'Ammān □, *Jordan* 74 D5
Al 'Assāfīyah, *Si. Arabia* ... 70 D3
Al 'Ayn, *Si. Arabia* 70 E3
Al 'Ayn, *U.A.E.* 71 E7
Al 'Ayn, *Iraq* 70 C5
Al 'Azīzīyah, *Iraq* 70 C5
Al Bāb, *Syria* 70 B3
Al Bad', *Si. Arabia* 70 D2
Al Bādī, *Iraq* 70 C4
Al Bahrah, *Kuwait* 70 D5
Al Baḥral Mayyit = Dead Sea,
  Asia 74 D4
Al Balqā' □, *Jordan* 74 C4
Al Barūk, J., *Lebanon* 74 B4
Al Baṣrah, *Iraq* 70 D5
Al Baṭhā, *Iraq* 70 D5
Al Batrūn, *Lebanon* 74 A4
Al Baydā, *Libya* 79 B10
Al Biqā □, *Lebanon* 74 A5
Al Bi'r, *Si. Arabia* 70 D3
Al Burayj, *Syria* 74 A5
Al Fadilī, *Si. Arabia* 71 E6
Al Fallūjah, *Iraq* 70 C4
Al Fāw, *Iraq* 71 D6
Al Fujayrah, *U.A.E.* 71 E8
Al Ghadaf, W. ➤, *Jordan* ... 74 D5
Al Ghammās, *Iraq* 70 D5
Al Ghazālah, *Si. Arabia* 70 E4
Al Ḥadīthah, *Iraq* 70 C4
Al Ḥadīthah, *Si. Arabia* 74 D6
Al Ḥadr, *Iraq* 70 C4
Al Hājānah, *Syria* 74 B5
Al Hajar al Gharbī, *Oman* ... 71 E8
Al Ḥāmad, *Si. Arabia* 70 D3
Al Hamdāniyah, *Syria* 70 C3
Al Ḥamīdīyah, *Syria* 74 A4
Al Ḥammār, *Iraq* 70 D5
Al Ḥamrā', *Si. Arabia* 70 E3
Al Ḥamzah, *Iraq* 70 D5
Al Ḥanākīyah, *Si. Arabia* ... 70 E4
Al Ḥasā, W. ➤, *Jordan* 74 D4
Al Ḥasakah, *Syria* 70 B4
Al Haydān ➤, *Jordan* 74 D4
Al Ḥayy, *Iraq* 70 C5
Al Ḥijānah, *Syria* 74 B5
Al Hillah, *Iraq* 70 C5
Al Ḥindīyah, *Iraq* 70 C5
Al Hirmil, *Lebanon* 74 A5
Al Hoceïma, *Morocco* 78 A5
Al Ḥudaydah, *Yemen* 75 E3
Al Ḥufūf, *Si. Arabia* 71 E6
Al Ḥumaydah, *Si. Arabia* ... 70 D2

Al Ḥunayy, *Si. Arabia* 71 E6
Al Īsāwīyah, *Si. Arabia* 70 D3
Al Jafr, *Jordan* 74 E5
Al Jāfūrah, *Si. Arabia* 71 E7
Al Jaghbūb, *Libya* 79 C10
Al Jahrah, *Kuwait* 70 D5
Al Jalāmīd, *Si. Arabia* 70 D3
Al Jamalīyah, *Qatar* 71 E6
Al Janūb □, *Lebanon* 74 B4
Al Jawf, *Libya* 79 D10
Al Jawf, *Si. Arabia* 70 D3
Al Jazirah, *Iraq* 70 C5
Al Jithāmīyah, *Si. Arabia* ... 70 E4
Al Jubayl, *Si. Arabia* 71 E6
Al Jubaylah, *Si. Arabia* 70 E5
Al Jubb, *Si. Arabia* 70 E4
Al Junaynah, *Sudan* 79 F10
Al Kabā'ish, *Iraq* 70 D5
Al Karak, *Jordan* 74 D4
Al Karak □, *Jordan* 74 E5
Al Kāẓimīyah, *Iraq* 70 C5
Al Khābūra, *Oman* 71 F8
Al Khafji, *Si. Arabia* 71 E6
Al Khalīl, *West Bank* 74 D4
Al Khāliṣ, *Iraq* 70 C5
Al Kharsānīyah, *Si. Arabia* .. 71 E6
Al Khaṣab, *Oman* 71 E8
Al Khawr, *Qatar* 71 E6
Al Khiḍr, *Iraq* 70 D5
Al Khiyām, *Lebanon* 74 B4
Al Khums, *Libya* 79 B8
Al Kiswah, *Syria* 74 B5
Al Kūfah, *Iraq* 70 C5
Al Kufrah, *Libya* 79 D10
Al Kuhayfīyah, *Si. Arabia* ... 70 E4
Al Kūt, *Iraq* 70 C5
Al Kuwayt, *Kuwait* 70 D5
Al Labwah, *Lebanon* 74 A5
Al Lādhiqīyah, *Syria* 70 C2
Al Līth, *Si. Arabia* 75 C3
Al Liwā', *Oman* 71 E8
Al Luḥayyah, *Yemen* 75 D3
Al Madīnah, *Iraq* 70 D5
Al Madīnah, *Si. Arabia* 70 E3
Al Mafraq, *Jordan* 74 C5
Al Mafraq □, *Jordan* 74 C5
Al Maḥmūdīyah, *Iraq* 70 C5
Al Majma'ah, *Si. Arabia* 70 E5
Al Makhruq, W. ➤, *Jordan* .. 74 D6
Al Makhūl, *Si. Arabia* 70 E4
Al Manāmah, *Bahrain* 71 E6
Al Maqwa', *Kuwait* 70 D5
Al Marj, *Libya* 79 B10
Al Maṭlā, *Kuwait* 70 D5
Al Mawjib, W. ➤, *Jordan* ... 74 D4
Al Mawṣil, *Iraq* 70 B4
Al Mayādin, *Syria* 70 C4
Al Mazār, *Jordan* 74 D4
Al Midhnab, *Si. Arabia* 70 E5
Al Minā', *Lebanon* 74 A4
Al Miqdādīyah, *Iraq* 70 C5
Al Mubarraz, *Si. Arabia* 71 E6
Al Mudawwarah, *Jordan* ... 74 F5
Al Mughayrā', *U.A.E.* 71 E7
Al Muḥarraq, *Bahrain* 71 E6
Al Mukallā, *Yemen* 75 E4
Al Mukhā, *Yemen* 75 E3
Al Musayjīd, *Si. Arabia* 70 E3
Al Musayyib, *Iraq* 70 C5
Al Muthanná □, *Iraq* 70 D5
Al Muwayh, *Si. Arabia* 80 C5
Al Muwaylih, *Si. Arabia* 70 E2
Al Owuho = Otukpa, *Nigeria* . 83 D6
Al Qā'im, *Iraq* 70 C4
Al Qādisīyah □, *Iraq* 70 D5
Al Qā'im, *Iraq* 70 C4
Al Qalībah, *Si. Arabia* 70 D3
Al Qāmishlī, *Syria* 70 B4
Al Qaryatayn, *Syria* 74 A6
Al Qaṣīm, *Si. Arabia* 70 E4
Al Qaṭ'ā, *Syria* 70 C4
Al Qaṭīf, *Si. Arabia* 71 E6
Al Qaṭrānah, *Jordan* 74 D5
Al Qaṭrūn, *Libya* 79 D9
Al Qayṣūmah, *Si. Arabia* ... 70 D5
Al Quds = Jerusalem, *Israel* . 74 D4
Al Qunayṭirah, *Syria* 74 C4
Al Qunfudhah, *Si. Arabia* ... 80 D5
Al Qurnah, *Iraq* 70 D5
Al Quṣayr, *Iraq* 70 D5
Al Quṣayr, *Syria* 74 A5
Al Qutayfah, *Syria* 74 B5
Al 'Ubaylah, *Si. Arabia* 75 C5
Al 'Udayliyah, *Si. Arabia* ... 71 E6
Al 'Ulā, *Si. Arabia* 70 E3
Al 'Uqayr, *Si. Arabia* 71 E6
Al 'Uwaynid, *Si. Arabia* 70 E5
Al 'Uwayqīlah, *Si. Arabia* ... 70 D4
Al 'Uyūn, *Ḥijāz, Si. Arabia* .. 70 E3
Al 'Uyūn, *Najd, Si. Arabia* .. 70 E4
Al 'Uzayr, *Iraq* 70 D5
Al Wajh, *Si. Arabia* 70 E3
Al Wakrah, *Qatar* 71 E6
Al Waqbah, *Si. Arabia* 70 D5
Al Wari'ah, *Si. Arabia* 70 E5
Ala, *Italy* 40 C8
Ala Dağ, *Turkey* 70 B2
Ala Dağları, *Turkey* 73 C10
Alabama □, *U.S.A.* 115 J2
Alabama ➤, *U.S.A.* 115 K2
Alabaster, *U.S.A.* 115 J2
Alaca, *Turkey* 72 B6
Alacaatlı, *Turkey* 47 B10
Alaçam, *Turkey* 72 B6
Alaçatı, *Turkey* 47 C8
Alachua, *U.S.A.* 115 L4
Alaejos, *Spain* 36 D5
Alaérma, *Greece* 49 C9
Alagir, *Russia* 35 J7
Alagna Valsésia, *Italy* 40 C4
Alagoa Grande, *Brazil* 125 E11

Alagoas □, *Brazil* 125 E11
Alagoinhas, *Brazil* 125 F11
Alagón, *Spain* 38 D3
Alagón ➤, *Spain* 36 F4
Alaior, *Spain* 48 B11
Alajero, *Canary Is.* 48 F2
Alajuela, *Costa Rica* 120 D3
Alakamisy, *Madag.* 89 C8
Alaknanda ➤, *India* 69 D8
Alakol, Ozero, *Kazakhstan* .. 60 B3
Alamarvdasht, *Iran* 71 E7
Alamata, *Ethiopia* 81 E4
Alameda, *Calif., U.S.A.* 110 H4
Alameda, *N. Mex., U.S.A.* .. 109 J10
Alaminos, *Phil.* 61 C3
Alamo, *U.S.A.* 111 J11
Alamo Crossing, *U.S.A.* 111 L13
Alamogordo, *U.S.A.* 109 K11
Álamos, *Mexico* 118 B3
Alamosa, *U.S.A.* 109 H11
Åland = Ahvenanmaa, *Finland* . 9 F19
Alandroal, *Portugal* 37 G3
Ålands hav, *Europe* 9 F18
Alange, Embalse d', *Spain* ... 37 G4
Alania = North Ossetia □, *Russia* 35 J7
Alanís, *Spain* 37 G5
Alanya, *Turkey* 70 B1
Alaotra, Farihin', *Madag.* ... 89 B8
Alapayevsk, *Russia* 52 D7
Alappuzha = Alleppey, *India* .. 66 Q10
Alar del Rey, *Spain* 36 C6
Alaraz, *Spain* 36 E5
Alarcón, Embalse de, *Spain* .. 38 F2
Alarobia-Vohiposa, *Madag.* .. 89 C8
Alaşehir, *Turkey* 47 C10
Alaska □, *U.S.A.* 100 B5
Alaska, G. of, *Pac. Oc.* 100 C5
Alaska Peninsula, *U.S.A.* 100 C4
Alaska Range, *U.S.A.* 100 B4
Álássio, *Italy* 40 E5
Älät, *Azerbaijan* 35 L9
Alatri, *Italy* 41 G10
Alatyr, *Russia* 34 C8
Alatyr ➤, *Russia* 34 C8
Alausí, *Ecuador* 124 D3
Álava □, *Spain* 38 C2
Alava, C., *U.S.A.* 108 B1
Alaverdi, *Armenia* 35 K7
Alavo = Alavus, *Finland* 9 E20
Alavus, *Finland* 9 E20
Alawoona, *Australia* 95 E3
'Alayh, *Lebanon* 74 B4
Alazani ➤, *Azerbaijan* 35 K8
Alba, *Italy* 40 D5
Alba □, *Romania* 29 D8
Alba Adriática, *Italy* 41 F10
Alba de Tormes, *Spain* 36 E5
Alba-Iulia, *Romania* 29 D8
Albac, *Romania* 28 D7
Albacete, *Spain* 39 F3
Albacete □, *Spain* 39 G3
Albacutya, L., *Australia* 95 F3
Albæk, *Denmark* 11 G4
Ålbæk Bugt, *Denmark* 11 G4
Albaida, *Spain* 39 G4
Albalate de las Nogueras, *Spain* . 38 E2
Albalate del Arzobispo, *Spain* . 38 D4
Alban, *France* 20 E6
Albanel, L., *Canada* 104 B5
Albania ■, *Europe* 44 E4
Albano Laziale, *Italy* 41 G9
Albany, *Australia* 93 G2
Albany, *Ga., U.S.A.* 115 K3
Albany, *N.Y., U.S.A.* 117 D11
Albany, *Oreg., U.S.A.* 108 D2
Albany, *Tex., U.S.A.* 113 J5
Albany ➤, *Canada* 104 B3
Albardón, *Argentina* 126 C2
Albarracín, *Spain* 38 E3
Albarracín, Sierra de, *Spain* . 38 E3
Albatera, *Spain* 39 G4
Albatross B., *Australia* 94 A3
Albegna ➤, *Italy* 41 F8
Albemarle, *U.S.A.* 115 H5
Albemarle Sd., *U.S.A.* 115 H7
Alberche ➤, *Spain* 36 F6
Alberdi, *Paraguay* 126 B4
Albères, Mts., *France* 20 F6
Alberga, The ➤, *Australia* ... 95 D2
Albersdorf, *Germany* 24 A5
Albert, *France* 19 C9
Albert, L., *Africa* 86 B3
Albert, L., *Australia* 95 F2
Albert Edward Ra., *Australia* . 92 C4
Albert Lea, *U.S.A.* 112 D8
Albert Nile ➤, *Uganda* 86 B3
Albert Town, *Bahamas* 121 B5
Alberta □, *Canada* 102 C6
Alberti, *Argentina* 126 D3
Albertinia, *S. Africa* 88 E3
Albertirsa, *Hungary* 28 C4
Alberton, *Canada* 105 C7
Albertville, *France* 21 C10
Albertville, *U.S.A.* 115 H2
Albi, *France* 20 E6
Albia, *U.S.A.* 112 E8
Albina, *Suriname* 125 B8
Albina, Ponta, *Angola* 88 B1
Albino, *Italy* 40 C6
Albion, *Mich., U.S.A.* 114 D3
Albion, *Nebr., U.S.A.* 112 E6
Albion, *Pa., U.S.A.* 116 E4
Albocácer, *Spain* 38 E5
Albolote, *Spain* 37 H7
Alborán, *Medit. S.* 37 K7
Alborea, *Spain* 39 F3
Ålborg, *Denmark* 11 G3
Ålborg Bugt, *Denmark* 11 H4
Alborz, Reshteh-ye Kūhhā-ye,
  Iran 71 C7

Albox, *Spain* 39 H2
Albufeira, *Portugal* 37 H2
Albula ➤, *Switz.* 25 J5
Albuñol, *Spain* 37 J7
Albuquerque, *U.S.A.* 109 J10
Albuquerque, Cayos de,
  Caribbean 120 D3
Alburg, *U.S.A.* 117 B11
Alburno, Mte., *Italy* 43 B8
Alburquerque, *Spain* 37 F4
Albury = Albury-Wodonga,
  Australia 95 F4
Albury-Wodonga, *Australia* .. 95 F4
Alcácer do Sal, *Portugal* 37 G2
Alcáçovas, *Portugal* 37 G2
Alcalá de Chivert, *Spain* 38 E5
Alcalá de Guadaira, *Spain* ... 37 H5
Alcalá de Henares, *Spain* ... 36 E7
Alcalá de los Gazules, *Spain* . 37 J5
Alcalá del Júcar, *Spain* 39 F3
Alcalá del Río, *Spain* 37 H5
Alcalá del Valle, *Spain* 37 J5
Alcalá la Real, *Spain* 37 H7
Álcamo, *Italy* 42 E5
Alcanadre, *Spain* 38 C2
Alcanadre ➤, *Spain* 38 D4
Alcanar, *Spain* 38 E5
Alcanede, *Portugal* 37 F2
Alcanena, *Portugal* 37 F2
Alcañices, *Spain* 36 D4
Alcaniz, *Spain* 38 D4
Alcântara, *Brazil* 125 D10
Alcántara, *Spain* 36 F4
Alcántara, Embalse de, *Spain* . 36 F4
Alcantarilla, *Spain* 39 H3
Alcaracejos, *Spain* 37 G6
Alcaraz, *Spain* 39 G2
Alcaraz, Sierra de, *Spain* 39 G2
Alcaudete, *Spain* 37 H6
Alcázar de San Juan, *Spain* .. 37 F7
Alcester, *U.K.* 15 E6
Alchevsk, *Ukraine* 33 H10
Alcira = Alzira, *Spain* 39 F4
Alcobaça, *Portugal* 37 F2
Alcobendas, *Spain* 36 E7
Alcolea del Pinar, *Spain* 38 D2
Alcora, *Spain* 38 E5
Alcorcón, *Spain* 36 E7
Alcoutim, *Portugal* 37 H3
Alcova, *U.S.A.* 108 E10
Alcoy, *Spain* 39 G4
Alcubierre, Sierra de, *Spain* . 38 D4
Alcublas, *Spain* 38 F4
Alcúdia, *Spain* 48 B10
Alcúdia, B. d', *Spain* 48 B10
Alcudia, Sierra de la, *Spain* . 37 G6
Aldabra Is., *Seychelles* 77 G8
Aldama, *Mexico* 119 C5
Aldan, *Russia* 53 D13
Aldan ➤, *Russia* 53 C13
Aldea, Pta. de la, *Canary Is.* . 48 G4
Aldeburgh, *U.K.* 15 E9
Alder Pk., *U.S.A.* 110 K5
Alderney, *U.K.* 15 H5
Aldershot, *U.K.* 15 F7
Åled, *Sweden* 11 H6
Aledo, *U.S.A.* 112 E9
Alefa, *Ethiopia* 81 E4
Aleg, *Mauritania* 82 B2
Alegranza, *Canary Is.* 48 E6
Alegranza, I., *Canary Is.* 48 E6
Alegre, *Brazil* 127 A7
Alegrete, *Brazil* 127 B4
Aleisk, *Russia* 52 D9
Aleksandriya = Oleksandriya,
  Kirovohrad, *Ukraine* 33 H7
Aleksandriya = Oleksandriya,
  Rivne, *Ukraine* 33 G4
Aleksandriyskaya, *Russia* ... 35 J8
Aleksandrov Gay, *Russia* ... 34 E9
Aleksandrov, *Russia* 32 D10
Aleksandrovac, *Serbia & M.* .. 44 C5
Aleksandrovac, *Serbia & M.* .. 44 B5
Aleksandrovka = Oleksandrivka,
  Ukraine 33 H7
Aleksandrovo, *Bulgaria* 45 C8
Aleksandrovsk-Sakhalinskiy,
  Russia 53 D15
Aleksandrów Kujawski, *Poland* . 31 F5
Aleksandrów Łódzki, *Poland* .. 31 G6
Aleksandry, Z., *Russia* 4 A10
Alekseyevka, *Samara, Russia* . 34 D10
Alekseyevka, *Voronezh, Russia* . 33 G10
Aleksin, *Russia* 32 E9
Aleksinac, *Serbia & M.* 44 C5
Além Paraíba, *Brazil* 127 A7
Alemania, *Argentina* 126 B2
Alemania, *Chile* 126 B2
Alençon, *France* 18 D7
Alenquer, *Brazil* 125 D8
Alenuihaha Channel, *U.S.A.* . 106 H17
Alépé, *Ivory C.* 82 D4
Aleppo = Ḥalab, *Syria* 70 B3
Aléria, *France* 21 F13
Alert, *Canada* 4 A4
Alès, *France* 21 D8
Aleşd, *Romania* 28 C7
Alessándria, *Italy* 40 D5
Ålestrup, *Denmark* 11 H3
Ålesund, *Norway* 9 E12
Alet-les-Bains, *France* 20 F6
Aletschhorn, *Switz.* 25 J4
Aleutian Is., *Pac. Oc.* 100 C2
Aleutian Trench, *Pac. Oc.* ... 96 C10
Alexander, *U.S.A.* 112 B3
Alexander, Mt., *Australia* ... 93 E3
Alexander Arch., *U.S.A.* 100 C6
Alexander Bay, *S. Africa* 88 D2
Alexander City, *U.S.A.* 115 J3
Alexander I., *Antarctica* 5 C17
Alexandra, *Australia* 95 F4
Alexandra, *N.Z.* 91 L2
Alexandra Falls, *Canada* 102 A5

Alexandria = El Iskandarîya, Egypt	80	H7
Alexandria, B.C., Canada	102	C4
Alexandria, Ont., Canada	117	A10
Alexandria, Romania	29	G10
Alexandria, S. Africa	88	E4
Alexandria, U.K.	13	F4
Alexandria, La., U.S.A.	113	K8
Alexandria, Minn., U.S.A.	112	C7
Alexandria, S. Dak., U.S.A.	112	D6
Alexandria, Va., U.S.A.	114	F7
Alexandria Bay, U.S.A.	117	B9
Alexandrina, L., Australia	95	F2
Alexandroúpolis, Greece	45	F9
Alexis →, Canada	105	B8
Alexis Creek, Canada	102	C4
Alfabia, Spain	48	B9
Alfambra, Spain	38	E3
Alfândega da Fé, Portugal	36	D4
Alfaro, Spain	38	C3
Alfaz del Pi, Spain	39	G4
Alfeld, Germany	24	D5
Alfenas, Brazil	127	A6
Alfiós →, Greece	46	D3
Alföld, Hungary	28	D5
Alfonsine, Italy	41	D9
Alford, Aberds., U.K.	13	D6
Alford, Lincs., U.K.	14	D8
Alfred, Maine, U.S.A.	117	C14
Alfred, N.Y., U.S.A.	116	D7
Alfreton, U.K.	14	D6
Alfta, Sweden	10	C10
Alga, Kazakhstan	52	E6
Algaida, Spain	48	B9
Algar, Spain	37	J5
Ålgård, Norway	9	G11
Algarinejo, Spain	37	H6
Algarve, Portugal	37	J2
Algeciras, Spain	37	J5
Algemesí, Spain	39	F4
Alger, Algeria	78	A6
Alger ✕ (ALG), Algeria	39	J8
Algeria ■, Africa	78	C6
Alghero, Italy	42	B1
Älghult, Sweden	11	G9
Algiers = Alger, Algeria	78	A6
Algoa B., S. Africa	88	E4
Algodonales, Spain	37	J5
Algodor →, Spain	36	F7
Algoma, U.S.A.	114	C2
Algona, U.S.A.	112	D7
Algonac, U.S.A.	116	D2
Algonquin △, Canada	104	C4
Algorta, Uruguay	128	C5
Alhama de Almería, Spain	37	J8
Alhama de Aragón, Spain	38	D3
Alhama de Granada, Spain	37	H7
Alhama de Murcia, Spain	39	H3
Alhambra, U.S.A.	111	L8
Alhaurín el Grande, Spain	37	J6
Alhucemas = Al Hoceïma, Morocco	78	A5
'Alī al Gharbī, Iraq	70	C5
'Alī ash Sharqī, Iraq	70	C5
Äli Bayramlı, Azerbaijan	35	L9
'Alī Khēl, Afghan.	68	C3
Ali Sahîh, Djibouti	81	E5
Alī Shāh, Iran	70	B5
Ália, Italy	42	E6
'Alīābād, Khorāsān, Iran	71	C8
'Alīābād, Kordestān, Iran	70	C5
'Alīābād, Yazd, Iran	71	D7
Aliaga, Spain	38	E4
Aliağa, Turkey	47	C8
Aliákmon →, Greece	44	F6
Alibo, Ethiopia	81	F4
Alibori →, Benin	83	C5
Alibunar, Serbia & M.	28	E5
Alicante, Spain	39	G4
Alicante □, Spain	39	G4
Alicante ✕ (ALC), Spain	39	G4
Alice, S. Africa	88	E4
Alice, U.S.A.	113	M5
Alice →, Queens., Australia	94	C3
Alice →, Queens., Australia	94	B3
Alice, Punta, Italy	43	C10
Alice Arm, Canada	102	B3
Alice Springs, Australia	94	C1
Aliceville, S. Africa	88	E4
Aliceville, U.S.A.	115	J1
Alicudi, Italy	43	D7
Aliganj, India	69	F8
Aligarh, Raj., India	68	G7
Aligarh, Ut. P., India	68	F8
Alīgūdarz, Iran	71	C6
Alijó, Portugal	36	D3
Alimnía, Greece	49	C9
Alingsås, Sweden	11	G6
Alipur, Pakistan	68	E4
Alipur Duar, India	67	F16
Aliquippa, U.S.A.	116	F4
Alishan, Taiwan	59	F13
Aliste →, Spain	36	D5
Alitus = Alytus, Lithuania	9	J21
Alivérion, Greece	46	C6
Aliwal North, S. Africa	88	E4
Alix, Canada	102	C6
Aljezur, Portugal	37	H2
Aljustrel, Portugal	37	H2
Alkamari, Niger	83	C7
Alkmaar, Neths.	17	B4
Allada, Benin	83	D5
All American Canal, U.S.A.	109	K6
Allagash →, U.S.A.	115	B11
Allah Dad, Pakistan	68	G2
Allahabad, India	69	G9
Allan, Canada	103	C7
Allanche, France	20	C6
Allanridge, S. Africa	88	D4
Allaqi, Wadi →, Egypt	80	C3
Allariz, Spain	36	C3
Allassac, France	20	C5
Ålleberg, Sweden	11	F7
Allegany, U.S.A.	116	D6
Allegheny →, U.S.A.	116	F5
Allegheny Mts., U.S.A.	114	G6
Allegheny Reservoir, U.S.A.	116	E6
Allègre, France	20	C7
Allègre, Pte., Guadeloupe	120	b
Allen, Bog of, Ireland	12	C5
Allen, L., Ireland	12	B3
Allendale, U.S.A.	115	J5
Allende, Mexico	118	B4
Allentown, U.S.A.	117	F9
Allentsteig, Austria	26	C8
Alleppey, India	66	Q10
Allepuz, Spain	38	E4
Aller →, Germany	24	C5
Alleynes B., Barbados	121	g
Alliance, Nebr., U.S.A.	112	D3
Alliance, Ohio, U.S.A.	116	F3
Allier □, France	19	F9
Allier →, France	19	F10
Alliford Bay, Canada	102	C2
Alligator Pond, Jamaica	120	a
Allinge, Denmark	11	J8
Alliston = New Tecumseth, Canada	116	B5
Alloa, U.K.	13	E5
Allones, France	18	D8
Allora, Australia	95	D5
Allos, France	21	D10
Alluitsup Paa, Greenland	101	B15
Alma, Canada	105	C5
Alma, Ga., U.S.A.	115	K4
Alma, Kans., U.S.A.	112	F6
Alma, Mich., U.S.A.	114	D3
Alma, Nebr., U.S.A.	112	E5
Alma Ata = Almaty, Kazakhstan	52	E8
Almacelles, Spain	38	D5
Almada, Portugal	37	G1
Almadén, Australia	94	B3
Almadén, Spain	37	G6
Almanor, L., U.S.A.	108	F3
Almansa, Spain	39	G3
Almanza, Spain	36	C5
Almanzor, Pico, Spain	36	E5
Almanzora →, Spain	39	H3
Almaş, Munţii, Romania	28	F7
Almassora, Spain	38	F4
Almaty, Kazakhstan	52	E8
Almazán, Spain	38	D2
Almeirim, Brazil	125	D8
Almeirim, Portugal	37	F2
Almelo, Neths.	17	B6
Almenar de Soria, Spain	38	D2
Almenara, Spain	38	F4
Almenara, Sierra de la, Spain	39	H3
Almendra, Embalse de, Spain	36	D4
Almendralejo, Spain	37	G4
Almere-Stad, Neths.	17	B5
Almería, Spain	37	J8
Almería □, Spain	39	H2
Almería, G. de, Spain	39	J2
Almetyevsk, Russia	34	C11
Älmhult, Sweden	11	H8
Almirante, Panama	120	E3
Almiropótamos, Greece	46	C6
Almirós, Greece	46	B4
Almirou, Kólpos, Greece	49	D6
Almodôvar, Portugal	37	H2
Almodóvar del Campo, Spain	37	G6
Almodóvar del Río, Spain	37	H5
Almond, U.S.A.	116	D7
Almont, U.S.A.	116	D1
Almonte, Canada	117	A8
Almonte, Spain	37	H4
Almora, India	69	E8
Almoradí, Spain	39	G4
Almorox, Spain	36	E6
Almoustarat, Mali	83	B5
Ålmsta, Sweden	10	E12
Almudévar, Spain	38	C4
Almuñécar, Spain	37	J7
Almunge, Sweden	10	E12
Almuradiel, Spain	37	G7
Alness, U.K.	13	D4
Almnouth, U.K.	14	B6
Alnwick, U.K.	14	B6
Aloi, Uganda	86	B3
Alon, Burma	67	H19
Alonissos-Voríai Sporades △, Greece	46	B6
Alor, Indonesia	63	F6
Alor Setar, Malaysia	65	J3
Álora, Spain	37	J6
Alosno, Spain	37	H3
Alot, India	68	H6
Aloysius, Mt., Australia	93	E4
Alpaugh, U.S.A.	110	K7
Alpe Apuane △, Italy	40	D7
Alpedrinha, Portugal	36	E3
Alpena, U.S.A.	114	C4
Alpes-de-Haute-Provence □, France	21	D10
Alpes-Maritimes □, France	21	E11
Alpha, Australia	94	C4
Alpha Cordillera, Arctic	4	A2
Alphen aan den Rijn, Neths.	17	B4
Alpiarça, Portugal	37	F2
Alpine, Ariz., U.S.A.	109	K9
Alpine, Calif., U.S.A.	111	N10
Alpine, Tex., U.S.A.	113	K3
Alps, Europe	6	F7
Alpu, Turkey	72	C4
Alqueta, Barragem do, Portugal	37	G3
Alrø, Denmark	11	J4
Als, Denmark	11	K3
Alsace □, France	19	D14
Alsask, Canada	103	C7
Alsasua, Spain	38	C2
Alsek →, U.S.A.	102	B1
Alsfeld, Germany	24	E5
Alsten, Norway	8	D15
Alstermo, Sweden	11	H9
Alston, U.K.	14	C5
Alta, Norway	8	B20
Alta, Sierra, Spain	38	E3
Alta Gracia, Argentina	126	C3
Alta Sierra, U.S.A.	111	K8
Altaelva →, Norway	8	B20
Altafjorden, Norway	8	A20
Altai = Aerhtai Shan, Mongolia	60	B4
Altamaha →, U.S.A.	115	K5
Altamira, Brazil	125	D8
Altamira, Chile	126	B2
Altamira, Mexico	119	C5
Altamira, Cuevas de, Spain	36	B6
Altamont, U.S.A.	117	D10
Altamura, Italy	43	B9
Altanbulag, Mongolia	60	A5
Altar, Mexico	118	A2
Altar, Desierto de, Mexico	118	B2
Altata, Mexico	118	C3
Altavista, U.S.A.	114	G6
Altay, China	60	B3
Altdorf, Switz.	25	J4
Alte Mellum, Germany	24	B4
Altea, Spain	39	G4
Altenberg, Germany	24	E9
Altenbruch, Germany	24	B4
Altenburg, Germany	24	E8
Altenkirchen, Mecklenburg-Vorpommern, Germany	24	A9
Altenkirchen, Rhld-Pfz., Germany	24	E3
Altenmarkt, Austria	26	D7
Alter do Chão, Portugal	37	F3
Altınoluk, Turkey	47	B8
Altınova, Turkey	47	B8
Altıntaş, Turkey	47	B12
Altınyaka, Turkey	47	E12
Altınyayla, Turkey	47	D11
Altiplano, Bolivia	122	E4
Altkirch, France	19	E14
Altmark, Germany	24	C7
Altmühl →, Germany	25	G7
Altmühltal △, Germany	25	G7
Altmunster, Austria	26	D6
Alto Adige = Trentino-Alto Adige □, Italy	41	B8
Alto Araguaia, Brazil	125	G8
Alto Cuchumatanes = Cuchumatanes, Sierra de los, Guatemala	120	C1
Alto del Carmen, Chile	126	B1
Alto del Inca, Chile	126	A2
Alto Garda Bresciano △, Italy	40	C7
Alto Ligonha, Mozam.	87	F4
Alto Molocue, Mozam.	87	F4
Alto Paraguai, Brazil	125	F7
Alto Paraguay □, Paraguay	126	A4
Alto Paraná □, Paraguay	127	B5
Alton, Canada	116	C4
Alton, U.K.	15	F7
Alton, Ill., U.S.A.	112	F9
Alton, N.H., U.S.A.	117	C13
Altona, Canada	103	D9
Altoona, U.S.A.	116	F6
Altötting, Germany	25	G8
Altstätten, Switz.	25	H5
Altun Kupri, Iraq	70	C5
Altun Shan, China	60	C3
Alturas, U.S.A.	108	F3
Altus, U.S.A.	113	H5
Alubijid, Phil.	61	G6
Alucra, Turkey	73	B8
Aluk, Sudan	81	F2
Alūksne, Latvia	9	H22
Alunda, Sweden	10	D12
Alunite, U.S.A.	111	K12
Aluoro →, Ethiopia	81	F3
Alupka, Ukraine	33	K8
Alushta, Ukraine	33	K8
Alusi, Indonesia	63	F8
Alustante, Spain	38	E3
Alva, U.S.A.	113	G5
Alvaiázere, Portugal	36	F2
Älvängen, Sweden	11	G6
Alvão △, Portugal	36	D3
Alvarado, Mexico	119	D5
Alvarado, U.S.A.	113	J6
Alvaro Obregón, Presa, Mexico	118	B3
Älvdalen, Sweden	10	C8
Alvear, Argentina	126	B4
Alverca, Portugal	37	G1
Alvesta, Sweden	11	H8
Alvin, U.S.A.	113	L7
Alvinston, Canada	116	D3
Alvito, Portugal	37	G3
Älvkarleby, Sweden	10	D11
Alvord Desert, U.S.A.	108	E4
Álvros, Sweden	10	B8
Älvsbyn, Sweden	8	D19
Alwar, India	68	F7
Alxa Zuoqi, China	56	E3
Alyangula, Australia	94	A2
Alyata = Älät, Azerbaijan	35	L9
Alyth, U.K.	13	E5
Alytus, Lithuania	9	J21
Alzada, U.S.A.	112	C2
Alzey, Germany	25	F4
Alzira, Spain	39	F4
Am Timan, Chad	79	F10
Amadeus, L., Australia	93	D5
Amadi, Dem. Rep. of the Congo	86	B2
Amâdi, Sudan	81	F3
Amadjuak L., Canada	101	B12
Amadora, Portugal	37	G1
Amagansett, U.S.A.	117	F12
Amager, Denmark	11	J6
Amagunze, Nigeria	83	D6
Amahai, Indonesia	63	E7
Amakusa-Shotō, Japan	55	H5
Åmål, Sweden	10	E6
Amalfi, Italy	43	B7
Amaliás, Greece	46	D3
Amalner, India	66	J9
Amamapare, Indonesia	63	E9
Amambaí, Brazil	127	A4
Amambaí →, Brazil	127	A5
Amambay □, Paraguay	127	A4
Amambay, Cordillera de, S. Amer.	127	A4
Amami-Guntō, Japan	55	L4
Amami-Ō-Shima, Japan	55	L4
Aman, Pulau, Malaysia	65	c
Amaná, L., Brazil	124	D6
Amanat →, India	69	G11
Amanda Park, U.S.A.	110	C3
Amangeldy, Kazakhstan	52	D7
Amantea, Italy	43	C9
Amapá, Brazil	125	C8
Amapá □, Brazil	125	C8
Amara, Sudan	81	E3
Amara □, Ethiopia	81	E4
Amarante, Brazil	125	E10
Amarante, Portugal	36	D2
Amaranth, Canada	103	C9
Amareleja, Portugal	37	G3
Amargosa →, U.S.A.	111	J10
Amargosa Range, U.S.A.	111	J10
Amári, Greece	49	D6
Amarillo, U.S.A.	113	H4
Amarkantak, India	69	H9
Amârna, Tell el', Sudan	80	B3
Amaro, Mte., Italy	41	F11
Amarpur, India	69	G12
Amarti, Eritrea	81	E5
Amarwara, India	69	H8
Amasra, Turkey	72	B5
Amassama, Nigeria	83	D6
Amasya, Turkey	72	B6
Amata, Australia	93	E5
Amatikulu, S. Africa	89	D5
Amatitlán, Guatemala	120	D1
Amatrice, Italy	41	F10
Amay, Belgium	17	D5
Amazon = Amazonas →, S. Amer.	125	D9
Amazonas □, Brazil	124	E6
Amazonas →, S. Amer.	125	D9
Amba Ferit, Ethiopia	81	E4
Ambah, India	68	F8
Ambahakily, Madag.	89	C7
Ambahita, Madag.	89	C8
Ambala, India	68	D7
Ambalavao, Madag.	89	C8
Ambanja, Madag.	89	A8
Ambararata, Madag.	89	B8
Ambarchik, Russia	53	C17
Ambarijeby, Madag.	89	A8
Ambaro, Helodranon', Madag.	89	A8
Ambato, Ecuador	124	D3
Ambato, Sierra de, Argentina	126	B2
Ambato Boeny, Madag.	89	B8
Ambatofinandrahana, Madag.	89	C8
Ambatolampy, Madag.	89	B8
Ambatomainty, Madag.	89	B8
Ambatomanoina, Madag.	89	B8
Ambatondrazaka, Madag.	89	B8
Ambatosoratra, Madag.	89	B8
Ambelón, Greece	46	B4
Ambenja, Madag.	89	B8
Amberg, Germany	25	F7
Ambergris Cay, Belize	119	D7
Amberley, N.Z.	91	K4
Ambert, France	20	C7
Ambidédi, Mali	82	C2
Ambikapur, India	69	H10
Ambikol, Sudan	80	C3
Ambilobé, Madag.	89	A8
Ambinanindrano, Madag.	89	C8
Ambinanitelo, Madag.	89	B8
Ambinda, Madag.	89	B8
Amble, U.K.	14	B6
Ambleside, U.K.	14	C5
Ambo, Peru	124	F3
Amboahangy, Madag.	89	C8
Ambodifototra, Madag.	89	B8
Ambodilazana, Madag.	89	B8
Ambodiriana, Madag.	89	B8
Ambohidratrimo, Madag.	89	B8
Ambohidray, Madag.	89	B8
Ambohimahamasina, Madag.	89	C8
Ambohimahasoa, Madag.	89	C8
Ambohimanga, Madag.	89	C8
Ambohimitombo, Madag.	89	C8
Ambohita, Madag.	89	A8
Amboise, France	18	E8
Ambon, Indonesia	63	E7
Ambondro, Madag.	89	D8
Amborompotsy, Madag.	89	C8
Amboseli △, Kenya	86	C4
Amboseli, L., Kenya	86	C4
Ambositra, Madag.	89	C8
Ambovombe, Madag.	89	D8
Amboy, U.S.A.	111	L11
Amboyna Cay, S. China Sea	62	C4
Ambridge, U.S.A.	116	F4
Ambriz, Angola	84	F2
Amchitka I., U.S.A.	100	C1
Amderma, Russia	52	C7
Amdhi, India	69	H9
Ameca, Mexico	118	C4
Ameca →, Mexico	118	C3
Amecameca, Mexico	119	D5
Ameland, Neths.	17	A5
Amélia, Italy	41	F9
Amendolara, Italy	43	C9
Amenia, U.S.A.	117	E11
American Falls, U.S.A.	108	E7
American Falls Reservoir, U.S.A.	108	E7
American Fork, U.S.A.	108	F8
American Highland, Antarctica	5	D6
American Samoa ☑, Pac. Oc.	91	B13
Americana, Brazil	127	A6
Americus, U.S.A.	115	K3
Amerigo Vespucci, Firenze ✕ (FLR), Italy	40	E8
Amersfoort, Neths.	17	B5
Amersfoort, S. Africa	89	D4
Amery Ice Shelf, Antarctica	5	C6
Ames, Spain	36	C2
Ames, U.S.A.	112	E8
Amesbury, U.S.A.	117	D14
Amet, India	68	G5
Amfíkia, Greece	46	C4
Amfilokhía, Greece	46	C3
Amfípolis, Greece	44	F7
Ámfissa, Greece	46	C4
Amga, Russia	53	C14
Amga →, Russia	53	C14
Amgu, Russia	53	E14
Amgun →, Russia	53	D14
Amherst, Canada	105	C7
Amherst, Mass., U.S.A.	117	D12
Amherst, N.Y., U.S.A.	116	D6
Amherst, Ohio, U.S.A.	116	E2
Amherst I., Canada	117	B8
Amherstburg, Canada	104	D3
Amiata, Mte., Italy	41	F8
Amidon, U.S.A.	112	B3
Amiens, France	19	C9
Amindaion, Greece	44	F5
Åminne, Sweden	11	G7
Amino, Ethiopia	81	G5
Aminuis, Namibia	88	C2
Amīrābād, Iran	70	C5
Amirante Is., Seychelles	50	K9
Amisk △, Canada	103	B9
Amisk L., Canada	103	C8
Amistad, U.S.A.	113	L4
Amistad, Presa de la, Mexico	118	B4
Amite, U.S.A.	113	K9
Amla, India	68	J8
Amlapura = Karangasem, Indonesia	63	J18
Amlia I., U.S.A.	100	C2
Amlwch, U.K.	14	D3
Amm Adam, Sudan	81	D4
'Ammān, Jordan	74	D4
'Ammān □, Jordan	74	D5
'Ammān ✕ (AMM), Jordan	74	D5
Ammanford, U.K.	15	F4
Ammassalik = Tasiilaq, Greenland	4	C6
Ammerån →, Sweden	10	A10
Ammersee, Germany	25	G7
Ammochostos = Famagusta, Cyprus	49	D12
Ammon, U.S.A.	108	E7
Amnat Charoen, Thailand	64	E5
Amnura, Bangla.	69	G13
Amo Jiang →, China	58	F3
Āmol, Iran	71	B7
Amorgós, Greece	47	E7
Amory, U.S.A.	115	J1
Amos, Canada	104	C4
Åmot, Norway	9	G13
Åmotfors, Sweden	10	E6
Amoy = Xiamen, China	59	E12
Ampanavoana, Madag.	89	B9
Ampang, Malaysia	65	L3
Ampanihy, Madag.	89	C7
Amparafaravola, Madag.	89	B8
Amparihy, Madag.	89	C8
Ampasinambo, Madag.	89	C8
Ampasindava, Helodranon', Madag.	89	A8
Ampasindava, Saikanosy, Madag.	89	A8
Ampenan, Indonesia	63	K18
Amper, Nigeria	83	D6
Amper →, Germany	25	G7
Ampezzo, Italy	41	B9
Amphoe Kathu, Thailand	65	a
Amphoe Thalang, Thailand	65	a
Ampitsikinana, Réunion	89	A8
Ampombiantambo, Madag.	89	A8
Amposta, Spain	38	E5
Ampotaka, Madag.	89	D7
Ampoza, Madag.	89	C7
Amqui, Canada	105	C6
Amravati, India	66	J10
Amreli, India	68	J4
Amrib, India	69	E8
Amritsar, India	68	D6
Amroha, India	69	E8
Amrum, Germany	24	A4
Amsterdam, Neths.	17	B4
Amsterdam, U.S.A.	117	D10
Amsterdam ✕ (AMS), Neths.	17	B4
Amsterdam, I. = Nouvelle-Amsterdam, Î., Ind. Oc.	3	F13
Amstetten, Austria	26	C7
Amudarya →, Uzbekistan	52	E6
Amundsen Gulf, Canada	100	A7
Amundsen-Scott, Antarctica	5	E
Amundsen Sea, Antarctica	5	D15
Amungen, Sweden	10	C9
Amuntai, Indonesia	62	E5
Amur →, Russia	53	D15
Amur, W. →, Sudan	80	D3
Amurang, Indonesia	63	D6
Amurrio, Spain	38	B1
Amursk, Russia	53	D14
Amusco, Spain	36	C6
Amvrakikós Kólpos, Greece	46	C2
Amvrosiyivka, Ukraine	33	J10
Amyderya = Amudarya →, Uzbekistan	52	E6
An Anbār □, Iraq	70	C4
An Bien, Vietnam	65	H5
An Hoa, Vietnam	64	E7
An Nabatīyah at Tahta, Lebanon	74	B4
An Nabk, Si. Arabia	70	D3
An Nabk, Syria	74	A5

An Nafūd, Si. Arabia ... 70 D4
An Najaf, Iraq ... 70 C5
An Nāşirīyah, Iraq ... 70 D5
An Nhon, Vietnam ... 64 F7
An Nîl □, Sudan ... 80 D3
An Nîl el Abyad □, Sudan ... 81 E3
An Nîl el Azraq □, Sudan ... 81 E3
An Nu'ayrīyah, Si. Arabia ... 71 E6
An Nu'mānīyah, Iraq ... 73 F11
An Nuwayb'ī, W. ➤, Si. Arabia ... 74 F3
An Thoi, Dao, Vietnam ... 65 H4
An Uaimh, Ireland ... 12 C5
Anabar ➤, Russia ... 53 B12
'Anabtā, West Bank ... 74 C4
Anaconda, U.S.A. ... 108 C7
Anacortes, U.S.A. ... 110 B4
Anacuao, Mt., Phil. ... 61 C4
Anadarko, U.S.A. ... 113 H5
Anadia, Portugal ... 36 E2
Anadolu, Turkey ... 72 C5
Anadyr, Russia ... 53 C18
Anadyr ➤, Russia ... 53 C18
Anadyrskiy Zaliv, Russia ... 53 C19
Anáfi, Greece ... 47 E7
Anafópoulo, Greece ... 47 E7
Anaga, Pta. de, Canary Is. ... 48 F3
Anagni, Italy ... 41 G10
'Ānah, Iraq ... 70 C4
Anaheim, U.S.A. ... 111 M9
Anahim Lake, Canada ... 102 C3
Anáhuac, Mexico ... 118 B4
Anakapalle, India ... 67 L13
Anakie, Australia ... 94 C4
Anaklia, Georgia ... 35 J5
Analalava, Madag. ... 89 A8
Analavoka, Madag. ... 89 C8
Análipsis, Greece ... 49 A3
Anambar ➤, Pakistan ... 68 D3
Anambas, Kepulauan, Indonesia ... 62 D3
Anambas Is. = Anambas,
  Kepulauan, Indonesia ... 62 D3
Anambra □, Nigeria ... 83 D6
Anamosa, U.S.A. ... 112 D9
Anamur, Turkey ... 70 B2
Anamur Burnu, Turkey ... 72 D5
Anan, Japan ... 55 H7
Anand, India ... 68 H5
Anánes, Greece ... 46 E6
Anantapur, India ... 66 M10
Anantnag, India ... 69 C6
Ananyiv, Ukraine ... 29 C14
Anapa, Russia ... 33 K9
Anapodháris ➤, Greece ... 49 E7
Anápolis, Brazil ... 125 G9
Anapu ➤, Brazil ... 125 D8
Anār, Iran ... 71 D7
Anārak, Iran ... 71 C7
Anarisfjällen, Sweden ... 10 A7
Anas ➤, India ... 68 H5
Anatolia = Anadolu, Turkey ... 72 C5
Anatsogno, Madag. ... 89 C7
Añatuya, Argentina ... 126 B3
Anaunethad L., Canada ... 103 A8
Anbyŏn, N. Korea ... 57 E14
Ancares ➤, Spain ... 36 C4
Ancares, Sierra de, Spain ... 36 C4
Ancaster, Canada ... 116 C5
Ancenis, France ... 18 E5
Anchor Bay, U.S.A. ... 110 G3
Anchorage, U.S.A. ... 100 B5
Anci, China ... 56 E9
Ancohuma, Nevado, Bolivia ... 124 G5
Ancón, Peru ... 124 F3
Ancona, Italy ... 41 E10
Ancud, Chile ... 128 E2
Ancud, G. de, Chile ... 128 E2
Ancy-le-Franc, France ... 19 E11
Andacollo, Argentina ... 126 D1
Andacollo, Chile ... 126 C1
Andaingo, Madag. ... 89 B8
Andalgalá, Argentina ... 126 B2
Åndalsnes, Norway ... 9 E12
Andalucía □, Spain ... 37 H6
Andalusia = Andalucía □, Spain ... 37 H6
Andalusia, U.S.A. ... 115 K2
Andaman Is., Ind. Oc. ... 50 H13
Andaman Sea, Ind. Oc. ... 62 B1
Andamooka Opal Fields,
  Australia ... 95 E2
Andapa, Madag. ... 89 A8
Andara, Namibia ... 88 B3
Andelot-Blancheville, France ... 19 D12
Andenes, Norway ... 8 B17
Andenne, Belgium ... 17 D5
Andéranboukane, Mali ... 83 B5
Andermatt, Switz. ... 25 J4
Andernach, Germany ... 24 E3
Andernos-les-Bains, France ... 20 D2
Anderslöv, Sweden ... 11 J7
Anderson, Alaska, U.S.A. ... 100 B5
Anderson, Calif., U.S.A. ... 108 F2
Anderson, Ind., U.S.A. ... 114 E3
Anderson, Mo., U.S.A. ... 113 G7
Anderson, S.C., U.S.A. ... 115 H4
Anderson ➤, Canada ... 100 B7
Anderstorp, Sweden ... 11 G7
Andes, U.S.A. ... 117 D10
Andes, Cord. de los, S. Amer. ... 124 H5
Andfjorden, Norway ... 8 B17
Andhra Pradesh □, India ... 66 L11
Andijon, Uzbekistan ... 52 E8
Andikíthira, Greece ... 46 F5
Andilamena, Madag. ... 89 B8
Andīmeshk, Iran ... 71 C6
Andímilos, Greece ... 46 E6
Andíparos, Greece ... 47 D7
Andípaxoi, Greece ... 46 B2
Andípsara, Greece ... 47 C7
Andírrion, Greece ... 46 C3
Andizhan = Andijon, Uzbekistan ... 52 E8
Andoain, Spain ... 38 B2
Andoany, Madag. ... 89 A8

Andohahela △, Madag. ... 89 C8
Andong, S. Korea ... 57 F15
Andongwei, China ... 57 G10
Andoom, Australia ... 94 A3
Andorra, Spain ... 38 E4
Andorra ■, Europe ... 20 F5
Andorra La Vella, Andorra ... 20 F5
Andover, U.K. ... 15 F6
Andover, Maine, U.S.A. ... 117 B14
Andover, Mass., U.S.A. ... 117 D13
Andover, N.J., U.S.A. ... 117 F10
Andover, N.Y., U.S.A. ... 116 D7
Andover, Ohio, U.S.A. ... 116 E4
Andøya, Norway ... 8 B16
Andradina, Brazil ... 125 H8
Andrahary, Mt., Madag. ... 89 A8
Andramasina, Madag. ... 89 B8
Andranopasy, Madag. ... 89 C7
Andranovory, Madag. ... 89 C7
Andratx, Spain ... 48 B9
Andreanof Is., U.S.A. ... 100 C2
Andreápol, Russia ... 32 D7
Andrews, S.C., U.S.A. ... 115 J6
Andrews, Tex., U.S.A. ... 113 J3
Andreyevka, Russia ... 34 D10
Ándria, Italy ... 43 A9
Andriamena, Madag. ... 89 B8
Andriandampy, Madag. ... 89 C8
Andriba, Madag. ... 89 B8
Andrijevica, Serbia & M. ... 44 D3
Andringitra △, Madag. ... 89 C8
Andrítsaina, Greece ... 46 D3
Androka, Madag. ... 89 C7
Ándros, Greece ... 46 D6
Andros I., Bahamas ... 120 B4
Andros Town, Bahamas ... 120 B4
Androscoggin ➤, U.S.A. ... 117 C14
Andselv, Norway ... 8 B18
Andújar, Spain ... 37 G6
Andulo, Angola ... 84 G3
Aneby, Sweden ... 11 G8
Anegada, Br. Virgin Is. ... 121 e
Anegada Passage, W. Indies ... 121 C7
Aného, Togo ... 83 D5
Anenni-Noi, Moldova ... 29 D14
Aneto, Pico de, Spain ... 38 C5
Anfu, China ... 59 D10
Ang Mo Kio, Singapore ... 65 d
Ang Thong, Thailand ... 64 E3
Ang Thong △, Thailand ... 65 H2
Ang Thong, Ko, Thailand ... 65 b
Angamos, Punta, Chile ... 126 A1
Angara ➤, Russia ... 53 D10
Angara-Débou, Benin ... 83 C5
Angarab, Ethiopia ... 81 E4
Angarsk, Russia ... 53 D11
Angas Hills, Australia ... 92 D4
Angaston, Australia ... 95 E2
Ånge, Sweden ... 10 B9
Ángel, Salto = Angel Falls,
  Venezuela ... 124 B6
Ángel de la Guarda, I., Mexico ... 118 B2
Angel Falls, Venezuela ... 124 B6
Ángeles, Phil. ... 61 D4
Ängelholm, Sweden ... 11 H6
Angels Camp, U.S.A. ... 110 G6
Ängelsberg, Sweden ... 10 E10
Anger ➤, Ethiopia ... 81 F4
Angereb ➤, Ethiopia ... 81 E4
Ångermanälven ➤, Sweden ... 10 B11
Ångermanland, Sweden ... 8 E18
Angermünde, Germany ... 24 B9
Angers, Canada ... 117 A9
Angers, France ... 18 E6
Angerville, France ... 19 D9
Ångesån ➤, Sweden ... 8 C20
Angikuni L., Canada ... 103 A9
Angkor, Cambodia ... 64 F4
Anglès, Spain ... 38 D7
Anglesey, Isle of □, U.K. ... 14 D3
Anglet, France ... 20 E2
Angleton, U.S.A. ... 113 L7
Anglin ➤, France ... 20 B4
Anglisidhes, Cyprus ... 49 E12
Anglure, France ... 19 D10
Angmagssalik = Tasiilaq,
  Greenland ... 4 C6
Ango, Dem. Rep. of the Congo ... 86 B2
Angoche, Mozam. ... 87 F4
Angoche, I., Mozam. ... 87 F4
Angol, Chile ... 126 D1
Angola, Ind., U.S.A. ... 114 E3
Angola, N.Y., U.S.A. ... 116 D5
Angola ■, Africa ... 85 G3
Angoulême, France ... 20 C4
Angoumois, France ... 20 C4
Angra dos Reis, Brazil ... 127 A7
Angrapa ➤, Russia ... 30 D8
Angren, Uzbekistan ... 52 E8
Angtassom, Cambodia ... 65 G5
Angu, Dem. Rep. of the Congo ... 86 B1
Anguang, China ... 57 B12
Anguilla ☑, W. Indies ... 121 C7
Anguo, China ... 56 E8
Angurugu, Australia ... 94 A2
Angus □, U.K. ... 13 E6
Anhanduí ➤, Brazil ... 127 A5
Anholt, Denmark ... 11 H5
Anhua, China ... 59 C8
Anhui □, China ... 59 B11
Anhwei = Anhui □, China ... 59 B11
Anichab, Namibia ... 88 C1
Anídhros, Greece ... 47 E7
Anié, Togo ... 83 D5
Animas, U.S.A. ... 109 H9
Anina, Romania ... 28 E6
Aninoasa, Romania ... 29 F9
Anivorano, Madag. ... 89 B8
Anjalankoski, Finland ... 9 F22

Anjar, India ... 68 H4
Anji, China ... 59 B12
Anjou, France ... 18 E6
Anjozorobe, Madag. ... 89 B8
Anju, N. Korea ... 57 E13
Anka, Nigeria ... 83 C6
Ankaboa, Tanjona, Madag. ... 89 C7
Ankang, China ... 56 H5
Ankara, Turkey ... 72 C5
Ankarafantsika △, Madag. ... 89 B8
Ankaramena, Madag. ... 89 C8
Ankaratra, Madag. ... 85 H9
Ankarsrum, Sweden ... 11 G10
Ankasakasa, Madag. ... 89 B7
Ankavandra, Madag. ... 89 B8
Ankazoabo, Madag. ... 89 C7
Ankazobe, Madag. ... 89 B8
Ankeny, U.S.A. ... 112 E8
Ankilimalinika, Madag. ... 89 C7
Ankilizato, Madag. ... 89 C8
Ankisabe, Madag. ... 89 B8
Anklam, Germany ... 24 B9
Ankober, Ethiopia ... 81 F4
Ankoro, Dem. Rep. of the Congo ... 86 D2
Ankororoka, Madag. ... 89 D8
Anlong, China ... 58 E5
Anlu, China ... 59 B9
Anmyŏn-do, S. Korea ... 57 F14
Ånn, Sweden ... 10 A6
Ann, C., U.S.A. ... 117 D14
Ann Arbor, U.S.A. ... 114 D4
Anna, Russia ... 34 E5
Anna, U.S.A. ... 113 G10
Annaba, Algeria ... 78 A7
Annaberg-Buchholz, Germany ... 24 E9
Annalee ➤, Ireland ... 12 B4
Annam, Vietnam ... 64 E7
Annamitique, Chaîne, Asia ... 64 D6
Annan, U.K. ... 13 G5
Annan ➤, U.K. ... 13 G5
Annapolis, U.S.A. ... 114 F7
Annapolis Royal, Canada ... 105 D6
Annapurna, Nepal ... 69 E10
Annean, L., Australia ... 93 E2
Anneberg, Sweden ... 11 G8
Annecy, France ... 21 C10
Annecy, Lac d', France ... 21 C10
Annemasse, France ... 19 F13
Annenskiy Most, Russia ... 32 B9
Anning, China ... 58 E4
Anniston, U.S.A. ... 115 J3
Annobón, Atl. Oc. ... 77 G4
Annonay, France ... 21 C8
Annot, France ... 21 E10
Annotto B., Jamaica ... 120 a
Annville, U.S.A. ... 117 F8
Annweiler, Germany ... 25 F3
Áno Arkhánai, Greece ... 47 F7
Áno Porróia, Greece ... 44 E7
Áno Síros, Greece ... 46 D6
Áno Viánnos, Greece ... 49 D7
Anorotsangana, Madag. ... 89 A8
Anosibe, Madag. ... 89 B8
Anou Mellene, Mali ... 83 B5
Anoumaba, Ivory C. ... 82 D4
Anóyia, Greece ... 49 D6
Anping, Hebei, China ... 56 E8
Anping, Liaoning, China ... 57 D12
Anpu Gang, China ... 58 G7
Anqing, China ... 59 B11
Anqiu, China ... 57 F10
Anren, China ... 59 D9
Ansager, Denmark ... 11 J2
Ansai, China ... 56 F5
Ansbach, Germany ... 25 F6
Anse la Raye, St. Lucia ... 121 f
Anseba ➤, Eritrea ... 81 D4
Ansfelden, Austria ... 26 C7
Anshan, China ... 57 D12
Anshun, China ... 58 D5
Ansião, Portugal ... 36 F2
Ansley, U.S.A. ... 112 E5
Ansó, Spain ... 38 C4
Ansoain, Spain ... 38 C3
Anson, U.S.A. ... 113 J5
Anson B., Australia ... 92 B5
Ansongo, Mali ... 83 B5
Ansongo-Ménaka △, Mali ... 83 B5
Ansonia, U.S.A. ... 117 E11
Anstruther, U.K. ... 13 E6
Ansudu, Indonesia ... 63 E9
Antabamba, Peru ... 124 F4
Antakya, Turkey ... 70 B3
Antalaha, Madag. ... 89 A9
Antalya, Turkey ... 72 D4
Antalya □, Turkey ... 47 E12
Antalya Körfezi, Turkey ... 72 D4
Antambohobe, Madag. ... 89 C8
Antanambao-Manampotsy,
  Madag. ... 89 B8
Antanambe, Madag. ... 89 B8
Antananarivo, Madag. ... 89 B8
Antananarivo □, Madag. ... 89 B8
Antanifotsy, Madag. ... 89 B8
Antanimbaribe, Madag. ... 89 C7
Antanimora, Madag. ... 89 C8
Antarctic Pen., Antarctica ... 5 C18
Antarctica ... 5 E3
Antelope, Zimbabwe ... 87 G2
Antequera, Paraguay ... 126 A4
Antequera, Spain ... 37 H6
Antero, Mt., U.S.A. ... 109 G10
Antevamena, Madag. ... 89 C7
Anthemoús, Greece ... 44 F7
Anthony, Kans., U.S.A. ... 113 G5
Anthony, N. Mex., U.S.A. ... 109 K10
Anti Atlas, Morocco ... 78 C4
Anti-Lebanon = Ash Sharqi, Al
  Jabal, Lebanon ... 74 B5
Antibes, France ... 21 E11
Antibes, C. d', France ... 21 E11

Anticosti, Î. d', Canada ... 105 C7
Antifer, C. d', France ... 18 C7
Antigo, U.S.A. ... 112 C10
Antigonish, Canada ... 105 C7
Antigua, Canary Is. ... 48 F5
Antigua, Guatemala ... 120 D1
Antigua, W. Indies ... 121 C7
Antigua & Barbuda ■, W. Indies ... 121 C7
Antilla, Cuba ... 120 B4
Antilles = West Indies,
  Cent. Amer. ... 121 D7
Antioch, U.S.A. ... 110 G5
Antioche, Pertuis d', France ... 20 B2
Antioquia, Colombia ... 124 B3
Antipodes Is., Pac. Oc. ... 96 M9
Antlers, U.S.A. ... 113 H7
Antoetra, Madag. ... 89 C8
Antofagasta, Chile ... 126 A1
Antofagasta □, Chile ... 126 A2
Antofagasta de la Sierra,
  Argentina ... 126 B2
Antofalla, Argentina ... 126 B2
Antofalla, Salar de, Argentina ... 126 B2
Anton, U.S.A. ... 113 J3
Antongila, Helodrano, Madag. ... 89 B8
Antonibé, Madag. ... 89 B8
Antonibé, Presqu'île d', Madag. ... 89 A8
Antonina, Brazil ... 127 B6
Antrain, France ... 18 D5
Antrim, U.K. ... 12 B5
Antrim, U.S.A. ... 116 F3
Antrim □, U.K. ... 12 B5
Antrim, Mts. of, U.K. ... 12 A5
Antrim Plateau, Australia ... 92 C4
Antrodoco, Italy ... 41 F10
Antropovo, Russia ... 34 A6
Antsakabary, Madag. ... 89 B8
Antsalova, Madag. ... 89 B7
Antsenavolo, Madag. ... 89 C8
Antsiafabositra, Madag. ... 89 B8
Antsirabe, Antananarivo, Madag. ... 89 B8
Antsirabe, Antsiranana, Madag. ... 89 A8
Antsirabe, Mahajanga, Madag. ... 89 B8
Antsiranana, Madag. ... 89 A8
Antsiranana □, Madag. ... 89 A8
Antsohihy, Madag. ... 89 A8
Antsohimbondrona Seranana,
  Madag. ... 89 A8
Antu, China ... 57 C15
Antwerp = Antwerpen, Belgium ... 17 C4
Antwerp, U.S.A. ... 117 B9
Antwerpen, Belgium ... 17 C4
Antwerpen □, Belgium ... 17 C4
Anupgarh, India ... 68 E5
Anuppur, India ... 69 H9
Anuradhapura, Sri Lanka ... 66 Q12
Anveh, Iran ... 71 E7
Anvers = Antwerpen, Belgium ... 17 C4
Anvers I., Antarctica ... 5 C17
Anwen, China ... 59 C13
Anxi, Fujian, China ... 59 E12
Anxi, Gansu, China ... 60 B4
Anxian, China ... 58 B5
Anxiang, China ... 59 C9
Anxious B., Australia ... 95 E1
Anyama, Ivory C. ... 82 D4
Anyang, China ... 56 F8
Anyer-Kidul, Indonesia ... 63 G11
Anyi, Jiangxi, China ... 59 C10
Anyi, Shanxi, China ... 56 G6
Anyuan, China ... 59 E10
Anyue, China ... 58 B5
Anza, U.S.A. ... 111 M10
Anze, China ... 56 F7
Anzhero-Sudzhensk, Russia ... 52 D9
Ánzio, Italy ... 42 A5
Ao Makham, Thailand ... 65 a
Ao Phangnga △, Thailand ... 65 a
Aoga-Shima, Japan ... 55 H9
Aoiz, Spain ... 38 C3
Aomen = Macau, China ... 59 F9
Aomori, Japan ... 54 D10
Aomori □, Japan ... 54 D10
Aonla, India ... 69 E8
Aoraki Mount Cook, N.Z. ... 91 K3
Aosta, Italy ... 40 C4
Aotearoa = New Zealand ■,
  Oceania ... 91 J6
Aoudéras, Niger ... 83 B6
Aoukâr, Mauritania ... 82 B3
Aozou, Couloir d', Chad ... 79 D9
Apa ➤, S. Amer. ... 126 A4
Apache, U.S.A. ... 113 H5
Apache Junction, U.S.A. ... 109 K8
Apalachee B., U.S.A. ... 115 L4
Apalachicola, U.S.A. ... 115 L3
Apalachicola ➤, U.S.A. ... 115 L3
Apam, Ghana ... 83 D4
Apapa, Nigeria ... 83 D5
Aparados da Serra △, Brazil ... 127 B5
Aparri, Phil. ... 61 B4
Apaporis ➤, Colombia ... 124 D5
Apateu, Romania ... 28 D6
Apatin, Serbia & M. ... 28 E4
Apatity, Russia ... 52 C4
Apatzingán, Mexico ... 118 D4
Apeldoorn, Neths. ... 17 B5
Apen, Germany ... 24 B3
Apennines = Appennini, Italy ... 40 D7
Aphrodisias, Turkey ... 47 D10
Apia, Samoa ... 91 A13
Apiacás, Serra dos, Brazil ... 124 E7
Apies ➤, S. Africa ... 89 D4
Apizaco, Mexico ... 119 D5
Apo, Mt., Phil. ... 63 C7
Apolakkiá, Greece ... 49 C9
Apolakkiá, Órmos, Greece ... 49 C9
Apolda, Germany ... 24 D7
Apollonia, Greece ... 46 E6
Apolo, Bolivia ... 124 F5
Aporé ➤, Brazil ... 125 G8

Apostle Is., U.S.A. ... 112 B9
Apostle Islands △, U.S.A. ... 112 B9
Apóstoles, Argentina ... 127 B4
Apostolos Andreas, C., Cyprus ... 49 D13
Apostolovo, Ukraine ... 33 J7
Apoteri, Guyana ... 124 C7
Appalachian Mts., U.S.A. ... 114 G6
Äppelbo, Sweden ... 10 D8
Appennini, Italy ... 40 D7
Appennino Ligure, Italy ... 40 D6
Appenzell-Ausser Rhoden □,
  Switz. ... 25 H5
Appenzell-Inner Rhoden □,
  Switz. ... 25 H5
Appiano, Italy ... 41 B8
Apple Hill, Canada ... 117 A10
Apple Valley, U.S.A. ... 111 L9
Appleby-in-Westmorland, U.K. ... 14 C5
Appledore, U.K. ... 15 F3
Appledore, U.S.A. ... 114 C1
Approuague ➤, Fr. Guiana ... 125 C8
Apricena, Italy ... 41 G12
Aprília, Italy ... 42 A5
Apsheronsk, Russia ... 35 H4
Apsley, Canada ... 116 B6
Apt, France ... 21 E9
Apuane, Alpi, Italy ... 40 D7
Apucarana, Brazil ... 127 A5
Apure ➤, Venezuela ... 124 B5
Apurimac ➤, Peru ... 124 F4
Apuseni, Munţii, Romania ... 28 D7
Āqā Jarī, Iran ... 71 D6
Aqaba = Al 'Aqabah, Jordan ... 74 F4
Aqaba, G. of, Red Sea ... 70 D2
'Aqaba, Khalīj al = Aqaba, G.
  of, Red Sea ... 70 D2
'Aqdā, Iran ... 71 C7
Aqīq, Sudan ... 80 D4
Aqīq, Khalīg, Sudan ... 80 D4
'Aqrah, Iraq ... 70 B4
Aqtaū, Kazakhstan ... 52 E6
Aqtöbe, Kazakhstan ... 52 D6
Aquidauana, Brazil ... 125 H7
Aquiles Serdán, Mexico ... 118 B3
Aquin, Haiti ... 121 C5
Aquitaine □, France ... 20 D3
Ar Rachidiya = Er Rachidia,
  Morocco ... 78 B5
Ar Rafīd, Syria ... 74 C4
Ar Raḥḥālīyah, Iraq ... 70 C4
Ar Ramādī, Iraq ... 70 C4
Ar Ramthā, Jordan ... 74 C5
Ar Raqqah, Syria ... 70 C3
Ar Rass, Si. Arabia ... 70 E4
Ar Rawshān, Si. Arabia ... 80 C5
Ar Rifā'ī, Iraq ... 70 D5
Ar Riyāḍ, Si. Arabia ... 70 E5
Ar Ru'ays, Qatar ... 71 E6
Ar Rukhaymīyah, Iraq ... 70 D5
Ar Ruṣāfah, Syria ... 70 C3
Ar Ruṭbah, Iraq ... 70 C4
Ara, India ... 69 G11
Ara Goro, Ethiopia ... 81 F5
Ara Tera, Ethiopia ... 81 F5
Arab, U.S.A. ... 115 H2
'Arab, Bahr el ➤, Sudan ... 81 F2
Arab, Khalīg el, Egypt ... 80 A2
Arab, Shatt al ➤, Asia ... 71 D6
'Araba, W. ➤, Egypt ... 80 J8
'Arabābād, Iran ... 71 C8
Araban, Turkey ... 72 D7
Arabatskaya Strelka, Ukraine ... 33 K8
Arabba, Italy ... 41 B8
Arabia, Asia ... 50 G8
Arabian Desert = Es Sahrâ' Esh
  Sharqīya, Egypt ... 80 B3
Arabian Gulf = Persian Gulf, Asia ... 71 E6
Arabian Sea, Ind. Oc. ... 50 H10
Araç, Turkey ... 72 B5
Aracaju, Brazil ... 125 F11
Aracati, Brazil ... 125 D11
Araçatuba, Brazil ... 127 A5
Aracena, Spain ... 37 H4
Aracena, Sierra de, Spain ... 37 H4
Aračinovo, Macedonia ... 44 E5
Araçuaí, Brazil ... 125 G10
'Arad, Israel ... 74 D4
Arad, Romania ... 28 D6
Arad □, Romania ... 28 D6
Arādān, Iran ... 71 C7
Aradhippou, Cyprus ... 49 E12
Arafura Sea, E. Indies ... 96 H5
Aragats, Armenia ... 35 K7
Aragón □, Spain ... 38 C4
Aragón ➤, Spain ... 38 C3
Aragona, Italy ... 42 F6
Araguacema, Brazil ... 125 E9
Araguaia ➤, Brazil ... 125 E9
Araguaína, Brazil ... 125 E9
Araguari, Brazil ... 125 G9
Araguari ➤, Brazil ... 125 C9
Araín, India ... 68 F6
Arak, Algeria ... 78 C6
Arāk, Iran ... 71 C6
Araka, Sudan ... 81 G3
Arakan Coast, Burma ... 67 K19
Arakan Yoma, Burma ... 67 K19
Arákhova, Greece ... 46 C4
Arakli, Turkey ... 73 B8
Araks = Aras, Rūd-e ➤, Asia ... 35 K9
Aral, Kazakhstan ... 52 E7
Aral Tengizi = Aral Sea, Asia ... 52 E7
Aralsk = Aral, Kazakhstan ... 52 E7
Aralskoye More = Aral Sea, Asia ... 52 E7
Aralsor, Ozero, Kazakhstan ... 35 F9
Aramac, Australia ... 94 C4
Aran I., Ireland ... 12 A3
Aran Is., Ireland ... 12 C2
Aranda de Duero, Spain ... 36 D7
Arandān, Iran ... 70 C5

Aranđelovac, Serbia & M. 44 B4
Aranjuez, Spain 36 E7
Aranos, Namibia 88 C2
Aransas Pass, U.S.A. 113 M6
Aranyaprathet, Thailand 64 F4
Araouane, Mali 82 B4
Arapahoe, U.S.A. 112 E5
Arapey Grande →, Uruguay 126 C4
Arapgir, Turkey 70 B3
Arapiraca, Brazil 125 E11
Arapongas, Brazil 127 A5
Ar'ar, Si. Arabia 70 D4
Araranguá, Brazil 127 B6
Araraquara, Brazil 125 H9
Araras, Serra das, Brazil 127 B5
Ararat, Armenia 73 C11
Ararat, Australia 95 F3
Ararat, Mt. = Ağrı Dağı, Turkey 70 B5
Araria, India 69 F12
Araripe, Chapada do, Brazil 125 E11
Araruama, L. de, Brazil 127 A7
Araxá, Brazil 125 G9
Araya, Pen. de, Venezuela 124 A6
Arba Gugu, Ethiopia 81 F5
Arba Minch, Ethiopia 81 F4
Arbat, Iraq 70 C5
Árbatax, Italy 42 C2
Arbi, Ethiopia 81 F4
Arbīl, Iraq 70 B5
Arboga, Sweden 10 E9
Arbois, France 19 F12
Arbore, Ethiopia 81 F4
Arboréa, Italy 42 C1
Arborfield, Canada 103 C8
Arborg, Canada 103 C9
Arbre du Ténéré, Niger 83 B7
Arbroath, U.K. 13 E6
Arbuckle, U.S.A. 110 F4
Arbus, Italy 42 C1
Arc →, France 21 C10
Arc-lès-Gray, France 19 E12
Arcachon, France 20 D2
Arcachon, Bassin d', France 20 D2
Arcade, Calif., U.S.A. 111 L8
Arcade, N.Y., U.S.A. 116 D6
Arcadia, Fla., U.S.A. 115 M5
Arcadia, La., U.S.A. 113 J8
Arcadia, Pa., U.S.A. 116 F6
Arcata, U.S.A. 108 F1
Arcévia, Italy 41 E9
Archangel = Arkhangelsk, Russia 52 C5
Archar, Bulgaria 44 C6
Archbald, U.S.A. 117 E9
Archena, Spain 39 G3
Archer →, Australia 94 A3
Archer B., Australia 94 A3
Archer Bend = Mungkan
  Kandju △, Australia 94 A3
Archers Post, Kenya 86 B4
Arches △, U.S.A. 109 G9
Archidona, Spain 37 H6
Archipel-de-Mingan △, Canada 105 B7
Archipélago Chinijo △,
  Canary Is. 48 E6
Archipélago Los Roques △,
  Venezuela 121 D6
Arci, Mte., Italy 42 C1
Arcidosso, Italy 41 F8
Arcipelago de la Maddalena △,
  Italy 42 A2
Arcipelago Toscano △, Italy 40 F7
Arcis-sur-Aube, France 19 D11
Arckaringa Cr. →, Australia 95 D2
Arco, Italy 40 C7
Arco, U.S.A. 108 E7
Arcos de Jalón, Spain 38 D2
Arcos de la Frontera, Spain 37 J5
Arcos de Valdevez, Portugal 36 D2
Arcot, India 66 N11
Arcozelo, Portugal 36 E3
Arctic Bay, Canada 101 A11
Arctic Ocean, Arctic 4 B18
Arctic Red River = Tsiigehtchic,
  Canada 100 B6
Arctowski, Antarctica 5 C18
Arda →, Bulgaria 45 E10
Arda →, Italy 40 C7
Ardabīl, Iran 71 B6
Ardabīl □, Iran 71 B6
Ardahan, Turkey 73 B10
Ardakān = Sepīdān, Iran 71 D7
Ardakān, Iran 71 C7
Ardala, Sweden 11 F7
Ardales, Spain 37 J6
Ardèche □, France 21 D8
Ardèche →, France 21 D8
Ardee, Ireland 12 C5
Arden, Canada 116 B8
Arden, Denmark 11 H3
Arden, Calif., U.S.A. 110 G5
Arden, Nev., U.S.A. 111 J11
Ardenne, Belgium 17 E5
Ardennes = Ardenne, Belgium 17 E5
Ardennes □, France 19 C11
Ardentes, France 19 F8
Arderin, Ireland 12 C4
Ardeşen, Turkey 73 B9
Ardestān, Iran 71 C7
Árdhas →, Greece 45 E10
Ardhéa, Greece 44 F6
Ardila →, Portugal 37 G3
Ardino, Bulgaria 45 E8
Ardivachar Pt., U.K. 13 D1
Ardlethan, Australia 95 E4
Ardmore, Okla., U.S.A. 113 H6

Ardmore, Pa., U.S.A. 117 G9
Ardnamurchan, Pt. of, U.K. 13 E2
Ardnave Pt., U.K. 13 F2
Ardon, Russia 35 J7
Ardore, Italy 43 D9
Ardres, France 19 B8
Ardrossan, Australia 95 E2
Ardrossan, U.K. 13 F4
Ards Pen., U.K. 12 B6
Arduan, Sudan 80 D3
Ardud, Romania 28 C7
Åre, Sweden 10 A7
Arecibo, Puerto Rico 121 d
Areia Branca, Brazil 125 E11
Arena, Pt., U.S.A. 110 G3
Arenal, Honduras 120 C2
Arenas = Las Arenas, Spain 36 B6
Arenas de San Pedro, Spain 36 E5
Arendal, Norway 9 G13
Arendsee, Germany 24 C7
Arenys de Mar, Spain 38 D7
Arenzano, Italy 40 D5
Areópolis, Greece 46 E4
Arequipa, Peru 124 G4
Arero, Ethiopia 81 G4
Arès, France 20 D2
Arévalo, Spain 36 D6
Arezzo, Italy 41 E8
Arga, Turkey 70 B3
Arga →, Spain 38 C3
Arga →, Turkey 70 B3
Argalastí, Greece 46 B5
Argamasilla de Alba, Spain 37 F7
Argamasilla de Calatrava, Spain 37 G6
Arganda, Spain 36 E7
Arganil, Portugal 36 E2
Argedeb, Ethiopia 81 F5
Argelès-Gazost, France 20 E3
Argelès-sur-Mer, France 20 F7
Argens →, France 21 E10
Argenta, Canada 102 C5
Argenta, Italy 41 D8
Argentan, France 18 D6
Argentário, Mte., Italy 41 F8
Argentat, France 20 C5
Argentera, Italy 40 D4
Argenteuil, France 19 D9
Argentia, Canada 105 C9
Argentina ■, S. Amer. 128 D3
Argentine Basin, S. Amer. 122 H5
Argentino, L., Argentina 128 G2
Argenton-Château, France 18 F6
Argenton-sur-Creuse, France 19 F8
Argeş □, Romania 29 F9
Argeş →, Romania 29 F11
Arghandab →, Afghan. 68 D1
Argheile, Ethiopia 81 F5
Argo, Sudan 80 D3
Argolikós Kólpos, Greece 46 D4
Argolís □, Greece 46 D4
Argonne, France 19 C12
Árgos, Greece 46 D4
Árgos Orestikón, Greece 44 F5
Argostólion, Greece 46 C2
Arguedas, Spain 38 C3
Arguello, Pt., U.S.A. 111 L6
Arguineguín, Canary Is. 48 G4
Argun, Russia 35 J7
Argun →, Russia 53 D13
Argun →, Russia 35 J7
Argungu, Nigeria 83 C5
Argus Pk., U.S.A. 111 K9
Argyle, L., Australia 92 C4
Argyll, U.K. 13 E4
Argyll & Bute □, U.K. 13 E3
Arhavi, Turkey 73 B9
Århus, Denmark 11 H4
Århus Amtskommune □,
  Denmark 11 H4
Ariadnoye, Russia 54 B7
Ariamsvlei, Namibia 88 D2
Ariano Irpino, Italy 43 A8
Aribinda, Burkina Faso 83 C4
Arica, Chile 124 G4
Arica, Colombia 124 D4
Arico, Canary Is. 48 F3
Arid, C., Australia 93 F3
Arida, Japan 55 G7
Ariège □, France 20 F5
Ariège →, France 20 E5
Arieş →, Romania 29 D8
Arihā, Israel 80 A4
Arilje, Serbia & M. 44 C4
Arílla, Ákra, Greece 49 A3
Arima, Trin. & Tob. 121 D7
Arinos →, Brazil 124 F7
Ario de Rosales, Mexico 118 D4
Aripo, Mt., Trin. & Tob. 125 K15
Aripuanã, Brazil 124 E6
Aripuanã →, Brazil 124 E6
Ariquemes, Brazil 124 E6
Arisaig, U.K. 13 E3
Arīsh, W. el →, Egypt 80 A3
Arissa, Ethiopia 81 E5
Aristazabal I., Canada 102 C3
Arivonimamo, Madag. 89 B8
Ariza, Spain 38 D2
Arizaro, Salar de, Argentina 126 A2
Arizona, Argentina 126 D2
Arizona □, U.S.A. 109 J8
Arizpe, Mexico 118 A2
Årjäng, Sweden 10 E6
Arjeplog, Sweden 8 D18
Arjepluovve = Arjeplog, Sweden 8 D18
Arjona, Colombia 124 A3
Arjona, Spain 37 H6
Arjuna, Indonesia 63 G15
Arka, Russia 53 C15
Arkadak, Russia 34 E6
Arkadelphia, U.S.A. 113 H8
Arkadhía □, Greece 46 D4

Arkaig, L., U.K. 13 E3
Arkalyk = Arqalyk, Kazakhstan 52 D7
Arkansas □, U.S.A. 113 H8
Arkansas →, U.S.A. 113 J9
Arkansas City, U.S.A. 113 G6
Arkaroola, Australia 95 E2
Árkathos →, Greece 46 B3
Árkhangelos, Greece 49 C10
Arkhangelsk, Russia 52 C5
Arkhangelskoye, Russia 34 E5
Arki, India 68 D7
Arkiko, Eritrea 81 D4
Arklow, Ireland 12 D5
Árkoi, Greece 47 D8
Arkona, Kap, Germany 24 A9
Arkösund, Sweden 11 F10
Arkport, U.S.A. 116 D7
Arktičeskiy, Mys, Russia 53 A10
Arkul, Russia 34 B10
Arkville, U.S.A. 117 D10
Árla, Sweden 10 E10
Arlanda, Stockholm ✈ (ARN),
  Sweden 10 E11
Arlanza →, Spain 36 C6
Arlanzón →, Spain 36 C6
Arlbergpass, Austria 26 D3
Arles, France 21 E8
Arli, Burkina Faso 83 C5
Arli △, Burkina Faso 83 C5
Arlington, S. Africa 89 D4
Arlington, N.Y., U.S.A. 117 E11
Arlington, Oreg., U.S.A. 108 D3
Arlington, S. Dak., U.S.A. 112 C6
Arlington, Tex., U.S.A. 113 J6
Arlington, Va., U.S.A. 114 F7
Arlington, Vt., U.S.A. 117 C11
Arlington, Wash., U.S.A. 110 B4
Arlington Heights, U.S.A. 114 D2
Arlit, Niger 78 E7
Arlon, Belgium 17 E5
Arltunga, Australia 94 C1
Armagh, U.K. 12 B5
Armagh □, U.K. 12 B5
Armagnac, France 20 E4
Armançon →, France 19 E11
Armando Bermudez △,
  Dom. Rep. 121 C5
Armavir, Russia 35 H5
Armenia, Colombia 124 C3
Armenia ■, Asia 35 K7
Armeniş, Romania 28 E7
Armenistís, Ákra, Greece 49 C9
Armentières, France 19 B9
Armidale, Australia 95 E5
Armilla, Spain 37 H7
Armorique △, France 18 D3
Armour, U.S.A. 112 D5
Armstrong, B.C., Canada 102 C5
Armstrong, Ont., Canada 104 B2
Armutlu, Bursa, Turkey 45 F12
Armutlu, Izmir, Turkey 47 C9
Arnaía, Greece 44 F7
Arnarfjörður, Iceland 8 D2
Arnaud →, Canada 101 B13
Arnauti, C., Cyprus 49 D11
Arnay-le-Duc, France 19 E11
Arnedillo, Spain 38 C2
Arnedo, Spain 38 C2
Arnett, U.S.A. 113 G5
Arnhem, Neths. 17 C5
Arnhem, C., Australia 94 A2
Arnhem B., Australia 94 A2
Arnhem Land, Australia 94 A1
Arníssa, Greece 44 F5
Arno →, Italy 40 E7
Arno Bay, Australia 95 E2
Arnold, U.K. 14 D6
Arnold, U.S.A. 110 G6
Arnoldstein, Austria 26 E6
Arnon →, France 19 E9
Arnot, Canada 103 B9
Arnøy, Norway 8 A19
Arnprior, Canada 117 A8
Arnsberg, Germany 24 D4
Arnsberger Wald △, Germany 24 D4
Arnstadt, Germany 24 E6
Aroab, Namibia 88 D2
Aroánia Óri, Greece 46 D4
Aroche, Spain 37 H4
Arochuku, Nigeria 83 D6
Arolsen, Germany 24 D5
Aron, India 68 G6
Aron →, France 19 F10
Arona, Canary Is. 48 F3
Arona, Italy 40 C5
Aroroy, Phil. 61 E5
Arpajon, France 19 D9
Arpajon-sur-Cère, France 20 D6
Arpaşu de Jos, Romania 29 E9
Arqalyk, Kazakhstan 52 D7
Arrah = Ara, India 69 G11
Arrah, Ivory C. 82 D4
Arraiolos, Portugal 37 G3
Arran, U.K. 13 F3
Arras, France 19 B9
Arrasate, Spain 38 B2
Arrats →, France 20 D4
Arreau, France 20 F4
Arrecife, Canary Is. 48 F6
Arrecifes, Argentina 126 C3
Arrée, Mts. d', France 18 D3
Arromanches-les-Bains, France 18 C6
Arronches, Portugal 37 F3

Arros →, France 20 E3
Arrow, L., Ireland 12 B3
Arrowhead, L., U.S.A. 111 L9
Arrowtown, N.Z. 91 L2
Arroyo de la Luz, Spain 37 F4
Arroyo Grande, U.S.A. 111 K6
Ars, Denmark 11 H3
Ars, Iran 70 B5
Ars-sur-Moselle, France 19 C13
Arsenault L., Canada 103 B7
Arsenev, Russia 54 B6
Arsi □, Ethiopia 81 F4
Arsiero, Italy 41 C8
Arsin, Turkey 73 B8
Arsk, Russia 34 B9
Ársunda, Sweden 10 D10
Árta, Greece 46 B3
Artà, Spain 48 B10
Arta □, Greece 46 B3
Arteaga, Mexico 118 D4
Arteche, Phil. 61 E6
Arteijo = Arteixo, Spain 36 B2
Arteixo, Spain 36 B2
Artem = Artyom, Azerbaijan 35 K10
Artem, Russia 54 C6
Artemovsk, Russia 53 D10
Artemovsk, Ukraine 33 H9
Artemovskiy, Russia 35 G5
Artenay, France 19 D8
Artern, Germany 24 D7
Artesa de Segre, Spain 38 D6
Artesia = Mosomane, Botswana 88 C4
Artesia, U.S.A. 113 J2
Arthington, Liberia 82 D2
Arthur, Canada 116 C4
Arthur →, Australia 95 G3
Arthur Cr. →, Australia 94 C2
Arthur Pt., Australia 94 C5
Arthur River, Australia 93 F2
Arthur's Pass, N.Z. 91 K3
Arthur's Pass △, N.Z. 91 K3
Arthur's Town, Bahamas 121 B4
Artigas, Antarctica 5 C18
Artigas, Uruguay 126 C4
Artik, Armenia 35 K6
Artillery L., Canada 103 A7
Artois, France 19 B9
Artotína, Greece 46 C4
Artrutx, C. de, Spain 48 B10
Artsyz, Ukraine 29 D14
Artvin, Turkey 73 B9
Artyom, Azerbaijan 35 K10
Aru, Kepulauan, Indonesia 63 F8
Aru Is. = Aru, Kepulauan,
  Indonesia 63 F8
Arua, Uganda 86 B3
Aruanã, Brazil 125 F8
Aruba ☑, W. Indies 121 D6
Arucas, Canary Is. 48 F4
Arudy, France 20 E3
Arun →, Nepal 69 F12
Arun →, U.K. 15 G7
Arunachal Pradesh □, India 67 F19
Arusha, Tanzania 86 C4
Arusha □, Tanzania 86 C4
Arusha △, Tanzania 86 C4
Arusha Chini, Tanzania 86 C4
Aruwimi →, Dem. Rep. of
  the Congo 86 B1
Arvada, Colo., U.S.A. 112 F2
Arvada, Wyo., U.S.A. 108 D10
Arve →, France 19 F13
Árvi, Greece 49 E7
Arviat, Canada 103 A10
Arvidsjaur, Sweden 8 D18
Arvika, Sweden 10 E6
Arvin, U.S.A. 111 K8
Arwal, India 69 G11
Arxan, China 60 B6
Aryd, Sweden 11 H8
Aryirádhes, Greece 49 B3
Aryiroúpolis, Greece 49 D6
Arys, Kazakhstan 52 E7
Arzachena, Italy 42 A2
Arzamas, Russia 34 C6
Arzgir, Russia 35 H7
Arzignano, Italy 41 C8
Arzúa, Spain 36 C2
Aš, Czech Rep. 26 A5
As Pontes de García Rodríguez,
  Spain 36 B3
Aş Şafā, Syria 74 B6
As Saffānīyah, Si. Arabia 71 E6
As Safīrah, Syria 70 B3
Aş Şahm, Oman 71 E8
As Sājir, Si. Arabia 70 E5
As Salamīyah, Syria 70 C3
As Salmān, Iraq 70 D5
As Salţ, Jordan 74 C4
As Sal'w'a, Qatar 71 E6
As Samāwah, Iraq 70 D5
As Samnayn, Syria 74 B5
As Sohar = Şuḥār, Oman 71 E8
As Sukhnah, Syria 70 C3
As Sulaymānīyah, Iraq 70 C5
As Sulaymī, Si. Arabia 70 E4
As Sulayyil, Si. Arabia 75 C4
As Summān, Si. Arabia 70 E5
As Suwaydā, Syria 74 C5
As Suwaydā □, Syria 74 C5
As Suwayq, Oman 71 F8
Aş Şuwayrah, Iraq 70 C5
Åsa, Sweden 11 G6
Asab, Namibia 88 D2
Asaba, Nigeria 83 D6
Asad, Buhayrat al, Syria 70 C3
Asadābād, Iran 73 E13
Asafo, Ghana 82 D4
Asahi-Gawa →, Japan 55 G6
Asahigawa, Japan 54 C11
Asale, L., Ethiopia 81 E5

Asamankese, Ghana 83 D4
Asan →, India 69 F8
Asansol, India 69 H12
Åsarna, Sweden 10 B8
Asayita, Ethiopia 81 E5
Asbe Teferi, Ethiopia 81 F5
Asbesberg, S. Africa 88 D3
Asbestos, Canada 105 C5
Asbury Park, U.S.A. 117 F10
Ascea, Italy 43 B8
Ascensión, Mexico 118 A3
Ascensión, B. de la, Mexico 119 D7
Ascension I., Atl. Oc. 77 G2
Aschach an der Donau, Austria 26 C7
Aschaffenburg, Germany 25 F5
Aschendorf, Germany 24 B3
Aschersleben, Germany 24 D7
Asciano, Italy 41 E8
Áscoli Piceno, Italy 41 F10
Áscoli Satriano, Italy 43 A8
Ascope, Peru 124 E3
Ascotán, Chile 126 A2
Aseb, Eritrea 81 E5
Åseda, Sweden 11 G9
Asela, Ethiopia 81 F4
Åsen, Sweden 10 C7
Asenovgrad, Bulgaria 45 D8
Aserradero, Mexico 118 C3
Asfeld, France 19 C11
Asfûn el Matâ'na, Egypt 80 B3
Asgata, Cyprus 49 E12
Ash Fork, U.S.A. 109 J7
Ash Grove, U.S.A. 113 G8
Ash Shabakah, Iraq 70 D4
Ash Shamāl □, Lebanon 74 A5
Ash Shāmīyah, Iraq 70 D5
Ash Shāriqah, U.A.E. 71 E7
Ash Sharmah, Si. Arabia 70 D2
Ash Sharqāṭ, Iraq 70 C4
Ash Sharqi, Al Jabal, Lebanon 74 B5
Ash Shawmari, J., Jordan 74 E5
Ash Shināfiyah, Iraq 70 D5
Ash Shu'bah, Si. Arabia 70 D5
Ash Shumlūl, Si. Arabia 70 E5
Ash Shūr'a, Iraq 70 C4
Ash Shurayf, Si. Arabia 70 E3
Ash Shuwayfāt, Lebanon 74 B4
Ashanti □, Ghana 83 D4
Ashau, Vietnam 64 D6
Ashbourne, U.K. 14 D6
Ashburn, U.S.A. 115 K4
Ashburton, N.Z. 91 K3
Ashburton →, Australia 92 D1
Ashcroft, Canada 102 C4
Ashdod, Israel 74 D3
Ashdown, U.S.A. 113 J7
Asheboro, U.S.A. 115 H6
Ashern, Canada 103 C9
Asherton, U.S.A. 113 L5
Asheville, U.S.A. 115 H4
Ashewat, Pakistan 68 D3
Asheweig →, Canada 104 B2
Ashford, Australia 95 D5
Ashford, U.K. 15 F8
Ashgabat, Turkmenistan 52 F6
Ashibetsu, Japan 54 C11
Ashikaga, Japan 55 F9
Ashington, U.K. 14 B6
Ashizuri-Uwakai △, Japan 55 H6
Ashizuri-Zaki, Japan 55 H6
Ashkarkot, Afghan. 68 C2
Ashkhabad = Ashgabat,
  Turkmenistan 52 F6
Áshkhāneh, Iran 71 B8
Ashland, Kans., U.S.A. 113 G5
Ashland, Ky., U.S.A. 114 F4
Ashland, Mont., U.S.A. 108 D10
Ashland, Ohio, U.S.A. 116 F2
Ashland, Oreg., U.S.A. 108 E2
Ashland, Pa., U.S.A. 117 F8
Ashland, Va., U.S.A. 114 G7
Ashland, Wis., U.S.A. 112 B9
Ashley, N. Dak., U.S.A. 112 B5
Ashley, Pa., U.S.A. 117 E9
Ashmore and Cartier Is., Ind. Oc. 92 B3
Ashmore Reef, Australia 92 B3
Ashmûn, Egypt 80 H7
Ashmyany, Belarus 9 J21
Ashokan Reservoir, U.S.A. 117 E10
Ashqelon, Israel 74 D3
Ashta, India 68 H7
Ashtabula, U.S.A. 116 E4
Ashton, S. Africa 88 E3
Ashton, U.S.A. 108 D8
Ashuanipi, L., Canada 105 B6
Ashville, U.S.A. 116 F6
'Āṣī →, Asia 72 D6
Asia 50 E11
Asia, Kepulauan, Indonesia 63 D8
Asiago, Italy 41 C8
Asifabad, India 66 K11
Asinara, Italy 42 A1
Asinara, G. dell', Italy 42 A1
Asino, Russia 52 D9
Asipovichy, Belarus 32 F5
'Asīr □, Si. Arabia 75 D3
Asir, Ras, Somali Rep. 75 E5
Aşkale, Turkey 73 C9
Askersund, Sweden 11 F8
Askham, S. Africa 88 D3
Askim, Norway 9 G14
Askja, Iceland 8 D5
Askøy, Norway 9 F11
Asl, Egypt 80 B3
Aslan Burnu, Turkey 47 C8
Aslanapa, Turkey 47 B11
Asmara = Asmera, Eritrea 81 D4
Asmera, Eritrea 81 D4
Asnæs, Denmark 11 J4

Åsnen, Sweden ... 11 H8
Aso Kuju △, Japan ... 55 H5
Åsola, Italy ... 40 C7
Asosa, Ethiopia ... 81 E3
Asoteriba, Jebel, Sudan ... 80 C4
Aspatria, U.K. ... 14 C4
Aspe, Spain ... 39 G4
Aspen, U.S.A. ... 109 G10
Aspendos, Turkey ... 72 D4
Aspermont, U.S.A. ... 113 J4
Aspet, France ... 20 E4
Aspiring, Mt., N.Z. ... 91 L2
Aspres-sur-Buëch, France ... 21 D9
Asprókavos, Ákra, Greece ... 49 B4
Aspromonte △, Italy ... 43 D8
Aspur, India ... 68 H6
Asquith, Canada ... 103 C7
Assab = Aseb, Eritrea ... 81 E5
Assâba, Massif de l', Mauritania ... 82 B2
Assagny △, Ivory C. ... 82 D4
Assaikio, Nigeria ... 83 D6
Assam □, India ... 67 G18
Assamakka, Niger ... 83 B6
Assateague Island △, U.S.A. ... 114 F8
Asse, Belgium ... 17 D4
Assémini, Italy ... 42 C1
Assen, Neths. ... 17 A6
Assens, Denmark ... 11 J3
Assini, Ivory C. ... 82 D4
Assiniboia, Canada ... 103 D7
Assiniboine →, Canada ... 103 D9
Assiniboine, Mt., Canada ... 102 C5
Assis, Brazil ... 127 A5
Assisi, Italy ... 41 E9
Ássos, Greece ... 46 C2
Assynt, L., U.K. ... 13 C3
Astaffort, France ... 20 D4
Astakídha, Greece ... 47 F8
Astakós, Greece ... 46 C3
Astana, Kazakhstan ... 52 D8
Āstāneh, Iran ... 71 B6
Astara, Azerbaijan ... 71 B6
Āstārā, Iran ... 73 C13
Asteroúsia, Greece ... 49 E7
Asti, Italy ... 40 D5
Astipálaia, Greece ... 47 E8
Astorga, Spain ... 36 C4
Astoria, U.S.A. ... 110 D3
Åstorp, Sweden ... 11 H6
Astrakhan, Russia ... 35 G9
Astudillo, Spain ... 36 C6
Asturias □, Spain ... 36 B5
Asturias ✈ (OVD), Spain ... 36 B4
Asunción, Paraguay ... 126 B4
Asunción Nochixtlán, Mexico ... 119 D5
Åsunden, Sweden ... 11 F9
Asutri, Sudan ... 81 D4
Aswa →, Uganda ... 86 B3
Aswa-Lolim △, Uganda ... 86 B3
Aswad, Ra's al, Si. Arabia ... 80 C4
Aswân, Egypt ... 80 C3
Aswan Dam = Sadd el Aali, Egypt ... 80 C3
Asyût, Egypt ... 80 B3
Asyûti, Wadi →, Egypt ... 80 B3
Aszód, Hungary ... 28 C4
At Ţafīlah, Jordan ... 74 E4
At Ţafīlah □, Jordan ... 74 E4
Aţ Ţa'if, Si. Arabia ... 75 C3
At Ta'mīm □, Iraq ... 70 C5
Aţ Ţīraq, Si. Arabia ... 70 E5
Aţ Ţubayq, Si. Arabia ... 70 D3
Atabey, Turkey ... 47 D12
Atacama □, Chile ... 126 B2
Atacama, Desierto de, Chile ... 126 A2
Atacama, Salar de, Chile ... 126 A2
Atakpamé, Togo ... 83 D5
Atalándi, Greece ... 46 C4
Atalaya, Peru ... 124 F4
Atalaya de Femes, Canary Is. ... 48 F6
Atami, Japan ... 55 G9
Atapupu, E. Timor ... 63 F6
Atâr, Mauritania ... 78 D3
Atarfe, Spain ... 37 H7
Atari, Pakistan ... 68 D6
Atascadero, U.S.A. ... 110 K6
Atasu, Kazakhstan ... 52 E8
Atatürk, Istanbul ✈ (IST), Turkey ... 45 F12
Atatürk Barajı, Turkey ... 73 D8
Atauro, E. Timor ... 63 F7
'Atbara, Sudan ... 80 D3
'Atbara, Nahr →, Sudan ... 80 D3
Atbasar, Kazakhstan ... 52 D7
Atça, Turkey ... 47 D10
Atchafalaya B., U.S.A. ... 113 L9
Atchison, U.S.A. ... 112 F7
Atebubu, Ghana ... 83 D4
Ateca, Spain ... 38 D3
Aterno →, Italy ... 41 F10
Āteshān, Iran ... 71 C7
Atessa, Italy ... 41 F11
Atfih, Egypt ... 80 J7
Ath, Belgium ... 17 D3
Athabasca, Canada ... 102 C6
Athabasca →, Canada ... 103 B6
Athabasca, L., Canada ... 103 B7
Athabasca Sand Dunes △, Canada ... 103 B7
Athboy, Ireland ... 12 C5
Athenry, Ireland ... 12 C3
Athens = Athínai, Greece ... 46 D5
Athens, Ala., U.S.A. ... 115 H2
Athens, Ga., U.S.A. ... 115 J4
Athens, N.Y., U.S.A. ... 117 D11
Athens, Ohio, U.S.A. ... 114 F4
Athens, Pa., U.S.A. ... 117 E8
Athens, Tenn., U.S.A. ... 115 H3
Athens, Tex., U.S.A. ... 113 J7
Atherley, Canada ... 116 B5
Atherton, Australia ... 94 B4
Athiéme, Benin ... 83 D5

Athienou, Cyprus ... 49 D12
Athínai, Greece ... 46 D5
Athínai ✈ (ATH), Greece ... 46 D5
Athlone, Ireland ... 12 C4
Athna, Cyprus ... 49 D12
Athol, U.S.A. ... 117 D12
Atholl, Forest of, U.K. ... 13 E5
Atholville, Canada ... 105 C6
Áthos, Greece ... 45 F8
Athy, Ireland ... 12 C5
Ati, Chad ... 79 F9
Ati, Sudan ... 81 E2
Atiak, Uganda ... 86 B3
Atienza, Spain ... 38 D2
Atiit, Sudan ... 81 F3
Atik L., Canada ... 103 B9
Atikaki △, Canada ... 103 C9
Atikameg →, Canada ... 104 B3
Atikokan, Canada ... 104 C1
Atikonak L., Canada ... 105 B7
Atimonan, Phil. ... 61 E4
Atitlán △, Cent. Amer. ... 119 E6
Atka, Russia ... 53 C16
Atka I., U.S.A. ... 100 C2
Atkarsk, Russia ... 34 E7
Atkinson, U.S.A. ... 112 D5
Atlanta, Ga., U.S.A. ... 115 J3
Atlanta, Tex., U.S.A. ... 113 J7
Atlantic, U.S.A. ... 112 E7
Atlantic City, U.S.A. ... 114 F8
Atlantic-Indian Basin, Antarctica ... 5 B4
Atlantic-Indian Ridge, Atl. Oc. ... 5 B3
Atlantic Ocean ... 2 E9
Atlas Mts. = Haut Atlas, Morocco ... 78 B4
Atlin, Canada ... 102 B2
Atlin △, Canada ... 102 B2
Atlin, L., Canada ... 102 B2
Atmore, U.S.A. ... 115 K2
Atoka, U.S.A. ... 113 H6
Átokos Nisís, Greece ... 46 C2
Atolia, U.S.A. ... 111 K9
Atrai →, Bangla. ... 69 G13
Atrak = Atrek →, Turkmenistan ... 71 B8
Ätran, Sweden ... 11 G6
Ätran →, Sweden ... 11 H6
Atrauli, India ... 68 E8
Atrek →, Turkmenistan ... 71 B8
Atri, Italy ... 41 F10
Atsiki, Greece ... 47 B7
Atsoum, Mts., Cameroon ... 83 D7
Atsuta, Japan ... 54 C10
Attalla, U.S.A. ... 115 H2
Attapu, Laos ... 64 E6
Attáviros, Greece ... 49 C9
Attawapiskat, Canada ... 104 B3
Attawapiskat →, Canada ... 104 B3
Attawapiskat L., Canada ... 104 B2
Attersee, Austria ... 26 D6
Attica, Ind., U.S.A. ... 114 E2
Attica, Ohio, U.S.A. ... 116 E2
Attichy, France ... 19 C10
Attigny, France ... 19 C11
Attika = Attikí □, Greece ... 46 D5
Attikamagen L., Canada ... 105 B6
Attikí □, Greece ... 46 D5
Attleboro, U.S.A. ... 117 E13
Attock, Pakistan ... 68 C5
Attopeu = Attapu, Laos ... 64 E6
Attu I., U.S.A. ... 100 C1
Attur, India ... 66 P11
Atuel →, Argentina ... 126 D2
Åtvidaberg, Sweden ... 11 F10
Atwater, U.S.A. ... 110 H6
Atwood, Canada ... 116 C3
Atwood, U.S.A. ... 112 F4
Atyraū, Kazakhstan ... 52 E6
Au Sable →, U.S.A. ... 116 B1
Au Sable →, U.S.A. ... 114 C4
Au Sable Forks, U.S.A. ... 117 B11
Au Sable Pt., U.S.A. ... 116 B1
Aubagne, France ... 21 E9
Aubarca, C. d', Spain ... 48 B7
Aube □, France ... 19 D11
Aube →, France ... 19 D10
Aubenas, France ... 21 D8
Aubenton, France ... 19 C11
Auberry, U.S.A. ... 110 H7
Aubigny-sur-Nère, France ... 19 E9
Aubin, France ... 20 D6
Aubrac, Mts. d', France ... 20 D7
Auburn, Ala., U.S.A. ... 115 J3
Auburn, Calif., U.S.A. ... 110 G5
Auburn, Ind., U.S.A. ... 114 E3
Auburn, Maine, U.S.A. ... 115 C10
Auburn, N.Y., U.S.A. ... 117 D8
Auburn, Nebr., U.S.A. ... 112 E7
Auburn, Pa., U.S.A. ... 117 F8
Auburn, Wash., U.S.A. ... 110 C4
Auburn Ra., Australia ... 95 D5
Auburndale, U.S.A. ... 115 L5
Aubusson, France ... 20 C6
Auce, Latvia ... 30 B9
Auch, France ... 20 E4
Auchi, Nigeria ... 83 D6
Auchterarder, U.K. ... 13 E5
Auchtermuchty, U.K. ... 13 E5
Auckland, N.Z. ... 91 G5
Auckland Is., Pac. Oc. ... 96 N8
Aude □, France ... 20 E6
Aude →, France ... 20 E7
Auden, Canada ... 104 B2
Auderville, France ... 18 C5
Audierne, France ... 18 D2
Audincourt, France ... 19 E13
Audo Ra., Ethiopia ... 81 F5
Audubon, U.S.A. ... 112 E7
Aue, Germany ... 24 E8
Auerbach, Germany ... 24 E8
Augathella, Australia ... 95 D4
Aughnacloy, U.K. ... 12 B5
Augrabies Falls, S. Africa ... 88 D3
Augrabies Falls △, S. Africa ... 88 D3

Augsburg, Germany ... 25 G6
Augsburg-Westliche Wälder △, Germany ... 25 G6
Augusta, Australia ... 93 F2
Augusta, Italy ... 43 E8
Augusta, Ark., U.S.A. ... 113 H9
Augusta, Ga., U.S.A. ... 115 J5
Augusta, Kans., U.S.A. ... 113 G6
Augusta, Maine, U.S.A. ... 101 D13
Augusta, Mont., U.S.A. ... 108 C7
Augustenborg, Denmark ... 11 K3
Augustów, Poland ... 30 E9
Augustus, Mt., Australia ... 93 D2
Augustus I., Australia ... 92 C3
Aukan, Eritrea ... 81 D5
Aukrug △, Germany ... 24 A5
Aukum, U.S.A. ... 110 G6
Auld, L., Australia ... 92 D3
Aulla, Italy ... 40 D6
Aulnay, France ... 20 B3
Aulne →, France ... 18 D2
Aulnoye-Aymeries, France ... 19 B10
Ault, France ... 18 B8
Ault, U.S.A. ... 112 E2
Aulus-les-Bains, France ... 20 F5
Aumale, France ... 19 C8
Aumont-Aubrac, France ... 20 D7
Auna, Nigeria ... 83 C5
Auning, Denmark ... 11 H4
Auponhia, Indonesia ... 63 E7
Aups, France ... 21 E10
Aur, Pulau, Malaysia ... 65 L5
Auraiya, India ... 69 F8
Aurangabad, Bihar, India ... 69 G11
Aurangabad, Maharashtra, India ... 66 K9
Auray, France ... 18 E4
Aurich, Germany ... 24 B3
Aurillac, France ... 20 D6
Auronzo di Cadore, Italy ... 41 B9
Aurora, Canada ... 116 C5
Aurora, S. Africa ... 88 E2
Aurora, Colo., U.S.A. ... 112 F2
Aurora, Ill., U.S.A. ... 114 E1
Aurora, Mo., U.S.A. ... 113 G8
Aurora, N.Y., U.S.A. ... 117 D8
Aurora, Nebr., U.S.A. ... 112 E6
Aurora, Ohio, U.S.A. ... 116 E3
Aurukun, Australia ... 94 A3
Aus, Namibia ... 88 D2
Ausable →, Canada ... 116 C3
Auschwitz = Oświęcim, Poland ... 31 H6
Austerlitz = Slavkov u Brna, Czech Rep. ... 27 B9
Austin, Minn., U.S.A. ... 112 D8
Austin, Nev., U.S.A. ... 108 G5
Austin, Tex., U.S.A. ... 113 K6
Austin, L., Australia ... 93 E2
Austin I., Canada ... 103 A10
Austra, Norway ... 8 D14
Austral Is. = Tubuai Is., French Polynesia ... 97 K13
Austral Seamount Chain, Pac. Oc. ... 97 K13
Australia ■, Oceania ... 96 K5
Australian Capital Territory □, Australia ... 95 F4
Australind, Australia ... 93 F2
Austria ■, Europe ... 26 E7
Austvågøy, Norway ... 8 B16
Auterive, France ... 20 E5
Authie →, France ... 19 B8
Authon-du-Perche, France ... 18 D7
Autlán, Mexico ... 118 D4
Autun, France ... 19 F11
Auvergne □, France ... 20 C7
Auvergne, Mts. d', France ... 20 C6
Auvézère →, France ... 20 C4
Auxerre, France ... 19 E10
Auxi-le-Château, France ... 19 B9
Auxonne, France ... 19 E12
Auzances, France ... 19 F9
Ava, U.S.A. ... 113 G8
Avallon, France ... 19 E10
Avalon, U.S.A. ... 111 M8
Avalon Pen., Canada ... 105 C9
Avanos, Turkey ... 70 B2
Avaré, Brazil ... 127 A6
Avawatz Mts., U.S.A. ... 111 K10
Avdan Dağı, Turkey ... 45 F13
Aveiro, Brazil ... 125 D7
Aveiro, Portugal ... 36 E2
Aveiro □, Portugal ... 36 E2
Avej, Iran ... 71 C6
Avellaneda, Argentina ... 126 C4
Avellino, Italy ... 43 B7
Avenal, U.S.A. ... 110 K6
Aversa, Italy ... 43 B7
Avery, U.S.A. ... 108 C6
Aves, I. de, W. Indies ... 121 C7
Aves, Is. las, Venezuela ... 121 D6
Avesnes-sur-Helpe, France ... 19 B10
Avesnois □, France ... 19 B10
Avesta, Sweden ... 10 D10
Aveyron □, France ... 20 D6
Aveyron →, France ... 20 D5
Avezzano, Italy ... 41 F10
Avgó, Greece ... 47 F7
Aviá Terai, Argentina ... 126 B3
Aviano, Italy ... 41 B9
Aviemore, U.K. ... 13 D5
Avigliana, Italy ... 40 C4
Avigliano, Italy ... 43 B8
Avignon, France ... 21 E8
Ávila, Spain ... 36 E6
Ávila □, Spain ... 36 E6
Avila, Sierra de, Spain ... 36 E5
Avila Beach, U.S.A. ... 111 K6
Avilés, Spain ... 36 B5
Avintes, Portugal ... 36 D2
Avionárion, Greece ... 46 C6

Avis, Portugal ... 37 F3
Avis, U.S.A. ... 116 E7
Avísio →, Italy ... 40 B8
Aviz = Avis, Portugal ... 37 F3
Avize, France ... 19 D11
Avoca, U.S.A. ... 116 D7
Avoca →, Australia ... 95 F3
Avoca →, Ireland ... 12 D5
Avola, Canada ... 102 C5
Avola, Italy ... 43 F8
Avon, U.S.A. ... 116 D7
Avon →, Australia ... 93 F2
Avon →, Bristol, U.K. ... 15 F5
Avon →, Dorset, U.K. ... 15 G6
Avon →, Warks., U.K. ... 15 E5
Avon Park, U.S.A. ... 115 M5
Avondale, Zimbabwe ... 87 F3
Avonlea, Canada ... 103 D8
Avonmore, Canada ... 117 A10
Avonmouth, U.K. ... 15 F5
Avramov, Bulgaria ... 45 D10
Avranches, France ... 18 D5
Avre →, France ... 18 D8
Avrig, Romania ... 29 E9
Avrillé, France ... 18 E6
Avtovac, Bos.-H. ... 44 C2
Awag el Baqar, Sudan ... 81 E3
A'waj →, Syria ... 74 B5
Awaji-Shima, Japan ... 55 G7
Awasa, Ethiopia ... 81 F4
Awasa, L., Ethiopia ... 81 F4
Awash, Ethiopia ... 81 F5
Awash △, Ethiopia ... 81 F5
Awash →, Ethiopia ... 81 E5
Awaso, Ghana ... 82 D4
Awatere →, N.Z. ... 91 J5
Awbārī, Libya ... 79 C8
Awbārī, Idehan, Libya ... 79 C8
Awe, L., U.K. ... 13 E3
Aweil, Sudan ... 81 F2
Awgu, Nigeria ... 83 D6
Awjilah, Libya ... 79 C10
Awka, Nigeria ... 83 D6
Ax-les-Thermes, France ... 20 F5
Axat, France ... 20 F6
Axe →, U.K. ... 15 F5
Axel Heiberg I., Canada ... 98 A10
Axim, Ghana ... 82 E4
Axintele, Romania ... 29 F11
Axiós →, Greece ... 44 F6
Axminster, U.K. ... 15 G4
Axvall, Sweden ... 11 F7
Ay, France ... 19 C11
Ayabaca, Peru ... 124 D3
Ayabe, Japan ... 55 G7
Ayacucho, Argentina ... 126 D4
Ayacucho, Peru ... 124 F4
Ayaguz, Kazakhstan ... 52 E9
Ayamé, Ivory C. ... 82 D4
Ayamonte, Spain ... 37 H3
Ayan, Russia ... 53 D14
Ayancık, Turkey ... 72 B6
Ayas, Turkey ... 72 B5
Ayaviri, Peru ... 124 F4
Aybastı, Turkey ... 72 B7
Aydın, Turkey ... 72 D2
Aydın □, Turkey ... 47 D9
Aydın Dağları, Turkey ... 47 C10
Ayelu, Ethiopia ... 81 E5
Ayenngré, Togo ... 83 D5
Ayer, U.S.A. ... 117 D13
Ayer Hitam, Malaysia ... 65 c
Ayerbe, Spain ... 38 C4
Ayer's Cliff, Canada ... 117 A12
Ayers Rock, Australia ... 93 E5
Ayiá, Greece ... 46 B4
Ayia Aikateríni, Ákra, Greece ... 49 A3
Ayía Ánna, Greece ... 46 C5
Ayía Dhéka, Greece ... 49 D6
Ayía Gálini, Greece ... 49 D6
Ayía Marína, Kásos, Greece ... 47 F8
Ayía Marína, Léros, Greece ... 47 E8
Ayía Napa, Cyprus ... 49 E13
Ayía Paraskeví, Greece ... 47 B8
Ayía Phyla, Cyprus ... 49 E12
Ayía Rouméli, Greece ... 46 F5
Ayía Varvára, Greece ... 49 D7
Ayiássos, Greece ... 47 B8
Áyioi Theódhoroi, Greece ... 47 B8
Áyion Óros □, Greece ... 45 F8
Áyios Amvrósios, Cyprus ... 49 D12
Áyios Andréas, Greece ... 46 D4
Áyios Evstrátios, Greece ... 46 B6
Áyios Ioánnis, Ákra, Greece ... 49 D7
Áyios Isídhoros, Greece ... 49 C9
Áyios Kiríkos, Greece ... 47 D8
Áyios Matthaíos, Greece ... 49 B3
Áyios Míronas, Greece ... 47 F7
Áyios Nikólaos, Greece ... 49 D7
Áyios Pétros, Greece ... 46 C2
Áyios Seryios, Cyprus ... 49 D12
Áyios Theodhoros, Cyprus ... 49 D13
Áyios Yeóryios, Greece ... 46 D5
Aykathonís, Greece ... 47 D8
Aykirikçi, Turkey ... 47 B12
Aylesbury, U.K. ... 15 F7
Aylmer, Canada ... 116 D4
Aylmer, L., Canada ... 100 B8
'Ayn, Wādī al, Oman ... 71 F7
Ayn Dār, Si. Arabia ... 71 E6
Ayn Zālah, Iraq ... 70 B4
Ayna, Spain ... 39 G2
Ayod, Sudan ... 81 F3
Ayolas, Paraguay ... 126 B4
Ayom, Sudan ... 81 F2
Ayon, Ostrov, Russia ... 53 C17
Ayora, Spain ... 39 F3
Ayorou, Niger ... 83 C5
'Ayoûn el 'Atroûs, Mauritania ... 82 B3

Ayr, Australia ... 94 B4
Ayr, Canada ... 116 C4
Ayr, U.K. ... 13 F4
Ayr →, U.K. ... 13 F4
Ayrancı, Turkey ... 72 D5
Ayrancılar, Turkey ... 47 C9
Ayre, Pt. of, I. of Man ... 14 C3
Aysha, Ethiopia ... 81 E5
Ayton, Australia ... 94 B4
Aytos, Bulgaria ... 45 D11
Aytoska Planina, Bulgaria ... 45 D11
Ayu, Kepulauan, Indonesia ... 63 D8
Ayutla, Guatemala ... 120 D1
Ayutla, Mexico ... 119 D5
Ayvacık, Turkey ... 72 C2
Ayvalık, Turkey ... 47 B8
Az Zabadānī, Syria ... 74 B5
Az Ẓāhirīyah, West Bank ... 74 D3
Az Ẓahrān, Si. Arabia ... 71 E6
Az Zarqā, Jordan ... 74 C5
Az Zarqā', U.A.E. ... 71 E7
Az Zarqā □, Jordan ... 74 C5
Az Zāwiyah, Libya ... 79 B8
Az Zībār, Iraq ... 70 B5
Az Zilfī, Si. Arabia ... 70 E5
Az Zubayr, Iraq ... 70 D5
Az Zuqur, Yemen ... 81 E5
Azad Kashmir □, Pakistan ... 69 C5
Azambuja, Portugal ... 37 F2
Azamgarh, India ... 69 F10
Azángaro, Peru ... 124 F4
Azaoua, Niger ... 83 B5
Azaouad, Mali ... 82 B4
Azaouak, Vallée de l', Mali ... 83 B5
Āžar Shahr, Iran ... 70 B5
Azara, Nigeria ... 83 D6
Azarān, Iran ... 70 B5
Āžārbāyjān = Azerbaijan ■, Asia ... 35 K9
Āžārbāyjān-e Gharbī □, Iran ... 70 B5
Āžārbāyjān-e Sharqī □, Iran ... 70 B5
Azare, Nigeria ... 83 C7
Azay-le-Rideau, France ... 18 E7
A'zāz, Syria ... 70 B3
Azbine = Aïr, Niger ... 83 B6
Azerbaijan ■, Asia ... 35 K9
Azerbaijchan = Azerbaijan ■, Asia ... 35 K9
Azezo, Ethiopia ... 81 E4
Azimganj, India ... 69 G13
Aznalcóllar, Spain ... 37 H4
Azogues, Ecuador ... 124 D3
Azores = Açores, Is. dos, Atl. Oc. ... 78 A1
Azov, Russia ... 35 G4
Azov, Sea of, Europe ... 33 J9
Azovskoye More = Azov, Sea of, Europe ... 33 J9
Azpeitia, Spain ... 38 B2
Azraq ash Shīshān, Jordan ... 74 D5
Aztec, U.S.A. ... 109 H10
Azúa de Compostela, Dom. Rep. ... 121 C5
Azuaga, Spain ... 37 G5
Azuara, Spain ... 38 D4
Azuer →, Spain ... 37 F7
Azuero, Pen. de, Panama ... 120 E3
Azuga, Romania ... 29 E10
Azul, Argentina ... 126 D4
Azusa, U.S.A. ... 111 L9
Azzano Décimo, Italy ... 41 C9

B

Ba Be △, Vietnam ... 64 A5
Ba Don, Vietnam ... 64 D6
Ba Dong, Vietnam ... 65 H6
Ba Ngoi = Cam Lam, Vietnam ... 65 G7
Ba Tri, Vietnam ... 65 G6
Ba Vi △, Vietnam ... 64 B5
Ba Xian = Bazhou, China ... 56 E9
Baa, Indonesia ... 63 F6
Baamonde, Spain ... 36 B3
Baardheere = Bardera, Somali Rep. ... 75 G3
Baarle-Nassau, Belgium ... 17 C4
Bab el Mandeb, Red Sea ... 75 E3
Baba, Bulgaria ... 44 D7
Bābā, Koh-i-, Afghan. ... 66 B5
Baba Burnu, Turkey ... 47 B8
Baba dag, Azerbaijan ... 35 K9
Bābā Kalū, Iran ... 71 D6
Babadag, Romania ... 29 F13
Babadağ, Turkey ... 47 D10
Babaeski, Turkey ... 45 E11
Babahoyo, Ecuador ... 124 D3
Babai = Sarju →, India ... 69 F9
Babana, Nigeria ... 83 C5
Babanusa, Sudan ... 81 E2
Babar, Indonesia ... 63 F7
Babar, Pakistan ... 68 D3
Babarkach, Pakistan ... 68 E3
Babayevo, Russia ... 32 C8
Babb, U.S.A. ... 108 B7
Babenhausen, Germany ... 25 F4
Bābeni, Romania ... 29 F9
Baberu, India ... 69 G9
Babi Besar, Pulau, Malaysia ... 65 L4
Babia Gora, Europe ... 31 J6
Babīl □, Iraq ... 70 C5
Babile, Ethiopia ... 81 F5
Babimost, Poland ... 31 F2
Babinda, Australia ... 94 B4
Babine, Canada ... 102 B3
Babine →, Canada ... 102 B3
Babine L., Canada ... 102 C3
Babiogórski △, Poland ... 31 J6
Babo, Indonesia ... 63 E8
Babócsa, Hungary ... 28 D2
Bābol, Iran ... 71 B7
Bābol Sar, Iran ... 71 B7

Baborów, *Poland* 31 H5
Babruysk, *Belarus* 33 F5
Babuhri, *India* 68 F3
Babuna, *Macedonia* 44 E5
Babura, *Nigeria* 83 C6
Babusar Pass, *Pakistan* 69 B5
Babushkin, *Russia* 60 A5
Babušnica, *Serbia & M.* 44 C6
Babuyan Chan., *Phil.* 61 B4
Babylon, *Iraq* 70 C5
Bač, *Serbia & M.* 28 E4
Bâc →, *Moldova* 29 D14
Bac Can, *Vietnam* 58 F5
Bac Giang, *Vietnam* 58 G6
Bac Lieu, *Vietnam* 65 H5
Bac Ninh, *Vietnam* 58 G6
Bac Phan, *Vietnam* 58 B5
Bac Quang, *Vietnam* 58 F5
Bacabal, *Brazil* 125 D10
Bacalar, *Mexico* 119 D7
Bacan, Kepulauan, *Indonesia* .. 63 E7
Bacarra, *Phil.* 61 B4
Bacău, *Romania* 29 D11
Bacău □, *Romania* 29 D11
Baccarat, *France* 19 D13
Bacerac, *Mexico* 118 A3
Băcești, *Romania* 29 D12
Bach Long Vi, Dao, *Vietnam* ... 64 B6
Bach Ma △, *Vietnam* 64 D6
Bacharach, *Germany* 25 E3
Bachhwara, *India* 69 G11
Bachuma, *Ethiopia* 81 F4
Bačina, *Serbia & M.* 44 C5
Back →, *Canada* 100 B9
Bačka Palanka, *Serbia & M.* ... 28 E4
Bačka Topola, *Serbia & M.* 28 E4
Bäckebo, *Sweden* 11 H10
Bäckefors, *Sweden* 11 F6
Bäckhammar, *Sweden* 10 E8
Bački Petrovac, *Serbia & M.* .. 28 E4
Backnang, *Germany* 25 G5
Baco, Mt., *Phil.* 61 E4
Bacolod, *Phil.* 61 F5
Bacqueville-en-Caux, *France* .. 18 C8
Bács-Kiskun □, *Hungary* 28 D4
Bácsalmás, *Hungary* 28 D4
Bacuag = Placer, *Phil.* 61 G6
Bacuk, *Malaysia* 65 J4
Bād, *Iran* 71 C7
Bad →, *U.S.A.* 112 C4
Bad Aussee, *Austria* 26 D6
Bad Axe, *U.S.A.* 116 C2
Bad Bergzabern, *Germany* 25 F3
Bad Berleburg, *Germany* 24 D4
Bad Bevensen, *Germany* 24 B6
Bad Bramstedt, *Germany* 24 B5
Bad Brückenau, *Germany* 25 E5
Bad Doberan, *Germany* 24 A7
Bad Driburg, *Germany* 24 D5
Bad Ems, *Germany* 25 E3
Bad Frankenhausen, *Germany* ... 24 D7
Bad Freienwalde, *Germany* 24 C10
Bad Goisern, *Austria* 26 D6
Bad Harzburg, *Germany* 24 D6
Bad Hersfeld, *Germany* 24 E5
Bad Hofgastein, *Austria* 26 D6
Bad Homburg, *Germany* 25 E4
Bad Honnef, *Germany* 24 E3
Bad Iburg, *Germany* 24 C4
Bad Ischl, *Austria* 26 D6
Bad Kissingen, *Germany* 25 E6
Bad Königshofen, *Germany* 25 E6
Bad Kreuznach, *Germany* 25 F3
Bad Krozingen, *Germany* 25 H3
Bad Laasphe, *Germany* 24 E4
Bad Lands, *U.S.A.* 112 D3
Bad Langensalza, *Germany* 24 D6
Bad Lauterberg, *Germany* 24 D6
Bad Leonfelden, *Austria* 26 C7
Bad Liebenwerda, *Germany* 24 D9
Bad Mergentheim, *Germany* 25 F5
Bad Münstereifel, *Germany* 24 E2
Bad Nauheim, *Germany* 25 E4
Bad Neuenahr-Ahrweiler,
   Germany 24 E3
Bad Neustadt, *Germany* 25 E6
Bad Oeynhausen, *Germany* 24 C4
Bad Oldesloe, *Germany* 24 B6
Bad Orb, *Germany* 25 E5
Bad Pyrmont, *Germany* 24 D5
Bad Reichenhall, *Germany* 25 H8
Bad Säckingen, *Germany* 25 H3
Bad Salzuflen, *Germany* 24 C4
Bad Salzungen, *Germany* 24 E6
Bad Schwartau, *Germany* 24 B6
Bad Segeberg, *Germany* 24 B6
Bad St. Leonhard, *Austria* 26 E7
Bad Tölz, *Germany* 25 H7
Bad Urach, *Germany* 25 G5
Bad Vöslau, *Austria* 27 D9
Bad Waldsee, *Germany* 25 H5
Bad Wildungen, *Germany* 24 D5
Bad Wimpfen, *Germany* 25 F5
Bad Windsheim, *Germany* 25 F6
Bad Zwischenahn, *Germany* 24 B4
Bada Barabil, *India* 69 H11
Badagara, *India* 66 P9
Badagri, *Nigeria* 83 D5
Badajós, L., *Brazil* 124 D6
Badajoz, *Spain* 37 G4
Badajoz □, *Spain* 37 G4
Badakhshān □, *Afghan.* 66 A7
Badalona, *Spain* 38 D7
Badalzai, *Afghan.* 68 E1
Badampahar, *India* 67 H15
Badanah, *Si. Arabia* 70 D4
Badarinath, *India* 69 D8
Badas, Kepulauan, *Indonesia* .. 62 D3
Baddo →, *Pakistan* 66 F4
Bade, *Indonesia* 63 F9
Badeggi, *Nigeria* 83 D6
Badéguichéri, *Niger* 83 C6

Baden, *Austria* 27 C9
Baden, *Switz.* 25 H4
Baden, *U.S.A.* 116 F4
Baden-Baden, *Germany* 25 G4
Baden-Württemberg □, *Germany* . 25 G4
Badgastein, *Austria* 26 D6
Badger, *Canada* 105 C8
Badger, *U.S.A.* 110 J7
Bādghīs □, *Afghan.* 66 B3
Badgingarra △, *Australia* 93 F2
Badgom, *India* 69 B6
Badia Polésine, *Italy* 41 C8
Badiar △, *Guinea* 82 C2
Badin, *Pakistan* 68 G3
Badinka ◌, *Mali* 82 C3
Badlands △, *U.S.A.* 112 D3
Badogo, *Mali* 82 C3
Badoumbé, *Mali* 82 C2
Badrah, *Iraq* 70 C5
Badrinath, *India* 69 D8
Badulla, *Sri Lanka* 66 R12
Badung, Selat, *Indonesia* 63 K18
Baena, *Spain* 37 H6
Baeza, *Spain* 37 H7
Bafang, *Cameroon* 83 D7
Bafatá, *Guinea-Biss.* 82 C2
Baffin B., *Canada* 101 A13
Baffin I., *Canada* 101 B12
Bafia, *Cameroon* 83 E7
Bafilo, *Togo* 83 D5
Bafing △, *Mali* 82 C2
Bafing →, *Mali* 82 C2
Bafliyūn, *Syria* 70 B3
Bafoulabé, *Mali* 82 C2
Bafoussam, *Cameroon* 83 D7
Bāfq, *Iran* 71 D7
Bafra, *Turkey* 72 B6
Bafra Burnu, *Turkey* 72 B7
Bāft, *Iran* 71 D8
Bafut, *Cameroon* 83 D7
Bafwasende, *Dem. Rep. of
   the Congo* 86 B2
Bagam, *Niger* 83 B6
Bagamoyo, *Tanzania* 86 D4
Bagan Datoh, *Malaysia* 65 L3
Bagan Serai, *Malaysia* 65 K3
Baganga, *Phil.* 61 H7
Bagani, *Namibia* 88 B3
Bagansiapiapi, *Indonesia* 62 D2
Bagasra, *India* 68 J4
Bagaud, *India* 68 H6
Bagawi, *Sudan* 81 E3
Bagbag, *Sudan* 81 D3
Bagdad, *U.S.A.* 111 L11
Bagdarin, *Russia* 53 D12
Bagé, *Brazil* 127 C5
Bagenalstown = Muine Bheag,
   Ireland 12 D5
Baggs, *U.S.A.* 108 F10
Bagh, *Pakistan* 69 C5
Baghain →, *India* 69 G9
Baghdād, *Iraq* 70 C5
Bagheria, *Italy* 42 D6
Baghlān, *Afghan.* 66 A6
Baghlān □, *Afghan.* 66 B6
Bagley, *U.S.A.* 112 B7
Bagnara Cálabra, *Italy* 43 D8
Bagnasco, *Italy* 40 D5
Bagnères-de-Bigorre, *France* .. 20 E4
Bagnères-de-Luchon, *France* ... 20 F4
Bagni di Lucca, *Italy* 40 D7
Bagno di Romagna, *Italy* 41 E8
Bagnoles-de-l'Orne, *France* ... 18 D6
Bagnols-sur-Cèze, *France* 21 D8
Bagnorégio, *Italy* 41 F9
Bago = Pegu, *Burma* 67 L20
Bagodar, *India* 69 G11
Bagrationovsk, *Russia* 9 J19
Bagrdan, *Serbia & M.* 44 B5
Baguio, *Phil.* 61 C4
Bağyurdu, *Turkey* 47 C9
Bagzane, Monts, *Niger* 83 B6
Bah, *India* 69 F8
Bahabón de Esgueva, *Spain* 36 D7
Bahadurganj, *India* 69 F12
Bahadurgarh, *India* 68 E7
Bahama, Canal Viejo de,
   W. Indies 120 B4
Bahamas ■, *N. Amer.* 121 B5
Bahār, *Iran* 73 E13
Baharampur, *India* 69 G13
Bahariya, El Wâhât al, *Egypt* . 80 B2
Baharu Pandan = Pandan,
   Malaysia .... 65 d
Bahawalnagar, *Pakistan* 68 E5
Bahawalpur, *Pakistan* 68 E4
Bahçe, *Turkey* 72 D7
Bahçecik, *Turkey* 45 F13
Baheri, *India* 69 E8
Bahgul →, *India* 69 F8
Bahi, *Tanzania* 86 D4
Bahi Swamp, *Tanzania* 86 D4
Bahía = Salvador, *Brazil* 125 F11
Bahia □, *Brazil* 125 F10
Bahía, Is. de la, *Honduras* ... 120 C2
Bahía Blanca, *Argentina* 126 D3
Bahía de Caráquez, *Ecuador* ... 124 D2
Bahía Honda, *Cuba* 120 B3
Bahía Laura, *Argentina* 128 F3
Bahía Negra, *Paraguay* 124 H7
Bahir Dar, *Ethiopia* 81 E4
Bahmanzād, *Iran* 71 D6
Bahr el Ahmar □, *Sudan* 80 D4
Bahr el Ghazâl □, *Sudan* 81 F2
Bahr el Jabal □, *Sudan* 81 G3
Bahraich, *India* 69 F9
Bahrain ■, *Asia* 71 E6
Bahror, *India* 68 F7
Bāhū Kalāt, *Iran* 71 E9
Bai, *Mali* 82 C4
Bai Bung, Mui = Ca Mau, Mui,
   Vietnam 65 H5

Bai Duc, *Vietnam* 64 C5
Bai Thuong, *Vietnam* 64 C5
Baia de Aramă, *Romania* 28 E7
Baia Mare, *Romania* 29 C8
Baia-Sprie, *Romania* 29 C8
Baião, *Brazil* 125 D9
Baïbokoum, *Chad* 79 G9
Baicheng, *China* 57 B12
Băicoi, *Romania* 29 E10
Baidoa, *Somali Rep.* 75 G3
Baie-Comeau, *Canada* 105 C6
Baie-St-Paul, *Canada* 105 C5
Baie-Trinité, *Canada* 105 C6
Baie Verte, *Canada* 105 C8
Baignes-Ste-Radegonde, *France* 20 C3
Baigneux-les-Juifs, *France* ... 19 E11
Baihar, *India* 69 H9
Baihe, *China* 56 H6
Baijnath, *India* 69 E8
Baikal, L. = Baykal, Oz., *Russia* . 53 D11
Baikunthpur, *India* 69 H10
Baile Atha Cliath = Dublin,
   Ireland 12 C5
Băile Govora, *Romania* 29 E9
Băile Herculane, *Romania* 28 F7
Băile Olănești, *Romania* 29 E9
Băile Tușnad, *Romania* 29 D10
Bailén, *Spain* 37 G7
Băilești, *Romania* 29 F8
Baima, *China* 58 A3
Bain-de-Bretagne, *France* 18 E5
Bainbridge, Ga., U.S.A.* 115 K3
Bainbridge, N.Y., U.S.A.* 117 D9
Baing, *Indonesia* 63 F6
Bainiu, *China* 56 H7
Baiona, *Spain* 36 C2
Bā'ir, *Jordan* 74 E5
Bairiki = Tarawa, *Kiribati* ... 96 G9
Bairin Youqi, *China* 57 C10
Bairin Zuoqi, *China* 57 C10
Bairnsdale, *Australia* 95 F4
Bais, *Phil.* 61 G5
Baisha, *China* 56 G7
Baissa, *Nigeria* 83 D7
Baitadi, *Nepal* 69 E9
Baixa Limia-Sierra do Xurés ◌,
   Spain 36 D2
Baiyin, *China* 56 F3
Baiyü, *China* 58 B2
Baiyu Shan, *China* 56 F4
Baiyuda, *Sudan* 80 D3
Baj Baj, *India* 69 H13
Baja, *Hungary* 28 D3
Baja, Pta., *Mexico* 118 B1
Baja California, *Mexico* 118 A1
Baja California □, *Mexico* 118 B2
Baja California Sur □, *Mexico* 118 B2
Bajag, *India* 69 H9
Bajamar, *Canary Is.* 48 F3
Bajana, *India* 68 H4
Bajatrejo, *Indonesia* 63 J17
Bajera, *Indonesia* 63 J18
Bājgīrān, *Iran* 71 B8
Bajimba, Mt., *Australia* 95 D5
Bajina Bašta, *Serbia & M.* 44 C3
Bajmok, *Serbia & M.* 28 E4
Bajo Nuevo, *Caribbean* 120 C4
Bajoga, *Nigeria* 83 C7
Bajool, *Australia* 94 C5
Bak, *Hungary* 28 D1
Bakar, *Croatia* 41 C11
Bakasi Pen., *Cameroon* 83 E6
Bakel, *Senegal* 82 C2
Baker, Calif., U.S.A.* 111 K10
Baker, Mont., U.S.A.* 112 B2
Baker, L., *Canada* 100 B10
Baker, Mt., U.S.A.* 108 B3
Baker City, *U.S.A.* 108 D5
Baker I., *Pac. Oc.* 96 G10
Baker I., *U.S.A.* 102 B2
Baker L., *Australia* 93 E4
Baker Lake, *Canada* 100 B10
Bakers Creek, *Australia* 94 C4
Bakers Dozen Is., *Canada* 104 A4
Bakersfield, Calif., U.S.A.* ... 111 K8
Bakersfield, Vt., U.S.A.* 117 B12
Bakhchysaray, *Ukraine* 33 K7
Bakhmach, *Ukraine* 33 G7
Bākhtarān, *Iran* 70 C5
Bākhtarān □, *Iran* 70 C5
Bakı, *Azerbaijan* 35 K9
Bakır →, *Turkey* 47 C9
Bakırdağı, *Turkey* 72 C6
Bakkafjörður, *Iceland* 8 C6
Baklan, *Turkey* 47 C11
Bako, *Ethiopia* 81 F4
Bako, *Ivory C.* 82 D3
Bakony, *Hungary* 28 C2
Bakony Forest = Bakony,
   Hungary 28 C2
Bakori, *Nigeria* 83 C6
Bakouma, *C.A.R.* 84 C4
Baksan, *Russia* 35 J6
Bakswaho, *India* 69 G8
Baku = Bakı, *Azerbaijan* 35 K9
Bakutis Coast, *Antarctica* 5 D15
Baky = Bakı, *Azerbaijan* 35 K9
Bala, *Canada* 116 A5
Bala, *Senegal* 82 C2
Bâlâ, *Turkey* 72 C5
Bala, *U.K.* 14 E4
Balabac I., *Phil.* 62 C5
Balabac Str., *E. Indies* 62 C5
Balabagh, *Afghan.* 68 B4
Bala'labek, *Lebanon* 74 B5
Balabalangan, Kepulauan,
   Indonesia 62 E5
Bălăcița, *Romania* 29 F8
Balad, *Iraq* 70 C5
Balad Rūz, *Iraq* 70 C5

Bālādeh, Fārs, *Iran* 71 D6
Bālādeh, Māzandaran, *Iran* 71 B6
Balaghat, *India* 66 J12
Balaghat Ra., *India* 66 K10
Balaguer, *Spain* 38 D5
Balakhna, *Russia* 34 B6
Balaklava, *Ukraine* 33 K7
Balakliya, *Ukraine* 33 H9
Balakovo, *Russia* 34 D8
Balamau, *India* 69 F9
Bālan, *Romania* 29 D10
Balancán, *Mexico* 119 D6
Balangir, *India* 67 J14
Balashov, *Russia* 34 E6
Balasinor, *India* 68 H5
Balasore = Baleshwar, *India* .. 67 J15
Balassagyarmat, *Hungary* 28 B4
Balât, *Egypt* 80 B2
Balaton, *Hungary* 28 D2
Balaton-Felvidéki △, *Hungary* . 28 D2
Balatonboglár, *Hungary* 28 D2
Balatonfüred, *Hungary* 28 D2
Balatonszentgyörgy, *Hungary* .. 28 D2
Balayan, *Phil.* 61 E4
Balazote, *Spain* 39 G2
Balbieriškis, *Lithuania* 30 D10
Balbigny, *France* 21 C8
Balbina, Reprêsa de, *Brazil* .. 124 D7
Balboa, *Panama* 120 E4
Balbriggan, *Ireland* 12 C5
Balcarce, *Argentina* 126 D4
Balcarres, *Canada* 103 C8
Bălcești, *Romania* 29 F8
Balchik, *Bulgaria* 45 C12
Balclutha, *N.Z.* 91 M2
Balcones Escarpment, *U.S.A.* .. 113 L5
Balçova, *Turkey* 47 C9
Bald Hd., *Australia* 93 G2
Bald I., *Australia* 93 F2
Bald Knob, *U.S.A.* 113 H9
Baldock L., *Canada* 103 B9
Baldwin, Mich., U.S.A.* 114 D3
Baldwin, Pa., U.S.A.* 116 F5
Baldwinsville, *U.S.A.* 117 C8
Baldy Mt., *U.S.A.* 108 B9
Baldy Peak, *U.S.A.* 109 K9
Bale, *Croatia* 41 C10
Bale, *Ethiopia* 81 F5
Baiyü, *China* 81 F5
Bale Mts. △, *Ethiopia* 81 F4
Baleares □, *Spain* 48 B10
Balearic Is. = Baleares, Is., *Spain* 48 B10
Baleine = Whale →, *Canada* 105 A6
Baleine, Petite R. de la →,
   Canada 104 A4
Băleni, *Romania* 29 E12
Baler, *Phil.* 61 D4
Baler Bay, *Phil.* 61 D4
Baleshare, *U.K.* 13 D1
Baleshwar, *India* 67 J15
Balezino, *Russia* 34 B11
Balfate, *Honduras* 120 C2
Bali, *Cameroon* 83 D7
Balí, *Greece* 49 D6
Bali, *India* 68 G5
Bali, *Indonesia* 63 J18
Bali □, *Indonesia* 63 J18
Bali, Selat, *Indonesia* 63 J17
Bali Sea, *Indonesia* 63 J17
Balia, S. Leone* 82 D2
Baliapal, *India* 69 J12
Baligród, *Poland* 31 J9
Balik Pulau, *Malaysia* .... 65 c
Balıkeşir, *Turkey* 47 B9
Balıkeşir □, *Turkey* 47 B9
Balıklıçeşme, *Turkey* 45 F11
Balikpapan, *Indonesia* 62 E5
Balimbing, *Phil.* 63 C5
Baling, *Malaysia* 65 K3
Balingen, *Germany* 25 G4
Baling, *Romania* 28 E6
Balintang Channel, *Phil.* 61 B4
Balipara, *India* 67 F18
Balkan Mts. = Stara Planina,
   Bulgaria 44 C7
Balkhash = Balqash, *Kazakhstan* 52 E8
Balkhash, Ozero = Balqash Köl,
   Kazakhstan 52 E8
Balla, *Bangla.* 67 G17
Ballachulish, *U.K.* 13 E3
Balladonia, *Australia* 93 F3
Ballaghaderreen, *Ireland* 12 C3
Ballarat, *Australia* 95 F3
Ballard, L., *Australia* 93 E3
Ballater, *U.K.* 13 D5
Ballé, *Mali* 82 B3
Ballena Gris = Ojo de Liebre ◌,
   Mexico 118 B2
Ballenas, Canal de, *Mexico* ... 118 B2
Balleny Is., *Antarctica* 5 C11
Balleroy, *France* 18 C6
Ballerup, *Denmark* 11 J6
Ballı, *Turkey* 45 F11
Ballia, *India* 69 G11
Ballina, *Australia* 95 D5
Ballina, *Ireland* 12 B2
Ballinasloe, *Ireland* 12 C3
Ballinger, *U.S.A.* 113 K5
Ballinrobe, *Ireland* 12 C2
Ballinskelligs B., *Ireland* ... 12 E1
Ballon, *France* 18 D7
Ballons des Vosges ◌, *France* . 19 E14
Ballsh, *Albania* 44 F3
Ballston Spa, *U.S.A.* 117 D11
Ballybunion, *Ireland* 12 D2
Ballycastle, *U.K.* 12 A5
Ballyclare, *U.K.* 12 B5
Ballyhaunis, *Ireland* 12 C3
Ballymena, *U.K.* 12 B5
Ballymoney, *U.K.* 12 A5
Ballymote, *Ireland* 12 B3
Ballynahinch, *U.K.* 12 B6

Ballyquintin Pt., *U.K.* 12 B6
Ballyshannon, *Ireland* 12 B3
Balmaceda, *Chile* 128 F2
Balmaseda, *Spain* 38 B1
Balmazújváros, *Hungary* 28 C6
Balmertown, *Canada* 103 C10
Balmoral, *Australia* 95 F3
Balmorhea, *U.S.A.* 113 K3
Balochistan = Baluchistan □,
   Pakistan 66 F4
Balonne →, *Australia* 95 D4
Balotra, *India* 68 G5
Balqash, *Kazakhstan* 52 E8
Balqash Köl, *Kazakhstan* 52 E8
Balrampur, *India* 69 F10
Balranald, *Australia* 95 E3
Balş, *Romania* 29 F9
Balsas, *Mexico* 119 D5
Balsas →, *Brazil* 125 E9
Balsas →, *Mexico* 118 D4
Bålsta, *Sweden* 10 E11
Balston Spa, *U.S.A.* 117 D11
Balta, *Romania* 28 F7
Balta, *Ukraine* 29 B14
Baltanás, *Spain* 36 D6
Bălți, *Moldova* 29 C12
Baltic Sea, *Europe* 9 H18
Baltîm, *Egypt* 80 H7
Baltimore, *Ireland* 12 E2
Baltimore, Md., U.S.A.* 114 F7
Baltimore, Ohio, U.S.A.* 116 G2
Baltit, *Pakistan* 69 A6
Baltiysk, *Russia* 9 J18
Baltrum, *Germany* 24 B3
Baluchistan □, *Pakistan* 66 F4
Balurghat, *India* 69 G13
Balvi, *Latvia* 9 H22
Balya, *Turkey* 47 B9
Bam, *Iran* 71 D8
Bama, *China* 58 E6
Bama, *Nigeria* 83 C7
Bamaga, *Australia* 94 A3
Bamaji L., *Canada* 104 B1
Bamako, *Mali* 82 C3
Bamba, *Mali* 83 B4
Bambara Maoundé, *Mali* 82 B4
Bambari, *C.A.R.* 84 C4
Bambaroo, *Australia* 94 B4
Bambey, *Guinea* 82 D2
Bamberg, *Germany* 25 F6
Bamberg, *U.S.A.* 115 J5
Bambesi, *Ethiopia* 81 F3
Bambili, *Dem. Rep. of the Congo* 86 B2
Bamboi, *Ghana* 82 D4
Bamburgh, *U.K.* 14 B6
Bamenda, *Cameroon* 83 D7
Bamfield, *Canada* 102 D3
Bāmīān □, *Afghan.* 66 B5
Bamiancheng, *China* 57 C13
Bamkin, *Cameroon* 83 D7
Bampūr, *Iran* 71 E9
Ban, *Burkina Faso* 82 C4
Ban Ao Tu Khun, *Thailand* ..... 65 a
Ban Ban, *Laos* 64 C4
Ban Bang Hin, *Thailand* 65 H2
Ban Bang Khu, *Thailand* .... 65 a
Ban Bang Rong, *Thailand* ...... 65 a
Ban Bo Phut, *Thailand* .... 65 b
Ban Chaweng, *Thailand* .... 65 b
Ban Chiang Klang, *Thailand* ... 64 C3
Ban Chik, *Laos* 64 D4
Ban Choho, *Thailand* 64 E4
Ban Dan Lan Hoi, *Thailand* 64 D2
Ban Don = Surat Thani, *Thailand* 65 H2
Ban Don, *Vietnam* 64 F6
Ban Don, Ao →, *Thailand* 65 H2
Ban Dong, *Thailand* 64 C3
Ban Hong, *Thailand* 64 C2
Ban Hua Thanon, *Thailand* ..... 65 b
Ban Kaeng, *Thailand* 64 D3
Ban Kantang, *Thailand* 65 J2
Ban Karon, *Thailand* .... 65 a
Ban Kata, *Thailand* .... 65 a
Ban Keun, *Laos* 64 C4
Ban Khai, *Thailand* 64 F3
Ban Kheun, *Laos* 64 B3
Ban Khlong Khian, *Thailand* ... 65 a
Ban Khlong Kua, *Thailand* 65 J3
Ban Khuan, *Thailand* .... 65 a
Ban Khuan Mao, *Thailand* 65 J2
Ban Ko Yai Chim, *Thailand* 65 G2
Ban Kok, *Thailand* 64 D4
Ban Laem, *Thailand* 64 F2
Ban Lamai, *Thailand* .... 65 b
Ban Lao Ngam, *Laos* 64 E6
Ban Le Kathe, *Thailand* 64 E2
Ban Lo Po Noi, *Thailand* ...... 65 a
Ban Mae Chedi, *Thailand* 64 C2
Ban Mae Laeng, *Thailand* 64 B2
Ban Mae Nam, *Thailand* .... 65 b
Ban Mae Sariang, *Thailand* 64 C1
Ban Mê Thuôt = Buon Ma Thuot,
   Vietnam 64 F7
Ban Mi, *Thailand* 64 E3
Ban Muong Mo, *Laos* 64 C4
Ban Na Bo, *Thailand* .... 65 b
Ban Na San, *Thailand* 65 H2
Ban Na Tong, *Laos* 64 B3
Ban Nam Bac, *Laos* 64 B4
Ban Nam Ma, *Laos* 64 A3
Ban Ngang, *Laos* 64 E6
Ban Nong Bok, *Laos* 64 D5
Ban Nong Boua, *Laos* 64 E6
Ban Nong Pling, *Thailand* 64 E3
Ban Pak Chan, *Thailand* 65 G2
Ban Patong, *Thailand* .... 65 a
Ban Phai, *Thailand* 64 D4
Ban Phak Chit, *Thailand* ...... 65 a
Ban Pong, *Thailand* 64 F2
Ban Rawai, *Thailand* .... 65 a

Ban Ron Phibun, *Thailand* 65 H2
Ban Sakhu, *Thailand* .... 65 a
Ban Sanam Chai, *Thailand* 65 J3
Ban Sangkha, *Thailand* 64 E4
Ban Tak, *Thailand* 64 D2
Ban Tako, *Thailand* 64 E4
Ban Tha Dua, *Thailand* 64 D2
Ban Tha Li, *Thailand* 64 D3
Ban Tha Nun, *Thailand* .... 65 a
Ban Tha Rua, *Thailand* .... 65 a
Ban Tha Yu, *Thailand* .... 65 a
Ban Thahine, *Laos* 64 E5
Ban Thong Krut, *Thailand* .... 65 b
Ban Xien Kok, *Laos* 64 B3
Ban Yen Nhan, *Vietnam* 64 B6
Banaba, *Kiribati* 96 H8
Banalia, *Dem. Rep. of the Congo* 86 B2
Banam, *Cambodia* 65 G5
Banamba, *Mali* 82 C3
Banana Is., *S. Leone* 82 D2
Bananal, I. do, *Brazil* 125 F8
Banaras = Varanasi, *India* ... 69 G10
Banas →, *Gujarat, India* 68 H4
Banas →, *Mad. P., India* 69 G9
Bânâs, Ras, *Egypt* 80 C4
Banaz, *Turkey* 47 C11
Banaz →, *Turkey* 47 C11
Banbridge, *U.K.* 12 B5
Banbury, *U.K.* 15 E6
Banchory, *U.K.* 13 D6
Banco, *Ethiopia* 81 F4
Bancroft, *Canada* 116 A7
Band, *Romania* 29 D9
Band Bonī, *Iran* 71 E8
Band Qīr, *Iran* 71 D6
Banda, *Mad. P., India* 69 G8
Banda, *Ut. P., India* 69 G9
Banda, Kepulauan, *Indonesia* .. 63 E7
Banda Aceh, *Indonesia* 62 C1
Banda Elat, *Indonesia* 63 F8
Banda Is. = Banda, Kepulauan,
  Indonesia 63 E7
Banda Sea, *Indonesia* 63 F7
Bandai-Asahi △, *Japan* 54 F10
Bandai-San, *Japan* 54 F10
Bandama →, *Ivory C.* 82 D3
Bandama Blanc →, *Ivory C.* ... 82 D3
Bandama Rouge →, *Ivory C.* ... 82 D4
Bandān, *Iran* 71 D9
Bandanaira, *Indonesia* 63 E7
Bandanwara, *India* 68 F6
Bandar = Machilipatnam, *India* . 67 L12
Bandar-e Abbās, *Iran* 71 E8
Bandar-e Anzalī, *Iran* 71 B6
Bandar-e Bushehr = Büshehr,
  Iran 71 D6
Bandar-e Chārak, *Iran* 71 E7
Bandar-e Deylam, *Iran* 71 D6
Bandar-e Emām Khomeynı, *Iran* . 71 D6
Bandar-e Lengeh, *Iran* 71 E7
Bandar-e Maqām, *Iran* 71 E7
Bandar-e Ma'shur, *Iran* 71 D6
Bandar-e Rīg, *Iran* 71 D6
Bandar-e Torkeman, *Iran* 71 B7
Bandar Lampung =
  Tanjungkarang Telukbetung,
  Indonesia 62 F3
Bandar Maharani = Muar,
  Malaysia 65 L4
Bandar Penggaram = Batu Pahat,
  Malaysia 65 M4
Bandar Seri Begawan, *Brunei* .. 62 C4
Bandar Sri Aman, *Malaysia* ... 62 D4
Bandawe, *Malawi* 87 E3
Bande, *Spain* 36 C3
Bandeira, Pico da, *Brazil* 127 A7
Bandera, *Argentina* 126 B3
Banderas, B. de, *Mexico* 118 C3
Bandhogarh, *India* 69 H9
Bandi →, *India* 68 F6
Bandiagara, *Mali* 82 C4
Bandikui, *India* 68 F7
Bandırma, *Turkey* 45 F11
Bandjarmasin = Banjarmasin,
  Indonesia 62 E4
Bandol, *France* 21 E9
Bandon, *Ireland* 12 E3
Bandon →, *Ireland* 12 E3
Bandula, *Mozam.* 87 F3
Bandundu, *Dem. Rep. of
  the Congo* 84 E3
Bandung, *Indonesia* 63 G12
Bané, *Burkina Faso* 83 C4
Băneasa, *Romania* 29 E12
Bāneh, *Iran* 70 C5
Bañeres, *Spain* 39 G4
Banes, *Cuba* 121 B4
Banff, *Canada* 102 C5
Banff, *U.K.* 13 D6
Banff △, *Canada* 102 C5
Banfora, *Burkina Faso* 82 C4
Bang Fai →, *Laos* 64 D5
Bang Hieng →, *Laos* 64 D5
Bang Krathum, *Thailand* 64 D3
Bang Lamung, *Thailand* 64 F3
Bang Mun Nak, *Thailand* 64 D3
Bang Pa In, *Thailand* 64 E3
Bang Rakam, *Thailand* 64 D3
Bang Saphan, *Thailand* 65 G2
Bang Thao, *Thailand* .... 65 a
Banganduni I., *India* 69 J13
Bangala Dam, *Zimbabwe* 87 G3
Bangalore, *India* 66 N10
Banganga →, *India* 68 F6
Bangangté, *Cameroon* 83 D7
Bangaon, *India* 69 H13
Bangassou, *C.A.R.* 84 D4
Banggai, *Indonesia* 63 E6
Banggai, Kepulauan, *Indonesia* . 63 E6
Banggai Arch. = Banggai,
  Kepulauan, *Indonesia* 63 E6

Banggi, *Malaysia* 62 C5
Banghāzī, *Libya* 79 B10
Bangjang, *Sudan* 81 E3
Bangka, *Sulawesi, Indonesia* .. 63 D7
Bangka, *Sumatera, Indonesia* .. 62 E3
Bangka, Selat, *Indonesia* 62 E3
Bangka-Belitung □, *Indonesia* .. 62 E3
Bangkalan, *Indonesia* 63 G15
Bangkinang, *Indonesia* 62 D2
Bangko, *Indonesia* 62 E2
Bangkok, *Thailand* 64 F3
Bangladesh ■, *Asia* 67 H17
Bangli, *Indonesia* 63 J18
Bangolo, *Ivory C.* 82 D3
Bangong Co, *India* 69 B8
Bangor, *Down, U.K.* 12 B6
Bangor, *Gwynedd, U.K.* 14 D3
Bangor, *Maine, U.S.A.* 101 D13
Bangor, *Pa., U.S.A.* 117 F9
Bangued, *Phil.* 61 C4
Bangui, *C.A.R.* 84 D3
Bangui, *Phil.* 61 B4
Banguru, *Dem. Rep. of the Congo* 86 B2
Bangweulu, L., *Zambia* 87 E3
Bangweulu Swamp, *Zambia* 87 E3
Banhine △, *Mozam.* 89 C5
Baní, *Dom. Rep.* 121 C5
Bani →, *Mali* 82 C4
Bani Bangou, *Niger* 83 B5
Banī Sa'd, *Iraq* 70 C5
Bania, *Ivory C.* 82 D4
Banihal Pass, *India* 69 C6
Banikoara, *Benin* 83 C5
Bāniyās, *Syria* 70 C3
Banja Luka, *Bos.-H.* 28 F2
Banjar, *India* 68 D7
Banjar →, *India* 69 H9
Banjarmasin, *Indonesia* 62 E4
Banjul, *Gambia* 82 C1
Banka, *India* 69 G12
Bankas, *Mali* 82 C4
Bankeryd, *Sweden* 11 G8
Banket, *Zimbabwe* 87 F3
Bankilaré, *Niger* 83 C5
Bankipore, *India* 67 G14
Banks I., *B.C., Canada* 102 C3
Banks I., *N.W.T., Canada* ... 100 A7
Banks Pen., *N.Z.* 91 K4
Banks Str., *Australia* 95 G4
Bankura, *India* 69 H12
Bankya, *Bulgaria* 44 D7
Banmankhi, *India* 69 G12
Bann →, *Arm., U.K.* 12 B5
Bann →, *L'derry., U.K.* 12 A5
Bannalec, *France* 18 E3
Banning, *U.S.A.* 111 M10
Banno, *Ethiopia* 81 G4
Bannockburn, *Canada* 116 B7
Bannockburn, *U.K.* 13 E5
Bannockburn, *Zimbabwe* 87 G2
Bannu, *Pakistan* 66 C7
Bano, *India* 69 H11
Bañolas = Banyoles, *Spain* ... 38 C7
Banon, *France* 21 D9
Baños de la Encina, *Spain* ... 37 G7
Baños de Molgas, *Spain* 36 C3
Bánovce nad Bebravou,
  Slovak Rep. 27 C11
Banovići, *Bos.-H.* 28 F3
Bansgaon, *India* 69 F10
Banská Bystrica, *Slovak Rep.* . 27 C12
Banská Štiavnica, *Slovak Rep.* 27 C11
Bansko, *Bulgaria* 44 E7
Banskobystrický □, *Slovak Rep.* 27 C12
Banswara, *India* 68 H6
Bantaeng, *Indonesia* 63 F5
Bantaji, *Nigeria* 83 D7
Bantayan, *Phil.* 61 F5
Banten □, *Indonesia* 63 G11
Bantry, *Ireland* 12 E2
Bantry B., *Ireland* 12 E2
Bantul, *Indonesia* 63 G14
Bantva, *India* 68 J4
Banya, *Bulgaria* 45 D8
Banyak, Kepulauan, *Indonesia* . 62 D1
Banyalbufar, *Spain* 48 B9
Banyo, *Cameroon* 83 D7
Banyoles, *Spain* 38 C7
Banyuls-sur-Mer, *France* 20 F7
Banyumas, *Indonesia* 63 G13
Banyuwangi, *Indonesia* 63 J17
Banzare Coast, *Antarctica* ... 5 C9
Bao Ha, *Vietnam* 58 F5
Bao Lac, *Vietnam* 64 A5
Bao Loc, *Vietnam* 65 G6
Bao'an = Shenzhen, *China* ... 59 F10
Baocheng, *China* 56 H4
Baode, *China* 56 E6
Baodi, *China* 57 E9
Baoding, *China* 56 E8
Baoji, *China* 56 G4
Baojing, *China* 58 C7
Baokang, *China* 59 B8
Baoshan, *Shanghai, China* ... 59 B13
Baoshan, *Yunnan, China* 58 E2
Baotou, *China* 56 D6
Baoxing, *China* 58 B4
Baoying, *China* 57 H10
Bap, *India* 68 F5
Bapatla, *India* 67 M12
Bapaume, *France* 19 B9
Bāqerābād, *Iran* 71 C6
Ba'qūbah, *Iraq* 70 C5
Baquedano, *Chile* 126 A2
Bar, *Serbia & M.* 44 D3
Bar, *Ukraine* 33 H4
Bar Bigha, *India* 69 G11
Bar Harbor, *U.S.A.* 115 C11
Bar-le-Duc, *France* 19 D12
Bar-sur-Aube, *France* 19 D11
Bar-sur-Seine, *France* 19 D11

Baritú △, *Argentina* 126 A3
Bâra, *Romania* 29 C12
Bara Banki, *India* 69 F9
Barabai, *Indonesia* 62 E5
Baraboo, *U.S.A.* 112 D10
Baracoa, *Cuba* 121 B5
Baradā →, *Syria* 74 B5
Baradero, *Argentina* 126 C4
Barāganul, *Romania* 29 F12
Barah →, *India* 68 F6
Barahona, *Dom. Rep.* 121 C5
Barahona, *Spain* 38 D2
Barail Range, *India* 67 G18
Barajas, Madrid ✈ (MAD), *Spain* 36 E7
Baraka, *Sudan* 81 E2
Baraka →, *Sudan* 80 D4
Barakaldo, *Spain* 38 B2
Barakar →, *India* 69 G12
Barakhola, *India* 67 G18
Barakot, *India* 69 J11
Barakpur, *India* 69 H13
Baralaba, *Australia* 94 C4
Baralla, *Spain* 36 C3
Baralzon L., *Canada* 103 B9
Barameiya, *Sudan* 80 D4
Baramula, *India* 69 B6
Baran, *India* 68 G7
Baran →, *Pakistan* 68 G3
Barañain, *Spain* 38 C3
Baranavichy, *Belarus* 33 F4
Barani, *Burkina Faso* 82 C4
Baranof, *U.S.A.* 102 B2
Baranof I., *U.S.A.* 100 C6
Baranów Sandomierski, *Poland* . 31 H8
Baranya □, *Hungary* 28 E3
Baraolt, *Romania* 29 D10
Barapasi, *Indonesia* 63 E9
Barasat, *India* 69 H13
Barat Daya, Kepulauan,
  Indonesia 63 F7
Barataria B., *U.S.A.* 113 L10
Barauda, *India* 68 H6
Baraut, *India* 68 E7
Barbacena, *Brazil* 127 A7
Barbados ■, *W. Indies* ..... 121 g
Barban, *Croatia* 41 C11
Barbària, C. de, *Spain* 48 C7
Barbaros, *Turkey* 45 F11
Barbastro, *Spain* 38 C5
Barbate de Franco, *Spain* ... 37 J5
Barberino di Mugello, *Italy* .. 41 E8
Barberton, *S. Africa* 89 D5
Barberton, *U.S.A.* 116 E3
Barbezieux-St-Hilaire, *France* . 20 C3
Barbosa, *Colombia* 124 B4
Barbourville, *U.S.A.* 115 G4
Barbuda, *W. Indies* 121 C7
Bârca, *Romania* 29 G8
Barcaldine, *Australia* 94 C4
Barcarrota, *Spain* 37 G4
Barcellona Pozzo di Gotto, *Italy* 43 D8
Barcelona, *Spain* 38 D7
Barcelona, *Venezuela* 124 A6
Barcelona □, *Spain* 38 D7
Barcelona ✈ (BCN), *Spain* ... 38 D7
Barceloneta, *Puerto Rico* ... 121 d
Barcelonnette, *France* 21 D10
Barcelos, *Brazil* 124 D6
Barcin, *Poland* 31 F4
Barclayville, *Liberia* 82 E3
Barcoo →, *Australia* 94 D3
Barcs, *Hungary* 28 E2
Barczewo, *Poland* 30 E7
Bârdā, *Azerbaijan* 35 K8
Bardaï, *Chad* 79 D9
Bardas Blancas, *Argentina* .. 126 D2
Bardawīl, Sabkhet el, *Egypt* .. 74 D2
Barddhaman, *India* 69 H12
Bardejov, *Slovak Rep.* 27 B14
Bardera, *Somali Rep.* 75 G3
Bardi, *Italy* 40 D6
Bardīyah, *Libya* 79 B10
Bardolino, *Italy* 40 C7
Bardonécchia, *Italy* 40 C3
Bardsey I., *U.K.* 14 E3
Bardstown, *U.S.A.* 114 G3
Bareilly, *India* 69 E8
Barela, *India* 69 H9
Barentin, *France* 18 C7
Barenton, *France* 18 D6
Barents Sea, *Arctic* 50 B7
Barentu, *Eritrea* 81 D4
Barfleur, *France* 18 C5
Barfleur, Pte. de, *France* ... 18 C5
Barga, *Italy* 40 D7
Bargara, *Australia* 94 C5
Bargas, *Spain* 36 F6
Bârgăului Bistriţa, *Romania* .. 29 C9
Barge, *Italy* 40 D4
Bargnop, *Sudan* 81 F2
Bargteheide, *Germany* 24 B6
Barguzin, *Russia* 53 D11
Barh, *India* 69 G11
Barhaj, *India* 69 F10
Barharwa, *India* 69 G12
Barhi, *India* 69 G11
Bari, *Italy* 43 A9
Bari Doab, *Pakistan* 68 D5
Bari Sadri, *India* 68 G6
Bari Sardo, *Italy* 42 C2
Barīdī, Ra's, *Si. Arabia* 70 E3
Barīm, *Yemen* 76 E8
Barinas, *Venezuela* 124 B4
Baring, C., *Canada* 100 B8
Baringo, L., *Kenya* 86 B4
Bârîs, *Egypt* 80 C3
Barisal, *Bangla.* 67 H17
Barisal □, *Bangla.* 67 H17
Barisan, Bukit, *Indonesia* ... 62 E2
Barito →, *Indonesia* 62 E4

Barjac, *France* 21 D8
Barjols, *France* 21 E10
Bark L., *Canada* 116 A7
Barka = Baraka →, *Sudan* ... 80 D4
Barkakana, *India* 69 H11
Barkam, *China* 58 B4
Barker, *U.S.A.* 116 C6
Barkley, L., *U.S.A.* 115 G2
Barkley Sound, *Canada* 102 D3
Barkly East, *S. Africa* 88 E4
Barkly Roadhouse, *Australia* . 94 B2
Barkly Tableland, *Australia* .. 94 B2
Barkly West, *S. Africa* 88 D3
Barkol, Wadi →, *Sudan* 80 D3
Barla Daği, *Turkey* 47 C12
Bârlad, *Romania* 29 D12
Bârlad →, *Romania* 29 E12
Barlee, L., *Australia* 93 E2
Barlee, Mt., *Australia* 93 D4
Barletta, *Italy* 43 A9
Barlinek, *Poland* 31 F2
Barlovento, *Canary Is.* 48 F2
Barlow L., *Canada* 103 A8
Barmedman, *Australia* 95 E4
Barmer, *India* 68 G4
Barmera, *Australia* 95 E3
Barmouth, *U.K.* 14 E3
Barna →, *India* 69 G10
Barnagar, *India* 68 H6
Barnala, *India* 68 D6
Barnard Castle, *U.K.* 14 C6
Barnaul, *Russia* 52 D9
Barnesville, *U.S.A.* 115 J3
Barnet □, *U.K.* 15 F7
Barneveld, *Neths.* 17 B5
Barneveld, *U.S.A.* 117 C9
Barneville-Cartevert, *France* .. 18 C5
Barnhart, *U.S.A.* 113 K4
Barnsley, *U.K.* 14 D6
Barnstaple, *U.K.* 15 F3
Barnstaple Bay = Bideford Bay,
  U.K. 15 F3
Barnsville, *U.S.A.* 112 B6
Barnwell, *U.S.A.* 115 J5
Baro, *Nigeria* 83 D6
Baro →, *Ethiopia* 81 F3
Baroda = Vadodara, *India* ... 68 H5
Baroda, *India* 68 G7
Baroe, *S. Africa* 88 E3
Baron Ra., *Australia* 92 D4
Barong, *China* 58 B2
Barotseland, *Zambia* 85 H4
Barouéli, *Mali* 82 C3
Barpeta, *India* 67 F17
Barques, Pt. Aux, *U.S.A.* .. 116 B2
Barquísimeto, *Venezuela* ... 124 A5
Barr, Ras el, *Egypt* 80 H7
Barr Smith Range, *Australia* . 93 E3
Barra, *Brazil* 125 F10
Barra, *U.K.* 13 E1
Barra, Sd. of, *U.K.* 13 D1
Barra de Navidad, *Mexico* .. 118 D4
Barra do Corda, *Brazil* 125 E9
Barra do Piraí, *Brazil* 127 A7
Barra Falsa, Pta. da, *Mozam.* . 89 C6
Barra Hd., *U.K.* 13 E1
Barra Mansa, *Brazil* 127 A7
Barraba, *Australia* 95 E5
Barrackpur = Barakpur, *India* . 69 H13
Barradale Roadhouse, *Australia* 92 D1
Barrafranca, *Italy* 43 E7
Barraigh = Barra, *U.K.* 13 E1
Barranca, *Lima, Peru* 124 F3
Barranca, *Loreto, Peru* 124 D3
Barranca del Cobre △, *Mexico* . 118 B3
Barrancabermeja, *Colombia* .. 124 B4
Barrancas, *Venezuela* 124 B6
Barrancos, *Portugal* 37 G4
Barranqueras, *Argentina* ... 126 B4
Barranquilla, *Colombia* 124 A4
Barraute, *Canada* 104 C4
Barre, Mass., *U.S.A.* 117 D12
Barre, Vt., *U.S.A.* 117 B12
Barreal, *Argentina* 126 C2
Barreiras, *Brazil* 125 F10
Barreirinhas, *Brazil* 125 D10
Barreiro, *Portugal* 37 G1
Barrême, *France* 21 E10
Barren, Nosy, *Madag.* 89 B7
Barretos, *Brazil* 125 H9
Barrhead, *Canada* 102 C6
Barrie, *Canada* 116 B5
Barrier Ra., *Australia* 95 E3
Barrière, *Canada* 102 C4
Barrington, *U.S.A.* 117 E13
Barrington L., *Canada* 103 B8
Barrington Tops, *Australia* .. 95 E5
Barringun, *Australia* 95 D4
Barro do Garças, *Brazil* 125 G8
Barron, *U.S.A.* 112 C9
Barrow, *U.S.A.* 100 A4
Barrow →, *Ireland* 12 D5
Barrow Creek, *Australia* ... 94 C1
Barrow I., *Australia* 92 D2
Barrow-in-Furness, *U.K.* ... 14 C4
Barrow Pt., *Australia* 94 A3
Barrow Pt., *U.S.A.* 98 B4
Barrow Ra., *Australia* 93 E4
Barrow Str., *Canada* 4 B3
Barruecopardo, *Spain* 36 D4
Barruelo de Santullán, *Spain* . 36 C6
Barry, *U.K.* 15 F4
Barry's Bay, *Canada* 116 A7
Barsalogho, *Burkina Faso* ... 83 C4
Barsat, *Pakistan* 69 A5
Barsham, *Syria* 70 C4
Barsi, *India* 66 K9
Barsinghausen, *Germany* ... 24 C5
Barsoi, *India* 67 G15
Barstow, *U.S.A.* 111 L9

Barth, *Germany* 24 A8
Barthélemy, Col, *Vietnam* ... 64 C5
Bartica, *Guyana* 124 B7
Bartin, *Turkey* 72 B5
Bartle Frere, *Australia* 94 B4
Bartlesville, *U.S.A.* 113 G7
Bartlett, *U.S.A.* 110 J8
Bartlett, L., *Canada* 102 A5
Bartolomeu Dias, *Mozam.* ... 87 G4
Barton, *U.S.A.* 117 B12
Barton upon Humber, *U.K.* .. 14 D7
Bartoszyce, *Poland* 30 D7
Bartow, *U.S.A.* 115 M5
Barú, Volcan, *Panama* 120 E3
Barumba, *Dem. Rep. of the Congo* 86 B1
Baruth, *Germany* 24 C9
Baruunsuu, *Mongolia* 56 C3
Barvinkove, *Ukraine* 33 H9
Barwani, *India* 68 H6
Barwice, *Poland* 30 E3
Barycz →, *Poland* 31 G3
Barysaw, *Belarus* 32 E5
Barysh, *Russia* 34 D8
Barzān, *Iraq* 70 B5
Bârzava, *Romania* 28 D6
Bas-Rhin □, *France* 19 D14
Bašaid, *Serbia & M.* 28 E5
Bāsa'idū, *Iran* 71 E7
Basal, *Pakistan* 68 C5
Basankusa, *Dem. Rep. of
  the Congo* 84 D3
Basarabeasca, *Moldova* 29 D13
Basarabi, *Romania* 29 F13
Basarabia = Bessarabiya,
  Moldova 33 J5
Basauri, *Spain* 38 B2
Basawa, *Afghan.* 68 B4
Bascuñán, C., *Chile* 126 B1
Basel, Euroairport ✈ (BSL),
  Europe 19 E14
Basel-Landschaft □, *Switz.* .. 25 H3
Basento →, *Italy* 43 B9
Bashākerd, Kühhā-ye, *Iran* .. 71 E8
Bashaw, *Canada* 102 C6
Bāshī, *Iran* 71 D6
Bashkir Republic =
  Bashkortostan □, *Russia* .. 52 D6
Bashkortostan □, *Russia* ... 52 D6
Bashtanivka, *Ukraine* 29 E14
Basibasy, *Madag.* 89 C7
Basilan I., *Phil.* 61 H5
Basilan Str., *Phil.* 61 H5
Basildon, *U.K.* 15 F8
Basile, Eq. Guin. 83 E6
Basilicata □, *Italy* 43 B9
Basim = Washim, *India* 66 J10
Basin, *U.S.A.* 108 D9
Basingstoke, *U.K.* 15 F6
Baška, *Croatia* 41 D11
Başkale, *Turkey* 73 C10
Baskatong, Rés., *Canada* ... 104 C4
Basle = Basel, *Switz.* 25 H3
Başmakçı, *Turkey* 47 D12
Basoda, *India* 68 H7
Basoko, *Dem. Rep. of the Congo* 86 B1
Basque, Pays, *France* 20 E2
Basque Provinces = País Vasco □,
  Spain 38 C2
Basra = Al Başrah, *Iraq* 70 D5
Bass Str., *Australia* 95 F4
Bassano, *Canada* 102 C6
Bassano del Grappa, *Italy* ... 41 C8
Bassar, *Togo* 83 D5
Bassas da India, Ind. Oc. 85 J7
Basse-Normandie □, *France* .. 18 D6
Basse-Pointe, *Martinique* ... 120 c
Basse Santa-Su, *Gambia* 82 C2
Basse-Terre, *Guadeloupe* ... 120 b
Basse Terre, *Trin. & Tob.* ... 125 K15
Bassein, *Burma* 67 L19
Basses, Pte. des, *Guadeloupe* 120 b
Basseterre, *St. Kitts & Nevis* . 121 C7
Bassett, *U.S.A.* 112 D5
Bassi, *India* 68 D7
Bassigny, *France* 19 E12
Bassikounou, *Mauritania* ... 82 B3
Bassila, *Benin* 83 D5
Bassum, *Germany* 24 C4
Båstad, *Sweden* 11 H6
Bastak, *Iran* 71 E7
Baştām, *Iran* 71 B7
Bastar, *India* 67 K12
Bastelica, *France* 21 F13
Basti, *India* 69 F10
Bastia, *France* 21 F13
Bastogne, *Belgium* 17 D5
Bastrop, La., *U.S.A.* 113 J9
Bastrop, Tex., *U.S.A.* 113 K6
Bat Yam, *Israel* 74 C3
Bata, Eq. Guin. 84 D1
Bata, *Romania* 28 D7
Bataan □, *Phil.* 61 D4
Batabanó, *Cuba* 120 B3
Batabanó, G. de, *Cuba* 120 B3
Batac, *Phil.* 61 B4
Batagai, *Russia* 53 C14
Batajnica, *Serbia & M.* 44 B4
Batak, *Bulgaria* 45 E8
Batala, *India* 68 D6
Batalha, *Portugal* 36 F2
Batama, *Dem. Rep. of the Congo* 86 B2
Batamay, *Russia* 53 C13
Batang, *China* 58 B2
Batang, *Indonesia* 63 G13
Batangas, *Phil.* 61 E4
Batanta, *Indonesia* 63 E8
Batatais, *Brazil* 127 A6
Batavia, *U.S.A.* 116 D6
Bataysk, *Russia* 33 J10
Batchelor, *Australia* 92 B5
Batdambang, *Cambodia* 64 F4

Batemans B., Australia ... 95 F5
Batemans Bay, Australia ... 95 F5
Bates Ra., Australia ... 93 E3
Batesburg-Leesville, U.S.A. ... 115 J5
Batesville, Ark., U.S.A. ... 113 H9
Batesville, Miss., U.S.A. ... 113 H10
Batesville, Tex., U.S.A. ... 113 L5
Bath, Canada ... 117 B8
Bath, U.K. ... 15 F5
Bath, Maine, U.S.A. ... 115 D11
Bath, N.Y., U.S.A. ... 116 D7
Bath & North East Somerset □, U.K. ... 15 F5
Batheay, Cambodia ... 65 G5
Bathsheba, Barbados ... 121 g
Bathurst, Australia ... 95 E4
Bathurst, Canada ... 105 C6
Bathurst, S. Africa ... 88 E4
Bathurst, C., Canada ... 100 A7
Bathurst B., Australia ... 94 A3
Bathurst Harb., Australia ... 95 G4
Bathurst I., Australia ... 92 B5
Bathurst I., Canada ... 98 B9
Bathurst Inlet, Canada ... 100 B9
Bati, Ethiopia ... 81 E5
Batie, Burkina Faso ... 82 D4
Batlow, Australia ... 95 F4
Batman, Turkey ... 70 B4
Baţn al Ghūl, Jordan ... 74 F4
Batna, Algeria ... 78 A7
Batobato = San Isidro, Phil. ... 61 H7
Batočina, Serbia & M. ... 44 B5
Batoka, Zambia ... 87 F2
Baton Rouge, U.S.A. ... 113 K9
Batong, Ko, Thailand ... 65 J2
Bátonyterenye, Hungary ... 28 C4
Batopilas, Mexico ... 118 B3
Batouri, Cameroon ... 84 D2
Båtsfjord, Norway ... 8 A23
Battambang = Batdambang, Cambodia ... 64 F4
Batticaloa, Sri Lanka ... 66 R12
Battipáglia, Italy ... 43 B7
Battle, U.K. ... 15 G8
Battle ➔, Canada ... 103 C7
Battle Creek, U.S.A. ... 114 D3
Battle Ground, U.S.A. ... 110 E4
Battle Harbour, Canada ... 105 B8
Battle Lake, U.S.A. ... 112 B7
Battle Mountain, U.S.A. ... 108 F5
Battlefields, Zimbabwe ... 87 F2
Battleford, Canada ... 103 C7
Battonya, Hungary ... 28 D6
Batu, Ethiopia ... 81 F4
Batu, Kepulauan, Indonesia ... 62 E1
Batu Caves, Malaysia ... 65 L3
Batu Ferringhi, Malaysia ... 65 c
Batu Gajah, Malaysia ... 65 K3
Batu Is. = Batu, Kepulauan, Indonesia ... 62 E1
Batu Pahat, Malaysia ... 65 M4
Batuata, Indonesia ... 63 F6
Batugondang, Tanjung, Indonesia ... 63 J17
Batukau, Gunung, Indonesia ... 63 J18
Batumi, Georgia ... 35 K5
Batur, Indonesia ... 63 J18
Batur, Gunung, Indonesia ... 63 J18
Baturaja, Indonesia ... 62 E2
Baturité, Brazil ... 125 D11
Baturiti, Indonesia ... 63 J18
Bau, Malaysia ... 62 D4
Baubau, Indonesia ... 63 F6
Baucau = Baucau, E. Timor ... 63 F7
Bauchi, Nigeria ... 83 C6
Bauchi □, Nigeria ... 83 C7
Baud, France ... 18 E3
Baudette, U.S.A. ... 112 A7
Bauer, C., Australia ... 95 E1
Bauhinia, Australia ... 94 C4
Baukau = Baucau, E. Timor ... 63 F7
Bauld, C., Canada ... 101 C14
Baume-les-Dames, France ... 19 E13
Baunatal, Germany ... 24 D5
Baunei, Italy ... 42 B2
Baure, Nigeria ... 83 C6
Bauru, Brazil ... 127 A6
Bausi, India ... 69 G12
Bauska, Latvia ... 9 H21
Bautino, Kazakhstan ... 35 H10
Bautzen, Germany ... 24 D10
Bauya, S. Leone ... 82 D2
Bavānāt, Iran ... 71 D7
Bavanište, Serbia & M. ... 28 F5
Bavaria = Bayern □, Germany ... 25 G7
Båven, Sweden ... 10 E10
Bavispe ➔, Mexico ... 118 B3
Bawdwin, Burma ... 67 H20
Bawean, Indonesia ... 62 F4
Bawku, Ghana ... 83 C4
Bawlake, Burma ... 67 K20
Bawolung, China ... 58 C3
Baxley, U.S.A. ... 115 K4
Baxoi, China ... 58 B1
Baxter, U.S.A. ... 112 B7
Baxter Springs, U.S.A. ... 113 G7
Baxter State ⊂, U.S.A. ... 115 B11
Bay, L. de, Phil. ... 61 D4
Bay City, Mich., U.S.A. ... 114 D4
Bay City, Tex., U.S.A. ... 113 L7
Bay Minette, U.S.A. ... 115 K2
Bay Roberts, Canada ... 105 C9
Bay St. Louis, U.S.A. ... 113 K10
Bay Springs, U.S.A. ... 113 K10
Bay View, N.Z. ... 91 H6
Baya, Dem. Rep. of the Congo ... 87 E2
Bayamo, Cuba ... 120 B4
Bayamón, Puerto Rico ... 121 d
Bayan Har Shan, China ... 60 C4
Bayan Hot = Alxa Zuoqi, China ... 56 E3
Bayan Lepas, Malaysia ... 65 c
Bayan Obo, China ... 56 D5

Bayan-Ovoo = Erdenetsogt, Mongolia ... 56 C4
Bayana, India ... 68 F7
Bayanaūyl, Kazakhstan ... 52 D8
Bayandalay, Mongolia ... 56 C2
Bayanhongor, Mongolia ... 60 B5
Bayard, N. Mex., U.S.A. ... 109 K9
Bayard, Nebr., U.S.A. ... 112 E3
Bayawan, Phil. ... 61 G5
Baybay, Phil. ... 61 F6
Bayburt, Turkey ... 73 B9
Baydhabo = Baidoa, Somali Rep. ... 75 G3
Bayelsa □, Nigeria ... 83 E6
Bayerische Alpen, Germany ... 25 H7
Bayerische Rhön △, Germany ... 25 E6
Bayerischer Spessart △, Germany ... 25 F6
Bayerischer Wald, Germany ... 25 G8
Bayern □, Germany ... 25 G7
Bayeux, France ... 18 C6
Bayfield, Canada ... 116 C3
Bayfield, U.S.A. ... 112 B9
Bayındır, Turkey ... 47 C9
Bayjī, Iraq ... 70 C4
Baykal, Oz., Russia ... 53 D11
Baykan, Turkey ... 70 B4
Baykonur = Bayqongyr, Kazakhstan ... 52 E7
Baynes Mts., Namibia ... 88 B1
Bayombong, Phil. ... 61 C4
Bayon, France ... 19 D13
Bayona = Baiona, Spain ... 36 C2
Bayonne, France ... 20 E2
Bayonne, U.S.A. ... 117 F10
Bayovar, Peru ... 124 E2
Bayqongyr, Kazakhstan ... 52 E7
Bayram-Ali = Bayramaly, Turkmenistan ... 52 F7
Bayramaly, Turkmenistan ... 52 F7
Bayramiç, Turkey ... 47 B8
Bayreuth, Germany ... 25 F7
Bayrischzell, Germany ... 25 H8
Bayrūt, Lebanon ... 74 B4
Bays, L. of, Canada ... 116 A5
Baysville, Canada ... 116 A5
Bayt Laḥm, West Bank ... 74 D4
Baytown, U.S.A. ... 113 L7
Bayun, Indonesia ... 63 J18
Bayzo, Niger ... 83 C5
Baza, Spain ... 37 H8
Bazar Dyuzi, Russia ... 35 K8
Bazardüzü = Bazar Dyuzi, Russia ... 35 K8
Bazaruk Karabulak, Russia ... 34 D8
Bazarnyy Syzgan, Russia ... 34 D8
Bazaruto △, Mozam. ... 89 C6
Bazaruto, I. do, Mozam. ... 89 C6
Bazas, France ... 20 D3
Bazhong, China ... 58 B6
Bazhou, China ... 56 E9
Bazmān, Kūh-e, Iran ... 71 D9
Beach, U.S.A. ... 112 B3
Beach City, U.S.A. ... 116 F3
Beachport, Australia ... 95 F3
Beachy Hd., U.K. ... 15 G8
Beacon, Australia ... 93 F2
Beacon, U.S.A. ... 117 E11
Beaconsfield, Australia ... 95 G4
Beagle, Canal, S. Amer. ... 128 H3
Beagle Bay, Australia ... 92 C3
Bealanana, Madag. ... 89 A8
Beals Cr. ➔, U.S.A. ... 113 J4
Beamsville, Canada ... 116 C5
Bear ➔, Calif., U.S.A. ... 110 G5
Bear ➔, Utah, U.S.A. ... 106 B4
Béar, C., France ... 20 F7
Bear I., Ireland ... 12 E2
Bear L., Canada ... 103 B9
Bear L., U.S.A. ... 108 F8
Beardmore, Canada ... 104 C2
Beardmore Glacier, Antarctica ... 5 E11
Beardstown, U.S.A. ... 112 F9
Bearma ➔, India ... 69 G8
Béarn, France ... 20 E3
Bearpaw Mts., U.S.A. ... 108 B9
Bearskin Lake, Canada ... 104 B1
Beas ➔, India ... 68 D6
Beas de Segura, Spain ... 37 G8
Beasain, Spain ... 38 B2
Beata, C., Dom. Rep. ... 121 C5
Beata, I., Dom. Rep. ... 121 C5
Beatrice, U.S.A. ... 112 E6
Beatrice, Zimbabwe ... 87 F3
Beatrice, C., Australia ... 94 A2
Beatton ➔, Canada ... 102 B4
Beatton River, Canada ... 102 B4
Beatty, U.S.A. ... 110 J10
Beaucaire, France ... 21 E8
Beauce, Plaine de la, France ... 19 D8
Beauceville, Canada ... 105 C5
Beaudesert, Australia ... 95 D5
Beaufort, France ... 21 C10
Beaufort, Malaysia ... 62 C5
Beaufort, N.C., U.S.A. ... 115 H7
Beaufort, S.C., U.S.A. ... 115 J5
Beaufort Sea, Arctic ... 98 B5
Beaufort West, S. Africa ... 88 E3
Beaugency, France ... 19 E8
Beauharnois, Canada ... 117 A11
Beaujeu, France ... 19 F11
Beaujolais, France ... 19 F11
Beaulieu ➔, Canada ... 102 A6
Beaulieu-sur-Dordogne, France ... 20 D5
Beaulieu-sur-Mer, France ... 21 E11
Beauly, U.K. ... 13 D4
Beauly ➔, U.K. ... 13 D4
Beaumaris, U.K. ... 14 D3
Beaumont, Belgium ... 17 D4
Beaumont, France ... 20 D4
Beaumont, U.S.A. ... 113 K7
Beaumont-de-Lomagne, France ... 20 E4
Beaumont-le-Roger, France ... 18 C7
Beaumont-sur-Sarthe, France ... 18 D7
Beaune, France ... 19 E11

Beaune-la-Rolande, France ... 19 D9
Beaupré, Canada ... 105 C5
Beaupréau, France ... 18 E6
Beauraing, Belgium ... 17 D4
Beaurepaire, France ... 21 C9
Beausejour, Canada ... 103 C9
Beauvais, France ... 19 C9
Beauval, Canada ... 103 B7
Beauvoir-sur-Mer, France ... 18 F4
Beauvoir-sur-Niort, France ... 20 B3
Beaver, Okla., U.S.A. ... 113 G4
Beaver, Pa., U.S.A. ... 116 F4
Beaver, Utah, U.S.A. ... 109 G7
Beaver ➔, B.C., Canada ... 102 B4
Beaver ➔, Ont., Canada ... 104 A2
Beaver ➔, Sask., Canada ... 103 B7
Beaver ➔, U.S.A. ... 113 G5
Beaver City, U.S.A. ... 112 E5
Beaver Creek, Canada ... 100 B5
Beaver Dam, U.S.A. ... 112 D10
Beaver Falls, U.S.A. ... 116 F4
Beaver Hill L., Canada ... 103 C10
Beaver I., U.S.A. ... 114 C3
Beaverhill L., Canada ... 102 C6
Beaverlodge, Canada ... 102 B5
Beaverstone ➔, Canada ... 104 B2
Beaverton, Canada ... 116 B5
Beaverton, U.S.A. ... 110 E4
Beawar, India ... 68 F6
Bebedouro, Brazil ... 127 A6
Bebera, Tanjung, Indonesia ... 63 K18
Beboa, Madag. ... 89 B7
Bebra, Germany ... 24 E5
Becan, Mexico ... 119 D7
Beccles, U.K. ... 15 E9
Bečej, Serbia & M. ... 28 E5
Beceni, Romania ... 29 E11
Becerreá, Spain ... 36 C3
Béchar, Algeria ... 78 B5
Bechyně, Czech Rep. ... 26 B7
Beckley, U.S.A. ... 114 G5
Beckum, Germany ... 24 D4
Beclean, Romania ... 29 C9
Bečov nad Teplou, Czech Rep. ... 26 A5
Bečva ➔, Czech Rep. ... 27 B10
Bédar, Spain ... 39 H3
Bédarieux, France ... 20 E7
Beddouza, Ras, Morocco ... 78 B4
Bedele, Ethiopia ... 81 F4
Bederkesa, Germany ... 24 B4
Bedeso, Ethiopia ... 81 F5
Bedford, Canada ... 117 A12
Bedford, S. Africa ... 88 E4
Bedford, U.K. ... 15 E7
Bedford, Ind., U.S.A. ... 114 F2
Bedford, Iowa, U.S.A. ... 112 E7
Bedford, Ohio, U.S.A. ... 116 E3
Bedford, Pa., U.S.A. ... 116 F6
Bedford, Va., U.S.A. ... 114 G6
Bedford, C., Australia ... 94 B4
Bedfordshire □, U.K. ... 15 E7
Bednja ➔, Croatia ... 41 B13
Bednodemyanovsk, Russia ... 34 D6
Bedok, Singapore ... 65 d
Bedónia, Italy ... 40 D6
Bedourie, Australia ... 94 C2
Bedum, Neths. ... 17 A6
Będzin, Poland ... 31 H6
Beebe Plain, Canada ... 117 A12
Beech Creek, U.S.A. ... 116 E7
Beef I., Br. Virgin Is. ... 121 e
Beelitz, Germany ... 24 C8
Beenleigh, Australia ... 95 D5
Be'er Menuha, Israel ... 70 D2
Be'er Sheva, Israel ... 74 D3
Beersheba = Be'er Sheva, Israel ... 74 D3
Beeskow, Germany ... 24 C10
Beesteekraal, S. Africa ... 89 D4
Beeston, U.K. ... 14 E6
Beetzendorf, Germany ... 24 C7
Beeville, U.S.A. ... 113 L6
Befale, Dem. Rep. of the Congo ... 84 D4
Befandriana, Mahajanga, Madag. ... 89 B8
Befandriana, Toliara, Madag. ... 89 C7
Befasy, Madag. ... 89 C7
Befotaka, Antsiranana, Madag. ... 89 A8
Befotaka, Fianarantsoa, Madag. ... 89 C8
Bega, Australia ... 95 F4
Bega, Canalul, Romania ... 28 E5
Bégard, France ... 18 D3
Beğendik, Turkey ... 45 F10
Begoro, Ghana ... 83 D4
Begusarai, India ... 69 G12
Behābād, Iran ... 71 C8
Behala, India ... 69 H13
Behara, Madag. ... 89 C8
Behbehān, Iran ... 71 D6
Behm Canal, U.S.A. ... 102 B2
Behshahr, Iran ... 71 B7
Bei Jiang ➔, China ... 59 F9
Bei'an, China ... 60 B7
Beibei, China ... 58 C6
Beichuan, China ... 58 B5
Beihai, China ... 58 G7
Beijing, China ... 56 E9
Beijing □, China ... 56 E9
Beilen, Neths. ... 17 B6
Beiliu, China ... 59 F8
Beilngries, Germany ... 25 F7
Beilpajah, Australia ... 95 E3
Beinn na Faoghla = Benbecula, U.K. ... 13 D1
Beipan Jiang ➔, China ... 58 E5
Beipiao, China ... 57 D11
Beira, Mozam. ... 87 F3
Beirut = Bayrūt, Lebanon ... 74 B4
Beiseker, Canada ... 102 C6
Beitaolaizhao, China ... 57 B13
Beitbridge, Zimbabwe ... 87 G3
Beiuş, Romania ... 28 D7

Beizhen = Binzhou, China ... 57 F10
Beizhen, China ... 57 D11
Beizhengzhen, China ... 57 B12
Beja, Portugal ... 37 G3
Béja, Tunisia ... 79 A7
Beja □, Portugal ... 37 H3
Bejaïa, Algeria ... 78 A7
Béjar, Spain ... 36 E5
Bejestān, Iran ... 71 C8
Bekçiler, Turkey ... 47 E11
Békés, Hungary ... 28 D6
Békés □, Hungary ... 28 D6
Békéscsaba, Hungary ... 28 D6
Bekilli, Turkey ... 47 C11
Bekily, Madag. ... 89 C8
Bekisopa, Madag. ... 89 C8
Bekitro, Madag. ... 89 C8
Bekodoka, Madag. ... 89 B8
Bekoji, Ethiopia ... 81 F4
Bekok, Malaysia ... 65 L4
Bekopaka, Madag. ... 89 B7
Bekwai, Ghana ... 83 D4
Bela, India ... 69 G10
Bela, Pakistan ... 68 F2
Bela, S. Africa ... 89 C4
Bela Crkva, Serbia & M. ... 28 F6
Bela Palanka, Serbia & M. ... 44 C6
Bela Vista, Brazil ... 126 A4
Bela Vista, Mozam. ... 89 D5
Belalcázar, Spain ... 37 G5
Belan ➔, India ... 69 G9
Belanovica, Serbia & M. ... 44 B4
Belarus ■, Europe ... 32 F4
Belau = Palau ■, Pac. Oc. ... 96 G5
Belavenona, Madag. ... 89 C8
Belawan, Indonesia ... 62 D1
Belaya ➔, Russia ... 52 C6
Belaya Glina, Russia ... 35 G5
Belaya Kalitva, Russia ... 35 F5
Belaya Tserkov = Bila Tserkva, Ukraine ... 33 H6
Belcești, Romania ... 29 C12
Belchatów, Poland ... 31 G6
Belcher Is., Canada ... 104 A3
Belchite, Spain ... 38 D4
Belden, U.S.A. ... 110 E5
Beled Weyne = Belet Uen, Somali Rep. ... 75 G4
Belém, Brazil ... 125 D9
Belén, Argentina ... 126 B2
Belén, Paraguay ... 126 A4
Belen, U.S.A. ... 109 J10
Belene, Bulgaria ... 45 C9
Beleni, Turkey ... 72 D7
Bélesta, France ... 20 F5
Belet Uen, Somali Rep. ... 75 G4
Belev, Russia ... 32 F9
Belevi, Turkey ... 47 C9
Belfair, U.S.A. ... 110 C4
Belfast, S. Africa ... 89 D5
Belfast, U.K. ... 12 B6
Belfast, Maine, U.S.A. ... 115 C11
Belfast, N.Y., U.S.A. ... 116 D6
Belfast L., U.K. ... 12 B6
Belfield, U.S.A. ... 112 B3
Belfort, France ... 19 E13
Belfort, Territoire de □, France ... 19 E13
Belfry, U.S.A. ... 108 D9
Belgaum, India ... 66 M9
Belgioioso, Italy ... 40 C6
Belgium ■, Europe ... 17 D4
Belgodère, France ... 21 F13
Belgorod, Russia ... 33 G9
Belgorod-Dnestrovskiy = Bilhorod-Dnistrovskyy, Ukraine ... 33 J6
Belgrade = Beograd, Serbia & M ... 44 B4
Belgrade, U.S.A. ... 108 D8
Belhaven, U.S.A. ... 115 H7
Beli Drim ➔, Europe ... 44 D4
Beli Manastir, Croatia ... 28 E3
Beli Timok ➔, Serbia & M. ... 44 C6
Bélice ➔, Italy ... 42 E5
Belimbing, Indonesia ... 63 J18
Belinskiy, Russia ... 34 D6
Belinyu, Indonesia ... 62 E3
Beliton Is. = Belitung, Indonesia ... 62 E3
Belitung, Indonesia ... 62 E3
Beliu, Romania ... 28 D6
Belize ■, Cent. Amer. ... 119 D7
Belize City, Belize ... 119 D7
Beljakovci, Macedonia ... 44 D5
Beljanica, Serbia & M. ... 44 B5
Belkovskiy, Ostrov, Russia ... 53 B14
Bell ➔, Canada ... 104 C4
Bell I., Canada ... 105 B8
Bell-Irving ➔, Canada ... 102 B3
Bell Peninsula, Canada ... 101 B11
Bell Ville, Argentina ... 126 C3
Bella, Italy ... 43 B8
Bella Bella, Canada ... 102 C3
Bella Coola, Canada ... 102 C3
Bella Unión, Uruguay ... 126 C4
Bella Vista, Corrientes, Argentina ... 126 B4
Bella Vista, Tucuman, Argentina ... 126 B2
Bellac, France ... 20 B5
Bellágio, Italy ... 40 C6
Bellaire, U.S.A. ... 116 F4
Bellária, Italy ... 41 D9
Bellary, India ... 66 M10
Bellata, Australia ... 95 D4
Belle-Chasse, U.S.A. ... 113 L10
Belle Fourche, U.S.A. ... 112 C3
Belle Fourche ➔, U.S.A. ... 112 C3
Belle Glade, U.S.A. ... 115 M5
Belle-Île, France ... 18 E3
Belle Isle, Canada ... 105 B8
Belle Isle, Str. of, Canada ... 105 B8
Belle Plaine, U.S.A. ... 112 E8

Belle Yella, Liberia ... 82 D3
Belledonne, France ... 21 C10
Bellefontaine, U.S.A. ... 114 E4
Bellefonte, U.S.A. ... 116 F7
Bellegarde, France ... 19 E9
Bellegarde-en-Marche, France ... 20 C6
Bellegarde-sur-Valserine, France ... 19 F12
Bellême, France ... 18 D7
Belleoram, Canada ... 105 C8
Belleplaine, Barbados ... 121 g
Belleville, Canada ... 116 B7
Belleville, France ... 19 F11
Belleville, Ill., U.S.A. ... 112 F10
Belleville, Kans., U.S.A. ... 112 F6
Belleville, N.Y., U.S.A. ... 117 C8
Belleville-sur-Vie, France ... 18 F5
Bellevue, Canada ... 102 D6
Bellevue, Idaho, U.S.A. ... 108 E6
Bellevue, Nebr., U.S.A. ... 112 E7
Bellevue, Ohio, U.S.A. ... 116 E2
Bellevue, Wash., U.S.A. ... 110 C4
Belley, France ... 21 C9
Bellin = Kangirsuk, Canada ... 101 B13
Bellingen, Australia ... 95 E5
Bellingham, U.S.A. ... 100 D7
Bellingshausen Sea, Antarctica ... 5 C17
Bellinzona, Switz. ... 25 J5
Bello, Colombia ... 124 B3
Bellows Falls, U.S.A. ... 117 C12
Bellpat, Pakistan ... 68 E3
Bellpuig d'Urgell, Spain ... 38 D6
Belluno, Italy ... 41 B9
Bellwood, U.S.A. ... 116 F6
Bélmez, Spain ... 37 G5
Belmont, Canada ... 116 D3
Belmont, S. Africa ... 88 D3
Belmont, U.S.A. ... 116 D6
Belmonte, Brazil ... 125 G11
Belmonte, Portugal ... 36 E3
Belmonte, Spain ... 39 F2
Belmopan, Belize ... 119 D7
Belmullet, Ireland ... 12 B2
Belo Horizonte, Brazil ... 125 G10
Belo-sur-Mer, Madag. ... 89 C7
Belo-Tsiribihina, Madag. ... 89 B7
Belogorsk = Bilohirsk, Ukraine ... 33 K8
Belogorsk, Russia ... 53 D13
Belogradchik, Bulgaria ... 44 C6
Belogradets, Bulgaria ... 45 C11
Beloha, Madag. ... 89 D8
Beloit, Kans., U.S.A. ... 112 F5
Beloit, Wis., U.S.A. ... 112 D10
Belokorovichi, Ukraine ... 33 G5
Belomorsk, Russia ... 52 C4
Belonia, India ... 67 H17
Belopolye = Bilopillya, Ukraine ... 33 G8
Belorechensk, Russia ... 35 H4
Belorussia = Belarus ■, Europe ... 32 F4
Beloslav, Bulgaria ... 45 C11
Belovo, Bulgaria ... 45 D8
Belovo, Russia ... 52 D9
Belovodsk, Ukraine ... 33 H10
Beloye More, Russia ... 52 C4
Belozem, Bulgaria ... 45 D9
Belozersk, Russia ... 32 B9
Belpasso, Italy ... 43 E7
Belpre, U.S.A. ... 114 F5
Belrain, India ... 69 E9
Belt, U.S.A. ... 108 C8
Beltana, Australia ... 95 E2
Belterra, Brazil ... 125 D8
Beltinci, Slovenia ... 41 B13
Belton, U.S.A. ... 113 K6
Belton L., U.S.A. ... 113 K6
Beltsy = Bălţi, Moldova ... 29 C12
Belturbet, Ireland ... 12 B4
Belukha, Russia ... 52 E9
Beluran, Malaysia ... 62 C5
Belušía, Slovak Rep. ... 27 B11
Belušić, Serbia & M. ... 44 C5
Belvedere Maríttimo, Italy ... 43 C8
Belvès, France ... 20 D5
Belvidere, Ill., U.S.A. ... 112 D10
Belvidere, N.J., U.S.A. ... 117 F9
Belvis de la Jara, Spain ... 36 F6
Belyando ➔, Australia ... 94 C4
Belyy, Russia ... 32 E7
Belyy, Ostrov, Russia ... 52 B8
Belyy Yar, Russia ... 52 D9
Belz, Ukraine ... 31 H11
Bełżec, Poland ... 31 H10
Belzig, Germany ... 24 C8
Belzoni, U.S.A. ... 113 J9
Bełżyce, Poland ... 31 G9
Bemaraha, Lembalemban' i, Madag. ... 89 B7
Bemarivo, Madag. ... 89 C7
Bemarivo, Antsiranana, Madag. ... 89 A9
Bemarivo ➔, Mahajanga, Madag. ... 89 B7
Bemavo, Madag. ... 89 C8
Bembéréke, Benin ... 83 C5
Bembesi, Zimbabwe ... 87 F2
Bembesi ➔, Zimbabwe ... 87 G2
Bembézar ➔, Spain ... 37 H5
Bembibre, Spain ... 36 C4
Bemetara, India ... 69 J9
Bemidji, U.S.A. ... 112 B7
Bemolanga, Madag. ... 89 B8
Ben, Iran ... 71 C6
Ben Cruachan, U.K. ... 13 E3
Ben Dearg, U.K. ... 13 D4
Ben En △, Vietnam ... 64 C5
Ben Hope, U.K. ... 13 C4
Ben Lawers, U.K. ... 13 E4
Ben Lomond, N.S.W., Australia ... 95 E5
Ben Lomond, Tas., Australia ... 95 G4
Ben Lomond, U.K. ... 13 E4
Ben Lomond △, Australia ... 95 G4
Ben Luc, Vietnam ... 65 G6

Ben Macdhui, *U.K.* 13 D5
Ben Mhor, *U.K.* 13 D1
Ben More, *Arg. & Bute, U.K.* ... 13 E2
Ben More, *Stirl., U.K.* 13 E4
Ben More Assynt, *U.K.* 13 C4
Ben Nevis, *U.K.* 13 E3
Ben Quang, *Vietnam* 64 D6
Ben Vorlich, *U.K.* 13 E4
Ben Wyvis, *U.K.* 13 D4
Bena, *Nigeria* 83 C6
Benalla, *Australia* 95 F4
Benalmádena, *Spain* 37 J6
Bénat, C., *France* 21 E10
Benavente, *Portugal* 37 G2
Benavente, *Spain* 36 C5
Benavides, *U.S.A.* 113 M5
Benavides de Órbigo, *Spain* ... 36 C5
Benbecula, *U.K.* 13 D1
Benbonyathe, *Australia* 95 E2
Bend, *U.S.A.* 108 D3
Bender Beila, *Somali Rep.* 75 F5
Bendery = Tighina, *Moldova* ... 29 D14
Bendigo, *Australia* 95 F3
Bendorf, *Germany* 24 E3
Benē Beraq, *Israel* 74 C3
Bénéna, *Mali* 82 C4
Benenitra, *Madag.* 89 C8
Benešov, *Czech Rep.* 26 B7
Benevento, *Italy* 43 A7
Benfeld, *France* 19 D14
Benga, *Mozam.* 87 F3
Bengal, Bay of, *Ind. Oc.* 67 M17
Bengalūru = Bangalore, *India* ... 66 N10
Bengbis, *Cameroon* 83 E7
Bengbu, *China* 57 H9
Benghazi = Banghāzī, *Libya* ... 79 B10
Bengkalis, *Indonesia* 62 D2
Bengkulu, *Indonesia* 62 E2
Bengkulu □, *Indonesia* 62 E2
Bengough, *Canada* 103 D7
Bengtsfors, *Sweden* 10 E6
Benguela, *Angola* 85 G2
Benguérua, I., *Mozam.* 89 C6
Benha, *Egypt* 80 H7
Beni, *Dem. Rep. of the Congo* ... 86 B2
Beni →, *Bolivia* 124 F5
Beni Mazâr, *Egypt* 80 B3
Beni Mellal, *Morocco* 78 B4
Beni Suef, *Egypt* 80 J7
Beniah L., *Canada* 102 A6
Benicarló, *Spain* 38 E5
Benicàssim, *Spain* 38 E5
Benicia, *U.S.A.* 110 G4
Benidorm, *Spain* 39 G4
Benin ■, *Africa* 83 D5
Benin →, *Nigeria* 83 D6
Benin, Bight of, *W. Afr.* 83 E5
Benin City, *Nigeria* 83 D6
Benisa, *Spain* 39 G5
Benitses, *Greece* 49 A3
Benjamin Aceval, *Paraguay* ... 126 A4
Benjamin Constant, *Brazil* 124 D4
Benjamin Hill, *Mexico* 118 A2
Benkelman, *U.S.A.* 112 E4
Benkovac, *Croatia* 41 D12
Bennett, *Canada* 102 B2
Bennett, L., *Australia* 92 D5
Bennetta, Ostrov, *Russia* 53 B15
Bennettsville, *U.S.A.* 115 H6
Bennichchāb, *Mauritania* 82 B1
Bennington, *N.H., U.S.A.* 117 D11
Bennington, *Vt., U.S.A.* 117 D11
Bénodet, *France* 18 E2
Benoni, *S. Africa* 89 D4
Benque Viejo del Carmen, *Belize* 119 D7
Bensheim, *Germany* 25 F4
Benson, *Ariz., U.S.A.* 109 L8
Benson, *Minn., U.S.A.* 112 C7
Bent, *Iran* 71 E8
Benteng, *Indonesia* 63 F6
Bentinck I., *Australia* 94 B2
Bentiu, *Sudan* 81 F2
Bento Gonçalves, *Brazil* 127 B5
Benton, *Ark., U.S.A.* 113 H8
Benton, *Calif., U.S.A.* 110 H8
Benton, *Ill., U.S.A.* 112 G10
Benton, *Pa., U.S.A.* 117 E8
Benton Harbor, *U.S.A.* 114 D2
Bentong, *Malaysia* 65 L3
Bentonville, *U.S.A.* 113 G7
Bentu Liben, *Ethiopia* 81 F4
Benue □, *Nigeria* 83 D6
Benue →, *Nigeria* 83 D6
Benxi, *China* 57 D12
Beo, *Indonesia* 63 D7
Beograd, *Serbia & M.* 44 B4
Beograd ✈ (BEG), *Serbia & M.* . 44 C4
Beoumi, *Ivory C.* 82 D3
Bepan Jiang →, *China* 58 E6
Beppu, *Japan* 55 H5
Beqaa Valley = Al Biqâ, *Lebanon* 74 A5
Ber Mota, *India* 68 H3
Berach →, *India* 68 G6
Beraketa, *Madag.* 89 C7
Berane, *Serbia & M.* 44 D3
Berat, *Albania* 44 F3
Berau, Teluk, *Indonesia* 63 E8
Beravina, *Madag.* 89 B8
Berber, *Sudan* 80 D3
Berbera, *Somali Rep.* 75 E4
Berbérati, *C.A.R.* 84 D3
Berbice →, *Guyana* 124 B7
Berceto, *Italy* 40 D6
Berchidda, *Italy* 42 B2
Berchtesgaden, *Germany* 25 H8
Berchtesgaden △, *Germany* ... 25 H8
Berck, *France* 19 B8
Berdichev = Berdychiv, *Ukraine* 33 H5
Berdsk, *Russia* 52 D9
Berdyansk, *Ukraine* 33 J9
Berdychiv, *Ukraine* 33 H5

Berea, *U.S.A.* 114 G3
Berebere, *Indonesia* 63 D7
Bereda, *Somali Rep.* 75 E5
Berehomet, *Ukraine* 29 B10
Berehove, *Ukraine* 28 B7
Berekum, *Ghana* 82 D4
Berenice, *Egypt* 80 C4
Berens →, *Canada* 103 C9
Berens I., *Canada* 103 C9
Berens River, *Canada* 103 C9
Beresford, *U.S.A.* 112 D6
Berestechko, *Ukraine* 33 G3
Bereşti, *Romania* 29 D12
Beretău →, *Romania* 28 C6
Berettyó →, *Hungary* 28 D6
Berettyóújfalu, *Hungary* 28 C6
Berevo, *Mahajanga, Madag.* ... 89 B7
Berevo, *Toliara, Madag.* 89 B7
Bereza = Byaroza, *Belarus* 33 F3
Berezhany, *Ukraine* 33 H3
Berezina = Byarezina →, *Belarus* 33 F6
Berezivka, *Ukraine* 33 J6
Berezna, *Ukraine* 33 G6
Bereznik, *Russia* 52 C5
Berezniki, *Russia* 52 D6
Berezovo, *Russia* 52 C7
Berezyne, *Ukraine* 29 D14
Berga, *Spain* 38 C6
Berga, *Sweden* 11 G10
Bergama, *Turkey* 47 B9
Bérgamo, *Italy* 40 C6
Bergara, *Spain* 38 B2
Bergby, *Sweden* 10 D11
Bergedorf, *Germany* 24 B6
Bergeforsen, *Sweden* 10 B11
Bergen,
  Mecklenburg-Vorpommern,
  Germany 24 A9
Bergen, *Niedersachsen, Germany* 24 C5
Bergen, *Neths.* 17 B4
Bergen, *Norway* 9 F11
Bergen, *U.S.A.* 116 C7
Bergen op Zoom, *Neths.* 17 C4
Bergerac, *France* 20 D4
Bergheim, *Germany* 24 E2
Bergholz, *U.S.A.* 116 F4
Bergisch Gladbach, *Germany* .. 17 D7
Bergisches Land △, *Germany* .. 24 E3
Bergkamen, *Germany* 24 D3
Bergkvara, *Sweden* 11 H10
Bergshamra, *Sweden* 10 E12
Bergsjö, *Sweden* 10 C11
Bergstrasse-Odenwald △,
  Germany 25 F1
Bergues, *France* 19 B9
Bergviken, *Sweden* 10 C10
Bergville, *S. Africa* 89 D4
Berhala, Selat, *Indonesia* 62 E2
Berhampore = Baharampur, *India* 69 G13
Berhampur = Brahmapur, *India* . 67 K14
Berheci →, *Romania* 29 E12
Bering Sea, *Pac. Oc.* 100 C1
Bering Strait, *Pac. Oc.* 100 B3
Beringovskiy, *Russia* 53 C18
Berisso, *Argentina* 126 C4
Berja, *Spain* 37 J8
Berkeley, *U.S.A.* 110 H4
Berkner I., *Antarctica* 5 D18
Berkovitsa, *Bulgaria* 44 C7
Berkshire, *U.S.A.* 117 D8
Berkshire Downs, *U.K.* 15 F6
Berlanga, *Spain* 37 G5
Berlenga, I., *Portugal* 37 F1
Berlin, *Germany* 24 C9
Berlin, *Md., U.S.A.* 114 F8
Berlin, *N.H., U.S.A.* 117 B13
Berlin, *N.Y., U.S.A.* 117 D11
Berlin, *Wis., U.S.A.* 114 D1
Berlin □, *Germany* 24 C9
Berlin L., *U.S.A.* 116 E4
Berlin Tegel ✈ (TXL), *Germany* 24 C9
Bermeja, *Sierra, Spain* 37 J5
Bermejo →, *Formosa, Argentina* 126 B4
Bermejo →, *San Juan, Argentina* 126 C2
Bermen, L., *Canada* 105 B6
Bermeo, *Spain* 38 B2
Bermillo de Sayago, *Spain* 36 D4
Bermuda ☑, *Atl. Oc.* 98 F13
Bern, *Switz.* 25 J3
Bern □, *Switz.* 25 J3
Bernalda, *Italy* 43 B9
Bernalillo, *U.S.A.* 109 J10
Bernardo de Irigoyen, *Argentina* 127 B5
Bernardo O'Higgins □, *Chile* .. 126 C1
Bernardsville, *U.S.A.* 117 F10
Bernasconi, *Argentina* 126 D3
Bernau, *Bayern, Germany* 25 H8
Bernau, *Brandenburg, Germany* . 24 C9
Bernay, *France* 18 C7
Bernburg, *Germany* 24 D7
Berndorf, *Austria* 26 D9
Berne = Bern, *Switz.* 25 J3
Berne □, *Switz.* 25 J3
Berner Alpen, *Switz.* 25 J3
Berneray, *U.K.* 13 D1
Bernier I., *Australia* 93 D1
Bernina, Piz, *Switz.* 25 J5
Bernkastel-Kues, *Germany* 25 F3
Beroroha, *Madag.* 89 C8
Béroubouay, *Benin* 83 C5
Beroun, *Czech Rep.* 26 B7
Berounka →, *Czech Rep.* 26 B7
Berre, Étang de, *France* 21 E9
Berre-l'Étang, *France* 21 E9
Berri, *Australia* 95 E3
Berriane, *Algeria* 78 B6
Berry, *Australia* 95 E5
Berry, *France* 19 F8
Berry Is., *Bahamas* 120 A4
Berryessa L., *U.S.A.* 110 G4
Berryville, *U.S.A.* 113 G8

Berseba, *Namibia* 88 D2
Bersenbrück, *Germany* 24 C3
Bershad, *Ukraine* 29 B14
Bershad, *U.S.A.* 112 A4
Berthold, *U.S.A.* 112 A4
Berthoud, *U.S.A.* 112 E2
Bertincourt, *France* 19 B9
Bertoua, *Cameroon* 84 D2
Bertraghboy B., *Ireland* 12 C2
Berwick, *U.S.A.* 117 E8
Berwick-upon-Tweed, *U.K.* ... 14 B6
Berwyn Mts., *U.K.* 14 E4
Beryslav, *Ukraine* 33 J7
Berzasca, *Romania* 28 F6
Berzence, *Hungary* 28 D2
Besal, *Pakistan* 69 B5
Besalampy, *Madag.* 89 B7
Besançon, *France* 19 E13
Besar, *Indonesia* 62 E5
Beshenkovichi, *Belarus* 32 E5
Beška, *Serbia & M.* 28 E5
Beslan, *Russia* 35 J7
Besna Kobila, *Serbia & M.* 44 D6
Besnard L., *Canada* 103 B7
Besni, *Turkey* 70 B3
Besor, N. →, *Egypt* 74 D3
Bessarabiya, *Moldova* 33 J5
Bessarabka = Basarabeasca,
  Moldova 29 D13
Bessèges, *France* 21 D8
Bessemer, *Ala., U.S.A.* 115 J2
Bessemer, *Mich., U.S.A.* 112 B9
Bessemer, *Pa., U.S.A.* 116 F4
Bessin, *France* 18 C6
Bessines-sur-Gartempe, *France* . 20 B5
Beswick, *Australia* 92 B5
Bet She'an, *Israel* 74 C4
Bet Shemesh, *Israel* 74 D4
Betafo, *Madag.* 89 B8
Betancuria, *Canary Is.* 48 F5
Betanzos, *Spain* 36 B2
Bétaré Oya, *Cameroon* 84 C2
Betatao, *Madag.* 89 B8
Bétera, *Spain* 39 F4
Bétérou, *Benin* 83 D5
Bethal, *S. Africa* 89 D4
Bethanien, *Namibia* 88 D2
Bethany, *Canada* 116 B6
Bethany, *U.S.A.* 112 E7
Bethel, *Alaska, U.S.A.* 100 B3
Bethel, *Conn., U.S.A.* 117 E11
Bethel, *Maine, U.S.A.* 117 B14
Bethel, *Vt., U.S.A.* 117 C12
Bethel Park, *U.S.A.* 116 F4
Béthenville, *France* 19 C11
Bethlehem = Bayt Laḥm,
  West Bank 74 D4
Bethlehem, *S. Africa* 89 D4
Bethlehem, *U.S.A.* 117 F9
Bethulie, *S. Africa* 88 E4
Béthune, *France* 19 B9
Béthune →, *France* 18 C8
Betioky, *Madag.* 89 C7
Betong, *Thailand* 65 K3
Betoota, *Australia* 94 D3
Betor, *Ethiopia* 81 E4
Betroka, *Madag.* 89 C8
Betsiamites, *Canada* 105 C6
Betsiamites →, *Canada* 105 C6
Betsiboka →, *Madag.* 89 B8
Bettendorf, *U.S.A.* 112 E9
Bettiah, *India* 69 F11
Bettna, *Sweden* 11 F10
Béttola, *Italy* 40 D6
Betul, *India* 66 J10
Betung, *Malaysia* 62 D4
Betws-y-Coed, *U.K.* 14 D4
Betxi, *Spain* 38 F4
Betzdorf, *Germany* 24 E3
Beuil, *France* 21 D10
Beulah, *Mich., U.S.A.* 114 C2
Beulah, *N. Dak., U.S.A.* 112 B4
Beuvron →, *France* 18 E8
Beveren, *Belgium* 17 C4
Beverley, *Australia* 93 F2
Beverley, *U.K.* 14 D7
Beverley Hills, *U.S.A.* 115 L4
Beverly, *U.S.A.* 117 D14
Beverly Hills, *U.S.A.* 111 L8
Beverungen, *Germany* 24 D5
Bevoalavo, *Madag.* 89 D7
Bewas →, *India* 69 H8
Bex, *Switz.* 25 J3
Bexhill, *U.K.* 15 G8
Bey Dağları, *Turkey* 47 E12
Beyānlū, *Iran* 70 C5
Beyazköy, *Turkey* 45 E11
Beyçayırı, *Turkey* 45 F10
Beydağ, *Turkey* 47 C10
Beyin, *Ghana* 82 D4
Beykoz, *Turkey* 45 E13
Beyla, *Guinea* 82 D3
Beynat, *France* 20 C5
Beyneu, *Kazakhstan* 52 E6
Beyoba, *Turkey* 47 C9
Beyoğlu, *Turkey* 45 E12
Beypazarı, *Turkey* 72 B4
Beyşehir, *Turkey* 72 D4
Beyşehir Gölü, *Turkey* 70 B1
Beytüşşebap, *Turkey* 73 D10
Bezdan, *Serbia & M.* 28 E3
Bezhetsk, *Russia* 32 D9
Béziers, *France* 20 E7
Bezwada = Vijayawada, *India* .. 67 L12
Bhabua, *India* 69 G10
Bhachau, *India* 66 H7
Bhadar →, *Gujarat, India* 68 H5
Bhadarwah, *India* 69 C6
Bhadgaon = Bhaktapur, *Nepal* . 69 F11
Bhadohi, *India* 69 G10
Bhadra, *India* 68 E6

Bhadrakh, *India* 67 J15
Bhadran, *India* 68 H5
Bhadravati, *India* 66 N9
Bhag, *Pakistan* 68 E2
Bhagalpur, *India* 69 G12
Bhagirathi →, *Uttaranchal, India* 69 D8
Bhagirathi →, *W. Bengal, India* . 69 H13
Bhakkar, *Pakistan* 68 D4
Bhakra Dam, *India* 68 D7
Bhaktapur, *Nepal* 69 F11
Bhamo, *Burma* 67 G20
Bhandara, *India* 66 J11
Bhanpura, *India* 68 G6
Bhanrer Ra., *India* 69 H8
Bhaptiahi, *India* 69 F12
Bharat = India ■, *Asia* 66 K11
Bharatpur, *Chhattisgarh, India* . 69 H9
Bharatpur, *Raj., India* 68 F7
Bharno, *India* 69 H11
Bharuch, *India* 66 J8
Bhatinda, *India* 68 D6
Bhatpara, *India* 69 H13
Bhattu, *India* 68 E6
Bhaun, *Pakistan* 68 C5
Bhaunagar = Bhavnagar, *India* . 66 J8
Bhavnagar, *India* 68 J8
Bhawari, *India* 68 G5
Bhayavadar, *India* 68 J4
Bhera, *Pakistan* 68 C5
Bhikangaon, *India* 68 J6
Bhilsa = Vidisha, *India* 68 H7
Bhilwara, *India* 68 G6
Bhima →, *India* 66 L10
Bhimbar, *Pakistan* 69 C6
Bhind, *India* 69 F8
Bhinga, *India* 69 F9
Bhinmal, *India* 68 G5
Bhiwandi, *India* 66 K8
Bhiwani, *India* 68 E7
Bhogava →, *India* 68 H5
Bhola, *Bangla.* 67 H17
Bholari, *Pakistan* 68 G3
Bhopal, *India* 68 H7
Bhubaneshwar, *India* 67 J14
Bhuj, *India* 68 H3
Bhumiphol Res., *Thailand* 64 D2
Bhusawal, *India* 66 J9
Bhutan ■, *Asia* 67 F17
Biafra, B. of = Bonny, Bight of,
  Africa 83 E6
Biak, *Indonesia* 63 E9
Biała, *Poland* 31 H4
Biała →, *Poland* 31 H7
Biała Piska, *Poland* 30 E9
Biała Podlaska, *Poland* 31 F10
Biała Rawska, *Poland* 31 G7
Białobrzegi, *Poland* 31 G7
Białogard, *Poland* 30 D2
Białowieski △, *Poland* 31 F10
Białowieża, *Poland* 31 F10
Biały Bór, *Poland* 30 E3
Białystok, *Poland* 31 E10
Biancavilla, *Italy* 43 E7
Bianco, *Italy* 43 D9
Biankouma, *Ivory C.* 82 D3
Biaora, *India* 68 H7
Bīārjmand, *Iran* 71 B7
Biaro, *Indonesia* 63 D7
Biarritz, *France* 20 E2
Bias, *Indonesia* 63 J18
Biasca, *Switz.* 25 J4
Biba, *Egypt* 80 J7
Bibai, *Japan* 54 C10
Bibbiena, *Italy* 41 E8
Bibby I., *Canada* 103 A10
Bibel →, *Spain* 36 C3
Biberach, *Germany* 25 G5
Bibiani, *Ghana* 82 D4
Bibungwa, *Dem. Rep. of
  the Congo* 86 C2
Bicaj, *Albania* 44 E4
Bicaz, *Romania* 29 D11
Bicazu Ardelean, *Romania* 29 D10
Bíccari, *Italy* 43 A8
Bicester, *U.K.* 15 F6
Bichena, *Ethiopia* 81 E4
Bicheno, *Australia* 95 G4
Bichia, *India* 69 H9
Bichvinta, *Georgia* 35 J5
Bickerton I., *Australia* 94 A2
Bicske, *Hungary* 28 C3
Bida, *Nigeria* 83 D6
Bidar, *India* 66 L10
Biddeford, *U.S.A.* 115 D10
Biddwara, *Ethiopia* 81 F4
Bideford, *U.K.* 15 F3
Bideford Bay, *U.K.* 15 F3
Bidhuna, *India* 69 F8
Bidor, *Malaysia* 65 K3
Bie, *Sweden* 10 E10
Bié, Planalto de, *Angola* 85 G3
Bieber, *U.S.A.* 108 F3
Biebrza →, *Poland* 31 E9
Biebrzański △, *Poland* 30 E9
Biecz, *Poland* 31 J8
Biel, *Switz.* 25 H3
Bielawa, *Poland* 31 H3
Bielefeld, *Germany* 24 C4
Bielersee, *Switz.* 25 H3
Biella, *Italy* 40 C5
Bielsk Podlaski, *Poland* 31 F10
Bielsko-Biała, *Poland* 31 J6
Bien Hoa, *Vietnam* 65 G6
Bienne = Biel, *Switz.* 25 H3
Bienville, L., *Canada* 104 A5
Bierné, *France* 18 E6
Bierun, *Poland* 31 J6
Bierutów, *Poland* 31 G4
Biescas, *Spain* 38 C4
Biese →, *Germany* 24 C7
Biesiesfontein, *S. Africa* 88 E2

Bieszczadzki △, *Poland* 31 J9
Bietigheim-Bissingen, *Germany* . 25 G5
Bieżuń, *Poland* 31 F6
Biferno →, *Italy* 41 G12
Big →, *Canada* 105 B8
Big B., *Canada* 105 A7
Big Bear City, *U.S.A.* 111 L10
Big Bear Lake, *U.S.A.* 111 L10
Big Belt Mts., *U.S.A.* 108 C8
Big Bend △, *U.S.A.* 113 L3
Big Bend Swaziland* 89 D5
Big Black →, *U.S.A.* 113 K9
Big Blue →, *U.S.A.* 112 F6
Big Creek, *U.S.A.* 110 H7
Big Cypress △, *U.S.A.* 115 M5
Big Cypress Swamp, *U.S.A.* ... 115 M5
Big Falls, *U.S.A.* 112 A8
Big Fork →, *U.S.A.* 112 A8
Big Horn Mts. = Bighorn Mts.,
  U.S.A. 108 D10
Big I., *Canada* 102 A5
Big Lake, *U.S.A.* 113 K4
Big Moose, *U.S.A.* 117 C10
Big Muddy Cr. →, *U.S.A.* 112 A2
Big Pine, *U.S.A.* 110 H8
Big Piney, *U.S.A.* 108 E8
Big Rapids, *U.S.A.* 114 D3
Big Rideau L., *Canada* 117 B8
Big River, *Canada* 103 C7
Big Run, *U.S.A.* 116 F6
Big Sable Pt., *U.S.A.* 114 C2
Big Salmon →, *Canada* 102 A2
Big Sand L., *Canada* 103 B9
Big Sandy, *U.S.A.* 108 B8
Big Sandy →, *U.S.A.* 114 F4
Big Sandy Cr. →, *U.S.A.* 112 F3
Big Sioux →, *U.S.A.* 112 D6
Big South Fork △, *U.S.A.* 115 G3
Big Spring, *U.S.A.* 113 J4
Big Stone City, *U.S.A.* 112 C6
Big Stone Gap, *U.S.A.* 115 G4
Big Stone L., *U.S.A.* 112 C6
Big Sur, *U.S.A.* 110 J5
Big Timber, *U.S.A.* 108 D9
Big Trout L., *Canada* 104 B2
Big Trout Lake, *Canada* 104 B2
Biga, *Turkey* 45 F11
Biga →, *Turkey* 45 F11
Bigadiç, *Turkey* 47 B10
Biganos, *France* 20 D3
Biggar, *Canada* 103 C7
Biggar, *U.K.* 13 F5
Bigge I., *Australia* 92 B4
Biggenden, *Australia* 95 D5
Biggleswade, *U.K.* 15 E7
Biggs, *U.S.A.* 110 F5
Bighorn, *U.S.A.* 108 C10
Bighorn →, *U.S.A.* 108 C10
Bighorn Canyon △, *U.S.A.* ... 108 D9
Bighorn L., *U.S.A.* 108 D9
Bighorn Mts., *U.S.A.* 108 D10
Bignona, *Senegal* 82 C1
Bigorre, *France* 20 E4
Bigstone L., *Canada* 103 C9
Biguglia, Étang de, *France* 21 F13
Bigwa, *Tanzania* 86 D4
Bihać, *Bos.-H.* 41 D12
Bihar, *India* 69 G11
Bihar □, *India* 69 G12
Biharamulo, *Tanzania* 86 C3
Biharamulo □, *Tanzania* 86 C3
Bihariganj, *India* 69 G12
Biharkeresztes, *Hungary* 28 C6
Bihor □, *Romania* 28 D7
Bihor, Munţii, *Romania* 28 D7
Bijagós, Arquipélago dos,
  Guinea-Biss. 82 C1
Bijaipur, *India* 68 F7
Bijapur, *Chhattisgarh, India* ... 67 K12
Bijapur, *Karnataka, India* 66 L9
Bījār, *Iran* 70 C5
Bijawar, *India* 69 G8
Bijeljina, *Bos.-H.* 28 F4
Bijelo Polje, *Serbia & M.* 44 C3
Bijie, *China* 58 D5
Bijnor, *India* 68 E8
Bikaner, *India* 68 E5
Bikapur, *India* 69 F10
Bikeqi, *China* 56 D6
Bikfayyā, *Lebanon* 74 B4
Bikin, *Russia* 53 E14
Bikin →, *Russia* 54 A7
Bikini Atoll, *Marshall Is.* 96 F8
Bikita, *Zimbabwe* 89 C5
Bikoué, *Cameroon* 83 E7
Bila Tserkva, *Ukraine* 33 H6
Bilanga, *Burkina Faso* 83 C4
Bilara, *India* 68 F5
Bilaspur, *Chhattisgarh, India* .. 69 H10
Bilaspur, *Punjab, India* 68 D7
Biläsuvar, *Azerbaijan* 73 C13
Bilauk Taungdan, *Thailand* ... 64 F2
Bilbao, *Spain* 38 B2
Bilbao ✈ (BIO), *Spain* 36 B8
Bilbeis, *Egypt* 80 H7
Bilbo = Bilbao, *Spain* 38 B2
Bilbor, *Romania* 29 C10
Bilche-Zolote, *Ukraine* 29 B10
Bilciureşti, *Romania* 29 F10
Bíldudalur, *Iceland* 8 D2
Bílé Karpaty, *Europe* 27 B11
Bileća, *Bos.-H.* 44 D3
Bilecik, *Turkey* 72 B4
Biłgoraj, *Poland* 31 H9
Bilgram, *India* 69 F9
Bilhaur, *India* 69 F9
Bilhorod-Dnistrovskyy, *Ukraine* 33 J6
Bilibino, *Russia* 53 C17
Bilibiza, *Mozam.* 87 E5
Bilisht, *Albania* 44 F5
Billabong Roadhouse, *Australia* 93 E2
Billdal, *Sweden* 11 G5

Billiluna, Australia 92 C4
Billings, U.S.A. 108 D9
Billiton Is. = Belitung, Indonesia 62 E3
Billsta, Sweden 10 A12
Billund, Denmark 11 J3
Bilma, Niger 79 E8
Bilo Gora, Croatia 28 E2
Biloela, Australia 94 C5
Bilohirsk, Ukraine 33 K8
Bilopillya, Ukraine 33 G8
Biloxi, U.S.A. 113 K10
Bilpa Morea Claypan, Australia 94 D3
Biltine, Chad 79 F10
Bilyarsk, Russia 34 C10
Bima, Indonesia 63 F5
Bimban, Egypt 80 C3
Bimbila, Ghana 83 D5
Bimini Is., Bahamas 120 A4
Bin Xian, Heilongjiang, China 57 B14
Bin Xian, Shaanxi, China 56 G5
Bin Yauri, Nigeria 83 C5
Bina-Etawah, India 68 G8
Bināb, Iran 71 B6
Binalbagan, Phil. 61 F5
Binalong, Australia 95 E4
Bīnālūd, Kūh-e, Iran 71 B8
Binatang = Bintangor, Malaysia 62 D4
Binche, Belgium 17 D4
Binchuan, China 58 E3
Binder, Chad 83 D7
Bindki, India 69 F9
Bindslev, Denmark 11 G4
Bindura, Zimbabwe 87 F3
Binefar, Spain 38 D5
Bingara, Australia 95 D5
Bingen, Germany 25 F3
Bingerville, Ivory C. 82 D4
Bingham, U.S.A. 115 C11
Binghamton, U.S.A. 117 D9
Bingöl, Turkey 70 B4
Bingöl Dağları, Turkey 73 C9
Bingsjö, Sweden 10 C9
Binh Dinh = An Nhon, Vietnam 64 F7
Binh Khe, Vietnam 64 F7
Binh Son, Vietnam 64 E7
Binhai, China 57 G10
Binic, France 18 D4
Binisatua, Spain 48 B11
Binjai, Indonesia 62 D3
Binji, Nigeria 83 C5
Binnaway, Australia 95 E4
Binongko, Indonesia 63 F6
Binscarth, Canada 103 C8
Binshangul Gumuz □, Ethiopia 81 E4
Bint Goda, Sudan 81 E3
Bintan, Indonesia 62 D2
Bintangor, Malaysia 62 D4
Bintulu, Malaysia 62 D4
Bintuni, Indonesia 63 E8
Binyang, China 58 F7
Binz, Germany 24 A9
Binzert = Bizerte, Tunisia 79 A7
Binzhou, China 57 F10
Bío Bío □, Chile 126 D1
Biograd na Moru, Croatia 41 E12
Biogradska Gora △, Serbia & M. 44 D3
Bioko, Eq. Guin. 83 E6
Biokovo, Croatia 41 E14
Bipindi, Cameroon 83 E7
Bir, India 66 K9
Bir, Ras, Djibouti 81 E5
Bîr Abu Hashim, Egypt 80 C3
Bîr Abu Minqar, Egypt 80 B2
Bîr Abu Muḥammad, Egypt 74 F3
Bi'r al Dabbāghāt, Jordan 74 E4
Bi'r Adal Deib, Sudan 80 C4
Bi'r al Butayyihat, Jordan 74 F4
Bi'r al Mārī, Jordan 74 E4
Bi'r al Qattār, Jordan 74 F4
Bîr 'Asal, Egypt 80 B3
Bir Atrun, Sudan 80 D2
Bîr Beiḍa, Egypt 74 E3
Bîr Diqnash, Egypt 80 A2
Bîr el 'Abd, Egypt 74 D2
Bîr el Basur, Egypt 80 B2
Bîr el Biarât, Egypt 74 F3
Bîr el Duweidar, Egypt 74 E1
Bîr el Garârât, Egypt 74 D2
Bîr el Gellaz, Egypt 80 A2
Bîr el Heisi, Egypt 74 F3
Bîr el Jafir, Egypt 74 E1
Bîr el Mâlḥi, Egypt 74 E2
Bîr el Shaqqa, Egypt 80 A2
Bîr el Thamâda, Egypt 74 E2
Bîr Fuad, Egypt 80 A2
Bîr Gebeil Ḥisn, Egypt 74 E2
Bi'r Ghadīr, Syria 74 A6
Bîr Haimur, Egypt 80 C3
Bîr Ḥasana, Egypt 74 E2
Bîr Hōōker, Egypt 80 H7
Bîr Kanayis, Egypt 80 C3
Bîr Kaseiba, Egypt 74 E2
Bîr Kerawein, Egypt 80 B2
Bîr Lahfân, Egypt 74 E2
Bîr Madkūr, Egypt 74 E1
Bîr Maql, Egypt 80 C3
Bîr Mîneiga, Sudan 80 C4
Bîr Misaha, Egypt 80 C2
Bîr Mogreïn, Mauritania 78 C3
Bîr Murr, Egypt 80 C3
Bi'r Muṭribah, Kuwait 70 D5
Bîr Nakheila, Egypt 74 E1
Bîr Qaţia, Egypt 74 E1
Bîr Qatrani, Egypt 80 A2
Bîr Ranga, Egypt 80 C4
Bîr Sahara, Egypt 80 C2
Bîr Seiyâla, Egypt 80 B3
Bîr Shalatein, Egypt 80 C3
Bîr Shebb, Egypt 80 C2
Bîr Shût, Egypt 80 C4
Bîr Terfawi, Egypt 80 C2
Bîr Umm Qubûr, Egypt 80 C3

Bîr Ungât, Egypt 80 C3
Bîr Za'farâna, Egypt 80 J8
Bîr Zeidûn, Egypt 80 B3
Biramféro, Guinea 82 C3
Biratnagar, Nepal 69 F12
Birawa, Dem. Rep. of the Congo 86 C2
Birch →, Canada 102 B6
Birch Hills, Canada 103 C7
Birch I., Canada 103 C9
Birch L., N.W.T., Canada 102 A5
Birch L., Ont., Canada 104 B1
Birch Mts., Canada 102 B6
Birch River, Canada 103 C8
Birchip, Australia 95 F3
Birchiş, Romania 28 E7
Bird, Canada 103 B10
Bird I. = Aves, I. de, W. Indies 121 C7
Bird I., Antarctica 5 B1
Birdsville, Australia 94 D2
Birdum Cr. →, Australia 92 C5
Birecik, Turkey 70 B3
Birein, Israel 74 E3
Bireuen, Indonesia 62 C1
Biri →, Sudan 81 F2
Birifo, Gambia 82 C2
Birigui, Brazil 127 A5
Birjand, Iran 71 C8
Birkenfeld, Germany 25 F3
Birkenhead, U.K. 14 D4
Birkerød, Denmark 11 J6
Birket Qârûn, Egypt 80 J7
Birkfeld, Austria 26 D8
Bîrlad = Bârlad, Romania 29 D12
Birmingham, U.K. 15 E6
Birmingham, U.S.A. 115 J2
Birmingham International ✈ (BHX), U.K. 15 E6
Birmitrapur, India 67 H14
Birni Ngaouré, Niger 83 C5
Birni Nkonni, Niger 83 C6
Birnin Gwari, Nigeria 83 C6
Birnin Kebbi, Nigeria 83 C5
Birnin Kudu, Nigeria 83 C6
Birobidzhan, Russia 53 E14
Birr, Ireland 12 C4
Birrie →, Australia 95 D4
Birsilpur, India 68 E5
Birsk, Russia 52 D6
Birštonas, Lithuania 30 D11
Birtle, Canada 103 C8
Birur, India 66 N9
Biryuchiy, Ukraine 33 J8
Biržai, Lithuania 9 H21
Birzebbugga, Malta 49 D2
Bisa, Indonesia 63 E7
Bisáccia, Italy 43 A8
Bisacquino, Italy 42 E6
Bisalpur, India 69 E8
Bisbee, U.S.A. 109 L9
Biscarrosse, France 20 D2
Biscarrosse et de Parentis, Étang de, France 20 D2
Biscay, B. of, Atl. Oc. 6 F5
Biscayne, B., U.S.A. 115 N5
Biscéglie, Italy 43 A9
Bischheim, France 19 D14
Bischofshofen, Austria 26 D6
Bischofswerda, Germany 24 D10
Bischwiller, France 19 D14
Biscoe Is., Antarctica 5 C17
Biscotasing, Canada 104 C3
Biševo, Croatia 41 F13
Bisha, Eritrea 81 D4
Bishah, W. →, Si. Arabia 80 C5
Bishan, China 58 C6
Bishkek, Kyrgyzstan 52 E8
Bishnupur, India 69 H12
Bisho, S. Africa 89 E4
Bishop, Calif., U.S.A. 110 H8
Bishop, Tex., U.S.A. 113 M6
Bishop Auckland, U.K. 14 C6
Bishop's Falls, Canada 105 C8
Bishop's Stortford, U.K. 15 F8
Bisignano, Italy 43 C9
Bisina, L., Uganda 86 B3
Biskra, Algeria 78 B7
Biskupiec, Poland 30 E7
Bismarck, U.S.A. 112 B4
Bismarck Arch., Papua N. G. 96 H7
Bismark, Germany 24 C7
Bismil, Turkey 70 B4
Biso, Uganda 86 B3
Bison, U.S.A. 112 C3
Bīsotūn, Iran 70 C5
Bispgården, Sweden 10 A10
Bissagos = Bijagós, Arquipélago dos, Guinea-Biss. 82 C1
Bissau, Guinea-Biss. 82 C1
Bissaula, Nigeria 83 D7
Bissikrima, Guinea 82 C2
Bissorã, Guinea-Biss. 82 C1
Bistcho L., Canada 102 B5
Bistreţ, Romania 29 G8
Bistrica = Ilirska-Bistrica, Slovenia 41 C11
Bistriţa, Romania 29 C9
Bistriţa →, Romania 29 D11
Bistriţa Năsăud □, Romania 29 C9
Bistriţei, Munţii, Romania 29 C10
Biswan, India 69 F9
Bisztynek, Poland 30 D7
Bitburg, Germany 25 F2
Bitche, France 19 C14
Bithynia, Turkey 72 B4
Bitlis, Turkey 70 B4
Bitola, Macedonia 44 E5
Bitolj = Bitola, Macedonia 44 E5
Bitonto, Italy 43 A9
Bitter Creek, U.S.A. 108 F9
Bitter L. = Buheirat-Murrat-el-Kubra, Egypt 80 H8
Bitterfeld, Germany 24 D8

Bitterfontein, S. Africa 88 E2
Bitterroot →, U.S.A. 108 C6
Bitterroot Range, U.S.A. 108 D6
Bitterwater, U.S.A. 110 J6
Bitti, Italy 42 B2
Bittou, Burkina Faso 83 C4
Biu, Nigeria 83 C7
Bivolari, Romania 29 C12
Bivolu, Vf., Romania 29 C10
Biwa-Ko, Japan 55 G8
Biwabik, U.S.A. 112 B8
Bixad, Romania 29 C8
Bixby, U.S.A. 113 H7
Biyang, China 56 H7
Biysk, Russia 52 D9
Bizana, S. Africa 89 E4
Bizen, Japan 55 G7
Bizerte, Tunisia 79 A7
Bjargtangar, Iceland 8 D1
Bjärnum, Sweden 11 H7
Bjästa, Sweden 10 A12
Bjelasica, Serbia & M. 44 D3
Bjelašnica, Bos.-H. 28 G3
Bjelovar, Croatia 41 C13
Bjerringbro, Denmark 11 H3
Bjørbo, Sweden 10 D8
Björneborg = Pori, Finland 9 F19
Björklinge, Sweden 10 D11
Björneborg, Sweden 10 E8
Bjørnevatn, Norway 8 B23
Bjørnøya, Arctic 4 B8
Bjursås, Sweden 10 D9
Bjuv, Sweden 11 H6
Bla, Mali 82 C3
Blace, Serbia & M. 44 C5
Blachownia, Poland 31 H5
Black →, Da →, Vietnam 58 G5
Black →, Canada 116 B5
Black →, Ariz., U.S.A. 109 K8
Black →, Ark., U.S.A. 113 H9
Black →, Mich., U.S.A. 116 D2
Black →, N.Y., U.S.A. 117 C8
Black →, Wis., U.S.A. 112 D9
Black Bay Pen., Canada 104 C2
Black Birch L., Canada 103 B7
Black Canyon of the Gunnison △, U.S.A. 109 G10
Black Diamond, Canada 102 C6
Black Duck →, Canada 104 A2
Black Forest = Schwarzwald, Germany 25 G4
Black Forest, U.S.A. 112 F2
Black Hd., Ireland 12 C2
Black Hills, U.S.A. 112 D3
Black I., Canada 103 C9
Black L., Canada 103 B7
Black L., Mich., U.S.A. 114 C3
Black L., N.Y., U.S.A. 117 B9
Black Lake, Canada 103 B7
Black Mesa, U.S.A. 113 G3
Black Mt. = Mynydd Du, U.K. 15 F4
Black Mts., U.K. 15 F4
Black Range, U.S.A. 109 K10
Black River, Jamaica 120 a
Black River Falls, U.S.A. 112 C9
Black Rock, Barbados 121 g
Black Sea, Eurasia 6 G12
Black Tickle, Canada 105 B8
Black Volta →, Africa 82 D4
Black Warrior →, U.S.A. 115 J2
Blackall, Australia 94 C4
Blackball, N.Z. 91 K3
Blackbull, Australia 94 B3
Blackburn, U.K. 14 D5
Blackburn with Darwen □, U.K. 14 D5
Blackdown Tableland △, Australia 94 C4
Blackfoot, U.S.A. 108 E7
Blackfoot →, U.S.A. 108 C9
Blackfoot River Reservoir, U.S.A. 108 E8
Blackpool, U.K. 14 D4
Blackpool □, U.K. 14 D4
Blackriver, U.S.A. 116 B1
Blacks Harbour, Canada 105 C6
Blacksburg, U.S.A. 114 G5
Blacksod B., Ireland 12 B1
Blackstone, U.S.A. 114 G7
Blackstone Ra., Australia 93 E4
Blackwater = West Road →, Canada 102 C4
Blackwater, Australia 94 C4
Blackwater →, Meath, Ireland 12 C4
Blackwater →, Waterford, Ireland 12 D4
Blackwater →, U.K. 12 B5
Blackwell, U.S.A. 113 G6
Blackwells Corner, U.S.A. 111 K7
Bladensburg △, Australia 94 C3
Blaenau Ffestiniog, U.K. 14 E4
Blaenau Gwent □, U.K. 15 F4
Blagaj, Bos.-H. 42 C1
Blagnac, France 20 E5
Blagnac, Toulouse ✈ (TLS), France 20 E5
Blagodarnoye = Blagodarnyy, Russia 35 H6
Blagodarnyy, Russia 35 H6
Blagoevgrad, Bulgaria 44 D7
Blagoveshchensk, Russia 53 D13
Blahkiuh, Indonesia 63 J18
Blain, France 18 E5
Blaine, Minn., U.S.A. 112 C8
Blaine, Wash., U.S.A. 110 B4
Blaine Lake, Canada 103 C7
Blair, U.S.A. 112 E6
Blair Athol, Australia 94 C4
Blair Atholl, U.K. 13 E5
Blairgowrie, U.K. 13 E5
Blairsden, U.S.A. 110 F6
Blairsville, U.S.A. 116 F5
Blaj, Romania 29 D8
Blakang Mati, Pulau, Singapore 65 d

Blake Pt., U.S.A. 112 A10
Blakely, Ga., U.S.A. 115 K3
Blakely, Pa., U.S.A. 117 E9
Blâmont, France 19 D13
Blanc, C., Spain 48 B9
Blanc, Mont, Europe 21 C10
Blanc-Sablon, Canada 105 B8
Blanca, B., Argentina 128 D4
Blanca Peak, U.S.A. 109 H11
Blanche, C., Australia 95 E1
Blanche, L., S. Austral., Australia 95 D2
Blanche, L., W. Austral., Australia 92 D3
Blanchisseuse, Trin. & Tob. 125 K15
Blanco, S. Africa 88 E3
Blanco, U.S.A. 113 K5
Blanco →, Argentina 126 C2
Blanco, C., Costa Rica 120 E2
Blanco, C., U.S.A. 108 E1
Blanda →, Iceland 8 D3
Blandford Forum, U.K. 15 G5
Blanding, U.S.A. 109 H9
Blanes, Spain 38 D7
Blangy-sur-Bresle, France 19 C8
Blanice →, Czech Rep. 26 B7
Blankaholm, Sweden 11 G10
Blankenberge, Belgium 17 C3
Blankenburg, Germany 24 D6
Blanquefort, France 20 D3
Blanquillo, Uruguay 127 C4
Blansko, Czech Rep. 27 B9
Blantyre, Malawi 87 F4
Blarney, Ireland 12 E3
Blasdell, U.S.A. 116 D6
Błaszki, Poland 31 G5
Blatná, Czech Rep. 26 B6
Blato, Croatia 41 F13
Blaubeuren, Germany 25 G5
Blaustein, Germany 25 G5
Blåvands Huk, Denmark 11 J2
Blaydon, U.K. 14 C6
Blaye, France 20 C3
Blaye-les-Mines, France 20 D6
Blayney, Australia 95 E4
Blaze, Pt., Australia 92 B5
Błażowa, Poland 31 J9
Bleckede, Germany 24 B6
Bled, Slovenia 41 B11
Bleiburg, Austria 26 E7
Blejeşti, Romania 29 F10
Blekinge, Sweden 9 H16
Blekinge län □, Sweden 11 H9
Blenheim, Canada 116 D3
Blenheim, N.Z. 91 J4
Bléone →, France 21 D10
Blérancourt, France 19 C10
Bletchley, U.K. 15 F7
Blida, Algeria 78 A6
Blidö, Sweden 10 E12
Blidsberg, Sweden 11 G7
Blieskastel, Germany 25 F3
Bligh Sound, N.Z. 91 L1
Blind River, Canada 104 C3
Blinisht, Albania 44 E3
Bliss, Idaho, U.S.A. 108 E6
Bliss, N.Y., U.S.A. 116 D6
Blissfield, U.S.A. 116 F3
Blitar, Indonesia 63 H15
Blitta, Togo 83 D5
Block I., U.S.A. 117 E13
Block Island Sd., U.S.A. 117 E13
Bloemfontein, S. Africa 88 D4
Bloemhof, S. Africa 88 D4
Blois, France 18 E8
Blomskog, Sweden 10 E6
Blomstermåla, Sweden 11 H10
Blönduós, Iceland 8 D3
Blongas, Indonesia 63 K19
Błonie, Poland 31 F7
Bloodvein →, Canada 103 C9
Bloody Foreland, Ireland 12 A3
Bloomer, U.S.A. 112 C9
Bloomfield, Canada 116 C7
Bloomfield, Iowa, U.S.A. 112 E8
Bloomfield, N. Mex., U.S.A. 109 H10
Bloomfield, Nebr., U.S.A. 112 D6
Bloomington, Ill., U.S.A. 112 E10
Bloomington, Ind., U.S.A. 114 F2
Bloomington, Minn., U.S.A. 112 C8
Bloomsburg, U.S.A. 117 F8
Bloomsbury, Australia 94 b4
Blora, Indonesia 63 G14
Blossburg, U.S.A. 116 E7
Blouberg, S. Africa 89 C4
Blountstown, U.S.A. 115 K3
Bludenz, Austria 26 D2
Blue Earth, U.S.A. 112 D8
Blue Hole △, Belize 120 C2
Blue Lagoon △, Zambia 87 F2
Blue Mesa Reservoir, U.S.A. 109 G10
Blue Mountain Lake, U.S.A. 117 C10
Blue Mountain Pk., Jamaica 120 a
Blue Mts., Jamaica 120 a
Blue Mts., Maine, U.S.A. 117 B14
Blue Mts., Oreg., U.S.A. 108 D4
Blue Mts., Pa., U.S.A. 117 F8
Blue Mud B., Australia 94 A2
Blue Nile = Nîl el Azraq →, Sudan 81 D3
Blue Rapids, U.S.A. 112 F6
Blue Ridge Mts., U.S.A. 115 G5
Blue River, Canada 102 C5
Bluefield, U.S.A. 114 G5
Bluefields, Nic. 120 D3
Bluff, Australia 94 C4
Bluff, N.Z. 91 M2
Bluff, U.S.A. 109 H9
Bluff Knoll, Australia 93 F2
Bluff Pt., Australia 93 E1
Bluffton, U.S.A. 114 E3
Blumenau, Brazil 127 B6
Blunt, U.S.A. 112 C5
Bly, U.S.A. 108 E3

Blyde River Canyon △, S. Africa 89 C5
Blyth, Canada 116 C3
Blyth, U.K. 14 B6
Blythe, U.S.A. 111 M12
Blytheville, U.S.A. 113 H10
Bo, S. Leone 82 D2
Bo Duc, Vietnam 65 G6
Bo Hai, China 57 E10
Bo Xian = Bozhou, China 56 H8
Boa Vista, Brazil 124 C6
Boac, Phil. 61 E4
Boaco, Nic. 120 D2
Bo'ai, China 56 G7
Boal, Spain 36 B4
Boalsburg, U.S.A. 116 F7
Boane, Mozam. 89 D5
Boardman, U.S.A. 116 E4
Bobadah, Australia 95 E4
Bobai, China 58 F7
Bobbili, India 67 K13
Bóbbio, Italy 40 D6
Bobcaygeon, Canada 116 B6
Böblingen, Germany 25 G5
Bobo-Dioulasso, Burkina Faso 82 C4
Bobolice, Poland 30 E3
Boboshevo, Bulgaria 44 D7
Bobov Dol, Bulgaria 44 D6
Bóbr →, Poland 31 F2
Bobraomby, Tanjon' i, Madag. 89 A8
Bobrinets, Ukraine 33 H7
Bobrov, Russia 34 E5
Bobrovitsa, Ukraine 33 G6
Bobruysk = Babruysk, Belarus 33 F5
Boby, Pic, Madag. 85 J9
Boca de Drago, Venezuela 125 K15
Bôca do Acre, Brazil 124 E5
Boca Raton, U.S.A. 115 M5
Bocanda, Ivory C. 82 D4
Bocas del Toro, Panama 120 E3
Boceguillas, Spain 36 D7
Bochnia, Poland 31 J7
Bocholt, Germany 24 D2
Bochum, Germany 24 D3
Bockenem, Germany 24 C6
Bočki, Poland 31 F10
Bocognano, France 21 F13
Bocoyna, Mexico 118 B3
Bocşa, Romania 28 E6
Boda, Dalarna, Sweden 10 C9
Böda, Kalmar, Sweden 11 G11
Boda, Västernorrland, Sweden 10 B10
Bodafors, Sweden 11 G8
Bodaybo, Russia 53 D12
Boddam, U.K. 13 B7
Boddington, Australia 93 F2
Bode Sadu, Nigeria 83 D5
Bodega Bay, U.S.A. 110 G3
Boden, Sweden 8 D19
Bodensee, Europe 25 H5
Bodenteich, Germany 24 C6
Bodhan, India 66 K10
Bodinga, Nigeria 83 C6
Bodmin, U.K. 15 G3
Bodmin Moor, U.K. 15 G3
Bodø, Norway 8 C16
Bodrog →, Hungary 28 B6
Bodrum, Turkey 47 D9
Bódva →, Hungary 28 B5
Boën, France 21 C8
Boende, Dem. Rep. of the Congo 84 E4
Boerne, U.S.A. 113 L5
Boesmans →, S. Africa 88 E4
Boffa, Guinea 82 C2
Bogalusa, U.S.A. 113 K10
Bogan →, Australia 95 D4
Bogan Gate, Australia 95 E4
Bogandé, Burkina Faso 83 C4
Bogantungan, Australia 94 C4
Bogata, U.S.A. 113 J7
Bogatić, Serbia & M. 44 B3
Boğazkale, Turkey 72 B6
Boğazlıyan, Turkey 72 C6
Bogen, Germany 25 G8
Bogense, Denmark 11 J4
Bogetići, Serbia & M. 44 D2
Boggabilla, Australia 95 D5
Boggabri, Australia 95 E5
Boggeragh Mts., Ireland 12 D3
Boglan = Solhan, Turkey 70 B4
Bognor Regis, U.K. 15 G7
Bogo, Phil. 61 F6
Bogodukhov = Bohodukhiv, Ukraine 33 G8
Bogol Manya, Ethiopia 81 G5
Bogong, Mt., Australia 95 F4
Bogor, Indonesia 63 G12
Bogoroditsk, Russia 32 F10
Bogorodsk, Russia 34 B6
Bogoso, Ghana 82 D4
Bogotá, Colombia 124 C4
Bogotol, Russia 52 D9
Bogou, Togo 83 C5
Bogra, Bangla. 67 G16
Boguchany, Russia 53 D10
Boguchar, Russia 35 F5
Bogué, Mauritania 82 B2
Boguslav, Ukraine 33 H6
Boguszów-Gorce, Poland 31 H3
Bohain-en-Vermandois, France 19 C10
Bohdan, Ukraine 29 B8
Bohemian Forest = Böhmerwald, Germany 25 F9
Bohinjska Bistrica, Slovenia 41 B11
Böhmerwald, Germany 25 F9
Bohmte, Germany 24 C4
Bohodukhiv, Ukraine 33 G8
Bohol □, Phil. 61 G6
Bohol Sea, Phil. 63 C6

Bohuslän, Sweden 11 F5
Boi, Nigeria 83 D6
Boi, Pta. de, Brazil 127 A6
Boiaçu, Brazil 124 D6
Boileau, C., Australia 92 C3
Boing'o, Sudan 81 F3
Boiro, Spain 36 C2
Boise, U.S.A. 108 E5
Boise City, U.S.A. 113 G3
Boissevain, Canada 103 D8
Bóite →, Italy 41 B9
Boitzenburg, Germany 24 B9
Boizenburg, Germany 24 B6
Bojador, C., W. Sahara 78 C3
Bojana →, Albania 44 E3
Bojano, Italy 43 A7
Bojanowo, Poland 31 G3
Bøjden, Denmark 11 J4
Bojnūrd, Iran 71 B8
Bojonegoro, Indonesia 63 G14
Boju, Nigeria 83 D6
Boka, Serbia & M. 28 E5
Boka Kotorska, Serbia & M. .. 44 D2
Bokala, Ivory C. 82 D4
Bokani, Nigeria 83 D6
Bokaro, India 69 H11
Boké, Guinea 82 C2
Bokhara →, Australia 95 D4
Bokkos, Nigeria 83 D6
Boknafjorden, Norway 9 G11
Bokora △, Uganda 86 B3
Bokoro, Chad 79 F9
Bokpyin, Burma 65 G2
Boksitogorsk, Russia 32 C7
Bol, Croatia 41 E13
Bolama, Guinea-Biss. 82 C1
Bolan →, Pakistan 68 E2
Bolan Pass, Pakistan 66 E5
Bolaños →, Mexico 118 C4
Bolaños de Calatrava, Spain .. 37 G7
Bolayır, Turkey 45 F10
Bolbec, France 18 C7
Boldājī, Iran 71 D6
Boldeşti-Scăeni, Romania 29 E11
Bole, China 60 B3
Bole, Ethiopia 81 F4
Bole, Ghana 82 D4
Bolekhiv, Ukraine 33 H2
Bolesławiec, Poland 31 G2
Bolgatanga, Ghana 83 C4
Bolgrad = Bolhrad, Ukraine .. 29 E13
Bolhrad, Ukraine 29 E13
Bolinao, Phil. 61 C3
Bolintin-Vale, Romania 29 F10
Bolívar, Argentina 126 D3
Bolivar, Mo., U.S.A. 113 G8
Bolivar, N.Y., U.S.A. 116 D6
Bolivar, Tenn., U.S.A. 113 H10
Bolivia ■, S. Amer. 124 G6
Bolivian Plateau = Altiplano,
  Bolivia 122 E4
Boljevac, Serbia & M. 44 C5
Bolkhov, Russia 32 F9
Bolków, Poland 31 H3
Bollebygd, Sweden 11 G6
Bollène, France 21 D8
Bollnäs, Sweden 10 C10
Bollon, Australia 95 D4
Bollstabruk, Sweden 10 B11
Bolmen, Sweden 11 H7
Bolobo, Dem. Rep. of the Congo 84 E3
Bologna, Italy 41 D8
Bologna ✈ (BLQ), Italy 41 D8
Bologoye, Russia 32 D8
Bolon, Ozero, Russia 60 B8
Bolonchenticul, Mexico 119 D7
Bolótana, Italy 42 B1
Boloven, Cao Nguyen, Laos .. 64 E6
Bolpur, India 69 H12
Bolsena, Italy 41 F8
Bolsena, L. di, Italy 41 F8
Bolshakovo, Russia 30 D8
Bolshaya Chernigovka, Russia 34 D10
Bolshaya Glushitsa, Russia ... 34 D10
Bolshaya Martynovka, Russia . 35 G5
Bolshaya Vradiyevka, Ukraine 33 J6
Bolshevik, Ostrov, Russia 53 B11
Bolshoy Anyuy →, Russia 53 C17
Bolshoy Begichev, Ostrov, Russia 53 B12
Bolshoy Kavkas = Caucasus
  Mountains, Eurasia 35 J7
Bolshoy Lyakhovskiy, Ostrov,
  Russia 53 B15
Bolshoy Tyuters, Ostrov, Russia 9 G22
Bolsward, Neths. 17 A5
Bolt Head, U.K. 15 G4
Boltaña, Spain 38 C5
Boltigen, Switz. 25 J3
Bolton, Canada 116 C5
Bolton, U.K. 14 D5
Bolton Landing, U.S.A. 117 C11
Bolu, Turkey 72 B4
Bolungavík, Iceland 8 C2
Boluo, China 59 F10
Bolvadin, Turkey 70 B1
Bolzano, Italy 41 B8
Bom Jesus da Lapa, Brazil ... 125 F10
Bomaderry, Australia 95 E5
Bomba, Australia 94 A1
Bombala, Australia 95 F4
Bombarral, Portugal 37 F1
Bombay = Mumbai, India 66 K8
Bombedor, Pta., Venezuela .. 125 L15
Bomboma, Dem. Rep. of
  the Congo 84 D3
Bombombwa, Dem. Rep. of
  the Congo 86 B2
Bomi Hills, Liberia 82 D2
Bomili, Dem. Rep. of the Congo 86 B2
Bømlo, Norway 9 G11
Bomokandi →, Dem. Rep. of
  the Congo 86 B2
Bomu →, C.A.R. 84 D4

Bon, C., Tunisia 76 C5
Bon Sar Pa, Vietnam 64 F6
Bonâb, Iran 73 D12
Bonaigarh, India 69 J11
Bonaire, Neth. Ant. 121 D6
Bonampak, Mexico 119 D6
Bonang, Australia 95 F4
Bonanza, Nic. 120 D3
Bonaparte Arch., Australia ... 92 B3
Boñar, Spain 36 C5
Bonar Bridge, U.K. 13 D4
Bonaventure, Canada 105 C6
Bonavista, Canada 105 C9
Bonavista, C., Canada 105 C9
Bonavista B., Canada 105 C9
Bondeno, Italy 41 D8
Bondo, Dem. Rep. of the Congo 86 B1
Bondoukou, Ivory C. 82 D4
Bondowoso, Indonesia 63 G15
Bone, Teluk, Indonesia 63 E6
Bonerate, Indonesia 63 F6
Bonerate, Kepulauan, Indonesia 63 F6
Bo'ness, U.K. 13 E5
Bonete, Cerro, Argentina 126 B2
Bong Son = Hoai Nhon, Vietnam 64 E7
Bonga, Ethiopia 81 F4
Bongabong, Phil. 61 E4
Bongor, Chad 79 F9
Bongouanou, Ivory C. 82 D4
Bonham, U.S.A. 113 J6
Boni, Mali 82 B4
Boni △, Kenya 86 C5
Bonifacio, France 21 G13
Bonifacio, Bouches de, Medit. S. 42 A2
Bonin Is. = Ogasawara Gunto,
  Pac. Oc. 96 E6
Bonke, Ethiopia 81 F4
Bonkoukou, Niger 83 C5
Bonn, Germany 24 E3
Bonnat, France 19 F8
Bonne Terre, U.S.A. 113 G9
Bonners Ferry, U.S.A. 108 B5
Bonnétable, France 18 D7
Bonneval, France 21 C11
Bonneval-sur-Arc, France 18 D8
Bonneville, France 19 F13
Bonney, L., Australia 95 F3
Bonnie Rock, Australia 93 F2
Bonny, Nigeria 83 E6
Bonny →, Nigeria 83 E6
Bonny, Bight of, Africa 83 E6
Bonny-sur-Loire, France 19 E9
Bonnyrigg, U.K. 13 F5
Bonnyville, Canada 103 C6
Bono, Italy 42 B2
Bonoi, Indonesia 63 E9
Bonorva, Italy 42 B1
Bontang, Indonesia 62 D5
Bontebok △, S. Africa 88 E3
Bonthe, S. Leone 82 D2
Bontoc, Phil. 61 C4
Bonyeri, Ghana 82 D4
Bonyhád, Hungary 28 D3
Bonython Ra., Australia 92 D4
Bookabie, Australia 93 F5
Booker, U.S.A. 113 G4
Boola, Guinea 82 D3
Booligal, Australia 95 E3
Boonah, Australia 95 D5
Boone, Iowa, U.S.A. 112 D8
Boone, N.C., U.S.A. 115 G5
Booneville, Ark., U.S.A. 113 H8
Booneville, Miss., U.S.A. 115 H1
Boonville, Calif., U.S.A. 110 F3
Boonville, Ind., U.S.A. 114 F2
Boonville, Mo., U.S.A. 112 F8
Boonville, N.Y., U.S.A. 117 C9
Boorabbin △, Australia 93 F4
Boorindal, Australia 95 E4
Boorowa, Australia 95 E4
Boosaaso = Bosaso, Somali Rep. 75 E4
Boothia, Gulf of, Canada 101 A11
Boothia Pen., Canada 100 A10
Bootle, U.K. 14 D4
Booué, Gabon 84 E2
Boppard, Germany 25 E3
Boquete, Panama 120 E3
Boquilla, Presa de la, Mexico . 118 B3
Boquillas del Carmen, Mexico 118 B4
Bor, Czech Rep. 26 B5
Bor, Russia 34 B7
Bor, Serbia & M. 44 B6
Bôr, Sudan 81 F3
Bor, Sweden 11 G8
Bor, Turkey 72 D6
Bor Mashash, Israel 74 D3
Borah Peak, U.S.A. 108 D7
Borang, Sudan 81 G3
Borås, Sweden 11 G6
Borāzjān, Iran 71 D6
Borba, Brazil 124 D7
Borba, Portugal 37 G3
Borborema, Planalto da, Brazil 122 D7
Borcea, Romania 29 F12
Borça, Turkey 73 B9
Bord Khūn-e Now, Iran 71 D6
Borda, C., Australia 95 F2
Bordeaux, France 20 D3
Bordeaux ✈ (BOD), France .. 20 D3
Borden, Australia 93 F2
Borden-Carleton, Canada ... 105 C7
Borden I., Canada 4 B2
Borden Pen., Canada 101 A11
Border Ranges △, Australia .. 95 D5
Borders = Scottish Borders □,
  U.K. 13 F6
Bordertown, Australia 95 F3
Borðeyri, Iceland 8 D3
Bordighera, Italy 40 E4
Bordj Fly Ste. Marie, Algeria .. 78 C5

Bordj-in-Eker, Algeria 78 D7
Bordj Omar Driss, Algeria 78 C7
Bore, Ethiopia 81 G4
Borehamwood, U.K. 15 F7
Borek Wielkopolski, Poland ... 31 G4
Borensberg, Sweden 11 F9
Borgå = Porvoo, Finland 9 F21
Borgarfjörður, Iceland 8 D7
Borgarnes, Iceland 8 D3
Børgefjellet, Norway 8 D15
Borger, Neths. 17 B6
Borger, U.S.A. 113 H4
Borgholm, Sweden 11 H10
Bórgia, Italy 43 D9
Borgo San Dalmazzo, Italy ... 40 D4
Borgo San Lorenzo, Italy 41 E8
Borgo Val di Taro, Italy 40 D6
Borgo Valsugana, Italy 41 B8
Borgomanero, Italy 40 C5
Borgorose, Italy 41 F10
Borgosésia, Italy 40 C5
Borhoyn Tal, Mongolia 56 C6
Bori, Nigeria 83 E6
Borikhane, Laos 64 C4
Borisoglebsk, Russia 34 E6
Borisov = Barysaw, Belarus ... 32 E5
Borisovka, Russia 33 G9
Borja, Peru 124 D3
Borja, Spain 38 D3
Borjas Blancas = Les Borges
  Blanques, Spain 38 D5
Borjomi, Georgia 35 K6
Børkop, Denmark 11 J3
Borkou, Chad 79 E9
Borkum, Germany 24 B2
Borlänge, Sweden 10 D9
Borley, C., Antarctica 5 C5
Borlu, Turkey 47 C10
Bormida →, Italy 40 D5
Bórmio, Italy 40 B7
Borna, Germany 24 D8
Borne Sulinowo, Poland 30 E3
Borneo, E. Indies 62 D5
Bornholm, Denmark 11 J8
Bornholms Amtskommune □,
  Denmark 11 J8
Bornhöved, Europe 11 J8
Borno □, Nigeria 83 C7
Bornos, Spain 37 J5
Bornova, Turkey 47 C9
Bornu Yassa, Nigeria 83 C7
Boro →, Sudan 81 F2
Borodino, Russia 29 D14
Borodino, Ukraine 29 E8
Borogontsy, Russia 53 C14
Boromo, Burkina Faso 82 C4
Boron, U.S.A. 111 L9
Borongan, Phil. 61 F6
Borotangba Mts., C.A.R. 81 F2
Borotou, Ivory C. 82 D3
Borovan, Bulgaria 44 C7
Borovichi, Russia 32 C7
Borovsk, Russia 32 E9
Borrby, Sweden 11 J8
Borrego Springs, U.S.A. 111 M10
Borriol, Spain 38 E4
Borroloola, Australia 94 B2
Borşa, Cluj, Romania 29 D8
Borşa, Maramureş, Romania .. 29 C9
Borsad, India 68 H5
Borsec, Romania 29 D10
Borshchiv, Ukraine 29 B11
Borsod-Abaúj-Zemplén □,
  Hungary 28 B6
Bort-les-Orgues, France 20 C6
Borth, U.K. 15 E3
Börtnan, Sweden 10 B7
Borūjerd, Iran 71 C6
Borynya, Ukraine 31 J10
Boryslav, Ukraine 31 J10
Boryspil, Ukraine 33 G6
Borzhomi = Borjomi, Georgia . 35 K6
Borzna, Ukraine 33 G7
Borzya, Russia 53 D12
Bosa, Italy 42 B1
Bosanska Dubica, Bos.-H. ... 41 C13
Bosanska Gradiška, Bos.-H. .. 28 E2
Bosanska Kostajnica, Bos.-H. . 41 C13
Bosanska Krupa, Bos.-H. 41 D13
Bosanski Brod, Bos.-H. 28 E2
Bosanski Novi, Bos.-H. 41 C13
Bosanski Petrovac, Bos.-H. ... 41 D13
Bosanski Šamac, Bos.-H. 28 E3
Bosansko Grahovo, Bos.-H. .. 41 D13
Bosaso, Somali Rep. 75 E4
Boscastle, U.K. 15 G3
Boscobelle, Barbados .... 121 g
Bose, China 58 F6
Boshan, China 57 F9
Boshof, S. Africa 88 D4
Boshrūyeh, Iran 71 C8
Bosilegrad, Serbia & M. 44 D6
Boskovice, Czech Rep. 27 B9
Bosna →, Bos.-H. 28 E3
Bosna i Hercegovina = Bosnia-
  Herzegovina ■, Europe ... 28 G2
Bosnia-Herzegovina ■, Europe 28 G2
Bosnik, Indonesia 63 E9
Bosobolo, Dem. Rep. of
  the Congo 84 D3
Bosporus = İstanbul Boğazı,
  Turkey 45 E13
Bosque Farms, U.S.A. 109 J10
Bossangoa, C.A.R. 84 C3
Bossé Bangou, Niger 83 C5
Bossier City, U.S.A. 113 J8
Bosso, Niger 83 C7
Bosso, Dallol →, Niger 83 C5
Bostan, Pakistan 68 D2
Bostānābād, Iran 70 B5
Bosten Hu, China 60 B3
Boston, U.K. 14 E7

Boston, U.S.A. 117 D13
Boston Bar, Canada 102 D4
Boston Mts., U.S.A. 113 H8
Bosumtwi, L., Ghana 83 D4
Bosut →, Croatia 28 E3
Boswell, Canada 102 D5
Boswell, U.S.A. 116 F5
Botad, India 68 H4
Botan →, Turkey 73 D10
Botene, Laos 64 D3
Botev, Bulgaria 45 D8
Botevgrad, Bulgaria 44 D7
Bothaville, S. Africa 88 D4
Bothnia, G. of, Europe 8 E19
Bothwell, Australia 95 G4
Bothwell, Canada 116 D3
Boticas, Portugal 36 D3
Botletle →, Botswana 88 C3
Botlikh, Russia 35 J8
Botna →, Moldova 29 D14
Botoroaga, Romania 29 F10
Botoşani, Romania 29 C11
Botoşani □, Romania 29 C11
Botou, Burkina Faso 83 C5
Botricello, Italy 43 D9
Botro, Ivory C. 82 D3
Botswana ■, Africa 88 C3
Bottineau, U.S.A. 112 A4
Bottnaryd, Sweden 11 G7
Bottrop, Germany 17 C6
Botucatu, Brazil 127 A6
Botwood, Canada 105 C8
Bou Djébéha, Mali 82 B4
Boū Rjeïmât, Mauritania 82 B1
Bouaflé, Ivory C. 82 D3
Bouaké, Ivory C. 82 D3
Bouar, C.A.R. 84 C3
Bouârfa, Morocco 78 B5
Boucaut B., Australia 94 A1
Bouches-du-Rhône □, France . 21 E9
Boucle de Baoulé △, Mali 82 C3
Boucles de la Seine Normande △,
  France 18 C7
Bouctouche, Canada 105 C7
Bougainville, C., Australia ... 92 B4
Bougainville I., Papua N. G. .. 96 H7
Bougainville Reef, Australia .. 94 B4
Bougie = Bejaïa, Algeria 78 A7
Bougouni, Mali 82 C3
Bouillon, Belgium 17 E5
Boukombé, Benin 83 C5
Boulal, Mali 82 B3
Boulazac, France 20 C4
Boulder, Colo., U.S.A. 112 E2
Boulder, Mont., U.S.A. 108 C7
Boulder City, U.S.A. 111 K12
Boulder Creek, U.S.A. 110 H4
Boulder Dam = Hoover Dam,
  U.S.A. 111 K12
Bouli, Mauritania 82 B2
Boulia, Australia 94 C2
Bouligny, France 19 C12
Boulogne →, France 18 E5
Boulogne-sur-Gesse, France .. 20 E4
Boulogne-sur-Mer, France ... 19 B8
Bouloire, France 18 E7
Boulouli, Mali 82 B3
Boulsa, Burkina Faso 83 C4
Boultoum, Niger 83 C7
Boûmdeïd, Mauritania 82 B2
Boun Neua, Laos 64 B3
Boun Tai, Laos 64 B3
Bouna, Ivory C. 82 D4
Boundary Peak, U.S.A. 110 H8
Boundiali, Ivory C. 82 D3
Boundou △, France 18 E8
Bountiful, U.S.A. 108 F8
Bounty Is., Pac. Oc. 96 M9
Boura, Mali 82 C4
Bourbon-Lancy, France 19 F10
Bourbon-l'Archambault, France 19 F10
Bourbonnais, France 19 F10
Bourbonne-les-Bains, France . 19 E12
Bourbourg, France 19 B9
Bourdel L., Canada 104 A5
Bourem, Mali 83 B4
Bourg, France 20 C3
Bourg-Argental, France 21 C8
Bourg-de-Péage, France 21 C9
Bourg-en-Bresse, France 19 F12
Bourg-Lastic, France 20 C6
Bourg-Madame, France 20 F5
Bourg-St-Andéol, France 21 D8
Bourg-St-Maurice, France ... 21 C10
Bourganeuf, France 20 C5
Bourges, France 19 E9
Bourget, Canada 117 A9
Bourget, Lac du, France 21 C9
Bourgneuf, B. de, France 18 E4
Bourgneuf-en-Retz, France ... 18 E5
Bourgogne △, France 19 F11
Bourgogne-Jallieu, France ... 21 C9
Bourgueil, France 18 E7
Bourke, Australia 95 E4
Bourne, U.K. 14 E7
Bournemouth, U.K. 15 G6
Bournemouth □, U.K. 15 G6
Bourou, Burkina Faso 83 C4
Bouse, U.S.A. 111 M13
Boussac, France 19 F9
Boussé, Burkina Faso 83 C4
Boussouma, Burkina Faso ... 83 C4
Boutilimit, Mauritania 82 B2
Boutonne →, France 20 C3
Bouvet I. = Bouvetøya, Antarctica 3 G10
Bouvetøya, Antarctica 3 G10
Bouxwiller, France 19 D14
Bouza, Niger 83 C6
Bouzonville, France 19 C13
Bova Marina, Italy 43 A8
Bovalino Marina, Italy 43 D9
Bovec, Slovenia 41 B10
Bovill, U.S.A. 108 C5

Bovino, Italy 43 A8
Bovril, Argentina 126 C4
Bow →, Canada 102 C6
Bow Island, Canada 102 D6
Bowbells, U.S.A. 112 A3
Bowdle, U.S.A. 112 C5
Bowelling, Australia 93 F2
Bowen, Argentina 126 D2
Bowen, Australia 94 J6
Bowen Mts., Australia 95 F4
Bowie, Ariz., U.S.A. 109 K9
Bowie, Tex., U.S.A. 113 J6
Bowkān, Iran 70 B5
Bowland, Forest of, U.K. 14 D5
Bowling Green, Ky., U.S.A. .. 114 G2
Bowling Green, Ohio, U.S.A. . 114 E4
Bowling Green, C., Australia .. 94 B4
Bowling Green Bay △, Australia 94 B4
Bowman, U.S.A. 112 B3
Bowman I., Antarctica 5 C8
Bowmanville = Clarington,
  Canada 116 C6
Bowmore, U.K. 13 F2
Bowral, Australia 95 E5
Bowraville, Australia 95 E5
Bowron →, Canada 102 C4
Bowron Lake △, Canada 102 C4
Bowser L., Canada 102 B3
Bowsman, Canada 103 C8
Bowwood, Zambia 87 F2
Box Cr. →, Australia 95 E3
Boxholm, Sweden 11 F9
Boxmeer, Neths. 17 C5
Boxtel, Neths. 17 C5
Boyabat, Turkey 72 B6
Boyalıca, Turkey 45 F13
Boyang, China 59 C11
Boyany, Ukraine 29 B11
Boyce, U.S.A. 113 K8
Boyd, L., Canada 104 B4
Boyle, Canada 102 C6
Boyle, Ireland 12 C3
Boyne →, Ireland 12 C5
Boyne City, U.S.A. 114 C3
Boynton Beach, U.S.A. 115 M5
Boyolali, Indonesia 63 G14
Boyoma, Chutes, Dem. Rep. of
  the Congo 86 B2
Boysen Reservoir, U.S.A. 108 E9
Boyuibe, Bolivia 124 G6
Boyup Brook, Australia 93 F2
Boz Burun, Turkey 45 F13
Boz Dağ, Turkey 47 D11
Boz Dağları, Turkey 47 C10
Bozburun, Turkey 47 E10
Bozcaada, Turkey 72 C2
Bozdoğan, Turkey 47 D10
Bozeman, U.S.A. 108 D8
Bozen = Bolzano, Italy 41 B8
Boževac, Serbia & M. 44 B5
Bozhou, China 56 H8
Bozkır, Turkey 72 D5
Bozkurt, Turkey 47 D11
Bozouls, France 20 D6
Bozoum, C.A.R. 84 C3
Bozova, Antalya, Turkey 47 D12
Bozova, Şanlıurfa, Turkey 73 D8
Bozovici, Romania 28 F7
Bozüyük, Turkey 47 B12
Bra, Italy 40 D4
Braås, Sweden 11 G9
Brabant □, Belgium 17 D4
Brabant L., Canada 103 B8
Brabrand, Denmark 11 H4
Brač, Croatia 41 E13
Bracadale, L., U.K. 13 D2
Bracciano, Italy 41 F9
Bracciano, L. di, Italy 41 F9
Bracebridge, Canada 116 A5
Brach, Libya 79 C8
Bracieux, France 18 E8
Bräcke, Sweden 10 B9
Brackettville, U.S.A. 113 L4
Brački Kanal, Croatia 41 E13
Bracknell, U.K. 15 F7
Bracknell Forest □, U.K. 15 F7
Brad, Romania 28 D7
Brádano →, Italy 43 B9
Bradenton, U.S.A. 115 M4
Bradford, Canada 116 B5
Bradford, U.K. 14 D6
Bradford, Pa., U.S.A. 116 E6
Bradford, Vt., U.S.A. 117 C12
Bradley, Ark., U.S.A. 113 J8
Bradley, Calif., U.S.A. 110 K6
Bradley Institute, Zimbabwe . 87 F3
Brady, U.S.A. 113 K5
Brædstrup, Denmark 11 J3
Braeside, Canada 117 A8
Braga, Portugal 36 D2
Braga □, Portugal 36 D2
Bragadiru, Romania 29 G10
Bragado, Argentina 126 D3
Braganca, Brazil 125 D9
Bragança, Portugal 36 D4
Bragança □, Portugal 36 D4
Bragança Paulista, Brazil 127 A6
Brahestad = Raahe, Finland .. 8 D21
Brahmanbaria, Bangla. 67 H17
Brahmani →, India 67 J15
Brahmapur, India 67 K14
Brahmaputra →, Asia 69 H13
Braich-y-pwll, U.K. 14 E3
Braidwood, Australia 95 F4
Brăila, Romania 29 E12
Brăila □, Romania 29 E12
Brainerd, U.S.A. 112 B7
Braintree, U.K. 15 F8
Braintree, U.S.A. 117 D14
Brak →, S. Africa 88 D3
Brake, Germany 24 B4

Brakel, *Germany* 24 D5
Bräkne-Hoby, *Sweden* 11 H9
Brakwater, *Namibia* 88 C2
Brålanda, *Sweden* 11 F6
Bramberg, *Germany* 25 E6
Bramdrupdam, *Denmark* 11 J3
Bramming, *Denmark* 11 J2
Brämön, *Sweden* 10 B11
Brampton, *Canada* 116 C5
Brampton, *U.K.* 14 C5
Bramsche, *Germany* 24 C3
Bramton I., *Australia* 94 J7
Branco →, *Brazil* 124 D6
Brandberg, *Namibia* 88 C1
Brandberg △, *Namibia* 88 C1
Brande, *Denmark* 11 J3
Brandenburg = Neubrandenburg,
  Germany 24 B9
Brandenburg, *Germany* 24 C8
Brandenburg □, *Germany* 24 C9
Brandfort, *S. Africa* 88 D4
Brando, *France* 21 F13
Brandon, *Canada* 103 D9
Brandon, *U.S.A.* 117 C11
Brandon B., *Ireland* 12 D1
Brandon Mt., *Ireland* 12 D1
Brandsen, *Argentina* 126 D4
Brandvlei, *S. Africa* 88 E3
Brandýs nad Labem, *Czech Rep.* 26 A7
Brănești, *Romania* 29 F11
Branford, *U.S.A.* 117 E12
Braniewo, *Poland* 30 D6
Bransfield Str., *Antarctica* .. 5 C18
Brańsk, *Poland* 31 F9
Branson, *U.S.A.* 113 G8
Brantford, *Canada* 116 C4
Brantôme, *France* 20 C4
Branxholme, *Australia* 95 F3
Branzi, *Italy* 40 B6
Bras d'Or L., *Canada* 105 C7
Brasher Falls, *U.S.A.* 117 B10
Brasil, Planalto, *Brazil* 122 E6
Brasiléia, *Brazil* 124 F5
Brasília, *Brazil* 125 G9
Brasília Legal, *Brazil* 125 D7
Braslaw, *Belarus* 9 J22
Braslovče, *Slovenia* 41 B12
Brașov, *Romania* 29 E10
Brașov □, *Romania* 29 E10
Brass, *Nigeria* 83 E6
Brass →, *Nigeria* 83 E6
Brassac-les-Mines, *France* ... 20 C7
Brasschaat, *Belgium* 17 C4
Brassey, Banjaran, *Malaysia* . 62 D5
Brassey Ra., *Australia* 93 E3
Brasstown Bald, *U.S.A.* 115 H4
Brastad, *Sweden* 11 F5
Brastavățu, *Romania* 29 G9
Bratan = Morozov, *Bulgaria* . 45 D9
Brateș, *Romania* 29 E11
Bratislava, *Slovak Rep.* 27 C10
Bratislava M.R. Štefánik ✈
  (BTS), *Slovak Rep.* 27 C10
Bratislavský □, *Slovak Rep.* . 27 C10
Bratsigovo, *Bulgaria* 45 D8
Bratsk, *Russia* 53 D11
Brattleboro, *U.S.A.* 117 D12
Bratunac, *Bos.-H.* 28 F4
Braunau, *Austria* 26 C6
Braunschweig, *Germany* 24 C6
Braunton, *U.K.* 15 F3
Bravicea, *Moldova* 29 C13
Brăviken, *Sweden* 11 F10
Bravo del Norte, Rio = Grande,
  Rio →, *U.S.A.* 113 N6
Brawley, *U.S.A.* 111 N11
Bray, *Ireland* 12 C5
Bray, Mt., *Australia* 94 A1
Bray-sur-Seine, *France* 19 D10
Brazeau →, *Canada* 102 C5
Brazil, *U.S.A.* 114 F2
Brazil ■, *S. Amer.* 125 F9
Brazilian Highlands = Brasil,
  Planalto, *Brazil* 122 E6
Brazo Sur →, *S. Amer.* 126 B4
Brazos →, *U.S.A.* 113 L7
Brazzaville, *Congo* 84 E3
Brčko, *Bos.-H.* 28 F3
Brda →, *Poland* 31 E5
Brdy, *Czech Rep.* 26 B6
Breaden, L., *Australia* 93 E4
Breaksea Sd., *N.Z.* 91 L1
Bream B., *N.Z.* 91 F5
Bream Hd., *N.Z.* 91 F5
Breas, *Chile* 126 B1
Breaza, *Romania* 29 E10
Brebes, *Indonesia* 63 G13
Brechin, *Canada* 116 B5
Brechin, *U.K.* 13 E6
Brecht, *Belgium* 17 C4
Breckenridge, *Colo., U.S.A.* . 108 G10
Breckenridge, *Minn., U.S.A.* . 112 B6
Breckenridge, *Tex., U.S.A.* .. 113 J5
Breckland, *U.K.* 15 E8
Břeclav, *Czech Rep.* 27 C9
Brecon, *U.K.* 15 F4
Brecon Beacons, *U.K.* 15 F4
Brecon Beacons △, *U.K.* 15 F4
Breda, *Neths.* 17 C4
Bredaryd, *Sweden* 11 G7
Bredasdorp, *S. Africa* 88 E3
Bredebro, *Denmark* 11 J2
Bredstedt, *Germany* 24 A4
Bree, *Belgium* 17 C5
Bregalnica →, *Macedonia* ... 44 E6
Bregenz, *Austria* 26 D2
Bregovo, *Bulgaria* 44 B6
Bréhal, *France* 18 D5
Bréhat, Î. de, *France* 18 D4
Breiðafjörður, *Iceland* 8 D2
Breil-sur-Roya, *France* 21 E11
Breisach, *Germany* 25 G3
Brejo, *Brazil* 125 D10

Bremen, *Germany* 24 B4
Bremen □, *Germany* 24 B4
Bremer Bay, *Australia* 93 F2
Bremer I., *Australia* 94 A2
Bremerhaven, *Germany* 24 B4
Bremerton, *U.S.A.* 110 C4
Bremervörde, *Germany* 24 B5
Brenes, *Spain* 37 H5
Brenham, *U.S.A.* 113 K6
Brenne, *France* 20 B5
Brenne →, *France* 20 B5
Brennerpass, *Austria* 26 D4
Breno, *Italy* 40 C7
Brent, *U.S.A.* 115 J2
Brenta →, *Italy* 41 C9
Brentwood, *U.K.* 15 F8
Brentwood, *Calif., U.S.A.* ... 110 H5
Brentwood, *N.Y., U.S.A.* 117 F11
Bréscia, *Italy* 40 C7
Breskens, *Neths.* 17 C3
Breslau = Wrocław, *Poland* . 31 G4
Bresle →, *France* 18 B8
Bressanone, *Italy* 41 B8
Bressay, *U.K.* 13 A7
Bresse, *France* 19 F12
Bressuire, *France* 18 F6
Brest, *Belarus* 33 F2
Brest, *France* 18 D2
Brest-Litovsk = Brest, *Belarus* 33 F2
Bretagne □, *France* 18 D3
Brețcu, *Romania* 29 D11
Bretenoux, *France* 20 D5
Breteuil, *Eure, France* 18 D7
Breteuil, *Oise, France* 19 C9
Breton, *Canada* 102 C6
Breton, Pertuis, *France* 20 B2
Breton Sd., *U.S.A.* 113 L10
Brett, C., *N.Z.* 91 F5
Bretten, *Germany* 25 F4
Breuil-Cervínia, *Italy* 40 C4
Brevard, *U.S.A.* 115 H4
Breves, *Brazil* 125 D8
Brewarrina, *Australia* 95 E4
Brewer, *U.S.A.* 115 C11
Brewer, Mt., *U.S.A.* 110 J8
Brewerville, *Liberia* 82 D2
Brewster, *N.Y., U.S.A.* 117 E11
Brewster, *Ohio, U.S.A.* 116 F3
Brewster, *Wash., U.S.A.* 108 B4
Brewster, Kap = Kangikajik,
  Greenland 4 B6
Brewton, *U.S.A.* 115 K2
Breyten, *S. Africa* 89 D5
Breza, *Bos.-H.* 28 F3
Brežice, *Slovenia* 41 C12
Březnice, *Czech Rep.* 26 B6
Breznik, *Bulgaria* 44 D6
Brezno, *Slovak Rep.* 27 C12
Brezoi, *Romania* 29 E9
Brezovica, *Serbia & M.* 44 D5
Brezovo, *Bulgaria* 45 D9
Briançon, *France* 21 D10
Briare, *France* 19 E9
Briático, *Italy* 43 D9
Bribie I., *Australia* 95 D5
Bribri, *Costa Rica* 120 E3
Briceni, *Moldova* 29 B12
Bricquebec, *France* 18 C5
Bridgefield, *Barbados* ...... 121 g
Bridgehampton, *U.S.A.* 117 F12
Bridgend, *U.K.* 15 F4
Bridgend □, *U.K.* 15 F4
Bridgeport, *Calif., U.S.A.* ... 110 G7
Bridgeport, *Conn., U.S.A.* ... 117 E11
Bridgeport, *Nebr., U.S.A.* ... 112 E3
Bridgeport, *Tex., U.S.A.* 113 J6
Bridger, *U.S.A.* 108 D9
Bridgeton, *U.S.A.* 114 F8
Bridgetown, *Australia* 93 F2
Bridgetown, *Barbados* ...... 121 g
Bridgetown, *Canada* 105 D6
Bridgewater, *Canada* 105 D7
Bridgewater, *Mass., U.S.A.* . 117 E14
Bridgewater, *N.Y., U.S.A.* .. 117 D9
Bridgewater, *C., Australia* .. 95 F3
Bridgewater-Gagebrook,
  Australia 95 G4
Bridgnorth, *U.K.* 15 E5
Bridgton, *U.S.A.* 117 B14
Bridgwater, *U.K.* 15 F5
Bridgwater B., *U.K.* 15 F4
Bridlington, *U.K.* 14 C7
Bridlington B., *U.K.* 14 C7
Bridport, *Australia* 95 G4
Bridport, *U.K.* 15 G5
Briec, *France* 18 D2
Brienne-le-Château, *France* .. 19 D11
Brienon-sur-Armançon, *France* 19 E10
Brienz, *Switz.* 25 J4
Brienzersee, *Switz.* 25 J3
Brière △, *France* 18 E4
Brig, *Switz.* 25 J3
Brigg, *U.K.* 14 D7
Brigham City, *U.S.A.* 108 F7
Bright, *Australia* 95 F4
Brighton, *Australia* 95 F2
Brighton, *Canada* 116 B7
Brighton, *Trin. & Tob.* 125 K15
Brighton, *U.K.* 15 G7
Brighton, *Colo., U.S.A.* 112 F2
Brighton, *N.Y., U.S.A.* 116 C7
Brignogan-Plage, *France* 18 D2
Brignoles, *France* 21 E10
Brihuega, *Spain* 38 E2
Brikama, *Gambia* 82 C1
Brilliant, *U.S.A.* 116 F4
Brilon, *Germany* 24 D4
Bríndisi, *Italy* 43 B10
Brinje, *Croatia* 41 D12
Brinkley, *U.S.A.* 113 H9
Brinnon, *U.S.A.* 110 C4
Brion, Î., *Canada* 105 C7

Brionne, *France* 18 C7
Brionski, *Croatia* 41 D10
Brioude, *France* 20 C7
Briouze, *France* 18 D6
Brisbane, *Australia* 95 D5
Brisbane →, *Australia* 95 D5
Brisighella, *Italy* 41 D8
Bristol, *U.K.* 15 F5
Bristol, *Conn., U.S.A.* 117 E12
Bristol, *Pa., U.S.A.* 117 F10
Bristol, *R.I., U.S.A.* 117 E13
Bristol, *Tenn., U.S.A.* 115 G4
Bristol, City of □, *U.K.* 15 F5
Bristol B., *U.S.A.* 100 C4
Bristol Channel, *U.K.* 15 F3
Bristol I., *Antarctica* 5 B1
Bristol L., *U.S.A.* 109 J5
Briston, *U.S.A.* 113 H6
Britain = Great Britain, *Europe* 6 E5
British Columbia □, *Canada* . 102 C3
British Indian Ocean Terr. =
  Chagos Arch. ☒, *Ind. Oc.* . 50 K11
British Isles, *Europe* 6 D4
British Virgin Is. ☒, *W. Indies* 121 e
Brits, *S. Africa* 89 D4
Britstown, *S. Africa* 88 E3
Britt, *Canada* 104 C3
Britton, *U.S.A.* 112 C6
Brive-la-Gaillarde, *France* ... 20 C5
Briviesca, *Spain* 36 C7
Brixen = Bressanone, *Italy* .. 41 B8
Brixham, *U.K.* 15 G4
Brnaze, *Croatia* 41 E13
Brnenský □, *Czech Rep.* 27 B9
Brno, *Czech Rep.* 27 B9
Broach = Bharuch, *India* 66 J8
Broad →, *U.S.A.* 115 J5
Broad Arrow, *Australia* 93 F3
Broad B., *U.K.* 13 C2
Broad Haven, *Ireland* 12 B2
Broad Law, *U.K.* 13 F5
Broad Sd., *Australia* 94 C4
Broadalbin, *U.S.A.* 117 C10
Broadback →, *Canada* 104 B4
Broadhurst Ra., *Australia* ... 92 D3
Broads △, *U.K.* 15 E9
Broads, The, *U.K.* 14 E9
Broadus, *U.S.A.* 112 C2
Broager, *Denmark* 11 K3
Broby, *Sweden* 11 H8
Broceni, *Latvia* 30 B9
Brochet, *Canada* 103 B8
Brochet, L., *Canada* 103 B8
Brocken, *Germany* 24 D6
Brockport, *U.S.A.* 116 C7
Brockton, *U.S.A.* 117 D13
Brockville, *Canada* 117 B9
Brockway, *Mont., U.S.A.* ... 112 B2
Brockway, *Pa., U.S.A.* 116 E6
Brocton, *U.S.A.* 116 D5
Brod, *Macedonia* 44 E5
Brodarevo, *Serbia & M.* 44 C3
Brodeur Pen., *Canada* 101 A11
Brodhead, Mt., *U.S.A.* 116 E7
Brodick, *U.K.* 13 F3
Brodnica, *Poland* 31 E6
Brody, *Ukraine* 33 G3
Brogan, *U.S.A.* 108 D5
Broglie, *France* 18 C7
Brok, *Poland* 31 F8
Broken Arrow, *U.S.A.* 113 G7
Broken Bow, *Nebr., U.S.A.* . 112 E5
Broken Bow, *Okla., U.S.A.* .. 113 H7
Broken Bow Lake, *U.S.A.* ... 113 H7
Broken Hill, *Australia* 95 E3
Broken River Ra., *Australia* . 94 K6
Brokind, *Sweden* 11 F9
Bromley □, *U.K.* 15 F8
Bromo, *Indonesia* 63 G15
Bromölla, *Sweden* 11 H8
Bromsgrove, *U.K.* 15 E5
Brønderslev, *Denmark* 11 G3
Brong-Ahafo □, *Ghana* 82 D4
Broni, *Italy* 40 C6
Bronkhorstspruit, *S. Africa* . 89 D4
Brønnøysund, *Norway* 8 D15
Bronte, *Italy* 43 E7
Brook Park, *U.S.A.* 116 E4
Brookhaven, *U.S.A.* 113 K9
Brookings, *Oreg., U.S.A.* ... 108 E1
Brookings, *S. Dak., U.S.A.* .. 112 C6
Brooklin, *Canada* 116 C6
Brooklyn Park, *U.S.A.* 112 C8
Brooks, *Canada* 102 C6
Brooks Range, *U.S.A.* 100 B5
Brooksville, *U.S.A.* 115 L4
Brookton, *Australia* 93 F2
Brookville, *U.S.A.* 114 F3
Broom, L., *U.K.* 13 D3
Broome, *Australia* 92 C3
Broons, *France* 18 D4
Brora, *U.K.* 13 C5
Brora →, *U.K.* 13 C5
Brørup, *Denmark* 11 J2
Brösarp, *Sweden* 11 J8
Brosna →, *Ireland* 12 C4
Broșteni, *Mehedinți, Romania* 28 F7
Broșteni, *Suceava, Romania* . 29 C10
Brothers, *U.S.A.* 108 E3
Brou, *France* 18 D8
Brouage, *France* 20 C2
Brough, *U.K.* 14 C5
Brough Hd., *U.K.* 13 B5
Broughton Island = Qikiqtarjuaq,
  Canada 101 B13
Broumov, *Czech Rep.* 27 A9
Brovary, *Ukraine* 33 G6
Brovst, *Denmark* 11 G3
Brown, L., *Australia* 93 F2
Brown, Pt., *Australia* 95 E1
Brown City, *U.S.A.* 116 C2

Brown Willy, *U.K.* 15 G3
Brownfield, *U.S.A.* 113 J3
Browning, *U.S.A.* 108 B7
Brownsville, *Oreg., U.S.A.* .. 108 D2
Brownsville, *Pa., U.S.A.* 116 F5
Brownsville, *Tenn., U.S.A.* .. 113 H10
Brownsville, *Tex., U.S.A.* ... 113 N6
Brownville, *U.S.A.* 117 C9
Brownwood, *U.S.A.* 113 K5
Browse I., *Australia* 92 B3
Bruas, *Malaysia* 65 K3
Bruce, Mt., *Australia* 92 D2
Bruce Pen., *Canada* 116 B3
Bruce Peninsula △, *Canada* . 116 A3
Bruce Rock, *Australia* 93 F2
Bruche →, *France* 19 D14
Bruchsal, *Germany* 25 F4
Bruck an der Leitha, *Austria* 27 C9
Bruck an der Mur, *Austria* .. 26 D8
Brue →, *U.K.* 15 F5
Bruges = Brugge, *Belgium* .. 17 C3
Brugg, *Switz.* 25 H4
Brugge, *Belgium* 17 C3
Bruin, *U.S.A.* 116 E5
Brûlé, *Canada* 102 C5
Brûlon, *France* 18 E6
Brumado, *Brazil* 125 F10
Brumath, *France* 19 D14
Brumunddal, *Norway* 9 F14
Bruneau, *U.S.A.* 108 E6
Bruneau →, *U.S.A.* 108 E6
Bruneck = Brunico, *Italy* ... 41 B8
Brunei = Bandar Seri Begawan,
  Brunei 62 C4
Brunei ■, *Asia* 62 D4
Brunflo, *Sweden* 10 A8
Brunico, *Italy* 41 B8
Brunna, *Sweden* 10 E11
Brunnen, *Switz.* 25 J4
Brunner, L., *N.Z.* 91 K3
Brunsbüttel, *Germany* 24 B5
Brunssum, *Neths.* 17 D5
Brunswick = Braunschweig,
  Germany 24 C6
Brunswick, *Ga., U.S.A.* 115 K5
Brunswick, *Maine, U.S.A.* .. 115 D11
Brunswick, *Md., U.S.A.* 114 F7
Brunswick, *Mo., U.S.A.* 112 F8
Brunswick, *Ohio, U.S.A.* ... 116 E3
Brunswick, Pen. de, *Chile* .. 128 G2
Brunswick B., *Australia* 92 C3
Brunswick Junction, *Australia* 93 F2
Bruntál, *Czech Rep.* 27 B10
Bruny I., *Australia* 95 G4
Brus Laguna, *Honduras* 120 C3
Brusartsi, *Bulgaria* 44 C7
Brush, *U.S.A.* 112 E3
Brushton, *U.S.A.* 117 B10
Brusio, *Switz.* 25 J6
Brusque, *Brazil* 127 B6
Brussel, *Belgium* 17 D4
Brussel ✈ (BRU), *Belgium* .. 17 D5
Brussels = Brussel, *Belgium* . 17 D4
Brussels, *Canada* 116 C3
Brusy, *Poland* 30 E4
Bruthen, *Australia* 95 F4
Bruxelles = Brussel, *Belgium* 17 D4
Bruyères, *France* 19 D13
Bruz, *France* 18 D5
Brwinów, *Poland* 31 F7
Bryagovo, *Bulgaria* 45 E9
Bryan, *Ohio, U.S.A.* 114 E3
Bryan, *Tex., U.S.A.* 113 K6
Bryan, Mt., *Australia* 95 E2
Bryanka, *Ukraine* 33 H10
Bryansk, *Bryansk, Russia* ... 33 F8
Bryansk, *Dagestan, Russia* .. 35 H8
Bryanskoye = Bryansk, *Russia* 35 H8
Bryce Canyon △, *U.S.A.* 109 H7
Bryne, *Norway* 9 G11
Bryson City, *U.S.A.* 115 H4
Bryukhovetskaya, *Russia* ... 33 K10
Brza Palanka, *Serbia & M.* . 44 B6
Brzeg, *Poland* 31 H4
Brzeg Dolny, *Poland* 31 G3
Brześć Kujawski, *Poland* 31 F5
Brzesko, *Poland* 31 J7
Brzeziny, *Poland* 31 G6
Brzozów, *Poland* 31 J9
Bsharri, *Lebanon* 74 A5
Bū Baqarah, *U.A.E.* 71 E8
Bu Craa, *W. Sahara* 78 C3
Bū Ḥasā, *U.A.E.* 71 F7
Bua, *Sweden* 11 G6
Bua Yai, *Thailand* 64 E4
Buapinang, *Indonesia* 63 E6
Buba, *Guinea-Biss.* 82 C2
Bubanza, *Burundi* 86 C2
Bubaque, *Guinea-Biss.* 82 C1
Bube, *Ethiopia* 81 F4
Būbiyān, *Kuwait* 71 D6
Buca, *Turkey* 47 C9
Bucak, *Turkey* 47 D12
Bucaramanga, *Colombia* ... 124 B4
Bucas Grande I., *Phil.* 61 G6
Bucasia, *Australia* 94 K7
Buccaneer Arch., *Australia* .. 92 C3
Buccino, *Italy* 43 B8
Bucco Reef, *Trin. & Tob.* ... 125 J16
Bucecea, *Romania* 29 C11
Buchach, *Ukraine* 33 H3
Buchan, *U.K.* 13 D7
Buchan Ness, *U.K.* 13 D7
Buchanan, *Canada* 103 C8
Buchanan, *Liberia* 82 D2
Buchanan, L., *Queens., Australia* 94 C4
Buchanan, L., *W. Austral.,
  Australia* 93 E3
Buchanan, L., *U.S.A.* 113 K5
Buchanan Cr. →, *Australia* . 94 B2

Buchans, *Canada* 105 C8
Bucharest = București, *Romania* 29 F11
Buchen, *Germany* 25 F5
Buchholz, *Germany* 24 B5
Buchloe, *Germany* 25 G6
Buchon, Pt., *U.S.A.* 110 K6
Buciumi, *Romania* 28 C8
Buck Hill Falls, *U.S.A.* 117 E9
Bückeburg, *Germany* 24 C5
Buckeye, *U.S.A.* 109 K7
Buckeye Lake, *U.S.A.* 116 G2
Buckhannon, *U.S.A.* 114 F5
Buckhaven, *U.K.* 13 E5
Buckhorn L., *Canada* 116 B6
Buckie, *U.K.* 13 D6
Buckingham, *Canada* 104 C4
Buckingham, *U.K.* 15 F7
Buckingham B., *Australia* ... 94 A2
Buckinghamshire □, *U.K.* ... 15 F7
Buckle Hd., *Australia* 92 B4
Buckleboo, *Australia* 95 E2
Buckley, *U.K.* 14 D4
Buckley →, *Australia* 94 C2
Bucklin, *U.S.A.* 113 G5
Bucks L., *U.S.A.* 110 F5
Bucquoy, *France* 19 B9
București, *Romania* 29 F11
București Otopeni ✈ (OTP),
  Romania 45 B10
Bucyrus, *U.S.A.* 114 E4
Budacu, Vf., *Romania* 29 C10
Budalin, *Burma* 67 H19
Budaörs, *Hungary* 28 C3
Budapest, *Hungary* 28 C3
Budapest □, *Hungary* 28 C3
Budapest ✈ (BUD), *Hungary* 28 C4
Budaun, *India* 69 E8
Budd Coast, *Antarctica* 5 C8
Buddusò, *Italy* 42 B2
Bude, *U.K.* 15 G3
Budennovsk, *Russia* 35 H7
Budești, *Romania* 29 F11
Budeyi, *Ukraine* 29 B14
Budge Budge = Baj Baj, *India* 69 H13
Budgewoi, *Australia* 95 E5
Budia, *Spain* 38 E2
Büdingen, *Germany* 25 E5
Budjala, *Dem. Rep. of the Congo* 84 D3
Budoni, *Italy* 42 B2
Búdrio, *Italy* 41 D8
Budva, *Serbia & M.* 44 D2
Budzyń, *Poland* 31 F3
Buea, *Cameroon* 83 E6
Buellton, *U.S.A.* 111 L6
Buena Esperanza, *Argentina* 126 C2
Buena Park, *U.S.A.* 111 M9
Buena Vista, *Colo., U.S.A.* .. 109 G10
Buena Vista, *Va., U.S.A.* ... 114 G6
Buena Vista Lake Bed, *U.S.A.* 111 K7
Buenaventura, *Colombia* ... 124 C3
Buenaventura, *Mexico* 118 B3
Buendía, Embalse de, *Spain* . 38 E2
Buenos Aires, *Argentina* 126 C4
Buenos Aires, *Costa Rica* ... 120 E3
Buenos Aires □, *Argentina* .. 126 D4
Buenos Aires, L., *Chile* 128 F2
Buffalo, *Mo., U.S.A.* 113 G8
Buffalo, *N.Y., U.S.A.* 116 D6
Buffalo, *Okla., U.S.A.* 113 G5
Buffalo, *S. Dak., U.S.A.* 112 C3
Buffalo, *Wyo., U.S.A.* 108 D10
Buffalo △, *U.S.A.* 113 G8
Buffalo →, *Canada* 102 A5
Buffalo →, *S. Africa* 89 D5
Buffalo Head Hills, *Canada* . 102 B5
Buffalo L., *Alta., Canada* ... 102 C6
Buffalo L., *N.W.T., Canada* . 102 A5
Buffalo Narrows, *Canada* ... 103 B7
Buffalo Springs △, *Kenya* .. 86 B4
Buffels →, *S. Africa* 88 D2
Buford, *U.S.A.* 115 H4
Bug = Buh →, *Ukraine* 33 J6
Bug →, *Poland* 31 F8
Buga, *Colombia* 124 C3
Bugala I., *Uganda* 86 C3
Buganda, *Uganda* 86 C3
Buganga, *Uganda* 86 C3
Bugasong, *Phil.* 61 F5
Bugeat, *France* 20 C5
Bugel, Tanjung, *Indonesia* .. 63 G14
Bugibba, *Malta* 49 D1
Bugojno, *Bos.-H.* 28 F2
Bugsuk, *Phil.* 62 C5
Buguma, *Nigeria* 83 E6
Bugun Shara, *Mongolia* 60 B5
Bugungu △, *Uganda* 86 B3
Buguruslan, *Russia* 52 D6
Buh →, *Ukraine* 33 J6
Buharkent, *Turkey* 47 D10
Buheirat-Murrat-el-Kubra, *Egypt* 80 H8
Buhera, *Zimbabwe* 89 B5
Bühl, *Germany* 25 G4
Buhl, *U.S.A.* 108 E6
Buhuși, *Romania* 29 D11
Bui △, *Ghana* 82 D4
Builth Wells, *U.K.* 15 E4
Buinsk, *Russia* 34 C9
Buir Nur, *Mongolia* 60 B6
Buis-les-Baronnies, *France* .. 21 D9
Buitrago del Lozoya, *Spain* .. 36 E7
Bujalance, *Spain* 37 H6
Bujanovac, *Serbia & M.* 44 D5
Bujaraloz, *Spain* 38 D4
Buje, *Croatia* 41 C10
Bujumbura, *Burundi* 86 C2
Bük, *Hungary* 28 C1
Buk, *Poland* 31 F3
Bukachacha, *Russia* 53 D12
Bukama, *Dem. Rep. of the Congo* 87 D2
Bukavu, *Dem. Rep. of the Congo* 86 C2
Bukene, *Tanzania* 86 C3
Bukhara = Bukhoro, *Uzbekistan* 52 F7

Bukhoro, *Uzbekistan* 52 F7
Bukima, *Tanzania* 86 C3
Bukit Badung, *Indonesia* 63 K18
Bukit Kerajaan, *Malaysia* . . . . . 65 c
Bukit Mertajam, *Malaysia* . . . . . 65 c
Bukit Ni, *Malaysia* . . . . 65 d
Bukit Panjang, *Singapore* . . . . . 65 d
Bukit Tengah, *Malaysia* . . . . . . 65 c
Bukittinggi, *Indonesia* 62 E2
Bükk, *Hungary* 28 B5
Bükki △, *Hungary* 28 B5
Bukoba, *Tanzania* 86 C3
Bukum, Pulau, *Singapore* . . . . . 65 d
Bukuru, *Nigeria* 83 D6
Bukuya, *Uganda* 86 B3
Būl, Kuh-e, *Iran* 71 D7
Bula, *Guinea-Biss.* 82 C1
Bula, *Indonesia* 63 E8
Bülach, *Switz.* 25 H4
Bulahdelah, *Australia* 95 E5
Bulan, *Phil.* 61 E5
Bulancak, *Turkey* 73 B8
Bulandshahr, *India* 68 E7
Bulanık, *Turkey* 73 C10
Būlāq, *Egypt* 80 B3
Bulawayo, *Zimbabwe* 87 G2
Buldan, *Turkey* 47 C10
Bulgar, *Russia* 34 C9
Bulgaria ■, *Europe* 45 D9
Bulgheria, Monte, *Italy* 43 B8
Bulgurca, *Turkey* 47 C9
Buli, Teluk, *Indonesia* 63 D7
Buliluyan, C., *Phil.* 61 G2
Bulim, *Singapore* . . . . 65 d
Bulki, *Ethiopia* 81 F4
Bulkley →, *Canada* 102 B3
Bull Shoals L., *U.S.A.* 113 G8
Bullaque →, *Spain* 37 G6
Bullas, *Spain* 39 G3
Bulle, *Switz.* 25 J3
Bulleringa △, *Australia* 94 B3
Bullhead City, *U.S.A.* 111 K12
Büllingen, *Belgium* 17 D6
Bullock Creek, *Australia* 94 B3
Bulloo →, *Australia* 95 D3
Bulloo L., *Australia* 95 D3
Bulls, *N.Z.* 91 J5
Bully-les-Mines, *France* 19 B9
Bulnes, *Chile* 126 D1
Bulqizë, *Albania* 44 E4
Bulsar = Valsad, *India* 66 J8
Bultfontein, *S. Africa* 88 D4
Bulukumba, *Indonesia* 63 F6
Bulun, *Russia* 53 B13
Bumba, *Dem. Rep. of the Congo* 84 D4
Bumbești-Jiu, *Romania* 29 E8
Bumbiri I., *Tanzania* 86 C3
Bumbuna, *S. Leone* 82 D2
Bumhpa Bum, *Burma* 67 F20
Bumi →, *Zimbabwe* 87 F2
Buna, *Kenya* 86 B4
Bunawan, *Phil.* 61 G6
Bunazi, *Tanzania* 86 C3
Bunbury, *Australia* 93 F2
Bunclody, *Ireland* 12 D5
Buncrana, *Ireland* 12 A4
Bundaberg, *Australia* 95 C5
Bünde, *Germany* 24 C4
Bundey →, *Australia* 94 C2
Bundi, *India* 68 G6
Bundjalung △, *Australia* 95 D5
Bundoran, *Ireland* 12 B3
Bundukia, *Sudan* 81 F3
Bung Kan, *Thailand* 64 C4
Bunga →, *Nigeria* 83 C6
Bungay, *U.K.* 15 E9
Bungil Cr. →, *Australia* 95 D4
Bungle Bungle = Purnululu △,
  Australia 92 C4
Bungo-Suidō, *Japan* 55 H6
Bungoma, *Kenya* 86 B3
Bungotakada, *Japan* 55 H5
Bungu, *Tanzania* 86 D4
Bunia, *Dem. Rep. of the Congo* . 86 B3
Bunji, *Pakistan* 69 B6
Bunkie, *U.S.A.* 113 K8
Bunnell, *U.S.A.* 115 L5
Buñol, *Spain* 39 F4
Bunsuru, *Nigeria* 83 C5
Buntok, *Indonesia* 62 E4
Bununu Dass, *Nigeria* 83 C6
Bununu Kasa, *Nigeria* 83 D6
Bunya Mts. △, *Australia* 95 D5
Bünyan, *Turkey* 72 C6
Bunyu, *Indonesia* 62 D5
Bunza, *Nigeria* 83 C5
Buol, *Indonesia* 63 D6
Buon Brieng, *Vietnam* 64 F7
Buon Ma Thuot, *Vietnam* 64 F7
Buong Long, *Cambodia* 64 F6
Buorkhaya, Mys, *Russia* 53 B14
Buqayq, *Si. Arabia* 71 E6
Buqbuq, *Egypt* 80 A2
Bur Acaba, *Somali Rep.* 75 G3
Būr Fu'ād, *Egypt* 80 H8
Būr Safāga, *Egypt* 70 E2
Būr Sa'īd, *Egypt* 80 H8
Būr Sūdān, *Sudan* 80 D4
Būr Taufiq, *Egypt* 80 J8
Bura, *Kenya* 86 C4
Burakin, *Australia* 93 F2
Buram, *Sudan* 81 E2
Burao, *Somali Rep.* 75 F4
Burāq, *Syria* 74 B5
Buraydah, *Si. Arabia* 70 E4
Burbank, *U.S.A.* 111 L8
Burda, *India* 68 G6
Burdekin →, *Australia* 94 B4
Burdur, *Turkey* 47 D12
Burdur □, *Turkey* 47 D12
Burdur Gölü, *Turkey* 47 D12
Burdwan = Barddhaman, *India* . 69 H12

Bure, Gojam, *Ethiopia* 81 E4
Bure, Ilubabor, *Ethiopia* 81 F4
Bure →, *U.K.* 14 E9
Büren, *Germany* 24 D4
Bureya →, *Russia* 53 E13
Burford, *Canada* 116 C4
Burg, *Germany* 24 C7
Burg auf Fehmarn, *Germany* . . . 24 A7
Burg el Arab, *Egypt* 80 H6
Burg et Tuyur, *Sudan* 80 C2
Burg Stargard, *Germany* 24 B9
Burgas, *Bulgaria* 45 D11
Burgas □, *Bulgaria* 45 D10
Burgaski Zaliv, *Bulgaria* 45 D11
Burgdorf, *Germany* 24 C6
Burgdorf, *Switz.* 25 H3
Burgeo, *Canada* 105 C8
Burgenland □, *Austria* 27 D9
Burgeo, *Canada* 105 C8
Burgersdorp, *S. Africa* 88 E4
Burges, Mt., *Australia* 93 F3
Burghausen, *Germany* 25 G8
Burghead, *U.K.* 13 D5
Búrgio, *Italy* 42 E6
Burglengenfeld, *Germany* 25 F8
Burgohondo, *Spain* 36 E6
Burgos, *Spain* 36 C7
Burgos □, *Spain* 36 C7
Burgstädt, *Germany* 24 E8
Burgsvik, *Sweden* 11 G12
Burguillos del Cerro, *Spain* . . . 37 G4
Burgundy = Bourgogne □, *France* 19 F11
Burhaniye, *Turkey* 47 B8
Burhanpur, *India* 66 J10
Burhi Gandak →, *India* 69 G12
Burhner →, *India* 69 H9
Buri Pen., *Eritrea* 81 D4
Burias I., *Phil.* 61 E5
Burica, Pta., *Costa Rica* 120 E3
Burien, *U.S.A.* 110 C4
Burigi △, *Tanzania* 86 C3
Burigi, L., *Tanzania* 86 C3
Burin, *Canada* 105 C8
Buriram, *Thailand* 64 E4
Burj Sāfitā, *Syria* 70 C3
Burji, *Ethiopia* 81 F4
Burkburnett, *U.S.A.* 113 H5
Burke →, *Canada* 94 C2
Burke Chan., *Canada* 102 C3
Burketown, *Australia* 94 B2
Burkina Faso ■, *Africa* 82 C4
Burk's Falls, *Canada* 104 C4
Burlada, *Spain* 38 C3
Burleigh Falls, *Canada* 116 B6
Burley, *U.S.A.* 108 E7
Burlingame, *U.S.A.* 110 H4
Burlington, *Canada* 116 C5
Burlington, Colo., *U.S.A.* 112 F3
Burlington, Iowa, *U.S.A.* 112 E9
Burlington, Kans., *U.S.A.* 112 F7
Burlington, N.C., *U.S.A.* 115 G6
Burlington, N.J., *U.S.A.* 117 F10
Burlington, Vt., *U.S.A.* 117 B11
Burlington, Wash., *U.S.A.* 110 B4
Burlington, Wis., *U.S.A.* 114 D1
Burlyu-Tyube, *Kazakhstan* 52 E8
Burma ■, *Asia* 67 J20
Burnaby I., *Canada* 102 C2
Burnet, *U.S.A.* 113 K5
Burney, *U.S.A.* 108 F3
Burnham, *U.S.A.* 116 F7
Burnham-on-Sea, *U.K.* 15 F5
Burnie, *Australia* 95 G4
Burnley, *U.K.* 14 D5
Burns, *U.S.A.* 108 E4
Burns Lake, *Canada* 102 C3
Burnside →, *Canada* 100 B9
Burnside, L., *Australia* 93 E3
Burnsville, *U.S.A.* 112 C8
Burnt, L., *Canada* 105 B7
Burnt River, *Canada* 116 B6
Burntwood →, *Canada* 103 B9
Burntwood L., *Canada* 103 B8
Burqān, *Kuwait* 70 D5
Burra, *Australia* 95 E2
Burra, *Nigeria* 83 C6
Burray, *U.K.* 13 C6
Burrel, *Albania* 44 E4
Burren △, *Ireland* 12 C3
Burren Junction, *Australia* 95 E4
Burriana, *Spain* 38 F4
Burrinjuck Res., *Australia* 95 F4
Burro, Serranías del, *Mexico* . . 118 B4
Burrow Hd., *U.K.* 13 G4
Burrum Coast △, *Australia* 95 D5
Burruyacú, *Argentina* 126 B3
Burry Port, *U.K.* 15 F3
Bursa, *Turkey* 45 F13
Burseryd, *Sweden* 11 G7
Burstall, *Canada* 103 C7
Burton, *Ohio, U.S.A.* 116 G3
Burton, S.C., *U.S.A.* 115 J5
Burton, L., *Canada* 104 B4
Burton upon Trent, *U.K.* 14 E6
Buru, *Indonesia* 63 E7
Burullus, Bahra el, *Egypt* 80 H7
Burûn, Râs, *Egypt* 74 D2
Burundi ■, *Africa* 86 C3
Bururi, *Burundi* 86 C2
Burutu, *Nigeria* 83 D6
Burwell, *U.S.A.* 112 E5
Burwick, *U.K.* 13 C5
Bury, *U.K.* 14 D5
Bury St. Edmunds, *U.K.* 15 E8
Buryatia □, *Russia* 53 D11
Buryn, *Ukraine* 33 G7
Burzenin, *Poland* 31 G5
Busalla, *Italy* 40 D5
Busango Swamp, *Zambia* 87 E2
Buşayrah, *Syria* 70 C4
Busca, *Italy* 40 D4
Bushat, *Albania* 44 E3

Būshehr, *Iran* 71 D6
Būshehr □, *Iran* 71 D6
Bushell, *Canada* 103 B7
Bushenyi, *Uganda* 86 C3
Bushire = Būshehr, *Iran* 71 D6
Bushtyna, *Ukraine* 29 B8
Busia, *Ghana* 82 C4
Businga, *Dem. Rep. of the Congo* 84 D4
Busko-Zdrój, *Poland* 31 H7
Busovača, *Bos.-H.* 28 F2
Buşra ash Shām, *Syria* 74 C5
Busselton, *Australia* 93 F2
Busseto, *Italy* 40 D7
Busser □, *Sudan* 81 F2
Bussière-Badil, *France* 20 C4
Bussolengo, *Italy* 40 C7
Bussum, *Neths.* 17 B5
Busteni, *Romania* 29 E10
Busto, C., *Spain* 36 B4
Busto Arsízio, *Italy* 40 C5
Busu Djanoa, *Dem. Rep. of
  the Congo* 84 D4
Busuanga I., *Phil.* 61 E3
Büsum, *Germany* 24 A4
Busungbiu, *Indonesia* 63 J17
Buta, *Dem. Rep. of the Congo* . 86 B1
Butare, *Rwanda* 86 C2
Butaritari, *Kiribati* 96 G9
Bute, *U.K.* 13 F3
Bute Inlet, *Canada* 102 C4
Butemba, *Uganda* 86 B3
Butembo, *Dem. Rep. of the Congo* 86 B2
Buteni, *Romania* 28 D7
Butera, *Italy* 43 E7
Butha Qi, *China* 60 B7
Butiaba, *Uganda* 86 B3
Butler, Mo., *U.S.A.* 112 F7
Butler, Pa., *U.S.A.* 116 F5
Buton, *Indonesia* 63 E6
Butte, Mont., *U.S.A.* 108 C7
Butte, Nebr., *U.S.A.* 112 D5
Butte Creek →, *U.S.A.* 110 F5
Butterworth = Gcuwa, *S. Africa* 89 E4
Butterworth, *Malaysia* . . . . . . 65 c
Buttevant, *Ireland* 12 D3
Buttfield, Mt., *Australia* 93 D4
Button B., *Canada* 103 B10
Buttonwillow, *U.S.A.* 111 K7
Butty Hd., *Australia* 93 F3
Butuan, *Phil.* 61 G6
Butuku-Luba, *Eq. Guin.* 83 E6
Butung = Buton, *Indonesia* . . . 63 E6
Buturlinovka, *Russia* 34 E5
Butzbach, *Germany* 25 E4
Bützow, *Germany* 24 B7
Buur Hakaba = Bur Acaba,
  Somali Rep. 75 G3
Buxa Duar, *India* 69 F13
Buxar, *India* 69 G10
Buxtehude, *Germany* 24 B5
Buxton, *U.K.* 14 D6
Buxy, *France* 19 F11
Buy, *Russia* 34 A5
Buynaksk, *Russia* 35 J8
Buyo, *Ivory C.* 82 D3
Buyo, L. de, *Ivory C.* 82 D3
Büyük Menderes →, *Turkey* . . . 47 D9
Büyükçekmece, *Turkey* 45 E12
Büyükkarıştıran, *Turkey* 45 E11
Büyükkemikli Burnu, *Turkey* . . . 45 F10
Büyükorhan, *Turkey* 47 B10
Büyükyoncalı, *Turkey* 45 E11
Buzançais, *France* 18 F8
Buzău, *Romania* 29 E11
Buzău □, *Romania* 29 E11
Buzău →, *Romania* 29 E12
Buzău, Pasul, *Romania* 29 E11
Buzen, *Japan* 55 H5
Buzet, *Croatia* 41 C10
Buzi →, *Mozam.* 87 F3
Buziaş, *Romania* 28 E6
Buzuluk, *Russia* 52 D6
Buzuluk →, *Russia* 34 E6
Buzzards B., *U.S.A.* 117 E14
Buzzards B., *U.S.A.* 117 E14
Bwana Mkubwe, *Dem. Rep. of
  the Congo* 87 E2
Bwindi △, *Uganda* 86 C2
Byala, Ruse, *Bulgaria* 45 C9
Byala, Varna, *Bulgaria* 45 D11
Byala Slatina, *Bulgaria* 44 C7
Byarezina →, *Belarus* 33 F6
Byaroza, *Belarus* 33 F3
Bychawa, *Poland* 31 G9
Byczyna, *Poland* 31 G5
Bydgoszcz, *Poland* 31 B4
Byelarus = Belarus ■, *Europe* . 32 F4
Byelorussia = Belarus ■, *Europe* 32 F4
Byers, *U.S.A.* 112 F2
Byesville, *U.S.A.* 116 G3
Byfield △, *Australia* 94 C5
Byford, *Australia* 93 F2
Bykhaw, *Belarus* 33 F6
Bykhov = Bykhaw, *Belarus* . . . 32 F6
Bykovo, *Russia* 34 E7
Bylas, *U.S.A.* 109 K8
Bylot, *Canada* 103 B10
Bylot I., *Canada* 101 A12
Byrd, C., *Antarctica* 5 C17
Byrock, *Australia* 95 E4
Byron, C., *Australia* 95 D5
Byron Bay, *Australia* 95 D5
Byrranga, Gory, *Russia* 53 B11
Byrranga Mts. = Byrranga, Gory,
  Russia 53 B11
Byrum, *Denmark* 11 G5
Byske, *Sweden* 8 D19
Byskeälven →, *Sweden* 8 D19
Bystrytsya, *Ukraine* 29 B9
Bystrzyca →, *Dolnośląskie,
  Poland* 31 G3
Bystrzyca →, *Lubelskie, Poland* 31 G9

Bystrzyca Kłodzka, *Poland* . . . 31 H3
Bytča, *Slovak Rep.* 27 B11
Bytkiv, *Ukraine* 29 B9
Bytom, *Poland* 31 H5
Bytom Odrzański, *Poland* 31 G2
Bytów, *Poland* 30 D4
Bzenec, *Czech Rep.* 27 C10
Bzura →, *Poland* 31 F7

C

Ca →, *Vietnam* 64 C5
Ca Mau, *Vietnam* 65 H5
Ca Mau, Mui, *Vietnam* 65 H5
Ca Na, *Vietnam* 65 G7
Caacupé, *Paraguay* 126 B4
Caaguazú □, *Paraguay* 127 B4
Caála, *Angola* 85 G3
Caamaño Sd., *Canada* 102 C3
Caazapá, *Paraguay* 126 B4
Caazapá □, *Paraguay* 127 B4
Cabadbaran, *Phil.* 61 G6
Cabalian = San Juan, *Phil.* 61 F6
Caballeria, C. de, *Spain* 48 A11
Cabana, *Spain* 36 B2
Cabañaquinta, *Spain* 36 B5
Cabanatuan, *Phil.* 61 D4
Cabañeros △, *Spain* 37 F6
Cabanes, *Spain* 38 E5
Cabano, *Canada* 105 C6
Čabar, *Croatia* 41 C11
Cabazon, *U.S.A.* 111 M10
Cabedelo, *Brazil* 125 E12
Cabeza del Buey, *Spain* 37 G5
Cabezón de la Sal, *Spain* 36 B6
Cabildo, *Chile* 126 C1
Cabimas, *Venezuela* 124 A4
Cabinda, *Angola* 84 F2
Cabinda □, *Angola* 84 F2
Cabinet Mts., *U.S.A.* 108 C6
Cabo Blanco, *Argentina* 128 F3
Cabo Frio, *Brazil* 127 A7
Cabo Pantoja, *Peru* 124 D3
Cabonga, Réservoir, *Canada* . . 104 C4
Cabool, *U.S.A.* 113 G8
Caboolture, *Australia* 95 D5
Cabora Bassa Dam = Cahora
  Bassa, Reprêsa de, *Mozam.* . 87 F3
Caborca, *Mexico* 118 A2
Cabot, Mt., *U.S.A.* 117 B13
Cabot Hd., *Canada* 116 A3
Cabot Str., *Canada* 105 C8
Cabra, *Spain* 37 H6
Cabra del Santo Cristo, *Spain* . 37 H7
Cábras, *Italy* 42 C1
Cabrera, *Spain* 48 B9
Cabrera △, *Spain* 39 F7
Cabrera, Sierra, *Spain* 36 C4
Cabri, *Canada* 103 C7
Cabriel →, *Spain* 39 F3
Cabugao, *Phil.* 61 C4
Cacabelos, *Spain* 36 C4
Caçador, *Brazil* 127 B5
Čačak, *Serbia & M.* 44 C4
Caçapava do Sul, *Brazil* 127 C5
Cáccamo, *Italy* 42 E6
Cacém, *Portugal* 37 G1
Cáceres, *Brazil* 124 G7
Cáceres, *Spain* 37 F4
Cáceres □, *Spain* 36 F5
Cache Bay, *Canada* 104 C4
Cache Cr. →, *U.S.A.* 110 G5
Cache Creek, *Canada* 102 C4
Cacheu, *Guinea-Biss.* 82 C1
Cachi, *Argentina* 126 B2
Cachimbo, Serra do, *Brazil* . . . 125 E7
Cachinal de la Sierra, *Chile* . . . 126 A2
Cachoeira, *Brazil* 125 F11
Cachoeira do Sul, *Brazil* 127 C5
Cachoeiro de Itapemirim, *Brazil* 127 A7
Cachopo, *Portugal* 37 H3
Cacine, *Guinea-Biss.* 82 C1
Cacoal, *Brazil* 124 F6
Cacólo, *Angola* 84 G3
Caconda, *Angola* 85 G3
Caddo, *U.S.A.* 113 H6
Cader Idris, *U.K.* 15 E4
Cadereyta, *Mexico* 118 B5
Cadí, Sierra del, *Spain* 38 C6
Cadí-Moixeró △, *Spain* 38 C6
Cadibarrawirracanna, L.,
  Australia 95 D2
Cadillac, *France* 20 D3
Cadillac, *U.S.A.* 114 C3
Cadiz, *Phil.* 61 F5
Cádiz, *Spain* 37 J4
Cadiz, Calif., *U.S.A.* 111 L11
Cadiz, Ohio, *U.S.A.* 116 F4
Cádiz □, *Spain* 37 J5
Cádiz, G. de, *Spain* 37 J3
Cadiz L., *U.S.A.* 109 J6
Cadney Park, *Australia* 95 D1
Cadomin, *Canada* 102 C5
Cadotte Lake, *Canada* 102 B5
Cadours, *France* 20 E5
Cadoux, *Australia* 93 F2
Caen, *France* 18 C6
Caernarfon, *U.K.* 14 D3
Caernarfon B., *U.K.* 14 D3
Caernarvon = Caernarfon, *U.K.* . 14 D3
Caerphilly, *U.K.* 15 F4
Caerphilly □, *U.K.* 15 F4
Caesarea, *Israel* 74 C3
Caetité, *Brazil* 125 F10
Cafayate, *Argentina* 126 B2

Cafu, *Angola* 88 B2
Cagayan →, *Phil.* 61 B4
Cagayan de Oro, *Phil.* 61 G6
Cagayan Is., *Phil.* 61 G4
Cagayan Sulu I., *Phil.* 61 H3
Cagli, *Italy* 41 E9
Cágliari, *Italy* 42 C2
Cágliari, G. di, *Italy* 42 C2
Cagnano Varano, *Italy* 41 G12
Cagnes-sur-Mer, *France* 21 E11
Caguán →, *Colombia* 124 D4
Caguas, *Puerto Rico* . . . . 121 d
Caha Mts., *Ireland* 12 E2
Cahama, *Angola* 88 B1
Caher, *Ireland* 12 D4
Cahersiveen, *Ireland* 12 E1
Cahora Bassa, L. de, *Mozam.* . . 87 F3
Cahora Bassa, Reprêsa de,
  Mozam. 87 F3
Cahore Pt., *Ireland* 12 D5
Cahors, *France* 20 D5
Cahul, *Moldova* 29 E13
Caì Bau, Dao, *Vietnam* 58 G6
Cai Nuoc, *Vietnam* 65 H5
Caia, *Mozam.* 87 F4
Caianda, *Angola* 87 E1
Caibarién, *Cuba* 120 B4
Caibiran, *Phil.* 61 F6
Caicara, *Venezuela* 124 B5
Caicó, *Brazil* 125 E11
Caicos Is., *Turks & Caicos* 121 B5
Caicos Passage, *W. Indies* . . . 121 B5
Caidian, *China* 59 B10
Căinari, *Moldova* 29 D14
Caird Coast, *Antarctica* 5 D1
Cairn Gorm, *U.K.* 13 D5
Cairngorm Mts., *U.K.* 13 D5
Cairngorms △, *U.K.* 13 D5
Cairnryan, *U.K.* 13 G3
Cairns, *Australia* 94 B4
Cairns L., *Canada* 103 C10
Cairo = El Qâhira, *Egypt* 80 H7
Cairo, Ga., *U.S.A.* 115 K3
Cairo, Ill., *U.S.A.* 113 G10
Cairo, N.Y., *U.S.A.* 117 D11
Cairo Montenotte, *Italy* 40 D5
Caithness, *U.K.* 13 C5
Caithness, Ord of, *U.K.* 13 C5
Caja de Muertos, I., *Puerto Rico* 121 d
Cajamarca, *Peru* 124 E3
Cajarc, *France* 20 D5
Cajàzeiras, *Brazil* 125 E11
Čajetina, Serbia & M. 44 C3
Çakirgol, *Turkey* 73 B8
Çakırlar, *Turkey* 47 E12
Čakovec, *Croatia* 41 B13
Çal, *Turkey* 47 C11
Cala, *Spain* 37 H4
Cala →, *Spain* 37 H4
Cala Cadolar, Punta de = Rotja,
  Pta., *Spain* 39 G6
Cala d'Or, *Spain* 48 B10
Cala en Porter, *Spain* 48 B11
Cala Figuera, C. de, *Spain* 48 B9
Cala Forcat, *Spain* 48 B10
Cala Major, *Spain* 48 B9
Cala Mezquida = Sa Mesquida,
  Spain 48 B11
Cala Millor, *Spain* 48 B10
Cala Ratjada, *Spain* 48 B10
Cala Santa Galdana, *Spain* . . . 48 B10
Calabanga, *Phil.* 61 E5
Calabar, *Nigeria* 83 E6
Calabogie, *Canada* 117 A8
Calabozo, *Venezuela* 124 B5
Calábria □, *Italy* 43 C9
Calábria △, *Italy* 43 C9
Calaburras, Pta. de, *Spain* 37 J6
Calaceite, *Spain* 38 D5
Calacuccia, *France* 21 F13
Calafat, *Romania* 28 G7
Calafate, *Argentina* 128 G2
Calafell, *Spain* 38 D6
Calahorra, *Spain* 38 C3
Calai, *France* 19 B8
Calais, *U.S.A.* 115 C12
Calakmul △, *Mexico* 119 D7
Calalaste, Cord. de, *Argentina* . 126 B2
Calama, *Brazil* 124 E6
Calama, *Chile* 126 A2
Calamar, *Colombia* 124 A4
Calamian Group, *Phil.* 61 F3
Calamocha, *Spain* 38 E3
Calamonte, *Spain* 37 G4
Calañas, *Spain* 37 H4
Calanda, *Spain* 38 E4
Calang, *Indonesia* 62 D1
Calángianos, *Italy* 42 B2
Calapan, *Phil.* 61 E4
Călărași, *Moldova* 29 C13
Călărași, *Romania* 29 F12
Călărași □, *Romania* 29 F12
Calasparra, *Spain* 39 G3
Calatafimi, *Italy* 42 E5
Calatayud, *Spain* 38 D3
Călăţele, *Romania* 28 D8
Calato = Kálathos, *Greece* 47 E10
Calauag, *Phil.* 61 E5
Calavà, C., *Italy* 43 D7
Calavite, C., *Phil.* 61 E4
Calayan, *Phil.* 61 B4
Calbayog, *Phil.* 61 E6
Calca, *Peru* 124 F4
Calcasieu L., *U.S.A.* 113 L8
Calcutta = Kolkata, *India* 69 H13
Calcutta, *U.S.A.* 116 F4
Caldas da Rainha, *Portugal* . . . 37 F1
Caldas de Reis, *Spain* 36 C2
Calder →, *U.K.* 14 D6
Caldera, *Chile* 126 B1

Caldera de Taburiente △,
  Canary Is. 48 F2
Caldwell, *Idaho, U.S.A.* 108 E5
Caldwell, *Kans., U.S.A.* 113 G6
Caldwell, *Tex., U.S.A.* 113 K6
Caledon, *S. Africa* 88 E2
Caledon →, *S. Africa* 88 E4
Caledon B., *Australia* 94 A2
Caledonia, *Canada* 116 C5
Caledonia, *U.S.A.* 116 D7
Calella, *Spain* 38 D7
Calemba, *Angola* 88 B2
Calen, *Australia* 94 J6
Calenzana, *France* 21 F12
Caletones, *Chile* 126 C1
Calexico, *U.S.A.* 111 N11
Calf of Man, *I. of Man* 14 C3
Calgary, *Canada* 102 C6
Calheta, *Madeira* 48 D2
Calhoun, *U.S.A.* 115 H3
Cali, *Colombia* 124 C3
Calicut, *India* 66 P9
Caliente, *U.S.A.* 109 H6
California, *Mo., U.S.A.* 112 F8
California, *Pa., U.S.A.* 116 F5
California □, *U.S.A.* 110 H7
California, Baja, *Mexico* 118 A1
California, Baja, T.N. = Baja
  California □, *Mexico* 118 B2
California, Baja, T.S. = Baja
  California Sur □, *Mexico* ... 118 B2
California City, *U.S.A.* 111 K9
California G. de, *Mexico* 118 B2
California Hot Springs, *U.S.A.* . 111 K8
Calilegua △, *Argentina* 126 B3
Călimănești, *Romania* 29 E9
Călimani, Munții, *Romania* 29 C10
Calingasta, *Argentina* 126 C2
Calipatria, *U.S.A.* 111 M11
Calistoga, *U.S.A.* 110 G4
Calitri, *Italy* 43 B8
Calitzdorp, *S. Africa* 88 E3
Callabonna, L., *Australia* 95 D3
Callac, *France* 18 D3
Callan, *Ireland* 12 D4
Callander, *U.K.* 13 E4
Callao, *Peru* 124 F3
Calles, *Mexico* 119 C5
Callicoon, *U.S.A.* 117 E9
Calling Lake, *Canada* 102 B6
Calliope, *Australia* 94 C5
Callosa de Ensarriá, *Spain* ... 39 G4
Callosa de Segura, *Spain* 39 G4
Calne, *U.K.* 15 F6
Calola, *Angola* 88 B2
Calolbon = San Andres, *Phil.* . 61 E6
Calonge, *Spain* 38 D8
Caloocan, *Phil.* 61 D4
Calore →, *Italy* 43 A7
Caloundra, *Australia* 95 D5
Calpe, *Spain* 39 G5
Calpella, *U.S.A.* 110 F3
Calpine, *U.S.A.* 110 F6
Calstock, *Canada* 104 C3
Caltabellotta, *Italy* 42 E6
Caltagirone, *Italy* 43 E7
Caltanissetta, *Italy* 43 E7
Çaltılıbük, *Turkey* 45 G12
Caluire-et-Cuire, *France* 19 G11
Calulo, *Angola* 84 G2
Caluso, *Italy* 40 C4
Calvados □, *France* 18 C6
Calvert →, *Australia* 94 B2
Calvert I., *Canada* 102 C3
Calvert Ra., *Australia* 92 D3
Calvi, *France* 21 F12
Calviá, *Spain* 39 F7
Calvillo, *Mexico* 118 C4
Calvinia, *S. Africa* 88 E2
Calvo, Mte., *Italy* 41 G12
Calwa, *U.S.A.* 110 J7
Calzada Almuradiel =
  Almuradiel, *Spain* 37 G7
Calzada de Calatrava, *Spain* .. 37 G7
Cam →, *U.K.* 15 E8
Cam Lam, *Vietnam* 65 G7
Cam Pha, *Vietnam* 58 G6
Cam Ranh, *Vietnam* 65 G7
Cam Xuyen, *Vietnam* 64 C6
Camabatela, *Angola* 84 F3
Camacha, *Madeira* 48 D3
Camacho, *Mexico* 118 C4
Camacupa, *Angola* 85 G3
Camagüey, *Cuba* 120 B4
Camaiore, *Italy* 40 E7
Camaná, *Peru* 124 G4
Camanche Reservoir, *U.S.A.* ... 110 G6
Camaquã, *Brazil* 127 C5
Camaquã →, *Brazil* 127 C5
Câmara de Lobos, *Madeira* 48 D3
Camararat, C., *France* 21 E10
Camarès, *France* 20 E6
Camaret-sur-Mer, *France* 18 D2
Camargo, *Mexico* 119 B5
Camargue, *France* 21 E8
Camargue △, *France* 21 E8
Camarillo, *U.S.A.* 111 L7
Camariñas, *Spain* 36 B1
Camarón, C., *Honduras* 120 C2
Camarones, *Argentina* 128 E3
Camas, *Spain* 37 H4
Camas, *U.S.A.* 110 E4
Camas Valley, *U.S.A.* 108 E2
Camballin, *Australia* 92 C3
Cambará, *Brazil* 127 A5
Cambay = Khambhat, *India* 68 H5
Cambay, G. of = Khambhat, G.
  of, *India* 66 J8
Cambil, *Spain* 37 H7
Cambo-les-Bains, *France* 20 E2
Cambodia ■, *Asia* 64 F5
Camborne, *U.K.* 15 G2

Cambrai, *France* 19 B10
Cambre, *Spain* 36 B2
Cambria, *U.S.A.* 110 K5
Cambrian Mts., *U.K.* 15 E4
Cambridge, *Canada* 116 C4
Cambridge, *Jamaica* .... 120 a
Cambridge, *N.Z.* 91 G5
Cambridge, *U.K.* 15 E8
Cambridge, *Mass., U.S.A.* 117 D13
Cambridge, *Minn., U.S.A.* 112 C8
Cambridge, *N.Y., U.S.A.* 117 C11
Cambridge, *Nebr., U.S.A.* 112 E4
Cambridge, *Ohio, U.S.A.* 116 F3
Cambridge Bay = Ikaluktutiak,
  Canada 100 B9
Cambridge G., *Australia* 92 B4
Cambridge Springs, *U.S.A.* 116 E4
Cambridgeshire □, *U.K.* 15 E7
Cambrils, *Spain* 38 D6
Cambuci, *Brazil* 127 A7
Cambundi-Catembo, *Angola* 84 G3
Camden, *Ala., U.S.A.* 115 K2
Camden, *Ark., U.S.A.* 113 J8
Camden, *Maine, U.S.A.* 115 C11
Camden, *N.J., U.S.A.* 117 G9
Camden, *N.Y., U.S.A.* 117 C9
Camden, *S.C., U.S.A.* 115 H5
Camden Sd., *Australia* 92 C3
Camdenton, *U.S.A.* 113 F8
Camelford, *U.K.* 15 G3
Cameron, *Ariz., U.S.A.* 109 J8
Cameron, *La., U.S.A.* 113 L8
Cameron, *Mo., U.S.A.* 112 F7
Cameron, *Tex., U.S.A.* 113 K6
Cameron Highlands, *Malaysia* .. 65 K3
Cameron Hills, *Canada* 102 B5
Cameroon ■, *Africa* 79 G7
Cameroun →, *Cameroon* 83 E6
Cameroun, Mt., *Cameroon* 83 E6
Cametá, *Brazil* 125 D9
Çamiçi Gölü, *Turkey* 47 D9
Camiguin □, *Phil.* 61 G6
Camiguin I., *Phil.* 61 B4
Camiling, *Phil.* 61 D4
Camilla, *U.S.A.* 115 K3
Caminha, *Portugal* 36 D2
Camino, *U.S.A.* 110 G6
Camira Creek, *Australia* 95 D5
Cammal, *U.S.A.* 116 E7
Cammarata, *Italy* 42 E6
Camocim, *Brazil* 125 D10
Camooweal, *Australia* 94 B2
Camooweal Caves △, *Australia* . 94 C2
Camopi, *Fr. Guiana* 125 C8
Camotes Is., *Phil.* 61 F6
Camotes Sea, *Phil.* 61 F6
Camp Borden, *Canada* 116 B5
Camp Hill, *U.S.A.* 116 F8
Camp Nelson, *U.S.A.* 111 J8
Camp Pendleton, *U.S.A.* 111 M9
Camp Verde, *U.S.A.* 109 J8
Camp Wood, *U.S.A.* 113 L5
Campagna, *Italy* 43 B8
Campana, *Argentina* 126 C4
Campana, I., *Chile* 128 F1
Campanário, *Madeira* 48 D2
Campanario, *Spain* 37 G5
Campânia □, *Italy* 43 B7
Campbell, *S. Africa* 88 D3
Campbell, *Calif., U.S.A.* 110 H5
Campbell, *Ohio, U.S.A.* 116 E4
Campbell I., *Pac. Oc.* 96 N8
Campbell L., *Canada* 103 A7
Campbell River, *Canada* 102 C3
Campbell Town, *Australia* 95 G4
Campbellford, *Canada* 116 B7
Campbellpur, *Pakistan* 68 C5
Campbellsville, *U.S.A.* 114 G3
Campbellton, *Canada* 105 C6
Campbelltown, *Australia* 95 E5
Campbeltown, *U.K.* 13 F3
Campeche, *Mexico* 119 D6
Campeche □, *Mexico* 119 D6
Campeche, Golfo de, *Mexico* ... 119 D6
Campello, *Spain* 39 G4
Câmpeni, *Romania* 28 D8
Camperdown, *Australia* 95 F3
Camperville, *Canada* 103 C8
Campi Salentina, *Italy* 43 B11
Câmpia Turzii, *Romania* 29 D8
Campidano, *Italy* 42 C1
Campíglia Maríttima, *Italy* ... 40 E7
Campillo de Altobuey, *Spain* .. 39 F3
Campillos, *Spain* 37 H6
Câmpina, *Romania* 29 E10
Campina Grande, *Brazil* 125 E11
Campinas, *Brazil* 127 A6
Campli, *Italy* 41 F10
Campo, *Spain* 38 C5
Campo de Criptana, *Spain* 37 F7
Campo de Gibraltar, *Spain* 37 J5
Campo Grande, *Brazil* 125 H8
Campo Maior, *Brazil* 125 D10
Campo Maior, *Portugal* 37 F3
Campo Mourão, *Brazil* 127 A5
Campo Túres, *Italy* 41 B8
Campobasso, *Italy* 43 A7
Campobello di Licata, *Italy* .. 42 E6
Campobello di Mazara, *Italy* .. 42 E5
Campofelice di Roccella, *Italy* . 42 E6
Campomarino, *Italy* 41 G12
Camporeale, *Italy* 42 E6
Camporrobles, *Spain* 38 F3
Campos, *Brazil* 127 A7
Campos Belos, *Brazil* 125 F9
Campos del Port, *Spain* 48 B10
Campos Novos, *Brazil* 127 B5
Camprodón, *Spain* 38 C7

Camptonville, *U.S.A.* 110 F5
Camptown, *U.S.A.* 117 E8
Câmpulung, *Argeş, Romania* ... 29 E10
Câmpulung, *Suceava, Romania* . 29 C10
Câmpuri, *Romania* 29 D11
Camrose, *Canada* 102 C6
Camsell Portage, *Canada* 103 B7
Çamyuva, *Turkey* 47 E12
Çan, *Turkey* 45 F11
Can Clavo, *Spain* 48 C7
Can Creu, *Spain* 48 C7
Can Gio, *Vietnam* 65 G6
Can Tho, *Vietnam* 65 G5
Canaan, *U.S.A.* 117 D11
Canada ■, *N. Amer.* 100 C10
Canada Basin, *Arctic* 4 B18
Cañada de Gómez, *Argentina* ... 126 C3
Canadian, *U.S.A.* 113 H4
Canadian →, *U.S.A.* 113 H7
Canajoharie, *U.S.A.* 117 D10
Çanakkale, *Turkey* 45 F10
Çanakkale □, *Turkey* 45 F10
Çanakkale Boğazı, *Turkey* 45 F10
Canal Flats, *Canada* 102 C5
Canalejas, *Argentina* 126 D2
Canals, *Argentina* 126 C3
Canals, *Spain* 39 G4
Canandaigua, *U.S.A.* 116 D7
Canandaigua L., *U.S.A.* 116 D7
Cananea, *Mexico* 118 A2
Canarias, Is., *Atl. Oc.* 48 F4
Canaries, *St. Lucia* .... 121 f
Canarreos, Arch. de los, *Cuba* . 120 B3
Canary Is. = Canarias, Is., *Atl. Oc.* . 48 F4
Canaseraga, *U.S.A.* 116 D7
Canatlán, *Mexico* 118 C4
Canaveral, *U.S.A.* 115 L5
Canaveral, C., *U.S.A.* 115 L5
Cañaverulas, *Spain* 38 E2
Canavieiras, *Brazil* 125 G11
Canberra, *Australia* 95 F4
Canby, *Calif., U.S.A.* 108 F3
Canby, *Minn., U.S.A.* 112 C6
Canby, *Oreg., U.S.A.* 110 E4
Cancale, *France* 18 D5
Canche →, *France* 19 B8
Cancún, *Mexico* 119 C7
Candanchu, *Spain* 38 C4
Çandarlı, *Turkey* 47 C8
Çandarlı Körfezi, *Turkey* 47 C8
Candas, *Spain* 36 B5
Candé, *France* 18 E5
Candela, *Italy* 43 A8
Candelaria, *Argentina* 127 B4
Candelaria, *Canary Is.* 48 F3
Candelario, *Spain* 36 E5
Candeleda, *Spain* 36 E5
Candelo, *Australia* 95 F4
Candi Dasa, *Indonesia* 63 J18
Candia = Iráklion, *Greece* 49 D7
Candia, Sea of = Crete, Sea of,
  Greece 47 E7
Candle L., *Canada* 103 C7
Candlemas I., *Antarctica* 5 B1
Cando, *U.S.A.* 112 A5
Candon, *Phil.* 61 C4
Canea = Khaniá, *Greece* 49 D6
Canelli, *Italy* 40 D5
Canelones, *Uruguay* 127 C4
Canet-Plage, *France* 20 F7
Cañete, *Chile* 126 D1
Cañete, *Peru* 124 F3
Cañete, *Spain* 38 E3
Cañete de las Torres, *Spain* .. 37 H6
Cangas, *Spain* 36 C2
Cangas de Narcea, *Spain* 36 B4
Cangas de Onís, *Spain* 36 B5
Cangnan, *China* 59 D13
Canguaretama, *Brazil* 125 E11
Canguçu, *Brazil* 127 C5
Canguçu, Serra do, *Brazil* 127 C5
Cangwu, *China* 59 F8
Cangxi, *China* 58 B5
Cangyuan, *China* 58 F2
Cangzhou, *China* 56 E9
Caniapiscau →, *Canada* 105 A6
Caniapiscau, L. de, *Canada* ... 105 B6
Canicattì, *Italy* 42 E6
Canicattini Bagni, *Italy* 43 E8
Caniles, *Spain* 37 H8
Canim Lake, *Canada* 102 C4
Canindeyú □, *Paraguay* 127 A5
Canino, *Italy* 41 F8
Canisteo, *U.S.A.* 116 D7
Canisteo →, *U.S.A.* 116 D7
Cañitas, *Mexico* 118 C4
Cañizal, *Spain* 36 D5
Canjáyar, *Spain* 37 H8
Çankırı, *Turkey* 72 B5
Cankuzo, *Burundi* 86 C3
Canmore, *Canada* 102 C5
Cann River, *Australia* 95 F4
Canna, *U.K.* 13 D2
Cannanore, *India* 66 P9
Cannes, *France* 21 E11
Canning Town = Port Canning,
  India 69 H13
Cannington, *Canada* 116 B5
Cannóbio, *Italy* 40 B5
Cannock, *U.K.* 15 E5
Cannon Ball →, *U.S.A.* 112 B4
Cannondale Mt., *Australia* 94 D4
Cannonsville Reservoir, *U.S.A.* . 117 D9
Cannonvale, *Australia* 94 J6
Canoas, *Brazil* 127 B5
Canoe L., *Canada* 103 B7
Canon City, *U.S.A.* 112 F2
Cañón de Rio Blanco △, *Mexico* . 119 D5
Cañón del Río Lobos △, *Spain* . 36 D7
Cañón del Sumidero △, *Mexico* . 119 D5
Canora, *Canada* 103 C8
Canosa di Púglia, *Italy* 43 A9

Canowindra, *Australia* 95 E4
Canso, *Canada* 105 C7
Cantabria □, *Spain* 36 B7
Cantabria, Sierra de, *Spain* .. 38 C2
Cantabrian Mts. = Cantábrica,
  Cordillera, *Spain* 36 C5
Cantábrica, Cordillera, *Spain* . 36 C5
Cantal □, *France* 20 C6
Cantal, Plomb du, *France* 20 C6
Cantanhede, *Portugal* 36 E2
Cantavieja, *Spain* 38 E4
Čantavir, *Serbia & M.* 28 E4
Cantemir, *Moldova* 29 D13
Canterbury, *Australia* 94 D3
Canterbury, *U.K.* 15 F9
Canterbury Bight, *N.Z.* 91 L3
Canterbury Plains, *N.Z.* 91 K3
Cantil, *U.S.A.* 111 K9
Cantillana, *Spain* 37 H5
Canton = Guangzhou, *China* ... 59 F9
Canton, *Ga., U.S.A.* 115 H3
Canton, *Ill., U.S.A.* 112 E9
Canton, *Miss., U.S.A.* 113 J9
Canton, *Mo., U.S.A.* 112 E9
Canton, *N.Y., U.S.A.* 117 B9
Canton, *Ohio, U.S.A.* 116 F3
Canton, *Pa., U.S.A.* 116 E8
Canton, *S. Dak., U.S.A.* 112 D6
Canton L., *U.S.A.* 113 G5
Cantù, *Italy* 40 C6
Canudos, *Brazil* 124 E7
Canumã →, *Brazil* 124 D7
Canutama, *Brazil* 124 E6
Canutillo, *U.S.A.* 109 L10
Canvey, *U.K.* 15 F8
Canyon, *U.S.A.* 113 H4
Canyon De Chelly △, *U.S.A.* ... 109 H9
Canyon of the Ancients △, *U.S.A.* . 109 H9
Canyonlands △, *U.S.A.* 109 G9
Canyonville, *U.S.A.* 108 E2
Cao Bang, *Vietnam* 58 F6
Cao He →, *China* 57 D13
Cao Lanh, *Vietnam* 65 G5
Cao Xian, *China* 56 G8
Cáorle, *Italy* 41 C9
Cap-aux-Meules, *Canada* 105 C7
Cap-Chat, *Canada* 105 C6
Cap-de-la-Madeleine, *Canada* .. 104 C5
Cap-Haïtien, *Haiti* 121 C5
Cap Pt., *St. Lucia* .... 121 f
Capac, *U.S.A.* 116 C2
Capáccio, *Italy* 43 B8
Capanaparo →, *Venezuela* 124 B5
Capánnori, *Italy* 40 E7
Capbreton, *France* 20 E2
Capdenac, *France* 20 D6
Capdepera, *Spain* 38 F8
Cape →, *Australia* 94 C4
Cape Arid △, *Australia* 93 F3
Cape Barren I., *Australia* 95 G4
Cape Breton Highlands △,
  Canada 105 C7
Cape Breton I., *Canada* 105 C7
Cape Charles, *U.S.A.* 114 G8
Cape Coast, *Ghana* 83 D4
Cape Cod △, *U.S.A.* 114 E10
Cape Coral, *U.S.A.* 115 M5
Cape Dorset, *Canada* 101 B12
Cape Fear →, *U.S.A.* 115 H6
Cape Girardeau, *U.S.A.* 113 G10
Cape Hatteras △, *U.S.A.* 115 H8
Cape Lee △, *Australia* 93 F3
Cape Lookout △, *U.S.A.* 115 H7
Cape May, *U.S.A.* 114 F8
Cape May Point, *U.S.A.* 114 F8
Cape Melville △, *Australia* ... 94 A3
Cape Mount □, *Liberia* 82 D2
Cape Peninsula △, *S. Africa* .. 88 E2
Cape Range △, *Australia* 92 D1
Cape Tormentine, *Canada* 105 C7
Cape Town, *S. Africa* 88 E2
Cape Tribulation △, *Australia* . 94 B4
Cape Verde ■, *Atl. Oc.* 77 E1
Cape Vincent, *U.S.A.* 117 B8
Cape York Peninsula, *Australia* . 94 A3
Capela, *Brazil* 125 F11
Capella, *Australia* 94 C4
Capendu, *France* 20 E6
Capestang, *France* 20 E7
Capesterre-Belle-Eau,
  Guadeloupe .... 120 b
Capesterre-de-Marie-Galante,
  Guadeloupe .... 120 b
Capim →, *Brazil* 125 D9
Capistrello, *Italy* 41 G10
Capitan, *U.S.A.* 109 K11
Capitán Arturo Prat, *Antarctica* . 5 C17
Capitol Reef △, *U.S.A.* 109 G8
Capitola, *U.S.A.* 110 H5
Capizzi, *Italy* 43 E7
Capoche →, *Mozam.* 87 F3
Capodichino, Nápoli ✈ (NAP),
  Italy 43 B7
Capoterra, *Italy* 42 C1
Cappadocia, *Turkey* 72 C6
Capraia, *Italy* 40 E6
Caprara, Pta., *Italy* 42 A1
Caprarola, *Italy* 41 F9
Capreol, *Canada* 104 C3
Caprera, *Italy* 42 A2
Capri, *Italy* 43 B7
Capricorn Group, *Australia* ... 94 C5
Capricorn Ra., *Australia* 92 D2
Caprino Veronese, *Italy* 40 C7
Caprivi Game △, *Namibia* 88 B3
Caprivi Strip, *Namibia* 88 B3
Captain's Flat, *Australia* 95 F4
Captieux, *France* 20 D3
Capulin Volcano △, *U.S.A.* ... 113 G3

Caracal, *Romania* 29 F9
Caracas, *Venezuela* 124 A5
Caracol, *Mato Grosso do Sul,
  Brazil* 126 A4
Caracol, *Piauí, Brazil* 125 E10
Caráglio, *Italy* 40 D4
Carajás, *Brazil* 125 E8
Carajás, Serra dos, *Brazil* ... 125 E8
Carangola, *Brazil* 127 A7
Caransebeş, *Romania* 28 E7
Carantec, *France* 18 D3
Caraquet, *Canada* 105 C6
Caras, *Peru* 124 E3
Caraş Severin □, *Romania* 28 E7
Caraşova, *Romania* 28 E6
Caratasca, L., *Honduras* 120 C3
Caratinga, *Brazil* 125 G10
Caraúbas, *Brazil* 125 E11
Caravaca de la Cruz, *Spain* ... 39 G3
Caravággio, *Italy* 40 C6
Caravela, *Guinea-Biss.* 82 C1
Caravelas, *Brazil* 125 G11
Caravelí, *Peru* 124 G4
Caravelle, Presqu'île de la,
  Martinique .... 120 c
Caràzinho, *Brazil* 127 B5
Carballino = O Carballiño, *Spain* . 36 C2
Carballo, *Spain* 36 B2
Carberry, *Canada* 103 D9
Carbó, *Mexico* 118 B2
Carbonara, C., *Italy* 42 C2
Carbondale, *Colo., U.S.A.* ... 108 G10
Carbondale, *Ill., U.S.A.* 113 G10
Carbondale, *Pa., U.S.A.* 117 E9
Carbonear, *Canada* 105 C9
Carboneras, *Spain* 39 J3
Carboneras de Guadazón, *Spain* . 38 F3
Carbónia, *Italy* 42 C1
Carcabuey, *Spain* 37 H6
Carcagente = Carcaixent, *Spain* . 39 F4
Carcaixent, *Spain* 39 F4
Carcajou, *Canada* 102 B5
Carcar, *Phil.* 61 F5
Carcarana →, *Argentina* 126 C3
Carcasse, C., *Haiti* 121 C5
Carcassonne, *France* 20 E6
Carcross, *Canada* 102 A2
Çardak, *Çanakkale, Turkey* 45 F10
Çardak, *Denizli, Turkey* 47 D11
Cardamon Hills, *India* 66 Q10
Cardeña, *Spain* 37 G6
Cárdenas, *Cuba* 120 B3
Cárdenas, *San Luis Potosí,
  Mexico* 119 C5
Cárdenas, *Tabasco, Mexico* 119 D6
Cardenete, *Spain* 38 F3
Cardiff, *U.K.* 15 F4
Cardiff □, *U.K.* 15 F4
Cardiff-by-the-Sea, *U.S.A.* ... 111 M9
Cardigan, *U.K.* 15 E3
Cardigan B., *U.K.* 15 E3
Cardinal, *Canada* 117 B9
Cardona, *Spain* 38 D6
Cardona, *Uruguay* 126 C4
Cardoner →, *Spain* 38 D6
Cardoso, Ilha do, *Brazil* 127 B5
Cardston, *Canada* 102 D6
Cardwell, *Australia* 94 B4
Careen L., *Canada* 103 B7
Carei, *Romania* 28 C7
Careme = Ciremay, *Indonesia* .. 63 G13
Carentan, *France* 18 C5
Carey, *U.S.A.* 108 E7
Carey, L., *Australia* 93 E3
Carey L., *Canada* 103 A8
Careysburg, *Liberia* 82 D2
Cargèse, *France* 21 F12
Carhaix-Plouguer, *France* 18 D3
Carhué, *Argentina* 126 D3
Caria, *Turkey* 47 D10
Cariacica, *Brazil* 125 H10
Cariati, *Italy* 43 C9
Caribbean Sea, *W. Indies* 121 D5
Cariboo Mts., *Canada* 102 C4
Caribou, *U.S.A.* 115 B12
Caribou →, *Man., Canada* 103 B10
Caribou →, *N.W.T., Canada* ... 102 A3
Caribou I., *Canada* 104 C2
Caribou Is., *Canada* 102 A6
Caribou L., *Man., Canada* 103 B9
Caribou L., *Ont., Canada* 104 B2
Caribou Mts., *Canada* 102 B5
Caribou River △, *Canada* 103 B9
Caribrod = Dimitrovgrad,
  Serbia & M. 44 C6
Carichic, *Mexico* 118 B3
Carigara, *Phil.* 61 F6
Carignan, *France* 19 C12
Carignano, *Italy* 40 D4
Carillo, *Mexico* 118 B4
Carinda, *Australia* 95 E4
Cariñena, *Spain* 38 D3
Carinhanha, *Brazil* 125 F10
Carinhanha →, *Brazil* 125 F10
Carini, *Italy* 42 D6
Cariño, *Spain* 36 B3
Cariñola, *Italy* 42 A6
Carinthia = Kärnten □, *Austria* . 26 E6
Caripito, *Venezuela* 124 A6
Carlet, *Spain* 39 F4
Carleton, Mt., *Canada* 105 C6
Carleton Place, *Canada* 117 A8
Carletonville, *S. Africa* 88 D4
Cârlibaba, *Romania* 29 C10
Carlin, *U.S.A.* 108 F5
Carlingford L., *U.K.* 12 B5
Carlinville, *U.S.A.* 112 F10
Carlisle, *U.K.* 14 C5
Carlisle, *U.S.A.* 116 F7
Carlisle B., *Barbados* .... 121 g
Carlisle I., *Australia* 94 J7
Carlit, Pic, *France* 20 F5

Carloforte, Italy 42 C1
Carlos Casares, Argentina 126 D3
Carlos Tejedor, Argentina 126 D3
Carlow, Ireland 12 D5
Carlow □, Ireland 12 D5
Carlsbad, Calif., U.S.A. 111 M9
Carlsbad, N. Mex., U.S.A. 113 J2
Carlsbad Caverns △, U.S.A. ... 113 J2
Carluke, U.K. 13 F5
Carlyle, Canada 103 D8
Carmacks, Canada 100 B6
Carmagnola, Italy 40 D4
Carman, Canada 103 D9
Carmarthen, U.K. 15 F3
Carmarthen B., U.K. 15 F3
Carmarthenshire □, U.K. 15 F3
Carmaux, France 20 D6
Carmel, U.S.A. 117 E11
Carmel-by-the-Sea, U.S.A. 110 J5
Carmel Valley, U.S.A. 110 J5
Carmelo, Uruguay 126 C4
Carmen, Colombia 124 B3
Carmen, Paraguay 127 B4
Carmen →, Mexico 118 A3
Carmen, I., Mexico 118 B2
Carmen de Patagones, Argentina 128 E4
Cármenes, Spain 36 C5
Carmensa, Argentina 126 D2
Carmi, Canada 102 D5
Carmi, U.S.A. 114 F1
Carmichael, U.S.A. 110 G5
Carmila, Australia 94 C4
Carmona, Costa Rica 120 E2
Carmona, Spain 37 H5
Carn Ban, U.K. 13 D4
Carn Eige, U.K. 13 D3
Carnamah, Australia 93 E2
Carnarvon, Australia 93 D1
Carnarvon, S. Africa 88 E3
Carnarvon □, Australia 94 C4
Carnarvon Ra., Queens., Australia 94 D4
Carnarvon Ra., W. Austral.,
    Australia 93 E3
Carnation, U.S.A. 110 C5
Carndonagh, Ireland 12 A4
Carnduff, Canada 103 D8
Carnegie, U.S.A. 116 F4
Carnegie, L., Australia 93 E3
Carnic Alps = Karnische Alpen,
    Europe 26 E6
Carniche Alpi = Karnische Alpen,
    Europe 26 E6
Carnot, C.A.R. 84 D3
Carnot, C., Australia 95 E2
Carnot B., Australia 92 C3
Carnoustie, U.K. 13 E6
Carnsore Pt., Ireland 12 D5
Caro, U.S.A. 114 D4
Carol City, U.S.A. 115 N5
Carolina, Brazil 125 E9
Carolina, Puerto Rico .... 121 d
Carolina, S. Africa 89 D5
Caroline I., Kiribati 97 H12
Caroline Is., Micronesia 96 G7
Caroni, Trin. & Tob. 125 K15
Caroni →, Venezuela 124 B6
Caronie = Nébrodi, Monti, Italy . 43 E7
Caroona, Australia 95 E5
Carpathians, Europe 6 F10
Carpaţii Meridionali, Romania . 29 E9
Carpentaria, G. of, Australia .. 94 A2
Carpentras, France 21 D9
Carpi, Italy 40 D7
Cărpineni, Moldova 29 D13
Carpinteria, U.S.A. 111 L7
Carpio, Spain 36 D5
Carr Boyd Ra., Australia 92 C4
Carrabelle, U.S.A. 115 L3
Carral, Spain 36 B2
Carranza, Presa V., Mexico ... 118 B4
Carrara, Italy 40 D7
Carrascal, Phil. 61 G6
Carrascosa del Campo, Spain .. 38 E2
Carrauntoohill, Ireland 12 D2
Carrick-on-Shannon, Ireland .. 12 C3
Carrick-on-Suir, Ireland 12 D4
Carrickfergus, U.K. 12 B6
Carrickmacross, Ireland 12 C5
Carrieton, Australia 95 E2
Carrington, U.S.A. 112 B5
Carrión →, Spain 36 D6
Carrión de los Condes, Spain .. 36 C6
Carrizal Bajo, Chile 126 B1
Carrizalillo, Chile 126 B1
Carrizo Cr. →, U.S.A. 113 G3
Carrizo Plain △, U.S.A. 110 K7
Carrizo Springs, U.S.A. 113 L5
Carrizozo, U.S.A. 109 K11
Carroll, U.S.A. 112 D7
Carrollton, Ga., U.S.A. 115 J3
Carrollton, Ill., U.S.A. 112 F9
Carrollton, Ky., U.S.A. 114 F3
Carrollton, Mo., U.S.A. 112 F8
Carrollton, Ohio, U.S.A. 116 F3
Carron →, U.K. 13 D4
Carron, L., U.K. 13 D3
Carrot →, Canada 103 C8
Carrot River, Canada 103 C8
Carrouges, France 18 D6
Carrù, Italy 40 D4
Carruthers, Canada 103 C7
Carsa Dek, Ethiopia 81 F4
Çarşamba, Turkey 72 B7
Carsoli, Italy 41 F10
Carson, Calif., U.S.A. 111 M8
Carson, N. Dak., U.S.A. 112 B4
Carson →, U.S.A. 110 F8
Carson City, U.S.A. 110 F7
Carson Sink, U.S.A. 108 G4
Cartagena, Colombia 124 A3
Cartagena, Spain 39 H4
Cartago, Colombia 124 C3

Cartago, Costa Rica 120 E3
Cártama, Spain 37 J6
Cartaxo, Portugal 37 F2
Cartaya, Spain 37 H3
Cartersville, U.S.A. 115 H3
Carterton, N.Z. 91 J5
Carthage, Tunisia 42 F3
Carthage, Ill., U.S.A. 112 E9
Carthage, Mo., U.S.A. 113 G7
Carthage, N.Y., U.S.A. 114 D8
Carthage, Tex., U.S.A. 113 J7
Cartier I., Australia 92 B3
Cartwright, Canada 105 B8
Caruaru, Brazil 125 E11
Carúpano, Venezuela 124 A6
Caruthersville, U.S.A. 113 G10
Carvin, France 19 B9
Carvoeiro, Brazil 124 D6
Carvoeiro, C., Portugal 37 F1
Cary, U.S.A. 115 H6
Casa, Pas de la = Envalira, Port
    d', Europe 38 C6
Casa Branca, Portugal 37 G2
Casa Grande, U.S.A. 109 K8
Casablanca, Chile 126 C1
Casablanca, Morocco 78 B4
Casacalenda, Italy 41 G11
Casalbordino, Italy 41 F11
Casale Monferrato, Italy 40 C5
Casalmaggiore, Italy 40 D7
Casalpusterlengo, Italy 40 C6
Casamance →, Senegal 82 C1
Casarano, Italy 43 B11
Casares, Spain 37 J5
Casas Ibáñez, Spain 39 F3
Casasimarro, Spain 39 F2
Casatejada, Spain 36 F5
Casavieja, Spain 36 E6
Cascada de Basaseachic △,
    Mexico 118 B3
Cascade, Idaho, U.S.A. 108 D5
Cascade, Mont., U.S.A. 108 C8
Cascade Locks, U.S.A. 110 E5
Cascade Ra., U.S.A. 110 D5
Cascade Reservoir, U.S.A. 108 D5
Cascais, Portugal 37 G1
Cascavel, Brazil 127 A5
Cáscina, Italy 40 E7
Casco B., U.S.A. 115 D10
Caselle Torinese, Italy 40 C4
Caserta, Italy 43 A7
Casey, Antarctica 5 C8
Caseyr, Raas = Asir, Ras,
    Somali Rep. 75 E5
Cashel, Ireland 12 D4
Casiguran, Phil. 61 C5
Casilda, Argentina 126 C3
Casimcea, Romania 29 F13
Casino, Australia 95 D5
Casiquiare →, Venezuela 124 C5
Casma, Peru 124 E3
Čáslav, Czech Rep. 26 B8
Casma, Slovak Rep. 27 D11
Cásola Valsénio, Italy 41 D8
Cásoli, Italy 41 F11
Caspe, Spain 38 D4
Casper, U.S.A. 108 E10
Caspian Depression, Eurasia .. 35 G9
Caspian Sea, Eurasia 52 E6
Cass Lake, U.S.A. 112 B7
Cassà de la Selva, Spain 38 D7
Cassadaga, U.S.A. 116 D5
Cassano allo Iónio, Italy 43 C9
Cassel, France 19 B9
Casselman, Canada 117 A9
Casselton, U.S.A. 112 B6
Cassiar, Canada 102 B3
Cassiar Mts., Canada 102 B2
Cassino, Italy 42 A6
Cassis, France 21 E9
Cassville, U.S.A. 113 G8
Castagneto Carducci, Italy 40 E7
Castaic, U.S.A. 111 L8
Castalia, U.S.A. 116 E2
Castanhal, Brazil 125 D9
Castara, Trin. & Tob. 125 J16
Casteggio, Italy 40 C6
Castejón de Monegros, Spain .. 38 D4
Castèl di Sangro, Italy 41 G11
Castèl San Giovanni, Italy 40 C6
Castèl San Pietro Terme, Italy . 41 D8
Castelbuono, Italy 43 E7
Castelfidardo, Italy 41 E10
Castelfiorentino, Italy 40 E7
Castelfranco Emilia, Italy 40 D8
Castelfranco Véneto, Italy 41 C8
Casteljaloux, France 20 D4
Castellabate, Italy 43 B7
Castellammare, G. di, Italy ... 42 D5
Castellammare del Golfo, Italy . 42 D5
Castellammare di Stábia, Italy . 43 B7
Castellamonte, Italy 40 C4
Castellane, France 21 E10
Castellaneta, Italy 43 B9
Castelli, Argentina 126 D4
Castelló de la Plana, Spain 38 F4
Castellón de la Plana □, Spain . 38 E4
Castellote, Spain 38 E4
Castelmáuro, Italy 41 G11
Castelnau-de-Médoc, France .. 20 C3
Castelnau-Magnoac, France .. 20 E4
Castelnaudary, France 20 E5
Castelnovo ne' Monti, Italy ... 40 D7
Castelnuovo di Val di Cécina,
    Italy 40 E7
Castelo, Brazil 127 A7
Castelo Branco, Portugal 36 F3
Castelo Branco □, Portugal ... 36 F3
Castelo de Paiva, Portugal 36 D2
Castelo de Vide, Portugal 37 F3
Castelsardo, Italy 42 B1
Castelsarrasin, France 20 D5

Casteltérmini, Italy 42 E6
Castelvetrano, Italy 42 E5
Casterton, Australia 95 F3
Castets, France 20 E2
Castiglion Fiorentino, Italy ... 41 E8
Castiglione del Lago, Italy 41 E9
Castiglione della Pescáia, Italy . 40 F7
Castiglione delle Stiviere, Italy . 40 C7
Castilblanco, Spain 37 F5
Castile, U.S.A. 116 D6
Castilla, Playa de, Spain 37 J4
Castilla-La Mancha □, Spain .. 6 H5
Castilla y Leon □, Spain 36 D6
Castillo de Locubín, Spain 37 H7
Castillon-en-Couserans, France 20 F5
Castillonès, France 20 D4
Castillos, Uruguay 127 C5
Castle Dale, U.S.A. 108 G8
Castle Douglas, U.K. 13 G5
Castle Rock, Colo., U.S.A. 112 F2
Castle Rock, Wash., U.S.A. ... 110 D4
Castlebar, Ireland 12 C2
Castlebay, U.K. 13 E1
Castleblaney, Ireland 12 B5
Castlederg, U.K. 12 B4
Castleford, U.K. 14 D6
Castlegar, Canada 102 D5
Castlemaine, Australia 95 F3
Castlepollard, Ireland 12 C4
Castlerea, Ireland 12 C3
Castlereagh →, Australia 95 E4
Castlereagh B., Australia 94 A2
Castletown, I. of Man 14 C3
Castletown Bearhaven, Ireland . 12 E2
Castor, Canada 102 C6
Castor →, Canada 104 B4
Castorland, U.S.A. 117 C9
Castres, France 20 E6
Castricum, Neths. 17 B4
Castries, St. Lucia .... 121 f
Castril, Spain 37 H8
Castro, Brazil 127 A6
Castro, Chile 128 E2
Castro Alves, Brazil 125 F11
Castro del Río, Spain 37 H6
Castro-Urdiales, Spain 36 B7
Castro Verde, Portugal 37 H2
Castrojeriz, Spain 36 C6
Castropol, Spain 36 B4
Castroreale, Italy 43 D8
Castrovíllari, Italy 43 C9
Castroville, U.S.A. 110 J5
Castuera, Spain 37 G5
Çat, Turkey 73 C9
Cat Ba △, Vietnam 64 B6
Cat Ba, Dao, Vietnam 64 B6
Cat I., Bahamas 121 B4
Cat L., Canada 104 B1
Cat Lake, Canada 104 B1
Cat Tien △, Vietnam 65 G6
Čata, Slovak Rep. 27 D11
Catacamas, Honduras 120 D2
Cataguases, Brazil 127 A7
Çatak, Turkey 73 C10
Catalão, Brazil 125 G9
Çatalca, Turkey 45 E12
Catalina, Canada 105 C9
Catalina, Chile 126 B2
Catalina, U.S.A. 109 K8
Catalonia = Cataluña □, Spain . 38 D6
Cataluña □, Spain 38 D6
Çatalzeytin, Turkey 72 B6
Catamarca, Argentina 126 B2
Catamarca □, Argentina 126 B2
Catanauan, Phil. 61 E5
Catanduanes □, Phil. 61 E6
Catanduva, Brazil 127 A6
Catánia, Italy 43 E8
Catánia, G. di, Italy 43 E8
Catanzaro, Italy 43 D9
Cataman, Phil. 61 E6
Catarman, Phil. 61 E6
Catatumbo-Bari △, Colombia .. 121 E5
Catbalogan, Phil. 61 F6
Cateel, Phil. 61 H7
Catembe, Mozam. 89 D5
Caterham, U.K. 15 F7
Cathcart, S. Africa 88 E4
Cathlamet, U.S.A. 110 D3
Catio, Guinea-Biss. 82 C1
Catlettsburg, U.S.A. 114 F4
Çatma Dağı, Turkey 47 C11
Catoche, C., Mexico 119 C7
Cátria, Mt., Italy 41 E9
Catriló, Argentina 126 D3
Catrimani, Brazil 124 C6
Catrimani →, Brazil 124 C6
Catskill, U.S.A. 117 D11
Catskill △, U.S.A. 117 D10
Catskill Mts., U.S.A. 117 D10
Catt, Mt., Australia 94 A1
Cattaraugus, U.S.A. 116 D6
Catterick, U.K. 14 C6
Cáttolica, Italy 41 E9
Cáttolica Eraclea, Italy 42 E6
Catuala, Angola 88 B2
Catuane, Mozam. 89 D5
Catur, Mozam. 87 E4
Catwick Is., Vietnam 65 G7
Cauca →, Colombia 124 B4
Caucaia, Brazil 125 D11
Caucasus Mountains, Eurasia . 35 J7
Caudete, Spain 39 G3
Caudry, France 19 B10
Caulnes, France 18 D4
Caulónia, Italy 43 D9
Caungula, Angola 84 F3
Caura →, Venezuela 124 B6
Cauresi →, Mozam. 87 F3
Căuşani, Moldova 29 D14
Causapscal, Canada 105 C6

Caussade, France 20 D5
Causse-Méjean, France 20 D7
Causses du Quercy △, France . 20 D5
Cauterets, France 20 F3
Cauvery →, India 66 P11
Caux, Pays de, France 18 C7
Cava de' Tirreni, Italy 43 B7
Cávado →, Portugal 36 D2
Cavagrande del Cassibile △, Italy 43 F8
Cavaillon, France 21 E9
Cavalaire-sur-Mer, France 21 E10
Cavalese, Italy 41 B8
Cavalier, U.S.A. 112 A6
Cavalla = Cavally →, Africa ... 82 E3
Cavallo, Î. de, France 21 G13
Cavally →, Africa 82 E3
Cavan, Ireland 12 B4
Cavan □, Ireland 12 C4
Cavárzere, Italy 41 C9
Çavdarhisar, Turkey 47 B11
Çavdır, Turkey 47 D11
Cave Creek, U.S.A. 109 K7
Cavenagh Ra., Australia 93 E4
Cavendish, Australia 95 F3
Caviana, I., Brazil 125 C8
Cavite, Phil. 61 D4
Cavnic, Romania 29 C8
Cavour, Italy 40 D4
Cavtat, Croatia 44 D2
Cawndilla L., Australia 95 E3
Cawnpore = Kanpur, India 69 F9
Caxias, Brazil 125 D10
Caxias do Sul, Brazil 127 B5
Çay, Turkey 72 C4
Cay Sal Bank, Bahamas 120 B4
Cayambe, Ecuador 124 C3
Çaycuma, Turkey 72 B5
Çayeli, Turkey 73 B9
Cayenne, Fr. Guiana 125 B8
Cayey, Puerto Rico .... 121 d
Caygören Barajı, Turkey 47 B10
Çayıralan, Turkey 72 C6
Caylus, France 20 D5
Cayman Brac, Cayman Is. 120 C4
Cayman Is. ☑, W. Indies 120 C3
Cayman Trough, Caribbean ... 98 H11
Cayres, France 20 D7
Cayuga, U.S.A. 117 D8
Cayuga L., U.S.A. 117 D8
Cazalla de la Sierra, Spain 37 H5
Căzăneşti, Romania 29 F12
Cazaubon, France 20 E3
Cazaux et de Sanguinet, Étang de,
    France 20 D2
Cazenovia, U.S.A. 117 D9
Cazères, France 20 E5
Cazin, Bos.-H. 41 D12
Čazma, Croatia 41 C13
Cazombo, Angola 85 G4
Cazorla, Spain 37 H7
Cazorla, Sierra de, Spain 37 G8
Cea →, Spain 36 C5
Ceamurlia de Jos, Romania ... 29 F13
Ceanannus Mor, Ireland 12 C5
Ceará = Fortaleza, Brazil 125 D11
Ceará □, Brazil 125 E11
Ceará Mirim, Brazil 125 E11
Ceauru, L., Romania 29 F8
Cebaco, I. de, Panama 120 E3
Cebollar, Argentina 126 B2
Cebollera, Sierra de, Spain ... 38 D2
Cebreros, Spain 36 E6
Cebu, Phil. 61 F5
Čečava, Bos.-H. 28 F2
Ceccano, Italy 42 A6
Cece, Hungary 28 D3
Cechi, Ivory C. 82 D4
Cecil Plains, Australia 95 D5
Cécina, Italy 40 E7
Cécina →, Italy 40 E7
Ceclavín, Spain 36 F4
Cedar →, U.S.A. 112 E9
Cedar City, U.S.A. 109 H7
Cedar Creek Reservoir, U.S.A. . 113 J6
Cedar Falls, Iowa, U.S.A. 112 D8
Cedar Falls, Wash., U.S.A. 110 C5
Cedar Key, U.S.A. 115 L4
Cedar L., Canada 103 C9
Cedar Rapids, U.S.A. 112 E9
Cedartown, U.S.A. 115 H3
Cedarvale, Canada 102 B3
Cedarville, S. Africa 89 E4
Cedeira, Spain 36 B2
Cedral, Mexico 118 C4
Cedrino →, Italy 42 B2
Cedro, Brazil 125 E11
Cedros, I. de, Mexico 118 B1
Cedros B., Trin. & Tob. 125 K15
Ceduna, Australia 95 E1
Cedynia, Poland 31 F1
Cée, Spain 36 C1
Ceerigaabo = Erigavo,
    Somali Rep. 75 E4
Cefalù, Italy 43 D7
Cega →, Spain 36 D6
Cegléd, Hungary 28 C4
Céglie Messápico, Italy 43 B10
Cehegín, Spain 39 G3
Cehu-Silvaniei, Romania 29 C8
Ceica, Romania 28 D7
Ceira →, Portugal 36 E2
Cekik, Indonesia 63 J17
Čelákovice, Czech Rep. 26 A7
Celano, Italy 41 F10
Celanova, Spain 36 C3
Celaque △, Honduras 120 D2
Celaya, Mexico 118 C4
Celebes = Sulawesi, Indonesia . 63 E6
Celebes Sea, Indonesia 63 D6
Čelić, Bos.-H. 28 F3
Celina, U.S.A. 114 E3

Celinac, Bos.-H. 28 F2
Celje, Slovenia 41 B12
Celldömölk, Hungary 28 C2
Celle, Germany 24 C6
Celorico da Beira, Portugal ... 36 E3
Celtic Sea, Atl. Oc. 6 E4
Çeltikçi, Turkey 47 D12
Çemişgezek, Turkey 73 C8
Cenderwasih, Teluk, Indonesia . 63 E9
Cengong, China 58 D7
Ceno →, Italy 40 D7
Centallo, Italy 40 D4
Centelles, Spain 38 D7
Center, N. Dak., U.S.A. 112 B4
Center, Tex., U.S.A. 113 K7
Centerburg, U.S.A. 116 F2
Centerville, Calif., U.S.A. 110 J7
Centerville, Iowa, U.S.A. 112 E8
Centerville, Pa., U.S.A. 116 F5
Centerville, Tenn., U.S.A. 115 H2
Centerville, Tex., U.S.A. 113 K7
Cento, Italy 41 D8
Central □ = Tsentralnyy □, Russia 34 D4
Central □, Ghana 83 D4
Central □, Kenya 86 C4
Central □, Malawi 87 E3
Central □, Zambia 87 E2
Central, Cordillera, Colombia .. 124 C4
Central, Cordillera, Costa Rica . 120 D3
Central, Cordillera, Dom. Rep. . 121 C5
Central, Cordillera, Phil. 61 C4
Central, Cordillera, Puerto Rico 121 d
Central African Rep. ■, Africa . 84 C4
Central America, America 98 H11
Central Butte, Canada 103 C7
Central City, Colo., U.S.A. ... 108 G11
Central City, Ky., U.S.A. 114 G2
Central City, Nebr., U.S.A. ... 112 E6
Central I., Kenya 86 B4
Central Island △, Kenya 86 B4
Central Kalahari △, Botswana . 88 C3
Central Makran Range, Pakistan 66 F4
Central Patricia, Canada 104 B1
Central Point, U.S.A. 108 E2
Central Russian Uplands, Europe 6 E13
Central Siberian Plateau, Russia 50 C14
Central Square, U.S.A. 117 C8
Centralia, Ill., U.S.A. 112 F10
Centralia, Mo., U.S.A. 112 F8
Centralia, Wash., U.S.A. 110 D4
Cenxi, China 59 F8
Ceotina →, Bos.-H. 44 C2
Cephalonia = Kefallinía, Greece . 46 C2
Čepin, Croatia 28 E3
Ceprano, Italy 42 A6
Ceptura, Romania 29 E11
Cepu, Indonesia 63 G14
Ceram = Seram, Indonesia 63 E7
Ceram Sea = Seram Sea,
    Indonesia 63 E7
Cerbère, France 20 F7
Cerbicales, Îs., France 21 G13
Cercal, Portugal 37 H2
Cerdaña, Spain 38 C6
Cère →, France 20 D5
Cerea, Italy 41 C8
Ceredigion □, U.K. 15 E3
Ceres, Argentina 126 B3
Ceres, S. Africa 88 E2
Ceres, U.S.A. 110 H6
Céret, France 20 F6
Cergy, France 19 C9
Cerignola, Italy 43 A8
Cerigo = Kíthira, Greece 46 E5
Cérilly, France 19 F9
Cerisiers, France 19 D10
Cerizay, France 18 F6
Çerkeş, Turkey 72 B5
Çerkezköy, Turkey 45 E12
Cerknica, Slovenia 41 C11
Cerkovica, Bulgaria 45 C8
Cermerno, Serbia & M. 44 C4
Çermik, Turkey 73 C8
Cerna, Romania 29 E13
Cerna →, Romania 29 F8
Cernavodă, Romania 29 F13
Cernay, France 19 E14
Cernik, Croatia 28 E2
Cerralvo, I., Mexico 118 C3
Cërrik, Albania 44 E3
Cerritos, Mexico 118 C4
Cerro Chato, Uruguay 127 C4
Cerro Corá △, Paraguay 127 A4
Cerro el Copey △, Venezuela .. 121 D7
Cerro Hoya △, Panama 120 E3
Cerro Saroche △, Venezuela ... 121 D6
Certaldo, Italy 40 E8
Cervaro →, Italy 43 A8
Cervati, Monte, Italy 43 B8
Cervelo, Spain 38 D6
Cervera, Spain 38 D6
Cervera de Pisuerga, Spain ... 36 C6
Cervera del Río Alhama, Spain . 38 C3
Cervéteri, Italy 41 F9
Cérvia, Italy 41 D9
Cervignano del Friuli, Italy ... 41 C10
Cervinara, Italy 43 A7
Cervione, France 21 F13
Cervo, Spain 36 B3
Cesarò, Italy 43 E7
Cesena, Italy 41 D9
Cesenático, Italy 41 D9
Cēsis, Latvia 9 H21
Česká Lípa, Czech Rep. 26 A7
Česká Třebová, Czech Rep. ... 27 B9
České Budějovice, Czech Rep. . 26 C7
České Velenice, Czech Rep. ... 26 C7
Českobudějovický □, Czech Rep. 26 B7
Českomoravská Vrchovina,
    Czech Rep. 26 B8
Český Brod, Czech Rep. 26 A7
Český Krumlov, Czech Rep. ... 26 C7

Český Těšín, *Czech Rep.* 27 B11
Česma →, *Croatia* 41 C13
Çeşme, *Turkey* 47 C8
Cessnock, *Australia* 95 E5
Cesson-Sévigné, *France* 18 D5
Cestas, *France* 20 D3
Cestos →, *Liberia* 82 D3
Cestos Sehnkwehn △, *Liberia* ... 82 D3
Cetate, *Romania* 28 F8
Cetin Grad, *Croatia* 41 C12
Cetina →, *Croatia* 41 E13
Cetinje, *Serbia & M.* 44 D2
Cetraro, *Italy* 43 C8
Ceuta, *N. Afr.* 78 A4
Ceva, *Italy* 40 D5
Cévennes, *France* 20 D7
Cévennes △, *France* 20 D7
Ceyhan, *Turkey* 70 B2
Ceyhan →, *Turkey* 72 D6
Ceylânpınar, *Turkey* 73 D9
Ceylon = Sri Lanka ■, *Asia* ... 66 R12
Cèze →, *France* 21 D8
Cha-am, *Thailand* 64 F2
Cha Pa, *Vietnam* 64 A4
Chabanais, *France* 20 C4
Chabeuil, *France* 21 D9
Chablais, *France* 19 F13
Chablis, *France* 19 E10
Chacabuco, *Argentina* 126 C3
Chachapoyas, *Peru* 124 E3
Chachoengsao, *Thailand* 64 F3
Chachran, *Pakistan* 66 E7
Chachro, *Pakistan* 68 G4
Chaco △, *Argentina* 126 B4
Chaco □, *Argentina* 126 B3
Chaco □, *Paraguay* 126 B4
Chaco →, *U.S.A.* 109 H9
Chaco Austral, *S. Amer.* 128 B4
Chaco Boreal, *S. Amer.* 124 H6
Chaco Central, *S. Amer.* 128 A4
Chaco Culture △, *U.S.A.* 109 H10
Chacon, C., *U.S.A.* 102 C2
Chad ■, *Africa* 79 F8
Chad, L. = Tchad, L., *Chad* 79 F8
Chadan, *Russia* 53 D10
Chadileuvú →, *Argentina* 126 D2
Chadiza, *Zambia* 87 E3
Chadron, *U.S.A.* 112 D3
Chadyr-Lunga = Ciadâr-Lunga,
  Moldova 29 D13
Chae Hom, *Thailand* 64 C2
Chae Son △, *Thailand* 64 C2
Chaem →, *Thailand* 64 C2
Chaeryŏng, *N. Korea* 57 E13
Chagai Hills = Chāh Gay Hills,
  Afghan. 66 E3
Chagda, *Russia* 53 D14
Chaghcharān, *Afghan.* 66 B4
Chagny, *France* 19 F11
Chagoda, *Russia* 32 C8
Chagos Arch. ⊠, *Ind. Oc.* 50 K11
Chagres △, *Panama* 120 E4
Chagrin Falls, *U.S.A.* 116 E3
Chaguanas, *Trin. & Tob.* 125 K15
Chāh Ākhvor, *Iran* 71 C8
Chāh Bahar, *Iran* 71 E9
Chāh-e Kavīr, *Iran* 71 C8
Chāh Gay Hills, *Afghan.* 66 E3
Chahar Burjak, *Afghan.* 66 D3
Chahār Maḥāll va Bakhtīārī □,
  Iran 71 C6
Chaibasa, *India* 67 H14
Chaillé-les-Marais, *France* 20 B2
Chainat, *Thailand* 64 E3
Chaiya, *Thailand* 65 H2
Chaiyaphum, *Thailand* 64 E4
Chaj Doab, *Pakistan* 68 C5
Chajari, *Argentina* 126 C4
Chak Amru, *Pakistan* 68 C6
Chaka, *Sudan* 81 G3
Chakar →, *Pakistan* 68 E3
Chakari, *Zimbabwe* 89 B4
Chake Chake, *Tanzania* 86 D4
Chakhānsūr, *Afghan.* 66 D3
Chakonipau, L., *Canada* 105 A6
Chakradharpur, *India* 69 H11
Chakrata, *India* 68 D7
Chakwal, *Pakistan* 68 C5
Chala, *Peru* 124 G4
Chalais, *France* 20 C4
Chalchihuites, *Mexico* 118 C4
Chalcis = Khalkís, *Greece* 46 C5
Châlette-sur-Loing, *France* ... 19 D9
Chaleur B., *Canada* 105 C6
Chalfant, *U.S.A.* 110 H8
Chalhuanca, *Peru* 124 F4
Chalindrey, *France* 19 E12
Chaling, *China* 59 D9
Chalisgaon, *India* 66 J9
Chalk River, *Canada* 104 C4
Chalky Inlet, *N.Z.* 91 M1
Challans, *France* 18 F5
Challapata, *Bolivia* 124 G5
Challis, *U.S.A.* 108 D6
Chalmette, *U.S.A.* 113 L10
Chalon-sur-Saône, *France* 19 F11
Chalonnes-sur-Loire, *France* .. 18 E6
Châlons-en-Champagne, *France* . 19 D11
Chālus, *France* 20 C4
Chālūs, *Iran* 71 B6
Cham, *Germany* 25 F8
Cham, Cu Lao, *Vietnam* 64 E7
Chama, *U.S.A.* 109 H10
Chamaicó, *Argentina* 126 D3
Chaman, *Pakistan* 66 D5
Chamba, *India* 68 C7
Chamba, *Tanzania* 87 E4
Chambal →, *India* 69 F8
Chamberlain, *U.S.A.* 112 D5
Chamberlain →, *Australia* 92 C4
Chamberlain L., *U.S.A.* 115 B11
Chambers, *U.S.A.* 109 J9

Chambersburg, *U.S.A.* 114 F7
Chambéry, *France* 21 C9
Chambeshi →, *Zambia* 84 G6
Chambly, *Canada* 117 A11
Chambord, *Canada* 105 C5
Chambord, *France* 19 E8
Chamboulive, *France* 20 C5
Chamchamal, *Iraq* 70 C5
Chamela, *Mexico* 118 D3
Chamical, *Argentina* 126 C2
Chamkar Luong, *Cambodia* 65 G4
Chamoli, *India* 69 D8
Chamonix-Mont Blanc, *France* .. 21 C10
Champa, *India* 69 H10
Champagne, *Canada* 102 A1
Champagne, *France* 19 D11
Champagnole, *France* 19 F12
Champaign, *U.S.A.* 114 E1
Champassak, *Laos* 64 E5
Champaubert, *France* 19 D10
Champawat, *India* 69 E9
Champdeniers-St-Denis, *France* . 20 B3
Champdoré, L., *Canada* 105 A6
Champeix, *France* 20 C7
Champion, *U.S.A.* 116 E4
Champlain, *U.S.A.* 117 B11
Champlain, L., *U.S.A.* 117 B11
Champlitte, *France* 19 E12
Champotón, *Mexico* 119 D6
Champua, *India* 69 H11
Chamusca, *Portugal* 37 F2
Chana, *Thailand* 65 J3
Chañaral, *Chile* 126 B1
Chanārān, *Iran* 71 B8
Chanasma, *India* 68 H5
Chancery Lane, *Barbados* ..... 121 g
Chanco, *Chile* 126 D1
Chand, *India* 69 J8
Chandan, *India* 69 G12
Chandan Chauki, *India* 69 E9
Chandannagar, *India* 69 H13
Chandausi, *India* 69 E8
Chandeleur Is., *U.S.A.* 113 L10
Chandeleur Sd., *U.S.A.* 113 L10
Chandigarh, *India* 68 D7
Chandil, *India* 69 H12
Chandler, *Australia* 95 D1
Chandler, *Canada* 105 C7
Chandler, *Ariz., U.S.A.* 109 K8
Chandler, *Okla., U.S.A.* 113 H6
Chandod, *India* 68 J5
Chandpur, *Bangla.* 67 H17
Chandrapur, *India* 66 K11
Chānf, *Iran* 71 E9
Chang, *Pakistan* 68 F3
Chang, Ko, *Thailand* 65 F4
Ch'ang Chiang = Chang Jiang →,
  China 59 B13
Chang Jiang →, *China* 59 B13
Changa, *India* 69 C7
Changanacheri, *India* 66 Q10
Changane →, *Mozam.* 89 C5
Changbai, *China* 57 D15
Changbai Shan, *China* 57 C15
Changchiak'ou = Zhangjiakou,
  China 56 D8
Ch'angchou = Changzhou, *China* . 59 B12
Changchun, *China* 57 C13
Changchunling, *China* 57 B13
Changde, *China* 59 C8
Changdo-ri, *N. Korea* 57 E14
Changfeng, *China* 59 A11
Changhai = Shanghai, *China* ... 59 B13
Changhua, *China* 59 B12
Changhua, *Taiwan* 59 E13
Changhŭng, *S. Korea* 57 G14
Changhŭngni, *N. Korea* 57 D15
Changi, *Singapore* .... 65 d
Changi, Singapore ✈ (SIN),
  Singapore 65 M4
Changjiang, *China* 64 C7
Changjin, *N. Korea* 57 D14
Changjin-chŏsuji, *N. Korea* 57 D14
Changle, *China* 59 E12
Changli, *China* 57 E10
Changling, *China* 57 B12
Changlun, *Malaysia* 65 J3
Changning, *Hunan, China* 59 D9
Changning, *Sichuan, China* 58 C5
Changning, *Yunnan, China* 58 E2
Changping, *China* 56 D9
Changsha, *China* 59 C9
Changshan, *China* 59 C12
Changshu, *China* 59 B13
Changshun, *China* 58 D6
Changtai, *China* 59 E11
Changting, *China* 59 E11
Changwu, *China* 56 G4
Changxing, *China* 59 B12
Changyang, *China* 59 B8
Changyi, *China* 57 F10
Changyŏn, *N. Korea* 57 E13
Changyuan, *China* 56 G8
Changzhi, *China* 56 F7
Changzhou, *China* 59 B12
Chanhanga, *Angola* 88 B1
Chania = Khaniá, *Greece* 49 D6
Chanlar = Xanlar, *Azerbaijan* ... 35 K8
Channapatna, *India* 66 N10
Channel Is., *U.K.* 15 H5
Channel Is., *U.S.A.* 111 M7
Channel Islands △, *U.S.A.* 111 L7
Channel-Port aux Basques,
  Canada 105 C8
Channel Tunnel, *Europe* 15 F9
Channing, *U.S.A.* 113 H3
Chantada, *Spain* 36 C3
Chanthaburi, *Thailand* 64 F4
Chantilly, *France* 19 C9
Chantonnay, *France* 18 F5
Chantrey Inlet, *Canada* 100 B10
Chanute, *U.S.A.* 113 G7
Chanza →, *Spain* 37 H3

Chao Hu, *China* 59 B11
Chao Phraya →, *Thailand* 64 F3
Chao Phraya Lowlands, *Thailand* . 64 E3
Chaocheng, *China* 56 F8
Chaohu, *China* 59 B11
Chaoyang, *Guangdong, China* .. 59 F11
Chaoyang, *Liaoning, China* 57 D11
Chaozhou, *China* 59 F11
Chapais, *Canada* 104 C5
Chapala, *Mozam.* 87 F4
Chapala, L. de, *Mexico* 118 C4
Chapayev, *Kazakhstan* 34 E10
Chapayevsk, *Russia* 34 D9
Chapecó, *Brazil* 127 B5
Chapel Hill, *U.S.A.* 115 H6
Chapleau, *Canada* 104 C3
Chaplin, *Canada* 103 C7
Chaplin L., *Canada* 103 C7
Chaplino, *Ukraine* 33 H9
Chaplygin, *Russia* 32 F11
Chapra = Chhapra, *India* 69 G11
Chara, *Russia* 53 D12
Charadai, *Argentina* 126 B4
Charagua, *Bolivia* 124 G6
Charambirá, Punta, *Colombia* .. 124 C3
Charaña, *Bolivia* 124 G5
Charantsavan, *Armenia* 35 K7
Charanwala, *India* 68 F5
Charata, *Argentina* 126 B3
Charcas, *Mexico* 118 C4
Charcot I., *Antarctica* 5 C17
Chard, *U.K.* 15 G5
Chardon, *U.S.A.* 116 E3
Chardzhou = Chärjew,
  Turkmenistan 52 F7
Charente □, *France* 20 C4
Charente →, *France* 20 C2
Charente-Maritime □, *France* .. 20 C3
Charenton-du-Cher, *France* 19 F9
Chari →, *Chad* 79 F8
Chārīkār, *Afghan.* 66 B6
Chariton →, *U.S.A.* 112 F8
Chärjew, *Turkmenistan* 52 F7
Charkhari, *India* 69 G8
Charkhi Dadri, *India* 68 E7
Charleroi, *Belgium* 17 D4
Charleroi, *U.S.A.* 116 F5
Charles, C., *U.S.A.* 114 G8
Charles City, *U.S.A.* 112 D8
Charles de Gaulle, Paris ✈
  (CDG), *France* 19 D9
Charles L., *Canada* 103 B6
Charles Town, *U.S.A.* 114 F7
Charleston, *Ill., U.S.A.* 114 F1
Charleston, *Miss., U.S.A.* 113 H9
Charleston, *Mo., U.S.A.* 113 G10
Charleston, *S.C., U.S.A.* 115 J6
Charleston, *W. Va., U.S.A.* ... 114 F5
Charleston L., *Canada* 117 B9
Charleston Peak, *U.S.A.* 111 J11
Charlestown, *Ireland* 12 C3
Charlestown, *S. Africa* 89 D4
Charlestown, *Ind., U.S.A.* 114 F3
Charlestown, *N.H., U.S.A.* 117 C12
Charlestown of Aberlour, *U.K.* . 13 D5
Charleville = Rath Luirc, *Ireland* . 12 D3
Charleville, *Australia* 95 D4
Charleville-Mézières, *France* .. 19 C11
Charlevoix, *U.S.A.* 114 C3
Charlieu, *France* 19 F11
Charlotte, *Mich., U.S.A.* 114 D3
Charlotte, *N.C., U.S.A.* 115 H5
Charlotte, *Vt., U.S.A.* 117 B11
Charlotte Amalie, *U.S. Virgin Is.* . 121 e
Charlotte Harbor, *U.S.A.* 115 M4
Charlotte L., *Canada* 102 C3
Charlottenberg, *Sweden* 10 E6
Charlottesville, *U.S.A.* 114 F6
Charlottetown, *Nfld. & L.,*
  Canada 105 B8
Charlottetown, *P.E.I., Canada* . 105 C7
Charlotteville, *Trin. & Tob.* 125 J16
Charlton, *Australia* 95 F3
Charlton, *U.S.A.* 112 E8
Charlton I., *Canada* 104 B4
Charmes, *France* 19 D13
Charny, *Canada* 105 C5
Charnyany, *Belarus* 31 G11
Charolles, *France* 19 F11
Chârost, *France* 19 F9
Charre, *Mozam.* 87 F4
Charroux, *France* 20 B4
Charsadda, *Pakistan* 68 B4
Charters Towers, *Australia* 94 C4
Chartres, *France* 18 D8
Chartreuse △, *France* 21 C9
Chascomús, *Argentina* 126 D4
Chasefu, *Zambia* 87 E3
Chashma Barrage, *Pakistan* ... 68 C4
Chasseneuil-sur-Bonnieure,
  France 20 C4
Chāt, *Iran* 71 B7
Chatal Balkan = Udvoy Balkan,
  Bulgaria 45 D10
Château-Arnoux-St-Auban,
  France 21 D10
Château-Chinon, *France* 19 E10
Château-d'Olonne, *France* 20 B2
Château-du-Loir, *France* 18 E7
Château-la-Vallière, *France* 18 E7
Château-Landon, *France* 19 D9
Château-Renard, *France* 19 E9
Château-Renault, *France* 18 E7
Château-Salins, *France* 19 D13
Château-Thierry, *France* 19 C10
Châteaubourg, *France* 18 D5
Châteaubriant, *France* 18 E5
Châteaudun, *France* 18 D8
Chateaugay, *U.S.A.* 117 B10
Châteaugiron, *France* 18 D5

Châteauguay, L., *Canada* 105 A5
Châteaulin, *France* 18 D2
Châteaumeillant, *France* 19 F9
Châteauneuf-du-Faou, *France* .. 18 D3
Châteauneuf-sur-Charente,
  France 20 C3
Châteauneuf-sur-Cher, *France* .. 19 F9
Châteauneuf-sur-Loire, *France* . 19 E9
Châteaurenard, *France* 21 E8
Châteauroux, *France* 19 F8
Châteauvillain, *France* 19 D11
Châteaux, Pte. des, *Guadeloupe* . 120 b
Châtelaillon-Plage, *France* 20 B2
Châtelguyon, *France* 20 C7
Châtellerault, *France* 18 F7
Châtelus-Malvaleix, *France* 19 F9
Chatham = Chatham-Kent,
  Canada 116 D2
Chatham = Miramichi, *Canada* . 105 C6
Chatham, *U.K.* 15 F8
Chatham, *U.S.A.* 117 D11
Chatham Is., *Pac. Oc.* 96 M10
Chatham-Kent, *Canada* 116 D2
Châtillon, *Italy* 40 C4
Châtillon-Coligny, *France* 19 E9
Châtillon-en-Diois, *France* 21 D9
Châtillon-sur-Indre, *France* ... 18 F8
Châtillon-sur-Loire, *France* ... 19 E9
Châtillon-sur-Seine, *France* ... 19 E11
Chatmohar, *Bangla.* 69 G13
Chatra, *India* 69 G11
Chatrapur, *India* 67 K14
Chats, L. des, *Canada* 117 A8
Chatsu, *India* 68 F6
Chatsworth, *Canada* 116 B4
Chatsworth, *Zimbabwe* 87 F3
Chattagam = Chittagong, *Bangla.* . 67 H17
Chattahoochee, *U.S.A.* 115 K3
Chattahoochee →, *U.S.A.* 115 K3
Chattanooga, *U.S.A.* 115 H3
Chatteris, *U.K.* 15 E8
Chaturat, *Thailand* 64 E3
Chau Doc, *Vietnam* 65 G5
Chaudes-Aigues, *France* 20 D7
Chauffailles, *France* 19 F11
Chaukan Pass, *Burma* 67 F20
Chaumont, *France* 19 D12
Chaumont-en-Vexin, *France* ... 19 C8
Chaumont-sur-Loire, *France* .. 18 E8
Chaunay, *France* 20 B4
Chauny, *France* 19 C10
Chausey, Îs., *France* 18 D5
Chaussin, *France* 19 F12
Chautauqua L., *U.S.A.* 116 D5
Chauvigny, *France* 18 F7
Chauvin, *Canada* 103 C6
Chaves, *Brazil* 125 D9
Chaves, *Portugal* 36 D3
Chawang, *Thailand* 65 H2
Chazelles-sur-Lyon, *France* ... 21 C8
Chazy, *U.S.A.* 117 B11
Cheb, *Czech Rep.* 26 A5
Cheboksarskoye Vdkhr., *Russia* . 34 B8
Cheboksary, *Russia* 34 B8
Cheboygan, *U.S.A.* 114 C3
Chebsara, *Russia* 32 C10
Chech, Erg, *Africa* 78 D5
Chechelnyk, *Ukraine* 29 B14
Chechen, Ostrov, *Russia* 35 J8
Chechenia □, *Russia* 35 J7
Checheno-Ingush Republic =
  Chechenia □, *Russia* 35 J7
Chechnya = Chechenia □, *Russia* . 35 J7
Chech'ŏn, *S. Korea* 57 F15
Chęciny, *Poland* 31 H7
Checotah, *U.S.A.* 113 H7
Chedabucto B., *Canada* 105 C7
Cheduba I., *Burma* 67 K18
Cheepie, *Australia* 95 D4
Chef-Boutonne, *France* 20 B3
Chegdomyn, *Russia* 53 D14
Chegga, *Mauritania* 78 C4
Chegutu, *Zimbabwe* 87 F3
Chehalis, *U.S.A.* 110 D4
Chehalis →, *U.S.A.* 110 D3
Cheile Nerei-Beusnita △,
  Romania 28 F6
Cheiron, Mt., *France* 21 E10
Cheju do, *S. Korea* 57 H14
Chekalin, *Russia* 32 E9
Chekhovo, *Russia* 30 D7
Chekiang = Zhejiang □, *China* .. 59 C13
Chel = Kuru, Bahr el →, *Sudan* . 81 F2
Chela, Sa. da, *Angola* 88 B1
Chelan, *U.S.A.* 108 C4
Chelan, L., *U.S.A.* 108 B3
Cheleken, *Turkmenistan* 52 F6
Cheleken Yarymadasy,
  Turkmenistan 71 B7
Chelforó, *Argentina* 128 D3
Chelkar = Shalqar, *Kazakhstan* . 52 E6
Chelkar Tengiz, Solonchak,
  Kazakhstan 52 E7
Chella, *Ethiopia* 81 F4
Chelles, *France* 19 D9
Chełm, *Poland* 31 G10
Chełmno, *Poland* 31 E5
Chelmsford, *U.K.* 15 F8
Chełmża, *Poland* 31 E5
Chelsea, *U.S.A.* 117 C12
Cheltenham, *U.K.* 15 F5
Chelva, *Spain* 38 F4
Chelyabinsk, *Russia* 52 D7
Chelyuskin, C. = Chelyuskin, Mys,
  Russia 53 B11
Chelyuskin, Mys, *Russia* 53 B11
Chemainus, *Canada* 110 B3
Chemba, *Mozam.* 85 H6
Chembar = Belinskiy, *Russia* ... 34 D6

Chemillé, *France* 18 E6
Chemnitz, *Germany* 24 E8
Chemult, *U.S.A.* 108 E3
Chen, Gora, *Russia* 53 C15
Chenab →, *Pakistan* 68 D4
Chenango Forks, *U.S.A.* 117 D9
Chencha, *Ethiopia* 81 F4
Chenchiang = Zhenjiang, *China* . 59 A12
Cheney, *U.S.A.* 108 C5
Cheng Xian, *China* 56 H3
Chengbu, *China* 59 D8
Chengcheng, *China* 56 G5
Chengchou = Zhengzhou, *China* . 56 G7
Chengde, *China* 57 D9
Chengdong Hu, *China* 59 A11
Chengdu, *China* 58 B5
Chenggong, *China* 58 E4
Chenggu, *China* 56 H4
Chenghai, *China* 59 F11
Chengjiang, *China* 58 E4
Chengkou, *China* 58 B7
Ch'engmai, *China* 64 C7
Ch'engtu = Chengdu, *China* 58 B5
Chengwu, *China* 56 G8
Chengxi Hu, *China* 59 A11
Chengyang, *China* 57 F11
Chenjiagang, *China* 57 G10
Chenkán, *Mexico* 119 D6
Chennai, *India* 66 N12
Chenôve, *France* 19 E12
Chenxi, *China* 59 C8
Chenzhou, *China* 59 E9
Cheo Reo, *Vietnam* 62 B3
Cheom Ksan, *Cambodia* 64 E5
Chepelare, *Bulgaria* 45 E8
Chepén, *Peru* 124 E3
Chepes, *Argentina* 126 C2
Chepo, *Panama* 120 E4
Chepstow, *U.K.* 15 F5
Chequamegon B., *U.S.A.* 112 B9
Cher □, *France* 19 E9
Cher →, *France* 18 E7
Chéradi, *Italy* 43 B10
Cherasco, *Italy* 40 D4
Cheraw, *U.S.A.* 115 H6
Cherbourg, *France* 18 C5
Cherdakly, *Russia* 34 C9
Cherdyn, *Russia* 52 C6
Cheremkhovo, *Russia* 53 D11
Cherepanovo, *Russia* 52 D9
Cherepovets, *Russia* 32 C9
Chergui, Chott ech, *Algeria* 78 B6
Cherikov = Cherykaw, *Belarus* . 33 F6
Cherkasy, *Ukraine* 33 H7
Cherkessk, *Russia* 35 H6
Cherlak, *Russia* 52 D8
Chernaya, *Russia* 53 B9
Chernelytsya, *Ukraine* 29 B10
Cherni, *Bulgaria* 44 D7
Chernigov = Chernihiv, *Ukraine* . 33 G6
Chernihiv, *Ukraine* 33 G6
Chernivetska □, *Ukraine* 29 B10
Chernivtsi, *Ukraine* 29 B10
Chernivtsi □, *Ukraine* 29 B13
Chernobyl = Chornobyl, *Ukraine* . 33 G6
Chernogorsk, *Russia* 53 D10
Chernomorskoye =
  Chornomorske, *Ukraine* 33 K7
Chernovtsy = Chernivtsi, *Ukraine* . 29 B10
Chernyakhovsk, *Russia* 9 J19
Chernyanka, *Russia* 33 G9
Chernysheyskiy, *Russia* 53 C12
Chernyshevskiy, *Russia* 53 C11
Chernyye Zemli, *Russia* 35 H8
Cherokee, *Iowa, U.S.A.* 112 D7
Cherokee, *Okla., U.S.A.* 113 G5
Cherokee Village, *U.S.A.* 113 G9
Cherokees, Grand Lake O' The,
  U.S.A. 113 G7
Cherrapunji, *India* 67 G17
Cherry Valley, *Calif., U.S.A.* .. 111 M10
Cherry Valley, *N.Y., U.S.A.* ... 117 D10
Cherskiy, *Russia* 53 C17
Cherskogo Khrebet, *Russia* 53 C15
Chertkovo, *Russia* 33 H11
Cherven, *Belarus* 32 F5
Cherven-Bryag, *Bulgaria* 45 C8
Chervonoarmiyske, *Ukraine* ... 29 E13
Chervonohrad, *Ukraine* 33 G3
Cherwell →, *U.K.* 15 F6
Cherykaw, *Belarus* 32 F6
Chesapeake, *U.S.A.* 114 G7
Chesapeake B., *U.S.A.* 114 G7
Cheshire □, *U.K.* 14 D5
Cheshskaya Guba, *Russia* 52 C5
Cheshunt, *U.K.* 15 F7
Chesil Beach, *U.K.* 15 G5
Chesley, *Canada* 116 B3
Cheste, *Spain* 39 F4
Chester, *U.K.* 14 D5
Chester, *Calif., U.S.A.* 108 F3
Chester, *Ill., U.S.A.* 113 G10
Chester, *Mont., U.S.A.* 108 B8
Chester, *Pa., U.S.A.* 114 F8
Chester, *S.C., U.S.A.* 115 H5
Chester, *Vt., U.S.A.* 117 C12
Chester, *W. Va., U.S.A.* 116 F4
Chester-le-Street, *U.K.* 14 C6
Chesterfield, *U.K.* 14 D6
Chesterfield, Is., *N. Cal.* 96 J7
Chesterfield Inlet, *Canada* 100 B10
Chesterton Range △, *Australia* . 95 D4
Chestertown, *U.S.A.* 117 C11
Chesterville, *Canada* 117 A9
Chestnut Ridge, *U.S.A.* 116 F5
Chesuncook L., *U.S.A.* 115 C11
Chéticamp, *Canada* 105 C7
Chetrosu, *Moldova* 29 B12
Chetumal, *Mexico* 119 D7
Chetumal, B. de, *Mexico* 119 D7
Chetwynd, *Canada* 102 B4
Chevanceaux, *France* 20 C3

Cheviot, The, *U.K.* 14 B5
Cheviot Hills, *U.K.* 14 B5
Cheviot Ra., *Australia* 94 D3
Chew Bahir, *Ethiopia* 81 G4
Chewelah, *U.S.A.* 108 B5
Chewore △, *Zimbabwe* 87 F2
Cheyenne, *Okla., U.S.A.* 113 H5
Cheyenne, *Wyo., U.S.A.* 112 E2
Cheyenne ➤, *U.S.A.* 112 C4
Cheyenne Wells, *U.S.A.* 112 F3
Cheyne B., *Australia* 93 F2
Chhabra, *India* 68 G7
Chhaktala, *India* 68 H6
Chhapra, *India* 69 G11
Chhata, *India* 68 F7
Chhatarpur, *Jharkhand, India* .. 69 G11
Chhatarpur, *Mad. P., India* 69 G8
Chhattisgarh □, *India* 69 J10
Chhep, *Cambodia* 64 F5
Chhindwara, *Mad. P., India* .. 69 H8
Chhindwara, *Mad. P., India* .. 69 H8
Chhlong, *Cambodia* 65 F5
Chhota Tawa ➤, *India* 68 H7
Chhoti Kali Sindh ➤, *India* .. 68 G6
Chhuikhadan, *India* 69 J9
Chhuk, *Cambodia* 65 G5
Chi ➤, *Thailand* 64 E5
Chiai, *Taiwan* 59 F13
Chiali, *Taiwan* 59 F13
Chiamboni, *Somali Rep.* 84 E8
Chianciano Terme, *Italy* 41 E8
Chiang Dao, *Thailand* 64 C2
Chiang Kham, *Thailand* 64 C3
Chiang Khan, *Thailand* 64 D3
Chiang Khong, *Thailand* 58 G3
Chiang Mai, *Thailand* 64 C2
Chiang Rai, *Thailand* 58 H4
Chiang Saen, *Thailand* 58 G3
Chianti, *Italy* 41 E8
Chiapa ➤, *Mexico* 119 D6
Chiapa de Corzo, *Mexico* 119 D6
Chiapas □, *Mexico* 119 D6
Chiaramonte Gulfi, *Italy* 43 E7
Chiaravalle, *Italy* 41 E10
Chiaravalle Centrale, *Italy* .. 43 D9
Chiari, *Italy* 40 C6
Chiatura, *Georgia* 35 J6
Chiautla, *Mexico* 119 D5
Chiávari, *Italy* 40 D6
Chiba, *Japan* 55 G10
Chiba □, *Japan* 55 G10
Chibabava, *Mozam.* 89 C5
Chibemba, *Cunene, Angola* 85 H2
Chibemba, *Huila, Angola* 88 B2
Chibi, *Zimbabwe* 89 C5
Chibia, *Angola* 85 H2
Chibougamau, *Canada* 104 C5
Chibougamau, L., *Canada* 104 C5
Chibuk, *Nigeria* 83 C7
Chibuto, *Mozam.* 89 C5
Chic-Chocs, Mts., *Canada* 105 C6
Chicacole = Srikakulam, *India* . 67 K13
Chicago, *U.S.A.* 114 E2
Chicago Heights, *U.S.A.* 114 E2
Chichagof I., *U.S.A.* 100 C6
Chichén-Itzá, *Mexico* 119 C7
Chicheng, *China* 56 D8
Chichester, *U.K.* 15 G7
Chichester Ra., *Australia* 92 D2
Chichibu, *Japan* 55 F9
Chichibu-Tama △, *Japan* 55 G9
Ch'ich'iharh = Qiqihar, *China* . 53 E13
Chicholi, *India* 68 H8
Chickasaw △, *U.S.A.* 113 H6
Chickasha, *U.S.A.* 113 H6
Chiclana de la Frontera, *Spain* .. 37 J4
Chiclayo, *Peru* 124 E3
Chico, *U.S.A.* 110 F5
Chico ➤, *Chubut, Argentina* .. 128 E3
Chico ➤, *Santa Cruz, Argentina* 128 G3
Chicomo, *Mozam.* 89 C5
Chicomostoc, *Mexico* 118 C4
Chicontepec, *Mexico* 119 C5
Chicopee, *U.S.A.* 117 D12
Chicoutimi, *Canada* 105 C5
Chicualacuala, *Mozam.* 89 C5
Chidambaram, *India* 66 P11
Chidenguele, *Mozam.* 89 C5
Chidley, C., *Canada* 101 B13
Chiducuane, *Mozam.* 89 C5
Chiede, *Angola* 88 B2
Chiefs Pt., *Canada* 116 B3
Chiem Hoa, *Vietnam* 64 A5
Chiemsee, *Germany* 25 H8
Chiengi, *Zambia* 87 D2
Chiengmai = Chiang Mai,
  Thailand 64 C2
Chienti ➤, *Italy* 41 E10
Chieri, *Italy* 40 C4
Chiers ➤, *France* 19 C11
Chiesa in Valmalenco, *Italy* .. 40 B6
Chiese ➤, *Italy* 40 C7
Chieti, *Italy* 41 F11
Chifeng, *China* 57 C10
Chigirin, *Ukraine* 33 H7
Chignecto B., *Canada* 105 C7
Chiguana, *Bolivia* 126 A2
Chigwell, *U.K.* 15 F8
Chiha-ri, *N. Korea* 57 E14
Chihli, G. of = Bo Hai, *China* .. 57 E10
Chihuahua, *Mexico* 118 B3
Chihuahua □, *Mexico* 118 B3
Chiili = Shīeli, *Kazakhstan* .. 52 E7
Chik Bollapur, *India* 66 N10
Chikmagalur, *India* 66 N9
Chikwawa, *Malawi* 87 F3
Chilac, *Mexico* 119 D5
Chilam Chavki, *Pakistan* 69 B6
Chilanga, *Zambia* 87 F2
Chilapa, *Mexico* 119 D5
Chilas, *Pakistan* 69 B6

Chilaw, *Sri Lanka* 66 R11
Chilcotin ➤, *Canada* 102 C4
Childers, *Australia* 95 D5
Childress, *U.S.A.* 113 H4
Chile ■, *S. Amer.* 128 D2
Chile Rise, *Pac. Oc.* 97 L18
Chilecito, *Argentina* 126 B2
Chilete, *Peru* 124 E3
Chilia, Brațul ➤, *Romania* 29 E14
Chililabombwe, *Zambia* 87 E2
Chilin = Jilin, *China* 57 C14
Chilka L., *India* 67 K14
Chilko ➤, *Canada* 102 C4
Chilko L., *Canada* 102 C4
Chillagoe, *Australia* 94 B3
Chillán, *Chile* 126 D1
Chillicothe, *Ill., U.S.A.* 112 E10
Chillicothe, *Mo., U.S.A.* 112 F8
Chillicothe, *Ohio, U.S.A.* 114 F4
Chilliwack, *Canada* 102 D4
Chilo, *India* 68 F5
Chiloane, I., *Mozam.* 89 C5
Chiloé, I. de, *Chile* 128 E2
Chilpancingo, *Mexico* 119 D5
Chiltern Hills, *U.K.* 15 F7
Chilton, *U.S.A.* 114 C1
Chilubi, *Zambia* 87 E3
Chilubula, *Zambia* 87 E3
Chilumba, *Malawi* 87 E3
Chilung, *Taiwan* 59 E13
Chilwa, L., *Malawi* 87 F4
Chimaltitán, *Mexico* 118 C4
Chimán, *Panama* 120 E4
Chimanimani, *Zimbabwe* 89 B5
Chimanimani △, *Zimbabwe* 87 F3
Chimay, *Belgium* 17 D4
Chimayo, *U.S.A.* 109 H11
Chimbay, *Uzbekistan* 52 E6
Chimborazo, *Ecuador* 124 D3
Chimbote, *Peru* 124 E3
Chimkent = Shymkent,
  Kazakhstan 52 E7
Chimoio, *Mozam.* 87 F3
Chimpembe, *Zambia* 87 D2
Chin □, *Burma* 67 J18
Chin Ling Shan = Qinling Shandi,
  China 56 H5
China, *Mexico* 119 B5
China ■, *Asia* 60 D6
China, Great Plain of, *Asia* .. 50 F15
China Lake, *U.S.A.* 111 K9
Chinan = Jinan, *China* 56 F9
Chinandega, *Nic.* 120 D2
Chinati Peak, *U.S.A.* 113 L2
Chincha Alta, *Peru* 124 F3
Chinchaga ➤, *Canada* 102 B5
Chinchilla, *Australia* 95 D5
Chinchilla de Monte Aragón,
  Spain 39 G3
Chinchorro, Banco, *Mexico* .. 119 D7
Chinchou = Jinzhou, *China* .. 57 D11
Chincoteague, *U.S.A.* 114 G8
Chinde, *Mozam.* 87 F4
Chindo, *S. Korea* 57 G14
Chindwin ➤, *Burma* 67 J19
Chineni, *India* 69 C6
Chinga, *Mozam.* 87 F4
Chingola, *Zambia* 87 E2
Chingole, *Malawi* 87 E3
Ch'ingtao = Qingdao, *China* .. 57 F11
Chinguetti, *Mauritania* 78 D3
Chingune, *Mozam.* 89 C5
Chinhae, *S. Korea* 57 G15
Chinhanguanine, *Mozam.* 89 D5
Chinhoyi, *Zimbabwe* 87 F3
Chini, *India* 68 D8
Chiniot, *Pakistan* 68 D5
Chínipas, *Mexico* 118 B3
Chinji, *Pakistan* 68 C5
Chinju, *S. Korea* 57 G15
Chinle, *U.S.A.* 109 H9
Chinmen, *Taiwan* 59 E13
Chinmen Tao, *Taiwan* 59 E12
Chinnampo = Namp'o, *N. Korea* 57 E13
Chino, *Japan* 55 G9
Chino, *U.S.A.* 111 L9
Chino Valley, *U.S.A.* 109 J7
Chinon, *France* 18 E7
Chinook, *U.S.A.* 108 B9
Chinsali, *Zambia* 87 E3
Chióggia, *Italy* 41 C9
Chíos = Khíos, *Greece* 47 C8
Chipata, *Zambia* 87 E3
Chiperceni, *Moldova* 29 C13
Chipinge, *Zimbabwe* 87 G3
Chipinge △, *Zimbabwe* 87 G3
Chipiona, *Spain* 37 J4
Chipley, *U.S.A.* 115 K3
Chipman, *Canada* 105 C6
Chipoka, *Malawi* 87 E3
Chippenham, *U.K.* 15 F5
Chippewa ➤, *U.S.A.* 112 C8
Chippewa Falls, *U.S.A.* 112 C9
Chipping Norton, *U.K.* 15 F6
Chiprovtsi, *Bulgaria* 44 C6
Chiputneticook Lakes, *U.S.A.* 115 C11
Chiquián, *Peru* 124 F3
Chiquibul △, *Belize* 120 C2
Chiquimula, *Guatemala* 120 D2
Chiquinquira, *Colombia* 124 B4
Chir ➤, *Russia* 35 F6
Chirala, *India* 66 M12
Chiramba, *Mozam.* 87 F3
Chirawa, *India* 68 E6
Chirchiq, *Uzbekistan* 52 E7
Chiredzi, *Zimbabwe* 89 C5
Chiricahua △, *U.S.A.* 109 K9
Chiricahua Peak, *U.S.A.* 109 L9
Chirikof I., *U.S.A.* 100 D8
Chiriquí, G. de, *Panama* 120 E3
Chiriquí, L. de, *Panama* 120 E3
Chirisa △, *Zimbabwe* 87 F2
Chirivira Falls, *Zimbabwe* 87 G3

Chirmiri, *India* 67 H13
Chirnogi, *Romania* 29 F11
Chirpan, *Bulgaria* 45 D9
Chirripó Grande, Cerro,
  Costa Rica 120 E3
Chirundu, *Zimbabwe* 89 B4
Chisamba, *Zambia* 87 E2
Chisapani Garhi, *Nepal* 67 F14
Chisasibi, *Canada* 104 B4
Ch'ishan, *Taiwan* 59 F13
Chisholm, *Canada* 102 C6
Chisholm, *U.S.A.* 112 B8
Chishtian Mandi, *Pakistan* .. 68 E5
Chishui, *China* 58 C5
Chishui He ➤, *China* 58 C5
Chisimaio, *Somali Rep.* 77 G8
Chisimba Falls, *Zambia* 87 E3
Chișinău, *Moldova* 29 C13
Chișinău ✈ (KIV), *Moldova* .. 29 C13
Chișineu Criș, *Romania* 28 D6
Chisone ➤, *Italy* 40 D4
Chisos Mts., *U.S.A.* 113 L3
Chistopol, *Russia* 34 C10
Chita, *Russia* 53 D12
Chitipa, *Malawi* 87 D3
Chitose, *Japan* 54 C10
Chitral, *Pakistan* 66 B7
Chitré, *Panama* 120 E3
Chittagong, *Bangla.* 67 H17
Chittagong □, *Bangla.* 67 G17
Chittaurgarh, *India* 68 G6
Chittoor, *India* 66 N11
Chitungwiza, *Zimbabwe* 87 F3
Chiusa, *Italy* 41 B8
Chiusi, *Italy* 41 E8
Chiva, *Spain* 39 F4
Chivasso, *Italy* 40 C4
Chivhu, *Zimbabwe* 87 F3
Chivilcoy, *Argentina* 126 C4
Chiwanda, *Tanzania* 87 E3
Chixi, *China* 59 G9
Chizarira, *Zimbabwe* 87 F2
Chizarira △, *Zimbabwe* 87 F2
Chizera, *Zambia* 87 E2
Chkalov = Orenburg, *Russia* .. 52 D6
Chkolovsk, *Russia* 34 B6
Chloride, *U.S.A.* 111 K12
Chlumec nad Cidlinou,
  Czech Rep. 26 A8
Chmielnik, *Poland* 31 H7
Cho Bo, *Vietnam* 58 G5
Cho-do, *N. Korea* 57 E13
Cho Phuoc Hai, *Vietnam* 65 G6
Choa Chu Kang, *Singapore* .. 65 d
Choba, *Kenya* 86 B4
Chobe △, *Botswana* 88 B4
Choch'iwŏn, *S. Korea* 57 F14
Chocianów, *Poland* 31 G2
Chociwel, *Poland* 30 E2
Chocolate Mts., *U.S.A.* 111 M11
Choctawhatchee ➤, *U.S.A.* .. 115 K3
Chodecz, *Poland* 31 F6
Chodov, *Czech Rep.* 26 A5
Chodziez, *Poland* 31 F3
Choele Choel, *Argentina* 128 D3
Choiseul, *St. Lucia* .... 121 f
Choix, *Mexico* 118 B3
Chojna, *Poland* 31 F1
Chojnice, *Poland* 30 E4
Chojnów, *Poland* 31 G2
Chōkai-San, *Japan* 54 E10
Choke Canyon L., *U.S.A.* 113 L5
Choke Mts., *Ethiopia* 81 E4
Chokurdakh, *Russia* 53 B15
Cholame, *U.S.A.* 110 K6
Cholet, *France* 18 E6
Cholguan, *Chile* 126 D1
Choluteca, *Honduras* 120 D2
Choluteca ➤, *Honduras* 120 D2
Chom Bung, *Thailand* 64 F2
Chom Thong, *Thailand* 64 C2
Choma, *Zambia* 87 F2
Cholomungma = Everest, Mt.,
  Nepal 69 E12
Chomun, *India* 68 F6
Chomutov, *Czech Rep.* 26 A6
Chon Buri, *Thailand* 64 F3
Chon Thanh, *Vietnam* 65 G6
Ch'onan, *S. Korea* 57 F14
Chone, *Ecuador* 124 D3
Chong Kai, *Cambodia* 64 F4
Chong Mek, *Thailand* 64 E5
Chong Phangan, *Thailand* .... 65 b
Chong Samui, *Thailand* ...... 65 b
Chongde, *China* 59 B13
Chŏngdo, *S. Korea* 57 G15
Chŏngha, *S. Korea* 57 F15
Chŏngjin, *N. Korea* 57 D15
Chŏngju, *S. Korea* 57 F14
Chŏngju, *N. Korea* 57 E13
Chongli, *China* 56 D8
Chongming, *China* 59 B13
Chongming Dao, *China* 59 B13
Chongqing, *Chongqing, China* 58 C6
Chongqing, *Sichuan, China* .. 58 B4
Chongqing Shi □, *China* 58 C6
Chongren, *China* 59 D11
Chonguene, *Mozam.* 89 C5
Chŏngŭp, *S. Korea* 57 G14
Chongyi, *China* 59 E10
Chongzuo, *China* 58 F6
Chonju, *S. Korea* 57 G14
Chonos, Arch. de los, *Chile* .. 128 F2
Chop, *Ukraine* 28 B7
Chopim ➤, *Brazil* 127 B5
Chor, *Pakistan* 68 G3
Chorbat La, *India* 69 B7
Chorley, *U.K.* 14 D5
Chornobyl, *Ukraine* 33 G6
Chornomorske, *Ukraine* 33 K7
Chorolque, Cerro, *Bolivia* 126 A2
Choroszcz, *Poland* 31 E9

Chorregon, *Australia* 94 C3
Chorro el Indio △, *Venezuela* . 121 E5
Chortkiv, *Ukraine* 33 H3
Ch'ŏrwon, *S. Korea* 57 E14
Chorzele, *Poland* 31 E7
Chorzów, *Poland* 31 H5
Chos-Malal, *Argentina* 126 D1
Ch'osan, *N. Korea* 57 D13
Choszczno, *Poland* 31 E2
Choteau, *U.S.A.* 108 C7
Chotěboř, *Czech Rep.* 26 B8
Chotila, *India* 68 H4
Chotta Udepur, *India* 68 H6
Chowchilla, *U.S.A.* 110 H6
Choybalsan, *Mongolia* 60 B6
Christchurch, *N.Z.* 91 K4
Christchurch, *U.K.* 15 G6
Christian I., *Canada* 116 B4
Christiana, *S. Africa* 88 D4
Christiansfeld, *Denmark* 11 J3
Christiansted, *U.S. Virgin Is.* . 121 C7
Christie B., *Canada* 103 A6
Christina ➤, *Canada* 103 B6
Christmas Cr. ➤, *Australia* .. 92 C4
Christmas I. = Kiritimati, *Kiribati* 97 G12
Christmas I., *Ind. Oc.* 96 J2
Christopher L., *Australia* 93 D4
Chrudim, *Czech Rep.* 26 B8
Chrzanów, *Poland* 31 H6
Chtimba, *Malawi* 87 E3
Chū = Shū, *Kazakhstan* 52 E8
Chū = Shū ➤, *Kazakhstan* 50 E10
Chu ➤, *Vietnam* 64 C5
Chu Lai, *Vietnam* 64 E7
Ch'uanchou = Quanzhou, *China* 59 E12
Chuankou, *China* 56 G6
Chubbuck, *U.S.A.* 108 E7
Chūbu □, *Japan* 55 F8
Chubu-Sangaku △, *Japan* 55 F8
Chubut ➤, *Argentina* 128 E3
Chuchi L., *Canada* 102 B4
Chuda, *India* 68 H4
Chudovo, *Russia* 32 C6
Chudskoye, Ozero, *Russia* 9 G22
Chūgoku □, *Japan* 55 G6
Chūgoku-Sanchi, *Japan* 55 G6
Chuguyev = Chuhuyiv, *Ukraine* 33 H9
Chugwater, *U.S.A.* 112 E2
Chuhuyiv, *Ukraine* 33 H9
Chukchi Sea, *Russia* 53 C19
Chukotskoye Nagorye, *Russia* 53 C18
Chula Vista, *U.S.A.* 111 N9
Chulucanas, *Peru* 124 E3
Chulym ➤, *Russia* 52 D9
Chum Phae, *Thailand* 64 D4
Chum Saeng, *Thailand* 64 E3
Chumar, *India* 69 C8
Chumbicha, *Argentina* 126 B2
Chumerna, *Bulgaria* 45 D9
Chumikan, *Russia* 53 D14
Chumphon, *Thailand* 65 G2
Chumuare, *Mozam.* 87 E3
Chumunjin, *S. Korea* 57 F15
Chuna ➤, *Russia* 53 D10
Chun'an, *China* 59 C12
Ch'unch'ŏn, *S. Korea* 57 F14
Chunchura, *India* 69 H13
Chunga, *Zambia* 87 F2
Chunggang-ŭp, *N. Korea* 57 D14
Chunghwa, *N. Korea* 57 E13
Ch'ungju, *S. Korea* 57 F14
Chungking = Chongqing, *China* . 58 C6
Chungli, *Taiwan* 59 E13
Ch'ungmu, *S. Korea* 57 G15
Chungt'iaoshan = Zhongtiao
  Shan, *China* 56 G6
Chungyang Shanmo, *Taiwan* .. 59 F13
Chunian, *Pakistan* 68 D6
Chunya, *Tanzania* 87 D3
Chunyang, *China* 57 C15
Chupara Pt., *Trin. & Tob.* 125 K15
Chuquibamba, *Peru* 124 G4
Chuquicamata, *Chile* 126 A2
Chur, *Switz.* 25 J5
Churachandpur, *India* 67 G18
Church Stretton, *U.K.* 15 E5
Churchill ➤, *Man., Canada* .. 103 B10
Churchill ➤, *Nfld. & L., Canada* 105 B7
Churchill, C., *Canada* 103 B10
Churchill Falls, *Canada* 105 B7
Churchill L., *Canada* 103 B7
Churchill Pk., *Canada* 102 B3
Churki, *India* 69 H10
Churu, *India* 68 E6
Churún Merú = Angel Falls,
  Venezuela 124 B6
Chushal, *India* 69 C8
Chuska Mts., *U.S.A.* 109 H9
Chusovoy, *Russia* 52 D6
Chute-aux-Outardes, *Canada* . 105 C6
Chuuronjang, *N. Korea* 57 D15
Chuvash Republic = Chuvashia □,
  Russia 34 C8
Chuvashia □, *Russia* 34 C8
Chuwārtah, *Iraq* 70 C5
Chuxiong, *China* 58 E3
Chuy, *Uruguay* 127 C5
Chuzhou, *China* 59 A12

Ciéagas del Catatumbo △,
  Venezuela 121 E5
Ciechanów, *Poland* 31 F7
Ciechanowiec, *Poland* 31 F9
Ciechocinek, *Poland* 31 F5
Ciego de Avila, *Cuba* 120 B4
Ciénaga, *Colombia* 124 A4
Cienfuegos, *Cuba* 120 B3
Cierp-Gaud, *France* 20 F4
Cíes, Is., *Spain* 36 C2
Cieszanów, *Poland* 31 H10
Cieszyn, *Poland* 31 J5
Cieza, *Spain* 39 G3
Çifteler, *Turkey* 72 C4
Cifuentes, *Spain* 38 E2
Cihanbeyli, *Turkey* 72 C5
Cihuatlán, *Mexico* 118 D4
Cijara △, *Spain* 37 F6
Cijara, Embalse de, *Spain* 37 F6
Cijulang, *Indonesia* 63 G13
Cilacap, *Indonesia* 63 G13
Çıldır, *Turkey* 73 B10
Çıldır Gölü, *Turkey* 73 B10
Cilento e Vallo di Diano △, *Italy* 43 B8
Cili, *China* 59 C8
Cilibia, *Romania* 29 E12
Cilicia, *Turkey* 72 D5
Cill Chainnigh = Kilkenny,
  Ireland 12 D4
Çilo Dağı, *Turkey* 73 D10
Cima, *U.S.A.* 111 K11
Cimarron, *Kans., U.S.A.* 113 G4
Cimarron, *N. Mex., U.S.A.* .. 113 G2
Cimarron ➤, *U.S.A.* 113 G6
Cimişlia, *Moldova* 29 D13
Cimone, Mte., *Italy* 40 D7
Çınar, *Turkey* 73 D9
Çınarcık, *Turkey* 45 F13
Cinca ➤, *Spain* 38 D5
Cincar, *Bos.-H.* 28 G2
Cincinnati, *U.S.A.* 114 F3
Cincinnatus, *U.S.A.* 117 D9
Çine, *Turkey* 47 D10
Ciney, *Belgium* 17 D5
Cíngoli, *Italy* 41 E10
Cinigiano, *Italy* 41 F8
Cinto, Mte., *France* 21 F12
Cintruénigo, *Spain* 38 C3
Ciocile, *Romania* 29 F12
Ciolănești din Deal, *Romania* . 29 F10
Ciorani, *Romania* 29 F11
Ciovo, *Croatia* 41 E13
Circeo, Mte., *Italy* 42 A6
Çırçır, *Turkey* 72 C7
Circle, *Alaska, U.S.A.* 100 B5
Circle, *Mont., U.S.A.* 112 B2
Circleville, *U.S.A.* 114 F4
Cirebon, *Indonesia* 63 G13
Ciremay, *Indonesia* 63 G13
Cirencester, *U.K.* 15 F6
Cireșu, *Romania* 28 F7
Cirey-sur-Vezouze, *France* .. 19 D13
Cirìe, *Italy* 40 C4
Cirium, *Cyprus* 49 E11
Cirò, *Italy* 43 C10
Cirò Marina, *Italy* 43 C10
Ciron ➤, *France* 20 D3
Cisco, *U.S.A.* 113 J5
Cislău, *Romania* 29 E11
Cisna, *Poland* 31 J9
Cisnădie, *Romania* 29 E9
Cisterna di Latina, *Italy* 42 A5
Cisternino, *Italy* 43 B10
Cistierna, *Spain* 36 C5
Citeli-Ckaro = Tsiteli-Tsqaro,
  Georgia 35 K8
Citlaltépetl = Orizaba, Pico de,
  Mexico 119 D5
Citrus Heights, *U.S.A.* 110 G5
Citrusdal, *S. Africa* 88 E2
Città della Pieve, *Italy* 41 F9
Città di Castello, *Italy* 41 E9
Città Sant' Angelo, *Italy* 41 F11
Cittadella, *Italy* 41 C8
Cittaducale, *Italy* 41 F9
Cittanova, *Italy* 43 D9
Ciuc, Munții, *Romania* 29 D11
Ciucaș, Vf., *Romania* 29 E10
Ciucea, *Romania* 28 D7
Ciuciulea, *Moldova* 29 C12
Ciuciuleni, *Moldova* 29 C13
Ciudad Altamirano, *Mexico* .. 118 D4
Ciudad Bolívar, *Venezuela* .. 124 B6
Ciudad Camargo, *Mexico* 118 B3
Ciudad de Valles, *Mexico* 119 C5
Ciudad del Carmen, *Mexico* .. 119 D6
Ciudad del Este, *Paraguay* .. 127 B5
Ciudad Delicias = Delicias,
  Mexico 118 B3
Ciudad Guayana, *Venezuela* .. 124 B6
Ciudad Guerrero, *Mexico* 118 B3
Ciudad Guzmán, *Mexico* 118 D4
Ciudad Juárez, *Mexico* 118 A3
Ciudad Madero, *Mexico* 119 C5
Ciudad Mante, *Mexico* 119 C5
Ciudad Obregón, *Mexico* 118 B3
Ciudad Real, *Spain* 37 G7
Ciudad Real □, *Spain* 37 G7
Ciudad Rodrigo, *Spain* 36 E4
Ciudad Victoria, *Mexico* 119 C5
Ciudadela, *Spain* 48 B10
Ciulnița, *Romania* 29 F12
Ciumeghiu, *Romania* 28 D6
Ciuperceni, *Romania* 28 F8
Civa Burnu, *Turkey* 72 B7
Cividale del Friuli, *Italy* 41 B10
Civita Castellana, *Italy* 41 F9
Civitanova Marche, *Italy* 41 E10
Civitavécchia, *Italy* 41 F8
Çivril, *Turkey* 47 C11
Çıvral, France 20 B4
Cixerri ➤, *Italy* 42 C1

Cixi, China 59 B13
Cizre, Turkey 70 B4
Cizur Mayor, Spain 38 C3
Clackmannanshire □, U.K. 13 E5
Clacton-on-Sea, U.K. 15 F9
Clain ➝, France 18 F7
Claire, L., Canada 102 B6
Clairton, U.S.A. 116 F5
Clairvaux-les-Lacs, France 19 F12
Claise ➝, France 20 B5
Clamecy, France 19 E10
Clanton, U.S.A. 115 J2
Clanwilliam, S. Africa 88 E2
Clara, Ireland 12 C4
Claraville, U.S.A. 111 K8
Clare, Australia 95 E2
Clare, U.S.A. 114 D3
Clare □, Ireland 12 D3
Clare ➝, Ireland 12 C2
Clare I., Ireland 12 C1
Claremont, Calif., U.S.A. 111 L9
Claremont, N.H., U.S.A. 117 C12
Claremont Pt., Australia 94 A3
Claremore, U.S.A. 113 G7
Claremorris, Ireland 12 C3
Clarence ➝, Australia 95 D5
Clarence ➝, N.Z. 91 K4
Clarence, I., Chile 128 G2
Clarence I., Antarctica 5 C18
Clarence Str., Australia 92 B5
Clarence Town, Bahamas 121 B5
Clarendon, Pa., U.S.A. 116 E5
Clarendon, Tex., U.S.A. 113 H4
Clarenville-Shoal Harbour,
    Canada 105 C9
Claresholm, Canada 102 D6
Clarie Coast, Antarctica 5 C9
Clarinda, U.S.A. 112 E7
Clarington, Canada 116 C6
Clarion, Iowa, U.S.A. 112 D8
Clarion, Pa., U.S.A. 116 E5
Clarion ➝, U.S.A. 116 E5
Clarion Fracture Zone, Pac. Oc. 98 H7
Clark, U.S.A. 112 C6
Clark, Pt., Canada 116 B3
Clark Fork, U.S.A. 108 B5
Clark Fork ➝, U.S.A. 108 B5
Clarkdale, U.S.A. 109 J7
Clarke City, Canada 105 B6
Clarke I., Australia 95 G4
Clarke Ra., Australia 94 J6
Clark's Fork ➝, U.S.A. 108 D9
Clark's Harbour, Canada 105 D6
Clarks Hill L., U.S.A. 115 J4
Clarks Summit, U.S.A. 117 E9
Clarksburg, U.S.A. 114 F5
Clarksdale, U.S.A. 113 H9
Clarksville, Ark., U.S.A. 113 H8
Clarksville, Tenn., U.S.A. 115 G2
Clarksville, Tex., U.S.A. 113 J7
Clatskanie, U.S.A. 110 D3
Claude, U.S.A. 113 H4
Claveria, Phil. 61 B4
Clay, U.S.A. 110 G5
Clay Center, U.S.A. 112 F6
Claypool, U.S.A. 109 K8
Claysburg, U.S.A. 116 F6
Claysville, U.S.A. 116 F4
Clayton, N. Mex., U.S.A. 113 G3
Clayton, N.Y., U.S.A. 117 B8
Clear, C., Ireland 12 E2
Clear, L., Canada 116 A7
Clear, L., Ireland 12 E2
Clear L., U.S.A. 110 F4
Clear Lake, U.S.A. 112 D8
Clear Lake, S. Dak., U.S.A. 112 C6
Clear Lake Reservoir, U.S.A. 108 F3
Clearfield, Pa., U.S.A. 116 E6
Clearfield, Utah, U.S.A. 108 F8
Clearlake, U.S.A. 108 G2
Clearlake Highlands, U.S.A. 110 G4
Clearwater, Canada 102 C4
Clearwater, U.S.A. 115 M4
Clearwater ➝, Alta., Canada 102 C6
Clearwater ➝, Alta., Canada 103 B6
Clearwater L., Canada 103 C9
Clearwater Lake △, Canada 103 C8
Clearwater Mts., U.S.A. 108 C6
Clearwater River △, Canada 103 B7
Cleburne, U.S.A. 113 J6
Clee Hills, U.K. 15 E5
Cleethorpes, U.K. 14 D7
Cleeve Cloud, U.K. 15 F6
Clelles, France 21 D9
Clemson, U.S.A. 115 H4
Clerke Reef, Australia 92 C2
Clermont, Australia 94 C4
Clermont, France 19 C9
Clermont, U.S.A. 115 L5
Clermont-en-Argonne, France 19 C12
Clermont-Ferrand, France 20 C7
Clermont-l'Hérault, France 20 E7
Clerval, France 19 E13
Clervaux, Lux. 17 D6
Cles, Italy 40 B8
Clevedon, U.K. 15 F5
Cleveland, Miss., U.S.A. 113 J9
Cleveland, Ohio, U.S.A. 116 E3
Cleveland, Okla., U.S.A. 113 G6
Cleveland, Tenn., U.S.A. 115 H3
Cleveland, Tex., U.S.A. 113 K7
Cleveland, C., Australia 94 B4
Cleveland, Mt., U.S.A. 108 B7
Cleveland Heights, U.S.A. 116 E3
Clevelândia, Brazil 127 B5
Clew B., Ireland 12 C2
Clewiston, U.S.A. 115 M5
Clifden, Ireland 12 C1
Clifden, N.Z. 91 M1
Cliffdell, U.S.A. 110 D5

Cliffy Hd., Australia 93 G2
Clifton, Australia 95 D5
Clifton, Ariz., U.S.A. 109 K9
Clifton, Colo., U.S.A. 109 G9
Clifton, Tex., U.S.A. 113 K6
Clifton Beach, Australia 94 B4
Climax, Canada 103 D7
Clinch ➝, U.S.A. 115 H3
Clingmans Dome, U.S.A. 115 H4
Clint, U.S.A. 109 L10
Clinton, B.C., Canada 102 C4
Clinton, Ont., Canada 116 C3
Clinton, N.Z. 91 M2
Clinton, Ark., U.S.A. 113 H8
Clinton, Conn., U.S.A. 117 E12
Clinton, Ill., U.S.A. 112 E10
Clinton, Ind., U.S.A. 114 F2
Clinton, Iowa, U.S.A. 112 E9
Clinton, Mass., U.S.A. 117 D13
Clinton, Miss., U.S.A. 113 J9
Clinton, Mo., U.S.A. 112 F8
Clinton, N.C., U.S.A. 115 H6
Clinton, Okla., U.S.A. 113 H5
Clinton, S.C., U.S.A. 115 H5
Clinton, Tenn., U.S.A. 115 G3
Clinton, Wash., U.S.A. 110 C4
Clinton C., Australia 94 C5
Clinton Colden L., Canada 100 B9
Clintonville, U.S.A. 112 C10
Clipperton, I., Pac. Oc. 97 F17
Clisham, U.K. 13 D2
Clisson, France 18 E5
Clitheroe, U.K. 14 D5
Clo-oose, Canada 110 B2
Cloates, Pt., Australia 92 D1
Clocolan, S. Africa 89 D4
Clodomira, Argentina 126 B3
Clogher Hd., Ireland 12 C5
Clonakilty, Ireland 12 E3
Clonakilty B., Ireland 12 E3
Cloncurry, Australia 94 C3
Cloncurry ➝, Australia 94 B3
Clondalkin, Ireland 12 C5
Clones, Ireland 12 B4
Clonmel, Ireland 12 D4
Cloppenburg, Germany 24 C4
Cloquet, U.S.A. 112 B8
Clorinda, Argentina 126 B4
Cloud Bay, Canada 104 C2
Cloud Peak, U.S.A. 108 D10
Cloudcroft, U.S.A. 109 K11
Cloverdale, U.S.A. 110 G4
Clovis, Calif., U.S.A. 110 J7
Clovis, N. Mex., U.S.A. 113 H3
Cloyes-sur-le-Loir, France 18 E8
Cloyne, Canada 116 B7
Cluj □, Romania 29 D8
Cluj-Napoca, Romania 29 D8
Clunes, Australia 95 F3
Cluny, France 19 F11
Cluses, France 19 F13
Clusone, Italy 40 C6
Clutha ➝, N.Z. 91 M2
Clwyd ➝, U.K. 14 D4
Clyde, Canada 102 C6
Clyde, N.Z. 91 L2
Clyde, U.S.A. 116 C8
Clyde ➝, U.K. 13 F4
Clyde, Firth of, U.K. 13 F3
Clyde Muirshiel △, U.K. 13 F4
Clyde River, Canada 101 A13
Clydebank, U.K. 13 F4
Clymer, N.Y., U.S.A. 116 D5
Clymer, Pa., U.S.A. 116 D5
Ćmielów, Poland 31 H8
Côa ➝, Portugal 36 D3
Coachella, U.S.A. 111 M10
Coachella Canal, U.S.A. 111 N12
Coahoma, U.S.A. 113 J4
Coahuayana ➝, Mexico 118 D4
Coahuila □, Mexico 118 B4
Coal ➝, Canada 102 B3
Coalane, Mozam. 87 F4
Coalcomán, Mexico 118 D4
Coaldale, Canada 102 D6
Coalgate, U.S.A. 113 H6
Coalinga, U.S.A. 110 J6
Coalisland, U.K. 12 B5
Coalville, U.K. 14 E6
Coalville, U.S.A. 108 F8
Coamo, Puerto Rico 121 d
Coari, Brazil 124 D6
Coast □, Kenya 86 C4
Coast Mts., Canada 102 C3
Coast Ranges, U.S.A. 110 G4
Coatbridge, U.K. 13 F4
Coatepec, Mexico 119 D5
Coatepeque, Guatemala 120 D1
Coatesville, U.S.A. 114 F8
Coaticook, Canada 117 A13
Coats I., Canada 101 B11
Coats Land, Antarctica 5 D1
Coatzacoalcos, Mexico 119 D6
Coba, Mexico 119 C7
Cobadin, Romania 29 F13
Cobalt, Canada 104 C4
Cobán, Guatemala 120 C1
Çobanlar, Turkey 47 C12
Cobar, Australia 95 E4
Cóbh, Ireland 12 E3
Cobija, Bolivia 124 F5
Cobleskill, U.S.A. 117 D10
Coboconk, Canada 116 B6
Cobourg, Canada 116 C6
Cobourg △, Australia 92 B5
Cobourg Pen., Australia 92 B5
Cobram, Australia 95 F4
Cóbué, Mozam. 87 E3
Coburg, Germany 25 E6
Coca, Spain 36 D6
Cocanada = Kakinada, India 67 L13
Cocentaina, Spain 39 G4

Cochabamba, Bolivia 124 G5
Cochem, Germany 25 E3
Cochemane, Mozam. 87 F3
Cochin, India 66 Q10
Cochin China = Nam-Phan,
    Vietnam 65 G6
Cochran, U.S.A. 115 J4
Cochrane, Alta., Canada 102 C6
Cochrane, Ont., Canada 104 C3
Cochrane, Chile 128 F2
Cochrane ➝, Canada 103 B8
Cochrane, L., Chile 128 F2
Cochranton, U.S.A. 116 E4
Cockburn, Australia 95 E3
Cockburn, Canal, Chile 128 G2
Cockburn I., Canada 104 C3
Cockburn Ra., Australia 92 C4
Cockermouth, U.K. 14 C4
Cocklebiddy, Australia 93 F4
Cockpit Country, The, Jamaica 120 a
Coco ➝, Cent. Amer. 120 D3
Coco, I. del, Pac. Oc. 97 G19
Cocoa, U.S.A. 115 L5
Cocobeach, Gabon 84 D1
Cocora, Romania 29 F12
Cocos, B., Trin. & Tob. 125 K15
Cocos Is., Ind. Oc. 96 J1
Cod, C., U.S.A. 114 D10
Codajás, Brazil 124 D6
Codigoro, Italy 41 D9
Codlea, Romania 29 E10
Codó, Brazil 125 D10
Codogno, Italy 40 C6
Codróipo, Italy 41 C10
Codru, Munții, Romania 28 D7
Cody, U.S.A. 108 D9
Coe Hill, Canada 116 B7
Coelemu, Chile 126 D1
Coen, Australia 94 A3
Coesfeld, Germany 24 D3
Cœur d'Alene, U.S.A. 108 C5
Cœur d'Alene L., U.S.A. 108 C5
Coevorden, Neths. 17 B6
Cofete, Canary Is. 48 F5
Coffeyville, U.S.A. 113 G7
Coffin B., Australia 95 E2
Coffin Bay, Australia 95 E2
Coffin Bay ➝, Australia 95 E2
Coffin Bay Peninsula, Australia 95 E2
Coffs Harbour, Australia 95 E5
Cofre de Perote △, Mexico 119 D5
Cofrentes, Spain 39 F3
Cogalnic ➝, Moldova 29 E14
Cogealac, Romania 29 F13
Coghinas ➝, Italy 42 B1
Coghinas, L. del, Italy 42 B2
Cognac, France 20 C3
Cogne, Italy 40 C4
Cogolin, France 21 E10
Cogolludo, Spain 38 E1
Cohocton, U.S.A. 116 D7
Cohocton ➝, U.S.A. 116 D7
Cohoes, U.S.A. 117 D11
Cohuna, Australia 95 F3
Coiba, I., Panama 120 E3
Coig ➝, Argentina 128 G3
Coigeach, Rubha, U.K. 13 C3
Coihaique, Chile 128 F2
Coimbatore, India 66 P10
Coimbra, Brazil 124 G7
Coimbra, Portugal 36 E2
Coimbra □, Portugal 36 E2
Coín, Spain 37 J6
Coipasa, Salar de, Bolivia 124 G5
Cojimies, Ecuador 124 C3
Cojocna, Romania 29 D8
Cojutepeque, El Salv. 120 D2
Čoka, Serbia & M. 28 E5
Cokeville, U.S.A. 108 E8
Colac, Australia 95 F3
Colatina, Brazil 125 G10
Colbeck, C., Antarctica 5 D13
Colborne, Canada 116 C7
Colby, U.S.A. 112 F4
Colchester, U.K. 15 F8
Cold L., Canada 103 C7
Coldstream, Canada 102 C5
Coldstream, U.K. 13 F6
Coldwater, Canada 116 B5
Coldwater, Kans., U.S.A. 113 G5
Coldwater, Mich., U.S.A. 114 E3
Colebrook, U.S.A. 117 B13
Coleman, U.S.A. 113 K5
Coleman ➝, Australia 94 B3
Colenso, S. Africa 89 D4
Coleraine, Australia 95 F3
Coleraine, U.K. 12 A5
Coleridge, L., N.Z. 91 K3
Colesberg, S. Africa 88 E4
Coleville, U.S.A. 110 G7
Colfax, Calif., U.S.A. 110 F6
Colfax, La., U.S.A. 113 K8
Colfax, Wash., U.S.A. 108 C5
Colhué Huapi, L., Argentina 128 F3
Colibași, Moldova 29 E13
Colibași, Romania 29 F9
Cólico, Italy 40 B6
Colico, Chile 126 A1
Coligny, France 19 F12
Coligny, S. Africa 89 D4
Colima, Mexico 118 D4
Colima □, Mexico 118 D4
Colima, Nevado de, Mexico 118 D4
Colina, Chile 126 C1
Colina do Norte, Guinea-Biss. 82 C2
Colinas, Brazil 125 E10
Colindres, Spain 36 B7
Coll, U.K. 13 E2
Collaguasi, Chile 126 A2
Collarada, Peña, Spain 38 C4
Collarenebri, Australia 95 D4
Colle di Val d'Elsa, Italy 40 E8
Collécchio, Italy 40 D7

Colleen Bawn, Zimbabwe 87 G2
College Park, U.S.A. 115 J3
College Station, U.S.A. 113 K6
Collesalvetti, Italy 40 E7
Collie, Australia 93 F2
Collier B., Australia 92 C3
Collier Ra., Australia 93 D2
Collier Range △, Australia 93 D2
Collina, Passo di, Italy 40 D7
Collingwood, Canada 116 B4
Collingwood, N.Z. 91 J4
Collins, Canada 104 B2
Collinsville, Australia 94 C4
Collipulli, Chile 126 D1
Collooney, Ireland 12 B3
Colmar, France 19 D14
Colmars, France 21 D10
Colmenar, Spain 37 J6
Colmenar de Oreja, Spain 36 E7
Colmenar Viejo, Spain 36 E7
Colo ➝, Australia 95 E5
Cologne = Köln, Germany 24 E2
Colom, I. d'en, Spain 48 B11
Coloma, U.S.A. 110 G6
Colomb-Béchar = Béchar, Algeria 78 B5
Colombey-les-Belles, France 19 D12
Colombey-les-Deux-Églises,
    France 19 D11
Colombia ■, S. Amer. 124 C4
Colombian Basin, S. Amer. 98 H12
Colombo, Sri Lanka 66 R11
Colomiers, France 20 E5
Colón, Buenos Aires, Argentina 126 C3
Colón, Entre Ríos, Argentina 126 C4
Colón, Cuba 120 B3
Colón, Panama 120 E4
Colón, Arch. de, Ecuador 97 H18
Colònia de Sant Jordi, Spain 48 B9
Colonia del Sacramento, Uruguay 126 C4
Colonia Dora, Argentina 126 B3
Colonial Beach, U.S.A. 114 F7
Colonie, U.S.A. 117 D11
Colonna, C., Italy 43 C10
Colonsay, Canada 103 C7
Colonsay, U.K. 13 E2
Colorado □, U.S.A. 109 G10
Colorado ➝, N. Amer. 109 L6
Colorado ➝, Argentina 128 D4
Colorado ➝, U.S.A. 113 L7
Colorado City, U.S.A. 113 J4
Colorado Plateau, U.S.A. 109 H8
Colorado River Aqueduct, U.S.A. 111 L12
Colorado Springs, U.S.A. 112 F2
Colotlán, Mexico 118 C4
Colstrip, U.S.A. 108 D10
Colton, U.S.A. 117 B10
Columbia, Ky., U.S.A. 114 G3
Columbia, La., U.S.A. 113 J8
Columbia, Miss., U.S.A. 113 K10
Columbia, Mo., U.S.A. 112 F8
Columbia, Pa., U.S.A. 117 F8
Columbia, S.C., U.S.A. 115 J5
Columbia, Tenn., U.S.A. 115 H2
Columbia ➝, N. Amer. 110 D2
Columbia, C., Canada 4 A4
Columbia, District of □, U.S.A. 114 F7
Columbia Basin, U.S.A. 108 C4
Columbia Falls, U.S.A. 108 B6
Columbia Mts., Canada 102 C5
Columbia Plateau, U.S.A. 108 D5
Columbiana, U.S.A. 116 F4
Columbretes, Is., Spain 38 F5
Columbus, Ga., U.S.A. 115 J3
Columbus, Ind., U.S.A. 114 F3
Columbus, Kans., U.S.A. 113 G7
Columbus, Miss., U.S.A. 115 J1
Columbus, Mont., U.S.A. 108 D9
Columbus, N. Mex., U.S.A. 109 L10
Columbus, Nebr., U.S.A. 112 E6
Columbus, Ohio, U.S.A. 114 F4
Columbus, Tex., U.S.A. 113 L6
Colusa, U.S.A. 110 F4
Colville, U.S.A. 108 B5
Colville ➝, U.S.A. 100 A4
Colville, C., N.Z. 91 G5
Colwood, Canada 110 B3
Colwyn Bay, U.K. 14 D4
Coma, Ethiopia 81 F4
Comácchio, Italy 41 D9
Comalcalco, Mexico 119 D6
Comallo, Argentina 128 E2
Comana, Romania 29 F11
Comanche, U.S.A. 113 K5
Comandante Ferraz, Antarctica 5 C18
Comănești, Romania 29 D11
Comarnic, Romania 29 E10
Comayagua, Honduras 120 D2
Combahee ➝, U.S.A. 115 J5
Combarbalá, Chile 126 C1
Combe Martin, U.K. 15 F3
Combeaufontaine, France 19 E12
Comber, Canada 116 D2
Comber, U.K. 12 B6
Combermere, Canada 116 A7
Comblain-au-Pont, Belgium 17 D5
Combourg, France 18 D5
Combrailles, France 19 F9
Combronde, France 20 C7
Comeragh Mts., Ireland 12 D4
Comet, Australia 94 C4
Comilla, Bangla. 67 H17
Comino, Malta 49 D1
Comino, C., Italy 42 B2
Cómiso, Italy 43 F7
Comitán, Mexico 119 D6
Commentry, France 19 F9
Commerce, Ga., U.S.A. 115 H4
Commerce, Tex., U.S.A. 113 J7

Commercy, France 19 D12
Committee B., Canada 101 B11
Commonwealth B., Antarctica 5 C10
Commoron Cr. ➝, Australia 95 D5
Communism Pk. = Kommunizma,
    Pik, Tajikistan 52 F8
Como, Italy 40 C6
Como, Lago di, Italy 40 B6
Comodoro Rivadavia, Argentina 128 F3
Comoé ➝, Ivory C. 82 D4
Comorâște, Romania 28 E6
Comorin, C., India 66 Q10
Comoro Is. = Comoros ■,
    Ind. Oc. 77 H8
Comoros ■, Ind. Oc. 77 H8
Comox, Canada 102 D4
Compiègne, France 19 C9
Comporta, Portugal 37 G2
Compostela, Mexico 118 C4
Comprida, I., Brazil 127 A6
Compton, Canada 117 A13
Compton, U.S.A. 111 M8
Comrat, Moldova 29 D13
Con Cuong, Vietnam 64 C5
Con Dao △, Vietnam 65 H6
Con Son, Vietnam 65 H6
Conakry, Guinea 82 D2
Conara, Australia 95 G4
Concarneau, France 18 E3
Conceição, Mozam. 87 F4
Conceição da Barra, Brazil 125 G11
Conceição do Araguaia, Brazil 125 E9
Concepción, Argentina 126 B2
Concepción, Bolivia 124 G6
Concepción, Chile 126 D1
Concepción, Mexico 119 D6
Concepción, Paraguay 126 A4
Concepción □, Chile 126 D1
Concepción ➝, Mexico 118 A2
Concepción, Est. de, Chile 128 G2
Concepción, L., Bolivia 124 G6
Concepción, Punta, Mexico 118 B2
Concepción del Oro, Mexico 118 C4
Concepción del Uruguay,
    Argentina 126 C4
Conception, Pt., U.S.A. 111 L6
Conception B., Canada 105 C9
Conception B., Namibia 88 C1
Conception I., Bahamas 121 B4
Concession, Zimbabwe 87 F3
Conchas Dam, U.S.A. 113 H2
Conches-en-Ouche, France 18 D7
Concho, U.S.A. 109 J9
Concho ➝, U.S.A. 113 K5
Conchos ➝, Chihuahua, Mexico 118 B4
Conchos ➝, Tamaulipas, Mexico 119 B5
Concord, Calif., U.S.A. 110 H4
Concord, N.C., U.S.A. 115 H5
Concord, N.H., U.S.A. 117 C13
Concordia, Argentina 126 C4
Concórdia, Brazil 124 D5
Concordia, Mexico 118 C3
Concordia, U.S.A. 112 F6
Concrete, U.S.A. 108 B3
Condamine, Australia 95 D5
Condat, France 20 C6
Conde, U.S.A. 112 C5
Condé-sur-Noireau, France 18 D6
Condeúba, Brazil 125 F10
Condobolin, Australia 95 E4
Condom, France 20 E4
Condon, U.S.A. 108 D3
Conegliano, Italy 41 C9
Conejera, I. = Conills, I. des,
    Spain 48 B9
Conejos, Mexico 118 B4
Conemaugh ➝, U.S.A. 116 F5
Conero △, Italy 41 E10
Confolens, France 20 B4
Confuso ➝, Paraguay 126 B4
Congaz, Moldova 29 D13
Congha, China 59 F9
Congjiang, China 58 E7
Congleton, U.K. 14 D5
Congo (Kinshasa) = Congo, Dem.
    Rep. of the ■, Africa 84 E4
Congo ■, Africa 84 E3
Congo ➝, Africa 84 F2
Congo, Dem. Rep. of the ■,
    Africa 84 E4
Congo Basin, Africa 84 E4
Congonhas, Brazil 127 A7
Congress, U.S.A. 109 J7
Conil de la Frontera, Spain 37 J4
Conills, I. des, Spain 48 B9
Coniston, Canada 104 C3
Conjeeveram = Kanchipuram,
    India 66 N11
Conklin, Canada 103 B6
Conklin, U.S.A. 117 D9
Conn, L., Ireland 12 B2
Connacht □, Ireland 12 C2
Conneaut, U.S.A. 116 E4
Connecticut □, U.S.A. 117 E12
Connecticut ➝, U.S.A. 117 E12
Connell, U.S.A. 108 C4
Connellsville, U.S.A. 116 F5
Connemara, Ireland 12 C2
Connemara △, Ireland 12 C2
Connerré, France 18 D7
Connersville, U.S.A. 114 F3
Connors Ra., Australia 94 C4
Conques, France 20 D6
Conquest, Canada 103 C7
Conrad, U.S.A. 108 B8
Conran, C., Australia 95 F4
Conroe, U.S.A. 113 K7
Conselheiro Lafaiete, Brazil 127 A7
Conselve, Italy 41 C8
Consett, U.K. 14 C6
Consort, Canada 103 C6

Constance = Konstanz, Germany 25 H5
Constance, L. = Bodensee, Europe 25 H5
Constanţa, Romania 29 F13
Constanţa □, Romania 29 F13
Constantia, U.S.A. 117 C8
Constantina, Spain 37 H5
Constantine, Algeria 78 A7
Constitución, Chile 126 D1
Constitución, Uruguay 126 C4
Constitucion de 1857 △, Mexico 118 A1
Consuegra, Spain 37 F7
Consul, Canada 103 D7
Contact, U.S.A. 108 F6
Contai, India 69 J12
Contamana, Peru 124 E4
Contarina, Italy 41 C9
Contas →, Brazil 125 F11
Contes, France 21 E11
Contoocook, U.S.A. 117 C13
Contra Costa, Mozam. 89 D5
Contres, France 18 E8
Contrexéville, France 19 D12
Contwoyto L., Canada 100 B8
Conversano, Italy 43 B10
Conway = Conwy, U.K. 14 D4
Conway = Conwy →, U.K. 14 D4
Conway, Australia 94 J6
Conway, Ark., U.S.A. 113 H8
Conway, N.H., U.S.A. 117 C13
Conway, S.C., U.S.A. 115 J6
Conway, C., Australia 94 J6
Conway, L., Australia 95 D2
Conwy □, U.K. 14 D4
Conwy →, U.K. 14 D4
Coober Pedy, Australia 95 D1
Cooch Behar = Koch Bihar, India 67 F16
Cooinda, Australia 92 B5
Cook, Australia 93 F5
Cook, U.S.A. 112 B8
Cook, B., Chile 128 H3
Cook, C., Canada 102 C3
Cook, Mt. = Aoraki Mount Cook, N.Z. 91 K3
Cook Inlet, U.S.A. 100 C4
Cook Is., Pac. Oc. 97 J12
Cook Strait, N.Z. 91 J5
Cookeville, U.S.A. 115 G3
Cookhouse, S. Africa 88 E4
Cookshire, Canada 117 A13
Cookstown, U.K. 12 B5
Cooksville, Canada 116 C5
Cooktown, Australia 94 B4
Coolabah, Australia 95 E4
Cooladdi, Australia 95 D4
Coolah, Australia 95 E4
Coolamon, Australia 95 E4
Coolgardie, Australia 93 F3
Coolidge, U.S.A. 109 K8
Coolidge Dam, U.S.A. 109 K8
Cooloola △, Australia 95 D5
Cooma, Australia 95 F4
Coon Rapids, U.S.A. 112 C8
Coonabarabran, Australia 95 E4
Coonamble, Australia 95 E4
Coonana, Australia 93 F3
Coondapoor, India 66 N9
Cooninie, L., Australia 95 D2
Cooper, U.S.A. 113 J7
Cooper Cr. →, Australia 95 D2
Cooperstown, N. Dak., U.S.A. 112 B5
Cooperstown, N.Y., U.S.A. 117 D10
Coorabie, Australia 93 F5
Coorong, The, Australia 95 F2
Coorow, Australia 93 E2
Cooroy, Australia 95 D5
Coos Bay, U.S.A. 108 E1
Coosa →, U.S.A. 115 J2
Cootamundra, Australia 95 E4
Cootehill, Ireland 12 B4
Copahue Paso, Argentina 126 D1
Copainalá, Mexico 119 D6
Copake Falls, U.S.A. 117 D11
Copalnic Mănăştur, Romania 29 C8
Copán, Honduras 120 D2
Cope, U.S.A. 112 F3
Cope, C., Spain 39 H3
Copenhagen = København, Denmark 11 J6
Copenhagen, U.S.A. 117 C9
Copertino, Italy 43 B11
Copiapó, Chile 126 B1
Copiapó →, Chile 126 B1
Coplay, U.S.A. 117 F9
Copp L., Canada 102 A6
Copparo, Italy 41 D8
Coppename →, Suriname 125 B7
Copper Harbor, U.S.A. 114 B2
Copper Queen, Zimbabwe 87 F2
Copperas Cove, U.S.A. 113 K6
Copperbelt □, Zambia 87 E2
Coppermine = Kugluktuk, Canada 100 B8
Coppermine →, Canada 100 B8
Copperopolis, U.S.A. 110 H6
Copşa Mică, Romania 29 D9
Coquet →, U.K. 14 B6
Coquille, U.S.A. 108 E1
Coquimbo, Chile 126 C1
Coquimbo □, Chile 126 C1
Corabia, Romania 29 G9
Coracora, Peru 124 G4
Coradal, Australia 95 D5
Coral, U.S.A. 116 F5
Coral Gables, U.S.A. 115 N5
Coral Harbour, Canada 101 B11
Coral Sea, Pac. Oc. 96 J7
Coral Springs, U.S.A. 115 M5
Coraopolis, U.S.A. 116 F4
Corato, Italy 43 A9
Corbeil-Essonnes, France 19 D9

Corbie, France 19 C9
Corbières, France 20 F6
Corbigny, France 19 E10
Corbin, U.S.A. 114 G3
Corbones →, Spain 37 H5
Corbu, Romania 29 F13
Corby, U.K. 15 E7
Corcaigh = Cork, Ireland 12 E3
Corcoran, U.S.A. 110 J7
Corcovado △, Costa Rica 120 E3
Cordele, U.S.A. 115 K4
Cordell, U.S.A. 113 H5
Cordenòns, Italy 41 C9
Cordes-sur-Ciel, France 20 D5
Córdoba, Argentina 126 C3
Córdoba, Mexico 119 D5
Córdoba, Spain 37 H6
Córdoba □, Argentina 126 C3
Córdoba □, Spain 37 G6
Córdoba, Sierra de, Argentina 126 C3
Cordon, Phil. 61 C4
Cordova, U.S.A. 100 B5
Corella, Spain 38 C3
Corella →, Australia 94 B3
Corfield, Australia 94 C3
Corfu = Kérkira, Greece 49 A3
Corfu ✈ (CFU), Greece 46 B1
Corfu, Str. of, Greece 49 A4
Corgo = O Corgo, Spain 36 C3
Cori, Italy 42 A5
Coria, Spain 36 F4
Coria del Río, Spain 37 H4
Corigliano Cálabro, Italy 43 C9
Coringa Is., Australia 94 B4
Corinth = Kórinthos, Greece 46 D4
Corinth, Miss., U.S.A. 115 H1
Corinth, N.Y., U.S.A. 117 C11
Corinth, G. of = Korinthiakós Kólpos, Greece 46 C4
Corinth Canal, Greece 46 D4
Corinto, Brazil 125 G10
Corinto, Nic. 120 D2
Cork, Ireland 12 E3
Cork □, Ireland 12 E3
Cork Harbour, Ireland 12 E3
Corlay, France 18 D3
Corleone, Italy 42 E6
Corleto Perticara, Italy 43 B9
Çorlu, Turkey 45 E11
Cormack L., Canada 102 A4
Cormòns, Italy 41 C10
Cormorant, Canada 103 C8
Cormorant L., Canada 103 C8
Corn Is. = Maíz, Is. del, Nic. 120 D3
Cornalvo △, Spain 37 F4
Cornélio Procópio, Brazil 127 A5
Corner Brook, Canada 105 C8
Corneşti, Moldova 29 C13
Corníglio, Italy 40 D7
Corning, Ark., U.S.A. 113 G9
Corning, Calif., U.S.A. 108 G2
Corning, Iowa, U.S.A. 112 E7
Corning, N.Y., U.S.A. 116 D7
Corno Grande, Italy 41 F10
Cornwall, Canada 117 A10
Cornwall, U.S.A. 117 F8
Cornwall □, U.K. 15 G3
Corny Pt., Australia 95 E2
Coro, Venezuela 124 A5
Coroatá, Brazil 125 D10
Corocoro, Bolivia 124 G5
Coroico, Bolivia 124 G5
Coromandel, N.Z. 91 G5
Coromandel Coast, India 66 N12
Corona, Calif., U.S.A. 111 M9
Corona, N. Mex., U.S.A. 109 J11
Coronach, Canada 103 D7
Coronada, U.S.A. 111 N9
Coronado, B. de, Costa Rica 120 E3
Coronados, Is. los, U.S.A. 111 N9
Coronation, Canada 102 C6
Coronation Gulf, Canada 100 B8
Coronation I., Antarctica 5 C18
Coronation Is., Australia 92 B3
Coronda, Argentina 126 C3
Coronel, Chile 126 D1
Coronel Bogado, Paraguay 126 B4
Coronel Dorrego, Argentina 126 D3
Coronel Oviedo, Paraguay 126 B4
Coronel Pringles, Argentina 126 D3
Coronel Suárez, Argentina 126 D3
Coronel Vidal, Argentina 126 D4
Coropuna, Nevado, Peru 124 G4
Çorovodë, Albania 44 F4
Corowa, Australia 95 F4
Corozal, Belize 119 D7
Corozal Pt., Trin. & Tob. 125 K15
Corps, France 21 D9
Corpus, Argentina 127 B4
Corpus Christi, U.S.A. 113 M6
Corpus Christi, L., U.S.A. 113 L6
Corral de Almaguer, Spain 36 F7
Corralejo, Canary Is. 48 F6
Corraun Pen., Ireland 12 C2
Corréggio, Italy 40 D7
Corrente, Brazil 125 F10
Corrèze □, France 20 C5
Corrèze →, France 20 C5
Corrib, L., Ireland 12 C2
Corridónia, Italy 41 E10
Corrientes, Argentina 126 B4
Corrientes □, Argentina 126 B4
Corrientes →, Argentina 126 C4
Corrientes →, Peru 124 D4
Corrientes, C., Colombia 124 B3
Corrientes, C., Cuba 120 B3
Corrientes, C., Mexico 118 C3
Corrigan, U.S.A. 113 K7
Corrigin, Australia 93 F2
Corry, U.S.A. 116 E5
Corse △, France 21 F13
Corse □, France 21 G13

Corse, C., France 21 E13
Corse-du-Sud □, France 21 G13
Corsica = Corse □, France 21 G13
Corsicana, U.S.A. 113 J6
Corte, France 21 F13
Corte Pinto, Portugal 37 H3
Cortegana, Spain 37 H4
Cortés, Mar de = California, G. de, Mexico 118 B2
Cortez, U.S.A. 109 H9
Cortina d'Ampezzo, Italy 41 B9
Cortland, N.Y., U.S.A. 117 D8
Cortland, Ohio, U.S.A. 116 E4
Cortona, Italy 41 E8
Corubal →, Guinea-Biss. 82 C2
Coruche, Portugal 37 G2
Çoruh →, Turkey 35 K5
Çorum, Turkey 72 B6
Corumbá, Brazil 124 G7
Corund, Romania 29 D10
Corunna = A Coruña, Spain 36 B2
Corvallis, U.S.A. 108 D2
Corvette, L. de la, Canada 104 B5
Corydon, U.S.A. 112 E8
Cosalá, Mexico 118 C3
Cosamaloapan, Mexico 119 D5
Cosenza, Italy 43 C9
Coşereni, Romania 29 F11
Coshocton, U.S.A. 116 F3
Cosmo Newberry, Australia 93 E3
Cosne-Cours-sur-Loire, France 19 E9
Coso Junction, U.S.A. 111 J9
Coso Pk., U.S.A. 111 J9
Cospeito, Spain 36 B3
Cosquín, Argentina 126 C3
Cossato, Italy 40 C5
Cossé-le-Vivien, France 18 E6
Cosson →, France 18 E8
Costa Blanca, Spain 39 G4
Costa Brava, Spain 38 D8
Costa del Sol, Spain 37 J6
Costa Dorada, Spain 38 D6
Costa Mesa, U.S.A. 111 M9
Costa Rica ■, Cent. Amer. 120 E3
Costa Smeralda, Italy 42 A2
Costeşti, Romania 29 F9
Costigliole d'Asti, Italy 40 D5
Cosumnes →, U.S.A. 110 G5
Coswig, Sachsen, Germany 24 D9
Coswig, Sachsen-Anhalt, Germany 24 D8
Cotabato, Phil. 61 H6
Cotagaita, Bolivia 126 A2
Côte d'Azur, France 21 E11
Côte-d'Ivoire = Ivory Coast ■, Africa 82 D4
Côte d'Or, France 19 E11
Côte-d'Or □, France 19 E11
Coteau des Prairies, U.S.A. 112 C6
Coteau du Missouri, U.S.A. 112 B4
Cotentin, France 18 C5
Côtes-d'Armor □, France 18 D4
Côtes de Meuse, France 19 C12
Côtes-du-Nord = Côtes-d'Armor □, France 18 D4
Cotiella, Spain 38 C5
Cotillo, Canary Is. 48 F5
Cotiujeni, Moldova 29 C13
Cotonou, Benin 83 D5
Cotopaxi, Ecuador 124 D3
Cotronei, Italy 43 C9
Cotswold Hills, U.K. 15 F5
Cottage Grove, U.S.A. 108 E2
Cottbus, Germany 24 D10
Cottonwood, U.S.A. 109 J7
Cotulla, U.S.A. 113 L5
Coubre, Pte. de la, France 20 C2
Couches, France 19 F11
Couço, Portugal 37 G2
Coudersport, U.S.A. 116 E6
Couedic, C. du, Australia 95 F2
Couëron, France 18 E5
Couesnon →, France 18 D5
Couhé, France 20 B4
Coulanges-sur-Yonne, France 19 E10
Coulee City, U.S.A. 108 C4
Coulman I., Antarctica 5 D11
Coulommiers, France 19 D10
Coulon →, France 21 E9
Coulonge →, Canada 104 C4
Coulonges-sur-l'Autize, France 20 B3
Coulounieix-Chamiers, France 20 C4
Coulterville, U.S.A. 110 H6
Council, U.S.A. 108 D5
Council Bluffs, U.S.A. 112 E7
Council Grove, U.S.A. 112 F6
Coupeville, U.S.A. 110 B4
Courantyne →, S. Amer. 124 B7
Courcelles, Belgium 17 D4
Courchevel, France 21 C10
Courçon, France 20 B3
Courmayeur, Italy 40 C3
Couronne, C., France 21 E9
Cours-la-Ville, France 19 F11
Coursan, France 20 E7
Courseulles-sur-Mer, France 18 C6
Courtenay, Canada 102 D4
Courtland, U.S.A. 110 G5
Courtright, Canada 116 D2
Coushatta, U.S.A. 113 J8
Coutances, France 18 C5
Coutras, France 20 C3
Coutts Crossing, Australia 95 D5
Couva, Trin. & Tob. 125 K15
Couvin, Belgium 17 D4
Covarrubias, Spain 36 C7
Covasna, Romania 29 E11
Covasna □, Romania 29 E10
Cove I., Canada 116 A3
Coventry, U.K. 15 E6
Covilhã, Portugal 36 E3

Covington, Ga., U.S.A. 115 J4
Covington, Ky., U.S.A. 114 F3
Covington, Okla., U.S.A. 113 G6
Covington, Tenn., U.S.A. 113 H10
Covington, Va., U.S.A. 114 G5
Cowal, L., Australia 95 E4
Cowan, L., Australia 93 F3
Cowan, L., Canada 103 C7
Cowangie, Australia 95 F3
Cowansville, Canada 117 A12
Coward Springs, Australia 95 D2
Cowcowing Lakes, Australia 93 F2
Cowdenbeath, U.K. 13 E5
Cowell, Australia 95 E2
Cowes, U.K. 15 G6
Cowichan L., Canada 110 B2
Cowlitz →, U.S.A. 110 D4
Cowra, Australia 95 E4
Cox, Spain 39 G4
Coxilha Grande, Brazil 127 B5
Coxim, Brazil 125 G8
Cox's Bazar, Bangla. 67 J17
Coyote Wells, U.S.A. 111 N11
Coyuca de Benítez, Mexico 119 D4
Coyuca de Catalan, Mexico 118 D4
Cozad, U.S.A. 112 E5
Cozes, France 20 C3
Cozumel, Mexico 119 C7
Cozumel, Isla, Mexico 119 C7
Crab Hill, Barbados 121 g
Cracow = Kraków, Poland 31 H6
Cracow, Australia 95 D5
Cradle Mt.-Lake St. Clair △, Australia 95 G4
Cradock, Australia 95 E2
Cradock, S. Africa 88 E4
Craig, U.S.A. 108 F10
Craigavon, U.K. 12 B5
Craigmore, Zimbabwe 87 G3
Craik, Canada 103 C7
Crailsheim, Germany 25 F6
Craiova, Romania 29 F8
Cramsie, Australia 94 C3
Cranberry L., U.S.A. 117 B10
Cranberry Portage, Canada 103 C8
Cranbrook, Australia 93 F2
Cranbrook, Canada 102 D5
Crandon, U.S.A. 112 C10
Crane, Oreg., U.S.A. 108 E4
Crane, Tex., U.S.A. 113 K3
Cranston, U.S.A. 117 E13
Craon, France 18 E6
Craonne, France 19 C10
Crapone-sur-Arzon, France 20 C7
Crasna, Romania 29 D12
Crasna →, Romania 28 C7
Crasnei, Munţii, Romania 29 C8
Crater L., U.S.A. 108 E2
Crater Lake △, U.S.A. 108 E2
Craters of the Moon △, U.S.A. 108 E7
Crateús, Brazil 125 E10
Crati →, Italy 43 C9
Crato, Brazil 125 E11
Crato, Portugal 37 F3
Craven, L., Canada 104 B4
Crawford, U.S.A. 112 D3
Crawfordsville, U.S.A. 114 E2
Crawley, U.K. 15 F7
Crazy Mts., U.S.A. 108 C8
Crean L., Canada 103 C7
Crécy-en-Ponthieu, France 19 B8
Crediton, Canada 116 C3
Crediton, U.K. 15 G4
Cree →, Canada 103 B7
Cree →, U.K. 13 G4
Cree L., Canada 103 B7
Creede, U.S.A. 109 H10
Creekside, U.S.A. 116 F5
Creel, Mexico 118 B3
Creemore, Canada 116 B4
Creighton, Canada 103 C8
Creighton, U.S.A. 112 D6
Creil, France 19 C9
Crema, Italy 40 C6
Cremona, Italy 40 C7
Crepaja, Serbia & M. 28 E5
Crépy, France 19 C10
Crépy-en-Valois, France 19 C9
Cres, Croatia 41 D11
Crescent City, U.S.A. 108 F1
Crescentino, Italy 40 C5
Crespino, Italy 41 D8
Crespo, Argentina 126 C3
Cresson, U.S.A. 116 F6
Crest, France 21 D9
Cresta, Mt., Phil. 61 C5
Crestline, Calif., U.S.A. 111 L9
Crestline, Ohio, U.S.A. 116 F2
Creston, Canada 102 D5
Creston, Calif., U.S.A. 110 K6
Creston, Iowa, U.S.A. 112 E7
Crestview, Calif., U.S.A. 110 H8
Crestview, Fla., U.S.A. 115 K2
Crêt de la Neige, France 19 F12
Crete = Kríti, Greece 49 D7
Crete, U.S.A. 112 E6
Crete, Sea of, Greece 47 E7
Créteil, France 19 D9
Creus, C. de, Spain 38 C8
Creuse □, France 19 F9
Creuse →, France 20 B4
Creutzwald, France 19 C13
Creuzburg, Germany 24 D6
Crèvecœur-le-Grand, France 19 C9
Crevillente, Spain 39 G4
Crewe, U.K. 14 D5
Crewkerne, U.K. 15 G5
Crianlarich, U.K. 13 E4
Criciúma, Brazil 127 B6
Cricova, Moldova 29 C13
Crieff, U.K. 13 E5
Crikvenica, Croatia 41 C11
Crimea □, Ukraine 33 K8

Crimean Pen. = Krymskyy Pivostriv, Ukraine 33 K8
Crimmitschau, Germany 24 E8
Cristuru Secuiesc, Romania 29 D10
Crişul Alb →, Romania 28 D6
Crişul Negru →, Romania 28 D6
Crişul Repede →, Romania 28 D5
Crivitz, Germany 24 B7
Crna →, Macedonia 44 E5
Crna Gora = Montenegro □, Serbia & M. 44 D3
Crna Gora, Macedonia 44 D5
Crna Reka = Crna →, Macedonia 44 E5
Crna Trava, Serbia & M. 44 D6
Crni Drim →, Macedonia 44 E4
Crni Timok →, Serbia & M. 44 C6
Crnoljeva Planina, Serbia & M. 44 D5
Črnomelj, Slovenia 41 C12
Croagh Patrick, Ireland 12 C2
Croatia ■, Europe 41 C13
Crocker, Banjaran, Malaysia 62 C5
Crockett, U.S.A. 113 K7
Crocodile = Krokodil →, Mozam. 89 D5
Crocodile Is., Australia 94 A1
Crocq, France 20 C6
Crodo, Italy 40 B5
Crohy Hd., Ireland 12 B3
Croisette, C., France 21 E9
Croisic, Pte. du, France 18 E4
Croix, L. La, Canada 104 C1
Croix, C., Australia 92 B5
Croker, C., Canada 116 B4
Croker I., Australia 92 B5
Cromarty, U.K. 13 D4
Cromer, U.K. 14 E9
Cromwell, N.Z. 91 L2
Cromwell, U.S.A. 117 E12
Cronat, France 19 F10
Crook, U.K. 14 C6
Crooked →, Canada 102 C4
Crooked →, U.S.A. 108 D3
Crooked I., Bahamas 121 B5
Crooked Island Passage, Bahamas 121 B5
Crookston, Minn., U.S.A. 112 B6
Crookston, Nebr., U.S.A. 112 D4
Crookwell, Australia 95 E4
Cropane-Micone △, Italy 43 D9
Crosby, U.K. 14 D4
Crosby, N. Dak., U.S.A. 112 A3
Crosby, Pa., U.S.A. 116 E6
Crosbyton, U.S.A. 113 J4
Crosía, U.S.A. 43 C9
Cross →, Nigeria 83 E6
Cross City, U.S.A. 115 L4
Cross Fell, U.K. 14 C5
Cross L., Canada 103 C9
Cross Lake, Canada 103 C9
Cross River □, Nigeria 83 D6
Cross River △, Nigeria 83 D6
Cross Sound, U.S.A. 100 C6
Crossett, U.S.A. 113 J9
Crosshaven, Ireland 12 E3
Crossville, U.S.A. 115 G3
Croswell, U.S.A. 116 C2
Croton-on-Hudson, U.S.A. 117 E11
Crotone, Italy 43 C10
Crow →, Canada 102 B4
Crow Agency, U.S.A. 108 D10
Crow Hd., Ireland 12 E1
Crowell, U.S.A. 113 J5
Crowley, U.S.A. 113 K8
Crowley, L., U.S.A. 110 H8
Crown Point, Ind., U.S.A. 114 E2
Crown Point, N.Y., U.S.A. 117 C11
Crown Pt., Trin. & Tob. 125 J16
Crownpoint, U.S.A. 109 J9
Crows Landing, U.S.A. 110 H5
Crows Nest, Australia 95 D5
Crowsnest Pass, Canada 102 D6
Croydon, Australia 94 B3
Croydon □, U.K. 15 F7
Crozet, Is., Ind. Oc. 3 G12
Crozon, France 18 D2
Cruz, C., Cuba 120 C4
Cruz Alta, Brazil 127 B5
Cruz Bay, U.S. Virgin Is. 121 e
Cruz de Incio, Spain 36 C3
Cruz del Eje, Argentina 126 C3
Cruzeiro, Brazil 127 A7
Cruzeiro do Oeste, Brazil 127 A5
Cruzeiro do Sul, Brazil 124 E4
Cry L., Canada 102 B3
Crystal Bay, U.S.A. 110 F7
Crystal Brook, Australia 95 E2
Crystal City, U.S.A. 113 L5
Crystal Falls, U.S.A. 114 B1
Crystal River, U.S.A. 115 L4
Crystal Springs, U.S.A. 113 K9
Csenger, Hungary 28 C7
Csongrád, Hungary 28 D5
Csongrád □, Hungary 28 D5
Csorna, Hungary 28 C2
Csurgo, Hungary 28 D2
Cu Lao Hon, Vietnam 65 G7
Cua Rao, Vietnam 64 C5
Cuácua →, Mozam. 87 F4
Cuamato, Angola 88 B2
Cuamba, Mozam. 87 E4
Cuando →, Angola 85 H4
Cuando Cubango □, Angola 88 B3
Cuangar, Angola 88 B2
Cuango = Kwango →, Dem. Rep. of the Congo 84 E3
Cuanza →, Angola 84 F2
Cuarto →, Argentina 126 C3
Cuatrociénegas, Mexico 118 B4
Cuauhtémoc, Mexico 118 B3
Cuba, Portugal 37 G3
Cuba, N. Mex., U.S.A. 109 J10
Cuba, N.Y., U.S.A. 116 D6
Cuba ■, W. Indies 120 B4

Cubango →, *Africa*   88 B3
Çubuk, *Turkey*   72 B5
Cuc Phuong △, *Vietnam*   64 B5
Cuchumatanes, Sierra de los,
  Guatemala   120 C1
Cuckfield, *U.K.*   15 F7
Cucuí, *Brazil*   124 C5
Cucurpe, *Mexico*   118 A2
Cúcuta, *Colombia*   124 B4
Cudalbi, *Romania*   29 E12
Cuddalore, *India*   66 P11
Cuddapah, *India*   66 M11
Cuddapan, L., *Australia*   94 D3
Cudillero, *Spain*   36 B4
Cue, *Australia*   93 E2
Cuéllar, *Spain*   36 D6
Cuenca, *Ecuador*   124 D3
Cuenca, *Spain*   38 E2
Cuenca □, *Spain*   38 F3
Cuenca, Serranía de, *Spain*   38 F3
Cuenca Alta del Manzanares △,
  Spain   36 E7
Cuerdo del Pozo, Embalse de la,
  Spain   38 D2
Cuernavaca, *Mexico*   119 D5
Cuero, *U.S.A.*   113 L6
Cuers, *France*   21 E10
Cueva de la Quebrada del
  Toro △, *Venezuela*   121 D6
Cuevas del Almanzora, *Spain*   39 H3
Cuevo, *Bolivia*   124 H6
Cugir, *Romania*   29 E8
Cugnaux, *France*   20 E5
Cuhai-Bakony →, *Hungary*   28 C2
Cuiabá, *Brazil*   125 G7
Cuiabá →, *Brazil*   125 G7
Cuijk, *Neths.*   17 C5
Cuilco, *Guatemala*   120 C1
Cuillin Hills, *U.K.*   13 D2
Cuillin Sd., *U.K.*   13 D2
Cuiseaux, *France*   19 F12
Cuito →, *Angola*   88 B3
Cuitzeo, L. de, *Mexico*   118 D4
Cujmir, *Romania*   28 F7
Cukai, *Malaysia*   65 K4
Culbertson, *U.S.A.*   112 A2
Culcairn, *Australia*   95 F4
Culebra, Isla de, *Puerto Rico*   121 d
Culebra, Sierra de la, *Spain*   36 D4
Culfa, *Azerbaijan*   73 C11
Culgoa →, *Australia*   95 D4
Culgoa Flood Plain △, *Australia*   95 D4
Culiacán, *Mexico*   118 C3
Culiacán →, *Mexico*   118 C3
Culik, *Indonesia*   63 J18
Culion, *Phil.*   61 F4
Cúllar, *Spain*   37 H8
Cullarin Ra., *Australia*   95 E4
Cullen, *U.K.*   13 D6
Cullen Pt., *Australia*   94 A3
Cullera, *Spain*   39 F4
Cullman, *U.S.A.*   115 H2
Cullompton, *U.K.*   15 G4
Culoz, *France*   21 C9
Culpeper, *U.S.A.*   114 F7
Culuene →, *Brazil*   125 F8
Culver, Pt., *Australia*   93 F3
Culverden, *N.Z.*   91 K4
Cumaná, *Venezuela*   124 A6
Cumaovası, *Turkey*   47 C9
Cumberland, B.C., *Canada*   102 D4
Cumberland, Ont., *Canada*   117 A9
Cumberland, *U.S.A.*   114 F6
Cumberland →, *U.S.A.*   115 G2
Cumberland, L., *U.S.A.*   115 G3
Cumberland Gap △, *U.S.A.*   115 G4
Cumberland I. *U.S.A.*   115 K5
Cumberland Is., *Australia*   94 J7
Cumberland Island △, *U.S.A.*   115 K5
Cumberland L., *Canada*   103 C8
Cumberland Pen., *Canada*   101 B13
Cumberland Plateau, *U.S.A.*   115 H3
Cumberland Sd., *Canada*   101 B13
Cumbernauld, *U.K.*   13 F5
Cumborah, *Australia*   95 D4
Cumbres de Majalca △, *Mexico*   118 B3
Cumbres de Monterrey △, *Mexico*   118 B4
Cumbres Mayores, *Spain*   37 G4
Cumbria □, *U.K.*   14 C5
Cumbrian Mts., *U.K.*   14 C5
Cumbum, *India*   66 M11
Cuminá →, *Brazil*   125 D7
Cummings Mt., *U.S.A.*   111 K8
Cummins, *Australia*   95 E2
Cumnock, *Australia*   95 E4
Cumnock, *U.K.*   13 F4
Cumpas, *Mexico*   118 B3
Cumplida, Pta., *Canary Is.*   48 F2
Çumra, *Turkey*   72 D5
Cunco, *Chile*   128 D2
Cuncumén, *Chile*   126 C1
Cunderdin, *Australia*   93 F2
Cunene →, *Angola*   88 B1
Cúneo, *Italy*   40 D4
Çüngüş, *Turkey*   70 B3
Cunillera, I. = Sa Conillera, *Spain*   48 C7
Cunlhat, *France*   20 C7
Cunnamulla, *Australia*   95 D4
Cuorgnè, *Italy*   40 C4
Cupar, *Canada*   103 C8
Cupar, *U.K.*   13 E5
Cupcini, *Moldova*   29 B12
Cupica, G. de, *Colombia*   124 B3
Ćuprija, *Serbia & M.*   44 C5
Curaçao, *Neth. Ant.*   121 D6
Curanilahue, *Chile*   126 D1
Curaray →, *Peru*   124 D4
Cure →, *France*   19 E10
Curepto, *Chile*   126 D1
Curiapo, *Venezuela*   124 B6
Curicó, *Chile*   126 C1
Curinga, *Italy*   43 D9

Curitiba, *Brazil*   127 B6
Curitibanos, *Brazil*   127 B5
Currabubula, *Australia*   95 E5
Currais Novos, *Brazil*   125 E11
Curralinho, *Brazil*   125 D9
Currant, *U.S.A.*   108 G6
Currawinya △, *Australia*   95 D3
Current →, *U.S.A.*   113 G9
Currie, *Australia*   95 F3
Currie, *U.S.A.*   108 F6
Curtea de Argeş, *Romania*   29 E9
Curtici, *Romania*   28 D6
Curtis, *U.S.A.*   112 E4
Curtis Group, *Australia*   95 F4
Curtis I., *Australia*   94 C5
Curuápanema →, *Brazil*   125 D7
Curuçá, *Brazil*   125 D9
Curuguaty, *Paraguay*   127 A4
Curup, *Indonesia*   62 E2
Cururupu, *Brazil*   125 D10
Curuzú Cuatiá, *Argentina*   126 B4
Curvelo, *Brazil*   125 G10
Cushing, *U.S.A.*   113 H6
Cushing, Mt., *Canada*   102 B3
Cusihuiriáchic, *Mexico*   118 B3
Cusna, Mte., *Italy*   40 D7
Cusset, *France*   19 F10
Custer, *U.S.A.*   112 D3
Cut Bank, *U.S.A.*   108 B7
Cutchogue, *U.S.A.*   117 E12
Cuthbert, *U.S.A.*   115 K3
Cutler, *U.S.A.*   110 J7
Cutro, *Italy*   43 C9
Cuttaburra →, *Australia*   95 D3
Cuttack, *India*   67 J14
Cuvier, C., *Australia*   93 D1
Cuvier I., *N.Z.*   91 G5
Cuxhaven, *Germany*   24 B4
Cuyahoga Falls, *U.S.A.*   116 E3
Cuyahoga Valley △, *U.S.A.*   116 E3
Cuyapo, *Phil.*   61 D4
Cuyo, *Phil.*   61 F4
Cuyo East Pass, *Phil.*   61 F4
Cuyo West Pass, *Phil.*   61 F4
Cuyuni →, *Guyana*   124 B7
Cuzco, *Bolivia*   124 H5
Cuzco, *Peru*   124 F4
Čvrsnica, *Bos.-H.*   28 G2
Cwmbran, *U.K.*   15 F4
Cyangugu, *Rwanda*   86 C2
Cybinka, *Poland*   31 F1
Cyclades = Kikládhes, *Greece*   46 E6
Cygnet, *Australia*   95 G4
Cynthiana, *U.S.A.*   114 F3
Cypress Hills, *Canada*   103 D7
Cypress Hills △, *Canada*   103 D7
Cyprus ■, *Asia*   49 E12
Cyrenaica, *Libya*   79 C10
Czaplinek, *Poland*   30 E3
Czar, *Canada*   103 C6
Czarna →, Łódzkie, *Poland*   31 G6
Czarna →, Świętokrzyskie,
  Poland   31 H8
Czarna Białostocka, *Poland*   31 E10
Czarna Woda, *Poland*   30 E5
Czarne, *Poland*   30 E3
Czarnków, *Poland*   31 F3
Czech Rep. ■, *Europe*   26 B8
Czechowice-Dziedzice, *Poland*   31 J5
Czempiń, *Poland*   31 F3
Czeremcha, *Poland*   31 F10
Czerniejewo, *Poland*   31 F4
Czersk, *Poland*   30 E4
Czerwieńsk, *Poland*   31 F2
Czerwionka-Leszczyny, *Poland*   31 H5
Częstochowa, *Poland*   31 H6
Człopa, *Poland*   31 E3
Człuchów, *Poland*   30 E4
Czyżew-Osada, *Poland*   31 F9

D

Da →, *Vietnam*   58 G5
Da Hinggan Ling, *China*   60 B7
Da Lat, *Vietnam*   65 G7
Da Nang, *Vietnam*   64 D7
Da Qaidam, *China*   60 C4
Da Yunhe →, *China*   57 G11
Da'an, *China*   57 B13
Daan Viljoen △, *Namibia*   88 C2
Dab'a, Ras el, *Egypt*   80 H6
Daba Shan, *China*   58 B7
Dabai, *Nigeria*   83 C6
Dabakala, *Ivory C.*   82 D4
Dabas, *Hungary*   28 C4
Dabat, *Ethiopia*   81 E4
Dabbagh, Jabal, *Si. Arabia*   70 E2
Dabhoi, *India*   68 H5
Dąbie, *Poland*   31 F5
Dabie Shan, *China*   59 B10
Dabilda, *Cameroon*   83 C7
Dabnou, *Niger*   83 C6
Dabo = Pasirkuning, *Indonesia*   62 E2
Dabola, *Guinea*   82 C2
Dabou, *Ivory C.*   82 D4
Daboya, *Ghana*   83 D4
Dabravolya, *Belarus*   31 F10
Dąbrowa Białostocka, *Poland*   30 E10
Dąbrowa Górnicza, *Poland*   31 H6
Dąbrowa Tarnowska, *Poland*   31 H7
Dabu, *China*   59 E11
Dabung, *Malaysia*   65 K4
Dabus →, *Ethiopia*   81 E4
Dacato →, *Ethiopia*   81 F5
Dacca = Dhaka, *Bangla.*   69 H14
Dacca = Dhaka □, *Bangla.*   69 G14
Dachau, *Germany*   25 G7
Dachstein, Hoher, *Austria*   26 D6

Dačice, *Czech Rep.*   26 B8
Dadanawa, *Guyana*   124 C7
Daday, *Turkey*   72 B5
Dade City, *U.S.A.*   115 L4
Dadhar, *Pakistan*   68 E2
Dadiya, *Nigeria*   83 D7
Dadra & Nagar Haveli □, *India*   66 J8
Dadri = Charkhi Dadri, *India*   68 E7
Dadu, *Pakistan*   68 F2
Dadu He →, *China*   58 C4
Daet, *Phil.*   61 D5
Dafang, *China*   58 D5
Dağ, *Turkey*   47 D12
Dagana, *Senegal*   82 B1
Dagash, *Sudan*   80 D3
Dagestan □, *Russia*   35 J8
Dagestanskiye Ogni, *Russia*   35 J9
Daggett, *U.S.A.*   111 L10
Daghestan Republic =
  Dagestan □, *Russia*   35 J8
Daghfeli, *Sudan*   80 D3
Dağlıq Qarabağ = Nagorno-
  Karabakh □, *Azerbaijan*   70 B5
Dagö = Hiiumaa, *Estonia*   9 G20
Dagu, *China*   57 E9
Daguan, *China*   58 D4
Dagupan, *Phil.*   61 C4
Daguragu, *Australia*   92 C5
Dahab, *Egypt*   80 B3
Dahlak △, *Eritrea*   81 D5
Dahlak Kebir, *Eritrea*   81 D5
Dahlenburg, *Germany*   24 B6
Dahlonega, *U.S.A.*   115 H4
Dahme, *Germany*   24 D9
Dahod, *India*   68 H9
Dahong Shan, *China*   59 B9
Dahra, *Senegal*   82 B1
Dahshûr, *Egypt*   80 J7
Dahūk, *Iraq*   70 B3
Dai Hao, *Vietnam*   64 C6
Dai-Sen, *Japan*   55 G6
Dai Shan, *China*   59 B14
Dai Xian, *China*   56 E7
Daicheng, *China*   56 E9
Daimiel, *Spain*   37 F7
Daingean, *Ireland*   12 C4
Daintree, *Australia*   94 B4
Daintree △, *Australia*   94 B4
Dair, J. ed, *Sudan*   81 E3
Dairût, *Egypt*   80 B3
Daisen-Oki △, *Japan*   55 G6
Daisetsu-Zan, *Japan*   54 C11
Daisetsu-Zan △, *Japan*   54 C11
Dajarra, *Australia*   94 C2
Dajin Chuan →, *China*   58 B3
Dak Dam, *Cambodia*   64 F6
Dak Nhe, *Vietnam*   64 E6
Dak Pek, *Vietnam*   64 E6
Dak Song, *Vietnam*   65 F6
Dak Sui, *Vietnam*   64 E6
Dakar, *Senegal*   82 C1
Dakhla, *W. Sahara*   78 D2
Dakhla, El Wâhât el-, *Egypt*   80 B2
Dakingari, *Nigeria*   83 C5
Dakor, *India*   68 H5
Dakoro, *Niger*   83 C6
Dakota City, *U.S.A.*   112 D6
Đakova, *Serbia & M.*   44 D4
Đakovica, *Croatia*   28 E3
Đakovo, *Croatia*   28 E3
Dalaba, *Guinea*   82 C2
Dalachi, *China*   56 F3
Dalai Nur, *China*   56 C9
Dālakī, *Iran*   71 D6
Dalälven →, *Sweden*   10 D10
Dalaman, *Turkey*   47 E10
Dalaman →, *Turkey*   47 E10
Dalandzadgad, *Mongolia*   56 C3
Dalap-Uliga-Darrit, *Marshall Is.*   96 G9
Dalarna, *Sweden*   10 D8
Dalarnas län □, *Sweden*   10 C8
Dālbandīn, *Pakistan*   66 E4
Dalbeattie, *U.K.*   13 G5
Dalbeg, *Australia*   94 C4
Dalbosjön, *Sweden*   11 F6
Dalby, *Australia*   95 D5
Dalby, *Sweden*   11 J7
Dalby Söderskog △, *Sweden*   11 J7
Dale City, *U.S.A.*   114 F7
Dale Hollow L., *U.S.A.*   115 G3
Dalga, *Egypt*   80 B3
Dalgān, *Iran*   71 E8
Dalhart, *U.S.A.*   113 G3
Dalhousie, *Canada*   105 C6
Dalhousie, *India*   68 C6
Dali, Shaanxi, *China*   56 G5
Dali, Yunnan, *China*   58 D3
Dalian, *China*   57 E11
Daliang Shan, *China*   58 D4
Daling He →, *China*   57 D11
Dāliyat el Karmel, *Israel*   74 C4
Dalj, *Croatia*   28 E3
Dalkeith, *U.K.*   13 F5
Dallas, Oreg., *U.S.A.*   108 D2
Dallas, Tex., *U.S.A.*   113 J6
Dalol, *Ethiopia*   81 E5
Dalmā, *U.A.E.*   71 E7
Dalmacija, *Croatia*   41 E13
Dalmas, L., *Canada*   105 B5
Dalmatia = Dalmacija, *Croatia*   41 E13
Dalmau, *India*   69 F9
Dalmellington, *U.K.*   13 F4
Dalnegorsk, *Russia*   53 E14
Dalnerechensk, *Russia*   53 E14
Dalnevostochnyy □, *Russia*   53 D13
Daloa, *Ivory C.*   82 D3
Dalou Shan, *China*   58 C6
Dalry, *U.K.*   13 F4
Dalrymple, L., *Australia*   94 C4
Dalrymple, Mt., *Australia*   94 K6
Dals Långed, *Sweden*   11 F6

Dalsjöfors, *Sweden*   11 G7
Dalsland, *Sweden*   11 F6
Daltenganj, *India*   69 H11
Dalton, *Mass., U.S.A.*   117 D11
Dalton, *Nebr., U.S.A.*   112 E3
Dalton-in-Furness, *U.K.*   14 C4
Dalupiri I., *Phil.*   61 B4
Dalvík, *Iceland*   8 D4
Dálvvadis = Jokkmokk, *Sweden*   8 C18
Dalwallinu, *Australia*   93 F2
Daly →, *Australia*   92 B5
Daly City, *U.S.A.*   110 H4
Daly L., *Canada*   103 B7
Daly River, *Australia*   92 B5
Daly Waters, *Australia*   94 B1
Dam Doi, *Vietnam*   65 H5
Dam Ha, *Vietnam*   64 B6
Daman, *India*   66 J8
Dāmaneh, *Iran*   71 C6
Damanhûr, *Egypt*   80 H7
Damant L., *Canada*   103 A7
Damanzhuang, *China*   56 E9
Damar, *Indonesia*   63 F7
Damaraland, *Namibia*   88 C2
Damascus = Dimashq, *Syria*   74 B5
Damaturu, *Nigeria*   83 C7
Damāvand, *Iran*   71 C7
Damāvand, Qolleh-ye, *Iran*   71 C7
Damba, *Angola*   84 F3
Dâmbovița □, *Romania*   29 F10
Dâmbovița →, *Romania*   29 F11
Dâmbovnic →, *Romania*   29 F10
Dame Marie, *Haiti*   121 C5
Dāmghān, *Iran*   71 B7
Dămienesti, *Romania*   29 D11
Damietta = Dumyât, *Egypt*   80 H7
Daming, *China*   56 F8
Damīr Qābū, *Syria*   70 B4
Dammam = Ad Dammām,
  Si. Arabia   71 E6
Dammarie-les-Lys, *France*   19 D9
Dammartin-en-Goële, *France*   19 C9
Damme, *Germany*   24 C4
Damodar →, *India*   69 H12
Damoh, *India*   69 H8
Dampier, *Australia*   92 D2
Dampier, Selat, *Indonesia*   63 E8
Dampier Arch., *Australia*   92 D2
Damrei, Chuor Phnum,
  Cambodia   65 G4
Damvillers, *France*   19 C12
Dan-Gulbi, *Nigeria*   83 C6
Dan Xian, *China*   64 C7
Dana, *Indonesia*   63 F6
Dana, L., *Canada*   104 B4
Dana, Mt., *U.S.A.*   110 H7
Danakil Desert, *Ethiopia*   81 E5
Danané, *Ivory C.*   82 D3
Danao, *Phil.*   61 F6
Danau Poso, *Indonesia*   63 E6
Danba, *China*   58 B3
Danbury, *U.S.A.*   117 E11
Danby L., *U.S.A.*   109 J6
Dand, *Afghan.*   68 D1
Dande △, *Zimbabwe*   87 F3
Dandeldhura, *Nepal*   69 E9
Dandeli, *India*   66 M9
Dandenong, *Australia*   95 F4
Dandîl, *Egypt*   80 J7
Dandong, *China*   57 D13
Danfeng, *China*   56 H6
Dangan Liedao, *China*   59 F10
Dangé-St-Romain, *France*   20 B4
Dângeni, *Romania*   29 C11
Danger Is. = Pukapuka, *Cook Is.*   97 J11
Danger Pt., *S. Africa*   88 E2
Danginport, *Indonesia*   63 K18
Dangla, *Ethiopia*   81 E4
Dangla Shan = Tanggula Shan,
  China   60 C4
Dangora, *Nigeria*   83 C6
Dangouadougou, *Burkina Faso*   82 D4
Dangrek, Phnom, *Thailand*   64 E5
Dangriga, *Belize*   119 D7
Dangshan, *China*   56 G9
Dangtu, *China*   59 B12
Dangyang, *China*   59 B8
Dani, *Burkina Faso*   83 C4
Daniel, *U.S.A.*   108 E8
Daniel's Harbour, *Canada*   105 B8
Danielskuil, *S. Africa*   88 D3
Danielson, *U.S.A.*   117 E13
Danilov, *Russia*   32 C11
Danilovgrad, *Serbia & M.*   44 D3
Danilovka, *Russia*   34 E7
Daning, *China*   56 F6
Danja, *Nigeria*   83 C6
Danjiangkou, *China*   59 A8
Danjiangkou Shuiku, *China*   59 A8
Dank, *Oman*   71 F8
Dankalwa, *Nigeria*   83 C7
Dankama, *Nigeria*   83 C6
Dankhar Gompa, *India*   66 C11
Dankov, *Russia*   32 F10
Danleng, *China*   58 B4
Danlí, *Honduras*   120 D2
Dannemora, *U.S.A.*   117 B11
Dannenberg, *Germany*   24 B7
Dannevirke, *N.Z.*   91 J6
Dannhauser, *S. Africa*   89 D5
Dansville, *U.S.A.*   116 D7
Danta, *India*   68 G5
Dantan, *India*   69 J12
Danube = Dunărea →, *Europe*   29 E14
Danvers, *U.S.A.*   117 D14
Danville, *Ill., U.S.A.*   114 E2
Danville, *Ky., U.S.A.*   114 G3
Danville, *Pa., U.S.A.*   117 F8
Danville, *Va., U.S.A.*   115 G6

Danville, *Vt., U.S.A.*   117 B12
Danyang, *China*   59 B12
Danzhai, *China*   58 D6
Danzig = Gdańsk, *Poland*   30 D5
Dão →, *Portugal*   36 E2
Dao Xian, *China*   59 E8
Daocheng, *China*   58 C3
Daoukro, *Ivory C.*   82 D4
Dapaong, *Togo*   83 C5
Dapchi, *Nigeria*   83 C7
Dapitan, *Phil.*   61 G5
Daqing Shan, *China*   56 D6
Daqu Shan, *China*   59 B14
Dar Banda, *Africa*   76 C4
Dar el Beida = Casablanca,
  Morocco   78 B4
Dar es Salaam, *Tanzania*   86 D4
Dar Mazār, *Iran*   71 D8
Dar'ā, *Syria*   74 C5
Dar'ā □, *Syria*   74 C5
Dārāb, *Iran*   71 D7
Daraban, *Pakistan*   68 D4
Darabani, *Romania*   29 B11
Daraina, *Madag.*   89 A8
Daraj, *Libya*   79 B8
Dārān, *Iran*   71 C6
Daravica, *Serbia & M.*   44 D4
Daraw, *Egypt*   80 C3
Dārayyā, *Syria*   74 B5
Darazo, *Nigeria*   83 C7
Darband, *Pakistan*   68 B5
Darband, Kūh-e, *Iran*   71 D8
Darbhanga, *India*   69 F11
D'Arcy, *Canada*   102 C4
Darda, *Croatia*   28 E3
Dardanelle, Ark., *U.S.A.*   113 H8
Dardanelle, Calif., *U.S.A.*   110 G7
Dardanelles = Çanakkale Boğazı,
  Turkey   45 F10
Dare →, *Ethiopia*   81 F5
Darende, *Turkey*   72 C7
Därestän, *Iran*   71 D8
Darfo, *Italy*   40 C7
Dârfûr, *Sudan*   79 F10
Dargai, *Pakistan*   68 B4
Dargan Ata, *Turkmenistan*   52 E7
Dargaville, *N.Z.*   91 F4
Dargol, *Niger*   83 C5
Darhan, *Mongolia*   60 B5
Darhan Muminggan Lianheqi,
  China   56 D6
Dari, *Sudan*   81 F3
Darica, *Turkey*   72 B3
Darién △, *Panama*   120 E4
Darién, G. del, *Colombia*   124 B3
Dariganga = Ovoot, *Mongolia*   56 B7
Darinskoye, *Kazakhstan*   34 E10
Darjeeling = Darjiling, *India*   69 F13
Darjiling, *India*   69 F13
Darkan, *Australia*   93 F2
Darkhana, *Pakistan*   68 D5
Darkhazīneh, *Iran*   71 D6
Darkot Pass, *Pakistan*   69 A5
Darling →, *Australia*   95 E3
Darling Downs, *Australia*   95 D5
Darling Ra., *Australia*   93 F2
Darlington, *U.K.*   14 C6
Darlington, *U.S.A.*   115 H6
Darlington □, *U.K.*   14 C6
Darlington, L., *S. Africa*   88 E4
Darlot, L., *Australia*   93 E3
Darłowo, *Poland*   30 D3
Dărmănești, Bacău, *Romania*   29 D11
Dărmănești, Suceava, *Romania*   29 C11
Darmstadt, *Germany*   25 F4
Darnah, *Libya*   79 B10
Darnall, *S. Africa*   89 D5
Darney, *France*   19 D13
Darnley, C., *Antarctica*   5 C6
Darnley B., *Canada*   100 B7
Daroca, *Spain*   38 D3
Darou-Mousti, *Senegal*   82 B1
Darr →, *Australia*   94 C3
Darra Pezu, *Pakistan*   68 C4
Darrequeira, *Argentina*   126 D3
Darrington, *U.S.A.*   108 B3
Darsser Ort, *Germany*   24 A8
Dart →, *U.K.*   15 G4
Dart, C., *Antarctica*   5 D14
Dartford, *U.K.*   15 F8
Dartmoor, *U.K.*   15 G4
Dartmoor △, *U.K.*   15 G4
Dartmouth, *Canada*   105 D7
Dartmouth, *U.K.*   15 G4
Dartmouth Res., *Australia*   95 D4
Dartuch, C. = Artrutx, C. de,
  Spain   48 B10
Daruvar, *Croatia*   28 E2
Darvaza, *Turkmenistan*   52 E6
Darvel, Teluk = Lahad Datu,
  Teluk, *Malaysia*   63 D5
Darwen, *U.K.*   14 D5
Darwendale, *Zimbabwe*   89 B5
Darwha, *India*   66 J10
Darwin, *Australia*   92 B5
Darwin, *U.S.A.*   111 J9
Darya Khan, *Pakistan*   68 D4
Daryoi Amu = Amudarya →,
  Uzbekistan   52 E6
Dās, *U.A.E.*   71 E7
Dashen, Ras, *Ethiopia*   81 E4
Dashetai, *China*   56 D5
Dashhowuz, *Turkmenistan*   52 E6
Dashkesan = Daşkäsän,
  Azerbaijan   35 K7
Dashköpri, *Turkmenistan*   71 B9
Dasht, *Iran*   71 B8
Dasht →, *Pakistan*   66 G2
Daska, *Pakistan*   68 C6
Daşkäsän, *Azerbaijan*   35 K7
Dasua, *Benin*   83 D5
Dasuya, *India*   68 D6

Datça, *Turkey* 47 E9
Datia, *India* 69 G8
Datian, *China* 59 E11
Datong, *Anhui, China* 59 B11
Datong, *Shanxi, China* 56 D7
Dattakhel, *Pakistan* 68 C3
Datteln, *Germany* 24 D3
Datu, Tanjung, *Indonesia* 62 D3
Datu Piang, *Phil.* 61 H6
Datuk, Tanjong = Datu, Tanjung, *Indonesia* 62 D3
Daua = Dawa ➤, *Africa* 81 G5
Daud Khel, *Pakistan* 68 C4
Daudnagar, *India* 69 G11
Daugava ➤, *Latvia* 9 H21
Daugavpils, *Latvia* 9 J22
Daulpur, *India* 68 F7
Daun, *Germany* 25 E2
Dauphin, *Canada* 103 C8
Dauphin, *U.S.A.* 116 F8
Dauphin L., *Canada* 103 C9
Dauphiné, *France* 21 C9
Daura, *Borno, Nigeria* 83 C7
Daura, *Katsina, Nigeria* 83 C6
Dausa, *India* 68 F7
Dāvaçi, *Azerbaijan* 35 K9
Davangere, *India* 66 M9
Davao, *Phil.* 61 H6
Davao G., *Phil.* 61 H6
Dāvar Panāh = Sarāvān, *Iran* 71 E9
Davenport, *Calif., U.S.A.* 110 H4
Davenport, *Iowa, U.S.A.* 112 E9
Davenport, *Wash., U.S.A.* 108 C4
Davenport Ra., *Australia* 94 C1
Daventry, *U.K.* 15 E6
David, *Panama* 120 E3
David City, *U.S.A.* 112 E6
David Gorodok = Davyd Haradok, *Belarus* 33 F4
Davidson, *Canada* 103 C7
Davis, *Antarctica* 5 C6
Davis, *U.S.A.* 110 G5
Davis Dam, *U.S.A.* 111 K12
Davis Inlet, *Canada* 105 A7
Davis Mts., *U.S.A.* 113 K2
Davis Sea, *Antarctica* 5 C7
Davis Str., *N. Amer.* 101 B14
Davo ➤, *Ivory C.* 82 D3
Davos, *Switz.* 25 J5
Davutlar, *Turkey* 47 D9
Davy L., *Canada* 103 B7
Davyd Haradok, *Belarus* 33 F4
Dawa ➤, *Africa* 81 G5
Dawaki, *Bauchi, Nigeria* 83 D6
Dawaki, *Kano, Nigeria* 83 C6
Dawei = Tavoy, *Burma* 64 E2
Dawes Ra., *Australia* 94 C5
Dawlish, *U.K.* 15 G4
Dawna Ra., *Burma* 64 D2
Dawros Hd., *Ireland* 12 B3
Dawson, *Canada* 100 B6
Dawson, *U.S.A.* 115 K3
Dawson, I., *Chile* 128 G2
Dawson B., *Canada* 103 C8
Dawson Creek, *Canada* 102 B4
Dawson Inlet, *Canada* 103 A10
Dawson Ra., *Australia* 94 C4
Dawu, *Hubei, China* 59 B9
Dawu, *Sichuan, China* 58 B3
Dax, *France* 20 E2
Daxian, *China* 58 B6
Daxin, *China* 58 F6
Daxindian, *China* 57 F11
Daxinggou, *China* 57 C15
Daxue Shan, *Sichuan, China* 58 B3
Daxue Shan, *Yunnan, China* 58 F2
Dayao, *China* 58 E3
Daye, *China* 59 B10
Dayet en Naharat, *Mali* 82 B4
Dayi, *China* 58 B4
Daylesford, *Australia* 95 F3
Dayong, *China* 59 C8
Dayr az Zawr, *Syria* 70 C4
Daysland, *Canada* 102 C6
Dayton, *Nev., U.S.A.* 110 F7
Dayton, *Ohio, U.S.A.* 114 F3
Dayton, *Pa., U.S.A.* 116 F5
Dayton, *Tenn., U.S.A.* 115 H3
Dayton, *Wash., U.S.A.* 108 C4
Dayton, *Wyo., U.S.A.* 108 D10
Daytona Beach, *U.S.A.* 115 L5
Dayu, *China* 59 E10
Dayville, *U.S.A.* 108 D4
Dazhu, *China* 58 B6
Dazkırı, *Turkey* 47 D11
Dazu, *China* 58 C5
De Aar, *S. Africa* 88 E3
De Biesbosch △, *Neths.* 17 C4
De Funiak Springs, *U.S.A.* 115 K2
De Grey ➤, *Australia* 92 D2
De Haan, *Belgium* 17 C3
De Hoge Veluwe △, *Neths.* 17 B5
De Hoop △, *S. Africa* 88 E3
De Kalb, *U.S.A.* 112 E10
De Kennemerduinen △, *Neths.* 17 B4
De Land, *U.S.A.* 115 L5
De Leon, *U.S.A.* 113 J5
De Panne, *Belgium* 17 C2
De Pere, *U.S.A.* 114 C1
De Queen, *U.S.A.* 113 H7
De Quincy, *U.S.A.* 113 K8
De Ridder, *U.S.A.* 113 K8
De Smet, *U.S.A.* 112 C6
De Soto, *U.S.A.* 112 F9
De Tour Village, *U.S.A.* 114 C4
De Witt, *U.S.A.* 113 H9
Dead Sea, *Asia* 74 D4
Deadwood, *U.S.A.* 112 C3
Deadwood L., *Canada* 102 B3
Deal, *U.K.* 15 F9
Deal I., *Australia* 95 F4
Dealesville, *S. Africa* 88 D4

De'an, *China* 59 C10
Dean ➤, *Canada* 102 C3
Dean, Forest of, *U.K.* 15 F5
Dean Chan., *Canada* 102 C3
Deán Funes, *Argentina* 126 C3
Dease ➤, *Canada* 102 B3
Dease L., *Canada* 102 B2
Dease Lake, *Canada* 102 B2
Death Valley, *U.S.A.* 111 J10
Death Valley △, *U.S.A.* 111 J10
Death Valley Jur.ction, *U.S.A.* 111 J10
Deauville, *France* 18 C7
Deba, *Spain* 38 B2
Deba Habe, *Nigeria* 83 C7
Debaltsevo, *Ukraine* 33 H10
Debao, *China* 58 F6
Debar, *Macedonia* 44 E4
Debark, *Ethiopia* 81 E4
Debden, *Canada* 103 C7
Dębica, *Poland* 31 H8
Dęblin, *Poland* 31 G8
Dębno, *Poland* 31 F1
Débo, L., *Mali* 82 B4
DeBolt, *Canada* 102 B5
Deborah East, L., *Australia* 93 F2
Deborah West, L., *Australia* 93 F2
Debrc, *Serbia & M.* 44 B3
Debre Birhan, *Etiopia* 81 F4
Debre Markos, *Ethiopia* 81 E4
Debre May, *Ethiopia* 81 E4
Debre Sina, *Ethiopia* 81 F4
Debre Tabor, *Ethiopia* 81 E4
Debre Zebit, *Ethiopia* 81 E4
Debre Zevit, *Ethiopia* 81 F4
Debrecen, *Hungary* 28 C6
Debrzno, *Poland* 30 E4
Dečani, *Serbia & M.* 44 D4
Decatur, *Ala., U.S.A.* 115 H2
Decatur, *Ga., U.S.A.* 115 J3
Decatur, *Ill., U.S.A.* 112 F10
Decatur, *Ind., U.S.A.* 114 E3
Decatur, *Tex., U.S.A.* 113 J6
Decazeville, *France* 20 D6
Deccan, *India* 66 L11
Deception Bay, *Australia* 95 D5
Deception I., *Antarctica* 5 C17
Deception L., *Canada* 103 B8
Dechang, *China* 58 D4
Deckerville, *U.S.A.* 116 C2
Decollatura, *Italy* 43 C9
Decorah, *U.S.A.* 112 D9
Deda, *Romania* 29 D9
Dedéagac = Alexandroúpolis, *Greece* 45 F9
Deder, *Ethiopia* 81 F5
Dedham, *U.S.A.* 117 D13
Dédougou, *Burkina Faso* 82 C4
Dedovichi, *Russia* 32 D5
Dedza, *Malawi* 87 E3
Dee ➤, *Aberds., U.K.* 13 D6
Dee ➤, *Dumf. & Gall., U.K.* 13 G4
Dee ➤, *Wales, U.K.* 14 D4
Deep B., *Canada* 102 A5
Deepwater, *Australia* 95 D5
Deer ➤, *Canada* 103 B10
Deer L., *Canada* 103 C10
Deer Lake, *Nfld. & L., Canada* 105 C8
Deer Lake, *Ont., Canada* 103 C10
Deer Lodge, *U.S.A.* 108 C7
Deer Park, *U.S.A.* 108 C5
Deer River, *U.S.A.* 112 B8
Deeragun, *Australia* 94 B4
Deerdepoort, *S. Africa* 88 C4
Deferiet, *U.S.A.* 117 B9
Defiance, *U.S.A.* 114 E3
Degana, *India* 68 F6
Dêgê, *China* 58 B2
Degebe ➤, *Portugcl* 37 G3
Degeberga, *Sweden* 11 J8
Dégelis, *Canada* 105 C6
Degema, *Nigeria* 83 E6
Degerfors, *Sweden* 10 E8
Degerhamn, *Sweden* 11 H10
Deggendorf, *Germany* 25 G8
Degh ➤, *Pakistan* 68 D5
Değirmendere, *Turkey* 45 F13
Deh Bīd, *Iran* 71 D7
Deh-e Shīr, *Iran* 71 D7
Dehaj, *Iran* 71 D7
Dehak, *Iran* 71 E9
Dehdez, *Iran* 71 D6
Dehej, *India* 68 J5
Dehestān, *Iran* 71 D7
Dehgolān, *Iran* 70 C5
Dehibat, *Tunisia* 79 B8
Dehlorān, *Iran* 70 C5
Dehnow-e Kühestān, *Iran* 71 E8
Dehra Dun, *India* 68 D8
Dehri, *India* 69 G11
Dehua, *China* 59 E12
Dehui, *China* 57 B13
Deim Zubeir, *Sudan* 81 F2
Deinze, *Belgium* 17 D3
Dej, *Romania* 29 C8
Deje, *Sweden* 10 E7
Dejiang, *China* 58 C7
Deka ➤, *Zimbabwe* 88 B4
Dekemhare, *Eritrea* 81 D4
Dekese, *Dem. Rep. of the Congo* 84 E4
Del Mar, *U.S.A.* 111 N9
Del Norte, *U.S.A.* 109 H10
Del Rio, *U.S.A.* 113 L4
Delai, *Sudan* 80 D4
Delambre I., *Australia* 92 D2
Delami, *Sudan* 81 E3
Delano, *U.S.A.* 111 K7
Delano Peak, *U.S.A.* 109 G7
Delareyville, *S. Africa* 88 D4
Delaronde L., *Canada* 103 C7

Delavan, *U.S.A.* 112 D10
Delaware, *U.S.A.* 114 E4
Delaware □, *U.S.A.* 114 F8
Delaware ➤, *U.S.A.* 117 G9
Delaware B., *U.S.A.* 114 F8
Delaware Water Gap △, *U.S.A.* 117 E10
Delay ➤, *Canada* 105 A5
Delčevo, *Macedonia* 44 E6
Delegate, *Australia* 95 F4
Delémont, *Switz.* 25 H3
Delevan, *U.S.A.* 116 D6
Delft, *Neths.* 17 B4
Delfzijl, *Neths.* 17 A6
Delgado, C., *Mozam.* 87 E5
Delgerhet, *Mongolia* 56 B6
Delgo, *Sudan* 80 C3
Delhi, *Canada* 116 D4
Delhi, *India* 68 E7
Delhi, *La., U.S.A.* 113 J9
Delhi, *N.Y., U.S.A.* 117 D10
Deli Jovan, *Serbia & M.* 44 B6
Delia, *Canada* 102 C6
Delice, *Turkey* 72 C6
Delicias, *Mexico* 118 B3
Delījān, *Iran* 71 C6
Déline, *Canada* 100 B7
Delisle, *Canada* 103 C7
Delitzsch, *Germany* 24 D8
Dell City, *U.S.A.* 109 L11
Dell Rapids, *U.S.A.* 112 D6
Delle, *France* 19 E14
Delmar, *U.S.A.* 117 D11
Delmenhorst, *Germany* 24 B4
Delnice, *Croatia* 41 C11
Delonga, Ostrova, *Russia* 53 B15
Deloraine, *Australia* 95 G4
Deloraine, *Canada* 103 D8
Delphi, *Greece* 46 C4
Delphi, *U.S.A.* 114 E2
Delphos, *U.S.A.* 114 E3
Delportshoop, *S. Africa* 88 D3
Delray Beach, *U.S.A.* 115 M5
Delsbo, *Sweden* 10 C10
Delta, *Colo., U.S.A.* 109 G9
Delta, *Utah, U.S.A.* 108 G7
Delta □, *Nigeria* 83 D6
Delta del Ebro, *Spain* 38 E5
Delta del Po, *Italy* 41 D9
Delta du Saloum △, *Senegal* 82 C1
Delta Dunărea △, *Romania* 29 E14
Delta Junction, *U.S.A.* 100 B5
Deltona, *U.S.A.* 115 L5
Delungra, *Australia* 95 D5
Delvada, *India* 68 J4
Delvinákion, *Greece* 46 B2
Delyatyn, *Ukraine* 29 B9
Demak, *Indonesia* 63 G14
Demanda, Sierra de la, *Spain* 38 C2
Demavend = Damāvand, Qolleh-ye, *Iran* 71 C7
Dembecha, *Ethiopia* 81 E4
Dembi, *Ethiopia* 81 F4
Dembia, *Dem. Rep. of the Congo* 86 B2
Dembidolo, *Ethiopia* 81 F3
Demchok, *India* 69 C8
Demer ➤, *Belgium* 17 D4
Demetrias, *Greece* 46 B5
Demidov, *Russia* 32 E6
Deming, *N. Mex., U.S.A.* 109 K10
Deming, *Wash., U.S.A.* 110 B4
Demini ➤, *Brazil* 124 D6
Demirci, *Turkey* 47 B10
Demirköprü Barajı, *Turkey* 47 C10
Demirköy, *Turkey* 45 E11
Demmin, *Germany* 24 B9
Demonte, *Italy* 40 D4
Demopolis, *U.S.A.* 115 J2
Dempo, *Indonesia* 62 E2
Demyansk, *Russia* 32 D7
Den Burg, *Neths.* 17 A4
Den Chai, *Thailand* 64 D3
Den Haag = 's-Gravenhage, *Neths.* 17 B4
Den Helder, *Neths.* 17 B4
Den Oever, *Neths.* 17 B5
Denain, *France* 19 B10
Denair, *U.S.A.* 110 H6
Denau, *Uzbekistan* 52 F7
Denbigh, *Canada* 116 A7
Denbigh, *U.K.* 14 D4
Denbighshire □, *U.K.* 14 D4
Dendang, *Indonesia* 62 E3
Dendermonde, *Belgium* 17 C4
Deneba, *Ethiopia* 81 F4
Deneba, *Ethiopia* 81 F4
Dengchuan, *China* 58 E3
Denge, *Nigeria* 83 C6
Dengfeng, *China* 56 G7
Dengi, *Nigeria* 83 D6
Dengkou, *China* 56 D4
Dengzhou, *China* 59 A9
Denham, *Australia* 93 E1
Denham, Mt., *Jamaica* 120 a
Denham Ra., *Australia* 94 C4
Denham Sd., *Australia* 93 E1
Denholm, *Canada* 103 C7
Denia, *Spain* 39 G5
Denial B., *Australia* 95 E1
Deniliquin, *Australia* 95 F3
Denison, *Iowa, U.S.A.* 112 E7
Denison, *Tex., U.S.A.* 113 J6
Denison Plains, *Australia* 92 C4
Denizli, *Turkey* 47 D11
Denizli □, *Turkey* 47 D11
Denman Glacier, *Antarctica* 5 C7
Denmark, *Australia* 93 F2
Denmark ■, *Europe* 11 J3
Denmark Str., *Atl. Oc.* 4 C6
Dennery, *St. Lucia* 121 f
Dennison, *U.S.A.* 116 F3
Denny, *U.K.* 13 E5

Denpasar, *Indonesia* 63 K18
Denpasar ✈ (DPS), *Indonesia* 63 K18
Denton, *Mont., U.S.A.* 108 C9
Denton, *Tex., U.S.A.* 113 J6
D'Entrecasteaux △, *Australia* 93 F2
D'Entrecasteaux, Pt., *Australia* 93 F2
Denu, *Ghana* 83 D5
Denver, *Colo., U.S.A.* 112 F2
Denver, *Pa., U.S.A.* 117 F8
Denver City, *U.S.A.* 113 J3
Deoband, *India* 68 E7
Deogarh, *India* 68 G5
Deoghar, *India* 69 G12
Deolali, *India* 66 K8
Deoli = Devli, *India* 68 G6
Deora, *India* 68 F4
Deori, *India* 69 H8
Deoria, *India* 69 F10
Deosai Mts., *Pakistan* 69 B6
Deosri, *India* 69 F14
Depalpur, *India* 68 H6
Deping, *China* 57 F9
Deposit, *U.S.A.* 117 D9
Depuch I., *Australia* 92 D2
Deputatskiy, *Russia* 53 C14
Dêqên, *China* 58 C2
Deqing, *China* 59 F8
Dera Ghazi Khan, *Pakistan* 68 D4
Dera Ismail Khan, *Pakistan* 68 D4
Derabugti, *Pakistan* 68 E3
Derawar Fort, *Pakistan* 68 E4
Derbent, *Russia* 35 J9
Derbent, *Turkey* 47 C10
Derby, *Australia* 92 C3
Derby, *U.K.* 14 E6
Derby, *Conn., U.S.A.* 117 E11
Derby, *Kans., U.S.A.* 113 G6
Derby, *N.Y., U.S.A.* 116 D6
Derby City □, *U.K.* 14 E6
Derby Line, *U.S.A.* 117 B12
Derbyshire □, *U.K.* 14 D6
Đerdap △, *Serbia & M.* 44 B6
Derdepoort, *S. Africa* 88 C4
Derecske, *Hungary* 28 C6
Dereham, *U.K.* 15 E8
Dereköy, *Turkey* 45 E11
Dereli, *Turkey* 73 B8
Derg ➤, *U.K.* 12 B4
Derg, L., *Ireland* 12 D3
Dergachi = Derhaci, *Ukraine* 33 G9
Dergaon, *India* 67 F19
Derhaci, *Ukraine* 33 G9
Derik, *Turkey* 73 D9
Derinkuyu, *Turkey* 72 C6
Dermott, *U.S.A.* 113 J9
Dêrong, *China* 58 C2
Derry = Londonderry, *U.K.* 12 B4
Derry = Londonderry □, *U.K.* 12 B4
Derry, *N.H., U.S.A.* 117 D13
Derry, *Pa., U.S.A.* 116 F5
Derryveagh Mts., *Ireland* 12 B3
Derudub, *Sudan* 80 D4
Derval, *France* 18 E5
Dervéni, *Greece* 46 C4
Derventa, *Bos.-H.* 28 F2
Derwent ➤, *Cumb., U.K.* 14 C4
Derwent ➤, *Derby, U.K.* 14 E6
Derwent ➤, *N. Yorks., U.K.* 14 D7
Derwent Water, *U.K.* 14 C4
Des Moines, *Iowa, U.S.A.* 112 E8
Des Moines, *N. Mex., U.S.A.* 113 G3
Des Moines ➤, *U.S.A.* 112 E9
Desa, *Romania* 28 G8
Desaguadero ➤, *Argentina* 126 C2
Desaguadero ➤, *Bolivia* 124 G5
Desante, *Ukraine* 29 E14
Desar, *Malaysia* 65 d
Descanso, Pta., *Mexico* 111 N9
Descartes, *France* 20 B4
Deschaillons-sur-St-Laurent, *Canada* 105 C5
Deschambault L., *Canada* 103 C8
Deschutes ➤, *U.S.A.* 108 D3
Dese, *Ethiopia* 81 E4
Deseado ➤, *Argentina* 128 F3
Desenzano del Garda, *Italy* 40 C7
Desert Center, *U.S.A.* 111 M11
Desert Hot Springs, *U.S.A.* 111 M10
Deshnok, *India* 68 F5
Desierto Central de Baja California △, *Mexico* 118 B2
Desna ➤, *Ukraine* 33 G6
Desnătui ➤, *Romania* 29 G8
Desolación, I., *Chile* 128 G2
Despeñaperros △, *Spain* 37 G7
Despeñaperros, Paso, *Spain* 37 G7
Despotovac, *Serbia & M.* 44 B5
Dessau, *Germany* 24 D8
Dessye = Dese, *Ethiopia* 81 E4
D'Estrees B., *Australia* 95 F2
Desuri, *India* 68 G5
Desvres, *France* 19 B8
Det Udom, *Thailand* 64 E5
Deta, *Romania* 28 E6
Dete, *Zimbabwe* 88 B4
Đetinja ➤, *Serbia & M.* 44 C4
Detmold, *Germany* 24 D4
Detour, Pt., *U.S.A.* 114 C2
Detroit, *U.S.A.* 116 D1
Detroit Lakes, *U.S.A.* 112 B7
Detva, *Slovak Rep.* 27 C12
Deurne, *Neths.* 17 C5
Deutsch-Luxemburgischer △, *Germany* 25 F2
Deutsche Bucht, *Germany* 24 A4
Deutschlandsberg, *Austria* 26 E8
Deva, *Romania* 28 E7
Devakottai, *India* 66 Q11
Devaprayag, *India* 69 D8

Dévaványa, *Hungary* 28 C5
Deveci Dağları, *Turkey* 72 B7
Devecikonağı, *Turkey* 45 G12
Devecser, *Hungary* 28 C2
Develi, *Turkey* 72 C6
Deventer, *Neths.* 17 B6
Deveron ➤, *U.K.* 13 D6
Devesel, *Romania* 28 F7
Devgadh Bariya, *India* 68 H5
Devikot, *India* 68 F4
Devils Den, *U.S.A.* 110 K7
Devils Lake, *U.S.A.* 112 A5
Devils Paw, *Canada* 102 B2
Devils Postpile △, *U.S.A.* 110 H7
Devils Tower △, *U.S.A.* 112 C2
Devils Tower Junction, *U.S.A.* 112 C2
Devin, *Bulgaria* 45 E8
Devine, *U.S.A.* 113 L5
Devizes, *U.K.* 15 F6
Devli, *India* 68 G6
Devnya, *Bulgaria* 45 C11
Devoll ➤, *Albania* 44 F4
Devon, *Canada* 102 C6
Devon □, *U.K.* 15 G4
Devon I., *Canada* 98 B11
Devonport, *Australia* 95 G4
Devonport, *N.Z.* 91 G5
Devrek, *Turkey* 72 B4
Devrekâni, *Turkey* 72 B5
Devrez ➤, *Turkey* 72 B6
Dewas, *India* 68 H7
Dewetsdorp, *S. Africa* 88 D4
Dewey, *Puerto Rico* 121 d
Dexing, *China* 59 C11
Dexter, *Maine, U.S.A.* 115 C11
Dexter, *Mo., U.S.A.* 113 G10
Dexter, *N. Mex., U.S.A.* 113 J2
Dey-Dey, L., *Australia* 93 E5
Deyang, *China* 58 B5
Deyhūk, *Iran* 71 C8
Deyyer, *Iran* 71 E6
Dezadeash L., *Canada* 102 A1
Dezfūl, *Iran* 71 C6
Dezhneva, Mys, *Russia* 53 C19
Dezhou, *China* 56 F9
Dhadhar ➤, *India* 69 G11
Dháfni, *Kríti, Greece* 49 D7
Dháfni, *Pelóponnisos, Greece* 46 D4
Dhahaban, *Si. Arabia* 80 C4
Dhahiriya = Aẕ Ẕāhirīyah, West Bank 74 D3
Dhahran = Aẕ Ẕahrān, *Si. Arabia* 71 E6
Dhak, *Pakistan* 68 C5
Dhaka, *Bangla.* 69 H14
Dhaka □, *Bangla.* 69 H14
Dhali, *Cyprus* 49 D12
Dhamási, *Greece* 46 B4
Dhampur, *India* 69 E8
Dhamtari, *India* 67 J12
Dhanbad, *India* 69 H12
Dhangarhi, *Nepal* 67 E12
Dhankuta, *Nepal* 69 F12
Dhar, *India* 68 H6
Dharampur, *India* 68 H6
Dharamsala = Dharmsala, *India* 68 C7
Dhariwal, *India* 68 D6
Dharla ➤, *Bangla.* 69 G13
Dharmapuri, *India* 66 N11
Dharmjaygarh, *India* 69 H10
Dharmsala, *India* 68 C7
Dharni, *India* 68 J7
Dharwad, *India* 66 M9
Dhasan ➤, *India* 69 G8
Dhaulagiri, *Nepal* 69 E10
Dhebar, L., *India* 68 G6
Dheftera, *Cyprus* 49 D12
Dhenkanal, *India* 67 J14
Dhenoúsa, *Greece* 47 D7
Dherinia, *Cyprus* 49 D12
Dheskáti, *Greece* 44 G5
Dhespotikó, *Greece* 46 E6
Dhestina, *Greece* 46 C4
Dhī Qār □, *Iraq* 70 D5
Dhíarrizos ➤, *Cyprus* 49 E11
Dhībān, *Jordan* 74 D4
Dhidhimótikhon, *Greece* 45 E10
Dhíkti Óros, *Greece* 49 D7
Dhilianáta, *Greece* 46 C2
Dhílos, *Greece* 47 D7
Dhilwan, *India* 68 D6
Dhimarkhera, *India* 69 H9
Dhimitsána, *Greece* 46 D4
Dhírfis Óros, *Greece* 46 C5
Dhodhekánisos, *Greece* 47 E8
Dhodhekánisos □, *Greece* 47 E8
Dhokós, *Greece* 46 D5
Dholiana, *Greece* 46 B2
Dholka, *India* 68 H5
Dhomokós, *Greece* 46 B4
Dhoraji, *India* 68 J4
Dhoxáton, *Greece* 45 E8
Dhragonísi, *Greece* 47 D7
Dhrangadhra, *India* 68 H4
Dhrápanon, Ákra, *Greece* 49 D6
Dhriopís, *Greece* 46 D6
Dhrol, *India* 68 H4
Dhuburi, *India* 67 F16
Dhule, *India* 66 J9
Di-ib, W. ➤, *Sudan* 80 C4
Di Linh, *Vietnam* 65 G7
Di Linh, Cao Nguyen, *Vietnam* 65 G7
Día, *Greece* 49 D7
Diabakania, *Guinea* 82 C2
Diablo, Mt., *U.S.A.* 110 H5
Diablo Range, *U.S.A.* 110 J5
Diafarabé, *Mali* 82 C4
Diala, *Mali* 82 C3
Dialakoto, *Senegal* 82 C2
Diallassagou, *Mali* 82 C4
Diamante, *Argentina* 126 C3

Diamante, *Italy* 43 C8
Diamante ➤, *Argentina* 126 C2
Diamantina, *Brazil* 125 G10
Diamantina △, *Australia* 94 C3
Diamantina ➤, *Australia* 95 D2
Diamantino, *Brazil* 125 F7
Diamond Bar, *U.S.A.* 111 L9
Diamond Harbour, *India* 69 H13
Diamond Is., *Australia* 94 B5
Diamond Mts., *U.S.A.* 108 G6
Diamond Springs, *U.S.A.* .. 110 G6
Dian Chi, *China* 58 E4
Dianalund, *Denmark* 11 J5
Dianbai, *China* 59 G8
Diancheng, *China* 59 G8
Dianjiang, *China* 58 B6
Diano Marina, *Italy* 40 E5
Dianra, *Ivory C.* 82 D3
Diapaga, *Burkina Faso* 83 C5
Diapangou, *Burkina Faso* 83 C5
Diariguila, *Guinea* 82 C2
Dībā, *U.A.E.* 71 E8
Dibai, *India* 68 E8
Dibaya-Lubue, *Dem. Rep. of the Congo* ... 84 E3
Dibbeen △, *Jordan* 74 C4
Dibete, *Botswana* 88 C4
Dibrugarh, *India* 67 F19
Dickens, *U.S.A.* 113 J4
Dickinson, *U.S.A.* 112 B3
Dickson, *U.S.A.* 115 G2
Dickson City, *U.S.A.* 117 E9
Dicle Nehri ➤, *Turkey* 73 D9
Dicomano, *Italy* 41 E8
Didesa, W. ➤, *Ethiopia* 81 F4
Didi, *Sudan* 81 F3
Didiéni, *Mali* 82 C3
Didsbury, *Canada* 102 C6
Didwana, *India* 68 F6
Die, *France* 21 D9
Diébougou, *Burkina Faso* 82 C4
Diecke, *Guinea* 82 D3
Diefenbaker, L., *Canada* 103 C7
Diego de Almagro, *Chile* ... 126 B1
Diego Garcia, *Ind. Oc.* 3 E13
Diekirch, *Lux.* 17 E6
Diéma, *Mali* 82 C3
Diembéring, *Senegal* 82 C1
Diemelsee △, *Germany* 24 D4
Dien Ban, *Vietnam* 64 E7
Dien Bien, *Vietnam* 58 G4
Dien Khanh, *Vietnam* 65 F7
Diepholz, *Germany* 24 C4
Dieppe, *France* 18 C8
Dierks, *U.S.A.* 113 H8
Diest, *Belgium* 17 D5
Dietikon, *Switz.* 25 H4
Dieulefit, *France* 21 D9
Dieuze, *France* 19 D13
Dif, *Somali Rep.* 75 G3
Differdange, *Lux.* 17 E5
Dig, *India* 68 F7
Digba, *Dem. Rep. of the Congo* . 86 B2
Digby, *Canada* 105 D6
Diggi, *India* 68 F6
Dighinala, *Bangla.* 67 H18
Dighton, *U.S.A.* 112 F4
Digna, *Mali* 82 C3
Digne-les-Bains, *France* 21 D10
Digoin, *France* 19 F11
Digor, *Turkey* 73 B10
Digos, *Phil.* 61 H6
Digranes, *Iceland* 8 C6
Digul ➤, *Indonesia* 63 F9
Digya △, *Ghana* 83 D5
Dihang = Brahmaputra ➤, *Asia* 69 H13
Dijlah, Nahr ➤, *Asia* 70 D5
Dijon, *France* 19 E12
Dikhil, *Djibouti* 81 E5
Dikili, *Turkey* 47 B8
Dikirnis, *Egypt* 80 H7
Dikkil = Dikhil, *Djibouti* .. 81 E5
Dikodougou, *Ivory C.* 82 D3
Diksmuide, *Belgium* 17 C2
Dikson, *Russia* 52 B9
Dikwa, *Nigeria* 83 C7
Dila, *Ethiopia* 81 F4
Dilek Yarimadisi △, *Turkey* . 47 D9
Dili, *E. Timor* 63 F7
Dilijan, *Armenia* 35 K7
Dilizhan = Dilijan, *Armenia* . 35 K7
Dilj, *Croatia* 28 E3
Dillenburg, *Germany* 24 E4
Dilley, *U.S.A.* 113 L5
Dilli = Delhi, *India* 68 E7
Dilling, *Sudan* 81 E2
Dillingen, *Bayern, Germany* . 25 G6
Dillingen, *Saarland, Germany* 25 F2
Dillingham, *U.S.A.* 100 C4
Dillon, *Canada* 103 B7
Dillon, *Mont., U.S.A.* 108 D7
Dillon, *S.C., U.S.A.* 115 H6
Dillon ➤, *Canada* 103 B7
Dillsburg, *U.S.A.* 116 F7
Dilly, *Mali* 82 C3
Dilolo, *Dem. Rep. of the Congo* 84 G4
Dilove, *Ukraine* 29 C9
Dimas, *Mexico* 118 C3
Dimashq, *Syria* 74 B5
Dimashq □, *Syria* 74 B5
Dimbaza, *S. Africa* 89 E4
Dimbokro, *Ivory C.* 82 D4
Dimboola, *Australia* 95 F3
Dîmbovița = Dâmbovița ➤, *Romania* ... 29 F11
Dimbulah, *Australia* 94 B4
Dimitrovgrad, *Bulgaria* 45 D9
Dimitrovgrad, *Russia* 34 C9
Dimitrovgrad, *Serbia & M.* .. 44 C6
Dimitrovo = Pernik, *Bulgaria* 44 D7
Dimmitt, *U.S.A.* 113 H3
Dimo, *Sudan* 81 F2

Dimona, *Israel* 74 D4
Dimovo, *Bulgaria* 44 C6
Dinagat, *Phil.* 61 F6
Dinajpur, *Bangla.* 67 G16
Dinan, *France* 18 D4
Dīnān Āb, *Iran* 71 C8
Dinant, *Belgium* 17 D4
Dinapur, *India* 69 G11
Dinar, *Turkey* 47 C12
Dīnār, Kūh-e, *Iran* 71 D6
Dinara Planina, *Croatia* 41 D13
Dinard, *France* 18 D4
Dinaric Alps = Dinara Planina, *Croatia* ... 41 D13
Dindanko, *Mali* 82 C3
Dinder △, *Sudan* 81 E4
Dinder, Nahr ed ➤, *Sudan* ... 81 E3
Dindigul, *India* 66 P11
Dindori, *India* 69 H9
Ding Xian = Dingzhou, *China* 56 E8
Dinga, *Pakistan* 68 G2
Dingalan, *Phil.* 61 D4
Dingbian, *China* 56 F4
Dingelstädt, *Germany* 24 D6
Dingle, *Ireland* 12 D1
Dingle, *Sweden* 11 F5
Dingle B., *Ireland* 12 D1
Dingmans Ferry, *U.S.A.* 117 E10
Dingnan, *China* 59 E10
Dingo, *Australia* 94 C4
Dingolfing, *Germany* 25 G8
Dingtao, *China* 56 G8
Dinguira, *Mali* 82 C2
Dinguiraye, *Guinea* 82 C2
Dingwall, *U.K.* 13 D4
Dingxi, *China* 56 G3
Dingxiang, *China* 56 E7
Dingyuan, *China* 59 A11
Dingzhou, *China* 56 E8
Dinh, Mui, *Vietnam* 65 G7
Dinh Lap, *Vietnam* 58 G6
Dinira △, *Venezuela* 121 E6
Dinokwe, *Botswana* 88 C4
Dinorwic, *Canada* 103 D10
Dinosaur △, *Canada* 102 C6
Dinosaur △, *U.S.A.* 108 F9
Dinuba, *U.S.A.* 110 J7
Diö, *Sweden* 11 H8
Dioïla, *Mali* 82 C3
Dioka, *Mali* 82 C2
Diongoï, *Mali* 82 C2
Diósgyör, *Hungary* 28 B5
Diosig, *Romania* 28 C7
Diougani, *Mali* 82 C4
Diouloulou, *Senegal* 82 C1
Dioura, *Mali* 82 C3
Diourbel, *Senegal* 82 C1
Dipalpur, *Pakistan* 68 D5
Diplo, *Pakistan* 68 G3
Dipolog, *Phil.* 61 G5
Dipperu △, *Australia* 94 C4
Dir, *Pakistan* 66 B7
Diré, *Mali* 82 B4
Dire Dawa, *Ethiopia* 81 F5
Diriamba, *Nic.* 120 D2
Dirk Hartog I., *Australia* .. 93 E1
Dirranbandi, *Australia* 95 D4
Disa, *India* 68 G5
Disa, *Sudan* 81 E3
Disappointment, C., *U.S.A.* . 108 C2
Disappointment, L., *Australia* 92 D3
Disaster B., *Australia* 95 F4
Discovery B., *Australia* 95 F3
Disentis Muster, *Switz.* 25 J4
Dishna, *Egypt* 80 B3
Disina, *Nigeria* 83 C6
Disko = Qeqertarsuaq, *Greenland* 101 B5
Disna = Dzisna ➤, *Belarus* .. 32 E5
Diss, *U.K.* 15 E9
Disteghil Sar, *Pakistan* 69 A6
Distrito Federal □, *Brazil* . 125 G9
Distrito Federal □, *Mexico* . 119 D5
Disûq, *Egypt* 80 H7
Diu, *India* 68 J4
Dīvāndarreh, *Iran* 70 C5
Dives ➤, *France* 18 C6
Dives-sur-Mer, *France* 18 C6
Divichi = Däväçi, *Azerbaijan* 35 K9
Divide, *U.S.A.* 108 D7
Dividing Ra., *Australia* 93 E2
Divinópolis, *Brazil* 125 H10
Divjake, *Albania* 44 F3
Divnoye, *Russia* 35 H6
Divo, *Ivory C.* 82 D3
Divriği, *Turkey* 73 C8
Dīwāl Kol, *Afghan.* 68 B2
Dixie Mt., *U.S.A.* 110 F6
Dixon, *Calif., U.S.A.* 110 G5
Dixon, *Ill., U.S.A.* 112 E10
Dixon Entrance, *U.S.A.* 100 C6
Dixville, *Canada* 117 A13
Diyadin, *Turkey* 73 C10
Diyālā □, *Iraq* 70 C5
Diyālā ➤, *Iraq* 70 C5
Diyarbakır, *Turkey* 70 B4
Diyodar, *India* 68 G4
Djakarta = Jakarta, *Indonesia* 63 G12
Djamba, *Angola* 88 B1
Djambala, *Congo* 84 E2
Djanet, *Algeria* 78 D7
Djawa = Jawa, *Indonesia* 62 F3
Djelfa, *Algeria* 78 B6
Djema, *C.A.R.* 86 A2
Djenné, *Mali* 82 C4
Djerba, I. de, *Tunisia* 79 B8
Djerid, Chott, *Tunisia* 78 B7
Djibo, *Burkina Faso* 83 C4
Djibouti, *Djibouti* 81 E5
Djibouti ■, *Africa* 81 E5
Djolu, *Dem. Rep. of the Congo* 84 D4
Djougou, *Benin* 83 D5
Djoum, *Cameroon* 84 D2

Djourab, Erg du, *Chad* 79 E9
Djugu, *Dem. Rep. of the Congo* . 86 B3
Djúpivogur, *Iceland* 8 D6
Djurås, *Sweden* 10 D9
Djurö △, *Sweden* 11 F7
Djursland, *Denmark* 11 H4
Dmitriya Lapteva, Proliv, *Russia* 53 B15
Dmitriyev Lgovskiy, *Russia* . 33 F8
Dmitrov, *Russia* 32 D9
Dmitrovsk-Orlovskiy, *Russia* 33 F8
Dnepr = Dnipro ➤, *Ukraine* .. 33 J7
Dneprodzerzhinsk = Dniprodzerzhynsk, *Ukraine* .. 33 H8
Dneprodzerzhinskoye Vdkhr. = Dniprodzerzhynske Vdskh., *Ukraine* ... 33 H8
Dnepropetrovsk = Dnipropetrovsk, *Ukraine* ... 33 H8
Dneprorudnoye = Dniprorudne, *Ukraine* ... 33 J8
Dnestr = Dnister ➤, *Europe* . 33 J6
Dnieper = Dnipro ➤, *Ukraine* 33 J7
Dniester = Dnister ➤, *Europe* 33 J6
Dnipro ➤, *Ukraine* 33 J7
Dniprodzerzhynsk, *Ukraine* .. 33 H8
Dniprodzerzhynske Vdskh., *Ukraine* ... 33 H8
Dnipropetrovsk, *Ukraine* 33 H8
Dniprorudne, *Ukraine* 33 J8
Dnister ➤, *Europe* 33 J6
Dnistrovskyy Lyman, *Ukraine* 33 J6
Dno, *Russia* 32 D5
Dnyapro = Dnipro ➤, *Ukraine* 33 J7
Doaktown, *Canada* 105 C6
Doan Hung, *Vietnam* 58 G5
Doany, *Madag.* 89 A8
Doba, *Chad* 79 G9
Dobandi, *Pakistan* 68 D2
Dobbiaco, *Italy* 41 B9
Dobbyn, *Australia* 94 B3
Dobele, *Latvia* 9 H20
Dobele □, *Latvia* 30 B10
Döbeln, *Germany* 24 D9
Doberai, Jazirah, *Indonesia* 63 E8
Dobiegniew, *Poland* 31 F2
Doblas, *Argentina* 126 D3
Dobo, *Indonesia* 63 F8
Doboj, *Bos.-H.* 28 F3
Dobra, *Dâmbovița, Romania* .. 29 F10
Dobra, *Hunedoara, Romania* .. 28 E7
Dobra, *Zachodnio-Pomorskie, Poland* ... 30 E2
Dobre Miasto, *Poland* 30 E7
Dobrich, *Bulgaria* 45 C11
Dobrinishta, *Bulgaria* 44 E7
Dobříš, *Czech Rep.* 26 B7
Dobrodzień, *Poland* 31 H5
Dobromyl, *Ukraine* 31 J9
Dobron, *Ukraine* 28 B7
Dobropole, *Ukraine* 33 H9
Dobrovolsk, *Russia* 30 D9
Dobruja, *Europe* 29 F13
Dobrush, *Belarus* 33 F6
Dobrzany, *Poland* 30 E2
Dobrzyń nad Wisłą, *Poland* .. 31 F6
Doc, Mui, *Vietnam* 64 D6
Docker River, *Australia* 93 D4
Docksta, *Sweden* 10 A12
Doctor Arroyo, *Mexico* 118 C4
Doda, *India* 69 C6
Doda, L., *Canada* 104 C4
Dodecanese = Dhodhekánisos, *Greece* ... 47 E8
Dodge City, *U.S.A.* 113 G5
Dodge L., *Canada* 103 B7
Dodgeville, *U.S.A.* 112 D9
Dodo, *Cameroon* 83 D7
Dodo, *Sudan* 81 F2
Dodola, *Ethiopia* 81 F4
Dodoma, *Tanzania* 86 D4
Dodoma □, *Tanzania* 86 D4
Dodona, *Greece* 46 B2
Dodori △, *Kenya* 86 C5
Dodsland, *Canada* 103 C7
Dodson, *U.S.A.* 108 B9
Doesburg, *Neths.* 17 B6
Doetinchem, *Neths.* 17 C6
Dog Creek, *Canada* 102 C4
Dog L., *Man., Canada* 103 C9
Dog L., *Ont., Canada* 104 C2
Doğanşehir, *Turkey* 72 C7
Dogliani, *Italy* 40 D4
Dogondoutchi, *Niger* 83 C5
Dogran, *Pakistan* 68 D5
Doğubayazıt, *Turkey* 70 B5
Doguéraoua, *Niger* 83 C6
Doha = Ad Dawḥah, *Qatar* 71 E6
Dohazari, *Bangla.* 67 H18
Dohrighat, *India* 69 F10
Doi, *Indonesia* 63 D7
Doi Inthanon △, *Thailand* ... 64 C2
Doi Khuntan △, *Thailand* 64 C2
Doi Luang, *Thailand* 64 C3
Doi Luang △, *Thailand* 64 C2
Doi Saket, *Thailand* 64 C2
Doi Suthep △, *Thailand* 64 C2
Doig ➤, *Nigeria* 83 D7
Dois Irmãos, Sa., *Brazil* ... 125 E10
Dojransko Jezero, *Macedonia* 44 E6
Dokkum, *Neths.* 17 A5
Dokri, *Pakistan* 68 F3
Dokuchayevsk, *Ukraine* 33 J9
Dol-de-Bretagne, *France* 18 D5
Dolac, *Serbia & M.* 44 D4
Dolak, Pulau, *Indonesia* 63 F9
Dolbeau-Mistassini, *Canada* . 105 C5
Dole, *France* 19 E12
Doleib, Wadi ➤, *Sudan* 81 E3
Dolenji Logatec, *Slovenia* .. 41 C11

Dolgellau, *U.K.* 14 E4
Dolgelley = Dolgellau, *U.K.* 14 E4
Dolhasca, *Romania* 29 C11
Dolianova, *Italy* 42 C2
Dolinskaya = Dolynska, *Ukraine* 33 H7
Dolj □, *Romania* 29 F8
Dollard, *Neths.* 17 A7
Dolna Banya, *Bulgaria* 44 D7
Dolni Chiflik, *Bulgaria* 45 D11
Dolni Dŭbnik, *Bulgaria* 45 C8
Dolnośląskie □, *Poland* 31 G3
Dolný Kubín, *Slovak Rep.* ... 27 B12
Dolo, *Ethiopia* 81 G5
Dolo, *Italy* 41 C9
Dolomites = Dolomiti, *Italy* 41 B8
Dolomiti, *Italy* 41 B8
Dolomiti Bellunesi △, *Italy* 41 B8
Dolores, *Argentina* 126 D4
Dolores, *Uruguay* 126 C4
Dolores, *U.S.A.* 109 H9
Dolores ➤, *U.S.A.* 109 G9
Dolovo, *Serbia & M.* 28 E5
Dolphin, C., *Falk. Is.* 128 G5
Dolphin and Union Str., *Canada* 100 B8
Dolsk, *Poland* 31 G4
Dolyna, *Ukraine* 29 B9
Dolynska, *Ukraine* 33 H7
Dolynske, *Ukraine* 29 C14
Dolzhanskaya, *Russia* 33 J9
Dom Pedrito, *Brazil* 127 C5
Doma, *Nigeria* 83 D6
Doma △, *Zimbabwe* 87 F3
Domaniç, *Turkey* 47 B11
Domariaganj ➤, *India* 69 F10
Domasi, *Malawi* 87 F4
Domažlice, *Czech Rep.* 26 B5
Dombarovskiy, *Russia* 52 D6
Dombås, *Norway* 9 E13
Dombasle-sur-Meurthe, *France* 19 D13
Dombes, *France* 21 C9
Dombóvár, *Hungary* 28 D3
Dombrád, *Hungary* 28 B6
Dome Fuji, *Antarctica* 5 D5
Domel I. = Letsôk-aw Kyun, *Burma* ... 65 G2
Domérat, *France* 19 F9
Domeyko, *Chile* 126 B1
Domeyko, Cordillera, *Chile* . 126 A2
Domfront, *France* 18 D6
Dominador, *Chile* 126 A2
Dominica ■, *W. Indies* 121 C7
Dominica Passage, *W. Indies* 121 C7
Dominican Rep. ■, *W. Indies* 121 C5
Dömitz, *Germany* 24 B7
Domme, *France* 20 D5
Domnești, *Romania* 29 E9
Domodóssola, *Italy* 40 B5
Domogled-Valea Cernei △, *Romania* ... 28 F7
Dompaire, *France* 19 D13
Dompierre-sur-Besbre, *France* 19 F10
Dompim, *Ghana* 82 D4
Domrémy-la-Pucelle, *France* 19 D12
Domville, Mt., *Australia* ... 95 D5
Domvraína, *Greece* 46 C4
Domžale, *Slovenia* 41 B11
Don ➤, *Russia* 33 J10
Don ➤, *Aberds., U.K.* 13 D6
Don ➤, *S. Yorks., U.K.* 14 D7
Don, C., *Australia* 92 B5
Don Benito, *Spain* 37 G5
Don Figuerero Mts., *Jamaica* 120 a
Don Sak, *Thailand* .... 65 b
Dona Ana = Nhamaabué, *Mozam.* ... 87 F4
Doña Mencía, *Spain* 37 H6
Donaghadee, *U.K.* 12 B6
Donald, *Australia* 95 F3
Donalda, *Canada* 102 C6
Donaldsonville, *U.S.A.* 113 K9
Donalsonville, *U.S.A.* 115 K3
Donau = Dunărea ➤, *Europe* . 29 E14
Donau ➤, *Austria* 27 C10
Donau Auen △, *Austria* 27 C9
Donaueschingen, *Germany* 25 H4
Donauwörth, *Germany* 25 G6
Doncaster, *U.K.* 14 D6
Dondo, *Mozam.* 87 F3
Dondo, Teluk, *Indonesia* 63 D6
Dondra Head, *Sri Lanka* 66 S12
Donduşeni, *Moldova* 29 B12
Donegal, *Ireland* 12 B3
Donegal □, *Ireland* 12 B4
Donegal B., *Ireland* 12 B3
Donets ➤, *Russia* 35 G5
Donets Basin, *Ukraine* 6 F13
Donetsk, *Ukraine* 33 J9
Dong Ba Thin, *Vietnam* 65 F7
Dong Dang, *Vietnam* 58 G6
Dong Giam, *Vietnam* 64 C5
Dong Ha, *Vietnam* 64 D6
Dong Hene, *Laos* 64 D5
Dong Hoi, *Vietnam* 64 D6
Dong Jiang ➤, *China* 59 F10
Dong Khe, *Vietnam* 58 A6
Dong Ujimqin Qi, *China* 56 B9
Dong Van, *Vietnam* 64 A5
Dong Xoai, *Vietnam* 65 G6
Donga, *Nigeria* 83 D7
Dong'an, *China* 59 D8
Dongara, *Australia* 93 E1
Dongbei, *China* 57 D13
Dongchuan, *China* 58 D4
Donges, *France* 18 E4
Dongfang, *China* 64 C7
Dongfeng, *China* 57 C13
Donggala, *Indonesia* 63 E5
Donggan, *China* 58 F5
Donggou, *China* 57 E13
Dongguan, *China* 59 F9
Dongguang, *China* 56 F9

Donghai Dao, *China* 59 G8
Dongjingcheng, *China* 57 B15
Dongkou, *China* 59 D8
Donglan, *China* 58 E6
Dongliu, *China* 59 B11
Dongmen, *China* 58 F6
Dongning, *China* 57 B16
Dongnyi, *China* 58 C3
Dongola, *Sudan* 80 D3
Dongping, *China* 56 G9
Dongsha Dao, *China* 59 G11
Dongshan, *China* 59 F11
Dongsheng = Ordos, *China* ... 56 E6
Dongtai, *China* 57 H11
Dongting Hu, *China* 59 C9
Dongtou, *China* 59 D13
Dongxiang, *China* 59 C11
Dongxing, *China* 59 C13
Dongyang, *China* 59 C13
Dongzhi, *China* 59 B11
Donington, C., *Australia* ... 95 E2
Doniphan, *U.S.A.* 113 G9
Donja Stubica, *Croatia* 41 C12
Donji Dušnik, *Serbia & M.* .. 44 C6
Donji Miholjac, *Croatia* 28 E3
Donji Milanovac, *Serbia & M.* 44 B6
Donji Vakuf, *Bos.-H.* 28 F2
Dønna, *Norway* 8 C15
Donna, *U.S.A.* 113 M5
Donnaconna, *Canada* 105 C5
Donnelly's Crossing, *N.Z.* .. 91 F4
Donnybrook, *Australia* 93 F2
Donnybrook, *S. Africa* 89 D4
Donora, *U.S.A.* 116 F5
Donostia = Donostia-San Sebastián, *Spain* ... 38 B3
Donostia-San Sebastián, *Spain* 38 B3
Donskoy, *Russia* 32 F10
Donsol, *Phil.* 61 E5
Donzère, *France* 21 D8
Donzy, *France* 19 E10
Doon ➤, *U.K.* 13 F4
Dora, L., *Australia* 92 D3
Dora Báltea ➤, *Italy* 40 C5
Dora Ripária ➤, *Italy* 40 C4
Doran L., *Canada* 103 A7
Dorchester, *U.K.* 15 G5
Dorchester, C., *Canada* 101 B12
Dordabis, *Namibia* 88 C2
Dordogne □, *France* 20 C4
Dordogne ➤, *France* 20 C4
Dordrecht, *Neths.* 17 C4
Dordrecht, *S. Africa* 88 E4
Dore ➤, *France* 20 C7
Dore, Mts. ➤, *France* 20 C6
Doré L., *Canada* 103 C7
Doré Lake, *Canada* 103 C7
Dorfen, *Germany* 25 G8
Dorgali, *Italy* 42 B2
Dori, *Burkina Faso* 83 C4
Doring ➤, *S. Africa* 88 E2
Doringbos, *S. Africa* 88 E2
Dorking, *U.K.* 15 F7
Dormaa-Ahenkro, *Ghana* 82 D4
Dormans, *France* 19 C10
Dormo, Ras, *Eritrea* 81 E5
Dornbirn, *Austria* 26 D2
Dornes, *France* 19 F10
Dornești, *Romania* 29 C11
Dornie, *U.K.* 13 D3
Dornoch, *U.K.* 13 D4
Dornoch Firth, *U.K.* 13 D4
Dornogovĭ □, *Mongolia* 56 C6
Doro, *Mali* 83 B4
Dorog, *Hungary* 28 C3
Dorogobuzh, *Russia* 32 E7
Dorohoi, *Romania* 29 C11
Döröö Nuur, *Mongolia* 60 B4
Dorr, *Iran* 71 C6
Dorre I., *Australia* 93 E1
Dorrigo, *Australia* 95 E5
Dorris, *U.S.A.* 108 F3
Dorset, *Canada* 116 A6
Dorset, *U.S.A.* 116 E4
Dorset □, *U.K.* 15 G5
Dorsten, *Germany* 24 D2
Dortmund, *Germany* 24 D3
Dortmund-Ems-Kanal ➤, *Germany* ... 24 D3
Dörtyol, *Turkey* 72 D7
Dorum, *Germany* 24 B4
Doruma, *Dem. Rep. of the Congo* 86 B2
Dorūneh, *Iran* 71 C8
Dos Bahías, C., *Argentina* .. 128 E3
Dos Hermanas, *Spain* 37 H5
Dos Palos, *U.S.A.* 110 J6
Döşemealtı, *Turkey* 47 D12
Dosso, *Niger* 83 C5
Dosso △, *Niger* 83 C5
Dothan, *U.S.A.* 115 K3
Doty, *U.S.A.* 110 D3
Douai, *France* 19 B10
Douako, *Guinea* 82 D2
Douala, *Cameroon* 83 E6
Douarnenez, *France* 18 D2
Doubabougou, *Mali* 82 C3
Double Island Pt., *Australia* 95 D5
Double Mountain Fork ➤, *U.S.A.* ... 113 J4
Doubrava ➤, *Czech Rep.* 26 A8
Doubs □, *France* 19 E13
Doubs ➤, *France* 19 F12
Doubtful Sd., *N.Z.* 91 L1
Doubtless B., *N.Z.* 91 F4
Doudeville, *France* 18 E6
Doué-la-Fontaine, *France* ... 18 E6
Douentza, *Mali* 82 C4
Douentza △, *Mali* 82 B4

Douglas, *Wyo., U.S.A.* 112 D2
Douglas Apsley △, *Australia* ... 95 G4
Douglas Chan., *Canada* 102 C3
Douglas Pt., *Canada* 116 B3
Douglasville, *U.S.A.* 115 J3
Doukáton, Ákra, *Greece* 46 C2
Doulevant-le-Château, *France* . 19 D11
Doullens, *France* 19 B9
Doumen, *China* 59 F9
Douna, *Mali* 82 C3
Dounreay, *U.K.* 13 C5
Dourada, Serra, *Brazil* 125 F9
Dourados, *Brazil* 127 A5
Dourados, Serra dos, *Brazil* .. 127 A5
Dourados →, *Brazil* 127 A5
Dourdan, *France* 19 D9
Douro →, *Europe* 36 D2
Douvaine, *France* 19 F13
Douvres-la-Délivrande, *France* . 18 C6
Douze →, *France* 20 E3
Dove →, *U.K.* 14 E6
Dove Creek, *U.S.A.* 109 H9
Dover, *Australia* 95 G4
Dover, *U.K.* 15 F9
Dover, *Del., U.S.A.* 114 F8
Dover, *N.H., U.S.A.* 117 C14
Dover, *N.J., U.S.A.* 117 F10
Dover, *Ohio, U.S.A.* 116 F3
Dover, Pt., *Australia* 93 F4
Dover, Str. of, *Europe* 15 G9
Dover-Foxcroft, *U.S.A.* 115 C11
Dover Plains, *U.S.A.* 117 E11
Dovey = Dyfi →, *U.K.* 15 E3
Dovhe, *Ukraine* 29 B8
Dovrefjell, *Norway* 9 E13
Dow Rūd, *Iran* 71 C6
Dowa, *Malawi* 87 E3
Dowagiac, *U.S.A.* 114 E2
Dowerin, *Australia* 93 F2
Dowgha'i, *Iran* 71 B8
Dowlatābād, *Iran* 71 D8
Down □, *U.K.* 12 B5
Downey, *Calif., U.S.A.* 111 M8
Downey, *Idaho, U.S.A.* 108 E7
Downham Market, *U.K.* 15 E8
Downieville, *U.S.A.* 110 F6
Downpatrick, *U.K.* 12 B6
Downpatrick Hd., *Ireland* 12 B2
Downsville, *U.S.A.* 117 D10
Downton, Mt., *Canada* 102 C4
Dowsārī, *Iran* 71 D8
Doyle, *U.S.A.* 110 E6
Doylestown, *U.S.A.* 117 F9
Dozois, Rés., *Canada* 104 C4
Dra Khel, *Pakistan* 68 F2
Drac →, *France* 21 C9
Dračevo, *Macedonia* 44 E5
Drachten, *Neths.* 17 A6
Drăgănești, *Moldova* 29 C13
Drăgănești, *Romania* 29 F9
Drăgănești-Olt, *Romania* 29 F9
Drăgănești-Vlașca, *Romania* ... 29 F10
Dragaš, *Serbia & M.* 44 D4
Drăgășani, *Romania* 29 F9
Dragichyn, *Belarus* 33 F3
Dragocvet, *Serbia & M.* 44 C5
Dragon's Mouth = Boca de
  Drago, *Venezuela* 125 K15
Dragovishtitsa, *Bulgaria* 44 D6
Draguignan, *France* 21 E10
Drahove, *Ukraine* 29 B8
Drain, *U.S.A.* 108 E2
Drake, *U.S.A.* 112 B4
Drake Passage, *S. Ocean* 5 B17
Drakensberg, *S. Africa* 89 D4
Dráma, *Greece* 45 E8
Dráma □, *Greece* 45 E8
Drammen, *Norway* 9 G14
Drangajökull, *Iceland* 8 C2
Dranov, Ostrov, *Romania* 29 F14
Dras, *India* 69 B6
Drau = Drava →, *Croatia* 28 E3
Drava →, *Croatia* 28 E3
Dravograd, *Slovenia* 41 B12
Drawa →, *Poland* 31 F2
Drawieński △, *Poland* 31 E2
Drawno, *Poland* 31 E2
Drawsko Pomorskie, *Poland* ... 30 E2
Drayton Valley, *Canada* 102 C6
Dreieich, *Germany* 25 E4
Dren, *Serbia & M.* 44 C4
Drenthe □, *Neths.* 17 B6
Drepanum, C., *Cyprus* 49 E11
Dresden, *Canada* 116 D2
Dresden, *Germany* 24 D9
Dreux, *France* 18 D8
Drezdenko, *Poland* 31 F2
Driffield, *U.K.* 14 C7
Driftwood, *U.S.A.* 116 E6
Driggs, *U.S.A.* 108 E8
Drin →, *Albania* 44 D3
Drin i Zi →, *Albania* 44 E4
Drina →, *Bos.-H.* 44 B3
Drincea →, *Romania* 28 F7
Drinjača →, *Bos.-H.* 28 F4
Drissa = Vyerkhnyadzvinsk,
  Belarus 32 E4
Drniš, *Croatia* 41 E13
Drøbak, *Norway* 9 G14
Drobeta-Turnu Severin, *Romania* 28 F7
Drobin, *Poland* 31 F6
Drochia, *Moldova* 29 B12
Drogheda, *Ireland* 12 C5
Drogichin = Dragichyn, *Belarus* 33 F3
Drogobych = Drohobych, *Ukraine* 31 J10
Drohiczyn, *Poland* 31 F9
Drohobych, *Ukraine* 31 J10
Droichead Atha = Drogheda,
  Ireland 12 C5
Droichead Nua, *Ireland* 12 C5
Droitwich, *U.K.* 15 E5
Drôme □, *France* 21 D9
Drôme →, *France* 21 D8

Dromedary, C., *Australia* 95 F5
Drömling ○, *Germany* 24 C7
Dromore, *U.K.* 12 B4
Dromore West, *Ireland* 12 B3
Dronero, *Italy* 40 D4
Dronfield, *U.K.* 14 D6
Dronne →, *France* 20 C3
Dronning Maud Land, *Antarctica* 5 D3
Dronninglund, *Denmark* 11 G4
Dronten, *Neths.* 17 B5
Dropt →, *France* 20 D3
Drosendorf, *Austria* 26 C8
Droué, *France* 18 D8
Drumbo, *Canada* 116 C4
Drumheller, *Canada* 102 C6
Drummond, *U.S.A.* 108 C7
Drummond I., *U.S.A.* 114 C4
Drummond Pt., *Australia* 95 E2
Drummond Ra., *Australia* 94 C4
Drummondville, *Canada* 104 C5
Drumright, *U.S.A.* 113 H6
Druskininkai, *Lithuania* 9 J20
Drut →, *Belarus* 33 F6
Druya, *Belarus* 32 E4
Druzhba, *Bulgaria* 45 C12
Druzhina, *Russia* 53 C15
Drvar, *Bos.-H.* 41 D13
Drvenik, *Croatia* 41 E13
Drwęca →, *Poland* 31 E5
Dry Harbour Mts., *Jamaica* ... 120 a
Dry Tortugas, *U.S.A.* 120 B3
Dryanovo, *Bulgaria* 45 D9
Dryden, *Canada* 103 D10
Dryden, *U.S.A.* 117 D8
Drygalski I., *Antarctica* 5 C7
Drysdale →, *Australia* 92 B4
Drysdale I., *Australia* 94 A2
Drysdale River △, *Australia* ... 92 B4
Drzewica, *Poland* 31 G7
Drzewiczka →, *Poland* 31 G7
Dschang, *Cameroon* 83 D7
Du Bois, *U.S.A.* 116 E6
Du Gué →, *Canada* 104 A5
Du He, *China* 59 A8
Du Quoin, *U.S.A.* 112 G10
Du'an, *China* 58 F7
Duanesburg, *U.S.A.* 117 D10
Duaringa, *Australia* 94 C4
Duarte, Pico, *Dom. Rep.* 121 D5
Ḍubā, *Si. Arabia* 70 E2
Dubai = Dubayy, *U.A.E.* 71 E7
Dubāsari, *Moldova* 29 C14
Dubāsari Vdkhr., *Moldova* 29 C13
Dubawnt →, *Canada* 103 A8
Dubawnt L., *Canada* 103 A8
Dubayy, *U.A.E.* 71 E7
Dubbo, *Australia* 95 E4
Dübendorf, *Switz.* 25 H4
Dubele, *Dem. Rep. of the Congo* 86 B2
Dübendorf, *Switz.* 25 H4
Dubica, *Croatia* 41 C13
Dublin, *Ireland* 12 C5
Dublin, *Ga., U.S.A.* 115 J4
Dublin, *Tex., U.S.A.* 113 J5
Dublin □, *Ireland* 12 C5
Dublin ✈ (DUB), *Ireland* 12 C5
Dubna, *Russia* 32 D9
Dubnica nad Váhom, *Slovak Rep.* 27 C11
Dubno, *Ukraine* 33 G3
Dubois, *U.S.A.* 108 D7
Dubossary = Dubāsari, *Moldova* 29 C14
Dubossary Vdkhr. = Dubāsari
  Vdkhr., *Moldova* 29 C13
Dubove, *Ukraine* 29 B8
Dubovka, *Russia* 35 F7
Dubovskoye, *Russia* 35 G6
Dubrajpur, *India* 69 H12
Dubréka, *Guinea* 82 D2
Dubrovitsa = Dubrovytsya,
  Ukraine 33 G4
Dubrovnik, *Croatia* 44 D2
Dubrovytsya, *Ukraine* 33 G4
Dubuque, *U.S.A.* 112 D9
Dubysa →, *Lithuania* 30 C10
Duchang, *China* 59 C11
Duchesne, *U.S.A.* 108 F8
Duchess, *Australia* 94 C2
Ducie I., *Pac. Oc.* 97 K15
Duck →, *U.S.A.* 115 G2
Duck Cr. →, *Australia* 92 D2
Duck Lake, *Canada* 103 C7
Duck Mountain, *Canada* 103 C8
Duckwall, Mt., *U.S.A.* 110 H6
Duderstadt, *Germany* 24 D6
Dudhi, *India* 67 G13
Dudinka, *Russia* 53 C9
Dudley, *U.K.* 15 E5
Dudwa, *India* 69 E9
Duékoué, *Ivory C.* 82 D3
Dueñas, *Spain* 36 D6
Duero = Douro →, *Europe* 36 D2
Dufftown, *U.K.* 13 D5
Dufourspitz, *Switz.* 25 K3
Dugi Otok, *Croatia* 41 D11
Dugo Selo, *Croatia* 41 C13
Duifken Pt., *Australia* 94 A3
Duisburg, *Germany* 24 D2
Duiwelskloof, *S. Africa* 89 C5
Dujiangyan, *China* 58 B4
Duk Fadiat, *Sudan* 81 F3
Duk Faiwil, *Sudan* 81 F3
Dukat, *Albania* 44 F3
Dūkdamīn, *Iran* 71 C8
Dukhān, *Qatar* 71 E6
Dukhovshchina, *Russia* 32 E7
Duki, *Pakistan* 66 D6
Dukla, *Poland* 31 J8
Duku, *Bauchi, Nigeria* 83 C7
Duku, *Sokoto, Nigeria* 83 C5
Dulag, *Phil.* 61 F6
Dulce, *U.S.A.* 109 H10

Dulce →, *Argentina* 126 C3
Dulce, G., *Costa Rica* 120 E3
Dulf, *Iraq* 70 C5
Dŭlgopol, *Bulgaria* 45 C11
Dulit, Banjaran, *Malaysia* 62 D4
Duliu, *China* 56 E9
Dullewala, *Pakistan* 68 D4
Dullstroom, *S. Africa* 89 D5
Dülmen, *Germany* 24 D3
Dulovo, *Bulgaria* 45 C11
Dulq Maghār, *Syria* 70 B3
Duluth, *U.S.A.* 112 B8
Dum Dum, *India* 69 H13
Dum Duma, *India* 67 F19
Dūmā, *Syria* 74 B5
Dumaguete, *Phil.* 61 G5
Dumai, *Indonesia* 62 D2
Dumaran, *Phil.* 61 F3
Dumas, *Ark., U.S.A.* 113 J9
Dumas, *Tex., U.S.A.* 113 H4
Dumayr, *Syria* 74 B5
Dumbarton, *U.K.* 13 F4
Dumbier, *Slovak Rep.* 27 C12
Dumbleyung, *Australia* 93 F2
Dumboa, *Nigeria* 83 C7
Dumbrăveni, *Romania* 29 D9
Dumfries, *U.K.* 13 F5
Dumfries & Galloway □, *U.K.* . 13 F5
Dumitrești, *Romania* 29 E11
Dumka, *India* 69 G12
Dumlupınar, *Turkey* 47 C12
Dümmer, *Germany* 24 C4
Dümmer ○, *Germany* 24 C4
Dumoine →, *Canada* 104 C4
Dumoine, L., *Canada* 104 C4
Dumont d'Urville, *Antarctica* .. 5 C10
Dumraon, *India* 69 G11
Dumyât, *Egypt* 80 H7
Dumyât, Masabb, *Egypt* 80 H7
Dún Dealgan = Dundalk, *Ireland* 12 B5
Dún Laoghaire, *Ireland* 12 C5
Dun-le-Palestel, *France* 19 F8
Dun-sur-Auron, *France* 19 F9
Dun-sur-Meuse, *France* 19 C12
Duna = Dunărea →, *Europe* .. 29 E14
Duna →, *Hungary* 28 E3
Duna-Drava △, *Hungary* 28 D3
Dunaföldvár, *Hungary* 28 D3
Dunagiri, *India* 69 D8
Dunaj = Dunărea →, *Europe* .. 29 E14
Dunaj →, *Slovak Rep.* 27 D11
Dunajec →, *Poland* 31 H7
Dunajská Streda, *Slovak Rep.* .. 27 C10
Dunakeszi, *Hungary* 28 C4
Dunapataj, *Hungary* 28 D4
Dunărea →, *Europe* 29 E14
Dunaszekcső, *Hungary* 28 D3
Dunaújváros, *Hungary* 28 D3
Dunav = Dunărea →, *Europe* .. 29 E14
Dunavațu de Jos, *Romania* ... 29 F14
Dunavtsi, *Bulgaria* 44 C6
Dunay, *Russia* 54 C6
Dunayivtsi, *Ukraine* 29 B11
Dunback, *N.Z.* 91 L3
Dunbar, *U.K.* 13 E6
Dunblane, *U.K.* 13 E5
Duncan, *Canada* 102 D4
Duncan, *Ariz., U.S.A.* 109 K9
Duncan, *Okla., U.S.A.* 113 H6
Duncan, L., *Canada* 104 B4
Duncan L., *Canada* 102 A6
Duncan Town, *Bahamas* 120 B4
Duncannon, *U.S.A.* 116 F7
Duncansby Head, *U.K.* 13 C5
Duncansville, *U.S.A.* 116 F6
Dundaga, *Latvia* 30 A9
Dundalk, *Canada* 116 B4
Dundalk, *Ireland* 12 B5
Dundalk, *U.S.A.* 114 F7
Dundalk Bay, *Ireland* 12 C5
Dundas = Uummannaq,
  Greenland 4 B4
Dundas = Uummannaq,
  Greenland 4 B5
Dundas, *Canada* 116 C5
Dundas, L., *Australia* 93 F3
Dundas Str., *Australia* 92 B5
Dundee, *S. Africa* 89 D5
Dundee, *U.K.* 13 E6
Dundee, *U.S.A.* 116 D8
Dundee City □, *U.K.* 13 E6
Dundgovĭ □, *Mongolia* 56 B4
Dundrum, *U.K.* 12 B6
Dundrum B., *U.K.* 12 B6
Dunedin, *N.Z.* 91 L3
Dunedin, *U.S.A.* 115 L4
Dunfermline, *U.K.* 13 E5
Dungannon, *Canada* 116 C3
Dungannon, *U.K.* 12 B5
Dungarpur, *India* 68 H5
Dungarvan, *Ireland* 12 D4
Dungarvan Harbour, *Ireland* .. 12 D4
Dungeness, *U.K.* 15 G8
Dungo, L. do, *Angola* 88 B2
Dungog, *Australia* 95 E5
Dungu, *Dem. Rep. of the Congo* 86 B2
Dungun, *Malaysia* 65 K4
Dungunâb, *Sudan* 80 C4
Dungunâb, Khalîg, *Sudan* 80 C4
Dunhua, *China* 57 C15
Dunhuang, *China* 60 B4
Dunk I., *Australia* 94 B4
Dunkassa, *Benin* 83 C5
Dunkeld, *Australia* 95 E4
Dunkeld, *U.K.* 13 E5
Dunkerque, *France* 19 A9
Dunkery Beacon, *U.K.* 15 F4
Dunkirk = Dunkerque, *France* . 19 A9
Dunkirk, *U.S.A.* 116 D5
Dunkuj, *Sudan* 81 E3

Dunkwa, *Central, Ghana* 82 D4
Dunkwa, *Central, Ghana* 83 D4
Dúnleary = Dún Laoghaire,
  Ireland 12 C5
Dunleer, *Ireland* 12 C5
Dunmanus B., *Ireland* 12 E2
Dunmanway, *Ireland* 12 E2
Dunmara, *Australia* 94 B1
Dunmore, *U.S.A.* 117 E9
Dunmore Hd., *Ireland* 12 D1
Dunmore Town, *Bahamas* 120 A4
Dunn, *U.S.A.* 115 H6
Dunnellon, *U.S.A.* 115 L4
Dunnet Hd., *U.K.* 13 C5
Dunning, *U.S.A.* 112 E4
Dunnville, *Canada* 116 D5
Dunolly, *Australia* 95 F3
Dunoon, *U.K.* 13 F4
Dunphy, *U.S.A.* 108 F5
Dunqul, *Egypt* 80 C3
Duns, *U.K.* 13 F6
Dunseith, *U.S.A.* 112 A4
Dunsmuir, *U.S.A.* 108 F2
Dunstable, *U.K.* 15 F7
Dunstan Mts., *N.Z.* 91 L2
Dunster, *Canada* 102 C5
Dunvegan, *U.K.* 13 D2
Dunvegan L., *Canada* 103 A7
Duolun, *China* 56 C9
Duong Dong, *Vietnam* 65 G4
Dupree, *U.S.A.* 112 C4
Dupuyer, *U.S.A.* 108 B7
Durack →, *Australia* 92 C4
Durack Ra., *Australia* 92 C4
Durağan, *Turkey* 72 B6
Durak, *Turkey* 47 B10
Durance →, *France* 21 E8
Durand, *U.S.A.* 112 C9
Durango, *Mexico* 118 C4
Durango, *U.S.A.* 109 H10
Durango □, *Mexico* 118 C4
Durankulak, *Bulgaria* 45 C12
Durant, *Miss., U.S.A.* 113 J10
Durant, *Okla., U.S.A.* 113 J6
Duratón →, *Spain* 36 D6
Durazno, *Uruguay* 126 C4
Durazzo = Durrës, *Albania* ... 44 E3
Durban, *France* 20 F6
Durban, *S. Africa* 89 D5
Durbuy, *Belgium* 17 D5
Dúrcal, *Spain* 37 J7
Đurđevac, *Croatia* 28 D2
Düren, *Germany* 24 E2
Durg, *India* 67 J12
Durgapur, *India* 69 H12
Durham, *Canada* 116 B4
Durham, *U.K.* 14 C6
Durham, *Calif., U.S.A.* 110 F5
Durham, *N.C., U.S.A.* 115 H6
Durham, *N.H., U.S.A.* 117 C14
Durham □, *U.K.* 14 C6
Durlești, *Moldova* 29 C13
Durmā, *Si. Arabia* 70 E5
Durmitor △, *Serbia & M.* 44 C2
Durness, *U.K.* 13 C4
Durrës, *Albania* 44 E3
Durrow, *Ireland* 12 D4
Dursey I., *Ireland* 12 E1
Dursley, *U.K.* 15 F5
Dursunbey, *Turkey* 47 B10
Durtal, *France* 18 E6
Duru, *Dem. Rep. of the Congo* 86 B2
Duru Gölü, *Turkey* 45 E12
Durusu, *Turkey* 45 E12
Durūz, Jabal ad, *Jordan* 74 C5
D'Urville, Tanjung, *Indonesia* . 63 E9
D'Urville I., *N.Z.* 91 J4
Duryea, *U.S.A.* 117 E9
Dūsh, *Egypt* 80 C3
Dushak, *Turkmenistan* 52 F7
Dushan, *China* 58 E6
Dushanbe, *Tajikistan* 52 F7
Dusheti, *Georgia* 35 J7
Dushore, *U.S.A.* 117 E8
Dusky Sd., *N.Z.* 91 L1
Dussejour, C., *Australia* 92 B4
Düsseldorf, *Germany* 24 D2
Düsseldorf Rhein-Ruhr ✈ (DUS),
  Germany 24 D2
Duszniki-Zdrój, *Poland* 31 H3
Dutch Harbor, *U.S.A.* 100 C3
Dutlwe, *Botswana* 88 C3
Dutsan Wai, *Nigeria* 83 C6
Dutton, *Canada* 116 D3
Dutton →, *Australia* 94 C3
Duved, *Sweden* 10 A6
Düvertepe, *Turkey* 47 B10
Duwayhin, Khawr, *U.A.E.* ... 71 E6
Duyun, *China* 58 D6
Düzağaç, *Turkey* 47 C12
Düzce, *Turkey* 72 B4
Dve Mogili, *Bulgaria* 45 C9
Dvina, Severnaya →, *Russia* .. 52 C5
Dvinsk = Daugavpils, *Latvia* . 9 J22
Dvor, *Croatia* 41 C13
Dvůr Králové nad Labem,
  Czech Rep. 26 A8
Dwarka, *India* 68 H3
Dwellingup, *Australia* 93 F2
Dwight, *Canada* 116 A5
Dwight, *U.S.A.* 114 E1
Dyakovo, *Ukraine* 29 B8
Dyatkovo, *Russia* 32 F8
Dyatlovo = Dzyatlava, *Belarus* 33 F3
Dyce, *U.K.* 13 D6
Dyer, C., *Canada* 101 B13
Dyer Bay, *Canada* 116 A3
Dyer Plateau, *Antarctica* 5 D17
Dyersburg, *U.S.A.* 113 G10

Dyfi →, *U.K.* 15 E3
Dyje →, *Czech Rep.* 27 C9
Dymer, *Ukraine* 33 G6
Dynów, *Poland* 31 J9
Dysart, *Australia* 94 C4
Dyviziya 29 E14
Dzerzhinsk, *Russia* 34 B6
Dzhalinda, *Russia* 53 D13
Dzhambul = Taraz, *Kazakhstan* 52 E8
Dzhankoy, *Ukraine* 33 K8
Dzhanybek, *Kazakhstan* 34 F8
Dzharylhach, Ostriv, *Ukraine* .. 33 J7
Dzhezkazgan = Zhezqazghan,
  Kazakhstan 52 E7
Dzhizak = Jizzakh, *Uzbekistan* . 52 E7
Dzhugdzur, Khrebet, *Russia* .. 53 D14
Dzhulynk, *Ukraine* 29 B14
Dzhuryn, *Ukraine* 29 B13
Dzhvari = Jvari, *Georgia* 35 J6
Działdowo, *Poland* 31 E7
Działoszyce, *Poland* 31 H7
Działoszyn, *Poland* 31 G5
Dzibilchaltún, *Mexico* 119 C7
Dzibilchaltun, *Yucatán, Mexico* . 119 C7
Dzierzgoń, *Poland* 30 E6
Dzierżoniów, *Poland* 31 H3
Dzilam de Bravo, *Mexico* 119 C7
Dzisna, *Belarus* 32 E5
Dzisna →, *Belarus* 32 E5
Dziwnów, *Poland* 30 D1
Dzungaria = Junggar Pendi, *China* 60 B3
Dzungarian Basin = Junggar
  Pendi, *China* 60 B3
Dzuumod, *Mongolia* 60 B5
Dzyarzhynsk, *Belarus* 32 F4
Dzyatlava, *Belarus* 32 F3

E

E.C. Manning △, *Canada* 102 D4
Eabamet L., *Canada* 104 B2
Eads, *U.S.A.* 112 F3
Eagar, *U.S.A.* 109 J9
Eagle, *Alaska, U.S.A.* 100 B5
Eagle, *Colo., U.S.A.* 108 G10
Eagle →, *Canada* 105 B8
Eagle Butte, *U.S.A.* 112 C4
Eagle Grove, *U.S.A.* 112 D8
Eagle L., *Canada* 103 D10
Eagle L., *Calif., U.S.A.* 108 F3
Eagle L., *Maine, U.S.A.* 115 B11
Eagle Lake, *Canada* 116 A6
Eagle Lake, *Maine, U.S.A.* ... 115 B11
Eagle Lake, *Tex., U.S.A.* 113 L6
Eagle Mountain, *U.S.A.* 111 M11
Eagle Nest, *U.S.A.* 109 H11
Eagle Pass, *U.S.A.* 113 L4
Eagle Pk., *U.S.A.* 110 G7
Eagle Pt., *Australia* 92 C3
Eagle River, *Mich., U.S.A.* ... 114 B1
Eagle River, *Wis., U.S.A.* 112 C10
Eaglehawk, *Australia* 95 F3
Eagles Mere, *U.S.A.* 117 E8
Ealing □, *U.K.* 15 F7
Ear Falls, *Canada* 103 C10
Earle, *U.S.A.* 113 H9
Earlimart, *U.S.A.* 111 K7
Earn →, *U.K.* 13 E5
Earn, L., *U.K.* 13 E4
Earnslaw, Mt., *N.Z.* 91 L2
Earth, *U.S.A.* 113 H3
Easley, *U.S.A.* 115 H4
East Anglia, *U.K.* 14 E9
East Angus, *Canada* 105 C5
East Antarctica, *Antarctica* ... 5 D7
East Aurora, *U.S.A.* 116 D6
East Ayrshire □, *U.K.* 13 F4
East Bengal, *Bangla.* 67 H17
East Beskids = Vychodné
  Beskydy, *Europe* 27 B15
East Brady, *U.S.A.* 116 F5
East C., *N.Z.* 91 G7
East Chicago, *U.S.A.* 114 E2
East China Sea, *Asia* 60 C7
East Coulee, *Canada* 102 C6
East Dereham = Dereham, *U.K.* 15 E8
East Dunbartonshire □, *U.K.* .. 13 F4
East Falkland, *Falk. Is.* 128 G5
East Grand Forks, *U.S.A.* 112 B6
East Greenwich, *U.S.A.* 117 E13
East Grinstead, *U.K.* 15 F8
East Hartford, *U.S.A.* 117 E12
East Helena, *U.S.A.* 108 C8
East Indies, *Asia* 50 K15
East Kilbride, *U.K.* 13 F4
East Lansing, *U.S.A.* 114 D3
East Liverpool, *U.S.A.* 116 F4
East London, *S. Africa* 89 E4
East Lothian □, *U.K.* 13 F6
East Main = Eastmain, *Canada* . 104 B4
East Northport, *U.S.A.* 117 F11
East Orange, *U.S.A.* 117 F10
East Pacific Ridge, *Pac. Oc.* ... 97 J17
East Palestine, *U.S.A.* 116 F4
East Pine, *Canada* 102 B4
East Point, *U.S.A.* 115 J3
East Providence, *U.S.A.* 117 E13
East Pt., *Br. Virgin Is.* ...... 121 e
East Retford = Retford, *U.K.* .. 14 D7
East Renfrewshire □, *U.K.* 13 F4
East Riding of Yorkshire □, *U.K.* 14 D7
East Rochester, *U.S.A.* 116 C7
East St. Louis, *U.S.A.* 112 F9
East Schelde = Oosterschelde →,
  Neths. 17 C4
East Sea = Japan, Sea of, *Asia* . 54 E7
East Siberian Sea, *Russia* 53 B17

East Stroudsburg, U.S.A. 117 E9
East Sussex □, U.K. 15 G8
East Tawas, U.S.A. 114 C4
East Timor ■, Asia 63 F7
East Toorale, Australia 95 E4
East Walker ➤, U.S.A. 110 G7
East Windsor, U.S.A. 117 F10
Eastbourne, N.Z. 91 J5
Eastbourne, U.K. 15 G8
Eastend, Canada 103 D7
Easter I. = Pascua, I. de, Chile . 97 K17
Eastern □, Ghana 83 D4
Eastern □, Kenya 86 C4
Eastern □, S. Leone 82 D2
Eastern Cape □, S. Africa 88 E4
Eastern Cr. ➤, Australia 94 C3
Eastern Ghats, India 66 N11
Eastern Group = Lau Group, Fiji 91 C9
Eastern Group, Australia 93 F3
Eastern Transvaal =
  Mpumalanga □, S. Africa ... 89 D5
Easterville, Canada 103 C9
Easthampton, U.S.A. 117 D12
Eastlake, U.S.A. 116 E3
Eastland, U.S.A. 113 J5
Eastleigh, U.K. 15 G6
Eastmain, Canada 104 B4
Eastmain ➤, Canada 104 B4
Eastmain, Canada 117 A12
Eastman, U.S.A. 115 J4
Easton, Md., U.S.A. 114 F7
Easton, Pa., U.S.A. 117 F9
Easton, Wash., U.S.A. 110 C5
Eastpointe, U.S.A. 116 D2
Eastport, U.S.A. 115 C12
Eastsound, U.S.A. 110 B4
Eaton, U.S.A. 112 E2
Eatonia, Canada 103 C7
Eatonton, U.S.A. 115 J4
Eatontown, U.S.A. 117 F10
Eatonville, U.S.A. 110 D4
Eau Claire, U.S.A. 112 C9
Eau Claire, L. à l', Canada ... 104 A5
Eauze, France 20 E4
Eban, Nigeria 83 D5
Ebbegebirge △, Germany 24 D3
Ebbw Vale, U.K. 15 F4
Ebeltoft, Denmark 11 H4
Ebeltoft Vig, Denmark 11 H4
Ebensburg, U.S.A. 116 F6
Ebensee, Austria 26 D6
Eber Gölü, Turkey 72 C4
Eberbach, Germany 25 F4
Eberswalde-Finow, Germany 24 C9
Ebetsu, Japan 54 C10
Ebey's Landing △, U.S.A. 110 B4
Ebian, China 58 C4
Ebingen, Germany 25 G5
Éboli, Italy 43 B8
Ebolowa, Cameroon 83 E7
Ebonyi □, Nigeria 83 D6
Ebrach, Germany 25 F6
Ébrié, Lagune, Ivory C. 82 D4
Ebro ➤, Spain 38 E5
Ebro, Embalse del, Spain 36 C7
Ebstorf, Germany 24 B6
Eceabat, Turkey 45 F10
Ech Chéliff, Algeria 78 A4
Echigo-Sammyaku, Japan 55 F9
Échirolles, France 21 C9
Echizen-Misaki, Japan 55 G7
Echmiadzin = Yejmiadzin,
  Armenia 35 K7
Echo Bay, N.W.T., Canada 100 B8
Echo Bay, Ont., Canada 104 C3
Echoing ➤, Canada 104 B1
Echterdingen, Stuttgart ✈ (STR),
  Germany 25 G5
Echternach, Lux. 17 E6
Echuca, Australia 95 F3
Ecija, Spain 37 H5
Eckental, Germany 25 F7
Eckernförde, Germany 24 A5
Eclipse I., Australia 93 G2
Eclipse Is., Australia 92 B4
Eclipse Sd., Canada 101 A11
Écommoy, France 18 E7
Écouché, France 18 D6
Ecrins △, France 21 D10
Ecuador ■, S. Amer. 124 D3
Écueillé, France 18 E8
Ed, Sweden 11 F5
Ed Dabbura, Sudan 80 D3
Ed Da'ein, Sudan 81 E2
Ed Damazin, Sudan 79 F12
Ed Dâmer, Sudan 80 D3
Ed Dar el Beida = Casablanca,
  Morocco 78 B4
Ed Debba, Sudan 80 D3
Ed-Déffa, Egypt 80 A2
Ed Deim, Sudan 81 E2
Ed Dueim, Sudan 81 E3
Edam, Canada 103 C7
Edam, Neths. 17 B5
Edane, Sweden 10 E6
Eday, U.K. 13 B6
Edd, Eritrea 81 E5
Eddrachillis B., U.K. 13 C3
Eddystone, U.K. 17 B5
Eddystone Pt., Australia 95 G4
Ede, Neths. 17 B5
Ede, Nigeria 83 D5
Édéa, Cameroon 83 E7
Edebäck, Sweden 10 D7
Edehon L., Canada 103 A9
Edelény, Hungary 28 B5
Eden, Australia 95 F4
Eden, N.C., U.S.A. 115 G6
Eden, N.Y., U.S.A. 116 D6
Eden, Tex., U.S.A. 113 K5
Eden ➤, U.K. 14 C4
Edenburg, S. Africa 88 D4

Edendale, S. Africa 89 D5
Edenderry, Ireland 12 C4
Edenton, U.S.A. 115 G7
Edenville, S. Africa 89 D4
Eder ➤, Germany 24 D5
Eder-Stausee, Germany 24 D4
Edewecht, Germany 24 B3
Edgar, U.S.A. 112 E6
Edgartown, U.S.A. 117 E14
Edge Hill, U.K. 15 E6
Edgefield, U.S.A. 115 J5
Edgeley, U.S.A. 112 B5
Edgemont, U.S.A. 112 D3
Edgeøya, Svalbard 4 B9
Édhessa, Greece 44 F6
Edievale, N.Z. 91 L2
Edina, Liberia 82 D2
Edina, U.S.A. 112 E8
Edinboro, U.S.A. 116 E4
Edinburg, U.S.A. 113 M5
Edinburgh, U.K. 13 F5
Edinburgh ✈ (EDI), U.K. 13 F5
Edinburgh, City of □, U.K. ... 13 F5
Edineţ, Moldova 29 B12
Edirne, Turkey 45 E10
Edirne □, Turkey 45 E10
Edison, U.S.A. 110 B4
Edithburgh, Australia 95 F2
Edmeston, U.S.A. 117 D9
Edmond, U.S.A. 113 H6
Edmonds, U.S.A. 110 C4
Edmonton, Australia 94 B4
Edmonton, Canada 102 C6
Edmund L., Canada 104 B1
Edmundston, Canada 105 C6
Edna, U.S.A. 113 L6
Edo □, Nigeria 83 D6
Edolo, Italy 40 B7
Edremit, Turkey 47 B9
Edremit Körfezi, Turkey 47 B8
Edsbro, Sweden 10 E12
Edsbyn, Sweden 10 C9
Edson, Canada 102 C5
Eduardo Castex, Argentina 126 D3
Edward ➤, Australia 95 F3
Edward, L., Africa 86 C2
Edward River, Australia 94 A3
Edward VII Land, Antarctica .. 5 E13
Edwards, Calif., U.S.A. 111 L9
Edwards, N.Y., U.S.A. 117 B9
Edwards Air Force Base, U.S.A. 111 L9
Edwards Plateau, U.S.A. 113 K4
Edwardsville, U.S.A. 117 E9
Edxná, Mexico 119 D6
Edzo, Canada 102 A5
Eeklo, Belgium 17 C3
Eferding, Austria 26 C7
Effigy Mounds △, U.S.A. 112 D9
Effingham, U.S.A. 114 F1
Eforie, Romania 29 F13
Ega ➤, Spain 38 C3
Égadi, Ísole, Italy 42 E5
Egan Range, U.S.A. 108 G6
Eganville, Canada 116 A7
Eger = Cheb, Czech Rep. 26 A5
Eger, Hungary 28 C5
Eger ➤, Hungary 28 C5
Egersund, Norway 9 G12
Egg L., Canada 103 B7
Eggegebirge Südlicher
  Teutoburger Wald △, Germany 24 D4
Eggenburg, Austria 26 C8
Eggenfelden, Germany 25 G8
Éghezée, Belgium 17 D4
Égletons, France 20 C6
Egmont, Canada 102 D4
Egmont □, N.Z. 91 H5
Egmont, C., N.Z. 91 H4
Egmont, Mt. = Taranaki, Mt.,
  N.Z. 91 H5
Egra, India 69 J12
Eğridir, Turkey 72 D4
Eğridir Gölü, Turkey 70 B1
Egtved, Denmark 11 J3
Egume, Nigeria 83 D6
Éguzon-Chantôme, France 19 F8
Egvekinot, Russia 53 C19
Egyek, Hungary 28 C5
Egypt ■, Africa 80 B3
Eha Amufu, Nigeria 83 D6
Ehime □, Japan 55 H6
Ehingen, Germany 25 G5
Ehrenberg, U.S.A. 111 M12
Ehrwald, Austria 26 D3
Eibar, Spain 38 B2
Eichstätt, Germany 25 G7
Eider ➤, Germany 24 A4
Eidsvold, Australia 95 D5
Eidsvoll, Norway 9 F14
Eifel, Germany 25 E2
Eiffel Flats, Zimbabwe 87 F3
Eiger, Switz. 40 B5
Eigg, U.K. 13 E2
Eighty Mile Beach, Australia . 92 C3
Eil, Somali Rep. 75 F4
Eil, L., U.K. 13 E3
Eildon, L., Australia 95 F4
Eilenburg, Germany 24 D8
Ein el Luweiqa, Sudan 81 E3
Einasleigh, Australia 94 B3
Einasleigh ➤, Australia 94 B3
Einbeck, Germany 24 D5
Eindhoven, Neths. 17 C5
Einsiedeln, Switz. 25 H4
Eire = Ireland ■, Europe 12 C4
Eiríksjökull, Iceland 8 D3
Eirunepé, Brazil 124 E5
Eiseb ➤, Namibia 88 C2
Eisenach, Germany 24 E6
Eisenberg, Germany 24 E7
Eisenerz, Austria 26 D7
Eisenhüttenstadt, Germany 24 C10

Eisenkappel, Austria 26 E7
Eisenstadt, Austria 27 D9
Eisfeld, Germany 25 E6
El Kere, Ethiopia 81 F5
Eisleben, Germany 24 D7
Eislingen, Germany 25 G5
Eivissa, Spain 48 C7
Eixe, Serra do, Spain 36 C4
Ejea de los Caballeros, Spain 38 C3
Ejeda, Madag. 89 C7
Ejura, Ghana 83 D4
Ejutla, Mexico 119 D5
Ekalaka, U.S.A. 112 C2
Ekenäs = Tammisaari, Finland . 9 F20
Ekenässjön, Sweden 11 G9
Ekerö, Sweden 10 E11
Eket, Nigeria 83 E6
Eketahuna, N.Z. 91 J5
Ekhínos, Greece 45 E9
Ekibastuz, Kazakhstan 52 D8
Ekiti □, Nigeria 83 D6
Ekoli, Dem. Rep. of the Congo 86 C1
Ekoln, Sweden 10 E11
Ekshärad, Sweden 10 D7
Eksjö, Sweden 11 G8
Ekuma ➤, Namibia 88 B2
Ekwan ➤, Canada 104 B3
Ekwan Pt., Canada 104 B3
El Aaiún, W. Sahara 78 C3
El Abanico, Chile 126 D1
El Abbasia, Sudan 81 E3
El 'Agrûd, Egypt 74 E3
El Ait, Sudan 81 E2
El 'Aiyat, Egypt 80 J7
El 'Alamein, Egypt 80 A2
El 'Aqaba, W. ➤, Egypt 74 E2
El 'Arag, Egypt 80 B2
El Arahal, Spain 37 H5
El Arīḥā, West Bank 74 D4
El 'Arîsh, Egypt 74 D2
El 'Arîsh, W. ➤, Egypt 74 D2
El Asnam = Ech Chéliff, Algeria 78 A4
El Astillero, Spain 36 B7
El Badâri, Egypt 80 B3
El Bahrein, Egypt 80 B2
El Ballâs, Egypt 80 B3
El Balyana, Egypt 80 B3
El Baqeir, Sudan 80 D3
El Barco de Ávila, Spain 36 E5
El Barco de Valdeorras = O
  Barco, Spain 36 C4
El Bauga, Sudan 80 D3
El Bawiti, Egypt 80 B2
El Bayadh, Algeria 78 B6
El Bierzo, Spain 36 C4
El Bluff, Nic. 120 D3
El Bonillo, Spain 39 G2
El Brûk, W. ➤, Egypt 74 E2
El Buheirat □, Sudan 81 F3
El Burgo de Osma, Spain 38 D1
El Cajon, U.S.A. 111 N10
El Campo, U.S.A. 113 L6
El Centro, U.S.A. 111 N11
El Cerro, Bolivia 124 G6
El Cerro de Andévalo, Spain .. 37 H4
El Compadre, Mexico 111 N10
El Coronil, Spain 37 H5
El Cuy, Argentina 128 D3
El Cuyo, Mexico 119 C7
El Dab'a, Egypt 80 H6
El Daheir, Egypt 74 D3
El Dátil, Mexico 118 B2
El Deir, Egypt 80 B3
El Dere, Somali Rep. 75 G4
El Descanso, Mexico 111 N10
El Desemboque, Mexico 118 A2
El Dilingat, Egypt 80 H7
El Diviso, Colombia 124 C3
El Djouf, Mauritania 78 D4
El Dorado, Ark., U.S.A. 113 J8
El Dorado, Kans., U.S.A. 113 G6
El Dorado, Venezuela 124 B6
El 'Ein, Sudan 81 D2
El Ejido, Spain 37 J8
El Escorial, Spain 36 E6
El Espinar, Spain 36 D6
El Faiyûm, Egypt 80 J7
El Fâsher, Sudan 81 E2
El Fashn, Egypt 80 J7
El Ferrol = Ferrol, Spain 36 B2
El Fifi, Sudan 81 E2
El Fuerte, Mexico 118 B3
El Ga'a, Sudan 81 E2
El Gal, Somali Rep. 75 E5
El Garef, Sudan 81 E3
El Gebir, Sudan 81 E2
El Gedida, Egypt 80 B2
El Geneina = Al Junaynah, Sudan 79 F10
El Geteina, Sudan 81 E3
El Gezira □, Sudan 81 E3
El Gîza, Egypt 80 J7
El Gogorrón △, Mexico 118 C4
El Goléa, Algeria 78 B6
El Grau, Spain 39 G4
El Guácharo △, Venezuela 121 D7
El Guache △, Venezuela 121 E6
El Hagiz, Sudan 81 D4
El Hâi, Egypt 80 J7
El Hammam, Egypt 80 A2
El Hawata, Sudan 81 E3
El Heiz, Egypt 80 B2
El Hideib, Sudan 81 E3
El Hilla, Sudan 81 E2
El 'Idisât, Egypt 80 B3
El Istiwa'iya, Sudan 79 G11
El Jadida, Morocco 78 B4
El Jardal, Honduras 120 D2
El Jebelein, Sudan 81 E3
El Kab, Sudan 80 D3
El Kabrît, G., Egypt 74 F2
El Kafr el Sharqi, Egypt 80 H7

El Kamlin, Sudan 81 D3
El Karaba, Sudan 80 D3
El Kere, Ethiopia 81 F5
El Khandaq, Sudan 80 D3
El Khârga, Egypt 80 B3
El Khartûm, Sudan 81 D3
El Khartûm □, Sudan 81 D3
El Khartûm Bahrî, Sudan 81 D3
El Kuntilla, Egypt 74 E3
El Laqâwa, Sudan 81 E2
El Leh, Ethiopia 81 G4
El Maestrazgo, Spain 38 E4
El Mafâza, Sudan 81 E3
El Maghra, Egypt 80 A2
El Mahalla el Kubra, Egypt ... 80 H7
El Mahârîq, Egypt 80 B3
El Maîmûn, Egypt 80 J7
El Maks el Bahari, Egypt 80 C2
El Malpais △, U.S.A. 109 J10
El Manshâh, Egypt 80 B3
El Mansûra, Egypt 80 H7
El Manzala, Egypt 80 H7
El Marâgha, Egypt 80 B3
El Masid, Sudan 81 D3
El Masnou, Spain 38 D7
El Matariya, Egypt 80 H8
El Meda, Ethiopia 81 F5
El Medano, Canary Is. 48 F3
El Metemma, Sudan 81 D3
El Milagro, Argentina 126 C2
El Minyâ, Egypt 80 B3
El Monte, U.S.A. 111 L8
El Montseny, Spain 38 D7
El Mreyyé, Mauritania 82 B3
El Niybo, Ethiopia 81 G4
El Obeid, Sudan 81 E3
El Odaiya, Sudan 81 E2
El Oro, Mexico 119 D4
El Oued, Algeria 78 B7
El Palmar △, Argentina 126 C4
El Palmito, Presa, Mexico 118 B3
El Paso, U.S.A. 109 L10
El Paso Robles, U.S.A. 110 K6
El Pedernoso, Spain 39 F2
El Pedroso, Spain 37 H5
El Pinacate y Gran Desierto de
  Altar = Gran Desierto del
  Pinacate △, Mexico 118 A2
El Pobo de Dueñas, Spain 38 E3
El Portal, U.S.A. 110 H7
El Porvenir, Mexico 118 A3
El Prat de Llobregat, Spain .. 38 D7
El Progreso, Honduras 120 C2
El Pueblito, Mexico 118 B3
El Pueblo, Canary Is. 48 F2
El Puente del Arzobispo, Spain 36 F5
El Puerto de Santa María, Spain 37 J4
El Qâhira, Egypt 80 H7
El Qantara, Egypt 74 E1
El Qasr, Egypt 80 B2
El Qubâba, Egypt 80 J7
El Quseima, Egypt 74 E3
El Qusîya, Egypt 80 B3
El Râshda, Egypt 80 B2
El Real, Panama 124 B3
El Reno, U.S.A. 113 H6
El Rey △, Argentina 126 A3
El Rîdisiya, Egypt 80 C3
El Rio, U.S.A. 111 L7
El Ronquillo, Spain 37 H4
El Roque, Pta., Canary Is. ... 48 F4
El Rosarito, Mexico 118 B2
El Rubio, Spain 37 H5
El Saff, Egypt 80 J7
El Saheira, W. ➤, Egypt 74 E2
El Salto, Mexico 118 C3
El Salvador ■, Cent. Amer. ... 120 D2
El Sauce, Nic. 120 D2
El Saucejo, Spain 37 H5
El Shallal, Egypt 80 C3
El Simbillawein, Egypt 80 H7
El Sueco, Mexico 118 B3
El Suweis, Egypt 80 J8
El Tabbîn, Egypt 80 J7
El Tamarâni, W. ➤, Egypt 74 E3
El Thamad, Egypt 74 F3
El Tigre, Venezuela 124 B6
El Tîh, Gebal, Egypt 74 F2
El Tîna, Egypt 80 H8
El Tîna, Khalîg, Egypt 74 D1
El Tofo, Chile 126 B1
El Tránsito, Chile 126 B1
El Tûr, Egypt 70 D2
El Turbio, Argentina 128 G2
El Uqsur, Egypt 80 B3
El Valle △, Spain 39 H3
El Venado, Mexico 118 C4
El Vendrell, Spain 38 D6
El Vergel, Mexico 118 B3
El Vigía, Venezuela 124 B4
El Viso del Alcor, Spain 37 H5
El Wabeira, Egypt 74 F2
El Wak, Kenya 86 B5
El Waqf, Egypt 80 B3
El Weguet, Ethiopia 81 F5
El Wuz, Sudan 81 D3
Elafónisos, Greece 46 E4
Élancourt, France 19 D8
Élassa, Greece 47 F8
Elassón, Greece 46 B4
Elat, Israel 74 F3
Eláthia, Greece 46 C4
Elâzığ, Turkey 70 B3
Elba, Italy 42 F7
Elba, U.S.A. 115 K2
Elbasan, Albania 44 E4
Elbe ➤, Europe 24 B4
Elbe-Seitenkanal, Germany 24 C6
Elbert, Mt., U.S.A. 109 G10
Elberton, U.S.A. 115 H4

Elbeuf, France 18 C8
Elbidtan, Turkey 70 B3
Elbing = Elbląg, Poland 30 D6
Elbistan, Turkey 72 C7
Elbląg, Poland 30 D6
Elbow, Canada 103 C7
Elbrus, Asia 35 J6
Elbufer-Drawehn △, Germany ... 24 B6
Elburz Mts. = Alborz, Reshteh-ye
  Kühhā-ye, Iran 71 C7
Elche, Spain 39 G4
Elche de la Sierra, Spain 39 G2
Elcho I., Australia 94 A2
Elda, Spain 39 G4
Elde ➤, Germany 24 B7
Eldon, Mo., U.S.A. 112 F8
Eldon, Wash., U.S.A. 110 C3
Eldora, U.S.A. 112 D8
Eldorado, Argentina 127 B5
Eldorado, Canada 116 B7
Eldorado, Mexico 118 C3
Eldorado, Ill., U.S.A. 114 G1
Eldorado, Tex., U.S.A. 113 K4
Eldorado Springs, U.S.A. 113 G8
Eldoret, Kenya 86 B4
Eldred, U.S.A. 116 E6
Elea, C., Cyprus 49 D13
Eleanora, Pk., Australia 93 F3
Elefantes ➤, Africa 89 C5
Elektrogorsk, Russia 32 E10
Elektrostal, Russia 32 E10
Elele, Nigeria 83 D6
Elena, Bulgaria 45 D9
Elephant Butte Reservoir, U.S.A. 109 K10
Elephant I., Antarctica 5 C18
Eleshnitsa, Bulgaria 44 E7
Eleşkirt, Turkey 73 C10
Eleuthera, Bahamas 120 B4
Elevsís, Greece 46 C5
Elevtheroúpolis, Greece 45 F8
Elgin, Canada 117 B8
Elgin, U.K. 13 D5
Elgin, Ill., U.S.A. 114 D1
Elgin, N. Dak., U.S.A. 112 B4
Elgin, Oreg., U.S.A. 108 D5
Elgin, Tex., U.S.A. 113 K6
Elgoibar, Spain 38 B2
Elgon, Mt., Africa 86 B3
Eliase, Indonesia 63 F8
Elikón, Greece 46 C4
Elim, Namibia 88 B2
Elim, S. Africa 88 E2
Elin Pelin, Bulgaria 44 D7
Elista, Russia 35 G7
Elizabeth, Australia 95 E2
Elizabeth, U.S.A. 117 F10
Elizabeth City, U.S.A. 115 G7
Elizabethton, U.S.A. 115 G4
Elizabethtown, Ky., U.S.A. ... 114 G3
Elizabethtown, N.Y., U.S.A. .. 117 B11
Elizabethtown, Pa., U.S.A. ... 117 F8
Elizondo, Spain 38 B3
Ełk, Poland 30 E9
Elk ➤, Canada 102 C5
Ełk ➤, Poland 30 E9
Elk ➤, U.S.A. 115 H2
Elk City, U.S.A. 113 H5
Elk Creek, U.S.A. 110 F4
Elk Grove, U.S.A. 110 G5
Elk Island △, Canada 102 C6
Elk Lake, Canada 104 C3
Elk Point, Canada 103 C6
Elk River, Idaho, U.S.A. 108 C5
Elk River, Minn., U.S.A. 112 C8
Elkedra ➤, Australia 94 C2
Elkhart, Ind., U.S.A. 114 E3
Elkhart, Kans., U.S.A. 113 G4
Elkhorn, Canada 103 D8
Elkhorn ➤, U.S.A. 112 E6
Elkhovo, Bulgaria 45 D10
Elkin, U.S.A. 115 G5
Elkins, U.S.A. 114 F6
Elkland, U.S.A. 116 E7
Elko, Canada 102 D5
Elko, U.S.A. 108 F6
Elkton, U.S.A. 116 C1
Ell, L., Australia 93 E4
Ellef Ringnes I., Canada 4 B2
Ellen, Mt., U.S.A. 117 B12
Ellenburg, U.S.A. 117 B11
Ellendale, U.S.A. 112 B5
Ellensburg, U.S.A. 108 C3
Ellenville, U.S.A. 117 E10
Ellerton, Barbados .... 121 g
Ellery, Mt., Australia 95 F4
Ellesmere, L., N.Z. 91 M4
Ellesmere I., Canada 98 B11
Ellesmere Port, U.K. 14 D5
Ellice Is. = Tuvalu ■, Pac. Oc. 96 H9
Ellicott City, U.S.A. 116 D6
Elliot, Australia 94 B1
Elliot, S. Africa 89 E4
Elliot Lake, Canada 104 C3
Elliotdale = Xhora, S. Africa 89 E4
Ellis, U.S.A. 112 F5
Elliston, Australia 95 E1
Ellisville, U.S.A. 113 K10
Ellon, U.K. 13 D6
Ellore = Eluru, India 67 L12
Ellsworth, Kans., U.S.A. 112 F5
Ellsworth, Maine, U.S.A. 115 C11
Ellsworth, Mts., Antarctica .. 5 D16
Elwangen, Germany 25 G6
Ellwood City, U.S.A. 116 F4
Elm, Switz. 25 J5
Elm-Lappwald △, Germany 24 C7
Elma, Canada 103 D9
Elma, U.S.A. 110 D3
Elmadağ, Turkey 72 C5
Elmalı, Turkey 47 E11

Elmhurst, *U.S.A.* 114 E2
Elmina, *Ghana* 83 D4
Elmira, *Canada* 116 C4
Elmira, *U.S.A.* 116 D8
Elmira Heights, *U.S.A.* 116 D8
Elmore, *Australia* 95 F3
Elmore, *U.S.A.* 111 M11
Elmshorn, *Germany* 24 B5
Elmvale, *Canada* 116 B5
Elne, *France* 20 F6
Elora, *Canada* 116 C4
Elos, *Greece* 46 E4
Eloúnda, *Greece* 49 D7
Eloy, *U.S.A.* 109 K8
Éloyes, *France* 19 D13
Elrose, *Canada* 103 C7
Elsdorf, *Germany* 24 E2
Elsie, *U.S.A.* 110 E3
Elsinore = Helsingør, *Denmark* . 11 H6
Elster →, *Germany* 24 D7
Elsterwerda, *Germany* 24 D9
Eltham, *N.Z.* 91 H5
Elton, *Russia* 35 F8
Elton, Ozero, *Russia* 35 F8
Eltville, *Germany* 25 E4
Eluru, *India* 67 L12
Elvas, *Portugal* 37 G3
Elven, *France* 18 E4
Elverum, *Norway* 9 F14
Elvire →, *Australia* 92 C4
Elvire, Mt., *Australia* 93 E2
Elvo →, *Italy* 40 C5
Elwell, L., *U.S.A.* 108 B8
Elwood, *Ind., U.S.A.* 114 E3
Elwood, *Nebr., U.S.A.* 112 E5
Elx = Elche, *Spain* 39 G4
Ely, *U.K.* 15 E8
Ely, *Minn., U.S.A.* 112 B9
Ely, *Nev., U.S.A.* 108 G6
Elyria, *U.S.A.* 116 E2
Elyrus, *Greece* 46 F5
Elz →, *Germany* 25 G3
Emådalen, *Sweden* 10 C8
Emāmrūd, *Iran* 71 B7
Emån →, *Sweden* 11 G10
Emba, *Kazakhstan* 52 E6
Emba →, *Kazakhstan* 52 E6
Embarcación, *Argentina* 126 A3
Embarras Portage, *Canada* ... 103 B6
Embetsu, *Japan* 54 B10
Embi = Emba, *Kazakhstan* 52 E6
Embi = Emba →, *Kazakhstan* .. 52 E6
Embóna, *Greece* 49 C9
Embrun, *France* 21 D10
Embu, *Kenya* 86 C4
Emden, *Germany* 24 B3
Emecik, *Turkey* 47 E9
Emerald, *Australia* 94 C4
Emerson, *Canada* 103 D9
Emet, *Turkey* 47 B11
Emi Koussi, *Chad* 79 D9
Emília-Romagna □, *Italy* 40 D8
Emilius, Mte., *Italy* 40 C4
Eminabad, *Pakistan* 68 C6
Emine, Nos, *Bulgaria* 45 D11
Emirdağ, *Turkey* 72 C4
Emissi, Tarso, *Chad* 79 D9
Emlenton, *U.S.A.* 116 E5
Emlichheim, *Germany* 24 C2
Emmaboda, *Sweden* 11 H9
Emmaus, *S. Africa* 88 D4
Emmaus, *U.S.A.* 117 F9
Emme →, *Switz.* 25 H3
Emmeloord, *Neths.* 17 B5
Emmen, *Neths.* 17 B6
Emmen, *Switz.* 25 H4
Emmendingen, *Germany* 25 G3
Emmental, *Switz.* 25 J3
Emmerich, *Germany* 24 D2
Emmet, *Australia* 94 C3
Emmetsburg, *U.S.A.* 112 D7
Emmett, *Idaho, U.S.A.* 108 E5
Emmett, *Mich., U.S.A.* 116 D2
Emmonak, *U.S.A.* 100 B3
Emo, *Canada* 103 D10
Emőd, *Hungary* 28 C5
Emona, *Bulgaria* 45 D11
Empalme, *Mexico* 118 B2
Empangeni, *S. Africa* 89 D5
Empedrado, *Argentina* 126 B4
Emperor Seamount Chain,
  Pac. Oc. 96 D9
Empoli, *Italy* 40 E7
Emporia, *Kans., U.S.A.* 112 F6
Emporia, *Va., U.S.A.* 115 G7
Emporium, *U.S.A.* 116 E6
Empress, *Canada* 103 C7
Empty Quarter = Rub' al Khālī,
  Si. Arabia 75 D4
Ems →, *Germany* 24 B3
Emsdale, *Canada* 116 A5
Emsdetten, *Germany* 24 C3
Emu, *China* 57 C15
Emu Park, *Australia* 94 C5
'En 'Avrona, *Israel* 74 K3
En Nahud, *Sudan* 81 E2
En Nofalab, *Sudan* 81 D3
Ena, *Japan* 55 G8
Enana, *Namibia* 88 B2
Enånger, *Sweden* 10 C11
Enard B., *U.K.* 13 C3
Enare = Inarijärvi, *Finland* ... 8 B22
Enarotali, *Indonesia* 63 E9
Encampment, *U.S.A.* 108 F10
Encantadas, Serra, *Brazil* 127 C5
Encarnación, *Paraguay* 127 B4
Encarnación de Diaz, *Mexico* . 118 C4
Enchi, *Ghana* 82 D4
Encinitas, *U.S.A.* 111 M9
Encino, *U.S.A.* 109 J11
Encounter B., *Australia* 95 F2
Encs, *Hungary* 28 B6

Endako, *Canada* 102 C3
Ende, *Indonesia* 63 F6
Endeavour Str., *Australia* 94 A3
Endelave, *Denmark* 11 J4
Enderby, *Canada* 102 C5
Enderby I., *Australia* 92 D2
Enderby Land, *Antarctica* 5 C5
Enderlin, *U.S.A.* 112 B6
Endicott, *U.S.A.* 117 D8
Endwell, *U.S.A.* 117 D8
Endyalgout I., *Australia* 92 B5
Eneabba, *Australia* 93 E2
Enewetak Atoll, *Marshall Is.* .. 96 F8
Enez, *Turkey* 45 F10
Enfer, Pte. d', *Martinique* .... 120 c
Enfield, *Canada* 105 D7
Enfield, *Conn., U.S.A.* 117 E12
Enfield, *N.H., U.S.A.* 117 C12
Engadin, *Switz.* 25 J6
Engaño, C., *Dom. Rep.* 121 C6
Engaño, C., *Phil.* 63 A6
Engaru, *Japan* 54 B11
Engcobo, *S. Africa* 89 E4
Engelberg, *Switz.* 25 J4
Engels, *Russia* 34 E8
Engemann L., *Canada* 103 B7
Engershatu, *Eritrea* 81 D4
England, *U.S.A.* 113 H9
England □, *U.K.* 15 E5
Englee, *Canada* 105 B8
Englehart, *Canada* 104 C4
Englewood, *U.S.A.* 112 F2
English →, *Canada* 103 C10
English Bazar = Ingraj Bazar,
  India 69 G13
English Channel, *Europe* 15 G6
English Company's Is., The,
  Australia 94 A2
English River, *Canada* 104 C1
Engures ezers, *Latvia* 30 A10
Enguri →, *Georgia* 35 J5
Enid, *U.S.A.* 113 G6
Enipévs →, *Greece* 46 B4
Enkhuizen, *Neths.* 17 B5
Enköping, *Sweden* 10 E11
Enle, *China* 58 F3
Enna, *Italy* 43 E7
Ennadai, *Canada* 103 A8
Ennadai L., *Canada* 103 A8
Ennedi, *Chad* 79 E10
Enngonia, *Australia* 95 D4
Ennigerloh, *Germany* 24 D4
Ennis, *Ireland* 12 D3
Ennis, *Mont., U.S.A.* 108 D8
Ennis, *Tex., U.S.A.* 113 J6
Enniscorthy, *Ireland* 12 D5
Enniskillen, *U.K.* 12 B4
Ennistimon, *Ireland* 12 D2
Enns, *Austria* 26 C7
Enns →, *Austria* 26 C7
Enontekiö, *Finland* 8 B20
Enosburg Falls, *U.S.A.* 117 B11
Enping, *China* 59 F9
Enriquillo, L., *Dom. Rep.* 121 C5
Enschede, *Neths.* 17 B6
Ensenada, *Argentina* 126 C4
Ensenada, *Mexico* 118 A1
Ensenada de los Muertos, *Mexico* 118 C2
Enshi, *China* 58 B7
Ensiola, Pta. de n', *Spain* 48 B9
Ensisheim, *France* 19 E14
Entebbe, *Uganda* 86 B3
Enterprise, *Canada* 102 A5
Enterprise, *Ala., U.S.A.* 115 K3
Enterprise, *Oreg., U.S.A.* 108 D5
Entorno de Doñana △, *Spain* .. 37 J4
Entraygues-sur-Truyère, *France* . 20 D6
Entre Ríos, *Bolivia* 126 A3
Entre Ríos □, *Argentina* 126 C4
Entrepeñas, Emba.se de, *Spain* . 38 E2
Entroncamento, *Portugal* 37 F2
Enugu, *Nigeria* 83 D6
Enugu □, *Nigeria* 83 D6
Enugu Ezike, *Nigeria* 83 D6
Enumclaw, *U.S.A.* 110 C5
Envalira, Port d', *Europe* 38 C6
Envermeu, *France* 18 C8
Enviken, *Sweden* 10 D9
Enying, *Hungary* 28 D3
Enza →, *Italy* 40 D7
Eólie, Ís., *Italy* 43 D7
Epanomí, *Greece* 44 F6
Epe, *Neths.* 17 B5
Epe, *Nigeria* 83 D5
Épernay, *France* 19 C10
Épernon, *France* 19 D8
Ephesus, *Turkey* 47 D9
Ephraim, *U.S.A.* 108 G8
Ephrata, *Pa., U.S.A.* 117 F8
Ephrata, *Wash., U.S.A.* 108 C4
Epidaurus Limera, *Greece* 46 E5
Épila, *Spain* 38 D3
Épinac, *France* 19 F11
Épinal, *France* 19 D13
Episkopi, *Cyprus* 49 E11
Episkopí, *Greece* 49 D6
Episkopi Bay, *Cyprus* 49 E11
Epitálion, *Greece* 46 D3
Eppan = Appiano, *Italy* 41 B8
Eppingen, *Germany* 25 F4
Epsom, *U.K.* 15 F7
Epukiro, *Namibia* 88 C2
Equatoria = El Istiwa'iya, *Sudan* 79 G11
Equatorial Guinea ■, *Africa* ... 84 D1
Er Hai, *China* 58 E3
Er Rachidia, *Morocco* 78 B5
Er Rahad, *Sudan* 81 E3
Er Rif, *Morocco* 78 A5
Er Rogel, *Sudan* 80 D4
Er Roseires, *Sudan* 81 E3

Er Rua'at, *Sudan* 81 E3
Eracela, *Italy* 41 C9
Erāwadī Myit = Irrawaddy →,
  Burma 67 M19
Erāwadī Myitwanya = Irrawaddy,
  Mouths of the, *Burma* 67 M19
Erba, *Italy* 40 C6
Erba, *Sudan* 80 D4
Erba, J., *Sudan* 80 C4
Erbaa, *Turkey* 72 B7
Erbeskopf, *Germany* 25 F3
Erbil = Arbīl, *Iraq* 70 B5
Erbu, *Ethiopia* 81 E3
Erçek, *Turkey* 70 B4
Erçiş, *Turkey* 73 C10
Erciyaş Dağı, *Turkey* 70 B2
Érd, *Hungary* 28 C3
Erdao Jiang →, *China* 57 C14
Erdek, *Turkey* 45 F11
Erdemli, *Turkey* 72 D6
Erdene = Ulaan-Uul, *Mongolia* . 56 B5
Erdenetsogt, *Mongolia* 56 C4
Erding, *Germany* 25 G7
Erdre →, *France* 18 E5
Erebus, Mt., *Antarctica* 5 D11
Erechim, *Brazil* 127 B5
Ereğli, *Konya, Turkey* 70 B2
Ereğli, *Zonguldak, Turkey* 72 B4
Erei, Monti, *Italy* 43 E7
Erenhot, *China* 56 C7
Eresma →, *Spain* 36 D6
Eressós, *Greece* 47 B7
Erfenisdam, *S. Africa* 88 D4
Erft →, *Germany* 24 D2
Erfurt, *Germany* 24 E7
Ergani, *Turkey* 70 B3
Ergel, *Mongolia* 56 C5
Ergene →, *Turkey* 45 E10
Ergeni Vozvyshennost, *Russia* . 35 G7
Érgli, *Latvia* 9 H21
Erhlin, *Taiwan* 59 F13
Eria →, *Spain* 36 C5
Eriba, *Sudan* 81 D4
Eriboll, L., *U.K.* 13 C4
Érice, *Italy* 42 D5
Erie, *U.S.A.* 116 D4
Erie, L., *N. Amer.* 116 D4
Erie Canal, *U.S.A.* 116 C7
Erieau, *Canada* 116 D3
Erigavo, *Somali Rep.* 75 E4
Erikoúsa, *Greece* 49 A3
Eriksdale, *Canada* 103 C9
Erímanthos, *Greece* 46 D3
Erimo-misaki, *Japan* 54 D11
Erin Pt., *Trin. & Tob.* 125 K15
Erinpura, *India* 68 G5
Eriskay, *U.K.* 13 D1
Erithraí, *Greece* 46 C5
Eritrea ■, *Africa* 81 E4
Erjas →, *Portugal* 36 F3
Erkelenz, *Germany* 24 D2
Erkner, *Germany* 24 C9
Erlangen, *Germany* 25 F6
Erldunda, *Australia* 94 D1
Ermelo, *Neths.* 17 B5
Ermelo, *S. Africa* 89 D4
Ermenek, *Turkey* 70 B2
Ermil, *Sudan* 81 E2
Ermióni, *Greece* 46 D5
Ermones, *Greece* 49 A3
Ernakulam, *India* 66 Q10
Erne →, *Ireland* 12 B3
Erne, Lower L., *U.K.* 12 B4
Erne, Upper L., *U.K.* 12 B4
Ernée, *France* 18 D6
Ernest Giles Ra., *Australia* ... 93 E3
Ernstberg, *Germany* 25 E2
Erode, *India* 66 P10
Eromanga, *Australia* 95 D3
Erongo, *Namibia* 88 C2
Erquy, *France* 18 D4
Erramala Hills, *India* 66 M11
Errer →, *Ethiopia* 81 F5
Errigal, *Ireland* 12 A3
Erris Hd., *Ireland* 12 B1
Ersekë, *Albania* 44 F4
Erskine, *U.S.A.* 112 B7
Erstein, *France* 19 D14
Ertholmene, *Denmark* 11 J9
Ertil, *Russia* 34 E5
Ertis = Irtysh →, *Russia* 52 C7
Eruh, *Turkey* 73 D10
Eruwa, *Nigeria* 83 D5
Ervy-le-Châtel, *France* 19 D10
Erwin, *U.S.A.* 115 G4
Eryuan, *China* 58 D2
Erzgebirge, *Germany* 24 E8
Erzin, *Russia* 53 D10
Erzincan, *Turkey* 70 B3
Erzurum, *Turkey* 70 B4
Es Caló, *Spain* 48 C8
Es Canar, *Spain* 48 B8
Es Mercadal, *Spain* 48 B11
Es Migjorn Gran, *Spain* 48 B11
Es Safiya, *Sudan* 81 D3
Es Sahrâ' Esh Sharqîya, *Egypt* . 80 B3
Es Sînâ', *Egypt* 74 F3
Es Sûkî, *Sudan* 81 E3
Es Vedrà, *Spain* 48 C7
Esan-Misaki, *Japan* 54 D10
Esashi, *Hokkaidō, Japan* 54 B11
Esashi, *Hokkaidō, Japan* 54 D10
Esbjerg, *Denmark* 11 J2
Esbo = Espoo, *Finland* 9 F21
Escalante, *U.S.A.* 109 H8
Escalante →, *U.S.A.* 109 H8
Escalón, *Mexico* 118 B4
Escambia →, *U.S.A.* 115 K2
Escanaba, *U.S.A.* 114 C2
Esch-sur-Alzette, *Lux.* 17 E6

Eschede, *Germany* 24 C6
Eschwege, *Germany* 24 D6
Eschweiler, *Germany* 24 E2
Escondido, *U.S.A.* 111 M9
Escravos →, *Nigeria* 83 D6
Escuinapa, *Mexico* 118 C3
Escuintla, *Guatemala* 120 D1
Eséka, *Cameroon* 83 E7
Eşen →, *Turkey* 47 E11
Esenguly, *Turkmenistan* 52 F6
Esens, *Germany* 24 B3
Esera →, *Spain* 38 C5
Eşfahān, *Iran* 71 C6
Eşfahān □, *Iran* 71 C6
Esfarāyen, *Iran* 71 B8
Esfideh, *Iran* 71 C8
Esgueva →, *Spain* 36 D6
Esh Sham = Dimashq, *Syria* ... 74 B5
Esh Shamâlîya □, *Sudan* 80 D2
Esha Ness, *U.K.* 13 A7
Eshan, *China* 58 E4
Esher, *U.K.* 15 F7
Eshkol △, *Israel* 74 D3
Eshowe, *S. Africa* 89 D5
Esiama, *Ghana* 82 E4
Esigodini, *Zimbabwe* 89 C4
Esil = Ishim →, *Russia* 52 D8
Esino →, *Italy* 41 E10
Esira, *Madag.* 89 C8
Esk →, *Cumb., U.K.* 13 G5
Esk →, *N. Yorks., U.K.* 14 C7
Eskān, *Iran* 71 E9
Esker, *Canada* 105 B6
Eskifjörður, *Iceland* 8 D7
Eskilsäter, *Sweden* 11 F7
Eskilstuna, *Sweden* 10 E10
Eskimalatya, *Turkey* 73 C8
Eskimo Point = Arviat, *Canada* . 103 A10
Eskişehir, *Turkey* 47 B12
Eskişehir □, *Turkey* 47 B12
Esla →, *Spain* 36 D4
Eslāmābād-e Gharb, *Iran* 70 C5
Eslāmshahr, *Iran* 71 C6
Eslöv, *Sweden* 11 J7
Eşme, *Turkey* 47 C10
Esmeraldas, *Ecuador* 124 C3
Esnagi L., *Canada* 104 C3
Espalion, *France* 20 D6
Espanola, *Canada* 104 C3
Espanola, *U.S.A.* 109 H10
Esparreguera, *Spain* 38 D6
Esparta, *Costa Rica* 120 E3
Espelkamp, *Germany* 24 C4
Esperance, *Australia* 93 F3
Esperance B., *Australia* 93 F3
Esperance Harbour □, *St. Lucia* 121 f
Esperanza, *Antarctica* 5 C18
Esperanza, *Argentina* 126 C3
Esperanza, *Phil.* 61 G6
Esperanza, *Puerto Rico* ...... 121 d
Espéraza, *France* 20 F6
Espichel, C., *Portugal* 37 G1
Espiel, *Spain* 37 G5
Espigão, Serra do, *Brazil* 127 B5
Espinazo, Sierra del = Espinhaço,
  Serra do, *Brazil* 125 G10
Espinhaço, Serra do, *Brazil* .. 125 G10
Espinho, *Portugal* 36 D2
Espinilho, Serra do, *Brazil* ... 127 B5
Espinosa de los Monteros, *Spain* 36 B7
Espírito Santo □, *Brazil* 125 H10
Espíritu Santo, *Vanuatu* 96 J8
Espíritu Santo, B. del, *Mexico* 119 D7
Espíritu Santo, I., *Mexico* 118 C2
Espita, *Mexico* 119 C7
Espiye, *Turkey* 73 B8
Espluga de Francolí, *Spain* ... 38 D6
Espoo, *Finland* 9 F21
España, Sierra de, *Spain* 39 H3
Espungabera, *Mozam.* 89 C5
Esquel, *Argentina* 128 E2
Esquina, *Argentina* 126 C4
Esquimalt, *Canada* 102 D4
Essaouira, *Morocco* 78 B4
Essebie, *Dem. Rep. of the Congo* 86 B3
Essen, *Belgium* 17 C4
Essen, *Germany* 24 D3
Essendon, Mt., *Australia* 93 E3
Essequibo →, *Guyana* 124 B7
Essex, *Canada* 116 D2
Essex, *Calif., U.S.A.* 111 L11
Essex, *N.Y., U.S.A.* 117 B11
Essex □, *U.K.* 15 F8
Essex Junction, *U.S.A.* 117 B11
Esslingen, *Germany* 25 G5
Essonne □, *France* 19 D9
Estaca de Bares, C. de, *Spain* . 36 B3
Estadilla, *Spain* 38 C5
Estados, I. de Los, *Argentina* . 128 G4
Estagel, *France* 20 F6
Eştahbānāt, *Iran* 71 D7
Estância, *Brazil* 125 F11
Estancia, *U.S.A.* 109 J10
Estārm, *Iran* 71 D8
Estarreja, *Portugal* 36 E2
Estats, Pic d', *Spain* 38 C6
Estcourt, *S. Africa* 89 D4
Este △, *Dom. Rep.* 121 C6
Estelí, *Nic.* 120 D2
Estella, *Spain* 38 C2
Estellencs, *Spain* 48 B9
Estena →, *Spain* 37 F6
Estepa, *Spain* 37 H6
Estepona, *Spain* 37 J5
Esterhazy, *Canada* 103 C8
Esternay, *France* 19 D10
Esterri d'Aneu, *Spain* 38 C6
Estevan, *Canada* 103 D8
Estevan Group, *Canada* 102 C3
Estherville, *U.S.A.* 112 D7

Estissac, *France* 19 D10
Eston, *Canada* 103 C7
Estonia ■, *Europe* 9 G21
Estoril, *Portugal* 37 G1
Estouk, *Mali* 83 B5
Estreito, *Brazil* 125 E9
Estrela, Serra da, *Portugal* ... 36 E3
Estrella, *Spain* 37 G7
Estremoz, *Portugal* 37 G3
Estrondo, Serra do, *Brazil* ... 125 E9
Esztergom, *Hungary* 28 C3
Et Tîdra, *Mauritania* 82 B1
Etah, *India* 69 F8
Étain, *France* 19 C12
Étampes, *France* 19 D9
Etanga, *Namibia* 88 B1
Étaples, *France* 19 B8
Etawah, *India* 69 F8
Etawney L., *Canada* 103 B9
Ete, *Nigeria* 83 D6
eThekwini = Durban, *S. Africa* . 89 D5
Ethel, *U.S.A.* 110 D4
Ethelbert, *Canada* 103 C8
Ethiopia ■, *Africa* 75 F3
Ethiopian Highlands, *Ethiopia* . 50 J7
Etili, *Turkey* 45 G10
Etive, L., *U.K.* 13 E3
Etna, *Italy* 43 E7
Etoile, *Dem. Rep. of the Congo* . 87 E2
Etosha △, *Namibia* 88 B2
Etosha Pan, *Namibia* 88 B2
Etowah, *U.S.A.* 115 H3
Étréchy, *France* 19 D9
Étrépagny, *France* 19 C8
Étretat, *France* 18 C7
Etropole, *Bulgaria* 45 D8
Ettelbruck, *Lux.* 17 E6
Ettlingen, *Germany* 25 G4
Ettrick Water →, *U.K.* 13 F6
Etuku, *Dem. Rep. of the Congo* . 86 C2
Etulia, *Moldova* 29 E13
Etzatlán, *Mexico* 118 C4
Etzná-Tixmucuy = Edzná, *Mexico* 119 D6
Eu, *France* 18 B8
Eubenangee Swamp △, *Australia* 94 B4
Euboea = Évvoia, *Greece* 46 C6
Eucla, *Australia* 93 F4
Euclid, *U.S.A.* 116 E3
Eucumbene, L., *Australia* 95 F4
Eudora, *U.S.A.* 113 J9
Eufaula, *Ala., U.S.A.* 115 K3
Eufaula, *Okla., U.S.A.* 113 H7
Eufaula L., *U.S.A.* 113 H7
Eugene, *U.S.A.* 108 E2
Eugowra, *Australia* 95 E4
Eulo, *Australia* 95 D4
Eungella △, *Australia* 94 C4
Eunice, *La., U.S.A.* 113 K8
Eunice, *N. Mex., U.S.A.* 113 J3
Eupen, *Belgium* 17 D6
Euphrates = Furāt, Nahr al →,
  Asia 70 D5
Eure □, *France* 18 C8
Eure →, *France* 18 C8
Eure-et-Loir □, *France* 18 D8
Eureka, *Canada* 4 B3
Eureka, *Calif., U.S.A.* 108 F1
Eureka, *Kans., U.S.A.* 113 G6
Eureka, *Mont., U.S.A.* 108 B6
Eureka, *Nev., U.S.A.* 108 G5
Eureka, *S. Dak., U.S.A.* 112 C5
Eureka, Mt., *Australia* 93 E3
Euroa, *Australia* 95 F4
Europa, Île, *Ind. Oc.* 85 J8
Europa, Picos de, *Spain* 36 B6
Europa, Pta. de, *Gib.* 37 J5
Europe 6 E10
Europoort, *Neths.* 17 C4
Euskirchen, *Germany* 24 E2
Eustis, *U.S.A.* 115 L5
Eutin, *Germany* 24 A6
Eutsuk L., *Canada* 102 C3
Evale, *Angola* 88 B2
Evans, *U.S.A.* 112 E2
Evans, L., *Canada* 104 B4
Evans City, *U.S.A.* 116 F4
Evans Head, *Australia* 95 D5
Evans Mills, *U.S.A.* 117 B9
Evansburg, *Canada* 102 C5
Evanston, *Ill., U.S.A.* 114 E2
Evanston, *Wyo., U.S.A.* 108 F8
Évaux-les-Bains, *France* 19 F9
Evaz, *Iran* 71 E7
Eveciler, *Afyon, Turkey* 47 C11
Eveciler, *Çanakkale, Turkey* ... 47 B8
Eveleth, *U.S.A.* 112 B8
Evensk, *Russia* 53 C16
Everard, L., *Australia* 95 E2
Everard Ranges, *Australia* 93 E5
Everest, Mt., *Nepal* 69 E12
Everett, *Pa., U.S.A.* 116 F6
Everett, *Wash., U.S.A.* 110 C4
Everglades △, *U.S.A.* 115 N5
Everglades, The, *U.S.A.* 115 N5
Everglades City, *U.S.A.* 115 N5
Evergreen, *Ala., U.S.A.* 115 K2
Evergreen, *Mont., U.S.A.* 108 B6
Everöd, *Sweden* 11 J8
Evertsberg, *Sweden* 10 C7
Evesham, *U.K.* 15 E6
Évian-les-Bains, *France* 19 F13
Évinos →, *Greece* 46 C3
Évisa, *France* 21 F12
Evje, *Norway* 9 G12
Évora, *Portugal* 37 G3
Évora □, *Portugal* 37 G3
Evowghlī, *Iran* 70 B5
Évreux, *France* 18 C8
Évritanía □, *Greece* 46 B3
Évron, *France* 18 D6

Évros □, *Greece* — 45 E10
Évros �, *Greece* — 72 B2
Evrótas ➤, *Greece* — 46 E4
Évry, *France* — 19 D9
Évvoia, *Greece* — 46 C6
Évvoia □, *Greece* — 46 C5
Evxinoúpolis, *Greece* — 46 B4
Ewe, L., *U.K.* — 13 D3
Ewing, *U.S.A.* — 112 D5
Ewo, *Congo* — 84 E2
Exaltación, *Bolivia* — 124 F5
Excelsior Springs, *U.S.A.* — 112 F7
Excideuil, *France* — 20 C5
Exe ➤, *U.K.* — 15 G4
Exeter, *Canada* — 116 C3
Exeter, *U.K.* — 15 G4
Exeter, *Calif., U.S.A.* — 110 J7
Exeter, *N.H., U.S.A.* — 117 D14
Exmoor, *U.K.* — 15 F4
Exmoor △, *U.K.* — 15 F4
Exmouth, *Australia* — 92 D1
Exmouth, *U.K.* — 15 G4
Exmouth G., *Australia* — 92 D1
Expedition △, *Australia* — 95 D4
Expedition Ra., *Australia* — 94 C4
Extremadura □, *Spain* — 37 F4
Exuma Sound, *Bahamas* — 120 B4
Eyasi, L., *Tanzania* — 86 C4
Eye Pen., *U.K.* — 13 C2
Eyemouth, *U.K.* — 13 F6
Eygues = Aigues ➤, *France* — 21 D8
Eygurande, *France* — 19 C9
Eyjafjörður, *Iceland* — 8 C4
Eymet, *France* — 20 D4
Eymoutiers, *France* — 20 C5
Eynesil, *Turkey* — 73 B8
Eyre (North), L., *Australia* — 95 D2
Eyre (South), L., *Australia* — 95 D2
Eyre Mts., *N.Z.* — 91 L2
Eyre Pen., *Australia* — 95 E2
Eysturoy, *Faeroe Is.* — 8 E9
Eyvānkī, *Iran* — 71 C6
Ez Zeidab, *Sudan* — 80 D3
Ezcaray, *Spain* — 38 C1
Eẓ̌erélis, *Lithuania* — 30 D10
Ezhou, *China* — 59 B10
Ezine, *Turkey* — 47 B8
Ezouza ➤, *Cyprus* — 49 E11

F

F.Y.R.O.M. = Macedonia ■, *Europe* — 44 E5
Fabala, *Guinea* — 82 D3
Fabens, *U.S.A.* — 109 L10
Fabero, *Spain* — 36 C4
Fåborg, *Denmark* — 11 J4
Fabriano, *Italy* — 41 E9
Făcăeni, *Romania* — 29 F12
Fachi, *Niger* — 79 E8
Fada, *Chad* — 79 E10
Fada-n-Gourma, *Burkina Faso* — 83 C5
Fadd, *Hungary* — 28 D3
Faddeyevskiy, Ostrov, *Russia* — 53 B15
Faddor, *Sudan* — 81 F3
Fadghāmī, *Syria* — 70 C4
Fadlab, *Sudan* — 80 D3
Faenza, *Italy* — 41 D8
Færoe Is. = Føroyar, *Atl. Oc.* — 8 F9
Fafa, *Mali* — 83 B5
Fafe, *Portugal* — 36 D2
Fagam, *Nigeria* — 83 C7
Făgăraș, *Romania* — 29 E9
Făgăraș, Munții, *Romania* — 29 E9
Fågelmara, *Sweden* — 11 H9
Fagerhult, *Sweden* — 11 G9
Fagersta, *Sweden* — 10 D9
Făget, *Romania* — 28 E7
Făget, Munții, *Romania* — 29 C8
Fagnano, L., *Argentina* — 128 G3
Fagnières, *France* — 19 D11
Faguibine, L., *Mali* — 82 B4
Fahlīān, *Iran* — 71 D6
Fahraj, *Kermān, Iran* — 71 D8
Fahraj, *Yazd, Iran* — 71 D7
Fai Tsi Long, *Vietnam* — 58 G6
Faial, *Madeira* — 48 D3
Fair Haven, *U.S.A.* — 114 D9
Fair Hd., *U.K.* — 12 A5
Fair Oaks, *U.S.A.* — 110 G5
Fairbanks, *U.S.A.* — 100 B5
Fairbury, *U.S.A.* — 112 E6
Fairfax, *U.S.A.* — 117 B11
Fairfield, *Ala., U.S.A.* — 115 J2
Fairfield, *Calif., U.S.A.* — 110 G4
Fairfield, *Conn., U.S.A.* — 117 E11
Fairfield, *Idaho, U.S.A.* — 108 E6
Fairfield, *Ill., U.S.A.* — 114 F1
Fairfield, *Iowa, U.S.A.* — 112 E9
Fairfield, *Tex., U.S.A.* — 113 K7
Fairford, *Canada* — 103 C9
Fairhope, *U.S.A.* — 115 K2
Fairlie, *N.Z.* — 91 L3
Fairmead, *U.S.A.* — 110 H6
Fairmont, *Minn., U.S.A.* — 112 D7
Fairmont, *W. Va., U.S.A.* — 114 F5
Fairmount, *Calif., U.S.A.* — 111 L8
Fairmount, *N.Y., U.S.A.* — 117 C8
Fairplay, *U.S.A.* — 109 G11
Fairport, *U.S.A.* — 116 C7
Fairport Harbor, *U.S.A.* — 114 E3
Fairview, *Canada* — 102 B5
Fairview, *Mont., U.S.A.* — 112 B2
Fairview, *Okla., U.S.A.* — 113 G5
Fairweather, Mt., *U.S.A.* — 102 B1
Faisalabad, *Pakistan* — 68 D5
Faith, *U.S.A.* — 112 C3
Faizabad, *India* — 69 F10

Fajardo, *Puerto Rico* — 121 d
Fajr, W. ➤, *Si. Arabia* — 70 D3
Fakenham, *U.K.* — 14 E8
Fåker, *Sweden* — 10 A8
Fakfak, *Indonesia* — 63 E8
Fakiya, *Bulgaria* — 45 D11
Fakobli, *Ivory C.* — 82 D3
Fakse, *Denmark* — 11 J6
Fakse Bugt, *Denmark* — 11 J6
Fakse Ladeplads, *Denmark* — 11 J6
Faku, *China* — 57 C12
Falaba, *S. Leone* — 82 D2
Falaise, *France* — 18 D6
Falaise, Mui, *Vietnam* — 64 C5
Falakrón Óros, *Greece* — 44 E7
Falam, *Burma* — 67 H18
Falces, *Spain* — 38 C3
Fălciu, *Romania* — 29 D13
Falcó, C. des, *Spain* — 48 C7
Falcón, Presa, *Mexico* — 119 B5
Falcon Lake, *Canada* — 103 D9
Falcon Reservoir, *U.S.A.* — 113 M5
Falconara Maríttima, *Italy* — 41 E10
Falcone, C. del, *Italy* — 42 B1
Falconer, *U.S.A.* — 116 D5
Faléa, *Mali* — 82 C2
Falémé ➤, *Senegal* — 82 C2
Falerum, *Sweden* — 11 F10
Faleshty = Fălești, *Moldova* — 29 C12
Fălești, *Moldova* — 29 C12
Falfurrias, *U.S.A.* — 113 M5
Falher, *Canada* — 102 B5
Falirakí, *Greece* — 49 C10
Falkenberg, *Germany* — 24 D9
Falkenberg, *Sweden* — 11 H6
Falkensee, *Germany* — 24 C9
Falkirk, *U.K.* — 13 F5
Falkirk □, *U.K.* — 13 F5
Falkland, *U.K.* — 13 E5
Falkland Is. ☑, *Atl. Oc.* — 128 G5
Falkland Sd., *Falk. Is.* — 128 G5
Falkonéra, *Greece* — 46 E5
Falköping, *Sweden* — 11 F7
Fall River, *U.S.A.* — 117 E13
Fallbrook, *U.S.A.* — 111 M9
Fallon, *U.S.A.* — 108 G4
Falls City, *U.S.A.* — 112 E7
Falls Creek, *U.S.A.* — 116 E6
Falmouth, *Jamaica* — 120 a
Falmouth, *U.K.* — 15 G2
Falmouth, *U.S.A.* — 117 E14
Falsa, Pta., *Mexico* — 118 B1
False B., *S. Africa* — 88 E2
Falso, C., *Honduras* — 120 C3
Falster, *Denmark* — 11 K5
Fălticeni, *Romania* — 29 C11
Falun, *Sweden* — 10 D9
Famagusta, *Cyprus* — 49 D12
Famagusta Bay, *Cyprus* — 49 D13
Famalé, *Niger* — 78 F6
Famatina, Sierra de, *Argentina* — 126 B2
Family L., *Canada* — 103 C9
Famoso, *U.S.A.* — 111 K7
Fan Xian, *China* — 56 G8
Fana, *Mali* — 82 C3
Fanad Hd., *Ireland* — 12 A4
Fanárion, *Greece* — 46 B3
Fandriana, *Madag.* — 89 C8
Fánes-Sénnes e Braies △, *Italy* — 41 B9
Fang, *Thailand* — 58 H2
Fang Xian, *China* — 59 A8
Fangaga, *Sudan* — 80 D4
Fangak, *Sudan* — 81 F3
Fangchang, *China* — 59 B12
Fangcheng, *China* — 56 H7
Fangchenggang, *China* — 58 G7
Fangliao, *Taiwan* — 59 F13
Fangshan, *China* — 56 E6
Fangzi, *China* — 57 F10
Fani i Madh ➤, *Albania* — 44 E4
Fanjakana, *Madag.* — 89 C8
Fanjiatun, *China* — 57 C13
Fannich, L., *U.K.* — 13 D4
Fannūj, *Iran* — 71 E8
Fanø, *Denmark* — 11 J2
Fano, *Italy* — 41 E10
Fanshi, *China* — 56 E7
Fao = Al Fāw, *Iraq* — 71 D6
Faqirwali, *Pakistan* — 68 E5
Fâqûs, *Egypt* — 80 H7
Far East = Dalnevostochnyy □, *Russia* — 53 C14
Far East, *Asia* — 50 E16
Fara in Sabina, *Italy* — 41 F9
Faradje, *Dem. Rep. of the Congo* — 86 B2
Farafangana, *Madag.* — 89 C8
Farāfirā, El Wâhât el-, *Egypt* — 80 B2
Farāh, *Afghan.* — 66 C3
Farāh □, *Afghan.* — 66 C3
Farahalana, *Madag.* — 89 A9
Faraid, Gebel, *Egypt* — 80 C4
Farako, *Ivory C.* — 82 D4
Faramana, *Burkina Faso* — 82 C4
Faranah, *Guinea* — 82 C2
Farasān, Jazāʾir, *Si. Arabia* — 75 D3
Farasan Is. = Farasān, Jazāʾir, *Si. Arabia* — 75 D3
Faratsiho, *Madag.* — 89 B8
Fardes ➤, *Spain* — 37 H7
Fareham, *U.K.* — 15 G6
Farewell, C., *N.Z.* — 91 J4
Farewell C. = Nunap Isua, *Greenland* — 101 C15
Färgelanda, *Sweden* — 11 F5
Farghona, *Uzbekistan* — 52 E8
Fār̄iah, W. al ➤, *West Bank* — 74 C4
Faribault, *U.S.A.* — 112 C8
Faridabad, *India* — 68 E6
Faridkot, *India* — 68 D6
Faridpur, *Bangla.* — 69 H13

Faridpur, *India* — 69 E8
Färila, *Sweden* — 10 C9
Farim, *Guinea-Biss.* — 82 C1
Farīmān, *Iran* — 71 C8
Farina, *Australia* — 95 E2
Fariones, Pta., *Canary Is.* — 48 E6
Fâriskûr, *Egypt* — 80 H7
Färjestaden, *Sweden* — 11 H10
Farkadhón, *Greece* — 46 B4
Farleigh, *Australia* — 94 K7
Farmakonisi, *Greece* — 47 D9
Farmerville, *U.S.A.* — 113 J8
Farmingdale, *U.S.A.* — 117 F10
Farmington, *Canada* — 102 B4
Farmington, *Calif., U.S.A.* — 110 H6
Farmington, *Maine, U.S.A.* — 115 C10
Farmington, *Mo., U.S.A.* — 113 G9
Farmington, *N.H., U.S.A.* — 117 C13
Farmington, *N. Mex., U.S.A.* — 109 H9
Farmington, *Utah, U.S.A.* — 108 F8
Farmington ➤, *U.S.A.* — 117 E12
Farmville, *U.S.A.* — 114 G6
Farne Is., *U.K.* — 14 B6
Färnebofjärden △, *Sweden* — 10 D10
Farnham, *Canada* — 117 A12
Farnham, Mt., *Canada* — 102 C5
Faro, *Brazil* — 125 D7
Faro, *Canada* — 100 B6
Faro, *Portugal* — 37 H3
Fårö, *Sweden* — 9 H18
Faro □, *Portugal* — 37 H2
Faro ✈ (FAO), *Portugal* — 37 H3
Fårösund, *Sweden* — 11 G13
Farquhar, C., *Australia* — 93 D1
Farrars Cr. ➤, *Australia* — 94 D3
Farrāshband, *Iran* — 71 D7
Farrell, *U.S.A.* — 116 E4
Farrokhī, *Iran* — 71 C8
Farruch, C. = Ferrutx, C., *Spain* — 48 B10
Fārs □, *Iran* — 71 D7
Fársala, *Greece* — 46 B4
Farsø, *Denmark* — 11 H3
Farson, *U.S.A.* — 108 E9
Farsund, *Norway* — 9 G12
Fartak, Râs, *Si. Arabia* — 70 D2
Fartak, Ra's, *Yemen* — 75 D5
Fârțănești, *Romania* — 29 E12
Fartura, Serra da, *Brazil* — 127 B5
Faru, *Nigeria* — 83 C6
Fārūj, *Iran* — 71 B8
Fårup, *Denmark* — 11 H3
Farvel, Kap = Nunap Isua, *Greenland* — 101 C15
Farwell, *U.S.A.* — 113 H3
Fāryāb □, *Afghan.* — 66 B4
Fasā, *Iran* — 71 D7
Fasano, *Italy* — 43 B10
Fashoda, *Sudan* — 81 F3
Fassa, *Mali* — 82 C3
Fastiv, *Ukraine* — 33 G5
Fastnet Rock, *Ireland* — 12 E2
Fastov = Fastiv, *Ukraine* — 33 G5
Fatagar, Tanjung, *Indonesia* — 63 E8
Fatehabad, *Haryana, India* — 68 E6
Fatehabad, *Ut. P., India* — 68 F8
Fatehgarh, *India* — 69 F8
Fatehpur, *Bihar, India* — 69 G11
Fatehpur, *Raj., India* — 68 E6
Fatehpur, *Ut. P., India* — 69 G9
Fatehpur, *Ut. P., India* — 69 F9
Fatehpur Sikri, *India* — 68 F6
Fatesh, *Russia* — 33 F8
Fathai, *Sudan* — 81 F3
Fathom Five △, *Canada* — 116 A3
Fatick, *Senegal* — 82 C1
Fatima, *Canada* — 105 C7
Fátima, *Portugal* — 37 F2
Fatoya, *Guinea* — 82 C3
Fatsa, *Turkey* — 72 B7
Faucille, Col de la, *France* — 19 F13
Faulkton, *U.S.A.* — 112 C5
Faulquemont, *France* — 19 C13
Faure I., *Australia* — 93 E1
Făurei, *Romania* — 29 E12
Fauresmith, *S. Africa* — 88 D4
Fauske, *Norway* — 8 C16
Favara, *Italy* — 42 E6
Faváritx, C. de, *Spain* — 48 B11
Faverges, *France* — 21 C10
Favignana, *Italy* — 42 E5
Favignana, I., *Italy* — 42 E5
Fawcett, Pt., *Australia* — 92 B5
Fawn ➤, *Canada* — 104 A2
Fawnskin, *U.S.A.* — 111 L10
Faxaflói, *Iceland* — 8 D2
Faxälven ➤, *Sweden* — 10 A10
Faya-Largeau, *Chad* — 79 E9
Fayd, *Si. Arabia* — 70 E4
Fayence, *France* — 21 E10
Fayette, *Ala., U.S.A.* — 115 J2
Fayette, *Mo., U.S.A.* — 112 F8
Fayetteville, *Ark., U.S.A.* — 113 G7
Fayetteville, *N.C., U.S.A.* — 115 H6
Fayetteville, *Tenn., U.S.A.* — 115 H2
Fayied, *Egypt* — 80 H8
Fayón, *Spain* — 38 D5
Fazao-Malfakassa △, *Togo* — 83 D5
Fazilka, *India* — 68 D6
Fazilpur, *Pakistan* — 68 E4
Feale ➤, *Ireland* — 12 D2
Fear, C., *U.S.A.* — 115 J7
Feather ➤, *U.S.A.* — 108 G3
Feather Falls, *U.S.A.* — 110 F5
Featherston, *N.Z.* — 91 J5
Featherstone, *Zimbabwe* — 87 F3
Fécamp, *France* — 18 C7
Fedala = Mohammedia, *Morocco* — 78 B4
Federación, *Argentina* — 126 C4
Féderal, *Argentina* — 128 C5

Federal Capital Terr. □, *Nigeria* — 83 D6
Federal Way, *U.S.A.* — 110 C4
Fedeshküh, *Iran* — 71 D7
Fehérgyarmat, *Hungary* — 28 C7
Fehmarn, *Germany* — 24 A7
Fehmarn Belt = Fehmarn Bælt, *Europe* — 11 K5
Fehmarn Belt = Fehmarn Bælt, *Europe* — 11 K5
Fei Xian, *China* — 57 G9
Feijó, *Brazil* — 124 E4
Feilding, *N.Z.* — 91 J5
Feira de Santana, *Brazil* — 125 F11
Feixi, *China* — 59 B11
Feixiang, *China* — 56 F8
Fejér □, *Hungary* — 28 C3
Fejø, *Denmark* — 11 K5
Feke, *Turkey* — 72 D6
Fekete ➤, *Hungary* — 28 E3
Felanitx, *Spain* — 48 B10
Feldbach, *Austria* — 26 E8
Feldberg, *Baden-W., Germany* — 25 H3
Feldberg, *Mecklenburg-Vorpommern, Germany* — 24 B9
Feldkirch, *Austria* — 26 D2
Feldkirchen, *Austria* — 26 E7
Felipe Carrillo Puerto, *Mexico* — 119 D7
Felixburg, *Zimbabwe* — 89 B5
Felixstowe, *U.K.* — 15 F9
Felletin, *France* — 20 C6
Fellingsbro, *Sweden* — 10 E9
Felton, *U.S.A.* — 110 H4
Feltre, *Italy* — 41 B8
Femer Bælt = Fehmarn Bælt, *Europe* — 11 K5
Femø, *Denmark* — 11 K5
Femunden, *Norway* — 9 E14
Fen He ➤, *China* — 56 G6
Fene, *Spain* — 36 B2
Fenelon Falls, *Canada* — 116 B6
Fener Burnu, *Turkey* — 47 E9
Feneroa, *Ethiopia* — 81 E4
Feng Xian, *Jiangsu, China* — 56 G9
Feng Xian, *Shaanxi, China* — 56 H4
Fengari, *Greece* — 45 F9
Fengcheng, *Jiangxi, China* — 59 C10
Fengcheng, *Liaoning, China* — 57 D13
Fengfeng, *China* — 56 F8
Fenggang, *China* — 58 D6
Fenghua, *China* — 59 C13
Fenghuang, *China* — 58 D7
Fengkai, *China* — 59 F8
Fengle, *China* — 59 B9
Fenglin, *Taiwan* — 59 F13
Fengning, *China* — 56 D9
Fengqing, *China* — 58 E2
Fengqiu, *China* — 56 G8
Fengrun, *China* — 57 E10
Fengshan, *Guangxi Zhuangzu, China* — 58 E7
Fengshan, *Guangxi Zhuangzu, China* — 58 E6
Fengshan, *Taiwan* — 59 F13
Fengshun, *China* — 59 F11
Fengtai, *Anhui, China* — 59 A11
Fengtai, *Beijing, China* — 56 E9
Fengxian, *China* — 59 B13
Fengxiang, *China* — 56 G4
Fengxin, *China* — 59 C10
Fengyang, *China* — 57 H9
Fengyi, *China* — 58 E3
Fengyuan, *Taiwan* — 59 E13
Fengzhen, *China* — 56 D7
Feno, C. de, *France* — 21 G12
Fenoarivo, *Fianarantsoa, Madag.* — 89 C8
Fenoarivo, *Fianarantsoa, Madag.* — 89 C8
Fenoarivo Afovoany, *Madag.* — 89 B8
Fenoarivo Atsinanana, *Madag.* — 89 B8
Fens, The, *U.K.* — 14 E7
Fensmark, *Denmark* — 11 J5
Fenton, *U.S.A.* — 114 D4
Fenxi, *China* — 56 F6
Fenyang, *China* — 56 F6
Fenyi, *China* — 59 D10
Feodosiya, *Ukraine* — 33 K8
Ferdows, *Iran* — 71 C8
Fère-Champenoise, *France* — 19 D10
Fère-en-Tardenois, *France* — 19 C10
Ferentino, *Italy* — 41 G10
Ferfer, *Somali Rep.* — 75 F4
Fergana = Farghona, *Uzbekistan* — 52 E8
Fergus, *Canada* — 116 C4
Fergus Falls, *U.S.A.* — 112 B6
Feričanci, *Croatia* — 28 E2
Ferihegy, Budapest ✈ (BUD), *Hungary* — 28 C4
Ferkéssédougou, *Ivory C.* — 82 D3
Ferlach, *Austria* — 26 E7
Ferland, *Canada* — 104 B2
Ferlo, Vallée du, *Senegal* — 82 B2
Ferlo-Nord △, *Senegal* — 82 B2
Ferlo-Sud △, *Senegal* — 82 B2
Fermanagh □, *U.K.* — 12 B4
Fermo, *Italy* — 41 E10
Fermont, *Canada* — 105 B6
Fermoselle, *Spain* — 36 D4
Fermoy, *Ireland* — 12 D3
Fernán Núñez, *Spain* — 37 H6
Fernández, *Argentina* — 126 B3
Fernandina Beach, *U.S.A.* — 115 K5
Fernando de Noronha, *Brazil* — 125 D12
Fernando Póo = Bioko, *Eq. Guin.* — 83 E6
Ferndale, *U.S.A.* — 108 B1
Fernie, *Canada* — 102 D5
Fernlees, *Australia* — 94 C4
Fernley, *U.S.A.* — 108 G4
Ferozepore = Firozpur, *India* — 68 D6
Férrai, *Greece* — 45 F10
Ferrandina, *Italy* — 43 B9
Ferrara, *Italy* — 41 D8

Ferrato, C., *Italy* — 42 C2
Ferreira do Alentejo, *Portugal* — 37 G2
Ferreñafe, *Peru* — 124 E3
Ferrerías, *Spain* — 48 B11
Ferret, C., *France* — 20 D2
Ferrette, *France* — 19 E14
Ferriday, *U.S.A.* — 113 K9
Ferriere, *Italy* — 40 D6
Ferrières, *France* — 19 D9
Ferro, Capo, *Italy* — 42 A2
Ferrol, *Spain* — 36 B2
Ferron, *U.S.A.* — 109 G8
Ferrutx, C., *Spain* — 48 B10
Ferryland, *Canada* — 105 C9
Fertile, *U.S.A.* — 112 B6
Fertőszentmiklós, *Hungary* — 28 C1
Fertőtavi △, *Hungary* — 28 C1
Fès, *Morocco* — 78 B5
Fessenden, *U.S.A.* — 112 B5
Festus, *U.S.A.* — 112 F9
Feté Bowé, *Senegal* — 82 C2
Fetești, *Romania* — 29 F12
Fethiye, *Turkey* — 47 E11
Fethiye Körfezi, *Turkey* — 47 E10
Fetlar, *U.K.* — 13 A8
Feuilles ➤, *Canada* — 101 C12
Feurs, *France* — 21 C8
Fez = Fès, *Morocco* — 78 B5
Fezzan, *Libya* — 79 C8
Fiambalá, *Argentina* — 126 B2
Fianarantsoa, *Madag.* — 89 C8
Fianarantsoa □, *Madag.* — 89 B8
Fiche, *Ethiopia* — 81 F4
Fichtelgebirge, *Germany* — 25 E7
Fichtelgebirge △, *Germany* — 25 E8
Ficksburg, *S. Africa* — 89 D4
Fidenza, *Italy* — 40 D7
Fiditi, *Nigeria* — 83 D5
Field ➤, *Australia* — 94 C2
Field I., *Australia* — 92 B5
Fieni, *Romania* — 29 E10
Fier, *Albania* — 44 F3
Fierzë, *Albania* — 44 D4
Fife □, *U.K.* — 13 E5
Fife Ness, *U.K.* — 13 E6
Fifth Cataract, *Sudan* — 80 D3
Figari, *France* — 21 G13
Figeac, *France* — 20 D6
Figeholm, *Sweden* — 11 G10
Figline Valdarno, *Italy* — 41 E8
Figtree, *Zimbabwe* — 87 G2
Figueira Castelo Rodrigo, *Portugal* — 36 E4
Figueira da Foz, *Portugal* — 36 E2
Figueiró dos Vinhos, *Portugal* — 36 F2
Figueres, *Spain* — 38 C7
Figuig, *Morocco* — 78 B5
Fihaonana, *Madag.* — 89 B8
Fiherenana, *Madag.* — 89 B8
Fiherenana ➤, *Madag.* — 89 C7
Fiji ■, *Pac. Oc.* — 91 C8
Fik, *Ethiopia* — 81 F5
Fika, *Nigeria* — 83 C7
Filabres, Sierra de los, *Spain* — 37 H8
Filabusi, *Zimbabwe* — 89 C4
Filadélfia, *Italy* — 43 D9
Fil'akovo, *Slovak Rep.* — 27 C12
Filey, *U.K.* — 14 C7
Filey B., *U.K.* — 14 C7
Filfla, *Malta* — 49 D1
Filiași, *Romania* — 29 F8
Filiátes, *Greece* — 46 B2
Filiatrá, *Greece* — 46 D3
Filicudi, *Italy* — 43 D7
Filingué, *Niger* — 83 C5
Filiouri ➤, *Greece* — 45 E9
Filipstad, *Sweden* — 10 E8
Filisur, *Switz.* — 25 J5
Fillmore, *Calif., U.S.A.* — 111 L8
Fillmore, *Utah, U.S.A.* — 109 G7
Filótion, *Greece* — 47 D7
Filottrano, *Italy* — 41 E10
Filtu, *Ethiopia* — 81 F5
Fina △, *Mali* — 82 C3
Finale Emília, *Italy* — 41 D8
Finale Lígure, *Italy* — 40 D5
Fiñana, *Spain* — 37 H8
Finch, *Canada* — 117 A9
Finch Hatton, *Australia* — 94 K6
Findhorn ➤, *U.K.* — 13 D5
Findlay, *U.S.A.* — 114 E4
Finger L., *Canada* — 104 B1
Finger Lakes, *U.S.A.* — 117 D8
Fíngoè, *Mozam.* — 87 E3
Finike, *Turkey* — 47 E12
Finike Körfezi, *Turkey* — 47 E12
Finiq, *Albania* — 44 G4
Finistère □, *France* — 18 D3
Finisterre = Fisterra, *Spain* — 36 C1
Finisterre, C. = Fisterra, C., *Spain* — 36 C1
Finke, *Australia* — 94 D1
Finke Gorge △, *Australia* — 92 D5
Finland ■, *Europe* — 8 E22
Finland, G. of, *Europe* — 9 G21
Finlay ➤, *Canada* — 102 B3
Finley, *Australia* — 95 F4
Finley, *U.S.A.* — 112 B6
Finn ➤, *Ireland* — 12 B4
Finnerödja, *Sweden* — 11 F8
Finnigan, Mt., *Australia* — 94 B4
Finniss, C., *Australia* — 95 E1
Finnmark, *Norway* — 8 B20
Finnsnes, *Norway* — 8 B18
Finspång, *Sweden* — 11 F9
Finsteraarhorn, *Switz.* — 25 J4
Finsterwalde, *Germany* — 24 D9
Fiora ➤, *Italy* — 41 F8
Fiordland △, *N.Z.* — 91 L1
Fiorenzuola d'Arda, *Italy* — 40 D6
Fīq, *Syria* — 74 C4

Firat = Furāt, Nahr al ➘, *Asia* .. 70 D5
Fire Island ○, *U.S.A.* 117 F11
Firebag ➘, *Canada* 103 B6
Firebaugh, *U.S.A.* 110 J6
Firedrake L., *Canada* 103 A8
Firenze, *Italy* 41 E8
Firenze Amerigo Vespucci ✈
(FLR), *Italy* 40 E8
Firenze Pisa ✈ (PSA), *Italy* .. 40 E7
Firenzuola, *Italy* 41 D8
Firk, Sha'ib ➘, *Iraq* 70 D5
Firmi, *France* 20 D6
Firminy, *France* 21 C8
Firozabad, *India* 69 F8
Firozpur, *India* 68 D6
Firozpur-Jhirka, *India* 68 F7
Fīrūzābād, *Iran* 71 D7
Fīrūzkūh, *Iran* 71 C7
Firvale, *Canada* 102 C3
Fish ➘, *Namibia* 88 D2
Fish ➘, *S. Africa* 88 E3
Fish River Canyon, *Namibia* ... 88 D2
Fisher, *Australia* 93 F5
Fisher B., *Canada* 103 C9
Fishers I., *U.S.A.* 117 E13
Fishguard, *U.K.* 15 E3
Fishing L., *Canada* 103 C9
Fishkill, *U.S.A.* 117 E11
Fismes, *France* 19 C10
Fisterra, *Spain* 36 C1
Fisterra, C., *Spain* 36 C1
Fitchburg, *U.S.A.* 117 D13
Fitz Roy, *Argentina* 128 F3
Fitzgerald, *Canada* 102 B6
Fitzgerald, *U.S.A.* 115 K4
Fitzgerald River △, *Australia* .. 93 F3
Fitzmaurice ➘, *Australia* 92 B5
Fitzroy ➘, *Queens., Australia* .. 94 C5
Fitzroy ➘, *W. Austral., Australia* 92 C3
Fitzroy, Mte., *Argentina* 128 F2
Fitzroy Crossing, *Australia* 92 C4
Fitzwilliam I., *Canada* 116 A3
Fiuggi, *Italy* 41 G10
Fiume = Rijeka, *Croatia* 41 C11
Fiumicino, Roma ✈ (FCO), *Italy* 41 G9
Five Points, *U.S.A.* 110 J6
Fivizzano, *Italy* 40 D7
Fizi, *Dem. Rep. of the Congo* .. 86 C2
Fjällbacka, *Sweden* 11 F5
Fjärdhundra, *Sweden* 10 E10
Fjellerup, *Denmark* 11 H4
Fjerritslev, *Denmark* 11 G3
Fjugesta, *Sweden* 10 E8
Flagstaff, *U.S.A.* 109 J8
Flagstaff L., *U.S.A.* 115 C10
Flaherty I., *Canada* 104 A4
Flåm, *Norway* 9 F12
Flambeau ➘, *U.S.A.* 112 C9
Flamborough Hd., *U.K.* 14 C7
Fläming, *Germany* 24 C8
Flaming Gorge ○, *U.S.A.* 108 F9
Flaming Gorge Reservoir, *U.S.A.* 108 F9
Flamingo, Teluk, *Indonesia* 63 F9
Flanders = Flandre, *Europe* 19 B9
Flandre, *Europe* 19 B9
Flandre-Occidentale = West-
Vlaanderen □, *Belgium* 17 D2
Flandre-Orientale = Oost-
Vlaanderen □, *Belgium* 17 C3
Flandreau, *U.S.A.* 112 C6
Flanigan, *U.S.A.* 110 E7
Flannan Is., *U.K.* 13 C1
Flåsjön, *Sweden* 8 D16
Flat ➘, *Canada* 102 A3
Flathead L., *U.S.A.* 108 C7
Flattery, C., *Australia* 94 A4
Flattery, C., *U.S.A.* 110 B2
Flatwoods, *U.S.A.* 114 F4
Fleetwood, *U.K.* 14 D4
Fleetwood, *U.S.A.* 117 F9
Flekkefjord, *Norway* 9 G12
Flemington, *U.S.A.* 116 E7
Flen, *Sweden* 10 E10
Flensburg, *Germany* 24 A5
Flers, *France* 18 D6
Flesherton, *Canada* 116 B4
Flesko, Tanjung, *Indonesia* 63 D6
Fleurance, *France* 20 E4
Fleurier, *Switz.* 25 J2
Fleurieu Pen., *Australia* 95 F2
Flevoland □, *Neths.* 17 B5
Flin Flon, *Canada* 103 C8
Flinders ➘, *Australia* 94 B3
Flinders B., *Australia* 93 F2
Flinders Group, *Australia* 94 A3
Flinders I., *S. Austral., Australia* 95 E1
Flinders I., *Tas., Australia* 95 G4
Flinders Ranges, *Australia* 95 E2
Flinders Reefs, *Australia* 94 B4
Flint, *U.K.* 14 D4
Flint, *U.S.A.* 114 D4
Flint ➘, *U.S.A.* 115 K3
Flint I., *Kiribati* 97 J12
Flintshire □, *U.K.* 14 D4
Fliseryd, *Sweden* 11 G10
Flix, *Spain* 38 D5
Flixecourt, *France* 19 B9
Floby, *Sweden* 11 F7
Floda, *Sweden* 11 G6
Flodden, *U.K.* 13 F6
Flogny-la-Chapelle, *France* 19 E10
Floodwood, *U.S.A.* 112 B8
Flora, *U.S.A.* 114 F1
Florac, *France* 20 D7
Florala, *U.S.A.* 115 K2
Florence = Firenze, *Italy* 41 E8
Florence, *Ala., U.S.A.* 115 H2
Florence, *Ariz., U.S.A.* 109 K8
Florence, *Colo., U.S.A.* 112 F2
Florence, *Oreg., U.S.A.* 108 E1
Florence, *S.C., U.S.A.* 115 H6

Florence, L., *Australia* 95 D2
Florencia, *Colombia* 124 C3
Florennes, *Belgium* 17 D4
Florensac, *France* 20 E7
Florenville, *Belgium* 17 E5
Flores, *Guatemala* 120 C2
Flores, *Indonesia* 63 F6
Flores I., *Canada* 102 D3
Flores Sea, *Indonesia* 63 F6
Floreşti, *Moldova* 29 C13
Floresville, *U.S.A.* 113 L5
Floriano, *Brazil* 125 E10
Florianópolis, *Brazil* 127 B6
Florida, *Cuba* 120 B4
Florida, *Uruguay* 127 C4
Florida □, *U.S.A.* 115 L5
Florida, Straits of, *U.S.A.* 120 B4
Florida B., *U.S.A.* 120 B3
Florida Keys, *U.S.A.* 115 N5
Florída, *Italy* 43 E8
Flórina, *Greece* 44 F5
Flórina □, *Greece* 44 F5
Florø, *Norway* 9 F11
Flower Station, *Canada* 117 A8
Flowerpot I., *Canada* 116 A3
Floydada, *U.S.A.* 113 J4
Fluk, *Indonesia* 63 E7
Flúmen ➘, *Spain* 38 D4
Flumendosa ➘, *Italy* 42 C2
Fluminimaggiore, *Italy* 42 C1
Flushing = Vlissingen, *Neths.* .. 17 C3
Fluviá ➘, *Spain* 38 C8
Flying Fish, C., *Antarctica* 5 D15
Foam Lake, *Canada* 103 C8
Foča, *Bos.-H.* 44 C2
Foça, *Turkey* 47 C8
Fochabers, *U.K.* 13 D5
Focşani, *Romania* 29 E12
Fodang, *China* 59 F9
Fodécontéa, *Guinea* 82 C2
Fóggia, *Italy* 43 A8
Foggo, *Nigeria* 83 C6
Foglia ➘, *Italy* 41 E9
Fogo, *Canada* 105 C9
Fogo I., *Canada* 105 C9
Fohnsdorf, *Austria* 26 D7
Föhr, *Germany* 24 A4
Foia, *Portugal* 37 H2
Foix, *France* 20 F5
Fojnica, *Bos.-H.* 28 G2
Fokino, *Russia* 32 F8
Fokís □, *Greece* 46 C4
Fokku, *Nigeria* 83 C5
Folda, *Nord-Trøndelag, Norway* 8 D14
Folda, *Nordland, Norway* 8 C16
Földeák, *Hungary* 28 D5
Folégandros, *Greece* 46 E6
Foley, *Botswana* 88 C4
Foley, *U.S.A.* 115 K2
Foleyet, *Canada* 104 C3
Folgefonni, *Norway* 9 F12
Foligno, *Italy* 41 F9
Folkestone, *U.K.* 15 F9
Folkston, *U.S.A.* 115 K5
Follansbee, *U.S.A.* 116 F4
Follónica, *Italy* 40 F7
Follónica, G. di, *Italy* 40 F7
Folsom L., *U.S.A.* 110 G5
Folteşti, *Romania* 29 E13
Fond-du-Lac, *Canada* 103 B7
Fond du Lac, *U.S.A.* 112 D10
Fond-du-Lac ➘, *Canada* 103 B7
Fonda, *U.S.A.* 117 D10
Fondi, *Italy* 42 A6
Fonfría, *Spain* 36 D4
Fongafale, *Tuvalu* 96 H9
Fonni, *Italy* 42 B2
Fonsagrada = A Fonsagrada,
Spain 36 B3
Fonseca, G. de, *Cent. Amer.* ... 120 D2
Font-Romeu-Odeillo-Via, *France* 20 F5
Fontaine-Française, *France* 19 E12
Fontainebleau, *France* 19 D9
Fontana, *U.S.A.* 111 L9
Fontas ➘, *Canada* 102 B4
Fonte Boa, *Brazil* 124 D5
Fontem, *Cameroon* 83 D6
Fontenay-le-Comte, *France* 20 B3
Fontenelle Reservoir, *U.S.A.* ... 108 E8
Fontur, *Iceland* 8 C6
Fonyód, *Hungary* 28 D2
Foochow = Fuzhou, *China* 59 D12
Foping, *China* 56 H5
Forbach, *France* 19 C13
Forbes, *Australia* 95 E4
Forbesganj, *India* 69 F12
Forcados, *Nigeria* 83 D6
Forcados ➘, *Nigeria* 83 D6
Forcalquier, *France* 21 E9
Forchheim, *Germany* 25 F7
Ford City, *Calif., U.S.A.* 111 K7
Ford City, *Pa., U.S.A.* 116 F5
Førde, *Norway* 9 F11
Ford's Bridge, *Australia* 95 D4
Fordyce, *U.S.A.* 113 J8
Forécariah, *Guinea* 82 D2
Forel, Mt., *Greenland* 98 C16
Foremost, *Canada* 102 D6
Forest, *Canada* 116 C3
Forest, *U.S.A.* 113 J10
Forest City, *Iowa, U.S.A.* 112 D8
Forest City, *N.C., U.S.A.* 115 H5
Forest City, *Pa., U.S.A.* 117 E9
Forest Grove, *U.S.A.* 110 E3
Foreste Casentinesi-Monte
Falterona-Campigna △, *Italy* . 41 E8
Foresthill, *U.S.A.* 110 F6
Forestier Pen., *Australia* 95 G4
Forestville, *Canada* 105 C6
Forestville, *Calif., U.S.A.* 110 G4

Forestville, *N.Y., U.S.A.* 116 D5
Forêt d'Orient ○, *France* 19 D11
Forez, Mts. du, *France* 20 C7
Forfar, *U.K.* 13 E6
Forillon △, *Canada* 105 C7
Forks, *U.S.A.* 110 C2
Forksville, *U.S.A.* 117 E8
Forlì, *Italy* 41 D9
Forman, *U.S.A.* 112 B6
Formazza, *Italy* 40 B5
Formby Pt., *U.K.* 14 D4
Formentera, *Spain* 48 C7
Formentor, C. de, *Spain* 48 B10
Former Yugoslav Republic of
Macedonia = Macedonia ■,
Europe 44 E5
Fórmia, *Italy* 42 A6
Formígine, *Italy* 40 D7
Formosa = Taiwan ■, *Asia* 59 F13
Formosa, *Argentina* 126 B4
Formosa, *Brazil* 125 G9
Formosa □, *Argentina* 126 B4
Formosa, Serra, *Brazil* 125 F8
Formosa B. = Ungwana B., *Kenya* 86 C5
Fornells, *Spain* 48 A11
Fornos de Algodres, *Portugal* .. 36 E3
Fornovo di Taro, *Italy* 40 D7
Føroyar, *Atl. Oc.* 8 F9
Forres, *U.K.* 13 D5
Forrest, *Australia* 93 F4
Forrest, Mt., *Australia* 93 D4
Forrest City, *U.S.A.* 113 H9
Fors, *Sweden* 10 D10
Forsayth, *Australia* 94 B3
Forshaga, *Sweden* 10 E7
Förslöv, *Sweden* 11 H6
Forsmo, *Sweden* 10 A11
Forssa, *Finland* 9 F20
Forst, *Germany* 24 D10
Forsvik, *Sweden* 11 F8
Forsyth, *U.S.A.* 108 C10
Fort Abbas, *Pakistan* 68 E5
Fort Albany, *Canada* 104 B3
Fort Ann, *U.S.A.* 117 C11
Fort Assiniboine, *Canada* 102 C6
Fort Augustus, *U.K.* 13 D4
Fort Beaufort, *S. Africa* 88 E4
Fort Benton, *U.S.A.* 108 C8
Fort Bragg, *U.S.A.* 108 G2
Fort Bridger, *U.S.A.* 108 F8
Fort Chipewyan, *Canada* 103 B6
Fort Clatsop ○, *U.S.A.* 110 D3
Fort Collins, *U.S.A.* 112 E2
Fort-Coulonge, *Canada* 104 C4
Fort Covington, *U.S.A.* 117 B10
Fort Davis, *U.S.A.* 113 K3
Fort-de-France, *Martinique* .... 120 c
Fort Defiance, *U.S.A.* 109 J9
Fort Dodge, *U.S.A.* 112 D7
Fort Edward, *U.S.A.* 117 C11
Fort Erie, *Canada* 116 D6
Fort Fairfield, *U.S.A.* 115 B12
Fort Frances, *Canada* 103 D10
Fort Franklin = Déline, *Canada* . 100 B7
Fort Garland, *U.S.A.* 109 H11
Fort George = Chisasibi, *Canada* 104 B4
Fort Good Hope, *Canada* 100 B7
Fort Hancock, *U.S.A.* 109 L11
Fort Hope, *Canada* 104 B2
Fort Irwin, *U.S.A.* 111 K10
Fort Kent, *U.S.A.* 115 B11
Fort Klamath, *U.S.A.* 108 E3
Fort Laramie, *U.S.A.* 112 D2
Fort Lauderdale, *U.S.A.* 115 M5
Fort Liard, *Canada* 102 A4
Fort Liberté, *Haiti* 121 C5
Fort Lupton, *U.S.A.* 112 E2
Fort MacKay, *Canada* 102 B6
Fort Macleod, *Canada* 102 D6
Fort McMurray, *Canada* 102 B6
Fort McPherson, *Canada* 100 B6
Fort Madison, *U.S.A.* 112 E9
Fort Meade, *U.S.A.* 115 M5
Fort Morgan, *U.S.A.* 112 E3
Fort Myers, *U.S.A.* 115 M5
Fort Nelson, *Canada* 102 B4
Fort Nelson ➘, *Canada* 102 B4
Fort Norman = Tulita, *Canada* . 100 B7
Fort Payne, *U.S.A.* 115 H3
Fort Peck, *U.S.A.* 108 B10
Fort Peck Dam, *U.S.A.* 108 C10
Fort Peck L., *U.S.A.* 108 C10
Fort Pierce, *U.S.A.* 115 M5
Fort Pierre, *U.S.A.* 112 C4
Fort Plain, *U.S.A.* 117 D10
Fort Portal, *Uganda* 86 B3
Fort Providence, *Canada* 102 A5
Fort Qu'Appelle, *Canada* 103 C8
Fort Resolution, *Canada* 102 A6
Fort Rixon, *Zimbabwe* 87 G2
Fort Ross, *U.S.A.* 110 G3
Fort Rupert = Waskaganish,
Canada 104 B4
Fort St. James, *Canada* 102 C4
Fort St. John, *Canada* 102 B4
Fort Saskatchewan, *Canada* 102 C6
Fort Scott, *U.S.A.* 113 G7
Fort Severn, *Canada* 104 A2
Fort Shevchenko, *Kazakhstan* .. 35 H10
Fort Simpson, *Canada* 102 A4
Fort Smith, *Canada* 102 B6
Fort Smith, *U.S.A.* 113 H7
Fort Stockton, *U.S.A.* 113 K3
Fort Sumner, *U.S.A.* 113 H2
Fort Thompson, *U.S.A.* 112 C5
Fort Union ○, *U.S.A.* 113 H2
Fort Valley, *U.S.A.* 115 J4
Fort Vermilion, *Canada* 102 B5
Fort Walton Beach, *U.S.A.* 115 K2
Fort Wayne, *U.S.A.* 114 E3
Fort William, *U.K.* 13 E3

Fort Worth, *U.S.A.* 113 J6
Fort Yates, *U.S.A.* 112 B4
Fort Yukon, *U.S.A.* 100 B5
Fortaleza, *Brazil* 125 D11
Fortescue ➘, *Australia* 92 D2
Forth ➘, *U.K.* 13 E5
Forth, Firth of, *U.K.* 13 E6
Fortore ➘, *Italy* 41 G12
Fortrose, *U.K.* 13 D4
Fortuna, *Spain* 39 G3
Fortuna, *Calif., U.S.A.* 108 F1
Fortuna, *N. Dak., U.S.A.* 112 A3
Fortune, *Canada* 105 C8
Fortune B., *Canada* 105 C8
Forūr, *Iran* 71 E7
Fos-sur-Mer, *France* 21 E8
Foshan, *China* 59 F9
Fosna, *Norway* 8 E14
Fosnavåg, *Norway* 9 E11
Foso, *Ghana* 83 D4
Fossano, *Italy* 40 D4
Fossil, *U.S.A.* 108 D3
Fossil Butte ○, *U.S.A.* 108 F8
Fossombrone, *Italy* 41 E9
Foster, *Canada* 117 A12
Foster ➘, *Canada* 103 B7
Fosters Ra., *Australia* 94 C1
Fostoria, *U.S.A.* 114 E4
Fotadrevo, *Madag.* 89 C8
Fougamou, *France* 18 E2
Fougères, *France* 18 D5
Foul Pt., *Sri Lanka* 66 Q12
Foula, *U.K.* 13 A6
Foulaba, *Mali* 82 C3
Foulness I., *U.K.* 15 F8
Foulpointe, *Madag.* 89 B8
Foulweather, C., *U.S.A.* 106 B2
Foumban, *Cameroon* 83 D7
Foumbot, *Cameroon* 83 D7
Foundiougne, *Senegal* 82 C1
Fountain, *U.S.A.* 112 F2
Fountain Springs, *U.S.A.* 111 K8
Fourchambault, *France* 19 E10
Fouriesburg, *S. Africa* 88 D4
Fourmies, *France* 19 B11
Fournás, *Greece* 46 B3
Foúrnoi, *Greece* 47 D8
Fours, *France* 19 F10
Fourth Cataract, *Sudan* 80 D3
Fouta Djallon, *Guinea* 82 C2
Foux, Cap-à-, *Haiti* 121 C5
Foveaux Str., *N.Z.* 91 M2
Fowey, *U.K.* 15 G3
Fowler, *Calif., U.S.A.* 110 J7
Fowler, *Colo., U.S.A.* 112 F3
Fowlers B., *Australia* 93 F5
Fowman, *Iran* 71 B6
Fox ➘, *Canada* 103 B10
Fox Creek, *Canada* 102 C5
Fox Lake, *Canada* 102 B6
Fox Valley, *Canada* 103 C7
Foxboro, *U.S.A.* 117 D13
Foxdale, *Australia* 94 J6
Foxe Basin, *Canada* 101 B12
Foxe Chan., *Canada* 101 B11
Foxe Pen., *Canada* 101 B12
Foxen, *Sweden* 10 E5
Foxton, *N.Z.* 91 J5
Foyle, Lough, *U.K.* 12 A4
Foynes, *Ireland* 12 D2
Foz, *Spain* 36 B3
Foz do Cunene, *Angola* 88 B1
Foz do Iguaçu, *Brazil* 127 B5
Frackville, *U.S.A.* 117 F8
Fraga, *Spain* 38 D5
Fraile Muerto, *Uruguay* 127 C5
Fram Basin, *Arctic* .... 4 A
Framingham, *U.S.A.* 117 D13
Frampol, *Poland* 31 H9
Franca, *Brazil* 125 H9
Francavilla al Mare, *Italy* 41 F11
Francavilla Fontana, *Italy* 43 B10
France ■, *Europe* 7 F6
Frances, *Australia* 95 F3
Frances ➘, *Canada* 102 A3
Frances L., *Canada* 102 A3
Franceville, *Gabon* 84 E2
Franche-Comté □, *France* 19 F12
Francis Case, L., *U.S.A.* 112 D5
Francisco Beltrão, *Brazil* 127 B5
Francisco I. Madero, Coahuila,
Mexico 118 B4
Francisco I. Madero, Durango,
Mexico 118 C4
Francistown, *Botswana* 89 C4
Francofonte, *Italy* 43 E7
François, *Canada* 105 C8
François L., *Canada* 102 C3
François Peron △, *Australia* 93 E1
Franeker, *Neths.* 17 A5
Frank Hann △, *Australia* 93 F3
Frankado, *Djibouti* 81 E5
Frankenberg, *Germany* 24 D4
Frankenhöhe △, *Germany* 25 F6
Frankenwald, *Germany* 25 E7
Frankenwald △, *Germany* 25 E7
Frankford, *Canada* 116 B7
Frankfort, *S. Africa* 89 D4
Frankfort, *Ind., U.S.A.* 114 E2
Frankfort, *Kans., U.S.A.* 112 F6
Frankfort, *Ky., U.S.A.* 114 F3
Frankfort, *N.Y., U.S.A.* 117 C9
Frankfurt, *Brandenburg,
Germany* 24 C10
Frankfurt, *Hessen, Germany* .. 25 E4
Frankfurt △ (FRA), *Germany* .. 25 E4
Fränkische Alb, *Germany* 25 F7
Fränkische Rezat ➘, *Germany* . 25 F7
Fränkische Saale ➘, *Germany* . 25 E5
Fränkische Schweiz, *Germany* . 25 F7

Fränkische Schweiz-
Veldensteiner Forst ○,
Germany 25 F7
Frankland ➘, *Australia* 93 G2
Franklin, *Ky., U.S.A.* 115 G2
Franklin, *La., U.S.A.* 113 L9
Franklin, *Mass., U.S.A.* 117 D13
Franklin, *N.H., U.S.A.* 117 C13
Franklin, *Nebr., U.S.A.* 112 E5
Franklin, *Pa., U.S.A.* 116 E5
Franklin, *Va., U.S.A.* 115 G7
Franklin, *W. Va., U.S.A.* 114 F6
Franklin B., *Canada* 100 B7
Franklin D. Roosevelt L., *U.S.A.* 108 B4
Franklin-Gordon Wild Rivers △,
Australia 95 G4
Franklin I., *Antarctica* 5 D11
Franklin L., *U.S.A.* 108 F6
Franklin Mts., *Canada* 100 B7
Franklin Str., *Canada* 100 A10
Franklinton, *U.S.A.* 113 K9
Franklinville, *U.S.A.* 116 D6
Franks Pk., *U.S.A.* 108 E9
Frankston, *Australia* 95 F4
Fränö, *Sweden* 10 B11
Fransfontein, *Namibia* 88 C2
Fränsta, *Sweden* 10 B10
Frantsa Iosifa, Zemlya, *Russia* . 52 A6
Franz, *Canada* 104 C3
Franz Josef Land = Frantsa Iosifa,
Zemlya, *Russia* 52 A6
Franz Josef Strauss, München ✈
(MUC), *Germany* 25 G7
Franzburg, *Germany* 24 A8
Frascati, *Italy* 41 G9
Fraser, *U.S.A.* 116 D2
Fraser ➘, *B.C., Canada* 102 D4
Fraser ➘, *Nfld. & L., Canada* .. 105 A7
Fraser, Mt., *Australia* 93 E2
Fraser I., *Australia* 95 D5
Fraser Lake, *Canada* 102 C4
Fraserburg, *S. Africa* 88 E3
Fraserburgh, *U.K.* 13 D6
Fraserdale, *Canada* 104 C3
Frashër, *Albania* 44 F4
Frasne, *France* 19 F13
Frătești, *Romania* 29 G10
Frauenfeld, *Switz.* 25 H4
Fray Bentos, *Uruguay* 126 C4
Fray Jorge △, *Chile* 126 C1
Frechilla, *Spain* 36 C6
Fredericia, *Denmark* 11 J3
Frederick, *Md., U.S.A.* 114 F7
Frederick, *Okla., U.S.A.* 113 H5
Frederick, *S. Dak., U.S.A.* 112 C5
Fredericksburg, *Pa., U.S.A.* 117 F8
Fredericksburg, *Tex., U.S.A.* ... 113 K5
Fredericksburg, *Va., U.S.A.* 114 F7
Fredericktown, *Mo., U.S.A.* 113 G9
Fredericktown, *Ohio, U.S.A.* ... 116 F2
Frederico I. Madero, Presa,
Mexico 118 B3
Frederico Westphalen, *Brazil* .. 127 B5
Fredericton, *Canada* 105 C6
Fredericton Junction, *Canada* .. 105 C6
Frederiksborg Amtskommune □,
Denmark 11 J6
Frederikshåb = Paamiut,
Greenland 101 B15
Frederikshamn = Hamina,
Finland 9 F22
Frederikshavn, *Denmark* 11 G4
Frederikssund, *Denmark* 11 J6
Frederiksted, *U.S. Virgin Is.* ... 121 C7
Frederiksværk, *Denmark* 11 J6
Fredonia, *Ariz., U.S.A.* 109 H7
Fredonia, *Kans., U.S.A.* 113 G7
Fredonia, *N.Y., U.S.A.* 116 D5
Fredriksberg, *Sweden* 10 D8
Fredrikstad, *Norway* 9 G14
Free State □, *S. Africa* 88 D4
Freehold, *U.S.A.* 117 F10
Freel Peak, *U.S.A.* 110 G7
Freeland, *U.S.A.* 117 E9
Freels, C., *Canada* 105 C9
Freeman, *Calif., U.S.A.* 111 K9
Freeman, *S. Dak., U.S.A.* 112 D6
Freeport, *Bahamas* 120 A4
Freeport, *Ill., U.S.A.* 112 D10
Freeport, *N.Y., U.S.A.* 117 F11
Freeport, *Ohio, U.S.A.* 116 F3
Freeport, *Pa., U.S.A.* 116 F5
Freeport, *Tex., U.S.A.* 113 L7
Freetown, *S. Leone* 82 D2
Frégate, L. de la, *Canada* 104 B5
Fregenal de la Sierra, *Spain* ... 37 G4
Fregene, *Italy* 41 G9
Fréhel, C., *France* 18 D4
Freiberg, *Germany* 24 E9
Freibourg = Fribourg, *Switz.* .. 25 J3
Freiburg, Baden-W., *Germany* . 25 H3
Freiburg, *Niedersachsen,
Germany* 24 B5
Freilassing, *Germany* 25 H8
Freire, *Chile* 128 D2
Freirina, *Chile* 126 B1
Freising, *Germany* 25 G7
Freistadt, *Austria* 26 C7
Freital, *Germany* 24 D9
Fréjus, *France* 21 E10
Fremantle, *Australia* 93 F2
Fremont, *Calif., U.S.A.* 110 H4
Fremont, *Mich., U.S.A.* 114 D3
Fremont, *Nebr., U.S.A.* 112 E6
Fremont, *Ohio, U.S.A.* 114 E4
Fremont ➘, *U.S.A.* 109 G8
French Cays = Plana Cays,
Bahamas 121 B5
French Creek ➘, *U.S.A.* 116 E5
French Guiana ☑, *S. Amer.* ... 125 C8

French Polynesia ☒, *Pac. Oc.* ... 97 K13
Frenchman Cr. ➤, *N. Amer.* ... 108 B10
Frenchman Cr. ➤, *U.S.A.* ... 112 E4
Frenštát pod Radhoštěm,
  Czech Rep. ... 27 B11
Fresco, *Ivory C.* ... 82 D3
Fresco ➤, *Brazil* ... 125 E8
Freshfield, C., *Antarctica* ... 5 C10
Fresnay-sur-Sarthe, *France* ... 18 D7
Fresnillo, *Mexico* ... 118 C4
Fresno, *U.S.A.* ... 110 J7
Fresno Alhandiga, *Spain* ... 36 E5
Fresno Reservoir, *U.S.A.* ... 108 B9
Freudenstadt, *Germany* ... 25 G4
Frévent, *France* ... 19 B9
Frew ➤, *Australia* ... 94 C2
Frewsburg, *U.S.A.* ... 116 D5
Freycinet △, *Australia* ... 95 G4
Freycinet Pen., *Australia* ... 95 G4
Freyming-Merlebach, *France* ... 19 C13
Freyung, *Germany* ... 25 G9
Fria, *Guinea* ... 82 C2
Fria, C., *Namibia* ... 88 B1
Friant, *U.S.A.* ... 110 J7
Frías, *Argentina* ... 126 B2
Fribourg, *Switz.* ... 25 J3
Fribourg □, *Switz.* ... 25 J3
Fridafors, *Sweden* ... 11 H8
Friday Harbor, *U.S.A.* ... 110 B3
Friedberg, *Bayern, Germany* ... 25 G6
Friedberg, *Hessen, Germany* ... 25 E4
Friedens, *U.S.A.* ... 116 F6
Friedland, *Germany* ... 24 B9
Friedrichshafen, *Germany* ... 25 H5
Friedrichskoog, *Germany* ... 24 A4
Friedrichstadt, *Germany* ... 24 A5
Friendship, *U.S.A.* ... 116 D6
Friesach, *Austria* ... 26 E7
Friesack, *Germany* ... 24 C8
Friesland □, *Neths.* ... 17 A5
Friesoythe, *Germany* ... 24 B4
Friggesund, *Sweden* ... 10 C10
Frillesås, *Sweden* ... 11 G6
Frinnaryd, *Sweden* ... 11 G8
Frio ➤, *U.S.A.* ... 113 L5
Frio, C., *Brazil* ... 122 F6
Friol, *Spain* ... 36 B3
Friona, *U.S.A.* ... 113 H3
Fristad, *Sweden* ... 11 G6
Fritch, *U.S.A.* ... 113 H4
Fritsla, *Sweden* ... 11 G6
Fritzlar, *Germany* ... 24 D5
Friuli-Venézia Giulia □, *Italy* ... 41 B9
Frobisher B., *Canada* ... 101 B13
Frobisher Bay = Iqaluit, *Canada* ... 101 B13
Frobisher L., *Canada* ... 103 B7
Frohavet, *Norway* ... 8 E13
Frohnleiten, *Austria* ... 26 D8
Frolovo, *Russia* ... 34 F6
Frombork, *Poland* ... 30 D6
Frome, *U.K.* ... 15 F5
Frome ➤, *U.K.* ... 15 G5
Frome, L., *Australia* ... 95 E2
Frome, The ➤, *Australia* ... 95 D2
Frómista, *Spain* ... 36 C6
Front Range, *U.S.A.* ... 106 C5
Front Royal, *U.S.A.* ... 114 F6
Fronteira, *Portugal* ... 37 F3
Frontera, *Canary Is.* ... 48 G2
Frontera, *Mexico* ... 119 D6
Fronteras, *Mexico* ... 118 A3
Frontignan, *France* ... 20 E7
Frosinone, *Italy* ... 42 A6
Frostburg, *U.S.A.* ... 114 F6
Frostisen, *Norway* ... 8 B17
Frouard, *France* ... 19 D13
Frøvi, *Sweden* ... 10 E9
Frøya, *Norway* ... 8 E13
Frumoasa, *Romania* ... 29 D10
Frunze = Bishkek, *Kyrgyzstan* ... 52 E8
Frunzivka, *Ukraine* ... 29 C14
Fruška Gora, *Serbia & M.* ... 28 E4
Fruška Gora, *Serbia & M.* ... 44 A3
Frutal, *Brazil* ... 125 H9
Frutigen, *Switz.* ... 25 J3
Frýdek-Místek, *Czech Rep.* ... 27 B11
Frýdlant, *Czech Rep.* ... 26 A8
Fryeburg, *U.S.A.* ... 117 B14
Fryvaldov = Jeseník, *Czech Rep.* ... 27 A10
Fthiótis □, *Greece* ... 46 C4
Fu Jiang ➤, *China* ... 58 C6
Fu Xian = Wafangdian, *China* ... 57 E11
Fu Xian, *China* ... 56 G5
Fu'an, *China* ... 59 D12
Fubian, *China* ... 58 B4
Fucécchio, *Italy* ... 40 E7
Fucheng, *China* ... 56 F9
Fuchou = Fuzhou, *China* ... 59 D12
Fuchū, *Japan* ... 55 G6
Fuchuan, *China* ... 59 E8
Fuchun Jiang ➤, *China* ... 59 B13
Fúcino, Piana del, *Italy* ... 41 F10
Fuding, *China* ... 59 D13
Fuencaliente, *Canary Is.* ... 48 F2
Fuencaliente, *Spain* ... 37 G6
Fuencaliente, Pta., *Canary Is.* ... 48 F2
Fuengirola, *Spain* ... 37 J6
Fuenlabrada, *Spain* ... 36 E7
Fuensalida, *Spain* ... 36 E6
Fuente-Álamo, *Spain* ... 39 G3
Fuente-Álamo de Murcia, *Spain* ... 39 H3
Fuente de Cantos, *Spain* ... 37 G4
Fuente del Maestre, *Spain* ... 37 G4
Fuente el Fresno, *Spain* ... 37 F7
Fuente Obejuna, *Spain* ... 37 G5
Fuente Palmera, *Spain* ... 37 H5
Fuentes de Andalucía, *Spain* ... 37 H5
Fuentes de Ebro, *Spain* ... 38 D4
Fuentes de León, *Spain* ... 37 G4
Fuentes de Oñoro, *Spain* ... 36 E4
Fuentesaúco, *Spain* ... 36 D5

Fuerte ➤, *Mexico* ... 118 B3
Fuerte Olimpo, *Paraguay* ... 126 A4
Fuerteventura, *Canary Is.* ... 48 F6
Fuerteventura ✈ (FUE),
  Canary Is. ... 48 F6
Fufeng, *China* ... 56 G5
Fuga I., *Phil.* ... 61 B4
Fugong, *China* ... 58 D2
Fugou, *China* ... 56 G8
Fugu, *China* ... 56 E6
Fuhai, *China* ... 60 B3
Fuḩaymī, *Iraq* ... 70 C4
Fuhlsbüttel, Hamburg ✈ (HAM),
  Germany ... 24 B5
Fuji, *Japan* ... 55 G9
Fuji-Hakone-Izu △, *Japan* ... 55 G9
Fuji-San, *Japan* ... 55 G9
Fuji-Yoshida, *Japan* ... 55 G9
Fujian □, *China* ... 59 E12
Fujinomiya, *Japan* ... 55 G9
Fujisawa, *Japan* ... 55 G9
Fujiyama, Mt. = Fuji-San, *Japan* ... 55 G9
Fukagawa, *Japan* ... 54 C11
Fukien = Fujian □, *China* ... 59 E12
Fukuchiyama, *Japan* ... 55 G7
Fukue-Shima, *Japan* ... 55 H4
Fukui, *Japan* ... 55 F8
Fukui □, *Japan* ... 55 G8
Fukuoka, *Japan* ... 55 H5
Fukuoka □, *Japan* ... 55 H5
Fukushima, *Japan* ... 54 F10
Fukushima □, *Japan* ... 54 F10
Fukuyama, *Japan* ... 55 G6
Fulacunda, *Guinea-Biss.* ... 82 C1
Fulda, *Germany* ... 24 E5
Fulda ➤, *Germany* ... 24 D5
Fulford Harbour, *Canada* ... 110 B3
Fuliang, *China* ... 59 C11
Fullerton, *Calif., U.S.A.* ... 111 M9
Fullerton, *Nebr., U.S.A.* ... 112 E6
Fulongquan, *China* ... 57 B13
Fülöpszállás, *Hungary* ... 28 D4
Fulton, *Mo., U.S.A.* ... 112 F9
Fulton, *N.Y., U.S.A.* ... 117 C8
Fuluälven ➤, *Sweden* ... 10 C7
Fulufjället, *Sweden* ... 10 C7
Fumay, *France* ... 19 C11
Fumel, *France* ... 20 D4
Fumin, *China* ... 58 E4
Funabashi, *Japan* ... 55 G10
Funafuti = Fongafale, *Tuvalu* ... 96 H9
Funäsdalen, *Sweden* ... 10 B6
Funchal, *Madeira* ... 48 D3
Funchal ✈ (FNC), *Madeira* ... 48 D3
Fundación, *Colombia* ... 124 A4
Fundão, *Portugal* ... 36 E3
Fundu Moldovei, *Romania* ... 29 C10
Fundulea, *Romania* ... 29 F11
Fundy △, *Canada* ... 105 C6
Fundy, B. of, *Canada* ... 105 D6
Funhalouro, *Mozam.* ... 89 C5
Funing, *Hebei, China* ... 57 E10
Funing, *Jiangsu, China* ... 57 H10
Funing, *Yunnan, China* ... 58 F5
Funiu Shan, *China* ... 56 H7
Funsi, *Ghana* ... 82 C4
Funtua, *Nigeria* ... 83 C6
Fuping, *Hebei, China* ... 56 E8
Fuping, *Shaanxi, China* ... 56 G5
Fuqing, *China* ... 59 E12
Fuquan, *China* ... 58 D6
Furano, *Japan* ... 54 C11
Furāt, Nahr al ➤, *Asia* ... 70 D5
Fürg, *Iran* ... 71 D7
Furmanov, *Russia* ... 34 B5
Furmanovo, *Kazakhstan* ... 34 F9
Furnás, *Spain* ... 48 B8
Furnas, Reprêsa de, *Brazil* ... 127 A6
Furneaux Group, *Australia* ... 95 G4
Furqlus, *Syria* ... 74 A6
Fürstenau, *Germany* ... 24 C3
Fürstenberg, *Germany* ... 24 B9
Fürstenfeld, *Austria* ... 26 D9
Fürstenfeldbruck, *Germany* ... 25 G7
Fürstenwalde, *Germany* ... 24 C10
Fürth, *Germany* ... 25 F6
Furth im Wald, *Germany* ... 25 F8
Furtwangen, *Germany* ... 25 G4
Furudal, *Sweden* ... 10 C9
Furukawa, *Japan* ... 54 E10
Furulund, *Sweden* ... 11 J7
Fury and Hecla Str., *Canada* ... 101 B11
Fusagasuga, *Colombia* ... 124 C4
Fuscaldo, *Italy* ... 43 C9
Fushan, *Shandong, China* ... 57 F11
Fushan, *Shanxi, China* ... 56 G6
Fushë Arrëz, *Albania* ... 44 D4
Fushë Krujë, *Albania* ... 44 E3
Fushun, *Liaoning, China* ... 57 D12
Fushun, *Sichuan, China* ... 58 C5
Fusong, *China* ... 57 C14
Füssen, *Germany* ... 25 H6
Fusui, *China* ... 58 F6
Futog, *Serbia & M.* ... 28 E4
Futuna, Wall. & F. Is. ... 91 B8
Fuwa, *Egypt* ... 80 H7
Fuxian Hu, *China* ... 58 E4
Fuxin, *China* ... 57 C11
Fuyang, *Anhui, China* ... 56 H8
Fuyang, *Zhejiang, China* ... 59 B12
Fuyang He ➤, *China* ... 56 E9
Fuying Dao, *China* ... 59 D13
Fuyu, *China* ... 57 B13
Fuyuan, *China* ... 58 E5
Füzesgyarmat, *Hungary* ... 28 D5
Fuzhou, *China* ... 59 D12
Fylde, *U.K.* ... 14 D5
Fyn, *Denmark* ... 11 J4
Fyne, L., *U.K.* ... 13 F3
Fyns Amtskommune □, *Denmark* ... 11 J4
Fynshav, *Denmark* ... 11 K3

G

Ga, *Ghana* ... 82 D4
Gaanda, *Nigeria* ... 83 C7
Gabarin, *Nigeria* ... 83 C7
Gabas ➤, *France* ... 20 E3
Gabela, *Angola* ... 84 G2
Gabès, *Tunisia* ... 79 B8
Gabès, G. de, *Tunisia* ... 79 B8
Gabgaba, W. ➤, *Egypt* ... 80 C3
Gabin, *Poland* ... 31 F6
Gabon ■, *Africa* ... 84 E2
Gaborone, *Botswana* ... 88 C4
Gabriels, *U.S.A.* ... 117 B10
Gābrīk, *Iran* ... 71 E8
Gabrovo, *Bulgaria* ... 45 D9
Gacé, *France* ... 18 D7
Găch Sār, *Iran* ... 71 B6
Gachsārān, *Iran* ... 71 D6
Gacko, *Bos.-H.* ... 44 C2
Gadag, *India* ... 66 M9
Gadamai, *Sudan* ... 81 D4
Gadap, *Pakistan* ... 68 G2
Gadarwara, *India* ... 69 H8
Gadebusch, *Germany* ... 24 B7
Gadein, *Sudan* ... 81 F2
Gadhada, *India* ... 68 J4
Gadwal, *India* ... 66 L10
Gadyach = Hadyach, *Ukraine* ... 33 G8
Găeşti, *Romania* ... 29 F10
Gaeta, *Italy* ... 42 A6
Gaeta, G. di, *Italy* ... 42 A6
Gaffney, *U.S.A.* ... 115 H5
Gafsa, *Tunisia* ... 78 B7
Gagarawa, *Nigeria* ... 83 C6
Gagaria, *India* ... 68 G4
Gagarin, *Russia* ... 32 E8
Gaggenau, *Germany* ... 25 G4
Gagino, *Russia* ... 34 C7
Gagliano del Capo, *Italy* ... 43 C11
Gagnef, *Sweden* ... 10 D9
Gagnoa, *Ivory C.* ... 82 D3
Gagnon, *Canada* ... 105 B6
Gagnon, L., *Canada* ... 103 A6
Gagra, *Georgia* ... 35 J5
Gahini, *Rwanda* ... 86 C3
Gahmar, *India* ... 69 G10
Gai Xian = Gaizhou, *China* ... 57 D12
Gaïdhouronísi, *Greece* ... 49 E7
Gail, *U.S.A.* ... 113 J4
Gail ➤, *Austria* ... 26 E6
Gaillac, *France* ... 20 E5
Gaillimh = Galway, *Ireland* ... 12 C2
Gaillon, *France* ... 18 C8
Gaines, *U.S.A.* ... 116 E7
Gainesville, *Fla., U.S.A.* ... 115 L4
Gainesville, *Ga., U.S.A.* ... 115 H4
Gainesville, *Mo., U.S.A.* ... 113 G8
Gainesville, *Tex., U.S.A.* ... 113 J6
Gainsborough, *U.K.* ... 14 D7
Gairdner, L., *Australia* ... 95 E2
Gairloch, *U.K.* ... 13 D3
Gairloch, L., *U.K.* ... 13 D3
Gaizhou, *China* ... 57 D12
Gaj, *Croatia* ... 28 E2
Gaj ➤, *Pakistan* ... 68 F2
Gakuch, *Pakistan* ... 69 A5
Galala, Gebel el, *Egypt* ... 80 J8
Galán, Cerro, *Argentina* ... 126 B2
Galana ➤, *Kenya* ... 86 C5
Galanta, *Slovak Rep.* ... 27 C10
Galapagar, *Spain* ... 36 E7
Galápagos = Colón, Arch. de,
  Ecuador ... 97 H18
Galashiels, *U.K.* ... 13 F6
Galatás, *Greece* ... 46 D5
Galați, *Romania* ... 29 E13
Galați □, *Romania* ... 29 E12
Galatia, *Turkey* ... 72 C5
Galatina, *Italy* ... 43 B11
Galátone, *Italy* ... 43 B11
Galax, *U.S.A.* ... 115 G5
Galaxídhion, *Greece* ... 46 C4
Galcaio, Somali Rep. ... 75 F4
Galdhøpiggen, *Norway* ... 9 F12
Galeana, *Chihuahua, Mexico* ... 118 A3
Galeana, *Nuevo León, Mexico* ... 118 A3
Galegu, *Sudan* ... 81 E4
Galela, *Indonesia* ... 63 D7
Galena, *U.S.A.* ... 100 B4
Galeota Pt., *Trin. & Tob.* ... 125 K16
Galera, *Spain* ... 39 H2
Galera Pt., *Trin. & Tob.* ... 121 D7
Galesburg, *U.S.A.* ... 112 E9
Galeton, *U.S.A.* ... 116 E7
Galga, *Ethiopia* ... 81 F4
Gali, *Georgia* ... 35 J5
Galicea Mare, *Romania* ... 29 F8
Galich, *Russia* ... 34 A6
Galiche, *Bulgaria* ... 44 C7
Galicia □, *Spain* ... 36 C3
Galíčica △, *Macedonia* ... 44 E4
Galilee = Hagalil, *Israel* ... 74 C4
Galilee, L., *Australia* ... 94 C4
Galilee, Sea of = Yam Kinneret,
  Israel ... 74 C4
Galim, *Cameroon* ... 83 D7
Galina Pt., *Jamaica* ... 120 a
Galinoporni, *Cyprus* ... 49 D13
Galion, *U.S.A.* ... 116 F2
Galiuro Mts., *U.S.A.* ... 109 K8
Galiwinku, *Australia* ... 94 A2
Gallabat, *Sudan* ... 81 E4
Gallan Hd., *U.K.* ... 13 C1
Gallarate, *Italy* ... 40 C5

Gallatin, *U.S.A.* ... 115 G2
Galle, *Sri Lanka* ... 66 R12
Gállego ➤, *Spain* ... 38 D4
Gallegos ➤, *Argentina* ... 128 G3
Galletti ➤, *Ethiopia* ... 81 F5
Galley Hd., *Ireland* ... 12 E3
Galliate, *Italy* ... 40 C5
Gallinas, Pta., *Colombia* ... 124 A4
Gallipoli = Gelibolu, *Turkey* ... 45 F10
Gallípoli, *Italy* ... 43 B10
Gallipolis, *U.S.A.* ... 114 F4
Gällivare, *Sweden* ... 8 C19
Gallneukirchen, *Austria* ... 26 C7
Gällö, *Sweden* ... 10 B9
Gallo, C., *Italy* ... 42 D6
Gallocanta, L. de, *Spain* ... 38 E3
Galloo I., *U.S.A.* ... 117 C8
Galloway, *U.K.* ... 13 F4
Galloway ∩, *U.K.* ... 13 F4
Galloway, Mull of, *U.K.* ... 13 G4
Gallup, *U.S.A.* ... 109 J9
Gallur, *Spain* ... 38 D3
Galoya, *Sri Lanka* ... 66 Q12
Galt, *U.S.A.* ... 110 G5
Galten, *Denmark* ... 11 H3
Galtür, *Austria* ... 26 E3
Galty Mts., *Ireland* ... 12 D3
Galtymore, *Ireland* ... 12 D3
Galva, *U.S.A.* ... 112 E9
Galve de Sorbe, *Spain* ... 38 D1
Galveston, *U.S.A.* ... 113 L7
Galveston B., *U.S.A.* ... 113 L7
Gálvez, *Argentina* ... 126 C3
Galway, *Ireland* ... 12 C2
Galway □, *Ireland* ... 12 C2
Galway B., *Ireland* ... 12 C2
Gam ➤, *Vietnam* ... 64 B5
Gamagōri, *Japan* ... 55 G8
Gamari, L., *Ethiopia* ... 81 E5
Gamawa, *Nigeria* ... 83 C7
Gamay, *Phil.* ... 61 E6
Gambaga, *Ghana* ... 83 C4
Gambat, *Pakistan* ... 68 F3
Gambela, *Ethiopia* ... 81 F3
Gambela △, *Ethiopia* ... 81 F3
Gambela-Hizboch □, *Ethiopia* ... 81 F3
Gambhir ➤, *India* ... 68 F6
Gambia ■, *W. Afr.* ... 82 C1
Gambia ➤, *W. Afr.* ... 82 C1
Gambier, *U.S.A.* ... 116 F2
Gambier, C., *Australia* ... 92 B5
Gambier Is., *Australia* ... 95 F2
Gambo, *Canada* ... 105 C9
Gamboli, *Pakistan* ... 68 E3
Gamboma, *Congo* ... 84 E3
Gamtoos ➤, *S. Africa* ... 88 E4
Gamka ➤, *S. Africa* ... 88 E3
Gamkab ➤, *Namibia* ... 88 D2
Gamla Uppsala, *Sweden* ... 10 E11
Gamleby, *Sweden* ... 11 G10
Gammon ➤, *Canada* ... 103 C9
Gammon Ranges △, *Australia* ... 95 E2
Gamo-Gofa, *Ethiopia* ... 81 F4
Gamou, *Niger* ... 83 C6
Gamtoos ➤, *S. Africa* ... 88 E4
Gan, *France* ... 20 E3
Gan Goriama, Mts., *Cameroon* ... 83 D7
Gan Jiang ➤, *China* ... 59 C11
Ganado, *U.S.A.* ... 109 J9
Gananita, *Sudan* ... 80 D3
Gananoque, *Canada* ... 117 B8
Ganăveh, *Iran* ... 71 D6
Gäncä, *Azerbaijan* ... 35 K8
Gancheng, *China* ... 64 C7
Gand = Gent, *Belgium* ... 17 C3
Ganda, *Angola* ... 85 G2
Gandajika, Dem. Rep. of
  the Congo ... 84 F4
Gandak ➤, *India* ... 69 G11
Gandava, *Pakistan* ... 68 E2
Gander, *Canada* ... 105 C9
Gander L., *Canada* ... 105 C9
Ganderkesee, *Germany* ... 24 B4
Ganderowe Falls, *Zimbabwe* ... 87 F2
Gandesa, *Spain* ... 38 D5
Gandhi Sagar, *India* ... 68 G6
Gandhinagar, *India* ... 68 H5
Gandi, *Nigeria* ... 83 C6
Gandía, *Spain* ... 39 G4
Gandino, *Italy* ... 40 C6
Gando, Pta., *Canary Is.* ... 48 G4
Gandole, *Nigeria* ... 83 D7
Gâneb, *Mauritania* ... 82 B2
Ganedidalem = Gani, *Indonesia* ... 63 E7
Ganetti, *Sudan* ... 80 D3
Ganga ➤, *India* ... 69 H14
Ganga Sagar, *India* ... 69 J13
Gangafani, *Mali* ... 82 C4
Gangan ➤, *India* ... 69 E8
Ganganagar, *India* ... 68 E5
Gangapur, *India* ... 68 F7
Gangara, *Niger* ... 83 C6
Gangaw, *Burma* ... 67 H19
Gangdisê Shan, *China* ... 67 D12
Ganges = Ganga ➤, *India* ... 69 H14
Ganges, *Canada* ... 102 D4
Ganges, *France* ... 20 E7
Ganges, Mouths of the, *India* ... 69 J14
Gånghester, *Sweden* ... 11 G7
Gangi, *Italy* ... 43 E7
Gângiova, *Romania* ... 29 G8
Gangoh, *India* ... 68 E7
Gangotri, *India* ... 69 D8
Gangtok, *India* ... 67 F16
Gangu, *China* ... 56 G3
Ganquan, *China* ... 56 F5
Gani, *Indonesia* ... 63 E7
Ganj, *India* ... 69 F8
Ganluc, *China* ... 58 C4
Gannan, *China* ... 57 B13
Gannat, *France* ... 19 F10
Gannett Peak, *U.S.A.* ... 108 E9
Ganquan, *China* ... 56 F5

Gänserndorf, *Austria* ... 27 C9
Ganshui, *China* ... 58 C6
Gansu □, *China* ... 56 G3
Ganta, *Liberia* ... 82 D3
Gantheaume, C., *Australia* ... 95 F2
Gantheaume B., *Australia* ... 93 E1
Ganye, *Nigeria* ... 83 D7
Ganyem = Genyem, *Indonesia* ... 63 E10
Ganyu, *China* ... 57 G10
Ganyushkino, *Kazakhstan* ... 35 G9
Ganzhou, *China* ... 59 E10
Gao, *Mali* ... 83 B5
Gao Xian, *China* ... 58 C5
Gao'an, *China* ... 59 C10
Gaochun, *China* ... 59 B12
Gaohe, *China* ... 59 F9
Gaohebu, *China* ... 59 B11
Gaokeng, *China* ... 59 D9
Gaolan Dao, *China* ... 59 G9
Gaoligong Shan, *China* ... 58 E2
Gaomi, *China* ... 57 F10
Gaoming, *China* ... 59 F9
Gaoping, *China* ... 56 G7
Gaotang, *China* ... 56 F9
Gaoua, *Burkina Faso* ... 82 C4
Gaoual, *Guinea* ... 82 C2
Gaoxiong = Kaohsiung, *Taiwan* ... 59 F13
Gaoyang, *China* ... 56 E8
Gaoyao, *China* ... 59 F9
Gaoyou, *China* ... 59 A12
Gaoyou Hu, *China* ... 57 H10
Gaoyuan, *China* ... 57 F9
Gaozhou, *China* ... 59 G8
Gap, *France* ... 21 D10
Gapan, *Phil.* ... 61 D4
Gapat ➤, *India* ... 69 G10
Gapuwiyak, *Australia* ... 94 A2
Gar, *China* ... 60 C2
Garabogazköl Aylagy,
  Turkmenistan ... 52 E6
Garachico, *Canary Is.* ... 48 F3
Garachiné, *Panama* ... 120 E4
Garafia, *Canary Is.* ... 48 F2
Garah, *Australia* ... 95 D4
Garajonay, *Canary Is.* ... 48 F2
Garamba △, Dem. Rep. of
  the Congo ... 86 B2
Garango, *Burkina Faso* ... 83 C4
Garanhuns, *Brazil* ... 125 E11
Garautha, *India* ... 69 G8
Garawe, *Liberia* ... 82 E3
Garba Tula, *Kenya* ... 86 B4
Garberville, *U.S.A.* ... 108 F2
Garbiyang, *India* ... 69 D9
Garbsen, *Germany* ... 24 C5
Gard □, *France* ... 21 E8
Gard ➤, *France* ... 21 E8
Garda, L. di, *Italy* ... 40 C7
Gardanne, *France* ... 21 E9
Gårdby, *Sweden* ... 11 H10
Garde L., *Canada* ... 103 A7
Gardelegen, *Germany* ... 24 C7
Garden City, *Ga., U.S.A.* ... 115 J5
Garden City, *Kans., U.S.A.* ... 113 G4
Garden City, *Tex., U.S.A.* ... 113 K4
Garden Grove, *U.S.A.* ... 111 M9
Gardēz, *Afghan.* ... 68 C3
Gardhíki, *Greece* ... 46 C3
Gardiner, *Maine, U.S.A.* ... 115 C11
Gardiner, *Mont., U.S.A.* ... 108 D8
Gardiners I., *U.S.A.* ... 117 E13
Gardner, *U.S.A.* ... 117 D13
Gardner Canal, *Canada* ... 102 C3
Gardnerville, *U.S.A.* ... 110 G7
Gardno, Jezioro, *Poland* ... 30 D4
Gardo, Somali Rep. ... 75 F4
Gardone Val Trómpia, *Italy* ... 40 C7
Gárdony, *Hungary* ... 28 C3
Garešnica, *Croatia* ... 41 C13
Garéssio, *Italy* ... 40 D5
Garey, *U.S.A.* ... 111 L6
Garfield, *U.S.A.* ... 108 C5
Garforth, *U.K.* ... 14 D6
Gargaliánoi, *Greece* ... 46 D3
Gargan, Mt., *France* ... 20 C5
Gargano □, *Italy* ... 41 G12
Gargett, *Australia* ... 94 K6
Gargouna, *Mali* ... 83 B5
Gargždai, *Lithuania* ... 30 C8
Garibaldi △, *Canada* ... 102 D4
Gariep, L., *S. Africa* ... 88 E4
Garies, *S. Africa* ... 88 E2
Garigliano ➤, *Italy* ... 42 A6
Garissa, *Kenya* ... 86 C4
Garkida, *Nigeria* ... 83 C7
Garko, *Nigeria* ... 83 C6
Garland, *Tex., U.S.A.* ... 113 J6
Garland, *Utah, U.S.A.* ... 108 F7
Garlasco, *Italy* ... 40 C5
Garliava, *Lithuania* ... 30 D10
Garlin, *France* ... 20 E3
Garm, *Tajikistan* ... 52 F8
Garmāb, *Iran* ... 71 C8
Garmisch-Partenkirchen,
  Germany ... 25 H7
Garmo, Qullai = Kommunizma,
  Pik, *Tajikistan* ... 52 F8
Garmsār, *Iran* ... 71 C7
Garner, *U.S.A.* ... 112 D8
Garnett, *U.S.A.* ... 112 F7
Garo Hills, *India* ... 69 G14
Garoe = Garowe, Somali Rep. ... 75 F4
Garonne ➤, *France* ... 20 C3
Garonne, Canal Latéral à la,
  France ... 20 D4
Garoowe = Garowe, Somali Rep. ... 75 F4
Garot, *India* ... 68 G6
Garoua, *Cameroon* ... 83 D7
Garpenberg, *Sweden* ... 10 D10
Garphyttan, *Sweden* ... 10 E8

Garrauli, *India* 69 G8
Garrel, *Germany* 24 C4
Garrigues, *France* 20 E7
Garrison, *Mont., U.S.A.* 108 C7
Garrison, *N. Dak., U.S.A.* 112 B4
Garrison Res. = Sakakawea, L.,
　U.S.A. 112 B4
Garron Pt., *U.K.* 12 A6
Garrovillas, *Spain* 37 F4
Garrucha, *Spain* 39 H3
Garry ➤, *U.K.* 13 E5
Garry, L., *Canada* 100 B9
Garsen, *Kenya* 86 C5
Gärsnäs, *Sweden* 11 J8
Garson L., *Canada* 103 B6
Garstang, *U.K.* 14 D5
Gartempe ➤, *France* 20 B4
Gartz, *Germany* 24 B10
Garu, *Ghana* 83 C4
Garu, *India* 69 H11
Garub, *Namibia* 88 D2
Garut, *Indonesia* 63 G12
Garvão, *Portugal* 37 H2
Garvie Mts., *N.Z.* 91 L2
Garwa, *India* 69 G10
Garwolin, *Poland* 31 G8
Gary, *U.S.A.* 114 E2
Garz, *Germany* 24 A9
Garzê, *China* 58 B3
Garzón, *Colombia* 124 C3
Gas-San, *Japan* 54 E10
Gasan Kuli = Esenguly,
　Turkmenistan 52 F6
Gascogne, *France* 20 E4
Gascogne, G. de, *Europe* 20 E2
Gascony = Gascogne, *France* ... 20 E4
Gascoyne ➤, *Australia* 93 D1
Gascoyne Junction, *Australia* ... 93 E2
Gascueña, *Spain* 38 E2
Gash, Wadi ➤, *Ethiopia* 81 D4
Gash-Setit △, *Eritrea* 81 D4
Gashagar, *Nigeria* 83 C7
Gashaka, *Nigeria* 83 D7
Gashaka-Gumti △, *Nigeria* ... 83 D7
Gasherbrum, *Pakistan* 69 B7
Gashua, *Nigeria* 83 C7
Gasparillo, *Trin. & Tob.* 125 K15
Gaspé, *Canada* 105 C7
Gaspé, C., *Canada* 105 C7
Gaspé Pen. = Gaspésie, Pén. de
　la, *Canada* 105 C6
Gaspésie △, *Canada* 105 C6
Gaspésie, Pén. de la, *Canada* ... 105 C6
Gassan, *Burkina Faso* 82 C4
Gassol, *Nigeria* 83 D7
Gasteiz = Vitoria-Gasteiz, *Spain* ... 38 C2
Gastonia, *U.S.A.* 115 H5
Gastoúni, *Greece* 46 D3
Gastoúri, *Greece* 46 B1
Gastre, *Argentina* 128 E3
Gästrikland, *Sweden* 10 D10
Gata, C., *Cyprus* 49 E12
Gata, C. de, *Spain* 39 J2
Gata, Sierra de, *Spain* 36 E4
Gataga ➤, *Canada* 102 B3
Gătaia, *Romania* 28 E6
Gatchina, *Russia* 32 C6
Gatehouse of Fleet, *U.K.* 13 G4
Gates, *U.S.A.* 116 C7
Gateshead, *U.K.* 14 C6
Gatesville, *U.S.A.* 113 K6
Gateway, *U.S.A.* 117 F11
Gaths, *Zimbabwe* 87 G3
Gatico, *Chile* 126 A1
Gâtinais, *France* 19 D9
Gâtine, Hauteurs de, *France* ... 20 B3
Gatineau, *Canada* 117 A9
Gatineau △, *Canada* 104 C4
Gatineau ➤, *Canada* 104 C4
Gattaran, *Phil.* 61 B4
Gattinara, *Italy* 40 C5
Gatton, *Australia* 95 D5
Gatun, L., *Panama* 120 E4
Gatwick, London ✈ (LGW), *U.K.* ... 15 F7
Gatyana, *S. Africa* 89 E4
Gau, *Fiji* 91 D8
Gaucín, *Spain* 37 J5
Gauer L., *Canada* 103 B9
Gauhati = Guwahati, *India* ... 67 F17
Gauja ➤, *Latvia* 9 H21
Gaula ➤, *Norway* 8 E14
Gauri Phanta, *India* 69 E9
Gausta, *Norway* 9 G13
Gauteng □, *S. Africa* 89 D4
Gāv Koshī, *Iran* 71 D8
Gāvakān, *Iran* 71 D7
Gavarnie, *France* 20 F3
Gavāter, *Iran* 71 E9
Gāvbandī, *Iran* 71 E7
Gavdhopoúla, *Greece* 49 E6
Gávdhos, *Greece* 49 E6
Gavi, *Italy* 40 D5
Gavião, *Portugal* 37 F3
Gaviota, *U.S.A.* 111 L6
Gävkhūnī, Bāţlāq-e, *Iran* 71 C7
Gävle, *Sweden* 10 D11
Gävleborgs län □, *Sweden* ... 10 C10
Gävlebukten, *Sweden* 10 D11
Gavorrano, *Italy* 40 F7
Gavray, *France* 18 D5
Gavrilov, Yam, *Russia* 32 D10
Gávrion, *Greece* 46 D6
Gawachab, *Namibia* 88 D2
Gawilgarh Hills, *India* 66 J10
Gawler, *Australia* 95 E2
Gawu, *Nigeria* 83 D6
Gaya, *India* 69 G11
Gaya, *Niger* 83 C5
Gaya, *Nigeria* 83 C6

Gayéri, *Burkina Faso* 83 C5
Gaylord, *U.S.A.* 114 C3
Gayndah, *Australia* 95 D5
Gaysin = Haysyn, *Ukraine* ... 29 B14
Gayvoron = Hayvoron, *Ukraine* ... 29 B14
Gaza, *Gaza Strip* 74 D3
Gaza □, *Mozam.* 89 C5
Gaza Strip ⊘, *Asia* 74 D3
Gazanjyk, *Turkmenistan* 71 B7
Gazaoua, *Niger* 83 C6
Gāzbor, *Iran* 71 D8
Gazi, *Dem. Rep. of the Congo* ... 86 B1
Gaziantep, *Turkey* 70 B3
Gazimağosa = Famagusta, *Cyprus* ... 49 D12
Gazipaşa, *Turkey* 72 D5
Gbarnga, *Liberia* 82 D3
Gbekebo, *Nigeria* 83 D5
Gboko, *Nigeria* 83 D6
Gbongan, *Nigeria* 83 D5
Gcoverega, *Botswana* 88 B3
Gcuwa, *S. Africa* 89 E4
Gdańsk, *Poland* 30 D5
Gdansk ✈ (GDN) *Poland* 30 D5
Gdańska, Zatoka, *Poland* 30 D6
Gdov, *Russia* 9 G22
Gdynia, *Poland* 30 D5
Geba ➤, *Guinea-Biss.* 82 C1
Gebe, *Indonesia* 63 D7
Gebeciler, *Turkey* 47 C12
Gebeit Mine, *Sudan* 80 C4
Gebel Abyad, *Sudan* 80 D2
Gebel Iweibid, *Egypt* 80 H8
Gebze, *Turkey* 45 F13
Gecha, *Ethiopia* 81 F4
Gedaref, *Sudan* 81 E4
Gedaref □, *Sudan* 81 E4
Gediz, *Turkey* 47 B11
Gediz ➤, *Turkey* 47 C8
Gedo, *Ethiopia* 81 F4
Gèdre, *France* 20 F4
Gedser, *Denmark* 11 K5
Gedung, Pulau, *Malaysia* .... 65 c
Geegully Cr. ➤, *Australia* ... 92 C3
Geel, *Belgium* 17 C4
Geelong, *Australia* 95 F3
Geelvink Chan., *Australia* ... 93 E1
Geelvink B. = Cenderwasih,
　Teluk, *Indonesia* 63 E9
Geesthacht, *Germany* 24 B6
Geidam, *Nigeria* 83 C7
Geikie ➤, *Canada* 103 B8
Geikie Gorge △, *Australia* ... 92 C4
Geilenkirchen, *Germany* 24 E2
Geili, *Sudan* 81 D3
Geisingen, *Germany* 25 H4
Geislingen, *Germany* 25 G5
Geistown, *U.S.A.* 116 F6
Geita, *Tanzania* 86 C3
Gejiu, *China* 58 F4
Gel ➤, *Sudan* 81 F2
Gel, Meydān-e, *Iran* 71 D7
Gel River, *Sudan* 81 F2
Gela, *Italy* 43 F7
Gela, G. di, *Italy* 43 F7
Gelahun, *Liberia* 82 D2
Gelang Patah, *Malaysia* ..... 65 d
Gelderland □, *Neths.* 17 B6
Geldern, *Germany* 24 D2
Geldrop, *Neths.* 17 C5
Geleen, *Neths.* 17 D5
Gelehun, *S. Leone* 82 D2
Gelembe, *Turkey* 47 B9
Gelemso, *Ethiopia* 81 F5
Gelendost, *Turkey* 72 C4
Gelendzhik, *Russia* 33 K10
Gelibolu, *Turkey* 45 F10
Gelibolu Yarımadası, *Turkey* ... 45 F10
Gelidonya Burnu, *Turkey* 72 D4
Gelnhausen, *Germany* 25 E5
Gelnica, *Slovak Rep.* 27 C13
Gelsenkirchen, *Germany* 24 D3
Gelting, *Germany* 24 A5
Gelugur, *Malaysia* .... 65 c
Gemas, *Malaysia* 65 L4
Gembloux, *Belgium* 17 D4
Gembu, *Nigeria* 83 D7
Gemena, *Dem. Rep. of the Congo* ... 84 D3
Gemerek, *Turkey* 70 C6
Gemla, *Sweden* 11 H8
Gemlik, *Turkey* 45 F13
Gemlik Körfezi, *Turkey* 45 F12
Gemona del Friuli, *Italy* 41 B10
Gemsa, *Egypt* 80 B3
Gemsbok △, *Botswana* 88 D3
Gemünden, *Germany* 25 E5
Genale ➤, *Ethiopia* 81 F4
Genç, *Turkey* 73 C9
Gençay, *France* 20 B4
Geneina, Gebel, *Egypt* 80 B3
General Acha, *Argentina* 126 D3
General Alvear, *Buenos Aires,
　Argentina* 126 D4
General Alvear, *Mendoza,
　Argentina* 126 D2
General Artigas, *Paraguay* ... 126 B4
General Belgrano, *Argentina* ... 126 D4
General Bernardo O'Higgins,
　Antarctica 5 C18
General Cabrera, *Argentina* ... 126 C3
General Cepeda, *Mexico* 118 B4
General Guido, *Argentina* 126 D4
General Juan Madariaga,
　Argentina 126 D4
General La Madrid, *Argentina* ... 126 D3
General MacArthur, *Phil.* 61 F6
General Martín Miguel de
　Güemes, *Argentina* 126 A3
General Paz, *Argentina* 126 B4
General Pico, *Argentina* 126 D3
General Pinedo, *Argentina* ... 126 B3
General Pinto, *Argentina* 126 C3
General Roca, *Argentina* 128 D3

General Santos, *Phil.* 61 H6
General Toshevo, *Bulgaria* ... 45 C12
General Trevino, *Mexico* 119 B5
General Trías, *Mexico* 118 B3
General Viamonte, *Argentina* ... 126 D3
General Villegas, *Argentina* ... 126 D3
Genesee, *Idaho, U.S.A.* 108 C5
Genesee, *Pa., U.S.A.* 116 E7
Geneseo, *Ill., U.S.A.* 112 E9
Geneseo, *N.Y., U.S.A.* 116 D7
Geneva = Genève, *Switz.* 25 J2
Geneva, *Ala., U.S.A.* 115 K3
Geneva, *N.Y., U.S.A.* 116 D8
Geneva, *Nebr., U.S.A.* 112 E6
Geneva, *Ohio, U.S.A.* 116 E4
Geneva, L. = Léman, L., *Europe* ... 25 J2
Geneva, L., *U.S.A.* 114 D1
Genève, *Switz.* 25 J2
Gengenbach, *Germany* 25 G4
Gengma, *China* 58 F2
Genichesk = Henichesk, *Ukraine* ... 33 J8
Genil ➤, *Spain* 37 H5
Genk, *Belgium* 17 D5
Genlis, *France* 19 E12
Gennargentu, Mti. del, *Italy* ... 42 B2
Gennes, *France* 18 E3
Genoa = Génova, *Italy* 40 D5
Genoa, *Australia* 95 F4
Genoa, *N.Y., U.S.A.* 117 D8
Genoa, *Nebr., U.S.A.* 112 E6
Genoa, *Nev., U.S.A.* 110 F7
Génova, *Italy* 40 D5
Génova ✈ (GOA), *Italy* 40 D5
Genriyetty, Ostrov, *Russia* 53 B16
Gent, *Belgium* 17 C3
Genteng, *Bali, Indonesia* 63 J17
Genteng, *Jawa, Indonesia* ... 63 G12
Genthin, *Germany* 24 C8
Genzano di Lucánia, *Italy* ... 43 B9
Genzano di Roma, *Italy* 41 G9
Geoagiu, *Romania* 29 E8
Geographe B., *Australia* 93 F2
Geographe Chan., *Australia* ... 93 D1
Geokchay = Göyçay, *Azerbaijan* ... 35 K8
Georg Forster, *Antarctica* ... 5 C4
Georg von Neumayer, *Antarctica* ... 5 D17
Georga, Zemlya, *Russia* 52 A5
George, *S. Africa* 88 E3
George ➤, *Canada* 105 A6
George, L., *N.S.W., Australia* ... 95 F4
George, L., *S. Austral., Australia* ... 95 F3
George, L., *W. Austral., Australia* ... 92 D3
George, L., *Uganda* 86 B3
George, L., *Fla., U.S.A.* 115 L5
George, L., *N.Y., U.S.A.* 117 C11
George Gill Ra., *Australia* ... 92 D5
George Pt., *Australia* 94 J6
George River = Kangiqsualujjuaq,
　Canada 101 C13
George Sound, *N.Z.* 91 L1
George Town, *Australia* 95 G4
George Town, *Bahamas* 120 B4
George Town, *Cayman Is.* 120 C3
George Town, *Malaysia* ...... 65 c
George V Land, *Antarctica* ... 5 C10
George VI Sound, *Antarctica* ... 5 D17
George West, *U.S.A.* 113 L5
Georgetown = Janjanbureh,
　Gambia 82 C2
Georgetown, *Australia* 94 B3
Georgetown, *Ont., Canada* ... 116 C5
Georgetown, *P.E.I., Canada* ... 105 C7
Georgetown, *Guyana* 124 B7
Georgetown, *Calif., U.S.A.* ... 108 G11
Georgetown, *Colo., U.S.A.* ... 108 G11
Georgetown, *Ky., U.S.A.* 114 F3
Georgetown, *N.Y., U.S.A.* ... 117 D9
Georgetown, *Ohio, U.S.A.* ... 114 F4
Georgetown, *S.C., U.S.A.* ... 115 J6
Georgetown, *Tex., U.S.A.* ... 113 K6
Georgia □, *U.S.A.* 115 K5
Georgia ■, *Asia* 35 J6
Georgia, Str. of, *Canada* 102 D4
Georgian B., *Canada* 116 A4
Georgian Bay Islands △, *Canada* ... 116 B5
Georgina ➤, *Australia* 94 C2
Georgina I., *Canada* 116 B5
Georgiyevsk, *Russia* 35 H6
Georgsmarienhütte, *Germany* ... 24 C4
Gera, *Germany* 24 E8
Geraardsbergen, *Belgium* 17 D3
Geral, Serra, *Brazil* 127 B6
Geral de Goiás, Serra, *Brazil* ... 125 F9
Geraldine, *U.S.A.* 108 C8
Geraldton, *Australia* 93 E1
Geraldton, *Canada* 104 C2
Gérardmer, *France* 19 D13
Gerçüş, *Turkey* 73 D9
Gerede, *Turkey* 72 B5
Gerês, Sierra do, *Portugal* ... 36 D3
Gereshk, *Afghan.* 66 D4
Geretsried, *Germany* 25 H7
Gérgal, *Spain* 39 H2
Gerik, *Malaysia* 65 K3
Gering, *U.S.A.* 112 E3
Gerlach, *U.S.A.* 108 F4
Gerlachovský štít, *Slovak Rep.* ... 27 B13
German Planina, *Macedonia* ... 44 D6
Germansen Landing, *Canada* ... 102 B4
Germantown, *U.S.A.* 113 M10
Germany ■, *Europe* 24 E6
Germencik, *Turkey* 47 D9
Germering, *Germany* 25 G7
Germersheim, *Germany* 25 F4
Germī, *Iran* 71 B6
Germiston, *S. Africa* 89 D4
Gernika-Lumo, *Spain* 38 B2
Gernsheim, *Germany* 25 F4
Gero, *Japan* 55 G8

Gerokgak, *Indonesia* 63 J17
Gerolzhofen, *Germany* 25 F6
Gerona = Girona, *Spain* 38 D7
Gerrard, *Canada* 102 C5
Gers □, *France* 20 E4
Gers ➤, *France* 20 D4
Gersfeld, *Germany* 24 E5
Gersthofen, *Germany* 25 G6
Gertak Sanggul, *Malaysia* ... 65 c
Gertak Sanggul, Tanjung,
　Malaysia .... 65 c
Gerung, *Indonesia* 63 K19
Gerze, *Turkey* 72 B6
Gerze, *China* 60 C3
Geseke, *Germany* 24 D4
Geser, *Indonesia* 63 E8
Gesso ➤, *Italy* 40 D4
Getafe, *Spain* 36 E7
Getinge, *Sweden* 11 H6
Gettysburg, *Pa., U.S.A.* 114 F7
Gettysburg, *S. Dak., U.S.A.* ... 112 C5
Getxo, *Spain* 38 B2
Getz Ice Shelf, *Antarctica* ... 5 D14
Gevaş, *Turkey* 73 C10
Gévaudan, *France* 20 D7
Gevgelija, *Macedonia* 44 E6
Gévora ➤, *Spain* 37 G4
Gewani, *Ethiopia* 81 E5
Gex, *France* 19 F13
Geyikli, *Turkey* 47 B8
Geyser, *U.S.A.* 108 C8
Geyserville, *U.S.A.* 110 G4
Geyve, *Turkey* 72 B4
Ghâbat el Arab = Wang Kai,
　Sudan 81 F2
Ghabeish, *Sudan* 81 E2
Ghaggar ➤, *India* 68 E6
Ghaghara ➤, *India* 69 G11
Ghaghat ➤, *Bangla.* 69 G13
Ghagra, *India* 69 H11
Ghagra ➤, *India* 69 F9
Ghalla, Wadi el ➤, *Sudan* ... 81 E2
Ghana ■, *W. Afr.* 83 D4
Ghansor, *India* 69 H9
Ghanzi, *Botswana* 88 C3
Gharb el Istiwa'iya □, *Sudan* ... 81 G3
Gharb Kordofân □, *Sudan* ... 81 E2
Gharbîya, Es Sahrâ el, *Egypt* ... 80 B2
Ghardaïa, *Algeria* 78 B6
Ghârib, G., *Egypt* 80 B3
Gharig, *Sudan* 81 E2
Gharyān, *Libya* 79 B8
G̱at, *Libya* 79 D8
Ghatal, *India* 69 H12
Ghatampur, *India* 69 F9
Ghats, Eastern, *India* 66 N11
Ghats, Western, *India* 66 N9
Ghatsila, *India* 69 H12
Ghaṭṭī, Si. Arabia* 70 D3
Ghawdex = Gozo, *Malta* 49 C1
Ghazal, Bahr el ➤, *Chad* 79 F9
Ghazâl, Bahr el ➤, *Sudan* ... 81 F3
Ghaziabad, *India* 68 E7
Ghazipur, *India* 69 G10
Ghazni, *Afghan.* 68 C3
Ghaznī □, *Afghan.* 66 C6
Ghedi, *Italy* 40 C7
Ghelari, *Romania* 28 E7
Ghent = Gent, *Belgium* 17 C3
Gheorghe Gheorghiu-Dej =
　Onești, *Romania* 29 D11
Gheorgheni, *Romania* 29 D10
Gherla, *Romania* 29 C8
Ghidigeni, *Romania* 29 D12
Ghilarza, *Italy* 42 B1
Ghimeş-Făget, *Romania* 29 D11
Ghīnah, Wādī al ➤, *Si. Arabia* ... 70 D3
Ghisonaccia, *France* 21 F13
Ghisoni, *France* 21 F13
Ghizao, *Afghan.* 68 C1
Ghizar ➤, *Pakistan* 69 A5
Ghot Ogrein, *Egypt* 80 A2
Ghotaru, *India* 68 F4
Ghotki, *Pakistan* 68 E3
Ghudāf, W. al ➤, *Iraq* 70 C4
Ghudāmis, *Libya* 77 C4
Ghudāmis □, *Libya* 79 B8
Ghughri, *India* 69 H9
Ghugus, *India* 66 K11
Ghulam Mohammad Barrage,
　Pakistan 68 G3
Ghūrīān, *Afghan.* 66 B2
Gia Dinh, *Vietnam* 65 G6
Gia Lai = Plei Ku, *Vietnam* ... 64 F7
Gia Nghia, *Vietnam* 65 G6
Gia Ngoc, *Vietnam* 64 E7
Gia Vuc, *Vietnam* 64 E7
Giannutri, *Italy* 40 F8
Giant Forest, *U.S.A.* 110 J8
Giant Mts. = Krkonoše,
　Czech Rep. 26 A8
Giant Sequoia △, *U.S.A.* 110 K8
Giants Causeway, *U.K.* 12 A5
Gianyar, *Indonesia* 63 K18
Giarabub = Al Jaghbūb, *Libya* ... 79 C10
Giarre, *Italy* 43 E8
Giaveno, *Italy* 40 C4
Gibara, *Cuba* 120 B4
Gibb River, *Australia* 92 C4
Gibbon, *U.S.A.* 112 E5
Gibe ➤, *Ethiopia* 81 F4
Gibellina Nuova, *Italy* 42 E5
Gibeon, *Namibia* 88 D2
Gibraltar ⊘, *Europe* 37 J5
Gibraltar, Str. of, *Medit. S.* ... 37 K5
Gibraltar Range △, *Australia* ... 95 D5
Gibson Desert, *Australia* 92 D4
Gibsons, *Canada* 102 D4
Gibsonville, *U.S.A.* 110 F6

Giddings, *U.S.A.* 113 K6
Gidole, *Ethiopia* 81 F4
Giebnegáisi = Kebnekaise,
　Sweden 8 C18
Gien, *France* 19 E9
Giengen, *Germany* 25 G6
Giessen, *Germany* 24 E4
Gīfān, *Iran* 71 B8
Gifatin, Geziret, *Egypt* 80 B3
Gifford Creek, *Australia* 24 C6
Gift Lake, *Canada* 102 B5
Gifu, *Japan* 55 G8
Gifu □, *Japan* 55 G8
Gigant, *Russia* 35 G5
Giganta, Sa. de la, *Mexico* ... 118 B2
Gigha, *U.K.* 13 F3
Gíglio, *Italy* 40 F7
Gignac, *France* 20 E7
Gigüela ➤, *Spain* 37 F7
Gijón, *Spain* 36 B5
Gil I., *Canada* 102 C3
Gila ➤, *U.S.A.* 109 K6
Gila Bend, *U.S.A.* 109 K7
Gila Bend Mts., *U.S.A.* 109 K7
Gila Cliff Dwellings △, *U.S.A.* ... 109 K9
Gīlān □, *Iran* 71 B6
Gilău, *Romania* 29 D8
Gilbert ➤, *Australia* 94 B3
Gilbert Is., *Kiribati* 96 G9
Gilbert River, *Australia* 94 B3
Gilead, *U.S.A.* 117 B14
Gilf el Kebîr, Hadabat el, *Egypt* ... 80 C2
Gilford I., *Canada* 102 C3
Gilgandra, *Australia* 95 E4
Gilgil, *Kenya* 86 C4
Gilgit, *India* 69 B6
Gilgit ➤, *Pakistan* 69 B6
Gili ➤, *Mozam.* 87 F4
Gilimanuk, *Indonesia* 63 J17
Giljeva Planina, *Serbia & M.* ... 44 C3
Gillam, *Canada* 103 B10
Gilleleje, *Denmark* 11 H6
Gillen, L., *Australia* 93 E3
Gilles, L., *Australia* 95 E2
Gillette, *U.S.A.* 112 C2
Gilliat, *Australia* 94 C3
Gillingham, *U.K.* 15 F8
Gilmer, *U.S.A.* 113 J7
Gilmore, L., *Australia* 93 F3
Gilroy, *U.S.A.* 110 H5
Gilo ➤, *Ethiopia* 81 F3
Gilort ➤, *Romania* 29 F8
Gilroy, *U.S.A.* 110 H5
Gilo ➤, *Ethiopia* 81 F3
Gimbi, *Ethiopia* 81 F4
Gimie, Mt, *St. Lucia* .... 121 f
Gimli, *Canada* 103 C9
Gimo, *Sweden* 10 D12
Gimone ➤, *France* 20 E5
Gimont, *France* 20 E4
Gin Gin, *Australia* 95 D5
Gināh, *Egypt* 80 B3
Gineifa, *Egypt* 80 H8
Gingin, *Australia* 93 F2
Gingindlovu, *S. Africa* 89 D5
Ginir, *Ethiopia* 81 F5
Ginosa, *Italy* 43 B9
Ginzo de Limia = Xinzo de Limia,
　Spain 36 C3
Gióia, G. di, *Italy* 43 D8
Gióia del Colle, *Italy* 43 B9
Gióia Táuro, *Italy* 43 D8
Gioiosa Iónica, *Italy* 43 D9
Gioiosa Marea, *Italy* 43 D7
Gióna, Óros, *Greece* 46 C4
Giovi, Passo dei, *Italy* 40 D5
Giovinazzo, *Italy* 43 A9
Gir Hills, *India* 68 J4
Girab, *India* 68 F4
Giráfi, W. ➤, *Egypt* 74 F3
Giraltovce, *Slovak Rep.* 27 B14
Girard, *Kans., U.S.A.* 113 G7
Girard, *Ohio, U.S.A.* 116 E4
Girard, *Pa., U.S.A.* 116 E4
Girdle Ness, *U.K.* 13 D6
Giresun, *Turkey* 73 B8
Girga, *Egypt* 80 B3
Giri ➤, *India* 68 D7
Giridih, *India* 69 G12
Girifalco, *Italy* 43 D9
Girne = Kyrenia, *Cyprus* 49 D12
Giro, *Nigeria* 83 C5
Giromagny, *France* 19 E13
Giron = Kiruna, *Sweden* 8 C19
Girona, *Spain* 38 D7
Girona □, *Spain* 38 C7
Gironde □, *France* 20 D3
Gironde ➤, *France* 20 C2
Gironella, *Spain* 38 C6
Girraween △, *Australia* 95 D5
Giru, *Australia* 94 B4
Girvan, *U.K.* 13 F4
Gisborne, *N.Z.* 91 H7
Gisenyi, *Rwanda* 86 C2
Gislaved, *Sweden* 11 G7
Gisors, *France* 19 C8
Gitega, *Burundi* 86 C2
Giuba = Jubba ➤, *Somali Rep.* ... 75 G3
Giugliano in Campania, *Italy* ... 43 B7
Giuleşti, *Romania* 41 F10
Giurgeni, *Romania* 29 F12
Giurgiu, *Romania* 29 G10
Giurgiu □, *Romania* 29 F10
Giurgiuleşti, *Moldova* 29 E13
Give, *Denmark* 11 J3
Givet, *France* 19 B11
Givors, *France* 19 C8
Givry, *France* 19 F11
Giyon, *Ethiopia* 81 F4
Giza = El Gîza, *Egypt* 80 J7
Gizhiga, *Russia* 53 C17
Gizhiginskaya Guba, *Russia* ... 53 C16
Giżycko, *Poland* 30 D8

Gizzeria, *Italy* ... 43 D9
Gjalicë e Lumës, Mal., *Albania* . 44 D4
Gjegjan, *Albania* ... 44 E4
Gjirokastër, *Albania* ... 44 F4
Gjoa Haven, *Canada* ... 100 B10
Gjøvik, *Norway* ... 9 F14
Gjuhës, Kep i, *Albania* ... 44 F3
Glace Bay, *Canada* ... 105 C8
Glacier △, *Canada* ... 102 C5
Glacier △, *U.S.A.* ... 108 B7
Glacier Bay △, *U.S.A.* ... 102 B1
Glacier Peak, *U.S.A.* ... 108 B3
Gladewater, *U.S.A.* ... 113 J7
Gladstone, *Queens., Australia* ... 94 C5
Gladstone, *S. Austral., Australia* . 95 E2
Gladstone, *Canada* ... 103 C9
Gladstone, *U.S.A.* ... 114 C2
Gladwin, *U.S.A.* ... 114 D3
Glafsfjorden, *Sweden* ... 10 E6
Glagah, *Indonesia* ... 63 J17
Głogów Małopolski, *Poland* ... 31 H8
Gláma, *Iceland* ... 8 D2
Glamis, *U.S.A.* ... 111 N11
Glamoč, *Bos.-H.* ... 41 D13
Glamorgan, Vale of □, *U.K.* ... 15 F4
Glamsbjerg, *Denmark* ... 11 J4
Glarus, *Switz.* ... 25 H5
Glarus □, *Switz.* ... 25 J5
Glasco, *Kans., U.S.A.* ... 112 F6
Glasco, *N.Y., U.S.A.* ... 117 D11
Glasgow, *U.K.* ... 13 F4
Glasgow, *Ky., U.S.A.* ... 114 G3
Glasgow, *Mont., U.S.A.* ... 108 B10
Glasgow, City of □, *U.K.* ... 13 F4
Glasgow International ✈ (GLA), *U.K.* ... 13 F4
Glaslyn, *Canada* ... 103 C7
Glastonbury, *U.K.* ... 15 F5
Glastonbury, *U.S.A.* ... 117 E12
Glauchau, *Germany* ... 24 E8
Glava, *Sweden* ... 10 E6
Glavice, *Croatia* ... 41 E13
Glazov, *Russia* ... 34 A11
Gleichen, *Canada* ... 102 C6
Gleisdorf, *Austria* ... 26 D8
Gleiwitz = Gliwice, *Poland* ... 31 H5
Glen, *U.S.A.* ... 117 B13
Glen Affric, *U.K.* ... 13 D3
Glen Canyon, *U.S.A.* ... 109 H8
Glen Canyon △, *U.S.A.* ... 109 H8
Glen Canyon Dam, *U.S.A.* ... 109 H8
Glen Coe, *U.K.* ... 13 E3
Glen Cove, *U.S.A.* ... 117 F11
Glen Garry, *U.K.* ... 13 D3
Glen Innes, *Australia* ... 95 D5
Glen Lyon, *U.S.A.* ... 117 E8
Glen Mor, *U.K.* ... 13 D4
Glen More △, *U.K.* ... 13 D5
Glen Moriston, *U.K.* ... 13 D4
Glen Robertson, *Canada* ... 117 A10
Glen Spean, *U.K.* ... 13 E4
Glen Ullin, *U.S.A.* ... 112 B4
Glénan, Îs. de, *France* ... 18 E3
Glenariff △, *Ireland* ... 12 A5
Glencoe, *Canada* ... 116 D3
Glencoe, *S. Africa* ... 89 D5
Glencoe, *U.S.A.* ... 112 C7
Glendale, *Ariz., U.S.A.* ... 109 K7
Glendale, *Calif., U.S.A.* ... 111 L8
Glendale, *Zimbabwe* ... 87 F3
Glendive, *U.S.A.* ... 112 B2
Glendo, *U.S.A.* ... 112 D2
Glenelg →, *Australia* ... 95 F3
Glenfield, *U.S.A.* ... 117 C9
Glengarriff, *Ireland* ... 12 E2
Glenmont, *U.S.A.* ... 116 F2
Glenmorgan, *Australia* ... 95 D4
Glenn, *U.S.A.* ... 110 F4
Glennallen, *U.S.A.* ... 100 B5
Glennamaddy, *Ireland* ... 12 C3
Glenns Ferry, *U.S.A.* ... 108 E6
Glenore, *Australia* ... 94 B3
Glenreagh, *Australia* ... 95 E5
Glenrock, *U.S.A.* ... 108 E11
Glenrothes, *U.K.* ... 13 E5
Glens Falls, *U.S.A.* ... 117 C11
Glenside, *U.S.A.* ... 117 F9
Glenties, *Ireland* ... 12 B3
Glenveagh △, *Ireland* ... 12 A3
Glenville, *U.S.A.* ... 114 F5
Glenwood, *Canada* ... 105 C9
Glenwood, *Ark., U.S.A.* ... 113 H8
Glenwood, *Iowa, U.S.A.* ... 112 E7
Glenwood, *Minn., U.S.A.* ... 112 C7
Glenwood, *Wash., U.S.A.* ... 110 D5
Glenwood Springs, *U.S.A.* ... 108 G10
Glettinganes, *Iceland* ... 8 D7
Glifádha, *Greece* ... 46 D5
Glimåkra, *Sweden* ... 11 H8
Glina, *Croatia* ... 41 C13
Glinojeck, *Poland* ... 31 F7
Gliwice, *Poland* ... 31 H5
Globe, *U.S.A.* ... 109 K8
Glodeanu Siliştea, *Romania* ... 29 F11
Glodeni, *Moldova* ... 29 C12
Glödnitz, *Austria* ... 26 E7
Gloggnitz, *Austria* ... 26 D8
Głogów, *Poland* ... 31 G3
Głogówek, *Poland* ... 31 H4
Glomma →, *Norway* ... 9 G14
Glorieuses, Is., *Ind. Oc.* ... 89 A8
Glóssa, *Greece* ... 46 B5
Glossop, *U.K.* ... 14 D6
Gloucester, *Australia* ... 95 E5
Gloucester, *U.K.* ... 15 F5
Gloucester, *U.S.A.* ... 117 D14
Gloucester I., *Australia* ... 94 J6
Gloucester Island △, *Australia* ... 94 J6
Gloucester Point, *U.S.A.* ... 114 G7
Gloucestershire □, *U.K.* ... 15 F5
Gloversville, *U.S.A.* ... 117 C10

Glovertown, *Canada* ... 105 C9
Głowno, *Poland* ... 31 G6
Głubczyce, *Poland* ... 31 H4
Glubokiy, *Russia* ... 35 F5
Glubokoye = Hlybokaye, *Belarus* 32 E4
Głuchołazy, *Poland* ... 31 H4
Glücksburg, *Germany* ... 24 A5
Glückstadt, *Germany* ... 24 B5
Glukhov = Hlukhiv, *Ukraine* ... 33 G7
Glusk, *Belarus* ... 33 F5
Głuszyca, *Poland* ... 31 H3
Glyngøre, *Denmark* ... 11 H2
Gmünd, *Kärnten, Austria* ... 26 E6
Gmünd, *Niederösterreich, Austria* 26 C8
Gmunden, *Austria* ... 26 D6
Gnarp, *Sweden* ... 10 B11
Gnesta, *Sweden* ... 10 E11
Gniew, *Poland* ... 30 E5
Gniewkowo, *Poland* ... 31 F5
Gniezno, *Poland* ... 31 F4
Gnjilane, *Serbia & M.* ... 44 D5
Gnoien, *Germany* ... 24 B8
Gnosjö, *Sweden* ... 11 G7
Gnowangerup, *Australia* ... 93 F2
Go Cong, *Vietnam* ... 65 G6
Gō-no-ura, *Japan* ... 55 H4
Goa, *India* ... 66 M8
Goa □, *India* ... 66 M8
Goalen Hd., *Australia* ... 95 F5
Goalpara, *India* ... 67 F17
Goaltor, *India* ... 69 H12
Goalundo Ghat, *Bangla.* ... 69 H13
Goaso, *Ghana* ... 82 D4
Goat Fell, *U.K.* ... 13 F3
Goba, *Ethiopia* ... 81 F4
Goba, *Mozam.* ... 89 D5
Gobabis, *Namibia* ... 88 C2
Göbel, *Turkey* ... 45 F12
Gobi, *Asia* ... 56 C6
Gobō, *Japan* ... 55 H7
Gobo, *Sudan* ... 81 F3
Göçbeyli, *Turkey* ... 47 B9
Goch, *Germany* ... 24 D2
Gochas, *Namibia* ... 88 C2
Godalming, *U.K.* ... 15 F7
Godavari →, *India* ... 67 L13
Godavari Pt., *India* ... 67 L13
Godbout, *Canada* ... 105 C7
Godda, *India* ... 69 G12
Godech, *Bulgaria* ... 44 C7
Goderich, *Canada* ... 116 C3
Goderville, *France* ... 18 C7
Godfrey Ra., *Australia* ... 93 D2
Godhavn = Qeqertarsuaq, *Greenland* ... 101 B14
Godhra, *India* ... 68 H5
Gödöllő, *Hungary* ... 28 C4
Godoy Cruz, *Argentina* ... 126 C2
Gods →, *Canada* ... 104 A1
Gods L., *Canada* ... 104 B1
Gods River, *Canada* ... 103 C10
Godthåb = Nuuk, *Greenland* ... 101 B14
Goeie Hoop, Kaap die = Good Hope, C. of, *S. Africa* ... 88 E2
Goéland, L. au, *Canada* ... 104 C4
Goélands, L. aux, *Canada* ... 105 A7
Goeree, *Neths.* ... 17 C3
Goes, *Neths.* ... 17 C3
Goffstown, *U.S.A.* ... 117 C13
Gogama, *Canada* ... 104 C3
Gogebic, L., *U.S.A.* ... 112 B10
Goggetti, *Ethiopia* ... 81 F4
Gogolin, *Poland* ... 31 H5
Gogonou, *Benin* ... 83 C5
Gogra = Ghaghara →, *India* ... 69 G11
Gogriâl, *Sudan* ... 81 F2
Gogti, *Ethiopia* ... 81 E5
Gohana, *India* ... 68 E7
Goharganj, *India* ... 68 H7
Goi →, *India* ... 68 H6
Goiânia, *Brazil* ... 125 G9
Goiás, *Brazil* ... 125 G8
Goiás □, *Brazil* ... 125 F9
Goio-Erê, *Brazil* ... 127 A5
Góis, *Portugal* ... 36 E2
Gojam, *Ethiopia* ... 81 E4
Gojeb, Wabi →, *Ethiopia* ... 81 F4
Gojō, *Japan* ... 55 G7
Gojra, *Pakistan* ... 68 D5
Gökçeada, *Turkey* ... 45 F9
Gökçedağ, *Turkey* ... 47 B10
Gökçen, *Turkey* ... 47 C9
Gökçeören, *Turkey* ... 47 C10
Gökçeyazı, *Turkey* ... 47 B9
Gökırmak →, *Turkey* ... 72 B6
Gökova, *Turkey* ... 47 D10
Gökova Körfezi, *Turkey* ... 47 E9
Göksu →, *Turkey* ... 72 D6
Göksun, *Turkey* ... 72 C7
Gökteik, *Burma* ... 67 H20
Göktepe, *Turkey* ... 47 D10
Gokurt, *Pakistan* ... 68 E2
Gokwe, *Zimbabwe* ... 89 B4
Gola, *India* ... 69 E9
Golakganj, *India* ... 69 F13
Golan Heights = Hagolan, *Syria* . 74 C4
Gołańcz, *Poland* ... 31 F4
Goläshkerd, *Iran* ... 71 E8
Golaya Pristen = Hola Pristan, *Ukraine* ... 33 J7
Gölbaşı, *Adiyaman, Turkey* ... 72 D7
Gölbaşı, *Ankara, Turkey* ... 72 C5
Golchikha, *Russia* ... 4 B12
Golconda, *U.S.A.* ... 108 F5
Gölcük, *Kocaeli, Turkey* ... 45 F13
Gölcük, *Niğde, Turkey* ... 72 C6
Gold, *U.S.A.* ... 116 E7
Gold Beach, *U.S.A.* ... 108 E1
Gold Coast, *W. Afr.* ... 83 E4
Gold Hill, *U.S.A.* ... 108 E2
Gold River, *Canada* ... 102 D3
Gołdap, *Poland* ... 30 D9

Goldberg, *Germany* ... 24 B8
Golden, *Canada* ... 102 C5
Golden B., *N.Z.* ... 91 J4
Golden Gate, *U.S.A.* ... 108 H2
Golden Gate Highlands △, *S. Africa* ... 89 D4
Golden Hinde, *Canada* ... 102 D3
Golden Lake, *Canada* ... 116 A7
Golden Spike △, *U.S.A.* ... 108 F7
Golden Vale, *Ireland* ... 12 D3
Goldendale, *U.S.A.* ... 108 D3
Goldfield, *U.S.A.* ... 109 H5
Goldsboro, *U.S.A.* ... 115 H7
Goldsand L., *Canada* ... 103 B8
Goldsmith, *U.S.A.* ... 113 K3
Goldsworthy, *Australia* ... 92 D2
Goldthwaite, *U.S.A.* ... 113 K5
Golegã, *Portugal* ... 37 F2
Goleniów, *Poland* ... 30 E1
Golestān □, *Iran* ... 71 B7
Golestānak, *Iran* ... 71 D7
Goleta, *U.S.A.* ... 111 L7
Golfito, *Costa Rica* ... 120 E3
Golfo Aranci, *Italy* ... 42 B2
Golfo di Orosei e del Gennargentu △, *Italy* ... 42 B2
Gölgeli Dağları, *Turkey* ... 47 D10
Gölhisar, *Turkey* ... 47 D11
Goliad, *U.S.A.* ... 113 L6
Golija, *Serbia & M.* ... 44 C2
Golija, *Serbia & M.* ... 44 C4
Golina, *Poland* ... 31 F5
Gölköy, *Turkey* ... 72 B7
Göllersdorf, *Austria* ... 26 C9
Gölmarmara, *Turkey* ... 47 C9
Golo →, *France* ... 21 F13
Gölova, *Turkey* ... 47 E12
Golpāyegān, *Iran* ... 71 C6
Gölpazarı, *Turkey* ... 72 B4
Golra, *Pakistan* ... 68 C5
Golspie, *U.K.* ... 13 D5
Golub-Dobrzyń, *Poland* ... 31 E6
Golubac, *Serbia & M.* ... 44 B5
Golyam Perelik, *Bulgaria* ... 45 E8
Golyama Kamchiya →, *Bulgaria* 45 C11
Goma, *Dem. Rep. of the Congo* ... 86 C2
Gomal Pass, *Pakistan* ... 68 D3
Gomati →, *India* ... 69 G10
Gombari, *Dem. Rep. of the Congo* 86 B2
Gombe, *Nigeria* ... 83 C7
Gömbe, *Turkey* ... 47 E11
Gombe □, *Nigeria* ... 83 C7
Gombe →, *Tanzania* ... 86 C3
Gombi, *Nigeria* ... 83 C7
Gomel = Homyel, *Belarus* ... 33 F6
Gomera, *Canary Is.* ... 48 F2
Gómez Palacio, *Mexico* ... 118 B4
Gomīshān, *Iran* ... 71 B7
Gommern, *Germany* ... 24 C7
Gomogomo, *Indonesia* ... 63 F8
Gomoh, *India* ... 67 H15
Gomotartsi, *Bulgaria* ... 44 B6
Gompa = Ganta, *Liberia* ... 82 D3
Gomphi, *Greece* ... 46 B3
Gonābād, *Iran* ... 71 C8
Gonaïves, *Haiti* ... 121 C5
Gonâve, G. de la, *Haiti* ... 121 C5
Gonâve, Île de la, *Haiti* ... 121 C5
Gonbad-e Kāvūs, *Iran* ... 71 B7
Gönc, *Hungary* ... 28 B6
Gonda, *India* ... 69 F9
Gondal, *India* ... 68 J4
Gonder, *Ethiopia* ... 81 E4
Gondia, *India* ... 66 J12
Gondola, *Mozam.* ... 87 F3
Gondomar, *Portugal* ... 36 D2
Gondrecourt-le-Château, *France* 19 D12
Gönen, *Balıkesir, Turkey* ... 45 F11
Gönen, *Isparta, Turkey* ... 47 D12
Gönen →, *Turkey* ... 45 F11
Gong Xian, *China* ... 58 C5
Gong'an, *China* ... 59 B9
Gongcheng, *China* ... 59 E8
Gongga Shan, *China* ... 58 C3
Gongguan, *China* ... 58 G7
Gonghe, *China* ... 60 C5
Gongola →, *Nigeria* ... 83 D7
Gongolgon, *Australia* ... 95 E4
Gongshan, *China* ... 58 D2
Gongtan, *China* ... 58 C7
Gongzhuling, *China* ... 57 C13
Goniadz, *Poland* ... 30 E9
Goniri, *Nigeria* ... 83 C7
Gonjo, *China* ... 58 B2
Gonnesa, *Italy* ... 42 C1
Gónnos, *Greece* ... 46 B4
Gonnosfanádiga, *Italy* ... 42 C1
Gonzaga, *Phil.* ... 61 B5
Gonzales, *Calif., U.S.A.* ... 110 J5
Gonzales, *Tex., U.S.A.* ... 113 L6
González Chaves, *Argentina* ... 126 D3
Good Hope, C. of, *S. Africa* ... 88 E2
Gooderham, *Canada* ... 116 B6
Goodhouse, *S. Africa* ... 88 D2
Gooding, *U.S.A.* ... 108 E6
Goodland, *U.S.A.* ... 112 F4
Goodlow, *Canada* ... 102 B4
Goodooga, *Australia* ... 95 D4
Goodsprings, *U.S.A.* ... 111 K11
Goole, *U.K.* ... 14 D7
Googowi, *Australia* ... 95 E4
Goomalling, *Australia* ... 93 F2
Goomeri, *Australia* ... 95 D5
Goonda, *Mozam.* ... 87 F3
Goondiwindi, *Australia* ... 95 D5
Goongarrie △, *Australia* ... 93 F3
Goongarrie, L., *Australia* ... 93 F3
Goonyella, *Australia* ... 94 C4
Goose →, *Canada* ... 105 B7
Goose Creek, *U.S.A.* ... 115 J5
Goose L., *U.S.A.* ... 108 F3

Gop, *India* ... 66 H6
Gopalganj, *India* ... 69 F11
Göppingen, *Germany* ... 25 G5
Gor, *Spain* ... 37 H8
Góra, *Dolnośląskie, Poland* ... 31 G3
Góra, *Mazowieckie, Poland* ... 31 F7
Góra Kalwaria, *Poland* ... 31 G8
Gorakhpur, *India* ... 69 F10
Goražde, *Bos.-H.* ... 28 G3
Gorbatov, *Russia* ... 34 B6
Gorbea, Peña, *Spain* ... 38 B2
Gorczański △, *Poland* ... 31 J7
Gorda, *U.S.A.* ... 110 K5
Gorda, Pta., *Canary Is.* ... 48 F2
Gorda, Pta., *Nic.* ... 120 D3
Gordan B., *Australia* ... 92 B5
Gordon, *U.S.A.* ... 112 D3
Gordon →, *Australia* ... 95 G4
Gordon L., *Alta., Canada* ... 103 B6
Gordon L., *N.W.T., Canada* ... 102 A6
Gordonvale, *Australia* ... 94 B4
Gore, *Ethiopia* ... 81 F4
Gore, *N.Z.* ... 91 M2
Gore Bay, *Canada* ... 104 C3
Görele, *Turkey* ... 73 B8
Goreme, *Turkey* ... 72 C6
Gorey, *Ireland* ... 12 D5
Gorg, *Iran* ... 71 D8
Gorgān, *Iran* ... 71 B7
Gorgona, *Italy* ... 40 E6
Gorgona, I., *Colombia* ... 124 C3
Gorgora, *Ethiopia* ... 81 E4
Gorham, *U.S.A.* ... 117 B13
Gori, *Georgia* ... 35 J7
Goriganga →, *India* ... 69 E9
Gorinchem, *Neths.* ... 17 C4
Goris, *Armenia* ... 73 C12
Goritsy, *Russia* ... 32 D9
Gorízia, *Italy* ... 41 C10
Gorj □, *Romania* ... 29 E8
Gorki = Horki, *Belarus* ... 32 E6
Gorki = Nizhniy Novgorod, *Russia* ... 34 B7
Gorkiy = Nizhniy Novgorod, *Russia* ... 34 B7
Gorkovskoye Vdkhr., *Russia* ... 34 B6
Gorleston, *U.K.* ... 15 E9
Gorlice, *Poland* ... 31 J8
Görlitz, *Germany* ... 24 D10
Gorlovka = Horlivka, *Ukraine* ... 33 H10
Gorman, *U.S.A.* ... 111 L8
Gorna Dzhumayo = Blagoevgrad, *Bulgaria* ... 44 D7
Gorna Oryakhovitsa, *Bulgaria* ... 45 C9
Gornja Radgona, *Slovenia* ... 41 B13
Gornja Tuzla, *Bos.-H.* ... 28 F3
Gornji Grad, *Slovenia* ... 41 B11
Gornji Milanovac, *Serbia & M.* ... 44 B4
Gornji Vakuf, *Bos.-H.* ... 28 G2
Gorno Ablanovo, *Bulgaria* ... 45 C9
Gorno-Altay □, *Russia* ... 52 D9
Gorno-Altaysk, *Russia* ... 52 D9
Gornyatskiy, *Russia* ... 35 F5
Gornyy, *Saratov, Russia* ... 34 E9
Gornyy, *Sib., Russia* ... 54 B6
Gorodenka = Horodenka, *Ukraine* ... 29 B10
Gorodets, *Russia* ... 34 B6
Gorodishche = Horodyshche, *Ukraine* ... 33 H6
Gorodnya = Horodnya, *Ukraine* 33 G6
Gorodok = Haradok, *Belarus* ... 32 E6
Gorodok = Horodok, *Ukraine* ... 33 H2
Gorodovikovsk, *Russia* ... 35 G5
Gorokhov = Horokhiv, *Ukraine* ... 33 G3
Gorokhovets, *Russia* ... 34 B6
Gorom Gorom, *Burkina Faso* ... 83 C4
Goromonzi, *Zimbabwe* ... 87 F3
Gorong, Kepulauan, *Indonesia* ... 63 E8
Gorongose →, *Mozam.* ... 89 C5
Gorongosa △, *Mozam.* ... 87 F3
Gorongosa, Sa. da, *Mozam.* ... 87 F3
Gorontalo, *Indonesia* ... 63 D6
Gorontalo □, *Indonesia* ... 63 D6
Goronyo, *Nigeria* ... 83 C6
Gorron, *France* ... 18 D6
Gorshechnoye, *Russia* ... 33 G10
Gort, *Ireland* ... 12 C3
Gortis, *Greece* ... 49 D6
Góry Bystrzyckie, *Poland* ... 31 H3
Goryachiy Klyuch, *Russia* ... 35 H4
Gorzkowice, *Poland* ... 31 G6
Górzno, *Poland* ... 31 E6
Gorzów Śląski, *Poland* ... 31 G5
Gorzów Wielkopolski, *Poland* ... 31 F2
Gosford, *Australia* ... 95 E5
Goshen, *Calif., U.S.A.* ... 110 J7
Goshen, *Ind., U.S.A.* ... 114 E3
Goshen, *N.Y., U.S.A.* ... 117 E10
Goshogawara, *Japan* ... 54 D10
Goslar, *Germany* ... 24 D6
Gospič, *Croatia* ... 41 D12
Gosport, *U.K.* ... 15 G6
Gossas, *Senegal* ... 82 C1
Gosse →, *Australia* ... 94 B1
Gossi, *Mali* ... 83 B4
Gossina, *Sudan* ... 81 F2
Gostivar, *Macedonia* ... 44 E4
Gostyń, *Poland* ... 31 G4
Gostynin, *Poland* ... 31 F6
Göta älv →, *Sweden* ... 11 G5
Göta kanal, *Sweden* ... 11 F9
Göteborg, *Sweden* ... 11 G5
Goteşti, *Moldova* ... 29 D13
Gotha, *Germany* ... 24 E6

Gothenburg = Göteborg, *Sweden* 11 G5
Gothenburg, *U.S.A.* ... 112 E4
Gothèye, *Niger* ... 83 C5
Gotland, *Sweden* ... 11 G12
Gotlands län □, *Sweden* ... 11 G12
Gotō-Rettō, *Japan* ... 55 H4
Gotse Delchev, *Bulgaria* ... 44 E7
Gotska Sandön, *Sweden* ... 9 G18
Gōtsu, *Japan* ... 55 G6
Gott Pk., *Canada* ... 102 C4
Góttero, Monte, *Italy* ... 40 D6
Göttingen, *Germany* ... 24 D5
Gottwald = Zmiyev, *Ukraine* ... 33 H9
Gottwaldov = Zlín, *Czech Rep.* ... 27 B10
Goubangzi, *China* ... 57 D11
Gouda, *Neths.* ... 17 B4
Goúdhoura, Ákra, *Greece* ... 49 E8
Goudiry, *Senegal* ... 82 C2
Goudoumaria, *Niger* ... 83 C7
Gouéké, *Guinea* ... 82 D3
Gough I., *Atl. Oc.* ... 2 G9
Gouin, Rés., *Canada* ... 104 C5
Gouitafla, *Ivory C.* ... 82 D3
Goulburn, *Australia* ... 95 E4
Goulburn Is., *Australia* ... 94 A1
Goulia, *Ivory C.* ... 82 C3
Goulimine, *Morocco* ... 78 C3
Goumbou, *Mali* ... 82 B3
Gouménissa, *Greece* ... 44 F6
Goundam, *Mali* ... 82 B4
Goúra, *Greece* ... 46 D4
Gourbassi, *Mali* ... 82 C2
Gourdon, *France* ... 20 D5
Gouré, *Niger* ... 83 C7
Gourin, *France* ... 18 D3
Gourits →, *S. Africa* ... 88 E3
Gourma-Rharous, *Mali* ... 83 B4
Goúrnais, *Greece* ... 49 D7
Gournay-en-Bray, *France* ... 19 C8
Gourock, *U.K.* ... 13 F4
Goursi, *Burkina Faso* ... 82 C4
Gouverneur, *U.S.A.* ... 117 B9
Gouviá, *Greece* ... 49 A3
Gouzon, *France* ... 19 F9
Governador Valadares, *Brazil* ... 125 G10
Governor's Harbour, *Bahamas* ... 120 A4
Govindgarh, *India* ... 69 G9
Gowan Ra., *Australia* ... 94 D4
Gowanda, *U.S.A.* ... 116 D6
Gower, *U.K.* ... 15 F3
Gowna, L., *Ireland* ... 12 C4
Goya, *Argentina* ... 126 B4
Göyçay, *Azerbaijan* ... 35 K8
Goyder Lagoon, *Australia* ... 95 D2
Goyllarisquisga, *Peru* ... 124 F3
Göynük, *Antalya, Turkey* ... 47 E12
Göynük, *Bolu, Turkey* ... 72 B4
Goz Beïda, *Chad* ... 79 F10
Goz Regeb, *Sudan* ... 81 D4
Gozo, *Malta* ... 49 C1
Graaff-Reinet, *S. Africa* ... 88 E3
Grabo, *Ivory C.* ... 82 D3
Grabow, *Germany* ... 24 B7
Grabów nad Prosną, *Poland* ... 31 G5
Gračac, *Croatia* ... 41 D12
Gračanica, *Bos.-H.* ... 28 F3
Graçay, *France* ... 19 E8
Gracias a Dios, C., *Honduras* ... 120 D3
Graciosa, I., *Canary Is.* ... 48 E6
Grad Sofiya □, *Bulgaria* ... 44 D7
Gradac, *Serbia & M.* ... 44 C3
Gradačac, *Bos.-H.* ... 28 F3
Gradeška Planina, *Macedonia* ... 44 E6
Gradets, *Bulgaria* ... 45 D10
Gradišče, *Slovenia* ... 41 B12
Grădiştea de Munte, *Romania* ... 29 E8
Grado, *Italy* ... 41 C10
Grado, *Spain* ... 36 B4
Grady, *U.S.A.* ... 113 H3
Graeca, Lacul, *Romania* ... 29 F11
Grafenau, *Germany* ... 25 G9
Gräfenberg, *Germany* ... 25 F7
Grafham Water, *U.K.* ... 15 E7
Grafton, *Australia* ... 95 D5
Grafton, *N. Dak., U.S.A.* ... 112 A6
Grafton, *W. Va., U.S.A.* ... 114 F5
Graham, *Canada* ... 104 C1
Graham, *U.S.A.* ... 113 J5
Graham, Mt., *U.S.A.* ... 109 K9
Graham Bell, Ostrov = Greem-Bell, Ostrov, *Russia* ... 52 A7
Graham I., *Canada* ... 102 C2
Graham Land, *Antarctica* ... 5 C17
Grahamstown, *S. Africa* ... 88 E4
Grahamsville, *U.S.A.* ... 117 E10
Grahovo, *Serbia & M.* ... 44 D2
Graie, Alpi, *Europe* ... 21 C11
Grain Coast, *W. Afr.* ... 82 E3
Grajagan, *Indonesia* ... 63 K17
Grajagan, Teluk, *Indonesia* ... 63 K17
Grajaú, *Brazil* ... 125 E9
Grajaú →, *Brazil* ... 125 D10
Grajewo, *Poland* ... 30 E9
Gramada, *Bulgaria* ... 44 C6
Gramat, *France* ... 20 D5
Grammichele, *Italy* ... 43 E7
Grámmos, Óros, *Greece* ... 44 F4
Grampian, *U.S.A.* ... 116 F6
Grampian Highlands = Grampian Mts., *U.K.* ... 13 E5
Grampian Mts., *U.K.* ... 13 E5
Grampians, The, *Australia* ... 95 F3
Gramsh, *Albania* ... 44 F4
Gran Canaria, *Canary Is.* ... 48 G4
Gran Chaco, *S. Amer.* ... 126 B3
Gran Desierto del Pinacate △, *Mexico* ... 118 A2
Gran Paradiso, *Italy* ... 40 C4
Gran Sasso d'Itália, *Italy* ... 41 F10
Gran Sasso e Monti Della Laga △, *Italy* ... 41 F10

Granada, *Nic.*	120	D2
Granada, *Spain*	37	H7
Granada, *U.S.A.*	113	F3
Granada □, *Spain*	37	H7
Granadilla de Abona, *Canary Is.*	48	F3
Granard, *Ireland*	12	C4
Granbury, *U.S.A.*	113	J6
Granby, *Canada*	117	A12
Granby, *U.S.A.*	108	F11
Grand →, *Canada*	116	D5
Grand →, *Mo., U.S.A.*	112	F8
Grand →, *S. Dak., U.S.A.*	112	C4
Grand Bahama I., *Bahamas*	120	A4
Grand Bank, *Canada*	105	C8
Grand Bassam, *Ivory C.*	82	D4
Grand Béréby, *Ivory C.*	82	E3
Grand-Bourg, *Guadeloupe*	120	b
Grand Canal = Yun Ho →, *China*	57	E9
Grand Canyon, *U.S.A.*	109	H7
Grand Canyon △, *U.S.A.*	109	H7
Grand Canyon-Parashant △, *U.S.A.*	109	H7
Grand Cayman, *Cayman Is.*	120	C3
Grand Centre, *Canada*	103	C6
Grand Cess, *Liberia*	82	E3
Grand Coulee, *U.S.A.*	108	C4
Grand Coulee Dam, *U.S.A.*	108	C4
Grand Falls, *Canada*	105	C6
Grand Falls-Windsor, *Canada*	105	C8
Grand Forks, *Canada*	102	D5
Grand Forks, *U.S.A.*	112	B6
Grand Gorge, *U.S.A.*	117	D10
Grand Haven, *U.S.A.*	114	D2
Grand I., *Mich., U.S.A.*	114	B2
Grand I., *N.Y., U.S.A.*	116	D6
Grand Island, *U.S.A.*	112	E5
Grand Isle, *La., U.S.A.*	113	L9
Grand Isle, *Vt., U.S.A.*	117	B11
Grand Junction, *U.S.A.*	109	G9
Grand L., *N.B., Canada*	105	C6
Grand L., *Nfld. & L., Canada*	105	C8
Grand L., *Nfld. & L., Canada*	105	B7
Grand L., *U.S.A.*	113	L8
Grand Lahou, *Ivory C.*	82	D3
Grand Lake, *U.S.A.*	108	F11
Grand-Lieu, L. de, *France*	18	E5
Grand Manan I., *Canada*	105	D6
Grand Marais, *Canada*	112	B9
Grand Marais, *U.S.A.*	114	B3
Grand-Mère, *Canada*	104	C5
Grand Popo, *Benin*	83	D5
Grand Portage, *U.S.A.*	112	B10
Grand Prairie, *U.S.A.*	113	J6
Grand Rapids, *Canada*	103	C9
Grand Rapids, *Mich., U.S.A.*	114	D2
Grand Rapids, *Minn., U.S.A.*	112	B8
Grand St-Bernard, Col du, *Europe*	25	K3
Grand Staircase-Escalante △, *U.S.A.*	109	H8
Grand Teton, *U.S.A.*	108	E8
Grand Teton △, *U.S.A.*	108	D8
Grand Union Canal, *U.K.*	15	E7
Grand-Vigie, Pte. de la, *Guadeloupe*	120	b
Grandas de Salime, *Spain*	36	B4
Grande →, *Jujuy, Argentina*	126	A2
Grande →, *Mendoza, Argentina*	126	D2
Grande →, *Bolivia*	124	G6
Grande →, *Bahia, Brazil*	125	F10
Grande →, *Minas Gerais, Brazil*	125	H8
Grande, B., *Argentina*	128	G3
Grande, Rio →, *U.S.A.*	113	N6
Grande Baleine, R. de la →, *Canada*	104	A4
Grande Cache, *Canada*	102	C5
Grande Casse, Pte. de la, *France*	21	C10
Grande-Entrée, *Canada*	105	C7
Grande Prairie, *Canada*	102	B5
Grande-Rivière, *Canada*	105	C7
Grande-Terre, *Guadeloupe*	120	b
Grande-Vallée, *Canada*	105	C6
Grandfalls, *U.S.A.*	113	K3
Grândola, *Portugal*	37	G2
Grandpré, *France*	19	C11
Grands Causses △, *France*	20	D6
Grands-Jardins △, *Canada*	105	C5
Grandview, *Canada*	103	C8
Grandview, *U.S.A.*	108	C4
Grandvilliers, *France*	19	C8
Graneros, *Chile*	126	C1
Grangemouth, *U.K.*	13	E5
Granger, *U.S.A.*	108	F9
Grängesberg, *Sweden*	10	D9
Grangeville, *U.S.A.*	108	D5
Granisle, *Canada*	102	C3
Granite City, *U.S.A.*	112	F9
Granite Falls, *U.S.A.*	112	C7
Granite L., *Canada*	105	C8
Granite Mt., *U.S.A.*	111	M10
Granite Pk., *U.S.A.*	108	D9
Graniteville, *U.S.A.*	117	B12
Granitola, C., *Italy*	42	F5
Granity, *N.Z.*	91	J3
Granja, *Brazil*	125	D10
Granja de Moreruela, *Spain*	36	D5
Granja de Torrehermosa, *Spain*	37	G5
Gränna, *Sweden*	11	F8
Granollers, *Spain*	38	D7
Grant, *U.S.A.*	112	E4
Grant, Mt., *U.S.A.*	108	G4
Grant City, *U.S.A.*	112	E7
Grant I., *Australia*	92	B5
Grant Range, *U.S.A.*	109	G6
Grantham, *U.K.*	14	E7
Grantown-on-Spey, *U.K.*	13	D5
Grants, *U.S.A.*	109	J10
Grantsville, *U.S.A.*	108	F7
Granville, *France*	18	D5
Granville, *N. Dak., U.S.A.*	112	A4
Granville, *N.Y., U.S.A.*	117	C11
Granville, *Ohio, U.S.A.*	116	F2
Granville L., *Canada*	103	B8
Graskop, *S. Africa*	89	C5
Gräsö, *Sweden*	10	D12
Grass →, *Canada*	103	B9
Grass Range, *U.S.A.*	108	C9
Grass River △, *Canada*	103	C8
Grass Valley, *Calif., U.S.A.*	110	F6
Grass Valley, *Oreg., U.S.A.*	108	D3
Grassano, *Italy*	43	B9
Grasse, *France*	21	E10
Grassflat, *U.S.A.*	116	F6
Grasslands △, *Canada*	103	D7
Grassy, *Australia*	95	G3
Gråsten, *Denmark*	11	K3
Grästorp, *Sweden*	11	F6
Gratkorn, *Austria*	26	D8
Graubünden □, *Switz.*	25	J5
Graulhet, *France*	20	E5
Graus, *Spain*	38	C5
Grave, Pte. de, *France*	20	C2
Gravelbourg, *Canada*	103	D7
Gravelines, *France*	19	A9
's-Gravenhage, *Neths.*	17	B4
Gravenhurst, *Canada*	116	B5
Gravesend, *Australia*	95	D5
Gravesend, *U.K.*	15	F8
Gravina in Púglia, *Italy*	43	B9
Gravois, Pointe-à-, *Haiti*	121	C5
Gravone →, *France*	21	G12
Gray, *France*	19	E12
Grayling, *U.S.A.*	114	C3
Grays, *U.K.*	15	F8
Grays Harbor, *U.S.A.*	108	C1
Grays L., *U.S.A.*	108	E8
Grays River, *U.S.A.*	110	D3
Grayvoron, *Russia*	33	G8
Graz, *Austria*	26	D8
Grdelica, *Serbia & M.*	44	D6
Greasy L., *Canada*	102	A4
Great Abaco I. = Abaco I., *Bahamas*	120	A4
Great Artesian Basin, *Australia*	94	C3
Great Australian Bight, *Australia*	93	F5
Great Bahama Bank, *Bahamas*	120	B4
Great Barrier I., *N.Z.*	91	G5
Great Barrier Reef, *Australia*	94	B4
Great Barrier Reef △, *Australia*	94	B4
Great Barrington, *U.S.A.*	117	D11
Great Basalt Wall △, *Australia*	94	B4
Great Basin, *U.S.A.*	108	G5
Great Basin △, *U.S.A.*	108	G6
Great Bear →, *Canada*	100	B7
Great Bear L., *Canada*	100	B7
Great Belt = Store Bælt, *Denmark*	11	J4
Great Bend, *Kans., U.S.A.*	112	F5
Great Bend, *Pa., U.S.A.*	117	E9
Great Blasket I., *Ireland*	12	D1
Great Britain, *Europe*	6	E5
Great Camanoe, *Br. Virgin Is.*	121	e
Great Codroy, *U.S.A.*	105	C8
Great Dividing Ra., *Australia*	94	C4
Great Driffield = Driffield, *U.K.*	14	C7
Great Exuma I., *Bahamas*	120	B4
Great Falls, *U.S.A.*	108	C8
Great Fish = Groot Vis →, *S. Africa*	88	E4
Great Guana Cay, *Bahamas*	120	B4
Great Inagua I., *Bahamas*	121	B5
Great Indian Desert = Thar Desert, *India*	68	F5
Great Karoo, *S. Africa*	88	E3
Great Khingan Mts. = Da Hinggan Ling, *China*	60	B7
Great Lake, *Australia*	95	G4
Great Lakes, *N. Amer.*	98	E11
Great Malvern, *U.K.*	15	E5
Great Miami →, *U.S.A.*	114	F3
Great Ormes Head, *U.K.*	14	D4
Great Ouse →, *U.K.*	14	E8
Great Palm I., *Australia*	94	B4
Great Pedro Bluff, *Jamaica*	120	a
Great Plains, *N. Amer.*	98	E9
Great Ruaha →, *Tanzania*	86	D4
Great Sacandaga L., *U.S.A.*	117	C10
Great Saint Bernard Pass = Grand St-Bernard, Col du, *Europe*	25	K3
Great Salt L., *U.S.A.*	108	F7
Great Salt Lake Desert, *U.S.A.*	108	F7
Great Salt Plains L., *U.S.A.*	113	G5
Great Sand Dunes △, *U.S.A.*	109	H11
Great Sandy △, *Australia*	95	D5
Great Sandy Desert, *Australia*	92	D3
Great Sangi = Sangihe, Pulau, *Indonesia*	63	D7
Great Scarcies →, *S. Leone*	82	D2
Great Skellig, *Ireland*	12	E1
Great Slave L., *Canada*	102	A5
Great Smoky Mts. △, *U.S.A.*	115	H4
Great Snow Mt., *Canada*	102	B4
Great Stour = Stour →, *U.K.*	15	F9
Great Victoria Desert, *Australia*	93	E4
Great Wall, *Antarctica*	5	C18
Great Wall, *China*	56	E5
Great Whernside, *U.K.*	14	C6
Great Yarmouth, *U.K.*	15	E9
Great Zab = Zāb al Kabīr →, *Iraq*	70	C4
Great Zimbabwe, *Zimbabwe*	87	G3
Greater Antilles, *W. Indies*	121	C5
Greater London □, *U.K.*	15	F7
Greater Manchester □, *U.K.*	14	D5
Greater St. Lucia Wetlands △, *S. Africa*	89	D5
Greater Sudbury = Sudbury, *Canada*	104	C3
Greater Sunda Is., *Indonesia*	62	F4
Grebbestad, *Sweden*	11	F5
Grebenka = Hrebinka, *Ukraine*	33	G7
Greco, C., *Cyprus*	49	E13
Greco, Mte., *Italy*	41	G10
Gredos, Sierra de, *Spain*	36	E6
Greece, *U.S.A.*	116	C7
Greece ■, *Europe*	46	B3
Greeley, *Colo., U.S.A.*	112	E2
Greeley, *Nebr., U.S.A.*	112	E5
Greem-Bell, Ostrov, *Russia*	52	A7
Green, *U.S.A.*	108	E2
Green →, *Ky., U.S.A.*	114	G2
Green →, *Utah, U.S.A.*	109	G9
Green B., *U.S.A.*	114	C2
Green Bay, *U.S.A.*	114	C2
Green C., *Australia*	95	F5
Green Cove Springs, *U.S.A.*	115	L5
Green Lake, *Canada*	103	C7
Green Mts., *U.S.A.*	117	C12
Green River, *Utah, U.S.A.*	109	G8
Green River, *Wyo., U.S.A.*	108	F9
Green Valley, *U.S.A.*	109	L8
Greenbank, *U.S.A.*	110	B4
Greenbush, *Mich., U.S.A.*	116	B1
Greenbush, *Minn., U.S.A.*	112	A6
Greene, *U.S.A.*	117	D9
Greenfield, *Calif., U.S.A.*	110	J5
Greenfield, *Calif., U.S.A.*	111	K8
Greenfield, *Ind., U.S.A.*	114	F3
Greenfield, *Iowa, U.S.A.*	112	E7
Greenfield, *Mass., U.S.A.*	117	D12
Greenfield, *Mo., U.S.A.*	113	G8
Greenfield Park, *Canada*	117	A11
Greenland ☑, *N. Amer.*	4	C5
Greenland Sea, *Arctic*	4	B7
Greenock, *U.K.*	13	F4
Greenore, *Ireland*	12	B5
Greenore Pt., *Ireland*	12	D5
Greenough, *Australia*	93	E1
Greenough →, *Australia*	93	E1
Greenough Pt., *Canada*	116	B3
Greenport, *U.S.A.*	117	E12
Greensboro, *Ga., U.S.A.*	115	J4
Greensboro, *N.C., U.S.A.*	115	G6
Greensburg, *Ind., U.S.A.*	114	F3
Greensburg, *Kans., U.S.A.*	113	G5
Greensburg, *Pa., U.S.A.*	116	F5
Greenstone Pt., *U.K.*	13	D3
Greenvale, *Australia*	94	B4
Greenville, *Liberia*	82	D3
Greenville, *Ala., U.S.A.*	115	K2
Greenville, *Calif., U.S.A.*	110	E6
Greenville, *Maine, U.S.A.*	115	C11
Greenville, *Mich., U.S.A.*	114	D3
Greenville, *Miss., U.S.A.*	113	J9
Greenville, *Mo., U.S.A.*	113	G9
Greenville, *N.C., U.S.A.*	115	H7
Greenville, *N.H., U.S.A.*	117	D13
Greenville, *N.Y., U.S.A.*	117	D10
Greenville, *Ohio, U.S.A.*	114	E3
Greenville, *Pa., U.S.A.*	116	E4
Greenville, *S.C., U.S.A.*	115	H4
Greenville, *Tenn., U.S.A.*	115	G4
Greenville, *Tex., U.S.A.*	113	J6
Greenwater Lake △, *Canada*	103	C8
Greenwich, *Conn., U.S.A.*	117	E11
Greenwich, *N.Y., U.S.A.*	117	C11
Greenwich, *Ohio, U.S.A.*	116	E2
Greenwich □, *U.K.*	15	F8
Greenwood, *Canada*	102	D5
Greenwood, *Ark., U.S.A.*	113	H7
Greenwood, *Ind., U.S.A.*	114	F2
Greenwood, *Miss., U.S.A.*	113	J9
Greenwood, *S.C., U.S.A.*	115	H4
Greenwood, Mt., *Australia*	92	B5
Gregbe, *Ivory C.*	82	D3
Gregory, *U.S.A.*	112	D5
Gregory →, *Australia*	92	C5
Gregory △, *Australia*	94	B2
Gregory, L., *S. Austral., Australia*	95	D2
Gregory, L., *W. Austral., Australia*	93	E2
Gregory Downs, *Australia*	94	B2
Gregory Ra., *Queens., Australia*	94	B3
Gregory Ra., *W. Austral., Australia*	92	D3
Greiffenberg, *Germany*	24	B9
Greifswald, *Germany*	24	A9
Greifswalder Bodden, *Germany*	24	A9
Grein, *Austria*	26	C7
Greiz, *Germany*	24	E8
Gremikha, *Russia*	52	C4
Grená, *Denmark*	11	H4
Grenada, *U.S.A.*	113	J10
Grenada ■, *W. Indies*	121	D7
Grenade, *France*	20	E5
Grenadier I., *U.S.A.*	117	B8
Grenadines, The, *St. Vincent*	121	D7
Grenchen, *Switz.*	25	H3
Grenen, *Denmark*	11	G4
Grenfell, *Australia*	95	E4
Grenfell, *Canada*	103	C8
Grenoble, *France*	21	C9
Grenville, C., *Australia*	94	A3
Grenville Chan., *Canada*	102	C3
Gréoux-les-Bains, *France*	21	E9
Gresham, *U.S.A.*	110	E4
Gresik, *Indonesia*	63	G15
Gretna, *U.K.*	13	F5
Greven, *Germany*	24	C3
Grevená, *Greece*	44	F5
Grevená □, *Greece*	44	F5
Grevenbroich, *Germany*	24	D2
Grevenmacher, *Lux.*	17	E6
Grevesmühlen, *Germany*	24	B7
Grevestrand, *Denmark*	11	J6
Grey →, *Canada*	105	C8
Grey →, *N.Z.*	91	K3
Grey, C., *Australia*	94	A2
Greybull, *U.S.A.*	108	D9
Greymouth, *N.Z.*	91	K3
Greystones, *Ireland*	12	C5
Greytown, *N.Z.*	91	J5
Greytown, *S. Africa*	89	D5
Gribanovskiy, *Russia*	34	E5
Gribbell I., *Canada*	102	C3
Gribës, Mal i, *Albania*	44	F3
Gridley, *U.S.A.*	110	F5
Griekwastad, *S. Africa*	88	D3
Griesheim, *Germany*	25	F4
Grieskirchen, *Austria*	26	C6
Griffin, *U.S.A.*	115	J3
Griffith, *Australia*	95	E4
Griffith, *Canada*	116	A7
Griffith I., *Canada*	116	B4
Grignols, *France*	20	D3
Grigoriopol, *Moldova*	29	C14
Grimaylov = Hrymayliv, *Ukraine*	33	H4
Grimes, *U.S.A.*	110	F5
Grimma, *Germany*	24	D8
Grimmen, *Germany*	24	A9
Grimsay, *U.K.*	13	D1
Grimsby, *Canada*	116	C5
Grimsby, *U.K.*	14	D7
Grímsey, *Iceland*	8	C5
Grimshaw, *Canada*	102	B5
Grimslöv, *Sweden*	11	H8
Grimstad, *Norway*	9	G13
Grindelwald, *Switz.*	25	J4
Grindsted, *Denmark*	11	J2
Grindstone I., *Canada*	117	B8
Grindu, *Romania*	29	F11
Grinnell, *U.S.A.*	112	E8
Grintavec, *Slovenia*	41	B11
Gris-Nez, C., *France*	19	B8
Grisolles, *France*	20	E5
Grisons = Graubünden □, *Switz.*	25	J5
Grisslehamn, *Sweden*	10	D12
Grmeč Planina, *Bos.-H.*	41	D13
Groais I., *Canada*	105	B8
Grobiņa, *Latvia*	30	B8
Groblersdal, *S. Africa*	89	D4
Grobming, *Austria*	26	D6
Grocka, *Serbia & M.*	44	B4
Gródek, *Poland*	31	E10
Grodno = Hrodna, *Belarus*	30	E10
Grodków, *Poland*	31	H4
Grodzisk Mazowiecki, *Poland*	31	F7
Grodzisk Wielkopolski, *Poland*	31	F3
Grodzyanka = Hrodzyanka, *Belarus*	32	F5
Groesbeck, *U.S.A.*	113	K6
Groix, *France*	18	E3
Groix, Î. de, *France*	18	E3
Grójec, *Poland*	31	G7
Gronau, *Niedersachsen, Germany*	24	C5
Gronau, *Nordrhein-Westfalen, Germany*	24	C3
Grong, *Norway*	8	D15
Grönhögen, *Sweden*	11	H10
Groningen, *Neths.*	17	A6
Groningen □, *Neths.*	17	A6
Groom, *U.S.A.*	113	H4
Groot →, *S. Africa*	88	E3
Groot Berg →, *S. Africa*	88	E2
Groot-Brakrivier, *S. Africa*	88	E3
Groot Karasberge, *Namibia*	88	D2
Groot-Kei →, *S. Africa*	89	E4
Groot Vis →, *S. Africa*	88	E4
Grootdrink, *S. Africa*	88	D3
Groote Eylandt, *Australia*	94	A2
Grootfontein, *Namibia*	88	B2
Grootlaagte →, *Africa*	88	C3
Grootvloer →, *S. Africa*	88	E3
Gros C., *Canada*	102	A6
Gros Islet, *St. Lucia*	121	f
Gros Morne △, *Canada*	105	C8
Gros Piton, *St. Lucia*	121	f
Gros Piton Pt., *St. Lucia*	121	f
Grósio, *Italy*	40	B7
Grosne →, *France*	19	F11
Grossa, Pta., *Spain*	48	B8
Grossenbrode, *Germany*	24	A7
Grossenhain, *Germany*	24	D9
Grosser Arber, *Germany*	25	F9
Grosser Plöner See, *Germany*	24	A6
Grosseto, *Italy*	41	F8
Grossgerungs, *Austria*	26	C7
Grossglockner, *Austria*	26	D5
Groswater B., *Canada*	105	B8
Groton, *Conn., U.S.A.*	117	E12
Groton, *N.Y., U.S.A.*	117	D8
Groton, *S. Dak., U.S.A.*	112	C5
Grottáglie, *Italy*	43	B10
Grottaminarda, *Italy*	43	A8
Grottammare, *Italy*	41	F10
Grouard Mission, *Canada*	102	B5
Grouin, Pte. du, *France*	18	D5
Groundhog →, *Canada*	104	C3
Grouw, *Neths.*	17	A5
Grove City, *U.S.A.*	116	E4
Grove Hill, *U.S.A.*	115	K2
Groveland, *U.S.A.*	110	H6
Grover City, *U.S.A.*	111	K6
Groves, *U.S.A.*	113	L8
Groveton, *U.S.A.*	117	B13
Groznjan, *Croatia*	41	C10
Groznyy, *Russia*	35	J7
Grubišno Polje, *Croatia*	28	E3
Grudovo = Sredets, *Bulgaria*	45	D11
Grudusk, *Poland*	31	E7
Grudziądz, *Poland*	30	E5
Gruinard B., *U.K.*	13	D3
Gruissan, *France*	20	E7
Grumo Áppula, *Italy*	43	A9
Grums, *Sweden*	10	E7
Grünberg, *Germany*	24	E4
Gründau, *Germany*	25	E5
Grundy Center, *U.S.A.*	112	D8
Grünstadt, *Germany*	25	F4
Gruppo di Tessa △, *Italy*	40	B8
Gruvberget, *Sweden*	10	C10
Gruver, *U.S.A.*	113	G4
Gruyères, *Switz.*	25	J3
Gruža, *Serbia & M.*	44	C4
Gryazi, *Russia*	33	F10
Gryazovets, *Russia*	32	C11
Grybów, *Poland*	31	J7
Grycksbo, *Sweden*	10	D9
Gryfice, *Poland*	30	E2
Gryfino, *Poland*	31	E1
Gryfów Śląski, *Poland*	31	G2
Grythyttan, *Sweden*	10	E8
Gstaad, *Switz.*	25	J3
Gua, *India*	67	H14
Gua Musang, *Malaysia*	65	K3
Guacanayabo, G. de, *Cuba*	120	B4
Guachipas →, *Argentina*	126	B2
Guadajoz →, *Spain*	37	H6
Guadalajara, *Mexico*	118	C4
Guadalajara, *Spain*	38	E1
Guadalajara □, *Spain*	38	E2
Guadalcanal, *Solomon Is.*	96	H8
Guadalcanal, *Spain*	37	G5
Guadalén →, *Spain*	37	G7
Guadales, *Argentina*	126	C2
Guadalete →, *Spain*	37	J4
Guadalhorce →, *Spain*	37	J6
Guadalimar →, *Spain*	37	G7
Guadalmena →, *Spain*	37	G8
Guadalmez →, *Spain*	37	G5
Guadalope →, *Spain*	38	D4
Guadalquivir →, *Spain*	37	J4
Guadalupe = Guadeloupe ☑, *W. Indies*	120	b
Guadalupe, *Mexico*	111	N10
Guadalupe, *Spain*	37	F5
Guadalupe, *U.S.A.*	111	L6
Guadalupe →, *Mexico*	111	N10
Guadalupe →, *U.S.A.*	113	L6
Guadalupe, Sierra de, *Spain*	37	F5
Guadalupe Bravos, *Mexico*	118	A3
Guadalupe I., *Pac. Oc.*	98	G8
Guadalupe Mts. △, *U.S.A.*	113	K2
Guadalupe Peak, *U.S.A.*	113	K2
Guadalupe y Calvo, *Mexico*	118	B3
Guadarrama, Sierra de, *Spain*	36	E7
Guadauta, *Georgia*	35	J5
Guadeloupe ☑, *Guadeloupe*	120	b
Guadeloupe ☑, *W. Indies*	120	b
Guadeloupe Passage, *W. Indies*	121	C7
Guadiamar →, *Spain*	37	J4
Guadiana →, *Portugal*	37	H3
Guadiana Menor →, *Spain*	37	H7
Guadiaro →, *Spain*	37	J5
Guadiato →, *Spain*	37	H5
Guadiela →, *Spain*	38	E2
Guadix, *Spain*	37	H7
Guafo, Boca del, *Chile*	128	E2
Guaico, *Trin. & Tob.*	125	K15
Guainía →, *Colombia*	124	C5
Guaíra, *Brazil*	127	A5
Guaíra □, *Paraguay*	126	B4
Guaitecas, Is., *Chile*	128	E2
Guajará-Mirim, *Brazil*	124	F5
Guajira, Pen. de la, *Colombia*	124	A4
Gualán, *Guatemala*	120	C2
Gualdo Tadino, *Italy*	41	E9
Gualeguay, *Argentina*	126	C4
Gualeguaychú, *Argentina*	126	C4
Gualequay →, *Argentina*	126	C4
Guam ☑, *Pac. Oc.*	96	F6
Guamini, *Argentina*	126	D3
Guamúchil, *Mexico*	118	B3
Guana I., *Br. Virgin Is.*	121	e
Guanabacoa, *Cuba*	120	B3
Guanacaste △, *Costa Rica*	120	D2
Guanacaste, Cordillera del, *Costa Rica*	120	D2
Guanaceví, *Mexico*	118	B3
Guanahani = San Salvador I., *Bahamas*	121	B5
Guanajay, *Cuba*	120	B3
Guanajuato, *Mexico*	118	C4
Guanajuato □, *Mexico*	118	C4
Guandacol, *Argentina*	126	B2
Guane, *Cuba*	120	B3
Guang'an, *China*	58	B6
Guangchang, *China*	59	D11
Guangde, *China*	59	B12
Guangdong □, *China*	59	F9
Guangfeng, *China*	59	C12
Guanghan, *China*	58	B5
Guangling, *China*	56	E8
Guangnan, *China*	58	E5
Guangning, *China*	59	F9
Guangrao, *China*	57	F10
Guangshui, *China*	59	B9
Guangshun, *China*	58	D6
Guangwu, *China*	56	F3
Guangxi Zhuangzu Zizhiqu □, *China*	58	F7
Guangyuan, *China*	58	A5
Guangze, *China*	59	D11
Guangzhou, *China*	59	F9
Guánica, *Puerto Rico*	121	d
Guanipa →, *Venezuela*	124	B6
Guanling, *China*	58	E5
Guannan, *China*	57	G10
Guantánamo, *Cuba*	121	B4
Guantánamo B., *Cuba*	121	C4
Guantao, *China*	56	F8
Guanyang, *China*	59	E8
Guanyun, *China*	57	G10
Guápiles, *Costa Rica*	120	D3
Guapo B., *Trin. & Tob.*	125	K15
Guaporé, *Brazil*	127	B5
Guaporé →, *Brazil*	124	F5
Guaqui, *Bolivia*	124	G5
Guara, Sierra de, *Spain*	38	C4
Guaramacal ☑, *Venezuela*	121	E5
Guarapari, *Brazil*	127	A7
Guarapuava, *Brazil*	127	B5
Guaratinguetá, *Brazil*	127	A6
Guaratuba, *Brazil*	127	B6
Guarda, *Portugal*	36	E3
Guarda □, *Portugal*	36	E3

Guardafui, C. = Asir, Ras,
  Somali Rep. 75 E5
Guardamar del Segura, *Spain* .. 39 G4
Guardavalle, *Italy* 43 D9
Guárdia Sanframondi, *Italy* .. 43 A7
Guardiagrele, *Italy* 41 F11
Guardo, *Spain* 36 C6
Guareña, *Spain* 37 G4
Guareña →, *Spain* 36 D5
Guárico □, *Venezuela* 124 B5
Guarujá, *Brazil* 127 A6
Guarulhos, *Brazil* 127 A6
Guarus, *Brazil* 127 A7
Guasave, *Mexico* 118 B3
Guasdualito, *Venezuela* 124 B4
Guastalla, *Italy* 40 D7
Guatemala, *Guatemala* 120 D1
Guatemala ■, *Cent. Amer.* ... 120 C1
Guatemala Trench, *Pac. Oc.* .. 98 H10
Guatopo △, *Venezuela* 121 D6
Guatuaro Pt., *Trin. & Tob.* .. 125 K16
Guaviare →, *Colombia* 124 C5
Guaxupé, *Brazil* 127 A6
Guayaguayare, *Trin. & Tob.* .. 125 K15
Guayama, *Puerto Rico* .... 121 d
Guayaquil, *Ecuador* 124 D3
Guayaquil, G. de, *Ecuador* .. 124 D2
Guaymas, *Mexico* 118 B2
Guba, *Dem. Rep. of the Congo* .. 87 E2
Guba, *Ethiopia* 81 E4
Gûbâl, Madîq, *Egypt* 80 B3
Gubat, *Phil.* 61 E6
Gúbbio, *Italy* 41 E9
Guben, *Germany* 24 D10
Gubin, *Poland* 31 G1
Gubio, *Nigeria* 83 C7
Gubkin, *Russia* 33 G9
Guča, *Serbia & M.* 44 C4
Gucheng, *China* 59 A8
Gudata = Guadauta, *Georgia* .. 35 J5
Gudbrandsdalen, *Norway* 9 F14
Guddu Barrage, *Pakistan* 66 E6
Gudenå →, *Denmark* 11 H4
Gudermes, *Russia* 35 J8
Gudhjem, *Denmark* 11 J8
Gudur, *India* 66 M11
Guebwiller, *France* 19 E14
Guecho = Getxo, *Spain* 38 B2
Guékédou, *Guinea* 82 D2
Guéle Mendouka, *Cameroon* .. 83 E7
Guelma, *Algeria* = Goulimine, *Morocco* 78 C4
Guelph, *Canada* 116 C4
Guémené-Penfao, *France* 18 E5
Guémené-sur-Scorff, *France* .. 18 D3
Guéné, *Benin* 83 C5
Guer, *France* 18 E4
Guérande, *France* 18 E4
Guéret, *France* 19 F8
Guérigny, *France* 19 E10
Guerneville, *U.S.A.* 110 G4
Guernica = Gernika-Lumo, *Spain* 38 B2
Guernsey, *U.K.* 15 H5
Guernsey, *U.S.A.* 112 D2
Guerrero □, *Mexico* 119 D5
Guessou-Sud, *Benin* 83 C5
Gueugnon, *France* 19 F11
Guéyo, *Ivory C.* 82 D3
Gughe, *Ethiopia* 81 F4
Gügher, *Iran* 71 D8
Guglionesi, *Italy* 41 G11
Guhakolak, Tanjung, *Indonesia* .. 63 G11
Gui Jiang →, *China* 59 F8
Guia, *Canary Is.* 48 F4
Guia de Isora, *Canary Is.* 48 F3
Guia Lopes da Laguna, *Brazil* .. 127 A4
Guiana Highlands, *S. Amer.* .. 122 C4
Guibéroua, *Ivory C.* 82 D3
Guichi, *China* 59 B11
Guider, *Cameroon* 83 D7
Guidiguir, *Niger* 83 C6
Guidimouni, *Niger* 83 C6
Guiding, *China* 58 D6
Guidong, *China* 59 D9
Guidónia-Montecélio, *Italy* .. 41 F9
Guiers, L. de, *Senegal* 82 B1
Guigang, *China* 58 F7
Guiglo, *Ivory C.* 82 D3
Guihulñgan, *Phil.* 61 F5
Guiiá, *Mozam.* 89 C5
Guijuelo, *Spain* 36 E5
Guildford, *U.K.* 15 F7
Guilford, *U.S.A.* 117 E12
Guilin, *China* 59 E8
Guillaume-Delisle, L., *Canada* 104 A4
Guillaumes, *France* 21 D10
Guillestre, *France* 21 D10
Guilvinec, *France* 18 E2
Güimar, *Canary Is.* 48 F3
Guimarães, *Portugal* 36 D2
Guimaras □, *Phil.* 61 F5
Guinda, *U.S.A.* 110 G4
Guinea, *U.S.A.* 76 F4
Guinea ■, *W. Afr.* 82 C2
Guinea, Gulf of, *Atl. Oc.* 83 E5
Guinea-Bissau ■, *Africa* 82 C2
Güines, *Cuba* 120 B3
Guingamp, *France* 18 D3
Guinguinéo, *Senegal* 82 C1
Guipavas, *France* 18 D2
Guiping, *China* 59 F8
Guipúzcoa □, *Spain* 38 B2
Guir, *Mali* 82 B4
Guirel, *Mauritania* 82 B3
Güiria, *Venezuela* 124 A6
Guiscard, *France* 19 C10
Guise, *France* 19 C10
Guitiriz, *Spain* 36 B3
Guitri, *Ivory C.* 82 D3
Guiuan, *Phil.* 61 F6
Guixi, *China* 59 C11
Guiyang, *Guizhou, China* 58 D6
Guiyang, *Hunan, China* 59 E9

Guizhou □, *China* 58 D6
Gujan-Mestras, *France* 20 D2
Gujar Khan, *Pakistan* 68 C5
Gujarat □, *India* 68 H4
Gujiang, *China* 59 D10
Gujranwala, *Pakistan* 68 C6
Gujrat, *Pakistan* 68 C6
Gukovo, *Russia* 35 F5
Gulbarga, *India* 66 L10
Gulbene, *Latvia* 9 H22
Gulf, The = Persian Gulf, *Asia* 71 E6
Gulf Islands △, *U.S.A.* 115 E2
Gulfport, *U.S.A.* 113 K10
Gulgong, *Australia* 95 E4
Gulin, *China* 58 C5
Gulistan, *Pakistan* 68 D2
Gull Lake, *Canada* 103 C7
Gullbrandstorp, *Sweden* 11 H6
Gullspång, *Sweden* 11 F8
Güllük, *Turkey* 47 D9
Güllük Daği △, *Turkey* 47 E12
Güllük Korfezi, *Turkey* 47 D9
Gulma, *Nigeria* 83 C5
Gulmarg, *India* 69 B6
Gülnar, *Turkey* 72 D5
Gülpınar, *Turkey* 47 B8
Gülşehir, *Turkey* 72 C6
Gulshad, *Kazakhstan* 52 E8
Gulu, *Uganda* 86 B3
Gülübovo, *Bulgaria* 45 D9
Gulud, J., *Sudan* 81 E2
Gulwe, *Tanzania* 86 D4
Gulyaypole = Hulyaypole,
  Ukraine 33 J9
Gumal →, *Pakistan* 68 D4
Gumbaz, *Pakistan* 68 D3
Gumel, *Nigeria* 83 C6
Gumiel de Hizán, *Spain* 36 D7
Gumla, *India* 69 H11
Gumlu, *Australia* 94 B4
Gumma □, *Japan* 55 F9
Gummersbach, *Germany* 24 D3
Gummi, *Nigeria* 83 C6
Gümüldür, *Turkey* 47 C9
Gümüşçay, *Turkey* 45 F11
Gümüşhacıköy, *Turkey* 72 B6
Gümüşhane, *Turkey* 73 B8
Gümüşsu, *Turkey* 47 C11
Gumzai, *Indonesia* 63 F8
Guna, *Ethiopia* 81 F4
Guna, *India* 68 G7
Gundelfingen, *Germany* 25 G6
Güney, *Burdur, Turkey* 47 D11
Güney, *Denizli, Turkey* 47 C11
Güneydoğu Toroslar, *Turkey* . 73 C9
Gunisao →, *Canada* 103 C9
Gunisao L., *Canada* 103 C9
Gunjyal, *Pakistan* 68 C4
Günlüce, *Turkey* 47 E10
Gunnarskog, *Sweden* 10 E6
Gunnbjørn Fjeld, *Greenland* . 4 C6
Gunnebo, *Sweden* 11 G10
Gunnedah, *Australia* 95 E5
Gunnewin, *Australia* 95 D4
Gunningbar Cr. →, *Australia* . 95 E4
Gunnison, *Colo., U.S.A.* 109 G10
Gunnison, *Utah, U.S.A.* 108 G8
Gunnison →, *U.S.A.* 109 G9
Gunpowder, *Australia* 94 B2
Guntakal, *India* 66 M10
Guntersville, *U.S.A.* 115 H2
Guntong, *Malaysia* 65 K3
Guntur, *India* 67 L12
Gunungapi, *Indonesia* 63 F7
Gunungsitoli, *Indonesia* 62 D1
Günz →, *Germany* 25 G6
Günzburg, *Germany* 25 G6
Gunzenhausen, *Germany* 25 F6
Guo He →, *China* 57 H9
Guoyang, *China* 56 H9
Gupis, *Pakistan* 69 A5
Gura Humorului, *Romania* ... 29 C10
Gura-Teghii, *Romania* 29 E11
Gurag, *Ethiopia* 81 F4
Gurahonț, *Romania* 28 D7
Gurdaspur, *India* 68 C6
Gurdon, *U.S.A.* 113 J8
Güre, *Balıkesir, Turkey* 47 B8
Güre, *Uşak, Turkey* 47 C11
Gurgaon, *India* 68 E7
Gürgentepe, *Turkey* 72 B7
Gurghiu, Munții, *Romania* ... 29 D10
Gurgueia →, *Brazil* 125 E10
Gurha, *India* 68 G4
Guri, Embalse de, *Venezuela* . 124 B6
Gurig △, *Australia* 92 B5
Gurin, *Nigeria* 83 D7
Gurjaani, *Georgia* 35 K7
Gurk →, *Austria* 26 E7
Gurkha, *Nepal* 69 E11
Gurley, *Australia* 95 D4
Gurnet Point, *U.S.A.* 117 D14
Guro, *Mozam.* 87 F3
Gürpınar, *Ist., Turkey* 45 F12
Gürpınar, *Van, Turkey* 73 C10
Gürsu, *Turkey* 45 F13
Gurué, *Mozam.* 87 F4
Gurun, *Malaysia* 65 K3
Gürün, *Turkey* 72 C7
Gurupá, *Brazil* 125 D8
Gurupá, I. Grande de, *Brazil* . 125 D8
Gurupi, *Brazil* 125 F9
Gurupí →, *Brazil* 125 D9
Guruwe, *Zimbabwe* 89 B5
Guryev = Atyraū, *Kazakhstan* 30 D7
Guryevsk, *Russia* 30 D7
Gus-Khrustalnyy, *Russia* 34 C5
Gusau, *Nigeria* 83 C6
Gusev, *Russia* 9 J20
Gushan, *China* 57 E12
Gushgy, *Turkmenistan* 52 F7

Gushi, *China* 59 A10
Gushiago, *Ghana* 83 D4
Gusinje, *Serbia & M.* 44 D3
Gusinoozersk, *Russia* 53 D11
Gúspini, *Italy* 42 C1
Güssing, *Austria* 27 D9
Gustavsberg, *Sweden* 10 E12
Gustavus, *U.S.A.* 102 B1
Gustine, *U.S.A.* 110 H6
Güstrow, *Germany* 24 B8
Gusum, *Sweden* 11 F10
Guta = Kolárovo, *Slovak Rep.* 27 D10
Gütersloh, *Germany* 24 D4
Gutha, *Australia* 93 E2
Guthalungra, *Australia* 94 B4
Guthrie, *Okla., U.S.A.* 113 H6
Guthrie, *Tex., U.S.A.* 113 J4
Gutian, *China* 59 D12
Guttenberg, *U.S.A.* 112 D9
Gutu, *Zimbabwe* 89 B5
Guwahati, *India* 67 F17
Guy Fawkes River △, *Australia* 95 D5
Guyana ■, *S. Amer.* 124 C7
Guyane française = French
  Guiana ☑, *S. Amer.* 125 C8
Guyang, *China* 56 D6
Guyenne, *France* 20 D4
Guymon, *U.S.A.* 113 G4
Guyra, *Australia* 95 E5
Guyuan, *Hebei, China* 56 D8
Guyuan, *Ningxia Huizu, China* 56 G4
Güzelbahçe, *Turkey* 47 C8
Güzelyurt = Morphou, *Cyprus* 49 D11
Guzhang, *China* 58 C7
Guzhen, *China* 57 H9
Guzmán, L. de, *Mexico* 118 A3
Gvardeysk, *Russia* 9 J19
Gvardeyskoye, *Ukraine* 33 K8
Gwa, *Burma* 67 L19
Gwaai, *Zimbabwe* 87 F2
Gwaai →, *Zimbabwe* 87 F2
Gwabegar, *Australia* 95 E4
Gwadabawa, *Nigeria* 83 C6
Gwādar, *Pakistan* 66 G3
Gwagwada, *Nigeria* 83 C6
Gwaii Haanas △, *Canada* 102 C2
Gwalior, *India* 68 F8
Gwanara, *Nigeria* 83 D5
Gwanda, *Zimbabwe* 87 G2
Gwandu, *Nigeria* 83 C5
Gwane, *Dem. Rep. of the Congo* 86 B2
Gwaram, *Nigeria* 83 C7
Gwarzo, *Nigeria* 83 C6
Gwasero, *Nigeria* 83 D5
Gwda →, *Poland* 31 E3
Gweebarra B., *Ireland* 12 B3
Gweedore, *Ireland* 12 A3
Gweru, *Zimbabwe* 87 F2
Gwi, *Nigeria* 83 D6
Gwinn, *U.S.A.* 114 B2
Gwio Kura, *Nigeria* 83 C7
Gwoza, *Nigeria* 83 C7
Gwydir →, *Australia* 95 D4
Gwynedd □, *U.K.* 14 E3
Gyandzha = Gäncä, *Azerbaijan* 35 K8
Gyaring Hu, *China* 60 C4
Gydanskiy Poluostrov, *Russia* 52 C8
Gympie, *Australia* 95 D5
Gyomaendrőd, *Hungary* 28 D5
Gyöngyös, *Hungary* 28 C4
Győr, *Hungary* 28 C3
Győr-Moson-Sopron □, *Hungary* 28 C2
Gypsum Pt., *Canada* 102 A6
Gypsumville, *Canada* 103 C9
Gyueshevo, *Bulgaria* 44 D6
Gyula, *Hungary* 28 D6
Gyumri, *Armenia* 35 K6
Gyzylarbat, *Turkmenistan* ... 52 F6
Gyzyletrek, *Turkmenistan* ... 71 B7
Gzhatsk = Gagarin, *Russia* ... 32 E8

H

Ha 'Arava →, *Israel* 74 E4
Ha Coi, *Vietnam* 58 G6
Ha Dong, *Vietnam* 58 G5
Ha Giang, *Vietnam* 58 F5
Ha Karmel △, *Israel* 74 C4
Ha Tien, *Vietnam* 65 G5
Ha Tinh, *Vietnam* 64 C5
Ha Trung, *Vietnam* 64 C5
Ha Yaek Chalong, *Thailand* .. 65 a
Haaksbergen, *Neths.* 17 B6
Haapsalu, *Estonia* 9 G20
Haarlem, *Neths.* 17 B4
Haast →, *N.Z.* 91 K2
Haast Bluff, *Australia* 92 D5
Hab →, *Pakistan* 68 G3
Hab Nadi Chauki, *Pakistan* .. 68 G2
Habahe, *China* 60 B3
Habaswein, *Kenya* 86 B4
Habay, *Canada* 102 B5
Habbānīyah, *Iraq* 70 C4
Ḥabbānīyah, Hawr al, *Iraq* .. 73 F10
Habichtswald △, *Germany* ... 24 D5
Habo, *Sweden* 11 G8
Haboro, *Japan* 54 B10
Habshān, *U.A.E.* 71 F7
Hachenburg, *Germany* 24 E3
Hachijō-Jima, *Japan* 55 H9
Hachinohe, *Japan* 54 D10
Hachiōji, *Japan* 55 G9
Hachōn, *N. Korea* 57 D15
Hacıbektaş, *Turkey* 72 C6
Hacılar, *Turkey* 72 C6
Hackås, *Sweden* 10 B8
Hackensack, *U.S.A.* 117 F10
Hackettstown, *U.S.A.* 117 F10

Hadali, *Pakistan* 68 C5
Hadarba, Ras, *Sudan* 80 C4
Hadarom □, *Israel* 74 E4
Ḥadd, Ra's al, *Oman* 75 C6
Haddington, *U.K.* 13 F6
Hadejia, *Nigeria* 83 C7
Hadejia →, *Nigeria* 83 C7
Ḥadera, *Israel* 74 C3
Ḥadera, N. →, *Israel* 74 C3
Haderslev, *Denmark* 11 J3
Hadhramaut = Ḥaḍramawt,
  Yemen 75 D4
Hadibou, *Yemen* 75 E5
Hadım, *Turkey* 72 D5
Hadong, S. *Korea* 57 G14
Ḥaḍramawt, *Yemen* 75 D4
Ḥaḍrānīyah, *Iraq* 70 C4
Hadrian's Wall, *U.K.* 14 B5
Hadsten, *Denmark* 11 H4
Hadsund, *Denmark* 11 H4
Hadyach, *Ukraine* 33 G8
Haeju, N. *Korea* 57 E13
Haenam, S. *Korea* 57 G14
Haenertsburg, S. *Africa* 89 C4
Hafar al Bāṭin, *Si. Arabia* .. 70 D5
Hafenlohr = Harbin, *China* .. 57 B14
Hafar al 'Aydā, *Si. Arabia* .. 70 E3
Hafit, *Oman* 71 F7
Hafizabad, *Pakistan* 68 C5
Haflong, *India* 67 G18
Hafnarfjörður, *Iceland* 8 D3
Haft Gel, *Iran* 71 D6
Hafun, Ras, *Somali Rep.* 75 E5
Hagby, *Sweden* 11 H10
Hagen, *Germany* 24 D3
Hagenow, *Germany* 24 B7
Hagerman, *U.S.A.* 113 J2
Hagerman Fossil Beds △, *U.S.A.* 108 E6
Hagerstown, *U.S.A.* 114 F7
Hagersville, *Canada* 116 D4
Hagetmau, *France* 20 E3
Hagfors, *Sweden* 10 D7
Hagi, *Japan* 55 G5
Hagolan, *Syria* 74 C4
Hagondange, *France* 19 C13
Hags Hd., *Ireland* 12 D2
Hague, The = 's-Gravenhage,
  Neths. 17 B4
Haguenau, *France* 19 D14
Hai Duong, *Vietnam* 58 G6
Hai'an, *Guangdong, China* ... 59 G8
Hai'an, *Jiangsu, China* 59 A13
Haicheng, *Fujian, China* 59 E11
Haicheng, *Liaoning, China* .. 57 D12
Haidar Khel, *Afghan.* 68 C3
Haidarābād = Hyderabad, *India* 66 L11
Haidargarh, *India* 69 F9
Haifa = Ḥefa, *Israel* 74 C4
Haifeng, *China* 59 F10
Haiger, *Germany* 24 E4
Haikou, *China* 60 D6
Ḥā'il, *Si. Arabia* 70 E4
Hailar, *China* 60 B6
Hailey, *U.S.A.* 108 E6
Haileybury, *Canada* 104 C4
Hailin, *China* 57 B15
Hailing Dao, *China* 59 G8
Hailong, *China* 57 C13
Hailuoto, *Finland* 8 D21
Haimen, *Guangdong, China* .. 59 F11
Haimen, *Jiangsu, China* 59 B13
Hainan □, *China* 60 E5
Hainaut □, *Belgium* 17 D4
Hainburg, *Austria* 27 C9
Haines, *Alaska, U.S.A.* 102 B1
Haines, *Oreg., U.S.A.* 108 D5
Haines City, *U.S.A.* 115 L5
Haines Junction, *Canada* 102 A1
Hainfeld, *Austria* 26 C8
Haining, *China* 59 B13
Haiphong, *Vietnam* 58 G6
Haitan Dao, *China* 59 E12
Haiti ■, *W. Indies* 121 C5
Haiya, *Sudan* 80 D4
Haiyan, *China* 59 B13
Haiyang, *China* 57 F11
Haiyuan, *Guangxi Zhuangzu,
  China* 58 F6
Haiyuan, *Ningxia Huizu, China* 56 F3
Haizhou, *China* 57 G10
Haizhou Wan, *China* 57 G10
Hajdú-Bihar □, *Hungary* 28 C6
Hajdúböszörmény, *Hungary* .. 28 C6
Hajdúdorog, *Hungary* 28 C6
Hajdúhadház, *Hungary* 28 C6
Hajdúnánás, *Hungary* 28 C6
Hajdúsámson, *Hungary* 28 C6
Hajdúszoboszló, *Hungary* 28 C6
Hajipur, *India* 69 G11
Ḥājjī Muḥsin, *Iraq* 70 C5
Ḥājjīābād, *Iran* 71 D7
Ḥājjīābād-e Zarrīn, *Iran* 71 C7
Hajnówka, *Poland* 31 F10
Hakansson, Mts., *Dem. Rep. of
  the Congo* 87 D2
Hakkâri, *Turkey* 70 B4
Hakkâri Dağları, *Turkey* 73 C10
Hakken-Zan, *Japan* 55 G7
Hakodate, *Japan* 54 D10
Hakos, *Namibia* 88 C2
Håksberg, *Sweden* 10 D9
Haku-San, *Japan* 55 F8
Haku-San □, *Japan* 55 F8
Hakui, *Japan* 55 F8
Hala, *Pakistan* 66 G6
Ḥalab, *Syria* 70 B3
Halabjah, *Iraq* 70 C5
Halaib, *Sudan* 80 C4
Halasa, *Sudan* 81 E3

Ḥālat 'Ammār, *Si. Arabia* ... 70 D3
Halba, *Lebanon* 74 A5
Halberstadt, *Germany* 24 D7
Halcombe, *N.Z.* 91 J5
Halcon, *Phil.* 63 B6
Halde Fjäll = Haltiatunturi,
  Finland 8 B19
Halden, *Norway* 9 G14
Haldensleben, *Germany* 24 C7
Haldia, *India* 67 H16
Haldimand, *Canada* 116 D5
Haldwani, *India* 69 E8
Hale →, *Australia* 94 C2
Halesowen, *U.K.* 15 E5
Halesworth, *U.K.* 15 E9
Haleyville, *U.S.A.* 115 H2
Half Assini, *Ghana* 82 D4
Halfmoon Bay, *N.Z.* 91 M2
Halfway →, *Canada* 102 B4
Halia, *India* 69 G10
Haliburton, *Canada* 116 A6
Halifax, *Australia* 94 B4
Halifax, *Canada* 105 D7
Halifax, *U.K.* 14 D6
Halifax, *U.S.A.* 116 F8
Halifax B., *Australia* 94 B4
Halifax I., *Namibia* 88 D2
Halîl →, *Iran* 71 E8
Halkirk, *U.K.* 13 C5
Hall Beach = Sanirajak, *Canada* 101 B11
Hall in Tirol, *Austria* 26 D4
Hall Pen., *Canada* 101 B13
Hall Pt., *Australia* 92 C3
Hallabro, *Sweden* 11 H9
Halland, *Sweden* 9 H15
Hallands län □, *Sweden* 11 H6
Hallands Väderö, *Sweden* 11 H6
Hallandsås, *Sweden* 11 H7
Hällbybrunn, *Sweden* 10 E10
Halle, *Belgium* 17 D4
Halle, *Nordrhein-Westfalen,
  Germany* 24 C4
Halle, *Sachsen-Anhalt, Germany* 24 D7
Hälleforsnäs, *Sweden* 10 E10
Hallein, *Austria* 26 D6
Hällekis, *Sweden* 11 F7
Hallen, *Sweden* 10 A8
Hallett, *Australia* 95 E2
Hallettsville, *U.S.A.* 113 L6
Hallim, S. *Korea* 57 H14
Hallingdalselvi →, *Norway* .. 9 F13
Hallock, *U.S.A.* 112 A6
Halls Creek, *Australia* 92 C4
Hallsberg, *Sweden* 10 E9
Hallstahammar, *Sweden* 10 E10
Hallstatt, *Austria* 26 D6
Hallstavik, *Sweden* 10 D12
Hallstead, *U.S.A.* 117 E9
Halmahera, *Indonesia* 63 D7
Halmeu, *Romania* 28 C8
Halmstad, *Sweden* 11 H6
Hals, *Denmark* 11 H4
Hälsingborg = Helsingborg,
  Sweden* 11 H6
Hälsingland, *Sweden* 10 C10
Halstad, *U.S.A.* 112 B6
Halstead, *U.K.* 15 F8
Haltern, *Germany* 24 D3
Haltiatunturi, *Finland* 8 B19
Halton □, *U.K.* 14 D5
Haltwhistle, *U.K.* 14 C5
Ḥālūl, *Qatar* 71 E7
Halvad, *India* 68 H4
Ḥalvān, *Iran* 71 C8
Ham, *France* 19 C10
Ham Tan, *Vietnam* 65 G6
Ham Yen, *Vietnam* 64 A5
Hamab, *Namibia* 88 D2
Hamad, *Sudan* 81 D3
Hamada, *Japan* 55 G6
Hamadān, *Iran* 71 C6
Hamadān □, *Iran* 71 C6
Ḥamāh, *Syria* 70 C3
Hamamatsu, *Japan* 55 G8
Hamar, *Norway* 9 F14
Hamâta, Gebel, *Egypt* 70 E2
Hambantota, *Sri Lanka* 66 R12
Hamber △, *Canada* 102 C5
Hamburg, *Germany* 24 B5
Hamburg, *Ark., U.S.A.* 113 J9
Hamburg, *N.Y., U.S.A.* 116 D6
Hamburg, *Pa., U.S.A.* 117 F9
Hamburg □, *Germany* 24 B5
Hamburg Fuhlsbüttel ✈ (HAM),
  Germany* 24 B5
Ḥamd, W. al →, *Si. Arabia* .. 70 E3
Hamden, *U.S.A.* 117 E12
Hamdibey, *Turkey* 47 B9
Häme, *Finland* 9 F20
Hämeenlinna, *Finland* 9 F21
Hamélé, *Ghana* 82 C4
Hamelin Pool, *Australia* 93 E1
Hameln, *Germany* 24 C5
Hamerkaz □, *Israel* 74 C3
Hamersley Ra., *Australia* ... 92 D2
Hamhung, N. *Korea* 57 E14
Hami, *China* 60 B4
Hamilton, *Australia* 95 F3
Hamilton, *Canada* 116 C5
Hamilton, *N.Z.* 91 G5
Hamilton, *U.K.* 13 F4
Hamilton, *Ala., U.S.A.* 115 H1
Hamilton, *Mont., U.S.A.* 108 C6
Hamilton, *Ohio, U.S.A.* 114 F3
Hamilton, *Tex., U.S.A.* 113 K5
Hamilton →, *Australia* 94 C2
Hamilton, L., *Australia* 95 D2
Hamilton City, *U.S.A.* 110 F4
Hamilton I., *Australia* 94 J6
Hamilton Inlet, *Canada* 105 D4
Hamilton Mt., *U.S.A.* 117 C10

Hamina, *Finland* 9 F22
Hamirpur, *H.P., India* 68 D7
Hamirpur, *Ut. P., India* 69 G9
Hamitabat, *Turkey* 45 E11
Hamlet, *U.S.A.* 115 H6
Hamley Bridge, *Australia* 95 E2
Hamlin = Hameln, *Germany* .. 24 C5
Hamlin, *N.Y., U.S.A.* 116 C7
Hamlin, *Tex., U.S.A.* 113 J4
Hamm, *Germany* 24 D3
Ḥammār, Hawr al, *Iraq* 70 D5
Hammarstrand, *Sweden* 10 A10
Hammelburg, *Germany* 25 E5
Hammeren, *Denmark* 11 J8
Hammerfest, *Norway* 8 A20
Hammerum, *Denmark* 11 H3
Hamminkeln, *Germany* 24 D2
Hammond, *Ind., U.S.A.* 114 E2
Hammond, *La., U.S.A.* 113 K9
Hammond, *N.Y., U.S.A.* 117 B9
Hammondsport, *U.S.A.* 116 D7
Hammonton, *U.S.A.* 114 F8
Hamneda, *Sweden* 11 H7
Hamoyet, Jebel, *Sudan* 80 D4
Hampden, *N.Z.* 91 L3
Hampshire □, *U.K.* 15 F6
Hampshire Downs, *U.K.* 15 F6
Hampton, *N.B., Canada* 105 C6
Hampton, *Ont., Canada* 116 C6
Hampton, *Ark., U.S.A.* 113 J8
Hampton, *Iowa, U.S.A.* 112 D8
Hampton, *N.H., U.S.A.* 117 D14
Hampton, *S.C., U.S.A.* 115 J5
Hampton, *Va., U.S.A.* 114 G7
Hampton Bays, *U.S.A.* 117 F12
Hampton Tableland, *Australia* .. 93 F4
Hamra, *Sweden* 10 C8
Hamrat esh Sheykh, *Sudan* 81 E2
Hamur, *Turkey* 73 C10
Hamyang, *S. Korea* 57 G14
Han Jiang →, *China* 59 F11
Han Shui, *China* 58 A7
Han Shui →, *China* 59 B10
Hanak, *Si. Arabia* 70 E3
Hanamaki, *Japan* 54 E10
Hanang, *Tanzania* 86 C4
Hanau, *Germany* 25 E4
Hanbogd = Ihbulag, *Mongolia* . 56 C4
Hançalar, *Turkey* 47 C11
Hâncești, *Moldova* 29 D13
Hancheng, *China* 56 G6
Hanchuan, *China* 59 B9
Hancock, *Mich., U.S.A.* 112 B10
Hancock, *N.Y., U.S.A.* 117 E9
Handa, *Japan* 55 G8
Handan, *China* 56 F8
Handeni, *Tanzania* 86 D4
Handlová, *Slovak Rep.* 27 C11
Handub, *Sudan* 80 D4
Handwara, *India* 69 B6
Hanegev, *Israel* 74 E4
Hanford, *U.S.A.* 110 J7
Hanford Reach △, *U.S.A.* 108 C4
Hang Chat, *Thailand* 64 C2
Hang Dong, *Thailand* 64 C2
Hangang →, *S. Korea* 57 F14
Hangayn Nuruu, *Mongolia* 60 B4
Hanggin Houqi, *China* 56 D4
Hanggin Qi, *China* 56 E5
Hangu, *China* 57 E9
Hangzhou, *China* 59 B13
Hangzhou Wan, *China* 59 B13
Hanhongor, *Mongolia* 56 C3
Ḥanīdh, *Si. Arabia* 71 E6
Ḥanīsh, *Yemen* 75 E3
Haniska, *Slovak Rep.* 27 C14
Hanjiang, *China* 59 E12
Hankinson, *U.S.A.* 112 B6
Hankö, *Finland* 9 G20
Hankou, *China* 59 B10
Hanksville, *U.S.A.* 109 G8
Hanle, *India* 69 C8
Hanmer Springs, *N.Z.* 91 K4
Hann →, *Australia* 92 C4
Hann, Mt., *Australia* 92 C4
Hanna, *Canada* 102 C6
Hanna, *U.S.A.* 108 F10
Hannah B., *Canada* 104 B4
Hannibal, *Mo., U.S.A.* 112 F9
Hannibal, *N.Y., U.S.A.* 117 C8
Hannik, *Sudan* 80 D3
Hannover, *Germany* 24 C5
Hanö, *Sweden* 11 H8
Hanöbukten, *Sweden* 11 J8
Hanoi, *Vietnam* 58 G5
Hanover = Hannover, *Germany* . 24 C5
Hanover, *Canada* 116 B3
Hanover, *S. Africa* 88 E3
Hanover, *N.H., U.S.A.* 117 C12
Hanover, *Ohio, U.S.A.* 116 F2
Hanover, *Pa., U.S.A.* 114 F7
Hanover, *I., Chile* 128 G2
Hans Lollik I., *U.S. Virgin Is.* .. 121 e
Hansdiha, *India* 69 G12
Hanshou, *China* 59 C8
Hansi, *India* 68 E6
Hanson, L., *Australia* 95 E2
Hanstholm, *Denmark* 11 G2
Hantsavichy, *Belarus* 33 F4
Hanumangarh, *India* 68 E6
Hanyin, *China* 58 A7
Hanzhong, *China* 56 H4
Hanzhuang, *China* 57 G9
Haora, *India* 69 H13
Haoxue, *China* 59 B9
Haparanda, *Sweden* 8 D21
Happy, *U.S.A.* 113 H4
Happy Camp, *U.S.A.* 108 F2
Happy Valley-Goose Bay,
 Canada 105 B7

Hapsu, *N. Korea* 57 D15
Hapur, *India* 68 E7
Ḥaql, *Si. Arabia* 74 F3
Har, *Indonesia* 63 F8
Har Hu, *China* 60 C4
Har-Ayrag, *Mongolia* 56 B5
Har Us Nuur, *Mongolia* 60 B4
Har Yehuda, *Israel* 74 D3
Ḥaraḍ, *Si. Arabia* 75 C4
Haradok, *Belarus* 32 E6
Häradsbäck, *Sweden* 11 H8
Haranomachi, *Japan* 54 F10
Harare, *Zimbabwe* 87 F3
Harbin, *China* 57 B14
Harbiye, *Turkey* 72 D7
Harbo, *Sweden* 10 D11
Harboør, *Denmark* 11 H2
Harbor Beach, *U.S.A.* 116 C2
Harbour Breton, *Canada* 105 C8
Harbour Deep, *Canada* 105 B8
Harburg, *Germany* 24 B5
Harburger Berge △, *Germany* .. 24 B5
Hårby, *Denmark* 11 J4
Harda, *India* 68 H7
Hardangerfjorden, *Norway* ... 9 F12
Hardangervidda, *Norway* 9 F12
Hardap □, *Namibia* 88 C2
Hardap Dam, *Namibia* 88 C2
Hardenberg, *Neths.* 17 B6
Harderwijk, *Neths.* 17 B5
Hardey →, *Australia* 92 D2
Hardin, *U.S.A.* 108 D10
Harding, *S. Africa* 89 E4
Harding Ra., *Australia* 92 C3
Hardisty, *Canada* 102 C6
Hardoi, *India* 69 F9
Hardwar = Haridwar, *India* ... 68 E8
Hardwick, *U.S.A.* 117 B12
Hardy, Pen., *Chile* 128 H3
Hardy, Pte., *St. Lucia* .... 121 f
Hare B., *Canada* 105 B8
Hareid, *Norway* 9 E12
Haren, *Germany* 24 C3
Harer, *Ethiopia* 81 F5
Harerge, *Ethiopia* 81 F5
Hareto, *Ethiopia* 81 F4
Harfleur, *France* 18 C7
Hargeisa, *Somali Rep.* 75 F3
Harghita □, *Romania* 29 D10
Harghita, Munții, *Romania* ... 29 D10
Hargshamn, *Sweden* 10 D12
Hari →, *Indonesia* 62 E2
Haria, *Canary Is.* 48 E6
Haridwar, *India* 68 E8
Harim, Jabal al, *Oman* 71 E8
Haringhata →, *Bangla.* 67 J16
Harīrūd →, *Asia* 66 A2
Härjedalen, *Sweden* 10 B7
Harlan, *Iowa, U.S.A.* 112 E7
Harlan, *Ky., U.S.A.* 115 G4
Hârlău, *Romania* 29 C11
Harlech, *U.K.* 14 E3
Harlem, *U.S.A.* 108 B9
Hårlev, *Denmark* 11 J6
Harlingen, *Neths.* 17 A5
Harlingen, *U.S.A.* 113 M6
Harlow, *U.K.* 15 F8
Harlowton, *U.S.A.* 108 C9
Harmancık, *Turkey* 47 B11
Harmånger, *Sweden* 10 C11
Harmil, *Eritrea* 81 D5
Harnai, *Pakistan* 68 D2
Harney Basin, *U.S.A.* 108 E4
Harney L., *U.S.A.* 108 E4
Harney Peak, *U.S.A.* 112 D3
Härnön, *Sweden* 10 B12
Härnösand, *Sweden* 10 B11
Haro, *Spain* 38 C2
Haroldswick, *U.K.* 13 A8
Harp L., *Canada* 105 A7
Harper, *Liberia* 82 E3
Harplinge, *Sweden* 11 H6
Harr, *Mauritania* 82 B2
Harrai, *India* 69 H8
Harrand, *Pakistan* 68 E4
Ḥarrat Khaybar, *Si. Arabia* ... 80 B5
Ḥarrat Nawāṣīf, *Si. Arabia* ... 80 C5
Harricana →, *Canada* 104 B4
Harriman, *U.S.A.* 115 H3
Harrington Harbour, *Canada* .. 105 B8
Harris, *U.K.* 13 D2
Harris, L., *Australia* 95 E2
Harris, Sd. of, *U.K.* 13 D1
Harris Pt., *Canada* 116 C2
Harrisburg, *Ill., U.S.A.* 113 G10
Harrisburg, *Nebr., U.S.A.* 112 E3
Harrisburg, *Pa., U.S.A.* 116 F8
Harrismith, *S. Africa* 89 D4
Harrison, *Ark., U.S.A.* 113 G8
Harrison, *Maine, U.S.A.* 117 B14
Harrison, *Nebr., U.S.A.* 112 D3
Harrison, *C., Canada* 105 B8
Harrison L., *Canada* 102 D4
Harrisonburg, *U.S.A.* 114 F6
Harrisonville, *U.S.A.* 112 F7
Harriston, *Canada* 116 C4
Harrisville, *Mich., U.S.A.* 116 B1
Harrisville, *N.Y., U.S.A.* 117 B9
Harrisville, *Pa., U.S.A.* 116 E5
Harrodsburg, *U.S.A.* 114 G3
Harrogate, *U.K.* 14 C6
Harrow □, *U.K.* 15 F7
Harrowsmith, *Canada* 117 B8
Harry S. Truman Reservoir,
 U.S.A. 112 F7
Harsefeld, *Germany* 24 B5
Harsewinkel, *Germany* 24 D4
Harsin, *Iran* 70 C5
Hârșova, *Romania* 29 F12
Harstad, *Norway* 8 B17
Harsud, *India* 68 H7

Hart, *U.S.A.* 114 D2
Hart, L., *Australia* 95 E2
Hartbees →, *S. Africa* 88 D3
Hartberg, *Austria* 26 D8
Hartford, *Conn., U.S.A.* 117 E12
Hartford, *Ky., U.S.A.* 114 G2
Hartford, *S. Dak., U.S.A.* 112 D6
Hartford, *Wis., U.S.A.* 112 D10
Hartford City, *U.S.A.* 114 E3
Hartland, *Canada* 105 C6
Hartland Pt., *U.K.* 15 F3
Hartlepool, *U.K.* 14 C6
Hartlepool □, *U.K.* 14 C6
Hartley Bay, *Canada* 102 C3
Hartmannberge, *Namibia* 88 B1
Hartney, *Canada* 103 D8
Hârtop, *Moldova* 29 D13
Harts →, *S. Africa* 88 D3
Hartselle, *U.S.A.* 115 H2
Hartshorne, *U.S.A.* 113 H7
Hartstown, *U.S.A.* 116 E4
Hartsville, *U.S.A.* 115 H5
Hartswater, *S. Africa* 88 D3
Hartwell, *U.S.A.* 115 H4
Harunabad, *Pakistan* 68 E5
Harvand, *Iran* 71 D7
Harvey, *Australia* 93 F2
Harvey, *Ill., U.S.A.* 114 E2
Harvey, *N. Dak., U.S.A.* 112 B5
Harwich, *U.K.* 15 F9
Haryana □, *India* 68 E7
Haryn →, *Belarus* 33 F4
Harz, *Germany* 24 D6
Harz △, *Germany* 24 D6
Harzgerode, *Germany* 24 D7
Hasa □, *Si. Arabia* 71 E6
Hasaheisa, *Sudan* 81 E3
Ḥasanābād, *Iran* 71 C7
Ḥasb, W. →, *Iraq* 70 D5
Hasdo →, *India* 69 J10
Haselünne, *Germany* 24 C3
Hashimoto, *Japan* 55 G7
Hashtjerd, *Iran* 71 C6
Haskell, *U.S.A.* 113 J5
Hasköy, *Turkey* 45 E10
Haslach, *Germany* 25 G4
Hasle, *Denmark* 11 J8
Haslemere, *U.K.* 15 F7
Haslev, *Denmark* 11 J5
Hasparren, *France* 20 E2
Hassa, *Turkey* 72 D7
Hassberge △, *Germany* 25 E6
Hassela, *Sweden* 10 B10
Hasselt, *Belgium* 17 D5
Hassfurt, *Germany* 25 E6
Hassi Messaoud, *Algeria* 78 B7
Hässleholm, *Sweden* 11 H7
Hassloch, *Germany* 25 F4
Hästholmen, *Sweden* 11 F8
Hastings, *N.Z.* 91 H6
Hastings, *U.K.* 15 G8
Hastings, *Mich., U.S.A.* 114 D3
Hastings, *Minn., U.S.A.* 112 C8
Hastings, *Nebr., U.S.A.* 112 E5
Hastings Ra., *Australia* 95 E5
Hästveda, *Sweden* 11 H7
Hat, *Ukraine* 28 B7
Hat Yai, *Thailand* 65 J3
Hatanbulag = Ergel, *Mongolia* . 56 C5
Hatay = Antalya, *Turkey* 72 D4
Hatch, *U.S.A.* 109 K10
Hatchet L., *Canada* 103 B8
Hațeg, *Romania* 28 E7
Hateruma-Shima, *Japan* 55 M1
Hatfield P.O., *Australia* 95 E3
Hatgal, *Mongolia* 60 A5
Hathras, *India* 68 F8
Hatia, *Bangla.* 67 H17
Ḥāṭibah, Ra's, *Si. Arabia* 80 C4
Hato Mayor, *Dom. Rep.* 121 C6
Hatta, *India* 69 G8
Hattah, *Australia* 95 E3
Hatteras, C., *U.S.A.* 115 H8
Hattiesburg, *U.S.A.* 113 K10
Hatvan, *Hungary* 28 C10
Hau Bon = Cheo Reo, *Vietnam* . 62 B3
Hau Duc, *Vietnam* 64 E7
Haugesund, *Norway* 9 G11
Haukipudas, *Finland* 8 D21
Haultain →, *Canada* 103 B7
Hauraki G., *N.Z.* 91 G5
Hausruck, *Austria* 26 C6
Haut Atlas, *Morocco* 78 B4
Haut-Jura △, *France* 19 F9
Haut-Languedoc △, *France* ... 20 E6
Haut Niger →, *Guinea* 82 C2
Haut-Rhin □, *France* 19 E14
Haute-Corse □, *France* 21 F13
Haute-Garonne □, *France* 20 E5
Haute-Loire □, *France* 20 C7
Haute-Marne □, *France* 19 D12
Haute-Normandie □, *France* .. 18 C7
Haute-Saône □, *France* 19 E13
Haute-Savoie □, *France* 21 C10
Haute-Vienne □, *France* 20 C5
Hautes-Alpes □, *France* 21 D10
Hautes Fagnes = Hohe Venn,
 Belgium 17 D6
Hautes Fagnes = Hohes Venn-
 Eifel △, *Europe* 24 E2
Hautes-Pyrénées □, *France* ... 20 F4
Hauteville-Lompnès, *France* .. 21 C9
Hautmont, *France* 19 B10
Hauts-de-Seine □, *France* 19 D9
Hauts Plateaux, *Algeria* 76 C4
Hauzenberg, *Germany* 25 G9
Havana = La Habana, *Cuba* .. 120 B3
Havant, *U.K.* 15 G7
Havârna, *Romania* 29 B11
Havasor = Kığızı, *Turkey* 70 B4
Havasu, L., *U.S.A.* 111 L12

Havdhem, *Sweden* 11 G12
Havel →, *Germany* 24 C8
Havelian, *Pakistan* 68 B5
Havelock, *Canada* 116 B7
Havelock, *N.Z.* 91 J4
Havelock, *U.S.A.* 115 H7
Haverfordwest, *U.K.* 15 F3
Haverhill, *U.K.* 15 E8
Haverhill, *U.S.A.* 117 D13
Haverstraw, *U.S.A.* 117 E11
Håverud, *Sweden* 11 F6
Havirga, *Mongolia* 56 B7
Havířov, *Czech Rep.* 27 B11
Havneby, *Denmark* 11 J2
Havran, *Turkey* 47 B9
Havre, *U.S.A.* 108 B9
Havre-Aubert, *Canada* 105 C7
Havre-St.-Pierre, *Canada* 105 B7
Havsa, *Turkey* 45 E10
Havza, *Turkey* 72 B6
Haw →, *U.S.A.* 115 H6
Hawaii □, *U.S.A.* 106 H16
Hawaii I., *Pac. Oc.* 106 J17
Hawaiian Is., *Pac. Oc.* 106 H17
Hawaiian Ridge, *Pac. Oc.* 97 E11
Hawarden, *U.S.A.* 112 D6
Hawea, L., *N.Z.* 91 L2
Hawera, *N.Z.* 91 H5
Hawick, *U.K.* 13 F6
Hawk Junction, *Canada* 104 C3
Hawke B., *N.Z.* 91 H6
Hawker, *Australia* 95 E2
Hawkesbury, *Canada* 104 C5
Hawkesbury I., *Canada* 102 C3
Hawkesbury Pt., *Australia* 94 A1
Hawkinsville, *U.S.A.* 115 J4
Hawley, *Minn., U.S.A.* 112 B6
Hawley, *Pa., U.S.A.* 117 E9
Ḥawrān, W. →, *Iraq* 70 C4
Hawsh Mūssá, *Lebanon* 74 B4
Hawthorne, *U.S.A.* 108 G4
Hay, *Australia* 95 E3
Hay →, *Australia* 94 C2
Hay, C., *Australia* 92 B4
Hay I., *Canada* 116 B4
Hay L., *Canada* 102 B5
Hay-on-Wye, *U.K.* 15 E4
Hay River, *Canada* 102 A5
Hay Springs, *U.S.A.* 112 D3
Haya = Tehoru, *Indonesia* ... 63 E7
Hayachine-San, *Japan* 54 E10
Hayange, *France* 19 C13
Haydarlı, *Turkey* 47 C12
Hayden, *U.S.A.* 108 F10
Haydon, *Australia* 94 B3
Hayes →, *Canada* 104 A1
Hayes Creek, *Australia* 92 B5
Hayle, *U.K.* 15 G2
Hayling I., *U.K.* 15 G7
Haymana, *Turkey* 72 C5
Haymen I., *Australia* 94 J6
Hayrabolu, *Turkey* 45 E11
Hays, *Canada* 102 C6
Hays, *U.S.A.* 112 F5
Haysyn, *Ukraine* 29 B14
Hayvoron, *Ukraine* 29 B14
Hayward, *Calif., U.S.A.* 110 H4
Hayward, *Wis., U.S.A.* 112 B9
Haywards Heath, *U.K.* 15 G7
Hazafon □, *Israel* 74 C4
Hazārān, Kūh-e, *Iran* 71 D8
Hazard, *U.S.A.* 114 G4
Hazaribag, *India* 69 H11
Hazaribag Road, *India* 69 G11
Hazebrouck, *France* 19 B9
Hazelton, *Canada* 102 B3
Hazelton, *U.S.A.* 112 B4
Hazen, *U.S.A.* 112 B4
Hazlehurst, *Ga., U.S.A.* 115 K4
Hazlehurst, *Miss., U.S.A.* 113 K9
Hazlet, *U.S.A.* 117 F10
Hazleton, *U.S.A.* 117 F9
Hazlett, L., *Australia* 92 D4
Hazro, *Turkey* 70 B4
He Xian, *Anhui, China* 59 B12
He Xian, *Guangxi Zhuangzu,
 China* 59 E8
Head of Bight, *Australia* 93 F5
Headlands, *Zimbabwe* 87 F3
Healdsburg, *U.S.A.* 110 G4
Healdton, *U.S.A.* 113 H6
Healesville, *Australia* 95 F4
Heany Junction, *Zimbabwe* ... 89 C4
Heard I., *Ind. Oc.* 3 G13
Hearne, *U.S.A.* 113 K6
Hearst, *Canada* 104 C3
Heart →, *U.S.A.* 112 B4
Heart's Content, *Canada* 105 C9
Heath, Pte., *Canada* 105 C7
Heathrow, London ✈ (LHR),
 U.K. 15 F7
Heavener, *U.S.A.* 113 H7
Hebbronville, *U.S.A.* 113 M5
Hebei □, *China* 56 E9
Hebel, *Australia* 95 D4
Heber, *U.S.A.* 111 N11
Heber City, *U.S.A.* 108 F8
Heber Springs, *U.S.A.* 113 H9
Hebert, *Canada* 103 C7
Hebgen L., *U.S.A.* 108 D8
Hebi, *China* 56 G8
Hebrides, *U.K.* 6 D4
Hebrides, Sea of the, *U.K.* ... 13 D2
Hebron = Al Khalīl, *West Bank* . 74 D4
Hebron, *Canada* 101 C13
Hebron, *N. Dak., U.S.A.* 112 B3
Hebron, *Nebr., U.S.A.* 112 E6
Heby, *Sweden* 10 E10
Hecate Str., *Canada* 102 C2

Heceta I., *U.S.A.* 102 B2
Hechi, *China* 58 E7
Hechingen, *Germany* 25 G4
Hechuan, *China* 58 B6
Hecla, *U.S.A.* 112 C5
Hecla I., *Canada* 103 C9
Hédé, *France* 18 D5
Hede, *Sweden* 10 B7
Hedemora, *Sweden* 10 D9
Hedensted, *Denmark* 11 J3
Hedesunda, *Sweden* 10 D10
Heerde, *Neths.* 17 B6
Heerenveen, *Neths.* 17 B5
Heerhugowaard, *Neths.* 17 B4
Heerlen, *Neths.* 17 D5
Ḥefa, *Israel* 74 C4
Ḥefa □, *Israel* 74 C4
Hefei, *China* 59 B11
Hefeng, *China* 59 C8
Hegalig, *Sudan* 81 E3
Hegang, *China* 60 B8
Heiban, *Sudan* 81 E3
Heichengzhen, *China* 56 F4
Heide, *Germany* 24 A5
Heidelberg, *Germany* 25 F4
Heidelberg, *S. Africa* 88 E3
Heidenau, *Germany* 24 E9
Heidenheim, *Germany* 25 G6
Heijing, *China* 58 E3
Heilbad Heiligenstadt, *Germany* . 24 D6
Heilbron, *S. Africa* 89 D4
Heilbronn, *Germany* 25 F5
Heiligenblut, *Austria* 26 D5
Heiligenhafen, *Germany* 24 A6
Heiligenjiang □, *China* 60 B7
Heilunkiang = Heilongjiang □,
 China 60 B7
Heimaey, *Iceland* 8 E3
Heinola, *Finland* 9 F22
Heinsberg, *Germany* 24 D2
Heinze Kyun, *Burma* 64 E1
Heishan, *China* 57 D12
Heishui, *Liaoning, China* 57 C10
Heishui, *Sichuan, China* 58 A4
Hejaz = Ḥijāz □, *Si. Arabia* .. 70 E3
Hejian, *China* 56 E9
Hejiang, *China* 58 C5
Hejin, *China* 56 G6
Hekimhan, *Turkey* 70 B3
Hekla, *Iceland* 8 E4
Hekou, *Guangdong, China* .. 59 F9
Hekou, *Yunnan, China* 58 F4
Hel, *Poland* 30 D5
Helagsfjället, *Sweden* 10 B6
Helan Shan, *China* 56 E3
Helechosa, *Spain* 37 F6
Helen Atoll, *Pac. Oc.* 63 D8
Helena, *Ark., U.S.A.* 113 H9
Helena, *Mont., U.S.A.* 108 C7
Helendale, *U.S.A.* 111 L9
Helensburgh, *U.K.* 13 E4
Helensville, *N.Z.* 91 G5
Helenvale, *Australia* 94 B4
Helgasjön, *Sweden* 11 H8
Helgeland, *Norway* 8 C15
Helgoland, *Germany* 24 A3
Heligoland = Helgoland,
 Germany 24 A3
Heligoland B. = Deutsche Bucht,
 Germany 24 A4
Heliopolis, *Egypt* 80 H7
Hella, *Iceland* 8 E3
Hellertown, *U.S.A.* 117 F9
Hellespont = Çanakkale Boğazı,
 Turkey 45 F10
Hellevoetsluis, *Neths.* 17 C4
Hellhole Gorge △, *Australia* .. 94 D3
Hellín, *Spain* 39 G3
Hells Canyon △, *U.S.A.* 108 D5
Hell's Gate △, *Kenya* 86 C4
Helmand □, *Afghan.* 66 D4
Helmand →, *Afghan.* 66 D2
Helme →, *Germany* 24 D7
Helmeringhausen, *Namibia* .. 88 D2
Helmond, *Neths.* 17 C5
Helmsdale, *U.K.* 13 C5
Helmsdale →, *U.K.* 13 C5
Helmstedt, *Germany* 24 C7
Helong, *China* 57 C15
Helper, *U.S.A.* 108 G8
Helsingborg, *Sweden* 11 H6
Helsinge, *Denmark* 11 H6
Helsingfors = Helsinki, *Finland* . 9 F21
Helsingør, *Denmark* 11 H6
Helsinki, *Finland* 9 F21
Helska, Mierzeja, *Poland* 30 D5
Helston, *U.K.* 15 G2
Helvellyn, *U.K.* 14 C4
Helwân, *Egypt* 80 J7
Hemel Hempstead, *U.K.* 15 F7
Hemet, *U.S.A.* 111 M10
Hemingford, *U.S.A.* 112 D3
Hemmingford, *Canada* 117 A11
Hempstead, *U.S.A.* 113 K6
Hemse, *Sweden* 11 G12
Hemsön, *Sweden* 10 B12
Henån, *Sweden* 11 F5
Henan □, *China* 56 H8
Henares →, *Spain* 36 E7
Henashi-Misaki, *Japan* 54 D9
Hendaye, *France* 20 E2
Hendek, *Turkey* 72 B4
Henderson, *Argentina* 126 D3
Henderson, *Ky., U.S.A.* 114 G2
Henderson, *N.C., U.S.A.* 115 G6
Henderson, *Nev., U.S.A.* 111 J12
Henderson, *Tenn., U.S.A.* ... 115 H1
Henderson, *Tex., U.S.A.* 113 J7
Hendersonville, *N.C., U.S.A.* . 115 H4
Hendersonville, *Tenn., U.S.A.* . 115 G2
Hendĭjān, *Iran* 71 D6

Hendorābī, *Iran* 71 E7
Heng Jiang, *China* 58 C5
Heng Xian, *China* 58 F7
Hengcheng, *China* 56 E4
Hëngchun, *Taiwan* 59 F13
Hengdaohezi, *China* 57 B15
Hengelo, *Neths.* 17 B6
Hengfeng, *China* 59 C10
Hengshan, *Hunan, China* 59 D9
Hengshan, *Shaanxi, China* .. 56 F5
Hengshui, *China* 56 F8
Hengyang, *China* 59 D9
Henichesk, *Ukraine* 33 J8
Hénin-Beaumont, *France* 19 B9
Henley-on-Thames, *U.K.* 15 F7
Henlopen, C., *U.S.A.* 114 F8
Hennan, *Sweden* 10 B9
Hennebont, *France* 18 E3
Hennenman, *S. Africa* 88 D4
Hennessey, *U.S.A.* 113 G6
Hennigsdorf, *Germany* 24 C9
Henri Pittier, *Venezuela* .. 121 D6
Henrietta, *U.S.A.* 113 J5
Henrietta, Ostrov = Genriyetty,
  Ostrov, *Russia* 53 B16
Henrietta Maria, C., *Canada* .. 104 A3
Henry, *U.S.A.* 112 E10
Henryetta, *U.S.A.* 113 H7
Henryville, *Canada* 117 A11
Hensall, *Canada* 116 C3
Henstedt-Ulzburg, *Germany* .. 24 B6
Hentiesbaai, *Namibia* 88 C1
Hentiyn Nuruu, *Mongolia* ... 60 B5
Henty, *Australia* 95 F4
Henzada, *Burma* 67 L19
Hephaestia, *Greece* 47 B7
Heping, *China* 59 E10
Heppner, *U.S.A.* 108 D4
Hepu, *China* 58 G7
Hepworth, *Canada* 116 B3
Heqing, *China* 58 D3
Hequ, *China* 56 E6
Heráðsflói, *Iceland* 8 D6
Heráðsvötn →, *Iceland* 8 D4
Heraklion = Iráklion, *Greece* .. 49 D7
Herald Cays, *Australia* 94 B4
Herāt, *Afghan.* 66 B3
Herāt □, *Afghan.* 66 B3
Hérault □, *France* 20 E7
Hérault →, *France* 20 E7
Herbault, *France* 18 E8
Herbert →, *Australia* 94 B4
Herbert River Falls △, *Australia* .. 94 B4
Herberton, *Australia* 94 B4
Herbertsdale, *S. Africa* ... 88 E3
Herbignac, *France* 18 E4
Herborn, *Germany* 24 E4
Herby, *Poland* 31 H5
Herceg-Novi, *Serbia & M.* .. 44 D2
Herchmer, *Canada* 103 B10
Herðubreið, *Iceland* 8 D5
Hereford, *U.K.* 15 E5
Hereford, *U.S.A* 113 H3
Herefordshire □, *U.K.* 15 E5
Hereke, *Turkey* 45 F13
Herencia, *Spain* 37 F7
Herentals, *Belgium* 17 C4
Herford, *Germany* 24 C4
Héricourt, *France* 19 E13
Herington, *U.S.A.* 112 F6
Herisau, *Switz.* 25 H5
Hérisson, *France* 19 F9
Herkimer, *U.S.A.* 117 D10
Herlong, *U.S.A.* 110 E6
Herm, *U.K.* 15 H5
Hermakivka, *Ukraine* 29 B11
Hermann, *U.S.A.* 112 F9
Hermannsburg, *Australia* ... 92 D5
Hermannsburg, *Germany* 24 C6
Hermanus, *S. Africa* 88 E2
Herment, *France* 20 C6
Hermidale, *Australia* 95 E4
Hermiston, *U.S.A.* 108 D4
Hermite, I., *Chile* 128 H3
Hermon, *U.S.A.* 117 B9
Hermon, Mt. = Shaykh, J. ash,
  Lebanon 74 B4
Hermosillo, *Mexico* 118 B2
Hernád →, *Hungary* 28 C6
Hernandarias, *Paraguay* 127 B5
Hernandez, *U.S.A.* 110 J6
Hernando, *Argentina* 126 C3
Hernando, *U.S.A.* 113 H10
Hernani, *Spain* 38 B3
Herndon, *U.S.A.* 116 F8
Herne, *Germany* 17 C7
Herne Bay, *U.K.* 15 F9
Herning, *Denmark* 11 H2
Heroica = Caborca, *Mexico* .. 118 A2
Heroica Nogales = Nogales,
  Mexico 118 A2
Heron Bay, *Canada* 104 C2
Herradura, Pta. de la, *Canary Is.* .. 48 F5
Herreid, *U.S.A.* 112 C4
Herrenberg, *Germany* 25 G4
Herrera, *Spain* 37 H6
Herrera de Alcántara, *Spain* .. 37 F3
Herrera de Pisuerga, *Spain* .. 36 C6
Herrera del Duque, *Spain* .. 37 F5
Herrestad, *Sweden* 11 F5
Herrin, *U.S.A.* 113 G10
Herriot, *Canada* 103 B8
Herrljunga, *Sweden* 11 F7
Hersbruck, *Germany* 25 F7
Herschel I., *Canada* 4 C1
Hershey, *U.S.A.* 117 F8
Hersonissos, *Greece* 49 D7
Herstal, *Belgium* 17 D5
Hertford, *U.K.* 15 F7
Hertfordshire □, *U.K.* 15 F7
's-Hertogenbosch, *Neths.* .. 17 C5

Hertsa, *Ukraine* 29 B11
Hertzogville, *S. Africa* ... 88 D4
Hervás, *Spain* 36 E5
Hervey B., *Australia* 94 C5
Herzberg, *Brandenburg, Germany* 24 D9
Herzberg, *Niedersachsen,*
  Germany 24 D6
Herzliyya, *Israel* 74 C3
Herzogenburg, *Austria* 26 C8
Heşār, *Fārs, Iran* 71 D6
Heşār, *Markazī, Iran* 71 C6
Hesdin, *France* 19 B9
Heshan, *China* 58 F7
Heshui, *China* 56 G5
Heshun, *China* 56 F7
Hesperia, *U.S.A.* 111 L9
Hesse = Hessen □, *Germany* .. 24 E4
Hessen □, *Germany* 24 E4
Hessenreuther und Manteler
  Wald △, *Germany* 25 F8
Hestra, *Sweden* 11 G7
Hetch Hetchy Aqueduct, *U.S.A.* .. 110 H5
Hettinger, *U.S.A.* 112 C3
Hettstedt, *Germany* 24 D7
Heuvelton, *U.S.A.* 117 B9
Heves, *Hungary* 28 C5
Heves □, *Hungary* 28 C5
Hewitt, *U.S.A.* 113 K6
Hexham, *U.K.* 14 C5
Hexi, *Yunnan, China* 58 E4
Hexi, *Zhejiang, China* 59 D12
Hexigten Qi, *China* 57 C9
Ḥeydarābād, *Iran* 71 D7
Heyuan, *China* 59 F10
Heywood, *Australia* 95 F3
Heze, *China* 56 G8
Hezhang, *China* 58 D5
Hi, Ko, *Thailand* .... 65 a
Hi Vista, *U.S.A.* 111 L9
Hialeah, *U.S.A.* 115 N5
Hiawatha, *U.S.A.* 112 F7
Hibbing, *U.S.A.* 112 B8
Hibbs B., *Australia* 95 G4
Hibernia Reef, *Australia* .. 92 B3
Hickman, *U.S.A.* 113 G10
Hickory, *U.S.A.* 115 H5
Hicks, Pt., *Australia* 95 F4
Hicks L., *Canada* 103 A9
Hicksville, *U.S.A.* 117 F11
Hida, *Romania* 29 C8
Hida-Gawa →, *Japan* 55 G8
Hida-Sammyaku, *Japan* 55 F8
Hidaka-Sammyaku, *Japan* 54 C11
Hidalgo, *Mexico* 119 C5
Hidalgo □, *Mexico* 119 C5
Hidalgo, Presa M., *Mexico* .. 118 B3
Hidalgo del Parral, *Mexico* .. 118 B3
Hiddensee, *Germany* 24 A9
Hieflau, *Austria* 26 D7
Hiendelaencina, *Spain* 38 D2
Hierro, *Canary Is.* 48 G1
Higashiajima-San, *Japan* ... 54 F10
Higashiōsaka, *Japan* 55 G7
Higgins, *U.S.A.* 113 G4
Higgins Corner, *U.S.A.* 110 F5
High Bridge, *U.S.A.* 117 F10
High Level, *Canada* 102 B5
High Point, *U.S.A.* 115 H6
High Prairie, *Canada* 102 B5
High River, *Canada* 102 C6
High Tatra = Tatry, *Slovak Rep.* .. 27 B13
High Veld, *Africa* 76 J6
High Wycombe, *U.K.* 15 F7
Highland □, *U.K.* 13 D4
Highland Park, *U.S.A.* 114 D2
Highmore, *U.S.A.* 112 C5
Highrock L., *Man., Canada* .. 103 B8
Highrock L., *Sask., Canada* .. 103 B7
Higüey, *Dom. Rep.* 121 C6
Hihya, *Egypt* 80 H7
Hiiumaa, *Estonia* 9 G20
Híjar, *Spain* 38 D4
Ḥijāz □, *Si. Arabia* 70 E3
Hijo = Tagum, *Phil.* 61 H6
Hikari, *Japan* 55 H5
Hikmak, Ras el, *Egypt* 80 A2
Hiko, *U.S.A.* 110 H11
Hikone, *Japan* 55 G8
Hikurangi, *Gisborne, N.Z.* .. 91 H6
Hikurangi, *Northland, N.Z.* .. 91 F5
Hildburghausen, *Germany* ... 24 E6
Hildesheim, *Germany* 24 C5
Hill →, *Australia* 93 F2
Hill City, *Idaho, U.S.A.* .. 108 E6
Hill City, *Kans., U.S.A.* .. 112 F5
Hill City, *S. Dak., U.S.A.* .. 112 D3
Hill Island L., *Canada* 103 A7
Hillaby, Mt., *Barbados* .... 121 g
Hillared, *Sweden* 11 G7
Hillcrest, *Barbados* .... 121 g
Hillcrest Center, *U.S.A.* .. 111 K8
Hillegom, *Neths.* 17 B4
Hillerød, *Denmark* 11 J6
Hillerstorp, *Sweden* 11 G7
Hillsboro, *Kans., U.S.A.* .. 112 F6
Hillsboro, *N. Dak., U.S.A.* .. 112 B6
Hillsboro, *Ohio, U.S.A.* ... 114 F4
Hillsboro, *Oreg., U.S.A.* .. 110 E4
Hillsboro, *Tex., U.S.A.* ... 113 J6
Hillsborough, *Grenada* 121 D7
Hillsborough Channel, *Australia* .. 94 J7
Hillsdale, *Mich., U.S.A.* .. 114 E3
Hillsdale, *N.Y., U.S.A.* ... 117 D11
Hillsport, *Canada* 104 C2
Hillston, *Australia* 95 E4
Hilo, *U.S.A.* 106 J17
Hilton, *U.S.A.* 116 C7
Hilton Head Island, *U.S.A.* .. 115 J5
Hilvan, *Turkey* 73 D8

Hilversum, *Neths.* 17 B5
Himachal Pradesh □, *India* .. 68 D7
Himalaya, *Asia* 69 E11
Himamaylan, *Phil.* 61 F5
Himatnagar, *India* 66 H8
Himeji, *Japan* 55 G7
Himi, *Japan* 55 F8
Ḥimṣ, *Syria* 74 A5
Ḥimṣ □, *Syria* 74 A6
Hinche, *Haiti* 121 C5
Hinchinbrook I., *Australia* .. 94 B4
Hinchinbrook Island △, *Australia* .. 94 B4
Hinckley, *U.K.* 15 E6
Hinckley, *U.S.A.* 112 B8
Hindaun, *India* 68 F7
Hindmarsh, L., *Australia* .. 95 F3
Hindsholm, *Denmark* 11 J4
Hindu Bagh, *Pakistan* 68 D2
Hindu Kush, *Asia* 66 B7
Hindupur, *India* 66 N10
Hines Creek, *Canada* 102 B5
Hinesville, *U.S.A.* 115 K5
Hinganghat, *India* 66 J11
Hingham, *U.S.A.* 108 B8
Hingir, *India* 69 J10
Hingoli, *India* 66 K10
Hinigaran, *Phil.* 61 F5
Hinis, *Turkey* 73 C9
Hinna = Imi, *Ethiopia* 81 F5
Hinna, *Nigeria* 83 C7
Hinnerup, *Denmark* 11 H4
Hinnøya, *Norway* 8 B16
Hinojosa del Duque, *Spain* .. 37 G5
Hinsdale, *U.S.A.* 117 D12
Hinterrhein →, *Switz.* 25 J5
Hinton, *Canada* 102 C5
Hinton, *U.S.A.* 114 G5
Hirado, *Japan* 55 H4
Hirakud Dam, *India* 67 J13
Hiran →, *India* 69 H8
Hirapur, *India* 69 G8
Hiratsuka, *Japan* 55 G9
Hirfanlı Barajı, *Turkey* ... 72 C5
Hiroo, *Japan* 54 C11
Hirosaki, *Japan* 54 D10
Hiroshima, *Japan* 55 G6
Hiroshima □, *Japan* 55 G6
Hirson, *France* 19 C11
Hirtshals, *Denmark* 11 G3
Hisar, *India* 68 E6
Hisarcık, *Turkey* 47 B11
Hisaria, *Bulgaria* 45 D8
Ḥisb, Sha'ib = Ḥasb, W. →, *Iraq* .. 70 D5
Ḥismá, *Si. Arabia* 70 D3
Hispaniola, *W. Indies* 121 C5
Hit, *Iraq* 70 C4
Hita, *Japan* 55 H5
Hitachi, *Japan* 55 F10
Hitchin, *U.K.* 15 F7
Hitoyoshi, *Japan* 55 H5
Hitra, *Norway* 8 E13
Hitzacker, *Germany* 24 B7
Hixon, *Canada* 102 C4
Ḥiyyon, N. →, *Israel* 74 E4
Hjalmar L., *Canada* 103 A7
Hjälmaren, *Sweden* 10 E9
Hjältevad, *Sweden* 11 G9
Hjo, *Sweden* 11 F8
Hjørring, *Denmark* 11 G3
Hjortkvarn, *Sweden* 11 F9
Hkakabo Razi, *Burma* 67 E20
Hlinsko, *Czech Rep.* 26 B8
Hlobane, *S. Africa* 89 D5
Hlohovec, *Slovak Rep.* 27 C10
Hluhluwe, *S. Africa* 89 D5
Hluhluwe △, *S. Africa* 89 D5
Hlukhiv, *Ukraine* 33 G7
Hlyboka, *Ukraine* 29 B10
Hlybokaye, *Belarus* 32 E4
Hnúšťa, *Slovak Rep.* 27 C12
Ho, *Ghana* 83 D5
Ho Chi Minh City = Thanh Pho
  Ho Chi Minh, *Vietnam* 65 G6
Ho Thuong, *Vietnam* 64 C5
Hoa Binh, *Vietnam* 58 G5
Hoa Da, *Vietnam* 65 G7
Hoa Hiep, *Vietnam* 65 G5
Hoai Nhon, *Vietnam* 64 E7
Hoang Lien Son, *Vietnam* ... 58 F4
Hoanib →, *Namibia* 88 B2
Hoare B., *Canada* 101 B13
Hoarusib →, *Namibia* 88 B2
Hobart, *Australia* 95 G4
Hobart, *U.S.A.* 113 H5
Hobbs, *U.S.A.* 113 J3
Hobbs Coast, *Antarctica* ... 5 D14
Hobe Sound, *U.S.A.* 115 M5
Hoboken, *U.S.A.* 117 F10
Hobro, *Denmark* 11 H3
Hoburgen, *Sweden* 11 H12
Hocalar, *Turkey* 47 C11
Hochfeld, *Namibia* 88 C2
Hochharz △, *Germany* 24 D6
Hochschwab, *Austria* 26 D8
Höchstadt, *Germany* 25 F6
Hockenheim, *Germany* 25 F4
Hodaka-Dake, *Japan* 55 F8
Hodeida = Al Ḥudaydah, *Yemen* .. 75 E3
Hodgeville, *Canada* 103 C7
Hodgson, *Canada* 103 C9
Hódmezővásárhely, *Hungary* .. 28 D5
Hodna, Chott el, *Algeria* .. 78 A6
Hodonín, *Czech Rep.* 27 C10
Hœdic, Î. de, *France* 18 E4
Hoek van Holland, *Neths.* .. 17 C4

Hoengsŏng, *S. Korea* 57 F14
Hoeryong, *N. Korea* 57 C15
Hoeyang, *N. Korea* 57 E14
Hof, *Germany* 25 E7
Hofgeismar, *Germany* 24 D5
Hofheim, *Germany* 25 E4
Hofmeyr, *S. Africa* 88 E4
Höfn, *Iceland* 8 D6
Hofors, *Sweden* 10 D10
Hofsjökull, *Iceland* 8 D4
Höfu, *Japan* 55 G5
Hogan Group, *Australia* 95 F4
Höganäs, *Sweden* 11 H6
Hogarth, Mt., *Australia* ... 94 C2
Hoggar = Ahaggar, *Algeria* .. 78 D7
Högsäter, *Sweden* 11 F6
Högsby, *Sweden* 11 G10
Högsjö, *Sweden* 10 E9
Hogsty Reef, *Bahamas* 121 B5
Hoh →, *U.S.A.* 110 C2
Hohe Acht, *Germany* 25 E3
Hohe Tauern, *Austria* 26 D5
Hohe Tauern △, *Austria* 26 D5
Hohe Venn, *Belgium* 17 D6
Hohenau, *Austria* 27 C9
Hohenems, *Austria* 26 D2
Hohenloher Ebene, *Germany* .. 25 F5
Hohenwald, *U.S.A.* 115 H2
Hohenwestedt, *Germany* 24 A5
Hoher Rhön = Rhön, *Germany* .. 24 E5
Hoher Vogelsberg △, *Germany* .. 24 E5
Hohes Venn-Eifel △, *Europe* .. 24 E2
Hohhot, *China* 56 D6
Hóhlakas, *Greece* 49 D9
Hohoe, *Ghana* 83 D5
Hoi An, *Vietnam* 64 E7
Hoi Xuan, *Vietnam* 58 G5
Hoisington, *U.S.A.* 112 F5
Højer, *Denmark* 11 K2
Hōjō, *Japan* 55 H6
Hok, *Sweden* 11 G8
Hökensås, *Sweden* 11 G8
Hökerum, *Sweden* 11 G7
Hokianga Harbour, *N.Z.* 91 F4
Hokitika, *N.Z.* 91 K3
Hokkaidō □, *Japan* 54 C11
Hol-Hol, *Djibouti* 81 E5
Hola Pristan, *Ukraine* 33 J7
Holbæk, *Denmark* 11 J5
Holbrook, *Australia* 95 F4
Holbrook, *U.S.A.* 109 J8
Holden, *U.S.A.* 108 G7
Holdenville, *U.S.A.* 113 H6
Holdrege, *U.S.A.* 112 E5
Holešov, *Czech Rep.* 27 B10
Holetown, *Barbados* .... 121 g
Holguín, *Cuba* 120 B4
Holíč, *Slovak Rep.* 27 C10
Holice, *Czech Rep.* 26 A8
Höljes, *Sweden* 10 D6
Hollabrunn, *Austria* 26 C9
Holland, *Mich., U.S.A.* 114 D2
Holland, *N.Y., U.S.A.* 116 D6
Hollandale, *U.S.A.* 113 J9
Holley, *U.S.A.* 116 C6
Hollfeld, *Germany* 25 F7
Hollidaysburg, *U.S.A.* 116 F6
Hollis, *U.S.A.* 113 H5
Hollister, *Calif., U.S.A.* .. 110 J5
Hollister, *Idaho, U.S.A.* .. 108 E6
Höllviken = Höllviksnäs, *Sweden* .. 11 J6
Höllviksnäs, *Sweden* 11 J6
Holly Hill, *U.S.A.* 115 L5
Holly Springs, *U.S.A.* 113 H10
Hollywood, *U.S.A.* 115 N5
Holman, *Canada* 100 A8
Hólmavík, *Iceland* 8 D3
Holmen, *U.S.A.* 112 D9
Holmes Reefs, *Australia* ... 94 B4
Holmsjö, *Sweden* 11 H9
Holmsjön, *Västernorrland,*
  Sweden 10 B10
Holmsjön, *Västernorrland,*
  Sweden 28 B9
Holmsland Klit, *Denmark* ... 11 J2
Holmsund, *Sweden* 8 E19
Holod, *Romania* 28 D7
Holovne, *Ukraine* 31 G11
Holozubyntsi, *Ukraine* 29 B11
Holroyd →, *Australia* 94 A3
Holstebro, *Denmark* 11 H2
Holsteinische Schweiz △,
  Germany 24 A6
Holsworthy, *U.K.* 15 G3
Holton, *Canada* 105 B8
Holton, *U.S.A.* 112 F7
Holtville, *U.S.A.* 111 N11
Holwerd, *Neths.* 17 A5
Holy I., *Angl., U.K.* 14 D3
Holy I., *Northumberland, U.K.* .. 14 B6
Holyhead, *U.K.* 14 D3
Holyoke, *Colo., U.S.A.* 112 E3
Holyoke, *Mass., U.S.A.* 117 D12
Holyrood, *Canada* 105 C9
Homa Bay, *Kenya* 86 C3
Homalin, *Burma* 67 G19
Homand, *Iran* 71 C8
Homathko →, *Canada* 102 C4
Homberg, *Germany* 24 D5
Hombori, *Mali* 83 B4
Homburg, *Germany* 25 F3
Home B., *Canada* 101 B13
Home Hill, *Australia* 94 B4
Homedale, *U.S.A.* 108 E5
Homer, *Alaska, U.S.A.* 100 C4
Homer, *La., U.S.A.* 113 J8
Homer City, *U.S.A.* 116 F5
Homert △, *Germany* 24 D4

Homestead, *Australia* 94 C4
Homestead, *U.S.A.* 115 N5
Homestead △, *U.S.A.* 112 E6
Homewood, *U.S.A.* 110 F6
Homoine, *Mozam.* 89 C6
Homoljske Planina, *Serbia & M.* .. 44 B5
Homorod, *Romania* 29 D10
Homs = Ḥimṣ, *Syria* 74 A5
Homyel, *Belarus* 33 F6
Hon Chong, *Vietnam* 65 G5
Hon Me, *Vietnam* 64 C5
Honan = Henan □, *China* 56 H8
Honaz, *Turkey* 47 D11
Honbetsu, *Japan* 54 C11
Honcut, *U.S.A.* 110 F5
Honda Bay, *Phil.* 61 G3
Hondarribia, *Spain* 38 B3
Hondeklipbaai, *S. Africa* .. 88 E2
Hondo, *Japan* 55 H5
Hondo, *U.S.A.* 113 L5
Hondo, Rio →, *Belize* 119 D7
Honduras ■, *Cent. Amer.* ... 120 D2
Honduras, G. de, *Caribbean* .. 120 C2
Hønefoss, *Norway* 9 F14
Honesdale, *U.S.A.* 117 E9
Honey L., *U.S.A.* 110 E6
Honfleur, *France* 18 C7
Høng, *Denmark* 11 J5
Hong →, *Vietnam* 58 F5
Hong Gai, *Vietnam* 58 G6
Hong He →, *China* 56 H8
Hong Hu, *China* 59 C9
Hong Kong □, *China* 59 F10
Hong'an, *China* 59 B10
Hongch'ŏn, *S. Korea* 57 F14
Honghai Wan, *China* 59 F10
Honghe, *China* 58 F4
Honghu, *China* 59 C9
Hongjiang, *China* 58 D7
Hongliu He →, *China* 56 F5
Hongor, *Mongolia* 56 B7
Hongsa, *Laos* 58 C3
Hongshui He →, *China* 58 F7
Hongsŏng, *S. Korea* 57 F14
Hongtong, *China* 56 F6
Honguedo, Détroit d', *Canada* .. 105 C7
Hongwon, *N. Korea* 57 E14
Hongya, *China* 58 C4
Hongyuan, *China* 58 A4
Hongze Hu, *China* 57 H10
Honiara, *Solomon Is.* 96 H7
Honiton, *U.K.* 15 G4
Honjō, *Japan* 54 E10
Honkorâb, Ras, *Egypt* 80 C4
Honningsvåg, *Norway* 8 A21
Hönö, *Sweden* 11 G5
Honolulu, *U.S.A.* 106 H16
Hontoria del Pinar, *Spain* .. 38 D1
Hood, Mt., *U.S.A.* 108 D3
Hood, Pt., *Australia* 93 F2
Hood River, *U.S.A.* 108 D3
Hoodsport, *U.S.A.* 110 C3
Hooge, *Germany* 24 A4
Hoogeveen, *Neths.* 17 B6
Hoogezand-Sappemeer, *Neths.* .. 17 A6
Hooghly = Hugli →, *India* .. 69 J13
Hooghly-Chinsura = Chunchura,
  India 69 H13
Hook Hd., *Ireland* 12 D5
Hook I., *Australia* 94 B4
Hook of Holland = Hoek van
  Holland, *Neths.* 17 C4
Hooker, *U.S.A.* 113 G4
Hooker Creek, *Australia* ... 92 C5
Hoonah, *U.S.A.* 102 B1
Hooper Bay, *U.S.A.* 100 B3
Hoopeston, *U.S.A.* 114 E2
Hoopstad, *S. Africa* 88 D4
Höör, *Sweden* 11 J7
Hoorn, *Neths.* 17 B5
Hoover, *U.S.A.* 115 J2
Hoover Dam, *U.S.A.* 111 K12
Hooversville, *U.S.A.* 116 F6
Hop Bottom, *U.S.A.* 117 E9
Hopa, *Turkey* 73 B9
Hope, *Canada* 102 D4
Hope, *Ariz., U.S.A.* 111 M13
Hope, *Ark., U.S.A.* 113 J8
Hope, L., *S. Austral., Australia* .. 95 D2
Hope, L., *W. Austral., Australia* .. 93 F3
Hope, Pt., *U.S.A.* 4 C17
Hope I., *Canada* 116 B4
Hope Town, *Bahamas* 120 A4
Hopedale, *Canada* 105 A7
Hopedale, *U.S.A.* 117 D13
Hopefield, *S. Africa* 88 E2
Hopei = Hebei □, *China* 56 E9
Hopelchén, *Mexico* 119 D7
Hopetoun, *Vic., Australia* .. 95 F3
Hopetoun, *W. Austral., Australia* .. 93 F3
Hopetown, *S. Africa* 88 D3
Hopevale, *Australia* 94 B4
Hopewell, *U.S.A.* 114 G7
Hopfgarten, *Austria* 26 D5
Hopkins, L., *Australia* 92 D4
Hopkinsville, *U.S.A.* 115 G2
Hopland, *U.S.A.* 110 G3
Hoquiam, *U.S.A.* 110 D3
Hora Hoverla, *Ukraine* 29 B9
Horasan, *Turkey* 73 B10
Horaždovice, *Czech Rep.* ... 26 B6
Horb, *Germany* 25 G4
Hörby, *Sweden* 11 J7
Horcajo de Santiago, *Spain* .. 38 F1
Horden Hills, *Australia* ... 92 D5
Horezu, *Romania* 29 E8
Horgen, *Switz.* 25 H4
Horgoš, *Serbia & M.* 28 D4
Hořice, *Czech Rep.* 26 A8
Horinchove, *Ukraine* 29 B8
Horinger, *China* 56 D6

I

Horki, *Belarus* 32 E6
Horlick Mts., *Antarctica* 5 E15
Horlivka, *Ukraine* 33 H10
Hormak, *Iran* 71 D9
Hormoz, *Iran* 71 E7
Hormoz, Jaz.-ye, *Iran* 71 E8
Hormozgān □, *Iran* 71 E8
Hormuz, Kūh-e, *Iran* 71 E7
Hormuz, Str. of, *The Gulf* 71 E8
Horn, *Austria* 26 C8
Horn, *Iceland* 8 C2
Horn, *Sweden* 11 G9
Horn ➤, *Canada* 102 A5
Horn, Cape = Hornos, C. de, *Chile* 128 H3
Horn Head, *Ireland* 12 A3
Horn I., *Australia* 94 A3
Horn Plateau, *Canada* 102 A5
Hornachuelos, *Spain* 37 H5
Hornavan, *Sweden* 8 C17
Hornbeck, *U.S.A.* 113 K8
Hornbrook, *U.S.A.* 108 F2
Hornburg, *Germany* 24 C6
Horncastle, *U.K.* 14 D7
Horndal, *Sweden* 10 D10
Hornell, *U.S.A.* 116 D7
Hornell L., *Canada* 102 A5
Hornepayne, *Canada* 104 C3
Horní Planá, *Czech Rep.* 26 C7
Hornings Mills, *Canada* 116 B4
Hornitos, *U.S.A.* 110 H6
Hornos, C. de, *Chile* 128 H3
Hornoy-le-Bourg, *France* 19 C8
Hornsea, *U.K.* 14 D7
Hornslandet, *Sweden* 10 C11
Hörnum, *Germany* 24 A4
Horobetsu = Noboribetsu, *Japan* 54 C10
Horodenka, *Ukraine* 29 B10
Horodnya, *Ukraine* 33 G6
Horodok, Khmelnytskyy, *Ukraine* 33 H4
Horodok, Lviv, *Ukraine* 33 H2
Horodyshche, *Ukraine* 33 H6
Horokhiv, *Ukraine* 33 G3
Horovice, *Czech Rep.* 26 B6
Horqin Youyi Qianqi, *China* 57 A12
Horqueta, *Paraguay* 126 A4
Horred, *Sweden* 11 G6
Horse Creek, *U.S.A.* 112 E3
Horse I., *Canada* 103 C9
Horse Is., *Canada* 105 B8
Horsefly L., *Canada* 102 C4
Horseheads, *U.S.A.* 116 D8
Horsens, *Denmark* 11 J3
Horsham, *Australia* 95 F3
Horsham, *U.K.* 15 F7
Horšovský Týn, *Czech Rep.* 26 B5
Horten, *Norway* 9 G14
Hortobágy ➤, *Hungary* 28 C6
Hortobágyi △, *Hungary* 28 C6
Horton, *U.S.A.* 112 F7
Horton ➤, *Canada* 100 B7
Horwood L., *Canada* 104 C3
Hosaina, *Ethiopia* 81 F4
Hose, Gunung-Gunung, *Malaysia* 62 D4
Hoseynābād, Khuzestān, *Iran* 71 C6
Hoseynābād, Kordestān, *Iran* 70 C5
Hoshangabad, *India* 68 H7
Hoshiarpur, *India* 68 D6
Hospet, *India* 66 M10
Hoste, I., *Chile* 128 H3
Hostens, *France* 20 D3
Hot, *Thailand* 64 C2
Hot Creek Range, *U.S.A.* 108 G6
Hot Springs, Ark., *U.S.A.* 113 H8
Hot Springs, S. Dak., *U.S.A.* 112 D3
Hot Springs △, *U.S.A.* 113 H8
Hotagen, *Sweden* 8 E16
Hotan, *China* 60 C2
Hotazel, *S. Africa* 88 D3
Hotchkiss, *U.S.A.* 109 G10
Hotham, C., *Australia* 92 B5
Hoting, *Sweden* 8 D17
Hotolisht, *Albania* 44 E4
Hotte, Massif de la, *Haiti* 121 C5
Hottentotsbaai, *Namibia* 88 D1
Houat, Î. de, *France* 18 E4
Houdan, *France* 19 D8
Houei Sai, *Laos* 58 G3
Houeillès, *France* 20 D4
Houffalize, *Belgium* 17 D5
Houghton, Mich., *U.S.A.* 112 B10
Houghton, N.Y., *U.S.A.* 116 D6
Houghton L., *U.S.A.* 114 C3
Houghton-le-Spring, *U.K.* 14 C6
Houhora Heads, *N.Z.* 91 F4
Houlton, *U.S.A.* 115 B12
Houma, *U.S.A.* 113 L9
Houndé, *Burkina Faso* 82 C4
Hourtin, *France* 20 C2
Hourtin-Carcans, Étang d', *France* 20 C2
Housatonic ➤, *U.S.A.* 117 E11
Houston, *Canada* 102 C3
Houston, Mo., *U.S.A.* 113 G9
Houston, Tex., *U.S.A.* 113 L7
Hout ➤, *S. Africa* 89 C4
Houtkraal, *S. Africa* 88 E3
Houtman Abrolhos, *Australia* 93 E1
Hovd, *Mongolia* 60 B4
Hove, *U.K.* 15 G7
Hovenweep △, *U.S.A.* 109 H9
Hoveyzeh, *Iran* 71 D6
Hovmantorp, *Sweden* 11 H9
Hövsgöl, *Mongolia* 56 C5
Hövsgöl Nuur, *Mongolia* 60 A5
Hovsta, *Sweden* 10 E9
Howakil, *Eritrea* 81 D5
Howar, Wadi ➤, *Sudan* 81 D2
Howard, *Australia* 95 D5
Howard, Pa., *U.S.A.* 116 F7
Howard, S. Dak., *U.S.A.* 112 C6

Howe, *U.S.A.* 108 E7
Howe, C., *Australia* 95 F5
Howe I., *Canada* 117 B8
Howell, *U.S.A.* 114 D4
Howick, *Canada* 117 A11
Howick, *S. Africa* 89 D5
Howick Group, *Australia* 94 A4
Howitt, L., *Australia* 95 D2
Howland I., *Pac. Oc.* 96 G10
Howrah = Haora, *India* 69 H13
Howth Hd., *Ireland* 12 C5
Hoy, *U.K.* 13 C5
Hoya, *Germany* 24 C5
Høyanger, *Norway* 9 F12
Hoyerswerda, *Germany* 24 D10
Hoylake, *U.K.* 14 D4
Hoyos, *Spain* 36 E4
Hpa-an = Pa-an, *Burma* 67 L20
Hpungan Pass, *Burma* 67 F20
Hradec Králové, *Czech Rep.* 26 A8
Hrádek, *Czech Rep.* 27 C9
Hranice, *Czech Rep.* 27 B10
Hrazdan, *Armenia* 35 K7
Hrebenka, *Ukraine* 33 G7
Hrodna, *Belarus* 30 E10
Hrodzyanka, *Belarus* 32 F5
Hron ➤, *Slovak Rep.* 27 D11
Hrubieszów, *Poland* 31 H10
Hrubý Jeseník, *Czech Rep.* 27 A10
Hrvatska = Croatia ■, *Europe* 41 C13
Hrymayliv, *Ukraine* 33 H4
Hrynyava, *Ukraine* 29 C9
Hsenwi, *Burma* 67 H20
Hsiamen = Xiamen, *China* 59 E12
Hsian = Xi'an, *China* 56 G5
Hsinchu, *Taiwan* 59 E13
Hsinhailien = Lianyungang, *China* 57 G10
Hsining = Xining, *China* 56 F5
Hsinying, *Taiwan* 59 F13
Hsopket, *Burma* 58 F2
Hsüchou = Xuzhou, *China* 57 G9
Hu Xian, *China* 56 G5
Hua Hin, *Thailand* 64 F2
Hua Xian, Henan, *China* 56 G8
Hua Xian, Shaanxi, *China* 56 G5
Hua'an, *China* 59 E11
Huab ➤, *Namibia* 88 B2
Huacheng, *China* 59 E10
Huachinera, *Mexico* 118 A3
Huacho, *Peru* 124 F3
Huade, *China* 56 D7
Huadian, *China* 57 C14
Huadu, *China* 59 F9
Huai Had △, *Thailand* 64 D5
Huai He ➤, *China* 59 A12
Huai Nam Dang △, *Thailand* 64 C2
Huai Yot, *Thailand* 65 J2
Huai'an, Hebei, *China* 56 D8
Huai'an, Jiangsu, *China* 57 H10
Huaibei, *China* 56 G9
Huaibin, *China* 59 A10
Huaide = Gongzhuling, *China* 57 C13
Huaidezhen, *China* 57 C13
Huaihua, *China* 58 D7
Huaiji, *China* 59 F9
Huainan, *China* 59 A11
Huaining, *China* 59 B11
Huairen, *China* 56 E7
Huairou, *China* 56 D9
Huaiyang, *China* 56 H8
Huaiyin, *China* 57 H10
Huaiyuan, Anhui, *China* 57 H9
Huaiyuan, Guangxi Zhuangzu, *China* 58 E7
Huajianzi, *China* 57 D13
Huajuapan de Leon, *Mexico* 119 D5
Hualapai Peak, *U.S.A.* 109 J7
Hualien, *Taiwan* 59 E13
Huallaga ➤, *Peru* 124 E3
Huambo, *Angola* 85 G3
Huan Jiang ➤, *China* 56 G5
Huan Xian, *China* 56 F4
Huancabamba, *Peru* 124 E3
Huancane, *Peru* 124 G5
Huancavelica, *Peru* 124 F3
Huancayo, *Peru* 124 F3
Huanchaca, *Bolivia* 124 H5
Huang Hai = Yellow Sea, *China* 57 G12
Huang He ➤, *China* 57 F10
Huang Xian, *China* 57 F11
Huangchuan, *China* 59 A10
Huanggang, *China* 59 B10
Huangguoshu, *China* 58 E5
Huangling, *China* 56 G5
Huanglong, *China* 56 G5
Huanglongtan, *China* 59 A8
Huangmei, *China* 59 B10
Huangpi, *China* 59 B10
Huangping, *China* 58 D6
Huangshan, *China* 59 C12
Huangshi, *China* 59 B10
Huangsongdian, *China* 57 C14
Huangyan, *China* 59 C13
Huangyangsi, *China* 59 D8
Huaning, *China* 58 E4
Huanjiang, *China* 58 E7
Huantai, *China* 57 F9
Huánuco, *Peru* 124 E3
Huaping, *China* 58 D3
Huaraz, *Peru* 124 E3
Huarmey, *Peru* 124 F3
Huarong, *China* 59 C9
Huascarán, *Peru* 124 E3
Huasco, *Chile* 126 B1
Huasco ➤, *Chile* 126 B1
Huasna, *U.S.A.* 111 K6
Huatabampo, *Mexico* 118 B3
Huauchinango, *Mexico* 119 C5
Huautla de Jiménez, *Mexico* 119 D5
Huaxi, *China* 58 D6
Huay Namota, *Mexico* 118 C4

Huayin, *China* 56 G6
Huayuan, *China* 58 C7
Huayun, *China* 58 B6
Huazhou, *China* 59 G8
Hubbard, Ohio, *U.S.A.* 116 E4
Hubbard, Tex., *U.S.A.* 113 K6
Hubbart Pt., *Canada* 103 B10
Hubei □, *China* 59 B9
Hubli, *India* 66 M9
Huch'ang, *N. Korea* 57 D14
Hucknall, *U.K.* 14 D6
Huddersfield, *U.K.* 14 D6
Hude, *Germany* 24 B4
Hudi, *Sudan* 80 D3
Hudiksvall, *Sweden* 10 C11
Hudson, *Canada* 104 B1
Hudson, Mass., *U.S.A.* 117 D13
Hudson, N.Y., *U.S.A.* 117 D11
Hudson, Wis., *U.S.A.* 112 C8
Hudson, Wyo., *U.S.A.* 108 E9
Hudson ➤, *U.S.A.* 117 F10
Hudson Bay, Nunavut, *Canada* 101 C11
Hudson Bay, Sask., *Canada* 103 C8
Hudson Falls, *U.S.A.* 117 C11
Hudson Mts., *Antarctica* 5 D16
Hudson Str., *Canada* 101 B13
Hudson's Hope, *Canada* 102 B4
Hue, *Vietnam* 64 D6
Huebra ➤, *Spain* 36 D4
Huedin, *Romania* 28 D8
Huehuetenango, *Guatemala* 120 C1
Huejúcar, *Mexico* 118 C4
Huélamo, *Spain* 38 E3
Huelgoat, *France* 18 D3
Huelma, *Spain* 37 H7
Huelva, *Spain* 37 H4
Huelva □, *Spain* 37 H4
Huelva ➤, *Spain* 37 H5
Huentelauquén, *Chile* 126 C1
Huércal-Overa, *Spain* 39 H3
Huerta, Sa. de la, *Argentina* 126 C2
Huertas, C. de las, *Spain* 39 G4
Huerva ➤, *Spain* 38 D4
Huesca, *Spain* 38 C4
Huesca □, *Spain* 38 C5
Huéscar, *Spain* 39 H2
Huetamo, *Mexico* 118 D4
Huete, *Spain* 38 E2
Hugh ➤, *Australia* 94 D1
Hughenden, *Australia* 94 C3
Hughes, *Australia* 93 F4
Hughesville, *U.S.A.* 117 E8
Hugli ➤, *India* 69 J13
Hugo, Colo., *U.S.A.* 112 F3
Hugo, Okla., *U.S.A.* 113 H7
Hugoton, *U.S.A.* 113 G4
Hui Xian = Huixian, *China* 56 G7
Hui Xian, *China* 56 H4
Hui'an, *China* 59 E12
Hui'anbu, *China* 56 F4
Huichang, *China* 59 E10
Huichapán, *Mexico* 119 C5
Huidong, Guangdong, *China* 59 F10
Huidong, Sichuan, *China* 58 D4
Huifa He ➤, *China* 57 C14
Huila, Nevado del, *Colombia* 124 C3
Huilai, *China* 59 F11
Huili, *China* 58 D4
Huimin, *China* 57 F9
Huinan, *China* 57 C14
Huinca Renancó, *Argentina* 126 C3
Huining, *China* 56 G3
Huinong, *China* 56 E4
Huisache, *Mexico* 118 C4
Huishui, *China* 58 D6
Huisne ➤, *France* 18 E7
Huiting, *China* 56 G9
Huitong, *China* 58 D7
Huixian, *China* 56 G7
Huixtla, *Mexico* 119 D6
Huize, *China* 58 D4
Huizhou, *China* 59 F10
Hukawng Valley, *Burma* 67 F20
Hukou, *China* 59 C11
Hüksan-chedo, *S. Korea* 57 G13
Hukuntsi, *Botswana* 88 C3
Hulayfa', *Si. Arabia* 70 E4
Hulin He ➤, *China* 57 B12
Hull = Kingston upon Hull, *U.K.* 14 D7
Hull, *Canada* 117 A9
Hull ➤, *U.K.* 14 D7
Hulst, *Neths.* 17 C4
Hultsfred, *Sweden* 11 G9
Hulun Nur, *China* 60 B6
Hulyaypole, *Ukraine* 33 J9
Huma, Tanjung, *Malaysia* 65 c
Humacao, *Puerto Rico* 121 d
Humahuaca, *Argentina* 126 A2
Humaitá, *Brazil* 124 E6
Humaitá, *Paraguay* 126 B4
Humansdorp, *S. Africa* 88 E3
Humara, J., *Sudan* 81 D3
Humbe, *Angola* 88 B1
Humber ➤, *U.K.* 14 D7
Humboldt, *Canada* 103 C7
Humboldt, Iowa, *U.S.A.* 112 D7
Humboldt, Tenn., *U.S.A.* 113 H10
Humboldt ➤, *U.S.A.* 108 F4
Humboldt Gletscher = Sermersuaq, *Greenland* 4 B4
Hume, *U.S.A.* 110 J8
Hume, L., *Australia* 95 F4
Humenné, *Slovak Rep.* 27 C14
Humphreys, Mt., *U.S.A.* 110 H8
Humphreys Peak, *U.S.A.* 109 J8
Humpolec, *Czech Rep.* 26 B8
Humptulips, *U.S.A.* 110 C3
Hūn, *Libya* 79 C9
Húnaflói, *Iceland* 8 D3
Hunan □, *China* 59 D9

Hunchun, *China* 57 C16
Hundested, *Denmark* 11 J5
Hundewali, *Pakistan* 68 D5
Hundred Mile House, *Canada* 102 C4
Hunedoara, *Romania* 28 E7
Hunedoara □, *Romania* 28 E7
Hünfeld, *Germany* 24 E5
Hung Yen, *Vietnam* 58 G6
Hungary ■, *Europe* 27 D12
Hungary, Plain of, *Europe* 6 F10
Hungerford, *Australia* 95 D3
Hüngnam, *N. Korea* 57 E14
Hungt'ou Hsü, *Taiwan* 59 G13
Huni Valley, *Ghana* 82 D4
Hunneberg, *Sweden* 11 F6
Hunnebostrand, *Sweden* 11 F5
Hunsberge, *Namibia* 88 D2
Hunsrück, *Germany* 25 F3
Hunstanton, *U.K.* 14 E8
Hunte ➤, *Germany* 24 B4
Hunter, *U.S.A.* 117 D10
Hunter I., *Australia* 95 G3
Hunter I., *Canada* 102 C3
Hunter Ra., *Australia* 95 E5
Hunters Road, *Zimbabwe* 87 F2
Huntingburg, *U.S.A.* 114 F2
Huntingdon, *Canada* 104 C5
Huntingdon, *U.K.* 15 E7
Huntingdon, *U.S.A.* 116 F6
Huntington, Ind., *U.S.A.* 114 E3
Huntington, N.Y., *U.S.A.* 117 F11
Huntington, Oreg., *U.S.A.* 108 D5
Huntington, Utah, *U.S.A.* 108 G8
Huntington, W. Va., *U.S.A.* 114 F4
Huntington Beach, *U.S.A.* 111 M9
Huntly, *N.Z.* 91 G5
Huntly, *U.K.* 13 D6
Huntsville, *Canada* 116 A5
Huntsville, Ala., *U.S.A.* 115 H2
Huntsville, Tex., *U.S.A.* 113 K7
Hunyani ➤, *Zimbabwe* 87 F3
Hunyuan, *China* 56 E7
Hunza ➤, *India* 69 B6
Huo Xian = Huozhou, *China* 56 F6
Huong Khe, *Vietnam* 64 C5
Huonville, *Australia* 95 G4
Huoqiu, *China* 59 A11
Huoshan, Anhui, *China* 59 A12
Huoshan, Anhui, *China* 59 B11
Huoshao Dao = Lü-Tao, *Taiwan* 59 F13
Huozhou, *China* 56 F6
Hupeh = Hubei □, *China* 59 B9
Hūr, *Iran* 71 D8
Hurbanovo, *Slovak Rep.* 27 D11
Hurd, C., *Canada* 116 A3
Hure Qi, *China* 57 C11
Hurezani, *Romania* 29 F8
Hurghada, *Egypt* 80 B3
Hurley, N. Mex., *U.S.A.* 109 K9
Hurley, Wis., *U.S.A.* 112 B9
Huron, Calif., *U.S.A.* 110 J6
Huron, Ohio, *U.S.A.* 116 E2
Huron, S. Dak., *U.S.A.* 112 C5
Huron, L., *U.S.A.* 116 B2
Huron East, *Canada* 116 C3
Hurricane, *U.S.A.* 109 H7
Hurso, *Ethiopia* 81 F5
Hurunge ➤, *Zimbabwe* 87 F2
Hurunui ➤, *N.Z.* 91 K4
Hurup, *Denmark* 11 H2
Húsavík, *Iceland* 8 C5
Huși, *Romania* 29 D13
Huskvarna, *Sweden* 11 G8
Hustadvika, *Norway* 8 E12
Hustontown, *U.S.A.* 116 F6
Hustopeče, *Czech Rep.* 27 C9
Husum, *Germany* 24 A5
Husum, *Sweden* 10 A13
Hutchinson, Kans., *U.S.A.* 113 F6
Hutchinson, Minn., *U.S.A.* 112 C7
Hutte Sauvage, L. de la, *Canada* 105 A7
Hüttenberg, *Austria* 26 E7
Hüttener Berge △, *Germany* 24 A5
Hutton, Mt., *Australia* 95 D4
Huwun, *Ethiopia* 81 G5
Huy, *Belgium* 17 D5
Huzhou, *China* 59 B13
Hvalpsund, *Denmark* 11 H3
Hvammstangi, *Iceland* 8 D3
Hvar, *Croatia* 41 E13
Hvarski Kanal, *Croatia* 41 E13
Hvítá ➤, *Iceland* 8 D3
Hvizdets, *Ukraine* 29 B10
Hwachŏn-chŏsuji, *S. Korea* 57 E14
Hwang Ho = Huang He ➤, *China* 57 F10
Hwange, *Zimbabwe* 87 F2
Hwange △, *Zimbabwe* 88 B4
Hyannis, Mass., *U.S.A.* 114 E10
Hyannis, Nebr., *U.S.A.* 112 E3
Hyargas Nuur, *Mongolia* 60 B4
Hybo, *Sweden* 10 C10
Hyde Park, *U.S.A.* 117 E11
Hyden, *Australia* 93 F2
Hyder, *U.S.A.* 102 B2
Hyderabad, *India* 66 L11
Hyderabad, *Pakistan* 68 G3
Hyères, *France* 21 E10
Hyères, Îs. d', *France* 21 F10
Hyesan, *N. Korea* 57 D15
Hyland ➤, *Canada* 102 B3
Hyltebruk, *Sweden* 11 H7
Hymia, *India* 69 C8
Hyndman Peak, *U.S.A.* 108 E6
Hyōgo □, *Japan* 55 G7
Hyrum, *U.S.A.* 108 F8
Hysham, *U.S.A.* 108 C10
Hythe, *U.K.* 15 F9
Hyūga, *Japan* 55 H5
Hyvinge = Hyvinkää, *Finland* 9 F21
Hyvinkää, *Finland* 9 F21

I-n-Gall, *Niger* 83 B6
I-n-Oudad, *Algeria* 83 A5
I-n-Ouzzal, *Algeria* 83 A5
I-n-Tadreft, *Niger* 83 B6
Iablanița, *Romania* 28 F7
Iaco ➤, *Brazil* 124 E5
Iacobeni, *Romania* 29 C10
Iakora, *Madag.* 89 C8
Ialomița ➤, *Romania* 29 F12
Ialomița □, *Romania* 29 F12
Ialoveni, *Moldova* 29 D13
Ialpug ➤, *Moldova* 29 E13
Ianca, *Romania* 29 E12
Iara, *Romania* 29 D8
Iarda, *Ethiopia* 81 E4
Iargara, *Moldova* 29 D13
Iași, *Romania* 29 C12
Iași □, *Romania* 29 C12
Íasmos, *Greece* 45 E9
Ib ➤, *India* 69 J10
Iba, *Phil.* 61 D3
Ibadan, *Nigeria* 83 D5
Ibagué, *Colombia* 124 C3
Iballë, *Albania* 44 D4
Ibănești, Botoșani, *Romania* 29 B11
Ibănești, Mureș, *Romania* 29 D9
Ibar ➤, *Serbia & M.* 44 C4
Ibaraki □, *Japan* 55 F10
Ibarra, *Ecuador* 124 C3
Ibba, *Sudan* 81 G2
Ibba, Bahr el ➤, *Sudan* 81 F2
Ibbenbüren, *Germany* 24 C3
Ibembo, *Dem. Rep. of the Congo* 86 B1
Ibera, L., *Argentina* 126 B4
Iberian Peninsula, *Europe* 6 H5
Iberville, *Canada* 117 A11
Iberville, Lac d', *Canada* 104 A5
Ibi, *Nigeria* 83 D6
Ibi, *Spain* 39 G4
Ibiá, *Brazil* 125 G9
Ibiapaba, Sa. da, *Brazil* 125 D10
Ibicuí ➤, *Brazil* 127 B4
Ibicuy, *Argentina* 126 C4
Ibiza = Eivissa, *Spain* 48 C7
Ibiza ✈ (IBZ), *Spain* 39 G6
Íblei, Monti, *Italy* 43 E7
Ibo, *Mozam.* 87 E5
Ibonma, *Indonesia* 63 E8
Ibotirama, *Brazil* 125 F10
Ibrāhīm ➤, *Lebanon* 74 A4
'Ibrī, *Oman* 71 F8
Ibriktepe, *Turkey* 45 E10
Ibshawâi, *Egypt* 80 J7
Ibu, *Indonesia* 63 D7
Ibusuki, *Japan* 55 J5
Iça ➤, *Brazil* 124 F3
Içana, *Brazil* 124 D5
Içana ➤, *Brazil* 124 D5
İçel = Mersin, *Turkey* 70 B2
Iceland ■, *Europe* 8 D4
Iceland Plateau, *Arctic* 4 C7
Ich'ang = Yichang, *China* 59 B8
Ichchapuram, *India* 67 K14
Ichhawar, *India* 68 H7
Ichihara, *Japan* 55 G10
Ichikawa, *Japan* 55 G9
Ichilo ➤, *Bolivia* 124 G6
Ichinohe, *Japan* 54 D10
Ichinomiya, *Japan* 55 G8
Ichinoseki, *Japan* 54 E10
Ichnya, *Ukraine* 33 G7
Icod, *Canary Is.* 48 F3
Ida Grove, *U.S.A.* 112 D7
Idabel, *U.S.A.* 113 J7
Idaga Hamus, *Ethiopia* 81 E4
Idah, *Nigeria* 83 D6
Idaho □, *U.S.A.* 108 D7
Idaho City, *U.S.A.* 108 E6
Idaho Falls, *U.S.A.* 108 E7
Idalia △, *Australia* 94 C3
Idanha-a-Nova, *Portugal* 36 F3
Idar-Oberstein, *Germany* 25 F3
Idensalmi = Iisalmi, *Finland* 8 E22
Idfû, *Egypt* 80 C3
Ídhi Oros, *Greece* 49 D6
Ídhra, *Greece* 46 D5
Idi, *Indonesia* 62 C1
Idiofa, *Dem. Rep. of the Congo* 84 E3
Idku, Bahra el, *Egypt* 80 H7
Idlib, *Syria* 70 C3
Idre, *Sweden* 10 C6
Idria, *U.S.A.* 110 J6
Idrija, *Slovenia* 41 C11
Idritsa, *Russia* 32 D5
Idutywa, *S. Africa* 89 E4
Ieper, *Belgium* 17 D2
Ierápetra, *Greece* 49 E7
Ierissós, *Greece* 44 F7
Ierissoú Kólpos, *Greece* 44 F7
Iernut, *Romania* 29 D9
Iesi, *Italy* 41 E10
Iešjávri, *Norway* 8 B21
Ifach, Peñón de, *Spain* 39 G5
Ifakara, *Tanzania* 84 F7
'Ifāl, W. al ➤, *Si. Arabia* 70 D2
Ifanadiana, *Madag.* 89 C8
Ife, *Nigeria* 83 D5
Iférouâne, *Niger* 83 B6
Iffley, *Australia* 94 B3
Ifon, *Nigeria* 83 D6
Iforas, Adrar des, *Africa* 83 B5
Ifould, L., *Australia* 93 F5
Iganga, *Uganda* 86 B3
Igarapava, *Brazil* 125 H9
Igarka, *Russia* 52 C9

Igatimi, Paraguay 127 A4
Igbetti, Nigeria 83 D5
Igbo-Ora, Nigeria 83 D5
Igboho, Nigeria 83 D5
Igbor, Nigeria 83 D6
Iğdır, Turkey 73 C11
Igelfors, Sweden 11 F9
Iggesund, Sweden 10 C11
Iglésias, Italy 42 C1
Igloolik, Canada 101 B11
Igluligaarjuk = Chesterfield Inlet, Canada 100 B10
Iglulik = Igloolik, Canada 101 B11
'Igma, Gebel el, Egypt 80 B3
Ignace, Canada 104 C1
Iğneada, Turkey 45 E11
Iğneada Burnu, Turkey 45 E12
Igoumenítsa, Greece 46 B2
Igra, Russia 34 B11
Iguaçu △, Brazil 127 B5
Iguaçu →, Brazil 127 B5
Iguaçu, Cat. del, Brazil 127 B5
Iguaçu Falls = Iguaçu, Cat. del, Brazil 127 B5
Iguala, Mexico 119 D5
Igualada, Spain 38 D6
Iguassu = Iguaçu →, Brazil 127 B5
Iguatu, Brazil 125 E11
Iguazú △, Argentina 127 B5
Iguidi, Erg, Africa 78 C4
Iharana, Madag. 89 A9
Ihbulag, Mongolia 56 C4
Iheya-Shima, Japan 55 L3
Ihiala, Nigeria 83 D6
Ihosy, Madag. 89 C8
Ihotry, Farihy, Madag. 89 C7
Ihugh, Nigeria 83 D6
Ii, Finland 8 D21
Ii-Shima, Japan 55 L3
Iida, Japan 55 G8
Iijoki →, Finland 8 D21
Iisalmi, Finland 8 E22
Iiyama, Japan 55 F9
Iizuka, Japan 55 H5
Ijebu-Igbo, Nigeria 83 D5
Ijebu-Ode, Nigeria 83 D5
IJmuiden, Neths 17 B4
Ijo älv = Iijoki →, Finland 8 D21
IJssel →, Neths. 17 B5
IJsselmeer, Neths. 17 B5
Ijuí, Brazil 127 B5
Ijuí →, Brazil 127 B5
Ikalamavony, Madag. 89 C8
Ikale, Nigeria 83 D6
Ikaluktutiak, Canada 100 B9
Ikang, Nigeria 83 E6
Ikara, Nigeria 83 C6
Ikare, Nigeria 83 D6
Ikaría, Greece 47 D8
Ikast, Denmark 11 H3
Ikeda, Japan 55 G6
Ikeja, Nigeria 83 D5
Ikela, Dem. Rep. of the Congo 84 E4
Ikerre-Ekiti, Nigeria 83 D6
Ikhtiman, Bulgaria 44 D7
Iki, Japan 55 H4
Ikimba L., Tanzania 86 C3
Ikire, Nigeria 83 D5
Ikizdere, Turkey 73 B9
Ikom, Nigeria 83 D6
Ikongo, Madag. 89 C8
Ikopa →, Madag. 89 B8
Ikorongo △, Tanzania 86 C3
Ikot Ekpene, Nigeria 83 D6
Ikparjuk = Arctic Bay, Canada 101 A11
Ikungu, Tanzania 86 C3
Ikurun, Nigeria 83 D5
Ila, Nigeria 83 D5
Ilagan, Phil. 61 C4
Ilaka, Madag. 89 B8
Ilām, Iran 70 C5
Ilam, Nepal 69 F12
Ilam □, Iran 70 C5
Ilan, Taiwan 59 E13
Ilanskiy, Russia 53 D10
Ilaro, Nigeria 83 D5
Ilatane, Niger 83 B5
Iława, Poland 30 E6
Ile →, Kazakhstan 52 E8
Île-à-la-Crosse, Canada 103 B7
Île-à-la-Crosse, Lac, Canada 103 B7
Île-de-France □, France 19 D9
Ileanda, Romania 29 C8
Ilebo, Dem. Rep. of the Congo 84 E4
Ilek, Russia 52 D6
Ilero, Nigeria 83 D5
Ilesha, Kwara, Nigeria 83 D5
Ilesha, Oyo, Nigeria 83 D5
Ilford, Canada 103 B9
Ilfracombe, Australia 94 C3
Ilfracombe, U.K. 15 F3
Ilgaz, Turkey 72 B5
Ilgaz Dağları, Turkey 72 B5
Ilgın, Turkey 72 C4
Ilha de Moçambique, Mozam. 87 F5
Ilhavo, Portugal 36 E2
Ilhéus, Brazil 125 F11
Ili = Ile →, Kazakhstan 52 E8
Ilia, Romania 28 E7
Ilia □, Greece 46 D3
Iliamna L., U.S.A. 100 C4
Iliç, Turkey 73 C8
Ilıca, Turkey 47 B9
Ilichevsk, Azerbaijan 73 C11
Iligan, Phil. 61 G6
Iligan Bay, Phil. 61 G6
Ilíki, L., Greece 46 C5
Ilin I., Phil. 61 E4
Iliodhrómia, Greece 46 B5
Ilion, U.S.A. 117 D9
Ilirska-Bistrica, Slovenia 41 C11
Ilkeston, U.K. 14 E6

Ilkley, U.K. 14 D6
Illampu = Ancohuma, Nevado, Bolivia 124 G5
Illana B., Phil. 61 H5
Illapel, Chile 126 C1
Ille-et-Vilaine □, France 18 D5
Ille-sur-Têt, France 20 F6
Illéla, Niger 83 C6
Iller →, Germany 25 G5
Illertissen, Germany 25 G6
Illescas, Spain 36 E7
Illetas, Spain 48 B9
Illichivsk, Ukraine 33 J6
Illiers-Combray, France 18 D8
Illimani, Nevado, Bolivia 124 G5
Illinois □, U.S.A. 112 E10
Illinois →, U.S.A. 112 F9
Illizi, Algeria 78 C7
Illkirch-Graffenstaden, France 19 D14
Íllora, Spain 37 H7
Ilm →, Germany 24 D7
Ilmajoki, Finland 9 E20
Ilmen, Ozero, Russia 32 C6
Ilmenau, Germany 24 E6
Ilo, Peru 124 G4
Ilobu, Nigeria 83 D5
Iloilo, Phil. 61 F5
Ilora, Nigeria 83 D5
Ilorin, Nigeria 83 D5
Ilovatka, Russia 34 E7
Ilovlya, Russia 35 F7
Ilovlya →, Russia 35 F7
Ilowa, Poland 31 G2
Ilubabor □, Ethiopia 81 F4
Ilva Mică, Romania 29 C9
Ilwaco, U.S.A. 110 D2
Ilwaki, Indonesia 63 F7
Ilyichevsk = Illichivsk, Ukraine 33 J6
Iłża, Poland 31 G8
Iłżanka →, Poland 31 G8
Imabari, Japan 55 G6
Imaloto →, Madag. 89 C8
Imamoğlu, Turkey 72 D6
Imandra, Ozero, Russia 52 C4
Imanombo, Madag. 89 C8
Imari, Japan 55 H4
Imasa, Sudan 80 D4
Imathía □, Greece 44 F6
Imatra, Finland 32 B5
Iménas, Mali 83 B5
imeni 26 Bakinskikh Komissarov = Neftçala, Azerbaijan 71 B6
imeni 26 Bakinskikh Komissarov, Turkmenistan 71 B7
Imeri, Serra, Brazil 124 C5
Imerimandroso, Madag. 89 B8
Imi, Ethiopia 81 F5
Imishly = Imişli, Azerbaijan 35 L9
Imişli, Azerbaijan 35 L9
Imlay, U.S.A. 108 F4
Imlay City, U.S.A. 116 D1
Immaseri, Sudan 81 D2
Immenstadt, Germany 25 H6
Immingham, U.K. 14 D7
Immokalee, U.S.A. 115 M5
Imo □, Nigeria 83 D6
Imo →, Nigeria 83 D6
Ímola, Italy 41 D8
Imotski, Croatia 41 E14
Imperatriz, Brazil 125 E9
Impéria, Italy 40 E5
Imperial, Canada 103 C7
Imperial, Calif., U.S.A. 111 N11
Imperial, Nebr., U.S.A. 112 E4
Imperial Beach, U.S.A. 111 N9
Imperial Dam, U.S.A. 111 N12
Imperial Reservoir, U.S.A. 111 N12
Imperial Valley, U.S.A. 111 N11
Imperieuse Reef, Australia 92 C2
Impfondo, Congo 84 D3
Imphal, India 67 G18
Imphy, France 19 F10
Imranlı, Turkey 73 C8
İmroz = Gökçeada, Turkey 45 F9
Imroz, Turkey 45 F9
Imst, Austria 26 D3
Imuris, Mexico 118 A2
Imuruan B., Phil. 63 B5
In Akhmed, Mali 83 B5
In Aleï, Mali 82 B4
In Delimane, Mali 83 B5
In Guezzam, Algeria 83 B6
In Koufi, Mali 83 B5
In Salah, Algeria 78 C6
In Tallak, Mali 83 B5
In Tebezas, Mali 83 B5
Ina, Japan 55 G8
Inagua △, Bahamas 121 B5
Inangahua, N.Z. 91 J3
Inanwatan, Indonesia 63 E8
Iñapari, Peru 124 F5
Inari, Finland 8 B22
Inarijärvi, Finland 8 B22
Inawashiro-Ko, Japan 54 F10
Inca, Spain 48 B9
Inca de Oro, Chile 126 B2
Incaguasi, Chile 126 B1
Ince Burun, Turkey 72 A6
Incekum Burnu, Turkey 72 D5
Incesu, Turkey 70 B2
Inch'ŏn, S. Korea 57 F14
Incio = Cruz de Incio, Spain 36 C3
Incirliova, Turkey 47 D9
Incline Village, U.S.A. 108 G4
Incomáti →, Mozam. 89 D5
Incudine, Mte., France 21 G13
Inda Silase, Ethiopia 81 E4
Indal, Sweden 10 B11
Indalsälven →, Sweden 10 B11
Indaw, Burma 67 G20

Indbir, Ethiopia 81 F4
Independence, Calif., U.S.A. 110 J8
Independence, Iowa, U.S.A. 112 D9
Independence, Kans., U.S.A. 113 G7
Independence, Ky., U.S.A. 114 F3
Independence, Mo., U.S.A. 112 F7
Independence Fjord, Greenland 4 A6
Independence Mts., U.S.A. 108 F5
Independenţa, Romania 29 E12
Index, U.S.A. 110 C5
India ■, Asia 66 K11
Indian →, U.S.A. 115 M5
Indian Cabins, Canada 102 B5
Indian Harbour, Canada 105 B8
Indian Head, Canada 103 C8
Indian Lake, U.S.A. 117 C10
Indian Ocean 50 K11
Indian Springs, U.S.A. 111 J11
Indiana, U.S.A. 116 F5
Indiana □, U.S.A. 114 F3
Indianapolis, U.S.A. 114 F2
Indianola, Iowa, U.S.A. 112 E8
Indianola, Miss., U.S.A. 113 J9
Indigirka →, Russia 53 B15
Indija, Serbia & M. 28 E5
Indio, U.S.A. 111 M10
Indira Gandhi Canal, India 68 F5
Indo-China, Asia 50 H14
Indonesia ■, Asia 62 F5
Indore, India 68 H6
Indramayu, Indonesia 63 G13
Indravati →, India 67 K12
Indre □, France 19 F8
Indre →, France 18 E7
Indre-et-Loire □, France 18 E7
Indulkana, Australia 95 D1
Indura, Belarus 30 E10
Indus →, Pakistan 68 G2
Indus, Mouths of the, Pakistan 68 H3
Inebolu, Turkey 72 B5
Inecik, Turkey 45 F11
Inegöl, Turkey 45 F13
Ineu, Romania 28 D6
Infantes = Villanueva de los Infantes, Spain 37 G7
Infiernillo, Presa del, Mexico 118 D4
Infiesto, Spain 36 B5
Ingelstad, Sweden 11 H8
Ingenio, Canary Is. 48 G4
Ingenio Santa Ana, Argentina 126 B2
Ingersoll, Canada 116 C4
Ingham, Australia 94 B4
Ingleborough, U.K. 14 C5
Inglewood, Queens., Australia 95 D5
Inglewood, Vic., Australia 95 F3
Inglewood, N.Z. 91 H5
Inglewood, U.S.A. 111 M8
Ingólfshöfði, Iceland 8 E5
Ingolstadt, Germany 25 G7
Ingomar, U.S.A. 108 C10
Ingonish, Canada 105 C7
Ingore, Guinea-Biss. 82 C1
Ingraj Bazar, India 69 G13
Ingrid Christensen Coast, Antarctica 5 C6
Ingul = Inhul →, Ukraine 33 J7
Ingulec = Inhulec, Ukraine 33 J7
Ingulets = Inhulets →, Ukraine 33 J7
Inguri = Enguri →, Georgia 35 J5
Ingushetia □, Russia 35 J7
Ingwavuma, S. Africa 89 D5
Inhaca, Mozam. 89 D5
Inhafenga, Mozam. 89 C5
Inhambane, Mozam. 89 C6
Inhambane □, Mozam. 89 C5
Inhaminga, Mozam. 87 F4
Inharrime, Mozam. 89 C6
Inharrime →, Mozam. 89 C6
Inhisar, Turkey 47 A12
Inhul →, Ukraine 33 J7
Inhulec, Ukraine 33 J7
Inhulets →, Ukraine 33 J7
Iniesta, Spain 39 F3
Ining = Yining, China 52 E9
Inírida →, Colombia 124 C5
Inishbofin, Ireland 12 C1
Inisheer, Ireland 12 C2
Inishfree B., Ireland 12 A3
Inishkea North, Ireland 12 B1
Inishkea South, Ireland 12 B1
Inishmaan, Ireland 12 C2
Inishmore, Ireland 12 C2
Inishowen Pen., Ireland 12 A4
Inishshark, Ireland 12 C1
Inishturk, Ireland 12 C1
Inishvickillane, Ireland 12 D1
Injibara, Ethiopia 81 E4
Injune, Australia 95 D4
Inklin →, Canada 102 B2
Inland Kaikoura Ra., N.Z. 91 J4
Inland Sea = Setonaikai, Japan 55 G6
Inle L., Burma 67 J20
Inlet, U.S.A. 117 C10
Inn →, Austria 26 C6
Innamincka, Australia 95 D3
Inner Hebrides, U.K. 13 E2
Inner Mongolia = Nei Monggol Zizhiqu □, China 56 D7
Inner Sound, U.K. 13 D3
Innerkip, Canada 116 C4
Innetalling I., Canada 104 A4
Innisfail, Australia 94 B4
Innisfail, Canada 102 C6
In'noshima, Japan 55 G6
Innsbruck, Austria 26 D4
Innviertel, Austria 26 C6
Inny →, Ireland 12 C4
Inongo, Dem. Rep. of the Congo 84 E3
Inoucdjouac = Inukjuak, Canada 101 C12
Inowrocław, Poland 31 F5
Inpundong, N. Korea 57 D14

Inscription, C., Australia 93 E1
Insein, Burma 67 L20
Insjön, Sweden 10 D9
Ińsko, Poland 30 E2
Însurăţei, Romania 29 F12
Inta, Russia 52 C6
Intendente Alvear, Argentina 126 D3
Intepe, Turkey 47 A8
Interlaken, Switz. 25 J3
Interlaken, U.S.A. 117 D8
International Falls, U.S.A. 112 A8
Intiyaco, Argentina 126 B3
Întorsura Buzăului, Romania 29 E11
Inukjuak, Canada 101 C12
Inútil, B., Chile 128 G2
Inuvik, Canada 100 B6
Inveraray, U.K. 13 E3
Inverbervie, U.K. 13 E6
Invercargill, N.Z. 91 M2
Inverclyde □, U.K. 13 F4
Inverell, Australia 95 D5
Invergordon, U.K. 13 D4
Inverloch, Australia 95 F4
Invermere, Canada 102 C5
Inverness, Canada 105 C7
Inverness, U.K. 13 D4
Inverness, U.S.A. 115 L4
Inverurie, U.K. 13 D6
Investigator Group, Australia 95 E1
Investigator Str., Australia 95 F2
Inya, Russia 52 D9
Inyanga, Zimbabwe 87 F3
Inyangani, Zimbabwe 87 F3
Inyantue, Zimbabwe 88 B4
Inyo Mts., U.S.A. 110 J9
Inyokern, U.S.A. 111 K9
Inza, Russia 34 D8
Inzhavino, Russia 34 D6
Iō-Jima, Japan 55 J5
Ioánnina, Greece 46 B2
Ioánnina □, Greece 46 B2
Iola, U.S.A. 113 G7
Ion Corvin, Romania 29 F12
Iona, U.K. 13 E2
Ione, U.S.A. 110 G6
Ionia, U.S.A. 114 D3
Ionian Is. = Iónioi Nísoi, Greece 46 C2
Ionian Sea, Medit. S. 6 H9
Iónioi Nísoi, Greece 46 C2
Iónion □, Greece 46 C2
Íos, Greece 47 E7
Iowa □, U.S.A. 112 D8
Iowa →, U.S.A. 112 E9
Iowa City, U.S.A. 112 E9
Iowa Falls, U.S.A. 112 D8
Iowa Park, U.S.A. 113 J5
Ipala, Tanzania 86 C3
Ipameri, Brazil 125 G9
Ipáti, Greece 46 C4
Ipatinga, Brazil 125 G10
Ipatovo, Russia 35 H6
Ipel' →, Europe 27 D11
Ipiales, Colombia 124 C3
Ipin = Yibin, China 58 C5
Ipiros □, Greece 46 B2
Ipixuna, Brazil 124 E4
Ipoh, Malaysia 65 K3
Ippy, C.A.R. 84 C4
Ipsala, Turkey 45 F10
Ipsárion, Óros, Greece 45 F8
Ipswich, Australia 95 D5
Ipswich, U.K. 15 E9
Ipswich, Mass., U.S.A. 117 D14
Ipswich, S. Dak., U.S.A. 112 C5
Ipu, Brazil 125 D10
Iqaluit, Canada 101 B13
Iquique, Chile 124 H4
Iquitos, Peru 124 D4
Irabu-Jima, Japan 55 M2
Iracoubo, Fr. Guiana 125 B8
Irafshān, Iran 71 E9
Irahuan, Phil. 61 G3
Irai, Brazil 127 B5
Iran ■, Asia 71 C7
Iran, Gunung-Gunung, Malaysia 62 D4
Iran, Plateau of, Asia 50 F9
Iran Ra. = Iran, Gunung-Gunung, Malaysia 62 D4
Īrānshahr, Iran 71 E9
Irapuato, Mexico 118 C4
Iraq ■, Asia 70 C5
Irati, Brazil 127 B5
Irbes saurums, Latvia 30 A9
Irbid, Jordan 74 C4
Irbid □, Jordan 74 C5
Iregua →, Spain 38 C7
Ireland ■, Europe 12 C4
Irele, Nigeria 83 D6
Irgiz, Bolshaya →, Russia 34 D9
Irhyangdong, N. Korea 57 D15
Iri, S. Korea 57 G14
Irian Jaya = Papua □, Indonesia 63 E9
Irié, Guinea 82 D3
Iriga, Phil. 61 E5
Iringa, Tanzania 86 D4
Iringa □, Tanzania 86 D4
Iriomote-Jima, Japan 55 M1
Iriona, Honduras 120 C2
Iriri →, Brazil 125 D8
Irish Republic ■, Europe 12 C4
Irish Sea, Europe 14 D3
Irkutsk, Russia 53 D11
Irlığanlı, Turkey 47 D11
Irma, Canada 103 C6
Iroise, Mer d', France 18 D2
Iron Baron, Australia 95 E2

Iron Gate = Portile de Fier, Europe 28 F7
Iron Knob, Australia 95 E2
Iron Mountain, U.S.A. 114 C1
Iron Range △, Australia 94 A3
Iron River, U.S.A. 112 B10
Irondequoit, U.S.A. 116 C7
Ironton, Mo., U.S.A. 113 G9
Ironton, Ohio, U.S.A. 114 F4
Ironwood, U.S.A. 112 B9
Ironwood Forest △, U.S.A. 109 K8
Iroquois, Canada 117 B9
Iroquois Falls, Canada 104 C3
Irosin, Phil. 61 E6
Irpin, Ukraine 33 G6
Irrara Cr. →, Australia 95 D4
Irrawaddy □, Burma 67 L19
Irrawaddy →, Burma 67 M19
Irrawaddy, Mouths of the, Burma 67 M19
Irricana, Canada 102 C6
Irshava, Ukraine 28 B8
Irsina, Italy 43 B9
Irtysh →, Russia 52 C7
Irumu, Dem. Rep. of the Congo 86 B2
Irún, Spain 38 B3
Irunea = Pamplona, Spain 38 C3
Irurzun, Spain 38 C3
Irvine, U.K. 13 F4
Irvine, Calif., U.S.A. 111 M9
Irvine, Ky., U.S.A. 114 G4
Irvinestown, U.K. 12 B4
Irving, U.S.A. 113 J6
Irvona, U.S.A. 116 F6
Irwin →, Australia 93 E1
Irymple, Australia 95 E3
Is, Jebel, Sudan 80 C4
Is-sur-Tille, France 19 E12
Isa, Nigeria 83 C6
Isa Khel, Pakistan 68 C4
Isaac →, Australia 94 C4
Isabel, U.S.A. 112 C4
Isabela, Phil. 61 H5
Isabela, Puerto Rico .... 121 d
Isabela, I., Mexico 118 C3
Isabela, Cord., Nic. 120 D2
Isabella Ra., Australia 92 D3
Isaccea, Romania 29 E13
Ísafjarðardjúp, Iceland 8 C2
Ísafjörður, Iceland 8 C2
Isagarh, India 68 G7
Isahaya, Japan 55 H5
Isaka, Tanzania 86 C3
Işalnița, Romania 29 F8
Isalo △, Madag. 89 C8
Isan →, India 69 F9
Isana = Içana →, Brazil 124 C5
Isangano △, Zambia 87 E3
Isanlu Makutu, Nigeria 83 D6
Isar →, Germany 25 G8
Ísari, Greece 46 D3
Isarco →, Italy 41 B8
Íscar, Spain 36 D6
Íschehisar, Turkey 47 C12
Íschia, Italy 42 B6
Isdell →, Australia 92 C3
Ise, Japan 55 G8
Ise-Shima △, Japan 55 G8
Ise-Wan, Japan 55 G8
Isefjord, Denmark 11 J5
Isel →, Austria 26 E5
Iseo, Italy 40 C7
Iseo, L. d', Italy 40 C7
Iseramagazi, Tanzania 86 C3
Isère □, France 21 C9
Isère →, France 21 D8
Iserlohn, Germany 24 D3
Isérnia, Italy 43 A7
Iseyin, Nigeria 83 D5
Isfahan = Eşfahān, Iran 71 C6
Ishëm, Albania 44 E3
Ishigaki-Shima, Japan 55 M2
Ishikari-Gawa →, Japan 54 C10
Ishikari-Sammyaku, Japan 54 C11
Ishikari-Wan, Japan 54 C10
Ishikawa □, Japan 55 F8
Ishim, Russia 52 D7
Ishim →, Russia 52 D8
Ishinomaki, Japan 54 E10
Ishioka, Japan 55 F10
Ishkuman, Pakistan 69 A5
Ishpeming, U.S.A. 114 B2
Isigny-sur-Mer, France 18 C5
Isıklı, Turkey 47 C11
Isıklı Dağı, Turkey 45 F11
Isil Kul, Russia 52 D8
Ísili, Italy 42 C2
Isiolo, Kenya 86 B4
Isiro, Dem. Rep. of the Congo 86 B2
Isisford, Australia 94 C3
Iskenderun, Turkey 70 B3
İskenderun Körfezi, Turkey 72 D6
İskilip, Turkey 72 B6
Iskŭr →, Bulgaria 45 C8
Iskŭr, Yazovir, Bulgaria 45 C8
Iskut →, Canada 102 B2
Isla →, U.K. 13 E5
Isla Coiba △, Panama 120 E3
Isla Cristina, Spain 37 H3
Isla de Salamanca △, Colombia 121 D5
Isla Gorge △, Australia 94 D4
Isla Tiburón y San Esteban △, Mexico 118 B2
Isla Vista, U.S.A. 111 L7
İslâhiye, Turkey 72 D7
Islam Headworks, Pakistan 68 E5
Islamabad, Pakistan 68 C5
Islamgarh, Pakistan 68 F4
Islamkot, Pakistan 68 G4
Islampur, India 69 G11
Island L., Canada 103 C10
Island Lagoon, Australia 95 E2
Island Pond, U.S.A. 117 B13

Islands, B. of, *Canada* ... 105 C8
Islands, B. of, *N.Z.* ... 91 F5
Islay, *U.K.* ... 13 F2
Isle →, *France* ... 20 D3
Isle aux Morts, *Canada* ... 105 C8
Isle of Wight □, *U.K.* ... 15 G6
Isle Royale △, *U.S.A.* ... 114 B1
Isleton, *U.S.A.* ... 110 G5
Ismail = Izmayil, *Ukraine* ... 29 E13
Ismâ'ilîya, *Egypt* ... 80 H8
Ismaning, *Germany* ... 25 G7
Isna, *Egypt* ... 80 B3
Isoanala, *Madag.* ... 89 C8
Isogstalo, *India* ... 69 B8
Ísola del Liri, *Italy* ... 41 G10
Ísola della Scala, *Italy* ... 40 C7
Ísola di Capo Rizzuto, *Italy* ... 43 D10
Isparta, *Turkey* ... 47 D12
Isperikh, *Bulgaria* ... 45 C10
Íspica, *Italy* ... 43 F7
Israel ■, *Asia* ... 74 D3
Isratu, *Eritrea* ... 81 D4
Issakly, *Russia* ... 34 C10
Issia, *Ivory C.* ... 82 D3
Issoire, *France* ... 20 C7
Issoudun, *France* ... 19 F8
Issyk-Kul, Ozero = Ysyk-Köl, *Kyrgyzstan* ... 52 E8
Ist, *Croatia* ... 41 D11
Istállós-kő, *Hungary* ... 28 B5
Istanbul, *Turkey* ... 45 E12
Istanbul □, *Turkey* ... 45 E12
Istanbul ✈ (IST), *Turkey* ... 45 F12
Istanbul Boğazı, *Turkey* ... 45 E13
Istiaía, *Greece* ... 46 C5
Istok, *Serbia & M.* ... 44 D4
Istokpoga, L., *U.S.A.* ... 115 M5
Istra, *Croatia* ... 41 C10
Istres, *France* ... 21 E8
Istria = Istra, *Croatia* ... 41 C10
Itá, *Paraguay* ... 126 B4
Itaberaba, *Brazil* ... 125 F10
Itabira, *Brazil* ... 125 G10
Itabirito, *Brazil* ... 127 A7
Itabuna, *Brazil* ... 125 F11
Itacaunas →, *Brazil* ... 125 E9
Itacoatiara, *Brazil* ... 124 D7
Itaipú, Reprêsa de, *Brazil* ... 127 B5
Itaituba, *Brazil* ... 125 D7
Itajaí, *Brazil* ... 127 B6
Itajubá, *Brazil* ... 127 A6
Itaka, *Tanzania* ... 87 D3
Itala →, *S. Africa* ... 89 D5
Italy ■, *Europe* ... 7 G8
Itamaraju, *Brazil* ... 125 G11
Itampolo, *Madag.* ... 89 C7
Itandrano, *Madag.* ... 89 C8
Itapecuru-Mirim, *Brazil* ... 125 D10
Itaperuna, *Brazil* ... 127 A7
Itapetininga, *Brazil* ... 127 A6
Itapeva, *Brazil* ... 127 A6
Itapicuru →, *Bahia, Brazil* ... 125 F11
Itapicuru →, *Maranhão, Brazil* ... 125 D10
Itapipoca, *Brazil* ... 125 D11
Itapuá □, *Paraguay* ... 127 B4
Itaquari, *Brazil* ... 127 A7
Itaquí, *Brazil* ... 126 B4
Itararé, *Brazil* ... 127 A6
Itatí, *Argentina* ... 126 B4
Itatiaia △, *Brazil* ... 127 A7
Itbayat, *Phil.* ... 61 A4
Itchen →, *U.K.* ... 15 G6
Itéa, *Greece* ... 46 C4
Itezhi Tezhi, L., *Zambia* ... 87 F2
Ithaca = Itháki, *Greece* ... 46 C2
Ithaca, *U.S.A.* ... 117 D8
Itháki, *Greece* ... 46 C2
Íti △, *Greece* ... 46 C4
Itiquira →, *Brazil* ... 125 G7
Itō, *Japan* ... 55 G9
Itoigawa, *Japan* ... 55 F8
Iton →, *France* ... 18 C8
Itonamas →, *Bolivia* ... 124 F6
Itri, *Italy* ... 42 A6
Itsa, *Egypt* ... 80 J7
Íttiri, *Italy* ... 42 B1
Ittoqqortoormiit, *Greenland* ... 4 B6
Itu, *Brazil* ... 127 A6
Itu, *Nigeria* ... 83 D6
Itu Aba I., *S. China Sea* ... 62 B4
Ituiutaba, *Brazil* ... 125 G9
Itumbiara, *Brazil* ... 125 G9
Ituna, *Canada* ... 103 C8
Itunge Port, *Tanzania* ... 87 D3
Iturbe, *Argentina* ... 126 A2
Ituri →, *Dem. Rep. of the Congo* ... 86 B2
Iturup, Ostrov, *Russia* ... 53 E15
Ituxi →, *Brazil* ... 124 E6
Ituyuro →, *Argentina* ... 126 A3
Itzehoe, *Germany* ... 24 B5
Ivahona, *Madag.* ... 89 C8
Ivaí →, *Brazil* ... 127 A5
Ivalo, *Finland* ... 8 B22
Ivalojoki →, *Finland* ... 8 B22
Ivanava, *Belarus* ... 33 F3
Ivančice, *Czech Rep.* ... 27 B9
Ivăneşti, *Romania* ... 29 D12
Ivangorod, *Russia* ... 32 C5
Ivanhoe, *Australia* ... 95 E3
Ivanhoe, *Calif., U.S.A.* ... 110 J7
Ivanhoe, *Minn., U.S.A.* ... 112 C6
Ivanhorod, *Ukraine* ... 29 B14
Ivanić Grad, *Croatia* ... 41 C13
Ivanjica, *Serbia & M.* ... 44 C4
Ivanjska, *Bos.-H.* ... 28 F2
Ivankoyskoye Vdkhr., *Russia* ... 32 D9
Ivano-Frankivsk, *Ukraine* ... 29 B9
Ivano-Frankovsk = Ivano-Frankivsk, *Ukraine* ... 29 B9
Ivanovo, *Russia* ... 32 D11

Ivanšćica, *Croatia* ... 41 B13
Ivato, *Madag.* ... 89 C8
Ivatsevichy, *Belarus* ... 33 F3
Ivaylovgrad, *Bulgaria* ... 45 E10
Ivinheima →, *Brazil* ... 127 A5
Ivinhema, *Brazil* ... 127 A5
Ivohibe, *Madag.* ... 89 C8
Ivory Coast, *W. Afr.* ... 82 E4
Ivory Coast ■, *Africa* ... 82 D4
Ivösjön, *Sweden* ... 11 H8
Ivrea, *Italy* ... 40 C4
Ivrindi, *Turkey* ... 47 B9
Ivujivik, *Canada* ... 101 B12
Ivybridge, *U.K.* ... 15 G4
Iwaizumi, *Japan* ... 54 E10
Iwaki, *Japan* ... 55 F10
Iwakuni, *Japan* ... 55 G6
Iwamizawa, *Japan* ... 54 C10
Iwanai, *Japan* ... 54 C10
Iwata, *Japan* ... 55 G8
Iwate □, *Japan* ... 54 E10
Iwate-San, *Japan* ... 54 E10
Iwo, *Nigeria* ... 83 D5
Iwonicz-Zdrój, *Poland* ... 31 J8
Ixiamas, *Bolivia* ... 124 F5
Ixopo, *S. Africa* ... 89 E5
Ixtepec, *Mexico* ... 119 D5
Ixtlán del Río, *Mexico* ... 118 C4
Iyal Bakhit, *Sudan* ... 81 E2
Iyo, *Japan* ... 55 H6
Izabal, L. de, *Guatemala* ... 120 C2
Izamal, *Mexico* ... 119 C7
Izberbash, *Russia* ... 35 J8
Izbica, *Poland* ... 31 H10
Izbica Kujawska, *Poland* ... 31 F5
Izbiceni, *Romania* ... 29 G9
Izena-Shima, *Japan* ... 55 L3
Izgrev, *Bulgaria* ... 45 C10
Izhevsk, *Russia* ... 52 D6
Izmayil, *Ukraine* ... 29 E13
Izmir, *Turkey* ... 47 C9
Izmir □, *Turkey* ... 47 C9
Izmir Adnan Menderes ✈ (ADB), *Turkey* ... 47 C9
Izmir Körfezi, *Turkey* ... 47 C8
Izmit = Kocaeli, *Turkey* ... 45 F13
Iznájar, *Spain* ... 37 H6
Iznalloz, *Spain* ... 37 H7
Iznik, *Turkey* ... 72 B3
Iznik Gölü, *Turkey* ... 45 F13
Izobil'nyy, *Russia* ... 35 H5
Izola, *Slovenia* ... 41 C10
Izra, *Syria* ... 74 C5
Iztochni Rodopi, *Bulgaria* ... 45 E9
Izu-Shotō, *Japan* ... 55 G10
Izúcar de Matamoros, *Mexico* ... 119 D5
Izumi-Sano, *Japan* ... 55 G7
Izumo, *Japan* ... 55 G6
Izyaslav, *Ukraine* ... 33 G4
Izyum, *Ukraine* ... 33 H9

J

Jaba, *Ethiopia* ... 81 F4
Jabal at Ta'ir, *Red Sea* ... 81 D5
Jabalón →, *Spain* ... 37 G6
Jabalpur, *India* ... 69 H8
Jabbūl, *Syria* ... 70 B3
Jabiru, *Australia* ... 92 B5
Jablah, *Syria* ... 70 C3
Jablanac, *Croatia* ... 41 D11
Jablanica, *Bos.-H.* ... 28 G2
Jablonec nad Nisou, *Czech Rep.* ... 26 A8
Jablonica, *Slovak Rep.* ... 27 C10
Jabłonowo Pomorskie, *Poland* ... 30 E6
Jablunkov, *Czech Rep.* ... 27 B11
Jaboatão, *Brazil* ... 125 E11
Jaboticabal, *Brazil* ... 127 A6
Jabukovac, *Serbia & M.* ... 44 B6
Jaca, *Spain* ... 38 C4
Jacareí, *Brazil* ... 127 A6
Jacarèzinho, *Brazil* ... 127 A6
Jackman, *U.S.A.* ... 115 C10
Jacksboro, *U.S.A.* ... 113 J5
Jackson, *Barbados* ... 121 g
Jackson, *Ala., U.S.A.* ... 115 K2
Jackson, *Calif., U.S.A.* ... 110 G6
Jackson, *Ky., U.S.A.* ... 114 G4
Jackson, *Mich., U.S.A.* ... 114 D3
Jackson, *Minn., U.S.A.* ... 112 D7
Jackson, *Miss., U.S.A.* ... 113 J9
Jackson, *Mo., U.S.A.* ... 113 G10
Jackson, *N.H., U.S.A.* ... 117 B13
Jackson, *Ohio, U.S.A.* ... 114 F4
Jackson, *Tenn., U.S.A.* ... 115 H1
Jackson, *Wyo., U.S.A.* ... 108 E8
Jackson B., *N.Z.* ... 91 K2
Jackson L., *U.S.A.* ... 108 E8
Jacksons, *N.Z.* ... 91 K3
Jackson's Arm, *Canada* ... 105 C8
Jacksonville, *Ala., U.S.A.* ... 115 J3
Jacksonville, *Ark., U.S.A.* ... 113 H8
Jacksonville, *Calif., U.S.A.* ... 110 H6
Jacksonville, *Fla., U.S.A.* ... 115 K5
Jacksonville, *Ill., U.S.A.* ... 112 F9
Jacksonville, *N.C., U.S.A.* ... 115 H7
Jacksonville, *Tex., U.S.A.* ... 113 K7
Jacksonville Beach, *U.S.A.* ... 115 K5
Jacmel, *Haiti* ... 121 C5
Jacob Lake, *U.S.A.* ... 109 H7
Jacobabad, *Pakistan* ... 68 E3
Jacobina, *Brazil* ... 125 F10
Jacques-Cartier →, *Canada* ... 105 C5
Jacques-Cartier, Dét. de, *Canada* ... 105 C7
Jacques-Cartier, Mt., *Canada* ... 105 C6
Jacuí →, *Ivory C.* ... 82 D4
Jacuí →, *Brazil* ... 127 C5
Jacumba, *U.S.A.* ... 111 N10

Jacundá →, *Brazil* ... 125 D8
Jade, *Germany* ... 24 B4
Jadebusen, *Germany* ... 24 B4
Jadovnik, *Serbia & M.* ... 44 C3
Jadraque, *Spain* ... 38 E2
Jaén, *Peru* ... 124 E3
Jaén, *Spain* ... 37 H7
Jaén □, *Spain* ... 37 H7
Jafarabad, *India* ... 68 J4
Jaffa = Tel Aviv-Yafo, *Israel* ... 74 C3
Jaffa, C., *Australia* ... 95 F2
Jaffna, *Sri Lanka* ... 66 Q12
Jaffray, *Canada* ... 103 D10
Jaffrey, *U.S.A.* ... 117 D12
Jagadhri, *India* ... 68 G7
Jagadishpur, *India* ... 69 G11
Jagdalpur, *India* ... 67 K13
Jagersfontein, *S. Africa* ... 88 D4
Jaghīn →, *Iran* ... 71 E8
Jagodina, *Serbia & M.* ... 44 B5
Jagraon, *India* ... 66 D9
Jagst →, *Germany* ... 25 F5
Jagtial, *India* ... 66 K11
Jaguariaíva, *Brazil* ... 127 A6
Jaguaribe →, *Brazil* ... 125 D11
Jaguey Grande, *Cuba* ... 120 B3
Jahanabad, *India* ... 69 G11
Jahazpur, *India* ... 68 G6
Jaijon, *India* ... 68 D7
Jailolo, *Indonesia* ... 63 D7
Jailolo, Selat, *Indonesia* ... 63 D7
Jaipur, *India* ... 68 F6
Jais, *India* ... 69 F9
Jaisalmer, *India* ... 68 F4
Jaisinghnagar, *India* ... 69 H8
Jaitaran, *India* ... 68 F5
Jaithari, *India* ... 69 H8
Jājarm, *Iran* ... 71 B8
Jajce, *Bos.-H.* ... 28 F2
Jakam →, *India* ... 68 H6
Jakarta, *Indonesia* ... 63 G12
Jakhal, *India* ... 68 E6
Jakhau, *India* ... 68 H3
Jakobstad = Pietarsaari, *Finland* ... 8 E20
Jakupica, *Macedonia* ... 44 E5
Jal, *U.S.A.* ... 113 J3
Jalālābād, *Afghan.* ... 68 B4
Jalalabad, *India* ... 69 F8
Jalalpur Jattan, *Pakistan* ... 68 C6
Jalama, *Sudan* ... 81 F3
Jalapa, *Guatemala* ... 120 D2
Jalapa Enríquez = Xalapa, *Mexico* ... 119 D5
Jalasjärvi, *Finland* ... 9 E20
Jalaun, *India* ... 69 F8
Jaldhaka →, *Bangla.* ... 69 F13
Jalesar, *India* ... 68 F8
Jaleswar, *Nepal* ... 69 F11
Jalgaon, *India* ... 66 J9
Jalībah, *Iraq* ... 70 D5
Jalingo, *Nigeria* ... 83 D7
Jalisco □, *Mexico* ... 118 D4
Jalkot, *Pakistan* ... 69 B5
Jallas →, *Spain* ... 36 C1
Jalna, *India* ... 66 K9
Jalón →, *Spain* ... 38 D3
Jalor, *India* ... 68 G5
Jalpa, *Mexico* ... 118 C4
Jalpaiguri, *India* ... 67 F16
Jaluit I., *Marshall Is.* ... 96 G8
Jalūlā, *Iraq* ... 70 C5
Jamaari, *Nigeria* ... 83 C6
Jamaica ■, *W. Indies* ... 120 a
Jamalpur, *Bangla.* ... 67 G16
Jamalpur, *India* ... 69 G12
Jamalpurganj, *India* ... 69 H13
Jamanxim →, *Brazil* ... 125 D7
Jambewangi, *Indonesia* ... 63 J17
Jambi, *Indonesia* ... 62 E2
Jambi □, *Indonesia* ... 62 E2
Jambusar, *India* ... 68 H5
James →, *S. Dak., U.S.A.* ... 112 D6
James →, *Va., U.S.A.* ... 114 G7
James B., *Canada* ... 104 B3
James Ranges, *Australia* ... 92 D5
James Ross I., *Antarctica* ... 5 C18
Jamesabad, *Pakistan* ... 68 G3
Jamestown, *Australia* ... 95 E2
Jamestown, *S. Africa* ... 88 E4
Jamestown, *N. Dak., U.S.A.* ... 112 B5
Jamestown, *N.Y., U.S.A.* ... 116 D5
Jamestown, *Pa., U.S.A.* ... 116 E4
Jamīlābād, *Iran* ... 71 C6
Jamiltepec, *Mexico* ... 119 D5
Jamira →, *India* ... 69 J13
Jamkhandi, *India* ... 66 L9
Jammerbugt, *Denmark* ... 11 G3
Jammu, *India* ... 68 C6
Jammu & Kashmir □, *India* ... 69 B7
Jamnagar, *India* ... 68 H4
Jamni →, *India* ... 69 G8
Jampur, *Pakistan* ... 68 E4
Jamrud, *Pakistan* ... 68 C4
Jämsä, *Finland* ... 9 F21
Jamshedpur, *India* ... 69 H12
Jamtara, *India* ... 69 H12
Jämtland, *Sweden* ... 8 E15
Jämtlands län □, *Sweden* ... 10 B7
Jan L., *Canada* ... 103 C8
Jan Mayen, *Arctic* ... 4 B7
Janakkala, *Finland* ... 9 F21
Janaúba, *Brazil* ... 125 G10
Jand, *Pakistan* ... 68 C5
Jandaq, *Iran* ... 71 C7
Jandía, *Canary Is.* ... 48 F5
Jandía △, *Canary Is.* ... 48 F5
Jandía, Pta. de, *Canary Is.* ... 48 F5
Jandola, *Pakistan* ... 68 C4
Jandowae, *Australia* ... 95 D5
Jándula →, *Spain* ... 37 G6
Janesville, *U.S.A.* ... 112 D10

Janga, *Ghana* ... 83 C4
Jangamo, *Mozam.* ... 89 C6
Janghai, *India* ... 69 G10
Janikowo, *Poland* ... 31 F5
Janin = Ioánnina □, *Greece* ... 46 B2
Janja, *Bos.-H.* ... 28 F4
Janjanbureh, *Gambia* ... 82 C2
Janjgir, *India* ... 69 J10
Janjina, *Croatia* ... 41 F14
Janjina, *Madag.* ... 89 C8
Janos, *Mexico* ... 118 A3
Jánoshalma, *Hungary* ... 28 D4
Jánosháza, *Hungary* ... 28 C2
Jánossomorja, *Hungary* ... 28 C2
Janów, *Poland* ... 31 H6
Janów Lubelski, *Poland* ... 31 H9
Janów Podlaski, *Poland* ... 31 F10
Janowiec Wielkopolski, *Poland* ... 31 F4
Januária, *Brazil* ... 125 G10
Janub □, *Sudan* ... 81 F2
Janub Dârfûr □, *Sudan* ... 81 E2
Janub Kordofân □, *Sudan* ... 81 E3
Janūb Sīnī □, *Egypt* ... 74 F2
Janubio, *Canary Is.* ... 48 F6
Janville, *France* ... 19 D8
Janzé, *France* ... 18 E5
Jaora, *India* ... 68 H6
Japan ■, *Asia* ... 55 G8
Japan, Sea of, *Asia* ... 54 E7
Japan Trench, *Pac. Oc.* ... 96 D6
Japen = Yapen, *Indonesia* ... 63 E9
Japla, *India* ... 69 G11
Japurá →, *Brazil* ... 124 D5
Jaquarão, *Brazil* ... 127 C5
Jaqué, *Panama* ... 120 E4
Jarābulus, *Syria* ... 70 B3
Jaraicejo, *Spain* ... 37 F5
Jaraíz de la Vera, *Spain* ... 36 E5
Jarama →, *Spain* ... 36 E7
Jaramānah, *Syria* ... 72 F7
Jarandilla, *Spain* ... 36 E5
Jaranwala, *Pakistan* ... 68 D5
Jarash, *Jordan* ... 74 C4
Jarash □, *Jordan* ... 74 C4
Jardim, *Brazil* ... 126 A4
Jardín →, *Spain* ... 39 G2
Jardine River △, *Australia* ... 94 A3
Jardines de la Reina, Arch. de los, *Cuba* ... 120 B4
Jargalang, *China* ... 57 C12
Jari →, *Brazil* ... 125 D8
Jarīr, W. al →, *Si. Arabia* ... 70 E4
Jārlāsa, *Sweden* ... 10 E11
Jarmen, *Germany* ... 24 B9
Järna, *Dalarna, Sweden* ... 10 D8
Järna, *Stockholm, Sweden* ... 10 E11
Jarnac, *France* ... 20 C3
Jarocin, *Poland* ... 31 G4
Jaroměř, *Czech Rep.* ... 26 A8
Jarosław, *Poland* ... 31 H9
Järpås, *Sweden* ... 11 F6
Järpen, *Sweden* ... 10 A7
Jarrahdale, *Australia* ... 93 F2
Jarrahi →, *Iran* ... 71 D6
Jarres, Plaine des, *Laos* ... 64 C4
Jarso, *Ethiopia* ... 81 F4
Jartai, *China* ... 56 E3
Jarud Qi, *China* ... 57 B11
Jarvis, *Canada* ... 116 D4
Jarvis I., *Pac. Oc.* ... 97 H12
Jarvorník, *Czech Rep.* ... 27 A10
Järvsö, *Sweden* ... 10 C10
Jarwa, *India* ... 69 F10
Jaša Tomić, *Serbia & M.* ... 28 E5
Jasdan, *India* ... 68 H4
Jashpurnagar, *India* ... 69 H11
Jasidih, *India* ... 69 G12
Jasień, *Poland* ... 31 G2
Jāsimīyah, *Iraq* ... 70 C5
Jasin, *Malaysia* ... 65 L4
Jāsk, *Iran* ... 71 E8
Jasło, *Poland* ... 31 J8
Jasmund △, *Germany* ... 24 A9
Jaso, *India* ... 69 G9
Jasper, *Alta., Canada* ... 102 C5
Jasper, *Ont., Canada* ... 117 B9
Jasper, *Ala., U.S.A.* ... 115 J2
Jasper, *Fla., U.S.A.* ... 115 K4
Jasper, *Ind., U.S.A.* ... 114 F2
Jasper, *Tex., U.S.A.* ... 113 K8
Jasper △, *Canada* ... 102 C5
Jasrasar, *India* ... 68 F5
Jastarnia, *Poland* ... 30 D5
Jastrebarsko, *Croatia* ... 41 C12
Jastrowie, *Poland* ... 30 E3
Jastrzębie Zdrój, *Poland* ... 31 J5
Jász-Nagykun-Szolnok □, *Hungary* ... 28 C5
Jászapáti, *Hungary* ... 28 C5
Jászárokszállás, *Hungary* ... 28 C4
Jászberény, *Hungary* ... 28 C4
Jászkisér, *Hungary* ... 28 C5
Jászladány, *Hungary* ... 28 C5
Jataí, *Brazil* ... 125 G8
Jati, *Pakistan* ... 68 G3
Jatibarang, *Indonesia* ... 63 G13
Jatiluwih, *Indonesia* ... 63 J18
Jatinegara, *Indonesia* ... 63 G12
Játiva = Xàtiva, *Spain* ... 39 G4
Jaú, *Brazil* ... 127 A6
Jauja, *Peru* ... 124 F3
Jaunpur, *India* ... 69 G10
Java = Jawa, *Indonesia* ... 62 F3
Java Sea, *Indonesia* ... 62 F3
Java Trench, *Ind. Oc.* ... 62 F3
Javalambre, Sa. de, *Spain* ... 38 E4

Jávea, *Spain* ... 39 G5
Jawa, *Indonesia* ... 62 F3
Jawa Barat □, *Indonesia* ... 63 G12
Jawa Tengah □, *Indonesia* ... 63 G14
Jawa Timur □, *Indonesia* ... 63 G15
Jawad, *India* ... 68 G6
Jawor, *Poland* ... 31 G3
Jaworzno, *Poland* ... 31 H6
Jaworzyna Śląska, *Poland* ... 31 H3
Jay Peak, *U.S.A.* ... 117 B12
Jaya, Puncak, *Indonesia* ... 63 E9
Jayanti, *India* ... 67 F16
Jayapura, *Indonesia* ... 63 E10
Jayawijaya, Pegunungan, *Indonesia* ... 63 E9
Jaynagar, *India* ... 67 F15
Jayrūd, *Syria* ... 70 C3
Jayton, *U.S.A.* ... 113 J4
Jāz Mūrīān, Hāmūn-e, *Iran* ... 71 E8
Jazminal, *Mexico* ... 118 C4
Jazzīn, *Lebanon* ... 74 B4
Jean, *U.S.A.* ... 111 K11
Jean Marie River, *Canada* ... 102 A4
Jean-Rabel, *Haiti* ... 121 C5
Jeanette, Ostrov = Zhannetty, Ostrov, *Russia* ... 53 B16
Jeannette, *U.S.A.* ... 116 F5
Jebāl Bārez, Kūh-e, *Iran* ... 71 D8
Jebba, *Nigeria* ... 83 D5
Jebel, Bahr el →, *Sudan* ... 81 F3
Jebel Dud, *Sudan* ... 81 E3
Jebel Qerri, *Sudan* ... 81 D3
Jedburgh, *U.K.* ... 13 F6
Jedda = Jiddah, *Si. Arabia* ... 75 C2
Jeddore L., *Canada* ... 105 C8
Jedlicze, *Poland* ... 31 J8
Jędrzejów, *Poland* ... 31 H7
Jedwabne, *Poland* ... 31 E9
Jeetzel →, *Germany* ... 24 B7
Jefferson, *Iowa, U.S.A.* ... 112 D7
Jefferson, *Ohio, U.S.A.* ... 116 E4
Jefferson, *Tex., U.S.A.* ... 113 J7
Jefferson, Mt., *Nev., U.S.A.* ... 108 G5
Jefferson, Mt., *Oreg., U.S.A.* ... 108 D3
Jefferson City, *Mo., U.S.A.* ... 112 F8
Jefferson City, *Tenn., U.S.A.* ... 115 G4
Jeffersontown, *U.S.A.* ... 114 F3
Jeffersonville, *U.S.A.* ... 114 F3
Jeffrey City, *U.S.A.* ... 108 E10
Jega, *Nigeria* ... 83 C5
Jeju = Cheju do, *S. Korea* ... 57 H14
Jēkabpils, *Latvia* ... 9 H21
Jekyll I., *U.S.A.* ... 115 K5
Jelcz-Laskowice, *Poland* ... 31 G4
Jelenia Góra, *Poland* ... 31 H2
Jelgava, *Latvia* ... 9 H20
Jelgava □, *Latvia* ... 30 B10
Jelica, *Serbia & M.* ... 44 C4
Jelli, *Sudan* ... 81 F3
Jelšava, *Slovak Rep.* ... 27 C13
Jemaja, *Indonesia* ... 65 L5
Jemaluang, *Malaysia* ... 65 L4
Jember, *Indonesia* ... 63 H15
Jembongan, *Malaysia* ... 62 C5
Jena, *Germany* ... 24 E7
Jena, *U.S.A.* ... 113 K8
Jenbach, *Austria* ... 26 D4
Jenīn, *West Bank* ... 74 C4
Jenkins, *U.S.A.* ... 114 G4
Jenner, *U.S.A.* ... 110 G3
Jennings, *U.S.A.* ... 113 K8
Jepara, *Indonesia* ... 63 G14
Jeparit, *Australia* ... 95 F3
Jequié, *Brazil* ... 125 F10
Jequitinhonha, *Brazil* ... 125 G10
Jequitinhonha →, *Brazil* ... 125 G11
Jerantut, *Malaysia* ... 65 L4
Jerejak, Pulau, *Malaysia* ... 65 c
Jérémie, *Haiti* ... 121 C5
Jerez, Punta, *Mexico* ... 119 C5
Jerez de García Salinas, *Mexico* ... 118 C4
Jerez de la Frontera, *Spain* ... 37 J4
Jerez de los Caballeros, *Spain* ... 37 G4
Jericho = El Arīḥā, *West Bank* ... 74 D4
Jericho, *Australia* ... 94 C4
Jerichow, *Germany* ... 24 C8
Jerid, Chott el = Djerid, Chott, *Tunisia* ... 78 B7
Jerilderie, *Australia* ... 95 F4
Jermyn, *U.S.A.* ... 117 E9
Jerome, *U.S.A.* ... 108 E6
Jerramungup, *Australia* ... 93 F2
Jersey, *U.K.* ... 15 H5
Jersey City, *U.S.A.* ... 117 F10
Jersey Shore, *U.S.A.* ... 116 E7
Jerseyville, *U.S.A.* ... 112 F9
Jerusalem, *Israel* ... 74 D4
Jervis B., *Australia* ... 95 F5
Jervis Inlet, *Canada* ... 102 C4
Jerzu, *Italy* ... 42 C2
Jesenice, *Slovenia* ... 41 B11
Jeseník, *Czech Rep.* ... 27 A10
Jesenké, *Slovak Rep.* ... 27 C13
Jesi = Iesi, *Italy* ... 41 E10
Jessnitz, *Germany* ... 24 D8
Jessore, *Bangla.* ... 67 H16
Jesup, *U.S.A.* ... 115 K5
Jesús Carranza, *Mexico* ... 119 D5
Jesús María, *Argentina* ... 126 C3
Jetmore, *U.S.A.* ... 112 F5
Jetpur, *India* ... 68 J4
Jeumont, *France* ... 19 B11
Jevnaker, *Norway* ... 9 F14
Jewett City, *U.S.A.* ... 117 E13
Jeypore, *India* ... 67 K13
Jeziorak, Jezioro, *Poland* ... 30 E6
Jeziorany, *Poland* ... 30 E7
Jeziorka →, *Poland* ... 31 F8

Jha Jha, *India* 69 G12
Jhaarkand = Jharkhand □, *India* 69 H11
Jhabua, *India* 68 H6
Jhajjar, *India* 68 E7
Jhal, *Pakistan* 68 E2
Jhal Jhao, *Pakistan* 66 F4
Jhalawar, *India* 68 G7
Jhalida, *India* 69 H11
Jhalrapatan, *India* 68 G7
Jhang Maghiana. *Pakistan* 68 D5
Jhansi, *India* 69 G8
Jhargram, *India* 69 H12
Jharia, *India* 69 H12
Jharkhand □, *India* 69 H11
Jharsuguda, *India* 67 J14
Jhelum, *Pakistan* 68 C5
Jhelum ➤, *Pakistan* 68 D5
Jhilmilli, *India* 69 H10
Jhudo, *Pakistan* 68 G3
Jhunjhunu, *India* 68 E6
Ji-Paraná, *Brazil* 124 F6
Ji Xian, *Hebei, China* 56 F8
Ji Xian, *Henan, China* 56 G8
Ji Xian, *Shanxi, China* 56 F6
Jiading, *China* 59 B13
Jiahe, *China* 59 E9
Jialing Jiang ➤, *China* 58 C6
Jiamusi, *China* 60 B8
Ji'an, *Jiangxi, China* 59 D10
Ji'an, *Jilin, China* 57 D14
Jianchang, *China* 57 D11
Jianchangying, *China* 57 D10
Jianchuan, *China* 58 D2
Jiande, *China* 59 C12
Jiang'an, *China* 58 C5
Jiangbei, *China* 58 C6
Jiangcheng, *China* 58 F3
Jiangchuan, *China* 58 E4
Jiangdi, *China* 58 D4
Jiangdu, *China* 59 A12
Jiange, *China* 58 A5
Jianghua, *China* 59 E8
Jiangjin, *China* 58 C6
Jiangkou, *China* 58 D7
Jiangle, *China* 59 D11
Jiangling, *China* 59 B9
Jiangmen, *China* 59 F9
Jiangning, *China* 59 B12
Jiangshan, *China* 59 C12
Jiangsu □, *China* 57 H11
Jiangxi □, *China* 59 D11
Jiangyan, *China* 59 A13
Jiangyin, *China* 59 B13
Jiangyong, *China* 59 E8
Jiangyou, *China* 58 B5
Jianhe, *China* 58 D7
Jianli, *China* 59 C9
Jianning, *China* 59 D11
Jian'ou, *China* 59 D12
Jianshi, *China* 58 B7
Jianshui, *China* 58 F4
Jianyang, *Fujian, China* 59 D12
Jianyang, *Sichuan, China* 58 B5
Jiao Xian = Jiaozhou, *China* 57 F11
Jiaohe, *Hebei, China* 56 E9
Jiaohe, *Jilin, China* 57 C14
Jiaojiang, *China* 59 C13
Jiaoling, *China* 59 E11
Jiaozhou, *China* 57 F11
Jiaozhou War, *China* 57 F11
Jiaozuo, *China* 56 G7
Jiashan, *China* 59 B13
Jiawang, *China* 57 G9
Jiaxiang, *China* 56 G9
Jiaxing, *China* 59 B13
Jiayi = Chiai, *Taiwan* 59 F13
Jiayu, *China* 59 C9
Jibiya, *Nigeria* 83 C6
Jibou, *Romania* 29 C8
Jibuti = Djibouti ■, *Africa* 81 E5
Jicarón, I., *Panama* 120 E3
Jičín, *Czech Rep.* 26 A8
Jiddah, *Si. Arabia* 75 C2
Jido, *India* 67 E19
Jieshou, *China* 56 H8
Jiexiu, *China* 56 F6
Jieyang, *China* 59 F11
Jigawa □, *Nigeria* 83 C6
Jiggalong, *Australia* 92 D3
Jigni, *India* 69 G8
Jihlava, *Czech Rep.* 26 B8
Jihlava ➤, *Czech Rep.* 27 C9
Jihlavský □, *Czech Rep.* 26 B8
Jihočeský □, *Czech Rep.* 26 B7
Jihomoravský □, *Czech Rep.* 27 B9
Jijiga, *Ethiopia* 75 F3
Jikamshi, *Nigeria* 83 C6
Jikau, *Sudan* 81 F3
Jilin, *China* 57 C14
Jilin □, *China* 57 C14
Jiloca ➤, *Spain* 38 D3
Jilong = Chilung, *Taiwan* 59 E13
Jim Thorpe, *U.S.A.* 117 F9
Jima, *Ethiopia* 81 F4
Jimbaran, Teluk, *Indonesia* 63 K18
Jimbolia, *Romania* 28 E5
Jimena de la Frontera, *Spain* 37 J5
Jiménez, *Mexico* 118 B4
Jimo, *China* 57 F11
Jin Jiang ➤, *China* 59 C10
Jin Xian = Jinzhou, *China* 56 E8
Jin Xian, *China* 57 E11
Jinan, *China* 56 F9
Jinchang, *China* 60 C5
Jincheng, *China* 56 G7
Jinchuan, *China* 58 B4
Jind, *India* 68 E7
Jindabyne, *Australia* 95 F4
Jindřichův Hradec, *Czech Rep.* 26 B8
Jing He ➤, *China* 56 G5

Jing Shan, *China* 59 B8
Jing Xian, *China* 59 B12
Jing'an, *China* 59 C10
Jingbian, *China* 56 F5
Jingchuan, *China* 56 G4
Jingde, *China* 59 B12
Jingdezhen, *China* 59 C11
Jingdong, *China* 58 E3
Jinggangshan, *China* 59 D10
Jinggu, *China* 58 F3
Jinghai, *China* 56 E9
Jinghong, *China* 58 G3
Jingjiang, *China* 59 A13
Jingle, *China* 56 E6
Jingmen, *China* 59 B9
Jingning, *China* 56 G3
Jingpo Hu, *China* 57 C15
Jingshan, *China* 59 B9
Jingtai, *China* 56 F3
Jingxi, *China* 58 F6
Jingxing, *China* 56 E8
Jingyang, *China* 56 G5
Jingyu, *China* 57 C14
Jingyuan, *China* 56 F3
Jingzhou, *China* 58 D7
Jingziguan, *China* 56 H6
Jinhua, *China* 59 C12
Jining, *Nei Mongol Zizhiqu, China* 56 D7
Jining, *Shandong, China* 56 G9
Jinja, *Uganda* 86 B3
Jinjang, *Malaysia* 65 L3
Jinji, *China* 56 F4
Jinjiang, *Fujian, China* 59 E12
Jinjiang, *Yunnan, China* 58 D3
Jinjini, *Ghana* 82 D4
Jinkou, *China* 59 B10
Jinkouhe, *China* 58 C4
Jinmen Dao, *China* 59 E12
Jinnah Barrage, *Pakistan* 66 C7
Jinning, *China* 58 E4
Jinotega, *Nic.* 120 D2
Jinotepe, *Nic.* 120 D2
Jinping, *Guizhou, China* 58 D7
Jinping, *Yunnan, China* 58 F4
Jinsha, *China* 58 D6
Jinsha Jiang ➤, *China* 58 C5
Jinshan, *China* 59 B13
Jinshi, *China* 59 C8
Jintan, *China* 59 B12
Jinxi, *Jiangxi, China* 59 D11
Jinxi, *Liaoning, China* 57 D11
Jinxian, *China* 59 C11
Jinxiang, *China* 56 G9
Jinyang, *China* 58 D4
Jinyun, *China* 59 C13
Jinzhai, *China* 59 B10
Jinzhou, *Hebei, China* 56 E8
Jinzhou, *Liaoning, China* 57 D11
Jiparaná ➤, *Brazil* 124 E6
Jipijapa, *Ecuador* 124 D2
Jiquilpan, *Mexico* 118 D4
Jishan, *China* 56 G6
Jishou, *China* 58 C7
Jishui, *China* 59 D10
Jisr ash Shughūr, *Syria* 70 C3
Jitarning, *Australia* 93 F2
Jitra, *Malaysia* 65 J3
Jiu ➤, *Romania* 29 G8
Jiudengkou, *China* 56 E4
Jiujiang, *Guangdong, China* 59 F9
Jiujiang, *Jiangxi, China* 59 C10
Jiuling Shan, *China* 59 C10
Jiulong = Kowloon, *China* 59 F10
Jiulong, *China* 58 C3
Jiutai, *China* 57 B13
Jiuxincheng, *China* 56 E8
Jiuyuhang, *China* 59 B12
Jixi, *Anhui, China* 59 B11
Jixi, *Heilongjiang, China* 57 B16
Jiyang, *China* 57 F9
Jiyuan, *China* 56 G7
Jīzān, *Si. Arabia* 75 D3
Jize, *China* 56 F8
Jizera ➤, *Czech Rep.* 26 A7
Jizl, Wādī al ➤, *Si. Arabia* 70 E3
Jizō-Zaki, *Japan* 55 G6
Jizzakh, *Uzbekistan* 52 E7
Joaçaba, *Brazil* 127 B5
Joal Fadiout, *Senegal* 82 C1
João Pessoa, *Brazil* 125 E12
Joaquín V. González, *Argentina* 126 B3
Jobat, *India* 68 H6
Jobourg, Nez de, *France* 18 C5
Jódar, *Spain* 37 H7
Jodhpur, *India* 68 F5
Jodiya, *India* 68 H4
Jõetsu, *Japan* 55 F9
Jœuf, *France* 19 C12
Jofane, *Mozam.* 89 C5
Jogbani, *India* 69 F12
Jõgeva, *Estonia* 9 G22
Jogjakarta = Yogyakarta, *Indonesia* 63 G14
Johannesburg, *S. Africa* 89 D4
Johannesburg, *U.S.A.* 111 K9
Johansfors, *Sweden* 11 H9
Johilla ➤, *India* 69 H9
John Crow Mts., *Jamaica* 120 a
John Day, *U.S.A.* 108 D4
John Day ➤, *U.S.A.* 108 D3
John Day Fossil Beds △, *U.S.A.* 108 D4
John D'Or Prairie, *Canada* 102 B5
John F. Kennedy International, New York ✈ (JFK), *U.S.A.* 117 F11
John H. Kerr Reservoir, *U.S.A.* 115 G6
John o' Groats, *U.K.* 13 C5
Johnnie, *U.S.A.* 111 J10
John's Ra., *Australia* 94 C1
Johnson, *Kans., U.S.A.* 113 G4
Johnson, *Vt., U.S.A.* 117 B12
Johnson City, *N.Y., U.S.A.* 117 D9

Johnson City, *Tenn., U.S.A.* 115 G4
Johnson City, *Tex., U.S.A.* 113 K5
Johnsonburg, *U.S.A.* 116 E6
Johnsondale, *U.S.A.* 111 K8
Johnsons Crossing, *Canada* 102 A2
Johnston, L., *Australia* 93 F3
Johnston Falls = Mambilima Falls, *Zambia* 87 E2
Johnston I., *Pac. Oc.* 97 F11
Johnstone Str., *Canada* 102 C3
Johnstown, *N.Y., U.S.A.* 117 C10
Johnstown, *Ohio, U.S.A.* 116 F2
Johnstown, *Pa., U.S.A.* 116 F6
Johor, Selat, *Asia* 65 d
Johor Bahru, *Malaysia* 65 d
Jõhvi, *Estonia* 9 G22
Joigny, *France* 19 E10
Joinville, *Brazil* 127 B6
Joinville, *France* 19 D12
Joinville I., *Antarctica* 5 C18
Jojutla, *Mexico* 119 D5
Jokkmokk, *Sweden* 8 C18
Jökulsá á Bru ➤, *Iceland* 8 D6
Jökulsá á Fjöllum ➤, *Iceland* 8 C5
Jolfā, *Āzarbājān-e Sharqī, Iran* 70 B5
Jolfā, *Esfahan, Iran* 71 C6
Joliet, *U.S.A.* 114 E1
Joliette, *Canada* 104 C5
Jolo, *Phil.* 61 J4
Jolon, *U.S.A.* 110 K5
Jomalig I., *Phil.* 61 D5
Jombang, *Indonesia* 63 G15
Jomda, *China* 58 B2
Jonava, *Lithuania* 9 J21
Jones Sound, *Canada* 4 B3
Jonesboro, *Ark., U.S.A.* 113 H9
Jonesboro, *La., U.S.A.* 113 J8
Jong ➤, *S. Leone* 82 D2
Jonglei, *Sudan* 81 F3
Jonglei □, *Sudan* 81 F3
Joniškis, *Lithuania* 9 H20
Jönköping, *Sweden* 11 G8
Jönköpings län □, *Sweden* 11 G8
Jonquière, *Canada* 105 C5
Jonsered, *Sweden* 11 G6
Jonzac, *France* 20 C3
Joplin, *U.S.A.* 113 G7
Jora, *India* 68 F6
Jordan, *Mont., U.S.A.* 108 C10
Jordan, *N.Y., U.S.A.* 117 C8
Jordan ■, *Asia* 74 E5
Jordan ➤, *Asia* 74 D4
Jordan Valley, *U.S.A.* 108 E5
Jordanów, *Poland* 31 J6
Jorhat, *India* 67 F19
Jörn, *Sweden* 8 D19
Jorong, *Indonesia* 62 E4
Jørpeland, *Norway* 9 G11
Jorquera ➤, *Chile* 126 B2
Jos, *Nigeria* 83 D6
Jos Plateau, *Nigeria* 83 D6
Jošanička Banja, *Serbia & M.* 44 C4
José Batlle y Ordóñez, *Uruguay* 127 C4
Joseni, *Romania* 29 D10
Joseph, L., *Nfld. & L., Canada* 105 B6
Joseph, L., *Ont., Canada* 116 A5
Joseph Bonaparte G., *Australia* 92 B4
Joshinath, *India* 69 D8
Joshinetsu-Kögen △, *Japan* 55 F9
Joshua Tree, *U.S.A.* 111 L10
Joshua Tree △, *U.S.A.* 111 M10
Josselin, *France* 18 E4
Jost Van Dyke, *Br. Virgin Is.* 121 e
Jostedalsbreen, *Norway* 9 F12
Jotunheimen, *Norway* 9 F13
Joubertberge, *Namibia* 88 B1
Joué-lès-Tours, *France* 18 E7
Jourdanton, *U.S.A.* 113 L5
Joutseno, *Finland* 32 B5
Jovellanos, *Cuba* 120 B3
Joyeuse, *France* 21 D8
Józefów, *Lubelskie, Poland* 31 H10
Józefów, *Mazowieckie, Poland* 31 F8
Ju Xian, *China* 57 F10
Juan Aldama, *Mexico* 118 C4
Juan Bautista Alberdi, *Argentina* 126 C3
Juan de Fuca Str., *Canada* 110 B3
Juan de Nova, *Ind. Oc.* 89 B7
Juan Fernández, Arch. de, *Pac. Oc.* 97 L20
Juan José Castelli, *Argentina* 126 B3
Juan L. Lacaze, *Uruguay* 126 C4
Juankoski, *Finland* 8 E23
Juárez, *Argentina* 126 D4
Juárez, *Mexico* 111 N11
Juárez, Sierra de, *Mexico* 118 A1
Juàzeiro, *Brazil* 125 E10
Juàzeiro do Norte, *Brazil* 125 E11
Juba = Giuba ➤, *Somali Rep.* 75 G3
Juba, *Sudan* 81 G3
Jubany, *Antarctica* 5 C18
Jubayl, *Lebanon* 74 A4
Jubbah, *Si. Arabia* 70 D4
Jubbal, *India* 68 D7
Jubbulpore = Jabalpur, *India* 69 H8
Jübek, *Germany* 24 A5
Jubga, *Russia* 35 H4
Jubilee L., *Australia* 93 E4
Juby, C., *Morocco* 78 C3
Júcar = Xúquer ➤, *Spain* 39 F4
Júcaro, *Cuba* 120 B4
Juchitán, *Mexico* 119 D5
Judaea = Har Yehuda, *Israel* 74 D3
Judenburg, *Austria* 26 D7
Judith ➤, *U.S.A.* 108 C9
Judith, Pt., *U.S.A.* 117 E13
Judith Gap, *U.S.A.* 108 C9
Juelsminde, *Denmark* 11 J4
Jugoslavia = Serbia & Montenegro ■, *Europe* 44 C4
Juigalpa, *Nic.* 120 D2
Juillac, *France* 20 C5

Juist, *Germany* 24 B2
Juiz de Fora, *Brazil* 127 A7
Jujuy □, *Argentina* 126 A2
Julesburg, *U.S.A.* 112 E3
Juli, *Peru* 124 G5
Julia Cr. ➤, *Australia* 94 C3
Julia Creek, *Australia* 94 C3
Juliaca, *Peru* 124 G4
Julian, *U.S.A.* 111 M10
Julian, L., *Canada* 104 B4
Julian Alps = Julijske Alpe, *Slovenia* 41 B11
Julianatop, *Suriname* 125 C7
Julianehåb = Qaqortoq, *Greenland* 101 B6
Jülich, *Germany* 24 E2
Julijske Alpe, *Slovenia* 41 B11
Julimes, *Mexico* 118 B3
Jullundur, *India* 68 D6
Julu, *China* 56 F8
Jumbo, *Zimbabwe* 87 F3
Jumbo Pk., *U.S.A.* 111 J12
Jumentos Cays, *Bahamas* 120 B4
Jumilla, *Spain* 39 G3
Jumla, *Nepal* 69 E10
Jumna = Yamuna ➤, *India* 69 G9
Junagadh, *India* 68 J4
Junction, *Tex., U.S.A.* 113 K5
Junction, *Utah, U.S.A.* 109 G7
Junction B., *Australia* 94 A1
Junction City, *Kans., U.S.A.* 112 F6
Junction City, *Oreg., U.S.A.* 108 D2
Junction Pt., *Australia* 94 A1
Jundah, *Australia* 94 C3
Jundiaí, *Brazil* 127 A6
Juneau, *U.S.A.* 102 B2
Junee, *Australia* 95 E4
Jungfrau, *Switz.* 25 J3
Junggar Pendi, *China* 60 B3
Jungshahi, *Pakistan* 68 G2
Juniata ➤, *U.S.A.* 116 F7
Junín, *Argentina* 126 C3
Junín de los Andes, *Argentina* 128 D2
Jūniyah, *Lebanon* 74 B4
Junlian, *China* 58 C5
Juntas, *Chile* 126 B2
Juntura, *U.S.A.* 108 E4
Jur, Nahr el ➤, *Sudan* 81 F2
Jura = Jura, Mts. du, *Europe* 19 F13
Jura = Schwäbische Alb, *Germany* 25 G5
Jura, *U.K.* 13 F3
Jura □, *France* 19 F12
Jura □, *Switz.* 25 H3
Jūra ➤, *Lithuania* 30 C9
Jura, Mts. du, *Europe* 19 F13
Jura, Sd. of, *U.K.* 13 F3
Jurbarkas, *Lithuania* 9 J20
Jurien, *Australia* 93 F2
Jurilovca, *Romania* 29 F13
Jūrmala, *Latvia* 9 H20
Jurong, *China* 59 B12
Jurong, *Singapore* 65 d
Juruá ➤, *Brazil* 124 D5
Juruena, *Brazil* 124 F7
Juruena ➤, *Brazil* 124 E7
Juruti, *Brazil* 125 D7
Jussey, *France* 19 E12
Justo Daract, *Argentina* 126 C2
Jutaí ➤, *Brazil* 124 D5
Jüterbog, *Germany* 24 D9
Juticalpa, *Honduras* 120 D2
Jutland = Jylland, *Denmark* 11 H3
Juventud, I. de la, *Cuba* 120 B3
Juvigny-sous-Andaine, *France* 18 D6
Juye, *China* 56 G9
Juzennecourt, *France* 19 D11
Jvari, *Georgia* 35 J6
Jwaneng, *Botswana* 85 J4
Jyderup, *Denmark* 11 J5
Jylland, *Denmark* 11 H3
Jyväskylä, *Finland* 9 E21

K

K2, *Pakistan* 69 B7
Ka ➤, *Nigeria* 83 C5
Kaap Plateau, *S. Africa* 88 D3
Kaapkruis, *Namibia* 88 C1
Kaapstad = Cape Town, *S. Africa* 88 E2
Kaba, *Guinea* 82 C2
Kabaena, *Indonesia* 63 F6
Kabala, *S. Leone* 82 D2
Kabale, *Uganda* 86 C3
Kabalo, *Dem. Rep. of the Congo* 86 D2
Kabambare, *Dem. Rep. of the Congo* 86 C2
Kabango, *Dem. Rep. of the Congo* 87 D2
Kabanjahe, *Indonesia* 62 D1
Kabankalan, *Phil.* 61 G5
Kabara, *Mali* 82 B4
Kabardinka, *Russia* 33 K10
Kabardino-Balkar Republic = Kabardino-Balkaria □, *Russia* 35 J6
Kabardino-Balkaria □, *Russia* 35 J6
Kabarega Falls = Murchison Falls, *Uganda* 86 B3
Kabasalan, *Phil.* 61 H5
Kabat, *Indonesia* 63 J17
Kabba, *Nigeria* 83 D6
Kabetogama, *U.S.A.* 112 A8
Kabi, *Niger* 83 C7
Kabin Buri, *Thailand* 64 E3
Kabinakagami L., *Canada* 104 C3
Kabinda, *Dem. Rep. of the Congo* 84 F4
Kabkabīyah, *Sudan* 80 D3
Kabompo, *Zambia* 87 E1
Kabompo ➤, *Zambia* 85 G4

Kabondo, *Dem. Rep. of the Congo* 87 D2
Kabongo, *Dem. Rep. of the Congo* 86 D2
Kabot, *Guinea* 82 C2
Kabou, *Togo* 83 D5
Kabr, *Sudan* 81 E2
Kabrousse, *Senegal* 82 C1
Kabūd Gonbad, *Iran* 71 B8
Kabugao, *Phil.* 61 B4
Kābul, *Afghan.* 68 B3
Kābul □, *Afghan.* 66 B6
Kābul ➤, *Pakistan* 68 C5
Kabunga, *Dem. Rep. of the Congo* 86 C2
Kaburuang, *Indonesia* 63 D7
Kabushiya, *Sudan* 81 D3
Kabwe, *Zambia* 87 E2
Kačanik, *Serbia & M.* 44 D5
Kačergine, *Lithuania* 30 D10
Kachchh, Gulf of, *India* 68 H3
Kachchh, Rann of, *India* 68 H4
Kachchhidhana, *India* 69 J8
Kachebera, *Zambia* 87 E3
Kachia, *Nigeria* 83 D6
Kachikau, *Botswana* 88 B3
Kachin □, *Burma* 58 D1
Kachira, L., *Uganda* 86 C3
Kachiry, *Kazakhstan* 52 D8
Kachisi, *Ethiopia* 81 F4
Kachnara, *India* 68 H6
Kachot, *Cambodia* 65 G4
Kaçkar, *Turkey* 73 B9
Kadan, *Czech Rep.* 26 A6
Kadan Kyun, *Burma* 64 F2
Kadanai ➤, *Afghan.* 68 D1
Kadarkút, *Hungary* 28 D2
Kadavu, *Fiji* 91 D8
Kade, *Ghana* 83 D4
Kadhimain = Al Kāzimīyah, *Iraq* 70 C5
Kadi, *India* 68 H5
Kadina, *Australia* 95 E2
Kadinhanı, *Turkey* 72 C5
Kadiolo, *Mali* 82 C4
Kadipur, *India* 69 F10
Kadirli, *Turkey* 70 B3
Kadiyevka = Stakhanov, *Ukraine* 33 H10
Kadodo, *Sudan* 81 E2
Kadoka, *U.S.A.* 112 D4
Kadom, *Russia* 34 C6
Kadoma, *Zimbabwe* 87 F2
Kādugli, *Sudan* 81 E2
Kaduna, *Nigeria* 83 C6
Kaduna □, *Nigeria* 83 C6
Kaduy, *Russia* 32 C9
Kaédi, *Mauritania* 82 B2
Kaélé, *Cameroon* 83 C7
Kaeng Khoï, *Thailand* 64 E3
Kaeng Kra Chan △, *Thailand* 64 F2
Kaeng Tana △, *Thailand* 64 E5
Kaesŏng, *N. Korea* 57 F14
Kāf, *Si. Arabia* 70 D3
Kafan = Kapan, *Armenia* 70 B5
Kafanchan, *Nigeria* 83 D6
Kafareti, *Nigeria* 83 C7
Kaffrine, *Senegal* 82 C1
Kafin, *Nigeria* 83 D6
Kafin Madaki, *Nigeria* 83 C6
Kafinda, *Zambia* 87 E3
Kafirévs, Ákra, *Greece* 46 C6
Kafr el Battikh, *Egypt* 80 H7
Kafr el Dauwâr, *Egypt* 80 H7
Kafr el Sheikh, *Egypt* 80 H7
Kafue, *Zambia* 87 F2
Kafue △, *Zambia* 87 F2
Kafue ➤, *Zambia* 85 H5
Kafue Flats, *Zambia* 87 F2
Kafulwe, *Zambia* 87 D2
Kaga, *Afghan.* 68 B4
Kaga Bandoro, *C.A.R.* 84 C3
Kagan, *Uzbekistan* 52 F7
Kagarko, *Nigeria* 83 D6
Kagawa □, *Japan* 55 G7
Kagera □, *Tanzania* 86 C3
Kagera ➤, *Uganda* 86 C3
Kağızman, *Turkey* 70 B4
Kagmar, *Sudan* 81 E3
Kagoshima, *Japan* 55 J5
Kagoshima □, *Japan* 55 J5
Kagul = Cahul, *Moldova* 29 E13
Kahak, *Iran* 71 B6
Kahama, *Tanzania* 86 C3
Kahan, *Pakistan* 68 E3
Kahang, *Malaysia* 65 L4
Kahayan ➤, *Indonesia* 62 E4
Kahe, *Tanzania* 86 C4
Kahnūj, *Iran* 71 E8
Kahoka, *U.S.A.* 112 E9
Kahoolawe, *U.S.A.* 106 H16
Kahramanmaraş, *Turkey* 70 B3
Kâhta, *Turkey* 73 D8
Kahul, Ozero, *Ukraine* 29 E13
Kahurangi △, *N.Z.* 91 J4
Kahuta, *Pakistan* 68 C5
Kahuzi-Biega △, *Dem. Rep. of the Congo* 86 C2
Kai, Kepulauan, *Indonesia* 63 F8
Kai Is. = Kai, Kepulauan, *Indonesia* 63 F8
Kai Kecil, *Indonesia* 63 F8
Kai Xian, *China* 58 B7
Kaiama, *Nigeria* 83 D5
Kaiapoi, *N.Z.* 91 K4
Kaieteur Falls, *Guyana* 124 C7
Kaifeng, *China* 56 G8
Kaihua, *China* 59 C12
Kaijiang, *China* 58 B6
Kaikohe, *N.Z.* 91 F4
Kaikoura, *N.Z.* 91 K4
Kailahun, *S. Leone* 82 D2
Kailash = Kangrinboqê Feng, *China* 69 D9
Kaili, *China* 58 D6
Kailu, *China* 57 C11

Kailua Kona, *U.S.A.* 106 J17
Kaimana, *Indonesia* 63 E8
Kaimanawa Mts., *N.Z.* 91 H5
Kaimganj, *India* 69 F8
Kaimur Hills, *India* 69 G10
Kainab →, *Namibia* 88 D2
Kainji Dam, *Nigeria* 83 D5
Kainji Lake △, *Nigeria* 83 C5
Kainji Res., *Nigeria* 83 C5
Kainuu, *Finland* 8 D23
Kaipara Harbour, *N.Z.* 91 G5
Kaiping, *China* 59 F9
Kaipokok B., *Canada* 105 B8
Kaira, *India* 68 H5
Kairana, *India* 68 E7
Kaironi, *Indonesia* 63 E8
Kairouan, *Tunisia* 79 A8
Kaiserslautern, *Germany* 25 F3
Kaiserstuhl, *Germany* 25 G3
Kaitaia, *N.Z.* 91 F4
Kaitangata, *N.Z.* 91 M2
Kaithal, *India* 68 E7
Kaitu →, *Pakistan* 68 C4
Kaiyang, *China* 58 D6
Kaiyuan, *Liaoning, China* ... 57 C13
Kaiyuan, *Yunnan, China* 58 F4
Kajaani, *Finland* 8 D22
Kajabbi, *Australia* 94 C3
Kajana = Kajaani, *Finland* .. 8 D22
Kajang, *Malaysia* 65 L3
Kajaran, *Armenia* 73 C12
Kajiado, *Kenya* 86 C4
Kajo Kaji, *Sudan* 81 G3
Kajuru, *Nigeria* 83 C6
Kaka, *Sudan* 81 E3
Kakabeka Falls, *Canada* 104 C2
Kakadu △, *Australia* 92 B5
Kakamas, *S. Africa* 88 D3
Kakamega, *Kenya* 86 B3
Kakanj, *Bos.-H.* 28 F3
Kakanui Mts., *N.Z.* 91 L3
Kakata, *Liberia* 82 D2
Kakdwip, *India* 69 J13
Kake, *Japan* 55 G6
Kake, *U.S.A.* 102 B2
Kakegawa, *Japan* 55 G9
Kakeroma-Jima, *Japan* 55 K4
Kakhib, *Russia* 35 J8
Kakhovka, *Ukraine* 33 J7
Kakhovske Vdskh., *Ukraine* .. 33 J7
Kakinada, *India* 67 L13
Kakisa →, *Canada* 102 A5
Kakisa L., *Canada* 102 A5
Kakogawa, *Japan* 55 G7
Kakum △, *Ghana* 83 D4
Kakwa →, *Canada* 102 C5
Kāl Gūsheh, *Iran* 71 D8
Kal Safīd, *Iran* 70 C5
Kala, *Nigeria* 83 C7
Kalaallit Nunaat = Greenland ☑,
 N. Amer. 4 C5
Kalabagh, *Pakistan* 68 C4
Kalabahi, *Indonesia* 63 F6
Kalabáka, *Greece* 46 B3
Kalabana, *Mali* 82 C3
Kalach, *Russia* 34 E5
Kalach na Donu, *Russia* 35 F6
Kaladan →, *Burma* 67 J18
Kaladar, *Canada* 116 B7
Kalahari, *Africa* 88 C3
Kalahari Gemsbok △, *S. Africa* . 88 D3
Kalajoki, *Finland* 8 D20
Kalakamati, *Botswana* 89 C4
Kalakan, *Russia* 53 D12
K'alak'unlun Shank'ou =
 Karakoram Pass, *Asia* 69 B7
Kalam, *Pakistan* 69 B5
Kalama, *Dem. Rep. of the Congo* 86 C2
Kalama, *U.S.A.* 110 E4
Kalámai, *Greece* 46 D4
Kalamariá, *Greece* 44 F6
Kalamazoo, *U.S.A.* 114 D3
Kalamazoo →, *U.S.A.* 114 D2
Kalambo Falls, *Tanzania* 87 D3
Kálamos, *Greece* 46 C5
Kálamos Nisís, *Greece* 46 C2
Kalan, *Turkey* 70 B3
Kalankalan, *Guinea* 82 C3
Kalannie, *Australia* 93 F2
Kalāntarī, *Iran* 71 C7
Kalao, *Indonesia* 63 F6
Kalaotoa, *Indonesia* 63 F6
Kälarne, *Sweden* 10 B10
Kalasin, *Thailand* 64 D4
Kālat, *Iran* 71 E8
Kalat, *Pakistan* 66 E5
Kalāteh, *Iran* 71 B7
Kalāteh-ye Ganj, *Iran* 71 E8
Kálathos, *Greece* 47 E10
Kalaus →, *Russia* 35 H7
Kalávrita, *Greece* 46 C4
Kalbarri, *Australia* 93 E1
Kalbarri △, *Australia* 93 E1
Kale, *Antalya, Turkey* 47 D10
Kale, *Denizli, Turkey* 47 D10
Kalecik, *Turkey* 72 B5
Kalegauk Kyun, *Burma* 67 M20
Kalehe, *Dem. Rep. of the Congo* 86 C2
Kalema, *Tanzania* 86 C3
Kalety, *Poland* 31 H5
Kalewa, *Burma* 67 H19
Kaleybar, *Iran* 70 B5
Kali →, *India* 69 F8
Kali Sindh →, *India* 68 G6
Kaliakra, Nos, *Bulgaria* 45 C12
Kalianda, *Indonesia* 62 F3
Kalibo, *Phil.* 61 F5
Kalima, *Dem. Rep. of the Congo* 86 C2
Kalimantan, *Indonesia* 62 E4
Kalimantan Barat ☐, *Indonesia* . 62 E4
Kalimantan Selatan ☐, *Indonesia* 62 E5
Kalimantan Tengah ☐, *Indonesia* 62 E4
Kalimantan Timur ☐, *Indonesia* . 62 D5
Kálimnos, *Greece* 47 D8
Kalimpong, *India* 69 F13
Kaliningrad, *Russia* 9 J19
Kaliningrad ✈ (KGD), *Russia* . 30 D7
Kalininsk, *Russia* 34 E7
Kalinkavichy, *Belarus* 33 F5
Kalinkovichi = Kalinkavichy,
 Belarus 33 F5
Kalinovik, *Bos.-H.* 44 C2
Kalipetrovo, *Bulgaria* 45 B11
Kalirrákhi, *Greece* 45 F8
Kaliro, *Uganda* 86 B3
Kalispell, *U.S.A.* 108 B6
Kalisz, *Poland* 31 G5
Kalisz Pomorski, *Poland* 31 E2
Kaliua, *Tanzania* 86 D3
Kalívia Thorikoú, *Greece* ... 46 D5
Kalix = Kalixälven →, *Sweden* . 8 D20
Kalix, *Sweden* 8 D20
Kalixälven →, *Sweden* 8 D20
Kalka, *India* 68 D7
Kalkan, *Turkey* 47 E11
Kalkarindji, *Australia* 92 C5
Kalkaska, *U.S.A.* 114 C3
Kalkfeld, *Namibia* 88 C2
Kalkfontein, *Botswana* 88 C3
Kalkım, *Turkey* 47 B9
Kalkrand, *Namibia* 88 C2
Kållandsö, *Sweden* 11 F7
Kallavesi, *Finland* 8 E22
Källby, *Sweden* 11 F7
Källered, *Sweden* 11 G6
Kallimasiá, *Greece* 47 C8
Kallinge, *Sweden* 11 H9
Kallithéa, *Greece* 46 D5
Kallmet, *Albania* 44 E3
Kalloní, *Greece* 47 B8
Kallonís, Kólpos, *Greece* ... 47 B8
Kallsjön, *Sweden* 8 E15
Kalmalo, *Nigeria* 83 C6
Kalmar, *Sweden* 11 H10
Kalmar län ☐, *Sweden* 11 G10
Kalmar sund, *Sweden* 11 H10
Kalmyk Republic = Kalmykia ☐,
 Russia 35 G8
Kalmykia ☐, *Russia* 35 G8
Kalmykovo, *Kazakhstan* 52 E6
Kalna, *India* 69 H13
Kalnai, *India* 69 H10
Kalocsa, *Hungary* 28 D4
Kalofer, *Bulgaria* 45 D8
Kalokhorio, *Cyprus* 49 E12
Kaloko, *Dem. Rep. of the Congo* 86 D2
Kalol, *Gujarat, India* 68 H5
Kalol, *Gujarat, India* 68 H5
Kalolímnos, *Greece* 47 D9
Kalomo, *Zambia* 87 F2
Kalonerón, *Greece* 46 D3
Kalpi, *India* 69 F8
Kaltag, *U.S.A.* 106 C8
Kaltern = Caldaro, *Italy* ... 41 B8
Kaltungo, *Nigeria* 83 D7
Kalu, *Pakistan* 68 G2
Kaluga, *Russia* 32 E9
Kalulushi, *Zambia* 87 E2
Kalundborg, *Denmark* 11 J5
Kalush, *Ukraine* 33 H3
Kałuszyn, *Poland* 31 F8
Kalutara, *Sri Lanka* 66 R12
Kalvarija, *Lithuania* 30 D10
Kalyan, *India* 66 K8
Kalyazin, *Russia* 32 D9
Kam, *Albania* 44 D4
Kam →, *Nigeria* 83 D7
Kama, *Dem. Rep. of the Congo* . 86 C2
Kama →, *Russia* 6 D16
Kamachumu, *Tanzania* 86 C3
Kamaishi, *Japan* 54 E10
Kamalia, *Pakistan* 68 D5
Kaman, *India* 68 F6
Kaman, *Turkey* 72 C5
Kamanjab, *Namibia* 88 B2
Kamapanda, *Zambia* 87 E1
Kamarán, *Yemen* 75 D3
Kamativi, *Zimbabwe* 88 B4
Kamba, *Nigeria* 83 C5
Kambalda, *Australia* 93 F3
Kambar, *Pakistan* 68 F3
Kambia, *S. Leone* 82 D2
Kambolé, *Togo* 83 D5
Kambolé, *Zambia* 87 D3
Kambos, *Cyprus* 49 D11
Kambove, *Dem. Rep. of
 the Congo* 87 E2
Kamchatka, Poluostrov, *Russia* . 53 D16
Kamchatka Pen. = Kamchatka,
 Poluostrov, *Russia* 53 D16
Kamchiya →, *Bulgaria* 45 C11
Kame Ruins, *Zimbabwe* 87 G2
Kamen, *Russia* 52 D9
Kamen-Rybolov, *Russia* 54 B6
Kamenica, *Serbia & M.* 44 C6
Kamenica, *Serbia & M.* 44 B3
Kamenice nad Lipou, *Czech Rep.* . 26 B8
Kamenjak, Rt, *Croatia* 41 D10
Kamenka = Kaminka, *Ukraine* . 33 H7
Kamenka, *Kazakhstan* 34 E7
Kamenka, *Penza, Russia* 34 D6
Kamenka, *Voronezh, Russia* .. 33 G10
Kamenka Bugskaya = Kamyanka-
 Buzka, *Ukraine* 33 G3
Kamenka Dneprovskaya =
 Kamyanka-Dniprovska,
 Ukraine 33 J8
Kamennomostskiy, *Russia* 35 H5
Kameno, *Bulgaria* 45 D11
Kamenolomni, *Russia* 35 G5
Kamensk-Shakhtinskiy, *Russia* . 35 F5
Kamensk Uralskiy, *Russia* ... 52 D7
Kamenskiy, *Russia* 34 E7
Kamenskoye, *Russia* 53 C17
Kamenyak, *Bulgaria* 45 C10
Kamenz, *Germany* 24 D10
Kameoka, *Japan* 55 G7
Kamiah, *U.S.A.* 108 C5
Kamień Krajeński, *Poland* ... 30 E4
Kamień Pomorski, *Poland* 30 E1
Kamienna →, *Poland* 31 G8
Kamienna Góra, *Poland* 31 H3
Kamieńsk, *Poland* 31 G6
Kamieskroon, *S. Africa* 88 E2
Kamilukuak L., *Canada* 103 A8
Kamin-Kashyrskyy, *Ukraine* .. 33 G3
Kaminak L., *Canada* 103 A10
Kamina, *Ukraine* 33 H7
Kaminoyama, *Japan* 54 E10
Kamiros, *Greece* 49 C9
Kamituga, *Dem. Rep. of
 the Congo* 86 C2
Kamla →, *India* 69 G12
Kamloops, *Canada* 102 C4
Kamnik, *Slovenia* 41 B11
Kamo, *Armenia* 35 K7
Kamo, *Japan* 54 F9
Kamoke, *Pakistan* 68 C6
Kamp →, *Austria* 26 C8
Kampala, *Uganda* 86 B3
Kampar, *Malaysia* 65 K3
Kampar →, *Indonesia* 62 D2
Kampen, *Neths.* 17 B5
Kampene, *Dem. Rep. of
 the Congo* 84 E5
Kamphaeng Phet, *Thailand* ... 64 D2
Kampinoski △, *Poland* 31 F7
Kampolombo, L., *Zambia* 87 E2
Kampong Chhnang, *Cambodia* .. 65 F5
Kampong Pengerang, *Malaysia* . 65 d
Kampong Punggai, *Malaysia* .. 65 d
Kampong Saom, *Cambodia* 65 G4
Kampong Saom, Chaak,
 Cambodia 65 G4
Kampong Tanjong Langsat,
 Malaysia .... 65 d
Kampong Telok Ramunia,
 Malaysia .... 65 d
Kampong To, *Thailand* 65 J3
Kampot, *Cambodia* 65 G5
Kampti, *Burkina Faso* 82 C4
Kampuchea = Cambodia ■, *Asia* . 64 F5
Kampung Air Putih, *Malaysia* . 65 K4
Kampung Jerangau, *Malaysia* . 65 K4
Kampung Raja, *Malaysia* 65 K4
Kampungbaru = Tolitoli,
 Indonesia 63 D6
Kamrau, Teluk, *Indonesia* ... 63 E8
Kamsack, *Canada* 103 C8
Kamsai, *Guinea* 82 C2
Kamskoye Ustye, *Russia* 34 C9
Kamuchawie L., *Canada* 103 B8
Kamui-Misaki, *Japan* 54 C10
Kamyanets-Podilskyy, *Ukraine* . 29 B11
Kamyanka-Buzka, *Ukraine* 33 G3
Kamyanka-Dniprovska, *Ukraine* . 33 J8
Kamyanets, *Belarus* 31 F10
Kamyanyuki, *Belarus* 31 F10
Kamyzyak, *Russia* 35 G9
Kanaaupscow, *Canada* 101 C12
Kanaaupscow →, *Canada* 104 B4
Kanab, *U.S.A.* 109 H7
Kanab →, *U.S.A.* 109 H7
Kanagi, *Japan* 54 D10
Kanairiktok →, *Canada* 105 A7
Kanália, *Greece* 46 B4
Kananga, *Dem. Rep. of the Congo* 84 F4
Kanash, *Russia* 34 C8
Kanaskat, *U.S.A.* 110 C5
Kanastraíon, Ákra = Palioúrion,
 Ákra, *Greece* 44 G7
Kanawha →, *U.S.A.* 114 F4
Kanazawa, *Japan* 55 F8
Kanchanaburi, *Thailand* 64 E2
Kanchenjunga, *Nepal* 69 F13
Kanchipuram, *India* 66 N11
Kańczuga, *Poland* 31 J9
Kandaghat, *India* 68 D7
Kandahar = Qandahār, *Afghan.* . 66 D4
Kandalaksha, *Russia* 52 C4
Kandangan, *Indonesia* 62 E5
Kandanghaur, *Indonesia* 63 G13
Kandanos, *Greece* 49 D5
Kandava, *Latvia* 30 A9
Kandavu = Kadavu, *Fiji* 91 D8
Kandhíla, *Greece* 46 D4
Kandhkot, *Pakistan* 68 E3
Kandhla, *India* 68 E7
Kandi, *Benin* 83 C5
Kandi, *India* 69 H13
Kandiaro, *Pakistan* 68 F3
Kandıra, *Turkey* 72 B4
Kandla, *India* 68 H4
Kandos, *Australia* 95 E4
Kandreho, *Madag.* 89 B8
Kandy, *Sri Lanka* 66 R12
Kane, *U.S.A.* 116 E6
Kane Basin, *Greenland* 98 B12
Kanel, *Senegal* 82 B2
Kaneohe, *U.S.A.* 106 H16
Kanevskaya, *Russia* 35 G4
Kanfanar, *Croatia* 41 C10
Kang, *Botswana* 88 C3
Kang Krung △, *Thailand* 65 H2
Kangaba, *Mali* 82 C3
Kangān, *Fārs, Iran* 71 E7
Kangān, *Hormozgān, Iran* 71 E8
Kangar, *Malaysia* 65 J3
Kangaré, *Mali* 82 C3
Kangaroo I., *Australia* 95 F2
Kangaroo Mts., *Australia* ... 94 C3
Kangasala, *Finland* 9 F21
Kangāvar, *Iran* 71 C6
Kangding, *China* 58 B3
Kangdong, *N. Korea* 57 E14
Kangean, Kepulauan, *Indonesia* . 62 F5
Kangean Is. = Kangean,
 Kepulauan, *Indonesia* 62 F5
Kangen →, *Sudan* 81 F3
Kanggye, *N. Korea* 57 D14
Kanggyŏng, *S. Korea* 57 F14
Kanghwa, *S. Korea* 57 F14
Kangikajik, *Greenland* 4 B6
Kangiqliniq = Rankin Inlet,
 Canada 100 B10
Kangiqsualujjuaq, *Canada* ... 101 C13
Kangiqsujuaq, *Canada* 101 B12
Kangiqtugaapik = Clyde River,
 Canada 101 A13
Kangirsuk, *Canada* 101 B13
Kangkar Chemaran, *Malaysia* . 65 d
Kangkar Sungai Tiram, *Malaysia* . 65 d
Kangkar Teberau, *Malaysia* .. 65 d
Kangnŭng, *S. Korea* 57 F15
Kangping, *China* 57 C12
Kangra, *India* 68 C7
Kangrinboqe Feng, *China* 69 D9
Kangto, *India* 67 F18
Kanhar →, *India* 69 G10
Kani, *Ivory C.* 82 D3
Kaniama, *Dem. Rep. of the Congo* 86 D1
Kaniapiskau = Caniapiscau →,
 Canada 105 A6
Kaniapiskau, L. = Caniapiscau, L.
 de, *Canada* 105 B6
Kanin, Poluostrov, *Russia* .. 52 C5
Kanin Nos, Mys, *Russia* 52 C5
Kanin Pen. = Kanin, Poluostrov,
 Russia 52 C5
Kaninë, *Albania* 44 F3
Kaniva, *Australia* 95 F3
Kanjiža, *Serbia & M.* 28 D5
Kanjut Sar, *Pakistan* 69 A6
Kankaanpää, *Finland* 9 F20
Kankakee, *U.S.A.* 114 E2
Kankakee →, *U.S.A.* 114 E1
Kankan, *Guinea* 82 C3
Kankendy = Xankändi,
 Azerbaijan 70 B5
Kanker, *India* 67 J12
Kankossa, *Mauritania* 82 B2
Kankroli, *India* 68 G5
Kannapolis, *U.S.A.* 115 H5
Kannauj, *India* 69 F8
Kannod, *India* 66 H10
Kano, *Japan* 83 C6
Kano ☐, *Nigeria* 83 C6
Kan'onji, *Japan* 55 G6
Kanoroba, *Ivory C.* 82 D3
Kanowit, *Malaysia* 62 D4
Kanoya, *Japan* 55 J5
Kanpetlet, *Burma* 67 J18
Kanpur, *India* 69 F9
Kansas ☐, *U.S.A.* 112 F6
Kansas →, *U.S.A.* 112 F7
Kansas City, *Kans., U.S.A.* . 112 F7
Kansas City, *Mo., U.S.A.* ... 112 F7
Kansenia, *Dem. Rep. of the Congo* 87 E2
Kansk, *Russia* 53 D10
Kansŏng, *S. Korea* 57 E15
Kansu = Gansu ☐, *China* 56 G3
Kantaphor, *India* 68 H7
Kantchari, *Burkina Faso* 83 C5
Kantché, *Niger* 83 C6
Kanté, *Togo* 83 D5
Kantemirovka, *Russia* 33 H10
Kantharalak, *Thailand* 64 E5
Kantli →, *India* 68 E6
Kantō ☐, *Japan* 55 F9
Kantō-Sanchi, *Japan* 55 G9
Kanturk, *Ireland* 12 D3
Kanuma, *Japan* 55 F9
Kanus, *Namibia* 88 D2
Kanye, *Botswana* 88 C4
Kanzenze, *Dem. Rep. of
 the Congo* 87 E2
Kanzi, Ras, *Tanzania* 86 D4
Kao Phara, *Thailand* .... 65 a
Kaohsiung, *Taiwan* 59 F13
Kaokoveld, *Namibia* 88 B1
Kaolack, *Senegal* 82 C1
Kaoshan, *China* 57 B13
Kapaa, *U.S.A.* 106 G15
Kapadvanj, *India* 68 H5
Kapan, *Armenia* 70 B5
Kapanga, *Dem. Rep. of the Congo* 84 F4
Kapchagai = Qapshaghay,
 Kazakhstan 52 E8
Kapela = Velika Kapela, *Croatia* . 41 C12
Kapéllo, Ákra, *Greece* 46 E5
Kapema, *Dem. Rep. of the Congo* 87 E2
Kapfenberg, *Austria* 26 D8
Kapi Dağı, *Turkey* 45 F11
Kapiri Mposhi, *Zambia* 87 E2
Kāpīsā ☐, *Afghan.* 66 B6
Kapiskau →, *Canada* 104 B3
Kapit, *Malaysia* 62 D4
Kapiti I., *N.Z.* 91 J5
Kaplan, *U.S.A.* 113 K8
Kaplice, *Czech Rep.* 26 C7
Kapoe, *Thailand* 65 H2
Kapoeta, *Sudan* 81 G3
Kápolnásnyék, *Hungary* 28 C3
Kapos →, *Hungary* 28 D2
Kaposvár, *Hungary* 28 D2
Kapowsin, *U.S.A.* 110 D4
Kappeln, *Germany* 24 A5
Kappelshamn, *Sweden* 11 G12
Kapps, *Namibia* 88 C2
Kaprije, *Croatia* 41 E12
Kangaroo I., *Australia* 95 F2
Kapsan, *N. Korea* 57 D15
Kapsukas = Marijampolė,
 Lithuania 9 J20
Kaptai L., *Bangla.* 67 H18
Kapuas →, *Indonesia* 62 E3
Kapuas Hulu, Pegunungan,
 Malaysia 62 D4
Kapuas Hulu Ra. = Kapuas Hulu,
 Pegunungan, *Malaysia* 62 D4
Kapulo, *Dem. Rep. of the Congo* . 87 D2
Kapunda, *Australia* 95 E2
Kapuni, *N.Z.* 91 H5
Kapurthala, *India* 68 D6
Kapuskasing, *Canada* 104 C3
Kapuskasing →, *Canada* 104 C3
Kapustin Yar, *Russia* 35 F7
Kaputar, *Australia* 95 E5
Kaputir, *Kenya* 86 B4
Kapuvár, *Hungary* 28 C2
Kara, *Russia* 52 C7
Karā, N. →, *Si. Arabia* 80 C5
Kara Ada, *Turkey* 47 E9
Kara Bogaz Gol, Zaliv =
 Garabogazköl Aylagy,
 Turkmenistan 52 E6
Kara Burun, *Turkey* 47 E9
Kara Kalpak Republic =
 Qoraqalpoghistan ☐,
 Uzbekistan 52 E6
Kara Kum, *Turkmenistan* 52 F6
Kara Sea, *Russia* 52 B7
Karaadilli, *Turkey* 47 C12
Karabiğa, *Turkey* 45 F11
Karabük, *Turkey* 72 B5
Karaburun, *Albania* 44 F3
Karaburun, *Turkey* 47 C8
Karabutak = Qarabutaq,
 Kazakhstan 52 E7
Karacabey, *Turkey* 45 F12
Karacakılavuz, *Turkey* 45 E11
Karacaköy, *Turkey* 45 E12
Karacasu, *Turkey* 47 D10
Karachala = Qaraçala, *Azerbaijan* 35 L9
Karachayevsk, *Russia* 35 J5
Karachey-Cherkessia ☐, *Russia* . 35 J5
Karachi, *Pakistan* 68 G2
Karad, *India* 66 L9
Karadirek, *Turkey* 47 C12
Karaga, *Ghana* 83 D4
Karaganda = Qaraghandy,
 Kazakhstan 52 E8
Karagayly = Qaraghayly,
 Kazakhstan 52 E8
Karaginskiy, Ostrov, *Russia* . 53 D17
Karagola Road, *India* 69 G12
Karagüney Dağları, *Turkey* .. 72 B6
Karahallı, *Turkey* 47 C11
Karaikal, *India* 66 P11
Karaikkudi, *India* 66 P11
Karaisali, *Turkey* 72 D6
Karaj, *Iran* 71 C6
Karak, *Malaysia* 65 L4
Karakalpakstan =
 Qoraqalpoghistan ☐,
 Uzbekistan 52 E6
Karakelong, *Indonesia* 63 D7
Karakitang, *Indonesia* 63 D7
Karakoçan, *Turkey* 73 C9
Karakol, *Kyrgyzstan* 52 E8
Karakoram Pass, *Asia* 69 B7
Karakoram Ra., *Pakistan* 69 B7
Karakurt, *Turkey* 73 B10
Karakuwisa, *Namibia* 88 B2
Karalon, *Russia* 53 D12
Karama, *Jordan* 74 D4
Karaman, *Balıkesir, Turkey* . 47 B9
Karaman, *Konya, Turkey* 70 B2
Karamanlı, *Turkey* 47 D11
Karamay, *China* 60 B3
Karambu, *Indonesia* 62 E5
Karamea Bight, *N.Z.* 91 J3
Karamnasa →, *India* 69 G10
Karamürsel, *Turkey* 45 F13
Karand, *Iran* 70 C5
Karanganyar, *Indonesia* 63 G13
Karangasem, *Indonesia* 63 J18
Karanja, *India* 66 J10
Karanjia, *India* 69 J11
Karankasso, *Burkina Faso* ... 82 C4
Karaova, *Turkey* 47 D9
Karapınar, *Turkey* 72 D5
Karasburg, *Namibia* 88 D2
Karasino, *Russia* 52 C9
Karasjok, *Norway* 8 B21
Karasu, *Turkey* 72 B4
Karasu →, *Turkey* 47 E12
Karasuk, *Russia* 52 D8
Karasuyama, *Japan* 55 F10
Karataş, *Adana, Turkey* 72 D6
Karataş, *Manisa, Turkey* 47 C10
Karataş Burnu, *Turkey* 72 D6
Karatau, Khrebet = Qarataū,
 Kazakhstan 52 E7
Karatoprak, *Turkey* 47 D9
Karatsu, *Japan* 55 H5
Karaul, *Russia* 52 B9
Karauli, *India* 68 F7
Karavastasë, L. e, *Albania* . 44 F3
Karávi, *Greece* 46 E5
Karavostasi, *Cyprus* 49 D11
Karawang, *Indonesia* 63 G12
Karawanken, *Europe* 26 C7
Karayazı, *Turkey* 73 C10
Karazhal, *Kazakhstan* 52 E8
Karbalā' , *Iraq* 70 C5
Kârböle, *Sweden* 10 C9
Karcag, *Hungary* 28 C5
Karcha →, *Pakistan* 69 B7
Karchana, *India* 69 G9
Karczew, *Poland* 31 F8
Kardam, *Bulgaria* 45 C12

Kardeljovo = Ploče, Croatia 41 E14
Kardhámila, Greece 47 C8
Kardhamíli, Greece 46 E4
Kardhítsa, Greece 46 B3
Kardhítsa □, Greece 46 B3
Kärdla, Estonia 9 G20
Kareeberge, S. Africa 88 E3
Kareha →, India 69 G12
Kareima, Sudan 80 D3
Karelia □, Russia 52 C4
Karelian Republic = Karelia □, Russia ... 52 C4
Karera, India 68 G8
Kārevāndar, Iran 71 E9
Kargasok, Russia 52 D9
Kargat, Russia 52 D9
Kargı, Turkey 72 B6
Kargil, India 69 B7
Kargopol, Russia 32 B10
Kargowa, Poland 31 F2
Karguéri, Niger 83 C7
Karhal, India 69 F8
Kariá, Greece 46 C2
Kariaí, Greece 45 F8
Kariān, Iran 71 E8
Karianga, Madag. 89 C8
Kariba, Zimbabwe 87 F2
Kariba, L., Zimbabwe 87 F2
Kariba Dam, Zimbabwe 87 F2
Kariba Gorge, Zambia 87 F2
Karibib, Namibia 88 C2
Karijini △, Australia 92 D2
Karimata, Kepulauan, Indonesia 62 E3
Karimata, Selat, Indonesia 62 E3
Karimata Is. = Karimata, Kepulauan, Indonesia ... 62 E3
Karimnagar, India 66 K11
Karimun Kecil, Pulau, Indonesia 65 d
Karimunjawa, Kepulauan, Indonesia ... 62 F4
Karin, Somali Rep. 75 E4
Káristos, Greece 46 C6
Karīt, Iran 71 C8
Kariya, Japan 55 G8
Kariyangwe, Zimbabwe 89 B4
Karjala, Finland 32 A5
Karkaralinsk = Qarqaraly, Kazakhstan ... 52 E8
Karkheh →, Iran 70 D5
Karkinitska Zatoka, Ukraine ... 33 K7
Karkinitskiy Zaliv = Karkinitska Zatoka, Ukraine ... 33 K7
Karkuk = Kirkūk, Iraq 70 C5
Karkur Tohl, Egypt 80 C2
Karl Liebknecht, Russia 33 G8
Karleby = Kokkola, Finland 8 E20
Karlholmsbruk, Sweden 10 D11
Karlino, Poland 30 D2
Karlivka, Ukraine 33 H8
Karlobag, Croatia 41 D12
Karlovac, Croatia 41 C12
Karlovarský □, Czech Rep. 26 A5
Karlovka = Karlivka, Ukraine .. 33 H8
Karlovo, Bulgaria 45 D8
Karlovy Vary, Czech Rep. 26 A5
Karlsbad = Karlovy Vary, Czech Rep. ... 26 A5
Karlsborg, Sweden 11 F8
Karlshamn, Sweden 11 H8
Karlskoga, Sweden 10 E8
Karlskrona, Sweden 11 H9
Karlsruhe, Germany 25 F4
Karlstad, Sweden 10 E7
Karlstad, U.S.A. 112 A6
Karlstadt, Germany 25 F5
Karma, Niger 83 C5
Karmėlava, Lithuania 30 D11
Karmi'el, Israel 74 C4
Karnak, Egypt 80 B3
Karnal, India 68 E7
Karnali →, Nepal 69 E9
Karnaphuli Res. = Kaptai L., Bangla. ... 67 H18
Karnaprayag, India 69 D8
Karnataka □, India 66 N10
Karnes City, U.S.A. 113 L6
Karnische Alpen, Europe 26 E6
Karnobat, Bulgaria 45 D10
Kärnten □, Austria 26 E6
Karo, Mali 82 C4
Karoi, Zimbabwe 87 F2
Karon, Ao, Thailand .... 65 a
Karonga, Malawi 87 D3
Karoo △, S. Africa 88 E3
Karoonda, Australia 95 F2
Karor, Pakistan 68 D4
Karora, Sudan 80 D4
Káros, Greece 47 E7
Karounga, Mali 82 B3
Karousádhes, Greece 46 A3
Karpacz, Poland 31 H2
Karpasia, Cyprus 49 D13
Kárpathos, Greece 47 F9
Kárpathos, Stenón, Greece 47 F9
Karpatsky △, Ukraine 29 B9
Karpenísion, Greece 46 C3
Karpuz Burnu = Apostolos Andreas, C., Cyprus ... 49 D13
Karpuzlu, Turkey 47 D9
Karratha, Australia 92 D2
Kars, Turkey 73 B10
Karsakpay, Kazakhstan 52 E7
Karsha, Russia 34 F10
Karshi = Qarshi, Uzbekistan ... 52 F7
Karsiyang, India 69 F13
Karsog, India 68 D7
Karst = Kras, Croatia 41 C10
Kartal, Turkey 45 F13
Kartál Óros, Greece 45 E9
Kartaly, Russia 52 D7
Kartapur, India 68 D6
Karthaus, U.S.A. 116 E6

Kartuzy, Poland 30 D5
Karufa, Indonesia 63 E8
Karuma △, Uganda 86 B3
Karumba, Australia 94 B3
Karumo, Tanzania 86 C3
Karumwa, Tanzania 86 C3
Kārūn →, Iran 71 D6
Karungu, Kenya 86 C3
Karup, Denmark 11 H3
Karviná, Czech Rep. 27 B11
Karwan →, India 68 F8
Karwar, India 66 M9
Karwendel △, Austria 26 D4
Karwi, India 69 G9
Kaş, Turkey 47 E11
Kasaba, Turkey 47 E11
Kasache, Malawi 87 E3
Kasai →, Dem. Rep. of the Congo 84 E3
Kasai-Oriental □, Dem. Rep. of the Congo ... 86 D1
Kasaji, Dem. Rep. of the Congo 87 E1
Kasama, Zambia 87 E3
Kasan-dong, N. Korea 57 D14
Kasane, Namibia 88 B3
Kasanga, Tanzania 87 D3
Kasanka △, Zambia 87 E3
Kasar, Ras, Sudan 80 D4
Kasaragod, India 66 N9
Kasba L., Canada 103 A8
Kāseh Garān, Iran 70 C5
Kasempa, Zambia 87 E2
Kasenga, Dem. Rep. of the Congo 87 E2
Kasese, Uganda 86 B3
Kasewa, Zambia 87 E2
Kasganj, India 69 F8
Kashabowie, Canada 104 C1
Kashaf, Iran 71 C9
Kashin, Russia 32 D9
Kashipur, India 69 E8
Kashira, Russia 32 E10
Kashiwazaki, Japan 55 F9
Kashk-e Kohneh, Afghan. 66 B3
Kashkū'īyeh, Iran 71 D7
Kāshmar, Iran 71 C8
Kashmir, Asia 69 C7
Kashmor, Pakistan 68 E3
Kashpirovka, Russia 34 D9
Kashun Noerh = Gaxun Nur, China ... 60 B5
Kasiari, India 69 H12
Kasimov, Russia 34 C5
Kasinge, Dem. Rep. of the Congo 86 D2
Kasiruta, Indonesia 63 E7
Kaskaskia →, U.S.A. 112 G10
Kaskattama →, Canada 103 B10
Kaskinen, Finland 9 E19
Kaskö = Kaskinen, Finland 9 E19
Kaslo, Canada 102 D5
Kasmere L., Canada 103 B8
Kasongo, Dem. Rep. of the Congo 86 C2
Kasongo Lunda, Dem. Rep. of the Congo ... 84 F3
Kásos, Greece 47 F8
Kásos, Stenón, Greece 47 F8
Kaspi, Georgia 35 K7
Kaspichan, Bulgaria 45 C11
Kaspiysk, Russia 35 J8
Kaspiyskiy, Russia 35 H8
Kassab ed Doleib, Sudan 81 E3
Kassaba, Egypt 80 C2
Kassalâ, Sudan 81 D4
Kassalâ □, Sudan 81 D4
Kassándra, Greece 44 F7
Kassándrinon, Greece 44 F7
Kassel, Germany 24 D5
Kassinger, Sudan 80 D3
Kassiópi, Greece 49 A3
Kasson, U.S.A. 112 C8
Kastamonu, Turkey 72 B5
Kastav, Croatia 41 C11
Kastélli, Greece 49 D5
Kastéllion, Greece 49 D7
Kastellórizon = Megiste, Greece 47 E11
Kástelos, Greece 47 E9
Kastellou, Ákra, Greece 47 F9
Kasterlee, Belgium 17 C4
Kastlösa, Sweden 11 H10
Kastóri, Greece 46 D4
Kastoría, Greece 44 F5
Kastoría □, Greece 44 F5
Kastorías, Límni, Greece 44 F5
Kastornoye, Russia 33 G10
Kastós, Greece 46 C2
Kastrosiká, Greece 46 B2
Kastrup, København ✈ (CPH), Denmark ... 11 J6
Kastsyukovichy, Belarus 32 F7
Kasulu, Tanzania 86 C3
Kasumi, Japan 55 G7
Kasumkent, Russia 35 K9
Kasungu, Malawi 87 E3
Kasungu △, Malawi 87 E3
Kasur, Pakistan 68 D6
Kata Tjuta = Olga, Mt., Australia 93 E5
Kataba, Zambia 87 F2
Katagum, Nigeria 83 C7
Katahdin, Mt., U.S.A. 115 C11
Katako Kombe, Dem. Rep. of the Congo ... 86 C1
Katákolon, Greece 46 D3
Katale, Tanzania 86 C3
Katanda, Katanga, Dem. Rep. of the Congo ... 86 D1
Katanda, Nord-Kivu, Dem. Rep. of the Congo ... 86 C2

Katanga □, Dem. Rep. of the Congo ... 86 D2
Katangi, India 66 J11
Katanning, Australia 93 F2
Katastári, Greece 46 D2
Katavi △, Tanzania 86 D3
Katavi Swamp, Tanzania 86 D3
Kateríni, Greece 44 F6
Katghora, India 69 H10
Katha, Burma 67 G20
Katherîna, Gebel, Egypt 70 D2
Katherine, Australia 92 B5
Katherine Gorge, Australia 92 B5
Kathi, India 68 J6
Kathiawar, India 68 H4
Kathikas, Cyprus 49 E11
Kathmandu = Katmandu, Nepal . 69 F11
Kathua, India 68 C6
Kati, Mali 82 C3
Katihar, India 69 G12
Katima Mulilo, Zambia 88 B3
Katimbira, Malawi 87 E3
Katingan = Mendawai →, Indonesia ... 62 E4
Katiola, Ivory C. 82 D3
Katlabukh, Özero, Ukraine 29 E14
Katlanovo, Macedonia 44 E5
Katmandu, Nepal 69 F11
Katni, India 69 H9
Káto Akhaïa, Greece 46 C3
Káto Arkhánai, Greece 49 D7
Káto Khorió, Greece 49 D7
Káto Pyrgos, Cyprus 49 D11
Káto Stavros, Greece 44 F7
Katokhí, Greece 46 C2
Katompe, Dem. Rep. of the Congo 86 D2
Katonga →, Uganda 86 B3
Katoomba, Australia 95 E5
Katoúna, Greece 46 C3
Katowice, Poland 31 H6
Katrancı Dağı, Turkey 47 D12
Katrine, L., U.K. 13 E4
Katrineholm, Sweden 10 E10
Katsepe, Madag. 89 B8
Katsina, Nigeria 83 C6
Katsina □, Nigeria 83 C6
Katsina Ala, Nigeria 83 D6
Katsina Ala →, Nigeria 83 D6
Katsumoto, Japan 55 H4
Katsuura, Japan 55 G10
Katsuyama, Japan 55 F8
Kattaviá, Greece 49 D9
Kattegat, Denmark 11 H5
Katthammarsvik, Sweden 11 G12
Katul, J., Sudan 81 E2
Katumba, Dem. Rep. of the Congo 86 D2
Katwa, India 69 H13
Katwijk, Neths. 17 B4
Kąty Wrocławskie, Poland 31 G3
Kauai, U.S.A. 106 H15
Kauai Channel, U.S.A. 106 H15
Kaub, Germany 25 E3
Kaudom △, Namibia 88 B3
Kaufbeuren, Germany 25 H6
Kaufman, U.S.A. 113 J6
Kauhajoki, Finland 9 E20
Kaukauna, U.S.A. 114 C1
Kaukauveld, Namibia 88 C3
Kaunakakai, U.S.A. 106 H16
Kaunas, Lithuania 9 J20
Kaunas ✈ (KUN), Lithuania 30 D11
Kaunia, Bangla. 69 G13
Kaunos, Turkey 47 E10
Kaura Namoda, Nigeria 83 C6
Kauru, Nigeria 83 C6
Kautokeino, Norway 8 B20
Kauwapur, India 69 F10
Kavacha, Russia 53 C17
Kavadarci, Macedonia 44 E6
Kavajë, Albania 44 E3
Kavak, Turkey 72 B7
Kavak Dağı, Turkey 47 D10
Kavaklı, Turkey 45 E11
Kavaklıdere, Turkey 47 D10
Kavalerovo, Russia 54 B7
Kavali, India 66 M12
Kaválla, Greece 45 F8
Kaválla □, Greece 45 F8
Kaválla Kólpos, Greece 45 F8
Kavār, Iran 71 D7
Kavarna, Bulgaria 45 C12
Kavi, India 68 H5
Kavimba, Botswana 88 B3
Kavīr, Dasht-e, Iran 71 C7
Kavkaz, Russia 33 K9
Kävlinge, Sweden 11 J7
Kavos, Greece 49 B4
Kavoúsi, Greece 47 F7
Kaw, Fr. Guiana 125 C8
Kawa, Sudan 81 E3
Kawagama L., Canada 116 A6
Kawagoe, Japan 55 G9
Kawaguchi, Japan 55 G9
Kawambwa, Zambia 87 D2
Kawanoe, Japan 55 G6
Kawardha, India 69 J9
Kawasaki, Japan 55 G9
Kawasi, Indonesia 63 E7
Kawerau, N.Z. 91 H6
Kawhia, N.Z. 91 H5
Kawhia Harbour, N.Z. 91 H5
Kawio, Kepulauan, Indonesia ... 63 D7
Kawnro, Burma 67 H21
Kawthaung, Burma 65 H2
Kawthoolei = Kayin □, Burma ... 67 L20
Kawthule = Kayin □, Burma 67 L20
Kaxholmen, Sweden 11 G8
Kaya, Burkina Faso 83 C4
Kayah □, Burma 67 K20
Kayalıköy Baraji, Turkey 45 E11
Kayan →, Indonesia 62 D5

Kaycee, U.S.A. 108 E10
Kayeli, Indonesia 63 E7
Kayenta, U.S.A. 109 H8
Kayes, Mali 82 C2
Kayı, Turkey 47 B12
Kayima, S. Leone 82 D2
Kayin □, Burma 67 L20
Kayoa, Indonesia 63 D7
Kayomba, Zambia 87 E1
Kaysatskoye, Russia 34 F8
Kayseri, Turkey 70 B2
Kaysville, U.S.A. 108 F8
Kaz Dağı, Turkey 47 B8
Kazachye, Russia 53 B14
Kazakhstan ■, Asia 52 E7
Kazan, Russia 34 C9
Kazan →, Canada 103 A9
Kazan-Rettō, Pac. Oc. 96 E6
Kazanlŭk, Bulgaria 45 D9
Kazanskaya, Russia 34 F5
Kazatin = Kozyatyn, Ukraine ... 33 H5
Kazaure, Nigeria 83 C6
Kazbek, Russia 35 J7
Kazi Magomed = Qazimämmäd, Azerbaijan ... 35 K9
Kazimierz Dolny, Poland 31 G8
Kazimierza Wielka, Poland 31 H7
Kazincbarcika, Hungary 28 B5
Kazlų Rūda, Lithuania 30 D10
Kaztalovka, Kazakhstan 34 F9
Kazuma Pan △, Zimbabwe 87 F2
Kazuno, Japan 54 D10
Kazym →, Russia 52 C7
Kcynia, Poland 31 F4
Ké-Macina, Mali 82 C3
Kéa, Greece 46 D6
Keady, U.K. 12 B5
Kearney, U.S.A. 112 E5
Kearny, U.S.A. 109 K8
Kearsage, Mt., U.S.A. 117 C13
Keban, Turkey 73 C8
Keban Baraji, Turkey 70 B3
Kebbi □, Nigeria 83 C5
Kébi, Ivory C. 82 D3
Kebnekaise, Sweden 8 C18
Kebri Dehar, Ethiopia 75 F3
Kebumen, Indonesia 63 G13
Kecel, Hungary 28 D4
Kechika →, Canada 102 B3
Keçiborlu, Turkey 47 D12
Kecskemét, Hungary 28 D4
Kedada, Ethiopia 81 F4
Kédainiai, Lithuania 9 J21
Kedarnath, India 69 D8
Kedgwick, Canada 105 C6
Kédhros Óros, Greece 49 D6
Kediri, Indonesia 63 G15
Kedjebi, Ghana 83 D5
Kédougou, Senegal 82 C2
Kędzierzyn-Koźle, Poland 31 H5
Keeler, U.S.A. 110 J9
Keeley L., Canada 103 C7
Keeling Is. = Cocos Is., Ind. Oc. 96 J1
Keelung = Chilung, Taiwan 59 E13
Keene, Canada 116 B6
Keene, Calif., U.S.A. 111 K8
Keene, N.H., U.S.A. 117 D12
Keene, N.Y., U.S.A. 117 B11
Keep River △, Australia 92 C4
Keeper Hill, Ireland 12 D3
Keer-Weer, C., Australia 94 A3
Keeseville, U.S.A. 117 B11
Keetmanshoop, Namibia 88 D2
Keewatin, Canada 103 D10
Keewatin →, Canada 103 B8
Kefa, Ethiopia 81 F4
Kefallinía, Greece 46 C2
Kefallinía □, Greece 46 C2
Kéfalos, Greece 47 E8
Kefamenanu, Indonesia 63 F6
Kefar Sava, Israel 74 C3
Keffi, Nigeria 83 D6
Keffin Hausa, Nigeria 83 C6
Keflavík, Iceland 8 D2
Keg River, Canada 102 B5
Kegaska, Canada 105 B7
Keheili, Sudan 80 D3
Kehl, Germany 25 G3
Keighley, U.K. 14 D6
Keila, Estonia 9 G21
Keimoes, S. Africa 88 D3
Keita, Niger 83 C6
Keitele, Finland 8 E22
Keith, Australia 95 F3
Keith, U.K. 13 D6
Keizer, U.S.A. 108 D2
Kejimkujik △, Canada 105 D6
Kejserr Franz Joseph Fd., Greenland ... 4 B6
Kekri, India 68 G6
Kelam, Ethiopia 81 G4
Kelamet, Eritrea 81 D4
Kelan, China 56 E6
Kelang = Klang, Malaysia 65 L3
Kelantan □, Malaysia 65 J4
Kelcyrë, Albania 44 F4
Kelekçi, Turkey 47 D11
Keles, Turkey 45 G13
Keleti-főcsatorna, Hungary 28 C6
Kelheim, Germany 25 G7
Kelkit, Turkey 73 B8
Kelkit →, Turkey 72 B7
Kellerberrin, Australia 93 F2
Kellett, C., Canada 4 B1
Kelleys I., U.S.A. 116 E2
Kellogg, U.S.A. 108 C5
Kells = Ceanannus Mor, Ireland 12 C5
Kelmė, Lithuania 30 C9
Kelmentsi, Ukraine 29 B11

Kelokedhara, Cyprus 49 E11
Kelowna, Canada 102 D5
Kelsey Creek, Australia 94 J6
Kelseyville, U.S.A. 110 G4
Kelso, N.Z. 91 L2
Kelso, U.K. 13 F6
Kelso, U.S.A. 110 D4
Keluang, Malaysia 65 L4
Kelvington, Canada 103 C8
Kem, Russia 52 C4
Kema, Indonesia 63 D7
Kemah, Turkey 70 B3
Kemaliye, Erzincan, Turkey 73 C8
Kemaliye, Manisa, Turkey 47 C10
Kemalpaşa, Turkey 47 C9
Kemano, Canada 102 C3
Kembolcha, Ethiopia 81 E4
Kemer, Antalya, Turkey 47 E12
Kemer, Burdur, Turkey 47 D12
Kemer, Muğla, Turkey 47 E11
Kemer Baraji, Turkey 47 D10
Kemerovo, Russia 52 D9
Kemeru △, Latvia 30 B10
Kemi, Finland 8 D21
Kemi älv = Kemijoki →, Finland 8 D21
Kemi träsk = Kemijärvi, Finland 8 C22
Kemijärvi, Finland 8 C22
Kemijoki →, Finland 8 D21
Kemmerer, U.S.A. 108 F8
Kemmuna = Comino, Malta 49 C1
Kemp, L., U.S.A. 113 J5
Kemp Land, Antarctica 5 C5
Kempas, Malaysia .... 65 d
Kempsey, Australia 95 E5
Kempt, L., Canada 104 C5
Kempten, Germany 25 H6
Kempton, Australia 95 G4
Kemptville, Canada 117 B9
Ken →, India 69 G9
Kenai, U.S.A. 100 B4
Kendai, India 69 H10
Kendal, Indonesia 63 G14
Kendal, U.K. 14 C5
Kendall, Australia 95 E5
Kendall, U.S.A. 115 N5
Kendall →, Australia 94 A3
Kendallville, U.S.A. 114 E3
Kendari, Indonesia 63 E6
Kendawangan, Indonesia 62 E4
Kende, Nigeria 83 C5
Kendi, Pulau, Malaysia .... 65 c
Kendrapara, India 67 J15
Kéndrevicës, Maja e, Albania .. 44 F3
Kendrew, S. Africa 88 E3
Kene Thao, Laos 64 D3
Kenedy, U.S.A. 113 L6
Kenema, S. Leone 82 D2
Keng Kok, Laos 64 D5
Keng Tawng, Burma 67 J21
Keng Tung, Burma 58 G2
Kengeja, Tanzania 86 D4
Kenhardt, S. Africa 88 D3
Kéniéba, Mali 82 C2
Kenitra, Morocco 78 B4
Kenli, China 57 F10
Kenmare, Ireland 12 E2
Kenmare, U.S.A. 112 A3
Kenmare River, Ireland 12 E2
Kennebago Lake, U.S.A. 117 A14
Kennebec, U.S.A. 112 D5
Kennebec →, U.S.A. 115 D11
Kennebunk, U.S.A. 117 C14
Kennedy, Zimbabwe 88 B4
Kennedy Ra., Australia 93 D2
Kennedy Range △, Australia 93 D2
Kenner, U.S.A. 113 L9
Kennet →, U.K. 15 F7
Kenneth Ra., Australia 93 D2
Kennett, U.S.A. 113 G9
Kennewick, U.S.A. 108 C4
Kenogami →, Canada 104 B3
Kenora, Canada 103 D10
Kenosha, U.S.A. 114 D2
Kensington, Canada 105 C7
Kent, Ohio, U.S.A. 116 E3
Kent, Tex., U.S.A. 113 K2
Kent, Wash., U.S.A. 110 C4
Kent, U.K. 15 F8
Kent Group, Australia 95 F4
Kent Pen., Canada 100 B9
Kentaū, Kazakhstan 52 E7
Kentland, U.S.A. 114 E2
Kenton, U.S.A. 114 E3
Kentucky □, U.S.A. 114 G3
Kentucky →, U.S.A. 114 F3
Kentucky L., U.S.A. 115 G2
Kentville, Canada 105 C7
Kentwood, U.S.A. 113 K9
Kenya ■, Africa 86 B4
Kenya, Mt., Kenya 86 C4
Keo Neua, Deo, Vietnam 64 C5
Keokuk, U.S.A. 112 E9
Keonjhargarh, India 69 J11
Kep, Cambodia 65 G5
Kep, Vietnam 64 B6
Kepala Batas, Malaysia .... 65 c
Kepez, Turkey 45 F10
Kepi, Indonesia 63 F9
Kepice, Poland 30 D3
Kępno, Poland 31 G4
Kepsut, Turkey 47 B10
Kerala □, India 66 P10
Kerama-Rettō, Japan 55 L3
Keran, Pakistan 69 B5
Keran △, Togo 83 C5
Keranyo, Ethiopia 81 F4
Kerao →, Sudan 81 E3
Keratéa, Greece 46 D5
Keraudren, C., Australia 92 C2

Kerava, Finland 9 F21
Kerch, Ukraine 33 K9
Kerchenskiy Proliv, Black Sea 33 K9
Kerchoual, Mali 83 B5
Kerempe Burnu, Turkey 72 A5
Keren, Eritrea 81 D4
Kerewan, Gambia 82 C1
Kerguelen, Ind. Oc. 3 G13
Keri, Greece 46 D2
Keri Kera, Sudan 81 E3
Kericho, Kenya 86 C4
Kerinci, Indonesia 62 E2
Kerki, Turkmenistan 52 F7
Kerkinítis, Límni, Greece 44 E7
Kérkira, Greece 49 A3
Kérkira □, Greece 46 B1
Kérkira ✈ (CFU), Greece 46 B1
Kerkouane, Tunisia 42 F4
Kerkrade, Neths. 17 D6
Kerma, Sudan 80 D3
Kermadec Is., Pac. Oc. 96 L10
Kermadec Trench, Pac. Oc. 96 L10
Kermān, Iran 71 D8
Kerman, U.S.A. 110 J6
Kermān □, Iran 71 D8
Kermān, Bīābān-e, Iran 71 D8
Kermānshāh = Bākhtarān, Iran 70 C5
Kermen, Bulgaria 45 D10
Kermit, U.S.A. 113 K3
Kern →, U.S.A. 111 K7
Kernhof, Austria 26 D8
Kernow = Cornwall □, U.K. 15 G3
Kernville, U.S.A. 111 K8
Keroh, Malaysia 65 K3
Kérou, Benin 83 C5
Kérouane, Guinea 82 D3
Kerpen, Germany 24 E2
Kerrera, U.K. 13 E3
Kerrobert, Canada 103 C7
Kerrville, U.S.A. 113 K5
Kerry □, Ireland 12 D2
Kerry Hd., Ireland 12 D2
Kersa, Ethiopia 81 F5
Kerulen →, Asia 60 B6
Kervo = Kerava, Finland 9 F21
Kerzaz, Algeria 78 C5
Kesagami →, Canada 104 B4
Kesagami L., Canada 104 B3
Keşan, Turkey 45 F10
Kesennuma, Japan 54 E10
Keshit, Iran 71 D8
Keşiş Dağ, Turkey 73 C8
Keskin, Turkey 72 C5
Kestell, S. Africa 89 D4
Kestenga, Russia 52 C4
Keswick, U.K. 14 C4
Keszthely, Hungary 28 D2
Ket →, Russia 52 D9
Keta, Ghana 83 D5
Keta Lagoon, Ghana 83 D5
Ketapang, Bali, Indonesia 63 J17
Ketapang, Kalimantan, Indonesia 62 E4
Ketchenery, Russia 35 G7
Ketchikan, U.S.A. 102 B2
Ketchum, U.S.A. 108 E6
Kete Krachi, Ghana 83 D4
Ketef, Khalîg Umm el, Egypt 70 F2
Keti Bandar, Pakistan 68 G2
Kétou, Benin 83 D5
Ketri, India 68 E6
Kętrzyn, Poland 30 D8
Kettering, U.K. 15 E7
Kettering, U.S.A. 114 F3
Kettle →, Canada 103 B11
Kettle Falls, U.S.A. 108 B4
Kettle Pt., Canada 116 C2
Kettleman City, U.S.A. 110 J7
Kęty, Poland 31 J6
Keuka L., U.S.A. 116 D7
Keuruu, Finland 9 E21
Kevelaer, Germany 24 D2
Kewanee, U.S.A. 112 E10
Kewaunee, U.S.A. 114 C2
Keweenaw B., U.S.A. 114 B1
Keweenaw Pen., U.S.A. 114 B2
Keweenaw Pt., U.S.A. 114 B2
Key Largo, U.S.A. 115 N5
Key West, U.S.A. 107 F10
Keyala, Sudan 81 G3
Keynsham, U.K. 15 F5
Keyser, U.S.A. 114 F6
Kezhma, Russia 53 D11
Kezi, Zimbabwe 89 C4
Kežmarok, Slovak Rep. 27 B13
Kgalagadi Transfrontier △, Africa 88 D3
Khabarovsk, Russia 53 E14
Khabr, Iran 71 D8
Khābūr →, Syria 70 C4
Khachmas = Xaçmaz, Azerbaijan 35 K9
Khachrod, India 68 H6
Khadari, W. el →, Sudan 81 E2
Khadro, Pakistan 68 F3
Khadyzhensk, Russia 35 H4
Khadzhilyangar, China 69 B8
Khaga, India 69 G9
Khagaria, India 69 G12
Khaipur, Pakistan 68 E5
Khair, India 68 F7
Khairabad, India 69 F9
Khairagarh, India 69 J9
Khairpur, Pakistan 68 F3
Khairpur Nathan Shah, Pakistan 68 F2
Khairwara, India 68 H5
Khaisor →, Pakistan 68 D3
Khajuri Kach, Pakistan 68 C3
Khakassia □, Russia 52 D9
Khakhea, Botswana 88 C3
Khalafābād, Iran 71 D6
Khalīlī, Iran 71 E7
Khalkhāl, Iran 71 B6
Khálki, Dhodhekánisos, Greece 47 E9

Khálki, Thessalía, Greece 46 B4
Khalkidhikí □, Greece 44 F7
Khalkís, Greece 46 C5
Khalmer Yu, Russia 52 C7
Khalûf, Oman 75 C6
Kham Keut, Laos 64 C5
Khamaria, India 69 H9
Khambhaliya, India 68 H3
Khambhat, India 68 H5
Khambhat, G. of, India 66 J8
Khamilonísion, Greece 47 F8
Khamīr, Iran 71 E7
Khamir, Yemen 75 D3
Khamsa, Egypt 74 E1
Khan →, Namibia 88 C2
Khān Abū Shāmat, Syria 74 B5
Khān Azād, Iraq 70 C5
Khān Mujiddah, Iraq 70 C4
Khān Shaykhūn, Syria 70 C3
Khān Yūnis, Gaza Strip 74 D3
Khanai, Pakistan 68 D2
Khānaqīn, Iraq 70 C5
Khānbāghī, Iran 71 B7
Khandra, Greece 47 F8
Khandwa, India 66 J10
Khandyga, Russia 53 C14
Khāneh, Iran 70 B5
Khanewal, Pakistan 68 D4
Khangah Dogran, Pakistan 68 D5
Khanh Duong, Vietnam 64 F7
Khaniá, Greece 49 D6
Khaniá □, Greece 49 D6
Khaniadhana, India 68 G8
Khanión, Kólpos, Greece 49 D5
Khanka, L., Asia 53 E14
Khankendy = Xankändi, Azerbaijan 70 B5
Khanna, India 68 D7
Khanozai, Pakistan 68 D2
Khanpur, Pakistan 68 E4
Khanty-Mansiysk, Russia 52 C7
Khao Laem, Thailand 64 E2
Khao Laem Res., Thailand 64 E2
Khao Luang, Thailand 65 H2
Khao Phlu, Thailand 65 b
Khao Pu-Khao Ya □, Thailand 65 J2
Khao Sam Roi Yot □, Thailand 65 F2
Khao Sok △, Thailand 65 H2
Khao Yai △, Thailand 64 E3
Khaoen Si Nakarin △, Thailand 64 E2
Khapalu, Pakistan 69 B7
Khapcheranga, Russia 53 E12
Kharabali, Russia 35 G8
Kharaghoda, India 68 H4
Kharagpur, India 69 H12
Kharan Kalat, Pakistan 66 E4
Kharānaq, Iran 71 C7
Kharda, India 66 K9
Khardung La, India 69 B7
Kharg = Khārk, Jazīreh-ye, Iran 71 D6
Khārga, El Wâhât-el, Egypt 80 B3
Khargon, India 66 J9
Khari →, India 68 G6
Kharian, Pakistan 68 C5
Kharit, Wadi el →, Egypt 80 C3
Khārk, Jazīreh-ye, Iran 71 D6
Kharkiv, Ukraine 33 H9
Kharkov = Kharkiv, Ukraine 33 H9
Kharmanli, Bulgaria 45 E9
Kharovsk, Russia 32 C11
Kharsawangarh, India 69 H11
Khartoum = El Khartûm, Sudan 81 D3
Khasan, Russia 54 C5
Khasavyurt, Russia 35 J8
Khāsh, Iran 66 E2
Khashm el Girba, Sudan 81 E4
Khashum, Sudan 81 E2
Khashuri, Georgia 35 J6
Khaskovo, Bulgaria 45 E9
Khaskovo □, Bulgaria 45 E9
Khatanga, Russia 53 B11
Khatanga →, Russia 53 B11
Khatauli, India 68 E7
Khatra, India 69 H12
Khātūnābād, Iran 71 D7
Khatyrka, Russia 53 C18
Khavda, India 68 H3
Khaybar, Ḥarrat, Si. Arabia 70 E4
Khayelitsha, S. Africa 85 L3
Khāzimiyah, Iraq 70 C4
Khazzân Jabal al Awliyâ, Sudan 81 D3
Khe Bo, Vietnam 64 C5
Khe Long, Vietnam 64 B5
Khe Sanh, Vietnam 64 D6
Khed Brahma, India 66 G8
Khekra, India 68 E7
Khemarak Phouminville, Cambodia 65 G4
Khemisset, Morocco 78 B4
Khemmarat, Thailand 64 D5
Khenāmān, Iran 71 D8
Khersān →, Iran 71 D6
Khérson, Greece 44 E9
Kherson, Ukraine 33 J7
Khersónisos Akrotíri, Greece 49 D6
Kheta →, Russia 53 B11
Khewari, Pakistan 68 F3
Khilchipur, India 68 G7
Khiliomódhion, Greece 46 D4
Khilok, Russia 53 D12
Khimki, Russia 32 E9
Khíos, Greece 47 C8
Khíos □, Greece 47 C8
Khirsadoh, India 69 H8
Khiuma = Hiiumaa, Estonia 9 G20
Khiva, Uzbekistan 52 E7
Khīyāv, Iran 70 B5
Khlebarovo, Bulgaria 45 C10
Khlong Khlung, Thailand 64 D2

Khmelnik, Ukraine 33 H4
Khmelnitskiy = Khmelnytskyy, Ukraine 33 H4
Khmelnytskyy, Ukraine 33 H4
Khmer Rep. = Cambodia ■, Asia 64 F5
Khoai, Hon, Vietnam 65 H5
Khodoriv, Ukraine 33 H3
Khodzent = Khŭjand, Tajikistan 52 E7
Khojak Pass, Afghan. 68 D2
Khok Kloi, Thailand 65 a
Khok Pho, Thailand 65 J3
Kholm, Russia 32 D6
Kholmsk, Russia 53 E15
Khomas Hochland, Namibia 88 C2
Khombole, Senegal 82 C1
Khomeyn, Iran 71 C6
Khomeynī Shahr, Iran 71 C6
Khomodino, Botswana 88 C3
Khon Kaen, Thailand 64 D4
Khong →, Cambodia 64 F5
Khong Sedone, Laos 64 E5
Khonu, Russia 53 C15
Khoper →, Russia 34 F6
Khor el 'Atash, Sudan 81 E3
Khóra, Greece 46 D3
Khóra Sfakíon, Greece 49 D6
Khorāsān □, Iran 71 C8
Khorat = Nakhon Ratchasima, Thailand 64 E4
Khorat, Cao Nguyen, Thailand 64 E4
Khorixas, Namibia 88 C1
Khorol, Ukraine 33 H7
Khorramābād, Khorāsān, Iran 71 C8
Khorramābād, Lorestān, Iran 71 C6
Khorrāmshahr, Iran 71 D6
Khorugh, Tajikistan 52 F8
Khosravī, Iran 71 D6
Khosrowābād, Khuzestān, Iran 71 D6
Khosrowābād, Kordestān, Iran 70 C5
Khost, Pakistan 68 D2
Khosūyeh, Iran 71 D7
Khotyn, Ukraine 29 B11
Khouribga, Morocco 78 B4
Khowst, Afghan. 68 C3
Khowst □, Afghan. 66 C6
Khoyniki, Belarus 33 G5
Khrami →, Georgia 35 K6
Khrenovoye, Russia 34 E5
Khrisoúpolis, Greece 45 F8
Khristianá, Greece 47 E7
Khrysokhou B., Cyprus 49 D11
Khtapodhiá, Greece 47 D7
Khu Khan, Thailand 64 E5
Khuan Wa, Thailand 65 a
Khudzhand = Khŭjand, Tajikistan 52 E7
Khuff, Si. Arabia 70 E5
Khūgīānī, Afghan. 68 D2
Khuis, Botswana 88 D3
Khuiyala, India 68 F4
Khŭjand, Tajikistan 52 E7
Khujner, India 68 H7
Khulna, Bangla. 67 H16
Khulna □, Bangla. 67 H16
Khulo, Georgia 35 K6
Khumago, Botswana 88 C3
Khūnsorkh, Iran 71 E8
Khunti, India 69 H11
Khūr, Iran 71 C8
Khurai, India 68 G8
Khurayş, Si. Arabia 71 E6
Khureit, Sudan 81 E2
Khurīyā Murīyā, Jazā'ir, Oman 75 D6
Khurja, India 68 E7
Khūrmāl, Iraq 70 C5
Khurr, Wādi al, Iraq 70 C4
Khūsf, Iran 71 C8
Khush, Afghan. 66 C3
Khushab, Pakistan 68 C5
Khust, Ukraine 29 B8
Khutse △, Botswana 88 C3
Khuzdar, Pakistan 68 F2
Khūzestān □, Iran 71 D6
Khvāf, Iran 71 C9
Khvājeh, Iran 70 B5
Khvānsār, Iran 71 D7
Khvatovka, Russia 34 D8
Khvor, Iran 71 C7
Khvorgū, Iran 71 E8
Khvormūj, Iran 71 D6
Khvoy, Iran 70 B5
Khvoynaya, Russia 32 C8
Khyber Pass, Afghan. 68 B4
Khyriv, Ukraine 28
Kiabukwa, Dem. Rep. of the Congo 87 D1
Kiama, Australia 95 E5
Kiamba, Phil. 61 H6
Kiambi, Dem. Rep. of the Congo 86 D2
Kiambu, Kenya 86 C4
Kiang West □, Gambia 82 C1
Kiangara, Madag. 89 B8
Kiangsi = Jiangxi □, China 59 D11
Kiangsu = Jiangsu □, China 57 H11
Kiáton, Greece 46 C4
Kibæk, Denmark 11 H2
Kibale □, Uganda 86 B3
Kibanga Port, Uganda 86 B3
Kibare, Mts., Dem. Rep. of the Congo 86 D2
Kibira △, Burundi 86 C3
Kibombo, Dem. Rep. of the Congo 86 C2
Kibondo, Tanzania 86 C3
Kibre Mengist, Ethiopia 81 F4
Kibumbu, Burundi 86 C2
Kibuye, Burundi 86 C2
Kibuye, Rwanda 86 C2
Kibwesa, Tanzania 86 D2
Kibwezi, Kenya 86 C4

Kicasalih, Turkey 45 E10
Kičevo, Macedonia 44 E4
Kichha, India 69 E8
Kichha →, India 69 E8
Kicking Horse Pass, Canada 102 C5
Kidal, Mali 83 B5
Kidderminster, U.K. 15 E5
Kidepo Valley △, Uganda 86 B3
Kidete, Tanzania 86 D4
Kidira, Senegal 82 C2
Kidnappers, C., N.Z. 91 H6
Kidsgrove, U.K. 14 D5
Kidston, Australia 94 B3
Kidugallo, Tanzania 86 D4
Kiel, Germany 24 A6
Kiel Canal = Nord-Ostsee-Kanal, Germany 24 A5
Kielce, Poland 31 H7
Kielder Water, U.K. 14 B5
Kieler Bucht, Germany 24 A6
Kiembara, Burkina Faso 82 C4
Kien Binh, Vietnam 65 H5
Kien Tan, Vietnam 65 G5
Kienge, Dem. Rep. of the Congo 87 E2
Kiessé, Niger 83 C5
Kifaya, Guinea 82 C2
Kiffa, Mauritania 82 B2
Kifisiá, Greece 46 C5
Kifissós →, Greece 46 C5
Kifrī, Iraq 70 C5
Kigali, Rwanda 86 C3
Kigarama, Tanzania 86 C3
Kigelle, Sudan 81 F3
Kigezi □, Uganda 86 C3
Kigoma □, Tanzania 86 D3
Kigoma-Ujiji, Tanzania 86 C3
Kigomasha, Ras, Tanzania 86 C4
Kığı, Turkey 70 B4
Kihei, U.S.A. 106 H16
Kihnu, Estonia 9 G21
Kii-Sanchi, Japan 55 G8
Kii-Suidō, Japan 55 H7
Kikaiga-Shima, Japan 55 K4
Kikinda, Serbia & M. 28 E5
Kikládhes, Greece 46 E6
Kikládhes □, Greece 46 D6
Kikwit, Dem. Rep. of the Congo 84 E3
Kil, Sweden 10 E7
Kilafors, Sweden 10 C10
Kilar, India 68 C7
Kilauea Crater, U.S.A. 106 J17
Kilbrannan Sd., U.K. 13 F3
Kilchu, N. Korea 57 D15
Kilcoy, Australia 95 D5
Kildare, Ireland 12 C5
Kildare □, Ireland 12 C5
Kileikli, Sudan 81 E2
Kilfinnane, Ireland 12 D3
Kilgore, U.S.A. 113 J7
Kilibo, Benin 83 D5
Kilifi, Kenya 86 C4
Kilimanjaro, Tanzania 86 C4
Kilimanjaro □, Tanzania 86 C4
Kilimli, Turkey 72 B4
Kilindini, Kenya 86 C4
Kilis, Turkey 70 B3
Kiliya, Ukraine 29 E14
Kilkee, Ireland 12 D2
Kilkeel, U.K. 12 B5
Kilkenny, Ireland 12 D4
Kilkenny □, Ireland 12 D4
Kilkieran B., Ireland 12 C2
Kilkís, Greece 44 F6
Kilkís □, Greece 44 F6
Killala, Ireland 12 B2
Killala B., Ireland 12 B2
Killaloe, Canada 116 A7
Killaloe, Ireland 12 D3
Killarney, Australia 95 D5
Killarney, Canada 103 D9
Killarney, Ireland 12 D2
Killarney △, Ireland 12 D2
Killary Harbour, Ireland 12 C2
Killdeer, U.S.A. 112 B3
Killeberg, Sweden 11 H8
Killeen, U.S.A. 113 K6
Killin, U.K. 13 E4
Killíni, Ilía, Greece 46 D3
Killíni, Korinthía, Greece 46 D4
Killorglin, Ireland 12 D2
Killybegs, Ireland 12 B3
Kilmarnock, U.K. 13 F4
Kilmez, Russia 34 B10
Kilmez →, Russia 34 B10
Kilmore, Australia 95 F3
Kilondo, Tanzania 87 D3
Kilosa, Tanzania 86 D4
Kilrush, Ireland 12 D2
Kilwa Kisiwani, Tanzania 87 D4
Kilwa Kivinje, Tanzania 87 D4
Kilwa Masoko, Tanzania 87 D4
Kilwinning, U.K. 13 F4
Kim, U.S.A. 113 G3
Kimaam, Indonesia 63 F9
Kimamba, Tanzania 86 D4
Kimba, Australia 95 E2
Kimball, Nebr., U.S.A. 112 E3
Kimball, S. Dak., U.S.A. 112 D5
Kimberley, Australia 92 C4
Kimberley, Canada 102 D5
Kimberley, S. Africa 88 D3
Kimberly, U.S.A. 108 E6
Kimch'aek, N. Korea 57 D15
Kimch'ŏn, S. Korea 57 F15
Kími, Greece 46 C6
Kimje, S. Korea 57 G14
Kimmirut, Canada 101 B13
Kímolos, Greece 46 E6
Kimovsk, Moskva, Russia 32 E9
Kimovsk, Tula, Russia 32 E10

Kimparana, Mali 82 C4
Kimpese, Dem. Rep. of the Congo 84 F2
Kimry, Russia 32 D9
Kimstad, Sweden 11 F9
Kinabalu, Gunung, Malaysia 62 C5
Kínaros, Greece 47 E8
Kinaskan L., Canada 102 B2
Kinbasket L., Canada 102 C5
Kincardine, Canada 116 B3
Kincolith, Canada 102 C3
Kinda, Dem. Rep. of the Congo 87 D2
Kindberg, Austria 26 D8
Kinde, U.S.A. 116 C2
Kinder Scout, U.K. 14 D6
Kindersley, Canada 103 C7
Kindia, Guinea 82 D2
Kindu, Dem. Rep. of the Congo 86 C2
Kinel, Russia 34 D10
Kineshma, Russia 34 B6
Kinesi, Tanzania 86 C3
King, L., Australia 93 F2
King, Mt., Australia 94 D4
King City, U.S.A. 110 J5
King Cr. →, Australia 94 C2
King Edward →, Australia 92 B4
King Frederick VI Land = Kong Frederik VI Kyst, Greenland 101 B15
King George B., Falk. Is. 128 G4
King George I., Antarctica 5 C18
King George Is., Canada 101 C11
King I. = Kadan Kyun, Burma 64 F2
King I., Australia 95 F3
King I., Canada 102 C3
King Leopold Ranges, Australia 92 C4
King of Prussia, U.S.A. 117 F9
King Sd., Australia 92 C3
King Sejong, Antarctica 5 C18
King William I., Canada 100 B10
King William's Town, S. Africa 88 E4
Kingait = Cape Dorset, Canada 101 B12
Kingaok = Bathurst Inlet, Canada 100 B9
Kingaroy, Australia 95 D5
Kingfisher, U.S.A. 113 H6
Kingirbān, Iraq 70 C5
Kingman, Ariz., U.S.A. 111 K12
Kingman, Kans., U.S.A. 113 G5
Kingoonya, Australia 95 E2
Kingri, Pakistan 68 D3
Kings →, U.S.A. 110 J7
Kings Canyon △, U.S.A. 110 J8
King's Lynn, U.K. 14 E8
Kings Mountain, U.S.A. 115 H5
Kings Park, U.S.A. 117 F11
King's Peak, U.S.A. 108 F8
Kingsbridge, U.K. 15 G4
Kingsburg, U.S.A. 110 J7
Kingscote, Australia 95 F2
Kingscourt, Ireland 12 C5
Kingsford, U.S.A. 114 C1
Kingsland, U.S.A. 115 K5
Kingsley, U.S.A. 112 D7
Kingsport, U.S.A. 115 G4
Kingston, Canada 117 B8
Kingston, Jamaica 120 a
Kingston, N.Z. 91 L2
Kingston, N.H., U.S.A. 117 D13
Kingston, N.Y., U.S.A. 117 E11
Kingston, Pa., U.S.A. 117 E9
Kingston, R.I., U.S.A. 117 E13
Kingston Pk., U.S.A. 111 K11
Kingston South East, Australia 95 F2
Kingston upon Hull, U.K. 14 D7
Kingston upon Hull □, U.K. 14 D7
Kingston-upon-Thames □, U.K. 15 F7
Kingstown, St. Vincent 121 D7
Kingstree, U.S.A. 115 J6
Kingsville, Canada 116 D2
Kingsville, U.S.A. 113 M6
Kingussie, U.K. 13 D4
Kingwood, U.S.A. 113 K7
Kınık, Antalya, Turkey 47 E11
Kınık, Izmir, Turkey 47 B9
Kinistino, Canada 103 C7
Kinkala, Congo 84 E2
Kinki □, Japan 55 H8
Kinleith, N.Z. 91 H5
Kinlochleven, U.K. 13 E4
Kinmount, Canada 116 B6
Kinna, Sweden 11 G6
Kinnairds Hd., U.K. 13 D6
Kinnared, Sweden 11 G7
Kinnarp, Sweden 11 F7
Kinnevikken, Sweden 11 F7
Kino, Mexico 118 B2
Kinoje →, Canada 104 B3
Kinomoto, Japan 55 G8
Kinoni, Uganda 86 C3
Kinoosao, Canada 103 B8
Kinross, U.K. 13 E5
Kinsale, Ireland 12 E3
Kinsale, Old Hd. of, Ireland 12 E3
Kinsha = Chang Jiang →, China 59 B13
Kinshasa, Dem. Rep. of the Congo 84 E3
Kinsley, U.S.A. 113 G5
Kinsman, U.S.A. 116 E4
Kinston, U.S.A. 115 H7
Kintampo, Ghana 83 D4
Kintore Ra., Australia 92 D4
Kinushseo →, Canada 104 A3
Kinuso, Canada 102 B5
Kinyangiri, Tanzania 86 C3
Kinzig →, Germany 25 G3
Kinzua, U.S.A. 116 E6
Kinzua Dam, U.S.A. 116 E6
Kióni, Greece 46 C2

Kiosk, Canada ... 104 C4
Kiowa, Kans., U.S.A. ... 113 G5
Kiowa, Okla., U.S.A. ... 113 H7
Kipahigan L., Canada ... 103 B8
Kipanga, Tanzania ... 86 D4
Kiparissía, Greece ... 46 D3
Kiparissiakós Kólpos, Greece ... 46 D3
Kipawa, L., Canada ... 104 C4
Kipembawe, Tanzania ... 86 D3
Kipengere Ra., Tanzania ... 87 D3
Kipili, Tanzania ... 86 D3
Kipini, Kenya ... 86 C5
Kipling, Canada ... 103 C8
Kipushi, Dem. Rep. of the Congo ... 87 E2
Kirane, Mali ... 82 B2
Kiranomena, Madag. ... 89 B8
Kiraz, Turkey ... 47 C10
Kirazlı, Turkey ... 45 F10
Kirchhain, Germany ... 24 E4
Kirchheim, Germany ... 25 G5
Kirchheimbolanden, Germany ... 25 F3
Kirchschlag, Austria ... 27 D9
Kireç, Turkey ... 47 B10
Kirensk, Russia ... 53 D11
Kirghizia = Kyrgyzstan ■, Asia ... 52 E8
Kirghizstan = Kyrgyzstan ■, Asia ... 52 E8
Kiribati ■, Pac. Oc. ... 96 H10
Kırıkhan, Turkey ... 72 D7
Kırıkkale, Turkey ... 72 C5
Kirillov, Russia ... 32 C10
Kirin = Jilin, China ... 57 C14
Kirinyaga = Kenya, Mt., Kenya ... 86 C4
Kirishi, Russia ... 32 C7
Kirishima Yaku △, Japan ... 55 J5
Kırka, Croatia ... 41 E12
Kırkağaç, Turkey ... 47 B9
Kirkby, U.K. ... 14 D5
Kirkby-in-Ashfield, U.K. ... 14 D6
Kirkby Lonsdale, U.K. ... 14 C5
Kirkby Stephen, U.K. ... 14 C5
Kirkcaldy, U.K. ... 13 E5
Kirkcudbright, U.K. ... 13 G4
Kirkee, India ... 66 K8
Kirkenes, Norway ... 8 B23
Kirkfield, Canada ... 116 B6
Kirkintilloch, U.K. ... 13 F4
Kirkjubæjarklaustur, Iceland ... 8 E4
Kirkkonummi, Finland ... 9 F21
Kirkland Lake, Canada ... 104 C3
Kırklareli, Turkey ... 45 E11
Kırklareli □, Turkey ... 45 E11
Kirksville, U.S.A. ... 112 E8
Kirkük, Iraq ... 70 C5
Kirkwall, U.K. ... 13 C6
Kirkwood, S. Africa ... 88 E4
Kirn, Germany ... 25 F3
Kirov, Kaluga, Russia ... 32 E8
Kirov, Kirov, Russia ... 52 D5
Kirovabad = Gäncä, Azerbaijan ... 35 K8
Kirovograd = Kirovohrad, Ukraine ... 33 H7
Kirovohrad, Ukraine ... 33 H7
Kirovskiy, Astrakhan, Russia ... 35 H9
Kirovskiy, Kamchatka, Russia ... 53 D16
Kirovskiy, Primorsk, Russia ... 54 B6
Kirriemuir, U.K. ... 13 E5
Kirsanov, Russia ... 34 D6
Kırşehir, Turkey ... 70 B2
Kirtachi, Niger ... 83 C5
Kirthar Range, Pakistan ... 68 F2
Kirtland, U.S.A. ... 109 H9
Kiruna, Sweden ... 8 C19
Kirundu, Dem. Rep. of the Congo ... 86 C2
Kirya, Russia ... 34 C8
Kiryū, Japan ... 55 F9
Kisa, Sweden ... 11 G9
Kisaga, Tanzania ... 86 C3
Kisalaya, Nic. ... 120 D3
Kisalföld, Hungary ... 28 C2
Kisámou, Kólpos, Greece ... 49 D5
Kisanga, Dem. Rep. of the Congo ... 86 B2
Kisangani, Dem. Rep. of the Congo ... 86 B2
Kisar, Indonesia ... 63 F7
Kisarawe, Tanzania ... 86 D4
Kisarazu, Japan ... 55 G9
Kisbér, Hungary ... 28 C3
Kishanganga →, Pakistan ... 69 B5
Kishanganj, India ... 69 F13
Kishangarh, Raj., India ... 68 F6
Kishangarh, Raj., India ... 68 F4
Kishi, Nigeria ... 83 D5
Kishinev = Chişinău, Moldova ... 29 C13
Kishiwada, Japan ... 55 G7
Kishtwar, India ... 69 C6
Kisielice, Poland ... 30 E6
Kisigo →, Tanzania ... 86 D3
Kisii, Kenya ... 86 C3
Kisiju, Tanzania ... 86 D4
Kisir, Turkey ... 73 B10
Kisizi, Uganda ... 86 C2
Kiskomárom = Zalakomár, Hungary ... 28 D2
Kiskörei-víztároló, Hungary ... 28 C5
Kiskőrös, Hungary ... 28 D4
Kiskundorozsma, Hungary ... 28 D5
Kiskunfélegyháza, Hungary ... 28 D4
Kiskunhalas, Hungary ... 28 D4
Kiskunmajsa, Hungary ... 28 D4
Kiskunsági △, Hungary ... 28 D4
Kislovodsk, Russia ... 35 J6
Kismayu = Chisimaio, Somali Rep. ... 77 G8
Kiso-Gawa →, Japan ... 55 G8
Kiso-Sammyaku, Japan ... 55 G8
Kisofukushima, Japan ... 55 G8
Kisoro, Uganda ... 86 C2
Kissidougou, Guinea ... 82 D2
Kissimmee, U.S.A. ... 115 L5
Kissimmee →, U.S.A. ... 115 M5

Kississing L., Canada ... 103 B8
Kissónerga, Cyprus ... 49 E11
Kissu, J., Sudan ... 80 C2
Kistanje, Croatia ... 41 E12
Kisújszállás, Hungary ... 28 C5
Kisumu, Kenya ... 86 C3
Kisvárda, Hungary ... 28 B7
Kiswani, Tanzania ... 86 C4
Kiswere, Tanzania ... 87 D4
Kit Carson, U.S.A. ... 112 F3
Kita, Mali ... 82 C3
Kitaibaraki, Japan ... 55 F10
Kitakami, Japan ... 54 E10
Kitakami-Gawa →, Japan ... 54 E10
Kitakami-Sammyaku, Japan ... 54 E10
Kitakata, Japan ... 54 F9
Kitakyūshū, Japan ... 55 H5
Kitale, Kenya ... 86 B4
Kitami, Japan ... 54 C11
Kitami-Sammyaku, Japan ... 54 B11
Kitangiri, L., Tanzania ... 86 C3
Kitaya, Tanzania ... 87 E5
Kitchener, Canada ... 116 C4
Kitee, Finland ... 32 A6
Kitega = Gitega, Burundi ... 86 C2
Kitengo, Dem. Rep. of the Congo ... 86 D1
Kitgum, Uganda ... 86 B3
Kíthira, Greece ... 46 E5
Kíthnos, Greece ... 46 D6
Kiti, Cyprus ... 49 E12
Kiti, C., Cyprus ... 49 E12
Kitimat, Canada ... 102 C3
Kitinen →, Finland ... 8 C22
Kitiyab, Sudan ... 81 D3
Kítros, Greece ... 44 F6
Kitsman, Ukraine ... 29 B10
Kitsuki, Japan ... 55 H5
Kittakittaooloo, L., Australia ... 95 D2
Kittanning, U.S.A. ... 116 F5
Kittatinny Mts., U.S.A. ... 117 F10
Kittery, U.S.A. ... 115 D10
Kittilä, Finland ... 8 C21
Kitui, Kenya ... 86 C4
Kitwanga, Canada ... 102 B3
Kitwe, Zambia ... 87 E2
Kitzbühel, Austria ... 26 D5
Kitzbühler Alpen, Austria ... 26 D5
Kitzingen, Germany ... 25 F6
Kivarli, India ... 68 G5
Kivertsi, Ukraine ... 33 G3
Kividhes, Cyprus ... 49 E11
Kivik, Sweden ... 11 J8
Kivotós, Greece ... 44 F5
Kivu, L., Dem. Rep. of the Congo ... 86 C2
Kiyev = Kyyiv, Ukraine ... 33 G6
Kiyevskoye Vdkhr. = Kyyivske Vdskh., Ukraine ... 33 G6
Kıyıköy, Turkey ... 45 E12
Kiziguru, Rwanda ... 86 C3
Kızıl Adalar, Turkey ... 45 F13
Kızıl Irmak →, Turkey ... 72 B6
Kizil Jilga, China ... 69 B8
Kizil Yurt, Russia ... 35 J8
Kızılcabölük, Turkey ... 47 D11
Kızılcadağ, Turkey ... 47 D11
Kızılcahamam, Turkey ... 72 B5
Kızılhisar, Turkey ... 72 D3
Kızılırmak, Turkey ... 72 B5
Kızılkaya, Turkey ... 47 D12
Kızılören, Turkey ... 47 C12
Kızıltepe, Turkey ... 70 B4
Kizimkazi, Tanzania ... 86 D4
Kizlyar, Russia ... 35 J8
Kizyl-Arvat = Gyzylarbat, Turkmenistan ... 52 F6
Kjellerup, Denmark ... 11 H3
Kjölur, Iceland ... 8 D4
Kladanj, Bos.-H. ... 28 F3
Kladnica, Serbia & M. ... 44 C4
Kladno, Czech Rep. ... 26 A7
Kladovo, Serbia & M. ... 44 B6
Klaeng, Thailand ... 64 F3
Klagenfurt, Austria ... 26 E7
Klaipėda, Lithuania ... 9 J19
Klaipėda □, Lithuania ... 30 C8
Klaksvík, Færoe Is. ... 8 E9
Klamath →, U.S.A. ... 108 F1
Klamath Falls, U.S.A. ... 108 E3
Klamath Mts., U.S.A. ... 108 F2
Klamono, Indonesia ... 63 E8
Klang, Malaysia ... 65 L3
Klanjec, Croatia ... 41 B12
Klappan →, Canada ... 102 B3
Klarälven →, Sweden ... 10 E7
Klässbol, Sweden ... 10 E6
Klatovy, Czech Rep. ... 26 B6
Klawer, S. Africa ... 88 E2
Klazienaveen, Neths. ... 17 B6
Klé, Mali ... 82 C3
Klecko, Poland ... 31 F4
Kleczew, Poland ... 31 F5
Kleena Kleene, Canada ... 102 C4
Klein-Karas, Namibia ... 88 D2
Klekovača, Bos.-H. ... 41 D13
Klembivka, Ukraine ... 29 B13
Klenoec, Macedonia ... 44 E4
Klenovec, Slovak Rep. ... 27 C12
Klerksdorp, S. Africa ... 88 D4
Kleszczele, Poland ... 31 F10
Kletnya, Russia ... 32 F7
Kletsk = Klyetsk, Belarus ... 33 F4
Kletskiy, Russia ... 35 F6
Kleve, Germany ... 24 D2
Klickitat, U.S.A. ... 108 D3
Klickitat →, U.S.A. ... 110 E5
Klidhes, Cyprus ... 49 D13
Klimovichi, Belarus ... 32 F6
Klin, Russia ... 32 D9
Klina, Serbia & M. ... 44 D4
Klinaklini →, Canada ... 102 C3
Klintehamn, Sweden ... 11 G12
Klintsy, Russia ... 33 F7

Klip →, S. Africa ... 89 D4
Klipdale, S. Africa ... 88 E2
Klippan, Sweden ... 11 H7
Klipplaat, S. Africa ... 88 E3
Klisura, Bulgaria ... 45 D8
Klishkivtsi, Ukraine ... 29 B11
Kljajićevo, Serbia & M. ... 28 E4
Ključ, Bos.-H. ... 41 D13
Kłobuck, Poland ... 31 H5
Klockestrand, Sweden ... 10 B11
Kłodawa, Poland ... 31 F5
Kłodzko, Poland ... 31 H3
Klong Wang Chao △, Thailand ... 64 D2
Klos, Albania ... 44 E4
Klosterneuburg, Austria ... 27 C9
Klosters, Switz. ... 25 J5
Klötze, Germany ... 24 C7
Klouto, Togo ... 83 D5
Kluane △, Canada ... 102 A1
Kluane L., Canada ... 100 B6
Kluczbork, Poland ... 31 H5
Klukwan, U.S.A. ... 102 B1
Klungkung, Indonesia ... 63 K18
Klyetsk, Belarus ... 33 F4
Klyuchevskaya, Gora, Russia ... 53 D17
Knäred, Sweden ... 11 H7
Knaresborough, U.K. ... 14 C6
Knee L., Man., Canada ... 104 A1
Knee L., Sask., Canada ... 103 B7
Knezha, Bulgaria ... 45 C8
Knight Inlet, Canada ... 102 C3
Knighton, U.K. ... 15 E4
Knights Ferry, U.S.A. ... 110 H6
Knights Landing, U.S.A. ... 110 G5
Knin, Croatia ... 41 D13
Knislinge, Sweden ... 11 H8
Knittelfeld, Austria ... 26 D7
Knivsta, Sweden ... 10 E11
Knjaževac, Serbia & M. ... 44 C6
Knob, C., Australia ... 93 F2
Knock, Ireland ... 12 C3
Knockmealdown Mts., Ireland ... 12 D4
Knokke-Heist, Belgium ... 17 C3
Knossós, Greece ... 49 D7
Knowlton, Canada ... 117 A12
Knox, U.S.A. ... 114 E2
Knox Coast, Antarctica ... 5 C8
Knoxville, Iowa, U.S.A. ... 112 E8
Knoxville, Pa., U.S.A. ... 116 E7
Knoxville, Tenn., U.S.A. ... 115 H4
Knud Rasmussen Land, Greenland ... 4 A5
Knysna, S. Africa ... 88 E3
Knyszyn, Poland ... 30 E9
Ko Kha, Thailand ... 64 C2
Ko Tarutao △, Thailand ... 65 J2
Ko Yao, Thailand ... 65 a
Koartac = Quaqtaq, Canada ... 101 B13
Koba, Indonesia ... 63 F8
Kobarid, Slovenia ... 41 B10
Kobayashi, Japan ... 55 J5
Kōbe, Japan ... 55 G7
Kobelyaky, Ukraine ... 33 H8
København, Denmark ... 11 J6
København ✈ (CPH), Denmark ... 11 J6
Københavns Amtskommune □, Denmark ... 11 J6
Kobenni, Mauritania ... 82 B3
Kōbi-Sho, Japan ... 55 M1
Koblenz, Germany ... 25 E3
Kobo, Ethiopia ... 81 E4
Kobryn, Belarus ... 33 F3
Kobuleti, Georgia ... 35 K5
Kobyletska Polyana, Ukraine ... 29 B9
Kobylin, Poland ... 31 G4
Kobyłka, Poland ... 31 F8
Kobylkino, Russia ... 34 C6
Koca →, Turkey ... 45 F11
Kocabaş, Turkey ... 47 D11
Kocaeli, Turkey ... 45 F13
Kocaeli □, Turkey ... 45 F13
Kočane, Serbia & M. ... 44 C5
Kočani, Macedonia ... 44 E6
Koçarlı, Turkey ... 47 D9
Koceljevo, Serbia & M. ... 44 B3
Kočevje, Slovenia ... 41 C11
Koch Bihar, India ... 67 F16
Kochang, S. Korea ... 57 G14
Kochas, India ... 69 G10
Kocher →, Germany ... 25 F5
Kochi = Cochin, India ... 66 Q10
Kōchi, Japan ... 55 H6
Kōchi □, Japan ... 55 H6
Kochiu = Gejiu, China ... 58 F4
Kock, Poland ... 31 G9
Kodarma, India ... 69 G11
Kode, Sweden ... 11 G5
Kodiak, U.S.A. ... 100 C4
Kodiak I., U.S.A. ... 100 C4
Kodinar, India ... 68 J4
Kodok, Sudan ... 81 F3
Kodori →, Georgia ... 35 J5
Kodyma, Ukraine ... 29 B14
Koedoesberge, S. Africa ... 88 E3
Koes, Namibia ... 88 D2
Kofçaz, Turkey ... 45 E11
Koffiefontein, S. Africa ... 88 D4
Kofiau, Indonesia ... 63 E7
Koforidua, Ghana ... 83 D4
Kōfu, Japan ... 55 G9
Kogaluc →, Canada ... 105 A7
Køge, Denmark ... 11 J6
Køge Bugt, Denmark ... 11 J6
Kogi □, Nigeria ... 83 D6
Kogin Baba, Nigeria ... 83 D7
Koh-i-Khurd, Afghan. ... 68 C1
Koh-i-Maran, Pakistan ... 68 E2
Kohat, Pakistan ... 68 C4
Kohima, India ... 67 G19

Kohkīlūyeh va Büyer Aḥmadi □, Iran ... 71 D6
Kohler Ra., Antarctica ... 5 D15
Kohlu, Pakistan ... 68 E3
Kohtla-Järve, Estonia ... 9 G22
Kohylnyk →, Ukraine ... 29 E14
Koi Sanjaq, Iraq ... 70 B5
Koillismaa, Finland ... 8 D23
Koin-dong, N. Korea ... 57 D14
Koinare, Bulgaria ... 45 C8
Koindu, S. Leone ... 82 D2
Kojetín, Czech Rep. ... 27 B10
Kojŏ, N. Korea ... 57 E14
Kojonup, Australia ... 93 F2
Kojūr, Iran ... 71 B6
Koka, Sudan ... 80 C3
Kokand = Qŭqon, Uzbekistan ... 52 E8
Kokas, Indonesia ... 63 E8
Kokava, Slovak Rep. ... 27 C12
Kokchetav = Kökshetaū, Kazakhstan ... 52 D7
Kokemäenjoki →, Finland ... 9 F19
Kokhma, Russia ... 34 B5
Koki, Senegal ... 82 B1
Kokkola, Finland ... 8 E20
Koko, Nigeria ... 83 C5
Koko Kyunzu, Burma ... 67 M18
Kokolopozo, Ivory C. ... 82 D3
Komomo, U.S.A. ... 114 E2
Kokoro, Niger ... 83 C5
Koksan, N. Korea ... 57 E14
Kökshetaū, Kazakhstan ... 52 D7
Koksoak →, Canada ... 101 C13
Kokstad, S. Africa ... 89 E4
Kokubu, Japan ... 55 J5
Kola, Indonesia ... 63 F8
Kola Pen. = Kolskiy Poluostrov, Russia ... 52 C4
Kolachi →, Pakistan ... 68 F2
Kolahoi, India ... 69 B6
Kolahun, Liberia ... 82 D2
Kolaka, Indonesia ... 63 E6
Kolar, India ... 66 N11
Kolar Gold Fields, India ... 66 N11
Kolaras, India ... 68 G6
Kolari, Finland ... 8 C20
Kolárovo, Slovak Rep. ... 27 D10
Kolašin, Serbia & M. ... 44 D3
Kolayat, India ... 66 F8
Kolbäck, Sweden ... 10 E10
Kolbäcksån →, Sweden ... 10 E10
Kolbermoor, Germany ... 25 H8
Kolbuszowa, Poland ... 31 H8
Kolchugino, Russia ... 32 D10
Koldegi, Sudan ... 81 E3
Kolding, Denmark ... 11 J3
Kolepom = Dolak, Pulau, Indonesia ... 63 F9
Kolguyev, Ostrov, Russia ... 52 C5
Kolhapur, India ... 66 L9
Kolia, Ivory C. ... 82 D3
Kolín, Czech Rep. ... 26 A8
Kolind, Denmark ... 11 H4
Kolkas rags, Latvia ... 9 H20
Kolkata, India ... 69 H13
Kölleda, Germany ... 24 D7
Kollum, Neths. ... 17 A6
Kolmanskop, Namibia ... 88 D2
Köln, Germany ... 24 E2
Kolno, Poland ... 30 E8
Koło, Poland ... 31 F5
Kołobrzeg, Poland ... 30 D2
Kolochava, Ukraine ... 29 B8
Kolokani, Mali ... 82 C3
Koloko, Burkina Faso ... 82 C3
Kolomna, Russia ... 32 E10
Kolomyya, Ukraine ... 29 B10
Kolondiéba, Mali ... 82 C3
Kolonodale, Indonesia ... 63 E6
Kolonowskie, Poland ... 31 H5
Kolosib, India ... 67 G18
Kolpashevo, Russia ... 52 D9
Kolpino, Russia ... 32 C6
Kolpny, Russia ... 33 F9
Kolskiy Poluostrov, Russia ... 52 C4
Kolsva, Sweden ... 10 E9
Kolubara →, Serbia & M. ... 44 B4
Koluszki, Poland ... 31 G6
Kolwezi, Dem. Rep. of the Congo ... 87 E2
Kolyma →, Russia ... 53 C17
Kolymskoye Nagorye, Russia ... 53 C16
Kôm Hamâda, Egypt ... 80 H7
Kôm Ombo, Egypt ... 80 C3
Komadugu Gana →, Nigeria ... 83 C7
Komandorskiye Is. = Komandorskiye Ostrova, Russia ... 53 D17
Komandorskiye Ostrova, Russia ... 53 D17
Komárno, Slovak Rep. ... 27 D11
Komárom, Hungary ... 28 C3
Komárom-Esztergom □, Hungary ... 28 C3
Komatipoort, S. Africa ... 89 D5
Komatou Yialou, Cyprus ... 49 D13
Komatsu, Japan ... 55 F8
Komatsushima, Japan ... 55 H7
Kombissiri, Burkina Faso ... 83 C4
Kombori, Burkina Faso ... 82 C4
Kombóti, Greece ... 46 B3
Komen, Slovenia ... 41 C10
Komenda, Ghana ... 83 D4
Komi □, Russia ... 52 C6
Komiža, Croatia ... 41 E13
Komló, Hungary ... 28 D3
Kommunarsk = Alchevsk, Ukraine ... 33 H10
Kommunizma, Pik, Tajikistan ... 52 F8
Komodo, Indonesia ... 63 F5
Komoé →, Ivory C. ... 82 D4

Komoran, Pulau, Indonesia ... 63 F9
Komoro, Japan ... 55 F9
Komotini, Greece ... 45 E9
Komovi, Serbia & M. ... 44 D3
Kompasberg, S. Africa ... 88 E3
Kompong Bang, Cambodia ... 65 F5
Kompong Cham, Cambodia ... 65 F5
Kompong Chhnang = Kompong Chnang, Cambodia ... 65 F5
Kompong Chikreng, Cambodia ... 64 F5
Kompong Kleang, Cambodia ... 64 F5
Kompong Luong, Cambodia ... 65 G5
Kompong Pranak, Cambodia ... 64 F5
Kompong Som = Kampong Saom, Cambodia ... 65 G4
Kompong Som, Chhung = Kampong Saom, Chaak, Cambodia ... 65 G4
Kompong Speu, Cambodia ... 65 G5
Kompong Sralau, Cambodia ... 64 E5
Kompong Thom, Cambodia ... 64 F5
Kompong Trabeck, Cambodia ... 64 F5
Kompong Trabeck, Cambodia ... 65 G5
Kompong Trach, Cambodia ... 65 G5
Kompong Tralach, Cambodia ... 65 G5
Komrat = Comrat, Moldova ... 29 D13
Komsberg, S. Africa ... 88 E3
Komsomolets, Ostrov, Russia ... 53 A10
Komsomolsk, Amur, Russia ... 53 D14
Komsomolsk, Ivanovo, Russia ... 32 D11
Komsomolskiy, Russia ... 34 C7
Kömür Burnu, Turkey ... 47 C8
Kon Tum, Vietnam ... 64 E7
Kon Tum, Plateau du, Vietnam ... 64 E7
Kona, Mali ... 82 C4
Konarhā □, Afghan. ... 66 B7
Konārī, Iran ... 71 D6
Konch, India ... 69 G8
Konde, Tanzania ... 86 C4
Kondiá, Greece ... 47 B7
Kondinin, Australia ... 93 F2
Kondoa, Tanzania ... 86 C4
Kondókali, Greece ... 49 A3
Kondopaga, Russia ... 32 A8
Kondratyevo, Russia ... 53 D10
Kondrovo, Russia ... 32 E8
Konduga, Nigeria ... 83 C7
Köneürgench, Turkmenistan ... 52 E6
Konevo, Russia ... 32 A10
Kong = Khong →, Cambodia ... 64 F5
Kong, Ivory C. ... 82 D4
Kong, Koh, Cambodia ... 65 G4
Kong Christian IX Land, Greenland ... 4 C6
Kong Christian X Land, Greenland ... 4 B6
Kong Frederik IX Land, Greenland ... 4 C5
Kong Frederik VI Kyst, Greenland ... 101 B15
Kong Frederik VIII Land, Greenland ... 4 B6
Kong Oscar Fjord, Greenland ... 4 B6
Kongeå →, Denmark ... 11 J2
Kongerslev, Denmark ... 11 H4
Kongju, S. Korea ... 57 F14
Konglu, Burma ... 67 F20
Kongola, Namibia ... 88 B3
Kongolo, Kasai-Or., Dem. Rep. of the Congo ... 86 D1
Kongolo, Katanga, Dem. Rep. of the Congo ... 86 D2
Kongoran, Sudan ... 81 F3
Kongoussi, Burkina Faso ... 83 C4
Kongsberg, Norway ... 9 G13
Kongsvinger, Norway ... 9 F15
Kongwa, Tanzania ... 86 D4
Koni, Dem. Rep. of the Congo ... 87 E2
Koni, Mts., Dem. Rep. of the Congo ... 87 E2
Koniakari, Mali ... 82 C2
Koniecpol, Poland ... 31 H6
Königs Wusterhausen, Germany ... 24 C9
Königsbrunn, Germany ... 25 G6
Königslutter, Germany ... 24 C6
Konin, Poland ... 31 F5
Konispol, Albania ... 44 G4
Kónitsa, Greece ... 46 A2
Konjic, Bos.-H. ... 28 G2
Konkiep, Namibia ... 88 D2
Konkouré →, Guinea ... 82 D2
Könnern, Germany ... 24 D7
Kono, S. Leone ... 82 D2
Konongo, Ghana ... 83 D4
Konosha, Russia ... 32 B11
Kōnosu, Japan ... 55 F9
Konotop, Ukraine ... 33 G7
Konsankoro, Guinea ... 82 D3
Końskie, Poland ... 31 G7
Konstancin-Jeziorna, Poland ... 31 F8
Konstantinovka = Kostyantynivka, Ukraine ... 33 H9
Konstantinovsk, Russia ... 35 G5
Konstantynów Łódzki, Poland ... 31 G6
Konstanz, Germany ... 25 H5
Kont, Iran ... 71 E9
Kontagora, Nigeria ... 83 C6
Kontcha, Cameroon ... 83 D7
Konya, Turkey ... 70 B2
Konya Ovası, Turkey ... 72 C5
Konz, Germany ... 25 F2
Konza, Kenya ... 86 C4
Koocanusa, L., Canada ... 108 B6
Kookynie, Australia ... 93 E3
Koolyanobbing, Australia ... 93 F2
Kooniba, Australia ... 95 E1
Koorawatha, Australia ... 93 F2
Koorda, Australia ... 93 F2
Kooskia, U.S.A. ... 108 C6
Kootenay △, Canada ... 102 C5
Kootenay →, U.S.A. ... 102 D5

Kootenay L., *Canada* 102 D5
Kootjieskolk, *S. Africa* 88 E3
Kopanovka, *Russia* 35 G8
Kopaonik, *Serbia & M.* 44 C4
Kopaonik △, *Serbia & M.* 44 C4
Kópavogur, *Iceland* 8 D3
Kopayhorod, *Ukraine* 29 B12
Koper, *Slovenia* 41 C10
Kopervik, *Norway* 9 G11
Kopet Dagh, *Asia* 71 B8
Kopi, *Australia* 95 E2
Köping, *Sweden* 10 E10
Köpingsvik, *Sweden* 11 H10
Kopište, *Croatia* 41 F13
Koplik, *Albania* 44 D3
Köpmanholmen, *Sweden* 10 A12
Kopparberg, *Sweden* 10 E9
Koppeh Dāgh = Kopet Dagh,
  Asia 71 B8
Koppies, *S. Africa* 89 D4
Koppom, *Sweden* 10 E6
Koprivlen, *Bulgaria* 44 E7
Koprivnica, *Croatia* 41 B13
Kopřivnice, *Czech Rep.* 27 B11
Koprivshtitsa, *Bulgaria* 45 D8
Köprübaşı, *Turkey* 47 C10
Kopychyntsi, *Ukraine* 33 H3
Kora △, *Kenya* 86 C4
Korab, *Macedonia* 44 E4
Korakiána, *Greece* 49 A3
Koral, *India* 68 J5
Korarou, L., *Mali* 82 B4
Korba, *India* 69 H10
Korbach, *Germany* 24 D4
Korbu, G., *Malaysia* 65 K3
Korçë, *Albania* 44 F4
Korčula, *Croatia* 41 F13
Korčulanski Kanal, *Croatia* ... 41 E13
Kord Kūy, *Iran* 71 B7
Kord Sheykh, *Iran* 71 D7
Kordestan = Kurdistan, *Asia* .. 73 D10
Kordestān □, *Iran* 70 C5
Kordofân, *Sudan* 79 F11
Koré Mayroua, *Niger* 83 C5
Korea, North ■, *Asia* 57 E14
Korea, South ■, *Asia* 57 G15
Korea Bay, *Korea* 57 E13
Korea Strait, *Asia* 57 H15
Korem, *Ethiopia* 81 E4
Korenevo, *Russia* 33 G8
Korenovsk, *Russia* 35 H4
Korets, *Ukraine* 33 G4
Korfantów, *Poland* 31 H4
Korgan, *Turkey* 72 B7
Korgus, *Sudan* 80 D3
Korhogo, *Ivory C.* 82 D3
Koribundu, *S. Leone* 82 D2
Korienzé, *Mali* 82 B4
Korinthía □, *Greece* 46 D4
Korinthiakós Kólpos, *Greece* .. 46 C4
Kórinthos, *Greece* 46 D4
Korioumé, *Mali* 82 B4
Koríssa, Límni, *Greece* 49 B3
Kōriyama, *Japan* 54 F10
Korkuteli, *Turkey* 47 D12
Kormakíti, C., *Cyprus* 49 D11
Körmend, *Hungary* 28 C1
Kornat, *Croatia* 41 E12
Kornat △, *Croatia* 41 E12
Korneshty = Corneşti, *Moldova* . 29 C13
Korneuburg, *Austria* 27 C9
Kórnik, *Poland* 31 F4
Koro, *Fiji* 91 C8
Koro, *Ivory C.* 82 D3
Koro, *Mali* 82 C4
Koro Sea, *Fiji* 91 C9
Köroğlu Dağları, *Turkey* 72 B5
Korogwe, *Tanzania* 86 D4
Koroleve, *Ukraine* 29 B8
Koronadal, *Phil.* 61 H6
Koróni, *Greece* 46 E3
Korónia, Limni, *Greece* 44 F7
Koronís, *Greece* 47 D7
Koronowo, *Poland* 31 E4
Koropets, *Ukraine* 29 B10
Koror, *Palau* 96 G5
Körös →, *Hungary* 28 D5
Körös Maros △, *Hungary* 28 C5
Köröstarcsa, *Hungary* 28 D6
Korosten, *Ukraine* 33 G5
Korostyshev, *Ukraine* 33 G5
Korotoyak, *Russia* 33 G10
Korraraika, Helodranon' i,
  Madag. 89 B7
Korsakov, *Russia* 53 E15
Korsberga, *Sweden* 11 G9
Korshiv, *Ukraine* 29 B10
Korshunovo, *Russia* 53 D12
Korsør, *Denmark* 11 J5
Korsun Shevchenkovskiy,
  Ukraine 33 H6
Korsze, *Poland* 30 D8
Korti, *Sudan* 80 D3
Kortrijk, *Belgium* 17 D3
Korucu, *Turkey* 47 B9
Korwai, *India* 68 G8
Koryakskoye Nagorye, *Russia* . 53 C18
Koryŏng, *S. Korea* 57 G15
Koryukovka, *Ukraine* 33 G7
Kos, *Greece* 47 E9
Kosa, *Ethiopia* 81 F4
Kosaya Gora, *Russia* 32 E9
Kościan, *Poland* 31 F3
Kościerzyna, *Poland* 30 D4
Kosciusko, *U.S.A.* 113 J10
Kosciuszko, Mt., *Australia* ... 95 F4
Kösely →, *Hungary* 28 C6
Kosha, *Sudan* 80 C3
Koshava, *Bulgaria* 44 B7
K'oshih = Kashi, *China* 60 C2
Koshiki-Rettō, *Japan* 55 J4

Kosi, *India* 68 F7
Kosi →, *India* 69 E8
Košice, *Slovak Rep.* 27 C14
Košický □, *Slovak Rep.* 27 C14
Kosiv, *Ukraine* 29 B10
Kosjerić, *Serbia & M.* 44 B3
Kösk, *Turkey* 47 D10
Koskinoú, *Greece* 49 C10
Koslan, *Russia* 52 C5
Kosmach, *Ukraine* 29 B9
Kosŏng, *N. Korea* 57 E15
Kosovo □, *Serbia & M.* 44 D4
Kosovo Polje, *Serbia & M.* ... 44 D4
Kosovska Kamenica, *Serbia & M.* 44 D5
Kosovska Mitrovica, *Serbia & M.* 44 D4
Kossou, L. de, *Ivory C.* 82 D3
Kosta, *Sweden* 11 H9
Kostajnica, *Croatia* 41 C13
Kostanjevica, *Slovenia* 41 C12
Kostenets, *Bulgaria* 44 D7
Koster, *S. Africa* 88 D4
Kôstî, *Sudan* 81 E3
Kostinbrod, *Bulgaria* 44 D7
Kostolac, *Serbia & M.* 44 B5
Kostopil, *Ukraine* 33 G4
Kostroma, *Russia* 32 D11
Kostromskoye Vdkhr., *Russia* . 32 D11
Kostrzyhivka, *Ukraine* 29 B10
Kostrzyn, *Lubuskie. Poland* ... 31 F1
Kostrzyn, *Wielkopolskie, Poland* 31 F4
Kostyantynivka, *Ukraine* 33 H9
Kostyukovichi = Kastsyukovichy,
  Belarus 32 F7
Koszalin, *Poland* 30 D3
Kőszeg, *Hungary* 28 C1
Kot Addu, *Pakistan* 68 D4
Kot Kapura, *India* 68 D6
Kot Moman, *Pakistan* 68 C5
Kot Sultan, *Pakistan* 68 D4
Kota, *India* 68 G6
Kota Barrage, *India* 68 G6
Kota Belud, *Malaysia* 62 C5
Kota Bharu, *Malaysia* 65 J4
Kota Kinabalu, *Malaysia* 62 C5
Kota Kubu Bharu, *Malaysia* ... 65 L3
Kota Tinggi, *Malaysia* 65 M4
Kotaagung, *Indonesia* 62 F2
Kotabaru, *Indonesia* 62 E5
Kotabumi, *Indonesia* 62 E2
Kotamobagu, *Indonesia* 63 D6
Kotcho L., *Canada* 102 B4
Kotdwara, *India* 69 E8
Kotel, *Bulgaria* 45 D10
Kotelnich, *Russia* 34 A9
Kotelnikovo, *Russia* 35 G6
Kotelnyy, Ostrov, *Russia* 53 B14
Kothari →, *India* 68 G6
Köthen, *Germany* 24 D7
Kothi, *Chhattisgarh, India* ... 69 H10
Kothi, *Mad. P., India* 69 G9
Kotiro, *Pakistan* 68 F2
Kotka, *Finland* 9 F22
Kotlas, *Russia* 52 C5
Kotlenska Planina, *Bulgaria* ... 45 D10
Kotli, *Pakistan* 69 C5
Kotma, *India* 69 H9
Kotmul, *Pakistan* 69 B6
Koton-Karifi, *Nigeria* 83 D6
Kotonkoro, *Nigeria* 83 C6
Kotor, *Serbia & M.* 44 D2
Kotor Varoš, *Bos.-H.* 28 F2
Kotoriba, *Croatia* 41 B13
Kotovo, *Russia* 34 E7
Kotovsk, *Russia* 34 D5
Kotovsk, *Ukraine* 33 J5
Kotputli, *India* 68 F7
Kotri, *Pakistan* 68 G3
Kótronas, *Greece* 46 E4
Kötschach-Mauthen, *Austria* .. 26 E6
Kotturu, *India* 66 M10
Kotuy →, *Russia* 53 B11
Kotyuzhany, *Ukraine* 29 B12
Kotzebue, *U.S.A.* 100 B3
Kouchibouguac △, *Canada* 105 C6
Koudougou, *Burkina Faso* 82 C4
Koufonísi, *Greece* 49 E8
Koufonísia, *Greece* 47 E7
Kougaberge, *S. Africa* 88 E3
Kouibli, *Ivory C.* 82 D3
Kouilou →, *Congo* 84 E2
Koula Moutou, *Gabon* 84 E2
Koulen = Kulen, *Cambodia* ... 64 F5
Koulikoro, *Mali* 82 C3
Koulourou →, *Greece* 49 A3
Koúm-bournoú, Ákra, *Greece* . 49 C10
Koumala, *Australia* 94 C4
Koumankou, *Mali* 82 C3
Koumbia, *Burkina Faso* 82 C4
Koumbia, *Guinea* 82 C2
Koumboum, *Guinea* 82 C2
Koumpenntoum, *Senegal* 82 C2
Koumra, *Chad* 79 G9
Koun-Fao, *Ivory C.* 82 D4
Koundara, *Guinea* 82 C2
Koundian, *Guinea* 82 C2
Koungheul, *Senegal* 82 C2
Kounradskiy, *Kazakhstan* 52 E8
Kountze, *U.S.A.* 113 K7
Koupéla, *Burkina Faso* 83 C4
Kourémalé, *Mali* 82 C3
Kouris →, *Cyprus* 49 E11
Kourou, *Fr. Guiana* 125 B8
Kourouba, *Mali* 82 C3
Kouroukoto, *Mali* 82 C3
Kourouma, *Burkina Faso* 82 C4
Kouroussa, *Guinea* 82 C3
Kourouninkoto, *Mali* 82 C3
Koussané, *Mali* 82 C2
Koussanar, *Senegal* 82 C2
Koussane, *Senegal* 82 C2
Kousséri, *Cameroon* 79 F8
Koutiala, *Mali* 82 C3

Kouto, *Ivory C.* 82 D3
Kouvé, *Togo* 83 D5
Kouvola, *Finland* 9 F22
Kovačica, *Serbia & M.* 28 E5
Kovel, *Ukraine* 33 G3
Kovin, *Serbia & M.* 28 F5
Kovrov, *Russia* 34 B5
Kowal, *Poland* 31 F6
Kowalewo Pomorskie, *Poland* . 31 E5
Kowanyama, *Australia* 94 B3
Kowloon, *China* 59 F10
Kowŏn, *N. Korea* 57 E14
Koyampattur = Coimbatore, *India* 66 P10
Köyceğiz, *Turkey* 47 E10
Köyceğiz Gölü, *Turkey* 47 E10
Koyulhisar, *Turkey* 72 B7
Koyunyeri, *Turkey* 45 F10
Koza, *Japan* 55 L3
Kozak, *Turkey* 47 B9
Kozan, *Turkey* 70 B2
Kozáni, *Greece* 44 F5
Kozáni □, *Greece* 44 F5
Kozara, *Bos.-H.* 41 D14
Kozara △, *Bos.-H.* 41 D13
Kozarac, *Bos.-H.* 41 D13
Kozelets, *Ukraine* 33 G6
Kozelsk, *Russia* 32 E8
Kozhikode = Calicut, *India* ... 66 P9
Koziegłowy, *Poland* 31 H6
Kozienice, *Poland* 31 G8
Kozje, *Slovenia* 41 B12
Kozloduy, *Bulgaria* 44 C7
Kozlovets, *Bulgaria* 45 C9
Kozlovka, *Russia* 34 C9
Kozlu, *Turkey* 72 B4
Kozluk, *Turkey* 73 C9
Koźmin, *Poland* 31 G4
Kozmodemyansk, *Russia* 34 B8
Kożuchów, *Poland* 31 G2
Kozyatyn, *Ukraine* 33 H5
Kpabia, *Ghana* 83 D4
Kpalimé, *Togo* 83 D5
Kpandae, *Ghana* 83 D4
Kpessi, *Togo* 83 D5
Kra, Isthmus of = Kra, Kho Khot,
  Thailand 65 G2
Kra, Kho Khot, *Thailand* 65 G2
Kra Buri, *Thailand* 65 G2
Kraai →, *S. Africa* 88 E4
Krabi, *Thailand* 65 H2
Kracheh, *Cambodia* 64 F6
Kragan, *Indonesia* 63 G14
Kragerø, *Norway* 9 G13
Kragujevac, *Serbia & M.* 44 B4
Krajenka, *Poland* 31 E3
Krakatau = Rakata, Pulau,
  Indonesia 62 F3
Krakatoa = Rakata, Pulau,
  Indonesia 62 F3
Krakor, *Cambodia* 64 F5
Kraków, *Poland* 31 H6
Kraków ✈ (KRK), *Poland* 31 H6
Kralanh, *Cambodia* 64 F4
Králíky, *Czech Rep.* 27 A9
Kraljevo, *Serbia & M.* 44 C4
Kralovéhradecký □, *Czech Rep.* 26 A8
Královský, *Slovak Rep.* 27 C14
Kralupy nad Vltavou, *Czech Rep.* 26 A7
Kramatorsk, *Ukraine* 33 H9
Kramfors, *Sweden* 10 B11
Kraniá, *Greece* 44 G5
Kraniá Elassónas, *Greece* 46 B4
Kranídhion, *Greece* 46 D5
Kranj, *Slovenia* 41 B11
Krankskop, *S. Africa* 89 D5
Krapina, *Croatia* 41 B12
Krapina →, *Croatia* 41 C12
Krapkowice, *Poland* 31 H4
Kras, *Croatia* 41 B11
Kraskino, *Russia* 53 E14
Krāslava, *Latvia* 32 E4
Kraslice, *Czech Rep.* 26 A5
Krasnaya Gorbatka, *Russia* ... 34 C5
Krasnaya Polyana, *Russia* 35 J5
Krasne, *Ukraine* 29 D14
Krasni Okny, *Ukraine* 29 C14
Kraśnik, *Poland* 31 H9
Krasnoarmeisk, *Ukraine* 33 H9
Krasnoarmeysk, *Russia* 34 E7
Krasnoarmeyskiy, *Russia* 35 G5
Krasnobrod, *Poland* 31 H10
Krasnodar, *Russia* 35 H4
Krasnodon, *Ukraine* 33 H10
Krasnogorskiy, *Russia* 34 B9
Krasnograd = Krasnohrad,
  Ukraine 33 H8
Krasnogvardeysk, *Uzbekistan* . 33 K8
Krasnogvardeyskoye, *Russia* .. 35 H5
Krasnohrad, *Ukraine* 33 H8
Krasnokutsk, *Ukraine* 33 G8
Krasnolesnyy, *Russia* 33 G10
Krasnoperekopsk, *Ukraine* ... 33 J7
Krasnorechenskiy, *Russia* 54 B7
Krasnoselkup, *Russia* 52 C9
Krasnoslobodsk, Mordvinia,
  Russia 34 C6
Krasnoslobodsk, Volgograd,
  Russia 35 E6
Krasnoturinsk, *Russia* 52 D7
Krasnoyarsk, *Russia* 53 D10
Krasnoyarskoye, *Russia* 35 D8
Krasnoye = Krasnyy, *Russia* .. 32 E6
Krasnoyilsk, *Ukraine* 33 K10
Krasnozavodsk, *Russia* 32 D10
Krasnoznamensk, *Russia* 30 D9
Krasny Sulin, *Russia* 33 J11
Krasnystaw, *Poland* 31 H10
Krasnyy, *Russia* 32 E6
Krasnyy Kholm, *Russia* 32 C9
Krasnyy Kut, *Russia* 34 E8
Krasnyy Liman, *Ukraine* 33 H9

Krasnyy Luch, *Ukraine* 33 H10
Krasnyy Profintern, *Russia* ... 32 D11
Krasnyy Yar, *Astrakhan, Russia* . 35 G9
Krasnyy Yar, *Samara, Russia* .. 34 D10
Krasnyy Yar, *Volgograd, Russia* . 34 E7
Krasnyye Baki, *Russia* 34 B7
Krasnyyoskolske Vdskh., *Ukraine* 33 H9
Kraszna →, *Hungary* 28 B7
Kratie = Kracheh, *Cambodia* .. 64 F6
Kratovo, *Macedonia* 44 D6
Krau, *Indonesia* 63 E10
Kravanh, Chuor Phnum,
  Cambodia 65 G4
Krefeld, *Germany* 24 D2
Krémaston, Límni, *Greece* 46 C3
Kremen, *Croatia* 41 D12
Kremenchuk, *Ukraine* 33 H7
Kremenchuksk Vdskh., *Ukraine* . 33 H7
Kremenets, *Ukraine* 33 G3
Kremennaya, *Ukraine* 33 H10
Kremges = Svitlovodsk, *Ukraine* 33 H7
Kremmen, *Germany* 24 C9
Kremmling, *U.S.A.* 108 F10
Kremnica, *Slovak Rep.* 27 C11
Krems, *Austria* 26 C8
Kremsmünster, *Austria* 26 C7
Kretinga, *Lithuania* 9 J19
Krettsy, *Russia* 32 C7
Kreuzberg, *Germany* 25 E5
Kreuztal, *Germany* 24 E4
Kría Vrísi, *Greece* 44 F6
Kribi, *Cameroon* 83 E6
Krichem, *Bulgaria* 45 D8
Krichev = Krychaw, *Belarus* .. 32 F6
Krim, *Slovenia* 41 C11
Kriós, Ákra, *Greece* 49 D5
Krishna →, *India* 67 M12
Krishnanagar, *India* 69 H13
Kristdala, *Sweden* 11 G10
Kristiansand, *Norway* 9 G13
Kristianstad, *Sweden* 11 H8
Kristiansund, *Norway* 8 E12
Kristiinankaupunki, *Finland* .. 9 E19
Kristinehamn, *Sweden* 10 E8
Kristinestad =
  Kristiinankaupunki, *Finland* . 9 E19
Kríti, *Greece* 49 D7
Kritsá, *Greece* 49 D7
Kriva →, *Macedonia* 44 D5
Kriva Palanka, *Macedonia* ... 44 D6
Krivaja →, *Bos.-H.* 28 F3
Krivelj, *Serbia & M.* 44 B6
Krivoy Rog = Kryvyy Rih,
  Ukraine = Kryvyy Rih,
  Ukraine 33 J7
Križevci, *Croatia* 41 B13
Krk, *Croatia* 41 C11
Krka △, *Croatia* 41 E12
Krka →, *Slovenia* 41 C12
Krkonoše, *Czech Rep.* 26 A8
Krkonoše △, *Czech Rep.* 26 A8
Krnov, *Czech Rep.* 27 A10
Krobia, *Poland* 31 G3
Krokeaí, *Greece* 46 E4
Krokek, *Sweden* 11 F10
Krokodil →, *Mozam.* 89 D5
Krokom, *Sweden* 10 A8
Krokowa, *Poland* 30 D5
Krolevets, *Ukraine* 33 G7
Kroměřiž, *Czech Rep.* 27 B10
Krompachy, *Slovak Rep.* 27 C13
Kromy, *Russia* 33 F8
Kronach, *Germany* 25 E7
Krong Kaoh Kong, *Cambodia* . 62 B2
Kronobergs län □, *Sweden* ... 11 H8
Kronprins Olav Kyst, *Antarctica* 5 C5
Kronprinsesse Märtha Kyst,
  Antarctica 5 D2
Kronshtadt, *Russia* 32 C5
Kroonstad, *S. Africa* 88 D4
Kröpelin, *Germany* 24 A7
Kropotkin, *Russia* 35 H5
Kropp, *Germany* 24 A5
Krosna, *Lithuania* 30 D10
Krośniewice, *Poland* 31 F6
Krosno, *Poland* 31 J8
Krosno Odrzańskie, *Poland* ... 31 F2
Krotoszyn, *Poland* 31 G4
Krotovka, *Russia* 34 D10
Kroussón, *Greece* 49 D6
Krrabë, *Albania* 44 E3
Krško, *Slovenia* 41 C12
Krstača, *Serbia & M.* 44 D4
Kruger △, *S. Africa* 89 C5
Krugersdorp, *S. Africa* 89 D4
Kruisfontein, *S. Africa* 88 E3
Krujë, *Albania* 44 E3
Krulevshchina = Krulyewshchyna,
  Belarus 32 E4
Krulyewshchyna, *Belarus* 32 E4
Krumbach, *Germany* 25 G6
Krumë, *Albania* 44 E4
Krumovgrad, *Bulgaria* 45 E9
Krupanj, *Serbia & M.* 44 B3
Krupina, *Slovak Rep.* 27 C11
Krupki, *Belarus* 32 E5
Kruševac, *Serbia & M.* 44 C5
Kruševo, *Macedonia* 44 E5
Krushelnyksya, *Ukraine* 31 J10
Krychaw, *Belarus* 32 F6
Krymsk, *Russia* 35 K10
Krymskiy Poluostrov = Krymskyy
  Pivostriv, *Ukraine* 33 K8
Krymskyy Pivostriv, *Ukraine* .. 33 K8
Krynica, *Poland* 31 J7
Krynica Morska, *Poland* 30 D6
Krynki, *Poland* 31 E10
Krynychne, *Ukraine* 29 E13
Kryvyy Rih, *Ukraine* 33 J7

Kryzhopil, *Ukraine* 29 B13
Krzepice, *Poland* 31 H5
Krzeszów, *Poland* 31 H9
Krzna →, *Poland* 31 F10
Krzywiń, *Poland* 31 G3
Krzyż Wielkopolski, *Poland* ... 31 F2
Ksar es Souk = Er Rachidia,
  Morocco 78 B4
Ksar el Kebir, *Morocco* 78 B4
Ksar es Souk = Er Rachidia,
  Morocco 78 B5
Książ Wielkopolski, *Poland* ... 31 F4
Kstovo, *Russia* 34 B7
Ku, W. el →, *Sudan* 81 E2
Kuah, *Malaysia* 65 J2
Kuala Belait, *Malaysia* 62 D4
Kuala Berang, *Malaysia* 65 K4
Kuala Dungun = Dungun,
  Malaysia 65 K4
Kuala Kangsar, *Malaysia* 65 K3
Kuala Kelawang, *Malaysia* ... 65 L4
Kuala Kerai, *Malaysia* 65 K4
Kuala Kerian, *Malaysia* ...... 65 c
Kuala Lipis, *Malaysia* 65 K4
Kuala Lumpur, *Malaysia* 65 L3
Kuala Nerang, *Malaysia* 65 J3
Kuala Pilah, *Malaysia* 65 L4
Kuala Rompin, *Malaysia* 65 L4
Kuala Selangor, *Malaysia* 65 L3
Kuala Sepetang, *Malaysia* ... 65 K3
Kuala Terengganu, *Malaysia* .. 65 K4
Kualajelai, *Indonesia* 62 E4
Kualakapuas, *Indonesia* 62 E4
Kualakurun, *Indonesia* 62 E4
Kualapembuang, *Indonesia* .. 62 E4
Kualasimpang, *Indonesia* 62 D1
Kuancheng, *China* 57 D10
Kuandang, *Indonesia* 63 D6
Kuandian, *China* 57 D13
Kuangchou = Guangzhou, *China* 59 F9
Kuanshan, *Taiwan* 59 F13
Kuantan, *Malaysia* 65 L4
Kuba = Quba, *Azerbaijan* 35 K9
Kuban →, *Russia* 33 K9
Kuban Depression =
  Prikubanskaya Nizmennost,
  Russia 35 H4
Kubenskoye, Ozero, *Russia* .. 32 C10
Kubokawa, *Japan* 55 H6
Kubrat, *Bulgaria* 45 C10
Kubu, *Indonesia* 63 J18
Kubutambahan, *Indonesia* ... 63 J18
Kucar, Tanjung, *Indonesia* ... 63 K18
Kučevo, *Serbia & M.* 44 B5
Kucha Gompa, *India* 69 B7
Kuchaman, *India* 68 F6
Kuchenspitze, *Austria* 26 D3
Kuchinda, *India* 69 J11
Kuchino-eruba-Jima, *Japan* .. 55 J5
Kuchino-Shima, *Japan* 55 K4
Kuchinotsu, *Japan* 55 H5
Kuchl, *Austria* 26 D6
Kuchurhan →, *Ukraine* 29 D14
Kucing = Kuching, *Malaysia* .. 62 D4
Kuçovë, *Albania* 44 F3
Küçükbahçe, *Turkey* 47 C8
Küçükköy, *Turkey* 47 B8
Küçükkuyu, *Turkey* 47 B8
Küçükmenderes →, *Turkey* .. 47 D9
Kud →, *Pakistan* 68 F2
Kuda, *India* 66 H7
Kudat, *Malaysia* 62 C5
Kudirkos Naumiestis, *Lithuania* 30 D9
Kudowa-Zdrój, *Poland* 31 H3
Kudus, *Indonesia* 63 G14
Kudymkar, *Russia* 52 D6
Kueiyang = Guiyang, *China* .. 58 D6
Kufra Oasis = Al Kufrah, *Libya* . 79 D10
Kufstein, *Austria* 26 D5
Kugaaruk = Pelly Bay, *Canada* . 101 B11
Kugluktuk, *Canada* 100 B8
Kugong I., *Canada* 104 A4
Kūhak, *Iran* 66 F3
Kuhan, *Pakistan* 68 E2
Kūhbonān, *Iran* 71 D8
Kühestak, *Iran* 71 E8
Kuhin, *Iran* 71 B6
Kūhīrī, *Iran* 71 E9
Kuhnsdorf, *Austria* 26 E7
Kūhpāyeh, *Eşfahan, Iran* 71 C7
Kūhpāyeh, *Kermān, Iran* 71 D8
Kūhrān, Kūh-e, *Iran* 71 E8
Kui Buri, *Thailand* 65 F2
Kuiseb →, *Namibia* 88 C1
Kuito, *Angola* 85 G3
Kuiu I., *U.S.A.* 102 B2
Kujang, *N. Korea* 57 E14
Kujawsko-Pomorskie □, *Poland* 30 E5
Kuji, *Japan* 54 D10
Kujū-San, *Japan* 55 H5
Kukava, *Ukraine* 29 B12
Kukawa, *Nigeria* 83 C7
Kukës, *Albania* 44 D4
Kukmor, *Russia* 34 B10
Kukup, *Malaysia* .... 65 d
Kukup, Pulau, *Malaysia* ..... 65 d
Kukvidze, *Russia* 34 E6
Kula, *Bulgaria* 44 C6
Kula, *Serbia & M.* 28 E4
Kula, *Turkey* 47 C10
Kulachi, *Pakistan* 68 D4
Kulai, *Malaysia* 65 M4
Kulaly, Ostrov, *Kazakhstan* ... 35 H10
Kulasekharapattana, *India* ... 66 Q11
Kulautuva, *Lithuania* 30 D10
Kuldīga □, *Latvia* 9 H19
Kuldja = Yining, *China* 60 B3
Kuldīga □, *Latvia* 32 E2
Kulebaki, *Russia* 34 C6
Kulen, *Cambodia* 64 F5
Kulen Vakúf, *Bos.-H.* 41 D13
Kulgam, *India* 69 C6

Kulgera, Australia 94 D1
Kulim, Malaysia 65 K3
Kulin, Australia 93 F2
Kulkayu = Hartley Bay, Canada . 102 C3
Kullen, Sweden 11 H6
Kulmbach, Germany 25 E7
Kūlob, Tajikistan 52 F7
Kulp, Turkey 73 C9
Kulpawn →, Ghana 83 D4
Kulsary, Kazakhstan 52 E6
Kulti, India 69 H12
Kulu, India 68 D7
Kulu, Turkey 72 C5
Kulumbura, Australia 92 B4
Kulunda, Russia 52 D8
Kulungar, Afghan. 68 C3
Kûlvand, Iran 71 D7
Kulwin, Australia 95 F3
Kulyab = Kūlob, Tajikistan 52 F7
Kuma →, Russia 35 H8
Kumafşarı, Turkey 47 D11
Kumaganum, Nigeria 83 C7
Kumagaya, Japan 55 F9
Kumai, Indonesia 62 E4
Kumalar Dağı, Turkey 47 C12
Kumamba, Kepulauan, Indonesia 63 E9
Kumamoto, Japan 55 H5
Kumamoto □, Japan 55 H5
Kumanovo, Macedonia 44 D5
Kumara, N.Z. 91 K3
Kumarina, Australia 93 D2
Kumasi, Ghana 82 D4
Kumba, Cameroon 83 E6
Kumbağ, Turkey 45 F11
Kumbakonam, India 66 P11
Kumbarilla, Australia 95 D5
Kumbhraj, India 68 G7
Kumbia, Australia 95 D5
Kumbo, Cameroon 83 D7
Kŭmch'ŏn, N. Korea 57 E14
Kumdok, India 69 C8
Kume-Shima, Japan 55 L3
Kumeny, Russia 34 A9
Kumharsain, India 68 D7
Kŭmhwa, S. Korea 57 E14
Kumi, Uganda 86 B3
Kumkale, Turkey 45 G10
Kumla, Sweden 10 E9
Kumluca, Turkey 47 E12
Kummerower See, Germany 24 B8
Kumo, Nigeria 83 C7
Kumo älv = Kokemäenjoki →,
    Finland 9 F19
Kumon Bum, Burma 67 F20
Kumylzhenskaya, Russia 34 F6
Kunágota, Hungary 28 D6
Kunashir, Ostrov, Russia 53 E15
Kunda, Estonia 9 G22
Kunda, India 69 G9
Kundar →, Pakistan 68 D3
Kundelungu △, Dem. Rep. of
    the Congo 87 E2
Kundelungu Ouest △, Dem. Rep.
    of the Congo 87 D2
Kundian, Pakistan 68 C4
Kundla, India 68 J4
Kung, Ao, Thailand .... 65 a
Kunga →, Bangla. 69 J13
Kungälv, Sweden 11 G5
Kunghit I., Canada 102 C2
Kungrad = Qŭnghirot, Uzbekistan 52 E6
Kungsängen, Sweden 10 E11
Kungsbacka, Sweden 11 G6
Kungsgård, Sweden 10 D10
Kungshamn, Sweden 11 F5
Kungsör, Sweden 10 E10
Kungur, Russia 52 D6
Kungurri, Australia 94 K6
Kunhar →, Pakistan 69 B5
Kunhegyes, Hungary 28 C5
Kuningan, Indonesia 63 G13
Kunlong, Burma 58 F2
Kunlun Shan, Asia 60 C3
Kunming, China 58 E4
Kunów, Poland 31 H8
Kunsan, S. Korea 57 G14
Kunshan, China 59 B13
Kunszentmárton, Hungary 28 D5
Kunszentmiklós, Hungary 28 C4
Kuntaur, Senegal 82 C2
Kununurra, Australia 92 C4
Kunwari →, India 69 F8
Kunya-Urgench = Köneürgench,
    Turkmenistan 52 E6
Künzelsau, Germany 25 F5
Kuopio, Finland 8 E22
Kupa →, Croatia 41 C13
Kupang, Indonesia 63 F6
Kupreanof I., U.S.A. 102 B2
Kupres, Bos.-H. 28 G2
Kupyansk, Ukraine 33 H9
Kupyansk-Uzlovoi, Ukraine ... 33 H9
Kuqa, China 60 B3
Kür →, Azerbaijan 73 C13
Kür Dili, Azerbaijan 71 B6
Kura = Kür →, Azerbaijan ... 73 C13
Kuranda, Australia 94 B4
Kuranga, India 68 H3
Kurashiki, Japan 55 G6
Kurayoshi, Japan 55 G6
Kürdämir, Azerbaijan 35 K9
Kurdistan, Asia 73 D10
Kŭrdzhali, Bulgaria 45 E9
Kure, Japan 55 G6
Küre, Turkey 72 B5
Küre Dağları, Turkey 72 B6
Kuressaare, Estonia 9 G21
Kurgan, Russia 52 D7
Kurganinsk, Russia 35 H5
Kurgannaya = Kurganinsk, Russia 35 H5
Kuri, India 68 F4

Kuria Maria Is. = Khurīyā Murīyā,
    Jazā'ir, Oman 75 D6
Kuridala, Australia 94 C3
Kurigram, Bangla. 67 G16
Kurikka, Finland 9 E20
Kuril Is. = Kurilskiye Ostrova,
    Russia 53 E15
Kuril Trench, Pac. Oc. 96 C7
Kurilsk, Russia 53 E15
Kurilskiye Ostrova, Russia 53 E15
Kurino, Japan 55 J5
Kurinskaya Kosa = Kür Dili,
    Azerbaijan 71 B6
Kurkur, Egypt 80 C3
Kurlovskiy, Russia 34 C5
Kurmuk, Sudan 81 E3
Kurnool, India 66 M11
Kuro-Shima, Kagoshima, Japan . 55 J4
Kuro-Shima, Okinawa, Japan .. 55 M2
Kuror, J., Sudan 80 C3
Kurow, N.Z. 91 L3
Kurów, Poland 31 G9
Kurram →, Pakistan 68 C4
Kurri Kurri, Australia 95 E5
Kurrimine, Australia 94 B4
Kursavka, Russia 35 H6
Kurshskaya Kosa △, Russia ... 30 C7
Kurshskiy Zaliv, Russia 9 J19
Kursk, Russia 33 G9
Kurşumlija, Serbia & M. 44 C5
Kurşumlijska Banja, Serbia & M. 44 C5
Kurşunlu, Bursa, Turkey 45 F13
Kurşunlu, Çankırı, Turkey 72 B5
Kurtalan, Turkey 73 D9
Kurtbey, Turkey 45 E10
Kuru, Sudan 81 F2
Kuru, Bahr el →, Sudan 81 F2
Kurucaşile, Turkey 72 B5
Kuruçay, Turkey 70 B3
Kuruktag, China 60 B3
Kuruman, S. Africa 88 D3
Kuruman →, S. Africa 88 D3
Kurume, Japan 55 H5
Kurun →, Sudan 81 F3
Kurunegala, Sri Lanka 66 R12
Kurya, Russia 52 C6
Kus Gölü, Turkey 45 F11
Kuşadası, Turkey 72 D2
Kuşadası Körfezi, Turkey 47 D8
Kusamba, Indonesia 63 K18
Kusatsu, Japan 55 F9
Kusawa L., Canada 102 A1
Kusel, Germany 25 F3
Kushaka, Nigeria 83 C6
Kushalgarh, India 68 H6
Kushchevskaya, Russia 35 G4
Kusheriki, Nigeria 83 C6
Kushikino, Japan 55 J5
Kushima, Japan 55 J5
Kushimoto, Japan 55 H7
Kushiro, Japan 54 C12
Kushiro-Gawa →, Japan 54 C12
Kushiro Shitsugen △, Japan ... 54 C12
Kūshk, Iran 71 D8
Kushka = Gushgy, Turkmenistan 52 F7
Kūshkī, Iran 70 C5
Kushnytsya, Ukraine 29 B8
Kushol, India 69 C7
Kushtia, Bangla. 67 H16
Kushum →, Kazakhstan 34 F10
Kuskokwim B., U.S.A. 100 C3
Kusmi, India 69 H10
Kussharo-Ko, Japan 54 C12
Kustanay = Qostanay,
    Kazakhstan 52 D7
Kut, Ko, Thailand 65 G4
Kuta, Indonesia 63 K18
Kütahya, Turkey 47 B12
Kütahya □, Turkey 47 B11
Kutaisi, Georgia 35 J6
Kutaraja = Banda Aceh,
    Indonesia 62 C1
Kutch, Gulf of = Kachchh, Gulf
    of, India 68 H3
Kutch, Rann of = Kachchh, Rann
    of, India 68 H4
Kutina, Croatia 41 C13
Kutiyana, India 68 J4
Kutjevo, Croatia 28 E2
Kutkashen, Azerbaijan 35 K8
Kutná Hora, Czech Rep. 26 B8
Kutno, Poland 31 F6
Kutse, Botswana 88 C3
Kuttabul, Australia 94 K6
Kutu, Dem. Rep. of the Congo .. 84 E3
Kutum, Sudan 81 E1
Kúty, Slovak Rep. 27 C10
Kuty, Ukraine 29 B10
Kuujjuaq, Canada 101 C13
Kuujjuarapik, Canada 104 A4
Kuŭp-tong, N. Korea 57 D14
Kuusamo, Finland 8 D23
Kuusankoski, Finland 9 F22
Kuvshinovo, Russia 32 D8
Kuwait = Al Kuwayt, Kuwait .. 70 D5
Kuwait ■, Asia 70 D5
Kuwana, Japan 55 G8
Kuwana →, India 69 F10
Kuybyshev = Samara, Russia .. 34 D10
Kuybyshev, Russia 52 D8
Kuybyshevo, Ukraine 33 J9
Kuybyshevskoye Vdkhr., Russia . 34 C9
Kuye He →, China 56 E6
Kūyeh, Iran 70 B5
Kuyucak, Turkey 47 D10
Kuyumba, Russia 53 C10
Kuzey Anadolu Dağları, Turkey 72 B7
Kuzmin, Serbia & M. 28 E4
Kuznetsk, Russia 34 D8
Kuzomen, Russia 52 C4
Kvænangen, Norway 8 A19

Kværndrup, Denmark 11 J4
Kvaløy, Norway 8 B18
Kvänum, Sweden 11 F7
Kvareli = Qvareli, Georgia 35 K7
Kvarner, Croatia 41 D11
Kvarnerič, Croatia 41 D11
Kvicksund, Sweden 10 E10
Kvillsfors, Sweden 11 G9
Kvismare kanal, Sweden 10 E9
Kvissleby, Sweden 10 B11
Kwa-Nobuhle, S. Africa 85 L5
Kwabhaca, S. Africa 89 E4
Kwakhanai, Botswana 88 C3
Kwakoegron, Suriname 125 B7
Kwale, Kenya 86 C4
Kwale, Nigeria 83 D6
KwaMashu, S. Africa 89 D5
Kwando →, Africa 88 B3
Kwangchow = Guangzhou, China 59 F9
Kwangdaeri, N. Korea 57 D14
Kwangju, S. Korea 57 G14
Kwango →, Dem. Rep. of
    the Congo 84 E3
Kwangsi-Chuang = Guangxi
    Zhuangzu Zizhiqu □, China .. 58 F7
Kwangtung = Guangdong □,
    China 59 F9
Kwara □, Nigeria 83 D6
Kwataboahegan →, Canada 104 B3
Kwatisore, Indonesia 63 E8
KwaZulu Natal □, S. Africa .. 89 D5
Kweichow = Guizhou □, China . 58 D6
Kwekwe, Zimbabwe 87 F2
Kwidzyn, Poland 30 E5
Kwiha, Ethiopia 81 E4
Kwinana New Town, Australia .. 93 F2
Kwisa →, Poland 31 G2
Kwoka, Indonesia 63 E8
Kwolla, Nigeria 83 D6
Kyabra Cr. →, Australia 95 D3
Kyabram, Australia 95 F4
Kyaikto, Burma 64 D1
Kyakhta, Russia 53 D11
Kyambura △, Uganda 86 C3
Kyancutta, Australia 95 E2
Kyaukpadaung, Burma 67 J19
Kyaukpyu, Burma 67 K18
Kyaukse, Burma 67 J20
Kybartai, Lithuania 30 D9
Kyburz, U.S.A. 110 G6
Kyelang, India 68 C7
Kyenjojo, Uganda 86 B3
Kyjov, Czech Rep. 27 B10
Kyle, Canada 103 C7
Kyle Dam, Zimbabwe 87 G3
Kyle of Lochalsh, U.K. 13 D3
Kyll →, Germany 25 F2
Kyllburg, Germany 25 E2
Kymijoki →, Finland 9 F22
Kymmene älv = Kymijoki →,
    Finland 9 F22
Kyneton, Australia 95 F3
Kynuna, Australia 94 C3
Kyō-ga-Saki, Japan 55 G7
Kyoga, L., Uganda 86 B3
Kyogle, Australia 95 D5
Kyom →, Sudan 81 F2
Kyongju, S. Korea 57 G15
Kyongpyaw, Burma 67 L19
Kyŏngsŏng, N. Korea 57 D15
Kyōto, Japan 55 G7
Kyōto □, Japan 55 G7
Kyparissovouno, Cyprus 49 D12
Kyperounda, Cyprus 49 E11
Kyrenia, Cyprus 49 D12
Kyrgyzstan ■, Asia 52 E8
Kyritz, Germany 24 C8
Kyrkhult, Sweden 11 H8
Kyrnasivka, Ukraine 29 B13
Kyrnychky, Ukraine 29 E14
Kyro älv = Kyrönjoki →, Finland 8 E19
Kyrönjoki →, Finland 8 E19
Kystatyam, Russia 53 C13
Kysucké Nové Mesto, Slovak Rep. 27 B11
Kytay, Ozero, Ukraine 29 E14
Kythréa, Cyprus 49 D12
Kyunhla, Burma 67 H19
Kyuquot Sound, Canada 102 D3
Kyūshū, Japan 55 H5
Kyūshū □, Japan 55 H5
Kyūshū-Sanchi, Japan 55 H5
Kyustendil, Bulgaria 44 D6
Kyusyur, Russia 53 B13
Kyyiv, Ukraine 33 G6
Kyyivske Vdskh., Ukraine 33 G6
Kyzyl, Russia 53 D10
Kyzyl Kum, Uzbekistan 52 E7
Kyzyl-Kyya, Kyrgyzstan 52 E8
Kyzyl-Orda = Qyzylorda,
    Kazakhstan 52 E7

L

La Albuera, Spain 37 G4
La Alcarria, Spain 38 E2
La Almarcha, Spain 38 F2
La Almunia de Doña Godina,
    Spain 38 D3
La Amistad △, Cent. Amer. .. 120 E3
La Asunción, Venezuela 124 A6
La Baie, Canada 105 C5
La Banda, Argentina 126 B3
La Bañeza, Spain 36 C5
La Barca, Mexico 118 C4
La Barge, U.S.A. 108 E8
La Bastide-Puylaurent, France .. 20 D7

La Baule, France 18 E4
La Belle, U.S.A. 115 M5
La Biche →, Canada 102 B4
La Biche, L., Canada 102 C6
La Bisbal d'Empordà, Spain .. 38 D8
La Blanquilla, Venezuela 121 D7
La Bomba, Mexico 118 A1
La Brea, Trin. & Tob. 125 K15
La Brède, France 20 D3
La Bresse, France 19 D13
La Bureba, Spain 36 C7
La Calera, Chile 126 C1
La Campana △, Chile 126 C1
La Campiña, Spain 37 H6
La Canal = Sa Canal, Spain .. 48 C7
La Cañiza = A Cañiza, Spain .. 36 C2
La Canourgue, France 20 D7
La Capelle, France 19 C10
La Carlota, Argentina 126 C3
La Carlota, Phil. 61 F5
La Carlota, Spain 37 H6
La Carolina, Spain 37 G7
La Ceiba, Honduras 120 C2
La Chaise-Dieu, France 20 C7
La Chapelle d'Angillon, France . 19 E9
La Chapelle-St-Luc, France ... 19 D11
La Chapelle-sur-Erdre, France .. 18 E5
La Charité-sur-Loire, France ... 19 E10
La Chartre-sur-le-Loir, France .. 18 E7
La Châtaigneraie, France 20 B3
La Châtre, France 19 F9
La Chaux-de-Fonds, Switz. ... 25 H2
La Chorrera, Panama 120 E4
La Ciotat, France 21 E9
La Clayette, France 19 F11
La Cocha, Argentina 126 B2
La Concepción, Panama 120 E3
La Concordia, Mexico 119 D6
La Coruña = A Coruña, Spain .. 36 B2
La Coruña □, Spain 36 B2
La Côte-St-André, France 21 C9
La Courtine, France 20 C6
La Crau, Bouches-du-Rhône,
    France 21 E8
La Crau, Var, France 21 E10
La Crescent, U.S.A. 112 D9
La Crete, Canada 102 B5
La Crosse, Kans., U.S.A. 112 F5
La Crosse, Wis., U.S.A. 112 D9
La Cruz, Costa Rica 120 D2
La Cruz, Mexico 118 C3
La Désirade, Guadeloupe .... 120 b
La Escondida, Mexico 118 C5
La Esmeralda, Paraguay 126 A3
La Esperanza, Cuba 120 B3
La Esperanza, Honduras 120 D2
La Estrada = A Estrada, Spain .. 36 C2
La Faouët, France 18 D3
La Fayette, U.S.A. 115 H3
La Fé, Cuba 120 B3
La Fère, France 19 C10
La Ferté-Bernard, France 18 D7
La Ferté-Gaucher, France 19 D10
La Ferté-Macé, France 18 D6
La Ferté-St-Aubin, France 19 E8
La Ferté-sous-Jouarre, France .. 19 D10
La Ferté-Vidame, France 18 D7
La Flèche, France 18 E6
La Follette, U.S.A. 115 G3
La Fregeneda, Spain 36 E4
La Fuente de San Esteban, Spain 36 E4
La Gacilly, France 18 E4
La Gineta, Spain 39 F2
La Grand'Combe, France 21 D8
La Grande, U.S.A. 108 D4
La Grande →, Canada 104 B5
La Grande-Motte, France 21 E8
La Grande Quatre, Rés., Canada 104 B5
La Grande Trois, Rés., Canada .. 104 B4
La Grange, Calif., U.S.A. 110 H6
La Grange, Ga., U.S.A. 115 J3
La Grange, Ky., U.S.A. 114 F3
La Grange, Tex., U.S.A. 113 L6
La Grave, France 21 C10
La Guaira, Venezuela 124 A5
La Guardia = A Guarda, Spain .. 36 D2
La Gudiña = A Gudiña, Spain .. 36 C3
La Guerche-de-Bretagne, France 18 E5
La Guerche-sur-l'Aubois, France 19 F10
La Habana, Cuba 120 B3
La Haute Vallée de Chevreuse △,
    France 19 D8
La Haye-du-Puits, France 18 C5
La Horra, Spain 36 D7
La Independencia, Mexico 119 D6
La Isabela, Dom. Rep. 121 C5
La Jonquera, Spain 38 C7
La Junta, U.S.A. 113 F3
La Laguna, Canary Is. 48 F3
La Libertad, Guatemala 120 C1
La Libertad, Mexico 118 B2
La Ligua, Chile 126 C1
La Línea de la Concepción, Spain 37 J5
La Loche, Canada 103 B7
La Londe-les-Maures, France .. 21 E10
La Lora, Spain 36 C7
La Loupe, France 18 D8
La Louvière, Belgium 17 D4
La Lune, Trin. & Tob. 125 K15
La Machine, France 19 F10
La Maddalena, Italy 42 A2
La Malbaie, Canada 105 C5
La Malinche △, Mexico 119 D5
La Mancha, Spain 39 F2
La Mariña, Spain 36 B3
La Martre, L., Canada 102 A5
La Mesa, U.S.A. 111 N9
La Misión, Mexico 118 A1
La Mothe-Achard, France 18 F5
La Motte-Chalançon, France .. 21 D9

La Motte-du-Caire, France 21 D10
La Motte-Servolex, France 21 C9
La Moure, U.S.A. 112 B5
La Muela, Spain 38 D3
La Mure, France 21 D9
La Negra, Chile 126 A1
La Oliva, Canary Is. 48 F6
La Orotava, Canary Is. 48 F3
La Oroya, Peru 124 F3
La Pacaudière, France 19 F10
La Palma, Canary Is. 48 F2
La Palma, Panama 120 E4
La Palma del Condado, Spain .. 37 H4
La Paloma, Chile 126 C1
La Pampa □, Argentina 126 D2
La Paragua, Venezuela 124 B6
La Paz, Entre Ríos, Argentina .. 126 C4
La Paz, San Luis, Argentina .. 126 C2
La Paz, Bolivia 124 G5
La Paz, Honduras 120 D2
La Paz, Mexico 118 C2
La Paz, Phil. 61 D4
La Paz Centro, Nic. 120 D2
La Pedrera, Colombia 124 D5
La Pérade, Canada 105 C5
La Perouse Str., Asia 54 B11
La Pesca, Mexico 119 C5
La Piedad, Mexico 118 C4
La Pine, U.S.A. 108 E3
La Plata, Argentina 126 D4
La Pobla de Lillet, Spain 38 C6
La Pobla de Segur, Spain 38 C5
La Pocatière, Canada 105 C5
La Pola de Gordón, Spain 36 C5
La Porta, France 21 F13
La Porte, Ind., U.S.A. 114 E2
La Porte, Tex., U.S.A. 113 L7
La Presanella, Italy 40 B7
La Puebla = Sa Pobla, Spain .. 48 B10
La Puebla de Cazalla, Spain .. 37 H5
La Puebla de los Infantes, Spain 37 H5
La Puebla de Montalbán, Spain . 36 F6
La Puebla del Río, Spain 37 H4
La Puerta de Segura, Spain ... 37 G8
La Purísima, Mexico 118 B2
La Push, U.S.A. 110 C2
La Quiaca, Argentina 126 A2
La Réole, France 20 D3
La Restinga, Canary Is. 48 G2
La Rioja, Argentina 126 B2
La Rioja □, Argentina 126 B2
La Rioja □, Spain 38 C2
La Robla, Spain 36 C5
La Roche-Bernard, France 18 E4
La Roche-Canillac, France ... 20 C5
La Roche-en-Ardenne, Belgium . 17 D5
La Roche-sur-Foron, France .. 19 F13
La Roche-sur-Yon, France 18 F5
La Rochefoucauld, France 20 C4
La Rochelle, France 20 B2
La Roda, Spain 39 F2
La Roda de Andalucía, Spain .. 37 H6
La Romana, Dom. Rep. 121 C6
La Ronge, Canada 103 B7
La Rumorosa, Mexico 111 N10
La Sabina = Sa Savina, Spain .. 48 C7
La Sagra, Spain 39 H2
La Salle, U.S.A. 112 E10
La Sanabria, Spain 36 C4
La Santa, Canary Is. 48 E6
La Sarre, Canada 104 C4
La Scie, Canada 105 C8
La Selva, Spain 38 C7
La Selva Beach, U.S.A. 110 J5
La Selva del Camp, Spain 38 D6
La Serena, Chile 126 B1
La Serena, Spain 37 G5
La Seu d'Urgell, Spain 38 C6
La Seyne-sur-Mer, France 21 E9
La Sila, Italy 43 C9
La Solana, Spain 37 G7
La Souterraine, France 19 F8
La Soufrière, St. Vincent 121 D7
La Spézia, Italy 40 D6
La Suze-sur-Sarthe, France ... 18 E7
La Tagua, Colombia 124 C4
La Teste-de-Buch, France 20 D2
La Tortuga, Venezuela 121 D6
La Tour-du-Pin, France 21 C9
La Tranche-sur-Mer, France .. 18 F5
La Tremblade, France 20 C2
La Trinité, Martinique .... 120 c
La Tuque, Canada 104 C5
La Unión, Chile 128 E2
La Unión, El Salv. 120 D2
La Unión, Mexico 118 D4
La Unión, Spain 39 H4
La Urbana, Venezuela 124 B5
La Vache Pt., Trin. & Tob. ... 125 K15
La Vall d'Uixó, Spain 38 F4
La Vecilla de Curveño, Spain .. 36 C5
La Vega, Dom. Rep. 121 C5
La Veleta, Spain 37 H7
La Venta, Mexico 119 D6
La Ventura, Mexico 118 C4
La Voulte-sur-Rhône, France .. 21 D8
Laa an der Thaya, Austria 27 C9
Laage, Germany 24 B8
Laaber, Grosse →, Germany .. 25 G8
Laage, Germany 24 B8
Laas Caanood = Las Anod,
    Somali Rep. 75 F4
Laatzen, Germany 24 C5
Laba →, Russia 35 H4
Labasa, Fiji 91 C8
Labason, Phil. 61 G5
Labastide-Murat, France 20 D5
Labastide-Rouairoux, France .. 20 E6
Labbézenga, Mali 83 B5
Labe = Elbe →, Europe 24 B4
Labé, Guinea 82 C2
Laberge, L., Canada 102 A1
Labin, Croatia 41 C11

Labinsk, *Russia* 35 H5
Labis, *Malaysia* 65 L4
Łabiszyn, *Poland* 31 F4
Labo, *Phil.* 61 D5
Laboe, *Germany* 24 A6
Laborec →, *Slovak Rep.* 27 C14
Laborie, *St. Lucia* .... 121 f
Labouheyre, *France* 20 D3
Laboulaye, *Argentina* 126 C3
Labrador, *Canada* 105 B7
Labrador City, *Canada* 105 B6
Labrador Sea, *Atl. Oc.* 101 C14
Lábrea, *Brazil* 124 E6
Labruguière, *France* 20 E6
Labuan, *Malaysia* 62 C5
Labuan, Pulau, *Malaysia* 62 C5
Labuha, *Indonesia* 63 E7
Labuhan, *Indonesia* 63 G11
Labuhanbajo, *Indonesia* 63 F6
Labuk, Telok, *Malaysia* 62 C5
Labyrinth, L., *Australia* 95 E2
Labytnangi, *Russia* 52 C7
Laç, *Albania* 44 E3
Lac-Bouchette, *Canada* 105 C5
Labrador City, *Canada* 105 C5
Lac La Biche, *Canada* 102 C6
Lac la Martre = Wha Ti, *Canada* 100 B8
Lac La Ronge △, *Canada* 103 B7
Lac-Mégantic, *Canada* 105 C5
Lac Thien, *Vietnam* 64 F7
Lacanau, *France* 20 D2
Lacanau, Étang de, *France* ... 20 D2
Lacantún →, *Mexico* 119 D6
Lacara →, *Spain* 37 G4
Lacaune, *France* 20 E6
Lacaune, Mts. de, *France* 20 E6
Laccadive Is. = Lakshadweep Is.,
　India 50 H11
Lacepede B., *Australia* 95 F2
Lacepede Is., *Australia* 92 C3
Lacerdónia, *Mozam.* 87 F4
Lacey, *U.S.A.* 110 C4
Lachhmangarh, *India* 68 F6
Lachi, *Pakistan* 68 C4
Lachine, *Canada* 104 C5
Lachlan →, *Australia* 95 E3
Lachute, *Canada* 104 C5
Lackawanna, *U.S.A.* 116 D6
Lackawaxen, *U.S.A.* 117 E10
Lacolle, *Canada* 117 A11
Lacombe, *Canada* 102 C6
Lacona, *U.S.A.* 117 C8
Láconi, *Italy* 42 C2
Laconia, *U.S.A.* 117 C13
Lacq, *France* 20 E3
Ladakh Ra., *India* 69 C8
Lądek-Zdrój, *Poland* 31 H3
Ládhon →, *Greece* 46 D3
Ladik, *Turkey* 72 B6
Ladismith, *S. Africa* 88 E3
Ladíspoli, *Italy* 41 G9
Lādīz, *Iran* 71 D9
Ladnun, *India* 68 F6
Ladoga, L. = Ladozhskoye Ozero,
　Russia 32 B6
Ladozhskoye Ozero, *Russia* ... 32 B6
Ladushkin, *Russia* 30 D7
Lady Elliott I., *Australia* 94 C5
Lady Grey, *S. Africa* 88 E4
Ladybrand, *S. Africa* 88 D4
Ladysmith, *Canada* 102 D4
Ladysmith, *S. Africa* 89 D4
Ladysmith, *U.S.A.* 112 C9
Ladyzhyn, *Ukraine* 29 B14
Lae, *Papua N. G.* 96 H6
Laem Hin Khom, *Thailand* .... 65 b
Laem Khat, *Thailand* .... 65 a
Laem Nga, *Thailand* .... 65 a
Laem Ngop, *Thailand* 65 F4
Laem Phan Wa, *Thailand* ...... 65 a
Laem Pho, *Thailand* 65 J3
Laem Phrom Thep, *Thailand* ... 65 a
Laem Riang, *Thailand* .... 65 a
Laem Sam Rong, *Thailand* ..... 65 b
Laem Son, *Thailand* .... 65 a
Laem Yamu, *Thailand* .... 65 a
Læsø, *Denmark* 11 G5
Læsø Rende, *Denmark* 11 G4
Lafayette, Colo., *U.S.A.* 112 F2
Lafayette, Ind., *U.S.A.* 114 E2
Lafayette, La., *U.S.A.* 113 K9
Lafayette, Tenn., *U.S.A.* 115 G2
Laferte →, *Canada* 102 A5
Lafia, *Nigeria* 83 D6
Lafiagi, *Nigeria* 83 D6
Laflèche, *Canada* 103 D7
Lafon, *Sudan* 81 F3
Lagan, *Sweden* 11 H7
Lagan →, *Sweden* 11 H6
Lagan →, *U.K.* 12 B6
Lagarfljót →, *Iceland* 8 D6
Lage, *Germany* 24 D4
Lågen →, *Oppland, Norway* ... 9 F14
Lågen →, *Vestfold, Norway* .. 9 G14
Lägerdorf, *Germany* 24 B5
Laghouat, *Algeria* 78 B6
Lagnieu, *France* 21 C9
Lagny-sur-Marne, *France* 19 D9
Lago, *Italy* 43 C9
Lago de Sanabria y Entorno △,
　Spain 36 C4
Lagôa, *Portugal* 37 H2
Lagoa do Peixe △, *Brazil* 127 C5
Lagoa Vermelha, *Brazil* 127 B5
Lagoaça, *Portugal* 36 D4
Lagodekhi, *Georgia* 35 K8
Lagónegro, *Italy* 43 B8
Lagonoy G., *Phil.* 61 E5
Lagos, *Nigeria* 83 D5
Lagos, *Portugal* 37 H2
Lagos □, *Nigeria* 83 D5
Lagos de Moreno, *Mexico* 118 C4

Lagrange, *Australia* 92 C3
Lagrange B., *Australia* 92 C3
Laguardia, *Spain* 38 C2
Laguépie, *France* 20 D5
Laguna, *Brazil* 127 B6
Laguna, *U.S.A.* 109 J10
Laguna Beach, *U.S.A.* 111 M9
Laguna de Duera, *Spain* 36 D6
Laguna de la Restinga △,
　Venezuela 121 D6
Laguna del Laja △, *Chile* 126 D1
Laguna del Tigre △, *Guatemala* 120 C1
Laguna Limpia, *Argentina* 126 B4
Lagunas, *Chile* 126 A2
Lagunas, *Peru* 124 E3
Lagunas de Chacahua △, *Mexico* 119 D5
Lagunas de Montebello △,
　Mexico 119 D6
Lagunas de Ruidera △, *Spain* . 39 G2
Lahad Datu, *Malaysia* 63 C5
Lahad Datu, Teluk, *Malaysia* . 63 D5
Lahan Sai, *Thailand* 64 E4
Lahanam, *Laos* 64 D5
Lahar, *India* 69 F8
Laharpur, *India* 69 F9
Lahat, *Indonesia* 62 E2
Lahewa, *Indonesia* 62 D1
Lāhījān, *Iran* 71 B6
Lahn →, *Germany* 25 E3
Lahnstein, *Germany* 25 E3
Laholm, *Sweden* 11 H7
Laholmsbukten, *Sweden* 11 H6
Lahore, *Pakistan* 68 D6
Lahr, *Germany* 25 G3
Lahri, *Pakistan* 68 E3
Lahti, *Finland* 9 F21
Lahtis = Lahti, *Finland* 9 F21
Laï, *Chad* 79 G9
Lai Chau, *Vietnam* 58 F4
Lai'an, *China* 59 A12
Laibin, *China* 58 F7
Laifeng, *China* 58 C7
L'Aigle, *France* 18 D7
Laignes, *France* 19 E11
L'Aiguillon-sur-Mer, *France* . 20 B2
Laila = Layla, *Si. Arabia* ... 75 C4
Laingsburg, *S. Africa* 88 E3
Lainioälven →, *Sweden* 8 C20
Lairg, *U.K.* 13 C4
Laishui, *China* 56 E8
Laissac, *France* 20 D6
Láives, *Italy* 41 B8
Laiwu, *China* 57 F9
Laixi, *China* 57 F11
Laiyang, *China* 57 F11
Laiyuan, *China* 56 E8
Laizhou, *China* 57 F10
Laizhou Wan, *China* 57 F10
Laja →, *Mexico* 118 C4
Lajere, *Nigeria* 83 C7
Lajes, *Brazil* 127 B5
Lajkovac, *Serbia & M.* 44 B4
Lajosmizse, *Hungary* 28 C4
Lak Sao, *Laos* 64 C5
Lakaband, *Pakistan* 68 D3
Lakamané, *Mali* 82 C3
Lake Alpine, *U.S.A.* 110 G7
Lake Andes, *U.S.A.* 112 D5
Lake Arthur, *U.S.A.* 113 K8
Lake Bindegolly △, *Australia* . 95 D3
Lake Cargelligo, *Australia* ... 95 E4
Lake Charles, *U.S.A.* 113 K8
Lake City, Colo., *U.S.A.* 109 G10
Lake City, Fla., *U.S.A.* 115 K4
Lake City, Mich., *U.S.A.* 114 C3
Lake City, Minn., *U.S.A.* 112 C8
Lake City, Pa., *U.S.A.* 116 D4
Lake City, S.C., *U.S.A.* 115 J6
Lake Cowichan, *Canada* 102 D4
Lake District △, *U.K.* 14 C4
Lake Elsinore, *U.S.A.* 111 M9
Lake Eyre △, *Australia* 95 D2
Lake Gairdner △, *Australia* .. 95 E2
Lake George, *U.S.A.* 117 C11
Lake Grace, *Australia* 93 F2
Lake Harbour = Kimmirut,
　Canada 101 B13
Lake Havasu City, *U.S.A.* 111 L12
Lake Hughes, *U.S.A.* 111 L8
Lake Isabella, *U.S.A.* 111 K8
Lake Jackson, *U.S.A.* 113 L7
Lake Junction, *U.S.A.* 108 D8
Lake King, *Australia* 93 F2
Lake Lenore, *Canada* 103 C8
Lake Louise, *Canada* 102 C5
Lake Malawi △, *Malawi* 87 E3
Lake Mburo △, *Uganda* 86 C3
Lake Mead △, *U.S.A.* 111 K12
Lake Meredith △, *U.S.A.* 113 H4
Lake Mills, *U.S.A.* 112 D8
Lake Nakura △, *Kenya* 86 C4
Lake Placid, *U.S.A.* 117 B11
Lake Pleasant, *U.S.A.* 117 C10
Lake Providence, *U.S.A.* 113 J9
Lake Roosevelt △, *U.S.A.* 108 C4
Lake St. Peter, *Canada* 116 A6
Lake Superior △, *Canada* 104 C3
Lake Torrens △, *Australia* ... 95 E2
Lake Village, *U.S.A.* 113 J9
Lake Wales, *U.S.A.* 115 M5
Lake Worth, *U.S.A.* 115 M5
Lakeba, *Fiji* 91 D9
Lakefield, *Canada* 116 B6
Lakefield △, *Australia* 94 B3
Lakehurst, *U.S.A.* 117 F10
Lakeland, *Australia* 94 B3
Lakeland, *U.S.A.* 115 M5
Lakemba = Lakeba, *Fiji* 91 D9
Lakeport, Calif., *U.S.A.* 110 F4
Lakeport, Mich., *U.S.A.* 116 C2
Lakes Entrance, *Australia* ... 95 F4
Lakeside, Ariz., *U.S.A.* 109 J9

Lakeside, Calif., *U.S.A.* 111 N10
Lakeside, Nebr., *U.S.A.* 112 D3
Lakeside, Ohio, *U.S.A.* 116 E2
Lakeview, *U.S.A.* 108 E3
Lakeville, *U.S.A.* 112 C8
Lakewood, Colo., *U.S.A.* 112 F2
Lakewood, N.J., *U.S.A.* 117 F10
Lakewood, N.Y., *U.S.A.* 116 D5
Lakewood, Ohio, *U.S.A.* 116 E3
Lakewood, Wash., *U.S.A.* 110 C4
Lakha, *India* 68 F4
Lakhaniá, *Greece* 49 D9
Lakhimpur, *India* 69 F9
Lakhnadon, *India* 69 H8
Lakhnau = Lucknow, *India* 69 F9
Lakhpat, *India* 68 H3
Laki, *Azerbaijan* 35 K8
Lakin, *U.S.A.* 113 G4
Lakitusaki →, *Canada* 104 B3
Lakki, *Pakistan* 68 C4
Lákkoi, *Greece* 49 D5
Lakonía □, *Greece* 46 E4
Lakonikós Kólpos, *Greece* 46 E4
Lakor, *Indonesia* 63 F7
Lakota, *Ivory C.* 82 D3
Lakota, *U.S.A.* 112 A5
Laksar, *India* 68 E8
Laksefjorden, *Norway* 8 A22
Lakselv, *Norway* 8 A21
Lakshadweep Is., *India* 50 H11
Lakshmanpur, *India* 69 H10
Lakshmikantapur, *India* 69 H13
Lala Musa, *Pakistan* 68 C5
Lalaghat, *India* 67 G18
Lalago, *Tanzania* 86 C3
Lalapanzi, *Zimbabwe* 87 F3
Lalapaşa, *Turkey* 45 E10
Lalbenque, *France* 20 D5
L'Albufera, *Spain* 39 F4
Lalganj, *India* 69 G11
Lalgola, *India* 69 G13
Lalī, *Iran* 71 C6
Lalibela, *Ethiopia* 81 E4
La'nga Co, *China* 67 D12
Lalín, *Spain* 36 C2
Lalin He →, *China* 57 B13
Lalinde, *France* 20 D4
Lalitapur, *Nepal* 69 F11
Lalitpur, *India* 69 G8
Lalkua, *India* 69 E8
Lalsot, *India* 68 F7
Lam, *Vietnam* 64 B6
Lam Pao Res., *Thailand* 64 D4
Lama Kara, *Togo* 83 D5
Lamaing, *Burma* 67 M20
Lamar, Colo., *U.S.A.* 112 F3
Lamar, Mo., *U.S.A.* 113 G7
Lamas, *Peru* 124 E3
Lamastre, *France* 21 D8
Lambach, *Austria* 26 C6
Lamballe, *France* 18 D4
Lambaréné, *Gabon* 84 E2
Lambasa = Labasa, *Fiji* 91 C8
Lambay I., *Ireland* 12 C5
Lambert Glacier, *Antarctica* .. 5 D6
Lambert's Bay, *S. Africa* 88 E2
Lambesc, *France* 21 E9
Lambeth, *Canada* 116 D3
Lámbia, *Greece* 46 D3
Lambomakondro, *Madag.* 89 C7
Lambro →, *Italy* 40 C6
Lambton Shores, *Canada* 116 C3
Lame, *Nigeria* 83 C6
Lame Deer, *U.S.A.* 108 D10
Lamego, *Portugal* 36 D3
Lamèque, *Canada* 105 C7
Lameroo, *Australia* 95 F3
Lamesa, *U.S.A.* 113 J4
Lamía, *Greece* 46 C4
Lamington △, *Australia* 95 D5
Lamitan, *Phil.* 61 H5
Lamon B., *Phil.* 61 D5
Lamont, *Canada* 102 C6
Lamont, Calif., *U.S.A.* 111 K8
Lamont, Wyo., *U.S.A.* 108 E10
Lampa, *Peru* 124 G4
Lampang, *Thailand* 64 C2
Lampasas, *U.S.A.* 113 K5
Lampazos de Naranjo, *Mexico* . 118 B4
Lampedusa, *Italy* .... 43 Pas?
Lampertheim, *Germany* 25 F4
Lampeter, *U.K.* 15 E3
Lampman, *Canada* 103 D8
Lamprechtshausen, *Austria* ... 26 D5
Lampung □, *Indonesia* 62 F2
Lamta, *India* 69 H9
Lamu, *Kenya* 86 C5
Lamy, *U.S.A.* 109 J11
Lan Xian, *China* 56 E6
Lan Yu = Hungt'ou Hsü, *Taiwan* 59 G13
Lanak La, *China* 69 B8
Lanak'o Shank'ou = Lanak La,
　China 69 B8
Lanao, L., *Phil.* 61 H6
Lanark, *Canada* 117 A8
Lanark, *U.K.* 13 F5
Lanbi Kyun, *Burma* 65 G2
Lancang, *China* 58 F2
Lancang Jiang →, *China* 58 G3
Lancashire □, *U.K.* 14 D5
Lancaster, *Canada* 117 A10
Lancaster, *U.K.* 14 C5
Lancaster, Calif., *U.S.A.* 111 L8
Lancaster, Ky., *U.S.A.* 114 G3
Lancaster, N.H., *U.S.A.* 117 B13
Lancaster, N.Y., *U.S.A.* 116 D6
Lancaster, Ohio, *U.S.A.* 114 F4
Lancaster, Pa., *U.S.A.* 117 F8

Lancaster, S.C., *U.S.A.* 115 H5
Lancaster, Wis., *U.S.A.* 112 D9
Lancaster Sd., *Canada* 101 A11
Lancelin, *Australia* 93 F2
Lanchow = Lanzhou, *China* 56 F2
Lanchyn, *Ukraine* 29 B9
Lanciano, *Italy* 41 F11
Lanco, *China* 57 F11
Łańcut, *Poland* 31 H9
Land Between the Lakes △,
　U.S.A. 115 G1
Landau, Bayern, *Germany* 25 G8
Landau, Rhld.-Pfz., *Germany* . 25 F4
Landeck, *Austria* 26 D3
Lander →, *Australia* 92 D5
Lander, *U.S.A.* 108 E9
Landerneau, *France* 18 D2
Landes □, *France* 20 E3
Landes de Gascogne △, *France* 20 D3
Landete, *Spain* 38 F3
Landi Kotal, *Pakistan* 68 B4
Landisburg, *U.S.A.* 116 F7
Landivisiau, *France* 18 D2
Landquart, *Switz.* 25 J5
Landrecies, *France* 19 B10
Land's End, *U.K.* 15 G2
Landsberg, *Germany* 25 G6
Landsborough Cr. →, *Australia* 94 C3
Landshut, *Germany* 25 G8
Landskrona, *Sweden* 11 J6
Landstuhl, *Germany* 25 F3
Landvetter, *Sweden* 11 G6
Lanesboro, *U.S.A.* 117 E9
Lanester, *France* 18 E3
Lanett, *U.S.A.* 115 J3
Lang Qua, *Vietnam* 64 A5
Lang Shan, *China* 56 D4
Lang Son, *Vietnam* 58 G6
Lang Suan, *Thailand* 65 H2
Langå, *Denmark* 11 H3
La'nga Co, *China* 67 D12
Lángádhás, *Greece* 44 F7
Langádhia, *Greece* 46 D4
Långan →, *Sweden* 10 A8
Langano, L., *Ethiopia* 81 F4
Langar, *Iran* 71 C9
Langara I., *Canada* 102 C2
Långås, *Sweden* 11 H6
Langdai, *China* 58 D5
Langdon, *U.S.A.* 112 A5
Länge Jan = Ölands södra udde,
　Sweden 11 H10
Langeac, *France* 20 C7
Langeais, *France* 18 E7
Langeb Baraka →, *Sudan* 80 D4
Langeberg, *S. Africa* 88 E3
Langeberge, *S. Africa* 88 D3
Langeland, *Denmark* 11 K4
Langelands Bælt, *Denmark* 11 K4
Langen, Hessen, *Germany* 25 F4
Langen, Niedersachsen, *Germany* 24 B4
Langenburg, *Canada* 103 C8
Langeneß, *Germany* 24 A4
Langenlois, *Austria* 26 C8
Langeoog, *Germany* 24 B3
Langeskov, *Denmark* 11 J4
Länghem, *Sweden* 11 G7
Langhirano, *Italy* 40 D7
Langholm, *U.K.* 13 F5
Langjökull, *Iceland* 8 D3
Langkawi, Pulau, *Malaysia* ... 65 J2
Langklip, *S. Africa* 88 D3
Langkon, *Malaysia* 62 C5
Langlade, St-P. & M. 105 C8
Langley, *Canada* 110 A4
Langnau, *Switz.* 25 J3
Langogne, *France* 20 D7
Langon, *France* 20 D3
Langøya, *Norway* 8 B16
Langreo, *Spain* 36 B5
Langres, *France* 19 E12
Langres, Plateau de, *France* . 19 E12
Langsa, *Indonesia* 62 D1
Långsele, *Sweden* 10 A11
Langtry, *U.S.A.* 113 L4
Langu, *Thailand* 65 J2
Langue de Barbarie △, *Senegal* 82 C1
Languedoc, *France* 20 E7
Languedoc-Roussillon □, *France* 20 E6
Langxi, *China* 59 B12
Langxiangzhen, *China* 56 E9
Langzhong, *China* 58 B5
Lanigan, *Canada* 103 C7
Lankao, *China* 56 G8
Länkäran, *Azerbaijan* 71 B6
Lanmeur, *France* 18 D3
Lannilis, *France* 18 D2
Lannion, *France* 18 D3
L'Annonciation, *Canada* 104 C5
Lanouaille, *France* 20 C5
Lanping, *China* 58 D2
Lansdale, *U.S.A.* 117 F9
Lansdowne, *Australia* 95 E5
Lansdowne, *Canada* 117 B8
Lansdowne, *India* 69 E8
Lansdowne House, *Canada* 104 B2
L'Anse, *U.S.A.* 114 B1
L'Anse au Loup, *Canada* 105 B8
L'Anse aux Meadows, *Canada* .. 105 B8
Lansford, *U.S.A.* 117 F9
Lanshan, *China* 59 E9
Lansing, *U.S.A.* 114 D3
Lanslebourg-Mont-Cenis, *France* 21 C10
Lanta Yai, Ko, *Thailand* 65 J2
Lantewa, *Nigeria* 83 C7
Lantian, *China* 56 G5
Lanus, *Argentina* 126 C4

Lanusei, *Italy* 42 C2
Lanuza, *Phil.* 61 G7
Lanxi, *China* 59 C12
Lanzarote, *Canary Is.* 48 F6
Lanzarote ✈ (ACE), *Canary Is.* 48 F6
Lanzhou, *China* 56 F2
Lanzo Torinese, *Italy* 40 C4
Lao →, *Italy* 43 C8
Lao Bao, *Laos* 64 D6
Lao Cai, *Vietnam* 58 F4
Laoag, *Phil.* 61 B4
Laoang, *Phil.* 61 E6
Laoha He →, *China* 57 C11
Laohekou, *China* 59 A8
Laois □, *Ireland* 12 D4
Laon, *France* 19 C10
Laona, *U.S.A.* 114 C1
Laos ■, *Asia* 64 D5
Lapa, *Brazil* 127 B6
Lapai, *Nigeria* 83 D6
Lapalisse, *France* 19 F10
Lapeer, *U.S.A.* 114 D4
Lapeyrade, *France* 20 D3
Lapithos, *Cyprus* 49 D12
Lapland = Lappland, *Europe* .. 8 B21
Laporte, *U.S.A.* 117 E8
Lapovo, *Serbia & M.* 44 B5
Lappeenranta, *Finland* 9 F23
Lappland, *Europe* 8 B21
Lappo = Lapua, *Finland* 8 E20
Laprida, *Argentina* 126 D3
Lapseki, *Turkey* 45 F10
Laptev Sea, *Russia* 53 B13
Lapua, *Finland* 8 E20
Lāpuş →, *Romania* 29 C8
Lāpuş, Munţii, *Romania* 29 C8
Lāpuşna, *Moldova* 29 D13
Łapy, *Poland* 31 F9
Laqiya Arba'in, *Sudan* 80 C2
Laqiya Umran, *Sudan* 80 D2
L'Aquila, *Italy* 41 F10
Lār, Āzarbājān-e Sharqī, *Iran* 70 B5
Lār, Fārs, *Iran* 71 E7
Larabanga, *Ghana* 82 D4
Laragne-Montéglin, *France* ... 21 D9
Laramie →, *U.S.A.* 112 E2
Laramie →, *U.S.A.* 108 F11
Laramie Mts., *U.S.A.* 112 E2
Laranjeiras do Sul, *Brazil* .. 127 B5
Larantuka, *Indonesia* 63 F6
Larat, *Indonesia* 63 F8
L'Arbresle, *France* 21 C8
Lärbro, *Sweden* 11 G12
Larde, *Mozam.* 87 F4
Larder Lake, *Canada* 104 C4
Lardhos, Ákra = Líndhos, Ákra,
　Greece 49 C10
Lardhos, Órmos, *Greece* 49 C10
Laredo, *Spain* 36 B7
Laredo, *U.S.A.* 113 M5
Laredo Sd., *Canada* 102 C3
Largentière, *France* 21 D8
L'Argentière-la-Bessée, *France* 21 D10
Largo, *U.S.A.* 115 M4
Largs, *U.K.* 13 F4
Lari, *Italy* 40 E7
Lariang, *Indonesia* 63 E5
Larimore, *U.S.A.* 112 B6
Larino, *Italy* 41 G11
Lárisa, *Greece* 46 B4
Lárisa □, *Greece* 46 B4
Larkana, *Pakistan* 68 F3
Larnaca, *Cyprus* 49 E12
Larnaca Bay, *Cyprus* 49 E12
Larne, *U.K.* 12 B6
Larned, *U.S.A.* 112 F5
Laroquebrou, *France* 20 D6
Larose, *U.S.A.* 113 L9
Larrimah, *Australia* 92 C5
Larsen Ice Shelf, *Antarctica* . 5 C17
Laruns, *France* 20 F3
Larvik, *Norway* 9 G14
Larzac, Causse du, *France* ... 20 E7
Las Alpujarras, *Spain* 39 J1
Las Animas, *U.S.A.* 112 F3
Las Anod, *Somali Rep.* 75 F4
Las Arenas, *Spain* 36 B6
Las Batuecas △, *Spain* 36 E4
Las Brenãs, *Argentina* 126 B3
Las Cabezas de San Juan, *Spain* 37 J5
Las Cañadas del Teide △,
　Canary Is. 48 F3
Las Cejas, *Argentina* 126 B3
Las Chimeneas, *Mexico* 111 N10
Las Cruces, *U.S.A.* 109 K10
Las Flores, *Argentina* 126 D4
Las Heras, *Argentina* 126 C2
Las Lajas, *Argentina* 128 D2
Las Lomitas, *Argentina* 126 A3
Las Marismas, *Spain* 37 H4
Las Minas, *Spain* 39 G3
Las Navas de la Concepción,
　Spain 37 H5
Las Navas del Marqués, *Spain* . 36 E6
Las Palmas, *Argentina* 126 B4
Las Palmas, *Canary Is.* 48 F4
Las Palmas →, *Mexico* 111 N10
Las Palmas ✈ (LPA), *Canary Is.* 48 G4
Las Palmas de Cocalán △, *Chile* 126 C1
Las Pedroñas, *Spain* 39 F2
Las Piedras, *Uruguay* 127 C4
Las Pipinas, *Argentina* 126 D4
Las Plumas, *Argentina* 128 E3
Las Rozas, *Spain* 36 E7
Las Tablas, *Panama* 120 E3
Las Termas, *Argentina* 126 B3
Las Toscas, *Argentina* 126 B4
Las Truchas, *Mexico* 118 D4
Las Varillas, *Argentina* 126 C3
Las Vegas, N. Mex., *U.S.A.* .. 109 J11
Las Vegas, Nev., *U.S.A.* 111 J11

Las Vegas McCarran
 International ✈ (LAS), U.S.A. 111 J11
Lasarte, Spain 38 B2
Lascano, Uruguay 127 C5
Lash-e Joveyn, Afghan. 66 D2
Lashburn, Canada 103 C7
Lashio, Burma 67 H20
Lashkar, India 68 F8
Łasin, Poland 30 E6
Lasíthi, Greece 49 D7
Lasíthi □, Greece 49 D7
Lāsjerd, Iran 71 C7
Lask, Poland 31 G6
Łaskarzew, Poland 31 G8
Laško, Slovenia 41 B12
Lassay-les-Châteaux, France 18 D6
Lassen Pk., U.S.A. 108 F3
Lassen Volcanic △, U.S.A. 108 F3
Last Mountain L., Canada 103 C7
Lastchance Cr. →, U.S.A. 110 E5
Lastoursville, Gabon 84 E2
Lastovo, Croatia 41 F13
Lastovski Kanal, Croatia 41 F14
Lat Yao, Thailand 64 E2
Latacunga, Ecuador 124 D3
Latakia = Al Lādhiqīyah, Syria 70 C2
Latchford, Canada 104 C4
Latehar, India 69 H11
Laterza, Italy 43 B9
Latham, Australia 93 E2
Lathen, Germany 24 C3
Lathi, India 68 F4
Lathrop Wells, U.S.A. 111 J10
Latiano, Italy 43 B10
Latina, Italy 42 A5
Latisana, Italy 41 C10
Latium = Lazio □, Italy 41 F9
Laton, U.S.A. 110 J7
Latorytsya →, Slovak Rep. 27 C14
Latouche Treville, C., Australia 92 C3
Latrobe, Australia 95 G4
Latrobe, U.S.A. 116 F5
Latrónico, Italy 43 B9
Latvia ■, Europe 9 H20
Lau, Nigeria 83 D7
Lau Group, Fiji 91 C9
Lauchhammer, Germany 24 D9
Lauda-Königshofen, Germany 25 F5
Lauenburg, Germany 24 B6
Lauenburgische Seen △, Germany 24 B6
Lauf, Germany 25 F7
Laughlin, U.S.A. 109 J6
Laujar de Andarax, Spain 39 H2
Laukaa, Finland 9 E21
Launceston, Australia 95 G4
Launceston, U.K. 15 G3
Laune →, Ireland 12 D2
Launglon Bok, Burma 64 F1
Laupheim, Germany 25 G5
Laura, Australia 94 B3
Laureana di Borrello, Italy 43 D9
Laurel, Miss., U.S.A. 113 K10
Laurel, Mont., U.S.A. 108 D9
Laurencekirk, U.K. 13 E6
Laurens, U.S.A. 115 H4
Laurentian Plateau, Canada 105 B6
Lauria, Italy 43 B8
Laurie L., Canada 103 B8
Laurinburg, U.S.A. 115 H6
Laurium, U.S.A. 114 B1
Lausanne, Switz. 25 J2
Laut, Indonesia 62 D3
Laut, Pulau, Indonesia 62 E5
Laut Kecil, Kepulauan, Indonesia 62 E5
Lauterbach, Germany 24 E5
Lauterecken, Germany 25 F3
Lautoka, Fiji 91 C7
Lauzès, France 20 D5
Lava →, Russia 30 D8
Lava Beds △, U.S.A. 108 F3
Lavagh More, Ireland 12 B3
Lavagna, Italy 40 D6
Laval, France 18 D6
Lavalle, Argentina 126 B2
Lavant Station, Canada 117 A8
Lāvar Meydān, Iran 71 D7
Lávara, Greece 45 E10
Lavardac, France 20 D4
Lavaur, France 20 E5
Lavelanet, France 20 F5
Lavello, Italy 43 A8
Laverton, Australia 93 E3
Lavis, Italy 40 B8
Lávkos, Greece 46 B5
Lavos, Portugal 36 E2
Lavradio, Portugal 37 G1
Lavras, Brazil 127 A7
Lavre, Portugal 37 G2
Lávrion, Greece 46 D6
Lávris, Greece 49 D6
Lavumisa, Swaziland 89 D5
Lavushi Manda △, Zambia 87 E3
Lawas, Malaysia 62 D5
Lawele, Indonesia 63 F6
Lawn Hill △, Australia 94 B2
Lawng Pit, Burma 67 G20
Lawqah, Si. Arabia 70 D4
Lawra, Ghana 82 C4
Lawrence, N.Z. 91 L2
Lawrence, Kans., U.S.A. 112 F7
Lawrence, Mass., U.S.A. 117 D13
Lawrenceburg, Ind., U.S.A. 114 F3
Lawrenceburg, Tenn., U.S.A. 115 H2
Lawrenceville, Ga., U.S.A. 115 J4
Lawrenceville, Pa., U.S.A. 116 E7
Laws, U.S.A. 110 H8
Lawton, U.S.A. 113 H5
Lawu, Indonesia 63 G14
Lawz, J. al, Si. Arabia 80 B4
Laxá, Sweden 11 F8
Laxford, L., U.K. 13 C3
Laxou, France 19 D13

Lay →, France 20 B2
Layla, Si. Arabia 75 C4
Laylān, Iraq 70 C5
Layon →, France 18 E6
Layton, U.S.A. 108 F7
Laytonville, U.S.A. 108 G2
Lazarevac, Serbia & M. 44 B4
Lazarevskoye, Russia 35 J4
Lazarivo, Madag. 89 C8
Lazdijai, Lithuania 30 D10
Lazio □, Italy 41 F9
Lazo, Moldova 29 C13
Lazo, Russia 54 C6
Le Beausset, France 21 E9
Le Bic, Canada 105 C6
Le Blanc, France 20 B5
Le Bleymard, France 20 D7
Le Bourgneuf-la-Forêt, France 18 D6
Le Bugue, France 20 D4
Le Cateau Cambrésis, France 19 B10
Le Caylar, France 20 E7
Le Chambon-Feugerolles, France 21 C8
Le Châtelet, France 19 F9
Le Chesne, France 19 C11
Le Cheylard, France 21 D8
Le Conquet, France 18 D2
Le Creusot, France 19 F11
Le Croisic, France 18 E4
Le Donjon, France 19 F10
Le Dorat, France 20 B5
Le François, Martinique 120 c
Le Gosier, Guadeloupe 120 b
Le Grand-Lucé, France 18 E7
Le Grand-Pressigny, France 18 F7
Le Grand-Quevilly, France 18 C8
Le Havre, France 18 C7
Le Lamentin, Martinique 120 c
Le Lavandou, France 21 E10
Le Lion-d'Angers, France 18 E6
Le Louroux-Béconnais, France 18 E6
Le Luc, France 21 E10
Le Lude, France 18 E7
Le Mans, France 18 E7
Le Marin, Martinique 120 c
Le Mars, U.S.A. 112 D6
Le Mayet-de-Montagne, France 19 F10
Le Mêle-sur-Sarthe, France 18 D7
Le Monastier-sur-Gazeille, France 20 D7
Le Monêtier-les-Bains, France 21 D10
Le Mont-Dore, France 20 C6
Le Mont-St-Michel, France 18 D5
Le Moule, Guadeloupe 120 b
Le Muy, France 21 E10
Le Palais, France 18 E3
Le Perthus, France 20 F6
Le Prêcheur, Martinique 120 c
Le Puy-en-Velay, France 20 C7
Le Robert, Martinique 120 c
Le St-Esprit, Martinique 120 c
Le Sueur, U.S.A. 112 C8
Le Teil, France 21 D8
Le Teilleul, France 18 D6
Le Theil, France 18 D7
Le Thillot, France 19 E13
Le Thuy, Vietnam 64 D6
Le Touquet-Paris-Plage, France 19 B8
Le Tréport, France 18 B8
Le Val-d'Ajol, France 19 E13
Le Verdon-sur-Mer, France 20 C2
Le Vigan, France 20 E7
Lea →, U.K. 15 F8
Leach, Cambodia 65 F4
Lead, U.S.A. 112 C3
Leader, Canada 103 C7
Leadville, U.S.A. 109 G10
Leaf →, U.S.A. 113 K10
Leaf Rapids, Canada 103 B9
Leamington, Canada 116 D2
Leamington, U.S.A. 108 G7
Leamington Spa = Royal
 Leamington Spa, U.K. 15 E6
Le'an, China 59 D10
Leandro Norte Alem, Argentina 127 B4
Leane, L., Ireland 12 D2
Learmonth, Australia 92 D1
Leask, Canada 103 C7
Leatherhead, U.K. 15 F7
Leavenworth, Kans., U.S.A. 112 F7
Leavenworth, Wash., U.S.A. 108 C3
Łeba, Poland 30 D4
Łeba →, Poland 30 D4
Lebach, Germany 25 F2
Lebak, Phil. 61 H6
Lebam, U.S.A. 110 D3
Lebane, Serbia & M. 44 D5
Lebanon, Ind., U.S.A. 114 E2
Lebanon, Kans., U.S.A. 112 F5
Lebanon, Ky., U.S.A. 114 G3
Lebanon, Mo., U.S.A. 113 G8
Lebanon, N.H., U.S.A. 117 C12
Lebanon, Oreg., U.S.A. 108 D2
Lebanon, Pa., U.S.A. 117 F8
Lebanon, Tenn., U.S.A. 115 G2
Lebanon ■, Asia 74 B5
Lebec, U.S.A. 111 L8
Lebedyan, Russia 33 F10
Lebedyn, Ukraine 33 G8
Lebel-sur-Quévillon, Canada 104 C4
Lebomboberge, S. Africa 89 D5
Lębork, Poland 30 D4
Lebrija, Spain 37 J4
Łebsko, Jezioro, Poland 30 D4
Lebu, Chile 126 D1
Leca da Palmeira, Portugal 36 D2
Lecce, Italy 43 B11
Lecco, Italy 40 C6
Lecco, L. di, Italy 40 C6
Lécera, Spain 38 D3
Lech, Austria 26 D3
Lech →, Germany 25 G6
Lechang, China 59 E9
Lechtaler Alpen, Austria 26 D3

Lecontes Mills, U.S.A. 116 E6
Lectoure, France 20 E4
Łęczna, Poland 31 G9
Łęczyca, Poland 31 F6
Ledesma, Spain 36 D5
Ledong, China 64 C7
Leduc, Canada 102 C6
Lee, U.S.A. 117 D11
Lee →, Ireland 12 E3
Lee Vining, U.S.A. 110 H7
Leech L., U.S.A. 112 B7
Leechburg, U.S.A. 116 F5
Leeds, U.K. 14 D6
Leeds, U.S.A. 115 J2
Leek, Neths. 17 A6
Leek, U.K. 14 D5
Leeman, Australia 93 E1
Leeper, U.S.A. 116 E5
Leesburg, U.S.A. 115 L5
Leesville, U.S.A. 113 K8
Leeton, Australia 95 E4
Leetonia, U.S.A. 116 F4
Leeu Gamka, S. Africa 88 E3
Leeuwarden, Neths. 17 A5
Leeuwin, C., Australia 93 F2
Leeuwin Naturaliste △, Australia 93 F2
Leeward Is., Atl. Oc. 121 C7
Lefka, Cyprus 49 D11
Lefkoniko, Cyprus 49 D12
Lefroy, Canada 116 B5
Lefroy, L., Australia 93 F3
Łęg →, Poland 31 H8
Leganés, Spain 36 K7
Legazpi, Phil. 61 E5
Lège-Cap-Ferret, France 20 D2
Lege Hida, Ethiopia 81 F5
Leghorn = Livorno, Italy 40 E7
Legionowo, Poland 31 F7
Legnago, Italy 41 C8
Legnano, Italy 40 C5
Legnica, Poland 31 G3
Legrad, Croatia 41 B13
Leh, India 69 B7
Lehigh Acres, U.S.A. 115 M5
Lehighton, U.S.A. 117 F9
Lehliu, Romania 29 F11
Lehre, Germany 24 C6
Lehrte, Germany 24 C5
Leho, Sudan 81 F3
Lehututu, Botswana 88 C3
Lei Shui →, China 59 D9
Leiah, Pakistan 68 D4
Leibnitz, Austria 26 E8
Leibo, China 58 C4
Leicester, U.K. 15 E6
Leicester City □, U.K. 15 E6
Leicestershire □, U.K. 15 E6
Leichhardt →, Australia 94 B2
Leichhardt Ra., Australia 94 C4
Leiden, Neths. 17 B4
Leie →, Belgium 17 C3
Leifers = Láives, Italy 41 B8
Leimen, Germany 25 F4
Leine →, Germany 24 C5
Leinefelde, Germany 24 D6
Leinster, Australia 93 E3
Leinster □, Ireland 12 C4
Leinster, Mt., Ireland 12 D5
Leipalingis, Lithuania 30 D10
Leipzig, Germany 24 D8
Leiria, Portugal 36 F2
Leiria □, Portugal 36 F2
Leirvik, Norway 9 G11
Leishan, China 58 D7
Leisler, Mt., Australia 92 D4
Leith, U.K. 13 F5
Leith Hill, U.K. 15 F7
Leitha →, Europe 27 D10
Leitrim, Ireland 12 B3
Leitrim □, Ireland 12 B4
Leitza, Spain 38 B3
Leiyang, China 59 D9
Leizhou, China 59 G8
Leizhou Bandao, China 58 G7
Leizhou Wan, China 59 G8
Lek →, Neths. 17 C4
Leka, Norway 8 D14
Lekáni, Greece 45 E8
Lekbibaj, Albania 44 D3
Lekeitio, Spain 38 B2
Lekhainá, Greece 46 D3
Lekoui, Burkina Faso 82 C4
Leksand, Sweden 10 D9
Lékva Óros, Greece 49 D6
Leland, Mich., U.S.A. 114 C3
Leland, Miss., U.S.A. 113 J9
Lelång, Sweden 10 E6
Leleque, Argentina 128 E2
Lelystad, Neths. 17 B5
Lem, Denmark 11 H2
Lema, Nigeria 83 C5
Lema Shilindi, Ethiopia 81 G5
Lemera, Dem. Rep. of the Congo 86 C2
Lemery, Phil. 61 E4
Lemhi Ra., U.S.A. 108 D7
Lemmer, Neths. 17 B5
Lemmon, U.S.A. 112 C3
Lemon Grove, U.S.A. 111 N9
Lemoore, U.S.A. 110 J7
Lempdes, France 20 C7
Lemvig, Denmark 11 H2
Lena →, Russia 53 B13
Lenart, Slovenia 41 B12
Lenartovce, Slovak Rep. 27 C13
Léndas, Greece 49 E6
Lendava, Slovenia 41 B13
Lendeh, Iran 71 D6

Lendinara, Italy 41 C8
Lengerich, Germany 24 C3
Lenggong, Malaysia 65 K3
Lenggries, Germany 25 H7
Lengshuijiang, China 59 D8
Lengshuitan, China 59 D8
Lengua de Vaca, Pta., Chile 126 C1
Lenhovda, Sweden 11 G9
Lenina, Kanal →, Russia 35 J7
Lenino, Ukraine 33 K8
Leninogorsk, Kazakhstan 52 D9
Leninsk, Russia 35 F7
Leninsk-Kuznetskiy, Russia 52 D9
Leninskoye, Russia 34 A8
Lenk, Switz. 25 J3
Lenkoran = Länkäran, Azerbaijan 71 B6
Lenmalu, Indonesia 63 E8
Lenne →, Germany 24 D3
Lennestadt, Germany 24 D4
Lennox, U.S.A. 112 D6
Lennoxville, Canada 117 A13
Leno, Italy 40 C7
Lenoir, U.S.A. 115 H5
Lenoir City, U.S.A. 115 H3
Lenore L., Canada 103 C8
Lenox, U.S.A. 117 D11
Lens, France 19 B9
Lensahn, Germany 24 A6
Lensk, Russia 53 C12
Lentekhi, Georgia 35 J6
Lenti, Hungary 28 D1
Lentini, Italy 43 E8
Lenwood, U.S.A. 111 L9
Lenya, Burma 62 B1
Lenzen, Germany 24 B7
Léo, Burkina Faso 82 C4
Leoben, Austria 26 D8
Leodhas = Lewis, U.K. 13 C2
Leola, U.S.A. 112 C5
Leominster, U.K. 15 E5
Leominster, U.S.A. 117 D13
León, France 20 E2
León, Mexico 118 C4
León, Nic. 120 D2
León, Spain 36 C5
León □, Spain 36 C5
Léon →, U.S.A. 113 K6
Leonardo da Vinci, Roma ✈
 (FCO), Italy 41 G9
Leonardtown, U.S.A. 114 F7
Leonardville, Namibia 88 C2
Leonberg, Germany 25 G5
Leonding, Austria 26 C7
Leonessa, Italy 41 F9
Leonforte, Italy 43 E7
Leongatha, Australia 95 F4
Leonídion, Greece 46 D4
Leonora, Australia 93 E3
Leopoldina, Brazil 127 A7
Leopoldsburg, Belgium 17 C5
Leoti, U.S.A. 112 F4
Leova, Moldova 29 D13
Leoville, Canada 103 C7
Lepe, Spain 37 H3
Lepel = Lyepyel, Belarus 32 E5
Lepenoú, Greece 46 C3
Leping, China 59 C11
Lépo, L. do, Angola 88 B2
Lepontine, Alpi, Italy 40 B5
Leppävirta, Finland 9 E22
Lepsény, Hungary 28 D3
Lequeitio = Lekeitio, Spain 38 B2
Lercara Friddi, Italy 42 E6
Lerdo, Mexico 118 B4
Léré, Chad 83 D7
Léré, Mali 82 B4
Lere, Bauchi, Nigeria 83 D6
Lere, Kaduna, Nigeria 83 C6
Leribe, Lesotho 89 D4
Lérici, Italy 40 D6
Lérida = Lleida, Spain 38 D5
Lérins, Îs. de, France 21 E11
Lerma, Spain 36 C7
Léros, Greece 47 D8
Lérouville, France 19 D12
Lerum, Sweden 11 G6
Lerwick, U.K. 13 A7
Leş, Romania 28 D6
Les Abrets, France 21 C9
Les Andelys, France 18 C8
Les Borges Blanques, Spain 38 D5
Les Cayes, Haiti 121 C5
Les Coteaux, Canada 117 A10
Les Essarts, France 18 F5
Les Herbiers, France 18 F5
Les Minquiers, Plateau des
 Chan. Is. 18 D4
Les Pieux, France 18 C5
Les Ponts-de-Cé, France 18 E6
Les Riceys, France 19 E11
Les Sables-d'Olonne, France 20 B2
Les Vans, France 21 D8
Lesbos = Lésvos, Greece 47 B8
L'Escala, Spain 38 C8
Leshan, China 58 C4
Leshwe △, Dem. Rep. of
 the Congo 87 E2
Lésina, Italy 41 G12
Lésina, L. di, Italy 41 G12
Lesjöfors, Sweden 10 E8
Lesko, Poland 31 B1
Leskov I., Antarctica 5 B1
Leskovac, Serbia & M. 44 C5
Leskovik, Albania 44 F4
Leśna, Poland 31 G2
Lesneven, France 18 D2
Leśnica, Poland 31 H5
Lešnica, Serbia & M. 44 B3

Lesnoye, Russia 32 C8
Lesopilnoye, Russia 54 A7
Lesotho ■, Africa 89 D4
Lesozavodsk, Russia 53 E14
Lesparre-Médoc, France 20 C3
Lessay, France 18 C5
Lesse →, Belgium 17 D4
Lesse et Lomme △, Belgium 17 D5
Lessebo, Sweden 11 H9
Lesser Antilles, W. Indies 121 D7
Lesser Slave L., Canada 102 B5
Lesser Sunda Is., Indonesia 63 F6
Lessines, Belgium 17 D3
Lester, U.S.A. 110 C5
Lester B. Pearson International,
 Toronto ✈ (YYZ), Canada 116 C5
Lestock, Canada 103 C8
Lesuer I., Australia 92 B4
Lesueur △, Australia 93 F2
Lésvos, Greece 47 B8
Leszno, Poland 31 G3
Letaba, S. Africa 89 C5
Letälven, Sweden 10 E8
Letchworth, U.K. 15 F7
Letea, Ostrov, Romania 29 E14
Lethbridge, Canada 102 D6
Lethem, Guyana 124 C7
Leti, Kepulauan, Indonesia 63 F7
Leti Is. = Leti, Kepulauan,
 Indonesia 63 F7
Letiahau →, Botswana 88 C3
Leticia, Colombia 124 D5
Leting, China 57 E10
Letjiesbos, S. Africa 88 E3
Letlhakane, Botswana 88 C4
Letlhakeng, Botswana 88 C3
Letong, Indonesia 62 D3
Letpadan, Burma 67 L19
Letpan, Burma 67 K19
Letsôk-aw Kyun, Burma 65 G2
Letterkenny, Ireland 12 B4
Leu, Romania 29 F9
Leucadia, U.S.A. 111 M9
Leucate, France 20 F7
Leucate, Étang de, France 20 F7
Leuchars, U.K. 13 E6
Leuk, Switz. 25 J3
Leușeni, Moldova 29 D13
Leuser, G., Indonesia 62 D1
Leutkirch, Germany 25 H6
Leuven, Belgium 17 D4
Leuze-en-Hainaut, Belgium 17 D3
Lev Tolstoy, Russia 32 F10
Levádhia, Greece 46 C4
Levan, Albania 44 F3
Levanger, Norway 8 E14
Levant, Î. du, France 21 E10
Lévanto, Italy 40 D6
Lévanzo, Italy 42 E5
Levelland, U.S.A. 113 J3
Leven, U.K. 13 E6
Leven, L., U.K. 13 E5
Leven, Toraka, Madag. 89 A8
Leveque C., Australia 92 C3
Leverano, Italy 43 B10
Leverkusen, Germany 24 D3
Levice, Slovak Rep. 27 C11
Lévico Terme, Italy 41 C8
Levie, France 21 G13
Levier, France 19 F13
Levin, N.Z. 91 J5
Lévis, Canada 105 C5
Levis, L., Canada 102 A5
Levítha, Greece 47 D8
Levittown, N.Y., U.S.A. 117 F11
Levittown, Pa., U.S.A. 117 F10
Levka, Bulgaria 45 E10
Levkás, Greece 46 C2
Levkímmi, Greece 49 B4
Levkímmi, Ákra, Greece 49 B4
Levkôsia = Nicosia, Cyprus 49 D12
Levoča, Slovak Rep. 27 B13
Levroux, France 19 F8
Levski, Bulgaria 45 C9
Levskigrad = Karlovo, Bulgaria 45 D9
Lewes, U.K. 15 G8
Lewes, U.S.A. 114 F8
Lewin Brzeski, Poland 31 H4
Lewis, U.K. 13 C2
Lewis →, U.S.A. 110 E4
Lewis, Butt of, U.K. 13 C2
Lewis Ra., Australia 92 D4
Lewis Range, U.S.A. 108 C7
Lewis Run, U.S.A. 116 E6
Lewisburg, Pa., U.S.A. 116 F8
Lewisburg, Tenn., U.S.A. 115 H2
Lewisburg, W. Va., U.S.A. 114 G5
Lewisporte, Canada 105 C8
Lewiston, Idaho, U.S.A. 108 C5
Lewiston, Maine, U.S.A. 115 C11
Lewistown, Mont., U.S.A. 108 C9
Lewistown, Pa., U.S.A. 116 F7
Lexington, Ill., U.S.A. 112 E10
Lexington, Ky., U.S.A. 114 F3
Lexington, Mich., U.S.A. 116 C2
Lexington, Mo., U.S.A. 112 F8
Lexington, N.C., U.S.A. 115 H5
Lexington, N.Y., U.S.A. 117 D10
Lexington, Nebr., U.S.A. 112 E5
Lexington, Ohio, U.S.A. 116 F2
Lexington, Tenn., U.S.A. 115 H1
Lexington, Va., U.S.A. 114 G6
Lexington Park, U.S.A. 114 F7
Leyburn, U.K. 14 C6
Leye, China 58 E6
Leyland, U.K. 14 D5
Leyre →, France 20 D2
Leyte □, Phil. 61 F6
Leyte Gulf, Phil. 61 F6

Leżajsk, Poland 31 H9
Lezay, France 20 B3
Lezhë, Albania 44 E3
Lezhi, China 58 B5
Lézignan-Corbières, France ... 20 E6
Lezoux, France 20 C7
Lgov, Russia 33 G8
Lhasa, China 60 D4
Lhazê, China 60 D3
Lhokkruet, Indonesia 62 D1
Lhokseumawe, Indonesia 62 C1
L'Hospitalet de Llobregat, Spain 38 D7
Li, Thailand 64 D2
Li Shui →, China 59 C9
Li Xian, Gansu, China 56 G3
Li Xian, Hebei, China 56 E8
Li Xian, Hunan, China 59 C8
Liádhoi, Greece 47 E8
Liancheng, China 59 E11
Liancourt Rocks = Tok-do, Asia 55 F5
Lianga, Phil. 61 G7
Liangcheng,
  Nei Monggol Zizhiqu, China . 56 D7
Liangcheng, Shandong, China . 57 G10
Liangdang, China 56 H4
Lianghe, China 58 E2
Lianghekou, China 58 C7
Liangping, China 58 B6
Liangpran, Indonesia 62 D4
Lianhua, China 59 D9
Lianjiang, Fujian, China 59 D12
Lianjiang, Guangdong, China .. 59 G8
Lianping, China 59 E10
Lianshan, China 59 E9
Lianshanguan, China 57 D12
Lianshui, China 57 H10
Lianyuan, China 59 D8
Lianyungang, China 57 G10
Lianzhou, China 59 E9
Liao He →, China 57 D11
Liaocheng, China 56 F8
Liaodong Bandao, China 57 E12
Liaodong Wan, China 57 D11
Liaoning □, China 57 D12
Liaotung, G. of = Liaodong Wan,
  China 57 D11
Liaoyang, China 57 D12
Liaoyuan, China 57 C13
Liaozhong, China 57 D12
Liapádhes, Greece 46 B1
Liard →, Canada 102 A4
Liard River, Canada 102 B3
Liari, Pakistan 68 G2
Libau = Liepāja, Latvia 9 H19
Libby, U.S.A. 108 B6
Libenge, Dem. Rep. of the Congo 84 D3
Liberal, U.S.A. 113 G4
Liberec, Czech Rep. 26 A8
Liberecký □, Czech Rep. 26 A8
Liberia, Costa Rica 120 D2
Liberia ■, W. Afr. 82 D3
Liberty, Mo., U.S.A. 112 F7
Liberty, N.Y., U.S.A. 117 E10
Liberty, Pa., U.S.A. 116 E7
Liberty, Tex., U.S.A. 113 K7
Libiąż, Poland 31 H6
Lībīya, Sahrā', Africa 79 C10
Libo, China 58 E6
Libobo, Tanjung, Indonesia ... 63 E7
Libode, S. Africa 89 E4
Libohovë, Albania 44 F4
Libourne, France 20 D3
Libramont, Belgium 17 E5
Librazhd, Albania 44 E4
Libreville, Gabon 84 D1
Libya ■, N. Afr. 79 C9
Libyan Desert = Lībīya, Sahrā',
  Africa 79 C10
Libyan Plateau = Ed-Déffa, Egypt 80 A2
Licantén, Chile 126 D1
Licata, Italy 42 E6
Lice, Turkey 73 C9
Licheng, China 56 F7
Lichfield, U.K. 15 E6
Lichinga, Mozam. 87 E4
Lichtenburg, S. Africa 88 D4
Lichtenfels, Germany 25 E7
Lichuan, Hubei, China 58 B7
Lichuan, Jiangxi, China 59 D11
Licking →, U.S.A. 114 F3
Licosa, Punta, Italy 43 B7
Licungo →, Mozam. 87 F4
Lida, Belarus 9 K21
Liden, Sweden 10 B10
Lidhoríkion, Greece 46 C4
Lidhult, Sweden 11 H7
Lidköping, Sweden 11 F7
Lido, Italy 41 C9
Lido, Niger 83 C5
Lido di Roma = Óstia, Lido di,
  Italy 41 G9
Lidzbark, Poland 31 E6
Lidzbark Warmiński, Poland ... 30 D7
Liebenwalde, Germany 24 C9
Lieberose, Germany 24 D10
Liebig, Mt., Australia 92 D5
Liebling, Romania 28 E6
Liechtenstein ■, Europe 25 H5
Liège, Belgium 17 D5
Liège □, Belgium 17 D5
Liegnitz = Legnica, Poland 31 G3
Lienart, Dem. Rep. of the Congo 86 B2
Lienyünchiangshih =
  Lianyungang, China 57 G10
Lienz, Austria 26 E5
Liepāja, Latvia 9 H19
Liepāja □, Latvia 30 B8
Liepājas ezers, Latvia 30 B8
Lier, Belgium 17 C4
Liernais, France 19 E11
Lieşti, Romania 29 E12
Liévin, France 19 B9

Lièvre →, Canada 104 C4
Liezen, Austria 26 D7
Liffey →, Ireland 12 C5
Lifford, Ireland 12 B4
Liffré, France 18 D5
Lifudzin, Russia 54 B7
Ligao, Phil. 61 E5
Lightning Ridge, Australia 95 D4
Lignano Sabbiadoro, Italy 41 C10
Ligny-en-Barrois, France 19 D12
Ligonha →, Mozam. 87 F4
Ligonier, U.S.A. 116 F5
Ligourion, Greece 46 D5
Ligueil, France 18 E7
Liguria □, Italy 40 D5
Ligurian Sea, Medit. S. 6 G7
Lihou Reefs and Cays, Australia 94 B5
Lihue, U.S.A. 106 H15
Lihué Calel △, Argentina 126 D2
Lijiang, China 58 D3
Likenäs, Sweden 10 D7
Likasi, Dem. Rep. of the Congo 87 E2
Likenäs, Sweden 10 D7
Likhoslavl, Russia 32 D8
Likhovskoy, Russia 33 H11
Likoma I., Malawi 87 E3
Likumburu, Tanzania 87 D4
L'Île-Bouchard, France 18 E7
L'Île-Rousse, France 21 F12
Liling, China 59 D9
Lilla Edet, Sweden 11 F6
Lille, France 19 B10
Lille Bælt, Denmark 11 J3
Lillebonne, France 18 C7
Lillehammer, Norway 9 F14
Lillesand, Norway 9 G13
Lillhärdal, Sweden 10 C8
Lillian Pt., Australia 93 E4
Lillo, Spain 36 F7
Lillooet, Canada 102 C4
Lillooet →, Canada 102 D4
Lilongwe, Malawi 87 E3
Liloy, Phil. 63 C6
Lim →, Bos.-H. 44 C3
Lim Chu Kang, Singapore ..... 65 d
Lima, Indonesia 63 E7
Lima, Peru 124 F3
Lima, Mont., U.S.A. 108 D7
Lima, Ohio, U.S.A. 114 E3
Lima →, Portugal 36 D2
Liman, Indonesia 63 G14
Liman, Russia 35 H8
Limanowa, Poland 31 J7
Limassol, Cyprus 49 E12
Limavady, U.K. 12 A5
Limay →, Argentina 128 D3
Limay Mahuida, Argentina 126 D2
Limbach-Oberfrohna, Germany 24 E8
Limbang, Brunei 62 D5
Limbara, Mte., Italy 42 B2
Limbaži, Latvia 9 H21
Limbdi, India 68 H4
Limbe, Cameroon 83 E6
Limburg, Germany 25 E4
Limburg □, Belgium 17 C5
Limburg □, Neths. 17 C5
Limedsforsen, Sweden 10 D7
Limeira, Brazil 127 A6
Limenária, Greece 45 F8
Limerick, Ireland 12 D3
Limerick, U.S.A. 117 C14
Limerick □, Ireland 12 D3
Limestone, U.S.A. 116 D6
Limestone →, Canada 103 B10
Limfjorden, Denmark 11 H3
Limia = Lima →, Portugal 36 D2
Limín Khersónisou, Greece 47 F7
Limingen, Norway 8 D15
Limmared, Sweden 11 G7
Limmen Bight, Australia 94 A2
Limmen Bight →, Australia ... 94 B2
Límni, Greece 46 C5
Límnos, Greece 47 B7
Limoges, Canada 117 A9
Limoges, France 20 C5
Limón, Costa Rica 120 E3
Limon, U.S.A. 112 F3
Limone Piemonte, Italy 40 D4
Limousin □, France 20 C5
Limousin, Plateaux du, France 20 C5
Limoux, France 20 E6
Limpopo □, S. Africa 89 C4
Limpopo →, Africa 89 D5
Limuru, Kenya 86 C4
Lin Xian, China 56 F6
Lin'an, China 59 B12
Linapacan I., Phil. 61 F3
Linapacan Str., Phil. 61 F3
Linares, Chile 126 D1
Linares, Mexico 119 C5
Linares, Spain 37 G7
Linaro, Capo, Italy 41 F8
Línas Mte., Italy 42 C1
Linate, Milano ✈ (LIN), Italy . 40 C6
Lincang, China 58 F3
Lincheng, China 56 F8
Linchuan, China 59 D11
Lincoln = Beamsville, Canada . 116 C5
Lincoln, Argentina 126 C3
Lincoln, N.Z. 91 K4
Lincoln, U.K. 14 D7
Lincoln, Calif., U.S.A. 110 G5
Lincoln, Ill., U.S.A. 112 E10
Lincoln, Kans., U.S.A. 112 F5
Lincoln, Maine, U.S.A. 115 C11
Lincoln, N.H., U.S.A. 117 B13
Lincoln, N. Mex., U.S.A. 109 K11
Lincoln, Nebr., U.S.A. 112 E6
Lincoln City, U.S.A. 108 D1
Lincoln Hav = Lincoln Sea, Arctic 4 A5
Lincoln Sea, Arctic 4 A5
Lincolnshire □, U.K. 14 D7
Lincolnshire Wolds, U.K. 14 D7

Lincolnton, U.S.A. 115 H5
Lind, U.S.A. 108 C4
Linda, U.S.A. 110 F5
Lindau, Germany 25 H5
Linden, Guyana 124 B7
Linden, Ala., U.S.A. 115 J2
Linden, Calif., U.S.A. 110 G5
Linden, Tex., U.S.A. 113 J7
Lindenhurst, U.S.A. 117 F11
Lindesberg, Sweden 10 E9
Lindesnes, Norway 9 H12
Líndhos, Greece 49 C10
Líndhos, Ákra, Greece 49 C10
Lindi, Tanzania 87 D4
Lindi □, Tanzania 87 D4
Lindi →, Dem. Rep. of the Congo 86 B2
Lindö, Sweden 11 F10
Lindome, Sweden 11 G6
Lindoso, Portugal 36 D2
Lindow, Germany 24 C8
Lindsay, Canada 116 B6
Lindsay, Calif., U.S.A. 110 J7
Lindsay, Okla., U.S.A. 113 H6
Lindsborg, U.S.A. 112 F6
Lindsdal, Sweden 11 H10
Line Islands, Pac. Oc. 97 H12
Linesville, U.S.A. 116 E4
Linfen, China 56 F6
Ling Xian, Hunan, China 59 D9
Ling Xian, Shandong, China ... 56 F9
Lingao, China 64 C7
Lingayen, Phil. 63 A6
Lingayen G., Phil. 61 C4
Lingbi, China 57 H9
Lingbo, Sweden 10 C10
Lingchuan, Guangxi Zhuangzu,
  China 59 E8
Lingchuan, Shanxi, China 56 G7
Lingen, Germany 24 C3
Lingga, Indonesia 62 E2
Lingga, Kepulauan, Indonesia . 62 E2
Lingga Arch. = Lingga,
  Kepulauan, Indonesia 62 E2
Linghem, Sweden 11 F9
Lingle, U.S.A. 112 D2
Lingqiu, China 56 E8
Lingshan, China 58 F7
Lingshi, China 56 F6
Lingshou, China 56 E8
Lingshui, China 64 C8
Lingtai, China 56 G4
Linguère, Senegal 82 B1
Lingui, China 59 E8
Lingwu, China 56 E4
Lingyuan, China 57 D10
Lingyun, China 58 E6
Linhai, China 59 C13
Linhares, Brazil 125 G10
Linhe, China 56 D4
Linjiang, China 57 D14
Linköping, Sweden 11 F9
Linkou, China 57 B16
Linli, China 59 C8
Linn, Mt., U.S.A. 110 F2
Linnhe, L., U.K. 13 E3
Linqi, China 56 G7
Linqing, China 56 F8
Linqu, China 57 F10
Linru, China 56 G7
Lins, Brazil 127 A6
Linshui, China 58 B6
Linstead, Jamaica .... 120 a
Linta →, Madag. 89 D7
Linth →, Switz. 25 H5
Linthal, Switz. 25 J5
Linton, Ind., U.S.A. 114 F2
Linton, N. Dak., U.S.A. 112 B4
Lintong, China 56 G5
Linwood, Canada 116 C4
Linwu, China 59 E9
Linxi, China 57 C10
Linxia, China 60 C5
Linxiang, China 59 C9
Linyi, China 57 G10
Linyanti →, Africa 88 B4
Linz, Austria 26 C7
Linz, Germany 24 E3
Linzhenzhen, China 56 F5
Linzi, China 57 F10
Lion, G. du, France 20 E7
Lionárisso, Cyprus 49 D13
Lioni, Italy 43 B8
Lions, G. of = Lion, G. du, France 20 E7
Lion's Den, Zimbabwe 87 F3
Lion's Head, Canada 116 B3
Liozno = Lyozna, Belarus 32 E6
Lipa, Phil. 61 E4
Lipali, Mozam. 87 F4
Lipany, Slovak Rep. 27 B13
Lípari, Italy 43 D7
Lípari, I., Italy 43 D7
Lípari, Is. = Eólie, Ís., Italy ... 43 D7
Lipcani, Moldova 29 B11
Lipetsk, Russia 33 F10
Lipiany, Poland 31 E1
Liping, China 58 D7
Lipkany = Lipcani, Moldova ... 29 B11
Lipljan, Serbia & M. 44 D5
Lipník nad Bečvou, Czech Rep. 27 B10
Lipno, Poland 31 F6
Lipova, Romania 28 D6
Lipovcy Manzovka, Russia 54 B5
Lipovets, Ukraine 33 H5
Lippe →, Germany 24 D2
Lippstadt, Germany 24 D4
Lipscomb, U.S.A. 113 G4
Lipsko, Poland 30 E10
Lipsói, Greece 47 D8
Liptovský Hrádok, Slovak Rep. 27 B12
Liptovský Mikuláš, Slovak Rep. 27 B12
Liptrap, C., Australia 95 F4

Lipu, China 59 E8
Liquillo, Sierra de, Puerto Rico . 121 d
Lira, Uganda 86 B3
Liri →, Italy 42 A6
Liria = Lliria, Spain 39 F4
Lisala, Dem. Rep. of the Congo 84 D4
Lisboa, Portugal 37 G1
Lisboa □, Portugal 37 F1
Lisboa ✈ (LIS), Portugal 37 G1
Lisbon = Lisboa, Portugal 37 G1
Lisbon, N. Dak., U.S.A. 112 B6
Lisbon, N.H., U.S.A. 117 B13
Lisbon, Ohio, U.S.A. 116 F4
Lisbon Falls, U.S.A. 115 D10
Lisburn, U.K. 12 B5
Lisburne, C., U.S.A. 4 C17
Liscannor B., Ireland 12 D2
Liscia →, Italy 42 A2
Lishe Jiang →, China 58 E3
Lishi, China 56 F6
Lishu, China 57 C13
Lishui, Jiangsu, China 59 B12
Lishui, Zhejiang, China 59 C12
Lisianski I., Pac. Oc. 96 E10
Lisichansk = Lysychansk, Ukraine 33 H10
Lisieux, France 18 C7
Liski, Russia 33 G10
L'Isle-Jourdain, Gers, France .. 20 E5
L'Isle-Jourdain, Vienne, France . 20 B4
L'Isle-sur-la-Sorgue, France ... 21 E9
Lisle-sur-Tarn, France 20 E5
Lismore, Australia 95 D5
Lismore, Ireland 12 D4
Lista, Norway 9 G12
Lister, Mt., Antarctica 5 D11
Liston, Australia 95 D5
Listowel, Canada 116 C4
Listowel, Ireland 12 D2
Lit, Sweden 10 A8
Lit-et-Mixe, France 20 D2
Litang, Guangxi Zhuangzu, China 58 F7
Litang, Sichuan, China 58 B3
Litang Qu →, China 58 C3
Litani →, Lebanon 74 B4
Litchfield, Calif., U.S.A. 110 E6
Litchfield, Conn., U.S.A. 117 E11
Litchfield, Ill., U.S.A. 112 F10
Litchfield, Minn., U.S.A. 112 C7
Litchfield △, Australia 92 B5
Litgow, Australia 95 E5
Líthinon, Ákra, Greece 49 E6
Lithuania ■, Europe 9 J20
Litija, Slovenia 41 B11
Lititz, U.S.A. 117 F8
Litókhoron, Greece 44 F6
Litoměřice, Czech Rep. 26 A7
Litomyšl, Czech Rep. 27 B9
Litschau, Austria 26 C8
Little Abaco, Bahamas 120 A4
Little Barrier I., N.Z. 91 G5
Little Belt Mts., U.S.A. 108 C8
Little Bighorn Battlefield △,
  U.S.A. 108 D10
Little Blue →, U.S.A. 112 F6
Little Buffalo →, Canada 102 A6
Little Cayman, Cayman Is. 120 C3
Little Churchill →, Canada ... 103 B9
Little Colorado →, U.S.A. 109 H8
Little Current, Canada 104 C3
Little Current →, Canada 104 B3
Little Falls, Minn., U.S.A. 112 C7
Little Falls, N.Y., U.S.A. 117 C10
Little Fork →, U.S.A. 112 A8
Little Grand Rapids, Canada .. 103 C9
Little Inagua I., Bahamas 121 B5
Little Karoo, S. Africa 88 E3
Little Khingan Mts. = Xiao
  Hinggan Ling, China 60 B7
Little Lake, U.S.A. 111 K9
Little Laut Is. = Laut Kecil,
  Kepulauan, Indonesia 62 E5
Little Mecatina = Petit-
  Mécatina →, Canada 105 B8
Little Minch, U.K. 13 D2
Little Missouri →, U.S.A. 112 B3
Little Ouse →, U.K. 15 E9
Little Rann, India 68 H4
Little Red →, U.S.A. 113 H9
Little River, N.Z. 91 K4
Little Rock, U.S.A. 113 H8
Little Ruaha →, Tanzania 86 D4
Little Sable Pt., U.S.A. 114 D2
Little Scarcies →, S. Leone ... 82 D2
Little Sioux →, U.S.A. 112 E6
Little Smoky →, Canada 102 C5
Little Snake →, U.S.A. 108 F9
Little Tobago, Trin. & Tob. 125 J16
Little Valley, U.S.A. 116 D6
Little Wabash →, U.S.A. 112 G1
Little White →, U.S.A. 112 D4
Little Zab = Zāb aş Şaghīr →,
  Iraq 70 C4
Littlefield, U.S.A. 113 J3
Littlehampton, U.K. 15 G7
Littleton, U.S.A. 117 B13
Litvínov, Czech Rep. 26 A6
Liu He →, China 57 D11
Liu Jiang →, China 58 F7
Liuba, China 56 H4
Liucheng, China 58 E7
Liugou, China 57 D10
Liuhe, China 57 C13
Liuheng Dao, China 59 C14
Liujiang, China 58 E7
Liukang Tenggaja = Sabalana,
  Kepulauan, Indonesia 63 F5
Liuli, Tanzania 87 E3
Liuwa Plain, Zambia 85 G4
Liuyang, China 59 C9
Liuzhou, China 58 E7

Liuzhuang, China 57 H11
Livada, Romania 28 C8
Livadherón, Greece 44 F5
Livadhia, Cyprus 49 E12
Livádhion, Greece 46 A4
Livarot, France 18 D7
Live Oak, Calif., U.S.A. 110 F5
Live Oak, Fla., U.S.A. 115 K4
Liveras, Cyprus 49 D11
Livermore, U.S.A. 110 H5
Livermore, Mt., U.S.A. 113 K2
Livermore Falls, U.S.A. 115 C11
Liverpool, Canada 105 D7
Liverpool, U.K. 14 D4
Liverpool, U.S.A. 117 C8
Liverpool Bay, U.K. 14 D4
Liverpool Ra., Australia 95 E5
Livigno, Italy 40 B7
Livingston, Guatemala 120 C2
Livingston, U.K. 13 F5
Livingston, Ala., U.S.A. 115 J1
Livingston, Calif., U.S.A. 110 H6
Livingston, Mont., U.S.A. 108 D8
Livingston, S.C., U.S.A. 115 J5
Livingston, Tenn., U.S.A. 115 G3
Livingston, Tex., U.S.A. 113 K7
Livingston, L., U.S.A. 113 K7
Livingston Manor, U.S.A. 117 E10
Livingstone, Zambia 87 F2
Livingstone Mts., Tanzania 87 D3
Livingstonia, Malawi 87 E3
Livno, Bos.-H. 28 G2
Livny, Russia 33 F9
Livonia, Mich., U.S.A. 114 D4
Livonia, N.Y., U.S.A. 116 D7
Livorno, Italy 40 E7
Livradois-Forez △, France 20 E7
Livramento, Brazil 127 C4
Livron-sur-Drôme, France 21 D8
Livyntsi, Ukraine 29 B11
Liwale, Tanzania 87 D4
Liwiec →, Poland 31 F8
Liwonde △, Malawi 87 E4
Lixi, China 58 D3
Lixian, China 58 B4
Lixoúrion, Greece 46 C2
Liyang, China 59 B12
Lizard I., Australia 94 A4
Lizard Pt., U.K. 15 H2
Lizzano, Italy 43 B10
Ljig, Serbia & M. 44 B4
Ljubija, Bos.-H. 41 D13
Ljubinje, Bos.-H. 44 D2
Ljubljana, Slovenia 41 B11
Ljubljana ✈ (LJU), Slovenia .. 41 B11
Ljubno, Slovenia 41 B11
Ljubovija, Serbia & M. 44 B3
Ljugarn, Sweden 11 G12
Ljung, Sweden 11 G7
Ljungan →, Sweden 10 B11
Ljungaverk, Sweden 10 B10
Ljungby, Sweden 11 H7
Ljungbyholm, Sweden 11 H10
Ljungdalen, Sweden 10 B6
Ljungsbro, Sweden 11 F9
Ljungskile, Sweden 11 F5
Ljusdal, Sweden 10 C10
Ljusfallshammar, Sweden 11 F9
Ljusnan →, Sweden 10 C11
Ljusne, Sweden 10 C11
Ljutomer, Slovenia 41 B13
Llagostera, Spain 38 D7
Llancanelo, Salina, Argentina . 126 D2
Llandeilo, U.K. 15 F4
Llandovery, U.K. 15 F4
Llandrindod Wells, U.K. 15 E4
Llandudno, U.K. 14 D4
Llanelli, U.K. 15 F3
Llanes, Spain 36 B6
Llangollen, U.K. 14 E4
Llanidloes, U.K. 15 E4
Llano, U.S.A. 113 K5
Llano →, U.S.A. 113 K5
Llano Estacado, U.S.A. 113 J3
Llanos, S. Amer. 124 C4
Llanos de Challe △, Chile 126 B1
Llanquihue, L., Chile 128 E1
Llanwrtyd Wells, U.K. 15 E4
Llebeig, C. des, Spain 48 B9
Lleida, Spain 38 D5
Lleida □, Spain 38 C6
Llentrisca, C., Spain 48 C7
Llera, Mexico 119 C5
Llerena, Spain 37 G5
Lleyn Peninsula, U.K. 14 E3
Llico, Chile 126 C1
Lliria, Spain 39 F4
Llobregat →, Spain 38 D7
Llodio, Spain 38 B2
Lloret de Mar, Spain 38 D7
Lloyd B., Australia 94 A3
Lloyd L., Canada 103 B7
Lloydminster, Canada 103 C7
Llucena del Cid, Spain 38 E4
Llucmajor, Spain 48 B9
Llullaillaco △, Chile 126 A2
Llullaillaco, Volcán, S. Amer. . 126 A2
Loa →, Vietnam 64 B5
Loa, U.S.A. 109 G8
Loa →, Chile 126 A1
Loaita I., S. China Sea 62 B4
Loange →, Dem. Rep. of
  the Congo 84 E4
Loano, Italy 40 D5
Lobatse, Botswana 88 D4
Löbau, Germany 24 D10
Lobenstein, Germany 24 E7
Lobería, Argentina 126 D4
Löberöd, Sweden 11 J7
Łobez, Poland 30 E2
Lobito, Angola 85 G2
Lobo →, Ivory C. 82 D3

Lobos, *Argentina* 126 D4
Lobos, I., *Mexico* 118 B2
Lobos, I. de, *Canary Is.* 48 F6
Łobżenica, *Poland* 31 E4
Loc Binh, *Vietnam* 64 B6
Loc Ninh, *Vietnam* 65 G6
Locarno, *Switz.* 25 J4
Loch Baghasdail = Lochboisdale,
  U.K. 13 D1
Loch Garman = Wexford, *Ireland* 12 D5
Loch Lomond and the
  Trossachs △, *U.K.* 13 E4
Loch Nam Madadh = Lochmaddy,
  U.K. 13 D1
Lochaber, *U.K.* 13 E3
Locharbriggs, *U.K.* 13 F5
Lochboisdale, *U.K.* 13 D1
Loche, L. La, *Canada* 103 B7
Lochem, *Neths.* 17 B6
Loches, *France* 18 E7
Lochgilphead, *U.K.* 13 E3
Lochinvar △, *Zambia* 87 F2
Lochinver, *U.K.* 13 C3
Lochmaddy, *U.K.* 13 D1
Lochnagar, *Australia* 94 C4
Lochnagar, *U.K.* 13 E5
Łochów, *Poland* 31 F8
Lochy, L., *U.K.* 13 E4
Lock, *Australia* 95 E2
Lock Haven, *U.S.A.* 116 E7
Lockeford, *U.S.A.* 110 G5
Lockeport, *Canada* 105 D6
Lockerbie, *U.K.* 13 F5
Lockhart, *U.S.A.* 113 L6
Lockhart, L., *Australia* 93 F2
Lockhart River, *Australia* 94 A3
Lockney, *U.S.A.* 113 H4
Lockport, *U.S.A.* 116 C6
Locminé, *France* 18 E4
Locri, *Italy* 43 D9
Locronan, *France* 18 D2
Lod, *Israel* 74 D3
Lodeinoye Pole, *Russia* 32 B7
Lodève, *France* 20 E7
Lodge Bay, *Canada* 105 B8
Lodge Grass, *U.S.A.* 108 D10
Lodgepole Cr. ➤, *U.S.A.* 112 E2
Lodhran, *Pakistan* 68 E4
Lodi, *Italy* 40 C6
Lodi, *Calif., U.S.A.* 110 G5
Lodi, *Ohio, U.S.A.* 116 E3
Lodja, *Dem. Rep. of the Congo* 86 C1
Lodosa, *Spain* 38 C2
Lödöse, *Sweden* 11 F6
Lodwar, *Kenya* 86 B4
Łódź, *Poland* 31 G6
Łódzkie □, *Poland* 31 G6
Loei, *Thailand* 64 D3
Loengo, *Dem. Rep. of the Congo* 86 C2
Loeriesfontein, *S. Africa* 88 E2
Lofa ➤, *Liberia* 83 D2
Lofa Mano △, *Liberia* 82 D2
Lofer, *Austria* 26 D5
Lofoten, *Norway* 8 B15
Lofsdalen, *Sweden* 10 B7
Lofsen ➤, *Sweden* 10 B7
Loftahammar, *Sweden* 11 G10
Loga, *Niger* 83 C5
Logan, *Iowa, U.S.A.* 112 E7
Logan, *Ohio, U.S.A.* 114 F4
Logan, *Utah, U.S.A.* 108 F8
Logan, *W. Va., U.S.A.* 114 G5
Logan, Mt., *Canada* 100 B5
Logandale, *U.S.A.* 111 J12
Logansport, *Ind., U.S.A.* 114 E2
Logansport, *La., U.S.A.* 113 K8
Logirim, *Sudan* 81 G3
Logo, *Sudan* 81 F3
Logone ➤, *Chad* 79 F9
Logroño, *Spain* 38 C2
Logrosán, *Spain* 37 F5
Løgstør, *Denmark* 11 H3
Løgumkloster, *Denmark* 11 J2
Lohals, *Denmark* 11 J4
Lohardaga, *India* 69 H11
Loharia, *India* 68 H6
Loharu, *India* 68 E6
Lohja, *Finland* 9 F21
Löhne, *Germany* 24 C4
Lohr, *Germany* 25 F5
Lohri Wah ➤, *Pakistan* 68 F2
Loi-kaw, *Burma* 67 K20
Loimaa, *Finland* 9 F20
Loir ➤, *France* 18 E6
Loir-et-Cher □, *France* 18 E8
Loire □, *France* 21 C8
Loire ➤, *France* 18 E4
Loire Anjou Touraine △, *France* 18 E6
Loire-Atlantique □, *France* ... 18 E5
Loiret □, *France* 19 E9
Loitz, *Germany* 24 B9
Loja, *Ecuador* 124 D3
Loja, *Spain* 37 H6
Loji = Kawasi, *Indonesia* 63 E7
Lojo = Lohja, *Finland* 9 F21
Løjt Kirkeby, *Denmark* 11 J3
Lojung, *China* 58 E7
Loka, *Sudan* 81 G3
Lokandu, *Dem. Rep. of the Congo* 86 C2
Lokeren, *Belgium* 17 C3
Lokgwabe, *Botswana* 88 C3
Lokhvitsa, *Ukraine* 33 G7
Lokichokio, *Kenya* 86 B3
Lokitaung, *Kenya* 86 B4
Lokkan tekojärvi, *Finland* 8 C22
Løkken, *Denmark* 11 G3
Loknya, *Russia* 32 D6
Loko, *Nigeria* 83 D6
Lokoja, *Nigeria* 83 D6
Lokot, *Russia* 33 F8
Lol ➤, *Sudan* 81 F2
Lola, *Guinea* 82 D3

Lola, Mt., *U.S.A.* 110 F6
Lolibai, Gebel, *Sudan* 81 G3
Lolimi, *Sudan* 81 G3
Loliondo, *Tanzania* 86 C4
Lolland, *Denmark* 11 K5
Lollar, *Germany* 24 E4
Lolo, *U.S.A.* 108 C6
Lolodorf, *Cameroon* 83 E7
Lom, *Bulgaria* 44 C7
Lom ➤, *Bulgaria* 44 C7
Lom Kao, *Thailand* 64 D3
Lom Sak, *Thailand* 64 D3
Loma, *U.S.A.* 108 C8
Loma Linda, *U.S.A.* 111 L9
Lomami ➤, *Dem. Rep. of
  the Congo* 86 B1
Lomas de Zamóra, *Argentina* . 126 C4
Lombadina, *Australia* 92 C3
Lombárdia □, *Italy* 40 C6
Lombardy = Lombárdia □, *Italy* 40 C6
Lombez, *France* 20 E4
Lomblen, *Indonesia* 63 F6
Lombok, *Indonesia* 62 F5
Lombok, Selat, *Indonesia* 63 K18
Lomé, *Togo* 83 D5
Lomela, *Dem. Rep. of the Congo* 84 E4
Lomela ➤, *Dem. Rep. of
  the Congo* 84 E4
Lomianki, *Poland* 31 F7
Lomma, *Sweden* 11 J7
Lommel, *Belgium* 17 C5
Lomond, *Canada* 102 C6
Lomond, L., *U.K.* 13 E4
Lomonosov Ridge, *Arctic* .... 4 A
Lomphat, *Cambodia* 64 F6
Lompobatang, *Indonesia* 63 F5
Lompoc, *Phil.* 61 L6
Łomża, *Poland* 31 E9
Lon, Ko, *Thailand* .... 65 a
Loncoche, *Chile* 128 D2
Londa, *India* 66 M9
Londiani, *Kenya* 86 C4
Londinières, *France* 18 C8
London, *Canada* 116 D3
London, *Ky., U.S.A.* 114 G3
London, *Ohio, U.S.A.* 114 F4
London, Greater □, *U.K.* 15 F7
London Gatwick ✈ (LGW), *U.K.* 15 F7
London Heathrow ✈ (LHR),
  U.K. 15 F7
London Stansted ✈ (STN), *U.K.* 15 F8
Londonderry, *U.K.* 12 B4
Londonderry □, *U.K.* 12 B4
Londonderry, C., *Australia* ... 92 B4
Londonderry, I., *Chile* 128 H2
Londres, *Argentina* 128 B3
Londrina, *Brazil* 127 A5
Lone Pine, *U.S.A.* 110 J8
Lonely Mine, *Zimbabwe* 89 B4
Long B., *U.S.A.* 115 J6
Long Beach, *Calif., U.S.A.* ... 111 M8
Long Beach, *N.Y., U.S.A.* ... 117 F11
Long Beach, *Wash., U.S.A.* .. 110 D2
Long Branch, *U.S.A.* 117 F11
Long Creek, *U.S.A.* 108 D4
Long Eaton, *U.K.* 14 E6
Long I., *Australia* 94 J6
Long I., *Bahamas* 121 B4
Long I., *Canada* 104 B4
Long I., *Ireland* 12 E2
Long I., *U.S.A.* 117 F11
Long Island Sd., *U.S.A.* 117 E12
Long L., *Canada* 104 C2
Long Lake, *U.S.A.* 117 C10
Long Point B., *Canada* 116 D4
Long Prairie ➤, *U.S.A.* 112 C7
Long Pt., *Canada* 116 D4
Long Range Mts., *Canada* 105 C8
Long Reef, *Australia* 92 B4
Long Spruce, *Canada* 103 B10
Long Str. = Longa, Proliv, *Russia* 4 C16
Long Thanh, *Vietnam* 65 G6
Long Xian, *China* 56 G4
Long Xuyen, *Vietnam* 65 G5
Longá, *Greece* 46 E3
Longa, Proliv, *Russia* 4 C16
Long'an, *China* 58 F6
Longarone, *Italy* 41 B9
Longbenton, *U.K.* 14 B6
Longboat Key, *U.S.A.* 115 M4
Longchang, *China* 58 C5
Longchi, *China* 58 C4
Longchuan, *Guangdong, China* 59 E10
Longchuan, *Yunnan, China* .. 58 E1
Longde, *China* 56 G4
Longeau, *France* 19 E12
Longford, *Australia* 95 G4
Longford, *Ireland* 12 C4
Longford □, *Ireland* 12 C4
Longhai, *China* 59 E11
Longhua, *China* 57 D9
Longhui, *China* 59 D8
Longido, *Tanzania* 86 C4
Longiram, *Indonesia* 62 E5
Longkou, *Jiangxi, China* 59 D10
Longkou, *Shandong, China* .. 57 F11
Longlac, *Canada* 104 C2
Longli, *China* 58 D6
Longling, *China* 58 E2
Longmeadow, *U.S.A.* 117 D12
Longmen, *China* 59 F10
Longming, *China* 58 F6
Longmont, *U.S.A.* 112 E2
Longnan, *China* 59 E10
Longnawan, *Indonesia* 62 D4
Longobucco, *Italy* 43 C9
Longreach, *Australia* 94 C3
Longshan, *China* 58 C7
Longsheng, *China* 59 E8

Longué-Jumelles, *France* 18 E6
Longueau, *France* 19 C9
Longueuil, *Canada* 117 A11
Longuyon, *France* 19 C12
Longvic, *France* 19 E12
Longview, *Tex., U.S.A.* 113 J7
Longview, *Wash., U.S.A.* 110 D4
Longwy, *France* 19 C12
Longxi, *China* 56 G3
Longyan, *China* 59 E11
Longyearbyen, *Svalbard* 4 B8
Longyou, *China* 59 C12
Longzhou, *China* 58 F6
Lonigo, *Italy* 41 C8
Löningen, *Germany* 24 C3
Lonoke, *U.S.A.* 113 H9
Lonquimay, *Chile* 128 D2
Lons-le-Saunier, *France* 19 F12
Lönsboda, *Sweden* 11 H8
Looe, *U.K.* 15 G3
Lookout, C., *Canada* 104 A3
Lookout, C., *U.S.A.* 115 H7
Loolmalasin, *Tanzania* 86 C4
Loon ➤, *Alta., Canada* 102 B5
Loon ➤, *Man., Canada* 103 B8
Loon Lake, *Canada* 103 C7
Loongana, *Australia* 93 F4
Loop Hd., *Ireland* 12 D2
Lop Buri, *Thailand* 64 E3
Lop Nor = Lop Nur, *China* ... 60 B4
Lop Nur, *China* 60 B4
Lopare, *Bos.-H.* 28 F3
Lopatin, *Russia* 35 J8
Lopatina, Gora, *Russia* 53 D15
Lopaye, *Sudan* 81 F3
Lopez, *Phil.* 61 E5
Lopez, *U.S.A.* 117 E8
Lopez, C., *Gabon* 84 E1
Lopphavet, *Norway* 8 A19
Loptra Aidhipsoú, *Greece* 46 C5
Lora ➤, *Afghan.* 66 D4
Lora, Hāmūn-i-, *Pakistan* 66 E4
Lora Cr. ➤, *Australia* 95 D2
Lora del Río, *Spain* 37 H5
Lorain, *U.S.A.* 116 E2
Loralai, *Pakistan* 68 D3
Lorca, *Spain* 39 H3
Lord Howe I., *Pac. Oc.* 96 L7
Lord Howe Ridge, *Pac. Oc.* .. 96 L8
Lordsburg, *U.S.A.* 109 K9
Lorestan □, *Iran* 71 C6
Loreto, *Brazil* 125 E9
Loreto, *Italy* 41 E10
Loreto, *Mexico* 118 B2
Lorgues, *France* 21 E10
Lorhosso, *Burkina Faso* 82 C4
Lorient, *France* 18 E3
Lõrinci, *Hungary* 28 C4
Lormi, *India* 69 H9
Lorn, *U.K.* 13 E3
Lorn, Firth of, *U.K.* 13 E3
Lorne, *Australia* 95 F3
Loronyo, *Sudan* 81 G3
Lorovouno, *Cyprus* 49 D11
Lörrach, *Germany* 25 H3
Lorraine □, *France* 19 D12
Lorraine □, *France* 19 D13
Los, *Sweden* 10 C9
Los, Îles de, *Guinea* 82 D2
Los Alamos, *Calif., U.S.A.* ... 111 L6
Los Alamos, *N. Mex., U.S.A.* . 109 J10
Los Alcornocales △, *Spain* .. 37 J5
Los Altos, *U.S.A.* 110 H4
Los Andes, *Chile* 126 C1
Los Angeles, *Chile* 126 D1
Los Angeles, *U.S.A.* 111 M8
Los Angeles, Bahia de, *Mexico* 118 B2
Los Angeles Aqueduct, *U.S.A.* 111 K9
Los Angeles International ✈
  (LAX), *U.S.A.* 111 M8
Los Banos, *U.S.A.* 110 H6
Los Barrios, *Spain* 37 J5
Los Blancos, *Argentina* 126 A3
Los Cardones △, *Argentina* .. 126 B2
Los Chiles, *Costa Rica* 120 D3
Los Corrales de Buelna, *Spain* 36 B6
Los Cristianos, *Canary Is.* ... 48 F3
Los Gallardos, *Spain* 39 H3
Los Gatos, *U.S.A.* 110 H5
Los Haïtises △, *Dom. Rep.* ... 121 C6
Los Hermanos Is., *Venezuela* . 121 D7
Los Islotes, *Canary Is.* 48 E6
Los Llanos de Aridane, *Canary Is.* 48 F2
Los Loros, *Chile* 126 B1
Los Lunas, *U.S.A.* 109 J10
Los Mochis, *Mexico* 118 B3
Los Monegros, *Spain* 38 D4
Los Nietos, *Spain* 39 H4
Los Olivos, *U.S.A.* 111 L6
Los Palacios, *Cuba* 120 B3
Los Palacios y Villafranca, *Spain* 37 H5
Los Reyes, *Mexico* 118 D4
Los Roques Is., *Venezuela* ... 121 D6
Los Santos de Maimona, *Spain* 37 G4
Los Teques, *Venezuela* 124 A5
Los Testigos, Is., *Venezuela* .. 124 A6
Los Vilos, *Chile* 126 C1
Los Yébenes, *Spain* 37 F7
Loskop Dam, *S. Africa* 89 D4
Løsning, *Denmark* 11 J3
Lossiemouth, *U.K.* 13 D5
Lossnen ➤, *Sweden* 10 B6
Lostwithiel, *U.K.* 15 G3
Lot □, *France* 20 D5
Lot ➤, *France* 20 D4
Lot-et-Garonne □, *France* ... 20 D4
Lota, *Chile* 126 D1
Lotagipi Swamp, *Sudan* 81 G3
Loţfābād, *Iran* 71 B8
Lothair, *S. Africa* 89 D5
Lotorp, *Sweden* 11 F9
Luang, Thale, *Thailand* 65 J3

Lötschbergtunnel, *Switz.* 25 J3
Löttorp, *Sweden* 11 G11
Lotung, *Taiwan* 59 E13
Lotubomo, *Congo* 84 E2
Loudéac, *France* 18 D4
Loudi, *China* 59 D8
Loudonville, *U.S.A.* 116 F2
Loudun, *France* 18 E7
Loue ➤, *France* 19 E12
Louga, *Senegal* 82 B1
Loughborough, *U.K.* 14 E6
Loughrea, *Ireland* 12 C3
Loughros More B., *Ireland* ... 12 B3
Louhans, *France* 19 F12
Louis Trichardt, *S. Africa* 89 C4
Louis XIV, Pte., *Canada* 104 B4
Louisa, *U.S.A.* 114 F4
Louisbourg, *Canada* 105 C8
Louise I., *Canada* 102 C2
Louiseville, *Canada* 104 C5
Louisiade Arch., *Papua N. G.* 96 J7
Louisiana, *U.S.A.* 112 F9
Louisiana □, *U.S.A.* 113 K9
Louisville, *Ky., U.S.A.* 114 F3
Louisville, *Miss., U.S.A.* 113 J10
Louisville, *Ohio, U.S.A.* 116 F3
Loulay, *France* 20 B3
Loulé, *Portugal* 37 H3
Louny, *Czech Rep.* 26 A6
Loup City, *U.S.A.* 112 E5
Loups Marins, Lacs des, *Canada* 104 A5
Lourdes, *France* 20 E3
Lourinhã, *Portugal* 37 F1
Lousã, *Portugal* 36 E2
Louta, *Burkina Faso* 82 C4
Louth, *Australia* 95 E4
Louth, *Ireland* 12 C5
Louth, *U.K.* 14 D7
Louth □, *Ireland* 12 C5
Loutrá Aidhipsoú, *Greece* 46 C5
Louvain = Leuven, *Belgium* .. 17 D4
Louviers, *France* 18 C8
Louwsburg, *S. Africa* 89 D5
Lovat ➤, *Russia* 32 C6
Loveč, *Serbia & M.* 44 D2
Lovćen △, *Serbia & M.* 44 D2
Lovech, *Bulgaria* 45 C8
Lovech □, *Bulgaria* 45 C8
Loveland, *U.S.A.* 112 E2
Lovell, *U.S.A.* 108 D9
Lovelock, *U.S.A.* 108 F4
Lóvere, *Italy* 40 C7
Lovestad, *Sweden* 11 J7
Loviisa, *Finland* 9 F22
Loving, *U.S.A.* 113 J2
Lovington, *U.S.A.* 113 J3
Lovisa = Loviisa, *Finland* 9 F22
Lovosice, *Czech Rep.* 26 A7
Lovran, *Croatia* 41 C11
Lovrin, *Romania* 28 E5
Lövstabruk, *Sweden* 10 D11
Lövstabukten, *Sweden* 10 D11
Low, L., *Canada* 104 B4
Low Pt., *Australia* 93 F4
Low Tatra = Nízké Tatry,
  Slovak Rep. 27 C12
Lowa, *Dem. Rep. of the Congo* 86 C2
Lowa ➤, *Dem. Rep. of the Congo* 86 C2
Lowell, *U.S.A.* 117 D13
Lowellville, *U.S.A.* 116 E4
Löwen ➤, *Namibia* 88 D2
Lower Alkali L., *U.S.A.* 108 F3
Lower Arrow L., *Canada* 102 D5
Lower Austria =
  Niederösterreich □, *Austria* . 26 C8
Lower California = Baja
  California, *Mexico* 118 A1
Lower Hutt, *N.Z.* 91 J5
Lower Lake, *U.S.A.* 110 G4
Lower Manitou L., *Canada* ... 103 D10
Lower Post, *Canada* 102 B3
Lower Red L., *U.S.A.* 112 B7
Lower Saxony =
  Niedersachsen □, *Germany* . 24 C4
Lower Tunguska = Tunguska,
  Nizhnyaya ➤, *Russia* 53 C9
Lower Zambezi △, *Zambia* .. 87 F2
Lowestoft, *U.K.* 15 E9
Lowgar □, *Afghan.* 66 B6
Łowicz, *Poland* 31 F6
Lowville, *U.S.A.* 117 C9
Loxton, *Australia* 95 E3
Loxton, *S. Africa* 88 E3
Loyalty Is. = Loyauté, Îs., *N. Cal.* 96 K8
Loyang = Luoyang, *China* 56 G7
Loyauté, Îs., *N. Cal.* 96 K8
Loyev = Loyew, *Belarus* 33 G6
Loyew, *Belarus* 33 G6
Loyoro, *Uganda* 86 B3
Lož, *Slovenia* 41 C11
Lozère □, *France* 20 D7
Loznica, *Serbia & M.* 44 B3
Lozova, *Ukraine* 33 H9

Luang Prabang, *Laos* 58 H4
Luangwa, *Zambia* 87 F3
Luangwa ➤, *Zambia* 87 E3
Luangwa Valley, *Zambia* 87 E3
Luanne, *China* 57 D9
Luanping, *China* 57 D9
Luanshya, *Zambia* 87 E2
Luapula □, *Zambia* 87 E2
Luapula ➤, *Africa* 87 D2
Luarca, *Spain* 36 B4
Luashi, *Dem. Rep. of the Congo* 87 E1
Luau, *Angola* 84 G4
Lubaczów, *Poland* 31 H10
Lubań, *Poland* 31 G2
Lubana, Ozero = Lubānas Ezers,
  Latvia 9 H22
Lubānas Ezers, *Latvia* 9 H22
Lubang, *Phil.* 61 E4
Lubang Is., *Phil.* 63 B6
Lubango, *Angola* 85 G2
Lubao, *Dem. Rep. of the Congo* 86 D2
Lubartów, *Poland* 31 G9
Lubawa, *Poland* 30 E6
Lübbecke, *Germany* 24 C4
Lübben, *Germany* 24 D9
Lübbenau, *Germany* 24 D9
Lubbock, *U.S.A.* 113 J4
Lübeck, *Germany* 24 B6
Lübecker Bucht, *Germany* ... 24 A6
Lubefu, *Dem. Rep. of
  the Congo* 86 C1
Lubelskie □, *Poland* 31 G9
Lubero = Luofu, *Dem. Rep. of
  the Congo* 86 C2
Luberon △, *France* 21 E9
Lubersac, *France* 20 C5
Lubicon L., *Canada* 102 B5
Lubień Kujawski, *Poland* 31 F6
Lubilash ➤, *Dem. Rep. of
  the Congo* 84 F4
Lubin, *Poland* 31 G3
Lublin, *Poland* 31 G9
Lubliniec, *Poland* 31 H5
Lubnān, Jabal, *Lebanon* 74 B4
Lubniewice, *Poland* 31 F2
Lubny, *Ukraine* 33 G7
Luboń, *Poland* 31 F3
Lubongola, *Dem. Rep. of
  the Congo* 86 C2
L'ubotín, *Slovak Rep.* 27 B13
Lubraniec, *Poland* 31 F5
Lubsko, *Poland* 31 G1
Lübtheen, *Germany* 24 B7
Lubuagan, *Phil.* 61 C4
Lubudi, *Dem. Rep. of the Congo* 84 F5
Lubudi ➤, *Dem. Rep. of
  the Congo* 87 D2
Lubukkinggau, *Indonesia* 62 E2
Lubuksikaping, *Indonesia* 62 D2
Lubumbashi, *Dem. Rep. of
  the Congo* 87 E2
Lubunda, *Dem. Rep. of the Congo* 86 D2
Lubungu, *Zambia* 87 E2
Lubuskie □, *Poland* 31 F2
Lubutu, *Dem. Rep. of the Congo* 86 C2
Luc An Chau, *Vietnam* 64 A5
Luc-en-Diois, *France* 21 D9
Lucan, *Canada* 116 C3
Lucania, Mt., *Canada* 100 B5
Lucas Channel, *Canada* 116 A3
Lucban, *Phil.* 61 D4
Lucca, *Italy* 40 C4
Lucé, *France* 18 D8
Luce Bay, *U.K.* 13 G4
Lucea, *Jamaica* .... 120 a
Lucedale, *U.S.A.* 115 K1
Lucena, *Phil.* 61 E4
Lucena, *Spain* 37 H6
Lučenec, *Slovak Rep.* 27 C12
Lucera, *Italy* 43 A8
Lucerne = Luzern, *Switz.* 25 H4
Lucerne, *U.S.A.* 110 F4
Lucerne Valley, *U.S.A.* 111 L10
Lucero, *Mexico* 118 A3
Luchena ➤, *Spain* 39 H3
Lucheng, *China* 56 F7
Lucheringo ➤, *Mozam.* 87 E4
Lüchow, *Germany* 24 C7
Luchuan, *China* 59 F8
Lucia, *U.S.A.* 110 J5
Lucinda, *Australia* 94 B4
Luckau, *Germany* 24 D9
Luckenwalde, *Germany* 24 C9
Luckhoff, *S. Africa* 88 D3
Lucknow, *Canada* 116 C3
Lucknow, *India* 69 F9
Luçon, *France* 20 B2
Lüda = Dalian, *China* 57 E11
Lüderitz, *Namibia* 88 D2
Lüderitzbaai, *Namibia* 88 D2
Ludhiana, *India* 68 D6
Ludian, *China* 58 C4
Luding Qiao, *China* 58 C4
Lüdinghausen, *Germany* 24 D3
Ludington, *U.S.A.* 114 D2
Ludlow, *U.K.* 15 E5
Ludlow, *Calif., U.S.A.* 111 L10
Ludlow, *Pa., U.S.A.* 116 E6
Ludlow, *Vt., U.S.A.* 117 C12
Ludus, *Romania* 29 D9
Ludvika, *Sweden* 10 D9
Ludwigsburg, *Germany* 25 G5
Ludwigsfelde, *Germany* 24 C9
Ludwigshafen, *Germany* 25 F4
Ludwigslust, *Germany* 24 B7
Ludza, *Latvia* 32 D4
Lueki, *Dem. Rep. of the Congo* 86 C2

Luena, *Dem. Rep. of the Congo* 87 D2
Luena, *Zambia* 87 E3
Luenha = Ruenya →, *Africa* 87 F3
Lüeyang, *China* 56 H4
Lufeng, *Guangdong, China* 59 F10
Lufeng, *Yunnan, China* 58 E4
Lufira →, *Dem. Rep. of the Congo* 87 D2
Lufkin, *U.S.A.* 113 K7
Lufupa, *Dem. Rep. of the Congo* 87 E1
Luga, *Russia* 32 C5
Luga →, *Russia* 32 C5
Lugano, *Switz.* 25 J4
Lugano, L. di, *Switz.* 40 C6
Lugansk = Luhansk, *Ukraine* 33 H10
Lugard's Falls, *Kenya* 86 C4
Lugela, *Mozam.* 87 F4
Lugenda →, *Mozam.* 87 E4
Lugh Ganana, *Somali Rep.* 75 G3
Lugnaquillia, *Ireland* 12 D5
Lugo, *Italy* 41 D8
Lugo, *Spain* 36 B3
Lugo □, *Spain* 36 C3
Lugoj, *Romania* 28 E6
Lugovoy = Qulan, *Kazakhstan* 52 E8
Luhansk, *Ukraine* 33 H10
Luhe, *China* 59 A12
Luhe →, *Germany* 24 B6
Luhuo, *China* 58 B3
Luiana, *Angola* 88 B3
Luichow Pen. = Leizhou Bandao, *China* 58 G7
Luimneach = Limerick, *Ireland* 12 D3
Luing, *U.K.* 13 E3
Luino, *Italy* 40 C5
Luís Correia, *Brazil* 125 D10
Luitpold Coast, *Antarctica* 5 D1
Luiza, *Dem. Rep. of the Congo* 84 F4
Luizi, *Dem. Rep. of the Congo* 86 D2
Luján, *Argentina* 126 C4
Lujiang, *China* 59 B11
Lukang, *Taiwan* 59 E13
Lukanga Swamp, *Zambia* 87 E2
Lukavac, *Bos.-H.* 28 F3
Lukenie →, *Dem. Rep. of the Congo* 84 E3
Lukhisaral, *India* 69 G12
Lŭki, *Bulgaria* 45 E8
Lukolela, *Dem. Rep. of the Congo* 86 D1
Lukosi, *Zimbabwe* 87 F2
Lukovë, *Albania* 44 G3
Lukovit, *Bulgaria* 45 C8
Łuków, *Poland* 31 G9
Lukoyanov, *Russia* 34 C7
Lukusuzi △, *Zambia* 87 E3
Luleå, *Sweden* 8 D20
Luleälven →, *Sweden* 8 D19
Lüleburgaz, *Turkey* 45 E11
Luliang, *China* 58 E4
Luling, *U.S.A.* 113 L6
Lulong, *China* 57 E10
Lulonga →, *Dem. Rep. of the Congo* 84 D3
Lulua →, *Dem. Rep. of the Congo* 84 E4
Lumajang, *Indonesia* 63 H15
Lumbala N'guimbo, *Angola* 85 G4
Lumberton, *U.S.A.* 115 H6
Lumsden, *Canada* 103 C8
Lumsden, *N.Z.* 91 L2
Lumut, *Malaysia* 65 K3
Lumut, Tanjung, *Indonesia* 62 E3
Luna, *India* 68 H3
Lunan, *China* 58 E4
Lunavada, *India* 68 H5
Lunca, *Romania* 29 C10
Lunca Corbului, *Romania* 29 F9
Lund, *Sweden* 11 J7
Lundazi, *Zambia* 87 E3
Lunderskov, *Denmark* 11 J3
Lundi →, *Zimbabwe* 87 G3
Lundu, *Malaysia* 62 D3
Lundy, *U.K.* 15 F3
Lune →, *U.K.* 14 C5
Lüneburg, *Germany* 24 B6
Lüneburg Heath = Lüneburger Heide, *Germany* 24 B6
Lüneburger Heide, *Germany* 24 B6
Lunel, *France* 21 E8
Lünen, *Germany* 24 D3
Lunenburg, *Canada* 105 D7
Lunéville, *France* 19 D13
Lunga →, *Zambia* 87 E2
Lungi Airport, *S. Leone* 82 D2
Lunglei, *India* 67 H18
Luni, *India* 68 G5
Luni →, *India* 68 G4
Luninets = Luninyets, *Belarus* 33 F4
Luning, *U.S.A.* 108 G4
Lunino, *Russia* 34 D7
Luninyets, *Belarus* 33 F4
Lunkaransar, *India* 68 E5
Lunsemfwa →, *Zambia* 87 E3
Lunsemfwa Falls, *Zambia* 87 E2
Luo He →, *China* 56 G6
Luocheng, *China* 58 E7
Luochuan, *China* 56 G5
Luoci, *China* 58 E4
Luodian, *China* 58 E6
Luoding, *China* 59 F8
Luofu, *Dem. Rep. of the Congo* 86 C2
Luohe, *China* 56 H8
Luojiang, *China* 58 B5
Luonan, *China* 56 G6
Luoning, *China* 56 G6
Luoshan, *China* 59 A10
Luotian, *China* 59 B10
Luoxiao Shan, *China* 59 D10
Luoyang, *China* 56 G7
Luoyuan, *China* 59 D12
Luozigou, *China* 57 C16
Lupanshui, *China* 58 D5
Lupeni, *Romania* 29 E8
Lupilichi, *Mozam.* 87 E4
Łupków, *Poland* 31 J9
Lupoing, *China* 58 E5
Luquan, *China* 58 E4
Luque, *Paraguay* 126 B4
Lúras, *Italy* 42 B2
Luray, *U.S.A.* 114 F6
Lure, *France* 19 E13
Lurgan, *U.K.* 12 B5
Lusaka, *Zambia* 87 F2
Lusaka □, *Zambia* 87 F2
Lusambo, *Dem. Rep. of the Congo* 86 C1
Lusangaye, *Dem. Rep. of the Congo* 86 C2
Luseland, *Canada* 103 C7
Lusenga Plain △, *Zambia* 87 D2
Lushan, *Henan, China* 56 H7
Lushan, *Sichuan, China* 58 B4
Lushi, *China* 56 G6
Lushnjë, *Albania* 44 F3
Lushoto, *Tanzania* 86 C4
Lushui, *China* 58 E2
Lüshun, *China* 57 E11
Lusignan, *France* 20 B4
Lusigny-sur-Barse, *France* 19 D11
Lusk, *U.S.A.* 112 D2
Lussac-les-Châteaux, *France* 20 B4
Lustenau, *Austria* 26 D2
Lūt, Dasht-e, *Iran* 71 D8
Luta = Dalian, *China* 57 E11
Lutherstadt Wittenberg, *Germany* 24 D8
Luton, *U.K.* 15 F7
Luton □, *U.K.* 15 F7
Łutselk'e, *Canada* 103 A6
Lutsk, *Ukraine* 33 G3
Lützow Holmbukta, *Antarctica* 5 C4
Lutzputs, *S. Africa* 88 D3
Luuq = Lugh Ganana, *Somali Rep.* 75 G3
Luverne, *Ala., U.S.A.* 115 K2
Luverne, *Minn., U.S.A.* 112 D6
Luvua, *Dem. Rep. of the Congo* 87 D2
Luvua →, *Dem. Rep. of the Congo* 86 D2
Luvuvhu →, *S. Africa* 89 C5
Luwegu →, *Tanzania* 87 D4
Luwuk, *Indonesia* 63 E6
Luxembourg, *Lux.* 17 E6
Luxembourg □, *Belgium* 17 E5
Luxembourg ■, *Europe* 7 F7
Luxembourg ✕ (LUX), *Lux.* 17 E6
Luxeuil-les-Bains, *France* 19 E13
Luxi, *Hunan, China* 59 C8
Luxi, *Yunnan, China* 58 E4
Luxi, *Yunnan, China* 58 E2
Luxor = El Uqsur, *Egypt* 80 B3
Luy-de-Béarn →, *France* 20 E3
Luy-de-France →, *France* 20 E3
Luyi, *China* 56 H8
Luz-St-Sauveur, *France* 20 F4
Luzern, *Switz.* 25 H4
Luzern □, *Switz.* 25 H3
Luzhai, *China* 58 E7
Luzhany, *Ukraine* 29 B10
Luzhi, *China* 58 D5
Luzhou, *China* 58 C5
Luziânia, *Brazil* 125 G9
Lužnice →, *Czech Rep.* 26 B7
Luzon, *Phil.* 61 D4
Luzon Strait, *Asia* 59 G13
Luzy, *France* 19 F10
Luzzi, *Italy* 43 C9
Lviv, *Ukraine* 33 H3
Lvov = Lviv, *Ukraine* 33 H3
Lwówek, *Poland* 31 F3
Lwówek Śląski, *Poland* 31 G2
Lyakhavichy, *Belarus* 33 F4
Lyakhovskiye, Ostrova, *Russia* 53 B15
Lyaki = Läki, *Azerbaijan* 35 K8
Lyal I., *Canada* 116 B3
Lyaskovets, *Bulgaria* 45 C9
Lyasnaya, *Belarus* 31 F10
Lybster, *U.K.* 13 C5
Lycaonia, *Turkey* 72 D5
Lychen, *Germany* 24 B9
Lychkova, *Russia* 32 D7
Lycia, *Turkey* 47 E11
Lyckebyån →, *Sweden* 11 H9
Lycksele, *Sweden* 8 D18
Lycosura, *Greece* 46 D4
Lydda = Lod, *Israel* 74 D3
Lydenburg, *S. Africa* 89 D5
Lydia, *Turkey* 47 C10
Łydynia →, *Poland* 31 F7
Lyell, *N.Z.* 91 J4
Lyell I., *Canada* 102 C2
Lyepyel, *Belarus* 32 E5
Lygnern, *Sweden* 11 G6
Lykens, *U.S.A.* 117 F8
Lyman, *Ukraine* 29 E14
Lyman, *U.S.A.* 108 F8
Lymanske, *Ukraine* 29 D14
Lyme B., *U.K.* 15 G4
Lyme Regis, *U.K.* 15 G5
Lymington, *U.K.* 15 G6
Łyna →, *Poland* 9 J19
Lynchburg, *U.S.A.* 114 G6
Lynd →, *Australia* 94 B3
Lynd Ra., *Australia* 95 D4
Lynden, *Canada* 116 C4
Lynden, *U.S.A.* 110 B4
Lyndhurst, *Australia* 95 E2
Lyndon →, *Australia* 93 D1
Lyndonville, *N.Y., U.S.A.* 116 C6
Lyndonville, *Vt., U.S.A.* 117 B12
Lyngen, *Norway* 8 B19
Lynher Reef, *Australia* 92 C3
Lynn, *U.S.A.* 117 D14
Lynn Lake, *Canada* 103 B8
Lynnwood, *U.S.A.* 110 C4
Lynton, *U.K.* 15 F4
Lyntupy, *Belarus* 9 J22
Lynx L., *Canada* 103 A7
Lyon, *France* 21 C8
Lyon St-Exupery ✕ (LYS), *France* 21 C9
Lyonnais, *France* 21 C8
Lyons = Lyon, *France* 21 C8
Lyons, *Ga., U.S.A.* 115 J4
Lyons, *Kans., U.S.A.* 112 F5
Lyons, *N.Y., U.S.A.* 116 C8
Lyons →, *Australia* 93 E2
Lyons Falls, *U.S.A.* 117 C9
Lyozna, *Belarus* 32 E6
Lys = Leie →, *Belgium* 17 C3
Lysá nad Labem, *Czech Rep.* 26 A7
Lysekil, *Sweden* 11 F5
Lyskovo, *Russia* 34 B7
Lystrup, *Denmark* 11 H4
Lysvik, *Sweden* 10 D7
Lysychansk, *Ukraine* 33 H10
Lytham St. Anne's, *U.K.* 14 D4
Lyttelton, *N.Z.* 91 K4
Lytton, *Canada* 102 C4
Lyuban, *Russia* 32 C6
Lyubertsy, *Russia* 32 E9
Lyubim, *Russia* 32 C11
Lyubimets, *Bulgaria* 45 E10
Lyuboml, *Ukraine* 31 G11
Lyubotyn, *Ukraine* 33 H8
Lyubytino, *Russia* 32 C7
Lyudinovo, *Russia* 32 F8

M

M.R. Gomez, Presa, *Mexico* 119 B5
M.R. Stefanik, Bratislava ✕ (BTS), *Slovak Rep.* 27 C10
Ma →, *Vietnam* 58 H5
Ma'adaba, *Jordan* 74 E4
Maamba, *Zambia* 88 B4
Ma'ān, *Jordan* 74 E4
Ma'ān □, *Jordan* 74 F5
Maanselkä, *Finland* 8 C23
Ma'anshan, *China* 59 B12
Maarianhamina, *Finland* 9 F18
Ma'arrat an Nu'mān, *Syria* 70 C3
Maas →, *Neths.* 17 C4
Maaseik, *Belgium* 17 C5
Maasin, *Phil.* 63 B6
Maastricht, *Neths.* 17 D5
Maave, *Mozam.* 89 C5
Mababe Depression, *Botswana* 88 B3
Mabalane, *Mozam.* 89 C5
Mabel L., *Canada* 102 C5
Mabenge, *Dem. Rep. of the Congo* 86 B1
Maberly, *Canada* 117 B8
Mabian, *China* 58 C4
Mabil, *Ethiopia* 81 E4
Mablethorpe, *U.K.* 14 D8
Mably, *France* 19 F11
Maboma, *Dem. Rep. of the Congo* 86 B2
Mabonto, *S. Leone* 82 D2
Mabrouk, *Mali* 83 B4
Mabuasehube ⌓, *Botswana* 88 D3
Mac Bac, *Vietnam* 65 H6
Macachín, *Argentina* 126 D3
Macaé, *Brazil* 127 A7
Macael, *Spain* 39 H2
McAlester, *U.S.A.* 113 H7
McAllen, *U.S.A.* 113 M5
MacAlpine L., *Canada* 100 B9
Macamic, *Canada* 104 C4
Macao = Macau, *China* 59 F9
Macão, *Portugal* 37 F3
Macapá, *Brazil* 125 C8
Macarao △, *Venezuela* 121 D6
McArthur →, *Australia* 94 B2
McArthur, Port, *Australia* 94 B2
Macau, *Brazil* 125 E11
Macau, *China* 59 F9
McBride, *Canada* 102 C4
McCall, *U.S.A.* 108 D5
McCamey, *U.S.A.* 113 K3
McCammon, *U.S.A.* 108 E7
McCauley I., *Canada* 102 C2
McCleary, *U.S.A.* 110 C3
Macclenny, *U.S.A.* 115 K4
Macclesfield, *U.K.* 14 D5
M'Clintock Chan., *Canada* 100 A9
McClintock Ra., *Australia* 92 C4
McCloud, *U.S.A.* 108 F2
McCluer I., *Australia* 92 B5
McClure, *U.S.A.* 116 F7
McClure, L., *U.S.A.* 110 H6
M'Clure Str., *Canada* 98 B8
McClusky, *U.S.A.* 112 B4
McComb, *U.S.A.* 113 K9
McConaughy, L., *U.S.A.* 112 E4
McCook, *U.S.A.* 112 E4
McCreary, *Canada* 103 C9
McCullough Mt., *U.S.A.* 111 K11
McCusker →, *Canada* 103 B7
McDame, *Canada* 102 B3
McDermitt, *U.S.A.* 108 F5
McDonald, *U.S.A.* 116 F4
Macdonald, L., *Australia* 92 D4
McDonald Is., *Ind. Oc.* 3 G13
MacDonnell Ranges, *Australia* 92 D5
MacDowell L., *Canada* 104 B1
Macduff, *U.K.* 13 D6
Maceda, *Spain* 36 C3
Macedonia, *U.S.A.* 116 E3
Macedonia ■, *Europe* 44 E5
Maceió, *Brazil* 125 E11
Maceira, *Portugal* 36 F2
Macenta, *Guinea* 82 D3
Macerata, *Italy* 41 E10
McFarland, *U.S.A.* 111 K7
McFarlane →, *Canada* 103 B7
Macfarlane, L., *Australia* 95 E2
McGehee, *U.S.A.* 113 J9
McGill, *U.S.A.* 108 G6
Macgillycuddy's Reeks, *Ireland* 12 E2
McGraw, *U.S.A.* 117 D8
McGregor, *U.S.A.* 112 D9
McGregor Ra., *Australia* 95 D3
McGuire, Mt, *Australia* 94 J6
Mach, *Pakistan* 66 E5
Māch Kowr, *Iran* 71 E9
Machado = Jiparaná →, *Brazil* 124 E6
Machagai, *Argentina* 126 B3
Machakos, *Kenya* 86 C4
Machala, *Ecuador* 124 D3
Machanga, *Mozam.* 89 C6
Machattie, L., *Australia* 94 C2
Machault, *France* 19 C11
Machava, *Mozam.* 89 D5
Machece, *Mozam.* 87 F4
Machecoul, *France* 18 F5
Macheke, *Zimbabwe* 89 B5
Macheng, *China* 59 B10
Machero, *Spain* 37 F6
Machhu →, *India* 68 H4
Machias, *Maine, U.S.A.* 115 C12
Machias, *N.Y., U.S.A.* 116 D6
Machichi →, *Canada* 103 B10
Machico, *Madeira* 48 D3
Machilipatnam, *India* 67 L12
Machiques, *Venezuela* 124 A4
Machupicchu, *Peru* 124 F4
Machynlleth, *U.K.* 15 E4
Macia, *Mozam.* 89 D5
Maciejowice, *Poland* 31 G8
McIlwraith Ra., *Australia* 94 A3
Măcin, *Romania* 29 E13
Macina, *Mali* 82 C4
McInnes L., *Canada* 103 C10
McIntosh, *U.S.A.* 112 C4
McIntosh L., *Canada* 103 B8
Macintosh Ra., *Australia* 93 E4
Macintyre →, *Australia* 95 D5
Macizo Galaico, *Spain* 36 C3
Mackay, *Australia* 94 K7
Mackay, *U.S.A.* 108 E7
MacKay →, *Canada* 102 B6
Mackay, L., *Australia* 92 D4
McKay Ra., *Australia* 92 D3
McKeesport, *U.S.A.* 116 F5
McKellar, *Canada* 116 A5
McKenna, *U.S.A.* 110 D4
Mackenzie, *Canada* 102 B4
McKenzie, *U.S.A.* 115 G1
Mackenzie →, *Australia* 94 C4
Mackenzie →, *Canada* 100 B6
McKenzie →, *U.S.A.* 108 D2
Mackenzie Bay, *Canada* 4 B1
Mackenzie City = Linden, *Guyana* 124 B7
Mackenzie Mts., *Canada* 100 B6
Mackinaw City, *U.S.A.* 114 C3
McKinlay, *Australia* 94 C3
McKinlay →, *Australia* 94 C3
McKinley, Mt., *U.S.A.* 100 B4
McKinley Sea, *Arctic* 4 A7
McKinney, *U.S.A.* 113 J6
Mackinnon Road, *Kenya* 86 C4
McKittrick, *U.S.A.* 111 K7
Macklin, *Canada* 103 C7
Macksville, *Australia* 95 E5
McLaughlin, *U.S.A.* 112 C4
Maclean, *Australia* 95 D5
McLean, *U.S.A.* 113 H4
McLeansboro, *U.S.A.* 112 F10
Maclear, *S. Africa* 89 E4
Maclear, C., *Malawi* 87 E3
Macleay →, *Australia* 95 E5
McLennan, *Canada* 102 B5
McLeod →, *Canada* 102 C5
MacLeod, B., *Canada* 103 A7
McLeod, L., *Australia* 93 D1
MacLeod Lake, *Canada* 102 C4
McLoughlin, Mt., *U.S.A.* 108 E2
McMechen, *U.S.A.* 116 G4
McMinnville, *Oreg., U.S.A.* 108 D2
McMinnville, *Tenn., U.S.A.* 115 H3
McMurdo Sd., *Antarctica* 5 D11
McMurray = Fort McMurray, *Canada* 102 B6
McMurray, *U.S.A.* 110 B4
Macodoene, *Mozam.* 89 C6
Macomb, *U.S.A.* 112 E9
Macomer, *Italy* 42 B1
Mâcon, *France* 19 F11
Macon, *Ga., U.S.A.* 115 J4
Macon, *Miss., U.S.A.* 115 J1
Macon, *Mo., U.S.A.* 112 F8
Macossa, *Mozam.* 87 F3
Macoun L., *Canada* 103 B8
Macovane, *Mozam.* 89 C6
McPherson, *U.S.A.* 112 F6
McPherson Pk., *U.S.A.* 111 L7
McPherson Ra., *Australia* 95 D5
Macquarie →, *Australia* 95 E4
Macquarie Harbour, *Australia* 95 G4
Macquarie Is., *Pac. Oc.* 96 N7
MacRobertson Land, *Antarctica* 5 D6
Macroom, *Ireland* 12 E3
MacTier, *Canada* 116 A5
Macubela, *Mozam.* 87 F4
Macugnaga, *Italy* 40 C4
Macuira △, *Colombia* 121 D5
Macuiza, *Mozam.* 87 F3
Macumba, The →, *Australia* 95 D2
Macuro, *Venezuela* 125 K15
Macusani, *Peru* 124 F4
Macuse, *Mozam.* 87 F4
Macuspana, *Mexico* 119 D6
Macusse, *Angola* 88 B3
Mada →, *Nigeria* 83 D6
Ma'dabā □, *Jordan* 74 D4
Madadeni, *S. Africa* 89 D5
Madagali, *Nigeria* 83 C7
Madagascar ■, *Africa* 89 C8
Madā'in Sālih, *Si. Arabia* 70 E3
Madama, *Niger* 79 D8
Madame, I., *Canada* 105 C7
Madan, *Bulgaria* 45 E8
Madaoua, *Niger* 83 C6
Madara, *Nigeria* 83 C7
Madaripur, *Bangla.* 67 H17
Madauk, *Burma* 67 L20
Madawaska, *Canada* 116 A7
Madawaska →, *Canada* 116 A8
Madaya, *Burma* 67 H20
Madbar, *Sudan* 81 F3
Maddalena, *Italy* 42 A2
Maddaloni, *Italy* 43 A7
Madeira, *Atl. Oc.* 48 D3
Madeira →, *Brazil* 124 D7
Madeleine, Îs. de la, *Canada* 105 C7
Maden, *Turkey* 73 C8
Madera, *Mexico* 118 B3
Madera, *Calif., U.S.A.* 110 J6
Madera, *Pa., U.S.A.* 116 F6
Madha, *India* 66 L9
Madhavpur, *India* 68 J3
Madhepura, *India* 69 F12
Madhubani, *India* 69 F12
Madhupur, *India* 69 G12
Madhya Pradesh □, *India* 68 J8
Madidi →, *Bolivia* 124 F5
Madikeri, *India* 66 N9
Madikwe ⌓, *S. Africa* 89 D5
Madill, *U.S.A.* 113 H6
Madimba, *Dem. Rep. of the Congo* 84 E3
Ma'din, *Syria* 70 C3
Madina, *Mali* 82 C3
Madinani, *Ivory C.* 82 D3
Madingou, *Congo* 84 E2
Madirovalo, *Madag.* 89 B8
Madison, *Calif., U.S.A.* 110 G5
Madison, *Fla., U.S.A.* 115 K4
Madison, *Ind., U.S.A.* 114 F3
Madison, *Nebr., U.S.A.* 112 E6
Madison, *Ohio, U.S.A.* 116 E3
Madison, *S. Dak., U.S.A.* 112 D6
Madison, *Wis., U.S.A.* 112 D10
Madison →, *U.S.A.* 108 D8
Madison Heights, *U.S.A.* 114 G6
Madisonville, *Ky., U.S.A.* 114 G2
Madisonville, *Tex., U.S.A.* 113 K7
Madista, *Botswana* 88 C4
Madiun, *Indonesia* 63 G14
Madoc, *Canada* 116 B7
Madol, *Sudan* 81 F2
Madon →, *France* 19 D13
Madona, *Latvia* 9 H22
Madonie, *Italy* 42 E6
Madonna di Campíglio, *Italy* 40 B7
Madra Dağı, *Turkey* 47 B9
Madrakah, Ra's al, *Oman* 75 D6
Madras = Chennai, *India* 66 N12
Madras = Tamil Nadu □, *India* 66 P10
Madras, *U.S.A.* 108 D3
Madre, Laguna, *U.S.A.* 113 M6
Madre, Sierra, *Phil.* 61 C5
Madre de Dios →, *Bolivia* 124 F5
Madre de Dios, I., *Chile* 128 G1
Madre del Sur, Sierra, *Mexico* 119 D5
Madre Occidental, Sierra, *Mexico* 118 B3
Madre Oriental, Sierra, *Mexico* 118 C5
Madri, *India* 68 G5
Madrid, *Spain* 36 E7
Madrid, *U.S.A.* 117 B9
Madrid □, *Spain* 36 E7
Madrid Barajas ✕ (MAD), *Spain* 36 E7
Madridejos, *Spain* 37 F7
Madrigal de las Altas Torres, *Spain* 36 D6
Madrona, Sierra, *Spain* 37 G6
Madroñera, *Spain* 37 F5
Madu, *Sudan* 81 E2
Madura, *Australia* 93 F4
Madura, *Indonesia* 63 G15
Madura, Selat, *Indonesia* 63 G15
Madurai, *India* 66 Q11
Madurantakam, *India* 66 N11
Madzhalis, *Russia* 35 J8
Mae Chan, *Thailand* 64 B2
Mae Hong Son, *Thailand* 64 C2
Mae Khlong →, *Thailand* 64 F3
Mae Phrik, *Thailand* 64 D2
Mae Ping △, *Thailand* 64 D2
Mae Ramat, *Thailand* 64 D2
Mae Rim, *Thailand* 64 C2
Mae Sot, *Thailand* 64 D2
Mae Suai, *Thailand* 58 H2
Mae Tha, *Thailand* 64 C2
Mae Wong △, *Thailand* 64 E2
Mae Yom △, *Thailand* 64 C3
Maebashi, *Japan* 55 F9
Maella, *Spain* 38 D5
Maesteg, *U.K.* 15 F4
Maestra, Sierra, *Cuba* 120 B4
Maevatanana, *Madag.* 89 B8
Mafeking = Mafikeng, *S. Africa* 88 D4
Mafeking, *Canada* 103 C8
Maféré, *Ivory C.* 82 D4
Mafeteng, *Lesotho* 88 D4
Maffra, *Australia* 95 F4
Mafia I., *Tanzania* 86 D4
Mafikeng, *S. Africa* 88 D4
Mafra, *Brazil* 127 B6
Mafra, *Portugal* 37 G1
Mafungabusi Plateau, *Zimbabwe* 87 F2
Magadan, *Russia* 53 D16
Magadi, *Kenya* 86 C4
Magadi, L., *Kenya* 86 C4
Magaliesburg, *S. Africa* 89 D4
Magallanes, Estrecho de, *Chile* 128 G2
Magaluf, *Spain* 39 F7
Magangué, *Colombia* 124 B4
Magaria, *Niger* 83 C6

Magburaka, *S. Leone* 82 D2
Magdalen Is. = Madeleine, Îs. de la, *Canada* 105 C7
Magdalena, *Argentina* 126 D4
Magdalena, *Bolivia* 124 F6
Magdalena, *Mexico* 118 A2
Magdalena, *U.S.A.* 109 J10
Magdalena →, *Colombia* 124 A4
Magdalena →, *Mexico* 118 A2
Magdalena, B., *Mexico* 118 C2
Magdalena, Llano de la, *Mexico* . 118 C2
Magdeburg, *Germany* 24 C7
Magdelaine Cays, *Australia* 94 B5
Magdub, *Sudan* 81 E2
Magee, *U.S.A.* 113 K10
Magelang, *Indonesia* 63 G14
Magellan's Str. = Magallanes, Estrecho de, *Chile* 128 G2
Magenta, *Italy* 40 C5
Magenta, L., *Australia* 93 F2
Magerøya, *Norway* 8 A21
Maggia →, *Switz.* 25 J4
Maggiorasca, Mte., *Italy* 40 D6
Maggiore, Lago, *Italy* 40 B5
Maggotty, *Jamaica* .... 120 a
Maghâgha, *Egypt* 80 B3
Maghama, *Mauritania* 82 B2
Magherafelt, *U.K.* 12 B5
Maghreb, *N. Afr.* 78 B5
Magione, *Italy* 41 E9
Magistralnyy, *Russia* 53 D11
Maglaj, *Bos.-H.* 28 F3
Magliano in Toscana, *Italy* 41 F8
Máglie, *Italy* 43 B11
Magnac-Laval, *France* 20 B5
Magnetic Pole (North), *Canada* . 4 A2
Magnetic Pole (South), *Antarctica* 5 C9
Magnísía □, *Greece* 46 B5
Magnitogorsk, *Russia* 52 D6
Magnolia, *Ark., U.S.A.* 113 J8
Magnolia, *Miss., U.S.A.* 113 K9
Magny-en-Vexin, *France* 19 C8
Mago △, *Ethiopia* 81 F4
Magog, *Canada* 117 A12
Magoro, *Uganda* 86 B3
Magoša = Famagusta, *Cyprus* .. 49 D12
Magouládhes, *Greece* 49 A3
Magoye, *Zambia* 87 F2
Magozal, *Mexico* 119 C5
Magpie, L., *Canada* 105 B7
Magrath, *Canada* 102 D6
Magre →, *Spain* 39 F4
Magrur, *Sudan* 81 E3
Magrur, Wadi →, *Sudan* 81 D2
Magta Lahjar, *Mauritania* 82 B2
Maguan, *China* 58 F5
Maguarinho, C., *Brazil* 125 D9
Magude, *Mozam.* 89 D5
Magurski △, *Poland* 31 J8
Magusa = Famagusta, *Cyprus* .. 49 D12
Maguse L., *Canada* 103 A9
Maguse Pt., *Canada* 103 A10
Magvana, *India* 68 H3
Magwe, *Burma* 67 J19
Magwe, *Sudan* 81 G3
Maha Sarakham, *Thailand* 64 D4
Mahābād, *Iran* 70 B5
Mahabharat Lekh, *Nepal* 69 E10
Mahabo, *Madag.* 89 C7
Mahadeo Hills, *India* 69 H8
Mahaffey, *U.S.A.* 116 F6
Mahagi, *Dem. Rep. of the Congo* 86 B3
Mahajamba →, *Madag.* 89 B8
Mahajamba, Helodranon' i, *Madag.* 89 B8
Mahajan, *India* 68 E5
Mahajanga, *Madag.* 89 B8
Mahajanga □, *Madag.* 89 B8
Mahajilo →, *Madag.* 89 B8
Mahakam →, *Indonesia* 62 E5
Mahalapye, *Botswana* 88 C4
Mahale Mts., *Tanzania* 86 D3
Mahale Mts. △, *Tanzania* 86 D2
Maḥallāt, *Iran* 71 C6
Māhān, *Iran* 71 D8
Mahan →, *India* 69 H10
Mahanadi →, *India* 67 J15
Mahananda →, *India* 69 G12
Mahanoro, *Madag.* 89 B8
Mahanoy City, *U.S.A.* 117 F8
Maharashtra □, *India* 66 J9
Mahasham, W. →, *Egypt* 74 E3
Mahasoa, *Madag.* 89 C8
Mahasolo, *Madag.* 89 B8
Mahattat ash Shīdīyah, *Jordan* . 74 F4
Mahattat 'Unayzah, *Jordan* 74 E4
Mahavavy →, *Madag.* 89 B8
Mahaxay, *Laos* 64 D5
Mahbubnagar, *India* 66 L10
Maḥḍah, *Oman* 71 E7
Mahdia, *Tunisia* 79 A8
Mahe, *India* 69 C8
Mahendragarh, *India* 68 E7
Mahenge, *Tanzania* 87 D4
Maheno, *N.Z.* 91 L3
Mahesana, *India* 68 H5
Maheshwar, *India* 68 H6
Mahgawan, *India* 69 F8
Mahi →, *India* 68 H5
Mahia Pen., *N.Z.* 91 H6
Mahilyow, *Belarus* 32 F6
Mahinerangi, L., *N.Z.* 91 L2
Mahmiya, *Sudan* 81 D3
Mahmud Kot, *Pakistan* 68 D4
Mahmudia, *Romania* 29 E14
Mahmudiye, *Turkey* 47 B12
Mahmutbey, *Turkey* 45 E12
Mahnomen, *U.S.A.* 112 B7
Mahoba, *India* 69 G8
Mahón = Maó, *Spain* 48 B11
Mahon, Menorca ✈ (MAH), *Spain* 38 F9

Mahone Bay, *Canada* 105 D7
Mahopac, *U.S.A.* 117 E11
Mahuta, *Nigeria* 83 C5
Mahuva, *India* 68 J4
Mahya Daği, *Turkey* 45 E11
Mai-Ndombe, L., *Dem. Rep. of the Congo* 84 E3
Mai-Sai, *Thailand* 58 G2
Mai Thon, Ko, *Thailand* ...... 65 a
Maia, *Portugal* 36 D2
Maia, *Spain* 38 B3
Maials, *Spain* 38 D5
Maïche, *France* 19 E13
Maicurú →, *Brazil* 125 D8
Máida, *Italy* 43 D9
Maidan Khula, *Afghan.* 68 C3
Maidenhead, *U.K.* 15 F7
Maidstone, *Canada* 103 C7
Maidstone, *U.K.* 15 F8
Maiduguri, *Nigeria* 83 C7
Maiella △, *Italy* 41 F11
Măieruş, *Romania* 29 E10
Maigatari, *Nigeria* 83 C6
Maignelay Montigny, *France* ... 19 C9
Maigo, *Phil.* 61 G5
Maigudo, *Ethiopia* 81 F4
Maihar, *India* 69 G9
Maijdi, *Bangla.* 67 H17
Maikala Ra., *India* 67 J12
Maiko △, *Dem. Rep. of the Congo* 86 C2
Mailani, *India* 69 E9
Maillezais, *France* 20 B3
Mailsi, *Pakistan* 68 E5
Main →, *Germany* 25 F4
Main →, *U.K.* 12 B5
Main Range △, *Australia* 95 D5
Main Ridge, *Trin. & Tob.* 125 J16
Mainburg, *Germany* 25 G7
Maine, *France* 18 D6
Maine □, *U.S.A.* 115 C11
Maine →, *Ireland* 12 D2
Maine-et-Loire □, *France* 18 E6
Maïne-Soroa, *Niger* 83 C7
Maingkwan, *Burma* 67 F20
Mainit, L., *Phil.* 61 G6
Mainland, *Orkney, U.K.* 13 C5
Mainland, *Shet., U.K.* 13 A7
Mainoru, *Australia* 94 A1
Mainpuri, *India* 69 F8
Maintal, *Germany* 25 E4
Maintenon, *France* 19 D8
Maintirano, *Madag.* 89 B7
Mainz, *Germany* 25 E4
Maipú, *Argentina* 126 D4
Maiquetía, *Venezuela* 124 A5
Máira →, *Italy* 40 D4
Mairabari, *India* 67 F18
Maisí, *Cuba* 121 B5
Maisí, Pta. de, *Cuba* 121 B5
Maitland, *N.S.W., Australia* ... 95 E5
Maitland, *S. Austral., Australia* . 95 E2
Maitland →, *Canada* 116 C3
Maitri, *Antarctica* 5 D3
Maiyema, *Nigeria* 83 C5
Maiyuan, *China* 59 E11
Maiz, Is. del, *Nic.* 120 D3
Maizuru, *Japan* 55 G7
Majalengka, *Indonesia* 63 G13
Majene, *Indonesia* 63 E5
Majete △, *Malawi* 87 F3
Majevica, *Bos.-H.* 28 F3
Maji, *Ethiopia* 81 F4
Majiang, *China* 58 D6
Majorca = Mallorca, *Spain* 48 B10
Maka, *Senegal* 82 C2
Makaha, *Zimbabwe* 89 B5
Makak, *Cameroon* 83 E7
Makalamabedi, *Botswana* 88 C3
Makale, *Indonesia* 63 E5
Makamba, *Burundi* 86 C2
Makari, *Cameroon* 83 C7
Makarikari = Makgadikgadi Salt Pans, *Botswana* 88 C4
Makarov Basin, *Arctic* .... 4 A
Makarovo, *Russia* 53 D11
Makarska, *Croatia* 41 E14
Makaryev, *Russia* 34 B6
Makasar = Ujung Pandang, *Indonesia* 63 F5
Makasar, Selat, *Indonesia* 63 E5
Makasar, Str. of = Makasar, Selat, *Indonesia* 63 E5
Makat, *Kazakhstan* 52 E6
Makedonija = Macedonia ■, *Europe* 44 E5
Makeni, *S. Leone* 82 D2
Makeyevka = Makiyivka, *Ukraine* 33 H9
Makgadikgadi →, *Botswana* ... 88 C3
Makgadikgadi Salt Pans, *Botswana* 88 C3
Makhachkala, *Russia* 35 J8
Makhado = Louis Trichardt, *S. Africa* 89 C4
Makharadze = Ozurgeti, *Georgia* 35 K5
Makhfar al Busayyah, *Iraq* 70 D5
Makhmūr, *Iraq* 70 C4
Makian, *Indonesia* 63 D7
Makindu, *Kenya* 86 C4
Makinsk, *Kazakhstan* 52 D8
Makiv, *Ukraine* 29 B11
Makiyivka, *Ukraine* 33 H9
Makkah, *Si. Arabia* 75 C2
Makkovik, *Canada* 105 A8
Makó, *Hungary* 28 D5
Mako, *Senegal* 82 C2
Makokou, *Gabon* 84 D2
Makongo, *Dem. Rep. of the Congo* 86 B2
Makoro, *Dem. Rep. of the Congo* 86 B2
Maków Mazowiecki, *Poland* ... 31 F8
Maków Podhalański, *Poland* ... 31 J6
Makrá, *Greece* 47 E7

Makrai, *India* 66 H10
Makran Coast Range, *Pakistan* . 66 G4
Makrana, *India* 68 F6
Makrany, *Belarus* 31 G11
Mákri, *Greece* 45 F9
Makriyialos, *Greece* 49 D7
Makū, *Iran* 70 B5
Makunda, *Botswana* 88 C3
Makung, *Taiwan* 59 F12
Makurazaki, *Japan* 55 J5
Makurdi, *Nigeria* 83 D6
Makūyeh, *Iran* 71 D7
Makwassie, *S. Africa* 88 D4
Makwiro, *Zimbabwe* 89 B5
Mâl, *Mauritania* 82 B2
Mala, Pta., *Panama* 120 E3
Mala Belozërka, *Ukraine* 33 J8
Malá Fatra △, *Slovak Rep.* 27 B12
Mala Kapela, *Croatia* 41 D12
Mała Panew →, *Poland* 31 H4
Mala Vyska, *Ukraine* 33 H6
Malabang, *Phil.* 61 H6
Malabar Coast, *India* 66 P9
Malabon, *Phil.* 61 D4
Malabu, *Nigeria* 83 D7
Malacca, Straits of, *Indonesia* . 65 L3
Malacky, *Slovak Rep.* 27 C10
Malad City, *U.S.A.* 108 E7
Maladeta, *Spain* 38 C5
Maladzyechna, *Belarus* 32 E4
Málaga, *Spain* 37 J6
Málaga □, *Spain* 37 J6
Malagarasi, *Tanzania* 86 D3
Malagarasi →, *Tanzania* 86 D2
Malagasy Rep. = Madagascar ■, *Africa* 89 C8
Malagón, *Spain* 37 F7
Malagón →, *Spain* 37 H3
Malahide, *Ireland* 12 C5
Malaimbandy, *Madag.* 89 C8
Malakal, *Sudan* 81 F3
Malakand, *Pakistan* 68 B4
Malakwal, *Pakistan* 68 C5
Malamala, *Indonesia* 63 E6
Malanda, *Australia* 94 B4
Malang, *Indonesia* 63 G15
Malangen, *Norway* 8 B18
Malanje, *Angola* 84 F3
Mälaren, *Sweden* 10 E11
Malargüe, *Argentina* 126 D2
Malartic, *Canada* 104 C4
Malaryta, *Belarus* 31 G11
Malatya, *Turkey* 70 B3
Malawi ■, *Africa* 87 E3
Malawi, L. = Nyasa, L., *Africa* . 87 E3
Malay Pen., *Asia* 65 J3
Malaya Belozërka = Mala Belozërka, *Ukraine* 33 J8
Malaya Vishera, *Russia* 32 C7
Malaya Viska = Mala Vyska, *Ukraine* 33 H6
Malaybalay, *Phil.* 61 G6
Malāyer, *Iran* 71 C6
Malaysia ■, *Asia* 65 K4
Malazgirt, *Turkey* 70 B4
Malbaza, *Niger* 83 C6
Malbon, *Australia* 94 C3
Malbooma, *Australia* 95 E1
Malbork, *Poland* 30 D6
Malcésine, *Italy* 40 C7
Malchin, *Germany* 24 B8
Malchow, *Germany* 24 B8
Malcolm, *Australia* 93 E3
Malcolm, Pt., *Australia* 93 F3
Malczyce, *Poland* 31 G3
Maldah, *India* 69 G13
Maldegem, *Belgium* 17 C3
Malden, *Mass., U.S.A.* 117 D13
Malden, *Mo., U.S.A.* 113 G10
Malden I., *Kiribati* 97 H12
Maldives ■, *Ind. Oc.* 50 J11
Maldon, *U.K.* 15 F8
Maldonado, *Uruguay* 127 C5
Maldonado, Punta, *Mexico* ... 119 D5
Malè, *Italy* 40 B7
Malé, *Maldives* 51 J11
Malé Karpaty, *Slovak Rep.* ... 27 C10
Maléa, Ákra, *Greece* 46 E5
Malegaon, *India* 66 J9
Malei, *Mozam.* 87 F4
Malek, *Sudan* 81 F3
Malek Kandī, *Iran* 70 B5
Malela, *Dem. Rep. of the Congo* 86 C2
Malema, *Mozam.* 87 E4
Máleme, *Greece* 49 D5
Malerkotla, *India* 68 D6
Máles, *Greece* 49 D7
Malesherbes, *France* 19 D9
Maleshevska Planina, *Europe* . 44 E7
Malesína, *Greece* 46 C5
Malestroit, *France* 18 E4
Malfa, *Italy* 43 D7
Malgobek, *Russia* 35 J7
Malgrat de Mar, *Spain* 38 D7
Malha, *Sudan* 81 E2
Malhargarh, *India* 68 G6
Malheur →, *U.S.A.* 108 D5
Malheur L., *U.S.A.* 108 E4
Mali, *Guinea* 82 C2
Mali ■, *Africa* 82 B4
Mali →, *Burma* 67 G20
Mali Kanal, *Serbia & M.* 28 E4
Mali Kyun, *Burma* 64 F2
Malibu, *U.S.A.* 111 L8
Maliku, *Indonesia* 63 E6
Malili, *Indonesia* 63 E6
Målilla, *Sweden* 11 G9
Malimba, Mts., *Dem. Rep. of the Congo* 86 D2

Malin Hd., *Ireland* 12 A4
Malin Pen., *Ireland* 12 A4
Malindi, *Kenya* 86 C5
Malines = Mechelen, *Belgium* . 17 C4
Malino, *Indonesia* 63 D6
Malinyi, *Tanzania* 87 D4
Malipo, *China* 58 F5
Maliq, *Albania* 44 F4
Malita, *Phil.* 63 C7
Maliwun, *Burma* 62 B1
Maliya, *India* 68 H4
Maljenik, *Serbia & M.* 44 C5
Malka Mari, *Kenya* 86 B5
Malkara, *Turkey* 45 F10
Małkinia Górna, *Poland* 31 F9
Malko Tūrnovo, *Bulgaria* 45 E11
Mallacoota Inlet, *Australia* 95 F4
Mallaig, *U.K.* 13 D3
Mallaoua, *Niger* 83 C6
Mallawan, *India* 69 F9
Mallawi, *Egypt* 80 B3
Mallemort, *France* 21 E9
Málles Venosta, *Italy* 40 B7
Mállia, *Greece* 49 D7
Mallión, Kólpos, *Greece* 49 D7
Mallorca, *Spain* 48 B10
Mallorytown, *Canada* 117 B9
Mallow, *Ireland* 12 D3
Malmback, *Sweden* 11 G8
Malmberget, *Sweden* 8 C19
Malmédy, *Belgium* 17 D6
Malmesbury, *S. Africa* 88 E2
Malmivaara = Malmberget, *Sweden* 8 C19
Malmköping, *Sweden* 10 E10
Malmö, *Sweden* 11 J7
Malmslätt, *Sweden* 11 F9
Malmyzh, *Russia* 34 B10
Malnaş, *Romania* 29 D10
Malo Konare, *Bulgaria* 45 D8
Maloarkhangelsk, *Russia* 33 F9
Malolos, *Phil.* 63 B6
Malolotja △, *Swaziland* 89 D5
Malombe L., *Malawi* 87 E4
Małomice, *Poland* 31 G2
Malone, *U.S.A.* 117 B10
Malong, *China* 58 E4
Małopolskie □, *Poland* 31 J7
Malorad, *Bulgaria* 44 C7
Måløy, *Norway* 9 F11
Maloyaroslovets, *Russia* 32 E9
Malpartida, *Spain* 37 F4
Malpaso, *Canary Is.* 48 G1
Malpelo, I. de, *Colombia* 124 C2
Malpica de Bergantiños, *Spain* . 36 B2
Malpur, *India* 68 H5
Malpura, *India* 68 F6
Mals = Málles Venosta, *Italy* .. 40 B7
Malta, *Idaho, U.S.A.* 108 E7
Malta, *Mont., U.S.A.* 108 B10
Malta ■, *Europe* 49 D2
Maltahöhe, *Namibia* 88 C2
Maltepe, *Turkey* 45 F13
Malton, *Canada* 116 C5
Malton, *U.K.* 14 C7
Maluku, *Indonesia* 63 E7
Maluku □, *Indonesia* 63 E7
Maluku Sea = Molucca Sea, *Indonesia* 63 E6
Maluku □, *Indonesia* 63 D7
Malumfashi, *Nigeria* 83 C6
Malung, *Sweden* 10 D7
Malungsfors, *Sweden* 10 D7
Maluwe, *Ghana* 82 D4
Malvan, *India* 66 L8
Malvern, *U.S.A.* 113 H8
Malvern Hills, *U.K.* 15 E5
Malvinas, Is. = Falkland Is. ☑, *Atl. Oc.* 128 G5
Malya, *Tanzania* 86 C3
Malye Derbety, *Russia* 35 G7
Malyn, *Ukraine* 33 G5
Malyy Lyakhovskiy, Ostrov, *Russia* 53 B15
Mama, *Russia* 53 D12
Mamadysh, *Russia* 34 C10
Mamanguape, *Brazil* 125 E11
Mamarr Mitlā, *Egypt* 74 E1
Mamasa, *Indonesia* 63 E5
Mambasa, *Dem. Rep. of the Congo* 86 B2
Mamberamo →, *Indonesia* ... 63 E9
Mambilima Falls, *Zambia* 87 E2
Mambirima, *Dem. Rep. of the Congo* 87 E2
Mambo, *Tanzania* 86 C4
Mambrui, *Kenya* 86 C5
Mamburao, *Phil.* 61 E4
Mameigwess L., *Canada* 104 B2
Mamers, *France* 18 D7
Mamfé, *Cameroon* 83 D6
Mammoth, *U.S.A.* 109 K8
Mammoth Cave △, *U.S.A.* ... 114 G3
Mamonovo, *Russia* 30 D6
Mamoré →, *Bolivia* 124 F5
Mamou, *Guinea* 82 C2
Mamoudzou, *Mayotte* 77 H8
Mampatá, *Guinea-Biss.* 82 C2
Mampikony, *Madag.* 89 B8
Mampong, *Ghana* 83 D4
Mamry, Jezioro, *Poland* 30 D8
Mamuju, *Indonesia* 63 E5
Mamuno, *Botswana* 88 C3
Mamuras, *Albania* 44 E3
Man, *Ivory C.* 82 D3
Man, I. of, *U.K.* 14 C3
Man-Bazar, *India* 69 H12
Man Na, *Burma* 67 H20
Mana →, *Fr. Guiana* 125 B8
Mana Pools △, *Zimbabwe* ... 87 F2

Manaar, G. of = Mannar, G. of, *Asia* 66 Q11
Manacapuru, *Brazil* 124 D6
Manacor, *Spain* 48 B10
Manado, *Indonesia* 63 D6
Managua, *Nic.* 120 D2
Managua, L. de, *Nic.* 120 D2
Manakara, *Madag.* 89 C8
Manali, *India* 68 C7
Manama = Al Manāmah, *Bahrain* 71 E6
Manambao →, *Madag.* 89 B7
Manambato, *Madag.* 89 A8
Manambolo →, *Madag.* 89 B7
Manambolosy, *Madag.* 89 B8
Mananara, *Madag.* 89 B8
Mananara →, *Madag.* 89 C8
Mananara △, *Madag.* 89 B8
Mananjary, *Madag.* 89 C8
Manankoro, *Mali* 82 C3
Manantenina, *Madag.* 89 C8
Manaos = Manaus, *Brazil* 124 D7
Manapire →, *Venezuela* 124 B5
Manapouri, *N.Z.* 91 L1
Manapouri, L., *N.Z.* 91 L1
Manaqil, *Sudan* 81 E3
Manār, Jabal, *Yemen* 75 E3
Manaravolo, *Madag.* 89 C8
Manas, *China* 60 B3
Manas →, *India* 67 F17
Manaslu, *Nepal* 69 E11
Manasquan, *U.S.A.* 117 F10
Manassa, *U.S.A.* 109 H11
Manatí, *Puerto Rico* .... 121 d
Manaung, *Burma* 67 K18
Manaus, *Brazil* 124 D7
Manavgat, *Turkey* 72 D4
Manawan L., *Canada* 103 B8
Manay, *Phil.* 61 H7
Manbij, *Syria* 70 B3
Mancha Real, *Spain* 37 H7
Manche □, *France* 18 C5
Manchegorsk, *Russia* 52 C4
Manchester, *U.K.* 14 D5
Manchester, *Calif., U.S.A.* ... 110 G3
Manchester, *Conn., U.S.A.* ... 117 E12
Manchester, *Ga., U.S.A.* 115 J3
Manchester, *Iowa, U.S.A.* ... 112 D9
Manchester, *Ky., U.S.A.* 114 G4
Manchester, *N.H., U.S.A.* ... 117 D13
Manchester, *N.Y., U.S.A.* ... 116 D7
Manchester, *Pa., U.S.A.* 117 F8
Manchester, *Tenn., U.S.A.* .. 115 H2
Manchester, *Vt., U.S.A.* 117 C11
Manchester International ✈ (MAN), *U.K.* 14 D5
Manchester L., *Canada* 103 A7
Manchhar L., *Pakistan* 68 F2
Manchuria = Dongbei, *China* .. 53 E16
Manchurian Plain, *China* 50 E16
Manciano, *Italy* 41 F8
Mancifa, *Ethiopia* 81 F5
Mand →, *India* 69 J10
Mand →, *Iran* 71 D7
Manda, *Ludewe, Tanzania* ... 87 E3
Manda, *Mbeya, Tanzania* ... 86 D3
Manda, *Mbeya, Tanzania* ... 87 D3
Mandabé, *Madag.* 89 C7
Mandaguari, *Brazil* 127 A5
Mandah = Töhöm, *Mongolia* . 56 B5
Mandal, *Norway* 9 G12
Mandala, Puncak, *Indonesia* .. 63 E10
Mandalay, *Burma* 67 J20
Mandale = Mandalay, *Burma* . 67 J20
Mandalgarh, *India* 68 G6
Mandalgovĭ, *Mongolia* 56 B4
Mandalī, *Iraq* 70 C5
Mandan, *U.S.A.* 112 B4
Mandaon, *Phil.* 61 E5
Mandar, Teluk, *Indonesia* 63 E5
Mándas, *Italy* 42 C2
Mandaue, *Phil.* 61 F5
Mandelieu-la-Napoule, *France* . 21 E10
Mandera, *Kenya* 86 B5
Mandeville, *Jamaica* .... 120 a
Mandi, *India* 68 D7
Mandi Dabwali, *India* 68 E6
Mandiana, *Guinea* 82 C3
Mandimba, *Mozam.* 87 E4
Mandioli, *Indonesia* 63 E7
Mandla, *India* 69 H9
Mandø, *Denmark* 11 J2
Mandorah, *Australia* 92 B5
Mandoto, *Madag.* 89 B8
Mandoúdhion, *Greece* 46 C5
Mándra, *Greece* 46 C5
Mandra, *Pakistan* 68 C5
Mandrákhi, *Greece* 47 E9
Mandritsara, *Madag.* 89 B8
Mandronarivo, *Madag.* 89 C8
Mandsaur, *India* 68 G6
Mandurah, *Australia* 93 F2
Mandúria, *Italy* 43 B10
Mandvi, *India* 68 H3
Mandya, *India* 66 N10
Mandzai, *Pakistan* 68 D2
Mané, *Burkina Faso* 83 C4
Manengouba, Mts., *Cameroon* . 83 E6
Manera, *Madag.* 89 C7
Manerbio, *Italy* 40 C7
Maneroo Cr. →, *Australia* ... 94 C3
Manfalût, *Egypt* 80 B3
Manfredónia, *Italy* 41 G13
Manfredónia, G. di, *Italy* 41 G13
Manga, *Burkina Faso* 83 C4
Manga, *Niger* 83 C7
Mangalia, *Romania* 29 G13
Mangalore, *India* 66 N9
Mangan, *India* 69 F13
Mangaung, *S. Africa* 85 K5

Mangawan, India 69 G9
Mangaweka, N.Z. 91 H5
Manggar, Indonesia 62 E3
Manggawitu, Indonesia 63 E8
Manggis, Indonesia 63 J18
Mangindrano, Madag. 89 A8
Mangla, Pakistan 68 C5
Mangla Dam, Pakistan 69 C5
Manglaur, India 68 E7
Mangnai, China 60 C4
Mango, Togo 83 C5
Mangoche, Malawi 87 E4
Mangoky →, Madag. 89 C7
Mangole, Indonesia 63 E6
Mangombe, Dem. Rep. of
   the Congo 86 C2
Mangonui, N.Z. 91 F4
Mangoro →, Madag. 89 B8
Mangrol, Mad. P., India 68 J4
Mangrol, Raj., India 68 G6
Mangualde, Portugal 36 E3
Mangueira, L. da, Brazil 127 C5
Mangum, U.S.A. 113 H5
Mangyshlak, Poluostrov,
   Kazakhstan 52 E6
Manhattan, U.S.A. 112 F6
Manhiça, Mozam. 89 D5
Mania →, Madag. 89 B8
Maniago, Italy 41 B9
Manica, Mozam. 89 B5
Manica □, Mozam. 89 B5
Manicaland □, Zimbabwe 87 F3
Manicoré, Brazil 124 E6
Manicouagan →, Canada 105 C6
Manicouagan, Rés., Canada 105 B6
Maniema □, Dem. Rep. of
   the Congo 86 C2
Manīfah, Si. Arabia 71 E6
Manifold, C., Australia 94 C5
Maniganggo, China 58 B2
Manigotagan, Canada 103 C9
Manigotagan →, Canada 103 C9
Manihari, India 69 G12
Manihiki, Cook Is. 97 J11
Manika, Plateau de la, Dem. Rep.
   of the Congo 87 E2
Manikpur, India 69 G9
Manila, Phil. 61 D4
Manila, U.S.A. 108 F9
Manila B., Phil. 61 D4
Manilla, Australia 95 E5
Manimpé, Mali 82 C3
Maningrida, Australia 94 A1
Maninian, Ivory C. 82 C3
Manipur □, India 67 G19
Manipur →, Burma 67 H19
Manisa, Turkey 47 C9
Manisa □, Turkey 47 C9
Manistee, U.S.A. 114 C2
Manistee →, U.S.A. 114 C2
Manistique, U.S.A. 114 C2
Manitoba □, Canada 103 B9
Manitoba, L., Canada 103 C9
Manitou, Canada 103 D9
Manitou, L., Canada 105 B6
Manitou Is., U.S.A. 114 C3
Manitou L., Canada 103 C7
Manitou Springs, U.S.A. 112 F2
Manitoulin I., Canada 104 C3
Manitouwadge, Canada 104 C2
Manitowoc, U.S.A. 114 C2
Manizales, Colombia 124 B3
Manja, Madag. 89 C7
Manjacaze, Mozam. 89 C5
Manjakandriana, Madag. 89 B8
Manjhand, Pakistan 68 G3
Manjil, Iran 71 B6
Manjimup, Australia 93 F2
Manjra →, India 66 K10
Mankato, Kans., U.S.A. 112 F5
Mankato, Minn., U.S.A. 112 C8
Mankayane, Swaziland 89 D5
Mankera, Pakistan 68 D4
Mankim, Cameroon 83 D7
Mankono, Ivory C. 82 D3
Mankota, Canada 103 D7
Manlay = Üydzin, Mongolia 56 B4
Manlleu, Spain 38 C7
Manmad, India 66 J9
Mann Ranges, Australia 93 E5
Manna, Indonesia 62 E2
Mannahill, Australia 95 E3
Mannar, Sri Lanka 66 Q11
Mannar, G. of, Asia 66 Q11
Mannar I., Sri Lanka 66 Q11
Mannheim, Germany 25 F4
Manning, Canada 102 B5
Manning, Oreg., U.S.A. 110 E3
Manning, S.C., U.S.A. 115 J5
Mannu →, Italy 42 C2
Mannu, C., Italy 42 B1
Mannum, Australia 95 E2
Mano, S. Leone 82 D2
Mano →, Liberia 82 D2
Mano River, Liberia 82 D2
Manoharpur, India 69 H11
Manokwari, Indonesia 63 E8
Manolás, Greece 46 C3
Manombo, Madag. 89 C7
Manono, Dem. Rep. of the Congo 86 D2
Manoppello, Italy 41 F11
Manosque, France 21 E9
Manotick, Canada 117 A9
Manouane →, Canada 105 C5
Manouane, L., Canada 105 B5
Manp'o, N. Korea 57 D14
Manpojin = Manp'o, N. Korea 57 D14
Manpur, Chhattisgarh, India 69 H10
Manpur, Mad. P., India 68 H6
Manresa, Spain 38 D6
Mansa, Gujarat, India 68 H5

Mansa, Punjab, India 68 E6
Mansa, Zambia 87 E2
Månsåsen, Sweden 10 A8
Mansehra, Pakistan 68 B5
Mansel I., Canada 101 B11
Mansfield, Australia 95 F4
Mansfield, U.K. 14 D6
Mansfield, La., U.S.A. 113 J8
Mansfield, Mass. U.S.A. 117 D13
Mansfield, Ohio, U.S.A. 116 F2
Mansfield, Pa., U.S.A. 116 E7
Mansfield, Mt., U.S.A. 117 B12
Mansilla de las Mulas, Spain 36 C5
Mansle, France 20 C4
Mansoa, Guinea-Biss. 82 C1
Manson Creek, Canada 102 B4
Manta, Ecuador 124 D2
Mantadia △, Madag. 89 B8
Mantalingajan, Mt., Phil. 61 G2
Mantare, Tanzania 86 C3
Manteca, U.S.A. 110 H5
Manteo, U.S.A. 115 H8
Mantes-la-Jolie, France 19 D8
Manthani, India 66 K11
Manti, U.S.A. 108 G8
Mantiqueira, Serra da, Brazil 127 A7
Manton, U.S.A. 114 C3
Mantorp, Sweden 11 F9
Mántova, Italy 40 C7
Mänttä, Finland 9 E21
Mantua = Mántova, Italy 40 C7
Manturovo, Russia 34 A7
Manu, Peru 124 F4
Manu →, Peru 124 F4
Manu'a Is., Amer. Samoa 91 B14
Manui, Indonesia 63 E6
Manukau, N.Z. 91 G5
Manuripi →, Bolivia 124 F5
Many, U.S.A. 113 K8
Manyara, L., Tanzania 86 C4
Manyas, Turkey 45 F11
Manyava, Ukraine 29 B9
Manych →, Russia 35 G5
Manych-Gudilo, Ozero, Russia 35 G6
Manyonga →, Tanzania 86 C3
Manyoni, Tanzania 86 D3
Manzai, Pakistan 68 C4
Manzala, Bahra el, Egypt 80 H7
Manzanar △, U.S.A. 110 J7
Manzanares, Spain 37 F7
Manzaneda, Spain 36 C3
Manzanillo, Cuba 120 B4
Manzanillo, Mexico 118 D4
Manzanillo, Pta., Panama 120 L4
Manzano Mts., U.S.A. 109 J10
Manẕarīyeh, Iran 71 C6
Manzhouli, China 60 B6
Manzini, Swaziland 89 D5
Mao, Chad 79 F9
Maó, Spain 48 B11
Maoke, Pegunungan, Indonesia 63 E9
Maolin, China 57 C12
Maoming, China 59 G8
Maopi T'ou, China 59 G13
Maouri, Dallol →, Niger 83 C5
Maoxian, China 58 B4
Maoxing, China 57 B13
Mapam Yumco, China 60 C3
Mapastepec, Mexico 119 D6
Mapia, Kepulauan, Indonesia 63 D8
Mapimí, Mexico 118 B4
Mapimí, Bolsón de, Mexico 118 B4
Maping, China 59 B9
Mapinga, Tanzania 86 D4
Mapinhane, Mozam. 89 C6
Maple Creek, Canada 103 D7
Maple Valley, U.S.A. 110 C4
Mapleton, U.S.A. 108 D2
Mapuera →, Brazil 124 D7
Mapulanguene, Mozam. 89 C5
Maputo, Mozam. 89 D5
Maputo □, Mozam. 89 D5
Maputo →, Mozam. 89 D5
Maputo, B. de, Mozam. 89 D5
Maqiaohe, China 57 B16
Maqnā, Si. Arabia 70 D2
Maquan He = Brahmaputra →,
   Asia 69 H13
Maqueda, Spain 36 E6
Maquela do Zombo, Angola 84 F3
Maquinchao, Argentina 128 E3
Maquoketa, U.S.A. 112 D9
Mar, Serra do, Brazil 127 B6
Mar Chiquita, L., Argentina 126 C3
Mar del Plata, Argentina 126 D4
Mar Menor, Spain 39 H4
Mara, Tanzania 86 C3
Mara □, Tanzania 86 C3
Maraã, Brazil 124 D5
Marabá, Brazil 125 E9
Maracá, I. de, Brazil 125 C8
Maracaibo, Venezuela 124 A4
Maracaibo, L. de, Venezuela 124 B4
Maracaju, Brazil 127 A4
Maracas Bay Village,
   Trin. & Tob. 125 K15
Maracay, Venezuela 124 A5
Maracena, Spain 37 H7
Maradi, Niger 83 C6
Marágheh, Iran 70 B5
Marāh, Si. Arabia 70 E5
Marahoue ○, Ivory C. 82 D3
Marais du Cotentin et du
   Bessin △, France 18 C5
Marais Poitevin, Val de Sèvre et
   Vendée △, France 20 B3
Marajó, I. de, Brazil 125 D9
Marākand, Iran 70 B5
Marakele △, S. Africa 89 A4
Maralal, Kenya 86 B4

Maralinga, Australia 93 F5
Maramaraereğlisi, Turkey 45 F11
Marambio, Antarctica 5 C18
Marampa, S. Leone 82 D2
Maran, Malaysia 65 L4
Marana, U.S.A. 109 K8
Maranboy, Australia 92 B5
Maranchón, Spain 38 D2
Marand, Iran 70 B5
Marang, Malaysia 65 K4
Maranguape, Brazil 125 D11
Maranhão = São Luís, Brazil 125 D10
Maranhão □, Brazil 125 E9
Marano, L. di, Italy 41 C10
Maranoa →, Australia 95 D4
Marañón →, Peru 124 D4
Marão, Mozam. 89 C5
Maraş = Kahramanmaraş, Turkey 70 B3
Mărăşeşti, Romania 29 E12
Maratea, Italy 43 C8
Marateca, Portugal 37 G2
Marathasa, Cyprus 49 E11
Marathókambos, Greece 47 D8
Marathon, Australia 94 C3
Marathon, Canada 104 C2
Marathón, Greece 46 C5
Marathon, N.Y., U.S.A. 117 D8
Marathon, Tex., U.S.A. 113 K3
Marathóvouno, Cyprus 49 D12
Maratua, Indonesia 63 D5
Maraval, Trin. & Tob. 125 K15
Maravatío, Mexico 118 D4
Marawi City, Phil. 61 G6
Marāwih, U.A.E. 71 E7
Marazliyivka, Ukraine 29 D15
Marbella, Spain 37 J6
Marble Bar, Australia 92 D2
Marble Falls, U.S.A. 113 K5
Marblehead, U.S.A. 117 D14
Marburg, Germany 24 E4
Marcal →, Hungary 28 C2
Marcali, Hungary 28 D2
Marcaria, Italy 40 C7
Mărcăuţi, Moldova 29 B12
March, U.K. 15 E8
Marche, France 20 B5
Marche □, Italy 41 E10
Marche-en-Famenne, Belgium 17 D5
Marchena, Spain 37 H5
Marches = Marche □, Italy 41 E10
Marchesale ○, Italy 43 D9
Marciana Marina, Italy 40 F7
Marcianise, Italy 43 A7
Marcigny, France 19 F11
Marcillat-en-Combraille, France 19 F9
Marck, France 19 B8
Marckolsheim, France 19 D14
Marco, U.S.A. 115 N5
Marcos Juárez, Argentina 126 C3
Mărculeşti, Moldova 29 C13
Marcus I. = Minami-Tori-Shima,
   Pac. Oc. 96 E7
Marcus Necker Ridge, Pac. Oc. 96 F9
Marcy, Mt., U.S.A. 117 B11
Mardan, Pakistan 68 B5
Mardarivka, Ukraine 29 C14
Mardin, Turkey 70 B4
Mårdsjö, Sweden 10 A9
Maréchia →, Italy 41 D9
Maree, L., U.K. 13 D3
Mareeba, Australia 94 B4
Mareetsane, S. Africa 88 D4
Maremma, Italy 41 F8
Maremma ○, Italy 40 F8
Maréna, Kayes, Mali 82 C2
Maréna, Koulikouro, Mali 82 C3
Marengo, U.S.A. 112 E8
Marennes, France 20 C2
Marerano, Madag. 89 C7
Marettimo, Italy 42 E5
Mareuil, France 20 C4
Marfa, U.S.A. 113 K2
Marfa Pt., Malta 49 D1
Marganets = Marhanets, Ukraine 33 J8
Margaret →, Australia 92 C4
Margaret Bay, Canada 102 C3
Margaret L., Canada 102 B5
Margaret River, Australia 93 F2
Margarita, I. de, Venezuela 124 A6
Margarítion, Greece 46 B2
Margaritovo, Russia 54 C7
Margate, S. Africa 89 E5
Margate, U.K. 15 F9
Margeride, Mts. de la, France 20 D7
Margherita di Savóia, Italy 43 A9
Margherita Pk., Uganda 86 B3
Marghita, Romania 28 C7
Margonin, Poland 31 F4
Margosatubig, Phil. 61 H5
Marguerite, Canada 102 C4
Marhanets, Ukraine 33 J8
Mari El □, Russia 34 B8
Mari Indus, Pakistan 68 C4
Mari Republic = Mari El □,
   Russia 34 B8
María, Sa. de, Spain 39 H2
María Elena, Chile 126 A2
María Grande, Argentina 126 C4
Maria I., N. Terr., Australia 94 A2
Maria I., Tas., Australia 95 G4
Maria Island △, Australia 95 G4
Maria van Diemen, C., N.Z. 91 F4
Mariager, Denmark 11 H3
Mariager Fjord, Denmark 11 H4
Mariakani, Kenya 86 C4
Mariala △, Australia 95 D4
Marian, Australia 94 K6
Marian L., Canada 102 A5
Mariana Trench, Pac. Oc. 96 F6
Marianao, Cuba 120 B3

Marianna, Ark., U.S.A. 113 H9
Marianna, Fla., U.S.A. 115 K3
Mariannelund, Sweden 11 G9
Mariánské Lázně, Czech Rep. 26 B5
Marias →, U.S.A. 108 C8
Mariato, Punta, Panama 120 E3
Mariazell, Austria 26 D8
Maribo, Denmark 11 K5
Maribor, Slovenia 41 B12
Marico →, Africa 88 C4
Maricopa, Ariz., U.S.A. 109 K7
Maricopa, Calif., U.S.A. 111 K7
Marîdî, Sudan 81 G2
Marîdî, Wadi →, Sudan 81 F2
Marié →, Brazil 124 D5
Marie Byrd Land, Antarctica 5 D14
Marie-Galante, Guadeloupe .... 120 b
Mariecourt = Kangiqsujuaq,
   Canada 101 B12
Mariefred, Sweden 10 E11
Mariehamn = Maarianhamina,
   Finland 9 F18
Marieholm, Sweden 11 J7
Mariembourg, Belgium 17 D4
Marienbad = Mariánské Lázně,
   Czech Rep. 26 B5
Marienberg, Germany 24 E9
Mariental, Namibia 88 C2
Marienville, U.S.A. 116 E5
Mariestad, Sweden 11 F7
Marietta, Ga., U.S.A. 115 J3
Marietta, Ohio, U.S.A. 114 F5
Marieville, Canada 117 A11
Mariga →, Nigeria 83 C6
Marignane, France 21 E9
Marihatag, Phil. 61 G7
Mariinsk, Russia 52 D9
Mariinskiy Posad, Russia 34 B8
Marijampolė, Lithuania 9 J20
Marijampolė □, Lithuania 30 D10
Marília, Brazil 127 A6
Marín, Spain 36 C2
Marina, U.S.A. 110 J5
Marinduque, Phil. 63 B6
Marine City, U.S.A. 116 D2
Marineo, Italy 42 E6
Marinette, U.S.A. 114 C2
Maringá, Brazil 127 A5
Marinha Grande, Portugal 36 F2
Marino, Italy 41 G9
Marion, Ala., U.S.A. 115 J2
Marion, Ill., U.S.A. 113 G10
Marion, Ind., U.S.A. 114 E3
Marion, Iowa, U.S.A. 112 E9
Marion, Kans., U.S.A. 112 F6
Marion, N.C., U.S.A. 115 H5
Marion, Ohio, U.S.A. 114 E4
Marion, S.C., U.S.A. 115 H6
Marion, Va., U.S.A. 115 G5
Marion, L., U.S.A. 115 J5
Mariposa, U.S.A. 110 H7
Mariscal Estigarribia, Paraguay 126 A3
Maritime Alps = Maritimes,
   Alpes, Europe 21 D11
Maritimes, Alpes, Europe 21 D11
Maritsa = Évros →, Greece 72 B2
Maritsá, Greece 49 C10
Mariupol, Ukraine 33 J9
Mariusa →, Venezuela 121 E7
Marīvān, Iran 70 C5
Marj 'Uyūn, Lebanon 74 B4
Marka = Merca, Somali Rep. 75 G3
Marka, Si. Arabia 80 D5
Markam, China 58 C2
Markaryd, Sweden 11 H7
Markdale, Canada 116 B4
Marked Tree, U.S.A. 113 H9
Markelsdorfer Huk, Germany 24 A7
Market Drayton, U.K. 14 E5
Market Harborough, U.K. 15 E7
Market Rasen, U.K. 14 D7
Markham, Canada 116 C5
Markham, Mt., Antarctica 5 E11
Marki, Poland 31 F8
Märkische Schweiz △, Germany 24 C10
Markkleeberg, Germany 24 D8
Markleeville, U.S.A. 110 G7
Markoupoulon, Greece 46 D5
Markovac, Serbia & M. 44 B5
Markovo, Russia 53 C17
Markoye, Burkina Faso 83 C5
Marks, Russia 34 E8
Marksville, U.S.A. 113 K8
Markt Schwaben, Germany 25 G7
Marktoberdorf, Germany 25 H6
Marktredwitz, Germany 25 F8
Marl, Germany 24 D3
Marla, Australia 95 D1
Marlbank, Canada 116 B7
Marlboro, Mass., U.S.A. 117 D13
Marlboro, N.Y., U.S.A. 117 E11
Marlborough, Australia 94 C4
Marlborough, U.K. 15 F6
Marlborough Downs, U.K. 15 F6
Marle, France 19 C10
Marlin, U.S.A. 113 K6
Marlow, Germany 24 A8
Marlow, U.K. 15 F7
Marlow, U.S.A. 113 H6
Marmagao, India 66 M8
Marmande, France 20 D4
Marmara, Turkey 45 F11
Marmara, Sea of = Marmara
   Denizi, Turkey 45 F12
Marmara Denizi, Turkey 45 F12
Marmara Gölü, Turkey 47 C10
Marmaris, Turkey 47 E10
Marmaris Limanı, Turkey 47 E10
Marmion, Mt., Australia 93 E2
Marmion L., Canada 104 C1
Marmolada, Mte., Italy 41 B8
Marmolejo, Spain 37 G6

Marmora, Canada 116 B7
Mármora, La, Italy 42 C2
Marnay, France 19 E12
Marne, Germany 24 B5
Marne □, France 19 D11
Marne →, France 19 D9
Marneuli, Georgia 35 K7
Maroala, Madag. 89 B8
Maroantsetra, Madag. 89 B8
Maroelaboom, Namibia 88 B2
Marofandilia, Madag. 89 C7
Marojejy △, Madag. 89 A8
Maromandia, Madag. 89 A8
Maromokotro, Madag. 89 A8
Marondera, Zimbabwe 87 F3
Maroni →, Fr. Guiana 125 B8
Marónia, Greece 45 F9
Maronne →, France 20 C5
Maroochydore, Australia 95 D5
Maroona, Australia 95 F3
Maros →, Hungary 28 D5
Marosakoa, Madag. 89 B8
Maroseranana, Madag. 89 B8
Maróstica, Italy 41 C8
Marotandrano, Madag. 89 B8
Marotaolana, Madag. 89 A8
Maroua, Cameroon 83 C7
Marovato, Madag. 89 B8
Marovoay, Madag. 89 B8
Marquard, S. Africa 88 D4
Marquesas Is. = Marquises, Îs.,
   French Polynesia 97 H14
Marquette, U.S.A. 114 B2
Marquis, St. Lucia .... 121 f
Marquise, France 19 B8
Marquises, Îs., French Polynesia 97 H14
Marra, Djebel, Sudan 79 F10
Marra, Gebel, Sudan 81 F2
Marracuene, Mozam. 89 D5
Marradi, Italy 41 D8
Marrakech, Morocco 78 B4
Marratxí, Spain 38 F7
Marrawah, Australia 95 G3
Marree, Australia 95 D2
Marrero, U.S.A. 113 L9
Marrimane, Mozam. 89 C5
Marromeu, Mozam. 89 B6
Marromeu →, Mozam. 89 B6
Marroquí, Punta, Spain 37 K5
Marrowie Cr. →, Australia 95 E4
Marrubane, Mozam. 87 F4
Marrúbiu, Italy 42 C1
Marrupa, Mozam. 87 E4
Mars Hill, U.S.A. 115 B12
Marsá 'Alam, Egypt 80 B3
Marsá Matrûh, Egypt 80 A2
Marsá Sha'b, Sudan 80 C4
Marsabit, Kenya 86 B4
Marsabit △, Kenya 86 B4
Marsala, Italy 42 E5
Marsalforn, Malta 49 C1
Mârşani, Romania 29 F9
Marsberg, Germany 24 D4
Marsciano, Italy 41 F9
Marsden, Australia 95 E4
Marseillan, France 20 E7
Marseille, France 21 E9
Marseille ✈ (MRS), France 21 E9
Marseilles = Marseille, France 21 E9
Marsh I., U.S.A. 113 L9
Marshall, Liberia 82 D2
Marshall, Ark., U.S.A. 113 H8
Marshall, Mich., U.S.A. 114 D3
Marshall, Minn., U.S.A. 112 C7
Marshall, Mo., U.S.A. 112 F8
Marshall, Tex., U.S.A. 113 J7
Marshall →, Australia 94 C2
Marshall Is. ■, Pac. Oc. 96 G9
Marshalltown, U.S.A. 112 D8
Marshbrook, Zimbabwe 89 B5
Marshfield, Mo., U.S.A. 113 G8
Marshfield, Vt., U.S.A. 117 B12
Marshfield, Wis., U.S.A. 112 C9
Marshūn, Iran 71 B6
Mársico Nuovo, Italy 43 B8
Märsta, Sweden 10 E11
Marstal, Denmark 11 K4
Marstrand, Sweden 11 G5
Mart, U.S.A. 113 K6
Marta →, Italy 41 F8
Martaban, Burma 67 L20
Martaban, G. of, Burma 67 L20
Martano, Italy 43 B11
Martapura, Kalimantan, Indonesia 62 E4
Martapura, Sumatera, Indonesia 62 E2
Marte, Nigeria 83 C7
Martel, France 20 D5
Martelange, Belgium 17 E5
Martellago, Italy 41 C9
Martés, Sierra, Spain 39 F4
Martfű, Hungary 28 C5
Martha's Vineyard, U.S.A. 117 E14
Martigné-Ferchaud, France 18 E5
Martigny, Switz. 25 J3
Martigues, France 21 E9
Martin, Slovak Rep. 27 B11
Martin, S. Dak., U.S.A. 112 D4
Martin, Tenn., U.S.A. 113 G10
Martin, L., Spain 38 D4
Martin, L., U.S.A. 115 J3
Martina, Italy 43 B10
Martina Franca, Italy 43 B10
Martinborough, N.Z. 91 J5
Martinez, Calif., U.S.A. 110 G4
Martinez, Ga., U.S.A. 115 J4
Martinique □, W. Indies .... 120 c
Martinique Passage, W. Indies 121 C7
Martinon, Greece 46 C5
Martinópolis, Brazil 127 A5
Martin's Bay, Barbados .... 121 g
Martins Ferry, U.S.A. 116 F4
Martinsberg, Austria 26 C8

Martinsburg, Pa., U.S.A. 116 F6
Martinsburg, W. Va., U.S.A. 114 F7
Martinsicuro, Italy 41 F10
Martinsville, Ind., U.S.A. 114 F2
Martinsville, Va., U.S.A. 115 G6
Marton, N.Z. 91 J5
Martorell, Spain 38 D6
Martos, Spain 37 H7
Martuni, Armenia 35 K7
Maru, Nigeria 83 C6
Marudi, Malaysia 62 D4
Maruf, Afghan. 66 D5
Marugame, Japan 55 G6
Marunga, Angola 88 B3
Marungu, Mts., Dem. Rep. of
     the Congo 86 D3
Marv Dasht, Iran 71 D7
Marvast, Iran 71 D7
Marvejols, France 20 D7
Marvel Loch, Australia 93 F2
Marwar, India 68 G5
Mary, Turkmenistan 52 F7
Maryborough = Port Laoise,
     Ireland 12 C4
Maryborough, Queens., Australia 95 D5
Maryborough, Vic., Australia .. 95 F3
Maryfield, Canada 103 D8
Maryland □, U.S.A. 114 F7
Maryland Junction, Zimbabwe .. 87 F3
Maryport, U.K. 14 C4
Mary's Harbour, Canada 105 B8
Marystown, Canada 105 C8
Marysville, Canada 102 D5
Marysville, Calif., U.S.A. 110 F5
Marysville, Kans., U.S.A. 112 F6
Marysville, Mich., U.S.A. 116 D2
Marysville, Ohio, U.S.A. 114 E4
Marysville, Wash., U.S.A. 110 B4
Maryville, Mo., U.S.A. 112 E7
Maryville, Tenn., U.S.A. 115 H4
Marzūq, Libya 79 C8
Masahunga, Tanzania 86 C3
Masai, Malaysia .... 65 d
Masai △, Kenya 86 C4
Masai Mara △, Kenya 86 C4
Masai Steppe, Tanzania 86 C4
Masaka, Uganda 86 C3
Masalembo, Kepulauan,
     Indonesia 62 F4
Masalima, Kepulauan, Indonesia 62 F5
Masallı, Azerbaijan 73 C13
Masamba, Indonesia 63 E6
Masan, S. Korea 57 G15
Masandam, Ra's, Oman 71 E8
Masasi, Tanzania 87 E4
Masaya, Nic. 120 D2
Masba, Nigeria 83 C7
Masbate, Phil. 61 E5
Máscali, Italy 43 E8
Mascara, Algeria 78 A6
Mascota, Mexico 118 C4
Masela, Indonesia 63 F7
Maseru, Lesotho 88 D4
Mashaba, Zimbabwe 87 G3
Mashābih, Si. Arabia 70 E3
Mashan, China 58 F7
Mashar, Sudan 81 F2
Mashatu △, Botswana 89 C4
Mashegu, Nigeria 83 D6
Masherbrum, Pakistan 69 B7
Mashhad, Iran 71 B8
Mashi, Nigeria 83 C6
Mashīz, Iran 71 D8
Māshkel, Hāmūn-i-, Pakistan .. 66 E3
Mashki Chāh, Pakistan 66 E3
Mashonaland, Zimbabwe 85 H6
Mashonaland Central □,
     Zimbabwe 89 B5
Mashonaland East □, Zimbabwe 89 B5
Mashonaland West □, Zimbabwe 89 B4
Mashrakh, India 69 F11
Mashtaga = Maştağa, Azerbaijan 35 K10
Masindi, Uganda 86 B3
Masindi Port, Uganda 86 B3
Maşīrah, Oman 75 C6
Maşīrah, Khalīj, Oman 75 C6
Masisi, Dem. Rep. of the Congo . 86 C2
Masjed Soleyman, Iran 71 D6
Mask, L., Ireland 12 C2
Maskin, Oman 71 F8
Maslen Nos, Bulgaria 45 D11
Maslinica, Croatia 41 E13
Masnou = El Masnou, Spain .. 38 D7
Masoala △, Madag. 89 B9
Masoala, Tanjon' i, Madag. ... 89 B9
Masoarivo, Madag. 89 B7
Masohi = Amahai, Indonesia .. 63 E7
Masomeloka, Madag. 89 C8
Mason, Nev., U.S.A. 110 G7
Mason, Tex., U.S.A. 113 K5
Mason City, U.S.A. 112 D8
Maspalomas, Canary Is. 48 G4
Maspalomas, Pta., Canary Is. .. 48 G4
Masqat, Oman 75 C6
Massa, Italy 40 D7
Massa Maríttima, Italy 40 E7
Massachusetts □, U.S.A. 117 D13
Massachusetts B., U.S.A. 117 D14
Massafra, Italy 43 B10
Massakory, Chad 79 F9
Massanella, Spain 48 B9
Massangena, Mozam. 89 C5
Massango, Angola 84 F3
Massat, France 20 F5
Massawa = Mitsiwa, Eritrea ... 81 D4
Massena, U.S.A. 117 B10
Massénya, Chad 79 F9
Masset, Canada 102 C2
Masseube, France 20 E4
Massiac, France 20 C7
Massiah Street, Barbados .... 121 g
Massif Central, France 20 D7
Massif des Bauges △, France .. 19 G13

Massigui, Mali 82 C3
Massillon, U.S.A. 116 F3
Massinga, Mozam. 89 C6
Massingir, Mozam. 89 C5
Masson-Angers, Canada 117 A9
Masson I., Antarctica 5 C7
Maştağa, Azerbaijan 35 K10
Mastanli = Momchilgrad, Bulgaria 45 E9
Masterton, N.Z. 91 J5
Mastic, U.S.A. 117 F12
Mástikho, Ákra, Greece 47 C8
Mastuj, Pakistan 69 A5
Mastung, Pakistan 66 E5
Mastūrah, Si. Arabia 80 C4
Masty, Belarus 32 F3
Masuda, Japan 55 G5
Masvingo, Zimbabwe 87 G3
Masvingo □, Zimbabwe 87 G3
Maswa △, Tanzania 86 C3
Maşyāf, Syria 70 C3
Maszewo, Poland 30 E2
Mat →, Albania 44 E3
Matabeleland, Zimbabwe 85 H5
Matabeleland North □,
     Zimbabwe 87 F2
Matabeleland South □,
     Zimbabwe 87 G2
Matachel →, Spain 37 G4
Matachewan, Canada 104 C3
Matadi, Dem. Rep. of the Congo 84 F2
Matagalpa, Nic. 120 D2
Matagami, Canada 104 C4
Matagami, L., Canada 104 C4
Matagorda B., U.S.A. 113 L6
Matagorda I., U.S.A. 113 L6
Matak, Indonesia 62 D3
Mátala, Greece 49 E6
Matam, Senegal 82 B2
Matameye, Niger 83 C6
Matamoros, Campeche, Mexico . 119 D6
Matamoros, Coahuila, Mexico .. 118 B4
Matamoros, Tamaulipas, Mexico 119 B5
Ma'ţan as Sarra, Libya 79 D10
Matandu →, Tanzania 87 D3
Matane, Canada 105 C6
Matang, China 58 F5
Matankari, Niger 83 C5
Matanomadh, India 68 H3
Matanzas, Cuba 120 B3
Matapa, Botswana 88 C3
Matapan, C. = Taínaron, Ákra,
     Greece 46 E4
Matapédia, Canada 105 C6
Matapo △, Zimbabwe 87 G2
Matara, Sri Lanka 66 S12
Mataram, Indonesia 63 K19
Matarani, Peru 124 G4
Mataranka, Australia 92 B5
Matarma, Râs, Egypt 74 E1
Mataró, Spain 38 D7
Matarraña →, Spain 38 D5
Mataruška Banja, Serbia & M. .. 44 C4
Matatiele, S. Africa 89 E4
Mataura, N.Z. 91 M2
Matehuala, Mexico 118 C4
Mateke Hills, Zimbabwe 87 G3
Matelot, Trin. & Tob. 125 K15
Matera, Italy 43 B9
Matese △, Italy 43 A7
Matese, Monti del, Italy 43 A7
Mátészalka, Hungary 28 C7
Matetsi, Zimbabwe 87 F2
Matfors, Sweden 10 B11
Matha, France 20 C3
Matheniko △, Uganda 86 B3
Mathis, U.S.A. 113 L6
Mathráki, Greece 49 A3
Mathura, India 68 F7
Mati, Phil. 61 H7
Matiakoali, Burkina Faso 83 C5
Matiali, India 69 F13
Matías Romero, Mexico 119 D5
Matibane, Mozam. 87 E5
Matiri Ra., N.Z. 91 J4
Matjiesfontein, S. Africa 88 E3
Matla →, India 69 J13
Matlamanyane, Botswana ... 88 B4
Matli, Pakistan 68 G3
Matlock, U.K. 14 D6
Matna, Sudan 81 E4
Mato Grosso □, Brazil 125 F8
Mato Grosso, Planalto do, Brazil 125 G8
Mato Grosso do Sul □, Brazil .. 125 G8
Matobo = Matapo △, Zimbabwe 87 G2
Matopo Hills, Zimbabwe 87 G2
Matopos, Zimbabwe 87 G2
Matosinhos, Portugal 36 D2
Matour, France 19 F11
Matroosberg, S. Africa 88 E2
Maţruḥ, Oman 75 C6
Matsena, Nigeria 83 C7
Matsesta, Russia 35 J4
Matsu Tao, Taiwan 59 E13
Matsue, Japan 55 G6
Matsum, Ko, Thailand ...... 65 b
Matsumae, Japan 54 D10
Matsumoto, Japan 55 F9
Matsusaka, Japan 55 G8
Matsuura, Japan 55 H4
Matsuyama, Japan 55 H6
Mattagami →, Canada 104 B3
Mattancheri, India 66 Q10
Mattawa, Canada 104 C4
Matterhorn, Switz. 25 K3
Mattersburg, Austria 27 D9
Matthew Town, Bahamas 121 B5
Matthews Ridge, Guyana 124 B6
Mattice, Canada 104 C3
Mattituck, U.S.A. 117 F12
Mattō, Japan 55 F8
Mattoon, U.S.A. 114 F1

Matuba, Mozam. 89 C5
Matucana, Peru 124 F3
Matūn = Khowst, Afghan. 68 C3
Matura B., Trin. & Tob. 125 K15
Maturín, Venezuela 124 B6
Matusadona △, Zimbabwe ... 87 F2
Matveyev Kurgan, Russia 33 J10
Matxitxako, C., Spain 38 B2
Mau, Mad. P., India 69 F8
Mau, Ut. P., India 69 G10
Mau, Ut. P., India 69 G9
Mau Escarpment, Kenya 86 C4
Mau Ranipur, India 69 G8
Maubeuge, France 19 B10
Maubourguet, France 20 E4
Maud, Pt., Australia 92 D1
Maude, Australia 95 E3
Maudin Sun, Burma 67 M19
Maués, Brazil 124 D7
Mauganj, India 67 G12
Maughold Hd., I. of Man 14 C3
Mauguio, France 20 E7
Maui, U.S.A. 106 H16
Maulamyaing = Moulmein,
     Burma 67 L20
Maule □, Chile 126 D1
Mauléon-Licharre, France ... 20 E3
Maumee, U.S.A. 114 E4
Maumee →, U.S.A. 114 E4
Maumere, Indonesia 63 F6
Maumusson, Pertuis de, France . 20 C2
Maun, Botswana 88 C3
Mauna Kea, U.S.A. 106 J17
Mauna Loa, U.S.A. 106 J17
Maungmagan Kyunzu, Burma . 64 E1
Maupin, U.S.A. 108 D3
Maure-de-Bretagne, France .. 18 E5
Maurepas, L., U.S.A. 113 K9
Maures, France 21 E10
Mauriac, France 20 C6
Maurice, L., Australia 93 E5
Mauricie △, Canada 104 C5
Maurienne, France 21 C10
Mauritania ■, Africa 78 E3
Mauritius ■, Ind. Oc. 77 J9
Mauron, France 18 D4
Maurs, France 20 D6
Mauston, U.S.A. 112 D9
Mauterndorf, Austria 26 D6
Mauvezin, France 20 E4
Mauzé-sur-le-Mignon, France . 20 B3
Mavli, India 68 G5
Mavrovë, Albania 44 F4
Mavrovo △, Macedonia 44 E4
Mavuradonha Mts., Zimbabwe . 87 F3
Mawa, Dem. Rep. of the Congo . 86 B2
Mawai, India 69 H9
Mawana, India 68 E7
Mawand, Pakistan 68 E3
Mawk Mai, Burma 67 J20
Mawlaik, Burma 67 H19
Mawlamyine = Moulmein, Burma 67 L20
Mawqaq, Si. Arabia 70 E4
Mawson Base, Antarctica ... 5 C6
Mawson Coast, Antarctica ... 5 C6
Max, U.S.A. 112 B4
Maxcanú, Mexico 119 C6
Maxesibeni, S. Africa 89 E4
Maxhamish L., Canada 102 B4
Maxixe, Mozam. 89 C6
Maxville, Canada 117 A10
Maxwell, U.S.A. 110 F4
Maxwelton, Australia 94 C3
May, C., U.S.A. 114 F8
May Pen, Jamaica .... 120 a
Maya →, Russia 53 D14
Maya Mts., Belize 119 D7
Mayaguana, Bahamas 121 B5
Mayagüez, Puerto Rico ..... 121 d
Mayahi, Niger 83 C6
Mayaky, Ukraine 29 C14
Mayals = Maials, Spain 38 D5
Mayāmey, Iran 71 B7
Mayang, China 58 D7
Mayanup, Australia 93 F2
Mayapán, Mexico 119 C7
Mayapan, Yucatán, Mexico ... 119 C7
Mayarí, Cuba 121 B4
Mayaro B., Trin. & Tob. 125 K16
Maybell, U.S.A. 108 F9
Maybole, U.K. 13 F4
Maychew, Ethiopia 81 E4
Maydān, Iraq 70 C5
Maydan, Ukraine 29 B8
Maydena, Australia 95 G4
Mayen, Germany 25 E3
Mayenne, France 18 D6
Mayenne □, France 18 D6
Mayenne →, France 18 E6
Mayer, U.S.A. 109 J7
Mayerthorpe, Canada 102 C5
Mayfield, Ky., U.S.A. 115 G1
Mayfield, N.Y., U.S.A. 117 C10
Mayhill, U.S.A. 109 K11
Maykop, Russia 35 H5
Maymyo, Burma 64 A1
Maynard, Mass., U.S.A. 117 D13
Maynard, Wash., U.S.A. 110 C4
Maynard Hills, Australia 93 E2
Mayne →, Australia 94 C3
Maynooth, Ireland 12 C5
Mayo, Canada 100 B6
Mayo □, Ireland 12 C2
Mayo Daga, Nigeria 83 D7
Mayo Faran, Nigeria 83 D7
Mayon Volcano, Phil. 61 E5
Mayor I., N.Z. 91 G6
Mayorga, Spain 36 C5
Mayotte ☑, Ind. Oc. 85 G9
Mayraira Pt., Phil. 61 B4
Maysān □, Iraq 70 D5

Mayskiy, Russia 35 J7
Maysville, U.S.A. 114 F4
Mayu, Indonesia 63 D7
Mayville, N. Dak., U.S.A. ... 112 B6
Mayville, N.Y., U.S.A. 116 D5
Mayya, Russia 53 C14
Mazabuka, Zambia 87 F2
Mazagán = El Jadida, Morocco . 78 B4
Mazagão, Brazil 125 D8
Mazamet, France 20 E6
Mazán, Peru 124 D4
Māzandarān □, Iran 71 B7
Mazapil, Mexico 118 C4
Mazara del Vallo, Italy 42 E5
Mazarrón, Spain 39 H3
Mazarrón, G. de, Spain 39 H3
Mazaruni →, Guyana 124 B7
Mazatán, Mexico 118 B2
Mazatenango, Guatemala ... 120 D1
Mazatlán, Mexico 118 C3
Mažeikiai, Lithuania 9 H20
Māzhān, Iran 71 C8
Mazinān, Iran 71 B8
Mazoe →, Mozam. 87 F3
Mazoe, Mozam. 87 F3
Mazowe, Zimbabwe 87 F3
Mazowieckie □, Poland 31 F8
Mazrūb, Sudan 81 E2
Mazu Dao, China 59 D12
Mazurian Lakes = Mazurski,
     Pojezierze, Poland 30 E7
Mazurski, Pojezierze, Poland .. 30 E7
Mazyr, Belarus 33 F5
Mbaba, Senegal 82 C1
Mbabane, Swaziland 89 D5
Mbagne, Mauritania 82 B2
M'bahiakro, Ivory C. 82 D4
Mbaïki, C.A.R. 84 D3
Mbala, Zambia 87 D3
Mbalabala, Zimbabwe 89 C4
Mbale, Uganda 86 B3
Mbalmayo, Cameroon 83 E7
Mbam →, Cameroon 83 E7
Mbamba Bay, Tanzania 87 E3
Mbandaka, Dem. Rep. of
     the Congo 84 D3
Mbanga, Cameroon 83 E6
Mbanza Congo, Angola 84 F2
Mbanza Ngungu, Dem. Rep. of
     the Congo 84 F2
Mbarangandu, Tanzania 87 D4
Mbarara, Uganda 86 C3
Mbashe →, S. Africa 89 E4
Mbatto, Ivory C. 82 D4
Mbenkuru →, Tanzania 87 D4
Mberengwa, Zimbabwe 87 G2
Mberengwa, Mt., Zimbabwe .. 87 G2
Mberubu, Nigeria 83 D6
Mbesuma, Zambia 87 E3
Mbeya, Tanzania 87 D3
Mbeya □, Tanzania 86 D3
Mbinga, Tanzania 87 E4
Mbini = Río Muni □, Eq. Guin. . 84 D2
Mboki, C.A.R. 81 F2
M'bonge, Cameroon 83 E6
Mboro, Senegal 82 B1
Mbour, Senegal 82 C1
Mbout, Mauritania 82 B2
Mbuji-Mayi, Dem. Rep. of
     the Congo 86 D1
Mbulu, Tanzania 86 C4
Mburucuyá, Argentina 126 B4
McCarran International, Las
     Vegas ✈ (LAS), U.S.A. . 111 J11
Mchinja, Tanzania 87 D4
Mchinji, Malawi 87 E3
McMurdo, Antarctica 5 D11
Mdantsane, S. Africa 85 L5
Mead, L., U.S.A. 111 J12
Meade, U.S.A. 113 G4
Meadow Lake, Canada 103 C7
Meadow Lake △, Canada ... 103 C7
Meadow Valley Wash →, U.S.A. 111 J12
Meadville, U.S.A. 116 E4
Meaford, Canada 116 B4
Mealhada, Portugal 36 E2
Mealy Mts., Canada 105 B8
Meander River, Canada 102 B5
Meares, C., U.S.A. 108 D2
Mearim →, Brazil 125 D10
Meath □, Ireland 12 C5
Meath Park, Canada 103 C7
Meaulne, France 19 F9
Meaux, France 19 D9
Mebechi-Gawa →, Japan ... 54 D10
Mebulu, Tanjung, Indonesia .. 63 K18
Mecanhelas, Mozam. 87 F4
Mecca = Makkah, Si. Arabia .. 75 C2
Mecca, U.S.A. 111 M10
Mechanicsburg, U.S.A. 114 F7
Mechanicville, U.S.A. 117 D11
Mechara, Ethiopia 81 F5
Mechelen, Belgium 17 C4
Mecheria, Algeria 78 B5
Mechernich, Germany 24 E2
Mechetinskaya, Russia 35 G5
Mecidiye, Turkey 45 F10
Mecitözü, Turkey 72 B6
Mecklenburg-Vorpommern □,
     Germany 24 B8
Mecklenburger Bucht, Germany 24 A7
Meconta, Mozam. 87 E4
Mecsek, Hungary 28 D3
Meda, Portugal 36 E3
Medan, Indonesia 62 D1
Médanos de Coro △, Venezuela 121 D6
Medanosa, Pta., Argentina ... 128 F3
Mede, Italy 40 C5
Médéa, Algeria 78 A6

Medeba, Bos.-H. 28 G4
Medellín, Colombia 124 B3
Medelpad, Sweden 10 B10
Medemblik, Neths. 17 B5
Mederdra, Mauritania 82 B1
Medford, Mass., U.S.A. 117 D13
Medford, Oreg., U.S.A. 108 E2
Medford, Wis., U.S.A. 112 C9
Medgidia, Romania 29 F13
Medi, Sudan 81 F3
Media Agua, Argentina 126 C2
Media Luna, Argentina 126 C2
Medianeira, Brazil 127 B5
Mediaş, Romania 29 D9
Medicina, Italy 41 D8
Medicine Bow, U.S.A. 108 F10
Medicine Bow Pk., U.S.A. ... 108 F10
Medicine Bow Ra., U.S.A. ... 108 F10
Medicine Hat, Canada 103 D6
Medicine Lake, U.S.A. 112 A2
Medicine Lodge, U.S.A. 113 G5
Medina = Al Madīnah, Si. Arabia 70 E3
Medina, N. Dak., U.S.A. 112 B5
Medina, N.Y., U.S.A. 116 C6
Medina, Ohio, U.S.A. 116 E3
Medina →, U.S.A. 113 L5
Medina de Pomar, Spain 36 C7
Medina de Ríoseco, Spain ... 36 D5
Medina del Campo, Spain ... 36 D6
Medina L., U.S.A. 113 L5
Medina Sidonia, Spain 37 J5
Medinaceli, Spain 38 D2
Medinipur, India 69 H12
Mediterranean Sea, Europe ... 6 H7
Médoc, France 20 C3
Medulin, Croatia 41 D10
Medveda, Serbia & M. 44 D5
Medvedevo, Russia 34 B8
Medveditsa →, Tver, Russia .. 32 D9
Medveditsa →, Volgograd, Russia 34 F6
Medvedok, Russia 34 B10
Medvezhi, Ostrava, Russia ... 53 B17
Medvezhyegorsk, Russia 52 C4
Medway →, U.K. 15 F8
Medway →, U.K. 15 F8
Medzev, Slovak Rep. 27 C13
Medzilaborce, Slovak Rep. ... 27 B14
Medžitlija, Macedonia 44 F5
Meekatharra, Australia 93 E2
Meeker, U.S.A. 108 F10
Meelpaeg Res., Canada 105 C8
Meersburg, Germany 25 H5
Meerut, India 68 E7
Meeteetse, U.S.A. 108 D9
Mega, Ethiopia 81 G4
Megáli Khorió, Greece 47 E9
Megálo Petalí, Greece 46 D6
Megalópolis, Greece 46 D4
Meganísi Nísís, Greece 46 C2
Mégara, Greece 46 D5
Megasini, India 69 J12
Megdhova →, Greece 46 B3
Megève, France 21 C10
Meghalaya □, India 67 G17
Meghezez, Ethiopia 81 F4
Meghna →, Bangla. 67 H17
Mégiscane, L., Canada 104 C4
Megiste, Greece 47 E11
Megra, Russia 32 B9
Mehadia, Romania 28 F7
Meharry, Mt., Australia 92 D2
Mehedeby, Sweden 10 D11
Mehedinți □, Romania 28 F7
Meheisa, Sudan 80 D3
Mehlville, U.S.A. 112 F9
Mehndawal, India 69 F10
Mehr Jān, Iran 71 C7
Mehrābād, Iran 70 B5
Mehrān, Iran 70 C5
Mehrīz, Iran 71 D7
Mehun-sur-Yèvre, France ... 19 E9
Mei Jiang →, China 59 E11
Mei Xian, China 56 G4
Meicheng, China 59 C12
Meichengzhen, China 59 C8
Meichuan, China 59 B10
Meigu, China 58 C4
Meiktila, Burma 67 J19
Meinerzhagen, Germany 24 D3
Meiningen, Germany 24 E6
Meira, Serra de, Spain 36 B3
Meiringen, Switz. 25 J4
Meishan, China 58 B4
Meissen, Germany 24 D9
Meissner, Germany 24 D5
Meissner-Kaufunger Wald △,
     Germany 24 D5
Meitan, China 58 D6
Meizhou, China 59 E11
Meja, India 69 G10
Mejillones, Chile 126 A1
Mekdela, Ethiopia 81 E4
Mekele, Ethiopia 81 E4
Mekhtar, Pakistan 66 D6
Meknès, Morocco 78 B4
Meko, Nigeria 83 D5
Mekong →, Asia 65 H6
Mekongga, Indonesia 63 E6
Mekrou →, Benin 83 C5
Mekvari = Kür →, Azerbaijan . 73 C13
Mel, Italy 41 B9
Melagiri Hills, India 66 N10
Melaka, Malaysia 65 L4
Melalap, Malaysia 62 C5
Mélambes, Greece 49 D6
Melanesia, Pac. Oc. 96 H7
Melaya, Indonesia 63 J17
Melbourne, Australia 95 F4
Melbourne, U.S.A. 115 L5
Melchor Múzquiz, Mexico ... 118 B4
Melchor Ocampo, Mexico ... 118 C4
Méldola, Italy 41 D9

Meldorf, *Germany* 24 A5
Melegnano, *Italy* 40 C6
Melenci, *Serbia & M.* 28 E5
Melenki, *Russia* 34 C5
Mélèzes ➤, *Canada* 104 A5
Melfi, *Italy* 43 B8
Melfort, *Canada* 103 C8
Melfort, *Zimbabwe* 87 F3
Melgaço, *Portugal* 36 C2
Melgar de Fernamental, *Spain* .. 36 C6
Melhus, *Norway* 8 E14
Melide, *Spain* 36 C2
Meligalá, *Greece* 46 D3
Melilla, *N. Afr.* 78 A5
Melilli, *Italy* 43 E8
Melipilla, *Chile* 126 C1
Mélissa, Ákra, *Greece* 49 D6
Mélissa Óros, *Greece* 47 D8
Melita, *Canada* 103 D8
Mélito di Porto Salvo, *Italy* .. 43 E8
Melitopol, *Ukraine* 33 J8
Melk, *Austria* 26 C8
Mellan Fryken, *Sweden* 10 E7
Mellansel, *Sweden* 8 E18
Mellbystrand, *Sweden* 11 H6
Melle, *France* 20 B3
Melle, *Germany* 24 C4
Mellen, *U.S.A.* 112 B9
Mellerud, *Sweden* 11 F6
Mellette, *U.S.A.* 112 C5
Mellid = Melide, *Spain* 36 C2
Mellieha, *Malta* 49 D1
Mellit, *Sudan* 81 E2
Mellrichstadt, *Germany* 24 E6
Melnik, *Bulgaria* 44 E7
Mělník, *Czech Rep.* 26 A7
Melnytsya Podilska, *Ukraine* .. 29 B11
Melo, *Uruguay* 127 C5
Melolo, *Indonesia* 63 F6
Melouprey, *Cambodia* 64 F5
Melrose, *Australia* 95 E4
Melrose, *U.K.* 13 F6
Melrose, Minn., *U.S.A.* 112 C7
Melrose, N. Mex., *U.S.A.* 113 H3
Melstone, *U.S.A.* 108 C10
Melsungen, *Germany* 24 D5
Melton Mowbray, *U.K.* 14 E7
Melun, *France* 19 D9
Melut, *Sudan* 81 E3
Melville, *Canada* 103 C8
Melville, C., *Australia* 94 A3
Melville, L., *Canada* 105 B8
Melville B., *Australia* 94 A2
Melville I., *Australia* 92 B5
Melville I., *Canada* 98 B8
Melville Pen., *Canada* 101 B11
Mélykút, *Hungary* 28 D4
Memaliaj, *Albania* 44 F3
Memba, *Mozam.* 87 E5
Memboro, *Indonesia* 63 F5
Memel = Klaipėda, *Lithuania* .. 9 J19
Memel, *S. Africa* 89 D4
Memmingen, *Germany* 25 H6
Mempawah, *Indonesia* 62 D3
Memphis, *Egypt* 80 J7
Memphis, Mich., *U.S.A.* 116 D2
Memphis, Tenn., *U.S.A.* 113 H10
Memphis, Tex., *U.S.A.* 113 H4
Memphremagog, L., *U.S.A.* 117 B12
Mena, *Ukraine* 33 G7
Mena, *U.S.A.* 113 H7
Mena ➤, *Ethiopia* 81 F5
Menai Strait, *U.K.* 14 D3
Ménaka, *Mali* 83 B5
Menan = Chao Phraya ➤,
    Thailand 64 F3
Menarandra ➤, *Madag.* 89 D7
Menard, *U.S.A.* 113 K5
Menawashei, *Sudan* 81 E1
Mende, *France* 20 D7
Mendebo Mts., *Ethiopia* 81 F4
Mendeleyev Ridge, *Arctic* 4 B17
Menden, *Germany* 24 D3
Menderes, *Turkey* 47 C9
Mendez, *Mexico* 119 B5
Mendhar, *India* 69 C6
Mendi, *Ethiopia* 81 F4
Mendip Hills, *U.K.* 15 F5
Mendocino, *U.S.A.* 108 G2
Mendocino, C., *U.S.A.* 108 F1
Mendota, Calif., *U.S.A.* 110 J6
Mendota, Ill., *U.S.A.* 112 E10
Mendoyo, *Indonesia* 63 J17
Mendoza, *Argentina* 126 C2
Mendoza □, *Argentina* 126 C2
Mene Grande, *Venezuela* 124 B4
Menemen, *Turkey* 47 C9
Menen, *Belgium* 17 D3
Menfi, *Italy* 42 E5
Mengdingjie, *China* 58 F2
Mengeš, *Slovenia* 41 B11
Menggala, *Indonesia* 62 E3
Menghai, *China* 58 G3
Mengíbar, *Spain* 37 H7
Mengjin, *China* 56 G7
Mengla, *China* 58 G3
Menglian, *China* 58 F2
Mengshan, *China* 59 E8
Mengyin, *China* 57 G9
Mengzhe, *China* 58 F3
Mengzi, *China* 58 F4
Menihek, *Canada* 105 B6
Menihek L., *Canada* 105 B6
Menin = Menen, *Belgium* 17 D3
Menindee, *Australia* 95 E3
Menindee L., *Australia* 95 E3
Meningie, *Australia* 95 F2
Menjangan, Pulau, *Indonesia* .. 63 J17
Menlo Park, *U.S.A.* 110 H4
Menominee, *U.S.A.* 114 C2

Menominee ➤, *U.S.A.* 114 C2
Menomonie, *U.S.A.* 112 C9
Menongue, *Angola* 85 G3
Menorca, *Spain* 48 B11
Menorca ✈ (MAH), *Spain* 38 F9
Mentakab, *Malaysia* 65 L4
Mentawai, Kepulauan, *Indonesia* 62 E1
Menton, *France* 21 E11
Mentor, *U.S.A.* 116 E3
Menzies, *Australia* 93 E3
Meob B., *Namibia* 88 C1
Me'ona, *Israel* 74 B4
Meoqui, *Mexico* 118 B3
Mepaco, *Mozam.* 87 F3
Meppel, *Neths.* 17 B6
Meppen, *Germany* 24 C3
Mequinenza, *Spain* 38 D5
Mequinenza, Embalse de, *Spain* . 38 D5
Mer, *France* 18 E8
Merabéllou, Kólpos, *Greece* .. 49 D7
Merak, *Indonesia* 63 F12
Meramangye, L., *Australia* ... 93 E5
Meran = Merano, *Italy* 41 B8
Merano, *Italy* 41 B8
Merate, *Italy* 40 C6
Merauke, *Indonesia* 63 F10
Merbein, *Australia* 95 E3
Merbuk, Gunung, *Indonesia* ... 63 J17
Merca, *Somali Rep.* 75 G3
Mercantour △, *France* 21 D10
Mercato Saraceno, *Italy* 41 E9
Merced, *U.S.A.* 110 H6
Merced ➤, *U.S.A.* 110 H6
Merced Pk., *U.S.A.* 110 H7
Mercedes, Buenos Aires,
    Argentina 126 C4
Mercedes, Corrientes, *Argentina* . 126 B4
Mercedes, San Luis, *Argentina* . 126 C2
Mercedes, *Uruguay* 126 C4
Mercedes, *U.S.A.* 113 M6
Merceditas, *Chile* 126 B1
Mercer, *N.Z.* 91 G5
Mercer, *U.S.A.* 116 E4
Mercer Island, *U.S.A.* 110 C4
Mercury, *U.S.A.* 111 J11
Mercy, C., *Canada* 101 B13
Merdrignac, *France* 18 D4
Mere, *U.K.* 15 F5
Meredith, C., *Falk. Is.* 128 G4
Meredith, L., *U.S.A.* 113 H4
Merefa, *Ukraine* 33 H9
Merei, *Romania* 29 E11
Merga = Nukheila, *Sudan* 80 D2
Mergui, *Burma* 64 F2
Mergui Arch. = Myeik Kyunzu,
    Burma 65 G1
Méribel-les-Allues, *France* .. 21 C10
Meriç, *Turkey* 45 E10
Meriç ➤, *Turkey* 45 F10
Mérida, *Mexico* 119 C7
Mérida, *Spain* 37 G4
Mérida, *Venezuela* 124 B4
Mérida, Cord. de, *Venezuela* .. 124 B4
Meriden, *U.K.* 15 E6
Meriden, *U.S.A.* 117 E12
Meridian, Calif., *U.S.A.* 110 F5
Meridian, Idaho, *U.S.A.* 108 E5
Meridian, Miss., *U.S.A.* 115 J1
Mérignac, *France* 20 D3
Merinaghène, *Senegal* 82 B1
Merinda, *Australia* 94 C4
Mering, *Germany* 25 G6
Meringa, *Nigeria* 83 C7
Merir, *Pac. Oc.* 63 D8
Merirumã, *Brazil* 125 C8
Merkel, *U.S.A.* 113 J5
Mermaid Reef, *Australia* 92 C2
Merowe, *Sudan* 80 D3
Merredin, *Australia* 93 F2
Merrick, *U.K.* 13 F4
Merrickville, *Canada* 117 B9
Merrill, Oreg., *U.S.A.* 108 E3
Merrill, Wis., *U.S.A.* 112 C10
Merrimack ➤, *U.S.A.* 117 D14
Merriman, *U.S.A.* 112 D4
Merritt, *Canada* 102 C4
Merritt Island, *U.S.A.* 115 L5
Merriwa, *Australia* 95 E5
Merry I., *Canada* 104 A4
Merryville, *U.S.A.* 113 K8
Mersa Fatma, *Eritrea* 81 E5
Mersch, *Lux.* 17 E6
Merse ➤, *Italy* 41 E8
Mersea I., *U.K.* 15 F8
Merseburg, *Germany* 24 D7
Mersey ➤, *U.K.* 14 D4
Merseyside □, *U.K.* 14 D4
Mersin, *Turkey* 70 B2
Mersing, *Malaysia* 65 L4
Merta, *India* 68 F6
Merta Road, *India* 68 F5
Merthyr Tydfil, *U.K.* 15 F4
Merthyr Tydfil □, *U.K.* 15 F4
Mértola, *Portugal* 37 H3
Mertzon, *U.S.A.* 113 K4
Méru, *France* 19 C9
Meru, *Kenya* 86 B4
Meru, *Tanzania* 86 C4
Meru △, *Kenya* 86 B4
Merville, *France* 19 B9
Méry-sur-Seine, *France* 19 D10
Merzifon, *Turkey* 72 B6
Merzig, *Germany* 25 F2
Mesa, *U.S.A.* 109 K8
Mesa Verde △, *U.S.A.* 109 H9
Mesagne, *Italy* 43 B10
Mesanagrós, *Greece* 49 C9
Mesaoría, *Cyprus* 49 D12
Mesarás, Kólpos, *Greece* 49 D6
Meschede, *Germany* 24 D4
Mescit, *Turkey* 73 B9
Mesfinto, *Ethiopia* 81 E4

Mesgouez, L., *Canada* 104 B5
Meshchovsk, *Russia* 32 E8
Meshed = Mashhad, *Iran* 71 B8
Meshoppen, *U.S.A.* 117 E8
Meshra er Req, *Sudan* 81 F2
Mesilinka ➤, *Canada* 102 B4
Mesilla, *U.S.A.* 109 K10
Meslay-du-Maine, *France* 18 E6
Mesocco, *Switz.* 25 J5
Mesolóngion, *Greece* 46 C3
Mesopotamia = Al Jazirah, *Iraq* . 70 C5
Mesopotamia, *U.S.A.* 116 E4
Mesopótamon, *Greece* 46 B2
Mesoraca, *Italy* 43 C9
Mésou Volímais = Volímai,
    Greece 46 D2
Mesquite, *U.S.A.* 109 H6
Messaad, *Algeria* 78 B6
Messac, *France* 18 E5
Messalo ➤, *Mozam.* 87 E4
Méssaména, *Cameroon* 83 E7
Messeue, *Greece* 46 D3
Messina = Musina, *S. Africa* .. 89 C5
Messina, *Italy* 43 D8
Messina, Str. di, *Italy* 43 D8
Messíni, *Greece* 46 D4
Messínia □, *Greece* 46 D3
Messiniakós Kólpos, *Greece* .. 46 E4
Messkirch, *Germany* 25 H5
Messlingen, *Sweden* 10 B6
Messonghi, *Greece* 49 B3
Mesta ➤, *Bulgaria* 44 E7
Mestá, Ákra, *Greece* 47 C7
Mestanza, *Spain* 37 G6
Mestre, *Italy* 41 C9
Mesudiye, *Turkey* 72 B7
Meta ➤, *S. Amer.* 124 B5
Meta Incognita Pen., *Canada* .. 101 B13
Metabetchouan, *Canada* 105 C5
Metairie, *U.S.A.* 113 L9
Metaline Falls, *U.S.A.* 108 A5
Metán, *Argentina* 126 B3
Metangula, *Mozam.* 87 E3
Metauro ➤, *Italy* 41 E10
Metema, *Ethiopia* 81 E4
Metengobalame, *Mozam.* 87 E3
Méthana, *Greece* 46 D5
Methóni, *Greece* 46 E3
Methven, *N.Z.* 91 K3
Metil, *Mozam.* 87 F4
Metkovets, *Bulgaria* 44 C7
Metković, *Croatia* 41 E14
Metlakatla, *U.S.A.* 100 C6
Metlika, *Slovenia* 41 C12
Metropolis, *U.S.A.* 113 G10
Métsovon, *Greece* 46 B3
Metu, *Ethiopia* 81 F4
Metz, *France* 19 C13
Metzingen, *Germany* 25 G5
Meulaboh, *Indonesia* 62 D1
Meung-sur-Loire, *France* 19 E8
Meureudu, *Indonesia* 62 C1
Meurthe ➤, *France* 19 D13
Meurthe-et-Moselle □, *France* . 19 D13
Meuse □, *France* 19 C12
Meuse ➤, *Europe* 17 D5
Meuselwitz, *Germany* 24 D8
Mexia, *U.S.A.* 113 K6
Mexiana, I., *Brazil* 125 D9
Mexicali, *Mexico* 111 N11
Mexican Plateau, *Mexico* 98 G9
Mexican Water, *U.S.A.* 109 H9
México, *Mexico* 119 D5
Mexico, Maine, *U.S.A.* 117 B14
Mexico, Mo., *U.S.A.* 112 F9
Mexico, N.Y., *U.S.A.* 117 C8
México □, *Mexico* 119 D5
Mexico ■, *Cent. Amer.* 118 C4
Mexico, G. of, *Cent. Amer.* .. 119 C7
Mexico B., *U.S.A.* 117 C8
Meydān-e Naftūn, *Iran* 71 D6
Meydani, Ra's-e, *Iran* 71 E8
Meyenburg, *Germany* 24 B8
Meymac, *France* 20 C6
Meymaneh, *Afghan.* 66 B4
Meyrueis, *France* 20 D7
Meyssac, *France* 20 C5
Meyzieu, *France* 21 C8
Mezdra, *Bulgaria* 44 C7
Mèze, *France* 20 E7
Mezen, *Russia* 52 C5
Mezen ➤, *Russia* 52 C5
Mézenc, Mt., *France* 21 D8
Mezeș, Munții, *Romania* 28 C8
Mezha ➤, *Russia* 32 E6
Mezhdurechenskiy, *Russia* 52 D7
Mézidon-Canon, *France* 18 C6
Mézières-en-Brenne, *France* .. 20 B5
Mézin, *France* 20 D4
Mezin, *France* 20 D4
Mezőberény, *Hungary* 28 D6
Mezőfalva, *Hungary* 28 D3
Mezőhegyes, *Hungary* 28 D5
Mezőkövácsháza, *Hungary* 28 D5
Mezőkövesd, *Hungary* 28 C5
Mézos, *France* 20 D2
Mezőtúr, *Hungary* 28 C5
Mezquital, *Mexico* 118 C4
Mezquitic, *Mexico* 118 C4
Mfolozi ➤, *S. Africa* 89 D5
Mgeta, *Tanzania* 87 D4
Mglin, *Russia* 33 F7
Mhlaba Hills, *Zimbabwe* 87 F3
Mhow, *India* 68 H6
Miahuatlán, *Mexico* 119 D5
Miajadas, *Spain* 37 F5
Miami, Fla., *U.S.A.* 115 N5
Miami, Okla., *U.S.A.* 113 G7
Miami, Tex., *U.S.A.* 113 H4
Miami Beach, *U.S.A.* 115 N5

Mian Xian, *China* 56 H4
Mianchi, *China* 56 G6
Miāndarreh, *Iran* 71 C7
Miāndowāb, *Iran* 70 B5
Miandrivazo, *Madag.* 89 B8
Miāneh, *Iran* 70 B5
Mianning, *China* 58 C4
Mianwali, *Pakistan* 68 C4
Mianyang, *China* 58 B5
Mianzhu, *China* 58 B5
Miaoli, *Taiwan* 59 E13
Miarinarivo, Antananarivo,
    Madag. 89 B8
Miarinarivo, Toamasina, *Madag.* 89 B8
Miariravaratra, *Madag.* 89 C8
Miass, *Russia* 52 D7
Miasteczko Krajeńskie, *Poland* . 31 E4
Miastko, *Poland* 30 E3
Mica, *S. Africa* 89 C5
Micăsasa, *Romania* 29 D9
Michalovce, *Slovak Rep.* 27 C14
Michigan □, *U.S.A.* 114 C3
Michigan, L., *U.S.A.* 114 D2
Michigan City, *U.S.A.* 114 E2
Michika, *Nigeria* 83 C7
Michipicoten I., *Canada* 104 C2
Michoacan □, *Mexico* 118 D4
Michurin, *Bulgaria* 45 D11
Michurinsk, *Russia* 34 D5
Mico, Pta., *Nic.* 120 D3
Micoud, St. Lucia .... 121 f
Micronesia, *Pac. Oc.* 96 G7
Micronesia, Federated States
    of ■, *Pac. Oc.* 96 G7
Mid-Oceanic Ridge, *Ind. Oc.* .. 96 M1
Midai, *Indonesia* 62 D3
Midale, *Canada* 103 D8
Middelburg, *Neths.* 17 C3
Middelburg, Eastern Cape,
    S. Africa 88 E4
Middelburg, Mpumalanga,
    S. Africa 89 D4
Middelfart, *Denmark* 11 J3
Middelpos, *S. Africa* 88 E3
Middelwit, *S. Africa* 88 C4
Middle Alkali L., *U.S.A.* 108 F3
Middle Bass I., *U.S.A.* 116 E2
Middle East, *Asia* 50 F7
Middle Fork Feather ➤, *U.S.A.* . 110 F5
Middle I., *Australia* 93 F3
Middle Loup ➤, *U.S.A.* 112 E5
Middle Sackville, *Canada* 105 D7
Middleboro, *U.S.A.* 117 E14
Middleburg, Fla., *U.S.A.* 115 K5
Middleburg, Pa., *U.S.A.* 116 F7
Middleburgh, *U.S.A.* 117 D10
Middlebury, *U.S.A.* 117 B11
Middlemount, *Australia* 94 C4
Middleport, N.Y., *U.S.A.* 116 C6
Middleport, Ohio, *U.S.A.* 114 F4
Middlesboro, *U.S.A.* 115 G4
Middlesbrough, *U.K.* 14 C6
Middlesbrough □, *U.K.* 14 C6
Middlesex, *Belize* 120 C2
Middlesex, N.J., *U.S.A.* 117 F10
Middlesex, N.Y., *U.S.A.* 116 D7
Middleton, *Australia* 94 C3
Middleton, *Canada* 105 D6
Middleton Cr. ➤, *Australia* .. 94 C3
Middletown, *U.K.* 12 B5
Middletown, Calif., *U.S.A.* .. 110 G4
Middletown, Conn., *U.S.A.* ... 117 E12
Middletown, N.Y., *U.S.A.* 117 E10
Middletown, Ohio, *U.S.A.* 114 F3
Middletown, Pa., *U.S.A.* 117 F8
Midge Point, *Australia* 94 J6
Midhurst, *U.K.* 15 G7
Midī, *Yemen* 81 D5
Midi, Canal du ➤, *France* 20 E5
Midi d'Ossau, Pic du, *France* . 20 F3
Midi-Pyrénées □, *France* 20 E5
Midland, *Australia* 93 F2
Midland, *Canada* 116 B5
Midland, Calif., *U.S.A.* 111 M12
Midland, Mich., *U.S.A.* 114 D3
Midland, Pa., *U.S.A.* 116 F4
Midland, Tex., *U.S.A.* 113 K3
Midlands □, *Zimbabwe* 87 F2
Midleton, *Ireland* 12 E3
Midlothian, *U.S.A.* 113 J6
Midlothian □, *U.K.* 13 F5
Midongy, Tangorombohitr' i,
    Madag. 89 C8
Midongy Atsimo, *Madag.* 89 C8
Midou ➤, *France* 20 E3
Midouze ➤, *France* 20 E3
Midsayap, *Phil.* 61 H6
Midu, *China* 58 E3
Midway Is., *Pac. Oc.* 96 E10
Midway Wells, *U.S.A.* 111 N11
Midwest, *U.S.A.* 107 B9
Midwest, Wyo., *U.S.A.* 108 E10
Midwest City, *U.S.A.* 113 H6
Midyat, *Turkey* 70 B4
Midzŏr, *Bulgaria* 44 C7
Mie □, *Japan* 55 G8
Miechów, *Poland* 31 H7
Miedwie, Jezioro, *Poland* 31 E1
Międzychód, *Poland* 31 G1
Międzylesie, *Poland* 31 H3
Międzyrzec Podlaski, *Poland* .. 31 G9
Międzyrzecz, *Poland* 31 F2
Międzyzdroje, *Poland* 30 E1
Miejska Górka, *Poland* 31 G3
Miélan, *France* 20 E4
Mielec, *Poland* 31 H8
Mienga, *Angola* 88 B2
Miercurea-Ciuc, *Romania* 29 D10
Miercurea Sibiului, *Romania* .. 29 E8
Mieres, *Spain* 36 B5
Mieroszów, *Poland* 31 H3

Mieso, *Ethiopia* 81 F5
Mieszkowice, *Poland* 31 F1
Mifflintown, *U.S.A.* 116 F7
Mifraz Ḥefa, *Israel* 74 C4
Migennes, *France* 19 E10
Migliarino, *Italy* 41 D8
Migliarino-San Rossore-
    Massaciuccoli △, *Italy* . 40 E7
Miguel Alemán, Presa, *Mexico* . 119 D5
Miguelturra, *Spain* 37 G7
Mihăileni, *Romania* 29 C11
Mihăilești, *Romania* 29 F10
Mihailovca, *Moldova* 29 D13
Mihalgazi, *Turkey* 47 A12
Mihaliçcik, *Turkey* 72 C4
Mihara, *Japan* 55 G6
Mihești de Cîmpie, *Romania* .. 29 D9
Mijas, *Spain* 37 J6
Mikese, *Tanzania* 86 D4
Mikha-Tskhakaya = Senaki,
    Georgia 35 J6
Mikhailovka = Mykhaylivka,
    Ukraine 33 J8
Mikhaylov, *Russia* 32 E10
Mikhaylovgrad = Montana,
    Bulgaria 44 C7
Mikhaylovka, *Russia* 34 E6
Mikhnevo, *Russia* 32 E9
Mikínai, *Greece* 46 D4
Mikkeli, *Finland* 9 F22
Mikkwa ➤, *Canada* 102 B6
Mikniya, *Sudan* 81 D3
Mikołajki, *Poland* 30 E8
Míkonos, *Greece* 47 D7
Mikrí Préspa, Límni, *Greece* .. 44 F5
Mikrón Dhérion, *Greece* 45 E10
Mikstat, *Poland* 31 G4
Mikumi, *Tanzania* 86 D4
Mikumi △, *Tanzania* 86 D4
Milaca, *U.S.A.* 112 C8
Milagro, *Ecuador* 124 D3
Milagros, *Phil.* 61 E5
Milan = Milano, *Italy* 40 C6
Milan, Mo., *U.S.A.* 112 E8
Milan, Tenn., *U.S.A.* 115 H1
Milange, *Mozam.* 87 F4
Milano, *Italy* 40 C6
Milano Linate ✈ (LIN), *Italy* . 40 C6
Milanoa, *Madag.* 89 A8
Milâs, *Turkey* 47 D9
Mílatos, *Greece* 49 D7
Milazzo, *Italy* 43 D8
Milbank, *U.S.A.* 112 C6
Milbanke Sd., *Canada* 102 C3
Milden, *Canada* 103 C7
Mildenhall, *U.K.* 15 E8
Mildmay, *Canada* 116 B3
Mildura, *Australia* 95 E3
Mile, *China* 58 E4
Miléai, *Greece* 46 B5
Miles, *Australia* 95 D5
Miles City, *U.S.A.* 112 B2
Milești, *Moldova* 29 C13
Milestone, *Canada* 103 D8
Mileto, *Italy* 43 D9
Miletto, Mte., *Italy* 43 A7
Miletus, *Turkey* 47 D9
Milevsko, *Czech Rep.* 26 B7
Milford, Calif., *U.S.A.* 110 E6
Milford, Conn., *U.S.A.* 117 E11
Milford, Del., *U.S.A.* 114 F8
Milford, Mass., *U.S.A.* 117 D13
Milford, N.H., *U.S.A.* 117 D13
Milford, Pa., *U.S.A.* 117 E10
Milford, Utah, *U.S.A.* 109 G7
Milford Haven, *U.K.* 15 F2
Milford Sd., *N.Z.* 91 L1
Milford Sound, *N.Z.* 91 L1
Milḩ, Baḩr al = Razzāzah,
    Buḩayrat ar, *Iraq* 70 C4
Milicz, *Poland* 31 G4
Milikapiti, *Australia* 92 B5
Miling, *Australia* 93 F2
Militello in Val di Catánia, *Italy* . 43 E7
Milk ➤, *U.S.A.* 108 B10
Milk, Wadi el ➤, *Sudan* 80 D3
Milk River, *Canada* 102 D6
Mill I., *Antarctica* 5 C8
Mill Valley, *U.S.A.* 110 H4
Millárs ➤, *Spain* 38 F4
Millau, *France* 20 D7
Millbridge, *Canada* 116 B7
Millbrook, *Canada* 116 B6
Millbrook, *U.S.A.* 117 E11
Mille Lacs, L. des, *Canada* .. 104 C1
Mille Lacs L., *U.S.A.* 112 B8
Milledgeville, *U.S.A.* 115 J4
Millen, *U.S.A.* 115 J5
Millennium I. = Caroline I.,
    Kiribati 97 H12
Miller, *U.S.A.* 112 C5
Millerovo, *Russia* 35 F5
Millersburg, Ohio, *U.S.A.* ... 116 F3
Millersburg, Pa., *U.S.A.* 116 F8
Millerton, *U.S.A.* 117 E11
Millerton L., *U.S.A.* 110 J7
Millet, St. Lucia .... 121 f
Millevaches, Plateau de, *France* . 20 C6
Millheim, *U.S.A.* 116 F7
Millicent, *Australia* 95 F3
Millington, *U.S.A.* 113 H10
Millinocket, *U.S.A.* 115 C11
Millmerran, *Australia* 95 D5
Millom, *U.K.* 14 C4
Mills L., *Canada* 102 A5
Millsboro, *U.S.A.* 116 G5
Millstream-Chichester △,
    Australia 92 D2
Milltown Malbay, *Ireland* 12 D2
Millville, *U.S.A.* 114 F8
Millville, Pa., *U.S.A.* 117 E8

Millwood L., *U.S.A.* 113 J8
Milna, *Croatia* 41 E13
Milne ➤, *Australia* 94 C2
Milo, *U.S.A.* 115 C11
Mílos, *Greece* 46 E6
Miłosław, *Poland* 31 F4
Milot, *Albania* 44 E3
Milparinka, *Australia* 95 D3
Miltenberg, *Germany* 25 F5
Milton, *N.S., Canada* 105 D7
Milton, *Ont., Canada* 116 C5
Milton, *N.Z.* 91 M2
Milton, *Calif., U.S.A.* 110 G6
Milton, *Fla., U.S.A.* 115 K2
Milton, *Pa., U.S.A.* 116 F8
Milton, *Vt., U.S.A.* 117 B11
Milton-Freewater, *U.S.A.* ... 108 D4
Milton Keynes, *U.K.* 15 E7
Milton Keynes □, *U.K.* 15 E7
Miluo, *China* 59 C9
Milverton, *Canada* 116 C4
Milwaukee, *U.S.A.* 114 D2
Milwaukee Deep, *Atl. Oc.* .. 121 C6
Milwaukie, *U.S.A.* 110 E4
Mim, *Ghana* 82 D4
Mimizan, *France* 20 D2
Mimoň, *Czech Rep.* 26 A7
Min Jiang ➤, *Fujian, China* . 59 E12
Min Jiang ➤, *Sichuan, China* 58 C5
Min Xian, *China* 56 G3
Mina Pirquitas, *Argentina* . 126 A2
Mīnā Su'ud, *Si. Arabia* 71 D6
Mīnā'al Aḥmadī, *Kuwait* 71 D6
Minago ➤, *Canada* 103 C9
Minaki, *Canada* 103 D10
Minamata, *Japan* 55 H5
Minami-Arapusa △, *Japan* ... 55 G9
Minami-Tori-Shima, *Pac. Oc.* 96 E7
Minas, *Uruguay* 127 C4
Minas, Sierra de las, *Guatemala* 120 C2
Minas Basin, *Canada* 105 C7
Minas de Riotinto, *Spain* .. 37 H4
Minas Gerais □, *Brazil* 125 G9
Minatitlán, *Mexico* 119 D6
Minbu, *Burma* 67 J19
Minchinabad, *Pakistan* 68 D5
Mincio ➤, *Italy* 40 C7
Minčol, *Slovak Rep.* 27 B13
Mindanao, *Phil.* 61 H6
Mindanao Sea = Bohol Sea, *Phil.* 63 C6
Mindanao Trench, *Pac. Oc.* . 61 F7
Mindel ➤, *Germany* 25 G6
Mindelheim, *Germany* 25 G6
Minden, *Canada* 116 B6
Minden, *Germany* 24 C4
Minden, *La., U.S.A.* 113 J8
Minden, *Nev., U.S.A.* 110 G7
Mindiptana, *Indonesia* 63 F10
Mindoro, *Phil.* 61 E4
Mindoro Str., *Phil.* 61 E4
Mine, *Japan* 55 G5
Minehead, *U.K.* 15 F4
Mineola, *N.Y., U.S.A.* 117 F11
Mineola, *Tex., U.S.A.* 113 J7
Mineral King, *U.S.A.* 110 J8
Mineral Wells, *U.S.A.* 113 J5
Mineralnyye Vody, *Russia* . 35 H6
Minersville, *U.S.A.* 117 F8
Minerva, *U.S.A.* 116 F3
Minervino Murge, *Italy* ... 43 A9
Minetto, *U.S.A.* 117 C8
Mingäçevir, *Azerbaijan* ... 35 K8
Mingäçevir Su Anbarı, *Azerbaijan* 35 K8
Mingan, *Canada* 105 B7
Mingechaur = Mingäçevir, *Azerbaijan* 35 K8
Mingechaurskoye Vdkhr. = Mingäçevir Su Anbarı, *Azerbaijan* 35 K8
Mingela, *Australia* 94 B4
Mingenew, *Australia* 93 E2
Mingera Cr. ➤, *Australia* . 94 C2
Minggang, *China* 59 A10
Mingguang, *China* 59 A11
Mingin, *Burma* 67 H19
Mingir, *Moldova* 29 D13
Minglanilla, *Spain* 39 F3
Minglun, *China* 58 E7
Mingo Junction, *U.S.A.* ... 116 F4
Mingorria, *Spain* 36 E6
Mingshan, *China* 58 B4
Mingteke Daban = Mintaka Pass, *Pakistan* 69 A6
Mingxi, *China* 59 D11
Mingyuegue, *China* 57 C15
Minho = Miño ➤, *Spain* 36 D2
Minhou, *China* 59 E12
Minićevo, *Serbia & M.* 28 G7
Minidoka, *U.S.A.* 108 E7
Minigwal, L., *Australia* .. 93 E3
Minilya ➤, *Australia* 93 D1
Minilya Roadhouse, *Australia* 93 D1
Minipi L., *Canada* 105 B7
Mink L., *Canada* 102 A5
Minkammen, *Sudan* 81 F3
Minna, *Nigeria* 83 D6
Minneapolis, *Kans., U.S.A.* 112 F6
Minneapolis, *Minn., U.S.A.* 112 C8
Minnedosa, *Canada* 103 C9
Minnesota □, *U.S.A.* 112 B8
Minnesota ➤, *U.S.A.* 112 C8
Minnewaukan, *U.S.A.* 112 A5
Minnipa, *Australia* 95 E2
Minnitaki L., *Canada* 104 C1
Mino, *Japan* 55 G8
Miño ➤, *Spain* 36 B2
Miño ➤, *Spain* 36 D2
Minoa, *Greece* 47 F7
Minorca = Menorca, *Spain* . 48 B11
Minot, *U.S.A.* 112 A4
Minqin, *China* 56 E2
Minqing, *China* 59 D12

Minsen, *Germany* 24 B3
Minsk, *Belarus* 32 F4
Mińsk Mazowiecki, *Poland* . 31 F8
Mintabie, *Australia* 95 D1
Mintaka Pass, *Pakistan* ... 69 A6
Minto, *Canada* 105 C6
Minto, L., *Canada* 104 A5
Minton, *Canada* 103 D8
Minturn, *U.S.A.* 108 G10
Minturno, *Italy* 42 A6
Minūf, *Egypt* 80 H7
Minusinsk, *Russia* 53 D10
Minutang, *India* 67 E20
Minya el Qamh, *Egypt* 80 H7
Minya Konka = Gongga Shan, *China* 58 C3
Mionica, *Bos.-H.* 28 F3
Mionica, *Serbia & M.* 44 B4
Miquelon, *Canada* 104 C4
Miquelon, *St-P. & M.* 105 C8
Mir, *Niger* 83 C7
Mīr Kūh, *Iran* 71 E8
Mīr Shahdād, *Iran* 71 E8
Mira, *Italy* 41 C9
Mira, *Portugal* 36 E2
Mira ➤, *Portugal* 37 H2
Mira por vos Cay, *Bahamas* 121 B5
Mirabella Eclano, *Italy* .. 43 A7
Mirador-Río Azul △, *Guatemala* 120 C2
Miraj, *India* 66 L9
Miram Shah, *Pakistan* 68 C4
Miramar, *Argentina* 126 D4
Miramar, *Mozam.* 89 C6
Miramas, *France* 21 E8
Mirambeau, *France* 20 C3
Miramichi, *Canada* 105 C6
Miramichi B., *Canada* 105 C7
Miramont-de-Guyenne, *France* 20 D4
Miranda, *Brazil* 125 H7
Miranda ➤, *Brazil* 124 G7
Miranda de Ebro, *Spain* ... 38 C2
Miranda do Corvo, *Portugal* 36 E2
Miranda do Douro, *Portugal* 36 D4
Mirande, *France* 20 E4
Mirandela, *Portugal* 36 D3
Mirándola, *Italy* 40 D8
Mirandópolis, *Brazil* 127 A5
Mirango, *Malawi* 87 E3
Mirani, *Australia* 94 K6
Mirano, *Italy* 41 C9
Miras, *Albania* 44 F4
Mirassol, *Brazil* 127 A6
Mirbāṭ, *Oman* 75 D5
Mirear, *Egypt* 80 C4
Mirebeau, *France* 18 F7
Mirebeau-sur-Bèze, *France* 19 E12
Mirecourt, *France* 19 D13
Mirgorod = Myrhorod, *Ukraine* 33 H7
Miri, *Malaysia* 62 D4
Miriam Vale, *Australia* ... 94 C5
Miribel, *France* 19 G11
Mirim, L., *S. Amer.* 127 C5
Mirnyy, *Russia* 53 C12
Miroč, *Serbia & M.* 44 B6
Mirokhan, *Pakistan* 68 F3
Mirond L., *Canada* 103 B8
Mirosławiec, *Poland* 30 E3
Mirpur, *Pakistan* 69 C5
Mirpur Batoro, *Pakistan* .. 68 G3
Mirpur Bibiwari, *Pakistan* 68 E2
Mirpur Khas, *Pakistan* 68 G3
Mirpur Sakro, *Pakistan* ... 68 G2
Mirria, *Niger* 83 C6
Mirsk, *Poland* 31 H2
Mirtağ, *Turkey* 70 B4
Miryang, *S. Korea* 57 G15
Mirzaani, *Georgia* 35 K8
Mirzapur, *India* 69 G10
Mirzapur-cum-Vindhyachal = Mirzapur, *India* 69 G10
Misantla, *Mexico* 119 D5
Misawa, *Japan* 54 D10
Miscou I., *Canada* 105 C7
Mish'āb, Ra's al, *Si. Arabia* 71 D6
Mishan, *China* 60 B8
Mishawaka, *U.S.A.* 114 E2
Mishbih, Gebel, *Egypt* 80 C3
Mishima, *Japan* 55 G9
Misión, *Mexico* 111 N10
Misiones □, *Argentina* 127 B5
Misiones □, *Paraguay* 126 B4
Miskah, *Si. Arabia* 70 E4
Miskitos, Cayos, *Nic.* 120 D3
Miskolc, *Hungary* 28 B5
Misoke, *Dem. Rep. of the Congo* 86 C2
Misool, *Indonesia* 63 E8
Mişrātah, *Libya* 79 B9
Missanabie, *Canada* 104 C3
Missinaibi ➤, *Canada* 104 B3
Missinaibi L., *Canada* 104 C3
Mission, *Canada* 102 D4
Mission, *S. Dak., U.S.A.* . 112 D4
Mission, *Tex., U.S.A.* 113 M5
Mission Beach, *Australia* . 94 B4
Mission Viejo, *U.S.A.* 111 M9
Missirah, *Senegal* 82 C1
Missisa L., *Canada* 104 B2
Mississagi ➤, *Canada* 104 C3
Mississauga, *Canada* 116 C5
Mississippi □, *U.S.A.* 113 J10
Mississippi ➤, *U.S.A.* 113 L10
Mississippi L., *Canada* ... 117 A8
Mississippi River Delta, *U.S.A.* 113 L9
Mississippi Sd., *U.S.A.* .. 113 K10
Missoula, *U.S.A.* 108 C7
Missouri □, *U.S.A.* 112 F8
Missouri ➤, *U.S.A.* 112 F9
Missouri City, *U.S.A.* 113 L7
Missouri Valley, *U.S.A.* .. 112 E7
Mist, *U.S.A.* 110 E3
Mistassibi ➤, *Canada* 105 B5

Mistassini ➤, *Canada* 105 C5
Mistassini, L., *Canada* ... 104 B5
Mistastin L., *Canada* 105 A7
Mistelbach, *Austria* 27 C9
Misterbianco, *Italy* 43 E8
Mistinibi, L., *Canada* 105 A7
Mistissini, *Canada* 105 C5
Mistretta, *Italy* 43 E7
Misty L., *Canada* 103 B8
Misurata = Miṣrātah, *Libya* 79 B9
Mît Ghamr, *Egypt* 80 H7
Mitatib, *Sudan* 81 D4
Mitchell, *Australia* 95 D4
Mitchell, *Canada* 116 C3
Mitchell, *Nebr., U.S.A.* .. 112 E3
Mitchell, *Oreg., U.S.A.* .. 108 D3
Mitchell, *S. Dak., U.S.A.* 112 D6
Mitchell ➤, *Australia* 94 B3
Mitchell, Mt., *U.S.A.* 115 H4
Mitchell and Alice Rivers △, *Australia* 94 B3
Mitchell Ranges, *Australia* 94 A2
Mitchelstown, *Ireland* 12 D3
Mitha Tiwana, *Pakistan* ... 68 C5
Mithi, *Pakistan* 68 G3
Mithrao, *Pakistan* 68 F3
Míthimna, *Greece* 47 B8
Mitilíni, *Greece* 47 B8
Mitilinoí, *Greece* 47 D8
Mito, *Japan* 55 F10
Mitrofanovka, *Russia* 33 H10
Mitrovica = Kosovska Mitrovica, *Serbia & M.* 44 D4
Mitsinjo, *Madag.* 89 B8
Mitsiwa, *Eritrea* 81 D4
Mitsiwa Channel, *Eritrea* . 81 D5
Mitsukaidō, *Japan* 55 F9
Mittagong, *Australia* 95 E5
Mittelberg, *Austria* 26 D3
Mittelfranken □, *Germany* . 25 F6
Mittellandkanal ➤, *Germany* 24 C4
Mittenwalde, *Germany* 24 C9
Mittersill, *Austria* 26 D5
Mitterteich, *Germany* 25 F8
Mittimatalik = Pond Inlet, *Canada* 101 A12
Mittweida, *Germany* 24 E8
Mitú, *Colombia* 124 C4
Mitumba, *Tanzania* 86 D3
Mitumba, Mts., *Dem. Rep. of the Congo* 86 D2
Mitwaba, *Dem. Rep. of the Congo* 87 D2
Mityana, *Uganda* 86 B3
Mixteco ➤, *Mexico* 119 D5
Miyagi □, *Japan* 54 E10
Miyah, W. el -, *Egypt* 80 C3
Miyah, W. el -, *Syria* 70 C3
Miyake-Jima, *Japan* 55 G9
Miyako, *Japan* 54 E10
Miyako-Jima, *Japan* 55 M2
Miyako-Rettō, *Japan* 55 M2
Miyakonojō, *Japan* 55 J5
Miyani, *India* 68 J3
Miyanoura-Dake, *Japan* 55 J5
Miyazaki, *Japan* 55 J5
Miyazaki □, *Japan* 55 J5
Miyazu, *Japan* 55 G7
Miyet, Bahr el = Dead Sea, *Asia* 74 D4
Miyi, *China* 58 D4
Miyoshi, *Japan* 55 G6
Miyun, *China* 56 D9
Miyun Shuiku, *China* 57 D9
Mizan Teferi, *Ethiopia* ... 81 F4
Mizdah, *Libya* 79 B8
Mizen Hd., *Cork, Ireland* . 12 E2
Mizen Hd., *Wicklow, Ireland* 12 D5
Mizhhirya, *Ukraine* 29 B8
Mizhi, *China* 56 F6
Mizil, *Romania* 29 F11
Mizoram □, *India* 67 H18
Mizpe Ramon, *Israel* 74 E3
Mizuho, *Antarctica* 5 D5
Mizusawa, *Japan* 54 E10
Mjällby, *Sweden* 11 H8
Mjöbäck, *Sweden* 11 G6
Mjölby, *Sweden* 11 F9
Mjörn, *Sweden* 11 G6
Mjøsa, *Norway* 9 F14
Mkata, *Tanzania* 86 D4
Mkhaya △, *Swaziland* 89 D5
Mkokotoni, *Tanzania* 86 D4
Mkomazi, *Tanzania* 86 C4
Mkomazi △, *Tanzania* 86 C3
Mkomazi ➤, *S. Africa* 89 E5
Mkulwe, *Tanzania* 87 D3
Mkumbi, Ras, *Tanzania* 86 D4
Mkushi, *Zambia* 87 E2
Mkushi River, *Zambia* 87 E2
Mkuze, *S. Africa* 89 D5
Mkuze △, *S. Africa* 89 D4
Mladá Boleslav, *Czech Rep.* 26 A7
Mladenovac, *Serbia & M.* .. 44 B4
Mlala Hills, *Tanzania* 86 D3
Mlange = Mulanje, *Malawi* . 87 F4
Mlanje, Pic, *Malawi* 85 H7
Mlava ➤, *Serbia & M.* 44 B5
Mława, *Poland* 31 E7
Mlawula △, *Swaziland* 89 D5
Mlinište, *Bos.-H.* 41 D13
Mljet, *Croatia* 41 F14
Mljet △, *Croatia* 41 F14
Mljetski Kanal, *Croatia* .. 41 F14
Młynary, *Poland* 30 D6
Mmabatho, *S. Africa* 88 D4
Mme, *Cameroon* 83 D7
Mnichovo Hradiště, *Czech Rep.* 26 A7
Mo i Rana, *Norway* 8 C16
Moa, *Cuba* 121 B4
Moa, *Indonesia* 63 F7
Moa ➤, *S. Leone* 82 D2
Moab, *U.S.A.* 109 G9
Moala, *Fiji* 91 D8
Moama, *Australia* 95 F3

Moamba, *Mozam.* 89 D5
Moapa, *U.S.A.* 111 J12
Moate, *Ireland* 12 C4
Moba, *Dem. Rep. of the Congo* 86 D2
Mobārakābād, *Iran* 71 D7
Mobaye, *C.A.R.* 84 D4
Mobayi, *Dem. Rep. of the Congo* 84 D4
Moberley Lake, *Canada* 102 B4
Moberly, *U.S.A.* 112 F8
Mobile, *U.S.A.* 115 K1
Mobile B., *U.S.A.* 115 K2
Mobridge, *U.S.A.* 112 C4
Moc Chau, *Vietnam* 64 B5
Moc Hoa, *Vietnam* 65 G5
Mocabe Kasari, *Dem. Rep. of the Congo* 87 D2
Moçambique, *Mozam.* 87 F5
Mocanaqua, *U.S.A.* 117 E8
Mochima △, *Venezuela* 121 D7
Mochudi, *Botswana* 88 C4
Mocimboa da Praia, *Mozam.* 87 E5
Mociu, *Romania* 29 D9
Möckeln, *Sweden* 11 H8
Mockfjärd, *Sweden* 10 D8
Moclips, *U.S.A.* 110 C2
Mocoa, *Colombia* 124 C3
Mococa, *Brazil* 127 A6
Mocorito, *Mexico* 118 B3
Moctezuma, *Mexico* 118 B3
Moctezuma ➤, *Mexico* 119 C5
Mocuba, *Mozam.* 87 F4
Mocúzari, Presa, *Mexico* .. 118 B3
Modane, *France* 21 C10
Modasa, *India* 68 H5
Modder ➤, *S. Africa* 88 D3
Modderrivier, *S. Africa* .. 88 D3
Módena, *Italy* 40 D7
Modena, *U.S.A.* 109 H7
Modesto, *U.S.A.* 110 H6
Módica, *Italy* 43 F7
Modimolle, *S. Africa* 89 C4
Mödling, *Austria* 27 C9
Modo, *Sudan* 81 F3
Modra, *Slovak Rep.* 27 C10
Modriča, *Bos.-H.* 28 F3
Moe, *Australia* 95 F4
Moebase, *Mozam.* 87 F4
Moëlan-sur-Mer, *France* ... 18 E3
Moengo, *Suriname* 125 B8
Moffat, *U.K.* 13 F5
Moga, *India* 68 D6
Mogadishu = Muqdisho, *Somali Rep.* 75 G4
Mogador = Essaouira, *Morocco* 78 B4
Mogadouro, *Portugal* 36 D4
Mogalakwena ➤, *S. Africa* . 89 C4
Mogami-Gawa ➤, *Japan* 54 E10
Mogán, *Canary Is.* 48 G4
Mogaung, *Burma* 67 G20
Mogente = Moixent, *Spain* . 39 G4
Mogho, *Ethiopia* 81 G5
Mogi das Cruzes, *Brazil* .. 127 A6
Mogi-Guaçu ➤, *Brazil* 127 A6
Mogi-Mirim, *Brazil* 127 A6
Mogielnica, *Poland* 31 G7
Mogige, *Ethiopia* 81 F4
Mogilev = Mahilyow, *Belarus* 32 F6
Mogilev-Podolskiy = Mohyliv-Podilskyy, *Ukraine* 29 B12
Mogilno, *Poland* 31 F4
Mogincual, *Mozam.* 87 F5
Mogliano Véneto, *Italy* ... 41 C9
Mogocha, *Russia* 53 D12
Mogok, *Burma* 67 H20
Mogollon Rim, *U.S.A.* 109 J8
Mógoro, *Italy* 42 C1
Moguer, *Spain* 37 H4
Mogumber, *Australia* 93 F2
Mohács, *Hungary* 28 E3
Mohales Hoek, *Lesotho* 88 E4
Mohall, *U.S.A.* 112 A4
Moḥammadābād, *Iran* 71 B8
Mohammedia, *Morocco* 78 B4
Mohana ➤, *India* 69 G11
Mohanlalganj, *India* 69 F9
Mohave, L., *U.S.A.* 111 K12
Mohawk ➤, *U.S.A.* 117 D11
Moheda, *Sweden* 11 G8
Mohenjodaro, *Pakistan* 68 F3
Moher, Cliffs of, *Ireland* 12 D2
Mohicanville Reservoir, *U.S.A.* 116 F3
Möhne ➤, *Germany* 24 D3
Mohoro, *Tanzania* 86 D4
Mohyliv-Podilskyy, *Ukraine* 29 B12
Moia, *Sudan* 81 F2
Moidart, L., *U.K.* 13 E3
Moinești, *Romania* 29 D11
Moira ➤, *Canada* 116 B7
Moires, *Greece* 49 D6
Moisaküla, *Estonia* 9 G21
Moisie, *Canada* 105 B6
Moisie ➤, *Canada* 105 B6
Moissac, *France* 20 D5
Moïta, *Portugal* 37 G2
Moixent, *Spain* 39 G4
Möja, *Sweden* 10 E12
Mojácar, *Spain* 39 H3
Mojados, *Spain* 36 D6
Mojave, *U.S.A.* 111 K8
Mojave △, *U.S.A.* 111 K11
Mojave Desert, *U.S.A.* 111 L10
Mojiang, *China* 58 F3
Mojo, *Ethiopia* 81 F4
Mojo, *Bolivia* 126 A2
Mojo, *Ethiopia* 81 F4
Mojokerto, *Indonesia* 63 G15
Mokai, *N.Z.* 91 H5

Mokambo, *Dem. Rep. of the Congo* 87 E2
Mokameh, *India* 69 G11
Mokau, *N.Z.* 91 H5
Mokelumne ➤, *U.S.A.* 110 G5
Mokelumne Hill, *U.S.A.* ... 110 G6
Mokhós, *Greece* 49 D7
Mokhotlong, *Lesotho* 89 D4
Möklinta, *Sweden* 10 D10
Mokhotlong, *India* 67 F19
Mokolo, *Cameroon* 83 C7
Mokolo ➤, *S. Africa* 89 C4
Mokopane, *S. Africa* 89 C4
Mokp'o, *S. Korea* 57 G14
Mokra Gora, *Serbia & M.* .. 44 D4
Mokronog, *Slovenia* 41 C12
Moksha ➤, *Russia* 34 C6
Mokshan, *Russia* 34 D7
Mokwa, *Nigeria* 83 D6
Mol, *Belgium* 17 C5
Mola di Bari, *Italy* 43 A10
Molale, *Ethiopia* 81 E4
Moláoi, *Greece* 46 E5
Molara, *Italy* 42 B2
Molat, *Croatia* 41 D11
Molchanovo, *Russia* 52 D9
Mold, *U.K.* 14 D4
Moldava nad Bodvou, *Slovak Rep.* 27 C14
Moldavia = Moldova ■, *Europe* 29 C13
Moldavia, *Romania* 29 D12
Molde, *Norway* 8 E12
Moldova ■, *Europe* 29 C13
Moldova Nouă, *Romania* 28 F6
Moldoveanu, Vf., *Romania* . 29 E9
Moldoviţa, *Romania* 29 C10
Mole ➤, *Ghana* 83 D4
Mole ➤, *U.K.* 15 F7
Mole Creek, *Australia* 95 G4
Molepolole, *Botswana* 88 C4
Molfetta, *Italy* 43 A9
Molina de Aragón, *Spain* .. 38 E3
Molina de Segura, *Spain* .. 39 G3
Moline, *U.S.A.* 112 E9
Molinella, *Italy* 41 D8
Molinos, *Argentina* 126 B2
Moliro, *Dem. Rep. of the Congo* 86 D3
Moliterno, *Italy* 43 B8
Molkom, *Sweden* 10 E7
Mölle, *Sweden* 11 H6
Molledo, *Spain* 36 B6
Mollendo, *Peru* 124 G4
Mollerin, L., *Australia* .. 93 F2
Mollerussa, *Spain* 38 D5
Mollina, *Spain* 37 H6
Mölln, *Germany* 24 B6
Mölltorp, *Sweden* 11 F8
Mölndal, *Sweden* 11 G6
Mölnlycke, *Sweden* 11 G6
Molochansk, *Ukraine* 33 J8
Molochnoye, Ozero, *Ukraine* 33 J8
Molodechno = Maladzyechna, *Belarus* 32 E4
Molodove, *Ukraine* 29 D14
Molokai, *U.S.A.* 106 H16
Molong, *Australia* 95 E4
Molopo ➤, *Africa* 88 D3
Mólos, *Greece* 46 C4
Molsheim, *France* 19 D14
Molson L., *Canada* 103 C9
Molteno, *S. Africa* 88 E4
Molu, *Indonesia* 63 F8
Molucca Sea, *Indonesia* ... 63 E6
Moluccas = Maluku, *Indonesia* 63 E7
Moma, *Dem. Rep. of the Congo* 86 C1
Moma, *Mozam.* 87 F4
Mombasa, *Kenya* 86 C4
Mombetsu, *Japan* 54 B11
Mombuey, *Spain* 36 C4
Momchilgrad, *Bulgaria* 45 E9
Momi, *Dem. Rep. of the Congo* 86 C2
Mompós, *Colombia* 124 B4
Møn, *Denmark* 11 K6
Mon □, *Burma* 67 L20
Mona, Canal de la = Mona Passage, *W. Indies* 121 C6
Mona, Isla, *Puerto Rico* .. 121 C6
Mona, Pta., *Costa Rica* ... 120 E3
Mona Passage, *W. Indies* .. 121 C6
Monaca, *U.S.A.* 116 F4
Monaco ■, *Europe* 21 E11
Monadhliath Mts., *U.K.* ... 13 D4
Monadnock, Mt., *U.S.A.* ... 117 D12
Monaghan, *Ireland* 12 B5
Monaghan □, *Ireland* 12 B5
Monahans, *U.S.A.* 113 K3
Monapo, *Mozam.* 87 E5
Monar, L., *U.K.* 13 D3
Monarch Mt., *Canada* 102 C3
Monashee Mts., *Canada* 102 C5
Monasterevin, *Ireland* 12 C4
Monastir = Bitola, *Macedonia* 44 E5
Moncada, *Phil.* 61 D4
Moncalieri, *Italy* 40 D4
Moncalvo, *Italy* 40 C5
Monção, *Portugal* 36 C2
Moncarapacho, *Portugal* ... 37 H3
Moncão, *Portugal* 36 C2
Moncayo, Sierra del, *Spain* 38 D3
Mönchengladbach, *Germany* . 24 D2
Monchique, *Portugal* 37 H2
Moncks Corner, *U.S.A.* 115 J5
Monclova, *Mexico* 118 B4
Moncontour, *France* 18 D4
Moncton, *Canada* 105 C7
Mondariz, *Spain* 36 C2
Mondego ➤, *Portugal* 36 E2
Mondego, C., *Portugal* 36 E2
Mondeville, *France* 18 C6
Mondo, *Indonesia* 63 E6
Mondolfo, *Italy* 41 E10
Mondoñedo, *Spain* 36 B3
Mondovì, *Italy* 40 D4
Mondragon, *Phil.* 61 E6

Mondragone, *Italy* 42 A6
Mondrain I., *Australia* 93 F3
Moneague, *Jamaica* .... 120 a
Monemvasía, *Greece* 46 E5
Monessen, *U.S.A.* 116 F5
Monesterio, *Spain* 37 G4
Monestier-de-Clermont, *France* .. 21 D9
Monett, *U.S.A.* 113 G8
Moneymore, *U.K.* 12 B5
Monfalcone, *Italy* 41 C10
Monflanquin, *France* 20 D4
Monforte, *Portugal* 37 F3
Monforte de Lemos, *Spain* 36 C3
Mong Cai, *Vietnam* 64 B6
Mong Hsu, *Burma* 58 G2
Mong Kung, *Burma* 67 J20
Mong Nai, *Burma* 67 J20
Mong Pawk, *Burma* 67 H21
Mong Ping, *Burma* 58 G2
Mong Ton, *Burma* 67 J21
Mong Wa, *Burma* 67 J22
Mong Yai, *Burma* 67 H21
Mongalla, *Sudan* 81 F3
Mongers, L., *Australia* 93 E2
Monghyr = Munger, *India* 69 G12
Mongibello = Etna, *Italy* 43 E7
Mongo, *Chad* 79 F9
Mongo →, *S. Leone* 82 D2
Mongolia ■, *Asia* 53 E10
Mongolia, Plateau of, *Asia* ... 50 E14
Mongonu, *Nigeria* 83 C7
Mongu, *Zambia* 85 H4
Mõngua, *Angola* 88 B2
Monifieth, *U.K.* 13 E6
Monistrol-sur-Loire, *France* .. 21 C8
Monkey Bay, *Malawi* 87 E4
Monkey Mia, *Australia* 93 E1
Monkey River Town, *Belize* 119 D7
Mońki, *Poland* 30 E9
Monkoto, *Dem. Rep. of the Congo* 84 E4
Monkton, *Canada* 116 C3
Monmouth, *U.K.* 15 F5
Monmouth, *Ill., U.S.A.* 112 E9
Monmouth, *Oreg., U.S.A.* 108 D2
Monmouthshire □, *U.K.* 15 F5
Mono L., *U.S.A.* 110 H7
Monolith, *U.S.A.* 111 K8
Monólithos, *Greece* 49 C9
Monongahela, *U.S.A.* 116 F5
Monópoli, *Italy* 43 B10
Monor, *Hungary* 28 C4
Monos I., *Trin. & Tob.* 125 K15
Monóvar, *Spain* 39 G4
Monreal del Campo, *Spain* 38 E3
Monreale, *Italy* 42 D6
Monroe, *Ga., U.S.A.* 115 J4
Monroe, *La., U.S.A.* 113 J8
Monroe, *Mich., U.S.A.* 114 E4
Monroe, *N.C., U.S.A.* 115 H5
Monroe, *N.Y., U.S.A.* 117 E10
Monroe, *Utah, U.S.A.* 109 G7
Monroe, *Wash., U.S.A.* 110 C5
Monroe, *Wis., U.S.A.* 112 D10
Monroe City, *U.S.A.* 112 F9
Monroeton, *U.S.A.* 117 E8
Monroeville, *Ala., U.S.A.* ... 115 K2
Monroeville, *Pa., U.S.A.* 116 F5
Monrovia, *Liberia* 82 D2
Mons, *Belgium* 17 D3
Møns Klint, *Denmark* 11 K6
Monsaraz, *Portugal* 37 G3
Monse, *Indonesia* 63 E6
Monségur, *France* 20 D4
Monsélice, *Italy* 41 C8
Mönsterås, *Sweden* 11 G10
Mont Cenis, Col du, *France* ... 21 C10
Mont-de-Marsan, *France* 20 E3
Mont-Joli, *Canada* 105 C6
Mont-Laurier, *Canada* 104 C4
Mont-Louis, *Canada* 105 C6
Mont Peko △, *Ivory C.* 82 D3
Mont-roig del Camp, *Spain* 38 D5
Mont-St-Michel, Le, *France* ... 18 D5
Mont Sangbe △, *Ivory C.* 82 D3
Mont-Tremblant △, *Canada* 104 C5
Montabaur, *Germany* 24 E3
Montagnac, *France* 20 E7
Montagnana, *Italy* 41 C8
Montagne d'Ambre △, *Madag.* .. 89 A8
Montagne de Reims △, *France* .. 19 C11
Montagu, *S. Africa* 88 E3
Montagu I., *Antarctica* 5 B1
Montague, *Canada* 105 C7
Montague, I., *Mexico* 118 A2
Montague Ra., *Australia* 93 E2
Montague Sd., *Australia* 92 B4
Montaigu, *France* 18 F5
Montalbán, *Spain* 38 E4
Montalbano Iónico, *Italy* 43 B9
Montalbo, *Spain* 38 F2
Montalcino, *Italy* 41 E8
Montalegre, *Portugal* 36 D3
Montalto, *Italy* 43 D8
Montalto di Castro, *Italy* ... 41 F8
Montalto Uffugo, *Italy* 43 C9
Montalvo, *U.S.A.* 111 L7
Montamarta, *Spain* 36 D5
Montana, *Bulgaria* 44 C7
Montaña, *Peru* 124 E4
Montana □, *Bulgaria* 44 C7
Montana □, *U.S.A.* 108 C9
Montaña Clara, I., *Canary Is.* . 48 E6
Montañas de Malaga △, *Spain* .. 37 J6
Montánchez, *Spain* 37 F4
Montargil, *Portugal* 37 F2
Montargis, *France* 19 E9
Montauban, *France* 20 D5
Montauk, *U.S.A.* 117 E13
Montauk Pt., *U.S.A.* 117 E13
Montbard, *France* 19 E11
Montbarrey, *France* 19 E12
Montbéliard, *France* 19 E13

Montblanc, *Spain* 38 D6
Montbrison, *France* 21 C8
Montcalm, Pic de, *France* 20 F5
Montceau-les-Mines, *France* ... 19 F11
Montcenis, *France* 21 B8
Montclair, *U.S.A.* 117 F10
Montcornet, *France* 19 C11
Montcuq, *France* 20 D5
Montdidier, *France* 19 C9
Monte Albán, *Mexico* 119 D5
Monte Alegre, *Brazil* 125 D8
Monte Azul, *Brazil* 125 G10
Monte-Carlo, *Monaco* 21 E11
Monte Caseros, *Argentina* 126 C4
Monte Comán, *Argentina* 126 C2
Monte Cristi, *Dom. Rep.* 121 C5
Monte Cucco △, *Italy* 41 E9
Monte Lindo →, *Paraguay* 126 A4
Monte Patria, *Chile* 126 C1
Monte Quemado, *Argentina* 126 B3
Monte Redondo, *Portugal* 36 F2
Monte Rio, *U.S.A.* 110 G4
Monte San Giovanni Campano,
   Italy 42 A6
Monte San Savino, *Italy* 41 E8
Monte Sant' Ángelo, *Italy* ... 41 G12
Monte Santu, C. ci, *Italy* ... 42 B2
Monte Sibillini △, *Italy* 41 F10
Monte Subasio △, *Italy* 41 E9
Monte Vista, *U.S.A.* 109 H10
Monteagudo, *Argentina* 127 B5
Montealegre del Castillo, *Spain* 39 G3
Montebello, *Canada* 104 C5
Montebello Iónico, *Italy* 43 E8
Montebello Is., *Australia* ... 92 D2
Montebelluna, *Italy* 41 C9
Montebourg, *France* 18 C5
Montecastrilli, *Italy* 41 F9
Montecatini Terme, *Italy* 40 E7
Montecito, *U.S.A.* 111 L7
Montecristo, *Italy* 40 F7
Montefalco, *Italy* 41 F9
Montefiascone, *Italy* 41 F9
Montefrío, *Spain* 37 H7
Montegiórgio, *Italy* 41 E10
Montego Bay, *Jamaica* .... 120 a
Montehermoso, *Spain* 36 E4
Montejícar, *Spain* 37 H7
Montélimar, *France* 21 D8
Montella, *Italy* 43 B8
Montellano, *Spain* 37 J5
Montello, *U.S.A.* 112 D10
Montemor-o-Novo, *Portugal* ... 37 G2
Montemor-o-Velho, *Portugal* .. 36 E2
Montemorelos, *Mexico* 119 B5
Montendre, *France* 20 C3
Montenegro, *Brazil* 127 B5
Montenegro □, *Serbia & M.* ... 44 D3
Montenero di Bisáccia, *Italy* . 41 G11
Montepuez, *Mozam.* 87 E4
Montepuez →, *Mozam.* 87 E5
Montepulciano, *Italy* 41 E8
Montereale, *Italy* 41 F10
Montereau-Faut-Yonne, *France* . 19 D9
Monterey, *U.S.A.* 110 J5
Monterey B., *U.S.A.* 110 J5
Montería, *Colombia* 124 B3
Monteros, *Argentina* 126 B2
Monterotondo, *Italy* 41 F9
Monterrey, *Mexico* 118 B4
Montes Azules △, *Mexico* 119 D6
Montes Claros, *Brazil* 125 G10
Montesano, *U.S.A.* 110 D3
Montesano sulla Marcellana, *Italy* 43 B8
Montesárchio, *Italy* 43 A7
Montescaglioso, *Italy* 43 B9
Montesilvano, *Italy* 41 F11
Montesinho, △, *Portugal* 36 D4
Montevarchi, *Italy* 41 E8
Montevideo, *Uruguay* 127 C4
Montevideo, *U.S.A.* 112 C7
Montezuma, *U.S.A.* 112 E8
Montezuma Castle △, *U.S.A.* .. 109 J8
Montfaucon, *France* 18 E5
Montfaucon-d'Argonne, *France* . 19 C12
Montfaucon-en-Velay, *France* .. 21 C8
Montfort-le-Gesnois, *France* .. 18 D7
Montfort-sur-Meu, *France* 18 D5
Montgenèvre, *France* 21 D10
Montgomery, *U.K.* 15 E4
Montgomery, *Ala., U.S.A.* 115 J2
Montgomery, *Pa., U.S.A.* 116 E8
Montgomery, *W. Va., U.S.A.* .. 114 F5
Montgomery City, *U.S.A.* 112 F9
Montguyon, *France* 20 C3
Monthermé, *France* 19 C11
Monthois, *France* 19 C11
Monthey, *Switz.* 25 J2
Monti, *Italy* 42 B2
Monti Lucrétili □, *Italy* 41 F9
Monti Picentini □, *Italy* 43 B8
Monti Simbruini □, *Italy* 41 G10
Monticelli d'Ongina, *Italy* .. 40 C6
Monticello, *Ark., U.S.A.* 113 J9
Monticello, *Ind., U.S.A.* 114 E2
Monticello, *Iowa, U.S.A.* 112 D9
Monticello, *Ky., U.S.A.* 115 G3
Monticello, *Minn., U.S.A.* ... 112 C8
Monticello, *Miss., U.S.A.* ... 113 K9
Monticello, *N.Y., U.S.A.* 117 E10
Monticello, *Utah, U.S.A.* 109 H9
Montichiari, *Italy* 40 C7
Montier-en-Der, *France* 19 D11
Montignac, *France* 20 C5
Montigny-les-Metz, *France* ... 19 C13
Montigny-sur-Aube, *France* ... 19 E11
Montijo, *Portugal* 37 G2
Montijo, *Spain* 37 G4
Montilla, *Spain* 37 H6
Montivilliers, *France* 18 C7

Montluçon, *France* 19 F9
Montmagny, *Canada* 105 C5
Montmarault, *France* 19 F9
Montmartre, *Canada* 103 C8
Montmédy, *France* 19 C12
Montmélian, *France* 21 C10
Montmirail, *France* 19 D10
Montmoreau-St-Cybard, *France* . 20 C4
Montmorillon, *France* 20 B4
Montmort-Lucy, *France* 19 D10
Monto, *Australia* 94 C5
Montoire-sur-le-Loir, *France* . 18 E7
Montóro al Vomano, *Italy* 41 F10
Montoro, *Spain* 37 G6
Montour Falls, *U.S.A.* 116 D8
Montoursville, *U.S.A.* 116 E8
Montpelier, *Idaho, U.S.A.* ... 108 E8
Montpelier, *Vt., U.S.A.* 117 B12
Montpellier, *France* 20 E7
Montpezat-de-Quercy, *France* .. 20 D5
Montpon-Ménestérol, *France* .. 20 D4
Montréal, *Canada* 117 A11
Montréal, *Aude, France* 20 E6
Montréal, *Gers, France* 20 E4
Montreal →, *Canada* 104 C3
Montreal L., *Canada* 103 C7
Montreal Lake, *Canada* 103 C7
Montredon-Labessonnié, *France* 20 E6
Montrésor, *France* 18 E8
Montret, *France* 19 F12
Montreuil, *Pas-de-Calais, France* 19 B8
Montreuil, *Seine-St-Denis, France* 19 D9
Montreuil-Bellay, *France* 18 E6
Montreux, *Switz.* 25 J2
Montrevel-en-Bresse, *France* .. 19 F12
Montrichard, *France* 18 E8
Montrose, *U.K.* 13 E6
Montrose, *Colo., U.S.A.* 109 G10
Montrose, *Pa., U.S.A.* 117 E9
Monts, Pte. des, *Canada* 105 C6
Montsalvy, *France* 20 D6
Montsant, Serra de, *Spain* ... 38 D6
Montsauche-les-Settons, *France* 19 E11
Montsec, Serra del, *Spain* ... 38 C5
Montseny □, *Spain* 38 D2
Montserrat, *Spain* 38 D6
Montserrat ☑, *W. Indies* 121 C7
Montuenga, *Spain* 36 D6
Montuiri, *Spain* 48 B9
Monywa, *Burma* 67 H19
Monza, *Italy* 40 C6
Monze, *Zambia* 87 F2
Monze, C., *Pakistan* 68 G2
Monzón, *Spain* 38 D5
Mooers, *U.S.A.* 117 B11
Mooi →, *S. Africa* 89 D5
Mooi River, *S. Africa* 89 D4
Moonah →, *Australia* 94 C2
Moonda, L., *Australia* 94 D3
Moonie, *Australia* 95 D5
Moonie →, *Australia* 95 D4
Moonta, *Australia* 95 E2
Moora, *Australia* 93 F2
Moorcroft, *U.S.A.* 112 C2
Moore →, *Australia* 93 F2
Moore, L., *Australia* 93 E2
Moore Park, *Australia* 94 C5
Moore River △, *Australia* ... 93 F2
Moorefield, *U.S.A.* 114 F6
Moores Res., *U.S.A.* 117 B13
Moorfoot Hills, *U.K.* 13 F5
Moorhead, *U.S.A.* 112 B6
Moormerland, *Germany* 24 B3
Moorpark, *U.S.A.* 111 L8
Moorreesburg, *S. Africa* 88 E2
Moorrinya △, *Australia* 94 C3
Moosburg, *Germany* 25 G7
Moose →, *Canada* 104 B3
Moose →, *U.S.A.* 117 C9
Moose Creek, *Canada* 117 A10
Moose Factory, *Canada* 104 B3
Moose Jaw, *Canada* 103 C7
Moose Jaw →, *Canada* 103 C7
Moose Lake, *Canada* 112 B8
Moose Mountain △, *Canada* ... 103 D8
Moosehead L., *U.S.A.* 115 C11
Mooselookmeguntic L., *U.S.A.* . 115 C10
Moosilauke, Mt., *U.S.A.* 117 B13
Moosomin, *Canada* 103 C8
Moosonee, *Canada* 104 B3
Moosup, *U.S.A.* 117 E13
Mopane, *S. Africa* 89 C4
Mopeia Velha, *Mozam.* 87 F4
Mopipi, *Botswana* 88 C3
Mopoi, *C.A.R.* 86 A2
Mopti, *Mali* 82 C4
Moqatta, *Sudan* 81 E4
Moqor, *Afghan.* 68 C2
Moquegua, *Peru* 124 G4
Mór, *Hungary* 28 C3
Mora, *Cameroon* 83 C7
Móra, *Portugal* 37 G2
Mora, *Spain* 37 F7
Mora, *Sweden* 10 C8
Mora, *Minn., U.S.A.* 112 C8
Mora, *N. Mex., U.S.A.* 109 J11
Mora →, *U.S.A.* 113 H2
Mora de Rubielos, *Spain* 38 E4
Mòra d'Ebre, *Spain* 38 D5
Mòra la Nova, *Spain* 38 D5
Morača →, *Serbia & M.* 44 D3
Moradabad, *India* 69 E8
Morafenobe, *Madag.* 89 B7
Morąg, *Poland* 30 E6
Moral de Calatrava, *Spain* ... 37 G7
Moraleja, *Spain* 36 E4
Moramanga, *Madag.* 89 B8
Moran, *Kans., U.S.A.* 113 G7
Moran, *Wyo., U.S.A.* 108 E8
Moranbah, *Australia* 94 C4
Morano Cálabro, *Italy* 43 C9

Morant Bay, *Jamaica* .... 120 a
Morant Cays, *Jamaica* 120 C4
Morant Pt., *Jamaica* .... 120 a
Morar, *India* 68 F8
Morar, L., *U.K.* 13 E3
Moratalla, *Spain* 39 G3
Moratuwa, *Sri Lanka* 66 R11
Morava →, *Slovak Rep.* 27 C9
Moravia, *U.S.A.* 117 D8
Moravian Hts. = Českomoravská
   Vrchovina, *Czech Rep.* 26 B8
Moravica →, *Serbia & M.* ... 44 C4
Moravița, *Romania* 28 E6
Moravské Třebová, *Czech Rep.* . 27 B9
Moravské Budějovice, *Czech Rep.* 26 B8
Morawa, *Australia* 93 E2
Morawhanna, *Guyana* 124 B7
Moray □, *U.K.* 13 D5
Moray Firth, *U.K.* 13 D5
Morbach, *Germany* 25 F3
Morbegno, *Italy* 40 B6
Morbi, *India* 68 H4
Morbihan □, *France* 18 E4
Mörbylånga, *Sweden* 11 H10
Morcenx, *France* 20 D3
Morcone, *Italy* 43 A7
Mordelles, *France* 18 D5
Morden, *Canada* 103 D9
Mordoğan, *Turkey* 47 C8
Mordovian Republic =
   Mordvinia □, *Russia* 34 C7
Mordovo, *Russia* 34 D5
Mordvinia □, *Russia* 34 C7
Mordy, *Poland* 31 F9
Morea, *Greece* 6 H10
Moreau →, *U.S.A.* 112 C4
Morecambe, *U.K.* 14 C5
Morecambe B., *U.K.* 14 C5
Moree, *Australia* 95 D4
Morehead, *U.S.A.* 114 F4
Morehead City, *U.S.A.* 115 H7
Morel →, *India* 68 F7
Morelia, *Mexico* 118 D4
Morella, *Australia* 94 C3
Morella, *Spain* 38 E4
Morelos, *Mexico* 118 B3
Morelos □, *Mexico* 119 D5
Morena, *India* 68 F8
Morena, Sierra, *Spain* 37 G7
Moreni, *Romania* 29 F10
Moreno Valley, *U.S.A.* 111 M10
Moresby I., *Canada* 102 C2
Morestel, *France* 21 C9
Moreton I., *Australia* 95 D5
Moreton Island △, *Australia* . 95 D5
Moreuil, *France* 19 C9
Morey, *Spain* 48 B10
Morez, *France* 19 F13
Morgan, *U.S.A.* 108 F8
Morgan City, *U.S.A.* 113 L9
Morgan Hill, *U.S.A.* 110 H5
Morganfield, *U.S.A.* 114 G2
Morganton, *U.S.A.* 115 H5
Morgantown, *U.S.A.* 114 F6
Morgenzon, *S. Africa* 89 D4
Morges, *Switz.* 25 J2
Morghak, *Iran* 71 D8
Morgongåva, *Sweden* 10 E10
Morhange, *France* 19 D13
Morhar →, *India* 69 G11
Mori, *Italy* 40 C7
Mori, *Japan* 54 C10
Moriarty, *U.S.A.* 109 J10
Moribaya, *Guinea* 82 D3
Morice L., *Canada* 102 C3
Moriki, *Nigeria* 83 C6
Morinville, *Canada* 102 C6
Morioka, *Japan* 54 E10
Moris, *Mexico* 118 B3
Morlaàs, *France* 20 E3
Morlaix, *France* 18 D3
Mörlunda, *Sweden* 11 G9
Mormanno, *Italy* 43 C8
Mormant, *France* 19 D9
Mornington, *Australia* 95 F4
Mornington, I., *Chile* 128 F1
Mornington I., *Australia* ... 94 B2
Mórnos →, *Greece* 46 C3
Moro, *Pakistan* 68 F2
Moro, *Sudan* 81 E3
Moro →, *Pakistan* 68 E2
Moro G., *Phil.* 61 H5
Morocco ■, *N. Afr.* 78 B4
Morogoro, *Tanzania* 86 D4
Morogoro □, *Tanzania* 86 D4
Moroleón, *Mexico* 118 C4
Morombe, *Madag.* 89 C7
Moron, *Argentina* 126 C4
Morón, *Cuba* 120 B4
Morón de Almazán, *Spain* 38 D2
Morón de la Frontera, *Spain* . 37 H5
Morona →, *Peru* 124 D3
Morondava, *Madag.* 89 C7
Morondo, *Ivory C.* 82 D3
Morongo Valley, *U.S.A.* 111 L10
Moroni, *Comoros Is.* 77 H8
Moroni, *U.S.A.* 108 G8
Moronou, *Ivory C.* 82 D4
Morotai, *Indonesia* 63 D7
Moroto, *Uganda* 86 B3
Moroto, Mt., *Uganda* 86 B3
Morozov, *Bulgaria* 45 D9
Morozovsk, *Russia* 35 F5
Morpeth, *U.K.* 13 B6
Morphou, *Cyprus* 49 D11
Morphou Bay, *Cyprus* 49 D11
Morrilton, *U.S.A.* 113 H8
Morrinhos, *Brazil* 125 G9
Morrinsville, *N.Z.* 91 G5
Morris, *Canada* 103 D9
Morris, *Ill., U.S.A.* 112 E10

Morris, *Minn., U.S.A.* 112 C7
Morris, *N.Y., U.S.A.* 117 D9
Morris, *Pa., U.S.A.* 116 E7
Morris, Mt., *Australia* 93 E5
Morris Jesup, Kap, *Greenland* . 4 A5
Morrisburg, *Canada* 117 B9
Morristown, *Ariz., U.S.A.* ... 109 K7
Morristown, *N.J., U.S.A.* ... 117 F10
Morristown, *N.Y., U.S.A.* ... 117 B9
Morristown, *Tenn., U.S.A.* .. 115 G4
Morrisville, *N.Y., U.S.A.* .. 117 D9
Morrisville, *Pa., U.S.A.* ... 117 F10
Morrisville, *Vt., U.S.A.* ... 117 B12
Morro, Pta., *Chile* 126 B1
Morro Bay, *U.S.A.* 110 K6
Morro del Jable, *Canary Is.* . 48 F5
Morro Jable, Pta. de, *Canary Is.* 48 F5
Morrocoy △, *Venezuela* 121 D6
Morrosquillo, G. de, *Colombia* 120 E4
Mörrum, *Sweden* 11 H8
Morrumbene, *Mozam.* 89 C6
Mörrumsån →, *Sweden* 11 H8
Mors, *Denmark* 11 H2
Morshansk, *Russia* 34 D5
Mörsil, *Sweden* 10 A7
Mortagne →, *France* 19 D13
Mortagne-au-Perche, *France* .. 18 D7
Mortagne-sur-Gironde, *France* . 20 C3
Mortagne-sur-Sèvre, *France* .. 18 F6
Mortain, *France* 18 D6
Mortara, *Italy* 40 C5
Morteau, *France* 19 E13
Morteros, *Argentina* 126 C3
Mortlach, *Canada* 103 C7
Mortlake, *Australia* 95 F3
Morton, *Tex., U.S.A.* 113 J3
Morton, *Wash., U.S.A.* 110 D4
Moruga, *Trin. & Tob.* 125 K15
Morundah, *Australia* 95 E4
Moruya, *Australia* 95 F5
Morvan, *France* 19 E11
Morvan □, *France* 19 E11
Morven, *Australia* 95 D4
Morvern, *U.K.* 13 E3
Morwell, *Australia* 95 F4
Moryń, *Poland* 31 F1
Morzine, *France* 19 F13
Mosalsk, *Russia* 32 E4
Mosbach, *Germany* 25 F5
Moščenice, *Croatia* 41 C11
Mosciano Sant' Ángelo, *Italy* . 41 F10
Moscos Is., *Burma* 64 E1
Moscow = Moskva, *Russia* 32 E9
Moscow, *Idaho, U.S.A.* 108 C5
Moscow, *Pa., U.S.A.* 117 E9
Mosel →, *Europe* 19 B14
Moselle = Mosel →, *Europe* . 19 B14
Moselle □, *France* 19 D13
Moses Lake, *U.S.A.* 108 C4
Mosgiel, *N.Z.* 91 L3
Moshaweng →, *S. Africa* 88 D3
Moshi, *Tanzania* 86 C4
Moshupa, *Botswana* 88 C4
Mosina, *Poland* 31 F3
Mosjøen, *Norway* 8 D15
Moskenesøya, *Norway* 8 C15
Moskenstraumen, *Norway* 8 C15
Moskva, *Russia* 32 E9
Moskva →, *Russia* 32 E10
Moslavačka Gora, *Croatia* ... 41 C13
Mosomane, *Botswana* 88 C4
Mosonmagyaróvár, *Hungary* ... 28 C2
Mošorin, *Serbia & M.* 28 E5
Mospino, *Ukraine* 33 J9
Mosquera, *Colombia* 124 C3
Mosquero, *U.S.A.* 113 H3
Mosqueruela, *Spain* 38 E4
Mosquitia, *Honduras* 120 C3
Mosquito Coast = Mosquitia,
   Honduras 120 C3
Mosquito Creek L., *U.S.A.* .. 116 E4
Mosquito L., *Canada* 103 A8
Mosquitos, G. de los, *Panama* . 120 E3
Moss, *Norway* 9 G14
Moss Vale, *Australia* 95 E5
Mossbank, *Canada* 103 D7
Mossburn, *N.Z.* 91 L2
Mosselbaai, *S. Africa* 88 E3
Mossendjo, *Congo* 84 E2
Mossgiel, *Australia* 95 E3
Mossingen, *Germany* 25 G5
Mossman, *Australia* 94 B4
Mossoró, *Brazil* 125 E11
Mossuril, *Mozam.* 87 E5
Most, *Czech Rep.* 26 A6
Mosta, *Malta* 49 D1
Mostaganem, *Algeria* 78 A6
Mostar, *Bos.-H.* 28 G2
Mostardas, *Brazil* 127 C5
Mostiska = Mostyska, *Ukraine* 31 J10
Móstoles, *Spain* 36 E7
Mosty = Masty, *Belarus* 32 F3
Mostyska, *Ukraine* 31 J10
Mosul = Al Mawşil, *Iraq* 70 B4
Mosûlpo, S. *Korea* 57 H14
Mota, *Ethiopia* 81 E4
Mota del Cuervo, *Spain* 39 F2
Mota del Marqués, *Spain* 36 D5
Motagua →, *Guatemala* 120 C2
Motala, *Sweden* 11 F9
Motaze, *Mozam.* 89 C5
Moţca, *Romania* 29 C11
Moth, *India* 69 G8
Motherwell, *U.K.* 13 F5
Motihari, *India* 69 F11
Motilla del Palancar, *Spain* . 39 F3
Motnik, *Slovenia* 41 B11
Motovun, *Croatia* 41 C10
Motozintla de Mendoza, *Mexico* 119 D6
Motril, *Spain* 37 J7
Motru, *Romania* 28 F7
Motru →, *Romania* 29 F8

Mott, U.S.A. 112 B3
Móttola, Italy 43 B10
Motueka, N.Z. 91 J4
Motueka →, N.Z. 91 J4
Motul, Mexico 119 C7
Mouchalagane →, Canada 105 B6
Moúdhros, Greece 47 B7
Mouding, China 58 E3
Moudjeria, Mauritania 82 B2
Moudon, Switz. 25 J2
Mouila, Gabon 84 E2
Moulamein, Australia 95 F3
Moule à Chique, C., St. Lucia 121 f
Moulianalá, Greece 49 D7
Moulins, France 19 F10
Moulmein, Burma 67 L20
Moulouya, O. →, Morocco 78 B5
Moultrie, U.S.A. 115 K4
Moultrie, L., U.S.A. 115 J5
Mound City, Mo., U.S.A. 112 E7
Mound City, S. Dak., U.S.A. 112 C4
Moúnda, Ákra, Greece 46 C2
Moundou, Chad 79 G9
Moundsville, U.S.A. 116 G4
Moung, Cambodia 64 F4
Mount Airy, U.S.A. 115 G5
Mount Albert, Canada 116 B5
Mount Aspiring △, N.Z. 91 L2
Mount Barker, S. Austral., Australia 95 F2
Mount Barker, W. Austral., Australia 93 F2
Mount Brydges, Canada 116 D3
Mount Burr, Australia 95 F3
Mount Carmel = Ha Karmel △, Israel 74 C4
Mount Carmel, Ill., U.S.A. 114 F2
Mount Carmel, Pa., U.S.A. 117 F8
Mount Charleston, U.S.A. 111 J11
Mount Clemens, U.S.A. 116 D2
Mount Coolon, Australia 94 C4
Mount Darwin, Zimbabwe 87 F3
Mount Desert I., U.S.A. 115 C11
Mount Dora, U.S.A. 115 L5
Mount Edziza △, Canada 102 B2
Mount Elgon △, E. Afr. 86 B3
Mount Field △, Australia 95 G4
Mount Fletcher, S. Africa 89 E4
Mount Forest, Canada 116 C4
Mount Gambier, Australia 95 F3
Mount Garnet, Australia 94 B4
Mount Holly, U.S.A. 117 G10
Mount Holly Springs, U.S.A. 116 F7
Mount Hope, N.S.W., Australia 95 E4
Mount Hope, S. Austral., Australia 95 E2
Mount Isa, Australia 94 C2
Mount Jewett, U.S.A. 116 E6
Mount Kaputar △, Australia 95 E5
Mount Kenya △, Kenya 86 C4
Mount Kilimanjaro △, Tanzania 86 C4
Mount Kisco, U.S.A. 117 E11
Mount Laguna, U.S.A. 111 N10
Mount Larcom, Australia 94 C5
Mount Lofty Ra., Australia 95 E2
Mount Magnet, Australia 93 E2
Mount Maunganui, N.Z. 91 G6
Mount Molloy, Australia 94 B4
Mount Morgan, Australia 94 C5
Mount Morris, U.S.A. 116 D7
Mount Pearl, Canada 105 C9
Mount Penn, U.S.A. 117 F9
Mount Perry, Australia 95 D5
Mount Pleasant, Iowa, U.S.A. 112 E9
Mount Pleasant, Mich., U.S.A. 114 D3
Mount Pleasant, Pa., U.S.A. 116 F5
Mount Pleasant, S.C., U.S.A. 115 J6
Mount Pleasant, Tenn., U.S.A. 115 H2
Mount Pleasant, Tex., U.S.A. 113 J7
Mount Pleasant, Utah, U.S.A. 108 G8
Mount Pocono, U.S.A. 117 E9
Mount Rainier △, U.S.A. 110 D5
Mount Revelstoke △, Canada 102 C5
Mount Robson △, Canada 102 C5
Mount St. Helens △, U.S.A. 110 D4
Mount Selinda, Zimbabwe 89 C5
Mount Shasta, U.S.A. 108 F2
Mount Signal, U.S.A. 111 N11
Mount Sterling, Ill., U.S.A. 112 F9
Mount Sterling, Ky., U.S.A. 114 F4
Mount Surprise, Australia 94 B3
Mount Union, U.S.A. 116 F7
Mount Upton, U.S.A. 117 D9
Mount Vernon, Ill., U.S.A. 114 F1
Mount Vernon, Ind., U.S.A. 112 F10
Mount Vernon, N.Y., U.S.A. 117 F11
Mount Vernon, Ohio, U.S.A. 116 F2
Mount Vernon, Wash., U.S.A. 110 B4
Mount William △, Australia 95 E4
Mountain Ash, U.K. 15 F4
Mountain Center, U.S.A. 111 M10
Mountain City, Nev., U.S.A. 108 F6
Mountain City, Tenn., U.S.A. 115 G5
Mountain Dale, U.S.A. 117 E10
Mountain Grove, U.S.A. 113 G8
Mountain Home, Ark., U.S.A. 113 G8
Mountain Home, Idaho, U.S.A. 108 E6
Mountain Iron, U.S.A. 112 B8
Mountain Pass, U.S.A. 111 K11
Mountain View, Ark., U.S.A. 113 H8
Mountain View, Calif., U.S.A. 110 H4
Mountain View, Hawaii, U.S.A. 106 J17
Mountain Village, U.S.A. 88 E4
Mountainair, U.S.A. 109 J10
Mountlake Terrace, U.S.A. 110 C4
Mountmellick, Ireland 12 C4
Mountrath, Ireland 12 D4
Moura, Australia 94 C4
Moura, Brazil 124 D6
Moura, Portugal 37 G3
Mourão, Portugal 37 G3
Mourdi, Dépression du, Chad 79 E10

Mourdiah, Mali 82 C3
Mourenx, France 20 E3
Mouri, Ghana 83 D4
Mourilyan, Australia 94 B4
Mourmelon-le-Grand, France 19 C11
Mourne →, U.K. 12 B4
Mourne Mts., U.K. 12 B5
Mourniaí, Greece 49 D6
Mournies = Mourniaí, Greece 49 D6
Mouscron, Belgium 17 D3
Moussoro, Chad 79 F9
Mouthe, France 19 F13
Moutier, Switz. 25 H3
Moûtiers, France 21 C10
Moutong, Indonesia 63 D6
Mouy, France 19 C9
Mouzáki, Greece 46 B3
Mouzon, France 19 C12
Movas, Mexico 118 B3
Moville, Ireland 12 A4
Mowandjum, Australia 92 C3
Moy →, Ireland 12 B2
Moyale, Kenya 81 G4
Moyamba, S. Leone 82 D2
Moyen Atlas, Morocco 78 B4
Moyne, L. le, Canada 105 A6
Moyo, Indonesia 62 F5
Moyobamba, Peru 124 E3
Moyyero →, Russia 53 C11
Moyynty, Kazakhstan 52 E8
Mozambique = Moçambique, Mozam. 87 F5
Mozambique ■, Africa 87 F4
Mozambique Chan., Africa 89 B7
Mozdok, Russia 35 J7
Mozdūrān, Iran 71 B9
Mozhaysk, Russia 32 E9
Mozhga, Russia 34 B11
Mozhnābād, Iran 71 C9
Mozirje, Slovenia 41 B11
Mozyr = Mazyr, Belarus 33 F5
Mpanda, Tanzania 86 D3
Mpésoba, Mali 82 C3
Mphoengs, Zimbabwe 89 C4
Mpika, Zambia 87 E3
Mpulungu, Zambia 87 D3
Mpumalanga, S. Africa 89 D5
Mpumalanga □, S. Africa 89 D5
Mpwapwa, Tanzania 86 D4
Mqanduli, S. Africa 89 E4
Mqinvartsveri = Kazbek, Russia 35 J7
Mrągowo, Poland 30 E8
Mramor, Serbia & M. 44 C5
Mrkonjić Grad, Bos.-H. 28 F2
Mrkopalj, Croatia 41 C11
Mrocza, Poland 31 E4
Msambansovu, Zimbabwe 87 F3
M'sila →, Algeria 78 A6
Msoro, Zambia 87 E3
Msta →, Russia 32 C6
Mstislavl = Mstsislaw, Belarus 32 E6
Mstsislaw, Belarus 32 E6
Mszana Dolna, Poland 31 J7
Mszczonów, Poland 31 G7
Mtama, Tanzania 87 E4
Mtamvuna →, S. Africa 89 E5
Mtilikwe →, Zimbabwe 87 G3
Mtsensk, Russia 32 F9
Mtskheta, Georgia 35 K7
Mtubatuba, S. Africa 89 D5
Mtwalume, S. Africa 89 E5
Mtwara-Mikindani, Tanzania 87 E5
Mu Gia, Deo, Vietnam 64 D5
Mu Ko Chang △, Thailand 65 G4
Mu Us Shamo, China 56 E5
Muang Chiang Rai = Chiang Rai, Thailand 58 H2
Muang Khong, Laos 64 E5
Muang Lamphun, Thailand 64 C2
Muang Mai, Thailand 65 a
Muang Pak Beng, Laos 58 H3
Muar, Malaysia 65 L4
Muarabungo, Indonesia 62 E2
Muaraenim, Indonesia 62 E2
Muarajuloi, Indonesia 62 E4
Muarakaman, Indonesia 62 E5
Muaratebo, Indonesia 62 E2
Muaratembesi, Indonesia 62 E2
Muaratewe, Indonesia 62 E4
Mubarakpur, India 69 F10
Mubarraz = Al Mubarraz, Si. Arabia 71 E6
Mubende, Uganda 86 B3
Mubi, Nigeria 83 C7
Mucajaí →, Brazil 124 C6
Muchachos, Roque de los, Canary Is. 48 F2
Mücheln, Germany 24 D7
Muchinga Mts., Zambia 87 E3
Muchkapskiy, Russia 34 E6
Muchuan, China 58 C5
Muck, U.K. 13 E2
Muckadilla, Australia 95 D4
Muckle Flugga, U.K. 13 A8
Mucur, Turkey 72 C6
Mucuri, Brazil 125 G11
Mucusso, Angola 88 B3
Muda, Canary Is. 48 F6
Mudanjiang, China 57 B15
Mudanya, Turkey 45 F12
Muddy Cr. →, U.S.A. 109 H8
Mudgee, Australia 95 E4
Mudjatik →, Canada 103 B7
Mudurnu, Turkey 72 B4
Muecate, Mozam. 87 E4
Mueda, Mozam. 87 E4
Mueller Ra., Australia 92 C4
Muende, Mozam. 87 E3
Muerto, Mar, Mexico 119 D6
Mufu Shan, China 59 C10
Mufulira, Zambia 87 E2
Mufumbiro Range, Africa 86 C2

Mugardos, Spain 36 B2
Muge →, Portugal 37 F2
Múggia, Italy 41 C10
Mughal Sarai, India 69 G10
Mughayrā', Si. Arabia 70 D3
Mugi, Japan 55 H7
Mugia = Muxía, Spain 36 B1
Mugila, Mts., Dem. Rep. of the Congo 86 D2
Muğla, Turkey 47 D10
Muğla □, Turkey 47 D10
Muglad, Sudan 81 E2
Mugu, Nepal 69 E10
Muhammad, Râs, Egypt 70 E2
Muhammad Qol, Sudan 80 C4
Muhammadabad, India 69 F10
Muhesi →, Tanzania 86 D4
Mühlacker, Germany 25 G4
Mühldorf, Germany 25 G8
Mühlhausen, Germany 24 D6
Mühlig Hofmann fjell, Antarctica 5 D3
Mühlviertel, Austria 26 C7
Muhos, Finland 8 D22
Muhu, Estonia 9 G20
Muhutwe, Tanzania 86 C3
Muine Bheag, Ireland 12 D5
Muir, L., Australia 93 F2
Muir of Ord, U.K. 13 D4
Mujnak = Muynak, Uzbekistan 52 E6
Muka, Tanjung, Malaysia 65 c
Mukacheve, Ukraine 28 B7
Mukachevo = Mukacheve, Ukraine 28 B7
Mukah, Malaysia 62 D4
Mukandwara, India 68 G6
Mukawwa, Geziret, Egypt 80 C4
Mukawwar, Sudan 80 C4
Mukdahan, Thailand 64 D5
Mukden = Shenyang, China 57 D12
Mukerian, India 68 D6
Mukhavets, Belarus 31 F10
Mukhtolovo, Russia 34 C6
Mukinbudin, Australia 93 F2
Mukishi, Dem. Rep. of the Congo 87 D1
Mukomuko, Indonesia 62 E2
Mukomwenze, Dem. Rep. of the Congo 86 D2
Muktsar, India 68 D6
Mukur = Moqor, Afghan. 68 C2
Mukutawa →, Canada 103 C9
Mukwela, Zambia 87 F2
Mula, Spain 39 G3
Mula →, Pakistan 68 F2
Mulange, Dem. Rep. of the Congo 86 C2
Mulanje, Malawi 87 F4
Mulanje, Mt., Malawi 87 F4
Mulchén, Chile 126 D1
Mulde →, Germany 24 D8
Mule Creek Junction, U.S.A. 112 D2
Muleba, Tanzania 86 C3
Mulejé, Mexico 118 B2
Muleshoe, U.S.A. 113 H3
Muletta, Gara, Ethiopia 81 F5
Mulgrave, Canada 105 C7
Mulhacén, Spain 37 H7
Mülheim, Germany 24 D2
Mulhouse, France 19 E14
Muli, China 58 D3
Muling, China 57 B16
Mull, U.K. 13 E3
Mull, Sound of, U.K. 13 E3
Mullaittivu, Sri Lanka 66 Q12
Mullen, U.S.A. 112 D4
Mullens, U.S.A. 114 G5
Muller, Pegunungan, Indonesia 62 D4
Mullet Pen., Ireland 12 B1
Mullewa, Australia 93 E2
Müllheim, Germany 25 H3
Mulligan →, Australia 94 D2
Mullingar, Ireland 12 C4
Mullins, U.S.A. 115 H6
Mullsjö, Sweden 11 G7
Mullumbimby, Australia 95 D5
Mulobezi, Zambia 87 F2
Mulroy B., Ireland 12 A4
Multan, Pakistan 68 D4
Mulumbe, Mts., Dem. Rep. of the Congo 87 D2
Mulungushi Dam, Zambia 87 E2
Mulvane, U.S.A. 113 G6
Mulwad, Sudan 80 D3
Mulwala, Australia 95 F4
Mumbai, India 66 K8
Mumbwa, Zambia 87 F2
Mumra, Russia 35 H8
Mun →, Thailand 64 E5
Muna, Indonesia 63 F6
Munabao, India 68 G4
Munamagi, Estonia 9 H22
Muncan, Indonesia 63 K18
Muncar, Indonesia 63 J17
München, Germany 25 G7
Müncheberg, Germany 24 C10
München, Germany 25 G7
Munchen-Gladbach = Mönchengladbach, Germany 24 D2
München International ✈ (MUC), Germany 25 G7
Muncho Lake, Canada 102 B3
Munch'ŏn, N. Korea 57 E14
Muncie, U.S.A. 114 E3
Muncoonie, L., Australia 94 D2
Mundabbera, Australia 95 D5
Munday, U.S.A. 113 J5
Münden, Germany 24 D5
Münden △, Germany 24 D5
Mundiwindi, Australia 92 D3
Mundo →, Spain 39 G2
Mundo Novo, Brazil 125 F10
Mundra, India 68 H3
Mundrabilla, Australia 93 F4
Munera, Spain 39 F2

Mungallala, Australia 95 D4
Mungallala Cr. →, Australia 95 D4
Mungana, Australia 94 B3
Mungaoli, India 68 G8
Mungari, Mozam. 87 F3
Mungbere, Dem. Rep. of the Congo 86 B2
Mungeli, India 69 H9
Munger, India 69 G12
Mungkan Kandju △, Australia 94 A3
Munich = München, Germany 25 G7
Munising, U.S.A. 114 B2
Munka-Ljungby, Sweden 11 H6
Munkebo, Denmark 11 J4
Munkedal, Sweden 11 F5
Munkfors, Sweden 10 E7
Münnerstadt, Germany 25 E6
Muñoz Gamero, Pen., Chile 128 G2
Munroe L., Canada 103 B9
Munsan, S. Korea 57 F14
Munster, France 19 D14
Munster □, Ireland 12 D3
Münster, Niedersachsen, Germany 24 C6
Münster, Nordrhein-Westfalen, Germany 24 D3
Munster □, Ireland 12 D3
Muntadgin, Australia 93 F2
Muntele Mare, Vf., Romania 29 D8
Muntok, Indonesia 62 E3
Munyama, Zambia 87 F2
Munzur Dağları, Turkey 73 C8
Muong Beng, Laos 58 G3
Muong Boum, Vietnam 58 F4
Muong Et, Laos 64 B5
Muong Hai, Laos 58 G3
Muong Hiem, Laos 64 B4
Muong Houn, Laos 58 G3
Muong Hung, Vietnam 58 G4
Muong Kau, Laos 64 E5
Muong Khao, Laos 64 C4
Muong Khoua, Laos 58 G4
Muong Liep, Laos 64 C3
Muong May, Laos 64 E6
Muong Ngeun, Laos 58 G3
Muong Ngoi, Laos 58 G4
Muong Nhie, Vietnam 58 F4
Muong Nong, Laos 64 D6
Muong Ou Tay, Laos 58 F3
Muong Oua, Laos 64 C3
Muong Peun, Laos 58 G4
Muong Phalane, Laos 64 D5
Muong Phieng, Laos 64 C3
Muong Phine, Laos 64 D6
Muong Sai, Laos 58 G3
Muong Saiapoun, Laos 64 C3
Muong Sen, Vietnam 64 C5
Muong Sing, Laos 58 G3
Muong Son, Laos 58 G4
Muong Soui, Laos 64 C4
Muong Va, Laos 58 G4
Muong Xia, Vietnam 64 B5
Muonio, Finland 8 C20
Muonio älv = Muonionjoki →, Finland 8 C20
Muonioälven = Muonionjoki →, Finland 8 C20
Muonionjoki →, Finland 8 C20
Muping, China 57 F11
Mupoi, Sudan 81 F2
Muqaddam, Wadi →, Sudan 80 D3
Muqdisho, Somali Rep. 75 G4
Mur →, Austria 27 E9
Mûr-de-Bretagne, France 18 D4
Muradiye, Manisa, Turkey 47 C9
Muradiye, Van, Turkey 73 C10
Murakami, Japan 54 E9
Murallón, Cerro, Chile 128 F2
Muranda, Rwanda 86 C2
Murang'a, Kenya 86 C4
Murashi, Russia 52 D5
Murat, France 20 C6
Murat →, Turkey 73 C9
Murat Dağı, Turkey 47 C11
Muratlı, Turkey 45 E11
Murato, France 21 F13
Murau, Austria 26 D7
Murava, Belarus 31 F11
Muravera, Italy 42 C2
Murayama, Japan 54 E10
Murça, Portugal 36 D3
Murchison →, Australia 93 E1
Murchison, Mt., Antarctica 5 D11
Murchison Falls, Uganda 86 B3
Murchison Falls △, Uganda 86 B3
Murchison Ra., Australia 94 C1
Murchison Rapids, Malawi 87 F3
Murcia, Spain 39 G3
Murcia □, Spain 39 H3
Murdo, U.S.A. 112 D4
Murdoch Pt., Australia 94 A3
Mürefte, Turkey 45 F11
Mureş □, Romania 29 D9
Mureş →, Romania 28 D5
Mureşul = Mureş →, Romania 28 D5
Muret, France 20 E5
Murewa, Zimbabwe 89 B5
Murfreesboro, N.C., U.S.A. 115 G7
Murfreesboro, Tenn., U.S.A. 115 H2
Murgab = Murghob, Tajikistan 52 F8
Murgab →, Turkmenistan 71 B9
Murgenella, Australia 92 B5
Murgeni, Romania 29 D13
Murgha Kibzai, Pakistan 68 D3
Murghob, Tajikistan 52 F8
Murgon, Australia 95 D5
Muri, India 69 H11
Muria, Indonesia 63 G14
Murias de Paredes, Spain 36 C4
Muriel Mine, Zimbabwe 87 F3
Müritz, Germany 24 B8
Müritz △, Germany 24 B8

Murliganj, India 69 G12
Murmansk, Russia 52 C4
Murnau, Germany 25 H7
Muro, France 21 F12
Muro, Spain 48 B10
Muro, C. de, France 21 G12
Muro de Alcoy, Spain 39 G4
Muro Lucano, Italy 43 B8
Murom, Russia 34 C6
Muroran, Japan 54 C10
Muros, Spain 36 C1
Muros y de Noya, Ría de, Spain 36 C1
Muroto, Japan 55 H7
Muroto-Misaki, Japan 55 H7
Murovani Kurylivtsi, Ukraine 29 B12
Murowana Goślina, Poland 31 F3
Murphy, U.S.A. 108 E5
Murphys, U.S.A. 110 G6
Murrat, Sudan 80 D2
Murrat Wells, Sudan 80 C3
Murray, Ky., U.S.A. 115 G1
Murray, Utah, U.S.A. 108 F8
Murray →, Australia 95 F2
Murray, L., U.S.A. 115 H5
Murray Bridge, Australia 95 F2
Murray Harbour, Canada 105 C7
Murray River △, Australia 95 E3
Murraysburg, S. Africa 88 E3
Murree, Pakistan 68 C5
Murrieta, U.S.A. 111 M9
Murro di Porco, Capo, Italy 43 F8
Murrumbidgee →, Australia 95 E3
Murrumburrah, Australia 95 E4
Murrurundi, Australia 95 E5
Murshid, Sudan 80 C3
Murshidabad, India 69 G13
Murska Sobota, Slovenia 41 B13
Murtle L., Canada 102 C5
Murtoa, Australia 95 F3
Murtosa, Portugal 36 E2
Murungu, Tanzania 86 C3
Mururoa, French Polynesia 97 K14
Murwara, India 69 H9
Murwillumbah, Australia 95 D5
Mürz →, Austria 26 D8
Mürzzuschlag, Austria 26 D8
Muş, Turkey 70 B4
Mûsa, Gebel, Egypt 70 D2
Musa Khel, Pakistan 68 D3
Mûsa Qal'eh, Afghan. 66 C4
Musafirkhana, India 69 F9
Musala, Bulgaria 44 D7
Musala, Indonesia 62 D1
Musan, N. Korea 57 C15
Musangu, Dem. Rep. of the Congo 87 E1
Musasa, Tanzania 86 C3
Musay'īd, Qatar 71 E6
Muscat = Masqat, Oman 75 C7
Muscatine, U.S.A. 112 E9
Musengezi = Unsengedsi →, Zimbabwe 87 F3
Musgrave Harbour, Canada 105 C9
Musgrave Ranges, Australia 93 E5
Mushie, Dem. Rep. of the Congo 84 E3
Mushin, Nigeria 83 D5
Musi →, Indonesia 62 E2
Musina, S. Africa 89 C5
Muskeg →, Canada 102 A4
Muskegon, U.S.A. 114 D2
Muskegon →, U.S.A. 114 D2
Muskegon Heights, U.S.A. 114 D2
Muskogee, U.S.A. 113 H7
Muskoka, L., Canada 116 B5
Muskwa →, Canada 102 B4
Muslīmiyah, Syria 70 B3
Musmar, Sudan 80 D4
Musofu, Zambia 87 E2
Musoma, Tanzania 86 C3
Musquaro, L., Canada 105 B7
Musquodoboit Harbour, Canada 105 D7
Musselburgh, U.K. 13 F5
Musselshell →, U.S.A. 108 C10
Mussidan, France 20 C4
Mussomeli, Italy 42 E6
Mussoorie, India 68 D8
Mussuco, Angola 88 B2
Mustafakemalpaşa, Turkey 45 F12
Mustang, Nepal 69 E10
Musters, L., Argentina 128 F3
Musudan, N. Korea 57 D15
Muswellbrook, Australia 95 E5
Muszyna, Poland 31 J7
Mût, Egypt 80 B2
Mut, Turkey 70 B2
Mutanda, Mozam. 89 C5
Mutanda, Zambia 87 E2
Mutare, Zimbabwe 87 F3
Muting, Indonesia 63 F10
Mutki = Mirtağ, Turkey 70 B4
Mutoko, Zimbabwe 89 B5
Mutoray, Russia 53 C11
Mutshatsha, Dem. Rep. of the Congo 87 E1
Mutsu, Japan 54 D10
Mutsu-Wan, Japan 54 D10
Muttaburra, Australia 94 C3
Muttalip, Turkey 47 B12
Mutton I., Ireland 12 D2
Mutuáli, Mozam. 87 E4
Mutum Biyu, Nigeria 83 D7
Muweilih, Egypt 74 E3
Muxía, Spain 36 B1
Muy Muy, Nic. 120 D2
Muyinga, Burundi 86 C3
Muynak, Uzbekistan 52 E6
Muzaffarabad, Pakistan 69 B5
Muzaffargarh, Pakistan 68 D4
Muzaffarnagar, India 68 E7
Muzaffarpur, India 69 F11
Muzafirpur, Pakistan 68 D3
Muzhi, Russia 52 C7
Muzillac, France 18 E4

Muzūra, *Egypt* 80 J7
Mvôlô, *Sudan* 81 F2
Mvuma, *Zimbabwe* 87 F3
Mvurwi, *Zimbabwe* 87 F3
Mwabvi ⌓, *Malawi* 87 F3
Mwadui, *Tanzania* 86 C3
Mwambo, *Tanzania* 87 E5
Mwandi, *Zambia* 87 F1
Mwanza, *Dem. Rep. of the Congo* 86 D2
Mwanza, *Tanzania* 86 C3
Mwanza, *Zambia* 87 F1
Mwanza □, *Tanzania* 86 C3
Mwaya, *Tanzania* 87 D3
Mweelrea, *Ireland* 12 C2
Mweka, *Dem. Rep. of the Congo* 84 E4
Mwenezi, *Zimbabwe* 87 G3
Mwenezi →, *Mozam.* 87 G3
Mwenga, *Dem. Rep. of the Congo* 86 C2
Mweru, L., *Zambia* 87 D2
Mweru Wantipa △, *Zambia* 87 D2
Mweza Range, *Zimbabwe* 87 G3
Mwilambwe, *Dem. Rep. of the Congo* 86 D2
Mwimbi, *Tanzania* 87 D3
Mwinilunga, *Zambia* 87 E1
My Tho, *Vietnam* 65 G6
Myajlar, *India* 68 F4
Myanaung, *Burma* 67 K19
Myanmar = Burma ■, *Asia* 67 J20
Myaungmya, *Burma* 67 L19
Myedna, *Belarus* 31 G10
Myeik Kyunzu, *Burma* 65 G1
Myers Chuck, *U.S.A.* 102 B2
Myerstown, *U.S.A.* 117 F8
Myingyan, *Burma* 67 J19
Myitkyina, *Burma* 67 G20
Myjava, *Slovak Rep.* 27 C10
Mykhaylivka, *Ukraine* 33 J8
Mykines, *Færoe Is.* 8 E9
Mykolayiv, *Ukraine* 33 J7
Mymensingh, *Bangla.* 67 G17
Mynydd Du, *U.K.* 15 F4
Mýrdalsjökull, *Iceland* 8 E4
Myrhorod, *Ukraine* 33 H7
Myrtle Beach, *U.S.A.* 115 J6
Myrtle Creek, *U.S.A.* 108 E2
Myrtle Point, *U.S.A.* 108 E1
Myrtou, *Cyprus* 49 D12
Mysia, *Turkey* 45 G11
Myślenice, *Poland* 31 J6
Myślibórz, *Poland* 31 F1
Mysłowice, *Poland* 31 H6
Mysore = Karnataka □, *India* 66 N10
Mysore, *India* 66 N10
Mystic, *U.S.A.* 117 E13
Myszków, *Poland* 31 H6
Myszyniec, *Poland* 30 E8
Mytishchi, *Russia* 32 E9
Mývatn, *Iceland* 8 D5
Mže →, *Czech Rep.* 26 B6
Mzimba, *Malawi* 87 E3
Mzimkulu →, *S. Africa* 89 E5
Mzimvubu →, *S. Africa* 89 E4
Mzuzu, *Malawi* 87 E3

N

Na Hearadh = Harris, *U.K.* 13 D2
Na Noi, *Thailand* 64 C3
Na Phao, *Laos* 64 D5
Na Sam, *Vietnam* 58 F6
Na San, *Vietnam* 64 B5
Na Thon, *Thailand* 65 b
Naab →, *Germany* 25 F8
Na'am, *Sudan* 81 F2
Na'am →, *Sudan* 81 F2
Naantali, *Finland* 9 F19
Naas, *Ireland* 12 C5
Nababeep, *S. Africa* 88 D2
Nabadwip = Navadwip, *India* 69 H13
Nabawa, *Australia* 93 E1
Nabberu, L., *Australia* 93 E3
Nabburg, *Germany* 25 F8
Naberezhnyye Chelny, *Russia* 34 C11
Nabeul, *Tunisia* 79 A8
Nabha, *India* 68 D7
Nabīd, *Iran* 71 D8
Nabire, *Indonesia* 63 E9
Nabisar, *Pakistan* 68 G3
Nabisipi →, *Canada* 105 B7
Nabiswera, *Uganda* 86 B3
Nāblus = Nābulus, *West Bank* 74 C4
Naboomspruit, *S. Africa* 89 C4
Nabou, *Burkina Faso* 82 C4
Nabua, *Phil.* 61 E5
Nābulus, *West Bank* 74 C4
Nacala, *Mozam.* 87 E5
Nacala-Velha, *Mozam.* 87 E5
Nacaome, *Honduras* 120 D2
Nacaroa, *Mozam.* 87 E4
Naches, *U.S.A.* 108 C3
Naches →, *U.S.A.* 110 D6
Nachicapau, L., *Canada* 105 A6
Nachingwea, *Tanzania* 87 E4
Nachna, *India* 68 F4
Náchod, *Czech Rep.* 26 A9
Nacimiento L., *U.S.A.* 110 K6
Naco, *Mexico* 118 A3
Nacogdoches, *U.S.A.* 113 K7
Nácori Chico, *Mexico* 118 B3
Nacozari, *Mexico* 118 A3
Nådendal = Naantali, *Finland* 9 F19
Nadi, *Fiji* 91 C7
Nadi, *Sudan* 80 D3
Nadiad, *India* 68 H5
Nădlac, *Romania* 28 D5
Nador, *Morocco* 78 B5
Nadur, *Malta* 49 C1
Nadūshan, *Iran* 71 C7
Nadvirna, *Ukraine* 29 B9
Nadvornaya = Nadvirna, *Ukraine* 29 B9
Nadym, *Russia* 52 C8
Nadym →, *Russia* 52 C8
Nærbø, *Norway* 9 G11
Næstved, *Denmark* 11 J5
Nafada, *Nigeria* 83 C7
Naft-e Safīd, *Iran* 71 D6
Naftshahr, *Iran* 70 C5
Nafud Desert = An Nafūd, *Si. Arabia* 70 D4
Nag Hammâdi, *Egypt* 80 B3
Naga, *Phil.* 61 E5
Nagahama, *Japan* 55 G8
Nagai, *Japan* 54 E10
Nagaland □, *India* 67 G19
Nagano, *Japan* 55 F9
Nagano □, *Japan* 55 F9
Nagaoka, *Japan* 55 F9
Nagappattinam, *India* 66 P11
Nagar →, *Bangla.* 69 G13
Nagar Parkar, *Pakistan* 68 G4
Nagasaki, *Japan* 55 H4
Nagasaki □, *Japan* 55 H4
Nagato, *Japan* 55 G5
Nagaur, *India* 68 F5
Nagda, *India* 68 H6
Nagercoil, *India* 66 Q10
Nagina, *India* 69 E8
Nagīneh, *Iran* 71 C8
Nagir, *Pakistan* 69 A6
Naglarby, *Sweden* 10 D9
Nagod, *India* 69 G9
Nagold, *Germany* 25 G4
Nagold →, *Germany* 25 G4
Nagoorin, *Australia* 94 C5
Nagorno-Karabakh □, *Azerbaijan* 70 B5
Nagornyy, *Russia* 53 D13
Nagoya, *Japan* 55 G8
Nagpur, *India* 66 J11
Nagua, *Dom. Rep.* 121 C6
Naguabo, *Puerto Rico* 121 d
Nagyatád, *Hungary* 28 D2
Nagyecsed, *Hungary* 28 C7
Nagykálló, *Hungary* 28 C6
Nagykanizsa, *Hungary* 28 D2
Nagykáta, *Hungary* 28 C4
Nagykőrös, *Hungary* 28 C4
Naha, *Japan* 55 L3
Nahan, *India* 68 D7
Nahanni △, *Canada* 102 A4
Nahanni Butte, *Canada* 102 A4
Nahargarh, *Mad. P., India* 68 G6
Nahargarh, *Raj., India* 68 G7
Nahariyya, *Israel* 70 C2
Nahāvand, *Iran* 71 C6
Nahe →, *Germany* 25 F3
Nahirne, *Ukraine* 29 E13
Nahîya, W. →, *Egypt* 80 B3
Nahuelbuta △, *Chile* 126 D1
Nai Yong, *Thailand* 65 a
Naicá, *Mexico* 118 B3
Naicam, *Canada* 103 C8
Naikoon ⌓, *Canada* 102 C2
Naila, *Germany* 25 E7
Naimisharanya, *India* 69 F9
Nain, *Canada* 105 A7
Nā'īn, *Iran* 71 C7
Naini Tal, *India* 69 E8
Nainpur, *India* 66 H12
Naintré, *France* 18 F7
Nainwa, *India* 68 G6
Naipu, *Romania* 29 F10
Nairn, *U.K.* 13 D5
Nairobi, *Kenya* 86 C4
Nairobi △, *Kenya* 86 C4
Naissaar, *Estonia* 9 G21
Naita, Mt., *Ethiopia* 81 F4
Naivasha, *Kenya* 86 C4
Naivasha, L., *Kenya* 86 C4
Najac, *France* 20 D5
Najaf = An Najaf, *Iraq* 70 C5
Najafābād, *Iran* 71 C6
Najd, *Si. Arabia* 75 B3
Nájera, *Spain* 38 C2
Najerilla →, *Spain* 38 C2
Najibabad, *India* 68 E8
Najin, *N. Korea* 57 C16
Najmah, *Si. Arabia* 71 E6
Najrān, *Si. Arabia* 75 D3
Naju, *S. Korea* 57 G14
Nakadōri-Shima, *Japan* 55 H4
Nakalagba, *Dem. Rep. of the Congo* 86 B2
Nakaminato, *Japan* 55 F10
Nakamura, *Japan* 55 H6
Nakano, *Japan* 55 F9
Nakano-Shima, *Japan* 55 K4
Nakashibetsu, *Japan* 54 C12
Nakfa, *Eritrea* 81 D4
Nakfa ⌓, *Eritrea* 81 D4
Nakha Yai, Ko, *Thailand* 65 a
Nakhichevan = Naxçıvan, *Azerbaijan* 70 B5
Nakhichevan Rep. = Naxçıvan □, *Azerbaijan* 52 F5
Nakhl, *Egypt* 74 F2
Nakhl-e Taqī, *Iran* 71 E7
Nakhodka, *Russia* 53 E14
Nakhon Nayok, *Thailand* 64 E3
Nakhon Pathom, *Thailand* 64 F3
Nakhon Phanom, *Thailand* 64 D5
Nakhon Ratchasima, *Thailand* 64 E4
Nakhon Sawan, *Thailand* 64 E3
Nakhon Si Thammarat, *Thailand* 65 H3
Nakhon Thai, *Thailand* 64 D3
Nakhtarana, *India* 68 H3
Nakina, *Canada* 104 B2
Nakło nad Notecią, *Poland* 31 E4
Nako, *Burkina Faso* 82 C4
Nakodar, *India* 68 D6
Nakskov, *Denmark* 11 K5
Naktong →, *S. Korea* 57 G15
Nakuru, *Kenya* 86 C4
Nakuru, L., *Kenya* 86 C4
Nakusp, *Canada* 102 C5
Nal, *Pakistan* 68 F2
Nal →, *Pakistan* 68 G1
Nalázi, *Mozam.* 89 C5
Nalchik, *Russia* 35 J6
Nałęczów, *Poland* 31 G9
Nalerigu, *Ghana* 83 C4
Nalgonda, *India* 66 L11
Nalhati, *India* 69 G12
Naliya, *India* 68 H3
Nallamalai Hills, *India* 66 M11
Nallıhan, *Turkey* 72 B4
Nalón →, *Spain* 36 B4
Nam Can, *Vietnam* 65 H5
Nam-ch'on, *N. Korea* 57 E14
Nam Co, *China* 60 C4
Nam Dinh, *Vietnam* 58 G6
Nam Du, Hon, *Vietnam* 65 H5
Nam Nao △, *Thailand* 64 D3
Nam Ngum Dam, *Laos* 64 C4
Nam-Phan, *Vietnam* 65 G6
Nam Phong, *Thailand* 64 D4
Nam Tha, *Laos* 58 G3
Nam Tok, *Thailand* 64 E2
Namacunde, *Angola* 88 B2
Namacurra, *Mozam.* 89 B6
Namak, Daryācheh-ye, *Iran* 71 C7
Namak, Kavir-e, *Iran* 71 C8
Namakzār, Daryācheh-ye, *Iran* 71 C9
Namaland, *Namibia* 88 C2
Namangan, *Uzbekistan* 52 E8
Namapa, *Mozam.* 87 E4
Namaqualand, *S. Africa* 88 E2
Namasagali, *Uganda* 86 B3
Namber, *Indonesia* 63 E8
Nambour, *Australia* 95 D5
Nambucca Heads, *Australia* 95 E5
Nambung △, *Australia* 93 F2
Namche Bazar, *Nepal* 69 F12
Namchonjŏm = Nam-ch'on, *N. Korea* 57 E14
Namecunda, *Mozam.* 87 E4
Nameponda, *Mozam.* 87 F4
Náměšť nad Oslavou, *Czech Rep.* 27 B9
Námestovo, *Slovak Rep.* 27 B12
Nametil, *Mozam.* 87 F4
Namew L., *Canada* 103 C8
Namgia, *India* 69 D8
Namhkam, *Burma* 58 E1
Namib Desert, *Namibia* 88 C2
Namib-Naukluft ⌓, *Namibia* 88 C2
Namibe, *Angola* 85 H2
Namibe □, *Angola* 88 B1
Namibia ■, *Africa* 88 C2
Namibwoestyn = Namib Desert, *Namibia* 88 C2
Namīn, *Iran* 73 C13
Namlea, *Indonesia* 63 E7
Namoi →, *Australia* 95 E4
Nampa, *U.S.A.* 108 E5
Nampala, *Mali* 82 B3
Namp'o, *N. Korea* 57 E13
Nampō-Shotō, *Japan* 55 J10
Nampula, *Mozam.* 87 F4
Namrole, *Indonesia* 63 E7
Namse Shankou, *China* 67 E13
Namsen →, *Norway* 8 D14
Namsos, *Norway* 8 D14
Namtok Chat Trakan △, *Thailand* 64 D3
Namtok Mae Surin △, *Thailand* 64 C2
Namtsy, *Russia* 53 C13
Namtu, *Burma* 67 H20
Namtumbo, *Tanzania* 87 E4
Namu, *Canada* 102 C3
Namur, *Belgium* 17 D4
Namur □, *Belgium* 17 D4
Namutoni, *Namibia* 88 B2
Namwala, *Zambia* 87 F2
Namwŏn, *S. Korea* 57 G14
Namysłów, *Poland* 31 G4
Nan, *Thailand* 64 C3
Nan →, *Thailand* 64 E3
Nan-ch'ang = Nanchang, *China* 59 C10
Nan Ling, *China* 59 E8
Nan Xian, *China* 59 C9
Nana, *Romania* 29 F11
Nana Kru, *Liberia* 82 E3
Nanaimo, *Canada* 102 D4
Nanam, *N. Korea* 57 D15
Nanan, *China* 59 E12
Nanango, *Australia* 95 D5
Nan'ao, *China* 59 F11
Nanao, *Japan* 55 F8
Nanbu, *China* 58 B6
Nanchang, *Jiangxi, China* 59 C10
Nanchang, *Kiangsi, China* 59 C10
Nancheng, *China* 59 D11
Nanching = Nanjing, *China* 59 A12
Nanchong, *China* 58 B6
Nanchuan, *China* 58 C6
Nancy, *France* 19 D13
Nanda Devi, *India* 69 D8
Nanda Kot, *India* 69 D9
Nandan, *China* 58 E6
Nandan, *Japan* 55 G7
Nanded, *India* 66 K10
Nandewar Ra., *Australia* 95 E5
Nandi = Nadi, *Fiji* 91 C7
Nandigram, *India* 69 H12
Nandurbar, *India* 66 J9
Nandyal, *India* 66 M11
Nanfeng, *Guangdong, China* 59 F8
Nanfeng, *Jiangxi, China* 59 D11
Nanga-Eboko, *Cameroon* 83 E7
Nanga Parbat, *Pakistan* 69 B6
Nangade, *Mozam.* 87 E4
Nangapinoh, *Indonesia* 62 E4
Nangarhār □, *Afghan.* 66 B7
Nangatayap, *Indonesia* 62 E4
Nangeya Mts., *Uganda* 86 B3
Nangis, *France* 19 D10
Nangong, *China* 56 F8
Nanhua, *China* 58 E3
Nanhuang, *China* 57 F11
Nanhui, *China* 59 B13
Nanjeko, *Zambia* 87 F1
Nanji Shan, *China* 59 D13
Nanjian, *China* 58 E3
Nanjiang, *China* 58 A6
Nanjing, *Fujian, China* 59 E11
Nanjing, *Jiangsu, China* 59 A12
Nanjirinji, *Tanzania* 87 D4
Nankana Sahib, *Pakistan* 68 D5
Nankang, *China* 59 E10
Nanking = Nanjing, *China* 59 A12
Nankoku, *Japan* 55 H6
Nanling, *China* 59 B12
Nanning, *China* 58 F7
Nannup, *Australia* 93 F2
Nanpan Jiang →, *China* 58 E6
Nanpara, *India* 69 F9
Nanpi, *China* 56 E9
Nanping, *Fujian, China* 59 D12
Nanping, *Henan, China* 59 C9
Nanri Dao, *China* 59 E12
Nanripe, *Mozam.* 87 E4
Nansei-Shotō = Ryūkyū-rettō, *Japan* 55 M3
Nansen Basin, *Arctic* 4 A10
Nansen Cordillera, *Arctic* 4 A
Nansen Sd., *Canada* 4 A3
Nanshan I., *S. China Sea* 62 B5
Nansio, *Tanzania* 86 C3
Nant, *France* 20 D7
Nanterre, *France* 19 D9
Nantes, *France* 18 E5
Nantiat, *France* 20 B5
Nanticoke, *U.S.A.* 117 E8
Nanton, *Canada* 102 C6
Nantong, *China* 59 A13
Nantou, *Taiwan* 59 F13
Nantua, *France* 19 F12
Nantucket I., *U.S.A.* 114 E10
Nantwich, *U.K.* 14 D5
Nanty Glo, *U.S.A.* 116 F6
Nanuque, *Brazil* 125 G10
Nanusa, Kepulauan, *Indonesia* 63 D7
Nanutarra Roadhouse, *Australia* 92 D2
Nanxi, *China* 58 C5
Nanxiong, *China* 59 E10
Nanyang, *China* 56 H7
Nanyi Hu, *China* 59 B12
Nanyuki, *Kenya* 86 B4
Nanzhang, *China* 59 B8
Nao, C. de la, *Spain* 39 G5
Naococane, L., *Canada* 105 B5
Náousa, *Imathía, Greece* 44 F6
Náousa, *Kikládhes, Greece* 47 D7
Naozhou Dao, *China* 59 G8
Napa, *U.S.A.* 110 G4
Napa →, *U.S.A.* 110 G4
Napanee, *Canada* 116 B8
Napanoch, *U.S.A.* 117 E10
Nape, *Laos* 64 C5
Nape Pass = Keo Neua, Deo, *Vietnam* 64 C5
Napier, *N.Z.* 91 H6
Napier Broome B., *Australia* 92 B4
Napier Pen., *Australia* 94 A2
Napierville, *Canada* 117 A11
Naples = Nápoli, *Italy* 43 B7
Naples, *U.S.A.* 115 M5
Napo, *China* 58 F5
Napo →, *Peru* 124 D4
Napoleon, *N. Dak., U.S.A.* 112 B5
Napoleon, *Ohio, U.S.A.* 114 E3
Nápoli, *Italy* 43 B7
Nápoli, G. di, *Italy* 43 B7
Nápoli Capodichino ✕ (NAP), *Italy* 43 B7
Napopo, *Dem. Rep. of the Congo* 86 B2
Naqâda, *Egypt* 80 B3
Naqadeh, *Iran* 73 D11
Naqb, Ra's an, *Jordan* 74 F4
Naqqāsh, *Iran* 71 C6
Nara, *Japan* 55 G7
Nara, *Mali* 82 B3
Nara □, *Japan* 55 G8
Nara Canal, *Pakistan* 68 G3
Nara Visa, *U.S.A.* 113 H3
Naracoorte, *Australia* 95 F3
Naradhan, *Australia* 95 E4
Naraini, *India* 69 G9
Narasapur, *India* 67 L12
Narathiwat, *Thailand* 65 J3
Narayanganj, *Bangla.* 67 H17
Narayanpet, *India* 66 L10
Narberth, *U.K.* 15 F3
Narbonne, *France* 20 E7
Narcea →, *Spain* 36 B4
Nardīn, *Iran* 71 B7
Nardò, *Italy* 43 B11
Narembeen, *Australia* 93 F2
Narendranagar, *India* 68 D8
Nares Str., *Arctic* 98 A13
Naretha, *Australia* 93 F3
Narew →, *Poland* 31 F7
Nari →, *Pakistan* 68 F2
Narin, *Afghan.* 66 A6
Narindra, Helodranon' i, *Madag.* 89 A8
Narita, *Japan* 55 G10
Nariva Swamp, *Trin. & Tob.* 125 K15
Närke, *Sweden* 10 E8
Narmada →, *India* 68 J5
Narman, *Turkey* 73 B9
Narmland, *Sweden* 9 F15
Narnaul, *India* 68 E7
Narni, *Italy* 41 F9
Naro, *Ghana* 82 C4
Naro Fominsk, *Russia* 32 E9
Narodnaya, *Russia* 6 B17
Narok, *Kenya* 86 C4
Narón, *Spain* 36 B2
Narooma, *Australia* 95 F5
Narowal, *Pakistan* 68 C6
Narrabri, *Australia* 95 E4
Narran →, *Australia* 95 D4
Narrandera, *Australia* 95 E4
Narrogin, *Australia* 93 F2
Narromine, *Australia* 95 E4
Narrow Hills ⌓, *Canada* 103 C8
Narsimhapur, *India* 69 H8
Narsinghgarh, *India* 68 H7
Nartes, L. e, *Albania* 44 F3
Nartkala, *Russia* 35 J6
Naruto, *Japan* 55 G7
Narva, *Estonia* 32 C5
Narva →, *Russia* 9 G22
Narva Bay = Narva Laht, *Estonia* 9 G19
Narva Laht, *Estonia* 9 G19
Narvik, *Norway* 8 B17
Narvskoye Vdkhr., *Russia* 32 C5
Narwana, *India* 68 E7
Narwiański △, *Poland* 31 F9
Naryan-Mar, *Russia* 52 C6
Narym, *Russia* 52 D9
Naryn, *Kyrgyzstan* 52 E8
Nasa, *Norway* 8 C16
Năsăud, *Romania* 29 C9
Naseby, *N.Z.* 91 L3
Naselle, *U.S.A.* 110 D3
Naser, Buheirat en, *Egypt* 80 C3
Nashua, *Mont., U.S.A.* 108 B10
Nashua, *N.H., U.S.A.* 117 D13
Nashville, *Ark., U.S.A.* 113 J8
Nashville, *Ga., U.S.A.* 115 K4
Nashville, *Tenn., U.S.A.* 115 G2
Našice, *Croatia* 28 E3
Nasielsk, *Poland* 31 F7
Nasik, *India* 66 K8
Nasipit, *Phil.* 61 G6
Nasir, *Sudan* 81 F3
Nasirabad, *India* 68 F6
Nasirabad, *Pakistan* 68 E3
Nasiriyah = An Nāṣirīyah, *Iraq* 70 D5
Naskaupi →, *Canada* 105 B7
Naso, *Italy* 43 D7
Naṣrābād, *Iran* 71 C6
Naṣriān-e Pā'īn, *Iran* 70 C5
Nass →, *Canada* 102 C3
Nassarawa, *Nigeria* 83 D6
Nassarawa □, *Nigeria* 83 D6
Nassau, *Bahamas* 120 A4
Nassau, *U.S.A.* 117 D11
Nassau, B., *Chile* 128 H3
Nasser, L. = Naser, Buheirat en, *Egypt* 80 C3
Nassian, *Ivory C.* 82 D4
Nässjö, *Sweden* 11 G8
Nastapoka →, *Canada* 104 A4
Nastapoka, Is., *Canada* 104 A4
Nasugbu, *Phil.* 61 D4
Näsum, *Sweden* 11 H8
Näsviken, *Sweden* 10 C10
Nata, *Botswana* 88 C4
Nata →, *Botswana* 88 C4
Natal, *Brazil* 125 E11
Natal, *Indonesia* 62 D1
Natal, *S. Africa* 85 K6
Natal Drakensberg ⌓, *S. Africa* 89 D4
Natalinci, *Serbia & M.* 28 F5
Naṭanz, *Iran* 71 C6
Natashquan, *Canada* 105 B7
Natashquan →, *Canada* 105 B7
Natchez, *U.S.A.* 113 K9
Natchitoches, *U.S.A.* 113 K8
Nathalia, *Australia* 95 F4
Nathdwara, *India* 68 G5
Nati, Pta., *Spain* 48 A10
Natimuk, *Australia* 95 F3
Nation →, *Canada* 102 B4
National City, *U.S.A.* 111 N9
Natitingou, *Benin* 83 C5
Natividad, I., *Mexico* 118 B1
Natkyizin, *Burma* 64 E1
Natron, L., *Tanzania* 86 C4
Natrona Heights, *U.S.A.* 116 F5
Natrûn, W. el →, *Egypt* 80 H7
Nättraby, *Sweden* 11 H9
Natukanaoka Pan, *Namibia* 88 B2
Natuna Besar, Kepulauan, *Indonesia* 62 D3
Natuna Is. = Natuna Besar, Kepulauan, *Indonesia* 62 D3
Natuna Selatan, Kepulauan, *Indonesia* 62 D3
Natural Bridge, *U.S.A.* 117 B9
Natural Bridges ⌓, *U.S.A.* 109 H8
Naturaliste, C., *Australia* 95 G4
Nau Qala, *Afghan.* 68 B3
Naucelle, *France* 20 D6
Nauders, *Austria* 26 E3
Nauen, *Germany* 24 C8
Naugatuck, *U.S.A.* 117 E11
Naujaat = Repulse Bay, *Canada* 101 B11
Naujoji Akmenė, *Lithuania* 30 B9
Naumburg, *Germany* 24 D7
Nā'ūr at Tunayb, *Jordan* 74 D4
Nauru ■, *Pac. Oc.* 96 H8
Naushahra = Nowshera, *Pakistan* 66 C8
Naushahro, *Pakistan* 68 F3
Naushon I., *U.S.A.* 117 E14
Nauta, *Peru* 124 D4
Nautanwa, *India* 67 F13
Naute ⌓, *Namibia* 88 D2
Nautla, *Mexico* 119 C5
Nava, *Mexico* 118 B4
Nava, *Spain* 36 B5
Nava del Rey, *Spain* 36 D5
Navadwip, *India* 69 H13
Navahermosa, *Spain* 37 F6
Navahrudak, *Belarus* 32 F3

Navajo Reservoir, *U.S.A.* **109 H10**
Navalcarnero, *Spain* **36 E6**
Navalmoral de la Mata, *Spain* ... **36 F5**
Navalvillar de Pela, *Spain* **37 F5**
Navan = An Uaimh, *Ireland* **12 C5**
Navapolatsk, *Belarus* **32 E5**
Navarin, Mys, *Russia* **4 C16**
Navarino, I., *Chile* **128 H3**
Navarra □, *Spain* **38 C3**
Navarre, *U.S.A.* **116 F3**
Navarro ➤, *U.S.A.* **110 F3**
Navas de San Juan, *Spain* **37 G7**
Navasota, *U.S.A.* **113 K6**
Navassa I., *W. Indies* **121 C5**
Nävekvarn, *Sweden* **11 F10**
Naver ➤, *U.K.* **13 C4**
Navia, *Spain* **36 B4**
Navia ➤, *Spain* **36 B4**
Navia de Suarna, *Spain* **36 C3**
Navibandar, *India* **68 J3**
Navidad, *Chile* **126 C1**
Naviraí, *Brazil* **127 A5**
Navlakhi, *India* **68 H4**
Navlya, *Russia* **33 F8**
Năvodari, *Romania* **29 F13**
Navoi = Nawoiy, *Uzbekistan* **52 E7**
Navojoa, *Mexico* **118 B3**
Navolato, *Mexico* **118 C3**
Návpaktos, *Greece* **46 C3**
Návplion, *Greece* **46 D4**
Navrongo, *Ghana* **83 C4**
Navsari, *India* **66 J8**
Nawa Kot, *Pakistan* **68 E4**
Nawab Khan, *Pakistan* **68 D3**
Nawabganj, *Ut. P., India* **69 F9**
Nawabganj, *Ut. P., India* **69 E8**
Nawabshah, *Pakistan* **68 F3**
Nawada, *India* **69 G11**
Nawakot, *Nepal* **69 F11**
Nawalgarh, *India* **68 F6**
Nawanshahr, *India* **69 C6**
Nawar, Dasht-i-, *Afghan.* **68 C3**
Nawi, *Sudan* **80 D3**
Nawoiy, *Uzbekistan* **52 E7**
Naxçıvan, *Azerbaijan* **70 B5**
Naxçıvan □, *Azerbaijan* **52 F5**
Náxos, *Greece* **47 D7**
Nay, *France* **20 E3**
Nay, Mui, *Vietnam* **62 B3**
Nāy Band, *Büshehr, Iran* **71 E7**
Nāy Band, *Khorāsān, Iran* **71 C8**
Nayakhan, *Russia* **53 C16**
Nayarit □, *Mexico* **118 C4**
Nayong, *China* **58 D5**
Nayoro, *Japan* **54 B11**
Nayyāl, W. ➤, *Si. Arabia* **70 D3**
Nazaré, *Brazil* **125 F11**
Nazaré, *Portugal* **37 F1**
Nazareth = Nazerat, *Israel* **74 C4**
Nazareth, *U.S.A.* **117 F9**
Nazas, *Mexico* **118 B4**
Nazas ➤, *Mexico* **118 B4**
Nazca, *Peru* **124 F4**
Naze, The, *U.K.* **15 F9**
Nazerat, *Israel* **74 C4**
Nāzik, *Iran* **70 B5**
Nazilli, *Turkey* **47 D10**
Nazko, *Canada* **102 C4**
Nazko ➤, *Canada* **102 C4**
Nazret, *Ethiopia* **81 F4**
Nazwa, *Oman* **75 C6**
Nchanga, *Zambia* **87 E2**
Ncheu, *Malawi* **87 E3**
Ndala, *Tanzania* **86 C3**
Ndalatando, *Angola* **84 F2**
Ndali, *Benin* **83 D5**
Ndareda, *Tanzania* **86 C4**
Ndélé, *C.A.R.* **84 C4**
Ndiael ○, *Senegal* **82 B1**
Ndikinimeki, *Cameroon* **83 E7**
N'Dioum, *Senegal* **82 B2**
Ndjamena, *Chad* **79 F8**
Ndola, *Zambia* **87 E2**
Ndoto Mts., *Kenya* **86 B4**
Nduguti, *Tanzania* **86 C3**
Ndumu ○, *S. Africa* **89 D5**
Néa Alikarnassós, *Greece* **47 F7**
Néa Ankhíalos, *Greece* **46 B4**
Néa Epídhavros, *Greece* **46 D5**
Néa Flippiás, *Greece* **46 B2**
Néa Ionia, *Greece* **46 B4**
Néa Kallikrátia, *Greece* **44 F7**
Néa Mákri, *Greece* **46 C5**
Néa Moudhaniá, *Greece* **44 F7**
Néa Péramos, *Attikí, Greece* **46 C5**
Néa Péramos, *Kaválla, Greece* ... **45 F8**
Néa Víssi, *Greece* **45 E10**
Néa Zíkhna, *Greece* **44 E7**
Neagh, Lough, *U.K.* **12 B5**
Neah Bay, *U.S.A.* **110 B2**
Neale, *L., Australia* **92 D5**
Neales, The ➤, *Australia* **95 D2**
Neamţ □, *Romania* **29 C11**
Neápolis, *Kozáni, Greece* **44 F5**
Neápolis, *Kríti, Greece* **49 D7**
Neápolis, *Lakonía, Greece* **46 E5**
Near Is., *U.S.A.* **100 C1**
Neath, *U.K.* **15 F4**
Neath Port Talbot □, *U.K.* **15 F4**
Nebbou, *Burkina Faso* **83 C4**
Nebelat el Hagana, *Sudan* **81 E2**
Nebine Cr. ➤, *Australia* **95 D4**
Nebitdag, *Turkmenistan* **52 F6**
Nebo, *Australia* **94 C4**
Nebolchy, *Russia* **32 C7**
Nebraska □, *U.S.A.* **112 E5**
Nebraska City, *U.S.A.* **112 E6**
Nébrodi, Monti, *Italy* **43 E7**
Necedah, *U.S.A.* **112 C9**
Nechako ➤, *Canada* **102 C4**
Neches ➤, *U.S.A.* **113 L8**

Nechisar △, *Ethiopia* **81 F4**
Neckar ➤, *Germany* **25 F4**
Neckartal-Odenwald ○, *Germany* **25 F5**
Necochea, *Argentina* **126 D4**
Neda, *Spain* **36 B2**
Nedelino, *Bulgaria* **45 E9**
Nedelišće, *Croatia* **41 B13**
Nédha ➤, *Greece* **46 D3**
Nedoboyivtsi, *Ukraine* **29 B11**
Needles, *U.S.A.* **111 L12**
Needles, *Canada* **102 D5**
Needles, The, *U.K.* **15 G6**
Neembucú □, *Paraguay* **126 B4**
Neemuch = Nimach, *India* **68 G6**
Neenah, *U.S.A.* **114 C1**
Neepawa, *Canada* **103 C9**
Neftçala, *Azerbaijan* **71 B6**
Neftegorsk, *Russia* **35 H4**
Neftekumsk, *Russia* **35 H7**
Nefyn, *U.K.* **14 E3**
Négala, *Mali* **82 C3**
Negapatam = Nagappattinam,
  India **66 P11**
Negara, *Indonesia* **63 J17**
Negaunee, *U.S.A.* **114 B2**
Negele, *Ethiopia* **81 F4**
Negev Desert = Hanegev, *Israel* . **74 E4**
Negoiul, Vf., *Romania* **29 E9**
Negombo, *Sri Lanka* **66 R11**
Negotin, *Serbia & M.* **44 B6**
Negotino, *Macedonia* **44 E6**
Negra, Peña, *Spain* **36 C4**
Negra, Pta., *Peru* **124 E2**
Negrais, C. = Maudin Sun, *Burma* **67 M19**
Negreşti, *Romania* **29 D12**
Negreşti-Oaş, *Romania* **29 C8**
Negril, *Jamaica* .... **120 a**
Negro ➤, *Argentina* **128 E4**
Negro ➤, *Brazil* **124 D7**
Negro ➤, *Uruguay* **127 C4**
Negros, *Phil.* **61 G5**
Negru Vodă, *Romania* **29 G13**
Neguac, *Canada* **105 C6**
Nehalem ➤, *U.S.A.* **110 E3**
Nehāvand, *Iran* **71 C6**
Nehbandān, *Iran* **71 D9**
Nehoiu, *Romania* **29 E11**
Nei Monggol Zizhiqu □, *China* .. **56 D7**
Neijiang, *China* **58 C5**
Neillsville, *U.S.A.* **112 C9**
Neilton, *U.S.A.* **108 C2**
Neiqiu, *China* **56 F8**
Neiva, *Colombia* **124 C3**
Neixiang, *China* **56 H6**
Nejanilini L., *Canada* **103 B9**
Nejd = Najd, *Si. Arabia* **75 B3**
Nejo, *Ethiopia* **81 F4**
Nekà, *Iran* **71 B7**
Nekemte, *Ethiopia* **81 F4**
Nêkheb, *Egypt* **80 B3**
Neksø, *Denmark* **11 J9**
Nelas, *Portugal* **36 E3**
Nelia, *Australia* **94 C3**
Nelidovo, *Russia* **32 D7**
Neligh, *U.S.A.* **112 D5**
Nelkan, *Russia* **53 D14**
Nellore, *India* **66 M11**
Nelson, *Canada* **102 D5**
Nelson, *N.Z.* **91 J4**
Nelson, *U.K.* **14 D5**
Nelson, *Ariz., U.S.A.* **109 J7**
Nelson, *Nev., U.S.A.* **111 K12**
Nelson ➤, *Canada* **103 C9**
Nelson, C., *Australia* **95 F3**
Nelson, Estrecho, *Chile* **128 G2**
Nelson Forks, *Canada* **102 B4**
Nelson House, *Canada* **103 B9**
Nelson L., *Canada* **103 B8**
Nelson Lakes △, *N.Z.* **91 J4**
Nelspoort, *S. Africa* **88 E3**
Nelspruit, *S. Africa* **89 D5**
Néma, *Mauritania* **82 B3**
Neman = Nemunas ➤, *Lithuania* **9 J19**
Neman, *Russia* **9 J20**
Neméa, *Greece* **46 D4**
Nemeiben L., *Canada* **103 B7**
Nemërçkë, Mal, *Albania* **44 F4**
Nemira, Vf., *Romania* **29 D11**
Nemiscau, *Canada* **104 B4**
Nemiscau, L., *Canada* **104 B4**
Nemours, *France* **19 D9**
Nemšová, *Slovak Rep.* **27 C11**
Nemunas ➤, *Lithuania* **9 J19**
Nemuro, *Japan* **54 C12**
Nemuro-Kaikyō, *Japan* **54 C12**
Nemyriv, *Ukraine* **31 H10**
Nen Jiang ➤, *China* **57 B13**
Nenagh, *Ireland* **12 D3**
Nenasi, *Malaysia* **65 L4**
Nene ➤, *U.K.* **15 E8**
Nénita, *Greece* **47 C8**
Nenjiang, *China* **60 B7**
Neno, *Malawi* **87 F3**
Neodesha, *U.S.A.* **113 G7**
Neokhórion,
  Aitolía kai Akarnanía, Greece . **46 C3**
Neokhórion, Árta, *Greece* **46 B3**
Néon Karlovásion, *Greece* **47 D8**
Néon Petrítsi, *Greece* **44 E7**
Neosho, *U.S.A.* **113 G7**
Neosho ➤, *U.S.A.* **113 H7**
Nepal ■, *Asia* **69 F11**
Nepalganj, *Nepal* **69 E9**
Nepalganj Road, *India* **69 E9**
Nephi, *U.S.A.* **108 G8**
Nephin, *Ireland* **12 B2**
Nepi, *Italy* **41 F9**
Nepomuk, *Czech Rep.* **26 B6**
Neptune, *U.S.A.* **117 F10**
Nera ➤, *Italy* **41 F9**
Nera ➤, *Romania* **28 F6**
Nérac, *France* **20 D4**

Nerang, *Australia* **95 D5**
Neratovice, *Czech Rep.* **26 A7**
Nerchinsk, *Russia* **53 D12**
Nereju, *Romania* **29 E11**
Nerekhta, *Russia* **32 D11**
Neresnytsya, *Ukraine* **29 B8**
Néret, L., *Canada* **105 B5**
Neretvanski Kanal, *Croatia* **41 E14**
Neringa, *Lithuania* **9 J19**
Neris ➤, *Lithuania* **9 J21**
Nerja, *Spain* **37 J7**
Nerl ➤, *Russia* **32 D11**
Nerpio, *Spain* **39 G2**
Nerva, *Spain* **37 H4**
Nervi, *Italy* **40 D6**
Neryungri, *Russia* **53 D13**
Nescopeck, *U.S.A.* **117 E8**
Nesebŭr, *Bulgaria* **45 D11**
Ness, L., *U.K.* **13 D4**
Ness City, *U.S.A.* **112 F5**
Nesterov, *Russia* **30 D9**
Nesterov, *Ukraine* **33 G2**
Nestórion, *Greece* **44 F5**
Néstos ➤, *Greece* **45 E8**
Nesvady, *Slovak Rep.* **27 D11**
Nesvizh = Nyasvizh, *Belarus* **33 F4**
Netanya, *Israel* **74 C3**
Netarhat, *India* **69 H11**
Nete ➤, *Belgium* **17 C4**
Netherdale, *Australia* **94 K6**
Netherlands ■, *Europe* **17 C5**
Netherlands Antilles ☑, *W. Indies* **124 A5**
Neto ➤, *Italy* **43 C10**
Netrang, *India* **68 J5**
Nettancourt, *France* **19 D11**
Nettetal, *Germany* **24 D2**
Nettilling L., *Canada* **101 B12**
Nettuno, *Italy* **42 A5**
Netzahualcoyotl, Presa, *Mexico* . **119 D6**
Neu-Isenburg, *Germany* **25 E4**
Neu-Ulm, *Germany* **25 G6**
Neubrandenburg, *Germany* **24 B9**
Neubukow, *Germany* **24 A7**
Neuburg, *Germany* **25 G7**
Neuchâtel, *Switz.* **25 J2**
Neuchâtel □, *Switz.* **25 J2**
Neuchâtel, Lac de, *Switz.* **25 J2**
Neudau, *Austria* **26 D9**
Neuenhagen, *Germany* **24 C9**
Neuenhaus, *Germany* **24 C2**
Neuf-Brisach, *France* **19 D14**
Neufahrn, *Bayern, Germany* **25 G8**
Neufahrn, *Bayern, Germany* **25 G7**
Neufchâteau, *Belgium* **17 E5**
Neufchâteau, *France* **19 D12**
Neufchâtel-en-Bray, *France* **18 C8**
Neufchâtel-sur-Aisne, *France* ... **19 C11**
Neuhaus, *Germany* **24 B6**
Neuillé-Pont-Pierre, *France* **18 E7**
Neuilly-St-Front, *France* **19 C10**
Neukalen, *Germany* **24 B8**
Neumarkt, *Germany* **25 F7**
Neumünster, *Germany* **24 A5**
Neung-sur-Beuvron, *France* **19 E8**
Neunkirchen, *Austria* **26 D9**
Neunkirchen, *Germany* **25 F3**
Neuquén, *Argentina* **128 D3**
Neuquén □, *Argentina* **126 D2**
Neuruppin, *Germany* **24 C8**
Neusäss, *Germany* **25 G6**
Neuse ➤, *U.S.A.* **115 H7**
Neusiedl, *Austria* **27 D9**
Neusiedler See, *Austria* **27 D9**
Neusiedler See-Seewinkel △,
  Austria **27 D9**
Neuss, *Germany* **24 D2**
Neussargues-Moissac, *France* ... **20 C7**
Neustadt, *Bayern, Germany* **25 F8**
Neustadt, *Bayern, Germany* **25 G8**
Neustadt, *Bayern, Germany* **25 F6**
Neustadt, *Bayern, Germany* **25 E7**
Neustadt, *Brandenburg, Germany* **24 C8**
Neustadt, *Hessen, Germany* **24 E5**
Neustadt, *Niedersachsen,
  Germany* **24 C5**
Neustadt, *Rhld.-Pfz., Germany* .. **25 F4**
Neustadt, *Sachsen, Germany* ... **24 D10**
Neustadt, *Schleswig-Holstein,
  Germany* **24 A6**
Neustadt, *Thüringen, Germany* .. **24 E7**
Neustrelitz, *Germany* **24 B9**
Neuvic, *France* **20 C6**
Neuville-sur-Saône, *France* **21 C8**
Neuvy-le-Roi, *France* **18 E7**
Neuvy-St-Sépulchre, *France* **19 F8**
Neuvy-sur-Barangeon, *France* ... **19 E9**
Neuwerk, *Germany* **24 B4**
Neuwied, *Germany* **24 E3**
Neva ➤, *Russia* **32 C6**
Nevada, *Iowa, U.S.A.* **112 D8**
Nevada, *Mo., U.S.A.* **113 G7**
Nevada □, *U.S.A.* **108 G5**
Nevada City, *U.S.A.* **110 F6**
Nevado, Cerro, *Argentina* **126 D2**
Nevado de Colima = Volcán de
  Colima △, *Mexico* **118 D4**
Nevado de Tres Cruces △, *Chile* . **126 B2**
Nevel, *Russia* **32 D5**
Nevers, *France* **19 E10**
Nevertire, *Australia* **95 E4**
Nevesinje, *Bos.-H.* **44 C2**
Neville, *Canada* **103 D7**
Nevinnomyssk, *Russia* **35 H6**
Nevis, *St. Kitts & Nevis* **121 C7**
Nevrokop = Gotse Delchev,
  Bulgaria **44 E7**
Nevşehir, *Turkey* **70 B2**
Nevskoye, *Russia* **30 D9**
New ➤, *U.S.A.* **114 F5**
New Aiyansh, *Canada* **102 B3**
New Albany, *Ind., U.S.A.* **114 F3**
New Albany, *Miss., U.S.A.* **113 H10**

New Albany, *Pa., U.S.A.* **117 E8**
New Amsterdam, *Guyana* **124 B7**
New Angledool, *Australia* **95 D4**
New Baltimore, *U.S.A.* **116 D2**
New Bedford, *U.S.A.* **117 E14**
New Berlin, *N.Y., U.S.A.* **117 D9**
New Berlin, *Pa., U.S.A.* **116 F8**
New Bern, *U.S.A.* **115 H7**
New Bethlehem, *U.S.A.* **116 F5**
New Bloomfield, *U.S.A.* **116 F7**
New Boston, *U.S.A.* **113 J7**
New Braunfels, *U.S.A.* **113 L5**
New Brighton, *N.Z.* **91 K4**
New Brighton, *U.S.A.* **116 F4**
New Britain, *Papua N. G.* **96 H7**
New Britain, *U.S.A.* **117 E12**
New Brunswick, *U.S.A.* **117 F10**
New Brunswick □, *Canada* **105 C6**
New Bussa, *Nigeria* **83 D5**
New Caledonia ☑, *Pac. Oc.* **96 K8**
New Castile = Castilla-La
  Mancha □, *Spain* **6 H5**
New Castle, *Ind., U.S.A.* **114 F3**
New Castle, *Pa., U.S.A.* **116 F4**
New City, *U.S.A.* **117 E11**
New Concord, *U.S.A.* **116 G3**
New Cumberland, *U.S.A.* **116 F4**
New Cuyama, *U.S.A.* **111 L7**
New Delhi, *India* **68 E7**
New Denver, *Canada* **102 D5**
New Don Pedro Reservoir, *U.S.A.* **110 H6**
New England, *U.S.A.* **107 B12**
New England, *N. Dak., U.S.A.* ... **112 B3**
New England Ra., *Australia* **95 E5**
New Forest, *U.K.* **15 G6**
New Galloway, *U.K.* **13 F4**
New Glasgow, *Canada* **105 C7**
New Guinea, *Oceania* **96 H5**
New Hamburg, *Canada* **116 C4**
New Hampshire □, *U.S.A.* **117 C13**
New Hampton, *U.S.A.* **112 D8**
New Hanover, *S. Africa* **89 D5**
New Hartford, *U.S.A.* **117 C9**
New Haven, *Conn., U.S.A.* **117 E12**
New Haven, *Mich., U.S.A.* **116 D2**
New Hazelton, *Canada* **102 B3**
New Hebrides = Vanuatu ■,
  Pac. Oc. **96 J8**
New Holland, *U.S.A.* **117 F8**
New Iberia, *U.S.A.* **113 K9**
New Ireland, *Papua N. G.* **96 H7**
New Jersey □, *U.S.A.* **114 E8**
New Kensington, *U.S.A.* **116 F5**
New Lexington, *U.S.A.* **114 F4**
New Liskeard, *Canada* **104 C4**
New London, *Conn., U.S.A.* **117 E12**
New London, *Ohio, U.S.A.* **116 E2**
New London, *Wis., U.S.A.* **112 C10**
New Madrid, *U.S.A.* **113 G10**
New Martinsville, *U.S.A.* **114 F5**
New Meadows, *U.S.A.* **108 D5**
New Melones L., *U.S.A.* **110 H6**
New Mexico □, *U.S.A.* **109 J10**
New Milford, *Conn., U.S.A.* **117 E11**
New Milford, *Pa., U.S.A.* **117 E9**
New Norcia, *Australia* **93 F2**
New Norfolk, *Australia* **95 G4**
New Orleans, *U.S.A.* **113 L9**
New Philadelphia, *U.S.A.* **116 F3**
New Plymouth, *N.Z.* **91 H5**
New Plymouth, *U.S.A.* **108 E5**
New Port Richey, *U.S.A.* **115 L4**
New Providence, *Bahamas* **120 A4**
New Quay, *U.K.* **15 E3**
New Radnor, *U.K.* **15 E4**
New Richmond, *Canada* **105 C6**
New Richmond, *U.S.A.* **112 C8**
New River Gorge △, *U.S.A.* **114 G5**
New Roads, *U.S.A.* **113 K9**
New Rochelle, *U.S.A.* **117 F11**
New Rockford, *U.S.A.* **112 B5**
New Romney, *U.K.* **15 G8**
New Ross, *Ireland* **12 D5**
New Salem, *U.S.A.* **112 B4**
New Scone = Scone, *U.K.* **13 E5**
New Siberian I. = Novaya Sibir,
  Ostrov, *Russia* **53 B16**
New Siberian Is. = Novosibirskiye
  Ostrova, *Russia* **53 B15**
New Smyrna Beach, *U.S.A.* **115 L5**
New South Wales □, *Australia* ... **95 E4**
New Tecumseth, *Canada* **116 B5**
New Town, *U.S.A.* **112 B3**
New Tredegar, *U.K.* **15 F4**
New Ulm, *U.S.A.* **112 C7**
New Waterford, *Canada* **105 C7**
New-Wes-Valley, *Canada* **105 C9**
New Westminster, *Canada* **110 A4**
New York, *U.S.A.* **117 F11**
New York □, *U.S.A.* **117 D9**
New York J.F. Kennedy
  International ✈ (JFK), *U.S.A.* . **117 F11**
New York Mts., *U.S.A.* **109 J6**
New Zealand ■, *Oceania* **91 J6**
Newaj ➤, *India* **68 G7**
Newala, *Tanzania* **87 E4**
Newark, *Del., U.S.A.* **114 F8**
Newark, *N.J., U.S.A.* **117 F10**
Newark, *N.Y., U.S.A.* **116 C7**
Newark, *Ohio, U.S.A.* **116 F2**
Newark International ✈ (EWR),
  U.S.A. **117 F10**
Newark-on-Trent, *U.K.* **14 D7**
Newark Valley, *U.S.A.* **117 D8**
Newberg, *U.S.A.* **108 D2**
Newberry, *Mich., U.S.A.* **114 B3**
Newberry, *S.C., U.S.A.* **115 H5**
Newberry Springs, *U.S.A.* **111 L10**
Newbridge = Droichead Nua,
  Ireland **12 C5**

Newburgh, *Canada* **116 B8**
Newburgh, *U.S.A.* **117 E10**
Newbury, *U.K.* **15 F6**
Newbury, *N.H., U.S.A.* **117 B12**
Newbury, *Vt., U.S.A.* **117 B12**
Newburyport, *U.S.A.* **115 D10**
Newcastle, *Australia* **95 E5**
Newcastle, *N.B., Canada* **105 C6**
Newcastle, *Ont., Canada* **104 D4**
Newcastle, *S. Africa* **89 D4**
Newcastle, *U.K.* **12 B6**
Newcastle, *Calif., U.S.A.* **110 G5**
Newcastle, *Wyo., U.S.A.* **112 D2**
Newcastle Emlyn, *U.K.* **15 E3**
Newcastle Ra., *Australia* **92 C5**
Newcastle-under-Lyme, *U.K.* ... **14 D5**
Newcastle-upon-Tyne, *U.K.* **14 C6**
Newcastle Waters, *Australia* **94 B1**
Newcastle West, *Ireland* **12 D2**
Newcomb, *U.S.A.* **117 C10**
Newcomerstown, *U.S.A.* **116 F3**
Newdegate, *Australia* **93 F2**
Newell, *Australia* **94 B4**
Newell, *U.S.A.* **112 C3**
Newfane, *U.S.A.* **116 C6**
Newfield, *U.S.A.* **117 D8**
Newfound L., *U.S.A.* **117 C13**
Newfoundland, *Canada* **105 C8**
Newfoundland □, *U.S.A.* **117 E9**
Newfoundland & Labrador □,
  Canada **105 B8**
Newhall, *U.S.A.* **111 L8**
Newhaven, *U.K.* **15 G8**
Newkirk, *U.S.A.* **113 G6**
Newlyn, *U.K.* **15 G2**
Newman, *Australia* **92 D2**
Newman, *U.S.A.* **110 H5**
Newmarket, *Canada* **116 B5**
Newmarket, *Ireland* **12 D2**
Newmarket, *U.K.* **15 E8**
Newmarket, *U.S.A.* **117 C14**
Newnan, *U.S.A.* **115 J3**
Newport, *Ireland* **12 C2**
Newport, *I. of W., U.K.* **15 G6**
Newport, *Newp., U.K.* **15 F5**
Newport, *Ark., U.S.A.* **113 H9**
Newport, *Ky., U.S.A.* **114 F3**
Newport, *N.H., U.S.A.* **117 C12**
Newport, *N.Y., U.S.A.* **117 C9**
Newport, *Oreg., U.S.A.* **108 D1**
Newport, *Pa., U.S.A.* **116 F7**
Newport, *R.I., U.S.A.* **117 E13**
Newport, *Tenn., U.S.A.* **115 H4**
Newport, *Vt., U.S.A.* **117 B12**
Newport, *Wash., U.S.A.* **108 B5**
Newport □, *U.K.* **15 F4**
Newport Beach, *U.S.A.* **111 M9**
Newport News, *U.S.A.* **114 G7**
Newport Pagnell, *U.K.* **15 E7**
Newquay, *U.K.* **15 G2**
Newry, *U.K.* **12 B5**
Newton, *Ill., U.S.A.* **112 F10**
Newton, *Iowa, U.S.A.* **112 E8**
Newton, *Kans., U.S.A.* **113 F6**
Newton, *Mass., U.S.A.* **117 D13**
Newton, *Miss., U.S.A.* **113 J10**
Newton, *N.C., U.S.A.* **115 H5**
Newton, *N.J., U.S.A.* **117 E10**
Newton, *Tex., U.S.A.* **113 K8**
Newton Abbot, *U.K.* **15 G4**
Newton Aycliffe, *U.K.* **14 C6**
Newton Falls, *U.S.A.* **116 E4**
Newton Stewart, *U.K.* **13 G4**
Newtonmore, *U.K.* **13 D4**
Newtown, *U.K.* **15 E4**
Newtownabbey, *U.K.* **12 B6**
Newtownards, *U.K.* **12 B6**
Newtownbarry = Bunclody,
  Ireland **12 D5**
Newtownstewart, *U.K.* **12 B4**
Newville, *U.S.A.* **116 F7**
Nexon, *France* **20 C5**
Neya, *Russia* **34 A6**
Neyrīz, *Iran* **71 D7**
Neyshābūr, *Iran* **71 B8**
Nezhin = Nizhyn, *Ukraine* **33 G6**
Nezperce, *U.S.A.* **108 C5**
Nezvysko, *Ukraine* **29 B10**
Ngabang, *Indonesia* **62 D3**
Ngabordamlu, Tanjung, *Indonesia* **63 F8**
N'Gage, *Angola* **84 F3**
Ngala, *Nigeria* **83 C7**
Ngambé, *Centre, Cameroon* **83 D7**
Ngambé, *Littoral, Cameroon* **83 E7**
Ngami Depression, *Botswana* ... **88 C3**
Ngamo, *Zimbabwe* **87 F2**
Ngangala, *Sudan* **81 G3**
Nganglong Kangri, *China* **67 C12**
Ngao, *Thailand* **64 C2**
Ngaoundéré, *Cameroon* **84 C2**
Ngapara, *N.Z.* **91 L3**
Ngara, *Tanzania* **86 C3**
Ngawi, *Indonesia* **63 G14**
Nghia Lo, *Vietnam* **58 G5**
Ngoboli, *Sudan* **81 G3**
Ngoma, *Malawi* **87 E3**
Ngomahura, *Zimbabwe* **87 G3**
Ngomba, *Tanzania* **87 D3**
Ngop, *Sudan* **81 F3**
Ngoring Hu, *China* **60 C4**
Ngorkou, *Mali* **82 B4**
Ngorongoro, *Tanzania* **86 C4**
Ngorongoro △, *Tanzania* **86 C3**
Ngozi, *Burundi* **86 C2**
Ngudu, *Tanzania* **86 C3**
Nguigmi, *Niger* **79 F8**
Nguila, *Cameroon* **83 E7**
Nguiu, *Australia* **92 B5**
Ngukurr, *Australia* **94 A1**
Ngunga, *Tanzania* **86 C3**
Nguru, *Nigeria* **83 C7**
Nguru Mts., *Tanzania* **86 D4**

Ngusi, Malawi 87 E3
Nguyen Binh, Vietnam 58 F5
Nha Trang, Vietnam 65 F7
Nhacoongo, Mozam. 89 C6
Nhamaabué, Mozam. 87 F4
Nhamundá →, Brazil 125 D7
Nhangulaze, L., Mozam. 89 C5
Nhill, Australia 95 F3
Nho Quan, Vietnam 58 G5
Nhulunbuy, Australia 94 A2
Nia-nia, Dem. Rep. of the Congo 86 B2
Niafounké, Mali 82 B4
Niagara, Canada 116 C5
Niagara Falls, Canada 116 C5
Niagara Falls, U.S.A. 116 C6
Niagara-on-the-Lake, Canada 116 C5
Niah, Malaysia 62 D4
Niamey, Niger 83 C5
Niandan-Koro, Guinea 82 C3
Nianforando, Guinea 82 D2
Niangara, Dem. Rep. of the Congo 86 B2
Niangbo, Ivory C. 82 D3
Niangoloko, Burkina Faso 82 C4
Niantic, U.S.A. 117 E12
Niaro, Sudan 81 E3
Nias, Indonesia 62 D1
Niassa △, Mozam. 87 E4
Niassa □, Mozam. 87 E4
Nibāk, Si. Arabia 71 E7
Nibe, Denmark 11 H3
Nicaragua ■, Cent. Amer. 120 D2
Nicaragua, L. de, Nic. 120 D2
Nicastro, Italy 43 D9
Nice, France 21 E11
Nice ✈ (NCE), France 21 E11
Niceville, U.S.A. 115 K2
Nichicun, L., Canada 105 B5
Nichinan, Japan 55 J5
Nicholas Channel, W. Indies 120 B3
Nicholasville, U.S.A. 114 G3
Nichols, U.S.A. 117 D8
Nicholson, Australia 92 C4
Nicholson, U.S.A. 117 E9
Nicholson →, Australia 94 B2
Nicholson L., Canada 103 A8
Nicholson Ra., Australia 93 E2
Nicholville, U.S.A. 117 B10
Nicobar Is., Ind. Oc. 50 J13
Nicola, Canada 102 C4
Nicolls Town, Bahamas 120 A4
Nicopolis, Greece 46 B2
Nicosia, Cyprus 49 D12
Nicosia, Italy 43 E7
Nicótera, Italy 43 D8
Nicoya, Costa Rica 120 D2
Nicoya, G. de, Costa Rica 120 E3
Nicoya, Pen. de, Costa Rica 120 E2
Nida, Lithuania 30 C8
Nidd →, U.K. 14 D6
Nidda, Germany 25 E5
Nidda →, Germany 25 E4
Nidwalden □, Switz. 25 J4
Nidzica, Poland 31 E7
Niebüll, Germany 24 A4
Nied →, Germany 19 C13
Niederaula, Germany 24 E5
Niederbayern □, Germany 25 G8
Niederbronn-les-Bains, France 19 D14
Niedere Tauern, Austria 26 D7
Niederlausitz, Germany 24 D9
Niederösterreich □, Austria 26 C8
Niedersachsen □, Germany 24 C4
Niedersächsisches Wattenmeer △, Germany 24 B3
Niekerkshoop, S. Africa 88 D3
Niellé, Ivory C. 82 C3
Niemba, Dem. Rep. of the Congo 86 D2
Niemen = Nemunas →, Lithuania 9 J19
Niemodlin, Poland 31 H4
Nienburg, Germany 24 C5
Niers →, Germany 24 D1
Niesky, Germany 24 D10
Nieszawa, Poland 31 F5
Nieu Bethesda, S. Africa 88 E3
Nieuw Amsterdam, Suriname 125 B7
Nieuw Nickerie, Suriname 125 B7
Nieuwoudtville, S. Africa 88 E2
Nieuwpoort, Belgium 17 C2
Nieves, Pico de las, Canary Is. 48 G4
Nièvre □, France 19 E10
Niga, Mali 82 C3
Niğde, Turkey 70 B2
Nigel, S. Africa 89 D4
Niger □, Nigeria 83 D6
Niger ■, W. Afr. 83 B7
Niger →, W. Afr. 83 D6
Niger Delta, Africa 83 E6
Nigeria ■, W. Afr. 83 D6
Nighasin, India 69 E9
Nightcaps, N.Z. 91 L2
Nigríta, Greece 44 F7
Nii-Jima, Japan 55 G9
Niigata, Japan 54 F9
Niigata □, Japan 55 F9
Niihama, Japan 55 H6
Niihau, U.S.A. 106 H14
Niimi, Japan 55 G6
Niitsu, Japan 54 F9
Níjar, Spain 39 J2
Nijil, Jordan 74 F4
Nijkerk, Neths. 17 B5
Nijmegen, Neths. 17 C5
Nijverdal, Neths. 17 B6
Nīk Pey, Iran 71 B6
Nike, Nigeria 83 D6
Nikiniki, Indonesia 63 F6
Nikísiani, Greece 45 F8
Nikítas, Greece 44 F7
Nikki, Benin 83 D5
Nikkō, Japan 55 F9
Nikkō △, Japan 55 F9
Nikolayev = Mykolayiv, Ukraine 33 J7

Nikolayevsk, Russia 34 E7
Nikolayevsk-na-Amur, Russia 53 D15
Nikolsk, Russia 34 D8
Nikolskoye, Russia 53 D17
Nikopol, Bulgaria 45 C8
Nikopol, Ukraine 33 J8
Niksar, Turkey 72 B7
Nīkshahr, Iran 71 E9
Nikšić, Serbia & M. 44 D2
Nîl, Nahr en →, Africa 80 H7
Nîl el Abyad →, Sudan 81 D3
Nîl el Azraq →, Sudan 81 D3
Nila, Indonesia 63 F7
Niland, U.S.A. 111 M11
Nile = Nîl, Nahr en →, Africa 80 H7
Nile Delta, Egypt 80 H7
Niles, Mich., U.S.A. 114 E2
Niles, Ohio, U.S.A. 116 E4
Nilüfer →, Turkey 45 F12
Nim Ka Thana, India 68 F6
Nimach, India 68 G6
Nimbahera, India 68 G6
Nîmes, France 21 E8
Nimfaíon, Ákra = Pínnes, Ákra, Greece 45 F8
Nimmitabel, Australia 95 F4
Nimule, Sudan 81 G3
Nimule △, Sudan 81 G3
Nin, Croatia 41 D12
Nīnawā, Iraq 70 B4
Nīnawā □, Iraq 70 B4
Nindigully, Australia 95 D4
Nineveh = Nīnawā, Iraq 70 B4
Ning Xian, China 56 G4
Ningaloo △, Australia 92 D1
Ning'an, China 57 B15
Ningbo, China 59 C13
Ningcheng, China 57 D10
Ningde, China 59 D12
Ningdu, China 59 D10
Ninggang, China 59 D9
Ningguo, China 59 B12
Ninghai, China 59 C13
Ninghua, China 59 D11
Ningi, Nigeria 83 C6
Ningjin, China 56 F8
Ningjing Shan, China 58 C2
Ninglang, China 58 D3
Ningling, China 56 G8
Ningming, China 58 F6
Ningnan, China 58 D4
Ningpo = Ningbo, China 59 C13
Ningqiang, China 56 H4
Ningshan, China 56 H5
Ningsia Hui A.R. = Ningxia Huizu Zizhiqu □, China 56 F4
Ningwu, China 56 E7
Ningxia Huizu Zizhiqu □, China 56 F4
Ningxiang, China 59 C9
Ningyang, China 56 G9
Ningyuan, China 59 E8
Ninh Binh, Vietnam 58 G5
Ninh Giang, Vietnam 64 B6
Ninh Hoa, Vietnam 64 F7
Ninh Ma, Vietnam 64 F7
Nini-Suhien △, Ghana 82 D4
Ninove, Belgium 17 D4
Nioaque, Brazil 127 A4
Niobrara, U.S.A. 112 D6
Niobrara →, U.S.A. 112 D6
Niokolo-Koba △, Senegal 82 C2
Niono, Mali 82 C3
Nionsamoridougou, Guinea 82 D3
Nioro du Rip, Senegal 82 C1
Nioro du Sahel, Mali 82 B3
Niort, France 20 B3
Nipawin, Canada 103 C8
Nipfjället, Sweden 10 C6
Nipigon, Canada 104 C2
Nipigon, L., Canada 104 C2
Nipishish L., Canada 105 B7
Nipissing, L., Canada 104 C4
Nipomo, U.S.A. 111 K6
Nipton, U.S.A. 111 K11
Niquelândia, Brazil 125 F9
Nīr, Iran 70 B5
Nirasaki, Japan 55 G9
Nirmal, India 66 K11
Nirmali, India 69 F12
Niš, Serbia & M. 44 C5
Nisa, Portugal 37 F3
Nişab, Si. Arabia 70 D5
Nişāb, Yemen 75 E4
Nišava →, Serbia & M. 44 C5
Niscemi, Italy 43 E7
Nishinomiya, Japan 55 G7
Nishino'omote, Japan 55 J5
Nishiwaki, Japan 55 G7
Nísiros, Greece 47 E9
Niška Banja, Serbia & M. 44 C6
Niskibi →, Canada 104 A2
Nisko, Poland 31 H9
Nisporeni, Moldova 29 C13
Nisqually →, U.S.A. 110 C4
Nissáki, Greece 49 A3
Nissan →, Sweden 11 H6
Nissum Bredning, Denmark 11 H2
Nissum Fjord, Denmark 11 H2
Nistru = Dnister →, Europe 33 J6
Nisutlin →, Canada 102 A2
Nitchequon, Canada 105 B5
Niterói, Brazil 127 A7
Nith →, Canada 116 C4
Nith →, U.K. 13 F5
Nitmiluk △, Australia 92 B5
Nitra, Slovak Rep. 27 C11
Nitra →, Slovak Rep. 27 D11
Nitriansky □, Slovak Rep. 27 C11
Nittenau, Germany 25 F8
Niuafo'ou, Tonga 91 B11
Niue, Cook Is. 97 J11
Niulan Jiang →, China 58 D4

Niut, Indonesia 62 D4
Niutou Shan, China 59 C13
Niuzhuang, China 57 D12
Nivala, Finland 8 E21
Nivelles, Belgium 17 D4
Nivernais, France 19 E10
Niwas, India 69 H9
Nixon, U.S.A. 113 L6
Nizamabad, India 66 K11
Nizamghat, India 67 E19
Nizhne Kolymsk, Russia 53 C17
Nizhneangarsk, Russia 53 D11
Nizhnegorskiy = Nyzhnohirskyy, Ukraine 33 K8
Nizhnekamsk, Russia 34 C10
Nizhneudinsk, Russia 53 D10
Nizhnevartovsk, Russia 52 C8
Nizhniy Chir, Russia 35 F6
Nizhniy Lomov, Russia 34 D6
Nizhniy Novgorod, Russia 34 B7
Nizhniy Tagil, Russia 52 D6
Nizhyn, Ukraine 33 G6
Nizina Mazowiecka, Poland 31 F8
Nizip, Turkey 70 B3
Nízké Tatry, Slovak Rep. 27 C12
Nízké Tatry △, Slovak Rep. 27 C12
Nízký Jeseník, Czech Rep. 27 B10
Nizza Monferrato, Italy 40 D5
Njakwa, Malawi 87 E3
Njanji, Zambia 87 E3
Njegoš, Serbia & M. 44 D2
Njinjo, Tanzania 87 D4
Njombe, Tanzania 87 D3
Njombe →, Tanzania 86 D3
Njurundabommen, Sweden 10 B11
Nkambe, Cameroon 83 D7
Nkana, Zambia 87 E2
Nkandla, S. Africa 89 D5
Nkawkaw, Ghana 83 D4
Nkayi, Zimbabwe 87 F2
Nkhotakota, Malawi 87 E3
Nkhotakota △, Malawi 87 E3
Nkongsamba, Cameroon 83 E6
Nkurenkuru, Namibia 88 B2
Nkwanta, Ghana 82 D4
Nmai →, Burma 58 F2
Noakhali = Maijdi, Bangla. 67 H17
Nobel, Canada 116 A4
Nobeoka, Japan 55 H5
Noblejas, Spain 36 F7
Noblesville, U.S.A. 114 E3
Noboribetsu, Japan 54 C10
Noce →, Italy 40 B8
Nocera Inferiore, Italy 43 B7
Nocera Umbra, Italy 41 E9
Noci, Italy 43 B10
Nocona, U.S.A. 113 J6
Nocrich, Romania 29 E9
Noda, Japan 55 G9
Nogales, Mexico 118 A2
Nogales, U.S.A. 109 L8
Nogaro, France 20 E3
Nogat →, Poland 30 D6
Nōgata, Japan 55 H5
Nogent, France 19 D12
Nogent-le-Rotrou, France 18 D7
Nogent-sur-Seine, France 19 D10
Noggerup, Australia 93 F2
Noginsk, Moskva, Russia 32 E10
Noginsk, Tunguska, Russia 53 C10
Nogoa →, Australia 94 C4
Nogoyá, Argentina 126 C4
Nógrád □, Hungary 28 C4
Noguera Pallaresa →, Spain 38 D5
Noguera Ribagorzana →, Spain 38 D5
Nohar, India 68 E6
Nohfelden, Germany 25 F3
Nohta, India 69 H8
Noia, Spain 36 C2
Noire, Montagne, France 20 E6
Noires, Mts., France 18 D3
Noirétable, France 20 C7
Noirmoutier, Î. de, France 18 F4
Noirmoutier-en-l'Île, France 18 F4
Nojane, Botswana 88 C3
Nojima-Zaki, Japan 55 G9
Nok Kundi, Pakistan 66 E3
Nok Ta Phao, Ko, Thailand 65 b
Nokaneng, Botswana 88 B3
Nokia, Finland 9 F20
Nokomis, Canada 103 C8
Nokomis L., Canada 103 B8
Nola, C.A.R. 84 D3
Nola, Italy 43 B7
Nolay, France 19 F11
Noli, C. di, Italy 40 D5
Nolinsk, Russia 34 B9
Noma Omuramba →, Namibia 88 B3
Nombre de Dios, Panama 120 E4
Nome, U.S.A. 100 B3
Nomo-Zaki, Japan 55 H4
Nonacho L., Canada 103 A7
Nonancourt, France 18 D8
Nonda, Australia 94 C3
None, Italy 40 D4
Nong Chang, Thailand 64 E2
Nong Het, Laos 64 C4
Nong Khai, Thailand 64 D4
Nong'an, China 57 B13
Nongoma, S. Africa 89 D5
Nongsa, Indonesia 65 d
Nonoava, Mexico 118 B3
Nonoava →, Mexico 118 B3
Nonthaburi, Thailand 64 F3
Nontron, France 20 C4
Nonza, France 21 F13
Noonamah, Australia 92 B5
Noondie, L., Australia 93 E2
Noord Brabant □, Neths. 17 C5
Noord Holland □, Neths. 17 B4
Noordbeveland, Neths. 17 C3
Noordoostpolder, Neths. 17 B5

Noordwijk, Neths. 17 B4
Noosa Heads, Australia 95 D5
Nootka I., Canada 102 D3
Nopiming △, Canada 103 C9
Nora, Eritrea 81 D5
Nora, Sweden 10 E9
Noralee, Canada 102 C3
Noranda = Rouyn-Noranda, Canada 104 C4
Norberg, Sweden 10 D9
Nórcia, Italy 41 F10
Norco, U.S.A. 111 M9
Nord-Kivu □, Dem. Rep. of the Congo 86 C2
Nord-Ostsee-Kanal, Germany 24 A5
Nord-Pas-de-Calais □, France 19 B9
Nordaustlandet, Svalbard 4 B9
Nordborg, Denmark 11 J3
Nordby, Denmark 11 J2
Norddeich, Germany 24 B3
Nordegg, Canada 102 C5
Norden, Germany 24 B3
Nordenham, Germany 24 B4
Norderney, Germany 24 B3
Norderstedt, Germany 24 B6
Nordfjord, Norway 9 F11
Nordfriesische Inseln, Germany 24 A4
Nordhausen, Germany 24 D6
Nordhorn, Germany 24 C3
Norðoyar, Faeroe Is. 8 E9
Nördinge-Nol, Sweden 11 G6
Nordingrå, Sweden 10 B12
Nordjyllands Amtskommune □, Denmark 11 G4
Nordkapp, Norway 8 A21
Nordkapp, Svalbard 4 A9
Nordkinnhalvøya, Norway 8 A22
Nördlicher Teutoburger Wald-Wiehengebirge △, Germany 24 C4
Nördlingen, Germany 25 G6
Nordrhein-Westfalen □, Germany 24 D3
Nordstrand, Germany 24 A4
Nordvik, Russia 53 B12
Nore →, Ireland 12 D4
Norfolk, Canada 116 D4
Norfolk, Nebr., U.S.A. 112 D6
Norfolk, Va., U.S.A. 114 G7
Norfolk □, U.K. 15 E8
Norfolk I., Pac. Oc. 96 K8
Norfork L., U.S.A. 113 G8
Norilsk, Russia 53 C9
Norma, Mt., Australia 94 C3
Normal, U.S.A. 112 E10
Norman, U.S.A. 113 H6
Norman →, Australia 94 B3
Norman Wells, Canada 100 B7
Normanby →, Australia 94 A3
Normandie-Maine △, France 18 D6
Normandin, Canada 104 C5
Normanhurst, Mt., Australia 93 E3
Normanton, Australia 94 B3
Normétal, Canada 104 C4
Norquay, Canada 103 C8
Norquinco, Argentina 128 E2
Norra Dellen, Sweden 10 C10
Norra Kvill □, Sweden 11 G9
Norra Ulvön, Sweden 10 A12
Norrahammar, Sweden 11 G8
Norrbottens län □, Sweden 8 C19
Nørre Åby, Denmark 11 J3
Nørre Alslev, Denmark 11 K5
Nørresundby, Denmark 11 G3
Norrhult-Klavreström, Sweden 11 G9
Norris Point, Canada 105 C8
Norristown, U.S.A. 117 F9
Norrköping, Sweden 11 F10
Norrland, Sweden 9 E16
Norrsundet, Sweden 10 D11
Norrtälje, Sweden 10 E12
Norseman, Australia 93 F3
Norsk, Russia 53 D14
Norte, Pta. del, Canary Is. 48 G2
Norte, Serra do, Brazil 124 F7
North, C., Canada 105 C7
North Adams, U.S.A. 117 D11
North America 98 F10
North Arm, Canada 102 A5
North Atlantic Ocean, Atl. Oc. 2 C7
North Augusta, U.S.A. 115 J5
North Ayrshire □, U.K. 13 F4
North Bass I., U.S.A. 116 E2
North Battleford, Canada 103 C7
North Bay, Canada 104 C4
North Belcher Is., Canada 104 A4
North Bend, Oreg., U.S.A. 108 E1
North Bend, Pa., U.S.A. 116 E7
North Bend, Wash., U.S.A. 110 C5
North Bennington, U.S.A. 117 D11
North Berwick, U.K. 13 E6
North Berwick, U.S.A. 117 C14
North C., Canada 105 C7
North C., N.Z. 91 F4
North Canadian →, U.S.A. 113 H7
North Canton, U.S.A. 116 F3
North Cape = Nordkapp, Norway 8 A21
North Cape = Nordkapp, Svalbard 4 A9
North Caribou L., Canada 104 B1
North Carolina □, U.S.A. 115 H6
North Cascades △, U.S.A. 108 B3
North Channel, Canada 104 C3
North Channel, U.K. 13 D4
North Charleston, U.S.A. 115 J6
North Chicago, U.S.A. 114 D2
North Creek, U.S.A. 117 C11
North Dakota □, U.S.A. 112 B5
North Downs, U.K. 15 F8
North East, U.S.A. 116 D5
North East Frontier Agency = Arunachal Pradesh □, India 67 F19
North East Lincolnshire □, U.K. 14 D7

North Eastern □, Kenya 86 B5
North Esk →, U.K. 13 E6
North European Plain, Europe 6 E10
North Foreland, U.K. 15 F9
North Fork, U.S.A. 110 H7
North Fork American →, U.S.A. 110 G5
North Fork Feather →, U.S.A. 110 F5
North Fork Grand →, U.S.A. 112 C3
North Fork Red →, U.S.A. 113 H5
North Frisian Is. = Nordfriesische Inseln, Germany 24 A4
North Gower, Canada 117 A9
North Hd., Australia 93 F1
North Henik L., Canada 103 A9
North Highlands, U.S.A. 110 G5
North Horr, Kenya 86 B4
North I., Kenya 86 B4
North I., N.Z. 91 H5
North Kingsville, U.S.A. 116 E4
North Kitui △, Kenya 86 C4
North Knife →, Canada 103 B10
North Koel →, India 69 G10
North Korea ■, Asia 57 E14
North Lakhimpur, India 67 F19
North Lanarkshire □, U.K. 13 F5
North Las Vegas, U.S.A. 111 J11
North Lincolnshire □, U.K. 14 D7
North Little Rock, U.S.A. 113 H8
North Loup →, U.S.A. 112 E5
North Luangwa △, Zambia 87 E3
North Magnetic Pole, Canada 4 A2
North Minch, U.K. 13 C3
North Moose L., Canada 103 C8
North Moose L., Man., Canada 103 C8
North Myrtle Beach, U.S.A. 115 J6
North Nahanni →, Canada 102 A4
North Olmsted, U.S.A. 116 E3
North Ossetia □, Russia 35 J7
North Pagai, I. = Pagai Utara, Pulau, Indonesia 62 E2
North Palisade, U.S.A. 110 H8
North Platte, U.S.A. 112 E4
North Platte →, U.S.A. 112 E4
North Pole, Arctic 4 A
North Portal, Canada 103 D8
North Powder, U.S.A. 108 D5
North Pt., Barbados 121 g
North Pt., Trin. & Tob. 125 J16
North Pt., U.S.A. 116 A1
North Rhine Westphalia = Nordrhein-Westfalen □, Germany 24 D3
North River, Canada 105 B8
North Ronaldsay, U.K. 13 B6
North Saskatchewan →, Canada 103 C7
North Sea, Europe 16
North Seal →, Canada 103 B9
North Somerset □, U.K. 15 F5
North Sporades = Vóriai Sporádhes, Greece 46 B5
North Sydney, Canada 105 C7
North Syracuse, U.S.A. 117 C8
North Taranaki Bight, N.Z. 91 H5
North Thompson →, Canada 102 C4
North Tonawanda, U.S.A. 116 C6
North Troy, U.S.A. 117 B12
North Truchas Pk., U.S.A. 109 J11
North Twin I., Canada 104 B4
North Tyne →, U.K. 14 B5
North Uist, U.K. 13 D1
North Vancouver, Canada 102 D4
North Vernon, U.S.A. 114 F3
North Wabasca L., Canada 102 B6
North Walsham, U.K. 14 E9
North West = Severo-Zapadnyy □, Russia 52 C4
North-West □, S. Africa 88 D4
North West C., Australia 92 D1
North West Christmas I. Ridge, Pac. Oc. 97 G11
North West Frontier □, Pakistan 68 C4
North West Highlands, U.K. 13 D4
North West River, Canada 105 B7
North Western □, Zambia 87 E2
North Wildwood, U.S.A. 114 F8
North York Moors, U.K. 14 C7
North York Moors △, U.K. 14 C7
North Yorkshire □, U.K. 14 C6
Northallerton, U.K. 14 C6
Northam, Australia 93 F2
Northam, S. Africa 88 C4
Northampton, Australia 93 E1
Northampton, U.K. 15 E7
Northampton, Mass., U.S.A. 117 D12
Northampton, Pa., U.S.A. 117 F9
Northamptonshire □, U.K. 15 E7
Northbridge, U.S.A. 117 D13
Northcliffe, Australia 93 F2
Northeast Providence Chan., W. Indies 120 A4
Northeim, Germany 24 D6
Northern = Limpopo □, S. Africa 89 C4
Northern □, Ghana 83 D4
Northern □, Malawi 87 E3
Northern □, S. Leone 82 D2
Northern □, Zambia 87 E3
Northern Areas □, Pakistan 69 A5
Northern Cape □, S. Africa 88 D3
Northern Circars, India 67 L13
Northern Indian L., Canada 103 B9
Northern Ireland □, U.K. 12 B5
Northern Light, L., Canada 104 C1
Northern Marianas ☑, Pac. Oc. 96 F6
Northern Mid-Atlantic Ridge, Atl. Oc. 4 D6
Northern Province □, S. Africa 89 C4
Northern Range, Trin. & Tob. 125 K15
Northern Territory □, Australia 92 D5
Northfield, Minn., U.S.A. 112 C8
Northfield, Vt., U.S.A. 117 B12
Northland □, N.Z. 91 F4
Northome, U.S.A. 112 B7

Northport, *Ala., U.S.A.* 115 J2
Northport, *Wash., U.S.A.* 108 B5
Northumberland □, *U.K.* 14 B6
Northumberland, C., *Australia* .. 95 F3
Northumberland Is., *Australia* .. 94 C4
Northumberland Str., *Canada* .. 105 C7
Northville, *U.S.A.* 117 C10
Northwest Providence Channel,
  W. Indies 120 A4
Northwest Territories □, *Canada* 100 B9
Northwich, *U.K.* 14 D5
Northwood, *Iowa, U.S.A.* 112 D8
Northwood, *N. Dak., U.S.A.* 112 B6
Norton, *U.S.A.* 112 F5
Norton, *Zimbabwe* 87 F3
Norton Sd., *U.S.A.* 100 B3
Nortorf, *Germany* 24 A5
Norwalk, *Calif., U.S.A.* 111 M8
Norwalk, *Conn., U.S.A.* 117 E11
Norwalk, *Iowa, U.S.A.* 112 E8
Norwalk, *Ohio, U.S.A.* 116 E2
Norway, *Mich., U.S.A.* 115 C10
Norway, *Mich., U.S.A.* 114 C2
Norway ■, *Europe* 8 E14
Norway House, *Canada* 103 C9
Norwegian Sea, *Atl. Oc.* 7 B6
Norwich, *Canada* 116 D4
Norwich, *U.K.* 15 E9
Norwich, *Conn., U.S.A.* 117 E12
Norwich, *N.Y., U.S.A.* 117 D9
Norwood, *Canada* 116 B7
Norwood, *U.S.A.* 117 B10
Noshiro, *Japan* 54 D10
Nosivka, *Ukraine* 33 G6
Nosovka = Nosivka, *Ukraine* 33 G6
Noṣratābād, *Iran* 71 D8
Noss Hd., *U.K.* 13 C5
Nossebro, *Sweden* 11 F6
Nossob ➤, *S. Africa* 88 D3
Nossombougou, *Mali* 82 C3
Nosy Barren, *Madag.* 85 H8
Nosy Be, *Madag.* 85 G9
Nosy Boraha, *Madag.* 89 B8
Nosy Lava, *Madag.* 89 A8
Nosy Varika, *Madag.* 89 C8
Noteć ➤, *Poland* 31 F2
Notikewin ➤, *Canada* 102 B5
Notio Aigaio = Notios Aiyaíon □,
  Greece 47 E7
Notios Aiyaíon □ 47 E7
Notios Evvoïkos Kólpos, *Greece* 46 C5
Noto, *Italy* 43 F8
Noto, G. di, *Italy* 43 F8
Notodden, *Norway* 9 G13
Notre Dame B., *Canada* 105 C8
Notre-Dame-de-Koartac =
  Quaqtaq, *Canada* 101 B13
Notre-Dame-des-Bois, *Canada* . 117 A13
Notre-Dame-d'Ivugivic = Ivujivik,
  Canada 101 B12
Notre-Dame-du-Nord, *Canada* . 104 C4
Notsé, *Togo* 83 D5
Nottawasaga B., *Canada* 116 B4
Nottaway ➤, *Canada* 104 B4
Nottingham, *U.K.* 14 E6
Nottingham, City of □, *U.K.* ... 14 E6
Nottingham I., *Canada* 101 B12
Nottinghamshire □, *U.K.* 14 D6
Nottoway ➤, *U.S.A.* 114 G7
Notwane ➤, *Botswana* 88 C4
Nouâdhibou, *Mauritania* 78 D2
Nouâdhibou, Ras, *Mauritania* .. 78 D2
Nouakchott, *Mauritania* 82 B1
Nouâmghâr, *Mauritania* 82 B1
Nouméa, *N. Cal.* 96 K8
Nouna, *Burkina Faso* 82 C4
Noupoort, *S. Africa* 88 E3
Nouveau Comptoir = Wemindji,
  Canada 104 B4
Nouvelle-Amsterdam, Î., *Ind. Oc.* 3 F13
Nouvelle-Calédonie = New
  Caledonia ☒, *Pac. Oc.* 96 K8
Nouzonville, *France* 19 C11
Nová Baňa, *Slovak Rep.* 27 C11
Nová Bystřice, *Czech Rep.* 26 B8
Nova Casa Nova, *Brazil* 125 E10
Nova Esperança, *Brazil* 127 A5
Nova Friburgo, *Brazil* 127 A7
Nova Gorica, *Slovenia* 41 C10
Nova Gradiška, *Croatia* 28 E2
Nova Iguaçu, *Brazil* 127 A7
Nova Iorque, *Brazil* 125 E10
Nova Kakhovka, *Ukraine* 33 J7
Nova Lamego, *Guinea-Biss.* 82 C2
Nova Lima, *Brazil* 127 A7
Nova Lusitânia, *Mozam.* 87 F3
Nova Mambone, *Mozam.* 89 C6
Nova Odesa, *Ukraine* 33 J6
Nová Paka, *Czech Rep.* 26 A8
Nova Pavova, *Serbia & M.* 28 F5
Nova Scotia □, *Canada* 105 C7
Nova Siri, *Italy* 43 B9
Nova Sofala, *Mozam.* 89 C5
Nova Ushytsya, *Ukraine* 29 B12
Nova Varoš, *Serbia & M.* 44 C3
Nova Venécia, *Brazil* 125 G10
Nova Zagora, *Bulgaria* 45 D10
Novaci, *Macedonia* 44 E5
Novaci, *Romania* 29 E8
Novaféltria, *Italy* 41 E9
Novannenskiy = Novoannenskiy,
  Russia 34 E6
Novar, *Canada* 116 A4
Novara, *Italy* 40 C5
Novato, *U.S.A.* 110 G4
Novaya Kakhovka = Nova
  Kakhovka, *Ukraine* 33 J7
Novaya Kazanka, *Kazakhstan* . 35 F9
Novaya Ladoga, *Russia* 32 B7
Novaya Lyalya, *Russia* 52 D7
Novaya Sibir, Ostrov, *Russia* ... 53 B16
Novaya Zemlya, *Russia* 52 B6
Nové Město, *Slovak Rep.* 27 C10

Nové Město na Moravě,
  Czech Rep. 26 B9
Nové Město nad Metují,
  Czech Rep. 27 A9
Nové Zámky, *Slovak Rep.* 27 C11
Novelda, *Spain* 39 G4
Novellara, *Italy* 40 D7
Noventa Vicentina, *Italy* 41 C8
Novgorod, *Russia* 32 C6
Novgorod-Severskiy = Novhorod-
  Siverskyy, *Ukraine* 33 G7
Novhorod-Siverskyy, *Ukraine* .. 33 G7
Novi Bečej, *Serbia & M.* 28 E5
Novi Iskar, *Bulgaria* 44 D7
Novi Kneževac, *Serbia & M.* ... 28 D5
Novi Lígure, *Italy* 40 D5
Novi Pazar, *Bulgaria* 45 C11
Novi Pazar, *Serbia & M.* 44 C4
Novi Sad, *Serbia & M.* 28 E4
Novi Slankamen, *Serbia & M.* .. 28 E5
Novi Travnik, *Bos.-H.* 28 F2
Novi Vinodolski, *Croatia* 41 C11
Novigrad, *Istra, Croatia* 41 C10
Novigrad, *Zadar, Croatia* 41 D12
Novigradsko More, *Croatia* 41 D12
Novo Hamburgo, *Brazil* 127 B5
Novo Ivanivka, *Ukraine* 29 E14
Novo Mesto, *Slovenia* 41 C12
Novo Miloševo, *Serbia & M.* ... 28 E5
Novo Remanso, *Brazil* 125 E10
Novoaleksandrovsk, *Russia* 35 H5
Novoaleksandrovskaya =
  Novoaleksandrovsk, *Russia* .. 35 H5
Novoaltaysk, *Russia* 52 D9
Novoannenskiy, *Russia* 34 E6
Novoazovsk, *Ukraine* 33 J10
Novocheboksarsk, *Russia* 34 B8
Novocherkassk, *Russia* 35 G5
Novodevichye, *Russia* 34 D9
Novogrudok = Navahrudak,
  Belarus 32 F3
Novohrad-Volynskyy, *Ukraine* . 33 G4
Novokachalinsk, *Russia* 54 B6
Novokhopersk, *Russia* 34 E5
Novokuybyshevsk, *Russia* 34 D9
Novokuznetsk, *Russia* 52 D9
Novomirgorod, *Ukraine* 33 H6
Novomoskovsk, *Russia* 32 E10
Novomoskovsk, *Ukraine* 33 H8
Novopolotsk = Navapolatsk,
  Belarus 32 E5
Novorossiysk, *Russia* 35 K9
Novorybnoye, *Russia* 53 B11
Novorzhev, *Russia* 32 D5
Novosej, *Albania* 44 E4
Novoselytsya, *Ukraine* 29 B11
Novoshakhtinsk, *Russia* 33 J10
Novosibirsk, *Russia* 52 D9
Novosibirskiye Ostrova, *Russia* 53 B15
Novosil, *Russia* 33 F9
Novosokolniki, *Russia* 32 D6
Novotitarovskaya, *Russia* 35 H4
Novotroitsk, *Russia* 52 D6
Novoukrayinka, *Ukraine* 33 H6
Novouljanovsk, *Russia* 34 C9
Novouzensk, *Russia* 34 E9
Novovolynsk, *Ukraine* 33 H11
Novovoronezhskiy, *Russia* 33 G10
Novoyavoriske, *Ukraine* 31 J10
Novozybkov, *Russia* 33 F6
Novska, *Croatia* 41 C14
Novvy Urengoy, *Russia* 52 C8
Nový Bor, *Czech Rep.* 26 A7
Novy Bug = Novyy Buh, *Ukraine* 33 J7
Nový Bydžov, *Czech Rep.* 26 A8
Novy Dvor, *Belarus* 31 F11
Nový Dwór Mazowiecki, *Poland* 31 F7
Nový Jičín, *Czech Rep.* 27 B11
Novyy Afon, *Georgia* 35 J5
Novyy Buh, *Ukraine* 33 J7
Novyy Oskol, *Russia* 33 G9
Novyy Port, *Russia* 52 C8
Now Shahr, *Iran* 71 B6
Nowa Deba, *Poland* 31 H8
Nowa Ruda, *Poland* 31 H3
Nowa Sarzyna, *Poland* 31 H9
Nowa Sól, *Poland* 31 G2
Nowata, *U.S.A.* 113 G7
Nowbarān, *Iran* 71 C6
Nowe, *Poland* 30 E5
Nowe Miasteczko, *Poland* 31 G2
Nowe Miasto, *Poland* 31 G7
Nowe Miasto Lubawskie, *Poland* 30 E6
Nowe Skalmierzyce, *Poland* 31 G4
Nowe Warpno, *Poland* 30 E1
Nowghāb, *Iran* 71 C8
Nowgong, *Assam, India* 67 F18
Nowgong, *Mad. P., India* 69 G8
Nowogard, *Poland* 30 E2
Nowogród, *Poland* 31 E8
Nowogród Bobrzanski, *Poland* . 31 G2
Nowogrodziec, *Poland* 31 G2
Nowra, *Australia* 95 E5
Nowshera, *Pakistan* 66 C8
Nowy Dwór Gdański, *Poland* .. 30 D6
Nowy Sącz, *Poland* 31 J7
Nowy Staw, *Poland* 30 D6
Nowy Targ, *Poland* 31 J7
Nowy Tomyśl, *Poland* 31 F3
Noxen, *U.S.A.* 117 E8
Noxon, *U.S.A.* 108 C6
Noyabr'sk, *Russia* 52 C8
Noyant, *France* 18 E7
Noyers, *France* 19 E10
Noyon, *France* 19 C9
Noyon, *Mongolia* 56 C2
Nozay, *France* 18 E5
Nqutu, *S. Africa* 89 D5
Nsanje, *Malawi* 87 F4
Nsawam, *Ghana* 83 D4
Nsomba, *Zambia* 87 E2

Nsukka, *Nigeria* 83 D6
Ntui, *Cameroon* 83 D7
Nu Jiang ➤, *China* 58 E2
Nu Shan, *China* 58 E2
Nuba Mts. = Nubah, Jibalan,
  Sudan 81 E3
Nubah, Jibalan, *Sudan* 81 E3
Nubia, *Africa* 76 D7
Nubian Desert = Nûbîya, Es
  Sahrâ en, *Sudan* 80 C3
Nûbîya, Es Sahrâ en, *Sudan* ... 80 C3
Nubledo, *Spain* 36 B5
Nuboai, *Indonesia* 63 E9
Nubra ➤, *India* 69 B7
Nucet, *Romania* 28 D7
Nueces ➤, *U.S.A.* 113 M6
Nueltin L., *Canada* 103 A9
Nueva Carteya, *Spain* 37 H6
Nueva Gerona, *Cuba* 120 B3
Nueva Palmira, *Uruguay* 126 C4
Nueva Rosita, *Mexico* 118 B4
Nueva San Salvador, *El Salv.* .. 120 D2
Nueva Tabarca, *Spain* 39 G4
Nuéve de Julio, *Argentina* 126 D3
Nuevitas, *Cuba* 120 B4
Nuevo, G., *Argentina* 128 E4
Nuevo Casas Grandes, *Mexico* 118 A3
Nuevo Guerrero, *Mexico* 119 B5
Nuevo Laredo, *Mexico* 119 B5
Nuevo León □, *Mexico* 118 C5
Nuevo Rocafuerte, *Ecuador* ... 124 D3
Nugget Pt., *N.Z.* 91 M2
Nugrus, Gebel, *Egypt* 80 C3
Nuhaka, *N.Z.* 91 H6
Nuits-St-Georges, *France* 19 E11
Nukey Bluff, *Australia* 95 E2
Nukheila, *Sudan* 80 D2
Nukhayb, *Iraq* 70 C4
Nuku'alofa, *Tonga* 91 E12
Nukus, *Uzbekistan* 52 E6
Nules, *Spain* 38 F4
Nullagine, *Australia* 92 D3
Nullagine ➤, *Australia* 92 D3
Nullarbor, *Australia* 93 F5
Nullarbor ➤, *Australia* 93 F2
Nullarbor Plain, *Australia* 93 F4
Numalla, L., *Australia* 95 D3
Numan, *Nigeria* 83 D7
Numata, *Japan* 55 F9
Numatinna ➤, *Sudan* 81 F2
Numaykoos Lake △, *Canada* .. 103 B9
Numazu, *Japan* 55 G9
Numbulwar, *Australia* 94 A2
Numfoor, *Indonesia* 63 E8
Numurkah, *Australia* 95 F4
Nunakuli, *U.S.A.* 105 A7
Nunap Isua, *Greenland* 101 C15
Nunavut □, *Canada* 101 D8
Nunda, *U.S.A.* 116 D7
Nuneaton, *U.K.* 15 E6
Nungarin, *Australia* 93 F2
Nungo, *Mozam.* 87 E4
Nungwe, *Tanzania* 86 C3
Nunivak I., *U.S.A.* 100 B3
Nunkun, *India* 69 C7
Núoro, *Italy* 42 B2
Nūrābād, *Iran* 71 E8
Nure ➤, *Italy* 40 C6
Nuremberg = Nürnberg, *Germany* 25 F7
Nuri, *Mexico* 118 B3
Nuri, *Sudan* 80 D3
Nuriootpa, *Australia* 95 E2
Nuristān □, *Afghan.* 66 B7
Nurlat, *Russia* 34 C10
Nurmes, *Finland* 8 E23
Nürnberg, *Germany* 25 F7
Nurpur, *Pakistan* 68 D4
Nurra, La, *Italy* 42 B1
Nurran, L. = Terewah, L.,
  Australia 95 D4
Nurrari Lakes, *Australia* 93 E5
Nurri, *Italy* 42 C2
Nürtingen, *Germany* 25 G5
Nurzec ➤, *Poland* 31 F9
Nus, *Italy* 40 C4
Nusa Barung, *Indonesia* 63 H15
Nusa Dua, *Indonesia* 63 K18
Nusa Kambangan, *Indonesia* .. 63 G13
Nusa Tenggara Barat □,
  Indonesia 62 F5
Nusa Tenggara Timur □,
  Indonesia 63 F6
Nusaybin, *Turkey* 73 D9
Nushki, *Pakistan* 68 E2
Nuuk, *Greenland* 101 B14
Nuwakot, *Nepal* 69 E10
Nuweiba', *Egypt* 70 D2
Nuwerus, *S. Africa* 88 E2
Nuweveldberge, *S. Africa* 88 E3
Nuyts, C., *Australia* 93 F5
Nuyts, Pt., *Australia* 93 G2
Nuyts Arch., *Australia* 95 E1
Nxai Pan △, *Botswana* 88 B3
Nxau-Nxau, *Botswana* 88 B3
Nyaake, *Liberia* 82 E3
Nyabing, *Australia* 93 F2
Nyack, *U.S.A.* 117 E11
Nyagan, *Russia* 52 C7
Nyahanga, *Tanzania* 86 C3
Nyahua, *Tanzania* 86 D3
Nyahururu, *Kenya* 86 B4
Nyaingentanglha Shan, *China* . 60 C4
Nyakanazi, *Tanzania* 86 C3
Nyakrom, *Ghana* 83 D4
Nyâlâ, *Sudan* 81 E1
Nyamandhlovu, *Zimbabwe* 87 F2
Nyambiti, *Tanzania* 86 C3
Nyamlell, *Sudan* 81 F2
Nyamwaga, *Tanzania* 86 C3
Nyandekwa, *Tanzania* 86 C3
Nyanding ➤, *Sudan* 81 F3
Nyandoma, *Russia* 32 B11

Nyanga △, *Zimbabwe* 87 F3
Nyangana, *Namibia* 88 B3
Nyanguge, *Tanzania* 86 C3
Nyankpala, *Ghana* 83 D4
Nyanza, *Rwanda* 86 C2
Nyanza □, *Kenya* 86 C3
Nyanza-Lac, *Burundi* 86 C2
Nyaponges, *Sudan* 81 F3
Nyasa, L., *Africa* 87 E3
Nyasvizh, *Belarus* 33 F4
Nyazura, *Zimbabwe* 87 F3
Nyazwidzi ➤, *Zimbabwe* 87 G3
Nyborg, *Denmark* 11 J4
Nybro, *Sweden* 11 H9
Nyda, *Russia* 52 C8
Nyeri, *Kenya* 86 C4
Nyerol, *Sudan* 81 F3
Nyhammar, *Sweden* 10 D8
Nyíka △, *Malawi* 87 E3
Nyinahin, *Ghana* 82 D4
Nyírádony, *Hungary* 28 C6
Nyírbátor, *Hungary* 28 C7
Nyíregyháza, *Hungary* 28 C6
Nykarleby = Uusikaarlepyy,
  Finland 8 E20
Nykøbing, Storstrøm, *Denmark*. 11 K5
Nykøbing, Vestsjælland, *Denmark* 11 J5
Nykøbing, Viborg, *Denmark* ... 11 H2
Nyköping, *Sweden* 11 F11
Nykroppa, *Sweden* 10 E8
Nykvarn, *Sweden* 10 E11
Nyland, *Sweden* 10 A11
Nylstroom = Modimolle, *S. Africa* 89 C4
Nymagee, *Australia* 95 E4
Nymboida ➤, *Australia* 95 D5
Nymburk, *Czech Rep.* 26 A8
Nynäshamn, *Sweden* 11 F11
Nyngan, *Australia* 95 E4
Nyoma Rap, *India* 69 C8
Nyoman = Nemunas ➤,
  Lithuania 9 J19
Nyon, *Switz.* 25 J2
Nyong ➤, *Cameroon* 83 E6
Nyons, *France* 21 D9
Nyou, *Burkina Faso* 83 C4
Nýrsko, *Czech Rep.* 26 B6
Nysa, *Poland* 31 H4
Nysa ➤, *Europe* 24 C10
Nysa Kłodzka ➤, *Poland* 31 H4
Nysäter, *Sweden* 10 E6
Nyslott = Savonlinna, *Finland* . 32 B5
Nyssa, *U.S.A.* 108 E5
Nystad = Uusikaupunki, *Finland* 9 F19
Nysted, *Denmark* 11 K5
Nyunzu, *Dem. Rep. of the Congo* 86 D2
Nyurba, *Russia* 53 C12
Nyzhankovychi, *Ukraine* 31 J9
Nyzhnohirskyy, *Ukraine* 33 K8
Nyzhny Vorota, *Ukraine* 29 B8
Nzébéla, *Guinea* 82 D3
Nzega, *Tanzania* 86 C3
Nzérékoré, *Guinea* 82 D3
Nzeto, *Angola* 84 F2
Nzilo, Chutes de, *Dem. Rep. of
  the Congo* 87 E2
Nzubuka, *Tanzania* 86 C3

O

O Barco, *Spain* 36 C4
O Carballiño, *Spain* 36 C2
O Corgo, *Spain* 36 C3
O Pino, *Spain* 36 C2
O Porriño, *Spain* 36 C2
Ō-Shima, *Japan* 55 G9
Oa, Mull of, *U.K.* 13 F2
Oacoma, *U.S.A.* 112 D5
Oahe, L., *U.S.A.* 112 C4
Oahe Dam, *U.S.A.* 112 C4
Oahu, *U.S.A.* 106 H16
Oak Harbor, *U.S.A.* 110 B4
Oak Hill, *U.S.A.* 114 G5
Oak Ridge, *U.S.A.* 115 G3
Oak View, *U.S.A.* 111 L7
Oakan-Dake, *Japan* 54 C12
Oakdale, *Calif., U.S.A.* 110 H6
Oakdale, *La., U.S.A.* 113 K8
Oakes, *U.S.A.* 112 B5
Oakesdale, *U.S.A.* 108 C5
Oakey, *Australia* 95 D5
Oakfield, *U.S.A.* 116 C6
Oakham, *U.K.* 15 E7
Oakhurst, *U.S.A.* 110 H7
Oakland, *U.S.A.* 110 H4
Oakley, *Idaho, U.S.A.* 108 E7
Oakley, *Kans., U.S.A.* 112 F4
Oakover ➤, *Australia* 92 D3
Oakridge, *U.S.A.* 108 E2
Oakville, *Canada* 116 C5
Oakville, *U.S.A.* 110 D3
Oamaru, *N.Z.* 91 L3
Oancea, *Romania* 29 E12
Oasi Faunistica di Vendicari △,
  Italy 43 F8
Oasis, *Calif., U.S.A.* 111 M10
Oasis, *Nev., U.S.A.* 110 H9
Oates Land, *Antarctica* 5 C11
Oatlands, *Australia* 95 G4
Oatman, *U.S.A.* 111 K12
Oaxaca, *Mexico* 119 D5
Oaxaca □, *Mexico* 119 D5
Ob ➤, *Russia* 52 C7
Oba, *Canada* 104 C3
Obala, *Cameroon* 83 E7
Obama, *Japan* 55 G7
Oban, *Nigeria* 83 D6

Oban, *U.K.* 13 E3
Obbia, Somali Rep. 75 F4
Obera, *Argentina* 127 B4
Oberammergau, *Germany* 25 H7
Oberasbach, *Germany* 25 F6
Oberbayern □, *Germany* 25 G7
Oberdrauburg, *Austria* 26 E5
Obere Donau △, *Germany* 25 G5
Oberer Bayerischer Wald △,
  Germany 25 F8
Oberfranken □, *Germany* 25 E7
Oberhausen, *Germany* 24 D2
Oberkirch, *Germany* 25 G4
Oberlausitz, *Germany* 24 D10
Oberlin, *Kans., U.S.A.* 112 F4
Oberlin, *La., U.S.A.* 113 K8
Oberlin, *Ohio, U.S.A.* 116 E2
Obernai, *France* 19 D14
Oberndorf, *Germany* 25 G4
Oberon, *Australia* 95 E4
Oberösterreich □, *Austria* 26 C7
Oberpfalz □, *Germany* 25 F8
Oberpfälzer Wald, *Germany* ... 25 F8
Oberpfälzer Wald △, *Germany* . 25 F8
Oberstdorf, *Germany* 25 H6
Obertyn, *Ukraine* 29 B10
Oberursel, *Germany* 25 E4
Oberwart, *Austria* 27 D9
Obi, *Indonesia* 63 E7
Obiaruku, *Nigeria* 83 D6
Óbidos, *Brazil* 125 D7
Óbidos, *Portugal* 37 F1
Obihiro, *Japan* 54 C11
Obilatu, *Indonesia* 63 E7
Obilnoye, *Russia* 35 G7
Obing, *Germany* 25 G8
Objat, *France* 20 C5
Obluchye, *Russia* 53 E14
Obo, *Cent. Afr. Rep.* 86 A2
Obo, Mt., *Uganda* 86 B3
Obock, *Djibouti* 81 E5
Obodivka, *Ukraine* 29 B14
Oborniki, *Poland* 31 F3
Oborniki Śląskie, *Poland* 31 G3
Oboyan, *Russia* 33 G9
Obozerskaya = Obozerskiy,
  Russia 52 C5
Obozerskiy, *Russia* 52 C5
Óbrenovac, *Serbia & M.* 44 B4
Obrovac, *Croatia* 41 D12
Obruk, *Turkey* 72 C5
Obrzycko, *Poland* 31 F3
Observatory Inlet, *Canada* 102 B3
Obshchi Syrt, *Russia* 6 E16
Obskaya Guba, *Russia* 52 C8
Obuasi, *Ghana* 83 D4
Obubra, *Nigeria* 83 D6
Obudu, *Nigeria* 83 D6
Obwalden □, *Switz.* 25 J4
Obzor, *Bulgaria* 45 D11
Ocala, *U.S.A.* 115 L4
Ocampo, *Chihuahua, Mexico* . 118 B3
Ocampo, *Tamaulipas, Mexico* . 119 C5
Ocaña, *Spain* 36 F7
Ocanomowoc, *U.S.A.* 112 D10
Occidental, Cordillera, *Colombia* 124 C3
Occidental, Grand Erg, *Algeria* 78 B6
Ocean City, *Md., U.S.A.* 114 F8
Ocean City, *N.J., U.S.A.* 114 F8
Ocean City, *Wash., U.S.A.* 110 C2
Ocean Falls, *Canada* 102 C3
Ocean I. = Banaba, *Kiribati* ... 96 H8
Ocean Park, *U.S.A.* 110 D2
Oceano, *U.S.A.* 111 K6
Oceanport, *U.S.A.* 117 F10
Oceanside, *U.S.A.* 111 M9
Ochagavía, *Spain* 38 C3
Ochakiv, *Ukraine* 33 J6
Ochamchira, *Georgia* 35 J5
Ochil Hills, *U.K.* 13 E5
Ocho Rios, *Jamaica* .... 120 a
Ochsenfurt, *Germany* 25 F6
Ochsenhausen, *Germany* 25 G5
Ocilla, *U.S.A.* 115 K4
Ockelbo, *Sweden* 10 D10
Ocmulgee ➤, *U.S.A.* 115 K4
Ocna Mureş, *Romania* 29 D8
Ocna Sibiului, *Romania* 29 E9
Ocnele Mari, *Romania* 29 E9
Ocniţa, *Moldova* 29 B12
Oconee ➤, *U.S.A.* 115 K4
Oconto, *U.S.A.* 114 C2
Oconto Falls, *U.S.A.* 114 C1
Ocosingo, *Mexico* 119 D6
Ocotal, *Nic.* 120 D2
Ocotlán, *Mexico* 118 C4
Ocotlán de Morelos, *Mexico* .. 119 D5
Ocreza ➤, *Portugal* 37 F3
Ócsa, *Hungary* 28 C4
Octeville, *France* 18 C5
Oda, *Ghana* 83 D4
Oda, *Japan* 55 G6
Oda, J., *Sudan* 80 C4
Ódáðahraun, *Iceland* 8 D5
Ódákra, *Sweden* 11 H6
Odate, *Japan* 54 D10
Odawara, *Japan* 55 G9
Odda, *Norway* 9 F12
Odder, *Denmark* 11 J4
Odei ➤, *Canada* 103 B9
Odemira, *Portugal* 37 H2
Ödemiş, *Turkey* 47 C9
Odendaalsrus, *S. Africa* 88 D4
Odensbacken, *Sweden* 10 E9
Odense, *Denmark* 11 J4
Odenwald △ = Neckartal-
  Odenwald △, *Germany* 25 F5
Odenwald, *Germany* 25 F5
Oder ➤, *Europe* 24 B10
Oder-Havel Kanal, *Germany* .. 24 C10
Oderzo, *Italy* 41 C9

Odesa, Ukraine 33 J6
Ödeshög, Sweden 11 F8
Odessa = Odesa, Ukraine ... 33 J6
Odessa, Canada 117 B8
Odessa, Tex., U.S.A. 113 K3
Odessa, Wash., U.S.A. 108 C4
Odiakwe, Botswana 88 C4
Odiel ➤, Spain 37 H4
Odintsovo, Russia 32 E9
Odiongan, Phil. 61 E4
Odobești, Romania 29 E12
Odolanów, Poland 31 G4
O'Donnell, U.S.A. 113 J4
Odorheiu Secuiesc, Romania .. 29 D10
Odoyevo, Russia 32 F9
Odra = Oder ➤, Europe ... 24 B10
Odra ➤, Spain 36 C6
Odžaci, Serbia & M. 28 E4
Odžak, Bos.-H. 28 E3
Odzi, Zimbabwe 89 B5
Odzi ➤, Zimbabwe 89 B5
Oebisfelde, Germany 24 C6
Oeiras, Brazil 125 E10
Oeiras, Portugal 37 G1
Oelrichs, U.S.A. 112 D3
Oelsnitz, Germany 25 E8
Oelwein, U.S.A. 112 D9
Oenpelli, Australia 92 B5
Oetz, Austria 26 D3
Of, Turkey 73 B9
Ofanto ➤, Italy 43 A9
Offa, Nigeria 83 D5
Offaly □, Ireland 12 C4
Offenbach, Germany 25 E4
Offenburg, Germany 25 G3
Officer, The ➤, Australia ... 93 E5
Offida, Italy 41 F10
Ofidhousa, Greece 47 E8
Ofotfjorden, Norway 8 B17
Ofunato, Japan 54 E10
Oga, Japan 54 E9
Oga-Hantō, Japan 54 E9
Ogaden, Ethiopia 75 F3
Ōgaki, Japan 55 G8
Ogallala, U.S.A. 112 E4
Ogasawara Gunto, Pac. Oc. ... 96 E6
Ogbomosho, Nigeria 83 D5
Ogden, U.S.A. 108 F7
Ogdensburg, U.S.A. 117 B9
Ogeechee ➤, U.S.A. 115 K5
Ogilby, U.S.A. 111 N12
Oglio ➤, Italy 40 C7
Oglio Nord △, Italy 40 C6
Oglio Sud △, Italy 40 C7
Ogmore, Australia 94 C4
Ognon ➤, France 19 E12
Ogoja, Nigeria 83 D6
Ogoki, Canada 104 B2
Ogoki ➤, Canada 104 B2
Ogoki L., Canada 104 B2
Ogoki Res., Canada 104 B2
Ogooué ➤, Gabon 84 E1
Ogosta ➤, Bulgaria 44 C7
Ogowe = Ogooué ➤, Gabon .. 84 E1
Ogr = Sharafa, Sudan 81 E2
Ograżden, Macedonia 44 E6
Ogre, Latvia 9 H21
Ogrein, Sudan 80 D3
Ogulin, Croatia 41 C12
Ogun □, Nigeria 83 D5
Ogurchinskiy, Ostrov,
　Turkmenistan 71 B7
Oguta, Nigeria 83 D6
Ogwashi-Uku, Nigeria 83 D6
Ogwe, Nigeria 83 E6
Ohai, N.Z. 91 L2
Ohakune, N.Z. 91 H5
Ohata, Japan 54 D10
Ohau, L., N.Z. 91 L2
Ohio □, U.S.A. 116 F2
Ohio ➤, U.S.A. 114 G1
Ohře ➤, Czech Rep. 26 A7
Ohre ➤, Germany 24 C7
Ohrid, Macedonia 44 E4
Ohridsko Jezero, Macedonia .. 44 E4
Ohrigstad, S. Africa 89 C5
Öhringen, Germany 25 F5
Oi Qu, China 58 C2
Oiapoque, Brazil 125
Oikou, China 57 E9
Oil City, U.S.A. 116 E5
Oil Springs, Canada 116 D2
Oildale, U.S.A. 111 K7
Oinousa, Greece 47 C8
Oise □, France 19 C9
Oise ➤, France 19 C9
Oiseaux du Djoudj △, Senegal . 82 B1
Oistins, Barbados .... 121 g
Oistins B., Barbados .... 121 g
Oita, Japan 55 H5
Oita □, Japan 55 H5
Oiticica, Brazil 125 E10
Ojacaliente, Mexico 118 C4
Ojai, U.S.A. 111 L7
Ojcowski △, Poland 31 H6
Ojinaga, Mexico 118 B4
Ojiya, Japan 55 F9
Ojo de Liebre △, Mexico ... 118 B2
Ojos del Salado, Cerro, Argentina 126 B2
Oka ➤, Russia 34 B7
Okaba, Indonesia 63 F9
Okahandja, Namibia 88 C2
Okanagan L., Canada 102 D5
Okanogan, U.S.A. 108 B4
Okanogan ➤, U.S.A. 108 B4
Okány, Hungary 28 D6
Okapi △, Dem. Rep. of the Congo 86 B2
Okaputa, Namibia 88 C2
Okara, Pakistan 68 D5
Okaukuejo, Namibia 88 B2
Okavango Delta, Botswana ... 88 B3

Okavango Swamp = Okavango
　Delta, Botswana 88 B3
Okaya, Japan 55 F9
Okayama, Japan 55 G6
Okayama □, Japan 55 G6
Okazaki, Japan 55 G8
Oke-Iho, Nigeria 83 D5
Okęcie, Warszawa ✈ (WAW),
　Poland 31 F7
Okeechobee, U.S.A. 115 M5
Okeechobee, L., U.S.A. 115 M5
Okefenokee △, U.S.A. 115 K4
Okefenokee Swamp, U.S.A. ... 115 K4
Okehampton, U.K. 15 G4
Okene, Nigeria 83 D6
Oker ➤, Germany 24 C6
Okha, India 68 H3
Okha, Russia 53 D15
Ókhi Óros, Greece 38 C6
Okhotsk, Russia 53 D15
Okhotsk, Sea of, Asia 53 D15
Okhotskiy Perevoz, Russia ... 53 C14
Okhtyrka, Ukraine 33 G8
Oki-Shotō, Japan 55 F6
Okiep, S. Africa 88 D2
Okigwi, Nigeria 83 D6
Okija, Nigeria 83 D6
Okinawa □, Japan 55 L4
Okinawa-Guntō, Japan 55 L4
Okinawa-Jima, Japan 55 L4
Okino-erabu-Shima, Japan ... 55 L4
Okitipupa, Nigeria 83 D5
Oklahoma □, U.S.A. 113 H6
Oklahoma City, U.S.A. 113 H6
Okmulgee, U.S.A. 113 H7
Oknitsa = Ocnița, Moldova ... 29 B12
Oko, W. ➤, Sudan 80 C4
Okolo, Uganda 86 B3
Okolona, U.S.A. 113 J10
Okombahe, Namibia 88 C2
Okonek, Poland 30 E3
Okotoks, Canada 102 C6
Okrika, Nigeria 83 E6
Oksibil, Indonesia 63 E10
Oktabrsk = Oktyabrsk,
　Kazakhstan 52 E6
Oktyabrsk, Kazakhstan 52 E6
Oktyabrsk, Russia 34 D9
Oktyabrskiy = Aktsyabrski,
　Belarus 33 F5
Oktyabrskiy, Russia 35 G5
Oktyabrskoy Revolyutsii, Ostrov,
　Russia 53 B10
Oktyabrskoye = Zhovtneve,
　Ukraine 33 J7
Okulovka, Russia 32 C7
Okuru, N.Z. 91 K2
Okushiri-Tō, Japan 54 C9
Okuta, Nigeria 83 D5
Okwa ➤, Botswana 88 C3
Ola, U.S.A. 113 H8
Ólafsfjörður, Iceland 8 C4
Ólafsvík, Iceland 8 D2
Olaine, Latvia 30 B10
Olancha, U.S.A. 111 J8
Olancha Pk., U.S.A. 111 J8
Olanchito, Honduras 120 C2
Öland, Sweden 11 H10
Ölands norra udde, Sweden ... 11 G11
Ölands södra udde, Sweden .. 11 H10
Olargues, France 20 E6
Olary, Australia 95 E3
Olascoaga, Argentina 126 D3
Olathe, U.S.A. 112 F7
Olavarría, Argentina 126 D3
Oława, Poland 31 H4
Olbernhau, Germany 24 E9
Ólbia, Italy 42 B2
Ólbia, G. di, Italy 42 B2
Olching, Germany 25 G7
Olcott, U.S.A. 116 C6
Old Bahama Chan. = Bahama,
　Canal Viejo de, W. Indies .. 120 B4
Old Baldy Pk. = San Antonio,
　Mt., U.S.A. 111 L9
Old Castile = Castilla y Leon □,
　Spain 36 D6
Old Crow, Canada 100 B6
Old Dale, U.S.A. 111 L11
Old Forge, N.Y., U.S.A. 117 C10
Old Forge, Pa., U.S.A. 117 E9
Old Perlican, Canada 105 C9
Old Shinyanga, Tanzania 86 C3
Old Speck Mt., U.S.A. 117 B14
Old Town, U.S.A. 115 C11
Old Washington, U.S.A. 116 F3
Old Wives L., Canada 103 C7
Oldbury, U.K. 15 F5
Oldcastle, Ireland 12 C4
Oldeani, Tanzania 86 C4
Oldenburg, Niedersachsen,
　Germany 24 B4
Oldenburg, Schleswig-Holstein,
　Germany 24 A6
Oldenzaal, Neths. 17 B6
Oldham, U.K. 14 D5
Oldman ➤, Canada 102 D6
Oldmeldrum, U.K. 13 D6
Olds, Canada 102 C6
Olduvai Gorge, Tanzania 86 C4
Olecko, Poland 30 D9
Oléggio, Italy 40 C5
Oleiros, Portugal 36 F3
Oleiros, Spain 36 B2
Olekma ➤, Russia 53 C13
Olekminsk, Russia 53 C13
Oleksandriya, Kirovohrad,
　Ukraine 33 H7
Oleksandriya, Rivne, Ukraine .. 33 G4
Oleksandrovka, Ukraine 33 H7

Olema, U.S.A. 110 G4
Olenek, Russia 53 C12
Olenek ➤, Russia 53 B13
Olenino, Russia 32 D7
Oléron, Î. d', France 20 C2
Olesk, Ukraine 31 G11
Oleśnica, Poland 31 G4
Olesno, Poland 31 H5
Olevsk, Ukraine 33 G4
Olga, Russia 53 E14
Olga, L., Canada 104 C4
Olga, Mt., Australia 93 E5
Ølgod, Denmark 11 J2
Olhão, Portugal 37 H3
Olhopil, Ukraine 29 B14
Olhovatka, Russia 30 D9
Olib, Croatia 41 D11
Oliena, Italy 42 B2
Oliete, Spain 38 D4
Olifants = Elefantes ➤, Africa . 89 C5
Olifants ➤, Namibia 88 C2
Olifantshoek, S. Africa 88 D3
Ólimbos, Greece 47 F9
Ólimbos, Óros, Greece 44 F6
Olímpia, Brazil 127 A6
Olimpos-Beydaglari △, Turkey . 47 E12
Olinda, Brazil 125 E12
Olite, Spain 38 C3
Oliva, Argentina 126 C3
Oliva, Spain 39 G4
Oliva, Punta del, Spain 36 B5
Oliva de la Frontera, Spain ... 37 G4
Olivares, Spain 38 F2
Olivehurst, U.S.A. 110 F5
Oliveira de Azeméis, Portugal .. 36 E2
Oliveira do Douro, Portugal ... 36 D2
Olivenza, Spain 37 G3
Oliver, Canada 102 D5
Oliver L., Canada 103 B8
Olivet, France 19 E8
Olkhovka, Russia 34 F7
Olkusz, Poland 31 H6
Ollagüe, Chile 126 A2
Olmedo, Spain 36 D6
Olmeto, France 21 G12
Olney, Ill., U.S.A. 114 F1
Olney, Tex., U.S.A. 113 J5
Olofström, Sweden 11 H8
Oloma, Cameroon 83 E7
Olomane ➤, Canada 105 B7
Olomouc, Czech Rep. 27 B10
Olomoucký □, Czech Rep. ... 27 B10
Olonets, Russia 32 B5
Olongapo, Phil. 61 D4
Olonne-sur-Mer, France 20 B2
Oloron, Gave d' ➤, France .. 20 E2
Oloron-Ste-Marie, France 20 E2
Olot, Spain 38 C7
Olovo, Bos.-H. 28 F3
Olovyannaya, Russia 53 D12
Oloy ➤, Russia 53 C16
Olsberg, Germany 24 D4
Olshammar, Sweden 11 F8
Olshanka, Ukraine 29 B13
Olshany, Ukraine 33 G8
Olsztyn, Poland 30 E7
Olsztynek, Poland 30 E7
Olt □, Romania 29 F9
Olt ➤, Romania 29 G9
Oltenița, Romania 29 F11
Olton, U.S.A. 113 H3
Oltu, Turkey 73 B9
Oluanpi, Taiwan 59 G13
Olula del Rio, Spain 39 H2
Olur, Turkey 73 B10
Olutanga, Phil. 61 H5
Olvega, Spain 38 D2
Olvera, Spain 37 J5
Olymbos, Cyprus 49 D12
Olympia, Greece 46 D3
Olympia, U.S.A. 110 D4
Olympic △, U.S.A. 110 C3
Olympic Dam, Australia 95 E2
Olympic Mts., U.S.A. 110 C3
Olympus, Cyprus 49 E11
Olympus, Mt. = Olimbos, Óros,
　Greece 44 F6
Olympus, Mt. = Uludağ, Turkey . 45 F13
Olympus, Mt., U.S.A. 110 C3
Olyphant, U.S.A. 117 E9
Om ➤, Russia 52 D8
Om Hajer, Eritrea 81 E4
Om Koi, Thailand 64 D2
Ōma, Japan 54 D10
Ōmachi, Japan 55 F8
Omae-Zaki, Japan 55 G9
Ōmagari, Japan 54 E10
Omagh, U.K. 12 B4
Omagh □, U.K. 12 B4
Omaha, U.S.A. 112 E7
Omak, U.S.A. 108 B4
Omalos, Greece 49 D5
Oman ■, Asia 75 C6
Oman, G. of, Asia 71 E8
Omaruru, Namibia 88 C2
Omaruru ➤, Namibia 88 C1
Omate, Peru 124 G4
Ombai, Selat, Indonesia 63 F6
Ombrone ➤, Italy 41 F8
Omdurmân, Sudan 81 D3
Omega, Italy 40 C5
Omemee, Canada 116 B6
Omeonga, Dem. Rep. of
　the Congo 86 C1
Ometepe, I. de, Nic. 120 D2
Ometepec, Mexico 119 D5
Ominato, Japan 54 D10
Ominéca ➤, Canada 102 B4
Omiš, Croatia 41 E13
Omišalj, Croatia 41 C11

Omitara, Namibia 88 C2
Ōmiya, Japan 55 G9
Omme Å ➤, Denmark 11 J2
Ommen, Neths. 17 B6
Ömnögovi □, Mongolia 56 C3
Omo △, Ethiopia 81 F4
Omo ➤, Ethiopia 81 F4
Omo Valley, Ethiopia 81 F4
Omodeo, L., Italy 42 B1
Omodhos, Cyprus 49 E11
Omoko, Nigeria 83 D6
Omolon ➤, Russia 53 C16
Omono-Gawa ➤, Japan 54 E10
Omsk, Russia 52 D8
Omsukchan, Russia 53 C16
Ōmu, Japan 54 B11
Omul, Vf., Romania 29 E10
Omulew ➤, Poland 31 E8
Ōmura, Japan 55 H4
Omuramba Omatako ➤,
　Namibia 88 B2
Omuramba Ovambo ➤, Namibia 88 B2
Ōmurta, Bulgaria 45 C10
Ōmuta, Japan 55 H5
Oña, Spain 36 C7
Onaga, U.S.A. 112 F6
Onalaska, U.S.A. 112 D9
Onancock, U.S.A. 114 G8
Onang, Indonesia 63 E5
Onaping L., Canada 104 C3
Oñati, Spain 38 B2
Onavas, Mexico 118 B3
Onawa, U.S.A. 112 D6
Oncócua, Angola 88 B1
Onda, Spain 38 F4
Ondaejin, N. Korea 57 D15
Ondangwa, Namibia 88 B2
Ondarroa, Spain 38 B2
Ondava ➤, Slovak Rep. 27 C14
Ondjiva, Angola 88 B2
Ondo, Nigeria 83 D5
Ondo □, Nigeria 83 D6
Öndörshil, Mongolia 56 B5
Öndörvarnes, Iceland 8 D1
One Tree, Australia 95 E3
Onega, Russia 52 C4
Onega ➤, Russia 6 C13
Onega, L. = Onezhskoye Ozero,
　Russia 32 B8
Oneida, U.S.A. 117 C9
Oneida L., U.S.A. 117 C9
O'Neill, U.S.A. 112 D5
Onekotan, Ostrov, Russia 53 E16
Oneonta, U.S.A. 117 D9
Onești, Romania 29 D11
Onezhskoye Ozero, Russia ... 32 B8
Ongarue, N.Z. 91 H5
Ongers ➤, S. Africa 88 E3
Ongerup, Australia 93 F2
Ongjin, N. Korea 57 F13
Ongkharak, Thailand 64 E3
Ongniud Qi, China 57 C10
Ongoka, Dem. Rep. of the Congo 86 C2
Ongole, India 66 M12
Ongon = Havirga, Mongolia ... 56 B7
Oni, Georgia 35 J6
Onida, U.S.A. 112 C4
Onilahy ➤, Madag. 89 C7
Onitsha, Nigeria 83 D6
Onoda, Japan 55 G5
Onpyŏng-ni, S. Korea 57 H14
Ons, I. de, Spain 36 C2
Onsala, Sweden 11 G6
Onslow, Australia 92 D2
Onslow B., U.S.A. 115 H7
Ontake-San, Japan 55 G8
Ontario, Calif., U.S.A. 111 L9
Ontario, Oreg., U.S.A. 108 D5
Ontario □, Canada 104 B2
Ontario, L., N. Amer. 116 C7
Ontinyent, Spain 39 G4
Ontonagon, U.S.A. 112 B10
Ontur, Spain 39 G3
Onyx, U.S.A. 111 K8
Oodnadatta, Australia 95 D2
Ooldea, Australia 93 F5
Oombulgurri, Australia 92 C4
Oorindi, Australia 94 C3
Oost-Vlaanderen □, Belgium .. 17 C3
Oostende, Belgium 17 C2
Oosterhout, Neths. 17 C4
Oosterschelde ➤, Neths. 17 C4
Oosterwolde, Neths. 17 B6
Ootacamund = Udagamandalam,
　India 66 P10
Ootsa L., Canada 102 C3
Op Luang △, Thailand 64 C2
Opaka, Bulgaria 45 C10
Opala, Dem. Rep. of the Congo . 86 C1
Opalenica, Poland 31 F3
Opan, Bulgaria 45 D9
Opanake, Sri Lanka 66 R12
Opasatika, Canada 104 C3
Opasquia △, Canada 104 B1
Opatija, Croatia 41 C11
Opatów, Poland 31 H8
Opava, Czech Rep. 27 B10
Opelika, U.S.A. 115 J3
Opelousas, U.S.A. 113 K8
Opémisca, L., Canada 104 C5
Opheim, U.S.A. 108 B10
Ophthalmia Ra., Australia ... 92 D2
Opi, Nigeria 83 D6
Opinaca ➤, Canada 104 B4
Opinaca, Rés., Canada 104 B4
Opinnagau ➤, Canada 104 B3
Opiscotéo, L., Canada 105 B6
Opobo, Nigeria 83 E6
Opochka, Russia 32 D5
Opoczno, Poland 31 G7
Opol, Phil. 61 G6

Opole, Poland 31 H4
Opole Lubelskie, Poland 31 G8
Opolskie □, Poland 31 H5
Oponono L., Namibia 88 B2
Oporto = Porto, Portugal ... 36 D2
Opotiki, N.Z. 91 H6
Opp, U.S.A. 115 K2
Oppdal, Norway 9 E13
Óppido Mamertina, Italy ... 43 D8
Opportunity, U.S.A. 108 C5
Oprișor, Romania 28 F8
Oprtalj, Croatia 41 C10
Opua, N.Z. 91 F5
Opunake, N.Z. 91 H4
Opuwo, Namibia 88 B1
Opuzen, Croatia 41 E14
Ora, Cyprus 49 E12
Oracle, U.S.A. 109 K8
Oradea, Romania 28 C6
Öræfajökull, Iceland 8 D5
Orahovac, Serbia & M. 44 D4
Orahovica, Croatia 28 E2
Orai, India 69 G8
Oraison, France 21 E9
Oral = Zhayyq ➤, Kazakhstan . 52 E6
Oral, Kazakhstan 34 E10
Oran, Algeria 78 A5
Orange, Australia 95 E4
Orange, France 21 D8
Orange, Calif., U.S.A. 111 M9
Orange, Mass., U.S.A. 117 D12
Orange, Tex., U.S.A. 113 K8
Orange, Va., U.S.A. 114 F6
Orange ➤, S. Africa 88 D2
Orange, C., Brazil 125 C8
Orange Cove, U.S.A. 110 J7
Orange Free State = Free State □,
　S. Africa 88 D4
Orange Grove, U.S.A. 113 M6
Orange Walk, Belize 119 D7
Orangeburg, U.S.A. 115 J5
Orangeville, Canada 116 C4
Orango, Guinea-Biss. 82 C1
Orani, Phil. 61 D4
Oranienburg, Germany 24 C9
Oranje = Orange ➤, S. Africa . 88 D2
Oranjemund, Namibia 88 D2
Oranjerivier, S. Africa 88 D3
Oranjestad, Aruba 121 D5
Orapa, Botswana 85 J5
Orarak, Sudan 81 F3
Oras, Phil. 61 E6
Orașje, Bos.-H. 28 E3
Orăștie, Romania 29 E8
Orava ➤, Slovak Rep. 27 B12
Orava, Vodna nádrž, Slovak Rep. 27 B12
Oravița, Romania 28 E6
Orb ➤, France 20 E7
Orba ➤, Italy 40 D5
Ørbæk, Denmark 11 J4
Orbe, Switz. 25 J2
Orbec, France 18 C7
Orbetello, Italy 41 F8
Órbigo ➤, Spain 36 C5
Orbisonia, U.S.A. 116 F7
Orbost, Australia 95 F4
Ørbyhus, Sweden 10 D11
Orcadas, Antarctica 5 C18
Orcas I., U.S.A. 110 B4
Orce, Spain 39 H2
Orce ➤, Spain 39 H2
Orchard City, U.S.A. 109 G10
Orchies, France 19 B10
Orchila, I., Venezuela 121 D6
Orchilla, Pta., Canary Is. 48 G1
Órcia ➤, Italy 41 F8
Orco ➤, Italy 40 C4
Orcutt, U.S.A. 111 L6
Ord, U.S.A. 112 E5
Ord ➤, Australia 92 C4
Ord, Mt., Australia 92 C4
Ordenes = Ordes, Spain 36 B2
Orderville, U.S.A. 109 H7
Ordes, Spain 36 B2
Ordesa y Monte Perido △, Spain 38 C4
Ording = St-Peter-Ording,
　Germany 24 A4
Ordos = Mu Us Shamo, China . 56 E5
Ordu, Turkey 72 B7
Ordubad, Azerbaijan 73 C12
Orduña, Álava, Spain 38 C2
Orduña, Granada, Spain ... 37 H7
Ordway, U.S.A. 112 F3
Ordzhonikidze, Ukraine 33 J8
Ore, Dem. Rep. of the Congo ... 86 B2
Ore Mts. = Erzgebirge, Germany 24 E8
Orebić, Croatia 41 F14
Örebro, Sweden 10 E9
Örebro län □, Sweden 10 E8
Orecchiella △, Italy 40 D7
Oregon, U.S.A. 112 D10
Oregon □, U.S.A. 108 E3
Oregon City, U.S.A. 110 E4
Oregon Dunes △, U.S.A. ... 108 E1
Öregrund, Sweden 10 D12
Öregrundsgrepen, Sweden ... 10 D12
Orekhov = Orikhiv, Ukraine .. 33 J8
Orekhovo-Zuyevo, Russia ... 32 E10
Orel, Russia 33 F9
Orel ➤, Ukraine 33 H8
Orellana, Peru 124 E3
Orellana, Canal de, Spain ... 37 F5
Orellana, Embalse de, Spain .. 37 F5
Orellana la Vieja, Spain 37 F5
Ören, Turkey 47 D9
Orenburg, Russia 52 D6
Orencik, Turkey 47 B11
Orense = Ourense, Spain 36 C3
Orense □, Spain 36 C3
Orestiás, Greece 45 E10
Orestos Pereyra, Mexico 118 B3

Øresund, Europe 11 J6
Orford Ness, U.K. 15 E9
Organ Pipe Cactus △, U.S.A. ... 109 K7
Organos, Pta. de los, Canary Is. . 48 F2
Organyà, Spain 38 C6
Orgaz, Spain 37 F7
Orgeyev = Orhei, Moldova 29 C13
Orhaneli, Turkey 45 G12
Orhaneli ➤, Turkey 45 G12
Orhangazi, Turkey 45 F13
Orhei, Moldova 29 C13
Orhon Gol ➤, Mongolia 60 A5
Óría, Italy 43 B10
Oriental, Cordillera, Colombia . 124 B4
Oriental, Grand Erg, Algeria ... 78 B7
Orientale □, Dem. Rep. of
  the Congo 86 B2
Oriente, Argentina 126 D3
Orihuela, Spain 39 G4
Orihuela del Tremedal, Spain .. 38 E3
Orikhiv, Ukraine 33 J8
Orikum, Albania 44 F3
Orillia, Canada 116 B5
Orinoco ➤, Venezuela 124 B6
Orion, Canada 103 D6
Oriskany, U.S.A. 117 C9
Orissa □, India 67 K14
Orissaare, Estonia 9 G20
Oristano, Italy 42 C1
Oristano, G. di, Italy 42 C1
Orizaba, Mexico 119 D5
Orizaba, Pico de, Mexico 119 D5
Orizare, Bulgaria 45 D11
Orjen, Bos.-H. 44 D2
Orjiva, Spain 37 J7
Orkanger, Norway 8 E13
Örkelljunga, Sweden 11 H7
Örken, Sweden 11 G9
Örkény, Hungary 28 C4
Orkla ➤, Norway 8 E13
Orkney, S. Africa 88 D4
Orkney □, U.K. 13 B5
Orkney Is., U.K. 13 B6
Orland, U.S.A. 110 F4
Orlando, U.S.A. 115 L5
Orlando, C. d', Italy 43 D7
Orléanais, France 19 E9
Orléans, France 19 E8
Orleans, U.S.A. 117 B12
Orléans, Î. d', Canada 105 C5
Orlice ➤, Czech Rep. 26 A8
Orlivka, Ukraine 29 E13
Orlov, Slovak Rep. 27 B13
Orlov Gay, Russia 34 E9
Orlová, Czech Rep. 27 B11
Orlovat, Serbia & M. 28 E5
Orly, Paris ✈ (ORY), France ... 19 D9
Ormara, Pakistan 66 G4
Ormea, Italy 40 D4
Ormília, Greece 44 F7
Ormoc, Phil. 61 F6
Ormond, N.Z. 91 H6
Ormond Beach, U.S.A. 115 L5
Ormož, Slovenia 41 B13
Ormskirk, U.K. 14 D5
Ormstown, Canada 117 A11
Ornans, France 19 E13
Orne □, France 18 D7
Orne ➤, France 18 C6
Orneta, Poland 30 D7
Ornö, Sweden 10 E12
Örnsköldsvik, Sweden 10 A12
Oro, N. Korea 57 D14
Oro ➤, Mexico 118 B3
Oro Grande, U.S.A. 111 L9
Oro Valley, U.S.A. 109 K8
Orobie, Alpi, Italy 40 B6
Orobie Bergamasche △, Italy .. 40 C6
Orobie Valtellinesi △, Italy 40 B6
Orocué, Colombia 124 C4
Orodara, Burkina Faso 82 C4
Orodo, Nigeria 83 D6
Orofino, U.S.A. 108 C5
Orol Dengizi = Aral Sea, Asia .. 52 E7
Oromíya □, Ethiopia 81 F5
Oromocto, Canada 105 C6
Oron, Nigeria 83 E6
Orono, Canada 116 C6
Orono, U.S.A. 115 C11
Oronsay, U.K. 13 E2
Oropesa, Spain 36 F5
Oroquieta, Phil. 61 G5
Orosei, Italy 42 B2
Orosei, G. di, Italy 42 B2
Orosháza, Hungary 28 D5
Oroszlány, Hungary 28 C3
Orotukan, Russia 53 C16
Oroville, Calif., U.S.A. 110 F5
Oroville, Wash., U.S.A. 108 B4
Oroville, L., U.S.A. 110 F5
Orrefors, Sweden 11 H9
Orroroo, Australia 95 E2
Orrviken, Sweden 10 A8
Orrville, U.S.A. 116 F3
Orsa, Sweden 10 C8
Orsara di Púglia, Italy 43 A8
Orsasjön, Sweden 10 C8
Orsha, Belarus 32 E6
Örsjö, Sweden 11 H9
Orsk, Russia 52 D6
Orşova, Romania 28 F7
Ørsted, Denmark 11 H4
Örsundsbro, Sweden 10 E11
Orta, L. d', Italy 40 C5
Orta Nova, Italy 43 A8
Ortaca, Turkey 47 E10
Ortakent, Turkey 47 D9
Ortaklar, Turkey 47 D9
Ortaköy, Çorum, Turkey 72 B6
Ortaköy, Niğde, Turkey 72 C6
Orte, Italy 41 F9
Ortegal, C., Spain 36 B3

Orthez, France 20 E3
Ortigueira, Spain 36 B3
Orting, U.S.A. 110 C4
Ortisei, Italy 41 B8
Ortles, Italy 40 B7
Ortón ➤, Bolivia 124 F5
Ortona, Italy 41 F11
Ortonville, U.S.A. 112 C6
Orūmīyeh, Iran 70 B5
Orūmīyeh, Daryācheh-ye, Iran . 70 B5
Orune, Italy 42 B2
Oruro, Bolivia 124 G5
Orust, Sweden 11 F5
Oruzgān □, Afghan. 66 C5
Orvault, France 18 E5
Orvieto, Italy 41 F9
Orwell, N.Y., U.S.A. 117 C9
Orwell, Ohio, U.S.A. 116 E4
Orwell ➤, U.K. 15 F9
Orwigsburg, U.S.A. 117 F8
Oryakhovo, Bulgaria 44 C7
Orynyn, Ukraine 29 B11
Orzinuovi, Italy 40 C6
Orzyc ➤, Poland 31 F8
Orzysz, Poland 30 E8
Osa ➤, Poland 30 E5
Osa, Pen. de, Costa Rica 120 E3
Osage, U.S.A. 112 D8
Osage ➤, U.S.A. 112 F9
Osage City, U.S.A. 112 F7
Osaka, Japan 55 G7
Osan, S. Korea 57 F14
Osawatomie, U.S.A. 112 F7
Osborne, U.S.A. 112 F5
Osby, Sweden 11 H7
Osceola, Ark., U.S.A. 113 H10
Osceola, Iowa, U.S.A. 112 E8
Oschatz, Germany 24 D9
Oschersleben, Germany 24 C7
Óschiri, Italy 42 B2
Oscoda, U.S.A. 116 B1
Osečina, Serbia & M. 44 B3
Osel = Saaremaa, Estonia 9 G20
Osery, Russia 32 E10
Osgoode, Canada 117 A9
Oshakati, Namibia 85 H3
Oshawa, Canada 116 C6
Oshigambo, Namibia 88 B2
Oshkosh, Nebr., U.S.A. 112 E3
Oshkosh, Wis., U.S.A. 112 C10
Oshmyany = Ashmyany, Belarus . 9 J21
Oshnovīyeh, Iran 70 B5
Oshogbo, Nigeria 83 D5
Oshtorīnān, Iran 71 C6
Oshwe, Dem. Rep. of the Congo . 84 E3
Osi, Nigeria 83 D6
Osieczna, Poland 31 G3
Osijek, Croatia 28 E3
Ósilo, Italy 42 B1
Ósimo, Italy 41 E10
Osintorf, Belarus 32 E6
Osipovichi = Asipovichy, Belarus . 32 F5
Osiyan, India 68 F5
Osizweni, S. Africa 89 D5
Oskaloosa, U.S.A. 112 E8
Oskarshamn, Sweden 11 G10
Oskarström, Sweden 11 H6
Oskélanéo, Canada 104 C4
Öskemen, Kazakhstan 52 E9
Oskol ➤, Ukraine 33 H9
Oslo, Norway 9 G14
Oslob, Phil. 61 G5
Oslofjorden, Norway 9 G14
Osmanabad, India 66 K10
Osmancık, Turkey 72 B6
Osmaniye, Turkey 70 B3
Osmanlı, Turkey 45 E10
Osmo, Sweden 10 F11
Osnabrück, Germany 24 C4
Ośno Lubuskie, Poland 31 F1
Osoblaha, Czech Rep. 27 A10
Osogovska Planina, Macedonia . 44 D6
Osor, Italy 41 D11
Osório, Brazil 127 B5
Osorno, Chile 128 E2
Osorno, Spain 36 C6
Osoyoos, Canada 102 D5
Osøyro, Norway 9 F11
Ospika ➤, Canada 102 B4
Osprey Reef, Australia 94 A4
Oss, Neths. 17 C5
Ossa, Mt., Australia 95 G4
Óssa, Óros, Greece 46 B4
Ossa de Montiel, Spain 39 G2
Ossabaw I., U.S.A. 115 K5
Osse ➤, France 20 D4
Osse ➤, Nigeria 83 D6
Ossi, Italy 42 B1
Ossining, U.S.A. 117 E11
Ossipee, U.S.A. 117 C13
Ossokmanuan L., Canada 105 B7
Ossora, Russia 53 D17
Ostashkov, Russia 32 D7
Östavall, Sweden 10 B9
Oste ➤, Germany 24 B5
Ostend = Oostende, Belgium .. 17 C2
Oster, Ukraine 33 G6
Österbotten = Pohjanmaa,
  Finland 8 E20
Osterburg, Germany 24 C7
Osterburg, U.S.A. 116 F6
Osterburken, Germany 25 F5
Österbybruk, Sweden 10 D11
Österbymo, Sweden 11 G9
Österdalälven ➤, Sweden 10 C7
Osterdalen, Norway 9 F14
Österfärnebo, Sweden 10 D10
Österforse, Sweden 10 A11
Östergötlands län □, Sweden .. 11 F9
Osterholz-Scharmbeck, Germany 24 B4
Østerild, Denmark 11 G2

Östermyra = Seinäjoki, Finland . 9 E20
Osterode, Germany 24 D6
Östersund, Sweden 10 A8
Östervåla, Sweden 10 D11
Ostfriesische Inseln, Germany .. 24 B3
Ostfriesland, Germany 24 B3
Östhammar, Sweden 10 D12
Óstia, Lido di, Italy 41 G9
Ostíglia, Italy 41 C8
Östmark, Sweden 10 D6
Östra Husby, Sweden 11 F10
Ostrava, Czech Rep. 27 B11
Ostravský □, Czech Rep. 27 B10
Ostróda, Poland 30 E6
Ostrogozhsk, Russia 33 G10
Ostroh, Ukraine 33 G4
Ostrołęka, Poland 31 E8
Ostrov, Bulgaria 45 C8
Ostrov, Czech Rep. 26 A5
Ostrov, Romania 29 F12
Ostrov, Russia 32 D5
Ostrów Lubelski, Poland 31 G9
Ostrów Mazowiecka, Poland ... 31 F8
Ostrów Wielkopolski, Poland .. 31 G4
Ostrowiec-Świętokrzyski, Poland 31 H8
Ostrožac, Bos.-H. 28 G2
Ostrzeszów, Poland 31 G4
Ostseebad Kühlungsborn,
  Germany 24 A7
Osttirol □, Austria 26 E5
Ostuni, Italy 43 B10
Osum ➤, Albania 44 F4
Ösüm ➤, Bulgaria 45 C8
Ōsumi-Kaikyō, Japan 55 J5
Ōsumi-Shotō, Japan 55 J5
Osun □, Nigeria 83 D5
Osuna, Spain 37 H5
Oswegatchie ➤, U.S.A. 117 B9
Oswego, U.S.A. 117 C8
Oswego ➤, U.S.A. 117 C8
Oswestry, U.K. 14 E4
Oświęcim, Poland 31 H6
Otaci, Moldova 29 B12
Otago □, N.Z. 91 L2
Otago Harbour, N.Z. 91 L3
Otaheite B., Trin. & Tob. 125 K15
Ōtake, Japan 55 G6
Otaki, N.Z. 91 J5
Otaru, Japan 54 C10
Otaru-Wan = Ishikari-Wan, Japan 54 C10
Otava ➤, Czech Rep. 26 B7
Otavalo, Ecuador 124 C3
Otavi, Namibia 88 B2
Otchinjau, Angola 88 B1
Otelec, Romania 28 E5
Otelnuk, L., Canada 105 A6
Oțelu Roșu, Romania 28 E7
Otero de Rey = Outeiro de Rei,
  Spain 36 B3
Othello, U.S.A. 108 C4
Othonoí, Greece 46 B1
Óthris, Óros, Greece 46 B4
Oti ➤, Togo 83 C5
Otjiwarongo, Namibia 88 C2
Otmuchów, Poland 31 H4
Otočac, Croatia 41 D12
Otoineppu, Japan 54 B11
Otok, Croatia 41 E13
Otopeni, Bucureşti ✈ (OTP),
  Romania 45 B10
Otorohanga, N.Z. 91 H5
Otoskwin ➤, Canada 104 B2
Otra ➤, Norway 9 G13
Otradnyy, Russia 34 D10
Otranto, Italy 43 B11
Otranto, C. d', Italy 43 B11
Otranto, Str. of, Italy 43 B11
Otrokovice, Czech Rep. 27 B10
Otse, S. Africa 88 D4
Ōtsu, Japan 55 G7
Ōtsuki, Japan 55 G9
Ottawa = Outaouais ➤, Canada 104 C5
Ottawa, Canada 117 A9
Ottawa, Ill., U.S.A. 112 E10
Ottawa, Kans., U.S.A. 112 F7
Ottawa Is., Canada 101 C11
Ottélé, Cameroon 83 E7
Ottensheim, Austria 26 C7
Otter Cr. ➤, U.S.A. 117 B11
Otter L., Canada 103 B8
Otterndorf, Germany 24 B4
Otterup, Denmark 11 J4
Otterville, Canada 116 D4
Ottery St. Mary, U.K. 15 G4
Otto Beit Bridge, Zimbabwe ... 87 F2
Ottosdal, S. Africa 88 D4
Ottumwa, U.S.A. 112 E8
Otu, Nigeria 83 D5
Otukpa, Nigeria 83 D6
Oturkpo, Nigeria 83 D6
Otway, B., Chile 128 G2
Otway, C., Australia 95 F3
Otwock, Poland 31 F8
Otyniya, Ukraine 29 B9
Ötztal Ache ➤, Austria 26 D3
Ötztaler Alpen, Austria 26 E3
Ou ➤, Laos 58 B4
Ou Neua, Laos 58 B3
Ou-Sammyaku, Japan 54 E10
Ouachita ➤, U.S.A. 113 K9
Ouachita, L., U.S.A. 113 H8
Ouachita Mts., U.S.A. 113 H7
Ouagadougou, Burkina Faso .. 83 C4
Ouahigouya, Burkina Faso 82 C4
Ouahran = Oran, Algeria 78 A5
Oualâta, Mauritania 82 B3
Ouallam, Niger 83 C5
Ouallene, Algeria 78 D6
Ouargaye, Burkina Faso 83 C5
Ouargla, Algeria 78 B7
Ouarkoye, Burkina Faso 82 C4
Ouarzazate, Morocco 78 B4

Ouassouas, Mali 83 B5
Ouatagouna, Mali 83 B5
Oubangi ➤, Dem. Rep. of
  the Congo 84 E3
Ouche ➤, France 19 E12
Ouddorp, Neths. 17 C3
Oude Rijn ➤, Neths. 17 B4
Oudeïka, Mali 83 B4
Oudenaarde, Belgium 17 D3
Oudon ➤, France 18 E6
Oudtshoorn, S. Africa 88 E3
Ouellé, Ivory C. 82 D4
Ouéme ➤, Benin 83 D5
Ouessa, Burkina Faso 82 C4
Ouessant, Î. d', France 18 D1
Ouesso, Congo 84 D3
Ouest, Pte. de l', Canada 105 C7
Ouezzane, Morocco 78 B4
Ougarou, Burkina Faso 83 C5
Oughterard, Ireland 12 C2
Ouidah, Benin 83 D5
Ouidi, Niger 83 C7
Ouistreham, France 18 C6
Oujda, Morocco 78 B5
Oujeft, Mauritania 82 A2
Oulainen, Finland 8 D21
Ould Yenjé, Mauritania 82 B2
Oullins, France 21 C8
Oulu, Finland 8 D21
Oulujärvi, Finland 8 D22
Oulujoki ➤, Finland 8 D21
Oulx, Italy 40 C3
Oum Chalouba, Chad 79 E10
Oum Hadjer, Chad 79 F9
Oumé, Ivory C. 82 D3
Ounasjoki ➤, Finland 8 C21
Ounguati, Namibia 88 C2
Ounianga Sérir, Chad 79 E10
Our ➤, Lux. 17 E6
Ouranópolis, Greece 44 F7
Ourârene, Niger 83 B6
Ouray, U.S.A. 109 G10
Ourcq ➤, France 19 C10
Ourense, Spain 36 C3
Ouricuri, Brazil 125 E10
Ourinhos, Brazil 127 A6
Ourique, Portugal 37 H2
Ouro Fino, Brazil 127 A6
Ouro Prêto, Brazil 127 A7
Ouro Sogui, Senegal 82 B2
Oursi, Burkina Faso 83 C4
Ourthe ➤, Belgium 17 D5
Ouse ➤, E. Susx., U.K. 15 G8
Ouse ➤, N. Yorks., U.K. 14 D7
Oust, France 20 F5
Oust ➤, France 18 E4
Outamba-Kilimi △, S. Leone .. 82 D2
Outaouais ➤, Canada 104 C5
Outardes ➤, Canada 105 C6
Outeiro de Rei, Spain 36 B3
Outer Hebrides, U.K. 13 D1
Outes = Serra de Outes, Spain . 36 C2
Outjo, Namibia 88 C2
Outlook, Canada 103 C7
Outokumpu, Finland 8 E23
Outreau, France 19 B8
Ouvèze ➤, France 21 E8
Ouyen, Australia 95 F3
Ouzouer-le-Marché, France ... 19 E8
Ovada, Italy 40 D5
Ovalau, Fiji 91 C8
Ovalle, Chile 126 C1
Ovamboland, Namibia 88 B2
Ovar, Portugal 36 E2
Overath, Germany 24 E3
Overflakkee, Neths. 17 C4
Overijssel □, Neths. 17 B6
Overland Park, U.S.A. 112 F7
Overton, U.S.A. 111 J12
Övertorneå, Sweden 8 C20
Överum, Sweden 11 F10
Ovid, U.S.A. 117 D8
Ovidiopol, Ukraine 33 J6
Ovidiu, Romania 29 F13
Oviedo, Spain 36 B5
Oviksfjällen, Sweden 10 A7
Oviši, Latvia 9 H19
Ovoot, Mongolia 56 B7
Övör Hangay □, Mongolia 56 B2
Ovoro, Nigeria 83 D6
Ovruch, Ukraine 33 G5
Övre Årdal, Norway 9 F12
Övre Fryken, Sweden 10 E7
Övruch, Ukraine 33 G5
Owaka, N.Z. 91 M2
Owambo = Ovamboland,
  Namibia 88 B2
Owasco L., U.S.A. 117 D8
Owase, Japan 55 G8
Owatonna, U.S.A. 112 C8
Owbeh, Afghan. 66 B3
Owego, U.S.A. 117 D8
Owen Falls Dam, Uganda 86 B3
Owen Sound, Canada 116 B4
Owens ➤, U.S.A. 110 J9
Owens L., U.S.A. 111 J9
Owensboro, U.S.A. 114 G2
Owerri, Nigeria 83 D6
Owl ➤, Canada 103 B10
Owo, Nigeria 83 D6
Owosso, U.S.A. 114 D3
Owyhee, U.S.A. 108 F5
Owyhee ➤, U.S.A. 108 E5
Owyhee, L., U.S.A. 108 E5
Ox Mts. = Slieve Gamph, Ireland 12 B3
Öxarfjörður, Iceland 8 C5
Oxbow, Canada 103 D8
Oxelösund, Sweden 11 F11
Oxford, N.Z. 91 K4
Oxford, U.K. 15 F6
Oxford, Mass., U.S.A. 117 D13
Oxford, Miss., U.S.A. 113 H10

Oxford, N.C., U.S.A. 115 G6
Oxford, N.Y., U.S.A. 117 D9
Oxford, Ohio, U.S.A. 114 F3
Oxford L., Canada 103 C9
Oxfordshire □, U.K. 15 F6
Oxía Nísís, Greece 46 C3
Oxie, Sweden 11 J7
Oxílithos, Greece 46 C6
Oxnard, U.S.A. 111 L7
Oxsjövalen, Sweden 10 B8
Oxus = Amudarya ➤, Uzbekistan 52 E6
Oya, Malaysia 62 D4
Oyama, Japan 55 F9
Oyambre △, Spain 36 B6
Oyem, Gabon 84 D2
Oyen, Canada 103 C6
Oykel ➤, U.K. 13 D4
Oymyakon, Russia 53 C15
Oyo, Nigeria 83 D5
Oyo □, Nigeria 83 D5
Oyonnax, France 19 F12
Oyster Bay, U.S.A. 117 F11
Ōyūbari, Japan 54 C11
Özalp, Turkey 73 C10
Ozamiz, Phil. 61 G5
Ozark, Ala., U.S.A. 115 K3
Ozark, Ark., U.S.A. 113 H8
Ozark, Mo., U.S.A. 113 G8
Ozark Plateau, U.S.A. 113 G9
Ozarks, L. of the, U.S.A. 112 F8
Ożarów, Poland 31 H8
Özd, Hungary 28 B5
Ozernoye, Russia 34 E10
Ozero Svityaz, Ukraine 31 G10
Ozersk, Russia 30 D8
Ozette L., U.S.A. 110 B2
Ozieri, Italy 42 B2
Ozimek, Poland 31 H5
Ozinki, Russia 34 E9
Ozona, U.S.A. 113 K4
Ozorków, Poland 31 G6
Ozren, Bos.-H. 28 G3
Ozuluama, Mexico 119 C5
Ozun, Romania 29 E10
Ozurgeti, Georgia 35 K5

P

Pa, Burkina Faso 82 C4
Pa-an, Burma 67 L20
Pa Mong Dam, Thailand 64 D4
Pa Sak ➤, Thailand 62 B2
Paamiut, Greenland 101 B15
Paar ➤, Germany 25 G7
Paarl, S. Africa 88 E2
Pab Hills, Pakistan 68 F2
Pabbay, U.K. 13 D1
Pabianice, Poland 31 G6
Pabna, Bangla. 67 G16
Pabo, Uganda 86 B3
Pacaja ➤, Brazil 125 D8
Pacaraima, Sa., S. Amer. 124 C6
Pacasmayo, Peru 124 E3
Paceco, Italy 42 E5
Pachhar, India 68 G7
Pachino, Italy 43 F8
Pachitea ➤, Peru 124 E4
Pachmarhi, India 69 H8
Pachpadra, India 66 G5
Pachuca, Mexico 119 C5
Pacific, Canada 102 C3
Pacific-Antarctic Ridge, Pac. Oc. 97 M16
Pacific Grove, U.S.A. 110 J5
Pacific Ocean 97 G14
Pacific Rim △, Canada 102 D3
Pacifica, U.S.A. 110 H4
Pacitan, Indonesia 63 H14
Packwood, U.S.A. 110 D5
Pacov, Czech Rep. 26 B8
Pacy-sur-Eure, France 18 C8
Padaido, Kepulauan, Indonesia . 63 E9
Padang, Indonesia 62 E2
Padang Endau, Malaysia 65 L4
Padangpanjang, Indonesia 62 E2
Padangsidempuan, Indonesia .. 62 D1
Padborg, Denmark 11 K3
Paddle Prairie, Canada 102 B5
Paddockwood, Canada 103 C7
Paderborn, Germany 24 D4
Padeş, Vf., Romania 28 E7
Padina, Romania 29 F12
Padma, India 69 G11
Pádova, Italy 41 C8
Padra, India 68 H5
Padrauna, India 69 F10
Padre I., U.S.A. 113 M6
Padre Island △, U.S.A. 113 M6
Padrón, Spain 36 C2
Padstow, U.K. 15 G3
Padua = Pádova, Italy 41 C8
Paducah, Ky., U.S.A. 114 G1
Paducah, Tex., U.S.A. 113 H4
Padul, Spain 37 H7
Paengnyŏng-do, S. Korea 57 F13
Paeroa, N.Z. 91 G5
Paesana, Italy 40 D4
Pafúri, Mozam. 89 C5
Paga, Ghana 83 C4
Pagadian, Phil. 61 H5
Pagai Selatan, Pulau, Indonesia 62 E2
Pagai Utara, Pulau, Indonesia . 62 E2
Pagalu = Annobón, Atl. Oc. ... 77 G4
Pagastikós Kólpos, Greece 46 B5
Pagatan, Indonesia 62 E5
Page, U.S.A. 109 H8
Pagégiai, Lithuania 30 C8

Pago Pago, *Amer. Samoa*   **91 B13**
Pagosa Springs, *U.S.A.*   **109 H10**
Pagwa River, *Canada*   **104 B2**
Pahala, *U.S.A.*   **106 J17**
Pahang →, *Malaysia*   **65 L4**
Pahiatua, *N.Z.*   **91 J5**
Pahokee, *U.S.A.*   **115 M5**
Pahrump, *U.S.A.*   **111 J11**
Pahute Mesa, *U.S.A.*   **110 H10**
Pai, *Thailand*   **64 C2**
Paicines, *U.S.A.*   **110 J5**
Paide, *Estonia*   **9 G21**
Paignton, *U.K.*   **15 G4**
Paiho, *Taiwan*   **59 F13**
Päijänne, *Finland*   **9 F21**
Pailani, *India*   **69 G9**
Pailin, *Cambodia*   **64 F4**
Paimpol, *France*   **18 D3**
Painan, *Indonesia*   **62 E2**
Painesville, *U.S.A.*   **116 E3**
Paint Hills = Wemindji, *Canada*   **104 B4**
Paint L., *Canada*   **103 B9**
Painted Desert, *U.S.A.*   **109 J8**
Paintsville, *U.S.A.*   **114 G4**
País Vasco □, *Spain*   **38 C2**
Paisley, *Canada*   **116 B3**
Paisley, *U.K.*   **13 F4**
Paisley, *U.S.A.*   **108 E3**
Paita, *Peru*   **124 E2**
Paiva →, *Portugal*   **36 D2**
Paizhou, *China*   **59 B9**
Pajares, *Spain*   **36 B5**
Pajares, Puerto de, *Spain*   **36 C5**
Pajęczno, *Poland*   **31 G5**
Pak Lay, *Laos*   **64 C3**
Pak Phanang, *Thailand*   **65 H3**
Pak Sane, *Laos*   **64 C4**
Pak Song, *Laos*   **64 E6**
Pak Suong, *Laos*   **58 H4**
Pakaur, *India*   **69 G12**
Pakenham, *Canada*   **117 A8**
Pákhnes, *Greece*   **49 D6**
Pakhuis, *S. Africa*   **88 E2**
Pakistan ■, *Asia*   **68 E4**
Pakkading, *Laos*   **64 C4**
Paklenica △, *Croatia*   **41 D12**
Pakokku, *Burma*   **67 J19**
Pakość, *Poland*   **31 F5**
Pakowki L., *Canada*   **103 D6**
Pakpattan, *Pakistan*   **68 D5**
Pakrac, *Croatia*   **28 E2**
Pakruojis, *Lithuania*   **30 C10**
Paks, *Hungary*   **28 D3**
Paktīā □, *Afghan.*   **66 C6**
Paktīkā □, *Afghan.*   **66 C6**
Pakwach, *Uganda*   **86 B3**
Pakxe, *Laos*   **64 E5**
Pal Lahara, *India*   **69 J11**
Pala, *Chad*   **79 G9**
Pala, *Dem. Rep. of the Congo*   **86 D2**
Pala, *U.S.A.*   **111 M9**
Palabek, *Uganda*   **86 B3**
Palacios, *U.S.A.*   **113 L6**
Palafrugell, *Spain*   **38 D8**
Palagiano, *Italy*   **43 B10**
Palagonía, *Italy*   **43 E7**
Palagruža, *Croatia*   **41 F13**
Palaiókastron, *Greece*   **49 D8**
Palaiokhóra, *Greece*   **49 D5**
Pálairos, *Greece*   **46 C2**
Palaiseau, *France*   **19 D9**
Palam, *India*   **66 K10**
Palamás, *Greece*   **46 B4**
Palamós, *Spain*   **38 D8**
Palampur, *India*   **68 C7**
Palamut, *Turkey*   **47 C9**
Palana, *Australia*   **95 F4**
Palana, *Russia*   **53 D16**
Palanan, *Phil.*   **61 C5**
Palanan Pt., *Phil.*   **61 C5**
Palandri, *Pakistan*   **69 C5**
Palanga, *Lithuania*   **9 J19**
Palangkaraya, *Indonesia*   **62 E4**
Palani Hills, *India*   **66 P10**
Palanpur, *India*   **68 G5**
Palapye, *Botswana*   **88 C4**
Palas, *Pakistan*   **69 B5**
Palas de Rei, *Spain*   **36 C3**
Palashi, *India*   **69 H13**
Palasponga, *India*   **69 J11**
Palatka, *Russia*   **53 C16**
Palatka, *U.S.A.*   **115 L5**
Palau, *Italy*   **42 A2**
Palau ■, *Pac. Oc.*   **96 G5**
Palauk, *Burma*   **64 F2**
Palawan, *Phil.*   **61 G3**
Palayankottai, *India*   **66 Q10**
Palazzo, Pte., *France*   **21 F12**
Palazzo San Gervásio, *Italy*   **43 B8**
Palazzolo Acréide, *Italy*   **43 E7**
Paldiski, *Estonia*   **9 G21**
Pale, *Bos.-H.*   **28 G3**
Paleleh, *Indonesia*   **63 D6**
Palembang, *Indonesia*   **62 E2**
Palencia, *Spain*   **36 C6**
Palencia □, *Spain*   **36 C6**
Palenque, *Mexico*   **119 D6**
Paleokastrítsa, *Greece*   **49 A3**
Paleometokho, *Cyprus*   **49 D12**
Palermo, *Italy*   **42 E6**
Palermo, *U.S.A.*   **108 G3**
Palermo × (PMO), *Italy*   **42 D6**
Palestina, *Chile*   **128 A3**
Palestine, *Asia*   **74 D4**
Palestine, *U.S.A.*   **113 K7**
Palestrina, *Italy*   **41 G9**
Paletwa, *Burma*   **67 J18**
Palghat, *India*   **66 P10**
Palgrave, Mt., *Australia*   **92 D2**
Pali, *India*   **68 G5**
Palikir, *Micronesia*   **96 G7**
Palinuro, *Italy*   **43 B8**

Palinuro, C., *Italy*   **43 B8**
Palioúrion, Ákra, *Greece*   **44 G7**
Palisades Reservoir, *U.S.A.*   **108 E8**
Paliseul, *Belgium*   **17 E5**
Palitana, *India*   **68 J4**
Palizada, *Mexico*   **119 D6**
Palk Bay, *Asia*   **66 Q11**
Palk Strait, *Asia*   **66 Q11**
Palkānah, *Iraq*   **70 C5**
Palkot, *India*   **69 H11**
Pallanza = Verbánia, *Italy*   **40 C5**
Pallarenda, *Australia*   **94 B4**
Pallasovka, *Russia*   **34 E8**
Pallës, Bishti i, *Albania*   **44 E3**
Pallinup →, *Australia*   **93 F2**
Pallisa, *Uganda*   **86 B3**
Pallu, *India*   **68 E6**
Palm Bay, *U.S.A.*   **115 L5**
Palm Beach, *U.S.A.*   **115 M6**
Palm Coast, *U.S.A.*   **115 L5**
Palm Desert, *U.S.A.*   **111 M10**
Palm Is., *Australia*   **94 B4**
Palm Springs, *U.S.A.*   **111 M10**
Palma, *Mozam.*   **87 E5**
Palma, B. de, *Spain*   **48 B9**
Palma de Mallorca, *Spain*   **48 B9**
Palma de Mallorca × (PMI), *Spain*   **39 F7**
Palma del Río, *Spain*   **37 H5**
Palma di Montechiaro, *Italy*   **42 E6**
Palma Soriano, *Cuba*   **120 B4**
Palmares, *Brazil*   **125 E11**
Palmarola, *Italy*   **42 B5**
Palmas, *Brazil*   **127 B5**
Palmas, C., *Liberia*   **82 E3**
Pálmas, G. di, *Italy*   **42 D1**
Palmdale, *U.S.A.*   **111 L8**
Palmeira das Missões, *Brazil*   **127 B5**
Palmeira dos Índios, *Brazil*   **125 E11**
Palmela, *Portugal*   **37 G2**
Palmer, *Antarctica*   **5 C17**
Palmer, *U.S.A.*   **100 B5**
Palmer →, *Australia*   **94 B3**
Palmer Arch., *Antarctica*   **5 C17**
Palmer Lake, *U.S.A.*   **112 F2**
Palmer Land, *Antarctica*   **5 D18**
Palmerston, *Australia*   **92 B5**
Palmerston, *Canada*   **116 C4**
Palmerston, *N.Z.*   **91 L3**
Palmerston North, *N.Z.*   **91 J5**
Palmerton, *U.S.A.*   **117 F9**
Palmetto, *U.S.A.*   **115 M4**
Palmi, *Italy*   **43 D8**
Palmira, *Argentina*   **126 C2**
Palmira, *Colombia*   **124 C3**
Palmyra = Tudmur, *Syria*   **70 C3**
Palmyra, Mo., *U.S.A.*   **112 F9**
Palmyra, N.Y., *U.S.A.*   **116 C7**
Palmyra, Pa., *U.S.A.*   **117 F8**
Palmyra Is., *Pac. Oc.*   **97 G11**
Palo Alto, *U.S.A.*   **110 H4**
Palo Seco, *Trin. & Tob.*   **125 K15**
Palo Verde, *U.S.A.*   **111 M12**
Palo Verde △, *Costa Rica*   **120 D2**
Paloich, *Sudan*   **81 E3**
Palomar Mt., *U.S.A.*   **111 M10**
Palompon, *Phil.*   **61 F6**
Palopo, *Indonesia*   **63 E6**
Palos, C. de, *Spain*   **39 H4**
Palos de la Frontera, *Spain*   **37 H4**
Palos Verdes, *U.S.A.*   **111 M8**
Palos Verdes, Pt., *U.S.A.*   **111 M8**
Pålsboda, *Sweden*   **10 E9**
Palu, *Indonesia*   **63 E5**
Palu, *Turkey*   **70 B3**
Paluke, *Liberia*   **82 D3**
Paluzza, *Italy*   **41 B10**
Palwal, *India*   **68 E7**
Pama, *Burkina Faso*   **83 C5**
Pama △, *Burkina Faso*   **83 C5**
Pamanukan, *Indonesia*   **63 G12**
Pamekasan, *Indonesia*   **63 G15**
Pamenang, *Indonesia*   **63 J19**
Pamiers, *France*   **20 E5**
Pamir, *Tajikistan*   **52 F8**
Pamlico →, *U.S.A.*   **115 H7**
Pamlico Sd., *U.S.A.*   **115 H8**
Pampa, *U.S.A.*   **113 H4**
Pampa de las Salinas, *Argentina*   **126 C2**
Pampanua, *Indonesia*   **63 E6**
Pampas, *Argentina*   **126 D3**
Pampas, *Peru*   **124 F4**
Pamphylia, *Turkey*   **72 D4**
Pamplona, *Colombia*   **124 B4**
Pamplona, *Spain*   **38 C3**
Pampoenpoort, *S. Africa*   **88 E3**
Pamukçu, *Turkey*   **47 B9**
Pamukkale, *Turkey*   **47 D11**
Pan de Azúcar △, *Chile*   **126 B1**
Pan Xian, *China*   **58 E5**
Pana, *U.S.A.*   **112 F10**
Panabo, *Phil.*   **61 H6**
Panaca, *U.S.A.*   **109 H6**
Panagyurishte, *Bulgaria*   **45 D8**
Panaitan, *Indonesia*   **63 G11**
Panaji, *India*   **66 M8**
Panamá, *Panama*   **120 E4**
Panama ■, *Cent. Amer.*   **120 E4**
Panamá, G. de, *Panama*   **120 E4**
Panama Canal, *Panama*   **120 E4**
Panama City, *U.S.A.*   **115 K3**
Panamint Range, *U.S.A.*   **111 J9**
Panamint Springs, *U.S.A.*   **111 J9**
Panão, *Peru*   **124 E3**
Panaon I., *Phil.*   **61 F6**
Panare, *Thailand*   **65 J3**
Panarea, *Italy*   **43 D8**
Panaro →, *Italy*   **41 D8**
Panay, *Phil.*   **61 F5**
Panay, G., *Phil.*   **63 B6**
Pančevo, *Serbia & M.*   **28 F5**

Panch'iao, *Taiwan*   **59 E13**
Panciu, *Romania*   **29 E12**
Pancorbo, Desfiladero, *Spain*   **36 C7**
Pâncota, *Romania*   **28 D6**
Panda, *Mozam.*   **89 C5**
Pandan, *Malaysia*   **65 d**
Pandan, *Antique, Phil.*   **61 F5**
Pandan, *Catanduanes, Phil.*   **61 D6**
Pandan, Selat, *Singapore*   **65 d**
Pandan Tampoi = Tampoi, *Malaysia*   **65 d**
Pandegelang, *Indonesia*   **63 G12**
Pandhana, *India*   **68 J7**
Pandharpur, *India*   **66 L9**
Pando, *Uruguay*   **127 C4**
Pando, L. = Hope, L., *Australia*   **95 D2**
Pando, *Indonesia*   **63 F5**
Pandokrátor, *Greece*   **49 A3**
Pandora, *Costa Rica*   **120 E3**
Pandrup, *Denmark*   **11 G3**
Panevéggio-Pale di San Martino △, *Italy*   **41 B8**
Panevėžys, *Lithuania*   **9 J21**
Panfilov, *Kazakhstan*   **52 E8**
Panfilovo, *Russia*   **34 E6**
Pang-Long, *Burma*   **67 H21**
Pang Sida △, *Thailand*   **64 E4**
Pang-Yang, *Burma*   **67 H21**
Panga, *Dem. Rep. of the Congo*   **86 B2**
Pangaíon Óros, *Greece*   **45 F8**
Pangalanes, Canal des = Ampangalana, Lakandranon', *Madag.*   **89 C8**
Pangani, *Tanzania*   **86 D4**
Pangani →, *Tanzania*   **86 D4**
Pangfou = Bengbu, *China*   **57 H9**
Pangil, *Dem. Rep. of the Congo*   **86 C2**
Pangkah, Tanjung, *Indonesia*   **63 G15**
Pangkajene, *Indonesia*   **63 E5**
Pangkalanbrandan, *Indonesia*   **62 D1**
Pangkalanbuun, *Indonesia*   **62 E4**
Pangkalpinang, *Indonesia*   **62 E3**
Pangnirtung, *Canada*   **101 B13**
Pangong Tso, *India*   **68 B8**
Panguitch, *U.S.A.*   **109 H7**
Pangutaran Group, *Phil.*   **61 H4**
Panhandle, *U.S.A.*   **113 H4**
Pani Mines, *India*   **68 H5**
Pania-Mutombo, *Dem. Rep. of the Congo*   **86 D1**
Panikota I., *India*   **68 J4**
Panipat, *India*   **68 E7**
Panjal Range = Pir Panjal Range, *India*   **68 C7**
Panjang, Hon, *Vietnam*   **65 H4**
Panjgur, *Pakistan*   **66 F4**
Panjim = Panaji, *India*   **66 M8**
Panjin, *China*   **57 D12**
Panjnad Barrage, *Pakistan*   **66 E7**
Panjnad →, *Pakistan*   **68 E4**
Panjwai, *Afghan.*   **68 D1**
Pankshin, *Nigeria*   **83 D6**
Panmunjŏm, *N. Korea*   **57 F14**
Panna, *India*   **69 G9**
Panna Hills, *India*   **69 G9**
Pannawonica, *Australia*   **92 D2**
Pannga, Tanjung, *Indonesia*   **63 K19**
Pannirtuuq = Pangnirtung, *Canada*   **101 B13**
Pano Akil, *Pakistan*   **68 F3**
Pano Lefkara, *Cyprus*   **49 E12**
Pano Panayia, *Cyprus*   **49 E11**
Panorama, *Brazil*   **127 A5**
Pánormon, *Greece*   **49 D6**
Pansemal, *India*   **68 J6**
Panshan = Panjin, *China*   **57 D12**
Panshi, *China*   **57 C14**
Pantanal, *Brazil*   **124 H7**
Pantanos de Centla △, *Mexico*   **119 D6**
Pantar, *Indonesia*   **63 F6**
Pante Macassar, *E. Timor*   **63 F6**
Pante Makasar = Pante Macassar, *E. Timor*   **63 F6**
Pantelleria, *Italy*   **42 F4**
Pantón, *Spain*   **36 C3**
Pánuco, *Mexico*   **119 C5**
Panyam, *Nigeria*   **83 D6**
Panyu, *China*   **59 F9**
Panzhihua, *China*   **58 D3**
Páola, *Italy*   **43 C9**
Paola, *Malta*   **49 D2**
Paola, *U.S.A.*   **112 F7**
Paonia, *U.S.A.*   **109 G10**
Paoting = Baoding, *China*   **56 E8**
Paot'ou = Baotou, *China*   **56 D6**
Paoua, *C.A.R.*   **84 C3**
Pápa, *Hungary*   **28 C2**
Papa Stour, *U.K.*   **13 A7**
Papa Westray, *U.K.*   **13 B6**
Papagayo →, *Mexico*   **119 D5**
Papagayo, G. de, *Costa Rica*   **120 D2**
Papakura, *N.Z.*   **91 G5**
Papantla, *Mexico*   **119 C5**
Papar, *Malaysia*   **62 C5**
Paparoa △, *N.Z.*   **91 K3**
Pápas, Ákra, *Greece*   **46 C3**
Papeete, *Tahiti*   **97 J13**
Papenburg, *Germany*   **24 B3**
Paphlagonia, *Turkey*   **72 B5**
Papigochic →, *Mexico*   **118 B3**
Paposo, *Chile*   **126 B1**
Papoutsa, *Cyprus*   **49 E12**
Papua □, *Indonesia*   **63 E9**
Papua New Guinea ■, *Oceania*   **96 H6**
Papudo, *Chile*   **126 C1**
Papuk, *Croatia*   **28 E2**
Papun, *Burma*   **67 K20**
Papunya, *Australia*   **92 D5**
Pará = Belém, *Brazil*   **125 D9**
Pará □, *Brazil*   **125 D8**
Paraburdoo, *Australia*   **92 D2**
Paracale, *Phil.*   **61 D5**

Paracatu, *Brazil*   **125 G9**
Paracel Is., *S. China Sea*   **62 A4**
Parachilna, *Australia*   **95 E2**
Parachinar, *Pakistan*   **68 C4**
Paraćin, *Serbia & M.*   **44 C5**
Paradas, *Spain*   **37 H5**
Paradela, *Spain*   **36 C3**
Paradip, *India*   **67 J15**
Paradise, Calif., *U.S.A.*   **110 F5**
Paradise, Nev., *U.S.A.*   **111 J11**
Paradise →, *Canada*   **105 B8**
Paradise Hill, *Canada*   **103 C7**
Paradise River, *Canada*   **105 B8**
Paradise Valley, *U.S.A.*   **108 F5**
Parado, *Indonesia*   **63 F5**
Paragould, *U.S.A.*   **113 G9**
Paragua →, *Venezuela*   **124 B6**
Paraguaçu →, *Brazil*   **125 F11**
Paraguaçu Paulista, *Brazil*   **127 A5**
Paraguaná, Pen. de, *Venezuela*   **124 A5**
Paraguarí, *Paraguay*   **126 B4**
Paraguarí □, *Paraguay*   **126 B4**
Paraguay ■, *S. Amer.*   **126 A4**
Paraguay →, *Paraguay*   **126 B4**
Paraíba = João Pessoa, *Brazil*   **125 E12**
Paraíba □, *Brazil*   **125 E11**
Paraíba do Sul →, *Brazil*   **127 A7**
Parainen, *Finland*   **9 F20**
Parak, *Iran*   **71 E7**
Parakhino Paddubye, *Russia*   **32 C7**
Parakou, *Benin*   **83 D5**
Paralimni, *Cyprus*   **49 D12**
Parálion-Astrous, *Greece*   **46 D4**
Paramaribo, *Suriname*   **125 B7**
Paramithiá, *Greece*   **46 B2**
Páramos del Batallón y La Negra △, *Venezuela*   **121 E5**
Paramushir, Ostrov, *Russia*   **53 D16**
Paran →, *Israel*   **74 E4**
Paraná, *Argentina*   **126 C3**
Paraná, *Brazil*   **125 F9**
Paraná □, *Brazil*   **127 A5**
Paraná →, *Argentina*   **126 C4**
Paranaguá, *Brazil*   **127 B6**
Paranaíba, *Brazil*   **125 G8**
Paranaíba →, *Brazil*   **125 H8**
Paranapanema →, *Brazil*   **127 A5**
Paranapiacaba, Serra do, *Brazil*   **127 A6**
Paranas, *Phil.*   **61 F6**
Paranavaí, *Brazil*   **127 A5**
Parang, Maguindanao, *Phil.*   **63 C6**
Parang, Sulu, *Phil.*   **61 J4**
Parângul Mare, Vf., *Romania*   **29 E8**
Paraparaumu, *N.Z.*   **91 J5**
Parápola, *Greece*   **46 E5**
Paraspóri, Ákra, *Greece*   **47 F9**
Paray-le-Monial, *France*   **19 F11**
Parbati →, Mad. P., *India*   **68 G7**
Parbati →, Raj., *India*   **68 F7**
Parbhani, *India*   **66 K10**
Parchim, *Germany*   **24 B7**
Parczew, *Poland*   **31 G9**
Pardes Hanna-Karkur, *Israel*   **74 C3**
Pardilla, *Spain*   **36 D7**
Pardo →, *Bahia, Brazil*   **125 G11**
Pardo →, Mato Grosso, *Brazil*   **127 A5**
Pardubice, *Czech Rep.*   **26 A8**
Pardubický □, *Czech Rep.*   **26 B8**
Pare, *Indonesia*   **63 G15**
Pare Mts., *Tanzania*   **86 C4**
Parecis, Serra dos, *Brazil*   **124 F7**
Paredes de Nava, *Spain*   **36 C6**
Paren, *Russia*   **53 C17**
Parent, *Canada*   **104 C5**
Parent, L., *Canada*   **104 C4**
Parentis-en-Born, *France*   **20 D2**
Parepare, *Indonesia*   **63 E5**
Parfino, *Russia*   **32 D6**
Párga, *Greece*   **46 B2**
Pargas = Parainen, *Finland*   **9 F20**
Pargo, Pta. do, *Madeira*   **48 D2**
Paria, G. de, *Venezuela*   **125 K14**
Pariaguán, *Venezuela*   **124 B6**
Paricutín, Cerro, *Mexico*   **118 D4**
Parigi, *Indonesia*   **63 E6**
Parika, *Guyana*   **124 B7**
Parikkala, *Finland*   **32 B5**
Parima, Serra, *Brazil*   **124 C6**
Parinari, *Peru*   **124 D4**
Pariñas, Pta., *S. Amer.*   **122 D2**
Parincea, *Romania*   **29 D12**
Parintins, *Brazil*   **125 D7**
Pariparit Kyun, *Burma*   **67 M18**
Paris, *Canada*   **116 C4**
Paris, *France*   **19 D9**
Paris, Idaho, *U.S.A.*   **108 E8**
Paris, Ky., *U.S.A.*   **114 F3**
Paris, Tenn., *U.S.A.*   **115 G1**
Paris, Tex., *U.S.A.*   **113 J7**
Paris, Ville de □, *France*   **19 D9**
Paris Charles de Gaulle × (CDG), *France*   **19 D9**
Paris Orly × (ORY), *France*   **19 D9**
Parish, *U.S.A.*   **117 C8**
Parishville, *U.S.A.*   **117 B10**
Park, *U.S.A.*   **110 B4**
Park City, *U.S.A.*   **113 G6**
Park Falls, *U.S.A.*   **112 C9**
Park Head, *Canada*   **116 B3**
Park Hills, *U.S.A.*   **113 G9**
Park Range, *U.S.A.*   **108 G10**
Park Rapids, *U.S.A.*   **112 B7**
Park River, *U.S.A.*   **112 A6**
Park Rynie, *S. Africa*   **89 E5**
Parkano, *Finland*   **9 E20**
Parker, Ariz., *U.S.A.*   **111 L12**
Parker, Pa., *U.S.A.*   **116 E5**
Parker Dam, *U.S.A.*   **111 L12**
Parkersburg, *U.S.A.*   **114 F5**

Parkes, *Australia*   **95 E4**
Parkfield, *U.S.A.*   **110 K6**
Parkhill, *Canada*   **116 C3**
Parkland, *U.S.A.*   **110 C4**
Parkston, *U.S.A.*   **112 D6**
Parksville, *Canada*   **102 D4**
Parla, *Spain*   **36 E7**
Pârlița, *Moldova*   **29 C12**
Parma, *Italy*   **40 D7**
Parma, *Idaho, U.S.A.*   **108 E5**
Parma, *Ohio, U.S.A.*   **116 E3**
Parma →, *Italy*   **40 D7**
Parnaguá, *Brazil*   **125 F10**
Parnaíba, *Brazil*   **125 D10**
Parnaíba →, *Brazil*   **125 D10**
Parnassós, *Greece*   **46 C4**
Párnis, *Greece*   **46 C5**
Párnitha △, *Greece*   **46 C5**
Párnon Óros, *Greece*   **46 D4**
Pärnu, *Estonia*   **9 G21**
Paroo →, *Australia*   **95 E3**
Páros, *Greece*   **47 D7**
Parowan, *U.S.A.*   **109 H7**
Parpaillon, *France*   **21 D10**
Parral, *Chile*   **126 D1**
Parras, *Mexico*   **118 B4**
Parrett →, *U.K.*   **15 F4**
Parris I., *U.S.A.*   **115 J5**
Parrsboro, *Canada*   **105 C7**
Parry I., *Canada*   **116 A4**
Parry Is., *Canada*   **98 B8**
Parry Sound, *Canada*   **116 A5**
Parsberg, *Germany*   **25 F7**
Parsęta →, *Poland*   **30 D2**
Parsnip →, *Canada*   **102 B4**
Parsons, *U.S.A.*   **113 G7**
Parsons Ra., *Australia*   **94 A2**
Partanna, *Italy*   **42 E5**
Partenio △, *Italy*   **43 B7**
Parthenay, *France*   **18 F6**
Partinico, *Italy*   **42 D6**
Partizánske, *Slovak Rep.*   **27 C11**
Partridge I., *Canada*   **104 A2**
Paru →, *Brazil*   **125 D8**
Parvān □, *Afghan.*   **66 B6**
Parvatipuram, *India*   **67 K13**
Parvatsar, *India*   **68 F6**
Påryd, *Sweden*   **11 H9**
Parys, *S. Africa*   **88 D4**
Pas, Pta. des, *Spain*   **48 C7**
Pas-de-Calais □, *France*   **19 B9**
Pasada, *Spain*   **36 B5**
Pasadena, *Canada*   **105 C8**
Pasadena, Calif., *U.S.A.*   **111 L8**
Pasadena, Tex., *U.S.A.*   **113 L7**
Pasaje, →, *Argentina*   **126 B3**
Paşalimanı, *Turkey*   **45 F11**
Pasar, *Indonesia*   **63 J17**
Pasay, *Phil.*   **61 D4**
Pascagoula, *U.S.A.*   **113 K10**
Pascagoula →, *U.S.A.*   **113 K10**
Paşcani, *Romania*   **29 C11**
Pasco, *U.S.A.*   **108 C4**
Pasco, Cerro de, *Peru*   **124 F3**
Pasco I., *Australia*   **92 D2**
Pascoag, *U.S.A.*   **117 E13**
Pascua, I. de, *Chile*   **97 K17**
Pasewalk, *Germany*   **24 B9**
Pasfield L., *Canada*   **103 B7**
Pasha →, *Russia*   **32 B7**
Pasinler, *Turkey*   **73 C9**
Pasir Mas, *Malaysia*   **65 J4**
Pasir Panjang, *Singapore*   **65 d**
Pasir Putih, *Malaysia*   **65 K4**
Pasirian, *Indonesia*   **63 H15**
Pasirkuning, *Indonesia*   **62 E2**
Påskallavik, *Sweden*   **11 G10**
Paskūh, *Iran*   **71 E9**
Pasłęk, *Poland*   **30 D6**
Pasłęka →, *Poland*   **30 D6**
Pasley, C., *Australia*   **93 F3**
Pašman, *Croatia*   **41 E12**
Pasni, *Pakistan*   **66 G3**
Paso Cantinela, *Mexico*   **111 N11**
Paso de Indios, *Argentina*   **128 E3**
Paso de los Libres, *Argentina*   **126 B4**
Paso de los Toros, *Uruguay*   **126 C4**
Paso Robles, *U.S.A.*   **109 J3**
Paspébiac, *Canada*   **105 C6**
Pasrur, *Pakistan*   **68 C6**
Passage West, *Ireland*   **12 E3**
Passaic, *U.S.A.*   **117 F10**
Passau, *Germany*   **25 G9**
Passero, C., *Italy*   **43 F8**
Passo Fundo, *Brazil*   **127 B5**
Passos, *Brazil*   **125 H9**
Passow, *Germany*   **24 B10**
Passy, *France*   **21 C10**
Pastavy, *Belarus*   **9 J22**
Pastaza →, *Peru*   **124 D3**
Pasto, *Colombia*   **124 C3**
Pastrana, *Spain*   **38 E2**
Pasuruan, *Indonesia*   **63 G15**
Pasym, *Poland*   **30 E7**
Pásztó, *Hungary*   **28 C4**
Patagonia, *Argentina*   **128 F3**
Patagonia, *U.S.A.*   **109 L8**
Patan = Lalitapur, *Nepal*   **69 F11**
Patan, Gujarat, *India*   **68 H5**
Patan, Maharashtra, *India*   **68 H5**
Patani, *Indonesia*   **63 D7**
Pătârlagele, *Romania*   **29 E11**
Pataudi, *India*   **68 E7**
Patchewollock, *Australia*   **95 F3**
Patchogue, *U.S.A.*   **117 F11**
Pate, *Kenya*   **86 C5**
Patea, *N.Z.*   **91 H5**
Pategi, *Nigeria*   **83 D6**
Patensie, *S. Africa*   **88 E3**
Paterna, *Spain*   **39 F4**
Paternion, *Austria*   **26 E6**

Paternò, Italy ... 43 E7
Pateros, U.S.A. ... 108 B4
Paterson, U.S.A. ... 117 F10
Paterson Ra., Australia ... 92 D3
Pathankot, India ... 68 C6
Pathein = Bassein, Burma ... 67 L19
Pathfinder Reservoir, U.S.A. ... 108 E10
Pathiu, Thailand ... 65 G2
Pathum Thani, Thailand ... 64 E3
Pati, Indonesia ... 63 G14
Patía →, Colombia ... 124 C3
Patiala, Punjab, India ... 68 D7
Patiala, Ut. P., India ... 69 F8
Patine Kouka, Senegal ... 82 C2
Patitírion, Greece ... 46 B5
Patkai Bum, India ... 67 F19
Pátmos, Greece ... 47 D8
Patna, India ... 69 G11
Patnos, Turkey ... 73 C10
Pato Branco, Brazil ... 127 B5
Patonga, Uganda ... 86 B3
Patos, Albania ... 44 F3
Patos, Brazil ... 125 E11
Patos, L. dos, Brazil ... 127 C5
Patos, Río de los →, Argentina ... 126 C2
Patos de Minas, Brazil ... 125 G9
Patquía, Argentina ... 126 C2
Pátrai, Greece ... 46 C3
Pátraikós Kólpos, Greece ... 46 C3
Patras = Pátrai, Greece ... 46 C3
Patrocínio, Brazil ... 125 G9
Pattada, Italy ... 42 B2
Pattani, Thailand ... 65 J3
Pattaya, Thailand ... 62 B2
Patten, U.S.A. ... 115 C11
Patterson, Calif., U.S.A. ... 110 H5
Patterson, La., U.S.A. ... 113 L9
Patterson, Mt., U.S.A. ... 110 G7
Patti, Punjab, India ... 68 D6
Patti, Ut. P., India ... 69 G10
Patti, Italy ... 43 D7
Pattoki, Pakistan ... 68 D5
Patton, U.S.A. ... 116 F6
Patuakhali, Bangla. ... 67 H17
Patuanak, Canada ... 103 B7
Patuca →, Honduras ... 120 D2
Patuca →, Honduras ... 120 C3
Patuca, Punta, Honduras ... 120 C3
Pătulele, Romania ... 28 F7
Pátzcuaro, Mexico ... 118 D4
Pau, France ... 20 E3
Pau, Gave de →, France ... 20 E2
Pauillac, France ... 20 C3
Pauk, Burma ... 67 J19
Paul I., U.S.A. ... 105 A7
Paul Smiths, U.S.A. ... 117 B10
Paulatuk, Canada ... 100 B7
Paulhan, France ... 20 E7
Paulistana, Brazil ... 125 E10
Paulo Afonso, Brazil ... 125 E11
Paulpietersburg, S. Africa ... 89 D5
Pauls Valley, U.S.A. ... 113 H6
Pauma Valley, U.S.A. ... 111 M10
Pauri, India ... 69 D8
Pāveh, Iran ... 70 C5
Pavelets, Russia ... 32 F10
Pavia, Italy ... 40 C6
Pavilion, U.S.A. ... 116 D6
Pavilly, France ... 18 C7
Pāvilosta, Latvia ... 9 H19
Pavlikeni, Bulgaria ... 45 C9
Pavlodar, Kazakhstan ... 52 D8
Pavlograd = Pavlohrad, Ukraine ... 33 H8
Pavlohrad, Ukraine ... 33 H8
Pavlovo, Russia ... 34 C6
Pavlovsk, Russia ... 34 E5
Pavlovskaya, Russia ... 35 G4
Pavlovskiy-Posad, Russia ... 32 E10
Pavullo nel Frignano, Italy ... 40 D7
Pawai, Pulau, Singapore ... 65 d
Pawayan, India ... 69 E9
Pawhuska, U.S.A. ... 113 G6
Pawling, U.S.A. ... 117 E11
Pawnee, U.S.A. ... 113 G6
Pawnee City, U.S.A. ... 112 E6
Pawtucket, U.S.A. ... 117 E13
Paximádhia, Greece ... 49 E6
Paxoí, Greece ... 46 B2
Paxton, Ill., U.S.A. ... 114 E1
Paxton, Nebr., U.S.A. ... 112 E4
Payakumbuh, Indonesia ... 62 E2
Payerne, Switz. ... 25 J2
Payette, U.S.A. ... 108 D5
Paymogo, Spain ... 37 H3
Payne Bay = Kangirsuk, Canada ... 101 B13
Payne L., Canada ... 101 C12
Paynes Find, Australia ... 93 E2
Paynesville, Liberia ... 82 D2
Paynesville, U.S.A. ... 112 C7
Pays de la Loire □, France ... 18 E6
Paysandú, Uruguay ... 126 C4
Payson, U.S.A. ... 109 J8
Paz →, Guatemala ... 120 D1
Paz, B. de la, Mexico ... 118 C2
Păzănăn, Iran ... 71 D6
Pazar, Turkey ... 73 B9
Pazarcık, Turkey ... 72 D7
Pazardzhik, Bulgaria ... 45 D8
Pazarköy, Turkey ... 47 B9
Pazarlar, Turkey ... 47 C11
Pazaryeri, Turkey ... 47 B11
Pazaryolu, Turkey ... 73 C10
Pazin, Croatia ... 41 C10
Pčinja →, Macedonia ... 44 E5
Pe Ell, U.S.A. ... 110 D3
Peabody, U.S.A. ... 117 D14
Peace →, Canada ... 102 B6
Peace Point, Canada ... 102 B6
Peace River, Canada ... 102 B5
Peach Springs, U.S.A. ... 109 J7

Peachland, Canada ... 102 D5
Peachtree City, U.S.A. ... 115 J3
Peak, The = Kinder Scout, U.K. ... 14 D6
Peak Charles △, Australia ... 93 F3
Peak District △, U.K. ... 14 D6
Peak Hill, N.S.W., Australia ... 95 E4
Peak Hill, W. Austral., Australia ... 93 E2
Peak Ra., Australia ... 94 C4
Peake Cr. →, Australia ... 95 D2
Peal de Becerro, Spain ... 37 H7
Peale, Mt., U.S.A. ... 109 G9
Pearblossom, U.S.A. ... 111 L9
Pearl →, U.S.A. ... 113 K10
Pearl City, U.S.A. ... 106 H16
Pearl Harbor, U.S.A. ... 106 H16
Pearl River = Zhu Jiang →, China ... 59 F9
Pearl River, U.S.A. ... 117 E10
Pearsall, U.S.A. ... 113 L5
Peary Land, Greenland ... 4 A6
Pease →, U.S.A. ... 113 H5
Peawanuck, Canada ... 101 C11
Pebane, Mozam. ... 87 F4
Pebas, Peru ... 124 D4
Pebble Beach, U.S.A. ... 110 J5
Peć, Serbia & M. ... 44 D4
Péccioli, Italy ... 40 E7
Pechea, Romania ... 29 E12
Pechenga, Russia ... 52 C4
Pechenizhyn, Ukraine ... 29 B9
Pechiguera, Pta., Canary Is. ... 48 F6
Pechnezhskoye Vdkhr., Ukraine ... 33 G9
Pechora, Russia ... 52 C6
Pechora →, Russia ... 52 C6
Pechorskaya Guba, Russia ... 52 C6
Pechory, Russia ... 9 H22
Pecica, Romania ... 28 D6
Pecka, Serbia & M. ... 44 B3
Pécora, C., Italy ... 42 C1
Pecos, U.S.A. ... 113 K3
Pecos →, U.S.A. ... 113 L3
Pécs, Hungary ... 28 D3
Pedder, L., Australia ... 95 G4
Peddie, S. Africa ... 89 E4
Pedernales, Dom. Rep. ... 121 C5
Pedies →, Cyprus ... 49 D12
Pedirka, Australia ... 95 D2
Pedra Azul, Brazil ... 125 G10
Pedreguer, Spain ... 39 G5
Pedreiras, Brazil ... 125 D10
Pedro Afonso, Brazil ... 125 E9
Pedro Cays, Jamaica ... 120 C4
Pedro de Valdivia, Chile ... 126 A2
Pedro Juan Caballero, Paraguay ... 127 A4
Pedro Muñoz, Spain ... 37 F8
Pedrógão Grande, Portugal ... 36 F2
Pee Dee →, U.S.A. ... 115 J6
Peebinga, Australia ... 95 E3
Peebles, U.K. ... 13 F5
Peekskill, U.S.A. ... 117 E11
Peel, I. of Man ... 14 C3
Peel →, Australia ... 95 E5
Peel →, Canada ... 100 B6
Peel Sd., Canada ... 100 A10
Peene →, Germany ... 24 A9
Peera Peera Poolanna L., Australia ... 95 D2
Peerless Lake, Canada ... 102 B6
Peers, Canada ... 102 C5
Pegasus Bay, N.Z. ... 91 K4
Peggau, Austria ... 26 D8
Pegnitz, Germany ... 25 F7
Pegnitz →, Germany ... 25 F6
Pego, Spain ... 39 G4
Pegu, Burma ... 67 L20
Pegu Yoma, Burma ... 67 K20
Pehčevo, Macedonia ... 44 E6
Pehlivanköy, Turkey ... 45 E10
Pehuajó, Argentina ... 126 D3
Pei Xian = Pizhou, China ... 56 G9
Peine, Chile ... 126 A2
Peine, Germany ... 24 C6
Peip'ing = Beijing, China ... 56 E9
Peipus, L. = Chudskoye, Ozero, Russia ... 9 G22
Peissenberg, Germany ... 25 H7
Peitz, Germany ... 24 D10
Peixe, Brazil ... 125 F9
Peixe →, Brazil ... 125 H8
Pek →, Serbia & M. ... 44 B5
Pekalongan, Indonesia ... 63 G13
Pekan, Malaysia ... 65 L4
Pekan Nenas, Malaysia ... 65 d
Pekanbaru, Indonesia ... 62 D2
Pekang, Taiwan ... 59 F13
Pekin, U.S.A. ... 112 E10
Peking = Beijing, China ... 56 E9
Pekutatan, Indonesia ... 63 J17
Péla, Guinea ... 82 D3
Pelabuhan Klang, Malaysia ... 65 L3
Pelabuhan Ratu, Teluk, Indonesia ... 63 G12
Pelabuhanratu, Indonesia ... 63 G12
Pélagos, Greece ... 46 B6
Pelaihari, Indonesia ... 62 E4
Pelat, Mt., France ... 21 D10
Pełczyce, Poland ... 31 E2
Peleaga, Vf., Romania ... 28 E7
Pelée, Mt., Martinique ... 120 c
Pelee, Pt., Canada ... 104 D3
Pelee I., Canada ... 116 E2
Pelekech, Kenya ... 86 B4
Peleng, Indonesia ... 63 E6
Pelican, Malaysia ... 65 d
Pélézi, Ivory C. ... 82 D3
Pelhřimov, Czech Rep. ... 26 B8
Pelican, U.S.A. ... 102 B1
Pelican L., Canada ... 103 C8
Pelican Narrows, Canada ... 103 B8
Pelister △, Macedonia ... 44 F5
Pelješac, Croatia ... 41 F14
Pelkosenniemi, Finland ... 8 C22

Pella, Greece ... 44 F6
Pella, S. Africa ... 88 D2
Pella, U.S.A. ... 112 E8
Péla □, Greece ... 44 F6
Pello, Finland ... 8 C21
Pellworm, Germany ... 24 A4
Pelly →, Canada ... 100 B6
Pelly Bay, Canada ... 101 B11
Peloponnese = Pelopónnisos □, Greece ... 46 D4
Pelopónnisos □, Greece ... 46 D4
Peloritani, Monti, Italy ... 43 D8
Pelorus Sd., N.Z. ... 91 J4
Pelotas, Brazil ... 127 C5
Pelotas →, Brazil ... 127 B5
Pelovo, Bulgaria ... 45 C8
Pelplin, Poland ... 30 E5
Pelvoux, Massif du, France ... 21 D10
Pemalang, Indonesia ... 63 G13
Pemanggil, Pulau, Malaysia ... 65 L5
Pematangsiantar, Indonesia ... 62 D1
Pemba, Mozam. ... 87 E5
Pemba, Zambia ... 87 F2
Pemba Channel, Tanzania ... 86 D4
Pemba I., Tanzania ... 86 D4
Pemberton, Australia ... 93 F2
Pemberton, Canada ... 102 C4
Pembina, U.S.A. ... 112 A6
Pembroke, Canada ... 104 C4
Pembroke, U.K. ... 15 F3
Pembrokeshire □, U.K. ... 15 F3
Pembrokeshire Coast △, U.K. ... 15 F2
Pen-y-Ghent, U.K. ... 14 C5
Peña, Sierra de la, Spain ... 38 C4
Peña de Francia, Sierra de la, Spain ... 36 E4
Penafiel, Portugal ... 36 D2
Peñafiel, Spain ... 36 D6
Peñaflor, Spain ... 37 H5
Peñalara, Spain ... 36 E7
Penamacôr, Portugal ... 36 E3
Penang = Pinang, Malaysia ... 65 c
Penápolis, Brazil ... 127 A6
Peñaranda de Bracamonte, Spain ... 36 E5
Peñarroya, Spain ... 38 E4
Peñarroya-Pueblonuevo, Spain ... 37 G5
Penarth, U.K. ... 15 F4
Peñas, C. de, Spain ... 36 B5
Penas, G. de, Chile ... 128 F2
Peñas de San Pedro, Spain ... 39 G3
Peñas del Chache, Canary Is. ... 48 E6
Peñausende, Spain ... 36 D5
Pench'i = Benxi, China ... 57 D12
Pend Oreille →, U.S.A. ... 108 B5
Pend Oreille, L., U.S.A. ... 108 C5
Pendálofon, Greece ... 44 F5
Pendembu, Eastern, S. Leone ... 82 D2
Pendembu, Northern, S. Leone ... 82 D2
Pender B., Australia ... 92 C3
Pendik, Turkey ... 45 F13
Pendjari △, Benin ... 83 C5
Pendjari →, Benin ... 83 C5
Pendleton, U.S.A. ... 108 D4
Pendra, India ... 69 H9
Peneda-Gerês △, Portugal ... 36 D2
Penedo, Brazil ... 125 F11
Penelokan, Indonesia ... 63 J18
Penetanguishene, Canada ... 116 B5
Penfield, U.S.A. ... 116 E6
Pengalengan, Indonesia ... 63 G12
Penge, Kasai-Or., Dem. Rep. of the Congo ... 86 D1
Penge, Sud-Kivu, Dem. Rep. of the Congo ... 86 C2
P'enghu Ch'üntou, Taiwan ... 59 F12
Penglai, China ... 57 F11
Pengshan, China ... 58 B4
Pengshui, China ... 58 C7
Penguin, Australia ... 95 G4
Pengxi, China ... 58 B5
Pengze, China ... 59 C11
Penhalonga, Zimbabwe ... 87 F3
Peniche, Portugal ... 37 F1
Penicuik, U.K. ... 13 F5
Penida, Nusa, Indonesia ... 63 K18
Peninnes, Alpes = Pennine, Alpi, Alps ... 25 J3
Peninsular Malaysia □, Malaysia ... 65 L4
Peñíscola, Spain ... 38 E5
Penitente, Serra do, Brazil ... 125 E9
Penkridge, U.K. ... 14 E5
Penmarch, France ... 18 E2
Penmarch, Pte. de, France ... 18 E2
Penn Hills, U.S.A. ... 116 F5
Penn Yan, U.S.A. ... 116 D7
Penna, Punta della, Italy ... 41 F11
Pennant, Canada ... 103 C7
Penne, Italy ... 41 F10
Penner →, India ... 66 M12
Pennine, Alpi, Alps ... 25 J3
Pennines, U.K. ... 14 C5
Pennington →, Nigeria ... 83 E6
Pennington, U.S.A. ... 110 F5
Pennino, Mte., Italy ... 41 E9
Pennsburg, U.S.A. ... 117 F9
Pennsylvania □, U.S.A. ... 114 E7
Penny, Canada ... 102 C4
Peno, Russia ... 32 D7
Penobscot →, U.S.A. ... 115 C11
Penobscot B., U.S.A. ... 115 C11
Penola, Australia ... 95 F3
Penong, Australia ... 93 F5
Penonomé, Panama ... 120 E3
Penrith, Australia ... 95 E5
Penrith, U.K. ... 14 C5
Penryn, U.K. ... 15 G2
Pensacola, U.S.A. ... 115 K2
Pensacola Mts., Antarctica ... 5 E1
Pense, Canada ... 103 C8
Penshurst, Australia ... 95 F3

Penticton, Canada ... 102 D5
Pentland, Australia ... 94 C4
Pentland Firth, U.K. ... 13 C5
Pentland Hills, U.K. ... 13 F5
Pentland Hills △, U.K. ... 13 F5
Penza, Russia ... 34 D7
Penzance, U.K. ... 15 G2
Penzberg, Germany ... 25 H7
Penzhino, Russia ... 53 C17
Penzhinskaya Guba, Russia ... 53 C17
Penzhou, China ... 58 B4
Penzlin, Germany ... 24 B9
Peoria, Ariz., U.S.A. ... 109 K7
Peoria, Ill., U.S.A. ... 112 E10
Pepacton Reservoir, U.S.A. ... 117 D10
Pepel, S. Leone ... 82 D2
Peski, Russia ... 34 E6
Pêso da Régua, Portugal ... 36 D3
Pesqueira, Brazil ... 125 E11
Pessac, France ... 20 D3
Pest □, Hungary ... 28 C4
Pestovo, Russia ... 32 C8
Pestravka, Russia ... 34 D9
Péta, Greece ... 46 B3
Petah Tiqwa, Israel ... 74 C3
Petalídhion, Greece ... 46 E3
Petaling Jaya, Malaysia ... 65 L3
Petaloudhes, Greece ... 49 C10
Petaluma, U.S.A. ... 110 G4
Pétange, Lux. ... 17 E5
Petaro, Pakistan ... 68 G3
Petatlán, Mexico ... 118 D4
Petauke, Zambia ... 87 E3
Petawawa, Canada ... 104 C4
Petén Itzá, L., Guatemala ... 120 C2
Peter I., Br. Virgin Is. ... 121 e
Peter I.s Øy, Antarctica ... 5 C16
Peter Pond L., Canada ... 103 B7
Peterbell, Canada ... 104 C3
Peterborough, Australia ... 95 E2
Peterborough, Canada ... 116 B6
Peterborough, U.K. ... 15 E7
Peterborough, U.S.A. ... 117 D13
Peterborough □, U.K. ... 15 E7
Peterculter, U.K. ... 13 D6
Peterhead, U.K. ... 13 D7
Peterlee, U.K. ... 14 C6
Petermann Ranges, Australia ... 92 E5
Petersburg, Alaska, U.S.A. ... 100 C6
Petersburg, Pa., U.S.A. ... 116 F6
Petersburg, Va., U.S.A. ... 114 G7
Petersburg, W. Va., U.S.A. ... 114 F6
Petersfield, U.K. ... 15 F7
Petershagen, Germany ... 24 C4
Petília Policastro, Italy ... 43 C9
Petit-Canal, Guadeloupe ... 120 b
Petit Goâve, Haiti ... 121 C5
Petit Jardin, Canada ... 105 C8
Petit Lac Manicouagan, Canada ... 105 B6
Petit-Mécatina →, Canada ... 105 B8
Petit-Mécatina, Î. du, Canada ... 105 B8
Petit Piton, St. Lucia ... 121 f
Petit-Saguenay, Canada ... 105 C5
Petit Saint Bernard, Col du, Italy ... 21 C10
Petitcodiac, Canada ... 105 C6
Petite Terre, Îles de la, Guadeloupe ... 120 b
Petitot →, Canada ... 102 A4
Petitsikapau L., Canada ... 105 B6
Petlad, India ... 68 H5
Peto, Mexico ... 119 C7
Petone, N.Z. ... 91 J5
Petorca, Chile ... 126 C1
Petoskey, U.S.A. ... 114 C3
Petra, Jordan ... 74 E4
Petra, Spain ... 48 B10
Petra, Ostrova, Russia ... 4 B13
Petra Velikogo, Zaliv, Russia ... 54 C6
Petrel = Petrer, Spain ... 39 G4
Petrella, Monte, Italy ... 42 A6
Petrer, Spain ... 39 G4
Petreto-Bicchisano, France ... 21 G12
Petrich, Bulgaria ... 44 E7
Petrified Forest △, U.S.A. ... 109 J9
Petrijanec, Croatia ... 41 B13
Petrila, Romania ... 29 E8
Petrinja, Croatia ... 41 C13
Petrodvorets, Russia ... 32 C5
Petrolândia, Brazil ... 125 E11
Petrolia, Canada ... 116 D2
Petrolina, Brazil ... 125 E10
Petropavl, Kazakhstan ... 52 D7
Petropavlovsk = Petropavl, Kazakhstan ... 52 D7
Petropavlovsk-Kamchatskiy, Russia ... 53 D16
Petropavlovskiy = Akhtubinsk, Russia ... 35 F8
Petrópolis, Brazil ... 127 A7
Petroşani, Romania ... 29 E8
Petrova Gora, Croatia ... 41 C12
Petrovac, Serbia & M. ... 44 B5
Petrovac, Serbia & M. ... 44 D3
Petrovaradin, Serbia & M. ... 28 E4
Petrovsk, Russia ... 34 D7
Petrovsk-Zabaykalskiy, Russia ... 53 D11
Petrovskaya, Russia ... 33 K9
Petrozavodsk, Russia ... 32 B6
Petrus Steyn, S. Africa ... 89 D4
Petrusburg, S. Africa ... 88 D4
Petzeck, Austria ... 26 E5
Peumo, Chile ... 126 C1
Peureulak, Indonesia ... 62 D1
Pevek, Russia ... 53 C18
Peveragno, Italy ... 40 D4
Peyrehorade, France ... 20 E2
Peyruis, France ... 21 D9
Pézenas, France ... 20 E7
Pezinok, Slovak Rep. ... 27 C10
Pfaffenhofen, Germany ... 25 G7

Pfälzerwald ◠, Germany 25 F5
Pfarrkirchen, Germany 25 G8
Pfeffenhausen, Germany 25 G7
Pforzheim, Germany 25 G4
Pfullendorf, Germany 25 H5
Pfungstadt, Germany 25 F4
Pha Taem △, Thailand 64 E5
Phagwara, India 66 D9
Phaistós, Greece 49 D6
Phala, Botswana 88 C4
Phalera = Phulera, India 68 F6
Phalodi, India 68 F5
Phalsbourg, France 19 D14
Phaluai, Ko, Thailand ...... 65 b
Phan, Thailand 64 C2
Phan Rang, Vietnam 65 G7
Phan Ri = Hoa Da, Vietnam 65 G7
Phan Thiet, Vietnam 65 G7
Phanae, Greece 47 C7
Phanat Nikhom, Thailand 64 F3
Phangan, Ko, Thailand 65 H3
Phangnga, Thailand 65 H2
Phangnga, Ao, Thailand ...... 65 a
Phanom Sarakham, Thailand 64 F3
Phaphund, India 69 F8
Pharenda, India 69 F10
Pharr, U.S.A. 113 M5
Phatthalung, Thailand 65 J3
Phayao, Thailand 64 C2
Phelps, U.S.A. 116 D7
Phelps L., Canada 103 B8
Phenix City, U.S.A. 115 J3
Phet Buri, Thailand 64 F2
Phetchabun, Thailand 64 D3
Phetchabun, Thiu Khao, Thailand ... 64 E3
Phetchaburi = Phet Buri, Thailand ... 64 F2
Phi Phi, Ko, Thailand 65 J2
Phiafay, Laos 64 E6
Phibun Mangsahan, Thailand ... 64 E5
Phichai, Thailand 64 D3
Phichit, Thailand 64 D3
Philadelphia, Miss., U.S.A. ... 113 J10
Philadelphia, N.Y., U.S.A. ... 117 B9
Philadelphia, Pa., U.S.A. ... 117 G9
Philip, U.S.A. 112 C4
Philippeville, Belgium 17 D4
Philippi, Greece 45 E8
Philippi, U.S.A. 114 F5
Philippi L., U.S.A. 94 C2
Philippine Sea, Pac. Oc. 50 H16
Philippines ■, Asia 61 F5
Philippolis, S. Africa 88 E4
Philippopolis = Plovdiv, Bulgaria ... 45 D8
Philipsburg, Canada 117 A11
Philipsburg, Mont., U.S.A. ... 108 C7
Philipsburg, Pa., U.S.A. ... 116 F6
Philipstown = Daingean, Ireland ... 12 C4
Philipstown, S. Africa 88 E3
Phillip I., Australia 95 F4
Phillips, U.S.A. 112 C9
Phillipsburg, Kans., U.S.A. ... 112 F5
Phillipsburg, N.J., U.S.A. ... 117 F9
Philmont, U.S.A. 117 D11
Philomath, U.S.A. 108 D2
Phimai, Thailand 64 E4
Phitsanulok, Thailand 64 D3
Phnom Dangrek, Thailand ... 62 B2
Phnom Penh, Cambodia 65 G5
Phnum Penh = Phnom Penh, Cambodia ... 65 G5
Phoenicia, U.S.A. 117 D10
Phoenix, Ariz., U.S.A. ... 109 K7
Phoenix, N.Y., U.S.A. ... 117 C8
Phoenix Is., Kiribati 96 H10
Phoenixville, U.S.A. 117 F9
Phon, Thailand 64 E4
Phon Tiou, Laos 64 D5
Phong ➤, Thailand 64 D4
Phong Saly, Laos 58 G4
Phong Tho, Vietnam 64 A4
Phonhong, Laos 64 C4
Phonum, Thailand 65 H2
Phosphate Hill, Australia ... 94 C2
Photharam, Thailand 64 F2
Phra Nakhon Si Ayutthaya, Thailand ... 64 E3
Phra Thong, Ko, Thailand ... 65 H2
Phrae, Thailand 64 C3
Phrom Phiram, Thailand ... 64 D3
Phrygia, Turkey 72 C4
Phu Chong-Na Yoi △, Thailand ... 64 E5
Phu Dien, Vietnam 64 C5
Phu Hin Rang Kla △, Thailand ... 64 D3
Phu Kradung △, Thailand ... 64 D3
Phu Loi, Laos 64 B4
Phu Luang △, Thailand ... 64 D3
Phu Ly, Vietnam 58 G5
Phu Phan △, Thailand ... 64 D4
Phu Quoc, Dao, Vietnam ... 65 G4
Phu Tho, Vietnam 58 G5
Phuc Yen, Vietnam 58 G5
Phuket, Thailand ...... 65 a
Phuket, Ko, Thailand ...... 65 a
Phul, India 68 D6
Phulad, India 68 G5
Phulchari, Bangla. 69 G13
Phulera, India 68 F6
Phulpur, India 69 G10
Phun Phin, Thailand 65 H2
Piacenza, Italy 40 C6
Piai, Tanjung, Malaysia ... 65 d
Pian Cr. ➤, Australia 95 E4
Pian-Upe ◠, Uganda 86 B3
Piana, France 21 F12
Pianella, Italy 41 F11
Pianosa, Puglia, Italy 41 F12
Pianosa, Toscana, Italy 40 F7
Piapot, Canada 103 D7
Pias, Portugal 37 G3
Piaseczno, Poland 31 F8
Piaski, Poland 31 G9

Piastów, Poland 31 F7
Piatra, Romania 29 G10
Piatra Craiului △, Romania ... 29 E10
Piatra Neamţ, Romania 29 D11
Piatra Olt, Romania 29 F9
Piauí □, Brazil 125 E10
Piauí ➤, Brazil 125 E10
Piave ➤, Italy 41 C9
Piazza Ármerina, Italy 43 E7
Pibor ➤, Sudan 81 F3
Pibor Post, Sudan 81 F3
Picardie □, France 19 C10
Picardie, Plaine de, France ... 19 C9
Picardy = Picardie □, France ... 19 C10
Picayune, U.S.A. 113 K10
Picerno, Italy 43 B8
Pichhor, India 69 G8
Pichilemu, Chile 126 C1
Pichor, India 68 G8
Pickerel L., Canada 104 C1
Pickering, U.K. 14 C7
Pickering, Vale of, U.K. ... 14 C7
Pickle Lake, Canada 104 B1
Pickwick L., U.S.A. 115 H1
Pico Bonito △, Honduras ... 120 C2
Pico Truncado, Argentina ... 128 F3
Picos, Brazil 125 E10
Picos de Europa △, Spain ... 36 B6
Picton, Australia 95 E5
Picton, Canada 116 B7
Picton, N.Z. 91 J5
Pictou, Canada 105 C7
Picture Butte, Canada 102 D6
Pictured Rocks ◠, U.S.A. ... 114 B2
Picún Leufú, Argentina ... 128 D3
Pidbuzh, Ukraine 31 J10
Pidurutalagala, Sri Lanka ... 66 R12
Piechowice, Poland 31 H2
Piedimonte Matese, Italy ... 43 A7
Piedmont = Piemonte □, Italy ... 40 D5
Piedmont, Ala., U.S.A. ... 115 J3
Piedmont, S.C., U.S.A. ... 107 D10
Piedra ➤, Spain 38 D3
Piedrabuena, Spain 37 G6
Piedrahita, Spain 36 E5
Piedralaves, Spain 36 E6
Piedras Blancas, Spain ... 36 B5
Piedras Negras, Mexico ... 118 B4
Piekary Śląskie, Poland ... 31 H5
Pieksämäki, Finland 9 E22
Piemonte □, Italy 40 D5
Pienaarsrivier, S. Africa ... 89 D4
Pieniężno, Poland 30 D7
Pieniński △, Europe 27 B13
Pieńsk, Poland 31 G2
Piercefield, U.S.A. 117 B10
Pierceland, Canada 103 C7
Piería □, Greece 44 F6
Pierpont, U.S.A. 116 E4
Pierre, U.S.A. 112 C4
Pierre-Buffière, France ... 20 C5
Pierre-de-Bresse, France ... 19 F12
Pierrefontaine-les-Varans, France ... 19 E13
Pierrefort, France 20 D6
Pierrelatte, France 21 D8
Pierreville, Trin. & Tob. ... 125 K16
Pieštany, Slovak Rep. 27 C10
Piesting ➤, Austria 27 C9
Pieszyce, Poland 31 H3
Piet Retief, S. Africa 89 D5
Pietarsaari, Finland 8 E20
Pietermaritzburg, S. Africa ... 89 D5
Pietersburg = Polokwane, S. Africa ... 89 C4
Pietragalla, Italy 43 B8
Pietrasanta, Italy 40 E7
Pietroșița, Romania 29 E10
Pietrosul, Vf., Maramureş, Romania ... 29 C9
Pietrosul, Vf., Suceava, Romania ... 29 C10
Pieve di Cadore, Italy 41 B9
Pieve di Teco, Italy 40 D4
Pievepélago, Italy 40 D7
Pigadhítsa, Greece 44 G5
Pigeon L., Canada 116 B6
Piggott, U.S.A. 113 G9
Pigna, Italy 40 E4
Pigüe, Argentina 126 D3
Pihani, India 69 F9
Pihlajavesi, Finland 9 F23
Pijijiapan, Mexico 119 D6
Pikalevo, Russia 32 C8
Pikangikum Berens, Canada ... 103 C10
Pikes Peak, U.S.A. 112 F2
Piketberg, S. Africa 88 E2
Pikeville, U.S.A. 114 G4
Pikou, China 57 E12
Pikwitonei, Canada 103 B9
Piła, Poland 31 E3
Pila, Spain 39 G3
Pilaía, Greece 44 F6
Pilanesberg △, S. Africa ... 88 D4
Pilani, India 68 E6
Pilar, Paraguay 126 B4
Pilar de la Horadada, Spain ... 39 H4
Pilat △, France 21 C8
Pilawa, Poland 31 G8
Pilaya ➤, Bolivia 124 H6
Pilcomayo ➤, Paraguay ... 126 B4
Pilgrim's Rest, S. Africa ... 89 C5
Pilgrimstad, Sweden 10 B9
Píli, Greece 47 E9
Pilibhit, India 69 E8
Pilica ➤, Poland 31 G8
Pilion, Greece 46 B5
Pilis, Hungary 28 C4
Pilisvörösvár, Hungary ... 28 C3
Pilkhawa, India 68 E7
Pilliga, Australia 95 E4
Pílos, Greece 46 E3

Pilot Mound, Canada 103 D9
Pilot Point, U.S.A. 113 J6
Pilot Rock, U.S.A. 108 D4
Pilštanj, Slovenia 41 B12
Piltene, Latvia 30 A8
Pilzno, Poland 31 J8
Pima, U.S.A. 109 K9
Pimba, Australia 95 E2
Pimenta Bueno, Brazil 124 F6
Pimentel, Peru 124 E3
Pina de Ebro, Spain 38 D4
Pinamalayan, Phil. 61 E4
Pinang, Malaysia ...... 65 c
Pinar, C. des, Spain 48 B10
Pinar del Río, Cuba 120 B3
Pınarbaşı, Çanakkale, Turkey ... 47 B8
Pınarbaşı, Kayseri, Turkey ... 72 C7
Pınarhisar, Turkey 45 E11
Pinatubo, Mt., Phil. 61 D3
Pincehely, Hungary 28 D3
Pinchang, China 58 B6
Pincher Creek, Canada ... 102 D6
Pinchi L., Canada 102 C4
Pinckneyville, U.S.A. ... 112 F10
Pindar, Australia 93 E2
Pindi Gheb, Pakistan 68 C5
Pindiga, Nigeria 83 D7
Pindos ➤, Greece 46 B3
Pindos Óros, Greece 46 B3
Pindus Mts. = Pindos Óros, Greece ... 46 B3
Pine ➤, B.C., Canada 102 B4
Pine ➤, Sask., Canada ... 103 B7
Pine, C., Canada 105 C9
Pine Bluff, U.S.A. 113 H9
Pine Bluffs, U.S.A. 112 E2
Pine City, U.S.A. 112 C8
Pine Creek, Australia ... 92 B5
Pine Cr. ➤, U.S.A. 116 E7
Pine Falls, Canada 103 C9
Pine Flat Res., U.S.A. ... 110 J7
Pine Grove, U.S.A. 117 F8
Pine Pass, Canada 102 B4
Pine Point, Canada 102 A6
Pine Ridge, U.S.A. 112 D3
Pine River, Canada 103 C8
Pine River, U.S.A. 112 B7
Pine Valley, U.S.A. 111 N10
Pinecrest, U.S.A. 110 G6
Pinedale, Calif., U.S.A. ... 110 J7
Pinedale, Wyo., U.S.A. ... 108 E9
Pinega ➤, Russia 52 C5
Pinehill, Australia 94 C4
Pinehouse L., Canada ... 103 B7
Pineimuta ➤, Canada ... 104 B1
Pinerolo, Italy 40 D4
Pineto, Italy 41 F11
Pinetop, U.S.A. 109 J9
Pinetown, S. Africa 89 D5
Pineville, U.S.A. 113 K8
Piney, France 19 D11
Ping ➤, Thailand 64 E3
Pingaring, Australia 93 F2
Pingba, China 58 D6
Pingbian, China 58 F4
Pingchuan, China 58 D3
Pingding, China 56 F7
Pingdingshan, China 56 H7
Pingdong, Taiwan 59 F13
Pingdu, China 57 F10
Pingelly, Australia 93 F2
Pingguo, China 58 F6
Pingguo, China 58 F6
Pinghe, China 59 E11
Pinghu, China 59 B13
Pingjiang, China 59 C9
Pingle, China 59 E8
Pingli, China 58 A7
Pingliang, China 56 G4
Pinglu, China 56 E7
Pingluo, China 56 E4
Pingnan, Fujian, China ... 59 D12
Pingnan, Guangxi Zhuangzu, China ... 59 F8
Pingquan, China 57 D10
Pingrup, Australia 93 F2
Pingshan, China 58 C5
Pingtan, China 59 E12
Pingtang, China 58 E6
Pingtung, Taiwan 59 F13
Pingwu, China 56 H3
Pingxiang, Guangxi Zhuangzu, China ... 58 F6
Pingxiang, Jiangxi, China ... 59 D9
Pingyao, China 56 F7
Pingyi, China 57 G9
Pingyin, China 56 F9
Pingyuan, Guangdong, China ... 59 E10
Pingyuan, Shandong, China ... 56 F9
Pingyuanjie, China 58 F4
Pinhal, Brazil 127 A6
Pinhal Novo, Portugal ... 37 G2
Pinheiro, Brazil 125 D9
Pinheiro Machado, Brazil ... 127 C5
Pinhel, Portugal 36 E3
Pini, Indonesia 62 D1
Piniós ➤, Ilía, Greece ... 46 D3
Piniós ➤, Tríkkala, Greece ... 46 B4
Pinjarra, Australia 93 F2
Pink Mountain, Canada ... 102 B4
Pinkafeld, Austria 27 D9
Pinnacles ◠, U.S.A. 110 J5
Pinnacles △, U.S.A. 110 J5
Pinnaroo, Australia 95 F3
Pinneberg, Germany 24 B5
Pínnes, Ákra, Greece ... 45 F8
Pinon Hills, U.S.A. 111 L9
Pinos, Mexico 118 C4
Pinos, Mt., U.S.A. 111 L7
Pinos Pt., U.S.A. 109 H3

Pinos Puente, Spain 37 H7
Pinotepa Nacional, Mexico ... 119 D5
Pinrang, Indonesia 63 E5
Pins, Pte. aux, Canada ... 116 D3
Pinsk, Belarus 33 F4
Pintados, Chile 124 H5
Pinyang, China 59 D13
Pinyug, Russia 52 C5
Pioche, U.S.A. 109 H6
Piombino, Italy 40 F7
Piombino, Canale di, Italy ... 40 F7
Pioner, Ostrov, Russia ... 53 B10
Pionerskiy, Russia 30 D7
Pionki, Poland 31 G8
Piorini, L., Brazil 124 D6
Piotrków Trybunalski, Poland ... 31 G6
Piove di Sacco, Italy ... 41 C9
Pip, Iran 71 E9
Pipar, India 68 F5
Pipar Road, India 68 F5
Piparia, Mad. P., India ... 68 H8
Piparia, Mad. P., India ... 68 J7
Pipéri, Greece 46 B6
Pipestone, U.S.A. 112 D6
Pipestone ➤, Canada ... 104 B2
Pipestone Cr. ➤, Canada ... 103 D8
Piplan, Pakistan 68 C4
Piploda, India 68 H6
Pipmuacan, Rés., Canada ... 105 C5
Pippingarra, Australia ... 92 D2
Pipriac, France 18 E5
Piqua, U.S.A. 114 E3
Piquiri ➤, Brazil 127 A5
Pir Panjal Range, India ... 68 C7
Pir Sohrāb, Iran 71 E9
Pira, Benin 83 D5
Piracicaba, Brazil 127 A6
Piracuruca, Brazil 125 D10
Piræus = Piraiévs, Greece ... 46 D5
Piraiévs, Greece 46 D5
Pirajuí, Brazil 127 A6
Piram I., India 68 J5
Piran = Piran, Slovenia ... 41 C10
Pirané, Argentina 126 B4
Pirano = Piran, Slovenia ... 41 C10
Pirapora, Brazil 125 G10
Pirawa, India 68 G7
Pircop, Bulgaria 45 D8
Pírgos, Ilía, Greece 46 D3
Pírgos, Kríti, Greece ... 47 F7
Pirgovo, Bulgaria 45 C9
Piribebuy, Paraguay 126 B4
Pirimapun, Indonesia ... 63 F9
Pirin ◠, Bulgaria 44 E7
Pirin Planina, Bulgaria ... 44 E7
Pirineos = Pyrénées, Europe ... 19 E3
Piripiri, Brazil 125 D10
Pirmasens, Germany 25 F3
Pirna, Germany 24 E9
Pirot, Serbia & M. 44 C6
Piru, Indonesia 63 E7
Piru, U.S.A. 111 L8
Piryatin = Pyryatyn, Ukraine ... 33 G7
Piryí, Greece 47 C7
Pisa, Italy 40 E7
Pisa ➤, Poland 31 E8
Pisa, Firenze ✈ (PSA), Italy ... 40 E7
Pisagne, Italy 40 C7
Pisagua, Chile 124 G4
Pisarovina, Croatia 41 C12
Pisco, Peru 124 F3
Piscu, Romania 29 E12
Písek, Czech Rep. 26 B7
Pishan, China 60 C2
Pishcha, Ukraine 31 G10
Pishchanka, Ukraine 29 B13
Pıshın, Iran 71 E9
Pishin, Pakistan 68 D2
Pishin Lora ➤, Pakistan ... 68 E1
Pisidia, Turkey 72 D4
Pising, Indonesia 63 F6
Pismo Beach, U.S.A. 111 K6
Piso, L., Liberia 82 D2
Pissis, Cerro, Argentina ... 126 B2
Pissos, France 20 D3
Pissouri, Cyprus 49 E11
Pisticci, Italy 43 B9
Pistóia, Italy 40 E7
Pistol B., Canada 103 A10
Pisuerga ➤, Spain 36 D6
Pisz, Poland 30 E8
Pit ➤, U.S.A. 108 F2
Pita, Guinea 82 C2
Pitarpunga, L., Australia ... 95 E3
Pitcairn I., Pac. Oc. 97 K14
Pitch L., Trin. & Tob. ... 125 K15
Piteå, Sweden 8 D19
Piteälven ➤, Sweden ... 8 D19
Piterka, Russia 34 E8
Piteşti, Romania 29 F9
Pithapuram, India 67 L13
Pithara, Australia 93 F2
Píthion, Greece 45 E10
Pithiviers, France 19 D9
Pithorāgarh, India 69 E9
Pithoro, Pakistan 68 G3
Pitigliano, Italy 41 F8
Pitkyaranta, Russia 32 B6
Pitlochry, U.K. 13 E5
Pitsilia, Cyprus 49 E12
Pitt I., Canada 102 C3
Pittsburg, Calif., U.S.A. ... 110 G5
Pittsburg, Kans., U.S.A. ... 113 G7
Pittsburg, Tex., U.S.A. ... 113 J7
Pittsburgh, U.S.A. 116 F5
Pittsfield, Ill., U.S.A. ... 112 F9
Pittsfield, Maine, U.S.A. ... 115 C11
Pittsfield, Mass., U.S.A. ... 117 D11
Pittsfield, N.H., U.S.A. ... 117 C13
Pittston, U.S.A. 117 E9

Pittsworth, Australia 95 D5
Pituri ➤, Australia 94 C2
Piura, Peru 124 E2
Piva ➤, Serbia & M. 44 C2
Pixley, U.S.A. 110 K7
Piyai, Greece 46 B3
Pizarra, Spain 37 J6
Pizhou, China 56 G9
Pizzo, Italy 43 D9
Placentia, Canada 105 C9
Placentia B., Canada 105 C9
Placer, Masbate, Phil. ... 61 F5
Placer, Surigao N., Phil. ... 61 G6
Placerville, U.S.A. 110 G6
Placetas, Cuba 120 B4
Plačkovica, Macedonia ... 44 E6
Plainfield, N.J., U.S.A. ... 117 F10
Plainfield, Ohio, U.S.A. ... 116 F3
Plainfield, Vt., U.S.A. ... 117 B12
Plains, Mont., U.S.A. ... 108 C6
Plains, Tex., U.S.A. 113 J3
Plainview, Nebr., U.S.A. ... 112 D6
Plainview, Tex., U.S.A. ... 113 H4
Plainwell, U.S.A. 114 D3
Plaisance, France 20 E4
Plaistow, U.S.A. 117 D13
Pláka, Greece 47 B7
Pláka, Ákra, Greece 49 D8
Plakenska Planina, Macedonia ... 44 E5
Planá, Czech Rep. 26 B5
Plana Cays, Bahamas 121 B5
Planada, U.S.A. 110 H6
Plancoët, France 18 D4
Plandište, Serbia & M. ... 28 E6
Plano, U.S.A. 113 J6
Plant City, U.S.A. 115 M4
Plaquemine, U.S.A. 113 K9
Plasencia, Spain 36 E4
Plaški, Croatia 41 C12
Plaster City, U.S.A. 111 N11
Plaster Rock, Canada ... 105 C6
Plastun, Russia 54 B8
Plasy, Czech Rep. 26 B6
Plata, Río de la, S. Amer. ... 126 C4
Plátani ➤, Italy 42 E6
Plátanos, Greece 49 D5
Plateau □, Nigeria 83 D6
Platí, Ákra, Greece 45 F8
Platte ➤, Mo., U.S.A. ... 112 F7
Platte ➤, Nebr., U.S.A. ... 112 E7
Platteville, U.S.A. 112 D9
Plattling, Germany 25 G8
Plattsburgh, U.S.A. 117 B11
Plattsmouth, U.S.A. 112 E7
Plau, Germany 24 B8
Plauen, Germany 24 E8
Plauer See, Germany 24 B8
Plav, Serbia & M. 44 D3
Plavinas, Latvia 9 H21
Plavnica, Serbia & M. ... 44 D3
Plavno, Croatia 41 D13
Plavsk, Russia 32 F9
Playa Blanca, Canary Is. ... 48 F6
Playa Blanca Sur, Canary Is. ... 48 F6
Playa de las Americas, Canary Is. ... 48 F3
Playa de Mogán, Canary Is. ... 48 G4
Playa del Inglés, Canary Is. ... 48 G4
Playa Esmeralda, Canary Is. ... 48 F5
Playgreen L., Canada ... 103 C9
Pleasant Bay, Canada ... 105 C7
Pleasant Hill, U.S.A. ... 110 H4
Pleasant Mount, U.S.A. ... 117 E9
Pleasanton, Calif., U.S.A. ... 110 H5
Pleasanton, Tex., U.S.A. ... 113 L5
Pleasantville, Calif., U.S.A. ... 114 F8
Pleasantville, Pa., U.S.A. ... 116 E5
Pléaux, France 20 C6
Plei Ku, Vietnam 64 F7
Plélan-le-Grand, France ... 18 D4
Pléneuf-Val-André, France ... 18 D4
Plenița, Romania 29 F8
Plenty ➤, Australia 94 C2
Plenty, B. of, N.Z. 91 G6
Plentywood, U.S.A. 112 A2
Plérin, France 18 D4
Plessisville, Canada 105 C5
Plestin-les-Grèves, France ... 18 D3
Pleszew, Poland 31 G4
Pleternica, Croatia 28 E2
Plétipi, L., Canada 105 B5
Pleven, Bulgaria 45 C8
Plevlja, Serbia & M. 44 C3
Plevna, Canada 116 B8
Plitvička Jezera △, Croatia ... 41 D12
Plješevica, Croatia 41 D12
Ploaghe, Italy 42 B1
Ploče, Croatia 41 E14
Płock, Poland 31 F6
Plöckenpass, Italy 41 B9
Plöckenstein, Germany ... 25 G9
Ploemeur, France 18 E3
Ploërmel, France 18 E4
Ploiești, Romania 29 F11
Plomárion, Greece 47 C8
Plombières-les-Bains, France ... 19 E13
Plomin, Croatia 41 C11
Plön, Germany 24 A6
Plonge, Lac la, Canada ... 103 B7
Płońsk, Poland 31 F7
Plopeni, Romania 29 E10
Plopișului, Munții, Romania ... 28 D7
Płoty, Poland 30 E2
Plouaret, France 18 D3
Plouay, France 18 E3
Ploučnice ➤, Czech Rep. ... 26 A7
Ploudalmézeau, France ... 18 D2
Plouescat, France 18 D2
Plougasnou, France 18 D3
Plougastel-Daoulas, France ... 18 D2

Plouguerneau, *France* 18 D2
Plouha, *France* 18 D4
Plouhinec, *France* 18 E2
Plovdiv, *Bulgaria* 45 D8
Plovdiv □, *Bulgaria* 45 D8
Plum, *U.S.A.* 116 F5
Plum I., *U.S.A.* 117 E12
Plumas, *U.S.A.* 110 F7
Plummer, *U.S.A.* 108 C5
Plumtree, *Zimbabwe* 87 G2
Plungė, *Lithuania* 9 J19
Pluvigner, *France* 18 E3
Plymouth, *Trin. & Tob.* 125 J16
Plymouth, *U.K.* 15 G3
Plymouth, *Calif., U.S.A.* 110 G6
Plymouth, *Ind., U.S.A.* 114 E2
Plymouth, *Mass., U.S.A.* 117 E14
Plymouth, *N.C., U.S.A.* 115 H7
Plymouth, *N.H., U.S.A.* 117 C13
Plymouth, *Pa., U.S.A.* 117 E9
Plymouth, *Wis., U.S.A.* 114 D2
Plympton-Wyoming, *Canada* ... 116 D2
Plynlimon = Pumlumon Fawr,
 U.K. 15 E4
Plyusa, *Russia* 32 C5
Plyusa →, *Russia* 32 C5
Plzeň, *Czech Rep.* 26 B6
Plzeňský □, *Czech Rep.* 26 B6
Pniewy, *Poland* 31 F3
Pô, *Burkina Faso* 83 C4
Pô △, *Burkina Faso* 83 C4
Po →, *Italy* 41 D9
Po, Foci del, *Italy* 41 D9
Po Hai = Bo Hai, *China* 57 E10
Pobé, *Benin* 83 D5
Pobé, *Burkina Faso* 83 C4
Pobeda, *Russia* 53 C15
Pobedy, Pik, *Kyrgyzstan* 52 E8
Pobiedziska, *Poland* 31 F4
Pobla de Segur, *Spain* 38 C5
Pobla de Segur, *Spain* 38 C5
Pobladura del Valle, *Spain* 36 C5
Pobra de Trives, *Spain* 36 C3
Pocahontas, *Ark., U.S.A.* 113 G9
Pocahontas, *Iowa, U.S.A.* 112 D7
Pocatello, *U.S.A.* 108 E7
Počátky, *Czech Rep.* 26 B8
Pochep, *Russia* 33 F7
Pochinki, *Russia* 34 C7
Pochinok, *Russia* 32 E7
Pöchlarn, *Austria* 26 C8
Pochutla, *Mexico* 119 D5
Pocito Casas, *Mexico* 118 B2
Pocking, *Germany* 25 G9
Pocomoke City, *U.S.A.* 114 F8
Poços de Caldas, *Brazil* 127 A6
Podbořany, *Czech Rep.* 26 A6
Poddębice, *Poland* 31 G5
Poděbrady, *Czech Rep.* 26 A8
Podensac, *France* 20 D3
Podenzano, *Italy* 40 D6
Podgorač, *Croatia* 28 E3
Podgorica, *Serbia & M.* 44 D3
Podgorie, *Albania* 44 F4
Podilska Vysochyna, *Ukraine* .. 29 B13
Podkarpackie □, *Poland* 31 H9
Podkova, *Bulgaria* 45 E9
Podlapača, *Croatia* 41 D12
Podlaskie □, *Poland* 31 E10
Podoleni, *Romania* 29 D11
Podolínec, *Slovak Rep.* 27 B13
Podolsk, *Russia* 32 E9
Podor, *Senegal* 82 B1
Podporozhye, *Russia* 32 B8
Podu Iloaiei, *Romania* 29 C12
Podu Turcului, *Romania* 29 D12
Podujevo, *Serbia & M.* 44 D5
Podyjí △, *Czech Rep.* 26 C8
Poel, *Germany* 24 B6
Pofadder, *S. Africa* 88 D2
Poggiardo, *Italy* 43 B11
Poggibonsi, *Italy* 40 E8
Póggio Mirteto, *Italy* 41 F9
Pogoanele, *Romania* 29 F12
Pogorzela, *Poland* 31 G4
Pogradec, *Albania* 44 F4
Pogranichnyy, *Russia* 54 B5
Poh, *Indonesia* 63 E6
P'ohang, S. *Korea* 57 F15
Pohjanmaa, *Finland* 8 E20
Pohnpei, *Micronesia* 96 G7
Pohořelá, *Slovak Rep.* 27 C13
Pohořelice, *Czech Rep.* 27 C9
Pohorje, *Slovenia* 41 B12
Pohri, *India* 68 G6
Poiana Mare, *Romania* 28 G8
Poiana Ruscăi, Munții, *Romania* 28 E7
Poiana Stampei, *Romania* 29 C10
Poinsett, C., *Antarctica* 5 C8
Point Arena, *U.S.A.* 110 G3
Point Baker, *U.S.A.* 102 B2
Point Edward, *Canada* 104 D3
Point Fortin, *Trin. & Tob.* 125 K15
Point Hope, *U.S.A.* 100 B3
Point L., *Canada* 100 B8
Point Lisas, *Trin. & Tob.* 125 K15
Point Pedro, *Sri Lanka* 66 Q12
Point Pelee △, *Canada* 116 E2
Point Pleasant, *N.J., U.S.A.* ... 117 F10
Point Pleasant, *W. Va., U.S.A.* . 114 F4
Point Reyes △, *U.S.A.* 110 G2
Pointe-à-Pitre, *Guadeloupe* ... 120 b
Pointe-au-Pic = La Malbaie,
 Canada 105 C5
Pointe-Claire, *Canada* 117 A11
Pointe-Gatineau, *Canada* 117 A9
Pointe-Noire, *Congo* 84 E2
Pointe Noire, *Guadeloupe* .... 120 b
Poio, *Spain* 36 C2
Poirino, *Italy* 40 D4
Poisonbush Ra., *Australia* 92 D3
Poissonnier Pt., *Australia* 92 C2

Poitiers, *France* 18 F7
Poitou, *France* 20 B3
Poitou-Charentes □, *France* ... 20 B4
Poix-de-Picardie, *France* 19 C6
Poix-Terron, *France* 19 C11
Pojoaque, *U.S.A.* 109 J11
Pokaran, *India* 66 F7
Pokataroo, *Australia* 95 D4
Pokhara, *Nepal* 69 E10
Pokhvistnevo, *Russia* 34 D11
Poko, *Dem. Rep. of the Congo* . 86 B2
Poko, *Sudan* 81 F3
Pokrov, *Russia* 32 E10
Pokrovsk, *Russia* 53 C13
Pokrovskoye, *Russia* 33 J10
Pola = Pula, *Croatia* 41 D10
Pola, *Russia* 32 D7
Pola de Allande, *Spain* 36 B4
Pola de Lena, *Spain* 36 B5
Pola de Siero, *Spain* 36 B5
Pola de Somiedo, *Spain* 36 B4
Polacca, *U.S.A.* 109 J8
Polan, *Iran* 71 E9
Pol'ana, *Slovak Rep.* 27 C12
Poland ■, *Europe* 31 G3
Polanica-Zdrój, *Poland* 31 H3
Połaniec, *Poland* 31 H8
Polanów, *Poland* 30 D3
Polar Bear △, *Canada* 104 A2
Polatlı, *Turkey* 72 C5
Polatsk, *Belarus* 32 E5
Polcura, *Chile* 126 D1
Police, *Poland* 30 E1
Police, *Poland* 30 E1
Polička, *Czech Rep.* 27 B9
Policoro, *Italy* 43 B9
Polignano a Mare, *Italy* 43 A9
Poligny, *France* 19 F12
Políkhnitos, *Greece* 47 B8
Polillo Is., *Phil.* 61 D4
Polillo Strait, *Phil.* 61 D4
Polis, *Cyprus* 49 D11
Polístena, *Italy* 43 D9
Políyiros, *Greece* 44 F7
Polk, *U.S.A.* 116 E5
Polkowice, *Poland* 31 G3
Polla, *Italy* 43 B8
Pollachi, *India* 66 P10
Pollença, *Spain* 48 B10
Pollença, B. de, *Spain* 48 B10
Póllica, *Italy* 43 B8
Pollino △, *Italy* 43 C9
Pollino, Mte., *Italy* 43 C9
Polna, *Russia* 32 C5
Polnovat, *Russia* 52 C7
Pology, *Ukraine* 33 J9
Polokwane, *S. Africa* 89 C4
Polonne, *Ukraine* 33 G4
Polonnoye = Polonne, *Ukraine* . 33 G4
Polski Trŭmbesh, *Bulgaria* 45 C9
Polsko Kosovo, *Bulgaria* 45 C9
Polson, *U.S.A.* 108 C6
Poltár, *Slovak Rep.* 27 C12
Poltava, *Ukraine* 33 H8
Põltsamaa, *Estonia* 9 G21
Polunochnoye, *Russia* 52 C7
Põlva, *Estonia* 9 G22
Polyana, *Ukraine* 28 B7
Polynesia, *Pac. Oc.* 97 F11
Polynésie française = French
 Polynesia ■, *Pac. Oc.* 97 K13
Pomarance, *Italy* 40 E7
Pomaro, *Mexico* 118 D4
Pombal, *Portugal* 36 F2
Pómbia, *Greece* 49 E6
Pomene, *Mozam.* 89 C6
Pomeroy, *Ohio, U.S.A.* 114 F4
Pomeroy, *Wash., U.S.A.* 108 C5
Pomézia, *Italy* 42 A5
Pomichna, *Ukraine* 33 H6
Pomona, *Australia* 95 D5
Pomona, *U.S.A.* 111 L9
Pomorie, *Bulgaria* 45 D11
Pomorskie □, *Poland* 30 D5
Pomorskie, Pojezierze, *Poland* . 30 E3
Pomos, *Cyprus* 49 D11
Pomos, C., *Cyprus* 49 D11
Pompano Beach, *U.S.A.* 115 M5
Pompei, *Italy* 43 B7
Pompey, *France* 19 D13
Pompeys Pillar, *U.S.A.* 108 D10
Pompeys Pillar △, *U.S.A.* 108 D10
Pompton Lakes, *U.S.A.* 117 F10
Ponape = Pohnpei, *Micronesia* . 96 G7
Ponask L., *Canada* 104 B1
Ponca, *U.S.A.* 112 D6
Ponca City, *U.S.A.* 113 G6
Ponce, *Puerto Rico* .... 121 d
Ponchatoula, *U.S.A.* 113 K9
Poncheville, L., *Canada* 104 B4
Pond, *U.S.A.* 111 K7
Pond Inlet, *Canada* 101 A12
Ponds, I. of, *Canada* 105 B8
Ponferrada, *Spain* 36 C4
Pongo, Wadi →, *Sudan* 81 F2
Poniatowa, *Poland* 31 G9
Poniec, *Poland* 31 G3
Ponikva, *Slovenia* 41 B12
Ponnani, *India* 66 P9
Ponoka, *Canada* 102 C6
Ponorogo, *Indonesia* 63 G14
Pons = Ponts, *Spain* 38 D6

Pons, *France* 20 C3
Ponsul →, *Portugal* 36 F3
Pont-à-Mousson, *France* 19 D13
Pont-Audemer, *France* 18 C7
Pont-Aven, *France* 18 E3
Pont Canavese, *Italy* 40 C4
Pont-d'Ain, *France* 19 F12
Pont-de-Roide, *France* 19 E13
Pont-de-Salars, *France* 20 D6
Pont-de-Vaux, *France* 19 F11
Pont-de-Veyle, *France* 19 F11
Pont-du-Château, *France* 19 G10
Pontacq, *France* 20 E3
Pontailler-sur-Saône, *France* .. 19 E12
Pontarlier, *France* 19 F13
Pontassieve, *Italy* 41 E8
Pontaumur, *France* 20 C6
Pontcharra, *France* 21 C10
Pontchartrain L., *U.S.A.* 113 K10
Pontchâteau, *France* 18 E4
Ponte da Barca, *Portugal* 36 D2
Ponte de Sor, *Portugal* 37 F2
Ponte dell'Ólio, *Italy* 40 D6
Ponte di Legno, *Italy* 40 B7
Ponte do Lima, *Portugal* 36 D2
Ponte-Leccia, *France* 21 F13
Ponte nelle Alpi, *Italy* 41 B9
Ponte Nova, *Brazil* 127 A7
Ponteareas, *Spain* 36 C2
Pontebba, *Italy* 41 B10
Ponteceso, *Spain* 36 B2
Pontecorvo, *Italy* 42 A6
Pontedeume, *Spain* 36 B2
Ponteix, *Canada* 103 D7
Pontevedra, *Spain* 36 C2
Pontevedra □, *Spain* 36 C2
Pontevedra, R. de →, *Spain* ... 36 C2
Pontevico, *Italy* 40 C7
Pontiac, *Ill., U.S.A.* 112 E10
Pontiac, *Mich., U.S.A.* 114 D4
Pontian Kechil, *Malaysia* ..... 65 d
Pontianak, *Indonesia* 62 E3
Pontine Is. = Ponziane, Ísole, *Italy* 42 B5
Pontine Mts. = Kuzey Anadolu
 Dağları, *Turkey* 72 B7
Pontínia, *Italy* 42 A6
Pontivy, *France* 18 D4
Pontoise, *France* 19 C9
Ponton →, *Canada* 102 B5
Pontorson, *France* 18 D5
Pontrémoli, *Italy* 40 D6
Pontrieux, *France* 18 D3
Ponts, *Spain* 38 D6
Pontypool, *Canada* 116 B6
Pontypool, *U.K.* 15 F4
Pontypridd, *U.K.* 15 F4
Ponza, *Italy* 42 B5
Ponziane, Ísole, *Italy* 42 B5
Poochera, *Australia* 95 E1
Poole, *U.K.* 15 G6
Poole □, *U.K.* 15 G6
Poona = Pune, *India* 66 K8
Pooncarie, *Australia* 95 E3
Poopelloe L., *Australia* 95 E3
Poopó, L. de, *Bolivia* 124 G5
Popayán, *Colombia* 124 C3
Poperinge, *Belgium* 17 D2
Popilta L., *Australia* 95 E3
Popina, *Bulgaria* 45 B10
Popio L., *Australia* 95 E3
Poplar, *U.S.A.* 112 A2
Poplar →, *Canada* 103 C9
Poplar Bluff, *U.S.A.* 113 G9
Poplarville, *U.S.A.* 113 K10
Popocatépetl, Volcán, *Mexico* . 119 D5
Popokabaka, *Dem. Rep. of
 the Congo* 84 F3
Pópoli, *Italy* 41 F10
Popovača, *Croatia* 41 C13
Popovo, *Bulgaria* 45 C10
Poppberg, *Germany* 25 F7
Poppi, *Italy* 41 E8
Poprad, *Slovak Rep.* 27 B13
Poprad →, *Slovak Rep.* 27 B13
Porali →, *Pakistan* 68 G2
Porbandar, *India* 68 J3
Porcher I., *Canada* 102 C2
Porcuna, *Spain* 37 H6
Porcupine →, *Canada* 103 B8
Porcupine →, *U.S.A.* 100 B5
Porcupine Gorge △, *Australia* . 94 C3
Pordenone, *Italy* 41 C9
Pordim, *Bulgaria* 45 C8
Poreč, *Croatia* 41 C10
Poretskoye, *Russia* 34 C8
Pori, *Finland* 9 F19
Póros, *Greece* 46 D5
Poroshiri-Dake, *Japan* 54 C11
Poroszló, *Hungary* 28 C5
Poroto Mts., *Tanzania* 87 D3
Porpoise B., *Antarctica* 5 C9
Porquerolles, Î. de, *France* 21 F10
Porrentruy, *Switz.* 25 H3
Porreres, *Spain* 48 B10
Porsangen, *Norway* 8 A21

Porsgrunn, *Norway* 9 G13
Port Alberni, *Canada* 102 D4
Port Alfred, *S. Africa* 88 E4
Port Alice, *Canada* 102 C3
Port Allegany, *U.S.A.* 116 E6
Port Allen, *U.S.A.* 113 K9
Port Alma, *Australia* 94 C5
Port Angeles, *U.S.A.* 110 B3
Port Antonio, *Jamaica* .... 120 a
Port Aransas, *U.S.A.* 113 M6
Port Arthur, *Australia* 95 G4
Port Arthur, *U.S.A.* 113 L8
Port au Choix, *Canada* 105 B8
Port au Port B., *Canada* 105 C8
Port-au-Prince, *Haiti* 121 C5
Port Augusta, *Australia* 95 E2
Port Austin, *U.S.A.* 116 B2
Port Bell, *Uganda* 86 B3
Port Bergé Vaovao, *Madag.* ... 89 B8
Port Blandford, *Canada* 105 C9
Port Broughton, *Australia* 95 E2
Port Burwell, *Canada* 116 D4
Port Canning, *India* 69 H13
Port-Cartier, *Canada* 105 B6
Port Chalmers, *N.Z.* 91 L3
Port Charlotte, *U.S.A.* 115 M4
Port Chester, *U.S.A.* 117 F11
Port Clements, *Canada* 102 C2
Port Clinton, *U.S.A.* 114 E4
Port Colborne, *Canada* 116 D5
Port Coquitlam, *Canada* 102 D4
Port Credit, *Canada* 116 C5
Port-Cros △, *France* 21 F10
Port Curtis, *Australia* 94 C5
Port d'Alcúdia, *Spain* 48 B10
Port Dalhousie, *Canada* 116 C5
Port d'Andratx, *Spain* 48 B9
Port Darwin, *Australia* 92 B5
Port Darwin, *Falk. Is.* 128 G5
Port Davey, *Australia* 95 G4
Port-de-Bouc, *France* 21 E8
Port-de-Paix, *Haiti* 121 C5
Port de Pollença, *Spain* 48 B10
Port de Sóller, *Spain* 48 B9
Port Dickson, *Malaysia* 65 L3
Port Douglas, *Australia* 94 B4
Port Dover, *Canada* 116 D4
Port Edward, *Canada* 102 C2
Port Elgin, *Canada* 116 B3
Port Elizabeth, *S. Africa* 88 E4
Port Ellen, *U.K.* 13 F2
Port-en-Bessin-Huppain, *France* 18 C6
Port Erin, *I. of Man* 14 C3
Port Essington, *Australia* 92 B5
Port Ewen, *U.S.A.* 117 E11
Port Fairy, *Australia* 95 F3
Port Fouâd = Bûr Fuad, *Egypt* . 80 H8
Port Gamble, *U.S.A.* 110 C4
Port-Gentil, *Gabon* 84 E1
Port Germein, *Australia* 95 E2
Port Gibson, *U.S.A.* 113 K9
Port Glasgow, *U.K.* 13 F4
Port Harcourt, *Nigeria* 83 E6
Port Hardy, *Canada* 102 C3
Port Harrison = Inukjuak, *Canada* 101 C12
Port Hawkesbury, *Canada* 105 C7
Port Hedland, *Australia* 92 D2
Port Henry, *U.S.A.* 117 B11
Port Hood, *Canada* 105 C7
Port Hope, *Canada* 116 C6
Port Hope, *U.S.A.* 116 C2
Port Hope Simpson, *Canada* .. 105 B8
Port Hueneme, *U.S.A.* 111 L7
Port Huron, *U.S.A.* 116 D2
Port Iliç, *Azerbaijan* 73 C13
Port Jefferson, *U.S.A.* 117 F11
Port Jervis, *U.S.A.* 117 E10
Port-Joinville, *France* 18 F4
Port Katon, *Russia* 33 J10
Port Kelang = Pelabuhan Klang,
 Malaysia 65 L3
Port Kenny, *Australia* 95 E1
Port-la-Nouvelle, *France* 20 E7
Port Laoise, *Ireland* 12 C4
Port Lavaca, *U.S.A.* 113 L6
Port Leyden, *U.S.A.* 117 C9
Port Lincoln, *Australia* 95 E2
Port Loko, *S. Leone* 82 D2
Port Louis, *France* 18 E3
Port-Louis, *Guadeloupe* ...... 120 b
Port Louis, *Mauritius* 77 H9
Port MacDonnell, *Australia* ... 95 F3
Port McNeill, *Canada* 102 C3
Port Macquarie, *Australia* 95 E5
Port Maria, *Jamaica* .... 120 a
Port Matilda, *U.S.A.* 116 F6
Port Mellon, *Canada* 102 D4
Port-Menier, *Canada* 105 C7
Port Moody, *Canada* 110 A4
Port Morant, *Jamaica* .... 120 a
Port Moresby, *Papua N. G.* ... 96 H6
Port Musgrave, *Australia* 94 A3
Port-Navalo, *France* 18 E4
Port Neches, *U.S.A.* 113 L8
Port Nolloth, *S. Africa* 88 D2
Port Nouveau-Québec =
 Kangiqsualujjuaq, *Canada* ... 101 C13
Port of Spain, *Trin. & Tob.* ... 125 K15
Port Orange, *U.S.A.* 115 L5
Port Orchard, *U.S.A.* 110 C4
Port Orford, *U.S.A.* 108 E1
Port Pegasus, *N.Z.* 91 M1
Port Perry, *Canada* 116 B6
Port Phillip B., *Australia* 95 F3
Port Pirie, *Australia* 95 E2
Port Renfrew, *Canada* 102 D4
Port Roper, *Australia* 94 A2
Port Rowan, *Canada* 116 D4

Port Safaga = Bûr Safâga, *Egypt* 70 E2
Port Sa'îd = Bûr Sa'îd, *Egypt* .. 80 H8
Port St. Joe, *U.S.A.* 115 L3
Port St. Johns = Umzimvubu,
 S. Africa 89 E4
Port-St-Louis-du-Rhône, *France* 21 E8
Port St. Lucie, *U.S.A.* 115 M5
Port-Ste-Marie, *France* 20 D4
Port Sanilac, *U.S.A.* 116 C2
Port Severn, *Canada* 116 B5
Port Shepstone, *S. Africa* 89 E5
Port Simpson, *Canada* 102 C2
Port Stanley = Stanley, *Falk. Is.* 128 G5
Port Stanley, *Canada* 116 D3
Port Sudan = Bûr Sûdân, *Sudan* 80 D4
Port Sulphur, *U.S.A.* 113 L10
Port-sur-Saône, *France* 19 E13
Port Talbot, *U.K.* 15 F4
Port Taufiq = Bûr Taufiq, *Egypt* 80 J8
Port Townsend, *U.S.A.* 110 B4
Port-Vendres, *France* 20 F7
Port Vila, *Vanuatu* 96 J8
Port Wakefield, *Australia* 95 E2
Port Washington, *U.S.A.* 114 D2
Portadown, *U.K.* 12 B5
Portaferry, *U.K.* 12 B6
Portage, *Pa., U.S.A.* 116 F6
Portage, *Wis., U.S.A.* 112 D10
Portage la Prairie, *Canada* 103 D9
Portageville, *U.S.A.* 113 G10
Portalegre, *Portugal* 37 F3
Portalegre □, *Portugal* 37 F3
Portales, *U.S.A.* 113 H3
Portarlington, *Ireland* 12 C4
Portbou, *Spain* 38 C8
Portel, *Portugal* 37 G3
Portela, Lisboa ✈ (LIS), *Portugal* 37 G1
Porter L., *N.W.T., Canada* 103 A7
Porter L., *Sask., Canada* 103 B7
Porterville, *S. Africa* 88 E2
Porterville, *U.S.A.* 110 J8
Portes-lès-Valence, *France* 21 D8
Porthcawl, *U.K.* 15 F4
Porthill, *U.S.A.* 108 B5
Porthmadog, *U.K.* 14 E3
Portile de Fier, *Europe* 28 F7
Portimão, *Portugal* 37 H2
Portishead, *U.K.* 15 F5
Portitei, Gura, *Romania* 29 F14
Portknockie, *U.K.* 13 D6
Portland, *N.S.W., Australia* ... 95 E5
Portland, *Vic., Australia* 95 F3
Portland, *Canada* 117 B8
Portland, *Conn., U.S.A.* 117 E12
Portland, *Maine, U.S.A.* 101 D12
Portland, *Mich., U.S.A.* 114 D3
Portland, *Oreg., U.S.A.* 110 D4
Portland, *Pa., U.S.A.* 117 F9
Portland, *Tex., U.S.A.* 113 M6
Portland ✈ (PDX), *U.S.A.* 110 E4
Portland, I. of, *U.K.* 15 G5
Portland B., *Australia* 95 F3
Portland Bight, *Jamaica* ..... 120 a
Portland Bill, *U.K.* 15 G5
Portland Canal, *U.S.A.* 102 B2
Portland Pt., *Jamaica* .... 120 a
Portmadoc = Porthmadog, *U.K.* 14 E3
Portmore, *Jamaica* .... 120 a
Porto, *France* 21 F12
Porto, *Portugal* 36 D2
Porto □, *Portugal* 36 D2
Porto, G. de, *France* 21 F12
Pôrto Alegre, *Brazil* 127 C5
Pôrto Azzurro, *Italy* 40 F7
Porto Cristo, *Spain* 48 B10
Pôrto de Móz, *Brazil* 125 D8
Porto Empédocle, *Italy* 42 E6
Pôrto Esperança, *Brazil* 124 G7
Pôrto Franco, *Brazil* 125 E9
Pôrto Lágos, *Greece* 45 E9
Pôrto Mendes, *Brazil* 127 A5
Pôrto Moniz, *Madeira* 48 D2
Pôrto Murtinho, *Brazil* 124 H7
Pôrto Nacional, *Brazil* 125 F9
Porto-Novo, *Benin* 83 D5
Pôrto San Giórgio, *Italy* 41 E10
Porto Sant' Elpídio, *Italy* 41 E10
Porto Santo, I. de, *Madeira* ... 78 B2
Porto Santo Stéfano, *Italy* 40 F8
Pôrto São José, *Brazil* 127 A5
Pôrto Seguro, *Brazil* 125 G11
Porto Tolle, *Italy* 41 D9
Pôrto Tórres, *Italy* 42 B1
Pôrto União, *Brazil* 127 B5
Pôrto Válter, *Brazil* 124 E4
Porto-Vecchio, *France* 21 G13
Pôrto Velho, *Brazil* 124 E6
Portobelo, *Panama* .... 120 a
Portoferráio, *Italy* 40 F7
Portogruaro, *Italy* 41 C9
Portola, *U.S.A.* 110 F6
Portomaggiore, *Italy* 41 D8
Portoscuso, *Italy* 42 C1
Portovénere, *Italy* 40 D6
Portoviejo, *Ecuador* 124 D2
Portpatrick, *U.K.* 13 G3
Portree, *U.K.* 13 D2
Portrush, *U.K.* 12 A5
Portsmouth, *Dominica* 121 C7
Portsmouth, *U.K.* 15 G6
Portsmouth, *N.H., U.S.A.* 115 D10
Portsmouth, *Ohio, U.S.A.* 114 F4
Portsmouth, *R.I., U.S.A.* 117 E13
Portsmouth, *Va., U.S.A.* 114 G7
Portsmouth □, *U.K.* 15 G6
Portsoy, *U.K.* 13 D6
Portstewart, *U.K.* 12 A5
Porttipahdan tekojärvi, *Finland* 8 B22
Portugal ■, *Europe* 36 F3
Portugalete, *Spain* 38 B1

Portumna, *Ireland* 12 C3
Portville, *U.S.A.* 116 D6
Porvenir, *Chile* 128 G2
Porvoo, *Finland* 9 F21
Porzuna, *Spain* 37 F6
Posada, *Italy* 42 B2
Posada →, *Italy* 42 B2
Posadas, *Argentina* 127 B4
Posadas, *Spain* 37 H5
Poschiavo, *Switz.* 25 J6
Posets, *Spain* 38 C5
Posht-e Badam, *Iran* 71 C7
Posídhion, Ákra, *Greece* 44 G7
Posidium, *Greece* 47 F9
Poso, *Indonesia* 63 E6
Posong, *S. Korea* 57 G14
Posse, *Brazil* 125 F9
Possession I., *Antarctica* 5 D11
Pössneck, *Germany* 24 E7
Possum Kingdom L., *U.S.A.* 113 J5
Post, *U.S.A.* 113 J4
Post Falls, *U.S.A.* 108 C5
Postavy = Pastavy, *Belarus* 9 J22
Poste-de-la-Baleine =
  Kuujjuarapik, *Canada* 104 A4
Postmasburg, *S. Africa* 88 D3
Postojna, *Slovenia* 41 C11
Poston, *U.S.A.* 111 M12
Postville, *Canada* 105 B8
Potamós, Andikíthira, *Greece* 46 F5
Potamós, Kíthira, *Greece* 46 E4
Potchefstroom, *S. Africa* 88 D4
Potcoava, *Romania* 29 F9
Poteau, *U.S.A.* 113 H7
Poteet, *U.S.A.* 113 L5
Potenza, *Italy* 43 B8
Potenza →, *Italy* 41 E10
Potenza Picena, *Italy* 41 E10
Poteriteri, L., *N.Z.* 91 M1
Potgietersrus = Mokopane,
  S. Africa 89 C4
Poti, *Georgia* 35 J5
Potiskum, *Nigeria* 83 C7
Potlogi, *Romania* 29 F10
Potomac →, *U.S.A.* 114 G7
Potosí, *Bolivia* 124 G5
Potosi Mt., *U.S.A.* 111 K11
Pototan, *Phil.* 61 F5
Potrerillos, *Chile* 126 B2
Potsdam, *Germany* 24 C9
Potsdam, *U.S.A.* 117 B10
Pottenstein, *Germany* 25 F7
Pottersville, *U.S.A.* 117 C11
Pottstown, *U.S.A.* 117 F9
Pottsville, *U.S.A.* 117 F8
Pottuvil, *Sri Lanka* 66 R12
P'otzu, *Taiwan* 59 F13
Pouancé, *France* 18 E5
Pouce Coupé, *Canada* 102 B4
Poughkeepsie, *U.S.A.* 117 E11
Pouilly-sur-Loire, *France* 19 E9
Poulaphouca Res., *Ireland* 12 C5
Poulsbo, *U.S.A.* 110 C4
Poultney, *U.S.A.* 117 C11
Poulton-le-Fylde, *U.K.* 14 D5
Pouso Alegre, *Brazil* 127 A6
Pout, *Senegal* 82 C1
Pouthisat, *Cambodia* 64 F4
Pouzauges, *France* 18 F6
Pova de Santa Iria, *Portugal* 37 G1
Považská Bystrica, *Slovak Rep.* 27 B11
Poverty B., *N.Z.* 91 H7
Povlen, *Serbia & M.* 44 B3
Póvoa de Lanhosa, *Portugal* 36 D2
Póvoa de Varzim, *Portugal* 36 D2
Povorino, *Russia* 34 E6
Povungnituk = Puvirnituq,
  Canada 101 B12
Powassan, *Canada* 104 C4
Poway, *U.S.A.* 111 N9
Powder →, *U.S.A.* 112 B2
Powder River, *U.S.A.* 108 E10
Powell, *U.S.A.* 108 D9
Powell, L., *U.S.A.* 109 H8
Powell River, *Canada* 102 D4
Powers, *U.S.A.* 114 C2
Powys □, *U.K.* 15 E4
Poyang Hu, *China* 59 C11
Poyarkovo, *Russia* 53 E13
Poysdorf, *Austria* 27 C9
Poza de la Sal, *Spain* 36 C7
Poza Rica, *Mexico* 119 C5
Pozantı, *Turkey* 72 D6
Požarevac, *Serbia & M.* 44 B5
Pozazal, Puerto, *Spain* 36 C6
Požega, *Croatia* 28 E2
Požega, *Serbia & M.* 44 C4
Poznań, *Poland* 31 F3
Poznań ✈ (POZ), *Poland* 31 F3
Pozo, *U.S.A.* 111 K6
Pozo Alcón, *Spain* 37 H8
Pozo Almonte, *Chile* 124 H5
Pozo Colorado, *Paraguay* 126 A4
Pozoblanco, *Spain* 37 G6
Pozzallo, *Italy* 43 F7
Pozzomaggiore, *Italy* 42 B1
Pozzuoli, *Italy* 43 B7
Pra →, *Ghana* 83 D4
Prabuty, *Poland* 30 E6
Prača, *Bos.-H.* 28 G3
Prachatice, *Czech Rep.* 26 B6
Prachin Buri, *Thailand* 64 E3
Prachuap Khiri Khan, *Thailand* 65 G2
Pradelles, *France* 20 D7
Prades, *France* 20 F6
Prado, *Brazil* 125 G11
Prado del Rey, *Spain* 37 J5
Præstø, *Denmark* 11 J6
Pragersko, *Slovenia* 41 B12
Prague = Praha, *Czech Rep.* 26 A7
Praha, *Czech Rep.* 26 A7

Praha ✈ (PRG), *Czech Rep.* 26 A7
Prahecq, *France* 20 B3
Prahova □, *Romania* 29 E10
Prahova →, *Romania* 29 F10
Prahovo, *Serbia & M.* 44 B6
Praia, *C. Verde Is.* 77 E1
Práia a Mare, *Italy* 43 C8
Praid, *Romania* 29 D10
Prainha, *Amazonas, Brazil* 124 E6
Prainha, *Pará, Brazil* 125 D8
Prairie, *Australia* 94 C3
Prairie City, *U.S.A.* 108 D4
Prairie Dog Town Fork →,
  U.S.A. 113 H5
Prairie du Chien, *U.S.A.* 112 D9
Prairies, L. of the, *Canada* 103 C8
Pramánda, *Greece* 46 B3
Prampram, *Ghana* 83 D5
Pran Buri, *Thailand* 64 F2
Prang, *Ghana* 83 D4
Prapat, *Indonesia* 62 D1
Prasonísi, Ákra, *Greece* 49 D9
Prästmon, *Sweden* 10 A11
Praszka, *Poland* 31 G5
Prata, *Brazil* 125 G9
Pratabpur, *India* 69 H10
Pratapgarh, *Raj., India* 68 G6
Pratapgarh, *Ut. P., India* 69 G9
Pratas Is. = Dongsha Dao, *China* 59 G11
Prato, *Italy* 40 E8
Prátola Peligna, *Italy* 41 F10
Prats-de-Mollo-la-Preste, *France* 20 F6
Pratt, *U.S.A.* 113 G5
Prattville, *U.S.A.* 115 J2
Pravdinsk, *Russia* 30 D8
Pravdinsk, *Russia* 34 B6
Pravets, *Bulgaria* 44 D7
Pravia, *Spain* 36 B4
Praya, *Indonesia* 62 F5
Pré-en-Pail, *France* 18 D6
Precipice △, *Australia* 95 D5
Precordillera, *Argentina* 126 C2
Predáppio, *Italy* 41 D8
Predazzo, *Italy* 41 B8
Predeal, *Romania* 29 E10
Predejane, *Serbia & M.* 44 D6
Preeceville, *Canada* 103 C8
Preetz, *Germany* 24 A6
Pregolya →, *Russia* 30 D7
Pregrada, *Croatia* 41 B12
Preiļi, *Latvia* 9 H22
Preko, *Croatia* 41 D12
Prelog, *Croatia* 41 B13
Prémery, *France* 19 E10
Premià de Mar, *Spain* 38 D7
Premont, *U.S.A.* 113 M5
Premuda, *Croatia* 41 D11
Prentice, *U.S.A.* 112 C9
Prenzlau, *Germany* 24 B9
Preobrazheniye, *Russia* 54 C6
Preparis North Channel, *Ind. Oc.* 67 M18
Preparis South Channel, *Ind. Oc.* 67 M18
Přerov, *Czech Rep.* 27 B10
Prescott, *Canada* 117 B9
Prescott, *Ariz., U.S.A.* 109 J7
Prescott, *Ark., U.S.A.* 113 J8
Prescott Valley, *U.S.A.* 109 J7
Preservation Inlet, *N.Z.* 91 M1
Preševo, *Serbia & M.* 44 D5
Presho, *U.S.A.* 112 D4
Presicce, *Italy* 43 C11
Presidencia de la Plaza, *Argentina* 126 B4
Presidencia Roque Saenz Peña,
  Argentina 126 B3
Presidente Epitácio, *Brazil* 125 H8
Presidente Hayes □, *Paraguay* 126 A4
Presidente Prudente, *Brazil* 127 A5
Presidio, *Mexico* 118 B4
Presidio, *U.S.A.* 113 L2
Preslav, *Bulgaria* 45 C10
Preslavska Planina, *Bulgaria* 45 C10
Prešov, *Slovak Rep.* 27 B14
Prešovský □, *Slovak Rep.* 27 B13
Prespa, *Bulgaria* 45 E8
Prespa, L. = Prespansko Jezero,
  Macedonia 44 F5
Prespansko Jezero *Macedonia* 44 F5
Presque I., *U.S.A.* 116 D4
Presque Isle, *U.S.A.* 115 B12
Prestatyn, *U.K.* 14 D4
Prestea, *Ghana* 82 D4
Presteigne, *U.K.* 15 E5
Přeštice, *Czech Rep.* 26 B6
Preston, *Canada* 116 C4
Preston, *U.K.* 14 D5
Preston, *Idaho, U.S.A.* 108 E8
Preston, *Minn., U.S.A.* 112 D8
Preston, C., *Australia* 92 D2
Prestonburg, *U.S.A.* 114 G4
Prestwick, *U.K.* 13 F4
Pretoria, *S. Africa* 89 D4
Preuilly-sur-Claise, *France* 18 F7
Préveza, *Greece* 46 C2
Préveza □, *Greece* 46 B2
Prey Veng, *Cambodia* 65 G5
Priazovskoye, *Ukraine* 33 J8
Pribilof Is., *U.S.A.* 100 C2
Priboj, *Serbia & M.* 44 C3
Příbram, *Czech Rep.* 26 B7
Price, *U.S.A.* 108 G8
Price I., *Canada* 102 C3
Prichard, *U.S.A.* 115 K1
Priego, *Spain* 38 E2
Priego de Córdoba, *Spain* 37 H6
Priekule, *Latvia* 9 H19
Priekule, *Lithuania* 30 C8
Prien, *Germany* 25 H8
Prienai, *Lithuania* 9 J20
Prieska, *S. Africa* 88 D3
Priest L., *U.S.A.* 108 B5

Priest River, *U.S.A.* 108 B5
Priest Valley, *U.S.A.* 110 J6
Prievidza, *Slovak Rep.* 27 C11
Prignitz, *Germany* 24 B7
Prijedor, *Bos.-H.* 41 D13
Prijepolje, *Serbia & M.* 44 C3
Prikaspiyskaya Nizmennost =
  Caspian Depression, *Eurasia* . 35 G9
Prikro, *Ivory C.* 82 D4
Prikubanskaya Nizmennost,
  Russia 35 H4
Prilep, *Macedonia* 44 E5
Priluki = Pryluky, *Ukraine* 33 G7
Prime Seal I., *Australia* 95 G4
Primorsk, *Russia* 30 D6
Primorsk, *Russia* 32 B5
Primorsko, *Bulgaria* 45 D11
Primorsko-Akhtarsk, *Russia* 33 J10
Primorskoye, *Ukraine* 33 J9
Primrose L., *Canada* 103 C7
Prince Albert, *Canada* 103 C7
Prince Albert, *S. Africa* 88 E3
Prince Albert △, *Canada* 103 C7
Prince Albert Mts., *Antarctica* 5 D11
Prince Albert Pen., *Canada* 100 A8
Prince Albert Sd., *Canada* 100 A8
Prince Alfred, C., *Canada* 4 B1
Prince Charles I., *Canada* 101 B12
Prince Charles Mts., *Antarctica* 5 D6
Prince Edward I. □, *Canada* 105 C7
Prince Edward Is., *Ind. Oc.* 3 G11
Prince Edward Pt., *Canada* 116 C8
Prince George, *Canada* 102 C4
Prince of Wales, C., *U.S.A.* 98 C3
Prince of Wales I., *Australia* 94 A3
Prince of Wales I., *Canada* 100 A10
Prince of Wales I., *U.S.A.* 100 C6
Prince Patrick I., *Canada* 4 B2
Prince Regent Inlet, *Canada* 4 B3
Prince Rupert, *Canada* 102 C2
Princes Town, *Trin. & Tob.* 125 K15
Princess Charlotte B., *Australia* 94 A3
Princess May Ranges, *Australia* 92 C4
Princess Royal I., *Canada* 102 C3
Princeton, *Canada* 102 D4
Princeton, *Calif., U.S.A.* 110 F4
Princeton, *Ill., U.S.A.* 112 E10
Princeton, *Ind., U.S.A.* 114 F2
Princeton, *Ky., U.S.A.* 114 G2
Princeton, *Mo., U.S.A.* 112 E8
Princeton, *N.J., U.S.A.* 117 F10
Princeton, *W. Va., U.S.A.* 114 G5
Principe, I. de, *Atl. Oc.* 76 F4
Principe da Beira, *Brazil* 124 F6
Prineville, *U.S.A.* 108 D3
Prins Harald Kyst, *Antarctica* 5 D4
Prinsesse Astrid Kyst, *Antarctica* 5 D3
Prinsesse Ragnhild Kyst,
  Antarctica 5 D4
Prinzapolca, *Nic.* 120 D3
Prior, C., *Spain* 36 B2
Priozersk, *Russia* 32 B6
Pripet = Prypyat →, *Europe* 33 G6
Pripet Marshes, *Europe* 33 F5
Pripyat Marshes = Pripet
  Marshes, *Europe* 33 F5
Pripyats = Prypyat →, *Europe* 33 G6
Prislop, Pasul, *Romania* 29 C9
Pristen, *Russia* 33 G9
Priština, *Serbia & M.* 44 D5
Pritzwalk, *Germany* 24 B8
Privas, *France* 21 D8
Priverno, *Italy* 42 A6
Privolzhsk, *Russia* 34 B5
Privolzhskaya Vozvyshennost,
  Russia 34 E7
Privolzhskiy, *Russia* 34 E8
Privolzhskiy □, *Russia* 34 B10
Privolzhye, *Russia* 34 D9
Priyutnoye, *Russia* 35 G6
Prizren, *Serbia & M.* 44 D4
Prizzi, *Italy* 42 E6
Prnjavor, *Bos.-H.* 28 F2
Probolinggo, *Indonesia* 63 G15
Prochowice, *Poland* 31 G3
Proctor, *U.S.A.* 117 C11
Proddatur, *India* 66 M11
Prodhromos, *Cyprus* 49 E11
Proença-a-Nova, *Portugal* 36 F3
Profítis Ilías, *Greece* 49 C9
Profondeville, *Belgium* 17 D4
Progreso, *Coahuila, Mexico* 118 B4
Progreso, *Yucatán, Mexico* 119 C7
Prokhladnyy, *Russia* 35 J7
Prokletije, *Albania* 44 D3
Prokopyevsk, *Russia* 52 D9
Prokuplje, *Serbia & M.* 44 C5
Proletarsk, *Russia* 35 G5
Proletarskaya = Proletarsk, *Russia* 35 G5
Prome, *Burma* 67 K19
Prophet →, *Canada* 102 B4
Prophet River, *Canada* 102 B4
Propriá, *Brazil* 125 F11
Propriano, *France* 21 G12
Proserpine, *Australia* 94 J6
Prosna →, *Poland* 31 F4
Prospect, *U.S.A.* 117 C9
Prosser, *U.S.A.* 108 C4
Prostějov, *Czech Rep.* 27 B10
Prostki, *Poland* 30 E9
Proston, *Australia* 95 D5
Proszowice, *Poland* 31 H7
Próti, *Greece* 46 D3
Provadiya, *Bulgaria* 45 C11
Provence, *France* 21 E9
Provence-Alpes-Côte d'Azur □,
  France 21 D10
Puerto de Cabrera, *Spain* 48 B9
Puerto de Gran Tarajal,
  Canary Is. 48 F6
Puerto de la Cruz, *Canary Is.* 48 F3
Providence, *Ky., U.S.A.* 114 G2
Providence, *R.I., U.S.A.* 117 E13
Providence Bay, *Canada* 104 C3
Providence Mts., *U.S.A.* 111 K11

Provencia, I. de, *Colombia* 120 D3
Proveniya, *Russia* 53 C19
Provins, *France* 19 D10
Provo, *U.S.A.* 108 F8
Provost, *Canada* 103 C6
Prozor, *Bos.-H.* 28 G2
Prrenjas, *Albania* 44 E4
Prudhoe Bay, *U.S.A.* 100 A5
Prudhoe I., *Australia* 94 C4
Prud'homme, *Canada* 103 C7
Prudnik, *Poland* 31 H4
Prüm, *Germany* 25 E2
Prundu, *Romania* 29 F11
Pruszcz Gdański, *Poland* 30 D5
Pruszków, *Poland* 31 F7
Prut →, *Romania* 29 E13
Pruzhany, *Belarus* 33 F3
Prvić, *Croatia* 41 D11
Prydz B., *Antarctica* 5 C6
Pryluky, *Ukraine* 33 G7
Pryor, *U.S.A.* 113 G7
Prypyat →, *Europe* 33 G6
Przasnysz, *Poland* 31 E7
Przedbórz, *Poland* 31 G6
Przedecz, *Poland* 31 F5
Przemków, *Poland* 31 G2
Przemyśl, *Poland* 31 J9
Przeworsk, *Poland* 31 H9
Przewóz, *Poland* 31 G1
Przhevalsk = Karakol, *Kyrgyzstan* 52 E8
Przysucha, *Poland* 31 G7
Psakhná, *Greece* 46 C5
Psará, *Greece* 47 C7
Psathoúra, *Greece* 46 B6
Psel →, *Ukraine* 33 H7
Pserimos, *Greece* 47 E9
Psíra, *Greece* 49 D7
Pskov, *Russia* 32 D5
Pskovskoye, Ozero, *Russia* 32 D5
Psunj, *Croatia* 28 E2
Pteleón, *Greece* 46 B4
Ptich = Ptsich →, *Belarus* 33 F5
Ptolemaís, *Greece* 44 F5
Ptsich →, *Belarus* 33 F5
Ptuj, *Slovenia* 41 B12
Ptujska Gora, *Slovenia* 41 B12
Pu Xian, *China* 56 F6
Pua, *Thailand* 64 C3
Puán, *Argentina* 126 D3
Pu'an, *China* 58 E5
Puan, *S. Korea* 57 G14
Pubei, *China* 58 F7
Pucallpa, *Peru* 124 E4
Pucheng, *China* 59 D12
Puchezh, *Russia* 34 B6
Pucheni, *Romania* 29 E10
Puchheim, *Germany* 25 G7
Pucioasa, *Romania* 29 E10
Pučišća, *Croatia* 41 E13
Puck, *Poland* 30 D5
Pucka, Zatoka, *Poland* 30 D5
Puçol, *Spain* 39 F4
Pudasjärvi, *Finland* 8 D22
Puding, *China* 58 D5
Pudozh, *Russia* 32 B9
Puducherri = Pondicherry, *India* 66 P11
Pudukkottai, *India* 66 P11
Puebla, *Mexico* 119 D5
Puebla □, *Mexico* 119 D5
Puebla de Alcocer, *Spain* 37 G5
Puebla de Don Fadrique, *Spain* 39 H2
Puebla de Don Rodrigo, *Spain* 37 F6
Puebla de Guzmán, *Spain* 37 H3
Puebla de la Calzada, *Spain* 37 G4
Puebla de Sanabria, *Spain* 36 C4
Puebla de Trives = Pobra de
  Trives, *Spain* 36 C3
Pueblo, *U.S.A.* 112 F2
Pueblo Hundido, *Chile* 126 B1
Puelches, *Argentina* 126 D2
Puelén, *Argentina* 126 D2
Puente Alto, *Chile* 126 C1
Puente-Genil, *Spain* 37 H6
Puente la Reina, *Spain* 38 C3
Puenteareas = Ponteareas, *Spain* 36 C2
Puentedeume = Pontedeume,
  Spain 36 B2
Puentes de Garcia Rodriguez =
  As Pontes de García
  Rodríguez, *Spain* 36 B3
Pu'er, *China* 58 F3
Puerca, Pta., *Puerto Rico* .... 121 d
Puerco →, *U.S.A.* 109 J10
Puerto Aisén, *Chile* 128 F2
Puerto Ángel, *Mexico* 119 D5
Puerto Arista, *Mexico* 119 D6
Puerto Armuelles, *Panama* 120 E3
Puerto Ayacucho, *Venezuela* 124 B5
Puerto Barrios, *Guatemala* 120 C2
Puerto Bermejo, *Argentina* 126 B4
Puerto Bermúdez, *Peru* 124 F4
Puerto Bolívar, *Ecuador* 124 D3
Puerto Cabello, *Venezuela* 124 A5
Puerto Cabezas, *Nic.* 120 D3
Puerto Cabo Gracias á Dios, *Nic.* 120 D3
Puerto Carreño, *Colombia* 124 B5
Puerto Castilla, *Honduras* 120 C2
Puerto Chicama, *Peru* 124 E3
Puerto Coig, *Argentina* 128 G3
Puerto Cortés, *Costa Rica* 120 E3
Puerto Cortés, *Honduras* 120 C2
Puerto Cumarebo, *Venezuela* 124 A5
Puerto de Alcudia = Port
  d'Alcúdia, *Spain* 48 B10
Puerto de Cabrera, *Spain* 48 B9
Puerto de Gran Tarajal,
  Canary Is. 48 F6
Puerto de la Cruz, *Canary Is.* 48 F3
Puerto de los Angeles △, *Mexico* 118 C3
Puerto de Mazarrón, *Spain* 39 H3
Puerto de Pozo Negro, *Canary Is.* 48 F6

Puerto de Sóller = Port de Sóller,
  Spain 48 B9
Puerto del Somosierra, *Spain* 36 D7
Puerto del Carmen, *Canary Is.* 48 F6
Puerto del Rosario, *Canary Is.* 48 F6
Puerto Deseado, *Argentina* 128 F3
Puerto Escondido, *Mexico* 119 D5
Puerto Heath, *Bolivia* 124 F5
Puerto Inírida, *Colombia* 124 C5
Puerto Juárez, *Mexico* 119 C7
Puerto La Cruz, *Venezuela* 124 A6
Puerto Leguízamo, *Colombia* 124 D4
Puerto Limón, *Colombia* 124 C4
Puerto Lobos, *Argentina* 128 E3
Puerto Lumbreras, *Spain* 39 H3
Puerto Madryn, *Argentina* 128 E3
Puerto Maldonado, *Peru* 124 F5
Puerto Manatí, *Cuba* 120 B4
Puerto Montt, *Chile* 128 E2
Puerto Morazán, *Nic.* 120 D2
Puerto Morelos, *Mexico* 119 C7
Puerto Natales, *Chile* 128 G2
Puerto Padre, *Cuba* 120 B4
Puerto Páez, *Venezuela* 124 B5
Puerto Peñasco, *Mexico* 118 A2
Puerto Pinasco, *Paraguay* 126 A4
Puerto Plata, *Dom. Rep.* 121 C5
Puerto Pollensa = Port de
  Pollença, *Spain* 48 B10
Puerto Princesa, *Phil.* 61 G3
Puerto Quepos, *Costa Rica* 120 E3
Puerto Real, *Spain* 37 J4
Puerto Rico, *Canary Is.* 48 G4
Puerto Rico ⬚, *W. Indies* .... 121 d
Puerto Rico Trench, *Atl. Oc.* 121 C6
Puerto San Julián, *Argentina* 128 F3
Puerto Sastre, *Paraguay* 126 A4
Puerto Serrano, *Spain* 37 J5
Puerto Suárez, *Bolivia* 124 G7
Puerto Vallarta, *Mexico* 118 C3
Puerto Wilches, *Colombia* 124 B4
Puertollano, *Spain* 37 G6
Pueyrredón, L., *Argentina* 128 F2
Púez Odle △, *Italy* 41 B8
Puffin I., *Ireland* 12 E1
Pugachev, *Russia* 34 D9
Pugal, *India* 68 E5
Puge, *China* 58 D4
Puge, *Tanzania* 86 C3
Puget Sound, *U.S.A.* 108 C2
Puget-Théniers, *France* 21 E10
Púglia □, *Italy* 43 A9
Pugödong, *N. Korea* 57 C16
Pugu, *Tanzania* 86 D4
Pūgūnzī, *Iran* 71 E8
Pui, *Romania* 28 E8
Puierși, *Romania* 29 D12
Puig Major, *Spain* 48 B9
Puigcerdà, *Spain* 38 C6
Puigmal, *Spain* 38 C7
Puigpunyent, *Spain* 48 B9
Puijiang, *China* 58 B4
Puisaye, Collines de la, *France* 19 E10
Puiseaux, *France* 19 D9
Pujehun, *S. Leone* 82 D2
Pujiang, *China* 59 C12
Pujols, *France* 20 D3
Pujon-chǒsuji, *N. Korea* 57 D14
Pukaki, *Cook Is.* 91 L3
Pukapuka, *Cook Is.* 97 J11
Pukaskwa △, *Canada* 104 C2
Pukatawagan, *Canada* 103 B8
Pukchin, *N. Korea* 57 D13
Pukch'ǒng, *N. Korea* 57 D15
Pukë, *Albania* 44 D3
Pukekohe, *N.Z.* 91 G5
Pukhrayan, *India* 69 F8
Pukou, *China* 59 A12
Pula, *Croatia* 41 D10
Pula, *Italy* 42 C1
Pulacayo, *Bolivia* 124 H5
Pulai, *Malaysia* .... 65 d
Pulandian, *China* 57 E11
Pularumpi, *Australia* 92 B5
Pulaski, *N.Y., U.S.A.* 117 C8
Pulaski, *Tenn., U.S.A.* 115 H2
Pulaski, *Va., U.S.A.* 114 G5
Pulau →, *Indonesia* 63 F9
Puławy, *Poland* 31 G8
Pulga, *U.S.A.* 110 F5
Pulicat L., *India* 66 N12
Pullman, *U.S.A.* 108 C5
Pulog, Mt., *Phil.* 61 C4
Pułtusk, *Poland* 31 F8
Pülümür, *Turkey* 73 C8
Pumlumon Fawr, *U.K.* 15 E4
Puná, I., *Ecuador* 124 D2
Punakaiki, *N.Z.* 91 K3
Punakha, *Bhutan* 67 F16
Punasar, *India* 68 F5
Punata, *Bolivia* 124 G5
Punch, *India* 69 C6
Punch →, *Pakistan* 69 C5
Punda Maria, *S. Africa* 89 C5
Pune, *India* 66 K8
P'ungsan, *N. Korea* 57 D15
Pungue, Ponte de, *Mozam.* 87 F3
Puning, *China* 59 F11
Punjab □, *India* 68 D7
Punjab □, *Pakistan* 68 D5
Puno, *Peru* 124 G4
Punpun →, *India* 69 G11
Punta, Cerro de, *Puerto Rico* .... 121 d
Punta Alta, *Argentina* 128 D4
Punta Arenas, *Chile* 128 G2
Punta de Díaz, *Chile* 126 B1
Punta del Hidalgo, *Canary Is.* 48 F3
Punta Gorda, *Belize* 119 D7
Punta Gorda, *U.S.A.* 115 M5
Punta Prieta, *Mexico* 118 B2
Punta Prima, *Spain* 48 B11

Punta Umbria, Spain ... 37 H4
Puntarenas, Costa Rica ... 120 E3
Punto Fijo, Venezuela ... 124 A4
Punxsatawney, U.S.A. ... 116 F6
Pupuan, Indonesia ... 63 J18
Puqi, China ... 59 C9
Puquio, Peru ... 124 F4
Pur →, Russia ... 52 C8
Puracé, Vol., Colombia ... 124 C3
Puračić, Bos.-H. ... 28 F3
Puralia = Puruliya, India ... 69 H12
Puranpur, India ... 69 E9
Purbeck, Isle of, U.K. ... 15 G5
Purcell, U.S.A. ... 113 H6
Purcell Mts., Canada ... 102 D5
Puri, India ... 67 K14
Purmerend, Neths. ... 17 B4
Purnia, India ... 69 G12
Purnululu △, Australia ... 92 C4
Pursat = Pouthisat, Cambodia ... 64 F4
Purukcahu, Indonesia ... 62 E4
Puruliya, India ... 69 H12
Purus →, Brazil ... 124 D6
Puruvesi, Finland ... 32 B5
Purvis, U.S.A. ... 113 K10
Pŭrvomay, Bulgaria ... 45 D9
Purwa, India ... 69 F9
Purwakarta, Indonesia ... 63 G12
Purwo, Tanjung, Indonesia ... 63 K18
Purwodadi, Indonesia ... 63 G14
Purwokerto, Indonesia ... 63 G13
Puryŏng, N. Korea ... 57 C15
Pusa, India ... 69 G11
Pusan, S. Korea ... 57 G15
Pushkin, Russia ... 32 C6
Pushkino, Moskva, Russia ... 32 D9
Pushkino, Saratov, Russia ... 34 E8
Püspökladány, Hungary ... 28 C6
Pustoshka, Russia ... 32 D5
Puszczykowo, Poland ... 31 F3
Putahow L., Canada ... 103 B8
Putao, Burma ... 67 F20
Putaruru, N.Z. ... 91 H5
Putbus, Germany ... 24 A9
Putian, China ... 59 E12
Putignano, Italy ... 43 B10
Puting, Tanjung, Indonesia ... 62 E4
Putlitz, Germany ... 24 B8
Putna, Romania ... 29 C10
Putna →, Romania ... 29 E12
Putnam, U.S.A. ... 117 E13
Putnok, Hungary ... 28 B5
Putorana, Gory, Russia ... 53 C10
Putrajaya, Malaysia ... 65 L3
Puttalam, Sri Lanka ... 66 Q11
Puttgarden, Germany ... 24 A7
Püttlingen, Germany ... 25 F7
Putumayo →, S. Amer. ... 124 D5
Putuo, China ... 59 C14
Putussibau, Indonesia ... 62 D4
Putyla, Ukraine ... 29 B10
Puvirnituq, Canada ... 101 B12
Puy-de-Dôme, France ... 20 C6
Puy-de-Dôme □, France ... 20 C7
Puy-l'Évêque, France ... 20 D5
Puyallup, U.S.A. ... 110 C4
Puyang, China ... 56 G8
Puylaurens, France ... 20 E6
Püzeh Rīg, Iran ... 71 E8
Puzhaykove, Ukraine ... 29 B14
Pwani □, Tanzania ... 86 D4
Pweto, Dem. Rep. of the Congo ... 87 D2
Pwllheli, U.K. ... 14 E3
Pyana →, Russia ... 34 C8
Pyapon, Burma ... 67 L19
Pyasina →, Russia ... 53 B9
Pyatigorsk, Russia ... 35 H6
Pyatykhatky, Ukraine ... 33 H7
Pydna, Greece ... 44 F6
Pyè = Prome, Burma ... 67 K19
Pyetrikaw, Belarus ... 33 F5
Pyhäjoki, Finland ... 8 D21
Pyinmana, Burma ... 67 K20
Pyla, C., Cyprus ... 49 E12
Pymatuning Reservoir, U.S.A. ... 116 E4
Pyŏktong, N. Korea ... 57 D13
P'yŏnggang, N. Korea ... 57 E14
P'yŏngt'aek, S. Korea ... 57 F14
P'yŏngyang, N. Korea ... 57 E13
Pyote, U.S.A. ... 113 K3
Pyramid L., U.S.A. ... 108 G4
Pyramid Pk., U.S.A. ... 111 J10
Pyramids, Egypt ... 80 J7
Pyrénées, Europe ... 20 F4
Pyrénées △, France ... 20 F3
Pyrénées-Atlantiques □, France ... 20 E3
Pyrénées-Orientales □, France ... 20 F6
Pyryatyn, Ukraine ... 33 G7
Pyrzyce, Poland ... 31 E1
Pyskowice, Poland ... 31 H5
Pytalovo, Russia ... 32 D4
Pyu, Burma ... 67 K20
Pyzdry, Poland ... 31 F4

Q

Qaanaaq, Greenland ... 4 B4
Qabirri →, Azerbaijan ... 35 K8
Qachasnek, S. Africa ... 89 E4
Qa'el Jafr, Jordan ... 74 E5
Qa'emābād, Iran ... 71 D9
Qā'emshahr, Iran ... 71 B7
Qagan Nur, China ... 56 C8
Qahar Youyi Zhongqi, China ... 56 D7
Qahremānshahr = Bākhtarān, Iran ... 70 C5
Qaidam Pendi, China ... 60 C4
Qajarīyeh, Iran ... 71 D6

Qala, Ras il, Malta ... 49 C1
Qala-i-Jadid = Spīn Būldak, Afghan. ... 68 D2
Qala Point = Qala, Ras il, Malta ... 49 C1
Qala Viala, Pakistan ... 68 D2
Qala Yangi, Afghan. ... 68 B2
Qal'at al Akhdar, Si. Arabia ... 70 E3
Qal'at Dīzah, Iraq ... 70 B5
Qal'at Şāliḥ, Iraq ... 70 D5
Qal'at Sukkar, Iraq ... 70 D5
Qalyûb, Egypt ... 80 H7
Qamani'tuaq = Baker Lake, Canada ... 100 B10
Qamdo, China ... 58 B1
Qamruddin Karez, Pakistan ... 68 D3
Qandahār, Afghan. ... 66 D4
Qandahār □, Afghan. ... 66 D4
Qapān, Iran ... 71 B7
Qapshaghay, Kazakhstan ... 52 E8
Qaqortoq, Greenland ... 101 B6
Qâra, Egypt ... 80 B2
Qara Qash →, China ... 69 B8
Qarabutaq, Kazakhstan ... 52 E7
Qaraçala, Azerbaijan ... 35 L9
Qaraghandy, Kazakhstan ... 52 E8
Qaraghayly, Kazakhstan ... 52 E8
Qārah, Si. Arabia ... 70 D4
Qarataū, Kazakhstan ... 52 E8
Qarataū, Kazakhstan ... 52 E7
Qardho = Gardo, Somali Rep. ... 75 F4
Qardud, Sudan ... 81 E2
Qareh →, Iran ... 70 B5
Qareh Tekān, Iran ... 71 B6
Qarqan He →, China ... 60 C3
Qarqaraly, Kazakhstan ... 52 E8
Qarrasa, Sudan ... 81 E3
Qarshi, Uzbekistan ... 52 F7
Qartabā, Lebanon ... 74 A4
Qaryat al Gharab, Iraq ... 70 D5
Qaryat al 'Ulyā, Si. Arabia ... 70 E5
Qasr 'Amra, Jordan ... 70 D3
Qaşr-e Qand, Iran ... 71 E9
Qasr Farâfra, Egypt ... 80 B2
Qatanā, Syria ... 74 B5
Qatar ■, Asia ... 71 E6
Qatlīsh, Iran ... 71 B8
Qattâra, Egypt ... 80 A2
Qattâra, Munkhafed el, Egypt ... 80 B2
Qattâra Depression = Qattâra, Munkhafed el, Egypt ... 80 B2
Qawām al Ḩamzah = Al Ḩamzah, Iraq ... 70 D5
Qāyen, Iran ... 71 C8
Qazaqstan = Kazakhstan ■, Asia ... 52 E7
Qazimämmäd, Azerbaijan ... 35 K9
Qazvin, Iran ... 71 B6
Qazvin □, Iran ... 71 B6
Qeissan, Sudan ... 81 E3
Qena, Egypt ... 80 B3
Qena, W. →, Egypt ... 80 B3
Qeqertarsuaq, Greenland ... 101 B5
Qeqertarsuaq, Greenland ... 101 B14
Qeshlāq, Iran ... 70 C5
Qeshm, Iran ... 71 E8
Qeys, Iran ... 71 E7
Qezel Owzen →, Iran ... 71 B6
Qezi'ot, Israel ... 74 E3
Qi Xian, China ... 56 G8
Qian Gorlos, China ... 57 B13
Qian Xian, China ... 56 G5
Qiancheng, China ... 58 D7
Qianjiang, Guangxi Zhuangzu, China ... 58 F7
Qianjiang, Hubei, China ... 59 B9
Qianjiang, Sichuan, China ... 58 C7
Qianshan, China ... 59 B11
Qianwei, China ... 58 C4
Qianxi, China ... 58 D6
Qianyang, Hunan, China ... 59 D8
Qianyang, Shaanxi, China ... 56 G4
Qianyang, Zhejiang, China ... 59 B12
Qiaojia, China ... 58 D4
Qichun, China ... 59 B10
Qidong, Hunan, China ... 59 D9
Qidong, Jiangsu, China ... 59 B13
Qijiang, China ... 58 C6
Qikiqtarjuaq, Canada ... 101 B13
Qila Safed, Pakistan ... 66 E2
Qila Saifullāh, Pakistan ... 68 D3
Qilian Shan, China ... 60 C4
Qimen, China ... 59 C11
Qin He →, China ... 56 G7
Qin Jiang →, Guangxi Zhuangzu, China ... 58 F7
Qin Jiang →, Jiangxi, China ... 59 D10
Qin Ling = Qinling Shandi, China ... 56 H5
Qin'an, China ... 56 G3
Qing Xian, China ... 56 E9
Qingcheng, China ... 57 F9
Qingdao, China ... 57 F11
Qingfeng, China ... 56 G8
Qinghai □, China ... 60 C4
Qinghai Hu, China ... 60 C5
Qinghecheng, China ... 57 D13
Qinghemen, China ... 57 D11
Qingjian, China ... 56 F6
Qingjiang = Huaiyin, China ... 57 H10
Qingliu, China ... 59 D11
Qinglong, China ... 58 E5
Qingping, China ... 58 D6
Qingpu, China ... 59 B13
Qingshui, China ... 56 H8
Qingshuihe, China ... 56 E6
Qingtian, China ... 59 C13
Qingtongxia Shuiku, China ... 56 F3
Qingxi, China ... 58 D7
Qingxu, China ... 56 F7
Qingyang, Anhui, China ... 59 B11
Qingyang, Gansu, China ... 56 F4
Qingyi Jiang →, China ... 58 C4
Qingyuan, Guangdong, China ... 59 F9

Qingyuan, Liaoning, China ... 57 C13
Qingyuan, Zhejiang, China ... 59 D12
Qingyun, China ... 57 F9
Qingzhen, China ... 58 D6
Qinhuangdao, China ... 57 E10
Qinling Shandi, China ... 56 H5
Qinshui, China ... 56 G7
Qinyang = Jiyuan, China ... 56 G7
Qinyuan, China ... 56 F7
Qinzhou, China ... 58 G7
Qionghai, China ... 64 C8
Qionglai, China ... 58 B4
Qionglai Shan, China ... 58 B4
Qiongzhou Haixia, China ... 64 B8
Qiqihar, China ... 53 E13
Qiraïya, W. →, Egypt ... 74 E3
Qiryat Ata, Israel ... 74 C4
Qiryat Gat, Israel ... 74 D3
Qiryat Mal'akhi, Israel ... 74 D3
Qiryat Shemona, Israel ... 74 B4
Qiryat Yam, Israel ... 74 C4
Qishan, China ... 56 G4
Qiubei, China ... 58 E5
Qixia, China ... 57 F11
Qiyang, China ... 59 D8
Qızlağac Körfäzi, Azerbaijan ... 71 B6
Qojūr, Iran ... 70 B5
Qom, Iran ... 71 C6
Qom □, Iran ... 71 C6
Qomolangma Feng = Everest, Mt., Nepal ... 69 E12
Qomsheh, Iran ... 71 D6
Qoraqalpoghistan □, Uzbekistan ... 52 E6
Qorveh, Iran ... 73 E12
Qostanay, Kazakhstan ... 52 D7
Qotūr, Iran ... 73 C11
Qu Jiang →, China ... 58 B6
Qu Xian, China ... 58 B6
Quabbin Reservoir, U.S.A. ... 117 D12
Quairading, Australia ... 93 F2
Quakenbrück, Germany ... 24 C3
Quakertown, U.S.A. ... 117 F9
Qualicum Beach, Canada ... 102 D4
Quambatook, Australia ... 95 F3
Quambone, Australia ... 95 E4
Quamby, Australia ... 94 C3
Quan Long = Ca Mau, Vietnam ... 65 H5
Quanah, U.S.A. ... 113 H5
Quang Ngai, Vietnam ... 64 E7
Quang Tri, Vietnam ... 64 D6
Quang Yen, Vietnam ... 58 G6
Quannan, China ... 59 E10
Quantock Hills, U.K. ... 15 F4
Quanzhou, Fujian, China ... 59 E12
Quanzhou, Guangxi Zhuangzu, China ... 59 E8
Qu'Appelle, Canada ... 103 C8
Quaqtaq, Canada ... 101 B13
Quaraí, Brazil ... 126 C4
Quarré-les-Tombes, France ... 19 E11
Quarteira, Portugal ... 37 H2
Quartu Sant'Élena, Italy ... 42 C2
Quartzsite, U.S.A. ... 111 M12
Quatsino Sd., Canada ... 102 C3
Quba, Azerbaijan ... 35 K9
Qūchān, Iran ... 71 B8
Queanbeyan, Australia ... 95 F4
Québec, Canada ... 105 C5
Québec □, Canada ... 105 C6
Quebrada del Condorito △, Argentina ... 126 C3
Quedlinburg, Germany ... 24 D7
Queen Alexandra Ra., Antarctica ... 5 E11
Queen Charlotte City, Canada ... 102 C2
Queen Charlotte Is., Canada ... 102 C2
Queen Charlotte Sd., Canada ... 102 C3
Queen Charlotte Strait, Canada ... 102 C3
Queen Elizabeth △, U.K. ... 13 E4
Queen Elizabeth △, Uganda ... 86 C3
Queen Elizabeth Is., Canada ... 98 B10
Queen Mary Land, Antarctica ... 5 D7
Queen Maud G., Canada ... 100 B9
Queen Maud Land = Dronning Maud Land, Antarctica ... 5 D3
Queen Maud Mts., Antarctica ... 5 E13
Queens Chan., Australia ... 92 C4
Queenscliff, Australia ... 95 F3
Queensland □, Australia ... 94 C3
Queenstown, Australia ... 95 G4
Queenstown, N.Z. ... 91 L2
Queenstown, Singapore ... 65 d
Queenstown, S. Africa ... 88 E4
Queets, U.S.A. ... 110 C2
Queguay Grande →, Uruguay ... 126 C4
Queimadas, Brazil ... 125 F11
Quelimane, Mozam. ... 87 F4
Quellón, Chile ... 128 E2
Quelpart = Cheju do, S. Korea ... 57 H14
Quemado, N. Mex., U.S.A. ... 109 J9
Quemado, Tex., U.S.A. ... 113 L4
Quemoy = Jinmen, Taiwan ... 59 E13
Quemú-Quemú, Argentina ... 126 D3
Quequén, Argentina ... 126 D4
Querétaro, Mexico ... 118 C4
Querétaro □, Mexico ... 118 C5
Querfurt, Germany ... 24 D7
Quérigut, France ... 20 F6
Querqueville, France ... 18 C5
Quesada, Spain ... 37 H7
Queshan, China ... 56 H8
Quesnel, Canada ... 102 C4
Quesnel →, Canada ... 102 C4
Quesnel L., Canada ... 102 C4
Questa, U.S.A. ... 109 H11
Questembert, France ... 18 E4
Quetico △, Canada ... 104 C1
Quetta, Pakistan ... 68 D2
Queyras △, France ... 21 D10
Quezaltenango, Guatemala ... 120 D1

Quezon City, Phil. ... 61 D4
Qufār, Si. Arabia ... 70 E4
Qui Nhon, Vietnam ... 64 F7
Quibaxe, Angola ... 84 F2
Quibdo, Colombia ... 124 B3
Quiberon, France ... 18 E3
Quiberon, Presqu'île de, France ... 18 E3
Quickborn, Germany ... 24 B5
Quiet L., Canada ... 102 A2
Quiindy, Paraguay ... 126 B4
Quila, Mexico ... 118 C3
Quilán, C., Chile ... 128 E2
Quilcene, U.S.A. ... 110 C4
Quilimarí, Chile ... 126 C1
Quilino, Argentina ... 126 C3
Quill Lakes, Canada ... 103 C8
Quillabamba, Peru ... 124 F4
Quillagua, Chile ... 126 A2
Quillaicillo, Chile ... 126 C1
Quillan, France ... 20 F6
Quillota, Chile ... 126 C1
Quilmes, Argentina ... 126 C4
Quilon, India ... 66 Q10
Quilpie, Australia ... 95 D3
Quilpué, Chile ... 126 C1
Quilua, Mozam. ... 87 F4
Quimilí, Argentina ... 126 B3
Quimper, France ... 18 E2
Quimperlé, France ... 18 E3
Quinault →, U.S.A. ... 110 C2
Quincy, Calif., U.S.A. ... 110 F6
Quincy, Fla., U.S.A. ... 115 K3
Quincy, Ill., U.S.A. ... 112 F9
Quincy, Mass., U.S.A. ... 117 D14
Quincy, Wash., U.S.A. ... 108 C4
Quines, Argentina ... 126 C2
Quinga, Mozam. ... 87 F5
Quingey, France ... 19 E12
Quintana de la Serena, Spain ... 37 G5
Quintana Roo □, Mexico ... 119 D7
Quintanar de la Orden, Spain ... 37 F7
Quintanar de la Sierra, Spain ... 38 D2
Quintanar del Rey, Spain ... 39 F3
Quinte West, Canada ... 116 B7
Quintero, Chile ... 126 C1
Quintin, France ... 18 D4
Quinto, Spain ... 38 D4
Quípar →, Spain ... 39 G3
Quirihue, Chile ... 126 D1
Quirindi, Australia ... 95 E5
Quirinópolis, Brazil ... 125 G8
Quiroga, Spain ... 36 C3
Quissac, France ... 21 E8
Quissanga, Mozam. ... 87 E5
Quissico, Mozam. ... 89 C5
Quitilipi, Argentina ... 126 B3
Quitman, U.S.A. ... 115 K4
Quito, Ecuador ... 124 D3
Quixadá, Brazil ... 125 D11
Quixaxe, Mozam. ... 87 F5
Qujing, China ... 58 E4
Qulan, Kazakhstan ... 52 E8
Qul'ân, Jazâ'ir, Egypt ... 70 E2
Qumbu, S. Africa ... 89 E4
Quneitra, Syria ... 74 B4
Qünghirot, Uzbekistan ... 52 E6
Qu'nyido, China ... 58 B2
Quoin I., Australia ... 92 B4
Quoin Pt., S. Africa ... 88 E2
Quorn, Australia ... 95 E2
Qüqon, Uzbekistan ... 52 E8
Qurein, Sudan ... 81 E3
Qurnat as Sawdā', Lebanon ... 74 A5
Qûs, Egypt ... 80 B3
Qusar, Azerbaijan ... 35 K9
Quşaybā', Si. Arabia ... 70 E4
Qusaybah, Iraq ... 70 C4
Quseir, Egypt ... 70 B3
Qūshchī, Iran ... 70 B5
Quthing, Lesotho ... 89 E4
Qūṭīābād, Iran ... 71 C6
Quwo, China ... 56 G6
Quyang, China ... 56 E8
Quynh Nhai, Vietnam ... 64 B4
Quyon, Canada ... 117 A8
Quzhou, China ... 59 C12
Quzi, China ... 56 F4
Qvareli, Georgia ... 35 K7
Qyzylorda, Kazakhstan ... 52 E7

R

Ra, Ko, Thailand ... 65 H2
Raab, Austria ... 26 C6
Raahe, Finland ... 8 D21
Raalte, Neths. ... 17 B6
Raasay, U.K. ... 13 D2
Raasay, Sd. of, U.K. ... 13 D2
Rab, Croatia ... 41 D11
Raba, Indonesia ... 63 F5
Rába →, Hungary ... 28 C2
Raba →, Poland ... 31 H7
Rabaçal →, Portugal ... 36 D3
Rabah, Nigeria ... 83 C6
Rabai, Kenya ... 86 C4
Rabak, Sudan ... 81 E3
Rabastens, France ... 20 E5
Rabastens-de-Bigorre, France ... 20 E4
Rabat = Victoria, Malta ... 49 C1
Rabat, Malta ... 49 D1
Rabat, Morocco ... 78 B4
Rabaul, Papua N. G. ... 96 H7
Rābigh, Si. Arabia ... 75 C2
Rabka, Poland ... 31 J6
Râbniţa, Moldova ... 29 C14
Rābor, Iran ... 71 D8
Rača, Serbia & M. ... 44 B4
Răcăciuni, Romania ... 29 D11

Răcășdia, Romania ... 28 F6
Racconigi, Italy ... 40 D4
Race, C., Canada ... 105 C9
Rach Gia, Vietnam ... 65 G5
Rachid, Mauritania ... 82 B2
Raciąż, Poland ... 31 F7
Racibórz, Poland ... 31 H5
Racichy, Belarus ... 30 E10
Racine, U.S.A. ... 114 D2
Rackerby, U.S.A. ... 110 F5
Radama, Nosy, Madag. ... 89 A8
Radama, Saikanosy, Madag. ... 89 A8
Radan, Serbia & M. ... 44 D5
Rădăuţi, Romania ... 29 C10
Rădăuţi-Prut, Romania ... 29 B11
Radbuza →, Czech Rep. ... 26 B6
Radcliff, U.S.A. ... 114 G3
Radeberg, Germany ... 24 D9
Radebeul, Germany ... 24 D9
Radeče, Slovenia ... 41 B12
Radekhiv, Ukraine ... 33 G3
Radekhov = Radekhiv, Ukraine ... 33 G3
Radenthein, Austria ... 26 E6
Radew →, Poland ... 30 D2
Radford, U.S.A. ... 114 G5
Radhanpur, India ... 68 H4
Radhwa, Jabal, Si. Arabia ... 70 E3
Radika →, Macedonia ... 44 E4
Radisson, Qué., Canada ... 104 B4
Radisson, Sask., Canada ... 103 C7
Radium Hot Springs, Canada ... 102 C5
Radlje ob Dravi, Slovenia ... 41 B12
Radnevo, Bulgaria ... 45 D9
Radnice, Czech Rep. ... 26 B6
Radnor Forest, U.K. ... 15 E4
Radolfzell, Germany ... 25 H4
Radom, Poland ... 31 G8
Radomir, Bulgaria ... 44 D6
Radomka →, Poland ... 31 G8
Radomsko, Poland ... 31 G6
Radomyshl, Ukraine ... 33 G5
Radomyśl Wielki, Poland ... 31 H8
Radoszyce, Poland ... 31 G7
Radoviš, Macedonia ... 44 E6
Radovljica, Slovenia ... 41 B11
Radstadt, Austria ... 26 D6
Răducăneni, Romania ... 29 D12
Raduša, Macedonia ... 44 D5
Radvanichy, Belarus ... 31 F11
Radviliškis, Lithuania ... 9 J20
Radville, Canada ... 103 D8
Raqwā, J., Si. Arabia ... 80 C4
Radymno, Poland ... 31 J9
Radzanów, Poland ... 31 F5
Radziejów, Poland ... 31 F5
Radzyń Chełmiński, Poland ... 30 E5
Radzyń Podlaski, Poland ... 31 G9
Rae, Canada ... 102 A5
Rae Bareli, India ... 69 F9
Rae Isthmus, Canada ... 101 B11
Raeren, Belgium ... 17 D6
Raeside, L., Australia ... 93 E3
Raetihi, N.Z. ... 91 H5
Rafaela, Argentina ... 126 C3
Rafah, Gaza Strip ... 74 D3
Rafai, C.A.R. ... 86 B1
Raffadali, Italy ... 42 E6
Raffili, Sudan ... 81 F2
Rafḩā, Si. Arabia ... 70 D4
Rafsanjān, Iran ... 71 D8
Raft Pt., Australia ... 92 C3
Râga, Sudan ... 81 F2
Raga →, Sudan ... 81 F2
Ragachow, Belarus ... 33 F6
Ragag, Sudan ... 81 E1
Ragama, Sri Lanka ... 66 R11
Ragged, Mt., Australia ... 93 F3
Ragged Pt., Barbados ... 121 g
Raghunathpalli, India ... 69 H11
Raghunathpur, India ... 69 H12
Raglan, N.Z. ... 91 G5
Ragusa, Italy ... 43 F7
Raha, Indonesia ... 63 E6
Rahad, Nahr ed →, Sudan ... 81 E3
Rahaeng = Tak, Thailand ... 64 D2
Rahatgarh, India ... 69 H8
Rahden, Germany ... 24 C4
Raheita, Eritrea ... 81 E5
Rahimyar Khan, Pakistan ... 68 E4
Rähjerd, Iran ... 71 C6
Rahole △, Kenya ... 86 B4
Rahon, India ... 68 D7
Raichur, India ... 66 L10
Raiganj, India ... 69 G13
Raigarh, India ... 67 J13
Raijua, Indonesia ... 63 F6
Raikot, India ... 68 D6
Railton, Australia ... 95 G4
Rainbow Bridge △, U.S.A. ... 109 H8
Rainbow Lake, Canada ... 102 B5
Rainier, U.S.A. ... 110 D4
Rainier, Mt., U.S.A. ... 110 D5
Rainy L., Canada ... 103 D10
Rainy River, Canada ... 103 D10
Raippaluoto, Finland ... 8 E19
Raipur, India ... 67 J12
Ra'is, Si. Arabia ... 80 C4
Raisen, India ... 68 H8
Raisio, Finland ... 9 F20
Raj Nandgaon, India ... 67 J12
Raj Nilgiri, India ... 69 J12
Raja, Ujung, Indonesia ... 62 D1
Raja Ampat, Kepulauan, Indonesia ... 63 E7
Rajahmundry, India ... 67 L12
Rajang →, Malaysia ... 62 D4
Rajanpur, Pakistan ... 68 E4
Rajapalaiyam, India ... 66 Q10
Rajasthan □, India ... 68 F5
Rajasthan Canal = Indira Gandhi Canal, India ... 68 F5

Rajauri, *India* 69 C6
Rajgarh, *Mad. P., India* 68 G7
Rajgarh, *Raj., India* 68 E6
Rajgarh, *Raj., India* 68 K6
Rajgir, *India* 69 G11
Rajgród, *Poland* 30 E9
Rajkot, *India* 68 H4
Rajmahal Hills, *India* 69 G12
Rajpipla, *India* 66 J8
Rajpur, *India* 68 H6
Rajpura, *India* 68 D7
Rajshahi, *Bangla.* 67 G16
Rajshahi □, *Bangla.* 69 G13
Rajula, *India* 68 J4
Rakaia, *N.Z.* 91 K4
Rakaia →, *N.Z.* 91 K4
Rakan, Ra's, *Qatar* 71 E6
Rakaposhi, *Pakistan* 69 A6
Rakata, Pulau, *Indonesia* 62 F3
Rakhiv, *Ukraine* 29 B9
Rakhni, *Pakistan* 68 D3
Rakhni →, *Pakistan* 68 E3
Rakhny-Lisovi, *Ukraine* 29 B13
Rakitnoye, *Russia* 54 B7
Rakitovo, *Bulgaria* 45 E8
Rakiura △, *N.Z.* 91 M1
Rakoniewice, *Poland* 31 F3
Rakops, *Botswana* 88 C3
Rakovica, *Croatia* 41 D12
Rakovník, *Czech Rep.* 26 A6
Rakovski, *Bulgaria* 45 D8
Rakvere, *Estonia* 9 G22
Raleigh, *U.S.A.* 115 H6
Ralja, *Serbia & M.* 44 B4
Ralls, *U.S.A.* 113 J4
Ralston, *U.S.A.* 116 E8
Ram →, *Canada* 102 A4
Rām Allāh, *West Bank* 74 D4
Rama, *Nic.* 120 D3
Ramacca, *Italy* 43 E7
Ramakona, *India* 69 J8
Ramales de la Victoria, *Spain* ... 36 B7
Rāmallāh = Rām Allāh,
  West Bank 74 D4
Raman, *Thailand* 65 J3
Ramanathapuram, *India* 66 Q11
Ramanetaka, B. de, *Madag.* 89 A8
Ramanujganj, *India* 69 H10
Ramat Gan, *Israel* 74 C3
Ramatlhabama, *S. Africa* 88 D4
Ramban, *India* 69 C6
Rambervillers, *France* 19 D13
Rambipuji, *Indonesia* 63 H15
Rambouillet, *France* 19 D8
Rame Hd., *Australia* 95 F4
Ramechhap, *Nepal* 69 F12
Ramenskoye, *Russia* 32 E10
Ramganga →, *India* 69 F8
Ramgarh, *Jharkhand, India* 69 H11
Ramgarh, *Raj., India* 68 F6
Ramgarh, *Raj., India* 68 F4
Rāmhormoz, *Iran* 71 D6
Ramīān, *Iran* 71 B7
Ramingining, *Australia* 94 A2
Ramla, *Israel* 74 D3
Ramlu, *Eritrea* 81 E5
Ramm = Rum, *Jordan* 74 F4
Ramm, Jabal, *Jordan* 74 F4
Râmna →, *Romania* 29 E12
Ramnad = Ramanathapuram,
  India 66 Q11
Ramnagar, *Jammu & Kashmir,
  India* 69 C6
Ramnagar, *Uttaranchal, India* .. 69 E8
Ramnäs, *Sweden* 10 E10
Râmnicu Sărat, *Romania* 29 E12
Râmnicu Vâlcea, *Romania* 29 E9
Ramon, *Russia* 33 G10
Ramona, *U.S.A.* 111 M10
Ramonville-St-Agne, *France* ... 20 E5
Ramore, *Canada* 104 C3
Ramos →, *Nigeria* 83 D6
Ramotswa, *Botswana* 88 C4
Rampur, *H.P., India* 68 D7
Rampur, *Mad. P., India* 68 H5
Rampur, *Ut. P., India* 69 E8
Rampur Hat, *India* 69 G12
Rampura, *India* 68 G6
Ramrama Tola, *India* 69 J8
Ramree I., *Burma* 67 K19
Rāmsar, *Iran* 71 B6
Ramsey, *I. of Man* 14 C3
Ramsey, *U.S.A.* 117 E10
Ramsey L., *Canada* 104 C3
Ramsgate, *U.K.* 15 F9
Ramsjö, *Sweden* 10 B9
Ramstein, *Germany* 25 F3
Ramtek, *India* 66 J11
Ramvik, *Sweden* 10 B11
Rana Pratap Sagar Dam, *India* .. 68 G6
Ranaghat, *India* 69 H13
Ranahu, *Pakistan* 68 G3
Ranau, *Malaysia* 62 C5
Rancagua, *Chile* 126 C1
Rance →, *France* 18 D5
Rancheria →, *Canada* 102 A3
Ranchester, *U.S.A.* 108 D10
Ranchi, *India* 69 H11
Rancho Cucamonga, *U.S.A.* 111 L9
Randalstown, *U.K.* 12 B5
Randan, *France* 19 F10
Randazzo, *Italy* 43 E7
Randers, *Denmark* 11 H4
Randers Fjord, *Denmark* 11 H4
Randfontein, *S. Africa* 89 D4
Randle, *U.S.A.* 110 D5
Randolph, *Mass., U.S.A.* 117 D13
Randolph, *N.Y., U.S.A.* 116 D6
Randolph, *Utah, U.S.A.* 108 F8
Randolph, *Vt., U.S.A.* 117 C12
Randsburg, *U.S.A.* 111 K9

Råneälven →, *Sweden* 8 D20
Rangae, *Thailand* 65 J3
Rangaunu B., *N.Z.* 91 F4
Rangeley, *U.S.A.* 117 B14
Rangeley L., *U.S.A.* 117 B14
Rangely, *U.S.A.* 108 F9
Ranger, *U.S.A.* 113 J5
Rangia, *India* 67 F17
Rangiora, *N.Z.* 91 K4
Rangitaiki →, *N.Z.* 91 G6
Rangitata →, *N.Z.* 91 K3
Rangitoto ke te tonga = D'Urville
  I., *N.Z.* 91 J4
Rangkasbitung, *Indonesia* 63 G12
Rangon →, *Burma* 67 L20
Rangoon, *Burma* 67 L20
Rangpur, *Bangla.* 67 G16
Rangsit, *Thailand* 64 F3
Ranibennur, *India* 66 M9
Raniganj, *Ut. P., India* 69 F9
Raniganj, *W. Bengal, India* ... 67 H15
Ranikhet, *India* 69 E8
Raniwara, *India* 66 G8
Rāniyah, *Iraq* 70 B5
Ranka, *India* 69 H10
Ranken →, *Australia* 94 C2
Rankin, *U.S.A.* 113 K4
Rankin Inlet, *Canada* 100 B10
Rankins Springs, *Australia* ... 95 E4
Rankweil, *Austria* 26 D2
Rannoch, L., *U.K.* 13 E4
Rannoch Moor, *U.K.* 13 E4
Ranobe, Helodrano' i, *Madag.* .. 89 C7
Ranohira, *Madag.* 89 C8
Ranomafana, Toamasina, Madag. .. 89 B8
Ranomafana, Toliara, Madag. 89 C8
Ranomafana △, *Madag.* 89 C8
Ranomena, *Madag.* 89 C8
Ranong, *Thailand* 65 H2
Ranotsara Nord, *Madag.* 89 C8
Ransa, *Iran* 71 C6
Ranski, *Indonesia* 63 E8
Rantabe, *Madag.* 89 B8
Rantauprapat, *Indonesia* 62 D1
Rantemario, *Indonesia* 63 E5
Rantoul, *U.S.A.* 114 E1
Ranum, *Denmark* 11 H3
Ranyah, W. →, *Si. Arabia* 80 C5
Raon l'Étape, *France* 19 D13
Raoping, *China* 59 F11
Raoyang, *China* 56 E8
Rap, Ko, *Thailand* .... 65 b
Rapa, *French Polynesia* 97 K13
Rapa Nui = Pascua, I. de, Chile .. 97 K17
Rapallo, *Italy* 40 D6
Rapar, *India* 68 H4
Rāpch, *Iran* 71 E8
Raper, C., *Canada* 101 B13
Rapid City, *U.S.A.* 112 D3
Rapid River, *U.S.A.* 114 C2
Rapla, *Estonia* 9 G21
Rapti →, *India* 69 F10
Rapu Rapu I., *Phil.* 61 E6
Raqaba ez Zarqa →, *Sudan* 81 F2
Raquette →, *U.S.A.* 117 B10
Raquette Lake, *U.S.A.* 117 C10
Rarotonga, *Cook Is.* 97 K12
Ra's al 'Ayn, *Syria* 70 B4
Ra's al Khaymah, *U.A.E.* 71 E7
Râs el Mâ, *Mali* 82 B4
Râs Ghârib, *Egypt* 80 B3
Râs Mallap, *Egypt* 80 B3
Râs Muhammad △, *Egypt* 80 B3
Rasca, Pta. de la, Canary Is. .. 48 G3
Rășcani, *Moldova* 29 C12
Raseiniai, *Lithuania* 9 J20
Rashad, *Sudan* 81 E3
Rashîd, *Egypt* 80 H7
Rashîd, Masabb, *Egypt* 80 H7
Rashmi, *India* 68 G6
Rasht, *Iran* 71 B6
Rasi Salai, *Thailand* 64 E5
Raška, *Serbia & M.* 44 C4
Râsnov, *Romania* 29 E10
Rason L., *Australia* 93 E3
Rașova, *Romania* 29 F12
Rasovo, *Bulgaria* 44 C7
Rasra, *India* 69 G10
Rasskazovo, *Russia* 34 D5
Rast, *Romania* 29 G8
Rastatt, *Germany* 25 G4
Rastede, *Germany* 24 B4
Răstolița, *Romania* 29 D9
Rasul, *Pakistan* 68 C5
Raszków, *Poland* 31 G4
Rat Buri, *Thailand* 64 F2
Rat Islands, *U.S.A.* 100 C1
Rat L., *Canada* 103 B9
Rätan, *Sweden* 10 B8
Ratangarh, *India* 68 E6
Raṭāwī, *Iraq* 70 D5
Rath, *India* 69 G8
Rath Luirc, *Ireland* 12 D3
Rathdrum, *Ireland* 12 D5
Rathenow, *Germany* 24 C8
Rathkeale, *Ireland* 12 D3
Rathlin I., *U.K.* 12 A5
Rathmelton, *Ireland* 12 A4
Ratibor = Racibórz, *Poland* ... 31 H5
Rätikon, *Austria* 26 D2
Ratingen, *Germany* 24 D2
Ratlam, *India* 68 H6
Ratnagiri, *India* 66 L8
Ratodero, *Pakistan* 68 F3
Raton, *U.S.A.* 113 G2
Rattaphum, *Thailand* 65 J3
Ratten, *Austria* 26 D8
Rattray Hd., *U.K.* 13 D7
Rättvik, *Sweden* 10 D9
Ratz, Mt., *Canada* 102 B2
Ratzeburg, *Germany* 24 B6

Raub, *Malaysia* 65 L3
Rauch, *Argentina* 126 D4
Raudales de Malpaso, *Mexico* .. 119 D6
Raufarhöfn, *Iceland* 8 C6
Raufoss, *Norway* 9 F14
Raukumara Ra., *N.Z.* 91 H6
Rauma, *Finland* 9 F19
Raumo = Rauma, *Finland* 9 F19
Raung, Gunung, *Indonesia* 63 J17
Raurkela, *India* 69 H11
Rausu-Dake, *Japan* 54 B12
Rāut →, *Moldova* 29 C14
Rava-Ruska, *Ukraine* 31 H10
Rava Russkaya = Rava-Ruska,
  Ukraine 31 H10
Ravalli, *U.S.A.* 108 C6
Ravānsar, *Iran* 70 C5
Ravanusa, *Italy* 42 E6
Rāvar, *Iran* 71 D8
Ravena, *U.S.A.* 117 D11
Ravenna, *Italy* 41 D9
Ravenna, *Nebr., U.S.A.* 112 E5
Ravenna, *Ohio, U.S.A.* 116 E3
Ravensburg, *Germany* 25 H5
Ravenshoe, *Australia* 94 B4
Ravensthorpe, *Australia* 93 F3
Ravenswood, *Australia* 94 C4
Ravenswood, *U.S.A.* 114 F5
Ravi →, *Pakistan* 68 D4
Ravna Gora, *Croatia* 41 C11
Ravna Reka, *Serbia & M.* 44 B5
Ravne na Koroškem, *Slovenia* .. 41 B11
Rawa Mazowiecka, *Poland* 31 G7
Rawalpindi, *Pakistan* 68 C5
Rawāndūz, *Iraq* 70 B5
Rawang, *Malaysia* 65 L3
Rawene, *N.Z.* 91 F4
Rawicz, *Poland* 31 G3
Rawka →, *Poland* 31 F7
Rawlinna, *Australia* 93 F4
Rawlins, *U.S.A.* 108 F10
Rawlinson Ra., *Australia* 93 D4
Rawson, *Argentina* 128 E3
Raxaul, *India* 69 F11
Ray, *U.S.A.* 112 A3
Ray, C., *Canada* 105 C8
Raya Ring, Ko, *Thailand* ...... 65 a
Rayadurg, *India* 66 M10
Rayagada, *India* 67 K13
Raychikhinsk, *Russia* 53 E13
Rāyen, *Iran* 71 D8
Rayleigh, *U.K.* 15 F8
Raymond, *Canada* 102 D6
Raymond, *Calif., U.S.A.* 110 H7
Raymond, *N.H., U.S.A.* 117 C13
Raymond, *Wash., U.S.A.* 110 D3
Raymondville, *U.S.A.* 113 M6
Raymore, *Canada* 103 C8
Rayón, *Mexico* 118 B2
Rayong, *Thailand* 64 F3
Rayville, *U.S.A.* 113 J9
Raz, Pte. du, *France* 18 D2
Razan, *Iran* 71 C6
Ražana, *Serbia & M.* 44 B3
Ražanj, *Serbia & M.* 44 C5
Razāzah, Buḩayrat ar, *Iraq* ... 70 C4
Razazah, L. = Razāzah, Buḩayrat
  ar, *Iraq* 70 C4
Razdelna, *Bulgaria* 45 C11
Razdel'naya = Rozdilna, Ukraine .. 29 D15
Razdolnoye, *Russia* 54 C5
Razdolnoye, *Ukraine* 33 K7
Razeh, *Iran* 71 C6
Razgrad, *Bulgaria* 45 C10
Razim, Lacul, *Romania* 29 F14
Razlog, *Bulgaria* 44 E7
Razmak, *Pakistan* 68 C3
Ré, Î. de, *France* 20 B2
Reading, *U.K.* 15 F7
Reading, *U.S.A.* 117 F9
Reading □, *U.K.* 15 F7
Realicó, *Argentina* 126 D3
Réalmont, *France* 20 E6
Ream, *Cambodia* 65 G4
Reata, *Mexico* 118 B4
Reay Forest, *U.K.* 13 C4
Rebais, *France* 19 D10
Rebi, *Indonesia* 63 F8
Rebiana, *Libya* 79 D10
Rebiana, Sahrâ', *Libya* 79 D10
Rebun-Tō, *Japan* 54 B10
Recanati, *Italy* 41 E10
Recaș, *Romania* 28 E6
Recco, *Italy* 40 D6
Recherche, Arch. of the, Australia .. 93 F3
Rechna Doab, *Pakistan* 68 D5
Rechytsa, *Belarus* 33 F6
Recife, *Brazil* 125 E12
Recklinghausen, *Germany* 17 C7
Reconquista, *Argentina* 126 B4
Recreo, *Argentina* 126 B2
Recz, *Poland* 31 E2
Red →, *U.S.A.* 113 K9
Red →, *N. Dak., U.S.A.* 100 C10
Red Bank, *U.S.A.* 117 F10
Red Bay, *Canada* 105 B8
Red Bluff, *U.S.A.* 108 F2
Red Bluff L., *U.S.A.* 113 K3
Red Cliffs, *Australia* 95 E3
Red Cloud, *U.S.A.* 112 E5
Red Creek, *U.S.A.* 117 C8
Red Deer, *Canada* 102 C6
Red Deer →, Alta., Canada 103 C7
Red Deer →, Man., Canada 103 C8
Red Deer L., *Canada* 103 C8
Red Hook, *U.S.A.* 117 E11
Red Indian L., *Canada* 105 C8
Red L., *Canada* 103 C10
Red Lake, *Canada* 103 C10
Red Lake Falls, *U.S.A.* 112 B6
Red Lake Road, *Canada* 103 C10

Red Lodge, *U.S.A.* 108 D9
Red Mountain, *U.S.A.* 111 K9
Red Oak, *U.S.A.* 112 E7
Red Rock, *Canada* 104 C2
Red Rock, L., *U.S.A.* 112 E8
Red Rocks Pt., *Australia* 93 F4
Red Sea, *Asia* 75 C2
Red Slate Mt., *U.S.A.* 110 H8
Red Sucker L., *Canada* 104 B1
Red Tower Pass = Turnu Roșu,
  P., *Romania* 29 E9
Red Wing, *U.S.A.* 112 C8
Reda, *Poland* 30 D5
Redang, *Malaysia* 65 K4
Redange, *Lux.* 17 E5
Redcar, *U.K.* 14 C6
Redcar & Cleveland □, *U.K.* ... 14 C7
Redcliff, *Canada* 103 C6
Redcliffe, *Australia* 95 D5
Redcliffe, Mt., *Australia* 93 E3
Reddersburg, *S. Africa* 88 D4
Redding, *U.S.A.* 108 F2
Redditch, *U.K.* 15 E6
Redfield, *U.S.A.* 112 C5
Redford, *U.S.A.* 117 B11
Redhead, Trin. & Tob. 125 K16
Redkino, *Russia* 32 D9
Redlands, *U.S.A.* 111 M9
Redmond, *Oreg., U.S.A.* 108 D3
Redmond, *Wash., U.S.A.* 110 C4
Redon, *France* 18 E4
Redonda, Antigua & B. 121 C7
Redondela, *Spain* 36 C2
Redondo, *Portugal* 37 G3
Redondo Beach, *U.S.A.* 111 M8
Redruth, *U.K.* 15 G2
Redvers, *Canada* 103 D8
Redwater, *Canada* 102 C6
Redwood, *U.S.A.* 108 F1
Redwood City, *U.S.A.* 110 H4
Redwood Falls, *U.S.A.* 112 C7
Ree, L., *Ireland* 12 C3
Reed, L., *Canada* 103 C8
Reed City, *U.S.A.* 114 D3
Reedley, *U.S.A.* 110 J7
Reedsburg, *U.S.A.* 112 D9
Reedsport, *U.S.A.* 108 E1
Reedsville, *U.S.A.* 116 F7
Reefton, *N.Z.* 91 K3
Rees, Germany 24 D2
Reese →, *U.S.A.* 108 F5
Refahiye, *Turkey* 73 C8
Reftele, Sweden 11 G7
Refugio, *U.S.A.* 113 L6
Rega →, *Poland* 30 D2
Regalbuto, *Italy* 43 E7
Regen, *Germany* 25 G9
Regen →, *Germany* 25 F8
Regensburg, *Germany* 25 F8
Regenstauf, *Germany* 25 F8
Reggâne = Zaouiet Reggâne,
  Algeria 78 C6
Reggello, *Italy* 41 E8
Réggio di Calábria, *Italy* 43 D8
Réggio nell'Emília, *Italy* 40 D7
Reghin, *Romania* 29 D9
Regina, *Canada* 103 C8
Regina Beach, *Canada* 103 C8
Registro, Brazil 127 A6
Reguengos de Monsaraz, Portugal .. 37 G3
Rehar →, *India* 69 H10
Rehoboth, *Namibia* 88 C2
Rehovot, *Israel* 74 D3
Rehli, india 69 H8
Reichenbach, *Germany* 24 E4
Reid, *Australia* 93 F4
Reidsville, *U.S.A.* 115 G6
Reigate, *U.K.* 15 F7
Reillo, *Spain* 38 F3
Reims, *France* 19 C11
Reina Adelaida, Arch., Chile ... 128 G2
Reina Sofía, Tenerife ✈ (TFS),
  Canary Is. 48 F3
Reinbek, *Germany* 24 B6
Reindeer →, *Canada* 103 B8
Reindeer I., *Canada* 103 C9
Reindeer L., *Canada* 103 B8
Reinga, C., *N.Z.* 91 F4
Reinosa, *Spain* 36 B6
Reitz, S Africa 89 D4
Reivilo, S. Africa 88 D3
Rejaf, Sudan 81 G3
Rejmyre, Sweden 11 F9
Rejowiec Fabryczny, Poland 31 G10
Reka →, *Slovenia* 41 C11
Rekovac, Serbia & M. 44 C5
Reliance, *Canada* 103 A7
Rémalard, France 18 D7
Remarkable, Mt., Australia 95 E2
Rembang, Indonesia 63 G14
Remedios, Panama 120 E3
Remeshk, iran 71 E8
Remetea, Romania 29 D10
Remich, Lux. 17 E6
Remiremont, France 19 D13
Remo, Ethiopia 81 F5
Remontnoye, Russia 35 G6
Remoulins, France 21 E8
Remscheid, Germany 17 C7
Ren Xian, China 56 F8
Rendang, Indonesia 63 J18
Rende, Italy 43 C9
Rendína, Greece 46 B3
Rendsburg, Germany 24 A5
Renfrew, Canada 117 A8
Renfrewshire □, U.K. 13 F4
Rengat, Indonesia 62 E2
Rengo, Chile 126 C1
Renhua, China 59 E9
Renhuai, China 58 D6

Reni, *Ukraine* 29 E13
Renk, *Sudan* 81 E3
Renmark, *Australia* 95 E3
Rennell Sd., *Canada* 102 C2
Renner Springs, *Australia* 94 B1
Rennes, *France* 18 D5
Rennie L., *Canada* 103 A7
Reno, *U.S.A.* 110 F7
Reno →, *Italy* 41 D9
Renovo, *U.S.A.* 116 E7
Renqiu, *China* 56 E9
Rens, *Denmark* 11 K3
Renshou, *China* 58 C5
Rensselaer, *Ind., U.S.A.* 114 E2
Rensselaer, *N.Y., U.S.A.* 117 D11
Rentería, *Spain* 38 B3
Renton, *U.S.A.* 110 C4
Réo, *Burkina Faso* 82 C4
Reocín, *Spain* 36 B6
Reotipur, *India* 69 G10
Répcelak, *Hungary* 28 C2
Republic, *Mo., U.S.A.* 113 G8
Republic, *Wash., U.S.A.* 108 B4
Republican →, *U.S.A.* 112 F6
Repulse B., *Australia* 94 J6
Repulse Bay, *Canada* 101 B11
Requena, *Peru* 124 E4
Requena, *Spain* 39 F3
Réquista, *France* 20 D6
Reșadiye = Datça, *Turkey* 47 E9
Reșadiye, *Turkey* 72 B7
Reșadiye Yarımadası, *Turkey* .. 47 E9
Resavica, *Serbia & M.* 44 B5
Resen, *Macedonia* 44 E5
Reserve, *U.S.A.* 109 K9
Resht = Rasht, *Iran* 71 B6
Resistencia, *Argentina* 126 B4
Reșița, *Romania* 28 E6
Resko, *Poland* 30 E2
Resolution I., *Canada* 101 B13
Resolution I., *N.Z.* 91 L1
Ressano Garcia, *Mozam.* 89 D5
Reston, *Canada* 103 D8
Reszel, *Poland* 30 D8
Retalhuleu, *Guatemala* 120 D1
Retenue, L. de, Dem. Rep. of
  the Congo 87 E2
Retezat △, *Romania* 28 E7
Retezat, Munții, *Romania* 28 E7
Retford, *U.K.* 14 D7
Rethel, *France* 19 C11
Rethem, *Germany* 24 C5
Réthímnon, *Greece* 49 D6
Réthímnon □, *Greece* 49 D6
Reti, *Pakistan* 68 E3
Retiche, Alpi, *Switz.* 25 J6
Retiers, *France* 18 E5
Retortillo, *Spain* 36 E4
Retournac, *France* 21 C8
Rétság, *Hungary* 28 C4
Réunion ☒, *Ind. Oc.* 77 J9
Reus, *Spain* 38 D6
Reuterstadt Stavenhagen,
  Germany 24 B8
Reutlingen, *Germany* 25 G5
Reutte, *Austria* 26 D3
Reval = Tallinn, *Estonia* 9 G21
Revel, *France* 20 E6
Revelganj, *India* 69 G11
Revelstoke, *Canada* 102 C5
Reventazón, *Peru* 124 E2
Revigny-sur-Ornain, *France* ... 19 D11
Revilla Gigedo, Is. de, Pac. Oc. .. 118 D2
Revin, *France* 19 C11
Revúca, *Slovak Rep.* 27 C13
Revuè →, *Mozam.* 87 F3
Rewa, *India* 69 G9
Rewari, *India* 68 E7
Rexburg, *U.S.A.* 108 E8
Rey, *Iran* 71 C6
Rey, I. del, *Panama* 120 E4
Rey Malabo, Eq. Guin. 83 E6
Reyðarfjörður, *Iceland* 8 D6
Reyes, *U.S.A.* 110 H3
Reyhanlı, *Turkey* 72 D7
Reykjahlíð, *Iceland* 8 D5
Reykjanes, *Iceland* 8 E2
Reykjavík, *Iceland* 8 D3
Reynolds Ra., *Australia* 92 D5
Reynoldsville, *U.S.A.* 116 E6
Reynosa, *Mexico* 119 B5
Rēzekne, *Latvia* 9 H22
Rezina, *Moldova* 29 C13
Rezovo, *Bulgaria* 45 D12
Rezvān, *Iran* 71 E8
Rgotina, *Serbia & M.* 44 B6
Rhamnus, *Greece* 46 C6
Rhayader, *U.K.* 15 E4
Rheda-Wiedenbrück, *Germany* ... 24 D4
Rhede, *Germany* 24 D2
Rhein →, *Europe* 17 C6
Rhein-Main-Donau-Kanal,
  Germany 25 F7
Rhein-Ruhr, Düsseldorf ✈
  (DUS), *Germany* 24 D2
Rhein-Taunus △, *Germany* 25 E4
Rhein-Westerwald △, *Germany* .. 24 E3
Rheinbach, *Germany* 24 E2
Rheine, *Germany* 24 C3
Rheinfelden, *Germany* 25 H3
Rheinhessen-Pfalz □, *Germany* . 25 F4
Rheinland-Pfalz □, *Germany* ... 25 E2
Rheinsberg, *Germany* 24 B8
Rhin = Rhein →, *Europe* 17 C6
Rhine = Rhein →, *Europe* 17 C6
Rhinebeck, *U.S.A.* 117 E11
Rhineland-Palatinate =
  Rheinland-Pfalz □, *Germany* . 25 E2
Rhinelander, *U.S.A.* 112 C10
Rhinns Pt., *U.K.* 13 F2

Rhino Camp, *Uganda* 86 B3
Rhir, Cap, *Morocco* 78 B4
Rho, *Italy* 40 C6
Rhode Island □, *U.S.A.* 117 E13
Rhodes = Ródhos, *Greece* 49 C10
Rhodope Mts. = Rhodopi Planina,
  Bulgaria 45 E8
Rhodopi Planina, *Bulgaria* 45 E8
Rhön, *Germany* 24 E5
Rhondda, *U.K.* 15 F4
Rhondda Cynon Taff □, *U.K.* ... 15 F4
Rhône □, *France* 21 C9
Rhône ➛, *France* 21 E8
Rhône-Alpes □, *France* 21 C9
Rhum, *U.K.* 13 E2
Rhyl, *U.K.* 14 D4
Ri-Aba, *Eq. Guin.* 83 E6
Ria Formosa △, *Portugal* 37 H3
Riachão, *Brazil* 125 E9
Riangnom, *Sudan* 81 F3
Riaño, *Spain* 36 C6
Rians, *France* 21 E9
Riansáres ➛, *Spain* 37 F7
Riasi, *India* 69 C6
Riau □, *Indonesia* 62 D2
Riau, Kepulauan, *Indonesia* 62 D2
Riau Arch. = Riau, Kepulauan,
  Indonesia 62 D2
Riaza, *Spain* 36 D7
Riaza ➛, *Spain* 36 D7
Riba de Saelices, *Spain* 38 E2
Riba-Roja de Turia, *Spain* 39 F4
Ribadavia, *Spain* 36 C2
Ribadesella, *Spain* 36 B5
Ribado, *Nigeria* 83 D7
Ribao, *Cameroon* 83 D7
Ribas = Ribes de Freser, *Spain* .. 38 C7
Ribas do Rio Pardo, *Brazil* 125 H8
Ribauè, *Mozam.* 87 E4
Ribble ➛, *U.K.* 14 D5
Ribe, *Denmark* 11 J2
Ribe Amtskommune □, *Denmark* 11 J2
Ribeauvillé, *France* 19 D14
Ribécourt-Dreslincourt, *France* .. 19 C9
Ribeira = Santa Uxía, *Spain* 36 C2
Ribeira Brava, *Madeira* 48 D2
Ribeirão Prêto, *Brazil* 127 A6
Ribemont, *France* 19 C10
Ribera, *Italy* 42 E6
Ribérac, *France* 20 C4
Riberalta, *Bolivia* 124 F5
Ribes de Freser, *Spain* 38 C7
Ribnica, *Slovenia* 41 C11
Ribnitz-Damgarten, *Germany* .. 24 A8
Ričany, *Czech Rep.* 26 B7
Riccarton, *N.Z.* 91 K4
Ríccia, *Italy* 43 A7
Riccione, *Italy* 41 E9
Rice, *U.S.A.* 111 L12
Rice L., *Canada* 116 B6
Rice Lake, *U.S.A.* 112 C9
Rich, C., *Canada* 116 B4
Richard Toll, *Senegal* 82 B1
Richards Bay, *S. Africa* 89 D5
Richardson ➛, *Canada* 103 B6
Richardson Lakes, *U.S.A.* 114 C10
Richardson Springs, *U.S.A.* 110 F5
Riche, C., *Australia* 93 F2
Richelieu, *France* 18 E7
Richey, *U.S.A.* 112 B2
Richfield, *U.S.A.* 109 G8
Richfield Springs, *U.S.A.* 117 D10
Richford, *U.S.A.* 117 B12
Richibucto, *Canada* 105 C7
Richland, *Ga., U.S.A.* 115 J3
Richland, *Wash., U.S.A.* 108 C4
Richland Center, *U.S.A.* 112 D9
Richlands, *U.S.A.* 114 G5
Richmond, *Australia* 94 C3
Richmond, *N.Z.* 91 J4
Richmond, *U.K.* 14 C6
Richmond, *Calif., U.S.A.* 110 H4
Richmond, *Ind., U.S.A.* 114 F3
Richmond, *Ky., U.S.A.* 114 G3
Richmond, *Mich., U.S.A.* 116 D2
Richmond, *Mo., U.S.A.* 112 F8
Richmond, *Tex., U.S.A.* 113 L7
Richmond, *Utah, U.S.A.* 108 F8
Richmond, *Va., U.S.A.* 114 G7
Richmond, *Vt., U.S.A.* 117 B12
Richmond Hill, *Canada* 116 C5
Richmond Ra., *Australia* 95 D5
Richtersveld △, *S. Africa* 88 D2
Richwood, *U.S.A.* 114 F5
Ricla, *Spain* 38 D3
Ridder = Leninogorsk,
  Kazakhstan 52 D9
Riddlesburg, *U.S.A.* 116 F6
Ridgecrest, *U.S.A.* 111 K9
Ridgefield, *Conn., U.S.A.* 117 E11
Ridgefield, *Wash., U.S.A.* 110 E4
Ridgeland, *U.S.A.* 115 J5
Ridgetown, *Canada* 116 D3
Ridgewood, *U.S.A.* 117 F10
Ridgway, *U.S.A.* 116 E6
Riding Mountain △, *Canada* .. 103 C9
Ridley, Mt., *Australia* 93 F3
Riebeek-Oos, *S. Africa* 88 E4
Ried, *Austria* 26 C6
Riedlingen, *Germany* 25 G5
Riedstadt, *Germany* 25 F4
Rienza ➛, *Italy* 41 B8
Riesa, *Germany* 24 D9
Riesi, *Italy* 43 E7
Riet ➛, *S. Africa* 88 D3
Rietavas, *Lithuania* 30 C8
Rietbron, *S. Africa* 88 E3
Rietfontein, *Namibia* 88 C3
Rieti, *Italy* 41 F9
Rieupeyroux, *France* 20 D6

Riez, *France* 21 E10
Rif = Er Rif, *Morocco* 78 A5
Riffe L., *U.S.A.* 110 D4
Rifle, *U.S.A.* 108 G10
Rift Valley, *Africa* 76 G7
Rift Valley ➛, *Kenya* 86 B4
Rīga, *Latvia* 9 H21
Rīga ✈ (RIX), *Latvia* 30 B10
Riga, G. of, *Latvia* 9 H20
Rigacikun, *Nigeria* 83 C6
Rīgān, *Iran* 71 D8
Rīgas Jūras Līcis = Riga, G. of,
  Latvia 9 H20
Rigaud, *Canada* 117 A10
Rigby, *U.S.A.* 108 E8
Rīgestān, *Afghan.* 66 D4
Riggins, *U.S.A.* 108 D5
Rignac, *France* 20 D6
Rigolet, *Canada* 105 B8
Rihand Dam, *India* 69 G10
Riihimäki, *Finland* 9 F21
Riiser-Larsen-halvøya, *Antarctica* 5 C4
Rijau, *Nigeria* 83 C6
Rijeka, *Croatia* 41 C11
Rijeka Crnojevića, *Serbia & M.* . 44 D3
Rijssen, *Neths.* 17 B6
Rika ➛, *Ukraine* 29 B8
Rike, *Ethiopia* 81 E4
Rikuchū-Kaigan △, *Japan* 54 E11
Rikuzentakada, *Japan* 54 E10
Rila, *Bulgaria* 44 D7
Rila Planina, *Bulgaria* 44 D7
Riley, *U.S.A.* 108 E4
Rima ➛, *Nigeria* 83 C6
Rimah, Wadi ar ➛, *Si. Arabia* .. 70 E4
Rimau, Pulau, *Malaysia* .... 65 c
Rimavská Sobota, *Slovak Rep.* .. 27 C13
Rimbey, *Canada* 102 C6
Rimbo, *Sweden* 10 E12
Rimersburg, *U.S.A.* 116 E5
Rimforsa, *Sweden* 11 F9
Rimi, *Nigeria* 83 C6
Rímini, *Italy* 41 D9
Rimouski, *Canada* 105 C6
Rimrock, *U.S.A.* 110 D5
Rinca, *Indonesia* 63 F5
Rincón de la Victoria, *Spain* 37 J6
Rincón de Romos, *Mexico* 118 C4
Rinconada, *Argentina* 126 A2
Rind ➛, *India* 69 G9
Ringarum, *Sweden* 11 F10
Ringas, *India* 68 F6
Ringe, *Denmark* 11 J4
Ringim, *Nigeria* 83 C6
Ringkøbing, *Denmark* 11 H2
Ringkøbing Amtskommune □,
  Denmark 11 H2
Ringkøbing Fjord, *Denmark* 11 H2
Ringsjön, *Sweden* 11 J7
Ringsted, *Denmark* 11 J5
Ringvassøy, *Norway* 8 B18
Ringwood, *U.S.A.* 117 E10
Rinía, *Greece* 47 D7
Rinjani, *Indonesia* 62 F5
Rinteln, *Germany* 24 C5
Río, Punta del, *Spain* 39 J2
Rio Branco, *Brazil* 124 E5
Río Branco, *Uruguay* 127 C5
Río Bravo ➛, *N. Amer.* 118 B4
Río Bravo del Norte ➛, *Mexico* 119 B5
Rio Brilhante, *Brazil* 127 A5
Rio Claro, *Brazil* 127 A6
Rio Claro, *Trin. & Tob.* 121 D7
Río Colorado, *Argentina* 128 D4
Río Cuarto, *Argentina* 126 C3
Rio das Pedras, *Mozam.* 89 C6
Rio de Janeiro, *Brazil* 127 A7
Rio de Janeiro □, *Brazil* 127 A7
Rio do Sul, *Brazil* 127 B6
Río Dulce ➛, *Guatemala* 120 C2
Río Gallegos, *Argentina* 128 G3
Río Grande, *Argentina* 128 G3
Rio Grande, *Brazil* 127 C5
Río Grande, *Mexico* 118 C4
Río Grande, *Nic.* 120 D3
Rio Grande, *Puerto Rico* ...... 121 d
Río Grande ➛, *U.S.A.* 113 N6
Río Grande City, *U.S.A.* 113 M5
Río Grande de Santiago ➛,
  Mexico 118 C3
Rio Grande do Norte □, *Brazil* . 125 E11
Rio Grande do Sul □, *Brazil* .. 127 C5
Río Hato, *Panama* 120 E3
Río Lagartos, *Mexico* 119 C7
Rio Largo, *Brazil* 125 E11
Rio Maior, *Portugal* 37 F2
Rio Marina, *Italy* 40 F7
Río Mulatos, *Bolivia* 124 G5
Río Muni □, *Eq. Guin.* 84 D2
Rio Negro, *Brazil* 127 B6
Río Pardo, *Brazil* 127 C5
Río Pilcomayo △, *Argentina* .. 126 B4
Río Platano △, *Honduras* 120 C3
Rio Rancho, *U.S.A.* 109 J10
Río Segundo, *Argentina* 126 C3
Río Tercero, *Argentina* 126 C3
Rio Tinto, *Portugal* 36 D2
Rio Verde, *Brazil* 125 G8
Río Verde, *Mexico* 119 C5
Rio Vista, *U.S.A.* 110 G5
Ríobamba, *Ecuador* 124 D3
Ríohacha, *Colombia* 124 A4
Riom, *France* 20 C7
Riom-ès-Montagnes, *France* 20 C6
Rion-des-Landes, *France* 20 E3
Rionero in Vúlture, *Italy* 43 B8
Rioni ➛, *Georgia* 35 J5
Ríos, *Spain* 36 D3
Ríosucio, *Colombia* 124 B3
Riou L., *Canada* 103 B7
Rioz, *France* 19 E13

Ripatransone, *Italy* 41 F10
Ripley, *Canada* 116 B3
Ripley, *Calif., U.S.A.* 111 M12
Ripley, *N.Y., U.S.A.* 116 D5
Ripley, *Tenn., U.S.A.* 113 H10
Ripley, *W. Va., U.S.A.* 114 F5
Ripoll, *Spain* 38 C7
Ripon, *U.K.* 14 C6
Ripon, *Calif., U.S.A.* 110 H5
Ripon, *Wis., U.S.A.* 114 D1
Riposto, *Italy* 43 E8
Risan, *Serbia & M.* 44 D2
Riscle, *France* 20 E3
Rishā', W. ar ➛, *Si. Arabia* 70 E5
Rishiri-Rebun-Sarobetsu △,
  Japan 54 B10
Rishiri-Tō, *Japan* 54 B10
Rishon le Ziyyon, *Israel* 74 D3
Risle ➛, *France* 18 C7
Risnjak △, *Croatia* 41 C11
Rison, *U.S.A.* 113 J8
Risør, *Norway* 9 G13
Rita Blanca Cr. ➛, *U.S.A.* 113 H3
Riti, *Nigeria* 83 D6
Ritter, Mt., *U.S.A.* 110 H7
Rittman, *U.S.A.* 116 F3
Ritzville, *U.S.A.* 108 C4
Riva del Garda, *Italy* 40 C7
Riva Lígure, *Italy* 40 E4
Rivadavia, *Buenos Aires,
  Argentina* 126 D3
Rivadavia, *Mendoza, Argentina* . 126 C2
Rivadavia, *Salta, Argentina* 126 A3
Rivadavia, *Chile* 126 B1
Rivarolo Canavese, *Italy* 40 C4
Rivas, *Nic.* 120 D2
Rive-de-Gier, *France* 21 C8
River Cess, *Liberia* 82 D3
River Jordan, *Canada* 110 B2
Rivera, *Argentina* 126 D3
Rivera, *Uruguay* 127 C4
Riverbank, *U.S.A.* 110 H6
Riverdale, *U.S.A.* 110 J7
Riverhead, *U.S.A.* 117 F12
Riverhurst, *Canada* 103 C8
Rivers, *Canada* 103 C8
Rivers □, *Nigeria* 83 E6
Rivers Inlet, *Canada* 102 C3
Riverside, *S. Africa* 88 E3
Riverside, *U.S.A.* 111 M9
Riverton, *Australia* 95 E2
Riverton, *Canada* 103 C9
Riverton, *N.Z.* 91 M2
Riverton, *U.S.A.* 108 E9
Riverton Heights, *U.S.A.* 110 C4
Rives, *France* 21 C9
Rivesaltes, *France* 20 F6
Riviera, *U.S.A.* 111 K12
Riviera di Levante, *Italy* 40 D6
Riviera di Ponente, *Italy* 40 D5
Rivière-au-Renard, *Canada* 105 C7
Rivière-du-Loup, *Canada* 105 C6
Rivière-Pentecôte, *Canada* 105 C6
Rivière-Pilote, *Martinique* ...... 120 c
Rivière St-Paul, *Canada* 105 B8
Rivière-Salée, *Martinique* ...... 120 c
Rivne, *Ukraine* 29 D14
Rivne, *Ukraine* 33 G4
Rívoli, *Italy* 40 C4
Rivoli B., *Australia* 95 F3
Rixheim, *France* 19 E14
Riyadh = Ar Riyāḍ, *Si. Arabia* .. 70 E5
Rize, *Turkey* 73 B9
Rizhao, *China* 57 G10
Rizokarpaso, *Cyprus* 49 D13
Rizzuto, C., *Italy* 43 D10
Rjukan, *Norway* 9 G13
Ro, *Greece* 47 E11
Roa, *Spain* 36 D7
Road Town, *Br. Virgin Is.* ...... 121 e
Roan Plateau, *U.S.A.* 108 G9
Roanne, *France* 19 F11
Roanoke, *Ala., U.S.A.* 115 J3
Roanoke, *Va., U.S.A.* 114 G6
Roanoke ➛, *U.S.A.* 115 H7
Roanoke I., *U.S.A.* 115 H8
Roanoke Rapids, *U.S.A.* 115 G7
Roatán, *Honduras* 120 C2
Robāṭ Sang, *Iran* 71 C8
Robāṭkarīm, *Iran* 71 C6
Robāṭkarīm □, *Iran* 71 B6
Robbins I., *Australia* 95 G4
Róbbio, *Italy* 40 C5
Robe ➛, *Australia* 92 D2
Robe, *Australia* 95 F2
Robert Lee, *U.S.A.* 113 K4
Robertsdale, *U.S.A.* 116 F6
Robertsganj, *India* 69 G10
Robertson, *S. Africa* 88 E2
Robertson I., *Antarctica* 5 C18
Robertson Ra., *Australia* 92 D3
Robertsport, *Liberia* 82 D2
Robertstown, *Australia* 95 E2
Roberval, *Canada* 105 C5
Robeson Chan., *N. Amer.* 4 A4
Robesonia, *U.S.A.* 117 F8
Robi, *Ethiopia* 81 F4
Robinson, *U.S.A.* 114 F2
Robinson ➛, *Australia* 94 B2
Robinson Ra., *Australia* 93 E2
Robinvale, *Australia* 95 E3
Robledo, *Spain* 39 G2
Roblin, *Canada* 103 C8
Roboré, *Bolivia* 124 G7
Robson, *Canada* 102 D5
Robson, Mt., *Canada* 102 C5
Robstown, *U.S.A.* 113 M6
Roca, C. da, *Portugal* 37 G1
Roca Partida, I., *Mexico* 118 D2
Rocamadour, *France* 20 D5
Rocas, I., *Brazil* 125 D12

Rocca San Casciano, *Italy* 41 D8
Roccadáspide, *Italy* 43 B8
Roccastrada, *Italy* 41 F8
Roccella Iónica, *Italy* 43 D9
Rocha, *Uruguay* 127 C5
Rochdale, *U.K.* 14 D5
Rochechouart, *France* 20 C4
Rochefort, *Belgium* 17 D5
Rochefort, *France* 20 C3
Rochefort-en-Terre, *France* 18 E4
Rochelle, *U.S.A.* 112 E10
Rocher River, *Canada* 102 A6
Rocheservière, *France* 18 F5
Rochester, *U.K.* 15 F8
Rochester, *Ind., U.S.A.* 114 E2
Rochester, *Minn., U.S.A.* 112 C8
Rochester, *N.H., U.S.A.* 117 C14
Rochester, *N.Y., U.S.A.* 116 C7
Rociu, *Romania* 29 F10
Rock ➛, *Canada* 102 A3
Rock Creek, *U.S.A.* 116 E4
Rock Falls, *U.S.A.* 112 E10
Rock Hill, *U.S.A.* 115 H5
Rock Island, *U.S.A.* 112 E9
Rock Rapids, *U.S.A.* 112 D6
Rock Sound, *Bahamas* 120 B4
Rock Springs, *Mont., U.S.A.* .. 108 C10
Rock Springs, *Wyo., U.S.A.* .. 108 F9
Rock Valley, *U.S.A.* 112 D6
Rockall, *Atl. Oc.* 6 D3
Rockdale, *Tex., U.S.A.* 113 K6
Rockdale, *Wash., U.S.A.* 110 C5
Rockeby = Mungkan Kandju △,
  Australia 94 A3
Rockefeller Plateau, *Antarctica* . 5 E14
Rockford, *U.S.A.* 112 D10
Rockglen, *Canada* 103 D7
Rockhampton, *Australia* 94 C5
Rockingham, *Australia* 93 F2
Rockingham, *U.S.A.* 115 H6
Rockingham B., *Australia* 94 B4
Rocklake, *U.S.A.* 112 A5
Rockland, *Canada* 117 A9
Rockland, *Idaho, U.S.A.* 108 E7
Rockland, *Maine, U.S.A.* 115 C11
Rockland, *Mich., U.S.A.* 112 B10
Rocklin, *U.S.A.* 110 G5
Rockmart, *U.S.A.* 115 H3
Rockport, *Mass., U.S.A.* 117 D14
Rockport, *Mo., U.S.A.* 112 E7
Rockport, *Tex., U.S.A.* 113 L6
Rocksprings, *U.S.A.* 113 K4
Rockville, *Conn., U.S.A.* 117 E12
Rockville, *Md., U.S.A.* 114 F7
Rockwall, *U.S.A.* 113 J6
Rockwell City, *U.S.A.* 112 D7
Rockwood, *Canada* 116 C4
Rockwood, *Maine, U.S.A.* 115 C11
Rockwood, *Tenn., U.S.A.* 115 H3
Rocky Ford, *U.S.A.* 112 F3
Rocky Gully, *Australia* 93 F2
Rocky Harbour, *Canada* 105 C8
Rocky Island L., *Canada* 104 C3
Rocky Lane, *Canada* 102 B5
Rocky Mount, *U.S.A.* 115 H7
Rocky Mountain △, *U.S.A.* .. 108 F11
Rocky Mountain House, *Canada* 102 C6
Rocky Mts., *N. Amer.* 108 G10
Rocky Point, *Namibia* 88 B2
Rocroi, *France* 19 C11
Rod, *Pakistan* 66 E3
Rødby, *Denmark* 11 K5
Rødbyhavn, *Denmark* 11 K5
Roddickton, *Canada* 105 B8
Rødding, *Denmark* 11 J3
Rödeby, *Sweden* 11 H9
Rødekro, *Denmark* 11 J3
Rodenkirchen, *Germany* 24 B4
Rodez, *France* 20 D6
Rodholívas, *Greece* 44 F7
Rodhópi □, *Greece* 45 E9
Rodhopoú, *Greece* 49 D5
Ródhos, *Greece* 49 C10
Ródhos ✈ (RHO), *Greece* 47 E10
Rodi Gargánico, *Italy* 41 G12
Rodna, *Romania* 29 C9
Rodnei, Munṭii, *Romania* 29 C9
Rodney, *Canada* 116 D3
Rodney, C., *N.Z.* 91 G5
Rodniki, *Russia* 34 B5
Rodonit, Kepi i, *Albania* 44 E3
Rodriguez, *Ind. Oc.* 3 E13
Roe ➛, *U.K.* 12 A5
Roebling, *U.S.A.* 117 F10
Roebourne, *Australia* 92 D2
Roebuck B., *Australia* 92 C3
Roermond, *Neths.* 17 C6
Roes Welcome Sd., *Canada* 101 B11
Roeselare, *Belgium* 17 D3
Rogachev = Ragachow, *Belarus* . 33 F6
Rogačica, *Serbia & M.* 44 B3
Rogagua, L., *Bolivia* 124 F5
Rogaška Slatina, *Slovenia* 41 B12
Rogatec, *Slovenia* 41 B12
Rogatica, *Bos.-H.* 28 G4
Rogatyn, *Ukraine* 33 H3
Rogdhia, *Greece* 49 D7
Rogers, *U.S.A.* 113 G7
Rogers City, *U.S.A.* 114 C4
Rogersville, *Canada* 105 C6
Roggan ➛, *Canada* 104 B4
Roggan L., *Canada* 104 B4
Roggeveldberge, *S. Africa* 88 E3
Roggiano Gravina, *Italy* 43 C9
Rogliano, *France* 21 F13
Rogliano, *Italy* 43 C9
Rogoaguado, L., *Bolivia* 124 F5
Rogojampi, *Indonesia* 63 J17
Rogoźno, *Poland* 31 F3
Rogue ➛, *U.S.A.* 108 E1

Rohan, *France* 18 D4
Róhda, *Greece* 49 A3
Rohnert Park, *U.S.A.* 110 G4
Rohri, *Pakistan* 68 F3
Rohri Canal, *Pakistan* 68 F3
Rohtak, *India* 68 E7
Roi Et, *Thailand* 64 D4
Roja, *Latvia* 9 H20
Rojas, *Argentina* 126 C3
Rojiṣte, *Romania* 29 F8
Rojo, C., *Mexico* 119 C5
Rokan ➛, *Indonesia* 62 D2
Rokel ➛, *S. Leone* 82 D2
Rokiškis, *Lithuania* 9 J21
Rokitno, *Russia* 33 G8
Rokycany, *Czech Rep.* 26 B6
Rolândia, *Brazil* 127 A5
Rolla, *U.S.A.* 113 G9
Rolleston, *Australia* 94 C4
Rollingstone, *Australia* 94 B4
Rom, *Sudan* 81 F3
Roma, *Australia* 95 D4
Roma, *Italy* 41 G9
Roma, *Sweden* 11 G12
Roma, *U.S.A.* 113 M5
Roma Fiumicino ✈ (FCO), *Italy* 41 G9
Romain, C., *U.S.A.* 115 J6
Romaine, *Canada* 105 B7
Romaine ➛, *Canada* 105 B7
Roman, *Bulgaria* 44 C7
Roman, *Romania* 29 D11
Roman-Kosh, Gora, *Ukraine* 33 K8
Romanche ➛, *France* 21 C9
Romang, *Indonesia* 63 F7
Români, *Egypt* 74 E1
Romania ■, *Europe* 29 D10
Romanija, *Bos.-H.* 28 G3
Romano, Cayo, *Cuba* 120 B4
Romans-sur-Isère, *France* 21 C9
Romanshorn, *Switz.* 25 H5
Rombari, *Sudan* 81 G3
Romblon, *Phil.* 61 E5
Rome = Roma, *Italy* 41 G9
Rome, *Ga., U.S.A.* 115 H3
Rome, *N.Y., U.S.A.* 117 C9
Rome, *Pa., U.S.A.* 117 E8
Rometta, *Italy* 43 D8
Romilly-sur-Seine, *France* 19 D10
Romney, *U.S.A.* 114 F6
Romney Marsh, *U.K.* 15 F8
Romny, *Ukraine* 33 G7
Rømø, *Denmark* 11 J2
Romodan, *Ukraine* 33 G7
Romodanovo, *Russia* 34 C7
Romont, *Switz.* 25 J2
Romorantin-Lanthenay, *France* . 19 E8
Romsdalen, *Norway* 9 E12
Romsey, *U.K.* 15 G6
Ron, *Vietnam* 64 D6
Rona, *U.K.* 13 D3
Ronan, *U.S.A.* 108 C6
Roncador, Cayos, *Colombia* 120 D3
Roncador, Serra do, *Brazil* 125 F8
Ronciglione, *Italy* 41 F9
Ronco ➛, *Italy* 41 D9
Ronda, *Spain* 37 J5
Ronda, Serranía de, *Spain* 37 J5
Rondane, *Norway* 9 F13
Rondônia □, *Brazil* 124 F6
Rondonópolis, *Brazil* 125 G8
Rong, Koh, *Cambodia* 65 G4
Rong Jiang ➛, *China* 58 E7
Rong Xian, *Guangxi Zhuangzu,
  China* 59 F8
Rong Xian, *Sichuan, China* 58 C5
Rong'an, *China* 58 E7
Rongchang, *China* 58 C5
Ronge, L. la, *Canada* 103 B7
Rongjiang, *China* 58 E7
Rongshui, *China* 58 E7
Rønne, *Denmark* 11 J8
Ronne Ice Shelf, *Antarctica* 5 D18
Ronneby, *Sweden* 11 H9
Ronnebyån ➛, *Sweden* 11 H9
Rönneshytta, *Sweden* 11 F9
Ronsard, C., *Australia* 93 E1
Ronse, *Belgium* 17 D3
Roodepoort, *S. Africa* 89 D4
Roof Butte, *U.S.A.* 109 H9
Rooiboklaagte ➛, *Namibia* 88 C3
Roorkee, *India* 68 E7
Roosendaal, *Neths.* 17 C4
Roosevelt, *U.S.A.* 108 F8
Roosevelt ➛, *Brazil* 124 E6
Roosevelt, Mt., *Canada* 102 B3
Roosevelt I., *Antarctica* 5 D12
Ropczyce, *Poland* 31 H8
Roper ➛, *Australia* 94 A2
Roper Bar, *Australia* 94 A1
Roque Pérez, *Argentina* 126 D4
Roquefort, *France* 20 D3
Roquemaure, *France* 21 D8
Roquetas de Mar, *Spain* 39 J2
Roquetes, *Spain* 38 E5
Roquevaire, *France* 21 E9
Roraima □, *Brazil* 124 C6
Roraima, Mt., *Venezuela* 124 B6
Røros, *Norway* 9 E14
Rorschach, *Switz.* 25 H5
Rosa, *Zambia* 87 D3
Rosa, L., *Bahamas* 121 B5
Rosa, Monte, *Europe* 40 C4
Rosal de la Frontera, *Spain* 37 H3
Rosalia, *U.S.A.* 108 C5
Rosamond, *U.S.A.* 111 L8
Rosans, *France* 21 D9
Rosário, *Brazil* 125 D10
Rosario, *Baja Calif., Mexico* .. 118 B1
Rosario, *Sinaloa, Mexico* 118 C3
Rosario, *Paraguay* 126 A4

Rosario de la Frontera, *Argentina* 126 B3
Rosario de Lerma, *Argentina* ... 126 A2
Rosario del Tala, *Argentina* ... 126 C4
Rosário do Sul, *Brazil* 127 C5
Rosario, *Mexico* 111 N9
Rosarno, *Italy* 43 D8
Rosas = Roses, *Spain* 38 C8
Roscoe, *U.S.A.* 117 E10
Roscoff, *France* 18 D3
Roscommon, *Ireland* 12 C3
Roscommon □, *Ireland* 12 C3
Roscrea, *Ireland* 12 D4
Rose →, *Australia* 94 A2
Rose Blanche-Harbour Le Cou,
  Canada 105 C8
Rose Pt., *Canada* 102 C2
Rose Valley, *Canada* 103 C8
Roseau, *Dominica* 121 C7
Roseau, *U.S.A.* 112 A7
Rosebery, *Australia* 95 G4
Rosebud, *S. Dak., U.S.A.* 112 D4
Rosebud, *Tex., U.S.A.* 113 K6
Roseburg, *U.S.A.* 108 E2
Rosedale, *U.S.A.* 113 J9
Rosehearty, *U.K.* 13 D6
Roseland, *U.S.A.* 110 G4
Rosemary, *Canada* 102 C6
Rosenberg, *U.S.A.* 113 L7
Rosendaël, *France* 19 A9
Rosenheim, *Germany* 25 H8
Roses, *Spain* 38 C8
Roses, G. de, *Spain* 38 C8
Roseto degli Abruzzi, *Italy* ... 41 F11
Rosetown, *Canada* 103 C7
Rosetta = Rashîd, *Egypt* 80 H7
Roseville, *Calif., U.S.A.* 110 G5
Roseville, *Mich., U.S.A.* 116 D2
Rosewood, *Australia* 95 D5
Roshkhvār, *Iran* 71 C8
Rosières-en-Santerre, *France* ... 19 C9
Rosignano Maríttimo, *Italy* ... 40 E7
Rosignol, *Guyana* 124 B7
Roşiori de Vede, *Romania* 29 F10
Rositsa, *Bulgaria* 45 C11
Rositsa →, *Bulgaria* 45 C9
Roskilde, *Denmark* 11 J6
Roskilde Amtskommune □,
  Denmark 11 J6
Roskovec, *Albania* 44 F3
Roslavl, *Russia* 32 F7
Rosmaninhal, *Portugal* 36 F3
Rosmead, *S. Africa* 88 E4
Røsnæs, *Denmark* 11 J4
Rosolini, *Italy* 43 F7
Rosporden, *France* 18 E3
Ross, *Australia* 95 G4
Ross, *N.Z.* 91 K3
Ross Béthio, *Mauritania* 82 B1
Ross Dependency, *Antarctica* ... 5 D12
Ross I., *Antarctica* 5 D11
Ross Ice Shelf, *Antarctica* 5 E12
Ross L., *U.S.A.* 108 B3
Ross-on-Wye, *U.K.* 15 F5
Ross River, *Australia* 94 C1
Ross River, *Canada* 102 A2
Ross Sea, *Antarctica* 5 D11
Rossall Pt., *U.K.* 14 D4
Rossan Pt., *Ireland* 12 B3
Rossano, *Italy* 43 C9
Rossburn, *Canada* 103 C8
Rosseau, *Canada* 116 A5
Rosseau, L., *Canada* 116 A5
Rosses, The, *Ireland* 12 A3
Rossignol L., *Canada* 104 B5
Rossignol L., *Canada* 105 D6
Rossland, *Canada* 102 D5
Rosslare, *Ireland* 12 D5
Rosslare Harbour, *Ireland* 12 D5
Rosslau, *Germany* 24 D8
Rosso, *Mauritania* 82 B1
Rosso, C., *France* 21 F12
Rossosh, *Russia* 33 G10
Røssvatnet, *Norway* 8 D16
Røst, *Norway* 8 C15
Rosthern, *Canada* 103 C7
Rostock, *Germany* 24 A8
Rostov, *Don, Russia* 33 J10
Rostov, *Yaroslavl, Russia* 32 D10
Rostrenen, *France* 18 D3
Roswell, *Ga., U.S.A.* 115 H3
Roswell, *N. Mex., U.S.A.* 113 J2
Rota, *Spain* 37 J4
Rotan, *U.S.A.* 113 J4
Rotenburg, *Hessen, Germany* ... 24 E5
Rotenburg, *Niedersachsen,*
  Germany 24 B5
Roth, *Germany* 25 F7
Rothaargebirge, *Germany* 24 D4
Rothaargebirge →, *Germany* ... 24 E4
Rothenburg ob der Tauber,
  Germany 25 F6
Rother →, *U.K.* 15 G8
Rothera, *Antarctica* 5 C17
Rotherham, *U.K.* 14 D6
Rothes, *U.K.* 13 D5
Rothesay, *Canada* 105 C6
Rothesay, *U.K.* 13 F3
Roti, *Indonesia* 63 F6
Rotja, Pta., *Spain* 39 G6
Roto, *Australia* 95 E4
Rotondo, Mte., *France* 21 F13
Rotoroa, L., *N.Z.* 91 J4
Rotorua, *N.Z.* 91 H6
Rotorua, L., *N.Z.* 91 H6
Rott →, *Germany* 25 G9
Rottenburg, *Germany* 25 G4
Rottenmann, *Austria* 26 D7
Rotterdam, *Neths.* 17 C4
Rotterdam, *U.S.A.* 117 D10
Rottne, *Sweden* 11 G8
Rottnest I., *Australia* 93 F2

Rottumeroog, *Neths.* 17 A6
Rottweil, *Germany* 25 G4
Rotuma, *Fiji* 96 J9
Roubaix, *France* 19 B10
Roubaix →, *France* 18 C8
Roudnice nad Labem, *Czech Rep.* 26 A7
Rouen, *France* 18 C8
Rouergue, *France* 20 D5
Rouillac, *France* 20 C3
Rouleau, *Canada* 103 C8
Round Mountain, *U.S.A.* 108 G5
Round Mt., *Australia* 95 E5
Round Rock, *U.S.A.* 113 K6
Roundup, *U.S.A.* 108 C9
Rousay, *U.K.* 13 B5
Rouses Point, *U.S.A.* 117 B11
Rouseville, *U.S.A.* 116 E5
Roussillon, *Isère, France* 21 C8
Roussillon, *Pyrénées-Or., France* 20 F6
Rouxville, *S. Africa* 88 E4
Rouyn-Noranda, *Canada* 104 C4
Rovaniemi, *Finland* 8 C21
Rovato, *Italy* 40 C7
Rovenki, *Ukraine* 33 H10
Rovereto, *Italy* 40 C8
Rovigo, *Italy* 41 C8
Rovinj, *Croatia* 41 C10
Rovno = Rivne, *Ukraine* 33 G4
Rovnoye, *Russia* 34 E8
Rovuma = Ruvuma →, *Tanzania* 87 E5
Row'ān, *Iran* 71 C6
Rowena, *Australia* 95 D4
Rowley Shoals, *Australia* 92 C2
Roxa, *Guinea-Biss.* 82 C1
Roxas, *Capiz, Phil.* 61 F5
Roxas, *Isabela, Phil.* 61 C4
Roxas, *Mind. Or., Phil.* 61 E4
Roxboro, *U.S.A.* 115 G6
Roxborough, *Trin. & Tob.* ... 125 J16
Roxburgh, *N.Z.* 91 L2
Roxbury, *U.S.A.* 116 F7
Roxen, *Sweden* 11 F9
Roy, *Mont., U.S.A.* 108 C9
Roy, *N. Mex., U.S.A.* 113 H2
Roy, *Utah, U.S.A.* 108 F7
Royal Canal, *Ireland* 12 C4
Royal Leamington Spa, *U.K.* .. 15 E6
Royal Natal △, *S. Africa* 89 D4
Royal Tunbridge Wells, *U.K.* .. 15 F8
Royale, Isle, *U.S.A.* 112 B10
Royan, *France* 20 C2
Roye, *France* 19 C9
Royston, *U.K.* 15 E7
Rožaj, *Serbia & M.* 44 D4
Różan, *Poland* 31 F8
Rozay-en-Brie, *France* 19 D9
Rozdilna, *Ukraine* 29 D15
Rozhnyativ, *Ukraine* 29 B9
Rozhyshche, *Ukraine* 33 G3
Rožmitál pod Třemšínem,
  Czech Rep. 26 B6
Rožňava, *Slovak Rep.* 27 C13
Rozogi, *Poland* 30 E8
Rozoy-sur-Serre, *France* 19 C11
Roztoczański △, *Poland* 31 H10
Rozzano, *Italy* 40 C6
Rrëshen, *Albania* 44 E3
Rrogozhinë, *Albania* 44 E3
Rtanj, *Serbia & M.* 44 C5
Rtishchevo, *Russia* 34 D6
Rúa = A Rúa, *Spain* 36 C3
Ruacaná, *Namibia* 88 B1
Ruaha △, *Tanzania* 86 D3
Ruahine Ra., *N.Z.* 91 H6
Ruapehu, *N.Z.* 91 H5
Ruapuke I., *N.Z.* 91 M2
Ruâq, W. →, *Egypt* 74 F2
Rub' al Khālī, *Si. Arabia* 75 D4
Rubeho Mts., *Tanzania* 86 D4
Rubezhnoye = Rubizhne, *Ukraine* 33 H10
Rubh a' Mhail, *U.K.* 13 F2
Rubha Hunish, *U.K.* 13 D2
Rubha Robhanais = Lewis, Butt
  of, *U.K.* 13 C2
Rubi, *Spain* 38 D7
Rubicon →, *U.S.A.* 110 G5
Rubicone →, *Italy* 41 D9
Rubik, *Albania* 44 E3
Rubino, *Ivory C.* 82 D4
Rubio, *Venezuela* 124 B4
Rubizhne, *Ukraine* 33 H10
Rubondo △, *Tanzania* 86 C3
Rubtsovsk, *Russia* 52 D9
Ruby L., *U.S.A.* 108 F6
Ruby Mts., *U.S.A.* 108 F6
Rubyvale, *Australia* 94 C4
Rucheng, *China* 59 E9
Ruciane-Nida, *Poland* 30 E8
Rüd Sar, *Iran* 71 B6
Ruda, *Sweden* 11 G10
Ruda Śląska, *Poland* 31 H5
Rudall, *Australia* 95 E2
Rudall →, *Australia* 92 D3
Rudall River △, *Australia* 92 D3
Rüdersdorf, *Germany* 24 C9
Rudewa, *Tanzania* 87 E3
Rudkøbing, *Denmark* 11 K4
Rudky, *Ukraine* 31 J10
Rudna, *Poland* 31 G3
Rudnik, *Bulgaria* 45 D11
Rudnik, *Poland* 31 H9
Rudnik, *Serbia & M.* 44 B4
Rudnya, *Russia* 32 E6
Rudnytsya, *Ukraine* 29 B13
Rudnyy, *Kazakhstan* 52 D7
Rudo, *Bos.-H.* 28 G4
Rudolfa, Ostrov, *Russia* 52 A6
Rudolstadt, *Germany* 24 E7
Rudong, *China* 59 A13
Rudozem, *Bulgaria* 45 E8
Rudyard, *U.S.A.* 114 B3
Rue, *France* 19 B8

Ruenya →, *Africa* 87 F3
Rufa'a, *Sudan* 81 E3
Rufiji →, *Tanzania* 86 D4
Rufino, *Argentina* 126 C3
Rufisque, *Senegal* 82 C1
Rufling Pt., *Br. Virgin Is.* .... 121 e
Rufunsa, *Zambia* 87 F2
Rugao, *China* 59 A13
Rugby, *U.K.* 15 E6
Rugby, *U.S.A.* 112 A5
Rügen, *Germany* 24 A9
Rügen □, *Germany* 24 A9
Rugles, *France* 18 D7
Ruhengeri, *Rwanda* 86 C2
Ruhla, *Germany* 24 E6
Ruhland, *Germany* 24 D9
Ruhnu, *Estonia* 9 H20
Ruhr →, *Germany* 24 D2
Ruhuhu →, *Tanzania* 87 E3
Rui'an, *China* 59 D13
Ruichang, *China* 59 C10
Ruidoso, *U.S.A.* 109 K11
Ruijin, *China* 59 E10
Ruili, *China* 58 E1
Ruivo, Pico, *Madeira* 48 D3
Ruj, *Bulgaria* 44 D6
Rujen, *Macedonia* 44 D6
Ruk, *Pakistan* 68 F3
Rukhla, *Pakistan* 68 C4
Ruki →, *Dem. Rep. of the Congo* 84 E3
Rukwa □, *Tanzania* 86 D3
Rukwa, L., *Tanzania* 86 D3
Rulhieres, C., *Australia* 92 B4
Rum = Rhum, *U.K.* 13 E2
Rum, *Jordan* 74 F4
Rum Cay, *Bahamas* 121 B5
Rum Jungle, *Australia* 92 B5
Ruma, *Serbia & M.* 28 E4
Ruma △, *Kenya* 86 C3
Rumāḥ, *Si. Arabia* 70 E5
Rumania = Romania ■, *Europe* 29 D10
Rumaylah, *Iraq* 70 D5
Rumbêk, *Sudan* 81 F2
Rumburk, *Czech Rep.* 26 A7
Rumford, *U.S.A.* 115 C10
Rumia, *Poland* 30 D5
Rumilly, *France* 21 C9
Rumoi, *Japan* 54 C10
Rumonge, *Burundi* 86 C2
Rumson, *U.S.A.* 117 F11
Rumuruti, *Kenya* 86 B4
Runan, *China* 56 H8
Runanga, *N.Z.* 91 K3
Runaway, C., *N.Z.* 91 G6
Runaway Bay, *Jamaica* ...... 120 a
Runcorn, *U.K.* 14 D5
Rundu, *Namibia* 88 B2
Rungwa, *Tanzania* 86 D3
Rungwa →, *Tanzania* 86 D3
Rungwa △, *Tanzania* 86 D3
Rungwe, *Tanzania* 87 D3
Rungwe, Mt., *Tanzania* 84 F6
Runka, *Nigeria* 83 C6
Runn, *Sweden* 10 D9
Runton Ra., *Australia* 92 D3
Ruokolahti, *Finland* 32 B5
Ruoqiang, *China* 60 C3
Rupa, *India* 67 F18
Rupar, *India* 68 D7
Rupat, *Indonesia* 62 D2
Rupea, *Romania* 29 D10
Rupen →, *India* 68 H4
Rupert, *U.S.A.* 108 E7
Rupert →, *Canada* 104 B4
Rupert B., *Canada* 104 B4
Rupert House = Waskaganish,
  Canada 104 B4
Rupsa, *India* 69 J12
Rur →, *Germany* 24 D1
Rurrenabaque, *Bolivia* 124 F5
Rus →, *Spain* 39 F2
Rusambo, *Zimbabwe* 87 F3
Rusape, *Zimbabwe* 87 F3
Ruschuk = Ruse, *Bulgaria* ... 45 C9
Ruse, *Bulgaria* 45 C9
Ruse □, *Bulgaria* 45 C10
Rusenski Lom △, *Bulgaria* ... 44 C7
Ruşeţu, *Romania* 29 F12
Rush, *Ireland* 12 C5
Rushan, *China* 57 F11
Rushden, *U.K.* 15 E7
Rushmore, Mt., *U.S.A.* 112 D3
Rushville, *Ill., U.S.A.* 112 E9
Rushville, *Ind., U.S.A.* 114 F3
Rushville, *Nebr., U.S.A.* 112 D3
Russas, *Brazil* 125 D11
Russell, *Canada* 103 C8
Russell, *Kans., U.S.A.* 112 F5
Russell, *N.Y., U.S.A.* 117 B9
Russell, *N.Z.* 91 F5
Russell Cave △, *U.S.A.* 115 H3
Russell L., *Man., Canada* 103 B8
Russell L., *N.W.T., Canada* .. 102 A5
Russellkonda, *India* 67 K14
Russellville, *Ala., U.S.A.* 115 H2
Russellville, *Ark., U.S.A.* 113 H8
Russellville, *Ky., U.S.A.* 115 G2
Rüsselsheim, *Germany* 25 F4
Russi, *Italy* 41 D9
Russia ■, *Eurasia* 53 C11
Russian →, *U.S.A.* 110 G3
Russkoye Ustie, *Russia* 4 B15
Rust, *Austria* 27 D9
Rustam Shahr, *Pakistan* 68 F2
Rustavi, *Georgia* 35 K7
Rustenburg, *S. Africa* 88 D4
Ruston, *U.S.A.* 113 J8
Rutana, *Burundi* 86 C3
Rute, *Spain* 37 H6

Ruteng, *Indonesia* 63 F6
Ruth, *U.S.A.* 116 C2
Rutherford, *U.S.A.* 110 G4
Rutland, *U.S.A.* 117 C12
Rutland □, *U.K.* 15 E7
Rutland Water, *U.K.* 15 E7
Rutledge →, *Canada* 103 A6
Rutledge L., *Canada* 103 A6
Rutqa, W. →, *Syria* 73 E9
Rutshuru, *Dem. Rep. of*
  the Congo 86 C2
Ruvo di Púglia, *Italy* 43 A9
Ruvu, *Tanzania* 86 D4
Ruvu →, *Tanzania* 86 D4
Ruvuma □, *Tanzania* 87 E4
Ruvuma →, *Tanzania* 87 E5
Ruwais, *U.A.E.* 71 E7
Ruwenzori, *Africa* 86 B2
Ruwenzori △, *Uganda* 86 B2
Ruya →, *Zimbabwe* 89 B5
Ruyigi, *Burundi* 86 C3
Ruyuan, *China* 59 E9
Ruzayevka, *Russia* 34 C7
Růzhevo Konare, *Bulgaria* ... 45 D8
Ružomberok, *Slovak Rep.* ... 27 B12
Ruzyně, Praha ✈ (PRG),
  Czech Rep. 26 A7
Rwanda ■, *Africa* 86 C3
Ryakhovo, *Bulgaria* 45 C10
Ryan, L., *U.K.* 13 G3
Ryazan, *Russia* 32 E10
Ryazhsk, *Russia* 32 F11
Rybache = Rybachye, *Kazakhstan* 52 E9
Rybachiy, *Russia* 30 C7
Rybachye, *Kazakhstan* 52 E9
Rybinsk, *Russia* 32 C10
Rybinskoye Vdkhr., *Russia* ... 32 C10
Rybnik, *Poland* 31 H5
Rybnitsa = Râbnița, *Moldova* .. 29 C14
Rybnoye, *Russia* 32 E10
Rychnov nad Kněžnou,
  Czech Rep. 27 A9
Rychwał, *Poland* 31 F5
Rycroft, *Canada* 102 B5
Ryd, *Sweden* 11 H8
Rydaholm, *Sweden* 11 H8
Ryde, *U.K.* 15 G6
Rydułtowy, *Poland* 110 D3
Ryczywół, *Poland* 31 G3
Rye, *U.K.* 15 G8
Rye →, *U.K.* 14 C7
Rye Bay, *U.K.* 15 G8
Rye Patch Reservoir, *U.S.A.* . 108 F4
Ryegate, *U.S.A.* 108 C9
Ryki, *Poland* 31 G8
Ryley, *Canada* 102 C6
Rylsk, *Russia* 33 G8
Rylstone, *Australia* 95 E4
Rymarów, *Poland* 31 J8
Ryn, *Poland* 30 E8
Ryn Peski, *Kazakhstan* 35 G9
Ryōtsu, *Japan* 54 E9
Rypin, *Poland* 31 E6
Ryssby, *Sweden* 11 H8
Rysy, *Europe* 27 B13
Ryūgasaki, *Japan* 55 G10
Ryukyu Is. = Ryūkyū-rettō, *Japan* 55 M3
Ryūkyū-rettō, *Japan* 55 M3
Rzepin, *Poland* 31 F1
Rzeszów, *Poland* 31 H8
Rzhev, *Russia* 32 D8

S

Sa, *Thailand* 64 C3
Sa Canal, *Spain* 48 C7
Sa Comillera, *Spain* 48 C7
Sa Dec, *Vietnam* 65 G5
Sa Dragonera, *Spain* 48 B9
Sa Mesquida, *Spain* 48 B11
Sa Pobla, *Spain* 38 F8
Sa Savina, *Spain* 48 C7
Sa'ādatābād, *Fārs, Iran* 71 D7
Sa'ādatābād, *Hormozgān, Iran* .. 71 D7
Sa'ādatābād, *Kermān, Iran* ... 71 D7
Saale →, *Germany* 24 D7
Saaler Bodden, *Germany* 24 A8
Saalfeld, *Germany* 24 E7
Saalfelden, *Austria* 26 D5
Saane →, *Switz.* 25 H3
Saar →, *Europe* 17 E6
Saar-Hunsrück △, *Germany* .. 25 F2
Saarbrücken, *Germany* 25 F2
Saarburg, *Germany* 25 F2
Saaremaa, *Estonia* 9 G20
Saarijärvi, *Finland* 9 E21
Saariselkä, *Finland* 8 B23
Saarland □, *Germany* 25 F2
Saarlouis, *Germany* 25 F2
Sab 'Ābar, *Syria* 70 C3
Saba, *W. Indies* 121 C7
Šabac, *Serbia & M.* 44 B3
Sabah □, *Malaysia* 62 C5
Sabak Bernam, *Malaysia* 65 L3
Sabalāna, Kepulauan, *Indonesia* 63 F5
Sábana de la Mar, *Dom. Rep.* . 121 C6
Sábanalarga, *Colombia* 124 A4
Sabang, *Indonesia* 62 C1
Săbăoani, *Romania* 29 C11
Sabará, *Brazil* 125 G10
Sabarmati →, *India* 68 H5
Sabáttis, *U.S.A.* 117 B10
Sabáudia, *Italy* 42 A6
Saberania, *Indonesia* 63 E9

Sabhah, *Libya* 79 C8
Sabi →, *India* 68 E7
Sabidana, J., *Sudan* 80 D4
Sabie, *S. Africa* 89 D5
Sabinal, *Mexico* 118 A3
Sabinal, *U.S.A.* 113 L5
Sabiñánigo, *Spain* 38 C4
Sabinar, Punta del, *Spain* 39 J2
Sabinas, *Mexico* 118 B4
Sabinas →, *Mexico* 118 B4
Sabinas Hidalgo, *Mexico* 118 B4
Sabine →, *U.S.A.* 113 L8
Sabine L., *U.S.A.* 113 L8
Sabine Pass, *U.S.A.* 113 L8
Sabinov, *Slovak Rep.* 27 B14
Sabinsville, *U.S.A.* 116 E7
Sabirabad, *Azerbaijan* 35 K9
Sablayan, *Phil.* 61 E4
Sable, *Canada* 105 A6
Sable, C., *Canada* 105 D6
Sable, C., *U.S.A.* 107 E10
Sable I., *Canada* 105 D8
Sablé-sur-Sarthe, *France* 18 E6
Sabonkafi, *Niger* 83 C6
Sabor →, *Portugal* 36 D3
Sabou, *Burkina Faso* 82 C4
Sabres, *France* 20 D3
Sabrina Coast, *Antarctica* 5 C9
Sabugal, *Portugal* 36 E3
Sabulubbek, *Indonesia* 62 E1
Sabuncu, *Turkey* 47 B12
Sabzevār, *Iran* 71 B8
Sabzvārān, *Iran* 71 D8
Sac City, *U.S.A.* 112 D7
Sacedón, *Spain* 38 E2
Săcele, *Romania* 29 E10
Sachigo →, *Canada* 104 A2
Sachigo, L., *Canada* 104 B1
Sachkhere, *Georgia* 35 J6
Sachsen □, *Germany* 24 E9
Sachsen-Anhalt □, *Germany* .. 24 D7
Sächsische Schweiz △, *Germany* 24 E9
Sacile, *Italy* 41 C9
Sackets Harbor, *U.S.A.* 117 C8
Sackville, *Canada* 105 C7
Saco, *Maine, U.S.A.* 115 D10
Saco, *Mont., U.S.A.* 108 B10
Sacramento, *U.S.A.* 110 G5
Sacramento →, *U.S.A.* 110 G5
Sacramento Mts., *U.S.A.* 109 K11
Sacramento Valley, *U.S.A.* ... 110 G5
Sacratif, C., *Spain* 37 J7
Săcueni, *Romania* 28 C7
Sada, *Spain* 36 B2
Sada-Misaki, *Japan* 55 H6
Sádaba, *Spain* 38 C3
Sadabad, *India* 68 F8
Sadani, *Tanzania* 86 D4
Sadao, *Thailand* 65 J3
Sadd el Aali, *Egypt* 80 C3
Saddle Mt., *U.S.A.* 110 E3
Sade, *Nigeria* 83 C7
Sadimi, *Dem. Rep. of the Congo* 87 D1
Sadiola, *Mali* 82 C2
Sa'dīyah, Hawr as, *Iraq* 73 F12
Sado, *Japan* 54 F9
Sado →, *Portugal* 37 G2
Sadon, *Burma* 67 G20
Sadon, *Russia* 35 J6
Sadovoye, *Russia* 35 G7
Sadra, *India* 68 H5
Sadri, *India* 68 G5
Sæby, *Denmark* 11 G4
Saegertown, *U.S.A.* 116 E4
Saelices, *Spain* 38 F2
Säffle, *Sweden* 11 F6
Safford, *U.S.A.* 109 K9
Saffron Walden, *U.K.* 15 E8
Safi, *Morocco* 78 B4
Şafiābād, *Iran* 71 B8
Safīd Dasht, *Iran* 71 C6
Safīd Kūh, *Afghan.* 66 B3
Safīd Rūd →, *Iran* 71 B6
Safipur, *India* 69 F9
Safonovo, *Russia* 32 E7
Safranbolu, *Turkey* 72 B5
Saft Rashîn, *Egypt* 80 J7
Şafwân, *Iraq* 70 D5
Sag Harbor, *U.S.A.* 117 F12
Saga, *Japan* 55 H5
Saga □, *Japan* 55 H5
Sagae, *Japan* 54 E10
Sagala, *Mali* 82 C3
Sagamartha = Everest, Mt., *Nepal* 69 F12
Sagamore, *U.S.A.* 116 F5
Sagar, *Karnataka, India* 66 M9
Sagar, *Mad. P., India* 69 H8
Sagara, L., *Tanzania* 86 D3
Sagay, *Phil.* 61 F5
Saginaw, *U.S.A.* 114 D4
Saginaw →, *U.S.A.* 114 D4
Saginaw B., *U.S.A.* 114 D4
Sagleipie, *Liberia* 82 D3
Saglouc = Salluit, *Canada* ... 101 B12
Sagŏ-ri, *S. Korea* 57 G14
Sagone, *France* 21 F12
Sagone, G. de, *France* 21 F12
Sagres, *Portugal* 37 J2
Sagua la Grande, *Cuba* 120 B3
Saguache, *U.S.A.* 109 G10
Saguaro △, *U.S.A.* 109 K8
Saguenay →, *Canada* 105 C5
Sagunt, *Spain* 38 F4
Sagunto = Sagunt, *Spain* 38 F4
Sagwara, *India* 68 H6
Sahaba, *Sudan* 80 D3

Sahagún, *Spain* 36 C5
Saham al Jawlān, *Syria* 74 C4
Sahamandrevo, *Madag.* 89 C8
Sahand, Kūh-e, *Iran* 70 B5
Sahara, *Africa* 78 D6
Saharan Atlas = Saharien, Atlas,
  Algeria 78 B6
Saharanpur, *India* 68 E7
Saharien, Atlas, *Algeria* 78 B6
Saharsa, *India* 69 G12
Sahasinaka, *Madag.* 89 C8
Sahaswan, *India* 69 E8
Sahel, *Africa* 78 E5
Sahel, Canal du, *Mali* 82 C3
Sahibganj, *India* 69 G12
Sāḩilīyah, *Iraq* 70 C4
Sahiwal, *Pakistan* 68 D5
Saḩneh, *Iran* 70 C5
Sahrawi = Western Sahara ■,
  Africa 78 D3
Sahuaripa, *Mexico* 118 B3
Sahuarita, *U.S.A.* 109 L8
Sahuayo, *Mexico* 118 C4
Šahy, *Slovak Rep.* 27 C11
Sai ➝, *India* 69 G10
Sai Buri, *Thailand* 65 J3
Sa'id Bundas, *Sudan* 79 G10
Sa'īdābād = Sīrjān, *Iran* 71 D7
Sa'īdābād, *Iran* 71 B7
Sa'īdīyeh, *Iran* 71 B6
Saidpur, *Bangla.* 67 G16
Saidpur, *India* 69 G10
Saidu, *Pakistan* 69 B5
Saignes, *France* 20 C6
Saigon = Thanh Pho Ho Chi
  Minh, *Vietnam* 65 G6
Saijō, *Japan* 55 H6
Saikai △, *Japan* 55 H4
Saikanosy Masoala, *Madag.* ... 89 B9
Saikhoa Ghat, *India* 67 F19
Saiki, *Japan* 55 H5
Sailana, *India* 68 H6
Saillans, *France* 21 D9
Sailolof, *Indonesia* 63 E8
Saimaa, *Finland* 9 F23
Saimbeyli, *Turkey* 72 D7
Saimen = Saimaa, *Finland* 9 F23
Şa'in Dezh, *Iran* 70 B5
St. Abb's Head, *U.K.* 13 F6
St-Affrique, *France* 20 E6
St-Agrève, *France* 21 C8
St-Aignan, *France* 18 C8
St. Alban's, *Canada* 105 C8
St. Albans, *U.K.* 15 F7
St. Albans, *Vt., U.S.A.* 117 B11
St. Albans, *W. Va., U.S.A.* ... 114 F5
St. Alban's Head, *U.K.* 15 G5
St. Albert, *Canada* 102 C6
St-Amand-en-Puisaye, *France* . 19 E10
St-Amand-les-Eaux, *France* ... 19 B10
St-Amand-Montrond, *France* ... 19 F9
St-Amarin, *France* 19 E14
St-Amour, *France* 19 F12
St-André-de-Cubzac, *France* ... 20 D3
St-André-les-Alpes, *France* ... 21 E10
St. Andrew's, *Canada* 105 C8
St. Andrews, *U.K.* 13 E6
St-Anicet, *Canada* 117 A10
St. Anns B., *Canada* 105 C7
St. Anthony, *Canada* 105 B8
St. Anthony, *U.S.A.* 108 E8
St-Antoine, *Canada* 105 C7
St-Antonin-Noble-Val, *France* . 20 D5
St. Arnaud, *Australia* 95 F3
St-Astier, *France* 20 C4
St-Aubin-du-Cormier, *France* .. 18 D5
St-Augustin, *Canada* 105 B8
St-Augustin ➝, *Canada* 105 B8
St. Augustine, *U.S.A.* 115 L5
St-Aulaye, *France* 20 C4
St. Austell, *U.K.* 15 G3
St-Avold, *France* 19 C13
St. Barbe, *Canada* 105 B8
St-Barthélemy, *W. Indies* 121 C7
St-Béat, *France* 20 F4
St. Bees Hd., *U.K.* 14 C4
St. Bees I., *Australia* 94 J7
St-Benoît-du-Sault, *France* 20 B5
St-Bonnet-en-Champsaur, *France* 21 D10
St-Brevin-les-Pins, *France* 18 E4
St-Brice-en-Coglès, *France* 18 D5
St. Bride's, *Canada* 105 C9
St. Brides B., *U.K.* 15 F2
St-Brieuc, *France* 18 D4
St-Calais, *France* 18 E7
St-Cast-le-Guildo, *France* 18 D4
St. Catharines, *Canada* 116 C5
St. Catherines I., *U.S.A.* 115 K5
St. Catherine's Pt., *U.K.* 15 G6
St-Céré, *France* 20 D5
St-Cergue, *Switz.* 25 J2
St-Cernin, *France* 20 C6
St-Chamond, *France* 21 C8
St. Charles, *Ill., U.S.A.* 114 E1
St. Charles, *Mo., U.S.A.* 112 F9
St. Charles, *Va., U.S.A.* 114 F7
St-Chély-d'Apcher, *France* 20 D7
St-Chinian, *France* 20 E6
St. Christopher-Nevis = St. Kitts
  & Nevis ■, *W. Indies* 121 C7
St-Ciers-sur-Gironde, *France* .. 20 C3
St-Clair, *Mich., U.S.A.* 116 D2
St. Clair, *Pa., U.S.A.* 117 F8
St. Clair ➝, *U.S.A.* 116 D2
St. Clair, L., *Canada* 104 D3
St. Clair, L., *U.S.A.* 116 D2
St. Clairsville, *U.S.A.* 116 F4
St-Claud, *France* 20 C4
St. Claude, *Canada* 103 D9
St-Claude, *France* 19 F12

St. Clears, *U.K.* 15 F3
St-Clet, *Canada* 117 A10
St. Cloud, *Fla., U.S.A.* 115 L5
St. Cloud, *Minn., U.S.A.* 112 C7
St. Cricq, C., *Australia* 93 E1
St. Croix, *U.S. Virgin Is.* 121 C7
St. Croix ➝, *U.S.A.* 112 C8
St. Croix Falls, *U.S.A.* 112 C8
St-Cyprien, *France* 20 F7
St-Cyr-sur-Mer, *France* 21 E9
St. David's, *Canada* 105 C8
St. David's, *U.K.* 15 F2
St. David's Head, *U.K.* 15 F2
St-Denis, *France* 19 D9
St-Dié, *France* 19 D13
St-Dizier, *France* 19 D11
St-Égrève, *France* 21 C9
St. Elias, Mt., *U.S.A.* 100 B5
St. Elias Mts., *N. Amer.* 102 A1
St-Eloy-les-Mines, *France* 19 F9
St-Émilion, *France* 20 D3
St-Étienne, *France* 21 C8
St-Étienne-de-Tinée, *France* .. 21 D10
St-Étienne-du-Rouvray, *France* 18 C8
St. Eugène, *Canada* 117 A10
St. Eustatius, *W. Indies* 121 C7
St-Exupery, Lyon ✈ (LYS),
  France 21 C9
St-Fargeau, *France* 19 E10
St-Félicien, *Canada* 104 C5
St-Florent, *France* 21 F13
St-Florent, G. de, *France* 21 F13
St-Florent-sur-Cher, *France* ... 19 F9
St-Florentin, *France* 19 E10
St-Flour, *France* 20 C7
St. Francis, *U.S.A.* 112 F4
St. Francis ➝, *U.S.A.* 113 H9
St. Francis, C., *S. Africa* 88 E3
St. Francisville, *U.S.A.* 113 K9
St-François, L., *Canada* 117 A10
St-Fulgent, *France* 18 F5
St-Gabriel, *Canada* 104 C5
St. Gallen = Sankt Gallen, *Switz.* 25 H5
St-Galmier, *France* 19 G11
St-Gaudens, *France* 20 E4
St-Gaultier, *France* 18 F8
St-Gengoux-le-National, *France* 19 F11
St-Geniez-d'Olt, *France* 20 D6
St. George, *Australia* 95 D4
St. George, *Canada* 105 C6
St. George, *S.C., U.S.A.* 115 J5
St. George, *Utah, U.S.A.* 109 H7
St. George, C., *Canada* 105 C8
St. George, C., *U.S.A.* 115 L3
St. George Ra., *Australia* 92 C4
St. Georges, *Canada* 105 C8
St-Georges, *France* 20 C5
St. George's, *Canada* 105 C8
St. George's, *Grenada* 121 D7
St. George's B., *Canada* 105 C8
St. George Basin, *N.S.W.,
  Australia* 95 F5
St. George Basin, *W. Austral.,
  Australia* 92 C4
St. George's Channel, *Europe* . 12 E6
St. Georges Hd., *Australia* ... 95 F5
St-Georges-lès-Baillargeaux,
  France 20 B4
St-Germain-de-Calberte, *France* 20 D7
St-Germain-en-Laye, *France* ... 19 D9
St-Germain-Lembron, *France* ... 20 C7
St-Gervais-d'Auvergne, *France* . 19 F9
St-Gervais-les-Bains, *France* .. 21 C10
St-Gildas, Pte. de, *France* ... 18 E4
St-Gilles, *France* 21 E8
St-Girons, *Ariège, France* 20 F5
St-Girons, *Landes, France* 20 E2
St. Gotthard P. = San Gottardo, P.
  del, *Switz.* 25 J4
St. Helena, *Atl. Oc.* 76 H3
St. Helena, *U.S.A.* 108 G2
St. Helena, Mt., *U.S.A.* 110 G4
St. Helena, B., *S. Africa* 88 E2
St. Helens, *Australia* 95 G4
St. Helens, *U.K.* 14 D5
St. Helens, *U.S.A.* 110 D4
St. Helens, Mt., *U.S.A.* 110 D4
St. Helier, *U.K.* 15 H5
St-Herblain, *France* 18 E5
St-Hilaire-du-Harcouët, *France* . 18 D5
St-Hippolyte, *France* 19 E13
St-Hippolyte-du-Fort, *France* .. 20 E7
St-Honoré-les-Bains, *France* ... 19 F10
St-Hubert, *Belgium* 17 D5
St-Hyacinthe, *Canada* 104 C5
St. Ignace, *U.S.A.* 114 C3
St. Ignace I., *Canada* 104 C2
St. Ignatius, *U.S.A.* 108 C6
St-Imier, *Switz.* 25 H2
St. Ives, *Cambs., U.K.* 15 E7
St. Ives, *Corn., U.K.* 15 G2
St-James, *France* 18 D5
St. James, *U.S.A.* 112 D7
St-Jean ➝, *Canada* 105 B7
St-Jean, L., *Canada* 105 C5
St-Jean-d'Angély, *France* 20 C3
St-Jean-de-Braye, *France* 19 E8
St-Jean-de-Luz, *France* 20 E2
St-Jean-de-Maurienne, *France* . 21 C10
St-Jean-de-Monts, *France* 18 F4
St-Jean-du-Gard, *France* 20 D7
St-Jean-en-Royans, *France* ... 21 C9
St-Jean-Pied-de-Port, *France* .. 20 E2
St-Jean-Port-Joli, *Canada* 105 C5
St-Jean-sur-Richelieu, *Canada* . 117 A11
St-Jérôme, *Canada* 104 C5
St. John, *Canada* 105 C6
St. John, *U.S.A.* 113 G5
St. John ➝, *Liberia* 82 D2
St. John ➝, *U.S.A.* 115 C12
St. John, C., *Canada* 105 C8
St. John I., *U.S. Virgin Is.* .. 121 e

St. John's, *Antigua & B.* 121 C7
St. John's, *Canada* 105 C9
St. Johns, *Ariz., U.S.A.* 109 J9
St. Johns, *Mich., U.S.A.* 114 D3
St. Johns ➝, *U.S.A.* 115 K5
St. John's Pt., *Ireland* 12 B3
St. Johnsbury, *U.S.A.* 117 B12
St. Johnsville, *U.S.A.* 117 D10
St-Joseph, *Martinique* .... 120 c
St. Joseph, *La., U.S.A.* 113 K9
St. Joseph, *Mo., U.S.A.* 112 F7
St. Joseph ➝, *U.S.A.* 114 D2
St. Joseph, I., *Canada* 104 C3
St. Joseph, L., *Canada* 104 B1
St-Jovite, *Canada* 104 C5
St-Juéry, *France* 20 E6
St-Julien-Chapteuil, *France* ... 21 C8
St-Julien-de-Vouvantes, *France* 18 E5
St-Julien-en-Genevois, *France* . 19 F13
St-Junien, *France* 20 C4
St-Just-en-Chaussée, *France* .. 19 C9
St-Just-en-Chevalet, *France* ... 20 C7
St. Kitts & Nevis ■, *W. Indies* 121 C7
St. Laurent, *Canada* 103 C9
St-Laurent-de-la-Salanque,
  France 20 F6
St-Laurent-du-Pont, *France* ... 21 C9
St-Laurent-en-Grandvaux, *France* 19 F12
St-Laurent-Médoc, *France* 20 C3
St. Lawrence, *Australia* 94 C4
St. Lawrence, *Canada* 105 C8
St. Lawrence ➝, *Canada* 105 C6
St. Lawrence, Gulf of, *Canada* . 105 C7
St. Lawrence I., *U.S.A.* 100 B3
St. Lawrence Islands △, *Canada* . 117 B9
St. Leonard, *Canada* 105 C6
St-Léonard-de-Noblat, *France* . 20 C5
St-Lewis ➝, *Canada* 105 B8
St-Lô, *France* 18 C5
St-Louis, *France* 19 E14
St-Louis, *Guadeloupe* .... 120 b
St-Louis, *Senegal* 82 B1
St. Louis, *U.S.A.* 112 F9
St. Louis ➝, *U.S.A.* 112 B8
St-Loup-sur-Semouse, *France* .. 19 E13
St. Lucia ■, *W. Indies* ...... 121 f
St. Lucia, L., *S. Africa* 89 D5
St. Lucia Channel, *W. Indies* . 121 D7
St. Maarten ☒, *W. Indies* 121 C7
St. Magnus B., *U.K.* 13 A7
St-Maixent-l'École, *France* ... 20 B3
St-Malo, *France* 18 D4
St-Malo, G. de, *France* 18 D4
St-Mandrier-sur-Mer, *France* .. 21 E9
St-Marc, *Haiti* 121 C5
St-Marcellin, *France* 21 C9
St-Marcouf, Îs., *France* 18 C5
St. Maries, *U.S.A.* 108 C5
St-Martin ☒, *W. Indies* 121 C7
St-Martin, C., *Martinique* .... 120 c
St. Martin, L., *Canada* 103 C9
St-Martin-de-Crau, *France* 21 E8
St-Martin-d'Hères, *France* 21 C9
St-Martin-Vésubie, *France* 21 D11
St. Martins, *Barbados* .... 121 g
St-Martory, *France* 20 E4
St. Mary Pk., *Australia* 95 E2
St. Marys, *Australia* 95 G4
St. Mary's, *Corn., U.K.* 15 H1
St. Mary's, *Orkney, U.K.* 13 C6
St. Marys, *Ga., U.S.A.* 115 K5
St. Marys, *Pa., U.S.A.* 116 E6
St. Mary's, C., *Canada* 105 C9
St. Mary's B., *Canada* 105 C9
St. Marys Bay, *Canada* 105 D6
St-Mathieu, Pte., *France* 18 D2
St. Matthew I., *U.S.A.* 100 B2
St. Maurice ➝, *Canada* 104 C5
St. Mawes, *U.K.* 15 G2
St-Maximin-la-Ste-Baume, *France* 21 E9
St-Médard-en-Jalles, *France* ... 20 D3
St-Méen-le-Grand, *France* 18 D4
St-Mihiel, *France* 19 D12
St. Moritz, *Switz.* 25 J5
St-Nazaire, *France* 18 E4
St. Neots, *U.K.* 15 E7
St-Nicolas-de-Port, *France* 19 D13
St-Niklaas, *Belgium* 17 C4
St-Omer, *France* 19 B9
St-Palais-sur-Mer, *France* 20 C2
St-Pamphile, *Canada* 105 C6
St-Pardoux-la-Rivière, *France* . 20 C4
St-Pascal, *Canada* 105 C6
St. Paul, *Canada* 102 C6
St. Paul, *France* 21 D10
St. Paul, *Minn., U.S.A.* 112 C8
St. Paul, *Nebr., U.S.A.* 112 E5
St-Paul ➝, *Canada* 105 B8
St. Paul ➝, *Liberia* 82 D2
St. Paul, I., *Ind. Oc.* 3 F13
St-Paul-de-Fenouillet, *France* . 20 F6
St. Paul I., *Canada* 105 C7
St-Paul-lès-Dax, *France* 20 E2
St-Péray, *France* 21 D8
St. Peter, *U.S.A.* 112 C8
St. Peter-Ording, *Germany* 24 A4
St. Peter Port, *U.K.* 15 H5
St. Peters, *N.S., Canada* 105 C7
St. Peters, *P.E.I., Canada* ... 105 C7
St. Petersburg = Sankt-Peterburg,
  Russia 32 C6
St. Petersburg, *U.S.A.* 115 M4
St-Philbert-de-Grand-Lieu,
  France 18 E4
St-Pie, *Canada* 117 A12
St-Pierre, *Martinique* .... 120 c
St-Pierre, *St.-P. & M.* 105 C8
St-Pierre, L., *Canada* 104 C5
St-Pierre-d'Oléron, *France* ... 20 C2

St-Pierre-en-Port, *France* 18 C7
St-Pierre-et-Miquelon ☒,
  N. Amer. 105 C8
St-Pierre-le-Moûtier, *France* .. 19 F10
St-Pierre-sur-Dives, *France* ... 18 C6
St-Pol-de-Léon, *France* 18 D3
St-Pol-sur-Mer, *France* 19 A9
St-Pol-sur-Ternoise, *France* ... 19 B9
St-Pons, *France* 20 E6
St-Pourçain-sur-Sioule, *France* . 19 F10
St-Priest, *France* 21 C8
St-Quay-Portrieux, *France* 18 D4
St-Quentin, *Canada* 105 C6
St-Quentin, *France* 19 C10
St-Rambert-d'Albon, *France* ... 21 C8
St-Raphaël, *France* 21 E10
St. Regis, *U.S.A.* 108 C6
St-Renan, *France* 18 D2
St-Saëns, *France* 18 C8
St-Savin, *France* 20 B4
St-Savinien, *France* 20 C3
St. Sebastien, Tanjon' i, *Madag.* 89 A8
St-Seine-l'Abbaye, *France* 19 E11
St-Sernin-sur-Rance, *France* ... 20 E6
St-Sever, *France* 20 E3
St-Siméon, *Canada* 105 C6
St. Simons I., *U.S.A.* 115 K5
St. Simons Island, *U.S.A.* 115 K5
St. Stephen, *Canada* 105 C6
St-Sulpice, *France* 20 E5
St-Sulpice-Laurière, *France* ... 20 B5
St-Sulpice-les-Feuilles, *France* 20 B5
St-Syprien = St-Cyprien, *France* 20 F7
St-Thégonnec, *France* 18 D3
St. Thomas, *Canada* 116 D3
St. Thomas I., *U.S. Virgin Is.* . 121 e
St-Tite, *Canada* 104 C5
St-Tropez, *France* 21 E10
St-Troud = St. Truiden, *Belgium* 17 D5
St. Truiden, *Belgium* 17 D5
St-Vaast-la-Hougue, *France* ... 18 C5
St-Valery-en-Caux, *France* 18 C7
St-Valéry-sur-Somme, *France* .. 19 B8
St-Vallier, *France* 19 F11
St-Vallier-de-Thiey, *France* ... 21 E10
St-Varent, *France* 18 F6
St. Vincent, G., *Australia* 95 F2
St. Vincent & the Grenadines ■,
  W. Indies 121 D7
St-Vincent-de-Tyrosse, *France* . 20 E2
St. Vincent Passage, *W. Indies* 121 D7
St-Vith, *Belgium* 17 D6
St-Vivien-de-Médoc, *France* ... 20 C2
St. Walburg, *Canada* 103 C7
St-Yrieix-la-Perche, *France* ... 20 C5
Ste-Adresse, *France* 18 C7
Ste-Agathe-des-Monts, *Canada* . 104 C5
Ste-Anne, *Guadeloupe* .... 120 b
Ste-Anne, L., *Canada* 105 B6
Ste-Anne-des-Monts-Tourelle,
  Canada 105 C6
Ste-Croix, *Switz.* 25 J2
Ste-Enimie, *France* 20 D7
Ste-Foy-la-Grande, *France* 20 D4
Ste. Genevieve, *U.S.A.* 112 G9
Ste-Hermine, *France* 20 B3
Ste-Livrade-sur-Lot, *France* ... 20 D4
Ste-Marguerite ➝, *Canada* 105 B6
Ste-Marie, *Canada* 105 C5
Ste-Marie, *Martinique* .... 120 c
Ste-Marie-aux-Mines, *France* .. 19 D14
Ste-Maure-de-Touraine, *France* 18 E7
Ste-Maxime, *France* 21 E10
Ste-Menehould, *France* 19 C11
Ste-Mère-Église, *France* 18 C5
Ste-Rose, *Guadeloupe* .... 120 b
Ste. Rose du Lac, *Canada* 103 C9
Ste-Savine, *France* 19 D11
Ste-Sigolène, *France* 21 C8
Saintes, *France* 20 C3
Saintes, Îs. des, *Guadeloupe* .. 120 b
Stes-Maries-de-la-Mer, *France* . 21 E8
Saintfield, *U.K.* 12 B6
Saintonge, *France* 20 C3
Saipan, *Pac. Oc.* 96 F6
Sairang, *India* 67 H18
Sairecábur, Cerro, *Bolivia* 126 A2
Saitama □, *Japan* 55 F9
Saiteli = Kadınhanı, *Turkey* ... 72 C5
Saiţi, *Moldova* 29 D14
Saiyid, *Pakistan* 68 C5
Saja-Besaya △, *Spain* 36 B6
Sajama, *Bolivia* 124 G5
Sajan, *Serbia & M.* 28 E5
Sajó ➝, *Hungary* 28 B5
Sajószentpéter, *Hungary* 28 B5
Sajum, *India* 69 C8
Sak ➝, *S. Africa* 88 E3
Sakaba, *Nigeria* 83 C6
Sakai, *Japan* 55 G7
Sakaide, *Japan* 55 G6
Sakaiminato, *Japan* 55 G6
Sakākah, *Si. Arabia* 70 D4
Sakakawea, L., *U.S.A.* 112 B4
Sakami ➝, *Canada* 104 B4
Sakami, L., *Canada* 104 B4
Sakania, *Dem. Rep. of the Congo* 87 E2
Sakaraha, *Madag.* 89 C7
Sakarya, *Turkey* 72 B4
Sakarya ➝, *Turkey* 72 B4
Sakashima-Guntō, *Japan* 55 M2
Sakassou, *Ivory C.* 82 D3
Sakata, *Japan* 54 E9
Sakchu, *N. Korea* 57 D13
Sakeny ➝, *Madag.* 89 C8
Sakété, *Benin* 83 D5
Sakha □, *Russia* 53 C13
Sakhalin, *Russia* 53 D15

Sakhalinskiy Zaliv, *Russia* 53 D15
Şāki, *Azerbaijan* 35 K8
Šiakiai, *Lithuania* 9 J20
Sakon Nakhon, *Thailand* 64 D5
Sakrand, *Pakistan* 68 F3
Sakri, *India* 69 F12
Sakrivier, *S. Africa* 88 E3
Sakskøbing, *Denmark* 11 K5
Sakti, *India* 69 H10
Sakuma, *Japan* 55 G8
Sakurai, *Japan* 55 G7
Saky, *Ukraine* 33 K7
Sal ➝, *Russia* 35 G5
Sala, *Eritrea* 81 D4
Šal'a, *Slovak Rep.* 27 C10
Sala, *Sweden* 10 E10
Sala ➝, *Eritrea* 81 D4
Sala Consilina, *Italy* 43 B8
Sala-y-Gómez, *Pac. Oc.* 97 K17
Salaberry-de-Valleyfield, *Canada* 117 A10
Salacgrīva, *Latvia* 30 A11
Salada, L., *Mexico* 109 K6
Saladas, *Argentina* 126 B4
Saladillo, *Argentina* 126 D4
Salado ➝, *Buenos Aires,
  Argentina* 126 D4
Salado ➝, *La Pampa, Argentina* 128 D3
Salado ➝, *Santa Fe, Argentina* 126 C3
Salado ➝, *Mexico* 113 M5
Salaga, *Ghana* 83 D4
Šalah, *Syria* 74 C5
Şalāḩ ad Dīn □, *Iraq* 70 C4
Sălaj □, *Romania* 28 C8
Sálakhos, *Greece* 49 C9
Salala, *Liberia* 82 D2
Salala, *Sudan* 80 C4
Salālah, *Oman* 75 D5
Salamanca, *Chile* 126 C1
Salamanca, *Spain* 36 E5
Salamanca, *U.S.A.* 116 D6
Salamanca □, *Spain* 36 E5
Salāmatābād, *Iran* 70 C5
Salamís, *Cyprus* 49 D12
Salamís, *Greece* 46 D5
Salar de Atacama, *Chile* 126 A2
Salar de Uyuni, *Bolivia* 124 H5
Sālard, *Romania* 28 C7
Salas, *Spain* 36 B4
Salas de los Infantes, *Spain* . 36 C7
Salatiga, *Indonesia* 63 G14
Salaverry, *Peru* 124 E3
Salawati, *Indonesia* 63 E8
Salaya, *India* 68 H3
Salayar, *Indonesia* 63 F6
Salazar ➝, *Spain* 38 C3
Salbris, *France* 19 E9
Salcia, *Romania* 29 G9
Sălciua, *Romania* 28 E8
Salcombe, *U.K.* 15 G4
Saldaña, *Spain* 36 C6
Saldanha, *S. Africa* 88 E2
Saldanha B., *S. Africa* 88 E2
Saldus, *Latvia* 9 H20
Saldus □, *Latvia* 30 B9
Sale, *Australia* 95 F4
Salé, *Italy* 40 D5
Sale ➝, *U.K.* 14 D5
Salé, *Morocco* 78 B4
Sale, *U.K.* 14 D5
Salekhard, *Russia* 52 C7
Salem, *India* 66 P11
Salem, *Ill., U.S.A.* 114 F1
Salem, *Ind., U.S.A.* 114 F2
Salem, *Mass., U.S.A.* 117 D14
Salem, *Mo., U.S.A.* 113 G9
Salem, *N.H., U.S.A.* 117 D13
Salem, *N.J., U.S.A.* 114 F8
Salem, *N.Y., U.S.A.* 117 C11
Salem, *Ohio, U.S.A.* 116 F4
Salem, *Oreg., U.S.A.* 108 D2
Salem, *S. Dak., U.S.A.* 112 D6
Salem, *Va., U.S.A.* 114 G5
Salemi, *Italy* 42 E5
Sälen, *Sweden* 10 C7
Salernes, *France* 21 E10
Salerno, *Italy* 43 B7
Salerno, G. di, *Italy* 43 B7
Salford, *U.K.* 14 D5
Salgir ➝, *Ukraine* 33 K8
Salgótarján, *Hungary* 28 B4
Salgueiro, *Brazil* 125 E11
Salibabu, *Indonesia* 63 D7
Salibea = Salybia, *Trin. & Tob.* 125 K15
Salida, *U.S.A.* 106 C5
Salies-de-Béarn, *France* 20 E3
Salihli, *Turkey* 72 C3
Salihorsk, *Belarus* 33 F4
Salima, *Malawi* 85 G6
Salina, *Italy* 43 D7
Salina, *Kans., U.S.A.* 112 F6
Salina, *Utah, U.S.A.* 109 G8
Salina Cruz, *Mexico* 119 D5
Salina di Margherita di Savoia △,
  Italy 43 A9
Salinas, *Brazil* 125 G10
Salinas, *Chile* 126 A2
Salinas, *Ecuador* 124 D2
Salinas, *U.S.A.* 110 J5
Salinas ➝, *Guatemala* 119 D6
Salinas ➝, *U.S.A.* 110 J5
Salinas, B. de, *Nic.* 120 D2
Salinas, Pampa de las, *Argentina* 126 C2
Salinas Ambargasta, *Argentina* 126 B3
Salinas de Hidalgo, *Mexico* .. 118 C4
Salinas Grandes, *Argentina* .. 126 C3
Salinas Pueblo Missions △, *U.S.A.* 109 J10
Saline ➝, *Ark., U.S.A.* 113 J8
Saline ➝, *Kans., U.S.A.* 112 F6
Saline di Trapani e Paceco △,
  Italy 42 E5
Salines, C. de ses, *Spain* ... 48 B10
Salinópolis, *Brazil* 125 D9

Salins-les-Bains, *France* 19 F12
Salir, *Portugal* 37 H2
Salisbury, *U.K.* 15 F6
Salisbury, *Md., U.S.A.* 114 F8
Salisbury I., *Canada* 101 B12
Salisbury, *N.C., U.S.A.* 115 H5
Salisbury Plain, *U.K.* 15 F6
Sălişte, *Romania* 29 E8
Salka, *Nigeria* 83 C5
Şalkhad, *Syria* 74 C5
Salkove, *Ukraine* 29 B14
Salla, *Finland* 8 C23
Sallanches, *France* 21 C10
Sallent, *Spain* 38 D6
Salles, *France* 20 D3
Salles-Curan, *France* 20 D6
Salling, *Denmark* 11 H2
Salliq = Coral Harbour, *Canada* .. 101 B11
Sallisaw, *U.S.A.* 113 H7
Sallom Junction, *Sudan* 80 D4
Salluit, *Canada* 101 B12
Salmås, *Iran* 70 B5
Salmerón, *Spain* 38 E2
Salmo, *Canada* 102 D5
Salmon, *U.S.A.* 108 D7
Salmon ➤, *Canada* 102 C4
Salmon ➤, *U.S.A.* 108 D5
Salmon Arm, *Canada* 102 C5
Salmon Gums, *Australia* 93 F3
Salmon River Mts., *U.S.A.* 108 D6
Salo, *Finland* 9 F20
Salò, *Italy* 40 C7
Salobreña, *Spain* 37 J7
Salome, *U.S.A.* 111 M13
Salon, *India* 69 F9
Salon-de-Provence, *France* 21 E9
Salonica = Thessaloníki, *Greece* . 44 F6
Salonta, *Romania* 28 D6
Salor ➤, *Spain* 37 F3
Salou, *Spain* 38 D6
Salou, C. de, *Spain* 38 D6
Saloum ➤, *Senegal* 82 C1
Salpausselkä, *Finland* 9 F22
Salsacate, *Argentina* 126 C2
Sálvora, I. de, *Spain* 36 C2
Salses, *France* 20 F6
Salsk, *Russia* 35 G5
Salso ➤, *Italy* 42 E6
Salsomaggiore Terme, *Italy* ... 40 D6
Salt, *Spain* 38 D7
Salt ➤, *Canada* 102 B6
Salt ➤, *U.S.A.* 109 K7
Salt L., The, *Australia* 95 E3
Salt Lake City, *U.S.A.* 108 F8
Salt Range, *Pakistan* 68 C5
Salta, *Argentina* 126 A2
Salta □, *Argentina* 126 A2
Saltara, *Italy* 41 E9
Saltash, *U.K.* 15 G3
Saltburn by the Sea, *U.K.* 14 C7
Saltcoats, *U.K.* 13 F4
Saltee Is., *Ireland* 12 D5
Saltfjellet, *Norway* 8 C16
Saltfjorden, *Norway* 8 C16
Saltholm, *Denmark* 11 J6
Saltillo, *Mexico* 118 B4
Salto, *Argentina* 126 C3
Salto, *Uruguay* 126 C4
Salto del Guairá, *Paraguay* ... 127 A5
Salton City, *U.S.A.* 111 M11
Salton Sea, *U.S.A.* 111 M11
Saltpond, *Ghana* 83 D4
Saltsburg, *U.S.A.* 116 F5
Saltsjöbaden, *Sweden* 10 E12
Saluda ➤, *U.S.A.* 115 H5
Salûm, *Egypt* 80 A2
Salûm, Khâlig el, *Egypt* 80 A2
Salur, *India* 67 K13
Saluzzo, *Italy* 40 D4
Salvador, *Brazil* 125 F11
Salvador, *Canada* 103 C7
Salvador, El ■, *Cent. Amer.* .. 120 D2
Salvador, L., *U.S.A.* 113 L9
Salvaterra de Magos, *Portugal* . 37 F2
Sálvora, I. de, *Spain* 36 C2
Salween ➤, *Burma* 67 L20
Salyan, *Azerbaijan* 52 F5
Salybia, *Trin. & Tob.* 125 K15
Salza ➤, *Austria* 26 D7
Salzach ➤, *Austria* 26 C5
Salzburg, *Austria* 26 D6
Salzburg □, *Austria* 26 D6
Salzgitter, *Germany* 24 C6
Salzkotten, *Germany* 24 D4
Salzwedel, *Germany* 24 C7
Sam, *India* 68 F4
Sam Neua, *Laos* 58 G5
Sam Ngao, *Thailand* 64 D2
Sam Rayburn Reservoir, *U.S.A.* . 113 K7
Sam Son, *Vietnam* 64 C5
Sam Teu, *Laos* 64 C5
Sama de Langreo = Langreo, *Spain* 36 B5
Samagaltay, *Russia* 53 D10
Samales Group, *Phil.* 61 J4
Samâlût, *Egypt* 80 B3
Samana, *India* 68 D7
Samana Cay, *Bahamas* 121 B5
Samandağı, *Turkey* 72 D6
Samandıra, *Turkey* 45 F13
Samanga, *Tanzania* 87 D4
Samangān □, *Afghan.* 66 B5
Samangwa, *Dem. Rep. of the Congo* 86 C1
Samani, *Japan* 54 C11
Samanli Dağları, *Turkey* 45 F13
Samar, *Phil.* 61 F6
Samara, *Russia* 34 D10
Samara ➤, *Russia* 34 D10
Samara ➤, *Ukraine* 33 H8
Samaria = Shōmrōn, *West Bank* . 74 C4
Samariá, *Greece* 49 D5

Samariá △, *Greece* 46 F5
Samarinda, *Indonesia* 62 E5
Samarkand = Samarqand, *Uzbekistan* 52 F7
Samarqand, *Uzbekistan* 52 F7
Sāmarrā', *Iraq* 70 C4
Samastipur, *India* 69 G11
Şamaxı, *Azerbaijan* 35 K9
Samba, *Dem. Rep. of the Congo* . 86 C2
Samba, *India* 69 C6
Sambalpur, *India* 67 J14
Sambar, Tanjung, *Indonesia* ... 62 E4
Sambas, *Indonesia* 62 D3
Sambava, *Madag.* 89 A9
Sambawizi, *Zimbabwe* 87 F2
Sambhal, *India* 69 E8
Sambhar, *India* 68 F6
Sambhar L., *India* 68 F6
Sambiase, *Italy* 43 D9
Sambir, *Ukraine* 31 J10
Sambor, *Cambodia* 64 F6
Samborombón, B., *Argentina* ... 126 D4
Sambuca di Sicília, *Italy* 42 E6
Samburu □, *Kenya* 86 B4
Samch'ŏk, *S. Korea* 57 F15
Samch'onp'o, *S. Korea* 57 G15
Same, *Tanzania* 86 C4
Samer, *France* 19 B8
Samfya, *Zambia* 87 E2
Sámi, *Greece* 46 C2
Şamkir, *Azerbaijan* 35 K8
Şamlı, *Turkey* 47 B9
Samnah, *Si. Arabia* 70 E4
Samo Alto, *Chile* 126 C1
Samoa ■, *Pac. Oc.* 91 B13
Samoan Is., *Pac. Oc.* 91 A13
Samobor, *Croatia* 41 C12
Samoëns, *France* 19 F13
Samokov, *Bulgaria* 44 D7
Šamorín, *Slovak Rep.* 27 C10
Samorogouan, *Burkina Faso* 82 C4
Sámos, *Greece* 47 D8
Samoš, *Serbia & M.* 28 E5
Samos, *Greece* 36 C3
Sámos □, *Greece* 47 D8
Samothráki = Mathráki, *Greece* . 49 A3
Samothráki, *Greece* 45 F9
Samoylovka, *Russia* 34 E6
Sampa, *Ghana* 82 D4
Sampacho, *Argentina* 126 C3
Sampalan, *Indonesia* 63 K18
Sampang, *Indonesia* 63 G15
Samper de Calanda, *Spain* 38 D4
Sampéyre, *Italy* 40 D4
Sampit, *Indonesia* 62 E4
Sampit, Teluk, *Indonesia* 62 E4
Samrong, *Cambodia* 64 E4
Samrong, *Thailand* 64 E3
Samsø, *Denmark* 11 J4
Samsø Bælt, *Denmark* 11 J4
Samsun, *Turkey* 72 B7
Samtredia, *Georgia* 35 J6
Samui, Ko, *Thailand* .... 65 b
Samur ➤, *Russia* 35 K9
Samurskiy Khrebet, *Russia* 35 K8
Samusole, *Dem. Rep. of the Congo* 87 E1
Samut Prakan, *Thailand* 64 F3
Samut Songkhram ➤, *Thailand* .. 62 B1
Samwari, *Pakistan* 68 E2
San, *Mali* 82 C4
San ➤, *Cambodia* 64 F5
San ➤, *Poland* 31 H8
San Adrián, *Spain* 38 C3
San Adrián, C. de, *Spain* 36 B2
San Agustin, C., *Phil.* 61 H7
San Agustín de Valle Fértil, *Argentina* 126 C2
San Ambrosio, *Pac. Oc.* 97 K20
San Andreas, *U.S.A.* 110 G6
San Andres, *Phil.* 61 E6
San Andrés, I. de, *Caribbean* . 120 D3
San Andrés del Rabanedo, *Spain* . 36 C5
San Andres Mts., *U.S.A.* 109 K10
San Andrés Tuxtla, *Mexico* 119 D5
San Angelo, *U.S.A.* 113 K4
San Anselmo, *U.S.A.* 110 H4
San Antonio, *Belize* 119 D7
San Antonio, *Chile* 126 C1
San Antonio, *Phil.* 61 D4
San Antonio, *N. Mex., U.S.A.* . 109 K10
San Antonio, *Tex., U.S.A.* 113 L5
San Antonio ➤, *U.S.A.* 113 L6
San Antonio, C., *Argentina* ... 126 D4
San Antonio, C. de, *Cuba* 120 B3
San Antonio, C. de, *Spain* 39 G5
San Antonio, Mt., *U.S.A.* 111 L9
San Antonio de los Baños, *Cuba* . 120 B3
San Antonio de los Cobres, *Argentina* 126 A2
San Antonio Oeste, *Argentina* . 128 E4
San Arcángelo, *Italy* 43 B9
San Ardo, *U.S.A.* 110 J6
San Augustín, *Canary Is.* 48 G4
San Augustine, *U.S.A.* 113 K7
San Bartolomé, *Canary Is.* 48 F6
San Bartolomé de Tirajana, *Canary Is.* 48 G4
San Bartolomeo in Galdo, *Italy* . 43 A8
San Benedetto del Tronto, *Italy* . 41 F10
San Benedetto Po, *Italy* 40 C7
San Benedicto, I., *Mexico* 118 D2
San Benito, *U.S.A.* 113 M6
San Benito ➤, *U.S.A.* 110 J5
San Benito Mt., *U.S.A.* 110 J6
San Bernardino, *U.S.A.* 111 L9
San Bernardino Mts., *U.S.A.* .. 111 L10
San Bernardino Str., *Phil.* ... 61 E6
San Bernardo, *Chile* 126 C1
San Bernardo, I. de, *Colombia* . 124 B3
San Blas, *Mexico* 118 B3

San Blas, Arch. de, *Panama* ... 120 E4
San Blas, C., *U.S.A.* 115 L3
San Bonifacio, *Italy* 41 C8
San Borja, *Bolivia* 124 F5
San Buenaventura = Ventura, *U.S.A.* 111 L7
San Buenaventura, *Mexico* 118 B4
San Carlos = Sant Carles, *Spain* . 48 B8
San Carlos, *Argentina* 126 C2
San Carlos, *Chile* 126 D1
San Carlos, *Baja Calif. S., Mexico* . 118 C2
San Carlos, *Coahuila, Mexico* . 118 B4
San Carlos, *Nic.* 120 D3
San Carlos, *Neg. Occ., Phil.* . 61 F5
San Carlos, *Pangasinan, Phil.* . 61 D4
San Carlos, *Uruguay* 127 C5
San Carlos, *U.S.A.* 109 K8
San Carlos, *Venezuela* 124 B5
San Carlos de Bariloche, *Argentina* 128 E2
San Carlos de Bolívar, *Argentina* . 128 D4
San Carlos de la Rápita = Sant Carles de la Ràpita, *Spain* . 38 E5
San Carlos del Zulia, *Venezuela* . 124 B4
San Carlos L., *U.S.A.* 109 K8
San Cataldo, *Italy* 42 E6
San Celoni = Sant Celoni, *Spain* . 38 D7
San Clemente, *Chile* 126 D1
San Clemente, *Spain* 39 F2
San Clemente, *U.S.A.* 111 M9
San Clemente I., *U.S.A.* 111 N8
San Cristóbal = Es Migjorn Gran, *Spain* 48 B11
San Cristóbal, *Argentina* 126 C3
San Cristóbal, *Dom. Rep.* 121 C5
San Cristóbal, *Venezuela* 124 B4
San Cristóbal de las Casas, *Mexico* . 119 D6
San Damiano d'Asti, *Italy* 40 D5
San Daniele del Friuli, *Italy* . 41 B10
San Diego, *Calif., U.S.A.* 111 N9
San Diego, *Tex., U.S.A.* 113 M5
San Diego, C., *Argentina* 128 G3
San Diego de la Unión, *Mexico* . 118 C4
San Diego International ✈ (SAN), *U.S.A.* 111 N9
San Dimitri, Ras, *Malta* 49 C1
San Dimitri Point = San Dimitri, Ras, *Malta* 49 C1
San Donà di Piave, *Italy* 41 C9
San Estanislao, *Paraguay* 126 A4
San Esteban de Gormaz, *Spain* . 38 D1
San Felice Circeo, *Italy* 42 A6
San Felice sul Panaro, *Italy* . 41 D8
San Felipe, *Chile* 126 C1
San Felipe, *Mexico* 118 A2
San Felipe, *Venezuela* 124 A5
San Felipe ➤, *U.S.A.* 111 M11
San Félix, *Pac. Oc.* 97 K20
San Fernando = Sant Ferran, *Spain* 48 C7
San Fernando, *Chile* 126 C1
San Fernando, *Baja Calif., Mexico* . 118 B1
San Fernando, *Tamaulipas, Mexico* 119 C5
San Fernando, *La Union, Phil.* . 61 C4
San Fernando, *Pampanga, Phil.* . 61 D4
San Fernando, *Spain* 37 J4
San Fernando, *Trin. & Tob.* ... 121 D7
San Fernando, *U.S.A.* 111 L8
San Fernando de Apure, *Venezuela* 124 B5
San Fernando de Atabapo, *Venezuela* 124 C5
San Fernando di Púglia, *Italy* . 43 A9
San Francisco, *Argentina* 126 C3
San Francisco, *U.S.A.* 110 H4
San Francisco ➤, *U.S.A.* 109 K9
San Francisco, C. de, *Colombia* . 122 C3
San Francisco, Paso de, *S. Amer.* . 126 B2
San Francisco de Macorís, *Dom. Rep.* 121 C5
San Francisco del Monte de Oro, *Argentina* 126 C2
San Francisco del Oro, *Mexico* . 118 B3
San Francisco International ✈ (SFO), *U.S.A.* 110 H4
San Francisco Javier = Sant Francesc de Formentera, *Spain* . 48 C7
San Fratello, *Italy* 43 D7
San Gabriel, *Chile* 126 C1
San Gabriel Mts., *U.S.A.* 111 L9
San German, *Puerto Rico* ...... 121 d
San Gimignano, *Italy* 40 E8
San Giórgio di Nogaro, *Italy* . 41 C10
San Giórgio Iónico, *Italy* 43 B10
San Giovanni Bianco, *Italy* ... 40 C6
San Giovanni in Fiore, *Italy* . 43 C9
San Giovanni in Persiceto, *Italy* . 41 D8
San Giovanni Rotondo, *Italy* .. 41 G12
San Giovanni Valdarno, *Italy* . 41 E8
San Giuliano Terme, *Italy* 40 E7
San Gorgonio Mt., *U.S.A.* 111 L10
San Gottardo, P. del, *Switz.* . 25 J4
San Gregorio, *Uruguay* 127 C4
San Gregorio, *U.S.A.* 110 H4
San Ignacio, *Belize* 119 D7
San Ignacio, *Bolivia* 124 G6
San Ignacio, *Mexico* 118 B2
San Ignacio, *Paraguay* 120 C2
San Ignacio ⌓, *Mexico* 118 B2
San Ignacio, L., *Mexico* 118 B2
San Ildefonso, C., *Phil.* 61 C5
San Isidro, *Argentina* 126 C4
San Isidro, *Phil.* 61 H7
San Jacinto, *U.S.A.* 111 M10
San Jaime = Sant Jaume, *Spain* . 48 B11
San Javier, *Misiones, Argentina* . 127 B4
San Javier, *Santa Fe, Argentina* . 126 C4

San Javier, *Bolivia* 124 G6
San Javier, *Chile* 126 D1
San Javier, *Spain* 39 H4
San Jerónimo Taviche, *Mexico* . 119 D5
San Joaquin, *U.S.A.* 110 J6
San Joaquin ➤, *U.S.A.* 110 G5
San Joaquin Valley, *U.S.A.* ... 110 J6
San Jon, *U.S.A.* 113 H3
San Jordi = Sant Jordi, *Spain* . 48 B9
San Jorge, *Argentina* 126 C3
San Jorge, B. de, *Mexico* 118 A2
San Jorge, G., *Argentina* 128 F3
San Jorge, G. de, *Spain* 38 C7
San José, *Costa Rica* 120 E3
San José, *Guatemala* 120 D1
San José, *Mexico* 118 C2
San Jose, *Mind. Occ., Phil.* .. 61 E4
San Jose, *Nueva Ecija, Phil.* . 61 D4
San Jose, *U.S.A.* 110 H5
San Jose ➤, *U.S.A.* 109 J10
San José de Buenavista, *Phil.* . 63 B6
San José de Chiquitos, *Bolivia* . 124 G6
San José de Feliciano, *Argentina* . 126 C4
San José de Jáchal, *Argentina* . 126 C2
San José de Mayo, *Uruguay* 126 C4
San José del Cabo, *Mexico* 118 C3
San José del Guaviare, *Colombia* . 124 C4
San Josep, *Spain* 48 C7
San Juan, *Argentina* 126 C2
San Juan, *Mexico* 118 C4
San Juan, *Phil.* 61 F6
San Juan, *Puerto Rico* .... 121 d
San Juan, *Trin. & Tob.* 125 K15
San Juan □, *Argentina* 126 C2
San Juan ➤, *Argentina* 126 C2
San Juan ➤, *Nic.* 120 D3
San Juan ➤, *U.S.A.* 109 H8
San Juan Bautista = Sant Joan Baptista, *Spain* 48 B8
San Juan Bautista, *Paraguay* .. 126 B4
San Juan Bautista, *U.S.A.* 110 J5
San Juan Bautista Valle Nacional, *Mexico* 119 D5
San Juan Capistrano, *U.S.A.* .. 111 M9
San Juan Cr. ➤, *U.S.A.* 110 J5
San Juan de Alicante, *Spain* .. 39 G4
San Juan de Guadalupe, *Mexico* . 118 C4
San Juan de la Costa, *Mexico* . 118 C2
San Juan de los Morros, *Venezuela* 124 B5
San Juan del Norte, *Nic.* 120 D3
San Juan del Norte, B. de, *Nic.* . 120 D3
San Juan del Río, *Mexico* 119 C5
San Juan del Sur, *Nic.* 120 D2
San Juan I., *U.S.A.* 110 B3
San Juan Island △, *U.S.A.* 110 B3
San Juan Mts., *U.S.A.* 109 H10
San Just, Sierra de, *Spain* ... 38 E4
San Justo, *Argentina* 126 C3
San Kamphaeng, *Thailand* 64 C2
San Lázaro, C., *Mexico* 118 C2
San Lázaro, Sa., *Mexico* 118 C3
San Leandro, *U.S.A.* 110 H4
San Leonardo de Yagüe, *Spain* . 38 D1
San Lorenzo = Sant Llorenç des Cardassar, *Spain* 48 B10
San Lorenzo, *Argentina* 126 C3
San Lorenzo, *Ecuador* 124 C3
San Lorenzo, *Paraguay* 126 B4
San Lorenzo ➤, *Mexico* 118 C3
San Lorenzo, I., *Mexico* 118 B2
San Lorenzo, Mte., *Argentina* . 128 F2
San Lorenzo de la Parrilla, *Spain* . 38 F2
San Lorenzo de Morunys = Sant Llorenç de Morunys, *Spain* . 38 C6
San Lucas, *Bolivia* 124 H5
San Lucas, *Baja Calif. S., Mexico* . 118 B2
San Lucas, *Baja Calif. S., Mexico* . 118 C3
San Lucas, *U.S.A.* 110 J5
San Lucas, C., *Mexico* 118 C3
San Lúcido, *Italy* 43 C9
San Luis, *Argentina* 126 C2
San Luis, *Cuba* 120 B3
San Luis, *Guatemala* 120 C2
San Luis, *Ariz., U.S.A.* 109 K6
San Luis, *Colo., U.S.A.* 109 H11
San Luis □, *Argentina* 126 C2
San Luis, I., *Mexico* 118 B2
San Luis, Sierra de, *Argentina* . 126 C2
San Luis de la Paz, *Mexico* ... 118 C4
San Luis Obispo, *U.S.A.* 111 K6
San Luis Potosí, *Mexico* 118 C4
San Luis Potosí □, *Mexico* 118 C4
San Luis Río Colorado, *Mexico* . 118 A2
San Manuel, *U.S.A.* 109 K8
San Marco, C., *Italy* 42 C1
San Marco Argentano, *Italy* ... 43 C9
San Marco in Lámis, *Italy* 41 G12
San Marcos, *Guatemala* 120 D1
San Marcos, *Mexico* 118 B2
San Marcos, *Calif., U.S.A.* ... 111 M9
San Marcos, *Tex., U.S.A.* 113 L6
San Marino, *San Marino* 41 E9
San Marino ■, *Europe* 41 E9
San Martín, *Antarctica* 5 C17
San Martín, *Argentina* 126 C2
San Martín ➤, *Bolivia* 124 F6
San Martín, L., *Argentina* 128 F2
San Martín de los Andes, *Argentina* 128 E2
San Martín de Valdeiglesias, *Spain* 36 E6
San Mateo = Sant Mateu, *Baleares, Spain* 48 B7
San Mateo = Sant Mateu, *Valencia, Spain* 38 E5
San Mateo, *Phil.* 61 C4
San Mateo, *U.S.A.* 110 H4
San Matías, *Bolivia* 124 G7

San Matías, G., *Argentina* 128 E4
San Miguel = Sant Miguel, *Spain* . 48 B7
San Miguel, *El Salv.* 120 D2
San Miguel, *Panama* 120 E4
San Miguel, *U.S.A.* 110 K6
San Miguel ➤, *Bolivia* 124 F6
San Miguel de Tucumán, *Argentina* 126 B2
San Miguel del Monte, *Argentina* . 126 D4
San Miguel I., *U.S.A.* 111 L6
San Miniato, *Italy* 40 E7
San Nicolás, *Canary Is.* 48 G4
San Nicolas, *Phil.* 61 B4
San Nicolás de los Arroyos, *Argentina* 126 C3
San Nicolas I., *U.S.A.* 111 M7
San Onofre, *U.S.A.* 111 M9
San Pablo, *Bolivia* 126 A2
San Pablo, *Phil.* 61 D4
San Pablo, *U.S.A.* 110 H4
San Páolo di Civitate, *Italy* . 41 G12
San Pedro, *Buenos Aires, Argentina* 126 C4
San Pedro, *Misiones, Argentina* . 127 B5
San Pedro, *Chile* 126 C1
San Pédro, *Ivory C.* 82 E3
San Pedro, *Mexico* 118 C2
San Pedro □, *Paraguay* 126 A4
San Pedro, *Chihuahua, Mexico* . 118 B3
San Pedro ➤, *Nayarit, Mexico* . 118 C3
San Pedro ➤, *U.S.A.* 109 K8
San Pedro, Pta., *Chile* 126 B1
San Pedro, Sierra de, *Spain* .. 37 F4
San Pedro Channel, *U.S.A.* 111 M8
San Pedro de Atacama, *Chile* .. 126 A2
San Pedro de Jujuy, *Argentina* . 126 A3
San Pedro de las Colonias, *Mexico* . 118 B4
San Pedro de Macorís, *Dom. Rep.* . 121 C6
San Pedro del Norte, *Nic.* 120 D3
San Pedro del Paraná, *Paraguay* . 126 B4
San Pedro del Pinatar, *Spain* . 39 H4
San Pedro Mártir, Sierra, *Mexico* . 118 A1
San Pedro Mártir, Sierra, *Mexico* . 118 A1
San Pedro Mixtepec, *Mexico* ... 119 D5
San Pedro Ocampo = Melchor Ocampo, *Mexico* 118 C4
San Pedro Sula, *Honduras* 120 C2
San Pietro, *Italy* 42 C1
San Pietro Vernótico, *Italy* .. 43 B11
San Quintín, *Mexico* 118 A1
San Rafael, *Argentina* 126 C2
San Rafael, *Calif., U.S.A.* ... 110 H4
San Rafael, *N. Mex., U.S.A.* .. 109 J10
San Rafael Mt., *U.S.A.* 111 L7
San Rafael Mts., *U.S.A.* 111 L7
San Ramón de la Nueva Orán, *Argentina* 126 A3
San Remo, *Italy* 40 E4
San Roque, *Argentina* 126 B4
San Roque, *Spain* 37 J5
San Rosendo, *Chile* 126 D1
San Saba, *U.S.A.* 113 K5
San Salvador, *El Salv.* 120 D2
San Salvador, *Spain* 48 B10
San Salvador de Jujuy, *Argentina* . 126 A3
San Salvador I., *Bahamas* 121 B5
San Sebastián = Donostia-San Sebastián, *Spain* 38 B3
San Sebastián, *Argentina* 128 G3
San Sebastián, *Puerto Rico* ... 121 d
San Sebastián de la Gomera, *Canary Is.* 48 F2
San Serra = Son Serra, *Spain* . 48 B10
San Servenino Marche, *Italy* .. 41 E10
San Severo, *Italy* 41 G12
San Simeon, *U.S.A.* 110 K5
San Simon, *U.S.A.* 109 K9
San Stéfano di Cadore, *Italy* . 41 B9
San Stino di Livenza, *Italy* .. 41 C9
San Telmo = Sant Telm, *Spain* . 48 B9
San Telmo, *Mexico* 118 A1
San Tiburcio, *Mexico* 118 C4
San Valentin, Mte., *Chile* 128 F2
San Vicente de Alcántara, *Spain* . 37 F3
San Vicente de la Barquera, *Spain* . 36 B6
San Vicente del Raspeig, *Spain* . 39 G4
San Vincenzo, *Italy* 40 E7
San Vito, *Costa Rica* 120 E3
San Vito, *Italy* 42 C2
San Vito, C., *Italy* 42 D5
San Vito al Tagliamento, *Italy* . 41 C9
San Vito Chietino, *Italy* 41 F11
San Vito dei Normanni, *Italy* . 43 B10
Sana', *Yemen* 75 D3
Sana ➤, *Bos.-H.* 41 C13
Sanaba, *Burkina Faso* 82 C4
Şanâfir, *Si. Arabia* 80 B3
Sanaga ➤, *Cameroon* 83 E6
Sanaloa, Presa, *Mexico* 118 C3
Sananda, *Indonesia* 63 E7
Sanand, *India* 68 H5
Sanandaj, *Iran* 70 C5
Sanandita, *Bolivia* 126 A3
Sanary-sur-Mer, *France* 21 E9
Sanawad, *India* 68 H7
Sancellas = Sencelles, *Spain* . 48 B9
Sancergues, *France* 19 E9
Sancerre, *France* 19 E9
Sancerrois, Collines du, *France* . 19 E9
Sancha He ➤, *China* 58 D6
Sanchahe, *China* 57 B14
Sánchez, *Dom. Rep.* 121 C6
Sanchor, *India* 68 G4
Sancoins, *France* 19 F9
Sancy, Puy de, *France* 20 C6
Sand ➤, *S. Africa* 89 C5
Sand Hills, *U.S.A.* 112 D4
Sand Lakes ⌓, *Canada* 103 B9
Sand Springs, *U.S.A.* 113 G6

Sanda, Japan 55 G7
Sandakan, Malaysia 62 C5
Sandan = Sambor, Cambodia 64 F6
Sandanski, Bulgaria 44 E7
Sandaré, Mali 82 C2
Sandared, Sweden 11 G6
Sandarne, Sweden 10 C11
Sanday, U.K. 13 B6
Sandefjord, Norway 9 G14
Sanders, U.S.A. 109 J9
Sanderson, U.S.A. 113 K3
Sandersville, U.S.A. 115 J4
Sandfire Roadhouse, Australia .. 92 C3
Sandfly L., Canada 103 B7
Sandfontein, Namibia 88 C2
Sandhammaren, C., Sweden .. 11 J8
Sandheads, The, India 69 J13
Sandía, Peru 124 F5
Sandıklı, Turkey 47 C12
Sandila, India 69 F9
Sandnes, Norway 9 G11
Sandnessjøen, Norway 8 C15
Sandoa, Dem. Rep. of the Congo .. 84 F4
Sandomierz, Poland 31 H8
Sândominic, Romania 29 D10
Sandover →, Australia 94 C2
Sandoway, Burma 67 K19
Sandoy, Faroe Is. 8 F9
Sandpoint, U.S.A. 108 B5
Sandray, U.K. 13 E1
Sandringham, U.K. 14 E8
Sandstone, Australia 93 E2
Sandu, China 58 E6
Sandusky, Mich., U.S.A. 116 C2
Sandusky, Ohio, U.S.A. 116 E2
Sandvig, Sweden 11 J8
Sandviken, Sweden 10 D10
Sandwich, C., Australia 94 B4
Sandwich B., Canada 105 B8
Sandwich B., Namibia 88 C1
Sandy, Oreg., U.S.A. 110 E4
Sandy, Pa., U.S.A. 116 E6
Sandy, Utah, U.S.A. 108 F8
Sandy Bay, Canada 103 B8
Sandy Bight, Australia 93 F3
Sandy C., Queens., Australia .. 94 C5
Sandy C., Tas., Australia 95 G3
Sandy Cay, Bahamas 121 B4
Sandy Cr. →, U.S.A. 108 F9
Sandy L., Canada 104 B1
Sandy Lake, Canada 104 B1
Sandy Valley, U.S.A. 111 K11
Sânfjällets △, Sweden 10 B7
Sanford, Fla., U.S.A. 115 L5
Sanford, Maine, U.S.A. 115 D10
Sanford, N.C., U.S.A. 115 H6
Sanford →, Australia 93 E2
Sanford, Mt., U.S.A. 100 B5
Sang-i-Masha, Afghan. 68 C2
Sanga, Mozam. 87 E4
Sanga →, Congo 84 E3
Sangamner, India 66 K9
Sanganeb Atoll △, Sudan 80 D4
Sangar, Afghan. 68 C1
Sangar, Russia 53 C13
Sangar Sarai, Afghan. 68 B4
Sangaredi, Guinea 82 C2
Sangarh →, Pakistan 68 D4
Sangasso, Mali 82 C3
Sangatte, France 19 B8
Sangay, Ecuador 124 D3
Sange, Dem. Rep. of the Congo .. 86 D2
Sangeang, Indonesia 63 F5
Sângeorz-Bâi, Romania 29 C9
Sanger, U.S.A. 110 J7
Sângera, Moldova 29 D13
Sangerhausen, Germany 24 D7
Sanggan He →, China 56 E9
Sanggau, Indonesia 62 D4
Sanghar, Pakistan 68 F3
Sangihe, Kepulauan, Indonesia .. 63 D7
Sangihe, Pulau, Indonesia 63 D7
Sangju, S. Korea 57 F15
Sangkapura, Indonesia 62 F4
Sangkhla, Thailand 64 E2
Sangkulirang, Indonesia 62 D5
Sangla, Pakistan 68 D5
Sangli, India 66 L9
Sangmélima, Cameroon 83 E7
Sangod, India 68 G7
Sangre de Cristo Mts., U.S.A. .. 113 G2
Sangre Grande, Trin. & Tob. .. 125 K15
Sangro →, Italy 41 F11
Sangrur, India 68 D6
Sangudo, Canada 102 C6
Sangue →, Brazil 124 F7
Sangüesa, Spain 38 C3
Sanguinaires, Is., France 21 G12
Sangzhi, China 59 C8
Sanhala, Ivory C. 82 C3
Sanibel, U.S.A. 115 M4
Sanikiluaq, Canada 101 C12
Sanin-Kaigan △, Japan 55 G7
Sanirajak, Canada 101 B11
Sanjawi, Pakistan 68 D3
Sanje, Uganda 86 C3
Sanjiang, China 58 E7
Sanjo, Japan 54 F9
Sankh →, India 69 H11
Sankt Andrä, Austria 26 E7
Sankt Augustin, Germany 24 E3
Sankt Blasien, Germany 25 H4
Sankt Gallen, Switz. 25 H5
Sankt Gallen □, Switz. 25 H5
Sankt Goar, Germany 25 E3
Sankt Ingbert, Germany 25 F3
Sankt Johann im Pongau, Austria .. 26 D6
Sankt Johann in Tirol, Austria .. 26 D5
Sankt Michel = Mikkeli, Finland .. 9 F22
Sankt-Peterburg, Russia 32 C6
Sankt Pölten, Austria 26 C8

Sankt Ulrich = Ortisei, Italy .. 41 B8
Sankt Valentin, Austria 26 C7
Sankt Veit an der Glan, Austria .. 26 E7
Sankt Wendel, Germany 25 F3
Sankt Wolfgang, Austria 26 D6
Sankuru →, Dem. Rep. of the Congo .. 84 E4
Sanliurfa, Turkey 70 B3
Sanlúcar de Barrameda, Spain .. 37 J4
Sanluri, Italy 42 C1
Sânmartin, Romania 29 D10
Sanmen, China 59 C13
Sanmenxia, China 56 G6
Sanming, China 59 D11
Sannaspos, S. Africa 88 D4
Sannicandro Gargánico, Italy .. 41 G12
Sânnicolau Mare, Romania 28 D5
Sannieshof, S. Africa 88 D4
Sannîn, J., Lebanon 74 B4
Sanniquellie, Liberia 82 D3
Sannûr, W. →, Egypt 80 B3
Sanok, Poland 31 J9
Sanquhar, U.K. 13 F5
Sans Souci, Trin. & Tob. .. 125 K16
Sansanding, Mali 82 C3
Sansepolcro, Italy 41 E9
Sansha, China 59 D13
Sanshui, China 59 F9
Sanski Most, Bos.-H. 41 D13
Sansui, China 58 D7
Sant Antoni Abat, Spain 48 C7
Sant Boi de Llobregat, Spain .. 38 D7
Sant Carles, Spain 48 B8
Sant Carles de la Ràpita, Spain .. 38 E5
Sant Celoni, Spain 38 D7
Sant Feliu de Guíxols, Spain .. 38 D8
Sant Feliu de Llobregat, Spain .. 38 D7
Sant Ferran, Spain 48 C7
Sant Francesc de Formentera, Spain .. 48 C7
Sant Jaume, Spain 48 B11
Sant Joan Baptista, Spain 48 B8
Sant Jordi, Ibiza, Spain 48 C7
Sant Jordi, Mallorca, Spain .. 48 B9
Sant Jordi, G. de, Spain 38 E6
Sant Llorenç de Morunys, Spain .. 38 C6
Sant Llorenç del Munt y l'Obac △, Spain 38 D3
Sant Llorenç des Cardassar, Spain .. 48 B10
Sant Mateu, Baleares, Spain .. 48 B7
Sant Mateu, Valencia, Spain .. 38 E5
Sant Miguel, Spain 48 B7
Sant Telm, Spain 48 B9
Sant' Ágata Militello, Italy .. 43 D7
Santa Agnés, Spain 48 B7
Santa Ana, Bolivia 124 F5
Santa Ana, El Salv. 120 D2
Santa Ana, Mexico 118 A2
Santa Ana, U.S.A. 111 M9
Sant' Ángelo Lodigiano, Italy .. 40 C6
Sant' Antíoco, Italy 42 C1
Santa Bárbara, Chile 126 D1
Santa Barbara, Honduras 120 D2
Santa Bárbara, Mexico 118 B3
Santa Bárbara, Spain 38 E5
Santa Barbara, U.S.A. 111 L7
Santa Bárbara, Mt., Spain .. 39 H2
Santa Barbara Channel, U.S.A. .. 111 L7
Santa Barbara I., U.S.A. 111 M7
Santa Catalina, Gulf of, U.S.A. .. 111 N9
Santa Catalina, I., Mexico .. 118 B2
Santa Catalina I., U.S.A. 111 M8
Santa Catarina □, Brazil 127 B6
Santa Catarina, I. de, Brazil .. 127 B6
Santa Caterina di Pittinuri, Italy .. 42 B1
Santa Caterina Villarmosa, Italy .. 43 E7
Santa Cecília, Brazil 127 B5
Santa Clara, Cuba 120 B4
Santa Clara, Calif., U.S.A. .. 110 H5
Santa Clara, Utah, U.S.A. .. 109 H7
Santa Clara, El Golfo de, Mexico 118 A2
Santa Clara de Olimar, Uruguay 127 C5
Santa Clarita, U.S.A. 111 L8
Santa Clotilde, Peru 124 D4
Santa Coloma de Farners, Spain 38 D7
Santa Coloma de Gramenet, Spain 38 D7
Santa Comba, Spain 36 B2
Santa Croce Camerina, Italy .. 43 F7
Santa Croce di Magliano, Italy .. 41 G11
Santa Cruz, Argentina 128 G3
Santa Cruz, Bolivia 124 G6
Santa Cruz, Chile 126 C1
Santa Cruz, Costa Rica 120 D2
Santa Cruz, Madeira 48 D3
Santa Cruz, Phil. 61 D4
Santa Cruz, U.S.A. 110 J4
Santa Cruz →, Argentina .. 128 G3
Santa Cruz de la Palma, Canary Is. 48 F2
Santa Cruz de la Palma ✈ (SPC), Canary Is. 48 F2
Santa Cruz de Mudela, Spain .. 37 G7
Santa Cruz de Tenerife, Canary Is. 48 F3
Santa Cruz del Norte, Cuba .. 120 B3
Santa Cruz del Retamar, Spain 36 E6
Santa Cruz del Sur, Cuba .. 120 B4
Santa Cruz do Rio Pardo, Brazil 127 A6
Santa Cruz do Sul, Brazil .. 127 B5
Santa Cruz I., U.S.A. 111 M7
Santa Cruz Is., Solomon Is. .. 96 J8
Santa Cruz Mts., Jamaica .. 120 a
Santa Domingo, Cay, Bahamas .. 120 B4
Sant' Egídio alla Vibrata, Italy .. 41 F10
Santa Elena, U.S.A. 120 C4
Santa Elena, C., Costa Rica .. 120 D2
Sant' Eufémia, G. di, Italy .. 43 D9
Santa Eulàlia des Riu, Spain .. 48 C8
Santa Fe, Argentina 126 C3

Santa Fe, Spain 37 H7
Santa Fe, U.S.A. 109 J11
Santa Fé □, Argentina 126 C3
Santa Fé do Sul, Brazil 125 H8
Santa Filomena, Brazil 125 E9
Santa Fiora, Italy 41 F8
Santa Gertrudis, Spain 48 C7
Santa Giustina, Italy 41 B9
Santa Inês, Brazil 125 F11
Santa Inés, Spain 37 G5
Santa Inés, I., Chile 128 G2
Santa Isabel, Argentina 126 D2
Santa Isabel, Pico, Eq. Guin. .. 83 E6
Santa Isabel do Morro, Brazil .. 125 F8
Santa Lucía, Corrientes, Argentina 126 B4
Santa Lucía, San Juan, Argentina 126 C2
Santa Lucía, Spain 39 H4
Santa Lucía, Uruguay 126 C4
Santa Lucia Range, U.S.A. .. 110 K5
Santa Magdalena, I., Mexico .. 118 C2
Santa Margarita, Argentina .. 126 D3
Santa Margarita, Spain 48 B10
Santa Margarita, U.S.A. 110 K6
Santa Margarita, I., Mexico .. 118 C2
Santa Margherita, Italy 42 D1
Santa Margherita Ligure, Italy .. 40 D6
Santa María, Argentina 126 B2
Santa Maria, Brazil 127 B5
Santa Maria, Phil. 61 C4
Santa Maria, U.S.A. 111 L6
Santa María →, Mexico .. 118 A3
Santa María, B. de, Mexico .. 118 B3
Santa Maria, C. de, Portugal .. 37 J3
Santa Maria Cápua Vétere, Italy .. 43 A7
Santa Maria da Feira, Portugal .. 36 E2
Santa Maria da Vitória, Brazil .. 125 F10
Santa Maria del Camí, Spain .. 48 B9
Santa Maria di Léuca, C., Italy .. 43 C11
Santa María la Real de Nieva, Spain 36 D6
Santa Marinella, Italy 41 F8
Santa Marta, Colombia 124 A4
Santa Marta, Sierra Nevada de, Colombia .. 124 A4
Santa Marta de Tormes, Spain .. 36 E5
Santa Marta Grande, C., Brazil .. 127 B6
Santa Marta Ortigueira, Ría de, Spain 36 B3
Santa Maura = Levkás, Greece .. 46 C2
Santa Monica, U.S.A. 111 M8
Santa Monica Mts. △, U.S.A. .. 111 L8
Santa Olalla, Huelva, Spain .. 37 H4
Santa Olalla, Toledo, Spain .. 36 E6
Santa Paula, U.S.A. 111 L7
Santa Pola, Spain 39 G4
Santa Ponça, Spain 48 B9
Santa Rita, U.S.A. 109 K10
Santa Rosa, La Pampa, Argentina 126 D3
Santa Rosa, San Luis, Argentina 126 C2
Santa Rosa, Brazil 127 B5
Santa Rosa, Calif., U.S.A. .. 110 G4
Santa Rosa, N. Mex., U.S.A. .. 113 H2
Santa Rosa and San Jacinto Mts. △, U.S.A. .. 111 M10
Santa Rosa de Copán, Honduras 120 D2
Santa Rosa de Río Primero, Argentina 126 C3
Santa Rosa del Sara, Bolivia .. 124 G6
Santa Rosa I., Calif., U.S.A. .. 111 M6
Santa Rosa I., Fla., U.S.A. .. 115 K2
Santa Rosa Range, U.S.A. .. 108 F5
Santa Rosalía, Mexico 118 B2
Santa Sylvina, Argentina 126 B3
Santa Tecla = Nueva San Salvador, El Salv. .. 120 D2
Santa Teresa, Argentina 126 C3
Santa Teresa, Australia 94 C1
Santa Teresa, Mexico 119 B5
Santa Teresa △, Uruguay 127 C5
Santa Teresa di Riva, Italy .. 43 E8
Santa Teresa Gallura, Italy .. 42 A2
Santa Uxía, Spain 36 C2
Santa Vitória do Palmar, Brazil .. 127 C5
Santa Ynez, U.S.A. 111 L6
Santa Ynez Mts., U.S.A. .. 111 L6
Santa Ysabel, U.S.A. 111 M10
Santadi, Italy 42 C1
Santaella, Spain 37 H6
Santai, China 58 B5
Santana, Madeira 48 D3
Sântana, Romania 28 D6
Santana, Coxilha de, Brazil .. 127 C4
Santana do Livramento, Brazil .. 127 C4
Santander, Spain 36 B7
Santander Jiménez, Mexico .. 119 C5
Santanilla, Is., Honduras 120 C3
Santanyí, Spain 48 B10
Santaquin, U.S.A. 108 G8
Santarcángelo di Romagna, Italy .. 41 D9
Santarém, Brazil 125 D8
Santarém, Portugal 37 F2
Santarém □, Portugal 37 F2
Santaren Channel, W. Indies .. 120 B4
Santee, U.S.A. 111 N10
Santee →, U.S.A. 115 J6
Santéramo in Colle, Italy 43 B9
Santerno →, Italy 41 D8
Santhià, Italy 40 C5
Santi-Quaranta = Sarandë, Albania 44 G3
Santiago, Brazil 127 B5
Santiago, Canary Is. 48 F2
Santiago, Chile 126 C1
Santiago, Panama 120 E3
Santiago, Phil. 61 C4
Santiago □, Chile 126 C1
Santiago →, Mexico .. 98 G9
Santiago →, Peru .. 124 D3
Santiago, Punta de, Eq. Guin. .. 83 E6
Santiago de Compostela, Spain .. 36 C2

Santiago de Cuba, Cuba 120 C4
Santiago de los Cabelleros, Dom. Rep. 121 C5
Santiago del Estero, Argentina .. 126 B3
Santiago del Estero □, Argentina 126 B3
Santiago del Teide, Canary Is. .. 48 F3
Santiago do Cacém, Portugal .. 37 G2
Santiago Ixcuintla, Mexico .. 118 C3
Santiago Papasquiaro, Mexico .. 118 C3
Santiaguillo, L. de, Mexico .. 118 C4
Santiguila, Mali 82 C3
Santillana, Spain 36 B6
Santisteban del Puerto, Spain .. 37 G7
Santo Amaro, Brazil 125 F11
Santo Anastácio, Brazil 127 A5
Santo André, Brazil 127 A6
Santo Ângelo, Brazil 127 B5
Santo Antônio do Içá, Brazil .. 124 D5
Santo Antônio do Leverger, Brazil 125 G7
Santo Domingo, Dom. Rep. .. 121 C6
Santo Domingo, Baja Calif., Mexico 118 A1
Santo Domingo, Baja Calif. S., Mexico 118 B2
Santo Domingo, Nic. 120 D3
Santo Domingo de la Calzada, Spain 38 C2
Santo Domingo de los Colorados, Ecuador 124 D3
Santo Domingo Pueblo, U.S.A. .. 109 J10
Santo Stéfano di Camastro, Italy .. 43 D7
Santo Tirso, Portugal 36 D2
Santo Tomás, Mexico 118 A1
Santo Tomás, Peru 124 F4
Santo Tomé, Argentina 127 B4
Santo Tomé de Guayana = Ciudad Guayana, Venezuela .. 124 B6
Santomera, Spain 39 G3
Santoña, Spain 36 B7
Santoríni = Thíra, Greece .. 47 E7
Santos, Brazil 127 A6
Santos, Sierra de los, Spain .. 37 G5
Santos Dumont, Brazil 127 A7
Sanur, Indonesia 63 K18
Sanwer, India 68 H6
Sanxenxo, Spain 36 C2
Sanyuan, China 56 G5
São Bartolomeu de Messines, Portugal 37 H2
São Bernardo do Campo, Brazil .. 127 A6
São Borja, Brazil 127 B4
São Brás de Alportel, Portugal .. 37 H3
São Carlos, Brazil 127 A6
São Cristóvão, Brazil 125 F11
São Domingos, Brazil 125 F9
São Domingos, Guinea-Biss. .. 82 C1
São Francisco, Brazil 125 G10
São Francisco →, Brazil .. 125 F11
São Francisco do Sul, Brazil .. 127 B6
São Gabriel, Brazil 127 C5
São Gonçalo, Brazil 127 A7
Sao Hill, Tanzania 87 D4
São João, Guinea-Biss. 82 C1
São João da Boa Vista, Brazil .. 127 A6
São João da Madeira, Portugal .. 36 E2
São João da Pesqueira, Portugal .. 36 D3
São João del Rei, Brazil 127 A7
São João do Araguaia, Brazil .. 125 E9
São João do Piauí, Brazil .. 125 E10
São Joaquim, Brazil 127 B6
São Joaquim △, Brazil 127 B6
São Jorge, Pta. de, Madeira .. 48 D3
São José do Norte, Brazil 127 C5
São José do Rio Prêto, Brazil .. 127 A6
São José dos Campos, Brazil .. 127 A6
São Leopoldo, Brazil 127 B5
São Lourenço, Brazil 127 A6
São Lourenço →, Brazil .. 125 G7
São Lourenço, Pta. de, Madeira .. 48 D3
São Lourenço do Sul, Brazil .. 127 C5
São Luís, Brazil 125 D10
São Luís Gonzaga, Brazil .. 127 B5
São Marcos →, Brazil .. 125 G9
São Marcos, B. de, Brazil .. 125 D10
São Martinho da Cortiça, Portugal 36 E2
São Mateus, Brazil 125 G11
São Mateus do Sul, Brazil .. 127 B5
São Miguel do Oeste, Brazil .. 127 B5
São Paulo, Brazil 127 A6
São Paulo □, Brazil 127 A6
São Paulo I., Atl. Oc. .. 2 D8
São Paulo de Olivença, Brazil .. 124 D5
São Pedro do Sul, Portugal .. 36 E2
São Roque, Madeira 48 D3
São Roque, C. de, Brazil .. 125 E11
São Sebastião, Brazil 127 A6
São Sebastião do Paraíso, Brazil .. 127 A6
São Teotónio, Portugal 37 H2
São Tomé, São Tomé & Príncipe .. 76 F4
São Tomé, C. de, Brazil .. 127 A7
São Tomé & Príncipe ■, Africa .. 77 F4
São Vicente, Brazil 127 A6
São Vicente, Madeira 48 D2
São Vicente, C. de, Portugal .. 37 H1
Saône →, France 19 G11
Saône-et-Loire □, France .. 19 F11
Saonek, Indonesia 63 E8
Sápai, Greece 45 E9
Sapam, Ao, Thailand .... 65 a
Sapanca, Turkey 72 B4
Saparua, Indonesia 63 E7
Sapele, Nigeria 83 D6
Sapelo I., U.S.A. 115 K5
Sapi △, Zimbabwe 87 F2
Sapiéntza, Greece 46 E3
Sapo △, Liberia 82 D3

Sapone, Burkina Faso 83 C4
Saposoa, Peru 124 E3
Sapotskina, Belarus 30 E10
Sapouy, Burkina Faso 83 C4
Sapphire, Australia 94 C4
Sappho, U.S.A. 110 B2
Sapporo, Japan 54 C10
Sapri, Italy 43 B8
Sapulpa, U.S.A. 113 H6
Saqqez, Iran 70 B5
Sar Dasht, Āzarbāyjān-e Gharbī, Iran 73 D11
Sar Dasht, Khuzestān, Iran .. 71 C6
Sar-e Pol □, Afghan. 66 B4
Sar Gachîneh = Yāsūj, Iran .. 71 D6
Sar Planina, Macedonia 44 E4
Sara, Burkina Faso 82 C4
Sara, Phil. 61 F5
Šara △, Serbia & M. 44 D5
Sara Buri = Saraburi, Thailand .. 64 E3
Sarāb, Iran 70 B5
Sarābādi, Iraq 70 C5
Saraburi, Thailand 64 E3
Saradiya, India 68 J4
Saraféré, Mali 82 B4
Saragossa = Zaragoza, Spain .. 38 D4
Saraguro, Ecuador 124 D3
Sarai Naurang, Pakistan 68 C4
Saraikela, India 69 H11
Saraiu, Romania 29 F13
Sarajevo, Bos.-H. 28 G3
Sarakhs, Turkmenistan 71 B9
Saran, Gunung, Indonesia .. 62 E4
Saranac, L., U.S.A. 117 B10
Saranac Lake, U.S.A. 117 B10
Saranda, Tanzania 86 D3
Sarandë, Albania 44 G3
Sarandí del Yi, Uruguay 127 C4
Sarandí Grande, Uruguay .. 126 C4
Sarangani B., Phil. 61 J6
Sarangani Is., Phil. 61 J6
Sarangarh, India 67 J13
Saransk, Russia 34 C7
Sarapul, Russia 52 D6
Sarasota, U.S.A. 115 M4
Sarata, Ukraine 29 D14
Saratoga, Calif., U.S.A. .. 110 H4
Saratoga, Wyo., U.S.A. .. 108 F10
Saratoga △, U.S.A. 117 D11
Saratoga Springs, U.S.A. .. 117 C11
Saratok, Malaysia 62 D4
Saratov, Russia 34 E7
Sarāvān, Iran 71 E9
Saravane, Laos 64 E6
Sarawak □, Malaysia 62 D4
Saray, Tekirdağ, Turkey .. 45 E11
Saray, Van, Turkey 73 C11
Saraya, Guinea 82 C2
Saraya, Senegal 82 C2
Saraycık, Turkey 47 B11
Sarayköy, Turkey 47 D10
Saraylar, Turkey 45 F11
Sarayönü, Turkey 72 C5
Sarbāz, Iran 71 E9
Sarbīsheh, Iran 71 C8
Sárbogárd, Hungary 28 D3
Sarca →, Italy 40 C7
Sarcelles, France 19 D9
Sarda →, India 67 F12
Sardarshahr, India 68 E6
Sardhana, India 68 E7
Sardina, Pta., Canary Is. 48 F4
Sardinia = Sardegna □, Italy .. 42 B1
Sardis, Turkey 47 C10
Sārdūīyeh = Dar Mazār, Iran .. 71 D8
Saren, Indonesia 63 J18
S'Arenal, Spain 48 B9
Sarentino, Italy 41 B8
Saréyamou, Mali 82 B4
Sargasso Sea, Atl. Oc. .. 97 D20
Sargodha, Pakistan 68 C5
Sarh, Chad 79 G9
Sarhala, Ivory C. 82 D3
Sārī, Iran 71 B7
Sari d'Orcino, France 21 F12
Sária, Greece 47 F9
Sária, India 69 J10
Sariab, Pakistan 68 D2
Sarıbeyler, Turkey 47 B9
Sarıgöl, Turkey 72 C3
Sarıkamış, Turkey 73 B10
Sarikei, Malaysia 62 D4
Sarıköy, Turkey 45 F11
Sarila, India 69 G8
Sarina, Australia 94 C4
Sariñena, Spain 38 D4
Sariwŏn, N. Korea 57 E13
Sarıyar Baraji, Turkey 72 B4
Sarıyer, Turkey 45 E13
Sarju →, India 69 F9
Sark, U.K. 15 H5
Sarkad, Hungary 28 D6
Sarkari Tala, India 68 F4
Şarkışla, Turkey 72 C7
Şarköy, Turkey 45 F11
Sarlat-la-Canéda, France .. 20 D5
Sărmașag, Romania 28 C7
Sărmașu, Romania 29 D9
Sarmi, Indonesia 63 E9
Sarmiento, Argentina 128 F3
Sarmizegetusa, Romania .. 28 E7
Särna, Sweden 10 C7
Sarnano, Italy 41 E10
Sarnen, Switz. 25 J4
Sarnia, Canada 116 D2
Sarno, Italy 43 B7

Sarnthein = Sarentino, *Italy* 41 B8
Särö, *Sweden* 11 G5
Sarolangun, *Indonesia* 62 E2
Saronikós Kólpos, *Greece* 46 D5
Saronno, *Italy* 40 C6
Saros Körfezi, *Turkey* 45 F10
Sárospatak, *Hungary* 28 B6
Sarpsborg, *Norway* 9 G14
Sarracín, *Spain* 36 C7
Sarralbe, *France* 19 D14
Sarre = Saar ➤, *Europe* 17 E6
Sarre, *Italy* 40 C4
Sarre-Union, *France* 19 D14
Sarreborg, *France* 19 D14
Sarreguemines, *France* 19 C14
Sarria, *Spain* 36 C3
Sarrión, *Spain* 38 E4
Sarro, *Mali* 82 C3
Sarstedt, *Germany* 24 C5
Sartène, *France* 21 G12
Sarthe □, *France* 18 D7
Sarthe ➤, *France* 18 E6
Sartilly, *France* 18 D5
Saruhanlı, *Turkey* 47 C9
Sărulești, *Romania* 29 F11
Saruna ➤, *Pakistan* 68 F2
Sárvár, *Hungary* 28 C1
Sarvar, *India* 68 F6
Sarvestān, *Iran* 71 D7
Särvfjället, *Sweden* 10 B7
Sárviz ➤, *Hungary* 28 D3
Sary-Tash, *Kyrgyzstan* 52 F8
Sarych, Mys, *Ukraine* 33 K7
Saryshagan, *Kazakhstan* 52 E8
Sarzana, *Italy* 40 D6
Sarzeau, *France* 18 E4
Sasan Gir, *India* 68 J4
Sasaram, *India* 69 G11
Sasebo, *Japan* 55 H4
Saser, *India* 69 B7
Saskatchewan □, *Canada* 103 C7
Saskatchewan ➤, *Canada* 103 C8
Saskatoon, *Canada* 103 C7
Saskylakh, *Russia* 53 B12
Saslaya △, *Nic.* 120 D2
Sasolburg, *S. Africa* 89 D4
Sasovo, *Russia* 34 C5
Sassandra, *Ivory C.* 82 E3
Sassandra ➤, *Ivory C.* 82 E3
Sássari, *Italy* 42 B1
Sassnitz, *Germany* 24 A9
Sasso Marconi, *Italy* 41 D8
Sassocorvaro, *Italy* 41 E9
Sassoferrato, *Italy* 41 E9
Sasstown, *Liberia* 82 E3
Sassuolo, *Italy* 40 D7
Sástago, *Spain* 38 D4
Sasyk, Ozero, *Ukraine* 29 E14
Sata-Misaki, *Japan* 55 J5
Satadougou, *Mali* 82 C2
Satakunda = Satakunta, *Finland* . 9 F20
Satakunta, *Finland* 9 F20
Satama-Soukoura, *Ivory C.* 82 D4
Satara, *India* 66 L8
Satara, *S. Africa* 89 C5
Satbarwa, *India* 69 H11
Sâtenäs, *Sweden* 11 F6
Säter, *Sweden* 10 D9
Satevó, *Mexico* 118 B3
Satilla ➤, *U.S.A.* 115 K5
Satmala Hills, *India* 66 J9
Satna, *India* 69 G9
Sator, *Bos.-H.* 41 D13
Sátoraljaújhely, *Hungary* 28 B6
Satpura Ra., *India* 66 J10
Satrup, *Germany* 24 A5
Satsuna-Shotō, *Japan* 55 K5
Sattahip, *Thailand* 64 F3
Satu Mare, *Romania* 28 C7
Satu Mare □, *Romania* 28 C8
Satui, *Indonesia* 62 E5
Satun, *Thailand* 65 J3
Saturnina ➤, *Brazil* 124 F7
Sauce, *Argentina* 126 C4
Sauceda, *Mexico* 118 B4
Saucillo, *Mexico* 118 B3
Sauda, *Norway* 9 G12
Sauðarkrókur, *Iceland* 8 D4
Saudi Arabia ■, *Asia* 70 B3
Saugeen ➤, *Canada* 116 B3
Saugerties, *U.S.A.* 117 D11
Saugues, *France* 20 D7
Saugus, *U.S.A.* 111 L8
Saujon, *France* 20 C3
Sauk Centre, *U.S.A.* 112 C7
Sauk Rapids, *U.S.A.* 112 C7
Saulgau, *Germany* 25 G5
Saulieu, *France* 19 E11
Sault, *France* 21 D9
Sault Ste. Marie, *Canada* 104 C3
Sault Ste. Marie, *U.S.A.* 101 D11
Saumlaki, *Indonesia* 63 F8
Saumur, *France* 18 E6
Saunders, *U.S.A.* 91 L3
Saunders I., *Antarctica* 5 B1
Saunders Point, *Australia* 93 E4
Sauri, *Nigeria* 83 C6
Saurimo, *Angola* 84 F4
Sausalito, *U.S.A.* 110 H4
Sauveterre-de-Béarn, *France* .. 20 E3
Sauzé-Vaussais, *France* 20 B4
Savá, *Honduras* 120 C2
Sava, *Italy* 43 B10
Sava ➤, *Serbia & M.* 28 F5
Savage, *U.S.A.* 112 B2
Savage I. = Niue, *Cook Is.* 97 J11
Savage River, *Australia* 95 G4
Savai'i, *Samoa* 91 A12
Savalou, *Benin* 83 D5
Savane, *Mozam.* 87 F4
Savanna, *U.S.A.* 112 D9

Savanna-la-Mar, *Jamaica* ...... 120 a
Savannah, *Ga., U.S.A.* 115 J5
Savannah, *Mo., U.S.A.* 112 F7
Savannah, *Tenn., U.S.A.* 115 H1
Savannah ➤, *U.S.A.* 115 J5
Savannakhet, *Laos* 64 D5
Savant L., *Canada* 104 B1
Savant Lake, *Canada* 104 B1
Săvârşin, *Romania* 28 D7
Savaştepe, *Turkey* 47 B9
Savé, *Benin* 83 D5
Save ➤, *France* 20 E5
Save ➤, *Mozam.* 89 C5
Sāveh, *Iran* 71 C6
Savelugu, *Ghana* 83 D4
Savenay, *France* 18 E5
Saverdun, *France* 20 E5
Săveni, *Romania* 29 C11
Saverne, *France* 19 D14
Savigliano, *Italy* 40 D4
Savigny-sur-Braye, *France* 18 E7
Sávio ➤, *Italy* 41 D9
Savnik, *Serbia & M.* 44 D3
Savo, *Finland* 8 E22
Savoie □, *France* 21 C10
Savona, *Italy* 40 D5
Savona, *U.S.A.* 116 D7
Savonlinna, *Finland* 32 B5
Savolax = Savo, *Finland* 8 E22
Savoy = Savoie □, *France* 21 C10
Savoy, *France* 21 C10
Savsat, *Turkey* 73 B10
Sävsjö, *Sweden* 11 G8
Savur, *Turkey* 70 B4
Sawahlunto, *Indonesia* 62 E2
Sawai, *Indonesia* 63 E7
Sawai Madhopur, *India* 68 G7
Sawang Daen Din, *Thailand* 64 D4
Sawankhalok, *Thailand* 64 D2
Sawara, *Japan* 55 G10
Sawatch Range, *U.S.A.* 109 G10
Sawel Mt., *U.K.* 12 B4
Sawi, *Thailand* 65 G2
Sawla, *Ghana* 82 D4
Sawmills, *Zimbabwe* 87 F2
Sawtooth □, *U.S.A.* 108 D6
Sawtooth Range, *U.S.A.* 108 E6
Sawu, *Indonesia* 63 F6
Sawu Sea, *Indonesia* 63 F6
Saxby ➤, *Australia* 94 B3
Saxmundham, *U.K.* 15 E9
Saxony = Sachsen □, *Germany* .. 24 E9
Saxony, Lower =
Niedersachsen □, *Germany* .. 24 C4
Saxton, *U.S.A.* 116 F6
Say, *Mali* 82 C4
Say, *Niger* 83 C5
Saya, *Nigeria* 83 D5
Sayabec, *Canada* 105 C6
Sayaboury, *Laos* 64 C3
Sayán, *Peru* 124 F3
Sayan, Vostochnyy, *Russia* 53 D10
Sayan, Zapadnyy, *Russia* 53 D10
Saydā, *Lebanon* 74 B4
Sayhandulaan = Oldziyt,
Mongolia 56 B5
Sayhūt, *Yemen* 75 D5
Saykhin, *Kazakhstan* 35 F8
Saylac = Zeila, *Somali Rep.* ... 75 E3
Saynshand, *Mongolia* 60 B6
Sayre, *Okla., U.S.A.* 113 H5
Sayre, *Pa., U.S.A.* 117 E8
Sayreville, *U.S.A.* 117 F10
Sayula, *Mexico* 118 D4
Sayward, *Canada* 102 C3
Sazanit, *Albania* 44 F3
Sázava ➤, *Czech Rep.* 26 B7
Sazin, *Pakistan* 69 B5
Sazlika ➤, *Bulgaria* 45 E9
Scaër, *France* 18 D3
Scafell Pike, *U.K.* 14 C4
Scalea, *Italy* 43 C8
Scalloway, *U.K.* 13 A7
Scalpay, *U.K.* 13 D3
Scandia, *Canada* 102 C6
Scandiano, *Italy* 40 D7
Scandicci, *Italy* 41 E8
Scandinavia, *Europe* 8 E16
Scansano, *Italy* 41 F8
Scapa Flow, *U.K.* 13 C5
Scappoose, *U.S.A.* 110 E4
Scarámia, Capo, *Italy* 43 F7
Scarba, *U.K.* 13 E3
Scarborough, *Trin. & Tob.* 121 D7
Scarborough, *U.K.* 14 C7
Scariff I., *Ireland* 12 E1
Scarp, *U.K.* 13 C1
Scarpe-Escaut △, *France* 19 B10
Scebeli, Wabi ➤, *Somali Rep.* .. 75 G3
Šćedro, *Croatia* 41 E13
Schaal See, *Germany* 24 B6
Schaalsee △, *Germany* 24 B6
Schaffhausen, *Switz.* 25 H4
Schagen, *Neths.* 17 B4
Schaghticoke, *U.S.A.* 117 D11
Schärding, *Austria* 26 C6
Scharhörn, *Germany* 24 B4
Scheessel, *Germany* 24 B5
Scheibbs, *Austria* 26 C8
Schelde ➤, *Belgium* 17 C4
Schell Creek Ra., *U.S.A.* 108 G6
Schellsburg, *U.S.A.* 116 F5
Schenectady, *U.S.A.* 117 D11
Schenevus, *U.S.A.* 117 D10
Scherfede, *Germany* 24 D5
Schesslitz, *Germany* 25 F7
Schiedam, *Neths.* 17 C4
Schiermonnikoog, *Neths.* 17 A6
Schiltigheim, *France* 19 D14
Schio, *Italy* 41 C8
Schiphol, Amsterdam ✈ (AMS),
Neths. 17 B4

Schladming, *Austria* 26 D6
Schlanders = Silandro, *Italy* 40 B7
Schlei ➤, *Germany* 24 A5
Schleiden, *Germany* 24 E2
Schleiz, *Germany* 24 E7
Schleswig, *Germany* 24 A5
Schleswig-Holstein □, *Germany* . 24 A5
Schlüchtern, *Germany* 25 E5
Schmalkalden, *Germany* 24 E6
Schmölln, *Germany* 24 E8
Schneeberg, *Austria* 26 D8
Schneeberg, *Germany* 24 E8
Schneverdingen, *Germany* 24 B5
Schœlcher, *Martinique* .... 120 c
Schoharie, *U.S.A.* 117 D10
Schoharie Cr. ➤, *U.S.A.* 117 D10
Scholls, *U.S.A.* 110 E4
Schönberg,
*Mecklenburg-Vorpommern,
Germany* 24 B6
Schönberg, *Schleswig-Holstein,
Germany* 24 A6
Schönbuch △, *Germany* 25 G5
Schönebeck, *Germany* 24 C7
Schongau, *Germany* 25 H6
Schöningen, *Germany* 24 C6
Schopfheim, *Germany* 25 H3
Schorndorf, *Germany* 25 G5
Schortens, *Germany* 24 B3
Schouten I., *Australia* 95 G4
Schouten Is. = Supiori, *Indonesia* 63 E9
Schouwen, *Neths.* 17 C3
Schramberg, *Germany* 25 G4
Schrankogel, *Austria* 26 D4
Schreiber, *Canada* 104 C2
Schrems, *Austria* 26 C8
Schrobenhausen, *Germany* 25 G7
Schroffenstein, *Namibia* 88 D2
Schroon Lake, *U.S.A.* 117 C11
Schruns, *Austria* 26 D2
Schuler, *Canada* 103 C6
Schumacher, *Canada* 104 C3
Schurz, *U.S.A.* 108 G4
Schuyler, *U.S.A.* 112 E6
Schuylerville, *U.S.A.* 117 C11
Schuylkill ➤, *U.S.A.* 117 G9
Schuylkill Haven, *U.S.A.* 117 F8
Schwabach, *Germany* 25 F7
Schwaben □, *Germany* 25 G6
Schwäbisch-Fränkischer Wald △,
Germany 25 G5
Schwäbisch Gmünd, *Germany* .. 25 G5
Schwäbisch Hall, *Germany* 25 F5
Schwäbische Alb, *Germany* 25 G5
Schwabmünchen, *Germany* 25 G6
Schwalmstadt, *Germany* 24 E5
Schwandorf, *Germany* 25 F8
Schwaner, Pegunungan, *Indonesia* 62 E4
Schwanewede, *Germany* 24 B4
Schwarmstedt, *Germany* 24 C5
Schwarze Elster ➤, *Germany* .. 24 D8
Schwarzenberg, *Germany* 24 E8
Schwarzrand, *Namibia* 88 D2
Schwarzwald, *Germany* 25 G4
Schwaz, *Austria* 26 D4
Schwechat, *Austria* 27 C9
Schwechat, Wien ✈ (VIA),
Austria 27 C9
Schwedt, *Germany* 24 B10
Schweinfurt, *Germany* 25 E6
Schweizer-Reneke, *S. Africa* ... 88 D4
Schwenningen = Villingen-
Schwenningen, *Germany* 25 G4
Schwerin, *Germany* 24 B7
Schweriner See, *Germany* 24 B7
Schwetzingen, *Germany* 25 F4
Schwyz, *Switz.* 25 H4
Schwyz □, *Switz.* 25 H4
Sciacca, *Italy* 42 F6
Scicli, *Italy* 43 F7
Sciliar △, *Italy* 41 B8
Scilla, *Italy* 43 D8
Scilly, Isles of, *U.K.* 15 H1
Scinawa, *Poland* 31 G3
Scione, *Greece* 44 G7
Scioto ➤, *U.S.A.* 114 F4
Scituate, *U.S.A.* 117 D14
Scobey, *U.S.A.* 112 A2
Scone, *Australia* 95 E5
Scone, *U.K.* 13 E5
Scordia, *Italy* 43 E7
Scoresbysund = Ittoqqortoormiit,
Greenland 4 B6
Scornicești, *Romania* 29 F9
Scotia, *Calif., U.S.A.* 108 F1
Scotia, *N.Y., U.S.A.* 117 D11
Scotia Sea, *Antarctica* 5 B18
Scotland, *Canada* 116 C4
Scotland □, *U.K.* 13 E5
Scott, *Antarctica* 5 D11
Scott, C., *Australia* 92 B4
Scott City, *U.S.A.* 112 F4
Scott Glacier, *Antarctica* 5 C8
Scott Is., *Antarctica* 5 C11
Scott Is., *Canada* 102 C3
Scott L., *Canada* 103 B7
Scott Reef, *Australia* 92 B3
Scottburgh, *S. Africa* 89 E5
Scottdale, *U.S.A.* 116 F5
Scottish Borders □, *U.K.* 13 F6
Scottsbluff, *U.S.A.* 112 E2
Scottsboro, *U.S.A.* 115 H3
Scottsburg, *U.S.A.* 114 F3
Scottsdale, *Australia* 95 G4
Scottsdale, *U.S.A.* 109 K7
Scottsville, *Ky., U.S.A.* 115 G2
Scottsville, *N.Y., U.S.A.* 116 C7
Scottville, *U.S.A.* 114 D2
Scranton, *U.S.A.* 117 E9
Scugog, L., *Canada* 116 B6
Sculeni, *Moldova* 29 C12

Scunthorpe, *U.K.* 14 D7
Scuol Schu.s, *Switz.* 25 J6
Scutari = Shkodër, *Albania* 44 D3
Scutari = Üsküdar, *Turkey* 45 F13
Seabrook, L., *Australia* 93 F2
Seaford, *U.K.* 15 G8
Seaford, *U.S.A.* 114 F8
Seaforth, *Australia* 94 J6
Seaforth, *Canada* 116 C3
Seaforth, L., *U.K.* 13 D2
Seaham, *U.K.* 14 C6
Seal ➤, *Canada* 103 B10
Seal L., *Canada* 105 B7
Sealy, *U.S.A.* 113 L6
Searchlight, *U.S.A.* 111 K12
Searcy, *U.S.A.* 113 H9
Searles L., *U.S.A.* 111 K9
Seascale, *U.K.* 14 C4
Seaside, *Calif., U.S.A.* 110 J5
Seaside, *Oreg., U.S.A.* 110 E3
Seaspray, *Australia* 95 F4
Seattle, *U.S.A.* 110 C4
Seattle-Tacoma International ✈
(SEA), *U.S.A.* 110 C4
Sebago, L., *U.S.A.* 117 C14
Sebago Lake, *U.S.A.* 117 C14
Sebastián Vizcaíno, B., *Mexico* . 118 B2
Sebastopol = Sevastopol, *Ukraine* 33 K7
Sebastopol, *U.S.A.* 110 G4
Sebba, *Burkina Faso* 83 C5
Sebderat, *Eritrea* 81 D4
Sébékoro, *Mali* 82 C3
Seben, *Turkey* 72 B4
Sebeş, *Romania* 29 E8
Sebeşului, Munţii, *Romania* 29 E8
Sebewaing, *U.S.A.* 114 D4
Sebezh, *Russia* 32 D5
Sebha = Sabhah, *Libya* 79 C8
Sébi, *Mali* 82 B4
Şebinkarahisar, *Turkey* 73 B8
Sebiş, *Romania* 28 D7
Sebnitz, *Germany* 24 E10
Sebring, *Fla., U.S.A.* 115 M5
Sebring, *Ohio, U.S.A.* 116 F3
Sebringville, *Canada* 116 C3
Sebta = Ceuta, *N. Afr.* 78 A4
Sebuku, *Indonesia* 62 E5
Sebuku, Teluk, *Malaysia* 62 D5
Sečanj, *Serbia & M.* 28 E5
Secchia ➤, *Italy* 40 C8
Sechelt, *Canada* 102 D4
Sechura, Desierto de, *Peru* 124 E2
Seclin, *France* 19 B10
Secondigny, *France* 18 F6
Sečovce, *Slovak Rep.* 27 C14
Secretary I., *N.Z.* 91 L1
Secunderabad, *India* 66 L11
Security-Widefield, *U.S.A.* 112 F2
Sedalia, *U.S.A.* 112 F8
Sedan, *France* 19 C11
Sedan, *U.S.A.* 113 G6
Sedano, *Spain* 36 C7
Sedbergh, *U.K.* 14 C5
Seddon, *N.Z.* 91 J5
Seddonville, *N.Z.* 91 J4
Sedé Boqér, *Israel* 74 E3
Sedeh, *Fārs, Iran* 71 D7
Sedeh, *Khorāsān, Iran* 71 C8
Séderon, *France* 21 D9
Sederot, *Israel* 74 D3
Sédhiou, *Senegal* 82 C1
Sedico, *Italy* 41 B9
Sedlčany, *Czech Rep.* 26 B7
Sedley, *Canada* 103 C8
Sedona, *U.S.A.* 109 J8
Sedova, Pik, *Russia* 52 B6
Sedro Woolley, *U.S.A.* 110 B4
Šeduva, *Lithuania* 30 C10
Sędziszów, *Poland* 31 H7
Sędziszów Małopolski, *Poland* .. 31 H8
Seebad Ahlbeck, *Germany* 24 B10
Seefeld in Tirol, *Austria* 26 D4
Seehausen, *Germany* 24 C7
Seeheim, *Namibia* 88 D2
Seeheim-Jugenheim, *Germany* . 25 F4
Seekoei ➤, *S. Africa* 88 E4
Seeley's Bay, *Canada* 117 B8
Seelow, *Germany* 24 C10
Sées, *France* 18 D7
Seesen, *Germany* 24 D6
Seevetal, *Germany* 24 B6
Seewinkel = Neusiedler See-
Seewinkel △, *Austria* 27 D9
Sefadu, *S. Leone* 82 D2
Seferihisar, *Turkey* 47 C8
Séfeto, *Mali* 82 C3
Sefwi Bekwai, *Ghana* 82 D4
Segamat, *Malaysia* 65 L4
Şegarcea, *Romania* 29 F8
Segbana, *Benin* 83 C5
Segbwema, *S. Leone* 82 D2
Seget, *Indonesia* 63 E8
Segezha, *Russia* 32 B4
Seghe, *Solomon Is.* (not listed)
Segorbe, *Spain* 38 F4
Segou, *Mali* 82 C3
Ségou, *Mali* 82 C3
Segovia = Coco ➤, *Cent. Amer.* . 120 D3
Segovia, *Spain* 36 E6
Segovia □, *Spain* 36 E6
Segré, *France* 18 E6
Segre ➤, *Spain* 38 D5
Segré, *Ivory C.* 82 D3
Séguéla, *Ivory C.* 82 D3
Séguénéga, *Burkina Faso* 83 C4
Seguin, *U.S.A.* 113 L6
Segundo ➤, *Argentina* 126 C3
Segura, Sierra de *Spain* 39 G2
Segura ➤, *Spain* 39 G4

Sehitwa, *Botswana* 88 C3
Sehlabathebe △, *Lesotho* 89 D4
Sehore, *India* 68 H7
Sehwan, *Pakistan* 68 F2
Şeica Mare, *Romania* 29 D9
Seil, *U.K.* 13 E3
Seiland, *Norway* 8 A20
Seilhac, *France* 20 C5
Seiling, *U.S.A.* 113 G5
Seille ➤, *Moselle, France* 19 C13
Seille ➤, *Saône-et-Loire, France* . 19 F11
Sein, Î. de, *France* 18 D2
Seinäjoki, *Finland* 9 E20
Seine ➤, *France* 18 C7
Seine, B. de la, *France* 18 C6
Seine-et-Marne □, *France* 19 D10
Seine-Maritime □, *France* 18 C7
Seine-St-Denis □, *France* 19 D9
Seini, *Romania* 29 C8
Seirijai, *Lithuania* 30 D10
Seistan = Sīstān, *Asia* 71 D9
Seistan, Daryācheh-ye = Sīstān,
Daryācheh-ye, *Iran* 71 D9
Sejerø, *Denmark* 11 J5
Sejerø Bugt, *Denmark* 11 J5
Seka, *Ethiopia* 81 F4
Sekayu, *Indonesia* 62 E2
Seke, *Tanzania* 86 C3
Sekenke, *Tanzania* 86 C3
Seki, *Turkey* 47 E11
Sekondi-Takoradi, *Ghana* 82 E4
Sekota, *Ethiopia* 81 E4
Seksna, *Russia* 32 C10
Sekudai, *Malaysia* .... 65 d
Sekuma, *Botswana* 88 C3
Selah, *U.S.A.* 108 C3
Selama, *Malaysia* 65 K3
Selárgius, *Italy* 42 C2
Selaru, *Indonesia* 63 F8
Selatan, Selat, *Malaysia* ...... 65 c
Selb, *Germany* 25 E8
Selby, *U.K.* 14 D6
Selby, *U.S.A.* 112 C4
Selca, *Croatia* 41 E13
Selçuk, *Turkey* 47 D9
Selden, *U.S.A.* 112 F4
Sele ➤, *Italy* 43 B7
Selebi-Pikwe, *Botswana* 89 C4
Selemdzha ➤, *Russia* 53 D13
Selendi, *Manisa, Turkey* 47 C10
Selendi, *Manisa, Turkey* 47 C9
Selenga = Selenge Mörön ➤,
Asia 60 A5
Selenge Mörön ➤, *Asia* 60 A5
Selenicë, *Albania* 44 F3
Selenter See, *Germany* 24 A6
Sélestat, *France* 19 D14
Seletan, Tanjung, *Indonesia* 62 E4
Selevac, *Serbia & M.* 44 B4
Sélibabi, *Mauritania* 82 B2
Seliger, Ozero, *Russia* 32 D7
Seligman, *U.S.A.* 109 J7
Şelim, *Turkey* 73 B10
Selīma, El Wâhât el, *Sudan* 80 C2
Selimiye, *Turkey* 47 D9
Selinda Spillway ➤, *Botswana* . 88 B3
Selinoús, *Greece* 46 D3
Selinsgrove, *U.S.A.* 116 F8
Selizharovo, *Russia* 32 D7
Selkirk, *Canada* 103 C9
Selkirk, *U.K.* 13 F6
Selkirk I. = Horse I., *Canada* .. 103 C9
Selkirk Mts., *Canada* 100 C8
Sellafield, *U.K.* 14 C4
Sellama, *Sudan* 81 E2
Selliá, *Greece* 49 D6
Sellières, *France* 19 F12
Sells, *U.S.A.* 109 L8
Sellye, *Hungary* 28 E2
Selma, *Ala., U.S.A.* 115 J2
Selma, *Calif., U.S.A.* 110 J7
Selma, *N.C., U.S.A.* 115 H6
Selmer, *U.S.A.* 115 H1
Selongey, *France* 19 E12
Selous ➤, *Tanzania* 88 D2
Selowandoma Falls, *Zimbabwe* . 87 G3
Selpele, *Indonesia* 63 E8
Selsey Bill, *U.K.* 15 G7
Seltso, *Russia* 32 F8
Seltz, *France* 19 D15
Selu, *Indonesia* 63 F8
Sélune ➤, *France* 18 D5
Selva = La Selva del Camp, *Spain* 38 D6
Selva, *Argentina* 126 B3
Selva Lancandona = Montes
Azules △, *Mexico* 119 D6
Selvas, *Brazil* 124 E5
Selwyn L., *Canada* 103 B8
Selwyn Mts., *Canada* 100 B6
Selwyn Ra., *Australia* 94 C3
Selyatyn, *Ukraine* 29 C10
Seman ➤, *Albania* 44 F3
Semarang, *Indonesia* 63 G14
Sembabule, *Uganda* 86 C3
Sembawang, *Singapore* .... 65 d
Sembung, *Indonesia* 63 J18
Şemdinli, *Turkey* 73 D11
Sémé, *Senegal* 82 B2
Semeih, *Sudan* 81 E3
Semenanjung Blambangan,
Indonesia 63 K17
Semenov, *Russia* 34 B7
Semenovka, Chernihiv, *Ukraine* . 33 F7
Semenovka, Kremenchuk,
Ukraine 33 H7
Semeru, *Indonesia* 63 H15
Semey, *Kazakhstan* 52 D9
Semikarakorskiy, *Russia* 35 G5
Semiluki, *Russia* 33 G10
Seminoe Reservoir, *U.S.A.* 108 F10

Seminole, Okla., U.S.A. 113 H6
Seminole, Tex., U.S.A. 113 J3
Seminole Draw →, U.S.A. 113 J3
Semipalatinsk = Semey, Kazakhstan 52 D9
Semirara Is., Phil. 61 F4
Semitau, Indonesia 62 D4
Semiyarka, Kazakhstan 52 D8
Semiyarskoye = Semiyarka, Kazakhstan 52 D8
Semmering P., Austria 26 D8
Semnān, Iran 71 C7
Semnān □, Iran 71 C7
Semporna, Malaysia 63 D5
Semuda, Indonesia 62 E4
Semur-en-Auxois, France 19 E11
Sen →, Cambodia 62 B3
Senā, Iran 71 D6
Sena, Mozam. 87 F4
Sena Madureira, Brazil 124 E5
Senador Pompeu, Brazil 125 E11
Senaki, Georgia 35 J6
Senang, Pulau, Singapore .... 65 d
Senanga, Zambia 85 H4
Senatobia, U.S.A. 113 H10
Sencelles, Spain 48 B9
Sendafa, Ethiopia 81 F4
Sendai, Kagoshima, Japan 55 J5
Sendai, Miyagi, Japan 54 E10
Sendai-Wan, Japan 54 E10
Senden, Bayern, Germany 25 G6
Senden, Nordrhein-Westfalen, Germany 24 D3
Sendhwa, India 68 J6
Sene →, Ghana 83 D4
Senec, Slovak Rep. 27 C10
Seneca, U.S.A. 115 H4
Seneca Falls, U.S.A. 117 D8
Seneca L., U.S.A. 116 D8
Senecaville L., U.S.A. 116 G3
Senegal ■, W. Afr. 82 C2
Sénégal →, W. Afr. 82 B1
Senegambia, Africa 76 E2
Senekal, S. Africa 89 D4
Senftenberg, Germany 24 D10
Senga Hill, Zambia 87 D3
Senge Khambab = Indus →, Pakistan 68 G2
Sengiley, Russia 34 D9
Sengua →, Zimbabwe 87 F2
Senhor-do-Bonfim, Brazil 125 F10
Senica, Slovak Rep. 27 C10
Senigállia, Italy 41 E10
Senio →, Italy 41 D9
Senirkent, Turkey 47 C12
Senise, Italy 43 B9
Senj, Croatia 41 D11
Senja, Norway 8 B17
Senkaku-Shotō, Japan 55 L1
Senkuang, Indonesia .... 65 d
Senlis, France 19 C9
Senmonorom, Cambodia 64 F6
Sennār, Sudan 81 E3
Sennar □, Sudan 81 E3
Senneterre, Canada 104 C4
Senno, Belarus 32 E5
Sénnori, Italy 42 B1
Seno, Laos 64 D5
Senonches, France 18 D8
Senorbì, Italy 42 C2
Senožeče, Slovenia 41 C11
Sens, France 19 D10
Senta, Serbia & M. 28 E5
Sentani, Indonesia 63 E10
Sentery = Lubao, Dem. Rep. of the Congo 86 D2
Sentinel, U.S.A. 109 K7
Šentjur, Slovenia 41 B12
Sentosa, Singapore .... 65 d
Senya Beraku, Ghana 83 D4
Seo de Urgel = La Seu d'Urgell, Spain 38 C6
Seohara, India 69 E8
Seonath →, India 69 J10
Seondha, India 69 F8
Seoni, India 69 H8
Seoni Malwa, India 68 H8
Seoul = Sŏul, S. Korea 57 F14
Sepīdān, Iran 71 D7
Sepo-ri, N. Korea 57 E14
Sępólno Krajeńskie, Poland 30 E4
Sepone, Laos 64 D6
Sępopol, Poland 30 D8
Sept-Îles, Canada 105 B6
Septemvri, Bulgaria 45 D8
Sepúlveda, Spain 36 D7
Sequeros, Spain 36 E4
Sequim, U.S.A. 110 B3
Sequoia △, U.S.A. 110 J8
Serafimovich, Russia 34 F6
Seraing, Belgium 17 D5
Serakhis →, Cyprus 49 D11
Seram, Indonesia 63 E7
Seram Sea, Indonesia 63 E7
Seranantsara, Madag. 89 B8
Serang, Indonesia 63 G12
Serangoon, Singapore .... 65 d
Serasan, Indonesia 62 D3
Seravezza, Italy 40 E7
Şerbettar, Turkey 45 E10
Serbia □, Serbia & M. 44 C4
Serbia & Montenegro ■, Europe 44 C4
Şercaia, Romania 29 E10
Serdo, Ethiopia 81 E5
Serdobsk, Russia 34 D7
Sered', Slovak Rep. 27 C10
Seredka, Russia 32 C5
Serednye, Ukraine 29
Şereflikoçhisar, Turkey 72 C5
Seregno, Italy 40 C6
Seremban, Malaysia 65 L3

Serengeti △, Tanzania 86 C3
Serengeti Plain, Tanzania 86 C4
Serenje, Zambia 87 E3
Seret →, Ukraine 29 B10
Sereth = Siret →, Romania 29 E12
Sergach, Russia 34 C7
Sergen, Turkey 45 E11
Sergino, Russia 52 C7
Sergipe □, Brazil 125 F11
Sergiyev Posad, Russia 32 D10
Seria, Brunei 62 D4
Serian, Malaysia 62 D4
Seriate, Italy 40 C6
Seribu, Kepulauan, Indonesia 62 F3
Sérifontaine, France 19 C8
Sérifos, Greece 46 D6
Sérignan, France 20 E7
Sérigny →, Canada 105 A6
Serik, Turkey 72 D4
Seringapatam Reef, Australia 92 B3
Serinhisar, Turkey 47 D11
Seririt, Indonesia 63 J17
Sermaize-les-Bains, France 19 D11
Sermata, Indonesia 63 F7
Sermersuaq, Greenland 4 B4
Sérmide, Italy 41 D8
Sernovodsk, Russia 34 D10
Sernur, Russia 34 B9
Serock, Poland 31 F8
Serón, Spain 39 H2
Seròs, Spain 38 D5
Serov, Russia 52 D7
Serowe, Botswana 88 C4
Serpa, Portugal 37 H3
Serpeddí, Punta, Italy 42 C2
Serpentara, Italy 42 C2
Serpentine Lakes, Australia 93 E4
Serpent's Mouth = Sierpe, Bocas de la, Venezuela 125 L15
Serpis →, Spain 39 G4
Serpneve, Ukraine 29 D14
Serpukhov, Russia 32 E9
Serra da Estrela △, Portugal 36 E3
Serra de Outes, Spain 36 C2
Serra do Navio, Brazil 125 C8
Serra San Bruno, Italy 43 D9
Serradilla, Spain 36 F4
Sérrai, Greece 44 E7
Sérrai □, Greece 44 E7
Serramanna, Italy 42 C1
Serranía San Luís △, Paraguay 126 A4
Serras d'Aire e Candeeiros △, Portugal 37 F2
Serravalle Scrívia, Italy 40 D5
Serre-Ponçon, L. de, France 21 D10
Serres, France 21 D9
Serrezuela, Argentina 126 C2
Serrinha, Brazil 125 F11
Sertã, Portugal 36 F2
Sertanópolis, Brazil 127 A5
Sêrtar, China 58 A3
Serua, Indonesia 63 F8
Serui, Indonesia 63 E9
Serule, Botswana 88 C4
Sérvia, Greece 44 F6
Serzedelo, Portugal 36 D2
Ses Salines, Spain 48 B10
Sese Is., Uganda 86 C3
Sesepe, Indonesia 63 E7
Sesfontein, Namibia 88 B1
Sesheke, Zambia 88 B3
Sésia →, Italy 40 C5
Sesimbra, Portugal 37 G1
S'Espalmador, Spain 48 C7
S'Espardell, Spain 48 C7
Sessa Aurunca, Italy 42 A6
S'Estanyol, Spain 48 B9
Sestao, Spain 38 B2
Sesto Calende, Italy 40 C5
Sesto San Giovanni, Italy 40 C6
Sestri Levante, Italy 40 D6
Sestriere, Italy 40 D3
Sestroretsk, Russia 32 B6
Sestrunj, Croatia 41 D11
Sestu, Italy 42 C2
Setana, Japan 54 C9
Sète, France 20 E7
Sete Lagôas, Brazil 125 G10
Sétif, Algeria 78 A7
Seto, Japan 55 G8
Setonaikai, Japan 55 G6
Setonaikai △, Japan 55 G6
Settat, Morocco 78 B4
Séttimo Torinese, Italy 40 C4
Setting L., Canada 103 C9
Settle, U.K. 14 C5
Settlement Pt., Bahamas 115 M6
Settlers, S. Africa 89 C4
Setúbal, Portugal 37 G2
Setúbal □, Portugal 37 G2
Setúbal, B. de, Portugal 37 G2
Seugne →, France 20 C3
Seul, Lac, Canada 104 B1
Seurre, France 19 F12
Sevan, Armenia 35 K7
Sevan, Ozero = Sevana Lich, Armenia 35 K7
Sevana Lich, Armenia 35 K7
Sevastopol, Ukraine 33 K7
Seven Sisters, Canada 102 C3
Sever →, Spain 37 F3
Sévérac-le-Château, France 20 D7
Severn →, Canada 104 A2
Severn →, U.K. 15 F5
Severn L., Canada 104 B1
Severnaya Zemlya, Russia 53 B10
Severo-Kurilsk, Russia 53 D16
Severo-Yeniseyskiy, Russia 53 C10
Severo-Zapadnyy □, Russia 52 C4
Severočeský □, Czech Rep. 26 A7

Severodonetsk = Syeverodonetsk, Ukraine 33 H10
Severodvinsk, Russia 52 C4
Severomoravský □, Czech Rep. 27 B10
Sevier, U.S.A. 109 G7
Sevier →, U.S.A. 109 G7
Sevier Desert, U.S.A. 108 G7
Sevier L., U.S.A. 108 G7
Sevilla, Spain 37 H5
Sevilla □, Spain 37 H5
Seville = Sevilla, Spain 37 H5
Sevlievo, Bulgaria 45 C9
Sevnica, Slovenia 41 B12
Sèvre-Nantaise →, France 18 E5
Sèvre-Niortaise →, France 20 B3
Sevsk, Russia 33 F8
Sewa →, S. Leone 82 D2
Sewani, India 68 E6
Seward, Alaska, U.S.A. 100 B5
Seward, Nebr., U.S.A. 112 E6
Seward, Pa., U.S.A. 116 F5
Seward Peninsula, U.S.A. 100 B3
Sewell, Chile 126 C1
Sewer, Indonesia 63 F8
Sewickley, U.S.A. 116 F4
Sexsmith, Canada 102 B5
Seychelles ■, Ind. Oc. 50 K9
Seyðisfjörður, Iceland 8 D6
Seydişehir, Turkey 72 D4
Seydvān, Iran 70 B5
Seyhan →, Turkey 70 B2
Seyhan Barajı, Turkey 72 D6
Seyitgazi, Turkey 47 B12
Seyitömer, Turkey 47 B11
Seym →, Ukraine 33 G7
Seymen, Turkey 45 E11
Seymour, Australia 95 F4
Seymour, S. Africa 89 E4
Seymour, Conn., U.S.A. 117 E11
Seymour, Ind., U.S.A. 114 F3
Seymour, Tex., U.S.A. 113 J5
Sfântu Gheorghe, Covasna, Romania 29 E10
Sfântu Gheorghe, Tulcea, Romania 29 F14
Sfântu Gheorghe, Braţul →, Romania 29 F14
Sfax, Tunisia 79 B8
Sha Xi →, China 59 D12
Sha Xian, China 59 D11
Shaanxi □, China 56 G5
Shaba = Katanga □, Dem. Rep. of the Congo 86 D2
Shaba △, Kenya 86 B4
Shaballe = Scebeli, Wabi →, Somali Rep. 75 G3
Shabla, Bulgaria 45 C12
Shabogamo L., Canada 105 B6
Shabunda, Dem. Rep. of the Congo 86 C2
Shache, China 60 C2
Shackleton Ice Shelf, Antarctica 5 C8
Shackleton Inlet, Antarctica 5 E11
Shādegān, Iran 71 D6
Shadi, China 59 D10
Shadi, India 69 C7
Shadrinsk, Russia 52 D7
Shadyside, U.S.A. 116 G4
Shaffa, Nigeria 83 C7
Shafter, U.S.A. 111 K7
Shaftesbury, U.K. 15 F5
Shagamu, Nigeria 83 D5
Shagram, Pakistan 69 A5
Shah Alizai, Pakistan 68 E2
Shah Bunder, Pakistan 68 G2
Shahabad, Punjab, India 68 D7
Shahabad, Raj., India 68 G7
Shahabad, Ut. P., India 69 F8
Shahadpur, Pakistan 68 G3
Shahba, Syria 74 C5
Shahdād, Iran 71 D8
Shahdād, Namakzār-e, Iran 71 D8
Shahdadkot, Pakistan 68 F2
Shahdol, India 69 H9
Shahe, China 56 F8
Shahganj, India 69 F10
Shahgarh, India 66 F6
Shahjahanpur, India 69 F8
Shahpur, India 68 H7
Shahpur, Baluchistan, Pakistan 68 E3
Shahpur, Punjab, Pakistan 68 C5
Shahpur Chakar, Pakistan 68 G3
Shahpura, Mad. P., India 69 H9
Shahpura, Raj., India 68 G6
Shahr-e Bābak, Iran 71 D7
Shahr-e Kord, Iran 71 C6
Shāhrakht, Iran 71 C9
Shahrig, Pakistan 68 D2
Shahukou, China 56 D7
Shaikhabad, Afghan. 68 B3
Shajapur, India 68 H7
Shakargarh, Pakistan 68 C6
Shakawe, Botswana 88 B3
Shaker Heights, U.S.A. 116 E3
Shakhty, Russia 35 G5
Shakhunya, Russia 34 B8
Shaki, Nigeria 83 D5
Shākir, Egypt 80 B3
Shaksam Valley, Asia 69 A7
Shala, L., Ethiopia 81 F4
Shali, Russia 35 J7
Shallow Lake, Canada 116 B3
Shalqar, Kazakhstan 52 E6
Shalskiy, Russia 32 B8
Shaluli Shan, China 58 B2
Shām, Iran 71 E8

Shām, Bādiyat ash, Asia 70 C3
Shamâl Bahr el Ghazal □, Sudan 81 F2
Shamâl Dârfûr □, Sudan 81 E2
Shamâl Kordofân □, Sudan 81 E3
Shamâl Sînî □, Egypt 74 E2
Shamattawa, Canada 104 A1
Shamattawa →, Canada 104 A2
Shambe, Sudan 81 F3
Shambe △, Sudan 81 F3
Shambu, Ethiopia 81 F4
Shamīl, Iran 71 E8
Shamkhor = Şämkir, Azerbaijan 35 K8
Shāmkūh, Iran 71 C8
Shamli, India 68 E7
Shamo = Gobi, Asia 56 C6
Shamo, L., Ethiopia 81 F4
Shamokin, U.S.A. 117 F8
Shamrock, U.S.A. 113 H4
Shamva, Zimbabwe 87 F3
Shan □, Burma 67 J21
Shan Xian, China 56 G9
Shanan →, Ethiopia 81 F5
Shanchengzhen, China 57 C13
Shāndak, Iran 71 D9
Shandon, U.S.A. 110 K6
Shandong □, China 57 G10
Shandong Bandao, China 57 F11
Shang Xian = Shangzhou, China 56 H5
Shanga, Nigeria 78 F6
Shangalowe, Dem. Rep. of the Congo 87 E2
Shangani, China 89 B4
Shangani →, Zimbabwe 87 F2
Shangbancheng, China 57 D10
Shangcheng, China 59 B10
Shangchuan Dao, China 59 G9
Shangdu, China 56 D7
Shanggao, China 59 C10
Shanghai, China 59 B13
Shanghai Shi □, China 59 B13
Shanghang, China 59 E11
Shanghe, China 57 F9
Shanglin, China 58 F7
Shangnan, China 56 H6
Shangqiu, China 56 G8
Shangrao, China 59 C11
Shangshui, China 60 C6
Shangsi, China 58 F6
Shangyou, China 59 E10
Shangyu, China 59 B13
Shangzhi, China 57 B14
Shangzhou, China 56 H5
Shanhetun, China 57 B14
Shani, Nigeria 83 C7
Shanklin, U.K. 15 G6
Shannon, N.Z. 91 J5
Shannon △, Australia 93 F2
Shannon →, Ireland 12 D2
Shannon, Mouth of the, Ireland 12 D2
Shannon Airport, Ireland 12 D3
Shansi = Shanxi □, China 56 F7
Shantar, Ostrov Bolshoy, Russia 53 D14
Shantipur, India 69 H13
Shantou, China 59 F11
Shantung = Shandong □, China 57 G10
Shanwei, China 59 F10
Shanxi □, China 56 F7
Shanyang, China 56 H5
Shanyin, China 56 E7
Shaodong, China 59 D8
Shaoguan, China 59 E9
Shaoshan, China 59 D9
Shaowu, China 59 D11
Shaoxing, China 59 C13
Shaoyang, Hunan, China 59 D8
Shaoyang, Hunan, China 59 D8
Shap, U.K. 14 C5
Shapinsay, U.K. 13 B6
Shaqq el Gi'eifer →, Sudan 81 D2
Shaqra', Si. Arabia 70 E5
Shaqrā', Yemen 75 E4
Sharafa, Sudan 81 E2
Sharafkhāneh, Iran 70 B5
Sharashova, Belarus 31 F11
Sharbot Lake, Canada 117 B8
Shari, Japan 54 C12
Sharjah = Ash Shāriqah, U.A.E. 71 E7
Shark B., Australia 93 E1
Shark Bay △, Australia 93 E1
Sharm el Sheikh, Egypt 80 B3
Sharon, Mass., U.S.A. 117 D13
Sharon, Pa., U.S.A. 116 E4
Sharon Springs, Kans., U.S.A. 112 F4
Sharon Springs, N.Y., U.S.A. 117 D10
Sharp Pt., Australia 94 A3
Sharpe L., Canada 104 B1
Sharpsville, U.S.A. 116 E4
Sharq el Istiwa'iya □, Sudan 81 G3
Sharya, Russia 34 A7
Shasha, Ethiopia 81 F4
Shashemene, Ethiopia 81 F4
Shashi, Botswana 89 C4
Shashi, China 59 B9
Shashi →, Africa 87 G2
Shasta, Mt., U.S.A. 108 F2
Shasta L., U.S.A. 108 F2
Shatawi, Sudan 81 E3
Shatsk, Russia 34 C5
Shatskyi △, Ukraine 31 G10
Shatt al Arab, Asia 71 D6
Shatura, Russia 32 E10
Shaumyani = Shulaveri, Georgia 35 K7
Shaunavon, Canada 103 D7
Shaver L., U.S.A. 110 H7
Shaw →, Australia 92 D2
Shaw I., Australia 94 J7
Shawanaga, Canada 116 A4
Shawangunk Mts., U.S.A. 117 E10

Shawano, U.S.A. 114 C1
Shawinigan, Canada 104 C5
Shawnee, U.S.A. 113 H6
Shay Gap, Australia 92 D3
Shayang, China 59 B9
Shaybārā, Si. Arabia 70 E3
Shayib el Banat, Gebel, Egypt 80 B3
Shaykh, J. ash, Lebanon 74 B4
Shaykh Miskīn, Syria 74 C5
Shaykh Sa'īd, Iraq 70 C5
Shchelkovo, Russia 32 E9
Shchigry, Russia 33 G9
Shchors, Ukraine 33 G6
Shchuchinsk, Kazakhstan 52 D8
She Xian, Anhui, China 59 C12
She Xian, Hebei, China 56 F7
Shebekino, Russia 33 G9
Shebele = Scebeli, Wabi →, Somali Rep. 75 G3
Sheboygan, U.S.A. 114 D2
Shebshi Mts., Nigeria 83 D7
Shediac, Canada 105 C7
Sheelin, L., Ireland 12 C4
Sheep Haven, Ireland 12 A4
Sheerness, U.K. 15 F8
Sheet Harbour, Canada 105 D7
Sheffield, U.K. 14 D6
Sheffield, Ala., U.S.A. 115 H2
Sheffield, Mass., U.S.A. 117 D11
Sheffield, Pa., U.S.A. 116 E5
Shehojele, Ethiopia 81 E4
Shehong, China 58 B5
Sheikh Idris, Sudan 81 E3
Sheikhpura, India 69 G11
Shek Hasan, Ethiopia 81 E4
Shekhupura, Pakistan 68 D5
Sheki = Şaki, Azerbaijan 35 K8
Shelburne, N.S., Canada 105 D6
Shelburne, Ont., Canada 116 B4
Shelburne, U.S.A. 117 B11
Shelburne B., Australia 94 A3
Shelburne Falls, U.S.A. 117 D12
Shelby, Mich., U.S.A. 114 D2
Shelby, Miss., U.S.A. 113 J9
Shelby, Mont., U.S.A. 108 B8
Shelby, N.C., U.S.A. 115 H5
Shelby, Ohio, U.S.A. 116 F2
Shelbyville, Ill., U.S.A. 112 F10
Shelbyville, Ind., U.S.A. 114 F3
Shelbyville, Ky., U.S.A. 114 F3
Shelbyville, Tenn., U.S.A. 115 H2
Sheldon, U.S.A. 112 D7
Sheldrake, Canada 105 B7
Shelengo, Khawr →, Sudan 81 E2
Shelikhova, Zaliv, Russia 53 D16
Shell Lakes, Australia 93 E4
Shellbrook, Canada 103 C7
Shellharbour, Australia 95 E5
Shelon →, Russia 32 C6
Shelter I, U.S.A. 117 E12
Shelton, Conn., U.S.A. 117 E11
Shelton, Wash., U.S.A. 110 C3
Shemakha = Şamaxi, Azerbaijan 35 K9
Shēmri, Albania 44 D4
Shemsi, Sudan 80 D2
Shen Xian, China 56 F8
Shenandoah, Iowa, U.S.A. 112 E7
Shenandoah, Pa., U.S.A. 117 F8
Shenandoah, Va., U.S.A. 114 F6
Shenandoah →, U.S.A. 114 F7
Shenchi, China 56 E7
Shendam, Nigeria 83 D6
Shendī, Sudan 81 D3
Shenge, S. Leone 82 D2
Shengfang, China 56 E9
Shēngjergj, Albania 44 E4
Shēngjin, Albania 44 E3
Shengzhou, China 59 C13
Shenjingzi, China 57 B13
Shenmu, China 56 E6
Shennongjia, China 59 B8
Shenqiu, China 56 H8
Shensi = Shaanxi □, China 56 G5
Shenyang, China 57 D12
Shenzhen, China 59 F10
Sheo, India 68 F4
Sheopur Kalan, India 66 G10
Shepetivka, Ukraine 33 G4
Shepetovka = Shepetivka, Ukraine 33 G4
Shepparton, Australia 95 F4
Sheppey, I. of, U.K. 15 F8
Shepton Mallet, U.K. 15 F5
Sheqi, China 56 H7
Sher Qila, Pakistan 69 A6
Sherab, Sudan 81 E1
Sherborne, U.K. 15 G5
Sherbro →, S. Leone 82 D2
Sherbro I., S. Leone 82 D2
Sherbrooke, N.S., Canada 105 C7
Sherbrooke, Qué., Canada 117 A13
Sherburne, U.S.A. 117 D9
Shereik, Sudan 80 D3
Shergarh, India 68 F5
Sherghati, India 69 G11
Sheridan, Ark., U.S.A. 113 H8
Sheridan, Wyo., U.S.A. 108 D10
Sheringham, U.K. 14 E9
Sherkin I., Ireland 12 E2
Sherkot, India 69 E8
Sherman, U.S.A. 113 J6
Sherpur, India 69 G10
Sherridon, Canada 103 B8
Sherwood Forest, U.K. 14 D6
Sherwood Park, Canada 102 C6
Sheslay →, Canada 102 B2
Shethanei L., Canada 103 B9
Shetland □, U.K. 13 A7
Shetland Is., U.K. 13 A7
Shetrunji →, India 68 J5

Shevchenkovo, *Ukraine* 29 E14
Shewa, *Ethiopia* 81 F4
Shewa Gimira, *Ethiopia* 81 F4
Sheyenne →, *U.S.A.* 112 B6
Shibām, *Yemen* 75 D4
Shibata, *Japan* 54 F9
Shibecha, *Japan* 54 C12
Shibetsu, *Japan* 54 B11
Shibîn el Kôm, *Egypt* 80 H7
Shibîn el Qanâtir, *Egypt* 80 H7
Shibing, *China* 58 D7
Shibogama L., *Canada* 104 B2
Shibushi, *Japan* 55 J5
Shicheng, *China* 59 D11
Shickshinny, *U.S.A.* 117 E8
Shickshock Mts. = Chic-Chocs,
  Mts., *Canada* 105 C6
Shidao, *China* 57 F12
Shidian, *China* 58 E2
Shido, *Japan* 55 G7
Shiel, L., *U.K.* 13 E3
Shield, C., *Australia* 94 A2
Shīeli, *Kazakhstan* 52 E7
Shifang, *China* 58 B5
Shiga □, *Japan* 55 G8
Shigu, *China* 58 D2
Shiguaigou, *China* 56 D6
Shihchiachuang = Shijiazhuang,
  China 56 E8
Shihezi, *China* 60 B3
Shijak, *Albania* 44 E3
Shijiazhuang, *China* 56 E8
Shijiu Hu, *China* 59 B12
Shikarpur, *India* 68 E8
Shikarpur, *Pakistan* 68 F3
Shikohabad, *India* 69 F8
Shikoku □, *Japan* 55 H6
Shikoku-Sanchi, *Japan* 55 H6
Shikotsu-Ko, *Japan* 54 C10
Shikotsu-Tōya △, *Japan* 54 C10
Shiliguri, *India* 67 F16
Shilka, *Russia* 53 D12
Shilka →, *Russia* 53 D13
Shillelagh, *Ireland* 12 D5
Shillington, *U.S.A.* 117 F9
Shillong, *India* 67 G17
Shilo, *West Bank* 74 C4
Shilong, *China* 59 F9
Shilou, *China* 56 F6
Shilovo, *Russia* 34 C5
Shimabara, *Japan* 55 H5
Shimada, *Japan* 55 G9
Shimane □, *Japan* 55 G6
Shimanovsk, *Russia* 53 D13
Shimba Hills △, *Kenya* 86 C4
Shimen, *China* 59 C8
Shimenjie, *China* 59 C11
Shimian, *China* 58 C4
Shimizu, *Japan* 55 G9
Shimodate, *Japan* 55 F9
Shimoga, *India* 66 N9
Shimoni, *Kenya* 86 C4
Shimonoseki, *Japan* 55 H5
Shimpuru Rapids, *Namibia* .. 88 B2
Shimsk, *Russia* 32 C6
Shin, L., *U.K.* 13 C4
Shinan, *China* 58 F7
Shinano-Gawa →, *Japan* 55 F9
Shināş, *Oman* 71 E8
Shīndand, *Afghan.* 66 C3
Shinglehouse, *U.S.A.* 116 E6
Shingū, *Japan* 55 H6
Shingwidzi, *S. Africa* 89 C5
Shinjō, *Japan* 54 E10
Shinkafe, *Nigeria* 83 C6
Shinshār, *Syria* 74 A5
Shinyanga, *Tanzania* 86 C3
Shinyanga □, *Tanzania* 86 C3
Shio-no-Misaki, *Japan* 55 H7
Shiogama, *Japan* 54 E10
Shiojiri, *Japan* 55 F8
Shipchenski Prokhod, *Bulgaria* . 45 D9
Shiping, *China* 58 F4
Shippagan, *Canada* 105 C7
Shippensburg, *U.S.A.* 116 F7
Shippenville, *U.S.A.* 116 E5
Shiprock, *U.S.A.* 109 H9
Shiqian, *China* 58 D7
Shiqma, N. →, *Israel* 74 D3
Shiquan, *China* 56 H5
Shiquan He = Indus →, *Pakistan* 68 G2
Shīr Kūh, *Iran* 71 D7
Shiragami-Misaki, *Japan* .. 54 D10
Shirakawa, *Fukushima, Japan* . 55 F10
Shirakawa, *Gifu, Japan* 55 F8
Shirane-San, *Gumma, Japan* . 55 F9
Shirane-San, *Yamanashi, Japan* . 55 G9
Shiraoi, *Japan* 54 C10
Shīrāz, *Iran* 71 D7
Shirbīn, *Egypt* 80 H7
Shire →, *Africa* 87 F4
Shiretoko-Misaki, *Japan* 54 B12
Shirinab →, *Pakistan* 68 D2
Shiriya-Zaki, *Japan* 54 D10
Shiroishi, *Japan* 54 F10
Shīrvān, *Iran* 71 B8
Shirwa, L. = Chilwa, L., *Malawi* . 87 F4
Shishi, *China* 59 E12
Shishou, *China* 59 C9
Shitai, *China* 59 B11
Shivpuri, *India* 68 G7
Shixian, *China* 57 C15
Shixing, *China* 59 E10
Shiyan, *China* 59 A8
Shiyata, *Egypt* 80 B2
Shizhu, *China* 58 C7
Shizong, *China* 58 E5
Shizuishan, *China* 56 E4
Shizuoka, *Japan* 55 G9
Shizuoka □, *Japan* 55 G9
Shklov = Shklow, *Belarus* 32 E6

Shklow, *Belarus* 32 E6
Shkodër, *Albania* 44 D3
Shkumbini →, *Albania* 44 E3
Shmidta, Ostrov, *Russia* 53 A10
Shō-Gawa →, *Japan* 55 F8
Shoal L., *Canada* 103 D9
Shoal Lake, *Canada* 103 C8
Shōdo-Shima, *Japan* 55 G7
Sholapur = Solapur, *India* .. 66 L9
Shomrōn, *West Bank* 74 C4
Shoreham by Sea, *U.K.* 15 G7
Shori →, *Pakistan* 68 E3
Shorkot Road, *Pakistan* 68 D5
Shoshone, *Calif., U.S.A.* .. 111 K10
Shoshone, *Idaho, U.S.A.* .. 108 E6
Shoshone L., *U.S.A.* 108 D8
Shoshone Mts., *U.S.A.* 108 G5
Shoshong, *Botswana* 88 C4
Shoshoni, *U.S.A.* 108 E9
Shostka, *Ukraine* 33 G7
Shou Xian, *China* 59 A11
Shouchang, *China* 59 C12
Shouguang, *China* 57 F10
Shouning, *China* 59 D12
Shouyang, *China* 56 F7
Show Low, *U.S.A.* 109 J9
Shpola, *Ukraine* 33 H6
Shpykiv, *Ukraine* 29 B13
Shreveport, *U.S.A.* 113 J8
Shrewsbury, *U.K.* 15 E5
Shri Mohangarh, *India* 68 F4
Shrirampur, *India* 69 H13
Shropshire □, *U.K.* 15 E5
Shū, *Kazakhstan* 52 E8
Shū →, *Kazakhstan* 50 E10
Shuangbai, *China* 58 E3
Shuangcheng, *China* 57 B14
Shuangfeng, *China* 59 D9
Shuanggou, *China* 57 G9
Shuangjiang, *China* 58 F2
Shuangliao, *China* 57 C12
Shuangshanzi, *China* 57 D10
Shuangyang, *China* 57 C13
Shuangyashan, *China* 60 B8
Shubra el Kheima, *Egypt* .. 80 H7
Shubra Khit, *Egypt* 80 H7
Shucheng, *China* 59 B11
Shugozero, *Russia* 32 C8
Shuguri Falls, *Tanzania* .. 87 D4
Shuiji, *China* 59 D12
Shuiye, *China* 56 F8
Shujalpur, *India* 68 H7
Shukpa Kunzang, *India* 69 B8
Shulan, *China* 57 B14
Shulaveri, *Georgia* 35 K7
Shule, *China* 60 C2
Shumagin Is., *U.S.A.* 100 C4
Shumen, *Bulgaria* 45 C10
Shumerlya, *Russia* 34 C8
Shumikha, *Russia* 52 D7
Shunchang, *China* 59 D11
Shunde, *China* 59 F9
Shungay, *Kazakhstan* 35 F8
Shuo Xian = Shuozhou, *China* . 56 E7
Shuozhou, *China* 56 E7
Shūr →, *Fārs, Iran* 71 D7
Shūr →, *Kermān, Iran* 71 D8
Shūr →, *Yazd, Iran* 71 D7
Shūr Āb, *Iran* 71 C6
Shūr Gaz, *Iran* 71 D8
Shūrāb, *Iran* 71 C8
Shūrjestān, *Iran* 71 D7
Shūsh, *Iran* 73 F13
Shūshtar, *Iran* 71 D6
Shuswap L., *Canada* 102 C5
Shuya, *Russia* 34 B5
Shuyang, *China* 57 G10
Shūzū, *Iran* 71 D7
Shwebo, *Burma* 67 H19
Shwegu, *Burma* 67 G20
Shweli →, *Burma* 67 H20
Shymkent, *Kazakhstan* 52 E7
Shyok, *India* 69 B8
Shyok →, *Pakistan* 69 B6
Shyroke, *Ukraine* 28 B8
Shyroke, *Ukraine* 29 E15
Si Chon, *Thailand* 65 H2
Si Kiang = Xi Jiang →, *China* . 59 F9
Si Lanna △, *Thailand* 64 C2
Si-ngan = Xi'an, *China* 56 G5
Si Prachan, *Thailand* 64 E3
Si Racha, *Thailand* 64 F3
Si Xian, *China* 57 H9
Siachen Glacier, *Asia* 69 B7
Siahaf →, *Pakistan* 68 E3
Siahan Range, *Pakistan* 66 F4
Siaksriindrapura, *Indonesia* . 62 D2
Sialkot, *Pakistan* 68 C6
Siam = Thailand ■, *Asia* .. 64 E4
Sian = Xi'an, *China* 56 G5
Sian Ka'an △, *Mexico* 119 D7
Sianów, *Poland* 30 D3
Siantan, *Indonesia* 62 D3
Siāreh, *Iran* 71 D9
Siargao I., *Phil.* 61 G7
Siari, *Pakistan* 69 B7
Siasi, *Phil.* 63 C6
Siasi I., *Phil.* 61 J4
Siátista, *Greece* 44 F5
Siau, *Indonesia* 63 D7
Šiauliai, *Lithuania* 9 J20
Šiauliai □, *Lithuania* 30 C10
Siazan = Siyäzän, *Azerbaijan* . 35 K9
Sîbâi, Gebel el, *Egypt* 70 E2
Sibang, *Indonesia* 63 K18
Sibayi, L., *S. Africa* 89 D5
Sibdu, *Sudan* 81 E2
Šibenik, *Croatia* 41 E12
Siberia = Sibirskiy □, *Russia* . 53 D10

Siberia, *Russia* 50 C13
Siberut, *Indonesia* 62 E1
Sibi, *Pakistan* 68 E2
Sibil = Oksibil, *Indonesia* .. 63 E10
Sibiloi △, *Kenya* 86 B4
Sibirskiy □, *Russia* 53 D10
Sibiti, *Congo* 84 E2
Sibiu, *Romania* 29 E9
Sibiu □, *Romania* 29 E9
Sibley, *U.S.A.* 112 D7
Sibolga, *Indonesia* 62 D1
Sibsagar, *India* 67 F19
Sibu, *Malaysia* 62 D4
Sibuco, *Phil.* 61 H5
Sibuguey B., *Phil.* 61 H5
Sibut, *C.A.R.* 84 C3
Sibutu, *Phil.* 63 D5
Sibutu Group, *Phil.* 61 J3
Sibutu Passage, *E. Indies* .. 63 D5
Sibuyan I., *Phil.* 61 E5
Sibuyan Sea, *Phil.* 61 E5
Sic, *Romania* 29 D8
Sicamous, *Canada* 102 C5
Sichuan □, *China* 58 B5
Sichuan Pendi, *China* 58 B5
Sicilia, *Italy* 43 E7
Sicily = Sicilia, *Italy* 43 E7
Sicily, Str. of 42 E4
Sicuani, *Peru* 124 F4
Sid, *Serbia & M.* 28 E4
Sidamo, *Ethiopia* 81 G4
Sidaouet, *Niger* 83 B6
Sidári, *Greece* 49 A3
Siddhapur, *India* 68 H5
Siddipet, *India* 66 K11
Sidensjö, *Sweden* 10 A12
Sidéradougou, *Burkina Faso* . 82 C4
Siderno, *Italy* 43 D9
Sidhauli, *India* 69 F9
Sídheros, Ákra, *Greece* 49 D8
Sidhi, *India* 69 G9
Sidhirókastron, *Greece* 44 E7
Sîdi Abd el Rahmân, *Egypt* .. 80 A2
Sîdi Barrâni, *Egypt* 80 A2
Sidi-bel-Abbès, *Algeria* 78 A5
Sîdi Haneish, *Egypt* 80 A2
Sidi Ifni, *Morocco* 78 C3
Sîdi Omar, *Egypt* 80 A1
Sidlaw Hills, *U.K.* 13 E5
Sidley, Mt., *Antarctica* 5 D14
Sidmouth, *U.K.* 15 G4
Sidmouth, C., *Australia* 94 A3
Sidney, *Canada* 102 D4
Sidney, *Mont., U.S.A.* 112 B2
Sidney, *N.Y., U.S.A.* 117 D9
Sidney, *Nebr., U.S.A.* 112 E3
Sidney, *Ohio, U.S.A.* 114 E3
Sidney Lanier, L., *U.S.A.* .. 115 H4
Sido, *Mali* 82 C3
Sidoarjo, *Indonesia* 63 G15
Sidon = Saydā, *Lebanon* 74 B4
Sidra, G. of = Surt, Khalīj, *Libya* . 79 B9
Siedlce, *Poland* 31 F9
Sieg →, *Germany* 24 E3
Siegburg, *Germany* 24 E3
Siegen, *Germany* 24 E4
Siem Pang, *Cambodia* 64 E6
Siem Reap = Siemreab, *Cambodia* . 64 F4
Siemiatycze, *Poland* 31 F9
Siemreab, *Cambodia* 64 F4
Siena, *Italy* 41 E8
Sieniawa, *Poland* 31 H9
Sieradz, *Poland* 31 G5
Sieraków, *Poland* 31 F2
Sierck-les-Bains, *France* .. 19 C13
Sierning, *Austria* 26 C7
Sierpc, *Poland* 31 F6
Sierpe, Bocas de la, *Venezuela* . 125 L15
Sierra Blanca, *U.S.A.* 109 L11
Sierra Blanca Peak, *U.S.A.* . 109 K11
Sierra City, *U.S.A.* 110 F6
Sierra Colorada, *Argentina* . 128 E3
Sierra de Aracena y Picas de
  Aroche △, *Spain* 37 H4
Sierra de Bahoruco △, *Dom. Rep.* . 121 C5
Sierra de Baza △, *Spain* .. 39 H2
Sierra de Castril △, *Spain* . 39 H2
Sierra de España △, *Spain* . 39 H3
Sierra de Grazalema △, *Spain* . 37 J5
Sierra de Gredos △, *Spain* . 36 E5
Sierra de Hornachuelos △, *Spain* . 37 H5
Sierra de Huétor △, *Spain* . 37 H7
Sierra de La Culata △, *Venezuela* 121 E5
Sierra de Lancandón △,
  Guatemala 120 C1
Sierra de las Nieves △, *Spain* . 37 J6
Sierra de las Quijadas △,
  Argentina 126 C2
Sierra de María-Los Vélez △,
  Spain 39 H2
Sierra de San Luis △, *Venezuela* . 121 D6
Sierra de Yeguas, *Spain* 37 H6
Sierra del São Mamede △,
  Portugal 37 F3
Sierra Gorda, *Chile* 126 A2
Sierra Madre, *Mexico* 119 D6
Sierra Mágina △, *Spain* 37 H7
Sierra Mojada, *Mexico* 118 B4
Sierra Nevada, *Spain* 37 H7
Sierra Nevada, *U.S.A.* 110 H8
Sierra Nevada △, *Spain* 37 H7
Sierra Nevada △, *Venezuela* . 121 E5
Sierra Nevada de Santa Marta △,
  Colombia 121 D5
Sierra Norte de Seville △, *Spain* . 37 H5
Sierra Subbéticas △, *Spain* . 37 H6
Sierra Vista, *U.S.A.* 109 L8
Sierras de Cardeña y Montoro △,
  Spain 37 G6

Sierras de Cazorla, Segura y las
  Villas △, *Spain* 39 J2
Sierraville, *U.S.A.* 110 F6
Sierre, *Switz.* 25 J3
Sifani, *Ethiopia* 81 E5
Sifié, *Ivory C.* 82 D3
Sífnos, *Greece* 46 E6
Sifton, *Canada* 103 C8
Sifton Pass, *Canada* 102 B3
Sigean, *France* 20 E6
Sighetu-Marmației, *Romania* . 29 C8
Sighișoara, *Romania* 29 D9
Sigiri, *Guinea* 82 C3
Sigli, *Indonesia* 62 C1
Siglufjörður, *Iceland* 8 C4
Sigmaringen, *Germany* 25 G5
Signa, *Italy* 40 E8
Signal, *U.S.A.* 111 L13
Signal de Botrang, *Belgium* . 17 D6
Signal Pk., *U.S.A.* 111 M12
Signy I., *Antarctica* 5 C18
Signy-l'Abbaye, *France* 19 C11
Sigsig, *Ecuador* 124 D3
Sigüenza, *Spain* 38 D2
Siguiri, *Guinea* 82 C3
Sigulda, *Latvia* 9 H21
Sihora, *India* 69 H9
Sihui, *China* 59 F9
Siikajoki →, *Finland* 8 D21
Siilinjärvi, *Finland* 8 E22
Siirt, *Turkey* 73 D9
Sijarira Ra. = Chizarira,
  Zimbabwe 87 F2
Sika, *India* 68 H3
Sikani Chief →, *Canada* 102 B4
Sikao, *Thailand* 65 J2
Sikar, *India* 68 F6
Sikasso, *Mali* 82 C3
Sikeston, *U.S.A.* 113 G10
Sikhote Alin, Khrebet, *Russia* . 53 E14
Sikhote Alin Ra. = Sikhote Alin,
  Khrebet, *Russia* 53 E14
Sikiá, *Greece* 44 F7
Síkinos, *Greece* 47 E7
Sikkim □, *India* 67 F16
Siklós, *Hungary* 28 E3
Sil →, *Spain* 36 C3
Silacayoapan, *Mexico* 119 D5
Šilalė, *Lithuania* 30 C9
Silandro, *Italy* 40 B7
Silawad, *India* 68 J6
Silay, *Phil.* 61 F5
Silba, *Croatia* 41 D11
Silchar, *India* 67 G18
Şile, *Turkey* 45 E13
Siler City, *U.S.A.* 115 H6
Silgarhi Doti, *Nepal* 69 E9
Silghat, *India* 67 F18
Sili, *Burkina Faso* 82 C4
Silifke, *Turkey* 70 B2
Siliguri = Shil guri, *India* . 67 F16
Siling Co, *China* 60 C3
Silistea Nouă, *Romania* 29 F10
Silistra, *Bulgaria* 45 B11
Silivri, *Turkey* 45 E12
Siljan, *Sweden* 10 D8
Siljansnäs, *Sweden* 10 D8
Silkeborg, *Denmark* 11 H3
Silkwood, *Australia* 94 B4
Silla, *Spain* 39 F4
Sillajhuay, Cordillera, *Chile* . 124 G5
Sillamäe, *Estonia* 9 G22
Sillé-le-Guillaume, *France* . 18 D6
Silleda, *Spain* 36 C2
Silloth, *U.K.* 14 C4
Silo, *Greece* 45 E9
Siloam Springs, *U.S.A.* 113 G7
Silopi, *Turkey* 73 D10
Silsbee, *U.S.A.* 113 K7
Siluko, *Nigeria* 83 D6
Šilutė, *Lithuania* 9 J19
Silvan, *Turkey* 73 C9
Silvani, *India* 69 H8
Silver City, *U.S.A.* 109 K9
Silver Cr. →, *U.S.A.* 108 E4
Silver Creek, *U.S.A.* 116 D5
Silver L., *U.S.A.* 110 G6
Silver Lake, *Calif., U.S.A.* . 111 K10
Silver Lake, *Oreg., U.S.A.* . 108 E3
Silverdalen, *Sweden* 11 G9
Silverton, *Colo., U.S.A.* .. 109 H10
Silverton, *Tex., U.S.A.* 113 H4
Silves, *Portugal* 37 H2
Silvi Marina, *Italy* 41 F11
Silvies →, *U.S.A.* 108 E4
Silvretta Bahari, *Egypt* 80 C3
Silwa Bahari, *Egypt* 80 C3
Silz, *Austria* 26 D3
Simaltala, *India* 69 G12
Simanggang = Bandar Sri Aman,
  Malaysia 62 D4
Simao, *China* 58 F3
Simard, L., *Canada* 104 C4
Şimareh →, *Iran* 73 F12
Simav, *Turkey* 47 B10
Simav →, *Turkey* 45 F12
Simav Dağları, *Turkey* 47 B10
Simba, *Tanzania* 86 C4
Simbach, *Germany* 25 G4
Simbirsk, *Russia* 34 C9
Simbo, *Tanzania* 86 C2
Simcoe, *Canada* 116 D4
Simcoe, L., *Canada* 116 B5
Simdega, *India* 69 H11
Simeonovgrad, *Bulgaria* 45 D9
Simeto →, *Italy* 43 E8
Simeulue, *Indonesia* 62 D1
Simferopol, *Ukraine* 33 K8
Sími, *Greece* 47 E9
Sími Valley, *U.S.A.* 111 L8

Simien Mts. △, *Ethiopia* 81 E4
Simikot, *Nepal* 69 E9
Simitli, *Bulgaria* 44 E7
Simla, *India* 68 D7
Simlångsdalen, *Sweden* 11 H7
Şimleu-Silvaniei, *Romania* . 28 C7
Simmern, *Germany* 25 F3
Simmie, *Canada* 103 D7
Simmler, *U.S.A.* 111 K7
Simnas, *Lithuania* 30 D10
Simo älv = Simojoki →, *Finland* . 8 D21
Simojoki →, *Finland* 8 D21
Simojovel, *Mexico* 119 D6
Simonette →, *Canada* 102 B5
Simonstown, *S. Africa* 88 E2
Simontornya, *Hungary* 28 D3
Simpang Empat, *Malaysia* .. 65 c
Simplonpass, *Switz.* 25 J4
Simplontunnel, *Switz.* 25 J4
Simpson Desert, *Australia* . 94 D2
Simpson Desert △, *Australia* . 94 C2
Simpson Pen., *Canada* 101 B11
Simpungdong, *N. Korea* 57 D15
Simrishamn, *Sweden* 11 J8
Simsbury, *U.S.A.* 117 E12
Simushir, Ostrov, *Russia* .. 53 E16
Sin Cowe I., *S. China Sea* .. 62 C4
Sinabang, *Indonesia* 62 D1
Sinadogo, *Somali Rep.* 75 F4
Sinai = Es Sînâ', *Egypt* 74 F3
Sinai, Mt. = Mûsa, Gebel, *Egypt* . 70 D2
Sinai Peninsula, *Egypt* 50 G7
Sinaia, *Romania* 29 E10
Sinaloa □, *Mexico* 118 C3
Sinaloa de Leyva, *Mexico* .. 118 B3
Sinalunga, *Italy* 41 E8
Sinan, *China* 58 D7
Sînandrei, *Romania* 28 E6
Sinarádhes, *Greece* 49 A3
Sincan, *Turkey* 72 B5
Sincanlı, *Turkey* 47 C12
Sincelejo, *Colombia* 124 B3
Sinch'ang, *N. Korea* 57 D15
Sinchang-ni, *N. Korea* 57 E14
Sinclair, *U.S.A.* 108 F10
Sinclair Mills, *Canada* 102 C4
Sinclair's B., *U.K.* 13 C5
Sinclairville, *U.S.A.* 116 D5
Sincorá, Serra do, *Brazil* .. 125 F10
Sind □, *Pakistan* 68 G3
Sind →, *Jammu & Kashmir, India* . 69 B6
Sind →, *Mad. P., India* 69 F8
Sind Sagar Doab, *Pakistan* . 68 D4
Sindal, *Denmark* 11 G4
Sindangan, *Phil.* 61 G5
Sindangbarang, *Indonesia* .. 63 G12
Sinde, *Zambia* 87 F2
Sindelfingen, *Germany* 25 G4
Sindh = Sind □, *Pakistan* .. 68 G3
Sındırgı, *Turkey* 47 B10
Sindou, *Burkina Faso* 82 C3
Sindri, *India* 69 H12
Sine →, *Senegal* 82 C1
Sinegorskiy, *Russia* 35 G5
Sinekli, *Turkey* 45 E12
Sinelnikovo = Synelnykove,
  Ukraine 33 H8
Sinendé, *Benin* 83 C5
Sines, *Portugal* 37 H2
Sines, C. de, *Portugal* 37 H2
Sineu, *Spain* 48 B10
Sinfra, *Ivory C.* 82 D3
Sing Buri, *Thailand* 64 E3
Singa, *Sudan* 81 E3
Singapore ■, *Asia* .... 65 d
Singapore, Straits of, *Asia* . 65 d
Singapore Changi ✈ (SIN),
  Singapore 65 M4
Singaraja, *Indonesia* 63 J18
Singen, *Germany* 25 H4
Singida, *Tanzania* 86 C3
Singida □, *Tanzania* 86 D3
Singitikós Kólpos, *Greece* .. 44 F7
Singkaling Hkamti, *Burma* .. 67 G19
Singkang, *Indonesia* 63 E6
Singkawang, *Indonesia* 62 D3
Singkep, *Indonesia* 62 E2
Singleton, *Australia* 95 E5
Singleton, Mt., *N. Terr., Australia* . 92 D5
Singleton, Mt., *W. Austral.,
  Australia* 93 E2
Singö, *Sweden* 10 D12
Singoli, *India* 68 G6
Singora = Songkhla, *Thailand* . 65 J3
Singosan, *N. Korea* 57 E14
Sinhüng, *N. Korea* 57 D14
Siniátsikon, Óros, *Greece* .. 44 F5
Siniscóla, *Italy* 42 B2
Sinj, *Croatia* 41 E13
Sinjai, *Indonesia* 63 F6
Sinjajevina, *Serbia & M.* .. 44 D3
Sinjār, *Iraq* 70 B4
Sinkat, *Sudan* 80 D4
Sinkiang Uighur = Xinjiang
  Uygur Zizhiqu □, *China* .. 60 B3
Sinmak, *N. Korea* 57 E14
Sínnai, *Italy* 42 C2
Sinnamary, *Fr. Guiana* 125 B8
Sinni →, *Italy* 43 B9
Sinnuris, *Egypt* 80 J7
Sinoie, Lacul, *Romania* 29 F13
Sinop, *Turkey* 72 A6
Sinor, *India* 68 J5
Sinp'o, *N. Korea* 57 E15
Sinsheim, *Germany* 25 F4
Sinsk, *Russia* 53 C13
Sinton, *U.S.A.* 113 L6
Sintra, *Portugal* 37 G1
Sintra-Cascais △, *Portugal* . 37 G1

Sinŭiju, *N. Korea* 57 D13
Sinyukha →, *Ukraine* 33 H6
Sinzig, *Germany* 24 E3
Sio →, *Hungary* 28 D3
Siocon, *Phil.* 61 H5
Siófok, *Hungary* 28 D3
Sion, *Switz.* 25 J3
Sion Mills, *U.K.* 12 B4
Sioux City, *U.S.A.* 112 D6
Sioux Falls, *U.S.A.* 112 D6
Sioux Lookout, *Canada* 104 B1
Sioux Narrows, *Canada* 103 D10
Sipalay, *Phil.* 61 G5
Sipan, *Croatia* 44 D1
Siparia, *Trin. & Tob.* 125 K15
Sipil Daği △, *Turkey* 47 C9
Siping, *China* 57 C13
Sipiwesk L., *Canada* 103 B9
Siple, *Antarctica* 5 D7
Sipovo, *Bos.-H.* 28 F2
Sipra →, *India* 68 H6
Sipura, *Indonesia* 62 E1
Siquia →, *Nic.* 120 D3
Siquijor, *Phil.* 61 G5
Siquirres, *Costa Rica* 120 D3
Şīr Abu Nu'ayr, *U.A.E.* 71 E7
Şīr Banī Yās, *U.A.E.* 71 E7
Sir Edward Pellew Group,
   Australia 94 B2
Sir Graham Moore Is., *Australia* . 92 B4
Sir James MacBrien, Mt., *Canada* . 100 B7
Sira →, *Norway* 9 G12
Siracusa, *Italy* 43 E8
Sirajganj, *Bangla.* 69 G13
Sirakoro, *Mali* 82 C3
Şiran, *Turkey* 73 B8
Sirasso, *Ivory C.* 82 D3
Sirathu, *India* 69 G9
Sīrdān, *Iran* 71 B6
Sirdaryo = Syrdarya →,
   Kazakhstan 52 E7
Sire, *Ethiopia* 81 F4
Siren, *U.S.A.* 112 C8
Sirente-Velino △, *Italy* 41 F10
Sirer, *Spain* 48 C7
Siret, *Romania* 29 C11
Siret →, *Romania* 29 E12
Sirghāyā, *Syria* 74 B5
Şiria, *Romania* 28 D6
Sirinath △, *Thailand* .... 65 a
Sirino, Mte., *Italy* 43 B8
Sīrjān, *Iran* 71 D7
Sirmaur, *India* 69 G9
Sírna, *Greece* 47 E8
Şırnak, *Turkey* 73 D10
Sirohi, *India* 68 G5
Sironj, *India* 68 G7
Síros, *Greece* 46 D6
Sirretta Pk., *U.S.A.* 111 K8
Sīrrī, *Iran* 71 E7
Sirsa, *India* 68 E6
Sirsa →, *India* 69 F8
Siruela, *Spain* 37 G5
Sisak, *Croatia* 41 C13
Sisaket, *Thailand* 64 E5
Sisante, *Spain* 39 F2
Sishen, *S. Africa* 88 D3
Sishui, *Henan, China* 56 G7
Sishui, *Shandong, China* 57 G9
Sisipuk L., *Canada* 103 B8
Sisophon, *Cambodia* 64 F4
Sisseton, *U.S.A.* 112 C6
Sissonne, *France* 19 C10
Sīstān, *Asia* 71 D9
Sīstān, Daryācheh-ye, *Iran* ... 71 D9
Sīstān va Balūchestān □, *Iran* .. 71 E9
Sisteron, *France* 21 D9
Sisters, *U.S.A.* 108 D3
Siswa Bazar, *India* 69 F10
Sitakili, *Mali* 82 C2
Sitamarhi, *India* 69 F11
Sitampiky, *Madag.* 89 B8
Sitapur, *India* 69 F9
Siteki, *Swaziland* 89 D5
Sitges, *Spain* 38 D6
Sithonía, *Greece* 44 F7
Sitía, *Greece* 49 D8
Sitka, *U.S.A.* 102 B1
Sitoti, *Botswana* 88 C3
Sitra, *Egypt* 80 B2
Sittang Myit →, *Burma* 67 L20
Sittard, *Neths.* 17 C5
Sittensen, *Germany* 24 B5
Sittingbourne, *U.K.* 15 F8
Sittona, *Eritrea* 81 E4
Sittoung = Sittang Myit →,
   Burma 67 L20
Sittwe, *Burma* 67 J18
Situbondo, *Indonesia* 63 G16
Siuna, *Nic.* 120 D3
Siuri, *India* 69 H12
Siutghiol, Lacul, *Romania* ... 29 F13
Sīvand, *Iran* 71 D7
Sivas, *Turkey* 70 B3
Sivaslı, *Turkey* 47 C11
Siverek, *Turkey* 70 B3
Sivrihisar, *Turkey* 72 C4
Sîwa, *Egypt* 80 B2
Sîwa, El Wâhât es, *Egypt* 80 B2
Siwa Oasis = Sîwa, El Wâhât es,
   Egypt 80 B2
Siwalik Range, *Nepal* 69 F10
Siwan, *India* 69 F11
Siwana, *India* 68 G5
Six Cross Roads, *Barbados* .. 121 g
Sixmilebridge, *Ireland* 12 D3
Sixth Cataract, *Sudan* 81 D3
Siyāl, Jazā'ir, *Egypt* 80 C4
Siyäzän, *Azerbaijan* 35 K9
Siziwang Qi, *China* 56 D6

Sjælland, *Denmark* 11 J5
Sjællands Odde, *Denmark* 11 J5
Sjenica, *Serbia & M.* 44 C3
Sjöbo, *Sweden* 11 J7
Sjötofta, *Sweden* 11 G7
Sjötorp, *Sweden* 11 F8
Sjumen = Shumen, *Bulgaria* .. 45 C10
Sjuntorp, *Sweden* 11 F6
Skadarsko Jezero, *Serbia & M.* .. 44 D3
Skadovsk, *Ukraine* 33 J7
Skælskør, *Denmark* 11 J5
Skærbæk, *Denmark* 11 J2
Skaftafell, *Iceland* 8 D5
Skagafjörður, *Iceland* 8 D4
Skagastølstindane, *Norway* ... 9 F12
Skagaströnd, *Iceland* 8 D3
Skagen, *Denmark* 11 G4
Skagern, *Sweden* 10 E8
Skagerrak, *Denmark* 11 G2
Skagit →, *U.S.A.* 110 B4
Skagway, *U.S.A.* 100 C6
Skala-Podilska, *Ukraine* 29 B11
Skala Podolskaya = Skala-
   Podilska, *Ukraine* 29 B11
Skalat, *Ukraine* 33 H3
Skalbmierz, *Poland* 31 H7
Skälderviken, *Sweden* 11 H6
Skalica, *Slovak Rep.* 27 C10
Skallingen, *Denmark* 11 J2
Skalni Dol = Kamenyak, *Bulgaria* . 45 C10
Skanderborg, *Denmark* 11 H3
Skåne, *Sweden* 11 J7
Skåne län □, *Sweden* 11 H7
Skaneateles, *U.S.A.* 117 D8
Skaneateles L., *U.S.A.* 117 D8
Skänninge, *Sweden* 11 F9
Skanör med Falsterbo, *Sweden* . 11 J6
Skantzoúra, *Greece* 46 B6
Skara, *Sweden* 11 F7
Skärblacka, *Sweden* 11 F9
Skardu, *Pakistan* 69 B6
Skåre, *Sweden* 10 E7
Skärhamn, *Sweden* 11 G5
Skarszewy, *Poland* 30 D5
Skaryszew, *Poland* 31 G8
Skarżysko-Kamienna, *Poland* . 31 G7
Skattkärr, *Sweden* 10 E7
Skattungbyn, *Sweden* 10 C8
Skawina, *Poland* 31 J6
Skebobruk, *Sweden* 10 E12
Skeena →, *Canada* 102 C2
Skeena Mts., *Canada* 102 B3
Skegness, *U.K.* 14 D8
Skeldon, *Guyana* 124 B7
Skeleton Coast, *Namibia* 85 H2
Skeleton Coast △, *Namibia* .. 88 C1
Skellefteå, *Sweden* 8 D19
Skellefteälven →, *Sweden* ... 8 D19
Skellefethamn, *Sweden* 8 D19
Skender Vakuf, *Bos.-H.* 28 F2
Skerries, The, *U.K.* 14 D3
Skhidnytsya, *Ukraine* 31 J10
Skhíza, *Greece* 46 E3
Skhoinoúsa, *Greece* 47 E7
Ski, *Norway* 9 G14
Skíathos, *Greece* 46 B5
Skibbereen, *Ireland* 12 E2
Skiddaw, *U.K.* 14 C4
Skidegate, *Canada* 102 C2
Skídhra, *Greece* 44 F6
Skien, *Norway* 9 G13
Skierniewice, *Poland* 31 G7
Skikda, *Algeria* 78 A7
Skillingaryd, *Sweden* 11 G8
Skillinge, *Sweden* 11 J8
Skilloura, *Cyprus* 49 D12
Skinári, Ákra, *Greece* 46 D2
Skinnskatteberg, *Sweden* 10 E9
Skipton, *U.K.* 14 D5
Skiring, C., *Senegal* 82 C1
Skirmish Pt., *Australia* 94 A1
Skiropoúla, *Greece* 46 C6
Skíros, *Greece* 46 C6
Skivarp, *Sweden* 11 J7
Skive, *Denmark* 11 H3
Skjálfandafljót →, *Iceland* ... 8 D5
Skjálfandi, *Iceland* 8 C5
Skjern, *Denmark* 11 J2
Skjoczów, *Poland* 31 J5
Škofja Loka, *Slovenia* 41 B11
Skoghall, *Sweden* 10 E7
Skogstorp, *Sweden* 10 E10
Skoki, *Poland* 31 F4
Skole, *Ukraine* 33 H2
Skópelos, *Greece* 46 B5
Skopí, *Greece* 49 D8
Skopin, *Russia* 32 F10
Skopje, *Macedonia* 44 D5
Skopje ✈ (SKP), *Macedonia* .. 44 E5
Skórcz, *Poland* 30 E5
Skørping, *Denmark* 11 H3
Skövde, *Sweden* 11 F7
Skovorodino, *Russia* 53 D13
Skowhegan, *U.S.A.* 115 C11
Skradin, *Croatia* 41 E12
Skrea, *Sweden* 11 H6
Skrunda, *Latvia* 30 B9
Skrwa →, *Poland* 31 F6
Skuleskogen △, *Sweden* 10 A12
Skull, *Ireland* 12 E2
Skultorp, *Sweden* 11 F7
Skultuna, *Sweden* 10 E10
Skunk →, *U.S.A.* 112 E9
Skuodas, *Lithuania* 9 H19
Skurup, *Sweden* 11 J7
Skutskär, *Sweden* 10 D11
Skvyra, *Ukraine* 33 H5
Skwierzyna, *Poland* 31 F2
Skye, *U.K.* 13 D2
Skykomish, *U.S.A.* 108 C3
Skyros = Skíros, *Greece* 46 C6

Skyttorp, *Sweden* 10 D11
Slade Pt., *Australia* 94 K7
Slættaratindur, *Færoe Is.* 8 E9
Slagelse, *Denmark* 11 J5
Slamet, *Indonesia* 63 G13
Slaney →, *Ireland* 12 D5
Slangberge, *S. Africa* 88 E3
Slano, *Croatia* 44 D1
Slănic, *Romania* 29 E10
Slantsy, *Russia* 32 C5
Slaný, *Czech Rep.* 26 A7
Śląskie □, *Poland* 31 H6
Slate Is., *Canada* 104 C2
Slatina, *Croatia* 28 E2
Slatina, *Romania* 29 F9
Slatina Timiş, *Romania* 28 E7
Slatington, *U.S.A.* 117 F9
Slaton, *U.S.A.* 113 J4
Slave →, *Canada* 102 A6
Slave Coast, *W. Afr.* 83 D5
Slave Lake, *Canada* 102 B6
Slave Pt., *Canada* 102 A5
Slavgorod, *Russia* 52 D8
Slavinja, *Serbia & M.* 44 C6
Slavkov u Brna, *Czech Rep.* .. 27 B9
Slavkovský Les △, *Czech Rep.* . 26 A5
Slavonija, *Europe* 28 E2
Slavonski Brod, *Croatia* 28 E3
Slavsk, *Russia* 30 C8
Slavska, *Ukraine* 29 B8
Slavskoye, *Russia* 30 D7
Slavuta, *Ukraine* 33 G4
Slavyanka, *Russia* 54 C5
Slavyanovo, *Bulgaria* 45 C8
Slavyansk = Slovyansk, *Ukraine* . 33 H9
Slavyansk-na-Kubani, *Russia* .. 33 K10
Sława, *Poland* 31 G3
Sławharad, *Belarus* 32 F6
Sławno, *Poland* 30 D3
Sławoborze, *Poland* 30 E2
Sleaford, *U.K.* 14 D7
Sleaford B., *Australia* 95 E2
Sleat, Sd. of, *U.K.* 13 D3
Sleeper Is., *Canada* 101 C11
Sleeping Bear Dunes △, *U.S.A.* . 114 C2
Sleepy Eye, *U.S.A.* 112 C7
Slemon L., *Canada* 102 A5
Slesin, *Poland* 31 F5
Slide Mt., *U.S.A.* 117 E10
Slidell, *U.S.A.* 113 K10
Sliema, *Malta* 49 D2
Slieve Aughty, *Ireland* 12 C3
Slieve Bloom, *Ireland* 12 C4
Slieve Donard, *U.K.* 12 B6
Slieve Gamph, *Ireland* 12 B3
Slieve Gullion, *U.K.* 12 B5
Slieve League, *Ireland* 12 B3
Slieve Mish, *Ireland* 12 D2
Slievenamon, *Ireland* 12 D4
Sligeach = Sligo, *Ireland* 12 B3
Sligo, *Ireland* 12 B3
Sligo, *U.S.A.* 116 E5
Sligo □, *Ireland* 12 B3
Sligo B., *Ireland* 12 B3
Slippery Rock, *U.S.A.* 116 E4
Slite, *Sweden* 11 G12
Slīteres △, *Latvia* 30 A9
Sliven, *Bulgaria* 45 D10
Slivnitsa, *Bulgaria* 44 D7
Sljeme, *Croatia* 41 C12
Sloan, *U.S.A.* 111 K11
Sloansville, *U.S.A.* 117 D10
Slobidka, *Ukraine* 29 B14
Slobozia, *Moldova* 29 D14
Slobozia, *Argeş, Romania* ... 29 F10
Slobozia, *Ialomiţa, Romania* . 29 F12
Slocan, *Canada* 102 D5
Słomniki, *Poland* 31 H7
Slonim, *Belarus* 33 F3
Slough, *U.K.* 15 F7
Slough □, *U.K.* 15 F7
Sloughhouse, *U.S.A.* 110 G5
Slovak Rep. ■, *Europe* 27 C13
Slovakia = Slovak Rep. ■, *Europe* . 27 C13
Slovakian Ore Mts. = Slovenské
   Rudohorie, *Slovak Rep.* 27 C12
Slovenia ■, *Europe* 41 C11
Slovenija = Slovenia ■, *Europe* . 41 C11
Slovenj Gradec, *Slovenia* 41 B12
Slovenska Bistrica, *Slovenia* .. 41 B12
Slovenské Konjice, *Slovenia* .. 41 B12
Slovenské Rudohorie,
   Slovak Rep. 27 C12
Slovenský Raj △, *Slovak Rep.* . 27 C12
Slovyansk, *Ukraine* 33 H9
Słowiński □, *Poland* 30 D4
Słubice, *Poland* 31 F1
Sluch →, *Ukraine* 33 G4
Sluis, *Neths.* 17 C3
Slünchev Bryag, *Bulgaria* 45 D11
Slunj, *Croatia* 41 C12
Słupca, *Poland* 31 F4
Słupia →, *Poland* 30 D3
Słupsk, *Poland* 30 D3
Slurry, *S. Africa* 88 D4
Slutsk, *Belarus* 33 F4
Slyne Hd., *Ireland* 12 C1
Slyudyanka, *Russia* 53 D11
Småland, *Sweden* 11 G9
Smålandsfarvandet, *Denmark* . 11 J5
Smålandsstenar, *Sweden* 11 G7
Smalltree L., *Canada* 103 A8
Smallwood Res., *Canada* 105 B7
Smarhon, *Belarus* 32 E14
Smarje, *Slovenia* 41 B12
Smartt Syndicate Dam, *S. Africa* . 88 E3
Smartville, *U.S.A.* 110 F5
Smeaton, *Canada* 103 C8
Smedby, *Sweden* 11 H10
Smederevo, *Serbia & M.* 44 B4

Smederevska Palanka,
   Serbia & M. 44 B4
Smedjebacken, *Sweden* 10 D9
Smela = Smila, *Ukraine* 33 H6
Smerwick Harbour, *Ireland* .. 12 D1
Smethport, *U.S.A.* 116 E6
Smidovich, *Russia* 53 E14
Śmigiel, *Poland* 31 F3
Smila, *Ukraine* 33 H6
Smilyan, *Bulgaria* 45 E8
Smith, *Canada* 102 B6
Smith Center, *U.S.A.* 112 F5
Smith River →, *U.S.A.* 108 F2
Smith Sd., *N. Amer.* 4 B4
Smithburne →, *Australia* 94 B3
Smithers, *Canada* 102 C3
Smithfield, *S. Africa* 89 E4
Smithfield, *N.C., U.S.A.* 115 H6
Smithfield, *Utah, U.S.A.* 108 F8
Smiths Falls, *Canada* 117 B9
Smithton, *Australia* 95 G4
Smithville, *Canada* 116 C5
Smithville, *U.S.A.* 113 K6
Smoky →, *Canada* 102 B5
Smoky Bay, *Australia* 95 E1
Smoky Hill →, *U.S.A.* 112 F6
Smoky Hills, *U.S.A.* 112 F5
Smoky Lake, *Canada* 102 C6
Smøla, *Norway* 8 E13
Smolensk, *Russia* 32 E7
Smolikas, Óros, *Greece* 44 F4
Smolník, *Slovak Rep.* 27 C13
Smolyan, *Bulgaria* 45 E8
Smooth Rock Falls, *Canada* .. 104 C3
Smoothstone L., *Canada* 103 C7
Smorgon = Smarhon, *Belarus* . 32 E14
Smotrych, *Ukraine* 29 B11
Smotrych →, *Ukraine* 29 B11
Smulți, *Romania* 29 E12
Smyadovo, *Bulgaria* 45 C11
Smygehamn, *Sweden* 11 J7
Smyrna = Izmir, *Turkey* 47 C9
Smyrna, *U.S.A.* 114 F8
Snæfell, *Iceland* 8 D6
Snaefell, *I. of Man* 14 C3
Snæfellsjökull, *Iceland* 8 D2
Snake →, *U.S.A.* 108 C4
Snake I., *Australia* 95 F4
Snake Range, *U.S.A.* 108 G6
Snake River Plain, *U.S.A.* ... 108 E7
Snasahögarna, *Sweden* 10 A7
Snåsavatnet, *Norway* 8 D14
Snedsted, *Denmark* 11 H2
Sneek, *Neths.* 17 A5
Sneeuberge, *S. Africa* 88 E3
Snejbjerg, *Denmark* 11 H2
Snelling, *U.S.A.* 110 H6
Snezhnoye, *Ukraine* 33 J10
Snežnik, *Slovenia* 41 C11
Śniadowo, *Poland* 31 E8
Sniardwy, Jezioro, *Poland* ... 30 E8
Śnieżka, *Europe* 26 A8
Snigirevka = Snihurivka, *Ukraine* . 33 J7
Snihurivka, *Ukraine* 33 J7
Snina, *Slovak Rep.* 27 C15
Snizort, L., *U.K.* 13 D2
Snøhetta, *Norway* 9 E13
Snohomish, *U.S.A.* 110 C4
Snoul, *Cambodia* 65 F6
Snow Hill, *U.S.A.* 114 F8
Snow Lake, *Canada* 103 C8
Snow Mt., *Calif., U.S.A.* 110 F4
Snow Mt., *Maine, U.S.A.* 117 A14
Snow Shoe, *U.S.A.* 116 E7
Snowbird L., *Canada* 103 A8
Snowdon, *U.K.* 14 D3
Snowdonia △, *U.K.* 14 D4
Snowdrift = Łutselk'e, *Canada* . 103 A6
Snowdrift →, *Canada* 103 A6
Snowflake, *U.S.A.* 109 J8
Snowshoe Pk., *U.S.A.* 108 B6
Snowtown, *Australia* 95 E2
Snowville, *U.S.A.* 108 F7
Snowy →, *Australia* 95 F4
Snowy Mt., *U.S.A.* 117 C10
Snowy Mts., *Australia* 95 F4
Snug Corner, *Bahamas* 121 B5
Snyatyn, *Ukraine* 29 B10
Snyder, *Okla., U.S.A.* 113 H5
Snyder, *Tex., U.S.A.* 113 J4
Soahanina, *Madag.* 89 B7
Soalala, *Madag.* 89 B8
Soaloka, *Madag.* 89 B8
Soamanonga, *Madag.* 89 C7
Soan →, *Pakistan* 68 C4
Soanierana-Ivongo, *Madag.* .. 89 B8
Soanindraniny, *Madag.* 89 B8
Şoarş, *Romania* 29 E9
Soavina, *Madag.* 89 C8
Soavinandriana, *Madag.* 89 B8
Sob →, *Ukraine* 29 B14
Soba, *Nigeria* 83 C6
Sobat, Nahr →, *Sudan* 81 F3
Soběslav, *Czech Rep.* 26 B7
Sobhapur, *India* 68 H8
Sobinka, *Russia* 32 E11
Sobótka, *Poland* 31 H3
Sobradinho, Reprêsa de, *Brazil* . 125 E10
Sobral, *Brazil* 125 D10
Sobrance, *Slovak Rep.* 27 C15
Soc Giang, *Vietnam* 58 F6
Soc Trang, *Vietnam* 65 H5
Soča →, *Europe* 26 E6
Socastee, *U.S.A.* 115 J6
Sochaczew, *Poland* 31 F7
Soch'e = Shache, *China* 60 C2
Sochi, *Russia* 35 J4
Société, Is. de la, *French Polynesia* . 97 J12
Society Is. = Société, Is. de la,
   French Polynesia 97 J12

Socompa, Portezuelo de, *Chile* . 126 A2
Socorro, *N. Mex., U.S.A.* 109 J10
Socorro, *Tex., U.S.A.* 109 L10
Socorro, I., *Mexico* 118 D2
Socotra, *Yemen* 75 E5
Socovos, *Spain* 39 G3
Socuéllamos, *Spain* 39 F2
Soda L., *U.S.A.* 109 J5
Soda Plains, *India* 69 B8
Soda Springs, *U.S.A.* 108 E8
Sodankylä, *Finland* 8 C22
Soddy-Daisy, *U.S.A.* 115 H3
Söderala, *Sweden* 10 C10
Söderåsen △, *Sweden* 11 H7
Söderbärke, *Sweden* 10 D9
Söderfors, *Sweden* 10 D11
Söderhamn, *Sweden* 10 C11
Söderköping, *Sweden* 11 F10
Södermanland, *Sweden* 9 G17
Södermanlands län □, *Sweden* . 10 E10
Södertälje, *Sweden* 10 E11
Sodiri, *Sudan* 81 E2
Sodo, *Ethiopia* 81 F4
Södra Dellen, *Sweden* 10 C10
Södra Finnskoga, *Sweden* ... 10 D6
Södra Sandby, *Sweden* 11 J7
Södra Ulvön, *Sweden* 10 B12
Södra Vi, *Sweden* 11 G9
Sodražica, *Slovenia* 41 C11
Sodus, *U.S.A.* 116 C7
Sodwana Bay △, *S. Africa* ... 89 D5
Soekmekaar, *S. Africa* 89 C4
Soest, *Germany* 24 D4
Soest, *Neths.* 17 B5
Sofádhes, *Greece* 46 B4
Sofala △, *Mozam.* 89 B5
Sofara, *Mali* 82 C4
Sofia = Sofiya, *Bulgaria* 44 D7
Sofia →, *Madag.* 89 B8
Sofievka, *Ukraine* 33 H7
Sofikón, *Greece* 46 D5
Sofiya, *Bulgaria* 44 D7
Sofiya □, *Bulgaria* 44 D7
Sofiya ✈ (SOF), *Bulgaria* 44 D7
Sōfu-Gan, *Japan* 55 K10
Sogakofe, *Ghana* 83 D5
Sogamoso, *Colombia* 124 B4
Sogār, *Iran* 71 E8
Sögel, *Germany* 24 C3
Sogndalsfjøra, *Norway* 9 F12
Søgne, *Norway* 9 G12
Sognefjorden, *Norway* 9 F11
Söğüt, *Bilecik, Turkey* 47 A12
Söğüt, *Burdur, Turkey* 47 D11
Söğüt Daği △, *Turkey* 47 D11
Söğütköy, *Turkey* 47 E10
Sögwipo, *S. Korea* 57 H14
Soh, *Iran* 71 C6
Sok →, *Russia* 34 D10
Sokal, *Ukraine* 33 G3
Söke, *Turkey* 47 D9
Sokelo, *Dem. Rep. of the Congo* . 87 D1
Sokhós, *Greece* 44 F7
Sokhumi, *Georgia* 35 J5
Soko Banja, *Serbia & M.* 44 C5
Sokodé, *Togo* 83 D5
Sokol, *Russia* 32 C11
Sokolac, *Bos.-H.* 28 G3
Sokółka, *Poland* 30 E10
Sokolo, *Ségou, Mali* 82 C3
Sokolo, *Sikasso, Mali* 82 C3
Sokolov, *Czech Rep.* 26 A5
Sokołów Małopolski, *Poland* .. 31 H9
Sokołów Podlaski, *Poland* ... 31 F9
Sokoły, *Poland* 31 F9
Sokoto, *Nigeria* 83 C6
Sokoto □, *Nigeria* 83 C6
Sokoto →, *Nigeria* 83 C5
Sokyrnytsya, *Ukraine* 29 B8
Sokyryany, *Ukraine* 29 B12
Sol Iletsk, *Russia* 52 D6
Sola →, *Poland* 31 H6
Solai, *Kenya* 86 B4
Solan, *India* 68 D7
Solander I., *N.Z.* 91 M1
Solano, *Phil.* 61 C4
Solapur, *India* 66 L9
Solca, *Romania* 29 C10
Solda Gölü, *Turkey* 47 D11
Soldănești, *Moldova* 29 C13
Soldeu, *Andorra* 38 C6
Soldotna, *U.S.A.* 100 B4
Soléa, *Cyprus* 49 D12
Solec Kujawski, *Poland* 31 E5
Soledad, *Colombia* 124 A4
Soledad, *U.S.A.* 110 J5
Soledad, *Venezuela* 124 B6
Solent, The, *U.K.* 15 G6
Solenzara, *France* 21 G13
Solesmes, *France* 19 B10
Solfonn, *Norway* 9 F12
Solhan, *Turkey* 70 B4
Soligorsk = Salihorsk, *Belarus* . 33 F4
Solihull, *U.K.* 15 E6
Solikamsk, *Russia* 52 D6
Solila, *Madag.* 89 C8
Solimões = Amazonas →,
   S. Amer. 125 D9
Solin, *Croatia* 41 E13
Solingen, *Germany* 24 D3
Sollebrunn, *Sweden* 11 F6
Sollefteå, *Sweden* 10 A11

Sollentuna, *Sweden* 10 E11
Sóller, *Spain* 48 B9
Solleron, *Sweden* 10 D8
Solling, *Germany* 24 D5
Solling-Vogler △, *Germany* 24 D5
Solnechnogorsk, *Russia* 32 D9
Solo →, *Indonesia* 63 G15
Solofra, *Italy* 43 B7
Sologne, *France* 19 E8
Solok, *Indonesia* 62 E2
Sololá, *Guatemala* 120 D1
Solomon, N. Fork →, *U.S.A.* ... 112 F5
Solomon, S. Fork →, *U.S.A.* ... 112 F5
Solomon Is. ■, *Pac. Oc.* 96 H7
Solon, *China* 60 B7
Solon Springs, *U.S.A.* 112 B9
Solor, *Indonesia* 63 F6
Solotcha, *Russia* 32 E10
Solothurn, *Switz.* 25 H3
Solothurn □, *Switz.* 25 H3
Solotvyn, *Ukraine* 29 B9
Solsona, *Spain* 38 C6
Solt, *Hungary* 28 D4
Šolta, *Croatia* 41 E13
Solṭānābād, *Khorāsān, Iran* ... 71 C8
Solṭānābād, *Khorāsān, Iran* ... 71 B8
Soltau, *Germany* 24 C5
Soltsy, *Russia* 32 C6
Solunska Glava, *Macedonia* 44 E5
Solvang, *U.S.A.* 111 L6
Solvay, *U.S.A.* 117 C8
Sölvesborg, *Sweden* 11 H8
Solway Firth, *U.K.* 14 C4
Solwezi, *Zambia* 87 E2
Sōma, *Japan* 54 F10
Soma, *Turkey* 47 B9
Somabhula, *Zimbabwe* 89 B4
Somali Pen., *Africa* 76 F8
Somali Rep. ■, *Africa* 75 F4
Somalia = Somali Rep. ■, *Africa* 75 F4
Sombernon, *France* 19 E11
Sombor, *Serbia & M.* 28 E4
Sombra, *Canada* 116 D2
Sombrerete, *Mexico* 118 C4
Sombrero, *Anguilla* 121 C7
Şomcuta Mare, *Romania* 29 C8
Somdari, *India* 68 G5
Someido △, *Spain* 36 B4
Somers, *U.S.A.* 108 B6
Somerset, *Ky., U.S.A.* 114 G3
Somerset, *Mass., U.S.A.* 117 E13
Somerset, *Pa., U.S.A.* 116 F5
Somerset □, *U.K.* 15 F5
Somerset East, *S. Africa* 88 E4
Somerset I., *Canada* 100 A10
Somerset West, *S. Africa* 88 E2
Somersworth, *U.S.A.* 117 C14
Somerton, *U.S.A.* 109 K6
Somerville, *U.S.A.* 117 F10
Someş →, *Romania* 28 C7
Someşul Mare →, *Romania* 29 C8
Somme □, *France* 19 C9
Somme →, *France* 19 B8
Somme, B. de la, *France* 18 B8
Sommen, *Jönköping, Sweden* 11 F8
Sommen, *Östergötland, Sweden* . 11 F9
Sommepy-Tahure, *France* 19 C11
Sommesous, *France* 19 D11
Sommières, *France* 21 E8
Somnath, *India* 68 J4
Somogy □, *Hungary* 28 D2
Somogyszob, *Hungary* 28 D2
Somoto, *Nic.* 120 D2
Sompolno, *Poland* 31 F5
Somport, Puerto de, *Spain* 38 C4
Son →, *India* 69 G11
Son Ha, *Vietnam* 64 E7
Son Hoa, *Vietnam* 64 F7
Son La, *Vietnam* 58 G4
Son Serra, *Spain* 48 B10
Son Servera, *Spain* 38 F8
Son Tay, *Vietnam* 58 G5
Soná, *Panama* 120 E3
Sonamarg, *India* 69 B6
Sonamukhi, *India* 69 H12
Sonar →, *India* 69 G8
Sŏnch'ŏn, *N. Korea* 57 E13
Sondags →, *S. Africa* 88 E4
Sóndalo, *Italy* 40 B7
Sondar, *India* 69 C6
Sønder Felding, *Denmark* 11 J2
Sønder Omme, *Denmark* 11 J2
Sønderborg, *Denmark* 11 K3
Sønderjyllands Amtskommune □,
    Denmark 11 J3
Sondershausen, *Germany* 24 D6
Sóndrio, *Italy* 40 B6
Sone, *Mozam.* 87 F3
Sonepur, *India* 67 J13
Song, *Nigeria* 83 D7
Song, *Thailand* 64 C3
Song Cau, *Vietnam* 64 F7
Song Xian, *China* 56 G7
Songan, *Indonesia* 63 J18
Sŏngch'ŏn, *N. Korea* 57 E14
Songea, *Tanzania* 87 E4
Songeons, *France* 19 C8
Songhua Hu, *China* 57 C14
Songhua Jiang →, *China* 60 B8
Songimvelo △, *S. Africa* 89 D5
Songjiang, *China* 59 B13
Songjin, *N. Korea* 57 D15
Songjŏng-ni, *S. Korea* 57 G14
Songkan, *China* 58 C6
Songkhla, *Thailand* 65 J3
Songming, *China* 58 E4
Songnim, *N. Korea* 57 E13
Songo, *Mozam.* 85 H6
Songo, *Sudan* 79 G10
Songpan, *China* 58 A4

Songtao, *China* 58 C7
Songwe, *Dem. Rep. of the Congo* 86 C2
Songwe →, *Africa* 87 D3
Songxi, *China* 59 D12
Songzi, *China* 59 B8
Sonhat, *India* 69 H10
Sonid Youqi, *China* 56 C7
Sonipat, *India* 68 E7
Sonkach, *India* 68 H7
Sonkovo, *Russia* 32 D9
Sonmiani, *Pakistan* 68 G2
Sonmiani B., *Pakistan* 68 G2
Sonnino, *Italy* 42 A6
Sono →, *Brazil* 125 E9
Sonoma, *U.S.A.* 110 G4
Sonora, *Calif., U.S.A.* 110 H6
Sonora, *Tex., U.S.A.* 113 K4
Sonora □, *Mexico* 118 B2
Sonora →, *Mexico* 118 B2
Sonoran Desert, *U.S.A.* 111 L12
Sonoyta, *Mexico* 118 A2
Sonqor, *Iran* 73 E12
Sŏnsan, *S. Korea* 57 F15
Sonseca, *Spain* 37 F7
Sonsonate, *El Salv.* 120 D2
Sonstorp, *Sweden* 11 F9
Sonthofen, *Germany* 25 H6
Soochow = Suzhou, *China* 59 B13
Sooke, *Canada* 110 B3
Sop Hao, *Laos* 58 G5
Sop Prap, *Thailand* 64 D2
Sopelana, *Spain* 38 B2
Sopi, *Indonesia* 63 D7
Sopo, Nahr →, *Sudan* 81 F2
Sopot, *Bulgaria* 45 D8
Sopot, *Poland* 30 D5
Sopot, *Serbia & M.* 44 B4
Sopotnica, *Macedonia* 44 E5
Sopron, *Hungary* 28 C1
Sopur, *India* 69 B6
Sør-Rondane, *Antarctica* 5 D4
Sora, *Italy* 41 G10
Sorah, *Pakistan* 68 F3
Söråker, *Sweden* 10 B11
Sorano, *Italy* 41 F8
Soraon, *India* 69 G9
Sorbas, *Spain* 39 H2
Sörbygden, *Sweden* 10 B10
Sore, *France* 20 D3
Sorel-Tracy, *Canada* 104 C5
Soresina, *Italy* 40 C6
Sörforsa, *Sweden* 10 C10
Sórgono, *Italy* 42 B2
Sorgues, *France* 21 D8
Sorgun, *Turkey* 72 C6
Soria, *Spain* 38 D2
Soria □, *Spain* 38 D2
Soriano, *Uruguay* 126 C4
Soriano nel Cimino, *Italy* 41 F9
Sorkh, Kuh-e, *Iran* 71 C8
Sorø, *Denmark* 11 J5
Soro, *Guinea* 82 C3
Soroca, *Moldova* 29 B13
Sorocaba, *Brazil* 127 A6
Soroki = Soroca, *Moldova* 29 B13
Sorong, *Indonesia* 63 E8
Soroni, *Greece* 49 C10
Soroti, *Uganda* 86 B3
Sørøya, *Norway* 8 A20
Sørøysundet, *Norway* 8 A20
Sorraia →, *Portugal* 37 G2
Sorrell, *Australia* 95 G4
Sorrento, *Italy* 43 B7
Sorsele, *Sweden* 8 D17
Sörsjön, *Sweden* 10 C7
Sorso, *Italy* 42 B1
Sorsogon, *Phil.* 61 E6
Sortavala, *Russia* 32 B6
Sortino, *Italy* 43 E8
Sortland, *Norway* 8 B16
Sorvizhi, *Russia* 34 B9
Sos del Rey Católico, *Spain* .. 38 C3
Sŏsan, *S. Korea* 57 F14
Soscumica, L., *Canada* 104 B4
Sösdala, *Sweden* 11 H7
Sosna →, *Russia* 33 F10
Sosnovka, *Kirov, Russia* 34 B10
Sosnovka, *Tambov, Russia* 34 D5
Sosnovyy Bor, *Russia* 32 C5
Sosnowiec, *Poland* 31 H6
Sospel, *France* 21 E11
Sossus Vlei, *Namibia* 88 C2
Šoštanj, *Slovenia* 41 B12
Sŏsura, *N. Korea* 57 C16
Sot →, *India* 69 F8
Sotkamo, *Finland* 8 D23
Soto del Barco, *Spain* 36 B4
Soto la Marina →, *Mexico* 119 C5
Soto y Amío, *Spain* 36 C5
Sotrondio, *Spain* 36 B5
Sotuta, *Mexico* 119 C7
Souanké, *Congo* 84 D2
Soubré, *Ivory C.* 82 D3
Souderton, *U.S.A.* 117 F9
Soúdha, *Greece* 49 D6
Soúdhas, Kólpos, *Greece* 49 D6
Souflíon, *Greece* 45 E10
Soufrière, *Guadeloupe* .... 120 b
Soufrière, *St. Lucia* .... 121 f
Soufrière Bay, *Dominica* ...... 121 f
Souillac, *France* 20 D5
Souilly, *France* 19 C12
Soukhouma, *Laos* 64 E5
Sŏul, *S. Korea* 57 F14
Soulac-sur-Mer, *France* 20 C2
Soulougou, *Burkina Faso* 83 C5
Soultz-sous-Forêts, *France* ... 19 D14
Sound, The = Øresund, *Europe* . 11 J6
Sound, The, *U.K.* 15 G3
Soúnion, Ákra, *Greece* 46 D6
Sources, Mt. aux, *Lesotho* 89 D4

Soure, *Brazil* 125 D9
Soure, *Portugal* 36 E2
Souris, *Man., Canada* 103 D8
Souris, *P.E.I., Canada* 105 C7
Souris →, *Canada* 112 A5
Sourou →, *Africa* 82 C4
Soúrpi, *Greece* 46 B4
Sousa, *Brazil* 125 E11
Sousel, *Portugal* 37 G3
Sousse, *Tunisia* 79 A8
Soustons, *France* 20 E2
Sout →, *S. Africa* 88 E2
South Africa ■, *Africa* 88 E3
South America 122 E5
South Atlantic Ocean 2 F8
South Aulatsivik I., *Canada* .. 105 A7
South Australia □, *Australia* . 95 E2
South Ayrshire □, *U.K.* 13 F4
South Baldy, *U.S.A.* 109 J10
South Bass I., *U.S.A.* 116 E2
South Bend, *Ind., U.S.A.* 114 E2
South Bend, *Wash., U.S.A.* 110 D3
South Boston, *U.S.A.* 115 G6
South Branch, *Canada* 105 C8
South Brook, *Canada* 105 C8
South Carolina □, *U.S.A.* 115 J5
South Charleston, *U.S.A.* 114 F5
South China Sea, *Asia* 62 C4
South Cumberland Is. △,
    Australia 94 J7
South Dakota □, *U.S.A.* 112 C5
South Deerfield, *U.S.A.* 117 D12
South Downs, *U.K.* 15 G7
South East C., *Australia* 95 G4
South-East Indian Rise, *Ind. Oc.* 5 B10
South East Is., *Australia* 93 F3
South Esk →, *U.K.* 13 E6
South Foreland, *U.K.* 15 F9
South Fork American →, *U.S.A.* 110 G5
South Fork Feather →, *U.S.A.* . 110 F5
South Fork Grand →, *U.S.A.* ... 112 C3
South Fork Republican →,
    U.S.A. 112 E4
South Georgia, *Antarctica* 128 G9
South Gloucestershire □, *U.K.* 15 F5
South Hadley, *U.S.A.* 117 D12
South Haven, *U.S.A.* 114 D2
South Henik L., *Canada* 103 A9
South Honshu Ridge, *Pac. Oc.* . 96 E6
South Horr, *Kenya* 86 B4
South I., *Kenya* 86 B4
South I., *N.Z.* 91 L3
South Indian Lake, *Canada* 103 B9
South Invercargill, *N.Z.* 91 M2
South Island △, *Kenya* 86 B4
South Kitui △, *Kenya* 86 C4
South Knife →, *Canada* 103 B10
South Koel →, *India* 69 H11
South Korea ■, *Asia* 57 G15
South Lake Tahoe, *U.S.A.* 110 G6
South Lanarkshire □, *U.K.* 13 F5
South Loup →, *U.S.A.* 112 E5
South Luangwa △, *Zambia* 87 E3
South Magnetic Pole, *Antarctica* 5 C9
South Milwaukee, *U.S.A.* 114 D2
South Molton, *U.K.* 15 F4
South Moose L., *Canada* 103 C8
South Nahanni →, *Canada* 102 A4
South Natuna Is. = Natuna
    Selatan, Kepulauan, *Indonesia* 62 D3
South Negril Pt., *Jamaica* .... 120 a
South Orkney Is., *Antarctica* . 5 C18
South Ossetia □, *Georgia* 35 J7
South Pagai, I. = Pagai Selatan,
    Pulau, *Indonesia* 62 E2
South Paris, *U.S.A.* 117 B14
South Pittsburg, *U.S.A.* 115 H3
South Platte →, *U.S.A.* 112 E4
South Pole, *Antarctica* .... 5 E
South Porcupine, *Canada* 104 C3
South Portland, *U.S.A.* 115 D10
South Pt., *Barbados* .... 121 g
South Pt., *U.S.A.* 116 B1
South River, *Canada* 104 C4
South River, *U.S.A.* 117 F10
South Ronaldsay, *U.K.* 13 C6
South Sandwich Is., *Antarctica* 5 B1
South Saskatchewan →, *Canada* . 103 C7
South Seal →, *Canada* 103 B9
South Shetland Is., *Antarctica* 5 C18
South Shields, *U.K.* 14 C6
South Sioux City, *U.S.A.* 112 D6
South Taranaki Bight, *N.Z.* ... 91 H5
South Thompson →, *Canada* 102 C4
South Twin I., *Canada* 104 B4
South Tyne →, *U.K.* 14 C5
South Uist, *U.K.* 13 D1
South West C., *Australia* 95 G4
South West C., *N.Z.* 91 M1
South Williamsport, *U.S.A.* ... 116 E8
South Yorkshire □, *U.K.* 14 D6
Southampton, *Canada* 116 B3
Southampton, *U.K.* 15 G6
Southampton, *U.S.A.* 117 F12
Southampton □, *U.K.* 15 G6
Southampton I., *Canada* 101 B11
Southaven, *U.S.A.* 113 H9
Southbank, *Canada* 102 C3
Southbridge, *N.Z.* 91 K4
Southbridge, *U.S.A.* 117 D12
Southend, *Canada* 103 B8
Southend-on-Sea, *U.K.* 15 F8
Southend-on-Sea □, *U.K.* 15 F8
Southern = Janub □, *Sudan* 81 F2
Southern = Yedebub Biheroch
    Bihereseboch na Hizboch □,
    Ethiopia 81 F4
Southern = Yuzhnyy □, *Russia* . 35 H5
Southern □, *Malawi* 87 F4

Southern □, *S. Leone* 82 D2
Southern □, *Zambia* 87 F2
Southern Alps, *N.Z.* 91 K3
Southern Cross, *Australia* 93 F2
Southern Indian L., *Canada* ... 103 B9
Southern Ocean, *Antarctica* ... 5 C6
Southern Pines, *U.S.A.* 115 H6
Southern Uplands, *U.K.* 13 F5
Southington, *U.S.A.* 117 E12
Southland □, *N.Z.* 91 L1
Southold, *U.S.A.* 117 E12
Southport, *Australia* 95 D5
Southport, *U.K.* 14 D4
Southport, *Fla., U.S.A.* 115 K3
Southport, *N.Y., U.S.A.* 116 D8
Southwest →, *Australia* 95 G4
Southwestern Pacific Basin,
    Pac. Oc. 5 A12
Southwold, *U.K.* 15 E9
Southwood △, *Australia* 95 D5
Soutpansberg, *S. Africa* 89 C4
Souvigny, *France* 19 F10
Sovata, *Romania* 29 D10
Soverato, *Italy* 43 D9
Sovetsk, *Kaliningrad, Russia* . 9 J19
Sovetsk, *Kirov, Russia* 34 B9
Sovetskaya Gavan = Vanino,
    Russia 53 E15
Sovicille, *Italy* 41 E8
Soweto, *S. Africa* 89 D4
Sōya-Kaikyō = La Perouse Str.,
    Asia 54 B11
Sōya-Misaki, *Japan* 54 B10
Soyaux, *France* 20 C4
Sozh →, *Belarus* 33 F6
Sozopol, *Bulgaria* 45 D11
Spa, *Belgium* 17 D5
Spain ■, *Europe* 7 H5
Spalding, *Australia* 95 E2
Spalding, *U.K.* 14 E7
Spangler, *U.S.A.* 116 F6
Spanish, *Canada* 104 C3
Spanish Fork, *U.S.A.* 108 F8
Spanish Town, *Br. Virgin Is.* . 121 e
Spanish Town, *Jamaica* .... 120 a
Sparks, *U.S.A.* 110 F7
Sparreholm, *Sweden* 10 E10
Sparta = Spárti, *Greece* 46 D4
Sparta, *Mich., U.S.A.* 114 D3
Sparta, *N.J., U.S.A.* 117 E10
Sparta, *Wis., U.S.A.* 112 D9
Spartanburg, *U.S.A.* 115 H5
Spartansburg, *U.S.A.* 116 E5
Spárti, *Greece* 46 D4
Spartivento, C., *Calabria, Italy* 43 E9
Spartivento, C., *Sard., Italy* 42 D1
Sparwood, *Canada* 102 D6
Spas-Demensk, *Russia* 32 E7
Spas-Klepiki, *Russia* 32 E11
Spassk Dalniy, *Russia* 53 E14
Spassk-Ryazanskiy, *Russia* 32 E11
Spátha, Ákra, *Greece* 49 D5
Spatsizi →, *Canada* 102 B3
Spatsizi Plateau Wilderness △,
    Canada 102 B3
Spean →, *U.K.* 13 E4
Spearfish, *U.S.A.* 112 C3
Spearman, *U.S.A.* 113 G4
Speculator, *U.S.A.* 117 C10
Speia, *Moldova* 29 D14
Speightstown, *Barbados* .... 121 g
Speke Gulf, *Tanzania* 86 C3
Spello, *Italy* 41 F9
Spence Bay = Taloyoak, *Canada* 100 B10
Spencer, *Idaho, U.S.A.* 108 D7
Spencer, *Iowa, U.S.A.* 112 D7
Spencer, *N.Y., U.S.A.* 117 D8
Spencer, *Nebr., U.S.A.* 112 D5
Spencer, *C., Australia* 95 F2
Spencer B., *Namibia* 88 D1
Spencer G., *Australia* 95 E2
Spencerville, *Canada* 117 B9
Spences Bridge, *Canada* 102 C4
Spennymoor, *U.K.* 14 C6
Spenser Mts., *N.Z.* 91 K4
Spentrup, *Denmark* 11 H4
Sperkhiós →, *Greece* 46 C4
Sperrin Mts., *U.K.* 12 B5
Spessart, *Germany* 25 F5
Spétsai, *Greece* 46 D5
Spey →, *U.K.* 13 D5
Speyer, *Germany* 25 F4
Spezand, *Pakistan* 68 E2
Spezzano Albanese, *Italy* 43 C9
Spiekeroog, *Germany* 24 B3
Spiez, *Switz.* 25 J3
Spíli, *Greece* 49 D6
Spilimbergo, *Italy* 41 B9
Spinalónga, *Greece* 49 D7
Spinazzola, *Italy* 43 B9
Spineni, *Romania* 29 F9
Spirit Lake, *U.S.A.* 110 D4
Spirit River, *Canada* 102 B5
Spiritwood, *Canada* 103 C7
Spišská Nová Ves, *Slovak Rep.* 27 C13
Spišské Podhradie, *Slovak Rep.* 27 B13
Spital, *Austria* 26 D7
Spithead, *U.K.* 15 G6
Spittal an der Drau, *Austria* . 26 E6
Spitzbergen = Svalbard, *Arctic* 51 B5
Spjelkavik, *Norway* 9 E12
Split, *Croatia* 41 E13
Split ✈ (SPU), *Croatia* 41 E13
Split L., *Canada* 103 B9
Split Lake, *Canada* 103 B9
Splitski Kanal, *Croatia* 41 E13
Splügenpass, *Switz.* 25 J5
Spofford, *U.S.A.* 113 L4
Spokane, *U.S.A.* 108 C5
Spoleto, *Italy* 41 F9

Spooner, *U.S.A.* 112 C9
Sporvy Navolok, Mys, *Russia* .. 52 B7
Sprague, *U.S.A.* 108 C5
Spratly I., S. China Sea 62 C4
Spratly Is., *S. China Sea* 62 C4
Spray, *U.S.A.* 108 D4
Spreča →, *Bos.-H.* 28 F3
Spree →, *Germany* 24 C9
Spreewald, *Germany* 24 D9
Spremberg, *Germany* 24 D10
Sprengisandur, *Iceland* 8 D5
Spring City, *U.S.A.* 117 F9
Spring Creek, *U.S.A.* 108 F6
Spring Garden, *U.S.A.* 110 F6
Spring Hall, *Barbados* .... 121 g
Spring Valley, *U.S.A.* 105 H6
Spring Mts., *U.S.A.* 109 H6
Spring Valley, *U.S.A.* 111 N10
Springbok, *S. Africa* 88 D2
Springboro, *U.S.A.* 116 E4
Springdale, *Canada* 105 C8
Springdale, *U.S.A.* 113 G7
Springe, *Germany* 24 C5
Springer, *U.S.A.* 113 G2
Springerville, *U.S.A.* 109 J9
Springfield, *Canada* 116 D4
Springfield, *N.Z.* 91 K3
Springfield, *Colo., U.S.A.* ... 113 G3
Springfield, *Ill., U.S.A.* 112 F10
Springfield, *Mass., U.S.A.* ... 117 D12
Springfield, *Mo., U.S.A.* 113 G8
Springfield, *Ohio, U.S.A.* 114 F4
Springfield, *Oreg., U.S.A.* ... 108 D2
Springfield, *Tenn., U.S.A.* ... 115 G2
Springfield, *Vt., U.S.A.* 117 C12
Springfontein, *S. Africa* 88 E4
Springhill, *Canada* 105 C7
Springhill, *U.S.A.* 113 J8
Springhouse, *Canada* 102 C4
Springs, *S. Africa* 89 D4
Springsure, *Australia* 94 C4
Springvale, *U.S.A.* 117 C14
Springville, *Calif., U.S.A.* .. 110 J8
Springville, *N.Y., U.S.A.* 116 D6
Springville, *Utah, U.S.A.* 108 F8
Springwater, *U.S.A.* 116 D7
Spruce-Creek, *U.S.A.* 116 F6
Spruce Knob-Seneca Rocks △,
    U.S.A. 114 F6
Spruce Mt., *U.S.A.* 117 B12
Spur, *U.S.A.* 113 J4
Spuž, *Serbia & M.* 44 D3
Spuzzum, *Canada* 102 D4
Squam L., *U.S.A.* 117 C13
Squamish, *Canada* 102 D4
Square Islands, *Canada* 105 B8
Squillace, G. di, *Italy* 43 D9
Squinzano, *Italy* 43 B11
Squires, Mt., *Australia* 93 E4
Srbac, *Bos.-H.* 28 E2
Srbica, *Serbia & M.* 44 D4
Srbija = Serbia □, *Serbia & M.* 44 C5
Srbobran, *Serbia & M.* 28 E4
Sre Ambel, *Cambodia* 65 G4
Sre Khtum, *Cambodia* 65 F6
Sre Umbell = Sre Ambel,
    Cambodia 65 G4
Srebrenica, *Bos.-H.* 28 F4
Sredinny Ra. = Sredinnyy
    Khrebet, *Russia* 53 D16
Sredinnyy Khrebet, *Russia* 53 D16
Središče, *Slovenia* 41 B13
Sredna Gora, *Bulgaria* 45 D8
Srednekolymsk, *Russia* 53 C16
Sredni Rodopi, *Bulgaria* 45 E8
Srednogorie, *Bulgaria* 45 D8
Śrem, *Poland* 31 F4
Sremska Mitrovica, *Serbia & M.* 28 F4
Sremski Karlovci, *Serbia & M.* 28 E4
Srepok →, *Cambodia* 64 F6
Sretensk, *Russia* 53 D12
Sri Lanka ■, *Asia* 66 R12
Srikakulam, *India* 67 K13
Srinagar, *India* 69 B6
Srinagarind Res., *Thailand* ... 64 E2
Środa Śląska, *Poland* 31 G3
Środa Wielkopolski, *Poland* ... 31 F4
Srono, *Indonesia* 63 J17
Srpska Crnja, *Serbia & M.* 28 E5
Srpski Itebej, *Serbia & M.* ... 28 E5
Staaten →, *Australia* 94 B3
Staaten River △, *Australia* ... 94 B3
Staberhuk, *Germany* 24 A7
Stade, *Germany* 24 B5
Stadskanaal, *Neths.* 17 A6
Stadtallendorf, *Germany* 24 E5
Stadthagen, *Germany* 24 C5
Stadtlohn, *Germany* 24 D2
Stadtroda, *Germany* 24 E7
Staffa, *U.K.* 13 E2
Staffanstorp, *Sweden* 11 J7
Stafford, *U.K.* 14 E5
Stafford, *U.S.A.* 113 G5
Stafford Springs, *U.S.A.* 117 E12
Staffordshire □, *U.K.* 14 E5
Stagnone, *Italy* 42 E5
Stagnone di Marsala △, *Italy* . 42 E5
Staines, *U.K.* 15 F7
Stainz, *Austria* 26 E8
Stakhanov, *Ukraine* 33 H10
Stalać, *Serbia & M.* 44 C5
Stalis, *Greece* 49 D7
Stallarholmen, *Sweden* 10 E11
Ställdalen, *Sweden* 10 E8
Stalowa Wola, *Poland* 31 H9
Stalybridge, *U.K.* 14 D5
Stamford, *Australia* 94 C3
Stamford, *U.K.* 15 E7
Stamford, *Conn., U.S.A.* 117 E11
Stamford, *N.Y., U.S.A.* 117 D10

Stamford, *Tex., U.S.A.* 113 **J5**
Stampriet, *Namibia* 88 **C2**
Stamps, *U.S.A.* 113 **J8**
Stančevo = Kalipetrovo, *Bulgaria* 45 **B11**
Standerton, *S. Africa* 89 **D4**
Standish, *U.S.A.* 114 **D4**
Stanford, *S. Africa* 88 **E2**
Stanford, *U.S.A.* 108 **C8**
Stånga, *Sweden* 11 **G12**
Stanger, *S. Africa* 89 **D5**
Stängselåsen = Salpausselkä,
   Finland 9 **F22**
Stanišić, *Serbia & M.* 28 **E4**
Stanislaus →, *U.S.A.* 110 **H5**
Stanisławów, *Poland* 31 **F8**
Stanley, *Australia* 95 **G4**
Stanley, *Falk. Is.* 128 **G5**
Stanley, *U.K.* 14 **C6**
Stanley, *Idaho, U.S.A.* 108 **D6**
Stanley, *N. Dak., U.S.A.* 112 **A3**
Stanley, *N.Y., U.S.A.* 116 **D7**
Stanley Mission, *Canada* 103 **B8**
Stanovoy Khrebet, *Russia* 53 **D13**
Stanovoy Ra. = Stanovoy
   Khrebet, *Russia* 53 **D13**
Stansmore Ra., *Australia* 92 **D4**
Stansted, London ✈ (STN), *U.K.* 15 **F8**
Stanthorpe, *Australia* 95 **D5**
Stanton, *U.S.A.* 113 **J4**
Stanwood, *U.S.A.* 110 **B4**
Staples, *U.S.A.* 112 **B7**
Stąporków, *Poland* 31 **G7**
Star City, *Canada* 103 **C8**
Star Lake, *U.S.A.* 117 **B9**
Stará Ľubovňa, *Slovak Rep.* 27 **B13**
Stara Moravica, *Serbia & M.* 28 **E4**
Stara Pazova, *Serbia & M.* 28 **F5**
Stara Planina, *Bulgaria* 44 **C7**
Stara Sil, *Ukraine* 31 **J9**
Stará Turá, *Slovak Rep.* 27 **C10**
Stara Ushytsya, *Ukraine* 29 **B12**
Stara Zagora, *Bulgaria* 45 **D9**
Starachowice, *Poland* 31 **G8**
Staraya Russa, *Russia* 32 **D6**
Starbuck I., *Kiribati* 97 **H12**
Starchiojd, *Romania* 29 **E11**
Starcke △, *Australia* 94 **A4**
Stargard Szczeciński, *Poland* ... 30 **E2**
Stari Bar, *Serbia & M.* 44 **D3**
Stari Trg, *Slovenia* 41 **C12**
Staritsa, *Russia* 32 **D8**
Starke, *U.S.A.* 115 **L4**
Starnberg, *Germany* 25 **H7**
Starnberger See, *Germany* 25 **H7**
Starobilsk, *Ukraine* 33 **H10**
Starodub, *Russia* 33 **F7**
Starogard Gdański, *Poland* 30 **E5**
Starokonstantinov =
   Starokonstyantyniv, *Ukraine* .. 33 **H4**
Starokonstyantyniv, *Ukraine* ... 33 **H4**
Starokozache, *Ukraine* 29 **D14**
Starominskaya, *Russia* 33 **J10**
Staroshcherbinovskaya, *Russia* .. 33 **J10**
Start Pt., *U.K.* 15 **G4**
Stary Sącz, *Poland* 31 **J7**
Staryy Biryuzyak, *Russia* 35 **H8**
Staryy Chartoriysk, *Ukraine* 33 **G3**
Staryy Krym, *Ukraine* 33 **K8**
Staryy Oskol, *Russia* 33 **G9**
Staryy Sambir, *Ukraine* 31 **J9**
Stassfurt, *Germany* 24 **D7**
Staszów, *Poland* 31 **H8**
State College, *U.S.A.* 116 **F7**
Stateline, *U.S.A.* 110 **G7**
Staten, I. = Estados, I. de Los,
   Argentina 128 **G4**
Staten I., *U.S.A.* 117 **F10**
Statesboro, *U.S.A.* 115 **J5**
Statesville, *U.S.A.* 115 **H5**
Statia = St. Eustatius, *W. Indies* . 121 **C7**
Stauffer, *U.S.A.* 111 **L7**
Staunton, *Ill., U.S.A.* 112 **F10**
Staunton, *Va., U.S.A.* 114 **F6**
Stavanger, *Norway* 9 **G11**
Staveley, *N.Z.* 91 **K3**
Stavelot, *Belgium* 17 **D5**
Stavern, *Norway* 9 **G14**
Stavoren, *Neths.* 17 **B5**
Stavropol, *Russia* 35 **H6**
Stavros, *Cyprus* 49 **D11**
Stavrós, *Greece* 49 **D6**
Stavrós, *Ákra, Greece* 49 **D6**
Stavroúpolis, *Greece* 45 **E8**
Stawell, *Australia* 95 **F3**
Stawell →, *Australia* 94 **C3**
Stawiski, *Poland* 30 **E9**
Stawiszyn, *Poland* 31 **G5**
Stayner, *Canada* 116 **B4**
Stayton, *U.S.A.* 108 **D2**
Steamboat Springs, *U.S.A.* 108 **F10**
Steblevë, *Albania* 44 **E4**
Steele, *U.S.A.* 112 **B5**
Steelton, *U.S.A.* 116 **F8**
Steen River, *Canada* 102 **B5**
Steens Mt., *U.S.A.* 108 **E4**
Steenwijk, *Neths.* 17 **B6**
Steep Pt., *Australia* 93 **E1**
Steep Rock, *Canada* 103 **C9**
Ştefan Vodă, *Moldova* 29 **D14**
Ştefăneşti, *Romania* 29 **C12**
Stefanie = Chew Bahir,
   Ethiopia 81 **G4**
Stefanie L. = Chew Bahir,
   Ethiopia 81 **G4**
Stefansson Bay, *Antarctica* 5 **C5**
Stege, *Denmark* 11 **K6**
Ştei, *Romania* 28 **D7**
Steiermark □, *Austria* 26 **D8**
Steigerwald, *Germany* 25 **F6**
Steigerwald △, *Germany* 25 **F6**
Steilacoom, *U.S.A.* 110 **C4**
Steilrandberge, *Namibia* 88 **B1**

Steinbach, *Canada* 103 **D9**
Steinfurt, *Germany* 24 **C3**
Steinhausen, *Namibia* 88 **C2**
Steinheim, *Germany* 24 **D5**
Steinhuder Meer, *Germany* 24 **C5**
Steinhuder Meer △, *Germany* .. 24 **C5**
Steinkjer, *Norway* 8 **D14**
Steinkopf, *S. Africa* 88 **D2**
Steinwald △, *Germany* 25 **F8**
Stellarton, *Canada* 105 **C7**
Stellenbosch, *S. Africa* 88 **E2**
Stelvio, Paso dello, *Italy* 40 **B7**
Stenay, *France* 19 **C12**
Stendal, *Germany* 24 **C7**
Stende, *Latvia* 30 **A9**
Stenhamra, *Sweden* 10 **E11**
Stenshuvud △, *Sweden* 11 **J8**
Stenstorp, *Sweden* 11 **F7**
Stenungsund, *Sweden* 11 **F5**
Steornabhaigh = Stornoway, *U.K.* 13 **C2**
Stepanakert = Xankändi,
   Azerbaijan 70 **B5**
Stepanavan, *Armenia* 35 **K7**
Stephens Creek, *Australia* 95 **E3**
Stephens I., *Canada* 102 **C2**
Stephens L., *Canada* 103 **B9**
Stephenville, *Canada* 105 **C8**
Stephenville, *U.S.A.* 113 **J5**
Stepnica, *Poland* 30 **E1**
Steppe, *Asia* 50 **D9**
Stereá Ellas □, *Greece* 46 **C4**
Sterkstroom, *S. Africa* 88 **E4**
Sterling, *Colo., U.S.A.* 112 **E3**
Sterling, *Ill., U.S.A.* 112 **E10**
Sterling, *Kans., U.S.A.* 112 **F5**
Sterling City, *U.S.A.* 113 **K4**
Sterling Heights, *U.S.A.* 114 **D4**
Sterling Run, *U.S.A.* 116 **E6**
Sterlitamak, *Russia* 52 **D6**
Sternberg, *Germany* 24 **B7**
Šternberk, *Czech Rep.* 27 **B10**
Stérnes, *Greece* 49 **D6**
Sterzing = Vipiteno, *Italy* 41 **B8**
Stettin = Szczecin, *Poland* 30 **E1**
Stettiner Haff, *Germany* 24 **B10**
Stettler, *Canada* 102 **C6**
Steubenville, *U.S.A.* 116 **F4**
Stevenage, *U.K.* 15 **F7**
Stevens Point, *U.S.A.* 112 **C10**
Stevenson, *U.S.A.* 110 **E5**
Stevenson →, *Australia* 95 **D2**
Stevenson L., *Canada* 103 **C9**
Stevensville, *U.S.A.* 108 **C6**
Stevns Klint, *Denmark* 11 **J6**
Stewart, *Canada* 102 **B3**
Stewart, *U.S.A.* 110 **F7**
Stewart →, *Canada* 100 **B6**
Stewart, C., *Australia* 94 **A1**
Stewart, I., *Chile* 128 **G2**
Stewart I., *N.Z.* 91 **M1**
Stewarts Point, *U.S.A.* 110 **G3**
Stewartville, *U.S.A.* 112 **D8**
Stewiacke, *Canada* 105 **C7**
Steynsburg, *S. Africa* 88 **E4**
Steyr, *Austria* 26 **C7**
Steyr →, *Austria* 26 **C7**
Steytlerville, *S. Africa* 88 **E3**
Stia, *Italy* 41 **E8**
Stigler, *U.S.A.* 113 **H7**
Stigliano, *Italy* 43 **B9**
Stigtomta, *Sweden* 11 **F10**
Stikine →, *Canada* 102 **B2**
Stilfontein, *S. Africa* 88 **D4**
Stilís, *Greece* 46 **C4**
Stillwater, *N.Z.* 91 **K3**
Stillwater, *Minn., U.S.A.* 112 **C8**
Stillwater, *N.Y., U.S.A.* 117 **D11**
Stillwater, *Okla., U.S.A.* 113 **G6**
Stillwater Range, *U.S.A.* 108 **G4**
Stillwater Reservoir, *U.S.A.* 117 **C9**
Stilo, Pta., *Italy* 43 **D9**
Stilwell, *U.S.A.* 113 **H7**
Stînga Nistrului □, *Moldova* ... 29 **C14**
Ştip, *Macedonia* 44 **E6**
Stíra, *Greece* 46 **C6**
Stirling, *Canada* 116 **B7**
Stirling, *U.K.* 13 **E5**
Stirling □, *U.K.* 13 **E4**
Stirling Ra., *Australia* 93 **F2**
Stirling Range △, *Australia* 93 **F2**
Stittsville, *Canada* 117 **A9**
Stjernøya, *Norway* 8 **A20**
Stjørdalshalsen, *Norway* 8 **E14**
Stockach, *Germany* 25 **H5**
Stockaryd, *Sweden* 11 **G8**
Stockerau, *Austria* 27 **C9**
Stockholm, *Sweden* 10 **E12**
Stockholm Arlanda ✈ (ARN),
   Sweden 10 **E11**
Stockholms län □, *Sweden* 10 **E12**
Stockport, *U.K.* 14 **D5**
Stocksbridge, *U.K.* 14 **D6**
Stockton, *Calif., U.S.A.* 110 **H5**
Stockton, *Kans., U.S.A.* 112 **F5**
Stockton, *Mo., U.S.A.* 113 **G8**
Stockton-on-Tees, *U.K.* 14 **C6**
Stockton-on-Tees □, *U.K.* 14 **C6**
Stockton Plateau, *U.S.A.* 113 **K3**
Stoczek Łukowski, *Poland* 31 **G8**
Stöde, *Sweden* 10 **B10**
Stoeng Treng, *Cambodia* 64 **F5**
Stoer, Pt. of, *U.K.* 13 **C3**
Stogovo, *Macedonia* 44 **E4**
Stoholm, *Denmark* 11 **H3**
Stoke-on-Trent, *U.K.* 14 **D5**
Stoke-on-Trent □, *U.K.* 14 **D5**
Stokes △, *Australia* 93 **E2**
Stokes Pt., *Australia* 95 **G3**
Stokes Ra., *Australia* 92 **C5**
Stokksnes, *Iceland* 8 **D6**
Stokmarknes, *Norway* 8 **B16**

Stolac, *Bos.-H.* 44 **C1**
Stolberg, *Germany* 24 **E2**
Stolbovoy, Ostrov, *Russia* 53 **B14**
Stolbtsy = Stowbtsy, *Belarus* ... 32 **F4**
Stolin, *Belarus* 33 **G4**
Stolnici, *Romania* 29 **F9**
Stomíon, *Greece* 49 **D5**
Ston, *Croatia* 41 **F14**
Stone, *U.K.* 14 **E5**
Stoneboro, *U.S.A.* 116 **E4**
Stonehaven, *U.K.* 13 **E6**
Stonehenge, *Australia* 94 **C3**
Stonehenge, *U.K.* 15 **F6**
Stonewall, *Canada* 103 **C9**
Stony L., *Man., Canada* 103 **B9**
Stony L., *Ont., Canada* 116 **B6**
Stony Point, *U.S.A.* 117 **E11**
Stony Pt., *U.S.A.* 117 **C8**
Stony Rapids, *Canada* 103 **B7**
Stony Tunguska = Tunguska,
   Podkamennaya →, *Russia* ... 53 **C10**
Stonyford, *U.S.A.* 110 **F4**
Stopnica, *Poland* 31 **H7**
Storå, *Sweden* 10 **E9**
Storå →, *Denmark* 11 **H2**
Stora Gla, *Sweden* 10 **E6**
Stora Le, *Sweden* 10 **E5**
Stora Lulevatten, *Sweden* 8 **C18**
Storavan, *Sweden* 8 **D18**
Stord, *Norway* 9 **G11**
Store Bælt, *Denmark* 11 **J4**
Store Heddinge, *Denmark* 11 **J6**
Store Mosse △, *Sweden* 11 **G7**
Storebro, *Sweden* 11 **G9**
Storfors, *Sweden* 10 **E8**
Storlien, *Sweden* 10 **A6**
Storm B., *Australia* 95 **G4**
Storm Lake, *U.S.A.* 112 **D7**
Stormberge, *S. Africa* 88 **E4**
Stormsrivier, *S. Africa* 88 **E3**
Stornoway, *U.K.* 13 **C2**
Storo, *Italy* 40 **C7**
Storozhinets = Storozhynets,
   Ukraine 29 **B10**
Storozhynets, *Ukraine* 29 **B10**
Storrs, *U.S.A.* 117 **E12**
Storsjön, *Gävleborg, Sweden* ... 10 **D10**
Storsjön, *Jämtland, Sweden* 10 **B7**
Storsjön, *Jämtland, Sweden* 10 **A8**
Storstrøms Amtskommune □,
   Denmark 11 **J5**
Storuman, *Sweden* 8 **D17**
Storuman, *Sweden* 8 **D17**
Storvätteshågna, *Sweden* 10 **B6**
Storvik, *Sweden* 10 **D10**
Storvreta, *Sweden* 10 **E11**
Stouffville, *Canada* 116 **C5**
Stoughton, *Canada* 103 **D8**
Stour →, *Dorset, U.K.* 15 **G6**
Stour →, *Kent, U.K.* 15 **F9**
Stour →, *Suffolk, U.K.* 15 **F9**
Stourbridge, *U.K.* 15 **E5**
Stout L., *Canada* 103 **C10**
Stove Pipe Wells Village, *U.S.A.* 111 **J9**
Støvring, *Denmark* 11 **H3**
Stow, *U.S.A.* 116 **E3**
Stowbtsy, *Belarus* 32 **F4**
Stowmarket, *U.K.* 15 **E9**
Strabane, *U.K.* 12 **B4**
Stracin, *Macedonia* 44 **D6**
Stradella, *Italy* 40 **C6**
Strahan, *Australia* 95 **G4**
Strajitsa, *Bulgaria* 45 **C9**
Strakonice, *Czech Rep.* 26 **B6**
Straldzha, *Bulgaria* 45 **D10**
Stralsund, *Germany* 24 **A9**
Strand, *S. Africa* 88 **E2**
Stranda, *Møre og Romsdal,*
   Norway 9 **E12**
Stranda, *Nord-Trøndelag, Norway* 8 **E14**
Strandby, *Denmark* 11 **G4**
Strangford L., *U.K.* 12 **B6**
Strängnäs, *Sweden* 10 **E11**
Stranraer, *U.K.* 13 **G3**
Strasbourg, *Canada* 103 **C8**
Strasbourg, *France* 19 **D14**
Strasburg, *Germany* 24 **B9**
Strǎşeni, *Moldova* 29 **C13**
Stråssa, *Sweden* 10 **E9**
Stratford, *Canada* 116 **C4**
Stratford, *N.Z.* 91 **H5**
Stratford, *Calif., U.S.A.* 110 **J7**
Stratford, *Conn., U.S.A.* 117 **E11**
Stratford, *Tex., U.S.A.* 113 **G3**
Stratford-upon-Avon, *U.K.* 15 **E6**
Strath Spey, *U.K.* 13 **D5**
Strathalbyn, *Australia* 95 **F2**
Strathaven, *U.K.* 13 **F4**
Strathcona □, *Canada* 102 **D3**
Strathmore, *Canada* 102 **C6**
Strathmore, *U.K.* 13 **E5**
Strathmore, *U.S.A.* 110 **J7**
Strathnaver, *Canada* 102 **C4**
Strathpeffer, *U.K.* 13 **D4**
Strathroy, *Canada* 116 **D3**
Strathy Pt., *U.K.* 13 **C4**
Strattanville, *U.S.A.* 116 **E5**
Stratton, *U.S.A.* 117 **A14**
Stratton Mt., *U.S.A.* 117 **C12**
Straubing, *Germany* 25 **G8**
Straumnes, *Iceland* 8 **C2**
Strausberg, *Germany* 24 **C9**
Strawberry →, *U.S.A.* 108 **F8**
Strážnice, *Czech Rep.* 27 **C10**
Streaky B., *Australia* 95 **E1**
Streaky Bay, *Australia* 95 **E1**
Streator, *U.S.A.* 112 **E10**
Středočeský □, *Czech Rep.* 26 **B7**
Streetsboro, *U.S.A.* 116 **E3**
Streetsville, *Canada* 116 **C5**

Strehaia, *Romania* 29 **F8**
Strelcha, *Bulgaria* 45 **D8**
Strelka, *Russia* 53 **D10**
Streng →, *Cambodia* 64 **F4**
Stresa, *Italy* 40 **C5**
Streymoy, *Færoe Is.* 8 **E9**
Strezhevoy, *Russia* 52 **C8**
Stříbro, *Czech Rep.* 26 **A6**
Strilky, *Ukraine* 31 **J9**
Strimón →, *Greece* 44 **F7**
Strimonikós Kólpos, *Greece* ... 44 **F7**
Strofádhes, *Greece* 46 **D3**
Stroma, *U.K.* 13 **C5**
Stromboli, *Italy* 43 **D8**
Stromeferry, *U.K.* 13 **D3**
Stromness, *U.K.* 13 **C5**
Strömsbruk, *Sweden* 10 **C11**
Stromsburg, *U.S.A.* 112 **E6**
Strömsnäsbruk, *Sweden* 11 **H7**
Strömstad, *Sweden* 11 **F5**
Strömsund, *Sweden* 8 **E16**
Strongilí, *Greece* 47 **E11**
Stróngoli, *Italy* 43 **C10**
Strongsville, *U.S.A.* 116 **E3**
Stronie Śląskie, *Poland* 31 **H3**
Stronsay, *U.K.* 13 **B6**
Stropkov, *Slovak Rep.* 27 **B14**
Stroud, *U.K.* 15 **F5**
Stroud Road, *Australia* 95 **E5**
Stroudsburg, *U.S.A.* 117 **F9**
Stroumbi, *Cyprus* 49 **E11**
Struer, *Denmark* 11 **H2**
Struga, *Macedonia* 44 **E4**
Strugi Krasnyye, *Russia* 32 **C5**
Strumica, *Macedonia* 44 **E6**
Strumica →, *Europe* 44 **E7**
Strumok, *Ukraine* 29 **E14**
Struthers, *Canada* 104 **C2**
Struthers, *U.S.A.* 116 **E4**
Stryama, *Bulgaria* 45 **D8**
Stryker, *U.S.A.* 108 **B6**
Stryków, *Poland* 31 **G6**
Stryy, *Ukraine* 33 **H2**
Strzegom, *Poland* 31 **H3**
Strzelce Krajeńskie, *Poland* 31 **F2**
Strzelce Opolskie, *Poland* 31 **H5**
Strzelecki Cr. →, *Australia* 95 **D2**
Strzelin, *Poland* 31 **H4**
Strzelno, *Poland* 31 **F5**
Strzybnica, *Poland* 31 **H5**
Strzyżów, *Poland* 31 **J8**
Stuart, *Fla., U.S.A.* 115 **M5**
Stuart, *Nebr., U.S.A.* 112 **D5**
Stuart →, *Canada* 102 **C4**
Stuart Bluff Ra., *Australia* 92 **D5**
Stuart L., *Canada* 102 **C4**
Stuart Ra., *Australia* 95 **D1**
Stubbekøbing, *Denmark* 11 **K6**
Stuben, *Austria* 26 **D3**
Studen Kladenets, Yazovir,
   Bulgaria 45 **E9**
Studenka, *Czech Rep.* 27 **B11**
Stugun, *Sweden* 10 **A9**
Stuhr, *Germany* 24 **B4**
Stull L., *Canada* 104 **B1**
Stung Treng = Stoeng Treng,
   Cambodia 64 **F5**
Stupart →, *Canada* 104 **A1**
Stupava, *Slovak Rep.* 27 **C10**
Stupino, *Russia* 32 **E10**
Sturgeon B., *Canada* 103 **C9**
Sturgeon Bay, *U.S.A.* 114 **C2**
Sturgeon Falls, *Canada* 104 **C4**
Sturgeon L., *Alta., Canada* 102 **B5**
Sturgeon L., *Ont., Canada* 104 **C1**
Sturgeon L., *Ont., Canada* 116 **B6**
Sturgis, *Canada* 103 **C8**
Sturgis, *Mich., U.S.A.* 114 **E3**
Sturgis, *S. Dak., U.S.A.* 112 **C3**
Sturkö, *Sweden* 11 **H9**
Stúrovo, *Slovak Rep.* 27 **D11**
Sturt △, *Australia* 95 **D3**
Sturt Cr. →, *Australia* 92 **C4**
Sturt Stony Desert, *Australia* .. 95 **D3**
Stutterheim, *S. Africa* 88 **E4**
Stuttgart, *Germany* 25 **G5**
Stuttgart, *U.S.A.* 113 **H9**
Stuttgart Echterdingen ✈ (STR),
   Germany 25 **G5**
Stuyvesant, *U.S.A.* 117 **D11**
Stykkishólmur, *Iceland* 8 **D2**
Styria = Steiermark □, *Austria* .. 26 **D8**
Styrsö, *Sweden* 11 **G5**
Su Xian = Suzhou, *China* 56 **H9**
Suakin, *Sudan* 80 **D4**
Suan, *N. Korea* 57 **E14**
Suaqui, *Mexico* 118 **B3**
Suar, *India* 69 **E8**
Subang, *Indonesia* 63 **G12**
Subansiri →, *India* 67 **F18**
Subarnarekha →, *India* 69 **H12**
Subayhah, *Si. Arabia* 70 **D3**
Subcetate, *Romania* 28 **E8**
Subi, *Indonesia* 62 **D3**
Subiaco, *Italy* 41 **G10**
Subotica, *Serbia & M.* 28 **D4**
Suca, *Ethiopia* 81 **F4**
Suceava, *Romania* 29 **C11**
Suceava □, *Romania* 29 **C11**
Suceava →, *Romania* 29 **C11**
Sucha-Beskidzka, *Poland* 31 **J6**
Suchań, *Poland* 31 **E2**
Suchitoto, *El Salv.* 120 **D2**
Suchou = Suzhou, *China* 59 **B13**
Suchow = Xuzhou, *China* 57 **G9**
Suchowola, *Poland* 30 **E10**
Suck →, *Ireland* 12 **C3**

Sucre, *Bolivia* 124 **G5**
Sućuraj, *Croatia* 41 **E14**
Sucuriú →, *Brazil* 125 **H8**
Sud, Pte. du, *Canada* 105 **C7**
Sud-Kivu □, *Dem. Rep. of*
   the Congo 86 **C2**
Sud-Ouest, Pte., *Canada* 105 **C7**
Suda →, *Russia* 32 **C9**
Sudak, *Ukraine* 33 **K8**
Sudan, *U.S.A.* 113 **H3**
Sudan ■, *Africa* 81 **E3**
Sudbury, *Canada* 104 **C3**
Sudbury, *U.K.* 15 **E8**
Sûdd, *Sudan* 81 **F3**
Sudeifel = Deutsch-
   Luxemburgischer △, *Germany* 25 **F4**
Süderbrarup, *Germany* 24 **A5**
Süderlügum, *Germany* 24 **A4**
Süderoogsand, *Germany* 24 **A4**
Sudeten Mts. = Sudety, *Europe* . 27 **A9**
Sudety, *Europe* 27 **A9**
Südheide △, *Germany* 24 **C6**
Suðuroy, *Færoe Is.* 8 **F9**
Sudi, *Tanzania* 87 **E4**
Sudirman, Pegunungan, *Indonesia* 63 **E9**
Sudiţi, *Romania* 29 **F12**
Sudogda, *Russia* 34 **C5**
Sudong, Pulau, *Singapore* ..... 65 **d**
Sudova Vyshnya, *Ukraine* 31 **J10**
Sudr, *Egypt* 80 **B3**
Sudzha, *Russia* 33 **G8**
Sue →, *Sudan* 81 **F2**
Sueca, *Spain* 39 **F4**
Süedinenie, *Bulgaria* 45 **D8**
Suemez I., *U.S.A.* 102 **B2**
Suez = El Suweis, *Egypt* 80 **J8**
Suez, G. of = Suweis, Khalîg el,
   Egypt 80 **J8**
Suez Canal = Suweis, Qanâ es,
   Egypt 80 **H8**
Suffield, *Canada* 102 **C6**
Suffolk, *U.S.A.* 114 **G7**
Suffolk □, *U.K.* 15 **E9**
Şugag, *Romania* 29 **E8**
Sugargrove, *U.S.A.* 116 **E5**
Sugarive →, *India* 69 **F12**
Suğla Gölü, *Turkey* 72 **D5**
Sugluk = Salluit, *Canada* 101 **B12**
Suhaia, Lacul, *Romania* 29 **G10**
Şuḩār, *Oman* 71 **E8**
Sühbaatar □, *Mongolia* 56 **B8**
Suhl, *Germany* 24 **E6**
Şuhut, *Turkey* 47 **C12**
Sui, *Pakistan* 68 **E3**
Sui Xian, *China* 56 **G8**
Suica, *Bos.-H.* 28 **G2**
Suichang, *China* 59 **C12**
Suichuan, *China* 59 **D10**
Suide, *China* 56 **F6**
Suifenhe, *China* 57 **B16**
Suihua, *China* 60 **B7**
Suijiang, *China* 58 **C4**
Suining, *Hunan, China* 59 **D8**
Suining, *Jiangsu, China* 57 **H9**
Suining, *Sichuan, China* 58 **B5**
Suiping, *China* 56 **H7**
Suippes, *France* 19 **C11**
Suir →, *Ireland* 12 **D4**
Suisun City, *U.S.A.* 110 **G4**
Suixi, *China* 59 **G8**
Suiyang, *Guizhou, China* 58 **D6**
Suiyang, *Heilongjiang, China* ... 57 **B16**
Suizhong, *China* 57 **D11**
Suizhou, *China* 59 **B9**
Sujangarh, *India* 68 **E6**
Sukabumi, *Indonesia* 63 **G12**
Sukadana, *Indonesia* 62 **E3**
Sukagawa, *Japan* 55 **F10**
Sukaraja, *Indonesia* 62 **E4**
Sukawati, *Indonesia* 63 **K18**
Sukch'ŏn, *N. Korea* 57 **E13**
Sukhindol, *Bulgaria* 45 **C9**
Sukhinichi, *Russia* 32 **E8**
Sukhona →, *Russia* 52 **D4**
Sukhothai, *Thailand* 64 **D2**
Sukhumi = Sokhumi, *Georgia* .. 35 **J5**
Sukkur, *Pakistan* 68 **F3**
Sukkur Barrage, *Pakistan* 68 **F3**
Sukovo, *Serbia & M.* 44 **D6**
Sukri →, *India* 68 **G4**
Sukumo, *Japan* 55 **H6**
Sukunka →, *Canada* 102 **B4**
Sula →, *Ukraine* 33 **H7**
Sula, Kepulauan, *Indonesia* 63 **E7**
Sulaco →, *Honduras* 120 **C2**
Sulaiman Range, *Pakistan* 68 **D3**
Sulak →, *Russia* 35 **J8**
Sūlār, *Iran* 71 **D6**
Sulawesi, *Indonesia* 63 **E6**
Sulawesi Sea = Celebes Sea,
   Indonesia 63 **D6**
Sulawesi Selatan □, *Indonesia* .. 63 **E6**
Sulawesi Tengah □, *Indonesia* .. 63 **E6**
Sulawesi Tenggara □, *Indonesia* . 63 **E6**
Sulawesi Utara □, *Indonesia* ... 63 **D6**
Sulechów, *Poland* 31 **G2**
Sulęcin, *Poland* 31 **F1**
Sulejów, *Poland* 31 **G6**
Sulejówek, *Poland* 31 **F8**
Süleymanlı, *Turkey* 47 **D9**
Sulima, *S. Leone* 82 **D2**
Sulina, *Romania* 29 **E14**
Sulina, Braţul →, *Romania* 29 **E14**
Sulingen, *Germany* 24 **C4**
Suliţa, *Romania* 29 **C11**
Sulitjelma, *Norway* 8 **C17**
Sułkowice, *Poland* 31 **J6**
Sullana, *Peru* 124 **D2**
Süller, *Turkey* 47 **C11**
Sullivan, *Ill., U.S.A.* 112 **F10**

Sullivan, Ind., U.S.A. 114 F2
Sullivan, Mo., U.S.A. 112 F9
Sullivan Bay, Canada 102 C3
Sullivan I. = Lanbi Kyun, Burma 65 G2
Sullom Voe, U.K. 13 A7
Sully-sur-Loire, France 19 E9
Sulmierzyce, Poland 31 G4
Sulmona, Italy 41 F10
Süloğlu, Turkey 45 E10
Sulphur, La., U.S.A. 113 K8
Sulphur, Okla., U.S.A. 113 H6
Sulphur Pt., Canada 102 A6
Sulphur Springs, U.S.A. 113 J7
Sultan, Canada 104 C3
Sultan, U.S.A. 110 C5
Sultan Dağları, Turkey 72 C4
Sultanhisar, Turkey 47 D10
Sultaniça, Turkey 45 F10
Sultaniye, Turkey 45 F12
Sultanpur, Mad. P., India 68 H8
Sultanpur, Punjab, India 68 D6
Sultanpur, Ut. P., India 69 F10
Sulu Arch., Phil. 61 J4
Sulu Sea, E. Indies 61 G4
Sülüklü, Turkey 72 C5
Sululta, Ethiopia 81 F4
Suluova, Turkey 72 B6
Suluq, Libya 79 B10
Sulzbach, Germany 25 F3
Sulzbach-Rosenberg, Germany . 25 F7
Sulzberger Ice Shelf, Antarctica   5 E13
Sumalata, Indonesia 63 D6
Sumampa, Argentina 126 B3
Sumatera, Indonesia 62 D2
Sumatera Barat □, Indonesia .. 62 E2
Sumatera Utara □, Indonesia .. 62 D1
Sumatra = Sumatera, Indonesia . 62 D2
Sumava △, Czech Rep. 26 C6
Sumba, Indonesia 63 F5
Sumba, Selat, Indonesia 63 F5
Sumbawa, Indonesia 62 F5
Sumbawa Besar, Indonesia 62 F5
Sumbawanga □, Tanzania 84 F6
Sumbe, Angola 84 G2
Sumbu △, Zambia 87 D3
Sumburgh Hd., U.K. 13 B7
Sumdeo, India 69 D8
Sumdo, China 69 B8
Sumedang, Indonesia 63 G12
Sümeg, Hungary 28 D2
Sumeih, Sudan 81 F2
Sumen = Shumen, Bulgaria 45 C10
Sumenep, Indonesia 63 G15
Sumgait = Sumqayıt, Azerbaijan   35 K9
Summer L., U.S.A. 108 E3
Summerland, Canada 102 D5
Summerside, Canada 105 C7
Summersville, U.S.A. 114 F5
Summerville, Ga., U.S.A. 115 H3
Summerville, S.C., U.S.A. 115 J5
Summit Lake, Canada 102 C4
Summit Peak, U.S.A. 109 H10
Sumner, Iowa, U.S.A. 112 D8
Sumner, Wash., U.S.A. 110 C4
Sumoto, Japan 55 G7
Šumperk, Czech Rep. 27 B9
Sumqayıt, Azerbaijan 35 K9
Sumter, U.S.A. 115 J5
Sumy, Ukraine 33 G8
Sun City, S. Africa 88 D4
Sun City, Ariz., U.S.A. 109 K7
Sun City, Calif., U.S.A. 111 M9
Sun City Center, U.S.A. 115 M4
Sun Lakes, U.S.A. 109 K8
Sun Valley, U.S.A. 108 E6
Sunagawa, Japan 54 C10
Sunan, N. Korea 57 E13
Sunart, L., U.K. 13 E3
Sunburst, U.S.A. 108 B8
Sunbury, Australia 95 F3
Sunbury, U.S.A. 117 F8
Sunchales, Argentina 126 C3
Suncho Corral, Argentina 126 B3
Sunch'ŏn, S. Korea 57 G14
Suncook, U.S.A. 117 C13
Sunda, Selat, Indonesia 62 F3
Sunda Is., Indonesia 96 H2
Sunda Str. = Sunda, Selat,
   Indonesia 62 F3
Sundance, Canada 103 B10
Sundance, U.S.A. 112 C2
Sundar Nagar, India 68 D7
Sundarbans, Asia 67 J16
Sundargarh, India 67 H14
Sundays = Sondags →, S. Africa 88 E4
Sunderland, Canada 116 B5
Sunderland, U.K. 14 C6
Sussex, Canada 117 E10
Sundown △, Australia 95 D5
Sundre, Canada 102 C6
Sunds, Denmark 11 H3
Sundsvall, Sweden 10 B11
Sundsvallsbukten, Sweden 10 B11
Sung Hei, Vietnam 65 G6
Sungai Acheh, Malaysia .... 65 c
Sungai Kolok, Thailand 65 J3
Sungai Lembing, Malaysia 65 L4
Sungai Petani, Malaysia 65 K3
Sungaigerong, Indonesia 62 E3
Sungailiat, Indonesia 62 E3
Sungaipenuh, Indonesia 62 E2
Sungari = Songhua Jiang →,
   China 60 B8
Sunghua Chiang = Songhua
   Jiang →, China 60 B8
Sungikai, Sudan 81 E2
Sungurlu, Turkey 72 B6
Sunja, Croatia 41 C13
Sunland Park, U.S.A. 109 L10
Sunnansjö, Sweden 10 D8
Sunndalsøra, Norway 9 E13

Sunne, Sweden 10 E7
Sunnemo, Sweden 10 E7
Sunnyside, U.S.A. 108 C3
Sunnyvale, U.S.A. 110 H4
Suntar, Russia 53 C12
Sunyani, Ghana 82 D4
Suomenselkä, Finland 8 E21
Suomussalmi, Finland 8 D23
Suoyarvi, Russia 32 A7
Supai, U.S.A. 109 H7
Supaul, India 69 F12
Superior, Ariz., U.S.A. 109 K8
Superior, Mont., U.S.A. 108 C6
Superior, Nebr., U.S.A. 112 E5
Superior, Wis., U.S.A. 112 B8
Superior, L., N. Amer. 104 C2
Supetar, Croatia 41 E13
Suphan Buri, Thailand 64 E3
Suphan Dağı, Turkey 70 B4
Supiori, Indonesia 63 E9
Suprasl, Poland 31 E10
Suprasl →, Poland 31 E9
Supung Shuiku, China 57 D13
Süq Suwayq, Si. Arabia 70 E3
Suqian, China 57 H10
Suqutra = Socotra, Yemen 75 E5
Şür, Lebanon 74 B4
Şür, Oman 75 C6
Sur, Pt., U.S.A. 110 J5
Sura →, Russia 34 C8
Surab, Pakistan 68 E2
Surabaja = Surabaya, Indonesia . 63 G15
Surabaya, Indonesia 63 G15
Surahammar, Sweden 10 E10
Suraia, Romania 29 E12
Surakarta, Indonesia 63 G14
Surakhany, Azerbaijan 35 K10
Şürany, Slovak Rep. 27 C11
Surat, Australia 95 D4
Surat, India 66 J8
Surat Thani, Thailand 65 H2
Suratgarh, India 68 E5
Suraż, Poland 31 F9
Surazh, Belarus 32 E6
Surazh, Russia 33 F7
Surduc, Romania 29 C8
Surduc Pasul, Romania 29 E8
Surdulica, Serbia & M. 44 D6
Surendranagar, India 68 H4
Surf, U.S.A. 111 L6
Surfers Paradise, Australia 95 D5
Surgères, France 20 B3
Surgut, Russia 52 C8
Süria, Spain 38 D6
Suriapet, India 66 L11
Surigao, Phil. 61 G6
Surigao Strait, Phil. 61 F6
Surin, Thailand 64 E4
Surin Nua, Ko, Thailand 65 H1
Surinam = Suriname ■, S. Amer. 125 C7
Suriname ■, S. Amer. 125 C7
Suriname →, Suriname 125 B7
Sürmaq, Iran 71 D7
Sürmene, Turkey 73 B9
Surovikino, Russia 35 F6
Surrey, Canada 110 A4
Surrey □, U.K. 15 F7
Sursand, India 69 F11
Sursar →, India 69 F12
Sursee, Switz. 25 H4
Sursk, Russia 34 D7
Surskoye, Russia 34 C8
Surt, Libya 79 B9
Surt, Khalīj, Libya 79 B9
Surtanahu, Pakistan 68 F4
Surte, Sweden 11 G6
Surtsey, Iceland 8 E3
Sürüç, Turkey 73 D8
Suruga-Wan, Japan 55 G9
Susa, Italy 40 C4
Süsā →, Denmark 11 J5
Sušac, Croatia 41 F13
Susak, Croatia 41 D11
Susaki, Japan 55 H6
Süsangerd, Iran 71 D6
Susanville, U.S.A. 108 F3
Susch, Switz. 25 J6
Suşehri, Turkey 73 B8
Sušice, Czech Rep. 26 B6
Susleni, Moldova 29 C13
Susner, India 68 H7
Susong, China 59 B11
Susquehanna, U.S.A. 117 E9
Susquehanna →, U.S.A. 117 G8
Susques, Argentina 126 A2
Sussex, Canada 105 C6
Sussex, U.S.A. 117 E10
Sussex, E. □, U.K. 15 G8
Sussex, W. □, U.K. 15 G7
Sustut →, Canada 102 B3
Susuman, Russia 53 C15
Susunu, Indonesia 63 E8
Susurluk, Turkey 47 B10
Susuz, Turkey 73 B10
Susz, Poland 30 E6
Sütçüler, Turkey 72 D4
Şuteşti, Romania 29 E12
Sutherland, S. Africa 88 E3
Sutherland, U.K. 13 C4
Sutherland, U.S.A. 112 E4
Sutherland Falls N.Z. 91 L1
Sutherlin, U.S.A. 108 E2
Suthri, India 68 H3
Sutjeska △, Bos.-H. 28 G3
Sutlej →, Pakistan 68 E4
Sutter, U.S.A. 110 F5
Sutter Creek, U.S.A. 110 G6
Sutton, Canada 117 A12
Sutton, Nebr., U.S.A. 112 E6
Sutton, W. Va., U.S.A. 114 F5

Sutton →, Canada 104 A3
Sutton Coldfield, U.K. 15 E6
Sutton in Ashfield, U.K. 14 D6
Sutton L., Canada 104 B3
Suttor →, Australia 94 C4
Suttsu, Japan 54 C10
Suva, Fiji 91 D8
Suva Gora, Macedonia 44 E5
Suva Planina, Serbia & M. 44 C6
Suva Reka, Serbia & M. 44 D4
Suvorov, Russia 32 E9
Suvorov Is. = Suwarrow Is.,
   Cook Is. 97 J11
Suvorove, Ukraine 29 E13
Suvorovo, Bulgaria 45 C11
Suwałki, Poland 30 D9
Suwana, Indonesia 63 K18
Suwannaphum, Thailand 64 E4
Suwannee →, U.S.A. 115 L4
Suwanose-Jima, Japan 55 K4
Suwarrow Is., Cook Is. 97 J11
Suwayq aş Şuqban, Iraq 70 D5
Suweis, Khalîg el, Egypt 80 J8
Suweis, Qanâ es, Egypt 80 H8
Suwŏn, S. Korea 57 F14
Suzdal, Russia 32 D11
Suzhou, Anhui, China 56 H9
Suzhou, Jiangsu, China 59 B13
Suzu, Japan 55 F8
Suzu-Misaki, Japan 55 F8
Suzuka, Japan 55 G8
Suzzara, Italy 40 D7
Svalbard, Arctic 51 B5
Svalbard Radio = Longyearbyen,
   Svalbard 4 B8
Svalöv, Sweden 11 J7
Svalyava, Ukraine 28 B7
Svaneke, Denmark 11 J9
Svängsta, Sweden 11 H8
Svanskog, Sweden 10 E6
Svappavaara, Sweden 8 C19
Svärdsjö, Sweden 10 D9
Svartå, Sweden 10 E8
Svartisen, Norway 8 C15
Svartvik, Sweden 10 B11
Svatove, Ukraine 33 H10
Svatovo = Svatove, Ukraine ... 33 H10
Svay Chek, Cambodia 64 F4
Svay Rieng, Cambodia 65 G5
Svealand □, Sweden 10 D9
Svedala, Sweden 11 J7
Sveg, Sweden 10 B8
Svendborg, Denmark 11 J4
Svenljunga, Sweden 11 G7
Svenstavik, Sweden 10 B8
Svenstrup, Denmark 11 H3
Sverdlovsk, Ukraine 33 H10
Sverdrup Is., Canada 98 B10
Svetac, Croatia 41 E12
Sveti Nikola, Prokhad, Europe . 44 C6
Sveti Nikole, Macedonia 44 E5
Sveti Rok, Croatia 41 D12
Svetlaya, Russia 54 A9
Svetlogorsk = Svyetlahorsk,
   Belarus 33 F5
Svetlograd, Russia 30 D7
Svetlograd, Russia 35 H6
Svetlovodsk = Svitlovodsk,
   Ukraine 33 H7
Svetlyy, Russia 30 D7
Svidník, Slovak Rep. 27 B14
Svilaja Planina, Croatia 41 E13
Svilajnac, Serbia & M. 44 B5
Svilengrad, Bulgaria 45 E10
Svir →, Russia 32 B7
Sviritsa, Russia 32 B7
Svishtov, Bulgaria 45 C9
Svislach, Belarus 31 E11
Svitava →, Czech Rep. 27 B9
Svitavy, Czech Rep. 27 B9
Svitlovodsk, Ukraine 33 H7
Svobodnyy, Russia 53 D13
Svoge, Bulgaria 44 D7
Svolvær, Norway 8 B16
Svratka →, Czech Rep. 27 B9
Svrljig, Serbia & M. 44 C6
Svyetlahorsk, Belarus 33 F5
Swabian Alps = Schwäbische Alb,
   Germany 25 G5
Swaffham, U.K. 15 E8
Swainsboro, U.S.A. 115 J4
Swakop →, Namibia 88 C2
Swakopmund, Namibia 88 C1
Swale →, U.K. 14 C6
Swan →, Australia 93 F2
Swan →, Canada 103 C8
Swan Hill, Australia 95 F3
Swan Hills, Canada 102 C5
Swan Is. = Santanilla, Is.,
   Honduras 120 C3
Swan L., Canada 103 C8
Swan Peak, U.S.A. 108 C7
Swan Ra., U.S.A. 108 C7
Swan River, Canada 103 C8
Swanage, U.K. 15 G6
Swansea, Australia 95 G4
Swansea, Canada 116 C5
Swansea, U.K. 15 F3
Swansea □, U.K. 15 F3
Swar →, Pakistan 69 B5
Swartberge, S. Africa 88 E3
Swartmodder, S. Africa 88 D3
Swartnossob →, Namibia 88 C2
Swartruggens, S. Africa 88 D4
Swarzędz, Poland 31 F4
Swastika, Canada 104 C3
Swatow = Shantou, China 59 F11
Swaziland ■, Africa 89 D5
Sweden ■, Europe 9 G16
Swedru, Ghana 83 D4

Sweet Home, U.S.A. 108 D2
Sweetgrass, U.S.A. 108 B8
Sweetwater, Nev., U.S.A. 110 G7
Sweetwater, Tenn., U.S.A. 115 H3
Sweetwater, Tex., U.S.A. 113 J4
Sweetwater →, U.S.A. 108 E10
Swellendam, S. Africa 88 E3
Swider →, Poland 31 F8
Świdnica, Poland 31 H3
Świdnik, Poland 31 G9
Świdwin, Poland 30 E2
Świebodzice, Poland 31 H3
Świebodzin, Poland 31 F2
Świecie, Poland 30 E5
Świerzawa, Poland 31 G2
Świętokrzyski △, Poland 31 H7
Świętokrzyskie □, Poland 31 H7
Świętokrzyskie, Góry, Poland .. 31 H7
Swift Current, Canada 103 C7
Swift Current →, Canada 103 C7
Swilly, L., Ireland 12 A4
Swindon, U.K. 15 F6
Swindon □, U.K. 15 F6
Swinemünde = Świnoujście,
   Poland 30 E1
Świnoujście, Poland 30 E1
Switzerland ■, Europe 25 J4
Swords, Ireland 12 C5
Swoyerville, U.S.A. 117 E9
Syasstroy, Russia 32 B7
Sychevka, Russia 32 E8
Syców, Poland 31 G4
Sydenham →, Canada 116 D2
Sydney, Australia 95 E5
Sydney, Canada 105 C7
Sydney L., Canada 103 C10
Sydney Mines, Canada 105 C7
Sydprøven = Alluitsup Paa,
   Greenland 101 B15
Sydra, G. of = Surt, Khalīj, Libya 79 B9
Syeverodonetsk, Ukraine 33 H10
Syke, Germany 24 C4
Sykesville, U.S.A. 116 E6
Syktyvkar, Russia 52 C6
Sylacauga, U.S.A. 115 J2
Sylarna, Sweden 8 E15
Sylhet, Bangla. 67 G17
Sylhet □, Bangla. 67 G17
Sylt, Germany 24 A4
Sylvan Beach, U.S.A. 117 C9
Sylvan Lake, Canada 102 C6
Sylvania, U.S.A. 115 J5
Sylvester, U.S.A. 115 K4
Sym, Russia 52 C9
Symón, Mexico 118 C4
Synelnykove, Ukraine 33 H8
Synevyr △, Ukraine 29 B8
Synevyrska Polyana, Ukraine .. 29 B8
Synnott Ra., Australia 92 C4
Synyak, Ukraine 28 B7
Syowa, Antarctica 5 C5
Syracuse, Kans., U.S.A. 113 G4
Syracuse, N.Y., U.S.A. 117 C8
Syracuse, Nebr., U.S.A. 112 E6
Syrdarya →, Kazakhstan 52 E7
Syria ■, Asia 70 C3
Syrian Desert = Shām, Bādiyat
   ash, Asia 70 C3
Sysslebäck, Sweden 10 D6
Syzran, Russia 34 D9
Szabolcs-Szatmár-Bereg □,
   Hungary 28 B6
Szadek, Poland 31 G5
Szamocin, Poland 31 E4
Szamos →, Hungary 28 B5
Szamotuły, Poland 31 F3
Száraz →, Hungary 28 D6
Szarvas, Hungary 28 D5
Százhalombatta, Hungary 28 C3
Szczawnica, Poland 31 J7
Szczebrzeszyn, Poland 31 H9
Szczecin, Poland 30 E1
Szczecinek, Poland 30 E3
Szczeciński, Zalew = Stettiner
   Haff, Germany 24 B10
Szczekociny, Poland 31 H6
Szczucin, Poland 31 H8
Szczuczyn, Poland 30 E9
Szczytna, Poland 31 H3
Szczytno, Poland 30 E7
Szechuan Basin = Sichuan Pendi,
   China 58 B5
Szechwan = Sichuan □, China .. 58 B5
Szécsény, Hungary 28 B4
Szeged, Hungary 28 D5
Szeghalom, Hungary 28 C6
Székesfehérvár, Hungary 28 C3
Szekszárd, Hungary 28 D3
Szendrő, Hungary 28 B5
Szentendre, Hungary 28 C3
Szentes, Hungary 28 D5
Szentgotthárd, Hungary 28 D1
Szentlőrinc, Hungary 28 D3
Szerencs, Hungary 28 B6
Szigetszentmiklós, Hungary ... 28 C3
Szigetvár, Hungary 28 D2
Szikszó, Hungary 28 B5
Szklarska Poręba, Poland 31 H2
Szkwa →, Poland 31 E8
Szlichtyngowa, Poland 31 G3
Szob, Hungary 28 C3
Szolnok, Hungary 28 C5
Szombathely, Hungary 28 C1
Szprotawa, Poland 31 G2
Sztum, Poland 30 E6
Sztutowo, Poland 30 D6
Szubin, Poland 31 E4
Szydłowiec, Poland 31 G7
Szypliszki, Poland 30 D10

T

Ta Khli Khok, Thailand 64 E3
Ta Lai, Vietnam 65 G6
Tab, Hungary 28 D3
Tabacal, Argentina 126 A3
Tabaco, Phil. 61 E5
Tabagné, Ivory C. 82 D4
Tābah, Si. Arabia 70 E4
Tabanan, Indonesia 63 K18
Tabankort, Niger 83 B5
Ţabas, Khorāsān, Iran 71 C9
Ţabas, Khorāsān, Iran 71 C8
Tabasará, Serranía de, Panama . 120 E3
Tabasco □, Mexico 119 D6
Tabāsīn, Iran 71 D8
Tabatinga, Serra da, Brazil 125 F10
Taber, Canada 102 D6
Taberg, Sweden 11 G8
Taberg, U.S.A. 117 C9
Tabla, Niger 83 C5
Tablas de Daimiel △, Spain ... 37 F7
Tablas I., Phil. 61 E5
Tablas Strait, Phil. 61 E4
Table B., Canada 105 B8
Table B., S. Africa 88 E2
Table Mt., S. Africa 88 E2
Table Rock L., U.S.A. 113 G8
Tabletop, Mt., Australia 94 C4
Tábor, Czech Rep. 26 B7
Tabora, Tanzania 86 D3
Tabora □, Tanzania 86 D3
Tabou, Ivory C. 82 E3
Tabrīz, Iran 70 B5
Tabuaeran, Kiribati 97 G12
Tabuenca, Spain 38 D3
Tabūk, Si. Arabia 70 D3
Taburno-Camposauro △, Italy .. 43 A7
Täby, Sweden 10 E12
Tacámbaro de Codallos, Mexico 118 D4
Tacheng, China 60 B3
Tach'i, Taiwan 59 E13
Tachia, Taiwan 59 E13
Tach'ing Shan = Daqing Shan,
   China 56 D6
Tachov, Czech Rep. 26 B5
Tácina →, Italy 43 D9
Tacloban, Phil. 61 F6
Tacna, Peru 124 G4
Tacoma, U.S.A. 110 C4
Tacuarembó, Uruguay 127 C4
Tademaït, Plateau du, Algeria .. 78 C6
Tadio, L., Ivory C. 82 D3
Tadjoura, Djibouti 81 E5
Tadjoura, Golfe de, Djibouti ... 81 E5
Tadmor, N.Z. 91 J4
Tadoule L., Canada 103 B9
Tadoussac, Canada 105 C6
Tadrés △, Niger 83 B6
Tadzhikistan = Tajikistan ■, Asia 52 F8
Taechŏn-ni, S. Korea 57 F14
Taegu, S. Korea 57 G15
Taegwan, N. Korea 57 D13
Taejŏn, S. Korea 57 F14
Taen, Ko, Thailand .... 65 b
Tafalla, Spain 38 C3
Tafar, Sudan 81 F2
Tafelbaai = Table B., S. Africa .. 88 E2
Tafermaar, Indonesia 63 F8
Tafī Viejo, Argentina 126 B2
Tafīhān, Iran 71 D7
Tafiré, Ivory C. 82 D3
Tafo, Ghana 83 D4
Tafresh, Iran 71 C6
Taft, Phil. 61 F6
Taft, U.S.A. 111 K7
Taftān, Kūh-e, Iran 71 D9
Taga Dzong, Bhutan 67 F16
Taganrog, Russia 33 J10
Taganrogskiy Zaliv, Russia 33 H10
Tagânt, Mauritania 82 B2
Tagatay, Phil. 61 D4
Tagbilaran, Phil. 61 G5
Tággia, Italy 40 E4
Tagish, Canada 102 A2
Tagish L., Canada 102 A2
Tagliacozzo, Italy 41 F10
Tagliamento →, Italy 41 C10
Táglio di Po, Italy 41 D9
Tago, Phil. 61 G7
Tagomago, Spain 48 B8
Tagounite, Mauritania 82 B3
Taguatinga, Brazil 125 F10
Tagudin, Phil. 61 C4
Tagum, Phil. 61 H6
Tagus = Tejo →, Europe 37 F2
Tahakopa, N.Z. 91 M2
Tahan, Gunung, Malaysia 65 K4
Tahat, Algeria 78 D7
Tāherī, Iran 71 E7
Tahiti, French Polynesia 97 J13
Tahlequah, U.S.A. 113 H7
Tahoe, L., U.S.A. 110 G6
Tahoe City, U.S.A. 110 F6
Tahoka, U.S.A. 113 J4
Taholah, U.S.A. 110 C2
Tahoua, Niger 83 C6
Tahrūd, Iran 71 D8
Tahsis, Canada 102 D3
Tahta, Egypt 80 B3
Tahtaköprü, Turkey 45 G13
Tahulandang, Indonesia 63 D7
Tahuna, Indonesia 63 D7
Taï △, Ivory C. 82 D3
Tai Hu, China 59 B12
Tai Rom Yen △, Thailand 65 H2

Tai Shan, China 57 F9
Tai'an, China 57 F9
Taibei = T'aipei, Taiwan 59 E13
Taibique, Canary Is. 48 G2
Taibus Qi, China 56 D8
Taicang, China 59 B13
T'aichung, Taiwan 59 E13
Taieri →, N.Z. 91 M3
Taigu, China 56 F7
Taihang Shan, China 56 G7
Taihape, N.Z. 91 H5
Taihe, Anhui, China 56 H8
Taihe, Jiangxi, China 59 D10
Taihu, China 59 B11
Taijiang, China 58 D7
Taikang, China 56 G8
Tailem Bend, Australia 95 F2
Tailfingen, Germany 25 G5
Tailuko, Taiwan 59 E13
Taimyr Peninsula = Taymyr, Poluostrov, Russia 53 B11
Tain, U.K. 13 D4
T'ainan, Taiwan 59 F13
Taínaron, Ákra, Greece 46 E4
Taining, China 59 D11
T'aipei, Taiwan 59 E13
Taiping, China 59 B12
Taiping, Malaysia 65 K3
Taipingzhen, China 56 H6
Tairbeart = Tarbert, U.K. 13 D2
Taishan, China 59 F9
Taishun, China 59 D12
Taita Hills, Kenya 86 C4
Taitao, Pen. de, Chile 128 F2
T'aitung, Taiwan 59 F13
Taivalkoski, Finland 8 D23
Taiwan ■, Asia 59 F13
Taiwan Strait, Asia 59 E12
Taixing, China 59 A13
Taiyara, Sudan 81 E3
Taÿetos Óros, Greece 46 D4
Taiyiba, Israel 74 C4
Taiyuan, China 56 F7
Taizhong = T'aichung, Taiwan 59 E13
Taizhou, China 59 A12
Taizhou Liedao, China 59 C13
Ta'izz, Yemen 75 E3
Tājābād, Iran 71 D7
Tajikistan ■, Asia 52 F8
Tajima, Japan 55 F9
Tajo = Tejo →, Europe 37 F2
Tajrīsh, Iran 71 C6
Tak, Thailand 64 D2
Takāb, Iran 70 B5
Takachiho, Japan 55 H5
Takachu, Botswana 88 C3
Takada, Japan 55 F9
Takahagi, Japan 55 F10
Takaka, N.Z. 91 J4
Takamatsu, Japan 55 G7
Takaoka, Japan 55 F8
Takapuna, N.Z. 91 G5
Takasaki, Japan 55 F9
Takatsuki, Japan 55 G7
Takaungu, Kenya 86 C4
Takayama, Japan 55 F8
Take-Shima, Japan 55 J5
Takefu, Japan 55 G8
Takengon, Indonesia 62 D1
Takeo, Japan 55 H5
Tåkern, Sweden 11 F8
Takeshima = Tok-do, Asia 55 F5
Tåkestān, Iran 71 C6
Taketa, Japan 55 H5
Takev, Cambodia 65 G5
Takh, India 69 C7
Takht-Sulaiman, Pakistan 68 D3
Takikawa, Japan 54 C10
Takla L., Canada 102 B3
Takla Landing, Canada 102 B3
Takla Makan = Taklamakan Shamo, China 60 C3
Taklamakan Shamo, China 60 C3
Taku →, Canada 102 B2
Takua Thung, Thailand 65 a
Takum, Nigeria 83 D6
Tal Halāl, Iran 71 D7
Tala, Uruguay 127 C4
Talachyn, Belarus 32 E5
Talacogan, Phil. 61 G6
Talagang, Pakistan 68 C5
Talagante, Chile 126 C1
Talak, Niger 83 B6
Talamanca, Cordillera de, Cent. Amer. 120 E3
Talant, France 19 E11
Talara, Peru 124 D2
Talas, Kyrgyzstan 52 E8
Talas, Turkey 72 C6
Talāta, Egypt 74 E1
Talata Mafara, Nigeria 83 C6
Talaud, Kepulauan, Indonesia 63 D7
Talaud Is. = Talaud, Kepulauan, Indonesia 63 D7
Talavera de la Reina, Spain 36 F6
Talavera la Real, Spain 37 G4
Talayan, Phil. 61 H6
Talayuela, Spain 36 F5
Talbandh, India 69 H12
Talbert, Sillon de, France 18 D3
Talbot, C., Australia 92 B4
Talbragar →, Australia 95 E4
Talca, Chile 126 D1
Talcahuano, Chile 126 D1
Talcher, India 67 J14
Talcho, Niger 83 C5
Taldy Kurgan = Taldyqorghan, Kazakhstan 52 E8
Taldyqorghan, Kazakhstan 52 E8
Tālesh, Iran 71 B6
Tālesh, Kūhhā-ye, Iran 71 B6

Talguharai, Sudan 80 D4
Tali Post, Sudan 81 F3
Taliabu, Indonesia 63 E6
Talibon, Phil. 63 B6
Talibong, Ko, Thailand 65 J2
Talihina, U.S.A. 113 H7
Talisayan, Phil. 61 G6
Taliwang, Indonesia 62 F5
Tall 'Afar, Iraq 70 B4
Tall Kalakh, Syria 74 A5
Talla, Egypt 80 B3
Talladega, U.S.A. 115 J2
Tallahassee, U.S.A. 115 K3
Tallangatta, Australia 95 F4
Tallard, France 21 D10
Tällberg, Sweden 10 D9
Tallering Pk., Australia 93 E2
Talli, Pakistan 68 E3
Tallinn, Estonia 9 G21
Tallmadge, U.S.A. 116 E3
Tallulah, U.S.A. 113 J9
Tălmaciu, Romania 29 E9
Talmont-St-Hilaire, France 20 B2
Talne, Ukraine 33 H6
Talnoye = Talne, Ukraine 33 H6
Talodi, Sudan 81 E3
Talovaya, Russia 34 E5
Taloyoak, Canada 100 B10
Talpa de Allende, Mexico 118 C4
Talparo, Trin. & Tob. 125 K15
Talsi, Latvia 9 H20
Talsi □, Latvia 30 A9
Taltal, Chile 126 B1
Taltson →, Canada 102 A6
Talwood, Australia 95 D4
Talyawalka Cr. →, Australia 95 E3
Tam Ky, Vietnam 64 E7
Tam Quan, Vietnam 64 E7
Tama, U.S.A. 112 E8
Tama △, Ethiopia 81 F4
Tamale, Ghana 83 D4
Taman, Russia 33 K9
Taman Negara △, Malaysia 65 K4
Tamani, Mali 82 C3
Tamano, Japan 55 G6
Tamanrasset, Algeria 78 D7
Tamaqua, U.S.A. 117 F9
Tamar →, U.K. 15 G3
Tamarinda, Spain 48 B10
Tamarite de Litera, Spain 38 D5
Tamashima, Japan 55 G6
Tamási, Hungary 28 D3
Tamaské, Niger 83 C6
Tamaulipas □, Mexico 119 C5
Tamaulipas, Sierra de, Mexico 119 C5
Tamazula, Mexico 118 C3
Tamazunchale, Mexico 119 C5
Tamba-Dabatou, Guinea 82 C2
Tambacounda, Senegal 82 C2
Tambelan, Kepulauan, Indonesia 62 D3
Tambellup, Australia 93 F2
Tambo, Australia 94 C4
Tambo de Mora, Peru 124 F3
Tambohorano, Madag. 89 B7
Tambora, Indonesia 62 F5
Tambov, Russia 34 D5
Tambre →, Spain 36 C2
Tambuku, Indonesia 63 G15
Tamburâ, Sudan 81 F2
Tâmchekket, Mauritania 82 B2
Tâmega →, Portugal 36 D2
Tamenglong, India 67 G18
Tamgué, Massif du, Guinea 82 C2
Tamiahua, L. de, Mexico 119 C5
Tamil Nadu □, India 66 P10
Tamis →, Serbia & M. 28 F5
Tamluk, India 69 H12
Tammerfors = Tampere, Finland 9 F20
Tammisaari, Finland 9 F20
Tämnaren, Sweden 10 D11
Tamo Abu, Pegunungan, Malaysia 62 D5
Tampa, U.S.A. 115 M4
Tampa, Tanjung, Indonesia 63 K19
Tampa B., U.S.A. 115 M4
Tampere, Finland 9 F20
Tampico, Mexico 119 C5
Tampin, Malaysia 65 L4
Tampoi, Malaysia 65 d
Tamsweg, Austria 26 D6
Tamu, Burma 67 G19
Tamuja →, Spain 37 F4
Tamworth, Australia 95 E5
Tamworth, Canada 116 B8
Tamworth, U.K. 15 E6
Tamyang, S. Korea 57 G14
Tan An, Vietnam 65 G6
Tan Chau, Vietnam 65 G5
Tan-Tan, Morocco 78 C3
Tana →, Kenya 86 C5
Tana →, Norway 8 A23
Tana, L., Ethiopia 81 E4
Tana River Primate △, Kenya 86 C5
Tanabe, Japan 55 H7
Tanafjorden, Norway 8 A23
Tanahbala, Indonesia 62 E1
Tanahgrogot, Indonesia 62 E5
Tanahjampea, Indonesia 63 F6
Tanahmasa, Indonesia 62 E1
Tanahmerah, Indonesia 63 F10
Tanakpur, India 69 E9
Tanakura, Japan 55 F10
Tanami, Australia 92 C4
Tanami Desert, Australia 92 C4
Tanana, U.S.A. 100 B4
Tananarive = Antananarivo, Madag. 89 B8
Tánaro →, Italy 40 D3
Tancheng, China 57 G10
Tanch'ŏn, N. Korea 57 D15
Tanda, Ut. P., India 69 F10

Tanda, Ut. P., India 69 E8
Tanda, Ivory C. 82 D4
Tandag, Phil. 61 G7
Tandaia, Romania 87 D3
Tandaué, Angola 88 B2
Tandil, Argentina 126 D4
Tandil, Sa. del, Argentina 126 D4
Tandlianwala, Pakistan 68 D5
Tando Adam, Pakistan 68 G3
Tando Allahyar, Pakistan 68 G3
Tando Bago, Pakistan 68 G3
Tando Mohommed Khan, Pakistan 68 G3
Tandou L., Australia 95 E3
Tandragee, U.K. 12 B5
Tandsjöborg, Sweden 10 C8
Tane-ga-Shima, Japan 55 J5
Taneatua, N.Z. 91 H6
Tanen Tong Dan = Dawna Ra., Burma 64 D2
Tanew →, Poland 31 H9
Tanezrouft, Algeria 78 D6
Tang, Koh, Cambodia 65 G4
Tang, Ra's-e, Iran 71 E8
Tang Krasang, Cambodia 64 F5
Tanga, Tanzania 86 D4
Tanga □, Tanzania 86 D4
Tanganyika, L., Africa 86 D3
Tangaza, Nigeria 83 C5
Tanger, Morocco 78 A4
Tangerang, Indonesia 63 G12
Tangerhütte, Germany 24 C7
Tangermünde, Germany 24 C7
Tanggu, China 57 E9
Tanggula Shan, China 60 C4
Tanghe, China 56 H7
Tanghla Range = Tanggula Shan, China 60 C4
Tangier = Tanger, Morocco 78 A4
Tangorin, Australia 94 C3
Tangorombohitr'i Makay, Madag. 89 C8
Tangshan, China 57 E10
Tangtou, China 57 G10
Tanguiéta, Benin 83 C5
Tangxi, China 59 C12
Tangyan He →, China 58 C7
Tanimbar, Kepulauan, Indonesia 63 F8
Tanimbar Is. = Tanimbar, Kepulauan, Indonesia 63 F8
Taninthari = Tenasserim, Burma 65 F2
Tanjay, Phil. 61 G5
Tanjong Malim, Malaysia 65 L3
Tanjong Pelepas, Malaysia 65 d
Tanjore = Thanjavur, India 66 P11
Tanjung, Indonesia 63 J19
Tanjung, Phil. 62 E5
Tanjung Tokong, Malaysia 65 c
Tanjungbalai, Indonesia 62 D1
Tanjungbatu, Indonesia 62 D5
Tanjungkarang Telukbetung, Indonesia 62 F3
Tanjungpandan, Indonesia 62 E3
Tanjungpinang, Indonesia 62 D2
Tanjungredeb, Indonesia 62 D5
Tanjungselor, Indonesia 62 D5
Tank, Pakistan 68 C4
Tankhala, India 68 J5
Tankwa-Karoo △, S. Africa 88 E2
Tännäs, Sweden 10 B6
Tannersville, U.S.A. 117 E9
Tannis Bugt, Denmark 11 G4
Tannu-Ola, Russia 53 D10
Tannum Sands, Australia 94 C5
Tano →, Ghana 82 D4
Tanon Str., Phil. 61 F5
Tanout, Niger 83 C6
Tanshui, Taiwan 59 E13
Tansilla, Burkina Faso 82 C4
Tanta, Egypt 80 H7
Tantoyuca, Mexico 119 C5
Tantung = Dandong, China 57 D13
Tanumshede, Sweden 11 F5
Tanunda, Australia 95 E2
Tanus, France 20 D6
Tanzania ■, Africa 86 D3
Tanzilla →, Canada 102 B2
Tao, Ko, Thailand 65 G2
Tao'an = Taonan, China 57 B12
Tao'er He →, China 57 B13
Taohua Dao, China 59 C14
Taolanaro, Madag. 89 D8
Taole, China 56 E4
Taonan, China 57 B12
Taormina, Italy 43 E8
Taos, U.S.A. 109 H11
Taoudenni, Mali 78 D5
Taoyuan, China 59 C8
T'aoyüan, Taiwan 59 E13
Tapa, Estonia 9 G21
Tapa Shan = Daba Shan, China 58 B7
Tapachula, Mexico 119 E6
Tapah, Malaysia 65 K3
Tapajós →, Brazil 125 D8
Tapaktuan, Indonesia 62 D1
Tapanahoni →, Suriname 125 C8
Tapanui, N.Z. 91 L2
Tapauá →, Brazil 124 E6
Tapes, Brazil 127 C5
Tapeta, Liberia 82 D3
Taphan Hin, Thailand 64 D3
Tapi →, India 66 J8
Tapia de Casariego, Spain 36 B4
Tapirapecó, Serra, Venezuela 124 C6
Tapo-Capara △, Venezuela 121 E5
Tapolca, Hungary 28 D2
Tapuae-o-Uenuku, N.Z. 91 K4
Tapul Group, Phil. 61 J4
Tapurucuará, Brazil 124 D5
Taqtaq, Iraq 70 C5
Taquara, Brazil 127 B5

Taquari →, Brazil 124 G7
Tara, Australia 95 D5
Tara, Canada 116 B3
Tara, Russia 52 D8
Tara, Zambia 87 F2
Tara △, Serbia & M. 44 C3
Tara →, Serbia & M. 44 C2
Taraba □, Nigeria 83 D7
Taraba →, Nigeria 83 D7
Tarābulus, Lebanon 74 A4
Tarābulus, Libya 79 B8
Taraclia, Taraclia, Moldova 29 E13
Taraclia, Tighina, Moldova 29 D14
Taradehi, India 69 H8
Tarajalejo, Canary Is. 48 F5
Tarakan, Indonesia 62 D5
Tarakit, Mt., Kenya 86 B4
Tarama-Jima, Japan 55 M2
Taran, Mys, Russia 9 J18
Taranagar, India 68 E6
Taranaki □, N.Z. 91 H5
Taranaki, Mt., N.Z. 91 H5
Tarancón, Spain 38 E1
Tarango, Italy 43 B10
Táranto, Italy 43 B10
Táranto, G. di, Italy 43 B10
Tarapacá, Colombia 124 D5
Tarapacá □, Chile 126 A2
Tarapoto, Peru 124 E3
Tarare, France 21 C8
Tararua Ra., N.Z. 91 J5
Tarascon, France 21 E8
Tarascon-sur-Ariège, France 20 F5
Tarashcha, Ukraine 33 H6
Tarauacá, Brazil 124 E4
Tarauacá →, Brazil 124 E5
Taravo →, France 21 G12
Tarawa, Kiribati 96 G9
Tarawera, N.Z. 91 H6
Tarawera, L., N.Z. 91 H6
Taraz, Kazakhstan 52 E8
Tarazona, Spain 38 D3
Tarazona de la Mancha, Spain 39 F3
Tarbagatay, Khrebet, Kazakhstan 52 E9
Tarbat Ness, U.K. 13 D5
Tarbela Dam, Pakistan 68 B5
Tarbert, Arg. & Bute, U.K. 13 F3
Tarbert, W. Isles, U.K. 13 D2
Tarbes, France 20 E4
Tarboro, U.S.A. 115 H7
Tărcău, Munţii, Romania 29 D11
Tarcento, Italy 41 B10
Tarcoola, Australia 95 E1
Tarcoon, Australia 95 E4
Tardets-Sorholus, France 20 E3
Tardoire →, France 20 C4
Taree, Australia 95 E5
Tarfa, W. el →, Egypt 80 B3
Tarfaya, Morocco 78 C3
Târgovişte, Romania 29 F10
Târgu Bujor, Romania 29 E12
Târgu Cărbuneşti, Romania 29 F8
Târgu Frumos, Romania 29 C12
Târgu-Jiu, Romania 29 E8
Târgu Lăpuş, Romania 29 C8
Târgu Mureş, Romania 29 D9
Târgu Neamţ, Romania 29 C11
Târgu Ocna, Romania 29 D11
Târgu Secuiesc, Romania 29 E11
Târguşor, Romania 29 F13
Târhăus, Vf., Romania 29 D11
Tarif, U.A.E. 71 E7
Tarifa, Spain 37 J5
Tarija, Bolivia 126 A3
Tarija □, Bolivia 126 A3
Tariku →, Indonesia 63 E9
Tarim Basin = Tarim Pendi, China 60 C3
Tarim He →, China 60 C3
Tarim Pendi, China 60 C3
Taritatu →, Indonesia 63 E9
Tarka →, S. Africa 88 E4
Tarkastad, S. Africa 88 E4
Tarkhankut, Mys, Ukraine 33 K7
Tarko Sale, Russia 52 C8
Tarkwa, Ghana 82 D4
Tarlac, Phil. 61 D4
Tarm, Denmark 11 J2
Tarma, Peru 124 F3
Tarn □, France 20 E6
Tarn →, France 20 D5
Tarn-et-Garonne □, France 20 D5
Tarna →, Hungary 28 C4
Târnava Mare →, Romania 29 D8
Târnava Mică →, Romania 29 D8
Târnăveni, Romania 29 D9
Tarnica, Poland 31 J9
Tarnobrzeg, Poland 31 H8
Tarnogród, Poland 31 H9
Tarnos, France 20 E2
Târnova, Moldova 29 B12
Târnova, Romania 28 E6
Tarnów, Poland 31 H8
Tarnowskie Góry, Poland 31 H5
Tärnsjö, Sweden 10 D10
Táro →, Italy 40 C7
Ţārom, Iran 71 D7
Taroom, Australia 95 D4
Taroudannt, Morocco 78 B4
Tarp, Germany 24 A5
Tarpon Springs, U.S.A. 115 L4
Tarquínia, Italy 41 F8
Tarragona, Spain 38 D6
Tarragona □, Spain 38 D6
Tarraleah, Australia 95 G4
Tarrasa = Terrassa, Spain 38 D7
Tàrrega, Spain 38 D6
Tarrytown, U.S.A. 117 E11
Târs, Denmark 11 G4
Tarshiha = Me'ona, Israel 74 B4

Tarsus, Turkey 70 B2
Tartagal, Argentina 126 A3
Tärtär, Azerbaijan 35 K8
Tärtär →, Azerbaijan 35 K8
Tartas, France 20 E3
Tartu, Estonia 9 G22
Ţarţūs, Syria 70 C2
Tarumizu, Japan 55 J5
Tarussa, Russia 32 E9
Tarutao = Ko Tarutao △, Thailand 65 J2
Tarutao, Ko, Thailand 65 J2
Tarutung, Indonesia 62 D1
Tarutyne, Ukraine 29 D14
Tarvísio, Italy 41 B10
Taseko →, Canada 102 C4
Tash-Kömür, Kyrgyzstan 52 E8
Tash-Kumyr = Tash-Kömür, Kyrgyzstan 52 E8
Tashauz = Dashhowuz, Turkmenistan 52 E6
Tashi Chho Dzong = Thimphu, Bhutan 67 F16
Ţashk, Daryācheh-ye, Iran 71 D7
Tashkent = Toshkent, Uzbekistan 52 E7
Tashtagol, Russia 52 D9
Tasiilaq, Greenland 4 C6
Tasikmalaya, Indonesia 63 G13
Tåsinge, Denmark 11 J4
Tåsjön, Sweden 8 D16
Taskan, Russia 53 C16
Tasker, Niger 83 C7
Taşköprü, Turkey 72 B6
Taşlâc, Moldova 29 C14
Tasman B., N.Z. 91 J4
Tasman Mts., N.Z. 91 J4
Tasman Pen., Australia 95 G4
Tasman Plateau, S. Ocean 5 A10
Tasman Sea, Pac. Oc. 96 L8
Tasmania □, Australia 95 G4
Tasnad, Romania 28 C7
Tassili n'Ajjer, Algeria 78 C7
Tassili Tin-Rerhoh, Algeria 83 A5
Tata, Hungary 28 C3
Tatabánya, Hungary 28 C3
Tatahouine, Tunisia 79 B8
Tataouine, Tunisia 79 B8
Tatar Republic = Tatarstan □, Russia 34 C10
Tatarbunary, Ukraine 29 E14
Tatarsk, Russia 52 D8
Tatarstan □, Russia 34 C10
Tateyama, Japan 55 G9
Tathlina L., Canada 102 A5
Tathra, Australia 95 F4
Tatinnai L., Canada 103 A9
Tatla L., Canada 102 C4
Tatlısu, Turkey 45 F11
Tatnam, C., Canada 103 B10
Tatra = Tatry, Slovak Rep. 27 B13
Tatranský △, Slovak Rep. 27 B13
Tatry, Slovak Rep. 27 B13
Tatshenshini →, Canada 102 B1
Tatsuno, Japan 55 G7
Tatta, Pakistan 68 G2
Tatuí, Brazil 127 A6
Tatum, U.S.A. 113 J3
Tat'ung = Datong, China 56 D7
Tatvan, Turkey 70 B4
Taubaté, Brazil 127 A6
Tauberbischofsheim, Germany 25 F5
Taucha, Germany 24 D8
Tauern-tunnel, Austria 26 D6
Taufikia, Sudan 81 F3
Taulé, France 18 D3
Taumarunui, N.Z. 91 H5
Taumaturgo, Brazil 124 E4
Taung, S. Africa 88 D3
Taungdwingyi, Burma 67 J19
Taunggyi, Burma 67 K19
Taungup, Burma 67 K19
Taungup Taunggya, Burma 67 K18
Taunsa, Pakistan 68 D4
Taunsa Barrage, Pakistan 68 D4
Taunton, U.K. 15 F4
Taunton, U.S.A. 117 E14
Taunus, Germany 25 E4
Taupo, N.Z. 91 H6
Taupo, L., N.Z. 91 H5
Tauragė, Lithuania 9 J20
Tauragė □, Lithuania 30 C9
Tauranga, N.Z. 91 G6
Tauranga Harb., N.Z. 91 G6
Taureau, Rés., Canada 104 C5
Taurianova, Italy 43 D9
Taurus Mts. = Toros Dağları, Turkey 70 B2
Tauste, Spain 38 D3
Tauz = Tovuz, Azerbaijan 35 K7
Tavas, France 47 D11
Tavastehus = Hämeenlinna, Finland 9 F21
Tavda, Russia 52 D7
Tavda →, Russia 52 D7
Taverns de la Valldigna, Spain 39 F4
Taveta, Tanzania 86 C4
Taveuni, Fiji 91 C9
Taviano, Italy 43 C11
Tavignano →, France 21 F13
Tavira, Portugal 37 H3
Tavistock, Canada 116 C4
Tavistock, U.K. 15 G3
Tavolara, Italy 42 B2
Távora →, Portugal 36 D3
Tavoy, Burma 64 E2
Tavşanlı, Turkey 47 B11
Taw →, U.K. 15 F3
Tawa →, India 68 H8
Tawas City, U.S.A. 114 C4
Tawau, Malaysia 62 D5
Taweisha, Sudan 81 E2

Tawitawi, *Phil.* 63 **B6**
Tawu, *Taiwan* 59 **F13**
Taxco de Alarcón, *Mexico* .. 119 **D5**
Taxila, *Pakistan* 68 **C5**
Tay △, *U.K.* 13 **E5**
Tay ➤, *U.K.* 13 **E5**
Tay, Firth of, *U.K.* 13 **E5**
Tay, L., *Australia* 93 **F3**
Tay, L., *U.K.* 13 **E4**
Tay Ninh, *Vietnam* 65 **G6**
Tayabamba, *Peru* 124 **E3**
Tayabas Bay, *Phil.* 61 **E4**
Taylakova, *Russia* 52 **D8**
Taylakovy = Taylakova, *Russia* . 52 **D8**
Taylor, *Canada* 102 **B4**
Taylor, *Nebr., U.S.A.* 112 **E5**
Taylor, *Pa., U.S.A.* 117 **E9**
Taylor, *Tex., U.S.A.* 113 **K6**
Taylor, Mt., *U.S.A.* 109 **J10**
Taylorville, *U.S.A.* 112 **F10**
Taymā, *Si. Arabia* 70 **E3**
Taymyr, Oz., *Russia* 53 **B11**
Taymyr, Poluostrov, *Russia* .. 53 **B11**
Tayport, *U.K.* 13 **E6**
Tayrona △, *Colombia* 121 **D5**
Tayshet, *Russia* 53 **D10**
Taytay, *Phil.* 61 **F3**
Tāyyebād, *Iran* 71 **C9**
Tāyyebād □, *Iran* 71 **C9**
Taz ➤, *Russia* 52 **C8**
Taza, *Morocco* 78 **B5**
Tāza Khurmātū, *Iraq* 70 **C5**
Tazawa-Ko, *Japan* 54 **E10**
Tazin, *Canada* 103 **B7**
Tazin L., *Canada* 103 **B7**
Tazovskiy, *Russia* 52 **C8**
Tbilisi, *Georgia* 35 **K7**
Tchad = Chad ■, *Africa* 79 **F8**
Tchad, L., *Chad* 79 **F8**
Tchaourou, *Benin* 83 **D5**
Tch'eng-tou = Chengdu, *China* .. 58 **B5**
Tchentlo L., *Canada* 102 **B4**
Tchetti, *Benin* 83 **D5**
Tchibanga, *Gabon* 84 **E2**
Tchien, *Liberia* 82 **D3**
Tchin Tabaraden, *Niger* 83 **B6**
Tch'ong-k'ing = Chongqing,
  China 58 **C6**
Tczew, *Poland* 30 **D5**
Te Anau, L., *N.Z.* 91 **L1**
Te Aroha, *N.Z.* 91 **G5**
Te Awamutu, *N.Z.* 91 **H5**
Te Ika a Maui = North I., *N.Z.* .. 91 **H5**
Te Kuiti, *N.Z.* 91 **H5**
Te-n-Dghâmcha, Sebkhet,
  Mauritania 82 **B1**
Te Puke, *N.Z.* 91 **G6**
Te Waewae B., *N.Z.* 91 **M1**
Te Wai Pounamu = South I., *N.Z.* 91 **L3**
Teaca, *Romania* 29 **D9**
Teague, *U.S.A.* 113 **K6**
Teano, *Italy* 43 **A7**
Teapa, *Mexico* 119 **D6**
Teba, *Spain* 37 **J6**
Tebakang, *Malaysia* 62 **D4**
Teberda, *Russia* 35 **J5**
Teberu, *Malaysia* .... 65 **d**
Tébessa, *Algeria* 78 **A7**
Tebicuary ➤, *Paraguay* 126 **B4**
Tebingtinggi, *Riau, Indonesia* .. 62 **E2**
Tebingtinggi, *Sumatera Utara,
  Indonesia* 62 **D1**
Tebulos, *Georgia* 35 **J7**
Tecate, *Mexico* 111 **N10**
Tecer Dağları, *Turkey* 72 **C7**
Tech ➤, *France* 20 **F7**
Techiman, *Ghana* 82 **D4**
Techirghiol, *Romania* 29 **F13**
Tecka, *Argentina* 128 **E2**
Tecomán, *Mexico* 118 **D4**
Tecopa, *U.S.A.* 111 **K10**
Tecoripa, *Mexico* 118 **B3**
Tecuala, *Mexico* 118 **C3**
Tecuci, *Romania* 29 **E12**
Tecumseh, *Canada* 116 **D2**
Tecumseh, *Mich., U.S.A.* 114 **D4**
Tecumseh, *Okla., U.S.A.* 113 **H6**
Tedzhen = Tejen, *Turkmenistan* .. 52 **F7**
Tees ➤, *U.K.* 14 **C6**
Tees B., *U.K.* 14 **C6**
Teeswater, *Canada* 116 **C3**
Tefé, *Brazil* 124 **D6**
Tefenni, *Turkey* 47 **D11**
Tegal, *Indonesia* 63 **G13**
Tegallalang, *Indonesia* 63 **J18**
Tegalsari, *Indonesia* 63 **J17**
Tegel, Berlin ✈ (TXL), *Germany* . 24 **C9**
Tegernsee, *Germany* 25 **H7**
Teggiano, *Italy* 43 **B8**
Tegid, L. = Bala, L., *U.K.* .. 14 **E4**
Tegina, *Nigeria* 83 **C6**
Tegucigalpa, *Honduras* 120 **D2**
Teguidda-i-n-Tessoum, *Niger* .. 83 **B6**
Tehachapi, *U.S.A.* 111 **K8**
Tehachapi Mts., *U.S.A.* 111 **L8**
Tehamiyam, *Sudan* 80 **D4**
Teheran = Tehrān, *Iran* 71 **C6**
Tehilla, *Sudan* 80 **D4**
Téhini, *Ivory C.* 82 **D4**
Tehoru, *Indonesia* 63 **E7**
Tehrān, *Iran* 71 **C6**
Tehrān □, *Iran* 71 **C6**
Tehri, *India* 69 **D8**
Tehuacán, *Mexico* 119 **D5**
Tehuantepec, *Mexico* 119 **D5**
Tehuantepec, G. de, *Mexico* .. 119 **D5**
Tehuantepec, Istmo de, *Mexico* . 119 **D6**
Teide, Pico de, *Canary Is.* .. 48 **F3**
Teifi ➤, *U.K.* 15 **E3**
Teign ➤, *U.K.* 15 **G4**
Teignmouth, *U.K.* 15 **G4**

Teiuș, *Romania* 29 **D8**
Teixeira Pinto, *Guinea-Biss.* 82 **C1**
Tejakula, *Indonesia* 63 **J18**
Tejam, *India* 69 **E9**
Tejen, *Turkmenistan* 52 **F7**
Tejen ➤, *Turkmenistan* 71 **B9**
Tejo ➤, *Europe* 37 **F2**
Tejon Pass, *U.S.A.* 111 **L8**
Tekamah, *U.S.A.* 112 **E6**
Tekapo, L., *N.Z.* 91 **K3**
Tekax, *Mexico* 119 **C7**
Teke, *Turkey* 45 **E13**
Tekeli, *Kazakhstan* 52 **E8**
Tekeze ➤, *Ethiopia* 81 **E4**
Tekija, *Serbia & M.* 44 **B6**
Tekirdağ, *Turkey* 45 **F11**
Tekirdağ □, *Turkey* 45 **E11**
Tekirova, *Turkey* 47 **E12**
Tekkali, *India* 67 **K14**
Tekke, *Turkey* 72 **B7**
Tekman, *Turkey* 73 **C9**
Tekoa, *U.S.A.* 108 **C5**
Tekong Besar, Pulau, *Singapore* . 65 **d**
Tel Aviv ✈ (TLV), *Israel* 74 **C3**
Tel Aviv-Yafo, *Israel* 74 **C3**
Tel Lakhish, *Israel* 74 **D3**
Tel Megiddo, *Israel* 74 **C4**
Tela, *Honduras* 120 **C2**
Telanaipura = Jambi, *Indonesia* . 62 **E2**
Telašćica △, *Croatia* 41 **E12**
Telavi, *Georgia* 35 **J7**
Telč, *Czech Rep.* 26 **B8**
Telciu, *Romania* 29 **C9**
Telde, *Canary Is.* 48 **G4**
Telegraph Creek, *Canada* 102 **B2**
Telekhany = Tsyelyakhany,
  Belarus 33 **F3**
Telemark, *Norway* 9 **G12**
Telén, *Argentina* 126 **D2**
Teleng, *Iran* 71 **E9**
Teleño, *Spain* 36 **C4**
Teleorman □, *Romania* 29 **G10**
Teleorman ➤, *Romania* 29 **G10**
Teles Pires ➤, *Brazil* 124 **E7**
Telescope Pk., *U.S.A.* 111 **J9**
Teletaye, *Mali* 83 **B5**
Telfer Mine, *Australia* 92 **C3**
Telford, *U.K.* 15 **E5**
Telford and Wrekin □, *U.K.* .. 14 **E5**
Telfs, *Austria* 26 **D4**
Télimélé, *Guinea* 82 **C2**
Teljo, J., *Sudan* 81 **E2**
Telkwa, *Canada* 102 **C3**
Tell City, *U.S.A.* 114 **G2**
Tellicherry, *India* 66 **P9**
Teloloapán, *Mexico* 119 **D5**
Telpos Iz, *Russia* 6 **C17**
Telsen, *Argentina* 128 **E3**
Telšiai, *Lithuania* 9 **H20**
Telšiai □, *Lithuania* 30 **C9**
Teltow, *Germany* 24 **C9**
Teluk Anson = Teluk Intan,
  Malaysia 65 **K3**
Teluk Bahang, *Malaysia* .... 65 **c**
Teluk Betung = Tanjungkarang
  Telukbetung, *Indonesia* .. 62 **F3**
Teluk Intan, *Malaysia* 65 **K3**
Teluk Kumbar, *Malaysia* .... 65 **c**
Telukbutun, *Indonesia* 62 **D3**
Telukdalem, *Indonesia* 62 **D1**
Tema, *Ghana* 83 **D5**
Temax, *Mexico* 119 **C7**
Temba, *S. Africa* 89 **D4**
Tembagapura, *Indonesia* 63 **E9**
Tembe, *Dem. Rep. of the Congo* . 86 **C2**
Tembe △, *S. Africa* 89 **D5**
Tembleque, *Spain* 36 **F7**
Temblor Range, *U.S.A.* 111 **K7**
Teme ➤, *U.K.* 15 **E5**
Temecula, *U.S.A.* 111 **M9**
Temerloh, *Malaysia* 62 **D2**
Teminabuan, *Indonesia* 63 **E8**
Temir, *Kazakhstan* 52 **E6**
Temirtau, *Kazakhstan* 52 **D8**
Temirtau, *Russia* 52 **D9**
Temiscamie ➤, *Canada* 105 **B5**
Témiscaming, *Canada* 104 **C4**
Témiscamingue, L., *Canada* .. 104 **C4**
Temnikov, *Russia* 34 **C6**
Temo ➤, *Italy* 42 **B1**
Temosachic, *Mexico* 118 **B3**
Tempe, *U.S.A.* 109 **K8**
Témpio Pausánia, *Italy* 42 **B2**
Tempiute, *U.S.A.* 110 **H11**
Temple, *U.S.A.* 113 **K6**
Temple B., *Australia* 94 **A3**
Templemore, *Ireland* 12 **D4**
Templeton, *U.S.A.* 110 **K6**
Templeton ➤, *Australia* 94 **C2**
Templin, *Germany* 24 **B9**
Tempoal, *Mexico* 119 **C5**
Temryuk, *Russia* 33 **K9**
Temska ➤, *Serbia & M.* 44 **C6**
Temuco, *Chile* 128 **D2**
Temuka, *N.Z.* 91 **L3**
Tenabo, *Mexico* 119 **C6**
Tenaha, *U.S.A.* 113 **K7**
Tenakee Springs, *U.S.A.* 102 **B1**
Tenali, *India* 67 **L12**
Tenancingo, *Mexico* 119 **D5**
Tenango, *Mexico* 119 **D5**
Tenasserim, *Burma* 65 **F2**
Tenasserim □, *Burma* 64 **F2**
Tenby, *U.K.* 15 **F3**
Tenda, Colle di, *France* 21 **D11**
Tendaho, *Ethiopia* 81 **E5**
Tende, *France* 21 **D11**
Tendelti, *Sudan* 81 **E3**
Tendrovskaya Kosa, *Ukraine* ... 33 **J6**

Tendukhera, *India* 69 **H8**
Teneguía, Volcanes de, *Canary Is.* . 48 **F2**
Teneida, *Egypt* 80 **B2**
Tenenkou, *Mali* 82 **C4**
Ténéré, *Niger* 83 **B7**
Tenerife, *Canary Is.* 48 **F3**
Tenerife, Pico, *Canary Is.* .. 48 **G1**
Tenerife Norte ✈ (TFN),
  Canary Is. 48 **F3**
Tenerife Sur ✈ (TFS), *Canary Is.* . 48 **F3**
Teng Xian, *Guangxi Zhuangzu,
  China* 59 **F8**
Teng Xian, *Shandong, China* .. 57 **G9**
Tengah, *Kepulauan, Indonesia* .. 62 **F5**
Tengchong, *China* 58 **E2**
Tengchowfu = Penglai, *China* .. 57 **F11**
Tenggarong, *Indonesia* 62 **E5**
Tenggol, Pulau, *Malaysia* .. 65 **K4**
Tengiz, Ozero, *Kazakhstan* .. 52 **D7**
Tenhult, *Sweden* 11 **G8**
Teniente Enciso △, *Paraguay* . 126 **A3**
Teniente Rodolfo Marsh,
  Antarctica 5 **C18**
Tenino, *U.S.A.* 110 **D4**
Tenkasi, *India* 66 **Q10**
Tenke, *Katanga, Dem. Rep. of
  the Congo* 87 **E2**
Tenke, *Katanga, Dem. Rep. of
  the Congo* 87 **E2**
Tenkodogo, *Burkina Faso* .. 83 **C4**
Tenna ➤, *Italy* 41 **E10**
Tennant Creek, *Australia* .. 94 **B1**
Tennessee □, *U.S.A.* 115 **H2**
Tennessee ➤, *U.S.A.* 114 **G1**
Teno, Pta. de, *Canary Is.* .. 48 **F3**
Tenom, *Malaysia* 62 **C5**
Tenosique, *Mexico* 119 **D6**
Tenryū-Gawa ➤, *Japan* 55 **G8**
Tenterden, *U.K.* 15 **F8**
Tenterfield, *Australia* 95 **D5**
Teo, *Spain* 36 **C2**
Teófilo Otoni, *Brazil* 125 **G10**
Tepa, *Indonesia* 63 **F7**
Tepalcatepec ➤, *Mexico* 118 **D4**
Tepecik, *Bursa, Turkey* 45 **F12**
Tepecik, *Kütahya, Turkey* .. 47 **B11**
Tepehuanes, *Mexico* 118 **B3**
Tepelenë, *Albania* 44 **F4**
Tepetongo, *Mexico* 118 **C4**
Tepic, *Mexico* 118 **C4**
Teplá, *Czech Rep.* 26 **B5**
Teplice, *Czech Rep.* 26 **A6**
Teplyk, *Ukraine* 29 **B14**
Tepoca, C., *Mexico* 118 **A2**
Tequila, *Mexico* 118 **C4**
Ter ➤, *Spain* 38 **C8**
Ter Apel, *Neths.* 17 **B7**
Téra, *Niger* 83 **C5**
Tera ➤, *Spain* 36 **D5**
Teraina, *Kiribati* 97 **G11**
Terakeka, *Sudan* 81 **F3**
Téramo, *Italy* 41 **F10**
Terang, *Australia* 95 **F3**
Terang, Teluk, *Indonesia* .. 63 **K19**
Terazit, Massif de, *Niger* .. 83 **A6**
Tercan, *Turkey* 73 **C9**
Tercero ➤, *Argentina* 126 **C3**
Terebovlya, *Ukraine* 33 **H3**
Teregova, *Romania* 28 **E7**
Tereida, *Sudan* 81 **E3**
Terek ➤, *Russia* 35 **J8**
Terepaima △, *Venezuela* .. 121 **E6**
Tereshka ➤, *Russia* 34 **E8**
Teresina, *Brazil* 125 **E10**
Terespol, *Poland* 31 **F10**
Teresva, *Ukraine* 29 **B8**
Terewah, L., *Australia* 95 **D4**
Terges ➤, *Portugal* 37 **H3**
Tergnier, *France* 19 **C10**
Teridgere Cr. ➤, *Australia* .. 95 **E4**
Terlizzi, *Italy* 43 **A9**
Terme, *Turkey* 72 **B7**
Termez = Termiz, *Uzbekistan* . 52 **F7**
Términi Imerese, *Italy* 42 **E6**
Términos, L. de, *Mexico* 119 **D6**
Termiz, *Uzbekistan* 52 **F7**
Térmoli, *Italy* 41 **F12**
Ternate, *Indonesia* 63 **D7**
Terneuzen, *Neths.* 17 **C3**
Terney, *Russia* 53 **E14**
Terni, *Italy* 41 **F9**
Ternitz, *Austria* 26 **D9**
Ternivka, *Ukraine* 29 **B14**
Ternopil, *Ukraine* 33 **H3**
Ternopol = Ternopil, *Ukraine* .. 33 **H3**
Terowie, *Australia* 95 **E2**
Terpní, *Greece* 44 **F7**
Terra Bella, *U.S.A.* 111 **K7**
Terra Nova △, *Canada* 105 **C9**
Terrace, *Canada* 102 **C3**
Terrace Bay, *Canada* 104 **C2**
Terracina, *Italy* 42 **A6**
Terralba, *Italy* 42 **C1**
Terrasini, *Italy* 42 **D6**
Terrassa, *Spain* 38 **D7**
Terrasson-la-Villedieu, *France* . 20 **C5**
Terre Haute, *U.S.A.* 114 **F2**
Terrebonne B., *U.S.A.* 113 **L9**
Terrell, *U.S.A.* 113 **J6**
Terrenceville, *Canada* 105 **C9**
Terry, *U.S.A.* 108 **C2**
Terryville, *U.S.A.* 117 **E11**
Terschelling, *Neths.* 17 **A5**
Tersko-Kumskiy Kanal, *Russia* .. 35 **H7**
Terter = Tärtär ➤, *Azerbaijan* .. 35 **K8**
Teruel, *Spain* 38 **E3**
Teruel □, *Spain* 38 **E4**
Tervel, *Bulgaria* 45 **C11**
Tervola, *Finland* 8 **C21**
Teryaweyna L., *Australia* .. 95 **E3**

Tešanj, *Bos.-H.* 28 **F3**
Teseney, *Eritrea* 81 **D4**
Tesha ➤, *Russia* 34 **C6**
Teshio, *Japan* 54 **B10**
Teshio-Gawa ➤, *Japan* 54 **B10**
Thayer, *U.S.A.* 113 **G8**
Tešica, *Serbia & M.* 44 **C5**
Tesiyn Gol ➤, *Mongolia* .. 60 **A4**
Teslić, *Bos.-H.* 28 **F2**
Teslin, *Canada* 102 **A2**
Teslin ➤, *Canada* 102 **A2**
Teslin L., *Canada* 102 **A2**
Tessalit, *Mali* 83 **A5**
Tessaoua, *Niger* 83 **C6**
Tessin, *Germany* 24 **A8**
Tessit, *Mali* 83 **B5**
Test ➤, *U.K.* 15 **G6**
Testa del Gargano, *Italy* .. 41 **G13**
Testigos, Is. Las, *Venezuela* . 121 **D7**
Tét, *Hungary* 28 **C2**
Tét ➤, *France* 20 **F7**
Tetachuck L., *Canada* 102 **C3**
Tetas, Pta., *Chile* 126 **A1**
Tete, *Mozam.* 87 **F3**
Tete □, *Mozam.* 87 **F3**
Teterev ➤, *Ukraine* 33 **G6**
Teterow, *Germany* 24 **B8**
Teteven, *Bulgaria* 45 **D8**
Tethul ➤, *Canada* 102 **A6**
Tetiyev, *Ukraine* 33 **H5**
Teton ➤, *U.S.A.* 108 **C8**
Tétouan, *Morocco* 78 **A4**
Tetovo, *Macedonia* 44 **D4**
Tetyushi, *Russia* 34 **C9**
Teuco ➤, *Argentina* 126 **B3**
Teulada, *Italy* 42 **D1**
Teulon, *Canada* 103 **C9**
Teun, *Indonesia* 63 **F7**
Teutoburger Wald, *Germany* .. 24 **C4**
Tevere ➤, *Italy* 41 **F9**
Tevere △, *Italy* 41 **G9**
Teverya, *Israel* 74 **C4**
Teviot ➤, *U.K.* 13 **F6**
Tewantin, *Australia* 95 **D5**
Tewkesbury, *U.K.* 15 **F5**
Texada I., *Canada* 102 **D4**
Texarkana, *Ark., U.S.A.* 113 **J8**
Texarkana, *Tex., U.S.A.* 113 **J7**
Texas, *Australia* 95 **D5**
Texas □, *U.S.A.* 113 **K5**
Texas City, *U.S.A.* 113 **L7**
Texel, *Neths.* 17 **A4**
Texline, *U.S.A.* 113 **G3**
Texoma, L., *U.S.A.* 113 **J6**
Teykovo, *Russia* 32 **D11**
Teza ➤, *Russia* 34 **B5**
Tezin, *Afghan.* 68 **B3**
Teziutlán, *Mexico* 119 **D5**
Tezpur, *India* 67 **F18**
Tezzeron L., *Canada* 102 **C4**
Tha-anne ➤, *Canada* 103 **A10**
Tha Deua, *Laos* 64 **D4**
Tha Deua, *Laos* 64 **C3**
Tha Pla, *Thailand* 64 **D3**
Tha Rua, *Thailand* 64 **E3**
Tha Sala, *Thailand* 65 **H2**
Tha Song Yang, *Thailand* .. 64 **D1**
Thaba Putsoa, *Lesotho* 89 **D4**
Thabana Ntlenyana, *Lesotho* .. 89 **D4**
Thabazimbi, *S. Africa* 89 **C4**
Thādiq, *Si. Arabia* 70 **E5**
Thai Binh, *Vietnam* 58 **G6**
Thai Muang, *Thailand* 65 **H2**
Thai Nguyen, *Vietnam* 58 **G5**
Thailand ■, *Asia* 64 **E4**
Thailand, G. of, *Asia* 65 **G3**
Thakhek, *Laos* 64 **D5**
Thal, *Pakistan* 68 **C4**
Thal Desert, *Pakistan* 68 **D4**
Thala La = Hkakabo Razi, *Burma* 67 **E20**
Thalabarivat, *Cambodia* 64 **F5**
Thallon, *Australia* 95 **D4**
Thalu, Ko, *Thailand* .... 65 **b**
Thalwil, *Switz.* 25 **H4**
Thames, *N.Z.* 91 **G5**
Thames ➤, *Canada* 116 **D2**
Thames ➤, *U.K.* 15 **F8**
Thames ➤, *U.S.A.* 117 **E12**
Thames Estuary, *U.K.* 15 **F8**
Thamesford, *Canada* 116 **C4**
Thamesville, *Canada* 116 **D3**
Than, *India* 68 **H4**
Than Uyen, *Vietnam* 64 **B4**
Thana Gazi, *India* 68 **F7**
Thandla, *India* 68 **H6**
Thane, *India* 66 **K8**
Thanesar, *India* 68 **D7**
Thanet, I. of, *U.K.* 15 **F9**
Thangoo, *Australia* 92 **C3**
Thanh Hoa, *Vietnam* 64 **C5**
Thanh Hung, *Vietnam* 65 **H5**
Thanh Pho Ho Chi Minh, *Vietnam* 65 **G6**
Thanh Thuy, *Vietnam* 64 **A5**
Thanjavur, *India* 66 **P11**
Thann, *France* 19 **E14**
Thano Bula Khan, *Pakistan* .. 68 **G2**
Thaolinta L., *Canada* 103 **A9**
Thaon-les-Vosges, *France* .. 19 **D13**
Thap Lan △, *Thailand* 64 **E4**
Thap Sakae, *Thailand* 65 **G2**
Thap Than, *Thailand* 64 **E2**
Thar Desert, *India* 68 **G4**
Tharad, *India* 68 **G4**
Thargomindah, *Australia* .. 95 **D3**
Tharrawaddy, *Burma* 67 **L19**
Tharthār, Buḥayrat ath, *Iraq* 70 **C4**
Tharthār, L. = Tharthār, Buḥayrat
  ath, *Iraq* 70 **C4**
Tharthār, W. ath ➤, *Iraq* .. 70 **C4**
Thasopoúla, *Greece* 45 **F8**
Thásos, *Greece* 45 **F8**

Thatcher, *Ariz., U.S.A.* 109 **K9**
Thatcher, *Colo., U.S.A.* 113 **G2**
Thaton, *Burma* 67 **L20**
Thau, Bassin de, *France* .. 20 **E7**
Thaungdut, *Burma* 67 **G19**
Thayer, *U.S.A.* 113 **G8**
Thayetmyo, *Burma* 67 **K19**
Thazi, *Burma* 67 **J20**
The Bight, *Bahamas* 121 **B4**
The Crane, *Barbados* .... 121 **g**
The Dalles, *U.S.A.* 108 **D3**
The Great Divide = Great
  Dividing Ra., *Australia* .. 94 **C4**
The Hague = 's-Gravenhage,
  Neths. 17 **B4**
The Pas, *Canada* 103 **C8**
The Range, *Zimbabwe* 87 **F3**
The Rock, *Australia* 95 **F4**
The Settlement, *Br. Virgin Is.* . 121 **e**
The Woodlands, *U.S.A.* 113 **K7**
Thebes = Thívai, *Greece* .. 46 **C5**
Thebes, *Egypt* 80 **B3**
Thedford, *U.S.A.* 112 **E4**
Theebine, *Australia* 95 **D5**
Thekulthili L., *Canada* 103 **A7**
Thelon ➤, *Canada* 103 **A8**
Thénezay, *France* 18 **F6**
Thenon, *France* 20 **C5**
Theodore, *Australia* 94 **C5**
Theodore, *Canada* 103 **C8**
Theodore, *U.S.A.* 115 **K1**
Theodore Roosevelt △, *U.S.A.* . 112 **B3**
Theodore Roosevelt L., *U.S.A.* . 109 **K8**
Thepha, *Thailand* 65 **J3**
Thérain ➤, *France* 19 **C9**
Theresa, *U.S.A.* 117 **B9**
Thermaïkós Kólpos, *Greece* .. 44 **F6**
Thérmi, *Greece* 47 **B8**
Thermopilís, *Greece* 46 **C4**
Thermopolis, *U.S.A.* 108 **E9**
Thermopylae P., *Greece* .. 46 **C4**
Thesprotía □, *Greece* 46 **B2**
Thessalía □, *Greece* 46 **B4**
Thessalon, *Canada* 104 **C3**
Thessaloníki, *Greece* 44 **F6**
Thessaloníki □, *Greece* 44 **F7**
Thessaloníki ✈ (SKG), *Greece* .. 44 **F7**
Thessaloníki, Gulf of =
  Thermaïkós Kólpos, *Greece* .. 44 **F6**
Thessaly = Thessalía □, *Greece* . 46 **B4**
Thetford, *U.K.* 15 **E8**
Thetford Mines, *Canada* 105 **C5**
Theun ➤, *Laos* 64 **C5**
Theunissen, *S. Africa* 88 **D4**
Thevenard, *Australia* 95 **E1**
Thiámis ➤, *Greece* 46 **B2**
Thiberville, *France* 18 **C7**
Thibodaux, *U.S.A.* 113 **L9**
Thicket Portage, *Canada* .. 103 **B9**
Thief River Falls, *U.S.A.* .. 112 **A6**
Thiel Mts., *Antarctica* 5 **E16**
Thiene, *Italy* 41 **C8**
Thiérache, *France* 19 **C10**
Thiers, *France* 20 **C7**
Thiès, *Senegal* 82 **C1**
Thiesi, *Italy* 42 **B1**
Thiet, *Sudan* 81 **F2**
Thika, *Kenya* 86 **C4**
Thikombia, *Fiji* 91 **B9**
Thille-Boubacar, *Senegal* .. 82 **B1**
Thimphu, *Bhutan* 67 **F16**
Þingvallavatn, *Iceland* 8 **D3**
Thionville, *France* 19 **C13**
Thíra, *Greece* 47 **E7**
Thirasía, *Greece* 47 **E7**
Third Cataract, *Sudan* 80 **D3**
Thirsk, *U.K.* 14 **C6**
Thiruvananthapuram =
  Trivandrum, *India* 66 **Q10**
Thisted, *Denmark* 11 **H2**
Thistle I., *Australia* 95 **F2**
Thívai, *Greece* 46 **C5**
Thiviers, *France* 20 **C4**
Thizy, *France* 19 **F11**
Þjórsá ➤, *Iceland* 8 **E3**
Thlewiaza ➤, *Canada* 103 **A10**
Thmar Puok, *Cambodia* 64 **F4**
Tho Vinh, *Vietnam* 64 **C5**
Thoa ➤, *Canada* 103 **A7**
Thoen, *Thailand* 64 **D2**
Thoeng, *Thailand* 64 **C3**
Thohoyandou, *S. Africa* 85 **J6**
Tholdi, *Pakistan* 69 **B7**
Thomas, *U.S.A.* 113 **H5**
Thomas, L., *Australia* 95 **D2**
Thomaston, *U.S.A.* 115 **J3**
Thomasville, *Ala., U.S.A.* .. 115 **K2**
Thomasville, *Ga., U.S.A.* .. 115 **K4**
Thomasville, *N.C., U.S.A.* .. 115 **H5**
Thompson, *Canada* 103 **B9**
Thompson, *U.S.A.* 117 **E9**
Thompson ➤, *Canada* 102 **C4**
Thompson ➤, *U.S.A.* 112 **F8**
Thompson Falls, *U.S.A.* 108 **C6**
Thompson Pk., *U.S.A.* 108 **F2**
Thompson Springs, *U.S.A.* .. 109 **G9**
Thompsontown, *U.S.A.* 116 **F7**
Thomson, *U.S.A.* 115 **J4**
Thomson ➤, *Australia* 94 **C3**
Thônes, *France* 21 **C10**
Thong Yang, *Thailand* ...... 65 **b**
Thonon-les-Bains, *France* .. 19 **F13**
Thorez, *Ukraine* 33 **H10**
Þórisvatn, *Iceland* 8 **D4**
Thornaby on Tees, *U.K.* .. 14 **C6**
Thornbury, *Canada* 116 **B4**
Thorne, *U.K.* 14 **D7**
Thornhill, *Canada* 102 **C3**
Thorold, *Canada* 116 **C5**
Þórshöfn, *Iceland* 8 **C6**
Thouarcé, *France* 18 **E6**
Thouars, *France* 18 **F6**

Thouet →, France ... 18 E6
Thouin, C., Australia ... 92 D2
Thousand Oaks, U.S.A. ... 111 L8
Thrace, Turkey ... 45 F10
Thrakikón Pélagos, Greece ... 45 F8
Three Forks, U.S.A. ... 108 D8
Three Gorges Dam, China ... 59 B8
Three Hills, Canada ... 102 C6
Three Hummock I., Australia ... 95 G3
Three Pagodas Pass, Asia ... 64 E2
Three Points, C., Ghana ... 82 E4
Three Rivers, Calif., U.S.A. ... 110 J8
Three Rivers, Tex., U.S.A. ... 113 L5
Three Sisters, U.S.A. ... 108 D3
Three Springs, Australia ... 93 E2
Throssell, L., Australia ... 93 E3
Throssell Ra., Australia ... 92 D3
Thrushton △, Australia ... 95 D4
Thuan Hoa, Vietnam ... 65 H5
Thubun Lakes, Canada ... 103 A6
Thueyts, France ... 21 D8
Thuin, Belgium ... 17 D4
Thuir, France ... 20 F6
Thule = Qaanaaq, Greenland ... 4 B4
Thule Air Base = Uummannaq, Greenland ... 4 B5
Thun, Switz. ... 25 J3
Thunder B., U.S.A. ... 116 B1
Thunder Bay, Canada ... 104 C2
Thunersee, Switz. ... 25 J3
Thung Salaeng Luang △, Thailand ... 64 D3
Thung Song, Thailand ... 65 H2
Thunkar, Bhutan ... 67 F17
Thuong Tra, Vietnam ... 64 D6
Thur →, Switz. ... 25 H5
Thurgau □, Switz. ... 25 H5
Thüringen □, Germany ... 24 D6
Thüringer Wald, Germany ... 24 E6
Thurles, Ireland ... 12 D4
Thurn P., Austria ... 26 D5
Thurrock □, U.K. ... 15 F8
Thursday I., Australia ... 94 A3
Thurso, Canada ... 104 C4
Thurso, U.K. ... 13 C5
Thurso →, U.K. ... 13 C5
Thurston I., Antarctica ... 5 D16
Thury-Harcourt, France ... 18 D6
Thutade L., Canada ... 102 B3
Thy, Denmark ... 11 H2
Thyborøn, Denmark ... 11 H2
Thyolo, Malawi ... 87 F4
Ti-n-Amzi →, Niger ... 83 B5
Ti-n-Barraouene, O. →, Africa ... 83 B5
Ti-n-Zaouatene, Algeria ... 83 B5
Ti Tree, Australia ... 94 C1
Tiadiaye, Senegal ... 82 C1
Tian Shan, Asia ... 60 B3
Tianchang, China ... 59 A12
Tiandeng, China ... 58 F6
Tiandong, China ... 58 F6
Tian'e, China ... 58 E6
Tianhe, China ... 58 E7
Tianjin, China ... 57 E9
Tiankoura, Burkina Faso ... 82 C4
Tianlin, China ... 58 E6
Tianmen, China ... 59 B9
Tianquan, China ... 58 B4
Tianshui, China ... 56 G3
Tiantai, China ... 59 C13
Tianyang, China ... 58 F6
Tianyar, Indonesia ... 63 J18
Tianzhen, China ... 56 D8
Tianzhu, China ... 58 D7
Tianzhuangtai, China ... 57 D12
Tiaret, Algeria ... 78 A6
Tiassalé, Ivory C. ... 82 D4
Tibagi, Brazil ... 127 A5
Tibagi →, Brazil ... 127 A5
Tibati, Cameroon ... 83 D7
Tibe, Ethiopia ... 81 F4
Tiber = Tevere →, Italy ... 41 G9
Tiberias = Teverya, Israel ... 74 C4
Tiberias, L. = Yam Kinneret, Israel ... 74 C4
Tibesti, Chad ... 79 D9
Tibet = Xizang Zizhiqu □, China ... 60 C3
Tibet, Plateau of, Asia ... 50 F12
Tibiao, Phil. ... 61 F5
Tibiri, Niger ... 83 C6
Ţibleş, Vf., Romania ... 29 C9
Ţibleşului, Munţii, Romania ... 29 C9
Tibnī, Syria ... 70 C3
Tibooburra, Australia ... 95 D3
Tibro, Sweden ... 11 F8
Tiburón, I., Mexico ... 118 B2
Ticao I., Phil. ... 61 E5
Tîchît, Mauritania ... 82 B3
Ticho, Ethiopia ... 81 F4
Ticino □, Switz. ... 25 J4
Ticino →, Italy ... 25 K5
Ticleni, Romania ... 29 F8
Ticonderoga, U.S.A. ... 117 C11
Ticul, Mexico ... 119 C7
Tidaholm, Sweden ... 11 F7
Tidan, Sweden ... 11 F8
Tiddim, Burma ... 67 H18
Tidioute, U.S.A. ... 116 E5
Tidjikja, Mauritania ... 82 B2
Tidore, Indonesia ... 63 D7
Tiébissou, Ivory C. ... 82 D3
Tiel, Neths. ... 17 C5
Tiel, Senegal ... 82 C1
Tieling, China ... 57 C12
Tielt, Belgium ... 17 C3
Tien Shan = Tian Shan, Asia ... 60 B3
Tien-tsin = Tianjin, China ... 57 E9
Tien Yen, Vietnam ... 64 B6
T'ienching = Tianjin, China ... 57 E9
Tienen, Belgium ... 17 D4
Tiénigbé, Ivory C. ... 82 D3

Tientsin = Tianjin, China ... 57 E9
Tieri, Australia ... 94 C4
Tierp, Sweden ... 10 D11
Tierra Amarilla, Chile ... 126 B1
Tierra Amarilla, U.S.A. ... 109 H10
Tierra Colorada, Mexico ... 119 D5
Tierra de Barros, Spain ... 37 G4
Tierra de Campos, Spain ... 36 C6
Tierra del Fuego, I. Gr. de, Argentina ... 128 G3
Tiétar →, Spain ... 36 F4
Tietê →, Brazil ... 127 A5
Tiffin, U.S.A. ... 114 E4
Tifton, U.S.A. ... 115 K4
Tifu, Indonesia ... 63 E7
Tighina, Moldova ... 29 D14
Tigil, Russia ... 53 D16
Tignish, Canada ... 105 C7
Tigray □, Ethiopia ... 81 E4
Tigre →, Peru ... 124 D4
Tigre →, Venezuela ... 124 B6
Tigris = Dijlah, Nahr →, Asia ... 70 D5
Tigveni, Romania ... 29 E9
Tigyaing, Burma ... 67 H20
Ţih, Gebel el, Egypt ... 80 B3
Tijara, India ... 68 F7
Tijuana, Mexico ... 111 N9
Tikal, Guatemala ... 120 C2
Tikal △, Guatemala ... 120 C2
Tikamgarh, India ... 69 G8
Tikaré, Burkina Faso ... 83 C4
Tikhoretsk, Russia ... 35 H5
Tikhvin, Russia ... 32 C7
Tikiraqjuaq = Whale Cove, Canada ... 103 A10
Tiko, Cameroon ... 83 E6
Tikrīt, Iraq ... 70 C4
Tiksi, Russia ... 53 B13
Tilamuta, Indonesia ... 63 D6
Tilburg, Neths. ... 17 C5
Tilbury, Canada ... 116 D2
Tilbury, U.K. ... 15 F8
Tilcara, Argentina ... 126 A2
Tilden, U.S.A. ... 112 D6
Tilemses, Niger ... 83 B5
Tilemsi, Vallée du, Mali ... 83 B5
Tilhar, India ... 69 F8
Tilichiki, Russia ... 53 C17
Tílissos, Greece ... 49 D7
Till →, U.K. ... 14 B5
Tillabéri, Niger ... 83 C5
Tillamook, U.S.A. ... 108 D2
Tillberga, Sweden ... 10 E10
Tillia, Niger ... 83 B5
Tillsonburg, Canada ... 116 D4
Tillyeria, Cyprus ... 49 D11
Tilogne, Senegal ... 82 B2
Tílos, Greece ... 47 E9
Tilpa, Australia ... 95 E3
Tilt →, U.K. ... 13 E5
Tilton, U.S.A. ... 117 C13
Tiltonsville, U.S.A. ... 116 F4
Tim, Denmark ... 11 H2
Timagami, L., Canada ... 104 C3
Timanfaya △, Canary Is. ... 48 F6
Timaru, N.Z. ... 91 L3
Timashevo, Russia ... 34 D10
Timashevsk, Russia ... 35 H4
Timau, Kenya ... 86 B4
Timbákion, Greece ... 49 D6
Timbedgha, Mauritania ... 82 B3
Timber Creek, Australia ... 92 C5
Timber Lake, U.S.A. ... 112 C4
Timber Mt., U.S.A. ... 110 H10
Timbo, Guinea ... 82 C2
Timbo, Liberia ... 82 D3
Timbuktu = Tombouctou, Mali ... 82 B4
Timeiaouine, Algeria ... 83 A5
Timétrine, Mts., Mali ... 83 B4
Timfi Óros, Greece ... 46 B2
Timfristós, Óros, Greece ... 46 C3
Timi, Cyprus ... 49 E11
Tîmia, Niger ... 83 B6
Timimoun, Algeria ... 78 C6
Timirist, Râs, Mauritania ... 82 B1
Timiş = Tamis →, Serbia & M. ... 28 F5
Timiş □, Romania ... 28 E6
Timişkaming, L. = Témiscamingue, L., Canada ... 104 C4
Timişoara, Romania ... 28 E6
Timmersdala, Sweden ... 11 F7
Timmins, Canada ... 104 C3
Timok →, Serbia & M. ... 44 B6
Timor, Asia ... 63 F7
Timor Leste = East Timor ■, Asia ... 63 F7
Timor Sea, Ind. Oc. ... 92 B4
Timrå, Sweden ... 10 B11
Tin Can Bay, Australia ... 95 D5
Tin Ethisane, Mali ... 83 B4
Tin Gornai, Mali ... 83 B4
Tin Mt., U.S.A. ... 110 J9
Tina →, S. Africa ... 89 E4
Tîna, Khalîg el, Egypt ... 80 A3
Tinaca Pt., Phil. ... 61 J6
Tinajo, Canary Is. ... 48 E6
Tinca, Romania ... 28 D6
Tindal, Australia ... 92 B5
Tindouf, Algeria ... 78 C4
Tinée →, France ... 21 E11
Tineo, Spain ... 36 B4
Tinfunque △, Paraguay ... 126 A3
Ting Jiang →, China ... 59 E11
Tinggi, Pulau, Malaysia ... 65 L5
Tinglev, Denmark ... 11 K3
Tingo Maria, Peru ... 124 E3
Tingrela, Ivory C. ... 82 C3
Tingsryd, Sweden ... 11 H9
Tingstäde, Sweden ... 11 G12
Tinh Bien, Vietnam ... 65 G5
Tinnevelly = Tirunelveli, India ... 66 Q10
Tinogasta, Argentina ... 126 B2

Tínos, Greece ... 47 D7
Tiñoso, C., Spain ... 39 H3
Tinpahar, India ... 69 G12
Tintina, Argentina ... 126 B3
Tintinara, Australia ... 95 F3
Tintioulé, Guinea ... 82 C3
Tinto →, Spain ... 37 H4
Tioga, N. Dak., U.S.A. ... 112 A3
Tioga, Pa., U.S.A. ... 116 E7
Tioman, Pulau, Malaysia ... 65 L5
Tione di Trento, Italy ... 40 B7
Tionesta, U.S.A. ... 116 E5
Tior, Sudan ... 81 F3
Tipongpani, India ... 67 F19
Tipperary, Ireland ... 12 D3
Tipperary □, Ireland ... 12 D4
Tipton, Calif., U.S.A. ... 110 J7
Tipton, Iowa, U.S.A. ... 112 E9
Tipton Mt., U.S.A. ... 111 K12
Tiptonville, U.S.A. ... 113 G10
Tīrān, Iran ... 71 C6
Tīrān, Si. Arabia ... 80 B3
Tiranë, Albania ... 44 E3
Tiranë ✈ (TIA), Albania ... 43 A12
Tirano, Italy ... 40 B7
Tiraspol, Moldova ... 29 D14
Tirdout, Mali ... 83 B4
Tire, Turkey ... 47 C9
Tirebolu, Turkey ... 73 B8
Tiree, U.K. ... 13 E2
Tiree, Passage of, U.K. ... 13 E2
Tîrgovişte = Târgovişte, Romania ... 29 F10
Tîrgu-Jiu = Târgu-Jiu, Romania ... 29 E8
Tîrgu Mureş = Târgu Mureş, Romania ... 29 D9
Tirich Mir, Pakistan ... 66 A7
Tiriolo, Italy ... 43 D9
Tiriro, Guinea ... 82 C3
Tiritiri o te Moana = Southern Alps, N.Z. ... 91 K3
Tírnavos, Greece ... 46 B4
Tirodi, India ... 66 J11
Tirol □, Austria ... 26 D3
Tirso →, Italy ... 42 C1
Tirstrup, Denmark ... 11 H4
Tiruchchirappalli, India ... 66 P11
Tirunelveli, India ... 66 Q10
Tirupati, India ... 66 N11
Tiruppur, India ... 66 P10
Tiruvannamalai, India ... 66 N11
Tisa, India ... 68 C7
Tisa →, Serbia & M. ... 28 E5
Tisdale, Canada ... 103 C8
Tishomingo, U.S.A. ... 113 H6
Tisjön, Sweden ... 10 D7
Tisnaren, Sweden ... 11 F9
Tišnov, Czech Rep. ... 27 B9
Tisovec, Slovak Rep. ... 27 C12
Tisza = Tisa →, Serbia & M. ... 28 E5
Tiszaföldvár, Hungary ... 28 D5
Tiszafüred, Hungary ... 28 C5
Tiszalök, Hungary ... 28 B6
Tiszavasvári, Hungary ... 28 C5
Tit-Ary, Russia ... 53 B13
Titaguas, Spain ... 38 F3
Titao, Burkina Faso ... 83 C4
Titel, Serbia & M. ... 28 E5
Tithwal, Pakistan ... 69 B5
Titicaca, L., S. Amer. ... 124 G5
Titisee, Germany ... 25 H4
Titiwa, Nigeria ... 83 C7
Tito, Italy ... 43 B8
Titova Korenica, Croatia ... 41 D12
Titu, Romania ... 29 F10
Titule, Dem. Rep. of the Congo ... 86 B2
Titusville, Fla., U.S.A. ... 115 L5
Titusville, Pa., U.S.A. ... 116 E5
Tivaouane, Senegal ... 82 C1
Tivat, Serbia & M. ... 44 D2
Tivedens △, Sweden ... 11 F8
Tiverton, U.K. ... 15 G4
Tívoli, Italy ... 41 G9
Tiyo, Eritrea ... 81 E5
Tizi-Ouzou, Algeria ... 78 A6
Tizimín, Mexico ... 119 C7
Tjæreborg, Denmark ... 11 J2
Tjällmo, Sweden ... 11 F9
Tjeggelvas, Sweden ... 8 C17
Tjieggelvas = Tjeggelvas, Sweden ... 8 C17
Tjirebon = Cirebon, Indonesia ... 63 G13
Tjluring, Indonesia ... 63 J17
Tjörn, Sweden ... 11 F5
Tkibuli = Tqibuli, Georgia ... 35 J6
Tkvarcheli = Tqvarcheli, Georgia ... 35 J5
Tlacotalpan, Mexico ... 119 D5
Tlahualilo, Mexico ... 118 B4
Tlaquepaque, Mexico ... 118 C4
Tlaxcala, Mexico ... 119 D5
Tlaxcala □, Mexico ... 119 D5
Tlaxiaco, Mexico ... 119 D5
Tlemcen, Algeria ... 78 B5
Tlumach, Ukraine ... 29 B10
Tłuszcz, Poland ... 31 F8
Tlyarata, Russia ... 35 J8
To Bong, Vietnam ... 64 F7
Toa Payoh, Singapore ... 65 d
Toad →, Canada ... 102 B3
Toad River, Canada ... 102 B3
Toamasina, Madag. ... 89 B8
Toamasina □, Madag. ... 89 B8
Toay, Argentina ... 126 D3
Toba, China ... 58 B1
Toba, Japan ... 55 G8
Toba, Danau, Indonesia ... 62 D1
Toba Kakar, Pakistan ... 68 D3
Toba Tek Singh, Pakistan ... 68 D5
Tobago, Trin. & Tob. ... 121 D7
Tobarra, Spain ... 39 G3
Tobelo, Indonesia ... 63 D7
Tobermory, Canada ... 116 A3

Tobermory, U.K. ... 13 E2
Tobin, U.S.A. ... 110 F5
Tobin, L., Australia ... 92 D4
Tobin L., Canada ... 103 C8
Toblach = Dobbiaco, Italy ... 41 B9
Toboali, Indonesia ... 62 E3
Tobol →, Russia ... 52 D7
Toboli, Indonesia ... 63 E6
Tobolsk, Russia ... 52 D7
Tobor, Senegal ... 82 C1
Tobruk = Tubruq, Libya ... 79 B10
Tobyhanna, U.S.A. ... 117 E9
Tobyl = Tobol →, Russia ... 52 D7
Tocantinópolis, Brazil ... 125 E9
Tocantins □, Brazil ... 125 F9
Tocantins →, Brazil ... 125 D9
Toccoa, U.S.A. ... 115 H4
Toce →, Italy ... 40 C5
Tochi →, Pakistan ... 68 C4
Tochigi, Japan ... 55 F9
Tochigi □, Japan ... 55 F9
Tocina, Spain ... 37 H5
Töcksfors, Sweden ... 10 E5
Toco, Trin. & Tob. ... 125 K16
Toconao, Chile ... 126 A2
Tocopilla, Chile ... 126 A1
Tocumwal, Australia ... 95 F4
Tocuyo →, Venezuela ... 124 A5
Todd →, Australia ... 94 C2
Todeli, Indonesia ... 63 E6
Todenyang, Kenya ... 86 B4
Todgarh, India ... 68 G5
Todi, Italy ... 41 F9
Todos os Santos, B. de, Brazil ... 125 F11
Todos Santos, Mexico ... 118 C2
Todtnau, Germany ... 25 H3
Toe Hd., U.K. ... 13 D1
Toecé, Burkina Faso ... 83 C4
Tofield, Canada ... 102 C6
Tofino, Canada ... 102 D3
Töfsingdalens △, Sweden ... 10 B6
Tofua, Tonga ... 91 D11
Tøgane, Japan ... 55 G10
Togba, Mauritania ... 82 B2
Togian, Kepulauan, Indonesia ... 63 E6
Togliatti, Russia ... 34 D9
Togo ■, W. Afr. ... 83 D5
Togtoh, China ... 56 D6
Tohma →, Turkey ... 72 C7
Tōhoku □, Japan ... 54 E10
Töhöm, Mongolia ... 56 B5
Toinya, Sudan ... 81 F2
Toiyabe Range, U.S.A. ... 108 G5
Tojikiston = Tajikistan ■, Asia ... 52 F8
Tojo, Indonesia ... 63 E6
Tōjō, Japan ... 55 G6
Tok, U.S.A. ... 100 B5
Tok-do, Asia ... 55 F5
Tokachi-Dake, Japan ... 54 C11
Tokachi-Gawa →, Japan ... 54 C11
Tokaj, Hungary ... 28 B6
Tokala, Indonesia ... 63 E6
Tōkamachi, Japan ... 55 F9
Tokanui, N.Z. ... 91 M2
Tokar, Sudan ... 80 D4
Tokara-Rettō, Japan ... 55 K4
Tokarahi, N.Z. ... 91 L3
Tokashiki-Shima, Japan ... 55 L3
Tokat, Turkey ... 72 B7
Tŏkch'ŏn, N. Korea ... 57 E14
Tokeland, U.S.A. ... 110 D3
Tokelau Is., Pac. Oc. ... 96 H10
Tokmak, Kyrgyzstan ... 52 E8
Tokmak, Ukraine ... 33 J8
Toko Ra., Australia ... 94 C2
Tokoro-Gawa →, Japan ... 54 B12
Tokuno-Shima, Japan ... 55 L4
Tokushima, Japan ... 55 G7
Tokushima □, Japan ... 55 H7
Tokuyama, Japan ... 55 G5
Tōkyō, Japan ... 55 G9
Tolaga Bay, N.Z. ... 91 H7
Tolbukhin = Dobrich, Bulgaria ... 45 C11
Toledo, Brazil ... 127 A5
Toledo, Spain ... 36 F6
Toledo, Ohio, U.S.A. ... 114 E4
Toledo, Oreg., U.S.A. ... 108 D2
Toledo, Wash., U.S.A. ... 108 C2
Toledo, Montes de, Spain ... 37 F6
Toledo Bend Reservoir, U.S.A. ... 113 K8
Tolentino, Italy ... 41 E10
Tolga, Australia ... 94 B4
Toliara, Madag. ... 89 C7
Toliara □, Madag. ... 89 C8
Tolima, Colombia ... 124 C3
Tolitoli, Indonesia ... 63 D6
Tolkmicko, Poland ... 30 D6
Tollarp, Sweden ... 11 J7
Tollensesee, Germany ... 24 B9
Tollhouse, U.S.A. ... 110 H7
Tolmachevo, Russia ... 32 C5
Tolmezzo, Italy ... 41 B10
Tolmin, Slovenia ... 41 B10
Tolna, Hungary ... 28 D3
Tolna □, Hungary ... 28 D3
Tolo, Teluk, Indonesia ... 63 E6
Tolochin = Talachyn, Belarus ... 32 E5
Tolosa, Spain ... 38 B2
Tolox, Spain ... 37 J6
Toluca, Mexico ... 119 D5
Tom Burke, S. Africa ... 89 C4
Tom Price, Australia ... 92 D2
Toma, Burkina Faso ... 82 C4
Tomah, U.S.A. ... 112 D9
Tomahawk, U.S.A. ... 112 C10
Tomai, Moldova ... 29 D13
Tomakomai, Japan ... 54 C10
Tomales, U.S.A. ... 110 G4
Tomales B., U.S.A. ... 110 G3

Tomar, Portugal ... 37 F2
Tómaros, Óros, Greece ... 46 B2
Tomarza, Turkey ... 72 C6
Tomashevka, Belarus ... 31 G10
Tomashpil, Ukraine ... 29 B13
Tomaszów Lubelski, Poland ... 31 H10
Tomaszów Mazowiecki, Poland ... 31 G7
Tomatlán, Mexico ... 118 D3
Tombador, Serra do, Brazil ... 124 F7
Tombe, Sudan ... 81 F3
Tombigbee →, U.S.A. ... 115 K2
Tombouctou, Mali ... 82 B4
Tombstone, U.S.A. ... 109 L8
Tombua, Angola ... 88 B1
Tomé, Chile ... 126 D1
Tomelilla, Sweden ... 11 J7
Tomelloso, Spain ... 37 F7
Tomini, Indonesia ... 63 D6
Tomini, Teluk, Indonesia ... 63 E6
Tominian, Mali ... 82 C4
Tomiño, Spain ... 36 D2
Tomintoul, U.K. ... 13 D5
Tomislavgrad, Bos.-H. ... 28 G2
Tomkinson Ranges, Australia ... 93 E4
Tommot, Russia ... 53 D13
Tomnop Ta Suos, Cambodia ... 65 G5
Tomo →, Colombia ... 124 B5
Toms Place, U.S.A. ... 110 H8
Toms River, U.S.A. ... 117 G10
Tomsk, Russia ... 52 D9
Tomtabacken, Sweden ... 11 G8
Tona, Spain ... 38 D7
Tonalá, Mexico ... 119 D6
Tonale, Passo del, Italy ... 40 B7
Tonantins, Brazil ... 124 D5
Tonasket, U.S.A. ... 108 B4
Tonawanda, U.S.A. ... 116 D6
Tonb, Iran ... 71 E7
Tonbridge, U.K. ... 15 F8
Tondano, Indonesia ... 63 D6
Tondela, Portugal ... 36 E2
Tønder, Denmark ... 11 K2
Tondi Kiwindi, Niger ... 83 C5
Tondibi, Mali ... 83 B4
Tondoro, Namibia ... 88 B2
Tone →, Australia ... 93 F2
Tone-Gawa →, Japan ... 55 F9
Tonekābon, Iran ... 71 B6
Tong Xian, China ... 56 E9
Tônga, Sudan ... 81 F3
Tonga ■, Pac. Oc. ... 91 D11
Tonga Trench, Pac. Oc. ... 96 J10
Tongaat, S. Africa ... 89 D5
Tong'an, China ... 59 E12
Tongareva, Cook Is. ... 97 H12
Tongariro △, N.Z. ... 91 H5
Tongatapu Group, Tonga ... 91 E12
Tongbai, China ... 59 A9
Tongcheng, Anhui, China ... 59 B11
Tongcheng, Hubei, China ... 59 C9
Tongchŏn-ni, N. Korea ... 57 E14
Tongchuan, China ... 56 G5
Tongdao, China ... 58 D7
Tongeren, Belgium ... 17 D5
Tonggu, China ... 59 C10
Tongguan, China ... 56 G6
Tonghae, S. Korea ... 57 F15
Tonghai, China ... 58 E4
Tonghua, China ... 57 D13
Tongjiang, China ... 58 B6
Tongjosŏn Man, N. Korea ... 57 E15
Tongking, G. of = Tonkin, G. of, Asia ... 60 E5
Tongliang, China ... 58 C6
Tongliao, China ... 57 C12
Tongling, China ... 59 B11
Tonglu, China ... 59 C12
Tongnae, S. Korea ... 57 G15
Tongnan = Anyue, China ... 58 B5
Tongobory, Madag. ... 89 C7
Tongoy, Chile ... 126 C1
Tongren, China ... 58 D7
Tongres = Tongeren, Belgium ... 17 D5
Tongsa Dzong, Bhutan ... 67 F17
Tongue, U.K. ... 13 C4
Tongue →, U.S.A. ... 112 B2
Tongwei, China ... 56 G3
Tongxiang, China ... 59 B13
Tongxin, China ... 56 F4
Tongyang, N. Korea ... 57 E14
Tongyu, China ... 57 B12
Tongzi, China ... 58 C6
Tonj, Sudan ... 81 F2
Tonj →, Sudan ... 81 F2
Tonk, India ... 68 F6
Tonkawa, U.S.A. ... 113 G6
Tonkin = Bac Phan, Vietnam ... 64 B5
Tonkin, G. of, Asia ... 60 E5
Tonle Sap, Cambodia ... 64 F4
Tonnay-Charente, France ... 20 C3
Tonneins, France ... 20 D4
Tonnerre, France ... 19 E10
Tönning, Germany ... 24 A4
Tono, Japan ... 54 E10
Tonosí, Panama ... 120 E3
Tons →, Haryana, India ... 68 D7
Tons →, Ut. P., India ... 69 F10
Tønsberg, Norway ... 9 G14
Tonto △, U.S.A. ... 109 K8
Tonya, Turkey ... 73 B8
Toobanna, Australia ... 94 B4
Toodyay, Australia ... 93 F2
Tooele, U.S.A. ... 108 F7
Toompine, Australia ... 95 D3
Toora, Australia ... 95 F4
Toora-Khem, Russia ... 53 D10
Toowoomba, Australia ... 95 D5
Top Springs, Australia ... 92 C5
Topalu, Romania ... 29 F13

Topaz, U.S.A. 110 G7
Topeka, U.S.A. 112 F7
Topl'a →, Slovak Rep. 27 C14
Topley, Canada 102 C3
Toplica →, Serbia & M. 44 C5
Toplița, Romania 29 D10
Topocalma, Pta., Chile 126 C1
Topock, U.S.A. 111 L12
Topola, Serbia & M. 44 B4
Topolčani, Macedonia 44 E5
Topol'čany, Slovak Rep. 27 C11
Topolnitsa →, Bulgaria 45 D8
Topolobampo, Mexico 118 B3
Topoloveni, Romania 29 F10
Topolovgrad, Bulgaria 45 D10
Topolvățu Mare, Romania 28 E6
Toppenish, U.S.A. 108 C3
Topraisar, Romania 29 F13
Topusko, Croatia 41 C12
Torà, Spain 38 D6
Tora Kit, Sudan 81 E3
Toraka Vestale, Madag. 89 B7
Torata, Peru 124 G4
Torbalı, Turkey 47 C9
Torbat-e Heydārīyeh, Iran 71 C8
Torbat-e Jām, Iran 71 C9
Torbay, Canada 105 C9
Torbay □, U.K. 15 G4
Torbjörntorp, Sweden 11 F7
Tordesillas, Spain 36 D6
Töreboda, Sweden 11 F8
Torekov, Sweden 11 H6
Torellò, Spain 38 C7
Toreno, Spain 36 C4
Torfaen □, U.K. 15 F4
Torgau, Germany 24 D8
Torgelow, Germany 24 B10
Torhamn, Sweden 11 H9
Torhout, Belgium 17 C3
Torhovytsya, Ukraine 29 B10
Tori, Ethiopia 81 F3
Tori-Shima, Japan 55 J10
Torigni-sur-Vire, France 18 C6
Torija, Spain 38 E1
Torin, Mexico 118 B2
Torino, Italy 40 C4
Torit, Sudan 81 G3
Torkamān, Iran 70 B5
Torkovichi, Russia 32 C6
Tormac, Romania 28 E6
Tormes →, Spain 36 D4
Tornado Mt., Canada 102 D6
Tornal'a, Slovak Rep. 27 C13
Torneå = Tornio, Finland 8 D21
Torneälven →, Europe 8 D21
Torneträsk, Sweden 8 B18
Tornio, Finland 8 D21
Tornionjoki = Torneälven →, Europe 8 D21
Tornquist, Argentina 126 D3
Toro, Baleares, Spain 48 B11
Toro, Zamora, Spain 36 D5
Torö, Sweden 11 F11
Toro □, Uganda 86 C3
Toro, Cerro del, Chile 126 B2
Toro Pk., U.S.A. 111 M10
Törökszentmiklós, Hungary 28 C5
Toronios Kólpos, Greece 44 F7
Toronto, Canada 116 C5
Toronto, U.S.A. 116 F4
Toronto Lester B. Pearson International ✈ (YYZ), Canada 116 C5
Toropets, Russia 32 D6
Tororo, Uganda 86 B3
Toros Dağları, Turkey 70 B2
Torpa, India 69 H11
Torquay, U.K. 15 G4
Torquemada, Spain 36 C6
Torrance, U.S.A. 111 M8
Torrão, Portugal 37 G2
Torre Annunziata, Italy 43 B7
Torre de Moncorvo, Portugal 36 D3
Torre del Campo, Spain 37 H7
Torre del Greco, Italy 43 B7
Torre del Mar, Spain 37 J6
Torre-Pacheco, Spain 39 H4
Torre Péllice, Italy 40 D4
Torreblanca, Spain 38 E5
Torrecampo, Spain 37 G6
Torrecilla en Cameros, Spain 38 C2
Torredembarra, Spain 38 D6
Torredonjimeno, Spain 37 H7
Torrejón de Ardoz, Spain 36 E7
Torrejoncillo, Spain 36 F4
Torrelaguna, Spain 36 E7
Torrelavega, Spain 36 B6
Torremaggiore, Italy 41 G12
Torremolinos, Spain 37 J6
Torrens, L., Australia 95 E2
Torrens Cr. →, Australia 94 C4
Torrens Creek, Australia 94 C4
Torrent, Spain 39 F4
Torrenueva, Spain 37 G7
Torreón, Mexico 118 B4
Torreperogil, Spain 37 G7
Torres, Brazil 127 B5
Torres, Mexico 118 B2
Torres Novas, Portugal 37 F2
Torres Strait, Australia 96 H6
Torres Vedras, Portugal 37 F1
Torrevieja, Spain 39 H4
Torrey, U.S.A. 109 G8
Torridge →, U.K. 15 G3
Torridon, L., U.K. 13 D3
Torrijos, Spain 36 F6
Tørring, Denmark 11 J3
Torrington, Conn., U.S.A. 117 E11
Torrington, Wyo., U.S.A. 112 D2
Torroella de Montgrì, Spain 38 C8
Torrox, Spain 37 J7
Torsås, Sweden 11 H9

Torsby, Sweden 10 D6
Torshälla, Sweden 10 E10
Tórshavn, Færoe Is. 8 E9
Torslanda, Sweden 11 G5
Torsö, Sweden 11 F7
Tortola, Br. Virgin Is. 121 e
Tórtoles de Esgueva, Spain 36 D6
Tortolì, Italy 42 C2
Tortona, Italy 40 D5
Tortorici, Italy 43 D7
Tortosa, Spain 38 E5
Tortosa, C., Spain 38 E5
Tortosendo, Portugal 36 E3
Tortue, I. de la, Haiti 121 B5
Tortuguero △, Costa Rica 120 D3
Tortum, Turkey 73 B9
Torūd, Iran 71 C7
Torul, Turkey 73 B8
Toruń, Poland 31 E5
Torun, Ukraine 29 B8
Tory I., Ireland 12 A3
Torysa →, Slovak Rep. 27 C14
Torzhok, Russia 32 D8
Torzym, Poland 31 F2
Tosa, Japan 55 H6
Tosa-Shimizu, Japan 55 H6
Tosa-Wan, Japan 55 H6
Toscana □, Italy 40 E8
Toscano, Arcipelago, Italy 40 F7
Toshkent, Uzbekistan 52 E7
Tosno, Russia 32 C6
Tossa de Mar, Spain 38 D7
Tösse, Sweden 11 F6
Tostado, Argentina 126 B3
Tostón, Pta. de, Canary Is. 48 F5
Tosu, Japan 55 H5
Tosya, Turkey 72 B6
Toszek, Poland 31 H5
Totana, Spain 39 H3
Totebo, Sweden 11 G10
Toteng, Botswana 88 C3
Tôtes, France 18 C8
Tótkomlós, Hungary 28 D5
Totma, Russia 52 C5
Totnes, U.K. 15 G4
Totness, Suriname 125 B7
Toto, Nigeria 83 D6
Totonicapán, Guatemala 120 D1
Totten Glacier, Antarctica 5 C8
Tottenham, Australia 95 E4
Tottenham, Canada 116 B5
Tottori, Japan 55 G7
Tottori □, Japan 55 G7
Touareg, Niger 83 A6
Touba, Ivory C. 82 D3
Touba, Senegal 82 C1
Toubkal, Djebel, Morocco 78 B4
Toucy, France 19 E10
Tougan, Burkina Faso 82 C4
Touggourt, Algeria 78 B7
Tougouri, Burkina Faso 83 C4
Tougué, Guinea 82 C2
Toukoto, Mali 82 C3
Toul, France 19 D12
Toulepleu, Ivory C. 82 D3
Toulon, France 21 E9
Toulouse, France 20 E5
Toulouse Blagnac ✈ (TLS), France 20 E5
Toummo, Niger 79 D8
Toumodi, Ivory C. 82 D3
Tounan, Taiwan 59 F13
Toungo, Niger → 83 D7
Toungoo, Burma 67 K20
Touques →, France 18 C7
Touraine, France 18 E7
Tourcoing, France 19 B10
Touriñán, C., Spain 36 B1
Tournai, Belgium 17 D3
Tournan-en-Brie, France 19 D9
Tournay, France 20 E4
Tournon-St-Martin, France 18 F7
Tournon-sur-Rhône, France 21 C8
Tournus, France 19 F11
Tours, France 18 E7
Toussora, Mt., C.A.R. 84 C4
Touwrivier, S. Africa 88 E3
Touws →, S. Africa 88 E3
Tovarkovskiy, Russia 32 F10
Tovste, Ukraine 29 B10
Tovuz, Azerbaijan 35 K7
Towada, Japan 54 D10
Towada-Hachimantai △, Japan 54 D10
Towada-Ko, Japan 54 D10
Towanda, U.S.A. 117 E8
Towang, India 67 F17
Tower, U.S.A. 112 B8
Towerhill Cr. →, Australia 94 C3
Towner, U.S.A. 112 A4
Townsend, U.S.A. 108 C8
Townshend I., Australia 94 C5
Townsville, Australia 94 B4
Towraghondi, Afghan. 66 B3
Towson, U.S.A. 114 F7
Towuti, Danau, Indonesia 63 E6
Toya-Ko, Japan 54 C10
Toyama, Japan 55 F8
Toyama □, Japan 55 F8
Toyama-Wan, Japan 55 F8
Toyapakeh, Indonesia 63 K18
Toyohashi, Japan 55 G8
Toyokawa, Japan 55 G8
Toyonaka, Japan 55 G7
Toyooka, Japan 55 G7
Toyota, Japan 55 G8
Tozeur, Tunisia 78 B7
Tozkhurmato, Iraq 70 C5
Tqibuli, Georgia 35 J6
Tqvarcheli, Georgia 35 J5
Trá Li = Tralee, Ireland 12 D2

Tra On, Vietnam 65 H5
Trabancos →, Spain 36 D5
Traben-Trarbach, Germany 25 F3
Trabzon, Turkey 73 B8
Tracadie-Sheila, Canada 105 C7
Tracy, Calif., U.S.A. 110 H5
Tracy, Minn., U.S.A. 112 C7
Tradate, Italy 40 C5
Trade Town, Liberia 82 D3
Trafalgar, C., Spain 37 J4
Traian, Brăila, Romania 29 E12
Traian, Tulcea, Romania 29 E13
Trail, Canada 102 D5
Trainor L., Canada 102 A4
Trákhonas, Cyprus 49 D12
Tralee, Ireland 12 D2
Tralee B., Ireland 12 D2
Tramore, Ireland 12 D4
Tramore B., Ireland 12 D4
Tran Ninh, Cao Nguyen, Laos 64 C4
Tranås, Sweden 11 F8
Tranbjerg, Denmark 11 H4
Trancas, Argentina 126 B2
Trancoso, Portugal 36 E3
Tranebjerg, Denmark 11 J4
Tranemo, Sweden 11 G7
Trang, Thailand 65 J2
Trangahy, Madag. 89 B7
Trangan, Indonesia 63 F8
Trangie, Australia 95 E4
Trångsviken, Sweden 10 A7
Trani, Italy 43 A9
Tranoroa, Madag. 89 C8
Tranqueras, Uruguay 127 C4
Transantarctic Mts., Antarctica 5 E12
Transilvania, Romania 29 D9
Transilvanian Alps = Carpații Meridionali, Romania 29 E9
Transnistria = Stînga Nistrului □, Moldova 29 C14
Transtrand, Sweden 10 C7
Transtrandsfjällen, Sweden 10 C6
Transylvania = Transilvania, Romania 29 D9
Trápani, Italy 42 D5
Trapper Pk., U.S.A. 108 D6
Traralgon, Australia 95 F4
Trarza, Mauritania 82 B2
Trasacco, Italy 41 G10
Trăscău, Munții, Romania 29 D8
Trasimeno, L., Italy 41 E9
Trasvase Tajo-Segura, Canal de, Spain 38 E2
Trat, Thailand 65 F4
Tratani →, Pakistan 68 E3
Traun, Austria 26 C7
Traunreut, Germany 25 H8
Traunsee, Austria 26 D6
Traunstein, Germany 25 H8
Traveller's L., Australia 95 E3
Travemünde, Germany 24 B6
Travers, Mt., N.Z. 91 K4
Traverse City, U.S.A. 114 C3
Travis, L., U.S.A. 113 K5
Travnik, Bos.-H. 28 F2
Trbovlje, Slovenia 41 B12
Trébbia →, Italy 40 C6
Trebel →, Germany 24 B9
Trébeurden, France 18 D3
Trebević, Bos.-H. 28 G3
Trebinje, Bos.-H. 44 D2
Trebisacce, Italy 43 C9
Trebišnjica →, Bos.-H. 44 D2
Trebišov, Slovak Rep. 27 C14
Trebižat →, Bos.-H. 41 E14
Trebnje, Slovenia 41 C12
Třeboň, Czech Rep. 26 B7
Trebonne, Australia 94 B4
Třebon̆sko △, Czech Rep. 26 B7
Trebujena, Spain 37 J4
Trecate, Italy 40 C5
Tregaron, U.K. 15 E4
Tregnago, Italy 41 C8
Tregrosse Is., Australia 94 B5
Tréguier, France 18 D3
Trégunc, France 18 E3
Treherne, Canada 103 D9
Tréia, Italy 41 E10
Treignac, France 20 C5
Treinta y Tres, Uruguay 127 C5
Treis-karden, Germany 25 E3
Treklyano, Bulgaria 44 D6
Trelawney, Zimbabwe 89 B5
Trélazé, France 18 E6
Trelew, Argentina 128 E3
Trélissac, France 20 C4
Trelleborg, Sweden 11 J7
Tremadog Bay, U.K. 14 E3
Trémiti, Italy 41 F12
Tremonton, U.S.A. 108 F7
Tremp, Spain 38 C5
Trenche →, Canada 104 C5
Trenčiansky □, Slovak Rep. 27 C11
Trenčín, Slovak Rep. 27 C11
Trenggalek, Indonesia 63 H14
Trenque Lauquen, Argentina 126 D3
Trent →, Canada 116 B7
Trent →, U.K. 14 D7
Trentino-Alto Adige □, Italy 40 B8
Trento, Italy 40 B8
Trenton = Quinte West, Canada 116 B7
Trenton, Mo., U.S.A. 112 E8
Trenton, N.J., U.S.A. 117 F10
Trenton, Nebr., U.S.A. 112 E4
Trepassey, Canada 105 C9
Trepuzzi, Italy 43 B11
Tres Arroyos, Argentina 126 D3
Três Corações, Brazil 127 A6
Três Lagoas, Brazil 125 H8

Tres Lomas, Argentina 126 D3
Tres Marías, Islas, Mexico 118 C3
Tres Montes, C., Chile 128 F1
Três Pinos, U.S.A. 110 J5
Três Pontas, Brazil 127 A6
Tres Puentes, Chile 126 B1
Tres Puntas, C., Argentina 128 F3
Três Rios, Brazil 127 A7
Tres Valles, Mexico 119 D5
Trasco, U.K. 15 H1
Treska →, Macedonia 44 E5
Treskavica, Bos.-H. 28 G3
Trespaderne, Spain 36 C7
Tresticklan △, Sweden 11 F5
Trets, France 21 E9
Treuchtlingen, Germany 25 G6
Treuenbrietzen, Germany 24 C8
Trevi, Italy 41 F9
Treviglio, Italy 40 C6
Trevínca, Peña, Spain 36 C4
Treviso, Italy 41 C9
Trévoux, France 21 C8
Trgovište, Serbia & M. 44 D6
Triabunna, Australia 95 G4
Triánda, Greece 49 C10
Triangle, Zimbabwe 89 C5
Triaucourt-en-Argonne, France 19 D12
Tribal Areas □, Pakistan 68 C4
Tribsees, Germany 24 A8
Tribulation, C., Australia 94 B4
Tribune, U.S.A. 112 F4
Tricárico, Italy 43 B9
Tricase, Italy 43 C11
Trichinopoly = Tiruchchirappalli, India 66 P11
Trichur, India 66 P10
Trida, Australia 95 E4
Trier, Germany 25 F2
Trieste, Italy 41 C10
Trieste, G. di, Italy 41 C10
Trigno →, Italy 41 F11
Trigueros, Spain 37 H4
Tríkeri, Greece 46 B5
Trikhonís, Límni, Greece 46 C3
Tríkkala, Greece 46 B3
Tríkkala □, Greece 46 B3
Trikomo, Cyprus 49 D12
Trikora, Puncak, Indonesia 63 E9
Trilj, Croatia 41 E13
Trillo, Spain 38 E2
Trim, Ireland 12 C5
Trincomalee, Sri Lanka 66 Q12
Trindade, Brazil 125 G9
Trindade, I., Atl. Oc. 2 F8
Třinec, Czech Rep. 27 B11
Trinidad, Bolivia 124 F6
Trinidad, Cuba 120 B4
Trinidad, Trin. & Tob. 121 D7
Trinidad, Uruguay 126 C4
Trinidad, U.S.A. 113 G2
Trinidad →, Mexico 119 D5
Trinidad & Tobago ■, W. Indies 121 D7
Trinitápoli, Italy 43 A9
Trinity, Canada 105 C9
Trinity →, Calif., U.S.A. 108 F2
Trinity →, Tex., U.S.A. 113 L7
Trinity B., Canada 105 C9
Trinity Hills, Trin. & Tob. 125 K15
Trinity Is., U.S.A. 100 C4
Trinity Range, U.S.A. 108 F4
Trinkitat, Sudan 80 D4
Trino, Italy 40 C5
Trinway, U.S.A. 116 F2
Trion, U.S.A. 117 H10
Triora, Italy 40 D4
Tripoli = Tarābulus, Lebanon 74 A4
Tripoli = Tarābulus, Libya 79 B8
Trípolis, Greece 46 D4
Tripolitania, N. Afr. 79 B8
Tripura □, India 67 H18
Tripylos, Cyprus 49 E11
Trischen, Germany 24 A4
Tristan da Cunha, Atl. Oc. 77 K2
Trisul, India 69 D8
Trivandrum, India 66 Q10
Trivento, Italy 41 G11
Trnava, Slovak Rep. 27 C10
Trnavský □, Slovak Rep. 27 C10
Troarn, France 18 C6
Trochu, Canada 102 C6
Trödely I., Canada 104 B4
Troezen, Greece 46 D5
Trogir, Croatia 41 E13
Troglav, Croatia 41 E13
Tróia, Italy 43 A8
Troilus, L., Canada 104 B5
Troina, Italy 43 E7
Trois-Pistoles, Canada 105 C6
Trois-Rivières, Canada 104 C5
Trois-Rivières, Guadeloupe 120 b
Troisdorf, Germany 24 E3
Troitsk, Russia 52 D7
Troitsk Pechorsk, Russia 52 C6
Troitskoye, Russia 35 G7
Trölladyngja, Iceland 8 D5
Trollhättan, Sweden 11 F6
Trollheimen, Norway 8 E13
Trombetas →, Brazil 125 D7
Tromsø, Norway 8 B18
Trona, U.S.A. 111 K9
Tronador, Mte., Argentina 128 E2
Trøndelag, Norway 8 D14
Trondheim, Norway 8 E14
Trondheimsfjorden, Norway 8 E14
Trönninge, Sweden 11 H6
Tronto →, Italy 41 F10

Troodos, Cyprus 49 E11
Troon, U.K. 13 F4
Tropea, Italy 43 D8
Tropic, U.S.A. 109 H7
Tropojë, Albania 44 D4
Trosa, Sweden 11 F11
Trostan, U.K. 12 A5
Trostberg, Germany 25 G8
Trostyanets, Ukraine 29 B14
Trostyanets, Ukraine 33 G8
Trou Gras Pt., St. Lucia 121 f
Trout →, Canada 102 A5
Trout L., N.W.T., Canada 102 A4
Trout L., Ont., Canada 103 C10
Trout Lake, Canada 102 B6
Trout Lake, U.S.A. 110 E5
Trout River, Canada 105 C8
Trout Run, U.S.A. 116 E7
Trouville-sur-Mer, France 18 C7
Trowbridge, U.K. 15 F5
Troy, Turkey 47 B8
Troy, Ala., U.S.A. 115 K3
Troy, Kans., U.S.A. 112 F7
Troy, Mo., U.S.A. 112 F9
Troy, Mont., U.S.A. 108 B6
Troy, N.Y., U.S.A. 117 D11
Troy, Ohio, U.S.A. 114 E3
Troy, Pa., U.S.A. 117 E8
Troyan, Bulgaria 45 D8
Troyes, France 19 D11
Trpanj, Croatia 41 E14
Trstenik, Serbia & M. 44 C5
Trubchevsk, Russia 33 F7
Truchas Peak, U.S.A. 113 H2
Trucial States = United Arab Emirates ■, Asia 71 F7
Truckee, U.S.A. 110 F6
Trudfront, Russia 35 H8
Trudovoye, Russia 54 C6
Trujillo, Honduras 120 C2
Trujillo, Peru 124 E3
Trujillo, Spain 37 F5
Trujillo, U.S.A. 113 H2
Trujillo, Venezuela 124 B4
Truk, Micronesia 96 G7
Trumann, U.S.A. 113 H9
Trumansburg, U.S.A. 117 D8
Trumbull, Mt., U.S.A. 109 H7
Trün, Bulgaria 44 D6
Trun, France 18 D7
Trundle, Australia 95 E4
Trung-Phan = Annam, Vietnam 64 E7
Truro, Canada 105 C7
Truro, U.K. 15 G2
Truskavets, Ukraine 33 H2
Trüstenik, Bulgaria 45 C8
Trustrup, Denmark 11 H4
Trutch, Canada 102 B4
Truth or Consequences, U.S.A. 109 K10
Trutnov, Czech Rep. 26 A8
Truxton, U.S.A. 117 D8
Truyère →, France 20 D6
Tryavna, Bulgaria 45 D9
Tryonville, U.S.A. 116 E5
Trzcianka, Poland 31 E3
Trzciel, Poland 31 F2
Trzcińsko Zdrój, Poland 31 F1
Trzebiatów, Poland 30 D2
Trzebiez, Poland 30 E1
Trzebnica, Poland 31 G4
Trzemeszno, Poland 31 F4
Tržič, Slovenia 41 B11
Tsagan Aman, Russia 35 G8
Tsamandás, Greece 46 B2
Tsandi, Namibia 88 B1
Tsaratanana, Madag. 89 B8
Tsaratanana △, Madag. 89 A8
Tsaratanana, Mt. de = Maromokotro, Madag. 89 A8
Tsarevo, Bulgaria 45 D9
Tsaritsáni, Greece 46 B4
Tsau, Botswana 88 C3
Tsavo East △, Kenya 86 C4
Tsavo West △, Kenya 86 C4
Tsebrykove, Ukraine 33 J6
Tsentralnyy □, Russia 34 D4
Tses, Namibia 88 D2
Tsetserleg, Mongolia 60 B5
Tsévié, Togo 83 D5
Tshabong, Botswana 88 D3
Tshane, Botswana 88 C3
Tshela, Dem. Rep. of the Congo 84 E2
Tshesebe, Botswana 89 C4
Tshibeke, Dem. Rep. of the Congo 86 C2
Tshibinda, Dem. Rep. of the Congo 86 C2
Tshikapa, Dem. Rep. of the Congo 84 F4
Tshilenge, Dem. Rep. of the Congo 86 D1
Tshinsenda, Dem. Rep. of the Congo 87 E2
Tshofa, Dem. Rep. of the Congo 86 D2
Tshwane = Pretoria, S. Africa 89 D4
Tshwane, Botswana 88 C3
Tsigara, Botswana 88 C4
Tsihombe, Madag. 89 D8
Tsiigehtchic, Canada 100 B6
Tsimlyansk, Russia 35 G6
Tsimlyansk Res. = Tsimlyanskoye Vdkhr., Russia 35 F6
Tsimlyanskoye Vdkhr., Russia 35 F6
Tsinan = Jinan, China 56 F9
Tsineng, S. Africa 88 D3
Tsínga, Greece 45 E8
Tsinghai = Qinghai □, China 60 C4
Tsingtao = Qingdao, China 57 F11
Tsingy de Bemaraha △, Madag. 89 B8
Tsingy de Namoroka △, Madag. 89 B8
Tsinjomitondraka, Madag. 89 B8
Tsiroanomandidy, Madag. 89 B8
Tsiteli-Tsqaro, Georgia 35 K8

Tsitondroina, Madag. 89 C8
Tsitsikamma △, S. Africa 88 E3
Tsivilsk, Russia 34 C8
Tsivory, Madag. 89 C8
Tskhinvali, Georgia 35 J7
Tsna →, Russia 34 C6
Tsnori, Georgia 35 K7
Tso Moriri, L., India 69 C8
Tsobis, Namibia 88 B2
Tsodilo Hill, Botswana 88 B3
Tsogttsetsiy = Baruunsuu,
  Mongolia 56 C3
Tsolo, S. Africa 89 E4
Tsomo, S. Africa 89 E4
Tsu, Japan 55 G8
Tsu L., Canada 102 A6
Tsuchiura, Japan 55 F10
Tsuen Wan, China 59 F10
Tsugaru-Kaikyō, Japan 54 D10
Tsumeb, Namibia 88 B2
Tsumis, Namibia 88 C2
Tsuruga, Japan 55 G8
Tsurugi-San, Japan 55 H7
Tsuruoka, Japan 54 E9
Tsushima, Gifu, Japan 55 G8
Tsushima, Nagasaki, Japan 55 G4
Tsuyama, Japan 55 G7
Tsvetkovo, Ukraine 33 H6
Tsyelyakhany, Belarus 33 F3
Tua →, Portugal 36 D3
Tual, Indonesia 63 F8
Tuam, Ireland 12 C3
Tuamotu Arch. = Tuamotu Is.,
  French Polynesia 97 J13
Tuamotu Is., French Polynesia . 97 J13
Tuamotu Ridge, Pac. Oc. 97 K14
Tuanfeng, China 59 B10
Tuanxi, China 58 D6
Tuao, Phil. 61 C4
Tuapse, Russia 35 H4
Tuas, Singapore .... 65 d
Tuatapere, N.Z. 91 M1
Tuba City, U.S.A. 109 H8
Tuban, Indonesia 63 G15
Tubani, Botswana 88 C3
Tubarão, Brazil 127 B6
Tūbās, West Bank 74 C4
Tubas →, Namibia 88 C2
Tübingen, Germany 25 G5
Tubruq, Libya 79 B10
Tubuai Is., French Polynesia .. 97 K13
Tuc Trung, Vietnam 65 G6
Tucacas, Venezuela 124 A5
T'uch'ang, Taiwan 59 E13
Tuchodi →, Canada 102 B4
Tuchola, Poland 30 E4
Tuchów, Poland 31 J8
Tuckanarra, Australia 93 E2
Tucson, U.S.A. 109 K8
Tucumán □, Argentina 126 B2
Tucumcari, U.S.A. 113 H3
Tucupita, Venezuela 124 B6
Tucuruí, Brazil 125 D9
Tucuruí, Reprêsa de, Brazil ... 125 D9
Tuczno, Poland 31 E3
Tudela, Spain 38 C3
Tudmur, Syria 70 C3
Tudor, L., Canada 105 A6
Tudora, Romania 29 C11
Tuella →, Portugal 36 D3
Tugela →, S. Africa 89 D5
Tuguegarao, Phil. 61 C4
Tugur, Russia 53 D14
Tui, Spain 36 C2
Tuineje, Canary Is. 48 F5
Tukangbesi, Kepulauan,
  Indonesia 63 F6
Tukarak I., Canada 104 A4
Tukayyid, Iraq 70 D5
Tūkh, Egypt 80 H7
Tukhlya, Ukraine 29 B8
Tukkae, Ao, Thailand .... 65 a
Tukobo, Ghana 82 D4
Tuktoyaktuk, Canada 100 B6
Tukums, Latvia 9 H20
Tukums □, Latvia 30 B10
Tukuyu, Tanzania 87 D3
Tula, Hidalgo, Mexico 119 C5
Tula, Tamaulipas, Mexico 119 C5
Tula, Nigeria 83 D7
Tula, Russia 32 E9
Tulancingo, Mexico 119 C5
Tulare, Serbia & M. 44 D5
Tulare, U.S.A. 110 J7
Tulare Lake Bed, U.S.A. 110 K7
Tularosa, U.S.A. 109 K10
Tulbagh, S. Africa 88 E2
Tulcán, Ecuador 124 C3
Tulcea, Romania 29 E13
Tulcea □, Romania 29 E13
Tulchyn, Ukraine 29 B13
Tūleh, Iran 71 C7
Tulemalu L., Canada 103 A9
Tulgheş, Romania 29 D10
Tuli, Zimbabwe 87 G2
Tulia, U.S.A. 113 H4
Tuliszków, Poland 31 F5
Tulita, Canada 100 B7
Ţūlkarm, West Bank 74 C4
Tulla, Ireland 12 D3
Tullahoma, U.S.A. 115 H2
Tullamore, Australia 95 E4
Tullamore, Ireland 12 C4
Tulle, France 20 C5
Tulln, Austria 26 C9
Tullow, Ireland 12 D5
Tullus, Sudan 81 E1
Tully, Australia 94 B4
Tully, U.S.A. 117 D8
Tulnici, Romania 29 E11
Tulovo, Bulgaria 45 D9

Tulsa, U.S.A. 113 G7
Tulsequah, Canada 102 B2
Tulu Milki, Ethiopia 81 F4
Tulu Welel, Ethiopia 81 F3
Tulua, Colombia 124 C3
Tuluceşti, Romania 29 E13
Tulun, Russia 53 D11
Tulungagung, Indonesia 63 H14
Tuma, Russia 32 E11
Tuma →, Nic. 120 D3
Tumacacori, U.S.A. 109 L8
Tumaco, Colombia 124 C3
Tumatumari, Guyana 124 B7
Tumba, Sweden 10 E11
Tumba, L., Dem. Rep. of
  the Congo 84 E3
Tumbarumba, Australia 95 F4
Tumbaya, Argentina 126 A2
Tumbes, Peru 124 D2
Tumbur, Sudan 81 G3
Tumbwe, Dem. Rep. of the Congo 87 E2
Tumby Bay, Australia 95 E2
Tumd Youqi, China 56 D6
Tumen, China 57 C15
Tumen Jiang →, China 57 C16
Tumeremo, Venezuela 124 B6
Tumkur, India 66 N10
Tump, Pakistan 66 F3
Tumpat, Malaysia 65 J4
Tumu, Ghana 82 C4
Tumucumaque, Serra, Brazil ... 125 C8
Tumut, Australia 95 F4
Tumwater, U.S.A. 110 C4
Tuna, India 68 H4
Tunadal, Sweden 10 B11
Tunapuna, Trin. & Tob. 125 K15
Tunas de Zaza, Cuba 120 B4
Tunbridge Wells = Royal
  Tunbridge Wells, U.K. 15 F8
Tunçbilek, Turkey 47 B11
Tunceli, Turkey 73 C8
Tuncurry, Australia 95 E5
Tundla, India 68 F8
Tundubai, Sudan 80 D2
Tunduru, Tanzania 87 E4
Tundzha →, Bulgaria 45 E10
Tungabhadra →, India 66 M11
Tungaru, Sudan 81 E3
Tungla, Nic. 120 D3
Tungsha Tao = Dongsha Dao,
  China 59 G11
Tungshih, Taiwan 59 E13
Tungsten, Canada 102 A3
Tunguska, Nizhnyaya →, Russia . 53 C9
Tunguska, Podkamennaya →,
  Russia 53 C10
Tunica, U.S.A. 113 H9
Tunis, Tunisia 78 A7
Tunis ✈ (TUN), Tunisia 42 F3
Tunisia ■, Africa 78 B6
Tunja, Colombia 124 B4
Tunkhannock, U.S.A. 117 E9
Tunliu, China 56 F7
Tunnel Creek △, Australia 92 C4
Tunnsjøen, Norway 8 D15
Tunø, Denmark 11 J4
Tunungayualok I., Canada 105 A7
Tunuyán, Argentina 126 C2
Tunuyán →, Argentina 126 C2
Tuo Jiang →, China 58 C5
Tuolumne, U.S.A. 110 H6
Tuolumne →, U.S.A. 110 H5
Tüp Ãghāj, Iran 70 B5
Tupã, Brazil 127 A5
Tupelo, U.S.A. 115 H1
Tupik, Russia 32 E7
Tupinambaranas, Brazil 124 D7
Tupiza, Bolivia 126 A2
Tupižnica, Serbia & M. 44 C6
Tupman, U.S.A. 111 K7
Tupper, Canada 102 B4
Tupper Lake, U.S.A. 117 B10
Tupungato, Cerro, S. Amer. ... 126 C2
Tuquan, China 57 B11
Túquerres, Colombia 124 C3
Tura, Russia 53 C11
Turabah, Ḥāʾil, Si. Arabia ... 70 D4
Turabah, Makkah, Si. Arabia .. 80 C5
Tūrān, Iran 71 C8
Turan, Russia 53 D10
Ţurayf, Si. Arabia 70 D3
Turbacz, Poland 31 J7
Turbe, Bos.-H. 28 F2
Turčianske Teplice, Slovak Rep. 27 C11
Turcoaia, Romania 29 E13
Turda, Romania 29 D8
Turek, Poland 31 F5
Turen, Venezuela 124 B5
Turfan = Turpan, China 60 B3
Turfan Basin = Turpan Hami,
  China 50 E12
Turfan Depression = Turpan
  Hami, China 50 E12
Turgeon →, Canada 104 C4
Tŭrgovishte, Bulgaria 45 C10
Turgut, Turkey 47 D10
Turgutlu, Turkey 47 C9
Turgwe →, Zimbabwe 89 C5
Turhal, Turkey 72 B7
Turia →, Spain 39 F4
Turiaçu, Brazil 125 D9
Turiaçu →, Brazil 125 D9
Turiec →, Slovak Rep. 27 B11
Turin = Torino, Italy 40 C4
Turka, Ukraine 31 J10
Turkana, L., Africa 86 B4
Türkeli, Turkey 45 F11
Turkestan = Türkistan,
  Kazakhstan 52 E7
Túrkeve, Hungary 28 C5
Turkey ■, Eurasia 72 C7

Turkey Creek, Australia 92 C4
Turki, Russia 34 D6
Türkistan, Kazakhstan 52 E7
Türkmenbashi, Turkmenistan ... 52 E6
Turkmenistan ■, Asia 52 F6
Türkmenli, Turkey 47 B8
Türkoğlu, Turkey 72 D7
Turks & Caicos Is. ☑, W. Indies 121 B5
Turks Island Passage, W. Indies 121 B5
Turku, Finland 9 F20
Turkwel →, Kenya 86 B4
Turlock, U.S.A. 110 H6
Turnagain →, Canada 102 B3
Turnagain, C., N.Z. 91 J6
Turneffe Is., Belize 119 D7
Turner, U.S.A. 108 B9
Turner Pt., Australia 94 A1
Turner Valley, Canada 102 C6
Turners Falls, U.S.A. 117 D12
Turnhout, Belgium 17 C4
Türnitz, Austria 26 D8
Turnor L., Canada 103 B7
Turnov, Czech Rep. 26 A8
Türnovo = Veliko Tŭrnovo,
  Bulgaria 45 C9
Turnu Măgurele, Romania 29 G9
Turnu Roşu, P., Romania 29 E9
Turobin, Poland 31 H9
Turpan, China 60 B3
Turpan Hami, China 50 E12
Turrès, Kala e, Albania 44 E3
Turriff, U.K. 13 D6
Tursāq, Iraq 70 C5
Tursi, Italy 43 B9
Turtle Head I., Australia 94 A3
Turtle Is., S. Leone 82 D2
Turtle L., Canada 103 C7
Turtle Lake, U.S.A. 112 B4
Turtleford, Canada 103 C7
Turuépano △, Venezuela 121 D7
Turukhansk, Russia 53 C9
Turzovka, Slovak Rep. 27 B11
Tuscaloosa, U.S.A. 115 J2
Tuscany = Toscana □, Italy ... 40 E8
Tuscarawas →, U.S.A. 116 F3
Tuscarora Mt., U.S.A. 116 F7
Tuscola, Ill., U.S.A. 114 F1
Tuscola, Tex., U.S.A. 113 J5
Tuscumbia, U.S.A. 115 H2
Tuskegee, U.S.A. 115 J3
Tustin, U.S.A. 111 M9
Tuszyn, Poland 31 G6
Tutak, Turkey 73 C10
Tutayev, Russia 32 D10
Tuticorin, India 66 Q11
Tutin, Serbia & M. 44 D4
Tutóia, Brazil 125 D10
Tutong, Brunei 62 D4
Tutova →, Romania 29 D12
Tutrakan, Bulgaria 45 B10
Tuttle Creek, L., U.S.A. 112 F6
Tuttlingen, Germany 25 H4
Tutuala, E. Timor 63 F7
Tutuila, Amer. Samoa 91 B13
Tutume, Botswana 85 J5
Tutun, Egypt 80 J7
Tututepec, Mexico 119 D5
Tuva □, Russia 53 D10
Tuvalu ■, Pac. Oc. 96 H9
Tuxer Alpen, Austria 26 D4
Tuxpan, Mexico 119 C5
Tuxtla Gutiérrez, Mexico 119 D6
Tuy = Tui, Spain 36 C2
Tuy An, Vietnam 64 F7
Tuy Duc, Vietnam 65 F6
Tuy Hoa, Vietnam 64 F7
Tuy Phong, Vietnam 65 G7
Tuya L., Canada 102 B2
Tuyen Hoa, Vietnam 64 D6
Tuyen Quang, Vietnam 58 G5
Tūysarkān, Iran 71 C6
Tuz Gölü, Turkey 72 C5
Tuz Khurmātū = Tozkhurmato,
  Iraq 70 C5
Tuzi, Serbia & M. 44 D3
Tuzigoot △, U.S.A. 109 J7
Tuzla, Bos.-H. 28 F3
Tuzlov →, Russia 33 J10
Tuzluca, Turkey 73 B10
Tuzly, Ukraine 29 E15
Tvååker, Sweden 11 G6
Tvardiţa, Moldova 29 D13
Tver, Russia 32 D8
Tvrdošin, Slovak Rep. 27 B12
Tvrdošovce, Slovak Rep. 27 C11
Tvŭrditsa, Bulgaria 45 D9
Twain, U.S.A. 110 E5
Twain Harte, U.S.A. 110 G6
Twardogóra, Poland 31 G4
Tweed, Canada 116 B7
Tweed →, U.K. 13 F6
Tweed Heads, Australia 95 D5
Tweedsmuir △, Canada 102 C3
Twentynine Palms, U.S.A. 111 L10
Twillingate, Canada 105 C9
Twin Bridges, U.S.A. 108 D7
Twin Falls, Canada 105 B7
Twin Falls, U.S.A. 108 E6
Twin Valley, U.S.A. 112 B6
Twinsburg, U.S.A. 116 E3
Twistringen, Germany 24 C4
Twitchell Reservoir, U.S.A. .. 111 L6
Two Harbors, U.S.A. 112 B9
Two Hills, Canada 102 C6
Two Rivers, U.S.A. 114 C2
Two Rocks, Australia 93 F2
Twofold B., Australia 95 F4
Tyachiv, Ukraine 33 H2
Tychy, Poland 31 H5
Tyczyn, Poland 31 J9

Tykocin, Poland 31 E9
Tyler, Minn., U.S.A. 112 C6
Tyler, Tex., U.S.A. 113 J7
Tyligul →, Ukraine 33 J6
Týn nad Vltavou, Czech Rep. .. 26 B7
Tynda, Russia 53 D13
Tyndall, U.S.A. 112 D6
Tyne →, U.K. 14 C6
Tyne & Wear □, U.K. 14 B6
Týnec nad Sázavou, Czech Rep. 26 B7
Tynemouth, U.K. 14 B6
Tyre = Sūr, Lebanon 74 B4
Tyresta △, Sweden 10 E12
Tyrifjorden, Norway 9 F14
Tyringe, Sweden 11 H7
Tyrnyauz, Russia 35 J6
Tyrol = Tirol □, Austria 26 D3
Tyrone □, U.K. 116 F6
Tyrone □, U.K. 12 B4
Tyrrell →, Australia 95 F3
Tyrrell, L., Australia 95 F3
Tyrrell L., Canada 103 A7
Tyrrhenian Sea, Medit. S. 6 G8
Tysfjorden, Norway 8 B17
Tysmenytsya, Ukraine 29 B9
Tystberga, Sweden 11 F11
Tytuvėnai, Lithuania 30 C10
Tyub Karagan, Mys, Kazakhstan 35 H10
Tyuleni, Ostrova, Kazakhstan . 35 H10
Tyuleniy, Russia 35 H8
Tyuleniy, Mys, Azerbaijan 35 K10
Tyumen, Russia 52 D7
Tywi →, U.K. 15 F3
Tywyn, U.K. 15 E3
Tzaneen, S. Africa 89 C5
Tzermiádhes, Greece 49 D7
Tzoumérka, Óros, Greece 46 B3
Tzukong = Zigong, China 58 C5

U

U Taphao, Thailand 64 F3
U.S.A. = United States of
  America ■, N. Amer. 106 C7
U.S. Virgin Is. ☑, W. Indies . 121 e
Uatumã →, Brazil 124 D7
Uaupés, Brazil 124 D5
Uaupés →, Brazil 124 C5
Uaxactún, Guatemala 120 C2
Ub, Serbia & M. 44 B4
Ubá, Brazil 127 A7
Uba, Nigeria 83 C7
Ubaitaba, Brazil 125 F11
Ubangi = Oubangi →, Dem. Rep.
  of the Congo 84 E3
Ubauro, Pakistan 68 E3
Ubaye →, France 21 D10
Ubayyiḍ, W. al →, Iraq 70 C4
Ube, Japan 55 H5
Úbeda, Spain 37 G7
Uberaba, Brazil 125 G9
Uberlândia, Brazil 125 G9
Überlingen, Germany 25 H5
Ubiaja, Nigeria 83 D6
Ubin, Pulau, Singapore .... 65 d
Ubolratna Res., Thailand 64 D4
Ubombo, S. Africa 89 D5
Ubon Ratchathani, Thailand ... 64 E5
Ubondo, Dem. Rep. of the Congo 86 C2
Ubort →, Belarus 33 F5
Ubrique, Spain 37 J5
Ubud, Indonesia 63 J18
Ubundu, Dem. Rep. of the Congo 86 C2
Ucayali →, Peru 124 D4
Uchab, Namibia 88 B2
Uchiura-Wan, Japan 54 C10
Uchquduq, Uzbekistan 52 E7
Uchte, Germany 24 C4
Uchur →, Russia 53 D14
Uckermark, Germany 24 B9
Ucluelet, Canada 102 D3
Uda →, Russia 53 D14
Udagamandalam, India 66 P10
Udainagar, India 68 H7
Udaipur, India 68 G5
Udaipur Garhi, Nepal 69 F12
Udala, India 69 J12
Udbina, Croatia 41 D12
Uddeholm, Sweden 10 D7
Uddevalla, Sweden 11 F5
Uddjaure, Sweden 8 D17
Uden, Neths. 17 C5
Udgir, India 66 K10
Udhampur, India 69 C6
Udi, Nigeria 83 D6
Udine, Italy 41 B10
Udmurtia □, Russia 52 D6
Udon Thani, Thailand 64 D4
Udupi, India 66 N9
Udvoy Balkan, Bulgaria 45 D10
Udzungwa, Tanzania 86 D4
Udzungwa Range, Tanzania 87 D4
Ueckermünde, Germany 24 B10
Ueda, Japan 55 F9
Uedineniya, Os., Russia 4 B12
Uele →, Dem. Rep. of the Congo 84 D4
Uelen, Russia 53 C19
Uelzen, Germany 24 C6
Uetersen, Germany 24 B5
Uetze, Germany 24 C6
Ufa, Russia 52 D6
Uffenheim, Germany 25 F6
Ugab →, Namibia 88 C1
Ugalla →, Tanzania 86 D3
Ugalla River △, Tanzania 86 D3
Uganda ■, Africa 86 B3
Ugento, Italy 43 C11

Ugep, Nigeria 83 D6
Ughelli, Nigeria 83 D6
Ugie, S. Africa 89 E4
Ugíjar, Spain 37 J7
Ugine, France 21 C10
Uglegorsk, Russia 53 E15
Uglich, Russia 32 D10
Ugljan, Croatia 41 D12
Ugljane, Croatia 41 E13
Ugra →, Russia 32 E9
Uğurchin, Bulgaria 45 C8
Uh →, Slovak Rep. 27 C15
Uherské Hradiště, Czech Rep. . 27 B10
Uherský Brod, Czech Rep. 27 B10
Úhlava →, Czech Rep. 26 B6
Uhlenhorst, Namibia 88 C2
Uhniv, Ukraine 31 H10
Uhrichsville, U.S.A. 116 F3
Uibhist a Deas = South Uist, U.K. 13 D1
Uibhist a Tuath = North Uist,
  U.K. 13 D1
Uig, U.K. 13 D2
Uíge, Angola 84 F2
Uijŏngbu, S. Korea 57 F14
Ŭiju, N. Korea 57 D13
Uinta Mts., U.S.A. 108 F8
Uis, Namibia 88 C1
Uitenhage, S. Africa 88 E4
Uithuizen, Neths. 17 A6
Ujazd, Poland 31 H5
Újfehértó, Hungary 28 C6
Ujh →, India 68 C6
Ujhani, India 69 F8
Uji-guntō, Japan 55 J4
Ujjain, India 68 H6
Ujście, Poland 31 E3
Ujszász, Hungary 28 C5
Ujung Pandang, Indonesia 63 F5
Uka, Russia 53 D17
Ukara I., Tanzania 86 C3
Uke-Shima, Japan 55 K4
Ukerewe I., Tanzania 86 C3
Ukholovo, Russia 34 D5
Ukhrul, India 67 G19
Ukhta, Russia 52 C9
Ukiah, U.S.A. 110 F3
Ukmergė, Lithuania 9 J21
Ukraine ■, Europe 33 H7
Ukwi, Botswana 88 C3
Ulaan-Uul, Mongolia 56 B6
Ulaanbaatar, Mongolia 53 E11
Ulaangom, Mongolia 60 A4
Ulaanjirem, Mongolia 56 B3
Ulamba, Dem. Rep. of the Congo 87 D1
Ulan Bator = Ulaanbaatar,
  Mongolia 53 E11
Ulan Erge, Russia 35 G7
Ulan Khol, Russia 35 H8
Ulan Ude, Russia 53 D11
Ulanów, Poland 31 H9
Ulaş, Sivas, Turkey 72 C7
Ulaş, Tekirdağ, Turkey 45 E11
Ulaya, Morogoro, Tanzania 86 D4
Ulaya, Tabora, Tanzania 86 C3
Ulcinj, Serbia & M. 44 E3
Ulco, S. Africa 88 D3
Ule älv = Oulujoki →, Finland . 8 D21
Ule träsk = Oulujärvi, Finland . 8 D21
Uleåborg = Oulu, Finland 8 D21
Ulefoss, Norway 9 G13
Ulëz, Albania 44 E4
Ulfborg, Denmark 11 H2
Ulhasnagar, India 66 K8
Uliastay, Mongolia 60 B4
Uljma, Serbia & M. 28 E6
Ulla →, Spain 36 C2
Ulladulla, Australia 95 F5
Ullapool, U.K. 13 D3
Ullared, Sweden 11 G6
Ulldecona, Spain 38 E5
Ullswater, U.K. 14 C5
Ullŭng-do, S. Korea 55 F5
Ulm, Germany 25 G5
Ulmarra, Australia 95 D5
Ulmeni, Buzău, Romania 29 E11
Ulmeni, Maramureş, Romania ... 29 C8
Ulonguè, Mozam. 87 E3
Ulricehamn, Sweden 11 G7
Ulrika, Sweden 11 F9
Ulsan, S. Korea 57 G15
Ulsta, U.K. 13 A7
Ulster □, U.K. 12 B5
Ulstrem, Bulgaria 45 D10
Ulubat Gölü, Turkey 45 F12
Ulubey, Turkey 47 C11
Uluborlu, Turkey 47 C12
Uluçınar, Turkey 72 D6
Uludağ, Turkey 45 F13
Uludağ △, Turkey 45 F13
Uludere, Turkey 73 D10
Uluguru Mts., Tanzania 86 D4
Ulukışla, Turkey 72 D6
Ulungur He →, China 60 B3
Uluru = Ayers Rock, Australia . 93 E5
Uluru-Kata Tjuta △, Australia . 93 E5
Ulutau, Kazakhstan 52 E7
Uluwatu, Indonesia 63 K18
Ulva, U.K. 13 E2
Ulverston, U.K. 14 C4
Ulverstone, Australia 95 G4
Ulya, Russia 53 D15
Ulyanovo, Russia 30 D9
Ulyanovsk = Simbirsk, Russia . 34 C9
Ulyasutay = Uliastay, Mongolia . 60 B4
Ulysses, U.S.A. 113 G4
Umag, Croatia 41 C10
Umala, Bolivia 124 G5
Uman, Ukraine 33 H6
Umaria, India 67 H12
Umarkot, Pakistan 66 G6
Umarpada, India 68 J5

Umatilla, *U.S.A.* 108 **D4**
Umbagog L., *U.S.A.* 117 **B13**
Umbakumba, *Australia* 94 **A2**
Umbértide, *Italy* 41 **E9**
Umbrella Mts., *N.Z.* 91 **L2**
Umbria □, *Italy* 41 **F9**
Umeå, *Sweden* 8 **E19**
Umeälven →, *Sweden* 8 **E19**
Umera, *Indonesia* 63 **E7**
Umfolozi ⌒, *S. Africa* 89 **D5**
Umfuli →, *Zimbabwe* 87 **F2**
Umfurudzi ⌒, *Zimbabwe* 87 **F3**
Umgusa, *Zimbabwe* 87 **F2**
Umm Urūmah, *Si. Arabia* ... 80 **B4**
Umka, *Serbia & M.* 44 **B4**
Umkomaas, *S. Africa* 89 **E5**
Umlazi, *S. Africa* 85 **L6**
Umm ad Daraj, J., *Jordan* ... 74 **C4**
Umm al Qaywayn, *U.A.E.* ... 71 **E7**
Umm Arda, *Sudan* 81 **D3**
Umm Bāb, *Qatar* 71 **E6**
Umm Badr, *Sudan* 81 **E2**
Umm Baiyud, *Sudan* 81 **E3**
Umm Bel, *Sudan* 81 **E2**
Umm Birkah, *Si. Arabia* 80 **B4**
Umm Boim, *Sudan* 81 **E2**
Umm Dam, *Sudan* 81 **E3**
Umm Debi, *Sudan* 81 **E3**
Umm Dubban, *Sudan* 81 **D3**
Umm Durman = Omdurmân,
 Sudan 81 **D3**
Umm el Fahm, *Israel* 74 **C4**
Umm Gafala, *Sudan* 81 **E2**
Umm Gimala, *Sudan* 81 **E2**
Umm Inderaba, *Sudan* 80 **D3**
Umm Keddada, *Sudan* 81 **E2**
Umm Koweika, *Sudan* 81 **E3**
Umm Lajj, *Si. Arabia* 70 **E3**
Umm Merwa, *Sudan* 80 **D3**
Umm Qantur, *Sudan* 81 **E3**
Umm Qurein, *Sudan* 81 **F2**
Umm Ruwaba, *Sudan* 81 **E3**
Umm Saiyala, *Sudan* 81 **D3**
Umm Shanqa, *Sudan* 81 **E2**
Umm Shutur, *Sudan* 81 **F3**
Umm Sidr, *Sudan* 81 **E2**
Umm Zehetir, *Egypt* 80 **J8**
Umnak I., *U.S.A.* 100 **C3**
Umniati →, *Zimbabwe* 87 **F2**
Umpqua →, *U.S.A.* 108 **E1**
Umreth, *India* 68 **H5**
Umtata, *S. Africa* 89 **E4**
Umuahia, *Nigeria* 83 **D6**
Umuarama, *Brazil* 127 **A5**
Umurbey, *Turkey* 45 **F10**
Umvukwe Ra., *Zimbabwe* ... 87 **F3**
Umzimvubu, *S. Africa* 89 **E4**
Umzingwane →, *Zimbabwe* .. 87 **G2**
Umzinto, *S. Africa* 89 **E5**
Una, *India* 68 **J4**
Una →, *Bos.-H.* 41 **D13**
Unac →, *Bos.-H.* 41 **D13**
Unadilla, *U.S.A.* 117 **D9**
Unalakleet, *U.S.A.* 100 **B3**
Unalaska, *U.S.A.* 100 **C3**
Unalaska I., *U.S.A.* 100 **C3**
'Unayzah, *Si. Arabia* 70 **E4**
'Unayzah, J., *Asia* 70 **C3**
Uncastillo, *Spain* 38 **C3**
Uncía, *Bolivia* 124 **G5**
Uncompahgre Peak, *U.S.A.* . 109 **G10**
Uncompahgre Plateau, *U.S.A.* 109 **G9**
Undara Volcanic ⌒, *Australia* . 94 **B3**
Unden, *Sweden* 11 **F8**
Underbool, *Australia* 95 **F3**
Undersaker, *Sweden* 10 **A7**
Unecha, *Russia* 33 **F7**
Ungarie, *Australia* 95 **E4**
Ungarra, *Australia* 95 **E2**
Ungava, Pén. d', *Canada* ... 101 **C12**
Ungava B., *Canada* 101 **C13**
Ungeny = Ungheni, *Moldova* . 29 **C12**
Unggi, *N. Korea* 57 **C16**
Ungheni, *Moldova* 29 **C12**
Unguala →, *Ethiopia* 81 **F5**
Ungwana B., *Kenya* 86 **C5**
Unguatiri, *Sudan* 81 **D4**
Uni, *Russia* 34 **B10**
União da Vitória, *Brazil* 127 **B5**
Uničov, *Czech Rep.* 27 **B10**
Uniejów, *Poland* 31 **G5**
Unije, *Croatia* 41 **D11**
Unimak I., *U.S.A.* 100 **C3**
Union, *Miss., U.S.A.* 113 **J10**
Union, *Mo., U.S.A.* 112 **F9**
Union, *S.C., U.S.A.* 115 **H5**
Union City, *Calif., U.S.A.* ... 110 **H4**
Union City, *N.J., U.S.A.* 117 **F10**
Union City, *Pa., U.S.A.* 116 **E5**
Union City, *Tenn., U.S.A.* ... 113 **G10**
Union Gap, *U.S.A.* 108 **C3**
Union Springs, *U.S.A.* 115 **J3**
Uniondale, *S. Africa* 88 **E3**
Uniontown, *U.S.A.* 114 **F6**
Unionville, *U.S.A.* 112 **E8**
Unirea, *Romania* 29 **F12**
United Arab Emirates ■, *Asia* . 71 **F7**
United Kingdom ■, *Europe* .. 7 **E5**
United States of America ■,
 N. Amer. 106 **C7**
Unity, *Canada* 103 **C7**
Universales, Mtes., *Spain* .. 38 **E3**
University Park, *U.S.A.* 109 **K10**
Unjha, *India* 68 **H5**
Unna, *Germany* 24 **D3**
Unnao, *India* 69 **F9**
Uno, Ilha, *Guinea-Biss.* 82 **C1**
Unsengedsi →, *Zimbabwe* .. 87 **F3**
Unst, *U.K.* 13 **A8**
Unstrut →, *Germany* 24 **D7**

Unterfranken □, *Germany* ... 25 **F5**
Unterschleissheim *Germany* . 25 **G7**
Unuk →, *Canada* 102 **B2**
Ünye, *Turkey* 72 **B7**
Unzen-Amakusa ⌒, *Japan* .. 55 **H5**
Unzha, *Russia* 34 **A7**
Unzha →, *Russia* 34 **B6**
Uozu, *Japan* 55 **F8**
Upata, *Venezuela* 124 **B6**
Upemba △, *Dem. Rep. of
 the Congo* 87 **D2**
Upemba, L., *Dem. Rep. of
 the Congo* 87 **D2**
Upernavik, *Greenland* 4 **B5**
Upington, *S. Africa* 88 **D3**
Upleta, *India* 68 **J4**
'Upolu, *Samoa* 91 **A13**
Upper □, *Ghana* 83 **C4**
Upper Alkali L., *U.S.A.* 108 **F3**
Upper Arrow L., *Canada* 102 **C5**
Upper Foster L., *Canada* 103 **B7**
Upper Hutt, *N.Z.* 91 **J5**
Upper Klamath L., *U.S.A.* ... 108 **E3**
Upper Lake, *U.S.A.* 110 **F4**
Upper Manzanilla, *Trin. & Tob.* . 125 **K15**
Upper Missouri River Breaks ⌒,
 U.S.A. 108 **C9**
Upper Musquodoboit, *Canada* 105 **C7**
Upper Red L., *U.S.A.* 112 **A7**
Upper Sandusky, *U.S.A.* 114 **E4**
Upper Volta = Burkina Faso ■,
 Africa 82 **C4**
Upphärad, *Sweden* 11 **F6**
Uppland, *Sweden* 10 **D12**
Upplands-Väsby *Sweden* 10 **E11**
Uppsala, *Sweden* 10 **E11**
Uppsala län □, *Sweden* 10 **D11**
Upshi, *India* 69 **C7**
Upstart, C., *Australia* 94 **B4**
Upton, *U.S.A.* 112 **C2**
Uqsuqtuuq = Gjoa Haven,
 Canada 100 **B10**
Ur, *Iraq* 70 **D5**
Urad Qianqi, *China* 56 **D5**
Urakawa, *Japan* 54 **C11**
Ural = Uralskiy □, *Russia* ... 52 **C7**
Ural = Zhayyq →, *Kazakhstan* 52 **E6**
Ural, *Australia* 95 **E4**
Ural Mts. = Uralskie Gory,
 Eurasia 52 **D6**
Uralla, *Australia* 95 **E5**
Uralsk = Oral, *Kazakhstan* .. 34 **E10**
Uralskie Gory, *Eurasia* 52 **D6**
Uralskiy □, *Russia* 52 **C7**
Urambo, *Tanzania* 86 **D3**
Urandangi, *Australia* 94 **C2**
Uranium City, *Canada* 103 **B7**
Uraricoera →, *Brazil* 124 **C6**
Urawa, *Japan* 55 **G9**
Uray, *Russia* 52 **C7**
'Uray'irah, *Si. Arabia* 71 **E6**
Urbana, *Ill., U.S.A.* 114 **E1**
Urbana, *Ohio, U.S.A.* 114 **E4**
Urbánia, *Italy* 41 **E9**
Urbel →, *Spain* 36 **C7**
Urbino, *Italy* 41 **E9**
Urbión, Picos de, *Spain* 38 **C2**
Urcos, *Peru* 124 **F4**
Urdinarrain, *Argentina* 126 **C4**
Urdos, *France* 20 **F3**
Urdzhar, *Kazakhstan* 52 **E9**
Ure →, *U.K.* 14 **C6**
Uren, *Russia* 34 **B7**
Ures, *Mexico* 118 **B2**
Urewera △, *N.Z.* 91 **H6**
Urfa = Şanlıurfa, *Turkey* ... 70 **B3**
Urganch, *Uzbekistan* 52 **E7**
Urgench = Urganch, *Uzbekistan* 52 **E7**
Ürgüp, *Turkey* 70 **B2**
Uri, *India* 69 **B6**
Uri □, *Switz.* 25 **J4**
Uribia, *Colombia* 124 **A4**
Uricani, *Romania* 28 **E8**
Uriondo, *Bolivia* 126 **A3**
Urique, *Mexico* 118 **B3**
Urique →, *Mexico* 118 **B3**
Urk, *Neths.* 17 **B5**
Urkiola ⌒, *Spain* 38 **B3**
Urla, *Turkey* 47 **C8**
Urlaţi, *Romania* 29 **F11**
Urmia = Orūmīyeh, *Iran* ... 70 **B5**
Uroševac, *Serbia & M.* 44 **D5**
Uroyan, Montañas de,
 Puerto Rico .... 121 **d**
Urshult, *Sweden* 11 **H8**
Uruaçu, *Brazil* 125 **F9**
Uruapan, *Mexico* 118 **D4**
Urubamba →, *Peru* 124 **F4**
Uruçara, *Brazil* 124 **D7**
Uruçuí, *Brazil* 125 **E10**
Uruguai →, *Brazil* 127 **B5**
Uruguaiana, *Brazil* 126 **B4**
Uruguay ■, *S. Amer.* 126 **C4**
Uruguay →, *S. Amer.* 126 **C4**
Urumchi = Ürümqi, *China* .. 52 **E9**
Ürümqi, *China* 52 **E9**
Urup →, *Russia* 35 **H5**
Urup, Ostrov, *Russia* 53 **E16**
Uryupinsk, *Russia* 34 **E5**
Urzhum, *Russia* 34 **B9**
Urziceni, *Romania* 29 **F11**
Usa →, *Russia* 52 **C6**
Uşak, *Turkey* 47 **C11**
Uşak □, *Turkey* 47 **C11**
Usakos, *Namibia* 88 **C2**
Ušće, *Serbia & M.* 44 **C4**
Usedom, *Germany* 24 **B10**
Usedom, *Germany* 24 **B10**
Useless Loop, *Australia* 93 **E1**
'Usfān, *Si. Arabia* 80 **C4**
Ush-Tobe, *Kazakhstan* 52 **E8**

Ushakova, Ostrov, *Russia* ... 4 **A12**
Ushakovo, *Russia* 30 **D7**
Ushant = Ouessant, Î. d', *France* 18 **D1**
Ushashi, *Tanzania* 86 **C3**
Ushat, *Sudan* 81 **F2**
'Ushayrah, *Si. Arabia* 80 **C5**
Ushibuka, *Japan* 55 **H5**
Ushuaia, *Argentina* 128 **G3**
Ushumun, *Russia* 53 **D13**
Ushytsya →, *Ukraine* 29 **B12**
Usk, *Canada* 102 **C3**
Usk →, *U.K.* 15 **F5**
Uska, *India* 69 **F10**
Üsküdar, *Turkey* 45 **F13**
Uslar, *Germany* 24 **D5**
Usman, *Russia* 33 **F10**
Usoke, *Tanzania* 86 **D3**
Usolye Sibirskoye, *Russia* .. 53 **D11**
Usoro, *Nigeria* 83 **D6**
Uspallata, P. de, *Argentina* . 126 **C2**
Uspenskiy, *Kazakhstan* 52 **E8**
Ussel, *France* 20 **C6**
Usson-du-Poitou, *France* ... 20 **B4**
Ussuri →, *Asia* 54 **A7**
Ussuriysk, *Russia* 53 **E14**
Ussurka, *Russia* 54 **B6**
Ust-Bolsheretsk, *Russia* 53 **D16**
Ust-Buzulukskaya, *Russia* .. 34 **E6**
Ust-Chaun, *Russia* 53 **C18**
Ust-Chorna, *Ukraine* 29 **B8**
Ust-Donetskiy, *Russia* 35 **G5**
Ust-Ilimsk, *Russia* 53 **D11**
Ust-Ishim, *Russia* 52 **D8**
Ust-Kamchatsk, *Russia* 53 **D17**
Ust-Kamenogorsk = Öskemen,
 Kazakhstan 52 **E9**
Ust-Khayryuzovo, *Russia* ... 53 **D16**
Ust-Kut, *Russia* 53 **D11**
Ust-Kuyga, *Russia* 53 **B14**
Ust-Labinsk, *Russia* 35 **H4**
Ust-Luga, *Russia* 32 **C5**
Ust-Maya, *Russia* 53 **C14**
Ust-Mil, *Russia* 53 **D14**
Ust-Nera, *Russia* 53 **C15**
Ust-Nyukzha, *Russia* 53 **D13**
Ust-Olenek, *Russia* 53 **B12**
Ust-Omchug, *Russia* 53 **C15**
Ust-Port, *Russia* 52 **C9**
Ust-Tsilma, *Russia* 52 **C6**
Ust Urt = Ustyurt Plateau, *Asia* . 52 **E6**
Ustaritz, *France* 20 **E2**
Ustecký □, *Czech Rep.* 26 **A7**
Uster, *Switz.* 25 **H4**
Ústí nad Labem, *Czech Rep.* . 26 **A7**
Ústí nad Orlicí, *Czech Rep.* . 27 **B9**
Ústica, *Italy* 42 **D6**
Ustinov = Izhevsk, *Russia* .. 52 **D6**
Ustka, *Poland* 30 **D3**
Ustroń, *Poland* 31 **J5**
Ustrzyki Dolne, *Poland* 31 **J9**
Ustyluh, *Ukraine* 31 **H11**
Ustyurt Plateau, *Asia* 52 **E6**
Ustyuzhna, *Russia* 32 **C9**
Usu, *China* 60 **B3**
Usuki, *Japan* 55 **H5**
Usulután, *El Salv.* 120 **D2**
Usumacinta →, *Mexico* 119 **D6**
Usumbura = Bujumbura, *Burundi* 86 **C2**
Usure, *Tanzania* 86 **C3**
Usutuo →, *Mozam.* 89 **D5**
Uta, *Indonesia* 63 **E9**
Utah □, *U.S.A.* 108 **G8**
Utah L., *U.S.A.* 108 **F8**
Utansjö, *Sweden* 10 **B11**
Utara, Selat, *Malaysia* ..... 65 **c**
Utarni, *India* 68 **F4**
Utatlan, *Guatemala* 120 **C1**
Ute Creek →, *U.S.A.* 113 **H3**
Utebo, *Spain* 38 **D3**
Utena, *Lithuania* 9 **J21**
Utete, *Tanzania* 86 **D4**
Uthai Thani, *Thailand* 64 **E3**
Uthal, *Pakistan* 68 **G2**
Utiariti, *Brazil* 124 **F7**
Utica, *N.Y., U.S.A.* 117 **C9**
Utica, *Ohio, U.S.A.* 116 **F2**
Utiel, *Spain* 39 **F3**
Utikuma L., *Canada* 102 **B5**
Utö, *Sweden* 10 **F12**
Utopia, *Australia* 94 **C1**
Utraula, *India* 69 **F10**
Utrecht, *Neths.* 17 **B5**
Utrecht, *S. Africa* 89 **D5**
Utrecht □, *Neths.* 17 **B5**
Utrera, *Spain* 37 **H5**
Utsjoki →, *Finland* 8 **B22**
Utsunomiya, *Japan* 55 **F9**
Uttar Pradesh □, *India* 69 **F9**
Uttaradit, *Thailand* 64 **D3**
Uttaranchal □, *India* 69 **D8**
Uttoxeter, *U.K.* 14 **E6**
Utuado, *Puerto Rico* .... 121 **d**
Uummannaq, *Greenland* ... 4 **B4**
Uummannaq, *Greenland* ... 4 **B5**
Uummannarsuaq = Nunap Isua,
 Greenland 101 **C15**
Uusikaarlepyy = Nykarleby,
 Finland 8 **E20**
Uusikaupunki, *Finland* 9 **F19**
Uva, *Russia* 34 **B11**
Uvac →, *Serbia & M.* 44 **C3**
Uvalde, *U.S.A.* 113 **L5**
Uvarovo, *Russia* 34 **E6**
Uvat, *Russia* 52 **D7**
Uvinza, *Tanzania* 86 **D3**
Uvira, *Dem. Rep. of the Congo* . 86 **C2**
Uvs Nuur, *Mongolia* 60 **A4**
'Uwairidh, Ḥarrat al, *Si. Arabia* . 70 **E3**
Uwajima, *Japan* 55 **H6**
Uwanda △, *Tanzania* 86 **D3**
Uweinat, Jebel, *Sudan* 80 **C1**
Uxbridge, *Canada* 116 **B5**

Uxin Qi, *China* 56 **E5**
Uxmal, *Mexico* 119 **C7**
Üydzin, *Mongolia* 56 **B4**
Uyo, *Nigeria* 83 **D6**
Üyüklü Tepe, *Turkey* 47 **D9**
Uyûn Mûsa, *Egypt* 74 **F1**
Uyuni, *Bolivia* 124 **H5**
Uzbekistan ■, *Asia* 52 **E7**
Uzen, Bolshoi →, *Kazakhstan* 35 **F9**
Uzen, Mal →, *Kazakhstan* .. 35 **F9**
Uzerche, *France* 20 **C5**
Uzès, *France* 21 **D8**
Uzh →, *Ukraine* 33 **G6**
Uzhgorod = Uzhhorod, *Ukraine* 28 **B7**
Uzhhorod, *Ukraine* 28 **B7**
Uzhok, *Ukraine* 28 **B7**
Užice, *Serbia & M.* 44 **C3**
Uzlovaya, *Russia* 32 **F10**
Üzümlü, *Turkey* 47 **E11**
Uzunköprü, *Turkey* 45 **E10**
Uzunkuyu, *Turkey* 47 **C8**

V

Vaal →, *S. Africa* 88 **D3**
Vaal Dam, *S. Africa* 89 **D4**
Vaalbos △, *S. Africa* 88 **D3**
Vaalwater, *S. Africa* 89 **C4**
Vaasa, *Finland* 8 **E19**
Vabre, *France* 20 **E6**
Vác, *Hungary* 28 **C4**
Vacaria, *Brazil* 127 **B5**
Vacaville, *U.S.A.* 110 **G5**
Vaccarès, Étang de, *France* . 21 **E8**
Vach = Vakh →, *Russia* 52 **C8**
Vache, Î. à, *Haiti* 121 **C5**
Väckelsång, *Sweden* 11 **H8**
Väddö, *Sweden* 10 **D12**
Väderstad, *Sweden* 11 **F8**
Vadnagar, *India* 68 **H5**
Vado Lígure, *Italy* 40 **D5**
Vadodara, *India* 68 **H5**
Vadsø, *Norway* 8 **A23**
Vadstena, *Sweden* 11 **F8**
Vaduz, *Liech.* 25 **H5**
Værøy, *Norway* 8 **C15**
Vágar, *Færøe Is.* 8 **E9**
Vaggeryd, *Sweden* 11 **G8**
Vagney, *France* 19 **D13**
Vagnhärad, *Sweden* 11 **F11**
Vagos, *Portugal* 36 **E2**
Vågsfjorden, *Norway* 8 **B17**
Váh →, *Slovak Rep.* 27 **D11**
Vahsel B., *Antarctica* 5 **D1**
Váhtjer = Gällivare, *Sweden* . 8 **C19**
Vaï, *Greece* 49 **D8**
Vaigach, *Russia* 52 **B6**
Vaiges, *France* 18 **D6**
Vaihingen, *Germany* 25 **G4**
Vail, *U.S.A.* 106 **C5**
Vailly-sur-Aisne, *France* 19 **C10**
Vaisali →, *India* 69 **F8**
Vaison-la-Romaine, *France* . 21 **D9**
Vakarel, *Bulgaria* 44 **D7**
Vakfıkebir, *Turkey* 73 **B8**
Vakh →, *Russia* 52 **C8**
Vakhtan, *Russia* 34 **B8**
Vál, *Hungary* 28 **C3**
Val-de-Marne □, *France* 19 **D9**
Val-d'Isère, *France* 21 **C10**
Val-d'Or □, *France* 19 **C9**
Val-d'Or, *Canada* 104 **C4**
Val Grande △, *Italy* 40 **B5**
Val Marie, *Canada* 103 **D7**
Val Thorens, *France* 21 **C10**
Valaam, *Russia* 32 **B6**
Valadares, *Portugal* 36 **D2**
Valahia, *Romania* 29 **F9**
Valais □, *Switz.* 25 **J3**
Valais, Alpes du, *Switz.* 25 **J3**
Valandovo, *Macedonia* 44 **E6**
Valašské Meziříčí, *Czech Rep.* 27 **B10**
Valáxa, *Greece* 46 **C6**
Válberg, *Sweden* 10 **E7**
Valbo, *Sweden* 10 **D10**
Valbondione, *Italy* 40 **B7**
Vălcani, *Romania* 28 **D5**
Vâlcea □, *Romania* 29 **F9**
Valchetta, *Argentina* 128 **E3**
Valdagno, *Italy* 41 **C8**
Valdahon, *France* 19 **E13**
Valdai Hills = Valdayskaya
 Vozvyshennost, *Russia* ... 32 **D7**
Valday, *Russia* 32 **D7**
Valdayskaya Vozvyshennost,
 Russia 32 **D7**
Valdeazogues →, *Spain* 37 **G6**
Valdecañas, Embalse de, *Spain* 36 **F5**
Valdemarsvik, *Sweden* 11 **F10**
Valdemoro, *Spain* 36 **E7**
Valdepeñas, *Spain* 37 **G7**
Valderaduey →, *Spain* 36 **D5**
Valderrobres, *Spain* 38 **E5**
Valdés, Pen., *Argentina* 128 **E4**
Valdez, *U.S.A.* 100 **B5**
Valdivia, *Chile* 128 **D2**
Valdobbiádene, *Italy* 41 **C8**
Valdosta, *U.S.A.* 115 **K4**
Valdoviño, *Spain* 36 **B2**
Valdres, *Norway* 9 **F13**
Vale, *Georgia* 35 **K6**
Vale, *U.S.A.* 108 **E5**
Vale of Glamorgan □, *U.K.* . 15 **F4**
Valea lui Mihai, *Romania* .. 28 **C7**
Valea Mărului, *Romania* ... 29 **E12**
Valemount, *Canada* 102 **C5**
Valença, *Brazil* 125 **F11**

Valença, *Portugal* 36 **C2**
Valença do Piauí, *Brazil* 125 **E10**
Valençay, *France* 19 **E8**
Valence, *France* 21 **D8**
Valence d'Agen, *France* 20 **D4**
Valencia, *Spain* 39 **F4**
Valencia, *Trin. & Tob.* 125 **K15**
Valencia, *U.S.A.* 109 **J10**
Valencia, *Venezuela* 124 **A5**
Valencia □, *Spain* 39 **F4**
Valencia ✈ (VLC), *Spain* ... 39 **F4**
Valencia, G. de, *Spain* 39 **F5**
Valencia de Alcántara, *Spain* 37 **F3**
Valencia de Don Juan, *Spain* 36 **C5**
Valencia I., *Ireland* 12 **E1**
Valenciennes, *France* 19 **B10**
Văleni, *Romania* 29 **F9**
Vălenii de Munte, *Romania* . 29 **E11**
Valensole, *France* 21 **E9**
Valentigney, *France* 19 **E13**
Valentim, Sa. do, *Brazil* 125 **E10**
Valentin, *Russia* 54 **C7**
Valentine, *U.S.A.* 113 **K2**
Valenza, *Italy* 40 **C5**
Valera, *Venezuela* 124 **B4**
Valga, *Estonia* 9 **H22**
Valguarnera Caropepe, *Italy* . 43 **E7**
Valier, *U.S.A.* 108 **B7**
Valinco, G. de, *France* 21 **G12**
Valjevo, *Serbia & M.* 44 **B3**
Valka, *Latvia* 9 **H21**
Valkeakoski, *Finland* 9 **F20**
Valkenswaard, *Neths.* 17 **C5**
Vall de Uxó = La Vall d'Uixó,
 Spain 38 **F4**
Valla, *Sweden* 10 **E10**
Valladolid, *Mexico* 119 **C7**
Valladolid, *Spain* 36 **D6**
Valladolid □, *Spain* 36 **D6**
Vallata, *Italy* 43 **A8**
Valldemossa, *Spain* 48 **B9**
Valle d'Aosta □, *Italy* 40 **C4**
Valle de Arán, *Spain* 38 **C5**
Valle de la Pascua, *Venezuela* 124 **B5**
Valle de las Palmas, *Mexico* . 111 **N10**
Valle de Santiago, *Mexico* .. 118 **C4**
Valle de Suchil, *Mexico* 118 **C4**
Valle de Zaragoza, *Mexico* .. 118 **B3**
Valle del Ticino ⌒, *Italy* 40 **C6**
Valle Fértil, Sierra del, *Argentina* 126 **C2**
Valle Gran Rey, *Canary Is.* .. 48 **F2**
Valle Hermoso, *Mexico* 119 **B5**
Valledupar, *Colombia* 124 **A4**
Vallehermoso, *Canary Is.* ... 48 **F2**
Vallejo, *U.S.A.* 110 **G4**
Vallenar, *Chile* 126 **B1**
Vallentuna, *Sweden* 10 **E12**
Valleraugue, *France* 20 **D7**
Vallet, *France* 18 **E5**
Valletta, *Malta* 49 **D2**
Valley Center, *U.S.A.* 111 **M9**
Valley City, *U.S.A.* 112 **B6**
Valley Falls, *Oreg., U.S.A.* .. 108 **E3**
Valley Falls, *R.I., U.S.A.* 117 **E13**
Valley of the Kings, *Egypt* .. 80 **B3**
Valley Springs, *U.S.A.* 110 **G6**
Valley View, *U.S.A.* 117 **F8**
Valley Wells, *U.S.A.* 111 **K11**
Valleyview, *Canada* 102 **B5**
Valli di Comácchio, *Italy* ... 41 **D9**
Vallimanca, Arroyo, *Argentina* 126 **D4**
Vallo della Lucánia, *Italy* ... 43 **B8**
Vallon-Pont-d'Arc, *France* .. 21 **D8**
Vallorbe, *Switz.* 25 **J2**
Valls, *Spain* 38 **D6**
Valmaseda = Balmaseda, *Spain* 38 **B1**
Valmiera, *Latvia* 9 **H21**
Valnera, *Spain* 36 **B7**
Valognes, *France* 18 **C5**
Valona = Vlorë, *Albania* 44 **F3**
Valongo, *Portugal* 36 **D2**
Valozhyn, *Belarus* 32 **E4**
Valpaços, *Portugal* 36 **D3**
Valparaíso, *Chile* 126 **C1**
Valparaíso, *Mexico* 118 **C4**
Valparaiso, *U.S.A.* 114 **E2**
Valparaíso □, *Chile* 126 **C1**
Valpovo, *Croatia* 28 **E3**
Valréas, *France* 21 **D9**
Vals, *Switz.* 25 **J5**
Vals →, *S. Africa* 88 **D4**
Vals, Tanjung, *Indonesia* ... 63 **F9**
Vals-les-Bains, *France* 21 **D8**
Valsad, *India* 66 **J8**
Valtellina, *Italy* 40 **B6**
Valuyki, *Russia* 33 **G10**
Valverde, *Canary Is.* 48 **G2**
Valverde del Camino, *Spain* . 37 **H4**
Valverde del Fresno, *Spain* . 36 **E4**
Vama, *Romania* 29 **C10**
Vamdrup, *Denmark* 11 **J3**
Vámhus, *Sweden* 10 **C8**
Vammala, *Finland* 9 **F20**
Vámos, *Greece* 49 **D6**
Van, *Turkey* 70 **B4**
Van, L. = Van Gölü, *Turkey* . 70 **B4**
Van Alstyne, *U.S.A.* 113 **J6**
Van Blommestein Meer,
 Suriname 125 **C7**
Van Buren, *Canada* 105 **C6**
Van Buren, *Ark., U.S.A.* 113 **H7**
Van Buren, *Maine, U.S.A.* .. 115 **B11**
Van Buren, *Mo., U.S.A.* 113 **G9**
Van Canh, *Vietnam* 64 **F7**
Van Diemen, C., *N. Terr.,
 Australia* 92 **B5**
Van Diemen, C., *Queens.,
 Australia* 94 **B2**
Van Diemen G., *Australia* .. 92 **B5**
Van Gölü, *Turkey* 70 **B4**
Van Horn, *U.S.A.* 113 **K2**

Van Ninh, *Vietnam* ... 64 F7
Van Rees, Pegunungan, *Indonesia* ... 63 E9
Van Wert, *U.S.A.* ... 114 E3
Van Yen, *Vietnam* ... 58 G5
Vanadzor, *Armenia* ... 35 K7
Vanavara, *Russia* ... 53 C11
Vancouver, *Canada* ... 102 D4
Vancouver, *U.S.A.* ... 110 E4
Vancouver, C., *Australia* ... 93 G2
Vancouver I., *Canada* ... 102 D3
Vancouver International ✈
  (YVR), *U.S.A.* ... 110 A3
Vanda = Vantaa, *Finland* ... 9 F21
Vandalia, *Ill., U.S.A.* ... 112 F10
Vandalia, *Mo., U.S.A.* ... 112 F9
Vanderbijlpark, *S. Africa* ... 89 D4
Vandergrift, *U.S.A.* ... 116 F5
Vanderhoof, *Canada* ... 102 C4
Vanderkloof Dam, *S. Africa* ... 88 E3
Vanderlin I., *Australia* ... 94 B2
Vänern, *Sweden* ... 11 F7
Vänersborg, *Sweden* ... 11 F6
Vang Vieng, *Laos* ... 64 C4
Vanga, *Kenya* ... 86 C4
Vangaindrano, *Madag.* ... 89 C8
Vanguard, *Canada* ... 103 D7
Vanino, *Russia* ... 53 E15
Vânju Mare, *Romania* ... 28 F7
Vanna, *Norway* ... 8 A18
Vännäs, *Sweden* ... 8 E18
Vannes, *France* ... 18 E4
Vanoise, Massif de la, *France* ... 21 C10
Vanrhynsdorp, *S. Africa* ... 88 E2
Vansbro, *Sweden* ... 10 D8
Vansittart B., *Australia* ... 92 B4
Vantaa, *Finland* ... 9 F21
Vanua Balavu, *Fiji* ... 91 C9
Vanua Levu, *Fiji* ... 91 C8
Vanuatu ■, *Pac. Oc.* ... 96 J8
Vanwyksvlei, *S. Africa* ... 88 E3
Vanzylsrus, *S. Africa* ... 88 D3
Vapnyarka, *Ukraine* ... 29 B13
Var □, *France* ... 21 E10
Var →, *France* ... 21 E11
Vara, *Sweden* ... 11 F6
Varades, *France* ... 18 E5
Varáita →, *Italy* ... 40 D4
Varallo, *Italy* ... 40 C5
Varāmīn, *Iran* ... 71 C6
Varāmīn □, *Iran* ... 71 B6
Varanasi, *India* ... 69 G10
Varangerfjorden, *Norway* ... 8 A23
Varangerhalvøya, *Norway* ... 8 A23
Varano, Lago di, *Italy* ... 41 G12
Varaždin, *Croatia* ... 41 B13
Varazze, *Italy* ... 40 D5
Varberg, *Sweden* ... 11 G6
Vardak □, *Afghan.* ... 66 B6
Vardar = Axiós →, *Greece* ... 44 F6
Varde, *Denmark* ... 11 J2
Varde Å →, *Denmark* ... 11 J2
Vardø, *Norway* ... 8 A24
Varel, *Germany* ... 24 B4
Varella, Mui, *Vietnam* ... 64 F7
Varėna, *Lithuania* ... 9 J21
Varennes-sur-Allier, *France* ... 19 F10
Varennes-Vauzelles, *France* ... 19 E10
Vareš, *Bos.-H.* ... 28 F3
Varese, *Italy* ... 40 C5
Vârfurile, *Romania* ... 28 D7
Vårgårda, *Sweden* ... 11 F6
Varginha, *Brazil* ... 127 A6
Vargön, *Sweden* ... 11 F6
Varillas, *Chile* ... 126 A1
Varkaus, *Finland* ... 9 E22
Värmdölandet, *Sweden* ... 10 E12
Värmeln, *Sweden* ... 10 E6
Värmlands län □, *Sweden* ... 10 E6
Värmlandsbro, *Sweden* ... 10 E7
Varna, *Bulgaria* ... 45 C11
Varna □, *Bulgaria* ... 45 C11
Värnamo, *Sweden* ... 11 G8
Varnsdorf, *Czech Rep.* ... 26 A7
Várpalota, *Hungary* ... 28 C3
Vars, *Canada* ... 117 A9
Vars, *France* ... 21 D10
Varto, *Turkey* ... 73 C9
Varvarin, *Serbia & M.* ... 44 C5
Varysburg, *U.S.A.* ... 116 D6
Varzaneh, *Iran* ... 71 C7
Varzi, *Italy* ... 40 D6
Varzo, *Italy* ... 40 B5
Varzy, *France* ... 19 E10
Vas □, *Hungary* ... 28 C1
Vasa = Vaasa, *Finland* ... 8 E19
Vasa Barris →, *Brazil* ... 125 F11
Vásárosnamény, *Hungary* ... 28 B7
Vascão →, *Portugal* ... 37 H3
Vaşcău, *Romania* ... 28 D7
Vascongadas = País Vasco □,
  Spain ... 38 C2
Vashkivtsi, *Ukraine* ... 29 B10
Vasht = Khāsh, *Iran* ... 66 E2
Vasilevichi, *Belarus* ... 33 F5
Vasilikón, *Greece* ... 46 C5
Vasilkov = Vasylkiv, *Ukraine* ... 33 G6
Vaslui, *Romania* ... 29 D12
Vaslui □, *Romania* ... 29 D12
Väsman, *Sweden* ... 10 D9
Vassar, *Canada* ... 103 D9
Vassar, *U.S.A.* ... 114 D4
Västerås, *Sweden* ... 10 E10
Västerbotten, *Sweden* ... 8 D18
Västerdalälven →, *Sweden* ... 10 D8
Västergötland, *Sweden* ... 11 F7
Västerhaninge, *Sweden* ... 10 E12
Västervik, *Sweden* ... 11 G10
Västmanland, *Sweden* ... 9 G16
Västmanlands län □, *Sweden* ... 10 E10
Vasto, *Italy* ... 41 F11

Västra Götalands Län □, *Sweden* ... 11 F6
Vasvár, *Hungary* ... 28 C1
Vasylivka, *Ukraine* ... 29 E13
Vasylkiv, *Ukraine* ... 33 G6
Vatan, *France* ... 19 E8
Vatersay, *U.K.* ... 13 E1
Váthia, *Greece* ... 46 E4
Vatican City ■, *Europe* ... 41 G9
Vaticano, C., *Italy* ... 43 D8
Vatili, *Cyprus* ... 49 D12
Vatin, *Serbia & M.* ... 28 E6
Vatnajökull, *Iceland* ... 8 D5
Vatoa, *Fiji* ... 91 D9
Vatólakkos, *Greece* ... 49 D5
Vatoloha, *Madag.* ... 89 B8
Vatra-Dornei, *Romania* ... 29 C10
Vatrak →, *India* ... 68 H5
Vättern, *Sweden* ... 11 F8
Vaucluse □, *France* ... 21 E9
Vaucouleurs, *France* ... 19 D12
Vaud □, *Switz.* ... 25 J2
Vaudreuil-Dorion, *Canada* ... 117 A10
Vaughn, *Mont., U.S.A.* ... 108 C8
Vaughn, *N. Mex., U.S.A.* ... 109 J11
Vaujours L., *Canada* ... 104 A5
Vaupés →, *Brazil* ... 124 C5
Vaupes □, *Colombia* ... 124 C4
Vauvert, *France* ... 21 E8
Vauxhall, *Canada* ... 102 C6
Vav, *India* ... 68 G4
Vavatenina, *Madag.* ... 89 B8
Vava'u, *Tonga* ... 91 D12
Vavoua, *Ivory C.* ... 82 D3
Vawkavysk, *Belarus* ... 33 F3
Vaxholm, *Sweden* ... 10 E12
Växjö, *Sweden* ... 11 H8
Våxtorp, *Sweden* ... 11 H7
Vaygach, Ostrov, *Russia* ... 52 C6
Váyia, *Greece* ... 46 C5
Váyia, Ákra, *Greece* ... 49 C10
Veaikevárri = Svappavaara,
  Sweden ... 8 C19
Vechelde, *Germany* ... 24 C6
Vechta, *Germany* ... 24 C4
Vechte →, *Neths.* ... 17 B6
Vecsés, *Hungary* ... 28 C4
Veddige, *Sweden* ... 11 G6
Vedea →, *Romania* ... 29 G10
Vedia, *Argentina* ... 126 C3
Vedrette di Ries-Aurina □, *Italy* ... 41 B9
Vedum, *Sweden* ... 11 F7
Veendam, *Neths.* ... 17 A6
Veenendaal, *Neths.* ... 17 B5
Vefsna →, *Norway* ... 8 D15
Vega, *Norway* ... 8 D14
Vega, *U.S.A.* ... 113 H3
Vega Baja, *Puerto Rico* ... 121 d
Vegadeo, *Spain* ... 36 B3
Vegorrítis, Límni, *Greece* ... 44 F5
Vegreville, *Canada* ... 102 C6
Veinge, *Sweden* ... 11 H7
Veisiejai, *Lithuania* ... 30 D10
Vejbystrand, *Sweden* ... 11 H6
Vejen, *Denmark* ... 11 J3
Vejer de la Frontera, *Spain* ... 37 J5
Vejle, *Denmark* ... 11 J3
Vejle Amtskommune □,
  Denmark ... 11 J3
Vejle Fjord, *Denmark* ... 11 J3
Vela Luka, *Croatia* ... 41 F13
Velas, C., *Costa Rica* ... 120 D2
Velasco, Sierra de, *Argentina* ... 126 B2
Velay, Mts. du, *France* ... 20 D7
Velbert, *Germany* ... 24 D3
Velddrif, *S. Africa* ... 88 E2
Velebit □, *Croatia* ... 41 D12
Velebit Planina, *Croatia* ... 41 D12
Velebitski Kanal, *Croatia* ... 41 D11
Veleka →, *Bulgaria* ... 45 D11
Velenje, *Slovenia* ... 41 B12
Veles, *Macedonia* ... 44 E5
Velestínon, *Greece* ... 46 B4
Vélez-Málaga, *Spain* ... 37 J6
Vélez Rubio, *Spain* ... 39 H2
Velhas →, *Brazil* ... 125 G10
Velika, *Croatia* ... 28 E2
Velika Gorica, *Croatia* ... 41 C13
Velika Kapela, *Croatia* ... 41 C12
Velika Kladuša, *Bos.-H.* ... 41 C12
Velika Kruša, *Serbia & M.* ... 44 D4
Velika Morava →, *Serbia & M.* ... 44 B5
Velika Plana, *Serbia & M.* ... 44 B5
Velikaya →, *Russia* ... 32 D5
Velikaya Kema, *Russia* ... 54 B8
Velikaya Lepetikha, *Ukraine* ... 33 J7
Veliké Kapušany, *Slovak Rep.* ... 27 C15
Velike Lašče, *Slovenia* ... 41 C11
Veliki Jastrebac, *Serbia & M.* ... 44 C5
Veliki Kanal, *Serbia & M.* ... 28 E4
Veliki Popović, *Serbia & M.* ... 44 B5
Velikiye Luki, *Russia* ... 32 D6
Veliko Gradište, *Serbia & M.* ... 44 B5
Veliko Tŭrnovo, *Bulgaria* ... 45 C9
Velikonda Range, *India* ... 66 M11
Vélingara, *Kolda, Senegal* ... 82 C2
Vélingara, *Louga, Senegal* ... 82 B2
Velingrad, *Bulgaria* ... 44 D7
Velino, Mte., *Italy* ... 41 F10
Velizh, *Russia* ... 32 E6
Velké Karlovice, *Czech Rep.* ... 27 B11
Velké Meziříčí, *Czech Rep.* ... 26 B9
Vel'ký Javorník, *Slovak Rep.* ... 27 B11
Vel'ký Krtíš, *Slovak Rep.* ... 27 C12
Vel'ký Meder, *Slovak Rep.* ... 27 D10
Vel'ký Tribeč, *Slovak Rep.* ... 27 C11
Velletri, *Italy* ... 42 A5
Vellinge, *Sweden* ... 11 J6
Vellmar, *Germany* ... 24 D5
Vellore, *India* ... 66 N11

Velsk, *Russia* ... 32 B11
Velten, *Germany* ... 24 C9
Veluwezoom △, *Neths.* ... 17 B6
Velva, *U.S.A.* ... 112 A4
Velvendós, *Greece* ... 44 F6
Velyka Mykhaylivka, *Ukraine* ... 29 C14
Velyki Luchky, *Ukraine* ... 28 B7
Velykyy Bereznyy, *Ukraine* ... 28 B7
Velykyy Bychkiv, *Ukraine* ... 29 C9
Vemb, *Denmark* ... 11 H2
Vemdalen, *Sweden* ... 10 B7
Ven, *Sweden* ... 11 J6
Venaco, *France* ... 21 F13
Venado Tuerto, *Argentina* ... 126 C3
Venafro, *Italy* ... 43 A7
Venarey-les-Laumes, *France* ... 19 E11
Venaría, *Italy* ... 40 C4
Venčane, *Serbia & M.* ... 44 B4
Vence, *France* ... 21 E11
Vendas Novas, *Portugal* ... 37 G2
Vendée □, *France* ... 18 F5
Vendée →, *France* ... 18 F5
Vendéen, Bocage, *France* ... 20 B2
Vendeuvre-sur-Barse, *France* ... 19 D11
Vendôme, *France* ... 18 E8
Vendrell = El Vendrell, *Spain* ... 38 D6
Vendsyssel, *Denmark* ... 11 G4
Vendychany, *Ukraine* ... 29 B12
Venelles, *France* ... 21 E9
Véneta, L., *Italy* ... 41 C9
Véneto □, *Italy* ... 41 C9
Venev, *Russia* ... 32 E10
Venézia, *Italy* ... 41 C9
Venézia, G. di, *Italy* ... 41 C10
Venezuela ■, *S. Amer.* ... 124 B5
Venezuela, G. de, *Venezuela* ... 124 A4
Vengurla, *India* ... 66 M8
Venice = Venézia, *Italy* ... 41 C9
Venice, *U.S.A.* ... 115 M4
Vénissieux, *France* ... 21 C8
Venjansjön, *Sweden* ... 10 D8
Venlo, *Neths.* ... 17 C6
Vennesla, *Norway* ... 9 G12
Venosa, *Italy* ... 43 B8
Venray, *Neths.* ... 17 C6
Venta →, *Latvia* ... 30 B9
Venta →, *Latvia* ... 30 A8
Venta de Baños, *Spain* ... 36 D6
Venta de Cardeña = Cardeña,
  Spain ... 37 G6
Ventana, Punta de la, *Mexico* ... 118 C3
Ventana, Sa. de la, *Argentina* ... 126 D3
Ventersburg, *S. Africa* ... 88 D4
Venterstad, *S. Africa* ... 88 E4
Ventimíglia, *Italy* ... 40 E4
Ventnor, *U.K.* ... 15 G6
Ventotene, *Italy* ... 42 B6
Ventoux, Mt., *France* ... 21 D9
Ventspils, *Latvia* ... 9 H19
Ventspils □, *Latvia* ... 30 A8
Ventuarí →, *Venezuela* ... 124 C5
Ventucopa, *U.S.A.* ... 111 L7
Ventura, *U.S.A.* ... 111 L7
Venus B., *Australia* ... 95 F4
Vera, *Argentina* ... 126 B3
Vera, *Spain* ... 39 H3
Veracruz, *Mexico* ... 119 D5
Veracruz □, *Mexico* ... 119 D5
Veraval, *India* ... 68 J4
Verbánia, *Italy* ... 40 C5
Verbicaro, *Italy* ... 43 C8
Verbier, *Switz.* ... 25 J3
Vercelli, *Italy* ... 40 C5
Verchovchevo, *Ukraine* ... 33 H8
Vercors △, *France* ... 21 D9
Verdalsøra, *Norway* ... 8 E14
Verde →, *Argentina* ... 128 E3
Verde →, *Goiás, Brazil* ... 125 G8
Verde →, *Mato Grosso do Sul,
  Brazil* ... 125 H8
Verde →, *Chihuahua, Mexico* ... 118 B3
Verde →, *Oaxaca, Mexico* ... 119 D5
Verde →, *Veracruz, Mexico* ... 118 C4
Verde →, *Paraguay* ... 126 A4
Verde →, *U.S.A.* ... 106 D4
Verde, Cay, *Bahamas* ... 120 B4
Verde Island Pass, *Phil.* ... 61 E4
Verden, *Germany* ... 24 C5
Verdhikoúsa, *Greece* ... 46 B3
Verdi, *U.S.A.* ... 110 F7
Verdon →, *France* ... 21 E10
Verdon △, *France* ... 21 E10
Verdun, *France* ... 19 C12
Verdun-sur-le-Doubs, *France* ... 19 F12
Vereeniging, *S. Africa* ... 89 D4
Verga, C., *Guinea* ... 82 C2
Vergara, *Uruguay* ... 127 C5
Vergato, *Italy* ... 40 D8
Vergemont Cr. →, *Australia* ... 94 C3
Vergennes, *U.S.A.* ... 117 B11
Vergt, *France* ... 20 C4
Verín, *Spain* ... 36 D3

Vermont □, *U.S.A.* ... 117 C12
Vermosh, *Albania* ... 44 D3
Vernadsky, *Antarctica* ... 5 C17
Vernal, *U.S.A.* ... 108 F9
Vernalis, *U.S.A.* ... 110 H5
Vernazza, *Italy* ... 40 D6
Verner, *Canada* ... 104 C3
Verneuil-sur-Avre, *France* ... 18 D7
Verneukpan, *S. Africa* ... 88 E3
Vernier, *Switz.* ... 25 J2
Vérnio, *Italy* ... 40 D8
Vernon, *Canada* ... 102 C5
Vernon, *France* ... 18 C8
Vernon, *U.S.A.* ... 113 H5
Vernonia, *U.S.A.* ... 110 E3
Vernouillet, *France* ... 18 D8
Véroia, *Greece* ... 44 F6
Verona, *Canada* ... 117 B8
Verona, *Italy* ... 40 C7
Verona, *U.S.A.* ... 112 D10
Verrès, *Italy* ... 40 C4
Versailles, *France* ... 19 D9
Versmold, *Germany* ... 24 C4
Vert, C., *Senegal* ... 82 C1
Vertou, *France* ... 18 E5
Vertus, *France* ... 19 D11
Verulam, *S. Africa* ... 89 D5
Verviers, *Belgium* ... 17 D5
Vervins, *France* ... 19 C10
Veržej, *Slovenia* ... 41 B13
Verzy, *France* ... 19 C11
Vescovato, *France* ... 21 F13
Veselí nad Lužnicí, *Czech Rep.* ... 26 B7
Veselie, *Bulgaria* ... 45 D11
Veselovskoye Vdkhr., *Russia* ... 35 G5
Veshenskaya, *Russia* ... 34 F5
Vesle →, *France* ... 19 C10
Vesoul, *France* ... 19 E13
Vesterålen, *Norway* ... 8 B16
Vestfjorden, *Norway* ... 8 C15
Vestmannaeyjar, *Iceland* ... 8 E3
Vestsjællands Amtskommune □,
  Denmark ... 11 J5
Vestspitsbergen, *Svalbard* ... 4 B8
Vestvågøy, *Norway* ... 8 B15
Vesuvio, *Italy* ... 43 B7
Vesuvius, Mt. = Vesuvio, *Italy* ... 43 B7
Vesyegonsk, *Russia* ... 32 C9
Veszprém, *Hungary* ... 28 C2
Veszprém □, *Hungary* ... 28 C2
Vésztő, *Hungary* ... 28 D6
Vetlanda, *Sweden* ... 11 G9
Vetluga, *Russia* ... 34 B7
Vetlugu →, *Russia* ... 34 B8
Vetluzhskiy, *Kostroma, Russia* ... 34 A7
Vetluzhskiy, *Nizhniy Novgorod,
  Russia* ... 34 B7
Vetovo, *Bulgaria* ... 45 C10
Vetralla, *Italy* ... 41 F9
Vetren, *Bulgaria* ... 45 D8
Vettore, Mte., *Italy* ... 41 F10
Veurne, *Belgium* ... 17 C2
Veveno →, *Sudan* ... 81 F3
Vevey, *Switz.* ... 25 J2
Vévi, *Greece* ... 44 F5
Veynes, *France* ... 21 D9
Veys, *Iran* ... 71 D6
Vézelay, *France* ... 19 E10
Vézelise, *France* ... 19 D13
Vézère →, *France* ... 20 D4
Vezhen, *Bulgaria* ... 45 D8
Vezirköprü, *Turkey* ... 72 B6
Vezzani, *France* ... 21 F13
Vi Thanh, *Vietnam* ... 65 H5
Viacha, *Bolivia* ... 124 G5
Viadana, *Italy* ... 40 D7
Viamão, *Brazil* ... 127 C5
Viana, *Brazil* ... 125 D10
Viana, *Spain* ... 38 C2
Viana do Alentejo, *Portugal* ... 37 G3
Viana do Bolo, *Spain* ... 36 C3
Viana do Castelo, *Portugal* ... 36 D2
Viana do Castelo □, *Portugal* ... 36 D2
Vianden, *Lux.* ... 17 E6
Viangchan = Vientiane, *Laos* ... 64 D4
Vianópolis, *Brazil* ... 125 G9
Viar →, *Spain* ... 37 H5
Viaréggio, *Italy* ... 40 E7
Viaur →, *France* ... 20 D5
Vibble, *Sweden* ... 11 G12
Vibo Valéntia, *Italy* ... 43 D9
Viborg, *Denmark* ... 11 H3
Viborg Amtskommune □,
  Denmark ... 11 H3
Vibraye, *France* ... 18 D7
Vic, *Spain* ... 38 D7
Vic, Étang de, *France* ... 20 E7
Vic-en-Bigorre, *France* ... 20 E4
Vic-Fezensac, *France* ... 20 E4
Vic-le-Comte, *France* ... 19 G10
Vic-sur-Cère, *France* ... 20 D6
Vícar, *Spain* ... 39 J2
Vicenza, *Italy* ... 41 C8
Vich = Vic, *Spain* ... 38 D7
Vichada →, *Colombia* ... 124 C5
Vichuga, *Russia* ... 34 B5
Vichy, *France* ... 19 F10
Vicksburg, *Ariz., U.S.A.* ... 111 M13
Vicksburg, *Miss., U.S.A.* ... 113 J9
Vico, *France* ... 21 F12
Vico, L. di, *Italy* ... 41 F9
Vico del Gargano, *Italy* ... 41 G12
Vicovu de Sus, *Romania* ... 29 C10
Victor, *India* ... 68 J4
Victor, *U.S.A.* ... 116 D7
Victor Harbor, *Australia* ... 95 F2
Victoria, *Argentina* ... 126 C3
Victoria, *Canada* ... 102 D4
Victoria, *Chile* ... 128 D2

Victoria, *Guinea* ... 82 C2
Victoria, *Malta* ... 49 C1
Victoria, *Phil.* ... 61 D4
Victoria, *Romania* ... 29 E9
Victoria, *Kans., U.S.A.* ... 112 F5
Victoria, *Tex., U.S.A.* ... 113 L6
Victoria □, *Australia* ... 95 F3
Victoria →, *Australia* ... 92 C4
Victoria, Grand L., *Canada* ... 104 C4
Victoria, L., *Africa* ... 86 C3
Victoria, L., *Australia* ... 95 E3
Victoria, Mt., *Burma* ... 67 J18
Victoria Beach, *Canada* ... 103 C9
Victoria de Durango = Durango,
  Mexico ... 118 C4
Victoria de las Tunas, *Cuba* ... 120 B4
Victoria Falls, *Zimbabwe* ... 87 F2
Victoria Harbour, *Canada* ... 116 B5
Victoria I., *Canada* ... 100 A8
Victoria L., *Canada* ... 105 C8
Victoria Ld., *Antarctica* ... 5 D11
Victoria Nile →, *Uganda* ... 86 B3
Victoria River, *Australia* ... 92 C5
Victoria Str., *Canada* ... 100 B9
Victoria West, *S. Africa* ... 88 E3
Victorias, *Phil.* ... 61 F5
Victoriaville, *Canada* ... 105 C5
Victorica, *Argentina* ... 126 D2
Victorville, *U.S.A.* ... 111 L9
Vicuña, *Chile* ... 126 C1
Vicuña Mackenna, *Argentina* ... 126 C3
Vidal, *U.S.A.* ... 111 L12
Vidal Junction, *U.S.A.* ... 111 L12
Vidalia, *U.S.A.* ... 115 J4
Vidamlya, *Belarus* ... 31 F10
Vidauban, *France* ... 21 E10
Videbæk, *Denmark* ... 11 H2
Videle, *Romania* ... 29 F10
Vídho, *Greece* ... 49 A3
Vidigueira, *Portugal* ... 37 G3
Vidin, *Bulgaria* ... 44 C6
Vidisha, *India* ... 68 H7
Vidra, *Romania* ... 29 E11
Viduša, *Bos.-H.* ... 44 D2
Vidzy, *Belarus* ... 9 J22
Viechtach, *Germany* ... 25 F8
Viedma, *Argentina* ... 128 E4
Viedma, L., *Argentina* ... 128 F2
Vieira do Minho, *Portugal* ... 36 D2
Vielha, *Spain* ... 38 C5
Viella = Vielha, *Spain* ... 38 C5
Vielsalm, *Belgium* ... 17 D5
Vienenburg, *Germany* ... 24 D6
Vieng Pou Kha, *Laos* ... 58 G3
Vienna = Wien, *Austria* ... 27 C9
Vienna, *Ill., U.S.A.* ... 113 G10
Vienna, *Mo., U.S.A.* ... 112 F9
Vienne, *France* ... 21 C8
Vienne □, *France* ... 20 B4
Vienne →, *France* ... 18 E7
Vientiane, *Laos* ... 64 D4
Vientos, Paso de los, *Caribbean* ... 121 C5
Vieques, Isla de, *Puerto Rico* ... 121 d
Vierge Pt., *St. Lucia* ... 121 f
Viernheim, *Germany* ... 25 F9
Viersen, *Germany* ... 24 D2
Vierwaldstättersee, *Switz.* ... 25 J4
Vierzon, *France* ... 19 E9
Vieste, *Italy* ... 41 G13
Vietnam ■, *Asia* ... 64 C6
Vieux-Boucau-les-Bains, *France* ... 20 E2
Vieux Fort, *St. Lucia* ... 121 f
Vif, *France* ... 21 C9
Vigan, *Phil.* ... 61 C4
Vigévano, *Italy* ... 40 C5
Vigia, *Brazil* ... 125 D9
Vigía Chico, *Mexico* ... 119 D7
Víglas, Ákra, *Greece* ... 49 D9
Vignemalle, *France* ... 20 F3
Vigneulles-lès-Hattonchâtel,
  France ... 19 D12
Vignola, *Italy* ... 40 D8
Vigo, *Spain* ... 36 C2
Vigo, Ría de, *Spain* ... 36 C2
Vigsø Bugt, *Denmark* ... 11 G2
Vihiers, *France* ... 18 E6
Vihowa, *Pakistan* ... 68 D4
Vihowa →, *Pakistan* ... 68 D4
Vijayawada, *India* ... 67 L12
Vijосе →, *Albania* ... 44 F3
Vík, *Iceland* ... 8 E4
Vika, *Sweden* ... 10 D8
Vikarbyn, *Sweden* ... 10 D9
Vikeke = Viqueque, *E. Timor* ... 63 F7
Viken, *Skåne, Sweden* ... 11 H6
Viken, *Västra Götaland, Sweden* ... 11 F8
Viking, *Canada* ... 102 C6
Vikmanshyttan, *Sweden* ... 10 D9
Vikna, *Norway* ... 8 D14
Víkos-Aoös △, *Greece* ... 44 F4
Vila da Maganja, *Mozam.* ... 87 F4
Vila de Rei, *Portugal* ... 36 F2
Vila do Bispo, *Portugal* ... 37 H2
Vila do Conde, *Portugal* ... 36 D2
Vila Franca de Xira, *Portugal* ... 37 G2
Vila Gamito, *Mozam.* ... 87 E3
Vila Gomes da Costa, *Mozam.* ... 89 C5
Vila Machado, *Mozam.* ... 87 F3
Vila Mouzinho, *Mozam.* ... 87 E3
Vila Nova de Famalicão, *Portugal* ... 36 D2
Vila Nova de Foz Côa, *Portugal* ... 36 D3
Vila Nova de Gaia, *Portugal* ... 36 D2
Vila Nova de Ourém, *Portugal* ... 36 F2
Vila Pouca de Aguiar, *Portugal* ... 36 D3
Vila Real, *Portugal* ... 36 D3
Vila Real □, *Portugal* ... 36 D3
Vila-real de los Infantes, *Spain* ... 38 F4
Vila Real de Santo António,
  Portugal ... 37 H3
Vila Vasco da Gama, *Mozam.* ... 87 E3
Vila Velha, *Brazil* ... 127 A7

Vila Viçosa, *Portugal* 37 G3
Vilafranca del Maestrat, *Spain* .. 38 E4
Vilafranca del Penedès, *Spain* .. 38 D6
Vilagarcía de Arousa, *Spain* ... 36 C2
Vilaine ➤, *France* 18 E4
Vilanandro, Tanjona, *Madag.* ... 89 B7
Vilanculos, *Mozam.* 89 C6
Vilanova de Castelló, *Spain* 39 F4
Vilanova i la Geltrú, *Spain* 38 D6
Vilar Formoso, *Portugal* 36 E4
Vilaseca, *Spain* 38 D6
Vilaseca-Salou = Vilaseca, *Spain* 38 D6
Vilbjerg, *Denmark* 11 H2
Vilcheka, Zemlya, *Russia* 4 A11
Vilches, *Spain* 37 G7
Vileyka, *Belarus* 32 E4
Vilhelmina, *Sweden* 8 D17
Vilhena, *Brazil* 124 F6
Viliya = Neris ➤, *Lithuania* ... 9 J21
Viljandi, *Estonia* 9 G21
Vilkaviškis, *Lithuania* 30 D10
Vilkija, *Lithuania* 30 C10
Vilkitskogo, Proliv, *Russia* 53 B11
Vilkovo = Vylkove, *Ukraine* ... 29 E14
Villa Abecia, *Bolivia* 126 A2
Villa Ahumada, *Mexico* 118 A3
Villa Ana, *Argentina* 126 B4
Villa Ángela, *Argentina* 126 B3
Villa Bella, *Bolivia* 124 F5
Villa Cañás, *Argentina* 126 C3
Villa Colón, *Argentina* 126 C2
Villa Constitución, *Argentina* .. 126 C3
Villa de María, *Argentina* 126 B3
Villa del Rio, *Spain* 37 H6
Villa Dolores, *Argentina* 126 C2
Villa Frontera, *Mexico* 118 B4
Villa Guillermina, *Argentina* .. 126 B4
Villa Hayes, *Paraguay* 126 B4
Villa Iris, *Argentina* 126 D3
Villa Juárez, *Mexico* 118 B4
Villa María, *Argentina* 126 C3
Villa Mazán, *Argentina* 126 B2
Villa Minozzo, *Italy* 40 D7
Villa Montes, *Bolivia* 126 A3
Villa Ocampo, *Argentina* 126 B4
Villa Ocampo, *Mexico* 118 B3
Villa Ojo de Agua, *Argentina* .. 126 B3
Villa San Giovanni, *Italy* 43 D8
Villa San José, *Argentina* 126 C4
Villa San Martín, *Argentina* ... 126 B3
Villa Santina, *Italy* 41 B9
Villa Unión, *Mexico* 118 C3
Villablino, *Spain* 36 C4
Villacarlos, *Spain* 48 B11
Villacarriedo, *Spain* 36 B7
Villacarrillo, *Spain* 37 G7
Villacastín, *Spain* 36 E6
Villach, *Austria* 26 E6
Villacidro, *Italy* 42 C1
Villada, *Spain* 36 C6
Villadiego, *Spain* 36 C6
Villadóssola, *Italy* 40 B5
Villafeliche, *Spain* 38 D3
Villafranca, *Spain* 38 C3
Villafranca de los Barros, *Spain* 37 G4
Villafranca de los Caballeros,
  Baleares 48 B10
Villafranca de los Caballeros,
  Toledo, Spain 37 F7
Villafranca del Cid = Vilafranca
  del Maestrat, *Spain* 38 E4
Villafranca del Panadés =
  Vilafranca del Penedès, *Spain* . 38 D6
Villafranca di Verona, *Italy* ... 40 C7
Villafranca Tirrena, *Italy* 43 D8
Villagrán, *Mexico* 119 C5
Villaguay, *Argentina* 126 C4
Villaharta, *Spain* 37 G6
Villahermosa, *Mexico* 119 D6
Villahermosa, *Spain* 39 G2
Villaines-la-Juhel, *France* 18 D6
Villajoyosa, *Spain* 39 G4
Villalba, *Spain* 36 B3
Villalba de Guardo, *Spain* 36 C6
Villalón de Campos, *Spain* 36 C5
Villalpando, *Spain* 36 D5
Villaluenga, *Spain* 36 E7
Villamanán, *Spain* 36 C5
Villamartín, *Spain* 37 J5
Villamayor de Santiago, *Spain* . 38 F2
Villablard, *France* 20 C4
Villanova Monteleone, *Italy* ... 42 B1
Villanueva, *U.S.A.* 113 H2
Villanueva de Castellón =
  Vilanova de Castelló, *Spain* .. 39 F4
Villanueva de Córdoba, *Spain* .. 37 G6
Villanueva de la Fuente, *Spain* . 39 G2
Villanueva de la Serena, *Spain* . 37 G5
Villanueva de la Sierra, *Spain* . 36 E4
Villanueva de los Castillejos,
  Spain 37 H3
Villanueva de los Infantes, *Spain* 37 G7
Villanueva del Arzobispo, *Spain* 39 G2
Villanueva del Fresno, *Spain* ... 37 G3
Villanueva y Geltrú = Vilanova i
  la Geltrú, *Spain* 38 D6
Villaputzu, *Italy* 42 C2
Villaquilambre, *Spain* 36 C5
Villar del Arzobispo, *Spain* 38 F4
Villar del Rey, *Spain* 37 F4
Villard-de-Lans, *France* 21 C9
Villarramiel, *Spain* 36 C6
Villarreal = Vila-real de los
  Infantes, *Spain* 38 F4
Villarrica, *Chile* 128 D2
Villarrica, *Paraguay* 126 B4
Villarrobledo, *Spain* 39 F2
Villarroya de la Sierra, *Spain* .. 38 D3
Villarrubia de los Ojos, *Spain* .. 37 F7
Villars-les-Dombes, *France* 19 F12
Villasayas, *Spain* 38 D2

Villaseca de los Gamitos =
  Villaseco de los Gamitos, *Spain* 36 D4
Villaseco de los Gamitos, *Spain* . 36 D4
Villasimíus, *Italy* 42 C2
Villastar, *Spain* 38 E3
Villatobas, *Spain* 36 F7
Villavicencio, *Argentina* 126 C2
Villavicencio, *Colombia* 124 C4
Villaviciosa, *Spain* 36 B5
Villazón, *Bolivia* 126 A2
Ville-Marie, *Canada* 104 C4
Ville Platte, *U.S.A.* 113 K8
Villedieu-les-Poêles, *France* ... 18 D5
Villefort, *France* 20 D7
Villefranche-de-Lauragais, *France* 20 E5
Villefranche-de-Rouergue, *France* 20 D6
Villefranche-du-Périgord, *France* 20 D5
Villefranche-sur-Saône, *France* . 21 C8
Villel, *Spain* 38 E3
Villemur-sur-Tarn, *France* 20 E5
Villena, *Spain* 39 G4
Villenauxe-la-Grande, *France* .. 19 D10
Villenave-d'Ornon, *France* 20 D3
Villeneuve-d'Ascq, *France* 19 B10
Villeneuve-l'Archevêque, *France* 19 D10
Villeneuve-lès-Avignon, *France* . 21 E8
Villeneuve-sur-Allier, *France* .. 19 F10
Villeneuve-sur-Lot, *France* 20 D4
Villeneuve-sur-Yonne, *France* .. 19 D10
Villeréal, *France* 20 D4
Villers-Bocage, *France* 18 C6
Villers-Cotterêts, *France* 19 C10
Villers-sur-Mer, *France* 18 C6
Villersexel, *France* 19 E13
Villerupt, *France* 19 C12
Villeurbanne, *France* 21 C8
Villiers, *S. Africa* 89 D4
Villingen-Schwenningen,
  Germany 25 G4
Villmanstrand = Lappeenranta,
  Finland 9 F23
Vilna, *Canada* 102 C6
Vilnius, *Lithuania* 9 J21
Vils, *Austria* 26 D3
Vils ➤, *Bayern, Germany* 25 G9
Vils ➤, *Bayern, Germany* 25 F7
Vilsbiburg, *Germany* 25 G8
Vilshofen, *Germany* 25 G9
Vilusi, *Serbia & M.* 44 D2
Vilvoorde, *Belgium* 17 D4
Vilyuy ➤, *Russia* 53 C13
Vilyuysk, *Russia* 53 C13
Vimianzo, *Spain* 36 B1
Vimioso, *Portugal* 36 D4
Vimmerby, *Sweden* 11 G9
Vimoutiers, *France* 18 D7
Vimperk, *Czech Rep.* 26 B6
Viña del Mar, *Chile* 126 C1
Vinarós, *Spain* 38 E5
Vincennes, *U.S.A.* 114 F2
Vincent, *U.S.A.* 111 L8
Vinchina, *Argentina* 126 B2
Vindelälven ➤, *Sweden* 8 E18
Vindeln, *Sweden* 8 D18
Vinderup, *Denmark* 11 H2
Vindhya Ra., *India* 68 H7
Vineland, *U.S.A.* 114 F8
Vineuil, *France* 18
Vinga, *Romania* 28 D6
Vingåker, *Sweden* 10 E9
Vinh, *Vietnam* 64 C5
Vinh Linh, *Vietnam* 64 D6
Vinh Long, *Vietnam* 65 G5
Vinh Yen, *Vietnam* 58 G5
Vinhais, *Portugal* 36 D3
Vinica, *Croatia* 41 B13
Vinica, *Macedonia* 44 E6
Vinica, *Slovenia* 41 C12
Vinita, *U.S.A.* 113 G7
Vinkovci, *Croatia* 28 E3
Vinnitsa = Vinnytsya, *Ukraine* . 33 H5
Vinnytsya, *Ukraine* 33 H5
Vinslöv, *Sweden* 11 H7
Vinson Massif, *Antarctica* 5 D16
Vintjärn, *Sweden* 10 D10
Vinton, Calif., *U.S.A.* 110 F6
Vinton, Iowa, *U.S.A.* 112 D8
Vinton, La., *U.S.A.* 113 K8
Vințu de Jos, *Romania* 29 D8
Viöl, *Germany* 24 A5
Vipava, *Slovenia* 41 C10
Vipiteno, *Italy* 41 B8
Viqueque, E. *Timor* 63 F7
Vir, *Croatia* 41 D12
Virac, *Phil.* 61 E6
Virachey, *Cambodia* 64 F6
Virachey △, *Cambodia* 64 E6
Virago Sd., *Canada* 102 C2
Viramgam, *India* 68 H5
Viranșehir, *Turkey* 70 B3
Virawah, *Pakistan* 68 G4
Virbalis, *Lith.* 30 D9
Virden, *Canada* 103 D8
Vire, *France* 18 D6
Vire ➤, *France* 18 C5
Vírgenes, C., *Argentina* 128 G3
Virgin ➤, *U.S.A.* 109 H6
Virgin Gorda, *Br. Virgin Is.* .. 121 e
Virgin Is. (British) ☑, *W. Indies* 121 e
Virgin Is. (U.S.) ☑, *W. Indies* . 121 e
Virgin Islands △, *U.S. Virgin Is.* 121 C7
Virginia, *S. Africa* 88 D4
Virginia, *U.S.A.* 112 B8
Virginia □, *U.S.A.* 114 G7
Virginia Beach, *U.S.A.* 114 G8
Virginia City, Mont., *U.S.A.* .. 108 D8
Virginia City, Nev., *U.S.A.* ... 110 F7
Virginia Falls, *Canada* 102 A3
Virginiatown, *Canada* 104 C4
Virje, *Croatia* 41 B13
Viroqua, *U.S.A.* 112 D9
Virovitica, *Croatia* 28 E2

Virpazar, *Serbia & M.* 44 D3
Virpur, *India* 68 J4
Virserum, *Sweden* 11 G9
Virton, *Belgium* 17 E5
Virudunagar, *India* 66 Q10
Virunga △, *Dem. Rep. of
  the Congo* 86 B2
Vis, *Croatia* 41 E13
Visalia, *U.S.A.* 110 J7
Visayan Sea, *Phil.* 61 F5
Visby, *Sweden* 11 G12
Viscount Melville Sd., *Canada* . 98 B9
Visé, *Belgium* 17 D5
Višegrad, *Bos.-H.* 28 G4
Viseu, *Brazil* 125 D9
Viseu, *Portugal* 36 E3
Viseu □, *Portugal* 36 E3
Vișeu de Sus, *Romania* 29 C9
Vishakhapatnam, *India* 67 L13
Vișina, *Romania* 29 G9
Vișineşti, *Moldova* 29 D13
Visingsö, *Sweden* 11 F8
Viskafors, *Sweden* 11 G6
Viskan ➤, *Sweden* 11 G6
Viški Kanal, *Croatia* 41 E13
Vislanda, *Sweden* 11 H8
Visnagar, *India* 68 H5
Višnja Gora, *Slovenia* 41 C11
Viso, Mte., *Italy* 40 D4
Viso del Marqués, *Spain* 37 G7
Visoko, *Bos.-H.* 28 G3
Visokoi I., *Antarctica* 5 B1
Visp, *Switz.* 25 J3
Vissefjärda, *Sweden* 11 H9
Visselhövede, *Germany* 24 C5
Vissenbjerg, *Denmark* 11 J4
Vista, *U.S.A.* 111 M9
Vistonikos, Órmos = Vistonís,
  Límni, Greece 45 E9
Vistonís, Límni, *Greece* 45 E9
Vistula = Wisła ➤, *Poland* 30 D5
Vit ➤, *Bulgaria* 45 C8
Vitanje, *Slovenia* 41 B12
Vitebsk = Vitsyebsk, *Belarus* .. 32 E6
Viterbo, *Italy* 41 F9
Vitez, *Bos.-H.* 28 F2
Viti Levu, *Fiji* 91 C7
Vitigudino, *Spain* 36 D4
Vitim, *Russia* 53 D12
Vitim ➤, *Russia* 53 D12
Vitina, *Bos.-H.* 41 E14
Vitina, *Greece* 46 D4
Vítkov, *Czech Rep.* 27 B10
Vitória, *Brazil* 125 H10
Vitória da Conquista, *Brazil* ... 125 F10
Vitória de São Antão, *Brazil* ... 125 E11
Vitoria-Gasteiz, *Spain* 38 C2
Vitosha △, *Bulgaria* 44 D7
Vitré, *France* 18 D5
Vitry-le-François, *France* 19 D11
Vitry-sur-Seine, *France* 19 D9
Vitsand, *Sweden* 10 D7
Vitsi, Óros, *Greece* 44 F5
Vitsyebsk, *Belarus* 32 E6
Vittaryd, *Sweden* 11 H7
Vitteaux, *France* 19 E11
Vittel, *France* 19 D12
Vittória, *Italy* 43 F7
Vittório Véneto, *Italy* 41 C9
Vittsjö, *Sweden* 11 H7
Viveiro, *Spain* 36 B3
Vivian, *U.S.A.* 113 J8
Viviers, *France* 21 D8
Vivonne, *France* 20 B4
Vizcaíno, Desierto de, *Mexico* . 118 B2
Vizcaíno, Sierra, *Mexico* 118 B2
Vizcaya □, *Spain* 38 B2
Vize, *Turkey* 45 E11
Vizianagaram, *India* 67 K13
Vizille, *France* 21 C9
Viziñada, *Croatia* 41 C10
Viziru, *Romania* 29 E12
Vizzini, *Italy* 43 E7
Vlaardingen, *Neths.* 17 C4
Vlǎdeasa, Vf., *Romania* 28 D7
Vladičin Han, *Serbia & M.* 44 D6
Vladikavkaz, *Russia* 35 J7
Vladimir, *Russia* 32 D11
Vladimir Volynskiy = Volodymyr-
  Volynskyy, *Ukraine* 33 G3
Vladimirci, *Serbia & M.* 44 B3
Vladimirovac, *Serbia & M.* ... 28 E5
Vladimirovka, *Russia* 35 F8
Vladimirovo, *Bulgaria* 44 C7
Vladimovka, *Kazakstan* 34 E10
Vladislavovka, *Ukraine* 33 K8
Vladivostok, *Russia* 53 E14
Vlǎhița, *Romania* 29 D10
Vlakhiótis, *Greece* 46 E4
Vlasenica, *Bos.-H.* 28 F3
Vlašić, *Bos.-H.* 28 F2
Vlašim, *Czech Rep.* 26 B7
Vlasinsko Jezero, *Serbia & M.* . 44 D6
Vlasotince, *Serbia & M.* 44 D6
Vlieland, *Neths.* 17 A4
Vlissingen, *Neths.* 17 C3
Vlorë, *Albania* 44 F3
Vlorë, Gjiri i, *Albania* 44 F3
Vltava ➤, *Czech Rep.* 26 A7
Vo Dat, *Vietnam* 65 G6
Vobarno, *Italy* 40 C7
Vocín, *Croatia* 28 E2
Vodice, *Croatia* 41 E12
Vodňany, *Czech Rep.* 26 B7
Vodnjan, *Croatia* 41 D10
Voe, *U.K.* 13 A7
Vogel Pk., *Nigeria* 83 D7
Vogelkop = Doberai, Jazirah,
  Indonesia 63 E8
Vogelsberg, *Germany* 24 E5
Voghera, *Italy* 40 D6

Vohibinany, *Madag.* 89 B8
Vohilava, *Madag.* 89 C8
Vohimarina = Iharana, *Madag.* . 89 A9
Vohimena, Tanjon' i, *Madag.* .. 89 D8
Vohipeno, *Madag.* 89 C8
Voi, *Kenya* 86 C4
Void-Vacon, *France* 19 D12
Voineşti, Iaşi, *Romania* 29 C12
Voineşti, Prahova, *Romania* ... 29 E10
Voiotía □, *Greece* 46 C5
Voiron, *France* 21 C9
Voisey B., *Canada* 105 A7
Voitsberg, *Austria* 26 D8
Vojens, *Denmark* 11 J3
Vojmsjön, *Sweden* 8 D17
Vojnić, *Croatia* 41 C12
Vojnik, *Italy* 41 B12
Vojvodina □, *Serbia & M.* 28 E5
Vokhtoga, *Russia* 32 C11
Volary, *Czech Rep.* 26 C6
Volborg, *U.S.A.* 112 C2
Volcán de Colima △, *Mexico* ... 118 D4
Volcano Is. = Kazan-Rettō,
  Pac. Oc. 96 E6
Volcans △, *Rwanda* 86 C2
Volcans d'Auvergne △, *France* . 20 C6
Volchansk = Vovchansk, *Ukraine* 33 G9
Volchya ➤, *Ukraine* 33 H8
Volda, *Norway* 9 E12
Volga ➤ Privolzhskiy □, *Russia* . 34 B10
Volga, *Russia* 32 C10
Volga ➤, *Russia* 35 G9
Volga Hts. = Privolzhskaya
  Vozvyshennost, *Russia* 34 E7
Volgodonsk, *Russia* 35 G6
Volgograd, *Russia* 35 F7
Volgogradskoye Vdkhr., *Russia* . 34 E8
Volgorechensk, *Russia* 34 B5
Volímai, *Greece* 46 D2
Volintiri, *Moldova* 29 D14
Volissós, *Greece* 47 C7
Volkach, *Germany* 25 F6
Völkermarkt, *Austria* 26 E7
Volkhov, *Russia* 32 C7
Volkhov ➤, *Russia* 32 B7
Völklingen, *Germany* 25 F2
Volkovysk = Vawkavysk, *Belarus* 33 F3
Volksrust, *S. Africa* 89 D4
Volnansk, *Ukraine* 33 H8
Volnovakha, *Ukraine* 33 J9
Volochanka, *Russia* 53 B10
Volodarsk, *Russia* 34 B6
Volodymyr-Volynskyy, *Ukraine* . 33 G3
Vologda, *Russia* 32 C10
Volokolamsk, *Russia* 32 D8
Volokonovka, *Russia* 33 G9
Volos, *Greece* 46 B4
Volosovo, *Russia* 32 C5
Volovets, *Ukraine* 29 B8
Volozhin = Valozhyn, *Belarus* .. 32 F10
Volsk, *Russia* 34 D8
Volta □, *Ghana* 83 D5
Volta ➤, *Ghana* 83 D5
Volta, L., *Ghana* 83 D5
Volta Blanche = White Volta ➤,
  Ghana 83 D4
Volta Redonda, *Brazil* 127 A7
Voltaire, C., *Australia* 92 B4
Volterra, *Italy* 40 E7
Voltri, *Italy* 40 D5
Volturno ➤, *Italy* 42 A6
Vólvi, L., *Greece* 44 F7
Volynǎ, *Czech Rep.* 26 B6
Volzhsk, *Russia* 34 C9
Volzhskiy, *Russia* 35 F7
Vondrozo, *Madag.* 89 C8
Vónitsa, *Greece* 46 C2
Vopnafjörður, *Iceland* 8 D6
Vóras Óros, *Greece* 44 F5
Vorbasse, *Denmark* 11 J3
Vorchdorf, *Austria* 26 C6
Vorderrhein ➤, *Switz.* 25 J5
Vordingborg, *Denmark* 11 J5
Vorë, *Albania* 44 E3
Voreio Aigaio = Vórios
  Aiyaíon □, *Greece* 47 C7
Voreppe, *France* 21 C9
Vórios Aiyaíon □, *Greece* 47 C7
Vórios Evvoïkos Kólpos, *Greece* . 46 C5
Vorkuta, *Russia* 52 C7
Vormsi, *Estonia* 9 G20
Vóroi, *Greece* 46 F6
Vorona ➤, *Russia* 34 E6
Voronezh, *Russia* 33 G10
Voronezh, *Ukraine* 33 G7
Voronezh ➤, *Russia* 33 G10
Vorontsovo-Aleksandrovskoye =
  Zelenokumsk, *Russia* 35 H6
Vorpommersche
  Boddenlandschaft △, *Germany* 24 A8
Vorskla ➤, *Ukraine* 33 H8
Võrts Järv, *Estonia* 9 G22
Võru, *Estonia* 9 H22
Vosges, *France* 19 D14
Vosges □, *France* 19 D13
Vosges du Nord △, *France* 19 D14
Voskopojë, *Albania* 44 F4
Voskresensk, *Russia* 32 E10
Voskresenskoye, *Russia* 34 B7
Voss, *Norway* 9 F12
Vostok, *Antarctica* 5 D8
Vostok I., *Kiribati* 97 J12
Votice, *Czech Rep.* 26 B7
Votsuri-Shima, *Japan* 55 M1
Vouga ➤, *Portugal* 36 E2
Vouillé, *France* 18 F7
Voúxa, Ákra, *Greece* 49 D5

Vouzela, *Portugal* 36 E2
Vouziers, *France* 19 C11
Vovchansk, *Ukraine* 33 G9
Vovchok, *Belarus* 31 F10
Voyageurs △, *U.S.A.* 112 A8
Vozhe, Ozero, *Russia* 32 B10
Vozhega, *Russia* 32 B11
Voznesensk, *Ukraine* 33 J6
Voznesenye, *Russia* 32 B8
Vrå, *Denmark* 11 G3
Vráble, *Slovak Rep.* 27 C11
Vračevšnica, *Serbia & M.* 44 B4
Vrakhnéïka, *Greece* 46 C3
Vrancea □, *Romania* 29 E11
Vrancei, Munții, *Romania* 29 E11
Vrangelya, Ostrov, *Russia* 53 B19
Vranica, *Bos.-H.* 28 G2
Vranje, *Serbia & M.* 44 D5
Vranjska Banja, *Serbia & M.* .. 44 D6
Vranov nad Topl'ou, *Slovak Rep.* 27 C14
Vransko, *Slovenia* 41 B11
Vransko Jezero, *Croatia* 41 E12
Vrapčište, *Macedonia* 44 E4
Vratsa, *Bulgaria* 44 C7
Vrbas, *Serbia & M.* 28 E4
Vrbas ➤, *Bos.-H.* 28 E2
Vrbnik, *Croatia* 41 C11
Vrbovec, *Croatia* 41 C13
Vrbovsko, *Croatia* 41 C12
Vrchlabí, *Czech Rep.* 26 A8
Vrede, *S. Africa* 89 D4
Vredefort, *S. Africa* 88 D4
Vreden, *Germany* 24 C2
Vredenburg, *S. Africa* 88 E2
Vredendal, *S. Africa* 88 E2
Vretstorp, *Sweden* 10 E8
Vrgorac, *Croatia* 41 E14
Vrhnika, *Slovenia* 41 C11
Vríði, *Ivory C.* 82 D4
Vrigstad, *Sweden* 11 G8
Vrindavan, *India* 68 F7
Vríses, *Greece* 49 D6
Vrnograč, *Bos.-H.* 41 C12
Vrondádhes, *Greece* 47 C8
Vrpolje, *Croatia* 28 E3
Vršac, *Serbia & M.* 28 E6
Vrsacki Kanal, *Serbia & M.* ... 28 E5
Vrútky, *Slovak Rep.* 27 B11
Vryburg, *S. Africa* 88 D3
Vryheid, *S. Africa* 89 D5
Vsetín, *Czech Rep.* 27 B11
Vu Liet, *Vietnam* 64 C5
Vúcha ➤, *Bulgaria* 45 D8
Vučitrn, *Serbia & M.* 44 D4
Vukovar, *Croatia* 28 E3
Vulcan, *Canada* 102 C6
Vulcan, *Romania* 29 E8
Vulcaneşti, *Moldova* 29 E13
Vulcano, *Italy* 43 D7
Vûlchedruma, *Bulgaria* 44 C7
Vulkaneshty = Vulcaneşti,
  Moldova 29 E13
Vunduzi ➤, *Mozam.* 87 F3
Vung Tau, *Vietnam* 65 G6
Vûrbitsa, *Bulgaria* 45 D10
Vurshets, *Bulgaria* 44 C7
Vutcani, *Romania* 29 D12
Vuya, *Sudan* 81 F2
Vuzlove, *Ukraine* 28 B7
Vwaza △, *Malawi* 87 E3
Vyartsilya, *Russia* 32 A6
Vyatka = Kirov, *Russia* 52 D5
Vyatka ➤, *Russia* 34 C10
Vyatskiye Polyany, *Russia* 34 B10
Vyazemskiy, *Russia* 53 E14
Vyazma, *Russia* 32 E8
Vyazniki, *Russia* 34 B6
Vyborg, *Russia* 32 B5
Vychegda ➤, *Russia* 52 C5
Vychodné Beskydy, *Europe* ... 27 B15
Vyerkhnyadzvinsk, *Belarus* ... 32 E4
Vyhoda, *Ukraine* 29 B8
Vyksa, *Russia* 34 C6
Vylkove, *Ukraine* 29 E14
Vylok, *Ukraine* 28 B7
Vynohradiv, *Ukraine* 28 B7
Vyrnwy, L., *U.K.* 14 E4
Vyshkiv, *Ukraine* 29 B8
Vyshkove, *Ukraine* 29 B8
Vyshniy Volochek, *Russia* 32 D8
Vyshza = imeni 26 Bakinskikh
  Komissarov, *Turkmenistan* .. 71 B7
Vškov, *Czech Rep.* 27 B9
Vysokaye, *Belarus* 31 F10
Vysoké Mýto, *Czech Rep.* 27 B9
Vysokovsk, *Russia* 32 D9
Vyšší Brod, *Czech Rep.* 26 C7
Vytegra, *Russia* 32 B9
Vyzhnytsya, *Ukraine* 29 B10
Vyzhnytsya △, *Ukraine* 29 B10

W

W du Benin △, *Benin* 83 C5
W du Burkina Faso △,
  Burkina Faso 83 C4
W du Niger △, *Niger* 83 C5
W.A.C. Bennett Dam, *Canada* .. 102 B4
Wa, *Ghana* 82 C4
Waal ➤, *Neths.* 17 C5
Waalwijk, *Neths.* 17 C5
Waat, *Sudan* 81 F3
Wabakimi △, *Canada* 104 B2
Wabana, *Canada* 105 C9
Wabasca ➤, *Canada* 102 B5
Wabasca-Desmarais, *Canada* .. 102 B6
Wabash, *U.S.A.* 114 E3
Wabash ➤, *U.S.A.* 114 G1

Wabi →, Ethiopia ... 81 F5
Wabigoon L., Canada ... 103 D10
Wabowden, Canada ... 103 C9
Wąbrzeźno, Poland ... 31 E5
Wabu Hu, China ... 59 A11
Wabuk Pt., Canada ... 104 A2
Wabush, Canada ... 105 B6
Wąchock, Poland ... 31 G8
Wächtersbach, Germany ... 25 E5
Waco, U.S.A. ... 113 K6
Waconichi, L., Canada ... 104 B5
Wad Ban Naqa, Sudan ... 81 D3
Wad Banda, Sudan ... 81 E2
Wad el Haddad, Sudan ... 81 E3
Wad en Nau, Sudan ... 81 E3
Wad Hamid, Sudan ... 81 D3
Wad Medanî, Sudan ... 81 E3
Wad Thana, Pakistan ... 68 F2
Wadai, Africa ... 76 E5
Wadayama, Japan ... 55 G7
Waddeneilanden, Neths. ... 17 A5
Waddenzee, Neths. ... 17 A5
Waddi, Chappal, Nigeria ... 83 D7
Waddington, U.S.A. ... 117 B9
Waddington, Mt., Canada ... 102 C3
Waddy Pt., Australia ... 95 C5
Wadebridge, U.K. ... 15 G3
Wadena, Canada ... 103 C8
Wadena, U.S.A. ... 112 B7
Wädenswil, Switz. ... 25 H4
Wadern, Germany ... 25 F2
Wadeye, Australia ... 92 B4
Wadhams, Canada ... 102 C3
Wādī as Sīr, Jordan ... 74 D4
Wadi Gemâl, Egypt ... 80 C4
Wadi Halfa, Sudan ... 80 C3
Wadi Rum △, Jordan ... 74 F4
Wadian, China ... 59 A9
Wadlew, Poland ... 31 G6
Wadowice, Poland ... 31 J6
Wadsworth, Nev., U.S.A. ... 108 G4
Wadsworth, Ohio, U.S.A. ... 116 E3
Waegwan, S. Korea ... 57 G15
Wafangdian, China ... 57 E11
Wafrah, Si. Arabia ... 70 D5
Wageningen, Neths. ... 17 C5
Wager B., Canada ... 101 B11
Wagga Wagga, Australia ... 95 F4
Waghete, Indonesia ... 63 E9
Wagin, Australia ... 93 F2
Wagner, U.S.A. ... 112 D5
Wagon Mound, U.S.A. ... 113 G2
Wagoner, U.S.A. ... 113 H7
Wągrowiec, Poland ... 31 F4
Wah, Pakistan ... 68 C5
Wahai, Indonesia ... 63 E7
Wahiawa, U.S.A. ... 106 H15
Wāḥid, Egypt ... 74 E1
Wahnai, Afghan. ... 68 C1
Wahni, Ethiopia ... 81 E4
Wahoo, U.S.A. ... 112 E6
Wahpeton, U.S.A. ... 112 B6
Waiau →, N.Z. ... 91 K4
Waibeem, Indonesia ... 63 E8
Waiblingen, Germany ... 25 G5
Waidhofen an der Thaya, Austria ... 26 C8
Waidhofen an der Ybbs, Austria ... 26 D7
Waigeo, Indonesia ... 63 E8
Waihi, N.Z. ... 91 G5
Waihou →, N.Z. ... 91 G5
Waika, Dem. Rep. of the Congo ... 86 C2
Waikabubak, Indonesia ... 63 F5
Waikaremoana, L., N.Z. ... 91 H6
Waikari, N.Z. ... 91 K4
Waikato →, N.Z. ... 91 G5
Waikerie, Australia ... 95 E3
Waikokopu, N.Z. ... 91 H6
Waikouaiti, N.Z. ... 91 L3
Wailuku, U.S.A. ... 106 H16
Waimakariri →, N.Z. ... 91 K4
Waimate, N.Z. ... 91 L3
Wainganga →, India ... 66 K11
Waingapu, Indonesia ... 63 F6
Waini →, Guyana ... 124 B7
Wainwright, Canada ... 103 C6
Waiouru, N.Z. ... 91 H5
Waipara, N.Z. ... 91 K4
Waipawa, N.Z. ... 91 H6
Waipiro, N.Z. ... 91 H7
Waipoua Forest, N.Z. ... 91 F4
Waipu, N.Z. ... 91 F5
Waipukurau, N.Z. ... 91 J6
Wairakei, N.Z. ... 91 H6
Wairarapa, L., N.Z. ... 91 J5
Wairoa, N.Z. ... 91 H6
Waitaki →, N.Z. ... 91 L3
Waitangi, N.Z. ... 91 F5
Waitara, N.Z. ... 91 H5
Waitomo Caves, N.Z. ... 91 H5
Waitsburg, U.S.A. ... 108 C5
Waiuku, N.Z. ... 91 G5
Wajima, Japan ... 55 F8
Wajir, Kenya ... 86 B5
Waka, Ethiopia ... 81 F4
Wakasa, Japan ... 55 G7
Wakasa-Wan, Japan ... 55 G7
Wakatipu, L., N.Z. ... 91 L2
Wakaw, Canada ... 103 C7
Wakayama, Japan ... 55 G7
Wakayama □, Japan ... 55 H7
Wake Forest, U.S.A. ... 115 H6
Wake I., Pac. Oc. ... 96 F8
WaKeeney, U.S.A. ... 112 F5
Wakefield, Jamaica ... 120 a
Wakefield, N.Z. ... 91 J4
Wakefield, U.K. ... 14 D6
Wakefield, Mass., U.S.A. ... 117 D13
Wakefield, Mich., U.S.A. ... 112 B10
Wakkanai, Japan ... 54 B10
Wakkerstroom, S. Africa ... 89 D5
Wakool, Australia ... 95 F3
Wakool →, Australia ... 95 F3

Wakre, Indonesia ... 63 E8
Wakuach, L., Canada ... 105 A6
Walamba, Zambia ... 87 E2
Wałbrzych, Poland ... 31 H3
Walbury Hill, U.K. ... 15 F6
Walcha, Australia ... 95 E5
Walcheren, Neths. ... 17 C3
Walcott, U.S.A. ... 108 F10
Wałcz, Poland ... 31 E3
Waldbröl, Germany ... 24 E3
Waldburg Ra., Australia ... 93 D2
Waldeck, Germany ... 24 D5
Walden, Colo., U.S.A. ... 108 F10
Walden, N.Y., U.S.A. ... 117 E10
Waldkirch, Germany ... 25 G3
Waldkirchen, Germany ... 25 G9
Waldkraiburg, Germany ... 25 G8
Waldport, U.S.A. ... 108 D1
Waldron, U.S.A. ... 113 H7
Waldviertel, Austria ... 26 C8
Walebing, Australia ... 93 F2
Walembele, Ghana ... 82 C4
Walensee, Switz. ... 25 H5
Wales □, U.K. ... 15 E3
Walewale, Ghana ... 83 C4
Walgett, Australia ... 95 E4
Walgreen Coast, Antarctica ... 5 D15
Walker, U.S.A. ... 112 B7
Walker, L., Canada ... 105 B6
Walker L., Canada ... 103 C9
Walker L., U.S.A. ... 108 G4
Walkerston, Australia ... 94 K7
Walkerton, Canada ... 116 B3
Wall, U.S.A. ... 112 D3
Walla Walla, U.S.A. ... 108 C4
Wallace, Idaho, U.S.A. ... 108 C6
Wallace, N.C., U.S.A. ... 115 H7
Wallaceburg, Canada ... 116 D2
Wallachia = Valahia, Romania ... 29 F9
Wallal, Australia ... 95 D4
Wallam Cr. →, Australia ... 95 D4
Wallambin, L., Australia ... 93 F2
Wallangarra, Australia ... 95 D5
Wallaroo, Australia ... 95 E2
Walldürn, Germany ... 25 F5
Wallenhorst, Germany ... 24 C4
Wallenpaupack, L., U.S.A. ... 117 E9
Wallingford, U.S.A. ... 117 E12
Wallis & Futuna, Is., Pac. Oc. ... 96 J10
Wallowa, U.S.A. ... 108 D5
Wallowa Mts., U.S.A. ... 108 D5
Walls, U.K. ... 13 A7
Walls of Jerusalem △, Australia ... 95 G4
Wallula, U.S.A. ... 108 C4
Wallumbilla, Australia ... 95 D4
Walmsley, L., Canada ... 103 A7
Walney, I. of, U.K. ... 14 C4
Walnut Canyon △, U.S.A. ... 109 J8
Walnut Creek, U.S.A. ... 110 H4
Walnut Ridge, U.S.A. ... 113 G9
Walpole, Australia ... 93 F2
Walpole, U.S.A. ... 117 D13
Wals, Austria ... 26 D5
Walsall, U.K. ... 15 E6
Walsenburg, U.S.A. ... 113 G2
Walsh, U.S.A. ... 113 G3
Walsh →, Australia ... 94 B3
Walsrode, Germany ... 24 C5
Walterboro, U.S.A. ... 115 J5
Walters, U.S.A. ... 113 H5
Waltershausen, Germany ... 24 E6
Waltham, U.S.A. ... 117 D13
Waltman, U.S.A. ... 108 E10
Walton, U.S.A. ... 117 D9
Walton-on-the-Naze, U.K. ... 15 F9
Walvis Bay, Namibia ... 88 C1
Walvisbaai = Walvis Bay, Namibia ... 88 C1
Wamba, Dem. Rep. of the Congo ... 86 B2
Wamba, Kenya ... 86 B4
Wamba, Nigeria ... 83 D6
Wamego, U.S.A. ... 112 F6
Wamena, Indonesia ... 63 E9
Wamsutter, U.S.A. ... 108 F9
Wamulan, Indonesia ... 63 E7
Wan Xian, China ... 56 E8
Wana, Pakistan ... 68 C3
Wanaaring, Australia ... 95 D3
Wanaka, N.Z. ... 91 L2
Wanaka, L., N.Z. ... 91 L2
Wan'an, China ... 59 D10
Wanapitei L., Canada ... 104 C3
Wandel Sea = McKinley Sea, Arctic ... 4 A7
Wandérama, Ivory C. ... 82 D4
Wanderer, Zimbabwe ... 87 F3
Wandhari, Pakistan ... 68 F2
Wanding, China ... 58 E2
Wandoan, Australia ... 95 D4
Wanfu, China ... 57 D12
Wang →, Thailand ... 64 D2
Wang Kai, Sudan ... 81 F2
Wang Noi, Thailand ... 64 E3
Wang Saphung, Thailand ... 64 D3
Wang Thong, Thailand ... 64 D3
Wanga, Dem. Rep. of the Congo ... 86 B2
Wangal, Indonesia ... 63 F8
Wanganella, Australia ... 95 F3
Wanganui, N.Z. ... 91 H5
Wangaratta, Australia ... 95 F4
Wangary, Australia ... 95 E2
Wangcang, China ... 58 A6
Wangcheng, China ... 59 C9
Wangdu, China ... 56 E8
Wangen, Germany ... 25 H5
Wangerooge, Germany ... 24 B3
Wangiwangi, Indonesia ... 63 F6
Wangjiang, China ... 59 B11
Wangmo, China ... 58 E6
Wangolodougou, Ivory C. ... 82 D3
Wangqing, China ... 57 C15
Wankaner, India ... 68 H4

Wanless, Canada ... 103 C8
Wanneroo, Australia ... 93 F2
Wannian, China ... 59 C11
Wanning, China ... 64 C8
Wanon Niwat, Thailand ... 64 D4
Wanquan, China ... 56 D8
Wanrong, China ... 56 G6
Wanshan, China ... 58 D7
Wanshengchang, China ... 58 C6
Wantage, U.K. ... 15 F6
Wanxian, China ... 58 B7
Wanyuan, China ... 58 A7
Wanzai, China ... 59 C10
Wapakoneta, U.S.A. ... 114 E3
Wapato, U.S.A. ... 108 C3
Wapawekka L., Canada ... 103 C8
Wapikopa L., Canada ... 104 B2
Wapiti →, Canada ... 102 B5
Wappingers Falls, U.S.A. ... 117 E11
Wapsipinicon →, U.S.A. ... 112 E9
Wapusk △, Canada ... 103 B10
Warab □, Sudan ... 81 F2
Warangal, India ... 66 L11
Waraseoni, India ... 69 J9
Waratah, Australia ... 95 G4
Waratah B., Australia ... 95 F4
Warburg, Germany ... 24 D5
Warburton, Vic., Australia ... 95 F4
Warburton, W. Austral., Australia ... 93 E4
Warburton, The →, Australia ... 95 D2
Warburton Ra., Australia ... 93 E4
Ward, N.Z. ... 91 J5
Ward →, Australia ... 95 D4
Ward Mt., U.S.A. ... 110 H8
Warden, S. Africa ... 89 D4
Wardha, India ... 66 J11
Wardha →, India ... 66 K11
Ware, Canada ... 102 B3
Ware, U.K. ... 15 F8
Ware, U.S.A. ... 117 D12
Waregem, Belgium ... 17 D3
Wareham, U.S.A. ... 117 E14
Waremme, Belgium ... 17 D5
Waren, Germany ... 24 B8
Warendorf, Germany ... 24 D4
Warialda, Australia ... 95 D5
Wariap, Indonesia ... 63 E8
Warin Chamrap, Thailand ... 64 E5
Warka, Poland ... 31 G8
Warkopi, Indonesia ... 63 E8
Warm Springs, U.S.A. ... 109 G5
Warman, Canada ... 103 C7
Warmbad = Bela Bela, S. Africa ... 89 C4
Warmbad, Namibia ... 88 D2
Warmińsko-Mazurskie □, Poland ... 30 D8
Warminster, U.K. ... 15 F5
Warminster, U.S.A. ... 117 F9
Warnemünde, Germany ... 24 A8
Warner Mts., U.S.A. ... 108 F3
Warner Robins, U.S.A. ... 115 J4
Warnow →, Germany ... 24 A8
Waroona, Australia ... 93 F2
Warracknabeal, Australia ... 95 F3
Warragul, Australia ... 95 F4
Warrego →, Australia ... 95 E4
Warrego Ra., Australia ... 94 C4
Warren, Australia ... 95 E4
Warren, Ark., U.S.A. ... 113 J8
Warren, Mich., U.S.A. ... 114 D4
Warren, Minn., U.S.A. ... 112 A6
Warren, Ohio, U.S.A. ... 116 E4
Warren, Pa., U.S.A. ... 116 E5
Warrenpoint, U.K. ... 12 B5
Warrensburg, Mo., U.S.A. ... 112 F8
Warrensburg, N.Y., U.S.A. ... 117 C11
Warrenton, S. Africa ... 88 D3
Warrenton, U.S.A. ... 110 D3
Warri, Nigeria ... 83 D6
Warrina, Australia ... 95 D2
Warrington, U.K. ... 14 D5
Warrington, U.S.A. ... 115 K2
Warrington □, U.K. ... 14 D5
Warrnambool, Australia ... 95 F3
Warroad, U.S.A. ... 112 A7
Warruwi, Australia ... 94 A1
Warsa, Indonesia ... 63 E9
Warsak Dam, Pakistan ... 68 B4
Warsaw = Warszawa, Poland ... 31 F8
Warsaw, Ind., U.S.A. ... 114 E3
Warsaw, N.Y., U.S.A. ... 116 D6
Warsaw, Ohio, U.S.A. ... 116 F3
Warstein, Germany ... 24 D4
Warszawa, Poland ... 31 F8
Warszawa ✈ (WAW), Poland ... 31 F7
Warta, Poland ... 31 G5
Warta →, Poland ... 31 F1
Warthe = Warta →, Poland ... 31 F1
Waru, Indonesia ... 63 E8
Warwick, Australia ... 95 D5
Warwick, U.K. ... 15 E6
Warwick, N.Y., U.S.A. ... 117 E10
Warwick, R.I., U.S.A. ... 117 E13
Warwickshire □, U.K. ... 15 E6
Wasaga Beach, Canada ... 116 B4
Wasagaming, Canada ... 103 C9
Wasatch Ra., U.S.A. ... 108 F8
Wasbank, S. Africa ... 89 D5
Wasco, Calif., U.S.A. ... 111 K7
Wasco, Oreg., U.S.A. ... 108 D3
Wase, Nigeria ... 83 D6
Waseca, U.S.A. ... 112 C8
Wasekamio L., Canada ... 103 B7
Wash, The, U.K. ... 14 E8
Washago, Canada ... 116 B5
Washburn, N. Dak., U.S.A. ... 112 B4
Washburn, Wis., U.S.A. ... 112 B9
Washim, India ... 66 J10
Washington, U.K. ... 14 C6
Washington, D.C., U.S.A. ... 114 F7
Washington, Ga., U.S.A. ... 115 J4
Washington, Ind., U.S.A. ... 114 F2
Washington, Iowa, U.S.A. ... 112 E9

Washington, Mo., U.S.A. ... 112 F9
Washington, N.C., U.S.A. ... 115 H7
Washington, N.J., U.S.A. ... 117 F10
Washington, Pa., U.S.A. ... 116 F4
Washington, Utah, U.S.A. ... 109 H7
Washington □, U.S.A. ... 108 C3
Washington Court House, U.S.A. ... 114 F4
Washington I., U.S.A. ... 114 C2
Washougal, U.S.A. ... 110 E4
Washpool △, Australia ... 95 D5
Wasian, Indonesia ... 63 E8
Wasilków, Poland ... 31 E10
Wasilla, U.S.A. ... 100 B5
Wasior, Indonesia ... 63 E8
Wāsiṭ □, Iraq ... 70 C5
Waskaganish, Canada ... 104 B4
Waskaiowaka, L., Canada ... 103 B9
Waskesiu Lake, Canada ... 103 C7
Wasserburg, Germany ... 25 G8
Wasserkuppe, Germany ... 24 E5
Wassy, France ... 19 D11
Waswanipi, Canada ... 104 C4
Waswanipi, L., Canada ... 104 C4
Watampone, Indonesia ... 63 E6
Watamu, Kenya ... 86 C5
Watarrka △, Australia ... 92 D5
Water Park Pt., Australia ... 94 C5
Water Valley, U.S.A. ... 113 H10
Waterberg Plateau △, Namibia ... 88 C2
Waterberge, S. Africa ... 89 C4
Waterbury, Conn., U.S.A. ... 117 E11
Waterbury, Vt., U.S.A. ... 117 B12
Waterbury L., Canada ... 103 B8
Waterdown, Canada ... 116 C5
Waterford, Canada ... 116 D4
Waterford, Ireland ... 12 D4
Waterford, Calif., U.S.A. ... 110 H6
Waterford, Pa., U.S.A. ... 116 E5
Waterford □, Ireland ... 12 D4
Waterford Harbour, Ireland ... 12 D5
Waterhen L., Canada ... 103 C9
Waterloo, Belgium ... 17 D4
Waterloo, Ont., Canada ... 116 C4
Waterloo, Qué., Canada ... 117 A12
Waterloo, S. Leone ... 82 D2
Waterloo, Ill., U.S.A. ... 112 F9
Waterloo, Iowa, U.S.A. ... 112 D8
Waterloo, N.Y., U.S.A. ... 116 D8
Watersmeet, U.S.A. ... 112 B10
Waterton Lakes △, Canada ... 102 D6
Watertown, Conn., U.S.A. ... 117 E11
Watertown, N.Y., U.S.A. ... 117 C9
Watertown, S. Dak., U.S.A. ... 112 C6
Watertown, Wis., U.S.A. ... 112 D10
Waterval-Boven, S. Africa ... 89 D5
Waterville, Canada ... 117 A13
Waterville, Maine, U.S.A. ... 115 C11
Waterville, N.Y., U.S.A. ... 117 D9
Waterville, Pa., U.S.A. ... 116 E7
Waterville, Wash., U.S.A. ... 108 C3
Watervliet, U.S.A. ... 117 D11
Wates, Indonesia ... 63 G14
Watford, Canada ... 116 D3
Watford, U.K. ... 15 F7
Watford City, U.S.A. ... 112 B3
Wathaman →, Canada ... 103 B8
Wathaman L., Canada ... 103 B8
Watheroo, Australia ... 93 F2
Watheroo △, Australia ... 93 F2
Wating, China ... 56 G4
Watkins Glen, U.S.A. ... 116 D8
Watling I. = San Salvador I., Bahamas ... 121 B5
Watonga, U.S.A. ... 113 H5
Watrous, Canada ... 103 C7
Watrous, U.S.A. ... 113 H2
Watsa, Dem. Rep. of the Congo ... 86 B2
Watseka, U.S.A. ... 114 E2
Watson, Australia ... 93 F5
Watson, Canada ... 103 C8
Watson Lake, Canada ... 102 A3
Watsontown, U.S.A. ... 116 E8
Watsonville, U.S.A. ... 110 J5
Wattiwarriganna Cr. →, Australia ... 95 D2
Wattwil, Switz. ... 25 H5
Watuata = Batuata, Indonesia ... 63 F6
Watubela, Kepulauan, Indonesia ... 63 E8
Watubela Is. = Watubela, Kepulauan, Indonesia ... 63 E8
Wau = Wâw, Sudan ... 81 F2
Waubamik, Canada ... 116 A4
Waubay, U.S.A. ... 112 C6
Wauchope, N.S.W., Australia ... 95 E5
Wauchope, N. Terr., Australia ... 94 C1
Wauchula, U.S.A. ... 115 M5
Waukarlycarly, L., Australia ... 92 D3
Waukegan, U.S.A. ... 114 D2
Waukesha, U.S.A. ... 114 D1
Waukon, U.S.A. ... 112 D9
Waupaca, U.S.A. ... 112 C10
Waupun, U.S.A. ... 112 D10
Waurika, U.S.A. ... 113 H6
Wausau, U.S.A. ... 112 C10
Wautoma, U.S.A. ... 112 C10
Wauwatosa, U.S.A. ... 114 D2
Waveney →, U.K. ... 15 E9
Waverley, N.Z. ... 91 H5
Waverly, Iowa, U.S.A. ... 112 D8
Waverly, N.Y., U.S.A. ... 117 E8
Wavre, Belgium ... 17 D4
Wâw, Sudan ... 81 F2
Wâw al Kabîr, Libya ... 79 C9
Wawa, Canada ... 104 C3
Wawa, Nigeria ... 83 D5
Wawa, Sudan ... 80 C3
Wawanesa, Canada ... 103 D9
Wawona, U.S.A. ... 110 H7
Waxahachie, U.S.A. ... 113 J6
Way, L., Australia ... 93 E3
Waycross, U.S.A. ... 115 K4
Wayi, Sudan ... 81 F3

Wayland, U.S.A. ... 116 D7
Wayne, Nebr., U.S.A. ... 112 D6
Wayne, W. Va., U.S.A. ... 114 F4
Waynesboro, Ga., U.S.A. ... 115 J4
Waynesboro, Miss., U.S.A. ... 115 K1
Waynesboro, Pa., U.S.A. ... 114 F7
Waynesboro, Va., U.S.A. ... 114 F6
Waynesburg, U.S.A. ... 114 F5
Waynesville, U.S.A. ... 115 H4
Waynoka, U.S.A. ... 113 G5
Wazirabad, Pakistan ... 68 C6
Wda →, Poland ... 30 E5
We, Indonesia ... 63 C1
Weald, The, U.K. ... 15 F8
Wear →, U.K. ... 14 C6
Weatherford, Okla., U.S.A. ... 113 H5
Weatherford, Tex., U.S.A. ... 113 J6
Weaverville, U.S.A. ... 108 F2
Webb City, U.S.A. ... 113 G7
Webequie, Canada ... 104 B2
Webo = Nyaake, Liberia ... 82 E3
Webster, Mass., U.S.A. ... 117 D13
Webster, N.Y., U.S.A. ... 116 C7
Webster, S. Dak., U.S.A. ... 112 C6
Webster City, U.S.A. ... 112 D8
Webster Springs, U.S.A. ... 114 F5
Weda, Indonesia ... 63 D7
Weda, Teluk, Indonesia ... 63 D7
Weddell I., Falk. Is. ... 128 G4
Weddell Sea, Antarctica ... 5 D1
Wedderburn, Australia ... 95 F3
Wedel, Germany ... 24 B5
Wedemark, Germany ... 24 C5
Wedgeport, Canada ... 105 D6
Wedza, Zimbabwe ... 87 F3
Wee Waa, Australia ... 95 E4
Weed, U.S.A. ... 108 F2
Weed Heights, U.S.A. ... 110 G7
Weedsport, U.S.A. ... 117 D8
Weedville, U.S.A. ... 116 E6
Weenen, S. Africa ... 89 D5
Weener, Germany ... 24 B4
Węgierska-Górka, Poland ... 31 J6
Węgliniec, Poland ... 31 G2
Węgorzewo, Poland ... 30 D8
Węgorzyno, Poland ... 30 E2
Węgrów, Poland ... 31 F9
Wehda □, Sudan ... 81 F3
Wei He →, Hebei, China ... 56 F8
Wei He →, Shaanxi, China ... 56 G6
Weichang, China ... 57 D9
Weichuan, China ... 56 G7
Weida, Germany ... 24 E8
Weiden, Germany ... 25 F8
Weifang, China ... 57 F10
Weihai, China ... 57 F12
Weil, Germany ... 25 H3
Weilburg, Germany ... 24 E4
Weilheim, Germany ... 25 H7
Weimar, Germany ... 24 E7
Weinan, China ... 56 G5
Weingarten, Germany ... 25 H5
Weinheim, Germany ... 25 F4
Weining, China ... 58 D5
Weipa, Australia ... 94 A3
Weir →, Australia ... 95 D4
Weir →, Canada ... 103 B10
Weir River, Canada ... 103 B10
Weirton, U.S.A. ... 116 F4
Weiser, U.S.A. ... 108 D5
Weishan, Shandong, China ... 57 G9
Weishan, Yunnan, China ... 58 E3
Weissenburg, Germany ... 25 F6
Weissenfels, Germany ... 24 D7
Weisswasser, Germany ... 24 D10
Weitra, Austria ... 26 C7
Weixi, China ... 58 D2
Weixin, China ... 58 D5
Weiyuan, China ... 56 G3
Weiz, Austria ... 26 D8
Weizhou Dao, China ... 58 G7
Wejherowo, Poland ... 30 D9
Wekusko L., Canada ... 103 C9
Welch, U.S.A. ... 114 G5
Weldya, Ethiopia ... 81 E4
Welega, Ethiopia ... 81 F3
Welford △, Australia ... 94 D3
Welkite, Ethiopia ... 81 F4
Welkom, S. Africa ... 88 D4
Welland, Canada ... 116 D5
Welland →, U.K. ... 15 E7
Wellesley Is., Australia ... 94 B2
Wellingborough, U.K. ... 15 E7
Wellington, Australia ... 95 E4
Wellington, Canada ... 116 C7
Wellington, N.Z. ... 91 J5
Wellington, S. Africa ... 88 E2
Wellington, Somst., U.K. ... 15 G4
Wellington, Telford & Wrekin, U.K. ... 15 E5
Wellington, Colo., U.S.A. ... 112 E2
Wellington, Kans., U.S.A. ... 113 G6
Wellington, Nev., U.S.A. ... 110 G7
Wellington, Ohio, U.S.A. ... 116 E2
Wellington, Tex., U.S.A. ... 113 H4
Wellington, I., Chile ... 128 F2
Wellington, L., Australia ... 95 F4
Wells, U.K. ... 15 F5
Wells, Maine, U.S.A. ... 117 C14
Wells, N.Y., U.S.A. ... 117 C10
Wells, Nev., U.S.A. ... 108 F6
Wells, L., Australia ... 93 E3
Wells, Mt., Australia ... 92 C4
Wells Gray △, Canada ... 102 C4
Wells-next-the-Sea, U.K. ... 14 E8
Wells River, U.S.A. ... 117 B12
Wellsboro, U.S.A. ... 116 E7
Wellsburg, U.S.A. ... 116 F4
Wellsville, N.Y., U.S.A. ... 116 D7
Wellsville, Ohio, U.S.A. ... 116 F4
Wellsville, Utah, U.S.A. ... 108 F8

Wellton, *U.S.A.* 109 K6
Welmel, Wabi ➤, *Ethiopia* 81 F5
Welo, *Ethiopia* 81 E4
Wels, *Austria* 26 C7
Welshpool, *U.K.* 15 E4
Welwyn Garden City, *U.K.* 15 F7
Wem, *U.K.* 14 E5
Wembere ➤, *Tanzania* 86 C3
Wemindji, *Canada* 104 B4
Wen Xian, *China* 56 G7
Wenatchee, *U.S.A.* 108 C3
Wenchang, *China* 64 C8
Wencheng, *China* 59 D13
Wenchi, *Ghana* 82 D4
Wenchow = Wenzhou, *China* 59 D13
Wenchuan, *China* 58 B4
Wenden, *U.S.A.* 111 M13
Wendeng, *China* 57 F12
Wendesi, *Indonesia* 63 E8
Wendo, *Ethiopia* 81 F4
Wendover, *U.S.A.* 108 F6
Weng'an, *China* 58 D6
Wengcheng, *China* 59 E9
Wengyuan, *China* 59 E10
Wenjiang, *China* 58 B4
Wenling, *China* 59 C13
Wenlock ➤, *Australia* 94 A3
Wenshan, *China* 58 F5
Wenshang, *China* 56 G9
Wenshui, *China* 56 F7
Wensleydale, *U.K.* 14 C6
Wensu, *China* 60 B3
Wensum ➤, *U.K.* 14 E8
Wentworth, *Australia* 95 E3
Wentzel L., *Canada* 102 B6
Wenut, *Indonesia* 63 E8
Wenxi, *China* 56 G6
Wenxian, *China* 56 H3
Wenzhou, *China* 59 D13
Weott, *U.S.A.* 108 F2
Wepener, *S. Africa* 88 D4
Werda, *Botswana* 88 D3
Werdau, *Germany* 24 E8
Werder, *Germany* 24 C8
Werdohl, *Germany* 24 D3
Wereilu, *Ethiopia* 81 E4
Weri, *Indonesia* 63 E8
Werneck, *Germany* 25 F6
Wernigerode, *Germany* 24 D6
Werra ➤, *Germany* 24 D5
Werrimull, *Australia* 95 E3
Werris Creek, *Australia* 95 E5
Wertach ➤, *Germany* 25 G6
Wertheim, *Germany* 25 F5
Wertingen, *Germany* 25 G6
Wesel, *Germany* 24 D2
Weser ➤, *Germany* 24 B4
Weser-Ems □, *Germany* 24 C3
Weserbergland, *Germany* 24 C5
Weserbergland Schaumburg
Hameln △, *Germany* 24 C5
Wesiri, *Indonesia* 63 F7
Weslemkoon L., *Canada* 116 A7
Wesleyville, *U.S.A.* 116 D4
Wessel, C., *Australia* 94 A2
Wessel Is., *Australia* 94 A2
Wesselburen, *Germany* 24 A4
Wessington Springs, *U.S.A.* 112 C5
West, *U.S.A.* 113 K6
West ➤, *U.S.A.* 117 D12
West Antarctica, *Antarctica* 5 D15
West Baines ➤, *Australia* 92 C4
West Bank ☑, *Asia* 74 C4
West Bend, *U.S.A.* 114 D1
West Bengal □, *India* 69 H13
West Berkshire □, *U.K.* 15 F6
West Beskids = Západné
Beskydy, *Europe* 27 B12
West Branch, *U.S.A.* 114 C3
West Branch Susquehanna ➤,
U.S.A. 117 F8
West Bromwich, *U.K.* 15 E6
West Burra, *U.K.* 13 A7
West Canada Cr. ➤, *U.S.A.* 117 C10
West Cape Howe, *Australia* 93 G2
West Chazy, *U.S.A.* 117 B11
West Chester, *U.S.A.* 117 G9
West Coast △, *Namibia* 88 C1
West Coast △, *S. Africa* 88 E2
West Columbia, *U.S.A.* 113 L7
West Covina, *U.S.A.* 111 L9
West Des Moines, *U.S.A.* 112 E8
West Dunbartonshire □, *U.K.* 13 F4
West End, *Bahamas* 120 A4
West Falkland, *Falk. Is.* 128 G5
West Fargo, *U.S.A.* 112 B6
West Farmington, *U.S.A.* 116 E4
West Fjord = Vestfjorden,
Norway 8 C15
West Fork Trinity ➤, *U.S.A.* 113 J6
West Frankfort, *U.S.A.* 112 G10
West Hartford, *U.S.A.* 117 E12
West Haven, *U.S.A.* 117 E12
West Hazleton, *U.S.A.* 117 F9
West Helena, *U.S.A.* 113 H9
West Hurley, *U.S.A.* 117 E10
West Ice Shelf, *Antarctica* 5 C7
West Indies, *Cent. Amer.* 121 D7
West Jordan, *U.S.A.* 108 F8
West Lorne, *Canada* 116 D3
West Lothian □, *U.K.* 13 F5
West Lunga ➤, *Zambia* 87 E1
West MacDonnell △, *Australia* 92 D5
West Memphis, *U.S.A.* 113 H9
West Midlands □, *U.K.* 15 E6
West Mifflin, *U.S.A.* 116 F5
West Milton, *U.S.A.* 116 E8
West Monroe, *U.S.A.* 113 J8
West Newton, *U.S.A.* 116 F5
West Nicholson, *Zimbabwe* 87 G2
West Palm Beach, *U.S.A.* 115 M5
West Plains, *U.S.A.* 113 G9

West Point, *N.Y., U.S.A.* 117 E11
West Point, *Nebr., U.S.A.* 112 E6
West Point, *Va., U.S.A.* 114 G7
West Pt. = Ouest, Pte. de l',
Canada 105 C7
West Pt., *Australia* 95 F2
West Road ➤, *Canada* 102 C4
West Rutland, *U.S.A.* 117 C11
West Schelde =
Westerschelde ➤, *Neths.* 17 C3
West Seneca, *U.S.A.* 116 D6
West Siberian Plain, *Russia* 50 C11
West Sussex □, *U.K.* 15 G7
West-Terschelling, *Neths.* 17 A5
West Valley City, *U.S.A.* 108 F8
West Virginia □, *U.S.A.* 114 F5
West-Vlaanderen □, *Belgium* 17 D2
West Walker ➤, *U.S.A.* 110 G7
West Wyalong, *Australia* 95 E4
West Yellowstone, *U.S.A.* 108 D8
West Yorkshire □, *U.K.* 14 D6
Westall, Pt., *Australia* 95 E1
Westbrook, *U.S.A.* 115 D10
Westbury, *Australia* 95 G4
Westby, *U.S.A.* 112 A2
Westend, *U.S.A.* 111 K9
Westerland, *Germany* 9 J13
Westerly, *U.S.A.* 117 E13
Western □, *Ghana* 82 D4
Western □, *Kenya* 86 B3
Western □, *S. Leone* 82 D2
Western □, *Zambia* 87 F1
Western Australia □ *Australia* 93 E2
Western Cape □, *S. Africa* 88 E3
Western Dvina = Daugava ➤,
Latvia 9 H21
Western Ghats, *India* 66 N9
Western Isles □, *U.K.* 13 D1
Western Sahara ■, *Africa* 78 D3
Western Samoa = Samoa ■,
Pac. Oc. 91 B13
Westernport, *U.S.A.* 114 F6
Westerschelde ➤, *Neths.* 17 C3
Westerstede, *Germany* 24 B3
Westerwald, *Germany* 24 E3
Westfield, *Mass., U.S.A.* 117 D12
Westfield, *N.Y., U.S.A.* 116 D5
Westfield, *Pa., U.S.A.* 116 E7
Westhill, *U.K.* 13 D6
Westhope, *U.S.A.* 112 A4
Westland △, *N.Z.* 91 K2
Westland Bight, *N.Z.* 91 K3
Westlock, *Canada* 102 C6
Westmar, *Australia* 95 D4
Westmeath □, *Ireland* 12 C4
Westminster, *U.S.A.* 114 F7
Westmont, *U.S.A.* 116 F6
Westmoreland, *Barbados* 121 g
Westmorland, *U.S.A.* 111 M11
Weston, *Oreg., U.S.A.* 108 D4
Weston, *W. Va., U.S.A.* 114 F5
Weston I., *Canada* 104 B4
Weston-super-Mare, *U.K.* 15 F5
Westover, *U.S.A.* 116 F6
Westport, *Canada* 117 B8
Westport, *Ireland* 12 C2
Westport, *N.Z.* 91 J3
Westport, *N.Y., U.S.A.* 117 B11
Westport, *Oreg., U.S.A.* 110 D3
Westport, *Wash., U.S.A.* 110 D2
Westray, *Canada* 103 C8
Westray, *U.K.* 13 B5
Westree, *Canada* 104 C3
Westville, *U.S.A.* 110 F6
Westwood, *U.S.A.* 108 F3
Wetar, *Indonesia* 63 F7
Wetaskiwin, *Canada* 102 C6
Wete, *Tanzania* 84 F7
Wetherby, *U.K.* 14 D6
Wethersfield, *U.S.A.* 117 E12
Wetteren, *Belgium* 17 D3
Wetzlar, *Germany* 24 E4
Wewoka, *U.S.A.* 113 H6
Wexford, *Ireland* 12 D5
Wexford □, *Ireland* 12 D5
Wexford Harbour, *Ireland* 12 D5
Weyburn, *Canada* 103 D8
Weyer Markt, *Austria* 26 D7
Weyhe, *Germany* 24 C4
Weyib ➤, *Ethiopia* 81 F5
Weymouth, *Canada* 105 D6
Weymouth, *U.K.* 15 G5
Weymouth, *U.S.A.* 117 D14
Weymouth, C., *Australia* 94 A3
Wha Ti, *Canada* 100 B8
Whakaari = White I., *N.Z.* 91 G6
Whakatane, *N.Z.* 91 G6
Whale ➤, *Canada* 105 A6
Whale Cove, *Canada* 103 A10
Whales, B. of, *Antarctica* 5 D12
Whalsay, *U.K.* 13 A8
Whangamata, *N.Z.* 91 G5
Whangamomona, *N.Z.* 91 H5
Whanganui △ *N.Z.* 91 H5
Whangarei, *N.Z.* 91 F5
Whangarei Harb., *N.Z.* 91 F5
Wharfe ➤, *U.K.* 14 D6
Wharfedale, *U.K.* 14 C5
Wharton, *N.J., U.S.A.* 117 F10
Wharton, *Pa., U.S.A.* 116 E6
Wharton, *Tex., U.S.A.* 113 L6
Wheatland, *Calif., U.S.A.* 110 F5
Wheatland, *Wyo., U.S.A.* 112 D2
Wheatley, *Canada* 116 D2
Wheaton, *Md., U.S.A.* 114 F7
Wheaton, *Minn., U.S.A.* 112 C6
Wheelbarrow Pk., *U.S.A.* 110 H10
Wheeler, *Oreg., U.S.A.* 108 D2
Wheeler, *Tex., U.S.A.* 113 H4
Wheeler ➤, *Canada* 105 A6
Wheeler L., *U.S.A.* 115 H2
Wheeler Pk. *N. Mex., U.S.A.* 109 H11

Wheeler Pk., *Nev., U.S.A.* 109 G6
Wheeler Ridge, *U.S.A.* 111 L8
Wheeling, *U.S.A.* 116 F4
Whernside, *U.K.* 14 C5
Whiskey Jack L., *Canada* 103 B8
Whiskeytown-Shasta-Trinity △,
U.S.A. 108 F2
Whistleduck Cr. ➤, *Australia* 94 C2
Whistler, *Canada* 102 C4
Whitby, *Canada* 116 C6
Whitby, *U.K.* 14 C7
White ➤, *Ark., U.S.A.* 113 J9
White ➤, *Ind., U.S.A.* 114 F2
White ➤, *S. Dak., U.S.A.* 112 D5
White ➤, *Tex., U.S.A.* 113 J4
White ➤, *Utah, U.S.A.* 108 F9
White ➤, *Vt., U.S.A.* 117 C12
White ➤, *Wash., U.S.A.* 110 C4
White, L., *Australia* 92 D4
White, L., *Canada* 117 A8
White, L., *U.S.A.* 113 L8
White B., *Canada* 105 C8
White Bird, *U.S.A.* 108 D5
White Butte, *U.S.A.* 112 B3
White City, *U.S.A.* 108 E2
White Cliffs, *Australia* 95 E3
White Hall, *U.S.A.* 112 F9
White Haven, *U.S.A.* 117 E9
White Horse, Vale of, *U.K.* 15 F6
White I., *N.Z.* 91 G6
White L., *Canada* 117 A8
White L., *U.S.A.* 113 L8
White Mountain Peak, *U.S.A.* 109 G4
White Mts., *Calif., U.S.A.* 110 H8
White Mts., *N.H., U.S.A.* 117 B13
White Mts., △, *Australia* 94 C4
White Nile = Nîl el Abyad ➤,
Sudan 81 D3
White Nile Dam = Khazzân Jabal
al Awliyâ, *Sudan* 81 D3
White Otter L., *Canada* 104 C1
White Pass, *U.S.A.* 110 D5
White Plains, *U.S.A.* 117 E11
White River, *Canada* 104 C2
White River, *S. Africa* 89 D5
White River, *U.S.A.* 112 D4
White Rock, *Canada* 110 A4
White Russia = Belarus ■,
Europe 32 F4
White Sands, *U.S.A.* 109 K10
White Sea = Beloye More, *Russia* 52 C4
White Sulphur Springs, *Mont.,*
U.S.A. 108 C8
White Sulphur Springs, *W. Va.,*
U.S.A. 114 G5
White Swan, *U.S.A.* 110 D6
White Volta ➤, *Ghana* 83 D4
Whitecliffs, *N.Z.* 91 K3
Whitecourt, *Canada* 102 C5
Whiteface Mt., *U.S.A.* 117 B11
Whitefield, *U.S.A.* 117 B13
Whitefish, *U.S.A.* 108 B6
Whitefish L., *Canada* 103 A7
Whitefish Point, *U.S.A.* 114 B3
Whitegull, L. = Goélands, L. aux,
Canada 105 A7
Whitehall, *Mich., U.S.A.* 114 D2
Whitehall, *Mont., U.S.A.* 108 D7
Whitehall, *N.Y., U.S.A.* 117 C11
Whitehall, *Wis., U.S.A.* 112 C9
Whitehaven, *U.K.* 14 C4
Whitehorse, *Canada* 102 A1
Whitemark, *Australia* 95 G4
Whiteplains, *Liberia* 82 D2
Whiteriver, *U.S.A.* 109 K9
Whitesand ➤, *Canada* 102 A5
Whitesands, *S. Africa* 88 E3
Whitesboro, *N.Y., U.S.A.* 117 C9
Whitesboro, *Tex., U.S.A.* 113 J6
Whiteshell △, *Canada* 103 D9
Whitesville, *U.S.A.* 116 D7
Whiteville, *U.S.A.* 115 H6
Whitewater, *U.S.A.* 114 D1
Whitewater Baldy, *U.S.A.* 109 K9
Whitewater L., *Canada* 104 B2
Whitewood, *Australia* 94 C3
Whitewood, *Canada* 103 C8
Whithorn, *U.K.* 13 G4
Whitianga, *N.Z.* 91 G5
Whitman, *U.S.A.* 117 D14
Whitney, *Canada* 116 A6
Whitney, Mt., *U.S.A.* 110 J8
Whitney Point, *U.S.A.* 117 D9
Whitstable, *U.K.* 15 F9
Whitsunday I., *Australia* 94 J7
Whitsunday Islands △, *Australia* 94 J7
Whitsunday Passage, *Australia* 94 J6
Whittier, *U.S.A.* 111 M8
Whittlesea, *Australia* 95 F4
Wholdaia L., *Canada* 103 A8
Whyalla, *Australia* 95 E2

Widgeegoara Cr. ➤, *Australia* 95 D4
Widgiemooltha, *Australia* 93 F3
Widnes, *U.K.* 14 D5
Więcbork, *Poland* 31 E4
Wiehengebirge = Nördlicher
Teutoburge· Wald-
Wiehengebirge △, *Germany* 24 C4
Wiehl, *Germany* 24 E3
Wiek, *Germany* 24 A9
Wielbark, *Poland* 30 E7
Wieleń, *Poland* 31 F3
Wielichowo, *Poland* 31 F3
Wieliczka, *Poland* 31 J7
Wielkopolski △, *Poland* 31 F3
Wielkopolskie □, *Poland* 31 F4
Wieluń, *Poland* 31 G5
Wien, *Austria* 27 C9
Wien ✕ (VIE), *Austria* 27 C9
Wiener Neustadt, *Austria* 27 D9
Wieprz ➤, *Poland* 31 G8
Wieprza ➤, *Poland* 30 D3
Wieruszów, *Poland* 31 G5
Wiesbaden, *Germany* 25 E4
Wiesental, *Germany* 25 F4
Wiesloch, *Germany* 25 F4
Wiesmoor, *Germany* 24 B3
Wieżyca, *Poland* 30 D5
Wigan, *U.K.* 14 D5
Wiggins, *Colo., U.S.A.* 112 E2
Wiggins, *Miss., U.S.A.* 113 K10
Wight, I. of □, *U.K.* 15 G6
Wigierski △, *Poland* 30 D10
Wigry, Jezioro, *Poland* 30 D10
Wigston, *U.K.* 15 E6
Wigton, *U.K.* 14 C4
Wigtown, *U.K.* 13 G4
Wigtown B., *U.K.* 13 G4
Wil, *Switz.* 25 H5
Wilamowice, *Poland* 31 J6
Wilber, *U.S.A.* 112 E6
Wilberforce, *Canada* 116 A6
Wilberforce, C., *Australia* 94 A2
Wilcannia, *Australia* 95 E3
Wilcox, *U.S.A.* 116 E6
Wildbad, *Germany* 25 G4
Wildeshausen, *Germany* 24 C4
Wildeshauser Geest △, *Germany* 24 C4
Wildon, *Austria* 26 E8
Wildrose, *U.S.A.* 111 J9
Wildspitze, *Austria* 26 E3
Wilga ➤, *Poland* 31 G8
Wilge ➤, *S. Africa* 89 D4
Wilhelm II Coast, *Antarctica* 5 C7
Wilhelmsburg, *Austria* 26 C8
Wilhelmshaven, *Germany* 24 B4
Wilhelmstal, *Namibia* 88 C2
Wilkes-Barre, *U.S.A.* 117 E9
Wilkes Land, *Antarctica* 5 D9
Wilkie, *Canada* 103 C7
Wilkinsburg, *U.S.A.* 116 F5
Wilkinson Lakes, *Australia* 93 E5
Willandra Creek ➤, *Australia* 95 E4
Willapa B., *U.S.A.* 108 C2
Willapa Hills, *U.S.A.* 110 D3
Willard, *N.Y., U.S.A.* 116 D8
Willard, *Ohio, U.S.A.* 116 E2
Willcox, *U.S.A.* 109 K9
Willemstad, *Neth. Ant.* 121 D6
Willet, *U.S.A.* 117 D9
William ➤, *Canada* 103 B7
William 'Bill' Dannely Res.,
U.S.A. 115 J2
William Creek, *Australia* 95 D2
Williams, *Australia* 93 F2
Williams, *Ariz., U.S.A.* 109 J7
Williams, *Calif., U.S.A.* 110 F4
Williams Harbour, *Canada* 105 B8
Williams Lake, *Canada* 102 C4
Williamsburg, *Ky., U.S.A.* 115 G3
Williamsburg, *Pa., U.S.A.* 116 F6
Williamsburg, *Va., U.S.A.* 114 G7
Williamson, *N.Y., U.S.A.* 116 C7
Williamson, *W. Va., U.S.A.* 114 G4
Williamsport, *U.S.A.* 116 E7
Williamston, *U.S.A.* 115 H7
Williamstown, *Australia* 95 F3
Williamstown, *Ky., U.S.A.* 114 F3
Williamstown, *Mass., U.S.A.* 117 D11
Williamstown, *N.Y., U.S.A.* 117 C9
Willimantic, *U.S.A.* 117 E12
Willingboro, *U.S.A.* 114 E8
Williston, *S. Africa* 88 E3
Williston, *Fla., U.S.A.* 115 L4
Williston, *N. Dak., U.S.A.* 112 A3
Williston L., *Canada* 102 B4
Willits, *U.S.A.* 108 G2
Willmar, *U.S.A.* 112 C7
Willmore Wilderness △, *Canada* 102 C5
Willoughby, *U.S.A.* 116 E3
Willow Bunch, *Canada* 103 D7
Willow L., *Canada* 102 A5
Willow Wall, The, *China* 57 C12
Willowick, *U.S.A.* 116 E3
Willowlake ➤, *Canada* 102 A4
Willowmore, *S. Africa* 88 E3
Willows, *U.S.A.* 110 F4
Willowvale = Gatyana, *S. Africa* 89 E4
Wills, L., *Australia* 92 D4
Wills Cr. ➤, *Australia* 94 C3
Wilsboro, *U.S.A.* 117 B11
Wilsonga, *Australia* 95 F2
Wilmette, *U.S.A.* 114 D2
Wilmington, *Australia* 95 E2
Wilmington, *Del., U.S.A.* 114 F8
Wilmington, *N.C., U.S.A.* 115 H7
Wilmington, *Ohio, U.S.A.* 114 F4
Wilmington, *Vt., U.S.A.* 117 D12
Wilmslow, *U.K.* 14 D5
Wilpena Cr. ➤, *Australia* 95 E2
Wilsall, *U.S.A.* 108 D8
Wilson, *N.C., U.S.A.* 115 H7

Wilson, *N.Y., U.S.A.* 116 C6
Wilson, *Pa., U.S.A.* 117 F9
Wilson ➤, *Australia* 92 C4
Wilson Bluff, *Australia* 93 F4
Wilson Inlet, *Australia* 93 G2
Wilsons Promontory, *Australia* 95 F4
Wilster, *Germany* 24 B5
Wilton, *Canada* 112 B4
Wilton ➤, *Australia* 94 A1
Wiltshire □, *U.K.* 15 F6
Wiltz, *Lux.* 17 E5
Wiluna, *Australia* 93 E3
Wimborne Minster, *U.K.* 15 G6
Wimereux, *France* 19 B8
Wimmera ➤, *Australia* 95 F3
Winam G., *Kenya* 86 C3
Winburg, *S. Africa* 88 D4
Winchendon, *U.S.A.* 117 D12
Winchester, *U.K.* 15 F6
Winchester, *Conn., U.S.A.* 117 E11
Winchester, *Idaho, U.S.A.* 108 C5
Winchester, *Ind., U.S.A.* 114 E3
Winchester, *Ky., U.S.A.* 114 G3
Winchester, *N.H., U.S.A.* 117 D12
Winchester, *Nev., U.S.A.* 111 J11
Winchester, *Tenn., U.S.A.* 115 H2
Winchester, *Va., U.S.A.* 114 F6
Wind ➤, *U.S.A.* 108 E9
Wind Cave △, *U.S.A.* 112 D3
Wind River Range, *U.S.A.* 108 E9
Windau = Ventspils, *Latvia* 9 H19
Windber, *U.S.A.* 116 F6
Winder, *U.S.A.* 115 J4
Windermere, *U.K.* 14 C5
Windhoek, *Namibia* 88 C2
Windischgarsten, *Austria* 26 D7
Windom, *U.S.A.* 112 D7
Windorah, *Australia* 94 D3
Window Rock, *U.S.A.* 109 J9
Windrush ➤, *U.K.* 15 F6
Windsor, *Australia* 95 E5
Windsor, *N.S., Canada* 105 D7
Windsor, *Ont., Canada* 116 D2
Windsor, *U.K.* 15 F7
Windsor, *Colo., U.S.A.* 112 E2
Windsor, *Conn., U.S.A.* 117 E12
Windsor, *Mo., U.S.A.* 112 F8
Windsor, *N.Y., U.S.A.* 117 D9
Windsor, *Vt., U.S.A.* 117 C12
Windsor & Maidenhead □, *U.K.* 15 F7
Windsorton, *S. Africa* 88 D3
Windward Is., *W. Indies* 121 D7
Windward Passage = Vientos,
Paso de los, *Caribbean* 121 C5
Winefred L., *Canada* 103 B6
Winejok, *Sudan* 81 F2
Winfield, *U.S.A.* 113 G6
Wingate Mts., *Australia* 92 B5
Wingham, *Australia* 95 E5
Wingham, *Canada* 116 C3
Winisk, *Canada* 104 A2
Winisk ➤, *Canada* 104 A2
Winisk L., *Canada* 104 B2
Wink, *U.S.A.* 113 K3
Winkler, *Canada* 103 D9
Winklern, *Austria* 26 E5
Winlock, *U.S.A.* 110 D4
Winneba, *Ghana* 83 D4
Winnebago, L., *U.S.A.* 114 D1
Winnecke Cr. ➤, *Australia* 92 C5
Winnemucca, *U.S.A.* 108 F5
Winnemucca L., *U.S.A.* 108 F4
Winnett, *U.S.A.* 108 C9
Winfield, *U.S.A.* 113 K8
Winfield, *Australia* 93 F2
Winnibigoshish, L., *U.S.A.* 112 B7
Winnipeg, *Canada* 103 D9
Winnipeg ➤, *Canada* 103 C9
Winnipeg, L., *Canada* 103 C9
Winnipeg Beach, *Canada* 103 C9
Winnipegosis, *Canada* 103 C9
Winnipegosis L., *Canada* 103 C9
Winnipesaukee, L., *U.S.A.* 117 C13
Winnisquam L., *U.S.A.* 117 C13
Winnsboro, *La., U.S.A.* 113 J9
Winnsboro, *S.C., U.S.A.* 115 H5
Winnsboro, *Tex., U.S.A.* 113 J7
Winokapau, L., *Canada* 105 B7
Winona, *Minn., U.S.A.* 112 C9
Winona, *Miss., U.S.A.* 113 J10
Winooski, *U.S.A.* 117 B11
Winooski ➤, *U.S.A.* 117 B11
Winschoten, *Neths.* 17 A7
Winsen, *Germany* 24 B6
Winsford, *U.K.* 14 D5
Winslow, *Ariz., U.S.A.* 109 J8
Winslow, *Wash., U.S.A.* 110 C4
Winsted, *U.S.A.* 117 E11
Winston-Salem, *U.S.A.* 115 G5
Winter Garden, *U.S.A.* 115 L5
Winter Haven, *U.S.A.* 115 M5
Winter Park, *U.S.A.* 115 L5
Winterberg, *Germany* 24 D4
Winterhaven, *U.S.A.* 111 N12
Winters, *U.S.A.* 110 G5
Wintersville, *U.S.A.* 116 F4
Winterswijk, *Neths.* 17 C6
Winterthur, *Switz.* 25 H4
Winthrop, *U.S.A.* 108 B3
Winton, *Australia* 94 C3
Winton, *N.Z.* 91 M2
Wipper ➤, *Germany* 24 D7
Wirrulla, *Australia* 95 E1
Wisbech, *U.K.* 15 E8
Wisconsin □, *U.S.A.* 112 C10
Wisconsin ➤, *U.S.A.* 112 D9
Wisconsin Rapids, *U.S.A.* 112 C10
Wisdom, *U.S.A.* 108 D7
Wishaw, *U.K.* 13 F5
Wishek, *U.S.A.* 112 B5
Wisła, *Poland* 31 J5
Wisła ➤, *Poland* 30 D5
Wisłok ➤, *Poland* 31 H9

Wisłoka ➤, Poland 31 H8
Wismar, Germany 24 B7
Wisner, U.S.A. 112 E6
Wissant, France 19 B8
Wissembourg, France 19 C14
Wisznice, Poland 31 G10
Witbank, S. Africa 89 D4
Witdraai, S. Africa 88 D3
Witham, U.K. 15 F8
Witham ➤, U.K. 14 E7
Withernsea, U.K. 14 D8
Witjira △, Australia 95 D2
Witkowo, Poland 31 F4
Witney, U.K. 15 F6
Witnica, Poland 31 F1
Witnossob ➤, Namibia 88 D3
Wittdün, Germany 24 A4
Witten, Germany 24 D3
Wittenberge, Germany 24 B7
Wittenburg, Germany 24 B7
Wittenheim, France 19 E14
Wittenoom, Australia 92 D2
Wittingen, Germany 24 C6
Wittlich, Germany 25 F2
Wittmund, Germany 24 B3
Wittow, Germany 24 A9
Wittstock Pen., Germany 24 B8
Witvlei, Namibia 88 C2
Witzenhausen, Germany 24 D5
Wkra ➤, Poland 31 F7
Władysławowo, Poland 30 D5
Wleń, Poland 31 G2
Wlingi, Indonesia 63 H15
Włocławek, Poland 31 F6
Włodawa, Poland 31 G10
Włoszczowa, Poland 31 H6
Woburn, U.S.A. 117 D13
Wodian, China 56 H7
Wodonga = Albury-Wodonga,
  Australia 95 F4
Wodzisław Śląski, Poland 31 H5
Wœrth, France 19 D14
Woinbogoin, China 58 A2
Woippy, France 19 C13
Wojcieszow, Poland 31 H2
Wokam, Indonesia 63 F8
Woking, U.K. 15 F7
Wokingham, U.K. 15 F7
Wokingham □, U.K. 15 F7
Wolbrom, Poland 31 H6
Wołczyn, Poland 31 G5
Woldegk, Germany 24 B9
Wolf ➤, Canada 102 A2
Wolf Creek, U.S.A. 108 C7
Wolf L., Canada 102 A2
Wolf Point, U.S.A. 112 A2
Wolfe I., Canada 117 B8
Wolfeboro, U.S.A. 117 C13
Wolfen, Germany 24 D8
Wolfenbüttel, Germany 24 C6
Wolfratshausen, Germany 25 H7
Wolfsberg, Austria 26 E7
Wolfsburg, Germany 24 C6
Wolgast, Germany 24 A9
Wolhusen, Switz. 25 H4
Wolin, Poland 30 E1
Woliński △, Poland 30 E1
Wollaston, Is., Chile 128 H3
Wollaston L., Canada 103 B8
Wollaston Lake, Canada 103 B8
Wollaston Pen., Canada 100 B8
Wollongong, Australia 95 E5
Wolmaransstad, S. Africa 88 D4
Wolmirstedt, Germany 24 C7
Wołomin, Poland 31 F8
Wołów, Poland 31 G3
Wolseley, S. Africa 88 E2
Wolsey, U.S.A. 112 C5
Wolstenholme, C., Canada 98 C12
Wolsztyn, Poland 31 F3
Wolvega, Neths. 17 B6
Wolverhampton, U.K. 15 E5
Wondai, Australia 95 D5
Wongalarroo L., Australia 95 E3
Wongan Hills, Australia 93 F2
Wŏnju, S. Korea 57 F14
Wonosari, Indonesia 63 G14
Wonosobo, Indonesia 63 G13
Wonowon, Canada 102 B4
Wŏnsan, N. Korea 57 E14
Wonthaggi, Australia 95 F4
Wood Buffalo △, Canada 102 B6
Wood Is., Australia 92 C3
Wood L., Canada 103 B8
Woodah I., Australia 94 A2
Woodbourne, U.S.A. 117 E10
Woodbridge, Canada 116 C5
Woodbridge, U.K. 15 E9
Woodburn, U.S.A. 108 D2
Woodenbong, Australia 95 D5
Woodend, Australia 95 F3
Woodford, Australia 95 D5
Woodfords, U.S.A. 110 G7
Woodlake, U.S.A. 110 J7
Woodland, Calif., U.S.A. 110 G5
Woodland, Maine, U.S.A. 115 C12
Woodland, Pa., U.S.A. 116 F6
Woodland, Wash., U.S.A. 110 E4
Woodland Caribou △, Canada . 103 C10
Woodlands, Singapore ...... 65 d
Woodridge, Canada 103 D9
Woodroffe, Mt., Australia 93 E5
Woods, L., Australia 94 B1
Woods, L. of the, Canada 103 D10
Woodstock, Australia 94 B4
Woodstock, N.B., Canada 105 C6
Woodstock, Ont., Canada 116 C4
Woodstock, U.K. 15 F6
Woodstock, Ill., U.S.A. 112 D10
Woodstock, Vt., U.S.A. 117 C12
Woodsville, U.S.A. 117 B13
Woodville, N.Z. 91 J5

Woodville, Miss., U.S.A. 113 K9
Woodville, Tex., U.S.A. 113 K7
Woodward, U.S.A. 113 G5
Woody, U.S.A. 111 K8
Woody ➤, Canada 103 C8
Woolacombe, U.K. 15 F3
Woolamai, C., Australia 95 F4
Wooler, U.K. 14 B5
Woolgoolga, Australia 95 E5
Woomera, Australia 95 E2
Woonsocket, R.I., U.S.A. 117 E13
Woonsocket, S. Dak., U.S.A. . 112 C5
Wooramel ➤, Australia 93 E1
Wooramel Roadhouse, Australia 93 E1
Wooster, U.S.A. 116 F3
Worcester, S. Africa 88 E2
Worcester, U.K. 15 E5
Worcester, Mass., U.S.A. 117 D13
Worcester, N.Y., U.S.A. 117 D10
Worcestershire □, U.K. 15 E5
Wörgl, Austria 26 D5
Workington, U.K. 14 C4
Worksop, U.K. 14 D6
Workum, Neths. 17 B5
Worland, U.S.A. 108 D10
Wormhout, France 19 B9
Worms, Germany 25 F4
Worsley, Canada 102 B5
Wörth, Germany 25 F8
Wortham, U.S.A. 113 K6
Wörther See, Austria 26 E7
Worthing, Barbados .... 121 g
Worthing, U.K. 15 G7
Worthington, Minn., U.S.A. .. 112 D7
Worthington, Pa., U.S.A. 116 F5
Wosi, Indonesia 63 E7
Wou-han = Wuhan, China 59 B10
Wousi = Wuxi, China 59 B13
Wowoni, Indonesia 63 E6
Wrangel I. = Vrangelya, Ostrov,
  Russia 53 B19
Wrangell, U.S.A. 102 B2
Wrangell Mts., U.S.A. 100 B5
Wrath, C., U.K. 13 C3
Wray, U.S.A. 112 E3
Wrekin, The, U.K. 15 E5
Wrens, U.S.A. 115 J4
Wrexham, U.K. 14 D4
Wrexham □, U.K. 14 D5
Wriezen, Germany 24 C10
Wright = Paranas, Phil. 61 F6
Wright, U.S.A. 112 D2
Wright Pt., Canada 116 C3
Wrightson, Mt., U.S.A. 109 L8
Wrightwood, U.S.A. 111 L9
Wrigley, Canada 100 B7
Wrocław, Poland 31 G4
Wronki, Poland 31 F3
Września, Poland 31 F4
Wschowa, Poland 31 G3
Wu Jiang ➤, China 58 C6
Wu'an, China 56 F8
Wubin, Australia 93 F2
Wubu, China 56 F6
Wuchang, China 57 B14
Wucheng, China 56 F9
Wuchuan, Guangdong, China . 59 G8
Wuchuan, Guizhou, China 58 C7
Wuchuan, Nei Monggol Zizhiqu,
  China 56 D6
Wudi, China 57 F9
Wuding, China 58 E4
Wuding He ➤, China 56 F6
Wudinna, Australia 95 E2
Wudu, China 56 H3
Wufeng, China 59 B8
Wugang, China 59 D8
Wugong Shan, China 59 D9
Wuhan, China 59 B10
Wuhe, China 57 H9
Wuhsi = Wuxi, China 59 B13
Wuhu, China 59 B12
Wujiang, China 59 B13
Wukari, Nigeria 83 D6
Wulajie, China 57 B14
Wulanbulang, China 56 D6
Wular L., India 69 B6
Wulehe, Ghana 83 D5
Wulian, China 57 G10
Wuliang Shan, China 58 E3
Wuliaru, Indonesia 63 F8
Wuling Shan, China 58 C7
Wulong, China 58 C6
Wulumuchi = Ürümqi, China . 52 E9
Wum, Cameroon 83 D7
Wuming, China 58 F7
Wun Rog, Sudan 81 F2
Wuning, China 59 C10
Wunnummin L., Canada 104 B2
Wunsiedel, Germany 25 E8
Wunstorf, Germany 24 C5
Wuntho, Burma 67 H19
Wupatki △, U.S.A. 109 J8
Wuping, China 59 E11
Wuppertal, Germany 24 D3
Wuppertal, S. Africa 88 E2
Wuqing, China 57 E9
Wurtsboro, U.S.A. 117 E10
Würzburg, Germany 25 F5
Wurzen, Germany 24 D8
Wushan, China 56 G3
Wushishi, Nigeria 83 D6
Wusuli Jiang = Ussuri ➤, Asia 54 A7
Wutach ➤, Germany 25 H4
Wutai, China 56 E7
Wuting = Huimin, China 57 F9
Wutonghaolai, China 57 C11
Wutongqiao, China 58 C4
Wuwei, Anhui, China 59 B11
Wuwei, Gansu, China 60 C5
Wuxi, Jiangsu, China 59 B13

Wuxi, Sichuan, China 58 B7
Wuxiang, China 56 F7
Wuxuan, China 58 F7
Wuxue, China 59 C10
Wuyang, China 56 H7
Wuyi, Hebei, China 56 F8
Wuyi, Zhejiang, China 59 C12
Wuyi Shan, China 59 D11
Wuyishan, China 59 D12
Wuyo, Nigeria 83 C7
Wuyuan, Jiangxi, China 59 C11
Wuyuan, Nei Monggol Zizhiqu,
  China 56 D5
Wuzhai, China 56 E6
Wuzhi Shan, China 64 C7
Wuzhong, China 56 E4
Wuzhou, China 59 F8
Wyaaba Cr. ➤, Australia 94 B3
Wyalkatchem, Australia 93 F2
Wyalusing, U.S.A. 117 E8
Wyandotte, U.S.A. 114 D4
Wyandra, Australia 95 D4
Wyangala, L., Australia 95 E4
Wyara, L., Australia 95 D3
Wycheproof, Australia 95 F3
Wye ➤, U.K. 15 F5
Wyemandoo, Australia 93 E2
Wyk, Germany 24 A4
Wymondham, U.K. 15 E9
Wymore, U.S.A. 112 E6
Wyndham, Australia 92 C4
Wyndham, N.Z. 91 M2
Wynne, U.S.A. 113 H9
Wynyard, Australia 95 G4
Wynyard, Canada 103 C8
Wyola L., Australia 93 E5
Wyoming = Plympton-Wyoming,
  Canada 116 D2
Wyoming □, U.S.A. 108 E10
Wyomissing, U.S.A. 117 F9
Wyong, Australia 95 E5
Wyrzysk, Poland 31 E4
Wyśmierzyce, Poland 31 G7
Wysoka, Poland 31 E4
Wysokie, Poland 31 H9
Wysokie Mazowieckie, Poland 31 F9
Wyszków, Poland 31 F8
Wyszogród, Poland 31 F7
Wytheville, U.S.A. 114 G5
Wyżyna Małopolska, Poland .. 31 H7

X

Xaafuun, Somali Rep. 75 E5
Xaçmaz, Azerbaijan 35 K9
Xai-Xai, Mozam. 89 D5
Xainza, China 60 C3
Xalapa, Mexico 119 D5
Xangongo, Angola 88 B2
Xankändi, Azerbaijan 70 B5
Xanlar, Azerbaijan 35 K8
Xanten, Germany 24 D2
Xánthi, Greece 45 E8
Xánthi □, Greece 45 E8
Xanthos, Turkey 47 E11
Xanxerê, Brazil 127 B5
Xapuri, Brazil 124 F5
Xar Moron He ➤, China 57 C11
Xarrë, Albania 44 G4
Xau, L., Botswana 88 C3
Xátiva, Spain 39 G4
Xavantina, Brazil 127 A5
Xenia, U.S.A. 114 F4
Xeropotamos ➤, Cyprus 49 E11
Xertigny, France 19 D13
Xhora, S. Africa 89 E4
Xhumo, Botswana 88 C3
Xi Jiang ➤, China 59 F9
Xi Xian, Henan, China 59 A10
Xi Xian, Shanxi, China 56 F6
Xia Xian, China 56 G6
Xiachengzi, China 57 B16
Xiachuan Dao, China 59 G9
Xiaguan, China 60 D5
Xiajiang, China 59 D10
Xiajin, China 56 F9
Xiamen, China 59 E12
Xi'an, China 56 G5
Xian Xian, China 56 E9
Xianfeng, China 58 C7
Xiang Jiang ➤, China 59 C9
Xiangcheng, Henan, China .. 56 H8
Xiangcheng, Henan, China .. 56 H7
Xiangcheng, Sichuan, China . 58 C2
Xiangdu, China 58 F6
Xiangfan, China 59 A9
Xianggang = Hong Kong □,
  China 59 F10
Xianghuang Qi, China 56 C7
Xiangning, China 56 G6
Xiangquan, China 56 F7
Xiangquan He = Sutlej ➤,
  Pakistan 68 E4
Xiangshan, China 59 C13
Xiangshui, China 57 G10
Xiangtan, China 59 D9
Xiangxiang, China 59 D9
Xiangyang, China 59 C9
Xiangyun, China 58 E3
Xiangzhou, China 58 F7
Xianju, China 59 C13
Xianning, China 59 C10
Xiannü He ➤, China 58 B3
Xiantao, China 59 B9
Xianyang, China 56 G5
Xianyou, China 59 E12
Xiao Hinggan Ling, China 60 B7
Xiao Xian, China 56 G9

Xiaofeng, China 59 B12
Xiaogan, China 59 B9
Xiaojin, China 58 B4
Xiaolan, China 59 F9
Xiaoshan, China 59 B13
Xiaoyi, China 56 F6
Xiapu, China 59 D12
Xiawa, China 57 C11
Xiayi, China 56 G9
Xichang, China 58 D4
Xichong, China 58 B5
Xichou, China 58 E5
Xichuan, China 56 H6
Xide, China 58 C4
Xiemahe, China 59 B8
Xieng Khouang, Laos 64 C4
Xifei He ➤, China 56 H9
Xifeng, Gansu, China 56 G4
Xifeng, Guizhou, China 58 D6
Xifeng, Liaoning, China 57 C13
Xifengzhen = Xifeng, China .. 56 G4
Xigazê, China 60 D3
Xihe, China 56 G3
Xihua, China 56 H8
Xilaganí, Greece 45 F9
Xiliao He ➤, China 57 C12
Xilin, China 58 E5
Xilókastron, Greece 46 C4
Ximana, Mozam. 87 F3
Xime, Guinea-Biss. 82 C2
Ximeng, China 58 F2
Xin Jiang ➤, China 59 C11
Xin Xian = Xinzhou, China .. 56 E7
Xinavane, Mozam. 89 D5
Xinbin, China 57 D13
Xincai, China 59 A10
Xinchang, China 59 C13
Xincheng, Guangxi Zhuangzu,
  China 58 E7
Xincheng, Jiangxi, China 59 D10
Xindu, China 58 B5
Xinfeng, Guangdong, China .. 59 E10
Xinfeng, Jiangxi, China 59 D11
Xinfeng, Jiangxi, China 59 E10
Xinfengjiang Skuiku, China .. 59 F10
Xing Xian, China 56 E6
Xing'an, Guangxi Zhuangzu,
  China 59 E8
Xingan, Jiangxi, China 59 D10
Xingcheng, China 57 D11
Xingguo, China 59 D10
Xinghe, China 56 D7
Xinghua, China 57 H10
Xinghua Wan, China 59 E12
Xinglong, China 57 D9
Xingning, China 59 E10
Xingping, China 56 G5
Xingren, China 58 E5
Xingshan, China 59 B8
Xingtai, China 56 F8
Xingu ➤, Brazil 125 D8
Xingwen, China 58 C5
Xingyang, China 56 G7
Xinhe, China 56 F8
Xinhua, China 59 D8
Xinhuang, China 58 D7
Xinhui, China 59 F9
Xining, China 60 C5
Xinjian, China 59 C10
Xinjiang, China 56 G6
Xinjiang Uygur Zizhiqu □, China 60 B3
Xinjie, China 58 D3
Xinjin = Pulandian, China 57 E11
Xinjin, China 58 B4
Xinkai He ➤, China 57 C12
Xinle, China 56 E8
Xinlitun, China 57 D12
Xinlong, China 58 B3
Xinmin, China 57 D12
Xinning, China 59 D8
Xinping, China 58 E3
Xinshao, China 59 D8
Xintai, China 57 G9
Xintian, China 59 E9
Xinxian, China 59 B10
Xinxiang, China 56 G7
Xinxing, China 59 F9
Xinyang, China 59 A10
Xinye, China 56 A9
Xinyi, China 59 F8
Xinyu, China 59 D10
Xinzhan, China 57 C14
Xinzheng, China 56 G7
Xinzhou, Hubei, China 59 B10
Xinzhou, Shanxi, China 56 E7
Xinzo de Limia, Spain 36 C3
Xiongyuecheng, China 57 D12
Xiping, Henan, China 56 H8
Xiping, Henan, China 56 H6
Xiping, Zhejiang, China 59 C12
Xique-Xique, Brazil 125 F10
Xisha Qundao = Paracel Is.,
  S. China Sea 62 A4
Xishui, Guizhou, China 58 C6
Xishui, Hubei, China 59 B10
Xitole, Guinea-Biss. 82 C2
Xiu Shui ➤, China 59 C10
Xiuning, China 59 C12
Xiuren, China 59 E8
Xiushan, China 58 C7
Xiushui, China 59 C10
Xiuwen, China 58 D6
Xiuyan, China 57 D12
Xixabangma Feng, China 67 E14
Xixia, China 56 H6
Xixiang, China 56 H4
Xiyang, China 56 F7
Xizang Zizhiqu □, China 60 C3
Xlendi, Malta 49 C1
Xochob, Mexico 119 D7
Xu Jiang ➤, China 59 D11
Xuan Loc, Vietnam 65 G6

Xuan'en, China 58 C7
Xuanhan, China 58 B6
Xuanhua, China 56 D8
Xuanwei, China 58 C5
Xuanzhou, China 59 B12
Xuchang, China 56 G7
Xudat, Azerbaijan 35 K9
Xuefeng Shan, China 59 D8
Xuejiaping, China 59 B8
Xun Jiang ➤, China 59 F8
Xun Xian, China 56 G8
Xundian, China 58 E4
Xunwu, China 59 E10
Xunyang, China 56 H5
Xunyi, China 56 G5
Xupu, China 59 D8
Xúquer ➤, Spain 39 F4
Xushui, China 56 E8
Xuwen, China 59 G8
Xuyen Moc, Vietnam 65 G6
Xuyong, China 58 C5
Xuzhou, China 57 G9
Xylophagou, Cyprus 49 E12

Y

Ya Xian, China 64 C7
Yaamba, Australia 94 C5
Ya'an, China 58 C4
Yaapeet, Australia 95 F3
Yabassi, Cameroon 83 E6
Yabelo, Ethiopia 81 G4
Yabelo △, Ethiopia 81 F4
Yablanitsa, Bulgaria 45 C8
Yablonovy Ra. = Yablonovyy
  Khrebet, Russia 53 D12
Yablonovyy Khrebet, Russia .. 53 D12
Yabluniv, Ukraine 29 B9
Yabluntsya, Ukraine 29 B9
Yabrai Shan, China 56 E2
Yabrūd, Syria 74 B5
Yabucoa, Puerto Rico ...... 121 d
Yacambú △, Venezuela 121 E6
Yacheng, China 64 C7
Yacuiba, Bolivia 126 A3
Yacuma ➤, Bolivia 124 F5
Yadgir, India 66 L10
Yadkin ➤, U.S.A. 115 H5
Yadrin, Russia 34 C8
Yaeyama-Rettō, Japan 55 M1
Yagaba, Ghana 83 C4
Yağcılar, Turkey 47 B10
Yagodnoye, Russia 53 C15
Yahila, Dem. Rep. of the Congo 86 B1
Yahk, Canada 102 D5
Yahotyn, Ukraine 33 G4
Yahuma, Dem. Rep. of the Congo 84 D4
Yahyalı, Turkey 72 C6
Yaita, Japan 55 F9
Yaiza, Canary Is. 48 F6
Yajiang, China 58 B3
Yajua, Nigeria 83 C7
Yakima, U.S.A. 108 C3
Yakima ➤, U.S.A. 108 C3
Yako, Burkina Faso 82 C4
Yakobi I., U.S.A. 102 B1
Yakoruda, Bulgaria 44 D7
Yakovlevka, Russia 54 B6
Yaku-Shima, Japan 55 J5
Yakumo, Japan 54 C10
Yakutat, U.S.A. 100 C6
Yakutia = Sakha □, Russia .. 53 C13
Yakutsk, Russia 53 C13
Yala, Thailand 65 J3
Yalboroo, Australia 94 J6
Yale, U.S.A. 116 C2
Yalgoo, Australia 93 E2
Yalgorup △, Australia 93 D2
Yalinga, C.A.R. 84 C4
Yalkubul, Punta, Mexico 119 C7
Yalleroi, Australia 94 C4
Yalobusha ➤, U.S.A. 113 J9
Yalong Jiang ➤, China 58 D3
Yalova, Turkey 45 F13
Yalpuh, Ozero, Ukraine 29 E13
Yalta, Ukraine 33 K8
Yalu Jiang ➤, China 57 E13
Yalvaç, Turkey 72 C4
Yam Ha Melah = Dead Sea, Asia 74 D4
Yam Kinneret, Israel 74 C4
Yamada, Japan 55 H5
Yamagata, Japan 54 E10
Yamagata □, Japan 54 E10
Yamaguchi, Japan 55 G5
Yamaguchi □, Japan 55 G5
Yamal, Poluostrov, Russia .. 52 B8
Yamal Pen. = Yamal, Poluostrov,
  Russia 52 B8
Yamanashi □, Japan 55 G9
Yamanie Falls △, Australia .. 94 B4
Yamba, Australia 95 D5
Yambarran Ra., Australia 92 C5
Yambéring, Guinea 82 C2
Yâmbiô, Sudan 81 G2
Yambol, Bulgaria 45 D10
Yamdena, Indonesia 63 F8
Yame, Japan 55 H5
Yamethin, Burma 67 J20
Yamma-Yamma, L., Australia 95 D3
Yamoussoukro, Ivory C. 82 D3
Yampa ➤, U.S.A. 108 F9
Yampi Sd., Australia 92 C3
Yampil, Moldova 33 H5
Yampol = Yampil, Moldova .. 33 H5
Yamrat, Nigeria 83 C6
Yamrukchal = Botev, Bulgaria 45 D8
Yamuna ➤, India 69 G9
Yamunanagar, India 68 D7

Yamzho Yumco, *China* 60 D4
Yan, *Nigeria* 83 C7
Yana ➤, *Russia* 53 B14
Yanagawa, *Japan* 55 H5
Yanai, *Japan* 55 H6
Yan'an, *China* 56 F5
Yanbian, *China* 58 D3
Yanbu 'al Baḥr, *Si. Arabia* ... 70 F3
Yanchang, *China* 56 F6
Yancheng, *Henan, China* 56 H8
Yancheng, *Jiangsu, China* 57 H11
Yanchep Beach, *Australia* 93 F2
Yanchi, *China* 56 F4
Yanchuan, *China* 56 F6
Yanco Cr. ➤, *Australia* 95 F4
Yandicoogina, *Australia* 92 D2
Yandoon, *Burma* 67 L19
Yanfeng, *China* 58 E3
Yanfolila, *Mali* 82 C3
Yang Xian, *China* 56 H4
Yang-Yang, *Senegal* 82 B1
Yangambi, *Dem. Rep. of the Congo* 86 B1
Yangbi, *China* 58 E2
Yangcheng, *China* 56 G7
Yangch'ü = Taiyuan, *China* ... 56 F7
Yangchun, *China* 59 F8
Yanggao, *China* 56 D7
Yanggu, *China* 56 F8
Yangjia, *China* 59 G8
Yangliuqing, *China* 57 E9
Yangon = Rangoon, *Burma* 67 L20
Yangping, *China* 59 B8
Yangpingguan, *China* 56 H4
Yangquan, *China* 56 F7
Yangshan, *China* 59 E9
Yangshuo, *China* 59 E8
Yangtse = Chang Jiang ➤, *China* 59 B13
Yangtze Kiang = Chang Jiang ➤, *China* 59 B13
Yangudi Rassa △, *Ethiopia* ... 81 E5
Yangxin, *China* 59 C10
Yangyang, *S. Korea* 57 E15
Yangyuan, *China* 56 D8
Yangzhong, *China* 59 A12
Yangzhou, *China* 59 A12
Yanhe, *China* 58 C7
Yanji, *China* 57 C15
Yanjin, *China* 58 C5
Yanjing, *China* 58 C2
Yankari △, *Nigeria* 83 D7
Yankton, *U.S.A.* 112 D6
Yanonge, *Dem. Rep. of the Congo* 86 B1
Yanqi, *China* 60 B3
Yanqing, *China* 56 D8
Yanshan, *Hebei, China* 57 E9
Yanshan, *Jiangxi, China* 59 C11
Yanshan, *Yunnan, China* 58 F5
Yanshou, *China* 57 B15
Yantabulla, *Australia* 95 D4
Yantai, *China* 57 F11
Yantarnyy, *Russia* 30 D6
Yanting, *China* 58 B5
Yanzhou, *China* 56 G9
Yao Noi, Ko, *Thailand* .... 65 a
Yao Xian, *China* 56 G5
Yao Yai, Ko, *Thailand* .... 65 a
Yao'an, *China* 58 E3
Yaodu, *China* 58 A5
Yaoundé, *Cameroon* 83 E7
Yaowan, *China* 57 G10
Yap, *Pac. Oc.* 96 G5
Yapen, *Indonesia* 63 E9
Yapen, Selat, *Indonesia* 63 E9
Yapero, *Indonesia* 63 E9
Yappar ➤, *Australia* 94 B3
Yaqui ➤, *Mexico* 118 B2
Yar-Sale, *Russia* 52 C8
Yaraka, *Australia* 94 C3
Yaransk, *Russia* 34 B8
Yarbasan, *Turkey* 47 C10
Yardımcı Burnu, *Turkey* 47 E12
Yare ➤, *U.K.* 15 E9
Yaremcha, *Ukraine* 29 B9
Yarensk, *Russia* 52 C5
Yarfa, *Si. Arabia* 80 C4
Yarí ➤, *Colombia* 124 D4
Yarkand = Shache, *China* 60 C2
Yarker, *Canada* 117 B8
Yarkhun ➤, *Pakistan* 69 A5
Yarlung Ziangbo Jiang = Brahmaputra ➤, *Asia* 69 H13
Yarmouth, *Canada* 105 D6
Yarmūk ➤, *Syria* 74 C4
Yarqa, W. ➤, *Egypt* 74 F2
Yarra Yarra Lakes, *Australia* . 93 E2
Yarram, *Australia* 95 F4
Yarraman, *Australia* 95 D5
Yarras, *Australia* 95 E5
Yartsevo, Sib., *Russia* 53 C10
Yartsevo, Smolensk, *Russia* .. 32 E7
Yarumal, *Colombia* 124 B3
Yasawa Group, *Fiji* 91 C7
Yaselda, *Belarus* 33 F4
Yass, *Australia* 95 E4
Yāsūj, *Iran* 71 D6
Yatakala, *Niger* 83 C5
Yass, *Turkey* 47 D10
Yates Center, *U.S.A.* 113 G7

Yathkyed L., *Canada* 103 A9
Yatsushiro, *Japan* 55 H5
Yatta Plateau, *Kenya* 86 C4
Yauco, *Puerto Rico* .... 121 d
Yavari ➤, *Peru* 124 D4
Yávaros, *Mexico* 118 B3
Yavatmal, *India* 66 J11
Yavne, *Israel* 74 D3
Yavoriv, *Ukraine* 31 J10
Yavorov = Yavoriv, *Ukraine* .. 31 J10
Yavuzeli, *Turkey* 72 D7
Yawatahama, *Japan* 55 H6
Yawri B., *S. Leone* 82 D2
Yaxi, *China* 58 D6
Yazd, *Iran* 71 D7
Yazd □, *Iran* 71 D7
Yazd-e Khvāst, *Iran* 71 D7
Yazıköy, *Turkey* 47 E9
Yazman, *Pakistan* 68 E4
Yazoo ➤, *U.S.A.* 113 J9
Yazoo City, *U.S.A.* 113 J9
Ybbs, *Austria* 26 C8
Ybycuí △, *Paraguay* 126 B4
Ybytyruzú △, *Paraguay* 127 B4
Yding Skovhøj, *Denmark* 11 J3
Ye, *Burma* 64 E1
Ye Xian, *China* 56 H7
Yebyu, *Burma* 64 E2
Yechŏn, *S. Korea* 57 F15
Yecla, *Spain* 39 G3
Yécora, *Mexico* 118 B3
Yedebub Biheroch Biheresebochna Hizboch □, *Ethiopia* ... 81 F4
Yedintsy = Edineţ, *Moldova* .. 29 B12
Yedseram ➤, *Nigeria* 83 C7
Yefremov, *Russia* 32 F10
Yeghegnadzor, *Armenia* 73 C11
Yegorlyk ➤, *Russia* 35 G5
Yegorlykskaya, *Russia* 35 G5
Yegoryevsk, *Russia* 32 E10
Yegros, *Paraguay* 126 B4
Yehbuah, *Indonesia* 63 J17
Yehuda, Midbar, *Israel* 74 D4
Yei, *Sudan* 81 G3
Yei, Nahr ➤, *Sudan* 81 F3
Yejmiadzin, *Armenia* 35 K7
Yekaterinburg, *Russia* 52 D7
Yelabuga, *Russia* 34 C11
Yelan, *Russia* 34 E6
Yelarbon, *Australia* 95 D5
Yelatma, *Russia* 34 C5
Yelets, *Russia* 33 F10
Yélimané, *Mali* 82 B2
Yelizavetgrad = Kirovohrad, *Ukraine* 33 H7
Yell, *U.K.* 13 A7
Yell Sd., *U.K.* 13 A7
Yellow Sea, *China* 57 G12
Yellowhead Pass, *Canada* 102 C5
Yellowknife, *Canada* 102 A6
Yellowknife ➤, *Canada* 102 A6
Yellowstone △, *U.S.A.* 108 D9
Yellowstone ➤, *U.S.A.* 112 B3
Yellowstone L., *U.S.A.* 108 D8
Yelnya, *Russia* 32 E7
Yelsk, *Belarus* 33 G5
Yelwa, *Nigeria* 83 C5
Yemen ■, *Asia* 75 E3
Yen Bai, *Vietnam* 58 G5
Yenagoa, *Nigeria* 83 E6
Yenakiyeve, *Ukraine* 33 H10
Yenakiyevo = Yenakiyeve, *Ukraine* 33 H10
Yenangyaung, *Burma* 67 J19
Yenbo = Yanbu 'al Baḥr, *Si. Arabia* 70 F3
Yenda, *Australia* 95 E4
Yende Millimou, *Guinea* 82 D2
Yendéré, *Burkina Faso* 82 C4
Yendi, *Ghana* 83 D4
Yéni, *Niger* 83 C5
Yenice, *Ankara, Turkey* 72 C5
Yenice, *Aydın, Turkey* 47 D10
Yenice, *Çanakkale, Turkey* ... 47 B9
Yenice, *Edirne, Turkey* 45 F10
Yenice ➤, *Turkey* 72 D6
Yenifoça, *Turkey* 47 C8
Yenihisar, *Turkey* 47 D9
Yeniköy, *Bursa, Turkey* 45 F13
Yeniköy, *Çanakkale, Turkey* .. 47 B8
Yeniköy, *Kütahya, Turkey* ... 47 C11
Yenipazar, *Turkey* 47 D10
Yenisaía, *Greece* 45 E8
Yenişehir, *Turkey* 45 F13
Yenisey ➤, *Russia* 52 B9
Yeniseysk, *Russia* 53 D10
Yeniseyskiy Zaliv, *Russia* 52 B9
Yennádhi, *Greece* 49 C9
Yenne, *France* 21 C9
Yenotayevka, *Russia* 35 G8
Yenyuka, *Russia* 53 D13
Yeo ➤, *U.K.* 15 G5
Yeo, L., *Australia* 93 E3
Yeo I., *Canada* 116 A3
Yeola, *India* 66 J9
Yeoryioúpolis, *Greece* 49 D6
Yeovil, *U.K.* 15 G5
Yepes, *Spain* 36 F7
Yeppoon, *Australia* 94 C5
Yeráki, *Greece* 46 D4
Yerbent, *Turkmenistan* 52 F6
Yerbogachen, *Russia* 53 C11
Yerevan, *Armenia* 35 K7
Yerington, *U.S.A.* 108 G4
Yerkesik, *Turkey* 47 D10
Yerköy, *Turkey* 72 C6
Yermak, *Kazakhstan* 52 D8
Yermo, *U.S.A.* 111 L10
Yerólakkos, *Cyprus* 49 D12
Yeropol, *Russia* 53 C17
Yerópotamos ➤, *Greece* 49 D6
Yeroskipos, *Cyprus* 49 E11

Yershov, *Russia* 34 E9
Yerushalayim = Jerusalem, *Israel* 74 D4
Yerville, *France* 18 C7
Yes Tor, *U.K.* 15 G4
Yesan, *S. Korea* 57 F14
Yeşilhisar, *Turkey* 72 C6
Yeşilırmak ➤, *Turkey* 72 B7
Yeşilkent, *Turkey* 72 D7
Yeşilköy, *Turkey* 45 F12
Yeşilova, *Turkey* 47 D11
Yeşilyurt, *Manisa, Turkey* ... 47 C10
Yeşilyurt, *Muğla, Turkey* 47 D10
Yesnogorsk, *Russia* 32 E9
Yeso, *U.S.A.* 113 H2
Yessentuki, *Russia* 35 H6
Yessey, *Russia* 53 C11
Yeste, *Spain* 39 G2
Yetman, *Australia* 95 D5
Yeu, Î. d', *France* 18 F4
Yevlakh = Yevlax, *Azerbaijan* . 35 K8
Yevlax, *Azerbaijan* 35 K8
Yevpatoriya, *Ukraine* 33 K7
Yevya ➤, *Russia* 33 J10
Yeysk, *Russia* 33 J10
Yezd = Yazd, *Iran* 71 D7
Yezerishche, *Belarus* 32 E5
Yhati, *Paraguay* 126 B4
Yhú, *Paraguay* 127 B4
Yi ➤, *Uruguay* 126 C4
Yi He ➤, *China* 57 G10
Yi Xian, *China* 59 C11
Yi Xian, *Hebei, China* 56 E8
Yi Xian, *Liaoning, China* 57 D11
Yialí, *Greece* 47 E9
Yialiás ➤, *Cyprus* 49 D12
Yi'allaq, G., *Egypt* 80 A3
Yialousa, *Cyprus* 49 D13
Yiáltra, *Greece* 46 C4
Yianisádhes, *Greece* 49 D8
Yiannitsa, *Greece* 44 F6
Yibin, *China* 58 C5
Yichang, *China* 59 B8
Yicheng, *Henan, China* 56 H7
Yicheng, *Shanxi, China* 56 G6
Yichuan, *China* 56 F6
Yichun, *Heilongjiang, China* . 60 B7
Yichun, *Jiangxi, China* 59 D10
Yidu, *China* 57 F10
Yidun, *China* 58 B2
Yifag, *Ethiopia* 81 E4
Yifeng, *China* 59 C10
Yihuang, *China* 59 D11
Yijun, *China* 56 G5
Yıldız Dağları, *Turkey* 45 E11
Yıldızeli, *Turkey* 72 C7
Yiliang, *Yunnan, China* 58 D5
Yiliang, *Yunnan, China* 58 E4
Yilong, *China* 58 B6
Yimen, *China* 58 E3
Yimianpo, *China* 57 B15
Yinchuan, *China* 56 E4
Yindarlgooda, L., *Australia* .. 93 F3
Ying He ➤, *China* 56 H9
Ying Xian, *China* 56 E7
Yingcheng, *China* 59 B9
Yingde, *China* 59 E9
Yingjiang, *China* 58 E1
Yingjing, *China* 58 B4
Yingkou, *China* 57 D12
Yingshan, *Henan, China* 59 B9
Yingshan, *Hubei, China* 59 B10
Yingshan, *Sichuan, China* 58 B6
Yingshang, *China* 59 A11
Yingtan, *China* 59 C11
Yining, *China* 52 E9
Yinjiang, *China* 58 C7
Yinmabin, *Burma* 67 H19
Yiofiros ➤, *Greece* 49 D7
Yioúra, *Nótios Aiyaíon, Greece* 46 D6
Yioúra, *Thessalía, Greece* 46 B6
Yipinglang, *China* 58 E3
Yirba Muda, *Ethiopia* 81 F4
Yirga Alem, *Ethiopia* 81 F4
Yirol, *Sudan* 81 F3
Yirrkala, *Australia* 94 A2
Yishan, *China* 58 E7
Yishui, *China* 57 G10
Yishun, *Singapore* .... 65 d
Yíthion, *Greece* 46 E4
Yitong, *China* 57 C13
Yiwu, *China* 59 C13
Yixing, *China* 59 B12
Yiyang, *Henan, China* 56 G7
Yiyang, *Hunan, China* 59 C9
Yiyang, *Jiangxi, China* 59 C11
Yizhang, *China* 59 E9
Yizheng, *China* 59 A12
Yli-Kitka, *Finland* 8 C23
Ylitornio, *Finland* 8 C20
Ylivieska, *Finland* 8 D21
Yngaren, *Sweden* 11 F10
Yoakum, *U.S.A.* 113 L6
Yob △, *Eritrea* 81 D4
Yobe □, *Nigeria* 83 C7
Yog Pt., *Phil.* 63 B6
Yogan, *Togo* 83 D5
Yoğuntaş, *Turkey* 45 E11
Yogyakarta, *Indonesia* 63 G14
Yogyakarta □, *Indonesia* 63 G14
Yoho △, *Canada* 102 C5
Yojoa, L. de, *Honduras* 120 D2
Yōju, *S. Korea* 57 F14
Yok Don △, *Vietnam* 64 F6
Yokadouma, *Cameroon* 84 D2
Yokkaichi, *Japan* 55 G8
Yoko, *Cameroon* 83 D7
Yokohama, *Japan* 55 G9
Yokosuka, *Japan* 55 G9
Yokote, *Japan* 54 E10
Yola, *Nigeria* 83 D7
Yolaina, Cordillera de, *Nic.* .. 120 D3

Yoloten, *Turkmenistan* 71 B9
Yom ➤, *Thailand* 62 A2
Yonago, *Japan* 55 G6
Yonaguni-Jima, *Japan* 55 M1
Yonan, *N. Korea* 57 F14
Yonezawa, *Japan* 54 F10
Yong Peng, *Malaysia* 65 L4
Yong Sata, *Thailand* 65 J2
Yongamp'o, *N. Korea* 57 E13
Yong'an, *China* 59 E11
Yongcheng, *China* 56 H9
Yongch'ŏn, *S. Korea* 57 G15
Yongchuan, *China* 58 C5
Yongchun, *China* 59 E12
Yongde, *China* 58 E2
Yongdeng, *China* 56 F2
Yongding, *China* 59 E11
Yŏngdŏk, *S. Korea* 57 F15
Yongding, *China* 59 D10
Yongfu, *China* 58 E7
Yonghe, *China* 56 F6
Yŏnghŭng, *N. Korea* 57 E14
Yongji, *China* 56 G6
Yongjia, *China* 59 C13
Yŏngju, *S. Korea* 57 F15
Yongkang, *Yunnan, China* ... 58 E2
Yongkang, *Zhejiang, China* .. 59 C13
Yongnian, *China* 56 F8
Yongning, *Guangxi Zhuangzu, China* 58 F7
Yongning, *Ningxia Huizu, China* 56 E4
Yongping, *China* 58 E2
Yongqing, *China* 56 E9
Yongren, *China* 58 D3
Yongshan, *China* 58 C4
Yongsheng, *China* 58 D3
Yongshun, *China* 58 C7
Yongtai, *China* 59 E12
Yŏngwŏl, *S. Korea* 57 F15
Yongxin = Jinggangshan, *China* . 59 D10
Yongxing, *China* 59 D9
Yongxiu, *China* 59 C10
Yongzhou, *China* 59 D8
Yonibana, *S. Leone* 82 D2
Yonkers, *U.S.A.* 117 F11
Yonne □, *France* 19 E10
Yonne ➤, *France* 19 D9
York, *Australia* 93 F2
York, *U.K.* 14 D6
York, *Ala., U.S.A.* 113 J10
York, *Nebr., U.S.A.* 112 E6
York, *Pa., U.S.A.* 114 F7
York, C., *Australia* 94 A3
York, City of □, *U.K.* 14 D6
York, Kap, *Greenland* 4 B4
York, Vale of, *U.K.* 14 C6
York Haven, *U.S.A.* 116 F8
York Sd., *Australia* 92 C4
Yorke Pen., *Australia* 95 E2
Yorkshire Dales △, *U.K.* 14 C5
Yorkshire Wolds, *U.K.* 14 C7
Yorkton, *Canada* 103 C8
Yorkville, *U.S.A.* 110 G3
Yoro, *Honduras* 120 C2
Yoron-Jima, *Japan* 55 L4
Yorosso, *Mali* 82 C4
Yos Sudarso, Pulau = Dolak, Pulau, *Indonesia* 63 F9
Yosemite △, *U.S.A.* 110 H7
Yosemite Village, *U.S.A.* 110 H7
Yoshino-Kumano △, *Japan* .. 55 H8
Yoshkar Ola, *Russia* 34 B8
Yŏsu, *S. Korea* 57 G14
Yotvata, *Israel* 74 F4
You Jiang ➤, *China* 58 F6
You Xian, *China* 59 D9
Youbou, *Canada* 110 B2
Youghal, *Ireland* 12 E4
Youghal B., *Ireland* 12 E4
Youkounkoun, *Guinea* 82 C2
Young, *Australia* 95 E4
Young, *Canada* 103 C7
Young, *Uruguay* 126 C4
Younghusband, L., *Australia* . 95 E2
Younghusband Pen., *Australia* . 95 F2
Youngstown, *Canada* 103 C6
Youngstown, N.Y., *U.S.A.* ... 116 C5
Youngstown, Ohio, *U.S.A.* .. 116 E4
Youngsville, *U.S.A.* 116 E5
Youngwood, *U.S.A.* 116 F5
Youxi, *China* 59 D12
Youyang, *China* 58 C7
Youyu, *China* 56 D7
Yozgat, *Turkey* 72 C6
Ypacaraí △, *Paraguay* 126 B4
Ypané ➤, *Paraguay* 126 A4
Yport, *France* 18 C7
Ypres = Ieper, *Belgium* 17 D2
Yreka, *U.S.A.* 108 F2
Yssingeaux, *France* 21 C8
Ystad, *Sweden* 11 J7
Ysyk-Köl, *Kyrgyzstan* 52 E8
Ythan ➤, *U.K.* 13 D7
Yu Jiang ➤, *China* 58 F7
Yu Shan, *Taiwan* 59 F13
Yu Xian = Yuzhou, *China* ... 56 G7
Yu Xian, *Hebei, China* 56 E8
Yu Xian, *Shanxi, China* 56 E7
Yuan Jiang ➤, *Hunan, China* . 59 C8
Yuan Jiang ➤, *Yunnan, China* . 58 F4
Yuan'an, *China* 59 B8
Yuanjiang, *Hunan, China* 59 C9
Yuanjiang, *Yunnan, China* ... 58 F4
Yüanli, *Taiwan* 59 E13
Yüanlin, *Taiwan* 59 F13
Yuanling, *China* 59 C8
Yuanmou, *China* 58 E3
Yuanqu, *China* 56 G6

Yuanyang, *Yunnan, China* 58 F4
Yuba ➤, *U.S.A.* 110 F5
Yuba City, *U.S.A.* 110 F5
Yūbari, *Japan* 54 C10
Yubdo, *Ethiopia* 81 F4
Yūbetsu, *Japan* 54 B11
Yubo, *Sudan* 81 F2
Yucatán □, *Mexico* 119 C7
Yucatán, Canal de, *Caribbean* . 120 B2
Yucatán, Península de, *Mexico* . 98 H11
Yucatan Basin, *Cent. Amer.* .. 98 H11
Yucatan Channel = Yucatán, Canal de, *Caribbean* 120 B2
Yucca, *U.S.A.* 111 L12
Yucca Valley, *U.S.A.* 111 L10
Yucheng, *China* 56 F9
Yuci, *China* 56 F7
Yudu, *China* 59 E10
Yuechi, *China* 58 B6
Yuendumu, *Australia* 92 D5
Yueqing, *China* 59 C13
Yueqing Wan, *China* 59 D13
Yuexi, *Anhui, China* 59 B11
Yuexi, *Sichuan, China* 58 C4
Yueyang, *China* 59 C9
Yugan, *China* 59 C11
Yugoslavia = Serbia & Montenegro ■, *Europe* ... 44 C4
Yuhuan, *China* 59 C13
Yühuan Dao, *China* 59 C13
Yujiang, *China* 59 C11
Yukhnov, *Russia* 32 E8
Yukon ➤, *U.S.A.* 100 B3
Yukon Territory □, *Canada* .. 100 B6
Yüksekova, *Turkey* 73 D11
Yukta, *Russia* 53 C11
Yukuhashi, *Japan* 55 H5
Yulara, *Australia* 93 E5
Yule ➤, *Australia* 92 D2
Yuleba, *Australia* 95 D4
Yuli, *Nigeria* 83 D7
Yüli, *Taiwan* 59 F13
Yulin, *Guangxi Zhuangzu, China* . 59 F8
Yülin, *Hainan, China* 65 C7
Yulin, *Shaanxi, China* 56 E5
Yuma, *Ariz., U.S.A.* 111 N12
Yuma, *Colo., U.S.A.* 112 E3
Yuma, B. de, *Dom. Rep.* 121 C6
Yumbe, *Uganda* 86 B3
Yumbi, *Dem. Rep. of the Congo* . 86 C2
Yumen, *China* 60 C4
Yumurtalık, *Turkey* 72 D6
Yun Gui Gaoyuan, *China* 58 E3
Yun Ho ➤, *China* 57 E9
Yun Ling, *China* 58 D2
Yun Xian, *Hubei, China* 59 A8
Yun Xian, *Yunnan, China* ... 58 E3
Yuna, *Australia* 93 E2
Yunak, *Turkey* 72 C4
Yunan, *China* 59 F8
Yuncheng, *Henan, China* 56 G8
Yuncheng, *Shanxi, China* ... 56 G6
Yunfu, *China* 59 F9
Yungas, *Bolivia* 124 G5
Yungay, *Chile* 126 D1
Yunhe, *China* 59 C12
Yunkai Dashan, *China* 59 F8
Yunlin, *Taiwan* 59 F13
Yunlong, *China* 58 E2
Yunmeng, *China* 59 B9
Yunnan □, *China* 58 E4
Yunquera de Henares, *Spain* . 38 E1
Yunt Dağı, *Turkey* 47 C9
Yunta, *Australia* 95 E2
Yunxi, *China* 56 H6
Yunxiao, *China* 59 F11
Yuping, *China* 58 D7
Yupukarri, *Guyana* 59 D15
Yuqing, *China* 58 D6
Yuraygir △, *Australia* 95 D5
Yurga, *Russia* 52 D9
Yurimaguas, *Peru* 124 E3
Yurkivka, *Ukraine* 29 B13
Yurubí △, *Venezuela* 121 D6
Yuryev-Polskiy, *Russia* 32 D10
Yuryevets, *Russia* 34 B6
Yuscarán, *Honduras* 120 D2
Yūsef, Bahr ➤, *Egypt* 80 B3
Yushan, *China* 59 C12
Yushanzhen, *China* 58 C7
Yushe, *China* 56 F7
Yushu, *Jilin, China* 57 B14
Yushu, *Qinghai, China* 60 C4
Yusufeli, *Turkey* 73 B9
Yutai, *China* 56 G9
Yutian, *China* 57 E9
Yuxarı Qarabağ = Nagorno-Karabakh □, *Azerbaijan* .. 70 B5
Yuxi, *China* 58 E4
Yuyao, *China* 59 B13
Yuzawa, *Japan* 54 E10
Yuzha, *Russia* 34 B6
Yuzhno-Sakhalinsk, *Russia* .. 53 E15
Yuzhnyy □, *Russia* 35 H5
Yuzhou, *China* 56 G7
Yvelines □, *France* 19 D8
Yverdon-les-Bains, *Switz.* ... 25 J2
Yvetot, *France* 18 C7
Yzeure, *France* 19 F10

Z

Zaanstad, *Neths.* 17 B4
Zāb al Kabīr ➤, *Iraq* 70 C4
Zāb aş Şaghīr ➤, *Iraq* 70 C4
Zabalj, *Serbia & M.* 28 E5
Żabari, *Serbia & M.* 44 B5
Zabarjad, *Egypt* 80 C4

Zabaykalsk, Russia ... 53 E12
Zabki, Poland ... 31 F8
Ząbkowice Śląskie, Poland ... 31 H3
Žabljak, Serbia & M. ... 44 C3
Zabłudów, Poland ... 31 F9
Žabno, Poland ... 31 H7
Zābol, Iran ... 71 D9
Zābol □, Afghan. ... 66 D5
Zābolī, Iran ... 71 E9
Zabolotiv, Ukraine ... 29 B10
Zabolottya, Ukraine ... 31 G11
Zabré, Burkina Faso ... 83 C4
Zábřeh, Czech Rep. ... 27 B9
Zabrze, Poland ... 31 H5
Zabuzhzhya, Ukraine ... 31 G10
Zabzuga, Ghana ... 83 D5
Zacapa, Guatemala ... 120 D2
Zacapu, Mexico ... 118 D4
Zacatecas, Mexico ... 118 C4
Zacatecas □, Mexico ... 118 C4
Zacatecoluca, El Salv. ... 120 D2
Zachary, U.S.A. ... 113 K9
Zachodnio-Pomorskie □, Poland ... 30 E2
Zacoalco, Mexico ... 118 C4
Zacualtipán, Mexico ... 119 C5
Zadar, Croatia ... 41 D12
Zadawa, Nigeria ... 83 C7
Zadetkyi Kyun, Burma ... 65 G2
Zadonsk, Russia ... 33 F10
Zafarqand, Iran ... 71 C7
Zafora, Greece ... 47 E8
Zafra, Spain ... 37 G4
Zagań, Poland ... 31 G2
Zagaoua, Chad ... 79 E10
Žagarė, Lithuania ... 30 B10
Zagazig, Egypt ... 80 H7
Zāgheh, Iran ... 71 C6
Zaglivérion, Greece ... 44 F7
Zagnanado, Benin ... 83 D5
Zagorá, Greece ... 46 B5
Zagorje, Slovenia ... 41 B11
Zagórów, Poland ... 31 F4
Zagórz, Poland ... 31 J9
Zagreb, Croatia ... 41 C12
Zagreb ✈ (ZAG), Croatia ... 41 C13
Zāgros, Kūhhā-ye, Iran ... 71 C6
Zagros Mts. = Zāgros, Kūhhā-ye, Iran ... 71 C6
Žagubica, Serbia & M. ... 44 B5
Zaguinaso, Ivory C. ... 82 C3
Zagyva →, Hungary ... 28 C5
Zahamena △, Madag. ... 89 B8
Zāhedān, Fārs, Iran ... 71 D7
Zāhedān, Sīstān va Balūchestān, Iran ... 71 D9
Zahlah, Lebanon ... 74 B4
Zahna, Germany ... 24 D8
Záhony, Hungary ... 28 B7
Zainsk, Russia ... 34 C11
Zaïre = Congo →, Africa ... 84 F2
Zaječar, Serbia & M. ... 44 C6
Zaka, Zimbabwe ... 89 C5
Zakamensk, Russia ... 53 D11
Zakarpatska □, Ukraine ... 29 B8
Zakataly = Zaqatala, Azerbaijan ... 35 K8
Zakháro, Greece ... 46 D3
Zakhodnaya Dzvina = Daugava →, Latvia ... 9 H21
Zākhū, Iraq ... 70 B4
Zákinthos, Greece ... 46 D2
Zákinthos □, Greece ... 46 D2
Zakopane, Poland ... 31 J6
Zakroczym, Poland ... 31 F7
Zákros, Greece ... 49 D8
Zala □, Hungary ... 28 D1
Zala →, Hungary ... 28 D1
Zalaegerszeg, Hungary ... 28 D1
Zalakomár, Hungary ... 28 D2
Zalalövő, Hungary ... 28 D1
Zalamea de la Serena, Spain ... 37 G5
Zalamea la Real, Spain ... 37 H4
Zalău, Romania ... 28 C8
Žalec, Slovenia ... 41 B12
Zaleshchiki = Zalishchyky, Ukraine ... 29 B10
Zalesye, Russia ... 30 D8
Zalew Wiślany, Poland ... 30 D6
Zalewo, Poland ... 30 E6
Zalingei, Sudan ... 79 F10
Zalishchyky, Ukraine ... 29 B10
Zama L., Canada ... 102 B5
Zambeke, Dem. Rep. of the Congo ... 86 B2
Zambeze →, Africa ... 87 F4
Zambezi = Zambeze →, Africa ... 87 F4
Zambezi, Zambia ... 85 G4
Zambezi △, Zimbabwe ... 87 F2
Zambézia □, Mozam. ... 87 F4
Zambia ■, Africa ... 87 F2
Zamboanga, Phil. ... 61 H5
Zambrów, Poland ... 31 F9
Zametchino, Russia ... 34 D6
Zamfara □, Nigeria ... 83 C6
Zamfara →, Nigeria ... 83 C5
Zamora, Mexico ... 118 D4
Zamora, Spain ... 36 D5
Zamora □, Spain ... 36 D5
Zamość, Poland ... 31 H10
Zamtang, China ... 58 A3
Zan, Ghana ... 83 D4
Záncara →, Spain ... 39 F1
Zandvoort, Neths. ... 17 B4
Zanesville, U.S.A. ... 116 G2
Zangābād, Iran ... 70 B5
Zangue →, Mozam. ... 87 F4
Zanján, Iran ... 71 B6
Zanján □, Iran ... 71 B6
Zanján →, Iran ... 71 B6
Zannone, Italy ... 42 B6
Zante = Zákinthos, Greece ... 46 D2

Zanthus, Australia ... 93 F3
Zanzibar, Tanzania ... 86 D4
Zaouiet El-Kala = Bordj Omar Driss, Algeria ... 78 C7
Zaouiet Reggâne, Algeria ... 78 C6
Zaoyang, China ... 59 A9
Zaozhuang, China ... 57 G9
Zap Suyu = Zāb al Kabīr →, Iraq ... 70 C4
Zapadna Morava →, Serbia & M. ... 44 C5
Zapadnaya Dvina = Daugava →, Latvia ... 9 H21
Zapadnaya Dvina, Russia ... 32 D7
Západné Beskydy, Europe ... 27 B12
Zapadni Rodopi, Bulgaria ... 44 E7
Západočeský □, Czech Rep. ... 26 B6
Zapala, Argentina ... 128 D2
Zapaleri, Cerro, Bolivia ... 126 A2
Zapata, U.S.A. ... 113 M5
Zapatón →, Spain ... 37 F4
Zaporizhzhya, Ukraine ... 33 J8
Zaporozhye = Zaporizhzhya, Ukraine ... 33 J8
Zaqatala, Azerbaijan ... 35 K8
Zara, Turkey ... 70 B3
Zaragoza, Coahuila, Mexico ... 118 B4
Zaragoza, Nuevo León, Mexico ... 119 C5
Zaragoza, Spain ... 38 D4
Zaragoza □, Spain ... 38 D4
Zarand, Kermān, Iran ... 71 D8
Zarand, Markazī, Iran ... 71 C6
Zărandului, Munții, Romania ... 28 D7
Zaranj, Afghan. ... 66 D2
Zarasai, Lithuania ... 9 J22
Zárate, Argentina ... 126 C4
Zarautz, Spain ... 38 B2
Zaraysk, Russia ... 32 E10
Zard, Kūh-e, Iran ... 71 C6
Zāreh, Iran ... 71 C6
Zari, Nigeria ... 83 C7
Zaria, Nigeria ... 83 C6
Żarki, Poland ... 31 H6
Zárkon, Greece ... 46 B4
Zarneh, Iran ... 70 C5
Zărnești, Romania ... 29 E10
Zárós, Greece ... 49 D6
Żarów, Poland ... 31 H3
Zarqā', Nahr az →, Jordan ... 74 C4
Zarrīn, Iran ... 71 C7
Zaruma, Ecuador ... 124 D3
Żary, Poland ... 31 G2
Zarza de Granadilla, Spain ... 36 E4
Zarzis, Tunisia ... 79 B8
Zas, Spain ... 36 B2
Zaskar →, India ... 69 B7
Zaskar Mts., India ... 69 C7
Zastavna, Ukraine ... 29 B10
Zastron, S. Africa ... 88 E4
Zatec, Czech Rep. ... 26 A6
Zator, Poland ... 31 J6
Zatyshshya, Ukraine ... 29 C14
Zavala, Bos.-H. ... 44 D1
Zavāreh, Iran ... 71 C7
Zave, Zimbabwe ... 89 B5
Zavetnoye, Russia ... 35 G6
Zavidovići, Bos.-H. ... 28 F3
Zavitinsk, Russia ... 53 D13
Zavodovski, I., Antarctica ... 5 B1
Zavolzhsk, Russia ... 34 B6
Zavolzhye, Russia ... 34 B6
Zawadzkie, Poland ... 31 H5
Zawichost, Poland ... 31 H8
Zawidów, Poland ... 31 G2
Zawiercie, Poland ... 31 H6
Zāwiyat al Bayḍā = Al Bayḍā, Libya ... 79 B10
Zāwyet Shammas, Egypt ... 80 A2
Zāwyet Um el Rakham, Egypt ... 80 A2
Zāwyet Ungeîla, Egypt ... 80 A2
Zāyā, Iraq ... 70 C5
Zāyandeh →, Iran ... 71 C7
Zaysan, Kazakhstan ... 52 E9
Zaysan, Oz., Kazakhstan ... 52 E9
Zayü, China ... 58 C1
Zazafotsy, Madag. ... 89 C8
Zázrivá, Slovak Rep. ... 27 B12
Zbarazh, Ukraine ... 33 H3
Zbąszyń, Poland ... 31 F2
Zbąszynek, Poland ... 31 F2
Zblewo, Poland ... 30 E5
Zbruch →, Ukraine ... 29 B11
Ždár nad Sázavou, Czech Rep. ... 26 B8
Zdolbuniv, Ukraine ... 33 G4
Ždrelo, Serbia & M. ... 44 B5
Zduńska Wola, Poland ... 31 G5
Zduny, Poland ... 31 G4
Zeballos, Canada ... 102 D3
Zebediela, S. Africa ... 89 C4
Zebila, Ghana ... 83 C4
Zeebrugge, Belgium ... 17 C3
Zeehan, Australia ... 95 G4
Zeeland □, Neths. ... 17 C3
Zeerust, S. Africa ... 88 D4
Żefat, Israel ... 74 C4
Zege, Ethiopia ... 81 E4
Zeggerene, Iracher, Mali ... 83 B5
Zégoua, Mali ... 82 C3
Zehdenick, Germany ... 24 C9
Zeil, Mt., Australia ... 92 D5
Zeist, Neths. ... 17 B5
Zeitz, Germany ... 24 D8
Zelechów, Poland ... 31 G8
Zelena, Ukraine ... 29 B9
Zelengora, Bos.-H. ... 44 C2
Zelenodolsk, Russia ... 34 C9
Zelenogorsk, Russia ... 32 B5
Zelenograd, Russia ... 32 D9
Zelenogradsk, Russia ... 9 J19
Zelenokumsk, Russia ... 35 H6
Železná Ruda, Czech Rep. ... 26 B6
Železnik, Serbia & M. ... 44 B4

Zelienople, U.S.A. ... 116 F4
Želiezovce, Slovak Rep. ... 27 C11
Zelina, Croatia ... 41 C13
Zell, Baden-W., Germany ... 25 H3
Zell, Rhld-Pfz., Germany ... 25 E3
Zell am See, Austria ... 26 D5
Zella-Mehlis, Germany ... 24 E6
Zelów, Poland ... 31 G6
Zeltweg, Austria ... 26 D7
Zémio, C.A.R. ... 86 A2
Zempléni-hegység, Hungary ... 28 B6
Zemplínska šírava, Slovak Rep. ... 27 C15
Zempoala, Mexico ... 119 D5
Zemun, Serbia & M. ... 44 B4
Zengbé, Cameroon ... 83 D7
Zengcheng, China ... 59 F9
Zenica, Bos.-H. ... 28 F2
Zenong, China ... 58 C3
Żepče, Bos.-H. ... 28 F3
Zeraf, Bahr ez →, Sudan ... 81 F3
Zerbst, Germany ... 24 D8
Zerków, Poland ... 31 F4
Zermatt, Switz. ... 25 J3
Zernez, Switz. ... 25 J6
Zernograd, Russia ... 35 G5
Zerqan, Albania ... 44 E4
Zestaponi, Georgia ... 35 J6
Zetel, Germany ... 24 B3
Zeulenroda, Germany ... 24 E7
Zeven, Germany ... 24 B5
Zevenaar, Neths. ... 17 C6
Zévio, Italy ... 40 C8
Zeya, Russia ... 53 D13
Zeya →, Russia ... 53 D13
Zeytinbaği, Turkey ... 45 F12
Zeytindağ, Turkey ... 47 C9
Zghartā, Lebanon ... 74 A4
Zgierz, Poland ... 31 G6
Zgorzelec, Poland ... 31 G2
Zgurița, Moldova ... 29 B13
Zhabinka, Belarus ... 31 F11
Zhabokrych, Ukraine ... 29 B13
Zhailma, Kazakhstan ... 52 D7
Zhambyl = Taraz, Kazakhstan ... 52 E8
Zhangaly, Kazakhstan ... 35 G10
Zhangaqazaly, Kazakhstan ... 52 E7
Zhangbei, China ... 56 D8
Zhangguangcai Ling, China ... 57 B15
Zhangping, China ... 59 E11
Zhangpu, China ... 59 E11
Zhangshu, China ... 59 C10
Zhangwu, China ... 57 C12
Zhangye, China ... 60 C5
Zhangzhou, China ... 59 E11
Zhanhua, China ... 57 F10
Zhanjiang, China ... 59 G8
Zhannetty, Ostrov, Russia ... 53 B16
Zhanyi, China ... 58 E4
Zhanyu, China ... 57 B12
Zhao'an, China ... 59 F11
Zhaocheng, China ... 56 F6
Zhaojue, China ... 58 C4
Zhaoping, China ... 59 E8
Zhaoqing, China ... 59 F9
Zhaotong, China ... 58 D4
Zhaoyuan, Heilongjiang, China ... 57 B13
Zhaoyuan, Shandong, China ... 57 F11
Zharkovskiy, Russia ... 32 E7
Zhashkiv, Ukraine ... 33 H6
Zhashui, China ... 56 H5
Zhayyq →, Kazakhstan ... 52 E6
Zhdanov = Mariupol, Ukraine ... 33 J9
Zhecheng, China ... 56 G8
Zhegao, China ... 59 B11
Zhejiang □, China ... 59 C13
Zheleznodorozhnyy, Russia ... 30 D8
Zheleznogorsk, Russia ... 33 F8
Zheleznogorsk-Ilimskiy, Russia ... 53 D11
Zheltyye Vody = Zhovti Vody, Ukraine ... 33 H7
Zhen'an, China ... 56 H5
Zhenba, China ... 58 A6
Zhenfeng, China ... 58 E5
Zheng'an, China ... 58 C6
Zhengding, China ... 56 E8
Zhenghe, China ... 59 D12
Zhengyang, China ... 59 A10
Zhengzhou, China ... 56 G7
Zhenhai, China ... 59 C13
Zhenjiang, China ... 59 A12
Zhenkang, China ... 58 F2
Zhenlai, China ... 57 B12
Zhenning, China ... 58 D5
Zhenping, Henan, China ... 56 H7
Zhenping, Shaanxi, China ... 58 B7
Zhenxiong, China ... 58 D5
Zhenyuan, Gansu, China ... 56 G4
Zhenyuan, Guizhou, China ... 58 D7
Zherdevka, Russia ... 34 E5
Zherebkove, Ukraine ... 29 C14
Zherong, China ... 59 D12
Zhetiqara, Kazakhstan ... 52 D7
Zhezqazghan, Kazakhstan ... 52 E7
Zhidan, China ... 56 F5
Zhigansk, Russia ... 53 C13
Zhigulevsk, Russia ... 34 D9
Zhijiang, Hubei, China ... 59 B8
Zhijiang, Hunan, China ... 58 D7
Zhijin, China ... 58 D5
Zhilinda, Russia ... 53 C12
Zhilino, Russia ... 30 D8
Zhitomir = Zhytomyr, Ukraine ... 33 G5
Zhizdra, Russia ... 32 F8
Zhlobin, Belarus ... 33 F6
Zhmerinka = Zhmerynka, Ukraine ... 33 H5
Zhmerynka, Ukraine ... 33 H5

Zhob, Pakistan ... 68 D3
Zhob →, Pakistan ... 68 C3
Zhodino = Zhodzina, Belarus ... 32 E5
Zhodzina, Belarus ... 32 E5
Zhokhova, Ostrov, Russia ... 53 B16
Zhongdian, China ... 58 D2
Zhongdong, China ... 58 F6
Zhongdu, China ... 58 E7
Zhongning, China ... 56 F3
Zhongshan, Antarctica ... 5 C6
Zhongshan, Guangdong, China ... 59 F9
Zhongshan, Guangxi Zhuangzu, China ... 59 E8
Zhongtiao Shan, China ... 56 G6
Zhongwei, China ... 56 F3
Zhongxiang, China ... 59 B9
Zhongyang, China ... 56 F6
Zhorany, Ukraine ... 31 G10
Zhoucun, China ... 57 F9
Zhouning, China ... 59 D12
Zhoushan, China ... 59 B14
Zhoushan Dao, China ... 59 C14
Zhouzhi, China ... 56 G5
Zhovti Vody, Ukraine ... 33 H7
Zhovtneve, Ukraine ... 31 H11
Zhovtneve, Ukraine ... 33 J7
Zhovtnevoye = Zhovtneve, Ukraine ... 33 J7
Zhu Jiang →, China ... 59 F9
Zhuanghe, China ... 57 E12
Zhucheng, China ... 57 G10
Zhugqu, China ... 56 H3
Zhuhai, China ... 59 F9
Zhuji, China ... 59 C13
Zhukovka, Russia ... 32 F7
Zhumadian, China ... 56 H8
Zhuo Xian = Zhuozhou, China ... 56 E8
Zhuolu, China ... 56 D8
Zhuozhou, China ... 56 E8
Zhuozi, China ... 56 D7
Zhushan, China ... 59 A8
Zhuxi, China ... 58 A7
Zhuzhou, China ... 59 D9
Zhvanets, Ukraine ... 29 B11
Zhytomyr, Ukraine ... 33 G5
Zi Shui →, China ... 59 C9
Žiar nad Hronom, Slovak Rep. ... 27 C11
Ziārān, Iran ... 71 B6
Ziarat, Pakistan ... 68 D2
Zibo, China ... 57 F10
Zichang, China ... 56 F5
Zidarovo, Bulgaria ... 45 D11
Zidi = Wandhari, Pakistan ... 68 F2
Ziębice, Poland ... 31 H4
Zielona Góra, Poland ... 31 G2
Zierikzee, Neths. ... 17 C3
Ziesar, Germany ... 24 C8
Zifta, Egypt ... 80 H7
Zigey, Chad ... 79 F9
Zigong, China ... 58 C5
Ziguinchor, Senegal ... 82 C1
Zihuatanejo, Mexico ... 118 D4
Zijin, China ... 59 F10
Zile, Turkey ... 72 B6
Žilina, Slovak Rep. ... 27 B11
Žilinský □, Slovak Rep. ... 27 B12
Zillah, Libya ... 79 C9
Zillertaler Alpen, Austria ... 26 D4
Zima, Russia ... 53 D11
Zimapán, Mexico ... 119 C5
Zimba, Zambia ... 87 F2
Zimbabwe, Zimbabwe ... 87 G3
Zimbabwe ■, Africa ... 87 F3
Zimi, S. Leone ... 82 D2
Zimnicea, Romania ... 29 G10
Zimovniki, Russia ... 35 G6
Zinave □, Mozam. ... 89 C5
Zinder, Niger ... 83 C6
Zinga, Tanzania ... 87 D4
Zíngaro △, Italy ... 42 D5
Zingst, Germany ... 24 A8
Ziniaré, Burkina Faso ... 83 C4
Zinnowitz, Germany ... 24 A9
Zion, U.S.A. ... 109 H7
Zirbitzkogel, Austria ... 26 D7
Zirc, Hungary ... 28 C2
Žiri, Slovenia ... 41 B11
Zirl, Austria ... 26 D4
Zirndorf, Germany ... 25 F6
Ziros, Greece ... 49 D8
Zirreh, Gowd-e, Afghan. ... 66 E3
Zisterdorf, Austria ... 27 C9
Zitácuaro, Mexico ... 118 D4
Žitava →, Slovak Rep. ... 27 C11
Žitište, Serbia & M. ... 28 E5
Zitong, China ... 58 B5
Žítsa, Greece ... 46 B2
Zittau, Germany ... 24 E10
Zitundo, Mozam. ... 89 D5
Živinice, Bos.-H. ... 28 F3
Ziwa Magharibi = Kagera □, Tanzania ... 86 C3
Ziway, L., Ethiopia ... 81 F4
Zixi, China ... 59 D11
Zixing, China ... 59 E9
Ziyang, Shaanxi, China ... 56 H5
Ziyang, Sichuan, China ... 58 B5
Ziyuan, China ... 59 D8
Ziyun, China ... 58 E6
Zizhong, China ... 58 C5
Zlarin, Croatia ... 41 E12
Zlatar, Croatia ... 41 B13
Zlatar, Serbia & M. ... 44 C3
Zlataritsa, Bulgaria ... 45 C9
Zlaté Moravce, Slovak Rep. ... 27 C11
Zlatibor, Serbia & M. ... 44 C3
Zlatitsa, Bulgaria ... 45 D8
Zlatna, Romania ... 29 D8
Zlatna Panega, Bulgaria ... 45 C8
Zlatni Pyasŭtsi, Bulgaria ... 45 C12
Zlatograd, Bulgaria ... 45 E9

Zlatoust, Russia ... 52 D6
Zletovo, Macedonia ... 44 E6
Zlín, Czech Rep. ... 27 B10
Zlínský □, Czech Rep. ... 27 B10
Złocieniec, Poland ... 30 E3
Złoczew, Poland ... 31 G5
Zlot, Serbia & M. ... 44 B5
Złotoryja, Poland ... 31 G2
Złotów, Poland ... 30 E4
Zmeinogorsk, Kazakhstan ... 52 D9
Żmigród, Poland ... 31 G3
Zmiyev, Ukraine ... 33 H9
Znamenka = Znamyanka, Ukraine ... 33 H7
Znamensk, Russia ... 30 D8
Znamyanka, Ukraine ... 33 H7
Żnin, Poland ... 31 F4
Znojmo, Czech Rep. ... 26 C9
Zobeyrī, Iran ... 70 C5
Zobia, Dem. Rep. of the Congo ... 86 B2
Zoetermeer, Neths. ... 17 B4
Zogang, China ... 58 C1
Zogno, Italy ... 40 C6
Zogqên, China ... 58 A2
Zolochev = Zolochiv, Ukraine ... 33 H3
Zolochiv, Ukraine ... 33 H3
Zolotonosha, Ukraine ... 33 H7
Zolotyy Potik, Ukraine ... 29 B10
Zomba, Malawi ... 87 F4
Zongo, Dem. Rep. of the Congo ... 84 D3
Zonguldak, Turkey ... 72 B4
Zongyang, China ... 59 B11
Zonqor Pt., Malta ... 49 D2
Zonza, France ... 21 G13
Zorgo, Burkina Faso ... 83 C4
Zorita, Spain ... 37 F5
Zorleni, Romania ... 29 D12
Zornitsa, Bulgaria ... 45 D10
Zorritos, Peru ... 124 D2
Żory, Poland ... 31 H5
Zorzor, Liberia ... 82 D3
Zossen, Germany ... 24 C9
Zou Xiang, China ... 56 G9
Zouar, Chad ... 79 D9
Zouérate = Zouîrât, Mauritania ... 78 D3
Zouîrât, Mauritania ... 78 D3
Zourika, Niger ... 83 B6
Zourma, Burkina Faso ... 83 C4
Zoutkamp, Neths. ... 17 A6
Zrenjanin, Serbia & M. ... 28 E5
Zuarungu, Ghana ... 83 C4
Zuba, Nigeria ... 83 D6
Zubayr, Yemen ... 81 D5
Zubtsov, Russia ... 32 D8
Zuénoula, Ivory C. ... 82 D3
Zuera, Spain ... 38 D4
Zufār, Oman ... 75 D5
Zug □, Switz. ... 25 H4
Zugersee, Switz. ... 25 H4
Zugspitze, Germany ... 25 H6
Zuid-Holland □, Neths. ... 17 C4
Zuidbeveland, Neths. ... 17 C3
Zuidhorn, Neths. ... 17 A6
Zújar, Spain ... 37 H8
Zújar →, Spain ... 37 G5
Zukowo, Poland ... 30 D5
Zula, Eritrea ... 81 D4
Zülpich, Germany ... 24 E2
Zumaia, Spain ... 38 B2
Zumárraga, Spain ... 38 B2
Zumbo, Mozam. ... 87 F3
Zummo, Nigeria ... 83 D7
Zumpango, Mexico ... 119 D5
Zungeru, Nigeria ... 83 D6
Zunhua, China ... 57 D9
Zuni, U.S.A. ... 109 J9
Zunyi, China ... 58 D6
Zuo Jiang →, China ... 58 F6
Zuozhou, China ... 58 F6
Županja, Croatia ... 28 E3
Žur, Serbia & M. ... 44 D4
Zurbāṭīyah, Iraq ... 70 C5
Zürich, Switz. ... 25 H4
Zürich □, Switz. ... 25 H4
Zürichsee, Switz. ... 25 H4
Zuromin, Poland ... 31 E6
Žut, Croatia ... 41 E12
Zutphen, Neths. ... 17 B6
Zuurberg △, S. Africa ... 88 E4
Zuwārah, Libya ... 79 B8
Züzan, Iran ... 71 C8
Žužemberk, Slovenia ... 41 C11
Zvenigorodka = Zvenyhorodka, Ukraine ... 33 H6
Zvenyhorodka, Ukraine ... 33 H6
Zverinogolovskoye, Russia ... 52 D7
Zvezdets, Bulgaria ... 45 D11
Zvishavane, Zimbabwe ... 87 G3
Zvolen, Slovak Rep. ... 27 C12
Zvonce, Serbia & M. ... 44 D6
Zvornik, Bos.-H. ... 28 F4
Zwedru = Tchien, Liberia ... 82 D3
Zweibrücken, Germany ... 25 F3
Zwelitsha, S. Africa ... 85 L5
Zwenkau, Germany ... 24 D8
Zwettl, Austria ... 26 C8
Zwickau, Germany ... 24 E8
Zwierzyniec, Poland ... 31 H9
Zwiesel, Germany ... 25 F9
Zwoleń, Poland ... 31 G8
Zwolle, Neths. ... 17 B6
Zwolle, U.S.A. ... 113 K8
Zychlin, Poland ... 31 F6
Zyrardów, Poland ... 31 F7
Zyryan, Kazakhstan ... 52 E9
Zyryanka, Russia ... 53 C16
Zyryanovsk = Zyryan, Kazakhstan ... 52 E9
Żywiec, Poland ... 31 J6
Zyyi, Cyprus ... 49 E12

KEY TO EUROPEAN MAP PAGES

 **Large scale maps**
(>1:2 500 000)

 **Medium scale maps**
(1:2 800 000 – 1:9 900 000)

 **Small scale maps**
(<1:10 000 000)

ICELAND

Arctic Circle

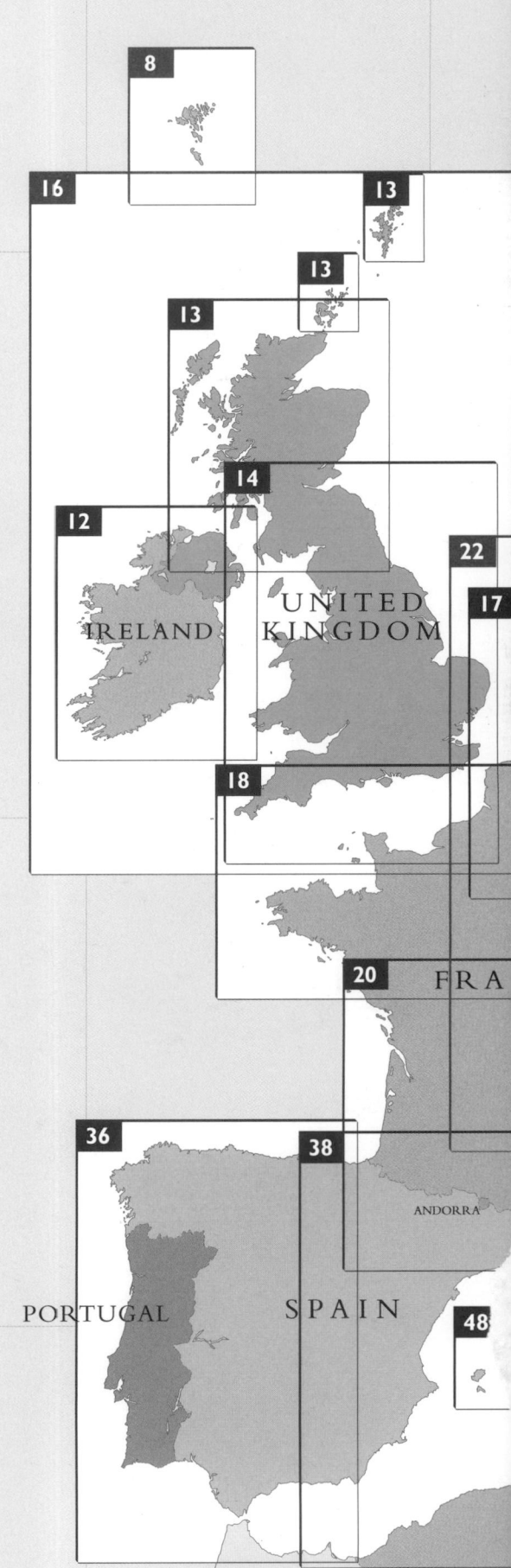

8

16   13

13

13

14

12   22

17

IRELAND   UNITED KINGDOM

18

20   FRA

36   38

ANDORRA

PORTUGAL   SPAIN   48

MOROCCO   A

WORLD COUNTRY INDEX

Afghanistan	66	
Albania	44	
Algeria	78	
Angola	84–85	
Argentina	126, 128	
Armenia	73	
Australia	92–95	
Austria	26–27	
Azerbaijan	73	
Bahamas	120–121	
Bahrain	71	
Bangladesh	67	
Barbados	121	
Belarus	32–33	
Belgium	17	
Belize	120	
Benin	83	
Bhutan	67	
Bolivia	124	
Bosnia-Herzegovina	41, 44	
Botswana	88	
Brazil	124–125, 127	
Brunei	62	
Bulgaria	44–45	
Burkina Faso	82–83	
Burma (Myanmar)	67	
Burundi	86	
Cambodia	64–65	
Canary Is.	48	
Cameroon	83, 84	
Canada	100–105	
Central African Republic	84	
Chad	79	
Chile	126–127, 128	
China	56–60	
Colombia	124	
Congo	84	
Congo, Dem. Rep. of the	84–85, 86–87	
Costa Rica	120	
Croatia	41	
Cuba	120–121	
Cyprus	49	
Czech Republic	26–27	
Denmark	11	
Djibouti	81	
Dominican Republic	121	
East Timor	63	
Ecuador	124	
Egypt	80	
El Salvador	120	
England	14–15	
Equatorial Guinea	84	
Eritrea	80–81	
Estonia	32	
Ethiopia	75, 81	
Fiji	91	
Finland	8–9	
France	18–21	
French Guiana	125	
Gabon	84	
Gambia	82	
Georgia	35	

Germany	24–25	
Ghana	82–83	
Greece	44–47	
Greenland	4	
Guadeloupe	120	
Guatemala	120	
Guinea	82	
Guinea-Bissau	82	
Guyana	124	
Haiti	121	
Honduras	120	
Hungary	28	
Iceland	8	
India	66–69	
Indonesia	62–63	
Iran	70–71, 73	
Iraq	70–71, 73	
Irish Republic	12	
Israel	74	
Italy	40–43	
Ivory Coast	82	
Jamaica	120	
Japan	54–55	
Jordan	74	
Kazakhstan	52	
Kenya	86	
Korea, North	57	
Korea, South	57	
Kuwait	70–71	
Kyrgyzstan	52	
Laos	64	
Latvia	32	
Lebanon	74	
Lesotho	89	
Liberia	82	
Libya	79	
Lithuania	32	
Luxembourg	17	
Macedonia	44	
Madagascar	89	
Malawi	87	
Malaysia	62–63, 65	
Mali	78, 82–83	
Malta	49	
Martinique	120	
Mauritania	78, 82	
Mexico	118–119	
Moldova	29	
Mongolia	60	
Morocco	78	
Mozambique	87, 89	
Namibia	88	
Nepal	69	
Netherlands	17	
New Zealand	91	
Nicaragua	120	
Niger	78–79, 83	
Nigeria	83	
Northern Ireland	12	
Norway	8–9	
Oman	75	

Pakistan	66, 68	
Panama	120	
Papua New Guinea	96	
Paraguay	126–127	
Peru	124	
Philippines	61	
Poland	30–31	
Portugal	36–37	
Puerto Rico	121	
Qatar	71	
Romania	28–29	
Russia	32–35, 52–53	
Rwanda	86	
St. Lucia	121	
Samoa	91	
Saudi Arabia	70–71, 75	
Scotland	13	
Senegal	82	
Serbia and Montenegro	28, 44	
Sierra Leone	82	
Singapore	65	
Slovak Republic	27	
Slovenia	41	
Solomon Is.	96	
Somali Republic	75	
South Africa	88–89	
Spain	36–39	
Sri Lanka	66	
Sudan	80–81	
Suriname	124–125	
Swaziland	89	
Sweden	8–9	
Switzerland	25	
Syria	70, 72–73	
Taiwan	59	
Tajikistan	52	
Tanzania	86–87	
Thailand	64–65	
Togo	83	
Tonga	91	
Trinidad and Tobago	125	
Tunisia	78–79	
Turkey	72–73	
Turkmenistan	52	
Uganda	86	
Ukraine	33	
United Arab Emirates	75	
United Kingdom	12–16	
USA	106–117	
Uruguay	126–127	
Uzbekistan	52	
Vanuatu	96	
Venezuela	124	
Vietnam	64–65	
Wales	14–15	
Yemen	75	
Zambia	85, 87	
Zimbabwe	87	